D1420926

THE OXFORD
COMPANION TO
ENGLISH
LITERATURE

THE OXFORD COMPANION TO ENGLISH LITERATURE

NEW EDITION

EDITED BY

MARGARET DRABBLE

GUILD PUBLISHING LONDON

This edition published 1985 by
Book Club Associates
by arrangement with Oxford University Press

© *Margaret Drabble and Oxford University Press, 1985*

Printed in Great Britain
by Richard Clay (The Chaucer Press), Ltd,
Bungay, Suffolk

PREFACE

In his introduction to the original *Oxford Companion to English Literature* (1932) Sir Paul Harvey stated that his volume would serve its purpose 'if it proves a useful companion to ordinary everyday readers of English literature', and such remains my hope of this new version. While the revision inevitably reflects the increasing specialization and professionalism of English studies, the chief virtue of a one-volume reference book of this nature must be that it can quickly, easily, and clearly satisfy the immediate curiosity of the common reader, and direct that reader, where appropriate, to further sources of information. There are now shelves of reference books (including many new *Companions*) that did not exist in Harvey's day, and there are occasions when they will supply answers that this volume can not, but this volume will remain, I hope, a starting point for some, and a comprehensive reply for many others.

Nevertheless, its scope is in some respects narrower than Harvey's. The decision having been made to keep the one-volume format, my first task was to decide what material to discard in order to make space for new entries and expansion of old ones. Ruthlessly, I resolved to drop most of Harvey's 'allusions commonly met with, or likely to be met with, in English literature', a field which Harvey conceded was infinitely expandable and highly contentious. So dollars and pieces of eight have gone, the Cinque Ports have gone, and so has the Doge of Venice, and many more items that may be found in Brewer's *Dictionary of Phrase and Fable*, which Harvey credits as the authority for many of his own entries. I have retained most of the entries on British and Irish mythology, but I have not even attempted to cover classical allusions—not because I assume everyone is familiar with them, but rather because they are so numerous that they can only be properly covered in a dictionary of classical mythology. It must, however, be acknowledged that fewer readers have the benefit of a classical education; the entries on classical authors have therefore been thoroughly revised and their links with and influences on English literature have been more strongly emphasized.

These, then, have been the major changes. I have in most other respects pursued the original policy of Harvey and his publishers, perhaps more closely than some would have done in my place: I have been highly conscious of the responsibility of revising a much-loved volume. This edition retains 'a list of English authors, literary works, and literary societies which have historical or present importance', and I have added to the list many past authors who have only recently received critical attention, and many modern authors born in or before 1939. Neither literary merit nor celebrity has been my only criterion. One or two writers famed for their lack of skill have been included (for example, William McGonagall and Amanda Ros now find a small place), and some who can only be considered obscure, but whose names nevertheless recur persistently through the network of literary history.

As in Harvey, the emphasis has been on primary information rather than on critical appreciation. Works and authors are described and characterized rather than judged, although some attempt has been made to place them in context, and to account for shifts in reputation and taste. The revised entry on the Metaphysical poets provides a classic example of recent change, but there are many other instances. On the other hand, some writers have maintained a remarkably steady reputation, and the coverage given to them has been little altered, although new bibliographical information has been added. Many of Harvey's plot summaries remain almost unchanged: they were brilliantly done in the first place, and many needed only the smallest adjustments. I now come to an area which has caused me some anxiety, and which deserves an explanation of its own—the question of Sir Walter Scott. Let me at once declare that the Scott entries are virtually unchanged, and that they are extensive. At various points I attempted to reduce them, and solicited help in reducing them, but all my efforts brought me to the same conclusion—that Harvey's Scott is so thorough, so scholarly, and so affectionate that it should stand more or less in its entirety. It will never be done again so well, and although Scott's popularity may have waned, his importance as a literary and historical figure remains enormous. It would have seemed a kind of vandalism to oust entries of such quality, and here they remain, a monument to Scott, to Harvey's admiration for Scott, and to the history of the novel.

I am highly conscious, as were my predecessors, that in choosing the names of the living for inclusion one is treading on dangerous ground, and I would like to make it clear that I have not been guided wholly by my own critical judgement or taste, but have deferred in many cases to the opinion either of the common reader or of the literary critic, with which I may not always have concurred. There are some names that have come into prominence too recently for me to take into consideration, and obviously there are also many writers born after 1939 who present themselves as candidates for any future revision. My choice of individual works for special notice or summary may well appear arbitrary, and indeed it is so, to some extent: there are occasions when I have given a plot summary of only one work by an author, hoping thereby to convey something of his or her distinctive quality, and not intending to imply it is the author's only major work. Consistency in coverage is an impossibility, and neither is the length of an entry an invariable guide to an author's importance. Some writers are easily described in a few phrases and represented by a few titles: others, not necessarily greater, have written more, and more variously, and require more space.

This volume does not contain only British authors and their works. It contains, like Harvey, clubs, coffee houses, literary societies, and a small selection of topographical references; it has entries on a limited number of printers, publishers, booksellers, and private presses. Authorship itself has not been narrowly defined: the reader will find here historians, critics, philosophers, scholars, and editors. There are entries on prizes, periodicals, newspapers, and literary agents. There are entries on non-literary figures famous in a literary context, from Penelope Rich to Ottoline Morrell. There are definitions of literary, artistic, and intellectual movements, from Acmeism to Vorticism, from Existentialism to the New Criticism, from Neoclassicism to Structuralism. Harvey, one suspects, did not much relish the task of defining movements, and with good reason: his entry on Realism was a classic of restraint. We have been more adventurous, and have thereby laid ourselves open to a good deal of ideological dispute, but in a good cause, it is hoped.

The coverage of foreign authors has been dictated largely by Harvey's own criterion; they are included 'as matter of allusion in English, not on any scale of merit which would satisfy students of those literatures'. A few have made their way on merit alone, but most have been treated in the context of English literature. In the entries for American authors, emphasis has been placed on Anglo-American connections and responses: the selection of contemporary American authors has been partly guided by British appraisals, which sometimes differ considerably from those current in the United States, although indisputably major figures have been included as a matter of course. There has been no attempt to provide comprehensive coverage of Commonwealth literature, although many individual new entries have been added. Titles have been given in English where it was felt that no purpose would be served (as with, for example, Russian) by including the original version: in other languages (e.g. French, German, and Italian) both the original version and a translation are given, except where a title is self-explanatory.

The volume also contains many new or radically different entries on artists and composers, seen in their relation to English literature. These, it is hoped, will not only be of use, but will also add to the interest and pleasure of those many readers who, as well as consulting reference books for information on particular points, also enjoy browsing from reference to reference.

In acknowledging my debts, I must begin with Sir Paul Harvey himself. My respect for his achievement has grown steadily, and I hope his admirers will not be too dismayed by the alterations I have made. I have always felt sustained by his original success, which gave me a solid framework on which to build and a sense that the task was, after all, finite and worth the doing. His work was most ably maintained and revised by Dorothy Eagle, who has been unfailingly helpful and generous to me. I have had the benefit of her advice and experience, and am most grateful to her for the trouble she has taken to help me: many of the additions dating from her revised editions have been carried over unaltered. My thanks are also due to those who advised and encouraged me at the very beginning: these include Professor Norman Davis, Professor John Carey, Dr Christopher Hill, Dr Roger Lonsdale, and P. N. Furbank, who managed to warn me of pitfalls and make constructive suggestions without making me lose my nerve.

My subsequent debts are manifold, and some are acknowledged in the list of contributors. I would like to thank all those who wrote to me with corrections and suggestions, many of which have been incorporated. I myself appealed for help to many people and institutions, and am particularly grateful to the staff of the British Library, the London Library, the Heath Library, Camden, and the Book Information Service of the National Book League. Christopher Hampton, K. M. Lea, Judith Landry, Harold Landry, Bob Gottlieb, Professor Pat Rogers, Professor John Vincent, Anthony Thwaite, Professor Claude Rawson, Professor Christopher Ricks, Salman Rushdie, Joan Winterkorn, Michael Schmidt, Barry Humphries, and Patrick Creagh are among those who have made valuable suggestions or endured my incessant questions. Subjects of entries have co-operated gallantly, and biographers have reduced two-volume works to a few hundred words at my request. Of my major contributors, I would like to offer particular thanks to Bernard O'Donoghue, who was responsible for the revision of all the Old and Middle English entries, and much else besides, and who responded to my appeals with the greatest courtesy and patience; and to Katherine Duncan-Jones and Henry Woudhuysen, who were jointly responsible for the entries covering the sixteenth century, and whose professionalism has been a help and an inspiration.

It is customary on these occasions to thank one's family, and mine here are more than formal. My sons Adam and Joseph and my daughter Rebecca responded nobly to my cries for help; they have worked as research assistants, chauffeurs, photocopy operators, and telephone answering machines, and I am very grateful to them all. I do not know how adequately to thank my husband Michael Holroyd, who married me and the *Companion* when it was half-way through its five-year-plan: the assistance he has given me has been invaluable, and I have made merciless use of his scholarship, his library, and his goodwill, all of which are remarkable.

Lastly, it is a great pleasure to thank my friend and assistant Jenny Stringer, who worked on the volume with me from start to finish, whose powers of organization saved me from wholesale confusion, and whose scrupulous attention to detail saved me and some of my contributors from many small (and not so small) errors. Her commitment to the task and enthusiasm for it at times exceeded even my own; without her I would at many points have despaired of reaching the end. I hope the volume will prove as great a source of interest to others as it has, over the years, to us.

Hampstead, London　　　　　　　　　　　　　　MARGARET DRABBLE
December 1984

CONTRIBUTORS

Rosemary Ashton (German), Jacques Berthoud, with Stephen Minta and Jack Dono-van (French), R. R. Bolgar (Classics), John Carey (Metaphysicals), Katherine Duncan-Jones (16th century), Barbara Garvin (Italian), Julian Graffy (Russian), Helen Langdon (Art), Bernard O'Donoghue (Old and Middle English), Michael Rose (Music), M. A. Stewart (18th-century philosophy), Sheila Sullivan (18th–19th-century topics), H. R. Woudhuysen (16th century).

Dawn Ades, Jonathan Barnes, John Batchelor, D. Berman, Alan Bold, F. Burns, Marilyn Butler, Humphrey Carpenter, Jeanne Clegg, Ursula Creagh, Hilary Dick-inson, P. Edwards, M. Erben, Penelope Fitzgerald, R. A. Foakes, V. Grosvenor Myer, P. S. Guptara, Alethea Hayter, L. Heyworth, R. V. Holdsworth, P. Holland, Richard Holmes, Ted Honderich, Michael Horovitz, J. D. Hunt, F. L. Huntley, P. Jones, Daniel Karlin, J. P. Kenyon, Mary Lago, Sarah Lawson, John Levitt, David Lodge, Philippa MacLiesh, Helen McNeill, P. Merchant, J. Milton, J. Moore, Brian Morris, R. Musgrave, W. Myers, Ira Nadel, Catherine Peters, Roy Porter, Lois Potter, Jocelyn Powell, Anthony Quinton, A. G. Rigg, R. Robbins, Geoffrey Robertson, M. Secrest, Roger Sharrock, R. D. Smith, Colin Smythe, Anthony Storr, Adam Swift, Jeremy Treglown, Stephen Wall, C. Webster, Stanley Wells, John Wilders, P. Wood.

The painting on the jacket, *A Lady Reading* by Gwen John, is reproduced by kind permission of Mr Ben John and Miss Sara John.

ABBREVIATIONS

a.	*ante*, before	ff.	and following
ad fin.	*ad finem*, near the end	*fl.*	*floruit*, flourished
ASPR	Anglo-Saxon Poetic Records	Fr.	French
b.	born	Gk.	Greek
BCP	Book of Common Prayer	Lat.	Latin
BM Cat.	British Museum Catalogue	l., ll.,	line, lines
Bk	Book	LXX	Septuagint
c.	*circa*, about	ME	Middle English
cent.	century	*MLR*	*Modern Language Review*
cf.	*confer*, compare	N. & Q.	*Notes and Queries*
CH	Companion of Honour	NT	New Testament
ch.	chapter	OE	Old English (Anglo-Saxon)
CHAL	Cambridge History of Ancient Literature	*OED*	*Oxford English Dictionary*
		OM	Order of Merit
CHEL	Cambridge History of English Literature	*op. cit.*	*opus citatum*, work quoted
		OS	Old Style dating, or calendar
d.	died	OT	Old Testament
DNB	*Dictionary of National Biography*	p., pp.	page, pages
EB	*Encyclopaedia Britannica*	*PEL*	*Periods of European Literature*
ed.	editor, or edited by	PMLA	Publications of the Modern Language Association of America
edn	edition		
EETS	Early English Texts Society	pron.	pronounced
OS	Original Series	Pt	Part
ES	Extra Series	*RES*	*Review of English Studies*
SS	Supplementary Series	*sc.*	*scilicet*, namely
	If no series is specified, the volume referred to is in the Original Series	STS	Scottish Texts Society
		s.v.	*sub verbo*, under the word
		TLS	*Times Literary Supplement*
EML	English Men of Letters	trans.	translation, or translated by
		vol.	volume

NOTE TO THE READER

NAMES in bold capital letters are those of real people; the headwords of all other entries are in bold upper and lower case: italics for the titles of novels, plays, and other full-length works; roman in quotation marks for individual short stories, poems, essays; ordinary roman type for fictional characters, terms, places, and so on. Entries are in simple letter-by-letter alphabetical order, with spaces, hyphens, and the definite or indefinite article ignored. This applies in all languages; but where a work written in English has a title in a foreign language, the article conditions its alphabetical ordering: 'L'Allegro' and 'La Belle Dame Sans Merci' are both listed under L, while *L'Avare* appears under *Avare, L'*. Names beginning with Mc or M' are ordered as though they were spelled Mac, St as though it were Saint, Dr as Doctor; but Mr and Mrs are ordered as they are spelled. An asterisk before a name, term, or title indicates that there is a separate entry for that subject, but it has been deemed unnecessary to place an asterisk before every occurrence of the name of Shakespeare. Where a person having his or her own entry is mentioned under another heading, the surname only is given unless there are entries for more than one person of the same name, when the initial or title is shown (*Auden, F. *Bacon, Dr *Johnson): the full name appears only where this is unavoidable in the interests of clarity (Richard *Graves, Robert *Graves). Where an author and a work are mentioned together, and each has an entry, only the title of the work carries an asterisk (Pope's *Dunciad*, Fielding's *Amelia*). Old spelling has been preferred, for both titles of works and quotations, except where its use might lead to confusion. For references to the works of Shakespeare the Alexander text has been used throughout.

A

Aaron's Rod, a novel by D. H. *Lawrence, published 1922.

The biblical Aaron was the brother of Moses, appointed priest by Jehovah, whose blossoming rod (Num. 17: 43–8) was a miraculous symbol of authority. In the novel Aaron Sisson, amateur flautist, forsakes his wife and his job as check-weighman at a colliery for a life of flute-playing, quest, and adventure in Bohemian and upper-class society. His flute is symbolically broken in the penultimate chapter as a result of a bomb explosion in Florence during political riots.

Aaron the Moor, a character in Shakespeare's *Titus Andronicus,* lover and accomplice of Tamora.

Abbey of Thelema, see THELEMA.

Abbey Theatre, Dublin, opened in 1904 with three one-act plays, two by W. B. *Yeats (*On Baile's Strand* and *Cathleen ni Houlihan*) and a comedy (*Spreading the News*) by Lady *Gregory. The theatre rapidly became a focus of the *Irish revival. In 1903 Miss A. E. *Horniman, a friend of Yeats from his London days, had been introduced by him to the Irish National Theatre Society, an amateur company led by F. J. and W. G. Fay, which had already produced several plays by contemporary Irish writers, including Yeats's *Cathleen* and G. *Russell's (Æ's) *Deirdre.* She decided to provide a permanent Dublin home for the Society (which had Yeats for its President) and took over the disused theatre of the Mechanics' Institute in Abbey Street (built on the site of a previous Theatre Royal), together with the old city morgue next door, and converted them into the Abbey Theatre, with Lady Gregory as holder of the patent. The company, led by the Fays, with Sarah Allgood as principal actress, turned professional in 1906, with Yeats, Lady Gregory, and J. M. *Synge as directors, and in 1907 successfully survived the riots provoked by Synge's *The Playboy of the Western World.* The Fays, who had become increasingly at loggerheads with Miss Horniman, Yeats, and the leading players, left in 1908. In 1909 Lady Gregory, as patentee, withstood strong pressure from the lord-lieutenant to withdraw *The Shewing-up of Blanco Posnet,* by G. B. *Shaw, before production; but the company staged it, almost uncut, knowing they might lose their patent. It was a great success and there was no more trouble with censorship.

Meanwhile Miss Horniman had become increasingly disenchanted with the company, and in 1910 did not renew her subsidy; however she offered the purchase of the theatre on generous terms, and Yeats and Lady Gregory became principal shareholders and managers. Over the years the early poetic dramas had been gradually replaced by more naturalistic prose works, written by *Colum, *Ervine, L. *Robinson, *O'Casey, and others. Robinson took over the management from Yeats in 1910 and with a short break continued until he became director in 1923. There were contentious but highly successful tours of Ireland, England, and the US.

After the First World War the Abbey's finances became perilous, although O'Casey's *Shadow of a Gunman* (1923), *Juno and the Paycock* (1924), and *The Plough and the Stars* (1926) brought some respite. In 1925 the Abbey received a grant from the new government of Eire, thus becoming the first state-subsidized theatre in the English-speaking world.

From the late 1930s more plays were performed in Gaelic, and actors were required to be bilingual. In 1951 the theatre was burned down, and the company played in the Queen's Theatre until the new Abbey opened in 1966.

ABBO OF FLEURY (?945–1004), a French theologian, author of the *Epitome de Vitis Romanorum Pontificum* and of lives of the saints. He was invited to England by *Oswald (bishop of Worcester and archbishop of York) to teach in his monastery of Ramsey; it was at the request of the monks of Ramsey, he tells us, that Abbo wrote his 'Life of St Edmund' which was the source for *Ælfric's famous sermon. Abbo became abbot of Fleury where he died; during his abbacy *Aristotle's *Categories* was commented on and his *Analytics* copied in Fleury.

Abbot, The, a novel by Sir W. *Scott, published 1820, a sequel to *The Monastery.*

The work is concerned with that period of the life of Mary Queen of Scots which she spent in imprisonment at Lochleven Castle, her escape, the rally of her supporters and their defeat at the battle of Langside, and her withdrawal across the border to England. With these historical events is woven the romantic story of Roland Graeme, or Roland Avenel, a spirited but hare-brained youth, over whose parentage hangs a certain mystery. After being brought up in the castle of Avenel as page to the Lady of Avenel, he is sent by the Regent Murray to act as page to Mary Stuart in her imprisonment, with directions to watch and report any attempt at escape. These directions he is prevented from carrying out by his own chivalrous loyalty, by the influence of his fanatical grandmother Magdalen Graeme, and by his love for Catherine Seyton, one of the queen's attendant ladies. Instead, he becomes an active agent in devising the queen's flight. The mystery of his birth is explained and he is found to be the heir of the house of Avenel. He is pardoned by the Regent and marries Catherine Seyton. The novel takes its title from the abbot of Kennaquhair, Edward Glendinning (Father Ambrose), brother of Sir Halbert Glendinning, the knight of Avenel (see MONASTERY).

Abbot of Misrule, see MISRULE, ABBOT OF.

Abbotsford, the name of Sir W. *Scott's property near Melrose on the Tweed, purchased in 1811.

Abbotsford Club, The, was founded in 1834 in memory of Sir W. *Scott, for the purpose of publishing materials bearing on the history or literature of any country dealt with in Scott's writings. It ceased its publications in 1865.

À BECKETT, Gilbert Abbott (1811–56), educated at Westminster School and called to the bar at Gray's Inn, was the editor of *Figaro in London* and on the original staff of *Punch. He was for many years a leader-writer on *The Times* and the *Morning Herald*, and was appointed a Metropolitan police magistrate in 1849. He wrote a large number of plays and humorous works, including a *Comic History of England* (1847–8), a *Comic History of Rome* (1852), and a *Comic Blackstone* (1846).

À BECKETT, Gilbert Arthur (1837–91), son of Gilbert Abbott *À Beckett, educated at Westminster School and Christ Church, Oxford, was, from 1879, like his father, a regular member of the staff of *Punch. He wrote, in collaboration with W. S. *Gilbert, the successful comedy *The Happy Land* (1873).

ABELARD, Peter (1079–1142), a native of Brittany, a brilliant disputant and lecturer at the schools of Ste Geneviève and Notre Dame in Paris, where *John of Salisbury was among his pupils. He was an advocate of rational theological enquiry, and his *Sic et Non* could be regarded as the first text in scholastic theology (see SCHOLASTICISM). He was primarily a dialectician rather than a theologian, though his theological views were declared heretical by the Council of Sens (1142) where he was vigorously opposed by St *Bernard. He was a student of Roscelin, who is noted as the first *Nominalist and against whose views Abelard

reacted. The pre-eminence of the University of Paris in the 12th cent. owes much to Abelard's popularity as a teacher. He fell in love with Héloïse, the niece of Fulbert, a canon of Notre Dame in whose house he lodged; she was a woman of learning and Abelard's pupil. Their love ended in a tragic separation and a famous correspondence. Héloïse died in 1163 and was buried in Abelard's tomb. Pope's poem *'Eloisa to Abelard' was published in 1717. See J. G. Sikes, *Peter Abailard* (1932).

ABERCROMBIE, Lascelles (1881–1938), began as a literary journalist in Liverpool, became successively lecturer in poetry at Liverpool University (1919–22), professor of poetry at Leeds (1922–9), and reader in English at Oxford. His first volume of verse, *Interludes in Poems*, appeared in 1908 and further volumes followed, including his collected *Poems* (1930) and the verse play *The Sale of St Thomas* (1931). Abercrombie contributed to *Georgian Poetry* and several of his verse plays appeared in *New Numbers*; R. *Brooke admired him as a lyric and dramatic poet of daring. His critical works included *Thomas Hardy* (1912) and *Principles of Literary Criticism* (1932). He was an eminent man of letters, but his work has received little serious attention in recent years.

Abessa, in Spenser's *Faerie Queene*, i. iii, the 'daughter of *Corceca* slow' (blindness of heart), and the personification of superstition.

Abigail, in 1 Sam. 25, the wife of Nabal and subsequently of David. The name came to signify a waiting-woman, from the name of the 'waiting gentlewoman' in *The Scornful Lady* by *Beaumont and Fletcher, so called possibly in allusion to the expression 'thine handmaid', so frequently applied to herself by the biblical Abigail.

Abora, Mount, in Coleridge's *'Kubla Khan', is perhaps to be identified with *Milton's Mt. Amara. See J. L. *Lowes, *The Road to Xanadu* (1927), pp. 374–5.

'Abou Ben Adhem', a poem by L. *Hunt.

Absalom and Achitophel, a poem by *Dryden, published 1681.

An allegory based on 2 Sam. 13–19, it deals with certain aspects of the Exclusion crisis, notably the intrigues of the earl of Shaftesbury and the ambition of the duke of Monmouth to replace James duke of York as Charles II's heir. Various public figures are represented under biblical names, notably Monmouth (Absalom), *Shaftesbury (Achitophel), the duke of *Buckingham (Zimri), Charles II (David), *Oates (Corah), and Slingsby Bethel, sheriff of London (Shimei). The poem concludes with a long speech by David vigorously but paradoxically affirming royalist principles, and asserting his determination to govern ruthlessly if he cannot do so mercifully.

In 1682 a second part appeared, mainly written by N. *Tate. However it contains 200 lines by Dryden, in which he attacks two literary and political enemies, *Shadwell as Og and *Settle as Doeg.

ABSE, Dannie (Daniel) (1923–), doctor and poet, born in Cardiff of a Welsh–Jewish family. His first volume of poetry, *After Every Green Thing* (1949), was followed by many others, including *Tenants of the House, Poems 1951–1956* (1957) and *Collected Poems 1948–1976* (1977); in a foreword to the latter he notes that his poems are increasingly 'rooted in actual experience', both domestic and professional. He has also published novels (one about a medical student), plays, and a volume of autobiography, *A Poet in the Family* (1974).

Absentee, The, a novel by M. *Edgeworth, first published 1812 in *Tales of Fashionable Life*.

This novel of (largely) Irish life was first written as a play, refused by *Sheridan, then turned into a novel. A swift, vivacious story, the greater part of which is in conversation, it begins with the extravagant London life of the absentee Irish landlord Lord Clonbrony and his ambitious, worldly wife. The author shows Lady Clonbrony's attempts to buy her way into high society, her contempt for her Irish origins, and her treatment of her son, Lord Colambre, who refuses to marry the heiress she provides for him. A sensible and distinguished young man, he gradually finds himself falling in love with his cousin Grace, and becomes increasingly appalled at his father's debts. He travels incognito to Ireland to visit the family estates and to see if his mother's dislike of Irish life is justified. Calling himself Evans, he visits the first of his father's estates, where he witnesses the dismissal, through a letter from Clonbrony, of the humane and honest agent Burke, who has been in much trouble with his master for not extorting sufficient income from the tenants and the land. The next estate is managed by the brothers Garraghty. Here the castle and church are half-ruined, the roads are rutted, the land is ill-farmed, and the tenants are treated with callous indifference; but Lord Clonbrony is satisfied because (in spite of the Garraghtys' embezzlement) money is forthcoming. Colambre discovers that both his mother and his cousin Grace are remembered with affection by the people of the estates. He returns to London and tells his father that he will himself pay off the debts, on condition that the Garraghtys are dismissed and the Clonbrony family returns to live on its Irish estates. After the sorting out of various troubles, he and Grace become engaged, his mother resigns herself to her return, and the family leave London to live in Ireland.

Absolute, Sir Anthony, and his son Captain Absolute, characters in Sheridan's *The Rivals*.

Absurd, Theatre of the, a term used to characterize the work of a number of European and American dramatists of the 1950s and early 1960s. As the term suggests, the function of such theatre is to give dramatic expression to the philosophical notion of the 'absurd', a notion that had received widespread diffusion following the publication of *Camus's essay *Le Mythe de Sisyphe* in 1942. To define the world as absurd is to recognize its fundamentally mysterious and indecipherable nature, and this recognition is frequently associated with feelings of loss, purposelessness, and bewilderment. To such feelings, the Theatre of the Absurd gives ample expression, often leaving the observer baffled in the face of disjointed, meaningless, or repetitious dialogues, incomprehensible behaviour, and plots which deny all notion of logical or 'realistic' development. But the recognition of the absurd nature of human existence also provided dramatists with a rich source of comedy, well illustrated in two early absurd plays, Ionesco's *La Cantatrice chauve*, written in 1948 (English trans., *The Bald Prima Donna*, 1958), and *Beckett's *En attendant Godot* (1952; trans. by the author, *Waiting for Godot*, 1954, subtitled 'A Tragicomedy in Two Acts'). The Theatre of the Absurd drew significantly on popular traditions of entertainment, on mime, acrobatics, and circus clowning, and, by seeking to redefine the legitimate concerns of 'serious' theatre, played an important role in extending the range of post-war drama. Amongst the dramatists associated with the Theatre of the Absurd are Arthur Adamov (1908–70), *Albee, Beckett, Camus, *Genet, Eugène Ionesco (1912–), Alfred Jarry (1873–1907), *Pinter, and Boris Vian (1920–59).

Académie française, a French literary academy, established by *Richelieu in 1634 to regulate and maintain the standards of the French language. One of its functions is the compilation and revision of a French dictionary, the first edition of which appeared in 1694 and the eighth in 1932–5. The Académie has, throughout its history, exercised a considerable influence on the course of French intellectual life.

Academy, The, a periodical founded in 1869 as 'a monthly record of literature, learning, science, and art' by a young Oxford don, Charles Edward Cutts Birch Appleton (1841–79), who edited it until his death, converting it in 1871 into a fortnightly and in 1874 into a weekly review. It included M. *Arnold, T. H. *Huxley, M. *Pattison, and the classical scholar John Conington (1825–69) among its early contributors. In 1896 it came under the control of Pearl Craigie ('J. O. *Hobbes'); she employed as editor C. Lewis Hind, who gave it a more popular colouring. After various vicissitudes and changes of title the *Academy* disappeared in the 1920s.

Academy, British, see BRITISH ACADEMY.

ACHEBE, Chinua (1930–), author, born and educated in Nigeria, where his father taught in a school under the Church Missionary Society. One of the most highly regarded of African writers in English, Achebe's reputation rests largely on his first four novels, which can be seen as a sequence re-creating Africa's journey from tradition to modernity. *Things Fall Apart* (1958) seems to derive from W. B. *Yeats its vision of history as well as its title; it was followed by *No Longer at Ease* (1960); *Arrow of God* (1964), a portrayal of traditional society at the time of its first confrontation with European society (a traditional society re-created in Achebe's novels by the use of Ibo legend and proverb); and *A Man of the People* (1966), which breaks new ground. Bitterness and disillusion lie just beneath the sparkling satiric surface, and the novel provides further evidence of Achebe's mastery of a wide range of language, from the English of Ibo-speakers and pidgin, to various levels of formal English.

Achitophel, name for the earl of *Shaftesbury in Dryden's *Absalom and Achitophel*.

ACKERLEY, J(oseph) R(andolph) (1896–1967), author, and for many years (1935–59) literary editor of *The Listener*, to which he attracted work from such distinguished contributors as E. M. *Forster and *Isherwood. *Hindoo Holiday* (1932) is based on his experiences as private secretary to an Indian maharajah; *My Dog Tulip* (1956) and his novel *We Think the World of You* (1960) both describe his intense relationship with his Alsatian dog. *My Father and Myself* (1968) is an account of his discovery of his apparently respectable father's extraordinary double life, the other side of which was described by Ackerley's half-sister Diana Petre in *The Secret Garden of Roger Ackerley* (1975); see also *My Sister and Myself: The Diaries of J. R. Ackerley* (1982), ed. F. *King.

ACKERMANN, Rudolph (1764–1834), German lithographer who settled in London and opened a print shop in the Strand in 1795. He played a major role in establishing lithography as a fine art, and published many handsome coloured-plate books with lithographs, hand-coloured aquatints, etc., in association with Prout, A. C. Pugin, *Rowlandson, and other artists. His publications include the *Repository of Arts, Literature, Fashions* etc. (1809–28); *The Microcosm of London* (3 vols, 1808–11), an antiquarian and topographical work by W. *Combe; and the gift-book annual *Forget-me-not*, of which the first issue appeared in 1825. Combe's *The Tour of Dr Syntax in search of the Picturesque* first appeared as 'The Schoolmaster's Tour' in Ackermann's *Poetical Magazine* (1809–11).

ACKLAND, Rodney (1908–), playwright, greatly admired but considered insufficiently frivolous by West End managements in the 1930s; he has been described as 'the English Chekhov', the only playwright of his generation to see how *Chekhov's revolutionary dramatic technique might be joined to the robust native tradition of mixing tragedy with comedy. His best early plays—*Strange Orchestra* (1931), *After October* (1936)—inhabit a world which recalls the seedy Bohemian gentility of the novels of J. *Rhys. *Birthday* (1934) is a study of hypocrisy and repression at work inside a comfortably respectable middle-class family. *The Dark River* (1941) is a grander and more sombre portrait of England in the shadow of the Second World War.

Acmeism, a school of Russian poetry, led by *Gumilev and Sergei Gorodetsky, and including among its members *Akhmatova and *Mandelstam. They gathered in a group called The Poets' Guild, organized by Gumilev in Oct. 1911. Their major concerns were the depiction of the concrete world of everyday reality with brevity and clarity and the precise and logical use of the poetic word. They declared themselves opposed to Symbolist mysticism and vagueness, and announced their forerunners as Shakespeare, *Villon, *Rabelais, and *Gautier.

Acrasia, in Spenser's *Faerie Queene*, II. xii, typifies Intemperance. She is captured and bound by Sir *Guyon, and her *Bower of Bliss destroyed.

Acres, Bob, a character in Sheridan's *The Rivals*.

Actes and Monuments *of these latter perillous dayes, touching matters of the Church*, popularly known as the *Book of Martyrs*, by *Foxe, first published in Latin at Strasburg 1559, printed in English 1563.

This enormous work, said to be twice the length of Gibbon's *Decline and Fall*, is a history of the Christian Church from the earliest times, with special reference to the sufferings of the Christian martyrs of all ages, but more particularly of the Protestant martyrs of Mary's reign. The book is, in fact, a violent indictment of 'the persecutors of God's truth, commonly called papists'. The author is credulous in his acceptance of stories of martyrdom and partisan in their selection. The work is written in a simple, homely style and enlivened by vivid dialogues between the persecutors and their victims. The title of the Latin version is *Rerum in ecclesia gestarum . . . maximarumque per Europam persecutionum . . . commentarii.*

Action française, L', an extreme right-wing political group which flourished in France between 1900 and 1940, monarchist, anti-Semitic, and Roman Catholic. The newspaper *L'Action française*, its organ, was founded and edited by two literary journalists and polemical writers, Charles Maurras (1868–1952) and Léon Daudet (1867–1942), a son of Alphonse *Daudet.

ACTON, Sir Harold Mario Mitchell (1904–), writer and aesthete, educated at Eton and Christ Church, Oxford, spent some years in the 1930s in Peking, and wrote several works on Chinese theatre and poetry. He later returned to settle at his family home at La Pietra, near Florence. He published several volumes of poems, including *Aquarium* (1923) and *This Chaos* (1930); fiction, which includes a novel set in Peking, *Peonies and Ponies* (1941), and *Tit for Tat and other tales* (1972, short stories); and historical studies, which include *The Last Medici* (1932) and *The Bourbons of Naples* (1957). He also published two volumes of autobiography, *Memoirs of an Aesthete* (1948) and *More Memoirs* (1970).

ACTON, Sir John Emerich Edward Dalberg, first Baron Acton (1834–1902), was born at Naples. His father was of a long-established Shropshire Roman Catholic family, his mother a German aristocrat; on his father's death, when John was three years old, she married Lord Leveson. He was thus brought up in a well-connected, wealthy, cosmopolitan world and was educated at Paris, Oscott, and Edinburgh. He studied history and criticism at Munich under Döllinger from 1848 to 1854, and with him visited Italy in 1857. He was Whig MP for Carlow (1859–65) and formed a friendship with *Gladstone. In the *Rambler* (converted under his direction to the *Home and Foreign Review*) he advocated Döllinger's proposed re-union of Christendom, but stopped the *Review* on the threat of a papal veto. He was strenuous in his opposition to the definition by the Catholic Church of the dogma of papal infallibility, and published his views in his *Letters from Rome on the Council* (1870). In 1874, in letters to *The Times*, he criticized Gladstone's pamphlet on 'The Vatican Decrees'. His literary activity was great, and took the form of contributions to the *North British Review*, the *Quarterly Review*, and the *English Historical Review* (which he helped to found), besides lectures and addresses. Lord Acton was appointed Regius professor of modern history at Cambridge in 1895, on which occasion he delivered a remarkable inaugural lecture on the study of history (reprinted in *Lectures on Modern History*, 1906). One of his principal works was the planning of the *Cambridge Modern History* (1899–1912).

ACTON BELL, see BRONTË, A.

Adam, the name given to a 12th-cent. Anglo-Norman play (also called the *Jeu d'Adam* and the *Mystère d'Adam*) in octosyllabics, surviving in one 13th-cent. manuscript from Tours. There are three scenes: the Fall and expulsion of Adam and Eve from Paradise; Cain and Abel; and a Prophets' Play (*Ordo Prophetarum*). It is generally thought that it was written in England *c.*1140 (though Bédier doubted it), and it is regarded as important for the evolution of the medieval *Mystery Plays in England. Although it contains Latin as well as the vernacular, and is enacted with rudimentary staging at the church door, the play is not good evidence for the evolution from liturgical to profane staging, displaying as it does a theatrical sophistication far beyond most of the later Mystery Plays. There is an English edition, ed. Paul Studer (1918); see also M. D. Legge, *Anglo-Norman Literature and its Background* (1963), pp. 311–21.

Adam, in Shakespeare's *As You Like It*, the faithful old servant who accompanies Orlando in exile.

Adamastor, (1) in *The Lusiads* (v. li) of *Camoëns, the spirit of the Cape of Storms (the Cape of Good Hope), who appears to Vasco Da *Gama and threatens all who dare venture into his seas; (2) the title of a poem by R. *Campbell.

Adam Bede, a novel by G. *Eliot, published 1859.

The plot was suggested by a story told to George Eliot by her Methodist aunt Elizabeth Evans of a confession of child-murder made to her by a girl in prison. The action takes place at the close of the 18th cent. Hetty Sorrel, pretty, vain, and self-centred, is the niece of the genial farmer Martin Poyser of Hall Farm. She is loved by Adam Bede, the village carpenter, a young man of dignity and character, but is deluded by the attentions of the young squire, Arthur Donnithorne, and is seduced by him, in spite of Adam's efforts to save her. Arthur breaks off relations with her, and Hetty, broken-hearted, agrees to marry Adam. But before the marriage she discovers she is pregnant, flies from home to seek Arthur, fails to find him, is arrested and convicted of infanticide, and saved from the gallows at the last moment, her sentence commuted to transportation through Arthur's intervention. In prison she is comforted by her cousin Dinah Morris, a Methodist preacher, whose strong, serious, and calm nature is contrasted with hers throughout the novel. In the last chapters, Adam discovers that Dinah loves him; his brother Seth, who had long and hopelessly loved Dinah, resigns to him with a fine unselfishness.

The novel was immediately acclaimed for its realism, for its picturesque portrayal of rural life, and for its humour; Mrs Poyser was greeted as a comic creation on the level of *Dickens's Sam Weller and Mrs Gamp. Some critics objected to its insistence on the 'startling horrors of rustic reality' (*Saturday Review) and its 'obstetric' details. H. *James in 1866 found Hetty Sorrel 'the most successful' of George Eliot's female figures.

Adam Bell, Clym of the Clough (or Cleugh), and William of Cloudesley, three noted outlaws, as famous for their skill in archery in Northern England as *Robin Hood and his fellows in the Midlands. They lived in the forest of Engelwood, not far from Carlisle, and are supposed to have been contemporary with Robin Hood's father. Clym of the Clough is mentioned in Jonson's *The Alchemist, I. ii; and in D'Avenant's *The Wits, II. i. There are ballads on the three outlaws in Percy's *Reliques (Adam Bell) and in *Child's collection. In these, William of Cloudesley, after having been captured by treachery, is rescued by his comrades. They surrender themselves to the king and are pardoned on William's shooting an apple placed on his little son's head.

Adam International Review, an irregular periodical of literature and the arts edited by Miron Grindea, published originally in Bucharest, and in England since 1941 (No. 152). Contributors have included *Auden, T. S. *Eliot, E. *Sitwell, R. *Graves, and many major European figures. Nos. 387–400 (1977) were devoted to a celebration of the *London Library.

ADAMOV, Arthur, see ABSURD, THEATRE OF THE.

Adams, Parson Abraham, a character in Fielding's *Joseph Andrews.

ADAMS, Henry Brooks (1838–1918), American man of letters, and grandson and great-grandson of presidents of the United States. He was born and brought up in Boston and educated at Harvard, and during the Civil War was in England, where his father Charles Francis Adams (1807–86) was minister. On his return he taught history at Harvard, edited the *North American Review, and, after moving to Washington, published two novels, Democracy (1880, anonymously) and Esther (1884, as 'Frances Snow Compton'). His ambitious History of the United States During the Administrations of Thomas Jefferson and James Madison appeared in 9 vols, 1889–91. He subsequently travelled widely in Europe; his Mont-Saint-Michel and Chartres (1904) is an interpretation of the spiritual unity of the 13th-cent. mind, which led to his autobiography, The Education of Henry Adams (1907), which describes the multiplicity of the 20th-cent. mind. In his Preface, he invokes the names of *Rousseau and *Franklin as predecessors in the field of autobiography, and proceeds (speaking of himself in the third person) to analyse the failures of his formal edu-

cation (which he describes as not only useless but harmful), the complexity of the 'multiverse' we now inhabit, and the predicament of modern man in an increasingly technological world. In Chapter XXV, 'The Dynamo and the Virgin', he contrasts the spiritual force that built Chartres with the dynamo: 'He began to feel the forty-foot dynamos as a moral force, much as the early Christians had felt the Cross . . .', and proceeds, in the final chapters, to define his own 'Dynamic Theory of History' and the acceleration of scientific progress. There are also interesting accounts of his residence in England, and of his 'diplomatic education' in the circle of Palmerston, Lord J. *Russell, and *Gladstone; and a lively description of an encounter (through his friend *Milnes) with *Swinburne, whom he likened to 'a tropical bird, high-crested, long-beaked, quick-moving . . . a crimson macaw among owls'.

ADAMS, Sarah Flower (1805–48), is remembered as a writer of hymns, including 'Nearer, my God, to Thee'. She also wrote Vivia Perpetua, a dramatic poem (1841).

ADCOCK, (Kareen) Fleur (1934–), poet, born in New Zealand, and educated partly in England, where she settled in 1963. Her volumes of poetry include The Eye of the Hurricane (1964), High Tide in the Garden (1971), The Inner Harbour (1979), and Selected Poems (1983). Predominantly ironic and domestic in tone, she suggests wider horizons through her evocations of travel and of varied landscapes. She edited the Oxford Book of Contemporary New Zealand Poetry (1983).

ADDISON, Joseph (1672–1719), the son of a dean of Lichfield, was educated at the Charterhouse with *Steele and at The Queen's College, Oxford, and Magdalen, of which he became a fellow. He was a distinguished classical scholar and attracted the attention of *Dryden by his Latin poems. He travelled on the Continent from 1699 to 1703, and his Dialogues upon the Usefulness of Ancient Medals (published posthumously) were probably written about this time. In 1705 he published The Campaign, a poem in heroic couplets in celebration of the victory of Blenheim. He was appointed undersecretary of state in 1706, and was MP from 1708 till his death. In 1709 he went to Ireland as chief secretary to Lord Wharton, the lord-lieutenant. He formed a close friendship with *Swift, Steele, and other writers and was a prominent member of the *Kit-Kat Club. Addison lost office on the fall of the Whigs in 1711. Between 1709 and 1711 he contributed a number of papers to Steele's *Tatler and joined with him in the production of *The Spectator in 1711–12. His *neo-classical tragedy *Cato was produced with much success in 1713, and during the same year he contributed to Steele's periodical *The Guardian and during 1714 to the revived Spectator. His prose comedy The Drummer (1715) proved a failure. On the return of the Whigs to power, Addison was again appointed chief secretary for Ireland, and started his political newspaper the Freeholder (1715–16). In 1716 he became a lord commissioner of trade, and married the countess of Warwick; the marriage was rumoured to be unsuccessful. In 1718 he retired from office with a pension of £1,500. His last year was marked by increasing tension in his friendship with Steele, as several of his papers in the Old Whig bear witness. Addison was buried in Westminster Abbey, and lamented in an elegy by *Tickell. He was satirized by Pope in the character of *'Atticus'.

Addison's prose was acclaimed by Dr *Johnson in his Life (1781) as 'the model of the middle style; on grave subjects not formal, on light occasions not groveling . . .', and Addison himself said, 'I shall be ambitious to have it said of me, that I have brought philosophy out of closets and libraries, schools and colleges, to dwell in clubs and assemblies, at tea-tables and coffee-houses.' He admired *Locke and did much to popularize his ideas. He attacked the coarseness of *Restoration literature, and introduced new, essentially middle-class, standards of taste and judgement; Bonamy Dobrée described him as 'The First Victorian'. One of his most original and influential contributions to the history of literary taste was his reassessment of the popular ballad, previously neglected as a form, in essays in the Spectator on *Chevy Chase and *The Children in the Wood.

Addison of the North, The, see MACKENZIE, H.

Adelphi, The, started in 1923 as a monthly journal under the editorship of J. M. *Murry, intended as a mouthpiece for D. H. *Lawrence and himself. On the verge of folding in 1927, it was resumed (with financial aid from readers) as The New Adelphi, but as a quarterly. Murry's editorship ended with a D. H. Lawrence memorial number in 1930, and the periodical was taken over by Max Plowman and Richard Rees, under the name The Adelphi, incorporating The New Adelphi, which ran until 1955. Contributors to the three series include W. B. *Yeats, T. S. *Eliot, A. *Bennett, H. G. *Wells, *Day-Lewis, *Orwell, and *Auden.

Admirable Crichton, The, see CRICHTON.

'Admiral Hosier's Ghost', see GLOVER, R.

ADOMNAN, St (c.625–704), abbot of Iona from 679, who *Bede says was the author of a work on 'The Holy Places' (Ecclesiastical History, v. 15, 21), and who is also credited with writing an extant Life of St *Columba.

Adonais, an elegy on the death of *Keats, by P. B. *Shelley written at Pisa, published 1821.

Composed in 55 Spenserian stanzas, the poem was inspired partly by the Greek elegies of *Bion and Moscus (both of which Shelley had translated) and partly by Milton's *Lycidas. Keats is lamented under the name of Adonais, the Greek god of beauty and fertility, together with other poets who had died young, such as *Chatterton, *Sidney, and *Lucan. His deathbed is attended by various figures, both allegorical and contemporary, including *Byron 'the Pilgrim of Eternity' (st. 30). Shelley, the atheist, accepts the physical facts of death, but insists on some form of Neoplatonic resurrection in the eternal Beauty of the universe, 'a portion of the loveliness | Which once he made more lovely' (st. 43). The style is deliberately grand and marmoreal—'a highly wrought piece of art'—and lacks intimacy. Yet Shelley strongly identified himself with Keats's sufferings, and in his Preface he attacks the Tory reviewers with a pen 'dipped in consuming fire'. The poem ends with astonishing clairvoyance: 'my spirit's bark is driven | Far from the shore . . .'

Adriana, in Shakespeare's *The Comedy of Errors, the jealous wife of Antipholus of Ephesus.

Adriano de Armado, see ARMADO.

Advancement of Learning, The, a philosophical treatise by F. *Bacon, published 1605, which, unlike most of Bacon's works, appeared in English, not Latin. Its two books are plausibly dated by *Spedding to 1603 and 1605 respectively.

The first book consists of a panegyric on the dignity and profitability of learning, and a defence of it against its various detractors. Bacon's criticisms of the fantastical learning of magicians, alchemists, and astrologers, of the contentious learning of the schoolmen, and of the delicate learning of the humanists anticipate his later analysis in the *Novum Organum. The second book is a highly elaborate survey and classification of the various kinds of learning, based on the relation of the three main parts of learning—history, poetry, and philosophy—to the three faculties of memory, imagination, and reason. After publishing the Novum Organum in 1620, Bacon prepared a revised and considerably expanded Latin translation of the Advancement, which was published in 1623 under the title De Dignitate et Augmentis Scientarum.

Adventurer, The, see HAWKESWORTH, J.

Adventures of a Younger Son, The, an autobiographical novel by E. J. *Trelawny, published 1831.

The work, which is part autobiography and part fiction, tells the story of the life of a handsome, buccaneering youth, a lawless daredevil, warped in youth by the harshness of his father, who deserts from the navy and takes to a life of wandering, during which he becomes involved in many wild escapades and desperate ventures, all narrated with freshness and vigour. Episodes involving *Shelley and *Byron are of particular biographical interest.

Adventures of Master F.J., The, by G. *Gascoigne, see F.J.

Adventures of Philip, The, the last complete novel by *Thackeray, published in the *Cornhill Magazine 1861–2.

The story is told by Arthur Pendennis, now a middle-aged married man. His young friend Philip is the son of a fashionable doctor, George Firmin, who, as George Brandon, was the seducer of Caroline Gann in *A Shabby Genteel Story. After abandoning Caroline, Firmin ran away with an heiress, Philip's mother, now dead. Firmin is being blackmailed by the disreputable parson Tufton Hunt, who performed the mock marriage ceremony with Caroline Gann and threatens to prove that the marriage was in fact valid. Caroline, calling herself Mrs Brandon, and known affectionately as 'the little Sister', is a nurse who has tended Philip through an attack of fever, and now looks on him as her own son. She refuses to give the evidence which will disinherit him. However Dr Firmin, having lost his own money and Philip's fortune, absconds to America, and Philip's cousin Agnes, daughter of a pretentious toady, Talbot Twysden, breaks off her engagement to Philip. While visiting Pendennis and his family in Boulogne, Philip comes across General Baynes, co-trustee with Dr Firmin of Philip's inheritance. Knowing that Baynes will be ruined by any financial claim on him, Philip does not pursue his legal rights. He falls in love with Baynes's daughter, Charlotte, and marries her in spite of her mother's fierce opposition. Philip is struggling to make a living as a journalist, and the young couple have very little to live on. Matters are not made easier by Philip's impetuous character and Charlotte's extravagance. However a happy ending is achieved through the device of a suddenly rediscovered will, made by Lord Ringwood, Philip's great-uncle. Philip, the only one of the haughty and capricious old man's relatives never to toady to him, has been left a large legacy.

Advocates' Library, now National Library of Scotland, see LIBRARIES.

Æ, see RUSSELL, G. W.

Aeglamour, (1) the *'Sad Shepherd' in Jonson's drama of that name; (2) a character in Shakespeare's *The Two Gentlemen of Verona.

Aeglogue, see ECLOGUE.

ÆLFRIC (c.955–c.1010), was a monk of Winchester (where he was a pupil of *Æthelwold),

Cerne Abbas, and Eynsham near Oxford where he was abbot. His chief works are the Catholic Homilies (990–2), largely drawn from the Church Fathers, and the Lives of the Saints (993–8), a series of sermons also mostly translated from Latin, employing skilfully the idiom of English and the alliteration and metrical organization of Old English poetry. Several other English works of his survive, all with an educational purpose; these include his Latin Grammar (his most popular work in the Middle Ages, judging by the number of manuscripts and by his being called 'Grammaticus' in the 17th and 18th cents); his Colloquy between a teacher and pupil on one side and various representatives of walks of life on the other: a ploughman, a shepherd, a hunter, and so on; and a translation of the Heptateuch, the first seven books of the Bible. Ælfric is the most prominent known figure in Old English literature and the greatest prose writer of his time; he is celebrated not only for his stylistic excellence but also for his educational principles and the breadth of his learning as a product of the 10th-cent. Benedictine Revival in England.

Catholic Homilies, Series 1, ed. N. Eliason and P. Clemoes (1966); Homilies of Ælfric: a Supplementary Collection, ed. J. C. Pope (EETS OS 259 and 260, 1967 and 1968); Ælfric's Catholic Homilies, Series 2. Text, ed. M. Godden (EETS SS 5, 1979).

ÆLFTHRYTH (Elfrida) (c.945–c.1000), the daughter of Ordgar, ealdorman of Devon, the second wife of King Edgar and the mother of Ethelred the Unready. She was said to have caused the death of her stepson Edward the Martyr, according to a story that first circulated in the late 11th cent. but for which there seems little evidence.

Ælla, an interlude or tragedy by *Chatterton, written in the winter of 1768–9, published 1777. Ælla, Chatterton's major fictitious character (with no historical basis) was introduced first in 'Songe toe Ella'; in Ælla he appears as Saxon 'warde' of Bristol Castle, newly married to Birtha, whose wedding celebrations are interrupted by news that the Danes have landed, and who is driven to a tragic death by the plotting of Celmonde, his rival in love. The piece is composed mainly in ten-lined stanzas, handled with considerable assurance and virtuosity, and contains one of Chatterton's most admired passages, the song of the minstrels beginning 'O! synge untoe mie roundelaie, | O! droppe the brynie teare wythe mee' (l. 961 ff.).

AENEAS SILVIUS PICCOLOMINI, see PICCOLOMINI, A. S.

Aeneid, The, see VIRGIL.

AESCHYLUS (525–456 BC), the earliest of the three great Athenian tragic poets. He has some claim to be regarded as an inventor of the genre, since, where there had previously been the chorus and only one actor, he introduced a second actor and subordinated choral song to the dialogue. He is noted for the scope and grandeur of his conceptions and style, but only seven of his many plays have survived, three of which form the famous trilogy the *Oresteia (Agamemnon, Choephoroe, Eumenides), which describes the murder of Agamemnon by his wife and his son's subsequent vengeance. Aeschylus was hardly known in England before T. *Stanley's edition of the plays in 1663. Milton gave some Aeschylean traits to *Samson Agonistes (1671) and in the next century the primitivists John Brown (1725) and William Duff (1770) praised Aeschylus' 'irregular greatness, wildness and enthusiasm'; but his true popularity dates from the 19th cent. and centres initially on the play Prometheus Bound. *Byron's 'Prometheus' (1816) was followed by Shelley's *Prometheus Unbound (1820), S. T. *Coleridge's essay On the Prometheus of Aeschylus (1825), and a translation of the play (1833) by Elizabeth Barrett (*Browning). Interest in the great cosmic rebel was a feature of the *Romantic Movement, but in the second half of the century there was only R. *Browning's outline of the legend in 'With Gerard de Lairesse' (1887) and *Bridges's Prometheus the Firegiver (1883). From *Landor on attention shifted rather to the Oresteia and has stayed there in the 20th cent., resulting in *O'Neill's Mourning becomes Electra (1930), a recasting of the Oresteia in terms suggested by Freudian psychology, and, less obviously, T. S. *Eliot's The Family Reunion (1939). See also Browning's *The Agamemnon of Aeschylus.

AESOP (6th cent. BC), to whom tradition attributes the authorship of the whole stock of Greek fables, is probably a legendary figure. The fables were orally transmitted for the most part, but some were put into verse by Babrius (3rd cent. AD), while some were translated into Latin by Phaedrus (1st cent. AD) and Avianus (? 4th cent. AD). They became known to the West in the Renaissance through the 14th-cent. prose version compiled by the Byzantine scholar Maximus Planudes. *Erasmus produced a Latin edition in 1513 which was then widely used in schools. Richard *Bentley's attack on the antiquity of the 'Aesopian' fables in his Dissertations (1697, 1699) was one of the notable contributions to the controversy satirized in Swift's *The Battle of the Books.

Aesthetic Movement, a movement which blossomed during the 1880s, heavily influenced by the *Pre-Raphaelites, *Ruskin, and *Pater, in which the adoption of sentimental archaism as the ideal of beauty was carried to extravagant lengths and often accompanied by affectation of speech and manner and eccentricity of dress. It and its followers (e.g. *Wilde) were much ridiculed in *Punch, in *Gilbert and Sullivan's Patience (1881), etc. See also ART FOR ART'S SAKE and GROSVENOR GALLERY.

ÆTHELWOLD, St (?908–84), born at Winchester, entered the monastery of Glastonbury, of which *Dunstan was abbot, and became dean there. He subsequently re-established a monastic house at Abingdon, introducing the strict Benedictine Rule from Fleury, and he was appointed bishop of Winchester (963) after Edgar became king of England and Dunstan archbishop of Canterbury (960). He co-operated with Dunstan and *Oswald in the Benedictine Reforms of his century, expelling the secular clergy from Winchester, Chertsey, Milton, and Ely, and replacing them with monks. He rebuilt the church at Peterborough and built a new cathedral at Winchester. He was an important figure too in the revival of learning, as his pupil *Ælfric testifies; most significantly, he translated the Rule of St Benedict (c.960), and wrote the Regularis Concordia, the code of the new English rule in the 10th-cent. Revival.

Aethiopica, a Greek romance by the 3rd-cent. AD Syrian Heliodorus of Emesa, displays the common characteristics of the genre in an extreme form: the hero and heroine are parted, and there is the usual emphasis on travel through strange lands as they seek each other and on the maintenance of chastity in the face of temptations and dangers. As often happens the intercalated stories have a 'realistic' character depicting Greek middle-class life, in sharp contrast to the romantic adventures that dominate the main narrative. The Aethiopica became widely known through *Amyot's French translation (1547) and *Underdowne's English version (1569), and its influence on the romantic novels of the next half-century was considerable: Sidney's *Arcadia, *Barclay's Argenis, *D'Urfé's L'Astrée, are all indebted to it.

Affectionate Shepheard, The, see BARNFIELD.

Affery, see FLINTWINCH.

Agamemnon of Aeschylus, The, a translation by R. *Browning, published 1877. It aroused controversy because of its uncompromising literalness, which Browning defended strongly in his preface, along with his spelling of Greek names ('Olumpos' for 'Olympus', etc.). The translation (or 'transcription', as Browning termed it) may be taken as an attack on the Hellenism of, e.g., M. *Arnold; by making his own version 'literally' unreadable, Browning countered Arnold's claim that the Greeks were masters of the 'grand style'.

Agape, in Spenser's *Faerie Queene, IV. ii. 41, the Fay, mother of Priamond, Diamond, and

Triamond, who, seeking to obtain for her children from the Fates

Long life, thereby did more prolong their paine.

The word in Greek means affection, charity.

AGATE, James Evershed (1877–1947), dramatic critic, was born in Lancashire, the son of a cotton manufacturer's agent; he was educated at Manchester Grammar School, then worked in his father's business for some years. He began to write for the *Manchester Guardian* in 1907, and later settled in London, where he wrote dramatic criticism for the *Sunday Times*. Agate also published novels and, more memorably, a nine-part autobiography, *Ego* (1935–48), in the form of a diary, recording his life in literary and theatrical London and describing the personalities of the day.

AGEE, James (1909–55), American novelist, poet, film critic, and screen-writer, best known for his semi-autobiographical novel *A Death in the Family* (1957), a moving account of a family in Tennessee shattered by the father's death in a car accident.

Agenda, a literary periodical of poetry, criticism, and translations, founded in 1959 and edited by William Cookson and Peter Dale. It has published work by D. *Jones, *MacDiarmid, and *Pound, as well as special issues devoted to their work, and has also championed W. *Lewis. Other contributors have included C. *Tomlinson, C. H. *Sisson, W. C. *Williams, M. *Hamburger, and B. *Bunting.

Agents, Literary. The role of literary agent—that is, of middleman between author and publisher—began to develop towards the end of the 19th cent., with A(lexander) P(ollock) Watt (1834–1914) frequently cited as the founder of the profession. Newspaper agencies and dramatic and lecture agents had existed earlier in the 19th cent., and the *Society of Authors had recently been founded to protect the rights of authors, but Watt appears to have been the first reputable literary agent, whose clients included *Hardy, *Kipling, and *Haggard. Other major figures in the early years were James Brand Pinker (1863–1922), who represented *Conrad and Arnold *Bennett and encouraged new authors, and American-born Curtis Brown (1866–1945). The influence of the agent was not universally acceptable; the Society of Authors was at first sceptical, as were some authors (including G. B. *Shaw) and many publishers, notably William Heinemann (1863–1920), who argued that an agent interfered with the natural relationship between author and publisher. But others spoke up well for the profession, including Bennett, who wrote in a letter to The Author (July 1913) that 'every author of large and varied output ought to put the whole of his affairs into the hands of a good agent', and by the end of the 1930s animosity had largely evaporated, all parties agreeing that agents could provide an indispensable service in terms of placing work, agreeing on contracts, sieving manuscripts, intervening in disputes, etc. See J. Hepburn, *The Author's Empty Purse and the Rise of the Literary Agent* (1968).

Age of Innocence, The, see WHARTON, E.

Age of Reason, The, by *Paine, published as a whole 1795; the first part appeared in 1793, but no copies are extant. The work was written in Paris at the height of the Terror, the second part during Paine's imprisonment when his own life was at risk. In it he states, 'I believe in one God, and no more', and proceeds to attack Christianity and the Bible: the Old Testament consists of 'obscene stories and voluptuous debaucheries', whereas the New is inconsistent, and the account of the Virgin Birth, for example (a passage that was found particularly shocking), merely 'hearsay upon hearsay'. He concludes with a plea for religious tolerance. The work was widely attacked as blasphemous and scurrilous, occasionally praised as blunt and plain; its apparent flippancy was certainly intended to be provocative, and long remained so.

Agnes Grey, a novel by A. *Brontë, published 1847.

It is the story of a rector's daughter who takes service as a governess, first with the Bloomfield family, whose undisciplined children are described as 'tigers' cubs', and then with the Murrays, where the conduct of her eldest charge, Rosalie, a heartless coquette, is contrasted with her own modest and gentle behaviour. Rosalie marries ambitiously and unhappily, but Agnes is happily united with Mr Weston, the curate, the only one to have shown kindness in her days of servitude. The novel is lightened by passages showing Agnes' warm response to the natural world and in particular her feeling for the sea, which forms the background for her final reunion with Mr Weston.

Agramant, in *Orlando Innamorato* and *Orlando Furioso,* the emperor of Africa, supreme ruler of the infidels and a descendant of Alexander the Great, who leads his hosts against Charlemagne.

Agravain, Sir, in the Arthurian legends the second son of King Lot of Orkney and Arthur's sister Morgawse, the brother of *Gawain, *Gareth, and *Gaheris. He conspires against Launcelot and discloses to Arthur Launcelot's love for Guinevere, and Launcelot kills him for this at Guinevere's door. He is called 'Agravayn a la Dure Mayn' (of the hard hand) in Sir *Gawain and the Green Knight* (l. 110) and *Chrétien's Perceval* (ll. 8139–40), and in the German *Parzifal* (dating from c.1205).

Agrican, in *Orlando Innamorato*, the king of Tartary to whom the hand of *Angelica has been promised. He besieges her in *Albracca and is slain by Orlando.

AGRIPPA, Henricus Cornelius, of Nettesheim (1486–1535), a scholar and writer on the occult sciences. He wrote *De Occulta Philosophia libri tres* (1529) and *De Vanitate Scientiarum* (1530), and argued against the persecution of witches. Jacke Wilton and the earl of Surrey meet him in the course of their travels (Nash, *The Unfortunate Traveller*). He is said to be the astrologer Her Trippa of *Rabelais's Third Book.

Aguecheek, Sir Andrew, in Shakespeare's *Twelfth Night*, a foolish knight whose name suggests that he is very thin. Touches of pathos include his best-known line 'I was adored once too' (II. iii. 170).

Ahab, (1) in the OT, 1 Kings 16: 28–22: 40, a king of Israel who married Jezebel: in Jeremiah 29: 21–2, a lying prophet; (2) a character in Melville's *Moby-Dick*.

Ahasuerus, see WANDERING JEW, THE.

Ahmed, Prince, *and the Fairy Peri-Banou*, the subject of one of the *Arabian Nights*. The three sons of a king were in love with his niece, the princess Nur-al-Nihar. The king promised her to whichever son should bring him the greatest marvel. Hussein, the eldest, secured a flying carpet which would transport whoever sat on it wherever he wished; Ali, the second, a spying-tube which permitted one to see whatever one desired; and Ahmed, the youngest, a magical apple the scent of which cured all disorders. The brothers met at an appointed place. The spying-tube revealed Nur-al-Nihar dying of a disorder; the carpet transported them to her presence; and the apple cured her. The king, still unable to choose between them, proposed a shooting match, in which Ahmed's arrow travelled so far that it could not be found, and Nur-al-Nihar was assigned to one of the other brothers. But Ahmed, seeking his arrow, encountered the beautiful fairy Peri-Banou, fell in love with her and married her.

Aids to Reflection, a religious and philosophical treatise by S. T. *Coleridge, published 1825.

As a result of his 'Thursday classes' at Highgate, Coleridge compiled this unsystematic collection of commentaries and aphorisms on selected passages from the 17th-cent. Anglican divine Archbishop Leighton. Intended primarily as a religious guide to young men and a work of biblical scholarship, it stresses the importance of Christianity as a 'personal revelation'. Another 'main object' was to develop further his famous distinction between Reason and Understanding, originally drawn from *Kant, as the

source respectively of 'Moral' and 'Prudential' action. The massive and frequently chaotic footnotes contain much fascinating literary material, such as discussions of symbolism and metaphor.

AIKEN, Conrad Potter (1889–1973), American author born in Georgia, brought up in Massachusetts, and educated at Harvard, where he was in the class of 1911 with T. S. *Eliot. He made the first of many journeys to Europe in 1911, and lived in England for extended periods in the early 1920s and mid-1930s, writing at one time as London correspondent for the *New Yorker* as 'Samuel Jeake, Jr.' His first volume of poetry, *Earth Triumphant* (1914), was followed by many others, including *The Jig of Forslin* (1916); *Senlin: A Biography* (1918); *John Deth* (1930); and *Preludes for Memnon* (1931). His long poems, which he described as 'symphonies', show the somewhat diffused and diffuse influence of his *Modernist contemporaries and friends. He also published several novels, which show a debt to *Joyce and *Freud, and his own desire to explore 'the fragmented ego'; these include *Blue Voyage* (1927) and *A Heart for the Gods of Mexico* (1939), both concerned with actual and metaphorical journeys. *Ushant* (1952) is a psychological autobiography, with portraits of *Lowry and of Eliot, who appears as 'Tsetse', an illustration of Aiken's fondness for pun and verbal invention. His short stories were collected in 1960, and his criticism, *A Reviewer's ABC*, in 1958. His *Selected Letters* were published in 1978.

His daughter, Joan Delano Aiken (1924–   ), is a well-known British novelist and writer of children's books.

AIKIN, Anna Laetitia, see BARBAULD.

AIKIN, John (1747–1822), physician, author, and Dissenter, and brother of Anna Laetitia *Barbauld, with whom he wrote *Evenings at Home* (6 vols., 1792–6), for children; he also wrote and collaborated with others in several volumes of memoirs and biography. The last decades of his life were spent in the Radical and Dissenting stronghold of Stoke Newington, and he was until 1806 literary editor of the *Monthly Magazine.

Aimwell, a character in Farquhar's *The Beaux' Stratagem.

AINGER, Alfred (1837–1904), a popular lecturer and preacher who was canon of Bristol (1887–1903), master of the Temple (1894–1904), author of a life of C. *Lamb (1882) and a life of *Crabbe (1903), and editor of Lamb's works (1883–1900).

AINSWORTH, William Harrison (1805–82), published his first novel *Rookwood*, romanticizing the career of Dick Turpin, in 1824, and followed it in 1839 with *Jack Sheppard*, exalting the life of another highwayman. These *'Newgate' novels were satirized by Thackeray in 1839-40 in *Catherine. Meanwhile in 1837 Ainsworth had published Crichton, the story of a swashbuckling Scot in France. From 1840 to 1842 he edited *Bentley's Miscellany, then from 1842 to 1853 Ainsworth's Magazine, and finally the *New Monthly Magazine. He wrote 39 novels, chiefly historical; the Lancashire group, beginning with The Lancashire Witches (1848) and ending with Mervyn Clithero (1857), cover 400 years of northern history. Among the most successful of the novels are Jack Sheppard, Guy Fawkes (1841), Old St Paul's (1841), Windsor Castle (1843), and The Lancashire Witches. His swift narrative and vivid scene-setting made him extremely popular, with enormous sales in the mid-century, but his reputation has not been sustained.

AKENSIDE, Mark (1721–70), poet and physician, the son of a butcher of Newcastle upon Tyne. He studied at Edinburgh and Leyden, where he met his friend and patron Jeremiah Dyson. His *Pleasures of Imagination (1744) was republished in a new version in 1757. He also wrote a number of odes and minor poems, many of them alluding to 'the banks of Tyne' where he composed them. His 'Hymn to the Naiads', written in 1746 and published in *Dodsley's Collection of Poems (1758), is a dazzling display of classical erudition, and other poems reveal his keen interest in the scientific theories of the *Enlightenment. His haughty and pedantic manner is said to have been satirized by Smollett in *Peregrine Pickle.

AKHMATOVA, Anna, pseudonym of Anna Andreevna Gorenko (1889–1966), Russian poet. She spent her childhood in Tsarskoe Selo, outside St Petersburg. In 1903 she met the poet *Gumilev, whom she married in 1910 and with whom she visited Paris, where she was drawn by Modigliani. Her first poetry was published in 1907. In 1911 she joined the Guild of Poets, the founders of Russian *Acmeism, along with Gumilev and *Mandelstam. She was divorced from Gumilev in 1918. Her collections of poetry Evening (1912), Rosary (1914), White Flock (1917), Plantain (1921), Anno Domini MCMXXI (1921), bringing Acmeist clarity to the delineation of personal feeling, won her enormous renown. No books of her poetry were published between 1923 and 1940, and she was increasingly attacked as 'out of step with the new age'. The arrest of her son, Lev Gumilev, in 1934 led her to write the first poem in her devastating cycle on the Stalinist terror, Requiem (first published in Munich in 1963). In 1940 the ban on her publication was lifted and From Six Books appeared. From 1940 until 1962 she worked on Poem without a hero, a complex analysis of her age and her relationship with it, in-cluding her significant meeting with *Berlin in 1945. In August 1946, along with the prose writer Mikhail Zoshchenko, she was singled out for attack by the Party during the post-war cultural freeze (*Stalin's cultural henchman, Andrei Zhdanov, notoriously called her poetic persona 'half-nun, half-whore'), and expelled from the Union of Writers. After Khrushchev's 'secret speech' of February 1956 the literary rehabilitation of Akhmatova began, though not all her poetry has yet been published in the Soviet Union. In 1962 she had a meeting in Leningrad with *Frost, and in 1965 she visited Oxford to be awarded an honorary D.Litt. Major translations of Akhmatova's work include Poems of Akhmatova (trans. Stanley Kunitz and Max Hayward, 1973) and Requiem and Poem Without a Hero (trans. D. M. *Thomas, 1976).

AKSAKOV, Sergei Timofeevich (1791–1859), Russian author, who in his autobiographical trilogy A Family Chronicle (1856), Recollections (1856), and The Childhood Years of Bagrov Grandson (1858, the second in the chronological scheme) depicted family life in a rural community, showing a passionate sympathy with nature. They remain extremely popular in Russia, and were translated by J. D. Duff as A Russian Gentleman (1915), A Russian Schoolboy (1917), and Years of Childhood (1915). Aksakov was a lifelong friend of *Gogol, whom he recalled in A History of my Acquaintance with Gogol (1855).

ALABASTER, William (1568–1640), an Elizabethan divine and Latin poet, was educated at Westminster and Trinity College, Cambridge. Between 1588 and 1592 he produced two notable poems in Latin; an unfinished epic on Queen Elizabeth, which has been preserved in manuscript, and of which Spenser said, 'Who lives that can match that heroick song?' (*Colin Clouts come home againe); and the tragedy Roxana, which Dr *Johnson thought contained the best Latin verse written in England before *Milton. In 1596 Alabaster became chaplain to Robert Devereux, earl of *Essex, and sailed with him to Cadiz. In 1597 he became a Roman Catholic (influenced by the same priest who temporarily converted *Jonson) and was arrested and deprived of Anglican orders. His sonnets (first published in 1959) were probably written about this time. Often written in the dramatic Petrarchan form, they are among the earliest *metaphysical poems of devotion and seem to have been composed during the course of a profound religious experience. It was, however, as a theologian that Alabaster was chiefly known in his own day. His first major essay in mystical theology, Apparatus in Revelationem Iesu Christi, was written in exile in the Low Countries and declared heretical by the Holy Office. He revolted from the Roman Church and by

1613–14 was again a Protestant, later becoming a doctor of divinity at Cambridge and chaplain to the king. In 1618 he married Katherine Fludd, a widow, and became brother-in-law to the celebrated physician and alchemist Robert *Fludd. After twenty years of vicissitudes his life now became settled and he devoted his later years to theological studies: De Bestia Apocalyptica (Delft, 1621), Ecce Sponsus Venit (1633), Spiraculum Tubarum (?1633). In 1635 he published a scholarly abridgement of Schindler's Hebrew lexicon.

Aladdin and the Wonderful Lamp, an *oriental tale generally regarded as belonging to the *Arabian Nights, but not contained in any MS of the collected tales.

Aladdin, the scapegrace son of a poor tailor in China, is employed by a Moorish sorcerer to obtain for him, from a subterranean cavern, a lamp possessing magic powers, but disappoints the sorcerer by retaining the lamp for himself. Discovering its power, he acquires great wealth and marries Bedr-el-Budur, the Sultan's daughter, for whom by means of the lamp he constructs a wonderful palace. The sorcerer, disguised as an itinerant merchant, recovers the lamp by offering 'new lamps for old', and whisks palace and princess off to Africa. Aladdin, pursuing, kills the magician, regains the lamp, and conveys palace and bride back to China.

A la recherche du temps perdu, a novel by M. *Proust, published in seven sections between 1913 and 1927. The English translation by C. K. Scott-Moncrieff, Remembrance of Things Past, appeared between 1922 and 1931; a fully revised version of this translation was published in 1981. The seven sections of the novel are: Du Côté de chez Swann (1913, Swann's Way), A l'ombre des jeunes filles en fleurs (1919, Within a Budding Grove), Le Côté de Guermantes (1920–1, The Guermantes Way), Sodome et Gomorrhe (1921–2, Cities of the Plain), La Prisonnière (1923, The Captive), Albertine disparue, now renamed La Fugitive (1925, The Sweet Cheat Gone), and Le Temps retrouvé (1927, Time Regained).

A la recherche is a novel of circular construction: it ends with the narrator Marcel's discovery of his artistic vocation, a discovery which will lead him to the writing of the book the reader has just experienced. The dominant tone of the work is one of loss, of despair at the apparent irrecoverability of the past experience and regret at the vanity of human relationships and of human endeavour seen in the perspective of the destructive power of time. The search proclaimed in the novel's title is, however, vindicated by the narrator's discovery that the past is, in fact, eternally alive in the unconscious, and that it may be rescued from oblivion, either through the chance operation of sensory per-

ception (the power of 'involuntary' memory) or through the agency of the work of art. But if the novel is thus fundamentally an account of an artistic vocation, the narrator's progress is characterized by a sustained analysis of a wide range of subjects: the psychology of family relationships and of sexual relations, both homosexual and heterosexual; the aesthetics of the novel, of music, and of painting; and the fluidity of contemporary French society, satirized through the rise of the rich and vulgar Madame Verdurin into the ranks of the declining Guermantes aristocracy.

Alastor, a visionary poem by P. B. *Shelley, largely written in Windsor Great Park in the late summer of 1815, published 1816. 'Alastor' is a transliteration from the Greek, meaning the 'evil spirit or demon of solitude', who pursues the Poet to his death because he will not be satisfied by domestic affections and 'human sympathy'. Composed in Miltonic blank verse, laboured but sometimes translucently descriptive, the poem reflects Shelley's early wanderings: it tells how the Poet left his 'alienated home', abandoned an 'Arab maiden', and vainly pursued his vision of ideal love 'through Arabie | And Persia, and the wild Carmanian waste' until he reached a remote river in the Indian Caucasus, where he died alone, exhausted, and unfulfilled. This rite de passage includes the dream of a 'veilèd maid' who dances with shimmering erotic intensity (ll. 129–222). The work is closely associated with Shelley's prose essays 'On Love' and 'On Life'.

ALBAN, St (d. ?304), the first British martyr, who is said to have been put to death under the edicts of Diocletian. While still a pagan, the story goes, he had sheltered in his house a Christian cleric by whom he was converted. Immediately after his conversion he was executed, accompanied by miracles, on a hill overlooking the Roman town of Verulamium, now St Albans.

Albany, Duke of, in Shakespeare's *King Lear, maintains his integrity in spite of marriage to the wicked *Goneril; in the Quarto text (1608) he speaks the closing lines of the play. Albany, according to *Holinshed, was the northern part of Britain, from the Humber to Caithness.

Albany, Albainn, Albin, Albania, ancient poetic names of Gaelic origin for the northern part of Britain.

ALBEE, Edward Franklin (1928–), American playwright, associated with the Theatre of the *Absurd, whose later explorations of sexual fantasy, frustration, and domestic anguish also recall the plays of T. *Williams. His works include the macabre one-act satiric comedy The American Dream (1961); the more naturalistic marital tragi-comedy of academe Who's Afraid of Virginia Woolf? (1962); Tiny Alice (1965), a fantasy of wealth and corruption; and *A Delicate Balance* (1966), a tragi-comedy set in a hard-drinking domestic environment.

ALBERTI, Leon Battista Degli (1404–72), Italian architect, scholar, and theorist, whose treatises on painting and sculpture (*Della Pittura*) and on architecture (*De Re Aedificatoria*; English trans., G. Leone, 1726) had a profound influence on Renaissance and subsequent architecture.

ALBERTUS MAGNUS (1193 or 1206–80), St Albert of Cologne, a Dominican friar who was a native of Swabia and a great *scholastic philosopher. He was an interpreter of Aristotle, whose doctrines he expounded at Cologne and Paris; he was the first Western thinker to outline the complete philosophy of Aristotle. *Aquinas was among his pupils. His wide learning earned for him the title 'Doctor Universalis', and his total *œuvre*, printed at Lyons in 1651, extends to twenty-one folio volumes of which six are commentaries on Aristotle. He also wrote an influential *Summa Theologiae*.

Albion, an ancient poetical name for Britain, perhaps derived from its white (Latin, *albus*) cliffs, visible from the coast of Gaul. *Blake frequently uses Albion as a personification of England, in such works as *Visions of the Daughters of Albion* (1793), *The Four Zoas* and *Jerusalem*, where he adapted the traditional presentation of England as a giant to his own mythological purposes. M. Horovitz's Penguin anthology *Children of Albion: Poetry of the 'Underground' in Britain* (1969) is a conscious tribute to Blake, as is A. *Henri's poem 'Mrs Albion You've Got a Lovely Daughter', which portrays Liverpool as 'Albion's most lovely daughter'.

Albions England, see WARNER, W.

Albracca, in *Orlando Innamorato*, the capital of *Galafron, king of Cathay, in which *Angelica is besieged by *Agrican.

Album Amicorum, an 'album of friends', the predecessor of the modern autograph album, popular from the 16th cent. with travelling students and scholars. Typically an entry would contain a biblical or classical motto, a personal device or coat of arms, a dedication and an autograph. There are many examples in the British Library.

Albumazar, see TOMKIS, T.

Alcaics, see METRE.

Alceste, see MISANTHROPE, LE.

Alchemist, The, a comedy by *Jonson, performed by the King's Men 1610, printed 1612, by many considered the greatest of his plays.

Lovewit, during an epidemic of the plague, leaves his house in Blackfriars in London in charge of his servant, Face. The latter, with Subtle, a fake alchemist and astrologer, and Dol Common, his consort, use the house as a place for fleecing a variety of victims. To Sir Epicure Mammon, a voluptuous knight, and Ananias and Tribulation Wholesome, fanatical Puritans, they promise the philosopher's stone, by which all metals may be turned to gold; to Dapper, a lawyer's clerk, a charm to win at gambling, bestowed by his aunt, the Queen of Fairy; to Drugger, a tobacconist, a magical way of designing his shop to improve trade; to Kastril, a country bumpkin who wants to learn the language of quarrelling, a rich marriage for his widowed sister, Dame Pliant. Surly, a gamester, sees through the fraud and attempts to expose it by presenting himself disguised as a Spaniard, but the dupes refuse to listen and drive him away. Lovewit's unexpected return puts Subtle and Dol to flight, and Face makes peace with his master by resourcefully marrying him to Dame Pliant.

Alcina, in *Orlando Innamorato* and *Orlando Furioso*, a witch who was mistress of an enchanted garden, and changed her lovers into beasts, stones, or trees. *Astolfo and *Rogero were among her prisoners.

Alcmena, see AMPHITRYON.

ALCOTT, Louisa M(ay) (1832–88), American author, born in Pennsylvania, the daughter of educationalist and Transcendentalist Bronson Alcott (1799–1888), friend of *Emerson and *Thoreau. From an early age she published sketches, stories, etc., to help support her impractical father and family, and achieved fame and financial security with *Little Women* (1868–9), which was followed by several other works in the same vein. She also wrote sensational novels and straight adult novels, and was involved in various reform movements, including women's suffrage.

ALCUIN (Albinus: English name Ealhwine) (735–804), theologian, man of letters, and the principal figure in the literary and educational programme of *Charlemagne in the 'Carolingian Renaissance'. He was born at York and educated in the Cloister School there under Archbishop Egbert. He met Charlemagne at Parma in 780, and settled on the Continent, becoming abbot of Tours in 796. He wrote liturgical, grammatical, hagiographical, and philosophical works, as well as numerous letters and poems in Latin, including an elegy on the destruction of Lindisfarne by the Danes. He was primarily an educationalist rather than an original thinker. He adapted *Tertullian's 'What has Athens to do with Jerusalem?' to ask his famous question about the inappropriateness of heroic writing in monasteries, 'Quid Hinieldus cum Christo?' (Ingeld being a character in *Beowulf).

But his enduring legacy was the Carolingian educational curricula and the Carolingian minuscule script developed in his writing school. (See also ANGLO-LATIN LITERATURE.)

See M. L. Laistner, *Thought and Letters in Western Europe, AD 500–900* (1957); E. S. Duckett, *Alcuin, Friend of Charlemagne* (1951).

Alcuin Club, The, exists to promote the study of Christian liturgy in general, and in particular the liturgies of the Anglican Communion. Founded in 1897, it produces one major volume of scholarship a year and occasional manuals of a practical nature.

Alcyon, in Spenser's *Daphnaïda* and *Colin Clout,* is Sir A. *Gorges, on whose wife's death the *Daphnaïda* is an elegy.

Aldclyffe, Cytherea, a character in Hardy's *Desperate Remedies.*

Aldersgate, originally Ealdredesgate, one of the old gates of London. From the old gatehouse J. *Day issued his editions of *Ascham's *The Scholemaster,* *Foxe's *Actes and Monuments,* and some of *Tyndale's works.

ALDHELM, St (*c.*639–709), the first bishop of Sherborne (705), was educated under *Theodore at Canterbury (671) and was a major figure in the intellectual movement led by him. He was the author of a number of Latin works which reveal a wide knowledge of Classical and Christian authors. His ornate and difficult vocabulary—his *verborum garrulitas*—shows the influence of Irish models. He was abbot of Malmesbury and built churches at Malmesbury, Bruton, and Wareham and monasteries at Frome and Bradford. His most important work is *De Septenario, the Letter to Acircius* (i.e. Aldfrith, king of Northumbria) which contains his own Latin riddles, the *Aenigmata.* Alfred says he was a popular vernacular poet but, as far as we know, none of this work survives. (See also ANGLO-LATIN LITERATURE.)

Ed. R. Ehwald, *Aldhelmi Opera* (1919).

Aldiborontiphoscophornio, see CHRONON-HOTONTHOLOGOS.

ALDINGTON, Richard (Edward Godfree) (1892–1962), educated at University College London, which he left without taking a degree. Early in his literary career he made the acquaintance of *Pound, who introduced him to Hilda *Doolittle (H.D.) whom he married in 1913, and of F. M. *Ford, for whom he worked briefly as secretary. He and H.D. both worked as editors on the Imagist periodical *The Egoist* and in 1915 Aldington's first volume of poetry, *Images 1910–1915,* was published by the Poetry Bookshop. (See IMAGISM.) Subsequent volumes include *Images of War* (1919) and *A Fool i' the Forest* (1925), which shows perhaps an excessive debt to *The Waste Land.* Aldington achieved

popular success with his first novel, *Death of a Hero* (1929, abridged; Paris, 1930, unexpurgated), based on his own war experiences. It relates the life and death of George Winterbourne, killed in action in 1918; the first two parts dwell on his youth and 'advanced' marriage, satirizing the complacency and frivolity of pre-war middle-class and Bohemian England, and Part Three is a horrifying description of life at the front in France. His later novels (*The Colonel's Daughter,* 1931; *All Men are Enemies,* 1933) made less impact. From 1928 Aldington lived mainly abroad, in France and the United States. Of his later works the best known are his biographies, which include *Portrait of a Genius, But . . .* (1950), a controversial life of D. H. *Lawrence, who had at one time been a close friend, and his even more controversial life of T. E. *Lawrence, *Lawrence of Arabia: a biographical enquiry* (1955), which caused a furore by its attack on Lawrence as an 'impudent mythomaniac'. This, in the view of Aldington's admirers, was the cause of his diminishing reputation and the decreasing availability of his works, which include many translations, an autobiography (*Life for Life's Sake,* 1941), and critical essays. His correspondence with *Durrell, *Literary Lifelines,* ed. I. S. MacNiven and H. T. Moore, was published in 1981.

ALDISS, Brian Wilson (1925–   ), novelist, short story writer, and critic, is best known for his works of *Science Fiction and his involvement with the cause of Science Fiction as a literary genre; he has edited many collections and anthologies and has written a history of the subject, *Billion Year Spree* (1973). His many works which employ classic devices—lost spaceships, threatened utopias, time-warps, etc. —include *Non-Stop* (1958), *Greybeard* (1964), and *Enemies of the System* (1978); his sense of the tradition is manifested in *Frankenstein Unbound* (1973), which pays tribute to his view of M. *Shelley's work as 'the first novel of the Scientific Revolution', 'a meeting with the Romantic and scientific', and which describes a meeting between an American from AD 2020 with the Shelleys, *Byron, and Frankenstein himself. Similarly, *Moreau's Other Island* (1980) picks up the theme of H. G. Wells's *The Island of Dr Moreau* (1896). *Helliconia Spring* (1982), *Helliconia Summer* (1983), and *Helliconia Winter* (1985) form an epic trilogy describing the evolution of a whole planetary system, in which each season lasts for centuries.

ALDRICH, Thomas Bailey (1836–1907), American author, born in Portsmouth, New Hampshire, the setting of his semi-autobiographical novel, *The Story of a Bad Boy* (1870). He contributed light, polished *vers de société* to various periodicals, including the *Atlantic Monthly,* which he edited from 1881 to 1890.

ALDUS MANUTIUS (1449–1515), Venetian scholar, printer, and publisher. Originally a teacher, he founded an academy at Venice for the study of Greek and Latin, and began editing and printing grammars and classical texts (many for the first time). His roman and italic type, which was cut by Francesco da Bologna, and his Greek types greatly influenced the design of printers' letters. He also popularized the use of small formats for learned books. Many subsequent publishing and printing ventures have been named after him, including W. *Pickering's pocket editions of poets, and J. M. Dent's 'Aldine Library', a series of reprints published 1938–9.

ALEXANDER, Peter (1893–1969), professor of English language and literature at Glasgow University (1935–63), editor of a standard one-volume edition of Shakespeare's works (1951) and a short account of his life (1964).

ALEXANDER, Sir William, earl of Stirling (?1567–1640), Scottish poet, courtier, and friend of *Drummond of Hawthornden, was secretary of state for Scotland from 1626 until his death. His chief poetical works are a collection of songs and sonnets, *Aurora* (1604), a long poem on *Doomsday* (1614) in eight-lined stanzas, and four tragedies on Darius, Croesus, Alexander, and Caesar, which are the source of some of the most striking lines in Webster's *The White Devil* and *The Duchess of Malfi*.

Alexander and Campaspe, see CAMPASPE.

'Alexander and Lodowick', 'the Two Faithful Friends, who were so like one another that none could know them asunder; wherein is declared how Lodowick married the Princess of Hungaria in Alexander's name and each night laid a naked sword between him and the princess, because he would not wrong his friend', an old *ballad in Evans's collection (1777). The story is referred to in *The Duchess of Malfi* (I. ii).

ALEXANDER OF HALES (1170/80–1245), a native of Gloucestershire, studied at Paris and taught theology there. For a short time he held various ecclesiastical appointments in England and he became archdeacon of Coventry. Returning to Paris he entered the Franciscan order and continued to teach theology, becoming the first member of this new order to hold the chair of theology there. He wrote glosses on the *Sententiae* of *Lombard. According to R. *Bacon the *Summa Theologica* which goes under his name was not by him but put together by other Franciscan theologians, partly drawing on his teachings. It influenced the Italian-born theologian Bonaventura (1217–74), who refers to it in 1250, and Alexander is important as evidencing a distinct Augustinian–Franciscan philosophical tradition in the first half of the 13th cent. In the later Middle Ages he was called the 'Doctor Irrefragabilis'.

Alexander's Feast, see DRYDEN, J.

ALEXANDER THE GREAT (356–323 BC), son of Philip II of Macedon and Olympias, born at Pella, and educated by *Aristotle, became king of Macedon in 336 BC upon the murder of his father. He caused the Greek states to nominate him to conduct the war against Persia and in 334 crossed the Hellespont. He captured the family of Darius and extended his conquests to Egypt, where he founded Alexandria; and, after completely defeating the Persians at the battle of Arbela in 331, to India. He married Roxana, the captive daughter of Oxyartes, a Bactrian prince, and a second wife, Barsine, daughter of Darius and Statira. He is said to have destroyed Persepolis, the capital of the Persian empire, at the instance of the courtesan Thais (331). He died of fever at Babylon when only 32 years old. His horse was named Bucephalus.

Alexander was made the centre of a cluster of medieval legends, comparable to the cycles concerning *Charlemagne and King *Arthur. The chief of the romances concerning him are the great French *Roman d'Alexandre* of the 12th cent., some 20,000 alexandrines, and the English *King Alisaunder* of the early 14th cent., 8,000 octosyllabic verses. The story of the rivalry of his two wives forms the subject of Lee's tragedy *The Rival Queens*.

ALEXANDER VI, see BORGIA, R.

Alexandrian Library, The, was formed at Alexandria during the reign of the Ptolemies (beginning with Ptolemy Soter, 323–283 BC). It is said to have contained at one time about 400,000 manuscripts, of which a part were accidentally burnt when Julius Caesar was besieged in Alexandria. The story that the library was destroyed by order of the Caliph Omar is without foundation.

Alexandria Quartet, see DURRELL, L.

Alexandrine, an iambic line of six feet, which is the French heroic verse, and in English is used, e.g., as the last line of the Spenserian stanza or as a variant in a poem of heroic couplets, rarely in a whole work. The name is derived from the fact that certain 12th- and 13th-cent. French poems on *Alexander the Great were written in this metre.

ALFIERI, Vittorio (1749–1803), Italian tragedian and poet. He gave up his own estates and, in his treatise *Della tirannide* (*On Tyranny*, 1789, written 1777) advocated the revolutionary overthrow of all tyrannies. In another, *Del principe e delle lettere* (*On the Prince and on Letters*, 1785–6), he argued for the independence of writers from court patronage. Between 1777 and 1789 he wrote 19 austerely concise tragedies on historical themes, of which the finest, *Saul* (1782), turns the king into a figure that may be compared with *Sturm und Drang* heroes. He hailed the French Revolution in the ode 'Parigi sbastigliata' ('Paris Unbastilled', 1789), but satirized its excesses in *Il misogallo* (*The Anti-Gaul*, 1793–9). His autobiography (*Vita*, 1803) is pre-Romantic both in its melancholy and in its strong-willed hatred of oppression. He was the devoted lover of the countess of Albany, wife of the Young Pretender.

ALFRED (the Great) (848–99), king of the West Saxons from 871 to his death, important in the history of literature for the revival of letters that he effected in his southern kingdom and as the beginner of a tradition of English prose translation (though there were some Northumbrian translations of Latin before him). He translated (before 896) the *Cura Pastoralis* of *Gregory with a view to the spiritual education of the clergy, and a copy of this was sent to each bishop. The preface to this translation refers to the decay of learning in England and indicates Alfred's resolve to restore it. He then translated (or had translated) the *Historia Adversus Paganos* of *Orosius, inserting the latest geographical information at his disposal, notably accounts of the celebrated voyages of the Norwegian Ohthere to the White Sea and of *Wulfstan in the Baltic, both of which are full of interesting detail. He had a translation made of *Bede's *Ecclesiastical History* with some omissions, but giving a West Saxon version of the Hymn of *Caedmon, and translated the *De Consolatione Philosophiae* of *Boethius, with some additions drawn from exegetes such as Remigius of Auxerre. The loose West-Saxon version of *Augustine's *Soliloquia* is also probably the work of Alfred. He composed a code of laws, drawing on the Mosaic and earlier English codes. The *Anglo-Saxon Chronicle, the systematic compilation of which began about 890, may represent in part his work or inspiration. The characteristic virtue of Alfred's style lies in his principle of idiomatic translation, 'sometimes sense for sense', which gives vividness to his English versions. The absence of this distinctive quality from the translation of Bede has led to the questioning of its authenticity as an Alfredian text. See Asser's *Life of Alfred*, in *Alfred the Great*, ed. S. Keynes and M. Lapidge (1983); E. S. Duckett, *Alfred the Great and his England* (1961).

Alfred, *a Masque*, containing 'Rule, Britannia', see THOMSON, J. (1700–48).

Algarsyf, one of the two sons of King Cambuscan, in *Chaucer's 'Squire's Tale' (see CANTERBURY TALES, II).

Algrind, in Spenser's *Shepheardes Calender*,

Edmund Grindal, archbishop of Canterbury, 1576–83.

Ali Baba and the Forty Thieves, an *oriental tale generally regarded as one of the *Arabian Nights*, but not included in any MS of these. The source from which Galland drew it is unknown.

Ali Baba and Kassim were two brothers in a town of Persia. Ali Baba one day, while collecting wood in the forest, observed forty robbers getting access to a cave by pronouncing the words, 'Open, Sesame!', whereupon a door in the rock opened. Using the same password he presently entered the cave, found it full of robbers' treasure, and brought home some sacks full of gold. He was soon compelled to reveal his discovery to Kassim, who in turn went to the cave, but forgot the password after entering it, and was unable to get out. He was discovered in the cave by the robbers, cut in quarters, and hung up in the cave. Ali Baba, coming to seek him, conveyed the body home, and in order to simulate a natural death, sent for an old cobbler to sew the quarters of the body together. Through this cobbler the thieves, determined to destroy the person who still knew their secret, eventually traced the house of Ali Baba, though at first their purpose was defeated by the ingenuity of Morgiana, Ali Baba's servant, who placed chalk-marks on the neighbouring doors similar to that by which the thieves had sought to recognize her master's. At last the captain of the thieves brought his men concealed in leather oil-jars to the house of Ali Baba, intending to kill him in the night, but was again defeated by Morgiana, who destroyed them with boiling oil; Ali Baba finally killed the captain himself.

'Alice Brand', a ballad in the 4th canto of Scott's *Lady of the Lake*, telling how Urgan 'a christened man', who has been carried off by the Elfin king and changed into a dwarf, is re-transformed into 'the fairest knight' by Alice Brand and is found to be her lost brother.

Alice's Adventures in Wonderland, a story for children by Lewis Carroll (see DODGSON), published 1865.

Originally entitled *Alice's Adventures Under Ground*, and written for his young friend Alice Liddell, it tells how Alice dreams she pursues a White Rabbit down a rabbit-hole to a world where she encounters such celebrated characters as the Duchess and the Cheshire Cat, the Mad Hatter and the March Hare, the King and Queen of Hearts, and the Mock Turtle. It contains the poems 'You are old, Father William', 'Beautiful Soup', and others, and Carroll's typographical experiment 'Fury and the Mouse', in the shape of a mouse's tail: it proved a lasting success and has been translated into many languages. See also THROUGH THE LOOKING-GLASS.

Alifanfaron, in medieval romance, the pagan

emperor of Taprobane, in love with the daughter of Pentapolin, the Christian king of the Garamantes. *Don Quixote takes two flocks of sheep for their opposing armies and attacks what he supposes to be the forces of Alifanfaron.

Alisaunder, see KING ALISAUNDER.

ALISON, Archibald (1757–1839), Scots episcopalian, father of Sir A. *Alison. He wrote *Essays on the Nature and Principles of Taste* (1790), a study of the role of the imagination and of the association of ideas in aesthetic perception. Alison claims that poetry and drama are distinctive in their capacity to present a 'unity of character or expression' not found either in daily life or narrative writing, and finds the appeal to mixed emotions in tragi-comedy 'utterly indefensible'. He thus thinks *Corneille a sounder dramatist than Shakespeare. The work went into six lifetime editions and influenced *Jeffrey. Alison's wife, Dorothea Gregory, grew up in the household of Mrs E. *Montagu.

ALISON, Sir Archibald (1792–1867), son of A. *Alison, educated at Edinburgh University and called to the Scottish bar, was a frequent contributor to *Blackwood's Magazine* and author of various historical works, including a *History of Europe during the French Revolution* (1833–42), and various legal works, including *Principles of the Criminal Law in Scotland* (1832) and *Practice of the Criminal Law in Scotland* (1833); he also wrote an autobiography, edited by his daughter and published in 1883.

Alison Wilson, in Scott's *Old Mortality*, the housekeeper of Silas Morton of Milnwood.

Allan-a-Dale, one of the companions of *Robin Hood, and the subject of a song in the 4th canto of Scott's *Rokeby*.

Allegory, a figurative narrative or description, conveying a veiled moral meaning; an extended metaphor. As C. S. *Lewis argues in *The Allegory of Love*, the medieval mind tended to think naturally in allegorical terms, and *Auerbach suggested that towards the end of the Middle Ages 'every kind of serious realism was in danger of being choked to death by the vines of allegory' (*Mimesis*, ch. 10). Nevertheless allegorical works of great vitality continued to be produced, ranging from Spenser's *Faerie Queene* and Bunyan's *Pilgrim's Progress*, both of which use personifications of abstract qualities, to Dryden's political allegory *Absalom and Achitophel*, which conceals real identities; and there are strongly allegorical elements in many more recent works, such as Hawthorne's *The Marble Faun* and V. Woolf's *Between the Acts*.

Allegory of Love, The, see LEWIS, C. S.

Allegra, daughter of *Byron and Claire Clairmont, Mary *Shelley's half-sister.

'Allegro, L' ', see 'L'ALLEGRO'.

Allen, Benjamin and Arabella, characters in Dickens's *Pickwick Papers*.

ALLEN, (Charles) Grant (Blairfindie) (1848–99), born in Canada, educated in America, France, and at Merton College, Oxford. He was a schoolmaster for several years and went to Jamaica, as professor of mental and moral philosophy, where he formulated his evolutionary system of philosophy based on the works of H. *Spencer. On his return to England he published *Physiological Aesthetics* (1877), which introduced his name to the leaders of thought in London, and he was soon contributing articles on popular scientific and other subjects to the *Cornhill and other journals. Next came *The Colour-sense* (1879), which won praise from A. R. *Wallace, C. *Darwin, and T. H. *Huxley. He began writing fiction, at first with stories for *Belgravia, later collected as *Strange Stories* (1884). His first novel, *Philista* (1884), was followed by nearly 30 books of fiction including his best-selling *The Woman Who Did* (1895), intended as a protest against the subjection of women. It is the tale of a woman of advanced views who believes that marriage is a barbarous institution, incompatible with the emancipation of women; she lives with the man she loves, bears his child, but is left alone, when he inconveniently dies, to endure the consequent social ostracism. Mrs Fawcett and other feminists condemned the novel and its author as 'not a friend but an enemy' of the movement.

ALLEN, Ralph (1694–1764), a man of humble origins who rose to considerable eminence and prosperity in Bath (where he was known as the 'Man of Bath'), and was generally beloved for his unobtrusive generosity, both public and private. Most notably (in the field of literature) he assisted the struggling *Fielding, who later portrayed him as Squire Allworthy in *Tom Jones* and dedicated *Amelia to him. After the novelist's death, Allen provided for the education and support of his children. *Pope praised him as one who did good 'by stealth'; S. *Richardson, *Pitt the elder, W. *Warburton, and Mrs *Delaney were among his friends. See B. Boyce, *The Benevolent Man* (1967).

ALLEN, William (1532–94), Cardinal, was educated at Oriel College. He left Oxford in 1561 and was instrumental in the founding of seminaries for the training of Roman Catholic missionaries at Douai, Rome (where life at the English College is vividly described by A. *Munday in *The English Romayne Lyfe*, 1582), and Valladolid. As well as his own controversial writings he inspired and was involved in the translation of the Douai-Rheims Bible (1582, 1609), for long the traditional Roman Catholic version of the Scriptures in the vernacular.

ALLESTREE, Richard (*fl.* 1618–43), see ALMANACS.

ALLESTREE, Richard (1619–81), see WHOLE DUTY OF MAN, THE.

ALLEYN, Edward (1566–1626), an actor (R. *Burbage's chief rival) and partner of *Henslowe, with whom he built the Fortune Theatre, Cripplegate. There he acted at the head of the Lord Admiral's company, playing among other parts the leading roles in Marlowe's *Tamburlaine, *Jew of Malta, and *Dr Faustus. He acquired great wealth, bought the manor of Dulwich, and built and endowed Dulwich College. His first wife was Henslowe's stepdaughter, his second the daughter of *Donne. He was a patron of *Dekker, John *Taylor (the 'water poet'), and other writers.

All for Love, or The World Well Lost, a tragedy by *Dryden produced and published 1678.
   Written in blank verse in acknowledged imitation of Shakespeare's *Antony and Cleopatra, it is Dryden's most performed and his best-known play. It concentrates on the last hours in the lives of its hero and heroine. In contrast to Shakespeare's play, it is an exemplary neo-classical tragedy, notable for its elaborately formal presentation of character, action, and theme. (See NEO-CLASSICISM.)

ALLIBONE, S. A., see CRITICAL DICTIONARY OF ENGLISH LITERATURE.

ALLINGHAM, William (1824–89), born in Co. Donegal, worked as a customs officer, first in Ireland, then in England, where he settled in 1863. His friends in the literary world included *Patmore, *Carlyle, D. G. *Rossetti, and notably *Tennyson; his diary, published in 1907, covers four decades and has many vivid portraits of his contemporaries. His first volume, *Poems*, appeared in 1850, and contains his best-known work 'The Fairies' ('Up the airy mountain'); it was followed by several others, including the long poem Laurence Bloomfield in Ireland (1864) and various collections and anthologies of verse for children, some with illustrations by Rossetti, *Millais, K. *Greenaway, and his wife Helen Paterson.

Alliteration, the commencement of two or more words in close connection with the same sound, as in e.g. G. M. *Hopkins's 'The Windhover':

I caught this morning morning's minion, kingdom
   of daylight's dauphin, dapple-dawn-drawn
   Falcon . . .

It was used to excess by many late 19th-cent. poets, notably *Swinburne, whose 'lilies and languors of virtue' and 'raptures and roses of vice' are characteristic examples from *'Dolores'. (See also ALLITERATIVE VERSE.)

Alliterative Prose, a tradition of Old and Middle English prose elevated in style by the employment of some of the techniques of *Alliterative Verse. Its most distinguished exponents are *Ælfric and *Wulfstan in Old English, and the writers of the *'Katherine Group' in Middle English. R. W. *Chambers, in his essay 'On the Continuity of English Prose from Alfred to More' (1932), saw this alliterative thread as a common factor in English writing from Old English to the Renaissance.

Alliterative Revival, a collective term for the group of alliterative poems written in the second half of the 14th cent. in which alliteration, which had been the formal basis of Old English poetry, was again used in poetry of the first importance (such as *Piers Plowman and Sir *Gawain and the Green Knight) as a serious alternative to the continental form, syllabic rhyming verse. Three views have been advanced to account for its emergence: (1) that it was a conscious return to traditional forms as politics became again more English than French, a nationalist movement like the attempted modern linguistic revivals in Wales or Ireland; (2) that it was merely a resurfacing of literature which had continued throughout the period since the conquest but had not been officially published; (3) that it was a straightforward development of the loose alliterative poetry of the previous century which the new movement only enhanced. The last view, argued by Thorlac Turville-Petre (*The Alliterative Revival*, 1977), is now thought the most persuasive. As well as their common formal elements, many of the poems are linked by a serious interest in contemporary politics and ethics (*Wynnere and Wastoure, Death and Liffe, The Parlement of the Three Ages, Piers Plowman).

Alliterative Verse, the native Germanic tradition of English poetry and the standard form in Old English up to the 11th cent., recurring in Middle English as a formal alternative to the syllable-counting, rhymed verse borrowed from French (see ALLITERATIVE REVIVAL). The Old English line was (normally) unrhymed, and made up of two distinct half-lines each of which contained two stressed syllables. The alliteration was always on the first stress of the second half-line, which alliterated with either, or both, of the stresses in the first half-line; e.g.

x   x   x
Nāp nihtscūa,   norþan snīwde   (*Seafarer, 31)

(The shade of night grew dark,   it snowed from
   the north).

In Middle English, even among the poets of the Revival, the alliterative rules were much less strict, although the alliteration was often very dense:

'I have lyved in londe', quod I, 'My name is Longe
Wille'   (*Piers Plowman B, xv. 152).

Nothing after Middle English could cate-
gorically be said to be 'Alliterative Verse', despite its recurrent use as a device throughout
English poetry, except perhaps for the rather
self-conscious revival of the form in this century
by such poets as *Auden and *Day-Lewis.

All Quiet on the Western Front, see
REMARQUE, E. M.

All's Lost by Lust, a tragedy by W. *Rowley,
acted by the Prince's Men c.1619, printed
1633. The story, taken from a legendary
episode in Spanish history, concerns Roderick,
king of Spain, his general Julianus, and Julianus's
daughter Jacinta, who is raped by Roderick and
later mutilated and murdered, along with her
father, by Roderick's Moorish successor. The
play remained popular throughout the 17th
cent., and was twice adapted during the Restoration. The story is also the subject of Landor's
*Count Julian (1812) and Southey's *Roderick
(1814).

All Souls College, Oxford, was founded by
Henry VI in 1438, with Archbishop *Chichele,
by whom the college was endowed, as co-
founder, to pray for the souls of all the faithful
and especially of those who fell in the wars
against France. It is a unique foundation, consisting of a warden and fellows (originally 40)
and no undergraduates; women have been admitted to membership since 1979.

All's Well that Ends Well, a comedy by
*Shakespeare, first printed in the First *Folio of
1623. It used to be thought to be the play referred to by *Meres as Loues labours wonne,
which would mean that it was written before
1598; but the Arden editor, G. K. Hunter,
assigns it to 1603–4, on the grounds of its
close affinity to *Measure for Measure. Both plays
are generally classified as 'tragi-comedies' or
'problem comedies'.

Its chief source is Boccaccio's *Decameron
(Day 3, Tale 9), which Shakespeare may have
read either in the translation by *Painter, or in
the French version by Antoine le Maçon. Bertram, the young count of Rousillon, on the death
of his father is summoned to the court of the
king of France, leaving his mother and with
her Helena, daughter of the famous physician
Gerard de Narbon. The king is sick of a disease
said to be incurable. Helena, who loves Bertram,
goes to Paris and effects his cure by means of a
prescription left by her father. As a reward she
is allowed to choose her husband and names
Bertram, who unwillingly obeys the king's
order to wed her. But under the influence of the
worthless braggart *Parolles, he at once takes
service with the duke of Florence, writing to
Helena that until she can get the ring from his
finger 'which never shall come off', and is with
child by him, she may not call him husband.
Helena, passing through Florence on a pilgrimage, finds Bertram courting Diana, the
daughter of her hostess there. Disclosing herself
as his wife to them, she obtains permission to
replace Diana at a midnight assignation with
Bertram, having that day caused him to be informed that Helena is dead. Thereby she obtains
from Bertram his ring, and gives him one that
the king had given her. Bertram returns to his
mother's house, where the king is on a visit. The
latter sees on Bertram's finger the ring that he
had given Helena, suspects Bertram of having
destroyed her, and demands an explanation on
pain of death. Helena herself now appears, explains what has passed, and claims that the conditions named in Bertram's letter have been
fulfilled. Bertram, filled with remorse, accepts
her as his wife. The sub-plot, concerning the
braggart Parolles, has been felt by some readers,
including Charles I, to dominate the play, and
in performance it has often done so.

All the Year Round, see HOUSEHOLD WORDS.

Allworth, Tom and Lady, characters in Massinger's A New Way to Pay Old Debts.

Allworthy, Squire, and his sister Bridget,
characters in Fielding's *Tom Jones. The character of Squire Allworthy was based on Fielding's
friends and benefactors R. *Allen and G.
*Lyttelton.

Alma (in Italian meaning 'soul', 'spirit'), in
Spenser's *Faerie Queene, II. ix, xi, represents the
virgin soul. She is the Lady of the House of
Temperance, where she is visited by Prince
*Arthur and Sir *Guyon, and defended against
her enemies by the former.

Almack's Assembly Rooms stood in King
Street, St James's, and were celebrated in the
18th and early 19th cents as the scene of social
functions. They were founded by one William
Almack (or Macall; d. 1781), who appears to
have come to London as valet to the duke of
Hamilton. Almack's was replaced as a social centre after 1863 by Willis's Rooms. Almack was
also founder of a gaming club, since converted
into *Brooks's.

Almanach de Gotha, a genealogical, diplomatic, and statistical gazetteer for all countries
of the world, first published by Justus Perthes de
Gotha in 1763, and appearing annually in
French ever since. It played a significant role in
defining an international aristocracy, particularly during the social upheavals of the 19th
and first half of the 20th cents.

Almanacs were, technically, tables of astronomical and astrological events of the coming
year, and as such had existed since antiquity;

with the advent of printing they proliferated, and by the 17th cent. in England were the most popular literary form, containing a wide range of material, from feast days, farming notes, tables of interest, to scurrilous verses and wild and colourful prophecies. They flourished particularly strongly from 1640 to 1700, when they engaged in political, social, and religious controversy, playing an active part in the ferment of the times. Well-known publishers and compilers of almanacs included Richard Allestree (active between 1618 and 1643, Derby and Coventry); the most famous of all, *Lilly; John Gadbury (1627–1704), astrologer and physician; John Partridge (1644–1715), who published almanacs from 1678; and Francis Moore, father of *Old Moore. In the 18th cent. growing scepticism and a declining interest in astrology led to a loss of vitality in the form, although Old Moore continued to be bought by the less educated classes in vast quantities, and still sells well today, as does the more prosaic reference book *Whitaker's Almanac* (see WHITAKER). See Bernard Capp, *Astrology and the Popular Press: English Almanacs 1500–1800* (1979) and Keith Thomas, *Religion and the Decline of Magic* (1971).

Almeria, the heroine of Congreve's *The Mourning Bride.*

Almeyda, a character in Dryden's *Don Sebastian.*

Almoran and Hamet, see HAWKESWORTH, J.

Alonso, the king of Naples in Shakespeare's *The Tempest* who helped Antonio depose Prospero. It is on the return from his daughter's wedding in Tunis that his ship is wrecked and that his son Ferdinand finds a bride in Miranda.

Alonzo the Brave and the Fair Imogine, a ballad by M. G. Lewis, which appears in *The Monk.*

Alph, in Coleridge's *'Kubla Khan',* the sacred river in Xanadu. For its connection with the river Alpheus and with the Nile, see J. L. *Lowes, The Road to Xanadu* (1927).

Alroy, a novel by B. *Disraeli, published 1833. This is the central novel of the group *Vivian Grey—Alroy—*Contarini Fleming; *Alroy*, the author wrote, represented 'my ideal ambition', and for it he deliberately invented 'a new style', which to modern readers may seem bizarre. Set in Azerbaijan in the 12th cent., this highly coloured romance of Hebrew chivalry, much influenced by *Byron, Sir W. *Scott, and the Old Testament, strives for an epic quality in the story of the noble Jewish conqueror Alrui, who becomes lord of the Levant, Egypt, Syria, and India. The supernatural, based on cabbalistic lore, plays an important part. Finally, corrupted by soft living, Alrui is conquered by the infidel Karasmé, and beheaded. The book was greatly admired by *Beckford, who wished for twenty volumes of it, but was refused for publication by John *Murray.

Altamont, Colonel Jack, alias Amory, alias Armstrong, in Thackeray's *Pendennis,* an escaped convict, father of Blanche Amory.

'Althea, To', a poem by *Lovelace.

ALTHUSSER, Louis, see MARXIST LITERARY CRITICISM.

Altisidora, in *Don Quixote,* the duchess's wanton damsel, who made love to the Don and then accused him of stealing her garters. She finally admitted that she was like the man who searched for the mule on which he was riding.

Alton Locke, Tailor and Poet: An Autobiography, a novel by C. *Kingsley, published 1850.
   The narrator, son of a small London tradesman and educated by a widowed Baptist mother, is apprenticed to a sweating tailor in whose workshop he experiences at first hand the miseries of the working classes and becomes imbued with the ideas of *Chartism; the material used in this section was first used by Kingsley in a stirring pamphlet, *Cheap Clothes and Nasty,* published earlier the same year. Locke's gift for poetry gains him the friendship first of an old Scottish bookseller, Saunders Mackaye, and then of a benevolent dean, his daughter Lillian (with whom he falls in love), and her cousin Eleanor. Under their influence he momentarily consents to the emasculation of his revolutionary poems before publication, a weakness he bitterly regrets. Roused by the taunts of his Chartist comrades, he undertakes a mission that involves him in a riot and is gaoled for three years. On emerging, he learns that Lillian is engaged to his prosperous time-serving cousin; he falls ill (and during his fever undergoes an interesting evolutionary dream, seeing himself transformed from a group of polyps through higher forms of life to man); is nursed by Eleanor, and by her converted from Chartism to Christian Socialism. He emigrates to America and dies on the voyage. The novel, despite its weaknesses, is a powerful social document, and had an impact similar to that of Disraeli's *Sybil* and Mrs Gaskell's *Mary Barton,* the latter of which Kingsley much admired.

Amadis of Gaul (*Amadís de Gaula*), a Spanish or Portuguese romance, written in the form in which we have it by Garcia de Montalvo in the second half of the 15th and printed early in the 16th cent., but taken from 'ancient originals' now lost, perhaps by Joham de Lobeira (1261–1325) or by Vasco de Lobeira (d. 1403), the materials of the story being of French source. Many continuations were written relating to the son and nephew of Amadis, Esplandian and Florisando.

Perion, king of Gaul (?Wales), falls in love with Elisena, daughter of Garinter, king of Lesser Britain; their child Amadis is cast away in a box on a river, and later washed ashore and reared by Gandales of Scotland. Until his identity is revealed he is known as 'The Child of the Sea'. He becomes the flower of chivalry and achieves wonderful feats of arms. He loves Oriana, daughter of Lisuarte, king of Great Britain, who is sought in marriage by the emperor of Rome and granted to him by her father, but rescued by Amadis, whence arises a great conflict. The emperor arrives with his fleet, but is defeated and killed. Amadis then comes to the succour of Lisuarte, reconciliation follows, and all ends happily.

The romance was translated into French by Herberay des Essarts in 1540, into English by *Munday (?1590), and an abridged version by *Southey appeared in 1803. *Amadis of Gaul* and *Palmerin of England* were two of the works specially excepted from the holocaust of romances of chivalry carried out by the curate and barber in *Don Quixote*.

Amadis of Greece, a Spanish continuation of the seventh book of *Amadis of Gaul*, of which Lisuarte of Greece, the grandson of Amadis, is the hero. The work is probably by Feliano de Silva (16th cent.).

Amara, Mt., a place in Abyssinia, where the kings of that country secluded their sons, to protect themselves from sedition (*Paradise Lost*, iv. 281). It figures as 'Amhara' in Johnson's *Rasselas*.

Amaryllis, the name given to a shepherdess by *Theocritus, *Virgil, and *Ovid. Spenser, in *Colin Clouts come home againe*, uses the name to signify Alice, one of the daughters of Sir John Spencer of Althorp. She became the countess of Derby for whom Milton wrote his *Arcades*.

Amaurote, or 'shadow city', the capital of More's *Utopia*. *Rabelais (II. xxiii) uses the name 'Amaurotes' for an imaginary people invaded by the Dipsodes.

Amazing Marriage, The, a novel by G. *Meredith, published 1895.

Carinthia and her brother Chillon are the children of Captain Kirby, the 'Old Buccaneer'. On his death they are left almost destitute and at the mercy of a miserly old uncle, Lord Levellier. Carinthia is a lovely, impetuous girl, a 'beautiful Gorgon', brought up in the wilds of the Austrian mountains. (The German and Austrian landscapes, memories of Meredith's happy school-days there, are lovingly described.) Lord Fleetwood, wealthy and arrogant, proposes to Carinthia during a dance on the first day he sees her, and is impulsively accepted. He soon repents

of his mad freak, and hopes that the girl has done the same, but he is grimly held to the engagement by Lord Levellier, who is anxious to be rid of his niece. Fleetwood consents to marry her, meets her at the church door, drives her straight to a prize-fight, and then abandons her at an inn. The eventual birth of her child only increases his resentment. She finds refuge at the Whitechapel home of the Woodseers, the father a minister among the poor, the son, Gower Woodseer (based on R. L. *Stevenson), a genial penniless philosopher. While walking in the Alps he had met Carinthia and Fleetwood, and become the devoted admirer of the girl and friend of her husband. He now contrives to show Fleetwood what he has lost. But Carinthia's feelings have changed and she, long dominated, now becomes the dominating partner; Fleetwood finds that she cannot be won back. She goes as an army nurse with her brother to the war in Spain, leaving Fleetwood to become a monk and eventually to die of his deprivations.

Ambassadors, The, a novel by H. *James, published 1903.

This is one of the novels in which, with much humour and delicacy of perception, the author depicts the reaction of different American types to the European environment. Chadwick Newsome, a young man of independent fortune, the son of Mrs Newsome of Woollett, Mass., a widow of overpowering virtue and perfection, has been living in Paris and is reported to have got entangled with a wicked woman. Mrs Newsome has decided to send out an ambassador to rescue Chad and bring him home. This ambassador is the elderly, amiable, guileless Strether, dependent on Mrs Newsome, for whom he entertains prodigious respect and to whom he has allowed himself to become engaged. The story describes Strether's evolution in the congenial atmosphere of Paris, his desertion to the side of Chad and the bewitching comtesse de Vionnet (he is convinced that the relation between them is virtuous), and his own mild flirtation with the pleasant cosmopolitan Maria Gostrey. Meanwhile his attitude and the disquieting report of Waymarsh, Strether's stolid and conscientious American friend, have caused dismay at Woollett, and Mrs Newsome sends out a fresh ambassador in the person of her daughter, the coldly glittering Sarah Pocock. The attempts to bamboozle Sarah utterly fail, and she presents her ultimatum—immediate return to America—to the delinquents Chad and Strether. Chad, exhorted by Strether, refuses to abandon the lady; and Strether is accordingly notified that all is over between him and Mrs Newsome. Then, and then only, an accident throws Strether unexpectedly into the company of Chad and Mme de Vionnet in circumstances which leave no doubt as to the nature of their real relations. Sadly disillusioned, but still insisting on the necessity of Chad's loyalty to Mme de Vionnet, Strether from a sense of duty turns his back on Paris.

Ambiguity, see SEVEN TYPES OF AMBIGUITY.

Ambit, a literary and artistic quarterly founded in 1959 by Dr Martin Bax, who has edited it in association with J. G. *Ballard, Edwin Brock, E. A. Markham, and others. Contributors have included P. *Porter, E. *Morgan, F. *Adcock, Jeff Nuttall, G. *Ewart, D. M. *Thomas, Ruth Fainlight, and many others.

AMBLER, Eric (1909–   ), writer of thrillers and screenplays, most of whose novels present an Englishman caught up in a network of European intrigue. They include *The Dark Frontier* (1936), *Epitaph for a Spy* (1938), *The Mask of Dimitrios* (1939), and *The Night-Comers* (1956).

Ambree, Mary, a legendary English heroine, supposed to have taken part in the siege of Ghent in 1584, when that town was held by the Spaniards. A ballad about her is included in Percy's *Reliques*, and she is referred to by *Jonson (*Epicene*, IV. ii; *Tale of a Tub*, I. iv; and *Fortunate Isles*) and other Elizabethan dramatists.

AMBROSE, St (*c*.340–97), born at Trèves, was a celebrated bishop of Milan (elected against his will by the people when still a catechumen), one of the Four Doctors of the Church, and a vigorous opponent of the *Arian heresy. He developed the use of music in Church services, restoring the ancient melodies and founding what is known as the Ambrosian chant (as opposed to the Gregorian chant, introduced two centuries later under *Gregory the Great). He composed several hymns, among which an old tradition includes the *Te Deum*, and he was a voluminous writer, though a great part of his output is no more than a translation of Greek fathers such as *Origen. He baptized St *Augustine and demonstrated the power of the Church by excluding the Emperor Theodosius from the cathedral at Milan until he repented and did penance for the massacre at Thessalonica (390).

Letters, trans. M. M. Beyenka (1954); F. H. Dudden, *St Ambrose. His Life and Times* (2 vols, 1935).

Ambrose, Father, in Scott's *The Abbot*, Edward Glendinning, abbot of Kennaquhair.

Ambrose's Tavern, the scene of the *Noctes Ambrosianae*, is loosely based on a real Edinburgh tavern of the same name, first described by *Lockhart in *Peter's Letters to his Kinsfolk*.

Ambrosio, the hero of M. G. Lewis's *The Monk*.

Ambrosian Library, The, at Milan, founded in 1609, was originally the private library of Cardinal Borromeo (1564–1631), archbishop of Milan, and was bequeathed by him to public uses. It was named after St *Ambrose, bishop of Milan.

Amelia, a novel by H. *Fielding, published 1752 (for 1751).

Joseph Andrews and *Tom Jones* end with the heroes and heroines about to embark on married life; in *Amelia* Captain and Mrs Booth have already enjoyed some happy years together, and the book is much concerned with married tenderness and family happiness. The character of Amelia, loving, forgiving, yet strong and spirited, is known to be a portrait of Fielding's wife Charlotte, who died in 1744, and the character of Captain Billy Booth clearly contains some elements of Fielding's own, although it altogether lacks his determination and industry. Certain incidents, such as that of Amelia's broken nose, are thought to refer to episodes in their life together. However, the novel is by no means an autobiography. Set in and against a London of almost unrelieved squalor, corruption, and violence, it opens in the court of the 'trading Justice', Justice Thrasher, who has the innocent, penniless Booth thrown into Newgate because he cannot bribe his way out of trouble. The filth and brutality of the prison, filled with sick, dying, and often innocent people, provides a sombre background against which Amelia's virtue shines. In prison Booth meets an old acquaintance, Miss Matthews, a courtesan who has the means to buy a clean cell and who invites Booth to share it with her. Although filled with remorse, he does so, and they exchange their stories. Booth describes his runaway marriage (in which he was assisted by the good parson Dr Harrison), his happiness with Amelia, their lives in the country, his soldiering, and Amelia's arrival in France when he was ill. There they had lived with the huge, pugnacious Colonel Bath and his sister, who had since married a Colonel James. James now bails out Booth, and takes Miss Matthews as his mistress. Booth begins a life of gambling, as he hangs about the haunts of the great and wealthy angling for a commission. Amelia's life is one of poverty and distress, but even when Booth fails to return from his gambling for her frugal but lovingly prepared meal of hashed mutton she does not upbraid him. And always, hovering in the background, is the kindly Dr Harrison, who protects and helps them as he can. 'My Lord', a flamboyant and menacing character who is never given a name, begins, with Colonel James, to lay plans to ensnare Amelia. The Booths' friendly landlady, Mrs Ellison (who is, unknown to Amelia, not only a cousin of My Lord's but also his procuress), arranges for Amelia to be attended at an oratorio by My Lord in disguise, and then introduces him as her cousin. My Lord becomes extremely agreeable, offers to acquire a command for Booth, and showers presents on Amelia's adored children. She then receives an invitation to a masquerade, but is sharply warned by a fellow-lodger, the learned widow Mrs Bennet, and she does not go. She learns that Mrs Bennet was once herself seduced by My Lord, after an invitation to a masquerade. After various other dangers and complications, during one of which Mrs Bennet, to Amelia's fury, succeeds in obtaining Booth's commission for her own new husband, the good Dr Harrison arrives, eventually pays off Booth's debts, and arranges for him to return to the farming life he loved. Amelia discovers that she is heiress to her mother's fortune, and the Booths retire to a happy and prosperous country life.

The book sold extremely well, but was attacked by many, led by *Richardson and *Smollett, and Fielding made alterations in later editions. It was his own favourite among all his books.

American Democrat, The, or Hints on the Social and Civic Relation of the United States of America, by J. F. *Cooper, published 1838. In this vigorous work Cooper examined and set forth, to the offence of his countrymen, the defects and dangers of democracy as it flourished in America.

American Senator, The, a novel by A. *Trollope, published 1877.

Elias Gotobed, senator for the fictional state of Mickewa, comes to England on a fact-finding tour, and finds 'irrational and salutary' English manners and customs more than he can understand. In this quiet exposition of country life in and around the town of Dillsborough, the love stories are highlighted. The first is a conventional Trollopean love-triangle, in which Mary Masters prefers her childhood sweetheart, Reginald Morton, to a neighbouring gentleman-farmer, Larry Twentyman. The second deals with Arabella Trefoil's pursuit of the wealthy Lord Rufford, despite a prior engagement to Reginald's cousin John.

American Taxation, On, a speech by E. *Burke, made in 1774 on a motion for the repeal of the American Tea Duty.

After dealing with the narrower arguments regarding the expediency of the proposal, Burke turns to a broad historical view of the subject, going back to the Navigation Act and explaining the course of British policy. He shows that the Tea Duty is at variance with the declarations of ministers and an 'exhaustless source of jealousy and animosity' without practical benefit. He exhorts the Government to abandon it. 'Do not burden the Americans with taxes. You were not used to do so from the beginning. Let this be your reason for not taxing. These are the arguments of states and kingdoms. Leave the rest to the schools.'

American Tragedy, An, a novel by T. *Dreiser.

Amiatinus Codex, the best extant MS of the Vulgate, so called from the abbey of Monte Amiata, to which it was presented. It was discovered in the 19th cent. to have been written in England, early in the 8th cent., at Wearmouth or Jarrow. It was probably copied from an Italian original. It is now in the *Laurentian Library at Florence.

AMIEL, Henri-Frédéric (1821–81), Swiss author. His remarkable diary was published first in part in 1883 (Fragments d'un journal intime, 2 vols) and translated by Mrs H. *Ward in 1885. It has since been re-edited and augmented.

Aminta, see TASSO.

Amintor, the hero of Beaumont and Fletcher's *The Maid's Tragedy.

AMIS, Kingsley (1922–), novelist and poet, was born in south London and educated at the City of London School and St John's College, Oxford. He lectured in Swansea, then Cambridge (1949–63). He published volumes of poetry, Bright November (1947) and A Frame of Mind (1953), but achieved popular success with his first novel, Lucky Jim (1954), whose hero, lower-middle-class radical lecturer Jim Dixon, with his subversive attitudes (anti-establishment, anti-pretension, anti-arts-and-crafts) was hailed as an *'angry young man'. Its setting in a provincial university was also indicative of a new development in fiction (see COOPER, W., LARKIN, BRAINE), a movement that Amis confirmed in That Uncertain Feeling (1955) and Take a Girl Like You (1960). I Like it Here (1958), a xenophobic and slight novel set in Portugal, displays Amis's deliberate cultivation, for comic effect, of a prejudiced and Philistine pose which was to harden into an increasingly conservative and hostile view of contemporary life and manners. His subsequent work is marked by much versatility; although best known for satiric comedy (One Fat Englishman, 1963, set in America; Ending Up, 1974, a savage study of old age; and Jake's Thing, 1978, a dissertation on middle-aged impotence and its causes), he has also successfully attempted many other genres. The Anti-Death League (1966), while in some respects offering the satisfaction of a conventional spy story, is a serious protest against God's inhumanity to man, and a tribute to 'the unaided and self-constituted human spirit, the final proof of the non-existence of God'. The Green Man (1969) is a novel of the supernatural, The Riverside Villas Murder (1973) an imitation of a classic detective story. Amis's enthusiasm for I. *Fleming's work expressed itself in The James Bond Dossier (1965) and Colonel Sun (1968), published under the pseudonym of Robert Markham. Among other anthologies he edited

The New Oxford Book of Light Verse (1978), and his *Collected Poems 1944–1979* appeared in 1979. (See also MOVEMENT, THE.)

Amis and Amiloun, a late 13th-cent. romance of 2,508 lines, adapted from an Anglo-Norman lay, about the virtue of friendship. Amis and Amiloun are two noble foster-brothers, bound in close friendship. Amiloun takes the place of Amis in a trial by combat and is punished for this deception with leprosy. Amis is told by an angel that only a bath made from the blood of his two children will cure the leprosy, and he provides this for his friend. At the end the children are brought back to life. *Morris and *Pater (in *Studies in the History of the Renaissance*) both tell the story as *Amis and Amile*. It was traditionally thought that the romance, while it was interesting and popular, was badly constructed, but criticism in the 1960s and 70s has argued its virtues. The standard edition is by MacEdward Leach (EETS OS 203, 1937).

Amlet, Mrs and Dick, characters in Vanbrugh's *The Confederacy*.

Amoret, in Spenser's *Faerie Queene*, III. vi, xii and IV. vii, daughter of the nymph Chrysogone and twin sister of *Belphoebe. She is 'Of grace and beautie noble Paragone', and has been married to Sir *Scudamour, but carried off immediately after by the enchanter *Busirane and imprisoned by him until released by *Britomart. *Timias loves her, but being reproved by Belphoebe leaves her. This incident refers to the displeasure of Queen Elizabeth at the relations of *Ralegh with Elizabeth Throckmorton.

Amoretti, a series of 88 sonnets by *Spenser, which have been thought to illustrate the course of his wooing of Elizabeth Boyle. His marriage to her was celebrated in *Epithalamion, which was printed with the *Amoretti* in 1595.

Amory, Blanche, a character in Thackeray's *Pendennis.

AMORY, Thomas (?1691–1788), was born in Ireland and educated in Dublin. He had some medical training, then spent the rest of his life as a leisured gentleman in Dublin and London. He worked for many years, by his own account, on a vast work on *The Ancient and Present State of Great Britain*, but the MS was accidentally burned. From his memory of it he assembled a rambling miscellany of travel and discourse, on his Unitarian beliefs, antiquities, medicine, landscape, and nature. This was to appear as a series, *Memoirs containing the Lives of Several Ladies of Great Britain*, but the first volume, published in 1755 and intermittently centred on Mrs Marinda Benlow, was the only one to appear. In it a visit to the Hebrides is followed by a lavish description of Green Island, to the west of St Kilda, which is inhabited by a society of learned and accomplished ladies, in a luxuriant setting of statuary and tropical vegetation. In 1756 and 1766 Amory published *The Life and Opinions of *John Buncle, Esq.*, in which the slim narrative of a journey through tremendous landscapes is filled out with impassioned discourse and marital adventure.

Amos Barton, *The Sad Fortunes of the Rev.*, see SCENES OF CLERICAL LIFE.

Amphialus, a character in Sidney's *Arcadia who has the bad luck always to injure those he loves.

Amphibrach, a foot consisting of a long between two short syllables.

Amphitryon, a comedy by *Dryden, produced and published 1690.

Adapted from the comedies of *Plautus and *Molière on the same subject, it represents the story of Jupiter's seduction of Alcmena in the guise of her husband Amphitryon. In this he is aided by Mercury, who is disguised as Amphitryon's slave Sosia. The cruel abuse of mortal love by the gods is in striking contrast to the play's uninhibited eroticism. The same story was adapted by *Giraudoux in his *Amphitryon 38* (1929).

Amurath (Murad), the name of several Turkish Sultans. Amurath III in 1574 murdered his brothers on succeeding to the throne, and his successor in 1596 did the same. Shakespeare in 2 *Henry IV* makes the newly acceded Henry V reassure his brothers with the words 'Not Amurath an Amurath succeeds, | But Harry Harry' (v. ii. 48).

Amyas Leigh, the hero of C. *Kingsley's *Westward Ho!*

Amyntas, in Spenser's *Colin Clouts come home againe*, may represent Ferdinando Stanley, earl of Derby.

AMYOT, Jacques (1513–93), a French writer, whose version of *Plutarch was translated into English by Sir T. *North.

Anabasis, see XENOPHON.

Anacoluthon (Greek, 'wanting sequence'), a sentence in which a fresh construction is adopted before the former is complete.

ANACREON (6th cent. BC), a Greek lyric poet who is supposed to have written extensively on love and wine, but only a handful of his genuine poems survive. A large collection of 'anacreontic' verse, of unknown origin, was printed for the first time in Paris in 1554; these verses were immediately imitated by the poets of the *Pléiade who popularized the genre. *Drayton, *Jonson, *Herrick, *Lovelace, *Cowley, all owed a debt to 'Anacreon'. In

1800 T. *Moore published a translation of the *Odes of Anacreon* in English verse.

Anacrusis, 'striking up', an additional syllable at the beginning of a line before the normal rhythm, e.g. the 'and' in the second of the following lines:

> Till danger's troubled night depart
> And the star of peace return.
>
> (T. *Campbell, 'Ye Mariners of England')

Analogy of Religion, *Natural and Revealed, to the Constitution and Course of Nature, The,* a treatise in defence of the Christian religion, by J. *Butler.

Analytical Review, The (1788–99), an important literary and radical periodical, published by J. *Johnson, which was an early influence in encouraging the growth of *Romanticism. *Gilpin's theories on the *picturesque, and some of *Wordsworth's early poems, were given sympathetic attention; the work of *Bowles, *Southey, *Lamb, and other young writers, was published. The *Review* attempted to comment, often fully, on every book published.

ANAND, Mulk Raj (1905–   ), Indian novelist, writing in English, who was born in Peshawar and educated at the Universities of Punjab and London. After the war he settled in Bombay, having published early work in *Criterion, *New Writing, and other English periodicals. Anand made his name with the novel *Untouchable* (1935), which recounts a day in the life of a street sweeper, roused to hopes of a classless and casteless society by *Gandhi (who advised Anand on the manuscript of the work). This was followed by other novels describing the lives of the poor, including *Coolie* (1936) and a trilogy (*The Village*, 1939; *Across the Black Waters*, 1940; *The Sword and the Sickle*, 1942) which describes the life of a rebellious and independent young Sikh peasant from the Punjab who fights for the British Army in the First World War. The best known of Anand's later works is *Private Life of an Indian Prince* (1953).

Ananias, the fanatical Anabaptist in Jonson's *The Alchemist.

Anapaest (Greek, 'reversed'), a reversed dactyl, a metrical foot composed of two short followed by a long syllable.

Anaphora, 'carrying back', the repetition of the same word or phrase in several successive clauses; for instance, 'Awake up, my glory; awake, lute and harp; I myself will awake right early' (Psalm 57: 9).

Anarchy, The Mask of, see MASK OF ANARCHY, THE.

Anastasius, see HOPE, T.

Anatomie of Abuses, The, see STUBBES, P.

Anatomy of Melancholy, The, by Robert *Burton, first published 1621, enlarged in successive editions between then and 1651.

In appearance the *Anatomy* is a medical work, in effect an affectionate satire on the inefficacy of human learning and endeavour. 'Melancholy' is never satisfactorily defined by the author, but embraces all the milder forms of mental illness. Burton finds it to be universally present in mankind, however, 'an inbred malady in every one of us', to avoid which we are advised: 'Be not solitary, be not idle.' The book is made up of a lengthy introduction and three 'partitions', the first on the nature, causes, and symptoms of melancholy, the second on its cure, and the third on two special forms—love-melancholy and religious melancholy. Burton was a learned man, and quotes and paraphrases an extraordinary range of authors, making his book a storehouse of anecdote and maxim. Its tone suits Burton's choice of pseudonym, 'Democritus Junior': *Democritus was 'the laughing philosopher'. The *Anatomy* made its author's reputation in his own lifetime, was admired by Dr *Johnson, and gave Keats the story for *'Lamia'.

Ancient Mariner, *The Rime of the,* a poem by S. T. *Coleridge, published 1798 in *Lyrical Ballads*.

An ancient mariner meets three gallants on their way to a marriage feast, and detains one of them in order to recount his story. He tells how his ship was drawn towards the South Pole by a storm. When the ship is surrounded by ice an albatross flies through the fog and is received with joy by the crew. The ice splits and the bird moves on with the ship; then inexplicably the mariner shoots it. For this act of cruelty a curse falls on the ship. She is driven north to the Equator and is becalmed under burning sun in a rotting sea. The albatross is hung round the neck of the hated mariner. A skeleton ship approaches, on which Death and Life-in-Death are playing dice, and when it vanishes all the crew die except the mariner. Suddenly, watching the beauty of the watersnakes in the moonlight, he blesses them—and the albatross falls from his neck. The ship sails home and the mariner is saved, but for a penance he is condemned to travel from land to land and to teach by his example love and reverence for all God's creatures. The activities of a parallel spirit world are described in marginal notes to the poem.

J. L. *Lowes, in *The Road to Xanadu* (1927), traces the sources of Coleridge's story and imagery. The poem was derided when it first appeared, but has since come to be regarded as one of the great poems of *Romanticism. R. P. *Warren re-interprets the symbolism of the poem, based on an opposition between Sun and Moon, in *Selected Essays* (1964).

Ancients and Moderns, *Quarrel of the*, see BATTLE OF THE BOOKS, THE.

Ancrene Wisse (often called *Ancrene Riwle*), a book of devotional advice, written for three sisters by a chaplain in about 1230. Seventeen manuscripts, whole or partial, survive: eleven in English (the language of the original), four in Latin, and two in French. It is admired as a work of great charm and expressiveness and regarded as the greatest prose work of the Early Middle English period. It has important linguistic and thematic connections with the group of texts known (from the subject of one of them) as the *'Katherine Group'. The book is divided into eight sections, each dealing in an accessible way with one division of the religious rule. E. J. Dobson (see below) believes that the work was written after 1215 and evolved in a series of revisions in the 1220s, and argues from an internal semi-acrostic on the name 'Brian of Lingen' that the author may have been an Augustinian priest connected with Wigmore Abbey in northwest Herefordshire, probably for the nuns of Limesbrook (or Lingbrook).

MS of Corpus Christi College, Cambridge, ed. J. R. R. *Tolkien (EETS 249, 1962); selections (Parts 6 and 7: on Penance, and on Love) ed. G. Shepherd (1959); translation by M. B. Salu (1956); E. J. Dobson, *The Origins of Ancrene Wisse* (1976).

ANDERSEN, Hans Christian (1805–75), Danish writer, born in Odense, the son of a cobbler and a washerwoman. His earliest ambitions were theatrical, and he trained as a singer and actor before achieving success as a playwright and novelist. From 1831 onwards he travelled widely in Europe, and remained a passionate traveller all his life, making his first visit to England in 1847. By this time he had already gained an international reputation for his fairy stories, which first appeared in Danish from 1835 onwards, and in English in 1846 in three separate translations, by Charles Boner, Mary Howitt, and Caroline Peachey. These stories, which include such haunting tales as 'The Little Mermaid', 'The Snow Queen', 'The Ugly Duckling', 'The Red Shoes', and 'The Emperor's New Clothes', were deeply rooted in Danish folklore, but were also shaped by Andersen's own psychological experiences and his at times morbidly acute sensitivity, and many of his narratives were wholly original. They were much admired by *Dickens, to whom Andersen dedicated *A Poet's Day Dreams* (1853) and with whom he stayed at Gad's Hill in 1857. Andersen's other works were also read and admired in England: E. B. *Browning wrote warmly to her future husband of his novel *The Improvisatore* (1845), and her last poem was written for him in 1861 shortly before her death. See also CHILDREN'S LITERATURE.

ANDERSON, Sherwood (1876–1941), American writer, born in Ohio, who made his name as a leading naturalistic writer with his third book, *Winesburg, Ohio* (1919), a collection of short stories illustrating life in a small town. He published other collections, including *The Triumph of the Egg* (1921) and *Death in the Woods* (1933), in which he continued to illustrate the frustrations of contemporary life, a theme also explored in his novels, which include *Poor White* (1920), *Dark Laughter* (1925), and the semi-autobiographical *Tar: A Midwest Childhood* (1926). His *Memoirs* (1942) and *Letters* (1953) were posthumously published.

'Andrea del Sarto', a poem by R. *Browning, included in *Men and Women.

Andrea of Hungary, *Giovanna of Naples* (1839), and *Fra Rupert* (1840), three plays forming a trilogy by W. S. *Landor. The plays deal with the marriage of Andrea, brother of King Lewis of Hungary, to Giovanna, queen of Naples, in the 14th cent.; his assassination brought about by the intrigues of the Hungarian monk Fra Rupert; the accusation brought against Giovanna of causing her husband's murder; the attempts, finally successful, to oust her from the throne; and the eventual exposure of Fra Rupert.

Andreas, an Old English poem of 1,722 lines divided into 15 fits, in the *Vercelli Book, based on a Latin version of the Greek Apocryphal *Acts of Andrew and Matthew amongst the Anthropophagi*. It was previously believed to be by *Cynewulf or by one of his followers influenced by *Beowulf, but it is now thought probable that *Andreas* is later than Cynewulf, towards the end of the 9th cent. See *Andreas and the Fates of the Apostles*, ed. K. R. Brooks (1961).

ANDREAS CAPELLANUS (*fl.* 1180s), is usually believed to have been a chaplain to *Marie de Champagne, though there is no historical evidence for him. His book *De Arte Honeste Amandi* (also entitled *De Amore*) is a handbook of procedure in love in three sections: Book One, concerned with the nature of love and procedure in it; Book Two, on how love can be retained; and Book Three, on the rejection of love. Andreas' work corresponds very closely to the writings of *Ovid on whom he often draws explicitly; especially influential are the *Ars Amatoria* and the *Remedia Amoris*. The whole work has a sceptical, Ovidian tone, and it has been very authoritative in the definitions of *Courtly Love from Gaston Paris to the present day. Its excessive authority in English discussion is attributable principally to the prominence given to it by C. S. *Lewis in *The Allegory of Love* (1936). It has been edited (in the original Latin) by P. G. Walsh (1982) and translated (with an excellent introduction) by J. J. Parry as *The Art of Courtly Love* (1941).

ANDREEV, Leonid Nikolaevich (1871–1919), Russian prose writer and dramatist who achieved great popularity in the early 20th cent. He spent his childhood in the provincial town of Orel, and then studied law at Moscow University. His first stories appeared in 1892. He worked as a court reporter and wrote journalistic satires, but his first major success was the story 'Bargamot and Garaska' (1898), which brought him to the attention of *Gorky. His first collection of stories (1901) was an enormous success. Among his most important stories are 'The Abyss' and 'In the Fog' (1902), which treat sexual themes with a new frankness, 'The Red Laugh' (1904), a response to the 'madness' of the Russo-Japanese War, and 'The Story of the Seven who were Hanged' (1908), which examines political terrorism. His major plays are *The Life of a Man* (1906), *Anathema* (1909), and *He Who Gets Slapped* (1915). Andreev opposed the October Revolution and died in exile in Finland. In 1919 he wrote 'S.O.S.', an appeal to Western nations to save Russia. 'The Red Laugh' was translated into English by A. Linden in 1905, and most of Andreev's work quickly received English translation.

ANDREWES, Lancelot (1555–1626), educated at Merchant Taylors' School and Pembroke Hall, Cambridge, was bishop successively of Chichester, Ely, and Winchester. He was renowned for his patristic learning and was one of the divines appointed to translate the Authorized Version of the *Bible. He was a major influence in forming a distinctively Anglican theology, reasonable in tone and based on sound scholarship: his friends included *Camden, *Selden, G. *Herbert, and *Casaubon. He was a highly popular preacher, and as a writer is remembered for his sermons, which in T. S. *Eliot's view 'rank with the finest English prose of their time' (*For Lancelot Andrewes*, 1928). The opening of Eliot's 'Journey of the Magi' ('A cold coming we had of it') is drawn from Andrewes's *Sermon 15: Of the Nativitie*. The sermons are in the *metaphysical style that preceded the plainer preaching of the Puritans and *Tillotson; they combine minute textual analysis, classical quotations, and verbal play with homely imagery and passages of powerful simplicity. His *Works* (11 vols, ed. Wilson and Bliss) appeared 1841–54 and a modern selection by G. M. Story in 1967.

ANDREW OF WYNTOUN, see WYNTOUN, ANDREW OF.

Androcles and the Lion; the story used by G. B. *Shaw in the play of that name appears first in *Gellius, v. 14.

Anecdotes of Painting in England, a work by Horace *Walpole, based on some 40 manuscript notebooks which he bought from the widow of the celebrated engraver *Vertue in 1758. The first two volumes appeared in 1762–3 and the third, with his *Catalogue of Engravers*, in 1765. The work surveys English art from medieval times to Walpole's own, and is at once a valuable and scholarly record and a reflection of Walpole's developing aesthetic taste.

Aneirin, The Book of, see ANEURIN.

Anelida and Arcite, an incomplete poem by *Chaucer in 357 lines. It is set, like 'The Knight's Tale' (*Canterbury Tales*, 1), in Theseus' Thebes and draws more on *Boccaccio's *Teseida* than on the sources it acknowledges, Statius and Corinna. The simple story tells of the faithlessness of Arcite to Queen Anelida in 210 lines of rhyme-royal, as a preface to the elaborate *Compleynt* of Anelida in 140 lines of varying and accomplished metrical patterns.

ANEURIN, or **ANEIRIN** (*fl.* ?600), a Welsh bard whose compositions are contained in a manuscript *Book of Aneirin* of the 13th cent. This contains the *Gododin*, an elegy on the Welsh chieftains who fell at Cattraeth at the hands of the Saxons, which contains one of the earliest mentions of King *Arthur (*c.*600).

Angelica, (1) in *Orlando Innamorato* and *Orlando Furioso*, the daughter of *Galafron, king of Cathay, the object of Orlando's love and the cause of his madness. For the story see under the above-named poems. Wordsworth in *The Prelude* (Bk. ix) refers to her 'thundering through the woods upon her palfrey'. See also *Paradise Regained*, iii. 341. (2) the heroine of Congreve's *Love for Love*; (3) the heroine of Thackeray's *The Rose and the Ring*.

Angel in the House, The, a sequence of poems by C. *Patmore. The first and second parts, *The Betrothal* and *The Espousals*, both in octosyllabic quatrains, were published 1854 and 1856 respectively; the third and fourth parts, *Faithful for Ever* (1860) and *The Victories of Love* (1861), both in octosyllabic couplets, were published as *The Victories of Love* in 1863.

The work is a celebration of married love, with lyrical and reflective passages linked by a narrative in which Felix courts and weds Honoria, a dean's daughter; in the last two parts Frederick, a rival for Honoria's hand, marries Jane and learns to love her before her early death. It was immensely popular with the Victorian public, though its mixture of high-flown sentiment and banal details about middle-class life made it the object of much mockery from more sophisticated authors like *Swinburne, and *Gosse referred to Patmore as 'this laureate of the tea-table, with his humdrum stories of girls that smell of bread and butter'. (*The Athenaeum*, June 1886). V. *Woolf, in a lecture on 'Professions for Women' (1931), spoke of the need for women writers to 'kill the Angel in the House'.

Angelo, the seemingly puritanical deputy to the duke in Shakespeare's *Measure for Measure.*

Angel Pavement, a novel by J. B. *Priestley.

Anglo-Latin Literature to 1422. From *Augustine's mission in 597 until the end of the 14th cent., the language of education and culture, in England as well as on the Continent, was Latin, even in the *Anglo-Saxon period when English enjoyed an unusual status. The leading names of this period were *Bede, *Aldhelm, and *Alcuin (the outstanding figure of the Carolingian Renaissance); poets continued to experiment with the cryptic 'hermeneutic' style.

From the Norman Conquest until the loss of Normandy in 1205 (the *Anglo-Norman period), the Channel might as well not have existed, and English men of letters had their education—and often their careers—as much in France as in England. *Geoffrey of Monmouth established a Trojan lineage for Britain and an Arthurian world for posterity, and enjoyed almost instantaneous success across Europe. The reign of Henry II saw English writers of European stature: Peter of Blois (c.1135–c.1205), *Map, *John of Salisbury. By the end of the 12th cent. England (or Wales) had also produced *Geoffrey de Vinsauf, *Giraldus Cambrensis, Alexander Neckam (d. 1217), and *Wireker (or de Longchamps). Their themes were unlimited: satire against the court was the common theme of the courtiers themselves. A genre of framed anecdote emerged in Map, John of Salisbury, Gervase of Tilbury (*fl.* 1180), and Giraldus Cambrensis. Some satire was personal, but most of it was directed against sin in general or institutions; the most brilliant was the *Speculum Stultorum* by Wireker of Canterbury. Metre varied from the established classical hexameter and elegiac couplet to the new rhythms, rhymed stanzas, and rhymed hexameters. The murder of *Becket produced a large literature of its own. In each genre England produced a master: in rhetoric Geoffrey de Vinsauf, in epic Joseph of Exeter (*fl.* 1190), and in *comoediae* the author of the *Babio*.

In the 13th cent. Anglo-Latin acquired a home-grown look. Two major secular poets were the rivals Michael of Cornwall (*fl.* 1250) and Henry of Avranches (*fl.* c.1230–62). A famous Englishman abroad was John of Garland (d. 1258), a prolific writer on all subjects. The arrival of the Franciscans in 1224 brought new inspiration and encouraged new poets, Walter of Wimborne (*fl.* late 12th cent.; already a prolific satirist) and John Pecham (d. 1292), later archbishop of Canterbury; although not a friar, John of Hoveden (d. 1275) was inspired by the same intense feelings for the Virgin and the Passion. Devotional literature continued in the 14th

cent., with the mysticism of *Rolle and the hymns of Richard Ledrede (d. 1360). From the Wars of the Barons onwards poems on topical events were popular—the fall of Gaveston, the wars of Edward I and III (e.g. 'John of Bridlington's *Prophecy*'), down to the life of Henry V.

Although *Gower wrote in Latin, French, and English, *Chaucer's choice of English alone indicated his sense that the vernacular was the language of the future. Historians and literary critics, such as Thomas Walsingham (early 15th cent.), Thomas Elmham (d. ?1428), and John Wethamstede (d. 1465), continued to write in Latin, but with an ever-diminishing audience. Any Latin poems after this time were of the classroom.

Anglo-Norman (or Anglo-French) designates the French language as spoken and written in the British Isles from the Norman Conquest until the 14th cent. It was a western type of French which, transplanted to Britain, developed characteristics of its own at an increasing rate. The earliest Anglo-Norman work of real literary merit, *The Voyage of St Brendan,* composed in the first half of the 12th cent., shows relatively few insular traits, whereas the French of the *Contes Moralisés* of Nicole Bozon (early 14th cent.) illustrates the disintegration of later Anglo-Norman. The French of *Gower in his *Mirour de l'Omme* is continental French, which was studied in its own right by Englishmen of the later medieval period. Anglo-Norman has many works of a moralizing nature as well as chronicles and practical works drawn from Latin sources. The *Mystère d'Adam* (see ADAM), the first French dramatic work of any moment, was almost certainly written in England. An Anglo-Norman type of French continued to be used for official documents and in English courts of law long after it had ceased to be spoken. See M. D. Legge, *Anglo-Norman Literature and its Background* (1963).

Anglo-Saxon. The Latin form of the word applies originally to the people and language of the Saxon race who colonized the southern parts of Britain (as distinct from the northern parts colonized by the Angles), to distinguish them from continental Saxons; hence, the 'Anglo' element is adverbial and the word does not mean, as was erroneously supposed, the combination of Angles and Saxons: i.e. the people and language of the whole of England. For the latter the term 'Old English' is more correct. The word became applied in the erroneous way very early; *Ælfric (c.1000) refers to the West Saxon he spoke as 'Englisc'. So the 'correct' distinction, made by the *OED* and enforced by modern scholars (especially at Oxford) between 'Old English' and 'Anglo-Saxon' is a somewhat pedantic one (the term 'Anglo-Saxon' is still used at

Cambridge, as in the 1941 book by the Chadwicks, *The Study of Anglo-Saxon*); since the revival of such studies in the 16th cent., 'Anglo-Saxon' has been used as the general term, without a sense of geographical distinction.

Anglo-Saxon Attitudes, a novel by Sir A. *Wilson.

Anglo-Saxon Chronicle, The, an early record in English of events in England from the beginning of the Christian era to 1154, surviving in seven manuscripts in which Plummer (see below) descried four groups: the Parker Chronicle, named from Archbishop Parker (1504–75); the Abingdon Chronicles; the Worcester Chronicle; and the Laud Chronicle, named from Archbishop *Laud (1573–1645), of which the most famous version is the Peterborough Chronicle. The most important and fullest are the Parker and Laud Chronicles. It is believed to have developed from the brief annalistic entries in Easter tables, and the entries up to 449 are as brief as the single-sentence Latin annals in those tables. The entries after 449 are sporadically more lengthy, and the most celebrated are those for 449 itself (the arrival of *Hengist and Horsa), for 755 (the story of Cynewulf and Cyneheard), for 893 to 897 (Alfred's last series of Danish wars), and for the disastrous years of Stephen's reign at the end of the Peterborough Chronicle. Most celebrated of all is the occurrence of the poem on the Battle of *Brunanburh (937); other lyrical passages of poetry or semi-poetry occur in the entries for 942, 959, 973 (in praise of King Edgar, ending in verse with his death in 975), 1011 (the martyrdom of Archbishop Aelfheah), and 1040 (the death of Prince Alfred). The organization of the Chronicle records in a more orderly way is attributed to *Alfred in the course of his literary ventures in the 890s. Editors and commentators have tended to look upon the Chronicle in too narrowly stylistic a spirit and to dismiss much of it as dry or cursory; but its importance in historical, linguistic, and literary terms is enormous.

C. Plummer, *Two of the Saxon Chronicles Parallel* (2 vols, 1892); G. N. Garmonsway, *The Anglo-Saxon Chronicle* (trans., 1953); D. Whitelock, D. C. Douglas, and S. I. Tucker (trans., 1961); A. Gransden, *Historical Writing in England c.550–c.1307* (1974), pp. 32–41.

Angria and Gondal, imaginary kingdoms invented by the *Brontë children, as a further development of games and stories inspired by a box of wooden soldiers brought home by their father in 1826. Early games created the Glass Town Confederacy on the west coast of Africa; the capital city, Glass Town or Verdopolis, owed much in its architecture to the engravings of J. *Martin. Later Emily and Anne broke away and invented the kingdom of Gondal, which was to

provide the setting for many of Emily's poems, including some of her finest; the initials and names attached to them (A.G.A., J. Brenzaida, R. Alcona, etc.) represent characters in the Gondal epic, of which no prose fragments remain. Charlotte and Branwell, in 1834, jointly created the kingdom of Angria, of which the principal characters were Alexander Percy, the earl of Northangerland, and Arthur Wellesley, marquis of Douro, later known as duke of Zamorna. Charlotte wrote many Angrian tales, most of them tragic and Byronic tales of passion; the tales of 1837–9 ('Julia', 'Mina Laury', 'Caroline Vernon', and 'Henry Hastings') foreshadow many of the themes of her mature novels. See F. E. Ratchford, *The Brontës' Web of Childhood* (1944).

Angry Young Men, a journalistic catch-phrase loosely applied to a number of British playwrights and novelists from the mid-1950s, including *Amis, J. *Osborne, *Sillitoe, and C. *Wilson, whose political views were radical or anarchic, and who described various forms of social alienation. It is sometimes said to derive from the title of a work by the Irish writer Leslie Paul, *Angry Young Man* (1951).

Angst, see KIERKEGAARD.

Animal Farm, a novel by G. *Orwell, published 1945.

It is a satire in fable form on Revolutionary and post-Revolutionary Russia, and, by extension, on all revolutions. The animals of Mr Jones's farm revolt against their human masters and drive them out, the pigs becoming the leaders. Eventually the pigs, dominated by Napoleon, their chief, become corrupted by power and a new tyranny replaces the old. The ultimate slogan runs 'All animals are equal but some animals are more equal than others.' Napoleon, ruthless and cynical, represents *Stalin, and Snowball, the idealist whom he drives out, *Trotsky. Boxer, the noble carthorse, stands for the strength, simplicity, and good nature of the common man.

Anima Poetae, see NOTEBOOKS, by S. T. *Coleridge.

'Annabel Lee', a poem by E. A. *Poe.

ANNA COMNENA (1083–?1148), historian, was the daughter of the Byzantine Emperor Alexius I, Comnenus. She tried in vain to usurp the succession from her brother to her husband, whose death in 1137 brought an end to her worldly ambitions. She retired to a monastery, where she wrote the *Alexiad*, a history in 15 books, and in the main part a panegyric about her father's life. She figures in Scott's *Count Robert of Paris*, and is the subject of a poem by *Cavafy.

Anna Karenina, a novel by *Tolstoy.

Annales Cambriae, a 10th-cent. series of Welsh annals, of interest for the information they offer about *Gildas and about some aspects of the *Arthur story, such as the Battle of Badon, which they place in 518, and the battle of Camlan in 539 in which, they say, Arthur and Modred fell.

Annalia Dubrensia, see COTSWOLD OLIMPICK GAMES.

Annals of the Parish, a novel by J. *Galt, published 1821.

In it the Revd Michael Balwhidder, a self-important old minister, chronicles with self-revealing irony the events, great and small, that affect the homely lives of the parishioners of Dalmailing in Ayrshire during the period 1760–1810. His solemn juxtaposition of national and domestic events is used with ludicrous effect. The book covers in some detail the social and economic changes affecting the people of the town, and is the source of the term 'utilitarian' adopted by J. S. *Mill.

Anne of Geierstein, or The Maiden of the Mist, a novel by Sir W. *Scott, published 1829.

The period of the story is the reign of Edward IV. The earl of Oxford and his son Arthur de Vere, exiled from England after the victory of the Yorkist party at Tewkesbury, are travelling on the Continent engaged in intrigues in the Lancastrian interest, under the name of Philipson and in the guise of merchants. Passing through Switzerland and overtaken by a storm in the mountains, they are hospitably entertained by Arnold Biederman, the Landamman or chief magistrate of Unterwalden, whose niece, the young countess Anne of Geierstein, rescues Arthur from death. The business of the Philipsons being with Charles the Bold, duke of Burgundy, they accompany Biederman and other Swiss delegates who are setting out to remonstrate with the duke against the outrages to which the Swiss have been subject at his hands. The Philipsons are seized by the cruel Archibald of Hagenbach, the duke's governor of the citadel of Brisach, and narrowly escape death, a fate only averted by a rising of the citizens against Hagenbach and his condemnation by the Vehmgericht and execution. The story is then occupied with the negotiations between Philipson (or Oxford), the duke of Burgundy, and Margaret of Anjou (Henry VI's queen), to secure the duke's assistance to the Lancastrian cause in return for the cession to him of Provence. These negotiations are interrupted by the utter defeat of the duke by the Swiss at Granson and Morat. After the duke's death at Nancy, Oxford and his son return to Geierstein, where Arthur marries Anne.

Apart from the vivid portrait of Charles the Bold and the picture of the court of René, the king of troubadours, the most interesting feature in the book is the description of the secret tribunal of the Vehmgericht, of which Anne's father, Count Albert of Geierstein (alias the Black Priest of St Paul's), is for the time being the chief figure. For this description Scott drew on *Goethe's Götz von Berlichingen, which he had translated.

Annot Lyle, a character in Scott's *Legend of Montrose.

Annual Register, The, an annual review of events of the past year, founded by *Dodsley and *Burke in 1758, which still survives. The first volume appeared on 15 May 1759, and was highly successful; *Prior described it as 'the best and most comprehensive of all the periodical works, without any admixture of their trash, or any tediousness of detail'. It also published poetry, literary articles, etc. Burke edited it anonymously for several years.

Annus Mirabilis, a poem in quatrains by *Dryden, published 1667.

Its subjects are the Dutch War (1665–6) and the Fire of London. Prefaced by 'Verses to her Highness and Dutchess' [of York], it indicates that even in the 1660s Dryden's optimism about the monarchy, mercantilism, and the *Royal Society (of which he was a fellow) did not preclude the oblique expression of an ironic vision of history.

Ann Veronica, see WELLS, H. G.

ANOUILH, Jean (1910–), French dramatist, author of some forty dramatic works and, from the mid-1930s, one of the most popular playwrights in France. Among his works are Le Bal des voleurs (1938; English trans., Thieves' Carnival, 1952), Antigone (1944; English trans., 1946), L'Invitation au château (1947; Ring Round the Moon, 1950), La Valse des toréadors (1952; The Waltz of the Toreadors, 1956), and a number of plays dealing with historical figures, including L'Alouette (1953; The Lark, 1955), on *Joan of Arc, Pauvre Bitos (1956; Poor Bitos, 1964), on Robespierre, and Becket ou l'honneur de Dieu (1959; Becket; or, The Honour of God, 1960), on *Becket.

ANSELM, St (1033–1109), a native of Aosta in northern Italy and a pupil of *Lanfranc at the abbey of Bec in Normandy, where he succeeded Lanfranc as prior. While he held this office he visited England, where William Rufus appointed him to the see of Canterbury, which had been vacant, in 1093, again in succession to Lanfranc. Anselm accepted the office with reluctance, and when the king again began to tyrannize over it he withdrew to Rome (1097), to return to England at the accession of Henry I (1100). He wrote many theological and philosophical works, the most famous of which are the Monologion, Proslogion, and Cur Deus Homo.

He was the cornerstone of the Augustinian tradition in the Middle Ages with its emphasis on Faith in search of Reason; the original title of his *Proslogion* was *Fides Quaerens Intellectum*. In this book is propounded the famous 'Ontological Argument': if God is defined as a Being than which no greater can be conceived of, then he must exist in reality since otherwise a Being of identical attributes with the further conceivable attribute of existence in reality would be greater. This argument has presented logical problems for philosophers ever since, including B. *Russell at one stage of his career.

Anselm of Canterbury, Works, trans. J. Hopkins and H. Richardson (Vol. i, 1974, contains *Monologion* and *Proslogion*); R. W. Southern, *St Anselm and His Biographer* (1963).

ANSON, George, Baron Anson (1697–1762), made his famous voyage round the world in 1740–4; an account of it compiled, according to the title page, by his chaplain Richard Walter appeared in 1748. It is the source of Cowper's poem *'The Castaway', which describes the fate of a seaman washed overboard while manning the shrouds.

ANSTEY, Christopher (1724–1805), is remembered as the author of the highly successful *New Bath Guide* (1766), later illustrated by *Cruikshank (1830), which consists of a series of letters in colloquial verse to and from several people, retailing the adventures of squire Blunderhead and his family in Bath. The manners of the fashionable town and its visitors are described with gaiety and good humour.

ANSTEY, F., the pseudonym of Thomas Anstey Guthrie (1856–1934), author of many novels of fantasy and humour and of innumerable comic sketches and stories. The great success of *Vice Versa* (1882), in which Mr Bultitude is magically transformed into his son, and vice versa, enabled Anstey to leave the bar in order to write. His long association with *Punch*, beginning in 1886, encouraged his skill in parody and burlesque; his series of *Voces Populi*, *Mr Punch's Pocket Ibsen*, and many others, became very popular. His many novels of magic, besides *Vice Versa*, include *Tourmalin's Time Cheques* (1891), *The Brass Bottle* (1900), and *In Brief Authority* (1915).

***Anthology, The* Greek**, a collection of some 6,000 short elegiac poems by more than 300 writers (7th cent. BC–10th cent. AD) originated in a collection by Meleager of Gadara ('The Garland of Meleager', *c*.60 BC) which grew by successive additions. In its fullest form it is substantially the collection of the Byzantine compiler Constantine Cephalas (10th cent. AD) and is known as the 'Palatine Anthology', as it was first discovered by *Salmasius in the Palatine Library at Heidelberg in 1607. The Palatine

MS was not however printed in its totality until 1813, though individual poems from it circulated in manuscript. Before the 19th cent. the *Anthology* was known for the most part through the abridgement produced by the 14th-cent. Byzantine scholar Maximus Planudes (the 'Planudean Anthology'), which was widely read and imitated during the Renaissance. There is an English translation of the *Anthology* by R. G. Macgregor (1864) and selected epigrams were translated by J. W. Mackail (1907).

Antigonus, a Sicilian lord in Shakespeare's *The Winter's Tale*, husband of *Paulina, and notable for his manner of death indicated by the stage direction '*Exit, pursued by a bear*' (III. iii. 58). Shakespeare took the name from *Plutarch; it was also used by Beaumont and Fletcher in *The Humorous Lieutenant*.

Anti-Jacobin, The (1797–8), a short-lived but remarkable journal founded by *Canning and a group of brilliant, high-spirited friends, including G. *Ellis and *Frere, to combat the Radical views supported by *The Monthly Magazine*, Coleridge's *The Watchman*, and other *Jacobin influences, and to deride their supporters. Edited by *Gifford, it was a political miscellany of strongly Tory outlook, which included much pungent parody and satire; 'The Needy Knife-Grinder', a parody of *Southey; 'The Loves of the Triangles', a parody of E. Darwin's *'The Loves of the Plants'; 'The Rovers', a burlesque on the romantic solemnities of German drama; and 'The New Morality', directed against French propaganda, are well known examples. *The Anti-Jacobin* came to an end in 1798, when many of its chief contributors moved on to the Tory *Quarterly Review*, but its crusade was continued briefly in enfeebled form by *The Anti-Jacobin Review and Magazine*.

Antinomian, one who maintains that the moral law is not binding upon Christians, under the 'law of grace'. A sect appeared in Germany in 1535 which was alleged to hold this opinion. (See HUTCHINSONIANS.)

Antipholus, the name of the twin brothers, sons of Egeon, in Shakespeare's *The Comedy of Errors*.

***Antiquary, The*,** a novel by Sir W. *Scott, published 1816.

A gallant young officer, known as Major Neville, on whose birth there is supposed to be the stain of illegitimacy, falls in love in England with Isabella Wardour, who, in deference to the prejudices of her father, Sir Arthur Wardour, repulses him. Under the assumed name of Lovel, he follows her to Scotland, falling in on the way with Jonathan Oldbuck, laird of Monkbarns, a learned and garrulous antiquary, and a neighbour of Sir Arthur. Lovel saves the lives of Sir Arthur and his daughter at the peril of his own, fights a duel with Hector M'Intyre, Oldbuck's impetuous nephew, and saves Sir Arthur from the ruin that his credulity and the impositions of the German charlatan Dousterswivel have brought on him. He finally turns out to be the son and heir of the earl of Glenallan, and all ends happily. The charm of the book, Scott's 'chief favourite among all his novels', lies in the character of the Antiquary, drawn according to Scott from a worthy friend of his boyish days (George Constable), but in which we may recognize a portrait or caricature of Scott himself; and in that of the shrewd, ironical and kindly old Edie Ochiltree, the king's bedesman.

Antistrophe, 'turning about', in a Greek chorus, the response to the strophe, recited as the chorus proceeded in the opposite direction to that followed in the strophe. The metre of strophe and antistrophe was the same.

Antonio, (1) the title character in Shakespeare's *The Merchant of Venice*, who opens the play with the words 'In sooth, I know not why I am so sad', and puts his wealth at the disposal of his friend *Bassanio; (2) the sea-captain who devotedly rescues the shipwrecked Sebastian in *Twelfth Night*; (3) the brother of Leonato in *Much Ado About Nothing*; (4) the father of *Proteus in *The Two Gentlemen of Verona*; (5) the usurping brother of *Prospero in *The Tempest*.

Antonio and Mellida, a two-part play by J. *Marston, printed 1602, probably acted two years earlier; it provided Jonson with materials for his ridicule of Marston in *The Poetaster*.

In Part I of the play Antonio, son of Andrugio, duke of Genoa, is in love with Mellida, daughter of Piero, duke of Venice. The two states are at war and Genoa has been defeated, and a price set in Venice on the heads of Antonio and Andrugio. Antonio, disguised as an Amazon, comes to Piero's court to see Mellida. Mellida flees with Antonio but is captured. Andrugio offers himself as a victim to Piero, who appears to relent and assents to the marriage of Antonio and Mellida, and the first part closes joyfully.

In Part II Piero reveals his true character. He kills Andrugio, contrives the dishonour of Mellida in order to prevent the match, plots the death of Antonio, and gains the hand of Andrugio's widow. Mellida dies broken-hearted. Antonio, urged by the ghost of his father, assumes the disguise of a fool and kills Piero.

Antony and Cleopatra, a tragedy by *Shakespeare probably written 1606-7, not printed until the First *Folio of 1623. Its chief source is the *Life of Antony* by *Plutarch, as translated by Sir T. *North, which Shakespeare followed extremely closely in places, as in Enobarbus's famous speech beginning: 'The barge she sat in, like a burnish'd throne, | Burn'd on the water' (II. ii. 195-6). Minor sources include the plays by the countess of *Pembroke and S. *Daniel.

The play presents Mark Antony, the great soldier and noble prince, at Alexandria, enthralled by the beauty of the Egyptian queen Cleopatra. Recalled by the death of his wife Fulvia and political developments, he tears himself from Cleopatra and returns to Rome, where the estrangement between him and Octavius Caesar is terminated by his marriage to Octavia, Caesar's sister, an event which provokes the intense jealousy of Cleopatra. But the reconciliation is short-lived, and Antony leaves Octavia and returns to Egypt. At the battle of Actium, the flight of the Egyptian squadron is followed by the retreat of Antony, pursued to Alexandria by Caesar. There, after a momentary success, Antony is finally defeated. On the false report of Cleopatra's death, he falls upon his sword. He is borne to the monument where Cleopatra has taken refuge and dies in her arms. Cleopatra, fallen into Caesar's power but determined not to grace his triumph, takes her own life by the bite of an asp. See also ALL FOR LOVE.

APELLES (*fl.* 330-320 BC), a Greek painter, famous in antiquity. The names and in some cases descriptions of thirty of his pictures are known, but as no ancient copies or imitations of them have survived, the quality of his work remains unknown. Born on the island of Cos, he won the favour of *Alexander the Great, who would not allow anyone else to paint his portrait and who is reputed to have given Apelles his mistress, Pancaspe (the *Campaspe of English literature), when the artist fell in love with her while painting her in the nude. After Alexander's death Apelles went to the court of Ptolemy I of Egypt, where he produced the 'Calumny' which *Botticelli tried to recreate on the basis of *Lucian's account. He was the inventor of the self-portrait, and some of the conventions he established—representing his sitters full or three-quarter face and, with more crowded compositions, stringing out his figures in a line—were widely copied during the Renaissance. Pancaspe is also supposed to have been the model for the masterpiece whose description inspired *Titian's Ellesmere Venus, where the nude and newly born Aphrodite is shown wringing out her hair in the shallows. Some authorities however bestow this honour on the famous courtesan Phryne.

Apemantus, the 'churlish philosopher' in Shakespeare's *Timon of Athens*.

Aphorism, a term transferred from the 'Aphorisms of Hippocrates' to other sententious statements of the principles of physical science, and later (e.g. in Coleridge's *Aids to Reflection*, which are divided into 'Aphorisms' and 'Comments') to statements of principles generally.

Thence it has come to mean any short pithy statement into which much thought or observation is compressed. J. S. *Mill wrote a fragment on aphorisms, and J. *Morley a short discourse on the same subject. See *The Oxford Book of Aphorisms* (1983), compiled by John Gross.

Apocalypse, The, from a Greek verb meaning 'to disclose', a 'revelation' or an 'unveiling', and the title given to the book of Revelation in the NT. The term 'apocalyptic literature' is used in a broader sense to describe prophetic writings generally, of a range which includes many of the works of *Blake, of *Yeats (e.g. 'The Second Coming'), D. *Lessing's *The Four-Gated City*, the 'disaster' novels of J. G. *Ballard, and other *Science Fiction writers, etc. D. *Lodge has described *Mailer's *The Armies of the Night* and *Barth's *Giles Goat-Boy*, as 'products of the apocalyptic imagination' (*The Novelist at the Crossroads*, 1971), a mode of imagination which many have seen as peculiarly strong in the 20th cent. when, in Mailer's words, 'reality is no longer realistic'. See also F. Kermode, *The Sense of an Ending* (1967), which discusses the implications for fictional narrative of the Judaeo-Christian view of history as linear, i.e. as possessing a beginning, a middle in which narrator and reader exist, and a necessarily different ending.

Apocrypha, The, in its special sense, those books included in the Septuagint and Vulgate versions of the OT which were not written in Hebrew and not counted genuine by the Jews, and which at the Reformation were excluded from the Sacred Canon by the Protestant party, as having no well-grounded claims to inspired authorship. They are 1 and 2 Esdras, Tobit, Judith, the Rest of Esther, the *Wisdom of Solomon, Ecclesiasticus, Baruch (with the Epistle of Jeremiah), the Song of the Three Holy Children, the History of Susanna, Bel and the Dragon, the Prayer of Manasses, 1 and 2 Maccabees.
   The texts of the Apocryphal Gospels, Acts, Epistles, and Apocalypses are printed in *The Apocryphal New Testament*, trans. M. R. *James (1924).

APOLLINAIRE, Guillaume (1880–1918), French poet, prose writer, and art critic. He was a prominent figure in the avant-garde in Paris during the early years of the 20th cent., and an ardent supporter of contemporary developments both in poetry and in painting (*Méditations esthétiques: les peintres cubistes*, 1913; English trans., 1944). His principal volumes of poetry are *Alcools* (1913, English trans., 1964), and *Calligrammes* (1918).

APOLLODORUS (2nd cent. BC), Athenian grammarian. He was known to have written

about the gods, and an extant treatise on mythology, the *Bibliotheca*, was attributed to him. First printed in 1555, this work was widely used in the second half of the 16th cent. and, directly or indirectly, provided *Jonson and *Milton with some of their mythological material.

APOLLONIUS RHODIUS (*fl.* end 3rd cent. BC), Alexandrian poet. He chose for his epic a conventionally heroic legend, 'The Voyage of the Argo', but he treated his subject with psychological insight, emphasized its romantic features, and left his readers keenly aware of his own presence as authoritative narrator. In short, he introduced into the genre many elements that were not found in *Homer. Apollonius had an important disciple in *Virgil. There are echoes of his verse in *Paradise Lost*, and he was naturally W. *Morris's main source for *The Life and Death of Jason*, but otherwise his influence on modern literature has been undeservedly small.

Apollyon, 'The Destroyer', the angel of the bottomless pit (Rev. 9: 11). He figures in Bunyan's *Pilgrim's Progress*.

Apologia pro Vita Sua, see NEWMAN, J. H.

Apologue, a fable conveying a moral lesson.

Apology for Poetry, An, see DEFENCE OF POETRY, A.

Apology for Smectymnuus, see SMECTYMNUUS.

Apology for the Life of **Mr Colley Cibber,** see CIBBER, C.

Apophthegm, a fable conveying a moral lesson.

Aposiopesis, a rhetorical artifice, in which the speaker comes to a sudden halt in the middle of a sentence, as if unable or unwilling to proceed.

Apostles, The, an exclusive intellectual society (officially 'The Cambridge Conversazione Society') formed in Cambridge in 1820, for the purpose of friendship and formal discussion. During the 19th cent. members included A. *Hallam, *Tennyson, *Milnes, and R. C. *Trench, and the 20th cent. saw a new age of brilliance, largely inspired by the influence of G. E. *Moore, with members such as *Keynes, *Strachey, B. *Russell, L. *Woolf, and E. M. *Forster. Members are elected for life.

Apostrophe (from Greek, 'to turn away'), a figure of speech in which the writer rhetorically addresses a dead or absent person or abstraction, e.g. 'Milton! thou shouldst be living at this hour' (*Wordsworth, 'London, 1802').

Appius, see VIRGINIA.

Appius and Virginia, (1) a tragedy traditionally attributed to *Webster, but by some authorities to *Heywood, in whole or part. R. *Brooke first seriously questioned the Webster attribution in 1913, and suggested Heywood; F. L. *Lucas in his 1927 edition of Webster argues for a distribution of scenes between the two playwrights; and A. M. Clark concludes in 'The Authorship of *Appius and Virginia*' (MLR, Jan. 1921) that Webster revised the play, but 'the bulk of the play is Heywood's alone'. The date of production is uncertain (?1603–34) and it appears not to have been printed until 1654. The plot is taken from the classical legend (see VIRGINIA) which forms one of the stories in Painter's *Palace of Pleasure*; (2) a tragedy by J. *Dennis.

Apprentice's Vade Mecum, The, a handbook by S. *Richardson.

APULEIUS (*c.* AD 125–after 170), North African rhetorician who rehashed Greek works for Latin readers. His treatise *De daemone Socratis* was an important source for that belief in 'middle spirits' supposedly existing as a form of life between men and angels, of which Prospero's Ariel and the sylphs in *The Rape of the Lock* can serve as examples. Apuleius' best-known work is his novel *Metamorphoses* or *The Golden Ass*. MSS of this proliferated from the 14th cent. onwards, and it became a quarry for the novella, for which its intercalated stories served as a model. *Boccaccio borrowed three and others appeared in the 15th-cent. *Cent nouvelles nouvelles*, both of which were translated into English. Generally, the adventures of the ass stand at the beginning of that *picaresque tradition which eventually produced *Tom Jones*. Special mention must be made, however, of one story, *Cupid and Psyche*.

AQUINAS, St Thomas (*c.*1225–74), an Italian philosopher and Dominican friar from Aquino in southern Italy, the greatest of the medieval Scholastic theologians. He represents in his writings, especially in the *Summa Theologica*, the culmination of Scholastic philosophy, the harmony of faith and reason, and in particular the reconciliation of Christian theology with Aristotelian philosophy (see SCHOLASTICISM). The *Summa*, which is unfinished, is a vast synthesis of the moral and political sciences, brought within a theological and metaphysical framework. He was called the 'Doctor Angelicus', and by his school companions 'the Dumb Ox'. His followers are called Thomists, and they are still an active school in contemporary philosophy, especially in France. He is a very important influence on *Dante's *Divina Commedia* whose philosophical framework is based on Aquinas (see *Paradiso*, x–xiii). His other major works are the *Summa Contra Gentiles* and a series of commentaries on *Aristotle. He promoted and used the translation of the works of Aristotle from Greek into Latin by William of Moerbeke. See

F. C. Copleston, *Aquinas* (1955); *Summa* trans. in 20 vols (1911–25), by Fathers of the Dominican Province.

Arabia Deserta, see DOUGHTY, C. M.

Arabian Nights Entertainments, or *The Thousand and One Nights*, is a collection of stories written in Arabic which were made known in Europe by the translation of Antoine Galland (1646–1715), whose version appeared between 1704 and 1717. An anonymous 'Grub Street' version appeared in English, 1705–8, and E. W. *Lane's bowdlerized version appeared in 1839–41. The first complete English translation was by John Payne (1842–1916), which appeared in a limited edition, 1882–4; this was followed by the most celebrated version, by Sir Richard *Burton (1885–8), which, despite its audacity, was a critical and financial success.

The tales derive from Indian, Persian, and Arabic sources. The framework (the story of the king who killed his wives successively on the morning after the consummation of their marriage, until he married the clever *Scheherazade, who saved her life by the tales she told him) is taken from a lost book of Persian fairy-tales, called *Hazar Afsanah* (A Thousand Tales), which was translated into Arabic *c.* AD 850; it is mentioned by the Arab encyclopaedist al-Mas'ūdī (d. AD 956). Other stories of different origins were added to this at various dates by professional story-tellers, and a standardized version collected by an unknown Egyptian editor appeared towards the end of the 18th cent. Burton believed that the earliest stories, including that of *Sindbad, dated back to the 8th cent., and the latest from the 16th cent.

The stories, dismissed by most Arab scholars as merely popular and no true part of classical Arabic literature, captivated the European imagination, and contributed greatly to the vogue for *oriental tales in the 18th and early 19th cents. (See also AHMED, HĀRŪN AR-RASHĪD, BARMECIDE.)

ARAGON, Louis (1897–1982), French poet, novelist, essayist, journalist, and political activist. He began his career under the influence of *Dada, and later became one of the leading exponents of *Surrealism. In 1919, with *Breton and Soupault, he founded the review *Littérature*, and in 1924, with Breton, *La Révolution surréaliste*. His first collections of poetry were *Feu de joie* (1920) and *Le Mouvement perpétuel* (1925). In 1927 he joined the Communist Party, and finally broke with the surrealist movement in 1932. During the Second World War he became one of the most popular of French Resistance poets, with *Le Crève-cœur* (1941), *Les Yeux d'Elsa* (1942), *Le Musée Grévin* (1943), and *La Diane française* (1945). His novels include *Le Paysan de Paris* (1926), *Les Cloches de Bâle* (1934, English trans., *The Bells of Basel*, 1936), *Les Beaux Quartiers* (1936,

Residential Quarter, 1938), and *La Semaine Sainte* (1958, *Holy Week*, 1961).

Aramis, see THREE MUSKETEERS, THE.

Araygnement of Paris, The, a pastoral play in verse by G. *Peele, published 1584.

It was written for and played before Queen Elizabeth, whose beauty and virtue are duly celebrated. Paris is tending his flocks on Ida, with Oenone his wife, when he is called on to decide to which of the three goddesses, Juno, Pallas, or Venus, the golden apple shall be awarded. He decides in favour of Venus, who carries away Paris, leaving Oenone disconsolate. Juno and Pallas arraign Paris before the gods of partiality in his judgement. The case is referred to Diana. She evades the delicate choice by awarding the apple to the nymph Eliza, 'our Zabeta fayre', i.e. Queen Elizabeth.

Arbaces, the passionate hero of Beaumont and Fletcher's *A King and no King*.

ARBER, Edward (1836–1912), began his career as an Admiralty clerk, 1854–78, but studied English literature at King's College, London, and in 1881 became professor of English at Mason College, Birmingham. He produced *English Reprints* (1868–71), *Transcripts of the Registers of the Company of Stationers of London, 1554–1640* (1875–94), and *Term Catalogues, 1668–1709* (1903–6).

ARBLAY, Madame d', see BURNEY, F.

ARBUCKLE, James (d. 1742), Irish poet, educated at Glasgow, where he clashed with the Calvinist authorities for his active part in politics and student dramatics. He espoused the philosophy of the third earl of *Shaftesbury. In association with *Hutcheson he wrote moral and aesthetic essays which were serialized in the *Dublin Weekly Journal* (1725–7) and later re-issued as *Hibernicus's Letters* (1729), and he attempted a short-lived Dublin periodical, *The Tribune*, in 1729. His student poetry was published in broadsheets or in *The Edinburgh Miscellany* (1720). He was at one time befriended by *Swift and in 1730 published the parody 'A Panegyric on the Reverend D–n S—t' formerly ascribed to Swift himself. Some classical translations and other manuscript poetry are now in the National Library of Wales.

ARBUTHNOT, John (1667–1735), was MD of St Andrews and from 1705 physician to Queen Anne, whose death was a blow to his prosperity. In 1711 he formed a close friendship with *Swift, and he was acquainted with most of the literary men of his day including *Pope, who in 1735 was to address to him one of his finest satirical epistles, generally known as *Prologue to the Satires*. Arbuthnot's *History of *John Bull*, a collection of pamphlets issued anonymously in 1712 advocating the termination of the war with France, was included in Pope and Swift's *Miscellanies* of 1727. In 1712 he also published a satiric pamphlet, *The Art of Political Lying*. He was a member of the *Scriblerus Club and principal author of the *Memoirs of *Martinus Scriblerus*, which were published with Pope's *Works* in 1741. He and Pope assisted *Gay in writing the unsuccessful comedy *Three Hours after Marriage* (1717). Many anonymous works were attributed to him, and he also wrote on mathematics and on medical matters; his *An Essay concerning the nature of Ailments* (1731) is a farsighted account of the importance of diet, though ironically he himself died of illnesses associated with overeating. He published one poem, *ΓΝΩΘΙ ΣΕΑΥΤΟΝ (Know Thyself*, 1734, anon.). He was a much loved figure, witty, kind-hearted, and absent-minded, and his satires are plain, clear, homely, and predominantly good-natured. Dr *Johnson described him as 'the most universal genius' (*Life and Works*, ed. G. A. Aitken, 1892).

ARC, Joan of, see JOAN OF ARC.

'Arcades, Part of an entertainment presented to the Countess Dowager of Darby at Harefield, by som Noble persons of her Family', by *Milton, written ?1630–?3 possibly at the suggestion of his friend Henry *Lawes, who wrote the music for the songs; published 1645.

This short piece consists of a song by nymphs and shepherds as they approach the seat of state of the countess, an address to them by the Genius of the Wood, and two further songs. The particular event which occasioned this celebration is not known.

Arcadia, a bleak and mountainous district in the central Peloponnese which became, thanks to references in *Virgil's *Eclogues*, the traditional and incongruous location of the idealized world of the *pastoral. Virgil himself was keenly aware of the clash between the realistic and idealizing purposes of the genre, and his use of the term may have reflected this awareness. But the writers who revived the pastoral in the Renaissance knew nothing about the real Arcadia and the idealized landscape reigns supreme in their work.

Arcadia, a series of verse eclogues connected by prose narrative, published 1504 by *Sannazar, occupied with the loves, laments, and other doings of various shepherds in Arcadia. The work, which was immensely popular, was a link between the *pastorals of *Theocritus and *Virgil and those of *Montemayor, *Sidney, *Spenser, and later writers.

Arcadia, The, a prose romance by Sir P. *Sidney, including poems and pastoral eclogues in a wide variety of verse forms. It exists in two versions: the first, completed by 1581, and much of it written at *Wilton, is known as the

Old Arcadia. Its survival as an independent work was discovered by Bertram Dobell in 1907. The second version, now known as the *New Arcadia*, was Sidney's radical revision, made about 1583–4 but never completed. It breaks down in the third of the original five books, having already run to twice the length of the original. It was this revised version which was first printed, on its own in 1590, with chapter divisions and summaries 'not of Sir *Philip Sidneis* dooing', and then in 1593 and thereafter with books iii–v of the *Old Arcadia* added to make a complete-seeming but hybrid work. It was the hybrid *Arcadia* only that was available to readers until the 20th cent.

The *Old Arcadia* is in five 'Books or Acts', sometimes quasi-dramatic in use of dialogue, interspersed with a large number of poems and songs. The first four books are followed by pastoral eclogues on themes linked or contrasted with the main narrative. The story is of the attempts of Arcadia's ruler, the foolish old duke Basilius, to prevent the fulfilment of an oracle by withdrawing to two rustic 'lodges' with his wife Gynecia and their daughters Pamela and Philoclea. Two young princes, Musidorus and Pyrocles, gain access to the retired court by disguising themselves as, respectively, a shepherd and an Amazon. A complicated series of intrigues ensues, with Basilius and Gynecia both falling in love with the disguised Pyrocles; Musidorus meanwhile becomes enmeshed with the family of Dametas, an ill-bred herdsman who has been made Pamela's guardian, his shrewish wife Miso, and foolish daughter Mopsa. Pyrocles succeeds in seducing Philoclea and Musidorus attempts to elope with Pamela, but their schemes go awry when Basilius appears to die of a potion believed by his wife to be an aphrodisiac, and Pyrocles and Philoclea are discovered in bed by Dametas. The climax of the narrative is a trial presided over by Euarchus, the just ruler of Macedon, who sentences Gynecia to be buried alive and Pyrocles and Musidorus to be executed. Their disguises and assumed names prevent Euarchus from recognizing the young men as his own son and nephew, but even when their identities are revealed he asserts that 'If rightly I have judged, then rightly have I judged mine own children.' The day is saved by Basilius' awakening from what turns out to have been only a sleeping potion. Among the minor characters Philisides, a melancholy gentleman-poet, is a version of Sidney himself. Strephon and Klaius, two shepherds in love with the mysterious Urania, recite two of the most elaborate love-complaints in the romance, the first being the double sestina 'Ye goat-herd gods, that love the grassy mountains'. Other memorable poems include the anatomical praise of Philoclea's beauties 'What tongue can her perfections tell', the echo poem in hexameters 'Fair rocks, goodly rivers, sweet woods, when shall I see peace?', the asclepiadics 'O sweet woods, the delight of solitariness', the beast-fable on tyranny 'As I my little flock on Ister bank', and the sonnet 'My true love hath my heart, and I have his.'

No new poems were added in the *New Arcadia*, but the method of narration was made far more complex, both stylistically and thematically. Major new characters include Basilius' wicked sister-in-law Cecropia and her well-meaning but unfortunate son Amphialus, who is in love with Philoclea. The first two books are enlarged by the addition of tournaments and courtly spectacles and by detailed accounts of the exploits of Pyrocles and Musidorus before they reached Arcadia. In the third revised book mock battles give way to real ones, after the two Arcadian princesses and the disguised Pyrocles have been taken captive by Cecropia; their sufferings in prison are powerfully described, in particular those of the patient and dignified Pamela, whose prayer in prison was later to be used by Charles I:

Let calamitie be the exercise, but not the overthrowe of my vertue: let their power prevaile, but prevaile not to destruction: let my greatnes be their praie: let my paine be the sweetnes of their revenge: let them (if so it seem good unto thee) vexe me with more and more punishment. But, ô Lord, let never their wickednes have such a hand, but that I may carie a pure minde in a pure bodie. (Bk. iii, ch. 6)

*Milton in *Eikonoklastes* attacked the monarch for his use of a prayer from a 'vain amatorious Poem'. The *New Arcadia* breaks off in mid-sentence just as rescue seems to be at hand for the imprisoned and besieged princesses.

The composite *Arcadia*, as printed from 1593 onwards, was attacked by *Hazlitt as 'one of the greatest monuments of the abuse of intellectual power upon record', mainly because of its prose style. T. S. *Eliot, more damningly still, called it 'a monument of dulness'. It was, however, a highly popular book throughout the 17th cent., and its plot material was frequently plundered by dramatists. Shakespeare based the Gloucester plot of *King Lear* on Sidney's story of 'the *Paphlagonian* unkinde king', and *Richardson took the name of his first heroine, Pamela, from Sidney's romance. In the later 20th cent. there have been signs that it is being appreciated again. C. S. *Lewis said that 'What a man thinks of it, far more than what he thinks of Shakespeare or Spenser or Donne, tests the depth of his sympathy with the sixteenth century.' Jean Robertson edited the *Old Arcadia* in 1973; an edition of the *New Arcadia* is in preparation.

Archer, (1) a character in Farquhar's *The Beaux' Stratagem*; (2) Isabel, the heroine of H. James's *The Portrait of a Lady*.

ARCHER, William (1856–1924), was born in Scotland, educated in Edinburgh, and spent large parts of his boyhood in Norway, where he became acquainted with the works of *Ibsen. He became a drama critic in London in 1879 and worked thereafter for various papers, exercising much influence. The establishment of Ibsen and of G. B. *Shaw owed much to his encouragement. He translated Ibsen's *Pillars of Society*, which became in 1880 the first Ibsen play to be produced in London, where it made little impression. Archer published *English Dramatists of Today* in 1882, a study of *Henry Irving* (1883), and *Masks or Faces?* (1888). In 1889 his translation of *A Doll's House* was produced, and gave rise to much antagonism, which increased with the production of *Ghosts* and *Hedda Gabler* in 1891. In 1890 Archer published a study of *Macready and then in 1891 his five-volume edition of Ibsen's prose dramas in translation (some with collaboration). He and his brother produced a translation of *Peer Gynt* in 1892 and Archer's own collected criticism, *A Theatre World*, appeared in 1897. The collected works of Ibsen appeared in 1906–7, and in the latter year Archer's detailed proposals, with *Granville-Barker, for a National Theatre. In 1919 he assisted with the establishment of the New Shakespeare Company at Stratford-upon-Avon. In *The Old Drama and the New* (1923) he pressed the merits of Ibsen, Shaw, and *Galsworthy, among others; and in the same year his own play, *The Green Goddess*, was produced with great success in the US and later in London.

Archetype, a word meaning prototype, or original pattern from which copies are made, and adapted by *Jung to mean 'a pervasive idea, image or symbol that forms part of the collective unconscious' (*OED* 1972 Supplement). Literary criticism with a Jungian slant has devoted itself to detecting archetypal figures in literature, and in myths, legends, and fairy-tales: e.g. The Divine Child, The Earth Mother, The Enchanted Prince. Jung himself described the archetypal qualities of many natural phenomena: e.g. a horse 'represents the non-human psyche, the subhuman, animal side, the unconscious' ('The Practical Use of Dream Analysis', Vol. 16, *Collected Works*), whereas the tree represents 'growth, life, unfolding of form in a physical and spiritual sense' ('The Philosophical Tree', Vol. 13, *Collected Works*).

Archgallo, see ARTEGAL.

Archimago, or **Archimage,** in Spenser's *Faerie Queene*, is the great enchanter, symbolizing Hypocrisy, who deceives *Una by assuming the appearance of the *Redcrosse Knight (I. i). His deceits are exposed and Archimago is 'layd full low in dungeon deepe' (I. xii. 36). From this he emerges in Bk II to seek vengeance on Sir *Guyon for what he has suffered at the hands of the Redcrosse Knight, and employs *Braggadochio for the purpose.

Arch-poet, The, the name given to the anonymous German writer of *Goliardic Latin poetry whose patron was Rainald of Dassel, arch-chancellor of Frederick Barbarossa and archbishop of Cologne. His best-known poem is the 'Confession' (see F. J. E. Raby, *The Oxford Book of Medieval Latin Verse*, 1959 etc., no. 183, pp. 263–6). The term was used by *Pope and *Fielding as equivalent to *poet laureate.

Arcite, see PALAMON AND ARCITE.

Arden, (1) a large forest in Warwickshire often referred to in romance literature. In Drayton's *Poly-Olbion* it extends from the Severn to the Trent (xiii. 16); (2) the forest which is the setting for the pastoral parts of Shakespeare's *As You Like It*, often assumed to be identical with (1) and perhaps so intended by Shakespeare, but actually based on the forest of Ardennes in what is now Belgium; (3) the surname of Shakespeare's mother Mary; (4), based on (1) and (2), the distinguishing name of a series of scholarly editions of Shakespeare's plays initiated by W. J. Craig and R. H. Case in 1899, and revised under the general editorship of Una Ellis-Fermor, H. F. Brooks, H. Jenkins, and Brian Morris from 1951 onwards.

ARDEN, John (1930–), playwright, born in Barnsley, Yorkshire, and educated at the Universities of Cambridge and Edinburgh, where he studied architecture. In 1957 (the year in which he married Margaretta D'Arcy) he had his first professional production, at the Royal Court, of *The Waters of Babylon*, a grotesque, satirical, sprawling play about a corrupt municipal lottery organized by a slum landlord. This was followed by *Live Like Pigs* (1958), dealing with social conflict and violence on a housing estate. *Serjeant Musgrave's Dance* (1959), set in a colliery town in the North of England in 1860–80, shows Musgrave, a deserter from the British army, attempting to exact revenge for the death of a colleague, but finding that violence breeds violence: as his co-deserter concludes, 'You can't cure the pox by further whoring.' Arden here mixes a rich, idiosyncratic, semi-historical prose with ballad and verse, as he does in *Armstrong's Last Goodnight* (1964), another fable about violence, set in the Border country in the 1530s, and figuring Sir D. *Lindsay as principal opponent of the freebooter John Armstrong of Gilnockie, whose hanging ends the play; Arden in a preface says he has composed a 'Babylonish dialect' based on the Scots of *Dunbar, *Henryson, and *MacDiarmid, inspired by A. *Miller's method in *The Crucible*. In a preface to *The Workhouse Donkey* (1963), a play about municipal corruption, Arden claims that 'the theatre must be catholic' and celebrate the Dionysian attributes of 'noise, disorder, drunkenness, lasciviousness, nudity, generosity, corruption, fertility and ease'. Widely praised as one of the most innovatory dramatists of the 1960s, his later plays (written with M. D'Arcy) have been less exuberant and ambiguous, and more deliberately socialist and doctrinaire. His first novel, *Silence Among the Weapons*, a rambling, picaresque work set in the 1st cent. BC, appeared in 1982.

Ardenne, The Fountain of, in Boiardo's **Orlando Innamorato*, had the power of changing to hate the love of those who drank its waters.

Arden of Feversham, *The Tragedy of Mr*, a play published 1592, author unknown. It has been attributed to Shakespeare, and its latest editor, M. L. Wine (1973), claims that internal stylistic evidence qualifies it for a place in the 'Shakespeare apocrypha'.

The play deals with the persistent and eventually successful attempts of Mistress Arden and her paramour Mosby to murder Arden: they hire two murderers, Black Will and Shakebag. The crime is discovered, and Mosby and Mrs Arden executed. The play's source is an account in *Holinshed of an actual murder committed in February 1551. *Lillo wrote a play on the same subject.

ARDIZZONE, Edward Jeffrey Irving (1900–79), painter, water-colourist, and printmaker, and one of the best known of 20th-cent. illustrators, of both adult and children's books.

Areopagitica: *a speech of Mr John Milton for the liberty of the unlicenc'd printing, to the Parliament of England*, by *Milton, published in 1644. The title is derived from the Areopagus, the hills of Ares near the Acropolis in Athens where the Upper Council met. This discourse, which was unlicensed and unregistered, was inspired partly by Parliament's attempts to suppress Milton's own pamphlet on divorce. Milton, addressing the 'Lords and Commons of England', attacks their recent order (1643) 'that no book . . . shall be henceforth printed unless the same be first approved and licensed by such . . . as shall be thereto appointed'. He shows, first, that licensing has been chiefly the practice of those whom the Presbyterians most detest, the Papacy and the Inquisition, whereas Moses, Daniel, and St Paul, by precept or example, enjoin freedom in the pursuit of learning. 'Prove all things, hold fast to that which is good.' Next, that promiscuous reading, constant testing, and diversity of opinion are necessary to the growth of virtue and knowledge. And thirdly, that the attempt to keep out evil doctrine by licensing is like 'the exploit of the gallant man who thought to pound up the crows by shutting the park gate'. Not only will licensing do no good, but it will be a grave discouragement to learning; he quotes the case of the imprisoned *Galileo. Milton builds his rhetoric to a magnificent exhortation to the 'Lords and Commons of

England' to consider 'what Nation it is whereof ye are, and whereof ye are governors: A Nation not slow and dull, but of a quick, ingenious and piercing spirit . . . Methinks I see in my mind a noble and puissant nation rousing herself like a strong man after sleep, and shaking her invincible locks. Methinks I see her as an eagle mewing her mighty youth . . .' Truth is stronger than falsehood, he concludes, and 'a gross conforming stupidity' more to be feared than new opinions.

Arethusa, (1) a legendary fountain in Ortygia, named after a nymph with whom the river-god Alpheus fell in love: she fled from him to Ortygia, where Artemis transformed her into a fountain, but Alpheus, flowing beneath the sea, was united with her; (2) a character in Beaumont and Fletcher's **Philaster*.

ARETINO, Pietro, or the Aretine (1492–1556), born at Arezzo in Italy, whence his name. He was author of five comedies and a tragedy, and also of satires and other works of a scandalous or licentious character. He is frequently mentioned in English works of the Elizabethan and later periods and differently appreciated, in comments ranging from 'It was one of the wittiest knaves God ever made' of Nashe (**The Unfortunate Traveller*) to 'that notorious ribald of Arezzo' of Milton (**Areopagitica*).

Argalia, in Boiardo's **Orlando Innamorato*, the brother of *Angelica.

Argan, the title character in *Molière's *Le Malade imaginaire*.

Argante, (1) in the *Brut* of *Laȝamon, *Morgan le Fay, of whose name it may be a corruption. She is the fairy queen to whom Arthur, after the last battle, is borne to be healed of his wounds in Avalon; (2) in Spenser's **Faerie Queene* (III. vii), a mighty and licentious giantess, typifying lust, daughter of Typhoeus the Titan.

Argantes, in Tasso's **Jerusalem Delivered*, a fierce Circassian, a champion on the pagan side, finally killed by Tancred.

Argentina, or Argentoratum, in imprints, Strasburg.

Argosy, The: (1) *a Magazine of Tales, Travels, Essays and Poems*, a periodical owned and edited 1865–87 by Mrs H. *Wood, who was herself a major contributor: it published work by many leading writers, including A. *Trollope, C. *Kingsley, and C. *Reade, and it survived until 1901; (2) *the World's Best Stories* (1926–40; as *The Argosy of Complete Stories*, 1940–74), consisted largely of reprints of work by established writers, including *Conrad, H. E. *Bates, *Maugham, *Sansom, and many others.

ARGYLE, Archibald Campbell, eighth earl,

first marquess of (1598–1661), who took a prominent part in the events in Scotland that contributed to the downfall of Charles I, figures in Scott's *The Legend of Montrose*, where his character is contrasted with that of his great rival, the earl of *Montrose. He was beheaded.

ARGYLE, John Campbell, second duke of (1678–1743), a prime agent in bringing about the union of England and Scotland and a distinguished military commander (he suppressed Mar's rising of 1715), figures in Scott's *The Heart of Midlothian*.

Arian heresy, named after its promulgator Arius, a Lybian priest born about the middle of the 3rd cent. and parish priest near Alexandria *c.*310, declared that God the Son, because begotten by the Father, must have an origin in time and therefore is not 'consubstantial' with the Father. This breach of the doctrine of the Trinity was condemned at the Council of Nicaea, summoned by Constantine in 325, which produced the Nicene Creed as the official declaration of the Church. Most of the 'barbarian' tribes who overran the Western Roman Empire (except the Franks, Angles, and Saxons) were converted by Arian preachers, so the heretical doctrine remained active up to the 6th cent. in the beliefs of such leaders as Alaric.

Ariel, (1) an airy spirit in Shakespeare's *The Tempest*, whom Prospero has released from bondage under the 'damn'd witch Sycorax' and employs as executor of his magical schemes; (2) a rebel angel in Milton's *Paradise Lost* (vi. 371); (3) in Pope's *Rape of the Lock* (ii. 53 ff.) the chief of the sylphs whose 'humbler Province is to tend the Fair'.

   Shakespeare's character (1) has inspired many later writers to identify the name 'Ariel' with poetic imagination. T. S. *Eliot called five Christmas poems (1927–54) 'Ariel poems', for instance, the first *Penguin paperback was *Maurois' life of *Shelley called *Ariel* (1935), and there have been several literary journals with 'Ariel' as title. See also PLATH, S.

Arioch, in Milton's *Paradise Lost* (vi. 371), one of the rebel angels.

ARIOSTO, Ludovico (1474–1535), born at Reggio, spent the greater part of his life at Ferrara and for many years was in the service, first of Cardinal Ippolito, and then of Duke Alfonso I, of Este. This family he exalted in his poem *Orlando Furioso*, published in its final form in 1532, the greatest of Italian romantic epics. He also wrote Italian and Latin lyrics, satires (known to *Wyatt), and four comedies, of which one, *I Suppositi* (1509), came through to Shakespeare's *The Taming of the Shrew* via Gascoigne's *Supposes*.

ARISTOPHANES (*c.*448–380 BC), Athenian comic dramatist whose satirical plays, the only surviving representatives of the Old Comedy, attacked individuals rather than types. Because of the difficulties of his language and the obscurity of his contemporary references, Aristophanes did not receive much attention in England until the 19th cent., which produced translations by B. H. Kennedy (*The Birds*, 1804), Thomas Mitchell, and *Frere. These were followed by versions by B. B. Rogers (1904 onwards), which were ingenious but failed to find favour with scholars; by G. *Murray; and by Dudley Fitts, whose version of *Lysistrata* was performed with considerable success in 1957 at the Royal Court. Other recent translations include A. H. Sommerstein's *Three Plays* (1973). The extant works of Aristophanes are *The Acharnians*; *The Knights*; *The Clouds*; *The Peace*; *The Wasps*; *The Birds*; *The Frogs* (of which the best known lines are the onomatopoeic chorus, 'Co-ax, co-ax, co-ax, Brekekekek co-ax'); *Plutus*; *Lysistrata* and *Ecclesiazusae*, both dealing with government by women; and *Thesmophoriazusae*, which presents the trial and conviction of *Euripides at the female festival of the Thesmophoria.

Aristophanes' Apology, *including a transcript from Euripides: being the last adventure of Balaustion,* a long poem in blank verse by R. *Browning, published 1875 as a sequel to *Balaustion's Adventure*.

   The core of the poem is a protracted argument between Balaustion and *Aristophanes as to the moral, social, and metaphysical value of the different aesthetics they espouse; Balaustion defending the visionary humanism of *Euripides, Aristophanes his own coarse realism. Part of Balaustion's argument consists in reading Euripides' play *Herakles* (whose plot, the madness of Herakles and his destruction of his family, constitutes the thematic focus of the poem). The poem is by no means the straightforward defence of Euripides by Browning that it has been taken to be: Balaustion, not Browning, is the speaker. The structure—a monologue containing the narrative of a dialogue and the reading of a play—is arguably Browning's profoundest exploration of the relation of poetic discourse to absolute values such as 'truth' or 'reality'. The poem also contains the remarkable fragment 'Thamuris marching', which reworks some of the material of '*Childe Roland to the Dark Tower Came'.

ARISTOTLE (384–322 BC), was born at Stagira, in Macedon, where his father was physician to the king Amyntas II. Sent to Athens in 367, he studied under *Plato for twenty years. Then after a period of travel he was appointed by Philip of Macedon to be tutor to the future *Alexander the Great in 342 and seven years later returned to Athens where he opened a school in the Lyceum, a grove outside the city. His extant works are believed to have been the notes he used for his lectures. They cover logic, ethics, metaphysics, physics, zoology, politics, rhetoric, and poetics. Transmitted through translations, they shaped the development of medieval thought first in the Arab world, then in the Latin West, where Aristotle came to be regarded as the source of all knowledge. His logical treatises won a central place in the curriculum during the 12th cent. Then after a brief struggle his ethical, metaphysical, and scientific works were harmonized with Christianity and constituted the subject-matter of higher education from the 13th to the 17th cent. They shaped the thinking of Englishmen writing in Latin from *Grosseteste to *Herbert of Cherbury, and their influence can be traced in *Spenser, *Donne, and occasionally in Sir T. *Browne. By the end of the 17th cent., however, the Aristotelian world-view had fallen out of favour except for the *Poetics. This treatise, virtually unknown during the Middle Ages, came into prominence in the middle of the 16th cent. and contributed to the rise of *Neo-classicism. It has left its mark on the critical writings of *Sidney, *Dryden, and even Dr *Johnson.

ARLEN, Michael (1895–1956), novelist, born Dikran Kuyumjian in Bulgaria of Armenian descent and educated at Malvern College and Edinburgh. He wrote many ornate and mannered novels of fashionable London life, but is chiefly remembered for his best-seller *The Green Hat* (1924). In 1928 he married and settled in the South of France, returning to London to offer his services during the war, where he was injured in a bombing raid. He eventually settled and died in New York.

Armado, Don Adriano de, a 'braggart' 'fantastical' Spaniard in Shakespeare's *Love's Labour's Lost*. His name is connected with the Spanish Armada of 1588.

Armida, in Tasso's *Jerusalem Delivered*, the niece of Hidraotes, king of Damascus, a powerful magician. She offered her services to the defenders of Jerusalem when it was besieged by the Christians under Godfrey de Bouillon, and going to the Christian camp lured away by her beauty many of the principal knights. She inveigled them by magic power into a delicious garden, where they were overcome by indolence. Among her captives were *Rinaldo of Este and *Tancred.

Armine, Ferdinand, the hero of *Henrietta Temple* by B. Disraeli.

Arminianism, the doctrine of James Arminius or Marmensen (d. 1609), a Dutch Protestant theologian, who put forth views opposed to those of *Calvin, especially on predestination,

refusing to hold God responsible for evil. In 1618–19 his doctrines were condemned by the synod of Dort; but they spread rapidly and were embraced, in whole or in part, by large sections of the Reformed Churches.

ARMSTRONG, John (1709–79), Scottish poet and physician, and friend of *Thomson (who portrayed him in *The Castle of Indolence*), *Smollett, and *Fuseli, with whom he made a continental tour in 1771. He is principally remembered for his didactic poem in blank verse *The Art of Preserving Health* (1744) and for a satirical epistle of literary criticism in heroic couplets, *Taste* (1753). He quarrelled with his friend *Wilkes over the latter's attacks on the Scots in *The North Briton*.

ARMSTRONG, William, known as Kinmont Willie (*fl.* 1596), a border moss-trooper, whose nickname is taken from his castle of Kinmont in Canonby, Dumfriesshire. He was captured in 1587 but escaped; he was imprisoned in 1596 at Carlisle, but was rescued by the Scottish warden. His fate is unknown. He is the hero of the ballad 'Kinmont Willie', included in Scott's *Minstrelsy of the Scottish Border*.

ARNE, Thomas Augustine (1710–78), English composer. He was the leading musical figure of the London theatre in the mid-18th cent., producing operas, *masques, and much incidental music for plays. His best-known opera, *Artaxerxes* (1762), was probably the most popular full-length English opera before the 20th cent.; the masque of *Alfred* (1740) added 'Rule Britannia' to the canon of English song; and his music for seven of Shakespeare's plays included some of the most famous of all English Shakespeare settings ('Where the bee sucks', 'When daisies pied', 'Fear no more the heat of the sun', and many others). For the Shakespeare Jubilee at Stratford-upon-Avon in 1769 he collaborated with *Garrick in an *Ode upon Dedicating a Building to Shakespeare*.

ARNOLD, Sir Edwin (1832–1904), won the *Newdigate Prize at Oxford in 1852, and was principal of the Poona College, Bombay Presidency, 1856–61. He then joined the staff of the *Daily Telegraph*, of which he became editor in 1873. He published several volumes of poems and translations, some from the Sanskrit, and is best remembered for his *The Light of Asia, or the Great Renunciation* (1879), a poem of eight books in blank verse, in which, in his own words, he attempted 'by the medium of an imaginary Buddhist votary to depict the life and character and indicate the philosophy of that noble hero and reformer, Prince Gautama of India, founder of Buddhism'.

ARNOLD, Matthew (1822–88), eldest son of Thomas *Arnold, was educated at Rugby, Winchester, and at Balliol College, Oxford, where he formed a close friendship with *Clough, and won the *Newdigate prize with a poem on Cromwell. He became a fellow of Oriel College, then in 1847 secretary to Lord Lansdowne. In 1851 he became an inspector of schools, in which capacity he served for 35 years, travelling extensively throughout England, and observing at first hand the social conditions that prompted much of his later critical work. His first volume of poems, *The Strayed Reveller, and Other Poems* (by 'A', 1849), contains 'The Forsaken Merman', 'The Sick King in Bokhara', and sonnets written at Balliol, including 'Shakespeare'. In 1851 he married Fanny Lucy Wightman, who was to bear six children, three of whom predeceased him. Part of 'Dover Beach' (1867) dates from his honeymoon, which continued on the Continent, and also inspired his 'Stanzas from the Grand Chartreuse' (1855). *Empedocles on Etna, and other Poems* appeared, also anonymously, in 1852; it contained *'Tristram and Iseult' and some of the 'Marguerite' poems, including 'Yes! in the sea of life enisled', now thought to have been addressed to Mary Calude of Ambleside, whom he had met while staying at the Arnold holiday home at Fox How. In 1853 appeared a volume of poems containing extracts from the earlier books, and *'Sohrab and Rustum', *'The Scholar-Gipsy', 'Memorial Verses to Wordsworth' (who had been a personal friend of the Arnolds), and 'Stanzas in Memory of the Author of "Obermann" ', which show how profoundly Arnold had been affected by *Senancour's novel and by the *mal du siècle* expressed by other European writers. His Preface discusses the problems of writing poetry in an 'age wanting in moral grandeur'. *Poems, Second Series*, including 'Balder Dead', appeared in 1855; *Merope, a Tragedy* in 1858; and *New Poems*, including *'Thyrsis', 'Rugby Chapel', and 'Heine's Grave', in 1867.

In his maturity Arnold turned increasingly to prose, writing essays on literary, educational, and social topics that established him as the leading critic of the day and which greatly influenced writers as diverse as Max *Weber, T. S. *Eliot, *Leavis, and R. *Williams. His lectures on translating *Homer, with his definition of 'the grand style' (delivered in 1860, while he was professor of poetry at Oxford) were published in 1861; *Essays in Criticism (First Series)* in 1865 (*Second Series*, 1888); *On the Study of Celtic Literature* (which caused Oxford to establish a chair of Celtic studies) in 1867; *Culture and Anarchy* in 1869; *Friendship's Garland* in 1871; *Literature and Dogma*, a study of the interpretation of the Bible, in 1873. In these and other works, Arnold sharply criticized the provincialism, *Philistinism, sectarianism, and utilitarian materialism of English life and culture, and argued that England needed more intellectual curiosity, more ideas, and a more comparative,

European outlook. The critic, he said, should be flexible, tactful, free of prejudice; his endeavour should be 'to see the object as in itself it really is'. His fame as a critic grew steadily, and in 1883 he delivered a series of lectures in America (undertaken partly to finance his feckless son Richard, who had inherited some of his father's early extravagances). He died in Liverpool, where he was awaiting the arrival of his daughter Lucy, who had married an American.

Special reference is due to Arnold's attempts to secure the improvement of education, particularly secondary education, in England. In 1859 and 1865 he visited the Continent to study educational systems, and produced reports (*The popular education of France*, 1861; *A French Eton*, 1864; *Schools and Universities on the Continent*, 1868), arguing that England badly needed more educational organization and could learn much from European models.

There is a biography by Park Honan (1981). *Poetical Works*, ed. C. B. Tinker and H. F. Lowry, 1950; *Poems*, ed. and annotated by K. Allott, 1965; *The Complete Prose Works of Matthew Arnold*, ed. R. H. Super, 1960–77.

ARNOLD, Thomas (1795–1842), educated at Winchester and Oxford, is remembered principally as the headmaster (1828–42) of *Rugby, which, through various reforms, he raised from a state of decline to the rank of a great public school. His concept of the public school had a profound and lasting influence, and he was held in great personal veneration by his pupils, who included his son Matthew *Arnold, *Clough, A. P. *Stanley, and T. *Hughes, author of *Tom Brown's Schooldays*. A Broad Churchman, he wrote in favour of church reform and Catholic emancipation, and attacked the Tractarians of the *Oxford Movement. He was the author of several works on Roman history, influenced by *Niebuhr, and was appointed Regius professor of modern history in 1841. The standard life is by A. P. Stanley, 1844.

Art and Letters, an illustrated quarterly edited by Frank Rutter, 1917–1920; from 1919 to 1920 with O. *Sitwell. It published T. S. *Eliot, W. *Lewis, A. *John, and Edward Wadsworth.

ARTAUD, Antonin (1896–1948), French actor, director, and dramatic theorist. In a series of manifestos, collected in *Le Théâtre et son double* (1938, English trans., *The Theatre and Its Double*, 1958), he called for a return to the primitive and the ritualistic in drama (enshrined in the frequently misunderstood notion of a 'Theatre of Cruelty'), in opposition to the realistic theatre of a dominant rationalist culture.

Artegal ('Archgallo' in Geoffrey), legendary king of Britain, son of the savage Morvidus and brother of Gorbonian whom he succeeds (described in *Geoffrey of Monmouth's *Historia*

Regum Britanniae, iii. 17). He was deposed for his crimes and replaced by his brother Elidurus the Dutiful; when he returned from exile Elidurus restored him to the throne. The story is the subject of *Wordsworth's poem 'Artegal and Elidure'.

Artegall, Sir, in Spenser's *Faerie Queene*, Bk v, the champion of Justice. *Britomart, to whom his image has been revealed by a magic mirror, is in love with him, and her quest of him ends in their union. Representing Lord Grey de Wilton, he undertakes the rescue of Irena (Ireland) from the tyrant Grantorto. Jointly with Prince *Arthur he slays the *Soldan (Philip II of Spain). His name perhaps signifies 'equal to Arthur'.

Arte of English Poesie, see PUTTENHAM, G.

Arte of Rhetorique, see WILSON, T.

Art for art's sake, a phrase associated with the aesthetic doctrine that art is self-sufficient and need serve no moral or political purpose. The phrase *l'art pour l'art* became current in France in the first half of the 19th cent. and *Gautier's formulation in his Preface to *Mademoiselle de Maupin* (1835), which denied that art could or should be in any way useful, was admired by *Pater, one of the leading influences on the English *'aesthetic' movement of the 1880s. (See WILDE, DOWSON, JOHNSON, L., SYMONS, A.) Pater in his conclusion to *The Renaissance* (1873) spoke of 'the desire of beauty, the love of art for art's sake'.

Artful Dodger, The, a member of Fagin's gang in Dickens's *Oliver Twist*.

Arthur, King. The romantic figure of King Arthur has probably some historical basis, and there is reason to think that, as *Nennius states, he was a chieftain or general (*dux bellorum*) in the 5th or 6th cent. The *Annales Cambriae* place the battle of Mount Badon, 'in which Arthur carried the cross of our Lord Jesus Christ on his shoulders', in 518, and the 'battle of Camlan, in which Arthur and Medraut fell' in 539. The contemporary chronicler *Gildas makes no mention of Arthur (though he refers to the battle of Badon), nor do some of the principal Welsh bards of the 6th and 7th cents. But there is mention of him in certain ancient poems contained in the *Black Book of Carmarthen* and more especially in the ancient Welsh romance *Kilhwch and Olwen*, where he figures with Kay, Bedivere, and Gawain (Gwalchmei). According to the *Arthur* of the marquis of Bath's manuscript (1428: ed. F. J. Furnivall EETS OS 2, 1864), he died in 542 after a reign of 22 years. He was said to be the father of Modred by his half-sister Morgawse; his sister was Anna. Guinevere was the daughter of Arthur's ally Leodegan. According to *Malory, the Grail was accomplished 454 years after the passing of Christ (i.e. in 487). The legend of the return of Arthur to rule Britain again is told by Malory and in the stanzaic *Le *Morte Arthur*. According to the alliterative *Morte Arthure*, he definitely died.

The Arthur of the cycle of legends first appears at length in the *Historia Regum Britanniae* of *Geoffrey of Monmouth. According to this, Arthur is the son of *Uther Pendragon and Ygaerne (Igraine), wife of Gorlois of Cornwall, whom Uther wins through Merlin's magic. At the age of 15 he becomes king and, with his sword Caliburn (Excalibur), slays Childric, defeats the heathen, and conquers Scotland, Ireland, Iceland, and Orkney. He marries Guanhamara, a noble Roman lady, and holds his court at Caerleon on the Usk. He is summoned to pay tribute to the emperor Lucius of Rome, resists, and declares war. Guanhamara and the kingdom are left in the charge of Modred, his nephew. On his way to Rome he slays the giant of St Michael's Mount; his ambassador Walwain (Gawain) defies the emperor and fights him bravely. When Arthur is about to enter Rome he is warned that Modred has seized Guanhamara and the kingdom. He returns with Walwain, who is slain on landing; Modred retreats to Cornwall where, with all his knights, he is slain in a final battle. Arthur is mortally wounded and is borne to the island of Avalon for the healing of his wounds, and Guanhamara becomes a nun. This version of Geoffrey's was developed by the 12th-cent. Norman writer *Wace; the Round Table is first mentioned by him as a device for the settlement of disputes over precedence; and Wace says that the wounded king is expected to return to rule the Britons again. Wace was the principal source of *Laȝamon's *Brut*, the first English version of the story which adds to both the magical and martial aspects. In Laȝamon, Arthur is borne off after the last battle at Camelford to *Argante (Morgan le Fay) in Avalon in a magic boat. The story was very significantly developed in the French *'Matter of Britain', by such writers as *Marie de France, *Chrètien de Troyes, and the authors of the 13th-cent. Vulgate prose cycles, and it became the centre of a mass of legends in several languages, most importantly German. Other characters—Merlin, Launcelot, and Tristram—gradually became associated with Arthur, and he himself is the central character only in the narratives describing his early years and his final battle and death; in the intervening tales his court is merely the starting-point for the adventures of various knights. Through the history of the legends Arthur himself is exceeded in excellence by first *Gawain and then *Launcelot. The story of Arthur as given here is the basis of Malory's *Morte D'Arthur* which was the most authoritative version of the legend in the English tradition. Malory's version gives great prominence to the exploits of the knights of the Round

Table, the quest of the Holy Grail, the love of Launcelot and Guinevere and the love of Tristram and Isoud. For other Arthurian writings, see TENNYSON, WILLIAM OF MALMESBURY, GLASTONBURY. See J. D. Bruce, *The Evolution of Arthurian Romance from the Beginnings down to the year 1300* (2 vols, 1923); R. W. Ackerman, *An Index of the Arthurian Names in Middle English* (1952); R. S. Loomis ed., *Arthurian Literature in the Middle Ages* (1959).

Arthur, Prince, in Spenser's *Faerie Queene*, symbolizes 'Magnificence' (?Magnanimity), in the Aristotelian sense of the perfection of all the virtues. He enters into the adventures of the several knights and brings them to a fortunate conclusion. His chief adventures are the slaying of the three-bodied monster *Geryoneo and the rescue from him of Belge (the Netherlands) (v. x, xi); and, jointly with *Artegall, the slaying of the *Soldan (Philip II) in his 'charret hye' (the Armada) (v. viii).

Arthour and of Merlin, Of, a later 13th-cent. non-alliterative romance in 9,938 lines of short rhyming couplets, preserved in the Auchinleck manuscript (four other manuscripts contain a lesser, variant version). It has been suggested that it may be by the same writer as *King Alisaunder* and *Richard Cœur de Lyon*. It probably comes from Kent, and it seems to derive from a French source related to the Vulgate *Merlin* cycle. The last two-thirds of the poem is taken up with a repetitive series of combats and minor battles. It has been edited by O. D. Macrae-Gibson, *Of Arthour and of Merlin* (EETS os 268, 1973).

Art nouveau, a decorative style that flourished throughout Europe and America from the 1880s to c.1914, characterized by asymmetry, sinuous lines, and a flame-like patterning of the surface; its motifs—the willowy, elongated, female figure with flowing locks and the fantastic curves of stylized flowers—are romantic and touched by *fin-de-siècle* decadence. In England art nouveau follows the Arts and Crafts movement and looks back to *Blake; the style tends to be sparser and more geometric than on the Continent. The first British works of art nouveau are a chair of 1881 and a title page to *Wren's City Churches* (1883) both by A. H. Mackmurdo (1851–1942). The 1890s were a brilliant period for the art nouveau book. Art-oriented literary periodicals played an important role; Mackmurdo's *The Century Guild Hobby Horse* (1884) was followed by *The Dial* (1889–97), *The Yellow Book* (1894–7), and *The Savoy* (1896–8). The most distinguished illustrators were *Beardsley, *Ricketts, L. *Housman, Charles Conder (1868–1909), and T. S. *Moore. In the 1900s the more geometric style of the Glasgow School—of whom Jessie M. King (1876–1949) was the most brilliant illustrator—dominated. The style lingered on in the 20th cent., in the decadent works of 'Alastair' (Hans Henning Voight, c.1889–1933) and in the fairy-tale illustrations of *Rackham and Edmund Dulac (1882–1953).

Art of Dining, The, see HAYWARD, B.

Art of English Poesie, *Observations in the,* an attack on the use of rhyme in English poetry by T. *Campion, to which S. Daniel replied in his *Defence of Ryme*.

Arts Council of Great Britain, The, was incorporated by royal charter in 1946 for the purpose of developing greater knowledge, understanding, and practice of the fine arts and to increase their accessibility to the public. It grew out of the war-time Council for the Encouragement of Music and the Arts, which began in 1940 with a grant of £25,000 from the Pilgrim Trust. The first chairman was Lord Macmillan; the vice-chairman and prime mover Dr Thomas Jones, CH. M. *Keynes was chairman from 1942 to 1945. See also under PATRONAGE.

Arveragus, the husband of Dorigen in Chaucer's 'Franklin's Tale'. See CANTERBURY TALES, 12.

Arviragus, the younger son of *Cymbeline, in Shakespeare's play of that name. He appears under the name of Cadwal. In Spenser's *Faerie Queene* (II. x. 51), Arviragus is Cymbeline's brother.

Aryan, a term formerly applied to the large family of languages now called *Indo-European.

Asaph, in the part of *Absalom and Achitophel* written by *Tate, is *Dryden, and refers to the Asaph of 1 Chron. 16: 4–7 and 25: 1, and the hereditary choir, the 'Sons of Asaph', who conducted the musical services of the Temple.

ASAPH, St (d. c.600), a pupil of St *Kentigern in his monastery at Llanelwy, and his successor as its prior. He was the first bishop of that see which took his name.

Ascent of F6, The, a play by W. H. *Auden and C. *Isherwood, published 1936, first performed 1937.

The central character, Michael Ransom, 'scholar and man of action', succumbs to his mother's persuasions and leads a mountaineering expedition up F6, a mysterious and haunted peak on the borders of disputed colonial territory; all his men die en route and he himself dies as he achieves his mission, destroyed by his own self-knowledge, having rejected (in conversation with a mystic Abbot, strongly reminiscent of *Hilton's *Lost Horizon*) the possibility of evasion and the contemplative life. A chorus of suburban Everyman, Mr A and Mrs A, comments in verse on his heroic exploits and their own dull lives. The Establishment figures (Ransom's brother, Sir James, and newspaper magnate Stagmantle) are presented satirically, the figures of the Mother and the comrades with more ambiguity; Ransom himself was in part modelled on T. E. *Lawrence, the Truly Strong Weak Man. The play is a parable about the nature of power and will and leadership, with both political and Freudian implications, and may be seen to reflect the growing apprehension of and attraction towards the 'strong man' at this period of the 1930s.

ASCHAM, Roger (1515/16–68), was educated at St John's College, Cambridge, where he distinguished himself in classics, becoming college reader in Greek in 1540. In 1545 he published *Toxophilus*, a treatise on archery. This delightful book, set in the form of a dialogue between Toxophilus (lover of shooting) and Philologus (lover of books), was immediately popular, gaining Ascham a royal pension of £10 a year. It provided the model for many later treatises in dialogue form, including *The Compleat Angler*. He succeeded Grindal as tutor to Princess Elizabeth in 1548, holding this post for less than two years. His brief encounter with Lady Jane Grey (then aged 13) in 1550 has inspired numerous paintings, plays, and other works, such as Landor's *'Imaginary Conversation'* between them. In 1550–3 he travelled on the Continent as secretary to Sir Richard Morison, English ambassador to Charles V, and on his return wrote his interesting *Report of Germany*. In 1554 he became Latin secretary to Queen Mary, being tacitly permitted to continue in his Protestantism, and he was renewed in this office under Elizabeth. He was afflicted by poverty in the last decade of his life; this was probably not caused, as *Camden claimed, by his addiction to dicing and cock-fighting, but by his responsibility for a large family which included his mother-in-law and her younger children. *The Scholemaster* was published posthumously by his widow in 1570. Its three most distinctive features are: Ascham's dislike of corporal punishment; the Ciceronian technique of double translation, from Latin into English and back again; and his attitude to Italy. While placing a high value on Italian language and culture, Ascham felt that it was a most dangerously corrupting country for English travellers: 'I was once in Italie my selfe; but I thanke God, my abode there, was but ix. dayes; And yet I sawe in that litle tyme, in one Citie, more libertie to sinne, than ever I hard tell of in our noble Citie of London in ix. yeare.' *The Scholemaster* was an immediate influence on Sidney's *Defence of Poetry*, as well as an important landmark in later educational theory. Ascham's English works are notable for their relaxed, personal style and for considerable economy of expression. Dr *Johnson wrote an anonymous *Life of Ascham* to accompany James Bennet's edition

of 1761. There has been no complete edition of Ascham's *Works* since J. A. Giles's in 1864–5, but Lawrence V. Ryan has edited *The Schoolmaster* (1967) and has written a detailed study of Ascham (1963).

Asclepiads, see METRE.

Ashendene Press, see PRIVATE PRESSES.

ASHFORD, Daisy (Mrs George Norman) (1881–1972), wrote *The Young Visiters*, a small comic masterpiece, while still a young child in Lewes. It was found in a drawer in 1919 and sent to Chatto and Windus, who published it in the same year with an introduction by J. M. *Barrie, who had first insisted on meeting the author in order to check that she was genuine. The book, a sparkling, misspelt, and unpunctuated view of High Life and the adventures of Ethel Monticue and her admirer Mr Salteena, has proved very popular.

Ashley Library, see LIBRARIES.

ASHMOLE, Elias (1617–92), antiquarian and astrologer, studied at Brasenose College, Oxford, and, as a Royalist, held several government appointments. His chief work was *The Institution, Laws and Ceremonies of the Order of the Garter* (1672), but he also edited work by Dr *Dee and was associated with *Lilly, whose autobiography appeared with Ashmole's *Memoirs* in the 1774 edition. In 1682 he presented his collection of curiosities, bequeathed to him by *Tradescant, to Oxford University, thus founding the Ashmolean Museum. A 5-vol. edition of his works by C. H. Josten, notes, correspondence, etc., appeared in 1966.

Ashmolean Museum, see ASHMOLE, E.

Ashton, Sir William, Lady, and Lucy, characters in Scott's *The Bride of Lammermoor*.

'Ash Wednesday', a poem by T. S. *Eliot.

Asolando, the last volume of poems by R. *Browning, published 1889. The title derives from a fanciful verb 'asolare', 'to disport in the open air, to amuse oneself at random', attributed to *Bembo at the time of his residence in Asolo, in northern Italy. Asolo had played an important part in Browning's life and work (see PIPPA PASSES).

The poems fall into three main groups: an opening series of love lyrics; a group of anecdotal poems and longer narratives; and a concluding group of meditative or reminiscent dramatic monologues. The 'Epilogue' to the volume, containing the famous self-description 'One who never turned his back but marched breast forward' etc., stands as a traditional proof of Browning's optimism; the 'Prologue' is better verse and a better guide. But the finest poem in the volume is undoubtedly 'Beatrice Signorini', the last of Browning's great poems about Italian painters.

Aspatia, a character in Beaumont and Fletcher's *The Maid's Tragedy.*

Asphodel, a genus of liliaceous plants, mostly native of southern Europe. The poets make it the flower of the Elysian fields (Homer, *Odyssey,* xi. 539) and connect it with the legend of Proserpine. The word 'daffodil' is a corruption of 'asphodel'.

Asseneth, in a variant of the story of Joseph and Potiphar's wife, is Potiphar's daughter, whom Joseph consents to marry if she will renounce her gods, which she does. An angel signifies approval and Pharaoh gives a feast to celebrate the nuptials. The story, perhaps of early Christian invention, was made the subject of a French prose romance, early in the 14th cent., by Jean de Vignay.

ASSER (d. 910), a monk of St David's, Pembrokeshire, who entered the household of King *Alfred (c. 885) and studied with him for six months of each year. He received the monasteries of Amesbury and Banwell, and later a grant of Exeter and its district; he was bishop of Sherborne (892–910). In 893 he wrote a Latin life of Alfred and a Chronicle of English History for the years 849 to 887. Since the only Alfredian translation he mentions is Wærferth's version of *Gregory's *Dialogues,* it is assumed that all other translations are later than 893, the date of Asser's *Life.* The authenticity of the *Life* has been questioned, some scholars believing the work to be an 11th-cent. forgery. But there seems to be no conclusive evidence that it does not belong to the 890s. There is an edition by W. H. Stevenson (1904).

Assonance, the correspondence or rhyming of one word with another in the accented and following vowels, but not in the consonants, as, e.g. in Old French versification. The term is now more broadly used to cover a wide range of vowel correspondences, from the deliberate reverberation of the last line of *Yeats's 'Byzantium'—'That dolphin-torn, that gong-tormented sea'—to the subtle echoes and repetitions of Keats in *'To Autumn': 'Then in a wailful choir the small gnats mourn | Among the river sallows, borne aloft | Or sinking as the light wind lives or dies.'

Astarte, the Phoenician goddess of love. This is the name which Byron gives to his half-sister Augusta *Leigh in his drama *Manfred.*

Astolat ('Ascolet') in the stanzaic Le *Morte Arthur), the place where Launcelot meets Elaine Le Blank, is, according to Malory's *Morte D'Arthur,* Guildford in Surrey. Elaine is 'The Fair Maid of Astolat' and Tennyson's *'Lady of Shalott'.

Astolfo, in *Orlando Innamorato* and *Orlando Furioso,* a courteous and graceful English knight, one of the suitors of *Angelica and at one time a prisoner of *Alcina. He receives from *Logistilla a magic horn, the blast of which fills its hearers with panic, and a book that tells him all he wishes to know. He gets possession of the hippogriff of *Rogero, and, with an Englishman's partiality for travel, flies about the world, relieves Prester John in Nubia of his troubles with harpies, visits Paradise, whence St John carries him in a chariot to the moon. There, in a valley, are collected all the things that are lost on earth, lost kingdoms, lost reputations, lost time, and in the heap he finds the lost wits of Orlando, which he restores to the crazy hero. As regards his description as an English knight, it appears that in the earlier French *chanson* he figures as *Estout de Langres,* or *Lengrois,* corrupted into *Lenglois* and *l'Englois* (F. J. Snell, in *PEL,* 'The Fourteenth Century').

Astraea, a name adopted by Afra *Behn under which she is ridiculed by *Pope.

Astraea Redux, see DRYDEN, J.

'Astrophel', a pastoral elegy, written by *Spenser in ?1591–5 on the death of Sir P. *Sidney, who was mortally wounded in 1586 at Zutphen. Spenser had previously lamented him in *'The Ruines of Time'. *Swinburne used the title for a volume of his poems in 1894.

Astrophel and Stella, a sequence of 108 sonnets and 11 songs by Sir P. *Sidney, written about 1582. They plot the unhappy love of Astrophel ('lover of a star') for Stella ('star'). As several sonnets make clear, e.g. 37, referring to one that 'Hath no misfortune, but that Rich she is', Stella is to be identified with Penelope *Rich; but the exact nature of Sidney's real, rather than poetic, relationship with her can never be known. Apart from snatching a kiss while she is asleep, Astrophel in the sequence achieves nothing, and the story breaks off—'That therewith my song is broken'—rather than being resolved. Poetically, however, the sonnets are an outstanding achievement, being written throughout in versions of the exacting Italian sonnet form, and displaying a striking range of tone, imagery, and metaphor. The best known is 31, 'With how sad steps, ô Moone, thou climb'st the skies'. There were two editions of *Astrophel and Stella* in 1591 which began a craze for sonnet sequences; from 1598 onwards it was included in editions of *The Arcadia.*

As You Like It, a comedy by *Shakespeare, registered 1599 but perhaps first written some years earlier, especially if the phrase 'it strikes a man more dead than a great reckoning in a little room' (III. iii. 9–12) refers to the death of *Marlowe. It was first printed in the *Folio of 1623. Firm evidence that it was performed before

James I at Wilton has never been found. Shakespeare's chief source was Lodge's *Rosalynde, but some notable characters, such as *Jaques and *Touchstone, have no original there.

Frederick has usurped the dominions of the duke his brother, who is living with his faithful followers in the forest of *Arden. Celia, Frederick's daughter, and Rosalind, the duke's daughter, living at Frederick's court, witness a wrestling match in which Orlando, son of Sir Rowland de Boys, defeats a powerful adversary, and Rosalind falls in love with Orlando and he with her. Orlando, who at his father's death has been left in the charge of his elder brother Oliver, has been driven from home by Oliver's cruelty. Frederick, learning that Orlando is the son of Sir Rowland, who was a friend of the exiled duke, has his anger against the latter revived, and banishes Rosalind from his court, and Celia accompanies her. Rosalind assumes a countryman's dress and takes the name Ganymede; Celia passes as Aliena his sister. They live in the forest of Arden, and fall in with Orlando, who has joined the banished duke. Ganymede encourages Orlando to pay suit to her as though she were his Rosalind. Oliver comes to the forest to kill Orlando, but is saved by him from a lioness, and is filled with remorse for his cruelty. He falls in love with Aliena, and their wedding is arranged for the next day. Ganymede undertakes to Orlando that she will by magic produce Rosalind at the same time to be married to him. When all are assembled in presence of the banished duke to celebrate the double nuptials, Celia and Rosalind put off their disguise and appear in their own characters. News is brought that Frederick the usurper, setting out to seize and destroy his brother and his followers, has been converted from his intention by 'an old religious man' and has made restitution of the dukedom.

Entertainment rather than plot dominates this play, however, much of it provided by the reflections of Jaques and Touchstone, and by the large number of songs, more than in any of Shakespeare's other plays, including such lyrics as 'Under the greenwood tree' (which *Hardy used as the title for a novel) and 'Blow, blow, thou winter wind' (both in II. vii).

Atalanta in Calydon, a poetic drama by *Swinburne, published 1865. It tells the story of the hunting of the wild boar sent by Artemis to ravage Calydon in revenge for its neglect of her: Meleager slays the boar, presents the spoils to the virgin athlete and huntress Atalanta, and then himself dies through the intervention of his mother Althaea. The work brought Swinburne fame, and was highly praised for its successful imitation of Greek models (though the subject had not been treated by any Greek dramatist); some critics pointed out its 'anti-theism', and W. M. *Rossetti compared it to Shelley's *Prometheus Unbound. *Ruskin described it as 'the

grandest thing ever yet done by a youth—though he is a Demoniac youth'. It is now chiefly remembered for the 'chorus' beginning 'When the hounds of spring are on winter's traces . . .'

Atalantis, The New, see MANLEY, MRS.

Atellan Fables were sketches depicting scenes from rustic life, presented on a crude stage with stock characters (the foolish old man, the rogue, the clown), and seem to have been the earliest form of drama to flourish in ancient Rome. It was imported from Campania where Oscan, a language akin to Latin, was spoken. The genre may have originated from the town of Atella as its name suggests, but the so-called Atellan fables seem to have been similar to the Phlyax farces which were popular at the time in the Greek-speaking world.

Athalie, a play by *Racine.

ATHANASIUS, St (c.296–373), bishop of Alexandria in the reign of the emperor Constantine and persecuted by him and by his successor Constantius II whose autocratic religious policies Athanasius strongly opposed. He was an uncompromising opponent of Arianism (see ARIAN HERESY) and defended the decisions of the Council of Nicaea (325), which he attended. His works include the influential De Incarnatione and a life of St Antony of Egypt. The Athanasian Creed, which begins with the words 'Quicunque vult', has been attributed to him.

Atheism, The Necessity of, a prose pamphlet by P. B. *Shelley and his friend T. J. *Hogg, published anonymously at Oxford, 1811. Using the sceptical arguments of *Hume and *Locke, the authors—then both undergraduates—smartly demolish the grounds for a rational belief in the Deity. The pamphlet ends with a flourishing 'Q.E.D.', as in a schoolboy's exercise, which caused great offence, as did its title. They were both expelled from the University for circulating the work to heads of colleges and to bishops, and 'contumacy' in refusing to answer questions about it. It is probably the first published statement of atheism in Britain.

Atheist's Tragedy, The, a tragedy by *Tourneur, printed 1611.

D'Amville, the 'atheist', desiring to increase the wealth of his family, wishes to marry his son to Castabella; she is betrothed to Charlemont, the son of his brother Montferrers, and D'Amville arranges that Charlemont shall go abroad on military service. During his absence D'Amville and Belforest, Castabella's father, achieve their purpose, aided by the lecherous Levidulcia, Belforest's second wife, and Castabella is married to the sickly and impotent Rousard; Charlemont, in one of the best-known speeches of the play, is falsely reported to have died at the siege of Ostend. ('Walking next day upon the fatal shore . . . ', II. I. 78 ff.) D'Amville then murders Montferrers. Charlemont, exhorted by his father's ghost to 'leave revenge unto the king of kings', now returns. D'Amville endeavours to procure his murder, but vengeance comes upon him in the death of his two sons, and he himself accidentally dashes out his own brains when raising the axe to execute Charlemont, held on a murder charge; he confesses his sins and dies, and Charlemont and Castabella are united, Charlemont expressing the 'anti-revenge' sentiment: 'Now I see | That patience is the honest man's revenge.' (See also REVENGE TRAGEDY.)

The play is generally considered inferior to *The Revenger's Tragedy*; T. S. *Eliot (who ascribes both plays to Tourneur), finds in it 'more regular verse, more conventional moralizing, more conventional scenes' (1930).

Athelstane of Coningsburgh, a character in Scott's *Ivanhoe*.

Athelston, a highly unhistorical but lively verse romance from about 1350, in 811 lines, whose only connection with the historical Athelstan (Alfred's grandson) is his being succeeded by a virtuous Edmund. The romance tells of the chance meeting in a forest of four messengers, one of whom, Athelston, becomes king of England, and the subsequent relations between the four. One becomes archbishop of Canterbury; one becomes earl of Dover, plots against the king, and is executed; and the fourth becomes earl of Stane and the father of Athelston's chosen successor Edmund. The poem is in the dialect of the north-east Midlands, but Trounce in his edition derives it from an Anglo-Norman metrical original.

See edition by A. M. Trounce (EETS 224, 1933; rev. 1951); *Medieval English Romances*, Part I, ed. A. V. C. Schmidt and N. Jacobs (1980).

Athenaeum, The (1828–1921), J. S. *Buckingham's literary review, followed a general monthly magazine of this name (1807–9). The founder wished the journal to become a true 'Athenaeum', the resort of thinkers, poets, orators, and other writers, and he attacked *The Quarterly Review* for the political bias of its literary criticism. Co-proprietors included at various times J. H. *Reynolds, T. *Hood, and A. *Cunningham. *Dilke was editor 1830–46, and the list of contributors in the 19th cent. included *Lamb, *Darley, *Hogg, *Hood, *Landor, *Carlyle, R. *Browning, *Lang, and *Pater. The scope of the review was enlarged in the 20th cent., but its contributors were no less eminent; they included *Hardy, K. *Mansfield, T. S. *Eliot, R. *Graves, *Blunden, V. *Woolf, and J. M. *Murry, who became editor in 1919. Its reputation and authority altered little during its long history. In 1921 it merged with the *Nation*, ran for 10 years as *Nation and Athenaeum*, and in 1931 was purchased by the *New Statesman*. See L. A. Marchand, *The Athenaeum* (1941).

Athenaeum Club, in London, was founded in 1824 as an association of persons of literary, scientific, and artistic attainments, patrons of learning, etc. Among its founders were the earls of Liverpool and Aberdeen, the marquess of Lansdowne, Sir W. *Scott, *Davy, *Faraday, *Croker, Sir T. *Lawrence, and T. *Moore. (There was an 'Athenaeum' at Rome, a university on the Capitoline, founded by the emperor Hadrian, for the promotion of science and literature.)

Athenian Gazette, later the *Athenian Mercury*, a periodical published by *Dunton, a question-and-answer paper designed to resolve 'the nice and curious questions proposed by the Ingenious', and thus a precursor of *Notes and Queries*. It first appeared in March 1691, and flourished until 1697, with Samuel Wesley (1662–1735), father of John *Wesley, as a partner. The queries ranged over a vast area, from the theological to the matrimonial, from the scientific to the literary, and it was praised and read by authors as diverse as *Halifax, *Swift, *Defoe, and *Temple.

Athos, Porthos, and Aramis, the *'Three Musketeers' in Dumas's novel of that name.

Atlantic Monthly, The, an American, and more particularly a New England, magazine of literature, the arts, and politics, founded in 1857. J. R. *Lowell was its first editor (1857–61) and O. W. *Holmes's contribution of *The Autocrat at the Breakfast-Table* added greatly to its early success. Lowell's distinguished successors included W. D. *Howells (1871–81) and T. B. *Aldrich (1881–90). It maintains its traditions, and continues to include many leading American men and women of letters among its contributors.

Atlantis, The New, see NEW ATLANTIS, THE.

Atom, The History and Adventures of an, a satire probably by T. *Smollett, published 1769.

The attribution to Smollett is on 18th-cent. rumour and internal evidence only. No references to it occur in his letters, in his wife's, or in those of his many correspondents, yet much of it seems to reflect what is known of Smollett's thoughts and feelings at the time. Strongly influenced by *Rabelais, the work is a violent political satire, largely couched in crude physiological terms, many of them scatological. The Atom, which in its various transmigrations has lived in the body of a Japanese in Japan, relates his experiences and observations to Nathaniel Peacock. Japan is a thin fiction for England, and the various Japanese politicians and figures of power represent Englishmen of the day; among many others, the demagogue Taycho is *Pitt, Fika-Kaka is Newcastle, and Yak-Strot the hated Bute. The 'mob' is characterized as sheeplike, malevolent, and stupid.

Atossa, the wife of Darius and mother of Xerxes, appears in *The Persians* of *Aeschylus. See also MORAL ESSAYS.

ATTERBURY, Francis (1662–1732), became bishop of Rochester in 1713 after holding various important preferments. He engaged in the *Phalaris controversy and in the theological and political disputes of the day, and was imprisoned in 1720 for alleged complicity in a Jacobite plot. He subsequently left the country and died in exile. He was a close friend of *Pope, *Swift, and other literary figures, and was one of the most noted preachers of his day; his *A Discourse occasioned by the Death of Lady Cutts* (1698) was delivered as the funeral sermon of the second wife of Baron Cutts (1661–1707); she died aged 18. His *Miscellaneous Works*, ed. J. Nichols, were published in 1789–98.

Attic, a form of Greek spoken in Athens during her period of literary pre-eminence, became later the basis of the common speech (κοινή) of the Greek-speaking East. Attic style was the product of a reaction against the turgid and aphoristic diction fashionable in the 1st cent. BC. Moulded on the great Athenian orators, it aimed at a dry, grammatically correct lucidity and was imitated in Rome where Brutus shone as its exponent.

Atticus, the character under which *Pope satirized *Addison in lines written in 1715, first published in 1723, and in a much altered version in Pope's *Epistle to Dr Arbuthnot* (1735), ll. 193–214. The original Atticus (109–32 BC), so called from his long residence in Athens, was a friend of Cicero.

Aubade (Provençal, *alba*; German, *Tagelied*), a dawn song, usually describing the regret of two lovers at their imminent separation. The form (which has no strict metrical pattern) flourished with the conventions of *Courtly Love (see the lament of Troilus, *Troilus and Criseyde*, III. i. 450, 'O cruel day') and survives in such modern examples as *Empson's 'Aubade' (1940), with its refrain, 'The heart of standing is you cannot fly'.

ATWOOD, Margaret (1939–), Canadian poet and novelist, born in Ottawa, who spent much of her early life in the northern Ontario and Quebec bush country. Her first volume of poetry, *The Circle Game*, appeared in 1966, to be followed by several others. Her first novel, *The Edible Woman* (1969), was followed by *Surfacing* (1972), *Lady Oracle* (1976), and *Life Before Man* (1979), all novels, and a controversial study of themes in Canadian literature, *Survival*

(1972). She also compiled *The New Oxford Book of Canadian Verse in English* (1983).

AUBREY, John (1626–97), antiquary and biographer, was born near Malmesbury, Wiltshire, the oldest surviving son of a well-to-do Herefordshire family. A lonely early childhood gave him delight in society, and he became familiar with many of the distinguished men of his time, including *Hobbes, whom he first met while still a boy in 1634. His education at Trinity College, Oxford, was interrupted by the Civil War. In 1648 he was the first to discover the ruins of Avebury, and devoted much time to archeological research, keenly deploring the neglect of antiquities; in 1662 he was nominated one of the original fellows of the *Royal Society. His *Miscellanies* (1696), a book of stories and folklore, was the only work completed and published in his lifetime. His 'Perambulation of Surrey', based on a tour in 1673, was included in Rawlinson's *Natural History and Antiquities of Surrey* (1719), and his *Natural History of Wiltshire* appeared (ed. J. Britton) in 1847, but he is chiefly remembered for his *Lives* of eminent people, much used (and in his view somewhat abused) by A. *Wood. He collected these over a period of years, constantly adding to his notes, deploring his own lack of method ('I now set things down tumultuarily, as if tumbled out of a Sack'), and depositing his manuscripts in the Ashmolean Museum in 1693. Early editions (1813, 1898) were bowdlerized. The *Lives* are a lively and heterogeneous mixture of anecdote, first-hand observation, folklore, and erudition, a valuable, open-minded, entertaining (if at times inaccurate) portrait of an age. Once convicted of credulity, Aubrey now appears more in the role of amateur anthropologist, as Oliver Lawson Dick argues in the full introduction to his 1949 edition. (See BIOGRAPHY.)

Auburn, see DESERTED VILLAGE, THE.

Aucassin and Nicolette, a 13th-cent. courtly story in northern French, composed in alternating prose and songs, now believed to be a loving pastiche of the excesses of courtly-love romances. The writer was probably a northern *jongleur* in the early part of the century, unfamiliar with the Provençal setting of the story. It is discussed or translated by *Swinburne, *Pater, and *Lang. The story tells of how Aucassin, the son of Count Garins of Beaucaire, loves Nicolette, a Saracen captive. Garins opposes their love and imprisons them both; but they escape and, after a series of adventures, they are married and become lord and lady of Beaucaire. There is an edition by M. Roques (1921); see also *Aucassin and Nicolette, and Other Tales*, ed. and trans. Pauline Matarasso (1971).

AUCHINLECK, see BOSWELL, J.

AUDEN, W(ystan) H(ugh) (1907–73), the youngest son of a doctor, was brought up in Birmingham and educated at Gresham's School, Holt. He began to be taken seriously as a poet while still at Christ Church, Oxford, where he was much influenced by Anglo-Saxon and Middle English poetry, but also began to explore the means of preserving 'private spheres' (through poetry) in 'public chaos'. Among his contemporaries, who were to share some of his left-wing near-Marxist response to the public chaos of the thirties, were *MacNeice, *Day-Lewis, and *Spender, with whom his name is often linked. (See PYLON POETS.) After Oxford, Auden lived for a time in Berlin; he returned to England in 1929 to work as a schoolteacher, but continued to visit Germany regularly, staying with his friend and future collaborator *Isherwood. His first volume, *Poems* (including some previously published in a private edition, 1928), was accepted for publication by T. S. *Eliot at Faber and Faber and appeared in 1930; it was well received and established him as the most talented voice of his generation. *The Orators* followed in 1932, and *Look Stranger!* in 1936. In 1932 he became associated with Rupert Doone's Group Theatre, which produced several of his plays (*The Dance of Death*, 1933; and, with Isherwood, *The Dog Beneath the Skin*, 1935; *The Ascent of F6*, 1936; *On the Frontier*, 1938); these owe something to the early plays of *Brecht. (See also EXPRESSIONISM.) Working from 1935 with the GPO Film Unit he became friendly with *Britten, who set many of his poems to music and later used Auden's text for his opera *Paul Bunyan*. In 1935 he married Erika Mann to provide her with a British passport to escape from Nazi Germany. A visit to Iceland with MacNeice in 1936 produced their joint *Letters from Iceland* (1937); *Journey to a War* (1939, with Isherwood) records a journey to China. Meanwhile in 1937 he had visited Spain for two months, to support the Republicans, but his resulting poem 'Spain' (1937) is less partisan and more detached in tone than might have been expected, and in January 1939 he and Isherwood left Europe for America (he became a US citizen in 1946) where he met Chester Kallman, who became his lifelong friend and companion. *Another Time* (1940), containing many of his most famous poems (including 'September 1939' and 'Lullaby'), was followed in 1941 by *The Double Man* (1941, published in London as *New Year Letter*), a long transitional verse epistle describing the 'baffling crime' of 'two decades of hypocrisy', rejecting political simplifications, accepting man's essential solitude, and ending with a prayer for refuge and illumination for the 'muddled heart'. From this time Auden's poetry became increasingly Christian in tone (to such an extent that he even altered some of his earlier work to bring it in line and disowned some of

his political pieces); this was perhaps not unconnected with the death in 1941 of his devout Anglo-Catholic mother, to whom he dedicated *For the Time Being: A Christmas Oratorio* (1944). This was published with *The Sea and the Mirror*, a series of dramatic monologues inspired by *The Tempest*. *The Age of Anxiety: A Baroque Eclogue* (1948) is a long dramatic poem, reflecting man's isolation, which opens in a New York bar at night, and ends with dawn on the streets.

Auden's absence during the war led to a poor reception of his works in England at that period, but the high quality of his later work reinstated him as an unquestionably major poet; in 1956 he was elected professor of poetry at Oxford, and in 1962 he became a Student (i.e. fellow) of Christ Church. His major later collections include *Nones* (1951, NY; 1952, London), *The Shield of Achilles* (1955), which includes 'Horae Canonicae' and 'Bucolics', and is considered by many his best single volume; and *Homage to Clio* (1960), which includes a high proportion of light verse. Auden had edited *The Oxford Book of Light Verse* in 1938, and subsequently many other anthologies, collections, etc.; his own prose criticism includes *The Enchafèd Flood* (1950, NY; 1951, London), *The Dyer's Hand* (1962, NY; 1963, London), and *Secondary Worlds* (1968, T. S. *Eliot Memorial lectures). He also wrote several librettos, notably for *Stravinsky's *The Rake's Progress* (1951, with Kallman). *About the House* (1965, NY; 1966, London), one of his last volumes of verse, contains a tender evocation of his life with Kallman at their summer home in Austria. Auden spent much of the last years of his life in Oxford, and died suddenly in Vienna.

Auden's influence on a succeeding generation of poets was incalculable, comparable only with that, a generation earlier, of *Yeats (to whom Auden himself pays homage in 'In Memory of W. B. Yeats', 1939). His progress from the engaged, didactic, satiric poems of his youth to the complexity of his later work offered a wide variety of models—the urbane, the pastoral, the lyrical, the erudite, the public, and the introspective mingle with great fluency. He was a master of verse form, and accommodated traditional patterns to a fresh, easy, and contemporary language. A life by Humphrey Carpenter was published in 1981; See also *The Auden Generation* by S. Hynes (1976).

Audrey, in Shakespeare's *As You Like It*, the country wench wooed and won by Touchstone.

AUDUBON, John James (1785–1851), an American ornithologist of French descent, noted for his remarkable pictures of birds. The colour prints of his *The Birds of America* were issued serially in London in 1827–38, and the accompanying text, 'Ornithological Biography', in which he was assisted, in 1831–9. He also published, again with assistance, *Viviparous Quadrupeds of North America* (plates 1842–5; text 1846–54). His important *Journal* appeared in 1929.

AUERBACH, Eric (1892–1957), born in Berlin, professor of Romance philology at Marburg from 1929 to 1935. Dismissed by the Nazis, he went to Istanbul, where he taught at the Turkish State University from 1936 to 1947; he then moved to the United States, and from 1950 was professor of French and Romance philology at Yale. He published several books on medieval literature, Christian symbolism, and methods of historical criticism; his best known work is *Mimesis: The Representation of Reality in Western Literature*, first published in German in 1946 (trans. 1953), a wide-ranging discussion taking texts from *Homer, through *Dante, Shakespeare, *Cervantes, etc., and ending with V. *Woolf, to explore the classical doctrine of levels of representation. He concludes that 'it was the story of Christ, with its ruthless mixture of everyday reality and the highest and most sublime tragedy, which conquered the classical rule of styles' in the Middle Ages, and contrasts this with the achievements of modern *Realism.

Aufidius, general of the Volscians, first enemy and then ally of *Coriolanus in Shakespeare's play of that name.

Augusta, the name used for London in Thomson's *The Seasons*.

Augusta, in imprints, Augsburg.

Augusta Leigh, *Byron's half-sister: see LEIGH.

Augustan Age, a term derived from the period of literary eminence under the Roman emperor Augustus (27 BC–AD 14) during which *Virgil, *Horace, and *Ovid flourished. In English literature it is generally taken to refer to the early and mid-18th cent., though the earliest usages date back to the reign of Charles II. Augustan writers (such as *Pope, *Addison, *Swift, and *Steele) greatly admired their Roman counterparts, imitated their works, and themselves frequently drew parallels between the two ages. *Goldsmith, in *The Bee*, in an 'Account of the Augustan Age in England' (1759), identifies it with the reign of Queen Anne, and the era of *Congreve, *Prior, and *Bolingbroke. See also NEO-CLASSICISM.

Augusta Trebocorum, in imprints, Strasburg. See also ARGENTINA.

Augusta Treverorum, in imprints, Trèves.

Augusta Trinobantum, in imprints, London.

AUGUSTINE, St (d. 26 May, between 604 and 609), first archbishop of Canterbury. He was prior of Pope *Gregory's monastery of St Andrew in Rome and in 596 was sent by that pope with some forty monks to preach the gospel in England arriving there in 597. He was favourably received by King Ethelbert of Kent who was afterwards converted and gave Augustine a see at Canterbury. Augustine was consecrated 'Bishop of the English' at Arles. He founded the monastery of Christ Church at Canterbury, and a number of other churches, none of which still survives. See M. Deanesly, *Augustine of Canterbury* (1964).

AUGUSTINE, St, of Hippo (354–430), born at Tagaste in Numidia (Constantine), his mother being Monica, already a devout Christian. He was trained as a rhetorician and abandoned the Christianity in which he had been brought up (though not baptized). He had an illegitimate son, Adeolatus. He was a Manichean for some time, but was converted (387) after hearing the sermons of *Ambrose, bishop of Milan, where Augustine taught rhetoric. The scene of his conversion is vividly described in his *Confessions* (c.400), which contains a celebrated account of his early life. He became bishop of Hippo (396) and was engaged in constant theological controversy, combating Manicheans, Donatists, and Pelagians. The most important of his numerous works is *De Civitate Dei*, 'The City of God' (413–27), a treatise in vindication of Christianity. His principal tenet was the immediate efficacy of grace, and his theology (which contains a significant *Neoplatonic element, probably from *Plotinus) remained an influence of profound importance on Franciscans, Cistercians, and others in the Middle Ages, when it was often characterized as being an alternative orthodoxy to the Dominican system of *Aquinas. His views on literature became standard in the Middle Ages, particularly as they are expressed in *De Doctrina Christiana*, and they are often cited as an authority by 20th-cent. 'exegetical' critics of medieval literature such as D. W. Robertson who are sometimes called 'Augustinian critics'.

Trans. D. W. Robertson, *De Doctrina Christiana* (1958); trans. R. H. Barrow, *The City of God* (1950); trans. F. J. Sheed, *Confessions* (1943); Peter R. L. Brown, *Augustine of Hippo, a biography* (1967).

'Auld Lang Syne', a song whose words were contributed by *Burns to the 5th vol. of James Johnson's *Scots Musical Museum* (1787–1803). It was not entirely of Burns's composition, but was taken down by him, he wrote, 'from an old man's singing'.

In fact the refrain, at least, had long been in print, and the first line and title appear in a poem by A. *Ramsey. Robert Aytoun (see under AYTOUN, W. E.) has also been credited with the original version.

'Auld Robin Gray', see LINDSAY, A.

Aurelia, Launcelot's love in Smollett's *Sir *Launcelot Greaves.*

Aurelia Allobrogum, in imprints, Geneva.

Aureng-Zebe, a tragedy by *Dryden, produced 1675, published 1676.

The plot is remotely based on the contemporary events by which Aureng-Zebe wrested the empire of India from his father and his brothers. The hero is a figure of exemplary rationality, virtue, and patience, whose stepmother lusts after him and whose father pursues the woman with whom Aureng-Zebe is himself in love. Apparently highly schematic in its organization, this last of Dryden's rhymed heroic plays evinces a deeply disturbing awareness of the anarchy and impotence which threaten every aspect of human life, emotional, moral, and political.

Aurora Leigh, described by its author E. B. *Browning as a 'novel in verse', published 1857, is the 11,000-line life-story of a woman writer. Her rejection of, and final reunion with, her philanthropist suitor Romney Leigh (and a melodramatic sub-plot in which a seamstress is trapped into a brothel) are less important than the poem's forceful and often witty speculations on the poet's mission, on social responsibilities, and on the position of women, its vivid impressionistic sketches of crowds and social groups, and its glimpses of dewy English countryside and luminous Italian landscapes.

AUSONIUS, Decimus Magnus (*c*. AD 310–90), Roman poet who taught grammar and rhetoric at Bordeaux and rose to high office under the emperor Gratian, who had been his pupil. His best poem, about a journey along the Moselle, shows a feeling for nature unusual in antiquity, but most of his verses are conventionally rhetorical. Some of them found a translator in T. *Stanley.

AUSTEN, Jane (1775–1817), born in the rectory at Steventon, Hampshire, was the sixth child in a family of seven. Her father, the Revd George Austen, was a cultivated man, comfortably prosperous, who taught Jane and encouraged her both in her reading and her writing. As a child and young woman she read widely, including, among novelists, *Fielding, *Sterne, *Richardson, and F. *Burney; and among poets, Sir W. *Scott, *Cowper, and her particular favourite, *Crabbe. Her life is notable for its lack of events; she did not marry, although she had several suitors, one of whom she accepted one evening, only to withdraw her acceptance the following morning. She lived in the midst of a lively and affectionate family, with occasional visits to Bath, London, Lyme, and her brothers' houses. Any references there may have been to private intimacies or griefs were excised from Jane's letters by her sister Cas-

sandra, after Jane's death, but the letters retain flashes of sharp wit and occasional coarseness that have startled some of her admirers. The letters cover the period 1796–1817, and her correspondents include Cassandra, her friend Martha Lloyd, and her nieces and nephews, to whom she confided her views on the novel (to Anna Austen, 9 Sept. 1814), '3 or 4 families in a Country Village is the very thing to work on'; (to J. Edward Austen, 16 Dec. 1816), 'the little bit (two Inches wide) of Ivory on which I work with so fine a brush, as produces little effect after much labour'. In 1801 the family moved to Bath, in 1806, after Mr Austen's death, to Southampton, and in 1809 to Chawton, again in Hampshire; for a few weeks before her death Jane lodged in Winchester, where she died of Addison's disease. The novels were written between the activities of family life, and the last three (*Mansfield Park, *Emma, and *Persuasion) are known to have been written in the busy family parlour at Chawton.

The Juvenilia, written in her early and mid-teens, are already incisive and elegantly expressed; *Love and Friendship* was written when she was fourteen, *A History of England* ('by a partial, ignorant and prejudiced historian') at fifteen; at sixteen *A Collection of Letters*; and sometime during those same years, *Lesley Castle*. *Lady Susan* is also an early work, written probably in 1793–4. Of the major novels, *Sense and Sensibility* was published in 1811, *Pride and Prejudice* in 1813, Mansfield Park in 1814, Emma in 1816, *Northanger Abbey and *Persuasion posthumously in 1818. They were, however, begun or completed in a different order. The youthful sketch *Elinor and Marianne* (1795–6) was followed in 1797 by *First Impressions*, which was refused without reading by the publisher Cadell; *Elinor and Marianne* was rewritten in 1797–8 as *Sense and Sensibility*. Northanger Abbey followed in 1798–9 and was in 1803 sold to the publishers Crosby and Sons who paid the author £10 but did not publish. In 1809 *Sense and Sensibility* was again revised for publication, and *First Impressions* was re-created and renamed *Pride and Prejudice*.

Between the writing of *Northanger Abbey* and the revision of *Sense and Sensibility* she wrote an unfinished novel, *The Watsons, probably begun in 1804 and abandoned in 1805, on her father's death—an event which may account for her comparatively long silence at this period. *Mansfield Park* was begun at Chawton in 1811, *Emma* in 1814, *Persuasion* in 1815; and in 1817, the year of her death, the unfinished *Sanditon. It is likely that although *Northanger Abbey* was, together with *Persuasion*, the last of the novels to be published, it was the earliest of the completed works as we now have them.

The novels were generally well received from publication onwards; the Prince Regent (whose librarian urged Miss Austen to write 'an historical romance, illustrative of the history of the august house of Coburg') kept a set of novels in each of his residences, and Sir W. *Scott praised her work in the *Quarterly Review in 1815; he later wrote of 'that exquisite touch which renders ordinary commonplace things and characters interesting'. There were, however, dissentient voices; C. *Brontë and E. B. *Browning found her limited, and it was not until the publication of J. E. Austen Leigh's Memoir in 1870 that a Jane Austen cult began to develop. Since then her reputation has remained consistently high, though with significant shifts of emphasis, some of them springing from D. W. Harding's seminal essay, 'Regulated Hatred: An Aspect of the Work of Jane Austen' (*Scrutiny, 1940), which presents her as a satirist more astringent than delicate, a social critic in search of 'unobtrusive spiritual survival' through her works. See Jane Austen: The Critical Heritage (1968), ed. B. C. Southam. The standard text of the novels (6 vols, 1923–54) is by R. W. Chapman, who also edited the letters (rev. 1952). See also M. Lascelles, Jane Austen, her mind and art (1939); D. *Cecil, A Portrait of Jane Austen (1978).

AUSTIN, Alfred (1835–1913), of a Roman Catholic family, was educated at Stonyhurst and Oscott College, but shortly abandoned his faith. Upon inheriting a fortune from his uncle, he gave up a career as a barrister for literature. An ardent imperialist and follower of *Disraeli, he became in 1883 joint editor with W. J. *Courthope of the newly founded National Review, and was its sole editor for eight years from 1887. Between 1871 and 1908 he published twenty volumes of verse, of little merit. A prose work, The Garden that I Love (1894), proved popular, and in 1896, to widespread mockery, Austin was made *poet laureate, shortly afterwards publishing in *The Times an unfortunate ode celebrating the Jameson Raid. Himself a waspish critic of his contemporaries, he was much derided and parodied as a poet. His Autobiography appeared in 1911. See N. B. Crowell, Alfred Austin, Victorian (1953).

AUSTIN, J(ohn) L(angshaw) (1911–60), educated at Shrewsbury and Balliol College, Oxford, White's professor of moral philosophy in Oxford, 1952–60. Though he published only a few technical articles in his lifetime, he had considerable influence as an exponent of the philosophical method which takes as its starting-point the careful elucidation of ordinary, non-philosophical language. One of his articles is 'Ifs and Cans' (1956, originally a *British Academy lecture). Two of his most important courses of lectures, Sense and Sensibilia and How to Do Things with Words, were published posthumously, both in 1962.

Authorized Version, see BIBLE, THE ENGLISH.

Authors, Society of, see SOCIETY OF AUTHORS, THE.

Autocrat of the Breakfast-Table, The, see HOLMES, O. W.

Autolycus, (1) in Greek mythology, a son of Hermes celebrated for his craft as a thief, who stole the flocks of his neighbours and mingled them with his own; (2) the roguish but charming pedlar in Shakespeare's *The Winter's Tale, so named because he is 'a snapper-up of unconsidered trifles'.

Avalon, in the Arthurian legends, one of the Celtic 'Isles of the Blest' (comparable to the classical 'Fortunate Isles'), to which Arthur is carried after his death. The name is variously explained as the island of apples (by *Geoffrey of Monmouth, among others) and as the island of Avalloc who ruled it with his daughters, including Morgan. *Glastonbury has also been identified as the burial-place of Arthur and hence with Avalon. For discussion, see R. S. Loomis in Arthurian Literature in the Middle Ages, ed. R. S. Loomis (1959), pp. 65–8.

Avare, L' (The Miser), one of *Molière's most famous comedies, acted 1668. Harpagon, the miser, and his son Cléante are rivals for the hand of Mariane. Cléante gets possession of the casket containing the miser's treasure, and gives his father, whom his loss has reduced to frenzy, the choice between Mariane and the casket. Harpagon chooses the casket and abandons Mariane to his son.

AVELLANEDA, Alonso Fernandez de, the name assumed by the author of the false Part II of *Don Quixote, issued in 1614. Cervantes's own Part II appeared in 1615.

Avenel, Mary, a character in Scott's *The Monastery and *The Abbot, and Julian, her uncle, a character in the former. Roland Avenel is the hero of the latter work. The White Lady of Avenel is a supernatural being introduced in The Monastery.

AVERROES (Abū 'l-Walīd Muḥammad bin Ahmad bin Rushd) (1126–98), a Muslim physician born at Cordova in Spain (Chaucer's Physician knows of him: *Canterbury Tales, General Prologue, 433), and a philosopher, the author of a famous Commentary on *Aristotle. He is placed in the Limbo of the Philosophers with *Avicenna by *Dante (Inferno, iv. 144). He is the inspiration for 'Latin Averroism' (1230 and afterwards), associated with Siger of Brabant, which regarded Aristotle as absolute in philosophy even when his view of things was not reconcilable with the absolute truth of Faith, a view which was repeatedly opposed (as by *Aquinas) and condemned (as by Tempier, 1277) until *Ockham in the 14th cent., when it became the unofficial norm. He is of immense importance as the conveyor of Aristotle back into the western tradition, and he attracted a great deal of attention. His view that the active intellect was separable and distinct from the passive was opposed by Aquinas in *De Unitate Intellectus.*

AVICENNA (Abū-'Ali al-Husayn bin Sīnā) (980–1037), a Persian physician (a capacity in which he was known to *Chaucer's Physician—General Prologue, 432—and Pardoner—CT, vi. 889) and philosopher, a voluminous writer who made Commentaries on *Aristotle and *Galen. His views of love have been said to be influential on the ideas of *Courtly Love, by A. J. Denomy in *The Heresy of Courtly Love* (1947), and he was a major influence on the development of 13th-cent. *scholasticism in his reordering of *Neoplatonism on an Aristotelian basis. *Dante places him with *Averroes in the Limbo of the Philosopher (*Inferno*, iv. 143).

Avon, the Sweet Swan of, *Shakespeare, born at Stratford-upon-Avon, first so called by Ben *Jonson in his commemorative poem in the First *Folio, 1623, 'To the memory of my beloved, The AUTHOR MR. WILLIAM SHAKESPEARE: AND what he hath left us'.

Awakening, The, a novel by K. *Chopin, published 1899.
Set in Grand Isle and New Orleans, it is the story of Edna Pontellier, a woman in her late twenties married to a successful Creole business man, leading a life of leisure which she finds vaguely dissatisfying. She dabbles in painting, unwilling to devote all her life to her children, and defies the convention of safe and permitted flirtation by committing adultery with one young man, though believing herself to be in love with another. On the last page she swims naked out to sea and presumably drowns, thus ambiguously asserting the individual's right to freedom.

Awkward Age, The, a novel by H. *James.

Awntyrs of Arthure at the *Terne Wathelyne, The* (The Adventures of Arthur at the Tarn Wadling, in Cumberland), an alliterative poem in 715 lines probably from the last quarter of the 14th cent. from the region of Cumberland or the Scottish Lowlands, surviving in five 15th-cent. manuscripts. It seems to have borrowed from the alliterative *Morte Arthure and from Sir *Gawain and the Green Knight. The romance is in two parts: in the first, while out hunting, Gawain and Gaynor (Guinevere) are visited by an apparition, from the lake, of Gaynor's mother who asks for thirty masses to be said for the relief of her suffering soul (a motif derived from the legend of the trental of St Gregory); the ghostly figure attacks the vices of Gawain, Arthur, and the court. This criticism

links the first to the second part of the poem set at Arthur's court in which a knight, Sir Galeron of Galway (Galloway), demands the return of lands which Arthur had confiscated and given to Gawain. Honour is satisfied: the knight's lands are returned, and Gaynor has the masses said for her mother. The poem (in complex 13-line stanzas) is impressively written and is one of the most admired alliterative poems.
It has been edited by R. Hanna (1974); see also J. Speirs, *Medieval English Poetry* (1957), pp. 252–62 (first part of poem).

Axel's Castle, a study of *Symbolist literature, by E. *Wilson.

Ayala's Angel, a novel by A. *Trollope, published 1881.
Egbert Dormer fails to provide for his daughters, and on his death Lucy and Ayala are farmed out to relations. The romantic Ayala has a high ideal of the man she wishes to marry, but must choose from the vulgar Captain Batsby, her callow cousin Tom Tringle, and ugly Jonathan Stubbs. Stubbs's persistence and good sense overcome all Ayala's objections, and he ends the novel transfigured into her 'Angel of Light'. Meanwhile the practical Lucy has attached herself to a penniless but deserving sculptor. Incidental interest derives from the matrimonial tribulations of the daughters of the wealthy Sir Thomas Tringle.

AYCKBOURN, Alan (1939–), playwright, born in London, whose first plays were produced at Scarborough, where he has since 1971 been artistic director of the Theatre-in-the-Round. His first London success, *Relatively Speaking* (1967, pub. 1968), was followed by many others, including *Absurd Person Singular* (1973, pub. 1974); *The Norman Conquests* (1974, pub. 1975; a trilogy with elaborately overlapping action covering the same period of time and the same events from different points of view); *Absent Friends* (1975, pub. 1975); and *Joking Apart* (1979, pub. 1979). The plays are comedies of suburban and middle-class life, showing a keen sense of social nuance and of domestic misery and insensitivity, and displaying the virtuosity of Ayckbourn's stagecraft; Benedict Nightingale (*An Introduction to Fifty Modern British Plays*, 1982) comments that they succeed as comedies despite 'an intricacy of plot better fitted to farce, and themes sometimes more suited to tragedy', and detects, in common with other critics, an increasingly sombre note in his work.

Ayenbite of Inwit, a devotional manual translated in 1340 by Dan Michel of Northgate, Canterbury, into English prose from the French moral treatise *Les Somme des Vices et des Vertues,* also known as *Le Somme le Roi* because it was composed for Philip III of France in 1279 by its author, the Dominican Frère Loren of Orleans. The French original may have been one of the sources for Chaucer's 'Parson's Tale' (*Canterbury Tales*, 24), and it is possible that the English version too was known to Chaucer. The manuscript claims to be in the author's hand, and it is full of elementary translating errors. The text has very little literary interest and is of note only as a specimen of the Kentish dialect in the 14th cent. It has been edited by R. Morris (EETS os 23, 1866), rev. P. O. Gradon (1965).

AYER, Sir A(lfred) J(ules) (1910–   ), educated at Eton and Christ Church, Oxford, Grote professor of mind and logic at University College London (1946–59), Wykeham professor of logic in the University of Oxford (1959–78). He is the author of *Language, Truth and Logic* (1936), which was the first exposition of logical positivism in the English language, *The Foundations of Empirical Knowledge* (1940), and *The Problem of Knowledge* (1956), as well as volumes of philosophical essays and histories of modern philosophy. He has, in these volumes, carried further the traditions of British empiricism.

Ayesha, (1) a novel by *Morier; (2) a novel by Sir R. *Haggard.

Aylwin, a novel by W. T. *Watts-Dunton.

Aymon, The Four Sons of, a medieval French romance telling of Charlemagne's struggle with these four noblemen, the eldest and most important of whom was *Rinaldo. The English prose version of the romance is founded on *Caxton's printed version (1489–91), there being no surviving manuscript. It has been edited by O. Richardson, EETS es 44 (1884, reprinted Kraus 1973).

Ayrshire Legatees, The, a novel by J. *Galt, published 1821.

The book largely takes the form of letters recording the adventures of a worthy Scottish minister, Dr Zachariah Pringle, and his family, in the course of a visit which they pay to London in order to take possession of a legacy. Their naïve comments on their experiences, and the comments of their friends in Scotland on the letters themselves, produce what is in effect a social satire, on travellers, on London society, and on the 'douce folk' at home.

AYTOUN, William Edmonstoune (1813–65), a descendant of the poet Sir Robert Aytoun (1570–1638), the reputed author of the lines on which Burns based *'Auld Lang Syne'. Educated at Edinburgh University, he divided his life between law and literature, becoming professor of *belles-lettres* at Edinburgh in 1845, and sheriff of Orkney in 1852. He is remembered for his share of the *Bon Gaultier ballads (1845), and for his *Lays of the Scottish Cavaliers*. The first of the lays appeared in *Blackwood's Magazine* in April 1843, and the volume was published in 1849. Modelled on Sir W. *Scott and *Macaulay, these patriotic ballad-romances, based on stories of *Montrose, Dundee, and other Scottish heroes, were extremely popular. Aytoun also wrote *Firmilian, or the Student of Badajoz* (1854), a mock-tragedy in which he parodied the poems of the *Spasmodic School; it played a decisive role in ending the vogue for such works.

B

Bab Ballads, a collection of humorous ballads by W. S. *Gilbert (who was called 'Bab' as a child by his parents), first published in *Fun*, 1866–71. They appeared in volume form as *Bab Ballads* (1869); *More Bab Ballads* (1873); *Fifty Bab Ballads* (1877).

Babbitt, a novel by S. *Lewis.

BABBITT, Irving (1865–1933), American critic and professor at Harvard, born in Ohio. He was, with Paul Elmer More (1864–1937), a leader of the New Humanism, a philosophical and critical movement of the 1920s which fiercely criticized *Romanticism, stressing the value of reason and restraint. His works include *The New Laokoon* (1910), *Rousseau and Romanticism* (1919), and *Democracy and Leadership* (1924). T. S. *Eliot, who described himself as having once been a disciple, grew to find Babbitt's concept of humanism inadequate as an alternative to religion, and described it (in an essay published in 1928 in *Forum*) as 'a product—a by-product—of Protestant theology in its last agonies'.

BABEL, Isaak Emmanuilovich (1894–?1941), Russian Jewish writer born in Odessa, the son of a shopkeeper. After an Orthodox Jewish upbringing, he arrived in Petrograd in 1915. *Gorky published Babel's first story in 1916. From 1917 Babel served as soldier and war correspondent, taking part in the Polish campaign with the First Cavalry in 1920. From this came his masterpiece, the collection of stories *Red Cavalry* (1923–5), which describes with harsh vigour the savagery of war and its paradoxical fascination for the intellectual Jewish narrator Lyutov. Many of Babel's other stories are loosely autobiographical ('The Story of My Dovecot', 'First Love'), but he also wrote a cycle of stories about a very different Jewish life, that of the Odessan gangster Benya Krik ('The King', 'How it was done in Odessa', and others). Neither his ornamentalist style nor his themes found favour with the Soviet authorities, and in the late 1920s he came under increasing pressure. This led to almost total artistic silence, but he was again attacked at the First Congress of the Union of Soviet Writers. He was arrested in 1939 and disappeared into the Soviet penal system: the date of his death is tentative. Like other writers, Babel was posthumously rehabilitated, and editions of his work appeared in the Soviet Union in the 1950s and 1960s, though his Jewishness would seem to be the reason for a tacit new ban on publication of his work. In the rest of the world his reputation as a master of the short story continues to grow. *Red Cavalry* was translated by J. Harland in 1929 and most of his work is available in English translation.

Babes in the Wood, The, see CHILDREN IN THE WOOD, THE.

Baboon, Lewis, see JOHN BULL.

Babylon, an old ballad, the plot of which is known 'to all branches of the Scandinavian race', of three sisters, to each of whom in turn an outlaw proposes the alternative of becoming a 'rank robber's wife' or death. The first two choose death and are killed by the outlaw. The third threatens the vengeance of her brother 'Baby Lon'. This is the outlaw himself, who thus discovers that he has unwittingly murdered his own sisters, and thereupon takes his own life. The ballad is in *Child's collection (1883–98).

Bacchius, see METRE.

BACH, German family of musicians, mainly of the 17th and 18th cents. Its greatest member, Johann Sebastian (1685–1750), since the revival of interest in his music in the early 19th cent. led by *Mendelssohn and, in England, Samuel Wesley, has become a central figure in British musical appreciation. Of his three famous sons, Wilhelm Friedemann (1710–84) and Carl Philipp Emanuel (1714–88) have been regarded as essentially German figures, but Johann Christian (the 18th and youngest child, 1735–82) settled in London in 1762 and became known as 'the English Bach'. His portrait was painted by his friend *Gainsborough and he was buried in St Pancras churchyard. He became music-master to the family of George III, and though his operas for London were in the prevailing Italian fashion (and language) he wrote various arias in English, a number of songs for *Vauxhall Gardens, and some settings of folk-songs.

Backbite, Sir Benjamin, one of the scandalmongers in Sheridan's **The School for Scandal*.

Bacon, Friar, see FRIER BACON AND FRIER BONGAY.

BACON, Francis, first baron Verulam and viscount St Albans (1561–1626), was the son of Sir Nicholas Bacon, lord keeper in Queen Elizabeth's reign, and Anne Cooke, a Puritan, sister to the wife of the Queen's chief minister, Burghley. Bacon was born in London, at York House in the Strand, and educated at Trinity College, Cambridge. He was admitted to Gray's Inn, became a barrister in 1582, and was elected to Parliament in 1584 for the first of several constituencies he was to represent. In search of advancement he exerted pressure on his uncle, Lord Burghley, but without much success. He was taken up by the Queen's favourite, Essex, in 1591. The large and vigorous part he played in securing Essex's conviction after his rebellion ten years later is hardly excused by the fact that he was not himself involved in it. After Elizabeth's death, and in spite of the settled enmity of *Coke, his worldly progress was rapid. He was appointed solicitor-general in 1607, attorney-general in 1613, lord keeper in 1617, and lord chancellor in 1618. James I's favourite, the 1st earl of *Buckingham, assisted his rise after Burghley's death in 1612. A few months after being created viscount St Albans in 1621, he was charged by way of petitions to the House of Commons with taking bribes as a judge. After self-abasingly admitting his guilt he was sentenced by the House of Lords to a huge fine, imprisonment in the Tower, disqualification from Parliament, and exclusion from the court. The fine was remitted and he spent only a couple of days in the Tower, but his public life was over. He occupied the last years with energetic study and writing. He married an heiress, Alice Barnham, and her money contributed to the splendour of his houses: Gornhambry at St Albans and York House, his London birthplace, which was extracted from him by Buckingham at the time of his disgrace.

Bacon's writings are of many different kinds, the largest and most influential body of his work being philosophical in a broad sense of the term. He saw this as all forming part of a massive system, never to be completed, called The Great Instauration. The first part, the 'division of the sciences', he carried out twice, first in English, in *The Advancement of Learning (1605), and then in Latin, in De Augmentis Scientiarum (1623). This systematic classification of all branches of knowledge, in which mechanical rigour of design is pleasantly mitigated by Jacobean digressiveness, has been the model for all subsequent enlightened (in other words, secular) constructions of its kind, such as those of the Encyclopédistes of the 18th cent. and the Comteans of the 19th. The second part is Bacon's theory of scientific method, 'true directions concerning the interpretation of nature', realized in his *Novum Organum of 1620. The third part, 'natural history', is represented by

several 'histories' of natural phenomena, such as the winds, and a general collection of odds and ends, the Sylva Sylvarum of 1627. The fourth part, the 'ladder of the intellect', intended to give examples of his new method in use, was never written, apart from a preface, nor was the fifth part, the 'anticipations of the new philosophy', which was to be the body of conclusions arrived at by ordinary procedures for temporary use until the true Baconian science came into being.

In his theory of scientific classification Bacon distinguishes knowledge of the natural world very sharply from knowledge of the supernatural and does not much conceal the fact of his exclusive interest in the former. He also criticizes three prevailing, but in his view unsatisfactory, ways of seeking to gain knowledge: the abstract disputation of the scholastics, the elegant insubstantiality of the humanists, and the preoccupation with marvels and monstrosities of the Renaissance occultists. In their place he proposes that nature's secrets should be unlocked, so that mankind can acquire power over its circumstances, by means of a mechanical routine of eliminative induction, making a gradual ascent from the level of the observably particular to the ever more general level of theory.

Many of Bacon's works lie outside the grand project of the Great Instauration. His *New Atlantis, published in 1627, a year after his death, describes a Utopian community, notable for the way it depends for its progress on collective scientific research. The *Essays, in various editions from 1597 to 1625, started as assemblages of aphorisms, held together only by a common subject, a chaos of bright ideas of a broadly Machiavellian tone. Bacon's History of Henry VII (1622) is not original so far as its raw material is concerned, but inaugurates a new era in being a genuinely explanatory account of its subject and not a mere chronicle. Bacon reflected about his own professional field, projecting an organized 'digest' of the law so as to extricate it from the obscurity of the common-law tradition, and he sketched his fundamental legal principles in Maxims of the Law (written in 1597). Nearly as popular in his own time as his Essays was his De Sapientia Veterum of 1609 (English translation 1619), in which rational messages are decoded from the myths and fables of antiquity.

Bacon's prose is rich, ornate, and supple. To a modern cast of mind there is a noticeable, but by no means unpleasing, contrast between the plainness of much of his matter and the ornamentation of his manner. He contributed as much as anyone to the depth of the contemporary division between art and science, but there is no sign of it in his own writing. The standard edition of his works is *Spedding's of 1857–9, which was followed by a Life and

Letters. *Macaulay's brilliant essay (*Edinburgh Review*, July 1837) is too hard on Bacon, at least on his philosophy.

BACON, Roger (1210/14–after 1292), the 'Doctor Mirabilis', a philosopher who studied at Oxford and Paris where he probably became Doctor before returning to England *c*.1250, at which time, probably, he joined the Franciscan order. It is likely that he remained at Oxford until *c*.1257 when he incurred the suspicions of the Franciscans and was sent under surveillance to Paris where he remained in confinement for ten years. He produced at the request of his friend Pope Clement IV (1265–8) Latin treatises on the sciences (grammar, logic, mathematics, physics, and modern philosophy); his great work is the *Opus Maius*, and he also completed an *Opus Minus* and an *Opus Tertium*. He was again in confinement for his heretical propositions, *c*.1278–92, and is said to have died and been buried at Oxford. He has been described as the founder of English philosophy. A conservative in theology, which he regarded as incomparably supreme among the arts, he advocated support for it from an appeal to experience rather than from the scholastic method of argument employed in the *Summa* of *Albertus Magnus and *Alexander of Hales. He begins by stating the chief causes of error to be ignorance of languages, especially Greek, bad Latin translations, and lack of knowledge of the natural sciences, especially mathematics. At the same time, his outlook remained partly mystical. His attack on the scholastic method was taken up again and developed by William of *Ockham in the next century. He was a man of immense learning, with a wide knowledge of the sciences and of languages: Greek, Hebrew, and Aramaic. He was also a practical scientist; he invented spectacles and indicated the method by which a telescope might be constructed. He was vulgarly regarded as a necromancer in the Middle Ages because of his interest in the new sciences, especially chemistry and alchemy.

Bacon and Bungay, (1) the rival publishers in Thackeray's *Pendennis*; (2) see FRIER BACON AND FRIER BONGAY.

Baconian Theory, the theory that F. *Bacon wrote the plays attributed to *Shakespeare. It was started in print in the mid-19th cent., and is based partly on (supposed) internal evidence in Shakespeare's plays (the knowledge displayed and the vocabulary), and partly on external circumstances (the obscurity of Shakespeare's own biography, and the assumption that the son of a Warwickshire husbandman was unlikely to be capable of such skilful creations). Some holders of the theory have found in the plays cryptograms in support of it, e.g. in the nonce-word 'honorificabilitudinitatibus' in *Love's Labour's Lost* (v.i), which has been rendered in Latin as 'These plays, F. Bacon's offspring, are preserved for the World'; the word, however, is found elsewhere as early as 1460. The best recent treatment of the topic is to be found in S. *Schoenbaum, *Shakespeare's Lives* (1970).

Badman, *The Life and Death of Mr*, an allegory by *Bunyan, published 1680.

The allegory takes the form of a dialogue, in which Mr Wiseman relates the life of Mr Badman, recently deceased, and Mr Attentive comments on it. The youthful Badman shows early signs of his vicious disposition. He beguiles a rich damsel into marriage and ruins her; sets up in trade and swindles his creditors by fraudulent bankruptcies and his customers by false weights; breaks his leg when coming home drunk; and displays a short-lived sickbed repentance. His wife dies of despair and Badman marries again, but his second wife is as wicked as he is and they part 'as poor as Howlets'. Finally Badman dies of a complication of diseases. The story is entertaining as well as edifying and has a place in the evolution of the English novel.

Badon, Mount, the scene of a battle connected with *Arthur, first mentioned by *Gildas without reference to Arthur. It was almost certainly a real battle, fought against the Saxons or Jutes by the Britons somewhere in the south of England. The *Annales Cambriae* give the date of the battle as 518, declaring that Arthur carried the cross of Christ as his standard there; but it is likely that this is merely an embellishment of Gildas. *Geoffrey of Monmouth identifies Badon as Bath; other authorities say it was Badbury near Wimborne.

BAEDEKER, Karl (1801–59), editor and publisher, of Essen, Germany. He started the issue of the famous guide-books in Koblenz, and this was continued by his son, Fritz, who transferred the business to Leipzig.

BAFFIN, William (?1584–1622), a navigator and discoverer, who was pilot in the Muscovy Company's expeditions of 1615 and 1616 in search of the North-West Passage, which resulted in the discovery of Baffin Bay. He was killed at the siege of Ormuz in the Persian Gulf. His accounts of his voyages were edited in 1881 for the *Hakluyt Society by C. R. Markham.

BAGE, Robert (1720–1801), Quaker, revolutionist, and a paper-maker by trade, was much influenced by *Rousseau and other French thinkers. He was the author of six novels: *Mount Henneth* (1781); *Barham Downs* (1784); *The Fair Syrian* (1787); *James Wallace* (1788); *Man as He Is* (1792); and *Hermsprong, or Man as He is Not* (1796). His original talent was much admired by Sir W. *Scott and other discerning critics. Scott included the first, second, and fourth of the works in the 'Ballantyne Novels'. *Hermsprong*, the most remarkable of Bage's works, is the story of a 'natural' man, brought up without the 'civilized' conventions of morality or religion, among American Indians (see PRIMITIVISM). Bage did not care to think of his works as 'novels', but rather as illustrations of certain views and attitudes.

BAGEHOT, Walter (1826–77), born in Langport, Somerset, educated at Bristol and University College London. He was called to the bar and then joined the shipping and banking business of his father. He contributed articles on economic, political, historical, and literary subjects to various periodicals, became joint editor with R. H. *Hutton of the *National Review* from 1855, and editor of the *Economist* from 1860 until his death. He was author of *The English Constitution* (1867; ed. R. H. S. Crossman, 1963), which takes the form of a philosophical discussion appraising the actual values of the elements of the constitution and has remained a classic introduction to the study of English politics, in spite of historical change. His *Physics and Politics* (1872) is 'an attempt to apply the principles of natural selection and inheritance to political society'. *Lombard Street* (1873) is a lively analysis of the money market of his day. Among his other works are *Biographical Studies* (1881) and *Literary Studies* (1879–95), which includes critical essays on Shakespeare, *Sterne, and the notable 'Wordsworth, Tennyson, and Browning, or Pure, Ornate, and Grotesque Art in English Poetry'. See *Collected Works,* ed. N. A. F. St John-Stevas (8 vols, 1965–) and *Life* by N. A. F. St John-Stevas (1959).

Bagford Ballads, The, illustrating the last years of the Stuarts' rule and the last years of the 17th cent., were published by the Ballad Society in 1878. They were assembled by John Bagford (1651–1716), originally a shoemaker, a book-collector who made for Robert Harley, first earl of Oxford, the collection of ballads that was subsequently acquired by the duke of *Roxburghe, and at the same time made a private collection for himself.

Bagnet, Mr and Mrs, characters in Dickens's *Bleak House.*

BAGNOLD, Enid Algerine (Lady Jones) (1889–1981), novelist and playwright, spent much of her early childhood in the West Indies, returning to England to Prior's Field, an intellectually progressive school run by the mother of A. *Huxley. She worked as nurse and ambulance driver during the First World War (see her *Diary without Dates,* 1917) and married in 1920, but continued to write and move in artistic and Bohemian circles, writing several novels, of which the best known and commercially most successful was *National Velvet* (1935, filmed 1944 with Elizabeth Taylor as the girl who wins the Grand National). Of her plays, the most successful was *The Chalk Garden* (1955). Her *Autobiography* was published in 1969.

Bagstock, Major Joe, a character in Dickens's *Dombey and Son.*

Baiardo, see BAYARD.

BAILEY, Nathan or Nathaniel (d. c.1742), author of the *Universal Etymological Dictionary* (1721), a forerunner of Dr *Johnson's, and very popular. Johnson used Bailey's *Dictionarium Britannicum* (1730), embracing the 1721 volume, while compiling his own work.

BAILEY, Philip James (1816–1902), after embarking on a career as a barrister at Lincoln's Inn, retired in 1836 to his father's house at Old Basset, near Nottingham, where he devoted three years to writing the original version of *Festus,* published in 1839. A second, much enlarged edition, appeared in 1845, and the final edition of 1889, which exceeded 40,000 lines, incorporated the greater part of three volumes of poetry that had appeared in the interval (*The Angel World,* 1850; *The Mystic,* 1855; *Universal Hymn,* 1867). *Festus* is Bailey's own version of the legend of Goethe's *Faust; it was also strongly influenced by *Paradise Lost. At one time it was immensely popular, admired for its 'fire of imagination' (E. B. *Browning), but, like the other works of the *Spasmodic school of which Bailey was considered the father, it is now almost unreadable. The story is similar to that of Faust; Lucifer receives permission from God to tempt Festus, and accompanies him through life, as does also Festus's guardian angel. It ends with the Last Judgement and the admission of Festus among the Elect Spirits. Bailey claimed it was 'a sketch of world-life and a summary of its combined moral and physical conditions, estimated on a theory of spiritual things opposed as far as possible to that of the . . . sceptic . . . in its general positions known as universalist'. (Preface to 50th anniversary edition.)

Bailiff's Daughter of Islington, The, an old ballad included in Percy's *Reliques. A squire's son loves the bailiff's daughter of Islington (probably the place of that name in Norfolk), but his friends send him to London bound as an apprentice. After seven years the lovers meet again and are united.

BAILLIE, Joanna (1762–1851), Scottish dramatist and poet, published in 1798 her first volume of *Plays on the Passions,* in which each drama displays the effect of one particular passion. *Basil,* on the subject of love, and *De Montfort,* on hatred, were the most successful; *De Montfort* was produced by *Kemble and Mrs

*Siddons in 1800. The volume brought her the friendship of Sir W. *Scott, who called her 'the immortal Joanna', but her dramas did not escape criticism. A second volume of the *Passions* appeared in 1802, *Miscellaneous Plays* in 1804, and a third *Passions* volume in 1812. Her most successful drama, *The Family Legend*, based on a bitter Scottish feud, was produced in 1810 with a Prologue by Scott and an Epilogue by *Mackenzie. Scott described it as a 'complete and decided triumph' and it established Miss Baillie as a literary and social success. Her poems *Fugitive Verses* (1790) and *Metrical Legends* (1821) show some lyrical and narrative skill, and a pleasing balance of humour and sentiment. Her house in Hampstead became a meeting place for many of the literary figures of her time.

BAILLIE, Robert (1599–1662), Scottish Presbyterian divine, who was with the Covenanters' army in 1639 and in 1640 went to London to draw up accusations against *Laud. His *Letters and Journals*, ed. D. Laing (1842), are valuable records of the Civil War.

Bailly, Harry, in Chaucer's *Canterbury Tales* the host of the Tabard Inn where the pilgrims meet in the General Prologue. We learn his name ('Herry Bailly') from the Cook's Prologue (l. 4,358) and he has been tentatively identified with an ostler of that name in the Subsidy Rolls for Southwark 1380/1 and perhaps with the Member of Parliament for Southwark 1376/7 and 1378/9. See account in Robinson's edition, note on l. 751, p. 668 (2nd edn). He initiates the story-telling competition which forms the basis of the work, and acts as master of ceremonies along the way.

BAIN, Alexander (1818–1903), son of a weaver, born in Aberdeen, left school when eleven years old to work in his father's trade, but continued his studies and obtained at 18 a bursary at Marischal College. He visited London and made the acquaintance of *Mill and *Carlyle. In 1860 he was appointed professor of logic in Aberdeen. His two principal philosophical works were *The Senses and the Intellect* (1855) and *The Emotions and the Will* (1859). His autobiography was published in 1904.

BAINBRIDGE, Beryl (1934–), novelist, born in Liverpool, and educated at the Merchant Taylors' School, Liverpool. She began her career as an actress, and her first novels (*A Weekend with Claude*, 1967; *Another Part of the Wood*, 1968) were little noticed, but in the 1970s a series of original and idiosyncratic works established her reputation. These include *The Dressmaker* (1973), *The Bottle Factory Outing* (1974), *Young Adolf* (1978), and *Winter Garden* (1980). Short, laconic, and rich in black comedy, they deal with the lives of characters at

once deeply ordinary and highly eccentric, in a world where violence and the absurd lurk beneath the daily routine of urban domesticity, evoked in carefully observed detail: in *Injury Time* (1977), for example, a quietly illicit dinner party becomes headline news when invaded by a gang of criminals on the run who take its guests hostage. The juxtaposition of the banal and the bizarre is also a feature of the dialogue, which shows a fine ear for the oddities of contemporary speech.

Baines, Constance and Sophia, characters in Bennett's *The Old Wives' Tale*.

Bajazet, or Bajayet, ruler of the Ottomans (1389–1402), overran the provinces of the Eastern empire and besieged Constantinople, but was interrupted by the approach of Timour (Tamerlane), and was defeated and taken prisoner by him. He figures in Marlowe's *Tamburlaine the Great* and Rowe's *Tamerlane*.

BAKER, Sir Samuel White (1821–93), traveller and big game hunter, explored Ceylon, where he established an agricultural settlement in Nuwara Eliya, superintended the construction of a railway across the Dobrudja, and in 1861 undertook the exploration of the Nile tributaries, during which he discovered and named Lake Albert Nyanza (Lake Albert). From 1869 to 1873 he commanded an expedition to the Equatorial Nile Basin and later travelled to Cyprus, Syria, India, Japan, and America. His adventures are vividly described in his works, which include *The Rifle and Hound in Ceylon* (1854), *The Nile Tributaries of Abyssinia* (1867), and *Ismailia* (1874).

Balaam, Sir, the subject of satire in Pope's *Moral Essays* (Ep. iii. 339–402), a religious and frugal citizen who, tempted by wealth, becomes a corrupt courtier. He has been tentatively identified as Thomas Pitt (1653–1726), grandfather of William *Pitt the elder.

'Balade of Charitie, The', one of the 'Thomas Rowley' poems, see CHATTERTON.

BALAKIREV, Mily Alexeevich (1837–1910), Russian composer. Early in his career, between 1858 and 1861, Balakirev wrote an overture and incidental music to *King Lear*, which he revised in 1902–5. On neither occasion does there seem to have been any stage production in mind, which was probably just as well since the music, though much of it imaginative and beautifully scored, is not always very practical: the Sennet which accompanies Lear's first entry in Act I is taken by Balakirev as the cue for a seven-minute piece laid out for a large military band on the stage as well as the orchestra in the pit. In itself, however, it is an impressive piece, and the overture, though little played, is unusually satisfying both as an interpretation of Shakespeare's tragedy and as a musical whole.

Balakirev was an aggressive, obstinate, and interfering character, and the acknowledged leader of the Russian nationalist school of composers. In this capacity it was he who pressed upon *Tchaikovsky the plan for a symphonic work based on *Romeo and Juliet (even going so far as to write a few sample bars for it himself), and who later bludgeoned the composer into writing the Manfred symphony, the *Byronic masterpiece of Tchaikovsky's later years.

Balan, see BALYN.

Balaustion's Adventure: *Including a Transcript from Euripides,* by R. *Browning, published 1871.

The story, suggested by a passage in *Plutarch's *Life of Nicias,* is set just after the defeat of the Athenian expedition against Sicily in 413 BC. A group of pro-Athenians from Rhodes, inspired by the young girl Balaustion, is intercepted on its voyage to Athens by a pirate ship and is forced to seek shelter in the harbour of Syracuse, where it is refused entry until it is discovered that Balaustion can recite a play by *Euripides, who was greatly admired in Sicily although neglected in his native Athens. The play is *Alcestis,* a performance of which Balaustion narrates, mingling with the text her own comments and descriptions. Browning is thus able to represent Euripides' play in his own interpretation, within the framework of another speaker's consciousness, a marriage of conventional drama with dramatic monologue which continues the experiment with form begun with *The Ring and the Book.* The plot of the *Alcestis,* with its concentration on the surpassing love of a woman for her husband and her rescue from Death by a heroic figure, has been thought to be modelled on Elizabeth Barrett (to whom there is a direct allusion at ll. 2,668–71), but personal references should not obscure Browning's long-standing preoccupation with the theme of literal and literary resurrection. Balaustion reappears in *Aristophanes' Apology.

Balbec, the name used by Proust for the seaside resort (Cabourg) in Normandy which is the scene of many of the incidents of *A la recherche du temps perdu.

BALBOA, Vasco Nuñez de (1475–1517), one of the companions of *Cortés, the conqueror of Mexico. He is said to have joined the expedition of 1510 to Darien as a stowaway. It was he who first, in 1513, discovered the Pacific Ocean, not Cortés, as *Keats supposed when he wrote:

> Or like stout Cortez when with eagle eyes
> He stared at the Pacific.

(Nor was Balboa silent on this occasion, as Keats makes Cortés. He exclaimed 'Hombre!') Balboa

was beheaded by Pedrarias, governor of Darien, on a charge of treason.

Balchristie, Jenny, in Scott's *The Heart of Midlothian,* the housekeeper of the laird of Dumbiedikes.

Balder, see DOBELL, S.

'Balder Dead', a poem by M. *Arnold.

Balderstone, Caleb, a character in Scott's *The Bride of Lammermoor.

BALDWIN, James (1924–), black American novelist, born in Harlem, the son of a preacher. His first novel, *Go Tell it on the Mountain* (1953), set in Harlem, was followed by several on a more international scale, dealing with both homosexuality and the situation of American blacks; they include *Giovanni's Room* (1956), *Another Country* (1962), and *Just Above my Head* (1979). He has also written short stories, political and autobiographical essays, and plays, including *Blues for Mister Charley* (1964).

BALDWIN, William, see MIRROR FOR MAGISTRATES, A.

BALE, John (1495–1563), bishop of Ossory, author of several religious plays, a history of English writers, and numerous polemical works in favour of the cause of the Reformation. He is notable in the history of the drama as having written *King John,* the first English historical play, or at least a bridge between the *morality and the historical play proper.

BALESTIER, Charles Wolcott (1861–91), American author and publisher, who visited England in 1888 to secure English manuscripts for Lovell, the publishing company which had issued his novel *A Fair Device* (1886). He became a director of Heinemann and Balestier, a firm which published English and American books on the Continent. He is remembered for his collaboration with *Kipling (who married his sister in 1892): he wrote the American chapters for *The Naulahka* (1892) and Kipling dedicated his *Barrack-Room Ballads* to him in the same year.

BALFOUR, Arthur James, first earl of Balfour (1848–1930), philosopher and distinguished statesman, educated at Eton and Trinity College, Cambridge, notable in a literary connection as the author of philosophic and other works, some of which attracted wide attention. These include *A Defence of Philosophic Doubt* (1879), *The Foundation of Belief* (1895), *Questionings on Criticism and Beauty* (*Romanes Lecture, 1909), *Decadence* (Henry *Sidgwick Memorial Lecture, 1908), *Theism and Humanism* (*Gifford Lectures, 1915), and *Theism and Thought* (Gifford Lectures, 1923). *Chapters of Autobiography* (1930, ed. Mrs Dugdale) is a fragment of autobiography. In 1893 he was president of the *Society for Psychical Research.

Balfour, David, a character in R. L. Stevenson's *Kidnapped and Catriona.

Balfour of Burley, John, a leader of the Cameronian sect, who figures in Scott's *Old Mortality.

Balin, see BALYN.

'Balin and Balan', one of Tennyson's *Idylls of the King, first published 1885. It is the story of two brothers who kill each other unwittingly, Balan mistaking for a demon the impassioned Balin, who is driven to frenzy by a conviction of Guinevere's adultery. (See BALYN.)

Baliol, Mrs Bethune, in the introduction to Scott's *Chronicles of the Canongate, the friend of Chrystal Croftangry, on whose recollections the latter draws for his stories.

BALIOL, John de (d. 1269), father of John de Baliol, king of Scotland (1292–6), founded Balliol College, Oxford, about 1263, as an act of penance imposed for having 'vexed and damnified' the churches of Tynemouth and Durham.

Balkan Trilogy, see MANNING, O.

BALL, John, the leader of the Peasants' Revolt of 1381. He is the subject of W. Morris's *A Dream of John Ball.

Ballad, originally a song intended as an accompaniment to a dance; hence a light, simple song of any kind, or a popular song, often one attacking persons or institutions. Broadside ballads, such as those hawked by Autolycus in *As You Like It, were printed on one side of a single sheet (a *'broadside' or 'broadsheet') and sold in the streets or at fairs. In the relatively recent sense, now most widely used, a ballad is taken to be a single, spirited poem in short stanzas, in which some popular story is graphically narrated (e.g. *Sir Patrick Spens), and in this sense of the word the oral tradition is an essential element, though there has been much discussion as to the origin and composition of the old English ballads. In the great collection of F. J. *Child, English and Scottish Popular Ballads (5 vols, 1882–98), the oldest ballad is *Judas (c.1300), with an uncharacteristically religious theme; ballads more traditionally deal with the pagan supernatural (e.g. *Tam Lin), with tragic love (e.g. *Barbara Allan), or with historical or semi-historical events, e.g. the Border ballads, or the *Robin Hood ballads. There was a notable awakening of interest in the form in Britain in the 18th cent., which led to the researches and collections of *Percy (*Reliques, 1765) and *Ritson, to the forgeries of *Chatterton and the adaptations of *Burns, and to the deliberate antiquarian imitations of *Tickell

(Lucy and Colin), Percy himself (The Hermit of Warkworth), Mallet (*'William and Margaret'), Goldsmith (*'The Hermit'), and others. Scott's *Minstrelsy of the Scottish Border is a mixture of traditional ballads, adaptations, and imitations, whereas the *Lyrical Ballads of *Wordsworth and *Coleridge manifests, in poems like 'The Idiot Boy' and the *Ancient Mariner, their own interpretation and development of the term. The form has continued to inspire poets, from *Keats (*'La Belle Dame Sans Merci') to W. *Morris, *Hardy, *Yeats, and *Causley, and flourishes in a popular folk form (see FRANKIE AND JOHNNY) as well as in a more literary guise. The ingredients of ballads, both ancient and modern, vary, but frequently include the use of a refrain (sometimes altered slightly at the end of each stanza, to advance the story), stock descriptive phrases, and simple, terse dialogue. See G. H. Gerould, The Ballad of Tradition (1932) and M. J. C. Hodgart, The Ballads (1950). (For 'ballad stanza' see METRE.)

Ballade, strictly a poem consisting of one or more triplets of seven- or (afterwards) eight-lined stanzas, each ending with the same line as refrain, and usually an envoy addressed to a prince or his substitute; e.g. *Chaucer's Compleynt of Venus. It was a dominant form in 14th- and 15th-cent. French poetry, and one of its great masters was *Villon. The form enjoyed a minor English revival in the late 19th cent. in the work of *Swinburne, *Henley, and *Dobson.

Balladino, Antonio, in Jonson's *The Case is Altered, the foolish writer of city pageants intended as a caricature of *Munday.

'Ballad of Bouillabaisse, The', a comic ballad by *Thackeray.

Ballad Opera, a theatrical and musical form, very popular in England in the 18th cent., in which the action of the play (usually comic) is carried in spoken prose, interspersed with songs set to traditional or currently familiar melodies. The first ballad opera is also the most famous, *The Beggar's Opera (1728) by John Gay, with music selected and arranged by J. C. Pepusch. Its immense success touched off a whole series of imitations, and the ballad opera became the main weapon of the English faction in its battle with the Italian operatic invaders, *Handel at their head. The vogue was short-lived, however, and began to decline at the end of the next decade, though it left an heir in the English comic opera of the later 18th cent.: works like *Arne and *Bickerstaffe's Thomas and Sally (1760) or Love in a Village (1762), or Linley and Sheridan's *The Duenna (1775), are still very near to the ballad opera in form and theatrical intention.

BALLANTYNE, James (1772–1833),

brother of John *Ballantyne, at first a solicitor, then a printer in Kelso, printed Scott's *Minstrelsy of the Scottish Border in 1802, and continued to print Scott's works. He transferred his press from Kelso to Edinburgh in 1802 and Scott became a partner in 1805. In 1809 he took a quarter share in the publishing and bookselling business of John Ballantyne and Co., started by his brother and Scott. Although his printing business was highly successful, he was bankrupted by the crash of Constable and Co. in 1826. Scott named him 'Aldiborontiphoscophornio' from a solemn character in Henry Carey's *Chrononhotonthologos.

BALLANTYNE, John (1774–1821), brother of James *Ballantyne, became in 1809 manager of the publishing firm started by himself and Sir W. *Scott. While his brother's printing business flourished, the publishing and bookselling firm did not, and was allowed to run down. Scott planned Ballantyne's Novelist's Library (1821–4) solely for Ballantyne's financial benefit, but only one volume was published before Ballantyne's death. Scott greatly enjoyed his flamboyant character, and named him 'Rigdumfunnidos', after a genial character in Carey's *Chrononhotonthologos.

BALLANTYNE, R(obert) M(ichael) (1825–94) was a nephew of the Ballantyne brothers (above). He began his career in the Hudson's Bay Company, and in 1848 published his adventurous diary, Hudson's Bay. He then returned and worked for *Constable's printing firm, and in 1856 published his first adventure story, Snowflakes and Sunbeams; or the Young Fur Traders (soon known only by its subtitle). After the success of The Coral Island in 1857 he became an extremely successful professional writer of stories for boys. In search of authentic background he travelled widely, visiting Norway, Canada, Algeria, and elsewhere, and working at various occupations, including fireman and miner. He wrote over 80 novels; his narrative skill, the interest of his settings, and the manly virtues of his heroes ensured their popularity well into this century. Among his best-known works are The Gorilla Hunters (1862) and Black Ivory (1873).

BALLARD, J(ames) G(raham) (1930–), born in Shanghai and educated at Cambridge, became known in the 1960s as the most prominent of the 'New Wave' *Science Fiction writers. His first short story was published in 1956 in New Worlds, a periodical to which he continued to contribute during the influential editorship of *Moorcock. His first novel, The Drowned World (1962), a 'catastrophe' novel in which the world turns into a vast swamp, was followed by several others, including High Rise (1975), a grim and surreal fantasy with mo-

ments of black comedy, about technological and human breakdown in a tower block; but he is generally more admired for the concentrated, powerful, occasionally lyrical prose and apocalyptic imagery of his short stories. His collections include The Terminal Beach (1964), The Disaster Area (1967), and Vermilion Sands (1971). In Empire of the Sun (1984) he turned away from science fiction to draw on his own war-time experiences in China.

Balmawhapple, The Laird of, Falconer by surname, a character in Scott's *Waverley.

Balnibarbi, in *Gulliver's Travels, the country, subject to the king of Laputa, of which Lagado is the capital, where in every town there is an academy of 'projectors', engaged on inventions for increasing the welfare of mankind, none of which come to perfection.

Balor, the chief of the *Fomors of Gaelic mythology. One of his eyes had the power of destroying whatever it looked on. The eye was put out and Balor himself slain by Lugh, the sun-god, at the great battle of Moytura.

Balthazar ('possessor of treasure'), (1) one of the three *Magi, represented as king of Chaldea; (2) the name assumed by Portia as a lawyer in Shakespeare's *The Merchant of Venice, also that of one of her servants.

Balyn (Balin Le Savage) and Balan, are the subjects of the second Book in Malory's *Morte D'Arthur (the second part of the first of Malory's Works in Vinaver's edition, headed 'The Knight with the two Swords' which refers to Balyn). The two are brothers who kill each other unknowingly after a series of linked adventures; Balyn is the more prominent, though the two are sometimes confused in Malory. Balyn deals King Pellam the *Dolorous Stroke which causes the Waste Land, a disaster which is redeemed by the Grail Quest. He also kills the *Lady of the Lake when she seeks his head as reward for giving Arthur *Excalibur.

BALZAC, Honoré de (1799–1850), French novelist, author of the great series of co-ordinated and interconnected novels and stories known collectively as the Comédie humaine. The 91 separate completed works—137 were planned—that make up the whole were written between 1827 and 1847. The Preface (1842) to the first collected edition (1842–8) of Balzac's works, which first applies the general title to them, sets out his grand design to give an authentic and comprehensive fictional representation of French society in the latter years of the 18th cent. and the first half of the 19th. Critical analysis was an essential part of his aim, and by bold analogies between the novelist's art and that of the natural scientist and the historian he claimed for his 'studies' the orderly method, seriousness of purpose, and intellectual scope of these disciplines. The novels were classified under three main heads: (1) *Études de mœurs* (by far the largest category, subdivided into those dealing with private, provincial, and country life, Paris, military matters, and politics); (2) *Études philosophiques*; (3) *Études analytiques*. The cast of the *Comédie humaine* comprises more than 2,000 characters, some of them, like the master-criminal Vautrin or the money-lender Gobseck, appearing at different stages of their careers in several novels. Characteristically, Balzac interests himself in the supernatural and the mysterious (especially in the *Études philosophiques*), in the operation of the passions, in the role of money in shaping personal and social relations, in the determining effect of environment on the individual, and, conversely, in the various courses taken by energy and ambition in pursuit of social fulfilment. A list of the masterpieces of the *Comédie humaine* would include: *La Peau de chagrin* (1831), *Illusions perdues* (1837–43), *Le Médecin de campagne* (1833), *La Rabouilleuse* (1840), *La Cousine Bette* (1846), and *Le Cousin Pons* (1847). The vitality of Balzac's creations and the breadth of his vision have led some (H. *James among them) to regard him as the greatest of novelists. His influence on later fiction has been immense, and his work is an essential reference-point in the history of the European novel.

Ban, in the Arthurian legends, king of Benwick in Brittany, brother of Bors and the father of *Launcelot.

Bananas, a literary periodical which ran from 1975 to 1981, edited by E. *Tennant (1975–9) then by Abigail Mozley (1979–81), with contributions from T. *Hughes, J. G. *Ballard, A. *Sillitoe, E. *Feinstein, Heathcote Williams, and others.

BANDELLO, Matteo (1485–1561), a Lombard who fled to France and was made bishop of Agen by Francis I, was the best writer of Italian short stories in the 16th cent. Many of his tales were translated by Belleforest into French (1564–82) and 13 of these French versions were rendered into English by Geoffrey Fenton in his *Certaine tragicall discourses* (1567). Painter's *Palace of Pleasure* includes 25 of Bandello's tales, nine translated from the Italian and sixteen from Belleforest. *Turberville included two in his *Tragical Tales* (1576). Bandello is the source of plots for many English plays, including *Much Ado about Nothing*, *Twelfth Night*, and *The Duchess of Malfi*.

Bangorian Controversy, a church controversy of the early years of George I, which followed a sermon by B. *Hoadly. The Anglican Church, committed to the hereditary principle of monarchy, found itself in difficulties on the death of Queen Anne and the succession of the Hanoverians; strict churchmen refused to take the oath of allegiance and became 'nonjurors'. Hoadly's sermon, preached before the king (and said to have been suggested by him) in 1717 and immediately published, was called 'The Nature of the Kingdom or Church of Christ' and its text was 'My kingdom is not of this world.' It attacked Church authority, establishing conscience and sincerity as guide and judge in religious matters. It provoked over 200 incensed replies, notably from *Law and T. *Sherlock.

BANIM, John (1798–1842), Irish novelist, dramatist, and poet, is chiefly remembered for his faithful drawing of Irish life and character contained in the highly successful *Tales by the O'Hara Family*, partly written with his brother Michael and published in 1825, 1826, and 1827. Several of the novels, later published separately, first appeared in the *Tales*. Novels chiefly written by John include *The Nowlans* (1833), *The Boyne Water* (1836), and *John Doe* (1842). His *Damon and Pythias*, a tragedy successfully performed in London in 1821, was followed by other successful dramas.

Michael Banim (1796–1874) claimed after his brother's death that he was himself responsible for 13 of their joint 24 works; according to his claim, his own books include *The Croppy* (1828), a sombre tale of the uprising of 1798, *The Mayor of Windy Gap* (1835), and *The Town of the Cascades* (1864).

BANKS, Sir Joseph (1743–1820), eminent explorer and naturalist, studied the flora of Newfoundland in 1766, accompanied *Cook round the world, and subsequently visited the Hebrides and Iceland. He became a member of Dr Johnson's literary *Club, and was president of the *Royal Society 1778–1820.

Bannatyne Club, The, was founded in 1823, with Sir W. *Scott as president, for the publication of old Scottish documents (see Lockhart's *Scott*, lviii). The club was dissolved in 1861. George Bannatyne (1545–1608), in whose honour it was named, was the compiler in 1568 of a large collection of Scottish poems.

BANNERMAN, Helen, see CHILDREN'S LITERATURE.

Bannockburn, near Stirling, the scene of the great battle in 1314, when Robert Bruce utterly routed the English under Edward II, and all Scotland was thereby lost to the latter. The battle is described in Scott's *Lord of the Isles*, vi.

Banquo, Scottish general and companion of *Macbeth in Shakespeare's play of that name, to whom the witches prophesy that his issue will be kings. According to *Holinshed he was the founder of the House of Stuart, and so an ancestor of James I and VI.

Bantam, Angelo Cyrus, in Dickens's *Pickwick Papers*, Grand Master of the Ceremonies at Bath.

Barabas, the *'Jew of Malta', in Marlowe's play of that name.

Barbara Allan, a Scottish *ballad included in Percy's *Reliques*, on the subject of the death of Sir John Grehme for unrequited love of Barbara Allan, and her subsequent remorse. *Barbara Allen's Cruelty,* another ballad on the same theme, is also in the *Reliques*.

Barbarian, see PHILISTINE.

BARBAULD, Mrs Anna Laetitia, *née* Aikin (1743–1824), published several popular volumes of prose for children with her brother John *Aikin, and edited *Collins (1794), *Akenside (1794), and *Richardson's correspondence (6 vols, 1804). After the suicide in 1808 of her mentally unstable husband, the Revd Rochemont Barbauld, she threw herself into increased literary activity, editing The British Novelists in 50 vols (1810). She was a friend of Mrs. H. *More, Mrs *Montagu, and a circle of dissenting radical intellectuals, and supported radical causes (*Corsica: an ode,* 1768; *Epistle to Wilberforce,* 1791). Her poem beginning 'Life, I know not what thou art' was much admired by *Wordsworth, but a more interesting production is her poem in heroic couplets, *Eighteen hundred and eleven* (1812), which foretells the decline of Britain's 'Midas dream' of wealth, and the rise of prosperity and culture in America, whose tourists will come to visit with nostalgia 'the gray ruin and the mouldering stone' of England.

BARBELLION, see CUMMINGS, B. F.

BARBEY-D'AUREVILLY, Jules-Amédée (1808–89), French novelist and critic. He earned his living by literary journalism, and his collected articles—at once brilliant, prejudiced, and prophetic—fill several volumes. His major novels, *L'Ensorcelée* (1854) and *Le Chevalier des Touches* (1864), and his short stories, *Les Diaboliques* (1874), excel in their evocation of the desolate Cotentin landscapes of his childhood and its ancient Catholic and Royalist traditions; and in their creation of proud, flamboyant, and tormented characters often susceptible to supernatural powers. His style combines spontaneity and elegance.

BARBOUR, John (*c.*1320–95), a Scottish poet, archdeacon of Aberdeen in 1357 and one of the auditors of the exchequer in 1372, 1382, and 1384. He probably studied and taught at Oxford and Paris. The only poem ascribed to him with certainty is *The Bruce (The Actes and Life of the Most Victorious Conquerour, Robert Bruce King of Scotland*), in over 13,000 lines, which dates from 1376; even if it is his, it has been argued that the poem was tampered with

by John Ramsay, the writer of both the manuscripts in which the poem survives (from 1487 and 1489). The poem is a verse chronicle of the deeds of Bruce and his follower James Douglas, and it contains a celebrated, graphic account of *Bannockburn. Of the three other works sometimes attributed to him, The Troy Book has been denied him on linguistic grounds; The Lives of the Saints (50 legends, certainly from Barbour's period and area of origin) is disputed; and The Buik of Alexander, a translation of two French romances may be his.

The Bruce, ed. W. W. Skeat in 4 vols (EETS ES 11, 21, 29, 55, 1870–89); The Bruce: a Selection, ed. A. Kinghorn (1960); The Bruce: a Selection, ed. A. N. Douglas (1964); The Buik of Alexander, ed. R. L. G. Ritchie (Saltire Society Classics, 4 vols, 1920–8).

Barchester Towers, a novel by A. *Trollope, published 1857, the second in the *'Barsetshire' series.

Archdeacon Grantly's hopes of succeeding his father as bishop of Barchester are dashed when an ineffectual evangelical, Dr Proudie, is set over him by a new Whig government. The novel is a record of the struggle for control of the diocese. Mrs Proudie, the bishop's overbearing wife, shows her strength when she selects Mr Quiverful as the future warden of Hiram's Hospital. Despite the efforts of Mr Slope, the bishop's oily chaplain, and Grantly, to push the claims of Mr Harding, Quiverful gains the appointment. When the old Dean dies, Slope, anxious to take his place, persuades a national newspaper to advertise his own merits, and the conflict with Mrs Proudie intensifies. Slope's marital ambitions, however, start to get in his way. His designs on the fortune of Mrs Bold, Harding's widowed daughter, are handicapped by his flirtation with the fascinating but penniless Signora Vesey-Neroni, and the scandal is his undoing. The Puseyite Dr Arabin succeeds to the deanery and marries Mrs Bold, while Mrs Proudie sees to it that Slope is dismissed from his chaplaincy.

Barchino, in imprints, Barcelona.

BARCLAY, Alexander (?1475–1552), poet, scholar, and divine, probably of Scottish birth, was successively a priest in the college of Ottery St Mary, Devonshire, a Benedictine monk at Ely, a Franciscan at Canterbury, and rector of All Hallows, Lombard Street, London. He translated Brant's *Narrenschiff* into English verse as *The Ship of Fools* (1509) and wrote his *Eclogues* at Ely (*c.*1513–14). He also translated a life of St George from *Mantuan and *Sallust's *Bellum Jugurthinum* (*c.*1520).

BARCLAY, John (1582–1621), a Scot born at Pont-à-Mousson in France, author of the extremely popular Latin romance *Argenis*

(1621), which refers to real historical events and personages under a veil of allegory. He also wrote *Euphormionis Satyricon* (?1603–7), a satire on the Jesuits in the form of a *picaresque novel, also in Latin.

BARCLAY, Robert (1648–90), Scottish Quaker whose *Apology for the True Christian Divinity* (1678) is a reasoned defence of Quakerism. His collected works, *Truth Triumphant*, with a preface by W. *Penn, were published in 1692.

Bard, The, a Pindaric ode by *Gray, published 1757, based on a tradition that Edward I ordered the violent suppression of the Welsh bards.

It opens with the surviving Bard's cursing of the conqueror as he and his army return from Snowdon in 1283; he laments his slaughtered comrades, whose ghosts prophesy the fate of the Plantagenets. The Bard then foretells the return of the house of Tudor and commits triumphant suicide. Johnson's dismissal of the poem (*Lives of the English Poets*, 1781) outraged its many admirers, who regarded it as a fine example of the *Sublime, and it exerted a considerable influence on the imagination of both poets and painters (e.g. *Blake and J. *Martin).

Bardell, Mrs, in Dickens's *Pickwick Papers*, Mr Pickwick's landlady, who sues him for breach of promise.

Bardolph, a red-nosed rogue who is a soldierly companion of *Falstaff in Shakespeare's *1* and *2* *Henry IV*; and in *Henry V* is hanged for robbing a French church shortly before the battle of Agincourt. In *The Merry Wives of Windsor* Falstaff finds him a post as tapster at the Garter Inn.

BARETTI, Giuseppe Marc'Antonio (1719–89), born at Turin, came to London in 1751 and, among other pursuits, taught Italian. One of his pupils was C. *Lennox, who introduced him to Dr *Johnson. The two became friends, and Baretti's standard work, *A Dictionary of the English and Italian Languages* (1760), was clearly influenced by Johnson's own dictionary. In 1768 he published *An Account of the Manners and Customs of Italy*, a riposte to the *Letters from Italy* by Samuel Sharp, which he considered a grossly unfair portrayal of his native land. In 1769 he was tried for stabbing a man in the street in self-defence; his acquittal was received with relief by his many eminent friends, who included *Reynolds, *Burke, and *Garrick. His *A Journey from London to Genoa* was published in 1770. In these and other works he stimulated interest in and understanding of Italian literature and culture. His *Easy Phraseology for the Use of Young Ladies* (1775) sprang from lessons in conversation with one of the daughters of Mrs

*Thrale, and was published with a preface by Johnson. An irascible man, Baretti finally quarrelled with Johnson over a game of chess.

BARHAM, R(ichard) H(arris) (1788–1845), held various preferments, including that of a minor canon of St Paul's. His *The Ingoldsby Legends: or mirth and marvels, by Thomas Ingoldsby esquire* were first published from 1837 in *Bentley's Miscellany* and *The New Monthly Magazine*, and first collected in 1840. Their lively rhythms and inventive rhymes, their comic and grotesque treatment of medieval legend, and their quaint narratives made them immensely popular. One of the best-known is the story of the Jackdaw of Rheims, who stole the archbishop's ring, was cursed, fell ill, but recovered when the curse was lifted, and became devout.

BARING, Maurice (1874–1945), was educated at Eton and Trinity College, Cambridge. Versatile, prolific, and successful, he produced articles, plays, biography, criticism, poetry, translations, stories and novels, and works on painting and music, amounting to some 50 vols. A gift for languages led him to the Foreign Office, and later as a reporter to the Russo-Japanese War. He is credited with having discovered *Chekhov's work in Moscow and helping to introduce it to the West. His *Landmarks in Russian Literature* appeared in 1910, *An Outline of Russian Literature* in 1914, and *The Oxford Book of Russian Verse* in 1924. Of his various novels 'C' (1924), *Cat's Cradle* (1925), *Daphne Adeane* (1926), and *The Coat without Seam* (1929), all set in his own high social world, were very successful, and are still well regarded for their acute, intimate portrait of the time. Baring's conversion to the Roman faith is reflected in two historical novels of Tudor times, *Robert Peckham* (1930) and *In my End is my Beginning* (1931). His novella *The Lonely Lady of Dulwich* (1934) is often held to be the best of his works.

BARING-GOULD, Sabine (1834–1924), travelled much on the Continent with his parents during his boyhood, then was educated at Clare College, Cambridge. In 1867 he married a mill girl, an experience described in his first novel *Through Fire and Flame* (1868). From 1881 until his death he was both squire and rector of Lew Trenchard in Devon. An extremely prolific writer and an enthusiastic if unscholarly antiquarian, he wrote dozens of works on travel, religion, folklore, local legend, and folksong, composed various hymns (including 'Onward Christian Soldiers') and published some 30 novels, of which the most celebrated, *Mehalah* (1880), was compared by *Swinburne to *Wuthering Heights*. He also wrote a life of R. S. *Hawker, *The Vicar* of *Morwenstow* (1876). See *Onward Christian Soldier* (1957), a life by W. Purcell.

BARKER, George Granville (1913–), poet, born in Essex of an English father and Irish mother, and educated (briefly) at the Regent Street Polytechnic. His first publication was *Thirty Preliminary Poems* (1933), which was followed by *Poems* (1935), *Calamiterror* (1937, a semi-political poem inspired by the Spanish Civil War), and *Lament and Triumph* (1940). In 1939 he taught in a Japanese university, then lived in America and Canada from 1940 and 1943; he then returned to England, though living for further periods in America and Italy. Subsequent volumes include *Eros in Dogma* (1944), *The True Confession of George Barker* (1950, augmented 1965), and *Collected Poems 1930–1965* (1965). Barker's earlier work is characteristically rhetorical, Dionysiac, and surreal, though some critics have suggested that he achieves disorder more by accident than intent; a neo-Romantic, associated with the *New Apocalypse, and a self-styled 'Augustinian anarchist', he has a marked penchant for puns, distortion, and abrupt changes of tone. His *True Confession*, written as he reached the age of 35, presents the poet as irreverent, defiant, offhand, Rabelaisian, and guilt-ridden at once ('this rather dreary | Joke of an autobiography'); its later stanzas, and works such as *Villa Stellar* (1978) and the long title-poem of *Anno Domini* (1983), have a more sombre, reflective, questioning tone, although they too have moments of exuberance.

BARKER, Harley Granville-, see GRANVILLE-BARKER, H.

Barkis, in Dickens's *David Copperfield*, the carrier, who sent a message by David to Clara Peggotty that 'Barkis is willin'.

Barlaam and Josaphat, a late 12th-cent. Anglo-Norman romance, interesting as a Christianized version of the legend of Buddha. It appears first in the works of John of Damascus (8th cent.). In the story Josaphat, the son of an Indian king, Abenner, is converted by the Christian hermit Barlaam. Abenner, after first being hostile to Christianity, is converted too before his death, whereupon Josaphat abdicates to become a hermit. See edition by J. Koch, *Altfranzösische Bibliothek*, i (1879).

BARLOW, Joel (1754–1812), American poet and diplomat, born in Connecticut, who is remembered as the author of *The Columbiad* (1787, originally published as *The Vision of Columbus* and revised and renamed in 1807), a lengthy patriotic epic in heroic couplets, and of the more enjoyable mock-epic, *The Hasty-Pudding* (1796). Barlow was one of the *'Hartford Wits', and was, like most of them, a graduate of Yale.

Barmecide, the patronymic of a family of princes ruling at Baghdad just before *Hārūn ar-Rashīd, concerning one of whom the story is told in the *Arabian Nights* (the story of the Barber's Sixth Brother) that he put a succession of imaginary dishes before a beggar pretending that they contained a sumptuous repast. The beggar, entering into the spirit of the jest, pretended to be intoxicated by the imaginary wine offered him, and fell upon his entertainer. Hence 'Barmecide' is used of one who offers illusory benefits. (See also JAFFAR.)

Barnaby Rudge, a novel by *Dickens published in 1841 as part of *Master Humphrey's Clock*. The earlier of Dickens's two historical novels, it is set at the period of the Gordon anti-popery riots of 1780, and Lord George Gordon himself appears as a character. Like the later *A Tale of Two Cities*, it contains powerful evocations of mob violence, culminating in the sack of Newgate: Dickens wrote, 'my object has been to convey an idea of multitudes, violence and fury; and even to lose my own dramatis personae in the throng . . . '

Reuben Haredale, a country gentleman, has been murdered, and the murderer never discovered. His brother Geoffrey Haredale, a Roman Catholic, and the smooth villain Sir John Chester (who models himself on Lord *Chesterfield) are enemies; Chester's son Edward is in love with Haredale's niece Emma, and the elders combine, despite their hatred, to thwart the match. The Gordon riots, secretly fomented by Chester, supervene. Haredale's house is burned and Emma carried off. Edward saves the lives of Haredale and Emma and wins Haredale's consent to his marriage with the latter. Haredale discovers the murderer of his brother, the steward Rudge, father of the half-witted Barnaby and the blackmailer of Barnaby's devoted mother Mrs Rudge. Rudge is hanged, Barnaby (who had been swept along as unwitting participant in the riots) is reprieved from the gallows at the last moment, and Chester is killed by Haredale in a duel.

The vivid description of the riots forms the principal interest of the book, which also displays Dickens's concern with the demoralizing effect of capital punishment in the character of Dennis the Hangman and Hugh, the savage ostler who turns out to be Chester's son. Other characters involved in the plot include the upright locksmith Gabriel Varden, with his peevish wife and their coquettish daughter Dolly; Simon Tappertit, his aspiring and anarchic apprentice, and Miggs, his mean and treacherous servant; John Willett, host of the Maypole Inn, and Joe, his gallant son, who finally wins Dolly; and Grip, Barnaby's raven.

Barnacles, The, in Dickens's *Little Dorrit*, types of government officials in the 'Circumlocution Office'.

BARNARD, Lady Anne, see LINDSAY, A.

Barnardine, in Shakespeare's *Measure for Measure*, a prisoner 'that apprehends death no more dreadfully but as a drunken sleep; careless, reckless, and fearless of what's past, present, or to come'.

Barnavelt, *Sir John van Olden*, a historical tragedy, probably by J. *Fletcher and *Massinger, acted in 1619, within months of the execution of its real-life protagonist. This remarkable play was discovered by A. H. Bullen among the MSS of the British Museum, and printed in his *Old English Plays* (1883, vol. ii). An edition by W. P. Frijlinck was published in 1922.

The play deals with contemporary events in Holland. Barnavelt, the great advocate, disturbed by the growing power of the Prince of Orange and the army, under cloak of a religious movement conspires against him and raises companies of burghers in the towns to resist the army. The plot is discovered, the companies disarmed, and Barnavelt's principal associates are captured. One of these, Leidenberch, confesses. Barnavelt, who by virtue of his great position is still left at liberty though suspect, upbraids him and tells him that death. is the only honourable course left to him. Leidenberch, in remorse, takes his own life. The Prince of Orange, who had hitherto counselled moderation, now convinced of the gravity of the conspiracy, advises severe measures. Barnavelt is arrested, tried, and executed.

BARNES, Barnabe (?1569–1609), son of the bishop of Durham, was educated at Brasenose College, Oxford. Early in 1598 he attempted to kill the recorder of Berwick with poisoned claret, but he successfully evaded sentence, living mainly in Durham. His sonnet sequence *Parthenophil and Parthenophe. Sonnettes, madrigals, elegies, and odes* had been published in 1593, and *A divine centurie of spirituall sonnets* in 1595. He published *Foure bookes of offices* in 1606, and in 1607 a vigorous Machiavellian drama, *The divils charter: a tragaedie conteining the Life and Death of Pope Alexander the Sixt*, said to have been performed before the king. It includes such melodramatic scenes as the murder of Lucrezia *Borgia with poisoned face wash. Though *Courthope described Barnes's poetry as 'a mixture of nonsense and nastiness', it is actually remarkable for its vigour and technical range. *Parthenophil and Parthenophe* was edited by V. A. Doyno in 1971.

BARNES, Djuna Chappell (1892–1982), American novelist, illustrator, short story writer, and playwright, born in Cornwall-on-Hudson; she studied art in New York, leading a Bohemian life in Greenwich Village, then moved to Paris. Her publications include *A Book* (1923), a volume of plays, poems, and stories; *Ryder* (1928), a novel dealing with a man, his mother, and his mistress; *Ladies Almanack* (1928, privately printed in Paris), an erotic 18th-cent. pastiche of lesbian life; *The Antiphon* (1958), a verse drama. She is best remembered for *Nightwood* (1936), a novel which T. S. *Eliot described in his preface as one that would 'appeal primarily to readers of poetry . . . ' and possessing 'a quality of horror and doom very nearly related to that of Elizabethan tragedy'. It evokes, in highly-wrought, high coloured prose, a nightmare cosmopolitan world (chiefly located in Paris and New York) peopled by tormented and mutually tormenting characters, linked by the enigmatic doctor, priest of the secret brotherhood of the City of Darkness; it mingles elements of *fin-de-siècle* decadence with premonitions of the neo-Gothic. Her *Selected Works* appeared in 1962.

BARNES, William (1801–86), born near Sturminster Newton, of a farming family, began work at the age of fourteen for a solicitor, then moved to Dorchester where he contributed poems to the local paper. He learned Greek, Latin, and music, taught himself wood-engraving, and in 1823 became a schoolmaster at Mere. He married in 1827 and in 1835 moved his flourishing school to Dorchester. He was deeply interested in grammar and language, studied French, Italian, Welsh, Hebrew, Hindustani, and other languages, and waged a lifelong campaign to rid English of classical and foreign influences, suggesting many 'Saxonized' alternatives, such as 'sun-print' for photograph and 'fall-time' for autumn. He registered as a 'Ten-Year' man at St John's, Cambridge, in 1838, to study for a BD degree (which he acquired in 1851), was ordained in 1848, and took up the living of Whitcombe, moving to Cambe in 1862. *Orra, a Lapland Tale* appeared in 1822 and his *Poems of rural life in the Dorset Dialect* in 1844; *Hwomely Rhymes* followed in 1859 and *Poems of Rural Life*, written in standard English, in 1868. His collected dialect poems appeared as *Poems of Rural Life in the Dorset Dialect* in 1879.

As well as his volumes of poetry, Barnes also contributed articles on archeology and etymology to the *Gentleman's Magazine* and, from 1852, to the *Retrospective Review*. He wrote text books, a primer of Old English (*Se Gefylsta*, 1849), *Philological Grammar* (1854), a *Grammar . . . of the Dorset Dialect* (1863), and other works reflecting his interest in philology and local history. He was one of the founders of the Dorchester Museum and as an old man became famed as a repository of old sentiments, customs, and manners.

According to his many admirers, who included *Tennyson, G. M. *Hopkins, *Hardy, and *Gosse, Barnes was a lyric poet of the first rank, but the difficulties presented by the Dorset dialect have greatly restricted his audience and contributed to the image of a quaint provincial versifier. His poems evoke the Dorset landscape, country customs (as in 'Harvest Hwome' and 'Woodcom' Feast'), and happy childhood, although his few poems of grief, such as 'Woak Hill' and 'The Wind at the Door', written after the death of his wife, are among his best. He was greatly interested in versification, prosody, and the techniques of verse (particularly in alliteration), and the wide variety of his forms much intrigued *Hardy; his noun-combinations ('heart-heaven', 'sun-sweep', and 'mind-sight') foreshadow Hopkins. The dialect poems for which he is best remembered were written largely between 1834 and 1867; his standard English poems, written before and after those dates, were preferred by his publisher, Macmillan, and by Hardy. Hardy wrote an affectionate portrait in the *Athenaeum on his death, and a poem, 'The Last Signal'. There is a Life by W. T. Levy, 1960.

Barney, in Dickens's *Oliver Twist*, a Jew, associate of Fagin.

BARNFIELD, Richard (1574–1627), was educated at Brasenose College, Oxford. He published *The Affectionate Shepheard* in 1594, *Cynthia, with certaine Sonnets* in 1595, and *The encomion of lady Pecunia* (the praise of money) in 1598. Two of his *Poems in divers humors* (1598) appeared also in *The Passionate Pilgrim* (1599) and were once attributed to Shakespeare, the better-known being the ode 'As it fell upon a day | In the merry month of May'. *The Affectionate Shepheard* is a pastoral (based on *Virgil's second eclogue) describing the love of Daphnis for Ganymede, and includes a rather surprising digression on the 'indecencie of mens long haire'. The twenty sonnets in *Cynthia* are also to Ganymede. Barnfield has the distinction of being the only Elizabethan poet other than Shakespeare to have addressed love sonnets to a man.

Baroque (from Portuguese *barroco*, Spanish *barrueco*, a rough or imperfect pearl), originally a term of abuse applied to 17th-cent. Italian art and that of other countries, especially Germany, influenced by Italy. It is characterized by the unclassical use of classical forms, and by the interpenetration of architecture, sculpture, and painting to produce grandiose and emotional effects.

In a literary context the word baroque is loosely used to describe highly ornamented verse or prose, abounding in extravagant conceits; it is rarely used of English writers (with the exception of the Italianate *Crashaw), but frequently applied to *Marino, whose name became synonymous with Marinism, and to Gongora, whose name supplied the term *Gongorism.

Barrack-Room Ballads, see KIPLING, R.

BARRÈS, Maurice (1862–1923), French novelist and essayist, deputy for Nancy (1889–93) and Paris (1906–23). Active in politics, Barrès was a committed nationalist—Boulangiste, anti-Dreyfusard, and militant of the Ligue de la patrie française. His reputation as a novelist rests largely upon his attempt to chronicle his times in three didactic trilogies. *Le Culte du moi* (*Sous l'oeil des Barbares*, 1888; *Un Homme libre*, 1889; *Le Jardin de Bérénice*, 1891) locates a source of moral energy in a sense of self that is at once disciplined and liberated. The spiritual benefits of a living relationship with one's regional patrimony of family, native environment, and inherited tradition become the focus of attention in *Le Roman de l'énergie nationale* (*Les Déracinés*, 1897; *L'Appel au soldat*, 1900; *Leurs figures*, 1902), which follows the fortunes of seven young men who leave Lorraine, Barrès' own province, to pursue their careers in Paris. *Les Bastions de l'Est* (*Au service de l'Allemagne*, 1905; *Colette Baudoche*, 1909; *Le Génie du Rhin*, 1921) explores the meeting of the French and German national characters in the eastern provinces of Alsace and Lorraine. *La Colline inspirée* (1913) presents the conflict between the Roman Catholic Church and a religious community rooted in regional consciousness.

BARRETT, Elizabeth, see BROWNING, E. B.

BARRIE, Sir J(ames) M(atthew) (1860–1937), born in Kirriemuir in Scotland, the son of a handloom weaver, educated at Dumfries and Edinburgh University. He began work with the *Nottinghamshire Journal*, an experience described in *When a Man's Single* (1888). In the same year he began his series of *'Kailyard School' stories and novels (for which he drew considerably on his mother's memories) based on the life of 'Thrums', his home town of Kirriemuir. These included *Auld Licht Idylls* (1888), *A Window in Thrums* (1889), and his highly successful *The Little Minister* (1891), a work which Barrie came to dislike. His first play, *Richard Savage*, was performed in London in the same year. In 1894 he married the actress Mary Ansell, divorce following in 1909. In 1896 he published his frankly adoring portrait of his mother, *Margaret Ogilvy*, and the first of his two most revealing books, *Sentimental Tommy*, followed in 1900 by *Tommy and Grizel*, which contains hints of *Peter Pan*. Meanwhile came his sentimental comedy *Quality Street*, performed in 1901, and in 1902 the enduring successful play *The Admirable Crichton* (see CRICHTON). *Peter Pan*, his internationally and abidingly famous children's play, grew from stories he had made up for the five sons of his friends Arthur and Sylvia Llewelyn Davies, to whom he gave a home on their parents' death. It was first performed in 1904 and was followed by a story, *Peter Pan in Kensington Gardens*, in 1906 and by the play in book form in 1911. Meanwhile a highly successful play with a political background, *What Every Woman Knows*, was performed in 1906. *Dear Brutus* (1917) and *Mary Rose* (1920) were the last of his successful dramas, *The Boy David* (1936) failing to capture attention. Several one-act plays, including *The Old Lady Shows her Medals* (1917) and *Shall We Join the Ladies?* (1921) were well received.

He was made a baronet, awarded the OM, and received several honorary degrees. His fame and success were considerable for the first half of this century, but his unfashionable whimsicality has come to obscure the best of his work. There is a Life by J. Dunbar (1970).

BARRINGTON, Daines (1727–1800), lawyer, antiquary, and naturalist and friend of G. *White, whose *Natural History of Selborne* takes the form of letters to Barrington and *Pennant.

BARROW, Isaac (1630–77), educated at Charterhouse, Felsted, and Trinity College, Cambridge, was successively professor of Greek at Cambridge, of geometry at Gresham College, and of mathematics at Cambridge, resigning the latter appointment in favour of his pupil I. *Newton. He became master of Trinity in 1672. His works include an *Exposition of the Creed, Decalogue and Sacraments* (1669) and a treatise on *The Pope's Supremacy* (published 1680). He was an able and thoughtful controversialist and his sermons, famed for their length, are lucid, humane, and carefully argued. His theological works were edited in 4 vols by *Tillotson (1683–9) and in 9 vols by A. Napier (1859).

BARROW, Sir John (1764–1848), travelled in China and South Africa, and as assistant secretary to the Admiralty revived the project to explore the Arctic for a North-West Passage. He wrote a number of works of history and travel, particularly relating to China and the Arctic, and contributed nearly 200 articles to the *Quarterly Review. He published *The Mutiny and Piratical Seizure of H.M.S. *Bounty in 1831; in 1846 *A History of Voyages into the Arctic Region*; and in 1847 an *Autobiographical Memoir*, containing an account of his many travels.

BARRY, Elizabeth (1658–1713), a celebrated actress who owed her entrance to the stage to the patronage of the earl of *Rochester. She created more than 100 roles, including Monimia in Otway's *The Orphan*, Belvidera in *Venice Preserv'd*, and Zara in *The Mourning

Bride. *Otway was passionately devoted to her, but she did not return his affection.

Barry Lyndon see LUCK OF BARRY LYNDON, THE.

Barsetshire Novels, The, of A. *Trollope are the following: *The Warden*, *Barchester Towers*, *Doctor Thorne*, *Framley Parsonage*, *The Small House at Allington*, and *The Last Chronicle of Barset*.

BARSTOW, Stan(ley) (1928–), novelist, born in Yorkshire, the son of a miner and educated at Ossett Grammar School. His first novel, *A Kind of Loving* (1960), is the first-person, present-tense narration of office-worker Vic Brown, trapped into marriage by his infatuation for small-minded Ingrid and harassed by his mother-in-law; it was followed by other vivid portrayals of Yorkshire life, including *Ask me Tomorrow* (1962) and *Joby* (1964), which contributed to the development of the regional novel associated with *Sillitoe, *Waterhouse (who adapted *A Kind of Loving* for the screen), *Braine, and others.

BARTH, John Simmons (1930–), American novelist, whose complex, experimental, elaborate novels include *The Sot-Weed Factor* (1960), *Giles Goat-Boy* (1966), and *Letters* (1979); all bear a highly ironic relationship to conventional realistic narrative, and their inventiveness and wit have been more admired in American academic circles than in Britain.

BARTHES, Roland, see STRUCTURALISM.

BARTHOLOMAEUS ANGLICUS (*fl.* 1230–50), also known as Bartholomew de Glanville, though the addition 'de Glanville' is most uncertain; a Minorite friar, professor of theology at Paris, and author of *De Proprietatibus rerum*, an encyclopaedia of the Middle Ages first printed *c.*1470. A 14th-cent. English version by John of *Trevisa was issued by *Wynkyn de Worde, *c.*1495.

Bartholomew, Massacre of St, the massacre of Huguenots throughout France ordered by Charles IX at the instigation of his mother Catherine de Médicis, and begun on the morning of the festival, 24 Aug. 1572.

Bartholomew Fair, a comedy by *Jonson, performed by the Lady Elizabeth's Men 1614, printed 1631.

The play is set at the fair which took place at Smithfield on 24 August, St Bartholomew's Day, and follows the fortunes of various visitors to it: Littlewit, a proctor, his wife Win-the-fight, his mother-in-law Dame Purecraft, and her mentor the ranting Puritan Zeal-of-the-land Busy, who come to eat roast pig; the rich simpleton Bartholomew Cokes, Wasp, his angry servant, and Grace Wellborn, who is unwillingly betrothed to Cokes; Justice Adam Overdo, who attends the fair in disguise in order to discover its 'enormities'; and two gallants, Quarlous and Winwife, who intend to jeer at the fair-people. Many mishaps and misunderstandings ensue, which result in Busy, Wasp, and Overdo being placed in the stocks, Cokes being robbed of all his possessions, including his future wife, who is won by Winwife, and Quarlous marrying Dame Purecraft. The play ends with the performance of a puppet-play written by Littlewit, in imitation of Marlowe's *Hero and Leander. Zeal-of-the-land Busy is defeated in a debate with one of the puppets about the morality of play-acting, and Overdo, reminded that he is 'but Adam, flesh and blood', agrees to renounce his censoriousness and invites everyone home to supper.

'Bartleby the Scrivener' (1856), a short story by H. *Melville. When the narrator, a New York lawyer, asks his scrivener (copier of legal documents) to help him, Bartleby replies, 'I would prefer not to', and with Bartleby's reiterated declaration what began as a humorous anecdote turns into a fable of existential refusal unto death.

BARTRAM, William (1739–1823), American Quaker naturalist and traveller, author of *Travels through North and South Carolina, Georgia, East and West Florida, the Cherokee Country, the Extensive Territories of the Moscogulges, or the Creek Confederacy, and the Country of the Chactaws* (1791), a travel book much admired by *Coleridge and *Wordsworth, both of whom drew on its descriptions of the natural wonders of the new world: for an account of echoes in the *Ancient Mariner, *'Kubla Khan', 'Ruth', and other poems, see J. L. *Lowes, *The Road to Xanadu* (1927).

Bas Bleu, see MORE, H.

BASHKIRTSEFF, Marie (Mariya Konstantinovna Bashkirtseva) (1859–84), Russian artist and diarist whose *Journal de Marie Bashkirtseff*, written in French and posthumously published in 1887, attained a great vogue by its morbid introspection and literary quality, and was translated into several languages (English trans. 1890, by Mathilde Blind).

Basic English, see RICHARDS, I. A.

Basilea, in imprints, Basle.

Basilikon Doron, see JAMES I AND VI.

Basilius, (1) the foolish old duke in Sidney's *Arcadia*; (2) in *Don Quixote*, the rival of Camacho.

BASKERVILLE, John (1706–75), English printer, first a writing-master in Birmingham. By 1754 he had established a printing office and type-foundry in Birmingham. His books are notable for the quality of presswork, type, and paper. His first book was a Latin *Virgil, 1757, followed by a *Milton in 1758. He was the first to use 'wove' (extra smooth) paper, and gave his pages a gloss by hot-pressing them after printing. In order to print the Book of *Common Prayer (3 edns, 1760–2) and the Bible (1763), Baskerville bought a nomination as supernumerary Printer to the University of Cambridge. His books are among the masterpieces of English printing; but they did not sell, and after his death his types were sold to *Beaumarchais for his great edition of *Voltaire (1784–9): they are still in existence, and some are in the possession of the *Cambridge University Press. See *The Survival of Baskerville's Punches* (1949) by J. G. Dreyfus. Baskerville gave his name to the roman typefaces based on his designs in current usage.

BASKETT, John (d. 1742), king's printer, was printer to the University of Oxford, 1711–42. He printed editions of the Book of *Common Prayer, and the *'Vinegar Bible' in two volumes (1716–17), of which it was said that it was 'a basketful of errors'.

BASSANI, Giorgio (1916–), Italian novelist and short story writer. His main theme is the onset of anti-Semitism in a provincial town. His best-known works are *Storie ferraresi* (1956; five of which are translated as *A Prospect of Ferrara*, 1962), and *Il giardino dei Finzi Contini* (*The Garden of the Finzi-Contini*, 1962).

Bassanio, in Shakespeare's *The Merchant of Venice*, an impoverished young man who is the lover of Portia.

Bassett, Count, a character in Vanbrugh and Cibber's *The Provok'd Husband*.

'Bastard, The', see SAVAGE, R.

Bastard, Philip the, the son of Sir Robert Falconbridge in Shakespeare's *King John. He is a lively commentator on events, and speaks the play's last lines:

Come the three corners of the world in arms,
And we shall shock them. Nought shall make us rue,
If England to itself do rest but true.

Bates, Charley, in Dickens's *Oliver Twist*, one of the pickpockets in Fagin's gang.

BATES, Henry Walter (1825–92), naturalist, who visited Pará with A. R. *Wallace in 1848 and the Amazons in 1851–9. His researches revealed over 8,000 species new to science. He published *The Naturalist on the Amazons* in 1863.

BATES, H(erbert) E(rnest) (1905–74), novelist and short story writer, born in Northamptonshire. With the encouragement of E. *Garnett (of whom he wrote a study, 1950) he published his first novel, *The Two Sisters* (1926), which launched him on a prolific career. His works include volumes of stories, *The Woman Who Had Imagination* (1934), *The Flying Goat* (1939), and *The Beauty of the Dead* (1940), and novels, *The Fallow Land* (1932), *Love for Lydia* (1952), and *The Darling Buds of May* (1958). Many of them were successfully televised. He also published three volumes of autobiography, *The Vanished World* (1969), *The Blossoming World* (1971), and *The World in Ripeness* (1972).

Bates, Miss and Mrs, characters in Jane Austen's *Emma*.

BATESON, F(rederick Noel) W(ilse) (1901–78), critic, scholar, and editor, educated at Charterhouse and Trinity College, Oxford. He edited the *Cambridge Bibliography of English Literature* (1940) and founded *Essays in Criticism*, which he edited from 1951 to 1974. His critical works include *Wordsworth: a reinterpretation* (1954) and *Essays in Critical Dissent* (1972).

Bath, in Somerset, is the site of a Roman spa, Aquae Sulis, probably built in the 1st and 2nd cents AD. The legendary prince Bladud was said to have discovered the hot springs. Much of the extensive Roman baths have been excavated, and fragments of a temple, as well as tombs, altars, etc., have been found. The King's Bath was built in 1597 and during the 17th cent. it was used for medicinal purposes.

In the 18th cent. Bath was transformed into a social resort by Richard ('Beau') *Nash, who became master of ceremonies, Ralph *Allen, who promoted the development of the city, and John Wood, father and son, who designed the Palladian public buildings and houses. It is the subject of very frequent literary allusion, having been visited among many others by Smollett, Fielding, Sheridan, F. Burney, Goldsmith, Southey, Landor, J. Austen, Wordsworth, Cowper, Scott, T. Moore, and Dickens. Its ruins seem to be the subject of the OE poem *Ruin*. It was once a cloth-making centre, and is mentioned in this connection by Chaucer (*Canterbury Tales*, Prologue 447, concerning the 'Wife of Bath').

Bath, Wife of, see CANTERBURY TALES, 6.

Bath Guide, *The New*, see ANSTEY, C.

Bathos (Greek, 'depth'). The current usage for 'descent from the sublime to the ridiculous' originates from *Pope's satire *Peri Bathous, or the art of sinking in poetry* (1727). The title was a travesty of *Longinus' essay *On the Sublime*.

Bathsheba Everdene, a character in Hardy's *Far from the Madding Crowd*.

Batrachomyomachia, or the *Battle of the Frogs and Mice*, a burlesque Greek epic which used at one time to be attributed to *Homer. It describes in Homeric style a battle between mice and frogs in which Zeus and Athena join. The taste for the mock-heroic which existed in the early years of the 18th cent. (if it was not of spontaneous growth) owed more to French and Italian models than to this third-rate classical poem. T. *Parnell's version of the *Batrachomyomachia* attacking *Dennis and *Theobald appeared in 1717, which was relatively late in the history of the genre.

Battle, Sarah, the subject of one of Lamb's *Essays of Elia*, 'Mrs Battle's Opinions on Whist'; a character drawn from Mrs Burney, wife of Admiral Burney and sister-in-law of F. *Burney.

Battle Abbey Roll, The, was probably compiled about the 14th cent. purporting to show the names of families that came over to England with William the Conqueror. The roll itself is not extant: the 16th-cent. versions by *Leland, *Holinshed, and Duchesne are all said to be imperfect and to contain names which have obviously no right there.

'Battle Hymn of the Republic, The', a patriotic hymn of the Federal party in the United States of America, written by Julia Ward Howe (1819–1910). She visited the army of the Potomac in 1861, and was invited to provide dignified words for the popular marching tune, 'John Brown's body lies a-mouldering in the grave' (see BROWN, JOHN). Her stanzas beginning 'Mine eyes have seen the glory of the coming of the Lord' were the result. The poem was first published in the *Atlantic Monthly* in 1862.

Battle of Alcazar, The, a play in verse by *Peele, published 1594.

It deals with the war between Sebastian, king of Portugal, and Abdelmelec, king of Morocco, who had recovered his kingdom from a usurper, Muly Mahamet. The latter invokes the assistance of Sebastian, offering to give up the kingdom of Morocco to him and to become his tributary. Sebastian sails with his fleet to Morocco and at the battle of Alcazar is killed, as are also Abdelmelec and Muly Mahamet, the latter being drowned while fleeing from the field. Sebastian is assisted in his expedition by the adventurer *Stukeley, who is likewise killed at the battle (which was fought in 1578). There survives an interesting contemporary 'plot', or playhouse summary, of this play which has been edited by W. W. *Greg. Though A. H. Bullen called the play 'tiresome windy stuff', it contains some remarkable passages, such as the description of the 'princely ospraie'.

'Battle of Hohenlinden, The', a poem by T. *Campbell, describing a battle in Bavaria in

1800, in which the French defeated the Austrians.

Battle of Maldon, see MALDON, BATTLE OF.

Battle of Otterbourne, see OTTERBOURNE, THE BATTLE OF.

Battle of the Books, The (*A Full and True Account of the Battel Fought last Friday, Between the Antient and the Modern Books in St James's Library*), a prose satire by *Swift, written 1697, when Swift was residing with Sir W. *Temple, published 1704.

Temple had written an essay on the comparative merits of 'Ancient and Modern Learning' (the subject at that time of an animated controversy in Paris), in which by his uncritical praise of the spurious *Epistles of *Phalaris* he had drawn on himself the censure of William Wotton and *Bentley. Swift, in his *Battle of the Books*, treats the whole question with satirical humour. The 'Battle' originates from a request by the moderns that the ancients shall evacuate the higher of the two peaks of Parnassus which they have hitherto occupied. The books that are advocates of the moderns take up the matter; but before the actual encounter a dispute arises between a spider living in the corner of the library and a bee that has got entangled in the spider's web. Aesop sums up the dispute: the spider is like the moderns who spin their scholastic lore out of their own entrails; the bee is like the ancients who go to nature for their honey. (The phrase 'Sweetness and Light' which Aesop uses to describe the contribution of the Ancients, in contrast with the 'Dirt and Poison' of the Moderns, was adopted by Arnold in *Culture and Anarchy*.) Aesop's commentary rouses the books to fury, and they join battle. The ancients, under the patronage of Pallas, are led by Homer, Pindar, Euclid, Aristotle, and Plato, with Sir W. Temple commanding the allies; the moderns by Milton, Dryden, Descartes, Hobbes, Scotus, and others, with the support of Momus and the malignant deity Criticism. The fight is conducted with great spirit. Aristotle aims an arrow at Bacon but hits Descartes. Homer overthrows Gondibert. Virgil encounters his translator Dryden, in a helmet nine times too big. Boyle transfixes Bentley and Wotton. On the whole the ancients have the advantage, but a parley ensues and the tale leaves the issue undecided.

Battle of the Frogs and Mice, see BATRACHO-MYOMACHIA.

Baucis and Philemon, a poem by *Swift, published 1709; Baucis and Philemon were the aged couple who entertained the gods unawares, and whose cottage was transformed by Zeus into a temple. In Swift's version, the couple entertain two hermits; their cottage becomes a church and Philemon the parson, an elevation described with some irony.

BAUDELAIRE,Charles (1821–67), French poet. His *Les Fleurs du mal* (1857), a series of 101 exquisitely crafted lyrics in a variety of metres, including many sonnets, is one of the great collections of French verse. It represents a determined attempt to create order and beauty, notably by the discovery of hidden relations or 'correspondences', in a world which is largely perceived as ugly and oppressive. In musical language and evocative images, the poet explores his own sense of isolation, exile, and sin, his boredom and melancholy, the transporting power of love, the attractions of evil and vice, the fascination and the degradation of Paris life. On publication of *Les Fleurs du mal* Baudelaire was fined and six of the poems were banned from subsequent editions as offensive to public morals; these were accordingly omitted from the second (1861) and the third, posthumous, edition (1868), by which time some 50 new poems had been added. Baudelaire's prose works include *Petits poèmes en prose (Le spleen de Paris)* (1869) and translations of *Poe's tales: *Histoires extraordinaires* (1856) and *Nouvelles histoires extraordinaires* (1857). He gave a detailed account of the effects of opium and hashish in *Les Paradis artificiels* (1860), which contains a commentary on the translated extracts from De Quincey's *Confessions of an English Opium Eater*. His reputation as a critic, which has increased steadily since his death, is now firmly established. Most of his critical writing, including essays on the Paris salons of 1845, 1846, and 1859, on *Delacroix, on such contemporary writers as *Gautier and *Flaubert, and on *Wagner, were collected in the posthumous volumes *Curiosités Esthétiques* and *L'Art romantique* (1868). His *Journaux intimes* were published in 1887.

Baviad, The, see GIFFORD, W.

BAX, Sir Arnold (1883–1953), English composer and writer. Though he was in fact of purely English ancestry, an early encounter with the poetry of *Yeats brought out a strong Celtic strain in Bax which remained a central characteristic of his creative personality. He spent much time in Ireland, and under the pseudonym 'Dermot O'Byrne' published novels, stories, and three volumes of poetry (a selection from the latter was reissued in 1979): in his early days in Dublin he was regarded as a novelist and poet as much as a composer.

Though his greatest achievement in the latter capacity was in symphonic and instrumental music, he was prolific in all forms, and from the early *Celtic Song Cycle* (1904, words by 'Fiona Macleod'—W. *Sharp) onwards he made many settings, both for solo voice and vocal ensembles, of texts from all periods of British literature, from anonymous medieval poetry to *Hardy,

*Housman, and *Colum. The autobiographical sketch *Farewell my Youth* (1943), published under his own name, is one of the best books of its kind by a musician.

BAXTER, Richard (1615–91), a Puritan divine who sided with Parliament and was a military chaplain during the Civil War. He was author of *The Saint's Everlasting Rest* (1650; the book that Mrs Glegg in *The Mill on the Floss* used to favour in a domestic crisis) and of *Call to the Unconverted* (1657), both of which played an important part in the Evangelical tradition in England and America. He contributed powerfully to the Restoration and had a bishopric offered to him, but soon after refusing it suffered much ill-treatment under Charles II and James II, being imprisoned in 1685–6 and fined by Judge *Jeffreys on the charge of libelling the Church in his *Paraphrase of the New Testament* (1685). His numerous writings include a lengthy autobiography, *Reliquiae Baxterianae* (1696) and several well-known hymns (e.g. 'Ye holy angels bright').

Bayard, or Baiardo, the magic horse given by Charlemagne to Renaud, son of Aymon, or *Rinaldo, which figures in *The Four Sons of *Aymon*, *Orlando Innamorato*, and *Orlando Furioso*. Bayard was formerly used as a mock-heroic allusive name for any horse, and also as a type of blind recklessness [OED].

Bayes, the name under which *Dryden is ridiculed in Buckingham's *The Rehearsal*.

BAYLE, Pierre (1647–1706), French Protestant scholar and philosopher, lived in Rotterdam from 1681, where his major work, the *Dictionnaire historique et critique*, was published (2 vols, 1695, 1697; 2nd, revised and enlarged, edn 1702). Most of the entries in the *Dictionnaire* were biographical articles on important personages of biblical, classical, and modern history, in the course of which, especially in the discursive footnotes, many theological and philosophical questions, some of them contentious, were subjected to rigorous critical analysis. Bayle's method rested on the systematic comparison of sources and scientific consideration of evidence. He deployed the erudition that made his work a source-book of historical and religious criticism in a humane and enquiring spirit, impatient of credulity, superstition, and intolerance. There were English translations of the *Dictionnaire* in 1710, 1734–8 (rev.), and 1734–41 (much enlarged, as *A General Dictionary, Historical and Critical*).

BAYLY, Nathaniel Thomas Haynes (1797–1839), was the author of many well-known and much ridiculed verses, including 'I'd be a butterfly' and 'She wore a wreath of roses'. He also wrote at great speed many pieces for the stage, including *Perfection* (1836), a successful farce.

Baynes, General, Mrs, and Charlotte, characters in Thackeray's *The Adventures of Philip*.

Bayona, see NAMANCOS.

Bazzard, Mr, in Dickens's *Edwin Drood*, Mr Grewgious's clerk.

BBC, The British Broadcasting Corporation, the national broadcasting authority, constituted in 1927. It succeeded the British Broadcasting Company, which had been formed in 1922.

BEACONSFIELD, earl of, see DISRAELI.

Beagle, **HMS,** see DARWIN, C.

Bean Lean, Donald, in Scott's *Waverley*, a Highland marauder.

BEARDSLEY, Aubrey Vincent (1872–98), illustrator and writer, notorious in the 1890s as the outstanding artist of *fin-de-siècle* decadence. His disturbingly erotic drawings develop rapidly from the murky sensuality of *Pre-Raphaelite medievalism to rococo wit and grace. Beardsley's most important illustrations are for *Wilde's *Salome* (1894), *Pope's *The Rape of the Lock* (1896), the *Lysistrata* of *Aristophanes (1896), and *Jonson's *Volpone* (1898). He was art editor of the *Yellow Book* in 1894; the Wilde scandal led to his dismissal in 1895; he then became art editor to the *Savoy*. Beardsley's most significant achievement as a writer is *The Story of Venus and Tannhauser*, a charmingly rococo and highly cultivated erotic romance. An expurgated version entitled *Under the Hill* was published in the *Savoy*; an unexpurgated edition was privately printed in 1907; it contains a cruel caricature of Wilde as 'Priapusa, the fat manicure and fardeuse'. In 1897 Beardsley, encouraged by J. *Gray and his friend Raffalovich, converted to Catholicism; he died of consumption. In 1916 his sister Mabel died of cancer; W. B. *Yeats, who had known them both, dedicated his sonnets *Upon a Dying Lady* to her.

Beast, Number of the, in Revelation 13: 18. The precise figures composing the number are uncertain, 666 or 616, but the former are generally adopted. It has been suggested that since each digit in 666 falls short by one of the perfect number seven, the number thereby symbolizes Antichrist. But it is more probably a cryptogram, of which no interpretation commanding general assent has yet been offered. One of the most likely rests on the fact that the letters of the name 'Nero Caesar' written in Hebrew represent numbers which added together make 666, or 616 if the name Nero is written as in Latin without a final *n*. Least probable are attempts to make the cipher represent some conspicuous character of modern history (Swete, *Apocrypha*).

Beat Generation, a phrase used to describe a group of American writers who emerged in the 1950s, and generally agreed to have been coined in this sense (with connotations of beatitude, disengagement, down-and-out 'street' language and experience, spontaneity, etc.) by *Kerouac. Influential texts include *Ginsberg's long poems, especially the apocalyptic elegies for the American Dream (*Howl*, 1955), and for his immigrant mother (*Kaddish*, 1960); the Shelleyan-futurist *Gasoline* (1958) and *Bomb* (1959) of Gregory Corso (1930–); the ecological *haiku and work-songs in *Riprap* (1959) and essays in *Earth House Hold* (1969) by Gary Snyder (1930–); the more humorously surreal *Pictures of the Gone World* (1955) and *A Coney Island of the Mind* (1958) of Lawrence Ferlinghetti (1919–); the laconic documentary collage novels of W. *Burroughs (*Junkie*, 1953; and *The Naked Lunch*, 1959), and his first 'cut-up' collation, *Minutes to Go* (1960, assembled in Paris with Corso, Brion Gysin, and Sinclair Beiles); and the analytic eye-witness accounts of Beat beginnings by novelist John Clellon Holmes (1926–), *Go* (1952), *The Horn* (1958), and *Nothing More to Declare* (1968). The beat emphasis was on escape from conventional, puritanical, middle-class (termed 'square') mores, towards visionary enlightenment and artistic improvisation, approached via (Zen) Buddhism and other echoes of religious confessional, such as Red Indian and Mexican Peyote cults; also through drive and accelerations charged by wheels, drugs, sex, drink, or talk. The experimental forms, metaphysical content, and provocative anti-intellectual, anti-hierarchical spirit of the movement spread across America and then beyond the English-speaking world, to be taken up by second and third generation writers (Yevtushenko, Voznesensky, Bob Dylan, the *Beatles, Wolf Biermann), evolving a 'counter-culture' which had a widespread and in many ways lasting impact. Foreshadowings of the Beat Generation have been claimed in writers as diverse as *Blake, *Whitman, *Rimbaud, *Melville, T. *Wolfe, Henry *Miller, and the *'Black Mountain' poets. For its reverberations in Britain see further under UNDERGROUND POETRY and JAZZ POETRY.

Beatles, The, a group of young working-class musicians from Liverpool (George Harrison, John Lennon, Paul McCartney, and 'Ringo' Starr), whose songs and life-style, from 1962 until their break-up in 1970, attracted a vast following, and not only from teenagers; many of their lyrics (e.g. 'Penny Lane', 'Eleanor Rigby', 'She's Leaving Home') have been highly praised, and they had a considerable influence on the success of the *Liverpool poets and the *Under-

ground poetry movement. *Larkin described their work as 'an enchanting and intoxicating hybrid of Negro rock-and-roll with their own adolescent romanticism', and 'the first advance in popular music since the War' (9 Oct. 1983).

Beatrice, (1) see DANTE; (2) heroine of Shakespeare's *Much Ado about Nothing*, who explains her sprightly temperament in the words 'there was a star danc'd, and under that was I born' (II. i. 303).

BEATTIE, James (1735–1803), professor of moral philosophy at Marischal College, Aberdeen. His *Essay on the Nature and Immutability of Truth* (1770) was an attempt to refute *Hume and *Berkeley. As a poet he is remembered for *The Minstrel*, a poem in Spenserian stanzas tracing 'the progress of a poetical Genius, born in a rude age, from the first dawning of fancy and reason'; Edwin, the son of a shepherd, a solitary and sensitive boy, finds his education in nature, in a manner that foreshadows Wordsworth's *Prelude*. Bk I appeared in 1771, Bk II in 1774, and they were many times reprinted, though the work remained unfinished.

Beau Brummell, see BRUMMELL.

Beauchamp's Career, a novel by G. *Meredith, published 1876.

In this novel of politics, much concerned with the contemporary state of Britain, Nevil Beauchamp begins his career as an idealistic young naval officer. In spite of his mildly subversive views on political and social questions, he earns the approval of his wealthy aristocratic uncle, Everard Romfrey, a traditionalist who detests radicals and their like. After the Crimean War, Nevil plunges into politics, stands unsuccessfully as a Radical candidate for Parliament, and becomes the friend of Dr Shrapnel, humanitarian, republican, and free-thinker, detestable to Mr Romfrey and his friends. In his rage at various rumours and misrepresentations, Romfrey horsewhips Shrapnel, incurring the fury of his nephew, who demands that his uncle apologize to his friend. This hopeless enterprise becomes an obsession with Nevil, who is also distracted by his own inconclusive love affairs, torn between his early passion for Renée de Crosnel, a spirited and intelligent young woman (now the unhappy wife of an elderly Frenchman), and his love for a soft and decorous English girl, Cecilia Halkett. Gallantry and indecision lose him Renée, who has fled from her husband; and he also loses Cecilia, who is married by her father to Nevil's dull second cousin. Harassed and unhappy, Nevil falls desperately ill, near to death. His danger moves his proud uncle to present himself at Shrapnel's cottage, where Nevil lies, and to offer his apology at last. Nevil recovers and marries Shrapnel's ward, Jenny Denham, a genial and sympathetic girl. But after a few months of happiness he is drowned trying to rescue an unknown child from the sea. Renée was Meredith's favourite among all his women characters.

Beau Geste, see WREN, P. C.

Beaumains ('Fair hands'), the nickname given contemptuously by Sir Kay, the Steward, to Gareth, the brother of Gawain, when as a probationer knight he is sent to work in the kitchens. See GARETH AND LYNETTE.

Beaumanoir, Sir Lucas, in Scott's *Ivanhoe*, Grand Master of the Knights Templars.

BEAUMARCHAIS, Pierre-Augustin Caron de (1732–99), French dramatist. He is remembered for two comedies of intrigue, *Le Barbier de Séville* (1775; English trans., *The Barber of Seville*, 1776), and *Le Mariage de Figaro* (1784; *The Marriage of Figaro*, 1785). The scheming and resourceful valet Figaro, hero of both plays, is presented with evident class-conscious sympathy, while the later play is quite openly anti-aristocratic in its implications. The plays respectively inspired operas by *Rossini (1816) and *Mozart (1786).

BEAUMONT, Sir Francis (1584–1616), was born at Grace-Dieu in Leicestershire, of an ancient family, and the third son of a justice of common pleas. He was educated at Broadgates Hall, Oxford, but took no degree, and was entered at the Inner Temple in 1600. The anonymous Ovidian poem *Salmacis and Hermaphroditus* (1602) has been attributed to him. He collaborated with *Fletcher in dramatic works from about 1606 to 1613 (for a list of their plays, see under FLETCHER, J.). His earliest known play, *The Woman Hater*, a Jonsonian comedy of humours, was probably performed 1605, published 1607: recent linguistic analysis assigns some scenes in it to Fletcher, whereas *The Knight of the Burning Pestle* (?1607) is now generally considered to be Beaumont's alone. Beaumont retired *c*.1613, when he married profitably and moved to Kent. He was buried in Westminster Abbey.

Dryden, in *Of Dramatick Poesy* (1668), pays tribute to the success of the Beaumont and Fletcher plays on the Restoration stage, and comments that both writers had 'great natural gifts improved by study; Beaumont especially being so accurate a judge of plays that Ben Jonson, while he lived, submitted all his writing to his censure, and, 'tis thought, used his judgement in correcting, if not contriving, all his plots.' Beaumont and *Jonson wrote one another commendatory verses, but Jonson's comment to *Drummond of Hawthornden (that Beaumont 'loved too much himself and his own verses') was less flattering. In the 17th cent. opinion tended to ascribe the tragic scenes in the collaborative effort to Beaumont, the comic

to Fletcher, but modern critics reject this neat division, and are themselves divided about attribution. (See under FLETCHER for further details.)

BEAUMONT, Sir George Howland (1753–1827), patron of art and friend and benefactor of *Wordsworth, who frequently visited him at Coleorton Hall; in his dedication to Sir George of his 1815 volume, Wordsworth wrote, 'some of the best pieces were composed under the shade of your own groves, upon the classic ground of Coleorton.' Sir W. *Scott described Beaumont as 'the man in the world most void of affectation', and said he 'understood Wordsworth's poetry, which is a rare thing' (*Journal*, 14 Feb. 1827). Beaumont also encouraged and supported *Coleridge and helped to procure his pension.

Beau Nash, see NASH, R.

Beauty and the Beast, a fairy-tale of which the best-known version was adapted by Mme de Beaumont from one of the *Contes marins* (4 vols, 1740–1) of Mme de Villeneuve. A somewhat similar story is included in the *Piacevoli Notti* of *Straparola.

Beauty ('la Belle') is the youngest and favourite daughter of a merchant, who suffers reverses. He sets out on a journey in the hope of restoring his shaken fortunes. Unlike her sisters, Beauty asks him to bring her back only a rose. The journey proves a failure, but on his return, in the beautiful garden of an apparently uninhabited palace, he plucks a rose for Beauty. The Beast, an ugly monster to whom the palace belongs, threatens him with death as the penalty for his theft unless he gives him his youngest daughter. Beauty sacrifices herself and goes to the Beast's palace and lives there. She is gradually filled with pity and affection for the Beast and finally consents to marry him, whereupon he turns into a beautiful prince, having been released from a magic spell by her virtue and courage.

BEAUVOIR, Simone de (1908–), French novelist and essayist. Her novels reflect the major preoccupations of the *Existentialist movement: *L'Invitée* (1943; English trans., *She Came to Stay*, 1949), *Le Sang des autres* (1944; *The Blood of Others*, 1948), *Les Mandarins* (1954; *The Mandarins*, 1956). Her feminist essay *Le Deuxième sexe* appeared in 1949 (*The Second Sex*, 1953), and she has published four volumes of autobiography, including *Mémoires d'une jeune fille rangée* (1958; *Memoirs of a Dutiful Daughter*, 1959) and *La Force de l'âge* (1960; *The Prime of Life*, 1962). See also FEMINIST CRITICISM and SARTRE.

Beaux' Stratagem, The, a comedy by *Farquhar, produced 1707.

Aimwell and Archer, two friends who have spent their inheritance, arrive at the inn at Litchfield, in search of the adventure that will rehabilitate their fortunes. To save money Archer pretends to be Aimwell's servant. There is much speculation as to who they are, and Boniface the landlord concludes that they are highwaymen. This curiosity is shared by Dorinda, daughter of the wealthy Lady Bountiful, who has fallen in love with Aimwell at first sight—in church—and Mrs Sullen, wife of Lady Bountiful's son, a drunken sot. Aimwell, thinking Dorinda a suitable prey, gets admission to Lady Bountiful's house on a pretext, with Archer, between whom and Mrs Sullen a mutual attraction has sprung up. An attack by rogues on the house is the occasion of the rescue of the ladies by Aimwell and Archer, and they both press the advantage thus gained. But Aimwell, who has passed himself off as his elder brother Lord Aimwell, smitten with remorse in presence of the trustfulness of Dorinda, confesses the fraud. At this moment Mrs Sullen's brother opportunely arrives, to rescue his sister from the brutality of Sullen. He brings news of the death of Aimwell's elder brother and of the accession of Aimwell to title and fortune. Sullen at the same time willingly agrees to the dissolution of his marriage, so that Mrs Sullen is free to marry Archer, and all ends happily.

BEAVERBROOK, William Maxwell ('Max') Aitken, first baron (1879–1964), newspaper proprietor, born in Canada, the son of a Presbyterian minister; he made a fortune as a financier, then came to England in 1910, and embarked on a career in politics. In 1916 (the year in which he became Lord Beaverbrook) he bought the *Daily Express*, launched the *Sunday Express* in 1918, and in 1923 gained control of the *Evening Standard*, of which his friend Arnold *Bennett became the influential reviewer; his drive for high circulation was immensely successful, and he became the most powerful figure in popular journalism, setting the stamp of his own flamboyant personality and prejudices on the papers he owned. He enjoyed controversy, from the 'Empire Crusade' of his early years to the anti-Common Market stand of his old age. His own works include *Canada in Flanders* (2 vols, 1915–17), *Politicians and the Press* (1925), *Politicians and the War* (2 vols, 1928, 1932, which provided much of the background for Bennett's novel *Lord Raingo*, 1926), and *The Decline and Fall of Lloyd George* (1963). According to A. J. P. *Taylor (*Beaverbrook*, 1972), E. *Waugh denied that Beaverbrook was the original of Lord *Copper in *Scoop* (1938), but he appears as Lord Ottercove in the novels of *Gerhardie, and suggested some of the characteristics of Sir Bussy Woodcock in *Wells's *The Autocracy of Mr Parham* (1930). (Wells to Beaverbrook: 'I wanted a man who had made money fast and had an original mind. You seem to be the only one who answers to that description in London.')

BECCARIA, Cesare (1738–94), Italian aristocrat and jurist, whose essay *Dei delitti e delle pene* (*Of Crimes and Punishments*, 1764), a masterpiece of the Italian Enlightment, inspired European schemes to improve prison systems, followed in England by *Bentham.

Beck, Madame, a character in *Villette* by C. Brontë.

Becket, a tragedy by *Tennyson, published 1884, based on the quarrel between Henry II and Thomas *Becket, interwoven with the story of Henry's love for Fair Rosamund.

BECKET, St Thomas (?1118–70), son of Gilbert Becket, of a Norman family of knights, was educated in London and Paris and subsequently studied canon law at Bologna and Auxerre. Henry II appointed him chancellor and made him his intimate friend and companion. In 1162 Thomas reluctantly became archbishop of Canterbury, an office which required him to become the champion of the rights of the Church which Henry was attempting to curtail. In particular he opposed the Constitutions of Clarendon (1164) which re-imposed the relations between Church and State that had prevailed in the time of William I. One measure in particular, that no clerical appeal to Rome could be made without the authority of the king, was contentious. Becket was exiled on the Continent for seven years; he returned to England in 1170 after a brief reconciliation with Henry was effected, but when the old arguments were revived he was assassinated on the king's orders in the cathedral at Canterbury on 29 Dec. 1170. The king, officially at least, claimed that his orders had been misinterpreted, and harmony with the Pope was only restored by his humiliation and flagellation at Avranche. Becket's shrine at Canterbury became the most famous in Christendom as a place where miracles were performed, and it was the objective of *Chaucer's pilgrims 200 years later. The story of Becket has been the subject of plays by *Tennyson, T. S. *Eliot (*Murder in the Cathedral*), and by *Anouilh in French. See H. *Belloc, *St Thomas of Canterbury* (1933). (See also ANGLO-LATIN LITERATURE.)

BECKETT, Samuel Barclay (1906–), was born at Foxrock, near Dublin, the second son of a quantity surveyor, and brought up as a Protestant by a mother whom he describes as 'profoundly religious'. He was educated at Portora Royal School, Enniskillen, and at Trinity College, Dublin, where he read English, French, and Italian. He then taught for two terms in Belfast before going to Paris as *lecteur d'anglais* at the École Normale Superieure; there in 1928 he met *Joyce, with whom he formed a lasting friendship. His first published work was an essay on Joyce (1929) and he assisted with the translation into French of the 'Anna Livia Plurabelle' section of *Finnegans Wake*. His first story, 'Assumption', appeared in *transition* (1929) and in 1930 he returned as lecturer to Trinity College, resigning after four terms to embark on five unsettled, solitary years in Germany, France, Ireland, and London, before settling permanently in France. During this period (aided by a small annuity) he reviewed, translated, published poems in various periodicals, and wrote a study of *Proust (1931). *More Pricks than Kicks* (1934, stories) was followed by several full-length novels, including *Murphy* (1938), a grimly entertaining Irish evocation of London life, and *Watt* (1953), both written in English. His trilogy *Molloy* (1951); *Malone Meurt* (1951; Beckett's own English version, *Malone Dies*, 1958); and *L'Innommable* (1953; *The Unnameable*, 1960) were all originally written in French, and all three are interior monologues or soliloquies, desolate, terminal, obsessional, irradiated with flashes of last-ditch black humour: *Malone Dies* opens with the characteristic sentence 'I shall soon be quite dead at last in spite of all', and the last volume trails away with ' . . . where I am, I don't know, I'll never know, in the silence you don't know, you must go on, I can't go on, I'll go on.' Beckett's highly distinctive, despairing, yet curiously exhilarating voice reached a wide audience and public acclaim with the Paris performance in 1953 of *En attendant Godot* (pub. 1952); the English version, *Waiting for Godot* (1955), also made a great impact, and from this time Beckett became widely known as a playwright associated with the Theatre of the *Absurd, whose use of the stage and of dramatic narrative and symbolism revolutionized drama in England and deeply influenced later playwrights, including *Pinter, *Fugard, and *Stoppard. Subsequent stage plays include *Fin de partie* (first performed in French at the Royal Court, 1957; English version, *Endgame*, pub. 1958), a one-act drama of frustration, irascibility, and senility, featuring blind Hamm and his attendant Clov, and Hamm's 'accursed progenitors', who spend the action in ashcans; *Krapp's Last Tape* (1958, pub. 1959), written for the Irish actor Patrick Magee, a monologue in which the shabby and aged Krapp attempts to recapture the intensity of earlier days by listening to recordings of his own younger self; *Happy Days* (1961, pub. 1961), which portrays Winnie buried to her waist in a mound, but still attached to the carefully itemized contents of her handbag; *Come and Go* (1966, pub. 1967), a stark 'dramaticule' with three female characters and a text of 121 words; the even more minimal *Breath* (1969), a 30-second play consisting only of a pile of rubbish, a breath, and a cry; and *Not I* (1973, pub. 1973), a brief, fragmented, disembodied monologue delivered by an actor of indeterminate sex of whom only the 'Mouth' is illuminated. Beckett has also written for television (*Eh Joe*, 1966) and, more frequently, for radio, and his *Collected Poems in English and French* was published in 1977. He was awarded the *Nobel Prize in 1969.

BECKFORD, William (1759–1844), son of a wealthy Lord Mayor of London, was an MP, a traveller, and a man of great wealth, who spent large sums in collecting curios and paintings and in the creation and decoration of Fonthill Abbey, a Gothic extravaganza, where he lived in almost complete and scandalous seclusion from 1796 until he was obliged, because of his extravagance, to sell it in 1822. He is remembered chiefly as the author of the *oriental tale *Vathek*, but he wrote several other works, including two books of travel, *Dreams, Waking Thoughts, and Incidents* (1783, suppressed by the author and revised 1834) and *Recollections of an Excursion to the Monastries of Alcobaca and Batalha* (1835), both of which reveal genuine powers of description and an ironic observance of customs and manners. See J. Lees-Milne, *William Beckford* (1976); A. B. Fothergill, *Beckford of Fonthill* (1979). (See also GOTHIC NOVEL; GOTHIC REVIVAL.)

Becky, see SHARP, REBECCA.

BEDDOES, Thomas Lovell (1803–49), educated at Charterhouse and Pembroke College, Oxford, was the son of the physician, radical, and writer Dr Thomas Beddoes (1760–1808), who had been friend and doctor of *Coleridge, *Wordsworth, and *Southey. Thomas also studied medicine and in 1835 settled at Zurich, living thereafter mostly abroad. He published in 1821 *The Improvisatore* and in 1822 *The Brides' Tragedy*. His most important work, *Death's Jest-Book, or the Fool's Tragedy*, was begun in 1825 and repeatedly altered at various times, not being published until 1850, after his death by suicide at Basle. It is in blank verse, heavily influenced by Elizabethan and Jacobean tragedy, and shows Beddoes's obsession with the macabre, the supernatural, and bodily decay; these interests were to appeal strongly to *fin-de-siècle* poets such as A. *Symons who compared Beddoes to *Baudelaire and *Poe, and wrote in praise, 'there is not a page without its sad, grotesque, gay or abhorrent imagery of the tomb . . . ' He is now best known for his shorter pieces, such as 'Dream Pedlary' ('If there were dreams to sell, | What would you buy?') and the lyrics which appear in *Death's Jest-Book* ('If thou wilt ease thine heart | Of love and all its smart'), although some of his blank verse has undeniable power and originality. His poetical works were edited by *Gosse in 1890 and 1928, and H. W. Donner's edition, *Plays and Poems* (1950), has a biographical introduction.

BEDE (Baeda, or 'The Venerable Bede') (673–735), historian and scholar, when young placed in the charge of *Benedict Biscop, the abbot of Wearmouth. From there he went in 682 to Jarrow in the care of its first abbot, Ceolfrid, and there he spent most of his life. He was a diligent teacher and scholar of Latin and Greek, and he had many pupils among the monks of Wearmouth and Jarrow. He was buried at Jarrow, but his remains were moved to Durham during the first half of the 11th cent. He was first called 'Venerabilis' during the 9th cent. His *Historia Ecclesiastica Gentis Anglorum* was finished in 731, by which time he had written nearly 40 works, mostly biblical commentaries. His early treatise *De Natura Rerum* was modelled on the *Origines* of *Isidore of Seville and contains rudimentary natural science, referring phenomena to natural causes. His other influential work of history is the *Lives of the Abbots*, which gives an account of the earlier abbots in the Northumbrian Revival such as Ceolfrid and *Benedict. There is a famous description of his death in a letter of St *Cuthbert. See *Bede. His Life, Times and Writings*, ed. A. H. Thompson (1935). (See also ANGLO-LATIN LITERATURE.)

BEDE, Cuthbert, see BRADLEY, E.

Bedevere, Sir, one of the most celebrated knights in the Arthurian legends, called earl of Normandy by *Laȝamon who also says he died in the Roman wars. According to *Malory only he and his brother Lucan, Arthur's butler, survived with Arthur the last battle against Modred; like Arthur Lucan dies after the battle. It was Bedevere who at Arthur's bidding threw *Excalibur into the lake and carried the king to the barge which bore him away to *Avalon.

BEDFORD, Sybille (1911–), author, born in Charlottenburg, the daughter of Maximilian von Schoenbeck, and educated privately in England, Italy, and France. *The Sudden View* (1953; reissued as *A Visit to Don Otavio*, 1960), a description of travels in Mexico, was followed by her best-known novel, *The Legacy* (1956), a sophisticated account, partly through a child's eyes, of the complex matrimonial and financial affairs of a wealthy German family in the years immediately preceding the First World War. *A Favourite of the Gods* (1962) and *A Compass Error* (1968), both novels with Jamesian echoes, were followed by a two-volume biography of A. *Huxley (1973, 1974).

Bedford Coffee-House stood at the north-east corner of Covent Garden. It described itself as 'the emporium of wit, the seat of criticism and the standard of taste', and gained in popularity in the 1730s with the decline of *Button's; it was frequented by actors and others, including *Garrick, *Foote, *Sheridan, *Hogarth, H. *Fielding, and *Collins. *The Connoisseur* (Jan. 1754) declared, 'This coffee-house is every

night crowded with men of parts. Almost everyone you meet is a polite scholar and a wit.'

Bedlam, a corruption of Bethlehem, applied to the Hospital of St Mary of Bethlehem, in Bishopsgate, London, founded as a priory in 1247, with the special duty of receiving and entertaining the clergy of St Mary of Bethlehem, the mother church, as often as they might come to England. In 1330 it is mentioned as 'an hospital', and in 1402 as a hospital for lunatics. In 1346 it was received under the protection of the City of London, and on the dissolution of the monasteries it was granted to the mayor and citizens. In 1547 it was incorporated as a royal foundation for the reception of lunatics. In 1675 a new hospital was built in Moorfields, and this in turn was replaced by a building in the Lambeth Road in 1815, now the Imperial War Museum.

From Bedlam are derived such expressions as *Tom o' Bedlam and Bess o' Bedlam for wandering lunatics, or beggars posing as lunatics.

Bee, The, see GOLDSMITH, O.

BEECHER, Henry Ward, see STOWE, H. E. B.

Beef-steak Club, The, was founded about 1876; the members used to dine in a room at Toole's Theatre, and moved, when this was demolished, to Green Street, Leicester Square. There was an earlier club of the same name. These are not to be confused with The Sublime Society of Beef Steaks (below).

Beef Steaks, The Sublime Society of, was founded in 1735 by J. *Rich, the manager of the Covent Garden Theatre. The society, which included many eminent persons, used to meet and dine in a room at the theatre, the name being derived from the beefsteaks served. When Covent Garden Theatre was burnt, the Society moved to the *Bedford Coffee-house, and later to the Lyceum Theatre.

Beelzebub, adapted from the Latin word used in the Vulgate to render both the Greek βεελζεβούλ of the received text of the NT, and the Hebrew 'baal-zᵉbub', 'fly-lord', mentioned in 2 Kings 1: 2 as 'God of Ekron'. The word βεελζεβούλ represents the Assyrian for 'lord of the high house', but was understood in NT times as 'lord of the underworld'. In Matt. 12: 24 Beelzebub is spoken of as 'prince of the devils'. Milton gives the name to one of the fallen angels, next to Satan in power (*Paradise Lost*, i. 79), and Golding adopted one version of it for the title of his novel *Lord of the Flies*.

BEER, Patricia (1924–), poet, was born in Devon, the daughter of a railway clerk and a mother who was a member of the Plymouth Brethren; she describes her background vividly in her autobiographical *Mrs Beer's House* (1968).

The legends and landscapes of the West Country also form the background for many of her poems (collections include *The Loss of the Magyar*, 1959; *The Estuary*, 1971; *Driving West*, 1975; *Selected Poems*, 1980), and her historical novel *Moon's Ottery* (1978) is set in Elizabethan Devon.

BEERBOHM, (Sir Henry) Max(imilian) (1872–1956), critic, essayist, and caricaturist, was born in London and educated at Charterhouse and Merton College, Oxford. He did not complete a degree but drew on Oxford for his one completed novel, *Zuleika Dobson* (1911), a fantasized distillation of the Oxford atmosphere of the 1890s. His writing, like his personality, was characterized by elegance and by a light but incisive touch in applying irony and wit to society's foibles and to the idiosyncrasies of writers, artists, and politicians. His first published book and collection of essays in this vein was somewhat audaciously entitled *The Works of Max Beerbohm* (1896), followed by *More* (1899), *Yet Again* (1909), *And Even Now* (1920). *A Christmas Garland* (1912) expertly parodied the literary styles of H. *James, *Wells, *Kipling, and other leading contemporary writers. His best short stories were collected in *Seven Men* (1919). As an associate in the 1890s of *Wilde and *Beardsley, of the *Rhymers' Club, the Bodley Head publishing circle, and the New English Art Club, he was well placed to observe and comment upon avant-garde tendencies of the period. As half-brother of the actor-manager Herbert Beerbohm Tree, Max had entrée into theatrical circles and was brilliant, if not always happy, as a dramatic critic of the *Saturday Review* from 1898 to 1912; he succeeded G. B. *Shaw, whose valedictory essay in that journal dubbed him 'the incomparable Max'. His dramatic criticism is collected in *Around Theatres* (1953) and *More Theatres* (1968). His caricatures, as elegant and as individual as his literary works, complement them with delicacy of line, witty captions, and unerring selection of salient characteristics. Among the best-known collections of these are *Caricatures of Twenty-Five Gentlemen* (1896), *The Poets' Corner* (1904), and *Rossetti and His Circle* (1922). In 1910 Max married the actress Florence Kahn and settled in Italy, his permanent home for the remainder of his life except for the periods of the two World Wars. During visits to England in the 1930s he began a new career as broadcaster; his commentaries on England then and now are collected in *Mainly on the Air* (1957).

BEETHOVEN, Ludwig van (1770–1827), German composer. Beethoven's immense reputation, well established during his own lifetime, has never really diminished, and more than 150 years after his death his works still provide the basis of the 'classical' musical repertory, whether in symphonic form, in chamber music, or on the piano. He has always had staunch supporters in England: the 9th Symphony was written in response to a commission from the Philharmonic Society of London, whose directors sent £100 for Beethoven's relief during the last months of his life; but he himself, though professing great admiration for the English and constantly planning visits to London, never succeeded in making any, and his purely musical connections with Britain are tenuous.

Between 1810 and 1816, taking over a task previously done by *Haydn, he made arrangements with accompaniment for piano trio of some 140 Scottish, Irish, and Welsh folksongs for the Edinburgh publisher George Thomson: many of these are beautiful, if not entirely in accord with modern views on the treatment of folk-song; in a few cases, where the publisher had omitted to send the words of the song with the tune, Beethoven misinterpreted the mood of the music with curious results. Apart from these, and the rather questionable play made with the tunes of 'God Save the King' and 'Rule Britannia' in the so-called Battle Symphony written to celebrate Wellington's victory at Vittoria, there is no other Beethoven composition that has any overt connection with English literature. According to Schindler, however, when he once asked Beethoven the 'meaning' of the stormy, dramatic first movement of the D minor Piano Sonata, Op. 31, No. 2, the composer replied, 'Read Shakespeare's *Tempest*'; and on another occasion Beethoven told Karl Amenda that, when writing the slow movement of his first string quartet (Op. 18, No. 1), he was 'thinking of the tomb scene in *Romeo and Juliet*'. The magnificent overture to *Coriolan*, though it is certainly worthy of Shakespeare's play (and indeed not unsuited to it), was in fact written for a play on the same theme by the Viennese poet H. J. von Collin. Collin also began a libretto for Beethoven based on Shakespeare's *Macbeth*, for which some music was sketched, probably in 1808; the project was abandoned when the poet died, though as late as 1822 the idea was still capable of producing a powerful reaction in the deaf and ageing composer.

BEETON, Mrs, *née* Isabella Mary Mayson (1836–65). Her famous book on *Household Management* (1861) first appeared in *The Englishwoman's Domestic Magazine* in 1859–61, covering cookery and other branches of domestic science. It has been frequently republished, sometimes in sections under varying titles.

Beggar's Bush, The, a drama by J. *Fletcher and *Massinger, possibly with scenes by

*Beaumont; it was probably performed 1622, published 1647.

Florez, the rightful heir of the earldom of Flanders, but ignorant of his rights and living as a rich merchant at Bruges, is in love with Bertha, who is heiress of Brabant, but has been stolen away and placed with the burgomaster of Bruges and is equally ignorant of her rights. Gerrard, father of Florez, who has been driven from Flanders, has concealed himself among the beggars near Bruges, is their king, and watches over the interests of Florez. Wolfort, the usurper, proposes to marry Bertha and restore her to her rights, thus obtaining possession of Brabant. He sends Hubert, one of his nobles, who is in love with Jacqueline, Gerrard's daughter, to effect his purpose. Hubert, however, joins the beggars, among whom Jacqueline is living, and plots with Gerrard to get Wolfort into their power. In this they are successful. The identity of Florez and Bertha is revealed and they are married.

The play has been admired for the intricacies of the plot, and for the realistic portrayal of its 'ragged regiment' of beggars, whose dialogue is enlivened by thieves' cant: *Coleridge, in his Table Talk (17 Feb. 1833), declared, 'I could read the Beggar's Bush from morning to night. How sylvan and sunshiny it is!'

Beggar's Daughter of Bednall Green, The, a ballad written in the reign of Elizabeth I and included in Percy's *Reliques.

Bessee is the fair daughter of a blind beggar, employed at the inn at Romford and courted by four suitors, a knight, a gentleman of good birth, a merchant of London, and the innkeeper's son. They all withdraw their suit on being referred by her to her father, except the knight. The old beggar gives her as dowry £3,000, two pounds for every one the knight puts down. It now appears that the beggar is Henry, son of Simon de Montfort, who has assumed the disguise of a beggar for safety.

The story forms the basis of *Chettle and *Day's The Blind-Beggar of Bednal-Green (1600, printed 1659). J. S. *Knowles also wrote a comedy called The Beggar's Daughter of Bethnal Green; and R. *Dodsley wrote a musical play, The Blind Beggar of Bethnal Green.

Beggar's Opera, The, a *ballad opera by J. *Gay, produced 1728.

The play arose out of *Swift's suggestion that a Newgate pastoral 'might make an odd pretty sort of thing'. The principal characters are Peachum, a receiver of stolen goods, who also makes a living by informing against his clients; his wife and his daughter Polly; Lockit, warder of Newgate, and his daughter Lucy; and Captain Macheath, a gallant highwayman. Polly falls in love with Macheath, who marries her. Peachum, furious at her folly, decides to place her in the

'comfortable estate of widowhood' by informing against Macheath, who is arrested and sent to Newgate. Here he makes a conquest of Lucy, and there ensues a spirited conflict between Lucy and Polly, the rival claimants of his heart. ('How happy could I be with either, | Were t'other dear charmer away!') In spite of her jealousy, Lucy procures Macheath's escape. The play, which combines burlesque of Italian opera and political satire (notably of Sir R. *Walpole) with some of Gay's most brilliant songs and scenes of genuine pathos was an unparalleled success, and is said to have brought Gay some £800. (It was said to have made Gay rich, and *Rich—the producer—gay.) It has been revived several times this century, and a *Brecht–Weill version was performed in 1928.

BEHAN, Brendan (1923–64), Irish playwright, born in Dublin, the son of a house-painter. He was arrested in 1939 for his involvement with the IRA, and his subsequent period of Borstal training is described in his autobiographical Borstal Boy (1958). His best-known works are The Hostage (1958), a sprawling tragi-comedy about an English soldier kidnapped and held hostage in a Dublin brothel, and The Quare Fellow (1959), set in an Irish prison on the eve of a hanging. Both were first directed in Britain by Joan Littlewood.

Behmenism, see BOEHME.

BEHN, Mrs Afra or Aphra, probably née Johnson (1640–89), was born in Kent and visited Surinam, then a British colony, in 1663 with members of her family. On her return to England the following year she married Behn, a city merchant probably of Dutch descent, who died within two years. She was employed in 1666 by Charles II as a spy in Antwerp in the Dutch war. Her first play, The Forced Marriage (1670), was followed by some 14 others, including her most popular, The Rover (in two parts, 1677–81), dealing with the adventures in Naples and Madrid of a band of English cavaliers during the exile of Charles II; its hero, the libertine Willmore, was said to be based on *Rochester, though another model may have been her lover John Hoyle, lawyer and son of the regicide Thomas Hoyle. The City Heiress (1682) is a characteristic satiric comedy of London life and, like Otway's *Venice Preserv'd, contains a caricature of *Shaftesbury. The Lucky Chance (1686) explores one of her favourite themes, the ill consequences of arranged and ill-matched marriages. Her friends included *Buckingham, *Etherege, *Dryden, and *Otway, and she was a staunch defender of the Stuart cause. She also wrote poems and novels and edited a Miscellany (1685). Her best remembered work is *Oroonoko, or the History of the Royal Slave, based on her visit to Surinam. Perhaps the earliest English philosophical novel, it deplores the slave trade and Christian hypocrisy, holding up for admiration the nobility and honour of its African hero. Despite her success she had even in her lifetime to contend with accusations of plagiarism and lewdness, attracted in her view by her sex, and as late as 1905, in an edition of her novels, Ernest Baker described her work as 'false, lurid and depraved'. V. Woolf in *A Room of One's Own* (1928) acclaims her as the first English woman to earn her living by writing, 'with all the plebeian virtues of humour, vitality and courage', and comments that she was buried 'scandalously but rather appropriately' in Westminster Abbey. See M. *Duffy, *The Passionate Shepherdess* (1977). (See RESTORATION.)

Belarius, in Shakespeare's *Cymbeline*, the banished lord who, under the name of Morgan, acts as foster-father to the king's two sons.

Belch, Sir Toby, in Shakespeare's *Twelfth Night*, a roistering humorous knight, uncle to Olivia.

Belford, John, the hero's principal correspondent in Richardson's *Clarissa*.

Belgravia, an illustrated monthly edited by M. E. *Braddon, which ran from 1866 to 1899, and published work by many well known writers, including *Hardy, Wilkie *Collins, *Harte, and *Ouida.

Belial, adapted from the Hebrew words b^eli-ya'al, means literally 'worthlessness' and 'destruction', but in Deut. 13: 13, and elsewhere, in the phrase 'sons of Belial', it is retained untranslated in the English version, as a proper name. It has thus come to mean the spirit of evil personified, and is used from early times as a name for the Devil or one of the fiends, and by Milton (*Paradise Lost*, i. 490) as the name of one of the fallen angels.

Believe As You List, a tragedy by *Massinger, acted 1631, not published until 1849. The original play was banned because it dealt with recent Spanish and Portuguese history. Massinger ingeniously transferred the story back to the safer days of the Roman empire.

Antiochus, king of lower Asia, returns years after his defeat and supposed death at the hands of the Romans. In his fight for recognition he is constantly opposed by the ruthless and indefatigable Roman envoy Flaminius. The Carthaginian senate is too frightened to back him, and Prusias, king of Bithynia, who at first shelters and encourages him, is intimidated into changing his mind. Antiochus, imprisoned and humiliated, refuses to deny his own identity, and is led out to death. The play is a fine study of the recurring conflict between nationalism and imperialism.

The MS of the play is one of the most interesting of those preserved from the earlier 17th

cent. It is in Massinger's own hand, and has been extensively worked over by the book-keeper of the King's Men to prepare it for performance.

Belinda, (1) a character in Vanbrugh's *The Provok'd Wife*; (2) the heroine of Pope's *The Rape of the Lock*; (3) the title of a novel by M. *Edgeworth; (4) a novel by H. *Belloc.

BELINSKY, Vissarion Grigorevich (1811–48), Russian literary critic whose influence on Russian and Soviet aesthetic theory has been immense. He was a prolific literary journalist in Moscow and St Petersburg from 1833 until his death. Particularly in his final years, he used literary criticism for the discussion of moral and social issues, and was thus the first in a continuing line of 'civic' critics. His major work is contained in *Literary Reveries* (1834), in numerous annual literary surveys, and in his work on *Pushkin and *Gogol, particularly the *Letter to Gogol* (1847). Belinsky wrote a long and interesting essay on *Hamlet (1838), and admired *Byron, Sir W. *Scott, and J. F. *Cooper. His work can be read in English in *Selected Criticism* (trans. Ralph Matlaw, 1962).

BELL, (Arthur) Clive (Heward) (1881–1962), art critic, educated at Cambridge where he came under the influence of G. E. *Moore and met members of what was to be the *Bloomsbury Group. In 1907 he married Vanessa Stephen (see BELL, V.). In 1910 he met R. *Fry, whose views contributed to his own theory of 'Significant Form', outlined in *Art* (1914), which held that form, independent of content, was the most important element in a work of art. With Fry, he was a champion of the Post-Impressionists. In *Civilization* (1928) he argued (with provocative and ironical undertones) that civilization, in itself artificial and characterized by tolerance, discrimination, reason, and humour, depended on the existence of a (not necessarily hereditary) leisured élite. His other works include *Old Friends: Personal Recollections* (1956).

BELL, Currer, Ellis, and Acton, see BRONTË, C., E., and A.

BELL, Gertrude Margaret Lowthian (1868–1926), the daughter of an ironmaster baronet, was educated at Lady Margaret Hall, Oxford, where she was the first woman ever to get a First in Modern History. At 23 she became engaged to a diplomat who died a few months later, and in middle life she was passionately attached to a married man who was killed at Gallipoli. After a dozen years of world travel and mountaineering, in which she distinguished herself by redoubtable first ascents in the Alps, she began her solitary travels as a field archaeologist in Syria, Asia Minor, and Mesopotamia. Her knowledge of the desert Arabs and Middle East politics caused her recruitment to the Arab

Bureau in Cairo in 1915, and later her appointment in Iraq as Oriental Secretary to the British High Commissioner. She died in Baghdad. Apart from important specialized archaeological works and political reports, her best-known books were *Safar Nameh: Persian Pictures* (1894), *The Desert and the Sown* (1907), and *Amurath to Amurath* (1911). In these, and in her brilliant *Letters* (1927) and diaries—largely quoted in *Gertrude Bell: from her Personal Papers*, ed. Elizabeth Burgoyne (1958 and 1961)—she vividly conveyed the landscapes and personalities of the desert, wittily recapturing in remembered dialogue the idiomatic flavour of the original; she was an accomplished linguist in Arabic and Persian, and published a translation of *Hafiz. See H. V. F. Winstone, *Gertrude Bell* (1978).

Bell, Laura, a character in Thackeray's *Pendennis*, who reappears as Laura Pendennis in *The Newcomes* and *The Adventures of Philip*.

BELL, Martin (1918–), poet, born in Southampton, educated at the University of Southampton. He was a member of the *Group; his *Collected Poems 1937–66* (1967) celebrates fellow poets, provincial school masters, the French symbolists, Groucho Marx, grand opera, and 'the shining rebels' of his pantheon, while satirizing conventional notions of patriotism and religion.

BELL, Vanessa, *née* Stephen (1879–1961), painter, and elder sister of V. *Woolf. She married Clive *Bell in 1907, was a central figure in the *Bloomsbury Group, and from *c.*1914 lived with the painter Duncan Grant (1885–1978).

Bellair, a character in Etherege's *The Man of Mode*.

Bellamira, a comedy by *Sir C. Sedley, produced 1687. Founded on *Terence's *Eunuchus*, it is coarse but lively. Dangerfield, a braggart and a bully, whose cowardice is exposed in an adventure similar to that of *Falstaff at Gadshill, is an amusing character.

BELLAMY, Edward (1850–98), American novelist and political theorist, born in Massachusetts, whose fame rests upon his popular *Utopian romance *Looking Backward: 2000–1887* (1888). Its hero, Julian West, a young Bostonian, falls into a hypnotic sleep in 1887 and wakes in the year 2000 to find great social changes. Squalor and injustice have disappeared, private capitalism has been replaced by public, and everyone works for and is a member of the state. The moral, social, and cultural benefits of the new system are everywhere apparent. This work had an immense vogue; a Nationalist Party was formed to advocate its principles, and Bellamy lectured widely and wrote other works to

further his views before dying of tuberculosis. He was widely read in Europe, and imitated by, among others, H. G. *Wells.

Bellario, (1) in Shakespeare's *The Merchant of Venice*, Portia's lawyer cousin; (2) the name assumed by the heroine of Beaumont and Fletcher's *Philaster*, when disguised as a page.

Bellaston, Lady, a character in Fielding's *Tom Jones*.

Bella Wilfer, a character in Dickens's *Our Mutual Friend*.

Belle, or Isopel, **Berners,** a character in Borrow's *Lavengro*, a beautiful Amazon who acts as second to Lavengro in his fight with the Flaming Tinman.

'Belle Dame Sans Merci, La', see LA BELLE DAME SANS MERCI.

BELLENDEN, or BALLANTYNE, John (*c.*1500–*c.*1548), Scottish poet and translator into Scots of *Livy.

Bellenden, Lady Margaret, Edith, and Major, characters in Scott's *Old Mortality*.

Bellerus, the name of a fabulous person introduced by Milton in his *Lycidas* to account for Bellerium, or Bolerium, the Roman name of Land's End, in Cornwall.

Belle's Stratagem, The, a comedy by Mrs H. *Cowley, produced 1780.
Doricourt returns from his travels to marry Letitia Hardy, whom he has not seen since his childhood, the match having been arranged by their parents. He finds her beautiful but lacking in animation; she falls in love with him at once. Distressed by his cold reception, she determines to win him by first disgusting him through the assumption of the manners of a country hoyden, and then conquering his heart by her sprightliness at a masquerade, and this scheme she successfully accomplishes.

BELLI, Giuseppe Gioachino (1791–1863), Italian poet, whose vernacular Roman sonnets (*I Sonetti*, ed. G. Vigolo, 1952) represent the outlook and customs of Roman plebeians. They were written between 1827 and 1849, but because of their blasphemous and erotic satire he kept them secret and seems to have tried to suppress them after the revolutionary threat of 1848–9. Some critics postulate an early liberal period up to this point, followed by Catholic reaction: it is more likely that Belli's intense questioning of the mysteries denotes that he was always fundamentally devout. His mask of ethnography, using sonnet-form not as the trajectory of his own feeling but as a sampling device for social reality, allows him to attribute forbidden thoughts to his interlocutors. In more than 2,000 sonnets he presents a *comédie humaine* that embraces the Bible, Roman history, ancient and modern, and the daily lives of characters ranging from Popes to prostitutes and ghetto Jews. For the sounds of 'Romanesque' he devised his own spelling, yet he is not a 'dialect' poet: his idiom is his own, using all the resources of literary Italian, as well as popular speech, to explore an extreme range of poetic registers. He also wrote some 45,000 verses in academic Italian, of little poetic value. First described in English by F. *Trollope, various of his works have been translated by E. *Morgan, by Harold Norse, and by A. *Burgess.

BELLINI, Vincenzo (1801–35), Italian composer and, with *Rossini and *Donizetti, one of the creators of the Italian operatic style in the 19th cent. His one treatment of a Shakespearian subject, *I Capuleti e i Montecchi* (1830), is based on *Romeo and Juliet. It is at least the 11th recorded operatic version of the subject, though the first to have any currency today, and like most of its predecessors is fairly remote from Shakespeare: the part of Romeo, as was quite common at this period of operatic history, was given to a female mezzo-soprano. Nevertheless, as the first fully mature work by the composer of *Norma* and *La Sonnambula*, it contains much beautiful music, and does convincingly express both the passion and the innocence of the lovers.

Bell Jar, The, a novel by S. *Plath, published 1963 under the pseudonym of Victoria Lucas, and under her own name in 1966.

It opens in New York in the summer of 1953 (the year of the execution of the Rosenbergs, an event which provides a recurrent motif) as the narrator, Esther Greenwood, a highly ambitious intelligent college girl from Boston, spends time working on a trainee programme for a women's magazine with a group of other award-winning young women, and throws herself recklessly into the dangers of city life. Her story is interwoven with recollections of her boyfriend, Yale medical student Buddy Willard, who represents in part the threats of the flesh, in part the dullness of the provincial existence she fears will engulf her. She returns home, suffers a nervous breakdown, undergoes ECT, attempts suicide, is kept in psychiatric care, and in the penultimate chapter succeeds in losing her virginity to a mathematics professor. At the end of the novel, after the suicide of one of her old friends and fellow inmates, she prepares to leave the asylum and return to college. The subject matter of the novel, which is written in a taut, controlled, colloquial yet poetic prose, is highly autobiographical.

BELLOC, Hilaire (Joseph Hilary Pierre) (1870–1953), was born in France, of part-French Catholic ancestry, and educated at *Newman's Oratory School and at Balliol College, Oxford. From 1906 to 1909, and again

in 1910, he was Liberal MP for Salford. He became a prolific and versatile writer of poetry and verses; essays on religious, social, and political topics; biography; travel; literary criticism; and novels. His first publications were, in 1896, *A Bad Child's Book of Beasts* and *Verses and Sonnets* (which he later withdrew); other books of verse included *Cautionary Tales* (1907) and *Sonnets and Verses* (1923). His most celebrated serious lyrics are probably 'Tarantella' ('Do you remember an inn, Miranda?') and 'Ha'nacker Hill'. He was an active journalist, literary editor of the *Morning Post* from 1906 to 1910, founder of the *Eye-witness* (1911), and writer of innumerable essays and reviews. His books attacking and satirizing Edwardian society (some with G. K. *Chesterton) include *Pongo and the Bull* (1910) and *The Servile State* (1912); of his many books propounding Catholicism, *Europe and Faith* (1920) was well regarded. His many biographies include *Danton* (1899), *Marie Antoinette* (1909), *Cromwell* (1927), and *Charles II* (1940); and his histories *The French Revolution* (1911) and a substantial *History of England* (1915). *The Cruise of the Nona* (1925), the most intimate of his books, contains many of his most personal reflections. His most successful book of travel, *The Path to Rome* (1902), which was published with his own sketches and illustrations, is an account of a journey which he undertook, largely on foot, from the valley of the Moselle to Rome; it is interspersed with anecdotes, reflections, and dialogues between 'Lector' and 'Auctor' and ends with his arrival; other travel books include *Sussex* (1906) and *The Pyrenees* (1909). Of the novels *Mr Clutterbuck's Election* (1908), *The Girondin* (1911), *The Green Overcoat* (1912), and *Belinda* (1928) were among the most highly regarded. The last, the author's favourite, is a brief and highly individual love story, related with romantic feeling but much irony as well. A biography by A. N. Wilson was published in 1984.

BELLOW, Saul (1915–), novelist, was born in Canada of Russian-Jewish parents, and educated from the age of 9 in Chicago, a city evoked in many of his works, including his first short novel *Dangling Man* (1944), a first-person account of a man waiting, unemployed, for his army draft. *The Victim* (1947) deals with the relationship between Jew and Gentile. *The Adventures of Augie March* (1953) opens in Chicago, 'that sombre city', and provides a lengthy, episodic, first-person account of Augie's progress from boyhood, moving to Mexico, then Paris. *Seize the Day* (1956), a novella, deals with middle-aged Wilhelm, still oppressed by his powerful father. *Henderson the Rain King* (1959), designed on a grand and mythic scale, records American millionaire Gene Henderson's quest for revelation and spiritual power in Africa, where he becomes rainmaker and heir to a kingdom. *Herzog* (1964) reveals the inner life of a Jewish intellectual, Moses Herzog, driven to the verge of breakdown by his second wife's adultery with his close friend; he writes unsent letters about himself and civilization to the living and the dead, seeking above all the intensity that drives so many of Bellow's characters. ('The soul requires intensity. At the same time virtue bores mankind.') *Dr Sammler's Planet* (1969), set in New York, reflects, through the one-eyed Polish-Jewish elderly survivor Sammler, on evolution and the future of civilization, combining metaphysical speculation with a vivid physical sense of daily city life. *Humboldt's Gift* (1974) is the story of Charlie Citrine, a successful writer and academic plagued by women, law-suits, and mafiosi, whose present career is interwoven with memories of the early success, failing powers, and squalid death of his friend Von Humboldt Fleischer, whose poetic destiny he fears he may inherit, together with his manuscripts. *The Dean's December* (1982) is a 'tale of two cities', both seen through the eyes of Albert Corde, who visits Bucharest to see his dying mother-in-law, where he reflects on the contrasts between the violence and corruption of Chicago and the bureaucratic chill of Eastern Europe; the novel has, like much of Bellow's work, a strongly apocalyptic note. Bellow has also written short stories, a play (*The Last Analysis*, 1964), and has lectured in many universities. He was awarded the *Nobel Prize in 1976.

Bells, The (1871), a dramatic adaptation by L. Lewis of *Le Juif polonais* by Erckmann-Chatrian, the story of a burgomaster haunted by the consciousness of an undiscovered murder that he has committed. It provided H. *Irving with one of his most successful parts.

Bells and Pomegranates, the covering title of a series of plays and collections of shorter dramatic poems by R. *Browning, published 1841–6, comprising *Pippa Passes (1841), *King Victor and King Charles (1842), *Dramatic Lyrics (1842), *The Return of the Druses (1843), *A Blot in the 'Scutcheon (1843), *Colombe's Birthday (1844), *Dramatic Romances and Lyrics (1845), and *Luria and A Soul's Tragedy (1846). The title baffled the critics; Elizabeth Barrett finally persuaded Browning to explain it in the last number, which he did by saying that it indicated 'an alternation, or mixture, of music with discoursing, sound with sense, poetry with thought; which looks too ambitious, thus expressed, so the symbol was preferred'. The 'symbol' derives from Exodus, 28: 33–4, where it relates to the ornamentation and embroidery of the High Priest's robe. The separate numbers were bound together and sold as a single volume after 1846.

Belmont, Portia's house in Shakespeare's *The Merchant of Venice*, first mentioned by *Bassanio in the words, 'In Belmont is a lady richly left.'

Belmont, Sir John, the heroine's father in F. Burney's *Evelina*.

Belphegor, the Septuagint and Vulgate form of the Moabitish 'Baal-peor' mentioned in Num. 25.

In *Machiavelli's *Novella di Belfagor* (probably written *c.*1518), the name is given to an arch-devil sent by Pluto to the world to investigate the truth of the complaints made by many souls reaching hell, that they have been sent there by their wives. Belphegor has orders to take a wife, arrives in Florence well provided with money and a retinue of devils as servants, and marries. But he is unable to put up with his wife's insolence and prefers to run away from her and return to hell. There are echoes of this legend in one of the stories of B. *Rich's *Farewell to the Militarie Profession* (1581), and in Jonson's *The Devil is an Ass* (1616). J. *Wilson produced a tragi-comedy, *Belphegor: or the Marriage of the Devil*, in 1677–8.

Belphoebe, in Spenser's *Faerie Queene*, the chaste huntress, daughter of the nymph Chrysogone and twin sister of *Amoret; she partly symbolizes Queen Elizabeth. Belphoebe puts *Braggadochio to flight (II. iii), finds herbs to heal the wounded *Timias ('whether it divine *Tobacco* were, | Or *Panachæa*, or *Polygony*', III. v), and rescues Amoret from *Corflambo (IV. vii).

Belshazzar's Feast, the feast made by Belshazzar the son of Nebuchadnezzar and the last king of Babylonia, at which his doom was foretold by writing on the wall, as interpreted by Daniel (Dan. 5). Belshazzar was killed in the sack of Babylon by Cyrus (538 BC). He is the subject of dramas by H. *More and *Milman, of R. *Landor's *The Impious Feast*, a poem by *Byron, and an oratorio by W. *Walton.

Belton Estate, The, a novel by A. *Trollope, published 1866.

Will Belton unexpectedly becomes the heir to an entailed estate in Somerset. On his first visit to Belton Castle he falls in love with the squire's daughter, Clara Amedroz, only to find that Clara has already promised herself to a luke-warm cousin, Captain Aylmer MP. When her father dies Clara, feeling bound by her engagement, goes to live for a trial period at Aylmer Park. But the family—particularly the ferociously condescending Lady Aylmer—find neither Clara's independence of mind nor her want of fortune to their liking. This inevitably leads to a quarrel with Captain Aylmer and, when Will Belton renews his suit, Clara is only too happy to accept the man to whom she has, all along, been attracted.

Belvidera, the heroine of Otway's *Venice Preserv'd.*

BELY, Andrei (Boris Nikolaevich Bugaev) (1880–1934), Russian novelist, poet, and literary theorist, a key figure in the Russian Symbolist movement. He was born in Moscow, the son of a professor of mathematics, and studied natural sciences, then literature, at Moscow University. He came under the influence of the philosopher Vladimir Solovyev and published his first work, the prose *Second Symphony,* in 1902. In 1903, after an extensive, exalted correspondence, he met *Blok, with whom he was to have a long 'inimical friendship', and for whose wife he conceived a complex passion. His first book of poetry, *Gold in Azure,* appeared in 1904. In the years between 1905 and 1910 he was prolific in the literary polemics about Symbolism. In 1912 he met the anthroposophist Rudolf Steiner, and after following him around Europe he settled in Dornach in 1914. In 1916 he returned to Russia, and after the Revolution he engaged in teaching both literature and anthroposophy. He spent from 1921 to 1923 in Berlin. On his return to Russia he began work on his memoirs, a major source for understanding this period of Russian literary history, which appeared as *On the Border of Two Centuries* (1931), *The Beginning of the Century* (1933), and *Between Two Revolutions* (1934). But it is above all on his novels that Bely's reputation as a pioneering and influential stylist is based. The first, *The Silver Dove* (1909), tells in a style reminiscent of *Gogol (whom Bely admired and about whom he wrote), the story of a young decadent poet who returns to 'the people' and becomes involved with a rural sect. His second novel, *Petersburg,* is generally considered to be his masterpiece, and was held by *Nabokov to be one of the four greatest prose works of the 20th cent. (along with *Ulysses,* *Kafka's *The Metamorphosis,* and *A la recherche du temps perdu*). The book went through a number of re-workings (1913–14, 1916, 1922). It is set in the revolution of 1905: against a background of hallucinatory St Petersburg, a group of radicals attempt the assassination of a senator. *Petersburg* is overwhelmingly concerned with questions of identity and consciousness, and the appearance of its definitive version the same year as *Joyce's *Ulysses* is a remarkable coincidence, for their shared interest in neologism, leitmotif, mythology, parody, and experiment has been much noted. Its reputation as an inaccessible masterpiece has at last been modified by the appearance of an excellent translation (by Robert Maguire and John Malmstad, 1978). Further novels by Bely include *Kotik Letaev* (1915–16), a fictionalized description of his consciousness when a very young child. After a long silence, a volume of Bely's poetry was published in Moscow in 1966, and the definitive *Petersburg* was re-published in 1981.

BEMBO, Pietro (1470–1547), Italian humanist, became bishop of Bergamo, a cardinal, and historiographer of Venice. He wrote prose and verse in Latin and Italian, his Italian being studiously modelled on Petrarchan Tuscan, as his Latin was on the Ciceronian. He was a devoted admirer of Lucrezia *Borgia, to whom he dedicated his dialogue on love, *Gl'Asolani* (1505); this work provided the title of R. *Browning's last volume of poems, *Asolando.* (Asolo is a small town north of Venice.) *Gl'Asolani,* modelled on *Plato's *Symposium,* also provided *Castiglione with the philosophical basis for his *Courtier* (in which Bembo himself figures prominently), and was useful to *Spenser in composing his *Fowre Hymnes.*

BENAVENTE Y MARTÍNEZ, Jacinto (1866–1954), Spanish playwright and critic, who was awarded the *Nobel Prize in 1922. He was the author of many satirical comedies (in all he wrote some 170 plays) which include *La noche del sábado* (1903, *Saturday Night*) and *Los intereses creados* (1907, *Vested Interests*).

Bend in the River, A, a novel by V. S. *Naipaul, published 1979.

It is the first-person narration of trader and store-keeper Salim, a Muslim from the east coast of Africa, whose family, of Indian origin, had been settled there for centuries. He buys a small business in a town in a French-speaking Central African state, and sets himself up there. The novel traces his personal relationships—with his servant Metty, the son of slaves from the coast; with the handsome, self-absorbed Indian couple Mahesh and Shoba, who win the Bigburger franchise; with village trader and reputed witch Zabeth and her *lycée*-educated son Ferdinand, who becomes Commissioner and rescues Salim from prosecution in the last chapter; with Indar, English-university-educated boyhood friend; with Nazruddin, entrepreneur from the coast who becomes a property-owner in Gloucester Road, London; with Father Huisman, whose knowledge of and veneration for African religion ends in assassination and decapitation; and with Raymond, white historian of Africa and adviser to the president, and his wife Yvette, with whom Salim has a violently sensual affair. It also charts the progress of the state itself, through revolution, counter-revolution, the nationalization of property (including Salim's), prosperity, and bloodshed, as the president attempts to combine new technology and new mythology in his image of the new Africa. Predominantly pessimistic in tone, with something of *Conrad's sense of the futility and corruptibility of human endeavour, the novel is an unsparing investigation of the cost of change and the meaning of culture, with some small comfort offered in the survival instincts of some of its characters.

Benedick, in Shakespeare's *Much Ado about Nothing*, a sworn bachelor who falls in love with *Beatrice; 'Benedict' has been used subsequently to refer to a newly-married erstwhile bachelor.

BENEDICT BISCOP, St (?628–89), a thegn of Oswiu, king of Northumbria, who after making two pilgrimages to Rome retired to the Isle of Lérins, where he adopted the monastic life. After two years he again went to Rome and was directed by the pope, Vitalian, to accompany Theodore of Tarsus from Rome to Canterbury. He was then appointed abbot of St Peter's, Canterbury (669), resigning the dignity two years later to visit Rome once more. During this journey he collected and brought back many volumes and relics. On his return he founded (in 674) the monastery of St Peter at the mouth of the River Wear, importing workmen to build a church of stone and to glaze the windows. Once more he went to Rome, bringing back a further store of books and relics. After this he founded the sister monastery of St Paul at Jarrow. He was buried in his church at Wearmouth, having left directions for the careful preservation of his library. He is regarded as one of the originators of the artistic and literary development of Northumbria in the next century, celebrated by *Bede in his *Lives of the Abbots* (716–20).

BENÉT, Stephen Vincent (1898–1943), American poet, born in Pennsylvania and educated at Yale. He is best known for his narrative poem of the Civil War, *John Brown's Body* (1928), and for some of the poems in *Ballads and Poems* (1931), including the popular 'American Names', with its resounding last line, 'Bury my heart at Wounded Knee'. He also wrote what he called 'bread-and-butter' novels and short stories, and worked as a screenwriter in Hollywood for some time. His folk opera *The Devil and Daniel Webster*, performed in 1939, for which he wrote the libretto, was based on his own short story (1937), and presents the successful appeal of the legendary *Webster against the devil's claim to the soul of New Hampshire farmer Jabez Stone.

Ben Gunn, a character in Stevenson's *Treasure Island*.

Ben-Hur: *A Tale of the Christ*, a historical novel, published 1880, about the early days of Christianity by Lew (Lewis) Wallace (1827–1905), an American novelist who had been a general in the Civil War.

'Benito Cereno' (1856), a short story by H. *Melville.
A gothic tale of white masters and implacable black revenge, it is set off the coast of Peru in 1799, where the amiable, condescendingly racist Yankee Captain Delano goes to the aid of a drifting slave-ship. Delano suspects piracy from the erratic Captain Benito Cereno and his devoted black servant Babo, when in fact the slaves have rebelled, enslaving Cereno and slaughtering their master Don Aranda, whose skeleton has been turned into a ghoulish figurehead with the slogan 'Follow Your Leader'. Cereno escapes with Delano, only to die later, and the recaptured slaves are executed, unrepentant. *Benito Cereno* was dramatized by R. *Lowell in 1967.

BENJAMIN, Walter, see MARXIST LITERARY CRITICISM.

BENLOWES, Edward (?1602–76), poet, was heir to a wealthy Catholic family, though he became a Protestant. He was a friend of *Quarles and P. *Fletcher in Oxford. His principal work was *Theophila, or Love's Sacrifice* (1652), in 13 cantos, celebrating the epic progress of the soul in learned, obscure, and occasionally grotesque conceits and language; it was praised by *D'Avenant but ridiculed by Samuel *Butler, *Pope, and *Warburton. A critical biography by H. Jenkins appeared in 1952.

Bennet, Mr and Mrs, Jane, Elizabeth, Mary, Kitty, and Lydia, characters in J. Austen's *Pride and Prejudice*.

BENNETT, Alan (1934–), dramatist and actor, born in Yorkshire and educated at Exeter College, Oxford. He made his name with the satirical review *Beyond the Fringe* (1960, pub. 1963, with Jonathan Miller and others), and his other works, most of which are satirical comedies, include *Forty Years On* (1968, pub. 1969), set in a public school, which has much fun at the expense of the *Bloomsbury Group, T. E. *Lawrence, and other fashionable cultural figures; *Getting On* (1971, pub. 1972); and *Habeas Corpus* (1973). A more sombre work, *The Old Country* (1977, pub. 1978), deals with the theme of exile through the life of an English spy in the Soviet Union; one of his many television plays, *An Englishman Abroad* (pub. 1982, broadcast 1983) deals with the same subject through a poignant evocation of Guy Burgess's real-life encounter in Moscow with the actress Coral Browne.

BENNETT, (Enoch) Arnold (1867–1931), novelist, born in Hanley, Staffordshire, was the son of a self-educated solicitor, destined to follow in his father's footsteps, but at the age of 21 he went to London where he worked as a clerk before establishing himself as a writer. His first stories were published in *Tit-Bits (1890) and the *Yellow Book (1895), and his first novel, *A Man from the North*, appeared in 1898. In 1893 he became assistant editor and subsequently editor of the periodical *Woman*, launching himself on a career of remarkable versatility. In 1902 he moved to Paris, returning to England to settle permanently in 1912 with his French wife Marguerite, from whom he later separated. In 1926 at the suggestion of his friend *Beaverbrook he began an influential weekly article on books for the *Evening Standard* which continued until his death from typhoid. He had a lifelong passion for the theatre and wrote several successful plays, notably *Milestones* (1912, with E. Knoblock, author of *Kismet*), but his fame rests chiefly on his novels and short stories, the best known of which were set in the Potteries of his youth, a region he re-created as the *'Five Towns'. Anna of the Five Towns* (1902), the story of a miser's daughter, shows clearly the influence of the French realists whom he much admired. *The Old Wives' Tale* (1908) was followed by the Clayhanger series (*Clayhanger*, 1910; *Hilda Lessways*, 1911; *These Twain*, 1916; *The Roll Call*, 1918). The novels portray the district with an ironic but affectionate detachment, describing provincial life and culture in documentary detail, and creating many memorable characters—Darius Clayhanger, the dictatorial printer who started work aged seven in a pot-bank, the monstrous but good-hearted Auntie Hamps, Edwin Clayhanger, frustrated architect, and Hilda Lessways, the independent and strong-willed young woman who marries Edwin. Two volumes of short stories, *The Grim Tale of the Five Towns* (1907) and *The Matador of the Five Towns* (1912), are set in the same region, as are several minor novels. Bennett shows a concern for obscure and ordinary lives which also manifests itself in the best novel of his later period, *Riceyman Steps* (1923), the story of a miserly second-hand bookseller, set in drab Clerkenwell. But he also wrote many entertaining lighter works, displaying a love of luxury and fantasy, among them *The Grand Babylon Hotel* (1902), *The Card* (1911), and *Mr Prohack* (1922). His *Journal*, begun in 1896, modelled partly on that of the *Goncourt brothers, was published in 1932–3 edited by Newman *Flower, and offers a striking portrait both of the period and of his own highly disciplined working life. Bennett's letters, ed. James Hepburn, were published in 3 vols (1966–70); there is a biography by Margaret Drabble (1974).

BENOÎT DE SAINTE-MAURE, a 12th-cent. *trouvère*, born probably at Sainte-Maure in Touraine and patronized by Henry II of England, for whom he composed a verse history of the dukes of Normandy. His best-known work is the *Roman de Troie*, based on the writings of *Dares Phrygius and *Dictys Cretensis. The *Roman* was translated into Latin prose by *Guido da Colonna, and thus served as a source on which many subsequent writers drew including *Boccaccio, followed by *Chaucer who is believed to have made con-

siderable direct use of Benoît. His works have been edited by L. Constance (6 vols, 1904–12).

BENSON, A(rthur) C(hristopher) (1862–1925), eldest surviving son of E. W. Benson (1829–96), archbishop of Canterbury, and brother of E. F. and R. H. *Benson, was from 1915 master of Magdalene College, Cambridge. He published many volumes of biography, family reminiscences, reflection, criticism, etc., and had a facility for writing public odes and verses, typified by his 'Land of Hope and Glory'. From 1897 until 1925 he kept a diary, amounting to five million words; extracts were published by *Lubbock in 1926, but the papers were locked away for 50 years. David Newsome makes use of them in his biography *On the Edge of Paradise: A. C. Benson, the Diarist* (1980, a work which reveals Benson's deeply depressive tendencies) and edited *Edwardian Excursions* (1981), selections from the manuscript covering 1898–1904.

BENSON, E(dward) F(rederic) (1867–1940), brother of A. C. and R. H. *Benson, was an extremely prolific and popular novelist, whose works include *Dodo* (1893, followed by other 'Dodo' novels) and *Queen Lucia* (1920, followed by other 'Lucia' novels), and various volumes of reminiscences (*As We Were*, 1930; *As We Are*, 1932, etc.) which are a rich source of anecdote. In his later years he lived at Lamb House, Rye, once the home of H. *James.

BENSON, R(obert) H(ugh) (1871–1914), younger brother of A. C. and E. F. *Benson, and like them an extremely prolific writer. He was ordained in 1895 but became a Roman Catholic in 1903, and most of his work consists of Catholic apologia: he wrote sensational apocalyptic novels (e.g. *The Lord of the World*, 1907), melodramatic historical novels (e.g. *Come Rack! Come Rope!*, 1912), and modern novels usually involving an impossible moral conundrum (e.g. *The Average Man*, 1913), and also published sermons, poems, etc. He was, briefly, a friend and collaborator of F. W. *Rolfe.

BENTHAM, Jeremy (1748–1832), educated at Westminster and The Queen's College, Oxford, was called to the bar at Lincoln's Inn, but found the practice of the law courts morally and intellectually distasteful; he set himself the task of working at and giving theoretical justification for a simple and equitable legal system. He published anonymously in 1776 *Fragment on Government*, in form a criticism of *Blackstone's *Commentaries*, in which he first sketched his theory of government. While in Russia, 1785–8, he wrote his *Defence of Usury* (1787) and a series of letters on a *Panopticon* (1791), a scheme for improving prison discipline. In 1789 he published *Introduction to Principles of Morals and Legislation* (which had first been printed in 1780). Besides these he produced a number of works on ethics, jurisprudence, logic, and political economy, his influence proving greatest in the first two of these spheres, but he did not care to publish; the vast mass of his papers were never properly prepared for publication. His only large work was the *Principles*; the rest were pamphlets. In the dissemination of his views Bentham was greatly assisted by his devoted disciple Etienne Dumont of Geneva, who compiled a number of treatises based on Bentham's manuscripts and published them between 1802 and 1825 in French. A considerable number of Bentham's published works are retranslations of Dumont.

It is in the *Fragment on Government* and more fully in the *Principles* that he enunciates the political and ethical theory of Utility by which he is best remembered. 'It is the greatest happiness of the greatest number that is the measure of right and wrong.' Pain and pleasure are the 'sovereign masters' governing man's conduct; 'it is for them alone to point out what we ought to do.' Pleasures and pains can be quantitatively measured according to their duration, intensity, certainty, and propinquity. When the pleasures and pains resulting from any act to all the members of the community affected have been measured by these standards, we are in a position to determine the moral quality of the act. The criterion of the goodness of a law is the principle of Utility, the measure in which it subserves the happiness to which every individual is equally entitled. The motive of an act always being self-interest, it is the business of law and education to make the sanctions sufficiently strong to induce the individual to subordinate his own happiness to that of the community. Bentham believed it possible that the quantitative value of pains and pleasures as motives of action could be minutely calculated, which would give scientific accuracy to morals and legislation.

Bentham did not share the theoretical views of the French revolutionists, and he criticized the *Declaration of the Rights of Man* in his *Anarchical Fallacies* (included in his collected works). His democratic views are expressed in his *Constitutional Code* (1830). His *Chrestomathia*, a series of papers on education, appeared in 1816. He also propounded a number of valuable reforms in the administration of English justice, which since his time have been applied. In 1824 with the assistance of J. *Mill he founded the *Westminster Review*, the organ of the philosophical radicals, which lasted until 1914. J. S. *Mill, in his essay *Bentham* in this same review (1838), gives an interesting summary of Bentham's notorious hostility to imaginative literature, quoting the aphorisms 'Quantity of pleasure being equal, push-pin is as good as poetry', and 'All poetry is mis-

representation', and criticizing Bentham's own involuted prose. True to his own utilitarian principles, Bentham left his body to be dissected and his skeleton, dressed in his own clothes, is still to be seen at University College London.

BENTLEY, Edmund Clerihew (1875–1956), son of a civil servant, was born in London and educated at St Paul's (where he became a lifelong friend of *Chesterton) and Merton College, Oxford. He was called to the bar, but made his career as a journalist on the *Daily News* and *Daily Telegraph*. In *Biography for Beginners* (1905) he invented the wittily absurd verse-form called *clerihew after his second name, and in *Trent's Last Case* (1913) he produced the prototype of the modern detective novel. See E. C. Bentley, *Those Days* (1940); introduction by B. R. Redman to *Trent's Case Book* (1953).

BENTLEY, Gerald Eades (1901–), American historian of 17th-cent. drama. His *The Jacobean and Caroline Stage* was published in seven vols between 1941 and 1968.

BENTLEY, Phyllis (1894–1977), novelist, born in Halifax, Yorkshire, and educated at the University of London. The West Riding forms the background for many of her interconnected regional novels, which include *Carr* (1929), about a manufacturer in the textile industry); *Inheritance* (1932, a family saga covering many decades); *A Modern Tragedy* (1934); and *Manhold* (1941, set in the 18th cent.). She also wrote on the *Brontës, and published an autobiography, *O Dreams, O Destinations* (1962).

BENTLEY, Richard (1662–1742), born at Oulton in Yorkshire, was educated at St John's College, Cambridge, and appointed by *Stillingfleet tutor to his son, 1683–9. He made his reputation as a scholar with his *Letter to Mill* (1691), a critical letter in Latin on the Greek dramatists, and the following year delivered the first *Boyle lectures, printed in 1693 as *The Folly and Unreasonableness of Atheism*. He became keeper of the king's libraries in 1694, and during 1697–9 was engaged in the famous Phalaris controversy, during which he proved the *Epistles of *Phalaris to be spurious (see BATTLE OF THE BOOKS) and queried the antiquity of *Aesop's fables. In 1699 he was appointed master of Trinity College, Cambridge, which he ruled with such despotic power that his mastership was a succession of quarrels, scandals, and litigation. Among his greatest critical works were his bold revisions of the texts of *Horace and Manilius; he was the last great classical scholar before the divergence of Greek and Latin studies. He was caricatured in *The Dunciad* (Bk. IV. 201 ff.) and elsewhere; *Pope's enmity was said to be based on Bentley's dismissal of his version of *Homer. Bentley's arbitrary revision of *Paradise Lost*, published in 1732 with over 800 suggested emendations, was based on the belief that Milton had been ill-served by an incompetent amanuensis and a careless editor; the quality of his proposals may be judged by his attempt at improving the last two lines of the epic:

Then hand in hand with social steps their way
Through Eden took with heavn'ly comfort cheer'd.

There is a life of Bentley by *Jebb (1882).

BENTLEY, Richard (1708–82), son of R. *Bentley (above), is remembered as the friend of Horace *Walpole and *Gray, and made a considerable contribution to the Gothic fantasy of *Strawberry Hill, designing chimney-pieces, ceilings, etc. He also illustrated Gray's poems in 1753 with designs described by *Clark as 'the most graceful monument to Gothic Rococo' (*The Gothic Revival*, 1928). He was idle and improvident, and lived for a while in Jersey to escape his creditors. Walpole quarrelled with him in 1761, and Bentley struggled on in London as a playwright and pamphleteer. (See also CHUTE.)

BENTLEY, Richard (1794–1871), learned the printing and publishing trades with his uncle, John *Nichols, and began in business on his own in 1819. He included T. *Moore, both *Disraelis, and *Dickens among his authors. In 1830 he joined with Henry *Colburn to found the firm of Colburn and Bentley, which in 1837 established *Bentley's Miscellany*, a magazine which was immensely successful. A cheap series of 'Standard Novels', comprising 127 volumes, was also popular. Bentley was succeeded in the business by his son George Bentley (1825–95), who introduced many novelists to the public, including Wilkie *Collins and Mrs H. *Wood.

Bentley's Miscellany (1837–69), a very successful periodical consisting of essays, stories, and poems, but mainly of fiction, begun by R. Bentley (above). *Dickens was the first editor, and *Oliver Twist* appeared in its pages in 1837–8. J. H. *Reynolds, *Hook, *Maginn, *Ainsworth, and later *Thackeray and *Longfellow were among its contributors. *Cruikshank and *Leech provided lively illustrations. In its early heyday the *Miscellany* covered, with biography or critical articles, all the important writers of the early 19th cent.

Benvolio, in Shakespeare's *Romeo and Juliet*, a cousin and friend of Romeo.

Benwick, Captain, a character in J. Austen's *Persuasion*.

Beowulf, an Old English poem of 3,182 lines, surviving in a 10th-cent. manuscript. It tells of two major events in the life of the Geatish hero Beowulf: the first when, in his youth, he fights and kills first Grendel, a monster who has been attacking Heorot, the hall of the Danish king Hrothgar, and then Grendel's mother who comes the next night to avenge her son; the second, 50 years later, when Beowulf, who has for a long time been king of the Geats, fights a dragon who has attacked his people, in a combat in which both Beowulf and the dragon are mortally wounded. The historical period of the poem's events can be dated in the 6th cent. from a reference to Beowulf's king Hygelac by the historian *Gregory of Tours; but much of the material of the poem is legendary and paralleled in other Germanic historical-mythological literature in Norse, Old English, and German.

Although it has been suggested that the date of the poem may be nearer to that of its manuscript in the 10th cent., the poem is generally dated in the 8th cent., perhaps in its second quarter, at a time when England was being won over from paganism to Christianity. This date is taken to account for the strong thread of Christian commentary which runs through the poem, seemingly inappropriate to the date of its historical events. The degree of Christian morality inherent in the poem has been one of the two principal critical talking points about *Beowulf*; the second is the consistency or otherwise of the poem's construction. W. P. *Ker (in *Epic and Romance*, 1896) regarded the monster stories as insignificant and the peripheral historical allusions as weighty and important. This view was most famously opposed by *Tolkien in 'The Monsters and the Critics' (1936) where he argued that it was precisely the superhuman opposition of the heathen monsters that elevated the poem to heroic stature, and that all the other allusions were related directly to the transient grandeur of Beowulf's life and battles with the monsters.

Beowulf is much the most important poem in Old English and it is the first major poem in a European vernacular language. But, apart from this pre-eminence in its period, the poem is remarkable for its sustained grandeur of tone and for the brilliance of its style, both in its rather baroque diction and in the association of the elements of its plot.

Ed. F. Klaeber (1922, etc.); C. L. Wrenn (1953; rev. W. F. Bolton, 1973); trans. E. T. Donaldson (1966); G. N. Garmonsway and others in *Beowulf and its Analogues* (1968); R. W. *Chambers, *Beowulf: an Introduction* (3rd edn. with supplement by C. L. Wrenn, 1959); L. E. Nicholson ed., *An Anthology of Beowulf Criticism* (1963).

Beppo: a Venetian story, a poem in *ottava rima* by Lord *Byron, published 1818.

This poem, the first in which Byron began to find the voice and style of *Don Juan*, was suggested to him by a mock-heroic romance by J. H. *Frere, and it marks a turning-point in his work. It tells, in the mock-heroic style, with great zest and irony, the story of a Venetian carnival, at which a lady's husband, Beppo, who has been absent for many years, returns in Turkish garb, and confronts her and her *cavaliere servente*. No tragedy follows, but full reconciliation, in what the narrator implies is the civilized Venetian manner, over a cup of coffee.

BÉRANGER, Pierre-Jean de (1780–1857), French poet. He gained a great reputation in the post-Napoleonic period for his popular songs, many of which display his sympathy for the oppressed and his hostility to the restored Bourbon monarchy. He published a series of *Chansons* from 1816 onwards, and from the 1830s to the end of the century his poetry was widely translated both in Britain and the US. *Thackeray wrote four 'Imitations of Béranger', including a version of 'Le Roi d'Yvetot', one of the best-known of Béranger's satirical poems.

Berenice, daughter of Agrippa I (grandson of Herod the Great), and wife of her uncle Herod, king of Chalcis. After his death in AD 48, she lived with her brother Agrippa II. She is the Bernice of Acts 25. Titus during his campaigns in Judaea fell in love with her and she accompanied him on his return to Rome. But the Romans disapproved of the connection and he dismissed her. The rupture of their relations is the subject of *Racine's *Bérénice* and of *Otway's *Titus and Berenice*.

BERENSON, Bernard (1865–1959), art historian and philosopher, born in Lithuania and educated in America. In 1887 he settled in Europe. In *Italian Painters of the Renaissance* (first published as separate essays, 1894–1907) he developed the theory that the 'tactile values' of a work of art, i.e. its ability to communicate a sense of form, stimulated in the spectator a state of increased awareness or 'life enhancement'. *Italian Pictures of the Renaissance* (1932) is a list of attributions and locations of all important Italian paintings of the Renaissance. He also wrote on history, aesthetics, and politics.

BERGER, John (1926–), novelist and art critic, born in London and educated at the Chelsea College of Art and Central School of Art. He became well known as a broadcaster and journalist holding Marxist views, and also published several novels: *A Painter of our Time* (1958), *The Foot of Clive* (1962), *Corker's Freedom* (1964), and *G* (*Booker Prize, 1972). Works of non-fiction include *A Fortunate Man* (1967), the story of a country doctor, and *Pig Earth* (1979), a study in stories, poems, and narrative of the plight of the French peasant facing the threat of migrant industrialized labour.

BERGERAC, Cyrano de, see CYRANO DE BERGERAC.

BERGSON, Henri (1859–1941), French philosopher, professor at the Collège de France from 1900 to 1921, awarded the *Nobel Prize for Literature in 1928. His major works, all of them clearly and vividly written and accessible to the non-specialist reader, are: *Essai sur les données immédiates de la conscience* (1889), *Matière et mémoire* (1896), *L'Évolution créatice* (1907), *Les Deux Sources de la morale et de la religion* (1932). In these studies Bergson elaborated a philosophical position in broad opposition to scientific materialism and positivism. Centring his enquiry on the self and its direct intuitions, he argued for the importance to a true understanding of experience of 'real duration', in contrast to measured time, as an immediate datum of consciousness which is intuitively perceived. Consciousness itself was above all the operation of memory, not mere habitual recollection but that pure memory which retains the totality of our conscious states, to be selected by the brain when necessary in order to guide spontaneous action in relation to what is about to happen. This conviction of the primacy of creative inner experience was extended to the cosmic plane in the notion of the *élan vital*, or vital impulse, which Bergson conceived as directing the evolutionary process towards ever new forms and increasingly complex states of organization. Thus the pre-eminent value in morals and religion of what is spiritual, creative, 'open', over what is formal, fixed, 'closed'. Bergson explored the aesthetics of comedy in *Le Rire: essai sur la signification du comique* (1900), where the comic is found to arise when we perceive in human actions those automatic, repetitive, or disjointed qualities that make against the essential spontaneity of life. Laughter is regarded as society's defence against such failure of adaptive power.

Berinthia, a character in Vanbrugh's *The Relapse* and Sheridan's *A Trip to Scarborough*.

BERKELEY, George (1685–1753), philosopher, was born at Dysart Castle in Co. Kilkenny, and educated at Kilkenny College and Trinity College, Dublin. He visited England in 1713 and became associated with *Steele, *Addison, *Pope, *Arbuthnot, *Swift, and others. He travelled abroad for the next seven years, and in 1728 went to America in connection with an abortive scheme for a missionary college in Bermuda. He was appointed dean of Derry in 1724 and bishop of Cloyne in 1734, remaining at Cloyne till 1752. He then retired to Oxford, where he died.

His chief philosophical works were *An Essay towards a New Theory of Vision* (1709, 1710, 1732), *A Treatise concerning the Principles of Human Knowledge* (1710, 1734), and *Three Dialogues between Hylas and Philonous* (1713, 1725, 1734). In 1712 he published controversial sermons on 'passive obedience' and a year later contributed essays against the Whig free-thinkers to *The Guardian*. His three-volume compilation *The Ladies Library* appeared in 1714. Returning to the attack on the free-thinkers and the defence of his own philosophy in the 1730s, he issued his dialogue *Alciphron* (1732, 1752) and *The Theory of Vision Vindicated and Explained* (1733). In 1734 he published *The Analyst*, criticizing *Newton's theory of fluxions; and in 1735–7 *The Querist*, dealing with questions of economic and social reform. *Siris*, a miscellany on the virtues of tar-water for the body and of a more mystical philosophy than that of his earlier years for the soul, appeared in 1744. The standard critical edition of Berkeley's works, ed. Luce and Jessop, was published in 1948–57; a defective supplement to Vol. I was added by the publishers of the 1979 reprint. A new critical edition of Berkeley's philosophical notebooks (G. H. Thomas) appeared in 1976.

In his works on vision, Berkeley seeks to show the mind-dependence of the ideas derived from sight, and explains their 'arbitrary' though constant connection with the more primary ideas of touch by analogy with the way in which written words 'signify' speech. His other philosophy is partly inspired by, and partly a reaction to, the work of *Locke (see ESSAY CONCERNING HUMAN UNDERSTANDING) and of Nicolas Malebranche, who accepted variant versions of *Descartes' dualism of spirit and matter which would logically lead, in Berkeley's view, to scepticism and atheism. Only particular things exist, and since these are only a complex of sensations, if we abstract from them that of which we have perception, nothing remains. The 'support' of ideas or sensations is percipient mind. The *esse* of material things is *percipi*. Locke's distinction between the primary and secondary qualities of bodies therefore has no validity; both are exclusively mind-dependent. Spirit is the only real cause or power. Of the existence of our own percipient mind we each have knowledge from experience. The existence of other finite spirits is inferred by analogy from their effects. For the same reason we believe in the existence of God, who speaks to us in the whole system of nature, through the sense-experiences produced in our minds in a regular and uniform manner. In redefining his philosophical position against the free-thinkers in *Alciphron*, Berkeley sees a fruitful parallel between the language of religion and the language of science; both use their artificial notations not as marks for non-spiritual realities, but in the formulation of general rules of practice for sentient beings.

Berkeley was a master both of English prose and of the dialogue form; he is remarkable for his lucidity, grace, and dignity of expression. Before leaving for America he wrote a set of 'Verses on the prospect of planting arts and learning in America', in which occurs the often quoted line, 'Westward the course of empire takes its way'.

BERKELEY, Sir Lennox (1903–), English composer. Of partly French descent, and a pupil of the distinguished French teacher Nadia Boulanger, Berkeley has always stood a little apart from the mainstream of English musical tradition. His earlier compositions are predominantly instrumental, and some of the best of his vocal works have texts from foreign sources (*Ronsard, St Teresa of Ávila, Greek songs); but there are several beautiful settings of English words, including two groups by *de la Mare, 5 *Songs* (1946) and *Songs of the Half-light* (1964), the latter with guitar accompaniment; 5 *Poems of W. H. Auden* (1958); *Herrick Songs* with accompaniment for harp (1974); and choral settings of *Crashaw, *Donne, *Herrick, *Bridges, and G. M. *Hopkins. For the stage he has written incidental music for *The Tempest* (1946) and *A Winter's Tale* (1960, also collected into an orchestral suite for concert performance), and four operas: *Nelson* (1954), on the grand scale, with a libretto by Alan Pryce-Jones; *Ruth* (1956), in three scenes, to a text by Eric Crozier; and two one-act operas, *A Dinner Engagement* (1954) and *Castaway* (1967), both with words by Paul Dehn. His son Michael (1948–) is also a composer.

BERKENHEAD, Sir John (1617–79), was the principal editor and writer of the influential royalist Oxford-based newsbook *Mercurius Aulicus* (1643–5), which was renowned for its cavalier insouciance and wit and condemned by its opponents as a 'Court Buffon', putting off everything with 'a jest and a jeer'. Berkenhead also wrote many pamphlets and much polite and satiric verse, including a mock-heroic piece called 'A Jolt', based on an incident when *Cromwell was thrown from his coach in Hyde Park. He is notable as one of the first writers to make a career in journalism, but he also maintained contact with the more fashionable world of letters, including among his friends K. *Philips and W. *Cartwright. A life by P. W. Thomas appeared in 1969, which describes him as 'a caricaturist of invention and exceptional acuteness' and credits him with raising journalistic standards. (See also NEWSPAPERS.)

BERLIN, Sir Isaiah (1909–), distinguished philosopher and historian of ideas, educated at St Paul's School and Corpus Christi College, Oxford, and later, among many other academic distinctions, Chichele professor of social and political theory (1957–67) and president of the *British Academy (1974–8). Berlin is best known as a political philosopher for his defence of liberalism and moral pluralism (see *Four Essays on Liberty*, 1969), views which, as historian of ideas, he has explored in his work on the recognition of the historical dimension of philosophical thought in, among others, *Vico and *Herder (*Vico and Herder*, 1976). His *Russian Thinkers* (1978), a collection of essays about the intelligentsia of 19th-cent. Russia, includes 'The Hedgehog and the Fox', a discussion of *Tolstoy focusing on the tension between monist and pluralist visions of the world and of history.

BERLIOZ, Hector (1803–69), French composer. Evidence of Berlioz's enthusiasm for English literature is scattered liberally through the list of his works. The early *Waverley*, *Rob Roy*, and *Roi Lear* overtures proclaim their origins clearly enough, though *Le Corsaire*, which seems to suggest *Byron in its final version (1852), began with a different title and later became *Le Corsaire rouge* (after J. F. *Cooper's *The Red Rover*). More specific in inspiration is the symphony with viola solo, *Harold en Italie* (1834), where the solo instrument, in Berlioz's own words, is treated as 'a kind of melancholy dreamer in the style of Byron's Childe Harold'. The *Neuf mélodies irlandaises* of 1830 (later renamed *Irlande*) are settings of poems by T. *Moore, and include a version of the *Elegy on the Death of Robert Emmet* that is one of Berlioz's most powerful songs. This setting appears to have been composed under the overwhelming impact of Berlioz's passion for Harriet Smithson, the Irish actress whom he had first seen as Ophelia in September 1827, in a performance of *Hamlet* which gave the composer his first experience of Shakespeare. Five years later, after many vicissitudes, Harriet became Berlioz's wife. But the effect of Shakespeare was instantaneous—'a voice out of the burning bush, amid the stormclouds, the thunder and the lightning of a poetry that was new to me . . .' For Berlioz, as for many of his contemporaries, Shakespeare was the supreme Romantic, and the inspiration he provided was a crucial factor in several of Berlioz's best works: first came the astonishingly original *Fantaisie sur la Tempête* (1830) which, in its earliest form, preceded the *Lear* overture by a year; it was later incorporated in the lyric monodrama *Lélio, ou le Retour à la Vie* (1832), a strange, intimately personal sequel to the *Symphonie Fantastique* in which the composer's Shakespearian obsession is worked out in a mixture of music and spoken monologue. Later *Hamlet* works include the magnificent 'Marche Funèbre' for the last scene, for orchestra with wordless chorus (1848), and a delicately written song, 'La mort d'Ophélie' (1842). Meanwhile the year 1839 had brought to fruition a work that he had been planning since the 1820s, the huge dramatic symphony *Roméo et Juliette*, a sprawling masterpiece that contains, along with much that is brilliant and original, the most deeply felt orchestral music

ever written on a Shakespearian theme. For his last composition Berlioz turned *Much Ado About Nothing* into a two-act comic opera, *Béatrice et Bénédict* (1862), compressing the action but retaining as much as he could of Shakespeare's dialogue; his music for it is witty and enchanting, though not perhaps his greatest. That title, at least in the operatic field, must be reserved for *Les Troyens*, the vast Virgilian epic which he finished in 1858 but never heard complete. Yet even here Shakespeare could not be excluded, and the words for the Love Duet in Act IV are drawn entirely from the last act of *The Merchant of Venice*: 'It is Shakespeare who is the real author of both words and music', wrote the composer. 'Strange that he, the poet of the North, should have intervened in the masterpiece of the poet of Rome . . . What singers, these two!'

'Bermudas', see MARVELL, A.

BERNANOS, Georges (1888–1948), French novelist and essayist. He emigrated to Brazil after Munich in 1936, returning to France with the Liberation in 1945. His novels, notably *Sous le soleil de Satan* (1926), *Journal d'un curé de campagne* (1936), and *Nouvelle Histoire de Mouchette* (1937), dramatize through the tormented lives of priests or outcasts an intensely religious vision of the world. His polemical attacks on 20th-cent. values, especially after the emergence of Fascist Spain and Germany, are scarcely less original. He has been widely translated into English, especially by P. Morris.

BERNARD, St (1090–1153), abbot of the Cistercian foundation of Clairvaux at the age of 24 and a developer of the Augustinian contemplative theological tradition with its emphasis on Faith rather than Reason, was one of the foremost figures of the 12th-cent. monastic Reformation. He preached the Second Crusade, and opposed the dialectical theological method of *Abelard which he had condemned at Soissons and Sens. The characteristic quality of his thought was a lively and personal mysticism; he developed and preached 'The Cistercian Programme', a progression from carnal to spiritual love which, in its literary application, became one of the most important elements of medieval poetry from the *troubadours to *Dante. In his mysticism the stress is on God's grace, according to the Augustinian school, rather than on the deliberate achievement of man's contemplative efforts which was the aspect emphasized by the *Neoplatonists and their followers in the prose mysticism of the 14th cent. See B. S. James, *St Bernard of Clairvaux* (1959).

BERNARD OF MORLAIX (12th cent.), a Benedictine monk of the monastery of Cluny in Burgundy who wrote the Latin poem 'De Contemptu Mundi', c.1140, a powerful satire. J. M. *Neale translated several of his hymns from part of Bernard's output.

Berners, Belle or Isopel, see BELLE BERNERS.

BERNERS, Lord (Gerald Hugh Tyrwhitt-Wilson), 14th Baron Berners (1883–1950), composer, novelist, painter, and conspicuous aesthete, perhaps best remembered for his ballet music of the 1920s and 1930s, notably *The Triumph of Neptune* (1926) with scenario by S. *Sitwell; he also wrote the music and designed the settings and costumes of the choral ballet *A Wedding Bouquet* (1936, text by G. *Stein). He published several novels, including *Far From the Madding War* (1941) and two volumes of memoirs, *First Childhood* (1934) and *A Distant Prospect* (1945).

BERNERS, John Bourchier, second baron (1467–1533), statesman and author. He was chancellor of the exchequer in 1516 and attended Henry VIII at the Field of the Cloth of Gold. He translated the *Chronicles* of *Froissart (1523–5); *Huon of Bordeaux* (probably printed before 1534); Guevara's *Il Libro Aureo di Marco Aurelio* (1535); and another Spanish work, the *Castell of Love* (printed 1549).

BERNERS, Juliana, see BOOK OF ST ALBANS.

BERNHARDT, Sarah (-Marie-Henriette) (1844–1923), French actress. In a career that spanned 60 years and took her to many parts of the world, including numerous appearances in London and New York, she attained great celebrity in both tragedy and comedy, and became renowned for a voice of extreme purity and beauty. Among her famous roles were Doña Sol in *Hugo's *Hernani*, Adrienne Lecouvreur in the play of the same name by Scribe and Legouvé, Phèdre in *Racine's tragedy, Marguerite in the younger *Dumas' *La Dame aux camélias*, several parts in plays by Sardou, and Napoleon's son in *Rostand's *L'Aiglon*. From 1899 she managed her own Théâtre Sarah Bernhardt, taking the role of Hamlet there. Her memoirs, *Ma double vie*, were published in 1907.

BERNI, Francesco (1496/7–1535), a Tuscan poet, author of facetious, burlesque compositions, whose style was imitated by Byron in his *Don Juan* and *Beppo*. Berni also wrote a recast of Boiardo's *Orlando Innamorato*, which for a long time was regarded as superior to the original.

Bernstein, Baroness, a character in Thackeray's *The Virginians*, formerly Beatrix Esmond in *The History of Henry Esmond*.

Berowne, or Biron, one of the three lords attending the King of France in Shakespeare's *Love's Labour's Lost*. From scoffing at love he becomes an extravagant lover of Rosaline, but she dismisses him at the end of the play to 'jest a twelvemonth in an hospital'.

BERRY, James (1924–), poet, born in Jamaica, who came to London in 1948 and worked until 1977 as an overseas telegraphist. Since then he has done much work in the field of multi-cultural education, and edited various anthologies, including *Bluefoot Traveller: An Anthology of Westindian Poets Of Britain* (1976), *Dance to a Different Drum* (1983, a Brixton Festival anthology), and *News from Babylon* (1984). His own collections include *Fractured Circles* (1979) and *Lucy's Letter and Loving* (1982). (See also JAZZ POETRY.)

Berry and Co., see YATES, D.

BERRYMAN, John (1914–72), American poet, was born John Smith in Oklahoma but took his stepfather's name after his father's suicide. Much of his poetry is anguished and confessional, exploring personal guilts and religious doubts, but it is also learned and often witty, and technically highly organized of idiosyncratic. His work includes *Poems* (1942), *The Dispossessed* (1948), and *Homage to Mistress Bradstreet* (1956), the last a complex biographical ode inspired by the first New England poet Anne *Bradstreet. *77 Dream Songs* (1964), with their imaginary and protean protagonist Henry, were completed by *His Toy, His Dream, His Rest* (1968), and together form his major work. He committed suicide in Minneapolis.

Bertram, count of Rousillon, in Shakespeare's *All's Well that Ends Well*, the reluctant husband of *Helena.

BERTRAM, Charles (1723–65), sometimes self-styled Charles Julius, literary forger, English teacher in a school for naval cadets at Copenhagen. He produced between 1747 and 1757 an alleged transcript of a manuscript work on Roman antiquities by Richard of *Cirencester, together with a copy of an ancient itinerary of Britain, at many points supplementing and correcting the itinerary of Antoninus. He also published works of *Gildas and *Nennius, with the text of his forgery and a commentary on it, at Copenhagen, 1757, and several philological works. His imposture was finally exposed by B. B. Woodward in the *Gentleman's Magazine*, 1866–7.

Bertram, Harry, a character in Scott's *Guy Mannering*.

Bertram, Sir Thomas and Lady, their sons Thomas and Edmund, and their daughters Julia and Maria, characters in J. Austen's *Mansfield Park*.

***Bertram;** or the Castle of St Aldobrand*, a tragedy

by C. R. *Maturin, produced with great success by *Kean, 1816. An overwrought drama, centred on a *Byronic hero, of love, madness, and suicide, it was the object of hostile criticism by Coleridge in his *Biographia Literaria.

Bertram Risingham, a character in Scott's *Rokeby.

BESANT, Mrs Annie, née Wood (1847–1933), after an unhappy marriage with a brother of Sir W. *Besant, became a secularist, a Fabian, a trade union organizer, and, in association with *Bradlaugh, an enthusiast for birth control. She then became a theosophist and pupil of Mme *Blavatsky, and an active supporter of the Indian nationalist movement.

BESANT, Sir Walter (1836–1901), educated at King's College, London, and Christ's College, Cambridge, published *Early French Poetry* (1868) and *The French Humourists* (1873). He was secretary to the Palestine Exploration Fund (1868–86) and with W. H. Palmer wrote *Jerusalem* (1871). From 1871 to 1882 Besant collaborated with J. *Rice and together they produced several best-selling novels, including *Ready-Money Mortiboy* (1872), *The Golden Butterfly* (1876), and *The Chaplain of the Fleet* (1881). He was deeply interested in the life of the poor, especially in the East End of London, and the terrible social conditions of industrial workers and draws attention to these in *All Sorts and Conditions of Men* (1882) and *Children of Gibeon* (1886); he stimulated the foundation of the People's Palace, Mile End (1887), for intellectual improvement and rational amusement. In 1884 he founded the *Society of Authors, and became editor of *The Author* in 1890; he defined the financial position of authors in *The Pen and the Book* (1899). His other books include the historical works *Rabelais* (1879) and *Captain Cook* (1890) and several histories of different parts of London. *A Survey of London* (1902–12) and his autobiography (1902) appeared posthumously.

Bess of Hardwick, Elizabeth Talbot, countess of Shrewsbury (c.1520–1608), daughter and co-heir of John Hardwick of Hardwick, Derbyshire. She is described as 'a woman of a masculine understanding and conduct; proud, furious, selfish, and unfeeling' (*Lodge). To her care and to that of her husband, the 6th earl of Shrewsbury, Mary Queen of Scots was entrusted in 1569 at Tutbury. She married her daughter to Charles Stuart, younger brother of Darnley (Arabella Stuart was the issue of the marriage), and was imprisoned in the Tower in consequence. She was herself four times married and inherited the fortunes of her four husbands, her income being estimated at £60,000. She built Chatsworth (not the present building) and Hardwick Hall.

Bessus, in Beaumont and Fletcher's *A King and no King*, a cowardly braggart.

Bessy, one of the stock characters, a man dressed as a woman, in the medieval *Sword-dance and in the *Mummers' Play.

Bestiaries, medieval treatises derived from the Greek *Physiologus*, which was a collection of about 50 fabulous anecdotes from natural (mostly animal) history, followed by a 'moralization' of the anecdotes for a Christian purpose. The Greek original dates from some time between the 2nd and 4th cents AD, and it was translated into many languages, most influentially Latin. In the 12th cent. additions began to be made to the Latin version from the popular encyclopedia of the Middle Ages, the *Etymologiae* of *Isidore of Seville. Those written in England in the 12th and 13th cents were often richly illustrated with miniatures. The Old English poems 'The Panther' and 'The Whale' are isolated examples of the kind; the Middle English Bestiary, coming from the north-east Midlands in the second half of the 13th cent., has 802 lines in various metres. Their method of moralization was influential on the relations between story and moral in many medieval texts, as well as being a popular source for such works as Sir T. Browne's *Pseudodoxia Epidemica.

F. McCulloch, *Medieval Latin and French Bestiaries* (1960); T. H. *White, *The Book of Beasts* (1954: a translation of a 12th-cent. Latin bestiary); Middle English version ed. R. Morris in *An Old English Miscellany* (EETS OS 49, 1872; reprinted 1927, pp. 1–25).

Bethgelert, meaning 'grave of Gelert'. According to a story traditional in the village at the foot of Snowdon, where Llewelyn the Great had his abode, Gelert was a hound given by King John to Llewelyn. On one occasion this favourite hound was missing when Llewelyn went hunting. On his return he found the hound smeared with blood, his child's bed in disorder, and the child not to be seen. Thinking that the hound had devoured the child, the father killed Gelert with his sword. The child, awakened by the hound's dying yell, cried out from under a heap of coverings, and under the bed was found a great wolf which the hound had slain.

The story is the subject of a ballad by William Robert Spencer (1769–1834, one of the many translators of Bürger's *Lenore), entitled 'Beth Gelert, or the Grave of the Greyhound', published in his *Poems* (1811). There are many similar stories, and *Baring-Gould in his *Curious Myths* discusses their origins, tracing them to Indian sources.

BETJEMAN, Sir John (1906–84), poet, born in Highgate, the son of a manufacturer of household articles; the name is of Dutch origin.

He was educated at Marlborough, which he disliked, and at Magdalen College, Oxford, where he became friendly with *Auden and *MacNeice, was encouraged by *Bowra, and adopted the pose of aesthete and bon viveur, while remaining, as he always maintained, essentially middle-class in his outlook. He left without taking a degree, worked briefly as a schoolmaster, then began to write, in 1931, for the *Architectural Review*; meanwhile he was beginning to publish poems in magazines ('Death in Leamington' appeared in the *London Mercury* in 1930), and his first collection of verse, *Mount Zion*, appeared in 1931. This was followed by other collections, including *Continual dew: a little book of bourgeois verse* (1937), *New bats in old belfries* (1945), *A few late chrysanthemums* (1954), and his extremely successful *Collected Poems* (1958, expanded 1962). His blank-verse autobiography, *Summoned by Bells* (1960), which covers his boyhood and life at Oxford, was followed by two more collections, *High and Low* (1976) and *A Nip in the Air* (1972). He was appointed poet laureate in 1972. His poetry, which has reached an unusually wide public (while numbering Auden and *Larkin amongst its advocates), is predominantly witty, urbane, satiric, and light of touch, a comedy of manners, place names, and contemporary allusions, but many have commented on the underlying melancholy, the chill of fear, the religion which dwells more on hope than faith; Larkin points to his 'heterogeneous world of farce and fury, where sports girls and old nuns jostle with town clerks and impoverished Irish peers' (*Observer*, 1983). In the preface to *Old Lights for New Chancels* (1940) Betjeman writes of his own 'topographical predilection' for 'suburbs and gaslights and Pont Street and Gothic Revival churches and mineral railways, provincial towns and garden cities', a predilection also displayed in his editing and writing of Shell Guides (some illustrated by his friend John Piper), and various works on architecture, beginning with *Ghastly Good Taste* (1933). Betjeman's popularity as a public personality and the apparent facility of his verse contributed to a neglect of his poetry in critical circles in the late 1950s and early sixties, when it was seen as lightweight, but it has since found new admirers in a second generation of readers and poets.

Betrothed, The, a novel by Sir W. *Scott, published 1825.

Though styled one of the 'Tales of the Crusaders', it has in fact little to do with these. The scene is laid in the Welsh Marches, in the reign of Henry II. Eveline Berenger, the sole child of a Norman baron, finds herself in grave peril when the fierce Welsh prince Gwenwyn besieges her father's castle of Garde Douloureuse, and the old warrior himself is killed in an imprudent sally. She is rescued by Hugo de Lacy, Constable of Chester, and under the influence of gratitude and of a vow made in the moment of danger, consents to be affianced to him, though his age commands her respect rather than her love, and he is under pledge moreover to set off immediately to the Crusade. Left to the care of his nephew, the gallant Damian whom she secretly loves, and exposed not only to malicious tongues but to the machinations of Randel, another de Lacy kinsman, Eveline spends the years of his absence in a position of much difficulty and danger. Hugo's return is only just in time to extricate Eveline and Damian from a position of the utmost peril; for they are charged with high treason, and accused moreover of taking a disloyal advantage of his absence to indulge their mutual love. The old Constable clears up the situation, releases Eveline from her pledge to him, and places her hand in that of Damian.

Betteredge, Gabriel, in Wilkie Collins's *The Moonstone*, the Verinders' steward and narrator of parts of the story.

BETTERTON, Mrs Mary (*c*.1637–1712), the wife of T. *Betterton, at first known on the stage as Mrs Saunderson, the first notable actress on the English stage (until 1660 female parts were taken by men or boys). Mrs Betterton was the first woman to act a series of Shakespeare's great female characters, such as Lady Macbeth, Ophelia, and Juliet.

BETTERTON, Thomas (1635–1710), the greatest actor in the Restoration, joined *D'Avenant's company at Lincoln's Inn Fields, and was associated in the management of the Dorset Garden Theatre from 1671. With most of his fellow-actors he revolted against the harsh management of C. Rich (father of John *Rich) and established a rival company at Lincoln's Inn Fields in 1695, opening with Congreve's *Love for Love*. In 1705 his company moved into the theatre erected by *Vanbrugh in the Haymarket. His 180 roles included Hamlet, Mercutio, Sir Toby Belch, Macbeth, Bosola (in the *Duchess of Malfi*), and Heartwell (in Congreve's *The Old Bachelor*). His dramas include the *Roman Virgin*, acted 1669, adapted from *Webster's *Appius and Virginia*; *The Prophetess* (1690), an opera from the *Prophetess* of *Beaumont and *Fletcher; *King *Henry IV* (1700, in which he played Falstaff) from Shakespeare; the *Amorous Widow* (1670), from *Molière's *George Dandin*. He was a man of high character, and much esteemed as an actor by his contemporaries.

BETTY, William Henry West (1791–1874), a phenomenally successful boy actor, known as 'The Young Roscius', in reference to the famous Roman actor. He made his début in Belfast at the age of twelve, playing four roles in four nights, one being that of Romeo. Proceeding to

Dublin, he added Hamlet, Prince Arthur, and other parts to his repertoire. He continued his success in Scotland, and arrived in London in 1804, aged thirteen. At Covent Garden he played many major roles, including Richard III and Macbeth; there were riots for admission, he was presented to the Royal Family, and the House of Commons suspended a sitting to enable MPs to see his Hamlet. His final appearance as a boy actor was in 1808. He then went to Cambridge to study, returning to the stage in 1812. But his career as an adult actor was not a success, and he finally retired, a very rich man, in 1824.

Between the Acts, the last novel of V. *Woolf, published shortly after her death in 1941. Although much of its composition was overshadowed by the war, it has a richness of invention missing from her previous work, *The Years*, and has been seen as her final statement on art as the transforming and unifying principle of life.

The action takes place at a middle-sized country house, Poyntz Hall, the home for a mere 120 years of the Oliver family, and Woolf's central metaphor is the enacting of a village pageant, which aspires to portray nothing less than the sweep of English history, by means of songs, tableaux, parody, pastiche, etc.; it ends by presenting the audience its own mirror-image, in the present, as a megaphoned voice demands how civilization could be built by 'orts, scraps and fragments like ourselves?' The pageant is directed by the sexually ambiguous Miss la Trobe, who represents the ever-dissatisfied artist ('A failure', she groans, at the end), and its scenes are interwoven with scenes in the lives of the audience; together, the illusion and the reality combine as a communal image of rural England, past and present—'a rambling capricious but somehow unified whole', as Woolf originally envisaged the novel.

Beulah, Land of, see Isaiah 62: 4. In Bunyan's *Pilgrim's Progress* it lies 'beyond the valley of the Shadow of Death and also out of the reach of Giant Despair'. Here the pilgrims were in sight of the Heavenly City, 'they heard continually the singing of birds and saw every day the flowers appear in the earth.' Beulah is also used in a similar sense by *Blake, to represent a state of Light (often associated with the third state of vision and sexual love): its symbol is the moon.

Beuves de Hanstone, see BEVIS OF HAMPTON.

Bevis of Hampton, a popular verse-romance from the late 13th or early 14th cent. in 4,620 lines (twelve-line tail-rhyme 1–474 and short couplets 475–end), based on a 12th-cent. Anglo-Norman *chanson de geste* entitled *Beuves de Hanstone* and on a subject popular throughout Europe, from Ireland, to Italy, to Russia. Bevis's mother, the wife of Guy, earl of Southampton, has her husband murdered, marries the murderer, and sells Bevis into slavery in the East. The rest of the story is taken up with Bevis's conversion and marriage to Josian, the daughter of the king of Arabia, and their adventures in Europe, England (where he kills the emperor of Germany, his father's murderer), and the East. The story is told in Drayton's *Poly-Olbion* (ii. 259); Bevis's sword was called 'Morglay' and his horse 'Arundel'.

Ed. E. Kölbing (EETS es 46, 48, 65, 1885–94; reprinted 1 vol., 1973); discussion in L. A. Hibbard, *Medieval Romances in England* (2nd edn, 1960, pp. 115–26).

Bevis, the Story of a Boy, a novel by R. *Jefferies, published 1882.

In this joyful evocation of a country childhood, revealing the secret world of two imaginative and adventurous boys, Bevis and Mark, Jefferies draws largely on his own boyhood in Wiltshire. The farm, the woods, the lake, become the Roman world (or any other world), the Unknown Island becomes the Hesperides, and the solemn games, adventures, and incidental terrors are played out in storm and sun, by day and under the stars, almost always out of doors.

BEWICK, Thomas (1753–1828), woodengraver, son of a Northumbrian farmer. He was apprenticed to, and subsequently partner of, Ralph Beilby (1744–1817), a metalengraver in Newcastle. He engraved blocks for *Gay's *Fables* (1779), *Select Fables* (1784), *A General History of Quadrupeds* (1790), *Fables of Aesop* (1818), the poems of *Goldsmith and T. *Parnell (1795), and other books; his most celebrated and successful work was *A History of British Birds* (1797, 1804). *Ruskin wrote of the 'flawless virtue, veracity, tenderness, the infinite humour of the man', and his vignettes of country life, as well as his close observations of animal life in its natural setting, were much admired by *Wordsworth, C. *Brontë, *Carlyle, and *Audubon, who visited him in his workshop in 1827. His *Memoir* (1862) is a vivid record of a north-country childhood and a craftsman's life.

BEYLE, Henri, see STENDHAL.

Beyond the Fringe, see SATIRE.

Bezae, Codex, see BIBLE, THE.

Bhagavadgita, one of the principal sacred writings of the Hindus, an episode in the great epic *Mahabharata* in which Krishna instructs and exhorts Arjuna before the battle of Kurukṣetra. It is a product of the Bhagavata or Vasudeva sect who worshipped Krishna as one of the principal incarnations of the supreme god Vishnu.

It probably dates from between the 5th and the 2nd cents BC, and has remained one of the most esteemed works of the religious literature of India. There is an edition with a commentary by R. C. Zaehner, published 1969.

Bianca, (1) sister of Katharina, the title character in Shakespeare's *The Taming of the Shrew*; (2) a Venetian courtesan, mistress of *Cassio, in his *Othello*.

Biathanatos, see DONNE, J.

Bible, The, (1) The Old Testament. The oldest surviving Hebrew text (Codex Babylonicus Petropolitanus) is comparatively recent, dating only from AD 916. It is a Masoretic text, i.e. one prepared by the guild of scholars called Masoretes (see MASORA). Of much earlier date (5th cent. BC) is the Samaritan text of the Pentateuch. We have also the Targums or Aramaic paraphrases, written at various times subsequent to the date when Aramaic superseded Hebrew as the language spoken by the Jews (shortly before the Christian era). The Greek version, known as the Septuagint, of the 3rd cent. BC is of far greater importance. Other translations into Greek were made in the 2nd cent. AD and were collected in parallel columns, together with the current Hebrew text and a revised text of the Septuagint, by *Origen in his Hexapla. This has perished with the exception of the revised Septuagint, of most of which we possess an 8th-cent. copy. In addition to the above, there was an old Latin version (known as Vetus Itala) of an early Greek translation, of which fragments alone remain, and which was superseded by Jerome's Latin text, known as the *Vulgate.

(2) The New Testament. Manuscripts in Greek, and manuscripts of translations from the Greek into Latin, Syriac, and Coptic are extant. The most important of these are the Greek, of which the chief are the Codex Vaticanus and the Codex Sinaiticus, uncial manuscripts of the 4th cent.; the Codex Bezae, containing the Greek text on the left-hand page and the Latin on the right, probably earlier than the 6th cent.; and the Codex Alexandrinus, an uncial of the 5th cent. Of the Latin versions there were, before Jerome undertook their revision in the Vulgate, two main types current respectively in Africa and Europe. Several manuscripts of these survive. Of the Vulgate text there are a large number of manuscripts, of which the best are Northumbrian (based on Italian originals), Irish, and Spanish. (See in this connection AMIATINUS CODEX and LINDISFARNE GOSPELS. See also BIBLE, THE ENGLISH; POLYGLOT BIBLE; COMPLUTENSIAN POLYGLOT; LUTHER; GUTENBERG; and ULFILAS.)

Bible, the English. Apart from paraphrases attributed to *Caedmon and the translation by *Bede of part of the Gospel of St John, the earliest attempts at translation into English of the Holy Scriptures are the 9th- and 10th-cent. glosses and versions of the Psalms, followed by the 10th-cent. glosses and versions of the Gospels (the Durham Book, or *Lindisfarne Gospels, and the West-Saxon Gospels), and *Aelfric's translation of the OT at the close of the same cent. After this little was done until the time of *Wyclif, to whom and his followers we owe the two 14th-cent. versions associated with his name, the first complete renderings into English of the Scripture. Of these two versions taken from the Latin text, which appeared about 1382 and 1388, it is doubtful how much was Wyclif's own work. The second, or revised version, was a great improvement on the first, and is a readable and correct translation.

*Tyndale was the first to translate the NT into English from the Greek text; this he probably did in Wittenberg, the translation being printed first at Cologne, and when this was interrupted, at Worms (1525–6). In 1530 his translation of the Pentateuch was printed at Marburg, followed by a translation of the Book of Jonah. These translations were made from the Hebrew, with reference also to the *Vulgate, *Erasmus's Latin version, and *Luther's Bible. The Authorised Version (see below) is essentially the text of Tyndale. The complete English Bible that bears the name of *Coverdale was printed in 1535. It is not a translation from the original texts, but probably from Luther's version, the Zurich Bible, and the Vulgate, with assistance from Tyndale's version. A second edition was issued in 1537. The Prayer Book text of the Psalms is largely Coverdale's version.

'Matthew's Bible' was issued in 1537, under the pseudonym of Thomas Matthew, by John Rogers (?1500–55). He was a friend of Tyndale, was converted to Protestantism, and prepared and annotated his version for publication. Rogers was burnt at Smithfield in Mary's reign.

'Taverner's Bible' was a revision of Matthew's. It appeared in 1539. Richard Taverner (?1505–75) was a religious author who was patronized by Wolsey and Cromwell, was sent to the Tower on the latter's fall, but subsequently obtained the favour of Henry VIII.

The 'Great Bible', also called 'Cranmer's Bible', was brought out in 1539 under the auspices of Henry VIII; Coverdale was placed by Cromwell in charge of its preparation. The printing of it was begun in Paris and finished in London.

Towards the end of Henry VIII's reign there were interdictions on the use of the Bible. During Mary's reign, the reformers took refuge, some in Frankfurt am Main, some in Geneva, where in 1560 appeared the Genevan or *'Breeches' Bible. It had a marginal commentary which proved agreeable to the Puritans.

In 1568 was published the 'Bishops' Bible', an edition promoted by Archbishop *Parker to counteract the popularity of the Calvinistic Genevan Bible; while Romanists made a translation, known as the Rheims and Douai version, which appeared, the NT in 1582, the OT in 1609–10. It is characterized by the frequent use of Latinisms.

The 'Authorized Version' arose out of a conference at Hampton Court, convened by James I in 1604, between the High Church and Low Church parties. The undertaking was proposed by Dr Reynolds, president of Corpus Christi College, Oxford, and was supported by the king. The revisers were 47 in number, divided into companies dealing with various sections of the Bible, and were drawn from the most eminent scholars and divines of the day. They were instructed to follow the text of the 'Bishops' Bible' wherever they could. The work of revision and retranslation occupied three years and a half, and the so-called 'Authorized Version' (it was not authorized by any official pronouncement) appeared in 1611. It is practically the version of Tyndale with some admixture from Wyclif. Two issues of it were made in 1611, known respectively as the 'He Bible' and the 'She Bible', because in the first the words in Ruth 3: 15 read 'and he went into the citie', and in the second 'and she went into the citie'. Modern bibles are based with slight variations on the 'She Bible'. Various editions of the Bible are named after eccentricities of wording or mistakes in the printed text; a few of the more important of these, such as 'Breeches Bible' and 'Vinegar Bible', are dealt with under their respective names.

In 1870 the Convocation of Canterbury appointed a committee to consider the question of revision, and as a consequence of their report two companies were constituted to revise the authorized versions of the OT and NT respectively. The Revised Text was published, of the NT in 1881, of the OT in 1885. That of the NT was unfavourably received, owing to many irritating and apparently unnecessary alterations of familiar passages. The Revised Version of the OT, though not altogether free from these, was in many respects an improvement on the Authorized text. In 1922 the Revd James Moffatt, Washburn professor of church history in the Union Theological Seminary, produced a 'New Translation of the New Testament', and in 1924 'The Old Testament, a new Translation', both of which caused much controversy. R. *Knox published a new translation of the Bible based on the Vulgate text; the NT in 1945 and the OT in 2 vols in 1949.

In 1947 a new translation of the Bible into modern English was undertaken by a Joint Committee of all the Churches (except the Roman Catholic) in the British Isles. The work was to be carried out by panels of translators for the OT, Apocrypha, and NT, with the help of literary advisers, and published by the University Presses of Oxford and Cambridge. The New English Bible NT was published in 1961 and the OT and Apocrypha in 1970.

Bible in Spain, The, a narrative of travel by *Borrow, published 1843.

Borrow travelled in Spain as distributor of Bibles for the British and Foreign Bible Society from 1835 to 1840, and this book purports to be an account of his adventures in a country racked by civil war. It is difficult to say how far the various incidents recounted actually occurred; but the vivid picture that the author gives of Spain is unquestionably realistic, and the work is one of the finest of English travel books.

Bibliographical Society, The, founded in 1892. Its *Transactions* were first published in 1893 (merged with *The Library* in 1920). The Society also published separate monographs, and in 1926 issued the invaluable *Short-Title Catalogue of English Books, 1475–1640* (work continued by *Wing). Volume 2 (I–Z) of a revised and enlarged version was published in 1976; Volume 1 is in progress.

Bibliography, Works of, see under BOHN; BRYDGES; CAMBRIDGE BIBLIOGRAPHY; DEWEY, M.; DIBDIN, T. F.; HAZLITT, W. C.; LANG; LOWNDES; MCKERROW; QUARITCH; SADLEIR; WATT, R.; WING, D. G.; and previous entry.

Bickerstaff, Isaac, a fictitious person invented by *Swift. A cobbler, John Partridge, claiming to be an astrologer, had published predictions in the form of an *almanac. Swift in the beginning of 1708 produced a parody entitled *Predictions for the ensuing year, by Isaac Bickerstaff*, in which he foretold the death of Partridge on 29 March. On 30 March he published a letter giving an account of Partridge's end. Partridge indignantly protested that he was still alive, but Swift retorted in a *Vindication* proving that he was really dead. Other writers took up the joke, and *Steele, when he launched *The Tatler* in 1709, adopted the name of Bickerstaff for the supposed author.

BICKERSTAFFE, Isaac (1733–?1808), an Irish playwright who arrived in London in 1755 and produced many successful comedies and opera librettos. His *Love in a Village* (1762), with music by *Arne, has a claim to be the first comic opera, and contains the well known song about the Miller of Dee ('There was a jolly miller once'). *The Maid of the Mill* (1765, with music by Samuel Arnold and others) was also very successful; Bickerstaffe acknowledged Richardson's *Pamela* as the source of his plot. *The Padlock, with music by *Dibdin, was performed in 1768, as was *Lionel and Clarissa*, which reappeared as *The School for Fathers* in 1772. *The Hypocrite* (1768, adapted from Molière's *Tartuffe* and *Cibber's *The Non-Juror*) contains the well known character of a hypocrite, Maw-worm. Bickerstaffe also wrote adaptations of *Wycherley and *Calderón, and a version of *Inkle and Yarico*. In 1772 Bickerstaffe fled to France, suspected of a homosexual offence, and spent the rest of his life in obscurity. *Garrick was implicated in the scandal in a lampoon, *Love in the Suds* by W. Kenrick (?1725–79), subtitled 'the lamentations of Roscius for the loss of his Nyky'. Long after Bickerstaffe's disappearance, his ex-colleague Dibdin was defending himself from the charge of plagiarizing his songs. Nothing is known of the circumstances of his death. See *The Dramatic Cobbler* (1971), a life by Peter Tasch.

Bidpai or *Pilpay, The Fables of*, or *Kalilah and Dimnah*, is the title of the Arabic version of a lost original of the *Panchatantra*, a celebrated Sanskrit collection of fables, the source of much European folklore. 'Bidpai' is a corruption of 'bidbah', the appellation of the chief scholar at the court of an Indian prince.

The fables were translated into many European languages, the first English version coming via the Italian in a version by Sir T. *North as *The Morall Philosophia of Doni* (1570). A recent version, *Kalila and Dimna: Selected Fables of Bidpai* (1980) by Ramsay Wood, has an introduction by D. *Lessing describing the history of the tales and their naturalization in other cultures.

BIERCE, Ambrose (1842–?1914), American writer, born in Ohio. He served in the Civil War, 1861–5, and afterwards became a prominent journalist, living and working for a time in England (1872–6). He returned to San Francisco, and later worked as a correspondent in Washington. He published much, and collected his writings together in 12 vols (1909–12), but is best known for his short stories, realistic, sardonic, and strongly influenced by *Poe. They were published in *Tales of Soldiers and Civilians* (1891), a title which was changed to *In the Midst of Life* (1892; rev. edn, 1898). Tired of life and America, he travelled to Mexico in 1913 and mysteriously disappeared, it is thought in the fighting of the Mexican Civil War.

Big Brother, in Orwell's *Nineteen Eighty-four*, is the head of the Party, who never appears in person, but whose dominating portrait in every public place, with the caption 'Big Brother is watching you', is inescapable.

Bildungsroman, the term applied to novels of 'education' (in the widest sense), of which many of the best examples are German. *Wieland's *Agathon* (1765–6) is usually thought of as the first example of the genre, but the best and most imitated was *Goethe's *Wilhelm Meisters Lehrjahre* (*Wilhelm Meister's Apprenticeship*, 1795–6), which became celebrated in England through *Carlyle's translation in 1824. Wilhelm provides the model of the innocent, inexperienced, well-meaning, but often foolish and erring, young man who sets out in life with either no aim in mind or the wrong one. By a series of false starts and mistakes and with help from well-disposed friends he makes in the course of his experiences, he finally reaches maturity and finds his proper profession. T. *Mann was Goethe's most distinguished successor with his philosophical novel *Der Zauberberg* (*The Magic Mountain*, 1924). The genre overlaps with the older type of the *picaresque novel, but is more philosophical. The German term *Bildungsroman* has been adopted in English criticism as a result of the fame during the 19th cent. of *Wilhelm Meister* and Carlyle's semi-fictional *Sartor Resartus* (1833–4).

Billickin, Mrs, in Dickens's *Edwin Drood*, a cousin of Mr Bazzard, who lets lodgings in Bloomsbury.

BILLINGS, Josh, see SHAW, H. W.

Billingsgate, the name of one of the gates of London on the river side, and hence of the fish market established there until Jan. 1982, when it was moved three miles down-river to the Isle of Dogs. It is perhaps derived from a personal name, Billing (cf. Billingshurst), and according to fable from Belinus, a legendary British king. There are frequent references in 17th-cent. literature to the abusive language of the Billingsgate market; hence foul language is itself called 'billingsgate'.

Billy Budd, Foretopman (written 1891, published 1924), a novella by H. *Melville, a symbolic tale built out of Melville's egalitarian meditations on the mutiny at Spithead in 1797 and a family story of how Melville's older brother presided over the court martial and execution of an insubordinate sailor.

Billy, 'the handsome sailor', wrongly accused by the satanic master-at-arms Claggart and unable to defend himself verbally because of a stammer, strikes Claggart dead. After being tried by the liberal Captain Vere, Billy is hanged, his last words being 'God bless Captain Vere!' Then, in apparently Christ-like apotheosis, 'the East was shot through with a soft glory as of the fleece of the Lamb of God', and the sailors question whether Billy has actually died. *Britten's setting of *Billy Budd* (1951) has become one of the most admired operas in the modern repertoire.

Billy Liar, see WATERHOUSE, K.

BINGHAM, Joseph (1668–1723), fellow of University College, Oxford. He withdrew from the university, being unjustly charged with preaching heretical doctrine, and became rector of Headbourne Worthy, near Winchester, where he wrote *Origines Ecclesiasticae, or the Antiquities of the Christian Church* (1709–22), a very learned work which long retained its authoritative character.

Bingley, Charles, and his sister, Caroline, characters in J. Austen's *Pride and Prejudice*.

Binks, Sir Bingo and Lady, characters in Scott's *St Ronan's Well*.

Binnorie, or *The Twa Sisters*, an old ballad, possibly of Scandinavian origin, in *Child's collection. Two sisters are in love with the same knight; the older drowns the younger, whose body drifts downstream to the mill. A harper makes a harp from her breastbone, strung with her hair, and when he visits her father's hall it sings in reproach 'Woe to my sister, false Helen!'

BINYON, (Robert) Laurence (1869–1945), educated at St Paul's and Trinity College, Oxford; he entered the British Museum where in 1909 he became assistant keeper in the department of prints and drawings. He published many works on art, chiefly English and oriental, *Painting in the Far East* (1908) being one of the best known. His dramas included *Attila* (1907) and *Arthur* (1923), the latter with music by *Elgar. His war poems include his much anthologized 'For the Fallen' ('. . . They shall grow not old, as we that are left grow old . . .'); two long odes, *The Sirens* (1924) and *The Idols* (1928), received much acclaim among traditionalists. The *Collected Poems* appeared in 1931, as did *Landscape in English Art and Poetry*. His last volume of verse, *The Burning of the Leaves*, was published posthumously in 1944, and *The Madness of Merlin*, the unfinished first part of a lengthy projected verse-drama, in 1947.

Biographia Literaria, a work of philosophical autobiography and Romantic literary criticism, by S. T. *Coleridge, published 1817.

Originally conceived in 1814 as a short explanatory Preface to the *Sibylline Leaves*, it rapidly expanded into a two-volume apologia for his 'literary life and opinions'. Part I is broadly autobiographical, describing Coleridge's friendship with *Southey and with the *Wordsworths at Stowey, and going on to trace his struggle with the 'dynamic philosophy' of *Kant, *Fichte, and *Schelling in Germany. The humorous narrative is gradually overwhelmed by Romantic metaphysics; ch. XIII contains his famous distinction between Fancy and Imagination. Part II is almost entirely critical, attacking Wordsworth's Preface to the *Lyrical Ballads* and then marvellously vindicating the poetry itself. Coleridge concentrates on the psychology of the creative process, and propounds

new theories of the origins of poetic language, metre, and form, as the interpenetration of 'passion and will' (ch. XV–XVIII). Other chapters discuss the poetry of Shakespeare, *Milton, *Daniel, G. *Herbert, etc., as exemplary of true 'Imagination' and the 'language of real life'. Though maddeningly unsystematic in structure, the book is a touchstone of Romantic criticism; it also gives some impression of Coleridge in full conversational flight.

Biography. The earliest biographies in England were written in Latin in the Middle Ages, largely to glorify saints or to commemorate and justify secular rulers, though some were enlivened by personal anecdotes. The Renaissance emphasis on man as an individual introduced a new approach, and the first biography in English, More's *The History of King *Richard the Thirde*, written about 1513, is denigratory rather than laudatory and was possibly intended as a warning to Henry VIII to avoid tyranny. It used more human detail and more first-hand information, quoted contemporary witnesses, and brought minor characters to life. Its dramatic quality served Shakespeare who used it as a source. The classic biographies of the mid-Tudor period are W. *Roper's life of *More, his father-in-law (Paris, 1626), and G. *Cavendish's life of Cardinal Wolsey, printed 1641 but previously circulated in manuscript; both had personal knowledge of their subjects, but confessed to a lack of it where necessary, thus striking a new and intimate note. The translation of *Plutarch's *Parallel Lives* (1st cent. AD) by Sir T. *North in 1579 was widely read, and had considerable influence, not only on Shakespeare, whose debt is well known. I. *Walton's lives of *Donne (1641), Sir Henry *Wotton (1651), Richard *Hooker (1665), George *Herbert (1670), and Bishop Sanderson (1678) show the biographer at work as a conscious artist, and *Aubrey's *Brief Lives* displays a passion for first-hand information and an interest in everyday details about the obscure as well as the famous. *Clarendon included valuable biographical portraits in his *History of the Rebellion and Civil Wars* (written between 1646 and 1670, published 1702–4). (His autobiography is written in the third person.) This period also produced the first two biographies by women: Lucy *Hutchinson and Margaret Cavendish, duchess of *Newcastle, both wrote lives of their husbands. But it was in the 18th cent. that the writing of biography came of age. The great masterpiece is Boswell's *The Life of Samuel *Johnson* (1791), celebrated for its intimacy, scholarly thoroughness, vividness, and dramatic artistry, but *Johnson himself was also a biographer, and his *Lives of the English Poets* (1779–81) is a classic work. His *Life of Mr Richard Savage*, previously published in 1744, is notable in that it is perhaps the first full life of a very unsuccessful man. The

19th cent. produced many biographies, but their authors were inhibited by a growing stress on 'seriousness' and respectability, with the result that few works approach the frankness of Boswell and Johnson, and most are written in a spirit of piety in order to improve rather than to inform or entertain: the moral purpose of *Smiles's *Lives of the Engineers* (1861–2), for example, is readily apparent. A distinguished exception is Mrs *Gaskell's biography of her friend Charlotte *Brontë (1857), which has been much admired as an honest and sensitive appreciation, and which involved its author in some scandal despite her efforts to abide by Victorian standards of reticence. Even more exceptional for its age was *Froude's life of *Carlyle, the frankness of which caused uproar. Biographers on the whole remained timidly unwilling to risk such opprobrium until *Strachey's *Eminent Victorians* (1918), by attacking Victorianism itself through its great institutions (the Church, the Public School, the Empire), revealed the worldliness, hypocrisy, and human oddity behind the public façade and ushered in a new age of free enquiry. The way was paved for the psychological, analytical (and, some would argue, reductive) approach of Strachey's many imitators and successors. The last decades have witnessed what has been described as the Golden Age of biography; *Shelley's biographer, Richard Holmes, has detected what he describes as 'the rise to power of a new literary genre', a view endorsed by R. *Gittings, biographer of *Keats and *Hardy, in his *The Nature of Biography* (1978). Classics of the new genre, which combine high scholarly standards with imaginative insight and narrative skill, include, notably, R. *Ellman's *Joyce (1959), George Painter's *Proust (2 vols, 1959, 1965), Leon Edel's Henry *James (3 vols, 1953–1962), and M. *Holroyd's Lytton Strachey (2 vols, 1967–8). Rapidly changing attitudes to revelation and discretion have greatly stimulated interest in the form (which has in itself contributed to the changing of attitudes); the publication of Nigel Nicolson's startlingly frank *Portrait of a Marriage* (see under SACKVILLE-WEST, V.) has been regarded as yet another landmark in biographical approach. (For psychobiography see ERIKSON.)

BION (*c.*100 BC), a Greek pastoral poet who is reputed to have been born in Smyrna and to have died prematurely in Sicily. His best-known work is a lament for Adonis, which was imitated by *Ronsard and other continental poets and of which echoes can be found in Shakespeare's *Venus and Adonis*, in *Lodge, and in Abraham Fraunce. Keats's *Hyperion* is indebted to its picture of Adonis, and it served as one of Shelley's models for *Adonais*. Later *Bridges' *Achilles in Scyros* took some of its detail from Bion's idyll.

Birds of America, The, (1) an ornithological

work by J. J. *Audubon; (2) the title of a novel by M. *McCarthy.

Birnam Wood, see MACBETH.

Biron, see BEROWNE.

BIRRELL, Augustine (1850–1933), chief secretary for Ireland, 1907–16, made his name as an author with a volume of lightweight essays, *Obiter Dicta* (1884), which he followed with other essays and works on *Hazlitt (1902), *Marvell (1905), and others. His son, Francis Birrell (1889–1935), journalist and dramatic critic, was associated with the *Bloomsbury Group.

Birthday Party, The, see PINTER, H.

BISHOP, Elizabeth (1911–79), American poet, born in Massachusetts, and brought up by her maternal grandparents in Nova Scotia after the death of her father and collapse of her mother. She was educated at Vassar, where in 1934 she met Marianne *Moore, with whose work her own has much affinity. She later travelled widely, finally settling in Brazil; the titles of some of her volumes (*North and South*, 1946; *Questions of Travel*, 1965; *Geography III*, 1976) reflect her preoccupation with place and movement, and her verse is reticent, objective, spare yet colloquial. Her *Complete Poems 1927–1979* appeared in 1983.

BISHOP, Sir Henry Rowley (1786–1855), English composer. At a rather poverty-stricken moment in English musical history, Bishop was highly regarded as a composer, particularly of songs and opera. The enormous list of his stage works, however, though it includes no less than eight pieces based on Sir W. *Scott (in every case served up for public consumption within a year of the first appearance of the novel), contains little or nothing that bears musical inspection today, and his name is remembered almost entirely for the song 'Home, Sweet Home'. The tune originally appeared as a 'Sicilian Air' in a volume of (presumably not very authentic) *National Airs* edited by Bishop in 1821, and was then re-used by its composer as the theme song of the opera *Clari* (1823), with words by J. H. *Payne.

BISHOP, John Peale (1892–1944), American poet and story writer, educated at Princeton with E. *Wilson and F. S. *Fitzgerald. His *Collected Essays* and *Collected Poems* were published in 1948.

'Bishop Blougram's Apology', a poem by R. Browning, included in *Men and Women*.

BIZET, Georges (1838–75), French composer. *La Jolie Fille de Perth*, very remotely based on Sir W. *Scott, was the fifth of seven completed operas by the composer of *Carmen*. The libretto was probably the worst Bizet ever set, but the press reviews after the first performance in 1867 were the best for any of his operas. The opera has not had much success since. Among Bizet's many unfinished operatic projects was a *Clarissa Harlowe*, after *Richardson, on which he was known to be working between 1870 and 1871, but the surviving sketches are fragmentary and there is no libretto.

BLACK, William (1841–98), Scottish novelist, an early member of the *'Kailyard School', whose first triumph was *A Daughter of Heth* (1871) followed by *The Strange Adventures of a Phaeton* (1872), *A Princess of Thule* (1873), *Madcap Violet* (1876), and *Macleod of Dare* (1879). He continued to write prolifically but without his earlier success.

Blackacre, The Widow, a character in Wycherley's *The Plain Dealer.*

Black Beauty, see SEWELL, A.; also CHILDREN'S LITERATURE.

Black Book of Carmarthen, The, a Welsh manuscript of the 12th cent., containing a collection of ancient Welsh poetry, interesting among other things for references to King *Arthur.

Black Book of the Admiralty, an ancient code of rules for the government of the navy, said to have been compiled in the reign of Edward III.

Black British Literature, a term applied to literature produced by black British writers, who are frequently held to include not only writers of Afro-Caribbean descent, but also people of Asian and other non-white, non-Anglo-Saxon origins.

The earliest black British writers belong to the 18th cent. *The Letters of the Late Ignatius Sancho* (1782, ed. P. Edwards, 1968) were published two years after his death; his correspondence with *Garrick and *Sterne shows his awareness of political issues and his love of family, and his contribution to the debate about slavery and the status of the African made his letters widely popular. Ottobah Cugoano's autobiographical *Thoughts and Sentiments* (1787) has anti-slavery passages which may be the work of another hand, or, more probably, be largely dependent on secondary material. *The Interesting Narrative of the Life of Olanudah Equiano* (1789) is considered the most literary achievement of the three, and went through eight English editions and one American by 1794.

Sake Deen Mahomed's *Travels* (Cork, 1794) depicts his life in India before his arrival in the British Isles in 1784, and his life thereafter; he eloped with a Cork girl and eventually settled in Brighton where he founded his famous medicated baths. These became very popular, and drew visitors from the Continent.

Mary Seacole's *Adventures* (1857; republished in 1984 as *Wonderful Adventures of Mrs Seacole in many lands*, ed. Z. Alexander and A. Dewjee) include an account of her early life in Jamaica and of her brave and voluntary service to Britain during the Crimean War, which earned her mentions in journalistic and military despatches. They reveal her as a strongly independent person, willing and able to confront the racism of her times.

Black British writing has flourished in the second half of the 20th cent. in a wide variety of traditional and experimental forms. Writers include Nirad C. Chaudhuri (1897–   ), Bengali author and journalist, perhaps best known for *The Autobiography of an Unknown Indian* (1951); British Guiana-born novelists E. A. Mittelholzer (1909–65), R. A. K. Heath (1926–   ), and W. *Harris; George *Lamming; V. S. *Naipaul and his novelist brother Shiva Naipaul (1945–   ); novelist Samuel Selvon (1923–   ) from Trinidad; novelists K. *Markandaya and Salman Rushdie (1947–   ), both born in India; playwrights Michael Abbensetts (1938–   ), born in British Guiana, and Mustapha Matura (1939–   ) from Trinidad; Nigerian-born novelist Buchi Emecheta (1944–   ); and West Indian-born poets J. *Berry, E. A. Markham (1939–   ), and Linton Kwesi Johnson (1952–   ).

Black Douglas, see DOUGLAS THE BLACK.

Black Dwarf, The, a novel by Sir W. *Scott, in *Tales of My Landlord, 1st series, published 1816.

The title character is a dwarf of extraordinary ugliness and strength who settles in a lonely spot in southern Scotland at the beginning of the 18th cent., builds himself a hovel of mighty stones, and acquires a reputation for supernatural powers. He is called Elshender the Recluse, or Elshie of the Mucklestanes, and his acrimonious speech suggests an excessively misanthropical disposition. Yet the story, of which the plot is slender, tells of his beneficent influence on events in his neighbourhood. A robber carries off Grace Armstrong, to the distress of her lover, the young farmer Hobbie Elliot, but she is immediately restored on the dwarf's intervention. He prevents the marriage of Isabella Vere with Sir Frederick Langley, to which her unwilling consent has been wrung by her father, the laird of Ellieslaw, for his own ends. It turns out that the dwarf is the rich Sir Edward Manley, the near kinsman of Isabella, a man embittered by his deformity and by his unhappy love for Isabella's mother; he has long been supposed dead and Ellieslaw is deeply indebted to him.

Blackfriars Theatre was built within the boundaries of the old Dominican monastery lying between Ludgate Hill and the river. The first theatre on the site was adapted for performances by Richard Farrant, master of the Children of Windsor Chapel in 1576; the second, in a different part of the old building, was bought and adapted by J. *Burbage in 1597, but was handed over to the Children of the Chapel because of local opposition. It reverted to James's son R. *Burbage in 1608. Shakespeare had a share in the new company that performed there. The building was demolished in 1655.

BLACKLOCK, Thomas (1721–91), 'the blind bard', was born in Dumfriesshire, the son of a bricklayer, and lost his sight when six months old. He published his first volume of poems in 1746, republished with an account by J. *Spence in 1754. He was befriended by *Hume, and in turn wrote in praise of *Burns, whom he received with kindness in Edinburgh. His poetry was, Dr *Johnson pointed out, largely derivative. There is an account of his meeting with Johnson in Boswell's *Journal of a Tour to the Hebrides. His collected poems with a life by H. *Mackenzie appeared in 1793.

BLACKMORE, Sir Richard (1654–1729), physician to Queen Anne, produced some indifferent poems of great length, heroic and epic, and Creation: a philosophical poem (1712) which was warmly praised by Dr *Johnson. He was one of the few poets added to *Lives of the English Poets by Johnson's own choice. Pope in *The Dunciad mocked his 'sonorous strain'.

BLACKMORE, R(ichard) D(oddridge) (1825–1900), son of a clergyman, was educated at Blundell's School, Tiverton, and at Exeter College, Oxford. He was called to the bar, but his occasional epileptic fits forced him to take up a country life, first as a schoolmaster, then as a fruit-grower at Teddington, where he lived till his death. His marriage to an Irishwoman, Lucy Maguire, though childless, was happy. He published several volumes of poems and translations from *Theocritus and *Virgil, but his fame rests almost entirely on one of his novels, *Lorna Doone (1869). He wrote 13 other novels, including Cradock Nowell (1866), The Maid of Sker (1872), Alice Lorraine (1875), and Springhaven (1887). These pastoral tales, stirring in incident and with a slightly grotesque humour, are often ill-constructed and prolix, and sometimes over-lush in style, but their great excellence is the intricacy of their descriptions of lovingly-observed climate, wild-life, and vegetation. Blackmore was a sincere and kindly but reserved and eccentric man, absorbed in his experimental fruit-farming. See Waldo H. Dunn, R. D. Blackmore, The Author of 'Lorna Doone', (1956); Kenneth Budd, The Last Victorian: R. D. Blackmore and His Novels, (1960).

Black Mountain Poets, a group of poets associated with Black Mountain College, an experimental liberal arts college founded in 1933 near Asheville, NC, which became in the early 1950s a centre of anti-academic poetic revolt. A leading figure was Charles Olson (1910–70), rector of the college from 1951 to 1956, whose Projective Verse (1950) was a form of manifesto, laying much emphasis on the dynamic energy of the spoken word and phrase and attacking the domination of syntax, rhyme, and metre. His students and followers included R. *Creeley, Robert Duncan (1919–), and Denise Levertov (1923–). The Black Mountain Review (1954–7; edited by Creeley) also published work by *Ginsberg and *Kerouac, thus heralding the *Beat Generation.

BLACKMUR, R(ichard) P(almer) (1904–65), American poet and critic, associated for many years with Princeton, where he was professor from 1948 to 1965. His critical works, which include The Expense of Greatness (1940), Language as Gesture (1952), and The Lion and the Honeycomb (1955), link him with the *New Criticism; he was one of the early champions of the art of W. *Stevens.

Blackpool, Stephen, a character in Dickens's *Hard Times.

Black Prince, The (1330–76), a name given (apparently by 16th-cent. chroniclers) to Edward, the eldest son of Edward III and father of Richard II. The origin of the title is unknown; it has been conjectured that it may have been because of the fear he inspired in battle (as at Poitiers in 1356) or because of his wearing black armour. His death led to a return to the domination of the English Court by *John of Gaunt, opposition to whom had been led by the Black Prince. See R. Barber, Edward, Prince of Wales and Aquitaine: a Biography of the Black Prince (1978).

BLACKSTONE, Sir William (1723–80), became the first Vinerian professor of English law at Oxford in 1758 and lectured there until 1766; his annual lectures became the basis of his Commentaries on the Laws of England (4 vols, 1765–9) which exerted a powerful influence, remained for many years the best historical account of English law, and is still regarded as a classic. It was criticized by *Bentham in his A Fragment on Government (1776) for its acceptance of the existing state of the law.

BLACKWOOD, Algernon (1869–1951), led an adventurous early life and when almost starving found work in journalism in New York—a period described in Episodes before Thirty (1923). His work included travel, adventure, humour, and some work of a semi-mystical nature, but the stories for which he is chiefly remembered deal in the psychic and macabre. The Empty House and other Ghost Stories appeared in 1906, at which time he was greatly encouraged by *Belloc. More than 30 books followed, culminating in *Tales of the Uncanny and Supernatural* (1949).

BLACKWOOD, William (1776–1834), Scots publisher, founder of the firm of William Blackwood and Son, and of the highly successful *Blackwood's (Edinburgh) Magazine* in the conduct of which he took a decided interest. He early recognized the talent of *Galt, whose *The Ayreshire Legatees* he published, and of S. *Ferrier. In 1810 he bought the *Edinburgh Encyclopaedia*, which he saw finally completed in 1830. His sons, in turn, became editors of *Blackwood's*; his son John (1818–79) was an admirer of G. *Eliot, published much of her work, and became a friend.

Blackwood's Magazine (1817–1980), or 'the Maga', was an innovating monthly periodical begun by W. *Blackwood as a Tory rival to the Whiggish *Edinburgh Review*. It began in April 1817 as *The Edinburgh Monthly Magazine* and in October that year continued as *Blackwood's Edinburgh Magazine* until Dec. 1905; from Jan. 1906 onwards it became *Blackwood's Magazine*. Although its politics were the same as those of the *Quarterly Review*, it was intended to be sharper, brighter, and less ponderous. The first editors were shortly replaced by *Lockhart, John *Wilson, and J. *Hogg, who gave the 'Maga' its forceful partisan tone. Its notoriety was early established with the publication in 1817 of the so-called *Chaldee MS, in which many leading Edinburgh figures were pilloried; and with the beginning, also in 1817, of the long series of attacks on the *'Cockney School of Poetry', directed chiefly against Leigh *Hunt, *Keats, and *Hazlitt. Blackwood had to pay damages more than once, notably to Hazlitt, for the venom of his writers' pens, and John *Murray gave up the London agency for the magazine in protest. *Blackwood's* did however give considerable support to *Wordsworth, *Shelley, *De Quincey, *Mackenzie, *Galt, Sir W. *Scott, and others, and did much to foster an interest in German literature. Unlike the *Edinburgh* and the *Quarterly* it published short stories and serialized novels. The *Noctes Ambrosianae*, though of ephemeral interest, was a highly popular series of sketches. Soon after 1830 the magazine became a purely literary review, and continued through the 19th cent. as a prosperous and respected literary miscellany, publishing *Conrad, *Noyes, *Lang, and many others. It continued, in a diminished form, until 1980.

BLAIR, Eric, see ORWELL, G.

BLAIR, Hugh (1718–1800), Scottish divine and professor of rhetoric in Edinburgh, is remembered for his famous sermons (5 vols, 1777–1801) and for his influential and often reprinted *Lectures on Rhetoric and Belles Lettres* (2 vols, 1784). He belonged to a distinguished literary circle which included *Hume, *Carlyle, Adam *Smith, and W. *Robertson. He was a warm defender of *Macpherson; his *A Critical Dissertation on the Poems of Ossian* (1763) found that *Fingal* possessed 'all the essential requisites of a true and regular epic'.

BLAIR, Robert (1699–1746), educated at Edinburgh and in Holland, was ordained minister of Athelstaneford in 1731. He published in 1743 *The Grave*, a didactic poem of the *graveyard school, consisting of some 800 lines of blank verse. It celebrates the horrors of death ('In that dread moment, how the frantic soul |Raves round the walls of her clay tenement'), the solitude of the tomb, the pains of bereavement, the madness of suicide, etc., ending more perfunctorily with thoughts of the Resurrection. It has passages of considerable power and, like Young's *Night Thoughts*, was illustrated by *Blake.

Blaise (Blays) dwelt in Northumberland and was the master of Merlin, according to *Malory and *Tennyson.

BLAKE, William (1757–1827), the third son of a London hosier, did not go to school, but was apprenticed to James Basire, engraver to the Society of *Antiquaries, and then became a student at the *Royal Academy. From 1779 he was employed as an engraver by the bookseller J. *Johnson, and in 1780 met *Fuseli and *Flaxman, the latter a follower of *Swedenborg, whose mysticism deeply influenced Blake. In 1782 he married Catherine Boucher, the daughter of a market-gardener; their marriage, although childless, was a lasting communion. Flaxman at this period introduced him to the progressive intellectual circle of the Revd A. S. Mathew and his wife (which included Mrs *Barbauld, H. *More, and Mrs E. *Montagu), and Mathew and Flaxman financed the publication of Blake's first volume, *Poetical Sketches* (1783). In 1784, with help from Mrs Mathew, he set up a print shop at 27 Broad Street, and at about the same period (although not for publication) wrote the satirical *An Island in the Moon*. He engraved and published his *Songs of Innocence* in 1789, and also *The Book of Thel*, both works which manifest the early phases of his highly distinctive mystic vision, and in which he embarks on the evolution of his personal mythology; years later (in *Jerusalem*) he was to state, through the character Los, 'I must Create a System, or be enslav'd by another Man's', words which have been taken by some to apply to his own need to escape from the fetters of 18th-cent. versification, as well as from the materialist philosophy (as he conceived it) of the *Enlightenment, and a Puritanical or repressive interpretation of Christianity. *The Book of Thel* presents the maiden Thel lamenting transience and mutability by the banks of the river of Adona; she is answered by the lily, the cloud, the worm, and the clod who assure her that 'He, who loves the lowly' cherishes even the meanest; but this relatively conventional wisdom is challenged by a final section in which Thel visits the house of Clay, sees the couches of the dead, and hears 'a voice of sorrow' breathe a characteristically Blakean protest against hypocrisy and restraint—'Why a tender curb upon the youthful, burning boy? Why a tender little curtain of flesh upon the bed of our desire?'—a message which sends Thel back 'with a shriek' to the vales of Har. The ambiguity of this much-interpreted poem heralds the increasing complexity of his other works which include *Tiriel* (written 1789, pub. 1874), which introduces the theme of the blind tyrannic father, 'the king of rotten wood, and of the bones of death', which reappears in different forms in many poems; *The Marriage of Heaven and Hell* (engraved c.1790–3), his principal prose work, a book of paradoxical aphorisms; and the revolutionary works *The French Revolution* (1791); *America: A Prophecy* (1793); and *Visions of the Daughters of Albion* (1793), in which he develops his attitude of revolt against authority, combining political fervour (he had met *Paine at Johnson's) and visionary ecstasy; Urizen, the deviser of moral codes (described as 'the stony law' of the Decalogue) and *Orc, the Promethean arch-rebel, emerge as principal characters in a cosmology that some scholars have related to that of *Gnosticism. By this time Blake had already established his poetic range; the long, flowing lines and violent energy of the verse combine with phrases of terse and aphoristic clarity and moments of great lyric tenderness, and he was once more to demonstrate his command of the lyric in *Songs of Experience* (1794) which includes 'Tyger! Tyger! burning bright', 'O Rose thou art sick', and other of his more accessible pieces.

Meanwhile the Blakes had moved to Lambeth in 1790; there he continued to engrave his own works and to write, evolving his mythology further in *The Book of *Urizen* (1794); *Europe, A Prophecy* (1794); *The Song of *Los* (1795); *The Book of Ahania* (1795); *The Book of Los* (1795); and *The Four Zoas* (originally entitled *Vala*, written and revised 1797–1804), and also working for the booksellers. In 1800 he moved to Felpham, Sussex, where he lived for three years, working for his friend and patron *Hayley, and working on *Milton* (1804–8); in 1803 he was charged at Chichester with high treason for having 'uttered seditious and treasonable expressions, such as "D-n the King, d-n all his subjects . . . " ', but was acquitted. In the same year he returned to London, to work on *Milton* and *Jerusalem: the Emanation of the Giant Albion* (written and etched, 1804–20). In 1805 he was commissioned by *Cromek to produce a set of

drawings for R. *Blair's poem *The Grave*, but Cromek defaulted on the contract, and Blake earned neither the money nor the public esteem he had hoped for, and found his designs engraved and weakened by another hand. This was symptomatic of the disappointment of his later years, when he appears to have relinquished expectations of being widely understood, and quarrelled even with some of the circle of friends who supported him. Both his poetry and his art had failed to find a sympathetic audience, and a lifetime of hard work had not brought him riches or even much comfort. His last years were passed in obscurity, although he continued to attract the interest and admiration of younger artists, and a commission in 1821 from the painter John Linnell produced his well known illustrations for the Book of Job, published in 1826. A later poem, 'The Everlasting Gospel', written about 1818, shows undiminished power and attack; it presents Blake's own version of Jesus, in a manner that recalls the paradoxes of *The Marriage of Heaven and Hell*, attacking the conventional 'Creeping Jesus', gentle, humble, and chaste, and stressing his rebellious nature, his forgiveness of the woman taken in adultery, his reversing of the stony law of Moses, praising 'the Naked Human form divine', and sexuality as the means whereby 'the Soul Expands its wing', and elevating forgiveness above the 'Moral Virtues'.

At Blake's death, general opinion held that he had been, if gifted, insane; *Wordsworth's verdict, according to C. *Robinson, was that 'There was no doubt that this poor man was mad, but there is something in the madness of this man which interests me more than the sanity of Lord Byron and Walter Scott', a view in some measure echoed by *Ruskin, who found his manner 'diseased and wild' but his mind 'great and wise'. It was not until A. *Gilchrist's biography of 1863 (significantly describing Blake as 'Pictor Ignotus') that interest began to grow. This was followed by an appreciation by *Swinburne (1868) and by W. M. *Rossetti's edition of 1874, which added new poems to the canon and established his reputation, at least as a lyric poet; his rediscovered engravings considerably influenced the development of *Art Nouveau. In 1893 *Yeats, a devoted admirer, produced with E. J. Ellis a three-vol. edition, with a memoir and an interpretation of the mythology, and the 20th cent. has seen an enormous increase in interest. The bibliographical studies and editions of G. *Keynes, culminating in *The Complete Writings of William Blake* (1966, 2nd edn), have added greatly to knowledge both of the man and his works, revealing him not only as an apocalyptic visionary but also as a writer of ribald and witty epigrams, a critic of spirit and originality, and an independent thinker who found his own way of resisting the orthodoxies of his age, and whose hostile response to the narrow vision and materialism (as he conceived it) of his *bêtes noires* Joshua *Reynolds, *Locke, and I. *Newton was far from demented, but in part a prophetic warning of the dangers of a world perceived as mechanism, with man as a mere cog in an industrial revolution. There have been many interpretative studies, relating his work to traditional Christianity, to the *Neoplatonic and Swedenborgian traditions, to Jungian *archetypes and to *Freudian and *Marxist theory; the Prophetic Books, once dismissed as incoherent, are now claimed by many as works of integrity as well as profundity. Recently, Blake has had a particularly marked influence on the *Beat generation and the English poets of the *Underground movement, hailed by both as liberator; *Auden earlier acclaimed him ('New Year Letter', 1941) as 'Self-educated Blake . . . ' who 'Spoke to Isaiah in the Strand | And heard inside each mortal thing | Its holy emanation sing'.

See also *The Life of William Blake* by Mona Wilson (1927, ed. G. Keynes, 1971) and *Blake Books* (1977) by G. E. Bentley Jnr., including annotated catalogues of his writings and scholarly works about him.

Blandamour, in Spenser's *Faerie Queene*, Bk. IV, a 'jollie youthfull knight', 'His fickle mind full of inconstancie', who consorts with *Paridell and *Duessa.

Blank Verse, verse without rhyme, especially the iambic pentameter of unrhymed heroic, the regular measure of English and dramatic and epic poetry, first used by *Surrey *c.*1540.

Blarney, a village near Cork. In the castle of Blarney there is an inscribed stone in a position difficult of access. The popular saying is that any one who kisses the 'Blarney stone' will ever after have 'a cajoling tongue and the art of flattery or of telling lies with unblushing effrontery' (Lewis, *Topographical Dictionary of Ireland,* quoted in *OED*).

Blast, see VORTICISM.

Blatant Beast, in Spenser's *Faerie Queene*, Bk. VI, a monster, the personification of the calumnious voice of the world, begotten of Envy and Detraction. Sir *Calidore pursues it, finds it despoiling monasteries and defiling the Church, overcomes it and chains it up. But finally it breaks the chain, 'So now he raungeth through the world againe.' Cf. QUESTING BEAST.

BLATCHFORD, Robert Peel Glanville (1851–1943), journalist and socialist, and son of a touring actor and actress; he wrote for the Manchester *Sunday Chronicle,* was one of the founders of the Manchester Fabian Society in 1890, and in 1891 left the *Sunday Chronicle* with four colleagues to start a socialist weekly,

The Clarion, in which appeared his series of articles, *Merrie England;* these appeared as a book in 1893, sold enormously, and made many converts to the cause of Socialism. His autobiography, *My Eighty Years,* appeared in 1931.

Blattergowl, Mr, in Scott's *The Antiquary,* the minister of Trotcosey and a neighbour of Mr Oldbuck.

BLAVATSKY, Madame Helena Petrovna (1831–91), a Russian whose adventurous career took her to Mexico, Europe, India, and Tibet. She became interested in spiritualism in New York in 1873, and in 1875 founded, with Col. H. S. Olcott and W. Q. Judge, the Theosophical Society, which she and Olcott re-established in India in 1879. It aimed to promote universal brotherhood, the study of Eastern literature and religion, and research into the unfamiliar laws of nature and the latent faculties of man. Despite widespread scepticism about her powers, she had many followers, including A. *Besant, and *Yeats in an account of his visits to her in London described her as 'a great passionate nature, a sort of female Dr Johnson' (*The Trembling of the Veil,* 1926). See SOCIETY FOR PSYCHICAL RESEARCH.

Bleak House, a novel by *Dickens, published in monthly parts 1852–3.

The book contains a vigorous satire on the abuses of the old court of Chancery, the delays and costs of which brought misery and ruin on its suitors. The tale centres in the fortunes of an uninteresting couple, Richard Carstone, a futile youth, and his amiable cousin Ada Clare. They are wards of the court in the case of Jarndyce and Jarndyce, concerned with the distribution of an estate, which has gone on so long as to become a subject of heartless joking as well as a source of great profit to those professionally engaged in it. The wards are taken to live with their kind elderly relative John Jarndyce. They fall in love and secretly marry. The weak Richard, incapable of sticking to any profession and lured by the will-o'-the-wisp of the fortune that is to be his when the case is settled, sinks gradually to ruin and death, and the case of Jarndyce and Jarndyce comes suddenly to an end on the discovery that the costs have absorbed the whole estate in dispute.

When Ada goes to live with John Jarndyce she is accompanied by Esther Summerson, a supposed orphan, one of Dickens's saints, and the narrative is partly supposed to be from her pen.

Sir Leicester Dedlock, a pompous old baronet, is devotedly attached to his beautiful wife. Lady Dedlock hides a dreadful secret under her haughty and indifferent exterior. Before her marriage she has loved a certain Captain Hawdon and has become the mother of a daughter, whom she believes dead. Hawdon is supposed to have perished at sea. In fact the daughter lives in the person of Esther Summerson, and

Hawdon in that of a penniless scrivener. The accidental sight of his handwriting in a legal document reveals to Lady Dedlock the fact of his existence, and its effect on her alerts the cunning old lawyer Tulkinghorn to the existence of a mystery. Lady Dedlock's inquiries bring her, through the medium of a wretched crossing-sweeper, Jo, to the burial-ground where her former lover's miserable career has just ended. Jo's unguarded revelation of his singular experience with this veiled lady sets Tulkinghorn on the track, until he possesses all the facts and tells Lady Dedlock that he is going to expose her next day to her husband. That night Tulkinghorn is murdered. Bucket, the detective, presently reveals to the baronet what Tulkinghorn had discovered, and arrests a former French maid of Lady Dedlock, a violent woman, who has committed the murder. Lady Dedlock, learning that her husband knows her secret, flies from the house in despair, and is found dead near the grave of her lover, in spite of the efforts of her husband and Esther to save her.

Much of the story is occupied with Esther's devotion to John Jarndyce; her acceptance of his offer of marriage from a sense of duty and gratitude, though she loves a young doctor, Woodcourt; Jarndyce's discovery of the state of her heart; and his surrender of her to Woodcourt.

There are a host of interesting minor characters, among whom may be mentioned Harold Skimpole (drawn 'in the light externals of character' from Leigh *Hunt), who disguises his utter selfishness under an assumption of childish irresponsibility; Mrs Jellyby, who sacrifices her family to her selfish addiction to professional philanthropy; Jo, the crossing-sweeper, who is chivied by the police to his death; Chadband, the pious, eloquent humbug; Turveydrop, the model of deportment; Krook, the 'chancellor' of the rag and bone department, who dies of spontaneous combustion; Guppy, the lawyer's clerk; Guster, the poor slavey; the law-stationer Snagsby; Miss Flite, the little lunatic lady who haunts the Chancery courts; and Jarndyce's friend, the irascible and generous Boythorn (drawn from W. S. *Landor).

For many of Dickens's contemporaries, this novel marked a decline in his reputation; individual characters (notably Jo and Bucket) were praised, but it was charged with verbosity and 'absolute want of construction'. Later readers, including G. B. *Shaw, *Chesterton, *Conrad, and *Trilling, have seen it as one of the high points of his achievement, and the herald of his last great phase.

Blefuscu, in Swift's *Gulliver's Travels, an island separated from Lilliput by a narrow channel.

Blenheim, Battle of (1704), at which Marl-borough defeated the French and Bavarians, was celebrated in poems by *Addison (The Campaign, 1705) and *Southey. Southey's version ('The Battle of Blenheim', 1798) is a sharply anti-militaristic ballad in which old Kaspar describes Marlborough's victory to his grandchildren, Peterkin and Wilhelmine; in spite of the bloodshed and carnage of the battle, it was (he repeatedly and ironically assures them) 'a famous victory'.

'Blessed Damozel, The', a poem by D. G. *Rossetti, of which the first version appeared in *The Germ (1850); many revised versions appeared subsequently.

In this poem, heavily influenced by *Dante, Rossetti describes the blessed damozel leaning out from the ramparts of Heaven, watching the worlds below and the souls mounting to God, and praying for union with her earthly lover in the shadow of the 'living mystic tree'. One of his earliest and most influential poems, it shows the *Pre-Raphaelite interest in medieval sacramental symbolism (she has three lilies in her hand, seven stars in her hair, and a white rose in her robe) and Rossetti's concept of an ideal *Platonic love, which he was to develop in later works. He also painted the same subject in later years.

BLESSINGTON, Marguerite, countess of (1789–1849), travelled on the Continent with her husband and with *D'Orsay, with whom she ultimately lived. She published A Journal of Conversations with Lord Byron (1832), which records in lively detail her encounters with *Byron in Italy, and is of great importance in any consideration of Byron's life abroad. She also wrote The Idler in Italy (1839) and The Idler in France (1841), as well as a number of novels.

Blifil, Master, a character in Fielding's *Tom Jones.

Blimber, Dr, and his daughter Cornelia, characters in Dickens's *Dombey and Son.

Blind Beggar of Bethnal Green, The, see BEGGAR'S DAUGHTER OF BEDNALL GREEN, THE.

Blind Harry, see HENRY THE MINSTREL.

BLISS, Sir Arthur (1891–1975), English composer. During the years after the First World War Bliss became known as something of an enfant terrible with works like Madam Noy (1918), a 'witchery' with words by E. H. W. Meyerstein, and Rout (1920), which uses nonsense syllables in the vocal part, but later compositions reverted to a more romantic idiom in the tradition of *Elgar, for whose music he had a great admiration. His first substantial setting of literary texts was the Pastoral: Lie strewn the white flocks (1928), which brings together poems by *Jonson, J. *Fletcher, *Poliziano, W. *Owen, R. *Nichols, and *Theocritus; the same catholic literary taste reappeared in the choral symphony *Morning Heroes* (1930), where words by *Homer, *Whitman, Li-Tai-Po, Owen, and Nichols provided the framework for a deeply personal expression of the composer's attitude to war. This work makes effective use of an orator against an orchestral background. The anthological approach returns in later choral works, and there are choral settings of individual poets, including a G. M. *Hopkins cantata, *The world is charged with the grandeur of God* (1969), and three short settings of *Day-Lewis.

In 1934–5 Bliss worked in close collaboration with *Wells on the music for the film *Things to Come*—the best-known of several film scores that he produced during the next 20 years. Works for the stage include incidental music for *The Tempest* (1921), in which tenor and bass voices, piano, trumpet, trombone, gongs, and five percussion instruments were scattered around the theatre, and a full-scale opera, *The Olympians* (1949), with a libretto by J. B. *Priestley.

Blithedale Romance, The, a novel by *Hawthorne, published 1852, and based on Hawthorne's own residence in 1841 at the *Transcendental co-operative community at Brook Farm.

It is narrated by a poet, Miles Coverdale, who visits Blithedale Farm, near Boston, where he meets the exotic, wealthy, and queenly Zenobia (said to be based on Margaret *Fuller, although she is mentioned by name in the text, possibly to warn readers against the identification), the philanthropic, but self-engrossed, inhuman, and fierce, social reformer Hollingsworth, and the gentle, delicate girl Priscilla. Coverdale broods on *Fourier, *Carlyle, and *Emerson, while both the women (who turn out to be half-sisters) fall in love with Hollingsworth; Zenobia is rejected and drowns herself, Hollingsworth marries Priscilla, and Coverdale remains a sceptical, solitary observer of mankind's aspirations and its disappointments.

BLIXEN, Karen Christentze, *née* Dinesen (1885–1962), Danish writer, who wrote mainly in English, under the name of 'Isak Dinesen'. Born at Rungsted, Denmark, she rebelled against bourgeois Danish society, studied art in Copenhagen, Paris, and Rome, then married her cousin, Baron Bror Blixen-Finecke, in 1914. They ran a coffee plantation in Kenya, which she continued to manage after her divorce; the story of this failed enterprise is told in *Out of Africa* (1937), written after her return to Denmark in 1931. From childhood she had interested herself in writing, working on sketches for stories, writing plays, and eventually contributing to periodicals, but her first major publication was *Seven Gothic Tales* (1934), a stylish collection exhibiting aristocratic hauteur, a neo-

Gothic use of fantasy, the macabre, and the bizarre, and manifesting her admiration for *fin-de-siècle* French decadence. This was followed by several other collections, which won her a considerable international reputation. See Judith Thurman, *Isak Dinesen: The Life of a Storyteller* (1982).

BLOK, Aleksandr Aleksandrovich (1880–1921), Russian Symbolist poet, playwright, and critic. Born into an academic St Petersburg family, he was one of a number of young poets influenced by the philosopher Vladimir Solovyev, from whom Blok took the central theme of his early poetry ('The Verses about the Beautiful Lady', 1901–2), Sophia, the feminine personification of Divine Wisdom. In 1903 he married Lyubov Dmitrievna Mendeleeva, whom he in some degree identified with this cult, and in 1904 he met *Bely. Loss of faith in his ideal, the experience of urban life, and the disillusionment following the débâcle of the Russo-Japanese War and the failure of the 1905 Revolution are all reflected in the gloom and pessimism of his second period (1904–8). Major works of these years are the narrative poem *The Night Violet* (1906), the cycles *The City* (1904–8), *The Snow Mask* (1907), and *Faina* (1906–8), and a bitter play satirizing his former ideals, *The Puppet Show* (1906). Some of Blok's most powerful work is contained in the cycles of his third period (1907–21), the urban poetry of *The Terrible World* (1907–16), *The Italian Verses* (1909), *Carmen* (1914), resulting from his love affair with the opera singer Lyubov Aleksandrovna Delmas, and *Native Land* (1907–16), which contains his late poems on the theme of Russia. Blok greeted the Russian Revolution romantically, as an expression of cosmic upheaval, and wrote his famous poem 'The Twelve', which ends with the image of Christ leading a band of Red Guards, in Jan. 1918 (trans. C. Bechhofer, 1920). After the revolution he took part in various state literary activities, but ceased to write poetry. His *Selected Poems* (trans. Jon Stallworthy and Peter France) appeared in 1970.

BLONDEL DE NESLE, a French *trouvère who wrote in Picardy in the late 12th cent. and whose poems keep very close to the terminology and spirit of the troubadours. A famous legend makes him a friend of *Richard Coeur de Lion: Richard, on his return from the Holy Land in 1192, was imprisoned in Austria. Blondel set out to find him and, when he sat under a window of the castle where Richard was imprisoned, he sang a song in French that he and the king had composed together; half-way through he paused, and Richard took up the song and completed it. Blondel returned to England and told of the king's whereabouts.

BLOOD, Thomas (?1618–80), an adventurer

who, among other exploits, headed an unsuccessful attempt to take Dublin Castle from the Royalists in 1663, and tried to steal the crown jewels from the Tower in 1671. He figures in Scott's *Peveril of the Peak.

Bloody Brother, The, or Rollo, Duke of Normandy, a play by J. *Fletcher, B. *Jonson, G. *Chapman, and P. *Massinger, performed c.1616, published 1639. It was very popular in the 17th cent. An edition by J. D. Jump was published in 1969.

The duke of Normandy has bequeathed his dukedom to his two sons Rollo and Otto. Rollo, the elder, a resolute and violent man, in order to secure the whole heritage, kills his brother and orders the immediate execution of all who refuse to further his ends, including his old tutor Baldwin. The latter's daughter Edith pleads for his life, and her beauty captivates Rollo, but his reprieve comes too late. Edith determines to avenge her father's death, and prepares to kill Rollo when he comes to woo her. His apparent repentance shakes her determination. While she hesitates, the brother of another of Rollo's victims enters and kills the tyrant. The scene between Latorch, Rollo's favourite, and the Astrologers was probably written by Jonson, as also part of Act IV, sc. i.

It contains the lyric 'Take, oh take those lips away', which occurs with certain changes in *Measure for Measure.

Bloom, Leopold Paula, and his wife Molly, characters in Joyce's *Ulysses.

BLOOMFIELD, Leonard (1887–1949), an American linguist whose book Language (1933) was a major influence on the development of 'Structural Linguistics', putting forward the idea that the analysis appropriate to a particular language must be inferred from its own structure, not brought to bear on it from general linguistic principles. The approach of the book is behaviourist and empiricist, arguing that a speech act is fully explained by the human needs that cause it to be made (though this full explanation is often not available). This approach, characterized as 'Bloomfieldian', prevailed in some circles up to the 1950s; it was opposed by *Chomsky, though the origins of his analyses of grammar lie in Bloomfield's system.

BLOOMFIELD, Robert (1766–1823), born in Suffolk, worked as a farm labourer and then as a shoemaker in London, enduring extreme poverty and often unable to afford the paper on which to write. He is remembered chiefly as author of The Farmer's Boy (1800, ed. *Lofft), which was illustrated with engravings by *Bewick and which related the life of Giles, an orphan farm labourer, throughout the seasons. A vogue for tales of rustic life led to the immense sale of 26,000 copies in under three years, and

translations into Italian and French. Bloomfield wrote various other tales in verse between 1802 and 1811, but died in penury.

Bloomsbury Group, the name given to a group of friends who began to meet about 1905–6; its original centre was 46 Gordon Square, Bloomsbury, which became in 1904 the home of V. *Bell and V. *Woolf (both then unmarried). It was to include, amongst others, *Keynes, *Strachey, D. *Garnett, D. Grant, E. M. *Forster, and R. *Fry. This informal association, based on friendship and interest in the arts, derived many of its attitudes from G. E. *Moore's Principia Ethica; 'By far the most valuable things . . . are . . . the pleasures of human intercourse and the enjoyment of beautiful objects; . . . it is they . . . that form the rational ultimate end of social progress.' Its members, many of whom were in conscious revolt against the artistic, social, and sexual restrictions of Victorian society, profoundly affected the development of the avant-garde in art and literature in Britain. Bloomsbury was attacked by *Leavis as dilettante and élitist, and its aims and achievements fell temporarily out of favour, but the late 1960s witnessed a great revival of interest and the publication of many critical and biographical studies (notably *Holroyd's two-volume life of Strachey, 1967–8) seeking to re-assess Bloomsbury's influence.

Blot in the 'Scutcheon, A, a tragedy in blank verse by R. *Browning, published in 1843 as no. V of *Bells and Pomegranates. It was produced at Drury Lane in 1843, ran for three nights, and caused a final rift between Browning and *Macready, who had rejected Browning's two previous plays and expressed doubts about the success of this one. Browning's friends accused Macready of sabotaging the production, and the quarrel was instrumental in Browning's decision to write no more stage plays. (See also COLOMBE'S BIRTHDAY.)

Set in an aristocratic household of the 18th cent., the play concerns the tragic outcome of an illicit love-affair between Mildred Tresham and Lord Henry Mertoun, although the central role is that of Mildred's brother and guardian, Lord Tresham.

Blougram, Bishop, see BISHOP BLOUGRAM'S APOLOGY.

BLOUNT, Martha (1690–1762), and her sister Teresa (b. 1688), were close friends of *Pope, who met them c.1705; he corresponded with both, and visited them at their family seat of Mapledurham. They were of an old Catholic family. Later he began to address his attentions more exclusively to the less attractive Martha, who was rumoured to be his mistress. He dedicated his Epistle . . . on the Characters of Women (*Moral Essays) to Martha, and also (almost certainly) 'To a Young Lady with the Works of Voiture'; 'To the Same on her Leaving the Town after the Coronation', which describes Zephalinda banished from social delights to 'old-fashion'd halls, dull aunts, and croaking rooks' was probably addressed to Teresa.

Blouzelinda, a shepherdess in *The Shepherd's Week* by J. Gay.

BLOW, Dr John (1649–1708), English composer and organist. At the age of 19 he became organist of Westminster Abbey, and from 1674 onwards was master of the Children of the Chapel Royal, where he exerted an important influence on a whole generation of English musicians and was 'Master to the famous Mr H. Purcell' (then some 15 years old). He was a prolific composer of church music and anthems for the Chapel Royal, and his many Court Odes include settings of *D'Urfey, N. *Tate, *Cowley, and *Dryden. To Blow also must go the credit for the composition of what is usually regarded as the first real English opera of which the music has survived in about 1684. Though described in the manuscript as a 'Masque for the Entertainment of the King', *Venus and Adonis* is in fact a true opera in miniature and antedates *Purcell's *Dido and Aeneas*, for which it was clearly an important model, by about five years. The librettist is unknown.

Blue Beard, a popular tale in an oriental setting, from the French of *Perrault, translated by Robert Samber (?1729).

A man of great wealth, but disfigured by a blue beard, and of evil reputation because he has married several wives who have disappeared, asks for the hand of Fatima, the younger of the two daughters of a neighbouring lady of quality. At last she is prevailed on to marry him. Blue Beard, called away on business, leaves the keys of all his treasures to his young wife, but strictly enjoins her not to make use of the key of a particular room. Overcome by curiosity, she opens this room and finds in it the bodies of Blue Beard's previous wives. Horror-struck, she drops the key, which becomes indelibly stained with blood. Blue Beard returns, discovers her disobedience and orders her death. She begs for a little delay, 'Sister Anne' sees her brothers arriving and Blue Beard is killed before he can carry out the sentence.

*Lang, in *Perrault's Popular Tales* (1888), discusses the many parallel stories found in other countries.

Blue Bird, The, see MAETERLINCK, M.

Blue Lagoon, The, a novel by H. de V. *Stacpoole.

Blue Stocking Circle, Blue Stocking Ladies; an informal group of intelligent, learned, and sociable women, which flourished in London in the second half of the 18th cent. The origin of the name almost certainly lies with the stockings of Benjamin Stillingfleet, who was too poor to possess fine evening clothes, and who came to the circle's evening receptions in his daytime stockings of blue worsted. Someone, traditionally Admiral Boscawen, transformed Stillingfleet's stockings into the collective name of the ladies who held the receptions. The group was of considerable size, but the chief hostesses and female members were Mrs *Vesey, Mrs *Montagu, Mrs *Carter, Mrs *Chapone, Mrs *Boscawen, Mrs *Delany, and, later, H. *More. *Swift wrote to Mrs Delany in 1734, 'A pernicious error prevails . . . that it is the duty of your sex to be fools.' Mrs Vesey, who was the first to try to show the world that many women were capable of rational conversation, held her first reception for men and women of both the fashionable and literary worlds in the early 1750s. As described later by Hannah More, the sole purpose of a Blue Stocking evening was to be conversation. There were no cards, and no refreshment other than tea, coffee, or lemonade. Learning was to be given free expression, but not be disfigured by pedantry; politics, scandal, and swearing were not allowed. The evenings became so popular that they were held not only by the circle's most famous hostesses but in the houses of Sir Joshua *Reynolds, Mrs *Thrale, the countess of Cork and Orrery, and many others. The company was divided evenly between men and women; among the most famous of the men in regular attendance were *Garrick, Horace *Walpole, Dr *Johnson, *Boswell, Reynolds, S. *Richardson, *Lyttleton, and *Beattie. Dr Johnson, who was largely ignored by the fashionable world, was lionized at any Blue Stocking evening, with duchesses, lords, knights, and ladies, in Boswell's words of 1781, 'four if not five deep around him'. Hannah More wrote a poem, *Bas Bleu* (1786), describing the charm of Blue Stocking society, and characterizing the chief of her friends. The expression 'Blue Stocking' seems to have been applied in the 18th cent. both affectionately and derisively, but it is now used only pejoratively to describe a pedantic, earnest woman.

Bluffe, Captain, a character in Congreve's *The Old Bachelor*.

Blumine, in Carlyle's *Sartor Resartus*, the lady with whom Herr *Teufelsdröckh falls in love (probably based on a Miss Margaret Gordon, whom Carlyle knew and admired before he met Jane Welsh).

BLUNDEN, Edmund Charles (1896–1974), born in London; his family moved soon after to Kent, the countryside of which was to become one of the chief subjects of his poetry. He was educated at Christ's Hospital and The Queen's College, Oxford. In 1914 he experienced war in the trenches and later wrote poems, such as 'Third Ypres' and 'Report on Experience', which have come to be regarded as among the best of their kind; memories of the war, and guilt at his own survival, became important themes in his later writing. In 1920 he published a small edition of MS poems of *Clare, whose work he rescued from obscurity. Volumes of poems largely of rural life (*The Waggoner*, 1920; *The Shepherd*, 1922; and *English Poems*, 1925), together with several slim limited editions, were followed by a spell teaching in Tokyo, and in 1928 by his best-known work, *Undertones of War*, which describes the double destruction of man and nature in Flanders. His first *Collected Poems* appeared in 1930, as did a biography of Leigh *Hunt. In 1931 he produced a collected edition of the work of W. *Owen. Further volumes of his own poems were collected as *Poems 1930–1940*; a study of *Hardy appeared in 1941, and a biography of *Shelley in 1946. After another period in Tokyo he published in 1950 a volume of poems, *After the Bombing*, more contemplative and searching than his previous work. In 1953 he was professor in Hong Kong, and in 1954 produced an edition of the poems of the almost unknown I. *Gurney. He was appointed professor of poetry at Oxford in 1966. Throughout his working life as a teacher and scholar he produced a wide variety of critical and editorial work, with an emphasis on Clare, the Romantics, and his fellow war-poets. Although heralded as one of the leaders of the *Georgians, Blunden belonged to no group; his precise natural imagery is, in his best work, fused with his own moods and attitudes, and with those of the country men and women who inhabit his landscapes. After many years in the making, his reputation stands high.

BLUNT, Wilfrid Scawen (1840–1922), poet, diplomat, traveller, anti-imperialist, and Arabist, married in 1869 Annabella King-Noel, *Byron's granddaughter; his own career as amorist appears to have been modelled on that of Byron, and his first volume of poetry, *Sonnets and Songs by Proteus* (1875, subsequently revised), passionately addresses various women. It was followed by several other volumes of verse, which include love lyrics, evocations of the Sussex countryside, and adaptations from the Arabic. He also wrote and agitated in support of Egyptian, Indian, and Irish independence, thus earning the approval of G. B. *Shaw (see the preface to *John Bull's Other Island*) and a brief spell in an Irish prison which inspired his sonnet sequence *In Vinculis* (1889). His many friends in the literary and political world included Lord *Lytton, *Curzon, *Morris, Lady *Gregory, A. *Meynell, and *Wilde, and in later years he received the homage of *Yeats and *Pound. *My Diaries* appeared in 2 vols, 1919–20, and there is a life by Elizabeth Longford, *A Passionate Pilgrimage* (1979).

BLYTHE, Ronald George (1922–   ), author, born in Suffolk, whose works include *The Age of Illusion* (1963), a study of England between the wars; *Akenfield: Portrait of an English Village* (1969), a study of an East Anglian village, evoked through a series of tape recordings of conversations with its inhabitants, linked by the author's own descriptions and interpretations; *The View in Winter: Reflections on Old Age* (1979), again based on tape-recorded interviews; and various critical and topographical studies.

BOADICEA, Bonduca, corrupt forms of the name Boudicca, queen of the Iceni in the east of Britain, who led a revolt against the Romans but was finally defeated by Suetonius Paulinus in AD 61 and killed herself.

Boar's Head Inn, celebrated in connection with *Falstaff, was in Eastcheap, and according to H. B. Wheatley (*London, Past and Present*, 1891) was 'destroyed in the Great Fire, rebuilt immediately after, and finally demolished . . . in 1831'. It is the subject of a paper in W. *Irving's *Sketch Book*, and provides the theme of one of *Goldsmith's essays, 'A Reverie at the Boar's-head-tavern in Eastcheap' originally published in 1760 in the *British Magazine*, in which the author imagines himself dozing by the fire and transported back in time to the days of Mistress Quickly and her guests.

Bobadill, Captain, the boastful, cowardly soldier in Jonson's *Every Man in his Humour*, a part several times acted by *Dickens in the 1840s.

Bob and Wheel, a metrical pattern used, for example, in Sir *Gawain and the Green Knight*, at the end of the strophes of the main narrative. The 'bob' is a short tag with one stress and the following 'wheel' is a quatrain of short lines rhyming ABAB:

```
. . . And al waz holȝ inwith,      nobot an olde cave
   Or a crevisse of an olde cragge,      he couþe hit
            noȝt deme
      wiþ spelle.
   'We! Lorde,' quoþ þe gentyle knyȝt,
   'Wheþer þis be þe grene chapelle?
   Here myȝt aboute mydnyȝt
   þe dele his matynnes tell!'
```
                                  (*Sir Gawain*, ll. 2,182–9)

Here the words 'with spelle' form the 'bob', leading into the 'wheel' of the quatrain.

BOCCACCIO, Giovanni (1313–75), Italian writer and humanist, was born at or near Florence, the son of a Florentine merchant. His formative years, from about 1325 until 1340, were spent in Naples, where he began his literary studies and wrote some of his first works. His outlook was greatly conditioned by the aristocratic society in which he moved and especially by his contacts with the Angevin court, but the tradition that he fell in love with Maria d'Aquino, illegitimate daughter of King Robert of Naples, is now discredited. He returned to Florence in 1340, and witnessed the ravages of the Black Death in 1348, described in the introduction to the first day of *The Decameron. From 1350 onwards the municipality of Florence employed him on various diplomatic missions. His friendship with *Petrarch—whom he first met in 1350—gave a powerful impetus to his classical studies, and his house became an important centre of humanist activity. He wrote a Life of *Dante and was the first to deliver a course of public lectures on the text of the *Divina Commedia (1373–4). Boccaccio's chief works, apart from The Decameron, were: Filocolo, a prose romance embodying the story of *Floris and Blancheflour; Filostrato, a poem on the story of Troilus and Cressida; Teseida, a poem on the story of Theseus, Palamon, and Arcite, which was translated by *Chaucer in the 'Knight's Tale'; Ameto, a combination of allegory and pastoral romance; the Amorosa visione, an uncompleted allegorical poem; Fiammetta, a psychological romance in prose, in which the woman herself recounts the various phases of her unhappy love; the Ninfale fiesolano, an idyll translated into English (from a French version) by an Elizabethan, John Goubourne. He also wrote a number of encyclopaedic works in Latin which were widely read in England: the De Genealogia deorum; the De claris mulieribus; and De casibus virorum illustrium, which was a source book for references to tragedy by Chaucer, by *Lydgate in The Fall of Princes, and for stories in *A Mirror for Magistrates. (See Willard Farnham: The Medieval Heritage of Elizabethan Tragedy, 1956.)

Boccaccio is an important figure in the history of literature, particularly of narrative fiction, and among the poets who found inspiration in his works were Chaucer, Shakespeare, *Dryden, *Keats, *Longfellow, and *Tennyson.

BODEL, Jean, see MATTER OF BRITAIN, FRANCE, ROME.

Bodleian Library, see BODLEY and LIBRARIES.

BODLEY, Sir Thomas (1545–1613), was educated at Geneva, whither his parents had fled during the Marian persecution, and subsequently at Magdalen College, Oxford. From 1588 to 1596 he was English diplomatic representative at The Hague. He devoted the rest of his life to founding at Oxford the great Bodleian Library (see LIBRARIES). It was opened in 1602. In 1609 Bodley endowed it with land in Berkshire and houses in London.

BOECE, see BOETHIUS.

BOECE, or **BOËTHIUS,** Hector (?1465–1536), a native of Dundee and a student in the University of Paris, where in the College of Montaigu with *Erasmus he became a professor.

In 1498 he was appointed first principal of the newly founded King's College in the University of Aberdeen. He published Latin lives of the bishops of Mortlach and Aberdeen (1522), and a Latin history of Scotland to the accession of James III (1526), the latter including many fabulous narratives, among others that of Macbeth and Duncan, which passed into *Holinshed's chronicles and thence to Shakespeare.

BOEHME, Jacob (1575–1624), a peasant shoemaker of Görlitz in Germany, a mystic. The essential features of his doctrine were that will is the original force, that all manifestation involves opposition, notably of God and nature, that existence emerges from a process of conflict between pairs of contrasted principles (light and darkness, love and anger, good and evil, and so forth) and that in this way the universe is to be seen as the revelation of God. The doctrine of Boehme strongly influenced W. *Law. English translations of Boehme's works, by various hands, appeared in 1645–62. A reprint of the works in English, ed. C. J. Barker, was published in 1910–24.

BOETHIUS, Anicius Manlius Severinus (c.475–525), was born at Rome and was consul in 510, in favour with the Goth Theodoric the Great who ruled over the city; but he incurred the suspicion of plotting against Gothic rule, was imprisoned and finally cruelly executed in 525 at Pavia. In prison he wrote the De Consolatione Philosophiae, his most celebrated work and one of the most translated works in history; it was translated into English in the 890s by *Alfred and in almost every generation up to the 18th cent. notably by *Chaucer (as Boece) and by *Elizabeth I into florid, *inkhorn language. It was translated into French by Jean de Meun, and was one of the most influential books of the Middle Ages. It is now generally believed that he was a Christian, though this is rarely explicit in the Consolation whose philosophy is broadly *Neoplatonic. Its form is 'Menippean Satire', i.e. alternating prose and verse. The verse often consists of a story told by *Ovid or *Horace, used to illustrate the philosophy being expounded—a relationship which was itself influential on medieval moral narrative. But the influence of the book is found everywhere in the work of Chaucer and his 15th-cent. followers. Before the Middle Ages, Boethius was of most importance for his translations of and commentaries on *Aristotle which provided the main part of what was known of Aristotle before the recovery of most of his writings from Arabic scholars in the 12th cent. The works he transmitted include the Categories, De Interpretatione, the Topics, and the Prior and Posterior Analytics. See C. S. *Lewis, The Discarded Image (1964), pp. 75–90; translation by R. Green (1962); H. R. Patch, The Tradition of Boethius (1935).

Boffin, Mr and Mrs, characters in Dickens's *Our Mutual Friend.*

BOHN, Henry George (1796–1884), publisher and bookseller, amassed a valuable collection of rare books and in 1841 published his *Guinea Catalogue,* an important early bibliographical work. In 1846 he started his popular *Standard Library* (followed by the *Scientific Library, Classical Library, Antiquarian Library,* etc.), the whole series numbering over 600 volumes. He was an accomplished scholar and translated several volumes for his 'Foreign Classics' series, compiled a *Dictionary of Quotations* (1867) and *A Bibliographical Account of the works of Shakespeare* (1864).

Bohun, Aubrey, in *A Year at Hartlebury,* by S. and B. Disraeli.

BOIARDO, Matteomaria (?1441–94), an Italian poet of the old chivalry, who drew on the legends of *Arthur and *Charlemagne for his principal work was the unfinished *Orlando Innamorato.*

BOILEAU, Nicholas Despreaux (1636–1711), French critic and poet. A friend of *Molière, *La Fontaine, and *Racine, legislator and model for French *neo-classicism at its apogee, he achieved legendary status in his lifetime. His dozen-odd epistles and satires and his *Art Poétique* (1674), a four-canto poem of great wit and elegance, establishing canons of taste and defining principles of composition and criticism, achieved international currency. *Dryden, *Pope, and *Addison regarded him as the supreme post-classical arbiter of literary judgement.

Bois–Guilbert, Sir Brian De, the fierce Templar in Scott's *Ivanhoe.*

BOITO, Arrigo (1842–1918), Italian composer, poet, and librettist. In spite of the distinction of his own two operas, *Mefistofele* and the unfinished *Nerone,* Boito's chief importance in musical history is as a producer of librettos for other composers. His first attempt, a version of *Hamlet* (1865) for Franco Faccio, already shows an exceptional sensitivity and ingenuity, and his two Shakespearian texts for *Verdi must be accounted among the best examples of this difficult literary form. *Otello* (1887) still makes some concessions to operatic convention, particularly in the treatment of Iago, but Boito's courageous decision to cut the whole of Shakespeare's first act cleverly tightens the dramatic structure and provides a superb operatic opening—as well as echoing, at a distance of over a hundred years, Dr *Johnson's criticism of the original play. *Falstaff,* based on *The Merry Wives of Windsor,* is a still more remarkable achievement: Boito was ruthless in his pruning of the rather incoherent plot, and in his determination 'to squeeze all the juice out of that enormous Shakespearian orange without letting useless pips slip through into the glass' he reduced Shakespeare's 25 scenes to six, at the same time filling out the figure of *Falstaff (generally acknowledged to be a little thin in *The Merry Wives*) with passages lifted wholesale from both parts of *Henry IV.*

Boke of Cupide, The, see CLANVOWE, J.

Boke of the Duchesse, The, see BOOK OF THE DUCHESS, THE.

Bold, John, a character in Trollope's *The Warden.* Mrs Bold, his widow, figures prominently in its sequel, *Barchester Towers,* and in *The Last Chronicle of Barset,* where she is the wife of Dean Arabin.

Bold Stroke for a Wife, A, a comedy by Mrs *Centlivre, produced 1718.
   Colonel Fainall, to win the consent of Obadiah Prim, the Quaker guardian of Anne Lovely, to his marriage with the latter, impersonates Simon Pure, 'a quaking preacher'. No sooner has he obtained it than the true Quaker arrives and proves himself 'the real Simon Pure', a phrase that was long in common use.

Boldwood, Farmer, a character in Hardy's *Far from the Madding Crowd.*

Bolingbroke, Henry, duke of Hereford, son of *John of Gaunt, deposes *Richard II in Shakespeare's play of that name, and becomes *Henry IV.

BOLINGBROKE, Henry St John, first Viscount (1678–1751), is sometimes said to have been educated at Eton and Christ Church, Oxford, but there is no record of his having attended either institution. It appears instead that he received his education at Sheriffhales Academy and at other Dissenting academies, although he subsequently sponsored legislation for the suppression of Nonconformist schools. He was elected to the House of Commons in 1701 for the riding of Wootton Basset, Wiltshire, a constituency represented previously by his father and his grandfather. In Parliament he soon became a leading figure in the Tory party; he distinguished himself by his eloquence in defending the interests of country or landed gentlemen in opposition to the financial or monied interests associated with the Whigs. He was appointed secretary of war in 1704 and secretary of state in 1710; his efforts as minister to wage war with France were hindered, he claimed, by the lack of support given Britain by other governments, a complaint given forceful expression by his friend *Swift in *The Conduct of the Allies* (1711). St John was made Viscount Bolingbroke in 1712; he took part in negotiating the Treaty of Utrecht in 1713; and he remained a dominant figure in the Tory party until the death of Queen Anne. After the accession of George I, Bolingbroke fled to France and declared his allegiance to the Pretender, James Stuart; he was convicted of high treason and his peerage was withdrawn. Bolingbroke lived in exile in France for the next decade. In an attempt to justify his conduct in the eyes of his fellow Tories he wrote *A Letter to Sir William Wyndham* in 1717; this long letter was widely circulated, but not published until after his death, in 1753. In France, Bolingbroke read widely and wrote several philosophical essays which reflect the influence of *Locke. These writings provoked the outrage of Dr *Johnson and others when they were published, also posthumously (in 1754), because of their scepticism concerning revealed religion. It has often been supposed that Pope's *An Essay on Man* (1734) was inspired by Bolingbroke's philosophical writings, but the influence appears to have been more personal than philosophical; the Renaissance Platonism which informs Pope's 'Essay' has no parallel in Bolingbroke's fragmentary philosophical works.

In 1723 Bolingbroke received a qualified pardon from the king; he was not allowed to resume his seat in the House of Lords, but he returned to England in 1725 to a life of political journalism in the company of Pope, Swift, *Gay, and *Lyttleton. In articles written for *The Craftsman* he attacked the policies and practices of the Walpole administration. He deplored, in particular, the practice of 'influence' or 'corruption' which allowed the administration to maintain power in Parliament by awarding offices, honours, and salaries to their supporters. Bolingbroke denounced this practice as a violation of the British constitution, which required the independence of Parliament from the crown. He appealed to Walpole and others to set aside their party differences of Whig and Tory and govern in a manner consistent with the constitution. These articles were collected in two volumes as *A Dissertation upon Parties* (1735) and *Remarks on the History of England* (1743). He retired to France in 1735, disenchanted with government and opposition alike in England. From his retreat he addressed letters on the need for an active and united opposition to corruption (*A Letter on the Spirit of Patriotism*, written in 1736) and on the role of a monarch in a free government (*The Idea of a Patriot King*, written in 1738). These essays, like his earlier political writings, reflect the influence of *Machiavelli and the classical republican tradition, particularly in their insistence on the importance of cultivating the public virtues of prudence, eloquence, and the spirit of liberty. The patriotic politician is enjoined to oppose the government in power, not for the satisfaction of his own ambitions, but out of a deeper allegiance to the constitution. The patriot king, like a Machiavellian prince, must be prepared to act,

when necessity requires, to bring the government back to its first principles; if corruption has attacked the constitution itself, the king may be obliged to reconstitute the state or found it anew. This classical republican or civic humanist perspective also appears in Bolingbroke's *Letters on the Study and Use of History*, also written in 1736-8, published in 1752. In this work he denounced contemporary English historical writing as merely antiquarian; he exhorted his readers to find in history illustrations and examples which would inspire men to higher standards of public and private virtue. Like his early philosophical fragments, these writings were circulated among his friends on the understanding they would not be published. His later years, following his return to England in 1743, were filled with acrimony on this account; he found that Pope had printed an edition of *The Idea of a Patriot King* and therefore he decided to publish the two essays on patriotism and a patriot king in 1749, with an introduction in which he denounced the perfidious conduct of his then deceased friend. Pope was defended by *Warburton, who was in turn excoriated by Bolingbroke in *A Familiar Epistle to the Most Impudent Man Living* (1749).

Bolingbroke's many posthumous publications excited intense controversy in the decade which immediately followed his death. The political essays published in his lifetime had a more lasting influence: in England, in the movement for parliamentary reform in the 18th and 19th cents; and, in America, on the ideas of John Adams, Thomas Jefferson, and other publicists and statesmen of the revolutionary era. See S. W. Jackman, *Man of Mercury* (1965); I. Kramnick, *Bolingbroke and his Circle* (1968); H. T. Dickinson, *Bolingbroke* (1970).

BÖLL, Heinrich (1917–), German author of novels and short stories, mostly on the subject of wartime and post-war Germany. He is highly acclaimed for his realistic portrayal of the social problems of a country recovering from guilt and defeat, for example in *Und sagte kein einziges Wort* (*And never Said a Word*, 1953) and *Billard um halb zehn* (*Billiards at half-past Nine*, 1959). His more recent works, such as *Gruppenbild mit Dame* (*Group Portrait with Lady*, 1971), *Die verlorene Ehre der Katherina Blum* (*The Lost Honour of Katharine Blum*, 1974), and *Fürsorgliche Belagerung* (*The Safety Net*, 1979), show a concern for topical problems like the hounding of individuals by the gutter press (*Katharina Blum*) and the coming to terms, private and public, with terrorism (*The Safety Net*). Böll received the *Nobel Prize for literature in 1972.

BOLT, Robert Oxton (1924–), born and educated in Manchester, worked in an insurance office, in the RAF and as a schoolmaster before his first West End success in 1957 with *Flowering*

Cherry (pub. 1958), a domestic drama about an insurance salesman incapable of fulfilling his own dreams of a better life. This was followed by *The Tiger and the Horse* (1960, pub. 1961), reflecting Bolt's own involvement with the campaign for nuclear disarmament, and *A Man for All Seasons* (1960, pub. 1960), his best-known work, based on the life of Sir T. *More. Other works include the screenplay of *Lawrence of Arabia* (1962), based on the exploits of T. E. *Lawrence. A recurrent theme is the conflict between private and public conscience, and although some critics have labelled his works as unadventurous and 'middlebrow', their simplicity and stagecraft have made them highly effective in performance.

Bolton, Fanny, a character in Thackeray's *Pendennis*.

Bombast, from 'cotton stuffing', a term used to describe verbose and exaggerated language.

Bombastes Furioso, a farce by W. B. *Rhodes, produced with great success in 1810 and published in the same year, and in an 1830 edition with illustrations by *Cruikshank.

Bombastus, in Butler's *Hudibras* (II. iii), refers to *Paracelsus.

BOND, (Thomas) Edward (1934–), playwright, born in north London, the son of an East Anglian labourer who had moved to London in search of work. Bond was educated at a secondary modern school, where his interest in the theatre was aroused by a performance of *Macbeth*; after leaving school early and working at a series of dead-end jobs, he began to write for the theatre. *The Pope's Wedding* was given a Sunday night performance at the Royal Court in 1962, and in 1965 his grim portrait of urban violence, *Saved*, in which a baby is stoned in its pram, aroused much admiration as well as a ban from the Lord Chamberlain. Other provocative works followed, including *Early Morning* (1969); *Lear* (1971, pub. 1972), a version of Shakespeare which stresses the play's physical cruelty; *The Sea* (1973), a black country-house comedy; *The Fool* (1975, published 1976), based on the life of *Clare; *Restoration* (1981), a Brechtian revolutionary historical drama with songs; and *Summer* (1982), set in a post-war Eastern European state. Bond's theatre is an outspoken indictment of capitalist society; his belief that violence occurs in 'situations of injustice' and that it therefore flourishes as 'a cheap consumer commodity' under capitalism, continues to arouse extreme responses from critics and audiences.

Bond, James, the debonair hero of the thrillers of I. *Fleming, and of their celluloid successors, repeatedly engaged, as '007, Licensed to Kill', in daring acts of espionage involving evil foreigners and dangerous and beautiful women, from which he invariably emerges triumphant.

Bondman, The, a tragi-comedy by *Massinger, acted 1623, published 1624.

A decadent and debauched aristocracy in Sicily has to import Timoleon to lead them into battle against the Carthaginians. Cleora, who despises the corruption of her society, is loved by Leosthenes, whose jealousy as he goes off to the wars makes her bind her eyes and swear she will not look at anyone until he returns. In the absence of the army, the oppressed slaves stage a rising under the leadership of the demagogue Marullo, but during the rising Marullo protects Cleora. When the army returns and eventually subdues the rebel slaves, Cleora rejects the suspicious, proud, and overbearing Leosthenes and to everyone's horror throws in her lot with the imprisoned leader of the slaves. Fortunately he turns out to be her former suitor Pisander.

This is one of the best of Massinger's tragi-comedies, with some well-developed characters and some fine satirical scenes. It is informed by his contempt for the arrogance of an effete aristocracy, which may well reflect Massinger's opinion of the ethics of the Jacobean court.

Bonduca, a tragedy by J. *Fletcher, probably performed 1613–14, published 1647.

The tragedy is based on the story of *Boadicea, as given by *Holinshed, but the principal character is her cousin, the wise, patriotic, chivalrous, and battle-hardened Caratach (*Caractacus), whose counsel to the vainglorious and impetuous Bonduca is disastrously ignored. After the defeat of the Britons in battle, Bonduca and her daughters defiantly commit suicide; the last act is devoted to the flight of Caratach and his young nephew Hengo, 'a brave boy', who is killed in a scene of much carefully contrived pathos (greatly admired by *Swinburne). Caratach survives, yielding to the 'brave courtesies' of the Romans, to be led off to Rome as a prisoner.

Bon Gaultier, the pseudonym (taken from *Rabelais) under which W. E. *Aytoun and T. *Martin published in 1845 *A Book of Ballads*, a collection of parodies and light poems. Among the authors parodied are *Tennyson (notably 'Locksley Hall', in 'The Lay of the Lovelorn') and E. B. *Browning (in 'The Rhyme of Sir Lancelot Bogle'). Martin also used the pseudonym in his contributions to *Tait's Magazine* and *Fraser's Magazine*.

Boniface, (1) the landlord of the inn in Farquhar's *The Beaux' Stratagem*; whence taken as the generic proper name of innkeepers; (2) in Scott's *The Monastery*, the abbot of Kennaquhair.

BONIFACE, St (680–755), 'the Apostle of Germany', whose original name is said to have been Wynfrith, was born at Kirton or Crediton in Devonshire, and educated at a monastery in Exeter and at Nursling near Winchester. He went to Rome in 718 and, with authority from Pope Gregory II, proceeded to Germany where he preached, established monasteries, and organized the Church. He was killed with his followers at Dokkum in Frisia. See ed. and trans. C. H. Talbot, *The Anglo-Saxon Missionaries in Germany* (1954).

Bonnivard, see PRISONER OF CHILLON, THE.

Bonny Dundee, see GRAHAM OF CLAVERHOUSE.

Bonthron, Anthony, in Scott's *The Fair Maid of Perth*, a villainous cut-throat, employed by Sir John Ramorny to murder Henry Smith and the duke of Rothsay.

Booby, Sir Thomas and Lady, and Squire Booby, characters in Fielding's *Joseph Andrews*.

Booker McConnell Prize for Fiction, a prize founded in 1969 and financed by Booker McConnell, a multinational conglomerate company, awarded annually to the best full-length novel published in the previous 12 months; its aim is to stimulate the kind of public interest aroused in France by the Prix *Goncourt. The winners have been P. H. Newby, Bernice Rubens, V. S. *Naipaul, J. *Berger, J. G. *Farrell, N. *Gordimer and Stanley Middleton (joint winners), R. P. *Jhabvala, D. *Storey, P. *Scott, I. *Murdoch, Penelope Fitzgerald, W. *Golding, Salman Rushdie, Thomas Keneally, and Anita Brookner.

Book of Martyrs, see ACTES AND MONUMENTS.

Book of St Albans, The, the last work issued by the press that was set up at St Albans about 1479, soon after *Caxton had begun to print at Westminster. It contains treatises on hawking and heraldry, and one on hunting by Dame Julians Barnes, probably the wife of the holder of the manor of Julians Barnes near St Albans. (The name Juliana Berners, and her identity as abbess of Sopwell in Hertfordshire, are 18th-cent. inventions.) The book is a compilation, not all by one hand. An edition printed by *Wynkyn de Worde in 1496 also included a treatise on 'Fishing with an Angle'. There is an edition by W. Blades (1901).

Book of Snobs, The, a collection of papers by *Thackeray, which first appeared in *Punch in 1846–7 under the title *The Snobs of England by One of Themselves*. When republished in 1848 some of the papers were omitted. Thackeray anatomized the various types of snobbery and pretentiousness to be found in the society of the time, 'Military Snobs', 'Country Snobs', and so on.

Book of the Duchess, The, a dream-poem in 1,334 lines by *Chaucer, probably written in 1369, in octosyllabic couplets. It is believed, in accordance with a long-standing tradition (which was questioned in the 1950s), to be an allegorical lament on the death of Blanche of Lancaster, the first wife of *John of Gaunt, who died in Sept. 1369.

The love-lorn poet falls asleep reading the story of Ceix (Seys) and Alcyone and follows a hunting party. He meets a knight in black who laments the loss of his lady. The knight tells of her virtue and beauty and of their courtship, and in answer to the dreamer's question declares her dead. The hunting party reappears and a bell strikes twelve, awakening the poet who finds his book still in his hand. The poem is one of Chaucer's earliest works, but it has great charm and accomplishment. It is founded on the French tradition of the dream as a vehicle for love poetry. 'A Complaynt of a Loveres Lyfe' by *Lydgate is based on it. For an account of the poem, see A. C. Spearing, *Medieval Dream-Poetry* (1976), pp. 49–73.

Bookseller, The, see WHITAKER, J.

Booksellers' Row, a name that was given to the old Holywell Street, which ran parallel to the Strand between St Clement Dane's and St Dunstan's, before the formation of the Aldwych at the end of the 19th cent.; so called from the number of second-hand booksellers that had shops there.

Bookselling, see MUMBY, F. A.

BOOTH, Charles (1840–1916), a successful shipowner, was author of a monumental inquiry into the condition and occupations of the people of London, of which the earlier part appeared as *Labour and Life of the People* in 1889, and the whole as *Life and Labour of the People of London* in 17 vols (1891–1902). Its object was to show 'the numerical relation which poverty, misery and depravity bear to regular earnings and comparative comfort, and to describe the general conditions under which each class lives'. He was aided in the survey by his wife's cousin, Beatrice *Webb, who gives an account of him and his work in *My Apprenticeship* (1926) and credits him with the introduction of the Old Age Pensions Act 1908.

BOOTH, William (1829–1912), popularly known as 'General' Booth', was the leader of the revivalist movement known from 1878 as the Salvation Army, which sprang from the Christian Mission which he founded in Whitechapel in 1865. Booth, the son of a failed speculative builder in Nottingham, was entirely ignorant of theology, but possessed of eloquence, fervour, and a sense of the practical and spiritual needs of the poor which made him a powerful force in social and religious life. G. B. Shaw's *Major Barbara* (perf. 1905) was based on first-hand knowledge of the Salvation Army.

Booth, William, the hero of Fielding's *Amelia*.

Boots Library, a circulating library (see LIBRARIES, CIRCULATING) established at the end of the 19th cent. by Nottingham businessman and philanthropist Jesse Boot (1850–1931). Unlike *Mudie's it catered largely for provincial and suburban subscribers, and by the mid-1930s was the largest of its kind, with over 400 branches. The stock was categorized as 'Light Romance', 'Family Stories', etc., and librarians were trained to make suggestions in line with the taste of their readers. *Betjeman in 'In Westminster Abbey' (1940) wrote

> Think of what our Nation stands for,
> Books from Boots, and country lanes . . .

See also Nicola Beauman, *A Very Great Profession; The Woman's Novel 1914–39* (1983).

Borderers, The, see WORDSWORTH, W.

Border Minstrelsy, see MINSTRELSY OF THE SCOTTISH BORDER.

BORGES, Jorge Luis (1899–   ), Argentinian writer, born in Buenos Aires and educated (1914–18) in Geneva; one of his grandmothers was English and from an early age he read English literature (notably the works of *Wilde, *De Quincey, R. L. *Stevenson, and *Chesterton). After some time in Spain, where he was associated with the Spanish literary movement *ultraísmo* (a form of Spanish *Expressionism), he returned in 1921 to Argentina, where for a time he championed the ultraist cause, partly through the periodical *Proa*. His first volume of poetry, *Fervor de Buenos Aires* (1923), was followed by many other volumes of verse and essays, but he is best known for his short stories, of which the first volume, *Historia universal de la infamia* (1935; *A Universal History of Infamy*), has been acclaimed as a landmark in Latin American literature and the first work of *Magic Realism. Originally published in an Argentinian evening paper, the stories recount the lives of real and fictitious criminals (some ascribed also to fictitious authors), and are an early illustration of Borges's enduring preoccupation with the relationship of fiction, truth, and identity; with violence; and with the puzzles of detective fiction. (With his friend Adolfo Bioy Casares he collaborated in several tales of crime and detection.) Subsequent collections of short stories included *Ficciones* (1945) and *El Aleph* (1949); the publication of a selection entitled *Labyrinths* in Paris in 1953 established his international reputation, and it was translated into English in 1962. Many of his best-known stories deal with the cyclical nature of time; they are themselves labyrinthine in form, metaphysical in their speculations, and often dreamlike in their endlessly reflected facets of reality and arcane knowledge. Borges worked as a librarian for some years in a municipal library (1938–46) and some of his stories (e.g. 'The Library of Babel' and 'Tlön, Uqbar, Orbis Tertius') take on the quality of a bibliographer's nightmare. Borges was relieved of this post for political reasons, but with the overthrow of the Peronist regime he became in 1955 the director of the National Library of Buenos Aires. By the 1950s, however, his eyesight was failing, and in his last years he was almost totally blind; in later years he wrote more poetry than prose, but a late collection of stories, *El informe de Brodie* (*Doctor Brodie's Report*) appeared in 1971.

BORGIA, Cesare (1476–1507), favourite son of Rodrigo *Borgia (Pope Alexander VI) and brother of Lucrezia *Borgia. Notorious for his crimes, he was at the same time a man of great military capacity and one of the early believers in the unity of Italy. His career is said to have inspired much of *Machiavelli's *Il Principe*. His power came to an end after his father's death; he fled to the court of Navarre, and was killed in the service of the king.

BORGIA, Lucrezia (1480–1519), daughter of Rodrigo (below) and sister of Cesare *Borgia. She was married when very young to Don Gasparo de Procida, but the marriage was annulled by her father and she was betrothed to Giovanni Sforza. This engagement was also cancelled by her father for political reasons, and Lucrezia was married to Alfonso of Aragon, a relative of the king of Naples. Alfonso was murdered by direction of Cesare Borgia and Lucrezia then married Alfonso d'Este, heir to the duke of Ferrara, being at the time 22. Her life thenceforth was peaceful, and when her husband reached the throne, her court became a centre for artists, poets, and men of learning, such as *Ariosto, *Titian, and *Aldus Manutius.

BORGIA, Rodrigo (1431–1503), Pope Alexander VI, a Spaniard by birth, and the father of Cesare and Lucrezia *Borgia, was elected to the pontificate in 1492. His policy was mainly directed towards the recovery of the Papal States and the unscrupulous promotion of the interests of his own family, though he was also a generous patron of the arts. The tradition that the Borgias possessed the secret of a mysterious and deadly poison has not been substantiated by historical research, but in England it captivated the Elizabethan imagination and is mentioned many times in the literature of the period. *The divils charter* by B. *Barnes is a *Machiavellian drama based on 'the Life and Death of Pope Alexander the Sixt', taken from *Guicciardini.

Born in Exile, see GISSING, G.

BORON, Robert de, a 12th–13th-cent. French poet who composed a trilogy (*Joseph d'Arimathie* in 3,514 lines; *Merlin*, a fragment of 502 lines; and *Perceval*) in which he developed the early history of the Holy *Grail in Britain, linking it with the Arthurian tradition. The works are dated *c*.1202 by P. Le Gentil (in *Arthurian Literature in the Middle Ages*, ed. R. S. Loomis, 1959, ch. 19). See D. C. Cabeen ed., *Critical Bibliography of French Literature* (i, 1952, by U. T. Holmes).

Borough, The, a poem by *Crabbe published 1810, in twenty-four 'letters', describing, with much penetration and accuracy of detail, the life and characters of the church, the school, the professions, the surroundings, the workhouse, the prisons, the sea, and other aspects of the town of Aldeburgh, Suffolk. The work, which is uneven in quality, took eight years to complete. Two of the most successful tales, concerning *Peter Grimes and *Ellen Orford, were combined in *Britten's opera *Peter Grimes* (1945).

BORROW, George Henry (1803–81), was educated at Edinburgh High School and at Norwich and was articled to a solicitor, but adopted literature as a profession. During his apprenticeship he edited *Celebrated Trials, and Remarkable Cases of Criminal Jurisprudence* (1825), an impressive piece of hack-work undertaken for a London publisher, and then travelled through England, France, Germany, Russia, Spain, and in the East, studying the languages of the countries he visited (though there is some suggestion that he exaggerated both his linguistic achievements and the extent of his travels). In Russia and Spain he acted as agent for the British and Foreign Bible Society. Finally he married a well-to-do widow and settled near Oulton Broad in Suffolk. He published a number of books based in part on his own life, experiences and travels: *The Zincali, or an account of the Gypsies in Spain* (1841), *The Bible in Spain* (1834), *Lavengro* (1851), *The Romany Rye* (1857), and *Wild Wales* (1862). His works have a peculiar picaresque quality, and contain vivid portraits of the extraordinary personages he encountered; his own personality also emerges with much force. Though physically robust and energetic he had suffered since his youth from bouts of manic depression that he referred to as 'the Horrors' which often temporarily frustrated him. In *Lavengro, The Romany Rye*, and *The Bible in Spain* fact is inextricably combined with fiction; and *Lavengro* he himself describes as 'a dream partly of study, partly of adventure'. The standard biography is by W. I. Knapp (2 vols, 1899); see also D. Williams, *A World of His Own* (1982).

Bors de Ganys, Sir, in *Malory, king of Gannes, brother of Lionel and Ban and cousin of *Launcelot. He was one of the three successful knights in the Quest of the Grail, after which he became a hermit at Glastonbury. He is sometimes confused with his father, King Bors of Gaul.

BOSCÁN DE ALMOGÁVER, Juan (*c*.1487–1542), a Spanish poet born at Barcelona, who did much to introduce Italian verse forms into the poetry of his country. He was an intimate friend of another Spanish poet, *Garcilaso de la Vega, and the two are mentioned together by Byron in *Don Juan* (i. 95).

BOSCAWEN, Mrs Frances (1719–1805), an eminent *Blue Stocking hostess, and the wife of Admiral Boscawen, who is traditionally supposed to have transformed Benjamin Stillingfleet's blue stockings into a name for his wife's learned and literary female friends. Hannah *More greatly admired Mrs Boscawen, finding her 'polite, learned, judicious and humble'; and in her poem *Bas Bleu* (1786) she accords her, with Mrs *Vesey and Mrs *Montagu, the 'triple crown' as the most successful of the Blue Stocking hostesses.

Bosola, a character in Webster's *The Duchess of Malfi.*

BOSSUET, Jacques Bénigne (1627–1704), French preacher. His reputation as the greatest French orator rests on his sermons, pronounced chiefly in the course of his duties as bishop of Meaux, and especially on his funeral orations, celebrating many of the greatest figures at the court of Louis XIV, including Henrietta Maria, wife of Charles I, Marie Thérèse, wife of Louis XIV, and the Grand Condé. His style was usually simple, direct, and dignified, but capable of rising to grandeur when dealing with the mysteries of mortality and faith. A dogmatist on principle (he defined a heretic as 'he who has an opinion'), he was involved in a number of notorious disputes with Protestants. These had some effect on English religious controversies of the time.

Bostonians, The, a novel by H. *James, published 1886.

Basil Ransom, a young lawyer fresh from Mississippi and the humiliations of the Civil War, has come north in search of a career. In Boston he calls on his cousin Olive Chancellor and her widowed sister, the girlishly arch Mrs Luna. Olive, a wealthy chill feminist, introduces him to a reformist group (acidly portrayed by James) at the house of the selfless and well-meaning Miss Birdseye. Selah Tarrant, a charlatan faith-healer and showman, is presenting his young daughter Verena. She is an 'inspirational' speaker, and while Basil Ransom is attracted by her prettiness Olive is intensely moved by the girl's performance, and sees her as a valuable instrument for the cause. She removes Verena from her unacceptable parents and sets about her education. Out for revenge rather than equality, she attempts to instil in the girl her own distrust and loathing for men. Ransom, contemptuous of reform and reformers, opens a battle for possession of Verena. Olive, full of hatred for Ransom and now passionately attached to the girl, tries to freeze him out. But Verena is now playing a double game. Attracted by Ransom and frightened by Olive's intensity, she has begun to doubt her role. As she is about to make her first public appearance Verena, schooled to be the banner of the suffragette movement, is carried off by Ransom, a mediocre young man who believes that woman's highest achievement is to be agreeable to men.

BOSWELL, James (1740–95), the eldest son of Alexander Boswell, Lord Auchinleck (pron. Affleck), a Scottish judge who took his title from the family estate in Ayrshire. He reluctantly studied law at Edinburgh, Glasgow, and Utrecht, his ambition being directed towards literature and politics, as was manifested by numerous pamphlets and verses which he published anonymously from 1760 onwards, many of them also expressing his love of the theatre. He was in London in 1762–3, where he met Dr *Johnson on 16 May 1763; he then went to Holland (where he met and courted *Zélide) and on through Europe to Italy. His extraordinary persistence in pursuit of the great achieved meetings with *Rousseau and *Voltaire; Rousseau inspired him with zeal for the cause of Corsican liberty, and he visited Corsica in 1765, establishing a lifelong friendship with General Paoli. On his return to Scotland he 'passed advocate' and was to practise there and in England for the rest of his life. His first substantial work, *An Account of Corsica* (1768), was followed in December of the same year by a book of essays 'in favour of the brave Corsicans' edited by Boswell; he was to remain loyal to this cause, creating a sensation by his appearance at the Shakespeare Jubilee in 1769 in Corsican dress. In this year he married his cousin Margaret Montgomerie, after a lengthy succession of attempted courtships and successful philanderings with others; she bore him several children. Although his family remained in Scotland, Boswell longed for the diversions of London, which he visited as frequently as possible, spending much time with Johnson, whose biography he already projected. They made their celebrated tour of Scotland and the Hebrides in 1773, in which year Boswell was elected a member of the *Club. From 1777 to 1783 he contributed a series of essays, as 'The Hypochondriack', to *The London Magazine*, on such subjects as drinking (a constant preoccupation), diaries, memory, and hypochondria. In 1782 his father (with whom his relationship had been complex and at times unhappy) died, and Boswell inherited the estate. His last meeting with Johnson was in 1784; his *Journal of a Tour of the Hebrides* appeared in 1785 after Johnson's death. The rest of Boswell's life was devoted to an unsuccessful

pursuit of a political career (he was recorder of Carlisle, 1788–90) and to the immense task of assembling materials for and composing his life of Johnson, a labour in which he was encouraged by *Malone. *The Life of Samuel *Johnson* appeared in 1791. Boswell's volatility, his promiscuity, his morbid fits of depression, his ambitions, and his emotional involvement in the affairs of his clients are frankly revealed in his letters (notably to his two old university friends, William Johnson Temple and John Johnston) and in private papers and journals, many of which were discovered at Malahide Castle and Fettercairn House; they cover his continental tour as well as his London visits, and have been edited, principally by F. A. Pottle, from 1928 in various volumes.

Botanic Garden, The, see DARWIN, E.

Bothie of Tober-na-Vuolich, The, see CLOUGH, A. H.

BOTHWELL, James Hepburn, fourth earl of (?1536–78), husband of Mary Queen of Scots, is the subject of a historical poem by W. E. *Aytoun (1856) and of a tragedy by *Swinburne (1874).

Bothwell, Sergeant, in Scott's *Old Mortality*, a soldier in Claverhouse's force, who claims the name of Francis Stewart.

BOTOLPH, or **BOTULF**, St (d. 680), an Englishman who studied in Germany and became a Benedictine monk. He founded a monastery at an unidentified place in East Anglia called Icanhoh (perhaps near the present town of Boston), which was destroyed by the Danes. He died, with a high reputation for sanctity, at Botolphstown (Boston). Four churches in London are dedicated to him, and he is also commemorated in Botolph's Lane and Botolph's Wharf.

Botteghe Oscure (literally 'dark shops'), a review edited in Rome by Marguerite Caetani, 1949–60, which established itself as a leading international periodical. The contributors, who included Dylan *Thomas, *Auden, *Bellow, *Grass, *Camus, *Montale, etc., were published in their own language.

BOTTICELLI, Sandro (c.1445–1510), Florentine painter, whose most famous paintings, *La Primavera* (c.1477–8) and *The Birth of Venus* (1485–90) were painted for the *Medici villas; they are complex allegories that reflect the humanist and classical interests of the time, and their power depends on Botticelli's compelling sense of feminine beauty and on the grace of his line. He also painted many altarpieces and portraits. His later works, perhaps in response to the teachings of *Savonarola, are wilder and more dramatic. By the time of his death Botticelli's decorative style had become old-fashioned and he is only rarely mentioned again before the 19th cent., when his popularity soared. *Pater's essay 'Sandro Botticelli' (1870) dwells on his sense of mystery and sadness—on the troubled, brooding faces of his 'peevish-looking' Madonnas, and on the cold light and grey water of *The Birth of Venus*. Pater's descriptions opened the eyes of English decadents to the painter's enigmatic beauty, and Botticelli became a cult figure. *Ruskin also rediscovered Botticelli, and copied his fresco *The Youth of Moses* (c.1482) in the Sistine Chapel.

Bottom, Nick, the weaver in Shakespeare's *Midsummer Night's Dream*. The name had no anatomical connotations in Shakespeare's time, but referred, here, to the clew on which thread was wound. A *'droll', *The Merry Conceited Humours of Bottom the Weaver*, adapted from Shakespeare's play, was printed in 1661.

BOTTOMLEY, Gordon (1874–1948), a bank clerk who became a prolific and successful poet and man of letters. His first volume of poems, *The Mickle Drede*, appeared in 1896, and his work was included in E. *Marsh's first volume of *Georgian Poetry* in 1912. He attempted the epic and sublime, as well as the lyric, and his *Poems of Thirty Years* (1925) show the marked influence of *Shelley. He hoped to promote a poetic revival in the theatre; of his poetic plays *King Lear's Wife* (1915) and *Gruach* (1921) were the most successful.

BOUCICAULT (originally Boursiquot), Dion(ysius Lardner) (1820–90), playwright, born in Dublin and educated at University College School, London, began his career as an actor and achieved great success with his comedy *London Assurance* (1841), written under the pseudonym of Lee Morton. He subsequently wrote and adapted some 200 plays, including *The Corsican Brothers* (1852, from the French), *The Poor of New York* (1857), *The Colleen Bawn; or the brides of Garryowen* (1860), *Arra-na-Pogue; or The Wicklow Wedding* (1864), and *The Shaughraun* (1874). One of the dominant figures of 19th-cent. theatre, his career was marked by spectacular successes and reverses, and he was responsible for important innovations, such as the introduction of a royalty from plays and copyright for dramatists in America. With the rise of realism and the emergence of *Ibsen and G. B. *Shaw, his work fell out of fashion, but it influenced *O'Casey, who praised his 'colour and stir', and some of his plays have been successfully revived. There is a life by R. Fawkes, 1979.

BOUDICCA, see BOADICEA.

Bouillabaisse, see BALLAD OF BOUILLABAISSE, THE.

BOUILLON, Godefroi de (Godfrey of Bouillon) (d. 1100), duke of Lower Lorraine, leader of the First Crusade and proclaimed 'Protector of the Holy Sepulchre' in 1099. He appears in Tasso's *Jerusalem Delivered* and in Scott's *Count Robert of Paris*.

Bounderby, Josiah, a character in Dickens's *Hard Times*.

Bountiful, Lady, a character in Farquhar's *The Beaux' Stratagem*.

Bounty, *The Mutiny and Piratical Seizure of H.M.S.*, by Sir J. *Barrow, published 1831.

HMS *Bounty*, which had been sent to the South Sea Islands to collect bread fuit trees, left Tahiti early in 1789 for the Cape of Good Hope and the West Indies. On 28 April of that year Fletcher Christian and others seized Lt Bligh, the commander, and placed him with eighteen loyal members of the crew in an open boat, which they cast adrift. The boat eventually reached Timor. Meanwhile the *Bounty* sailed east with twenty-five of the crew to Tahiti, where sixteen were put ashore. These men were later arrested and many of them were drowned when HMS *Pandora* sank. Fletcher Christian and eight of his companions, together with some Tahitians, went on and settled on Pitcairn Island. There they founded a colony, of which Alexander Smith (now calling himself John Adams) became the leader, and which was eventually taken under the protection of the British government. These famous events form part of Byron's poem *'The Island', and have been the subject of books and films.

Boustrophedon, from the Greek words meaning 'ox turning', written alternately from right to left and left to right, like the course of the plough in successive furrows, as in various ancient inscriptions in Greek and other languages.

Bouts-rimés, 'The bouts-rimez were the favourites of the French nation for a whole age together . . . They were a List of Words that rhyme to one another, drawn up by another Hand, and given to a Poet, who was to make a poem to the Rhymes in the same Order that they were placed upon the list.' Addison, *Spectator*, No. 60.

Bovary, Madame, the chief work of *Flaubert.

BOWDLER, Thomas (1754–1825), MD of Edinburgh, published in 1818 his *Family Shakespeare*, dedicated to the memory of Mrs *Montagu, who had published a much respected essay *On the Genius of Shakespeare* in 1769. As is shown by his Prefaces, Bowdler's love and admiration of Shakespeare were profound; nevertheless he believed that nothing 'can afford an excuse for profaneness or obscenity; and if these could be obliterated, the transcendant genius of the poet would undoubtedly shine with more unclouded lustre.' Profanity he found only a small problem; 'God' as an expletive is always replaced by 'Heaven', and other brief passages and exclamations cut. But he confessed to enormous trouble with the endless indecency scattered throughout the plays. His method was to cut, not to substitute; he in fact added almost nothing except prepositions and conjunctions. But the cutting is severe; for instance, Juliet's speech of longing for Romeo, 'Gallop apace . . .', is cut from 30 lines to 15, and many of her Nurse's comments have gone; in Lear's speech of madness, 'Aye, every inch a king . . . ' 22 lines of verse are cut to seven. Bowdler found 1 and 2 *Henry IV 'the most difficult of all the histories for family reading'. Doll Tearsheet is entirely removed, but Bowdler apologizes that even with the omission of many obscenities he could not achieve 'perfect delicacy of sentiment'. *Measure for Measure he found contained so many indecent expressions interwoven with the text that he could do nothing better than to print, with a warning, *Kemble's version for the stage. He admits failure with *Othello ('unfortunately little suited to family reading'), and recommends transferring it 'from the parlour to the cabinet'.

Bowdler's work was extremely successful, and went through many editions. He executed similar excisions on Gibbon's *Decline and Fall. With the verb 'to bowdlerize', or expurgate, Dr Bowdler joins the small band of those who have given their names to the language.

BOWEN, Elizabeth Dorothea Cole (1899–1973), Anglo-Irish novelist and short story writer. Born in Dublin, she spent much of her childhood at the family home in Co. Cork which she inherited in 1930 and described in *Bowen's Encounters.* She married Alan Cameron, and they lived for ten years in London, vividly evoked in many of her works; her skill in describing landscape, both urban and rural, and her sensitivity to changes of light and season are distinguishing features of her prose. Her novels include *The Hotel* (1927), *The Last September* (1929), *The House in Paris* (1935), *A World of Love* (1955), and *Eva Trout* (1969). The best-known are probably *The Death of the Heart* (1938) and *The Heat of the Day* (1949). The first (which clearly demonstrates her debt to H. *James) is the story of Portia, a 16-year-old orphan whose dangerous innocence threatens the precarious, sophisticated London lives of her half-brother Thomas and his wife Anna, and who is herself threatened by her love for the glamorously despairing young Eddy, a young admirer of Anna; the second centres on the tragic war-time love affair of Stella Rodney and Robert Kelway, and their reactions to the revelation, through the sinister Harrison, that the latter is a spy. The war inspired many of Elizabeth Bowen's best short stories, including 'Mysterious Kôr' (*Penguin *New Writing,* 1944); A. *Wilson in his introduction to her *Collected Stories* (1980)

praised her as one of the great writers of the blitz. Other stories (e.g. the title story of *The Cat Jumps,* 1934) reveal subtle deployment of the supernatural. She writes most confidently of the upper middle and middle classes, but within that social range her perceptions of change are acute; her works already strike the reader with a powerful sense of period, through their accurate detail and keen response to atmosphere. See V. Glendinning, *Elizabeth Bowen: Portrait of a Writer* (1977).

BOWEN, Marjorie, the best-known pseudonym of Gabrielle Margaret Vere Campbell (1886–1952), prolific writer of historical novels, children's stories, etc.; G. *Greene in his essay 'The Lost Childhood' (1951, included in *Collected Essays,* 1969) claims that her first novel, *The Viper of Milan* (1906), so affected his imagination that it inspired him to be a writer and supplied him 'once and for all with a subject'.

Bower of Bliss, The, in Spenser's *Faerie Queene* (II. xii), the home of *Acrasia, demolished by Sir *Guyon.

BOWERS, Fredson (1905–), bibliographer and textual critic, author of the classic short study *On Editing Shakespeare and the Elizabethan Dramatists* (1955). *Dekker, *Beaumont and *Fletcher, and *Marlowe are among the dramatists he has edited.

Bowge of Courte, The, an allegorical poem in seven-lined stanzas by *Skelton, satirizing court life (c.1498). The word 'bowge' is a corrupt form of 'bouche', meaning court rations, from the French 'avoir bouche à cour', to have free board at the king's table.

BOWLES, William Lisle (1762–1850), educated at Westminster and Trinity College, Oxford, was vicar of Bremhill and a canon of Salisbury. He is remembered chiefly for his *Fourteen Sonnets* published in 1789. His work was greatly admired by the youthful *Coleridge (who in 1796 dedicated his *Poems* to Bowles), as well as by *Lamb, *Southey, and many others. *Byron, however, describes him as 'the maudlin prince of mournful sonneteers', and was roused to further anger by Bowles's strictures on *Pope, of whom Bowles published an edition in 1806.

Bowling, Tom, (1) a character in Smollett's *Roderick Random*; (2) see DIBDIN, C.

BOWRA, (Sir Cecil) Maurice (1898–1971), scholar and critic, from 1922 a fellow and from 1938 until 1970 warden of Wadham College, Oxford, where his wit, hospitality, and energy made him a legendary figure and earned him the gratitude and friendship of many, including *Connolly and *Betjeman; Betjeman in *Summoned by Bells* recalls the 'learning lightly worn' and 'The fusillade of phrases. "I'm a man | More dined against than dining." ' Bowra published various works on and translations of Greek literature, notably *Pindar, and edited *The Oxford Book of Greek Verse in Translation* (1938) and two books of Russian verse in translation (1943, 1948): *The Heritage of Symbolism* (1943) and *The Creative Experiment* (1949) are both commentaries on modern literature.

Bows, Mr, a character in Thackeray's *Pendennis*, a crippled fiddler who teaches Miss Fotheringay to act and Fanny Bolton to sing.

BOWYER, William (1699–1777), 'the learned printer', was printer of votes of the House of Commons (1729), printer to the *Royal Society (1761), and to the House of Lords (1767). He published his *Origin of Printing* in 1774.

Bowzybeus, a drunken swain, the subject of the last pastoral in *The Shepherd's Week* by J. Gay.

Box and Cox, a farce by J. M. *Morton, adapted from two French vaudevilles, published 1847.

Box is a journeyman printer, Cox a journeyman hatter. Mrs Bouncer, a lodging-house keeper, has let the same room to both, taking advantage of the fact that Box is out all night and Cox out all day to conceal from each the existence of the other. Discovery comes when Cox unexpectedly gets a holiday. Indignation follows, and complications connected with a widow to whom both have proposed marriage; and finally a general reconciliation.

Boy and the Mantle, The, a ballad included in Percy's *Reliques*, which tells how a boy visits King Arthur's court at 'Carleile', and tests the chastity of the ladies there by means of his mantle, a boar's head, and a golden horn. Sir Cradock's (Cradoc's) wife alone successfully undergoes the ordeal.

Boy Bishop, one of the choirboys formerly elected at the annual 'Feast of Boys' in certain cathedrals, to walk in a procession of the boys to the altar of the Innocents or of the Holy Trinity, and perform the office on the eve and day of the Holy Innocents, the boys occupying the canons' stalls in the cathedral during the service. Provision for this is made in the Sarum Office (see E. K. *Chambers, *The Medieval Stage*, App. M). The custom dates from the 13th cent. and lasted until the Reformation. Boy Bishops were appointed also in religious houses and in schools.

BOYDELL, John (1719–1804), engraver and publisher, who with his nephew Josiah Boydell opened their Shakespeare Gallery in Pall Mall in 1789. Originally it contained 34 paintings of subjects from Shakespeare, by many of the most famous artists of the day, including J. *Wright of Derby (Prospero's Cell); *Fuseli (scenes from *A Midsummer Night's Dream*, *Macbeth*, and *Hamlet*) and Joshua *Reynolds (Henry VI at the deathbed of Beaufort). The collection was later expanded, and many engravings of the works were sold.

BOYER, Abel (1667–1729), a French Huguenot who settled in England in 1689. He published a yearly register of political and other occurrences, and a periodical, *The Political State of Great Britain* (1711–29). He also brought out an English-French and a French-English dictionary, a *History of William III* (3 vols, 1702–3) and a *History of the life and reign of Queen Ann* (1722). He translated into English the memoirs of *Gramont (1714) and *Racine's *Iphigénie*.

BOYLE, Charles, see PHALARIS, EPISTLES OF.

BOYLE, John, fifth earl of Orrery (1707–62), son of Charles Boyle (1676–1731), was an intimate friend of *Swift, *Pope, and Dr *Johnson. His *Remarks on the Life and Writings of Dr Jonathan Swift* were written in a series of letters to his son Hamilton at Christ Church, Oxford, and published in 1751. These letters give a critical account of Swift's character, his life, his relations with Stella and Vanessa, and his friendship with Pope and others—*Gay, P. *Delany, and Dr Young, 'his intimate friends, whom he loved sincerely'. Orrery discusses Swift's work: poetry, political writings, letters, *Gulliver's Travels, *The Tale of a Tub, etc. Although he deplores Swift's misanthropy 'which induced him peevishly to debase mankind, and even to ridicule human nature itself' (Letter VI), he says that the character at which Swift aimed and which he deserved was that of 'an enemy to tyranny and oppression in any shape whatever' (Letter XVII).

BOYLE, Robert (1627–91), was fourteenth child of Richard Boyle, first earl of Cork, educated at Eton and privately. While touring in Switzerland as a teenager he experienced a conversion, which caused him to devote the rest of his life to science and good works. He eschewed marriage, wrote prolifically, and became the dominant figure in English science between F. *Bacon and I. *Newton. Robert Hooke was his technical assistant in experiments on the air which led to the first formulation of 'Boyle's Law'. Boyle's 'corpuscularianism', a rendering of the mechanical philosophy, exercised great influence throughout Europe. Among his more popular scientific writings *The Sceptical Chymist* (1661) is the best known and *The Origin of Forms and Qualities* (1666) anticipates much of the philosophy of *Locke. Among his early writings were the romances *Seraphic Love* and *The Martyrdom of Theodora*, the latter of which was turned into an opera libretto for *Handel. These exercises in moralizing find their echoes in many of Boyle's religious and philosophical writings. Samuel *Butler and *Swift wrote parodies of his *Occasional Reflections* (1665), a work which also supplied Swift with one of the central story-lines in *Gulliver's Travels*. The monotonous acres of Boyle's works are occasionally relieved by a colourful expression.

Boyle paid for the translation of the New Testament into Irish and other languages, supported evangelical schemes abroad, and in his Will made provision for the foundation of a series of annual lectures in defence of natural and revealed religion. The first series of Boyle Lectures was delivered by Richard *Bentley in 1692. The influence of these lectures was at its peak during the first 20 years; especially important were the lectures delivered by Bentley, John Harris, S. *Clarke, William Whiston, John Woodward, and William Derham, all of whose statements of natural theology were published as substantial volumes.

BOYLE, Roger, first earl of Orrery (1621–79), author of *Parthenissa* (1654–65), the first English romance in the style of *La Calprenède and M. de *Scudéry, which deals with the prowess and vicissitudes of Artabanes, a Median prince, and his rivalry with Surena, an Arabian prince, for the love of Parthenissa. Boyle also wrote a *Treatise on the Art of War* (1677), two comedies, and some rhymed tragedies, which include *Mustapha* (1665), based on Mlle de Scudéry's *Ibrahim* and the history of *Knolles. His plays were edited in 2 vols by W. S. Clark, 1937.

Boyle Lectures, see BOYLE, ROBERT.

'Boy's Song, A', probably the best-known of the ballads of J. *Hogg.

'Boy stood on the burning deck, The', see HEMANS, F. D.

Boythorn, a character in Dickens's *Bleak House*.

BOZ, the pseudonym used by *Dickens in his contributions to the *Morning Chronicle* and in the *Pickwick Papers*, 'was the nickname of a pet child, a younger brother, whom I had dubbed Moses, in honour of the Vicar of Wakefield; which being facetiously pronounced . . . became Boz' (Dickens, Preface to *Pickwick Papers*, 1847 edn).

Brabantio, in Shakespeare's *Othello*, the father of Desdemona.

Bracebridge Hall, a collection of tales and sketches by W. *Irving.

BRACEGIRDLE, Anne (?1673/4–1748), a famous actress, the friend of *Congreve, to the success of whose comedies on stage she largely contributed. She also created Belinda in Vanbrugh's *The Provok'd Wife*, and played Portia,

Desdemona, Ophelia, Cordelia, and Mrs Ford. She was finally eclipsed by Mrs *Oldfield in 1707 and retired from the stage. The age of 85, registered when she was buried in Westminster Abbey, is probably mistaken.

Brachiano, a character in Webster's *The White Devil*.

BRACKENBRIDGE, Hugh Henry (1748–1816), American novelist, poet, and lawyer, born in Scotland, and educated at the College of New Jersey (later Princeton). His satirical novel *Modern Chivalry*, published in instalments from 1792 to 1815, gives a good description of men and manners during the early days of the American republic, and manifests Brackenbridge's allegiance to the robust tradition of the English novel in *Smollett and *Fielding.

BRACTON, BRATTON, or BRETTON, Henry de (d. 1268), a judge and ecclesiastic, was author of the famous treatise *De Legibus et Consuetudinibus Angliae*, the first attempt at a complete treatise on the laws and customs of England. He also left a 'Note-book' containing some 2,000 legal cases with comments.

Bracy, Sir Maurice De, in Scott's *Ivanhoe*, one of Prince John's knights, a suitor for the hand of Rowena.

Bradamante, in *Orlando Innamorato* and *Orlando Furioso*, a maiden warrior, sister of *Rinaldo. She fights with the great *Rodomont. *Rogero comes to her assistance and falls in love with her. *Spenser owed much to Bradamante in fashioning his Britomart in *The Faerie Queene*.

BRADBROOK, Muriel Clara (1909–), scholar, educated at Girton College, Cambridge, of which she was mistress from 1968 to 1976. Known primarily as an Elizabethan scholar, her works range from *Themes and Conventions of Elizabethan Tragedy* (1935, rev. 1980) and a study of the *School of Night (1936) to *The Rise of the Common Player* (1962), in which she examines the social implications of drama as a performing art, but she has also written on *Conrad, M. *Lowry, V. *Woolf, T. S. *Eliot, and other 20th-cent. literary figures. Her *Collected Papers* (2 vols) appeared in 1982.

BRADBURY, Malcolm Stanley (1932–), critic and novelist, born in Sheffield, and educated at the universities of Leicester, London, and Manchester; he held several academic appointments, and in 1970 became professor of American studies at the University of East Anglia. His critical works include *Possibilities: essays on the state of the novel* (1973) and (with J. W. McFarlane) *Modernism* (1976), and studies of E. *Waugh (1962) and *Bellow (1982); his approach combines a respect for pluralism with an admiration for the experiments and fictive devices of the American novel and of British writers such as *Fowles. His first three novels are satirical *Campus novels, though with widely differing backgrounds; *Eating People is Wrong* (1959) relates the amorous and pedagogic adventures of ageing liberal humanist Professor Treece in a second-rate redbrick provincial university; *Stepping Westward* (1965) is set in the mid-west of America; and *The History Man* (1975) is set in the new plate-glass university of Watermouth, where the ambivalent figure of the ambitious Dr Howard Kirk manipulates wife, colleagues, students, lovers, and academic politics with a fine sense of the historical moment. *Rates of Exchange* (1983) takes academic linguist Dr Petworth on a British Council lecture tour to an Eastern European country where there is no British Council; the novel's imagery and plot spring from *Structuralist concepts of culture, and it is a witty and satiric commentary on cultural exchange.

BRADDON, Mary Elizabeth (1837–1915), privately educated, was an actress for three years in order to support herself and her mother. She met John Maxwell, a publisher of periodicals, in 1860, and acted as stepmother to his five children before marrying him in 1874 upon the death of his insane wife; she had six children by him. She published several works, including *Garibaldi and other poems* (1861), before the appearance of the sensational *Lady Audley's Secret* (1862, first serialized in *Robin Goodfellow* and *The Sixpenny Magazine*), which won her fame and fortune. The bigamous pretty blonde heroine, who deserts her child, murders her husband, and contemplates poisoning her second husband, shocked Mrs *Oliphant who credited Miss Braddon as 'the inventor of the fair-haired demon of modern fiction'. The novel has been dramatized, filmed, and translated and remained in print throughout the author's life. She published a further 74 inventive, lurid novels including the successful *Aurora Floyd* (1863), *The Doctor's Wife* (1864), *Henry Dunbar* (1864), and *Ishmael* (1884) and edited several magazines including *Belgravia* and *Temple Bar*. She was often attacked for corrupting young minds by making crime and violence attractive, but she won some notable admirers including *Bulwer-Lytton, *Hardy, *Stevenson, and *Thackeray. (See SENSATION, NOVEL OF.)

BRADLAUGH, Charles (1833–91), social reformer and advocate of free thought, who, after being employed in various occupations, became a lecturer and pamphleteer on many popular causes, under the name 'Iconoclast'. His voice was to be heard on platforms throughout the country and in the *National Reformer* (of which he became proprietor) which was a chief outlet for his friend James *Thomson's poems. He was elected MP for Northampton in 1880, but was unseated having been refused the right to make affirmation of allegiance instead of taking the parliamentary oath; he was re-elected in 1881, but it was not until 1886 that he took his seat, having agreed finally to take the oath. He became a popular debater in the House. He was engaged in several lawsuits to maintain freedom of the press. In association with Mrs *Besant, he republished a pamphlet *The Fruits of Philosophy* advocating birth control, which led to a six-month prison sentence and a £200 fine; the conviction was quashed on appeal.

BRADLEY, A(ndrew) C(ecil) (1851–1935), brother of F. H. *Bradley, was professor of literature at Liverpool, then Glasgow, and from 1901 to 1906 professor of poetry at Oxford. He is particularly remembered for his contributions to Shakespearian scholarship; his best-known works are *Shakespearean Tragedy* (1904) and *Oxford lectures on poetry* (1909). L. C. *Knights in his essay 'How many children had Lady Macbeth?' (1933) represented a new generation of critics in his mockery of Bradley's 'detective interest' in plot and emphasis on 'character' as a detachable object of study, but Bradley's works retain their interest and some admirers.

BRADLEY, Edward (1827–89), educated at University College, Durham (which suggested his pseudonym, 'Cuthbert Bede'), and rector of various country livings, is remembered as the author of *The Adventures of Mr Verdant Green* (1853–7), a novel which traces the Oxford career of a gullible young undergraduate, fresh from Warwickshire, from his freshman days to graduation and marriage. It was reprinted in 1982 with an introduction by A. *Powell. Bradley also contributed extensively to periodicals, illustrated his own works, and drew for *Punch.

BRADLEY, F(rancis) H(erbert) (1846–1924), brother of A. C. *Bradley, and fellow of Merton College, Oxford, published *Ethical Studies* in 1876, perhaps most notable for its essay on 'My Station and its Duties', and *Principles of Logic* in 1883. His *Appearance and Reality* (1893) was considered an important philosophical discussion of contemporary metaphysical thought; Bradley was greatly concerned to draw attention in England to continental philosophy, and particularly to Hegelianism. *Essay on Truth and Reality* appeared in 1914. He was admired by T. S. *Eliot, who noted that his own prose style was 'closely . . . formed on that of Bradley'. See R. Wollheim, *F. H. Bradley* (1959).

BRADLEY, Dr Henry (1845–1923), philologist, is principally remembered for his work on the *Oxford English Dictionary* with which he was associated for forty years, from

1884. He became second editor in 1887 and succeeded James *Murray as senior editor on Murray's death in 1915. Among Bradley's works may be mentioned the successful *The Making of English* (1904, rev. 1968). A memoir of Bradley by *Bridges is prefixed to *Collected Papers of Henry Bradley* (1928).

BRADSHAW, Henry (1831–86), bibliographer, scholar, antiquary, and librarian of the University of Cambridge (1867–86) where he reformed the department of early printed books and manuscripts. He published treatises on typographical and antiquarian subjects, including some important original discoveries.

Bradshaw's Railway Guide was first published in 1839 in the form of Railway Time Tables by George Bradshaw (1801–53), a Quaker engraver and printer. These developed into *Bradshaw's Monthly Railway Guide* in 1841 and it continued to be published until May 1961.

BRADSTREET, Anne (*c*.1612–72), American poet, was born in England and emigrated with her father Thomas Dudley and husband Simon Bradstreet in 1630, settling first at Ipswich, then in North Andover, Massachusetts. She had eight children. Her poems were published in London without her knowledge in 1650, under the title *The Tenth Muse Lately Sprung Up in America*, and a posthumous second edition with her own corrections and additions was published in Boston (1678). She admired and was influenced by *Quarles and Sylvester's translation of *Du Bartas, and her work was highly praised in her own time. Her later and shorter poems are now more highly regarded than her longer philosophical and historical discourses, and she has received much attention both as a woman writer and as the first poet of the New World. *Berryman pays tribute to her in his poem *Homage to Mistress Bradstreet* (1956).

Bradwardine, The Baron of, and Rose, characters in Scott's *Waverley*.

BRADWARDINE, Thomas (*c*.1280–1349), Oxford theologian appointed archbishop of Canterbury immediately before his death of the plague in August 1349. His *De Causa Dei* reasserted the primacy of faith and divine grace in opposition to the rationalist sceptics (whom he characterized as New Pelagians) of the tradition of *Ockham and *Holcot. Like his direct contemporary *Fitzralph he was a member of the circle of Richard de Bury. He has been called a Determinist and a preacher of Predestination because of his insistence on the involvement of God's will as a primary cause in every action of the human will, the independence of which is thus reduced. The effect of this, as of the arguments of his opponents, was to destroy the

13th-cent. synthesis of Faith and Reason, but in this case giving the primacy unconditionally to Faith/Theology over Reason/Philosophy. See G. Leff, *Bradwardine and the Pelagians* (1957).

BRAGG, Melvyn (1939–), novelist, journalist, and broadcaster, brought up in Cumberland, which forms the setting of several of his works, and educated at Wadham College, Oxford. He is best known as a presenter of arts programmes on television, in which medium he has made a sustained effort to present literature to a wide public in a popular and informal manner.

Braggadochio, in Spenser's *Faerie Queene*, the typical braggart. His adventures and final exposure and humiliation occur in Bks. II. iii; III. viii, x; IV. iv, v, ix; V. iii. Cf. *Trompart.

BRAHMS, Johannes (1833–97), German composer. With the exception of a few Shakespeare songs in German translations, Brahms made no settings of any texts drawn from English literature. Though twice invited to accept an honorary doctorate at Cambridge, he never in fact visited England—largely because he hated the sea and did not like the idea of crossing the Channel.

BRAILLE, Louis (1809–52), the French inventor, himself blind, of a system of reading for the blind. This consists of embossed characters printed on special paper, recognizable by touch and formed by varying combinations of six dots.

BRAINE, John Gerard (1922–), novelist, born and educated in Bradford, was for many years a librarian in the north of England. His first novel, *Room at the Top* (1957), set in a small Yorkshire town, was an instant success, and its hero, Joe Lampton, was hailed as another of the provincial *'angry young men' of the 1950s. Lampton, a ruthless opportunist working at the Town Hall, seduces and marries the wealthy young Susan Browne, despite his love for an unhappily married older woman. *Life at the Top* (1962) continues the story of his success and disillusion. Braine's later novels express his increasing hostility to the radical views with which he was once identified.

Brainworm, the wily, high-spirited servant in Jonson's *Every Man in his Humour*.

Bramble, Matthew and Tabitha, characters in Smollett's *Humphry Clinker*.

Brambletye House, see SMITH, H.

Bramine's Journal, The, see ELIZA, JOURNAL TO.

Brandon, (1) Colonel, a character in J. Austen's *Sense and Sensibility*; (2) George, the assumed name of George Firmin in Thackeray's *A

Shabby Genteel Story; (3) Mrs, a character in Thackeray's *The Adventures of Philip*.

Branghtons, The, in Fanny Burney's *Evelina*, the heroine's vulgar relatives.

Brangwane (Bragwaine, Bregwaine), the maid-servant of Isoud (Isolde); see TRISTRAM AND ISOUD.

BRANTÔME, Pierre de Bourdeilles, seigneur de (*c.*1534–1614), French memorialist. His career as an officer and courtier offered him every opportunity to observe the private conduct of the great figures of the day. His memoirs (pub. posth., 1665) include the notorious *Vie des dames galantes*, which repeat the scandals of court intrigues in a lively and uncensorious style.

Branwen, see MABINOGION.

Brasenose College, Oxford, was founded in 1509, replacing an earlier Brasenose Hall. In 1344 a part of the students of Oxford migrated for a time to Stamford, where they occupied a house known as Brasenose Hall, on the door of which was a brass knocker shaped like a nose. The knocker remained at Stamford until 1890, when it was acquired by the College. It was this knocker which probably gave its name to the Hall, although it has been maintained that the origin of Brasenose is to be sought in 'brasinium', a brewery.

Brass, (1) a character in Vanbrugh's *The Confederacy*; (2) Sampson and his sister Sally, characters in Dickens's *The Old Curiosity Shop*.

BRATHWAITE, Edward Kamau (1930–), poet, born in Barbados, was educated there and at Pembroke College, Cambridge. From 1955 to 1962 he taught in Ghana, then returned to the West Indies. He has written works on West Indian history and culture, and his volumes of poetry include *The Arrivants, A New World Trilogy* (1973), which consists of *Rights of Passage* (1967), *Masks* (1968), and *Islands* (1969). The poem explores the complex Caribbean heritage and search for identity, using (but not exclusively) vernacular rhythms and diction; its references range from Afro-Caribbean religious beliefs to cricket matches at the Oval. *Mother Poem* (1977) and *Sun Poem* (1982) are the first two parts of a trilogy about Barbados, 'most English of West Indian islands'.

Brave New World, a novel by A. *Huxley, published 1932.

It is a fable about a world state in the 7th cent. AF (after Ford), where social stability is based on a scientific caste system. Human beings, graded from highest intellectuals to lowest manual workers, hatched from incubators and brought up in communal nurseries, learn by methodical conditioning to accept their social destiny. The action of the story develops round Bernard Marx, an unorthodox and therefore unhappy Alpha-Plus (something had presumably gone wrong with his antenatal treatment), who visits a New Mexican Reservation and brings a Savage back to London. The Savage is at first fascinated by the new world, but finally revolted, and his argument with Mustapha Mond, World Controller, demonstrates the incompatibility of individual freedom and a scientifically trouble-free society.

In *Brave New World Revisited* (1958) Huxley reconsiders his prophecies and fears that some of these may be coming true much sooner than he thought.

BRAWNE, Fanny (1800–65), the young woman with whom *Keats fell in love in 1818. To what extent she returned or understood his passion for her (expressed in many of his letters and several poems) is not clear, but some kind of engagement took place, and after his death she wore mourning for him for several years. She married in 1833. His letters to her were published in 1878 and in the collected edition of 1937; hers to his sister, also called Fanny, were published in 1937.

Bray, Madeline, a character in Dickens's *Nicholas Nickleby*.

Bray, Vicar of, see VICAR OF BRAY.

Brazen, Captain, a character in Farquhar's *The Recruiting Officer*.

Bread and Cheese Club, a New York literary society founded by J. F. *Cooper *c.*1822.

BRECHT, Bertolt (1898–1956), German dramatist and poet. After emigrating (to the United States, where he collaborated on translations and productions of his plays with Eric Bentley and Charles Laughton), he settled in 1949 in East Berlin, where he founded and directed the Berliner Ensemble. After his death his widow, the actress Helene Weigel, directed the company until she died in 1971. Brecht's early plays, e.g. *Baal* (1922) and *Trommeln in der Nacht* (*Drums in the Night*, 1922) show kinship with *Expressionism. *Mann ist Mann* (*Man is Man*, 1927) anticipates Brecht's later systematic development of his famous 'alienation effect', and *Die Dreigroschenoper* (*The Threepenny Opera*, 1928), his version of *The Beggar's Opera*, was one of the theatrical successes of Weimar Germany, not least in the bourgeois circles which were satirized in the work. His theory of 'epic theatre' rejected Aristotelian principles, regarded a play as a series of loosely connected scenes, dispensed with dramatic climaxes, and used songs to comment on the action. The theory is best illustrated in *Leben des Galilei* (*The Life of Galileo*, 1937–9), *Der Gute Mensch von Sezuan* (*The Good Woman of Setzuan*, 1938–41), *Mutter Courage* (*Mother Courage,*

1941), based on a story by *Grimmelshausen, and *Der kaukasische Kreidekreis* (*The Caucasian Chalk Circle*, 1948). All these plays call for highly stylized acting which, like his general theory of drama, expounded in its most mature form in his essay *Kleines Organon für das Theater* (*Little Treatise on the Theatre*, 1949), discards the notion that drama should seek to create the illusion of reality. Some of Brecht's plays, e.g. *Die heilige Johanna der Schlachthöfe* (*St Joan of the Stockyards*, 1929–30), have a particularly direct anti-capitalist theme, and others, e.g. *Der aufhaltsame Aufstieg des Arturo Ui* (*The Resistible Rise of Arturo Ui*, 1941), combine this with the theme of Hitlerism. The didactic plays of the period around 1930, e.g. *Der Jasager/Der Neinsager* (*He who said Yes/He who said No*) and *Die Massnahme* (*The Measures Taken*), are closely connected with the interests of the Communist Party, with which Brecht was intimately associated from the late 1920s. He was never a member of the Party, however, and his relations with it, even in his last years in East Berlin, became rather uncertain. Since the first visit of the Berliner Ensemble to London in 1956, Brecht's plays have been produced frequently in Britain. British playwrights of the 1960s, particularly *Bond and *Arden and, more recently, Howard Brenton (1942–   ), are clearly influenced by Brecht's radical approach, in theme and treatment, to drama. Brecht was also an outstanding lyric poet.

Breck, Alan, a character in R. L. Stevenson's *Kidnapped* and *Catriona*.

Breeches Bible, The, a name given to the edition of the English Bible printed at Geneva in 1560 (see BIBLE, THE ENGLISH), in allusion to the version adopted therein at Gen. 3: 7, 'They sewed fig leaves together, and made themselves breeches.'

BRENAN, Gerald (Edward Fitz-Gerald Brenan) (1894–   ), author born in Malta, who lived in Spain from 1920 and wrote various works on Spanish literature, including *The Literature of the Spanish People* (1951) and a study of St *John of the Cross (1972). He was friendly with several members of the *Bloomsbury Group, as he records in his autobiographies *A Life of One's Own* (1962) and *Personal Record* (1974).

BRENDAN, St (?484–?577), of the monastery of Clonfert in Ireland, about whom grew up a tradition of legendary voyages as a Christianized version of the Old Irish genre *imram*, describing sea-adventures; other examples are 'The Voyage of Bran' and 'The Voyage of Maeldune' of which the latter too was Christianized. The *Navigatio Sancti Brandani* is one of the earliest substantial texts in *Anglo-Norman, but there are earlier Latin versions,

none from before the 10th cent. The legends of Brendan have been revived in popularity at various times, for example by M. *Arnold. The most familiar stories are those of the meeting with Judas cooling himself on a rock on Christmas night, a privilege allowed him once a year; and of the landing on a whale, mistaking it for an island, and its being aroused by the lighting of a fire. A traditional Irish story credits Brendan with reaching America nearly a thousand years before Columbus, a theory of which the credibility was put to the test in the 1970s, with doubtful results.

See Lady *Gregory, *The Voyages of Saint Brendan the Navigator and Stories of the Saints of Ireland* (1906/7) ed. C. Smythe, 1973.

Brer Fox and **Brer Rabbit,** the chief characters in *Uncle Remus*. See HARRIS, J. C.

BRETON, André (1896–1966), French poet, essayist, and critic, one of the founders of *Surrealism. He collaborated with Philippe Soupauit on *Les Champs magnétiques* of 1919, an early experiment in automatic writing, and he wrote his first Surrealist Manifesto in 1924, followed by two others in 1930 and 1942. He was instrumental in the direction of two surrealist periodicals, *La Révolution surréaliste* (1924–30) and *Le Surréalisme au service de la révolution* (1930–3). He produced a number of volumes of poetry, including *Clair de terre* (1923), *Le Revolver à cheveux blancs* (1932), and *L'Air de l'eau* (1934), as well as narrative works, *Nadja* (1928; English trans., 1960), *Les Vases communicants* (1932), and *L'Amour fou* (1937). His theoretical essays are collected in *Les Pas perdus* (1924), *Point du jour* (1934), and *La Clé des champs* (1953). He was also the author of a volume on art, *Le Surréalisme et la peinture* (1928).

BRETON, Nicholas (?1555–1626), educated at Oxford, was the author of a miscellaneous collection of satirical, religious, romantic, and political writings in verse and prose. His stepfather was George *Gascoigne. From about 1576 he seems to have settled in London, and between 1575 and 1622 he published well over 50 books including: *The Wil of Wit, Wits Wil, or Wils Wit* (c.1582); *The Pilgrimage To Paradise, Joyned With The Countesse of Penbrookes love* (1592); *Wits Trenchmour* (a dialogue on angling, 1597); *The Figure of Foure, Or A Handfull of sweet Flowers* (c.1597); *Pasquils Mad-Cap* (1600); *The Soules Heavenly Exercise* (1601); *Olde mad-cappes new Gally-mawfry* (1602); *Fantasticks: Serving for A Perpetuall Prognostication* (a collection of observations on men and nature arranged calendar-wise, c.1604); *The Honour of Valour* (1605); *The Good And The Badde, Or Descriptions of the Worthies and Unworthies of this Age* (1616); *Conceyted Letters, Newly Layde Open* (1618). His best poetry is to be found among his short lyrics in *Englands Helicon* (1600) and in his volume of pastoral poetry *The Passionate Shepheard* (1604). His works were edited by *Grosart in 1879, and poems not included by Grosart were edited, with much information about his works, by Jean Robertson in 1952.

Breton Lays, in English literature of the Middle English period, are short stories in rhyme like those of *Marie de France; the English examples are by no means a clearly-defined group, and they often owe their identification to the fact that they say they are Breton lays, or that the same story is told by Marie in French. See EMARÉ, SIR ORFEO, SIR DEGARÉ; the other English examples are *Sir Landeval, Lai le Freine, The Erle of Tolous, Sir Gowther,* Chaucer's 'The Franklin's Tale' (*Canterbury Tales,* 12) and *Gower's 'Tale of Rosiphilee' (*Confessio Amantis,* Book IV). See T. C. Rumble ed., *The Breton Lays in Middle English* (1965); M. J. Donovan, *The Breton lay: a guide to Varieties* (1969).

Bretton, John, a character in *Villette* by C. Brontë, introduced in the opening chapters as Graham Bretton.

Brewer's Dictionary of Phrase and Fable, by the Revd Ebenezer Cobham Brewer (1810–97), first published 1870, regularly revised. It contains explanations and origins of the familiar and unfamiliar in English phrase and fable, including colloquial and proverbial phrases, embracing archaeology, history, religion, the arts, science, mythology, fictitious characters and titles, etc.

Briana, in Spenser's *Faerie Queene* (VI. i), the mistress of a castle who takes a toll of ladies' locks and knights' beards to make a mantle for her lover Crudor.

Bridal of Triermain, The, a poem by Sir W. *Scott, published 1813. It is a romance of love and magic, telling of the quest of Roland de Vaux, lord of Triermain, for the maid Gyneth, daughter of King Arthur and the fay Guendolen, and her rescue from the spell that Merlin has laid on her.

Bridehead, Sue, a character in Hardy's *Jude the Obscure.*

Bride of Abydos, The, a poem by Lord *Byron, published 1813, 'a Turkish tale', as Byron called it, in which the beautiful Zuleika, daughter of the Pasha Giaffir, is destined, by her father's order, to marry the rich, elderly Bey of Carasman, whom she has never seen. Tenderly she confesses her grief to her beloved brother Selim. He takes her to his grotto, where he reveals himself in magnificent pirate garb and declares he is not her brother but her cousin. He begs her to share his future, but Giaffir and his soldiers arrive and Selim is killed. Zuleika dies of grief. In the original unpublished version Selim and Zuleika are not cousins, but half-brother and sister.

Bride of Lammermoor, The, a novel by Sir W. *Scott, published 1819 in *Tales of My Landlord,* 3rd series.

Lord Ravenswood, deprived of his title for the part he had taken in the Civil War of 1689, and dispossessed of his estate in East Lothian by the legal chicanery of Sir William Ashton, a clever upstart lawyer who has attained the office of Lord Keeper, dies in a fit of fury against the man whom he regards as the author of his ruin. His son, the fiery sombre Master of Ravenswood, inherits his hatred, and, as sole possession, the ruinous tower of Wolf's Crag. Chance leads to his saving the life of his enemy, Sir William Ashton, and of Lucy Ashton, his daughter; he and Lucy fall deeply in love. Political changes raise the friends of Ravenswood to power, and the timid Sir William thinks it advisable to conciliate Ravenswood, which he does so effectually that the latter overcomes his desire for vengeance and becomes secretly betrothed to Lucy Ashton. Lady Ashton, a violent and domineering woman who has hitherto been absent from her home, now returns, learns the state of affairs, and contemptuously dismisses Ravenswood, who proceeds on a foreign mission after having renewed his pledge to Lucy. Lady Ashton now sets about breaking her daughter's spirit and obliging her to marry a husband of her own choice, the Laird of Bucklaw. The gentle Lucy appears at last to yield, only stipulating that she shall write to Ravenswood and obtain his release from her pledge. The letter is intercepted by her mother, and Lucy in despair consents to the fixing of the wedding day, convinced that her lover has abandoned her. Immediately after the ceremony Ravenswood appears, and challenges Lucy's brother and her husband to duels. The same night, Lucy stabs her husband, is found insane, and shortly after dies. Ravenswood, galloping furiously along the shore to meet his antagonists, is swallowed up in a quicksand.

One of the characters in the book is Caleb Balderstone, the old butler of Ravenswood, determined to maintain in the eyes of the world the fallen dignity of the family, who resorts for this purpose to the most absurd devices.

Brideshead Revisited, a novel by E. *Waugh, published 1945.

Narrated by Charles Ryder, it describes his emotional involvement with an ancient aristocratic Roman Catholic family, which grows from his meeting as an undergraduate at Oxford the handsome, whimsical younger son, Sebastian Flyte, already an incipient alcoholic. Through Sebastian Charles meets his mother, the devout Lady Marchmain, who refuses to divorce Lord Marchmain, exiled to Venice with his mistress; the heir, Lord Brideshead; and the sisters Julia and Cordelia. Lady Marchmain attempts to enlist Charles's support in preventing Sebastian's drinking, but Sebastian finally escapes to North Africa, where, after his mother's death, he becomes some kind of saintly down-and-out. Meanwhile Charles, now an unhappily married but successful artist, falls in love with Julia, also unhappily married; they both plan to divorce and begin a new life, but the power of the Church reclaims Julia, and they part forever. The narrative is set in a war-time framework of prologue and epilogue, in which Charles is billeted in Brideshead, the great country house which had once dominated his imagination. In a 1959 preface, Waugh (for whom this novel marked a departure from his earlier satiric style) said that his theme was 'the operation of divine grace on a group of diverse but closely connected characters', but also conceded that the book was 'infused with a kind of gluttony, for food and wine, for the splendours of the recent past, and for rhetorical and ornamental language, which now with a full stomach I find distasteful'; these aspects contributed greatly to the success of the lavish, lengthy, nostalgic television adaptation, shown in 1980.

Bridgenorth, Major and Alice, characters in Scott's *Peveril of the Peak*.

'Bridge of Sighs, The', a poem by T. *Hood, published 1843, one of the most popular of his serious works. It is a morbid and ostensibly compassionate elegy on the suicide by drowning of a 'Fallen Woman', a favourite Victorian theme, which dwells in some detail on her youth and beauty, her penitence for her 'evil behaviour', and on the 'cold inhumanity' of the world which cast her out.

BRIDGES, Robert (1844–1930), educated at Eton and Corpus Christi College, Oxford, afterwards studied medicine at St Bartholomew's Hospital, and he continued to practise until 1881. At Oxford he met G. M. *Hopkins, who became a close and influential friend, and whose complete poems Bridges eventually published in 1918. Bridges' first book, *Poems*, was published in 1873, and further volumes, with additional poems, followed over many years. *The Growth of Love*, a sonnet sequence, appeared in 1876 with some success, and in an enlarged form in 1890. Two long poems followed, *Prometheus the Firegiver* (1883) and *Eros and Psyche* (1885). Between 1885 and 1894 he wrote eight plays. He wrote two influential essays, *Milton's Prosody* (1893) and *John Keats* (1895); and between 1895 and 1908 wrote the words for four works by H. *Parry. He was much interested in the musical settings of words, and edited several editions of the *Yattendon Hymnal* from 1895 onwards. In 1898 appeared the first of the six volumes of his *Poetical Works* (1898–1905). His poetry appeared in one volume in 1912, and

received great critical and popular acclaim. The following year he was appointed poet laureate, and became one of the founders of the *Society for Pure English, many of whose Tracts he wrote or edited. For many years he was closely connected with the Oxford University Press, which he advised on many matters of style, phonetics, spelling, and typography. In 1916 he published a highly successful anthology of prose and verse, *The Spirit of Man*, which included six poems by Hopkins, little of whose work had yet been published. *October and other Poems* appeared in 1920, *New Verse* in 1925, and then in 1929 *The Testament of Beauty*, a long poem, in four books, on his spiritual philosophy, which he regarded as the culmination of his work as a poet, and which met with high acclaim and sold extremely well. His lyric verse has been much anthologized, and some of it (including 'London Snow', 'A Passer-by', 'Asian Birds', and 'A Dead Child') has become widely known. His collected prose works, mostly on poets and various literary topics, were published between 1927 and 1936.

Bridges' general reputation does not stand as high as it once did; but his 'inward and retired deliberation' (in the words of C. *Williams); his veneration for 'the master Reason'; the simplicity of his diction; and his adventurous experiments in metre and prosody are still respected.

BRIDIE, James, pseudonym of Osborne Henry Mavor (1888–1951), son of a Glasgow engineer, who trained and practised as a doctor; questions of medical ethics and practice appear frequently in his plays. He began his career as a playwright with a cheerful morality, *The Sunlight Sonata*, with Tyrone Guthrie in Glasgow in 1928; *The Anatomist* (1930), a comedy on the grave-robbers Burke and Hare, established his name. His plays fall roughly into four groups: those on biblical themes, such as *Tobias and the Angel* (1930), *Jonah and the Whale* (1932), and *Susannah and the Elders* (1937); those with medical themes, such as *A Sleeping Clergyman* (1933); portrait plays, including *Mr Bolfry* (1943); and experimental, symbolist, and partly poetic plays such as *Daphne Laureola* (1949) and his last play, the dark, foreboding *The Baikie Charivari* (1952). Many of Bridie's dramas, with their bold characterization, lively debate, and humour, are reminiscent of *Morality plays. Bridie assisted in the establishment of the Glasgow Citizen's Theatre in 1943, founded the first College of Drama in Scotland in 1950, and worked diligently for various artistic enterprises such as the Edinburgh Festival. His modest autobiography, *One Way of Living*, appeared in 1939.

BRIEUX, Eugène (1858–1932), French dramatist of contemporary morals, championed as 'the greatest writer France has produced since Molière' by G. B. *Shaw, whose wife translated his *Maternité* in *Three Plays by Brieux* (1913, with an introduction by Shaw). A second volume, *Woman on Her Own, False Gods and The Red Robe: Three Plays by Brieux* (1916), has translations by Mrs Shaw, J. B. Fagan, and A. B. Miall and an introduction by Brieux.

Brigadore, in Spenser's *Faerie Queene*, the horse of Sir *Guyon, stolen by *Braggadochio (v. iii. 34).

Briggs, (1) a character in Fanny Burney's *Cecilia*, drawn in some respects from the sculptor Nollekens; (2) Miss, a character in Thackeray's *Vanity Fair*, companion first to Miss Crawley and then to Becky.

BRIGHOUSE, H., see HOBSON'S CHOICE.

BRIGHT, John (1811–89), son of a Rochdale miller, renowned political agitator and orator, prominent member of the Anti-Corn Law League, and with *Cobden a leading representative of the emergence of the manufacturing class in England after the 1832 *Reform Bill. He was successively MP for Durham (1843), Manchester, and Birmingham, and held various posts in *Gladstone's governments, from 1868 onwards.

Brighton Rock, a novel by G. *Greene, published 1938.

Set in Brighton in the criminal underworld of gang warfare and protection rackets, it describes the brief and tragic career of 17-year-old Pinkie, 'The Boy', whose ambition is to run a gang to rival that of the wealthy and established Colleoni. He murders a journalist called Hale, marries a 16-year-old girl, the downtrodden Rose (like himself a Roman Catholic), to prevent her giving evidence in court against him, and is driven to further crimes and eventual death by the almost casual pursuit of Ida, a justice-seeking acquaintance of Hale. Pinkie's corruption and Rose's innocence are shown as in some way complementary, and the vigorous, fun-loving, stout-drinking, single-minded Ida is not portrayed with sympathy; the novel (originally described by Greene as 'an entertainment') foreshadows the religious complexity and ambiguities of later works, and Greene later claimed to regret the detective story element of the opening section (*Ways of Escape*, 1980, Ch. 2).

'Brigs of Ayr, The', a poem by *Burns, published 1786, in which the old and new bridges at Ayr speak to each other, and to the poet, of their respective merits and of their history.

BRILLAT-SAVARIN, Anthelme (1755–1826), French jurist and magistrate, author of the gastronomic classic *Physiologie du goût ou Méditations sur la gastronomie transcendente* (1825).

BRINK, André Philippus (1935–), South African novelist and playwright, educated at the University of Potchefstroom and at the Sorbonne, who writes in both English and Afrikaans, and translates into Afrikaans. His novels, which have encountered troubles with the censor in South Africa because of their open criticisms of apartheid, include *Looking on Darkness* (1974; in Afrikaans, 1973, *Kennis van die aand*), *Rumour of Rain* (1978), *A Dry White Season* (1979), and *A Chain of Voices* (1982).

Brisk, a voluble coxcomb in Congreve's *The Double Dealer*.

Brisk, Fastidious, a foppish courtier in Jonson's *Every Man out of his Humour*.

Britannia, or, according to the sub-title, *A chorographicall description of the most flourishing Kingdomes of England, Scotland, and Ireland, and the Ilands adioyning, out of the depth of Antiquitie*, by W. *Camden, published in Latin 1586, the sixth (much enlarged) edition appearing in 1607. It was translated in 1610 by *Holland. It is in effect a guide-book of the country, county by county, replete with archaeological, historical, physical, and other information.

Britannia's Pastorals, see BROWNE, W.

British Academy, a society, incorporated in 1902, for the promotion of the study of the moral and political sciences, including history, philosophy, law, political economy, archaeology, and philology. It publishes Proceedings, administers endowments for a number of annual lectures, encourages archaeological and oriental research, etc. Its first secretary was Sir I. *Gollancz.

British Association for the Advancement of Science, The, held its first meeting at York in 1831. Its object is the promotion and diffusion of science, and the encouragement of intercourse of scientists.

British Library, see LIBRARIES.

British Magazine, The, a periodical miscellany founded in 1759 by *Newbery, which ran from Jan. 1760 to Dec. 1767. It was edited by *Smollett, and one of its principal contributors was *Goldsmith. It published a large amount of fiction (including a serialization of Smollett's *The Life and Adventures of *Sir Launcelot Greaves*, 1760–1), and also reviews, essays, etc.

British Museum, Bloomsbury, occupies the site of the old Montagu House, which was acquired in 1753 to house the library and collection of curiosities of Sir H. *Sloane. These were from time to time enormously increased, notably by the purchase of the *Harleian MSS, the gift by George II and George IV of royal libraries, the purchase of the Elgin Marbles, and the acquisition of Egyptian antiquities (including the Rosetta Stone), and of the Layard Assyrian collections. The new buildings, designed by Sir Robert Smirke, were erected in 1823–47, and the great reading-room, designed by *Panizzi, the librarian, was opened in 1857.

Britomart, the heroine of Bk III of Spenser's *Faerie Queene,* the daughter of King Ryence of Britain and the female knight of chastity. She has fallen in love with *Artegall, whose image she has seen in a magic mirror, and the poet recounts her adventures in her quest for him. She is the most powerful of several types of Queen Elizabeth in the poem.

Briton, The, a weekly periodical conducted in 1762 by *Smollett in Lord Bute's interest. Wilkes's *North Briton was started in opposition to it.

BRITTAIN, Vera Mary (1893–1970), writer, pacifist, and feminist. The daughter of a wealthy manufacturer, she was brought up in the north of England, and educated at Somerville College, Oxford. Her education was interrupted by the First World War, during which she served as a VAD nurse, and which caused the death of her fiancé in France. *Testament of Youth* (1933) is a moving account of her girlhood and struggle for education (she came under the influence of O. *Schreiner while still at school) and of her war experiences. She returned to Oxford after the war, where she formed a close friendship with Winifred *Holtby, recorded in *Testament of Friendship* (1940). She also published various volumes of poetry, fiction, essays, etc.

BRITTEN, (Edward) Benjamin (1913–76), English composer. Skilful judgement in the choice of literary texts and an exceptional sensitivity in the setting of words were characteristic features of Britten's musical production, in many cases ideally served by the artistry and clear diction of the tenor Peter Pears, for whose voice much of Britten's music was designed. Early works like the *Serenade* for tenor, horn, and strings (1943), or the *Spring Symphony* (1949), already brought together poems ranging from an anonymous medieval dirge through *Spenser, *Jonson, and *Herrick to *Blake, *Keats, *Tennyson, and *Auden, each interpreted with an inventiveness and intensity that were something altogether new in the musical setting of English poetry. Britten's friendship with Auden resulted in a number of Auden settings during the thirties and early forties (*Our Hunting Fathers, On this Island, Hymn to Saint Cecilia,* and other lesser pieces), as well as the composer's first opera, *Paul Bunyan* (1941). This was withdrawn and not revived until 1976, but Britten's second venture in this form, *Peter Grimes* (1945), established him at once as an opera composer of real importance, the first to emerge in this country since *Handel or *Purcell. The choice of *Crabbe's poem as a subject, with its 'outsider' protagonist, and Britten's concern with the problems of innocence and misunderstanding, set a trend that was to be followed in later works: *Billy Budd* (1951), for instance, with a libretto drawn from *Melville's story by E. M. *Forster, or *The Turn of the Screw* (1954), after the chilling tale by H. *James. The latter work is described as a 'chamber opera', a form to which Britten had turned after *Peter Grimes,* partly for economic reasons: *The Rape of Lucretia* (1946) was the first example of this move towards simplification which was to lead, at the other end of his career, to the three *Parables for Church Performance,* stylized pieces on the model of the Japanese *Nōh-play, all with librettos by *Plomer (1964, 1966, 1968). Plomer had also provided the text for Britten's ill-starred 'coronation' opera *Gloriana* (1953); later operas in the more traditional sense included *A Midsummer Night's Dream* (1960), with a libretto compiled from Shakespeare by the composer and Pears, *Owen Wingrave,* after Henry James (1970), and *Death in Venice,* after T. *Mann (1973). On a smaller scale Britten made a number of finely judged solo settings of individual poets: *The Holy Sonnets of John Donne* (1945), *Winter Words* (*Hardy, 1953), *Songs and Proverbs of William Blake* (1965), *Who Are These Children?* (*Soutar, 1969), as well as cycles from *Rimbaud, *Michelangelo, *Hölderlin, *Pushkin, and *Waley's translations from the Chinese, and a series of five *Canticles* (spread between 1947 and 1975) with texts from *Quarles, the Chester Miracle Play, E. *Sitwell, and two from T. S. *Eliot. But the most substantial use of the English language, outside the operas, is in the *War Requiem* (1962), written to celebrate the dedication of the new cathedral at Coventry built to replace the church destroyed by bombs in 1940. The Latin Mass for the Dead is here punctuated by settings for solo voice of poems by W. *Owen, and the implications and ironies of these juxtapositions, as well as the emotional expressiveness of the music itself, create a work whose immediate universality of appeal is comparable only to *Peter Grimes* in Britten's output.

Broad Church, a popular term especially current in the latter half of the 19th cent. for those in the Church of England who sought to interpret the creeds in a broad and liberal manner, and whose theological beliefs lay between Low and High Churchmen. The expression was used by A. P. *Stanley in one of his sermons, about 1847, though the term appears to have originally been proposed by A. H. *Clough. The existence of the Broad Church school owes much to the influence of T. *Arnold and to Romantic philosophy as interpreted by *Coleridge who earned the title of 'Father of the Broad Church Movement'. Other characteristic representatives of the school were T. *Hughes, *Jowett, *Pattison, and most of the other writers for *Essays and Reviews. Their successors are more commonly known as Modernists.

Broadside, a sheet of paper printed on one side only, forming one large page; a term generally used of *ballads, etc., so printed.

Brobdingnag, see GULLIVER'S TRAVELS.

Broceliande, a legendary region adjoining Brittany, in the Arthurian legends, where *Merlin lies. *Wace in his *Roman de Rou* says that he made a disappointing visit there (i.e. to Brecheliant in Brittany) and found nothing (ii. 6395 ff.); there is a legendary Tomb of Merlin there still. Broceliande is made the magical forest of Calogrenant's story in *Chrétien's *Yvain.*

Broken Heart, The, a tragedy by J. *Ford, printed 1633.

The scene is Sparta. Penthea, who was betrothed to Orgilus whom she loved, has been forced by her brother Ithocles to marry the jealous and contemptible Bassanes, who makes her life so miserable that presently she goes mad and dies. Ithocles returns, a successful general, and is honourably received by the king. He falls in love with Calantha, the king's daughter, and she with him, and their marriage is sanctioned by the king. Orgilus, to avenge the fate of Penthea, of which he has been the witness, entraps Ithocles and kills him. During a feast, Calantha hears, in close succession, of the deaths of Penthea, of her father, and of Ithocles. She dances on, apparently unmoved. When the feast is done, she sentences Orgilus to death, and herself dies brokenhearted.

Spartan values (courage, endurance, self-control) dominate the action, and the characters represent abstractions rather than individuals. The grave, formal, stately language, and emblematic imagery make it Ford's finest dramatic achievement.

BROME, Alexander (1620–66), a Royalist poet and friend of I. *Walton and *Cotton, both of whom addressed verses to him. He wrote many attacks on the Rump Parliament, including a ballad entitled *Bumm-foder: or wastepaper proper to wipe the nations rump with* (?1660). He also translated *Horace, wrote songs, and was the author of one comedy, *The Cunning Lovers* (1654).

BROME, Richard (c.1590–1652/3) was servant or perhaps secretary to *Jonson, whose friendship he afterwards enjoyed and whose influence is clear in his works, as is that of *Dekker. *The Northern Lass,* his first extant play, was printed in 1632. *The Sparagus Garden* (a place to which more or less reputable persons resorted to eat asparagus and otherwise amuse themselves), a comedy of manners, was acted in 1635. *The City Witt* was printed in 1653. *The Joviall Crew,* his best and latest play, was acted in 1641, often revived, and later turned into an operetta. Fifteen in all of his plays survive, including romantic dramas in the manner of *Fletcher and *Middleton.

BRONTË, Anne (1820–49), sister of Charlotte and Emily *Brontë, was educated largely at home, where, as the youngest of the motherless family, she was much under the Wesleyan influence of her Aunt Branwell, who is thought to have encouraged her tendency to religious melancholy. As a child she was particularly close to Emily; together they invented the imaginary world of Gondal, the setting of many of their dramatic poems. Anne accompanied Charlotte to Roe Head in 1836–7, and became governess to the Ingham family at Blake Hall in 1839; from 1841 to 1845 she was governess to the Robinson family at Thorp Green Hall, near York. Her brother Branwell joined her there as tutor in 1843, and became disastrously involved with Mrs Robinson. Anne's recollections of her experiences with the over-indulged young children and the worldly older children of these two households are vividly portrayed in *Agnes Grey* (1847). The novel appeared under the pseudonym Acton Bell, as did a selection of her poems, together with those of her sisters, in 1846. Her second novel, *The Tenant of Wildfell Hall* (1848), portrays in Arthur Huntingdon a violent drunkard clearly to some extent drawn from Branwell; Charlotte, in her 'Biographical Notice' (1850) felt obliged to comment that 'the choice of subject was an entire mistake', and insists that her sister's nature was 'naturally sensitive, reserved and dejected'. Anne died at Scarborough, where she was buried. There is a life by W. Gérin (1959).

BRONTË, (Patrick) Branwell (1817–48), the brother of Charlotte, Emily, and Anne *Brontë, as a boy was much involved with his sisters' literary efforts, and collaborated with Charlotte in creating the imaginary world of *Angria. His ambitions as a painter and writer were frustrated; he took to drink and opium, and after a brief spell as a tutor became assistant clerk to a railway company, but was dismissed in 1842 for culpable negligence. In 1843 he joined Anne at Thorp Green Hall as tutor, but became emotionally involved with his employer's wife, Mrs Robinson. The affair ended disastrously, and he returned to Haworth in 1845, where his rapid decline and death caused much suffering to his family.

BRONTË, Charlotte (1816–55), daughter of Patrick Bontë, an Irishman, perpetual curate of

Haworth, Yorkshire, from 1820 until his death in 1861. Charlotte's mother died in 1821, leaving five daughters and a son to the care of their aunt, Elizabeth Branwell. Four of the daughters were sent to a Clergy Daughters' School at Cowan Bridge (which Charlotte portrayed as Lowood in *Jane Eyre*), an unfortunate step which Charlotte believed to have hastened the death in 1825 of her two elder sisters and to have permanently impaired her own health. The surviving children pursued their education at home; they read widely, and became involved in a rich fantasy life that owes much to their admiration of *Byron, Sir W. *Scott, the *Arabian Nights*, the *Tales of the Genii*, and the engravings of J. *Martin. They began to write stories, to produce microscopic magazines in imitation of their favourite *Blackwood's Magazine*, and Charlotte and Branwell collaborated in the increasingly elaborate invention of the imaginary kingdom of *Angria, Emily and Anne in the invention of Gondal. (For a discussion of the juvenilia, see F. E. Ratchford, *The Brontës' Web of Childhood*, 1941.) In 1831–2 Charlotte was at Miss Wooler's school at Roe Head, whither she returned as a teacher in 1835–8, and where she met her two close friends, Ellen Nussey and Mary Taylor. In 1839 she was a governess with the Sidgwick family, near Skipton, and in 1841 with the White family at Rawdon. In 1842 she went with Emily to study languages at the Pensionnat Heger in Brussels; they were recalled at the end of the year by their aunt's death, and in 1843 Charlotte, whose thirst for wider experience was much greater than her sister's, returned alone for a further year. She fell deeply in love with M. Heger, who failed to respond to the letters she wrote to him after her return to Haworth; a project to establish her own school, with her sisters, also failed. In 1845 she 'discovered' (or so she alleged) the poems of Emily, and, convinced of their quality, projected a joint publication; a volume of verse entitled *Poems by Currer, Ellis, and Acton Bell* (the pseudonyms of Charlotte, Emily, and Anne) appeared in 1846, but did not sell and received little attention. By this time each had finished a novel; Charlotte's first,*The Professor*, never found a publisher in her lifetime, but Emily's *Wuthering Heights* and Anne's *Agnes Grey* were accepted by Thomas Newby in 1847 and published in 1848. Undeterred by her own rejections, Charlotte immediately began *Jane Eyre* (in Manchester, where her father was undergoing an operation for cataract); it was published in 1847 by Smith, Elder and achieved immediate success, arousing much speculation about its authorship. To quell the suspicion (encouraged by the unscrupulous Newby) that the Bell pseudonyms concealed but one author, Charlotte and Anne visited Smith, Elder in July 1848 and made themselves known.

She was not able to enjoy her success and the many invitations now extended to her; Branwell, whose wildness and intemperance had caused the sisters much distress, died in Sept. 1848, Emily in Dec. of the same year, and Anne the following summer. Through this tragic period she persevered with the composition of *Shirley*, which appeared in 1849. The loneliness of her later years was alleviated by friendship with Mrs *Gaskell, whom she met in 1850 and who was to write her biography (1857). In the same year she prepared and published a memorial edition of *Wuthering Heights* and *Agnes Grey*, with a preface to the former, a 'Biographical Notice of Ellis and Acton Bell', and a further selection of hitherto unpublished poems. *Villette*, founded on her memories of Brussels, appeared in 1853. Although her identity was by this time well known in the literary world, she continued to publish as Currer Bell. In 1854, after much persistence on his part and hesitation on hers, she married her father's curate, A. B. Nicholls, but died a few months later of an illness probably associated with pregnancy. 'Emma', a fragment, was published in 1860 in the *Cornhill Magazine* with an introduction by *Thackeray, and many of her juvenile works have subsequently been published, adding to our knowledge of the intense creativity of her early years. In her lifetime, Charlotte was the most admired of the Brontë sisters, although she came in for some criticism (which deeply wounded her) on the grounds of alleged 'grossness' and emotionalism, considered particularly unbecoming in a clergyman's daughter: M. *Arnold wrote in a letter (1853) that her mind contained 'nothing but hunger, rebellion and rage', and H. *Martineau offended her by claiming that *Villette* dealt excessively with 'the need of being loved', and was passionately anti-Catholic. More widespread, however, was praise for her depth of feeling and her courageous realism, and her works continue to hold high popular and critical esteem. The standard biographies are E. Gaskell, *The Life of Charlotte Brontë* (1857), and W. Gérin, *Charlotte Brontë: The Evolution of Genius* (1967): see also *The Brontës: their lives, friendships and correspondence* (4 vols, ed. T. J. Wise and J. A. Symington, 1932).

BRONTË, Emily Jane (1818–48), sister of Charlotte and Anne *Brontë, briefly attended the school at Cowan Bridge with Charlotte in 1824–5, and was then educated largely at home, where she was particularly close to Anne, with whom she created the imaginary world of Gondal, the setting for many of her finest dramatic poems. She was at Roe Head in 1835, but suffered from homesickness and returned after a few months to Haworth; she was even more intensely attached than her sisters to the moorland scenery of home, which her work evokes so vividly. She was for a time in 1837 governess at Law Hill, near Halifax, and in 1842 went to Brussels with Charlotte to study languages, but returned on her aunt's death at the end of the year to Haworth, where she spent the rest of her brief life. In 1845 Charlotte 'discovered' Emily's poems, and projected a joint publication, *Poems, by Currer, Ellis and Acton Bell*, which appeared in 1846. **Wuthering Heights* was written between Oct. 1845 and June 1846, and published by T. C. Newby after some delay in Dec. 1847. Unlike Charlotte's **Jane Eyre*, it met with more incomprehension than recognition, and it was only after Emily's death (of consumption) that it became widely acknowledged as a masterpiece; in her posthumous 'Biographical Notice' (1850) Charlotte felt obliged to comment on the 'horror of great darkness' that seemed to her to brood over the work. Emily's response to her apparent lack of success, like so much in her character, remains enigmatic. Unlike Charlotte, she had no close friends, wrote few letters, and had few but strong loyalties; the vein of violence (exemplified in the story of her subduing the dog Keeper with her bare hands), of stoicism, and of mysticism in her personality have given rise to many legends but few certainties. She is now established as much the most considerable poet of the three sisters, and one of the most original poets of the century, remembered for her lyrics (e.g. 'The night is darkening round me') for her passionate invocations from the world of Gondal ('Remembrance', 'The Prisoner') and her apparently more personal visionary moments ('No coward soul is mine'). *Wuthering Heights*, which was at first regarded as excessively morbid and violent, was gradually re-assessed, and by 1899 Mrs H. *Ward was praising Emily's masterly fusion of romance and realism at the expense of Charlotte's shrill didacticism; 20th-cent. critics, including David *Cecil and Q. D. Leavis, have opened new areas of debate about the book's poetic and moral structure, and her imaginative powers are now frequently described as Shakespearian. There is a life by W. Gérin, 1971.

Brooke, Mr, and his nieces Dorothea and Celia, characters in G. Eliot's **Middlemarch*.

BROOKE, Frances (1724–89), spent some years with her husband in Quebec, but the rest of her life as a writer in London. She conducted *The Old Maid* in 1755–6, then in 1760 published *Letters from Juliet Lady Catesby*, translated from Riccoboni, in which intricate currents of feeling are carefully traced. The highly successful *History of Lady Julia Mandeville* followed in 1763, relating the tragic story of the trusting and artless Harry and Lady Julia. It is a book of considerable pessimism, in which the virtuous do not prosper but die. *The History of Emily Montague* (1769), set in Quebec and the frozen Canadian winter, relates the tremulous love

story of Emily with Edward Rivers. In 1777 came *The Excursion*, which exposes the superficial nature of 'good breeding'. Young Lord Melvile's education in correct behaviour is displayed confusingly at odds with the generous impulses of his heart. Frances Brooke wrote several works of history and translation, and various dramatic works, including the tragedies *Virginia* (1756) and the *Siege of Sinope* (1781); she enjoyed a continuing success with a musical play, *Rosina*, in 1783 onwards.

BROOKE, Henry (1703–83), was educated in Dublin, attended the Temple, and returned in 1740 to Dublin, where he then chiefly lived. While in London he became a friend of *Pope and other literary men. In 1735 he published *Universal Beauty*, a poem which was thought to have greatly influenced E. *Darwin's *The Botanic Garden*. Encouraged by *Garrick, he wrote several plays, but his tragedy *Gustavus Vasa* (1739) was prohibited on the grounds that the villain resembled Sir R. *Walpole. In 1765–70 he published his highly successful *The Fool of Quality*, and in 1774 another novel, *Juliet Grenville*, both of which are notable for their looseness of structure and for a sustained tone of high sensibility. Brooke wrote much on Irish subjects, and advocated a relaxation of the anti-Catholic laws.

BROOKE, Jocelyn (1908–66), novelist, educated at Bedales and Worcester College, Oxford, who worked at various jobs and spent some time as a regular soldier after serving during the war with the Royal Army Medical Corps. His works include the semi-autobiographical trilogy *The Military Orchid* (1948), *A Mine of Serpents* (1949), and *The Goose Cathedral* (1950), which recall his school and army days; the first uses as its central symbol his search for the vanished military orchid and the pastoral 'Land of Lost Content', and concludes that it has 'gone with scarlet and pipe-clay, with Ouida's guardsmen and Housman's lancers; gone with the concept of soldiering as a chivalric and honourable calling'. His other works include two volumes of poems, *December Spring* (1946) and *The Elements of Death* (1952), and the novel *The Image of a Drawn Sword* (1950).

BROOKE, Rupert Chawner (1887–1915), was born at Rugby, where his father was a master at the school and where he was educated. A young man of remarkable beauty and charm, he won a scholarship to King's College, Cambridge, where he spent five years as a leader of the literary world. He began to publish poems in journals in 1909, the year in which he settled at Granchester (about which he later wrote his celebrated poem) and also travelled in Germany. *Poems 1911* was well received, as was his work in the first and second volumes of **Georgian Poetry*, edited by his friend E. *Marsh. In 1912 he won a fellowship to King's; wrote a stark one-act play, *Lithuania*; and suffered a serious breakdown, which led him in 1913 to travel in the US, Canada, and the Pacific, where, in Tahiti, he wrote 'Tiara Tahiti' and other poems, often thought to be among his best. In 1914 he joined the RNVR and took part in the Antwerp expedition. His five 'War Sonnets', which included 'The Soldier' ('If I should die'), appeared in *New Numbers* early in 1915. The ecstatic reception they received made him the nation's poet of war, a reputation further enhanced by the posthumous publication of *1914 and Other Poems* in 1915. Brooke was then dispatched to the Dardanelles, but he died of blood-poisoning on the way and was buried on Scyros. His dazzling reputation survived for many years, but is now chiefly valued for his highly accomplished lighter verse, such as 'The Old Vicarage, Granchester' and 'Heaven'; for the Tahiti poems; for a few sonnets (other than the war sequence); and for an intriguing last fragment 'I strayed about the deck'. His work on the dramatist *Webster was published in 1916, as were his *Letters from America*; the *Collected Poems*, with a memoir by Edward Marsh, appeared in 1918, and further poems were added in the *Poetical Works* edited by G. *Keynes in 1946. A biography by C. *Hassall was published in 1964.

BROOKE-ROSE, Christine (1926–), novelist and critic, and professor of English language and literature at the University of Paris from 1975. She is best known for her experimental novels (which have some affinity with the *nouveau roman*); these include *Out* (1964), *Such* (1966), *Between* (1968), and *Thru* (1975).

Brook Farm Institute, see TRANSCENDENTAL CLUB.

Brooks's, a club founded by *Almack in the middle of the 18th cent. It was originally in Pall Mall, and the present clubhouse dates from 1778. In its early days it was a noted gambling centre, and was much associated with the names of C. J. *Fox and *Sheridan. Horace *Walpole writes of it to Sir H. *Mann on 2 Feb. 1770, 'The young men of the age lose five, ten, fifteen thousand pounds in an evening there.'

BROPHY, Brigid Antonia (1929–), novelist, daughter of the author John Brophy (1899–1965), and wife of the art historian Michael Levey, was educated at St Hugh's College, Oxford. Her novels include *Hackenfeller's Ape* (1953), *Flesh* (1962), *The Snow Ball* (1962), and *In Transit* (1969), in the last of which the narrator, waiting in an airport lounge, explores his/her own identity through a series of reflections, verbal fantasies, and typographical experiments. Her non-fiction works (which, like her fiction, express her interest in opera and the visual arts) include *Black and White: a portrait of Aubrey Beardsley* (1968) and a life of *Firbank, *Prancing Novelist* (1973). She has also written plays and short stories, and been actively involved in the campaign for *Public Lending Right.

Brothers, The, a comedy by R. *Cumberland, produced 1769.

The younger Belfield has been dispossessed of his estate by his brother, who has left his wife, Violetta, and is now courting Belfield's own sweetheart Sophia, from whom Belfield has been forcibly parted. A privateer, wrecked on the coast, turns out to have on board both the younger Belfield and Violetta. Their unexpected arrival frustrates the designs of the elder brother, and the lovers are reunited.

Brothers' Club, founded by *Bolingbroke in 1711 at the inspiration of *Swift 'to advance conversation and friendship' and assist deserving authors and wits. It was composed of members of the Tory Ministry and some of their supporters, and included Swift, *Prior, *Arbuthnot, Harley's son Lord Orrery, and others.

BROUGHAM, Henry Peter, Baron Brougham and Vaux (1778–1868), educated at Edinburgh High School and University, rose to be lord chancellor. He was a man of tremendous activity. His legal career was of the highest distinction, and included the defence of Queen Caroline in 1820, but he also took an important part in the founding of London University, and vigorously promoted the Mechanics' Institute and the Society for the Diffusion of Useful Knowledge. In the history of literature he is remembered principally as one of the founders, with *Jeffrey and Sydney *Smith, of the *Edinburgh Review* in 1802. He also wrote *Observations on the Education of the People* (1825); *Historical Sketches of Statesmen in the Time of George III* (1839–43); *Demosthenes upon the Crown*, translated (1840); and *The Life and Times of Lord Brougham*, published posthumously in 1871. He is said to have been the author of the disparaging article on *Hours of Idleness* in the *Edinburgh Review* of Jan. 1808, an article which provoked Byron into writing *English Bards and Scotch Reviewers*. Of the many squibs written on Brougham's character and activities, the most famous is the lampoon in Peacock's *Crotchet Castle*, where Brougham appears as the 'learned friend' who 'is for doing all the world's business as well as his own.'

The brougham, a one-horse closed carriage, with two or four wheels, is named after him.

'Brougham Castle, Song at the Feast of', a poem by *Wordsworth, composed in 1807. See under SHEPHERD, LORD CLIFFORD, THE.

BROUGHTON, Rhoda (1840–1920), the daughter of a clergyman, who spent many years in Oxford with her widowed sister. Her many light, witty novels of country-house and town life, with their lively and articulate heroines, gained her a reputation for audacity of which a younger and more outspoken generation deprived her—to her own private amusement. She began her career with the three- and two-decker novels that were still popular (*Not wisely, but too well*, 1867; *Cometh up as a flower*, 1867; *Nancy*, 1873), but was possibly more at home with the form of her later short, sharp, observant one-volume novels, which include *Mrs Bligh* (1892), *Dear Faustina* (1897), *Lavinia* (1902, which boldly presents an anti-Boer War hero, fond of old lace), and *A Waif's Progress* (1905). G. B. *Shaw described her as 'the first to give us sincere pictures of the girls who drift from womanhood with some obsolete schooling and no training whatever . . . eventually suffering the doom of the unfit' ('Fact and Fiction').

Browdie, John, in Dickens's *Nicholas Nickleby*, a bluff, kind-hearted Yorkshireman, who befriends Nicholas and Smike.

Brown, Father, in G. K. *Chesterton's detective stories, a Roman Catholic priest, highly successful in the detection of crime by intuitive methods.

BROWN, Charles Brockden (1771–1810), acclaimed as the first professional American author, was born in Philadelphia, and worked briefly as a lawyer before writing the four *Gothic novels for which he is remembered, *Wieland* (1798), *Arthur Mervyn* (1799), *Ormond* (1799), and *Edgar Huntly* (1799). Although obviously indebted to *Godwin and A. *Radcliffe, these were pioneer works which gave Gothic romance an American setting, and Brown's psychological interest in obsession, seduction, madness, and cruelty made him a precursor of *Poe. He was admired in England, notably by Sir W. *Scott and *Keats, and *Shelley was so affected by him that he playfully named many of his friends after Brown's heroes and heroines; *Peacock was to write, 'nothing so blended itself with the structure of [Shelley's] interior mind as the creations of Brown.'

BROWN, Curtis, see AGENTS, LITERARY.

BROWN, George Douglas, see DOUGLAS, GEORGE.

BROWN, George Mackay (1921–), Scottish poet, novelist, playwright, and short story writer, born and brought up in Orkney, educated at the University of Edinburgh. His volumes of poetry include *Loaves and Fishes* (1959), *The Year of the Whale* (1969), and *Selected Poems* (1977); he has also published several collections of short stories, two novels (*Greenvoe*, 1972; *Magnus*, 1973), and other works including *An Orkney Tapestry* (1969), a medley of prose and verse, history, legend, and anecdote. Although versatile in the variety of its literary forms, all his work springs from a deep local source, and is rooted in Norse saga, island folklore, and the cycle of rural life.

BROWN, John (1800–59), commemorated in the well known marching song 'John Brown's Body' and in *Whittier's poem 'John Brown of Osawatomie', migrated in 1855 from Ohio to Kansas, where he became a leader of the anti-slavery movement. On the night of 16 Oct. 1859, at the head of a small party of his followers, he seized the arsenal of Harper's Ferry, Virginia, intending to arm the slaves and start an uprising. He was quickly captured, tried by the Virginia authorities, and hanged at Charlestown.

The author of the song is unknown, but it is most frequently attributed to Thomas B. Bishop (1835–1905) of Portland; set to an old Methodist hymn-tune, it became the most popular marching song of the Federal forces. (See also BATTLE HYMN OF THE REPUBLIC.)

BROWN, Dr John (1810–82), Edinburgh physician and essayist, most of whose writings are contained in his three volumes of *Horae Subsecivae* (1858–82), including *Marjorie Fleming* and the memorable dog story *Rab and his Friends*.

BROWN, Lancelot (1716–83), landscape architect, known as 'Capability' Brown because he was reputed to tell patrons that their estates had 'great capabilities'. Notable among his creations are the lake at Blenheim and the park at Chatsworth. Although attacked by later devotees of the *Picturesque, he was a key figure in its development, and his landscapes were deliberately fashioned to evoke the landscapes of *Claude.

BROWN, Pete, see JAZZ POETRY.

BROWN, Thomas (1663–1704), satirist, educated at Christ Church, Oxford, where he wrote 'I do not love you, Dr Fell' (see FELL). He later settled in London as Tory pamphleteer, translator, and hack writer. See B. Boyce, *Tom Brown of Facetious Memory* (1939).

BROWN, T(homas) E(dward) (1830–97), born in the Isle of Man and educated there and at Oxford, was second master at Clifton 1864–93. He published *Betsy Lee*, *A Foc's'le Yarn* (1873), *Foc's'le Yarns* (1881), and other books of verse, most of it in the Manx dialect, and dealing with Manx life. His collected poems were issued in 1900 and reprinted in 1952 (2 vols) with a memoir by *Quiller-Couch, originally published in 1930.

BROWNE, Charles Farrar (1834–67), American humorous moralist, born in Maine, who wrote under the pseudonym 'Artemus Ward'. He purported to describe the experiences of a travelling showman, using, like 'Josh Billings' (H. W. *Shaw), his own comic phonetic spelling. He became a contributor to *Punch and died in England.

BROWNE, Hablot Knight (1815–82), under the pseudonym 'Phiz', illustrated some of the works of *Dickens, *Surtees, *Smedley, etc.

BROWNE, Robert, see BROWNISTS.

BROWNE, Sir Thomas (1605–82), was born in London and educated at Winchester and Pembroke College, Oxford. He toured Ireland before studying medicine at Montpellier and Padua, and received a doctorate from Leiden. After writing *Religio Medici—first published without his consent in 1642—he settled in Norwich in about 1637 to practise medicine, remaining there for the rest of his life. In 1646 appeared his most learned and ambitious work, *Pseudodoxia Epidemica, commonly known as Vulgar Errors. In the 1650s he wrote for friends the shorter tracts *Hydriotaphia or Urn Burial, *The Garden of Cyrus, and A Letter to a Friend (published 1690), the latter overlapping in content with Christian Morals, a sententious piece said by his daughter Elizabeth to be a continuation of Religio Medici; it was first published in 1716 and re-edited in 1756 by Dr *Johnson, who prefaced it with a substantial 'Life'. Certain Miscellany Tracts, on a wide range of topics in human and natural history, were also published posthumously. He was knighted in 1671 by Charles II, and lies buried in the church of St Peter Mancroft, Norwich.

BROWNE, William (?1590–1645), was born in Tavistock and educated at Exeter College, Oxford. He published Britannia's Pastorals (Bks I and II, 1613, 1616), a fluent but desultory narrative poem dealing with the loves and woes of Marina, Celia, etc., in couplets interspersed with lyrics; Bk III, unfinished, remained in manuscript until 1852. He contributed to The Shepheard's Pipe (1614) with *Wither and others. Among various epitaphs he wrote the well-known lines on the dowager countess of Pembroke, 'Sidney's sister, Pembroke's mother' (attributed to *Jonson in Whalley's edition of that poet, 1756.) His poetry displays genuine love and observation of nature, and its sensuous richness influenced *Keats; he was also admired by Milton, whose *'L'Allegro' and *Lycidas contain echoes and imitations.

BROWNING, Elizabeth Barrett (1806–61), eldest of the twelve children of Edward Moulton Barrett, whose wealth was derived from Jamaican plantations, spent her childhood at Hope End in Herefordshire. Although largely self-educated at home, she learnt much from correspondence with her scholarly neighbours U. *Price and Hugh Stuart Boyd, became deeply versed in the classics and in prosodic theory, and later published translations from ancient and Byzantine Greek poetry. In 1832 the Barrett family moved to Sidmouth, and in 1835 to London; in 1838 Elizabeth Barrett, seriously ill as a result of a broken blood-vessel, was sent to Torquay and here, two years later, her eldest brother Edward was drowned, to her lifelong grief. She returned to London, still an invalid, in 1841. In 1845 Robert *Browning began a correspondence with her which led to their meeting and to an engagement, necessarily secret since the tyrannical Mr Barrett ruled his adult sons and daughters as though they were still children and forbade any of them to marry. In Sept. 1846 Browning and Elizabeth Barrett were secretly married and left for Italy. Casa Guidi in Florence became their base for the rest of Mrs Browning's life, though they paid long visits to Rome, Siena, Bagni di Lucca, Paris, and London. Their only child, Robert Wiedemann (known as Penini), was born in 1849. Throughout her married life Mrs Browning was passionately interested in Italian and French politics and an ardent partisan of Italian unity. She also became fascinated by spiritualism, though this—unlike her political enthusiasms—played no part in her poetry. Her intensely happy fifteen years of marriage ended with her death in Browning's arms.

Mrs Browning's juvenilia, The Battle of Marathon (1820), An Essay on Mind (1826), and a translation of Prometheus Bound, with other poems (1833), appeared anonymously, the first two were privately printed at her father's expense. The Seraphim, and Other Poems (1838) was her first work to gain critical and public attention. Her next set of Poems (1844) was so highly regarded that, when *Wordsworth died in 1850, her name was widely canvassed as his most appropriate successor as poet laureate. Throughout her married life her poetic reputation stood higher than Browning's in general contemporary opinion, though her progressive social ideas and her audacious prosodic experiments—perhaps the most appealing aspects of her work to many 20th-cent. readers—were considered alarming by readers in her own day. Her *Sonnets from the Portuguese first appeared in a collected edition of her poems in 1850; Casa Guidi Windows, on the theme of Italian liberation, in 1851; and her magnum opus, *Aurora Leigh, in 1857. The stridently political Poems Before Congress (1860) injured her popularity. Last Poems, issued posthumously in 1862, contained some of her best-known lyrics. Since her death many volumes of her spirited and engaging letters, including her exchange of love letters with Browning and her correspondence with such friends as M. R. *Mitford and *Haydon, have been published. The Brownings were friends with Ruskin, Carlyle, Tennyson, Thackeray, Landor, Rossetti, Hawthorne, and many other famous contemporaries, on all of whom

Mrs Browning's large-mindedness, vivid intelligence, and quietly sympathetic manner made a lifelong impression. There are biographies by Dorothy Hewlett (1953) and G. B. Taplin (1957).

BROWNING, Oscar (1837–1923), was a pupil of W. J. *Cory at Eton, and from 1860 to 1875 was himself assistant master there. He was then a history lecturer at King's College, Cambridge, where he became a legendary figure: fat, vain, snobbish, and quarrelsome, he nevertheless commanded considerable loyalty from his favoured pupils, and enjoyed his own somewhat ridiculous reputation and the anecdotes he inspired. For accounts of his personality, see E. F. *Benson's *As We Were* (1930) and A. C. *Benson's *Memories and Friends* (1924). He published various historical and biographical works, including a life of G. *Eliot (1890), whom he had known since his Eton days. There is a life by I. Anstruther (1983).

BROWNING, Robert (1812–89), the son of Robert Browning (d. 1866), a clerk in the Bank of England, and Sarah Anna Wiedemann (d. 1849), of German-Scottish descent, was brought up with his only sister Sarianna in Camberwell in south-east London, receiving his education mainly in his father's large (6,000 vols) and eclectic library. The contrasting influences of his boyhood were those of his reading (particularly of *Shelley, *Byron, and *Keats) and of his mother's strong Nonconformist piety. He wrote a volume of lyric poems, *Incondita*, at the age of 12, but subsequently destroyed them: two survive. In 1828 he enrolled at London University, but dropped out in his second term. His first published poem, *Pauline, appeared anonymously in 1833 and attracted little notice. Browning travelled to Russia in 1834 and made his first trip to Italy in 1838. *Paracelsus (1835) was a critical success, as a result of which Browning formed several important friendships, notably with J. *Forster and *Macready, who persuaded him to write for the stage; he also met *Carlyle, *Dickens, and *Tennyson. In 1837 his play *Strafford was produced at Covent Garden. He next published *Sordello (1840), whose hostile reception eclipsed his reputation for over twenty years, and the series of plays and collections of shorter poems called *Bells and Pomegranates* (1841–6). He began corresponding with Elizabeth Barrett (see BROWNING, E. B.) in Jan. 1845 when, after returning from his second trip to Italy, he read and admired her 1844 *Poems*. He met her first in 1845; their relationship attracted the increasing disapproval of her father, and they finally married and eloped to Italy in Sept. 1846. They lived mainly in Italy (first in Pisa and then in Florence) until Elizabeth's death in 1861. They had one child, Robert Wiedemann Barrett Browning

('Pen', 1849–1913). In 1850 Browning published *Christmas-Eve and Easter Day* and in 1855 the masterpiece of his middle period, *Men and Women*, which, together with *Dramatis Personae* (1864), began to revive his reputation; the revival was completed by the triumph of *The Ring and the Book* (1868–9), though Browning was never to achieve the commercial success of Tennyson. Meanwhile he had returned to England after the death of Elizabeth; from 1866, after his father died, he lived with his sister, generally spending the 'season' in London, and the rest of the year in the country or abroad. He formed a wide circle of acquaintance in London society, and was awarded an honorary degree by Oxford University, and an honorary fellowship by Balliol College, Oxford, whose master *Jowett was a close friend. The Browning Society was founded in 1881. Browning's publications after *The Ring and the Book* were: *Balaustion's Adventure* (1871), *Prince Hohenstiel-Schwangau* (1871), *Fifine at the Fair* (1872), *Red Cotton Night-Cap Country* (1873), *Aristophanes' Apology* (1875), *The Inn Album* (1875), *Pacchiarotto . . . with Other Poems* (1876), *The Agamemnon of Aeschylus* (1877), *La Saisiaz* and *The Two Poets of Croisic* (1878), *Dramatic Idyls* (1879), *Dramatic Idyls, Second Series* (1880), *Jocoseria* (1883), *Ferishtah's Fancies* (1884), *Parleyings with Certain People of Importance in their Day* (1887) and *Asolando* (1889, published on 12 Dec., the day of Browning's death). Browning issued collections of his work in 1849, 1863, 1868, and 1888–9. The most recent collected edition (1981) contains Browning's fugitive pieces, of which the most notable are the fine unfinished poem known as 'Aeschylus' Soliloquy', the sonnet 'Helen's Tower', 'Gerousios Oinos', the sonnet 'Why I am a Liberal', and the sonnet 'To Edward Fitzgerald' (a savage attack after Browning read a disparaging reference to his wife in one of *Fitzgerald's posthumously published letters). Browning's only prose works of importance are two 'essays' on *Chatterton (1842) and *Shelley (1852), the first in the form of a review (of a book on another subject) and the second as the introduction to a collection of letters of Shelley (which turned out to be forgeries). His correspondence with Elizabeth Barrett has been published, along with other separate volumes of letters; a collected edition is in progress. Browning died in Venice and is buried in Westminster Abbey.

Brownists, adherents of the ecclesiastical principles of Robert Browne (?1550–?1633), who preached c.1578 denouncing the parochial system and ordination, whether by bishops or by presbytery. About 1580 he, with Robert Harrison, collected a congregation at Norwich, which they called 'the church', but which was familiarly known as 'the Brownists'. He finally submitted to the bishop of Peterborough and became for 40 years rector of Achurch in Northamptonshire. He is regarded as the founder of Congregationalism.

BROWNJOHN, Alan Charles (1931–), poet, born in London and educated at Merton College, Oxford, who taught in various schools and other institutions from 1953 to 1979, before becoming a full-time writer. An early booklet of poems, *Travellers Alone* (1954), and his first volume, *The Railings* (1961), were followed by several other volumes, and a *Collected Poems 1952–83* was published in 1983. Brownjohn's poetry is, characteristically, goodhumoured, ironic, and urbane, and, in P. *Porter's phrase, it unites 'wit and civic responsibility' in its survey of contemporary social, domestic, and literary life. He has also written for children (*Brownjohn's Beasts*, 1970) and edited several anthologies.

Brownlow, Mr, a character in Dickens's *Oliver Twist*.

BRUCE, James (1730–94), African traveller, educated at Harrow, was author of an interesting narrative of his *Travels to discover the source of the Nile* (he discovered that of the Blue Nile), and of his visit to Abyssinia, published in 1790. His veracity, long doubted, was established by *Burton, *Speke, and *Baker.

Bruce, The, see BARBOUR, J.

BRUEGEL, Pieter (*c*.1525/30–69), Netherlandish genre, landscape, and religious painter, a prolific designer of engravings and a brilliant draughtsman. Little is known about his early life; he visited Italy some time between 1551 and 1553 when he made some remarkable drawings of the Alps. He first became known for his allegorical and satirical prints and his paintings crowded with little figures, that look back to the demonic imagery of Bosch. Much of this imagery is drawn from proverb and folklore—reflecting a contemporary literary interest—and a parallel is often drawn between his *Netherlandish Proverbs* (1559; Berlin, Staatliche Museen) and *Rabelais' *Gargantua and Pantagruel* (Bk V, ch. 22) (1564). In 1565 Bruegel painted his most famous works, great cosmic landscapes representing *The Months*, and in 1566–8 his celebrated scenes of rustic genre, the *Peasant Wedding Feast* (Vienna, Kunsthistorisches Museum). His latest works, e.g. *The Blind leading the Blind* (1568, Naples, Capodimonte), are tragic indictments of the human condition. From the early 17th cent. Bruegel was thought of as 'Peasant Bruegel', a naïve painter of comic genre. In our own century his art has been rediscovered, his contacts with humanist scholars stressed, and his profound knowledge of man emphasized. He has been the subject of a vast amount of scholarly literature and virulent controversy, and his paintings have inspired poets, including American poets, W. C. *Williams and Joseph Langland (1917–), and, notably, W. H. *Auden, in his 'Musée des Beaux Arts', on the *Fall of Icarus*.

BRUMMELL, George Bryan (1778–1840), generally called Beau Brummell, a friend of the prince regent (George IV) and leader of fashion in London. He died in poverty at Caen.

Brunanburh, a poem in Old English, included in four manuscripts of the *Anglo-Saxon Chronicle* under the year 937, dealing with the battle fought in that year at Brunanburh between the English under Athelstan, the grandson of Alfred, and the Danes under Anlaf from Dublin, supported by the Scots led by Constantine II and the Welsh. The site of the battle is unknown, but it is thought to be somewhere on the west coast of Britain between Chester and Dumfries. The poem is a triumphant celebration of the deeds of Athelstan and his brother and successor Edmund, in their defeat of the invaders. *Tennyson wrote a verse translation (*Ballads and Other Poems*, 1880). There is an edition by A. Campbell (1938).

Brunhild, see BRYNHILD.

BRUNO, Giordano (?1548–1600), Italian philosopher (who saw God as the unity reconciling spirit and matter), born at Nola. He was in early life a Dominican friar, but broke from his order and wandered about Europe teaching his philosophical doctrines or embodying them in dialogues and verse (some of them dedicated to *Sidney, under whose auspices he visited Oxford). He finally quarrelled with one of the Mocenigos, by whom he was employed at Venice, was denounced to the Inquisition, condemned to death, and burnt. See F. *Yates, *Giordano Bruno and the Hermetic Tradition* (1964). His writings were much admired by *Joyce, who mystified his friends by enigmatic references to 'the Nolan'.

Brut, or **Brutus,** legendary founder of the British race. *Geoffrey of Monmouth states that Walter, archdeacon of Oxford, gave him an ancient book in the British tongue containing an account of the kings of Britain from Brutus to Cadwallader. This Brutus was son of Sylvius, grandson of Ascanius and great-grandson of Aeneas. Having had the misfortune to kill his father, he collected a remnant of the Trojan race and brought them to England (uninhabited at the time 'except by a few giants'), landing at Totnes. He founded Troynovant or New Troy (later known as London) and was the progenitor of a line of British kings including Bladud, *Gorboduc, Ferrex and Porrex, *Lud, *Cymbeline, *Coel, *Vortigern, and *Arthur. The name 'Troynovant' is a back-formation from 'Trinovantes', the name of the powerful British tribe that lived north and east of London. Drayton, in his *Poly-Olbion* (i. 312), relates the legend, and *Selden, in his *Illustrations* to that work, discusses its probability.

His name came to be used to mean 'chronicle of the Britons', by Geoffrey of Monmouth's followers such as *Wace and *Laȝamon after Geoffrey began his history of the kings of Britain with him. No doubt the phonetic echo (cf. Romulus/Rome) led to the adoption of this eponymous progenitor for the Britons.

Brut, The Prose, a long English version, translated between 1350 and 1380, of the Anglo-Norman prose *Brut* which extends up to 1333. Over 100 copies of the English are extant. It has a strong Lancastrian bias which differentiates it from the 15th-cent. *Brut*, composed in London *c.*1461 and pro-York. See above and the discussions in A. Gransden, *Historical Writing in England II* (1982), pp. 73–7 and pp. 220 ff.

Brute, Sir John and Lady, characters in Vanbrugh's *The Provok'd Wife*.

Brutus: in Shakespeare's *Julius Caesar*, Decius Brutus is one of the conspirators. Marcus Brutus is the idealistic friend of Caesar who is persuaded by *Cassius to join the conspiracy. Caesar receives his wound from Brutus with the legendary words 'Et tu, Brute?—Then fall, Caesar!' (III. i. 76). Antony's tribute to Brutus after his death as 'the noblest Roman of them all' (V. v. 68) is well known. The internal deliberations of Brutus have been seen as precursors of those of *Hamlet, hero of what was probably Shakespeare's next play.

BRYAN, Sir Francis (d. 1550), poet, soldier, and diplomatist, was Henry VIII's permanent favourite, held various court posts, and was sent on diplomatic missions. He behaved discreditably in the matter of the execution of his cousin Anne Boleyn, and accepted a pension vacated by one of her accomplices. Cromwell, in writing of this circumstance to Gardiner and Wallop, calls him 'the vicar of hell', which became a popular nickname. It is to this, no doubt, that Milton in the *Areopagitica* refers when he writes, 'I name not him for posterities sake, whom *Harry* the 8. nam'd in merriment his Vicar of hell.' He was a friend of *Wyatt, who addressed his third satire to him. Bryan contributed to *Tottel's *Miscellany* and his poetry was highly valued in his day, but is now undiscoverable.

BRYANT, William Cullen (1794–1878), American poet, born in Massachusetts. He first practised law, but then entered journalism, and was for 50 years editor of the New York *Evening Post*. He began to make a name as a poet as early as 1817, when his Wordsworthian blank verse meditation 'Thanatopsis' was published in the *North American Review*, and confirmed his reputation with *Poems* (1821), which contains his well-known 'To a Waterfowl', 'The Yellow Violet', and 'Green River'. His next volume, *Poems* (1832), which contains 'The Death of the Flowers' and 'To the Fringed Gentian', was followed by several other collections of less importance. Although limited in range, his poetry has simplicity and dignity, and some delicate observations of the natural world.

BRYCE, James, Viscount (1838–1922), educated at the High School and University of Glasgow, Trinity College, Oxford, and Heidelberg, was Regius professor of civil law at Oxford, 1870–93, and held a number of high political and diplomatic posts including chief secretary for Ireland (1905–6) and ambassador to the USA (1907–13). Bryce published works on various subjects, including the two notable volumes *The Holy Roman Empire* (1864) and *The American Commonwealth* (1888).

BRYDGES, Sir Samuel Egerton (1762–1837), devoted his life to literary work and considered himself to be a great writer, but he was successful only as a bibliographer. He published his valuable *Censura Literaria* in 1805–9 and 1815; *The British Bibliographer* in 1810–14; and *Restituta: or Titles, Extracts, and Characters of Old Books in English Literature Revived* in 1814–16. Of his novel *Arthur Fitz-Albini* (1798) J. *Austen mildly observed, 'there is a very little story.' His *Autobiography, Times, Opinions, Contemporaries of Sir Egerton Brydges* (1835) is a confused and opinionated narrative of little interest.

BRYHER, the pseudonym, adopted from the name of one of the Isles of Scilly, of (Annie) Winifred Ellerman (1894–1983), novelist, poet, and patron of the arts. The daughter of a wealthy shipping magnate, she lived for many years at Geneva; her friends in the literary world included the *Sitwells, and notably, H. *Doolittle, whom she met in 1918, and whom she both protected and dominated for years.

Brynhild, or **Brunhild,** one of the principal characters in the *Vǫlsunga saga* and the *Niebelungenlied*.

BUCHAN, John, first Baron Tweedsmuir (1875–1940), born in Perth, the son of a minister, was educated at Glasgow and Brasenose College, Oxford, and while still at Oxford published a novel (*Sir Quixote of the Moors*, 1895) and essays (*Scholar Gipsies*, 1896), and contributed to the *Yellow Book. From 1901 to 1903 he was in South Africa with the High Commission working on reconstruction after the Boer War, and later combined a literary career with a career in public life, culminating with the post of governor-general of Canada, 1935–40. He wrote many non-fiction works, including lives of *Montrose (1913) and *Scott (1932), but is remembered for his adventure stories, most of which feature a recurring group of heroes (Richard Hannay, Sandy Arbuthnot, Peter Pienaar, Edward Leithen, etc.); favoured settings include Scotland, the Cotswolds, and South Africa, although the last, *Sick Heart River* (1941), prefiguring his own death, is set in the icy wastes of Canada. The stories are packed with action, often involving elaborate cross-country chases; the characterization is simple, the landscapes are lovingly evoked. The most popular include *The Thirty-nine Steps* (1915; filmed by Hitchcock, 1935), *Greenmantle* (1916), *Mr Standfast* (1918), and *John Macnab* (1925). There is a life by Janet Adam Smith (1965).

BUCHANAN, George (1506–82), born near Killearn in Stirlingshire, studied at St Andrews and Paris, and became tutor to a natural son of James V. He satirized the Franciscans, thus provoking Cardinal Beaton, and was imprisoned at St Andrews. Escaping, he went to the Continent, became a professor at Bordeaux, where he had *Montaigne among his pupils, and in 1547 was invited to teach in the university of Coimbra, but was imprisoned by the Inquisition, 1549–51. After some years in France he returned to Scotland and professed himself a Protestant. He became a bitter enemy of *Mary Queen of Scots, in consequence of the murder of Darnley, and vouched that the Casket Letters were in her handwriting. He wrote his *Detectio Mariae Reginae* in 1571. He was tutor to James VI and I during 1570–8. Chief among his many writings are his Latin poem *De Sphaera*, an exposition of the Ptolemaic system as against that advocated by *Copernicus, and his Latin *Rerum Scoticarum Historia* (1582), which for long was regarded as a standard authority. His first elegy 'Quam misera sit conditio docentium literas humaniores Lutetiae', describes the hard lot of the student at Paris. There is a life of him by I. D. McFarlane (1981).

BUCHANAN, Robert Williams (1841–1901), poet, essayist, novelist, and playwright, the son of a socialist and secularist tailor who owned several socialist journals in Glasgow. He came to London in 1860 and made a name for himself as a man of letters, but his many novels, poems, and plays are now forgotten, and he is remembered largely for his attacks on *Swinburne (whom he called unclean, morbid, and sensual, and satirized in a poem 'The Session of the Poets' in the *Spectator*, 1866) and on *Pre-Raphaelites, principally D. G. *Rossetti, whom he attacked in 'The Fleshly School of Poetry' in the *Contemporary Review* (1871) under the pseudonym 'Thomas Maitland'. After Rossetti's death he recanted in an essay in *A Look Round Literature* (1887), in which he declared that Rossetti 'uses amatory forms and carnal images to express ideas which are purely and remotely spiritual . . .'

Bucket, Inspector, the detective in Dickens's *Bleak House.*

BUCKHURST, Lord, see SACKVILLE, T. and C.

BUCKINGHAM, George Villiers, first duke of (1592–1628), the favourite of James I, by whom he was familiarly known as 'Steenie', figures in Scott's *The Fortunes of Nigel*. He was assassinated by John Felton.

BUCKINGHAM, George Villiers, second duke of (1628–87), a prominent figure in the reign of Charles II and an influential member of the *Cabal, was the Zimri of Dryden's *Absalom and Achitophel*. He was the author of verses, satires, and the burlesque *The Rehearsal*, which was much performed in the 18th cent. with topical additions and substitutions. Famed for his debauchery and amorous adventures, as well as for the vicissitudes of his public life, he died miserably at Kirby Moorside; the death of 'this lord of useless thousands' in 'the worst inn's worst room' is described by Pope in a famous passage in his *Epistle III* (*Moral Essays*). He also figures in Scott's *Peveril of the Peak*.

BUCKINGHAM, James Silk (1786–1855), author and traveller, and founder of the *Athenaeum*.

Buckingham, Complaint of, see COMPLAINT OF BUCKINGHAM.

Buckingham, duke of, in Shakespeare's *Richard III*, acts as Richard's ally in murdering Lord *Hastings and in elevating him to the throne, but defects to the support of *Richmond after his master fails to reward him. The line 'Off with his head! So much for Buckingham' occurs in C. *Cibber's adaptation (1700), which was the stage version generally used until H. *Irving's production in 1877.

Bucklaw, The Laird of, Frank Hayston, a character in Scott's *The Bride of Lammermoor.*

BUCKLE, Henry Thomas (1821–62), received no school or college training, but inherited money from his father and devoted himself to travelling on the Continent, where he acquired several languages and became a radical free-thinker. He was also among the world's strongest chess-players in the 1840s, giving up serious play in favour of writing. The first volume of his *History of Civilization in England* appeared in 1857 and the second in 1861. These were only to be introductory portions of a far larger work, which the author's premature death of typhoid at Damascus prevented him from executing. Buckle criticized the methods of previous historians and sought to establish a scientific basis, arguing that changing phenomena have unchanging laws and that the growth of civilization in various countries depended on the interrelated factors of climate, food production, population, and wealth. The work achieved great success, was much admired by C. *Darwin, and gained an international reputation; it was particularly admired in Russia. See J. M. Robertson, *Buckle and his Critics* (1895).

Bucolic, see ECLOGUE.

BUDÉ, Guillaume (1467–1540), French humanist. He did important work in Roman law and in numismatics, but was primarily celebrated for his contribution to Greek scholarship, notably the *Commentarii linguae graecae* (1529). He did much to encourage the revival of classical learning in France, was instrumental in the founding of what was to become the Collège de France, and, as royal librarian under Francis I, laid the basis for the future Bibliothèque Nationale.

BUDGELL, Eustace (1686–1737), a cousin of *Addison, a miscellaneous writer who contributed to *The Spectator* and is mocked by Pope in *The Dunciad* and other works. He lost money in the *South Sea Company, became involved in various lawsuits, and eventually committed suicide.

BUFFON, Georges-Louis Leclerc, comte de (1707–88), French naturalist, curator of the Jardin du Roi and author of the monumental *Histoire naturelle, générale et particulière* in 36 vols (1749–88), for which he enjoyed immense public esteem during his lifetime. The *Natural History*, which was completed after Buffon's death in eight additional vols (1788–1804) by E. de Lacépède, aimed at a comprehensive view of living creatures in their environment and included (in *Théorie de la terre*, 1749, and *Époques de la nature*, 1778) reconstructions of the geological periods of the earth. Buffon's method combines detailed observation with bold generalization and poetic vision: both his descriptions of animals and his hypothetical accounts of geological epochs are vividly and imaginatively rendered. He refused to enter into the controversy aroused by his conception of the earth's history, maintaining deistic views and the unity of all creation with man as its centre and crown. Buffon was a notable stylist. His ideals of order, harmony, and decorum are set out in his *Discours sur le style* (1753), originally his address on being received into the *Académie française, later published as a supplement to the *Natural History*; it contains the celebrated dictum: '*Le style, c'est l'homme même.*'

Buffone, Carlo, in Jonson's *Every Man out of his Humour*, 'a public scurrilous profane jester', from the Italian *buffone*, 'jester', the origin of the English 'buffoon'.

Bufo, a character in *Pope's *Epistle to Dr Arbuthnot* (ll. 230–48), a patron of the arts 'fed with soft Dedication all day long' who may represent some of the traits of the earl of Halifax and of *Dodington.

Bug Bible, a name given to versions of the English Bible (Coverdale's and Matthew's) in which the words in Psalm 91: 5 are translated, 'thou shalt not be afraid for any bugs by night'. (See BIBLE, THE ENGLISH.)

Bukton, the dedicatee of an 'Envoy' by *Chaucer, probably dating from 1396. It is not certain which (if either) of two claimants in modern scholarship is Chaucer's subject.

BULGAKOV, Mikhail Afanasevich (1891–1940), Russian prose writer and dramatist, born in Kiev, the son of a professor at the theological academy. He studied medicine and began his literary career by writing stories drawn from his experience as a doctor. After the revolution he worked in Moscow as a journalist and wrote satirical and humorous stories and plays. In the late 1920s he came under increasing pressure from party-oriented critics. He wrote a letter to *Stalin on 28 March 1930 asking permission to emigrate. Instead, Stalin intervened to get Bulgakov's play *The Days of the Turbins* re-staged, and the theme of the writer and the state became his key subject until his early death. His major works include stories: 'The Adventures of Chichikov' (1922, evidence of his great admiration for *Gogol), 'The Fatal Eggs' (1924), 'The Heart of a Dog' (1925); novels: *The White Guard* (1925, a sympathetic portrait of a White family in Kiev after the Revolution), *The Theatrical Novel* (*Black Snow*) (1936–7); and plays: *The Days of the Turbins* (1925–6), an adaptation of *The White Guard*), *Flight* (1925–8), *A Cabal of Hypocrites* (*Molière*) (1930–6). His masterpiece, *The Master and Margarita* (1928–40, not published until 1966–7), is a Faustian tale of the devil's appearance in contemporary Moscow and his relationship with a writer and his beloved.

BULL, John (?1562–1628), English composer and keyboard player. Unusually for his period, Bull wrote no songs, no madrigals, and only a few sacred vocal compositions; his works for organ and virginals, however, are among the most important of their day. The latter seem to have included a modest *Ayre* which, the original manuscript being lost, now exists only in a 19th-cent. copy; it bears an interesting resemblance to the tune of *'God Save the King', and has often been claimed as the origin of the British national anthem. Any connection with pugnacious British nationalism stops with his name—and in fact Bull left England in 1613, in official disgrace, and never returned.

Bull, John, see JOHN BULL.

Bull-dog Drummond, see SAPPER.

BULLOUGH, Geoffrey (1901–82), scholar and head of the department of English at King's College, London (1946–68). His principal works were an edition of *Greville's poems and plays (1939) and his definitive account of the *Narrative and Dramatic Sources of Shakespeare* (8 vols, 1957–75).

Bulstrode, Mr, a character in G. Eliot's *Middlemarch.*

BULWER-LYTTON, Edward George Earle Lytton, first Baron Lytton (1803–73), son of General Bulwer, who added his mother's surname to his own when he inherited Knebworth in 1843. Educated at Trinity College, Cambridge, he embarked on a career in politics as MP for St Ives and a keen Reform member in 1831; he was subsequently MP for Lincoln and in 1858–9 secretary for the colonies. He financed his extravagant life as a man of fashion by a versatile and prolific literary output, publishing either anonymously or under the name of Bulwer Lytton. His first success, *Pelham: or the adventures of a gentleman* (1828), was of the *Fashionable school, a lively novel set in an aristocratic social and political world, bearing some resemblance to Disraeli's recent *Vivian Grey*; it brought him considerable acclaim and established his reputation as a wit and dandy. Sir W. *Scott found it 'easy and gentleman-like' but complained of 'a slang tone of morality which is immoral'. His *'Newgate' novels were more in the 'reforming' manner of *Godwin, e.g. *Paul Clifford* (1830), about a philanthropic highwayman, and *Eugene Aram* (1832), about a repentant murderer. He also wrote novels of domestic life, such as *The Caxtons: a family picture* (1849); many popular *historical novels, including *The Last Days of Pompeii* (1834), in which the panoramic splendours show his admiration for J. *Martin, *Rienzi, the last of the Roman Tribunes* (1835), and *The Last of the Barons* (1843); tales of the occult, including *Zanoni* (1842) and *A Strange Story* (1862); and a *science fiction fantasy, *The Coming Race* (1871). Other novels include *Falkland* (1827), *The Disowned* and *Devereux* (1829), *Godolphin* (1833), *Ernest Maltravers* (1837), *Harold, the last of the Saxons* (1848), *My Novel, or Varieties in English Life* (1853), *What Will He Do With It?* (1858), *Kenelm Chillingly* (1873), and *The Parisians* (1873, unfinished). He was also editor of the *New Monthly Magazine, 1831–3, and the author of three plays, *The Lady of Lyons, or Love and Pride*, a romantic comedy first performed in 1838; *Richelieu, or the Conspiracy*, a historical play in blank verse performed in 1839; and *Money*, a comedy performed in 1840, all of which have been successfully revived. He published several volumes of verse, including his earliest *Byronic tale, *Ismael* (1820); *The New Timon* (1846), an anonymous

satirical poem in which he attacked *Tennyson as 'School-Miss Alfred', thus aggravating previous criticisms and stinging Tennyson into a bitter response in verse, mocking Lytton as a rouged and padded fop; and an epic, *King Arthur* (1848–9). Bulwer-Lytton made many enemies in his career, which was not helped by his disastrous marriage and separation from his wife Rosina in 1836; he was the frequent butt of *Fraser's Magazine*, of *Lockhart, and of *Thackeray. Nevertheless he had powerful friends and admirers, including *Disraeli and *Dickens, and his works, though now little read, span many of the changes in 19th-cent. fiction and are thus of considerable sociological interest.

Bumble, the beadle in Dickens's *Oliver Twist*, a type of the consequential, domineering parish official.

Bumby, Mother, a fortune-teller frequently alluded to by the Elizabethan dramatists. *Lyly wrote a Terentian comedy entitled, *Mother Bombie* (1594), which is, says *Hazlitt, 'very much what its name would import, old, quaint, and vulgar', 'little else than a tissue of absurd mistakes, arising from the confusion of the different characters one with another, like another Comedy of Errors, and ends in their being (most of them), married . . . to the persons they particularly dislike'.

Bumppo, Natty, see COOPER, J. F.

BUNBURY, Henry William (1750–1811), amateur artist and caricaturist, had many friends in the literary world, and in 1771 married Catherine Horneck, *Goldsmith's 'Little Comedy'.

Bunbury, an imaginary character introduced by Wilde in *The Importance of being Earnest.*

Bunce, Jack, alias Altamont, ex-actor and pirate in Scott's *The Pirate.*

Buncle Esq., John, see JOHN BUNCLE.

BUNGAY, Thomas, known as 'Friar Bungay' (*fl.* 1290), a Franciscan, who was divinity lecturer of his order in Oxford and Cambridge. He was vulgarly accounted a magician and is frequently referred to in that capacity. (See FRIER BACON AND FRIER BONGAY.)

BUNIN, Ivan Alekseevich (1870–1953), Russian prose-writer and poet. The son of gentry from Voronezh in central Russia, he worked as a young man as assistant editor of a provincial newspaper. His first poem was published in 1887, his first stories in the early 1890s, and his first collection of prose, *To the Edge of the World*, in 1897. In the early years of the 20th cent. he attained great popularity. Love and rural life are prominent themes, and he was a consistent opponent of *Modernism. Among his best works of the period are *The Village* (1910), *Sukhodol* (1911), and *The Gentleman from San Francisco* (1914). In these years he travelled widely in Europe, Asia, and Africa. Totally opposed to the October revolution, he left Russia in 1918, eventually reaching France and permanent exile. *The Accursed Days* (1925) is a diary of the post-revolutionary period, *The Life of Arsenev* (1927–9) an autobiographical novel. In 1933 Bunin became the first Russian to win the *Nobel Prize for literature. His final volume of stories, *Dark Avenues*, appeared in 1946. Bunin's reputation has risen continuously since his death. He is the Russian translator of *Byron's *Cain*, *Manfred*, and *Heaven and Earth*, *Longfellow's *The Song of Hiawatha*, and *Tennyson's *Lady Godiva*. There have been a number of translations of Bunin's work into English since the first, *The Gentleman from San Francisco and Other Stories*, translated by D. H. *Lawrence, S. S. Koteliansky, and L. *Woolf (1922).

Bunsby, Captain John, a character in Dickens's *Dombey and Son*, a friend of Captain Cuttle.

Bunthorne, Reginald, the principal male character in Gilbert and Sullivan's opera *Patience*, a 'fleshly poet', in whose person the *Aesthetic Movement of the 1880s was caricatured.

BUNTING, Basil (1900–), poet, born in Northumberland, worked in Paris as a sub-editor on the *Transatlantic Review* and in the 1930s followed *Pound to Italy, where he met *Yeats and the American poet Louis Zukofsky (1904–78). During and after the Second World War he worked in Persia, returning to Newcastle to work on a local paper. Although he had been published abroad (*Redimiculum Matellarum*, Milan, 1930; *Poems*, Texas, 1950) and had a considerable reputation among younger American poets as an important figure in the modernist movement, he was virtually unknown in his own country until the appearance of his long, semi-autobiographical, and deeply Northumbrian poem *Briggflatts* (1966), which firmly established his presence. His *Collected Poems* (1968) includes translations ('Overdrafts') from Latin and Persian.

BUNYAN, John (1628–88), born at Elstow, near Bedford, the son of a brazier, learned reading and writing at the village school and was early set to his father's trade. He was drafted into the parliamentary army and was stationed at Newport Pagnell, 1644–6, an experience perhaps reflected in *The Holy War*. In 1649 he married his first wife, who introduced him to two religious works, Dent's *Plain Man's Pathway to Heaven* and Bayly's *Practice of Piety*; these, the Bible, the Prayer Book, and Foxe's *Actes and Monumentes* (or *Book of Martyrs*) were his principal reading matter. In 1653 he joined a Nonconformist church in Bedford, preached there, and came into conflict with the Quakers, against whom he published his first writings, *Some Gos-*

pel Truths Opened (1656) and *A Vindication* (1657). He married his second wife Elizabeth c.1659, his first having died c.1656 leaving four children. He was arrested in Nov. 1660 for preaching without a licence, and spent most of the next twelve years in Bedford gaol. During the first half of this period he wrote nine books, the principal of which was *Grace Abounding to the Chief of Sinners* (1666). In 1665 appeared *The Holy City, or the New Jerusalem*, inspired by a passage in the book of Revelation. In 1672 he published *A Confession of my Faith, and a Reason of my Practice*. After his release in 1672 he was appointed pastor at the same church, but was again imprisoned for a short period in 1676, during which he probably finished the first part of *The Pilgrim's Progress*, which had been partly written during the latter years of the first imprisonment. The first part was published in 1678, and the second, together with the whole work, in 1684. His other principal works are *The Life and Death of Mr *Badman* (1680), and *The Holy War* (1682). Bunyan preached in many parts, but was not further molested. There are recent editions of his more important works by R. Sharrock, who also wrote a biography.

Burana, Carmina, see CARMINA BURANA.

BURBAGE, James (c.1530–97), actor, was a joiner by trade. He was one of the earl of Leicester's players in 1572. He leased land in Shoreditch (1576), on which he erected, of wood, the first building in England specially intended for plays. In 1596 he acquired a house in Blackfriars, and converted it into the *Blackfriars Theatre. He lived in Halliwell Street, Shoreditch, 1576–97. The first English playhouse is mentioned in an order of council, Aug. 1577, and was known as 'The Theatre'; the fabric was removed, c. Dec. 1598, to the Bankside and set up as the *Globe Theatre.

BURBAGE, Richard (?1567–1619), actor, was son of James *Burbage, from whom he inherited a share in the *Blackfriars Theatre and an interest in the *Globe Theatre. He acted as a boy at the Theatre in Shoreditch and rose to be an actor of chief parts, 1595–1618, in plays by Shakespeare, *Jonson, and *Beaumont and *Fletcher. He excelled in tragedy. Burbage lived in Halliwell Street, Shoreditch, 1603–19. He is known also as a painter in oil-colours and is known to have collaborated with Shakespeare on an 'impresa', a tilting shield for the earl of Rutland, in 1613.

Burbon, Sir, in Spenser's *Faerie Queene* (v. xi), represents Henry of Navarre.

BURCHFIELD, Robert William (1923–), born in New Zealand, editor from 1957 onwards of *A Supplement to the *Oxford English Dictionary*.

BURCKHARDT, Jacob (1818–97), Swiss historian born in Basle, who is principally known in Britain for his great work *Die Kultur der Renaissance in Italien* (1860, trans. as *The Civilization of the Renaissance in Italy*, 1929, 1951), a survey which discusses the arts, politics, philosophy, etc. of the period and propounds the view that it was at this time that man, previously conscious of himself 'only as a member of a race, people, party, family or corporation', became aware of himself as 'a spiritual *individual*'. This concept of the Italian Renaissance has been both highly influential and much attacked, as has Burckhardt's wide historical pessimism; some, however, have seen him as a precursor of *Existentialism.

Burden, the refrain or chorus of a song, a set of words recurring at the end of each verse, or the dominant theme of a song or poem.

BÜRGER, Gottfried August, see LENORE and WILD HUNTSMAN, THE.

BURGESS, Anthony (John Anthony Burgess Wilson) (1917–), novelist, born in Manchester, of a Catholic family, and educated at the University of Manchester. His original ambitions were musical, and his varied early career included some years (1954–60) as an education officer in the colonial service in Malaya and Borneo. During this period he wrote his first three novels, set in the Far East, *Time for a Tiger* (1956), *The Enemy in the Blanket* (1958), and *Beds in the East* (1959; published together as *The Malayan Trilogy* in 1972). *A Clockwork Orange* (1962), an alarming vision of violence, high technology, and authoritarianism, appeared in a film version by Stanley Kubrick in 1971. His many other works include his comic trilogy about the gross and fitfully inspired poet Enderby (*Inside Mr Enderby*, 1963, under the pseudonym 'Joseph Kell'; *Enderby Outside*, 1968; *The Clockwork Testament*, 1974), which traces the literary, amorous, and digestive misfortunes and triumphs of Enderby in England, Rome, Tangiers, and New York, and displays a fine flair for pastiche, satiric social comment, and verbal invention. *Earthly Powers* (1980) is a long and ambitious first-person novel, narrated by a successful octogenarian homosexual writer, Kenneth Toomey, in which real and fictitious characters mingle to produce an international panorama of the 20th cent. Burgess has also written critical works, notably on *Joyce; composed many orchestral works; written screenplays and television scripts, innumerable reviews, and a biography of Shakespeare (1970).

BURGON, John William (1813–88), became dean of Chichester in 1876. He is remembered as the author of the poem 'Petra' (1845), which contains the well-known line 'A rose-red city— "half as old as time" '.

BURGOYNE, Sir John (1722–92), nicknamed 'Gentleman Johnny', remembered principally as the general who was forced to capitulate to the Americans at Saratoga in 1777, was the author of a clever and successful comedy *The Heiress* (1786), in which the vulgarity of the rich Alscrip family is contrasted with the native good breeding of Clifford, Lord Gayville, and his sister; while the temporary humiliation of the virtuous heroine Miss Alton, who is driven to take service in the Alscrip family until she is discovered to be an heiress and Clifford's sister, provides a sentimental interest. He also wrote *The Maid of the Oaks* (1774), a cheerful little comedy of country life. He figures in G. B. *Shaw's play *The Devil's Disciple* (1900).

Burgundy, duke of, the 'wat'rish' suitor of *Cordelia in Shakespeare's *King Lear*.

'Burial of Sir John Moore, The', see WOLFE, C.

BURIDAN (late 12th cent.), a French natural scientist to whom is attributed the sophism of the ass equally pressed by hunger and thirst and placed between a bundle of hay and a pail of water, who must die of hunger and thirst, having no determining motive to direct him to one or the other. 'Like Buridan's ass between two bundles of hay' is said of a person undecided between two courses of action, who adopts neither. According to tradition Buridan was thrown into the Seine in a sack (*Villon, *Ballade*).

BURKE, Edmund (1729–97), the second son of an Irish Protestant attorney and a Catholic mother, was educated at Trinity College, Dublin, and came to London in 1750, where he entered the Middle Temple. He was more interested in literature than the law, and was to make many lasting friendships with eminent literary and artistic figures, including Dr *Johnson (of whose *Club he was a founding member), *Goldsmith, *Reynolds, *Garrick, and the *Blue Stocking Circle. In 1756 he married Jane Nugent, and in the same year published **A Vindication of Natural Society* and in 1757 *A Philosophical Enquiry into the *Sublime and the Beautiful*. In 1759 with *Dodsley he started the *Annual Register* to which he contributed until 1788; in the same year he became private assistant to W. G. ('Single-Speech') *Hamilton, with whom he remained until 1765, when he transferred his services to the marquis of Rockingham and was elected MP for Wendover. He first spoke in the House in 1766 on the American question, and during the following years vehemently attacked the Tory government. In 1768 he purchased an estate at Beaconsfield for a considerable sum, which aroused allegations (still debated) about speculations with East India stock. He published his *Observations on a late Publication on the *Present State of the Nation* in 1769, and his *Thoughts on the Cause of the *Present Discontents* in 1770. In

1773 he visited France, where he met Mme du *Deffand, *Diderot, and the *Encyclopaedists, and saw Marie Antionette, a vision that was to inspire, years later, some of the best-known passages of *Reflections on the *Revolution in France* (1790). In 1774 he became MP for Bristol, and made his speeches *On *American Taxation* (1774) and *On *Conciliation with America* (11 March 1775, shortly before the war with America began). His *Letter to the Sheriffs of Bristol* was written in 1777, and his powerful speech against employing Indians in the war was made in 1780. His championship of free trade with Ireland and Catholic emancipation lost him his seat in Bristol in 1780; he became MP for Malton in 1781, in which year, in the midst of a busy political life, he found time to respond generously to *Crabbe, who appealed to him for patronage. His attacks on the conduct of the American war contributed to North's resignation in 1783. Burke became paymaster of the forces in 1782, resigned with Fox, and returned to the same office (the highest he ever held) under the coalition government. He took an active part in the investigation of the affairs of the East India Company; his famous speeches on the East India Bill and *On the Nabob of Arcot's Private Debts* were delivered in 1783 and 1785, and he opened the case for the impeachment of *Hastings in 1788. In the same year he supported *Wilberforce in advocating abolition of the slave trade. The French Revolution prompted his *Reflections* and other important works, including *An Appeal from the New to the Old Whigs* (1791), a defence against the charge of inconsistency in his attitude to the French and the Americans, and *Letters on a *Regicide Peace* (1795–7). He retired in 1794 and received a pension from the ministry, for which he was criticized, chiefly by the duke of Bedford and earl of Lauderdale; he defended himself in his *A Letter to a Noble Lord* (1796), in which he alludes movingly to the death of his only son Richard in 1794.

Burke's political life was devoted to five 'great, just and honourable causes': the emancipation of the House of Commons from the control of George III and the 'King's friends'; the emancipation of the American colonies; the emancipation of Ireland; the emancipation of India from the misgovernment of the East India Company; and opposition to the atheistical Jacobinism displayed in the French Revolution. For his support of this last cause he was bitterly attacked by those who considered he had betrayed his earlier faith in political liberty (e.g. *Paine, *Godwin, *Bentham, and James *Mill), and his friend Goldsmith, a Tory, described him earlier in 1774 in a celebrated mock-epitaph as one who 'born for the universe, narrowed his mind, | And to party gave up what was meant for mankind' (*Retaliation, 1774). Yet as writer and orator he won admiration from all sides

(although, paradoxically, many of his best speeches were failures and were said to have emptied the House). *Macaulay, at one point describing his later style as 'ungracefully gorgeous' (1837), also declared him the 'greatest man since Milton'; M. *Arnold considered that he was 'so great, because, almost alone in England, he brings thought to bear upon politics, he saturates politics with thought' (1864). Wordsworth in *The Prelude saluted him as one who 'declares the vital power of social ties | Endeared by custom', in which role he also, according to his biographer *Morley, had considerable influence on the political thought of *Coleridge.

His works were published in 16 vols, 1803–27; his correspondence in 9 vols, ed. T. W. Copeland, 1958–70; there are lives by J. Prior (1824), J. Morley (1879), and P. Magnus (1939), among others.

Burke's Peerage, properly *A Genealogical and Heraldic History of the Peerage and Baronetage of the United Kingdom*, first compiled by John Burke and published in 1826. Since 1847 it has been published annually.

BURLEIGH, or **BURGHLEY,** William Cecil, Lord (1520–98), lord treasurer under Queen Elizabeth, and her chief minister. He had previously been secretary to Lord Protector Somerset; secretary of state, 1550–3; and employed in negotiations by Queen Mary. He is introduced in Sheridan's *The Critic, where, in Puff's tragedy, he comes on the stage and shakes his head, being too much occupied with cares of state to talk, whence the expression, 'Burleigh's nod'.

Burlesque, from the Italian *burla,* ridicule, mockery, a literary composition or dramatic representation which aims at exciting laughter by the comical treatment of a serious subject or the caricature of the spirit of a serious work. Notable examples of burlesque in English literature are Butler's *Hudibras and Sheridan's *The Rehearsal.

BURNABY, Frederick Gustavus (1842–85), cavalry officer and traveller. His greatest adventure, a ride across the Russian steppes, resulted in his best-selling *A Ride to Khiva* (1876) and warned Gladstone of Russia's expansionist aims. The young H. *James in reviewing the work (American *Nation*) described the author as 'opaque in intellect but indomitable in muscle'. It was followed by the successful *On Horseback through Asia Minor* (1877). *A Ride across the Channel* (1882) was written after a perilous flight to Normandy in a balloon. Burnaby was killed by an Arab spear-thrust in Abu Klea during the Nile expedition.

BURNAND, Sir Francis Cowley (1836–1917), was a regular contributor to *Punch from 1863, and his series 'Happy Thoughts' (1866) was very popular. He was editor of *Punch*, 1880–1906. He wrote many burlesques and adaptations of French farces, and his operetta *Cox and Box*, with music by *Sullivan, adapted from J. M. Morton's *Box and Cox*, was performed in 1867.

BURNE-JONES, Sir Edward Coley (1833–98), painter and designer, born in Birmingham, and educated at Oxford, where he came under the influence of *Morris and, through him, of D. G. *Rossetti, under whom he studied painting. He was much impressed by the medieval worlds of *Malory and of K. H. *Digby's *The Broad Stone of Honour* (1822), and later by the Italian Primitive painters; his best-known works (e.g. *King Cophetua and the Beggar Maid*, 1884) tend to portray women with a characteristic willowy, dreamlike beauty. He designed tapestry and stained glass for Morris and Co., and illustrations for the Kelmscott Press.

Burnell the Ass, the hero of the *Speculum Stultorum* by *Wireker. Burnell, who represents the monk who is dissatisfied with his lot, is an ass who wants a longer tail. He goes to Salerno and Paris to study, and finally loses his tail altogether. In the course of his travels he hears the tale that Chaucer alludes to in 'The Nun's Priest's Tale' (CT VII. 3,312–16; see CANTERBURY TALES, 20): the priest's son Gandulf breaks a cock's leg by throwing a stone at it. Later, on the morning when he is to be ordained, the cock fails to crow in time to rouse him and he loses his benefice.

BURNET, Gilbert (1643–1715), educated at Marischal College, Aberdeen, was a popular preacher, a latitudinarian and a Whig. He refused four bishoprics before he was 29, and in 1674 was dismissed from the post of king's chaplain for his outspoken criticisms of Charles II. He went to the Continent, and in 1686 to The Hague, where he became an adviser of William of Orange. He became bishop of Salisbury in 1689. His account of the death-bed repentance of *Rochester, *Some Passages in the Life and Death of the right honourable John Wilmot Earl of Rochester*, appeared in 1680 and his *History of the Reformation in England* in 3 vols, 1679, 1681, 1715. His best-known work, *The History of My Own Times*, is a mixture of history, autobiography, and anecdote, and was published posthumously (2 vols, 1724, 1734). Other works include *Memoires of the . . . Dukes of Hamilton* (1677) and *Life of Sir Matthew Hale* (1682). The standard biography is by T. E. S. Clarke and H. C. Foxcroft, 1907.

BURNET, Thomas (?1635–1715), a Yorkshire divine and master of the Charterhouse. He was the author of *The Theory of the Earth* (2 vols, 1684–90), translated by himself from the Latin and edited by B. Willey, 1965. It is an imaginative and romantic cosmogony, suggested to him by a voyage across the Alps. It contains, particularly in the third book, descriptive passages that are highly sonorous and magniloquent. The work was much praised by Addison in No. 146 of *The Spectator*.

BURNETT, Frances (Eliza) Hodgson (1849–1924), a prolific author, who wrote many novels and other books for adults, but is remembered for her work for children; in particular for the immensely successful (but much derided) *Little Lord Fauntleroy* (1886), whose character was based on her second son, Vivian, and whose velvet suit began an abiding fashion; and for *The Secret Garden* (1911), a widely admired children's classic about a spoilt, ill-tempered orphan, Mary, who finds an abandoned garden. While trying to revive it she encounters Colin, her sickly and hysterical cousin; as they work in the garden together he achieves health and she happiness. (See CHILDREN'S LITERATURE.)

BURNEY, Dr Charles (1726–1814), organist, musical historian, and minor composer, was the friend of *Garrick, Joshua *Reynolds, Dr *Johnson, and many members of aristocratic and literary society. He was the father of Fanny *Burney. He wrote a *History of Music*, published in four vols, 1776–89. He also wrote accounts of the travels he made in France, Italy, Germany, and the Low Countries in order to collect material for the work. (See also under MUSIC, LITERATURE OF.)

BURNEY, Charles (1757–1817), son of Dr *Burney, was famous in his time as a classical scholar. After his death the British Museum bought his library of over 13,000 volumes, which included classical books and manuscripts and the largest extant collection of early English newspapers.

BURNEY, Fanny (Frances, Mme d'Arblay) (1752–1840), daughter of Dr *Burney, lived in her youth in the midst of that London society which included Dr *Johnson, *Burke, *Reynolds, *Garrick, the *Blue Stocking Circle, and many members of the aristocracy. In 1778 she published anonymously her first novel *Evelina* and the revelation of its authorship brought her immediate fame. She published *Cecilia* in 1782, and in 1786 was appointed second keeper of the robes to Queen Charlotte. Her health was never good, but she lived a busy family and social life, much of which is reflected in her novels. In 1793 she married General d'Arblay, a French refugee in England. In 1796 she published *Camilla*. She and her husband were interned by Napoleon and lived in France from 1802 to 1812. *The Wanderer* (1814) was not a success. In 1832 she edited the *Memoirs* of her father. She was a prodigious writer of lively letters and journals; her *Early Diary 1768–1778*, which includes attractive sketches of Johnson, Garrick, and many others, was published in 1889, and her later *Diary and Letters . . . 1778–1840*, with a vivid account of her life at court, in 1842–6.

Her three major novels take as their theme the entry into the world of a young girl of beauty and understanding but no experience, and expose her to circumstances and events that develop her character; they display, with a satirical eye and a sharp ear for dialogue, the various social levels and the varied company in which she finds herself. Her novels were enjoyed and admired by J. *Austen, among many others. A complete edition of her letters and journals (10 vols, 1972–81) appeared under the general editorship of Joyce Hemlow, who also wrote a life, *The History of Fanny Burney* (1958).

'Burning Babe, The', see SOUTHWELL, R.

BURNS, Robert (1759–96), was one of seven children born to a cotter near Alloway in Ayrshire. His father moved his family from one unprofitable farm to another, but he was determined that his sons should be well educated. At various schools Robert was given a thorough grounding in English, including classic authors from Shakespeare onwards, and a knowledge of French and mathematics. He read voraciously for himself, and began to write occasional verses when he was still at school. His spare time was fully employed on the ailing farm as labourer and ploughman. The experience of poverty and injustice as a youth no doubt increased his belief in the equality of men, which led him to become an ardent supporter of the early days of the French Revolution. After his father's death in 1784 he and his brother Gilbert continued to farm, now at Mossgiel in the parish of Mauchline, which is often mentioned in the poems he was now beginning to write in some quantity. To this period at Mossgiel belong *'The Cotter's Saturday Night', 'To a *Mouse', 'To a Mountain Daisy', *'Holy Willie's Prayer', the Epistles to Labraik, *'The Holy Fair', and many others. He was much influenced at this time by Mackenzie's novel *The Man of Feeling*, a book he loved 'next to the Bible'. In 1785 he met Jean Armour, who was eventually to become his wife, but continued his long series of entanglements with women, many of whom are mentioned in his poems (for instance, Alison Begbie as 'Mary Morison', Mary Campbell in 'To Mary in Heaven').

In this and the following year he wrote prolifically, but his problems, both financial and domestic, became so acute that he thought of emigrating to Jamaica. However he sent his poems to a publisher in Kilmarnock, and when *Poems, chiefly in the Scottish Dialect* appeared in 1786 it was an immediate success. Burns found himself fêted by the literary and aristocratic society of Edinburgh, not only for his poetic skills but because he appeared, in Mackenzie's words as 'a Heaven-taught ploughman'. His attractive appearance and his gregarious temperament led him into a life of dissipation and amorous complexity. In 1787 he met Mrs M'Lehose, with whom he corresponded at length in high-flown terms, addressing her as 'Clarinda', signing himself 'Sylvander'. He was encouraged to write in the rhetorical and sentimental fashion of the day, and in this mode wrote a great deal—'The Lament', 'Despondency', and 'Address to Edinburgh' are examples—but fortunately his own characteristic voice was not subdued. A second edition of the *Poems* appeared in 1786, and Burns was asked if he would help to collect old Scottish songs for *The Scots Musical Museum*. He responded with an energy and enthusiasm that were to last until his death. He collected, amended, and wrote some 200 songs, which include many of his best-known lyrics, such as *'Auld Lang Syne', *'O my luve's like a red, red rose', *'Ye Banks and Braes', and *'Scots wha hae'. In 1787 he travelled in the Highlands and the Borders, collecting tunes and words, and contributed in 1792 to *Select Scottish Airs*. For all this work he took no money, regarding it as his patriotic duty. He did, however, continue to write and publish work of his own.

In 1788 he finally married Jean Armour, and settled on a poor farm at Ellisland, near Dumfries. A year later he eventually secured a post as an Excise officer, and in 1791 relinquished his farming life with relief and moved to Dumfries. Farming had always been a source of strain and anxiety to him, and he never, in *Wordsworth's words, 'walked in glory and in joy | Following his plough along the mountainside'. Also in 1791 he published his last major poem, *'Tam o' Shanter'. Turning against the French at last, he joined the Dumfries Volunteers in 1795, dying the following year of rheumatic heart disease.

Burns wrote with equal facility in correct 18th-cent. English and in his native Scots. In some of his songs, most notably in 'The Cotter's Saturday Night', English and Scots are both used. The Scottish poems owe much to Scottish song, to the early Scottish poets (such as *Ramsay), and to the 18th-cent. poet *Fergusson. His songs, his satires, his animal poems, and his verse-letters, together with his one narrative poem 'Tam o' Shanter' contain the best of his work. His work was much admired by his contemporaries, and *Lamb declared that in his own youth 'Burns was the god of my idolatry.' His popularity with his fellow-countrymen is reflected in celebrations held all over the world on 'Burns Night', 25 Jan., his birthday. His

Poems and Songs (with music) were edited in 3 vols, 1968, by J. Kinsley; see also D. Daiches, *Robert Burns* (1950, rev. 1966) and R. T. Fitzhugh, *Robert Burns, the man and the poet* (1970).

BURROUGHS, Edgar Rice (1875–1950), American novelist and writer of *Science Fiction, remembered principally for his adventure stories about Tarzan, who first appeared in *Tarzan of the Apes* (1914) and who rapidly gained popularity as hero of many sequels, films, radio programmes, and comic strips. Tarzan is the son of a British aristocrat, abandoned in the jungle as a baby and reared by apes.

BURROUGHS, William Seward (1914–   ), American novelist, best known for his frank accounts of life as a drug addict (*Junkie*, 1953; *The Naked Lunch*, 1959), for his experiments with collage technique, and for his obsession with the underworld and homosexual fantasy (*Nova Express*, 1964; *The Wild Boys*, 1971). See also under BEAT GENERATION.

BURTON, Sir Richard Francis (1821–90), explorer, swordsman, anthropologist, and linguist, and one of the most flamboyant characters of his day, left Oxford without graduating and in 1842 joined the Indian army. He left India in 1849, and subsequent travels took him to the forbidden city of Mecca (which he visited in disguise), to Africa on several expeditions, to the Crimea, to Salt Lake City (where he studied the Mormons), and as consul to Brazil, Damascus (1869–71), and Trieste (1871) where he died. He published over 40 volumes of travel, including his *Personal Narrative of a Pilgrimage to El-Medinah and Meccah* (1855–6) and *The Lake Regions of Central Africa* (1860); several volumes of folklore; two of poetry; and translations from Latin and Portuguese. He was a formidable linguist, speaking 25 languages and many more dialects. He is best remembered for his unexpurgated versions of the *Arabian Nights* (1885–8), *The Kama Sutra* (1883), *The Perfumed Garden* (1886, from the French), and other works of Arabian erotology. His interest in sexual behaviour and deviance (which he shared with his friends *Milnes and *Swinburne) and his detailed, frank, and valuable ethnographical notes led him to risk prosecution many times under the Obscene Publications Act of 1857, and his more erotic works were published secretly or privately. On his death his wife Isabel destroyed his papers and diaries, including the manuscript of his translation from the original Arabic of *The Perfumed Garden*, on which he had been working for 14 years.

BURTON, Robert (1577–1640), educated at Nuneaton and Sutton Coldfield schools and Brasenose College and Christ Church, Oxford,

rector of Segrave, Leicestershire. He was author of *The Anatomy of Melancholy*.

BURY, Richard de (1281–1345), named from his birthplace, Bury St Edmunds, was tutor to Edward III when Prince of Wales, became bishop of Durham, and is celebrated as a patron of learning and a collector of books. He wrote *Philobiblon*, a Latin autobiographical sketch of a lover of letters, first printed in 1473 and edited by M. Maclagan (1960). An English translation was published in the edition by E. C. Thomas (1888, 1903).

BUSBY, Richard (1606–95), educated at Westminster and Christ Church, Oxford, was a famous headmaster of *Westminster School from 1638 to 1695. Among his pupils were *Dryden, *Locke, *Atterbury, and *Prior.

Busie Body, The, a comedy by S. *Centlivre, produced 1709.

Sir George Airy and Miranda are in love with one another, but her guardian, Sir Francis Gripe, has the design of marrying her himself and believes that she loves him. The devices by which his intentions are defeated, and those by which Charles, Gripe's son, secures the hand of Isabinda, whom her father intends for a Spanish merchant, occupy the play. The character of Marplot, whose well-meant but misdirected interference constantly endangers the course of true love, has enriched the language with a name for the blundering busybody.

Busirane, in Spenser's *Faerie Queene* (III. xi and xii) the 'vile Enchaunter' symbolizing unlawful love. He is stricken down by *Britomart in his castle and forced to release *Amoret. On the door of one of the rooms of the castle was written:

> Be bold, be bold, and every where Be bold;

but on another iron door,

> Be not too bold.

Buskin, a word existing in many European languages, whose ultimate derivation is unknown. The special source of the English word is likewise uncertain. It is the word used for the high thick-soled boot (*cothurnus*) worn by actors in ancient Athenian tragedy, frequently contrasted with the 'sock' (*soccus*) or low shoe worn by comedians. Hence it is applied figuratively to the style or spirit of tragedy, the tragic vein. 'To put on the buskins', to write tragedy [*OED*].

Bussy D'Ambois, a tragedy by *Chapman, written ?1604, published 1607. The most famous of Chapman's plays, it was very popular in its day, and was revived at the Restoration, when *Dryden savagely attacked it in terms that nevertheless suggest its dramatic power: 'when I had taken up what I supposed a fallen star, I found I had been cozened with a jelly: nothing but a cold dull mass, which glittered no longer than it was shooting; a dwarfish thought, dressed up in gigantic words . . .' (1681).

Bussy D'Ambois (in real life, Louis de Bussy-d'Ambois), a man of insolence and fiery courage, is raised from poverty and introduced to the court of Henri III of France by Monsieur, brother of the king, his protector. He quarrels with the king's courtiers, of whom he kills three in an encounter, and even with the duc de Guise. He wins the favour of Tamyra, wife of Montsurry (Montsoreau); Monsieur, who also desires Tamyra, betrays Bussy to Montsurry. Montsurry by torture forces Tamyra to lure Bussy into a trap; he is overpowered and killed, dying defiantly on his feet. ('Here like a Roman statue I will stand | Till death hath made me marble.') Chapman's sequel is *The Revenge of Bussy D'Ambois.*

The story is the same as that told by *Dumas père in *La Dame de Monsoreau* (1846); both writers make the same alteration of historical fact, which was that not Monsieur but the king, who detested Bussy, revealed Bussy's amour to Montsoreau.

BUTLER, Lady Eleanor, see LLANGOLLEN, THE LADIES OF.

BUTLER, Joseph (1692–1752), was son of a Presbyterian linen-draper at Wantage, and was educated at Oriel College, Oxford. A youthful correspondence with S. *Clarke on natural theology was published in 1716. In 1736 he was brought into prominence by being appointed clerk of the closet to the queen, and in 1738 bishop of Bristol, from which he was translated to Durham in 1750.

His reputation stemmed from the publication in 1726 of *Fifteen Sermons* preached at the Rolls Chapel, in which he defines his moral philosophy, affirming an intuitional theory of virtue. While recognizing benevolence and a due degree of self-love as elements in virtuous conduct, he regards conscience as governing and limiting them by considerations, not of happiness or misery, but of right and wrong. In 1736 appeared his *Analogy of Religion,* a defence of the Christian religion against the Deists, in which Butler argues that belief in immortality, revelation, and miracles is as reasonable as the beliefs upon which natural religion is founded. Appended to this work are two further essays: 'Of Personal Identity' contains influential criticism of *Locke and more particularly Anthony *Collins; and 'Of the Nature of Virtue' counteracts the incipient utilitarianism found in some other philosophers of the moral sense tradition.

Butler, The Revd Reuben, a character who marries Jeanie Deans in Scott's *The Heart of Midlothian.*

BUTLER, Samuel ('Hudibras') (1613–80),

born at Strensham, a hamlet south of Worcester, the son of a farmer, and educated at the King's School, Worcester. He is said to have served as a clerk to a local justice of the peace and later to have become secretary to the countess of Kent. By 1661 he was steward at Ludlow Castle to Richard Vaughan, earl of Carbery. The most significant event in an otherwise obscure life was the publication in 1663 of his *Hudibras,* which instantly became the most popular poem of its time. It was probably as a result of its success that he became secretary to the second duke of *Buckingham. In 1677 he was awarded an annual pension of £100 by Charles II, but by then he himself appears to have given currency to the complaint that, though a loyal satirist, he had been left to endure his old age in poverty. He wrote a number of shorter satirical poems, including 'The Elephant in the Moon', an attack on the *Royal Society, and a great many prose 'Characters'. See *Hudibras,* ed. John Wilders (1967); *Characters,* ed. C. W. Daves (1970); *Prose Observations,* ed. Hugh de Quehen (1980); *Hudibras Parts I and II and Selected Other Writings,* ed. Wilders and de Quehen (1973).

BUTLER, Samuel (1835–1902), the son of a clergyman and grandson of a bishop, was educated at Shrewsbury and St John's College, Cambridge. Religious doubts prevented his taking holy orders and in 1859 he went to New Zealand, where he achieved success as a sheep-farmer. *A First Year in Canterbury Settlement* (1863), compiled by his father from Samuel's letters, was published in 1863 in a New Zealand journal and became the core of *Erewhon.* He returned to England in 1864 and settled in Clifford's Inn, where he began to study painting (at which he worked for ten years) and exhibited occasionally at the Royal Academy. In 1872 he published *Erewhon,* anonymously, which enjoyed a brilliant but brief success. In 1873 appeared *The Fair Haven,* an elaborate and ironic attack on the Resurrection, which brought him encouragement from C. *Darwin and L. *Stephen. A journey to Canada in 1874–5 inspired his well known poem 'A Psalm of Montreal', first printed in the *Spectator in May 1878, in which he laments (with the refrain: 'O God! O Montreal!') the Canadian philistinism that relegated a Greek statue of a Discobolus to a room in the Natural History Museum used by a taxidermist, who explained that the statue was 'vulgar' because 'he hath neither vest nor pants to cover his lower limbs.'

Between 1877 and 1890 Butler produced a series of works of scientific controversy, many of them directed against certain aspects of Darwinism, in particular C. *Darwin's theory of natural selection: they include *Evolution, Old and New* (1879), *Unconscious Memory* (1880), and three articles on 'The Deadlock in Darwinism' (*The Universal Review,* 1890). Butler's espousal of the cause of *Lamarck and creative evolution won him the praise of G. B. *Shaw in his preface to *Back to Methuselah* (1921); Shaw also praised Butler's outspoken views on religion and the 'importance of money' in his preface to *Major Barbara* (1907).

In 1881 Butler published *Alps and Sanctuaries of Piedmont and the Canton Ticino*, the first of several animated works on art and travel. He experimented with musical composition, including a comic pastoral oratorio, *Narcissus* (1888), written in collaboration with his great friend Festing Jones. In 1896 appeared his *The Life and Letters of Dr Samuel Butler*, his revered grandfather, who had been headmaster, bishop, and geographer. A long interest in *Homer led to his theory of the feminine authorship of the *Odyssey* and its origin at Trapini in Sicily. *The Authoress of the 'Odyssey'* appeared in 1897, and translations of the *Iliad* and the *Odyssey* into vigorous colloquial prose in 1898 and 1900. A quirky study, *Shakespeare's Sonnets Reconsidered*, appeared in 1899, and *Erewhon Revisited* in 1901. Butler's most revealing work, on which he had been labouring for many years, was his semi-autobiographical novel, *The Way of All Flesh*, published posthumously in 1903. He left six large Notebooks, full of incident, self-revelation, and ideas; selections of these were published by Festing Jones in 1912.

BUTOR, Michel (1926–   ), French novelist and one of the creators of the *nouveau roman*; notable in an English context for his novel *L'Emploi du temps* (1957; English trans., *Passing Time*, 1961), a remarkable evocation of Manchester, where Butor worked for a year as an export clerk.

Button's Coffee House, the rival of *Will's, stood in Russell Street, Covent Garden; Button was an old servant of *Addison's, and the house was frequented by *Dryden, Addison, *Steele, and *Pope. It declined in popularity after Addison's death and Steele's retirement to Wales.

Buzfuz, Mr Serjeant, in Dickens's *Pickwick Papers*, counsel for the plaintiff in Bardell v. Pickwick.

BYATT, A(ntonia) S(usan) (1936–   ), novelist and critic, born in Sheffield, the daughter of a barrister, and educated at The Mount School, York, and Newnham College, Cambridge. Her first novel, *Shadow of a Sun* (1964), describes the efforts of Anna to escape from the shadow of her novelist father; *The Game* (1967) also explores the influence of art on life through the relationship of two sisters, one an Oxford don, the other a popular novelist. Her most substantial work, *The Virgin in the Garden* (1978), is set largely in the Coronation year of 1953; the second Elizabethan Golden Age is celebrated by a performance at a Yorkshire country house

of a new verse drama by public schoolmaster Alexander Wedderburn, in which schoolgirl Frederica Potter plays the role of the Virgin Queen. Rich in complex allegorical allusions to *Spenser, *Ralegh, *Shakespeare, and many others, the novel also provides a realistic and vivid portrait of the Potter family, and of provincial life in the 1950s.

By-Ends, Mr, in Bunyan's *Pilgrim's Progress*, 'a very arch fellow, a downright hypocrite; one that would be religious, which way ever the world went: but so cunning, that he would be sure never to lose or suffer for it'.

BYRD, William (1543–1623), English composer. Byrd was the father figure of Elizabethan music, a pupil and colleague of *Tallis (whose career stretched back into the reign of Henry VIII) and in his turn the teacher of *Morley and Tomkins, and very probably Philips, *Weelkes, and *Bull, as well. He composed prolifically in all forms: the largest section of his output is devoted to sacred music, for both Anglican and Catholic rites, but there is an impressive list of secular vocal works as well. In comparison with some of his later Elizabethan successors (*Wilbye, to take an extreme case) he appears a very universal genius.

Though he lived and composed well into the reign of James I, Byrd's musical character was formed essentially in the early part of Elizabeth's, and when the Italian *madrigal arrived in England in the 1580s and 1590s he treated it with circumspection. He experimented with the form in *Psalmes, Sonets and Songs* of 1588, and again in *Songs of Sundrie Natures* in the following year, though the pieces he produced are mostly based on earlier traditions and have little of the new Italian model about them; neither these pieces, nor the later *Psalmes, Songs and Sonnets* (1611), were called 'madrigals' by Byrd himself, the title being foisted on them by the scholars of the 19th cent. He kept all his life a preference for the poetry of his earlier days: *Sidney's name appears as an author from time to time, along with *Ralegh, *Dyer, and minor figures like Geoffry Whitney, William Hunnis, and *Churchyard, but the majority of the texts he set, as is usual at this period, remain obstinately anonymous.

BYROM, John (1692–1763), born near Manchester, was educated at Merchant Taylors' School and at Trinity College, Cambridge, under the reign of *Bentley, in whose defence he wrote, and to whose daughter he may have addressed *A Pastoral*, published in *The Spectator*, 1714. He invented his own system of shorthand or 'tychygraphy', had many varied literary, linguistic, religious, and scientific interests, and was from 1724 a fellow of the *Royal Society; his varied acquaintance included *Hartley, the *Wesleys, J. *Butler, and, notably, *Law, of whom he left interesting accounts in his *Private Journals and literary remains*, published in 1854–7. Byrom had Jacobite sympathies and was, like Law, a non-juror; he was the author of the ambiguously loyal toast, beginning 'God bless the King! I mean the Faith's Defender . . .' His *Miscellaneous Poems* (1773) include some curious versifications of Law's *Serious Call*, which amused Law, and the well-known hymn 'Christians, awake! Salute the happy morn'. His *Journals* give the impression of a light-hearted and good-natured man paradoxically attracted to the mysticism of writers like *Boehme, *Malebranche, Tauler, and Suso (the latter both disciples of *Eckhart).

BYRON, George Gordon, sixth baron (1788–1824), son of Captain John Byron, 'Mad Jack', who eloped with and married Lady Carmarthen, and had by her a daughter, Augusta, who was to be of great importance in Byron's life. As his second wife Captain Byron married Catherine Gordon of Gight, an impetuous Scot, who became Byron's mother. The boy was born with a club-foot, which (it is generally supposed) had a profound affect on his future temperament. Mary *Shelley was to write, 'No action of Lord Byron's life—scarce a line he has written—but was influenced by his personal defect.' Pursued by creditors, the family moved in 1789 to Aberdeen, where Byron was educated until he was ten. His father died in 1791, and the fifth baron's grandson was killed in 1794; so when the baron himself died in 1798, Byron inherited the title. He and his mother moved south, visited his future inheritance, the dilapidated Gothic Newstead Abbey, and Byron was eventually sent to Harrow School. Staying at Newstead in 1802 he probably first met his half-sister, Augusta. In 1805, an extremely handsome young man, he went up to Cambridge, where he attended intermittently to his studies between extravagant debauches there and in London. His first published collection of poems, *Hours of Idleness*, appeared in 1807, and was bitterly attacked by *Brougham in the *Edinburgh Review*. Byron avenged himself in 1809 with his satire *English Bards and Scotch Reviewers*. In 1808 he returned to Newstead, in 1809 took his seat in the House of Lords, then left for the first of his prolonged travels abroad. Between 1809 and 1811 he visited Portugal, Spain, Malta, Greece, and the Levant. In 1809 he began the poem that was to become *Childe Harold* and completed two cantos; he wrote one of his most famous lyrics, *'Maid of Athens'; he swam the Hellespont; and he became fired with the wish, which was to lead to his return and death, that Greece should be freed from the Turks.

In England again in 1811 he again met Augusta. In that year, and in 1813, he spoke effectively on liberal themes in the House of Lords.

His first great literary triumph came with the publication of the first two cantos of *Childe Harold's Pilgrimage* in March 1812. He was lionized by aristocratic and literary London, survived a hectic love-affair with Lady Caroline *Lamb, and became the constant companion of Augusta. In 1813 he wrote *The Bride of Abydos* in a week, and *The Corsair* in ten days: *The Giaour* appeared in the same year. In 1814 Augusta gave birth to a daughter, who was generally supposed to be Byron's and was almost certainly so. In the same year he wrote *Lara. After a long and hesitant courtship he married in 1815 Lady Melbourne's daughter, Annabella Milbanke. In the same year their daughter Ada was born, and Byron published *Hebrew Melodies. But his debts were accumulating, doubts were cast upon his sanity, and public horror at the rumours of his incest was rising. Annabella left him to live with her parents, and a legal separation was eventually arranged.

Ostracized and deeply embittered, Byron left England in 1816, never to return, and travelled to Geneva, where the *Shelleys and Claire Claremont had rented a villa. Here Byron wrote *The Prisoner of Chillon*, and Claire became his mistress. He wrote two acts of *Manfred, Canto III of *Childe Harold, and several shorter poems, but after four months left for Italy. His daughter by Claire, Allegra, was born in Jan. 1817 in England. While living a riotous life in Venice in the same year, he devised and published an Armenian dictionary and wrote the third act of *Manfred*. While travelling to Rome he passed Tasso's cell, which inspired his *Lament of Tasso, and in Rome he began the IVth and last Canto of *Childe Harold*. He returned to Venice and there wrote *Beppo, his first work in the ironic, colloquial style which was to lead him to *Don Juan. Newstead Abbey was at last sold, and Byron was free of financial worries. In 1818 he wrote *Mazeppa, and began *Don Juan*, the first two Cantos of which were published in 1819 by John *Murray, reluctantly and anonymously, and which were denounced in *Blackwood's as 'a filthy and impious poem'. However it was much admired by *Goethe, a fact which Byron found greatly encouraging. In this year he met Teresa, Countess Guiccioli, to whom he became deeply attached. They lived first in Venice, then he followed her and her household to Ravenna, where he wrote *The Prophecy of Dante*. In 1820 he continued with Cantos III and IV of *Don Juan*, wrote *Marino Faliero, and became deeply involved with the cause of the Italian patriots. Teresa left her husband for Byron in 1821, and Shelley rented houses in Pisa both for Byron and for the Gambas, Teresa's family. While at Ravenna and Pisa that year Byron became deeply interested in drama, and wrote *The Two Foscari, *Sardanapalus, *Cain, the unfinished *Heaven and Earth, and the unfinished *The Deformed Transformed. He thought well of his dramatic works and regretted they were not better received. In the same productive year he also wrote *The Vision of Judgement and continued with Don Juan. The death in 1822 of his daughter Allegra, whom he had continually failed to visit, was a great grief to him. With the Gambas he left Pisa for Leghorn, where Leigh *Hunt joined them. Hunt and Byron co-operated in the production of *The Liberal magazine, the three issues of which contained successively The Vision of Judgement, Heaven and Earth, and a translation from *Pulci. Now in Genoa, Byron wrote *Werner, and was much preoccupied with Don Juan and with thoughts of Greece. In 1823 he wrote The Age of Bronze, a satirical poem on the Congress of Vienna, and *The Island, but he had come to feel that action was more important than poetry, and he told Lady *Blessington, 'I have a presentiment I shall die in Greece.' By July he was ready to sail, and Goethe sent him good wishes in verse. In Jan. 1824, after various mishaps and escapes, he arrived at Missolonghi. He formed the 'Byron Brigade' and gave large sums of money, and great inspiration, to the insurgent Greeks, but he was dismayed by their disarray. Before he saw any serious military action he died of fever in April. Memorial services were held all over Greece, but his body was refused by the deans of both Westminster and St Paul's. After his old friend *Hobhouse had arranged for the coffin to lie in state for a few days in London, it was interred in the family vault at Hucknall Torkhard, near Newstead.

Byron's poetry, although widely condemned on moral grounds, and frequently attacked by critics, was immensely popular in England and even more so abroad. He noted in his Journal in 1822 that his sales were better in Germany, France, and America than at home. Much of his poetry and drama exerted great influence on *Romanticism. His legacy of inspiration in European poetry, music, the novel, opera, and painting, has been immense. B. *Russell wrote that 'As a myth his importance, especially on the continent, was enormous.'

He was an indefatigable writer of letters and journals, many of which (T. *Moore asserted) were written with an eye to publication. They provide a brilliantly vivid commentary both on his own life and on the times in which he lived. Moore's life was published in 1830 (Letters and Journals of Lord Byron, with notices of his life, 2 vols) and a 3-vol. biography by L. A. Marchand was published in 1958. Marchand also edited the letters (11 vols, 1973–81) and the Complete Poetical Works (3 vols, 1980–1) are edited by J. J. McGann.

Byron, Harriet, the heroine of Richardson's *Sir Charles Grandison.

BYRON, John (1723–86), as a midshipman on the Wager, one of the ships of *Anson's squadron in his famous voyage, was wrecked on an island off the coast of Chile in 1741. His 'Narrative' of the shipwreck, published in 1768, was used by his grandson Lord *Byron in his description of the storm and wreck in *Don Juan.

BYRON, Robert (1905–41), travel writer, Byzantinist, and aesthete, educated at Eton and Merton College, Oxford. His works include The Station (1928), The Byzantine Achievement (1929), and The Appreciation of Architecture (1932), but he is chiefly remembered for his classic study The Road to Oxiana (1937), a record in the form of diary jottings of a journey from Venice through the Middle East and Afghanistan to India in search of the origins of Islamic architecture and culture; it contains passages that, in the opinion of travel writer Bruce Chatwin (in a 1981 introduction), place him in 'the rank of Ruskin'. Byron died when his ship was hit by a torpedo.

Byron, The Conspiracy and Tragedy of Charles Duke of, a two-part play by *Chapman, published 1608.

The play deals with the intrigues of Charles Gontaut, duc de Biron, a brave soldier who had fought successfully and been nobly rewarded by Henri IV of France, but whose overweening ambition made him disloyal to the king. His plots are discovered, he asks forgiveness, and is pardoned. But his restless ambition makes him prepare a new conspiracy, which is revealed to the king. He is arrested and condemned to death. He professes his innocence and is reduced to frenzy and despair when he realizes that he is to die.

Byronic, characteristic of or resembling *Byron or his poetry; that is, contemptuous of and rebelling against conventional morality, or defying fate, or possessing the characteristics of Byron's romantic heroes, or imitating his dress and appearance; as *Meredith describes it, 'posturing statuesque pathetic'; or in the words of *Macaulay, 'a man proud, moody, cynical, with defiance on his brow, and misery in his heart, a scorner of his kind, implacable in revenge, yet capable of deep and strong affection'.

BYWATER, Ingram (1840–1914), educated at University College School and King's College School, London, and at The Queen's College, Oxford, and a fellow of Exeter College, was an eminent Greek scholar. He succeeded *Jowett as Regius professor of Greek in 1893. He had acquired a European reputation by his edition (1877) of the Fragments of *Heraclitus. His monumental edition of the Poetics of *Aristotle appeared in 1909. He made important contributions to the OED, and guided the critical methods of the editors of the long series of Oxford Classical Texts.

Byzantine, the word used to designate the art,

and especially the architecture, developed in the eastern division of the Roman Empire. This eastern division endured from the partition of the Empire between the two sons of Theodosius in AD 395 to the capture of Constantinople, its capital, formerly known as Byzantium, by the Turks in 1453. Byzantine architecture is distinguished by its use of the round arch, cross, circle, dome, and rich mosaic ornament. St Mark's at Venice is a prominent example. Byzantium stands as an important symbol in the poems of *Yeats ('Sailing to Byzantium', 'Byzantium'), where it appears to represent the undying world of art, contrasted with the 'fury and the mire of human veins'; but the word 'byzantine' is also sometimes used (with reference to history rather than art) to convey a sinister sense of oriental intrigue.

C

Cabal, from the Hebrew word *qabbalah* (see CABBALA), a secret intrigue of a sinister character formed by a small body of persons, or a small body of persons engaged in such an intrigue; in British history applied specially to the five ministers of Charles II who signed the treaty of alliance with France for war against Holland in 1672; these were Clifford, Arlington, *Buckingham, Ashley (see SHAFTESBURY, 1st earl of) and Lauderdale, the initials of whose names thus arranged happened to form the word 'cabal' [*OED*].

Cabbala, from the Hebrew *qabbalah*, tradition, a Jewish tradition of the mystical interpretation of the Scriptures, a reaction from the rationalism of the school of *Maimonides, developed between the 9th and 13th cents, comprising the 'Sepher Yezirah' ('Book of Creation') and the 'Zohar' ('Splendour'). These mystic doctrines included the existence of 'Sephiroth', realized abstractions or emanations, by which the infinite entered into relations with the finite; and the belief that the letters of the biblical text, converted into numbers, may be manipulated in such a way as to reveal hidden truths. There is perhaps a trace of this in the number of the *Beast in Rev. 13: 18.

CABLE, George Washington (1844–1925), American novelist, author of stories of the old Creole society of Louisiana, including *Old Creole Days* (1879), *The Grandissimes* (1880), and *Madame Delphine* (1881).

Cade, Jack, Rebellion of, a popular revolt by the men of Kent in June and July 1450, Yorkist in sympathy, against the misrule of Henry VI and his council. Its intent was more to reform political administration than to create social upheaval, as the revolt of 1381 had attempted. Its leader Jack Cade, who is said to have been Irish, took the name Mortimer and marched triumphantly into London where his followers beheaded Say, the lord treasurer. After a fight on London Bridge, Cade was abandoned by his followers, whereupon he retreated into Sussex where he was killed. He appears as a character in Shakespeare's 2 *Henry VI*.

Cadenus and Vanessa, a poem by *Swift, written in 1713 for Esther Vanhomrigh ('Vanessa'). It is the narrative, in mock classical form, of the author's relations with 'Vanessa' and an apology for his conduct. 'Cadenus' is an obvious anagram of 'Decanus', dean. Miss Vanhomrigh evidently took no exception to his statement of the facts, since she preserved the poem and desired it to be published. It appeared in 1726, three years after her death.

Cadwal, in Shakespeare's *Cymbeline*, the name of Cymbeline's younger son *Arviragus during his childhood in Wales.

CADWALLADER, (1) the son of Cadwallon, died in 689 according to *Geoffrey of Monmouth. He is the last of the British kings of England, according to the various *Bruts* which conclude with him. After his day, which was characterized by plague and desolation, the British would be called Welsh (foreign) and the Saxons rule instead in England, until the time prophesied by *Merlin for the return of a British king. He joined Penda (according to Geoffrey, Cadwallader's maternal uncle) against Eadwine, the Anglican king of Northumbria; (2) a character in Smollett's *Peregrine Pickle*; (3) a Mrs Cadwallader figures in George Eliot's *Middlemarch*.

CAEDMON (*fl*. 670), entered the monastery of Streaneshalch (Whitby) between 658 and 680, when already an elderly man. He is said by *Bede to have been an unlearned herdsman who received suddenly, in a vision, the power of song, and later put into English verse passages translated to him from the Scriptures. The name Caedmon cannot be explained in English, and has been conjectured to be Celtic (an adaptation of the British Catumanus). In 1655 François Dujon (Franciscus Junius) published at Amsterdam from the unique Bodleian MS Junius II (*c*.1000) long scriptural poems, which he took to be those of Caedmon. These are *Genesis*, *Exodus*, *Daniel*, and *Christ and Satan*, but they cannot be the work of Caedmon. The only work which can be attributed to him is the short 'Hymn of Creation', quoted by Bede, which survives in several manuscripts of Bede in various dialects.

Caelia, in Spenser's *Faerie Queene* (I. x) the Lady of the House of Holiness, mother of Fidelia, Speranza, and Charissa (Faith, Hope, and Charity).

Caerleon, see CARLIOUN.

CAESAR, Gaius Julius (102/100–44 BC), Roman politician who in his middle forties surfaced as a general of genius. Victor in the factional struggles that destroyed the Republic, and eventually dictator, he prepared the ground for six centuries of imperial rule. He was also a writer of exceptional ability and has left a lucid account of his campaigns in his *Commentaries*. Since he cuts an attractive figure in the correspondence of *Cicero (the principal contemporary source for the events of his lifetime) and is praised by the biographers and historians who served his imperial successors, and since he had for good measure a love affair with Cleopatra, the most spectacularly fascinating woman of his day, later ages came to look upon him as a superman and, in spite of attacks from opponents of autocracy, this larger-than-life reputation has clung to him to the present time. The *Commentaries on the Gallic War* were translated in part by A. *Golding (1565) and C. Edmundes (1600), but they were read in the original by every English schoolboy, and mentions of Caesar abound in English literature. *Dryden for example cites his opinions repeatedly. But the true signposts to the nature of his reputation are Shakespeare's *Julius Caesar* (*c*.1600) and *Shaw's *Caesar and Cleopatra* (1901). It is in these that we have the time-honoured Caesarian legend.

Caesar and Pompey, a Roman tragedy by *Chapman, published 1631, but written between 1599 and 1607.

It deals with the contention of Caesar and Pompey, the events leading to the battle of Pharsalus (48 BC), the murder of Pompey, and the suicide of Cato of Utica. The latter is the real hero of the play, of which the motto is 'Only a just man is a free man'.

Caesaraugusta, in imprints, Saragossa.

Caesura, in Greek and Latin prosody, the division of a metrical foot between two words, especially in certain recognized places near the middle of the line; in English prosody, a pause about the middle of a metrical line, generally indicated by a pause in the sense.

Café Royal, a French-style café-restaurant at 68 Regent Street, which was for several decades from the 1880s onwards the haunt of artists and writers and the scene of many artistic gatherings, scandals, and celebrations. Its habitués included *Whistler, *Wilde, *Dowson, A. *Symons, *Crowley, F. *Harris, *Firbank, *Beerbohm, and G. B. *Shaw; it appeared in the novels of D. H. *Lawrence (as The Café Pompadour, in *Women in Love), of *Maugham, Arnold *Bennett, E. *Waugh, and others, and was painted and sketched by *Beardsley, Sickert, and others. Its famous Brasserie closed in 1951. See *Café Royal: Ninety Years of Bohemia* (1955) by G. Deghy and K. Waterhouse.

Cain: a Mystery, a poetic drama by *Byron, published 1821.

Cain, revolting against the heavy toil imposed upon him because of another's fault and bewildered how to reconcile the world he knows with the goodness of an omnipotent God, becomes a willing pupil of Lucifer and questions him about the problems of existence. Lucifer's teaching, exposing the ways of God to man, confirms Cain in his revolt, and in a fit of passion at Abel's devotion to Jehova, and the barbaric blood-sacrifice on Abel's altar, he strikes his brother and kills him. Remorse and punishment follow, and Cain becomes an exile and a wanderer. The audacity of the poem aroused intense indignation, and the publisher, John *Murray, was threatened with prosecution. Byron strongly denied that the views of either Cain or Lucifer represented his own.

CAINE, (Sir Thomas Henry) Hall (1853–1931), novelist, of Manx and Cumberland parentage, who worked as teacher, architect's assistant, and journalist in his early years. In 1878 he delivered a lecture at the Free Library in Liverpool on D. G. *Rossetti, which brought him into correspondence with the poet; Caine was befriended by Rossetti, and spent the last few months of Rossetti's life as his housemate: see Caine's *Recollections of Dante Gabriel Rossetti* (1882). He edited an anthology, *Sonnets of Three Centuries* (1882), in which all three Rossettis and W. B. *Scott were well represented. He then turned his attention to fiction, and wrote many novels of wide popularity and a somewhat sensational reputation, many of them centred in the Isle of Man; they include *The Shadow of a Crime* (1885), *The Deemster* (1887), *The Bondman* (1890), *The Scapegoat* (1891), *The Manxman* (1894), *The Christian* (1897), *The Eternal City* (1901), *The Prodigal Son* (1904), *The White Prophet* (1909), *The Woman Thou Gavest Me* (1913). *My Story*, a narrative of the early years of Cain's literary career, appeared in 1908.

CAIRD, Edward (1835–1908), philosopher, educated at Greenock Academy, at the Universities of Glasgow and St Andrews, and at Balliol College, Oxford, where *Jowett was his tutor, and T. H. *Green a close friend. He became professor of moral philosophy at Glasgow in 1866, and in 1893 succeeded Jowett as master of Balliol. His work on *Kant and *Hegel was important in its day, and his *Gifford Lectures on *The Evolution of Religion* were published in 1893.

Caius, Dr, a French physician in Shakespeare's *The Merry Wives of Windsor*. Kent in *King Lear* makes an enigmatic reference to 'your servant Caius' (v. iii. 283). Neither character appears to carry any allusion to the real life Dr John Caius, refounder of Gonville and Caius College, Cambridge.

Caius (pron. 'Keys') **College,** Cambridge (full

title, Gonville and Caius College), was formerly Gonville Hall, which was founded by Edmund Gonville in 1348. John Caius or Kay (1510–73), scholar and physician to Edward VI and Mary, who was educated at Gonville Hall, refounded and enlarged it as Caius College in 1557, and was master, 1559–73.

Calantha, the heroine of Ford's *The Broken Heart.*

CALDERÓN DE LA BARCA, Pedro (1600–81), the great Spanish dramatist and successor of Lope de *Vega, was born in Madrid and educated at Salamanca. After a turbulent early life he was ordained priest in 1651; he enjoyed royal favour, and in 1663 became chaplain of honour to the king. He wrote some 120 plays—tragedies, comedies of manners, histories, philosophical dramas—and, in later life, more than 70 highly regarded *autos sacramentales,* allegorical religious plays with subjects from mythology and the Old and New Testaments, dramatizing aspects of faith. Of his secular plays, one of the best known is *El alcalde de Zalamea* (c.1643), in which the peasant-mayor takes revenge on the captain who has seduced his daughter and is rewarded by Philip II by being made mayor for life. Other works include *La vida es sueño* (1635), a baroque philosophical romance which he also rewrote as an *auto,* and *El mágico prodigioso* (1637), a religious drama set in the reign of Diocletian. E. *Fitzgerald translated eight of his plays (1853, 1865), and there are more literal translations by D. F. MacCarthy (1853–70). R. *Campbell's translation of *El médico de su honra* (1635), a play about the apparently justified murder of a falsely suspected wife, was published in 1960 as *The Surgeon of his Honour.*

Caleb Balderstone, a character in Scott's *The Bride of Lammermoor.*

Caleb Williams (*Things as they are: or The Adventures of Caleb Williams*), a novel by W. *Godwin, published 1794. This work is remarkable as an early example of the propagandist novel, as a novel of pursuit, crime, and detection, and as a psychological study. It was designed to show 'the tyranny and perfidiousness exercised by the powerful members of the community against those who are less privileged than themselves'. A provocative preface to the original edition was withdrawn.

It is related in the first person by its eponymous hero. The first part of the book deals with the misdeeds of Tyrrel, an arrogant and tyrannical country squire, who ruins a tenant on his estate, Hawkins, for refusing to yield to one of his whims, and drives to the grave his niece Miss Melville for refusing to marry a boor of his selection. In the course of these events he comes into conflict with the idealistic and benevolent Falkland, a neighbouring squire, knocks him down in public, and is shortly after found murdered. Suspicion falls on Falkland but is diverted to Hawkins and his son, who are tried and executed. From this time Falkland becomes eccentric and solitary. Caleb Williams, the self-educated son of humble parents, is appointed his secretary, and convinces himself that Falkland is in fact Tyrrel's murderer. The remainder of the book concerns Falkland's unrelenting persecution of Williams, despite Williams's devotion to his employer and refusal to betray his secret. Williams is imprisoned on a false charge of robbing his employer, escapes, but is tracked by Falkland's agents until, in despair, he lays a charge of murder against Falkland, is confronted with him, and, although he has no proof to offer, through his generosity and sincerity wins from the murderer a confession of guilt. Godwin's original ending was radically different; in it Falkland maintains his innocence and Williams ends, nearly demented, in jail. *Hazlitt paid tribute to the power of the narrative when he wrote, 'no one ever began *Caleb Williams* that did not read it through.' Godwin reinforces his political points by documentary references in footnotes to such works as the *Newgate Calendar and *John Howard's *The State of the Prisons in England and Wales, 1770–80.* The edition by David McCracken (1970) has the alternative ending printed as appendix.

Caledonia, the Roman name for the northern part of Britain, hence used poetically for Scotland.

Calendar, the system according to which the beginning and length of the year are fixed.

The Julian Calendar is that introduced by Julius Caesar in 46 BC, in which the ordinary year has 365 days, and every fourth year is a leap year of 366 days, the months having the names, order, and length still retained. This was known as 'Old Style' when the Gregorian Calendar was introduced.

The Gregorian Calendar is the modification of the preceding, adapted to bring it into closer conformity with astronomical data and the natural course of the seasons, and to rectify the error already contracted by its use. This modification was introduced by Pope Gregory XIII in 1582, and adopted in Great Britain in 1752 (see CHESTERFIELD). It was known as 'New Style'. The error, due to the fact that the Julian year of 365¼ days (allowing for leap years) was 11 minutes 10 seconds too long, amounted in 1752 to 11 days, such that in order to correct this, 2 Sept. was in that year followed by 14 Sept., while century years were to be leap years only when divisible by 400 (e.g. 1600, 2000). See also USSHER and Appendix III.

Calendar of Modern Letters, The (1925–7), a literary periodical, first a monthly, then a quarterly, edited by E. *Rickword and Douglas Garman. It published fiction by D. H. *Lawrence, *Pirandello, A. E. *Coppard, *Gerhardi, and others; in its critical articles (some in a series called 'Scrutinies') it praised Lawrence and T. F. *Powys, faintly praised S. T. *Warner and others, condemned the 'non-combatant' and uncommitted critical attitudes of *Gosse and the grossness of Arnold *Bennett, found the products of *Bloomsbury to be on the whole frivolous and sentimental, and praised the critical approach of I. A. *Richards. *Towards Standards of Criticism: Selections from the Calendar of Modern Letters* was published in 1933 with an introduction by *Leavis, who credited the periodical with having established 'the critical basis for appreciating Mr Eliot, Mr Pound and their successors'. *Scrutiny* upheld many of its attitudes.

CALENIUS, Walter (d. 1151), a name used by *Bale for a writer who was archdeacon of Oxford, 1115–38. This Walter, according to *Geoffrey of Monmouth, brought from Brittany the Celtic chronicle which Geoffrey professed to translate. 'Calena' being, in the bastard Latin of the 16th cent., used for Oxford, Bale meant by 'Calenius' only Walter of Oxford. He is sometimes confused with later archdeacons of Oxford, Walter of Coutances (1183) and Walter *Map.

Caliban, in Shakespeare's *The Tempest, is described in the *Folio 'Names of the Actors' as 'a salvage and deformed slave'. His name probably derives either from 'Carib' or 'cannibal'. Son of the witch *Sycorax and the original possessor of *Prospero's island, he is only semi-human, but has often been portrayed attractively in modern productions: the poetic qualities of his speeches have facilitated this.

'Caliban upon Setebos', a poem by R. Browning, included in *Dramatis Personae*.

Caliburn, see EXCALIBUR.

Calidore, Sir, the Knight of Courtesy, the hero of Bk VI of Spenser's *Faerie Queene*. He pursues and chains the *Blatant Beast. One of Keats's earliest poems, the fragment 'Young Calidore is paddling o'er the lake' (1816), was inspired by him.

Calista, the heroine of Rowe's *The Fair Penitent*, in which the 'gay Lothario' figures as her lover.

Calisto and Melibea, see CELESTINA.

CALLIMACHUS (c.310–after 246 BC), perhaps the finest of Hellenistic poets and a scholar who worked in the library at Alexandria. Much admired by Roman poets in the 1st cent. BC— *Catullus imitated his poem on the 'Lock of Berenice'—he was admired also by the By-

zantines. But many of his works were lost in the upheavals of the 13th cent., and his manuscript tradition has preserved only six hymns, sixty epigrams, and a number of fragments. A difficult author, Callimachus found few readers until the end of the 17th cent., after which a number of editions appeared including one to which Richard *Bentley contributed (1697). He was imitated by *Akenside in his 'Hymn to the Naiads'. One of his epigrams served as a model for W. J. *Cory's 'They told me Heraclitus . . .' (1845), and material of a mythological sort drawn from his hymns can be found in Tennyson's *'Tiresias' and *Bridges' *Prometheus the Firegiver* (1883). Papyrus discoveries since 1910 have enlarged modern knowledge of his texts.

Callista, a religious novel by J. H. *Newman.

Call of the Wild, The, a story by J. *London.

CALPRENÈDE, Gauthier de Costes de la, see LA CALPRENÈDE.

CALVERLEY, Charles Stuart (born Blayds, assumed Calverley from 1852) (1831–84), became a barrister of the Inner Temple, but his career was hindered by the effects of a serious skating accident. He became known under the initials C.S.C. as a writer of light verse, parodies, and translations, some of which now bring to mind the works of *Betjeman. *Verses and Translations* appeared in 1862, *Fly Leaves* in 1872.

Calves' Head Club, an association formed at the end of the 17th cent. to ridicule Charles I, calves' heads being used to represent the monarch and his courtiers on the anniversary of his execution. The club was suppressed in 1735.

CALVIN (from Calvinus, the Latinized form of Cauvin), Jean (1509–64), French theologian and reformer. Born of a well-to-do middle-class family, he studied canon and civil law, became interested in Greek and Hebrew, and by 1533 was giving signs of commitment to the doctrines of the Reformers. In 1536 he published the first (Latin) edition of his *Institution de la religion chrétienne* in Basle, and settled in Geneva, establishing moral and political ascendency over that city in 1541. In addition to continuous revisions of his *Institution* (the French version was published in 1541), he produced a succession of influential pamphlets, sermons, commentaries, and letters. The *Institution* was conceived as a defence of the Reformed Faith. It repudiated scholastic methods of argument in favour of deductions from biblical authority and the moral nature of man, and it advocated the doctrines of sin and grace—with the attendant doctrine of predestination derived from St Paul—at the expense of salvation by works. Calvin was an unswerving opponent of episcopacy, favouring the voice of independent congregations. The influence of his ideas in 16th- and 17th-cent. England can scarcely be exaggerated. The clarity, conciseness, energy, and austerity of his use of the vernacular mark a significant advance in the development of French prose.

CALVINO, Italo (1923–), Italian novelist and short-story writer. His first work, *Il sentiero dei nidi di ragno* (*The Path of the Nest of Spiders*, 1947), which deals with the resistance against Fascism, is one of the main novels of *neo-realism. In his later work he explored the limits of realism by delving into fantasy and myth, and by his punctilious description of minute fragments of life. He has written three allegorical novels: *Il visconte dimezzato* (*The Cloven Viscount*, 1952), *Il barone rampante* (*Baron in the Trees*, 1957), which plays with the 'reality' of *Richardson and *Fielding, and *Il cavaliere inesistente* (*The Non-Existent Knight*, 1959), which plays with conventions of Renaissance chivalrous epic. His critique of neo-capitalism emerges in such novels as *La speculazione edilizia* (*Building Speculation*, 1957). His later novels move into fabulous realms—for example, *Le città invisibili* (*Invisible Cities*, 1972); but in *Palomar* (1983) he reverts to exploring the minutest details of experience. His inventive ironic fantasies are comparable to those of *Borges. (See also MAGIC REALISM.)

Camacho, in *Don Quixote* (II. xx, xxi), a rich farmer of La Mancha, who prepares a splendid feast in anticipation of his wedding with Quiteria, of whom, however, he is deprived by a stratagem of his rival Basilius.

Cambalo, one of the two sons of King Cambuscan, in Chaucer's 'Squire's Tale: see CANTERBURY TALES, 11; see also Cambell (below) for the continuation of his story in Spenser's *Faerie Queene*.

Cambell, or Cambello, the name given by Spenser in *The Faerie Queene*, IV. iii, to *Cambal, whose tale he borrows from 'Dan Chaucer, well of English undefyled', and completes. Cambell is brother of *Canacee, for whom there are many suitors. It is arranged that the strongest of these, three brothers, shall fight with Cambell and the lady be awarded to the victor. Two of the brothers are defeated: the contest between the third, *Triamond, and Cambell is undecided, each wounding the other. They are reconciled by Cambina, Triamond's sister; Canacee is awarded to Triamond and Cambell marries Cambina. The magic ring of Canacee in the 'Squire's Tale' reappears in the *Faerie Queene*, with the power of healing wounds.

Camber (Kamber), according to legend one of the sons of Brutus (see BRUT), the legendary first king of Britain. Camber is supposed to have given his name to Cambria (Wales), but this is in fact a Latinized derivative of *Cymry* (Welsh-men). See *Geoffrey of Monmouth's *History*, ii. 1.

CAMBRENSIS, Giraldus, see GIRALDUS CAMBRENSIS.

Cambridge Bibliography of English Literature, an invaluable reference work in four volumes, edited by F. W. *Bateson, published 1940, with a supplement, edited by George Watson, 1957. It was succeeded by the *New Cambridge Bibliography of English Literature* of which Vol. I (600–1660) appeared in 1974; Vol. II (1660–1800) in 1971; Vol. III (1800–1900) in 1969, all edited by Watson. Vol. IV (1900–50), edited by I. R. Williams, appeared in 1972, and Vol. V (the Index), compiled by J. D. Pickles, in 1977.

Cambridge Platonists, a group of Anglican divines who had close connections with Cambridge University and tried to promote a rational form of Christianity in the tradition of *Hooker and *Erasmus. The group included Benjamin Whichcote (1609–83), appointed provost of King's College by Parliament (1644) and dispossessed at the Restoration (1660). His writings, mostly sermons and letters, were published posthumously. Posthumous publication was the fate also of the only volume (*Select Discourses*, 1660) produced by Whichcote's pupil, John Smith (1618–52): M. *Arnold said that his sermon 'On the Excellency and Nobleness of True Religion' contained all that ordinands needed to know outside of the Bible. Henry More (1614–87) remained all his life a fellow of Christ's College refusing all preferment. His early poetry in *Psychozoia Platonica* (1642) has some remarkable as well as some remarkably awkward passages. His prose works (eleven were published during his lifetime) are profound, complex, overloaded with learning, and their interpretation is made difficult by More's conflicting attitudes. He attacked superstition but had himself a keen taste for the occult; he wanted to simplify religion so that all could understand it, but was bitterly opposed to the emotional fervour that had most appeal for the uneducated; at one time he was full of praise for *Descartes, later he censured him as a materialist. Ralph Cudworth (1617–88) master successively of Clare Hall (1645) and Christ's College (1654) had a more lucid style and more logical mind, and his major work, *The True Intellectual System of the Universe* (1678), must be regarded as the group's most detailed manifesto. Another fellow of Emmanuel College often included in the group was Nathaniel Culverwell (d. 1651), but his outlook differed from that of the rest, being more Calvinist and Aristotelian.

The aims of the group were to combat materialism, which was finding a forceful exponent in T. *Hobbes, and to reform religion by freeing it from fanaticism and controversy.

Drawing inspiration from *Plato and *Plotinus, they maintained that Sense reveals only appearances, Reality consists in 'intelligible forms' which are 'not impressions printed on the soul without, but ideas vitally protended or actively exerted from within itself'. They held furthermore that Revelation, the Rational Order of the Universe and human Reason were all in harmony, so that to search for Truth was to search for God. They rejected the Calvinist doctrine that human nature was deeply corrupt, capable of salvation only through the action of a Divine Grace granted to some and withheld from others, and saw Man as 'deiform', able to advance towards perfection through Reason and the imitation of Christ. Reason for the Cambridge Platonists was not just power of critical thought, but to function effectively had to result in virtuous behaviour. Truth and Goodness were inseparable.

These doctrines were presented in a rhetorical, quotation-laden, often verbose, late Renaissance manner which has masked their revolutionary character, but it is evident that they prepared the way for the *Deism of the 18th cent. The odd fact that Cudworth's daughter was one of *Locke's patrons was in a way symbolic.

Cambridge University, in terms of English studies, has been particularly linked with the names of I. A. *Richards and F. R. *Leavis. See PRACTICAL CRITICISM.

Cambridge University Press. Books were first printed at Cambridge in 1521–2 by John Siberch (John Lair of Siegburg), a friend of *Erasmus. A charter was granted to the University by Henry VIII in 1534 authorizing the printing of books there, but not until 1583 was the first university Printer, Thomas Thomas, appointed. The undertaking was opposed by the *Stationers' Company as an infringement of their privilege, but the University finally vindicated its rights. The activity of the Press was developed under the influence of R. *Bentley (1662–1742) when the present system of control by a Syndicate, or committee of senior academics, was instituted. The Press evolved from the original system under which licensed printers did some work for the University, through a partnership with a dynasty of printer-publishers (the Clays) to full control, by the Syndicate and its permanent staff, of its own large printing-house and world-wide publishing business, issuing schoolbooks, textbooks, works of learning and reference, journals, Bibles, and prayer-books as part of the University's charitable function of fostering 'education, learning, religion, and research'. With a history of continuous activity since 1584, the Press claims to be the oldest printer-publisher in England, perhaps in the world. The Press has been a notable scientific publisher from I. *Newton and *Ray

through Rutherford, Schrodinger, Sherrington to the present day. *Jebb's and *Housman's editions of classical authors, Ventris and Chadwick on the decipherment of Mycenean Greek, Needham on *Science and Civilisation in China*, Runciman's *History of the Crusades*, C. S. *Lewis and F. R. *Leavis on literature, indicate the range and level of publication. The most obviously 'Cambridge' publication is the great range of collaborative histories first planned by *Acton (Cambridge Ancient History, Cambridge Medieval History, Cambridge Modern History) and extended since his death (Economic Histories of Europe, History of Africa, of China, of Japan, of Latin America, of Iran, of India). The principle of large-scale collaborative history has also been applied to English literature, and a history of American literature is planned.

Cambuscan, in Chaucer's 'Squire's Tale' (see CANTERBURY TALES, 11), a king of Tartary.

Cambyses, King, subject of a tragedy (1569) by T. *Preston, which illustrates the transition from the morality play to the historical tragedy. It is founded on the story of Cambyses (king of Persia) in Herodotus; its bombastic grandiloquence became proverbial and is referred to in 1 *Henry IV*, II. iv: 'I must speak in passion, and I will do it in King Cambyses' vein.' Among the characters are three comic villains, Ruff, Huff, and Snuff, who figure again in the *Martin Marprelate controversy in the course of Lyly's *Pappe with an Hatchet*.

CAMDEN, William (1551–1623), antiquary and historian, was educated at Christ's Hospital, St Paul's School, and Magdalen College, Broadgates Hall, and Christ Church, Oxford. In 1593 he was appointed headmaster of *Westminster School; one of his pupils was *Jonson, who said that he owed Camden 'All that I am in arts, all that I know'. He made tours of antiquarian research up and down England, publishing his *Britannia* in 1586, of which the sixth, greatly enlarged, edition appeared in 1607. In 1615 he published *Annales . . . regnante Elizabetha . . . ad annum 1589*, a civic history; the second part was published posthumously in 1629. He founded a chair of ancient history in Oxford. He wrote principally in Latin, but his *Britannia* was translated into English by *Holland in 1610, and his *Annales*, by other hands, in 1625, 1630, and 1635.

Camden Society, founded in 1838 in honour of W. *Camden, for the purpose of publishing documents relating to the early history and literature of the British empire. In 1897 it was amalgamated with the *Royal Historical Society.

The Cambridge Camden Society was founded by *Neale in 1839 for the study of ecclesiology. Its name was afterwards changed to The Ecclesiological Society, still in existence.

Camelot, the seat of King Arthur's court, is said by *Malory to be Winchester. It may be Camelford in Somerset, the name actually given it by *Laȝamon; Selden, following Drayton's *Poly-Olbion, identifies it as South Cadbury in Somerset, and *Leland says he found traces of Arthur in Queen's Camel in Somerset which (he says) was previously called Camelot. Loomis says it is a fusion of Avallon, the location of Arthur's last battle, and Caerleon in South Wales. Colchester has also claimed it. See R. S. Loomis, *Arthurian Tradition and Chrétien de Troyes* (1949), pp. 480–1.

CAMERON, (John) Norman (1905–53), poet, born in India of Scottish parents. He was educated in Edinburgh and at Oriel College, Oxford, worked (1929–32) as an education officer in Nigeria, then (after staying in Majorca with Robert *Graves) returned to England, where he worked for an advertising agency. During and immediately after the war (until 1947) he worked in government propaganda with the British forces in Italy and Austria. His poems were published in periodicals during the 1930s, principally in *New Verse*; his collections include *The Winter House* (1935) and *Forgive me, Sire* (1950). His *Collected Poems* were published posthumously in 1957 with an introduction by Graves. His poems are brief, lucid, and concentrated, built usually on a single image or parable: Dylan *Thomas wrote (in an undated letter to Henry Treece), 'A poem by Cameron *needs* no more than one image; it moves around one idea, from one logical point to another, making a full circle. A poem by myself *needs* a host of images . . .'

CAMERON, Julia Margaret, *née* Pattle (1815–79), photographer, born in Calcutta, into an artistic and well-connected family; she had many friends in the literary world, and her portraits of *Carlyle, *Tennyson, *Jowett, Anne Thackeray *Ritchie, and many others are outstanding: one of the most celebrated is of her niece, Mrs Herbert Duckworth, later the wife of L. *Stephen and mother of V. *Woolf. She lived from 1860 till 1875 at Freshwater, Isle of Wight, and many of her photographs were designed to illustrate poetic works, notably her neighbour Tennyson's; she was also fond of allegorical and symbolic subjects which she composed in a style strongly influenced by the *Pre-Raphaelites. Unconventional and striking in dress and manner, she was described by Lady Ritchie as 'a woman of noble plainness'.

Cameronians, the followers of Richard Cameron (d. 1680), a noted Scottish Covenanter and field preacher who rejected the indulgence granted to Nonconforming ministers

and formally renounced allegiance to Charles II. His followers afterwards constituted the 'Reformed Presbyterian Church of Scotland'.

Camilla, or a *Picture of Youth*, a novel by F. *Burney, published 1796.

The author always insisted this was not a novel but a *work*, in which characters and morals were to be put into action. It relates the stories of a group of young people, the lively and beautiful Camilla Tyrold, her sisters, and her exotic, selfish cousin Indiana Lynmere; and centres on the love affair of Camilla herself and her eligible, but cool and judicious, suitor Edgar Mandlebert. Its happy consummation is delayed over five volumes by intrigues, contretemps, and misunderstandings, many of them designed to exhibit the virtues and failings of Camilla, or to test and improve her character. The book, especially in its earlier volumes, contains humour, inventive incident, and lively characterization, especially of some of the minor characters such as the grotesque tutor Dr Orkborne, the fop Sir Sedley Clarendel, and Camilla's uncle Sir Hugh Tyrold.

Camillo, in Shakespeare's *The Winter's Tale*, a Sicilian lord.

Camiola, the heroine of Massinger's *The Maid of Honour*.

Camlann, according to the 9th-10th-cent. *Annales Cambriae* the place of the battle in 537 in which *Arthur and Medraut (Modred) fell. It may possibly be Slaughter or Bloody Bridge on the River Camel, near Camelford in Somerset; *Malory, a very long time after the historical sources, says the battle was near Salisbury and the sea.

CAMOËNS (or **CAMÕES**), Luis de (1524–80), a Portuguese poet of Galician stock, who led a troubled and adventurous life, losing an eye in service against the Moors, suffering imprisonment, and being shipwrecked off the coast of Cochin China, among other misfortunes. He died miserably in Lisbon. He wrote plays, sonnets, and lyrics, but is remembered outside his own country for his great epic poem *Os Lusiades* (1572), the *Lusiads*. Its subject is the history of Portugal, and it celebrates the descendants of Lusus, the legendary founder of Lusitania, or Portugal, and more particularly the exploits of Vasco da *Gama, the Portuguese navigator. In ten cantos of eight-lined stanzas, it follows the voyages of Gama, interweaving the past and present history of the nation; it contains such well-known episodes as the story of *Iñez de Castro (Canto III); the tournament of 'the Twelve of England', in which the duke of Lancaster arranges combat between English and Portuguese knights (Canto VI); and the arrival of Gama's men at the Isle of Love (possibly Zanzibar) (Canto IX), where Gama is allegorically wedded to Tethys, the sea goddess. Sir Richard *Burton, who translated much of Camoëns, praised this last section as 'the most charming pictures ever painted by [his] rich and amorous fancy—pictures which a Tasso might have imitated but not excel' (1881). There are other English translations by Sir Richard Fanshawe (1655, a spirited version in stanza form); W. J. Mickle (1776, in heroic couplets); and J. J. Aubertin (1878, in stanza form).

Campaspe, a prose comedy by *Lyly, published 1584 under the title *Alexander, Campaspe and Diogenes.* Alexander the Great, enamoured of his Theban captive Campaspe, gives her freedom and engages *Apelles to paint her portrait. Apelles and Campaspe fall in love, and when the portrait is finished Apelles spoils it so as to have occasion for further sittings. Alexander suspects the truth and by a trick makes him reveal it. He surrenders Campaspe to Apelles and returns to his wars, saying 'It were a shame *Alexander* should desire to commaund the world, if he could not commaund himselfe.' The play includes the charming lyric, '*Cupid* and my *Campaspe* playd, | At Cardes for kisses . . .' The story of Alexander, Campaspe, and Apelles is told in *Pliny's *Natural History*, xxxv. 10.

CAMPBELL, Joseph (1879–1944), Irish poet, who published some of his works under the Irish version of his name, Seosamh MacCathmhaoil. He was born in Belfast, spent some years in London as secretary of the Irish National Literary Society, was later interned as a Republican in Ireland, and spent some years in America. Most of his lyrics and ballads are based on Irish legend and folklore; his collections include *The Garden of Bees* (1905), *The Gilly of Christ* (1907), and *Earth of Cualann* (1917). His *Collected Poems*, with an introduction by A. *Clarke, was published in 1963.

CAMPBELL, (Ignatius) Roy(ston Dunnachie) (1901–57), born in Natal, came to England in 1918. In 1924 he published, to great acclaim, *The Flaming Terrapin*, an exuberant allegorical narrative of the Flood, in which the terrapin represents energy and rejuvenation. Returning to South Africa, he founded in 1926 with *Plomer a satirical literary magazine, *Voorslag* ('Whiplash', 1926–7), which he and Plomer wrote largely by themselves until joined by *van der Post; in 1928 he published *The Wayzgoose*, a satire on South African life. Now living in Provence, he published *Adamastor* (1930), and in 1931 *The Georgiad*, a long, biting attack on the *Bloomsbury group. *Flowering Reeds* (1933), a book of gentler lyrics, was followed in 1934 by his first autobiography, *Broken Record*, a swashbuckling narrative of adventure and blatantly Fascist opinions. In 1935 he became a Roman Catholic and fought for Franco in Spain. His next book of verse, *Mithraic Em-*

blems, appeared in 1936, and in 1939 a long poem, *Flowering Rifle*, a noisily pro-Fascist work which brought him much opprobrium. During the Second World War he fought in Africa, and in 1941 published *Sons of the Mistral*, a selection of his best poems. His *Collected Poems* appeared in 1950. *Light on a Dark Horse* (1951) is a second autobiography, propagating his legend. He did much translation in the course of his life, chiefly from French and Spanish, and in 1952 published an important study and translation of *García Lorca. He was killed in a car crash in Portugal. See P. Alexander, *Roy Campbell* (1982).

CAMPBELL, Thomas (1777–1844), son of a Glasgow merchant, was educated at Glasgow University and closely associated with the founding of the University of London (now University College London) in the late 1820s. He published *The Pleasures of Hope in 1799, *Gertrude of Wyoming* in 1809, *Theodric, and other poems* in 1824, and *The Pilgrim of Glencoe, and other poems* in 1842. He was immensely popular in his own day, but is now chiefly remembered for his war-songs, *'The Battle of Hohenlinden', 'The Battle of the Baltic', and 'Ye Mariners of England'; and for his ballads, such as 'The Soldier's Dream', 'Lord Ullin's Daughter', 'Lochiel's Warning', and 'Lines on Revisiting a Scene in Argyllshire'.

CAMPION, St Edmund (1540–81), fellow of St John's College, Oxford (1557), went to Douai in 1571 and graduated there, and joined the Jesuits in 1573. He returned to England in 1580, preached privately in London, was arrested in 1581, sent to the Tower, examined under torture, and executed. He was beatified in 1886 and canonized in 1970. E. *Waugh published a life of him (1935).

CAMPION, Thomas (1567–1620), poet, musician, and doctor, was educated at Cambridge and Gray's Inn; he studied medicine in middle age, receiving an MD from the University of Caen in 1605. Five songs by him were appended to the unauthorized *Astrophel and Stella in 1591; in 1595 he published his Latin *Poemata* and between 1601 and 1617 four *Bookes of Ayres*, with many settings composed by himself, and his *Songs of Mourning* for Prince Henry. His *Observations in the Art of English Poesie* were published in 1602, defending classical metres against 'the vulgar and unarteficiall custome of riming'. The treatise includes such beautiful illustrative poems as 'Rose-cheekt Lawra, come'. In the early years of James I's reign he wrote a number of court masques. His poems and the *Observations* were edited by W. R. Davis in 1967.

Campo-Basso, count of, an Italian captain in the army of Charles the Bold of Burgundy, who figures in Scott's *Quentin Durward* and *Anne of Geierstein*.

Campus Novel, a novel set on a university campus; most are written by novelists who are also (temporarily or permanently) academics, and notable English examples include *Amis's Lucky Jim* (1954), D. *Lodge's Changing Places* (1975), and *Bradbury's The History Man* (1975).

CAMUS, Albert (1913–60), French novelist, dramatist, and essayist. He was born in Algeria, which provides the setting for many of his works. Through his novels *L'Étranger* (1942, English trans., *The Outsider*, 1946), *La Peste* (1947, *The Plague*, 1948), *Le Mythe de Sisyphe* (1942, *The Myth of Sisyphus*, 1955), and *L'Homme révolté* (1951, *The Rebel*, 1953), he explored the implications of the 'absurd' nature of the human condition. His novel *La Chute* appeared in 1956 (*The Fall*, 1957), and in 1957 his collection of short stories *L'Exil et le royaume* (*Exile and the Kingdom*, 1958). He wrote a number of plays, including *Caligula* (1944, trans. 1948), and several adaptations for the stage, including one from *Faulkner's Requiem for a Nun*. He was awarded the *Nobel Prize for literature in 1957. (See also ABSURD, THEATRE OF THE.)

Canacee, the daughter of King Cambuscan in Chaucer's 'Squire's Tale' (see CANTERBURY TALES, 11) and in Spenser's *Faerie Queene*, Bk IV.

CANALETTO, (Giovanni Antonio Canal) (1697–1768), Venetian architectural painter, and the son of a painter of theatrical scenery. He was associated for more than 30 years with Joseph Smith, merchant, collector, and, from 1744, the English consul in Venice (whose collection is now in the Royal Collection), and with other English patrons, and worked in England from 1746 to c.1756. He painted Windsor, Warwick Castle, and Syon House, but most of his English views were of London and the Thames.

Candide, see VOLTAIRE.

Candour, Mrs, one of the scandal-mongers in Sheridan's *The School for Scandal*.

CANETTI, Elias (1905–), born in Bulgaria of a Spanish- and German-speaking Jewish family, was educated largely in Zurich and Frankfurt, and gained a doctorate in chemistry at the University of Vienna. In 1939 he came to London where he has since been based. His best-known work, a novel, was published as *Die Blendung* in 1935, and in an English translation by C. V. Wedgwood as *Auto da Fé* in 1946. Inspired by the burning of the Palace of Justice in Vienna in 1927, it centres on Peter Kien, a Sinologist, who lives for his books, and finally sets fire to his own library. Canetti's sociological study of crowd behaviour *Masse und Macht*

(1960) appeared as *Crowds and Power* in 1962. He has also published plays, essays, and two volumes of autobiography (*Die gerettete Zunge*, 1977; *Die Fackel im Ohr*, 1980). In 1981 he was awarded the *Nobel Prize for literature.

CANNING, George (1770–1827), Tory statesman and author, was educated at Eton and Christ Church, Oxford. He was appointed foreign secretary in 1822 and prime minister in 1827. Apart from his political speeches (published 1828), he is remembered in a literary connection as founder of and contributor to *The Anti-Jacobin*, the chief object of which was to ridicule the Revolutionary party. He was also a frequent and influential contributor to the *Quarterly Review* and a witty literary parodist. His *Poems* were published in 1823.

Canongate, *Chronicles of the,* see CHRONICLES OF THE CANONGATE.

'Canon's Yeoman's Tale, The', see CANTERBURY TALES, 22.

Canterbury Tales, The, *Chaucer's most celebrated work probably designed about 1387 and extending to 17,000 lines in prose and verse of various metres (though the predominant form is the rhyming couplet). The General Prologue describes the meeting of 29 pilgrims in the Tabard Inn in Southwark (in fact they add up to 31; it has been suggested that the prioress's 'preestes three' in line 164 may be an error since only one 'Nun's Priest' is mentioned in the body of the work). Detailed pen-pictures are given of 21 of them, vividly described but perhaps corresponding to traditional lists of the orders of society, clerical and lay (see J. Mann, *Chaucer and Medieval Estates Satire*, 1973). The host (see BAILLY, HARRY) proposes that the pilgrims should shorten the road by telling four stories each, two on the way to Canterbury and two on the way back; he will accompany them and award a free supper on their return to the teller of the best story. The work is incomplete; only 23 pilgrims tell stories, and there are only 24 stories told altogether (Chaucer tells two). In the scheme the stories are linked by narrative exchanges between the pilgrims and by prologues and epilogues to the tales; but this aspect of the work is also very incomplete. It is uncertain even, in what order the stories are meant to come; the evidence of the manuscripts and of geographical references is conflicting, as is the scholarly interpretation of that evidence. The order that follows is that of the Ellesmere MS, followed in the best complete edition of Chaucer, F. N. Robinson's (2nd edn, 1957, which is now being revised).

(1) 'The Knight's Tale', a shortened version of the *Teseida* of *Boccaccio, the story of the love of Palamon and Arcite, prisoners of Theseus king of Athens, for Emelye, sister of Hippolyta

queen of the Amazons, whom Theseus has married. The rivals compete for her in a tournament. Palamon is defeated, but Arcite, the favourite of Mars, at the moment of his triumph is thrown and injured by his horse through the intervention of Venus and Saturn, and dies. Palamon and Emelye, after prolonged mourning for Arcite, are united. Robinson follows the Ellesmere division of the tale into four books, but it is not so divided in all the manuscripts. An interesting interpretation of the tale as ironic is given by Terry Jones in *Chaucer's Knight* (1978).

(2) 'The Miller's Tale', a ribald story of the deception, first of a husband (a carpenter) through the prediction of a second flood, and secondly of a lover who expects to kiss the lady's lips but kisses instead her 'nether eye'. He avenges himself on her lover for this humiliation with a red-hot ploughshare. The Tale has been said to be a parody of a courtly-love story.

(3) 'The Reeve's Tale' is a *fabliau about two clerks who are robbed by a miller of some of the meal which they take to his mill to be ground, and who take their vengeance by sleeping with the miller's wife and daughter. There are two manuscript versions of a French analogue in Bryan and Dempster, *Sources and Analogues of Chaucer's Canterbury Tales* (1941), pp. 126–47, 'Le meunier at les II clers'. In Chaucer's context, it is an obvious rejoinder to the miller's tale of the duping of a carpenter, the reeve's profession.

(4) 'The Cook's Tale' of Perkyn Revelour only extends to 58 lines before it breaks off. It is another ribald fabliau which ends with the introduction of a prostitute, and it has been suggested that Chaucer may have decided that the occurrence of three indecent tales together was unbalanced. The tale of *Gamelyn, not by Chaucer, is introduced for the cook in some manuscripts. The cook himself, Roger (by nickname traditionally Hodge) of Ware (I. 4,336), has been identified with an attested cook of that name. See Robinson, p. 688 and introduction to Fragment IX, p. 762.

(5) 'The Man of Law's Tale' is the story of Constance, daughter of a Christian emperor of Rome, who marries the Sultan of Syria on condition that he become a Christian and who is cast adrift in a boat because of the machinations of the Sultan's jealous mother. It is a frequently told medieval story, paralleled by the romance *Emaré and by *Gower's Constance story in *Confessio Amantis*, ii. 587 ff.; there is argument about the priority of Chaucer's and Gower's versions. It is certain, at least, that Chaucer's is based on a passage in the early 14th-cent. Anglo-Norman Chronicle by *Trivet. Both Trivet's and Gower's versions are in Bryan and Dempster.

(6) 'The Wife of Bath's Tale' is preceded by an 856-line prologue in which she condemns celibacy by describing her life with her five late husbands, in the course of which Chaucer draws widely on the medieval anti-feminist tradition, especially on Jean de Meun's *La Vielle* (the Duenna) in the *Roman de la rose*. After this vigorous, learned, and colourful narrative, the following tale, though appropriate, seems rather flat. It is the story of 'the loathly lady' (paralleled by Gower's 'Tale of Florent' in *Confessio Amantis*, i. 1,396 ff., and by the romance *Weddynge of Sir Gawen and Dame Ragnell*, edited in D. B. Sands, *Middle English Verse Romances*, pp. 323–47) in which a knight is asked to answer the question, 'what do women most desire?' The correct answer, 'sovereignty', is told him by a hideous old witch on condition that he marry her; when he does she is restored to youth and beauty. Since Kittredge (*Chaucer and his Poetry*, 1915, p. 185 ff.) is has generally been thought that this Prologue-Tale sets in motion a discussion of marriage, 'The Marriage Group', which is taken up (after interruptions) by the clerk, the merchant, and the franklin (see 9, 10, 12, below).

(7) 'The Friar's Tale' tells how a summoner meets the devil dressed as a yeoman and they agree to share out what they are given. They come upon a carter who curses his horse, commending it to the devil; the summoner asks the devil why he does not take the horse thus committed to him and the devil replies that it is because the commendation does not come from the heart. Later they visit an old woman from whom the summoner attempts to extort twelve pence, whereupon she commends *him* to the devil. The devil carries him off to Hell because her curse was from the heart. The story is widely attested in popular tradition, and its motif is referred to as *ex corde*, 'from the heart'. Chaucer's exact source is not known, but it is clear that the friar tells it to enrage the summoner on the pilgrimage, who interrupts the narrative and rejoins with a scurrilous and discreditable story about a friar.

(8) 'The Summoner's Tale' tells of a greedy friar who undertakes to divide a deathbed legacy amongst his community; he receives a fart and has to devise an ingenious stratagem to divide it with perfect justice.

(9) 'The Clerk's Tale', which the poet tells us he took from *Petrarch, was translated into Latin by the latter from the Italian version of Boccaccio in *The Decameron* (Day 10, Tale 10). Boccaccio was the first writer (in 1353) to take the story from popular currency, and there are several versions of the story in Italian, Latin, and French before Chaucer's (indeed it is clear that Chaucer's version is rather more dependent on a French prose version then on Petrarch's Latin). The story tells of patient Griselda and her trials by her husband, the Marquis Walter. Chaucer's version has more hints of criticism of the relentless husband than any of his predecessors (except Boccaccio, whose narrator frowns

on Gualtieri's 'strange desire' to try his wife's obedience). Apologists for 'The Marriage Group' (see 6 above) regard the tale as a response to the Wife of Bath, partly because the Clerk concludes with an expression of good will towards her (IV. 1,170 ff.).

(10) 'The Merchant's Tale', in which the Merchant, prompted by the tale of Griselda's extreme obedience, tells his 'Tale' of January and May, the old husband with his young wife, and the problems with obedient fidelity involved in this relationship. After a lengthy review of the pros and cons of taking a young wife, January ignores the good advice of Justinus in favour of the time-serving opinion of Placebo and marries May. When he goes blind she makes love to her suitor Damyan in a pear-tree round which January wraps his arms. Pluto mischievously restores January's sight at this point, but Proserpine inspires May to explain that the restoration of his sight was brought about by her activities in the pear-tree and that this had been their purpose. Critics have argued about the relative proportions of mordancy and humour in the tale; see E. Talbot Donaldson in Speaking of Chaucer (1970), pp. 30–45. There are parallels to the various sections of the story in French, Latin, Italian, and German (see D. S. Brewer ed., Medieval Comic Tales, 1973, German no. 3 and Latin, (0)).

(11) 'The Squire's Tale', of Cambuscan, king of Tartary, to whom on his birthday an envoy from the king of Arabia brings magic gifts, including a ring for the king's daughter Canace, which enables her to understand the language of birds. A female falcon tells Canace the story of her own desertion by a tercelet. The tale is incomplete but it seems likely that Chaucer meant to finish it, judging from the fact that there is no suggestion that it is unfinished in the laudatory words of the Franklin that follow it (V. 673 ff.). The precise origin of the tale is unknown, but a number of parallels are suggested by H. S. V. Jones in Bryan and Dempster pp. 357–76.

(12) 'The Franklin's Tale', of Dorigen, wife of Arveragus, who to escape the assiduity of her lover, the squire Aurelius, makes her consent depend upon an impossible condition, that all the rocks on the coast of Brittany be removed. When this condition is realized by the aid of a magician, the lover, from a generous remorse, releases her from her promise. Chaucer states that the tale is taken from a *'Breton Lay', but that this is lost; if this is true, the original is lost. There are a number of parallels in medieval literature, of which the closest is Boccaccio's Il Filocolo, Question 4. See N. R. Hayely, Chaucer's Boccaccio (1980).

(13) 'The Physician's Tale' tells of Virginia who, at her own request, is killed by her father to escape the designs of the corrupt judge Apius. The original source is *Livy's History, and this

is what Chaucer cites, though his version seems to rely principally on the Roman de la rose, ll. 5,589–658, by Jean de Meun.

(14) 'The Pardoner's Tale' follows a prologue in which he declares his own covetousness, and takes covetousness as its theme, relating it to other sins: drunkenness, gluttony, gambling, and swearing. Three rioters set out to find Death who has killed their companion; a mysterious old man tells them they will find him under a particular tree, but when they get there they find instead a heap of gold. By aiming to cheat each other in possessing the gold they kill each other. The character of the Pardoner in the prologue here is related to Faus-Semblant (False-Seeming) in Jean de Meun's part of the Roman de la rose, ll. 11,065–972 (a section corresponding to the Middle English Romaunt of the Rose, Fragment C, lines 6,061 ff.: Robinson, pp. 621 ff.). There are many analogues for the tale, in Latin, Italian, and German, but Chaucer's exact source, if he had one, is not known.

(15) 'The Shipman's Tale'. There is a similar story in The Decameron (Day 8, Tale 1). The wife of a niggardly merchant asks the loan of a hundred francs from a priest to buy finery. The priest borrows the sum from the merchant and hands it to the wife, and the wife grants him her favours. On the merchant's return from a journey the priest tells him that he has repaid the sum to the wife, who cannot deny receiving it.

(16) 'The Prioress's Tale' tells of the murder of a child by Jews because he sings a Marian hymn while passing through their quarter and of the discovery of his body because of its continued singing of the hymn after death. There are a great many parallels for the story. Some critics, perhaps anachronistically, see the bland story as a comment on the uncritical nature of the prioress.

(17) 'Chaucer's Tale of Sir Thopas' is a witty and elegant parody of the contemporary romance, both in its subject and in the unsubstantiality of its *tail-rhyme form. Its butts are no doubt general; but it can perhaps be taken to have special reference to the heroes it catalogues (VII. 898–900): Horn Child, the legend of Ypotys, *Bevis of Hampton, *Guy of Warwick, the unidentified Pleyndamour, and *Libeaus Desconsus. It is closest, it has been argued, to the last of these.

(18) When the Host interrupts the tale of Sir Thopas, Chaucer moves to the opposite extreme with a heavy prose homily, 'The Tale of Melibeus'. This story of the impetuous Melibeus and his wise wife Prudence dates from Italy in the 1240s, when the story was written in Latin prose for his third son by Albertano of Brescia. Chaucer's immediate source was the 1336 version in French prose by Renaud de Louens.

(19) 'The Monk's Tale' is composed of a number of 'tragedies' of persons fallen from high estate, taken from different authors and arranged

on the model of Boccaccio's *De casibus virorum illustrium*. The tale is in eight-lined stanzas.

(20) 'The Nun's Priest's Tale' is related to the French cycle of Renart (see REYNARD), telling of a fox that beguiled a cock by praising his father's singing and was in turn beguiled by him into losing him by pausing to boast at his victory. The mock-heroic story is full of rhetoric and *exempla*, and it is one of the most admired of the Tales, regarded as the most typically 'Chaucerian' in tone and content. The fable is very familiar, but the parallels to Chaucer's treatment of it are not very close (see Kate Petersen, *On the Sources of the 'Nonne Prestes Tale'*, 1898). The famous ending of the tale invites the reader to 'take the morality' of the Tale in spite of its apparent lightness of substance, on the grounds that St Paul says everything has *some* moral; this invitation has been taken with surprising solemnity by many critics.

(21) 'The Second Nun's Tale', in rhymeroyal, is perhaps translated from the life of St Cecilia in the *Golden Legend* of Jacobus de Voragine. It describes the miracles and martyrdom of the noble Roman maiden Cecilia and her husband Valerian.

(22) 'The Canon's Yeoman's Tale' is told by a character who joins the pilgrims at this late stage (VIII. 554 ff.) with his master, the suspicious Canon whose alchemical skills the yeoman praises. The first 200 lines of the Tale tells of the Alchemist's arcane practice and its futility, before proceeding to the Tale proper which tells of how an alchemical canon (who is *not* his master, he protests, perhaps suggesting that it is) tricks a priest out of £40 by pretending to teach him the art of making precious metals. The dishonesty of the alchemists was much discussed and condemned in the 14th cent.; there is a close analogue to Chaucer's story in one of the *Novelle* of Sercambi (included in Bryan and Dempster, pp. 694–5). The most significant literary parallel, of course, is Jonson's *The Alchemist*.

(23) 'The Manciple's Tale' is the fable of the tell-tale crow, told by many authors from *Ovid in *Metamorphoses* (ii. 531–62) onwards. Phebus (Phoebus) has a crow which is white and can speak. It reveals to Phebus the infidelity of his wife (nameless in Chaucer, but Coronis in Ovid and most of the writers who follow him) and Phebus kills her in a rage. Then, in remorse, he plucks out the crow's white feathers, deprives it of speech and throws it 'unto the devel', which is why crows are now black. A very similar version of the story is told in Gower's *Confessio Amantis* (iii. 768–835), and there are other examples by *Machaut and in the *Ovide Moralisé* (c.1324). As well as these, J. A. Work in Bryan and Dempster edits as analogues a story from *The Seven Sages of Rome* which does not name Phebus and which exchanges the fates of wife and bird, as well as some sententious parallels from *Boethius and Jean de Meun.

(24) 'The Parson's Tale' which concludes the work (and was, no doubt, meant to, even if the main body of the *Tales* is incomplete) is a long prose treatise, ostensibly on Penitence but dealing at most length with the *Seven Deadly Sins. The two principal sources are Raymund de Pennaforte's *Summa* (dating from the 1220s) for the sections on Penitence, and Guilielmus Peraldus' *Summa Vitiorum* (probably from the 1250s) for the Seven Deadly Sins.

Most manuscripts have 'The Parson's Tale' leading straight into Chaucer's closing 'Retracciouns' in which he takes leave of his book. He asks forgiveness of God for his 'translacions and enditynges of worldly vanities', including 'The Tales of Caunterbury, thilke that sownen into (i.e. tend towards) synne'. But this rhetorical conclusion need not be read as a revocation of his work by the poet; following St Augustine's *Retractationes*, many medieval works end by distancing the writer from the non-spiritual elements in his work: the Author's Epilogue in *The Decameron* and Chaucer's *Troilus* are other familiar examples. See N. F. Blake, *The Canterbury Tales, edited from the Hengwrt Manuscript* (1980); R. Schoeck and J. Taylor ed., *Chaucer Criticism*, Vol. 1 (1960); H. Cooper, *The Structure of the Canterbury Tales* (1983).

Canto, a subdivision of a long narrative or epic poem, employed in the works of *Dante, *Ariosto, *Tasso, and others; *Spenser was the first to employ the term in English.

CANUTE (Cnutr), a Dane who was king of England 1016–35. The old legend of his failing to repel the sea is told by Holinshed, VII. xiii, after *Henry of Huntingdon (who may have invented it) and *Gaimar.

Canute, The Song of, a famous early English ballad stated to have been composed and sung by the king as he rowed past Ely, and recorded by a monk of Ely in 1166. It begins

Merie sungen the munechis binnen Ely
Tha Cnut ching reu ther by.

Can you Forgive Her?, a novel by A. *Trollope, published 1864–5, the first in the *'Palliser' series.

Alice Vavasor, a girl of independent spirit and means, is engaged to the 'paragon' John Grey but, seemingly distressed by his perfection, she jilts him in favour of her less reputable cousin George Vavasor. George's finances and expectations are in a parlous state, and Alice uses her means to help him to a political career. George is disinherited by his grandfather. Ruined, and having lost his parliamentary seat, George takes ship for America, pausing only to make a murderous attack on Mr Grey. When, after a suitable interval, John Grey proposes again to Alice, he is accepted. This part of the novel's plot derives from a play in blank verse, *The Noble Jilt*, written by Trollope in 1850.

Interwoven with this story is the account of the early married life of Alice's friend Lady Glencora. Lady Glencora has made a splendid match with Plantagenet Palliser, nephew and heir of the old duke of Omnium, but remains in love with the handsome wastrel Burgo Fitzgerald. When she meets Burgo at Lady Monk's ball, Glencora is tempted to elope with him, but is dissuaded by the timely arrival of Mr Palliser. Palliser decides to take his wife out of harm's way, and arranges an extensive foreign tour, despite the fact that his political ambitions have just been crowned with an offer of the post of chancellor of the exchequer. On the Continent Plantagenet and Glencora come to a better understanding, and the novel ends with the birth of an heir.

There is a comic sub-plot, dealing with the efforts of a rich widow, Alice's Aunt Greenow, to dispose of her heart and fortune.

Capability Brown, see BROWN, L.

ČAPEK, Karel (1890–1938), Czech novelist and dramatist, born in Bohemia, the son of a doctor, and educated at the universities of Paris, Berlin, and Prague. He and his brother, painter and stage-designer Josef Čapek (1887–1945), began to write plays together *c.*1910; the best-known of their joint works is *The Insect Play* (1921), a satire on human society and totalitarianism. Čapek's best-known independent work was *R.U.R.* (1920, first performed in England in 1923), a play set 'on a remote island in 1950–60'. The title stands for 'Rossum's Universal Robots', and the concept of the mechanical robot (a word coined from the Czech 'robota', meaning drudgery) opened up a whole new vein of *Science Fiction, as well as adding a word to the English language. In Čapek's play the robots, having acquired human emotions, rebel against their servile status and destroy their masters. His other plays include *The Makropulos Affair* (1923), a play about longevity with some similarity to G. B. *Shaw's *Back to Methuselah* (which Čapek had not at the time read) in which he arrives at conclusions in his own view diametrically opposed to Shaw's. Čapek also wrote several Wellsian Utopian romances, such as *The Manufacture of the Absolute* (1923) and *War with the Newts* (1936); a trilogy of more realistic novels, *Hordubal*, *The Meteor*, and *An Ordinary Life* (1933–4); and various travel books and essays, including *Letters from England* (1923).

CAPELL, Edward (1713–81), Shakespearian commentator. His edition of Shakespeare in 10 vols (1768) was the first to be based on complete and careful collations of all the old copies, and it is his arrangement of the lines that is now usually followed. His *Commentary, Notes and Various Readings to Shakespeare*, begun in 1774, was published in 3 vols in 1783. Capell was responsible for the first full scholarly discussion of Shakespeare's sources, and for the first attempt to establish the relationship between the *Folios and Quartos; he supported the authenticity of the three parts of *Henry VI, *Titus Andronicus, *Love's Labour's Lost, and *The Taming of the Shrew. He was attacked by *Malone and *Steevens, but the soundness of his judgement makes his edition of lasting value.

CAPGRAVE, John (1393–1464), an Augustinian friar who spent most of his life in the friary at King's Lynn. He wrote a number of theological and historical works in Latin, the chief of which were his *Nova Legenda Angliae*, *De Illustribus Henriciis*, and *Vita Humfredi Ducis Glocestriae*. In English he wrote lives of St Gilbert of Sempringham and St Catharine of Alexandria, and a small body of unremarkable poetry. His most significant English work is his *Chronicle* of English history up to AD 1417, which is marked by simplicity and lucidity of style.

Chronicle of England, ed. F. C. Hingeston (1858); EETS os *St Katharine* (ed. C. Horstmann, 100, 1893); *St Augustine* and *St Gilbert of Sempringham* (ed. J. Munro, 140, 1910); *The Solace of Pilgrimes* (ed. C. A. Mills, 1911).

CAPOTE, Truman (1924–84), American author, born in New Orleans, whose work ranges from the light-hearted story of playgirl Holly Golightly in *Breakfast at Tiffany's* (1958) to the grim investigation *In Cold Blood* (1966), a 'non-fiction novel' or work of *faction, in which Capote recreated the brutal multiple murder of a whole Kansas family by two ex-convicts, and traces the lives of the murderers to the moment of their execution.

Captain Nemo, see NEMO.

Captain Singleton, Adventures of, see SINGLETON.

Capulets, in Shakespeare's *Romeo and Juliet, the noble Veronese house (the Cappelletti) to which Juliet belongs, hostile to the family of the Montagues (the Montecchi).

Carabas, Marquess of, a character in (1) the fairy tale of *Puss in Boots*; (2) a song by *Béranger; (3) Disraeli's *Vivian Grey*; (4) Thackeray's *Book of Snobs*.

CARACTACUS, or **CARADOC,** king of the Silures in the west of Britain during the reign of Claudius, was defeated by the Romans and fled to Cartimandua, queen of the Brigantes, who betrayed him. He was taken a prisoner to Rome in AD 51, where his noble spirit so pleased the emperor that he pardoned and released him. He figures as Caratach in Fletcher's *Bonduca. W. *Mason wrote a play *Caractacus*.

CARADOC, see CARACTACUS.

Carbonek, see CORBENIC.

Cardenio, a lost play by Shakespeare, probably in collaboration with *Fletcher, acted at Court in 1613. *Theobald in his play *Double Fals'hood* (1728) claimed to have made use of an old prompt copy of *Cardenio,* but this has never been seen since and Theobald's version lacks Shakespearian touches. It may be assumed, however, that Shakespeare's play, like Theobald's, was based on the story of Cardenio and Lucinda in *Don Quixote* (Part 1, ch. 24–8); Cardenio is the Ragged Knight, who, driven mad by the loss of his loved Lucinda, haunts the Sierra Morena, and is eventually reunited with her.

Cardinal, The, a tragedy by J. *Shirley, acted 1641, printed 1652.

This was the first play Shirley wrote for the King's Men, and both he and his contemporaries thought it his best work. The Duchess Rosaura, a young widow, wants to marry Alvarez, but the diabolical Cardinal, chief adviser to the King, has forced her into a contract with his nephew Columbo. She tricks Columbo into releasing her from this contract, but on the night of her wedding to Alvarez a group of masquers (Columbo and his followers in disguise) kill the bridegroom during a dance. The Duchess feigns madness and plots revenge. Columbo is killed in a duel by Hernando, a soldier who has been wronged by him. The final scene is a series of tricks. The vengeful Cardinal attempts to rape the Duchess and is stabbed by Hernando, who has been in hiding. Hernando then kills himself. The Cardinal declares that he has already poisoned the Duchess and offers her an antidote, drinking it himself as a sign of good faith. He then reveals that the 'antidote' was a poison, which he took in the belief that his wounds were mortal; a doctor tells him that they were not. The King sums up by wishing that rulers had more trustworthy advisers.

CARDUCCI, Giosuè (1835–1907), Italian poet and classicist, winner of the *Nobel Prize (1906). His poetry celebrates Italy's classical heritage at the expense of Romanticism and the Church. His early hymn to Satan ('A Satana', 1863) is republican in spirit, but he was to become poet laureate in middle age. Some of his best poems are in *Rime nuove* (*New Rhymes*, 1861–7); *Odi barbare* (*Barbarian Odes*, 1873–89), based on classical quantitative metre, and *Rime e ritmi* (*Rhymes and Rhythms*, 1887–9).

Carducis, the hero of *Venetia* by B. *Disraeli.

Carduel, see CARLIOUN.

Careless Husband, The, a comedy by C. *Cibber, performed and published 1704 (imprint 1705).

Sir Charles Easy, who neglects his wife and carries on an intrigue with her maid Edging and with Lady Graveairs, discovers that his wife is aware of his infidelities and is moved to reconciliation by her tolerance and virtue. The coquette Lady Betty Modish is led to accept the suit of the honourable Lord Morelove (contrasted with the boastful and immoral Lord Foppington) by a plot to excite her jealousy, followed by reproaches from Sir Charles. In his dedication, Cibber claims that he has set out to avoid coarseness and to imitate the conversation of the polite world, and the work was praised for its 'elegant dialogue', though harsher critics maintained that Cibber knew little of the social milieu he described.

Caretaker, The, a play by H. *Pinter, performed and published in 1960.

One of Pinter's characteristically enigmatic dramas, it is built on the interaction of three characters, the tramp Davies and the brothers Aston and Mick. Aston has rescued Davies from a brawl and brought him back to a junk-filled room, in which he offers Davies a bed and, eventually, an ill-defined post as caretaker, although it emerges that the flat actually belongs to his brother. The characters reveal themselves in inconsequential dialogue and obsessional monologue. The paranoid Davies is worried about his papers, the Blacks, gas leaks, and getting to Sidcup; Aston reveals that he has suffered headaches ever since undergoing electric shock treatment for his 'complaint'; Mick, the youngest, is alternately bully, cajoler, and materialist visionary, with dreams of transforming the room into a fashionable penthouse. In the end both brothers turn on Davies, after he has tried to play the one off against the other, and evict him. The dialogue is at once naturalistic and surreal; the litany of London place names (Finsbury Park, Shepherd's Bush, Putney) and of decorator's jargon (charcoal-grey worktops, teak veneer) serves to highlight the no-man's-land in which the characters in fact meet.

CAREW (pron. Carey), Thomas (1594/5–1640), son of a master in chancery, was educated at Oxford and became secretary to Sir Dudley Carleton at Venice and subsequently at The Hague. He won the favour of Charles I, was appointed to an office at court, and received an estate from him. His elegy for *Donne was published with Donne's poems in 1633, his masque *Coelum Britannicum* (with settings by I. *Jones) was performed before the king in 1634, and his *Poems* appeared in 1640. He was a close friend of *Suckling and one of the best-known of the *Cavalier poets; his works include many graceful, witty, and often cynical songs and lyrics, and several longer poems, including the erotic 'A Rapture', and 'To Saxham', a country house poem in the genre of *Jonson's 'To Penshurst', by whom, with Donne, he was much influenced. The standard edition of his work is by R. Dunlap, 1949.

CAREY, Henry (?1687–1743), wrote farces, operas, and burlesques, and is remembered as the author of *Chrononhotonthologos*, as the inventor of the nick-name 'Namby Pamby' for Ambrose *Philips, and as the author of the words and music of 'Sally in our Alley'. His burlesque opera *The Dragon of Wantley* was performed with much success in 1737.

Carker, James, a character in Dickens's *Dombey and Son*.

Carleton, Memoirs of Captain, see MEMOIRS OF CAPTAIN CARLETON.

CARLETON, William (1794–1869), born in Tyrone, the son of a peasant farmer; he wrote many stories of Irish peasant life, both melancholy and humorous. Traits and Stories of the Irish Peasantry (1830–5) was followed by Tales of Ireland in 1834. His novels include Fardorougha, the Miser (1839), a powerful study of an Irish farmer and usurer, torn between avarice and his love for his son; and Black Prophet (1847), a bleak story of the potato famine.

Carlioun (sometimes Carduel), in Malory's *Morte D'Arthur*, the city where Arthur was crowned and held his court, probably Caerleon-upon-Usk, though in places Carlisle appears to be meant.

CARLISLE, Frederick Howard, fifth earl of (1748–1825), Chancery guardian to *Byron and attacked by him in *English Bards and Scotch Reviewers*. His tragedy The Father's Revenge was praised by Dr *Johnson and Horace *Walpole.

Carlos, Don, the deformed son of Philip II of Spain. The marriage of the latter with Elizabeth of France, who had been affianced to Don Carlos, forms the subject of Otway's tragedy *Don Carlos and of *Verdi's opera.

Carlton Club, was founded in 1831 by the duke of *Wellington and his political friends. It is a political club for men of Conservative opinions. It moved to its present house in St James's Street after the bombing of the previous premises in Pall Mall in 1940.

CARLYLE, Alexander (1722–1805), nick-named 'Jupiter', educated at Edinburgh University, Glasgow, and Leiden, a minister and leader of the Scottish 'Broad Church' party, was author of an interesting autobiography (printed 1860) which refers to various notable events and personalities of the period.

CARLYLE, Jane Baillie Welsh (1801–66), born in Haddington, East Lothian, the daughter of a doctor. She showed considerable powers both of intellect and of character while still at school, and in 1821 was introduced by her former tutor Edward Irving to Thomas *Carlyle. Together and by correspondence she and Carlyle studied German literature, he effectively taking on the role of tutor, then of lover; they were married in 1826. Much of her energy during her married life was devoted to domestic chores and to the humouring and protection of a temperamental husband, but she is nevertheless remembered as one of the best letter-writers in the English language, witty, caustic, and observant, and as a literary hostess who impressed all who met her. Her vast circle of friends, acquaintances, and correspondents included Mazzini, R. *Browning, *Tennyson, J. *Forster, and G. *Jewsbury (who spent much time with Jane Carlyle during her husband's years of obsession with Lady Ashburton), but many of her best letters were written to her relatives in Edinburgh and Liverpool and, most notably, to Thomas himself, with whom she corresponded copiously during their temporary separations. Her kindness and generosity are as remarkable as her wit; one of her most famous letters, about the loneliness of her life at Craigenputtock, was written to cheer a dissatisfied schoolmistress in Carlisle who aspired to be a writer (Letter to Mary Smith, Jan. 1857). Her subjects include personalities, travels, books, and notably, her servants; she commented, 'I think, talk, and write about my servants as much as Geraldine [Jewsbury] does about her lovers.' Various collections and selections of her letters have been published, including editions by J. A. *Froude (1883), Leonard Huxley (1924), and T. Scudder (1931).

CARLYLE, Thomas (1795–1881), was born at Ecclefechan, in Dumfriesshire, the son of a stonemason; his parents were serious, industrious, and devout, and belonged to a Dissenting branch of the Presbyterian church. Carlyle, intended by them and by himself for the ministry, was educated at Annan Academy and at the University of Edinburgh, where, affected by the legacy of the *Scottish Enlightenment, he abandoned this resolve; he taught for a while at Annan and Kirkcaldy and then took to literary work, tutoring and reviewing. He studied German literature; his life of *Schiller appeared in the *London Magazine in 1823–4 and was separately published in 1825; his translations of *Goethe's Wilhelm Meister's Apprenticeship and Wilhelm Meister's Travels appeared in 1824 and 1827 respectively, the latter being included in his anthology of selections from German authors, German Romance (4 vols, 1827). In 1826 he married Jane Welsh (see above) and after two years in Edinburgh they moved for financial reasons to her farm at Craigenputtock, an isolated dwelling on the lonely moors of Nithsdale. 'Sayings of the Times', an attack on *Utilitarianism, appeared in

1829 in the *Edinburgh Review*; *Sartor Resartus* followed in *Fraser's Magazine* in 1833–4, a highly idiosyncratic and personal work which showed his great debt to German philosophy and literature. In 1834 the Carlyles moved to Cheyne Walk, Chelsea, where he worked on his *History of the *French Revolution*, which appeared in 1837; the manuscript of the first volume was accidentally used to light a fire while on loan to J. S. *Mill, but with characteristic perseverance Carlyle rewrote it. This work, somewhat to his own surprise, established Carlyle's reputation, and he from this time onward strengthened the position that made him known as 'the Sage of Chelsea'. His series of lectures, *On *Heroes, Hero-Worship and the Heroic in History*, delivered in 1840 and published in 1841, attracted glittering and fashionable audiences, and taught him to distrust (and indeed to abandon) his own blend of 'prophecy and play-acting'; it also brought him and his wife many new and influential friends. In *Chartism* (1839) and *Past and Present* (1843) Carlyle applied himself to what he called 'the Condition-of-England question', attacking both *laissez-faire* and the dangers of revolution it encouraged, castigating an economic and political climate where Cash Payment had become 'the sole nexus between man and man', and manifesting with more passion than consistency a sympathy with the industrial poor which heralded the new novels of social consciousness of the 1840s (see GASKELL, E. and DISRAELI, B.). His evocation in *Past and Present* of medieval conditions at the time of Abbot Samson (see JOCELIN DE BRAKELOND) provided a new perspective on machinery and craftsmanship that was pursued by *Ruskin and W. *Morris, but Carlyle, unlike some of his followers, turned increasingly away from democracy towards the kind of feudalism which he saw expressed in the rule of the 'Strong Just Man'. His 'Occasional discourse on the nigger question' (1849) and *Latter-day Pamphlets* (1850) express his anti-democratic views in an exaggerated form. His admiration for *Cromwell was expressed in his edition of *Oliver Cromwell's letters and speeches* (2 vols, 1845), and for *Frederick the Great of Prussia in a lengthy biography, some 14 years in preparation, which appeared in 1858–65, 6 vols. A more modest and, to 20th-cent. tastes, more readable work, a life of his friend *Sterling (with some remarkable reminiscences of *Coleridge) appeared in 1851.

Jane Carlyle died in 1866, a blow which he said 'shattered my whole existence into immeasurable ruin', and he thereafter wrote little of importance. He gave her papers and letters in 1871, with ambiguous instructions, to his friend and disciple J. A. *Froude, who published them after Carlyle's death, in 1883; Froude also published Carlyle's *Reminiscences* (1881) and a four-vol. biography (1882–4). These posthumous publications caused much controversy, largely by breaking the conventions of Victorian *biography (against which Carlyle had himself fulminated) to suggest marital discord and sexual inadequacy on Carlyle's part.

Carlyle's influence as social prophet and critic, and his prestige as historian, were enormous during his lifetime; G. *Eliot in the *Leader* (1855) wrote 'there is hardly a superior or active mind of this generation that has not been modified by Carlyle's writings', and he was later described by *Yeats in his *Autobiography* as 'the chief inspirer of self-educated men in the 'eighties and early 'nineties'. In the 20th cent. his reputation waned, partly because his trust in authority and admiration of strong leaders were interpreted as foreshadowings of Fascism. His prose, which had always presented difficulties, became more obscure with the lapse of time; his violent exclamatory rhetoric, his italics and Teutonic coinages, and his eccentric archaisms and strange punctuation were already known by the late 1850s as 'Carlylese'; H. *Martineau described him as 'the greatest mannerist of the age', and *Aytoun ridiculed him, along with the *Spasmodics, for 'dislocating language'. But many of his coinages have become accepted as part of the language, and his work continues to attract scholars and biographers. Many different collections and editions of his letters have been published, and *The Collected Letters of Thomas and Jane Carlyle*, ed. C. R. Sanders and K. J. Fielding (7 vols, 1970–) is in progress.

CARMAN, William Bliss (1861–1929), Canadian poet, cousin of C. G. D. *Roberts, born in New Brunswick; he was once the best-known of the group of poets that came to maturity after the federation and expressed the developing national consciousness. His works, which display a buoyant love of nature and the open road, include *Low Tide on the Grand Pré* (1893) and three series of *Songs from Vagabondia* (1894, 1897, 1901), the last group written in collaboration with American poet Richard Hovey (1864–1900).

Carmarthen, The Black Book of, see BLACK BOOK OF CARMARTHEN, THE.

Carmelide (Camylyard in *Malory), the realm of King Leodegan (Lodegraunce in Malory), the father of Guinevere. Like many other Arthurian places, it is localized both in Cornwall and in the North.

Carmina Burana, a compilation of 228 Latin and German poems, discovered in the monastery of Benediktbeuern in 1803, whence it is also known as the 'Benediktbeuern manuscript'. It was probably written *c*.1230, perhaps in Carinthia, and is the work of three compilers. It contains works of three kinds, corresponding to the categories of poetry written by the 12th-cent. troubadours: moral-satirical poems; love poems; and poems of camaraderie, many of them drinking-songs. It is the most important collection of *Goliardic Latin poetry in particular, and contains poems by many identified poets: Walter of Chatillon, Hugh of Orleans, the *Archpoet, and Philip the Chancellor, for example. Carl Orff used a selection for his scenic cantata *Carmina Burana* (1935–6). The standard edition is by Hilka, Schumann, and B. Bischoff (1930–70).

CARNEGIE, Andrew (1835–1919), the son of a damask-linen weaver of Dunfermline, was taken when a child to America by his parents who emigrated thither during the 'hungry forties'. At the age of 13 he began work in a cotton factory. Later, by his energy and shrewd speculative investment, he became enormously rich and one of the foremost ironmasters of the United States. In 1900 he published *The Gospel of Wealth*, maintaining that a 'man who dies rich dies disgraced', and set about the distribution of his surplus wealth. From a literary point of view, the most important of his many benefactions was his provision of public libraries in Great Britain and the United States, on condition that the local authorities provided site and maintenance. (See LIBRARIES, PUBLIC.)

Caro, Avice, the name of three women, of successive generations, in Hardy's *The Well-Beloved*.

Carol, a word whose etymology is obscure, and of which the earliest meaning appears to be a round dance; thence a song, originally the song of joy sung at Christmas time in celebration of the Nativity. The first known collection of Christmas carols was printed by *Wynkyn de Worde in 1521.

Caroline, Queen, (1) consort of George II, figures in Scott's *The Heart of Midlothian* and is prominent in the memoirs of the time; (2) consort of George IV, figures in *Byron's poems, etc.

CARPENTER, Edward (1844–1929), educated at Cambridge, where he became fellow of Trinity Hall and curate to F. D. *Maurice. In 1874 he abandoned fellowship and orders and moved north, working for some years as University Extension lecturer before settling at Millthorpe, near Chesterfield, where he pursued, by precept and example, his own concept of Socialism and communal fellowship, in a manner much influenced by *Thoreau and also by *Ruskin and W. *Morris. He wrote and lectured in support of varied progressive causes (sexual reform, women's rights, clean air, antivivisection, industrial reorganization, etc.), and his own life-style and revolt against middle-class convention (expressed by sandals, vegetarianism, overt homosexuality, praise of manual labour and the working man) became an important

symbol of liberation for many, including E. M. *Forster. Of his many writings the best remembered is probably his long poem *Towards Democracy* (published in 4 parts, 1883–1902), in which he expresses his millenarian sense of the cosmic consciousness and 'spiritual democracy', and of the march of humanity towards 'freedom and joy'; both manner and content are much influenced by *Whitman and the *Bhagavadgita. His autobiography, *My Days and Dreams*, was published in 1916; see also C. Tsuzuki, *Edward Carpenter, Prophet of Human Fellowship* (1980).

CARPENTER, John (?1370–?1441), town clerk of London, 1417–38, was a generous patron and a friend of *Whittington and of *Pecock. *Hoccleve wrote a ballad to him, appealing for money. He compiled the *Liber Albus*, a valuable collection of records of the City of London, and he left lands for educational purposes, from which the City of London School was founded. See *Liber Albus*, ed. H. T. Riley (1859); T. Brewer, *Memoir of the Life and Times of John Carpenter* (1856).

CARRACCI, Annibale (1560–1609), the greatest of a family of Bolognese painters, who, after the excesses of *Mannerism, restored to Italian art both the clarity of the classical tradition and the glowing, sensuous colours of Venice. His best work is the decoration of the Farnese Gallery (1595–1604) which, for the next two centuries, was deservedly as famous as *Raphael's Farnesina or the Sistine ceiling. Annibale was much admired in literary England in the 18th and early 19th centuries; parallels have been drawn between his paintings and the poetry of *Dryden and of *Pope. Fielding, in *Joseph Andrews*, caricatures him as Hannibal Scratchi.

Carrasco, Samson, in *Don Quixote*, a bachelor of the University of Salamanca, a little mirth-loving man, who, in order to cure Don Quixote of his folly, disguises himself as the Knight of the Mirrors, overcomes him in combat, and requires him to return home and abstain from chivalric exploits for a year.

CARROLL, Lewis, see DODGSON, C. L.

CARSON, Rachel (1907–64), American zoologist, educated at Johns Hopkins University, who is remembered as a pioneer ecologist and popularizer of scientific information. Her works include *The Sea Around Us* (1951), *The Edge of the Sea* (1955), and *Silent Spring* (1963), a powerful attack on the indiscriminate use of pesticides and weed-killers.

CARTER, Angela, see MAGIC REALISM.

CARTER, Mrs Elizabeth (1717–1806), a noted member of the *Blue Stocking Circle; with a persistence that won the praise of V. Woolf in *A Room of One's Own* she learned Latin, Greek, and Hebrew in childhood with her brothers, later acquiring French, Italian, German, Portuguese, and Arabic. Dr *Johnson thought her one of the best Greek scholars he had known. In 1738 she published her early poems, and Johnson, as a high honour, invited her to contribute to *The Rambler, for which she wrote numbers 44 and 100. She made various translations, and spent seven years on her translation of *Epictetus, which appeared with great success in 1758 and gained her a European reputation. She was not herself a hostess, and she was notably unfashionable in dress, but she was loved and revered in Blue Stocking society.

Carton, Sydney, a character in Dickens's *A Tale of Two Cities.

CARTWRIGHT, Thomas (1536–1603), was a leading Puritan theologian educated at St John's College, Cambridge. A Marian exile, he left the country three times during Queen Elizabeth's reign and was deprived of his *Lady Margaret professorship. He died before he could fully represent his Presbyterian views to James I.

CARTWRIGHT, William (1611–43), Oxford scholar, preacher, poet and dramatist, one of the 'sons' of *Jonson. His most successful play, The Royal Slave, was performed before Charles I in 1636, and revived by professional players at Hampton Court at the queen's request. The 1651 edition of his works, Comedies, Tragicomedies, with other poems, was prefaced by over 50 commendatory verses from fellow royalists.

CARY, Henry Francis (1772–1844), educated at Oxford, was an assistant librarian at the British Museum from 1826 to 1837. He translated Dante's *Divina Commedia, producing with his translation the first Italian text of Dante to be printed in England. The Inferno appeared in 1805, and together with the Purgatorio and the Paradiso in 1814. *Coleridge praised 'the severity and learned simplicity' of Cary's diction, and the work became well known. He wrote a series of appreciative articles (collected in 1846) on the early French poets, then little regarded, in *The London Magazine.

CARY, (Arthur) Joyce (Lunel) (1888–1957), novelist, born in Londonderry, was educated at Clifton College and Oxford, and studied art in Edinburgh and Paris. He took part in the Balkan War (1912–13), joined the Nigerian political service in 1913, and served with the Nigerian regiment in the Cameroons campaign, 1915–16. In 1920 he returned to England and devoted himself to writing. His early 'African' novels, Aissa Saved (1932), An American Visitor (1933), The African Witch (1936), and Mister Johnson (1939), show with shrewd sympathy the relations between Africans and their British administrators. His major work consists of two

trilogies; Herself Surprised (1941), To Be a Pilgrim (1942), and The Horse's Mouth (1944), chiefly concerned with the life of the artist Gulley Jimson; and Prisoner of Grace (1952), Except the Lord (1953), and Not Honour More (1955), a study of politics. The major theme of the novels, which exhibit a vast range of characters, is the necessity for individual freedom and choice. Two further novels are studies of childhood: Charley is my Darling (1940) and the semi-autobiographical A House of Children (1941). Cary also wrote political studies, such as Power in Men (1939) and The Case for African Freedom (1941); poetry, including Marching Soldier (1945) and The Drunken Sailor (1947); a study in aesthetics, Art and Reality (1958); short stories, such as Spring Song and Other Stories (1960); and an unfinished novel with a religious theme, The Captive and the Free (1959). A biography by J. W. Noble appeared in 1973.

CARY, Lucius, see FALKLAND.

CARYLL, John (1625–1711), diplomatist and secretary to Mary of Modena, was the author of a tragedy, The English Princess: or the death of Richard III (1667), and a comedy, Sir Salomon (1670). His nephew, also John Caryll (?1666–1736), was a friend and correspondent of Pope, to whom he suggested the subject of *The Rape of the Lock.

CASABIANCA, Louis (1755–98), a Corsican naval officer who perished with his little son at the battle of Aboukir. He is the subject of a well known poem by Mrs *Hemans.

CASANOVA, Giacomo (1725–98), Italian autobiographer. In the course of an adventurous life throughout Western Europe he wrote a number of historical works in Italian, but his reputation rests on the posthumously published Mémoires (12 vols, 1826–38) written in French. These are primarily an account of an extraordinary succession of sexual encounters, but they also provide an intimate portrait of the manners of the age and achieve considerable psychological consistency.

Casaubon, Mr, a leading character in G. Eliot's *Middlemarch.

CASAUBON, Isaac (1559–1614), French classical scholar, born in Geneva of Huguenot refugee parents; professor of Greek at the Academy of Geneva, 1582–96; professor of classical letters at the University of Montpellier, 1597–9; sub-librarian at the Royal Library in Paris, 1605–10. From 1610 until his death he lived in London, receiving a pension from James I and becoming naturalized in 1611. Casaubon published critical editions and commentaries on the works of a number of ancient authors, chiefly Greek, including *Theophrastus (1592) and the Hellenistic writer of the 2nd cent. AD, Athenaeus

(1597). He projected a major work of church history in the form of a criticism of the 'Annals' of the Italian Roman Catholic Baronius, but only the first volume (*De rebus sacris et ecclesiasticis exercitationes XVI ad Baronii annales*, 1614) was finished when he died. He left a diary in Latin of his daily activities, the *Ephemerides*. There is a life of Casaubon by *Pattison (1875).

Casby, Christopher and Flora, characters in Dickens's *Little Dorrit.

Casca, one of the conspirators in Shakespeare's *Julius Caesar*, who affects a blunt and surly manner of speech.

Case is Altered, The, a comedy by *Jonson, performed *c.*1597–8, printed 1609.

Count Ferneze, who has lost his infant son Camillo when Vicenza was captured by the French general Chamont, sees his elder son Paulo go off to the wars against the same Chamont, under the care of his general Maximilian. Paulo is taken prisoner, but on the other hand Maximilian brings back Chamont and his friend Gasper captive. It is agreed that Gasper shall return and effect an exchange between Paulo and Chamont, but Gasper impersonates Chamont, and Chamont himself departs. The trick is discovered, and Ferneze is on the point of executing Gasper, when Chamont returns with Paulo, and it is moreover discovered that Gasper is Ferneze's son Camillo. There is also a farcical subplot, involving the attempts made by the clowns Juniper, Onion, and Christophero to steal the daughter and the treasure of the supposed beggar Jacques de Prie. The play seems to have been published without Jonson's permission, for he omitted it from the folio of his works.

Casket Letters, letters supposed to have passed between *Mary Queen of Scots and *Bothwell, and to have established her complicity in the murder of Darnley. They were repudiated by the queen as forgeries, but it was threatened that they would be used as evidence against her. They disappeared before the end of the 16th cent. and have never been recovered.

CASLON, William (1692–1766), was the first English typefounder to make a complete range of Roman and Italic types of his own design, besides cutting Greek and exotic scripts. From 1725 onwards his types superseded those hitherto imported from abroad in English printing, and they are still in use. His foundry was carried on by his descendants until 1872.

Cassell's Weekly, a periodical founded in 1923, and at first edited by N. *Flower; after 32 issues it was taken over by T. P. *O'Connor, and changed its title to *T.P.'s and Cassell's Weekly*, which ran until 1929. It published work by E. M. *Forster, Arnold *Bennett, *Wells, and others.

Cassio, Michael, in Shakespeare's *Othello*, a sophisticated Florentine who at the opening of the play has just been appointed as Othello's lieutenant.

Cassius, in Shakespeare's *Julius Caesar*, friend of *Brutus and leader of the conspiracy against Caesar, who voices his suspicions in the lines:

Yond Cassius has a lean and hungry look;
He thinks too much. Such men are dangerous.

Cassivelaunus (called 'Cassibelan' in Shakespeare's *Cymbeline I. i. 30), according to *Geoffrey of Monmouth's *History* (iv. 1–11) the brother and successor of *Lud as King of Britain, led the resistance to Julius Caesar's second invasion (54 BC). He was defeated and sued for peace, and (according to Geoffrey) is buried at York. His successor as king was Tenvantius, duke of Cornwall, whose son and successor was Cymbeline.

Castalio, a character in Otway's *The Orphan.

'Castaway, The', a poem by *Cowper, written 1799, published 1803. It is based on an incident from *Anson's *Voyage Round the World*. Cowper depicts with tragic power the suffering of a seaman swept overboard and awaiting death by drowning. Mr Ramsay in V. Woolf's *To the Lighthouse* is given to declaiming its last lines: 'We perish'd, each alone: | But I beneath a rougher sea, | And whelm'd in deeper gulphs than he.'

CASTELNUOVO-TEDESCO, Mario (1895–1968), Italian composer. His enormous musical output contains an unusually high proportion of Shakespearian works, including operas on *The Merchant of Venice (1956) and *All's Well that Ends Well (1958), and an impressive series of Shakespeare overtures: *La bisbetica domata* (1933), *Il mercante di Venezia* (1933), *Giulio Cesare* (1934), *Il raconto d'inverno* (1934), *A Midsummer Night's Dream (1940), *King John (1941), *Antony and Cleopatra (1947), *The Tragedy of *Coriolanus (1947), *Much Ado about Nothing (1953), *As You Like It (1953), and four dances for *Love's Labour's Lost (1953). Several of these have had considerable success, but greater musical interest perhaps attaches to the *33 Shakespeare . Songs* (1921–5), in which an original and eclectic mind produces settings that are both varied and unconventional. There is also a set of *28 Shakespeare Sonnets* (1944–7) and a chamber opera, *The Importance of Being Earnest*, after *Wilde (1962).

CASTELVETRO, Ludovico (1505–71), Italian scholar and critic from Modena, best known for his commentary on Aristotle's *Poetics (1750, 1756), which included a Greek text, an Italian translation, and a critical discussion. His views on the *Unities, more rigid than Aristotle's own, had considerable influence on the development of neo-classical theory.

CASTIGLIONE, Baldassare (1478–1529), Italian humanist, chiefly known for his prose dialogues *Il libro del cortegiano* (1528), translated into English as *The Courtyer* (1561) by *Hoby. In these dialogues, which take place at the court of Urbino and are presided over by the duchess, nineteen men and four women (all historical characters) discuss the qualifications for the ideal courtier, who should unite ethical and intellectual virtues, military and sporting prowess, and yet display his talents with an easy grace and nonchalance. The book ends with a discussion of love by *Bembo, describing the 'ladder' whereby the lover ascends from love of one person to love of the abstract good. The work had much influence on the literature of England, e.g. on *Surrey, *Wyatt, *Sidney, *Spenser, and Shakespeare; and later on W. B. *Yeats, whose poem 'In memory of Major Robert Gregory', for example, laments the 'soldier, scholar, horseman' as 'our Sidney and our perfect man'. See also Ruth Kelso, *The doctrine of the English gentleman in the sixteenth century* (1929).

Castle Dangerous, a novel by Sir W. *Scott, published 1831 in *Tales of My Landlord*, 4th series.

The story deals with the defence in 1306 of Douglas Castle by Sir John de Walton, assisted by the young knight Aymer de Valence, on behalf of the king of England, against the forces of Robert the Bruce and Sir James Douglas ('The Black Douglas'). The Lady Augusta de Berkely, a noble and beautiful young Englishwoman, has offered her hand and fortune to the English knight who will hold it for a year and a day. In a spirit of frolic she herself goes in disguise, with an aged minstrel, Bertram, to the neighbourhood of the castle. Here she is in danger of being treated as a spy by Sir John, before he discovers her identity, and then is captured by the Douglas and offered to Sir John in exchange for the castle. Sir John's embarrassment is solved by the arrival of orders to surrender the castle, and the lady is restored to her lover.

Castle of Indolence, The, a poem in Spenserian stanzas by J. *Thomson published 1748.

According to Patrick Murdoch, Thomson's biographer, the poem grew out of 'a few detached stanzas, in the way of raillery on himself and some of his friends' written in 1733 (*Works*, 1762). It consists of two cantos, of which the first describes the castle of the wizard Indolence, into which he entices weary pilgrims who sink into torpor amidst luxurious ease; Thomson draws sketches of various real people, including himself, his patron *Lyttleton, Patrick Murdoch, and J. *Armstrong. The inmates, becoming diseased, are thrown into a dungeon to languish. The second canto describes the conquest of the castle by the knight of Arts and Industry. *Wordsworth, amongst many others, praised its harmonious verse and pure diction.

Castle of Otranto, The; *a Gothic Story*, by Horace *Walpole, published 1765.

The first of the true *'Gothic' novels, this was an immediate success, and has run to over 150 editions since its original publication. Walpole wrote of its composition, 'I gave rein to my imagination; visions and passions choked me.' The narrative is filled with ghosts, vaults, giants, living statues, mysterious appearances, and violent emotions of terror, anguish, and love. Walpole's fear of ridicule led him to publish the first edition anonymously, with an elaborate preface describing the author as 'Onuphrio Muralto', an Italian canon of Otranto, writing somewhere between the 11th and 13th cents.

Prince Manfred, the tyrant of Otranto, has a devoted wife, Hippolita; a son, Conrad; and a daughter, Matilda. At his wedding to Isabella of Vicenza, Conrad is crushed to death by a vast, black-plumed helmet, which belongs to the nearby statue of the Old Prince, Alfonso the Good. A bold young man in the crowd is accused of causing Conrad's death and imprisoned beneath the helm. Manfred, distracted by a cryptic prophecy, determines that he must have an heir to Otranto. Wildly he decrees that he will divorce Hippolita and marry Isabella, at which the portrait of his grandfather descends accusingly from the wall, beckons him away, and vanishes. Meanwhile the terrified Isabella tries to escape through a gloomy vault at night, where she is assisted by the mysterious young man who has escaped from the helm. Manfred begins a frenzied search for Isabella, only to be confronted by Friar Jerome, who has given the girl sanctuary in his nearby monastery. The young man, Theodore, now accused of being Isabella's lover, is discovered to be Jerome's son, and Jerome is revealed as the count of Falconara. The black plumes wave, and Frederic of Vicenza arrives, demanding Isabella and the resignation of Manfred. But Isabella has vanished from the monastery. Matilda secretly frees and arms Theodore, who rescues Isabella in an eerie forest cave and wounds her father, whom he mistakes for an enemy. When all are again gathered at the castle he relates the story of his destitute and wandering life, and Jerome confirms that Theodore's mother was indeed the daughter of Alfonso. Both Isabella and Matilda have now come to love Theodore. Matilda refuses as passionately to be given to Frederic as Isabella refuses to accept Manfred. Blood runs from the nose of Alfonso's statue. On hearing a rumour that Isabella is with Theodore in the churchyard, Manfred rushes thither, and stabs the woman— only to find it is his daughter, Matilda. His grief, and Hippolita's, is terrible. The walls of the castle fall, and the giant image of Alfonso rises to heaven. Manfred reveals that he poisoned Alfonso in order to gain Otranto. He and Hippolita retire to the religious life, and eventually Isabella marries Theodore, the new and rightful Prince.

Castle of Perseverance, The, a *morality play in 3,700 lines, dating from the first quarter of the 15th cent., one of the group (the others are *Mankind* and *Wisdom*) known as *Macro* plays from their 18th-cent. owner. It is the earliest surviving complete Morality. A huge play, divided into four parts, it is of interest as an exhaustive compendium of such morality features as a battle between vices and virtues, a mixture of allegorical (Backbiter) and diabolical (Belyal) figures, and the enactment of Death and Judgement; but it is also highly significant in the history of English theatre, largely because of a diagrammatic representation of the Castle-mound as 'Theatre in the Round' which its staging requires. There is an edition by P. Happé in *Four Morality Plays* (1979); see also R. Southern, *The Medieval Theatre in the Round* (2nd edn, 1975).

Castle Perilous, in *Malory the castle of the lady Lyonesse in which she is held captive by Ironsyde before her release by Gareth of Orkney. (See GARETH AND LYNETTE.)

Castle Rackrent, a novel by M. *Edgeworth, published 1800.

This work may be regarded as the first fully developed *historical novel and the first true *regional novel in English. Set, according to the title-page, 'Before the year 1782', the characters, the life of the country, and the speech, are unmistakably Irish. It is a brief, high-spirited work, narrated in his old age by the devoted Thady Quirk, steward to three generations of Rackrents. This racy character, for whom the Rackrents could do no wrong, was based (the author wrote) on her father's steward, John Langan, who 'seemed to stand beside me and dictate'. The rattling narrative begins with the wild life of the hard-drinking Sir Patrick, 'inventor of raspberry whisky', who lived before Thady's time. He was succeeded by the litigious and debt-ridden Sir Murtagh, a skinflint who died of a fury. His brother Sir Kit, who inherits, brings to the castle his unfortunate English Jewish wife, who has 'never seen a peat-stack or a bog' and who, after many arguments over sausages, diamonds, and other matters, is shut up in the Castle for seven years, until her gambling husband is killed in a duel. Meanwhile the cunning young lawyer Jason Quirk, Thady's son, is gathering more and more of the family's affairs into his hands. The next heir, Sir Condy, is an ardent, extravagant politician, who tosses a coin to decide whether to marry the rich Isabella Moneygawl or the pretty Judy M'Quirk

(Thady's grandniece). He marries Isabella and, keeping lavish open house in their tumbledown castle, they finally exhaust the last resources of the Rackrents. When the bailiffs arrive Isabella flees and Jason Quirk is found to own almost everything. The Castle is sold and Condy amuses himself by feigning death at his own wake. When he eventually dies Isabella contests the property, but Jason (who is hated by the countrymen but admired by his father) emerges as a 'high gentleman with estates and a fortune'.

Miss Edgeworth wrote the book without her father's knowledge, and it is one of the few he did not 'edit'. The second half, relating to Sir Condy, was not written until two years after the first.

CASTLEREAGH, Robert Stewart, Viscount Castlereagh (1769–1822), was chief secretary for Ireland 1799–1801, when he secured the passing of the Act of Union. During a long political life he discharged many high offices. As foreign secretary from 1812 to 1822 he took a leading part in the European settlement at the Congress of Vienna and after Waterloo, restraining the Allies from retaliation on France. He was greatly disliked by many of the young writers of his day, who felt that he opposed the cause of liberty. There is, for instance, a virulent attack on him in the Dedication to Byron's *Don Juan*; and Shelley, in *The Mask of Anarchy* (which was provoked by the massacre of Peterloo, 1819), wrote:

> I met Murder on the way—
> He had a mask like Castlereagh.

Castlewood, Thomas, third Viscount, and his wife Isabel; Francis, fourth Viscount, his wife Rachel, his daughter Beatrix, and his son Frank, characters in Thackeray's *The History of Henry Esmond*. Also Eugene, earl of Castlewood, in Thackeray's *The Virginians*.

Catcher in the Rye, The, see SALINGER, J. D.

Catch–22, a comic, satirical, surreal, and apocalyptic novel by J. *Heller, published in 1961, which describes the ordeals and exploits of a group of American airmen based on a small Mediterranean island during the Italian campaign of the Second World War, and in particular the reactions of Captain Yossarian, the protagonist. The title of the novel has passed into the language to describe a situation of deadlock, composed of two mutually exclusive sets of conditions: the original instance in the novel of 'Catch–22', defined in ch. 5, concerns pilot Orr, Yossarian's room-mate. According to Doc Daneeka, 'Orr was crazy and could be grounded. All he had to do was ask; and as soon as he did, he would no longer be crazy and would have to fly more missions. Orr would be crazy to fly more missions and sane if he didn't, but if he was sane he had to fly them. If he flew them he was crazy and didn't have to; but if he didn't want to he was sane and had to.' Yossarian is deeply impressed by the 'elliptical precision' of this catch, which he compares to 'good modern art'.

Catharsis, a much-disputed term used by Aristotle in his *Poetics*, where he speaks of the function of tragedy which should succeed in 'arousing pity and fear in such a way as to accomplish a catharsis (i.e. purgation) of such emotions'. Aristotle here seems to be responding to *Plato's view that poetic drama improperly fed the passions by a counter-suggestion that on the contrary it helped to cleanse and release them. The concept has been redefined by generations of critics, including *Castelvetro, G. E. *Lessing, *Goethe, and *Schopenhauer, and Milton gives his own interpretation in his preface to *Samson Agonistes: 'Tragedy . . . said by Aristotle to be of power by raising pity and fear, or terror, to purge the mind of those and such like passions, that is to temper and reduce them to just measure with a kind of delight, stirr'd up by reading or seeing those passions well imitated'.

CATHER, Willa Sibert (1876–1947), American novelist, born in Virginia, but brought up from the age of eight in Nebraska, and educated at the University of Nebraska. After a period of teaching and journalism, during which she published her first book of poems, *April Twilights* (1903), and a book of short stories, *The Troll Garden* (1905), she worked on the staff, then as editor, of *McClure's Magazine* in New York from 1906 to 1912. Her first novel, *Alexander's Bridge* (1912), was followed by *O Pioneers!* (1913), about a Swedish immigrant family struggling to establish itself in the Nebraskan prairies; *The Song of the Lark* (1915), a study of the professional dedication of an opera singer, Thea Kronberg; *My Ántonia* (1918), the story of an immigrant girl from Bohemia, settled in Nebraska, narrated by her childhood friend Jim Burden; and *One of Ours* (1922). *A Lost Lady* (1923) is a delicate, double-edged evocation of elegant, warm-hearted Marian Forrester, married to the ageing railroad builder Captain Forrester in the small and dwindling town of Sweet Water in the Midwest; she is observed by her admirer from boyhood, Niel Hebert, who watches as she becomes the mistress of Forrester's friend Ellinger, then, after the Captain's death, the apparent victim of a destructive rising young business man, Ivy Peters; but, with characteristic subtlety of plot, she escapes both Sweet Water and Niel's condemnation. Miss Cather's range and complexity are further demonstrated in *The Professor's House* (1925), a rich and suggestive work which contrasts the middle-aged disillusion of Professor St Peter with his memories of his favourite student, the brilliant explorer and inventor Tom Outland, whose haunting dis-

covery of an ancient New Mexican cliff city is recorded in Book Two of the novel; New Mexico also provides the vividly pictorial setting for another major work, *Death Comes for the Archbishop* (1927), a historical novel based on the French Catholic mission of Father Latour, and his years of work with the peasant population. Her other works include two studies of the dangers and rewards of unconventionality: *My Mortal Enemy* (1926), in which Myra Henshawe lives to regret her runaway marriage and fallen fortunes, and *Lucy Gayheart* (1935), the story of a music student caught in the tension between the values of her home town and the values of the artistic world. The dual impulse towards exploration and cultivation, towards art and domesticity, towards excitement and safety, is a constant theme in Miss Cather's work, treated with much flexibility and a marked lack of didacticism; she was a pioneer not only in her treatment of the frontiers of the West, but also in her development of the American novel. She records her own debt to another pioneer, S. O. *Jewett, in *Not Under Forty* (1936). See also E. K. Brown, *Willa Cather: A Critical Biography* (1953).

Catherine, a novel by *Thackeray, published serially in *Fraser's Magazine*, 1839–40.

Thackeray took the outine of the story of the murderess Catherine Hayes from the *Newgate Calendar, and deliberately made his novel as grim and sordid as possible, in reaction against the popular 'Newgate novels' of *Bulwer-Lytton, *Ainsworth, and others. However the lively ironic characterization of the heroine and two invented characters, her seducer Galgenstein and his companion Corporal Brock, transcend the original intention.

Catherine de Bourgh, Lady, a character in J. Austen's *Pride and Prejudice.

CATHERINE OF GENOA, St (1447–1510), born at Genoa of an illustrious family, felt an early vocation to a convent life, but was refused on account of her youth. Her marriage to Giuliano Adorno was unhappy. She became an outstanding mystic, and wrote 'Dialogues of the Soul and Body' and a 'Treatise on Purgatory' (published in *Vita e dottrina*, 1551). See the definitive biographical study by F. *von Hugel, *The Mystical Element of Religion* (1908). She is commemorated on 15 Sept.

CATHERINE OF SIENA, St (1347–80), an Italian saint. Her holiness of life and gift of diplomacy were so famous that she was called upon to mediate between Pope Urban VI and the Florentines in 1378. It was through her persuasion that Gregory XI returned from Avignon to Rome. Her extensive correspondence with popes and princes, instinct with religious fervour, was published in 1860. She is commemorated on 30 April.

Catiline, a Roman tragedy by *Jonson, performed 1611, based principally on *Sallust's *Catiline* and *Cicero's orations.

The play concerns the events of the year 63 BC, when Catiline organized a conspiracy to overthrow the existing government and to renew with the aid of Sulla's veterans the scenes of bloodshed which Rome had recently seen. Cicero and Antonius were elected consuls, and Catiline, secretly encouraged by Caesar and Crassus, prepared for a rising. Cicero, warned by Fulvia, the mistress of one of the conspirators, of the intention to assassinate him as a first step in the movement, summons the senate and accuses Catiline, who leaves Rome and joins the troops raised by his adherents at Faesulae. Cicero obtains evidence of the guilt of the conspirators through the ambassadors of the Allobroges, and submits it to the senate, which condemns them to death. Catiline falls in the decisive engagement between his troops and those of the government commanded by Petreius.

The play's first performance was a notorious failure, as Jonson noted in an angrily defensive preface to the printed text.

CATNACH, James (1792–1841), a publisher in Seven Dials, London. He issued at a very low price a large number of chapbooks, ballads, and broadsides, many of them about crimes, highwaymen, and executions, which throw much light on his period.

Cato, a tragedy by *Addison, produced 1713.

It deals with the death of Cato the republican, who commits suicide rather than submit to the dictator Caesar; love interest is added by the devotion of Juba, Cato's Numidian ally, to Cato's daughter Marcia. Dr *Johnson described it as 'rather a poem in dialogue than a drama', but it proved popular on stage and was frequently performed; it owed its success partly to the political intentions imputed to it.

Cat on a Hot Tin Roof, a play by T. *Williams.

Catriona, see KIDNAPPED.

CATULLUS, Gaius Valerius (c.84–c.54 BC), was one of the most versatile of Roman poets, writing love poems, elegies, and satirical epigrams with equal success. He was also among the first to introduce into Latin the mannered style of the Hellenistic school. His work remained virtually unknown during the Middle Ages, but after a manuscript of his poems had come to light at Verona in the 14th cent. he exercised an extensive, if imprecise, influence. He left his mark on *Campion's *Bookes of Ayres*, on *Jonson's songs, and generally on *Herrick and *Lovelace. Leigh *Hunt translated his *Attis*

(1810) and *Tennyson, visiting Sirmione where Catullus once had a house, wrote his pathetic 'Frater Ave atque Vale'. There are few direct echoes of Catullus' work, but poets all over Europe were stimulated by his freshness and simplicity.

CAUDWELL, Christopher, pseudonym of Christopher St John Sprigg (1907–37), Marxist literary critic who joined the Communist Party in 1935 and the International Brigade in 1936; he was killed in Spain. He published poems, novels (under both real and pen name), and many books on aircraft, but is known for his critical works *Illusion and Reality* (1937) and *Studies in a Dying Culture* (1938). These attempted to define a Marxist theory of art and called on writers of the thirties to commit themselves to the culture of the revolutionary proletariat. (See MARXIST LITERARY CRITICISM.)

Cauline, Sir, the subject of a ballad included in Percy's *Reliques*. A young knight at the court of the king of Ireland falls in love with Christabelle, the king's daughter, is banished, returns in disguise and slays a grim 'Soldan' giant who is a suitor for the princess, but is himself mortally wounded. Christabelle dies of a broken heart.

CAUSLEY, Charles (1917–   ), poet, born in Launceston, Cornwall, where he was educated and where, after six wartime years in the Royal Navy, he himself became a teacher. He began writing in the navy. His first collection of verse, *Farewell, Aggie Weston* (1951), was followed by several others, including *Survivor's Leave* (1953), *Union Street* (1957), *Johnny Alleluia* (1961), *Underneath the Water* (1968), and *Figgie Hobbin* (1970). His interest in and understanding of children is expressed in various collections of children's stories and anthologies of verse. His poetry is marked by a powerful simplicity of diction and rhythm, and shows the influence of popular songs (when young he played the piano in a dance band) and the ballad tradition. Innocence is a recurrent theme, and his admiration for *Clare is the direct inspiration of several poems. Religious and seafaring images, often interwoven, are also characteristic. His own selection of *Collected Poems 1951–75* appeared in 1975.

CAVAFY, Constantine (1863–1933), poet, born in Alexandria of Greek parents from Constantinople. His father, who died in 1870, was a partner in an export firm with branches in England and Alexandria, and Constantine was at school in England between the ages of nine and sixteen. On the collapse of the family business the Cavafys returned to Alexandria, where Constantine spent the rest of his life, living quietly with his mother, then alone, and working for many years as clerk in the ministry of public works. He published two privately printed pamphlets of verse, in 1904 and 1910, and later distributed his work to friends in broadsheets; his local reputation grew, but recognition from the English-reading world was achieved largely through the influence of E. M. *Forster, who met him in Alexandria in 1917 and maintained a long friendship and correspondence. His poems, all fairly short, are both lyrical and colloquial, ranging from the personal confession to the dramatic monologue, and in subject matter treating historical themes and characters (Julian the Apostate, Mark Antony, the fall of Constantinople) with great verve and originality, homosexual themes with frankness, and contemporary Alexandrian café life with realism and a strong sense of place. There have been several translations, including versions by J. Mavrogordato (1951), Rae Dalven (1961), and E. Keeley and P. Sherrard (1975).

Cavalier, Memoirs of a, see MEMOIRS OF A CAVALIER.

Cavaliers, a name given to supporters of Charles I in the Civil War, derived from the Italian for horseman or knight and carrying overtones of courtly gallantry. 'Cavalier lyrics' is the term applied to lyrics by *Carew, *Lovelace, *Suckling, and *Herrick (the last of whom was not a courtier) and to work similar in tone and style. These poets were not a formal group, but all were influenced by *Jonson and like him paid little attention to the sonnet; their lyrics on the whole are distinguished by short lines, precise but idiomatic diction, and an urbane and graceful wit. In 'The Line of Wit' (Revaluation, 1936) *Leavis states that the line 'runs from Ben Jonson (and Donne) through Carew and Marvell to Pope'.

CAVE, Edward (1691–1754), who called himself 'Sylvanus Urban', was the son of a Rugby cobbler. He became a London printer and publisher, chiefly remembered as the founder of * The Gentleman's Magazine, to which his friend Dr *Johnson contributed extensively. Cave handled * The Rambler at a loss between 1750 and 1752, and between 1739 and 1775 published nine of Johnson's *Lives of the English Poets.

CAVENDISH, George (?1499–?1561), a gentleman of Thomas Wolsey's household, and author of a remarkable biography of the cardinal (The Life and Death of Cardinal Wolsey), in which with much art he contrasts the magnificence of the cardinal's life with his subsequent disgrace, and indicates 'the wonderouse mutabilitie of vayn honours . . . And the tykkyll trust to worldly prynces'. It was first printed in 1641, but was previously circulated in manuscript.

CAVENDISH, Margaret, see NEWCASTLE.

Cave of Mammon, see MAMMON, THE CAVE OF.

Cawdor, Thane of, at the beginning of Shakespeare's *Macbeth, is condemned to death for treachery by *Duncan and his title bestowed on Macbeth.

Caxon, Jacob, in Scott's * The Antiquary, hairdresser at Fairport, employed by Jonathan Oldbuck.

CAXTON, William (c.1422–91), born in Kent, the first English printer, and a prominent merchant. After apprenticeship in London he spent 30 years in the Low Countries. From 1465 to 1469 he was governor of the English merchants at Bruges, and he successfully negotiated commercial treaties with the dukes of Burgundy. He began translating the Recuyell of the Historyes of Troye (printed in Bruges, 1473–4) but did not finish it until 1471 in Cologne because he became secretary to the household of Margaret of Burgundy, the sister of Edward IV, in 1469. After his return to Bruges from Cologne (where he probably worked in a printing-house), he presented the book to Margaret and next printed, also in Bruges with the calligrapher Colard Mansion, * The Game and Playe of the Chesse. He set up a press at Westminster in 1476—his first dated book printed there is The Dictes or Sayengis of the Philosophres (1477)—and printed about 100 books, a number of them his own translations from French. He used eight founts of type, the first of which he brought from Bruges, and he began to use woodcut illustrations c.1480. His translations contributed to the development of 15th-cent. prose style, though his own style is somewhat rambling and ill-constructed, manifesting the weaknesses of the elaboration of courtly writing without its virtues. It was his modified version of *Malory that appeared as Malory's work before the discovery of the Winchester manuscript by W. F. Oakeshott in 1934.

Ed. W. J. B. Crotch, Caxton's Prologues and Epilogues (EETS os 176, 1927; reprinted 1957); N. F. Blake, Caxton and his World (1969), Caxton's Own Prose (1973); ed. N. F. Blake, Selections from William Caxton (1973).

Caxtons, The, a novel by *Bulwer-Lytton.

CECIL, David (Lord Edward Christian David Gascoyne) (1902–), scholar and biographer, was educated at Eton and Christ Church, Oxford, and was Goldsmiths' professor of English literature at Oxford, 1948–69. His many works include a study of *Cowper (1929), a life of Melbourne (2 vols, 1939, 1954), a study of *Hardy (1943), Two Quiet Lives (1948; studies of T. *Gray and D. *Osborne), The Cecils of Hatfield House (1973), A Portrait of Jane Austen (1978), and A Portrait of Charles Lamb (1983), all of which combine scholarly attention to detail with accessibility to the general reader.

Cecilia, or *Memoirs of an Heiress*, a novel by F. *Burney, published 1782.

This was the second of Fanny Burney's novels, and she wished it to be 'true to life'. Cecilia Beverley has inherited a large fortune on the condition that her future husband takes her name. Until she comes of age she is required to live with one of her three guardians. The first is Harrel, a gambler, who, failing in his attempt to exploit his ward, kills himself, the second is the vulgar and avaricious Briggs, the third, the Hon. Compton Delvile, is a man of arrogant family pride. Cecilia and his son Mortimer fall deeply in love with one another; but old Delvile is furious at the idea that his son should exchange his name for Cecilia's. However, a marriage is arranged on the basis that Cecilia will renounce her fortune and Delvile keep his name. But the plan is defeated by the crafty Monckton, whom Cecilia has regarded as a friend, but who hopes to win both her and her fortune when his wife dies. Monckton's treachery is exposed; Cecilia, who has been driven to madness and almost to death by her tribulations, marries her beloved Mortimer; and old Delvile is eventually reconciled to the match.

The novel was immensely successful; Dr *Johnson admired 'the general Power of the whole', and *Burke praised the humour, the sentiment, the moral tone, and the dialogue.

Cedric the Saxon, one of the principal characters in Scott's *Ivanhoe*.

Ceix and Alceone, see GOWER, J., and BOOK OF THE DUCHESS, THE.

CELAN, Paul, the pseudonym of Paul Anschel (1920–70), poet, born in Czernowitz, Bukovina (then in Romania) of a Jewish family; both his parents died in an extermination camp, and he was interned for two years in a Romanian labour camp. He settled in Paris in 1950, and finally drowned himself in the Seine. He wrote in German, and translations into English include *Nineteen Poems* (1972, by M. *Hamburger), *Selected Poems* (1972, Hamburger and C. Middleton), and *Poems* (1980), selected, translated and introduced by Hamburger.

Celestial City, in Bunyan's *Pilgrim's Progress*, signifying Heaven.

Celestina, or the *Tragi-Comedy of Calisto and Melibea*, a Spanish novel in dialogue which has had several stage adaptations. The first known edition appeared about 1499, in 16 acts, and a later version, in 1502, in 21 acts. It is reasonably certain that Acts II–XVI were written by Fernando de *Rojas, although the authorship of Act I and the later additions is still disputed.

The work is essentially dramatic, and marks an important stage in the literary history of Spain and of Europe. Though, as Mabbe, its translator, observes, 'some part of it seemeth somewhat more obscene than may suit with a civil style', it is an extremely vivid, entertaining work, one of the first to present romance in everyday life. The reader is brought into disreputable, but admirably depicted, company. The principal characters are Calisto, a young gentleman of birth and fortune; Melibea, a modest and romantic young lady; Celestina, a crafty wise old bawd; Parmeno and Sempronio, the rascally braggart servants of Calisto; and Elicia and Areusa, two wenches. Calisto casually meeting Melibea falls violently in love with her, but is, from her modesty, sharply repulsed. On the advice of one of his servants he calls in the aid of Celestina, who deflects Melibea from the path of virtue and brings about a general catastrophe. Celestina is murdered by Parmeno and Sempronio for a share in the reward that she has received, and they are punished with death for their crime. Calisto is killed in one of his secret meetings with Melibea, and she in despair kills herself.

An excellent and racy, if exuberantly diffuse, translation into English prose, *The Spanish Bawd*, was made by *Mabbe, and published in 1631. The early part of *Celestina* was translated into English verse by *Rastell, provided with a happy ending, and published, about 1530, as 'A new comody in englyshe in maner of an interlude', better known as 'An Interlude of Calisto and Melebea'. It is one of the first English dramatic works that approach true comedy. A new translation by P. Hartnoll appeared in 1959, and one by J. M. Cohen in 1964.

Rojas's borrowings from *Petrarch are discussed in A. D. Deyemond, *The Petrarchan Sources of La Celestina* (1961).

Celia, in Shakespeare's *As You Like It*, daughter to Duke Frederick, who chooses to share *Rosalind's banishment in the Forest of *Arden, adopting the name Aliena.

Célimène, see MISANTHROPE, LE.

CÉLINE, Louis-Ferdinand (1894–1961), pseudonym of L.-F. Destouches, French novelist. His first novel, *Voyage au bout de la nuit* (1932, English trans. John Marks, 1934), describing the experiences and opinions of an unsavoury and truculent slum doctor during and after the First World War, earned him the reputation of a right-wing misanthrope. His later novels, including *Mort à crédit* (1936), *D'un château l'autre* (1957), and *Nord* (1960), have drawn increasingly respectful critical attention to the systematic indecorousness of his narratives, to the nightmare power of his vision, and to the profligate resourcefulness of his language.

CELLINI, Benvenuto (1500–71), a Florentine goldsmith and sculptor, and author of one of the most vivid and interesting autobiographies ever written. It was first published (dedicated to

Richard Boyle) at Naples in 1730; English translations include that by T. Roscoe (1791–1871), and one by J. A. *Symonds, published 1888. Cellini combined the characters of artist and bravo; he was arrogant, passionate, conceited, and vainglorious. His autobiography gives a vivid account of the personalities and events of his time, including the Sack of Rome (1527), in which he took part; he also describes artistic techniques such as bronze casting. He went to France and worked for Francis I.

Celtic Twilight, The, a collection of stories by *Yeats, published 1893, illustrating the mysticism of the Irish and their belief in fairies, ghosts, and spirits. It has since become a generic phrase (slightly ironical) for the whole *Irish revival in literature.

Cenci, The, a verse tragedy by P. B. *Shelley, largely written at Livorno, in summer 1819, published 1819 and 1821.

The melodramatic plot is taken from the true story of Beatrice Cenci, who was tried and executed for the murder of her father, count Francesco Cenci, at Rome in 1599. Shelley was attracted by the themes of incest and atheism: the play concentrates on the Iago-like evil of the count and the inner sufferings of Beatrice, whose justification men seek with 'restless and anatomizing casuistry'. Shelley claimed to have been influenced by the dramatic style of *Calderón, but in fact the play is indebted to Shakespeare for much of its construction and language: Beatrice's great speech on the prospect of death, 'So young to go | Under the obscure, cold, rotting, wormy ground!' (v. 4) is based on Claudio's in *Measure for Measure* (III. i). Surprisingly Shelley hoped for a popular theatrical success at Drury Lane or Covent Garden; the play was eventually produced in Paris a century later.

Censorship, see APPENDIX I.

CENTLIVRE, Susannah (1669–1723), actress and dramatist, after an adventurous early career married in 1706 Joseph Centlivre, cook to Queen Anne. He appears to have been her third husband. Her early plays appeared under the name Susannah Carroll, taken from her second husband. An ardent Whig, she was a friend of *Farquhar, *Steele, and *Rowe, and it may have been her mockery of priests and Catholicism that earned her a place in Pope's *The Dunciad.* She wrote 19 plays, chiefly comedies, between 1700 and 1722, the best being comedies of intrigue and manners. *The Gamester* (1705, based to some extent on Regnard's *Le Joueur*) shows Valere torn between his love of Angelica and of gambling: in a dramatic scene she, disguised as a beau, wins from him her own picture as a stake, and thus leads him to repentance. *The Wonder: A Woman Keeps a Secret* (1714) provided *Garrick with one of his most successful parts, and *The Busie Body* (1709) and *A Bold Stroke for a Wife* (1718) were also frequently revived.

Cent nouvelles nouvelles, Les, a collection of French tales, loosely modelled on Boccaccio's *Decameron, and written down probably between 1464 and 1467. The tales, predominantly licentious in character, were related at the court of Philip, duke of Burgundy, some by the duke himself, most by members of his household.

Century Guild Hobby Horse, The, see ART NOUVEAU.

Cerdon, the name (meaning 'craftsman') of a cobbler who appears with the bear-baiting mob in Butler's *Hudibras.

Certain Sonnets, 32 sonnets and poems by Sir P. *Sidney appended to editions of the *Arcadia from 1598 onwards. The last two sonnets are rejections of secular love, the second beginning:

> Leave me ô Love, which reachest but to dust,
> And thou my mind aspire to higher things:
> Grow rich in that which never taketh rust:
> What ever fades, but fading pleasure brings.

In the 19th cent. editors used, incorrectly, to append these two sonnets to *Astrophel and Stella.

CERVANTES SAAVEDRA, Miguel de (1547–1616), the great Spanish novelist and dramatist, was born in Alcalá of an ancient but impoverished family, and was wounded, losing for life the use of his left hand, at the battle of Lepanto (1571). He was taken by pirates in 1575, and spent the next five years as a prisoner at Algiers. The remainder of his life was, for the greater part, occupied with a struggle to earn a livelihood from literature and humble government employment. His first attempt at fiction was a pastoral novel, *La Galatea* (1585), which was followed by his masterpiece, *Don Quixote, of which the first part was published in 1605, the second in 1615. He also wrote a number of plays (16 of which survive), a collection of highly accomplished short stories (*Novelas ejemplares,* 1613), and a tale of adventure, *Persiles y Sigismunda,* published posthumously in 1617. J. *Fletcher drew largely on these last two for the plots of his plays.

CÉZANNE, Paul (1839–1906), French painter, born at Aix-en-Provence. He was a friend of *Zola until the publication of Zola's novel *L'Œuvre* (1886) in which Cézanne and the Impressionists were slighted. At first closely connected with the Impressionists, Cézanne became more and more concerned with the rendering of solidity by the simplification of forms. His work was the starting point for the development of *Cubism.

Chabot, The Tragedy of, a tragedy by *Chapman, probably revised and added to by *Shirley, written between 1611 and 1622, published 1639.

Philip de Chabot, high admiral of France under Francis I, a loyal servant of the king, incurs the enmity of Montmorency the high constable, Poyet the chancellor, and their faction. By fearless insistence on his innocence he infuriates the king, is accused on trumped-up charges, and found guilty of high treason by the judges under pressure from the chancellor. The king pardons him and discovers the misconduct of the chancellor, who is tried and sentenced. But Chabot's heart is broken by the unjust treatment he has suffered and he dies.

Chace, The, see SOMERVILE, W.

Chadband, a character in Dickens's *Bleak House.

Chaffanbrass, Mr, a character in Trollope's novels *The Three Clerks, *Orley Farm, and *Phineas Redux, a celebrated Old Bailey barrister of slovenly and unprepossessing appearance, whose speciality is the successful defence of the apparently indefensible criminal.

Chainmail, Mr, a character in Peacock's *Crotchet Castle. He believes the 12th cent. to be the best period in 'English History'.

Chaldee MS, The; a Translation from an Ancient Chaldee Manuscript, published in *Blackwood's Magazine 1817. The article, purporting to be an ancient manuscript and written in pseudo-biblical prose, describes the conflict between the two Edinburgh publishers *Blackwood and *Constable (owners, respectively, of Blackwood's and *The Edinburgh Review), and contains many venomous descriptions of wellknown Edinburgh figures. Its publication created a furore. Although anonymous, the piece was conceived by *Hogg, who later admitted he supplied 'the kernal', and was written by John *Wilson and *Lockhart, who, according to Hogg, were the 'young lions of Edinburgh' who added the 'devilry'. Blackwood had to pay damages, but the circulation of the 'Maga' rose.

CHALKHILL, John (d. 1642), entered Trinity College, Cambridge, in 1610, and was the author of a pastoral Thealma and Clearchus, published 1683 with a preface by I. *Walton, and reproduced in *Saintsbury's Caroline Poets, vol. ii (1906), and of other verse included in *The Compleat Angler.

Challenger, Professor George Edward, hero of The Lost World and other stories of Sir A. C. *Doyle, a distinguished zoologist and anthropologist of great vitality and violent temper.

CHALMERS, Thomas (1780–1847), became professor of moral philosophy at St Andrews in 1823, and of theology at Edinburgh in 1828. From his early days as a minister in Glasgow he was known as one of the most formidable orators of the Scottish pulpit; he was a pioneer of popular education and an intellectual defender of Christianity. His chief importance lies in his leadership of the movement which led to the disruption of the Scottish Established Church and the founding of the Free Church of Scotland in 1843; he became its first moderator. His many works, mainly on natural theology and social economy, included 'The Adaptation of External Nature to the Moral and Intellectual Constitution of Man' (1833, the first of the Bridgewater Treatises).

CHAMBERLAYNE, Edward (1616–1703), tutor to the duke of Grafton and to Prince George of Denmark, was author of Angliae Notitia, or the Present State of England (1669), a handbook of social and political conditions which met with extraordinary success and was enlarged by his son, John Chamberlayne.

CHAMBERLAYNE, William (1619–89), was a physician at Shaftesbury in Dorset. He published a play, Love's Victory (1658), but remembered for his Pharonnida (1659), a heroic romance in five books of rhymed couplets, recounting the adventures of the knight Argalia, his beloved Pharonnida, and the villainous Almanzor. *Saintsbury summarizes its incoherent plot, in his preface to his edition (Caroline Poets, vol. i, 1905). *Southey admired its 'sublimity of thought and beauty of expression'.

CHAMBERS, Sir E(dmund) K(erchever) (1866–1954), Shakespearean scholar and dramatic historian, educated at Marlborough and Corpus Christi College, Oxford, entered the education department of the civil service in 1892 where he remained until 1926. During this time he contributed articles to the *Academy and the *Athenaeum and in 1904–5 he was dramatic critic of the Outlook and the Academy. His major works of dramatic history, which began as 'a little book about Shakespeare', grew into the monumental The Medieval Stage (2 vols, 1903), The Elizabethan Stage (4 vols, 1923), and William Shakespeare: A Study of the Facts and Problems (2 vols, 1930). His scholarly achievements are the more remarkable for being the fruits of his spare time. As well as editions of all Shakespeare's plays for the Red Letter Shakespeare and an important lecture on 'The Disintegration of Shakespeare' (1924) he published Arthur of Britain (1927), a synthesis and reassessment based on available evidence; biographies of *Coleridge (1938) and M. *Arnold (1947); editions of *Donne, *Milton, *Beaumont and *Fletcher, among others; and the Oxford Book of Sixteenth Century Verse (1932).

CHAMBERS, Ephraim (d. 1740), educated

at Kendal grammar school, published his *Cyclo-paedia*, the first true English encyclopaedia (which has no connection with the current *Chambers's Encyclopaedia*) in 1728. It had some influence on *Johnson's *Dictionary*. (See also ENCYCLOPÉDIE.)

CHAMBERS, R(aymond) W(ilson) (1874–1942), born in Staxton, Yorkshire, graduated from University College London (1894), and was afterwards librarian and (in succession to W. P. *Ker) Quain professor there (1922–41). The range of his scholarly interests extended from Old English to the Renaissance; his most celebrated works are *Widsith* (1912); *Beowulf: an Introduction to the Study of the Poem* (1921), which remained for 60 years the authoritative study of the poem's background; *On the Continuity of English Prose from Alfred to More* (1932), tracing a chronological line between his two major interests; *Thomas More* (1935); and *Man's Unconquerable Mind* (1939), a collection of essays of which the most striking are on *Langland, *More, and the Philologists of UCL. He became president of the *Philological Society in 1933. He died at Swansea after evacuation to Wales in the Second World War. A memorial lecture to him was endowed at London University; the first lecture, on Chambers himself, was given in 1951 by C. J. Sisson.

CHAMBERS, Robert (1802–71), founded with his brother the publishing firm of W. and R. Chambers, Edinburgh, and wrote and issued a number of books on Scottish history, biography, and literature. He established *Chambers's Journal* in 1832, and his firm issued *Chambers's Encyclopedia*, which was begun in 1859, completed in 1868, and has been through many subsequent editions. He wrote and published anonymously in 1844 *Vestiges of the Natural History of Creation* in which he maintained a theory of biological evolution produced by the action of universal and progressive natural law. Though found odious by churchmen and incompetent by scientists, the *Vestiges* was immensely influential in popularizing an evolutionary view of nature.

Chambers's Encyclopaedia, see CHAMBERS, R.

Chambers's Journal (originally *Chambers's Edinburgh Journal*), one of the most popular of the 19th-cent. journals of literature, science, and the arts, founded by R. *Chambers in 1832. It changed its name in 1854, and survived until 1938.

CHAMISSO, Adelbert von (1781–1838), German zoologist and poet, chiefly remembered for his story *Peter Schlemihls wundersame Geschichte* (*The Strange Story of Peter Schlemihl*): see SCHLEMIHL.

Chamont, one of the principal characters in Otway's *The Orphan*.

Champion, The, which ran from 1739 to 1741, was an anti-Jacobite, opposition journal written largely by H. *Fielding. In its columns Captain Hercules Vinegar, his wife, and their two sons, discourse in various forms of essays, sermons, sketches, and letters on the political, social, and domestic problems of the day. *The Champion* contains some of the best of Fielding's journalistic work.

Chance, a novel by J. *Conrad.

Chances, The, a play by J. *Fletcher, almost certainly his unaided work, written ?c.1617, printed 1647. The plot is based on one of *Cervantes' *Novelas ejemplares*; the 'chances' are the coincidences by which Constantia, who is eloping with the duke of Ferrara, and the duke himself, are brought into a number of complications, from which they are extracted by Don John and Don Frederick, two Spanish gallants, Dame Gillian their landlady at Bologna, and Peter Vecchio, a wizard. It was very popular after the Restoration, and was adapted by *Buckingham (1682), whose version was in turn successfully adapted by *Garrick.

CHANDLER, Raymond (1888–1959), American writer of thrillers and detective stories, born in Chicago but brought up from the age of seven in England, where he was educated at Dulwich College. He returned to America in 1912 and settled in California, where he worked for an oil company before embarking on a career as a writer. Many of his early stories were published in the 1930s in *Black Mask*, a magazine founded in 1920 by *Mencken and *Nathan; his first novel, *The Big Sleep* (1939), introduced his detective narrator, cool, attractive, wise-cracking, lonely tough guy, Philip Marlowe, who owes something to Chandler's admiration for *Hammett. Later works include *Farewell, my Lovely* (1940), *The High Window* (1942), *The Lady in the Lake* (1943), and *The Long Goodbye* (1954), all of which were filmed. His works have been greatly admired by British intellectuals; in an appreciation (*Harper's*, 1948) *Auden spoke for many when he wrote that Chandler's thrillers were 'serious studies of a criminal milieu, the Great Wrong Place, and his powerful but extremely depressing books should be read and judged, not as escape literature, but as works of art.'

CHANDOS, Sir John (d. 1370), English soldier, 'the flower of all chivalry' (*Froissart). He fought at the siege of Cambrai, 1337, at Crécy, 1346, and at Poitiers, 1356, where he saved the life of the *Black Prince. Edward III granted him a manor in Lincolnshire and lands in the Cotentin, and in 1360 appointed him his regent and lieutenant in France. He died of wounds in a battle near Poitiers and the French king declared that Sir John alone could have made the peace permanent between England and France.

Sir John was one of the founders of the Order of the Garter, and one of the 25 original knights.

Changeling, The, a tragedy by T. *Middleton and W. *Rowley, printed 1653, but acted as early as 1622.

Beatrice-Joanna, daughter of the governor of Alicant, is ordered by her father to marry Alonzo de Piracquo. She falls in love with Alsemero, and in order to avoid the marriage employs the ill-favoured villain De Flores, whom she detests but who cherishes a passion for her, to murder Alonzo. To the horror of Beatrice, De Flores exacts the reward he had lusted for. Beatrice is now to marry Alsemero. To escape detection she arranges that her maid Diaphanta shall take her place on the wedding night; and to remove a dangerous witness, De Flores then kills the maid. The guilt of Beatrice and De Flores is revealed to Alsemero, and they are both brought before the governor, whereupon they take their own lives. The title of the play is taken from the sub-plot, in which Antonio disguises himself as a crazy changeling in order to get access to Isabella, wife of the keeper of a madhouse. The main plot is taken from John Reynolds's *God's revenge against Murther* (1621).

CHANNING, William Ellery (1780–1842), an American Unitarian clergyman, much involved in the Unitarian controversy, *c*.1815. He exercised a marked influence on American intellectual life, and is considered a forerunner of the *Transcendentalists. His *Remarks on American Literature* (1830) calls for a literary Declaration of Independence. His many pamphlets on slavery, pacifism, social questions, etc., are included in his collected *Works* (6 vols, 1841–3).

His nephew, also William Ellery Channing (1818–1901), poet and Transcendentalist, contributed frequently to *The Dial* and is remembered largely as the friend of *Emerson (who first brought his poetry to public attention) and of *Thoreau, whose biography Channing wrote. His first volume of verse, *Poems* (1843), was followed by several others. Thoreau referred to Channing's poetic style as 'sublime-slipshod'.

Chanson de Roland, see ROLAND and CHANSONS DE GESTE.

Chansons de geste, epic poems in Old French embodying legends which had grown up about earlier historical figures. The earliest extant versions are from the 12th cent. and use the legends to embody problems and difficulties of feudal society: either the stresses within the feudal system itself caused by conflicting loyalties, as in *Raoul de Cambrai* and *Girart de Roussillon*; or those caused by the impact of the Crusades on feudalism, as in the *Chanson de Guillaume* and,

above all, in the *Chanson de Roland* (see ROLAND). These epics gradually grew into three cycles, first delineated by Bertran de Bar-sur-Aube, a writer of two such poems in the early 13th cent.: firstly, the *geste du roi*, those dealing with the *Charlemagne of legend and his knights; secondly, those dealing with Charlemagne's rebellious vassals, the *geste de Doon de Mayence*; and thirdly, the William of Orange cycle, the *geste de Garin de Monglane*. The genre followed the usual development of narrative literature during the Old French period: the earliest poems, the *Roland* and *Gormont and Isembart*, are heroic; the 12th-cent. poems, with William of Orange as their hero, are more realistic; the later poems have courtly and marvellous elements in them, and lose the tragic seriousness of the earlier works. Similarly, the later ones become more elaborate in style, while the early poems were written in a simple, formulaic style of great dramatic force. The only parallel English poems are those concerned with Charlemagne, such as the fragmentary Middle English *Song of Roland* (see FERUMBRAS and OTUEL). See K. Voretsch, *Introduction to the Study of Old French Literature* (English trans., 1931).

Chanticleer, the cock in *Reynard the Fox*, and in Chaucer's 'The Nun's Priest's Tale' (see CANTERBURY TALES, 20) as Chauntecleer.

Chapbook, a modern name applied by book-collectors and others to specimens of the popular literature which was formerly circulated by itinerant dealers or chapmen, consisting chiefly of small pamphlets of popular tales, ballads, tracts, etc. They were illustrated with wood-blocks, and consisted of 16 pages octavo or 24 pages duodecimo, and were sold generally at a penny to sixpence. They reproduced old romances, such as *Bevis of Hampton* and *Guy of Warwick*, or such stories as *'John Gilpin'*, *Robinson Crusoe*, or nursery rhymes and fairy-tales. They were issued in great numbers throughout the 18th cent.

Chapel, Children of the, see PAUL'S, CHILDREN OF.

CHAPMAN, George (?1559–1634), was born near Hitchin, in Hertfordshire. His Homeric translations suggest that he had a university education, possibly at Oxford, if A. *Wood is to be believed. His young manhood may have been spent as a soldier in France and the Netherlands. After more than a decade as a professional playwright he began to pursue courtly patrons, with limited success, and turned to his major work of translating Homer, completed in 1616. Minor works of translation occupied him until his death, which seems to have been in poverty.

Chapman's earliest published works were non-dramatic poems: *The Shadow of Night* (1594), a pair of complex Neoplatonic poems on night and day; *Ovid's Banquet of Sense* (1595), an allegorical account of *Ovid's courtship of Corinna; and his completion of Marlowe's *Hero and Leander* (1598). Seven comedies are extant: *The Blind Beggar of Alexandria* (1598), *An Humorous Day's Mirth* (1599), *All Fools* (1605), *The Gentleman Usher* and *Monsieur D'Olive* (1606), *May-Day* (1611), and *The Widow's Tears* (1612). He collaborated with *Jonson and John *Marston on a further comedy, *Eastward Hoe*, in 1605, which led to a short period of imprisonment for Jonson and Chapman because of its anti-Scottish satire. The tragedies consist of two two-part plays, *Bussy D'Ambois* (1607) and *The Revenge of Bussy D'Ambois* (1613), *The Conspiracy of Charles, Duke of *Byron* and *The Tragedy of Byron* (1608), and one single play, *Caesar and Pompey* (1631). *The Tragedy of *Chabot* (1639) appears to be a Chapman tragedy revised by James *Shirley. Chapman also collaborated with *Fletcher, Jonson, and *Massinger in writing *The Bloody Brother* (c.1616, pub. 1639). The first of his Homeric translations, *Seven Books of the Iliads*, appeared in 1598 in a hasty publication devised to mark the earl of Essex's embarkation for Ireland; twelve books of the *Iliad* appeared in 1608; the complete *Iliad* and *Odyssey* were published together in 1616 as *The Whole Works of Homer; Prince of Poetts*. Jonson praised Chapman as second only to himself as a writer of *masques, though all that survives is *The Memorable Mask* (1613), presented in the Middle Temple and Lincoln's Inn to celebrate the marriage of Princess Elizabeth.

Chapman's literary reputation has often sprung from peripheral associations rather than direct knowledge. *Keats's sonnet beginning 'Much have I travell'd in the realms of gold' has commended Chapman's Homer to generations of readers who have not themselves 'looked into' it. He was long the favourite candidate for the 'rival poet' referred to in Shakespeare's *Sonnets*. 'The proud full sail of his great verse' of Sonnet 86 was linked with the distinctive 14-syllable lines of Chapman's *Iliad*, and the 'affable familiar ghost' of the same sonnet with the spirit of Homer, by which Chapman claimed to be directly inspired. In more recent times Chapman has been seen as a crucial figure in a secret society of freethinkers called the *School of Night, of which Marlowe, *Harriot, and Matthew Roydon were also members. Though there are links between Chapman and all these figures, it is not now thought that they took such a formal shape. As poet and dramatist, Chapman is most often seen as a genius manqué, whose learning and energy were never sufficiently disciplined. T. S. *Eliot called him 'potentially the greatest artist' of the Elizabethan dramatists. Perhaps the only lines of Chapman's poetry that are still well known are these from *Bussy D'Ambois*:

Man is a torch borne in the wind; a dream
But of a shadow, summ'd with all his substance.

His complete plays were edited by T. M. Parrott (1910, 1914), and a few individual plays have appeared in the Revels Plays series. P. Bartlett had edited the *Poems* (1941) and Allardyce Nicoll the Homer (1957). There is a pamphlet on him by M. C. *Bradbrook (1977).

CHAPMAN, Guy, see JAMESON, S.

CHAPMAN, John (1821–94), the son of a Nottingham druggist and shopkeeper, moved to London early in life and established himself as a publisher and editor. He published G. *Eliot's translation of Strauss in 1846, and she stayed in his home and literary headquarters at 142 Strand in 1851; in the same year he purchased the *Westminster Review*, of which she became assistant editor, and for which she wrote regularly. Chapman edited the *Review* continuously for 43 years until his death. A strikingly handsome man and a notorious philanderer, married to a wife considerably older than himself, Chapman was a conspicuous figure in literary London; *Carlyle, commending him to R. *Browning in 1851, wrote that he had 'real enthusiasm (tho' a soft and slobbery) in him'. He qualified as a physician in 1857 and wrote various medical works, but appears to have been something of a quack. He died in Paris. His diaries for 1851 and 1860 survive, which, edited by G. S. Haight (*George Eliot and John Chapman, with Chapman's Diaries*), shed considerable light on both their personalities.

Chapman and Hall, a publishing company founded in 1830 at 186 Strand, London, by Edward Chapman and William Hall. It owed much of its success to its early association with *Dickens (*Pickwick Papers* having originated in a suggestion from Hall) and published many distinguished and popular authors, including *Carlyle, *Kingsley, Mrs *Gaskell, and *Trollope. G. *Meredith was for a time literary director, and Arthur Waugh, father of Evelyn *Waugh, became chairman and managing director in 1902 and wrote a history of the firm (*A Hundred Years of Publishing*, 1930). The firm was sold to Methuen in 1938, and scientific and technical books now appear under its imprint.

CHAPONE, Mrs (Hester) (1721–1801), a famous member of the *Blue Stocking circle, was a precocious child who learned French, Italian, Latin, music, and drawing to a high standard. *Johnson invited her to contribute to *The Rambler*, of which No. 10 is partly hers. She published her verse tales in 1750–3, her essays in 1773–7, and her *Letters on the Improvement of the Mind* (1773), addressed to Mrs *Montagu, was much admired as a work on education. All her works were highly regarded and went into many editions. Although 30 years younger, she was a particular friend of S. *Richardson, who called her 'little spit-fire' and with whom she discussed his female characters; Mrs *Delany asserted that Mrs Chapone was the model for one or two of Richardson's heroines. Her *Works* and *Posthumous Works* appeared in 1807.

Characteristics of Women, see JAMESON, A. B.

Characters of Shakespeare's Plays, essays by W. *Hazlitt, published 1817.

The characters are often analysed in some detail, but without much reference to their function in the drama as a whole. Hazlitt's general observations are often acute, and his enthusiasm for his subject is very evident.

Character-writing. Books of 'characters' were popular in the 17th cent., and many were based, though some loosely, on *Theophrastus translated by *Casaubon in 1592 and by Healey (printed 1616, but previously circulated). The first was published in 1608 by J. *Hall, followed by *Overbury in 1614, the *Satirical Essays, Characters and Others* of J. *Stephens in 1615, Geffray Mynshul's *Certain Characters and Essays of Prison and Prisoners* in 1618, Earle's *Microcosmographie* (1628), Richard Brathwaite's *Whimzies* (1631), and others. The 'characters' gave generalized but detailed descriptions of behaviour and appearance of a class or type; they were on the whole short, succinct, pointed, and less discursive than the essay, also a popular literary form of the period. See B. Boyce, *The Theophrastan Character in England to 1642* (1947) and Gwendolen Murphy, *Bibliography of English Character Books 1608–1700* (1925).

Charalois, the hero of Massinger's *The Fatal Dowry.*

'Charge of the Light Brigade, The', a poem by *Tennyson, first published in the *Examiner* in 1854 only weeks after the famous charge (25 Oct. 1854) at Balaclava, near Sebastopol, during which owing to a misunderstood order, 247 officers and men out of 637 were killed or wounded. The line 'Someone had blundered', suggested by a phrase in a report in *The Times*, was omitted from the version published in 1855 (*Maud, and Other Poems*) but later reinstated.

CHARKE, Mrs Charlotte (1713–c.1760), the youngest child of Colley *Cibber, early displayed a fondness for masculine dress and pursuits, was widowed in 1737 after an early marriage to a violinist, and pursued a varied career as waiter, pastry cook, strolling player, etc. Her *Narrative of the Life of Mrs Charlotte Charke* (1755) vividly describes her family background and later misfortunes.

CHARLEMAGNE (742–814), king of the Franks (768) and crowned by Pope Leo III as Emperor of the West (800), the son of Pepin the Short. He and his *Paladins are the subject

of numerous *chansons de geste*, of which the *Chanson de Roland* is the most famous (see ROLAND). Of the three groups of French *chansons de geste* concerned with Charlemagne, only the first, the *geste du roi*, is represented in English, in such romances as *Otuel, Sir *Ferumbras,* and *The Sege of Melayne.* As well as being the subject of romances, Charlemagne is of significance in English literature for the tradition of learning he established at his court (led by the Northumbrian *Alcuin) which King *Alfred copied a century later. See P. Wolff, *The Awakening of Europe* (English trans. A. Carter, 1968).

Charlemont, a character in Tourneur's *The Atheist's Tragedy.*

CHARLES, duc d'Orléans (1394–1465), French poet, and a member of the French royal family. He fought at the battle of Agincourt in 1415, was captured, and held prisoner in England until 1440. On his return to France he established his court at Blois, where he received many literary figures. He is often considered to be the last important poet in the French courtly tradition; he wrote numerous ballades, chansons, complaintes, and rondeaux. A large number of English poems, many of which are versions of Charles's French lyrics, are also probably to be attributed to him.

CHARLES XII, king of Sweden 1682–1718, and a great military commander, who led his forces successfully against the northern coalition. He captured the capital of Poland from Augustus the Elector of Saxony, and invaded Russia, defeating Peter the Great at Narva (1700) and being in turn totally defeated at Poltava in 1709, after which he retreated to Turkey. He returned in 1714 to Stralsund, which alone remained to him of his continental possessions, but was driven thence to Sweden. He was killed at Frederikshald in a war with Norway. His life was written by *Voltaire. Johnson (*The Vanity of Human Wishes*) says of him:

> He left the name at which the world grew pale,
> To point a moral or adorn a tale.

(See also MAZEPPA.)

CHARLES THE BOLD, duke of Burgundy (1433–77), married Margaret of York, sister of Edward IV. He was severely defeated by the Swiss at Granson and Morat, and killed in an engagement with them before Nancy. He figures in Scott's *Anne of Geierstein* and *Quentin Durward.*

CHARLETON, Dr Walter (1619–1707), fellow of the *Royal Society. His *Chorea Gigantium* (1655) attempted to demonstrate that Stonehenge was a Danish coronation site and prompted one of *Dryden's finest early poems, 'To my Honour'd Friend, Dr Charleton'

(1663), in which royalist, scientific, commercial, patriotic, and religious sentiments are subtly interwoven.

Charley's Aunt, a highly popular farce by (Walter) Brandon Thomas (1856–1914), produced in 1892 and still performed.

Charmian, in Shakespeare's *Antony and Cleopatra* and Dryden's *All for Love,* Cleopatra's chief waiting woman. In Shakespeare she laments her dead mistress as 'A lass unparallel'd' (v. ii. 314).

Charmond, Felice, a character in Hardy's *The Woodlanders.*

CHARRIÈRE, Madame de, see ZÉLIDE.

Charteris, Sir Patrick, the provost of Perth, in Scott's *The Fair Maid of Perth.*

CHARTIER, Alain (c.1385–c.1435), French poet and prose writer. His most famous poem was *La Belle Dame sans mercy* (1424), a story of unrequited love in 800 octosyllabic lines; an English translation, falsely ascribed to *Chaucer, appeared c.1526. His most famous prose work, the *Quadrilogue invectif* of 1422, is a bitter attack on the divisions within French society and a passionate appeal for national unity. His Latin prose work *De vita curiali,* a disillusioned account of court life, was translated into English by *Caxton.

Chartist Movement, a chiefly working-class political movement between 1837 and 1848, arose as a result of the *Reform Bill of 1832, which had excluded the working classes from political rights for lack of the necessary property qualification. Their six-point 'People's Charter' consisted of: Universal Suffrage, Vote by Ballot, Annually Elected Parliaments, Payment for Members of Parliament, Abolition of the Property Qualification, and Equal Electoral Districts. The movement had an enormous following but failed through poor leadership, though the points eventually became law between 1860 and 1914, except for Annually Elected Parliaments. The movement was alluded to by novelists of the mid-19th cent. who were concerned with the Condition of the People question, in particular B. Disraeli in *Sybil, and C. Kingsley in *Alton Locke; and also by *Carlyle in his essay 'Chartism'. See D. Thompson, *The Chartists* (1984).

Chase, The, see SOMERVILE, W.

Chaste Mayd in Cheap-side, A, by T. *Middleton, written 1613, printed 1630, now widely believed his best comedy.

The play centres on the attempt of the dissolute Sir Walter Whorehound to pass off his mistress as his niece (the 'Chaste Maid') and to marry her to the foolish pedantic son of Yellowhammer, a rich goldsmith; while Whorehound himself is to marry Yellowhammer's daughter Moll. The first part of the plot succeeds, but the second fails. For Moll and the resourceful young Touchwood are in love with one another, and their attempts to evade the parents and get married, though repeatedly foiled, are finally successful.

CHATEAUBRIAND, François-René, vicomte de (1768–1848), one of the major figures of early French Romanticism. He achieved great celebrity with *Le Génie du Christianisme* (1802), a work of Christian apologetic which accompanied and contributed to the post-revolutionary religious revival in France. It argues with great eloquence for the emotional and imaginative appeal of religion to the deepest instincts of man's nature. 'Of all the religions that have ever existed'—thus the author sums up his thesis—'the Christian religion is the most poetical, the most favourable to freedom, art and letters; the modern world owes all to it, from agriculture to the abstract sciences.' From this work Chateaubriand detached two fragments, inspired in part by his stay in America (1791), which he published separately: *Atala* (1801), the tragic romance, set in Louisiana, of the Indian maiden Atala and her lover Chactas; and *René* (1805), the story of a young European devoured by a secret sorrow (his temperament and early circumstances resemble the author's) who flies to the solitudes of America to find solace for profound melancholy and unsatisfied longings. Both had a wide and enthusiastic reception. *Les Martyrs* (1809) is a prose epic of early Christianity. *Mémoires d'outre-tombe* (1849–50), his posthumously published autobiography, now regarded as his most accomplished work, gives a penetrating and brilliantly written account of the author's life against the varied background of an age of political upheaval. Between 1793 and 1800 Chateaubriand lived in exile in England, mainly in London, where he published an *Essai sur les révolutions* (1797). Under Louis XVIII he returned to London in 1822 as French ambassador.

CHATHAM, earl of, see PITT, W.

CHATTERTON, Thomas (1752–70), the posthumous son of a Bristol lay clerk and schoolmaster, began to write verse while still at school at Colston's Hospital; one of his earliest poems is a satire, 'Apostate Will', composed in 1764. He left school aged 14 and was apprenticed to an attorney. In 1768 he published in *Felix Farley's Bristol Journey* a passage of pseudo-archaic prose, of which he claimed to have discovered the original in a chest in St Mary Redcliffe. This attracted the attention of various local antiquaries, for whom he provided fake documents, pedigrees, deeds, etc. He had by this time already written some of his 'Rowley' poems, including his 'Bristowe Tragedie'; these purported to be the work of an imaginary 15th-cent. Bristol poet, Thomas Rowley, a monk and friend of William Canynge, a historical Bristol merchant. He also fabricated prose correspondence between the two and other background documents. He offered some of the poems (without success) to *Dodsley in Dec. 1768; in 1765 Dodsley had published Percy's *Reliques, a work which greatly encouraged the growing interest in antique and *primitive poetry. In March 1769 Chatterton sent to Horace *Walpole a short treatise on painting 'bie T. Rowleie', which Walpole temporarily accepted as authentic. In the same month he published in the *Town and Country Magazine* the first of seven Ossianic pieces in poetic prose, 'Ethelgar. A Saxon poem', though he took care in this and similar pieces to avoid using the Scottish background of *Macpherson. The only Rowleian piece published in Chatterton's life was 'Elinoure and Juga', which appeared in the same periodical in May 1769. In April 1770 he went to London, writing home at first 'in high spirits', and claiming 'great encouragement' from Dodsley and others, but within four months he committed suicide by taking arsenic, apparently reduced to despair by poverty. He wrote a good deal in these last months, including a burletta, *The Revenge* (no record of performance); the satirical 'Kew Gardens', modelled on the satires of Charles *Churchill; and one of his finest Rowleian pieces, 'An Excelente Balade of Charitie'. The Rowley poems were first published in 1777 by Thomas Tyrwhitt, and a year later Thomas *Warton publicly raised doubts of their authenticity; the controversy raged for decades, and Rowley continued to find champions until *Skeat's edition of 1871.

Chatterton's life, work, and tragic death had a powerful effect on the *Romantic imagination; *Wordsworth wrote of him as 'the marvellous Boy, | The sleepless Soul that perished in his pride', and *Keats, who dedicated *Endymion* to his memory, described him in a letter as 'the purest writer in the English Language. He has no French idioms or particles, like Chaucer— 'tis genuine English Idiom in English words.' In his Rowley poems Chatterton employs a variety of verse forms, including Spenserian stanzas, rhyme-royal, and the ballad; notable among them are his *Pindaric 'Songe to Ella' in which Ella (or, as often, Ælla) makes his first appearance, and 'Ælla' itself, 'a tragycal enterlude'. The famous painting of *The Death of Chatterton* (1856) in the Tate Gallery by Henry Wallis, much admired by *Ruskin, is not based on any authentic portrait or likeness, as none survived. The fullest life is by E. H. W. Meyerstein (1930), and there is a 2-vol. edition of the *Complete Works*, ed. D. S. Taylor and B. B. Hoover (1971).

CHAUCER, Geoffrey (*c*.1343–1400), was the son of John Chaucer (*c*.1312–68), a London vintner. The date of his birth has been much argued, all views now placing it between 1339 and 1346. In 1357 he served with Lionel, afterwards duke of Clarence. In 1359 he was in France with Edward III's invading army, was taken prisoner, and ransomed. He married, perhaps in 1366, Philippa, the daughter of Sir Paon Roet of Hainault and the sister of *John of Gaunt's third wife, Katherine Swynford. Philippa died in 1387 and Chaucer enjoyed Gaunt's patronage throughout his life. He held a number of positions at court and in the king's service, and he travelled abroad on numerous occasions on diplomatic missions; as well as missions to France, he made a journey to Genoa and Florence in 1372–3 in the course of which he could theoretically have met *Boccaccio and (slightly more plausibly) *Petrarch. He was sent on to France and Lombardy in 1378. In 1374 he was appointed controller of customs in the port of London and leased his house over Aldgate. He was knight of the shire for Kent in 1386 and probably lived in Kent for most of the rest of his life. His last official position was deputy forester in the King's Forest at Petherton in Somerset (1391–8 at least) and it is possible that he lived there for some time. He was buried in the Poets' Corner of Westminster Abbey where a monument was erected to him in 1555. The known facts of his life are well summarized in F. N. Robinson's edition of Chaucer's *Works* (2nd edn, 1957), pp. xix–xxviii. His writings develop through his career from a period of French influence in the late 1360s (of which the culmination was *The Book of the Duchess* in about 1370), through his 'middle period' of both French and Italian influences (including *The House of Fame* in the 1370s and the mature Italian–influenced works of which the most important is *Troilus and Criseyde, c*.1385), to the last period of most of *The Canterbury Tales* and his short lyrics; but this chronology is not very enlightening. His prose works include a translation of *Boethius (*Boece*) and the complicated *A Treatise on the Astrolabe*, written to 'little Lewis', probably the poet's son. Portraits of Chaucer occur in three places: in the Ellesmere MSS (now in the Huntington Library and the basis of most modern editions); in the manuscript of *Troilus and Criseyde* in Corpus Christi College, Cambridge; and in *Hoccleve's *The Regement of Princes*, beside lines 4,995–6 (in several manuscripts: the best is the one dating from Hoccleve's time, British Museum Harley 4866, edited by Furnivall for EETS es 72).

For a good brief selection of the immense bibliography on Chaucer (up to 1972), see 'Chaucer: a Select Bibliography' by L. D. Benson in *Geoffrey Chaucer*, ed. D. S. Brewer (1974), pp. 352–72 (the book is in general a good source of commentary on Chaucer and his works). See also M. C. Crow and C. C. Olson, *Chaucer Life Records* (1966); C. Muscatine *Chaucer and the French Tradition* (1957); B. Rowland, *A Companion to Chaucer Studies* (rev. edn, 1979).

Chaucerians, Scottish, the name traditionally given to a very diverse group of 15th- and 16th-cent. Scottish writers who show some influence from *Chaucer, although the debt is now regarded as negligible or indirect in most cases. See JAMES I (of Scotland); KINGIS QUAIR, THE; HENRYSON; DUNBAR; DOUGLAS, GAWIN.

Chaucer Society, founded in 1868 by *Furnivall, for the purpose of collecting materials for the study of *Chaucer.

Chauntecleer, see CHANTICLEER.

CHAWORTH, Mary Anne, later Mrs Chaworth-Musters, the young cousin with whom *Byron fell in love in his youth, and who is the first of the women described in his poem *'The Dream'.

Cheeryble Brothers, Ned and Charles, characters in Dickens's *Nicholas Nickleby*.

CHEEVER, John (1912–82), American novelist, whose sophisticated, ironic novels and short stories (many published in the *New Yorker*) satirize affluent suburban New England life, and have gained a growing following in England. His novels include *The Wapshot Chronicle* (1957), *The Wapshot Scandal* (1964), *Bullet Park* (1969), and *Falconer* (1977).

CHEKE, Sir John (1514–57), fellow of St John's College, tutor to Edward VI, and subsequently the first Regius professor of Greek at Cambridge. He was imprisoned by Queen Mary, 1553–4. He was an eminent scholar and, though he wrote little in the vernacular (but many Latin translations from the Greek), was influential in promoting a simple style of English prose. He is referred to ('O soul of *Sir John Cheek*') in *Milton's Sonnet XI, 'A Book was writ of late'.

CHEKHOV, Anton Pavlovich (1860–1904), Russian dramatist and short story writer. He studied medicine in Moscow, where be began writing short humorous stories for journals. Among the greatest of his mature stories are 'A Dreary Story' (1889), 'Ward No. Six' (1892), 'My Life' (1896), 'Ionych' and the trilogy 'The Man in a Case', 'Gooseberries', and 'About Love' (all 1898), and 'The Lady with the Little Dog' (1899). Chekhov's first successful play was *Ivanov* (1887), and he then wrote several light one-act comedies. His status as a dramatist, however, rests on his four late plays. *The Seagull* (1895) was produced at the State Theatre of St Petersburg, but its originality was badly understood by the actors and the first night was a disaster. After this Chekhov's plays were staged by the Moscow Art Theatre, founded by Konstantin Stanislavsky and Vladimir Nemirovich-Danchenko in 1898. A triumphant new production of *The Seagull* was followed by *Uncle Vanya* (1900), *Three Sisters* (1901), and *The Cherry Orchard* (1904). These productions established the Art Theatre's reputation and style. In 1901 Chekhov married the Art Theatre actress Olga Knipper. Another actor to appear in the Art Theatre's Chekhov productions was Vsevolod Meyerhold, whose own later anti-naturalistic, anti-Stanislavskian productions of the plays were probably more true to the intentions of a playwright who had always chafed at Stanislavskian naturalism.

Chekhov's success and influence in England has been immense. Since 1903 most of his work has been translated. The first major translation is that by C. *Garnett, *The Tales of Tchehov* (1916–22) and *The Plays of Tchehov* (1923–4). The major modern translation is that by Ronald Hingley, *The Oxford Chekhov* (9 vols, 1964–80). The first English productions of his plays were George Calderon's staging of *The Seagull* in Glasgow in 1909 and the Incorporated Stage Society's 1911 London production of *The Cherry Orchard*, much admired by Arnold *Bennett. E. M. *Forster, V. *Woolf, *Gerhardie, J. M. *Murry (who placed him above *Joyce and *Proust), and especially K. *Mansfield were among early admirers. Katherine Mansfield's stories are held to be the main channel through which his work influenced England, and her letters are full of expressions of her temperamental sympathy for him. G. B. *Shaw declared that reading Chekhov's plays made him want to tear up his own, and he went on to write *Heartbreak House* as a tribute to him. He is also held to have influenced E. *Bowen, *O'Faolain, *Maugham, H. E. *Bates, *Ackland, and others. Chekhov's work is characterized by its subtle blending of naturalism and symbolism; by its sympathetic, humane, but acutely observed portraits of a threatened upper class stifled by inactivity and ennui; and above all by its unique combination of comedy, tragedy, and pathos, and the sensitivity of its movement from one mode to another.

CHÉNIER, André-Marie (1762–94), French poet, born in Constantinople of mixed French and Greek parentage. He played an active part as a political journalist during the French revolution, was arrested in March 1794, and died on the guillotine. His poetry remained unpublished in his lifetime, but the example of his life and death made a considerable impression on subsequent generations; the first collected edition of his poems, in 1819, gained wide popularity, exercising an influence on the Romantic and *Parnassian movements. His poetry reveals his affinities with the classical world, particularly with the elegiac verse of the Greek *Anthology, and his involvement in the social and political issues of the revolution.

'**Cherry**' and 'Fair Star', the pseudonyms under which S. and B. Disraeli published *A Year at Hartlebury*.

Cherry and Merry, in Dickens's *Martin Chuzzlewit*, Pecksniff's daughters, Charity and Mercy.

Cherry and the Slae, The, see MONTGOMERIE, A.

Cheshire Cheese, The, 'an ancient eating-house in Fleet Street' where the *Rhymers Club met for some years in the 1880s and 90s; it is described by *Yeats in his autobiography *The Trembling of the Veil* (1922): he also celebrated 'Poets with whom I learned my trade, | Companions of the Cheshire Cheese' in his poem 'The Grey Rock' (*Responsibilities*, 1914).

Chester, Sir John, and Edward his son, characters in Dickens's *Barnaby Rudge*.

CHESTERFIELD, Philip Dormer Stanhope, fourth earl of (1694–1773), was the son of Lady Elizabeth Savile, for whom *Halifax had written his 'Advice to a Daughter' (1688). He was a distinguished statesman and diplomatist, ambassador at The Hague 1728–32 and lord lieutenant of Ireland 1745–6. He was keenly interested in the literary world, and in his youth was a friend of *Pope, *Gay, and *Arbuthnot. He wrote political tracts, contributed to *The World*, and was responsible for securing the adoption of the New Style Gregorian *calendar in 1751, but is chiefly remembered for his 'Letters' to his natural son Philip Stanhope (1732–68), which were written (not for publication) almost daily from 1737 onwards. These consist largely of instruction in etiquette and the worldly arts, and became after publication (by the son's widow in 1774) a handbook of good manners; it appears that the young man was shy and awkward, and his father is full of useful advice about deportment (laughter occasions 'a shocking distortion of the face' and should be avoided), conversation, approaches to women (described as 'children of larger growth'), etc. Although widely admired, the letters increasingly attracted criticism, as the century became less cynical and more sentimental; Dr *Johnson declared that they 'teach the morals of a whore and the manners of a dancing-master' and *Cowper, in his 'Progress of Error', described their author as 'Graybeard corrupter of our listening youth'. After his son's death Chesterfield turned his attention to his godson, also Philip, his letters to whom were published by Lord Carnarvon in 1890. A complete edition of all his letters by B. Dobrée appeared in 1932. Chesterfield is also remembered in connection

with Johnson's *Dictionary*. Johnson had addressed the *Plan* of that work to Chesterfield but it was received with neglect, probably unintentional; on publication of the *Dictionary* Chesterfield wrote two papers in *The World* commending it. Thereupon on 7 Feb. 1755 Johnson addressed to him the famous letter in which he bitterly rejected a notice which 'had it been early, had been kind; but it has been delayed till I am indifferent, and cannot enjoy it till I am solitary, and cannot impart it; till I am known, and do not want it.' Chesterfield received this with good nature, and would show it to visitors with admiration. Johnson's own hostility softened over the years.

Chester Plays, see MYSTERY PLAYS.

CHESTERTON, G(ilbert) K(eith) (1874–1936), born on Camden Hill, London, and educated (with his friend E. C. *Bentley) at St Paul's School, made his name in journalism (according to him 'the easiest of all professions') writing (with *Belloc) for *The Speaker*, in which both took a controversial, anti-Imperial, pro-Boer line on the Boer war; his long and fruitful friendship with Belloc earned them both, from G. B. *Shaw, the twin nickname of 'Chesterbelloc'. His first novel, *The Napoleon of Notting Hill* (1904), a fantasy set in a future in which London is plunged into a strange mixture of medieval nostalgia and street warfare, develops his political attitudes, glorifying the little man, the colour and romance of 'Merry England', and attacking big business, technology, and the monolithic state. These themes echo through his fiction, which includes *The Man who was Thursday: a nightmare* (1908), an alarming but rollicking fantasy with a surreal anarchist background which attacks fin-de-siècle pessimism, and his many volumes of short stories, of which the best known are those which feature Father Brown, an unassuming East Anglian Roman Catholic priest, highly successful in the detection of crime by intuitive methods, who first appears in *The Innocence of Father Brown* (1911); Chesterton himself became a Roman Catholic in 1922. He published several volumes of verse; his most characteristic poems (with some exceptions, such as 'The Donkey', from *The Wild Knight*, 1900, and 'Lepanto', from *Poems*, 1915) tend to celebrate the Englishness of England, the nation of Beef and Beer, e.g. 'The Secret People' (1915) and 'The Rolling English Road' (1914).

Chesterton also wrote literary criticism, including works on R. *Browning (1903), *Dickens (1906), and Shaw (1910), and many volumes of political, social, and religious essays, including *Heretics* (1905), *Orthodoxy* (1909) and *The Everlasting Man* (1925); also an *Autobiography* (1936). He contributed regularly to the *Eye Witness*, later the *New Witness* (1911–

23), of Belloc and his brother Cecil Chesterton (1879–1918), and edited it from 1925 (when it was revived as *G.K.'s Weekly*) until his death. Much of his vast output has proved ephemeral, but Chesterton's vigour, idiosyncrasies, optimism, puns, and paradoxes celebrate the oddity of life and the diversity of people and places with a peculiar and at times exhilarating violence. Recent selections of his non-fiction prose and his short stories have been edited, with introductions, by, respectively, *Auden (1970) and *Amis (1972), and there is a life by Maisie Ward (1944).

CHESTRE, Thomas, see SIR LAUNFAL.

CHETTLE, Henry (*c.*1560–?1607), the son of a London dyer, was apprenticed to a printer and was for a time a partner in a printing business. Upon its failure he took to writing plays, of which he is reputedly the author of about 13 and the joint author of considerably more (including *The Blind-Beggar of Bednal-Green*, with J. *Day). The only extant play attributed to him alone is *The Tragedy of Hoffman* (*c.*1603), dealing with the story of a Danish pirate who is executed and the revenge and execution of his son. He edited *Greenes Groats-Worth of Witte in 1592, and wrote two satirical pamphlets, *Kind Harts Dreame* (?1593) and *Piers Plainnes seauen yeares Prentiship* (1595). He also published *Englandes Mourning Garment*, an elegy on Queen Elizabeth, in 1603.

Chevy Chase, *The Ballad of*, one of the oldest of the English ballads, probably dates in its primitive form from the 15th cent. Its subject is the rivalry of the neighbouring families of Percy and Douglas, heightened by the national quarrel between England and Scotland. Percy, earl of Northumberland, has vowed to hunt for three days across the Scottish border 'maugre the doughty Douglas'. The two parties meet and fight, there is great slaughter on both sides, and both Percy and Douglas are killed (cf. OTTER-BOURNE). The ballad is quoted with notes by *Addison in the *Spectator* (Nos. 21 and 25, 1711) and is included in Percy's *Reliques*.

Chiaroscuro, originally, the style of pictorial art in which only the light and shade, and not the various colours, are represented, and still used chiefly in this sense. It is used figuratively in poetic and literary contexts in the sense of mingled clearness and obscurity, light and gloom, praise and blame, etc.

Chiasmus, a figure of speech by which the order of the words in the first of two parallel clauses is reversed in the second, e.g. 'He saved others; himself he cannot save.'

CHICHELE, or **CHICHELEY,** Henry (?1362–1443), archbishop of Canterbury, son of a yeoman of Higham Ferrers, Northampton-shire. He was educated at Winchester and New College, Oxford, and became archbishop in 1414. He founded the Chichele chest in Oxford University for the relief of poor students, built a house for Cistercians in Oxford, and was co-founder with Henry VI of All Souls College. There is a Life by A. Duck (Latin 1617; expanded in English 1699).

Chicken Soup with Barley, see WESKER TRILOGY.

Chickerell, Ethelberta, a character in Hardy's *The Hand of Ethelberta*.

CHIFFINCH, William (1602–88), the confidential agent of Charles II, page of the bedchamber, figures in Scott's *Peveril of the Peak*.

CHILD, Francis James (1825–96), American scholar and professor of English literature at Harvard. He edited *Spenser (5 vols, 1855) and wrote a pioneering study of *Chaucer (*Observations on the Language of Chaucer*, 1863), but is most widely known for his great collection of *English and Scottish Popular Ballads* (5 vols, 1882–98). (See BALLAD.)

Childe, in 'Childe Harold', 'Childe Roland', etc., signifies a youth of gentle birth, and is used as a kind of title. In the 13th and 14th cents 'child' appears to have been applied to a young noble awaiting knighthood.

Childe Harold's Pilgrimage, a poem by *Byron, of which the first two cantos appeared in 1812, Canto III in 1816, and Canto IV in 1818.

The poem describes the travels, experiences, and reflections of a pilgrim, Childe Harold, whose life and journeyings correspond in many ways to Byron's own. Byron, however, denied that he identified himself with Harold, and wrote in his Preface that the pilgrim 'was never intended as an example'. The pilgrim, who is characterized as a melancholy, defiant outcast, is the first of the truly *'Byronic' heroes in the author's work; Harold's histrionic character appears with little variation in such poems as *The Corsair*, *Lara*, *Manfred*, and other works. The first two cantos describe how the pilgrim, sated with his past life of sin and pleasure, finds distraction in his travels through Portugal, Spain, the Ionian Islands, and Albania. In Canto III, written six years after I and II, the pilgrim travels to Belgium, the Rhine, the Alps, and the Jura. His reflections on nature, on his own states of mind, and on events and people of the public world are more skilfully blended than in the earlier cantos. The historical associations of the places he visits lead to reflections on, particularly, the Spanish war, Napoleon and Waterloo, and *Rousseau and Julie. Byron wrote that when he was composing this canto, soon after his departure from England in 1816, he was 'half mad . . . between metaphysics, mountains, lakes, love unextinguishable, thoughts unutterable . . .' In Canto IV the device of the pilgrim is abandoned and the poet speaks directly, in a long meditation on time and history, on Venice, *Petrarch and Arqua, *Tasso and Ferrara, *Boccaccio and Florence, Rome and her great men, ending with a passage on the eternal symbol of the sea.

The poem enjoyed tremendous success. After the publication of Cantos I and II in March 1812 Byron wrote, 'I woke one morning and found myself famous.' The work was nevertheless vigorously satirized by Peacock in *Nightmare Abbey, and Byron himself felt that by the time he had finished Canto IV he and 'the moderns' were on the wrong lines, and he came to dislike the work as in 'the false exaggerated style of youth'.

Childe Roland, in an old Scottish ballad, a son of King Arthur. His sister, Burd Ellen, is carried away by the fairies to the castle of the king of Elfland. Aided by the instructions of Merlin, Childe Roland makes his way into the castle and rescues his sister.

> Child Rowland to the dark tower came,
> His word was still 'Fie, foh, and fum,
> I smell the blood of a British man.'
> (Shakespeare, *King Lear*, III. iv)

*Halliwell (*Nursery Rhymes*) thinks that Shakespeare is here quoting from two different compositions, the first line from a ballad about Roland, the second and third from the story of *Jack the Giant-killer.

'Childe Roland to the Dark Tower Came', a poem by R. *Browning, published in *Men and Women*. The title derives from a snatch of song recited by Edgar in *King Lear* (see above).

A knight errant crosses a nightmare landscape in search of the Dark Tower (or has been deceived into doing so; it is not clear which); he eventually reaches the Tower and blows his horn defiantly at its foot. The poem ends with the title phrase, and there is no indication of what happened next. Because the story is told by the knight himself, the poem's form raises insoluble problems of interpretation, and the poem is both profoundly satisfying as a dream narrative and profoundly disturbing as an impenetrable allegory—of life, of art, or of both. Browning consistently refused to explain the poem, saying simply that it had come upon him as a dream. The intensity of the poem's language remained unsurpassed in Browning's work until the fragment known as 'Thamuris marching' appeared in *Aristophanes' Apology*.

CHILDERS, (Robert) Erskine (1870–1922), writer and political activist, was from 1895 a Clerk in the House of Commons, served in the Boer War, and then devoted himself to Irish affairs. In 1920 he settled in Ireland and in 1921 was appointed director of publicity for the Irish republicans. In 1922 he was court-martialled and shot by firing squad. As a writer he is remembered for his novel *The Riddle of the Sands* (1903), a sea story about two amateur British yachtsmen sailing in the Baltic who discover German preparations for an invasion of England.

Childe Waters, one of the most beautiful of the old ballads, celebrating the constancy of Ellen to Childe Waters, her heartless lover, whom she serves as a page, receiving cruel and degrading treatment. Her child is born in a stable, where she is tending her master's horse. He hears her singing a lullaby and wishing herself dead, relents, and marries her. The ballad is in Percy's *Reliques*.

Child of the Jago, A (1896), a novel by A. *Morrison, describes the boyhood of Dick Perrott in an East End slum off Shoreditch High Street, and gives a vivid account of the violent crime of the neighbourhood known in real life as 'The Nichol'. Dicky's good instincts are frustrated by the environment, his father is hanged for murder, and he dies aged 17 in a street fight. In an 1897 preface Morrison rejected the label of 'realist', but his work belongs to the same school as that of G. *Moore and resembles the early *Maugham.

Children in the Wood, The, popularly known as the story of the Babes in the Wood, is the subject of an old ballad, included in *Percy's and *Ritson's collections.

A Norfolk gentleman leaves his property to his infant son and daughter and gives the children into his brother's charge; the wicked uncle plans to acquire the property by making away with them. He hires two ruffians to slay them in a wood. One of these, more tender-hearted than the other, repents and kills his fellow, then abandons the children in the wood. The children perish, and a robin covers them with leaves. The surviving ruffian confesses, and the wicked uncle dies miserably.

Children of the Chapel of Paul's, see PAUL'S, CHILDREN OF.

Children of the New Forest, The, see MARRYAT, F.

Children's Literature. As early as the 15th cent. *'courtesy books', such as *The Babees' Book*, provided children with instruction on behaviour; but for entertainment, then as in the next century, they had to turn to adult books such as *Aesop or collections of legends. It was not until the 17th cent. that books were specifically written for children, and then the stories (such as James Janeway's *A Token for Children* in 1671) were sternly moralistic. Children read Bunyan's *Pilgrim's Progress* (1678–84), Defoe's

Robinson Crusoe (1719), Swift's *Gulliver's Travels* (1726), and other works primarily written for adults; but it was not until well into the 18th cent., when (largely under the influence of *Locke and *Rousseau) education became more humane, that the first books appeared designed to attract and please children. In 1745 *Newbery opened a children's bookshop (described in *The Vicar of Wakefield*, and remembered by Leigh *Hunt), and wrote many of the volumes he sold; at the same time Thomas Boreman produced, from 1740, tiny, attractive booklets called *Gigantick Histories*. Crude *chapbooks of alphabets, rhymes, and fairy-tales began to abound, and more serious didactic works, such as T. *Day's *The History of Sandford and Merton* (1783-9) and M. *Edgeworth's *Moral Tales* (1801), achieved great popularity. With the publication in 1814 of J. D. Wyss's *The Swiss Family Robinson* and in 1818-47 of Mrs *Sherwood's *History of the Fairchild Family*, the demand for children's books of quality was firmly established, and the various categories into which they still group themselves (adventure, school stories, family sagas, animal stories, fantasy, and so on) began to be distinguished. The perennial argument as to whether children should read fairy-tales was stimulated by the publication of *German Popular Stories* by the brothers *Grimm in 1823, and the stories of *Andersen in 1846; Thackeray's *The Rose and the Ring* (1855) is a gentle satire of fairy-story conventions. Adventure stories for boys were produced from the 1840s and 1850s onwards by *Marryat, R. M. *Ballantyne, *Henty, and many others. School stories were established by Thomas *Hughes's *Tom Brown's Schooldays* (1857) and F. W. Farrar's *Eric, or Little by Little* (1858); family sagas by C. M. *Yonge's *The Daisy Chain* (1856) and by the American L. M. Alcott, with *Little Women* (1868); and animal stories by A. *Sewell's *Black Beauty* (1877). During the rest of the century many of the abiding classics of children's literature appeared, which included C. Kingsley's *The Water-Babies* (1863), *Alice's Adventures in Wonderland* (1865) by Lewis Carroll (C. L. *Dodgson), Mrs *Molesworth's *The Tapestry Room* (1879), and R. *Jefferies's *Bevis* (1882). R. L. *Stevenson's *Treasure Island* in 1883 was one of the first adventure stories with no obvious didactic purpose. In 1886 F. H. *Burnett's *Little Lord Fauntleroy* achieved immense success; soon after appeared Stevenson's *Kidnapped* (1886) and *Catriona* (1893), *Haggard's *King Solomon's Mines* (1885), *Kipling's *Jungle Books* (1894-5), and the first of E. *Nesbit's long line of successes, *The Story of the Treasure-Seekers* (1899). Also in 1899 appeared *Little Black Sambo*, the first of a popular and vividly illustrated series by Helen Bannerman (1862/3-1946); she, with Beatrix *Potter (whose *Peter Rabbit* appeared in 1902), did much to establish the book in which pictures

and text are of equal importance. The increasing demand for children's fiction was manifested not only in a vast amount of work of lesser quality, but also in Kipling's *Puck of Pook's Hill* (1906), *Grahame's *The Wind in the Willows* (1908), F. H. Burnett's *The Secret Garden* (1911); the first of the 'Dr Dolittle' books by Hugh Lofting (1886-1947) appeared in 1920, *Martin Pippin in the Apple Orchard* by E. *Farjeon in 1921, A. A. *Milne's *Winnie-the-Pooh* in 1926, and the first of A. *Uttley's 'Little Grey Rabbit' books in 1929. The first of *Ransome's 'Swallows and Amazons' series appeared in 1930, and Noel Streatfeild (1895–   ) established the 'career' novel with *Ballet Shoes* in 1936. *Tolkien restimulated the tradition of fantasy with *The Hobbit* (1937).

Since about 1950 the publishing of fiction for children has been a vast industry, with specialist guides and reviewers and many annual prizes and medals, including the Newbery Medal, the Carnegie Medal, and the Eleanor Farjeon Medal; together with the Kate Greenaway Medal for illustration. The dividing line between fiction written for older children and that written for adults has become rigidly defined, as has the distinction between writing for boys and writing for girls; allegations of racism have been levelled against many old favourites, including those by Lofting and Bannerman, and children's writers and publishers have attempted to cultivate increased sensitivity towards issues of racism and sexism. Straight adventure stories and school stories have declined in popularity, but in the flourishing field of fantasy work of a high standard has been produced by C. S. *Lewis, Alan Garner (1934–), Philippa Pearce (1920–   , among many others. The historical novels of Rosemary Sutcliff (1920–) and Leon Garfield (1921–) should also be mentioned, as should the daily-life novels of Nina Bawden (1925–).

The history of verse written for children is much briefer. The 16th-cent. manuals of instruction, such as the *Booke in Englyssh Metre*, were often written in pleasing verse, but the first identifiable children's poet was probably *Watts, whose memorable jingles, *Divine Songs for Children*, proved immensely popular from 1715. At about this time collections of nursery rhymes began to appear. Ann and Jane *Taylor, whose first book, *Original Poems for Infant Minds*, included 'Twinkle, twinkle little star', were extremely successful in 1804 and thereafter. The *Butterfly's Ball and the Grasshopper's Feast* (1806), a *jeu d'esprit* by *Roscoe, produced scores of imitations. R. *Browning's 'The Pied Piper of Hamelin' was published in 1842, *Lear's *Book of Nonsense* (followed by many other verses) in 1846, and R. L. Stevenson's *A Child's Garden of Verses* in 1885. Verse in this century has included distinguished work by *Belloc, *De La

Mare, A. A. Milne, Robert *Graves, Ted *Hughes, and *Causley, among others.

Chillingworth, Roger, in Hawthorne's *The Scarlet Letter*, the name assumed by Hester Prynne's husband.

CHILLINGWORTH, William (1602–44), a scholar and fellow of Trinity College, Oxford, embraced Romanism and went to Douai in 1630, but abjured that creed in 1634. He was one of the literary coterie that gathered round *Falkland at Great Tew, and was the author of the controversial work *The Religion of the Protestants a safe Way to Salvation* (1637).

Chillip, Dr, in Dickens's *David Copperfield*, the physician who attended Mrs Copperfield at the hero's birth.

Chillon, *The Prisoner of*, see PRISONER OF CHILLON, THE.

Chimène, or Ximena, the wife of the *Cid.

Chimes, The, a Christmas book by *Dickens, published 1845.

It is the story of a nightmare or vision in which Toby Veck, porter and runner of errands, under the influence of the goblins of the church bells and a dish of tripe, witnesses awful misfortunes befalling his daughter, a vision happily dissipated at the end; together with some social satire on justices, aldermen, and the like, in the persons of Sir Joseph Bowley and Mr Chute.

Chingachgook (pron. 'chicago'), the Indian chief in the 'Leatherstocking' series of tales of Indian life of J. F. *Cooper.

Chips with Everything, see WESKER, A.

Chivery, Mr and 'Young John', characters in Dickens's *Little Dorrit*.

Chloe, the name under which Pope satirizes Lady Suffolk, mistress of George II (*Moral Essays*, ii. 157), although in other verses and letters he shows her much respect.

The 'Chloe' or 'Cloe' in Horace *Walpole's letters was the duke of Newcastle's French cook Clouet.

Choice, The, see POMFRET, J.

CHOMSKY, Noam (1928–), professor of modern languages and linguistics at Massachusetts Institute of Technology, after *Saussure the most important figure in modern linguistics. Two of his books, in particular, proposed a radically new view of the nature and analysis of language: *Syntactic Structures* (1957) and *Aspects of the Theory of Syntax* (1965). Following on from the systems of grammatical analysis developed by L. *Bloomfield and Chomsky's teacher Zellig Harris, Chomsky's 'generative grammar' proposes a set of 'deep structure' grammatical rules which produce a set of sentences at the 'surface structure' of language. A grammar of a language would be a set of rules which generates 'all and only the correct sentences of the language'. The significance of his emphasis is that it brings linguistic analysis closer to analyses of mental operations such as are conducted by psychologists and logicians; his approach has more in common, in some of its aspects, with 17th-cent. 'Cartesian' notions of 'Universal Grammar' than with the taxonomic endeavours of pre-Saussurean philology.

Eds. J. P. B. Allen and P. Van Buren, *Chomsky: Selected Readings* (1971); N. Chomsky, *Reflections on Language* (1975); J. Lyons, *Chomsky* (1970).

CHOPIN, Fryderyk Franciszek (1810–49), Polish composer. Chopin, who lived in Paris from the age of 21 onwards, was one of the central figures of the musical Romantic movement. The circumstances of his life, and his notorious liaison with the novelist G. *Sand, combined with the poetry of his piano playing and the strong emotional appeal of his compositions, made him a legend in his own time; after his death he came to be seen as the archetype of the consumptive Romantic artist, and his slighter works were on the piano in many Victorian drawing rooms. His music is a great deal better than this popular image suggests, particularly in the larger works not aimed at the aristocratic salons of which he was so assiduous a frequenter, and its influence on later composers was profound. Unlike most of his contemporaries, however, he never tried to relate his music to literary, pictorial, or autobiographical themes, and his few songs are written entirely to Polish texts.

CHOPIN, Kate, *née* O'Flaherty (1850–1904), daughter of an Irish immigrant father and Creole mother; she was born in St Louis, Missouri, and brought up in a largely female household. She married Oscar Chopin, a Creole, and went to live in New Orleans, Louisiana, spending her summers at Grand Isle, a fashionable resort off the south coast. Her husband's business did not prosper and he returned to the family plantation in the Cane River district, where he died of swamp fever in 1882, leaving her with six children to support. After paying off his debts she returned to St Louis and began to write, using as material her memories of New Orleans and of Cane River, the latter providing material for three collections of short stories. She was originally acclaimed as a 'local colourist', but has won posthumous recognition principally for *The Awakening*, first published in 1899, when it was greeted as scandalous and morbid. Discouraged from writing more full-length fiction, she turned to poems, essays, and short stories until her death from a brain haemorrhage. Interest in her largely neglected work increased from the late 1940s; in 1962 E. *Wilson devoted six pages of *Patriotic Gore* to it, and she has since attracted much attention from feminist scholars.

Choriamb, a metrical foot of four syllables, the first and last long, the two others short. A choree is a *trochee.

Chowder, Tabitha's dog in Smollett's *Humphry Clinker.*

CHRÉTIEN DE TROYES (*fl.* 1170–90), regarded as the greatest of the writers of courtly romances, wrote in French in the second half of the 12th cent. He is believed to have written a romance of *Tristan*, but four complete romances of his survive, all written in octosyllabic rhyming couplets: *Erec and Enide* (*c.*1170); *Cligés* (*c.*1176); *Yvain* (*c.*1177–81); and *Lancelot*, or *Le Chevalier de la Charrette* (*c.*1177–81): the last 1,000 of the 7,000-odd lines of the latter were written by Godefroy de Lagny. As well as these four he left incomplete the lengthy *Perceval* or *Le Conte du Graal* (1181–90) of which 9,234 lines survive. There are also two short *trouvère* poems by him, and he lists at the beginning of *Cligés* a number of other complete, mostly Ovidian, poems. All that is known for certain of the writer is that he lived and worked for some time at the court of *Marie de Champagne. His influence on all subsequent Arthurian literature, including English, is general rather than particular, but the English romance *Iwain and Gawain* is a loose translation of his *Yvain*. The qualities required of a courtly lover were partly inferred from *Lancelot* by G. Paris in 1883 (see COURTLY LOVE).

There is an English translation of the four completed romances by W. W. Comfort (Everyman, 1914, etc.). For general discussion and reference to French editions, see 'Chrétien de Troyes' by Jean Frappier, in R. S. Loomis, ed., *Arthurian Literature in the Middle Ages* (1959), pp. 157–91.

'Christabel', a poem by S. T. *Coleridge, published 1816.

The poem is unfinished. The first part was written at Nether Stowey in 1797, the second (which contains Lake District local colour) at Keswick in 1800; Coleridge made plans for Part III but was unable to continue with it. It is a medieval romance of the supernatural, written in what is sometimes referred to as 'Christabel metre'—that is, in four-foot couplets, mostly iambic and anapaestic, used with immense variety, so that the line length varies from seven syllables to ten or eleven.

Christabel, praying at night in a wood for her betrothed lover, discovers the fair Geraldine in distress and takes her to the castle of her father, Sir Leoline. Geraldine claims to have been abducted from her home by five warriors, and to be the daughter of Sir Leoline's estranged friend

Sir Roland of Vaux. She shares Christabel's chamber for the night, and bewitches her as they lie in one another's arms. In the morning she meets Sir Leoline, who vows reconciliation with her father and vengeance on the 'reptile souls' of her abductors. Christabel, who has seen Geraldine's true malignant serpent nature, is at first silenced by the spell placed upon her, but manages to implore her father to send Geraldine away, although she can offer no explanation for this plea. Sir Leoline, offended by his daughter's insult to a guest, turns from her to Geraldine, and so the poem ends. The imagery throughout is strongly sexual, and the theme would appear to be connected with the corruption and seduction of innocence. To Coleridge's disappointment, Wordsworth did not include the poem in the second edition of the *Lyrical Ballads*. Coleridge's sources have been traced by A. Nethercot, *The Road to Tryermaine* (1939).

Christ and Satan, an Old English poem of 733 lines in three sections, found in the *Junius manuscript. Clubb, in his 1925 edn, dated the work (more exactly than seems justified) 790–830, and said it was of Anglian origin. Like many of the poems in the Junius manuscript, it used to be attributed to *Caedmon, but it is now said to be a mixture of his 'school' and that of *Cynewulf. The subjects of the three sections are: Satan's lament for his fall; the *Harrowing of Hell; and the temptation of Christ by Satan.

Christ Church, Oxford, a college begun by Cardinal Wolsey (it was to be called 'Cardinal College'), and taken over after his fall and established by Henry VIII in 1546. Among famous men educated there were *Locke, John *Wesley, *Pusey, and *Gladstone. Christ Church is at the same time the cathedral of Oxford, the cathedral being within the walls of the college and serving as its chapel.

Christian and **Christiana,** the hero of Bunyan's *The Pilgrim's Progress* and his wife, who is introduced in the second part.

Christian, Edward, a character in Scott's *Peveril of the Peak.*

Christian Hero, The. An *Argument proving that no Principles but those of Religion are Sufficient to make a great Man,* a treatise by *Steele, published 1701.

Finding, as the author tells us, military life 'exposed to much Irregularity', he wrote this little work 'with a design to fix upon his own Mind a strong Impression of Virtue and Religion, in opposition to a stronger Propensity towards unwarrantable Pleasures'. In it he stresses the value of the Bible as a moral guide and the failure of Stoic philosophy. The treatise ends with a comparison between Louis XIV and William III, and includes a significant passage recommending, in contrast with the immorality that pervaded most of the writings of the day, a chivalrous attitude towards women. The work is important as one of the first signs of a change of tone in the English literature of the period. (See also STOICISM.)

Christian Morals, see BROWNE, T.

Christian Year, The, see KEBLE, J.

CHRISTIE, Dame Agatha, *née* Miller (1890–1976), born and brought up in Torquay, was educated at home, and in 1914 married Archibald Christie. During the First World War she worked as a hospital dispenser, which gave her a knowledge of poisons which was to be useful when she started writing detective stories. Her marriage broke up in 1926, and in 1930 she married the archaeologist Max Mallowan, whom she accompanied on his excavations of sites in Syria and Iraq. Her first detective novel, *The Mysterious Affair at Styles* (1920), introduced Hercule Poirot, the Belgian detective who appeared in many subsequent novels (her other main detective being the elderly spinster Miss Marple). In the next 56 years she wrote 66 detective novels, among the best of which are *The Murder of Roger Ackroyd* (1926), *Murder on the Orient Express* (1934), *Death on the Nile* (1937), and *Ten Little Niggers* (1939). She also wrote six novels under the pseudonym Mary Westmacott, two self-portraits (*Come Tell Me How You Live*, 1946; *An Autobiography*, 1977), and several plays, including *The Mousetrap*, which has run continuously in London for more than 30 years. Her prodigious international success seems due to her matchless ingenuity in contriving plots, sustaining suspense and misdirecting the reader, to her ear for dialogue, and brisk, unsentimental commonsense and humour. Her style is undistinguished and her characterization slight, but sufficient for the exigencies of the form. See R. Barnard, *A Talent to Deceive* (1980); C. Osborne, *The Life and Crimes of Agatha Christie* (1982).

CHRISTINE DE PISAN (*c.*1364–*c.*1430), French poet and prose writer. She produced a large number of works, including courtly ballades, rondeaux, and virelais, moral and didactic poems, a biography of Charles V, and several specifically feminist works, such as *L'Epistre au dieu d'amours* (1399), an eloquent denunciation of anti-feminist attitudes, *La Cité des dames* (1405, English trans. 1521), and *Le Livre des trois vertus* (1406). A number of English translations of her work appeared in the late 15th and early 16th cents and a new translation of *La Cité des dames* by Earle Jeffrey Richards, *The Book of the City of Ladies*, was published in 1983 with a foreword by Marina Warner, in which she relates 'the *querelle des femmes*—the woman question in late 14th- and early 15th-cent.

France' to 'today's debate about the equality of women'.

Christis Kirk on the Green, an old Scottish poem, doubtfully attributed to James I or James V of Scotland, in nine-lined stanzas with a 'bob' after the eighth line, descriptive of the rough fun, dancing, and love-making of a village festival or 'wappinshaw'. Two additional cantos were composed by *Ramsay.

Christmas Carol, A, a Christmas book by *Dickens, published 1843.

Scrooge, an old curmudgeon, receives on Christmas Eve a visit from the ghost of Marley, his late partner in business, and beholds a series of visions of the past, present, and future, including one of what his own death will be like unless he is quick to amend his ways. As a result of this he wakes up on Christmas morning an altered man. He sends a turkey to his ill-used clerk Bob Cratchit, positively enjoys subscribing to Christmas charities, and generally behaves like the genial old fellow that he has become.

Christmas-Eve and Easter-Day, a poem by R. *Browning, published 1850. The poem is in two parts, in octosyllabic metre, with an irregular rhyme-scheme. The first part, 'Christmas-Eve', in the form of a narrative combining realistic and visionary elements, accepts that denominational religion is an imperfect medium for divine truth, but emphasizes the need to choose the best method of worship according to one's lights; the second part, 'Easter-Day', in the form of an imagined dialogue, examines the difficulties of holding to the Christian faith at all, and argues that the condition of doubt is, in fact, essential to the existence of human faith. The poem, the first to appear after Browning's marriage, shows the influence of E. B. *Browning's strong intellectual and emotional engagement with religious polemic, acting on Browning's own Nonconformist upbringing.

Christ's Hospital, London, the most famous of the Blue-Coat or charity schools, was founded under a charter of Edward VI as a school for poor children, in buildings that before the dissolution had belonged to the Grey Friars. *Coleridge, *Lamb, and Leigh *Hunt were educated there.

Christs Teares over Jerusalem, a tract by T. *Nashe, published 1593. Nashe here figures as a religious reformer. He applies Christ's prophecy of the fall of Jerusalem as a warning to sinful London and analyses with his usual vigour the vices and abuses of contemporary society.

Christs Victorie and Triumph, see FLETCHER, GILES (the younger).

Chronicle Play, a type of drama popular in the 1590s and the early 17th cent., in which scenes from the life of a monarch or famous historical character were depicted. Examples are Shakespeare's *Henry V* and *Henry VIII*, the Sir Thomas *More play and *Dekker and *Webster's *Sir Thomas Wyat*.

Chronicles, see under ANGLO–SAXON CHRONICLE, ANNALES CAMBRIAE, ASSER, BEDE, CAMDEN, CAPGRAVE, CIRENCESTER, EADMER, FABYAN, FLORENCE OF WORCESTER, GEOFFREY OF MONMOUTH, GILDAS, GIRALDUS CAMBRENSIS, HALL, E., HARRISON, W., HOLINSHED, HOVEDEN, JOCELIN DE BRAKELOND, NENNIUS, PETERBOROUGH CHRONICLE, RICHARD THE THIRDE, ROBERT OF GLOUCESTER, SPEED, STOW, VERGIL, WACE, WILLIAM OF MALMESBURY, WILLIAM OF NEWBURGH, WYNTOUN, A.

Chronicles of the Canongate, The, an inclusive title for Sir W. Scott's novels *The Highland Widow*, *The Two Drovers*, and *The Fair Maid of Perth*, to which the author attached the fiction that they were written by Mr Chrystal Croftangry, who draws on the recollections of his old friend Mrs Bethune Baliol, a resident in the Canongate, Edinburgh. Mr Croftangry's own story, notable among Scott's shorter sketches, forms an introduction to the *Chronicles*.

Chrononhotonthologos, a burlesque of contemporary drama by H. *Carey, 'the Most Tragical Tragedy that ever was Tragediz'd by any Company of Tragedians', acted 1734.
Chrononhotonthologos is king of Queerummania, and two of the characters are Aldiborontiphoscophornia and Rigdum-Funnidos, names which Sir W. *Scott gave to James and John *Ballantyne, on account of the pomposity of the one and the fun and cheerfulness of the other.

Chrysal, or the Adventures of a Guinea, see JOHNSTONE, C.

Chrysaor, in Spenser's *Faerie Queene* (v. i. 9 and v. xii. 40), the sword of Justice, wielded by Sir *Artegall. The Chrysaor of Greek mythology was a son of Poseidon and Medusa.

CHRYSOSTOM, St John (*c*.345–407), a Greek father of the Church, born at Antioch in Syria; he was baptized in 370 and spent ten years in the desert in ascetical study. He became bishop of Constantinople where he preached so eloquently against the vices of the city and its empress Eudoxia that he was condemned by a packed synod and banished to Nicaea. His name means 'Golden-mouth', in tribute to his eloquent preaching; in his writings he stressed the ascetical element in religion and the need for personal study of the Scriptures. Amongst his many writings the most celebrated are his Commentaries on the Gospel of St Matthew and on the Epistles to the Romans and Corinthians, all translated in *A Library of the Father of the Holy*

Catholic Church (J. H. Parker, 1852, etc.). See also D. Attwater, *St John Chrysostom* (1939).

Chuffey, in Dickens's *Martin Chuzzlewit*, Anthony Chuzzlewit's old clerk.

CHURCH, Richard Thomas (1893–1972), poet, novelist and essayist, who worked in the department of customs and excise before devoting himself to literary journalism. He published many volumes of verse from 1917 onwards, mainly of a Georgian tone, and also both adult and children's fiction. He also published three volumes of autobiography, 1956–64.

CHURCH, Richard William (1815–90), dean of St Paul's. In 1838 he was elected a fellow of Oriel College, Oxford, where he met *Newman, and became a supporter of the *Oxford Movement. He was author of lives of St *Anselm (1870), *Spenser (1879), and *Bacon (1884) and published numerous essays and sermons. His *The Oxford Movement, Twelve Years, 1833–1845* (1891) is a notable interpretation of the history of the movement.

CHURCHILL, Caryl (1938–), playwright, born in London and educated in Montreal and at Lady Margaret Hall, Oxford. Most of her plays, predominantly radical and feminist in tone, have been performed at the Royal Court Theatre, in association with the *English Stage Company: they include *Owners* (1972, pub. 1973), a satire on property and capitalism; *Light Shining in Buckinghamshire* (1976, pub. 1978); *Cloud Nine* (1979, pub. 1979); *Top Girls* (1982, with an all–female cast); and *Softcops* (1984, with an all–male cast). She has also written radio and television plays.

CHURCHILL, Charles (1732–64), the son of a poor clergyman, educated at Westminster and St John's College, Cambridge. His university career was interrupted by an early marriage, and he was ordained 'through need, not choice' in 1756, succeeding his father as curate at St John's, Westminster. He was oppressed by poverty until the publication of *The Rosciad* and *The Apology* (both 1761), which brought him fame and between £750 and £1,000. He increasingly abandoned the church, leading a worldly and dissipated life, and by 1762 was a close friend of *Wilkes, writing for his paper *The North Briton* and attacking his opponents in satiric verse. *The Prophecy of Famine* (1763) is a mock-pastoral and a powerful satiric attack on Bute, J. *Home, and other Scots. Other targets were *Smollett (*The Author*, 1763); *Hogarth (*The Epistle to William Hogarth*, 1763, inspired by Hogarth's caricature of Wilkes); *The Duellist* (1764, an attack on Samuel Martin, who had wounded Wilkes in a duel); *The Candidate* (1764, directed against Lord Sandwich, *'Jemmy Twitcher') and *The Times* (1764), a more generalized attack on vice and homosexuality. *Gotham* (1764), which his old school friend *Cowper found a 'noble and beautiful poem', describes Churchill as Patriot King (see BOLINGBROKE) of an ideal state. Its heroic couplets mark the transition to the softer usages of the later 18th cent. (Gotham, a village near Nottingham, was traditionally famed for the simplicity of its inhabitants.) Churchill died young at Boulogne on his way to visit Wilkes in France; Wilkes promised to edit his papers, but neglected to do so. His admirers included *Boswell (who defended him from Dr *Johnson's attacks, and discounted his violent prejudice against the Scots), Cowper, and *Byron, but, as Boswell predicted, his dependence on topical references has led to his neglect. His poems were edited, with a short life, by J. Laver (2 vols, 1933) and by D. Grant (1956).

Churchill, Frank, a character in J. Austen's *Emma.*

CHURCHILL, Winston (1871–1947), Missouri-born American novelist, whose historical romances were in their day immensely popular; nearly all of them had titles which begin with the letter 'C', and they include *The Crisis* (1901), *The Crossing* (1904), and *Coniston* (1906).

CHURCHILL, Rt. Hon. Sir Winston Leonard Spencer (1874–1965), eldest son of Lord Randolph Churchill (third son of the 7th duke of Marlborough). He entered the army in 1895 and served in Cuba, India, Egypt, and the Sudan; was present as a war correspondent at Spion Kop, Diamond Hill, etc.; and served in France as Lt.-Col. in 1916. He was under-secretary of state for the colonies, 1906–8; president of the board of trade, 1908–10; home secretary, 1910–11; first lord of the Admiralty, 1911–15; secretary of state for war, 1918–21; for the colonies, 1921–2; chancellor of the exchequer 1924–9; prime minister, 1940–5 and 1951–5. Among his publications are: *The Story of the Malakand Field Force* (1898), *The River War* (1899), *London to Ladysmith via Pretoria* (1900), *Ian Hamilton's March* (1900), *Lord Randolph Churchill* (1906–7), *My African Journey* (1908), *Liberalism and the Social Problem* (1909), *The World Crisis* (4 vols, 1923–9), *My Early Life* (1930), *Marlborough* (1933–8), *War Speeches 1940–5* (1946), *The Second World War* (6 vols, 1948–54), and *A History of the English-speaking Peoples* (4 vols, 1956–8). He was awarded the *Nobel Prize in 1953. Vols 1 and 2 of the official biography, by his son Randolph Churchill (1911–68), appeared in 1966–7; Martin Gilbert succeeded as official biographer (Vol. 3, 1971–   ).

CHURCHYARD, Thomas (?1520–1604), at one time page to Henry Howard, earl of *Sur-

rey, lived a wandering life, partly as a soldier in Scotland, Ireland, France, and the Low Countries, partly as a hanger-on of the court and the nobility. He published, before 1553, *A myrrour for man.* Between 1560 and 1603 he issued a multitude of broadsheets and small volumes in verse and prose, several containing autobiographical pieces and notices of current events. His best-known works are *Shores Wife* (1563), in the *Mirror for Magistrates*, and the *Generall Rehearsall of Warres* (1579), in which he made use of his own experience as a soldier. Spenser in his *Colin Clout* refers to Churchyard as 'old Palemon . . . That sung so long untill quite hoarse he grew'.

CHUTE, John (1701–76), friend and correspondent of Horace *Walpole, whom he met in Florence in 1740. He remodelled his own family estate, The Vyne, in Hampshire, and contributed greatly to the creation of *Strawberry Hill. Walpole referred to him as 'my oracle in taste, the standard to whom I submitted my trifles, and the genuis that presided over poor Strawberry!' (letter to *Mann, 27 May 1776). He has been credited with more fidelity to antiquity than his fellow connoisseur, the more fantastic Richard *Bentley.

CIBBER, Mrs (1714–66), actress, see under CIBBER, T.

CIBBER, Colley (1671–1757), son of Caius Cibber the sculptor, was educated at Grantham School and became an actor in 1690. His first play, *Love's Last Shift* (1696), of which *Congreve said that 'it has only in it a great many things that were like wit, that in reality were not wit', introduced the character of Sir Novelty Fashion, who was transformed into Lord Foppington in Vanbrugh's *The Relapse.* Cibber wrote in his varied theatrical career many plays and adaptations, notably *She Would and She Would Not* (1702), *The Careless Husband* (1704), both comedies, and a successful adaptation of Shakespeare's *Richard III* (1700). The *Non-Juror* (1717), a comedy based on Molière's *Tartuffe*, was ridiculed by *Pope in a pamphlet, and Cibber became the hero of Pope's *Dunciad in its final edition, after becoming poet laureate in 1730. He attracted many enemies by his rudeness and vanity, and as a writer was more concerned with theatrical effect than with literary merit, but nevertheless made a significant contribution to 18th-cent. drama, particularly to the genre of *sentimental comedy; his plays were highly praised by *Smollett and *Walpole, and Samuel Derrick in 1759 described *The Careless Husband* as 'not only the best comedy in the English but in any other language'. In 1740 Cibber published his autobiography, *An Apology for the Life of Mr Colley Cibber, Comedian*, which gives a vivid picture of the theatrical life of the time, and contains striking portraits of

*Betterton, Mrs *Bracegirdle, and others. His reference in this work to *Fielding as 'a broken wit' provoked the already hostile playwright-turned-novelist to yet more satire, notably in the opening chapter of *Joseph Andrews*. A biography, *Mr Cibber of Drury Lane* by R. H. Barker, was published in 1939.

CIBBER, Theophilus (1703–58), son of Colley *Cibber, actor and hack-writer, was born during the Great Storm and had an appropriately stormy career. His wildness and eccentricities provoked much scandal, as did his marriage in 1734 to Susanna Maria Arne (1714–66), sister of Dr *Arne. She became with his encouragement a distinguished tragic actress, but he also encouraged for mercenary reasons her relationship with a well-to-do lover, John Sloper, and all three became involved in disgrace and a notorious lawsuit in 1738. Her career recovered but his was ruined, and after struggling along in minor roles he was drowned in another storm on the way to keep an engagement at the Smock Alley Theatre in Dublin.

CICERO, Marcus Tullius (106–43 BC), referred to sometimes as Tully, was the most influential of Roman prose writers. Born into a rich provincial family, he studied philosophy as well as rhetoric and law. Early success as a pleader and as a politician led to his becoming consul in 63 BC when he suppressed the conspiracy of Catiline. He supported the senatorial party against Julius *Caesar. After the assassination of Caesar he attacked Mark Antony in a series of speeches and was put to death. His influence on later ages has been remarkable for its variety. His writings left their mark on ethics, epistemology, and political thought, on men's ideals of conduct, on the development of oratory and letter-writing, on literary style, the popularity of paradox, and the viability of Latin as an international language. During the Middle Ages Cicero figured primarily as a master of rhetoric. The textbook *De Inventione* remained the best-known of his works and was imitated by *Alcuin. But some importance must be assigned to the *De Amicitia*, which served Aelred of Rievaulx and others as a model for disquisitions on Christian love, and also to the few erudite scholars who even at this early stage attempted to copy Cicero's style. It was enthusiasm for a more systematic form of such imitation that distinguished the Renaissance, when it had the result of popularizing for a time the Ciceronian period with writers like *Ascham and when it had the additional result of promoting that Ciceronianism deplored by G. *Harvey, which destroyed Latin as an international language by insisting on its limitations to the words and idioms that Cicero had employed. The Renaissance also paid careful attention to Cicero the thinker. His works

contributed substantially to the late 16th-cent. revival of *Stoicism and Scepticism. Cicero stood behind *Hume's systematic doubt as he stood behind the half-hearted republicanism that led up to the French revolution.

Cid, The (c.1030–99), the favourite hero of Spain in whose story history and myth are difficult to disentangle. Rodrigo Díaz de Bivar, el Cid Campeador ('el Seyd', the lord, 'Campeador', champion), of a noble Castilian family, rose to fame by his prowess in the war between Sancho of Castile and Sancho of Navarre, and in conflicts with the Moors. Having incurred the jealousy of Alphonso, king of Castile, he was banished and became a soldier of fortune, fighting at times for the Christians, at others for the Moors. His principal feat was the capture of Valencia from the Moors after a siege of nine months. He died of grief at the defeat of his force.

In myth his character has been glorified into a type of knightly and Christian virtue and patriotic zeal. His achievements are narrated in the *Poema del Cid* of the 12th cent. (the most important of early Spanish poems, some 3,700 irregular lines), in the Spanish Chronicle of the 13th cent., and in numerous ballads. The chronicles relating to him were translated by R. *Southey (1808). The Cid is the subject of the most famous drama of *Corneille. The Cid's horse was called Babieca, and his wife Ximena.

Cid Hamet ben Engeli, an imaginary Arabian author to whom *Cervantes attributes the story of *Don Quixote*.

Cider with Rosie, see LEE, L.

Cinderella, a fairy-tale, from the French of *Perrault, translated by Robert Samber (?1729).

The gentle Cinderella is cruelly used by her stepmother and two stepsisters, and when her household drudgery is done, sits at the corner of the hearth in the cinders, whence her name. Her stepsisters having gone to a ball, she is left crying at home. Her fairy godmother arrives, provides her with beautiful clothes, a coach made out of a pumpkin, and six horses transformed from mice, and sends her to the ball, on condition that she returns before the stroke of twelve. The prince falls in love with her. She hurries away at midnight, losing one of her tiny glass slippers (*pantoufle de verre*; perhaps *verre* should be *vair*, minever), and resumes her humble garb at the fireside. The prince has search made for her and announces that he will marry her whom the slipper fits. To the discomfiture of the stepsisters the slipper is found to fit only Cinderella, who produces the fellow to it from her pocket, and marries the prince.

*Lang, in *Perrault's Popular Tales* (1888), discusses the analogous stories which exist in the folklore of various countries. Various operas have been based on this fairy-tale, including *Rossini's La Cenerentola (1817), and it is one of the most popular subjects for Christmas pantomimes.

CINTHIO, Giambattista Giraldi (1504–73), born at Ferrara, the author of the Hecatommithi, or 'hundred tales', told after the manner of Boccaccio's *Decameron by ten ladies and gentlemen sailing to Marseilles after the sack of Rome in 1527. Some of these were incorporated by Painter in his *Palace of Pleasure, providing the plots of Shakespeare's *Othello and *Measure for Measure, and of plays by *Beaumont and *Fletcher and *Shirley. His nine tragedies and his treatise on tragedy had a decisive influence on the development of 16th–cent. drama in Italy; his first and most famous play, Orbecche (1541), showing divine retribution on the royal house of Persia, was closely modelled on *Seneca's Thyestes, and was full of Senecan blood and horrors. *Praz claims in The Flaming Heart (1958) that 'Cinthio provides the link between the Senecan tyrant and the Elizabethan villain', but P. R. Horne in The Tragedies of Giambattista Cinthio Giraldi (1962) questions this view.

Circulating Libraries, see LIBRARIES, CIRCULATING.

Circumlocution Office, the type of a government department, satirized in Dickens's *Little Dorrit.

CIRENCESTER, Richard of (d. ?1401), a monk of St Peter's, Westminster, who compiled a Speculum Historiale, AD 447–1066. See BERTRAM, C.

Citizen Comedy, an early 17th-cent. type of play, usually set in contemporary London and dealing with the common life of the middle classes. Jonson's *Bartholomew Fair and Middleton's *A Chaste Mayd in Cheap-side are examples of the genre.

Citizen of the World, The, by *Goldsmith, a collection of 119 letters purporting to be written by or to an imaginary philosophic Chinaman, Lien Chi Altangi, residing in London. They first appeared as Chinese Letters in Newbery's *Public Ledger between Jan. 1760 and Aug. 1761, and were republished under the above title in 1762.

They are a series of whimsical or satirical comments on English life and manners, with character sketches and episodes strung on a slender thread of narrative. The best-known character sketches are those of the 'Man in Black', a covert philanthropist, son of a good-hearted but feckless clergyman, which may contain hints of a self-portrait (Letters 26 and 27) and 'Beau' Tibbs, an affected nonentity who claims acquaintance with the great and whose wife, 'at once a slattern and a coquette', talks of countesses while she washes shirts (Letters 54 and 55).

City Heiress, The, a comedy by A. *Behn.

City Madam, The, a comedy by *Massinger, acted 1632, printed 1658.

The wife and daughters of Sir John Frugal have become proud and extravagant as a result of their wealth. When the girls drive away their suitors, Sir Maurice Lacy and Mr Plenty, by setting exorbitant conditions for marriage, Sir John decides to teach them a lesson and at the same time test the character of his brother, Luke, a ruined prodigal whom he has taken into his house where he occupies a servile position, feigning virtue and humility. The merchant pretends to retire to a monastery, handing over his property and the management of his family to Luke, who then acts with great harshness to Lady Frugal and her daughters and Sir John's debtors and apprentices. Sir John returns with Lacy and Plenty disguised as Indians, and exposes Luke's hypocrisy. He is welcomed by his family, who promise to reform their ways.

City of Destruction, in Bunyan's *Pilgrim's Progress, typifies the state of the worldly and irreligious.

'City of Dreadful Night, The', see under THOMSON, J. (1834–82).

City Witt, The, or the Woman Wears the Breeches, a comedy by *Brome, printed 1653, one of the best of Brome's comedies.

Crasy, a young citizen, has been ruined by his generous and easy-going disposition, and is cursed moreover with a virago for a mother-in-law, Mrs Pyannet Sneakup. From her he gets no mercy in his misfortune, and the friends whom he has helped in the past turn from him when he comes to them for assistance. His wife indulges her amorous proclivities as soon as he leaves her. He determines to show them all that his past good nature was not due to want of wit and, disguising himself in various characters, plays on their several vices to extort from them the money and jewels he has lent them or they have stolen from him. Aided by his servant Jeremy, who passes himself off as the rich widow Tryman, he contrives a marriage between the latter and his malignant brother-in-law, a drubbing for each of his wife's would-be lovers, and humiliation for his mother-in-law. The pedant Sarpego, with his comically apposite snatches of Latin, who refuses to repay him a loan of ten pounds, does not escape his share of punishment.

'Civil Disobedience', see THOREAU, H. D.

Civilization of the Renaissance in Italy, The, see BURCKHARDT, J.

Civil Wars between the two Houses of York and Lancaster, The, an epic poem by S. *Daniel, of which the first four books appeared in 1595. The complete work, comprising eight books, was published 1609. It contains some 900 eight-lined stanzas, of a grave and philosophic cast and marked by strong patriotism. The first book deals with the period from the Conquest to Hereford's rising against Richard II, the remaining seven with that from the Wars of the Roses to the accession of Edward IV and his marriage with Lady Elizabeth Grey.

CLAIRMONT, Claire (1798–1879), daughter of Mary Clairmont, who became William *Godwin's second wife. She accompanied Mary *Godwin, her stepsister, on Mary's elopement with *Shelley, and in spite of pursuit remained with them on the Continent, thus giving rise to many of the calumnies directed against Shelley. She returned to London with the Shelleys in 1816, fell in love with *Byron, and when he went to Switzerland induced the Shelleys to follow him with her. Byron's daughter Allegra was born to her in 1817. In 1818 Byron demanded the baby, offering to acknowledge and educate her. Strongly against her will, and against the advice of Shelley, Claire surrendered the child. Much to her distress, Byron in 1821 placed the child in a convent near Ravenna, where she died of a fever in 1822. Claire's subsequent life was spent in Russia, Italy, and Paris.

Clandestine Marriage, The, a comedy by *Colman the elder and *Garrick, performed 1766; it caused a rift between the two collaborators when Garrick refused to take the role of Lord Ogleby.

Lovewell, the clerk of Mr Sterling, a wealthy and purse-proud London merchant, has secretly married his employer's younger daughter Fanny. The father has arranged a marriage between his elder daughter and Sir John Melvil, nephew of Lord Ogleby, who accepts the alliance for mercenary reasons. Ogleby and Melvil arrive at Sterling's house to make the final arrangements, when Melvil suddenly reveals his aversion to the proposed match and his passion for the more attractive Fanny. The latter repels his advances, but hesitates to reveal her marriage. Melvil turns to Mr Sterling and induces him, for a financial consideration, to allow him to transfer his suit to Fanny. But now Mrs Heidelberg, Mr Sterling's wealthy sister (whose eccentric speech foreshadows that of Mrs *Malaprop), intervenes, resenting the affront to the family, and orders Fanny to be packed off from the house. Fanny in despair applies to the amorous old Ogleby, who, mistaking her inarticulate confession for a declaration of love for himself, announces that he himself will marry her, thereby increasing the confusion. Finally a lover is discovered in Fanny's bedroom, and the household assemble outside the door for the exposure of the villain. When he turns out to be Lovewell, Lord Ogleby

good-naturedly intervenes on behalf of the guilty couple and all ends well.

CLANVOWE, Sir John (d. 1391), possibly born in Hergyst, Hereford, and died near Constantinople, a diplomat and a member of the king's household. He was one of the Lollard Knights, and the author of the pacifist and puritanical work *The Two Ways.* He was a friend of *Chaucer, and he may also have been the author of *The Cuckoo and the Nightingale or The Boke of Cupide,* an elegant debate-poem in 290 lines which was included by *Skeat in his *Chaucerian and Other Pieces.* The manuscript ends *Explicit Clanvowe,* but this may just as well refer to Sir John's son Thomas (d. 1410). *Wordsworth translated it, and it was said in the 19th cent. to be 'one of the prettiest things in Medieval Literature'.

Ed. V. J. Scattergood, *The Works of Sir John Clanvowe* (1975) (i.e. *The Two Ways* and *The Cuckoo and the Nightingale*); K. B. McFarlane, *Lancastrian Kings and Lollard Knights* (1972), pp. 165 ff., 197 ff., 230 ff.

Clapham Sect, the name given by Sydney *Smith to a group of Evangelical and anti-slave-trade philanthropists, centred on Clapham, whose members included *Wilberforce, Zachary Macaulay (father of T. B. *Macaulay), the scholar and pamphleteer Granville Sharp, and the Thornton family, ancestors of E. M. *Forster.

Clara Douglas, the heroine of Bulwer-Lytton's comedy *Money.*

Clare, Angel, a character in Hardy's *Tess of the D'Urbervilles.*

CLARE, John (1793–1864), poet, the son of a labourer, was born in Helpstone, Northamptonshire, a neighbourhood to which he remained deeply attached, where he worked as hedge-setter and day labourer. In 1820 he published *Poems Descriptive of Rural Life and Scenery,* and in the same year married Martha Turner, having parted from his first love, Mary Joyce, a sorrow which troubled him throughout his life. His successful first volume was followed by *The Village Minstrel* (1821), *The Shepherd's Calendar* (1827), and *The Rural Muse* (1835). In 1832 he left his native cottage for Northborough, only four miles away, but the move, to one so deeply attached to place, was disturbing, and reinforced the theme of loss in his work. In 1837 he was admitted as insane to an asylum in High Beach, Epping, whence he escaped in 1841, walking home to Northamptonshire in the delusion that he would there be reunited with Mary, to whom he thought himself married. He was once more certified insane, and spent the rest of his life in Northampton General Asylum where he was allowed much freedom. The declining sales of his work may have contributed to his mental troubles, for by the 1830s the vogue for rural poetry and 'ploughman' poets such as *Burns and R. *Bloomfield was passing; and Clare's work remained little read until this century, when various new editions of his poetry, autobiographical prose, and letters made it available once more, together with much previously unpublished work. Clare is now recognized as a poet of great truth and power; his much anthologized asylum poems have perhaps tended to obscure the real nature of his gifts, and recently more attention has been paid to his highly personal evocations of landscape and place. His best poems ('Remembrances', 'The Flitting', 'Decay') demonstrate a complex sensibility and fine organization, and have been variously read as laments for lost love and talent, for the death of rural England, or for lost innocence. Unlike many poets from a similar background, he never succumbed to the taste of his patrons for artificial poetic diction (although he greatly admired James *Thomson) and insisted to his publisher John *Taylor that he would continue to write in his own language, dialect, and idiosyncratic grammar. Many poets, including E. *Blunden, G. *Grigson, and C. *Day-Lewis, have written of their admiration for his work and contributed towards his fuller recognition. His *Poems* (1935), *Prose* (1951), and *Letters* (1951) were edited by J. W. and A. Tibble; *The Shepherd's Calendar*, ed. E. Robinson and G. Summerfield, appeared in 1964; and his *Later Poems* (ed. E. Robinson and D. Powell, with M. Grainger) in 1984.

CLARENDON, Edward Hyde, earl of (1609–74), was educated at Magdalen Hall, Oxford, and later studied law. He entered Parliament in 1640 and at first sided with the popular party, but as a strong Anglican he was from 1641 onwards one of the chief supporters and advisers of the king. He followed Prince Charles into exile to Scilly and Jersey, where he began his History. At the Restoration he returned as lord chancellor and played a leading role in reorganizing the country, but fell out of favour, partly through the ill-success of the Dutch war; he was impeached in 1667 and fled to France, where he spent his last years revising and completing his history and writing his own life. He died at Rouen. His daughter Anne Hyde had in 1660 married the future James II.

The History—*The True Historical Narrative of the Rebellion and Civil Wars in England*—was first printed from a transcript under the supervision of Clarendon's son in 1702–4, but the first true text was edited by W. D. Macray (6 vols, 1888). His autobiography, *The Life of Edward, Earl of Clarendon*, appeared in 1759. The *History of the Rebellion* (as it is frequently known) is a composite work, put together from material written at different periods and in widely differing circumstances, and is uneven in accuracy

and penetration, but it remains a classic work, in part written with an eye on posterity, for publication when 'the passion, rage and fury of this time shall be forgotten'. It is also an important contribution to the art of *biography and autobiography, and memorable for its portraits of figures as varied as *Falkland, *Godolphin, *Laud, and *Strafford. Clarendon also wrote a history of the Irish rebellion, of lesser interest, published in 1721. A useful volume of *Selections from Clarendon*, ed. G. Huehns, appeared in 1955, and was reprinted with an introduction by H. Trevor-Roper in 1978.

Clarendon's works were presented to the University of Oxford by his heirs, and from the profits of the History a new printing-house, which bears his name, was built for the *Oxford University Press.

Clarendon Press, see OXFORD UNIVERSITY PRESS.

Clarion, The, a socialist weekly which ran from 1891 to 1932, founded by R. *Blatchford, his brother Montague Blatchford, A. M. Thompson, and E. F. Fay.

Clarissa: or The History of a Young Lady, an *epistolary novel by S. *Richardson, published 1748 (for 1747)–1749, in 8 vols. About one-third of the work (which is in all over a million words) consists of the letters of Clarissa and Lovelace, mainly written to Anna Howe and John Belford respectively, but there are over 20 correspondents in all, displaying many points of view and variations in style.

Lovelace, a handsome, dashing rake, is courting Arabella Harlowe, the elder sister of Clarissa. The Harlowes are an acquisitive, ambitious, 'narrow-souled' family, and when Lovelace transfers his affections to Clarissa they decide he is not good enough and that Clarissa must marry the wealthy Solmes, whom she detests. When she refuses she is locked up and humiliated. Lovelace, cleverly representing himself as her deliverer, plays on her fears, convinces her that he is forwarding her reconciliation with her family, and persuades her to escape under his protection to London. There he establishes her in a superior brothel, which she at first supposes to be respectable lodgings. She unwaveringly resists his advances and he, enraged by her intransigence, is also attracted by it and finds his love and respect for her increase. Her emotions are likewise deeply confused; she is fascinated by his charm and wit, but distrusts him and refuses his eventual proposals of marriage. In his growing insistence, Lovelace overreaches himself, interfering with her letters, deceiving her over a supposed emissary from her family, violently assaulting her, and cunningly ensnaring her after her escapes. As she unhappily but stubbornly resists, he becomes more obsessive in his determination to conquer, and makes an attempt to rape her. He claims to believe her resistance is no more than prudery and that, once subdued, she will turn to him: 'Is not *this* the hour of her trial—And in *her*, of the trial of the virtue of her whole Sex, so long premeditated, so long threatened?—Whether her frost be frost indeed? Whether her virtue be principle?' (Vol. 5, Letter 31). To Clarissa chastity represents identity, and the climax of her tragedy comes when Lovelace, abetted by the women of the house, drugs and rapes her, an event he reports in one of the shortest letters of the work: 'And now, Belford, I can go no farther. The affair is over. Clarissa lives.' (Vol. 5, Letter 32.)

Slowly Clarissa loses grip of her reason, and Lovelace realizes that he has lost the very dominance he had hoped to establish. Cut off from family, friends, and even correspondence, Clarissa eventually escapes, only to find herself trapped in a debtor's prison. She is rescued by Belford, who looks after her with affectionate care. Lovelace is overwhelmed by remorse. Clarissa recovers her sanity, but almost ceases to write, and her long decline and Christian preparation for death are reported largely in letters by Belford. After her death her cousin, Colonel Morden, kills Lovelace in a duel. Because of its great length, the novel has been more admired than read, but it has always been held in high critical esteem; the characters of the protagonists are developed with great subtlety, and the irresoluble nature of their conflict takes on an emblematic and tragic quality unique for its author and its period.

CLARK, Lord Kenneth Mackenzie (1903–83), author, art historian, and public official. The only child of wealthy and neglectful parents, he was educated at Winchester (where he aspired to be an artist) and at Oxford, where he turned to art history. His first book, *The Gothic Revival* (1928), was hailed as original and audacious; his approach, derived from *Ruskin and also from *Berenson (with whom he studied), was interpretative rather than pedantic. He was director of the National Gallery from 1934 to 1945, and held many other public posts in later life. Other publications include a study of *Leonardo da Vinci (1939), *Landscape into Art* (1949), and his major work, *The Nude: A Study of Ideal Art* (1953); also two volumes of autobiography, *Another Part of the Wood* (1974) and *The Other Half* (1977). His television series *Civilization*, published in book form in 1969, was popular with a very large audience.

CLARKE, Arthur C(harles) (1917–), prolific and popular writer of *Science Fiction, whose great technical expertise in the realm of aeronautics and astronautics is manifested both in his fiction, which includes *Childhood's End* (1953), *The City and the Stars* (1956), *The Nine Billion Names of God* (1967), and *2001: A space*

odyssey (1968), and in his many non-fiction works on space travel.

CLARKE, Austin (1896–1974), Irish poet and verse dramatist, born in Dublin, and educated at the Jesuit Belvedere College and University College, Dublin (in the footsteps of *Joyce). He worked for some 15 years in England as journalist and book reviewer, returning to Dublin in 1937. He published some 18 volumes of poetry, from his first, *The Vengeance of Fionn* (1917, a narrative poem based on the story of Diarmid and *Grainne), to his *Collected Poems* of 1974. His early work is much influenced by *Yeats and the *Celtic Twilight, but much of his later work is sharply satiric and highly critical of his own nation's attitudes; in form it is subtle and complex, with an unobtrusive technical expertise. Clarke was also greatly interested in verse drama; he founded the Dublin Verse-Speaking Society in 1938, which developed into the Lyric Theatre Company and performed many of his own plays as well as those of *Bottomley, T. S. *Eliot, and others. Clarke's plays are rooted in medieval Irish legend, but many have pantomime or farcical elements; he considered that the tradition of verse drama at the *Abbey Theatre had suffered through too much solemnity. His *Collected Plays* were published in 1963. He also wrote three prose romances, various works on Irish literature, and two autobiographical volumes, *Twice round the Black Church* (1962) and *A Penny in the Clouds* (1968).

CLARKE, Charles Cowden- (1787–1877), the son of *Keats's enlightened schoolmaster, and a close friend of the poet. Keats's 'Epistle to Charles Cowden-Clarke' is full of affection and gratitude. Cowden-Clarke lectured frequently between 1834 and 1856 on Shakespeare and general literature, and many of his lectures were published. With his wife, Mary Victoria Cowden-Clarke (below), he produced editions of Shakespeare, G. *Herbert, and other poets. Also with his wife he wrote *Recollections of Writers* (1878), a lively and valuable collection of reminiscences of their close friends Keats, *Lamb, Mary *Lamb, Leigh *Hunt, Douglas *Jerrold, and *Dickens.

CLARKE, Marcus Andrew Hislop (1846–81), emigrated to Australia in 1863. He spent four years on a sheep station in Victoria before settling as a journalist in Melbourne writing critical columns for most of the leading journals. He is remembered for his celebrated novel *For the Term of his Natural Life* (1874), a powerful and sympathetic portrayal of an Australian penal settlement, and his shorter stories of Australian life. Plagued by financial worries during his short life, he devoted most of his talents to writing plays and pantomimes.

CLARKE, Mary Victoria Cowden- (1809–98), was the joint author, with her husband Charles Cowden-Clarke (above), of *Recollections of Writers*, and the author of the excellent *Complete Concordance to Shakespeare*, published in monthly parts in 1844–5.

CLARKE, Samuel (1675–1729), educated at Caius College, Cambridge, metaphysician, moralist, and a defender of rational theology; although a critic of the *Deists, he had sympathy with some of their teaching. He believed that there exists in the nature of things, an immutable agreement or harmony of certain things and circumstances, apparent to the understanding. Clarke's principal works were his *Boyle lectures delivered in 1704 and 1705, published 1705–6, *A Demonstration of the Being and Attributes of God* and *A Discourse concerning the Unchangeable Obligation of Natural Religion*.

CLARKSON, Laurence (1615–67), a pamphleteer whose spiritual autobiography *The Lost Sheep Found* (1660) charts his progress through many religious affiliations; from his Church of England boyhood in Lancashire he became Anabaptist, Seeker, Ranter, and finally *Muggletonian, suffering imprisonment for his views. His tracts, written with originality, force, and feeling, shed an interesting light on the adventurous and speculative ideas of the age: in *A Single Eye All Light, No Darkness*, he argued that all things, even sin, are from God: 'What act soever is done by thee in light and love, is light and lovely, though it be that act called adultery' (1650).

Classicism, Classic, are terms used in several different and at times overlapping senses. A 'literary classic' is a work considered first-rate or excellent of its kind, and therefore standard, fit to be used as a model or imitated; a series such as the *World's Classics includes work from many different genres, including poetry, fiction, autobiography, biography, letters, and history. More narrowly, 'classicism' may be taken to denote the deliberate imitation of the works of antiquity, and in this sense is often qualified as *'Neo-classicism', which flourished in England in the late 17th and 18th cents. An elaboration of this concept leads to a distinction between Classicism and *Romanticism; the Romantic movement, which dominated the early 19th cent., and which saw itself in part as a revolt against Classicism, led in turn to a reaction at the beginning of the 20th cent. from writers such as T. S. *Eliot and T. E. *Hulme, whose concern was to stress man's limitations rather than his perfectibility and illimitable aspirations, and who emphasized the virtues of formal restraint in literature rather than the virtues of inspiration and exuberance.

The shades of meaning which the terms have acquired lead at times to apparent confusion: when one speaks of the drama of *Racine and *Corneille as 'classical', and the drama of *Shakespeare or *Hugo as 'romantic', one is not depriving Shakespeare or Hugo of classic status, nor suggesting that Shakespeare himself had any sense of such a contrast; whereas Hugo wrote as a conscious rebel against classicism. *Auden and Dylan *Thomas, near-contemporaries, are frequently described as exemplars of, respectively, the classical and the romantic in modern poetry, and both are widely considered classics of their own period and aesthetic approach. The use of the phrase 'a minor classic', raises yet more problems of definition, indicating the adaptability rather than the precision of the term.

CLAUDEL, Paul (1868–1955), French poet and dramatist. He spent 40 years abroad as a diplomat, mostly in the United States, South America, and the Far East. Converted to Catholicism in 1886, he expressed a passionate and dogmatic personality in a form of versification he made uniquely his own: the long magniloquent phrases of the so-called *verset claudélien* which he forged out of the prose of *Rimbaud's *Les Illuminations* and the Old Testament. His major plays, *L'Annonce faite à Marie* (1912) and *Le Soulier de Satin* (1928–9), and poems, *Cinq grandes Odes* (1910) and *La Cantate à troix voix* (1913), exerted a strong influence on the following generation of poets, notably Pierre-Jean Jouve, but left very little mark on English writing.

CLAUDE LORRAIN (1600–82), landscape painter from Lorrain, who worked mainly in Rome. He was the first artist to be inspired by the beauty of the Roman Campagna, and the myths and legends associated with it. In the 18th cent. the English traveller on the *Grand Tour, newly alive to the beauty of the Alps and of Italy, was deeply moved by Claude's idyllic landscapes and his nostalgic vision of lost splendour; many of his pictures and engravings after them were brought to England. Here they influenced the way both artists and writers looked at all kinds of natural beauty. By the 1720s poets like James *Thomson and J. *Dyer, frequently invoke Claude's name to suggest a Virgilian serenity that contrasts with the wildness of *Rosa's landscapes; in 1748 Thomson wrote in *The Castle of Indolence*, 'What'er Lorrain light touched with softening hue | Or savage Rosa dashed, or learned Poussin drew'. Landscape gardeners emulated Claude's compositions, and they were important to the theory of the *Picturesque. From the 1760s picturesque travel became popular; enthusiasts looked at the Lake District as though it were a sequence of pictures by Claude or Salvator Rosa. Thomas *Gray carried a 'Claude glass', a blackened convex mirror which enabled the traveller to pick out an instant 'Claudian' view. Romantic poets responded more intensely to the strange, elusive beauty of Claude's late works. In 1786 Joshua *Reynolds had written that Claude conducts us 'to the tranquillity of Arcadian scenes and fairyland'. The 'fairyland' beauty of the *Enchanted Castle* (London, National Gallery) moved both *Hazlitt and *Keats, and Keats was directly inspired by it. Claude's reputation waned with *Ruskin, who saw him as a pallid precursor of the more passionate *Turner.

CLAUDIAN (Claudius Claudianus) (*fl. c.* AD 395–404), the last great Latin poet to be a pagan was born in Alexandria and wrote in Rome. His short epic *De raptu Proserpinae* influenced Spenser's account of the garden of Proserpina (*Faerie Queene*, II. vii. 52) and was translated by Leonard Digges (1607). One of his shorter works, the idyll on the 'Old Man of Verona' was translated by *Cowley.

Claudio, (1) the lover of Hero in Shakespeare's *Much Ado about Nothing*; (2) the brother of Isabella and betrothed husband of Julietta in his *Measure for Measure*; best remembered for his speech on the fear of death beginning, 'Ay, but to die, and go we know not where' (III. i).

Claudius, in Shakespeare's *Hamlet*, brother of old Hamlet and husband of his widow *Gertrude. Shakespeare may have taken his name from the incestuous Roman Emperor Claudius.

CLAVELL, John (1603–42), was a highwayman, condemned to death and then pardoned (1627). He published a metrical autobiography, *Recantation of an ill led Life* (1628), which begins 'Stand and Deliver to your observation | Right serious thoughts', and proceeds to describe the highway law and organization of thieves. *The Soddered Citizen*, a comedy of which he was reputed author, was performed by the King's Men *c.*1630.

CLAVERHOUSE, Graham of, see GRAHAM OF CLAVERHOUSE.

Clavering, Sir Francis and Lady, characters in Thackeray's *Pendennis*.

Claverings, The, a novel by A. *Trollope, published 1867.
   Harry Clavering is a gentleman–engineer who becomes engaged to his master's daughter, steady Florence Burton. Julia Brabazon, an old flame, returns to London newly widowed after marrying the dissipated Lord Ongar for money. Harry is called in to protect her from the machinations of the sycophantic Sophie Gordeloup and the scheming Count Pateroff, and Lady Ongar offers to renew their old engagement, but Harry remains true to Florence. He gets his reward when his rich relations go to their fate in a fishing accident in the North Sea, and he becomes heir to the Clavering fortunes.

Clayhanger, see BENNETT, ARNOLD.

Claypole, Noah, in Dickens's *Oliver Twist*, a fellow apprentice of the hero in the establishment of Mr Sowerberry, the undertaker, and subsequently one of Fagin's gang of thieves.

Cleanness (or *Purity*), an alliterative poem in 1,812 lines from the second half of the 14th cent., the only manuscript of which is the famous Cotton Nero A x which is also the sole manuscript of *Pearl, *Patience, and Sir *Gawain and the Green Knight*. It deals with three subjects from the Scriptures and is hardly more than a vigorous paraphrase of them: the Flood, the destruction of Sodom and Gomorrah, and the fall of Belshazzar. It has some passages of great power, such as the denunciation of Sodom and the description of the destruction of Babylon. Modern critical practice usually treats the four poems in the manuscript as the work of a single author, regarding *Cleanness* as the earliest on grounds of quality (*Pearl* comes first in the manuscript). There is an edition by J. J. Anderson (1977).

Cleishbotham, Jedediah, schoolmaster and parish clerk of Gandercleugh, who, by a fiction of Sir W. Scott, sold to publishers the *Tales of My Landlord*. These were supposed to have been composed by his assistant schoolmaster Peter Pattieson from the stories told by the landlord of the Wallace Inn at Gandercleugh. (See introduction to *The Black Dwarf*.)

CLELAND, John (1709–89), was educated at Westminster School, became consul in Smyrna, worked in the East India Company in Bombay, and spent much time in wandering and travel. Although *Memoirs of a Woman of Pleasure* (often known as *Fanny Hill*), published 1748–9, had an enormous sale, and brought his publisher £10,000, it brought him only 20 guineas. He was summoned before the Privy Council for indecency, but discharged. In 1751 he published the *Memoirs of a Coxcomb*, and in 1764 *The Surprises of Love*. He wrote various plays, engaged in much journalistic work, and between 1766 and 1769 published three philological studies, with special references to Celtic.

CLEMENS, S. L., see TWAIN, M.

Clementine Vulgate, see VULGATE.

CLEMENT OF ALEXANDRIA (b. *c.* AD 160), a Greek Father of the Church, born in Alexandria, and the first to apply Greek culture and philosophy to the exposition of Christianity. Of his four surviving works, the *Exhortation to the Greeks* is an attempt to convert the Greeks to Christianity, influenced by the Platonist Christian exegete Philo. See R. B. Tollinton, *Clement of Alexandria. A Study in Christian Liberalism* (2 vols, 1914).

Clennam, Arthur and Mrs, characters in Dickens's *Little Dorrit.*

CLEMO, Jack (Reginald John) (1916–), poet, born at St Austell, Cornwall, the son of a clay-worker. From childhood he suffered from poor eyesight and, subsequently, deafness, eventually becoming completely blind. He published a novel, *Wilding Graft* (1948), an autobiography, *Confession of Rebel* (1949), and several volumes of poetry, including *The Clay Verge* (1951) and *The Echoing Tip* (1971), which evoke with a kind of visionary grimness the tormented landscapes of the clay pits, and express his own Calvinist faith.

Cleon, (1) governor of Tarsus in Shakespeare's *Pericles*; (2) title of a poem by R. Browning, included in *Men and Women.*

Cleopatra, a tragedy in blank verse by S. *Daniel, published 1594.

It is on the Senecan model, and deals with the story of Cleopatra after the death of Antony. Octavius Caesar endeavours to persuade her to leave the monument that she had caused to be built, in order that he may have her to grace his triumph. Feigning to yield, she asks permission first to sacrifice to the ghost of Antonius. After the performance of the rites she dines with great magnificence, and by her order a basket of figs is brought her which contains an asp. With this she does herself to death. Her son Caesarion about the same time is murdered at Rhodes and the race of the Ptolemies becomes extinct.

Clerihew, an epigrammatic verse-form invented by Edmund Clerihew *Bentley, consisting of two rhymed couplets, usually dealing with the character or career of a well-known person, e.g.

> Sir James Jeans
> Always says what he means;
> He is really perfectly serious
> About the Universe being Mysterious.

'Clerk's Tale, The', see CANTERBURY TALES, 9.

Cleveland, Captain Clement, a character in Scott's *The Pirate.*

CLEVELAND, John (1613–58), *Cavalier poet, was born in Loughborough, the son of a clergyman, and educated at Cambridge, but joined the king's camp in Oxford during the civil war as an active royalist; he wrote there one of his best-known satires 'The Rebel Scot', which contains the couplet commended by Dr *Johnson, 'Had Cain been Scot, God would have changed his doom | Not forced him wander, but confined him home.' Although criticized during his life as an academic and coterie poet, his works were highly popular, and 25 editions (none, apparently, with his supervision) appeared between 1647 and 1700.

*Dryden's opinion of him as one 'who gives us common thoughts in abstruse words' eventually prevailed, but the 20th-cent. revival of interest in the *Metaphysicals and in political satire has led to more serious consideration. An edition by B. Morris and E. Withington appeared in 1967.

Cliché, French, 'a stereotype block', a stock expression which by constant use has become hackneyed and lost its sharp edge.

CLIFFORD, Lord, The Shepherd, see SHEPHERD, LORD CLIFFORD, THE.

CLIFFORD, Martin, see HAMILTON, C.

CLIVE, Mrs Caroline Archer (1801–73), wrote chiefly under the initial 'V'. She was lame from an early age and the consequent privations of her infirmity were often reflected in her verse. Her first volume of poems, *IX Poems by V* (1840), attracted high praise, but her reputation rests on her powerful novel *Paul Ferroll* (1855); the hero murders his wife who had prevented him from marrying the woman he loved, escapes suspicion, and marries his true love, who, after 18 years of happy marriage, dies of shock when Paul Ferroll voluntarily confesses his crime in order to save innocent suspects. By substituting villain for hero, *Paul Ferroll* was a forerunner of the purely sensational novel (see SENSATION, NOVEL OF). *Why Paul Ferroll killed his Wife* (1860) was less successful. Mrs Clive was accidentally burned to death while writing in her boudoir.

CLIVE, Kitty (Catherine) (1711–85), the celebrated comic actress, renowned for her red face and vulgar good nature, was a close friend of Horace *Walpole, and his neighbour at *Strawberry Hill, where he gave her for life a small house called Little Strawberry Hill, later known as Cliveden.

CLIVE, Robert, Baron Clive of Plassey (1725–74), who avenged the tragedy of the Black Hole of Calcutta in 1757 at the victory of Plassey, was later governor of Bengal, a position from which he resigned in 1767. His conduct in India was subjected in 1772–3 to a parliamentary inquiry which resulted substantially in his favour. He died by his own hand, though perhaps intentionally.

Clockmaker, The, see HALIBURTON, T. C.

Cloddipole, one of the rustics in Gay's *The Shepherd's Week.*

Cloister and the Hearth, The, a novel by C. *Reade, published 1861.

The story is set in the 15th cent. Gerard, the son of a mercer living in Tergou in Holland, is destined to enter the Church, but falls in love with Margaret Brandt, whose father is an impoverished scholar suspected of sorcery. They become betrothed, but the burgomaster Ghysbrecht, together with Gerard's scheming brothers and his outraged father, prevent the marriage and succeed in having the young man imprisoned. He contrives to escape and finds Margaret, but he is relentlessly pursued and has to leave Holland. He travels through Germany and Burgundy to Italy, encountering many dangers and hardships and meeting all conditions of men, from bishop to beggar, in palace, monastery, road, and tavern: the richness and complexity of detail is intended to assist the sense of 'reality' sought by the author. While he is in Italy Gerard hears of Margaret's death; not realizing the news is a trick, he throws himself in despair into a world of gambling, drinking, and women. Margaret meanwhile has borne his son and lives in wretchedness at his loss. Eventually sickened by his life, Gerard renounces the world, takes his vows as a Dominican monk, and in the guise of Father Clement travels slowly back to Holland. He is overjoyed to find Margaret alive, but agonized at his predicament, for his love for her is as strong as ever. Because of his son he allows himself to return to her and becomes accepted as the vicar of Gouda. The pain of his struggles to remain true to his vows slowly subsides, and he and Margaret achieve a peace in which passion is subsumed in the love of God. However, when she is dying, both confess to each other the strength of their human love. Their son, the end of the story indicates, is the future philosopher *Erasmus.

The novel was based on Reade's short story 'A Good Fight' (published in *Once a Week* in 1859), in which the fight refers to the struggle against sexual feeling, a theme common in Reade's work. The novel arose from his discovery, in 'a musty chronicle' (the *Colloquia* and the letters of Erasmus), of the story of Erasmus's father, an obscure cleric.

Clorin, in *The Faithful Shepherdess* by J. Fletcher.

Clorinda, in Tasso's *Jerusalem Delivered*, a leader of the pagan forces, the daughter of the king of Ethiopia, who had been lost as a baby in the forest and suckled by a tigress. Tancred, who has fallen in love with her, wounds her fatally and unwittingly in a night attack, and she pleads for baptism before dying in his arms.

Cloten, the clownish son of the queen in Shakespeare's *Cymbeline*.

Cloud-cuckoo-land (Nephelococcygia), an imaginary city built in the air in *The Birds* of *Aristophanes.

Cloud of Unknowing, The, a mystical prose work, probably from the North-East Midlands, dating from the second half of the 14th cent., and one of the most admired products of the Middle English mystical tradition. Its popularity is indicated by its survival in 17 manuscripts;

the author was presumably a priest, though no more certain identification of him has resulted from the many recent speculations about him. He also wrote *The Book of Privy Counselling*, *The Epistle of Prayer*, and *Denis Hid Divinity*, in the opinion of most commentators; it is likely that three other works linked with the *Cloud* in the various manuscripts are by him too: *Benjamin Minor*, *The Epistle of Discretion in Stirrings*, and *Of Discerning of Spirits*. None of the other works or translations has the same life or cogency in argument of the *Cloud* itself. Ed. P. Hodgson (EETS 218, 1944; rev. 1958); trans. C. Wolters (1961).

CLOUGH, Arthur Hugh (1819–61), son of a Liverpool cotton merchant, was a pupil at T. *Arnold's Rugby, and a scholar at Balliol College, Oxford. He took a second and told Dr Arnold in June 1841 'I have failed.' He became a fellow of Oriel, but resigned; he became principal of University Hall, London, then an examiner in the Education Office. His career was inconclusive, and he was tormented by doubt when the Rugby indoctrination was challenged by the religious ferment of Oxford. Yet out of religious doubt and minutely-analysed uncertainties Clough wrote lasting poetry, and *Gosse called his 'the sympathetic modern accent'. He died in Florence, and M. Arnold's *'Thyrsis' was written to commemorate his death.

The Bothie of Tober-na-Vuolich (1848) originally published as *The Bothie of Toper-na-fuosich*, is a poem in hexameters about a student reading party in Scotland. Philip falls in love with Elspie, a peasant who represents 'work, mother earth, and the objects of living'. There is no place for them in English society, so 'they rounded the globe to New Zealand'. M. Arnold said the poem had 'freshness, life, naturalness . . . the true Homeric ring'.

'Amours de Voyage' (first published in the *Atlantic Monthly*, 1858) is similar in form, but *epistolary. Claude, travelling in Rome at the time of the siege, is paralysed by 'terrible notions of duty', unable to form political commitment or to respond to Rome, which he finds 'rubbishy'. (Of St Peter's, 'Alas, Bernini has filled it with sculpture.') He cannot follow his impulse to court Mary, whose mother 'grates the fastidious ear with a slightly mercantile accent'. Clough wrote in a letter, 'Poetry should deal more than at present it usually does with general wants and ordinary feelings.'

Clough is also remembered for 'Dipsychus' (published posthumously, 1865), a Faustian dialogue set in Venice in which the tempting spirit describes the protagonist as 'An o'ergrown baby, sucking at the dugs | Of instinct dry long since'. The best-known of his shorter poems, sharply contrasted, are 'Say not the struggle nought availeth' and the satirical 'The Latest Decalogue', both published posthumously in *Poems, 1862*, with a Memoir by F. T. *Palgrave.

Club, The (sometimes known later as the Literary Club), was an informal group founded by Dr *Johnson at the suggestion of Joshua *Reynolds in the winter of 1763–4. It met at the Turk's Head, Soho, and the nine original members included *Goldsmith and *Burke; those elected later included *Percy (elected 1765), *Garrick and *Boswell (1773), C. J. *Fox and *Steevens (1774), Adam *Smith (1775), *Banks (1778), and *Malone (1782).

Clumsy, Sir Tunbelly, a character in Vanbrugh's *The Relapse* and Sheridan's *A Trip to Scarborough*.

Clutterbuck, Captain Cuthbert, a fictitious personage supposed to be concerned with the publication of some of Sir W. Scott's novels, e.g. *The Monastery*.

Clym of the Clough, see ADAM BELL.

CNUT, CNUTR, see CANUTE.

Coart, Couwaert, or Cuwaert, the name of the hare in *Reynard the Fox*.

Coavinses, in Dickens's *Bleak House*, see NECKETT.

COBB, Richard Charles (1917–), historian and author, educated at Merton College, Oxford, became professor of modern history at Oxford in 1973. Most of his works deal with French history and sociology and provide an evocative, eclectic portrayal of French life and culture; they include *Reactions to the French Revolution* (1972), *Death in Paris 1795–1801* (1978), and *Promenades* (1980). *Still Life* (1983) is a memoir of his childhood in Tunbridge Wells.

COBBE, Frances Power (1822–1908), philanthropist and author of works mainly on religious and social questions. She was a strong theist, supporter of women's rights, a prominent anti–vivisectionist, and became associated with Mary Carpenter in her ragged school and reformatory work. Her numerous writings include *The Theory of Intuitive Morals* (1855–7), *Broken Lights* (1864), *Darwinism in Morals* (1872), and *The Duties of Women* (1881). Her travels in Italy and the East are described in *Italics* (1864) and *Cities of the Past* (1864). Her autobiography appeared in 1904.

COBBETT, William (1763–1835), the son of a farmer near Farnham, and self-educated, enlisted as a soldier and served in New Brunswick from 1784 to 1791. He obtained his discharge, brought an accusation of peculation against some of his former officers, and in 1792 retired, first to France then to America, to avoid prosecution. There he published in 1796 *The Life and Adventures of Peter Porcupine*, a pro-

vocatively pro-British work, and in 1801 his *Works*, critical of America. He returned to England in 1800, and became an anti-Radical journalist, founding and writing *Cobbett's *Political Register* from 1802. Soon, however, as a result of what he observed, his views began to change, and from about 1804 he wrote more and more positively in the Radical interest, suffering two years' imprisonment for his attack on flogging in the army. He published *Parliamentary Debates*, afterwards taken over by *Hansard, and *State Trials*; wrote an entertaining English grammar (1817); and a number of books on economic subjects. At the same time he was farming in Hampshire and later in Surrey. From 1817 to 1819 he was again in America. The reflections assembled in 1830 as *Rural Rides* began to appear in the *Political Register* from 1821. His *History of the Protestant "Reformation" in England and Ireland* appeared in 1824; his *Advice to Young Men* in 1829. He became MP for Oldham in 1832. Throughout his life he was an avid reader and a prolific writer. He wrote with perspicuity and vigour, in a prose style commended by *Hazlitt as 'plain, broad, downright English', and he produces without artifice (particularly in *Rural Rides*) an engaging and idiosyncratic portrait of himself. There are biographies by G. D. H. *Cole (1924) and G. Spater (1982).

COBDEN, Richard (1804–65), son of a Sussex farmer, settled in Manchester in 1832. He was the foremost leader of the Anti-Corn Law League, and contributed powerfully to the repeal of the Corn Laws in 1846. He was an apostle of free trade and negotiated the commercial treaty with France, 1859. He was successively MP for Stockport (1841), the West Riding of Yorkshire, and Stockdale.

COCCAI, Merlin, see FOLENGO, T.

COCKBURN, Alison, *née* Rutherford (*c.* 1712– 94), Scots poet and song-writer, whose lively soirées brought together most of the literary talent of 18th-cent. Edinburgh. She was friendly with *Hume, was admired by *Burns, and was on close terms with the family of Sir W. *Scott, to whom she was distantly related. She wrote one of the well known versions of 'The Flowers of the Forest'. (See also ELLIOT, J.)

COCKBURN, Catharine, *née* Trotter (1679– 1749), had her first tragedy, *Agnes de Castro*, performed at the Theatre Royal, Drury Lane, when she was 15 and published a year later. She made the acquaintance of *Congreve, and wrote four other stage works and occasional poetry. She developed an interest in philosophy and published several works in explication and defence of the writings of *Locke, both during and after Locke's life. In later life she wrote on moral philosophy and in defence of S. *Clarke.

COCKBURN, Henry Thomas, Lord Cockburn (1779–1854), was educated in Edinburgh. He shared with *Jeffrey the leadership of the Scottish bar for many years. His *Memorials of his Times* (1856) gives a vivid account of literary circles in Edinburgh, and includes descriptions of *Brougham, Jeffrey, John *Wilson, Sydney *Smith, and the founding of the *Edinburgh Review*. His *Life of Jeffrey* was published in 1852.

Cocke Lorells Bote, a popular verse satire of the early 16th cent. in which types of the various tradesfolk take ship and sail through England. The captain of the 'Bote' is Cocke Lorell, a tinker and probably a historical personage. It is an interesting picture of low life.

Cockney School, a term apparently first used in *Blackwood's Magazine* in Oct. 1817, when *Lockhart and his associates began a series of attacks 'On the Cockney School of Poetry'. Leigh *Hunt was the chief target, but *Hazlitt and *Keats were also objects of frequent derision. The Londoners, all of humble origin, were contrasted with the great writers, all of whom 'have been men of some rank', and Hunt was particularly singled out for his 'low birth and low habits'. The virulence of the attacks, which described the writers as 'the vilest vermin' and of 'extreme moral depravity', was sustained over several years, and included the cruel and famous passages on Keats's *Endymion* in 1818. After his death Keats was described as a man 'who had left a decent calling [i.e. pharmacy] for the melancholy trade of Cockney-poetry'.

Cocktail Party, The, a comedy by T. S. *Eliot.

Cock Lane Ghost, a supposed ghost to which were attributed mysterious noises heard at 33 Cock Lane, Smithfield, in 1762. They were discovered to be due to the imposture of one William Parsons and his daughter. Dr *Johnson took part in the investigation of the mystery, and wrote a brief 'Account of the Detection of the Imposture in Cock-Lane', published in *The Gentleman's Magazine* (Feb. 1762). Charles *Churchill seized the opportunity to attack him in his satire *The Ghost* (1762) for credulity, and, more woundingly, for his long delays in producing his edition of Shakespeare.

Cocoa-tree Club, in St James's Street, originally a chocolate house of the same name dating from the early 18th cent. After being a Tory centre and subsequently, in 1745, a resort of the Jacobite party, it became a fashionable club where, as Horace *Walpole's letters attest, there was gambling for high stakes. 'At the Cocoa-tree Lord Stavordale, not one-and-twenty, lost eleven thousand last Tuesday, but recovered it by one great hand at hazard' (1770).

COCTEAU, Jean (1889–1963), French poet, novelist, dramatist, film director, and critic. He was prominently associated with *modernism in literature, art, music, ballet, and the cinema, collaborating with many of the leading figures in Europe, such as Diaghilev, *Picasso, and *Stravinsky. He produced numerous volumes of poetry; novels, including *Le Grand Écart* (1923, English trans. *The Grand Ecart*, 1925) and *Les Enfants terribles* (1929, English trans. 1930, and, as *Children of the Game*, 1955); several sketches for ballets, including *Parade* (1917); films, such as *La Belle et la bête* (1945); and plays, including *Orphée* (1926, English trans. 1933) and *La Machine infernale* (1934, *The Infernal Machine*, 1936), a reworking of the Oedipus myth.

Codex, a manuscript volume e.g. of one of the ancient manuscripts of the Scriptures, or of the ancient classics [OED]. See entries under AMIATINUS CODEX and BIBLE (*Codex Bezae, Codex Vaticanus, Codex Alexandrinus*, etc.).

Codlin and Short, in Dickens's *The Old Curiosity Shop*, travel about the country with a Punch and Judy show. Thomas Codlin is a surly misanthrope; Short (real name Harris familiarly known as 'Short Trotters') is a cheerful little man.

CODRINGTON, Christopher (1668–1710), born in Barbados, and educated at Christ Church, Oxford, became captain-general of the Leeward Islands in 1697. He spent the last years of his life in study on his Barbados estates, which he bequeathed to the Society for the Propagation of the Gospel, for the foundation of a college in Barbados. He also left his books and £10,000 to All Souls College, Oxford, a bequest out of which was founded the Godrington Library.

Coel (King Cole of the nursery rhyme) was duke of Colchester who, according to *Geoffrey of Monmouth's *History* (v. 6), became king of Britain for a short time. He was succeeded by the Roman Constantius who married Coel's daughter Helen, thus transferring the kingship into Roman hands. See *Chesterton's parodies in 'Variations on an Air Composed on Having to Appear in a Pageant as Old King Cole', in *New Poems* (1932).

Coelebs in Search of a Wife, a novel by H. *More, published 1809. The book, which was immensely successful, consists of a collection of sharp social sketches and moral precepts, strung together by the hero's search for a wife, who must possess the qualities stipulated by his departed parents.

Coffee Houses were first introduced in the time of the Commonwealth; the first recorded in England was in Oxford in 1650 (mentioned by A. *Wood), and the first in London was in 1652, in St Michael's Alley, off Cornhill, at the Sign of Pasqua Rosee. They were much frequented in the 17th and 18th cents for political and literary discussions, circulation of news, etc. Their decline during the 18th cent. has been in part attributed to the increasing popularity of clubs (see CLUB, THE, BROTHERS CLUB, KIT-CAT CLUB, COCOA-TREE CLUB). There is an interesting description of coffee houses in *Macaulay's History of England, ch. III. See also Aytoun Ellis, The Penny Universities (1956) and B. Lillywhite, London Coffee Houses (1963). For individual coffee houses see BEDFORD, BUTTON'S, DON SALTERO'S, GARRAWAY'S, GRECIAN, JONATHAN'S, SLAUGHTER'S, TOM'S, WHITE'S, WILL'S.

COKE, Sir Edward (1552–1634), educated at Norwich and Trinity College, Cambridge, and a barrister of the Inner Temple, was advanced by Burghley's influence to be attorney-general, to the disappointment of F. *Bacon, whose lifelong rival he was. He became chief justice of the Common Pleas in 1606 and of the King's Bench in 1613. Here he quarrelled incessantly with the Court of Chancery and was dismissed by the king in 1616. Gardiner calls his dismissal a 'turning point' in the relations of king and Parliament. Coke's fame as a legal author rests on his eleven volumes of Reports (1600–15), and his Institutes (1628–44) in which he recast, explained, and defended the common law rules.

COKE, Lady Mary (1726–1811), a daughter of John, duke of Argyll, the reluctant wife of Edward, viscount Coke. An eccentric and striking woman, she was a friend of Horace *Walpole, who accompanied the second edition of his *The Castle of Otranto with a sonnet addressed to her. Her entertaining Letters and Journals were privately printed (1889–96).

Cokes, Bartholomew, the simpleton in Jonson's *Bartholomew Fair, 'an esquire of Harrow'.

'Colbeck, The Dancers of', see HANDLYNG SYNNE.

Colbrand, see GUY OF WARWICK.

COLBURN, Henry (d. 1855), a very successful publisher who founded the *New Monthly Magazine in 1814 and the *Literary Gazette in 1817, and who published the fashionable and profitable novels of Lady *Morgan and T. *Hook. He was the first to publish *Evelyn's Diary, in 1818, and *Pepys's newly-deciphered Diaries in 1825. In 1830 he went into partnership with Richard *Bentley and together they published a successful series of Standard Novelists (1835–41). He died a very rich man.

Cold Comfort Farm, the first novel of Stella Gibbons (1902–   ), a witty and highly successful parody of the earthy primitive school of regional fiction popular at the beginning of the century (by e.g. Sheila Kaye-Smith, 1887–1956; M. *Webb; and D. H. *Lawrence).

Flora Poste visits her relatives the Starkadders

in Sussex, and finds herself in a household of seething emotion, gloom, and rural intrigue, which she proceeds to reform. The descriptive 'purple passages' common to the genre are obligingly marked with asterisks by the author, after the method 'perfected by the late Herr *Baedeker'.

Cole, King, see COEL.

COLE, G(eorge) D(ouglas) H(oward) (1889–1959), Fabian economist, was converted to Socialism after reading W. *Morris's News from Nowhere. Educated at St Paul's School and Balliol College, he subsequently held important academic posts at Oxford. He became prominent immediately before the First World War as a leading exponent of guild socialism (as opposed to the bureaucratic socialism of B. and S. *Webb), and published in 1913 his first major work, The World of Labour. During the 1930s he was acknowledged as the most prolific writer on the intellectual history of British Socialism in articles in the *New Statesman and in his works, which included A History of Socialist Thought (1953–8). He was married to Margaret Postgate (sister of Raymond Postgate) with whom he collaborated in detective fiction.

COLENSO, John William (1814–83), a mathematician who became bishop of Natal, where he pioneered the writing of Zulu. He was denounced for his strong views on Zulu polygamy in relation to Christian conversion and for applying the Christian ethic to the problem of race relations in southern Africa. In 1861 he issued his commentary St Paul's Epistle to the Romans, which aroused a storm of controversy by its repudiation of much orthodox sacramental theology and its denial of everlasting punishment; further protest was aroused by his The Pentateuch and the Book of Joshua Critically Examined (1862–79) which challenged the traditional historical accuracy and authorship of these books. In 1863 he was deposed by Bishop Gray of Capetown, but Colenso denied his jurisdiction and, by a series of judicial decisions, secured possession of the see.

COLERIDGE, Hartley (1796–1849), the unworldly eldest son of S. T. *Coleridge, who inherited many of his father's gifts, including verbal eloquence, but achieved little, losing his Oxford fellowship for intemperance and failing as a schoolmaster. In 1833 he published Poems, Songs and Sonnets (the sonnets of which were much praised), and in the same year his unfinished Biographia Borealis, retitled Worthies of Yorkshire and Lancashire in 1836. He contributed to *Blackwood's Magazine, the *London Magazine and other literary journals, and in 1840 published his edition, with brief biographies, of *Massinger and *Ford. His Essays and Marginalia, edited by his brother Derwent, were published posthumously in 1851. He spent his childhood and the latter part of his life in the Lake District, where he died. He is the subject of two important poems by his father, *'Frost at Midnight' and 'The Nightingale'.

COLERIDGE, Mary (1861–1907), the great-great-niece of S. T. *Coleridge, published her first volume of verse, *Fancy's Following*, with the encouragement of *Bridges in 1896, and a second, *Fancy's Guerdon*, in 1897. Two sonnets, 'True to myself am I' and 'Go in the deepest, darkest dead of night' have been much anthologized. Her first novel, an original and fantastical romance *The Seven Sleepers of Ephesus* (1893), was praised by R. L. *Stevenson but achieved little success; her second, *The King with Two Faces* (1897), a historical romance centring on Gustavus III of Sweden, was well received. She contributed extensively to various journals, such as the *Monthly Review* and the *Cornhill*. In 1900 she published *Non Sequitur*, a collection of lively and ironic essays; her unpublished remains appeared as *Gathered Leaves* in 1910.

COLERIDGE, Samuel Taylor (1772–1834), poet, critic, and philosopher of *Romanticism. Youngest son of the vicar of Ottery St Mary, Devon, he was destined for the church. A temperamental, dreamy child, he was sent away after his father's early death to Christ's Hospital school, London, where his precocious classical reading and powers of 'inspired' talk (which never left him) attracted a circle of young admirers, including Leigh *Hunt and the future essayist *Lamb. At Jesus College, Cambridge (1792–4), a brilliant career in classics was diverted by French revolutionary politics, heavy drinking, and an unhappy love-affair, which led Coleridge to enlist in desperation in the 15th Light Dragoons under the name of Comerbache. He was bought out under an 'insanity' clause by his brother, but did not take a degree.

In the summer of 1794 an undergraduate walking-tour through Oxford brought him the passionate friendship of *Southey, and together they invented *Pantisocracy, a scheme to set up a commune in New England. Coleridge now published his first poetry in the *Morning Chronicle*, a series of sonnets to eminent radicals including *Godwin and J. *Priestley. To finance Pantisocracy, he and Southey gave political lectures in Bristol and collaborated on a verse-drama, *The Fall of Robespierre* (1794); they also simultaneously courted and married two sisters, Sara and Edith Fricker. After quarrelling with Southey over money and politics, Coleridge retired with Sara to a cottage at Clevedon, where their first son Hartley (above), named after the philosopher David *Hartley, was born. Here Coleridge edited a radical Christian journal, *The Watchman*, which ran for ten issues; and published *Poems on Various Subjects* (1796),

which included the 'Monody on the Death of Chatterton' and 'The Eolian Harp'. He considered entering the Unitarian ministry and preached throughout the West Country; he also took opium in periods of sickness and depression.

In June 1779 Coleridge walked to Racedown, Dorset, where he met *Wordsworth and his sister Dorothy. The intense friendship that sprang up between the three shaped their lives for the next 14 years and proved one of the most creative partnerships in English Romanticism. It was based on a mutual love of poetry, critical discussion, and hill-walking; and an empassioned response to the political and social problems of the age. Between July 1797 and Sept. 1798 they lived and worked intimately together; the Coleridges at Nether Stowey, Somerset, and the Wordsworths two miles away at Alfoxden, on the edge of the Quantock hills, where they were visited by Lamb, *Hazlitt, and others. Here Coleridge wrote a moving series of blank verse 'conversation' poems, addressed to his friends: 'Fears in Solitude', 'This Lime Tree Bower My Prison', 'The Nightingale', and *'Frost at Midnight'. He also composed his celebrated opium-vision, *'Kubla Khan'. At Wordsworth's suggestion, Coleridge wrote 'The Rime of the *Ancient Mariner', which recounts a nightmare sea-voyage with powerful metaphysical overtones; and started three other ballads, of which the best is *'Christabel', a tale of spiritual seduction set in a medieval castle. A selection from their work appeared as the *Lyrical Ballads* (1798), intended as an 'experiment' in English poetry, which after a poor critical reception, achieved a revolution in literary taste and sensibility.

Disenchanted with political developments ('France: an Ode'), Coleridge now turned towards Germany, where he spent ten months (1798–9), partly in the company of the Wordsworths, studying *Kant, *Schiller, and *Schelling. Returned to London, he translated Schiller's verse play *Wallenstein*, engaged in journalism for D. *Stuart of *The Morning Post*, and first began to plan a great work on metaphysics. In 1800 he moved to the Lake District with the Wordsworths, but his marriage was increasingly unhappy and he had fallen disastrously in love with Wordsworth's future sister-in-law Sara Hutchinson, as recorded in 'Love' (1799) and other 'Asra' poems. His use of opium now became a crippling addiction. Many of these difficulties are examined in the brilliant and emotional *'Dejection: an Ode' (1802). During these years he also began to compile his *Notebooks*, daily meditations on his life, writing, and dreams, which have proved among his most enduring and moving works. In 1804 Coleridge went abroad alone, the first of many attempts to restore his health and remake his career: he worked for two years as secretary to the governor of wartime Malta, and later travelled through Sicily and Italy. In 1807 he separated from his wife and went to live again with the Wordsworths and Sara Hutchinson at Colerton, Leicestershire: here Wordsworth first read 'The Poem to Coleridge' which became *The Prelude. In 1808, though ill, Coleridge began his series of Lectures on Poetry and Drama, which he continued sporadically over the next decade to audiences including *Keats and *Byron, and which as his *Shakespearian Criticism introduced new concepts of 'organic' form and dramatic psychology. In 1809–10 he wrote and edited with Sara Hutchinson's help a second periodical, *The Friend, 'a literary, moral, and political weekly paper' that ran for 28 issues: it contains the seeds of all his mature philosophic criticism. The intellectual effort, combined with the struggle against opium, shattered his circle of friends: Sara left for Wales, Dorothy grew estranged, he quarrelled irrevocably with Wordsworth. Coleridge fled to London, where between 1811 and 1814 he was on the verge of suicide, sustained only by his friends the Morgans, who took him to live in Calne, Wiltshire. Nevertheless he continued lecturing and journalism, and his play *Remorse, a melodrama of the Spanish Inquisition, had a succès d'estime at Drury Lane (1813). After a physical and spiritual crisis at the Greyhound Inn, Bath, in the winter of 1813–14, Coleridge achieved a rebirth of his Christian beliefs, openly admitted his opium addiction, submitted himself to a series of medical régimes, and began slowly to write again. To this period belong the touching prose 'commentary' printed in the margins of the 'Mariner'; his essay 'on the Principles of Genial Criticism', adapted from Kant; and his *Biographia Literaria (1817), a major work of poetic criticism, philosophy, and humorous autobiography.

In the spring of 1816 Coleridge found permanent harbour in the household of Dr James Gillman, a young surgeon living at Highgate, London, where he remained for the rest of his life. His by now almost legendary reputation among the younger Romantics was assured by Christabel and Other Poems (1816), which included for the first time 'Kubla Khan', and 'The Pains of Sleep'; it was published partly through *Byron's influence. Sibylline Leaves, the first edition of his collected poems, was published in 1817 and expanded in 1828 and 1834; *Zapolya in 1817. He became the centre of a new circle of young disciples: *Carlyle christened him 'the Sage of Highgate', and Lamb—who dedicated the *Essays of Elia to him—described him as 'an archangel slightly damaged'.

His remaining prose works had a more openly social and religious slant: his two Lay Sermons (1816, 1817) were addressed to the 'Higher' and 'Middle' classes on questions of reform and moral responsibility. A final 3-vol. edition of

The Friend added his 'Treatise on Method', originally written as an introduction to the Encyclopaedia Metropolitana, which makes a Baconian attempt to explain the growth of knowledge itself. His *Aids to Reflection (1825) had a fruitful influence on *Sterling, *Kingsley, and the young Christian Socialists; while his Church and State (1830), a short monograph on the concept of a national 'Culture' and the 'clerisy' responsible for it, was taken up by M. *Arnold and *Newman. Coleridge also gave lectures on general literature and philosophy, which have survived in the form of notes and shorthand reports.

All these later works develop Coleridge's leading critical ideas, concerning Imagination and Fancy; Reason and Understanding; Symbolism and Allegory; Organic and Mechanical Form; Culture and Civilization. The dialectical way he expresses them is one of his clearest debts to German Romantic philosophy, and represents a decisive counterattack against British *Utilitarianism. His final position is that of a Romantic conservative and Christian radical, who strangely foreshadows much of the spiritual 'anxiety' of European *Existentialism. He also wrote some haunting late poems, 'Youth and Age', 'Limbo', 'Work Without Hope', and 'Constancy to an Ideal Object'. He died of heart failure at 3, The Grove, Highgate. The last echoes of his inspired conversation were captured in Table Talk (1836).

Coleridge has been variously criticized as a political turn-coat, a drug addict, a plagiarist, and a mystic humbug, whose wrecked career left nothing but a handful of magical early poems. But the shaping influence of his highly imaginative criticism is now generally accepted, and his position (with his friend Wordsworth) as one of the two great progenitors of the English Romantic spirit is assured. Nothing has re-established him as a creative artist more than the modern editions of his Letters (6 vols, 1956–71), and his Notebooks (3 vols, 1957–). There is a religious and metaphysical dimension to all his best work, both poetry and prose, which has the inescapable glow of the authentic visionary.

Modern biographies include those by E. K. *Chambers (1938), Walter Jackson Bate (1968), and Molly Lefebure (1974). Hazlitt's superb essay 'On My First Acquaintance with Poets' (1823) is indispensable.

COLERIDGE, Sara (1802–52), daughter of S. T. *Coleridge, grew up largely without her father in the company of *Southey and his family and of the *Wordsworths. She was, in Wordsworth's words, 'remarkably clever'; she read widely and acquired six languages. She married her cousin, Henry Nelson Coleridge, and after his death continued with the labour of editing and annotating her father's papers, which she performed with such skill that much of her work still stands. In 1822 she translated Dobrizhoffer's Latin *Account of the Abipones* and in 1825 the *Memoirs* of the Chevalier Bayard. *Pretty Lessons for Good Children* appeared in 1834, and in 1837 her long fantastical poem 'Phantasmion', set in the Lake country of her childhood and relating in the manner of a fairytale the story of Phantasmion and Iarine. She was greatly esteemed in London literary society, and was the friend of *Macaulay, the *Carlyles, and *de Vere, among many others. The lively and engaging *Memoir and Letters*, published by her daughter in 1873, provides much information on the literary and personal lives of the Coleridges, the Wordsworths, and the Southeys. She appears, with Dora Wordsworth and Edith Southey, in Wordsworth's poem 'The Triad' (1828).

COLET, John (1466–1519), born in London of rich parentage, one of the principal Christian Humanists of his day in England. He studied at Oxford and in Italy, and he lectured at Oxford on the New Testament from 1496 to 1504, *Erasmus being among his audience. As dean of St Paul's (1505) he founded and endowed St *Paul's School, writing for it a Latin Grammar for which *Lily, the first headmaster, wrote the Syntax; from this work and others is derived the grammar authorized by Henry VIII, which was known from 1758 as the *Eton Latin Grammar. He was a famous preacher and lecturer, a pioneer of the Reformation in England. He first came to notice with his lectures on the Epistles of St Paul at Oxford in 1497–8 which draw on *Neoplatonism from *Plotinus to Pseudo-*Dionysius to *Pico della Mirandola. He was a vitriolic and powerful opponent of *Scholasticism, of ecclesiastical abuses, and of foreign wars. He was a friend of Erasmus and *More. See biography by J. H. Lupton (1887), who also edited the 1497–8 *Expositions*, on St Paul to the Romans and on the First Epistle to the Corinthians.

COLETTE, (Sidonie Gabrielle) (1873–1954), French novelist. Having achieved success in the music-hall of the 1890s, she established her reputation as a writer with *Chéri* (1920) and *La Fin de Chéri* (1926), narratives evoking the tragic passion of a young man and an older woman. The short, intense *récits* which she made her speciality include *La Maison de Claudine* (1922), *Le Blé en herbe* (1923), *Sido* (1929), *La Naissance du jour* (1932), *Le Képi* (1943), and *Gigi* (1943). They express a sensibility shaped by the style of the *belle époque* and informed by a sensual responsiveness to the life of nature and the world of childhood. She continues to hold attention for the vividness and precision of her insights into the crises of womanhood. She has been variously translated into English, notably by E. McLeod and R. Stenhouse.

Colin and Lucy, see LUCY AND COLIN.

Colin Clout, the name adopted by *Spenser in *The Shepheardes Calender* and *Colin Clouts come home againe*. Colin Clout is also the name of a rustic in Gay's *The Shepherd's Week*. See also COLLYN CLOUTE.

Colin Clouts come home againe, an allegorical pastoral written by *Spenser on his return to Kilcolman after his visit to London of 1589–91, published 1595. It was dedicated to *Ralegh 'in part of paiment of the infinite debt in which I acknowledge my selfe bounden unto you, for your singular favours and sundrie good turnes shewed to me at my late being in England'.

The poem describes in allegorical form how Ralegh visited Spenser in Ireland and induced him to come to England 'his *Cynthia* to see'— i.e. the queen. There is a charming description of the sea voyage; after which the poet tells of the glories of the queen and her court and the beauty of the ladies who frequent it. Then follows a bitter attack on the envies and intrigues of the court. The poem ends with a definition of true love and a tribute to Colin's proud mistress *Rosalind.

Colkitto, 'or Macdonnel, or Galasp', in Milton's first *Tetrachordon* sonnet, was the lieutenant-general of the marquis of Montrose in his campaign on behalf of Charles I. He was called Alexander Macdonnel, MacColkittoch, MacGillespie, that is, Alexander Macdonnel, the son of Colkittoch, the son of Gillespie (Galasp). He figures in Scott's *The Legend of Montrose*.

Colleen Bawn, The (meaning 'the fair girl'), a play adapted in 1860 by *Boucicault from a novel, *The Collegians*, by *Griffin.

Collegians, The, see GRIFFIN.

Collegiate Ladies, in Jonson's *Epicene*, a coterie of domineering women 'between courtiers and country madams, who live from their husbands and give entertainment to all the wits and braveries [beaux] of the time'. Wycherley copied them for Lady Fidget and her cronies in *The Country Wife*.

COLLIER, Jeremy (1650–1726), a nonjuring clergyman who refused to swear the oath to William and Mary and was outlawed in 1696 for publicly absolving on the scaffold two of those found guilty of plotting to assassinate William III. He became a non-juring bishop in 1713. He is chiefly remembered for his *Short View of the Immorality and Profaneness of the English Stage* (1698), in which he attacked *Dryden, *Wycherley, *Congreve, *Vanbrugh, *D'Urfey, and *Otway, complaining particularly of profanity in stage dialogue and mockery of the clergy. The work created a great impact; Congreve and D'Urfey were prosecuted, *Betterton and Mrs *Bracegirdle were fined, and several of the poets replied, though not very effectively. Although the kind of play to which Collier objected continued to flourish, notably in the work of Congreve, Vanbrugh, and *Farquhar, its days were numbered, and Collier contributed towards the climate that produced the 'reformed' drama of C. *Cibber and his successors. (See also RESTORATION COMEDY.) Collier published a learned *Ecclesiastical History of Great Britain* in 1708–14.

COLLIER, John (1901–80), was poetry editor of *Time and Tide* during the 1920s and 1930s, but is remembered as a novelist and writer of fantastic stories combining satire with the macabre and the supernatural. His best-known novel is *His Monkey Wife* (1930), describing the marriage between a repatriated explorer and his pet chimpanzee. In 1935 he moved to the US and made his living as a screen-writer in Hollywood. *The John Collier Reader* (1972) is an anthology of his major stories with an introduction by A. *Burgess.

COLLIER, John Payne (1789–1883), antiquarian, whose achievements first received public attention with *The History of English dramatic poetry to the time of Shakespeare: and Annals of the Stage to the Restoration* (1831) which contained valuable new documentary information but was contaminated with his own fabrications, the first of his insidious literary frauds. He dedicated the *History* to the duke of Devonshire (then lord chamberlain) who showed his appreciation by entrusting to him his library and making him his literary adviser. He was also given free access to Lord Ellesmere's manuscripts at Bridgewater House. In 1840 he founded the Shakespeare Society for which he published many rare works including *The Memoirs of Edward Alleyn* (1841); as director of the Society many rare documents were made available to him on which he based his researches and forgeries. But it was his falsifications of the marginal corrections of the so-called Perkins Folio (a Second *Folio of Shakespeare's plays dated 1632, with a possibly forged signature of Tho. Perkins on its cover) that finally brought him discredit.

Doubt was cast on the nature and extent of Collier's frauds by D. Ganzel in a biography, *Fortune and Men's Eyes* (1982), but see Arthur Freeman, *TLS*, 22 April 1983, and following correspondence for a full discussion of Ganzel's claims.

COLLINGWOOD, R(obin) G(eorge) (1889–1943), philosopher and archaeologist. He was educated by his father before going to Rugby and University College, Oxford, and in 1935 became professor of metaphysical philosophy in Oxford. He combined philosophy with the history and archaeology of Roman Britain. His chief work in the latter field was *Roman Britain and the English Settlements* (with J. N. L. Myres,

1936). In his vigorous *Autobiography* (1939) and *The Idea of History* (1946) he maintained the identity of philosophy and history. Earlier books included an *Essay on Philosophical Method* (1933) and *The Principles of Art* (1938).

COLLINS, Anthony (1676–1729), free-thinker, was born at Heston, Middlesex, and educated at Eton and King's College, Cambridge. In 1703 he became intimate with *Locke. His debate on immortality with S. *Clarke—each man issuing four pamphlets (1707–8)—established his reputation as a leading freethinker. His materialistic theory of mind is satirized in the *Memoirs of *Martinus Scriblerus* (1741). The boldly insinuating *Discourse of Free-thinking* (1713), his best-known work, drew angry replies from Richard *Bentley, *Berkeley, *Steele, Whiston, *Hoadley, and, in *Mr C . . . s Discourse . . . , put into plain English* (1713), from *Swift.

Collins's classic defence of determinism, *A Philosophical Inquiry*, appeared in 1717. Between 1720 and 1721 he collaborated with Trenchard and Gordon on the anti-clerical periodical *The Independent Whig*. In *Grounds and Reasons of the Christian Religion* (1724) he contests the messianic prophecies. Overtly or covertly, Collins attacked nearly every part of Christian theology; T. H. *Huxley described him as 'the Goliath of Freethinking'.

COLLINS, Arthur (?1690–1760), genealogist and bookseller, was author of various memoirs and biographies and of *The Peerage of England* (1709, enlarged editions 1735 and 1756) and *The Baronettage of England* (1720).

COLLINS, John Churton (1848–1908), lecturer and critic, educated at Balliol College, Oxford. He was known in literary circles for his long pursuit of the academic recognition of English in the university curriculum, and for his arguments in favour of the conjunct study of English and classical literature, which drew support from M. *Arnold, T. H. *Huxley, and *Swinburne, who became a close friend and correspondent. His frequent and often controversial articles appeared in the *Quarterly Review, the *Pall Mall Gazette, and other journals. His efforts were rewarded when in 1893 a final honours school was established at Oxford, and in 1904 when he became professor of English literature at Birmingham. He edited the works of *Tourneur (1878), of R. *Greene (1905), and Lord *Herbert of Cherbury's poems (1881); his critical works included *Ephemera Critica* (1891) and *Voltaire, Montesquieu and Rousseau in England* (1908). He was found drowned at Oulton Broad.

COLLINS, (William) Wilkie (1824–89), elder son of the landscape painter William Collins, was named after his godfather, the painter

David Wilkie, a friend of his father. He was educated for a few years at private schools in London, but gained his real education on a two-year tour of Italy with his family, 1836–8. He worked briefly for a tea importer and was later called to the bar, but never practised. His first book, a biography of his father, was published in 1848, and he later wrote numerous articles and short stories for Dickens's periodicals *Household Words* and *All The Year Round* and for other journals, a book about a walking tour in Cornwall, and a number of moderately successful plays; but his reputation rests on his novels. His first was *Antonina* (1850), a historical novel about the fall of Rome; but with *Basil* (1852) he found his true métier as an expert in mystery, suspense, and crime. His finest work in this genre, the Novel of *Sensation, was written in the 1860s, when he produced *The Woman in White* (1860), *No Name* (1862), *Armadale* (1866), and *The Moonstone* (1868). Between 1870 and his death he produced 15 more novels of deteriorating quality, though he never lost his popularity with the general public. The falling-off was possibly due to ill-health—he suffered severely from gout—and to his addiction to opium for the last 27 years of his life. He never married, but lived for many years with Caroline Graves, whom he first saw at a mysterious mid-night encounter of which he made use in *The Woman in White*. By another woman, Martha Rudd, he had three illegitimate children. His home throughout his life was in London, but he travelled extensively in France and Italy (often with *Dickens) and undertook a lecture tour in the US in 1873–4. He was a close friend and collaborator of Dickens from 1851 to Dickens's death; among his other friends were D. *Jerrold, *Lear, Augustus Egg, C. *Reade, G. *Eliot and G. H. *Lewes, and Frederic and Nina Lehmann.

Collins wrote the first full-length detective stories in English, and set a mould for the genre which has lasted for a century. He excelled at constructing ingenious and meticulous plots, and made interesting experiments in narrative technique. His characterization was sometimes perfunctory, but many of his novels contain vivid and sympathetic portraits of physically abnormal individuals—the blind, deaf, crippled, deformed, obese. In his later less successful novels, such as *The New Magdalen* and *The Law and The Lady*, he attacked various social abuses with more enthusiasm than skill provoking *Swinburne's gibe,

What brought good Wilkie's genius nigh perdition?
Some demon whispered—'Wilkie! have a mission'.

Contemporary critics, though often attacking him for offending their notions of propriety, rated his powers very highly, and a huge public in Britain, America, and most European countries (his books were widely translated) was gripped by his narrative gifts. There is a biography by Kenneth Robinson (1951); see also *Wilkie Collins: the Critical Heritage*, ed. Norman Page (1974).

COLLINS, William (1721–59), the son of a Chichester hatter, was educated at Winchester (where he first met his friend J. *Warton) and Oxford, and published his *Persian Eclogues* (1742) while an undergraduate. He moved to London in the 1740s, where he met James *Thomson, *Armstrong, and Dr *Johnson, and embarked on many abortive literary enterprises. His *Odes on Several Descriptive and Allegoric Subjects* (1746, dated 1747) made little impression at the time, but was to have considerable influence; the volume includes his well-known 'Ode to Evening' and 'How sleep the Brave', and odes to Pity, Fear, Simplicity, and other abstractions. The last work published in his lifetime was an ode on the death of Thomson (1749), and in 1750 he presented an unfinished draft of his *Ode on the Popular Superstitions of the Highlands* (published 1788) to J. *Home. Thereafter he suffered increasingly from severe melancholia, and died in Chichester, where he had been living for some time. Johnson in his *Lives of the English Poets* commented on his wildness and extravagance, which produced harshness and obscurity as well as 'sublimity and splendour', but later poets responded more eagerly to his lyrical intensity and to his conception of poetry as visionary and sacred (see SUBLIME); with *Gray he was one of the dominant influences of the later 18th cent.

The first collected edition was by John *Langhorne (1765, with memoir): the standard modern edition is by R. Lonsdale (1977, with Gray), and a biography by P. L. Carver was published in 1967.

Collins, William, a character in J. Austen's *Pride and Prejudice*, a pompous, silly, and self-satisfied young clergyman, excessively obsequious to persons of high social station. The fulsome letter of thanks that he addresses to Mr Bennet (ch. xxiii, though the text is not given) after his stay with the family has led to his name being colloquially associated with such 'bread-and-butter' letters.

COLLIS, John Stewart (1900–84), the son of an Irish solicitor, was, like his brother Maurice Stewart Collis (1889–1973), a writer of biographies and other works, but is remembered largely for *While Following the Plough* (1946) and *Down to Earth* (1947: as one volume, *The Worm Forgives the Plough*, 1973), works inspired by the years he spent working as a farm labourer in Dorset and Sussex during the Second World War. His autobiography, *Bound upon a Course* (1971), brought him belated recognition as a pioneer in the ecological movement, who wrote with imagination and authenticity of rural life.

Collyn Clout, a satirical poem by *Skelton, directed against ecclesiastical abuses, written about 1521. See also COLIN CLOUT.

COLMAN, George, the elder (1732–94), was born in Florence, the son of the British envoy there, and educated at Westminster, where he was a schoolfellow of *Cowper and Bonnell Thornton (1724–68); with the latter he edited *The Connoisseur* (1754–6). He was called to the bar in 1757, but devoted himself increasingly to the theatre, partly through the influence of his friend *Garrick, with whom he collaborated in writing *The Clandestine Marriage* (1766), which caused a rift between them when Garrick refused to appear as Lord Ogleby. He was manager of Covent Garden, 1767–74, and of the Haymarket, 1777–89. He wrote many plays, including *Polly Honeycombe* (1760), *The Jealous Wife* (1761), and *Tit for Tat* (1786), adapted Shakespeare and *Beaumont and *Fletcher for the stage, and translated the comedies of *Terence (1765). He was elected to Dr Johnson's literary *Club in 1768. R. B. Peake's *Memoirs of the Colman Family* appeared in 1841.

COLMAN, George, the younger (1762–1836), son of the above, was educated at Westminster and the universities of Oxford and Aberdeen. He made his name with the musical romantic comedy *Inkle and Yarico* in 1787, which was followed by other sentimental and humorous operettas. Among many other dramatic works, *The Iron Chest* of 1796 is a dramatization of *Caleb Williams* by Godwin. Colman's comedy of contemporary life. *The Heir-at-Law* (1797), became famous for the character of Dr Pangloss, a greedy, pompous pedant. *John Bull* (1803) contains a sketch of the supposed British character in Job Thornberry.

Colombe's Birthday, a play in blank verse by R. *Browning, published in 1844 as no. VI of *Bells and Pomegranates*. In the aftermath of his quarrel with *Macready (see BLOT IN THE 'SCUTCHEON, A) Browning wrote the play for his rival *Kean, whose wife was to have taken the title role; but Kean's wish to delay the production for a year or more decided Browning to withdraw and publish it: he never wrote for the stage again. The play ran for seven nights at the Haymarket theatre in 1853 with Browning's friend Helen Faucit (see STRAFFORD) in the title role: it had a critical success. The play (whose events are unhistorical) is set in 17th-cent. Germany, on the day that Colombe is to celebrate her birthday and the first anniversary of her accession to the duchy of Juliers and Cleves.

Colon ('farmer'), a member of the bear-baiting mob in Butler's *Hudibras.

Colonel Jack, *The History and Remarkable Life*

of Colonel Jacque, Commonly Call'd, a romance of adventure by *Defoe, published 1722.

The supposed narrator, abandoned by his parents in childhood, falls into bad company and becomes a pickpocket. His profession grows distasteful to him, he enlists, and presently deserts to avoid being sent to serve in Flanders. He is kidnapped, sent to Virginia, and sold to a planter. He is promoted to be an overseer, is given his liberty, becomes himself a planter, and acquires much wealth. He returns home and has a series of unfortunate matrimonial adventures, but finally ends in prosperity and repentance.

Colonia, Colonia Agrippina, Colonia Claudia, or Colonia Ubiorum, in imprints, Cologne; Colonia Allobrogum, Geneva; Colonia Munatiana, Basle; Colonia is also an imprint for Naples.

COLONNA, Vittoria (1492–1547), granddaughter of Frederick, duke of Urbino, and devoted wife (although early widowed) of the marquis of Pescara. She was remarkable in a dissolute age for her stainless character and the admiration and friendship of many great men, including *Sannazar, *Castiglione, *Bembo, *Tasso, and *Michelangelo.

Colophon, from Gk. κολοφών, summit, 'finishing touch', the inscription or device, sometimes pictorial or emblematic, placed at the end of a book or manuscript, and containing the title, the scribe's or printer's name, the date and place of printing, etc.; now the publisher's imprint, or logotype, usually found on the title-page and often on the spine of a book.

COLUM, Padraic (1881–1972), Irish poet and playwright, born in Co. Longford, where his father was master of a workhouse, and educated at Trinity College, Dublin, where he met *Joyce, who became a close friend. Prominent amongst the younger members of the *Irish Revival, he wrote several plays for the *Abbey Theatre, including *Thomas Muskerry* (1910), which was strongly attacked for its gloomily realistic Ibsenite portrayal of Irish life. His first collection of poems, *Wild Earth* (1907), was followed by many others (*Collected Poems*, 1953) and by works on Irish and Hawaiian folklore. He contributed a preface to Joyce's *Anna Livia Plurabelle* (1928), and he and his wife Mary wrote a memoir, *Our Friend James Joyce* (1958).

COLUMBA, or **COLUMCILLE,** St (521–97), a recluse of Glasnevin, near Dublin, and the founder of churches in Derry and other places. He went to Scotland in 563 and founded the monastery of Iona, from which the conversion of Scotland and Northumbria by the Celtic Church proceeded. The book of his miracles was written by *Adomnan of Iona. See W. D. Simpson, *The Historical St Columba* (1927).

Columbine, a character in Italian *commedia dell'arte*, the daughter of *Pantaloon and mistress of *Harlequin, which has been transferred to our pantomime or harlequinade.

COLVIN, Sir Sidney (1845–1927), critic of art and literature, educated at Trinity College, Cambridge, was Slade professor of fine art at Cambridge 1873–85, director of the Fitzwilliam Museum in 1876, and keeper of the department of prints and drawings at the British Museum 1883–1912. Besides contributing many articles to periodicals, mainly on the history and criticism of art, he published several volumes including lives of W. S. *Landor (1881) and *Keats (1887). He was honorary secretary of the Society of Dilettanti, 1891–6, moved in artistic and literary circles, and corresponded with some of the most eminent intellectuals of his day (see E. V. *Lucas, *The Colvins and their Friends*, 1928). He edited the Edinburgh edition of R. L. *Stevenson's works (1894–7) and *The Letters of R. L. Stevenson* (1899 and 1911) and in 1895 published the *Vailima Letters* written to him by Stevenson, 1890–4.

COMBE, William (1741–1823), educated at Eton, published a number of metrical satires, including *The Diaboliad* (1776), directed against Lord Irnham; and many other works in prose and verse, including *The Devil upon Two Sticks in England* (1790) and *The Microcosm of London* (1808). He is particularly remembered for the verses that he wrote to accompany *Rowlandson's coloured plates and drawings of the adventures of 'Dr Syntax'. The first of these works, *The Tour of Dr Syntax in search of the Picturesque*, a parody of the popular books of picturesque travels of the day, and particularly of the works of *Gilpin, appeared in *Ackerman's *Poetical Magazine* in 1809, and in 1812 as a book which went into many editions. Dr Syntax is the grotesque figure of a clergyman and schoolmaster, who sets out during the holidays, on his old horse Grizzle, to 'make a TOUR and WRITE IT', and meets with a series of absurd misfortunes. This was followed in 1820 by *The Second Tour of Dr Syntax in search of Consolation* (for the loss of his wife) and in 1821 by *The Third Tour of Dr Syntax in search of a Wife*. The three Tours were collected in 1826. Combe also wrote the letterpress for Rowlandson's *The English Dance of Death* (1815–16), *The Dance of Life* (1816), and *Johnny Quae Genus* (1822), another Syntax story.

Combray, the name used by Proust for the country town (Illiers, near Chartres) described in the early volumes of *A la recherche du temps perdu*.

Comédie humaine, La, see BALZAC.

Comedy had its roots in a fertility ritual that in ancient Greece was an occasion for crude satire aimed at named persons. Already during the lifetime of its supreme exponent, *Aristophanes, such personal abuse became unacceptable, and an Athenian law of 414 BC forced the replacement of individuals by fictional types as targets for attack. Aristotle defined Comedy as written about persons of minor importance whom their faults rendered ridiculous. This 'New Comedy', known to us through the Latin adaptations of *Plautus and *Terence, had a restricted range of characters: grumbling middle-aged men and women, young lovers, boastful soldiers, parasites, prostitutes, slaves. Superseded by *Mime under the Roman Empire, classical comedy vanished from the stage during the Middle Ages when a homespun variety of farce was preferred, but was performed again in Italy at the end of the 15th cent. and soon gave rise to Italian imitations, of which *Machiavelli's *Mandragola* is the best-known. The great comic playwrights of the late 16th and 17th cents, Shakespeare, Lope de *Vega, *Jonson, *Molière, drew on both the classical tradition and medieval farce, some adding a poetic dimension, others making their plays vehicles of social criticism. Writers in *Restoration England and the 18th cent. followed the pattern set by their predecessors, widening the range of characters and making use of sentiment and realism. But after the Romantic period serious comedy blended inextricably with the realist drama that explored the problems of everyday life. Only light comedy survived as a distinct genre akin to farce. See also SENTIMENTAL COMEDY.

Comedy, The Divine, see DIVINA COMMEDIA, LA.

Comedy of Errors, The, a comedy by *Shakespeare, acted at Gray's Inn 1594, though possibly written as early as 1590, first printed in the First *Folio (1623).

Syracuse and Ephesus being at enmity, any Syracusan found in Ephesus is put to death unless he can pay a ransom of 1,000 marks. Egeon, an old Syracusan merchant, has been arrested in Ephesus and on the duke's order explains how he came there. He and his wife Emilia had twin sons, exactly alike and each named Antipholus; the parents had purchased twin slaves, also exactly alike, each named Dromio, who attended on their sons. Having in a shipwreck been separated, with the younger son and one Dromio, from his wife and the other son and slave, Egeon had never seen them since. The younger son (Antipholus of Syracuse) on reaching manhood had gone (with his Dromio) in search of his brother and mother and had no more been heard of, though Egeon had now sought him for five years over the world, coming at last to Ephesus.

The duke, moved by this tale, gives Egeon till evening to find the ransom. Now, the elder Antipholus (Antipholus of Ephesus), with one of the Dromios, has been living in Ephesus since his rescue from shipwreck and is married. Antipholus of Syracuse and the other Dromio have arrived there that very morning. Each twin retains the same confusing resemblance to his brother as in childhood. From this the comedy of errors results. Antipholus of Syracuse is summoned home to dinner by Dromio of Ephesus; he is claimed as husband by the wife of Antipholus of Ephesus, the latter being refused admittance to his own house, because he is supposed to be already within; and Antipholus of Syracuse falls in love with Luciana, his brother's wife's sister. Finally Antipholus of Ephesus is confined as a lunatic, and Antipholus of Syracuse takes refuge from his brother's jealous wife in a convent.

Meanwhile evening has come and Egeon is led to execution. As the duke proceeds to the place of execution, Antipholus of Ephesus appeals to him for redress. Then the abbess of the convent presents Antipholus of Syracuse, also claiming redress. The simultaneous presence of the two brothers explains the numerous misunderstandings. Egeon recovers his two sons and his liberty, and the abbess turns out to be his lost wife Emilia.

COMENIUS, John Amos (Jan Komenský), (1592–1670), Moravian educational reformer, chiliast, and pansophist, completed his studies in Heidelberg in 1614 and was ordained in 1618. He gained European fame in 1633 with the publication of *Janua linguarum reserata*, published in England as *The Gates of Tongues unlocked and opened*. In 1637 *Hartlib published *Conatum Comenianorum praeludia* (in 1639 as *Pansophiae Prodromus* and in 1642 in English as *A Reformation of Schools*). Comenius visited London in 1641, where he wrote *Via Lucis*, then travelled in northern and middle Europe, finally settling in Amsterdam, where he wrote his last great work, *De rerum humanorum emendatione consultatio catholica*, much of which was presumed lost until 1934 and which was published in its entirety in 1966. His *Orbis Sensualium pictus*, with a Latin and German text, appeared in 1658, and was published in English in 1659 as *Comenius's Visible World*, the first school-book consistently to use pictures in the learning of languages. He believed in a system of universal wisdom, and his most lasting contribution was in the field of pedagogy.

COMESTOR, Petrus (d. 1179), from Troyes in Champagne, named 'the feeder' because of his voracity in studying books. He was the author of a *Historia Scholastica*, a collection of scriptural narratives with commentary which was very popular throughout the Middle Ages

in a French translation, and was one of the first of the very many commentators on the *Sententiae* of *Peter Lombard. He became chancellor of the University of Paris in 1164. His work was familiar to *Chaucer, and *Dante places him among the Doctors of the Church in the Heaven of the Sun (*Paradiso*, xii. 134) as 'Pietro Mangiadore'.

Comical Revenge, The, or *Love in a Tub*, a comedy by *Etherege, acted 1664.

The serious part of the plot, in heroic couplets, deals with the rivalry of Lord Beaufort and Colonel Bruce for the hand of Graciana. A duel ensues. Bruce is defeated, tries to kill himself in despair, is cured of his wound, and consoled with Graciana's sister. The comic and farcical part, in prose, centres on the French valet Dufoy, who for his impudence is confined by his fellow servants in a tub. His master Sir Frederick Frolick, a debonair libertine, is courted by a rich widow; he cajoles her out of £200 and finally marries her. There is a foolish country knight, Sir Nicholas Cully, whom two rogues cozen out of £1,000. The knaves and the fool are exposed, and for punishment married off against their will and expectation.

Comics, Comic Strips, flourished from the end of the 19th cent. with *Ally Sloper's Half-Holiday* (1884–1923), widely acknowledged as the publication that established the form, although comic strips had appeared earlier in papers such as *The Graphic* (1869–1932); Edwin John Brett's *The Boys of England* (1866–99, a highly successful mixture of fiction, 'sport, travel, fun and instruction'); and *Funny Folks* (1874–94; 'A Weekly Budget of Funny Pictures'). Ally Sloper was a sharp, gin-drinking, working-class anti-hero, the first regular character in the comic world. The growing boom continued with such publications as *Comic Cuts* (1890–1953) and *Chips* (1890–1953); *The Gem* (1907–39) and *The Magnet* (1908–40; see HAMILTON, C.); with boys' adventure comics such as *Adventure* (1921–61), *Wizard* (1922–63) and *Hotspur* (1933–59); and with *Beano* (1938–   ) and *Dandy* (1937–   ), both still flourishing with many of their original characters. *Rainbow* (1914–56), with its hero Tiger Tim, was the first coloured comic designed exclusively for children, and described itself as 'The Children's Paper Parents Approve of', whereas *Chips* less loftily called itself 'The "Kid" 's Quietener, Father's Comfort, and Mother's Joy'. The battle between the subversively entertaining and the morally improving continued; Rupert Bear, who first appeared in the *Daily Express* on 8 Nov. 1920 (the creation of Mary Tourtel, distinguished by being written in rhyming couplets) was on the side of the angels, as was Dan Dare in *Eagle*. The founding of *Eagle* in 1950 by Lancashire vicar Marcus

Morris was directly prompted by the growing infiltration of American horror comics, and it aimed to combine high moral values with the thrills of space adventure; the original series came to an end in 1969, but Dan Dare himself survives in *2000 AD*. For a history of British and American comics, see *The Penguin Book of Comics* (1967, rev. 1971) by George Perry and Alan Aldridge.

'Coming of Arthur, The', one of Tennyson's *Idylls of the King* published 1869. It describes the newly-crowned Arthur's first meeting with Guinevere, and their marriage.

Coming Race, The, a novel by *Bulwer-Lytton, published 1871.

The narrator describes his visit to a subterranean race of superior beings that long ago took refuge, possibly from the biblical flood, in the depths of the earth. There they have evolved a highly sophisticated civilization, with the aid of a form of energy called Vril, which has great powers of destruction as well as great utility. Much of the novel is devoted to a satiric account of the narrator's own democratic society, of which he is initially proud, and to praise of the underground society, which has no war, no crime, and no inequality, and where women are stronger than men and free to choose their own mates. This involves the narrator in some embarrassing situations with his host's daughter Zee; he convinces her that he would never be happy in her world, and she returns him to the upper earth, aided by her mechanical Vril-powered wings. 'Love is swifter than Vril' is one of her more romantic statements. He is left to prophesy the death of the human race at the hands of 'our inevitable destroyers'. The sublime subterranean landscapes recall the paintings of J. *Martin, whose work Bulwer-Lytton much admired, and a memory of the novel lingers on in the trade name of the product 'Bovril', derived from 'Vril'.

Commedia dell'arte, Italian popular character comedy, in which masked professional actors improvised on a traditional plot. It developed in the 16th cent., probably from the 'Commedia erudita' (Renaissance learned comedy, following *Plautus and *Terence), but some critics postulate an even earlier origin in the mime of the popular Latin *Atellan fables. Its main characters came to be fixed into farcical types (e.g. Harlequin, Pulcinella, Pantaloon, Columbine). It was dying out by the 18th cent. when *Goldoni refreshed its types with a richer psychology.

Commines, Philippe de (*c.*1445–1511), French chronicler. He served in a diplomatic capacity under Charles the Bold of Burgundy, and subsequently under Louis XI and Charles VIII of France. His *Mémoires*, first published in 1524–8, are in two parts, the first dealing with the reign of Louis XI, the second with Charles VIII's Italian campaign. They were first translated into English by Thomas Danett (1596), and were the inspiration for Scott's *Quentin Durward*.

Common, Dol, one of the cheaters in Jonson's *Volpone*.

Common Prayer, *The Book of*, was evolved in the 16th cent. to meet the popular need for aids to devotion (not entirely satisfied by the *Primers) and the demand for the use of the vernacular in church services. Its development was gradual. The Sarum breviary was reissued in 1541 and ordered to be used throughout the province of Canterbury 1542. The reading in churches of a chapter of the Bible in English, and the Litany in English (probably the work of *Cranmer), were introduced in 1544, and an English communion service in 1548. About the same time the Primers were revised, and the King's Primer issued in 1545 in the interest of uniformity; it included the English Litany. Cranmer and a commission each drafted a scheme for a prayer book, and these were discussed in Edward VI's reign, leading to the successive issue of the Prayer Books of 1549 and 1552. In the latter the form of the *Book of Common Prayer* was practically settled, though a revision was made under Elizabeth (1559), minor changes under James I, and the final text is that of 1662. As it stands the Prayer Book represents largely the work of Cranmer; N. *Ridley may perhaps claim some share.

Alternative forms of service in contemporary language were published in 1980 and recommended for general use in church services in preference to the 1662 Prayer Book. This gave rise to vigorous argument, inside and outside the Church of England, as to the respective merits of attempting to improve the congregation's understanding of the liturgy and of preserving its traditions and literary qualities.

Common Reader, The, the title of two collections of essays by V. *Woolf, taken from Dr Johnson's life of Gray in *Lives of the English Poets*, which concludes with a famous paragraph in praise of the *Elegy: 'In the character of his Elegy I rejoice to concur with the common reader . . . The *Church-yard* abounds with images which find a mirrour in every mind, and with sentiments to which every bosom returns an echo.'

Commonwealth of Oceana, The, a political work by J. *Harrington, published 1656 and dedicated to *Cromwell; in form it is part historical analysis, part *Utopia, and part a written constitution.

Harrington analyses the events leading to the Civil War (particularly the decay of the feudal system and the new allegiances of freeholders), using both historical and fictional names; Ethelred and *Coke appear as themselves, whereas Oceana is England, the Normans become the Neustrians, Henry VII becomes Panurgus, etc. He then proceeds to draw up a plan for an ideal republic, under the leadership of the Archon, Olphaus Megaletor, an idealized Cromwell figure. He expresses his admiration for the republics of Greece and Rome and for the Venetian republic, and frequently invokes *Machiavelli as 'the only politician of later ages'. His own proposals include the dividing of the great estates, a two-chamber system, indirect election by ballot, rotation in office, a popularly elected poet laureate, and a National Theatre: 'An equal commonwealth . . . is a government established upon an equal agrarian, arising into the superstructures or three orders, the senate debating and proposing, the people resolving, and the magistracy executing by an equal rotation through the suffrage of the people given by the ballot.' Overall, he proposes a carefully worked-out system of checks and balances, far from Utopian in its concept of human nature, which *Hume was to describe as 'the only valuable model of a commonwealth that has yet been offered to the public'. Harrington's *Oceana* is an intended contrast to Hobbes's *Leviathan*, to which he frequently refers: Hobbes, says *Aubrey, 'remained silent' on the subject.

COMNENA and COMNENUS, see ANNA COMNENA.

Complaint, a poetic form derived from the Latin *planctus*, bewailing the vicissitudes of life (as in *Hoccleve's *Complaint*) or addressed to a more particular end (such as *Chaucer's 'Complaint to his Purse'). The form is particularly common in poems up to the Renaissance; thereafter the terms *'elegy' and 'lament' were used.

Complaint, The, or *Night Thoughts on Life, Death, and Immortality*, see NIGHT THOUGHTS.

Complaint of Buckingham, The, a poem by T. *Sackville, contributed by him to *A Mirror for Magistrates*.
  Henry Stafford, duke of Buckingham, after his rebellion against Richard III, takes refuge with a dependant, Humfrey Banastair. Banastair betrays him to the king and Buckingham is executed. As his corpse lies on the ground it raises its head and heaps curses on Banastair and his children.

'Complaint of Rosamund', a poem by S. *Daniel in rhyme-royal appended to *Delia*.

Complaynt to the King, see LINDSAY, D.

Compleat Angler, The, or *the Contemplative Man's Recreation*, a discourse on fishing by I. *Walton, first published 1653, the second much enlarged edition 1655, 5th edn. with a continuation by *Cotton, 1676.

It takes the form of a dialogue, at first between the author Piscator (a fisherman), Auceps (a fowler), and Venator (a hunter), each commending his own recreation, in which Auceps is silenced and Venator becomes a pupil of the angle; then between Piscator and Venator alone. The author instructs his pupil in the art of catching various kinds of freshwater fish, with directions for dressing some of them for the table. The five days' fishing expedition along the river Lea also contains interludes of verse and song, angling anecdotes, moral reflections, and snatches of mythology and folklore. In Cotton's continuation Piscator and Viator (who turns out to be Venator) fish along the river Dove which divides Derbyshire and Staffordshire; there are fuller instructions for making of artificial flies (Walton was not an experienced fly-fisher) and descriptions of the picturesque scenery of the district.
  Walton's various sources include *The Treatise of Fishing with an Angle* (**The Book of St Albans*, 1496) and an anonymous book, *The Art of Angling* (in which Piscator and Viator both appear), published in 1577, of which the only known copy was discovered in 1954.

Complutensian Polyglot Bible, The, the earliest complete polyglot Bible, containing the Hebrew, Septuagint, and Vulgate texts, a Hebrew dictionary, etc., prepared at the expense of Cardinal *Ximenes in the early part of the 16th cent., at Alcalá in Spain (of which town Complutum is the ancient name). The special Greek type used has formed the basis of modern Greek type-design (Proctor types and others). It has been called the finest Greek type ever designed.

COMPTON-BURNETT, Dame Ivy (1884–1969), novelist, who embarked on a serious career as a writer only with *Pastors and Masters* (1925), which meant that she had in some ways less in common with the *Modernism of her contemporaries than with the post-war generation of novelists such as E. *Waugh and *Powell, whose brittle, deflationary wit, irony, and satirical exuberance are reflected especially in early works like *Brother and Sisters* (1929) or *More Women Than Men* (1933). But her highly condensed and abstracted novels, composed almost entirely in dialogue, were so unlike anyone else's that their impact was often compared to that of *post-impressionism in painting. They are all dated round about the turn of the century and set in large, gloomy, generally dilapidated houses full of servants, children, and dependent relatives. Each family is ruled in almost complete isolation from the outside world by a more or less tyrannical parent or grandparent: hence the consistently high rate of domestic crime ranging from adultery, incest, and child abuse to murder and fraud. Dame Ivy held that 'nothing is so corrupting as power', and her inward-looking, self-contained, and heavily monitored high Victorian households provided her with an ideal environment in which to examine the misuse of power together with the violence and misery hat follow.

Her personal life was effectively destroyed by the First World War and, when she eventually recovered from a protracted physical and emotional breakdown in the early 1920s, she found herself increasingly preoccupied with the eruption of passionate and disruptive forces smouldering beneath the smooth surface of a deceptively calm and well-ordered society. Her chief formative influences were G. *Eliot (imitated with unhappy results in Dolores, 1911, and afterwards crucially rejected), the Greek tragic dramatists, and S. *Butler. After 1925 she published another 18 novels (A House and Its Head, 1935, A Family and a Fortune, 1939, and Manservant and Maidservant, 1947, are perhaps outstanding); and her achievement has been well summed up by A. *Wilson: 'In the age of the concentration camp, when, from 1935 or so to 1947, she wrote her very best novels, no writer did more to illumine the springs of human cruelty, suffering and bravery.' See H. Spurling, Ivy When Young. The Early Life of I. Compton-Burnett 1884–1919 (1974) and Secrets of a Woman's Heart. The Later Life of I. Compton-Burnett 1920–1969 (1984).

COMTE, Auguste (1798–1857), French philosopher, was in early life (1817–24) secretary to C. H. de *Saint–Simon, with whom he shared the conviction that throughout history the mind and political institutions had evolved in close relation, that a new phase of mental development had been entered, and that opinion needed to be prepared for the orderly acceptance of the consequent reorganization of society. Comte accordingly set himself to frame a general system of human conceptions as they had developed to their existing state: such is the plan of his Cours de philosophie positive (6 vols, 1830–42). The Système de politique positive (4 vols, 1851–4) gave a fuller treatment of political philosophy and its applications. The main departments of human knowledge, Comte argued, passed of necessity through three successive phases: the theological, the metaphysical, and the positive. This was the 'Law of the Three States' and it applied to the historical progress of the mind and to the development of the individual mind alike. The positive or scientific state, which had been attained but not brought to completion, was the 'normal' or final state of humanity. It was characterized by the abandonment of the search for absolute causes and the recognition of the 'laws of succession and relation' that govern phenomena as the true object of knowledge. Comte illustrated his primary law by studying the history of what he

called the six 'fundamental' sciences, classifying them in the order in which they had reached the positive state: Mathematics, Astronomy, Physics, Chemistry, Biology, Sociology—a series that indicated the dependence of each on all those preceding, their decreasing generality and simplicity (or, conversely, their increasing speciality and complexity), and their progressive human importance.

The object of Comte's synthesis was to prepare the way for bringing the science of social phenomena, Sociology, into its final, positive, state and so lay the foundations of a social and political system proper to the age of industry. Temporal power was to be vested in a self-perpetuating élite of industrial chiefs. A separate spiritual authority would be established in the form of a priesthood with the duty of educating and informing opinion in the general truths of the positive philosophy and their practical corollaries, and of administering a formal religion centred on the cult of Humanity (conceived as a Great Being composed of those men and women, past, present, and to come, whose lives had been, were, or would be devoted to human progress or well-being). A preponderant place was to be given in the organization of religious and social life to the influence of women on the feelings, in order to foster altruism, the basis of the Comtean morality, expressed in the motto: 'Live for Others'.

Besides his two major works, Comte published several shorter ones intended for general instruction including: Discours sur l'ensemble du positivisme (1848, trans. J. H. Bridges, A General View of Positivism, 1865) and Catéchisme positiviste (1852). His principal English followers were F. *Harrison, E. S. Beesly, J. H. Bridges, and Richard Congreve. The Cours de philosophie positive was condensed, with the author's approval, in English translation by H. *Martineau (The Positive Philosophy of Auguste Comte, 2 vols, 1853); the Système de politique positive was translated by Harrison, Bridges, and others as The System of Positive Polity (4 vols, 1875–7). G. H. *Lewes provided an exposition of the leading ideas of the Cours in Comte's Philosophy of the Sciences (1853). J. S. *Mill gave a critical account of Comte's thought in Auguste Comte and Positivism (1865); Lettres inédites de John Stuart Mill à Auguste Comte was published in Paris in 1899.

Comus, A Maske presented at Ludlow Castle, 1634: on Michaelmasse night, before the Right Honorable John Earl of Bridgewater, Lord President of Wales, by *Milton, first printed, anonymously and untitled, 1637.

This work was written at Hammersmith at the suggestion of Milton's friend H. *Lawes; its purpose was to celebrate the earl of Bridgewater's entry on the presidency of Wales and the Marches, and the roles of the Lady and her two brothers were taken by his daughter Alice, aged 15, and her 11- and 9-year-old brothers. Although described as a 'masque', *Comus* depends little on spectacle and has been better defined as a *pastoral drama. Comus himself is a pagan god invented by Milton, son of Bacchus and Circe, who waylays travellers and transforms their faces to those of wild beasts by means of a magic liquor. The Lady, benighted in a forest and separated from her brothers, comes across Comus in the guise of a shepherd; he leads her off to his cottage, offering protection. The brothers appear and are told what has happened by the Attendant Spirit Thyrsis, also disguised as a shepherd; he warns them of the magic power of Comus and gives them a root of the plant Haemony as protection. The scene changes to 'a stately Palace', where Comus with his rabble tempts the Lady to drink his magic potion, and with much eloquence urges her not to be 'cosen'd with that same vaunted name Virginity'. She defends herself and Chastity with such spirit that even Comus feels her possessed of 'some superior power'. At this point the brothers burst in and disperse the crew. Unfortunately they have not secured the wand of Comus and are unable to release the Lady from her enchanted chair, which provides an opportunity for Thyrsis to invoke *Sabrina, goddess of the neighbouring river Severn, in the lovely song 'Sabrina Fair, | Listen where thou art sitting'. She arrives, the Lady is freed, and the Lady and her brothers are returned to Ludlow and presented to their parents. The richness and variety of the poetry which moves from blank verse to rhymed octosyllabics to song, and the abundance and grace of the pastoral, pagan, and Christian allusions combine with an Elizabethan freshness and Spenserian charm, though the action has been justly but somewhat irrelevantly criticized as 'a dramatised debate' (E. Welsford, *The Court Masque*, 1927).

Conachar, in Scott's *The Fair Maid of Perth*, the Highland apprentice of Simon Glover.

Conan, in the legends relating to *Finn (Fingal), 'in some respects a kind of Thersites, but brave and daring even to rashness' (author's notes to *Waverley*). Having visited the infernal regions, he received a cuff from the Arch-fiend, which he instantly returned with the words 'blow for blow'.

CONAN DOYLE, Arthur, see DOYLE, A. C.

Conceit, an elaborate metaphor comparing two apparently dissimilar objects or emotions, often with an effect of shock or surprise. The *Petrarchan conceit, much imitated by Elizabethan sonneteers and both used and parodied by Shakespeare, usually evoked the qualities of the disdainful mistress and the devoted lover, often in highly exaggerated terms; the *Metaphysical

conceit, as used by *Donne and his followers, applied wit and ingenuity to, in the words of Dr *Johnson, 'a combination of dissimilar images, or discovery of occult resemblances in things apparently unlike' e.g. Donne's famous comparison of two lovers to a pair of compasses.

Conchubar, or **Conchobar** (pron. Conachoor), in the Ulster cycle of Irish mythology, king of Ulster, see CUCHULAIN and DEIRDRE.

***Conciliation with America,** On*, by *Burke, speech made in the House of Commons on 22 March 1775.

This, one of Burke's greatest speeches, was a last effort to find a peaceful solution of the difference with the American colonies. Burke's proposal is to restore order and repose to the empire 'by restoring the former unsuspecting confidence of the colonies in the mother country'. He rejects the use of force, as inapplicable to the 'fierce spirit of liberty' prevailing in the English colonies. He traces the 'capital sources' from which this spirit has grown up, descent, religion, remoteness of situation; and propounds three options, to change this spirit, to prosecute it as criminal, to comply with it as necessary. He shows the first two courses to be impossible or inexpedient. He dismisses American representation in Parliament as impracticable. He finds the solution in the taxation of America through grants by the local legislatures and not by imposition. His trust is in America's interest in the British constitution: 'My hold of the colonies is in the close affection which grows from common names, from kindred blood, from similar privileges, and equal protection.' 'Magnanimity in politics is not seldom the truest wisdom; and a great empire and little minds go ill together.'

Concrete Poetry, a term used to describe a kind of experimental poetry developed in the 1950s and flourishing in the 1960s, which dwells primarily on the visual aspects of the poem (although two other forms of concrete poetry, the kinetic and the phonetic, have also been distinguished). An international movement was officially launched at the National Exhibition of concrete art in São Paulo in 1956; a Brazilian 'Pilot Plan' or manifesto, published in 1958, stated that 'concrete poetry begins by being aware of graphic space as structural agent'. Concrete poets experiment with typography, graphics, the 'ideogram concept', computer poems, collage, etc., and in varying degrees acknowledge influence from *Dada, Hans Arp, Schwitters, Malevich, and other visual artists. Ian Hamilton Finlay (1925–), one of the leading Scottish exponents, expresses his own affinity with 17th-cent. *emblems and poems such as G. *Herbert's 'Easter Wings', which use the shape as well as the sense of a poem to convey meaning. E. *Morgan, also a Scot, has written a variety of concrete poems, which were criticized by some devotees of the form as being 'too verbal'. Mary Ellen Solt in 'A World Look at Concrete Poetry' (*Hispanic Arts*, Vol. 1, Nos 3 and 4, 1968) declares that 'the concrete poet seeks to relieve the poem of its centuries-old burden of ideas, symbolic reference, ailusion and repetitious emotional content.' Others claim a less radical role, pointing to Herbert, *Blake, Carroll (C. L. *Dodgson), *Pound's use of Chinese characters, and E. E. *Cummings as evidence of a long tradition of typographical experiment. See *TLS*, 29 March 1968 and *An Anthology of Concrete Poetry* (1967), ed. Emmett Williams.

CONDELL, Henry, see HEMING, J.

CONDER, Charles, see ART NOUVEAU.

CONDILLAC, Etienne, abbé de (1715–80), French philosopher. His *Essai sur l'origine des connaissances humaines* (1746, 1771) and *Traité des sensations* (1754, 1778), carry the empiricism of *Locke to a systematic extreme, deriving all subsequent operations of the mind, including the ideas of God and of the immortality of the soul, from their alleged origin in sensation. He polarized Enlightenment opinion against Cartesian metaphysics.

Condition of England, see CARLYLE, T.

CONDORCET, Jean Antoine Nicolas Caritat, marquis de (1743–94), see PHILOSOPHES.

Coney-Catching, see ROGUE LITERATURE.

Confederacy, The, a comedy by *Vanbrugh, produced 1705, adapted from Dancourt's *Les Bourgeoises à la mode.*

Gripe and Moneytrap, two rich usurers, are niggardly husbands, and Gripe's wife Clarissa, in order to pay her debts, is obliged to pawn her necklace with Mrs Amlet. Mrs Amlet has a knave of a son, Dick, who passes himself off as a colonel, and is trying to win by fair means or foul the hand of Gripe's daughter Corinna, assisted in the plot by Brass, who acts as his footman, and by Flippanta, Clarissa's maid. Meanwhile Gripe falls in love with Moneytrap's wife and Moneytrap falls in love with Gripe's wife. This the ladies communicate to each other and contrive to turn to their mutual advantage. By their directions, Brass and Flippanta, who act as go-betweens, extract £250 apiece from the would-be lovers to relieve their ladies' immediate necessities. The two couples take tea together, each of the four pleased with the course of events, but the pawned necklace brings about a general exposure. Clarissa has told her husband that she has lost it, and he has warned the goldsmiths to look out for it. Dick has stolen it from his mother and sent Brass to try and sell it. The goldsmith to whom Brass offers it now brings it to Gripe. Dick's true character and the

pawning of the necklace are thus brought to light. But all ends well, Corinna agreeing to take Dick despite all, and Mrs Amlet endowing him with £10,000.

Confessio Amantis, see GOWER, J.

Confessions, see AUGUSTINE, ST (OF HIPPO) and ROUSSEAU.

Confessions of a Justified Sinner, see PRIVATE MEMOIRS AND CONFESSIONS OF A JUSTIFIED SINNER by J. Hogg.

Confessions of an English Opium Eater, by *De Quincey, published 1822 (enlarged version 1856).

De Quincey's study of his own opium addiction and its psychological effects traces how childhood and youthful experiences are transformed, under the influence of opium, into symbolical and revealing dreams. The central experience for subsequent dream-formations was his childhood loss of his sister, duplicated by the disappearance of the 15-year-old prostitute Ann, who befriended him during his months of homeless near-starvation in London. The euphoric reveries of the early stages of his addiction and the appalling nightmares of the later stages are described in sonorous and haunting prose, and the work, first appearing in the *London Magazine* in 1821, conferred instant literary fame on De Quincey, whose first book it was. In 1856 he greatly extended the *Confessions* for a collected edition of his works, but thereby blunted its effect.

Confidence-Man: His Masquerade, The (1857), a novel by H. *Melville.

A comic allegory set on the ironically named Mississippi steamboat *Fiddle*, Melville's last novel shows a cross-section of mid-century America and, through them, humanity, being gulled by a satanic trickster who magically metamorphoses into the shape appropriate to his victim's desires. Melville's nihilist fable expresses a profound philosophical and social pessimism.

Confidential Clerk, The, a comedy by T. S. *Eliot.

CONFUCIUS, the Latinized form of K'ung fu-tzu (551–479 BC), meaning 'Master K'ung', who has been revered by the Chinese as their greatest sage.

He was born in the state of Lu in present-day Shantung. Little is known for certain about his life. He felt that the remedy for the moral and political evils of a divided China lay in conserving the culture of the sage founders of the Chou dynasty (1030–256 BC). Failing to secure acceptance of his doctrines at any of the courts he visited, he became a teacher of moral and political wisdom, mainly to young men who were potential statesmen. He has been revered not only for his lofty ideals, but also because he was traditionally (but mistakenly) regarded as author or editor of the oldest among the Thirteen Classics, which later provided China with her staple educational diet and became required reading for aspirants to the mandarinate. This heterogeneous corpus of history, poetry, ethics, and works on ritual, divination, etc., includes the *Analects*, which contains the most authentic of the Master's sayings, and the *Book of Mencius*, comprising the teachings of the most famous later Confucian.

Confucianism became systematized during the Han dynasty (206 BC–AD 220). Despite the rivalry of *Taoism and Buddhism (which entered China in the 1st cent. AD), it formed the dominant ideology of China throughout most of its history down to the close of the empire in 1911. Dominating the educational system, it moulded moral beliefs and political practices. Although Confucius's own teachings were entirely secular and largely concerned with goodness, justice, loyalty, filial piety, and other virtues practised in human relationships, a cult of Confucius developed. The term Confucianism has sometimes also been loosely applied to religious practices coloured by Confucianist ritual (e.g. ancestor-worship) or sponsored by the Confucian state (e.g. the religious functions of the Emperor).

CONGREVE, William (1670–1729), born at Bardsey, near Leeds, of an ancient family. Because his father was commander of the garrison at Youghal, he was educated at Kilkenny school and Trinity College, Dublin, at both of which he was a fellow student of *Swift. He entered the Middle Temple, but soon gave up law for literature, published a novel of intrigue, *Incognita* (1691), and in 1693 suddenly achieved fame with his comedy *The Old Bachelor*. Of his other comedies, *The Double Dealer* was published in 1694 (first performed 1693), *Love for Love* in 1695, and *The Way of the World* in 1700. In these Congreve shows himself the master of *Restoration comedy, studying the social pressures on love and marriage with wit and subtlety. His one tragedy, *The Mourning Bride*, was produced in 1697. In 1698 he replied to the attack made on him in the *Short View* of Jeremy *Collier. After 1700 he wrote comparatively little for the stage; he was by then in comfortable circumstances, holding more than one government post, and enjoying general admiration and the friendship of men like Swift, *Steele, and *Pope. He was visited by *Voltaire, and had an affair with the duchess of Marlborough, who bore him a daughter. He was throughout the friend of Mrs *Bracegirdle. He was buried at Westminster Abbey.

Coningsby, a novel by B. *Disraeli, published 1844.

In the preface to the Hughenden edition of his novels in 1870 Disraeli declares that his purpose in the trilogy *Coningsby*—*Sybil*—*Tancred* was to describe the influence of the main political parties on the condition of the people, and to indicate how those conditions might be improved. His theme is that the Crown must govern justly and the Church inspire. His purpose was avowedly political, and he chose the novel as the most effective influence on public opinion. *Coningsby* celebrates the new Tories of the 'Young England' set, whose opposition to Whiggery and whose concern at the treatment of the poor and the injustice of the franchise is strongly reflected in the narrative.

The high-spirited and generous Coningsby, whose parents both die, is sent to Eton by his wealthy and powerful grandfather, Lord Monmouth, who represents the old type of oppressive Tory aristocrat. There Coningsby becomes the friend, and saves the life of, Oswald Millbank, who is the son of an energetic Lancashire manufacturer, detested by Monmouth. At Cambridge and thereafter Coningsby develops political and social ideals far removed from those of his grandfather, and meanwhile falls in love with Oswald's sister Edith. His behaviour so angers Monmouth that when the old man dies Coningsby finds he has been disinherited. He has to forgo his life of affluence and set to work in the Inns of Court. Gradually Millbank, who had been opposed to Coningsby's marriage to his daughter, begins to realize the young man's worth; he helps him to stand for Parliament and sees him returned. Edith and Coningsby are married and Coningsby's fortunes are restored.

The vigorous portrait of Lord Monmouth is based on Lord Hertford, who was also the model for *Thackeray's Lord Steyne. Sidonia, the wise old Jew who appears also in *Tancred*, reflects aspects of Lord Rothschild; and Rigby, possibly the most unpleasant of all Disraeli's characters, is based on J. W. *Croker. *Coningsby* was immensely successful and came to be regarded as a manifesto for Young England.

Connecticut Wits, see HARTFORD WITS.

Connoisseur, The, a periodical edited by G. *Colman the elder, and journalist and wit Bonnell Thornton (1724–68). It ran from Jan. 1754 to Sept. 1756, and *Cowper was among its contributors.

CONNOLLY, Cyril Vernon (1903–74), educated at Eton and Balliol College, Oxford, became a journalist and critic, and a regular contributor to the *New Statesman; he was literary editor of the *Observer, 1942–3, and was for many years a weekly reviewer for the *Sunday Times. In 1939, with *Spender, he founded *Horizon, and edited it until it closed in 1950. His only novel, *The Rock Pool* (Paris,

1936; London, 1947), is a satiric extravaganza with echoes of *Firbank and E. *Waugh; it describes the adventures of a young literary stockbroker in Trou-sur-Mer, an artistic expatriate colony on the French Riviera. His works include *Enemies of Promise* (1938), critical essays, with an autobiographical section, 'A Georgian Boyhood', vividly recalling his schooldays (and the distinctive Etonian literary tradition of light verse, *Pre-Raphaelite-style Homer, etc.); *The Unquiet Grave* (1944), subtitled 'A Word Cycle' and published under the pseudonym of Palinurus (the drowned pilot of the *Aeneid*), which consists of aphorisms, reflections, etc.; and various collections of essays (*The Condemned Playground*, 1945, which displays his gift for parody; *Previous Convictions*, 1963; *The Evening Colonnade*, 1973, and others). Connolly's favourite themes include the dangers of early success and the hazardous lure of literary immortality, but he also celebrated the ephemeral pleasure of food, wine, and travel. A biography by David Pryce-Jones was published in 1983.

CONQUEST, (George) Robert (Acworth) (1917–   ), poet, historian, and critic, educated at Winchester and Magdalen College, Oxford, who edited the important and controversial anthology *New Lines (1956). His publications include *Poems* (1955), *Between Mars and Venus* (1962), *Arias from a Love Opera* (1969), and several works on the USSR.

CONRAD, Joseph (Teodor Josef Konrad Korzeniowski) (1857–1924), novelist and short story writer, born of Polish parents in the Russian-dominated Ukraine. His father's political sympathies caused the family to be exiled to Volagda in northern Russia, where Conrad's mother died when he was seven. After their return to Poland his father also died and Conrad was taken under the wing of his uncle, Thaddeus Bobrowski, who was to be a continuing influence on his life. From an early age he longed to go to sea and in 1874 he went to Marseilles, embarked on a French vessel, and began the career as a sailor which was to supply so much material for his writing. In 1886 he became a British subject and a master mariner and in 1894, after twenty years at sea, he settled in England and devoted himself to writing. He published his first novel at the age of 38, writing in English, his third language.

In 1895 Conrad married Jessie George, by whom he was to have two sons, and his novel *Almayer's Folly* appeared in the same year. This was followed by *An Outcast of the Islands* (1896), in which there is still evidence of his struggle with both technique and the English language; but with *The Nigger of the Narcissus* (1897) and *Lord Jim* (1900) he showed himself a master of his craft. The sea continued to suppply the setting for most of his novels and short stories. His

narrative technique is characterized by a skilful use of breaks in time–sequence and he uses a narrator, Marlow, who provides a commentary on the action not unlike that of a Greek chorus. Conrad has been called an Impressionist and the movement of the stories, of the images and emotions, are portrayed through each character's private vision of reality. He collaborated with F. M. *Ford on *The Inheritors* (1900) and *Romance* (1903), but eventual disagreements brought their association to an end. *Typhoon* (1902) was followed by a major work, *Nostromo* (1904), an imaginative novel which again explores one of Conrad's chief preoccupations—man's vulnerability and corruptibility. In *'Heart of Darkness' (1902) one of his best-known short stories, Conrad had carried this issue to a terrifying conclusion. *The Secret Agent* (1907) and *Under Western Eyes* (1911) are both novels with political themes, the latter set in Switzerland and Russia and centred on the tragedy of student Razumov, caught up in the treachery and violence of revolution. Although warmly supported by E. *Garnett and the agent J. B. Pinker, and praised by Arnold *Bennett, *Galsworthy, H. *James, and other influential men of letters, Conrad's work was generally ill-received by both critics and public alike, and he was plagued with money problems. Some of his stories were serialized in *Blackwood's Magazine*, but it was the novel *Chance* (1913) that brought Conrad his first popular and financial success; it is the story of Flora de Barral, lonely daughter of a crooked financier, and combines the attractions of a sea background with the theme of Romantic love and more female interest than is usual with Conrad. His other major works include *Youth* (1902), *The Mirror of the Sea* (1906), *Victory* (1915), *The Shadow Line* (1917), *The Rescue* (1920), and *The Rover* (1923). Conrad's autobiography, *A Personal Record*, appeared in book form in 1912 and his unfinished novel *Suspense* was published in 1925.

By the time of his death, Conrad was well established in the literary world as one of the leading *Modernists; a decline of interest in the 1930s was followed by increasing scholarly and critical attention, pioneered in part by a study in 1941 by M. C. *Bradbrook, and by an essay in the same year by *Leavis in *Scrutiny (later reprinted in *The Great Tradition*) in which Conrad is placed 'among the very great novelists in the language'. See J. Baines, *Joseph Conrad: A Critical Biography* (1960); F. R. Karl, *Joseph Conrad: The Three Lives* (1979) and Z. Najder, *Joseph Conrad. A Chronicle* (1983).The first volume of his *Collected Letters 1861–1897*, ed. F. Karl and L. Davis, was published in 1983.

Conrade of Montserrat, a character in Scott's *The Talisman*, based on the historical Conrad of Montferrat.

Conscience, Mr, in Bunyan's *The Holy War*, the Recorder of the city of Mansoul, deposed from his office during the tyranny of Diabolus.

Conscious Lovers, The, the last comedy of *Steele, based on the *Andria* of *Terence, performed 1722.

Young Bevil is, at his father's desire, about to marry Lucinda, daughter of the wealthy Mr Sealand. But he loves Indiana, an orphan whom he met destitute and friendless in a foreign town and has honourably supported. Not wishing to oppose his father openly, he makes known to Lucinda his aversion to the proposed match, the more readily as he knows his friend Myrtle loves her. In doing this he offends Myrtle, is challenged to a duel, and declines, thus exhibiting the folly of duelling, a favourite theme with Steele. Indiana turns out to be a lost daughter of Mr Sealand, who is happy to bestow her on Bevil; Myrtle gains Lucinda. The play, with its high moral tone, was a success, and considerably influenced the drift towards *sentimental comedy in England and in France.

CONSTABLE, Archibald (1774–1827), a Scots publisher whom Sir W. *Scott described as 'of uncommon importance to literature'. He was an expert in antiquarian books, yet he also possessed a flair for choosing contemporary authors and he published most of Scott's early work. He established the highly successful *Edinburgh Review* in 1802, paying his contributors handsomely, and bought the *Encyclopaedia Britannica* in 1812. Yet in 1826 he went bankrupt, heavily involving Scott in his debts. He was an enthusiast for the new concept of cheap books, and in 1827 established Constable's Miscellany, a series of volumes on literature, art, and science.

CONSTABLE, Henry (1562–1613), was educated at St John's College, Cambridge, embraced Roman Catholicism, and withdrew to Paris. He published *Diana*, a volume of sonnets, in 1592; it was republished in 1594 with additions by other poets. He was sent as papal envoy to Edinburgh in 1599 and pensioned by the French king. He came to London in 1603, was imprisoned in the Tower in 1604, and released the same year. He died at Liège. Verses by him were embodied in various collections, among others in *Englands Helicon*. His poems were edited by Joan Grundy in 1960. Many of his sonnets are modelled on or translated from sonnets by Desportes.

CONSTABLE, John (1776–1837), landscape painter, born at East Bergholt, Suffolk, the son of a miller. His interest in transient effects of light and his rural subjects, often with East Anglian settings, departed from the standards of classical landscape. His works develop from the tranquillity of the early exhibited landscapes (*The Haywain*, 1821, National Gallery, London) to the sombre drama of *Hadleigh Castle* (1829, Tate Gallery, London). Constable's relationship with the Romantic poets has been much discussed by scholars; he is linked to them by his passionate feeling for the simplest facts of nature and by his sense of their moral power. Yet Constable disliked the Lake District, where he met *Wordsworth and *Coleridge in 1806; although he admired the *'Ancient Mariner', his tastes were generally more traditional—for *Cowper and *Gray, whose *Elegy* he illustrated, and for Thomson's *The Seasons* and R. *Bloomfield's *The Farmer's Boy* (1802)—and lines from these works sometimes accompanied his pictures. Constable was a friend of Joseph Farington, of J. T. Smith, of Sir G. *Beaumont, and of Charles Leslie; Leslie's *The Life of John Constable* was published in 1843 and remains a standard work. (See ROMANTICISM.)

Constance, (1) the heroine of 'The Man of Law's Tale' in Chaucer's *Canterbury Tales*, 5; (2) in Shakespeare's *King John*, the mother of Arthur, the king's nephew.

Constance of Beverley, a character in Scott's *Marmion*.

Constant, a character in Vanbrugh's *The Provok'd Wife*.

CONSTANT, Benjamin (Henri-Benjamin Constant de Rebecque) (1767–1830), French novelist, political philosopher, and politician, born at Lausanne of a family of French Protestant origins, had his university education at Oxford (briefly), in Germany, and at Edinburgh. He was intermittently in Paris after 1795 and held office under the Consulate, but went into exile in 1803. From Hanover he published the anti-Napoleonic pamphlet 'De l'esprit de conquête et de l'usurpation' (1813). His political career in the Liberal opposition begins after the Restoration. Constant is remembered for the political and religious treatises *De la religion considérée dans sa source, ses formes et ses développements* (5 vols, 1824–31), but much more for the literary masterpiece *Adolphe* (first published in London in 1816) a short novel of psychological analysis reflecting at some points his own liaison with Mme de *Staël. His *Journaux intimes*, first published in 1895, appeared in a complete edition in 1952; his *Cahier rouge*, recounting the first 20 years of his life, in 1907, and *Cécile*, the fragment of an autobiographical novel, in 1951. (See also ZÉLIDE.)

Constant Couple, The, or a Trip to the Jubilee, a farcical comedy by *Farquhar, produced 1699, which was very successful owing chiefly to the amusing character of Sir Harry Wildair, 'an airy gentleman, affecting humorous gaiety and freedom in his behaviour'. It had a less successful sequel in *Sir Harry Wildair* (1701).

Contarini Fleming: a Psychological Romance, a novel by B. *Disraeli, published 1832.

This novel, which remained Disraeli's own favourite, was the last in the group *Vivian Grey—*Alroy—Fleming, although it was published before *Alroy*. In the preface to the 1845 edition of his novels, Disraeli describes how in this book he developed 'my poetic character' and attempted to provide a complete picture of the development of a poet. In making his hero the son of both Saxon and Venetian lineage, living in 'a northern court', Disraeli attempts to show the effects on character of North and South. Contarini is an impetuous, handsome boy, whose visions of beauty and freedom make him rebellious at school, from which he runs away. His kindly father sends him to a university, where he wins prizes, and then introduces him to society, where his wit and moody brilliance bring him great success. But society palls and, after various wild adventures in the northern forests, he eventually finds his way to Venice, the home of his mother's family, where he is captivated by the beauty of the city and where he meets his lovely cousin, Alceste, whom he marries. She dies within a year and to calm his grief he again takes up his travels, passing through Italy, Andalusia, Greece, the Holy Land, and Egypt, before returning to an estate near Naples, where he intends to live in solitude in 'the study and creation of the beautiful'. The influence of *Goethe's *Wilhelm Meister* and of the *'Byronic' hero are clearly evident. The novel (described by a contemporary reviewer as 'a *Childe Harold* in prose') lost money to begin with, but was admired by Goethe and *Heine, as well as by *Beckford.

Contemporary Review, The, was founded in 1866 and was edited for many years by Sir Percy Bunting. It covered religious, political, and literary subjects; in 1955 it incorporated *The Fortnightly*, and now deals largely with current affairs.

Conversation, A complete Collection of polite and ingenious, by *Swift, published 1738.

In this entertaining work Swift good-humouredly satirizes the stupidity, coarseness, and attempted wit of the conversation of fashionable people. In three dialogues he puts into the mouth of various characters, Lord Sparkish, Miss Notable, Lady Smart, Tom Neverout, etc., samples of questions and answers, proverbial sayings, and repartees, fitted, as he explains in the amusing introduction, 'to adorn every kind of discourse that an assembly of English ladies and gentlemen, met together for their mutual entertainment, can possibly want'. The work was published under the pseudonym of 'Simon Wagstaff, Esq.'

CONWAY, Anne, Viscountess (d. 1679), metaphysical writer and friend of Henry More

(see CAMBRIDGE PLATONISTS). Her posthumous *Principles of the most Ancient and Modern Philosophy* (Latin 1790, English 1692) influenced *Leibniz.

COOK, Eliza (1818–89), largely self-educated, began writing verse at an early age. Her first volume, *Lays of a Wild Harp* (1835), appeared when she was 17. Encouraged by early success, she began contributing regularly to periodicals including the *Weekly Dispatch*, in which her most popular poem 'The Old Armchair' first appeared in 1837. Her poems were characterized by an unaffected domestic sentiment which appealed strictly to popular uncultured tastes. She conducted *Eliza Cook's Journal* from 1849, but her failing health caused its demise in 1854. Her complete poetical works were published in 1870.

COOK, James (1728–79), celebrated circumnavigator, left records of his three principal voyages in *An Account of a Voyage round the World 1768–71* (1773), compiled by J. Hawkesworth from the journals of Cook and his botanist *Banks (Cook's own journal of this voyage was edited by Wharton in 1893); *A Voyage towards the South Pole . . . 1772–3* (1777); *A Voyage to the Pacific Ocean . . . 1776–1780* (1784, the third vol. by Capt. T. King). Passages from Cook's second volume provided sources for the story and imagery of Coleridge's *'Ancient Mariner' (see J. L. *Lowes, *The Road to Xanadu*, 1927). Cook was murdered by natives in Hawaii.

'Cook's Tale, The', see CANTERBURY TALES, 4.

Coole Park, Co. Galway, home of Lady *Gregory, famous as the headquarters of the *Irish Revival. Summer home of W. B. *Yeats for nearly 20 years, it was the subject of many of his poems, notably 'In the Seven Woods', 'Coole Park, 1929', and 'Coole Park and Ballylee, 1931'. Guests who carved their names on its famous autograph tree (a copper beech) included G. B. *Shaw, J. M. *Synge, W. B. Yeats, J. B. *Yeats, A. *John, G. W. *Russell (Æ), and D. *Hyde. The house, described by Lady Gregory in *Coole* (1931, enl. 1971), was pulled down in 1941.

COOPER, James Fenimore (1789–1851), born in New Jersey, spent his youth partly on the family estate at Cooperstown on Otsego Lake (NY), partly in the merchant marine (after dismissal from Yale), partly in the American navy. He then settled down as a country proprietor and writer of novels. His second book *The Spy* (1821), a stirring tale of the American revolution, brought him into prominence. *The Pioneers* (1823) was the first of his best-known group of novels, *Leather-Stocking Tales*, called after the deerskin leggings of their hero, pioneer scout Natty Bumppo (alias 'Deerslayer', 'Pathfinder', or 'Hawkeye'); the sequels were *The Last of the Mohicans* (1826), *The Prairie* (1827), *The Pathfinder* (1840), and *The Deerslayer* (1841). They deal with adventures of the frontier and give a vivid picture of Red Indian and pioneer life; *Parkman, in an 1852 appreciation, echoes the familiar comparison with Sir W. *Scott and, despite some reservations about the loquacity of the characters, the bloodthirstiness of some of the scenes, and improbabilities of plot, finds his descriptions 'instinct with life, with the very spirit of the wilderness; they breathe the sombre poetry of solitude and danger.'

From 1826 to 1833 Cooper travelled in Europe, and on his return appeared several highly critical accounts of European society, including *England, with Sketches of Society in the Metropolis* (1837; which nevertheless contains some appreciative comments, notably of the famous breakfasts of S. *Rogers); this was violently attacked in Britain, notably by *Lockhart. Cooper was, however, also deeply critical of American democracy, and expressed his conservative opinions directly in *The American Democrat* (1838) and fictionally in *Homeward Bound* and *Home as Found* (both 1838). Among his many other works the scholarly *The History of the Navy of the United States* (1839); *Satanstoe* (1845), a historical novel of manners; and *The Crater* (1848) could be mentioned to illustrate his fertility and variety. A collection of *Letters and Journals* (6 vols, ed. J. F. Beard) appeared in 1960–8. See also two influential essays by D. H. *Lawrence, in *Studies in Classic American Literature* (1923), which provoked a continuing discussion of Cooper's role as myth-maker.

COOPER, William, pseudonym of Harry Summerfield Hoff (1910–   ), who taught physics in a Leicester school before the war, during which period he published novels under his own name. After the war he embarked on a career in government service, and the civil service features in much of his work, as it does in that of his friend and colleague C. P. *Snow. His most influential novel, *Scenes from Provincial Life* (1950, reissued in 1969 with a preface by M. *Bradbury) was hailed as seminal by *Braine and other writers of the 1950s, who also chose provincial, anarchic but ambitious, lower-middle-class heroes, and a low-key realist tone, in what some have seen as a reaction against *Modernism. (See also ANGRY YOUNG MEN.) It was followed in 1961 by *Scenes from Married Life*, and in 1982 by *Scenes from Metropolitan Life*, originally written as the middle volume of the trilogy. In these novels Joe Lunn narrates with comic irony his own story, from his schoolmaster days in a nameless provincial city when his mistress, Myrtle, is trying to marry him, through the immediate post-war years in London when he is trying to marry Myrtle, to his successful marriage to schoolmistress Elspeth; his

affairs and career are contrasted with those of his colleague, confidant, and fellow novelist, Robert. A sequel, *Scenes from Later Life*, appeared in 1983.

Cooper's Hill, see DENHAM, J.

COPERNICUS, Latinized form of the surname of Nicolas KOPPERNIK (1473–1543), astronomer, native of Torun, Poland, who propounded in his *De Revolutionibus* (1543) the theory that the planets, including the earth, move in orbits round the sun as centre, in opposition to *Ptolemy's earlier geocentric theory. Only after a century of fierce debate was the superiority of the heliocentric theory accepted in the scientific and scholarly world.

Cophetua, King, a legendary king in Africa, who cared nothing for women until he saw a beggar maid 'all in gray', with whom he fell in love. He married her and together they lived 'a quiet life during their princely reign'. The tale is told in one of the ballads included in Percy's *Reliques*, where the maid's name is given as Penelophon. Shakespeare, in *Love's Labour's Lost* (IV. i), gives it as Zenelophon. There are other references to the story in Shakespeare's *Romeo and Juliet* (II. i) and in 2 *Henry IV* (V. iii), in Jonson's *Every Man in his Humour* (III. iv), and in *Tennyson's 'The Beggar Maid' (1842).

Copmanhurst, Clerk of, otherwise Friar Tuck, in Scott's *Ivanhoe*.

COPPARD, A(lfred) E(dgar) (1878–1957), the son of a tailor, who worked through many jobs before he became a full-time writer, and supplemented his meagre earnings with money prizes won through his athletic skills. His first collection of short stories, *Adam and Eve and Pinch Me* (1921), established his name and led to much encouragement, including that of F. M. *Ford. His first book of verse, *Hips and Haws*, appeared in 1922, and thereafter he produced a book of stories or verses almost every year until the early 1950s. The first part of an autobiography, *It's Me O Lord*, was published posthumously in 1957. The deceptive simplicity of Coppard's stories conceals a widely admired technical skill; many of the most characteristic tales are set in robust country backgrounds, and display a deep sympathy for the oddity and misfit.

COPPE, Abiezer (1619–72), a Ranter, preacher, mystic, and pamphleteer, famed for his eccentric behaviour (he preached naked in the streets of London, denouncing the rich); his two *Fiery Flying Rolls* (1649) are charged with fervour and compassion, and are written in a highly original poetic prose described by Christopher *Hill (*The World Turned Upside Down*, 1972) as 'unlike anything else in the seventeenth century'.

Copper, Lord, the domineering newspaper magnate in E. Waugh's *Scoop*. His foreign editor Salter is given to saying 'Definitely, Lord Copper' when he was right, and 'Up to a point, Lord Copper' when he was wrong.

Copyright, see APPENDIX II.

Copyright Libraries may, under the Copyright Act, 1911, claim a free copy of any book published in Britain. There are six: the British Library, London; the Bodleian, Oxford; the University Library, Cambridge; the National Library of Wales, Aberystwyth; the National Library of Scotland, Edinburgh; and Trinity College, Dublin: see under LIBRARIES.

Corah, name for Titus *Oates in Dryden's *Absalom and Achitophel*.

Coral Island, The, see BALLANTYNE, R. M.

Coranto, or current of news, the name applied to periodical news-pamphlets issued between 1621 and 1641 (their publication was interrupted 1632–8) containing foreign intelligence taken from foreign papers. They were one of the earliest forms of English journalism, and were followed by the *newsbook. See also NEWS-PAPERS, ORIGINS OF.

Corbaccio, the deaf old miser in Jonson's *Volpone*.

Corbenic, the castle where the *Grail is found in the Arthurian legends. R. S. Loomis (*The Grail From Celtic Myth to Christian Symbol*, 1963) believes that the name may be a miswriting for 'Corbenoit', blessed horn, which was one of the archetypal ingredients (the horn of Bran) in the Grail story, misunderstood as *cor(s)*, body (of Christ). However this may be, there is little evidence of any awareness of this etymological archetype in any of the surviving Grail stories.

CORBETT, or **CORBET,** Richard (1582–1635), was the son of Vincent Corbet, a Surrey gardener, of whom *Jonson said in an elegy, 'His mind as pure and neatly kept | As were his nourseries . . . ' Richard was educated at Westminster and Christ Church, Oxford, became chaplain to James I and, later bishop first of Oxford, then of Norwich. He was generous, witty, and eloquent, and his poetry—*Certain Elegant Poems* (1647) and *Poetica Stromata* (1648)—ranges from the entertaining traveller's story of 'Iter Boreale' and the ironical verses on 'The Distracted Puritane' to the charming little poem 'To his son, Vincent Corbet' on his third birthday. His best-known poem is probably 'A Proper New Ballad, entitled The Fairies Farewell' which begins 'Farewell, rewards and fairies'. He also addressed some amusing lines to *Coryate after the latter's return from a journey in Europe. He pronounced the funeral oration

for *Bodley. An edition of his poems, edited by J. A. W. Bennett and H. R. Trevor-Roper, was published in 1955.

Corceca, in Spenser's *Faerie Queene* (I. iii. 18), 'blindness of heart', an old blind woman, mother of *Abessa (Superstition).

Cordelia, in Shakespeare's *King Lear*, the youngest of the king's three daughters.

CORELLI, Marie, pseudonym of Mary Mackay (1855–1924), studied music and turned to fiction at the age of 30 with her first novel, *A Romance of Two Worlds* (1886), which was followed by many more romantic melodramas. She hypnotized her public with her exuberant imagination and her far-fetched theories on anything from morality to radioactive vibrations. She achieved outstanding success at the turn of the century, *Gladstone and *Wilde being among her admirers, but her popularity turned to ridicule long before her death. Her other novels include *Barabbas* (1893), *The Sorrows of Satan* (1895), *The Mighty Atom* (1896), *The Master Christian* (1900), *Temporal Power* (1902), *The Young Diana* (1918), and *The Secret Power* (1921).

Corflambo, in Spenser's *Faerie Queene* (IV. vii and viii), 'a mightie man . . . Ryding upon a Dromedare on hie, | Of stature huge, and horrible of hew', symbolizes lust. He carries off *Amoret, who is released from him by *Timias and *Belphoebe. He is slain by Prince *Arthur.

CORIAT, Thomas, see CORYATE.

Corineus, see GOGMAGOG.

Corinthian Tom, a character in *Egan's *Life in London*.

Coriolanus, a play by *Shakespeare first printed in the *Folio (1623), in which, before the late insertion of *Troilus and Cressida*, it seems to have been placed first of the tragedies. In order of composition, however, it was probably Shakespeare's last tragedy, written about 1608. Its source is *North's version of *Plutarch's 'Life of Caius Martius Coriolanus'. The play has never been a very popular one, but in the 20th cent. its political and military themes have stimulated some interest; see for instance the two poems by T. S. *Eliot yoked by the title *Coriolan*. The opening scene, in which Menenius Agrippa tells the citizens of Rome a fable of the body's members rebelling against itself, was a popular Renaissance allegory of the state.

Caius Marcius, a proud Roman general, performs wonders of valour in a war against the Volscians, and captures the town Corioli, receiving in consequence the surname Coriolanus. On his return it is proposed to make him consul, but his arrogant and outspoken contempt of the Roman rabble makes him unpopular with the fickle crowd, and the tribunes of the people have no difficulty in securing his banishment. He goes to the Volscian general, Aufidius, his enemy of long standing, is received with delight, and leads the Volscians against Rome to effect his revenge. He reaches the walls of the city, and the Romans, to save it from destruction, send emissaries, old friends of Coriolanus, to propose terms, but in vain. Finally his mother Volumnia, his meek wife Valeria, and his son come to beseech him to spare the city and he yields to the eloquence of his mother, suspecting that by so doing he has signed his own death warrant: makes a treaty favourable to the Volscians, and returns with them to Antium, a Volscian town. Here Aufidius turns against him, accusing him of betraying the Volscian interests, and with the assistance of conspirators of his faction, publicly kills Coriolanus.

Corisande, Lady, in *Lothair by B. Disraeli.

CORNEILLE, Pierre (1616–84), French dramatist. Born in a family of magistrates, he was educated at a Jesuit school, studied the law, and practised in the Rouen magistrature until 1630. Although the 33 plays that make up his *œuvre* exploited every dramatic genre available to him, he is best known as the creator of French classical tragedy. Elements of tragic form, including the observation of the *unities and the use of the alexandrine, had been evolving in the work of his predecessors, but he gave this form its appropriate content by confining the action of the play to a conflict between passion and duty at a point of moral crisis. His first great play, *Le Cid* (1637), inspired by Spanish drama (see CID), achieved a triumph which provoked a cabal, and eventually an adverse judgement by the *Académie française. After a period of discouragement, he followed *Le Cid* with three further masterpieces: *Horace* (1640), dramatizing a conflict between domestic and patriotic imperatives; *Cinna* (1641), exploring the tensions between justice and mercy; and *Polyeucte* (1643), presenting the dilemma of a Christian martyr caught between the desire for glory and the prompting of affection. Corneille's world is a heroic one, but the heroism is grounded in psychological and social reality. The magnifications of tragedy are qualified by comic and even pastoral perspectives; and the aim of the drama remains less to exalt his audience than to show it the facts of its own nature. He exerted a powerful influence on the English dramatists of the *Restoration, particularly *Dryden. The best 17th-cent. translations are by Katherine *Philips (the 'matchless Orinda').

Cornelia, a tragedy translated by T. *Kyd from a Senecan play by Robert Garnier, published 1594. It appeared in the following year under the title *Pompey the Great, his faire Corneliaes Tragedie*.

It deals with the story of Cornelia, daughter of Metellus Scipio and wife of Pompey the Great. The latter, after the battle of Pharsalus, is killed on the way to Egypt. Scipio assembles new forces, but after being defeated by Caesar at Thaspus in Africa and again at sea stabs himself. The play largely consists of Cornelia's lamentations for her misfortunes.

Cornelia, a character in Webster's *The White Devil.

CORNFORD, Frances (1886–1960), poet, born in Cambridge where she spent most of her life. She published several volumes of verse but is best known for her triolet 'To a Fat Lady Seen from a Train', with its curiously memorable though undistinguished lines 'O why do you walk through the fields in gloves, | Missing so much and so much? | O fat white woman whom nobody loves'. Her *Collected Poems* appeared in 1954. She was a granddaughter of C. *Darwin and mother of J. *Cornford.

CORNFORD, John (1915–36), poet, the son of Frances *Cornford and the distinguished scholar Francis M. Cornford. By the time he enrolled at the London School of Economics in 1933 he had become heavily involved with radical politics and Communism. In 1936 he was the first Englishman to enlist against Franco in the Spanish Civil War, and was killed in action the same year. His poems had been published in various periodicals (*New Writing, The Cambridge Review, The Student Vanguard*) and were collected with various prose pieces, mainly political, in *John Cornford: A Memoir*, ed. Pat Sloan, 1938.

Cornhill Magazine, The (1860–1975), a literary periodical of consistently high quality, began with *Thackeray as editor and specialized in the serialization of novels. Trollope's *Framley Parsonage* was succeeded by the novels of, among others, Mrs *Gaskell, *Reade, G. *Eliot, and *Hardy; many poems of *Tennyson, R. *Browning, and *Swinburne first appeared in it, as well as work by *Ruskin, *MacDonald, and another of its editors, L. *Stephen. It continued in this century to publish the work of many major writers, both creative and critical.

Cornhill to Cairo, see NOTES OF A JOURNEY FROM CORNHILL TO GRAND CAIRO.

Corn Law Rhymer, see ELLIOTT, E.

Corno di Bassetto, the name under which G. B. *Shaw wrote his music criticism. See also under MUSIC, LITERATURE OF.

CORNWALL, Barry, pseudonym of Brian Waller Proctor (1787–1874), practised as a solicitor and barrister in London, and was made a commissioner in lunacy. He began to contribute to *The Literary Gazette* in 1815 and became a friend of Leigh *Hunt, *Lamb, and later *Dickens. Under his pseudonym he enjoyed great popular success, particularly as a writer of songs and lyrics. His *Dramatic Scenes* (1819) was praised by Lamb, and his poem *Marcian Collona* (1820), a verse tale of madness and passion, was well received by the public. However, *Keats and *Shelley were disparaging about his work, and *Darley complained of Cornwall's 'eternal cud of rose-leaves'. In 1821 *Macready successfully produced Cornwall's one drama, *Mirandola*. His *English Songs* appeared in 1832, and he also wrote biographies of Lamb and *Kean.

Corridors of Power, The, see SNOW, C. P.

Corsair, The, a poem by Lord *Byron, published 1814.

Conrad, a pirate chief, a *'Byronic' character of many vices but with the virtue of chivalry, receives warning that the Turkish Pacha is preparing to descend upon his island. He takes leave of his beloved Medora, arrives at the Pacha's rallying-point, and introduces himself as a dervish escaped from the pirates. However his plans go amiss, and he is wounded and taken prisoner, but not before he has rescued Gulnare, the chief slave in the Pacha's harem, from imminent death. She falls in love with him, and finally brings him a dagger with which he may kill the Pacha in his sleep. Conrad revolts from such an act, whereupon she herself kills the Pacha and escapes with Conrad. When they arrive at the pirate island Conrad finds Medora dead from grief at the reported killing of her lover. Conrad disappears and is never heard of again: but see LARA.

CORSO, Gregory, see BEAT GENERATION.

Cortegiano, Il, see CASTIGLIONE.

CORTÉS, Hernando (1485–1547), the conqueror of Mexico. He entered Mexico City in 1519. It was not he but *Balboa who was the first European to gaze on the Pacific (see *Keats's sonnet 'On first looking into Chapman's Homer').

Corvino, one of Volpone's would-be heirs in Jonson's *Volpone*.

CORVO, Baron, see ROLFE, F. W.

CORY, William Johnson (1823–92), assistant master at Eton, 1845–72. On leaving he changed his name from Johnson to Cory. He published various educational works, but is best remembered for his volume of poems *Ionica* (1858), and in particular for the translation that it contains of the epigram of Heraclitus of Halicarnassus by *Callimachus, 'They told me Heraclitus, they told me you were dead.' He also wrote the 'Eton Boating Song', published 1865.

His letters and journals were edited by F. Warre-Cornish (1897).

CORYATE, Thomas (?1577–1617), the son of a rector of Odcombe, whose fame as a traveller was legendary in his lifetime and long outlasted it. He travelled in 1608 through France, Italy, Switzerland, Germany, and Holland, mainly on foot. He published in 1611 a long narrative of his travels entitled *Coryats Crudities*, a much shorter sequel, and *The Odcombian Banquet*, a reprint of the verses printed with the *Crudities*. In 1612 he set out overland to India, travelling through Constantinople, Palestine, Mesopotamia, and reaching Agra in 1616. He died at Surat. A letter of his from the court of the Great Mogul is printed by *Purchas, and this and another letter from the East are included in a compilation called *Thomas Coriate Traveller for the English Wits: Greeting*. Coryate wrote in an extravagant and euphuistic style ('He is a great and bold carpenter of words', said *Jonson), and was well known as an eccentric and amusing character; there are many references to him in 17th-cent. literature. See M. Strachan, *The Life and Adventures of Thomas Coryate* (1962).

Corydon, a shepherd who figures in the *Idylls* of *Theocritus and the *Eclogues* of *Virgil, and whose name has become conventional in pastoral poetry.

Coryphaeus, the leader of a chorus in the Attic drama.

Cosmos, see HUMBOLDT, A. VON.

Costard, a clown in Shakespeare's *Love's Labour's Lost*.

Costigan, Captain and Emily (Miss Fotheringay), characters in Thackeray's *Pendennis*.

Coterie, a sophisticated avant-garde periodical, edited by Chapman Hall, of which six numbers appeared in 1919–20, and a seventh, edited by Russell Green, in 1920. It was superseded by *New Coterie* (1925–7), handsomely illustrated, with covers by William Roberts. Contributors included D. H. *Lawrence, T. S. *Eliot, A. *Huxley, E. *Sitwell, and R. *Aldington.

COTGRAVE, Randle (d. ?1634), author of a famous French-English dictionary published 1611. He was a scholar of St John's College, Cambridge. He had a wide knowledge not only of French and French literature, but of the slang of the day and also of natural history. *Urquhart relied largely upon his dictionary for the translation of *Rabelais.

Cotswold Olimpick Games, yearly celebrations held during Whit week on the hillside above Chipping Campden in Gloucestershire. With James I's permission, they were first organized in 1612 by Robert Dover (1582–1652), of Cambridge and Gray's Inn, using traditional pastimes and customs such as horse-racing, coursing, wrestling, backsword fighting, leaping, and dancing, and were commemorated in *Annalia Dubrensia* (1636), a collection of poems by 34 writers including *Drayton, *Jonson, T. *Randolph, and T. *Heywood. The frontispiece portrays Robert Dover, mounted, wearing the king's clothes, in front of his castle, with the games in progress. Suspended during the Civil War, the games were later continued as Dover's Meeting until 1852. The games are described in *Somervile's *Hobbinol* (1740), originally 'The Wicker Chair' (1708), and in Richard *Graves's *The Spiritual Quixote* (1773). They were again revived in 1963 and are held annually on the Friday of Spring Bank Holiday week on Dover's Hill.

'Cotter's Saturday Night, The', a poem by *Burns, published 1786. The verses describing the cotter's home, and the introduction of the daughter's young man, are in Scots, while those expounding religious and patriotic themes are in English.

COTTLE, Joseph (1770–1853), a bookseller of Bristol, who published the *Lyrical Ballads* and other work by *Wordsworth, *Coleridge, and *Southey. He was the author of a poem, 'Malvern Hills', published 1798, and edited with Southey the works of *Chatterton in 1803. His brother Amos Cottle (?1768–1800) translated, probably from Latin, the Edda of Saemund, published in 1797 under the title of *Icelandic Poetry*. The verse is limp, and *Byron wrote of him, 'Amos Cottle strikes the lyre in vain' (*English Bards and Scotch Reviewers*, l. 396).

COTTON, Charles (1630–87), of Beresford Hall, Staffordshire, was the son of Charles Cotton, a close friend of *Wotton, *Donne, *Selden, and other writers; the younger Charles was himself a friend of *Lovelace and of I. *Walton. He wrote the dialogue between Piscator and Viator which forms the second part in the 5th edn of *The Compleat Angler* (1676), and published in 1664 *Scarronides*, a burlesque of *Virgil (which *Pepys found 'extraordinary good'), and in 1665 a burlesque of *Lucian. His translation of *Montaigne, closer but less colourful than *Florio's, appeared in 1685. His *topographical poem *The Wonders of the Peake* (1681) celebrates the beauties and curiosities of the Peak district (the seventh wonder being Chatsworth). Cotton's love of his native landscapes and particularly of 'fair Dove, princess of rivers' is also expressed in many of his *Poems on Several Occasions* (1689). *Wordsworth and *Coleridge both admired his work, making particular mention of 'Ode upon Winter' and 'The Retirement'. Cotton also wrote love poems, some addressed to his first wife Isabella, sister of

Colonel Hutchinson (see HUTCHINSON, L.). His poems were edited by J. Buxton in 1958.

COTTON, Sir Robert Bruce (1571–1631), educated at Westminster School and Jesus College, Cambridge, was an antiquary and collector of manuscripts and coins. He gave the free use of his library to *Bacon, *Camden, *Ralegh, *Selden, *Speed, *Ussher, and other scholars, and sent a gift of manuscripts to the Bodleian Library on its foundation. He joined the parliamentary party and published various political tracts. The Cottonian Library, largely composed of works rescued from the dissolved monasteries, was left to the nation by Sir John Cotton (1621–1701), grandson of Sir Robert; it was placed in Essex House, then in Ashburnham House, where it suffered severely from fire in 1731. It was removed to the British Museum in 1753. It includes such treasures as the *Lindisfarne Gospels and other splendid biblical MSS such as the Codex Purpureus, the MS of *Beowulf, and the famous MS that includes *Pearl and Sir *Gawain and the Green Knight.

Count Alarcos, The Tragedy of, a verse play by B. *Disraeli, published 1839.
   Set in 13th-cent. Burgos and based on a Spanish ballad, the play recounts with much violence and intrigue the career of the wicked Alarcos, whose ambitious love for the cruel Infanta Solisa leads him to the murder of his loving and gentle wife. Written in flamboyant blank verse, the play was not staged until 1868, when its author was prime minister.

Countess Cathleen, The, a play in blank verse by *Yeats, published 1892. It is based on the story of Countess Kathleen O'Shea, told in Yeats's compilation *Fairy and Folk Tales of the Irish Peasantry* (1888). The scene is laid 'in Ireland in old times' at a period of famine. The people sell their souls to the demons for food. The countess does all she can to relieve their needs, till the demons steal their wealth. Finally she sells her own soul to the demons for a great sum, sacrificing her hope of salvation for the people. But at the end she is forgiven, for her intention was good. The play was first performed in Dublin in 1899, and marked the beginning of the *Irish Revival in the theatre.

Count Julian, a tragedy by W. S. *Landor, published 1812. The drama relates the vengeance taken by Count Julian, a Spanish nobleman, on Roderigo the king, who has seduced Julian's daughter; and Julian's fate. The story, which is told from the point of view of Julian, is also treated in Southey's *Roderick* and in a different form by Rowley in *All's Lost by Lust.

Count Robert of Paris, a novel by Sir W. *Scott, published 1831, the year before the author's death. This was one of the *Tales of my Landlord, 4th series, the last of the Waverley

Novels. It was written in ill health and betrays the decline of his powers.

The scene is Constantinople in the days of the Emperor Alexius Comnenus (1081–1118), and the story centres in the arrival there of the first crusaders, and in a plot of Nicephorus Briennius, the husband of *Anna Comnena, to dethrone his father-in-law. Anna Comnena herself figures largely in the novel and provides some of its best pages. Count Robert of Paris, a proud and valiant Frankish knight, and his Amazonian wife Brenhilda, are among the crusaders. When they pay homage to the emperor, Count Robert grossly insults him by seating himself on his throne. He thereby arouses the wrath of Hereward, an English soldier of the emperor's Varangian guard. The count and his wife, by a device of the emperor's, are detained as hostages for the crusaders when these cross to Asia; the count is thrown into prison and rescued by the chivalrous Hereward. Meanwhile his wife Brenhilda is exposed to the unwelcome attentions of Briennius and challenges him to a duel, agreeing to surrender herself to him if defeated. When the time for the duel comes, Count Robert presents himself in her stead, and as Briennius fails to appear, Hereward fights on his behalf. He is defeated, but his life is spared by the count in consideration of his past services. Hereward attaches himself to the count, having discovered his old Saxon love, Bertha, in the countess's waiting-woman.

Country Wife, The, a comedy by *Wycherley, published and probably first performed 1675. It is now considered by many to be his finest play, a sharp satiric attack on social and sexual hypocrisy and greed and on the corruption of town manners, but even in the author's time (see his own jokes on the subject in *The Plain Dealer*) was attacked for its alleged obscenity. *Garrick's version, The Country Girl (1766), aimed to remove the original's 'immorality' and 'obscenity', and with them cut the character of Horner, a central figure of the plot, a witty libertine who spreads a false report that he is impotent as a result of an operation for the pox, and thus gains access to the favours of various women, each of whom believes he has sacrificed reputation for her sake.

The main plot concerns Mr Pinchwife, who comes to London for the marriage of his sister Alithea, bringing with him his artless young wife Margery; his excessive warnings against wrongdoing put ideas into her head, and she is eventually seduced by Horner, innocently protesting the while that she is merely behaving as town ladies do. Alithea's suitor Sparkish loses her to a new lover, Harcourt, through the opposite fault of excessive credulity. Pinchwife's conclusion, as he apparently accepts the excuse of Horner's impotence, is 'Cuckolds like Lovers shou'd themselves deceive.'

Coup de théâtre, an unexpected and sensational turn in a play.

Courcy, Lord and Lady de, and their sons and daughters, characters in A. *Trollope's *Barsetshire series of novels, types of a worldly, selfseeking, heartless aristocracy.

Courier, The, an evening newspaper of high repute in the early part of the 19th cent., under the management of D. *Stuart. *Coleridge, *Wordsworth, *Lamb, and *Southey were among its occasional contributors, and *Galt was at one time its editor.

COURTELINE, Georges, the name by which Georges Moinaux (1858–1929) is generally known: French humorous journalist and playwright who ridiculed French officialdom, civil and military, and French legal absurdities in a number of satirical sketches and short plays containing sharp observation of contemporary life and manners, e.g. Messieurs les ronds-de-cuir (1893, English trans. The Bureaucrats, 1928), Les Gaîetés de l'escadron (1886), Le Train de 8h. 47 (1888), Un Client sérieux (1897).

Courtesy Literature, as a distinct literary genre teaching courtiers and others good manners and morals, was imported into England through works such as Il Cortegiano of *Castiglione (translated by *Hoby in 1561), Il Galateo of Giovanni della Casa (translated by Robert Peterson in 1576) and Stefano Guazzo's La Civil Conversatione (Bks I–III translated by G. *Pettie in 1581, Bk IV by B. *Yonge in 1586). One of the most popular native examples of this type of writing was H. Peacham's The Compleat Gentleman (1622).

COURTHOPE, William John (1842–1917), educated at Harrow and Corpus Christi and New College, Oxford, became a civil service commissioner and professor of poetry at Oxford. His important contributions to English literature include the last 5 vols of the standard edition of *Pope's works, including a Life (1871–89), and a History of English Poetry (1895–1910). Among his other works were Ludibria Lunae (1869), a satirical burlesque on women's rights, Paradise of Birds (1870), and The Country Town and other Poems (1920).

Courtier, The (Il Cortegiano), see CASTIGLIONE.

Courtly Love. The term 'amour courtois' was coined by Gaston Paris in 1883 in the course of an essay on the Lancelot of *Chrétien de Troyes, to describe the conception of love developed by the Provençal troubadours in the 12th cent., which had become the central theme of lyric and epic poetry in France and Germany by 1200. Its relation of lover to adored lady was modelled on the dependence of feudal follower on his lord; the love itself was a religious passion, ennobling, ever unfulfilled, and ever increasing. The common (though not universal) requirement of non-fulfilment meant that the love was usually pre-marital or extra-marital. A code of practice for courtly lovers, *De Arte Honeste Amandi* (c.1185), was written by *Andreas Capellanus, who may have been a chaplain at the court of *Marie de Champagne. Though the poetry of the troubadours is the first definable occurrence of the phenomenon in western Europe, many aspects of courtly love are much older and have affinities with the poetry of *Ovid and with the religious terminology of love used by Arabic writers. From its beginnings in Provence the writing of this kind of poetry had spread to northern France and to the German *Minnesingers and epic by 1200; the most influential works in the 13th cent. were the *Roman de la rose* (Guillaume de Lorris, c.1230 and Jean de Meun c.1275), and the lyric poems of the *dolce stil nuovo* in Italy at the end of the century; Guinicelli, Cavalcanti, and *Dante's *Vita Nuova*. Though the elements of courtly love are found in many places in medieval and Renaissance English literature, it is never the central theme of medieval English poetry, probably because it only reached England in the period of its decadence, after the mid-13th cent. and mostly as presented through the sceptical satire of writers such as Jean de Meun. See P. Dronke, *Medieval Latin and the Rise of the European Love-Lyric* (1968), R. Boase, *The Origin and Meaning of Courtly Love* (1977); B. O'Donoghue, *The Courtly Love Tradition* (1982).

Court of Love, an institution said to have existed in Provence and Languedoc in the 12th cent., principally on the authority of *Andreas Capellanus, at which a noble tribunal of lords and ladies made pronouncements on cases of love. No doubt such courts, like that of *Marie de Champagne claimed by Andreas, were largely a literary fiction or a later post-literary development.

Court of Love, The, an early 15th-cent. allegorical poem in 1,442 lines of rhyme-royal, once doubtfully attributed to *Chaucer and included by *Skeat in his *Chaucerian and Other Pieces*, published as vol. 7 of his large edition of Chaucer (pp. 409–47). It is in the tradition of the *Roman de la rose*, describing the visit of the poet to the Court of Venus and the love scenes he saw portrayed there, and ending with a May-day concert of birds when they sing descants on the opening words of psalms. It claims to be the work of 'Philogenet of Cambridge, clerk'.

Covent Garden, in London, the old Convent Garden of Westminster. At the dissolution of the monasteries it passed into the hands of the Russell family, who built Bedford House north of the Strand and laid out the garden for building, with the market as the centre. I. *Jones built St Paul's Church there, and the piazza that runs

along two sides of the market-place. Many celebrated people lived in Covent Garden (Sir K. *Digby, *Kneller, *Lely, Zoffany, Lady M. W. *Montagu, among others), and the *Bedford, *Will's, and *Button's coffee-houses were in the neighbourhood. Covent Garden is frequently mentioned in 17th- and 18th-cent. literature, generally as a centre of dissipation. It remained the principal wholesale market in London for vegetables, fruit, and flowers until the 1970s, and was then rebuilt as a shopping centre with boutiques, cafés, etc.

The first Covent Garden Theatre was opened by J. *Rich in 1732. It was burnt down in 1808, and its successor in 1856. In these, many famous actors were seen, including *Garrick, the *Kembles, Mrs *Siddons, and *Macready. The new theatre (by Barry) opened in 1858 has been the principal home in England of grand opera.

Covent-Garden Journal, The, a periodical issued twice a week during 1752 by H. *Fielding, containing some of the best work of his journalistic career. Under the name of Sir Alexander Drawcansir, Censor of Great Britain, Fielding attacks political abuses, scandal, hypocrisy, meanness, sexual morality, fashion, and many other targets. It contained an attack on Smollett's *Peregrine Pickle* and *Roderick Random*, to which that author replied in a slanderous pamphlet, *A Faithful Narrative of . . . *Habbakuk Hilding, Justice, Dealer, and Chapman*.

COVENTRY, Francis (1725–54), from 1751 perpetual curate at Edgware, was the author of *The History of Pompey the Little: or the Life and adventures of a Lap-Dog* (1751), a satire in the form of the life of a dog 'born A.D. 1735 at Bologna in Italy, a Place famous for Lap-Dogs and Sausages'. He undergoes many vicissitudes, passing from one owner to another of very diverse stations; Lady M. W. *Montagu in a letter to her daughter declared it 'a real and exact representation of Life as it is now acted in London'. An edition by R. A. Day appeared in 1974.

Coventry Miracle Plays, or *Ludus Coventriae*, see MYSTERY PLAYS.

COVERDALE, Miles (1488–1568), studied at Cambridge, was ordained priest in 1514, and adopted Lutheran views. He translated at Antwerp, apparently in the pay of Jacob van Meteren, the *Bible and *Apocrypha from German and Latin versions with the aid of *Tyndale's New Testament. His translation was first printed at Marsburg; a modified version was issued in 1537. Coverdale also superintended the printing of the Great Bible of 1539 (see under BIBLE, THE ENGLISH) He was bishop of Exeter in 1551–3, and was allowed to leave England in 1554 after Queen Mary's accession. He was in England again in 1559, published his last book, *Let-*

ters of Saintes, in 1564, and was rector of St Magnus, London Bridge, from 1563 to 1566. His collected works, which include translations of theological tracts and German hymns, were published in 1844–6. If he was in fact (which has been questioned) the translator of the version of the Bible attributed to him, he is entitled to the credit for much of the noble language of the Authorized Version, and in particular for the Prayer-Book version of the Psalter.

Coverdale, Miles, the narrator of Hawthorne's novel * *The Blithedale Romance*.

Coverley, Sir Roger de, a character described in * *The Spectator*, a member of the Spectator Club, 'a gentleman of Worcestershire, of ancient descent, a baronet. His great-grandfather was inventor of that famous country-dance which is called after him. He is a gentleman that is very singular in his behaviour, but his singularities proceed from his good sense . . . It is said he keeps himself a batchelor, by reason he was crossed in love by a perverse beautiful widow of the next county to him.' (No. 2, by *Steele.) He figures in a number of *Spectator* papers by both *Addison and Steele, and is pictured at home, at church, at the assizes, in town, etc. His death is reported in No. 517, by Addison.

COWARD, Noël (1899–1973), actor, dramatist, and composer, was born in Teddington, Middlesex, the son of a piano salesman and an ambitious mother who from an early age encouraged his theatrical aspirations. His first play was performed in 1917, but he achieved fame with *The Vortex* (1924) in which he himself appeared as Nicky Lancaster, a young drug-addict tormented by his mother's adulteries. More characteristic of his talent were his comedies *Fallen Angels* (1925), *Hay Fever* (1925, about the eccentric, theatrical, guest-confusing, self-regarding Bliss family), *Private Lives* (1933, about two disastrous inter-connected second marriages), *Design for Living* (1933, about a successful *ménage à trois*), and *Blithe Spirit* (1941), which features the hearty medium, Madame Arcati, and Elvira, a predatory ghost. The smart sophistication, technical accomplishment, and convention-defying morality (or amorality) of these pieces captured the public of the day, but another and more sentimental side of Coward was revealed in his patriotic works (*Cavalcade*, 1931) and war-time screenplays such as *Brief Encounter* (1944) and *This Happy Breed* (1942). After the war Coward continued to write prolifically; his plays were less well received, to his own surprise, and he was outspoken about his contempt for the new *kitchen sink school of realism and for the 'pretentious symbolism' of *Beckett. He had a new lease of life as cabaret entertainer at the Café de Paris, London, and in Las Vegas; then, in 1963, a revival of *Private Lives* at Hampstead

Theatre Club precipitated a new wave of interest in Coward's work and many more revivals, including prestige productions at the National Theatre. Coward was knighted in 1970, and died in Jamaica. He also published volumes of verse, short stories, a novel (*Pomp and Circumstance*, 1960), and two volumes of autobiography. *The Noel Coward Diaries* (1982, ed. G. Payn and Sheridan Morley) which cover his life from 1941 to 1969, are an entertaining fund of theatrical gossip, criticism of fellow playwrights, and admiring comments on the royal family.

COWLEY, Abraham (1618–67), was the posthumous son of a London stationer, King's scholar at Westminster, and scholar and fellow of Trinity College, Cambridge. His precocity is shown by 'Pyramus and Thisbe', a verse romance written when he was 10 years old, and 'Constantia and Philetus', written two years later (both included in *Poetical Blossomes*, 1633). *Loves Riddle*, a pastoral drama, and *Naufragium Joculare*, a Latin comedy, appeared in 1638. On the outbreak of the Civil War Cowley left Cambridge for Oxford where he contributed to the Royalist cause by writing a satire, *The Puritan and the Papist* (1643), and a political epic, *The Civil War*. (Bk I of *The Civil War* was published in 1679; the two other books were presumed lost until recently discovered and edited.) In 1644 he left Oxford for Paris, where he was in the service of Henry Jermyn at the court of Henrietta Maria. In 1654 he returned to England, apparently as a Royalist spy, and was imprisoned briefly in 1655; however, his conduct at this time, together with various remarks in the Preface to *Poems* (1656), gave rise to doubts in certain quarters about his continuing loyalty to the Royalist cause. At the Restoration he was disappointed in his expectation of a reward for his services, though the earl of St Albans and the duke of Buckingham combined to provide him with a competence. He spent the last years of his life in retirement, at Barnes and later Chertsey. On his death Charles II bestowed on him the epitaph, 'That Mr Cowley had not left a better man behind him in England.' He is buried in Westminster Abbey.

His principal works, besides those mentioned above, are *The Mistress* (1647), a collection of love poems; 'Miscellanies' in *Poems* (1656); also in the same collection 'Davideis', an epic on the biblical history of David, and 'Pindarique Odes' (see PINDARIC ODES), in which he introduces the irregular ode imitated by *Dryden and others; *Ode, upon the Blessed Restoration* (1660); and *Verses on Several Occasions* (1663). His prose works, marked by grace and simplicity of style, include *A Proposition for the Advancement of Learning* (1661), *The Visions and Prophecies concerning England* (1661), and some 'Essays', notably one 'Of My Self' containing interesting particulars of his early life (first published in *The Works*, 1668). His plays include *The Guardian* (1650), written to entertain the prince of Wales on his visit to Cambridge in 1642, which he later revised as *Cutter of Coleman Street* (1663).

Cowley's life was written by his friend and literary executor *Sprat and is prefixed to *The Works* (1668).

COWLEY, Hannah, *née* Parkhouse (1743–1809), wrote a number of comedies and two tedious tragedies; her comedies include *The Runaway* (1776), *A Bold Stroke for a Husband* (1783), and her most successful, *The Belle's Stratagem,* performed 1780. They tend to preach the importance of marriage and the domestic virtues. She also wrote long narrative romances, and corresponded as 'Anna Matilda' in poetry in *The World* with Robert Merry (see DELLA CRUSCANS), a correspondence satirized by *Gifford.

COWPER, William (1731–1800), elder son of the rector of Great Berkhamsted, Hertfordshire, whose mother died when he was six. He was educated at a private school (where he was bullied) and at Westminster, where he was a contemporary of Charles *Churchill and W. *Hastings. He was called to the bar in 1754. Sensitive and hypochondriac by nature as a child, he began to suffer from severe depression, and when called for examination for a disputed clerkship in the House of Lords he broke down completely and attempted suicide; his illness may have been aggravated by the failure of his hope of marrying his cousin, Theodora Cowper. From this time he was subject to periods of acute melancholia which took a religious form; he felt himself cast out of God's mercy, and wrote later in his moving autobiographical *Memoir* (*c.*1767, pub. 1816), 'conviction of sin and expectation of instant judgement never left me.' He spent some months in Dr Cotton's Collegium Insanorum at St Albans, and turned increasingly to evangelical Christianity for consolation. In 1765 he became a boarder (in his own words, 'a sort of adopted son') in the home of the Revd Morley Unwin at Huntingdon, and on Morley's death moved with Mary, his widow, to Olney.

There he came under the influence of J. *Newton, the evangelical curate, with whom he wrote *Olney Hymns* (1779); his contributions include 'God moves in a mysterious way' and 'Oh, for a closer walk with God'. He became engaged to Mrs Unwin, but suffered another period of severe depression and made another suicide attempt; he spent a year with the Newtons before returning to Mrs Unwin's home. A calmer period followed, during which at her suggestion he wrote his satires ('Table Talk', 'The Progress of Error', 'Truth', 'Expostulation', 'Hope', 'Charity', 'Conversation', and 'Retirement') which were published in 1782 with several shorter poems (including 'Verses supposed to be written by Alexander Selkirk'; see SELKIRK, A.); in the same year he wrote *John Gilpin* and in 1783–4 his best-known long poem *The Task* (1785), both subjects suggested by his new friend and neighbour Lady Austen. The volume in which these appeared also contained 'Tirocinium', a vigorous attack on public schools. In 1786 he moved with Mrs Unwin to Weston Underwood, where he wrote various poems published after his death, including the unfinished 'Yardley-Oak' (admired by *Wordsworth), the verses 'On the Loss of the Royal George' ('Toll for the brave . . . '), 'To Mary', and 'The Poplar-Field'. His translation of *Homer, published in 1791, was not successful. From 1791 Mrs Unwin suffered a series of paralytic strokes; she died in 1796, leaving Cowper in severe depression from which he never fully recovered.

He wrote *'The Castaway' shortly before his death; like many of his poems it deals with man's isolation and helplessness. Storms and shipwrecks recur in his work as images of the mysterious ways of God, and Cowper's search for a retired and quiet life of simple domestic and rural pleasures gave him little sense of permanent security. Yet his poems and his much-admired letters (published posthumously) have been highly valued for their intimate portrait of tranquillity and for their playful and delicate wit. His sympathetic feelings for nature (expressed in the lines from *The Task* admired by J. *Austen's Fanny Price, 'Ye fallen avenues! Once more I mourn, | Your fate unmerited') presage *Romanticism, and his use of blank verse links that of James *Thomson with that of *Wordsworth. He was also, like his evangelical friends, a champion of the oppressed, and wrote verses on *Wilberforce and the slave trade. Whether religion was cause or cure of his depression has been much disputed; the sense of guilt and paranoia displayed in his *Memoir* has much in common with that in Bunyan's *Grace Abounding. A life by his friend W. *Hayley was published 1803–4; see also *The Stricken Deer* (1929) by David *Cecil and a critical biography by M. Quinlan (1953). Cowper's *Letters and Prose Writings,* ed. J. King and C. Ryskamp, appeared in 3 vols, 1979–82.

Cox and Box, see BURNAND, F.

Crab, in Shakespeare's *Two Gentlemen of Verona,* Launce's dog. He appears to be a small lap-dog, whose name suggests the size and sourness of a crab-apple.

CRABBE, George (1754–1832), was born in Aldeburgh, Suffolk, where his father was a collector of salt-duties. He was apprenticed to a doctor and during that time, in 1775, he published *Inebriety,* a derivative but vigorous poem on the evils of drink. During his apprenticeship he met Sarah Elmy (the 'Mira' of his poems and journals), whom he married ten years later. He then began to practise as the parish doctor in Aldeburgh, meanwhile writing, reading, and studying botany. In 1770 he determined on a career in writing and went to London, where he became almost destitute before he was generously befriended by *Burke. On Burke's advice, and with his literary help, he published *The Library* (1781), a poem in the manner of *Pope containing the author's reflections on books and reading. Burke introduced Crabbe to influential friends, including *Fox, *Reynolds, and Dr *Johnson, and encouraged him to take orders. In 1781 he became curate at Aldeburgh, then from 1782 to 1785 was chaplain to the duke of Rutland at Belvoir, where he found stimulating company and leisure for writing. In 1783, after advice and revision from Burke and Johnson, he published *The Village*, a poem in heroic couplets which established his reputation and made plain his revulsion from the conventions of the *pastoral and the myth of the Golden Age, painting instead a grim, detailed picture of rural poverty and of a blighted, infertile landscape, described with a botanist's precision.

In the same year he married Sarah Elmy, and in 1785 published a satirical (and probably early) work, *The Newspaper*. A long interval followed, during which he published nothing of importance, although he wrote and destroyed several unpublished novels, and during which he held (1789–1814) a living at Muston, Leicestershire, from which he was absent 1792–1805, living in Suffolk. In 1807 appeared a volume containing his previous works, some new shorter poems, *The Parish Register* (which revealed his gift as a narrative poet), and another, atypical, narrative in 55 eight-line stanzas, 'Sir Eustace Grey', set in a madhouse, in which Sir Eustace relates, to a 'Physician' and a 'Visitor', the tale of his guilt (he had killed his wife's lover in a duel) and his subsequent demented hallucinations. Alethea Hayter, in *Opium and the Romantic Imagination* (1968), relates the peculiarly vivid dream descriptions to Crabbe's opium-taking, a habit he had adopted in 1790 on a doctor's recommendation.

In 1810 he published *The Borough*, a poem in 24 'letters' in which he illustrates the life of a country town (based on Aldeburgh), and which includes the tales of *'Peter Grimes' and *'Ellen Orford'. This was followed in 1812 by *Tales in Verse*. In 1813 Sarah died at Muston, after a depressive illness, and Crabbe began to visit London more frequently. In 1814 he was appointed vicar of Trowbridge, and in 1819 published *Tales of the Hall*, a series of varied stories. He visited Sir W. *Scott in Edinburgh in 1822 and became his friend. He died in Trowbridge and much unpublished work was found, some of which (for instance 'The Equal Marriage' and 'Silford Hall') was published in a collected edition in 1834; later discoveries appeared in *New Poems* (1960) ed. A. Pollard. The standard edn of the poems is by A. Ward, 3 vols, 1905–7.

Throughout the upheaval represented by the *Romantic movement, Crabbe persisted in his precise, closely observed, realistic portraits of rural life and landscape, writing mainly in the heroic couplets of the *Augustan age, and attempting to

> paint the cot
> As Truth will paint it, and as Bards will not.
>
> *(The Village)*

*Byron called him 'Nature's sternest painter yet the best', Scott called him 'the English Juvenal', and he was the favourite poet of J. Austen. See *The Life of George Crabbe by his Son* (1834, with the *Poetical Works*, and 1947 with an introduction by E. *Blunden) and *George Crabbe* (1977) by T. Barcham.

Crabshaw, a character in Smollett's *Sir *Launcelot Greaves*.

CRACHERODE, Clayton Mordaunt (1730–99), scholar and book-collector. Inherited wealth enabled him to acquire a fine collection of books and prints, which he bequeathed to the British Museum. His special interest was in early editions of the classics and the Silver Age of Latin, as well as in the art of early printing.

Craftsman, The, a periodical started in Dec. 1726 by Nicholas Amhurst ('Caleb D'Anvers'), to which *Bolingbroke contributed his 'Remarks upon the History of England' (Sept. 1730–May 1731) and his 'Dissertation upon Parties' (1733). William Pulteney, later earl of Bath, was another leading contributor. Its title was intended to indicate Sir R. *Walpole as a 'man of craft'; and its essence (so far as it was political) lay in its opposition to Walpole and his cabinets.

CRAIG, (Edward Henry) Gordon (1872–1966), artist, actor, wood-engraver, writer, and stage-designer, the son of Edward William Godwin and Ellen *Terry; he chose his own name, Craig, from the island Ailsa Craig. He began his career as an actor, then edited *The Page* (1898–1901), a periodical in which he published his own woodcuts. After directing in London he moved to the Continent, where he developed his avant-garde, anti-realist stage and lighting designs; in 1905 in Berlin he formed a liaison with the dancer Isadora Duncan, who bore him a child. (This was only one of many similar episodes in his colourful emotional life.) In the same year he published his first book, *The Art of the Theatre*, which was further expanded as *On the Art of the Theatre* (1911); several other works on the same subject followed, including *Towards a New Theatre* (1913). In 1908 in Florence he founded a theatre magazine, *The Mask*, which he edited (with a wartime interlude) until 1929.

His radical ideas on design and stagecraft had considerable influence in both Europe and America, and his wood engravings contributed to a revival of the art. His memoirs of his early years, *Index to the Story of my Days*, were published in 1957.

Craigdallie, in Scott's *The Fair Maid of Perth*, the bailie of Perth.

CRAIGIE, Sir William Alexander (1867–1957), lexicographer and philologist, co-editor of the *Oxford English Dictionary* and its first *Supplement*, co-editor (1925–44) of the *Dictionary of American English*, editor (1919–55) of the *Dictionary of the Older Scottish Tongue*, and a notable contributor to Anglo-Norman, Frisian, and Icelandic philology.

CRAIK, Mrs (Dinah Maria Mulock) (1826–87), a prolific writer of novels, poems, children's books, fairy-tales, essays, and short stories. A novel, *The Ogilvies* (1846), followed by *Olive* (1850), established her name, but she wrote nine further novels before *John Halifax, Gentleman* (1856), the great and prolonged success for which she is chiefly remembered. Her short stories were collected under the title *Avillion* in 1853 and her *Collected Poems* appeared in 1881. She was awarded a Civil List pension in 1864, but put it aside for authors less fortunate than herself.

Crambo poem, one designed to exhaust the possible rhymes with someone's name. See MOLLY MOG.

CRANE, (Harold) Hart (1899–1932), American poet, born in Ohio. He published two volumes of verse, *White Buildings* (1926) and *The Bridge* (1930), the latter an obscure but powerful work which explores the 'Myth of America', with many echoes of *Whitman; its national symbols include Brooklyn Bridge itself, invoked in its Proem, and such historical and legendary characters as Columbus, *Rip Van Winkle, *Pocahontas, who, the poet explains, is 'mythological nature-symbol chosen to represent the physical body of the continent, or the soul'. Crane was an alcoholic, and committed suicide by jumping from a steamer in the Caribbean after spending some time in Mexico. His *Complete Poems and Selected Letters and Prose*, ed. B. Weber, appeared in 1960, and his correspondence with Y. *Winters was published in 1978.

CRANE, Stephen (1871–1900), American writer, born in New Jersey, the son of a Methodist minister. He worked as a journalist in New York before attempting to publish his first novel, *Maggie: A Girl of the Streets* (1893), which was too grim to find a readership. His next work, *The Red Badge of Courage* (1895), a study of an inexperienced soldier (Henry Flem-

ing) and his reactions to the ordeal of battle during the American Civil War, although based on no personal experience of war was hailed as a masterpiece of psychological realism, and Crane found himself working as a war reporter in Mexico, Cuba, and Greece. He came to England (where his novel had been even more warmly greeted than in the US) in 1897, already ill with tuberculosis; he developed a close friendship with *Conrad (to whose work his own was compared), and met many other literary figures, including H. G. *Wells, who described his short story 'The Open Boat' (1898; which was based on personal experience of shipwreck) as 'an imperishable gem'. He died in Baden-Baden, almost immediately after his arrival, having been rushed there for a cure by his common-law wife Cora Stewart. His other works include two volumes of free verse, short stories, and sketches; his *Letters* (ed. R. W. Stallman and Lillian Gilkes) were published in 1960.

CRANE, Walter (1845–1915), designer, illustrator, painter, and writer. Crane is most famous for his coloured picture books for children and for his flower books; some of these he wrote himself. He cherished ambitions as a philosophical painter and poet, and developed the themes of his allegorical pictures—*The Roll of Fate* (1882), *The Bridge of Life* (1884)—in accompanying poems. His most elaborate work, *The Sirens Three*, was published in the *English Illustrated Magazine* (1885), with his own decorations. Crane, deeply influenced by W. *Morris, played an important role in the Arts and Crafts Movement; he was convinced of the value of the crafts and of good design and discussed his belief in *The Claims of Decorative Art* (1892). In the 1880s he became a socialist, and created many designs, cartoons, and verses for the socialist cause. His lectures on art education were published as *The Bases of Design* (1898) and *Line and Form* (1900). His toy books were praised by J. K. *Huysmans.

Cranford, a novel by Mrs *Gaskell, published serially in *Household Words*, 1851–3.

Cranford, a series of linked sketches of life among the ladies of a quiet country village in the 1830s, is based on Knutsford in Cheshire where Mrs Gaskell spent her childhood. It centres on the formidable Miss Deborah Jenkyns and her gentle sister Miss Matty, daughters of the former rector. Moments of drama are provided by the death of the genial Captain Brown, run over by a train when saving the life of a child; by the panic caused in the village by rumours of burglars; by the surprising marriage of the widowed Lady Glenmire with the vulgar Mr Hoggins, the village surgeon; by the failure of a bank which ruins Miss Matty, and her rescue by the fortunate return from India of her long-lost brother Peter. But the greatest charm of

Cranford, which has kept it unfailingly popular, is its amused but loving portrayal of the old-fashioned customs and 'elegant economy' of a delicately observed group of middle-aged figures in a landscape.

CRANMER, Thomas (1489–1556), arch-bishop of Canterbury, was a fellow of Jesus College, Cambridge. He propounded views in favour of the divorce of Henry VIII from Catherine of Aragon, was appointed to the arch-bishopric in 1533, and maintained the king's claim to be the supreme head of the Church of England. He supervised the production of the first prayer-book of Edward VI, 1549; prepared the revised prayer-book of 1552; and prom-ulgated the 42 articles of religion (afterwards reduced to 39) in the same year. To meet the need for suitable sermons, he contributed to and probably edited the first book of *Homilies* issued in 1547. In Queen Mary's reign he was condemned for heresy by Cardinal Pole, recently appointed archbishop of Canterbury, and degraded in 1556. He signed six documents admitting the supremacy of the pope and the truth of all Roman Catholic doctrine except tran-substantiation, in vain; he was burned at the stake, repudiating these admissions, on 21 March 1556 at Oxford, holding his right hand (which had written his recantation) steadily in the flames, that it might be the first burnt. He compiled a *Reformatio Legum Ecclesiasticarum* (1550), which was published in a translation by W. Haddon and J. *Cheke in 1571, and wrote on Anglican discipline and theology; but his chief title to fame is that of being the principal author of the English liturgy.

CRASHAW, Richard (1612/13–49), poet, lost both mother and stepmother before he was 9, and his father, a noted Puritan divine, died in 1626. He was educated at Charterhouse and Pembroke Hall, Cambridge, where he came under the influence of High Church friends in-cluding *Ferrar, whom he visited at *Little Gid-ding. From 1635 to 1643 he was a fellow of Peterhouse. He became a Catholic convert *c.*1645 and fled to Paris, where his friend *Cow-ley persuaded Queen Henrietta Maria to interest herself on his behalf. Through her influence he moved to Italy, first as attendant on Cardinal Palotta, then in 1649 in a minor post at the Santa Casa of Loreto, where he died shortly after. His principal work was the *Steps to the Temple* (1646), a collection of religious poems influenced by *Marino and the Spanish mystics, which has been acclaimed as the height of baroque in English poetry. To this was attached a secular section, the *Delights of the Muses,* con-taining 'Music's Duel', a paraphrase of the Latin of Strada, in which nightingale and lute-player contend until the former fails and dies: also 'Wishes. To his (supposed) Mistresse', which be-

gins 'Who'er she be | That not impossible she'. His best-known poems are those addressed to St *Theresa, the 'Hymne' beginning 'Love, thou art absolute, sole Lord | Of life and death' and 'The Flaming Hart', the second of which was added to the 2nd edn of 1648 and printed in an expanded version in the posthumous collection *Carmen Deo Nostro* (1652). Both celebrate the bliss of martyrdom in characteristically baroque imagery of doves, darts, hearts, and 'delicious wounds'. The extravagant conceits of 'The Weeper', addressed to Mary Magdalen, were much ridiculed in subsequent periods. *Praz (*The Flaming Heart,* 1958) describes his work as 'the literary counterpart, though a minor one, to Rubens's apotheoses, Murillo's languors and El Greco's ecstasies'.

Cratchit, Bob, a character in Dickens's *A Christmas Carol.*

Crawford, Lord, in Scott's *Quentin Durward,* the commander of the Scottish Archers of the Guard.

Crawford, Henry and Mary, characters in J. Austen's *Mansfield Park.*

CRAWFORD, Isabella Valancy (1850–87), Canadian poet, born in Dublin, who lived from the age of eight in Canada. Her narrative poem of the western settlement, 'Malcolm's Katie' (1884), has been admired for its descriptions of forest scenery. Her *Collected Poems* were pub-lished in 1905.

Crawley, (1) the Revd Josiah, one of the most memorable characters in A. Trollope's 'Barset-shire' novels, figuring most prominently in *The Last Chronicle of Barset* and also in *Framley Par-sonage*; (2) Sir Pitt, his sister Miss Crawley, his sons Pitt and Rawdon, characters in Thackeray's *Vanity Fair.*

Craye, Col. Horace de, a character in Mere-dith's *The Egoist.*

CRAYON, Geoffrey, pseudonym of W. *Irv-ing.

Creakle, in Dickens's *David Copperfield,* the bullying headmaster of the hero's first school.

CREELEY, Robert (1926–), American poet and lecturer, and one of the *Black Moun-tain group; he edited (1954–7) the *Black Moun-tain Review.* His verse is plainer, more personal, less rhetorical than that of his associates; his *Col-lected Poems 1945–1975* was published in 1983.

CREEVEY, Thomas (1768–1838), was Whig MP successively for Thetford and Appleby. *The Creevey Papers* (ed. Sir H. Maxwell), published 1903, consisting of letters to his stepdaughter Elizabeth Ord, extracts from his journal, and letters to Creevey from various important per-sons, are interesting for their gossip and the light they throw on the characters of prominent persons and on the society of the later Georgian era. He was in Brussels for some years from 1814 and left a classic first-hand account of the city at the time of Waterloo. In Creevey's old age, when the Whigs were in power, he held office as treasurer of ordnance and afterwards as treasurer of Greenwich Hospital. Charles Greville in the *Greville Memoirs, 20 Feb. 1838) refers to Creevey's cheerful and sociable disposition; he was at once 'perfectly happy and exceedingly poor'. See also Creevey's Life and Times (1934), ed. J. Gore, a further selection with commentary.

CREIGHTON, Mandell (1843–1901), educated at Merton College, Oxford, where he became fellow and tutor, devoting himself to ecclesiastical, Italian, and Byzantine history. He was ordained in 1870 and was vicar of Embleton from 1875 to 1884, when he was elected to the chair of ecclesiastical history at Cambridge. During this time he continued his important History of the Papacy during the period of the Reformation (5 vols, 1882–94). He was first editor of the English Historical Review, from 1886, and was selected bishop of Peterborough in 1891 and of London in 1897. His other works include The Tudors and the Reformation (1876), The Age of Elizabeth (1876), and lives of Simon de Montfort (1876), Cardinal Wolsey (1888), and Queen Elizabeth (1896). His Life and Letters by his widow appeared in 1904.

Cremorne Gardens, in Chelsea, were a popular place of entertainment during the middle of the 19th cent., but became notorious for irregularities and were closed in 1877.

Crescent and the Cross, The, see WARBURTON, ELIOT.

Cresseid, see TESTAMENT OF CRESSEID, THE; **Cressida**, see TROILUS AND CRESSIDA; see also TROILUS AND CRISEYDE.

Cretic, see METRE.

CRÈVECŒUR, Michel-Guillaume de (1735–1813), known as J. Hector St John de Crèvecœur, was born at Caen in France of a good but impoverished family. He emigrated to Canada and served under Montcalm, then moved south, landing at New York in 1759 and taking American citizenship in 1765. He then settled in Orange County, New York State, where for several idyllic years he farmed, until the revolution obliged him to flee to Europe. These years were the basis of his famous work, much admired by the Romantics, Letters from an American Farmer (published in London 1782) which describe rural life and customs with simplicity, artistry, and vigour; the third essay is on the subject of 'What is an American?' D. H. *Lawrence commented on his role as myth-

maker in Studies in Classic American Literature (1923), and described him as the 'emotional prototype' of the American (as distinct from *Franklin, 'the real practical prototype').

Crewler, the Revd Horace and Mrs, characters in Dickens's *David Copperfield, the parents of Sophy, whom Traddles marries.

CRICHTON, James, 'The Admirable' (1560–82), Scots adventurer, scholar, linguist, and poet, who served in the French army, travelled in Italy, and died in a brawl in Mantua. His colourful career is recounted by *Urquhart and is the subject of a historical novel by H. *Ainsworth. *Barrie's play The Admirable Crichton concerns a polymath manservant cast away with his employers on a desert island.

Cricket on the Hearth, The, a Christmas book by *Dickens, published 1846.

John Peerybingle, carrier, and his much younger wife, Dot, are as happy a couple as possible, although the venomous old Tackleton, who himself is about to marry the young May Fielding, throws suspicion on Dot's sincerity. This suspicion appears to be disastrously verified when an eccentric old stranger takes up his abode with the Peerybingles and is discovered one day by John, metamorphosed into a bright young man by the removal of his wig, in intimate conversation with Dot. By the fairy influence of the Cricket on the Hearth John is brought to the decision to pardon her offence, which he attributes to the incompatibility of their ages and temperaments. But there turns out to be no occasion for forgiveness, for the bright young man is an old friend, the lover of May Fielding, believed dead, who has turned up just in time to prevent her marrying Tackleton. Among the other characters are Caleb Plummer and his blind daughter Bertha, the toy-makers; and Tilly Slowboy, most loving and incompetent of nurses.

Crimsworth, William, the hero of C. Brontë's *The Professor.

Criseyde, see TROILUS AND CRISEYDE.

Crisparkle, the Revd Septimus, a character in Dickens's *Edwin Drood.

Crispinus, a false poet in Jonson's *The Poetaster, in part a caricature of J. *Marston.

Criterion, The (1922–39), an influential literary periodical launched as a quarterly and edited by T. S. *Eliot; *The Waste Land appeared in its first issue. It became the New Criterion in 1926, and in 1927, briefly, The Monthly Criterion, but then reverted to its original title and quarterly publication. It included poems, essays, short stories, and reviews, and published work by *Pound, *Empson, *Auden, *Spender, *Grigson, etc.; it also introduced the work of *Proust, *Valéry, *Cocteau, and other European writers. Eliot disowned any particular programme, claiming that his magazine represented a 'tendency', 'toward something which, for want of a better name, we may call classicism', but later critics have detected in the *Criterion* a sympathy towards Fascist ideology. Despite this, it continued to enjoy immense literary prestige until it closed in 1939 under the pressure of what Eliot described as 'a depression of spirits' induced by 'the present state of public affairs'.

Critic, The, or a Tragedy Rehearsed, a comedy by R. B. *Sheridan, produced 1779.

Based on Buckingham's *The Rehearsal*, *The Critic* is an exuberant burlesque on the problems of producing a play. The work under rehearsal by its distraught producer is 'The Spanish Armada', a ludicrous parody of the modish tragic drama of the day (see, for example, CUMBERLAND, R.; COLMAN, G.). Mr Puff, the author of 'The Spanish Armada' and an enterprising promoter of literary wares, has invited to the rehearsal Dangle and Sneer, two savage and inept theatre critics, and Sir Fretful Plagiary (a caricature of Cumberland). His absurd historical drama, written in both the bombastic and the sentimental styles, introduces Sir Walter Ralegh, Sir Christopher Hatton, the earl of Leicester, Lord Burleigh, and others, at the time when the armada is approaching. Meanwhile Tilburina, the daughter of the governor of Tilbury Fort, complicates the plot with her love for Don Ferolo Whiskerandos, a Spanish prisoner. The action of the main play, including the solemn discussions by the author and his guests, their confused involvement with the rehearsal, and continual interruptions by producer, actors, and stage hands, continues with undiminished vivacity to the end.

Critical Dictionary of English Literature, A, from the earliest accounts . . . to the middle of the Nineteenth Century, by Samuel Austin Allibone (1816–89), first published in the US in 1858 and in London in 1859. In the editor's words, 'the fruits of many years of anxious research and conscientious toil', this vast work, the first of its kind on a comprehensive scale, includes biographical entries for 30,000 authors and entries for an even greater number of books. The aim was to direct the public to 'the Best Works of the Best Authors', and each book of any note is described with generous extracts from contemporary reviews and other critical writing. The interpretation of 'English Literature' is wide, as the 'Best Books' for doctors, lawyers, merchants, farmers, etc., were also included. The work was highly successful, with a new edition in 1871, and two supplements in 1891.

Critical Quarterly, The, a literary review founded in 1959 and edited by C. B. Cox and E. A. Dyson. It publishes essays, reviews, and poetry, and contributors have included A. *Wilson, P. *Larkin, D. *Davie, D. J. *Enright, W. *Empson, S. *Heaney, and others.

Critical Review, The (1756–90), a Tory and Church journal, founded in opposition to the liberal *Monthly Review. Much of its space was devoted to public affairs, but it also provided full and balanced reviews of a wide range of books. Dr *Johnson thought well of it and contributed many articles, as did *Goldsmith. It was edited from 1756 to 1759 by *Smollett, who proved a controversial editor.

Criticism, Schools of, see under FEMINIST CRITICISM; FREUDIAN CRITICISM; MARXIST LITERARY CRITICISM; NEW CRITICISM; PRACTICAL CRITICISM; and STRUCTURALISM. See also JUNG, C. G., ARCHETYPE.

Croaker, a character in Goldsmith's *The Good-Natur'd Man.

CROCE, Benedetto (1866–1952), Italian philosopher, historian, and critic. His aesthetics and criticism, published in his journal La Critica from 1903 to 1944, were profoundly influential in Italy before the Second World War. His most influential work is Estetica come scienza dell'espressione e linguistica generale (Aesthetics as the Science of Expression and General Linguistics, 1902). Central to all phases of his thought is the concept of art as a 'lyrical intuition'. His best criticism is in Poesia popolare e poesia d'arte (Popular Poetry and Literary Poetry, 1933), an original interpretation of Italian literary history from the 14th to the 16th cents; in his essay on Ariosto, Shakespeare, Corneille (1920); and in La poesia (Poetics, 1936). His historical works include detailed analysis, as in Storia d'Europa nel secolo XIX (History of Europe in the 19th Century, 1932), as well as theory, such as La storia come pensiero e come azione (History as Thought and as Action, 1938), which asserts that History is always the history of freedom.

CROCKETT, S. R., see KAILYARD SCHOOL.

Crockford, Crockford's Clerical Directory, first published 1857. A book of reference for facts relating to the clergy and the Church of England.

Crockford's, a famous gambling club established in 1827 at 50 St James's Street, London, by William Crockford (1775–1844); it is now in Curzon Street. Crockford was originally a fishmonger; he amassed £1,200,000 out of the club in a few years.

Croft, Admiral and Mrs, characters in J. Austen's *Persuasion.

Croftangry, Chrystal, see CHRONICLES OF THE CANONGATE.

CROKER, John Wilson (1780–1857), was an MP, secretary to the admiralty, and a prominent Tory politician. He was a regular contributor to the *Quarterly Review*, in which he made very plain his Tory and Anglican stance, even in his literary reviews, and for which he acted as an important link with circles of political power. Known for his bitter opposition to most of the younger writers of his day, he became (and has remained) notorious for his criticism of Keats's *Endymion* in 1818. *Shelley (in his Preface to *Adonais) and *Byron (in his jingle 'Who killed John Keats?') established the belief, still quoted, that Croker's review hastened the death of the poet. Yet Croker's views on *Endymion*, although blinkered and ungenerous, were considerably more temperate than those of *Lockhart in *Blackwood's, and there is some justice in his comments on Keats's diction and versification. Croker was a painstaking scholar, and an expert on the 18th cent. His books include *An Intercepted Letter from Canton* (1804), a satire on Dublin society; a reliable edition of Boswell's *Life of Samuel *Johnson*, in 1831, and in the same year *Military Events of the French Revolution of 1830*; and *Essays on the Early Period of the French Revolution* (1857). He was a much hated man, caricatured in three contemporary novels; Peacock's *Melincourt* (1817); Lady *Morgan's *Florence Macarthy* (1818); and Disraeli's *Coningsby* (1844); and was detested by his lifelong enemy *Macaulay 'more than cold boiled veal'. It appears that he was the originator of the political term 'Conservative', which first appeared in an article of his in the *Quarterly Review* in Jan. 1830. *The Croker Papers*, published 1884, cover Croker's political life 1808–32 and are of considerable historical interest.

CROKER, Thomas Crofton (1798–1854), an Irish antiquary who worked in the admiralty, was probably the first collector to regard national and folk stories as a literary art. *Researches in the South of Ireland* appeared in 1824; *Fairy Legends and Traditions in the South of Ireland*, which delighted Sir W. *Scott and was very successful, in 1825–8; *Legends of the Lakes* 1829; and *Popular Songs of Ireland* in 1839. These works, together with Croker's many contributions to literary and antiquarian journals, provide a rich source of information on Irish folklore.

CROLY, George (1780–1860), educated at Trinity College, Dublin, and rector of St Stephen's Walbrook, was author of *Paris in 1815* (1817), a work which owes much to Byron's *Childe Harold; Catiline* (1822), a tragedy; *May Fair* (1827), a satire; and, most notably, *Salathiel* (1829), a romance of the *Wandering Jew, Rome under Nero, and the siege of Jerusalem by Titus. *Marston* followed in 1846, a romance to which the French revolution and the Napoleonic wars provide the background. He published numerous other narrative and romantic poems, as well as religious and historical works. Byron in *Don Juan* refers to Croly as 'the Revd Rowley Powley'.

CROMEK, Robert Hartley (1720–1812), engraver, appears also to have been a shifty literary speculator who made many enemies, notably *Blake. He published *Reliques of Burns* in 1808, and in 1810 a volume of *Select Scottish Songs* by *Burns. In the same year he published *Remains of Nithsdale and Galloway Song*, much of which consisted of the poems of A. *Cunningham, which the author had disguised as ancient songs. It seems probable that Cromek knew of and ignored the deception. Blake expressed his enmity in the couplet, 'A petty, sneaking knave I knew | O! Mr Cr——, how do ye do?'

Crome Yellow, see HUXLEY, A.

CROMWELL, Oliver (1599–1658), soldier, politician, general, and from 1653 to 1658 Lord Protector, was the subject of innumerable contemporary pamphlets, satires, odes, and panegyrics. *Marvell's 'An Horatian Ode upon Cromwell's Return from Ireland', written in 1650 and his *The First Anniversary of the Government under his Highness the Lord Protector* (1655) are notable expressions of balanced admiration for Cromwell's 'active star'; 'If these the times, then this must be the man.' *Milton, who was Latin secretary to the newly formed Council of State from 1649, appealed to him in the sonnet 'Cromwell, our chief of men' as the defender of conscience and liberty, and *Waller (his cousin) wrote in praise of his government and foreign policy. *D'Avenant's plays *The Cruelty of the Spaniards in Peru* (1658) and *The History of Sir Francis Drake* (1659) were intended to support Cromwell's war against Spain. After his death Cromwell was variously depicted by writers and historians as honest patriot, 'frantic enthusiast' (*Hume), corrupt hypocrite, and true Englishman: *Carlyle in his lecture on the 'Hero as King' (1840) and his *Letters and Speeches of Oliver Cromwell* (1845) praised him as a Puritan hero, God-sent to save England, grappling 'like a giant, face to face, heart to heart, with the naked truth of things'.

CROMWELL, Thomas, earl of Essex (?1485–1540), secretary to Cardinal Wolsey and subsequently to Henry VIII, and his chief adviser in ecclesiastical matters. He was the principal promoter of the dissolution of the monasteries. He negotiated Henry's marriage with Anne of Cleves, and the failure of this match and of the policy that underlay it, coupled with the intense unpopularity of the minister, led to his downfall. A bill of attainder was passed and Cromwell was executed.

Cromwell, *The True Chronicle Historie of the*

whole life and death of Thomas Lord, a play published in 1602 and stated in the title to have been 'written by W.S.' It was included in the 3rd and 4th Shakespeare Folios (1663 and 1685). The play has little merit and is certainly not by Shakespeare.

CRONIN, A(rchibald) J(oseph) (1896–1981), born in Dunbartonshire, studied medicine in Glasgow, then practised as a doctor for some years before devoting himself to an extremely successful career as a middle-brow novelist whose works reached an even wider audience through film and television: his best-known novels (e.g. *The Stars Look Down*, 1935; *The Citadel*, 1937) combine in their subject-matter the appeal of medicine and of mining, reflecting his own early experiences as a doctor in South Wales.

Crosbie, Adolphus, a character in A. *Trollope's *The Small House at Allington*.

'Crossing the Bar', a poem in four stanzas by Lord *Tennyson, written Oct. 1889 while crossing the Solent and published that year. It is published as the last poem in most editions of Tennyson's work, in accordance with his own wishes.

Crossjay Patterne, a character in Meredith's *The Egoist*.

Crotchet Castle, a satire by *Peacock, published 1831.

As in most of Peacock's books, the story assembles a group of theorists at a country house, such as Mr Skionar (who resembles *Coleridge), Mr MacQuedy (a Scottish economist who suggests J. R. MacCulloch), Mr Chainmail (who wants to revive the Middle Ages, possibly based on the historian Samuel Rush Meyrick, 1783–1848), and others. The Revd Dr Folliott, though more amiable and learned than Peacock's previous clerics, is also mocked for his bigoted conservatism. The dinner-table conversations at Crotchet Castle turn on the clash between Folliott's Toryism and MacQuedy's progressivism. The guests take a journey by river and canal to Wales, reminiscent of a trip Peacock took up the Thames with *Shelley in 1815. In Lady Clarinda, Peacock supplies the most spirited and cynical of his heroines. She has a foil in the romantic Susannah Touchandgo, who retires to a simple life in Wales after her father, a banker, absconds. The book ends with an assault by the mob on Mr Chainmail's 12th-cent. castle, an ironic comment on the more visionary schemes to solve the troubles of the age of reform.

Crow, a volume of poetry by Ted *Hughes.

Crowdero (meaning 'fiddler', because he plays on a 'crowd' or 'fiddle'), a member of the bear-baiting mob in Butler's *Hudibras*.

Crowe, Captain, a character in Smollett's *Sir *Launcelot Greaves*.

CROWE, William, see LEWESDON HILL.

CROWLEY, 'Aleister' (really Edward Alexander) (1875–1947), son of a rich brewer turned Plymouth Brother, was a diabolist and a bad but prolific poet who claimed to be the *Beast from the Book of Revelation. He joined the Order of the Golden Dawn, a group of theosophists involved in Cabbalistic magic, of which *Yeats was a member, and precipitated its dissolution when it rejected his claims to ascend to a higher spiritual grade. See *The Confessions of Aleister Crowley* (1971), ed. John Symonds and Kenneth Grant.

CROWNE, John (?1640–?1703), probably the son of an emigrant to Nova Scotia, where he appears to have spent some of his youth. A prose romance, *Pandion and Amphigenia* (1665), was followed by his first comedy, *The Country Wit* (1675), containing the character of Sir Mannerly Shallow, subsequently developed into *Sir Courtly Nice in the play of that name (1685). He wrote several other comedies, a court masque, *Calisto* (1675), and eleven tragedies, including the two-part rhymed *The Destruction of Jerusalem* (1677), *Thyestes* (1681), and *Caligula* (1698). The success of the tragedies is said to have owed much to expensive and elaborate scenery. He was part author, with *Dryden and *Shadwell of *Notes and Observations*, a satirical attack on *The Empress of Morocco* by *Settle. Although Crowne was a favourite of Charles II, *Dennis said that he had 'a mortal aversion to the court'; he himself claimed in his later years that his plays were 'successful, and yet clean'.

Croyland, or **Crowland, History, The,** a chronicle of the 14th or 15th cent., printed by Savile in 1596 and for long erroneously attributed to Ingulf, abbot of Croyland (d. 1109), secretary to William the Conqueror. It was shown by Sir F. *Palgrave and others to be a forgery of the 15th cent.

CRUDEN, Alexander (1701–70), born in Aberdeen, established a bookshop in London in 1732 and in 1737 published his *Biblical Concordance*; its later editions (1761 and 1769) remain standard works of reference. His eccentricities verged on insanity, and he believed himself in later life called upon to reform the nation.

CRUIKSHANK, George (1792–1878), illustrator and caricaturist, son of Isaac Cruikshank, also a caricaturist. His vast amount of work was largely in political caricature, but among the books he illustrated were: Burns's *'The Jolly Beggars' in 1823; *Grimm's *Popular Stories* in 1824–6; Cowper's *John Gilpin* in 1828;

Rhodes's *Bombastes Furioso* in 1830; Defoe's *Robinson Crusoe* in 1831; *Sketches by Boz* in 1836, which began a long association with Dickens including the illustrations to *Oliver Twist* in 1837; Scott's *Waverley* in 1836–9; *Ainsworth's The Tower of London* in 1840; *Thackeray's Legend of the Rhine* in 1845; H. B. *Stowe's Uncle Tom's Cabin* in 1853. In 1835 he became the editor of *The Comic Almanack*, a predecessor of *Punch*.

Crummles, Mr Vincent, Mrs, and Ninetta ('the infant phenomenon'), characters in Dickens's *Nicholas Nickleby*.

Cruncher, Jerry, a character in Dickens's *A Tale of Two Cities*.

Crusoe, Robinson, see ROBINSON CRUSOE.

Cry, the Beloved Country, a novel by Alan Paton, published 1948. Paton (1903–   ) was educated at the University of Natal, and was National President of the South African Liberal Party until it was declared illegal in 1968.

The Revd Stephen Kumalo sets off from his impoverished homeland at Ndotasheni, Natal, for Johannesburg, in search of his sister Gertrude and his son Absalom. He finds Gertrude has turned to prostitution, and Absalom has murdered the son of a white farmer, James Jarvis. Absalom is convicted and condemned to death, and Kumalo returns home with Gertrude's son and Absalom's pregnant wife. The novel ends with the reconciliation of Jarvis and Kumalo, and Jarvis's determination to rise above tragedy by helping the poor black community. The book is a moving plea for racial understanding and co-operation.

C.S.C., see CALVERLEY, C. S.

Cuala Press, a *private press founded in 1902 at Dundrum, Co. Dublin, by Elizabeth and Lily Yeats, sisters of W. B. *Yeats, to stimulate local crafts and employment. It was originally called the Dun Emer Press, changing its name in 1908, and it flourished as the Cuala Press until the late 1940s, publishing work by Yeats, *Synge, *Gogarty, Lady *Gregory, etc.

Cubism, a movement in art developed by *Picasso and Georges Braque (1882–1963): the first Cubist pictures were exhibited in 1907. In Analytical Cubism forms are broken down into simple geometric shapes, various views of an object being shown together. In Synthetic Cubism, which developed c.1912, fragments of objects, such as newspapers and matches, are often incorporated in the paintings (collages).

Cuchulain (pron. Choolin), one of the principal heroes of the Ulster cycle of Irish mythology, the nephew or ward of Conchubar, king of Ulster. He is supposed to have lived in the 1st cent. AD. His birth was miraculous, and he showed his strength and prowess at an early age. While still a child he killed the terrible watchdog of the smith Culain and compensated the owner by undertaking to guard his house in the dog's place, whence the name of Cuchulain, signifying 'Culain's hound'. Of his numerous feats of valour, which won him the love of many women, the chief was his defence of Ulster, single-handed, against Medb (pron. Maeve), queen of Connaught, who attacked it in order to carry off the Brown Bull of Cuaiigne (pron. Cooley). Cuchulain was killed, aged 27, by Lugaid, son of a king of Ulster, and the daughters of Calatin the wizard, in vengence for their fathers whom Cuchulain had slain.

A series of the legends about him have been translated by Lady *Gregory (*Cuchulain of Muirthemne*). He figures in *Macpherson's Ossianic poems as 'Cuthullin'.

Cuckoo and the Nightingale, The, see CLANVOWE. J.

Cuddie Headrigg, in Scott's *Old Mortality*, the ploughman in Lady Margaret Bellenden's service.

Cuddy, a herdsman or shepherd, in *The Shepheardes Calender* of Spenser and *The Shepherd's Week* of Gay.

CUDWORTH, Ralph (1617–88), see CAMBRIDGE PLATONISTS.

Cuff, Sergeant, the detective in W. Collins's *The Moonstone*.

CULPEPER, Nicholas (1616–54), apothecary, Puritan, and republican, conducted a campaign against the monopoly of the College of Physicians, and in 1649 published an English translation of the college's *Pharmacopoeia*, thus making its contents available for the first time to the poor who could not afford doctors' fees. Both this work and his *The English Physician Enlarged, or the Herbal* (1653) sold in vast quantities, but his infringement of the monopoly made him many enemies and he was the object of much slander and abuse.

Culture and Anarchy, a collection of essays by M. *Arnold, published 1869. This work contains many of Arnold's central critical arguments.

The first chapter is devoted to his concept of culture as 'sweetness and light', a phrase adopted from Swift's *The Battle of the Books*; Arnold presents culture as the classical ideal of human perfection, rather than 'a smattering of Greek and Latin'. Subsequent chapters set forward his definitions of Barbarians, *Philistines, and the Populace, and contrast the spirit of Hebraism (as manifested in primitive Christianity and Protestantism) with that of Hellenism, with its aim of seeing 'things as they really are'; both are important contributions to human development and should not be mutually exclusive.

CULVERWEL, Nathaniel (d. 1651), see CAMBRIDGE PLATONISTS.

CUMBERLAND, Richard (1732–1811), educated at Westminster School and Cambridge, was the author of a number of highly successful *sentimental comedies, of which *The West Indian* and *The Brothers* are the most interesting. He also wrote tragedies; two novels, *Arundel* (1789) and *Henry* (1795); a translation of the *Clouds* of *Aristophanes; and an autobiography. Cumberland is caricatured by *Sheridan as Sir Fretful Plagiary in *The Critic.*

CUMBERLAND, William Augustus, duke of (1721–65), third son of George II, and in command of the English army at Culloden (1746); known as 'the Butcher' on account of the severity with which he stamped out disaffection among the Highlanders. He figures in Scott's *Waverley.*

CUMMINGS, Bruce Frederick (1889–1919), diarist and biologist, born in Barnstaple, known under his pseudonym of W. N. P. Barbellion as the author of a diary covering the years 1903–17, *The Journal of a Disappointed Man,* which was published in 1919 with an introduction by H. G. *Wells, who described it as a 'specimen, carefully displayed and labelled' of 'a recorded unhappiness'. It is largely an account of the author's struggle with an illness (diagnosed as disseminated sclerosis) that made him increasingly introspective; he alternates between moods of elation, egotism, self disgust, and physical nausea, leading more and more of a substitute existence through his diaries, and noting that 'as I became more static and moribund, they become more active and aggressive.' He clearly intended publication, and modelled his work to some extent on the immensely successful diary of M. *Bashkirtseff ('She is impressionable, volatile, passionate—ill! So am I.'); the last entry was made on 21 Oct. 1917, after which 'Barbellion's' death was recorded, but in fact Cummings survived to see his own work published, and his *A Last Diary* (1920, ed. A. J. and H. R. Cummings) covers the last two years of his life.

CUMMINGS, E(dward) E(stlin) (1894–1962), American poet, born in Cambridge, Massachusetts, and educated at Harvard. His first book, *The Enormous Room* (1922), an account of his three-month internment in a French detention camp in 1917, won him an immediate international reputation for its brilliant prose and its iconoclastic views, with *Dos Passos, Robert *Graves, T. E. *Lawrence, and V. Larbaud among its earliest admirers. In 1923 appeared *Tulips and Chimneys,* the first of 12 volumes of poetry. Strongly influenced by the English

Romantic poets, by *Swinburne, and by *Pound, and marked by *Dada and the jazz age, the early poems attracted attention more for their experimental typography and technical skill than for their considerable lyric power; the frankness of his vocabulary and the sharpness of his satire also created some scandal. In *Eimi* (1933), a typographically difficult but enthralling journal of a trip to Russia, he broke in disillusion from his earlier socialist leanings, and thenceforth his work reflected his increasingly reactionary social and political views. His later lyrics, on the other hand, achieved a greater depth and simplicity. His other works include essays, plays, and *Tom* (1935), a satirical ballet based on H. B. *Stowe's *Uncle Tom's Cabin.* Cummings opened new perspectives for an entire generation of American and British poets, including *Auden and *Spender. His *Complete Poems: 1910–1962* was published in 1980.

CUNNINGHAM, Alan (1784–1842), born in Dumfriesshire, was apprenticed to his brother as a stonemason. As a boy he walked in *Burns': funeral procession. He was an avid reader, and became a friend of J. *Hogg. In 1809 *Cromek was collecting songs in Scotland, and Cunningham, when he found his own poems were not acceptable, profited from the vogue for *primitivism by disguising them as old Scottish songs, many of which Cromek then published in 1810 as *Remains of Nithsdale and Galloway Song.* Cromek persuaded him to come to London, and introduced him to Sir Francis Chantrey, whose secretary he became. He was soon a frequent contributor to the *London Magazine* and to *Blackwood's.* He published *Traditional Tales of the English and Scottish Peasantry* in 1822; *The Songs of Scotland* in 1825; various romantic tales between 1826 and 1836; *Lives of the most eminent British Painters, Sculptors, and Architects* in 1829–33; and in 1834 an edition of Burns. Several of his poems and ballads, such as 'A wet sheet and a flowing sea' and 'Hame, hame, hame', which were very popular in his lifetime, are still remembered.

CUNNINGHAM, John (1729–73), the son of a Dublin wine-cooper, wrote a successful farce, *Love in a Mist* (1747), then came to England and joined a group of travelling players, though it appears he had little talent as an actor. He also wrote contemplative pastoral verse imitative of *Gray and *Shenstone (*Poems chiefly pastoral,* 1766). He died in Newcastle upon Tyne.

CUNNINGHAME GRAHAM, Robert Bontine (1852–1936), horseman, writer, anti-imperialist, and social reformer, was the son of a Scottish laird and a half-Spanish mother. During a flamboyant and varied career he was a rancher in Argentina, an outspoken MP (he was imprisoned after Bloody Sunday, 1887), and a traveller in remote parts of the world, particularly in Spanish America where he gained an intimate knowledge of gaucho life and of the older civilization surviving from the period of Spanish rule. His many stories, books, and articles include remarkable and exotic tales of travel. *Mogreb-el-Acksa* (1898) recounts his attempt to reach the forbidden city of Tarudant in Morocco; G. B. *Shaw in his preface to *Captain Brassbound's Conversion* claimed it as his inspiration for the play, and it was also much admired by *Conrad. Other titles include *Thirteen Stories* (1900), *Success* (1902), *Scottish Stories* (1914), and *The Horses of the Conquest* (1930); he also wrote several volumes of Latin-American history. See A. F. Tschiffely, *Don Roberto* (1937), an account of Graham's life and their friendship, and Alexander Maitland, *Robert and Gabriela Cunninghame Graham* (1984).

CUNOBELIN (Cymbeline), a king of Britain in the early years of the Christian era, and father of *Caractacus.

Cup, The, a tragedy by Lord *Tennyson, produced 1881. Tennyson was disappointed in H. *Irving's portrayal of 'my Synorix, who is a subtle blend of Roman refinement and intellectuality, and barbarian, self-satisfied sensuality'.

Cupid and Campaspe, see CAMPASPE.

Cupid and Psyche, the allegorical centrepiece of the *Golden Ass* of *Apuleius, in which the author blends a familiar folk-tale depicting an enchanted suitor and his abandoned bride with a Hellenistic epyllion about the god of love which has some of the trappings of a philosophical myth. Psyche, daughter of a king, is beloved by Cupid, who visits her nightly, but remains invisible, forbidding her to attempt to see him: one night she takes a lamp and looks at him as he sleeps, and agitated by his beauty lets fall a drop of hot oil on his shoulder. He departs in wrath, leaving her solitary and remorseful. Like the hero of the novel in which her tale is set, Psyche has forfeited her happiness through misplaced curiosity, and has to regain it through painful wanderings. The irony evident in the treatment of the gods and the rich decoration of the setting of certain scenes betray an indebtedness to a Hellenistic original, while many elements of the fable—the magic palace, the enchantress (Venus) to whom the hero (Cupid) is in thrall, the tasks the heroine has to perform and the animals that aid her—belong to the world of the folk-tale. Apuleius' story has been retold by W. *Browne (*Britannia's Pastorals* Bk 3), by S. *Marmion (*Cupid and Psyche*), by W. *Morris (**The Earthly Paradise*), and by *Bridges (*Eros and Psyche*). Pater's *Marius the Epicurean* provides a prose version. Milton's *Comus* (1,003–11) contains a reference to

Apuleius' story and *Keats's 'Ode to Psyche' owes a debt to it.

Cure for a Cuckold, A, a comedy by J. *Webster and W. *Rowley, possibly with T. *Heywood, brought out in 1661.

It deals with the love-affairs of two couples, Bonville and Annabel, and Lessingham and Clare; and contains a notable duel scene on Calais sands.

Curious Impertinent, The (or *The Fatal Curiosity*), an episode in *Don Quixote* (I. xxx–xxxv) which provided the plot for more than one English 17th-cent. drama. Anselmo, having married the beautiful Camilla, urges his friend Lothario to test her virtue. Lothario, at first reluctant, yields to the constant pressure of his friend. Camilla's lapse encourages the licentiousness of her maid Leonela, which leads to the discovery of her mistress's infidelity, the death of Anselmo and Lothario, and Camilla's retirement to a convent.

CURLL, Edmund (1683–1747), a bookseller and pamphleteer who specialized in scandalous biographies, seditious pamphlets, pirated works, and pornography; he was imprisoned in 1724 for publishing *Venus in the Cloister: or the Nun in her Smock* (a characteristic title), though he denied that it was his. He made many enemies in the literary world, including *Pope, who pilloried him in *The Dunciad*. Pope was involved in various manœuvres to encourage Curll to publish an unauthorized edition of his letters (which he did, in 1735), in order to appear himself to be pushed into publishing the authentic versions. Curll is also mentioned in *Swift's poem 'On the Death of Dr Swift'. A life by R. Straus, *The Unspeakable Curll*, appeared in 1927.

CURRER BELL, see BRONTË, C.

Curse of Kehama, The, a narrative poem by R. *Southey, published 1810, relating the story of Kehama, the cruel Raja of the world, and the peasant Ladurlad, who is cursed for his endeavour to protect his daughter Kailyal from the lust of Arvalan, Kehama's son. After many vicissitudes, based on complex Hindu mythology, Kehama finds himself under the dominion of the lord of Hell, while Ladurlad and Kailyal are transported to heaven. Mme de *Staël, writing to *Byron on the subject of *oriental tales, refers to 'Southey's unsaleables'.

Cursor Mundi, a northern poem dating from about 1300 surviving in seven manuscripts of about 24,000 short lines, supplemented in most of them by another 6,000 or so lines of devotional material. It is founded on the works of late 12th-cent. Latin writers who wrote various pseudo-histories made up of hagiographic, legendary, and biblical material. This poem covers mankind's spiritual history from the Creation to the Last Judgement, divided into Seven Ages, and is a very successful, readable piece of popular instruction. It has been edited by R. Morris (EETS os, 7 vols, 1874–93).

CURZON, Robert, 14th Baron Zouche (1810–72), was author of a *Visit to the Monasteries of the Levant* (1849), a record of his travels undertaken in search of manuscripts to Mount Athos, Greece, Palestine, and Egypt, *An Account of the most Celebrated Libraries of Italy* (1854), and *Armenia* (1854).

CURZON OF KEDLESTON, George Nathaniel, marquess (1859–1925), educated at Eton and Balliol College, Oxford, was MP for Southport (1886), viceroy of India (1899–1905), chancellor of Oxford University (1907), and secretary of state for foreign affairs, 1918–22. He travelled widely, and the results were embodied in the authoritative *Persia and the Persian* (1892), and in books on the Far East and Asiatic Russia. His energy, pomposity, and enjoyment of the splendour and formality of official life have made him a legendary figure.

Custance, the widow in Udall's *Ralph Roister Doister*.

Custom of the Country, The, (1) a tragicomedy by J. *Fletcher and P. *Massinger, composed between 1619 and 1622, and derived from the *Persiles y Sigismunda* of *Cervantes. Famed for its obscenity, it was described by *Dryden as containing more bawdry than any Restoration play, and *Pepys declared it 'of all the plays that ever I did see, the worst—having neither plot, language, nor anything in the earth that is acceptable' (2 Jan. 1667). The plot is set in motion when Count Clodio, an Italian governor, claims his *droit de seigneur* ('the custom of the country') from Zenocia on her marriage to Arnoldo; she, Arnoldo, and Arnoldo's brother Rutilio escape by sea, but Zenocia is captured by a Portuguese captain and placed in service in Lisbon with Hippolita, who subsequently falls in love with Arnoldo and seeks Zenocia's destruction. There is an elaborately interwoven sub-plot involving Rutilio, his adventures in a brothel, and a duel. An adaptation by Nicholas Wright, with the action set in Southern Africa, was performed in 1983; (2) a witty and satiric novel by E. *Wharton in which a beautiful, energetic, destructive, and ambitious American, Udine Spragg, works her way to wealth and power through a succession of marriages—to Ralph Marvell, of the old New York aristocracy; to Marquis Raymond de Chelles, of the French aristocracy; and finally to billionaire Elmer Moffatt of Apex City, Kansas, who is revealed to have been her first husband in a secret marriage.

Cute, Alderman, a character in Dickens's *The

Chimes, said to be intended for Sir Peter Laurie, the City magistrate.

CUTHBERT, St (d. 687), in his youth kept sheep on the hills near the Lauder, a tributary of the Tweed. He entered the monastery of Melrose, of which he became prior. In course of time he was sent to fill the post of abbot of Lindisfarne, on which the monastery of Melrose then depended; and after several years, feeling himself called to a life of perfect solitude, he retired to the small island of Farne. In 684, at a synod held under St Theodore, archbishop of Canterbury, he was selected for the see of Lindsfarne, and to overcome his unwillingness to accept it King Egfrith himself, accompanied by the bishop of the Picts, visited him on his island. After two years, feeling death approaching, he retired to the solitude of his island, and died in his cell on 20 March (his feast day) 687. His body, which was said to have remained for many years in a state of incorruption and was carried away by the monks when they were driven by the Danes from Lindisfarne, was finally buried in Durham cathedral.

Cuttle, Captain Edward, a character in Dickens's *Dombey and Son*. His favourite expression is, 'When found, make a note of.' (See NOTES AND QUERIES.)

Cyder, see PHILIPS, J.

Cymbeline, a play by *Shakespeare, first published in the Folio of 1623. It may have been written in 1609/10; *Forman saw a performance of it, perhaps at the Globe, probably in April 1611. Its sources are *Holinshed, *A Mirror for Magistrates, and perhaps Boccaccio's *Decameron (see also PHILASTER). Though included among the tragedies in the First *Folio the play is now generally classified as a 'romance', and is more highly regarded than it was by Dr *Johnson, who said that 'To remark the folly of the fiction, the absurdity of the conduct, the confusion of the names and manners of different times, and the impossibility of the events in any system of life, were to waste criticism upon unresisting imbecility, upon faults too evident for detection, and too gross for aggravation.' The play was much loved in the 19th cent., however; *Tennyson died with a copy of it on the coverlet of his bed. G. B. *Shaw wrote an emended version of the long fifth act, published in 1938 under the title *Cymbeline Refinished*.

Imogen, daughter of Cymbeline, King of Britain, has secretly married Leonatus Posthumus, a 'poor but worthy gentleman'. The queen, Imogen's stepmother, determined that her clownish son Cloten shall marry Imogen, reveals the secret marriage to the king, who banishes Posthumus. In Rome Posthumus boasts of Imogen's virtue and makes a wager with

Iachimo that if he can seduce Imogen he shall have a diamond ring that Imogen had given him. Iachimo is repulsed by Imogen, but by hiding in her bedchamber he observes details of Imogen's room and her body which persuade Posthumus of her infidelity, and he receives the ring. Posthumus writes to his servant Pisanio directing him to kill Imogen; but Pisanio instead provides her with male disguise, sending a bloody cloth to Posthumus to deceive him that the deed is done. Under the name Fidele Imogen becomes a page to Bellarius and the two lost sons of Cymbeline, Guiderius and Arviragus, living in a cave in Wales. Fidele sickens and is found as dead by the brothers, who speak the dirge 'Fear no more the heat o'th'sun'. Left alone she revives, only to discover at her side the headless corpse of Cloten which she believes, because of his borrowed garments, to be that of her husband Posthumus. A Roman army invades Britain; Imogen falls into the hands of the general Lucius and becomes his page. The Britons defeat the Romans, thanks to the super-human valour in a narrow lane of Bellarius and his two sons aided by the disguised Posthumus. However Posthumus, pretending to be a Ro-man, is subsequently taken prisoner and has a vision in gaol of his family and Jupiter, who leaves a prophetic document with him. Lucius pleads with Cymbeline for the life of Fidele/Imogen: moved by something familiar in her appearance, he spares her life and grants her a favour. She asks that Iachimo be forced to tell how he came by the ring he wears. Posthumus, learning from this confession that his wife is innocent but believing her dead, is in despair till Imogen reveals herself. The king's joy at recovering his daughter is intensified when Bellarius restores to him his two lost sons, and the scene ends in a general reconciliation. Posthumus's words to Imogen on being reconciled with her, 'Hang there like fruit, my soul, | Till the tree die!' were described by Tennyson as 'the tenderest lines in Shakespeare'.

Cymochles, in Spenser's *Faerie Queene* (II. v, vi, and viii), 'a man of rare redoubted might', 'given all to lust and loose living', the husband of *Acrasia* and brother of *Pyrochles*. He sets out to avenge on Sir *Guyon the supposed death of his brother, but *Phaedria intervenes. He is finally slain by Prince *Arthur.

Cymodoce, one of the Nereids. Cymodoce is the name of the mother of Marinell in Spenser's *Faerie Queene* (IV. xii). *Swinburne's 'Garden of Cymodoce' in *Songs of the Springtides* is the island of Sark.

CYNEWULF, probably a Northumbrian or Mercian poet of the late 8th or 9th century. At one time a great number of Old English poems were attributed to him (notably *Andreas, *Guthlac A and B, *The Phoenix, and *The

Dream of the Rood), but modern scholarship restricts attribution to the four poems in the *Exeter Book and the *Vercelli Book which end with his name in runes. The poems are *Juliana, Elene, The Fates of the Apostles,* and *Christ II* (the last is a poem on the Ascension in the Exeter Book placed between poems on the Incarnation and on the Last Judgement, the three together being taken as a composite poem, *Christ*). *Elene* is the story of the finding of the Cross by St Helena, the mother of the emperor Constantine.

Trans. C. W. Kennedy, *The Poems of Cyne-wulf* (1910: reprinted 1949; contains the attrib-uted as well as the signed poems); K. Sisam, 'Cynewulf and his Poetry' (*Studies in the History of Old English Literature*, 1953, ch. 1); *Juliana,* ed. R. Woolf (1955).

Cynthia, a poem by R. *Barnfield.

Cynthia, (1) a name for Artemis or Diana, from Mount Cynthus in Delos, where Artemis was born, and used poetically to denote the Moon; (2) the name given by the Roman poet *Propertius to his mistress; (3) deriving from (1), a name used by *Spenser (in *Colin Clouts come home againe), *Ralegh, and others to denote Elizabeth I as virgin moon-goddess; (4) in Congreve's *The Double Dealer, the daughter of Sir Paul Plyant, affianced to Mellefont; (5) in Mrs Gaskell's *Wives and Daughters, Cynthia Kirkpatrick, stepsister of Molly Gibson.

Cynthia, Ocean's Love to, a poem by *Ralegh reflecting on his shifting relationship with Elizabeth I. The title plays on Ralegh's name (Walter/Water). Spenser in *Colin Clouts come home againe (1595) referred to Ralegh's author-ship of

> a lamentable lay . . .
> Of Cynthia the Ladie of the sea,
> Which from her presence faultlesse him debard.

Ralegh may have written a longer poem or sequence of poems on this theme; what survives in Ralegh's own hand is a 522-line piece 'the 21th: and last booke of the Ocean to Scinthia'. Cf. Walter Oakeshott, *The Queen and the Poet* (1960).

Cynthia's Revels, an allegorical comedy by *Jonson, performed 1600, printed 1601.
The play satirizes various court vices re-presented by characters whose names typify their failings: Argurion, money; Asotus, prodigality; Anaides, impudence; Hedon, voluptuousness; Moria, folly; Phantaste, frivolity; Philautia, self-love; Amorphus, who has 'lost his shape' through too much travel. Having drunk of the Fountain of Self-Love (the sub-title of the play), the court-iers are emboldened to appear before Queen Cynthia in a masque devised by the wise poet Crites, in which each character is made to im-personate his complementary virtue. With the

aid of Mercury, who had been sent by Jove to purge the court, Crites exposes the masquers, and as a penance they are sent on a pilgrimage to drink the waters of Mount Helicon, the fountain of truth. The song of Hesperus in Act V, 'Queen and huntress, chaste and fair', is one of Jonson's most beautiful lyrics.

Cypress, Mr, a character in Peacock's *Nightmare Abbey*, a caricature of *Byron.

Cypresse Grove, A, see DRUMMOND OF HAWTHORNDEN.

CYRANO DE BERGERAC, Savinien (1619–55), a French soldier and duellist, whom a wound in the Spanish War turned into a dramatist and novelist. He is the subject of a highly successful play by *Rostand.

D

Dacier, the Hon. Percy, a character in Meredith's *Diana of the Crossways*.

Dacres, and his daughter May, in *The Young Duke*, by B. Disraeli.

Dactyl, a metrical foot consisting of one long followed by two short syllables, or of one accented followed by two unaccented (derived from the three joints of the finger, δάκτυλος). See METRE.

Dada (Fr. 'hobby-horse' a name chosen at random from a dictionary), a movement in art and literature founded c.1916 in Zurich and more or less simultaneously in New York. The movement's aim was nihilistic, a denial of sense or order; it lasted until the mid-1920s, with Paris as its centre from 1920. Writers connected with Dada included Tristan Tzara, who appears as a character in Stoppard's *Travesties*, which is set in Zurich during the First World War. Notable among Dada artists were Hans Arp, Marcel Duchamp, and Man Ray.

DADD, Richard (1817–86), English painter, who is best known for his fairy pictures filled with meticulous, tiny detail. They follow Joshua *Reynolds, *Fuseli, and Joseph Noel Paton in illustrating scenes from *A Midsummer Night's Dream* and *The Tempest*. Dadd went mad in 1843 and murdered his father; he spent the rest of his life in Bethlehem Hospital and in Broadmoor. His most famous work is *The Fairy Fellers Master-Stroke* (1855–64, Tate Gallery, London); a recently discovered MS poem (dated 1865) explains its subject in detail.

'Daffodils' ('I wandered lonely as a cloud'), an untitled poem by *Wordsworth, written 1804, published 1807, possibly the most popular and anthologized of all Wordsworth's poems.

Dagon, the national deity of the ancient Philistines, represented as half man, half fish (Judges 16: 23; 1 Sam, 5: 1–5; Milton, *Paradise Lost*, i. 462 and *Samson Agonistes*).

DAICHES, David (1912–), scholar and author, educated at George Watson's College, Edinburgh, and Edinburgh University. He has held various academic posts and written on a wide variety of subjects: his works include studies of R. L. *Stevenson (1947), *Burns (1950), and Sir W. *Scott (1971); a *Critical History of English Literature* (4 vols, 1960); *Scotch Whisky* (1969); and two autobiographical works which vividly evoke his unusual childhood as son of a Jewish scholar and rabbi in Edinburgh (*Two Worlds*, 1957; *Was; a pastime from time past*, 1975).

Daily Courant, The, the first English daily newspaper, started in March 1702. It contained foreign intelligence, translated from foreign newspapers. It lasted till 1735. (See NEWSPAPERS, ORIGINS OF.)

Daily Express, The, a daily paper founded in 1900 by Sir A. *Pearson.

Daily News, The, was founded by *Dickens in 1845 as a Liberal rival to the *Morning Chronicle; the first issue appeared on 21 Jan. 1846. Dickens himself edited the paper for 17 numbers only, then handed over to John *Forster. Among notable contributors and members of its staff at various times may be mentioned H. *Martineau, *Lang, G. B. *Shaw, *Wells, Arnold *Bennett, and the eminent war correspondent Archibald Forbes (1839–1900). It became the *News Chronicle* in 1930, having absorbed the *Daily Chronicle*, and survived under this title until 1960.

Daily Telegraph, The, founded in 1855, was the first daily paper to be issued in London at a penny. Its enterprising character and rather highly coloured style proved so successful that for a time it enjoyed a larger circulation than any other English newspaper, and in its early days, with T. *Hunt as assistant editor, its political views were Radical. After a period of decline in the early 20th cent., circulation recovered in the 1930s; in 1937 the *Morning Post* was at its own request amalgamated. The *Sunday Telegraph* was added in 1961. Among famous members of its staff have been G. A. *Sala, Sir E. *Arnold, and Edward Dicey (1832–1911).

Dairyman's Daughter, The, a moral rustic tale by L. *Richmond, published 1809. The work had an enormous circulation, reaching two million copies in England, apart from translations into many European languages and a wide sale in America.

Daisy Miller, one of H. *James's most popular stories, published 1879, dramatized by James 1883.

Daisy Miller travels to Europe with her wealthy, commonplace mother, and in her innocence and audacity offends convention and seems to compromise her reputation. She dies in Rome of malaria. She is one of the most notable and charming of James's portrayals of 'the American girl'.

Dale, (1) Laetitia, a character in Meredith's *The Egoist*; (2) Lily, the heroine of A. *Trollope's novel *The Small House at Allington*, and an important character in *The Last Chronicle of Barset*.

D'ALEMBERT, or Dalembert, Jean le Rond (1717–83), see PHILOSOPHES and ENCYCLOPÉDIE.

Dalgarno, Lord, a character in Scott's *The Fortunes of Nigel*.

Dalgetty, Dugald, a character in Scott's *The Legend of Montrose*.

DALI, Salvador Felipe Jacinto (1904–   ), Spanish painter, stage designer, and writer, born in Figueras, Catalonia, and from 1929 associated with the *Surrealist movement. He has also written a novel, *Hidden Faces* (1944), and several volumes of flamboyant autobiography.

Dalila, see DELILAH.

DALRYMPLE, Sir David, Lord Hailes (1726–92), Scottish jurist, historian, and antiquarian, was a friend of *Boswell, Dr *Johnson, and Horace *Walpole. He published much, including his *Annals of Scotland* (1776, 1779, 1797), a valuable study of Scottish history which Johnson much admired. He was also keenly interested in ancient Scottish poems and ballads, and corresponded with *Percy on this subject.

DAMIEN, Father, see STEVENSON, R. L.

Damoetas, (1) a shepherd in the *Idylls* of *Theocritus and the *Eclogues* of *Virgil; (2) a character in Sidney's *Arcadia*, a base herdsman who has become a royal favourite; (3) an old shepherd (representing a Cambridge academic?) in Milton's *Lycidas*.

Damon, a shepherd singer in *Virgil's eighth *Eclogue*; a name adopted by poets for a rustic swain. Cf. *Epitaphium Damonis*, *Milton's Latin elegy on his friend *Diodati.

Damon and Pithias, a rhymed play by R. *Edwards, acted probably 1564, printed 1571.

Damon and Pithias, Pythagorean Greeks, visit Syracuse, and the former is presently arrested on a baseless charge of spying and conspiring against Dionysius the tyrant of Syracuse, who orders his execution. Damon obtains a respite of two months to return home in order to settle his affairs, Pythias offering himself as security for his return. Damon is delayed and arrives when Pythias is just about to be put to death. They contend which shall be executed,

each striving to save the other. Dionysius, impressed with their mutual loyalty, pardons Damon and asks to be admitted to their brotherhood.

In the original classical legend it is Phintias (of which 'Pythias' is a corruption), not Damon, who is sentenced, and Damon goes bail for him.

DAMPIER, William (1652–1715), navigator, explorer, and buccaneer, who travelled to South America, Yucatan, the Pacific, Australia, and the East Indies in the course of an adventurous career which ended in some disgrace, after accusations of brutality and drunkenness. His accounts of his travels, written in a lively and straightforward style and showing precise scientific observation, were extremely popular, and heralded an era of great interest in travel and voyage literature. (*New Voyage round the World*, 1697; *Voyages and Descriptions*, 1698; *A Voyage to New Holland*, 1703–9; edited by J. *Masefield in 2 vols, 1906.) Dampier also figures in W. *Rogers's journal of his privateering expedition during which *Selkirk was rescued from Juan Fernandez. (See also ROBINSON CRUSOE.)

D'Amville, the 'atheist' in Tourneur's *The Atheist's Tragedy*.

DANA, Richard Henry (1815–82), son of the poet and journalist Richard Henry Dana (1787–1879), born in Massachusetts, broke off his education at Harvard to embark as a common sailor, hoping to recover from 'a weakness of the eyes', and is remembered for his realistic and lively account of his voyage from Boston around Cape Horn to California, published anonymously in 1840 as *Two Years Before the Mast*.

Dance of Death, or *danse macabre* (or *danse macabré*), gave expression to the sense especially prominent in the 15th cent. (perhaps as a consequence of the plague and the preaching of the mendicant friars) of the ubiquity of Death the leveller. The Dance appears to have first taken shape in France, as a mimed sermon in which figures typical of various orders of society were seized and haled away each by its own corpse (not, as later, by the personification of Death). The earliest known painting of the Dance, accompanied by versified dialogues between living and dead, was made in 1424 in the cemetery of the Innocents in Paris, and the German artists (including *Holbein) who later depicted it appear to have drawn inspiration from French sources. The origin of the word *macabre* or *macabré* has been the subject of many conjectures, such as that the latter is a corruption of Old French *Macabé*, to refer to a mystery play in which the Apocryphal killing of the Maccabees by Antiochus was represented.

Dance to the Music of Time, A, see POWELL, A.

Dandie Dinmont, in Scott's *Guy Mannering*, a sturdy hospitable Liddesdale farmer and the owner of a special breed of terriers.

Dandin, George, the hero of a comedy of that name by *Molière, a tradesman who marries a noble's daughter and suffers many humiliations in consequence. *'Vous l'avez voulu, George Dandin'*, is his frequent comment on his situation.

DANE, Clemence, the pseudonym of Winifred Ashton (1888–1965), playwright and novelist, whose first play, *A Bill of Divorcement* (1921), had a success never quite matched by her later works (*Will Shakespeare*, 1921, a blank verse drama; *Wild Decembers*, 1932, a play about the *Brontës). Her novels include *Regiment of Women* (1917) and *Legend* (1919).

Dangerfield, a character in (1) Sedley's *Bellamira*; (2) Scott's *Peveril of the Peak*; (3) *The Ginger Man* by *Donleavy.

Dangle, a character in Sheridan's *The Critic*.

'Daniel', an Old English poem of 764 lines found in the *Junius manuscript, paraphrasing the Old Testament Book of Daniel. See F. A. Blackburn ed., *Exodus and Daniel: Two Old English Poems* (1907).

DANIEL, Charles Henry Olive (1836–1919), scholar, fellow, and provost of Worcester College, Oxford, is remembered for his lifelong interest in printing. He established a private press at Oxford, where he used the *Fell types and produced some fine examples of typography, including plays and poems of *Bridges.
    The 'Daniel Mark', sometimes called the 'Misit Mark', the special note of the press, represents Daniel in the lions' den with the motto: 'Misit Angelum suum' ('He sent his Angel').
    See *The Daniel Press 1845–1919* (1921), a memorial volume compiled by his friends.

DANIEL, Samuel (1563–1619), the son of a music–master, entered Magdalen Hall, Oxford, in 1579, and after visiting Italy, where he met the pastoral poet *Guarini, he became tutor to William Herbert, third earl of Pembroke, and later to Lady Anne Clifford, daughter of the countess of Cumberland. In 1592 he published *Delia*, a collection of sonnets inspired by *Tasso and Desportes, to which was appended the 'Complaint of Rosamund'. Spenser mentioned him by name in *Colin Clouts come home againe*, praising *Delia*, but predicting that

> most me seemes, thy accent will excell,
> In Tragick plaints and passionate mischance.

Daniel made the transition to tragedy forthwith, his next work being *Cleopatra* (1594), a

Senecan tragedy closely related to the countess of Pembroke's *Antonie*, itself translated from Garnier in 1590. *'Musophilus: Containing a generall defence of learning' appeared in 1599. In 1603 he welcomed James I's accession with a *Panegyrike Congratulatorie*, and published also his verse 'Epistles' and *A Defence of Ryme*, the last being a reply to T. *Campion's *Observations in the Art of English Poesie*. His career as a court poet developed with his masques and plays, *The Vision of the 12 Goddesses* (1604), *The Queen's Arcadia* (1605), *Tethys' Festival* (1610), and *Hymen's Triumph* (1614). Early in 1604 he became licenser for the Children of the Queen's Revels, but he gave over this lucrative office in April 1605. This may have been because of the row caused by his second tragedy *Philotas*, performed in the autumn of 1604, which was held—perhaps justly—to allude closely and sympathetically to the rebellion of the earl of *Essex in 1600. Daniel affixed an 'Apology', claiming that any resemblance to the Essex affair was purely coincidental, when the play was published in 1605. His position at court appears to have recovered thereafter. His weightiest work was his *Civil Wars*, a verse epic on the Wars of the Roses. Four books appeared in 1595, and the complete eight books in 1609. A prose history of England from the Romans to Edward III, *The Collection of the History of England*, was his last work. *Jonson called Daniel 'a good honest Man, . . . but no poet'; other contemporaries esteemed him, such as W. *Browne who called him 'Well-languag'd Danyel'. In later times his greatest admirers have been in the Romantic period: *Lamb, *Wordsworth, and *Coleridge were among those who read him appreciatively, the last finding his style and language as 'pure and manly' as Wordsworth's own. The bibliographical complexity of Daniel's texts, combined with a decline in admiration for his plain manner, may account for the lack of any complete edition of his works since *Grosart's of 1885–96.

Daniel Deronda, a novel by G. *Eliot, published 1876, the last of her novels.
    Gwendolen Harleth, high-spirited, self-confident, and self-centred, marries Henleigh Grandcourt, an arrogant, selfish, and cold-hearted man of the world, for his money and his position, to save her mother, sisters, and herself from destitution and in spite of the fact that she knows of the existence of (and has indeed met) Lydia Glasher, who has had a long-standing affair with Grandcourt, and children by him. She rejects Mrs Glasher's appeals and threats, and suffers in consequence in terms of guilt and a sense of her husband's increasing power over her. In her misery she comes increasingly under the influence of Daniel Deronda, who becomes her spiritual adviser.

He is an idealistic young man, whose own parentage is involved in mystery; it is gradually revealed that he is not, as he had assumed, an illegitimate cousin of Grandcourt's, but the son of a Jewish singer of international renown. This discovery strengthens his bonds with Mirah, a young Jewish singer whom he has saved from drowning, and her brother Mordecai, an intellectual Jewish nationalist. Gwendolen's husband is drowned at Genoa, in a manner that leaves her feeling partly guilty for his death; she confesses to Deronda, but shortly discovers to her initial despair that he is to marry Mirah and devote himself to the Jewish cause and the founding of a Jewish national home. Notable among the minor characters is Klesmer, the musician, who persuades Gwendolen that her talent as a singer, though acceptable in an amateur, would not repay training, thus unwittingly pushing her towards her disastrous marriage. One of the themes of the novel is the nature of professional and artistic dedication, explored through Gwendolen's dilettante expectations, Klesmer's seriousness and insistence on constant application, Mirah's acceptance of a hard–working but less than illustrious career, and the passionate and self–glorifying commitment of Deronda's mother, who had been obliged to sacrifice her own child to her success.

The Jewish plot has been severely handled by critics, by H. *James (*Daniel Deronda: A Conversation*, 1876) for being 'at bottom cold', and by *Leavis (*The Great Tradition*, 1948) as 'embarrassingly fervid'. Leavis also traces the debt of James in * *The Portrait of a Lady*.

Dannisburgh, Lord, a character in Meredith's *Diana of the Crossways*, drawn from Lord Melbourne.

D'ANNUNZIO, Gabriele (1863–1938), Italian novelist, playwright, and poet. An irredentist nationalist, he effectively urged the entry of Italy into the First World War on the side of the Allies, and himself took part in spectacular exploits by sea and air. In 1919, with a small volunteer force, he occupied Fiume where he remained as dictator until 1921. One of his novels, *Il piacere* (*The Child of Pleasure*, 1890), is one of the significant texts of European Decadence. His later novels, which include *Trionfo della morte* (*Triumph of Death*, 1894) and *Il fuoco* (*The Flame of Life*, 1900), were strongly influenced by Nietzschean ideas. Some of his plays were set to music, one in French, *Le Martyre de Saint Sébastien* (1911), by *Debussy, and *Parisina* (1913) by Mascagni. His best play is *La figlia di Iorio* (*Iorio's Daughter*, 1904), set in his native Abruzzi. D'Annunzio is at his best in his lyrics in *Alcyone* and in *Maia*, part of a four-volume collection entitled *Laudi* (*Praises*, 1904). As a poet he was influenced by *Symbolism and the *Pre-Raphaelites. His prose style was admired by *Joyce.

DANTE ALIGHIERI (1265–1321), was born at Florence of a Guelf family. The circumstances of his early life are obscure, but we know that in 1277 he was formally betrothed to his future wife, Gemma Donati, and that in 1289 he took part in military operations against Arezzo and Pisa. During this early period of his life he fell in love with the girl whom he celebrates under the name of Beatrice in the *Vita nuova* and the *Divina Commedia*. Her identity has been much discussed, but the generally accepted view is that she was Bice Portinari, who became the wife of Simone de' Bardi. When she died, in 1290, Dante was grief-stricken and sought consolation in the study of philosophy. In 1295 he became active in the political life of Florence. In June 1300 he was one of the municipal priors who banished the leaders of the White and Black Guelf factions, and in Oct. 1301 he was one of the three envoys sent to Rome to negotiate with Boniface VIII. He was never to set foot in Florence again, for during his absence the Blacks seized power and Dante, whose sympathies were with the Whites, became the victim of political reprisals and was for the rest of his life to lead a wandering existence. He died at Ravenna, where he had for some years found refuge.

The precise dating of Dante's works presents problems as yet unsolved. The first in order of composition (apart from his earliest lyric poems) was the *Vita nuova*, written in the period 1290–4, in which Dante brings together 31 poems, most of them relating to his love for Beatrice. A linking prose narrative tells the story of his love and interprets the poems from the standpoint of one who has come to see his beloved as the instrument of his spiritual salvation. There is a translation by D. G. *Rossetti (1861). The *Convivio* or *Banquet*, is an unfinished philosophical work, planned as a series of 14 treatises, each in the form of a prose commentary on one of Dante's own *canzoni*. The four completed treatises, written between 1304 and 1308, draw on numerous philosophical sources, but principally on *Aristotle. The Latin treatise *De vulgari eloquentia*, begun shortly before the *Convivio*, is also unfinished. The completed part consists of an enquiry into the form of vernacular language most suitable for lofty poetry, followed by the beginning of a discussion of the technique of the *canzone*. It is a pioneering work in the field of linguistic history. The *Monarchia*, written in the period 1309–12, is a Latin treatise on the universal empire and the relations between emperor and pope. It is very uncertain when Dante began his masterpiece, the *Divina Commedia*. (See entry under this heading for his influence on English writers.) It may have been begun as early as 1307, or possibly not until 1314 or later, and was finished just before his death.

Daphnaïda, an elegy by *Spenser closely

modelled on Chaucer's *Book of the Duchess. See ALCYON.

Daphnis and Chloe is the finest of Greek romances and the only one that has a purely pastoral character. Written by an otherwise unknown Longus it belongs probably to the end of the 2nd cent. AD and describes how two youngsters waken to sexual desire, fall in love, and eventually marry. Regarded as pornographic throughout its history since it contains a description of the sexual act, the work has not received the critical attention to which its charm and genuine artistry entitle it. It was translated from *Amyot's French version by Angel Day (1587) and from the original Greek by George Thornley (1657). G. *Moore produced a modern translation in 1924. The story provided the subject of a ballet with music by Ravel and choreography by Fokine, composed for Diaghilev and first performed in 1912.

Dapper, the clerk in Jonson's *The Alchemist who is gagged and locked in the privy for most of the play.

d'ARBLAY, Mme, see BURNEY, F.

Darcy, Fitzwilliam and his sister Georgiana, characters in J. Austen's *Pride and Prejudice.

Dares Phrygius, a Trojan priest mentioned by *Homer (Iliad, V. 9). He was supposed to have been the author of an account of the fall of Troy of which a Latin prose version is extant. This work, De excidio Troiae, dating probably from the 5th cent. AD, provided, together with the complementary history of *Dictys Cretensis, the only detailed account of the Trojan War available in the medieval West. Everything written about Troy before the middle of the 17th cent. was to some extent dependent, directly or indirectly, on the narratives of Dares and Dictys.

Dark as the Grave Wherein my Friend is Laid, a novel by M. *Lowry, based on a journey to Mexico taken in 1945-6 and published posthumously in 1968. The title is taken from *Cowley's elegy 'On the Death of Mr William Harvey'.

Darkness at Noon, a novel by A. *Koestler, published 1940, translated from German.

It deals with the arrest, imprisonment, trial, and execution of N. S. Rubashov in an unnamed dictatorship over which 'No. 1' presides. Koestler describes Rubashov as 'a synthesis of the lives of a number of men who were victims of the so-called Moscow trials', and the novel did much to draw attention to the nature of *Stalin's régime.

DARLEY, George (1795-1846), born in Dublin, was the eldest of the seven children of a merchant, and was educated at Trinity College,

Dublin. He settled in London in 1821, and earned his living by writing textbooks on mathematics and as dramatic critic for *The London Magazine and later as art critic for *The Athenaeum; he was a forerunner in the English rediscovery of early Italian painting. His first published poem was The Errors of Ecstasie (1822). Sylvia, a pastoral drama which was the most successful of his works in his own lifetime, followed in 1827. Many of his lyrics were published in magazines, the best known being Syren Songs, 'Serenade of a Loyal Martyr' (which may have influenced *Meredith's 'Love in the Valley'), and 'It is not Beauty I demand', a 17th-cent. pastiche which F. T. *Palgrave included in his Golden Treasury under the impression that it was a genuine Caroline poem. Darley also published two historical plays, Thomas à Becket and Ethelstan. His finest work was his unfinished Nepenthe, privately printed 1835, an allegory of the imagination in excesses of joy or melancholy, partly inspired by *Milton, *Shelley, and *Keats, but containing some remarkable lyrics and passages of wild fantasy and highly skilled versification.

Darley suffered all his life from a very severe stammer, which cut him off from most social activities, and he also had recurring headaches, probably some form of migraine. He never married, and his life was reclusive, but his friends—who included *Lamb, H. F. *Cary, *Clare, A. *Cunningham, *Milnes, and *Carlyle—admired him as an amiable, high minded, and unjustly neglected poet, though he made some enemies by his virulent dramatic criticism. See C. C. Abbott, The Life and Letters of George Darley (1928); Selected Poems of George Darley, with an introduction and notes by Anne Ridler (1979).

DARLING, Frank Fraser (1903–), naturalist and pioneer ecologist, educated at Edinburgh University. He is the author of many authoritative books on subjects concerning the relationship of man to his environment and man's responsibility to nature. His 1969 Reith Lectures have been published as Wilderness and Plenty (1970).

Darnay, Charles, a character in Dickens's *A Tale of Two Cities.

D'Artagnan, one of the heroes of A. Dumas père's *The Three Musketeers.

Dartle, Rosa, a character in Dickens's *David Copperfield.

DARWIN, Charles Robert (1809–82), born at Shrewsbury, grandson of E. *Darwin, was educated at Edinburgh University and Christ's College, Cambridge. He embarked in 1831 with *Fitzroy as naturalist on the Beagle, bound for South America, returned in 1836, and published in 1839 his Journal of Researches into *the Geology and Natural History of the various countries visited by H.M.S. Beagle*. His great work *On the Origin of Species by means of Natural Selection* appeared in 1859. Darwin had received from A. R. *Wallace a manuscript containing a sketch of his theory. Building upon the Uniformitarian geology of Charles Lyell (1797–1875), which supposed a very great antiquity for the earth and slow, regular change, Darwin argued for a natural, not divine, origin of species. In the competitive struggle for existence, creatures possessing advantageous mutations would be favoured, eventually evolving into new species. In the 'survival of the fittest' (a phrase coined by H. *Spencer, but accepted by Darwin) organic descent was achieved by natural selection, by analogy with the artificial selection of the stockbreeder. An agnostic, Darwin saw no higher moral or religious ends in evolution, only chance and necessity. Other evolutionists, such as Wallace and Spencer, by contrast, identified evolution with progress. Darwin's book gave rise to intense opposition, but found distinguished supporters in T. H. *Huxley, Lyell, and Sir Joseph Hooker (1817–1911); the reverberation of his ideas can be seen throughout the literature of the second half of the 19th cent. In *The Descent of Man* (1871) Darwin discussed sexual selection, and argued that man too had evolved, from the higher primates, whereas Wallace made man a partial exception to this rule. Despite religious and humanist fears, evolutionism in general quickly won acceptance, but natural selection, Darwin's evolutionary mechanism, foundered for want of an adequate theory of inheritance until the rediscovery of Mendelian genetics, which led to the emergence of the modern evolutionary synthesis in the 1920s. A dedicated naturalist, Darwin also wrote extensively on barnacles, earthworms, and orchids, and was a pioneer observer of animal behaviour. *The Life and Letters of Darwin*, edited by his son Francis Darwin, appeared 1887–8, and several further volumes of letters have also been published.

DARWIN, Erasmus (1731–1802), educated at Cambridge, spent part of his life as a physician at Lichfield, where he established a botanical garden. Declaring that 'the general design . . . is to enlist imagination under the banner of Science', he embodied the botanical system of *Linnaeus in his long poem *The Loves of the Plants*, published 1789. The work reappeared as Part II of *The Botanic Garden* (1791), of which Part I was 'The Economy of Vegetation'. The poem is in heroic couplets, in imitation of *Pope. The goddess of Botany, descending to earth, expounds various natural phenomena throughout the four cantos of Part I, while Part II describes 'the Ovidian metamorphosis of the flowers, with their floral harems', stamens and pistils figuring as beaux and belles. The work

contains an interesting embryonic theory of evolution, similar in many ways to that developed by the poet's grandson, C. *Darwin. The poem was ridiculed by *Canning and *Frere in 'The Loves of the Triangles', published in *The Anti-Jacobin* in 1798. In his prose *Zoonomia* (in which *Wordsworth found the story of Goody Blake), published 1794–6, Darwin further describes the laws of organic life, both plant and animal, on an evolutionary principle. His heretical views on creation brought him into some disrepute. Anna *Seward published *Memoirs* of him in 1804, and his grandson Charles published a life in 1887.

DARYUSH, Elizabeth (1887–1977), poet, daughter of R. *Bridges. Her volumes of poetry include *Verses* (1930), *Verses, Third Book* (1933), *The Last Man, and other poems* (1936), and *Verses, Seventh Book* (1971); her *Collected Poems*, published in 1976 with an introduction by D. *Davie, was an attempt to recover her work from what several poets (including Y. *Winters and R. *Fuller) saw as undeserved neglect. Her experiments with syllabics show an affinity with the *sprung rhythm of G. M. *Hopkins, and her poetry has also been compared to that of *Hardy.

DASENT, Sir George Webbe (1817–96), educated at Magdalen Hall, Oxford, spent four years in Stockholm from 1841 studying Scandinavian literature and northern mythology. In 1845 he joined the staff of *The Times* and in 1853 became professor of English literature at King's College, London. He devoted much of his life to the popularization of Scandinavian literature and the interpretation of Icelandic sagas, publishing many translations. Among his publications are *Prose, or the Younger Edda* (1842), dedicated to *Carlyle, who had encouraged him, the *Grammar of the Icelandic or Old Norse Tongue* (1843), *Popular Tales from the Norse* (1859), and *The Story of Burnt Njal* (1861).

Dashwood, Mrs, her daughters Elinor, Marianne, and Margaret, and their stepbrother John, characters in J. Austen's *Sense and Sensibility*.

Datchery, Dick, the name assumed by one of the characters in Dickens's *Edwin Drood*; his identity is not revealed when the fragment ends.

D'AUBIGNÉ, Théodore-Agrippa (1552–1630), French Huguenot leader and writer. After participating in the wars of religion and witnessing the accession of Henry IV, he withdrew to his Poitou domains in 1593 and, in order to escape further persecution, to Geneva in 1620. Soldier, architect, administrator, scholar, and poet, he was one of the complete men of his age. His literary output is as varied as it is innovatory. His early love lyrics, *Printemps* (first pub. 1874), are passionate and 'metaphysical'; his epic poem *Les Tragiques* (1616) is a violent and visionary representation of the fate of the Huguenots in 16th–cent. France; his *Histoire Universelle* (1616–20) is a personal and historical narrative of religious and political events in France between 1550 and 1601; his burlesque novels, *Adventures du baron de Faeneste* (1617) and *Confession de Sancy* (pub. 1660), satirize religious absurdity and vice; and his autobiography, *Sa vie à ses enfants*, justifies the course of a tumultuous life.

DAUDET, Alphonse (1840–97), French novelist, best known for his charming sketches of life in his native Provence (*Lettres de mon moulin*, 1869) and as the creator of Tartarin, the character who is the sum and epitome of those qualities supposed to make up the meridional temperament, combining the powers of self-deception and enthusiasm for adventure of Don Quixote with the timidity of Sancho Panza. His comic exploits are related in *Tartarin de Tarascon* (1872), *Tartarin sur les Alpes* (1885), *La Défense de Tarascon* (1886), and *Port Tarascon* (1890). The novel in two parts, *Le petit chose* (1868), is semi-autobiographical. Daudet's other novels, which make up the bulk of his output, portray the social and professional life of Paris in a broadly *Naturalistic vein, e.g. *Fromont jeune et Risler aîné* (1874), *Le Nabab* (1877), *Numa Roumestan* (1881), *Sapho* (1884).

DAUMIER, Honoré (1808–79), French painter and lithographer. More than 4,000 of his political and satirical cartoons were published in *Charivari*, *Caricature*, and *Le Figaro*.

Dauphine Eugenie, Sir, the hero of Jonson's *Epicene*.

D'AVENANT, Sir William (1606–68), born and educated in Oxford, was rumoured to be the natural son of Shakespeare. His first play, *The Tragedy of Albovine*, was printed in 1629 but probably never performed; *The Cruel Brother* was performed in 1627, printed 1630. In 1630–2 he was gravely ill with syphilis, a subject referred to in his own works and in the jests of others; his first play on his recovery was probably his comic masterpiece *The Wits*, performed 1633, printed 1636. In 1638 he succeeded to *Jonson's pension as unofficial *poet laureate, then actively supported Charles I in the Civil War and was knighted by him in 1643 at the siege of Gloucester. In 1645 he visited Paris, where he met *Hobbes, to whom he addressed his *Preface* (1650) to *Gondibert* (1651). He was imprisoned in the Tower, 1650–2, and is said to have been saved by *Milton. With *The Siege of Rhodes* (1656) he simultaneously evaded the ban on stage-plays and produced one of the earliest English operas (but see also FLECKNOE), with an entertainment that combined music and in-

struction. After the Restoration he and T. *Killigrew the elder obtained patents from Charles II giving them the monopoly of acting in London; his charter for the Duke's House, Lincoln's Inn, was later transferred to Covent Garden. Among the innovations of the period were movable scenery and the use of actresses. In conjunction with *Dryden D'Avenant adapted various of Shakespeare's plays to suit the taste of the day, among them *The Tempest* (1667); he is satirized with Dryden in Buckingham's *The Rehearsal*. His poems and songs (which include 'The lark now leaves his watry nest') were edited by A. M. Gibbs in 1972.

Davers, Lady, a character in Richardson's *Pamela*.

DAVID, Elizabeth, *née* Gwynne (1913–), writer on food and cookery, whose early works (*A Book of Mediterranean Food*, 1950; *French Country Cooking*, 1951; *Italian Food*, 1954) were read avidly by a generation brought up on a wartime diet; they were enjoyed for their new recipes, for their loving descriptions of continental meals, and for gastronomic quotations from H. *James, *Smollett, *Marinetti, etc. She has become respected for her serious, indeed scholarly, approach to the history of gastronomy.

David, Song to, see SMART.

David and Fair Bethsabe, *The Love of King*, a play in blank verse by *Peele, printed 1599. Its sources are mainly scriptural, offering a highly poeticized account of King David's seduction of Bethsabe (Bathsheba) and the death of his son Absalon.

David Copperfield, a novel by *Dickens, published 1849–50. 'Of all my books,' wrote Dickens, 'I like this the best', and it has always been a favourite with a wide public. It is (in some of its details) Dickens's veiled autobiography.

David Copperfield is born at Blunderstone (of which the original is the village of Blundeston) in Suffolk, soon after the death of his father. His mother, a gentle, weak woman, marries again, and her second husband Mr Murdstone, by cruelty disguised as firmness and abetted by Miss Murdstone his sister, drives her to an early grave. Young Copperfield, who has proved recalcitrant, is sent to school, where he is bullied by the tyrannical headmaster Creakle, but makes two friends in the brilliant and fascinating Steerforth and the good-humoured plodding Traddles. Thence he is sent to menial employment in London, where he lives a life of poverty and misery, enlivened by his acquaintance with the mercurial and impecunious Mr Micawber and his family. He runs away and walks penniless to Dover to throw himself on the mercy of his aunt Betsey Trotwood, an eccentric old lady who had renounced all interest in him from his birth because, contrary to her firm expectation, he had been born a boy instead of a girl. He is kindly received and given a new home, which he shares with an amiable lunatic, Mr Dick. This poor gentleman is perpetually engaged on a memorial regarding his affairs, but is unable to complete it owing to the inevitable intrusion into it of King Charles's head. Copperfield continues his education at Canterbury, living in the house of Miss Trotwood's lawyer Mr Wickfield, whose daughter Agnes, a girl of exceptionally sweet and high-minded disposition, exercises a powerful influence on the rest of his life. He then enters Doctors' Commons, being articled to Mr Spenlow, of the firm of Spenlow and Jorkins. Meanwhile he has come again into touch with Steerforth, whom, ignorant of his true character, he introduces to the family of his old nurse Clara Peggotty, married to Barkis the carrier. The family consists of Mr Peggotty, a Yarmouth fisherman, his nephew Ham, and the latter's cousin Little Em'ly, a pretty, simple girl whom Ham is about to marry. The remaining inmate of Mr Peggotty's hospitable home is Mrs Gummidge, another dependant and a widow, whose peevish laments for her forlorn condition are patiently borne by Mr Peggotty. Steerforth induces Em'ly to run away with him, thereby producing intense misery in the Peggotty household. Mr Peggotty sets out to find her, following her through many countries, and finally recovering her after she had been cast off by Steerforth. The latter's crime also brings unhappiness to his mother and to her protégée Rosa Dartle, who has long loved Steerforth with all the suppressed violence of a passionate nature. The tragedy finds its culmination in the shipwreck and drowning of Steerforth, and the death of Ham in trying to save him.

Meanwhile Copperfield, blind to the affection of Agnes Wickfield, marries Dora Spenlow, a pretty empty-headed child, and becomes famous as an author. Dora dies after a few years of married life and Copperfield, at first disconsolate, awakens to a growing appreciation and love of Agnes. Her father has fallen into the toils of a villainous and cunning clerk, Uriah Heep, who under the cloak of fawning humility has obtained complete control over him, reduced him to the verge of imbecility, and nearly ruined him. Uriah also aspires to marry Agnes. But his misdeeds, which include forgery and theft, are exposed by Micawber, employed as his clerk, with the assistance of Traddles, now a barrister. Uriah is last seen in prison, under a life sentence. Copperfield marries Agnes. Mr Peggotty, with Em'ly and Mrs Gummidge, is found prospering in Australia, where Mr Micawber, relieved of his debts, appears finally as a much-esteemed colonial magistrate.

'Davideis', see COWLEY, A.

David Simple, *The Adventures of, in Search of a Real Friend*, a novel by S. *Fielding, published 1744, and described by the author as 'a Moral Romance'. This was one of the earliest novels (published four years after Richardson's *Pamela*) to examine minutely what the author's brother, Henry *Fielding, described in his Preface to her book as 'the Mazes, Windings, and Labyrinths' of the heart.

David discovers that his beloved younger brother, with the aid of two trusted family servants, has defrauded him of his inheritance. Horrified by this deceit, he sets out on a quest to see if he can find a true and honest friend. Everywhere he encounters self-seeking, hypocrisy, and dishonesty; his friend Mr Orgueil is unmasked by Mr Spatter, Mr Spatter is exposed by Mr Varnish, Mr Varnish by David himself. Eventually he meets Cynthia, who has been excluded from her share of her father's fortune and is harshly treated by her mistress. He also encounters a brother and sister, Valentine and Camilla, whose scheming stepmother has alienated their father's affection from them. The four friends, all of whom have suffered because of their trusting innocence, live together in rich, happy companionship; in time David is married to Camilla and Valentine to Cynthia. David shares his fortune with them, and Valentine and Camilla are reconciled with their father.

In the sombre *Volume the Last* (1753) both couples face dire financial loss. Once again friends prove cruel and false, the terrible figure of Mrs Orgueil hovers malevolently, and the crushing of the innocent moves remorselessly on. There is no happy release, and by the end only Cynthia and one of David's children survive.

DAVIDSON, John (1857–1909), a reluctant schoolmaster in Scotland from 1872 to 1899, settled in London in the latter year, having already published several plays. He contributed to the *Yellow Book*, and his collection of verse *Fleet Street Eclogues* (1893), which showed a genuine poetic gift, was followed by several others. Between 1901 and 1908 he wrote a series of 'Testaments' expounding in blank verse a materialistic and rebellious philosophy, described very fully in the introduction to *The Theatrocrat God and Mammon*, an intended trilogy of which the first two parts were published in 1907. T. S. *Eliot expressed his debt to Davidson's use of 'dingy urban images' and colloquial idiom in a preface to a selection, edited 1961 by M. Lindsay, singling out for particular praise his best-known ballad, the defiant and satiric 'Thirty Bob a Week'.

DAVIDSON, Thomas, see FABIAN SOCIETY.

DAVIE, Donald Alfred (1922–), poet and critic, born in Barnsley, and educated at Barnsley Holgate Grammar School and at Cambridge, where he was much influenced by the ethos of F. R. *Leavis and the Cambridge English school; he describes his ambiguous feelings towards this heritage in his memoirs, *These the Companions* (1982). His critical work *Purity of Diction in English Verse* (1952) expressed many of the anti-Romantic, anti-Bohemian ideals of the *Movement and of his fellow contributors to *New Lines*. His volumes of poetry include *Brides of Reason* (1955), *A Winter Talent* (1957), *Essex Poems* (1969), and *In the Stopping Train* (1977); two volumes of collected poems appeared in 1972 (1950–70) and 1983 (1971–83). His poems are philosophical, speculative, and erudite, manifesting a mind that (in his own phrase) 'moves most easily and happily among abstractions', yet they also vividly evoke the various landscapes of his travels and academic appointments, from Ireland to California, from Essex to Italy, and show a marked rejection of the English provincialism which characterized some of his friends from the Movement. Davie has also written on Sir W. *Scott (1961), *Pound (1964), *Hardy (1972), and others, and adapted the *Pan Tadeusz* of *Mickiewicz in *The Forests of Lithuania* (1959).

DAVIES, John (?1565–1618), of Hereford, poet and writing-master. He published several volumes of verse, epitaphs, and epigrams, etc., including *Microcosmos* (1603), *The Muse's Sacrifice*, containing the famous 'Picture of an Happy Man' (1612), and *Wits Bedlam* (1617). Some of his epigrams, most of which are contained in *The Scourge of Folly* (?1611), are valuable for their notices of *Jonson, *Fletcher, and other contemporary poets.

DAVIES, Sir John (1569–1626), a Wiltshire man of good family, was educated at Winchester and at The Queen's College, Oxford; he became solicitor- and attorney-general for Ireland, and was subsequently appointed Lord Chief Justice of the King's Bench as a reward for maintaining the legality of Charles I's forced loans. He died before taking up this office. His *Orchestra Or a Poeme of Dauncing*, published in 1596, describes the attempts of the suitor Antinous to persuade Penelope to dance with him, giving a long account of the antiquity and universality of dancing. The *Hymnes of Astraea* and *Nosce Teipsum* both appeared in 1599: the latter, written in quatrains, is a philosophical poem on the nature of man and the nature and immortality of the soul. His *Epigrammes* and *Gullinge Sonnets* reflect his keen and satirical interest in the contemporary scene. His poems were edited by Robert Krueger in 1975.

DAVIES, Thomas (?1712–85), actor and bookseller who, according to his friend Dr *Johnson, was driven from the stage by Churchill's attack in *The Rosciad*—'he mouths a sentence as curs mouth a bone.' He introduced *Boswell to Johnson in his bookshop in Russell Street, Covent Garden, in 1763. An amiable and sociable man, he appears frequently in Boswell's *Life*, often as the recipient of help from Johnson, who encouraged him to write his lively life of *Garrick (1780), himself supplying information about Garrick's early years.

DAVIES, W(illiam) H(enry) (1871–1940), born in his grandfather's house in Newport, went as a young man to America, where he spent several years on the road, returning after a brief trip home to seek his fortune in the Klondike. On the second visit he lost a leg in an accident, an experience recounted in a few laconic paragraphs in his *The Autobiography of a Super-Tramp*, published in 1908 with a preface by G. B. *Shaw, who did much to encourage the young poet and who interested himself in Davies's first volume, *The Soul's Destroyer and other poems* (1905). This was followed by several other volumes, and growing praise from writers such as E. *Thomas; he made many friends in the literary and artistic world. His best-known poems record his sharp and intense response to the natural world. In 1923 he married a girl much younger than himself, and he tells the story of his extraordinary courtship in *Young Emma*, posthumously published in 1980. His *Complete Poems*, with an introduction by O. *Sitwell, appeared in 1963.

DAVISON, Francis, see POETICAL RHAPSODY, A.

DAVY, Sir Humphry (1778–1829), professor of chemistry at the Royal Institution, who greatly advanced knowledge of chemistry and magnetism and invented the miner's safety-lamp. In early youth he assisted his friend *Cottle, Wordsworth's publisher, in correcting the proofs of *Lyrical Ballads*. His collected works, prose and verse, with a memoir by his brother, were published in 1839–40. Among these is a brief dialogue, *Salmonia, or Days of Fly-fishing, by an Angler* (1828), reminiscent of I. *Walton's book. Davy was a friend of Sir W. *Scott and there is a pleasing account in *Lockhart's *Life of Scott* of Davy's visits to Abbotsford.

Daw, Sir John, in Jonson's *Epicene*, a cowardly braggart who pretends to learning.

Dawson, Jemmy, the hero of a ballad by *Shenstone. He was one of the Manchester rebels who supported the Young Pretender, and was drawn, hanged, and quartered on Kennington Common in 1746.

Day, Fancy, a character in Hardy's *Under the Greenwood Tree*.

DAY, DAYE, or **DAIE**, John (1522–84), the foremost English printer of the reign of Elizabeth I. He published Protestant devotional books under Edward VI and was imprisoned by

Queen Mary; later he held lucrative monopolies for the psalms in metre, the catechism, and the ABC, printed the first church music book in English (1560), and the first English edition of Foxe's *Actes and Monuments* (or *Book of Martyrs*) (1563). He was patronized by M. *Parker, at whose behest he was the first to print Old English, having type made for it.

DAY, John (*c*.1574–*c*.1640), playwright, collaborated with *Dekker and others in a number of plays. Of his own extant works *The Isle of Gulls*, suggested by Sidney's *Arcadia*, appeared in 1606, and *Law Trickes* and *Humour out of Breath* in 1608. His best work, *The Parliament of Bees*, appeared perhaps in 1607, although the earliest extant copy is of 1641. It is a dramatic allegory or masque, containing a series of 'characters' of different bees with their virtues and vices, and ending with Oberon's Star Chamber, where he pronounces penalties on the offenders, the wasp, the drone, and the humble bee. It is a charming and inventive piece; the lines 'When of a sudden, listening, you shall hear | A noise of horns and hunting, which shall bring | Acteon to Diana in the spring' suggested a passage of *The Waste Land* to T. S. *Eliot. Day's works were collected by A. H. Bullen, 1881. The *Parnassus Plays* have been doubtfully attributed to Day.

DAY, Thomas (1748–89), an admirer of *Rousseau and a friend of R. L. Edgeworth (1744–1817, father of Maria *Edgeworth), was keenly interested in educational theory and natural upbringing; he was the author of the celebrated children's book *The History of Sandford and Merton* (3 vols, 1783–9), which was intended to illustrate the doctrine that many may be made good by instruction and by an appeal to reason. It consists of a series of episodes in which the rich and objectionable Tommy Merton is contrasted with the upright and tender-hearted Harry Sandford, a farmer's son; eventually Tommy is reformed, partly through the intervention of their tutor, Mr Barlow. Despite its didacticism, this work was very popular, went through many editions, and was translated into several languages. Day also wrote *The History of Little Jack* (1787), the story of a young wild boy suckled by goats. He himself died from a fall from an unbroken colt.

DAY-LEWIS, Cecil (1904–72) (who wrote as C. Day Lewis), born in Ireland, the son of a Church of Ireland minister; the family moved to England in 1905 and his mother died three years later. He was educated at Sherborne and Wadham College, Oxford, where he was befriended by *Bowra and became associated with a group of young left-wing poets, of which *Auden was the acknowledged leader, and with whom he edited *Oxford Poetry* (1927). (The nick-name 'MacSpaunday' was coined by R.

*Campbell: see also PYLON POETS.) He worked for some years as a schoolmaster and was politically active during the 1930s, writing for the *Left Review*, supporting the *Left Book Club, speaking at meetings, etc.; he joined the Communist Party in 1936 and in 1937 edited a socialist symposium, *The Mind in Chains*, with contributions from *Upward, *Madge, R. *Warner, and others. These preoccupations are not reflected in his earliest verse (e.g. *Beechen Vigil*, 1925), but become apparent in *Transitional Poem* (1929), *From Feathers to Iron* (1931), and *The Magnetic Mountain* (1933) which have a strong revolutionary flavour, prophesying a new dawn: 'We shall expect no birth–hour without blood.' The title poem of *A Time to Dance* (1935) more ambiguously celebrates in verse strongly reminiscent of G. M. *Hopkins the heroic flight of Parer and M'Intosh to Australia. The poor reception of *Noah and the Waters* (1936), a verse morality play about the class struggle, may have encouraged him to turn from political poetry to the more personal and pastoral themes of his later years. During the thirties he also embarked, under the pseudonym of 'Nicholas Blake', on a successful career as a writer of *detective fiction; his first work in this genre, *A Question of Proof* (1935), introducing his Audenesque detective Nigel Strangeways, was followed by some twenty others. *The Friendly Tree* (1936) was the first of three largely autobiographical novels.

In 1938 he moved with his family to Musbury, Devon; his poetry of this period (*Overtures to Death*, 1938; *Poems in Wartime*, 1940) reflect its obvious concerns. He also published in 1940 the first of his translations, a version of *Virgil's *Georgics*, before working for some time for the Ministry of Information. From this time (despite an emotional private life), he became an increasingly establishment figure (having already endured much mockery from *Grigson for joining the Book Society Committee in 1937); he delivered the Clark lectures in Cambridge in 1946 (*The Poetic Image*, 1947), broadcast frequently, gave recitals, sat on committees, judged awards, etc., meanwhile consolidating his literary reputation with a translation of *Valéry (1946), further translations of Virgil (*The Aeneid*, 1952; *The Eclogues*, 1963), and collections of original verse, including *An Italian Visit* (1953), recording a journey with R. *Lehmann, and incidentally describing his own generation as 'an odd lot; sceptical yet susceptible, | Dour though enthusiastic, horizon-addicts and future-fans . . . ' He was professor of poetry at Oxford from 1951 to 1956, the first poet of distinction to hold the post since M. *Arnold, and in 1968 was appointed poet laureate. His autobiography *The Buried Day* (1960) is much amplified by a biography by Sean Day-Lewis, the elder son of his first marriage, published in 1980, a detailed, questioning account of his father's 'divided heart' and search for identity.

Day of Doom, The, see WIGGLESWORTH, M.

Dead Sea Scrolls, the popular name for the remains of the once considerable collection of Hebrew and Aramaic MSS discovered in caves at the NW end of the Dead Sea between 1947 and 1956. Although no one MS is intact and many exist only in fragments, nearly all the books of the canonical OT are represented, as well as apocryphal books and some works not previously known. The Scrolls belonged to the library of the Jewish community at Qumran about the beginning of the Christian era, and it is probable that most of them were written there, between 20 BC and AD 70. It is presumed that they were hidden in the caves for safety. The Scrolls are important in being almost the only surviving MS material in Hebrew and Aramaic from this period and have a valuable bearing on the study of OT texts. They also provide a first-hand account of Jewish life and thought contemporary with the beginning of Christianity.

Deane, Mr and Lucy, characters in G. Eliot's *The Mill on the Floss.*

Deans, David, and his daughters Jeanie and Effie, the principal characters in Scott's *The Heart of Midlothian.*

'Death and Dr Hornbook', a satirical poem by *Burns, published 1786. Dr Hornbook was a doctor in Burns's parish of Mauchline. In the poem the poet meets Death, who describes to him the knavery and quackery of the doctor.

Death Comes for the Archbishop, a historical novel by W. *Cather; the title is based on a work by *Holbein.

Death of a Hero, see ALDINGTON, R.

Death's Jest-Book, see BEDDOES, T. L.

De Bourgh, Lady Catherine, a character in J. Austen's *Pride and Prejudice.*

DEBUSSY, (Achille-)Claude (1862–1918), French composer. Two of Debussy's *Préludes* for piano claim inspiration from English literature, *La danse de Puck* (Book 1) and *Hommage à S. Pickwick Esq.* (Book 2); the former, and better, piece has perhaps more relevance to its subject than the latter (in spite of the rather ingenuous use of 'God Save the King'), but it should be borne in mind that Debussy often chose the titles for his Preludes after he had written them. The only English poet he ever set was D. G. *Rossetti, whose *The Blessed Damozel* provided the text for the early cantata *La damoiselle élue* (1888): a second Rossetti setting, a translation of *Willow-wood* by Pierre Louÿs, was never finished. At about the same period the composer was enthusiastically considering an opera from

As You Like It, but this was soon shelved in favour of *Maeterlinck's *Pelléas et Mélisande* (which fitted him like a glove), and in the event Shakespeare is represented in Debussy's output only by two short instrumental pieces (*Fanfare* and *Le Sommeil de Lear*) out of seven sketched for a production of *King Lear* in Paris in 1904. In a field very much closer to *Pelléas,* Debussy later worked intensively on a project for two short operas based on *Poe, *The Fall of the House of Usher* and *The Devil in the Belfry.* The influence of Poe on Debussy (like that of *Swinburne) was an early and important one; in 1889 he had begun a symphonic work on *Usher* (now lost), and the preoccupation with this story, in particular, continued to near the end of his life.

Decameron, The, a collection of tales from many sources by *Boccaccio, written probably over many years, but assembled in their definitive form between 1349 and 1351.

Florence being visited by the plague in 1348, seven young ladies and three young men leave the city for neighbouring villas, the beauty of which is described, and spend part of each of ten days (whence the title) in amusing one another with stories, each person telling one tale on each day, so that there are 100 tales in all. The work had much influence on English literature, notably on *Chaucer (though possibly indirectly, through a translation: Chaucer nowhere mentions Boccaccio in any of his works); many of the tales were incorporated in Painter's *Palace of Pleasure.* A credible case has been made by H. G. Wright for *Florio as the translator of the first English version of *The Decameron* (1620); see his *Boccaccio in England from Chaucer to Tennyson* (1957).

Decline and Fall, the first novel of E. *Waugh, published with great success in 1928.

It recounts the chequered career of Paul Pennyfeather, sent down from Scone College, Oxford, for 'indecent behaviour', as the innocent victim of a drunken orgy. Thus forced to abandon a career in the church, he becomes a schoolmaster at Llanabba Castle, where he encounters headmaster Fagan and his daughters, the dubious, bigamous, and reappearing Captain Grimes, and young Beste-Chetwynde, whose glamorous mother Margot carries him off to the dangerous delight of high society. They are about to be married when Paul is arrested at the Ritz and subsequently imprisoned for Margot's activities in the white slave trade, a sentence he bears stoically on the grounds that 'anyone who has been to an English public school will always feel comparatively at home in prison'; however, Margot (now Margot Metroland) arranges his escape, and he returns incognito but under his own name ('a *very* distant cousin') to resume his theological studies at Scone.

Decline and Fall of the Roman Empire, *The*

History of the, a work by *Gibbon, vol. i of the first (quarto) edition published 1776, vols ii and iii 1781, and the last three vols 1788.

This, the most celebrated historical work in English literature, falls into three divisions, as defined by the author in the preface, according to a plan that expanded during composition: from the age of Trajan and the Antonines to the subversion of the western Empire; from the reign of Justinian in the East to the establishment of the second or German Empire of the West, under *Charlemagne; from the revival of the western Empire to the taking of Constantinople by the Turks. It thus covers a period of about 13 centuries, and comprehends such vast subjects as the establishment of Christianity, the movements and settlements of the Teutonic tribes, the conquests of the Muslims, and the crusades. It traces in fact the connection of the ancient world with the modern.

Gibbon's great erudition, breadth of treatment, and powerful organization render this a lasting monument, of substantial accuracy as well as elegance. His measured and dignified prose is cool, lucid, and enlivened by ironic wit, much of it aimed at the early Church and the credulity and barbarism that overwhelmed the noble Roman virtues he so much admired. J. B. Bury's editions (1896–1900, 1909–14, 1926–9) are supplemented with notes incorporating subsequent research, but most of Gibbon's scholarship remains unchallenged.

De Croye, Isabelle and Hameline, characters in Scott's *Quentin Durward.*

Dedalus, Stephen, a character in J. Joyce's *A Portrait of the Artist as a Young Man* and *Ulysses.*

Dedlock, Sir Leicester, Lady, and Volumnia, characters in Dickens's *Bleak House.*

DEE, Dr John (1527–1608), mathematician and astrologer, was educated at St John's College, Cambridge, and travelled in Europe in 1548–51. He became a fellow of Trinity College, Cambridge, where the stage effects he introduced into a performance of the *Peace* of *Aristophanes procured him his lifelong reputation of being a magician, which was confirmed by his erudition and practice of crystallomancy and astrology. He wrote *Monas Hieroglyphica* (1564); a preface to the first English translation of Euclid (1570); and *General and Rare Memorials pertayning to the perfect Art of Navigation* (1577). He was a profoundly learned scholar and hermeticist, but also a sham. Among the many who consulted him on astrological matters were Sir P. *Sidney and Sir E. *Dyer. Many books survive from his remarkable library. There is a life of him by P. J. French (1972).

DEEPING, (George) Warwick (1877–1950), prolific and successful novelist, who caught the popular imagination with *Sorrell and Son*

(1925), the story of a wounded ex-officer who takes a job as under-porter in a hotel to earn money to ensure an appropriate private education for his son Christopher, where he will not be exposed to 'class hatred' or 'the sneers of the new young working-class intellectuals' in the social war that Sorrell envisages.

Deerbrook, a novel by H. *Martineau.

Deerslayer, The, a novel by J. F. *Cooper.

Defarge, M. and Mme, characters in Dickens's *A Tale of Two Cities.*

Defence of All Learning, see MUSOPHILUS.

Defence of Poetry, A, an essay by P. *Sidney written in 1579–80. *Gosson's *Schoole of Abuse,* dedicated to Sidney in 1579, may have helped to stimulate the composition of the *Defence,* but Sidney's chief aim was probably to write an English vindication of literature to match the many recently written on the Continent in Italian, French, and Latin. Two editions of the work appeared posthumously in 1595: one, published by Ponsonby, bore the title *The Defence of Poesie* and the other, published by Olney, *An Apologie for Poetrie.* Most modern editors have preferred the first title both because Ponsonby was the official publisher of Sidney's remains and because Sidney in the opening paragraph speaks of being moved 'to make a pitiful defence of poor poetry'.

Sidney expounds the antiquity of poetry in all cultures, 'whose milk by little and little enabled them to feed afterwards of tougher knowledges'. He demonstrates its superiority to philosophy or history as a means of teaching virtue. After defining and distinguishing the 'parts, kinds, or species' of poetry, vindicating each in turn, he digresses to England: he sees contemporary poetry as having reached a low ebb, with little to be admired since *Chaucer, but affirms with prophetic confidence that major poetry in every genre, including drama, can be written in the English language. *A Defence of Poetry* is remarkable for the lightness of Sidney's style and the catholicity of his examples, often drawn from experience:

I never heard the old song of Percy and Douglas that I found not my heart moved more than with a trumpet; and yet is it sung but by some blind crowder, with no rougher voice than rude style. (See CHEVY CHASE.)

The poetic qualities of the essay in themselves illustrate the power of imaginative writing:

Nature never set forth the earth in so rich tapestry as divers poets have done; neither with so pleasant rivers, fruitful trees, sweet-smelling flowers, nor whatsoever else may make the too much loved earth more lovely. Her world is brazen, the poets only deliver a golden.

Defence of Poetry, The, an essay by P. B. *Shelley, written at Pisa 1821, first published

1840. It was begun as a light-hearted reply to his friend Peacock's magazine article, *'The Four Ages of Poetry', which humorously argued that the best minds of the future must turn to economic and social sciences, rather than poetry. In vindicating the role of poetry in a progressive society, and defending the whole notion of imaginative literature and thinking (not just 'poetry') within an industrial culture, Shelley came to write his own poetic *credo* with passionate force and conviction. Against a background of classical and European literature, he discusses in some detail the nature of poetic thought and inspiration; the problems of translation; the value of erotic writing; the connections between poetry and politics; and the essentially *moral* nature of the imagination—an emphasis he drew from *Coleridge.

Throughout, Shelley associates poetry with social freedom and love. He argues that the 'poetry of life' provides the one sure response to the destructive, isolating, alienating, 'accumulating and calculating processes' of modern civilization; 'the creative faculty to imagine that which we know'. There are superb literary evocations of the Greeks, *Dante, and *Milton.

The essay is not a regular treatise. It draws on many of Shelley's earlier prefaces and essays, notably *A Philosophical View of Reform. Though diffuse in places, it frequently sharpens to epigrammatic point: 'the great instrument of moral good is the imagination'; 'the freedom of women produced the poetry of sexual love'; and the famous peroration, ending 'Poets are the unacknowledged legislators of the world'—which must be read in context and which echoes in part the argument of Imlac in Johnson's *Rasselas.

Defence of Ryme, a treatise by S. *Daniel written in reply to T. *Campion's *Observations in the Art of English Poesie.*

DEFFAND, Mme du, Marie de Vichy-Chamrond (1697–1780), a French literary hostess, whose salon was frequented by *Montesquieu, D'Alembert, and others, and who became blind in later life. Horace *Walpole was her close friend, and a large number of her letters to him survive (ed. Mrs Paget Toynbee, 1912). Walpole's letters to her were destroyed by his request.

DE FILIPPO, Eduardo (1900–84), Italian playwright and actor, who draws on Naples, his native city, for his themes, characters and language. His major plays are: *Filumena Marturano* (*Filumena*, 1946), *Le bugie hanno le gambe lunghe* (*Lies Have Long Legs*, 1947), *La grande paura* (*The Great Fear*, 1948), *Sabato, domenica, lunedì* (*Saturday, Sunday, Monday*, 1959).

DEFOE, Daniel (1660–1731), born in London, the son of James Foe, a butcher. He changed his name to Defoe from *c.*1695. He attended Morton's academy for Dissenters at Newington Green with a view to the ministry, but by the time he married Mary Tuffley in 1683/4 he was established as a hosiery merchant in Cornhill, having travelled in France, Spain, the Low Countries, and possibly Italy and Germany; he was absorbed by travel throughout his life. He took part in Monmouth's rebellion, and in 1688 joined the advancing forces of William III. His first important signed work was *An Essay upon Projects* (1697), followed by *The True-Born Englishman* (1701), an immensely popular satirical poem attacking the prejudice against a king of foreign birth and his Dutch friends. In 1702 appeared *The Shortest Way with Dissenters*, a notorious pamphlet in which Defoe, himself a Dissenter, ironically demanded the total and savage suppression of dissent; for this he was fined, imprisoned (May–Nov. 1703), and pilloried. While in prison he wrote his *Hymn to the Pillory*, a mock-Pindaric ode which was sold in the streets to sympathetic crowds. Meanwhile various business projects (the breeding of civet cats, marine insurance, a brick works) had come to grief, and Defoe's fortunes were revived by *Harley, the Tory politician, who arranged a pardon and employed him as a secret agent; between 1703 and 1714 Defoe travelled around the country for Harley and Godolphin gathering information and testing the political climate. Defoe wrote many pamphlets for Harley, and in 1704 began *The Review; in the same year appeared his pamphlet *Giving Alms no Charity* and in 1706 his *True Relation of the Apparition of one Mrs Veal*, a vivid report of a current ghost story. Certain anti-Jacobite pamphlets in 1712–13 led to his prosecution by the Whigs and to a brief imprisonment. He now started a new trade journal, *Mercator*, in place of *The Review*. In 1715 he was convicted of libelling Lord Annesley (by implying that he was a Jacobite); he escaped punishment through the intervention of Townshend, the Whig secretary of state.

Defoe was an extremely versatile and prolific writer, and produced some 560 books, pamphlets, and journals, many anonymously or pseudonymously, but the works for which he is best known belong to his later years. *Robinson Crusoe* appeared in 1719, the *Farther Adventures* following a few months later. The next five years saw the appearance of his most important works of fiction: *Life and Adventures of Mr Duncan Campbell*, the deaf and dumb conjurer, and *Captain *Singleton* in 1720; *Moll Flanders, A Journal of the *Plague Year, The History of Peter the Great*, and *Colonel Jack* in 1722; *Roxana, the *Memoirs of a Cavalier* (now considered to be certainly by Defoe), his tracts on Jack *Sheppard, and *A New Voyage round the World* in 1724; *The Four Voyages of Capt. George Roberts* in 1726. The *Memoirs of Captain George Carleton* (1728) were probably largely by his hand.

His *Tour through the Whole Island of Great Britain*, a guide-book in 3 vols (1724–6), is a vivid first-hand account of the state of the country, gleaned from his many travels, the last of which he appears to have taken in 1722. His last principal works were *The Complete English Tradesman* (1726), *Augusta Triumphans* (1728), *A Plan of the English Commerce* (1728), and *The Complete English Gentleman*, not published until 1890. He died in his lodgings in Ropemaker's Alley, Moorfields, and was buried in what is now Bunhill Fields. Defoe's influence on the evolution of the English novel was enormous, and many regard him as the first true novelist. He was a master of plain prose and powerful narrative, with a journalist's curiosity and love of realistic detail; his peculiar gifts made him one of the greatest reporters of his time, as well as a great imaginative writer who in *Robinson Crusoe* created one of the most familiar and resonant myths of modern literature.

Deformed Transformed, The, an unfinished poetic drama by Lord *Byron, published 1824.

Count Arnold is a hideous hunchback, made miserable by his deformity. A stranger, the Devil in disguise, offers to change his shape, and calls up the forms of Caesar, Alcibiades, and others to tempt him. Arnold chooses the form of Achilles, and the stranger takes the hunchback shape of Arnold, whom he follows as a servant. Part II presents the sack of Rome in 1527, in which Arnold distinguishes himself. Here the fragment ends.

Degaré, Sir, a metrical romance in 1,073 lines of short couplets from the early 14th cent. in a south Midland dialect, one of the Middle English Breton lays.

Degaré, the son of a princess of Brittany who has been raped by a knight, is abandoned in a forest with a purse of money, a letter of directions, and a pair of gloves which are to fit the lady that he is to marry. The poem recounts Degaré's prowess in the course of his searches for his parents. The lady that the gloves fit is, in the event, his own mother who recognizes him with joy as her son immediately after their wedding ceremony and before its consummation. Rosemary Woolf makes the interesting suggestion that the romance may be a medievalizing of Oedipus, as *Sir *Orfeo* is of Orpheus. The name is probably a corruption of 'l'esgaré', 'the lost one' (apparently punned on in line 214, 'almost lost it is'), and is thought to be the origin of 'Diggory'. See edns by W. H. French and C. B. Hale, *Middle English Metrical Romances* (1930), i. 287–320, and in *Medieval English Romances*, Part Two (1980) ed. A. V. C. Schmidt and N. Jacobs.

'Deil, Address to the', a satirical poem by *Burns, published 1786. In vigorous, familiar terms the poet scolds the Devil for all the trouble he causes in the world.

Deiphobus, a son of Priam of Troy, who married *Helen after the death of his brother Paris. He was betrayed by her and slain by Menelaus. In Shakespeare's *Troilus and Cressida* his role is minimal (IV. i).

Deirdre, the heroine of the tale of 'The Sons of Usnach' (pron. 'Usna'), one of the 'Three Sorrowful Stories of Erin'. She was the daughter of Fedlimid, harper to King Conchubar (pron. Conachoor) of Ulster, and Cathbad the Druid prophesied that her beauty would bring banishment and death to heroes. Conchubar destined her for his wife and had her brought up in solitude. But she accidentally saw and fell in love with Naoise (or Naisi; pron. 'Neesha' as in 'Portlaoise'), the son of Usnach, who with his brothers carried her off to Scotland. They were lured back by Conchubar and treacherously slain, and Deirdre took her own life. See Lady *Gregory, *Cuchulain of Muirthemne*, and the dramas on Deirdre by G. W. *Russell (Æ), *Synge, and *Yeats.

Deirdre of the Sorrows, see SYNGE, J. M., and under DEIRDRE.

Deism, or 'natural religion', the belief in a Supreme Being as the source of finite existence, with rejection of revelation and the supernatural doctrines of Christianity.

The Deists, who came into prominence at the end of the 17th and during the 18th cent. (the word in English dates from the 1680s), were much influenced by the views of Lord *Herbert of Cherbury, often known as 'the father of Deism'. They include Charles Blount (1654–93), *Toland (author of *Christianity not Mysterious*, 1696), Matthew Tindal (1657–1733, author of *Christianity as old as the Creation*, 1730), Anthony *Collins (author of *A Discourse of freethinking*, 1713), Thomas Chubb (1679–1747), and the third earl of *Shaftesbury. *Locke, who rejected the label of Deist, nevertheless contributed significantly to the movement with his *Reasonableness of Christianity* (1695). One of the most cogent refutations was by J. *Butler in his *Analogy of Religion* (1736), in which he argues that natural religion is no more credible and acceptable than revealed religion.

'Dejection: An Ode', an autobiographical poem by S. T. *Coleridge, first published in the *Morning Post*, 1802.

Originally composed as a much longer verse-letter to his beloved Sara Hutchinson (Asra), it describes the loss of his poetical powers, the dulling of his response to Nature, the breakdown of his marriage, and the paralysing effect of metaphysics (or opium). Paradoxically this is achieved in verse of great emotional intensity and metrical brilliance. *Wordsworth partly answered it in his *'Intimations of Immortality' ode.

DEKKER, Thomas (?1570–1632), was born and mainly lived in London, the manners of which his writings vividly illustrate. He suffered from poverty and was several times imprisoned for debt, briefly in 1598–9 and from 1612 for a period of nearly seven years; the six prison chapters added in 1616 to his prose work *Lanthorne and Candle-light* (first version 1608), and *Dekker his Dreame* (1620), evoke his own experiences of imprisonment. Despite this he is held to have been of a cheerful, good-natured temperament. He was engaged by *Henslowe about 1595 to write plays (over 40 of which are now lost) in collaboration with *Drayton, *Jonson, J. *Webster, and many others.

He published *The Shoemaker's Holiday* and *Old Fortunatus*, comedies, in 1600. Having been ridiculed, jointly with J. *Marston, by Jonson in *The Poetaster*, he retorted in *Satiromastix* (presumably in collaboration with Marston), a play produced in 1601; it is assumed that Jonson, Marston, and Dekker planned to quarrel in order to advertise themselves as literary figures. His other principal plays are *The Honest Whore*, of which Part I, in collaboration with *Middleton, appeared in 1604 and Part II, written 1604/5, in 1630; *Patient Grissil* (1603), written in collaboration with *Chettle and Haughton; *The Witch of Edmonton*, written in collaboration with Ford and Rowley in 1621, first published 1658. He also collaborated with Webster in *Westward Hoe* (written 1604, published 1607) and *Northward Hoe* (written 1605, published 1607), with Middleton in *The Roaring Girle* (written 1604–10, published 1611), and with Massinger in *The Virgin Martyr* (written 1620, published 1622). His tragi-comedy *Match mee in London*, written 1604/5, was published 1631. Dekker also wrote pageants, tracts, and pamphlets. His pamphlet *The Wonderfull yeare* (1603) is a poignant description of London during the plague of that year; it was used by Defoe for his *Journal of the *Plague Year*. *Newes from Hell* (1606) is an imitation of *Nashe; *The Guls Hornebooke* (1609) is a satirical book of manners.

Dekker's work is noted for its realistic and vivid portrayal of daily London life, both domestic and commercial, for its sympathy with the poor and oppressed, including animals tortured for man's amusement, and for its prevailing cheerfulness, though E. D. Pendry in an introduction to a selection of prose works (1967) stresses that he could be tough and bitter as well as whimsical. His dramatic works were collected by R. H. Shepherd, 1873, and edited by F. T. Bowers in 4 vols, 1953–61.

DELACROIX, Eugène (1798–1863), French painter, a leader of the Romantic movement.

His Journal (published 1893–5) gives a vivid account of his personality, his methods of work, and the artistic life of Paris. Delacroix visited England in 1825; he wrote enthusiastically of performances of Shakespeare, who, with *Byron and Sir W. *Scott, inspired many of his pictures; he shared the Romantic passion for *Hamlet. His love of the exotic East was stimulated by Byron's poetry and by the poet's death in Greece.

DELAFIELD, E. M., the pen-name of Edmée Elizabeth Monica Dashwood, née De La Pasture (1890–1943), novelist, journalist, magistrate, and pillar of the Women's Institute, whose many popular novels include *The Diary of a Provincial Lady* (1930), a gentle satire of a middle-class life of laundry lists, cooks, and visits from the vicar.

DE LA MARE, Walter (1873–1956), was born in Kent of well-to-do parents and attended St Paul's Choir School. At sixteen he began to work for an oil company, where he stayed for twenty years. In his mid-twenties he began to contribute poems and stories to various magazines, and in 1902, under the name of Walter Ramal, published *Songs of Childhood*, a volume which attracted little notice. Subsequently de la Mare published many volumes of poetry for both adults and children including, for adults, *The Listeners*, his first successful book, in 1912; *The Veil* in 1921; various volumes of *Collected Poems*; *The Burning Glass* in 1945; and two long visionary poems, 'The Traveller' (1946) and 'The Winged Chariot' (1951). Among many volumes for children were *Peacock Pie* (1913), *Tom Tiddler's Ground* (1932), and *Bells and Grass* (1941). Several collections were amalgamated in *Collected Rhymes and Verses* (1970) and *Collected Poems* (1979). De la Mare's highly individual prose works include the novels *Henry Brocken* (1904), in which the hero encounters writers of the past; *The Return* (1910), an eerie story of spirit possession, and in the same year a very successful children's story, *The Three Mulla-Mulgars* (later *The Three Royal Monkeys*); 'The Almond Tree' (in *The Riddle*, 1923), in which an uncomprehending child relates the events of his parents' breaking marriage; and the celebrated *Memoirs of a Midget* (1921), describing the world of the minute Miss M. Many volumes of short stories, often arresting and bizarre, for both adults and children, include *Broomsticks* (1925), *The Lord Fish* (1933), and *The Scarecrow* (1945). De la Mare's highly successful anthologies, incorporating long prefaces and commentaries, include *Come Hither* (1923), a widely admired collection for children; *Behold this Dreamer* (1939); and *Love* (1943). Essays and critical work include studies of R. *Brooke (1919) and Lewis Carroll—C. L. *Dodgson— (1932), and an edition of C. *Rossetti in 1930.

Remembered chiefly as a poet, for both adults and children, de la Mare was fluent, highly inventive, technically skilful, and unaffected by fashion. In his favourite themes of childhood, fantasy, and the numinous, commonplace objects and events are invested with mystery, and often with an undercurrent of melancholy. He was awarded the CH in 1948, the OM in 1953, and is buried in St Paul's Cathedral.

DELANE, John Thaddeus (1817–79), educated at King's College, London, and Magdalen Hall, Oxford, the famous editor of *The Times, 1841–77. He was caricatured by Trollope in *The Warden as 'Tom Towers'.

DELANEY, Shelagh (1939–), playwright, born in Salford, left school at 16 and is known for A Taste of Honey which she wrote when she was 17 after seeing *Rattigan's play Variations on a Theme. It was presented by Joan Littlewood in 1958 and was hailed as a landmark in the new school of *'kitchen sink' realism, a movement partly inspired by reaction against the drawing-room drama of Rattigan and *Coward.

DELANY, Mrs Mary, née Granville (1700–88), a member of the *Blue Stocking circle, who became a friend and correspondent of *Swift, married her friend Patrick *Delany in 1743, and knew many other eminent literary figures, including *Pope, *Burke, and Horace *Walpole. She was a favourite of the royal family, and introduced Fanny *Burney to court. Her Autobiography and Correspondence (1861–2, 6 vols, ed. Lady Llanover) gives a spirited account of 18th-cent. court, literary, and social life.

DELANY, Patrick (?1685–1768), Irish divine, friend of *Swift, husband of Mary *Delany. He was the author of Observations upon Lord Orrery's Remarks on the Life and Writings of Dr Jonathan Swift (1754), a series of letters, signed 'J.R.', written in an attempt to correct what he describes as 'the very mistaken and erroneous accounts [of Swift] that have been published'. See BOYLE, J.

DE LA RAMÉE, Marie Louise, see OUIDA.

DE LA ROCHE, Mazo (1885–1961), Canadian novelist, born in Ontario, best known as the author of the 'Jalna' novels, so named after the first of the series, Jalna (1927).

Delectable Mountains, in Bunyan's *Pilgrim's Progress, 'Emmanuel's Land', within sight of the *Celestial City.

DELEDDA, Grazia (1871–1936), Italian novelist and winner of the *Nobel prize (1926). She is, with *Verga, a major writer of *verismo. Her best novels, drawn from her Sardinian background, are Elias Portolu (The Woman and the Priest, 1900, English trans. 1928, introduction by D. H. *Lawrence), Canne al vento (Canes in

the Wind, 1913), Cenere (Ashes, 1903), and an autobiographical novel, Cosima (1937).

Delia, a collection of sonnets by S. *Daniel.

Delilah (Dalila in Milton's *Samson Agonistes), in Judges 16, a woman of the valley of Sorek, loved by Samson; she persuaded him to tell her the secret of his strength and (by cutting off his hair) betrayed him to the Philistines. In Milton's version she is Samson's wife.

DELIUS, Frederick (1862–1934), English composer. In spite of his German descent and the fact that he spent most of his mature life in France, there is an undeniably English quality about much of Delius's music, which (partly owing to the advocacy of Sir Thomas Beecham) has always been appreciated more in England than anywhere else. His operas generally have libretti either by himself or based on foreign authors (Keller, Jacobsen), but there are several settings of English and American poets among his other vocal works, particularly those with chorus and orchestra which contain some of his best music. A lifelong enthusiasm for *Whitman produced the texts for Sea Drift (1904), regarded by many as Delius's finest achievement, and also for two late works, Songs of Farewell (1930) and the Idyll: Once I passed through a populous city (1932). Two settings of *Dowson, Songs of Sunset (1907) and Cynara (begun in 1907 as part of the preceding, but only completed in 1929), draw out the nostalgic element in Delian romanticism. There are some early settings for solo voice of *Shelley and *Tennyson (1891) and a beautiful setting of W. E. *Henley (A Late Lark, 1925). In later life Delius became blind and totally paralysed: the last work he completed with his own hand was the extensive incidental music for *Flecker's Hassan (1923), after which all his later works were taken down to dictation by the young Yorkshireman Eric Fenby, who has left a moving account of this astonishing and arduous labour of love.

Della Crusca, the name of a literary academy established in Florence in 1582, with the principal object of purifying the Italian language. The first edition of its dictionary appeared in 1612.

Della Cruscans, a band of poets, led by Robert Merry (1755–98), who produced affected, sentimental, and highly ornamented verse towards the end of the 18th cent. After a wandering and varied career, Merry lived in Florence from 1784 to 1787 as a member of the *Della Crusca academy. With Mrs *Piozzi and others he produced in 1785 a Miscellany, in which he signed his work 'Della Crusca'. 'Anna Matilda' (H. *Cowley) was another copious writer of the school, who contributed with Merry and others to the British Album in 1790, a volume which proved very successful until the publication in 1791 of *Gifford's *The Baviad*, a savage satire on the Della Cruscans, followed by *The Maeviad* in 1795, part of which was also directed against them.

DELONEY, Thomas (?1560–1600), was a silk-weaver by trade, whose place of birth and education are unknown, though he was certainly able to translate from Latin. He wrote broadside ballads on popular subjects, including three early ones on the defeat of the Armada in 1588. He is now best known for his four works of prose fiction, originally published between 1597 and 1600: *Jack of Newberie*; *The gentle craft* and *The gentle craft. The second part*; and *Thomas of Reading*. His fiction celebrates the virtues and self-advancement of hard-working craftsmen, especially in the cloth trade, and has been much admired in modern times for its effective use of dialogue. *The gentle craft* includes the story of Simon *Eyre, the shoemaker's apprentice who became Lord Mayor and founder of Leadenhall, which was adapted by Dekker in *The Shoemaker's Holiday*. The scene in *Thomas of Reading* in which the host and hostess of the tavern screw their courage up before murdering Thomas Cole has been seen as an analogue to *Macbeth*.

Deloraine, William of, a character in Scott's *The Lay of the Last Minstrel*.

Delphi, in imprints, Delft.

Delvile, Mortimer, the hero of F. Burney's *Cecilia*.

Demetrius, (1) in Shakespeare's *Titus Andronicus*, younger son of *Tamora the Goth, one of the rapists of *Lavinia; (2) one of the young lovers in his *A Midsummer Night's Dream*; (3) Demetrius Fannius in Jonson's *The Poetaster*, a satirical portrait of *Dekker; (4) lover of Celia in Fletcher's *The Humorous Lieutenant*. From classical times onwards the name seems to have had villainous associations.

DEMOCRITUS (b. c.460 BC), a celebrated Greek philosopher, born at Abdera. He wrote on the natural sciences, mathematics, morals, and music. He advanced (with Leucippus) the theory that the world was formed by the concourse of atoms, the theory subsequently expounded by *Lucretius and confirmed and developed by recent scientific discovery. *Juvenal speaks of him as ever laughing at the follies of mankind, and he is sometimes known as the 'laughing philosopher' in opposition to the melancholy *Heraclitus.

DEMOCRITUS JUNIOR, the pseudonym of Robert *Burton.

Demogorgon was mentioned only once in classical times, casually in an obscure commentary (where it may be a misreading for Demiourgon). He found a place in *Boccaccio's *Genealogia Deorum*, but it was *Prometheus Unbound* that gave him a character and a role. The name may have attracted *Shelley because it is compounded of 'Demos' (people) and 'Gorgo' (the name of some terrifying demigods) and so fitted his conception of Necessity and particularly that Historical Necessity which he thought would bring about an initially alarming but ultimately beneficial social revolution.

DE MONTHERLANT, Henri, see MONTHERLANT, H. DE.

DE MORGAN, William Frend (1839–1917), educated at University College London, at first devoted his attention to art and in particular to the production of stained glass and glazed pottery, working for a time in association with his friend W. *Morris; he published two treatises on the craft of pottery. He was particularly successful with decorative tiles, but ill health brought this pursuit to an end, and at the age of 67 he embarked somewhat casually on the writing of fiction, his first and best novel, *Joseph Vance* (1906), proving to his astonishment a great success. It is the rambling but entertaining tale of a drunken builder's son befriended by a middle-class family, who graduates from Oxford and becomes an engineer and inventor. This was followed by several others; the last two, *The Old Madhouse* (1919) and *The Old Man's Youth* (1921), left unfinished on his death, were skilfully completed by his widow, the artist Evelyn de Morgan. See A. M. D. W. Stirling, *William de Morgan and his Wife* (1922).

DEMOSTHENES (c.383–322 BC), Athenian orator who was regarded by ancient critics as the best of Greek prose writers. His reputation rested, however, on the excellence of his style rather than on the interest of his subject-matter. His ideals were lofty, his policies statesmanlike, but he does not surprise by his originality or by subtle insights. T. *Wilson, who translated his *Philippics* (1570), said that they were 'Most nedefull to be redde in these daungerous dayes of all them that loue their Countries libertie'. Sir P. *Sidney thought him most worthy to be imitated. Dr *Johnson pictured him speaking to brutes. Edited a great number of times during the 19th cent., he must be regarded as a scholar's author and not a favourite with the general public.

Dempster, Mr and Janet, characters in G. Eliot's 'Janet's Repentance' (see SCENES OF CLERICAL LIFE).

DENHAM, Sir John (1615–69), was born in Dublin and educated at Trinity College, Oxford. A royalist, he was forced to surrender Farnham Castle, of which he was governor, in 1642, fled to the Continent in 1648, and was appointed surveyor-general of works at the Restoration. His tragedy *The Sophy*, set in the

Turkish court, was performed in 1641, and he also published occasional verses, satires, and a free translation from *Virgil (*The Destruction of Troy*, 1656). He is chiefly known for his *topographical poem *Cooper's Hill*, piratically published 1642, an early and influential example of what was to become a very popular genre. (See Pope's WINDSOR FOREST.) It combines descriptions of scenery with moral, historical, and political reflections, and contains the well-known address to the Thames, 'O, could I flow like thee', which was singled out for praise by Dr *Johnson for its economy of language, smoothness, and sweetness. *Dryden also praised his work highly, as 'majestic' and 'correct'. His poetry (and notably his use of the heroic couplet) played an important part in the transition from what were seen as the rugged eccentricities of the *Metaphysicals to the neo-classicism of the *Augustan age. (See also WALLER.)

Denis Duval, *Thackeray's last, unfinished, novel, published in the *Cornhill Magazine* 1864.

The story begins in Rye, in the second half of the 18th cent. The narrator, Denis Duval, grows up in a colony of French Protestant refugees. A French noblewoman, Mme de Saverne, escapes from the persecution of her husband and comes to England with the help of the sinister Chevalier de la Motte, who was intended to become the villain of the novel. She takes refuge with her old nurse, Denis's mother, and Denis falls in love with her little daughter Agnes. Denis has to leave home and go to sea after he has exposed the smuggling activities of his grandfather and the treasonable behaviour of de la Motte, and the fragment ends at this point. Thackeray intended Denis to encounter a series of adventures at sea, and to return to rescue Agnes from the machinations of de la Motte.

Dennis, in Dickens's *Barnaby Rudge*, the hangman and one of the leaders of the no-Popery riots.

DENNIS, John (1657–1734), a son of a saddler, was educated at Harrow and Caius College, Cambridge. He was a poet and dramatist, but is best known for his criticism, which combines a respect for *neo-classical theory with a passion for the *Sublime (particularly as manifested by *Milton), and with a dislike for the new *sentimental comedy. He declared that the 'Rules of *Aristotle' were 'nothing but Nature and Good Sense reduc'd to a Method', maintaining that *Paradise Lost was not so much 'against the Rules' as 'above them all'. His critical works (ed. E. N. Hooker, 2 vols, 1939–43) include *The Advancement and Reformation of Modern Poetry* (1701), *The Grounds of Criticism in Poetry* (1704), and *An Essay on the Genius and Writings of Shakespeare* (1712). His tragedies include *Appius and Virginia*, unsuccessfully produced in 1709, which was mocked by Pope in his *Essay on Criticism* ('Appius reddens at each word you speak', l. 585); this started a feud between the two writers, their interchanges including Pope's *Narrative of Dr Robert Norris . . .* (1713) and Dennis's *Remarks upon Mr Pope's Homer* (1717). Dennis also features as 'Sir Tremendous' in Pope's *Three Hours after Marriage* (1717), 'tremendous' being one of his favourite terms of praise. But Pope accepted and acted upon some of his critical comments, and shortly before Dennis's poverty-stricken death wrote a prologue for his benefit performance.

DENNIS, Nigel Forbes (1912–), novelist, playwright, journalist, and critic, born in Surrey, but educated abroad, in Southern Rhodesia and Germany. He worked for many years in America, where his first novel, *Boys and Girls Come out to Play* (1949), is largely set. His best-known work is *Cards of Identity* (1955), a satiric fantasy set in an English country house, which comments harshly but with much incidental comedy on post-war social change and insecurity and the ease with which the human personality can be controlled. *A House In Order* (1966) is a more abstract, Kafkaesque treatment of the problem of identity in which the imprisoned narrator, confined to a greenhouse, tries to ignore the world at war outside by cultivating his own garden. Dennis also published three plays, several critical works, and was for some time co-editor of *Encounter.

Dennison, Jenny, in Scott's *Old Mortality*, the attendant on Edith Bellenden.

Denouement, the unravelling of the plot, the final solution, in a drama or novel; *Aristotle's λύσις.

DENT, J. M., see EVERYMAN'S LIBRARY.

De Nugis Curialium, see MAP; also the subtitle of the *Policraticus* of *John of Salisbury.

Deor, an Old English poem from the 9th or 10th cent. in the *Exeter Book, of 42 lines divided into seven unequal sections and containing the refrain 'that passed; so can this'. Deor seems to be a minstrel who has fallen out of favour and consoles himself by considering the past misfortunes of others such as Wayland the Smith, Theodoric, and Hermanric. It is one of the group of poems in the Exeter Book referred to as 'elegies', short poems whose theme is usually the transience and unreliability of the world, sometimes (though not in *Deor*) ending with a Christian consolation. See edition by Kemp Malon (4th edn, 1966).

De Profundis, 'Out of the depths', the first two words of the Latin version of Psalm 130. It is the title of the prose apologia of *Wilde.

'Deputy', in Dickens's *Edwin Drood*, the

nearest thing to a name acknowledged by the imp who attends on Durdles.

DE QUINCEY, Thomas (1785–1859), second son of a linen merchant, was born in Manchester and educated at schools in Bath and Winkfield, ending at Manchester Grammar School from which he ran away to the homeless wanderings in Wales and London which he was to describe in *Confessions of an English Opium Eater*. He afterwards went to Worcester College, Oxford, and—having made the acquaintance of *Coleridge and *Wordsworth—settled at Grasmere in the cottage formerly occupied by the Wordsworths. In 1804, while at Oxford, he had begun to take opium, and from 1812 he became an addict. In 1817 he married Margaret Simpson, daughter of a local farmer, by whom he had eight children, and in the following year, having by then exhausted his private fortune, he started to earn a living by journalism. *Confessions of an English Opium Eater*, by which he made his name, was published in 1822. For the next 30 years he earned a precarious living, mainly in Edinburgh, by tales, articles and reviews, mostly in *Blackwood's* and *Tait's*, including *Klosterheim* (1832), *Recollections of the Lake Poets* (1834–9), 'Sketches . . . from the Autobiography of an English Opium Eater' (1834–41, later entitled *Autobiographic Sketches*), 'Suspiria de Profundis' (1845), and 'The English Mail Coach' (1849). A collected edition of his works, *Selections Grave and Gay*, was started under his supervision in 1853, and occupied him until his death.

Since nearly all De Quincey's work was journalism, written under pressure to support his family, it is more remarkable for brilliant *tours de force* such as 'On the Knocking on the Gate in "Macbeth" ', 'On Murder Considered as One of the Fine Arts', and 'The Revolt of the Tartars', than for sustained coherence. Eclectic learning, pungent black humour sometimes degenerating into facetiousness, a stately but singular style, distinguish all his writing. His impressionistic reminiscences both of his own childhood and of his literary contemporaries are memorably vivid. His greatest, though never completed, achievement was his psychological study of the faculty of dreaming in 'Suspiria de Profundis' and 'The English Mail Coach', in which he traced—twenty-five years before Freud was born—how childhood experiences and sufferings are crystallized in dreams into symbols which can form and educate the dreamer's personality, and can also give birth to literature, either as poetry or as 'impassioned prose', as De Quincey called his own climaxes of imagery. His influence, both on other writers such as *Poe and *Baudelaire (half of whose *Paradis artificiels* is a direct translation from De Quincey) and on ordinary readers tempted to experiment with opium, has been immense and sometimes malign. See E. Sackville-West, *A Flame in Sun-*

light: The Life and Work of Thomas de Quincey (1936); H. A. Eaton, *Thomas de Quincey* (1936).

Derby, countess of, wife of the seventh earl, who as 'queen' of the Isle of Man figures in Scott's *Peveril of the Peak*.

DERRIDA, Jacques, see STRUCTURALISM and MARXIST LITERARY CRITICISM.

Derriman, Festus, a character in Hardy's *The Trumpet Major*.

'Der wilde Jäger', see WILD HUNTSMAN, THE.

DESAI, Anita (1937–), novelist and short story writer, born in India and educated in Delhi; her father was Bengali, her mother German. Her elegant and lucid novels, which vividly evoke the atmosphere, society, and landscapes of India, include *Fire on the Mountain* (1977) and *Clear Light of Day* (1980). *Games at Twilight* (1978) is a collection of short stories, and her works for children include *The Village by the Sea* (1982).

DESANI, G. V. (1909–), Indian writer, born in Nairobi, Kenya; he lived in Britain during the Second World War, where he became a regular lecturer and broadcaster. His prose-poem *Hali* (1950) was published with a preface by E. M. *Forster, but he is known principally for his eccentric and inventive novel, *All about H. Hatterr* (1948), in which Hatterr, son of a European merchant seaman and 'an Oriental, a Malay Peninsula-resident lady, a steady non-voyaging non-Christian human', seeks wisdom from the seven sages of India. This was revised and republished in 1972 with an introduction by A. *Burgess.

DESCARTES, René (1596–1650), French philosopher and mathematician. After a period of extensive travelling he went into studious retirement, first in Paris until 1629, then in Holland until 1649 when he accepted an invitation to visit Sweden, where he died. His main works are: *Discours de la méthode* (printed as an introduction to the conclusions of his scientific research in 1637), *Méditations philosophiques* (originally published in Latin in 1641), *Principia philosophiae* (1644), and *Traité des passions de l'âme* (1649). They have exerted a unique influence on European thought. Philosophically his starting point is the problem of certainty posed by *Montaigne's radical scepticism: in other words, the necessity of a method productive of reliable propositions. Rejecting the accumulated preconceptions of the past ('systematic doubt'), he proposes to reconstruct the whole of philosophy on the basis of a few self-evident intuitions, such as the existence of the self in consciousness ('cogito ergo sum') and of elementary logical truths, such as the principle of non-contradiction. From these premisses he attempts to deduce the existence of God as guarantor of the reliability of the perceptible world, and thus of its susceptibility to scientific analysis. As a mathematician (he made major contributions to algebraic notation and co-ordinate geometry), he considered mathematical reasoning to be applicable to the whole of science. Although his astronomical theories were demolished by I. *Newton, his reduction of matter to the quantifiable has remained fundamental to science. In epistemology and ethics, his rigorous dualism (between mind and body) has been immensely influential, though it has come under suspicion in recent years. He is generally regarded as the founder of modern philosophy.

DESCHAMPS, Eustache (*c.*1346–*c.*1406), French poet. He was a disciple of *Guillaume de Machaut, influential in the development of the *ballade*, and the writer of the first treatise on poetry in French. He addressed one of his 'Balades de moralitez' to *Chaucer, whom he styled 'grand translateur'.

Desdemona, the heroine of Shakespeare's *Othello*.

Deserted Village, The, a poem by *Goldsmith, published 1770, in which he evokes the idyllic pastoral life of Auburn, 'loveliest village of the plain', in its days of prosperous peace, now over; the poet laments the growth of trade, the demand for luxuries, and the mercantile spirit which have depopulated such villages and driven 'a bold peasantry, their country's pride' to emigration. *Boswell attributes the last four lines to Dr *Johnson. Auburn was long identified with Lissoy, where Goldsmith spent much of his childhood, but is now believed to be a composite portrait, based also on Goldsmith's observations of the declining English countryside. Goldsmith's idealized descriptions of a happy rural community provoked a protest in Crabbe's *The Village* and have also been the focus for much discussion of the Tory view of a Golden Age.

Despair, Giant, in Bunyan's *Pilgrim's Progress*, imprisons Christian and Hopeful in *Doubting Castle.

Desperate Remedies, a novel by *Hardy, published 1871.

This was the first of Hardy's published novels. Cytherea Gray, who loves and is loved by Edward Springrove, becomes lady's maid to Miss Aldclyffe. The contrivances of Miss Aldclyffe, the discovery that Edward is already engaged, and the need to support a sick brother, drive Cytherea to marry Aeneas Manston, Miss Aldclyffe's villainous and illegitimate son, whose first wife is supposed to have perished in a fire. As soon as she is married Cytherea discovers that Edward is free from his engagement and that Aeneas's wife is probably still alive. In-

genious investigations reveal that Aeneas murdered his first wife in order to gain Cytherea. He hangs himself in his cell and the lovers are united.

Destiny, a novel by S. *Ferrier, published 1831.

The earnest evangelical tone of the book almost overwhelms the sense of comedy shown in her other novels. The story relates, in a complex plot, the fortunes of the various members of the Malcolm family: Glenroy, a Highland chief, married to the London-bred Lady Elizabeth Waldegrave, who finds the conditions of Scottish life so intolerable she leaves him; Glenroy's poor but worthy cousin Captain Malcolm, and his son Ronald; another cousin, the misanthrope Inch-Orran, who disappoints Glenroy by leaving his estate to Ronald and his father; Glenroy's nephew Reginald, who becomes engaged to Edith, the Chief's daughter, then jilts her to marry her half-sister; and Ronald, who disappears after a shipwreck in order to leave his father in possession of the Inch-Orran property, and returns, after years away, to marry the jilted Edith.

DE TABLEY, Lord, see WARREN, J. B. L.

Detective Fiction. In the detective story, or 'whodunit', a crime (generally, though not necessarily, murder) is committed by one of a group of people; the puzzle of the criminal's identity is finally solved, through a process of investigation, observation, and deduction, by an expert detective, who may be either police or private. It is a genre distinct from that of the crime novel, in which the criminal's identity is known from the start, and the interest consists in observing his psychology and his attempts to escape justice; from the 'hidden secret' novel (see SENSATION, NOVEL OF), in which a mystery, generally sinister though not necessarily criminal, is gradually revealed without deductive process; from the spy, conspiracy, or gang story, which is concerned with a battle of wits and violence between two sides known to the reader from the start; and from the suspense story, in which it is generally the innocent who are attempting to escape from the criminals. All these categories overlap, and many authors write in more than one of them, but the first is the classic form. The generic terms 'thriller' and 'mystery' are now too blurred for descriptive use.

Although crime novels such as Godwin's *Caleb Williams* and hidden secret novels such as Dickens's *Bleak House* have been allocated to the British ancestry of the detective story, its real progenitor is generally agreed to be *Poe's 'Chevalier Dupin' stories. In England Wilkie Collins's *The Moonstone* (1868) was the prototype for the full-length detective novel. Detective fiction, and the image of the superhumanly intelligent detective Sherlock Holmes and his auxiliary Watson, reached world-wide popularity in the novels and short stories of

A. C. *Doyle. Short detective stories, of which G. K. *Chesterton's 'Father Brown' stories were the other outstanding example, remained in the ascendant until E. C. *Bentley, in *Trent's Last Case* (1913), introduced in a full-length novel more spacious characterization and the gentlemanly amateur detective, setting the pattern for the next quarter-century of detective novels, generally regarded as the Golden Age of the genre.

During this period rules of fair play between author and reader in the game of puzzle-solving were formulated, and generally adhered to; law and order were always finally vindicated, and crime punished. Scientific and technical expertise (as in R. Austin Freeman and Freeman Wills Croft), locked room puzzles (in which John Dickson Carr specialized), ingeniously recondite murder weapons such as daggers of ice or trained killer bees, murder by the least likely suspect (as in A. *Christie's *Murder of Roger Ackroyd* where the narrator is the criminal, or her *Murder on the Orient Express* where the entire cast of suspects collaborate in the crime), were characteristics of Golden Age detective novels. Leading authors were D. L. *Sayers (who also made useful contributions to the history and criticism of the genre), Christie, H. C. Bailey, and Anthony Berkeley (who as Francis Iles also pioneered the crime novel genre), and, in the 1930s, Margery Allingham, Michael Innes (pseudonym of J. I. M. *Stewart), Ngaio *Marsh, and Nicholas Blake (pseudonym of C. *Day-Lewis).

After the Second World War, the American school of tough detective fiction began to erode the classic British genre, and some of the younger writers—disapproving of what were seen as the snobbery, nostalgia, and lack of social concern in the Golden Age detective story—turned to writing crime and spy stories, in which the conflict between justice and the criminal was no longer seen entirely from one side. Those, including Michael Gilbert, Elizabeth Ferrars, H. R. F. Keating, Ellis Peters, and P. D. James, who have remained faithful to the classic formula, have mostly abandoned the amateur detective and rely less on ingenious murder methods and more on realistic characterization. Exotic settings in the distant past, in remote countries, or in specialized milieux such as Dick Francis's racing world, are often deployed. A new sub-genre is the 'police procedural', whose chief English exponent is J. J. Marric (pseudonym of John Creasey), in which a complete police unit investigates concurrently a series of separate crimes. See Howard Haycraft, *Murder for Pleasure: The Life and Times of the Detective Story* (1942); Julian Symons, *Bloody Murder: From the Detective Story to the Crime Novel, A History* (1972).

Deus ex machina, 'God from the machine', an unexpected event or intervention in a play or novel, which resolves a difficult situation. When a god was introduced in the ancient Greek drama, he was brought on to the stage by some mechanical means ($\mu\eta\chi\alpha\nu\dot{\eta}$). *Euripides was particularly fond of the device.

De Vere, Arthur, alias Arthur Philipson, son of the earl of Oxford, a character in Scott's *Anne of Geierstein*.

DE VERE, Aubrey Thomas (1814–1902), born in Co. Limerick, the son of Sir Aubrey de Vere (1788–1846, himself a poet), was educated at Trinity College, Dublin. He came early under the influence of *Wordsworth and *Coleridge and had many friends in the literary world, including *Tennyson, Sir H. *Taylor, the *Brownings, and *Ruskin; in 1851, in the footsteps of his friend *Newman, he was received into the Roman Catholic church. His voluminous works include *The Waldenses, or the Fall of Rora, with other Poems* (1842); *English Misrule and Irish Misdeeds* (1848), which displays Irish sympathies, as do many of his works; and *Recollections* (1897). He is the subject of a memoir by W. G. *Ward. See also M. P. Reilly, *Aubrey de Vere: Victorian Observer* (1956).

DE VERE, Edward, see OXFORD.

Devereux, a novel by *Bulwer-Lytton.

DEVEREUX, Robert, see ESSEX.

Devil is an Ass, The, a comedy by *Jonson, acted by the King's Men 1616, printed 1631.

Fitzdottrel, a foolish country squire, is cheated out of his estate by Meercraft, a 'projector', who parades various fantastic schemes for making money and deludes him with the promise that he will make him duke of Drowndland through a project for land reclamation. When Fitzdottrel finds he has made over his estate to the wrong person, he pretends to be bewitched in order to have the contract declared void, but eventually confesses to the fraud. He then learns that Wittipol and Manly, who had intrigued to seduce his wife, have out of admiration for her virtue safeguarded his estate. A secondary plot concerns Pug, a minor devil who has been allowed by Satan to try his hand at iniquity on earth for a day and is taken on by Fitzdottrel as a servant. He finds himself completely outdone in wickedness by human knaves, is sent to Newgate, and returns to hell baffled.

Devils, The, a play by J. *Whiting, based on A. *Huxley's *The Devils of Loudon*.

'Devil's Thoughts, The', a satirical poem by S. T. *Coleridge and R. *Southey, published 1799, describing the Devil going walking and enjoying the sight of the vices of men. The poem was imitated by *Byron in his 'Devil's Drive', and by *Shelley in his 'Devil's Walk'.

Devil upon Two Sticks in England, The, a continuation by W. *Combe, published 1790, of *Le Sage's *Le Diable boiteux*. S. *Foote also wrote a farce called *The Devil upon Two Sticks*, produced 1768.

DEWEY, John (1859–1952), American philosopher, one of the leaders of the Pragmatist school, and educationist, born in Vermont. His chief works are: *Critical Theory of Ethics* (1891), *Studies in Logical Theory* (1903), *Democracy and Education* (1916), *Human Nature and Conduct* (1922).

DEWEY, Melvil (1851–1931), American librarian, invented the Dewey decimal system of library cataloguing.

Dewy, Dick, a character in Hardy's *Under the Greenwood Tree*.

Dial, The, (1) (1840–4), the literary organ of the American Transcendental movement (see TRANSCENDENTAL CLUB), of which M. *Fuller was editor; she was succeeded by *Emerson. It contained contributions by *Thoreau. (2) (1889–97) (Nos 1–5), a literary and artistic periodical edited by *Ricketts and Charles Shannon. The 'Dial Group' also included T. S. *Moore and Lucien Pissarro (1863–1944). (3) (1880–1929), a literary monthly founded in Chicago, which moved in 1918 to New York. In its last decade it was one of the most important international periodicals, publishing work by T. S. *Eliot, *Yeats, D. H. *Lawrence, *Pound, *Cummings, *Aiken, and many others. Scofield Thayer was editor from 1925. It was expensively printed and paid well; *Connolly described it as 'the most successful of eclectic magazines, rich, discerning . . .' with 'a distinct impression of modishness in its later numbers as the twenties entered their sleek decline' ('Little Magazines', 1964, printed in *The Evening Colonnade*, 1973).

Diall of Princes, the title of the translation by Sir T. *North of Guevara's *El Relox de Principes*, published 1557.

Dialogues concerning Natural Religion, a treatise on natural theology by *Hume, written in the 1750s and published posthumously 1779. The work is modelled on *Cicero's *De Natura Deorum*. It portrays in 18th-cent. terms the conflict between scientific theism and philosophical scepticism, on the question of whether the human mind is capable of inferring the nature of the source of order in the universe

Dialogues of the Dead, Four, by *Prior, written 1721, imaginary conversations on the model set by *Lucian and perhaps directly suggested by *Fénelon's *Dialogues des Morts* (1712–30). The first is between 'Charles the Emperor and Clenard the Grammarian' on the subject of greatness; the second is between 'Mr John Lock

and Seigneur de Montaigne'; the third between 'The Vicar of Bray and Sir Thomas More'; and the fourth between 'Oliver Cromwell and his Porter'.

*Lyttleton also wrote *Dialogues of the Dead* (1760).

Dialogus de Scaccario, or *Dialogue of the Exchequer*, is the work of Richard Fitz-Nigel, treasurer of England from 1195 or 1196 to 1198, and bishop of London 1189–98. It takes the form of a dialogue in Latin between teacher and pupil, and is one of the principal sources of our knowledge of the Norman administration in England before Magna Carta.

Diana, a volume of sonnets by H. *Constable.

Diana, a character in Shakespeare's *All's Well that Ends Well*.

Diana of the Crossways, a novel by G. *Meredith, published 1885.

The story has a foundation in the probably baseless rumour that *Sheridan's granddaughter Caroline Norton had, while Melbourne's mistress, passed on information about the repeal of the Corn Laws. After the family's protests Meredith included a note that the work 'is to be read as fiction'.

The beautiful and impulsive Irish girl Diana Merion marries Mr Warwick, a man incapable of understanding the remarkable qualities of his wife. Her innocent indiscretions arouse his jealousy and he brings an action for divorce, citing Lord Dannisburgh (drawn from Melbourne), which he loses. Percy Dacier, a rising young politician, falls in love with Diana, but when she is about to live with him, openly and rashly, the dangerous illness of her friend Lady Dunstane recalls her sense of duty and propriety. Dacier perseveres, and she is once more on the point of joining him when he discovers that an important political secret which he had confided to her has been passed to a London newspaper. He does not believe her protestations, and after much pain they part. Diana's husband dies, and after a time she becomes the wife of her steady and faithful adorer Thomas Redworth, who, without being brilliant, has the wit and understanding to appreciate her.

DIAPER, William (1685–1717), poet, born in Somerset, wrote *Nereides: or, Sea-Eclogues* (1712), in which the speakers are mermen and mermaids and the landscapes subaqueous; *Swift found them 'very pretty' (*Journal to Stella*, 12 March 1712) and briefly interested himself in Diaper's career in the church. He also wrote *Dryades* (1712) and a *topographical poem, 'Brent' (printed 1754), and translated Part 1 of Oppian's *Halieuticks*, a Greek didactic poem on fish and fishing. See *Complete Works*, ed. D. Broughton (1952).

Diarmid, or **Diarmait O'Duibhne,** in the legends relating to the Irish hero *Finn, the lover of *Grainne.

Diary of a Country Parson, The, see WOODFORDE, J.

Diary of a Nobody, The, by G. and W. *Grossmith, published 1892.

Charles Pooter's diary covers fifteen months of his life in the early 1890s. His entries, describing the events of his life with his wife Carrie in Brickfield Terrace, Holloway, reveal in cumulative detail the society of anxious gentility in which he lives. Pooter emerges as worthy, deferential, and acutely sensitive to minor humiliations, such as those he suffers at the Mansion House reception or the Volunteer Ball. The wide variety of people who impinge upon him include his son, the 'fast' young Lupin, and his shocking Daisy Mutlar; the revered superior, Mr Perkup; the fashionable spiritualist, Mrs James of Sutton, who unsettles Carrie; the noisy Gowing, the fatuous Padge, cheeky errand boys, and tiresome servants. Text and illustrations reveal much precise contemporary background, including the details of clothes, the plaster antlers and splayed fans of the décor, the new fad for the bicycle, the fashion for imitations of Sir H. *Irving, and the admired slang and popular songs of the time. *Belloc's assertion that Pooter was 'an immortal achievement' is not often challenged.

DIBDIN, Charles (1745–1814), actor, dramatist, and song-writer, born at Southampton, who is best remembered for his sea songs, including 'The Lass that Loved a Sailor' and 'Tom Bowling', said to have been inspired by his brother Tom, a naval captain who died at Cape Town in 1780. He wrote many musical entertainments (including *The Waterman,* 1774) and dramatic monologues; also an autobiography, *The Professional Life of Mr Dibdin . . .with the words of six hundred songs* (4 vols, 1803), in which he describes his relations with *Garrick and others. His son Charles (1768–1833), by the actress Harriet Pitt, was also a playwright; his son Thomas John (1771–1841) composed some 2,000 songs, many attributed to his father.

DIBDIN, Thomas Frognall (1776–1847), nephew of Charles *Dibdin, educated at Oxford, was a renowned bibliographer and librarian to Lord Spencer at Althorp. He published his *Introduction to the Knowledge of Rare and Valuable Editions of the Greek and Latin Classics* in 1802, and in 1809 his *Bibliomania* ('a bibliographical romance'), which did much to stimulate interest in old books and rare editions. Dibdin became the first secretary of the bibliophiles' *Roxburghe Club when it was founded in 1812. *A Bibliographical, Antiquarian, and Picturesque Tour in France and Germany* was published in 1821,

and his *Library Companion* in 1824. In his *Bibliophobia* (1832) he comments with surprise on the respectful manner of the publisher John *Murray to his authors, and examines the depressed state of the book trade. *Reminiscences of a Literary Life* followed in 1836, and his *Bibliographical, Antiquarian, and Picturesque Tour in the Northern Counties of England* in 1838.

DICEY, Albert Venn (1835–1922), educated at Balliol College, Oxford, under *Jowett, became fellow of Trinity College, Oxford, in 1860 and was called to the bar in 1863. He played a leading part in political controversy and wrote extensively against Irish Home Rule, publishing in 1886 *England's Case against Home Rule.* As Vinerian professor of English law at Oxford (1882–1909), he published his three most influential works; the *Introduction to the Study of the Law of the Constitution* (1885), a classic treatise which has endured redefinition by modern authorities; *Conflict of Laws* (1896); and *Law and Opinion in the Nineteenth Century* (1905). Dicey's intellectual reputation was at its peak in his own lifetime but has since declined.

Dick, Mr, the amiable lunatic in Dickens's *David Copperfield.*

DICKENS, Charles John Huffham (1812–70), born in Portsmouth, the son of a clerk in the Navy pay office, spent the happiest period of his boyhood in Chatham; this was followed by a period of intense misery which deeply affected him, during which his father was imprisoned for debt in the Marshalsea and he himself (aged 12) worked in a blacking warehouse. Memories of this painful period inspired much of his fiction, notably the early chapters of *David Copperfield.* He then worked as an office boy; studied shorthand; and became reporter of debates in the Commons for the *Morning Chronicle.* He contributed to the *Monthly Magazine* (1833–5), to the *Evening Chronicle* (1835), and to other periodicals the articles subsequently republished as *Sketches by 'Boz', Illustrative of Every-Day Life and Every-Day People* (1836–7); these attracted much attention and led to an approach from *Chapman and Hall which resulted in the creation of Mr Pickwick, and the publication in twenty monthly numbers (beginning April 1836) of *The Posthumous Papers of the Pickwick Club,* published in volume form in 1837 when Dickens was only 25 years old. (See PICKWICK PAPERS.) After a slow start the series achieved immense popularity, and Dickens, with his young wife Catherine Hogarth, embarked on a promising future, courted by publishers, admired by the public, and befriended by celebrities. On Christmas Day 1836 he met John *Forster, who became his close friend and biographer.

In 1837 (a year overshadowed by the death of his much-loved sister-in-law Mary) *Oliver

Twist began to appear in monthly numbers in *Bentley's Miscellany*, a new periodical of which Dickens was the first editor. It was followed by *Nicholas Nickleby*, also in monthly numbers. In 1840 a new weekly was launched, written wholly by Dickens, called *Master Humphrey's Clock*; it was originally intended to carry short sketches as well as instalments of the full-length novels *The Old Curiosity Shop* (1840–1) and his long-deliberated *Barnaby Rudge* (1841), but the novels proved so popular that the linking by 'Master Humphrey' was dropped. In 1842 he and his wife visited America, where he was rapturously received. His first impressions were favourable, but disillusion followed and his *American Notes* (1842) caused much offence in America, as did his portrayal of American stereotypes in *Martin Chuzzlewit* (1843–4). While in America he advocated international copyright and the abolition of slavery.

The sales of *Martin Chuzzlewit* were disappointing, but the demands of the public and his own growing family were met by the success of *A Christmas Carol* (1843), the first of a series of Christmas books (*The Chimes, *The Cricket on the Hearth, The Battle of Life,* and *The Haunted Man*), works described by him as 'a whimsical sort of masque intended to awaken loving and forebearing thoughts'. In 1844 he paid a long visit to Italy, which produced 'Pictures from Italy' contributed to the *Daily News*, a new Radical paper founded by Dickens in 1846 and briefly edited by him. He wrote *Dombey and Son* (1848) during a visit to Switzerland in 1846. In 1850 he started the weekly periodical *Household Words*; in 1859 it was incorporated into *All the Year Round*, which he continued to edit until his death. In this he published much of his later writings, including the Christmas stories that replaced the Christmas books. *David Copperfield* appeared in monthly numbers in 1849–50; *Bleak House* in 1852–3; and *A Child's History of England* (a work which manifests his own historical bias: his heroes were Alfred and Cromwell) appeared irregularly, 1851–3. *Hard Times* appeared in 1854, *Little Dorrit* in 1855–7, *A Tale of Two Cities* in 1859, *Great Expectations* in 1860–1, and *Our Mutual Friend* in 1864–5.

During these years of intense productivity he also found time for his large family, for a vast circle of friends, and for philanthropic enterprises, at times combined with his passion for amateur theatricals; it was a fund-raising performance of Wilkie *Collins's The Frozen Deep* in 1857, in aid of *Jerrold's family, that introduced him to the young actress Ellen Ternan. His admiration for her further strained his deteriorating relationship with his wife, and he and Catherine separated in 1858. He defied scandal, protested his own innocence (and that of his sister-in-law Georgina, for many years his devoted housekeeper, whose name gossip had also

linked with his), and continued to appear in public, distracting himself from domestic sorrow by throwing his restless energy into public readings of his own works. These, though immensely successful, were physically and emotionally exhausting. He revisited America in 1867–8, delivered a series of readings there, and on his return continued to tour the provinces. He died suddenly in 1870, leaving unfinished his last novel, *The Mystery of *Edwin Drood*.

Dickens captured the popular imagination as no other novelist had done and, despite some murmurs against his sensationalism and sentimentality and his inability to portray women other than as innocents or grotesques, he was also held in high critical esteem, admired by contemporaries as varied as Queen *Victoria and *Dostoevsky. But it was not until this century that he began to attract serious academic attention; see in particular 'Charles Dickens' in *Inside the Whale*, G. *Orwell (1940), *The Dickens World*, H. House (1941), and 'Dickens: the Two Scrooges', E. *Wilson (1941). Later criticism has tended to praise the complexity of the sombre late works at the expense of the high-spirited humour and genius for caricature traditionally labelled 'Dickensian'. Mention should also be made of the series of distinguished illustrators inseparably connected with his work, which includes H. K. *Browne ('Phiz'), *Leech, *Cruikshank, G. Cattermole, and S. L. Fildes; also of his collaboration with Wilkie Collins in various stories which appeared in *Household Words*.

J. Forster, *The Life of Dickens* (1872–4); Edgar Johnson, *Charles Dickens: His Tragedy and Triumph* (1952); G. H. Ford, *Dickens and his Readers: Aspects of Novel Criticism since 1836* (1955); P. A. W. Collins, *Dickens and Crime* (1962); *Dickens: The Critical Heritage*, ed. P. Collins (1971).

DICKENSON, John (*fl.* 1591–8), was a minor Elizabethan writer and poet. His *Arisbas* (1594) is a euphuistic romance and *The Shepheardes Complaint* (1598), written in English hexameters with connecting prose passages, is reminiscent of Sidney's *Arcadia*. His *Greene in Conceipt. New Raised from his Grave* (1598) tells the 'Tragique Historie of faire Valeria of London'.

DICKINSON, Emily Elizabeth (1830–86), American poet, born in Amherst, Massachusetts, the daughter of a successful lawyer. She was educated at Amherst Academy (1834–47) and Mount Holyoake (1847–8); during her early years she was lively, witty, and sociable, but from her mid-twenties she gradually withdrew into an inner world, eventually, in her forties, refusing to leave her home, and avoiding all contact with strangers, although she maintained intimate correspondences with people she never saw face to face. Her emotional life remains mysterious, despite much speculation about a possible disappointed love affair, for which one candidate is the Revd Charles Wadsworth, with whom she corresponded and who twice visited her; another is Samuel Bowles, editor of the *Springfield Republican*, to whom she sent and addressed many poems. She wrote poetry from girlhood onward, but only seven poems out of nearly 2,000 are known to have been published during her lifetime, and those appeared anonymously and much edited. She at one stage actively sought publication, but her contemporaries found her work bewildering, and she appears to have accepted her lot as an unrecognized writer—her 'Barefoot-Rank'. From *c.*1858 she assembled many of her poems in packets or 'fascicles', which were discovered after her death; a selection, arranged and edited by Mabel Loomis Todd and T. W. Higginson, appeared in 1890. Full publication was delayed by family difficulties, but eventually other editions and volumes of letters appeared, restoring her individual punctuation and presentation. At first regarded as an eccentric minor poet, she is now considered a major writer of startling originality. Her work presents recurrent themes—a mystic apprehension of the natural world, a preoccupation with poetic vocation, fame, death, and immortality—and is expressed in a rhetoric and language of her own, cryptic, elliptical, and at times self-dramatizing and hyperbolic. Her imagery reflects an intense and painful inner struggle over many years; she refers to herself as 'the queen of Calvary', and her verse is full of allusions to volcanoes, shipwrecks, funerals, storms, imprisonments, and other manifestations of natural and human violence. Her simultaneous conviction of isolation and 'election' was dramatized in her way of life, which is vividly described in a two-volume biography by R. B. Sewall, published in 1974.

Dictionary. The origins of the English dictionary are found in the late 16th cent. when people became aware of the two levels of English ('learned', 'literary', **'inkhorn', distinct from 'spoken', 'popular') to an extent that made it desirable to gloss one in the other's terms, as previously Latin or French had been glossed by English. Cawdrey's *Table Alphabeticall of Hard Words* (1604), containing about 3,000 words, might be called the first English dictionary; Henry Cockeram's *English Dictionarie* (1623) translates hard words to easy as well as easy to hard. The first major English dictionary was N. *Bailey's *Universal Etymological English Dictionary* (1721), which had more entries than its famous successor Dr *Johnson's Dictionary (1755). Johnson's Dictionary is one of the two great landmarks in English lexicographical history; Johnson illustrates his words in practice, and attempts to indicate the connotations of words, as well as offering their exact meaning. A number of 19th-cent. dictionaries attempted to develop these empirical tendencies in Johnson. But the second great landmark is the greatest dictionary of any modern language, **The Oxford English Dictionary* (1884–1928), edited by J. A. H. *Murray, H. *Bradley, W. A. *Craigie, and C. T. *Onions: The *OED* attempts to give a full history of the development of all English words since the 12th cent., with full illustrative quotations, ordered according to the principal distinct senses of the word. It is being updated by a series of supplements under the editorship of R. W. *Burchfield. The possibility of a dictionary organized on synchronic, rather than historical, principles was brought closer when in 1984 the *OED* files began to be converted into a computerized database. The other major English language dictionary is N. *Webster's dictionary of American English (1828; *Third New International Dictionary*, 1961), the Third being controversial on its appearance for its omission of indications of inferior usage in categories such as 'slang', 'obscene', etc. See J. A. H. Murray, *The Evolution of English Lexicography* (1900); J. R. Hulbert, *Dictionaries, British and American* (1955); J. H. Sledd and G. J. Kolb, *Dr Johnson's Dictionary* (1955); T. Starnes and G. E. Noyes, *The English Dictionary from Cawdry to Johnson* (1946); E. L. McAdam and G. Milne eds., *Johnson's Dictionary: A Modern Selection* (1963); H. D. Weinbrot ed., *New Aspects of Lexicography* (1972).

Dictionary of National Biography, The, designed and published by George *Smith, was begun in 1882 with Sir L. *Stephen as editor. It included in its original form biographies of all national notabilities from earliest times to 1900. The work has been continued by the publishing of decennial supplements. Stephen was succeeded in the editorship by Sir Sidney *Lee. Their names appear jointly on the title-pages of vols xxii–xxvi (1890), and Lee's name alone from vol. xxvii till 1911. In 1917 the Dictionary was transferred to the *Oxford University Press. The 1912–21 volume was edited by H. W. C. Davis and J. R. H. Weaver; 1922–30 by J. R. H. Weaver; 1931–40 by L. G. Wickham Legg; 1941–50 by L. G. Wickham Legg and E. T. Williams; 1951–60 by E. T. Williams and Helen Palmer; 1961–70 by E. T. Williams and C. S. Nicholls. The *Concise DNB* is in two parts: Part 1, epitome of the *DNB* from earliest times to 1900, and Part 2, epitome of the supplements, 1901–70.

Dictionary of the English Language, A, see JOHNSON'S DICTIONARY.

DICTYS CRETENSIS is the supposed author of a diary of the Trojan War which we possess in Latin. In the preface, written in the 4th cent. AD, Lucius Septimius claims that he translated the work from a Greek version prepared for Nero from a Phoenician original. Dictys claims to have been present at the siege of Troy as a companion of the Cretan Idomeneus. Like the narrative of *Dares Phrygius his diary is probably a fabrication, but the two were the chief sources of medieval Trojan legends.

Diddler, Jeremy, the chief character in James Kenney's farce *Raising the Wind* (1803). Jeremy's habit of continually borrowing small sums which he does not pay back probably gave rise to the present sense of the verb 'diddle'—to cheat or deceive.

DIDEROT, Denis (1713–84), French philosopher and man of letters. The son of a prosperous artisan, he became a leading member of the *Enlightenment. He began by translating *Shaftesbury (1745), and continued to maintain his interest in English culture, publishing an influential appreciation of S. *Richardson (1761). He also wrote two mediocre sentimental dramas, *Le Fils naturel* (1757) and *Le Père de famille* (1758) which demonstrate his faith in the dramatic viability of bourgeois domestic subjects, a theory influenced by *Lillo; he also adapted E. *Moore's prose tragedy *The Gamester*, as *Est-il bon? Est-il méchant?* (which was never performed). He developed a scientific empiricism which, far from turning him into a mere experimenter, served only to stimulate the originality of his thought. His *Pensées sur l'interprétation de la nature* (1754), for example, anticipated evolutionary ideas on the nature and origin of life. In 1746 he assumed what became, in effect, a twenty-year editorship of the *Encyclopédie. He closed his literary career with a number of seminal narratives, notably *Le neveu de Rameau* (1761, later translated by *Goethe) and *Jacques le fataliste* (1773, a work influenced by *Sterne), which explore the complexities of the relations between psychology and morality.

Dido Queene of Carthage, *The Tragedie of,* written by *Marlowe and *Nashe, possibly while they were at Cambridge together. It was performed at unknown dates by the Children of the Queen's Chapel, and published in 1594. It is closely based on Virgil's *Aeneid* (Bks I, II, and IV), depicting Dido's failure to persuade Aeneas to stay with her in Carthage and her subsequent suicide.

Dies Irae, 'Day of wrath', the first words of one of the greatest medieval Latin hymns, authorship of which is attributed to Thomas of Celano (d. *c.*1255), the biographer of St *Francis.

Dietrich of Bern, the name given in the *Nibelungenlied to Theodoric, a great king of the Ostrogoths (*c.*454–526), who invaded Italy and decisively defeated Odoacer at Verona (Bern) in 489. He was the hero of the German epics of the 13th cent. and of the Teutonic race in general, and the centre round which clustered many legends.

DIGBY, Sir Kenelm (1603–65), was author, diplomatist, naval commander (who defeated the French and Venetian fleets in Scanderoon harbour, 1628), and one of the first members of the *Royal Society; he discovered the necessity of oxygen to the life of plants, but less scientifically believed in the curing of wounds by 'powder of sympathy'. In 1625 he secretly married the celebrated beauty Venetia Stanley, and gives an account, under disguised names, of his wooing in his *Private Memoirs* (published 1827); her situation is said to have provided the plot of *Shirley's *The Wedding*, and her death in 1633 was lamented by *Jonson, *Habington, and others. He published a criticism of Browne's *Religio Medici in 1643, and wrote 'Of Bodies' and 'Of the Immortality of Man's Soul' in the same year. A life by R. T. Petersson appeared in 1956.

DIGBY, Kenelm Henry (1800–80), educated at Trinity College, Cambridge, was author of *The Broad Stone of Honour* (1822), a study of chivalry, and *Mores Catholici* (1831–42).

Digby Plays, The, three late Mystery plays from East Anglia, probably dating from the early 16th cent., bearing on them the name or initials of Myles Blomefeld (1525–1603), a collector of books from Bury St Edmunds. These long plays are outcrops from the Mystery Cycles, found with non–literary material in Digby MS 133. They are *Mary Magdalen, The Conversion of St Paul*, and *The Killing of the Children of Israel*; all of them, but especially *Mary Magdalen*, have considerable literary and theatrical interest. They have been edited by D. C. Baker, J. L. Murphy, and L. B. Hall Jr. (EETS OS 283, 1982).

Dilettanti, Society of the, originally founded about 1732 as a dining society by some gentlemen of wealth and position who had travelled in Italy, soon devoted itself to the patronage of the fine arts. It has chiefly encouraged the study of classical archaeology. See Lionel Cust's history of the society (1898).

DILKE, Sir Charles Wentworth (1843–1911), radical statesman, educated at Trinity Hall, Cambridge, and later called to the bar. He became Member of Parliament for Chelsea in 1868 and held offices under *Gladstone. On his father's death in 1869 he inherited the baronetcy and the proprietorship of the *Athenaeum and *Notes and Queries. He was the author of *Greater Britain* (1868), a record of his travels through English-speaking countries; *Problems of Greater Britain* (1890), an account of questions dealing with the Empire; and *The Fall of Prince Florestan of Monaco* (1874), a political satire. In 1885 he married the widow of Mark *Pattison (*née* Emilia Francis Strong, 1840–1904, historian of French art and author of *Claude Lorrain*, 1884; *The Shrine of Death*, 1886; etc.). It has been suggested that Dilke might have succeeded Gladstone but for his connection with a divorce scandal (Crawford v. Crawford and Dilke) which led to his defeat and temporary retirement in 1886. He was returned Member for the Forest of Dean in 1892. See R. Jenkins, *Sir Charles Dilke, A Victorian Tragedy* (1958).

DILLON, Wentworth, fourth earl of Roscommon (?1633–85), educated at Caen, author of a blank-verse translation of *Horace's *Ars Poetica* (1680) and an *Essay on Translated Verse* (1684). He was the first critic publicly to praise *Paradise Lost.

Dimmesdale, the Revd Arthur, a character in Hawthorne's *The Scarlet Letter.

Dinas Vawr, *The War-Song of*, see MISFORTUNES OF ELPHIN, THE.

DINESEN, Isak, see BLIXEN, K.

Dinmont, see DANDIE DINMONT.

DIODATI, Charles (d. 1638), schoolfellow and close friend of *Milton, and son of an Italian Protestant settled in London. Milton addressed to him two Latin elegies and mourned him in the pastoral *Epitaphium Damonis* (?1640).

DIODORUS SICULUS, a Greek historian of the latter half of the 1st cent. BC. The surviving portion of his history of the world was translated into Latin by Poggio, and Bks I–V, which gave an account of Egypt, Assyria, and early Greece, were widely read in the 16th and 17th cents. *Skelton produced a translation into English, and there are references to it in D. *Lindsay, *Kirke, *Milton, and even W. *Morris.

DIOGENES LAERTIUS, a Greek historian of philosophy of the early 3rd cent. AD. He presented philosophers as heroic figures, so that his lives, like *Plutarch's, served as an admirable source of moral examples.

DIONYSIUS THE AREOPAGITE, (1) a disciple of St Paul, passingly mentioned (Acts 17: 34); (2) more importantly, a 5th-cent. Neoplatonic writer (now known as Pseudo-Dionysius) claimed to be this disciple, in an attempt to give canonical authority to elements of mysticism and *Neoplatonism which he attempted to introduce, with considerable success. His works, the most important of which was *The Divine Names*, first appeared in 532. This work, and the Commentary on it by Maximus the Confessor (580–662), was very influential on *Scotus Erigena and on the whole medieval mystical tradition. The 14th-cent. mystical prose work *Deonise Hid Divinite* (EETS

OS 231, 1949, ed. P. Hodgson) is founded on him, as its name suggests.

Dionyza, in Shakespeare's *Pericles*, wife of Cleon, governor of Tarsus, to whom Pericles entrusts his daughter *Marina.

'Dipsychus', a poem by *Clough.

Discourse concerning the original and progress of Satire, A, by *Dryden.
The Discourse was published with *The Satires* (1693) of *Juvenal and *Persius, translated by various hands, among them Dryden's. Less impressive for its scholarship (which is not, however, negligible) than for its broad sense of the principles underlying literary and social history, it distinguishes between 'Varronian', 'Horatian', and 'Juvenalian' satire in a way that has considerably influenced criticism of Dryden's own satirical works and that of his Augustan successors.

Discoverie of Witchcraft, The, see SCOT, R.

Discoveries made upon Men and Matter, see TIMBER.

Disowned, The, a novel by *Bulwer-Lytton.

DISRAELI, Benjamin (1804–81), first earl of Beaconsfield, politician, prime minister, and novelist; only his literary career is here outlined. The oldest son of I. *D'Israeli, Benjamin attended private schools in and near London, but acquired much of his education in his father's extensive library. When he was fifteen he wrote a short tale, *A True Story*, which Leigh *Hunt published in the *Indicator* in 1820. At seventeen he was articled in Lincoln's Inn but was more interested in the literary world inhabited by his father. He was to attempt an ambitious variety of literary forms (epic, verse tragedy, and satire, among others) before he settled on the novel. In 1826, with profits from speculative ventures in the Americas, he and John *Murray established a daily paper, the *Representative*, in opposition to *The Times*, and the organization was well advanced when the boom collapsed and Disraeli withdrew; the new paper survived for seven months at great loss. *Vivian Grey*, his first novel, was no doubt partly written (as were some others) to pay off debts. It was published anonymously in 1826 and its considerable success encouraged him to provide a continuation in 1827. In the same year he published *Popanilla*. Between 1828 and 1831 he travelled in Spain and Italy, and made much use of these, and of subsequent travels in Albania, the Levant, and Egypt, in future novels. In 1831 he published *The Young Duke*, followed by *Contarini Fleming* (1832) and *Alroy* (1833), which together with *Vivian Grey* (in the order Grey—Alroy—Fleming) formed his first trilogy. In 1833 appeared the burlesque *Ixion in Heaven*; in 1834 a light political satire, *The Infernal Marriage*, and the brief but highly coloured *Rise of Iskander*, set in warring Albania; his one long, serious but unsuccessful attempt at poetry, *The Revolutionary Epic*, in blank verse; and an anonymous novel, written with his sister Sarah, *A Year at Hartlebury*, whose authorship he never admitted. *A Vindication of the English Constitution* (which contained several of the ideas developed later in *Coningsby* and *Sybil*) appeared in 1835; the *Junius*-inspired *Letters of Runnymede*, together with *The Spirit of Whiggism*, in 1836; and in those years also various stories in *Heath's Book of Beauty*.

By 1834 Disraeli had established himself in the highest social and political society, which was vividly reflected in his next two novels, *Henrietta Temple* and *Venetia*, both love stories and both published in 1837. A verse play, *The Tragedy of *Count Alarcos*, appeared in 1839, but caused little interest. The trilogy for which Disraeli is most renowned, *Coningsby* (1844), *Sybil* (1845), and *Tancred* (1847), was written, he declared, because it was through novels that he felt he could best influence public opinion, and they may be regarded as the first truly political novels in English. The first two, much of which are concerned with the conditions of the urban and rural poor, were particularly successful, and certain attitudes expressed in them foreshadowed future social legislation. In 1852 Disraeli published *Lord George Bentinck: a Political Biography*, which was well received. He published no more novels for over twenty years, until *Lothair* in 1870. The first collected edition of the novels, with an illuminating Preface by the author, was published in the same year. *Endymion* (1880), his last completed novel, for which he was offered the enormous sum of £10,000, was set in the period of his youth. He died when he had completed only nine brief chapters of the intriguing *Falconet*.

Disraeli declared 'My works are my life' and that anyone wishing to know him would find him there. Many of the characters were intended as portraits of prominent men and women of the time. A combination of fascination and amused contempt for high society, both social and political; a clever vein of irony; shrewd observation of personal and political manœuvre; an apparently genuine sympathy for poverty and oppression; a skill in the characterization of clever women and of tender relationships between parents and children; and a brisk readability characterized his novels. But a deficiency of creative power, revealed in much feeble characterization, and long passages of rhetorical and philosophic musing, has meant that in spite of their original popularity his novels have never received high critical acclaim. Even in his own time they were popular rather than admired; *Wordsworth, for instance, described them as 'trashy' and *Trollope found them 'spurious'. Disraeli's famous comment, 'When I want to read a novel I write one', was made on the publication of *Daniel Deronda* in 1876.

D'ISRAELI, Isaac (1766–1848), the father of B. *Disraeli, was descended from a Levantine Jewish family who had settled in Italy. He had hoped to become a creative writer, but instead turned largely to literary history. In 1791 he published the first volume of *Curiosities of Literature*, the sixth and last volume of which appeared in 1834. It was the first of several discursive and entertaining collections. His most remarkable and original work was *The Literary Character* (1795), in which he attempts to identify the qualities of temperament common to creative writers. *Byron's annotations and encouragement led to an expanded version of the book. *Calamities of Authors* followed in 1813, *Quarrels of Authors* in 1814. His study in five vols of *The Life and Reign of Charles I* appeared in 1828–30, and *Amenities of Literature* in 1840. He also published several novels and essays, and his works were much read and enjoyed, notably by Byron, who found them both amusing and instructive.

Dissertation upon Parties, A, see BOLINGBROKE, H. ST J.

Dissociation of Sensibility, a phrase coined by T. S. *Eliot in an essay entitled 'The Metaphysical Poets' (1921), to describe the 'something which happened to the mind of England between the time of Donne or Lord Herbert of Cherbury and the time of Tennyson and Browning; it is the difference between the intellectual poet and the reflective poet.' Eliot suggests that by an increasing refinement of language, accompanied by an increasing crudity of feeling (*Gray is cruder than *Marvell), thought became separated from feeling. The *metaphysical poets, like the Elizabethan and Jacobean dramatists, 'possessed a mechanism of sensibility which could devour any kind of experience . . . A thought to Donne was an experience; it modified his sensibility' . . . 'in the seventeenth century a dissociation of sensibility set in, from which we have never recovered.' The phrase became extremely fashionable, to Eliot's own surprise, and has given rise to much discussion; it is now more generally regarded as a comment on Eliot's own creative problems and innovations than as an objective historical analysis.

Dithyramb, a lyric poem in a lofty style with a flute accompaniment in the Phrygian mode. Supposedly invented by Arion (7th cent. BC) it was originally antistrophic and sung in honour of Bacchus. Later dithyrambs were monostrophic and could be addressed to other gods.

Diurnalls, see NEWSBOOKS.

Divan, a collection of short lyrics by *Hāfiz.

Diversions of Purley, "Επεα πτερόεντα or, see
TOOKE, J.

Dives and Pauper, a lengthy prose dialogue
from 1405–10, dealing with poverty and the
Ten Commandments.

Divina Commedia, the greatest work of
*Dante, comprising the *Inferno*, the *Purgatorio*,
and the *Paradiso*, in *terza rima* (lines of eleven
syllables, arranged in groups of three and rhyming a b a b c b c d c).

The *Inferno* is a description of Hell, conceived
as a graduated conical funnel, to the successive
circles of which the various categories of sinners
are assigned. The *Purgatorio* is a description of
Purgatory, a mountain rising in circular ledges,
on which are the various groups of repentant
sinners. At the top of the mountain is the Earthly
Paradise, where Dante encounters Beatrice. In
his visit to Hell and Purgatory, Dante has for
guide the poet *Virgil, and there he sees and
converses with his lost friends or former foes.
The *Paradiso* is a vision of a world of beauty,
light, and song, where the Poet's guide is
Beatrice. The poem is not only an exposition
of the future life, but a work of moral edification, replete with symbolism and allusions based
on Dante's wide knowledge of philosophy,
astronomy, natural science, and history.

Dante's name first occurs in English in
*Chaucer, and that of Beatrice in *Sidney;
Dante was read and admired in the 17th cent. by
*Milton, Jeremy *Taylor, and Sir T. *Browne,
among others. The first acknowledged translation was by the artist Jonathan Richardson in
1719, a blank verse version of the famous Ugolino episode (*Inferno*, Canto 33), which remained a favourite with translators, including T.
*Gray; it was also the subject of one of *Blake's
illustrations. However, Dante was by no means
always highly regarded or even read in the 18th
cent.; Horace *Walpole in a letter to *Mason
(25 June 1782) referred to him as 'extravagant,
absurd, disgusting, in short a Methodist parson
in Bedlam'. His reputation rose in the 19th cent.
with the admiration of *Byron, *Shelley, *Carlyle, and others, and with the enthusiasm of political refugees such as *Foscolo and Gabriele
Rossetti. (See *Dante in English Literature from
Chaucer to Cary*, by Paget Toynbee, 2 vols,
1909.) In the 20th cent. he profoundly influenced T. S. *Eliot; his essay *Dante* (1929) and
the many references and quotations in his poetry
brought Dante to the attention of a new
readership. Eliot particularly praises his universality, his 'visual imagination', and his power
to make 'the spiritual visible'.

Among well known translations are those of
H. F. *Cary (1805–14, blank verse); *Longfellow (1867, blank terzine); P. H. Wicksteed
(1899, prose); H. F. Tozer (1904, prose); G. L.
Bickersteth (1932–55, *terza rima*); L. *Binyon

(1933–43, *terza rima*); J. D. Sinclair (1939–46,
prose); D. L. *Sayers (1949–62, *terza rima*); and
C. H. *Sisson (1980, unrhymed verse). For a
detailed account of Dante's translators, see G. F.
Cunningham, *The Divine Comedy in English*
(2 vols, 1965–6).

Divio, in imprints, Dijon.

Divorce, *The Doctrine and Discipline of*, the first
of *Milton's Divorce Tracts.

DIXON, Richard Watson (1833–1900), educated at Pembroke College, Oxford, where he
became the intimate friend of *Burne-Jones and
W. *Morris, and was closely involved in the
*Pre-Raphaelite movement before marriage and
various preferments distanced him from his early
life. He became a minor canon in Carlisle in
1868 and published, despite difficulties of access
to libraries, an important *History of the Church of
England from the abolition of the Roman jurisdiction*
(1878–1902). His original and striking poetry
found few but discriminating admirers, including *Bridges and G. M. *Hopkins; his correspondence with Hopkins (ed. C. C. Abbott,
1935), covering the years 1878–88, in which
the two poets offer each other support and encouragement, is of great interest. His long narrative poem *Mano* (1883), set in the year AD 999
as the world awaits the Millennium, recounts in
terza rima the adventures of Mano, a Norman
knight, but as a poet Dixon is now better remembered for his shorter pieces ('Dream', 'The
Wizard's Funeral'), reprinted with a memoir by
Bridges in a selection in 1909. See J. Sambrook,
A Poet Hidden (1962).

DNB, see DICTIONARY OF NATIONAL BIOGRAPHY.

Dobbin, Colonel William, a character in
Thackeray's *Vanity Fair*.

DOBELL, Sydney Thompson (1824–74),
published in 1850 *The Roman*, a dramatic poem
inspired by sympathy with oppressed Italy
which had some success, and in 1854 *Balder*, one
of the most extreme productions of the *Spasmodic school. This lengthy dramatic poem, of
which only the first part was completed, describes the inner turmoil and aspirations of a
young poet, who has taken his bride and baby
daughter to live in 'a tower gloomy and ruinous'
while he plans his great work. His search for the
ultimate experience of death is rewarded by the
death of his baby in mysterious circumstances;
his wife Amy goes mad; and finally, unable to
witness her sufferings, Balder kills her. Balder's
destructive egoism so shocked readers that Dobell prefaced a second edition with an explanation, claiming that his hero was not held
up for admiration, but as a warning. Balder's
lines 'Ah! Ah! Ah! | Ah! Ah! Ah! Ah! Ah! Ah!
Ah! Ah! Ah! Ah!' demonstrate the violent in-
coherence of which the school was capable, and
which was so ridiculed by *Aytoun, but the

poem nevertheless contains some notable lyric passages. In 1855 Dobell published (jointly with Alexander *Smith) *Sonnets on the War* and in 1856 *England in Time of War*, which contains the ballad with the refrain 'O Keith of Ravelston' ('A Nuptial Eve'), much admired by D. G. *Rossetti.

DOBSON, Henry Austin (1840–1921), educated at Beaumaris Grammar School and at Strasbourg, entered the Board of Trade, where he served from 1856 to 1901, with *Gosse as close friend and colleague. He was an accomplished writer of verse of the lighter kind, with a particular fondness for French forms such as the triolet and the rondeau; many of his best-known poems evoke the courtly elegance of French society of the 18th cent. as portrayed, notably, by *Watteau. His collections include *Vignettes in Rhyme* (1873), *Proverbs in Porcelain* (1877), and *At the Sign of the Lyre* (1885). His knowledge of the 18th cent. was also displayed in prose biographies of *Hogarth (1879), *Steele (1886), *Goldsmith (1888), Horace *Walpole (1890), S. *Richardson (1902), and F. *Burney (1903). Under the title of *Four Frenchwomen* (1890) he published essays on Charlotte Corday, Mme Roland, the Princesse de Lamballe, and Mme de Genlis. He also published three series of *Eighteenth Century Vignettes* (1892–4–6), besides several volumes of collected essays. See *Austin Dobson* (1928) by Alban Dobson, with essays by Gosse and *Saintsbury.

Doctor, etc., The, a miscellany by R. *Southey, published 1834–47 (7 vols).

It consists of a series of essays and observations on a great variety of subjects, reflecting Southey's wide range of reading and interests. It differs from a commonplace book in that the articles are connected, somewhat loosely, by the story of an imaginary Dr Dove of Doncaster and his horse Nobs. It is an original and often humorous work, which was never finished, and is chiefly renowned for containing the nursery story of 'The Three Bears'.

Doctor Angelicus, *Aquinas; **Invincibilis,** *Ockham; **Irrefragabilis,** Alexander of *Hales; **Mirabilis,** Roger *Bacon; **Subtilis,** *Duns Scotus; **Universalis,** *Albertus Magnus.

Dr Faustus, *The tragical history of,* a drama in blank verse and prose by *Marlowe, published 1604 and, in a radically different version known as the 'B-text', 1616. The earliest known performance was by the Lord Admiral's men in 1594. It is perhaps the first dramatization of the medieval legend of a man who sold his soul to the Devil, and who became identified with a Dr Faustus, a necromancer of the 16th cent. The legend appeared in the *Faustbuch*, first published at Frankfurt in 1587, and was translated into English as *The historie of the damnable life, and deserved death of Doctor John Faustus*. Marlowe's play follows this translation in the general outline of the story, though not in the conception of the principal character, who from a mere magician becomes, under the poet's hand, a man athirst for infinite power, ambitious to be 'great Emperor of the world'.

Faustus, weary of the sciences, turns to magic and calls up Mephistopheles, with whom he makes a compact to surrender his soul to the Devil in return for 24 years of life; during these Mephistopheles shall attend on him and give him whatsoever he demands. Then follows a number of scenes in which the compact is executed, notable among them the calling up of Helen of Troy, where Faustus addresses Helen in the well-known line: 'Was this the face that launched a thousand ships . . . ' The anguish of mind of Faustus as the hour for the surrender of his soul draws near is poignantly depicted. Both in its end and in the general conception of the character of Faustus, the play thus differs greatly from the *Faust* of *Goethe.

Doctor Fell, see FELL.

Dr Syntax, see COMBE, W.

Doctor Thorne, a novel by A. *Trollope, published 1858, the third of the *'Barsetshire' series.

Dr Thorne's brother seduced the sister of a Greshambury stonemason, Roger Scatcherd, and was killed by him. Dr Thorne adopts the child of this liaison, hushes up the circumstances of her birth, and introduces her to the best local circles. There she meets and falls in love with Frank Gresham, heir to the Greshambury estate. The estate is heavily mortgaged, and the leading creditor happens to be Sir Roger Scatcherd, the former stonemason, who has now served his prison term, married, and made money as a railway contractor. It seems incumbent upon Frank to marry wealth, and release the property from embarrassment, and he half-heartedly sets about courting Miss Dunstable, whose money rests in patent medicine. Sir Roger Scatcherd dies of drink and his dissipated son Louis almost immediately follows him, leaving the Scatcherd fortunes without an heir. Thorne reveals Mary's true identity and, as Scatcherd's next of kin, she inherits. The marriage with Frank can now proceed, and Frank's maternal relatives, the de Courcys, gloss over Mary's illegitimacy, especially since one of their number, the Lady Amelia, has recently married an obsequious lawyer. The temporizing of the grandiloquent de Courcys in the marriage-mart forms the secondary plot of the novel.

The plot of *Doctor Thorne* was suggested to the author by his brother, T. A. Trollope.

DODD, William (1729–77), a popular preacher and the king's chaplain whose extravagance and debts led him to forge a bond in the name of his former pupil, the 5th Lord Chesterfield. Despite the efforts of Dr *Johnson and others, he was convicted and hanged. His many works include *The Beauties of Shakespeare* (1752) and *Thoughts in Prison* (1777).

DODDRIDGE, Philip (1702–51), a Nonconformist divine, was a celebrated hymnwriter and author of *The Rise and Progress of Religion in the Soul* (1745), a much reprinted work notable for its literary as well as its devotional quality. He also published in 1747 *Some Remarkable Passages in the Life of Col. James Gardiner*, the reformed rake and colonel of dragoons (1688–1745) who became a religious enthusiast, was killed at Prestonpans, and figures in Scott's *Waverley*.

DODGSON, Charles Lutwidge (1832–98), celebrated under his pseudonym Lewis Carroll, the third in a family of eleven children of considerable literary and artistic interests; they produced family magazines which display Dodgson's love of parody, acrostics, and other word games and puzzles; he was later to invent many educational board games. He was educated at Rugby and Christ Church, Oxford, where he became a lecturer in mathematics in 1855. His most famous work, *Alice's Adventures in Wonderland* (1865) originated in a boat trip with the young daughters of H. G. *Liddell, Lorina, Alice, and Edith; it was for Alice that he expanded an impromptu story into book form. *Through the Looking-Glass and What Alice Found There* followed in 1871: both volumes were illustrated by *Tenniel. One reviewer attributed the success of these works to the fact that, unlike most children's books of the period, they had no moral and did not teach anything. Dodgson's other works include *Phantasmagoria and other poems* (1869), *The Hunting of the Snark* (1876), and *Sylvie and Bruno* (1889, vol. 2, 1893, both parts expanded from a short story, 'Bruno's Revenge', published in *Aunt Judy's Magazine*, 1867). The most valuable of his various mathematical treatises is his light-hearted defence of Euclid, *Euclid and His Modern Rivals* (1879). Dodgson was also a keen amateur photographer, with a particular interest in photographing little girls, whose friendship he valued highly; he also took some striking portraits of the sons of his friend *Tennyson. His diaries were edited by R. L. Green (2 vols, 1953), his letters by M. N. Cohen with R. L. Green (2 vols, 1979), and there is a life by Anne Clark (1979).

DODINGTON, George Bubb (1691–1762), a time-serving politician who attained high office and a peerage (as Baron Melcombe) was author of a Diary, published posthumously in 1784, which throws much light on the venal politics of his day. It was edited in 1965 in 2 vols by J. Carswell and L. A. Dralle as *The Political Journal of George Bubb Dodington*.

Dodington was also a patron of the arts, and in particular of James *Thomson, E. *Young, and H. *Fielding, who dedicated *Jonathan Wild* to him: in this guise he may be the *Bufo of Pope's satire. He also appears in a poem by R. *Browning (*Parleyings with Certain People*, 1887).

Dods, Meg, in Scott's *St Ronan's Well*, the landlady of the Cleikum Inn.

DODSLEY, Robert (1703–64), wrote several poems while a footman in the service of the Hon. Mrs Lowther, including *Servitude* (anon., 1729) and *The Muse in Livery: or the footman's miscellany* (1732). He was encouraged by his employer and other fashionable patrons, and in 1735 set up as a bookseller (with assistance from *Pope) at 'Tully's Head' in Pall Mall; his brother James (1724–97) became a partner and eventually succeeded him. He wrote several plays, including a tragedy, *Cleone* (1758), a musical play, *The Blind Beggar of Bethnal Green* (1741), and *The Toyshop, a dramatic Satire* (1735). But he is chiefly remembered as the publisher of works by Pope, Dr *Johnson, E. *Young, *Goldsmith, T. *Gray, *Akenside, and *Shenstone and of the *Select Collection of Old Plays* (12 vols, 1744) and *A collection of poems, by several hands* (1748–58, revised and continued by Pearch, 1775). His *Collection* in particular was a classic and influential statement of mid-18th-cent. taste. In 1758 he founded, in conjunction with *Burke, *The Annual Register*. He also has the credit of having suggested the compiling of a dictionary to Dr Johnson. See R. Strauss, *Dodsley: poet, publisher and playwright* (1910).

Dodson and Fogg, in Dickens's *Pickwick Papers*, Mrs Bardell's attorneys.

Doeg, Dryden's name for *Settle in *The Second Part of *Absalom and Achitophel*.

Dogberry and Verges, in Shakespeare's *Much Ado about Nothing*, constables. Dogberry is a precursor of Mrs *Malaprop in his gift for misapplying words.

Doggerel, comic or burlesque, or trivial, mean, or irregular verse. The derivation is unknown, but cf. DOG-LATIN [*OED*].

DOGGETT, Thomas (c.1670–1721), Dublin-born comic actor, joint manager of the Haymarket, and subsequently of Drury Lane Theatre, and friend of *Congreve and C. *Cibber.

Dog-Latin, bad unidiomatic Latin ' "Nescio quid est materia cum me", Sterne writes to one of his friends (in dog-Latin, and very sad dog-Latin too)'; *Thackeray, *The English Humorists of the Eighteenth Century*, vi. Cf. DOGGEREL.

Dolabella, a character in Shakespeare's *Antony and Cleopatra*, and in Dryden's *All for Love*.

Dol Common, one of the cheaters in Jonson's *The Alchemist*.

Doll Tearsheet, Falstaff's tavern mistress in Shakespeare's 2 *Henry IV*.

Dolly Dialogues, The, see HAWKINS, A. H.

Dolly Varden, a character in Dickens's *Barnaby Rudge*.

Dolon, in Spenser's *Faerie Queene* (v. vi), 'A man of subtill wit and wicked minde', who tries to entrap *Britomart.

'Dolores', a poem in anapaests by *Swinburne, included in *Poems and Ballads* (1866).

One of his most notorious works, it addresses Dolores, 'Our Lady of Pain', in a profane hymn to perverse and cruel sensual delights, and contains some of his most parodied lines, e.g. 'the lilies and languors of virtue' and 'the raptures and roses of vice'. It clearly shows Swinburne's obsession with erotic pain and the image of a 'splendid and sterile' *femme fatale*, and, with other poems in the volume ('Faustine', 'Anactoria', 'Les Noyades', 'Laus Veneris', etc.), understandably provoked violent abuse. It was also much admired by many, including *Ruskin, who is said to have exclaimed during a recitation 'How beautiful! How divinely beautiful!'

Dolorous Stroke, The, the stroke dealt by *Balyn to King Pellam in Bk II of Malory's *Morte D'Arthur* (in 'The Knight with the two Swords', the second book in the first of the *Works* in Vinaver's edition). It causes the devastation of three kingdoms and the deaths of the people in Pellam's castle, and Merlin prophesies that its disastrous effect will only be cured by the achievement of the Grail by *Galahad. Merlin links in an obscure way this slight narrative event with the whole decline of the world of Arthur, and the story is the starting point of the anthropological investigation in J. L. Weston's *From Ritual to Romance* (1920).

Dombey and Son, *Dealings with the Firm of,* a novel by *Dickens, published 1847–8.

When the story opens Mr Dombey, the rich, proud, frigid head of the shipping house of Dombey and Son, has just been presented with a son and heir, Paul, and his wife dies. The father's love and ambition are centred in the boy, an odd, delicate, prematurely old child, who is sent to Dr Blimber's school, under whose strenuous discipline he sickens and dies; the death of the little Dombey moved the nation nearly as much as the death of Little Nell in *The Old Curiosity Shop*, though later chapters were seen by many as a disappointment. Dombey neglects his devoted daughter Florence, and the estrangement is increased by the death of her brother. Walter Gay, a good–hearted youth in Dombey's employment, falls in love with her, but is sent to the West Indies by Dombey, who

disapproves of their relationship. He is shipwrecked and believed drowned. Dombey marries again—a proud and penniless young widow, Edith Granger, but his arrogant treatment drives her into the arms of his villainous manager Carker, with whom she flies to France. They are pursued, Carker meets Dombey in a railway station, falls in front of a train, and is killed. (As Humphry House points out in *The Dickens World*, 1941, the effect of the railways on English life and the changing landscape is a dominant theme in the novel.) The house of Dombey fails; Dombey has lost his fortune, his son, and his wife; Florence has been driven by ill-treatment to fly from him, and has married Walter Gay, who has survived his shipwreck. Thoroughly humbled, Dombey lives in desolate solitude till Florence returns to him, and at last finds the way to his heart.

Among the other notable characters in the book are Solomon Gills, the nautical instrument-maker and uncle of Gay, and his friend Cuttle, the genial old sea-captain; Susan Nipper, Florence's devoted servant; Toots, the innocent and humble admirer of Florence; Joe Bagstock, the gouty retired Major; and 'Cousin Feenix', the good-natured aristocrat.

Domesday Book, 'the Book of the day of assessment', is the name applied since the 12th cent. to the record of the great inquest or survey of the lands of England made by order of William the Conqueror in 1086. It contains a record of the ownership, area, and value of lands, and of the numbers of tenants, livestock, etc. The manuscript is in the Public Record Office in London.

DOMETT, Alfred (1811–87), is remembered as a friend of R. *Browning, who lamented his departure for New Zealand in 1842 in 'Waring'. Domett remained in New Zealand until 1871, and was prime minister there for a brief period; on his return Browning encouraged the publication of his long poem about Maori life, *Ranolf and Amohia, a South-Sea day dream* (1872). Their correspondence was edited in 1906 by F. G. Kenyon.

Dominic, Father, a character in Dryden's *The Spanish Fryar*.

Don, Arabella, a character in Hardy's *Jude the Obscure*.

DONATUS, Aelius (4th cent. AD), a grammarian who taught at Rome and had St *Jerome among his pupils. He was the author of a Latin grammar, *Ars Grammatica*, known as the 'Donet' or 'Donat', which has served as the basis of later works. A 'Donet' is hence used for an introduction to, or the elements of, any art or science. It is mentioned in *Piers Plowman*, A, v. 123, and other early English works.

Don Carlos, a tragedy by *Otway, in rhymed verse, produced 1676.

Philip II, king of Spain, having married Elizabeth of Valois, who had been affianced to his son Don Carlos, is stirred to jealousy by their mutual affection. This jealousy is inflamed by the machinations of Ruy Gomez and his wife the duchess of Eboli, till he believes in their guilty relations; he causes the queen to be poisoned and Don Carlos takes his own life, the king discovering too late their innocence.

DONIZETTI, Gaetano (1797–1848), Italian composer and, with *Rossini and *Bellini, one of the creators of the Italian operatic style of the 19th cent. Sir W. *Scott and *Byron are the two English authors represented on Donizetti's list of 68 operas, both figures dear to the heart of 19th-cent. *Romanticism, and both regularly pillaged by composers in search of subjects for operatic treatment; often with scant respect for the original: in *Parisina* (1833) the main events of Byron's poem are fairly used as a framework for Felice Romani's libretto, but in *Marino Faliero* (1835) the primary source is a play by the French author Casimir Delavigne and only the secondary Byron's tragedy. In the case of *Il diluvio universale* (1830) the connection with Byron's biblical verse drama *Heaven and Earth* (1822) is even more remote, as it is with Scott in *Elisabetta, o il Castello di Kenilworth* (1829), where the original novel had already been filtered through two French stage adaptations, *Hugo's *Amy Robsart* and Scribe's *Leicester* (itself written as a libretto for Auber). But *Lucia di Lammermoor* (1835) is a different matter. The plot, though—or perhaps because—ruthlessly pruned (Cammarano cut all but six of the novel's thirty characters, including a promising operatic villain in Lucy's mother), remains a strong version of one of Scott's most dramatic stories, and Donizetti, though making some concessions to the operatic conventions of his day, treated it with passion and considerable insight. *Lucia,* which at once became extremely popular, has come to be regarded as the archetype of Italian Romantic opera, and must certainly be accounted the best of all operas on a subject from Scott.

DON JOHN OF AUSTRIA, see JOHN OF AUSTRIA.

Don Juan, according to a Spanish story apparently first dramatized by Gabriel *Téllez (who wrote under the name 'Tirso da Molina') in *El burlador de Sevilla,* and subsequently by *Molière in *Le Festin de pierre* and in *Mozart's *Don Giovanni,* was Don Juan Tenorio, of Seville. Having attempted to ravish Doña Anna, the daughter of the commander of Seville, he is surprised by the father, whom he kills in a duel. A statue of the commander is erected over his tomb. Juan and his cowardly servant Leporello visit the tomb, when the statue is seen to move its head. Juan jestingly invites it to a banquet. The statue comes, seizes Juan, and delivers him to devils. Don Juan is the proverbial heartless and impious seducer. His injured wife is Elvira.

Don Juan is also the subject of plays by *Shadwell (*The Libertine*), *Goldoni, *Pushkin, and *Montherlant, and of a poem by *Byron (see below). For R. *Browning's Don Juan see FIFINE AT THE FAIR, and for *Shaw's see MAN AND SUPERMAN. Molière's version was translated by Christopher Hampton (pub. 1974). *The Joker of Seville* (pub. 1978) by *Walcott is an adaptation of *El Burlador de Sevilla,* based on R. *Campbell's blank verse translation.

Don Juan, an unfinished epic satire in *ottava rima* by Lord *Byron, published 1819–24.

Don Juan, a young gentleman of Seville, is sent abroad by his mother at the age of 16, in disgrace after an intrigue. His ship is wrecked and the passengers take to the long-boat. After many tribulations, in the course of which first Juan's spaniel and then his tutor are eaten by the crew, Juan is cast up on a Greek island. He is restored to life by Haidée, the daughter of a Greek pirate, and the pair fall in love. The father, who is supposed dead, returns, finds the lovers together, and captures the fighting Juan, who is put in chains on one of the pirate's ships. He is then sold as a slave in Constantinople to a sultana who has fallen in love with him. He arouses her jealousy and is threatened with death, but escapes to the Russian army, which is besieging Ismail. Because of his gallant conduct he is sent with dispatches to St Petersburg, where he attracts the favour of the Empress Catherine, who sends him on a political mission to England. The last cantos (the 'English cantos') of the unfinished work are taken up with a satirical description of social conditions in England and with the love affairs of Juan.

With *Beppo Byron had found in *ottava rima* a new form for his new voice, and he adopted it for *Don Juan.* He told his publisher, John *Murray, 'I *have* no plan . . . the Soul of such writing is its licence . . .', but he did undoubtedly intend a longer work than the one which was cut short by his death, after 16 cantos and a fragment of a 17th. He wished the poem to be 'a little quietly facetious upon everything'. Almost every serious passage is abruptly punctured; as *Hazlitt wrote, after the 'intoxication' comes 'the splashing of the soda–water'. The outspoken wit and satire are especially directed at hypocrisy in all its forms, at social and sexual conventions, and at sentimentality. There are many attacks on the objects of Byron's scorn, among them *Southey, *Coleridge, *Wordsworth, *Wellington, Lord Londonderry, and many others. The poet told Lady *Blessington in 1823 that 'there are but two sentiments to which I am constant—a strong love of liberty, and a detestation of cant.'

Both sentiments receive full expression in the poem.

Don Juan himself is a charming, handsome young man, who delights in succumbing to the beautiful women he meets, but his character is little more than the connecting thread in a long social comedy, a poetical novel, of satirical fervour and wit. The first two cantos were ill-received by the critics, who called them 'an insult and an outrage' and 'a filthy and impious poem', but the work became increasingly successful with the general public and was much admired by *Goethe, who translated a part of it.

DONLEAVY, J(ames) P(atrick) (1926–), novelist, born in Brooklyn of Irish parents, educated at Trinity College, Dublin, and an Irish citizen since 1967. He is best known for *The Ginger Man* (1955), a comic and bawdy account, much influenced by *Joyce, of Sebastian Dangerfield's adventures as a law student in Dublin. His other works include *A Singular Man* (1964), *The Beastly Beatitudes of Balthazar B* (1968), and *The Destinies of Darcy Dancer, Gentleman* (1977), all novels, and several plays, including *Fairy Tales of New York* (1960) and various stage adaptations of his own novels.

DONNE, John (1572–1631), related on his mother's side to Sir T. *More, was born into a devout Catholic family, his uncle Jasper Heywood being the leader of the Jesuit mission in England. His father, a prominent member of the London Ironmongers' Company, died when Donne was four, and six months later his mother married a Catholic physician, Dr John Syminges. Educated at home by Catholic tutors, Donne went at the age of 11 to Hart Hall, Oxford (now Hertford College), favoured by Catholics because it had no chapel, so that recusancy attracted less notice. He may later have transferred to Cambridge, but his religion debarred him from taking a degree in either university. In 1589–91 he may have travelled on the Continent, to Italy and Spain, but little is known of his adolescence before his admission as a law student to Lincoln's Inn from Thavies Inn in May 1592. In 1593 his younger brother Henry died in prison after being arrested for harbouring a Catholic priest. Somewhere about this time Donne apparently renounced his Catholic faith. He was one of the gentlemen volunteers who sailed with *Essex to sack Cadiz (1596) and with *Ralegh to hunt the Spanish treasure ships off the Azores (1597). His poems 'The Storm' and 'The Calm' commemorate these voyages. His comrades-in-arms included Thomas, elder son of Sir Thomas Egerton, Lord Keeper of the Great Seal, and through his influence Donne became Egerton's secretary. In 1601 he was elected MP for Brackley, Northants, an Egerton seat. He forfeited his chance of a civil career,

however, when late in 1601 he secretly married Ann More, Lady Egerton's niece and daughter of a Surrey landowner. He was dismissed from Egerton's service and briefly imprisoned. Donne's next 14 years were marked by fruitless attempts to live down his disgrace and find responsible employment. At first he depended on the charity of friends and of his wife's relations, living with his ever-growing family in a cottage at Mitcham. In 1612 he moved to a London house owned by his patron, Sir Robert Drury of Hawstead, Suffolk, whom he had accompanied on his continental travels. In honour of Sir Robert's dead child Elizabeth, whom Donne had never met, he wrote his extravagant *Anniversaries*. Other friends and patrons in these years were Sir Walter Chute, with whom Donne went to the Continent in 1605–6, Sir Henry Goodyer, probably Donne's closest friend, to whom many of his surviving letters are addressed, Lucy, countess of Bedford, Magdalen Herbert (mother of G. *Herbert), and Sir Robert Ker, Viscount Rochester (later earl of Somerset), to whom Donne offered his services in the infamous Essex divorce case. Despite Ker's good offices, James I persisted in the view that Donne was unfit for confidential employment and urged him to enter the church, which he did in 1615. James made him a chaplain-in-ordinary and forced Cambridge to grant him a DD, much to the anger of the university, where he was regarded as a careerist. In the church Donne became a pluralist, being presented by powerful friends to livings at Keyston, Sevenoaks, and Blunham, and holding in addition the divinity readership at Lincoln's Inn. His wife died in 1617 at the age of 33, after giving birth to their 12th child, and the following year Donne went as chaplain to the earl of Doncaster in his embassy to the German princes. His 'Hymn to Christ at the Author's last going into Germany', full of apprehension of death, was written before this journey. In 1621 Donne successfully courted the favour of the new reigning favourite, the duke of *Buckingham, and procured the deanery of St Paul's. One of the most celebrated preachers of his age, as well as its greatest non-dramatic poet, he died on 31 March 1631, having first, as his earliest biographer I. *Walton records, had his portrait drawn wearing his shroud and standing on a funeral urn, as he would appear when rising from the grave at the Last Judgement.

Donne's earliest poems, his Satires and Elegies, belong to the 1590s. His unfinished satirical epic 'The Progress of the Soul' bears the date 1601, and some at least of his Holy Sonnets were probably written in 1610–11. His 'Songs and Sonnets' are, however, largely impossible to date even approximately. Many of them may well have been written after his marriage. His poems were collected by his son John and published in 1633 (second, enlarged, edn 1635). Of his prose works, *Pseudo-Martyr*, an attack on Catholics who had died for their faith, and an attempt to gain royal favour by encouraging surviving Catholics to take the oath of allegiance to James, was published in 1610; *Ignatius His Conclave*, a scurrilous onslaught on the Jesuits, in 1611. *Biathanatos*, a defence of suicide, to which Donne confessed a 'sickely inclination', was probably written at this time, but its subject matter made it unpublishable until after his death. His *Essays in Divinity* (1651) were composed in preparation for his ordination and the *Devotions* (1624) were assembled in less than a month from notes made during a near-fatal fever. His sermons appeared after his death in three volumes, *LXXX Sermons* (1640), *Fifty Sermons* (1649), and *XXVI Sermons* (1660). These were edited by his son John and based on texts which Donne himself prepared from his rough preaching notes during two periods of rest in the country in 1625 and 1630. See also META-PHYSICAL POETS.

R. C. Bald, *John Donne: A Life* (1970); J. Carey, *John Donne: Life, Mind and Art* (1981); *Elegies and Songs and Sonnets* (ed. H. *Gardner, 1965); *Divine Poems* (ed. H. Gardner, 1952; 2nd edn, 1978); *Satires, Epigrams and Verse Letters* (ed. W. Milgate, 1967); *Epithalamions, Anniversaries and Epicedes* (ed. W. Milgate, 1978); *Paradoxes and Problems* (ed. H. Peters, 1980); *Ignatius His Conclave* (ed. T. S. Healy, SJ, 1969); *Essays in Divinity* (ed. E. M. Simpson, 1952); *Devotions upon Emergent Occasions* (ed. J. Sparrow, 1923); *Sermons* (ed. G. R. Potter and E. M. Simpson, 10 vols, 1953–62). There is no collected edition of Donne's letters, the best available approach to it still being E. *Gosse, *Life and Letters* (2 vols, 1899).

Donnithorne, Arthur, a character in G. Eliot's *Adam Bede*.

Don Quixote de la Mancha, a satirical romance by *Cervantes, published 1605, a second part appearing 1615. Cervantes gave to his work initially the form of a burlesque of the ballads and romances of chivalry (see AMADIS OF GAUL and PALMERIN OF ENGLAND), which were already beginning to lose their popularity. But he soon ceased to write mere burlesque, as the character of his hero developed and deepened, and his work acquired the richness and profundity that have made it one of the most popular classics ever written.

Don Quixote, a poor gentleman of La Mancha, a man of gentle and amiable disposition and otherwise sane, has had his wits disordered by inordinate devotion to the tales of chivalry, and imagines himself called upon to roam the world in search of adventures on his old horse, Rosinante, and accoutred in rusty armour, accompanied by a squire in the shape of the rustic Sancho Panza, a curious mixture of shrewdness

and credulity, whom he lures with the prospect of the governorship of the island of Barataria. Quixote conforms to chivalric tradition by electing a good–looking girl of a neighbouring village as the mistress of his heart, under the style of Dulcinea del Toboso, an honour of which she is entirely unaware. To the disordered imagination of the knight the most commonplace objects assume fearful or romantic forms, and he is consequently involved in the most absurd adventures, as in the famous episode (Pt I, ch. viii) when he tilts at windmills, imagining them to be giants. Finally one of his friends, the bachelor Samson Carrasco, in order to force him to return home, disguises himself as a knight, overthrows Don Quixote, and requires him to abstain for a year from chivalrous exploits. This period Don Quixote resolves to spend as a shepherd, living a pastoral life, but, falling sick on his return to his village, after a few days he dies. The plot also contains several lengthy digressions, including the story of the *Curious Impertinent, and the story of *Cardenio and Lucinda.

After the appearance of the first part of *Don Quixote* in 1605, a continuation was issued by a writer who styled himself Alonso Fernandez de Avellaneda, a forgery which stimulated Cervantes to write his own second part. The book was translated into English as early as 1616, by Thomas Shelton, and in 1700–3 by *Motteux; J. M. Cohen's Penguin Classic version first appeared in 1950. *Don Quixote* supplied the plots of several 17th-cent. English plays, and inspired and continues to inspire innumerable imitations. *Unamuno described Don Quixote and Quixotism as the genius of the Spanish nation, but he has also been adopted by many other countries.

Don Saltero's Coffee House, founded by John Salter, one-time servant of Sir H. *Sloane, about 1690; it stood in Cheyne Walk, Chelsea, and Salter (encouraged by Sloane) turned it into a museum of curios, in which he also operated as barber and tooth-drawer. There is a lively account by *Steele in *The Tatler*, No. 34, 1709, of him as 'a Sage of thin and meagre Countenance'. The coffee house was still in existence when *Carlyle moved into Cheyne Walk in 1834, although it lost its eccentric character after Salter's death *c.*1728.

Don Sebastian, a tragi-comedy by *Dryden, produced 1689, published 1691.

The play is based on the legend that King Sebastian of Portugal survived the battle of Alcazar. He and the princess Almeyda, with whom he is in love, are captured by Muley Moloch, who spares their lives until he discovers that they have secretly married. In love with Almeyda himself, he orders Dorax, a renegade Portuguese nobleman, to execute Sebastian, but Dorax, once Sebastian's favourite, refuses to do so. Muley

Moloch is killed in a revolt, but Sebastian and Almeyda then discover that their marriage is incestuous, and they renounce each other and their thrones. However, they do not renounce the memory of their love, which is subsumed in ecstatic and total submission to the decrees of an inscrutable Providence. Counterpointing this main plot is a notably erotic and earthy sub-plot. The play is Dryden's most complex dramatic treatment of a number of important political, sexual, and religious themes.

Doolittle, Eliza, the flower seller in Shaw's *Pygmalion.*

DOOLITTLE, Hilda (1886–1961), who wrote as 'H.D.', was born in Bethlehem, Pennsylvania, and in 1911 followed her friend *Pound to Europe, where both became leading members of the Imagist movement (see IMAGISM). She married *Aldington in 1913, but the marriage was not a success. Her several volumes of poetry, from her first, *Sea Garden* (1916), to her last, the quasi-epic *Helen in Egypt* (1961), show a deep involvement with classical mythology, a mysticism in part influenced by her Moravian ancestry, a sharp, spare use of natural imagery, and interesting experiments with *vers libre.* She also published several novels, including *Bid Me to Live* (1960), a *roman-à-clef* about her *Bloomsbury years, and *Tribute to Freud* (1965), an account of her analysis by Freud in 1933. See Barbara Guest, *Herself Defined: The Poet H.D. and her World* (1984).

Doomsday Book, see DOMESDAY BOOK.

Dora Spenlow, in Dickens's *David Copperfield,* the hero's 'child-wife'.

Dorax, a character in Dryden's *Don Sebastian.*

DORÉ, (Louis Auguste) Gustave (1832–83), French illustrator and caricaturist, who became well known in London both for his illustrations of the Bible (1866) and for his drawings and engravings of London life, done in 1869–71, which appeared in B. *Jerrold's *London* (1872); they show many aspects of the city, but dwell on the picturesque clutter and squalor of the poorer districts. Doré also did a series of steel engravings for Tennyson's *Idylls of the King* (1868–9), and illustrated Coleridge's *Ancient Mariner* (1875) and the works of *Dante, *Balzac, *Ariosto, *Cervantes, and many others. For many years his works were on permanent exhibition at the Doré Gallery in Bond Street, which opened in 1867. The 'agreeable terror' of his illustrations appealed to generations of children. A life by Jerrold was published in 1891.

Doric, an adjective from Doris, a small district south of Thessaly from which the Dorians, one of the four Greek tribes, were conventionally supposed to have emigrated to the Peloponnese about the 12th cent. BC. Archaeological evidence has failed so far to support this traditional theory, but a people speaking a common dialect (Dorian) was certainly dominant in southern and western Greece in historical times. Since the Dorians were regarded as uncivilized by the Athenians, 'Doric' came to mean 'rustic' in English and was applied particularly to the language of Northumbria and the Lowlands of Scotland, and also to the simplest of the three orders in architecture.

Dorigen, the heroine of 'The Franklin's Tale' in Chaucer's *Canterbury Tales,* 12.

Dorimant, a character in Etherege's *The Man of Mode* based on *Rochester.

Dorothea, St, a Christian martyr who suffered in the persecution under Diocletian (303). Her story forms the subject of *The Virgin Martyr* by Massinger and Dekker.

Dorothea Brooke, the heroine of G. Eliot's *Middlemarch.*

D'ORSAY, Count Alfred Guillaume Gabriel (1801–52), a Frenchman who, coming to London in 1821, soon made himself famous as wit, dandy, and artist. He was adopted by the earl and countess of Blessington. In 1823, with his benefactors, he travelled to Genoa, where he met *Byron and made a rapid pencil sketch of the poet which has survived. In 1827 he married Lady Harriet Gardiner, Lord Blessington's daughter by a former marriage, but a separation took place almost immediately. He was prominent in the society of Gore House, at which Lady *Blessington entertained literary, political, and artistic London.

DORSET, earl of, see SACKVILLE, C., and SACKVILLE, T.

DOS PASSOS, John Roderigo (1896–1970), American novelist, born in Chicago and educated at Harvard, who served in Europe during the First World War as a member of the French ambulance service. His first important novel, *Three Soldiers* (1921), which has war as its subject, was followed by many others, as well as poetry, essays, travel writings, memoirs, and plays, which include *The Garbage Man* (1925); *Airways Inc.* (1929); and *Fortune Heights* (1933), published in 1934 as *Three Plays.* He is chiefly remembered for his novels *Manhattan Transfer* (1925), a collective portrait in hundreds of fictional episodes of life in New York City, and *U.S.A.* (1938), a trilogy composed of *The 42nd Parallel* (1930), *1919* (1932), and *The Big Money* (1936). *U.S.A.* tries to capture, through a diversity of fictional techniques, the variety and intensity of American life in the first decades of the 20th cent.; it presents various interlocking and parallel narratives, against a panoramic collage of real-life events, snatches of newsreel and popular song, advertisements, etc., with a commentary by the author as 'The Camera Eye'.

DOSTOEVSKY, Fyodor Mikhailovich (1821–81), Russian prose writer. Born in Moscow, he studied from 1838 to 1843 at the St Petersburg Engineering Academy. His first published work, a translation of *Balzac's Eugénie Grandet*, appeared in 1844, followed by his first original work, the short story 'Poor Folk' (1846), 'The Double' (1846), 'White Nights' (1848), and other short prose pieces. In April 1849 Dostoevsky was arrested as a member of the socialist Petrashevsky circle. After a macabre mock execution, he was sent to a Siberian penal settlement for four years, to be followed by four years as a private soldier. During his imprisonment he underwent a religious crisis, rejecting the Socialism and progressive ideas of his early years, and replacing them by a belief in the Russian Orthodox Church and the Russian people. His next publication, *The Village of Stepanchikovo*, appeared only in 1859. Then came *Notes from the House of the Dead* (1860–1), based on his period of imprisonment, which, along with the novel *The Insulted and the Injured* (1861), appeared in the journal *Time*, which he founded with his brother Mikhail. In 1862 he travelled abroad, visiting England, France, Germany, and Italy. His views on Western Europe are recorded in *Winter Notes on Summer Impressions* (1863). In London, which he describes as 'Baal', centre of world capitalism, he saw the Crystal Palace of the 1862 World Exhibition, an image he was to use to express the corruption of the modern scientific world in *Notes from Underground* and other works. Another impression reflected in his later work was his horror at the poverty of Whitechapel and the prostitutes of the Haymarket. In London he also visited *Herzen and Bakunin. In 1863 *Time* was suppressed. Dostoevsky made further trips abroad throughout the 1860s. The series of brilliant works which followed, *Notes from Underground* (1864), *Crime and Punishment* (1866), *The Idiot* (1868), *The Devils* (1872), *An Adolescent* (*A Raw Youth*, 1875), and *The Brothers Karamazov* (1880), are those on which his reputation is based. In them Dostoevsky reveals extraordinary powers of character analysis, considers profound religious and political ideas, showing himself to be a significant and powerful thinker, and develops the Russian novel, both through the use of urban settings and by his gift for narrative tension. Among English writers Dostoevsky admired Shakespeare, Sir W. *Scott, *Byron, and in particular *Dickens, who had been known and translated in Russia since around 1838. In his Omsk prison Dostoevsky read *Pickwick Papers* and *David Copperfield*. His letters and notebooks are full of references to Dickens, and they share an interest in such major subjects as the city, children, crime, and the suffering of the innocent.

Notes from the House of the Dead was translated into English in 1881, and many of Dostoevsky's novels appeared in English in the 1880s. R. L. *Stevenson was an early admirer, saying in 1886 of *Crime and Punishment*, 'The greatest book I have read in ten years . . . Many find it dull: Henry James could not finish it: all I can say is, it nearly finished me. It was like having an illness.' Its influence on *Dr *Jekyll and Mr Hyde* (1886) is apparent, but in general the response of late 19th-cent. England to Dostoevsky was cool. The main impact of his work in England followed the appearance of *Baring's *Landmarks in Russian Literature* (1910), *Murry's *Fyodor Dostoevsky* (1916), and above all the translations by C. *Garnett (1912–20). Opposition to Dostoevsky remained strong, however, led by H. *James, *Galsworthy, *Conrad, and D. H. *Lawrence ('I don't like Dostoievsky . . . he is like the rat, slithering along in hate.') During the 20th cent. Dostoevsky has become the Russian writer most widely read and influential in England.

Dotheboys Hall, in Dickens's *Nicholas Nickleby*, the school conducted by Mr Squeers.

Douai Bible, SEE BIBLE, THE ENGLISH.

Double Dealer, The, a comedy by *Congreve, produced 1693, published 1694.

The entire action of the play takes place in Lord Touchwood's house in the three hours after dinner on the night before Mellefont, nephew and prospective heir of Lord Touchwood, is about to marry Cynthia, daughter of Sir Paul Plyant. Lady Touchwood, a passionate and promiscuous woman, is in love with Mellefont; and, because he rejects her advances, she determines to prevent the match and ruin him in Touchwood's esteem. She finds a confederate in Maskwell, the Double Dealer, who has been her lover, pretends to be Mellefont's friend, and aspires to cheat him of Cynthia and get her for himself. He leads Plyant to suspect an intrigue between Mellefont and Lady Plyant, and Touchwood an intrigue between Mellefont and Lady Touchwood; and contrives that Touchwood shall find Mellefont in the latter's chamber. Mellefont is disinherited and Cynthia is to be made over to Maskwell. The plot, however, here goes wrong. Touchwood informs Lady Touchwood of Maskwell's intention to marry Cynthia. This awakens her jealousy. She upbraids Maskwell and is overheard by Touchwood, who now perceives Maskwell's treachery, and defeats his final attempt to carry off Cynthia.

Double Deceit, The, or *The Cure for Jealousy,* a comedy by W. *Popple.

Double Marriage, The, SEE MASSINGER, T.

Doubting Castle, in Bunyan's *Pilgrim's Progress*, the castle of Giant Despair.

DOUCE, Francis (1757–1834), antiquary and book-collector. His *Illustrations of Shakspeare* (1807) was a pioneering assemblage of sources and analogues, and he published a large number of learned articles, but his most lasting achievement was his personal collection of books, manuscripts (including the famous illuminated 'Douce Apocalypse'), and coins, which he bequeathed to the Bodleian Library, Oxford.

DOUGHTY, Charles Montagu (1843–1926), educated at Caius College, Cambridge, is principally remembered for his remarkable record of *Travels in Arabia Deserta*, carried out in 1876–8, first published 1888, republished 1921 with an introduction by T. E. *Lawrence. It is notable for its extraordinary and eccentric style: Doughty disapproved of 'Victorian prose', and mingled his own with Chaucerian and Elizabethan English and Arabic. Attempts to revive interest in his equally eccentric poetry, by invoking comparisons with G. M. *Hopkins, have failed, and his volumes of verse, which include the epic *The Dawn in Britain* (6 vols, 1906), *Adam Cast Forth* (a sacred drama, 1908), and *Mansoul, or the Riddle of the World* (1920), are largely forgotten. A life by D. G. *Hogarth was published in 1928.

Douglas, a romantic tragedy by J. *Home, based on a Scottish ballad, and first performed in Edinburgh in 1756, where it caused violent controversy and protests from those who believed it improper for a minister of the church to write for the stage. *Hume and Adam *Smith supported it; it was a great success, and frequently revived.

Old Norval, a shepherd, brings up the infant son of Douglas, supposed dead by his mother, now Lady Randolph. Young Norval saves Lord Randolph's life, and is reunited with his mother, only to be slain through the machinations of Randolph's heir, Glenalvon; his mother in despair hurls herself (off-stage) from a cliff.

DOUGLAS, Lord Alfred Bruce (1870–1945), poet, and friend of *Wilde, whom he met in 1891, and who addressed to him his letter from prison, *De Profundis*. Douglas translated Wilde's *Salome* from French to English (1894), and published several volumes of verse which show a distinctly minor talent, although his sonnets have had their admirers. He was editor of the *Academy* from 1907 to 1910. He also wrote various defensive accounts of his relationship with Wilde, including *Oscar Wilde and myself* (1914) and the less extreme *Oscar Wilde: a summing up* (1940); his autobiography appeared in 1929. Douglas was much given to litigation, and in 1924 was imprisoned for a libel on W. S. *Churchill. *Bernard Shaw and Alfred Douglas: A Correspondence* (1982, ed. M. Hyde) admirably illustrates Douglas's weaknesses and *Shaw's forebearance.

DOUGLAS, the Black, (1) Sir James Douglas (?1286–1330) who, in 1319, in the days of Robert Bruce and Edward II, invaded England and plundered the towns and villages of the north. He three times destroyed an English garrison in his castle of Douglas, and it is on one of these incidents that Scott bases the story of *Castle Dangerous*. (2) Sir William Douglas, lord of Nithsdale (d. ?1392), illegitimate son of Archibald, third earl of Douglas; (3) for the 'Degenerate Douglas!' addressed in a sonnet by *Wordsworth, see OLD Q.

Douglas, Ellen, heroine of Scott's *Lady of the Lake*.

DOUGLAS, Gawin, or Gavin (?1475–1522), Scottish poet and bishop of Dunkeld, was third son of Archibald, fifth earl of Angus. He wrote an allegorical poem, *The Palice of Honour* (first published ?1553), and *King Hart*, a homiletic allegory (first printed 1786), has also been attributed to him. He was best known for his translation of the *Aeneid* (*Eneados*, with prologues, 1553), the earliest translation of the classics into English, or rather, as he commented (Prologue I, ll. 117–18), into 'Scottis'. He was one of the first to draw the distinction between *Scots and 'Inglis', and unlike many of his contemporaries, he wrote only in the vernacular. Earlier versions of the *Aeneid* and *The Palice of Honour* existed but have disappeared. His works were edited by John Small of Edinburgh in 1874, and his shorter poems by P. J. Bawcutt (1967) who also wrote a critical study (1976). *Pound, among others, admired him, saying that 'he gets more out of Virgil than any other translator', and there is evidence that his version was used by *Surrey and T. *Sackville.

DOUGLAS, George, the pseudonym of George Douglas Brown (1869–1902), the son of an Ayrshire farmer, who was educated at Glasgow University and Balliol College, Oxford. He settled in London where he wrote magazine and boys' fiction, In 1901 he published *The House with the Green Shutters* which received high critical acclaim and was described as 'a masterpiece' by J. B. *Priestley. The work, written from a standpoint of realism in contrast with the sentimental view of Scotland depicted by *'Kailyard School', is set in the village of Barbie and describes the rise of the tyrannical, dullminded John Gourlay who builds his business on his feckless wife's dowry. His house, which becomes the 'passion of his life', gives him a sense of triumph over the village, but his world finally collapses with the failure of his business and the disgrace of his son, and retribution falls. Brown died suddenly the year after the novel's publication, leaving other works unfinished.

DOUGLAS, (George) Norman (1868–1952), novelist and essayist, who spent much of his life abroad, principally in Italy. He is chiefly remembered for his travel books about Capri, Tunisia, and Calabria, published as *Siren Land* (1911), *Fountains in the Sand* (1912), and *Old Calabria* (1915), and for his novel *South Wind* (1917), which celebrates the pleasures of the hedonistic life on the island of Nepenthe. In the 1920s and 1930s he was a well-known figure in the expatriate literary community of Florence, where his account of his quarrel with D. H. *Lawrence, *D. H. Lawrence and Maurice Magnus: a plea for better manners*, was published in 1924. There is a life by M. Holloway (1976).

DOUGLAS, Keith Castellain (1920–44), was educated at Christ's Hospital and Merton College, Oxford, where *Blunden was his tutor. His verses began to appear in periodicals in the 1930s, but the only volume published in his lifetime was *Selected Poems* (1943). He was killed in Normandy, and inevitably is remembered largely as a war poet, whose descriptions of war-time Cairo and desert fighting and whose contemplations of death ('Simplify me when I'm dead') show a rapidly maturing energy and simplicity of diction. His vivid experimental narrative of desert warfare, *Alamein to Zem Zem*, was published posthumously in 1946; his *Collected Poems* appeared in 1951, ed. J. Waller and G. S. Fraser. A selection with an introduction by Ted *Hughes appeared in 1964 and the *Complete Poems* in 1979, edited by Desmond Graham, who published a life in 1974.

Douglas Tragedy, The, a ballad included in Sir W. Scott's *Minstrelsy of the Scottish Border*, the story of the carrying off of Lady Margaret by Lord William Douglas. They are pursued by her father and seven brothers, who fall in the ensuing fight. Douglas dies of his wounds and she does not survive him.

Dousterswivel, Herman, a character in Scott's *The Antiquary*.

Dove Cottage, a short distance from the north-east shore of Grasmere, taken by *Wordsworth and his sister at the end of 1799 when they migrated to the Lakes. They occupied it till the end of 1807.

DOVER, Captain Robert, see COTSWOLD OLIMPICK GAMES.

'Dover Beach', a poem by M. *Arnold.

Doves Press, see PRIVATE PRESSES.

DOW, Alexander (d. 1779), joined the army in India, where he spent much of his life. In 1768 he joined the fashion for *Oriental tales with *Tales . . . of Inatulla of Delhi*, a series of flamboyant and ribald stories which met with some success. In the same year he published *The History of Hindostan*; two dramas, *Zingis* and *Sethona*, followed in 1769 and 1774.

DOWDEN, Edward (1843–1913), educated at Queen's College, Cork, and Trinity College, Dublin, where he became professor of English literature in 1867. He was a noted Shakespearian scholar and made his reputation with the publication of *Shakspere: A Critical Study of His Mind and Art* (1875) which influenced future approaches to Shakespearian biography. This was followed by *Shakspere* (1877), a primer, and editions of single plays. He wrote other volumes of criticism, a life of *Shelley (1887), short biographies of *Southey, R. *Browning, and *Montaigne, and published editions of *Spenser and other English poets.

Dowel (Dobet, Dobest), see PIERS PLOWMAN.

DOWLAND, John (1563–1626), English composer and lutenist, generally considered the greatest of all English song-writers. On failing to receive one of the vacant posts of lutenist to Queen Elizabeth in 1594 he travelled abroad, visiting various German and Italian courts and returning to England in 1597, when he issued *The First Booke of Songes or Ayres of Foure Partes with Tableture for the Lute*, the earliest and most popular book of its kind. Being passed over again for a court post, he went back to Germany and by 1598 was lutenist at the court of Christian IV of Denmark. *The Second Booke of Songs or Ayres* (1600) and *The Third and Last Booke of Songs* (1603) were both published during his absence from London, but by 1606 he was permanently back in England where he brought out a fourth collection of songs, *A Pilgrimes Solace*, in 1612. By now he was famous as a lute composer all over Europe, above all for the widely disseminated song 'Flow, my teares' (1600), later arranged for instruments as the *Lachrymae* pavane and several times referred to in contemporary literature under that title: he was at last appointed lutenist to James I, though he appears to have written little of importance after this date.

A few of the texts set by Dowland are known to be by courtly amateurs like Sir F. *Greville, Sir E. *Dyer, or the earls of *Essex, Cumberland, or Pembroke and there is an occasional poem by *Donne or *Peele. But many more have texts by unknown authors: in the best of them and particularly in the tragic ones like 'In darknesse let mee dwell', 'Sorrow, stay', or 'Flow, my teares', music and words are fused in a singleness of conception that is hard to parallel.

Down with Knavery, see HEY FOR HONESTY.

Dowsabel, an English form of the Latin female name Dulcibella, used generically for a sweetheart.

DOWSON, Ernest Christopher (1867–1900), born in Kent, the son of ailing and impoverished parents. After erratic schooling he went in 1886 to The Queen's College, Oxford, where he read widely and made many friends, including L. P. *Johnson, but left without taking his degree. He assisted with his father's dwindling docking business, and established himself in the London society of *Beardsley, *Le Gallienne, *Wilde, and their friends. He contributed poems to the *Yellow Book, the *Savoy, and the anthologies published by the *Rhymers' Club, and in 1891 met 'Missie', Adelaide Foltinowicz, a girl of twelve, who later became an important symbol of lost love and innocence in his verse. He enjoyed a widely varied literary and social life between drawing-rooms, taverns, and the *Café Royal; his feelings for the Roman Catholic Church, into which he was received c.1891–2, appear to have been as much aesthetic as religious. Both his parents were now suffering from advanced tuberculosis and in 1895 they committed suicide within months of each other. Dowson's stories Dilemmas appeared in 1894, and at about that time he began to move restlessly between London, France, Ireland, and back again, living an ever wilder and more intemperate life. The first of his two books of poetry, Verses (containing his celebrated 'Non Sum Qualis Eram', better known as 'Cynara'), appeared in 1896, and his second, Decorations (half of which consists of his experiments with 'prose poems'), in 1899. His one-act verse play The Pierrot of the Minute was published in 1897.

The poems, which display much variety in stanza and prosody, group themselves chiefly into love poetry, including 'Cynara'; devotional poems, of which 'Nuns of the Perpetual Adoration' and 'Carthusians' are perhaps the most successful; poems of the natural world, such as 'Breton Afternoon'; and above all poems of ennui and world-weariness, such as the well known 'Vitae Summa Brevis' ('They are not long, the days of wine and roses'), 'To One in Bedlam', and several translations and adaptations of *Verlaine. See also ART FOR ART'S SAKE. There is a life by M. Longaker (1944, rev. 1967); see also Ernest Dowson 1888–97: reminiscences (1914) by his friend and fellow poet Victor Plarr.

DOYLE, Arthur Conan (1859–1930), educated at Stoneyhurst and Edinburgh, became a doctor and practised at Southsea, 1882–90. He is chiefly remembered for his widely celebrated creation of the subtle, hawk-eyed amateur detective Sherlock Holmes, whose brilliant solutions to a wide variety of crimes began in A Study in Scarlet (1887), continued through a long line of stories, chiefly in the *Strand Magazine, and were collected in The Adventures of Sherlock Holmes (1892), The Memoirs of Sherlock Holmes (1894), The Hound of the Baskervilles (1902), and other works. His friend and foil, the stolid Dr Watson with whom he shares rooms in Baker Street, attends him throughout most of his adventures. As well as his 'Holmes' stories, Doyle wrote a long series of historical and other romances. Notable among them are Micah Clarke (1889), The White Company (1891), The Exploits of Brigadier Gerard (1896), the first of many 'Gerard' tales, Rodney Stone (1896), and The Lost World (1912), the first of a series of stories dominated by Professor Challenger. In 1902 Doyle wrote an influential pamphlet, 'The War in South Africa', which was much translated; and later many books on public themes, including a long history of the Flanders campaign in the First World War. His one-act play Waterloo provided Sir H. *Irving in 1894 with one of his most successful parts. In 1926 Doyle published his History of Spiritualism, one of several books he wrote on the subject, in which he was greatly interested.

DOYLE, Sir Francis Hastings Charles (1810–88), fellow of All Souls and professor of poetry at Oxford, published several volumes of verse, which include the patriotic military ballads 'The Loss of the Birkenhead' and 'The Private of the Buffs'.

DOYLE, Richard (1824–83), illustrator, the son of the caricaturist John Doyle (1797–1868) and uncle of A. C. *Doyle. He worked for *Punch and designed the cover (with Mr Punch, Toby, and a margin of nymphs, goblins, and satyrs) that lasted from 1844 to 1956. He illustrated chiefly fairy stories, including *Ruskin's The King of the Golden River (1851) and W. *Allingham's In Fairyland (1870), and also some of *Dickens's Christmas Books; and published books of annotated drawings, including The Foreign Tour of Brown, Jones and Robinson (1854), whose comic adventures in England and on the Rhine he had depicted in Punch.

Drab, term used first by C. S. *Lewis (English Literature in the Sixteenth Century, Introduction) to denote poetry and prose of the later medieval period until the early Renaissance: 'a period in which, for good or ill, poetry has little richness either of sound or images'. Although Lewis claimed that the term was not dyslogistic, it has generally been used, by Lewis and by later critics, to characterize works of the Tudor period which are unappealing to a modern ear. Typically, 'Drab' poets wrote in strongly rhythmical verse forms such as *poulter's measure, making use of alliteration and of poetic 'fillers' such as 'eke', and employed few Latinate words. An example from *Tottel's Miscellany illustrates these features:

I know under the grene serpent how he lurkes.
The hammer of the restles forge I wote eke how it wurkes.
I know and can by roate the tale that I would tel:
But oft the wurdes come forth awrie of him that loueth wel.

Yet many so-called 'Drab' writers, such as

*Wyatt, have been much admired in modern times. The Tudor translators of *Seneca's plays were highly regarded by T. S. *Eliot, who edited the Tenne Tragedies in 1927; and many other 'Drab' translations were of crucial importance for the later Renaissance in England, such as Sir T. *Hoby's version of *Castiglione's Il Cortegiano (1561) and A. *Golding's of *Ovid's Metamorphoses (1567).

Dracula, a novel by B. *Stoker, published 1897, the most famous of all tales of vampirism. The story is told through the diaries of a young solicitor, Jonathan Harker, his fiancée Mina, her friend Lucy Westenra, and Dr John Seward, the superintendent of a large lunatic asylum at Purfleet, in Essex. It begins with Harker's journey to Count Dracula's eerie castle in Transylvania, in connection with the Count's purchase of Carfax, an ancient estate adjoining Dr Seward's asylum. After various horrifying experiences as an inmate of the castle, Jonathan makes his way to a ruined chapel, where he finds 50 great wooden boxes filled with earth recently dug from the graveyard of the Draculas, in one of which the Un-Dead Count is lying, gorged with blood. These boxes are shipped from Varna to Whitby and thence to Carfax. Dracula disembarks at Whitby in the shape of a wolf, having dispatched the entire ship's crew en route, and proceeds to vampirize Lucy who, despite multiple blood transfusions and the occult precautions of Dr Seward's old teacher Professor Van Helsing, dies drained of blood but remains Un-Dead until staked through the heart. The rest of the book tells of the attempt to save Mina from Dracula's insidious advances and of the search for the boxes of earth, his only refuge between sunrise and sunset. All but one of these are neutralized with fragments of the Host. The last, with Dracula in it, is followed by Van Helsing and the others back to Transylvania where, after a thrilling chase, the Count is beheaded and stabbed through the heart, at which his body crumbles to dust.

Dracula—tall and thin, with his beaky nose, pointed ears, cruel and sensual features, and 'peculiarly sharp white teeth' protruding over his lips—has been the subject of many films, the most notable being F. W. Murnau's silent Nosferatu (1922) and Tod Browning's early talkie Dracula (1931).

Dragon of Wantley, The, a humorous ballad, probably of the 17th cent., satirizing the old verse romances. It tells of a Yorkshire dragon that devoured children and cattle, and was killed by Moore of Moore Hall. It was included in Percy's *Reliques, which provides the following key: Wantley is Wharncliffe, Yorkshire; Sir Francis Wortley is the dragon, who was in conflict with his parishioners over tithes; Moore is the attorney who takes the parishioners' part.

*Carey's burlesque opera The Dragon of Wantley was performed in 1734.

DRAKE, Sir Francis (?1540–96), circumnavigator and admiral, was born near Tavistock, Devonshire. His early sea career is uncertain, but he was undoubtedly engaged in the Guinea trade with Sir John *Hawkins. He commanded the Judith in Hawkins's ill-fated expedition to San Juan de Ulúa of 1567, and made three voyages to the West Indies in 1570–2. In 1577 he set out in the Pelican (afterwards renamed the Golden Hind) for the river Plate, sailed through the Straits of Magellan, plundered Valparaiso, rounded the Cape of Good Hope, and completed the circumnavigation of the world. He was knighted by Elizabeth on his return in 1581. Under a commission from Elizabeth he plundered Santiago and burnt Vigo in 1585, and took San Domingo and Cartagena. In 1587 he destroyed a Spanish armament in the harbour of Cadiz. Drake, as vice-admiral, commanded one of the divisions of the English fleet against the Armada. He was subsequently associated with Sir John Norris in an expedition which in 1589 plundered Coruña and destroyed much Spanish shipping. Drake died in Jan. 1596 off Portobello in the course of an unsuccessful expedition to the West Indies; Hawkins had died on the same expedition a few weeks earlier. The narratives of some of his expeditions figure in *Hakluyt and *Purchas, and he became the hero of many legends. *Newbolt assimilated Drake's achievements into the public school ideal in his popular poem 'Drake's Drum' (1895).

Dramatic Idyls, a volume of six poems, of medium length, four of them in the same metre, by R. *Browning, published 1879. After the publication of a sequel (below), the collection was called 'Dramatic Idyls, First Series'. The spelling 'Idyl' differentiated the poems from *Tennyson's 'Idylls'. The poems are among the finest of Browning's later period, particularly 'Iván Ivànovitch', a story based on a Russian folk-tale of a woman who threw her children to the wolves in order to save her own life. The collection has a notable unity of tone, and focuses on human behaviour in conditions of extreme stress.

Dramatic Idyls, Second Series, a volume of six poems by R. *Browning, published 1880 and influenced by the success of the 1879 volume (above). Although the collection does not have the unity of the first series, it demonstrates Browning's continuing interest and vitality in the dramatic monologue form, notably 'Clive'.

Dramatic irony, or Tragic irony, a figure of speech in which what is said by the characters in a play has a different and more serious meaning to the audience who are more aware than are the characters concerned of the catastrophe which is either impending or has occurred. As, for example, Duncan's speech in *Macbeth* on arriving at Macbeth's castle, where his murder has already been planned, or Macbeth's 'Fail not our feast' to Banquo when he has arranged Banquo's murder for that same evening.

Dramatic Lyrics, a collection of poems by R. *Browning, published 1842 and No. III of *Bells and Pomegranates*. Browning's publisher, *Moxon, persuaded him to vary the format of the series, which had been intended to consist solely of plays. The collection included some of Browning's best-known poems such as 'My Last Duchess', 'Porphyria's Lover', and 'The Pied Piper of Hamelin'. For Browning's later reclassification of the poems in this collection, see under MEN AND WOMEN.

Dramatic monologue, generally, a poem delivered as though by a single imagined person, frequently but not always to an imagined auditor: the speaker is not to be identified with the poet, but is dramatized, usually ironically, through his or her own words. The tradition of the verse epistle may be seen to have contributed to the development of the dramatic monologue, which found one of its most accomplished exponents in R. *Browning ('My Last Duchess', 1842; 'Caliban upon Setebos', 1864). The form was employed by many 19th- and 20th-cent. poets, including *Tennyson, *Hardy, *Kipling, *Frost, *Pound, and T. S. *Eliot.

Dramatic Romances and Lyrics, a collection of poems by R. *Browning, published 1845 as No. VII of *Bells and Pomegranates*. Many of the poems were revised before publication in consultation with Elizabeth Barrett (*Browning), whom Browning was courting at the time. The collection included some of Browning's best-known poems, such as 'How They Brought the Good News from Ghent to Aix', 'The Lost Leader', and 'The Flight of the Duchess'. For Browning's later re-classification of the poems in this collection, see under MEN AND WOMEN.

Dramatis Personae, a collection of poems by R. *Browning, published 1864, of which a few had been published previously, but most were new. They were marked by Browning's grief after the death of his wife (see BROWNING, E. B.) in 1861, and by his searching examination of the relation of human to divine love, especially as it concerns the nature of belief. A striking unity of theme and structure makes the collection an intermediate stage in Browning's development between *Men and Women and *The Ring and the Book*. Several of the poems are anthology favourites—notably 'Rabbi Ben Ezra' and 'Prospice'—but the heart of the collection are the long dramatic monologues such as 'A

Death in the Desert', 'Caliban upon Setebos', and 'Mr Sludge,"the Medium" '.

DRAPER, Mrs Elizabeth (1744–78), the wife of Daniel Draper (an official of the East India Company), with whom *Sterne fell in love in 1767 and to whom he wrote the *Journal to *Eliza* and *Letters of Yorick to Eliza*.

DRAPER, Ruth (1884–1956), American diseuse. Her dramatic monologues, written by herself, which delighted audiences throughout the English-speaking world, were witty and lively, frequently ironical, sometimes touching, and portrayed women of every age and class. As a young woman she received advice and encouragement from H. *James, who wrote a monologue for her in 1913, featuring a socially ambitious American in London society, but she never performed it, preferring to work with her own material. A collection of her monologues is printed in *The Art of Ruth Draper* (1960) by M. D. Zabel.

Drapier's Letters, The, a series of pamphlets published by *Swift in 1724. The word 'Drapier' = 'Draper'.

A patent had been granted to the duchess of Kendal for supplying copper coins for use in Ireland, and by her had been sold to a certain William Wood for £10,000. The profit on the patent would have been apparently some £25,000. In 1723 the Irish Houses of Parliament voted addresses protesting against the transaction, and Swift took up the cudgels on behalf of the Irish. Writing in the character of a Dublin draper, he published a series of four letters in which he prophesies ruin to the Irish if 'Wood's half-pence' were admitted into circulation, and he addressed a fifth letter of protest, also signed Drapier, to Viscount *Molesworth. The letters produced an immense effect and the government was forced to abandon the project and compensate Wood; Swift was thus established as an Irish national hero. Two more Drapier letters, written at the same period, one addressed to 'Lord Chancellor Middleton' and the other to 'both Houses of Parliament', were published in 1735: for details see the Clarendon edition, H. Davis (1935).

Drawcansir, a character in Buckingham's *The Rehearsal*, parodying Almanzor in Dryden's *The Conquest of Granada*; he appears briefly in the last act in a mock-heroic stage battle, and according to the stage directions, 'kills 'em all on both sides'. *Carlyle, in his history of *Frederick the Great, refers to the 'terrific Drawcansir figures' of the French revolution, 'of enormous whiskerage, unlimited command of gunpowder . . . and even a certain heroism, stage-heroism . . .'

DRAWCANSIR, Sir Alexander, pseudonym

of H. *Fielding, under which he contributed to the *Covent Garden Journal.

DRAYTON, Michael (1563–1631), was born at Hartshill, in Warwickshire. His early life was probably spent in the service of Sir Henry Goodere of Polesworth, whose daughter Anne is generally identified with the lady he was to address as 'Idea'. Little is known of Drayton's personal life, though dedications and epistles reveal his circle to have included such friends as *Stow, *Camden, *Jonson, and W. *Drummond. He died in comparative poverty, but was buried in Westminster Abbey, where Lady Anne Clifford, countess of Dorset, paid for his handsome monument.

He was an extremely prolific writer, producing historical, *topographical, and religious verse, as well as odes, sonnets, and satires. He revised and tinkered with his early work repeatedly, not always to good effect. His earliest work was *The Harmonie of the Church*, paraphrases from the OT and Apocrypha (1591). In 1593 he published *Idea. The Shepheards Garland*, eclogues in the Spenserian manner including praise of Queen Elizabeth (in the Third Eglog) and lament for the death of *Sidney (in the Fourth). Drayton's *Ideas Mirrour*, a sonnet sequence, was published in 1594; in its final version, entitled *Idea* (1619), it included the famous sonnet 'Since there's no help, come let us kiss and part'. His poems on legendary and historical figures began c.1593 with *Peirs Gaveston*, followed by *Matilda* (1594), *Robert, Duke of Normandy* (1596), and *Mortimeriados* (1596), later revised as *The Barrons Warres* (1603). *Englands Heroicall Epistles* (1597) was modelled on *Ovid's *Heroides*; it consists of twelve pairs of verse letters exchanged by lovers from English history, such as Henry II and Fair Rosamond, Edward IV and Jane Shore, Lord Gilford Dudley and Lady Jane Grey. Another Ovidian poem was *Endimion and Phoebe* (1595), a minor source for Keats's *Endymion. Among later works, *The Owle*, an obscure satire, appeared in 1604; *Odes* in 1606. This innovatory collection included 'To the Virginian voyage' and 'To the Cambro-britans and theyr harp', his 'Ballad of Agincourt', which opens with the lines:

Fayre stood the winde for *France*
When we our sailes advaunce.

He later wrote a narrative poem on the same subject, *The Battaile of Agincourt* (1627), which Jonson professed to admire; the same volume also included *The Miseries of Queene Margarite*, *Nimphidia, The Court of Fayrie*, and the interesting epistle to Henry Reynolds 'Of Poets and Poesie'. Drayton's largest project, the great topographical poem on England, *Poly-Olbion*, was completed in 1622, the first part having appeared in 1612. His *Works* have been definitively edited in six volumes by J. W. Hebel, K. Tillotson, and B. H. Newdigate (1931–41, rev. 1961).

'Dream, The', a poem by Lord *Byron, written 1816, describing his long love for his cousin Mary Chaworth and the disaster of his marriage to Annabella Milbanke.

Dream of Gerontius, The, see NEWMAN, J. H.

Dream of John Ball, A, a historical socialist fantasy by W. *Morris, published in *Commonweal*, Nov. 1886–Jan. 1887, in volume form 1888. It takes the form of a dream in which the narrator is carried back to the time of the early stages of the peasants' revolt in 1381; he encounters the 'hedge-priest' John Ball, and in their final night-long dialogue Morris both satirizes the 19th-cent. present and offers hope for a future when men 'shall see things as they verily are' and rise in successful protest against their exploitation.

Dream of the Rood, an Old English poem of 156 lines, found in the 10th-cent. *Vercelli Book, in three parts: a description of the poet's vision of the cross and the address to him by the cross describing the Crucifixion (paralleled in part by the Northumbrian Runic inscriptions on the 8th-cent. *Ruthwell Cross in Dumfriesshire); a homiletic address to the dreamer by the cross; and a declaration of faith and confidence in Heaven by the dreamer himself. There has been much argument about the coherence of the poem; it seems likely that, as it stands, it was composed in one piece, drawing on an earlier cross *prosopopoeia* related to the tradition of riddles in Old English and Latin. The poem is greatly admired for the devotional simplicity of its first, narrative section, and for the ingenious web of imagery upon which it is constructed. There are editions by B. Dickins and A. S. C. Ross (rev. 1963) and M. Swanton (1970).

DREISER, Theodore Herman Albert (1871–1945), American novelist, born in Indiana, the son of a devout Catholic German immigrant father, and brought up in semi-poverty. He left his family at the age of fifteen for Chicago, and after various jobs became a journalist, meanwhile writing his first novel, *Sister Carrie* (1900), a powerful account of a young working girl's rise to the 'tinsel and shine' of worldly success, and of the slow decline of her lover and protector Hurstwood. It was withheld from circulation by its publishers, who were apprehensive about Dreiser's frank and amoral treatment of Carrie's sexuality and ambition, and he continued work as a hack journalist until the greater success of *Jennie Gerhardt* (1911), again a novel of a working girl's betterment through liaisons. This was followed by the first parts of a trilogy about an unscrupulous business magnate, Frank Cowperwood (*The Financier*, 1912; *The Titan*, 1914; *The Stoic* was published posthumously in 1947). *The Genius* (1915) is a study of an artist, with much autobiographical material. *An American Tragedy* (1925) is the story of Clyde Griffiths, son of unworldly, evangelist parents, who escapes from them to what seems to him the vastly more exciting and colourful life of a bell-boy in a Kansas City hotel; he moves to New York State to work in a collar factory, and when his girl friend Roberta becomes pregnant he drowns her, possibly accidentally in the event, though after much anguished premeditation, and is tried and condemned to death. Dreiser's many other works include *Dreiser Looks at Russia* (1928, written after travels in Russia), *Tragic America* (1931), and *America is Worth Saving* (1941), which express the growing faith in Socialism that replaced the nihilistic naturalism and pessimism of his earlier works. Dreiser has frequently been described as a clumsy stylist, with a weak sense of structure; even his supporter and friend H. L. *Mencken thought *Sister Carrie* a poorly balanced narrative, but the power, originality, first-hand observations, and moral independence of his work has ensured him a lasting readership and a serious reputation as an artist. One of his earliest English admirers was Arnold *Bennett, whose review of *Sister Carrie* in the **Academy* was notably more favourable and enlightened than the American reviews.

'**Dreme, The**', see LINDSAY, D.

DREYFUS, Alfred (1859–1935), a captain in the French army, subject of a notorious judicial miscarriage. In 1894 an unsigned official letter, addressed to the German military attaché in Paris and listing a number of documents which were to be sent to him, was purloined from the German embassy and handed to the French ministry of war. The similarity of the handwriting to that of Dreyfus, a Jew who held an appointment at the ministry, led to his arrest, trial, and sentence to imprisonment for life on Devil's Island off the coast of Guiana. In 1896 Colonel Picquart of the Secret Service came upon evidence indicating that the true criminal was a Major Esterhazy. But opposition involving the use of forgery, intimidation, and a violent anti-Semitic press campaign was raised against a retrial. In the course of this controversy *Zola published his famous letter, entitled J'accuse', in the newspaper *L'Aurore* (Jan. 1898), and was condemned in consequence to a year's imprisonment. Dreyfus was pardoned by the government in 1899 after a second trial had reaffirmed his guilt. It was not until 1906 that the second verdict was quashed by the Court of Appeal, and Dreyfus reintegrated into the army. The controversy gave rise to the term *Dreyfusard*, to signify a supporter of the innocence of Dreyfus. Extracts from the papers of Colonel Schwartzkoppen, the German military attaché in Paris at the time, confirming Esterhazy's guilt, appeared in 1930.

DRINKWATER, John (1882–1937), the son of a schoolmaster, became a prolific poet, dramatist, critic, and actor. His first volume of *Poems* appeared in 1903, and his work appeared in all five volumes of **Georgian Poetry*, and was collected in 1933 in *Summer Harvest*. In 1907 he founded the company which later became the Birmingham Repertory Theatre, and he wrote many plays, including *Abraham Lincoln* (1918), *Oliver Cromwell* (1921), *Mary Stuart* (1922), and a successful comedy *Bird in Hand* (1927). He also wrote stories and plays for children, and accomplished much critical work, including histories of literature, and produced critical studies of (among others) W. *Morris, *Swinburne, Lord *Byron, *Cromwell, *Pepys, and Shakespeare. Two volumes of an unfinished autobiography, *Inheritance* and *Discovery*, appeared in 1931 and 1932.

DROESHOUT, Martin (1601–*c*.1650), engraver of the portrait of Shakespeare on the title–page of the First *Folio (1623). *Schoenbaum says: 'How he obtained the commission we do not know—perhaps his fee was as modest as his gifts' (*William Shakespeare: A Documentary Life*, 1975, p.258).

DROLLS, or **DROLL-HUMOURS**, in Commonwealth days when stage plays were forbidden, were farces or comic scenes adapted from existing plays or invented by the actors, produced generally at fairs or in taverns. A few drolls, which are supposed to have been adapted and performed by an actor named Robert Cox, were published in 1655, but most were published after the Restoration by Francis Kirkman in *The Wits, or Sport upon Sport* (two parts, 1662, 1673). 'Bottom the Weaver', which was published separately in 1661, is described on the title page as having been 'often publickely acted by some of his majesties comedieans, and lately, privately, presented by several apprentices for their harmless recreation'. It is not known how many of the other drolls achieved performance.

Dromio, the name of the twin slaves in Shakespeare's **The Comedy of Errors*.

Drugger, Abel, the credulous tobacconist of Jonson's **The Alchemist*. The character was one of *Garrick's most famous parts, and his success prompted Francis Gentleman's *The Tobacconist* (1770), an adaptation in which Drugger becomes the hero.

Druidism, see STUKELEY, W.

DRUMMOND, Henry, see IRVINGITES.

DRUMMOND OF HAWTHORNDEN, William (1585–1649), was born at the manor of Hawthornden near Edinburgh, educated at

Edinburgh University, then travelled in Europe, acquiring a broad education and familiarity with the works of poets in many languages, including *Du Bartas, *Ronsard, *Tasso, and *Marino; he settled on his estate on his return, *c.*1610, where he had an imposing library, and eventually turned to literature himself. His works include pamphlets and verses in the Royalist cause, laments for the early death of his betrothed in 1614/15 (he did not marry until 1632), satires and hymns, and a history of Scotland 1423–1524, first published in 1655. His best-known prose work was *A Cypresse Grove* (1623), a meditation on death. He was a correspondent of *Drayton, and in the winter of 1618/19 was visited by *Jonson, an event recorded in his Conversations, with many of Jonson's often-quoted comments on his fellow poets. Jonson found Drummond's own poetry 'smelled too much of the schools', but some of his shorter pieces show originality and power. Drummond's poems were edited by E. *Phillips in 1656; there is a critical edition by L. E. Kastner (1913), and later studies by A. Joly (1934) and F. R. Fogle (1952).

Drury Lane, London, was so called from the Drury family, who had a large house there from Tudor times. The Theatre Royal, Drury Lane, was originally a cock-pit, converted into a theatre in the time of James I. It was rebuilt by T. *Killigrew (1612–83), to whom Charles II granted a patent in 1662, again by Sir C. *Wren in 1674, and again in 1812, when the reopening was celebrated in *Rejected Addresses. Junius Brutus Booth, *Garrick, Mrs *Siddons, J. P. *Kemble, and *Kean are among the famous actors who have appeared there. In the 19th cent. it was the great house of Christmas pantomimes, and after the Second World War many successful American musicals were staged there including *Oklahoma!* (1947) and *South Pacific* (1951), both by Rodgers and Hammerstein, and *My Fair Lady* (1958, adapted from Shaw's *Pygmalion).

Dryasdust, Dr Jonas, a fictitious character, a prosy antiquarian, to whom Sir W. *Scott addresses the prefaces of some of his novels.

DRYDEN, John (1631–1700), was educated at Westminster School under Busby and at Trinity College, Cambridge. He inherited a small estate, but supported himself mainly by his writing. His first major poem was the *Heroique Stanza's* (1658) on the death of Cromwell: he later celebrated the king's return with *Astraea Redux* and *To His Sacred Majesty.* Other poems were addressed to Sir Robert Howard, whose sister Lady Elizabeth Dryden married in 1663; the earl of *Clarendon, *Charleton, and Lady Castlemaine. He also published a long poem in quatrains, *Annus Mirabilis* (1667), but most of his early writing was for the theatre and included

several rhymed heroic plays, *The Indian Queen* (1664), *The Indian Emperour* (1665), *Tyrannick Love* (1669), and *The Conquest of Granada* in two parts (1670). He also wrote comedies, *The Wild Gallant* (1663), *The Rival Ladies* (1664), *Sir Martin Mar-all* (1667, in collaboration with the duke of *Newcastle), *An Evening's Love* (1668), and a perceptive adaptation of *The Tempest* (1667). He was most original, however, with his tragi-comedies, *Secret Love* (1667), *Marriage à-la-Mode* (1672), *The Assignation* (1672), and a second Shakespeare adaptation, *Troilus and Cressida* (1679). All these plays, together with adaptations of *Paradise Lost,* under the title *The State of Innocence, and the Fall of Man* (1667) and of *Oedipus* (1679, with N. *Lee), reveal Dryden's considerable interest in philosophical and political questions. He became poet laureate in 1668, and historiographer royal in 1670.

Dryden constantly defended his own literary practice. His first major critical work was *Of Dramatick Poesie* (1668). Subsequent essays include *A Defence of an Essay* (1668), Preface to *An Evening's Love* (1671), *Of Heroick Plays* (1672), *Heads of an Answer* (to *Rymer, 1711) and Preface to *Troilus and Cressida* (1679). *Aureng-Zebe* (1675) was his best heroic play. The prologue, however, denounces rhyme in serious drama, and his next play, *All for Love* (1678), was in blank verse. At the same time he reverted to an earlier high evaluation of *Jonson. This flexibility as critic and dramatist left him vulnerable to attack. He was represented as Bayes in *The Rehearsal* (1671) by *Buckingham, and physically assaulted in 1679, possibly at the instigation of *Rochester. But his principal opponent was *Shadwell, whom Dryden ridiculed in *MacFlecknoe* (1682). Other poems in which he develops his critical principles include many notably fluent prologues and epilogues and poems about, or addressed to, fellow-writers and artists, notably Lee, *Roscommon, *Oldham, *Congreve, and *Kneller.

The constitutional crisis of the late 1670s troubled Dryden greatly. Three plays, *The Duke of Guise* (1679, written with Lee), *Mr Limberham* (1679), and *The Spanish Fryar* (1681) and his prologues and epilogues, testify to this His interest in religion also heightened at thi time. He produced his most celebrated satires in the early 1680s, *Absalom and Achitophel* (1681), *The Medall* (1682), and 200 lines for N. *Tate's *The Second Part of Absalom and Ach itophel* (1682), as well as *Religio Laici* (1682) a defence of the Anglican *via media.* However following the accession of James II Dryden be came a Catholic and wrote *The Hind and th Panther* (1687) in support of his new co religionists. At the death of Charles II he at tempted a *pindaric ode, *Threnodia Augustali* (1685), the first of several poems in this form notably *To the Pious Memory . . . of Mrs Ann

Killigrew (1686), *A Song for Saint Cecilia's Day* (1687), 'An Ode, on the death of Mr Henry Purcell' (1696), and *Alexander's Feast* (1697), which was later incorporated into **Fables Ancient and Modern* (1700). Dryden also wrote numerous witty elegant songs for his many plays.

In 1688 he lost both his court offices and returned to the theatre. Two of his late plays, **Don Sebastian* (1689) and **Amphitryon* (1690), are excellent; *Cleomenes* (1692) is intellectually impressive; and only *Love Triumphant* (1694) is a failure; but Dryden was tired of the theatre and turned to the politically less compromising work of translating. His immense and splendid achievements in this field include translations of small pieces from **Theocritus and **Horace, and more substantial passages from **Homer, **Lucretius, **Persius, **Juvenal, **Ovid, **Boccaccio, and **Chaucer, as well as the whole of **Virgil. His version of the *Georgics* is especially magnificent. In all these translations he made frequent but subtle allusions to his Jacobite principles. He also returned to criticism, notably in Preface to the *Sylvae* (1685), **'A Discourse concerning the Original and Progress of Satire' (1693), Dedication to *Examen Poeticum* (1693), and Dedication of the *Aeneis* (1697). His culminating and most impressive achievement both as critic and translator was *Fables Ancient and Modern*, which should be read as a whole, and to which 'The Secular Masque' (1700) is a wise and noble coda. He was buried in Westminster Abbey. (See also RESTORATION.)

Other works by Dryden include:

Plays: *Amboyna* (1673), and two operas, *Albion and Albanius* (1685) and *King Arthur* (1691);

Poems: 'Upon the death of Lord Hastings' (1649), *Britannia Rediviva* (1688), *Eleonora* (1696);

Prose Works: *His Majesty's Declaration Defended* (1681), *Life of Plutarch* (1683), *Vindication of The Duke of Guise* (1683), *Character of St Evrémond* (1692), *Character of Polybius* (1693), *Life of Lucian* (1711), translations of Maimbourg's *The History of the League* (1684), Bouhours' *Life of St Francis Xavier* (1686), Du Fresnoy's *De Arte Graphica* (1695).

The standard complete edition of Dryden's works is that of Sir W. *Scott (18 vols, 1808, with life as vol. 1; rev. edn by *Saintsbury, 18 vols, 1882–93). This is being replaced by The *William Andrews Clark Edition of Dryden's Works*, ed. E. N. Hooker, H. T. Swedenberg Jr, et al. (1956–). Other editions include *Dramatic Works*, ed. M. Summers (6 vols, 1931–2); *Poems*, ed. J. Kinsley (4 vols, 1958), *Of Dramatic Poesy, and other Critical Essays*, ed. G. Watson (2 vols, 1962). See also T. S. *Eliot, *Homage to John Dryden* (1924); C. E. Ward, *The Life of John Dryden* (1961); W. Myers, *Dryden* (1973).

DU BARTAS, Guillaume de Salluste, Seigneur (1544–90), French poet. He published a number of moral epics, including *Judith* (1574, English trans. 1584), but his most famous work was the creation epic *La Semaine* (1578, complete English trans. by *Sylvester, *Devine Weekes and Workes*, 1605). Partly because of his Protestant convictions, he was more influential in England than in France; *Spenser, *Sidney, and *Milton were familiar with his work, either in the original or through translation.

DU BELLAY, Joachim (1522–60), French poet. In 1549 he published *La Deffence et illustration de la langue françoyse*, the manifesto of the *Pléiade, and, in 1549–50, the first French sonnet sequence, *L'Olive*. He spent the years 1553–7 in Rome, and on his return to France published two further sequences, *Les Antiquitez de Rome* and *Les Regrets*, and also a sequence of 15 sonnets which he appended to the *Antiquitez*. *Spenser's versions (as *The Visions of Bellay*) appeared in the *Complaints* of 1591; an earlier form of the *Visions* appeared in the *Theatre for Worldlings* of 1569.

DU BOIS, William Edward Burghardt (1868–1963), black American author, social reformer, and activist, whose many historical and sociological studies include *The Souls of the Black Folk* (1903), a collection of essays which criticizes Booker T. *Washington for being insufficiently militant about black rights. He became increasingly radical and anti-imperial during his long career, and in the year before his death moved to Ghana and became a citizen of that country.

DUBOS, Abbé Jean-Baptiste (1670–1742), diplomat, historian, critic, was perpetual secretary of the *Académie française from 1722 until his death. He was friend of *Bayle, whose philosophical scepticism he found increasingly congenial, and of *Locke, whose *Essay*, in Coste's French translation, he helped to publicize at the beginning of the century. His 'Réflexions critiques sur la poésie et sur la peinture' was published in Paris in 1719 and in an English translation in 1748. For at least fifty years it was the most influential work of its kind in Europe. Among French writers who owed much to it were *Voltaire and later *Taine, while in Britain *Hume followed Dubos closely in his essay 'Of the Standard of Taste' (1757).

Dubos's confessedly eclectic work was a temperate defence of the moderns in the debate between the ancients and the moderns. He grounds his view on a discussion of six main questions: (a) the nature of poetic or pictorial beauty; (b) the relations between beauty and conformity to rules; (c) how the arts influence each other; (d) the qualities needed by great artists; (e) how artistic reputations are established; (f) why some ages seem to be more artistically fertile than others. Dubos argues that the arts are valued for the pleasure they are designed to provide; those best able to judge are not critics, scholars, or fellow artists, but the public, who rely on their inner conviction or sixth sense. The main task of reason is to justify the verdicts already delivered by sentiment, by finding out which features of a work cause pleasure. Genuine sentiment is immune to specious reasoning. Dubos also holds that taste is influenced more by physical than social factors, as can be seen by the effects of age and physiology. Later writers sought to examine Dubos's unanalysed notion of pleasure, and the respective roles of thought and feeling, or reason and sentiment, in the experience, appreciation, and judgement of art.

DUBRIC, or **DUBRICIUS, St** (d. 612), the reputed founder of the bishopric of Llandaff, said by *Geoffrey of Monmouth to have crowned *Arthur king of Britain at Silchester, and to have been archbishop of Caerleon. He is mentioned in Tennyson's *'The Coming of Arthur'.

Duchess of Malfi, The (*The Tragedy of the Dutchesse of Malfy*), by *Webster, written 1612/13, printed 1623. The story is taken from one of *Bandello's novelle, through Painter's *Palace of Pleasure*, and also shows the influence of Sidney's *Arcadia*.

The duchess, a high-spirited and high-minded widow, reveals her love for the honest Antonio, steward at her court, and secretly marries him, despite the warnings of her brothers, Ferdinand, duke of Calabria, and the Cardinal, and immediately after informing them that she has no intention of remarrying. Their resistance appears to be induced by consideration for their high blood, and by, as Ferdinand later asserts, a desire to inherit her property; there is also a strong suggestion of Ferdinand's repressed incestuous desire for her. The brothers place in her employment as a spy the cynical ex-galley-slave Bosola, who betrays her to them; she and Antonio fly and separate. She is captured and is subjected by Ferdinand and Bosola to fearful mental tortures, including the sight of the feigned corpse of her husband and the attendance of a group of madmen; finally she is strangled with two of her children and Cariola, her waiting woman. Retribution overtakes the murderers: Ferdinand goes mad, imagining himself a wolf ('A very pestilent disease . . . they call licanthropia'); the Cardinal is killed by the now remorseful Bosola, and Bosola by Ferdinand. Bosola has already killed Antonio, mistaking him for the Cardinal. The humanity and tenderness of the scenes between the Duchess, Antonio, and their children; the pride and dignity of the Duchess in her suffering ('I am Duchesse of Malfy still'); and individual lines such as the celebrated 'Cover her face: Mine eyes dazell: she di'd yong' have long been admired, but until recently critics have been less happy about the overall structure, the abrupt changes in tone and the bloodbath of the last act; 20th-cent. critics and directors have been more sympathetic towards the satire and the black farce in the play, and there have been many notable revivals, emphasizing T. S. *Eliot's point that Webster's 'verse is essentially dramatic verse, written for the theatre by a man with a very acute sense of the theatre' (1941).

DUCK, Stephen (1705–56), was born in Wiltshire and began his working life as a farm labourer. Almost entirely self-educated, he took to writing verse, and through Lord Macclesfield came to the notice of Queen Caroline, who gave him a pension and made him a yeoman of the guard in 1733. In 1746 he took Holy Orders but drowned himself four years later in a fit of despondency. According to J. *Spence (in a life attached to *Poems on several occasions*, 1736) his early reading consisted largely of *Milton, whose lofty blank verse he feared to emulate, and of the *Spectator*. His best-known poem, *The thresher's labour* (in heroic couplets), is a vividly realistic portrayal of the unremitting toil of the labourer's life, but his less successful works degenerate into conventional pastoral and artificial diction. (See also PRIMITIVISM.)

DUDLEY, Robert, earl of Leicester (?1532–88), courtier and favourite of Queen Elizabeth I. Uncle of Sir P. *Sidney he was a notable patron of writers and poets, including *Spenser. His personal power and ambitions provoked much hatred and a tradition of literary attacks, the most famous of which is Sir W. Scott's *Kenilworth*.

Duenna, The, a comic opera-play by R. B. *Sheridan, produced 1775. The play contains much music, a great deal of which consists of pleasant airs familiar to the audiences of the time.

Don Jerome, an irascible father, is determined his daughter Louisa shall marry a rich Jew, Isaac. Louisa, however, is in love with Antonio, who is far from rich. Jerome discovers that the duenna is acting as an intermediary between Louisa and Antonio, dismisses the duenna, and locks up Louisa. Louisa, disguised as the duenna, escapes from the house, leaving the duenna to take her place. Isaac is duped into marrying the duenna, and inadvertently into bringing Antonio and Louisa together.

Duessa, in Spenser's *Faerie Queene*, the daughter of Deceit and Shame, Falsehood in general, in Bk I signifies in particular the Roman Catholic Church, and in Bk v. ix, Mary Queen of Scots.

DUFFY, Sir Charles Gavan (1816–1903), Irish nationalist and Australian statesman, was born in Monaghan, Ireland, the son of a journalist. He is remembered in a literary connection as having started in 1842, with two barristers, Thomas Osborne Davis and John Dillon, a journal called *The Nation*, for which he gathered a brilliant staff of 'Young Irelanders' and in which he proclaimed the cause of national unity and emancipation. *The Nation* was suppressed on political grounds in 1848–9, then revived, but Duffy, disillusioned, sold it and emigrated to Australia in 1855, rising to political prominence there. His works include *Young Ireland, 1840–50* (1880–3) and *My Life in Two Hemispheres* (1898). He returned to Europe in 1880 and settled at Nice. *Yeats, describing a return visit by Duffy as elder statesman to Ireland, says that 'in all his writings, in which there is so much honesty, so little rancour, there is not one sentence . . . distinguished because of its thought or music', and gives an account of the gap between the two generations of Irish nationalists. (*Autobiographies*, Book 2.)

DUFFY, Maureen Patricia (1933–   ), writer, educated at King's College, London. She has published plays, poetry, and non-fiction (including a life of A. *Behn, *The Passionate Shepherdess*, 1977), but is perhaps best known as a novelist. Her first novel, *That's How It Was* (1962), is a moving autobiographical account of her childhood and of her relationship with her mother, who died of tuberculosis when she was 14. It was followed by several others, some of which deal frankly and with dignity with the subject of homosexuality; they include *The Paradox Players* (1967), *Wounds* (1969), *Capital* (1975), and *Londoners* (1983), a sardonic but poignant view of the writer's lot in the contemporary cosmopolitan bedsitter London of Earl's Court; the sex of the narrator, Al, is left intentionally ambiguous.

DUGDALE, Sir William (1605–86), garter king-at-arms, and author of *The Antiquities of Warwickshire* (1656), a topographical history that set new standards of fullness and accuracy for the genre and inspired, amongst others, A. *Wood. His *Monasticon Anglicanum*, written in collaboration with Roger Dodsworth, an account of the English monastic houses, appeared in 3 vols, 1655–73. In 1658 he published his *History of St Paul's Cathedral*, and in 1662 *The History of the Imbanking and Drayning of divers Fenns and Marshes*, which incidentally gives much information of antiquarian and historical interest. He also wrote *Origines Judicales* (1666), a history of English laws, law-courts, and kindred matters, and *The Baronage of England* (1675–6).

DUJARDIN, Édouard, see SYMBOLISM and STREAM OF CONSCIOUSNESS.

Duke of Milan, The, a tragedy by *Massinger, printed 1623, one of his earliest independent plays and a popular one. It is based on the story of Herod and Marianne as told by Josephus.

Lodovico Sforza, duke of Milan, has, in the war between the Emperor Charles and the king of France, allied himself with the latter. On their defeat, he goes to surrender himself to Charles, but, fearing for his life, leaves a written instruction with his wicked favourite Francisco to put his beloved wife Marcelia to death if he himself is killed. Francisco, seeking to corrupt Marcelia in revenge for the dishonouring of his own sister Eugenia by Sforza, reveals the existence of the warrant to her, but fails to move her chastity and only incenses her against the duke, so that on his return after a reconciliation with Charles she receives him coldly. This, coupled with accusations from various quarters of his wife's intimacy with Francisco, makes the duke suspicious of her. Francisco now tells Sforza that Marcelia made amorous advances to him, which so inflames the duke with anger that he stabs her to death; dying, she reveals the truth, leaving her husband distracted with remorse. Francisco flees, then returns to court disguised as a Jewish doctor, and undertakes to restore Marcelia to life. He is discovered and tortured, but not before he succeeds in poisoning the duke.

Duke's Children, The, a novel by A. *Trollope, published 1880, the last novel in the *'Palliser' series.

The duchess of Omnium encourages Frank Tregear, a young Conservative with little fortune, in his suit to her daughter Lady Mary Palliser, but after the death of the duchess Tregear has no one to plead his cause with the Liberal duke, and the match is broken off. Meanwhile the duke shows mounting concern at the behaviour of his eldest son and heir, Lord Silverbridge. After being sent down from Oxford, Silverbridge immerses himself in London club–life, and becomes well known for his interest in the turf. He becomes part-owner, with the unsavoury Major Tifto, of a racehorse waggishly named 'The Prime Minister', and loses £70,000 betting on its performances in the Derby and St Leger. The duke pays his son's debts and hints that marriage might help him to settle down in life, whereupon Silverbridge admits his involvement with an impoverished cousin of Tregear's, Lady Mabel Grex. Tregear finds a seat in Parliament, finally convincing the duke of his political and personal integrity. The duke sanctions his marriage to Lady Mary, and is prepared to encourage Silverbridge's marriage to Lady Mabel, when he discovers that his son has fallen in love with the brilliant American Isabel Boncassen. Although the duke finds it hard to reconcile himself to the idea of a wedding between a future duke of Omnium and a girl whose family has risen from obscurity in two generations, even though Mr Boncassen is a respected scholar, Silverbridge's determination and Isabel's charm make him give way gracefully in the end.

Dulcinea del Toboso, the name given by

*Don Quixote to the peasant girl Alonza Lorenzo, whom he elects to be mistress of his heart. Hence the English use of the name Dulcinea for a sweetheart.

Dumaine, in Shakespeare's *Love's Labour's Lost,* one of the three lords attending the king of Navarre.

DUMAS, Alexandre (1802–70), French novelist and playwright, known as 'Dumas *père*'. One of the pioneers of the Romantic theatre in France, he achieved great popularity with a series of colourful, swiftly-moving dramas mostly on historical subjects, including: *Henry III et sa cour* (1829), *Antony* (1831, dealing with contemporary social life), *La Tour de Nesle* (1832), and *Kean* (1836, in which the English tragedian is the central character of a comedy). The historical novels on which his reputation now chiefly rests began to appear serially at prodigious speed around 1840. *Les Trois Mousquetaires* (1844–5; see THREE MUSKETEERS, THE), *Vingt ans après* (1845), and *Le Vicomte de Bragelonne* (1848–50), set in the 17th cent., follow the adventures of d'Artagnan, who comes from Gascony to Paris in the reign of Louis XIII to join the king's musketeers, and shares the fortunes and exploits of three of them, Athos, Porthos, and Aramis, over twenty years. The action of other novels is laid against the wars of religion in 16th-cent. France (e.g. *La Reine Margot,* 1845) or the period of the late 18th cent. and the revolution (e.g. *Le Collier de la reine,* 1849–50; *La comtesse de Charny,* 1852–5). His masterpiece of mystery and adventure, *Le Comte de *Monte Cristo* (1844–5), recounts the elaborate vengeance of Edmond Dantès, falsely accused as a Bonapartiste conspirator in 1815, and imprisoned for many years in the Château d'If. Dumas' astonishing energy also found expression in numerous books of travel, 22 volumes of *Mémoires* (1852–5), several children's stories, and a *Grand Dictionnaire de cuisine* (1872, posthumous).

DUMAS, Alexandre (1824–95), known as 'Dumas *fils*', son of the above, French novelist and playwright. His first, and most remarkable, venture into the theatre was *La Dame aux camélias* (1852), a dramatization of his own novel (1848) of the same title. The story of the love, doomed by social disapproval, of the reformed courtesan Marguerite Gautier for the respectable Armand Duval, it held the stage with great success for half a century. Thereafter Dumas *fils* turned to the writing of social-problem dramas, such as *Le Demi-monde* (1855), *Le Fils naturel* (1858), *Les Idées de Madame Aubray* (1867), *L'Etrangère* (1876).

DU MAURIER, Dame Daphne (1907–   ), novelist and granddaughter of George *du Maurier, was born in London and educated in Paris, but many of her popular novels and period romances, including her most famous, *Rebecca* (1938), are set in the West Country where she spent much of her life.

DU MAURIER, George Louis Palmella Busson (1834–96), artist and writer, born in Paris. He spent his childhood there and in London, and became between 1856 and 1860 an art student in Paris and Antwerp. He began to contribute drawings to illustrated editions of Mrs *Gaskell, *Meredith, *Hardy, and H. *James, among others. In 1865 he began to write humorous verse, including 'The History of the Jack Sprats', and a parody of W. *Morris's ballads, 'The Legend of Camelot', with mock *Pre-Raphaelite illustrations. In 1891 he published his first novel, *Peter Ibbetson,* largely based on his early childhood in Paris, and turning on two supernaturally related dreams. His next novel,*Trilby,* for which he is still remembered, appeared in 1894; its vast fame and success continued for many years. *The Martian,* a story based on school life, appeared posthumously in 1897.

Dumbello, Lady, in A. Trollope's *Barsetshire series of novels, the married name of Griselda, daughter of Archdeacon Grantly.

Dumbiedikes, The Laird of, in Scott's *The Heart of Midlothian,* (1) the grasping landlord of the widow Butler and Davie Deans; (2) Jock Dumbie, his son, Jeanie Deans's silent suitor.

Dumb Show, a piece of silent action or stage business, especially in the Elizabethan and Jacobean theatre, where speech is expected but not actually delivered. These shows, such as the one before the play scene in *Hamlet* or Revenge's in *The Spanish Tragedy,* suggest by mime and symbolism what is shortly to take place and its meaning.

DUNBAR, William (?1456–?1513), Scottish poet and priest, was an MA of St Andrews (1479). He was wrecked off Zeeland while carrying out a diplomatic mission for James IV; in 1500 he was awarded a royal pension. He wrote 'The Thrissill and the Rois', his first great poem, in 1503; 'The Dance of the Sevin Deidly Synnis', part of 'Fasternis Evin in Hell', in 1507; and at about the same time 'The Goldyn Targe', the 'Lament for the Makaris', and 'The Tretis of the Tua Mariit Wemen and the Wedo', as well as numerous minor pieces. The poem which opens 'London, thou art of townes A per se' is not now thought to be Dunbar's, but he did write 'To Aberdein', celebrating Queen Margaret Tudor's entry into the town in 1511. He probably fell at the battle of *Flodden; certainly no poems indubitably by him survive from a date later than 1513.

'The Thrissill and the Rois' is a political allegory in rhyme-royal, the Rose representing Margaret Tudor, married to James IV, the

Thistle. The 'Tua Mariit Wemen and the Wedo' (widow), a visionary dialogue in which the three interlocutors relate their experiences of marriage, is a satire on women reminiscent of Chaucer's Wife of Bath's Prologue in the *Canterbury Tales. 'The Goldyn Targe' is an allegory in which the poet, appearing in a dream before the court of Venus, is wounded by the arrows of Beauty in spite of the shield ('targe') of Reason. In 'The Dance of the Sevin Deidly Synnis' the poet in a trance sees the fiend Mahoun call a dance of unshriven outcasts, who are characterized with great vigour. The 'Lament for the Makaris' may also relate to the tradition of the *Dance of Death. It is a powerful elegy for the transitoriness of things, with its refrain '*Timor mortis conturbat me*', and in particular for the deaths of Dunbar's fellow poets, including *Chaucer, *Gower, and *Henryson. Dunbar's satirical energy and Rabelaisian humour are particularly well displayed in 'The Flyting of Dunbar and Kennedie'. See, ed. J. Kinsley, *Poems* (1979); biography by J. W. Baxter (1952); T. Scott, *Dunbar: a critical exposition of the poems* (1966).

Duncan, king of Scotland in Shakespeare's *Macbeth*; murdered in his sleep by Macbeth.

DUNCAN, Robert, see BLACK MOUNTAIN POETS.

Dunciad, The, a mock-heroic satire by *Pope, of which three books were published anonymously in 1728. Its authorship was acknowledged in 1735. The *New Dunciad* was published in 1742, and forms the fourth book of the complete work as it appeared in 1743. The poem had been under preparation for some years and its issue was determined by the criticisms of Pope's edition of Shakespeare contained in *Theobald's *Shakespeare Restored*. Theobald was made the hero of the poem in its earlier form, but in the final edition of 1743 C. *Cibber was enthroned in his stead. The satire is directed against 'Dulness' in general, and in the course of it all the authors who have earned Pope's condemnation are held up to ridicule. But the work is not confined to personal abuse, for literary vices receive their share of exposure. The argument of the poem is as follows.

Bk I. The reign of Dulness is described. Bayes (i.e. Cibber) is shown debating whether he shall betake himself to the church, or gaming, or party-writing, but is carried off by the goddess and anointed king in the place of *Eusden, the poet laureate, who has died.

Bk II. This solemnity is graced by games, in which poets, critics, and booksellers contend. There are races, with various accidents, in which booksellers pursue the phantom of a poet; exercises for the poets; and finally a test for the critics, to decide whether they can hear the works of two authors read aloud without sleep-ing. But presently spectators, critics, and all fall fast asleep.

Bk III. The king, slumbering with his head on the lap of the goddess, is transported to the Elysian shades, where, under the guidance of *Settle, he sees visions of the past and future triumphs of the empire of Dulness, how this shall extend to the theatres and the court, the arts and the sciences.

Bk IV. The realization of these prophecies is described, and the subjugation of the sciences and universities to Dulness, the growth of indolence, the corruption of education, and the consummation of all in the restoration of night and chaos.

Dun Cow, Book of the, an Irish manuscript of the 11th cent. containing mythological romances. A fragment of it survives, containing in particular many of the feats of *Cuchulain.

Dun Cow of Dunsmore, a monstrous animal slain by *Guy of Warwick.

Dun in the Mire, where 'Dun' (originally a dun horse) is a quasi-proper name for any horse, an old Christmas game (also called 'drawing Dun out of the mire'), in which the horse in the mire is represented by a heavy log, and the players compete to lift and carry it off.

If thou art Dun, we'll draw thee from the mire.
    (Shakespeare, *Romeo and Juliet, I. iv. 41)

Dunmow Flitch, according to an ancient custom of the manor of Dunmow in Essex, a side of bacon given to any married couple who after twelve months of marriage could swear that they had maintained perfect harmony and fidelity during that time. The antiquity of the custom is shown by the reference to it in the Prologue to Chaucer's 'Wife of Bath's Tale' (*Canterbury Tales, 6):

The bacoun was nought fet for hem, I trowe,
That some men fecche in Essex at Dunmowe.

The custom is said to have been instituted by Robert Fitz-Walter in 1244 and is still observed.

DUNN, Nell (1936–), novelist and playwright, whose early novels *Up the Junction* (1963) and *Poor Cow* (1967) showed a sensitive ear for working-class dialogue and an uninhibited approach to female sexuality. Her other works include *The Only Child* (1978, a tale of the rich) and *Steaming* (perf. 1981), a comedy with an all-female cast set in a Turkish bath.

DUNNE, J(ohn) W(illiam) (1875–1949), pioneer aircraft designer and author of the widely-read *An Experiment with Time* (1927) and *The Serial Universe* (1934), in which he outlined a theory of time to account for such phenomena as precognition, previsional dreaming, etc. He quotes in support *Wells's *The Time Machine*, but Wells was to reply that Dunne had taken his concept of 'duration as a dimension of space' too seriously. Dunne's concept proved a useful dramatic device to J. B. *Priestley in his 'Time' plays, and is mentioned with interest by G. *Greene (who asks if it is possible for novelists to draw their symbols from the future as well as from the past: see *Ways of Escape*, ch. 3).

DUNSANY, Edward John Moreton Drax Plunkett, 18th Baron (1878–1957), of Anglo-Irish parentage, was associated with the *Irish revival, and a friend of *Yeats, *Gogarty, and Lady *Gregory. His first book of (non-Celtic) mythological tales, *The Gods of Pegana* (1905), was illustrated by S. H. Sime, whose weird *fin-de-siècle* drawings were to accompany many subsequent fantasies, including *The Book of Wonder* (1912) and *The Blessing of Pan* (1927). Dunsany's first play, *The Glittering Gate*, was performed at the *Abbey Theatre in 1909; this and many later plays show the influence of *Maeterlinck's not dissimilar vein of fantasy. His short plays were popular with the Little Theatre movement in America, and his full-length *If* (an *oriental tale) was a success in London in 1921. In more realistic vein, Dunsany wrote the popular 'Jorkens' stories, beginning with *The Travel Tales of Mr Joseph Jorkens* (1931). He also wrote novels, essays, verse, and a series of autobiographies. See Mark Amory, *Lord Dunsany* (1972).

DUNS SCOTUS, John (c.1266 or 1270–1308), the 'Doctor Subtilis', a Scottish Franciscan who entered the order at Dumfries in 1278. He lectured on the *Sententiae* of *Peter Lombard at Oxford, probably 1300–4, and at Paris, probably 1304–5. He was among those expelled from Paris by Philip the Fair in 1305, and he died at Cologne, probably on 8 Nov. 1308. His principal works were his two series of commentaries on the *Sententiae*, the *Reportata Parisiensia* (?1306) and the *Opus Oxoniense* (?1297); most of the reconstruction of his thought is based on the latter. He wrote many other works in his brief lifetime, though many of those attributed to him are, at least in part, of disputed authorship (such as the *De Anima* and the important, advanced *Theoremata*); the uncertainty of the states in which the manuscripts of his work survive, combined with the extreme sophistication of his thought, make detailed understanding of his systematic beliefs very difficult. His principal significance in the history of *Scholasticism is that he drove the first wedge between theology and philosophy (a split which widened throughout the 14th cent.), with his emphasis on the separation (already noted by Thomas *Aquinas) between God as necessary Being from all contingent Beings, and (shifting away from Aquinas) the impossibility of arguing from the latter to the former. Although this emphasis, together with his

associated Augustinian-Franciscan stress on faith and will rather than reason, distinguishes him from the synthesis of Aquinas, he resembles him in the employment of an emphatically *Realist metaphysics in the theory of Essences, and in his incorporation of a good deal of Aristotle into his metaphysics. He was much influenced too by Arabic philosophers, especially *Avicenna, with their emphasis on Being as the metaphysical object. His great significance is that he straddles the dividing-line between 13th-cent. system-building and 14th-cent. scepticism. The word 'dunce', first in the sense of 'a maker of impossibly ingenious distinctions', derives from him (Aquinas was called 'the dumb ox'); some of his formal metaphysical distinctions were referred to by G. M. *Hopkins in his development of a poetic psychology, and it has been argued by John MacQueen that Scotus was an influence on *Langland. His works have been edited by Vives (26 vols, 1891–5).

DUNSTAN, St (c.910–88), born at Glastonbury of a noble family, was educated by Irish scholars there. He became a favourite with King Athelstan, but withdrew from the court in disfavour and stayed with his kinsman Ælfheah (Elphege) who became bishop of Winchester in 934 and who persuaded Dunstan to take monastic vows. He is also said to have practised the arts of metal-working, painting, and transcribing. He was restored to favour by King Edmund who appointed him abbot of Glastonbury (939). He made it a famous school, restoring it spiritually and materially. He was one of the chief advisers of kings Edmund and Eadred (who succeeded in 946); but when King Eadwig succeeded Eadred, he incurred his disfavour (according to a traditional story, by rebuking the king for his lasciviousness with two 'loose women' at his coronation) and retired to Flanders in disgrace in 956. Edgar recalled him and appointed him bishop of Worcester (957), London (959), and Canterbury (960). Dunstan set about restoring and reforming English monasteries (as Ælfric says) and making the Danes an integral part of the nation. He averted civil war by crowning Edward the Martyr in 975, and he foretold to King Ethelred the Unready the calamities which would befall the nation because of Edward's murder. In his last years the onus of the revival was carried by his successors and colleagues, Æthelwold and *Oswald. See D. Knowles, *The Monastic Order in England* (1940); J. A. Robinson, *The Times of St Dunstan* (1923).

DUNTON, John (1659–1733), a publisher and bookseller who between 1691 and 1697 issued the *Athenian Gazette* (afterwards *Athenian Mercury*), dealing with philosophical and scientific matters, and incorporating a quiz in the form of questions sent in by readers. He also wrote many political pamphlets and *The Life and Errors of John Dunton* (1705).

Dupin, the detective in the detective tales of *Poe.

Durandarte, a hero of Spanish legend and ballad, killed at Roncesvalles. See *Don Quixote* (II. xxiii). He is the subject of a ballad by M. G. *Lewis.

D'Urberville, Alec, a character in Hardy's *Tess of the D'Urbervilles.*

Durdles, the stonemason in Dickens's *Edwin Drood.*

DÜRER, Albrecht (1471–1528), German painter and engraver, the son of a Hungarian goldsmith who had settled in Nuremberg. His close friendship with the great humanist scholar Willibald Pirkheimer stimulated his interest in the new learning of the Renaissance; he made two journeys to Italy and introduced to the north the ideals and forms which he encountered there. He wrote treatises on proportion and artistic theory, as well as a diary of a visit to the Netherlands. His woodcuts include the *Apocalypse* (1498); his most famous engravings—and those which have fascinated literary men—are *Knight, Death and the Devil* (1513) and *Melencolia* (1514). Panofsky, in his classic analysis of its iconography, has described the *Melencolia* as 'a spiritual self-portrait'. In 1636 Arundel, a passionate collector of Dürer, bought the Pirkheimer library with many books illuminated by the artist. The northern Renaissance roused little enthusiasm in 18th-cent. England, but interest revived in the 19th cent.; James *Thomson's *City of Dreadful Night* contains a long description of the *Melencolia.* Both *Ruskin and G. *Eliot admired Dürer; Ruskin tended to prefer *Holbein's realism, but was fascinated by Dürer's melancholy, and in *Modern Painters* drew an interesting comparison between Dürer and *Rosa. T. *Mann's *Dr Faustus* draws much of its imagery from Dürer's works. See E. Panofsky, *The Life and Art of Albrecht Dürer* (1943).

D'URFÉ, Honoré (1567–1625), French novelist. He is remembered chiefly for *L'Astrée* (published in four parts, 1607, 1610, 1619, and, posthumously, 1627), a sentimental romance in a pastoral setting celebrating the virtues of a refined life. Regarded as the first French novel, it enjoyed great popularity, influencing English playwrights under Charles I. It was praised by *La Fontaine and *Rousseau for the sensitivity of its natural descriptions.

D'URFEY, Thomas (1653–1723), a French Huguenot by descent, familiarly known as Tom Durfey, wrote a large number of songs, tales, satires, melodramas, and farces. A friend of Charles II and James II, he was still writing in the reign of Queen Anne, and was one of the most familiar figures of the day, given to singing his own songs in public. His comedies include *Madame Fickle* (1676), *The Virtuous Wife* (1679), and the more sentimental *Love for Money* (1691). He was attacked by Jeremy *Collier and replied in a comedy, *The Campaigners* (1698), with an unrepentant prose preface. His works include many adaptations: *Bussy d'Ambois, *Cymbeline (as *The Injured Princess*), and a three–part dramatization of *Don Quixote* (1694–6) with music by *Purcell. His *Wit and Mirth, or Pills to purge Melancholy* (6 vols, 1719–20) is an interesting collection of songs and ballads.

Durham, Constantia, a character in Meredith's *The Egoist.*

Durindana, or Durandal, the sword of *Roland or *Orlando, which had been that of Hector of Troy.

DURKHEIM, Émile (1858–1917), French sociologist. His significance as a major figure in modern sociology proceeds from his attempt to establish sociology as a science. His studies of criminality (*De la division du travail social,* 1893), of suicide (*Le Suicide,* 1897), and of magic (*Les Formes élémentaires de la vie religieuse,* 1912) served to mark out the sociological field and to determine the nature of the sociological fact. In 1898 he founded *L'Année sociologique,* the first sociological review.

DURRELL, Lawrence George (1912–   ), poet, novelist, and travel writer, born in India; he returned to England in his late teens, and thereafter travelled widely, living in Paris in the 1930s, and then for much of his life in the eastern Mediterranean. Although he began to write and publish both verse and prose when very young (his first pamphlet of verse appeared in 1931, his first novel, *Pied piper of lovers,* in 1935) his work made little impact for some years. He was first recognized as a poet: his collections include *A private country* (1943); *Cities, plains and people* (1946); *On seeing to presume* (1948); *The Tree of Idleness* (1955). His *Collected Poems* appeared in 1960. His first novel of interest, *The Black Book: an Agon,* heavily influenced by Henry *Miller, published in Paris in 1938, did not appear in Britain until 1973; it is a mildly pornographic fantasia, peopled by prostitutes and failed artists, intended by the author as 'a savage charcoal sketch of spiritual and sexual etiolation'. It was with the publication of *Justine* (1957), the first volume of his *Alexandria Quartet,* that Durrell achieved fame: *Balthazar* and *Mountolive* followed in 1958, and *Clea* in 1960. Set in Alexandria during the period just before the Second World War, the first three novels cover roughly the same period of time and the same events, while *Clea* advances the action in time; the central topic, according to Durrell, is 'an investigation of modern love'. Principal characters include the narrator L. G. Darley, his Greek mistress Melissa, the British ambassador Mountolive, the British intelligence agent Pursewarden, the artist Clea, and Justine (who is Jewish) and her wealthy Coptic husband Nessim. All are bound together in a web of political and sexual intrigue: each novel reveals different aspects of the truth. The style is ornate, lyrical, and sensual, perhaps too much so for English tastes, as the *Quartet* tends to be more highly regarded abroad than in Britain. Durrell's later novels, which include *Tunc* (1968), *Nunquam* (1970), *Monsieur* (1974), and *Constance* (1982), show even greater disregard for British respect for realism. His best-known travel books are his three 'island' books, *Prospero's Cell* (1945), based on his pre-war years in Corfu; *Reflections on a Marine Venus* (1953), based on his experiences as Information Officer in Rhodes, 1945–6; and *Bitter Lemons* (1957), on Cyprus.

Lawrence Durrell's brother, the zoologist Gerald Malcolm Durrell (1925–   ), is also a writer, well known for his popular accounts of animal life and his own zoo on Jersey: titles include *The Overloaded Ark* (1953), *My Family and Other Animals* (1956), *Island Zoo* (1961).

DÜRRENMATT, Friedrich (1921–   ), Swiss dramatist, a writer of grotesque black comedy, because he thinks that since the Second World War tragedy is a form no longer applicable to our modern 'upside-down world'. His best-known plays are *Der Besuch der alten Dame* (*The Visit*, 1956) and *Die Physiker* (*The Physicists*, 1962). Both are absurdist dramas dealing with power and responsibility, the first with reference to money, the second on the theme of the criminality of atomic physics. Dürrenmatt has also written many radio plays and some critical essays.

Dusty Answer, a novel by R. *Lehmann; the title is taken from Meredith's *Modern Love*.

Dutch Courtezan, The, a comedy by *Marston, printed 1605.

Young Freevill, being about to marry Beatrice, daughter of Sir Hubert Subboys, determines to break his connection with Franceschina, the Dutch courtesan. He introduces the latter to his self-righteous friend Malheureux, who becomes violently enamoured of her. She consents to gratify his passion if he will kill Freevill, and bring proof of the deed in the shape of a ring given to him by Beatrice. Freevill consents to help him; a pretended quarrel is arranged, Freevill disappears, and Malheureux takes the ring to Franceschina, who hastens to communicate the news to old Freevill and Sir Hubert Subboys. Malheureux is arrested for the murder of Freevill and sentenced to death. At the last moment young Freevill appears, and begs forgiveness for the device that he has adopted to cure his friend of his passion. Franceschina is condemned to be whipped and gaoled.

DVOŘÁK, Antonin (1841–1904), Czech composer. Dvořák, primarily a symphonic composer, made only one essay at an English literary theme, the concert overture *Othello* (1892): this is a splendidly dramatic piece, designed by the composer to a very definite programme, though its exact relevance to the details of Shakespeare's play are not always clear. England gave Dvořák his first opportunity to conduct outside Bohemia, and he received a warm welcome on his first visit to London in 1884, but the choral works commissioned as a result of the visit make no use of English literary sources. But the three-year visit to America which produced, among other works, the 9th Symphony *From the New World*, was also responsible for a cantata *The American Flag* to words by Rodman Drake (1893), which seems in the end to have been Dvořák's only setting of the English language.

DYCE, Alexander (1798–1869), scholar, who edited a large number of the works of Shakespeare and his contemporaries. His editions include the works of G. *Peele (1828–39), T. *Middleton (1840), *Beaumont and *Fletcher (1843–6), *Marlowe (1850), J. *Ford (1869), R. *Greene (1831, 1861), and J. *Webster (1830, 1857). As well as producing a full edition of Shakespeare's works (1857, 1864–7) he was the first editor of *Sir Thomas *More (1844). He left his valuable collection of books and manuscripts to the Victoria and Albert Museum.

DYCK, Sir Anthony van, see VAN DYCK, SIR A.

DYER, Sir Edward (1543–1607), was educated either at Broadgates Hall or Balliol College, Oxford. He was introduced at court by the earl of *Leicester, and took part in the queen's entertainment at Woodstock in 1575. The most famous poem attributed to him, *'My mind to me a kingdom is', is probably not his work. Few authentic poems have survived: those which do show him to be a rather old-fashioned courtly poet. One of the best of his surviving poems is his elegy on his close friend Sir P. *Sidney, which begins 'Silence augmenteth griefe', printed in *The Phoenix Nest* (1593). There is an account of his life and works by R. M. Sargent (1935).

DYER, George (1755–1841), educated at Christ's Hospital and Emmanuel College, Cambridge, was usher at Dedham Grammar School and later at a school in Northampton. He published his *Poems* in 1792, and various critical essays from time to time. He is principally remembered as a friend of *Lamb, who writes of him as a gentle and kindly eccentric. He is the subject of Lamb's essay 'Amicus Redivivus' in *The Last Essays of Elia*, which describes how

Dyer, departing from Lamb's cottage in Islington, marched absent–mindedly into the nearby river and disappeared. His rescue and resuscitation are affectionately described.

DYER, John (1699–1757), Welsh poet, briefly educated at Westminster. He studied law, then painting (with Jonathan Richardson), and eventually became a clergyman. He is remembered chiefly for his *topographical poem in tetrameter couplets, *Grongar Hill* (1726), which describes the scenery of the river Towy. He also wrote *The Ruins of Rome* (1740) and *The Fleece* (1757), a poem about the wool trade, which contains fine early industrial and pastoral landscapes, as well as much practical information. Dr *Johnson and many others scorned *The Fleece* for its prosaic subject and prolix manner, but *Wordsworth admired it greatly, addressed a sonnet to Dyer ('Bard of the Fleece . . .'), and in his notes to *The Excursion* comments 'He wrote at a time when machinery was first beginning to be introduced, and his benevolent heart prompted him to augur from it nothing but good.'

DYLAN, Bob (1941–), pseudonym of American singer-songwriter Robert Allen Zimmerman: see BEAT GENERATION.

Dynasts, The; an epic-drama of the War with Napoleon, in three Parts, nineteen Acts and one hundred and thirty scenes, by T. *Hardy, published in three parts, 1904, 1906, 1908.

This vast and original work, for which Hardy had read extensively, was shaping itself in his mind for nearly 30 years before he began to publish it. It is written partly in blank verse, partly in a variety of other metres, and partly in prose. The events of history with which it deals are recounted in the descriptive passages and stage directions. The work centres on the tragic figure of Napoleon. Part I opens with the year 1805, and Napoleon's threat of invasion. It presents the House of Commons discussing the re-

peal of the Defence Act, Napoleon's coronation at Milan, the preparations at Boulogne for the invasion of England, the battles of Ulm and Austerlitz, Trafalgar, the death of Nelson, and the death of Pitt.

Part II covers the defeat of the Prussians at Jena, the meeting of Napoleon and Alexander at Tilsit, the battle of Wagram, the fall of Godoy and the abdication of the king of Spain, and war in Spain, the divorce of Josephine, and Napoleon's marriage with Marie Louise.

Part III presents the Russian expedition of 1812, the British victories in the Pyrenees, the battle of Leipzig, Napoleon's abdication, his return from Elba, the ball in Brussels, Quatre-Bras, and Waterloo. Accompanying the major scenes are small vignettes, seen at close quarters, showing how these great events affected English rustics in Wessex, private soldiers, camp followers, and other ordinary people. Above them all, supernatural spectators of the terrestrial action, are impersonated abstractions, or Intelligences; the Ancient Spirit of the Years, the Spirit of the Pities, the Spirits Sinister and Ironic, and the Spirit of Rumour, with their attendant choruses, the Shade of the Earth, and the Recording Angels. Above all is the Immanent Will, the force, unconscious and heedless, that moves the world. They are introduced not, as the author is careful to point out in his Preface, 'as a systematized philosophy warranted to lift "the burthen of the mystery" of this unintelligible world' but to give by their comments a universal significance to the particular events recounted.

After the experience of the First World War Hardy felt that he should not have ended the work with a glimpse of hope for mankind. The drama was intended 'simply for mental performance', but scenes from it were produced in London in 1914, when Rebecca *West found it 'one of the greatest plays' that had been seen on the English stage. The cinematic nature of the work has often been noted.

E

EADMER (d. ?1124), a monk of Canterbury who wrote a Latin chronicle of the events of his own time down to 1122, *Historia Novorum in Anglia*, a biography of his friend and leader *Anselm, and an early Marian work, the *Liber de Excellentia Beatae Mariae*. The *Historia* and the life of Anselm were edited together by M. Rule (Rolls Series 1881, 1884).

EAGLETON, Terry, see MARXIST LITERARY CRITICISM.

Eames, Johnny, a character in A. *Trollope's novels *The Small House at Allington* and *The Last Chronicle of Barset*.

Earine, the shepherdess loved by Aeglamour in Jonson's *The Sad Shepherd*.

EARLE, John (?1601–65), a member of *Falkland's circle at Great Tew, became tutor to Prince Charles in 1641, served him as chaplain during his exile in France, and after the Restoration became bishop of Worcester, then Salisbury, in which roles he defended persecuted Nonconformists. *Microcosmographie* (1628) was a collection of character sketches, chiefly by his hand, based on the model of *Theophrastus, though some of them are responses to the harsher and more satiric 'characters' of *Overbury (e.g. his 'Good Old Man', compared with Overbury's 'Old Man'). He analyses varied social and moral types, ranging from the plain country fellow to the pot poet, with wit, sympathy, and insight. (See CHARACTER-WRITING.)

Early English Texts Society, founded in 1864 by *Furnivall for the publication of Early and Middle English texts.

Earnshaw, Catherine, Hindley, and Hareton, characters in Emily Brontë's *Wuthering Heights*.

Earthly Paradise, The, a poem by W. *Morris, published 1868–70, consisting of a prologue and 24 tales, in Chaucerian metres.

The prologue tells how a company of Norsemen, fleeing from the pestilence, set sail in search of the fabled Earthly Paradise 'across the western sea where none grow old'. They are disappointed in their quest and return after long wanderings, 'shrivelled, bent and grey', to a 'nameless city in a distant sea' where the ancient Greek gods are still worshipped. They are hospitably received and there spend their remaining years. Twice in each month they meet their hosts at a feast and a tale is told, alternately by

one of the elders of the city and one of the wanderers. The tales of the former are on classical subjects (Atalanta, Perseus, the Apples of the Hesperides, etc.), those of the latter from Norse and other medieval subjects, including 'The Lovers of Gudrun', a version of the *Laxdæla* saga. Between the tales are interpolated lyrics describing the changing seasons, and the whole work is prefaced by an Apology which contains some of Morris's best known (and in a sense most misleading) lines, in which he describes himself as 'the idle singer of an empty day', 'born out of my due time'. Although the plan of the work owes a debt to *The Canterbury Tales*, it is almost entirely static, and its narrators undifferentiated; highly popular in its day, it has since been seen as symptomatic of the weaknesses of Victorian late Romanticism.

Earwicker, Humphrey Chimpden, a character in Joyce's *Finnegans Wake*.

Eastern, see ORIENTAL.

East Lynne, see WOOD, E.

Eastward hoe, a comedy by G. *Chapman, *Jonson, and J. *Marston, printed 1605, having been previously performed by the Children of the Revels at the Blackfriars. A passage derogatory to the Scots (III. iii. 40–7) gave offence at court, and Chapman and Jonson were imprisoned, but released on the intercession of powerful friends. The play is particularly interesting for the light it throws on London life of the time. Like Dekker's *Shoemaker's Holiday*, it gives a sympathetic picture of a tradesman.

The plot contrasts the careers of the virtuous and idle apprentices, Golding and Quicksilver, of the goldsmith Touchstone; and the fates of his two daughters, the modest Mildred, who marries the industrious Golding, and the immodest Gertrude who, in order to ride in her own coach, marries the penniless adventurer Sir Petronel Flash. Golding soon rises to the dignity of a deputy alderman, while Sir Petronel, having sent off his lady in a coach to an imaginary castle of his and filched her dowry, sets off for Virginia, accompanied by the prodigal Quicksilver, who has robbed his master. They are wrecked on the Isle of Dogs, and brought up before Golding, the deputy alderman. After some days in prison, where their mortifications lead them to repent, they are released at Golding's intercession.

Eatanswill, the scene of the parliamentary elections in Dickens's *Pickwick Papers*.

Eblana, in imprints, Dublin.

Eboracum, in imprints, York.

Ebuda, in *Orlando Furioso*, the island west of Scotland on which *Angelica was exposed to the Orc.

Ecclesiastical History of Bede, see HISTORIA ECCLESIASTICA.

Ecclesiastical Politie, Of the Laws of, see LAWS OF ECCLESIASTICAL POLITIE.

Echidna, in Spenser's *Faerie Queene* (VI. vi), is the mother of the *Blatant Beast. In Greek mythology, a monster, half woman and half snake.

ECKERMANN, Johann, see GOETHE.

ECKHARD, Johannes (?1260–1327), known as 'Meister Eckhard', a German Dominican who was conferred Doctor by Boniface VIII but was later summoned before the bishop of Cologne and obliged to recant some of his opinions. He is regarded as the founder of German Mysticism and one of its greatest exponents. English trans. by J. M. Clark included in his *Meister Eckhart: an Introduction* (1957).

Eclogue, the term for a short pastoral poem, comes from ἐκλογή (a choice), the title given in Greek to collections of elegant extracts. The Latinized form *ecloga* was used, however, for any short poem and attached itself particularly to *Virgil's pastorals which their author had called *bucolica*, a name commonly applied to the Idylls (εἰδύλλα—short descriptive poems) of *Theocritus that Virgil had imitated. The terms eclogue, bucolic, and idyll have been widely used as synonyms, except that grammarians have made an effort to confine 'eclogue' to poems in dialogue form. The alternative spelling 'aeglogue' was prompted by a mistaken derivation from the Greek αἴξ, a goat.

Eclogues, The, of A. *Barclay, written *c*. 1513–14, are interesting as the earliest English *pastorals, anticipating *Spenser. They are moral and satirical in character, dealing with such subjects as the evils of a court life and the happiness of the countryman's lot. They are modelled upon *Mantuan and the *Miseriae Curialium* of *Piccolomini.

ECO, Umberto (1932–), Italian semiologist. His main works are: *Thema: omaggio a Joyce* (*Themes: Homage to Joyce*, 1958, tape with music by Luciano Berio), *La struttura assente* (*The Absent Structure*, 1968), *Le forme del contenuto* (*The Forms of Content*, 1971), *A Theory of Semiotics* (1975), *Opera aperta* (*The Open Work*, 1962), and a historical thriller, *Il nome della rosa* (*The Name of the Rose*, 1981). He has influenced the development of European semiotics (see SAUSSURE).

Economist, The, a weekly financial and commercial review founded in 1843. James Wilson was its first editor. It advocated free trade and the repeal of the corn laws and took up a sound attitude in opposition to the reckless railway speculation of the middle of the century. Among its later editors was *Bagehot, Wilson's son-in-law.

It remains a specialist review, and was considerably modernized under the successful editorship of Alastair Burnet (1965–74). The contributions remain anonymous.

Ector, Sir, in Malory's *Morte D'Arthur*, the knight to whom the infant King Arthur was entrusted. He was father of Sir *Kay, the steward.

Ector de Marys, Sir, in *Malory, the illegitimate son of King *Ban of Benwick and half-brother of *Launcelot. It is he who, in the last section of the *Morte D'Arthur*, finds Launcelot dead and utters his great lament over him.

Edda, an Old Norse name of uncertain meaning given to a 13th-cent. poetic manual written by Snorri *Sturluson, known as the Prose, Younger, or Snorra Edda. The same name was applied in the 17th cent. to a manuscript collection of poems, the Poetic or Elder Edda. The Prose Edda is divided into a Prologue and three parts: the 'Gylfaginning', or Deluding of Gylfi, a series of mythological stories in the form of a dialogue between one Gylfi and the Norse gods; the 'Skáldskaparmál', or Poetic Diction, in which Snorri illustrates the elaborate diction of *Skaldic Verse, retelling many myths and legends; and the 'Háttatal', or List of Metres, a long poem each strophe of which exemplifies a different Norse metre. Snorri's work is valuable for the stories it enshrines, the verses it has preserved, and Snorri's own gifts as a story-teller. The Poetic Edda was compiled in about 1270, but some of the poems in it undoubtedly belong to a much earlier age. The poems fall into two groups: heroic lays about legendary Germanic heroes such as Sigurðr and Helgi; and mythological lays, such as the Vǫluspá, a history of the Norse gods from creation to apocalypse, and the Hávamál, the words of the High One, Oðinn. *Auden wrote free translations of many Eddaic lays. See *The Prose Edda of Snorri Sturluson*, trans. J. I. Young (1954); *The Poetic Edda*, Vol. I: *Heroic Poems*, ed. U. Dronke (1969– , parallel trans.); *Norse Poems* by W. H. *Auden and P. B. Taylor (1981); E. O. G. Turville-Petre, *Origins of Icelandic Literature* (1953).

EDDY, Mrs Mary Baker Glover (1821–1910), born at Bow, New Hampshire. She was the founder of Christian Science, the doctrine of which she expounded in *Science and Health with Key to the Scriptures* (1875); the Christian Science Association was formed the following year.

EDEN, Emily (1797–1869), daughter of William Eden, first Baron Auckland, moved in prominent Whig circles and was a close friend of Melbourne. When Melbourne appointed her brother governor-general of India in 1835, she accompanied him, travelled with him, and acted as his hostess, which she continued to do after his return until his death in 1849. She published *Portraits of the People and Princes of India* (1844) and *Up the Country* (1866); *Letters from India* appeared in 1872, and a collection of her letters edited by her great-niece Violet Dickinson in 1919. Her two novels *The Semi-detached House* (1859, anon.) and *The Semi-attached Couple* (1860, by 'E.E.'), written some 30 years earlier, both deal with fashionable society, and combine shrewd perception, wit, and good nature; their plots and characterization owe much to J. *Austen, whom she greatly admired and frequently mentions. They are a valuable record of social life, shedding a revealing light on attitudes to marriage, politics, and manners, and have been several times reprinted, most recently in 1979.

Edgar, (1) in Shakespeare's *King Lear*, the legitimate son of Gloucester, who for much of the play (II. iii–IV. i) is disguised as the bedlam beggar 'poor Tom'; (2) the Master of Ravenswood, hero of Scott's *The Bride of Lammermoor*.

Edge-hill, see JAGO, R.

EDGEWORTH, Maria (1768–1849), was the eldest daughter of the first wife of Richard Lovell Edgeworth (1744–1817), a wealthy Irish landlord of a large estate in Co. Longford, who was to marry three more wives after the death of Maria's mother in 1773 and to father in all 22 children. He was an eccentric, radical, and inventive man, deeply interested in the practical applications of science and in education: his friends included E. *Darwin, Mrs *Barbauld, and T. *Day. His influence on Maria was profound; he frequently 'edited' her work (which involved cutting, correcting, and occasionally contributing passages), managed her literary career, and imparted to her many of his own enthusiasms. They wrote together *Practical Education* (1798), a treatise which owes much to *Rousseau, although its tone is less theoretical.

Maria spent her infancy in Ireland, received some schooling in England, and when she was 15 returned to live the rest of her life with her family in Ireland. Her first publication was *Letters to Literary Ladies* (1795), a plea for women's education. From then on she wrote prolifically for some 40 years and established a high reputation. She visited London in 1803, when she was fêted by the literary world, meeting, among others, *Byron, Sydney *Smith, Joanna *Baillie, and Crabb *Robinson. She visited Sir W. *Scott at Abbotsford in 1823, and he returned the visit in Ireland in 1825. He greatly admired her work, described her as 'the great Maria', and acknowledged his debt to her Irish novels in the Preface to his 'Waverley' edition of 1829. J. *Austen sent her a copy of *Emma*, and later admirers included *Macaulay, *Thackeray, *Ruskin, and *Turgenev.

Although not generally regarded as a novelist of the first rank, Miss Edgeworth appears to have initiated, in *Castle Rackrent*, both the first fully developed *regional novel and the first true *historical novel in English, pointing the way to the historical/regional novels of Scott. Her writings fall into three groups: those based on Irish life (considered her finest), *Castle Rackrent* (1800) and *The Absentee* (first published in *Tales of Fashionable Life* in 1812) together with the lesser *Ormond* (1817); those depicting contemporary English society, such as *Belinda* (1801—commended by the heroine of *Northanger Abbey*), *Leonora* (1806), *Patronage* (1814), and *Helen* (1834); and her many popular lessons and stories for and about children, including *The Parent's Assistant* (1796–1800), *Moral Tales* (1801), *Popular Tales* (1804), and *Harry and Lucy Concluded* (1825). See M. S. Butler, *Maria Edgeworth* (1972).

Edinburgh Review, The (1802–1929), a quarterly periodical, established by F. *Jeffrey, Sydney *Smith, and H. *Brougham, and originally published by A. *Constable. It succeeded immediately in establishing a prestige and authority which (shared with *The Quarterly Review*) lasted for over a century. *Carlyle described it as 'a kind of Delphic oracle'. Under the influence of its first editor, Jeffrey, its politics became emphatically Whig, but although it was anxious for reform in many spheres an effort was made to hold a balanced view. Only a section of the journal was reserved for literature, but the views expressed there were highly influential and the few books selected for review were very fully considered. Although Jeffrey perceived the genius of *Keats, his veneration for 18th-cent. literature led him to notorious and scathing denouncements of *Wordsworth, *Coleridge, and *Southey as the 'Lake School'. Between Jeffrey's resignation in 1829 and the demise of the *Review* in 1929 contributions were published from almost all the major writers and critics of the 19th and early 20th cents.

Edith of Lorn, the heroine of Scott's *The Lord of the Isles*.

Edith Plantagenet, The Lady, kinswoman of Richard I, a character in Scott's *The Talisman.*

Edmund, in Shakespeare's *King Lear,* the villainously self-seeking bastard son of the earl of Gloucester.

Edward, a fine old Scottish ballad of domestic tragedy, included in Percy's *Reliques* and beginning:

> Why does your brand sae drop wi' blude,
> Edward, Edward?

Edward II, a tragedy in blank verse by *Marlowe probably first performed 1592, published 1594.

It deals with the recall by Edward II, on his accession, of his favourite, Piers Gaveston; the revolt of the barons and the capture and execution of Gaveston; the period during which Spenser (Hugh le Despenser) succeeded Gaveston as the king's favourite; the estrangement of Queen Isabella from her husband; her rebellion, supported by her paramour Mortimer, against the king; the capture of the latter, his abdication of the crown, and his murder in Berkeley Castle. The play was an important influence on Shakespeare's *Richard II.*

Edward III, *The Raigne of King,* a historical play, published 1596, of uncertain authorship, attributed by some, at least in part, to Shakespeare.

The two first acts are concerned mainly with the dishonourable wooing of the countess of Salisbury by the king, who is finally brought to a sense of shame by her determination to kill herself if he pursues his suit. The rest is occupied with the French wars.

Edwardian, strictly, of the reign of Edward VII, but the term is commonly used (in contrast with 'Victorian') of the years 1900–14. H. G. *Wells, who stands in a symbolic relation to the Edwardian period as *Wilde stood in a symbolic relation to the 1890s, wrote that Queen Victoria sat on England like a great paper-weight, and that after her death things blew all over the place. This expresses well the excitement, the new sense of freedom, and the lack of direction, in Wells himself and in Arnold *Bennett, *Galsworthy, E. M. *Forster, and other liberal writers of the period. It was an era of outstanding achievement in the theatre (with G. B. *Shaw and *Granville-Barker) and, especially, in the novel, notably in the great works of H. *James's last phase and the radical experiments of *Conrad (and his collaborator F. M. *Ford). At the same time strongly traditional themes in the writing of the period—the Empire as a source of national pride, the countryside as the custodian of national values, the upper-class house-party representing the whole of English life—support the still current alternative sense of the word 'Edwardian', referring to a period of sunlit prosperity and opulent confidence preceding the cataclysm of the Great War.

EDWARDS, Jonathan (1703–58), born in Connecticut, the philosopher, ardent divine, and formidable preacher who provoked the fervent religious revival in New England known as the 'Great Awakening'. In his *Treatise Concerning Religious Affections* (1746) he nicely discriminated between the state of grace and the state of worldliness; and his attempt to make this distinction a criterion of fitness to receive the Eucharist led to his dismissal from the charge of the church of Northampton, Mass., in 1750. He was then for six years a missionary to the Indians. His principal philosophical work, *A Careful and Strict Enquiry into the Modern Prevailing Notions of . . . Freedom of Will* (1754), in which he attacked from a predestinarian standpoint the *Arminian view of liberty, occasioned *Boswell's remark that 'the only relief I had was to forget it', and Dr *Johnson's aphorism, 'All theory is against the freedom of the will; all experience for it.' (Boswell, *Life of Johnson,* ed. G. B. Hill, iii. 291, 1778.)

EDWARDS, Richard (?1523–66), of Corpus Christi College and Christ Church, Oxford, was master of the children of the Chapel Royal, 1561. He composed *Palamon and Arcite* (now lost) for Queen Elizabeth's entertainment at Oxford, 1566. *The Excellent Comedie of . . . *Damon and Pithias* (printed 1571) is his only extant play. He was the compiler of the *Paradyse of Dainty Devises,* published after his death (1576).

'Edwin and Angelina', see HERMIT, THE.

Edwin Drood, *The mystery of,* an unfinished novel by *Dickens, published 1870.

The fathers of Edwin Drood and Rosa Bud, both widowers, have before their deaths betrothed their young children to one another. The orphan Rosa has been brought up in Miss Twinkleton's school at Cloisterham (Rochester), where Edwin, also an orphan, has an uncle, John Jasper, the precentor of the cathedral, to whom he is devoted and who appears to return the devotion. It is understood that the two young people are to marry as soon as Edwin comes of age, although this very understanding has been fatal to love between them. Jasper, a sinister and hypocritical character, gives Rosa music lessons and loves her passionately, but inspires her with terror and disgust. There now come upon the scene two other orphans, Neville and Helena Landless. Neville and Edwin at once become enemies, for Neville admires Rosa and is disgusted at Edwin's unappreciative treatment of her. This enmity is secretly fomented by Jasper and there is a violent quarrel between the young men. On the last of Edwin's periodical visits to Cloisterham before the time of his anticipated marriage, Rosa and he recognize that this marriage will not be for their happiness and break off the engagement. That same night Edwin disappears under circumstances pointing to foul play and suggesting that he has been murdered by Neville Landless, a theory actively supported by Jasper. But Jasper receives with uncontrollable symptoms of dismay the intelligence that the engagement of Edwin and Rosa had been broken off before Edwin's disappearance, and this betrayal of himself is noted by Mr Grewgious, Rosa's eccentric, good-hearted guardian. Neville is arrested but, as the body of Edwin is not found, is released untried. He is ostracized by public opinion and is obliged to hide himself as a student in London. The remainder of the fragment of the novel is occupied with the continued machinations of Jasper against Neville and his pursuit of Rosa, who in terror of him flies to her guardian in London; with the countermoves prepared by Mr Grewgious, assisted by the amiable minor canon Mr Crisparkle and a new ally, the retired naval officer Mr Tartar; also with the proceedings of the mysterious Mr Datchery, directed against Jasper. Of the solution or catastrophe intended by the author no hint exists, beyond those which the fragment itself contains, and the statement as to the broad lines of the plot given by J. *Forster. There have been many conjectures, turning mainly on two points: whether Edwin Drood had in fact been murdered or had miraculously survived; and who was Datchery. It has been suggested, for instance, that Datchery was Drood himself, or Tartar, or Grewgious, or Grewgious's clerk Bazzard, or Helena Landless, in disguise.

Mention should also be made of some notable characters: the fatuous Mr Sapsea, auctioneer and mayor; Mr Honeythunder, the bullying 'philanthropist'; the grim stonemason Durdles and his attendant imp 'Deputy'.

There have been several attempts at continuations, from *John Jasper's Secret* (1871–2) by H. Morford and others, to recent versions such as one by Leon Garfield (1980) and one contained in *The Decoding of Edwin Drood* (1980) by C. Forsyte. For further interpretations, see *A Reader's Guide to Charles Dickens* (1973) by P. *Hobsbaum, *The Wound and the Bow* (1941) by E. *Wilson, and an article by W. W. Robson in the *TLS*, 11 Nov.1983.

EGAN, Pierce, the elder (1772–1849), is remembered as the author of *Life in London; or the Day and Night Scenes of Jerry Hawthorn Esq. and Corinthian Tom*, issued in monthly numbers from 1820 (the completed book in 1821), illustrated by George and Robert *Cruikshank. The book is a description of the life of the 'man about town' of the day, interesting for the light it throws on the manners of the period and for the many slang phrases it introduces. In 1824

Egan began the issue of a weekly paper, *Pierce Egan's Life in London and Sporting Guide*, which subsequently developed into the sporting journal *Bell's Life in London*. His son, also Pierce Egan (1814–80), was associated with him in several of his works, and wrote a vast number of novels.

Egeon, in Shakespeare's *The Comedy of Errors*, the Syracusan merchant who is father of the Antipholus twins.

EGERTON, George, the pen-name of Mary Chavelita Dunne (1859–1945), short story writer, born in Australia of Irish-Welsh parentage and brought up in Ireland. Her adventurous early life included an elopement to Norway and two marriages, the first to George Egerton Clairemont, the second in 1901 to a theatrical agent, Reginald Golding Bright. Her first volume of short stories, *Keynotes* (1893), published by John *Lane with a cover by *Beardsley, created something of a sensation with its echoes of Scandinavian realism and portraits of the *New Woman; it was dedicated to *Hamsun, with whom she had fallen briefly in love and whose novel *Hunger* she later (1899) translated. Other works include *Discords* (1894) and *The Wheel of God* (1898). See T. de Vere White, *A Leaf from the Yellow Book* (1958).

EGERTON, Sir Thomas, Baron Ellesmere and Viscount Brackley (?1540–1617), was lord chancellor from 1603 till his death. He befriended F. *Bacon. *Donne was his secretary for four years (1597–1602) and S. *Daniel and J. *Owen addressed poems to him. He left judicial and legal treatises in manuscript. It was to his third wife that Milton's *Arcades* was addressed.

EGGLESTON, Edward (1837–1902), itinerant Methodist preacher and author, born in Indiana, USA. His fame rests on *The Hoosier Schoolmaster* (1871), in which he attempted to depict faithfully and realistically the people of backwoods Indiana.

Eglantine, or **Eglentyne,** Madame, the Prioress in Chaucer's *Canterbury Tales*.

Egoist, The, a novel by G. *Meredith, published 1879.

The central character, the Egoist himself, is Sir Willoughby Patterne, rich and handsome, with a high position in the county, but totally blind to his own arrogance and to the needs of the women he loves. Laetitia Dale, an intelligent young woman but past her first bloom, has loved him for many years, and his vanity has been flattered. But the dashing Constantia Durham is a greater prize, and she accepts his proposal. However, she soon discerns the true Sir Willoughby and elopes with Harry Oxford, an officer in the hussars, thus bringing Willoughby his first bewildering humiliation. Soon he discovers the qualities he required in Clara Middleton, the daughter of an elderly scholar (said to be a sketch of Meredith's first father-in-law, *Peacock), whose passion for wine overwhelms even his affection for his daughter. Clara, bewitched by Willoughby's charm and surroundings, becomes engaged to him, but soon perceives his intention of directing and moulding her; her attempts to free herself from the entanglements of the engagement form the main theme of the book. Clara envies but cannot emulate Constantia, and Willoughby struggles frantically against an incredible second jilting. Clara is meanwhile seeing more and more of Vernon Whitford, a poor and earnest young scholar (based on L. *Stephen), who lives at Patterne and is tutor to young Crossjay, son of a poor relation, an officer of the marines. The spirited Crossjay is finally the means of Clara's release, for he unintentionally overhears Willoughby, seriously shaken by Clara's wish to be free, seeking a way out of his humiliation by proposing to Laetitia Dale, a proposal which she, with sad dignity, refuses. So Willoughby finds himself once more and trebly humiliated. However, in the end his persistence achieves the reluctant Laetitia, and Clara marries Vernon Whitford. The sharp compressed dialogue of the last chapters is among Meredith's most brilliant.

Egoist, The, originally *The New Freewoman: An Individualist Review,* founded by Harriet Shaw Weaver and Dora Marsden. It published articles on modern poetry and the arts, and from being a feminist paper became, under the influence of *Pound and others, a mouthpiece for the Imagist poets (see IMAGISM). It ran from 1914 to the end of 1919, first fortnightly and then monthly, with *Aldington as assistant editor, followed by T. S. *Eliot in 1917. Miss Marsden and Miss Weaver succeeded each other as nominal editors and it was due to Miss Weaver that Joyce's *Portrait of the Artist as a Young Man* was published serially in the magazine in 1914–15.

Egotistical Sublime, a phrase coined by *Keats to describe his version of *Wordsworth's distinctive genius. See under NEGATIVE CAPABILITY, and see also ROMANTICISM.

Egremont, Charles, the hero of *Sybil* by B. Disraeli.

Eikon Basilike, the Pourtraicture of His Sacred Majestie in His Solitudes and Sufferings, a book of which Dr John Gauden (1605–62), bishop of Worcester, claimed authorship. It purported to be meditations by Charles I, and was long so regarded; it was published about the date of his execution, 30 Jan. 1649 (1648 OS), and appealed so strongly to popular sentiment that 47 editions of it were published, and Parliament

thought it necessary to issue a reply, *Milton's *Eikonoklastes* (1649). ('Eikon Basilike' means 'royal image' and 'Eikonoklastes' 'image breaker'.) *Eikonoklastes* takes the *Eikon* paragraph by paragraph in an effort to refute it: it also attacks the 'miserable, credulous and deluded' public with much vigour. Gauden's claim, which was not made known until 1690, is discussed at length in F. F. Madan's *A New Bibliography of the Eikon Basilike* (1950).

Eikonoklastes, see EIKON BASILIKE.

EINHARD (?770–?840), a Frankish noble in the service of *Charlemagne, who wrote the famous biography of the emperor, *Vita Caroli Magni.*

Eisteddfod, a Welsh word meaning 'session', the annual congress of Welsh bards.

E.K., see KIRKE, E.

Elaine (variously spelt), in Malory's *Morte D'Arthur,* is the name of several ladies whose identities sometimes overlap: (1) Elaine Le Blank, the daughter of Sir Bernard of Astolat and known as the Fair Maid of Astolat (*Tennyson's Shalott), who falls in love with Launcelot and dies for love of him (see LAUNCELOT OF THE LAKE); (2) Elayne the Fair or Sans Pere (Peerless), the daughter of King Pelles and the mother, by Launcelot, of *Galahad; (3) Elayne the sister of Morgawse and Morgan le Fay in the opening pages of Malory; (4) Elayne the wife of King *Ban and mother of *Launcelot; (5) Elayne the daugher of King Pellinore.

Élan vital, a phrase coined by *Bergson to describe the vital impulse which he believed directed evolutionary growth. See also under MAN AND SUPERMAN.

Elayne, see ELAINE.

Elder Brother, The, a drama by J. *Fletcher, written *c.*1625, probably with *Massinger, who completed it about 1635 (after Fletcher's death). The story is suggested in part by *Overbury's Theophrastian 'character' of 'An Elder Brother' (1614).

Lewis, a French lord, proposes to marry his daughter Angelina to one of the sons of Brisac, a country gentleman. Charles, the heir of Brisac, devoted to study, declines marriage; and Brisac thereupon proposes that Angelina shall marry the younger brother, Eustace, and that Charles shall be induced to surrender the bulk of his inheritance to Eustace, who eagerly falls in with the proposal. The plan is in a fair way of accomplishment, when Charles sees Angelina and they fall in love. Eustace, a poor-spirited courtier, is routed, and after various complications the lovers are united.

Elder Statesman, The, a comedy by T. S. *Eliot.

ELEANOR OF AQUITAINE (1122–1204), the granddaughter of the first troubadour whose work survives, Guilhem IX of Aquitaine, and inheritor of the kingdom of Aquitaine, married for her inheritance by Louis VII of France in 1137. She had two daughters by him before their divorce (encouraged by her enemy St *Bernard of Clairvaux who deplored the southern worldliness that she brought to the Parisian court) in 1152. She was immediately remarried to Henry Plantagenet of Anjou, the future Henry II of England, to whom she bore eight children including the future *Richard I (b. 1157) and, the youngest, the future King John (b. 1166). After the death of Henry II in 1189 she was regent of England in the absence of her son Richard until his death in 1199. She was an immensely influential patron of the arts, particularly in her patronage of the development of courtly poetry in Poitiers, a function carried on by her daughter *Marie de Champagne. Among others she brought the troubadour Bernart de Ventadorn (*fl.* 1170s) to Poitiers, perhaps fuelling troubadour influence on more northerly French poetry.

Eleatic, the name used to describe the philosophy of Parmenides (d. *c.*450 BC) and Zeno (*fl.* *c.*460 BC), who lived or were born at Elea, an ancient Greek city on the west coast of south Italy. These philosophers held that the real universe is a single, indivisible, eternal, unchanging whole, and the only subject of knowledge; what is mutable and perishable, and phenomena such as motion, are illusions, and about them we can have only conjectures.

Elegant Extracts, see KNOX, V.

Elegiac, (1) in prosody, the metre consisting of a dactylic *hexameter and *pentameter, as being the metre appropriate to elegies; (2) generally, of the nature of an *elegy.

Elegy, from the Greek, the word has been variously used with reference to different periods of English. In Old English a group of short poems in the *Exeter Book whose subject is the transience of the world, sometimes relieved by Christian consolation, are called elegies (see WANDERER; SEAFARER; DEOR; RUIN). From the 16th cent. onwards the term was used for a reflective poem (*Coleridge called it the kind of poetry 'natural to the reflective mind') by poets such as *Donne; later it was applied particularly to poems of mourning (from Milton's *Lycidas), and the general reflective poem, as written by Coleridge and *Yeats, is sometimes called 'reverie'. The great English mourning elegies are Lycidas (for E. *King), Shelley's *Adonais (for *Keats), Tennyson's *In Memoriam (for A. H. *Hallam), M. Arnold's *Thyrsis (for *Clough) and *Hopkins's Wreck of the Deutschland. T. Gray's *Elegy Written in a Country Church-Yard is a general poem of mourning, combined with the reflective mode. (See ELEGIAC.)

'Elegy on the Death of a Mad Dog', a poem by Goldsmith, from * The Vicar of Wakefield.

Elegy Written in a Country Church-Yard, a meditative poem in quatrains by T. *Gray, published 1751, but begun some years earlier. The churchyard is perhaps that of Stoke Poges, where Gray often visited members of his family. The poem, which contains some of the best-known lines in English literature, reflects on the obscure destinies of the villagers who lie buried ('Full many a flower is born to blush unseen') and then describes the supposed death of the melancholy and unknown author. Critics have related the closing stanzas both to Gray's fears about his own poetic destiny, and to the early death of his friend Richard *West in 1742.

Elene, see CYNEWULF.

'Elephant in the Moon, The', see BUTLER, S. (1613–80).

ELFRIDA, see ÆLFTHRYTH.

ELGAR, Sir Edward William (1857–1934), English composer. He was by far the most important figure in English music between the death of *Handel and the First World War, and created an individual musical style in which high Romanticism and deep emotional sensitivity are blended with an unmistakably English quality of inspiration and, on occasion, a direct popular appeal. The two works that first confirmed his position were the so-called Enigma Variations (1899) and The Dream of Gerontius (1900), a setting of the greater part of *Newman's poem which came to be recognized as a landmark in the history of the English oratorio. The later oratorios, The Apostles (1903) and The Kingdom (1906), designed as parts of a trilogy of which the third oratorio (The Last Judgement) was never completed, had texts selected from the Bible by the composer himself. But Elgar's greatest claim to fame is as a symphonic composer, and in this field he left two works of specific literary relevance: the concert overture Froissart (1890), his first orchestral work of interest, is a fairly generalized tribute to chivalry, but the masterly Symphonic Study Falstaff (1913), at the other end of his symphonic career, has a precise and detailed programme, and must come high on any list of musical works inspired by Shakespeare. (It is perhaps worth noting Elgar's insistence that his subject here is not the Falstaff of The Merry Wives of Windsor, and therefore of *Verdi's opera, but the subtler figure of Henry IV and V.)

Apart from the early Sea Pictures (1899), attractive settings of relatively undistinguished poems, Elgar's songs for solo voice are not of great importance, but there are a number of beautiful choral pieces and a curiously auto-biographical setting of *O'Shaughnessy's 'Ode' *The Music Makers* (1912). Works like *Fringes of the Fleet* (poems by *Kipling) and *The Spirit of England* (*Binyon) belong to the period of the First World War and, with the immense success of 'Land of Hope and Glory' (words by A. C. *Benson) and the *Pomp and Circumstance* style as a whole, have contributed to a popular image of Elgar far removed from the sensitive and reserved figure of fact. A truer idea of his later life is suggested by his close friendship with G. B. *Shaw and, encouraged by Shaw, his plans for an opera, *The Spanish Lady*, to be drawn from Jonson's *The Devil is an Ass*. Of this project only sketches and a couple of songs remain.

Elia, see ESSAYS OF ELIA.

Elidure, see ARTEGAL.

ELIOT, George (Mary Ann, later Marian, Evans) (1819–80), was the youngest surviving child of Robert Evans, agent for an estate in Warwickshire. In her girlhood she was par-ticularly close to her brother Isaac, from whom she was later estranged. At school she became a convert to Evangelicalism; she was freed from this by the influence of Charles Bray, a free-thinking Coventry manufacturer (a develop-ment which temporarily alienated her father), but remained strongly influenced by religious concepts of love and duty; her works contain many affectionate portraits of Dissenters and clergymen. She pursued her education rig-orously, reading widely, and devoted herself to completing a translation of *Strauss's *Life of Jesus*, which appeared without her name in 1846. In 1850 she met J. *Chapman, and became a contributor to the *Westminster Re-view*; she moved to 142 Strand, London, in 1851, as a paying guest in the Chapmans' home, where her emotional attachment to him proved an embarrassment. She became assistant editor to the *Westminster Review* in 1851, and in the same year met *Spencer, for whom she also developed strong feelings which were not reciprocated, though the two remained friends. In 1854 she published a translation of *Feuer-bach's *Essence of Christianity*; she endorsed his view that religious belief is an imaginative necessity for man and a projection of his interest in his own species, a heterodoxy of which the readers of her novels only gradually became aware. At about the same time she joined G. H. *Lewes in a union without legal form (he was already married) that lasted until his death; they travelled to the Continent in that year and set up house together on their return. He was to be a constant support throughout her working life and their relationship, although its irregularity caused her much anxiety, was gradually accepted

by their friends. 'The Sad Fortunes of the Rev. Amos Barton', the first of the *Scenes of Clerical Life*, appeared in *Blackwood's Magazine* in 1857, followed by 'Mr Gilfil's Love-Story' and 'Janet's Repentance'; these at once attracted praise for their domestic realism, pathos, and humour, and speculation about the identity of 'George Eliot', who was widely supposed to be a clergyman or possibly a clergyman's wife. She began *Adam Bede* (1859) in 1858; it was received with great enthusiasm and at once established her as a leading novelist. *The Mill on the Floss* appeared in 1860 and *Silas Marner* in 1861. In 1860 she visited Florence, where she conceived the idea of *Romola*, and returned to do further research in 1861; it was published in the *Cornhill* in 1862–3. John Blackwood, son of William *Blackwood, was unable to meet her terms; by this time she was earning a considerable income from her work. *Felix Holt, The Radical* appeared in 1866. She trav-elled in Spain in 1867, and her dramatic poem *The Spanish Gypsy* (conceived on an earlier visit to Italy, and inspired by *Tintoretto) appeared in 1868. *Middlemarch* was published in in-stalments in 1871–2 and *Daniel Deronda*, her last great novel, in the same way in 1874–6. She was now at the height of her fame, and widely recognized as the greatest living English novelist, admired by readers as diverse as *Tur-genev, H. *James, and Queen *Victoria. In 1878 Lewes died. Her *Impressions of Theo-phrastus Such* appeared in 1879, and in 1880 she married the 40-year-old John Walter Cross, whom she had met in Rome in 1869 and who had become her financial adviser. The marriage distressed many of her friends, but brought the consolation of a congratulatory note from her brother Isaac, who had not communicated with her since 1857. She died seven months later.

After her death her reputation declined some-what, and L. *Stephen indicated much of the growing reaction in an obituary notice (1881) which praised the 'charm' and autobiographical elements of the early works, but found the later novels painful and excessively reflective. V. *Woolf defended her in an essay (1919) which declared *Middlemarch* to be 'one of the few English novels written for grown-up people', but critics like David *Cecil and Oliver Elton continued to emphasize the division between her creative powers and supposedly damaging intellect. In the late 1940s a new generation of critics, led by *Leavis (*The Great Tradition*, 1948), introduced a new respect for and under-standing of her mature works; Leavis praises her 'traditional moral sensibility', her 'luminous intelligence', and concludes that she 'is not as transcendently great as Tolstoy, but she *is* great, and great in the same way'.

As well as the novels for which she is re-membered, she wrote various poems, including 'O may I join the choir invisible' (1867),

'Agatha' (1869), *Brother and Sister* (1869), a sonnet sequence recalling her happy childhood, 'The Legend of Jubal' (1870), and 'Armgart' (1871); also the short stories 'The Lifted Veil' (1859) and 'Brother Jacob' (1864). Her letters and journals were edited by Cross (3 vols, 1885); her complete letters were edited by G. S. Haight (7 vols, 1954–6), who also wrote a life (1968).

ELIOT, T(homas) S(tearns) (1888–1965), a major figure in English literature since the 1920s. He was born at St Louis, Missouri, and educated at Harvard, the Sorbonne, and Merton College, Oxford, where he pursued a doctoral thesis on F. H. *Bradley begun at Harvard. In 1914 he met *Pound, who encouraged him to settle in England; in June 1915 he married Vivien Haigh-Wood, and in the same month his poem 'The Love Song of J. Alfred Prufrock' appeared (also with Pound's encouragement) in *Poetry*. Eliot taught briefly during the war, then in 1917 began to work for Lloyds Bank; from 1917 he was also assistant editor of *The Egoist*. His first volume of verse, *Prufrock and other Observations* (1917), was followed by *Poems* (1919), hand-printed by L. and V. *Woolf at the *Hogarth Press; these struck a new note in modern poetry, satiric, allusive, cosmopolitan, at times lyric and elegiac. In 1922 Eliot founded a new quarterly, *The Criterion*; in the first issue appeared, with much éclat, *The Waste Land*, which established him decisively as the voice of a disillusioned generation. In 1925 he left Lloyds and became a director of Faber and Faber, where he built up a list of poets (*Auden, G. *Barker, Pound, *Spender, etc.; see also FABER BOOK OF MODERN VERSE) which represented the mainstream of the modern movement in poetry in England: from this time he was regarded as a figure of great cultural authority, whose influence was more or less inescapable.

In 1927 he became a British subject and a member of the Anglican church; his pilgrimage towards his own particular brand of High Anglicanism may be charted in his poetry through 'The Hollow Men' (1925), with its broken asseverations of faith, through 'The Journey of the Magi' (1927) and 'Ash-Wednesday' (1930), to its culminating vision in *Four Quartets* (1935–42). His prose also shows the same movement; for example, the title essay of *For Lancelot Andrewes* (1928) praises tradition, prayer, and liturgy, and points away from 'personality' towards hierarchy and community, and in the preface to this collection he describes himself as 'classical in literature, royalist in politics, and Anglo-Catholic in religion'. The same preoccupation with tradition continued to express itself in his critical works, and developed in part from the concept of *'dissociation of sensibility' which he had formulated in 1921. (See also here HULME, whose views influenced Eliot.)

In the 1930s Eliot began his attempt to revive poetic drama. *Sweeney Agonistes* (1932), an 'Aristophanic fragment' which gives, in syncopated rhythms, a satiric impression of the sterility of proletarian life, was followed by a pageant play, *The Rock* (1934), *Murder in the Cathedral* (1935), *The Family Reunion* (1939), and three 'comedies': *The Cocktail Party* (1950), *The Confidential Clerk* (1954), and *The Elder Statesman* (1959). These last were not wholly successful attempts to clothe profound ideas in the garb of a conventional West End play. Eliot's classic book of verse for children, *Old Possum's Book of Practical Cats* (1939), which reveals an aspect of his character that claimed the influence of *Lear, achieved a considerable stage success in a musical adaptation, *Cats*, in 1981.

Eliot was equally influential as critic and poet, and in his combination of literary and social criticism may be called the M. *Arnold of the 20th cent. Among his critical works may be mentioned: *The Sacred Wood: Essays on Poetry and Criticism* (1920) (which contains the essay on *Hamlet, coining the phrase *'objective correlative'); *The Use of Poetry and the Use of Criticism* (1933); *Elizabethan Essays* (1934); *The Idea of a Christian Society* (1940); *Notes Towards a Definition of Culture* (1948); *Poetry and Drama* (1951); *On Poets and Poetry* (1957). *Leavis, himself much influenced by Eliot, has pointed out the vital connections between Eliot's creative work and critical attitude (in, e.g., his revaluation of *Donne, *Marvell, Elizabethan and Jacobean verse drama, *Milton, *Dryden, and his praise of *Dante, *Laforgue, and the French Symbolists): 'Eliot's best, his important criticism has an immediate relation to his technical problems as the poet who, at that moment in history, was faced with "altering expression" ' ('T. S. Eliot's Stature as Critic', *Commentary*, Nov. 1958).

Eliot was formally separated from his first wife (whose ill health, both physical and mental, had caused him much stress and misery) in 1932–3; she died in 1947. The following year he was awarded the *Nobel Prize for literature and the Order of Merit. He married his second wife, Valerie Fletcher, in 1957. See *The Waste Land*, with biographical introduction by Valerie Eliot (1971), and Helen Gardner, *The Composition of Four Quartets* (1978). See also *T. S. Eliot* (1984) by P. Ackroyd.

Elision, the suppression of a vowel or syllable in pronouncing.

Elissa, (1) a name borne by Dido; (2) in Spenser's *Faerie Queene* (II. ii.), one of the two 'froward sisters' of the sober *Medina.

Eliza (Mrs Elizabeth Draper), see DRAPER.

Eliza, The Journal to, by L. *Sterne, written 1767, first published 1904.

The *Journal*, also called by Sterne the *Bramine's Journal*, was kept intermittently between mid-April and Nov. of 1767, and describes with fulsome pathos, often in the persona of Yorick, sometimes as 'Bramin' to 'Bramine', his love for the young Mrs Elizabeth *Draper and his torment at their separation. She was the wife of an official of the East India Company, and Sterne knew her for only a few months before she returned to her husband in India. The first instalments of the *Journal*, sent abroad to Eliza, appear to have been lost, and Sterne never attempted to publish the remainder, which was not discovered until 1851. At the time of its writing Sterne was also engaged on *A Sentimental Journey*, in which Eliza is often invoked and extolled, but the lachrymose *Journal* exhibits little of the verve of *A Sentimental Journey*. The work contains puzzling passages of Sterne's self-plagiarism, including a section copied almost exactly from a love-letter to his wife written 30 years before.

ELIZABETH I (1533–1603), a daughter of *Henry VIII, and queen of England from 1558 to 1603. She was celebrated by the greatest poets of her age, including *Spenser, *Ralegh, and *Shakespeare, under such names as *Cynthia and *Gloriana (with many allusions to her semi-mythological role as Virgin Queen) and has been the subject of innumerable plays, novels, romances, and biographies. She was famed for her ready wit and for the stirring eloquence called forth in, for example, her speech at Tilbury on the approach of the Spanish Armada. She also wrote poetry, which was highly praised by her courtiers and by *Puttenham, who used one of her few undisputed works ('The doubt of future foes', on the conspiracies of *Mary Queen of Scots) as an example of rhetoric in his *Art of English Poesy*. Her verses, which include six undisputed lyrics and epigrams, various doubtful attributions, and translations from *Boethius, *Horace, and *Plutarch, were edited by L. Bradner (1964).

Elizabeth and her German Garden, see VON ARNIM, E.

Elizabethan Literature, a name often applied vaguely to the literature produced in the reigns of Elizabeth I and the first Stuarts. See under DRAB and GOLDEN.

Ellen, the heroine of the ballad of *Childe Waters*.

'Ellen Alleyn', the pseudonym under which C. *Rossetti produced her earlier poems.

Ellen Douglas, the 'Lady of the Lake' in *Scott's poem of that name.

'Ellen Orford', one of the tales in Crabbe's *The Borough*. It tells the story of a courageous woman, who, after a neglected childhood, is seduced and abandoned. Her child turns out to be an idiot, her husband dies, and his death is followed by the deaths of their children. She becomes a teacher but blindness forces her to retire, and she finds consolation in her trust in God. She appears in *Britten's opera *Peter Grimes*.

ELLESMERE, Lord, see EGERTON, SIR T.

Ellieslaw, Richard Vere, laird of, and his daughter Isabella, characters in Scott's *The Black Dwarf*.

Elliot, Hobbie or Halbert, a character in Scott's *The Black Dwarf*.

ELLIOT, Jean (1727–1805), third daughter of Sir Gilbert Elliot of Minto, was author of the most popular version of the old lament for Flodden, 'The Flowers of the Forest', beginning 'I've heard them lilting at our ewe-milking'. It was written c.1763, and published by *Herd in 1776. Another popular version was written by A. *Cockburn.

Elliot, Sir Walter, his daughters Elizabeth, Anne, and Mary, and his heir William Walter Elliot, characters in J. Austen's *Persuasion*.

ELLIOTT, Ebenezer (1781–1849), became a master-founder in Sheffield, and is remembered as the 'Corn Law Rhymer'. In 1829 he published *The Village Patriarch*, in which Enoch Wray, an old blind mason, reflects upon rural life and the bitter poverty brought about by cruelty and injustice. *Carlyle, writing in *The Edinburgh Review* in 1832, found great interest in the poem, and 'a manful tone of reason and determination'—but nevertheless urged Elliott to abandon poetry for prose. *Corn Law Rhymes* (1830) is a collection of simple poems which employ both satire and pathos in fiercely condemning the Bread Tax. The book was immensely successful, at a time when sales of poetry were very low. Some of Elliott's poems are of genuine quality, and his themes of poverty and oppression are deeply felt. His collected works were published in 1846.

Elliott, Kirstie, Robert, Gilbert, Clement, and Andrew, characters in R. L. Stevenson's *Weir of Hermiston*.

Ellipsis, the leaving out from a sentence words necessary to express the sense completely.

ELLIS, George (1753–1815), was one of the talented group who, with *Canning and *Frere, founded and contributed to *The Anti-Jacobin* in 1797. His *Poetical Tales by Sir Gregory Gander* appeared in 1778, and his contributions to the Whig *Rolliad* in 1784, but his most important works were his translations and selections from Middle English verse: *Early English Poets* (1803) and *Specimens of Early English Romances in Metre* (1805).

ELLIS, Henry Havelock (1859–1939), born in Croydon, Surrey, spent some early years studying and teaching in Australia. He returned to London in 1879 and eventually qualified as a physician, although much distracted by his literary pursuits. These included reviewing, translating, and editing the unexpurgated *Mermaid Series of Elizabethan dramatists (1887–9) and the Contemporary Science Series. In 1884 he met Olive *Schreiner, who became an intimate friend and who shared his interest in progressive thought, particularly in the realm of sexuality, the subject with which he is most closely identified; other friends included E. *Carpenter, Arthur *Symons, and the advocate of birth control, Margaret Sanger. His 'new marriage' to the equally progressive (and lesbian) Edith Lees (1861–1916) was not wholly successful. An energetic if not entirely fearless pioneer in the field of sexology, his works (which include *The New Spirit*, 1890; *Sexual Inversion*, 1897, with J. A. *Symonds; *Affirmations*, 1898; *The Dance of Life*, 1923; and his autobiographical *My Life*, 1939, as well as many other volumes on the psychology of sex, marriage, censorship, social hygiene, etc.) had a considerable and liberating influence. He had many followers, although the scientific accuracy of his investigations has been questioned, and he damaged his own reputation by indiscriminate publication and by his apparent misunderstandings of *Freud. See P. Grosskurth, *Havelock Ellis* (1980)

ELLIS BELL, see BRONTË, E.

ELLISON, R. W., see INVISIBLE MAN.

ELLMANN, Richard (1918–), scholar and biographer, born in Michigan and educated at Yale University and Trinity College, Dublin. In 1970 he became Goldsmiths' professor of English literature at Oxford. His publications include *Yeats: The Man and the Mask* (1948, rev. 1979) and several works on *Joyce, including notably his monumental, imaginative, and revelatory biography, *James Joyce* (1959, rev. 1982), which made a highly influential contribution to the new conception of the art of *biography that developed at this period. He also edited the *New Oxford Book of American Verse* (1976).

ELLWOOD, Thomas (1639–1713), Quaker and friend of Milton, whose chance comment on *Paradise Lost*, 'Thou has said much here of paradise lost, but what has thou to say of paradise found?' suggested the subject of *Paradise Regained*.

'Eloisa to Abelard', a heroic epistle by *Pope, published 1717. Pope's version of the tragic love of Héloïse and *Abelard was highly popular; it portrays Héloïse, in a Gothic seclusion of 'grots and caverns', still tormented by passionate love, unable to renounce for God the memory of 'unholy joy'.

Elshender the Recluse, Canny Elshie, or the Wise Wight of Mucklestane-Moore, the *'Black Dwarf' in Scott's novel of that name.

ELSTOB, Elizabeth (1683–1756), born in Newcastle upon Tyne, was a pioneer in Anglo-Saxon studies, as was her brother William (1673–1715). After his death poverty obliged her to set up a school in Evesham, then to become governess to the children of the duchess of Portland. Her publications include *An English-Saxon homily on the birthday of St Gregory* (1709) and *The rudiments of grammar for the English-Saxon tongue, first given in English; with an apology for the study of northern antiquities* (1715). See also HICKES, G.

Elton, the Revd Philip, a character in J. Austen's *Emma*.

ÉLUARD, Paul (1895–1952), French poet, prominent exponent of *surrealism from 1919 to 1938. He collaborated with Max Ernst on *Les Malheurs des immortels* (1922) and with *Breton on *L'Immaculée Conception* (1930). Among his volumes of surrealist poetry are *Les Dessous d'une vie ou la pyramide humaine* (1926), *Capitale de la douleur* (1926), *L'Amour, la Poésie* (1929), *La Vie immédiate* (1932), *La Rose publique* (1934), and *Les Yeux fertiles* (1936). He broke with the surrealist movement in the late 1930s, and joined the Communist Party in 1942. He became one of the leading writers of the French Resistance (*Poésie et vérité*, 1942; *Au rendez-vous allemand*, 1944).

Elvira, (1) the wife of *Don Juan; (2) the heroine of *Dryden's *The Spanish Fryar*; (3) the mistress of Pizarro in *Sheridan's play *Pizarro*.

ELYOT, Sir Thomas (c.1490–1546), author of the *Boke named the Governour*, published in 1531, a treatise on education and politics which displays the influence at this time of the classics, and Plato in particular, and illustrates the evolution of English prose. To this book Elyot owed his appointment as ambassador to Charles V. He wrote a number of other works, including *The Doctrinall of Princis* (c.1533), translated from Isocrates, *The Image of Governance* (first published 1540), *The Castel of Helth* (c.1536), an important manual of health, and Platonic dialogues and compilations from the Fathers. His translations did much to popularize the classics in England. His *Dictionary* (Latin and English, 1538) was the first book published in England to bear this title. There is a life by S. E. Lehmberg, 1960.

Emaré, a mid-14th-cent. verse romance of 1,035 lines in a north-east Midland dialect, written in twelve-line tail-rhyme stanzas. It is a Breton lay (on the grounds that its introduction says it is) on the model of the repeatedly told Constance story; the name 'esmaré' could be a variant of the French word for 'tried', 'troubled'. The area of origin of the only manuscript might suggest a connection with the version of the story told by Nicholas *Trivet earlier in the 14th cent.; he was the first to call the heroine Constance. Emaré, like Constance, is repeatedly cast adrift, in this case first by order of her unnatural father and later by her mother-in-law, as was traditional in the story. At the end she is reunited with her lost son and her penitent husband. It has been edited by W. H. French and C. B. Hale, in *Middle English Metrical Romances* (1930), I. 421–55.

Emblem book. In its widest sense, an emblem is a visual representation carrying a symbolic meaning: hence, *Yeats's 'tower | Emblematical of the night' ('Dialogue of Self and Soul'). Most often, however, the word refers to a genre of verbal–pictorial art which is particularly associated with the Renaissance. One source of this genre was the belief that Egyptian hieroglyphics had been symbols rather than part of a language; this view was derived from the *Hieroglyphics* of Horapollo (or Horus Apollo), a Greek manuscript discovered in 1419, which was generally thought to be the work of an Egyptian in the 2nd or 4th cent. AD. Other important sources were the *Physiologus* and the epigrams of the Greek *Anthology*.

The first emblem book, the *Emblematum liber* of Alciati (or Alciato), was published in 1531. Each emblem consists of a motto, a symbolic picture, and an explanatory set of verses called an epigram. This format is followed by most other emblem books. All three parts of an emblem contribute to its meaning: e.g. Alciati's picture of a bee-hive in a helmet, together with the motto *Ex bello pax* and the explanatory epigram, means that the weapons of war may be turned into the works of peace. Writers often borrowed one another's pictures and wrote new verses which reinterpreted them. In *A Theatre for Worldlings* (1569) *Spenser translated verses from *Petrarch and *Du Bellay which had been used for a Dutch emblem book, but the translation was printed without the original plates. The earliest English emblem book to contain illustrations as well as verses was Geoffrey Whitney's (?1548–?1601) *A Choice of Emblemes* (1586), which distinguished three categories: natural, historical, and moral. The 17th cent. produced many religious emblem books, of which the most famous English example was the *Emblems* of Quarles (1635). The children's figures of these emblem books represent Divine Love (God) and Earthly Love (Man); they have been derived from the Cupid figures of earlier love emblems. A *Collection of Emblemes*, also illustrated, was published by G. *Wither, 1634–5.

The poetry of some religious poets of the period, such as G. *Herbert and H. *Vaughan, is sometimes described as emblematic, though their books were not illustrated. *Bunyan also wrote an emblem book without pictures (*A Book for Boys and Girls*, 1686). By then the form had already gone out of fashion; it enjoyed something of a revival in the Victorian period.

Emblems, a book of short devotional poems by *Quarles, first published 1635 and much reprinted; it was adapted from two Jesuit *emblem books, *Typus Mundi* (1627) and Herman Hugo's *Pia Desideria*. The poems are in various metres, each based on some scriptural text, and some in the form of dialogues, e.g. between Eve and the Serpent, between Jesus and the Soul, and between the Flesh and the Spirit. The engravings are mostly by William Marshall (*fl.* 1630–50).

Emelye, the lady loved by Palamon and Arcite in Chaucer's 'The Knight's Tale' (see CANTERBURY TALES, I). She figures as Emilia in *The Two Noble Kinsmen*.

EMERSON, Ralph Waldo (1803–82), American philosopher and poet, born in Boston, the son of a Unitarian minister who died when he was eight, leaving him and four other brothers (one mentally retarded) to the care of their mother and aunt, in straitened circumstances. He was educated at Harvard, studied theology, was ordained, and became a pastor in Boston, but resigned his charge (shortly after the death of his first wife) because he felt unable to believe in the sacrament of the Lord's Supper. Dejected and with uncertain prospects, he departed in 1832 for Europe, and in 1833 visited England, where he met *Coleridge and *Wordsworth, and notably *Carlyle, who after a day's intensive conversation at Craigenputtock became a lifelong friend and correspondent. On his return to America Emerson embarked on a career as lecturer, evolving the new quasi-religious concept of *Transcendentalism, which found written expression in his essay *Nature* (1836): 'Nature is the incarnation of thought. The world is the mind precipitated.' This form of mystic idealism and Wordsworthian reverence for nature ('What is a farm but a mute gospel?') was immensely influential in American life and thought, and Emerson, like his friend Carlyle, was revered as a sage. In 1835 he married and settled in Concord; his 1837 Harvard address, 'The American Scholar', urged America (as *Channing had recently done) to assert its intellectual independence: 'We have listened too long to the courtly muses of Europe.' *The Dial*, founded in 1840, was edited by Emerson from 1842 to 1844, and published many of his gnomic, rough-hewn, but frequently striking poems, including 'The Problem' and 'Woodnotes'. His first volume of essays (1841) contains 'Self-Reliance' ('Whoso would be a man, must

be a nonconformist . . . A foolish consistency is
the hobgoblin of little minds'); 'Compensation';
and 'The Over-Soul', which proposes a mystic
Unity 'within which every man's particular
being is contained and made one with all other'.
His second *Essays* (1844) contains 'The Poet',
in which he urges the 'incomparable materials'
of America, 'our log-rolling, our stumps and
their politics, our fisheries, our Negroes and Indians . . . America is a poem in our eyes; its
ample geography dazzles the imagination, and
it will not wait long for metres.' This challenge
was to be met by one of Emerson's most devoted
disciples, *Whitman, although other American
writers, including *Melville and *Hawthorne,
deplored what they perceived as his cloudy rhetoric and empty optimism.

In 1845 Emerson delivered the lectures later
published in 1850 as *Representative Men*; these
studies of *Plato, *Swedenborg, Napoleon, and
others owe something to Carlyle's concept of
the Hero. In 1847 he revisited England on a
lecture tour, staying in London in the home
of his publisher, J. *Chapman; he was greatly
admired in this country and his *English Traits*
(1865), a perceptive study of the English
national character, won him more readers. On his
return to America he was actively engaged in the
anti-slavery campaign, and continued to lecture
and write (including poems and prose for *The
Atlantic Monthly*) until, in his last decade, he
gradually lost his mental powers and became a
quiet blank. Of his many later works, mention
should be made of his moving tribute to his
friend and follower *Thoreau (1862) in which,
after a warm appreciation, he mildly deplored
Thoreau's want of ambition, a comment which
takes on an ironic light in view of Emerson's
current neglect as a writer and Thoreau's great
and continuing influence. A definitive edition of
Emerson's *Collected Works*, ed. R. E. Spiller and
others (Vol. I, 1971) is in progress, as is a complete edition of the *Journals* and *Notebooks*
(1960–).

Emilia, (1) in Shakespeare's *Othello*, the
plain-spoken wife of *Iago. In Cyprus she waits
on Desdemona and shares her confidence, most
memorably in the 'willow-song scene' (IV. iii);
(2) the lady loved by Palamon and Arcite in
Chaucer's 'The Knight's Tale' (see EMELYE), who
also figures in *The Two Noble Kinsmen*; (3)
Peregrine's love in Smollett's *Sir *Launcelot
Greaves*.

Emilia in England, see SANDRA BELLONI.

Emilia Viviani, see EPIPSYCHIDION.

Eminent Victorians, a biographical work by
L. *Strachey.

Em'ly, Little, a character in Dickens's *David
Copperfield*.

Emma, a novel by J. Austen, begun 1814, published 1816.

Emma, a clever, pretty, and self-satisfied
young woman, is the daughter, and mistress of
the house, of Mr Woodhouse, an amiable old
valetudinarian. Her former governess and companion, Anne Taylor, beloved of both father and
daughter, has just left them to marry a neighbour, Mr Weston. Missing Miss Taylor's companionship, Emma takes under her wing Harriet
Smith, parlour-boarder at the school in the
neighbouring village of Highbury. Harriet, a
pretty, pliant girl of 17, is the daughter of unknown parents. Emma's active mind sets to
work on schemes for Harriet's advancement, but
her interfering and injudicious attempts lead in
the end to considerable mortification. She first
prevents Harriet from accepting an offer of marriage from Robert Martin, an eligible young
farmer, as being beneath her. This tampering
greatly annoys Mr Knightley, the bachelor
owner of Donwell Abbey, who is Emma's
brother-in-law and one of the few people able
to see that she has faults. Emma has hope of
arranging a match between Harriet and Mr
Elton, the young vicar, only to find that Elton
despises Harriet and has the presumption to aspire to her own hand. Frank Churchill, the son
of Mr Weston by a former marriage, an attractive but thoughtless young man, now comes
to visit Highbury. Emma first supposes him in
love with herself, but presently thinks that Harriet might attract him, and encourages her not
to despair. This encouragement, however, is
misunderstood by Harriet, who assumes it is
directed, not at Frank Churchill, in whom she
has no interest, but at the great Mr Knightley
himself, with whom Emma is half unwittingly
in love. Emma then suffers the double mortification of discovering, first, that Frank Churchill
is already engaged to Jane Fairfax, niece of Miss
Bates, who lives in the village; and second, that
Harriet has hopes, which appear on the surface
to have some foundation, of supplanting her in
Mr Knightley's affections. However, Mr
Knightley in the end proposes to the humbled
and repentant Emma, and Harriet is happily consoled with Robert Martin.

The novel is generally considered Jane
Austen's most accomplished work, and the one
which most fully realizes her own recommendation of '3 or 4 families in a Country Village' as 'the very thing to work on'. Minor
characters include the vulgar Mrs Elton, with
her frequent references to her 'cara sposo' and
her brother-in-law's seat at Maple Grove, and
the garrulous old maid Miss Bates, who lives
with her widowed mother and enjoys 'a most
uncommon degree of popularity for a woman
neither young, handsome, rich nor married', and
who becomes the occasion of one of Emma's
educational moments at the celebrated outing to
Box Hill (ch. 43) when Emma is reprimanded

by Mr Knightley for making a joke at Miss Bates's expense.

EMPEDOCLES (*c*.484–*c*.424 BC), a Greek scientist, philosopher, and democratic politician who lived in Agrigentum in Sicily. He was responsible for demonstrating the existence of air, used experimentation in medicine, and taught that the universe was in a state of unending change thanks to the contrary action of Love, which united the four elements, and Strife, which drove them apart. He must have been an impressive character, judging by the number of legends about him. He was supposed to work miracles, controlling the winds and raising the dead, and to have met his death plunging into the crater of Etna. The opposition of Love and Strife is mentioned by Spenser (*Faerie Queene*, IV. x). The legend of Empedocles' death is referred to in *Paradise Lost* (iii. 471), by *Lamb in 'All Fools' Day', and by *Meredith in *Empedocles*; but the finest work it inspired is M. Arnold's *Empedocles on Etna* (1852) which shows the conflict between sensuous emotion and disciplined thought.

Empedocles on Etna, a dramatic poem by M. *Arnold, published anonymously 1852.

Arnold portrays the philosopher *Empedocles, who committed suicide by throwing himself into the crater of Etna, on the verge of his last act: his physician friend Pausanias tries to cheer him, accompanied by songs from the unseen harp-player Callicles. Empedocles expresses his intellectual doubts, dismissing the reassuring platitudes of religion and philosophy; man's yearning for joy, calm, and enlightenment is in itself no proof that these things exist or can be attained. He dismisses Pausanias, grieves over his own 'dwindling faculty of joy', concludes that he is man no more, but 'a naked, eternally restless mind', and finally, in a kind of triumph, concluding that at least he has been ever honest in his doubts, hurls himself to his death.

EMPSON, Sir William (1906–84), poet and critic, educated at Winchester and Magdalene College, Cambridge, where he studied mathematics, then English under I. A. *Richards. He taught at universities in China and Japan, and subsequently became professor of English at Sheffield. He published two volumes of verse, *Poems* (1935) and *The Gathering Storm* (1940): *Collected Poems* (revised) appeared in 1955. His criticism includes *Seven Types of Ambiguity* (1930), *Some Versions of Pastoral* (1935), *The Structure of Complex Words* (1951), and *Milton's God* (1961). Empson's poetry is extremely difficult, making use of analytical argument and imagery drawn from modern physics and mathematics; a technical virtuoso, he offered (in his own words) 'a sort of puzzle interest', and employed metaphysical conceits and linguistic, metrical, and syntactical complexities. *Wain praised his 'passion, logic and formal beauty', which widely influenced younger writers, particularly those associated with the *Movement. *Using Biography* (1984), a posthumous collection of essays, 1958–82, constitutes a spirited attack on the *New Criticism's neglect of the biographical element in literary interpretation.

Encounter, a political, cultural, and literary review, founded in 1953, and originally edited by S. *Spender and Irving Kristol; subsequently by Melvin J. Lasky, F. Kermode, A. *Thwaite, N. *Dennis, and others. D. W. Brogan, in an anthology selected from its first ten years, described it as 'a *journal de combat* . . . the organ of protest against the *trahison des clercs*', and its political tone at this period reflected some of the Anglo-American anti-Soviet spirit of the Cold War. But it was also the vehicle for N. *Mitford's celebrated formulation of the 'U' and 'Non-U' concept (1955), and C. P. *Snow pursued the *Two Cultures controversy in its pages (1959–60). It has also published poetry by R. *Lowell, *Plath, *Roethke, *Auden, *Larkin, *Amis, and many others, and articles by *Koestler, *Popper, *Naipaul, etc.

Encyclopaedia Britannica. The word encyclopaedia means instruction in the whole circle of learning. Among early precursors of the *EB* may be mentioned *Le Grand Dictionnaire* (1674) of Louis Moréri (1643–80), the *Dictionnaire historique et critique* (1697) of *Bayle (1647–1706), the *Cyclopaedia* (1728) of Ephraim *Chambers, and the great French *Encyclopédie* of the 18th cent.

The first *Encyclopaedia Britannica* was issued by a 'Society of Gentlemen in Scotland' in numbers (1768–71), the editor being William Smellie, a printer, afterwards secretary of the Society of Scottish Antiquaries. It was a dictionary of the arts and sciences. The second edition (1777–84), in ten vols, added history and biography. The third edition, in 15 vols, appeared in 1788–97; and the fourth edition, in 20 vols, in 1801–10. The undertaking was taken over by Constable in 1812, and the copyright sold after the failure of that house in 1826. After some further editions it passed to Cambridge University for the publication in 1910–11 of the eleventh edition in 28 vols [EB]. The tenth and eleventh editions were by Hugh Chisholm. The fourteenth edition, under the editorship-in-chief of J. L. Garvin, was published in London and New York in 1929. Since then a system of continuous revision has replaced the making of new editions. (See also CHAMBERS'S ENCYCLOPAEDIA.)

Encyclopaedists, the collaborators in the *Encyclopédie* of *Diderot and D'Alembert.

Encyclopédie, L', a dictionary of universal knowledge published between 1751 and 1776 in 35 vols under the editorship of *Diderot, with (until 1758) D'Alembert as his chief assistant, and with the leading intellectuals of the age, including *Voltaire, *Montesquieu, *Rousseau, *Buffon, and *Turgot, as contributors. It attempted nothing less than the provision of a rational explanation for all aspects of existence, and it can be regarded as the most representative monument of the *Enlightenment. Its attacks on superstition and credulity attracted the hostility of church and state. Something of the historical significance of the work can be gauged from the fact that the original investment of one million francs produced a profit of 300 per cent.

Endimion, *The Man in the Moone,* an allegorical prose play by *Lyly, published 1591.

Endimion abandons Tellus (the earth) in consequence of a hopeless passion for Cynthia (the moon). Tellus conspires with the witch Dipsas against Endimion, who is sent to sleep for 40 years. Cynthia breaks the spell and releases Endimion with a kiss. The dramatic element is slight, the allegory perhaps relating to the rivalry between *Elizabeth I (Cynthia) and *Mary Queen of Scots (Tellus), and the favour of Elizabeth for Leicester (Endimion).

End of the Affair, The, a novel by G. *Greene.

Endymion, a poem in four books, by *Keats, written 1817, published 1818.

The poem tells, with a wealth of epithet and invention, the story of Endymion, 'the brain-sick shepherd-prince' of Mount Latmos, who falls in love with Cynthia, the moon, and descends to the depths of the earth to find her. There he encounters a real woman, Phoebe, and giving up his pursuit of the ideal he falls in love with her. She, however, turns out to be none other than Cynthia, who, after luring him, weary and perplexed, through 'cloudy phantasms', bears him away to eternal life. With the main story are woven the legends of Venus and Adonis, of Glaucus and Scylla, and of Arethusa. The poem includes in Bk I the well-known 'Hymn to Pan', and in Bk IV the roundelay 'O sorrow'.

In his preface Keats describes the work as 'a feverish attempt, rather than a deed accomplished'. It is a work, rich in luxuriant imagery, of an immature genius, the product of sensation rather than thought. The allegory, which is sometimes obscure, appears to represent the poet pursuing ideal perfection, and distracted from his quest by human beauty. The work was violently attacked in the *Quarterly Review and in *Blackwood's, in which *Lockhart described the poem as one of 'calm, settled, imperturbable drivelling idiocy'.

Endymion, a novel by B. *Disraeli, published 1880.

This was the last of Disraeli's novels, set in an earlier period of his life between about 1830

and the early 1850s, and describing with vivacity the political and social scene of that time, as well as the antagonism between Whig and Tory, the power of the great political hostesses, the *Tractarians, railway-mania, the Chartists, and the story of Louis Napoleon as 'Florestan'. There are many other identifications: Lord Palmerston appears as the engaging Lord Roehampton; Lady Jersey as the relentless Zenobia; Bismark as Ferroll, Cardinal Manning as Penruddock, Rothschild as Mr Neuchatel; *Cobbett and *Cobden combine in Job Thornberry, *Thackeray (in revenge for his *Codlingsby*) is satirized as St Barbe.

Endymion, a reflective, sweet-natured boy, is the twin of the fiery, ambitious Myra, and the book is much concerned with their close relationship. Their father, Pitt Ferrars, is a rising young politician, who is enabled to move in the highest social circles in the expectation of a great inheritance, and of soon achieving Cabinet rank. When neither comes to him he kills himself, leaving his family almost destitute. Endymion obtains a clerkship at Somerset House, and after Myra has rejected Penruddock, because of her bond with Endymion, she obtains a place as companion to Adriana Neuchatel, the daughter of a kindly Jewish banker. Myra's beauty and wit bring her great success in society and she marries Lord Roehampton, who finds the retiring Endymion a place as secretary to a Cabinet Minister. The young man becomes deeply interested in the plight of the poor, and in Manchester becomes a friend of Job Thornberry, a bold young Radical and political economist. Throughout the novel there are rumblings of social unrest, and reports of incendiaries. Eventually Endymion is persuaded by Myra, and by Lady Montfort (whom he loves), to enter Parliament. After the death of Lord Roehampton Myra marries the exiled monarch Florestan and, reluctantly parting from her brother, goes to live abroad. When she too is free, Endymion marries Lady Montfort. On the death of the Prime Minister Endymion is asked to form the next government, and Myra returns to visit him in his triumph.

Enemy, The, a periodical which ran to three issues, 1927–9, edited and largely written by W. *Lewis.

ENGELS, Friedrich (1820–95), German philosopher, the son of a factory owner who supervised his father's business in Manchester. He wrote influential essays on the social and political conditions in Britain in the 1840s, including *The Condition of the Working Class in England* (1845), in which he praised *Carlyle as the only British writer to take account (in *Past and Present,* 1843) of the atrocious working conditions of the urban poor. Engels collaborated with *Marx, whom he helped to support when the latter settled in London in 1849, in writing

The German Ideology (1845–6, but not published until 1932), a critique of German philosophy as lacking in social application; the *Manifesto of the Communist Party* (1848); and their great work, *Das Kapital*, the third volume of which Engels completed after Marx's death.

Much has been extrapolated about Engels's views on literary theory from two letters, both written to aspiring novelists: in the first, written to Minna Kautsky in 1885, he says he is by no means opposed to literature designed to further social or political ideas (*Tendenzpoesie*), but that he believes 'the thesis must spring forth from the situation and action itself, without being explicitly displayed.' The second, written in English to Margaret Harkness in 1888 on receipt of a copy of her proletarian novel *A City Girl*, criticizes her work for being 'not quite realistic enough' . . . 'Realism, to my mind, implies, besides the truth of detail, the truthful reproduction of typical characters under typical circumstances . . . In *City Girl*, the working class appears as a passive mass, incapable of helping itself . . . ': but he reiterates that 'the more the opinions of the author remain hidden, the better the work of art.' These letters have been taken both to justify and to oppose the necessity for political commitment in art. (See also MARXIST LITERARY CRITICISM.)

Englands Helicon, a miscellany of Elizabethan verse, published in 1600, with additions in 1614, edited by H. E. Rollins (1935). It is the best collection of lyrical and pastoral poetry of the Elizabethan age, and includes pieces by *Sidney, *Spenser, *Drayton, R. *Greene, T. *Lodge, *Ralegh, *Marlowe, and others.

England's Parnassus, a collection of extracts from contemporary poets, by R. Allott, published in 1600.

English, the Germanic language spoken in England which takes its name from the Angles (who first committed their dialect to writing) and was extended to refer to all the dialects of the vernacular, Saxon and Jutish too. Old English (formerly *Anglo-Saxon) is the English language of the period ending soon after the Norman Conquest (*c.*1100–50); Middle English is used to describe the language from then to about 1500; Modern English, founded on the dialect of the East Midlands in Middle English, extends from 1500 to the present day.

English Association, founded in 1906 to promote the teaching and advanced study of the English language and of English literature, and to unite all those who are interested in these subjects. In the 1970s the Association founded a series of sixth-form conferences for third year A-level students.

English Bards and Scotch Reviewers, a satirical poem by Lord *Byron, published 1809.

Angered by contemptuous criticism of his *Hours of Idleness*, by *Brougham in the *Edinburgh Review*, Byron wrote this vigorous satire, in which he attacks not only *Jeffrey, the editor of the *Review*, but *Southey, Sir W. *Scott, *Wordsworth, *Coleridge, and other poets and poetasters of *Romanticism, at the same time holding up to admiration *Dryden, *Pope, *Burns, *Crabbe, *Campbell, *Rogers, and others who wrote in the classical tradition of the 18th cent.

English Comic Writers, The, by W. *Hazlitt, published 1819.

The essays cover a wide range of humorous dramatists, poets, novelists, and essayists, from Elizabethan times to the late 18th cent., and are marked by Hazlitt's characteristic vigour and enjoyment.

Englishman's Magazine, The (1831–3), an original and ambitious literary monthly, edited by E. *Moxon, which published poems, criticism, and essays, as well as notes on drama, music, and art. It published the work of the unknown young *Tennyson, as well as that of *Hood, *Lamb, Leigh *Hunt, *Clare, A. H. *Hallam, and others. It vigorously supported *Wordsworth and the *'Cockney School', defending them against *Blackwood's, the *Quarterly, and similar journals. Unusually for the time, more than half the contributions were signed. The *Englishman's* seems to have been killed by John *Wilson's scathing comments in *Blackwood's* on Hallam's effusive article proclaiming the genius of Tennyson.

English Place-Name Society, founded in 1923 to carry out the survey of English place-names inaugurated under the auspices of the *British Academy in 1922. The survey is published county by county.

English Review, The, a periodical founded in 1908 through the inspiration of a group of writers including *Conrad, H. G. *Wells, and E. *Garnett, with the purpose, in the words of its first editor F. M. *Ford (then Hueffer) of 'giving imaginative literature a chance in England'. It was backed at first by Arthur Marwood, the 'heavy Yorkshire squire' and friend of Ford, from whom Ford drew many of the characteristics of Christopher Tietjens in *Parade's End*. The first issue, in which appeared *Hardy's poem 'A Sunday Morning Tragedy', was published in Dec. 1908. The period of Ford's editorship (until Feb. 1910) was one of great distinction: Ford published work by established writers such as Arnold *Bennett, *Galsworthy, H. *James, and Wells, and by newcomers such as D. H. *Lawrence and W. *Lewis, amongst others. He was, however, impractical by temperament, ran the *Review* into financial difficulties, and was replaced by Austin Harrison, who remained editor until 1923. It was eventually merged with the *National Review*.

English Stage Company, an organization founded in 1956 by George Devine (1910–66) to present modern plays and encourage new dramatists; its home is the Royal Court Theatre, London. Its first production was A. *Wilson's *The Mulberry Bush* (2 April 1956), and it subsequently produced important new work by *Osborne, *Wesker, *Arden, *Bond, *Logue, *Storey, *Orton, *Jellicoe, N. F. *Simpson, *Beckett, Christopher Hampton, Heathcote Williams, David Hare, E. A. Whitehead, Brian Friel, *Fugard, Mustapha Matura, Caryl *Churchill, Howard Barker, Howard Brenton, and others. (See also KITCHEN SINK DRAMA.)

English Traits, see EMERSON, R. W.

English Traveller, The, a romantic drama by T. *Heywood, written c.1624, printed 1633.

Geraldine, returning from his travels, finds that the lady he loves has been married to Wincot, an old gentleman to whom he is under obligations. He and the lady bind themselves, she that she will marry him after Wincot's death, he that he will remain single till then. A plot by his treacherous friend Delavil leads to Geraldine's discovery that Delavil has seduced Wincot's wife. Heart-broken, Geraldine decides to leave the country. Before doing so he attends a farewell feast given him by Wincot. Wincot's wife hypocritically taxes him with his desertion of her, whereupon he reveals his discovery and upbraids her as an adulteress. She, in contrition and despair, dies.

There is a humorous under-plot, borrowed from the *Mostellaria* of *Plautus: the prodigal son who wastes his father's substance during the latter's absence on a voyage, the father's unexpected return, the tricks of a resourceful servant to postpone the discovery of the prodigal's doings, and the final pardon and general reconciliation.

'Enid', see IDYLLS OF THE KING, THE.

Enitharmon, in the mystical books of *Blake, the female counterpart and emanation of *Los, who represents Time, as she represents Space. She also represents Inspiration. She is the mother of the rebellious *Orc. See under URIZEN, THE BOOK OF, and EUROPE: A PROPHECY.

Enjambment, a technical term in verse, signifying the carrying on of the sense of a line or couplet into the next.

Enlightenment, a term (originally taken from the German *Aufklärung*) generally used to describe the philosophic, scientific, and rational spirit, the freedom from superstition, the scepticism and faith in religious tolerance of much of 18th-cent. Europe. The ancestors of the movement were *Descartes, *Locke, *Shaftesbury,

and *Newton. *Voltaire, *Rousseau, *Condorcet, and *Buffon were associated with the Enlightenment in the minds of English readers, as was one of its great monuments, *L'*Encyclopédie*. The *Encyclopaedia Britannica* was in part a product of the distinct and important intellectual movement sometimes described as the *Scottish Enlightenment. In England many writers and poets echo or develop the educational and political ideas of the Enlightenment, including *Godwin, *Shelley, E. *Darwin, *Akenside, and the *Edgeworths. *Blake subscribed to the politics of the Enlightenment, but not to what he saw as the 'single vision' of Newtonian materialism. *Paine was much influenced by the politics of the French Enlightenment and his *The Rights of Man* and the American Declaration of Independence were also characteristic products. On a more literary level, some have seen a connection between the philosophy of the Enlightenment, the growth of literary realism, and the rise of the novel: *Romanticism was in part a reaction.

ENNIUS, Quintus (239–169 BC), the father of Roman poetry, an Italian from Calabria, he introduced scansion by quantity, the hexameter, and many Homeric devices, so that his *Annals* have been called an epic though they do not centre on a single complete action. The 550 lines that have survived from his work show him to have achieved a rugged grandeur. *Dryden mentions him a number of times in his critical essays, stressing *Virgil's debt to him and comparing him to *Chaucer.

Enobarbus (Domitius Ahenobarbus), close companion and friend of Antony in Shakespeare's *Antony and Cleopatra*, who deserts him for Octavius Caesar after his fortunes have declined (IV. v). It is he who describes Antony's first meeting with Cleopatra in the famous 'barge' speech (II. ii).

Enoch Arden, a narrative poem by *Tennyson, published 1864; the story was suggested by his friend *Woolner.

Enoch Arden, Philip Ray, and Annie Lee are children together in a little seaport town; both boys love Annie, but Enoch wins and marries her. They live happily for some years, until Enoch is compelled through temporary adversity to go as boatswain in a merchantman. He is shipwrecked, and for more than ten years nothing is heard of him; Annie, consulting her Bible for a sign, puts her finger on the text 'Under the palm tree', which, after a dream, she interprets to mean that he is in heaven. She marries Philip, who has long watched over her. Tennyson then turns to Enoch on his desert island, which is described in a fine, clear, bright Parnassian passage, and contrasted with the 'dewy meadowy morning-breath of England' for which he yearns. He is rescued and returns home, but when he discovers that Annie has remarried does not reveal himself, resolving that she shall not know of his return until after his death. The last lines—'And when they buried him the little port | Had seldom seen a costlier funeral'—have caused much offence to some, but others have found them to echo a curiously ambiguous attitude to Providence which pervades the whole poem.

Enquiry concerning Human Understanding, see HUME, D.

Enquiry into the Present State of Polite Learning, An, a treatise by *Goldsmith, published 1759.

This was Goldsmith's first considerable piece of writing, in which he examines the causes of the decline of 'polite learning' from ancient times, through the dark ages, to its present state in Italy, Germany, Holland, France, and England, with perfunctory references to Spain and the Scandinavian countries. He attributes the alleged decay in England to the low status of the writer, driven to hack-work for the booksellers through lack of patronage—'We keep him poor, and yet revile his poverty'; also to the 'disgusting solemnity' and lack of comic spirit among poets, the restrictive conditions of the theatre, and the carping of critics. His attack on theatrical managers and actors offended *Garrick, and (according to T. *Davies) he toned it down for the second edition of 1774.

ENRIGHT, D(ennis) J(oseph) (1920–), poet, born in Leamington and educated at Leamington College and Downing College, Cambridge. He taught English literature for 25 years, mainly in the East; many of his poems are set in Japan, Egypt, Singapore, and Germany, and concern cultural differences and misunderstandings, themes which he also explores in various critical essays and in his autobiographical *Memoirs of a Mendicant Professor* (1969). His first collection of verse, *The Laughing Hyena and other poems* (1953), was followed by several others, including *Bread rather than Blossoms* (1956), *Addictions* (1962), *Sad Ires* (1975), and *A Faust Book* (1979; a sequence of poems on the *Faust legend). His *Collected Poems*, with new poems, appeared in 1981. He has also published novels for children (*The Joke Shop*, 1976; *Wild Ghost Chase*, 1978; *Beyond Land's End*, 1979) and various other prose works, including *The World of Dew: Aspects of Living Japan* (1955), *Insufficient Poppy* (1960, a novel), and works of criticism, including *Man is an Onion* (1972, collected reviews and essays). His anthology *Poets of the 1950s* (1955) brought together many of the poets to appear in R. Conquest's *New Verse, and in his preface to his anthology *The Oxford Book of Contemporary Verse 1945–1980* (1980) he reasserted the claims of 'the poetry of civility, passion, and order'

against those of the confessional mode, as written by R. *Lowell, *Berryman, and others. His own work is predominantly detached and ironic in tone (although by no means impersonal) and wide ranging in its subject matter. He also edited *The Oxford Book of Death* (1983).

Entail, The, a novel by J. *Galt, published 1823, a satire on the corrupting effects of greed.

Claud Walkinshaw, a successful packman, cruelly disinherits his eldest son in favour of his second, who is a half-wit. Walkinshaw is thereby enabled to recover the ancestral property of his family. The disastrous consequences of his act recoil upon himself, and on his children and grandchildren. As a study in obsession the book is powerful, and it was admired by *Byron.

Eōthen, see KINGLAKE, A. W.

Ephesus, Seven Sleepers of, see SEVEN SLEEPERS OF EPHESUS.

Epic, a poem that celebrates in the form of a continuous narrative the achievements of one or more heroic personages of history or tradition. Among the great epics of the world may be mentioned the *Iliad, *Odyssey, and *Aeneid* of classical, and the *Mahābhārata* and *Rāmāyaṇa* of Hindu literature; the *Chanson de *Roland; the *Poema del Cid* (see CID, THE); Milton's *Paradise Lost; Boiardo's *Orlando Innamorato; Ariosto's *Orlando Furioso; Tasso's *Gerusalemme Liberata; and *Camoëns' *Lusiads*.

Epicene, or *The Silent Woman,* a comedy by *Jonson, acted by the Children of the Queen's Revels 1609–10, printed 1616.

Morose, an egotistic old bachelor with a pathological aversion to noise, proposes to disinherit his nephew Sir Dauphine Eugenie, whom he suspects of ridiculing him, by marrying and producing children, provided he can find a silent woman. Cutbeard, his barber, has found such a one in Epicene. Immediately after the wedding Epicene proceeds to torment her husband by turning into a loquacious shrew, and his agony is increased when Dauphine and his friends Truewit and Clerimont arrive with a rowdy party of guests and musicians to celebrate the marriage. Among the guests are a henpecked bearward, Captain Otter, and his Amazonian wife, the *Collegiate Ladies, and two boastful knights, Amorous La Foole and John Daw, whose cowardice is exposed when Truewit tricks them into fighting a duel. Driven frantic by the hubbub, and having unsuccessfully sought grounds for divorce from a parson and canon lawyer (in fact impostors planted by Dauphine, who chatter interminably to no purpose), Morose accepts Dauphine's offer to rid him of Epicene for £500 a year and the reversion of his property. Whereupon Dauphine pulls off Epicene's wig and reveals that, unknown to everyone else, including the audience, she is a boy whom he has trained for the part. *Dryden thought this play the most perfectly plotted of all comedies.

Epic Simile, an extended simile which compares one composite action with another, often with a digressive effect; it originates in *Homer, and was imitated by *Virgil, *Dante, and, in English, notably by *Milton. It is frequently parodied by *Fielding.

EPICTETUS (*c*. AD 60–after 100), a *Stoic philosopher, said to have been a freedman, poor and lame. He wrote nothing himself; the *Encheiridion*, or collection of his principles, was compiled by his disciple Arrian. Epictetus held health, pleasure, possessions to be of no account. Virtue alone mattered, and that resided in the will which should direct man to abstain and endure. The *Encheiridion* was translated from the Greek by John Healey (1610). It influenced *Chapman and was praised by *Dryden, although he found it dry reading. Not surprisingly, however, it was one of M. *Arnold's favourite works.

EPICURUS (341–279 BC), the founder of the school of philosophy that bears his name, after teaching in various places settled finally in Athens. Some fragments of his writings survive, but his ideas are perhaps best studied in the *De rerum natura* of *Lucretius. Epicurus adopted the atomic theory of *Democritus but postulated an indeterminacy in the movement of his atoms which allowed him to believe in free will. In ethics he regarded the absence of pain—ἀγαραξία or peace of mind—as the greatest good. Conventional moralists tended to describe him as a contemptible pleasure-seeker, but his life had been marked by rigorous abstinence from greed, lust, and anger, a fact which made Sir T. *Browne defend his reputation (*Pseudodoxia*, 7. 17). Epicureanism in a modified form, amounting perhaps to no more than a gentlemanly avoidance of over-rigid principles, was common at the end of the 17th cent. It found its high priest in the French exile *Sainte-Evremond, for whose translated essays *Dryden wrote an appreciative preface (1692).

Epigram, originally an inscription, usually in verse, e.g. on a tomb; hence a short poem ending in a witty turn of thought; hence a pointed or antithetical saying.

Epigrams, The, a collection of poems by *Jonson, printed 1616, including 'Inviting a Friend to Supper', 'On My First Son', 'The Famous Voyage', and addresses to *Donne and King James.

Epiphany, 'manifestation', usually used in a Christian context to refer to the festival commemorating the manifestation of Christ to the Gentiles in the persons of the Magi (celebrated on 6 Jan., or Twelfth Night); but adapted by *Joyce to describe the sudden 'revelation of the whatness of a thing', the moment in which 'the soul of the commonest object seems to us radiant'. He uses the word in this sense in *Stephen Hero*, an early draft of *A Portrait of the Artist as a Young Man*. These 'sudden spiritual manifestations' have been detected by critics in other revelatory moments in Joyce's work, and in the work of other writers; they bear some similarity to the 'spots of time' described by Wordsworth in *The Prelude* (see Bk XI, ll. 208 ff.).

Epipsychidion, an autobiographical poem by P. B. *Shelley written at Pisa in 1821, and published there anonymously in the same year.

Composed in couplets of breathless energy, the poem celebrates Shelley's lifelong search for the eternal image of Beauty, in the earthly form of his various wives, mistresses, and female friends: notably Harriet Westbrook, Mary *Shelley, Claire *Clairmont, and Emilia Viviani—to whom the work is addressed: 'In many mortal forms I rashly sought | The Shadow of that idol of my thought.' Though drawing on the courtly love and planetary imagery of *Petrarch and *Dante, the work is passionately sexual as well as Platonic: it ends with an invitation to Emilia to elope to 'an isle under Ionian skies, | Beautiful as a wreck of Paradise'. There is an attack on conventional marriage, 'the dreariest and longest journey', and praise of 'Free' or 'True' Love (ll. 148–73). Yet despite its blaze of amorous rhetoric, the poem is partly also a study of the creative process itself.

The title remains a puzzle: perhaps from the *epi-psyche*, the 'soul out of my soul', or beloved; or perhaps with ironic reference to the *epithalamium*, the conventional marriage song. A close biographical reading reveals much sly humour.

Epistolae Obscurorum Virorum (*Epistles of Obscure Men*), published 1515–17, an anonymous collection of letters in medieval Latin purporting to be written by various bachelors and masters in theology to Ortuinus Gratius, a famous opponent of the new learning, in which they incidentally expose themselves to ridicule and to scurrilous charges. The letters are attributed principally to Ulrich von Hutten (1488–1523), soldier, humanist, and supporter of *Luther, and were written in connection with the celebrated *Reuchlin–*Pfefferkorn controversy.

Epistolary novel, a story written in the form of letters, or letters with journals, and usually presented by an anonymous author masquerading as 'editor'. The first notable example in English, written entirely in epistolary form, was a translation from the French in 1678, *Letters of a Portuguese Nun*. In 1683 A. *Behn published *Love-letters between a Nobleman and his Sister*, and many similar tales of illicit love and love-manuals followed. Thus when *Richardson, the first and perhaps greatest master of the form, came to write *Pamela* (1741) he felt a duty to rescue the novel from its tainted reputation. The immediacy of the epistolary form lends itself to intense subjective analysis, but also to charges of implausible absurdity (fully exploited by Fielding in *Shamela*). Between the 1740s and about 1800, when the form chiefly flourished, it was employed not only by Richardson but by *Smollett, *Bage, J. *Moore (the elder), and F. *Burney, among many others. After 1800 both M. *Edgeworth and J. *Austen experimented with the form, as did *Swinburne and H. *James, among others; it is now rarely adopted, but W. *Golding's *Rites of Passage* (1980) provides an interesting variation in the form of an epistolary journal. (See also NOVEL, RISE OF THE.)

Epithalamion, a hymn by *Spenser, perhaps in celebration of his marriage with Elizabeth Boyle in 1594. The poem was printed with the *Amoretti* in 1595. Its beauty of composition has always been much admired, and in 1960, Kent Hieatt (in his *Short time's endless monument*) demonstrated that its 24 stanzas represent the hours of Midsummer Day.

Epithalamium, or **Epithalamion**, a poem or song written to celebrate a marriage. The form flourished in the Renaissance, one of the most notable examples being Spenser's *Epithalamion*.

Eponymous, that gives his name to anything, used for example of the mythical personages from whose names the names of places or peoples are reputed to be derived. It is now most frequently used in the phrase, 'the eponymous hero/heroine' of a work: e.g. *Tom Jones or *Clarissa.

Eppie, in G. Eliot's *Silas Marner*, the daughter of Cass and adopted child of Silas.

ERASMUS, Desiderius (*c.*1467–1536), the great Dutch humanist, was born at Rotterdam. Under pressure of his guardians he became an Augustinian monk, but thanks to the protection of the bishop of Cambrai was allowed to leave the cloister and travel extensively in Europe. He came more than once to England, where he was welcomed by the great scholars of the day, *More, *Colet and *Grocyn, and was induced by *Fisher to lecture at Cambridge on Greek from 1511 to 1514. He was a friend and patron of *Holbein, whom he introduced to More, and by whom he was painted several times. He received from Archbishop Warham the benefice of Aldington in Kent and, on resigning it, a pension which was continued until his death. His principal works were a new edition of the Greek New Testament (1516), followed by Latin

paraphrases (1517–24); *Encomium Moriae* (*The Praise of Folly*, 1511, a satire written at the suggestion of More, principally directed against theologians and Church dignitaries); *Enchiridion Militis Christiani* (1503, a manual of simple piety according to the teaching of Jesus Christ, which was translated perhaps by *Tyndale into English, and also into other languages; *Institutio Christiani Principis* (*Education of a Christian Prince*); the vivid and entertaining *Colloquia* and letters furnishing autobiographical details and pictures of contemporary life, which were drawn upon by C. Reade in *The Cloister and the Hearth* and by Sir W. Scott in *Anne of Geierstein*. His *Adagia* (1500), a collection of Latin and Greek proverbs traced to their source with witty comments, one of the first works of the new learning, was much drawn upon by *Rabelais and by many English writers. His many editions and translations of the Bible, early Christian authors, and the classics revolutionized European literary culture. Erasmus prepared the way for the Reformation by his writings. With the movement itself he sympathized at first, but he refused to intervene either for or against *Luther at the time of the Diet of Worms, although invoked by both sides. He urged moderation on both and disclaimed sympathy with Luther's violence and extreme conclusions, and at a later stage (1524, in his tract on 'Free Will') entered into controversy with him. The standard edition of the letters of Erasmus (11 vols, 1906–47) was edited by P. S. and H. M. Allen.

ERCELDOUNE, Thomas of, called also the Rhymer and Learmont (*fl.* ?1220–?97), seer and poet, is mentioned in the chartulary (1294) of the Trinity House of Soltra as having inherited lands in Erceldoune, a Berwickshire village. He is said to have predicted the death of Alexander III, king of Scotland, and the battle of Bannockburn, and is the traditional source of many (fabricated) oracles, one of which 'foretold' the accession of James VI to the English throne. He is the reputed author of a poem on the *Tristram story, which Sir W. *Scott considered genuine; it probably emanated from a French source. The romance of 'True Thomas' and the 'ladye gaye', popularly attributed to him, may be placed after 1401 (ed. J. A. H. *Murray, 1875).

Erewhon (e–re–whon, an anagram of 'nowhere'), a satirical novel by S. *Butler, published anonymously 1872.

The narrator (whose name is revealed in *Erewhon Revisited* as Higgs) crosses a range of mountains and comes upon the undiscovered country of Erewhon. He is first thrown into gaol, where he is helped by his beautiful girl gaoler, Yram. On his release he is lodged with Mr Nosnibor (Robinson) and his family. In this society morality is equated with health and beauty, and crime with illness. The Unborn select their parents, who have to endure their selection. The Musical Banks produce a currency which is venerated but not used. The development of machinery, which had at one stage threatened to usurp human supremacy, had led to a civil war and is now forbidden. The country is ruled by so-called philosophers and prophets, whom Higgs sees to be merely faddists and fanatics. When he is threatened with prosecution for contracting measles, Higgs announces that he will visit the air-god and end the terrible drought; with Nosnibor's daughter Arowhena, he escapes in a balloon to England, where they marry. The story, which was written over a period of ten years, had its origin in Butler's article 'Darwin among the Machines', published in New Zealand in 1863.

Erewhon Revisited, a sequel to *Erewhon,* by S. *Butler, published 1901.

John, the son of Higgs and Arowhena, is the writer of this account of his father's return to Erewhon. After 20 years Higgs finds that his ascent in the balloon has become that of a god, the Sunchild, in a sun-chariot, his conversation has become the basis of sacred texts, a temple has been built to him at Sunchildiston, and that the new religion is organized by two cynical exploiters, professors Hanky and Panky. Once again Higgs's life is threatened, but again he escapes and, after further bewildered wanderings in Erewhon, returns, half unhinged, to England.

Eric, or, Little by Little, see FARRAR, F. W.

ERIGENA, see SCOTUS ERIGENA.

ERIKSON, Eric Homburger (1902–   ), psychoanalyst, born in Frankfurt-am-Main and educated at the Vienna Psychoanalytic Institute and at Harvard. He settled in the US in 1933. His works include *Childhood and Society* (1950), *Insight and Responsibility* (1964), and *Gandhi's Truth: on the origins of militant nonviolence* (1969). His biography of *Luther, *Young Man Luther* (1958), is an example of psycho-biography—that is, a clinical biography in which he applies to Luther 'the first Protestant at the end of the age of absolute faith, insights developed by Freud, the first psychoanalyst at the end of the era of absolute reason', and discusses in analytic terms Luther's adolescent identity crisis, his 'fit in the choir' and 'revelation on the tower', his obscenity and coprophilic attacks on the Pope, and other aspects of his personality and psychic history.

Erin, the ancient name of Ireland.

Erl-King, the German *Erl-könig* (alder-king), an erroneous rendering of the Danish *eller-konge,* king of the elves, a malignant goblin who, in German legend and in *Goethe's poem on the subject, haunts the Black Forest and lures people,

particularly children, to destruction. Goethe's poem was the foundation of one of *Schubert's best-known songs ('Erlkönig', written 1816), and was translated by Sir W. *Scott.

Ernani, see HERNANI.

Ernest Maltravers, a novel by *Bulwer-Lytton.

ERNULF, or **ERNULPHUS** (1040–1124), bishop of Rochester, supposed compiler of the *Textus Roffensis,* a collection of laws, papal decrees, and documents relating to the church of Rochester. The comprehensive curse or excommunication of Ernulphus figures in Bk III, chs x, xi of Sterne's *Tristram Shandy.

Eros, in Shakespeare's *Antony and Cleopatra, is the faithful attendant of Antony, and kills himself to avoid killing his master.

Erse, a term formerly used for Irish Gaelic (i.e. Irish) or occasionally (and inaccurately, since the term is the Lowland Scots word for Irish) for Scots Gaelic.

ERVINE, St John Greer (1883–1971), playwright and novelist, was born in Belfast of a long-established Ulster family. Many of his early plays (including *Mixed Marriage,* 1911; *The Magnanimous Lover,* 1912; and *John Ferguson,* 1915) were performed at the *Abbey Theatre in its realist phase, and dealt with themes of religious violence and conflict in Northern Ireland. Ervine later moved to England, where he wrote as drama critic for the *Morning Post and the *Observer, and achieved his first West End success with *The First Mrs Fraser* (1929), which was followed by many other popular comedies. He also published several novels, and studies of C. S. *Parnell (1925), General *Booth (1934), and G. B. *Shaw (1956).

ESENIN, Sergei Aleksandrovich (1895–1925), Russian poet. The son of a peasant from central Russia, Esenin first visited Moscow in 1911. The themes of his first collection of poems, *Memorial Service* (1915), religious Russia and the village, are those associated with his early success. He greeted the October Revolution as bringing peace and land to the peasants. He signed the Imaginist Declaration in Jan. 1919. (Though the Imaginists were aware of *Pound and English *Imagism, links between them are very tenuous.) Major themes in his later years were urban hooliganism and the death of the Russian village. He married the dancer Isadora Duncan in 1922 and visited the United States with her. His last years were characterized by disillusionment, drunkenness, and excess and he committed suicide, writing his last poem in his own blood. He fell out of favour in the USSR until after the Second World War, but is now one of the most popular Russian poets. The major English translation is that of Geoffrey Thurley, *Confessions of a Hooligan* (1973).

Esmond, see HISTORY OF HENRY ESMOND, THE.

Esmond, Beatrix, a character in Thackeray's *The History of Henry Esmond* and, as Baroness Bernstein, in *The Virginians*.

Esoteric, a word used by *Lucian, who attributes to *Aristotle a classification of his own works into 'esoteric', i.e. designed for, or appropriate to, an inner circle of advanced or privileged disciples, and 'exoteric', i.e. popular, untechnical. Later writers use the word to designate the secret doctrines said to have been taught by *Pythagoras to a select few of his disciples; it has come to denote any work restricted to a narrow, informed audience.

Esperanto, an artificial language for universal use invented (*c.*1887) by a Polish physician, Dr L. L. Zamenhof.

Espriella, see SOUTHEY, R.

Esprit de l'escalier, French, a tardy wit, which thinks of a smart retort or witticism too late, when its owner is going downstairs on his way out of the house.

ESQUEMELING, EXQUEMELING, or OEXMELIN, Alexander Olivier, a Dutch physician, who lived with the buccaneers, 1668–74, and published an account of them (including Sir Henry Morgan, 1635–88, a Glamorgan-born buccaneer who later became deputy governor of Jamaica) and their doings. This was translated into Spanish, French, and English: there is a recent translation by A. Brown, *The Buccaneers of America* (1969).

Essay concerning Human Understanding, a philosophical treatise by *Locke, published 1690 (2nd edn, 1694; 4th, 1700; 5th, 1706; all with large additions).

The Essay is an examination of the nature of the human mind and its powers of understanding. Locke begins in Bk I by rejecting the doctrine of 'innate ideas', maintaining that all knowledge is based on experience. The objects of understanding are termed by him *ideas*, and Bk II provides an account of the origin, sorts, and extent of our ideas. The source of ideas is *experience*, the observation of external objects or of the internal operations of the mind, i.e. sensation or reflection. Sensation is always of a quality. Qualities are either primary—extension, figure, mobility, and number; or secondary, not really belonging to things but imputed to them, depending on our subjective perception, and inscrutably connected with the primary qualities, which alone really belong to things. A number of simple ideas being constantly found to go together, the mind is led to suppose a substratum for them, and this we call *substance*, but we have

no other idea of its nature. We are equally ignorant of spiritual substance, the substratum of the operations of the mind: we do not even know whether material or spiritual substance are the same or different. The idea of cause or power is derived from experience, principally of the workings of the mind; this discussion of power leads Locke into a long and subtle account of the 'freedom of the will'.

In Bk III Locke discusses language. He holds that words have meaning insofar as they stand for ideas in the mind; distinguishing between 'real' and 'nominal' essence, he argues that terms for natural kinds (e.g. 'gold', 'horse') can express only nominal essences or sets of ideas; they cannot latch on to the real essences or hidden constitutions of the things themselves, which may always remain beyond our grasp.

Bk IV defines knowledge as the perception of the agreement or disagreement of ideas. It is either intuitive and direct, demonstrative (through the interposition of a third idea), or 'sensitive', i.e. based upon perception. Knowledge in matters of real existence is limited to two certainties, of our own existence, by intuition, and of the existence of God, by demonstration. We have a lesser degree of certainty of the existence of finite beings without us, for which we must rely on sensitive knowledge. If the mind perceives nothing but its own ideas, how can we know that they agree with the things themselves? Locke advances various arguments for the possibility of 'real' knowledge (i.e. knowledge about real things), but points out that even if we admit its validity, this knowledge is narrowly limited: we know only of the existence together, here and now, of collections of simple ideas; we cannot demonstrate the necessity of their co-existence. There are therefore very few general propositions, carrying with them undoubted certainty, to be made concerning substances; a perfect science of natural bodies is unattainable. Experience and history is all we can attain to, from which we may derive advantages of ease and health. Knowledge at once general and real must be, not of the relations of ideas to reality, but of ideas to each other, as, e.g., in mathematics, and also, Locke oddly thought, in ethics (though on the latter point he is more doubtful in his *Reasonableness of Christianity*). The faculty that God has given us in place of clear knowledge is judgement, whereby the mind takes a proposition to be true or false without demonstration. Locke discusses the relations of faith and reason. Unlike F. *Bacon and *Hobbes, he holds that faith is nothing but the firm assent of the mind, which should not be accorded to anything except for good reason. Revelation must be judged by reason. But the field of knowledge being so limited, it must be supplemented by faith, and this is the basis of his *Reasonableness of Christianity* (1695).

Essay on Criticism, a didactic poem in heroic

couplets by *Pope, published anonymously 1711. It begins with an exposition of the rules of taste and the authority to be attributed to the ancient writers on the subject. The laws by which a critic should be guided are then discussed, and instances are given of critics who have departed from them. The work is remarkable as having been written when Pope was only 21.

Essay on Man, a philosophical poem in heroic couplets by *Pope, published 1732–4, part of a larger poem projected but not completed.

It consists of four epistles addressed to *Bolingbroke, and perhaps to some extent inspired by his fragmentary philosophical writings. Its objective is to vindicate the ways of God to man; to prove that the scheme of the universe is the best of all possible schemes, in spite of appearances of evil, and that our failure to see the perfection of the whole is due to our limited vision. 'Partial Ill' is 'universal Good', and 'self-love and social' are both directed to the same end: 'All are but parts of one stupendous whole | Whose body Nature is, and God the soul.' The epistles deal with man's relations to the universe, to himself as an individual, to society, and to happiness. D. *Stewart thought the *Essay* 'the noblest specimen of philosophical poetry which our language affords' (*Active and Moral Powers*, 1828), but Dr *Johnson commented, 'Never were penury of knowledge and vulgarity of sentiment so happily disguised.' Pope's attempts to prove that 'Whatever is, is right' recall the efforts of Pangloss in *Voltaire's *Candide*.

Essay on the Learning of Shakespeare, An, by Richard Farmer (1735–97), published 1767. This brief volume consists of a forceful presentation of Farmer's views, and a scornful refutation of his opponents', on the subject of Shakespeare's knowledge of languages, ancient and modern. Farmer's conclusion is that Shakespeare's studies were 'most demonstratively confined to Nature and his own Language'.

Essays, The, or *Counsels, Civill and Morall,* of F. *Bacon, are collections of reflections and generalizations, and extracts from previous authors, woven together, for the most part, into counsels for the successful conduct of life and the management of men.

Three editions of the essays were published in Bacon's lifetime. The first, 1597, contained ten essays; the second, 1612, contained thirty-eight essays; and the third, 1625, contained fifty-eight. Of these some deal with questions of state policy, such as the essay on 'Greatness of Kingdoms'; some with personal conduct, such as those on 'Wisdom for a Man's Self' and 'Cunning'; some on abstract subjects, such as 'Truth', 'Death', and 'Unity'; while some reveal Bacon's delight in Nature, such as the pleasant essay on 'Gardens'.

Essays and Reviews, a collection of essays on religious subjects from a *Broad Church standpoint published in 1860. Among them were M. *Pattison's 'Tendencies of Religious Thought in England 1688–1750' and *Jowett's 'The interpretation of Scripture'. The other essayists were the Revd H. B. Wilson (editor), Frederick Temple, Rowland Williams, Baden Powell, and C. W. Goodwin. A meeting of the bishops, urged on by Samuel Wilberforce, in 1861 denounced the book for its liberalism. Williams and Wilson were condemned to deprivation for a year, but were acquitted on appeal. The *Essays* were finally synodically condemned in 1864.

Essays Contributed to the Edinburgh Review, *Critical and Historical,* by T. B. *Macaulay, a collection published in 1843 and later editions. The essays deal with literary and historical subjects, taking the form not so much of a review as of a general survey of the subject of the book discussed; topics include (with dates of original publication) *Milton (1825), *Machiavelli (1827), *Croker's edition of Boswell (1831), Horace *Walpole (1833), *Chatham (1834 and 1844), Sir F. *Bacon (1837), Sir W. *Temple (1838), *Clive (1840), W. *Hastings (1841), and *Addison (1843).

Essays in Criticism, three series of essays by M. *Arnold, published in 1865, 1888, and 1910. The title was adopted by F. W. *Bateson for a periodical founded in 1951, in which he intended to combine 'social relevance' and 'scholarly standards', and in which the influence both of Arnold himself and of *Scrutiny may be detected.

Essays of Elia, The, miscellaneous essays by C. *Lamb, of which the first series appeared in the *London Magazine between 1820 and 1823, in which latter year they appeared as a separate volume. *The Last Essays of Elia* was published in 1833. Lamb adopted the name Elia, which was that of a former Italian clerk at the South Sea House, ostensibly to save the embarrassment of his brother John, who worked at that same place, but also, one must suppose, for literary reasons. The essays are all cast as if written by Elia, but they are not reliably autobiographical, even when seeming so. The fanciful, old-fashioned character of the narrator is maintained throughout. He is, in Lamb's words, 'a bundle of prejudices' with a strong liking for the whimsical, the quaint, and the eccentric. The tone is never didactic or seriously philosophical, and all the more disturbing aspects of life are avoided. The style is very literary and carefully wrought, filled with archaisms and with echoes of Lamb's master *Sterne. Some of the best-known essays were: 'Some of the Old Benchers of the Inner Temple'; 'Christ's Hospital'; 'The South Sea House'; 'Mrs Battle's Opinions on Whist'; 'Dream Children'; and 'A Dissertation on Roast

Pig'. The collected essays of 1823 did not sell well, to Lamb's great discouragement. A falling off in the quality of the *Last Essays* is very apparent.

ESSEX, Robert Devereux, second earl of (1566–1601), was the stepson of Queen *Elizabeth's old favourite the earl of *Leicester. He was regarded as the natural successor to *Sidney, whose widow he married in 1590. A period of intense and lucrative favour in the 1590s culminated in his despatch to Ireland in March 1599 to suppress Tyrone's rebellion. Shakespeare referred optimistically in *Henry V (v. Prologue 29–34) to the successful return of 'the General of our gracious Empress', but in fact Essex's return was sudden and ignominious. He came back without leave, having panicked at his lack of success, and after almost a year of house arrest he made an abortive attempt at rebellion in the City of London in Feb. 1601. A special performance of Shakespeare's *Richard II*, showing a monarch willingly abdicating an unpopular rule, had been among the activities by which Essex and his friends fomented discontent. Essex was executed on 25 Feb., the episode casting a dark shadow over the last 18 months of Elizabeth's reign. He was a literary patron of some discernment, and himself wrote poems of which a small handful have survived. L. *Strachey's *Elizabeth and Essex* (1928) is a highly coloured and highly readable fictionalization; among many more recent biographies is Robert Lacey's *An Elizabethan Icarus* (1971).

Estella, a character in Dickens's *Great Expectations*.

Esther Lyon (or **Bycliffe**), the heroine of G. Eliot's *Felix Holt*.

Esther Summerson, a character in Dickens's *Bleak House*, and narrator of part of the story.

Esther Waters, a novel by G. *Moore, published 1894.

It is the story of the life of a religiously minded girl, a Plymouth Sister, driven from home into service at 17 by a drunken stepfather. She obtains a situation at Woodview, the house of the Barfields, where a racing-stable is kept, and all above- and below-stairs (except Mrs Barfield, a Plymouth Sister like Esther) are wrapped up in gambling on races. There, in a moment of weakness, she is seduced by a fellow servant and deserted. She has to leave her place, though kindly treated by Mrs Barfield. Then follows a poignant tale of poverty, hardship, and humiliation: the lying-in hospital, service as wet-nurse, other miserable situations, even the workhouse, in the mother's brave struggle to rear her child. Her seducer re-enters her life, marries her, and makes a good husband. But he is a bookmaker and publican; exposure to weather at the races ruins his health and trouble

with the authorities over betting at his public house causes the latter to be closed. He dies, and leaves his wife and son penniless. Finally Esther returns to Woodview, where she finds peace at last with Mrs Barfield, now a widow, living alone and impoverished in a corner of the old house.

ESTIENNE, in Latin Stephanus, the name of a family of French printers and scholars. Henri Estienne (d. 1520), of a Provençal family, came to Paris in 1502 and founded a printing-house. His son Robert (1503–59) was printer to Francis I, and printed a number of important works and compiled the best Latin dictionary of the time, *Thesaurus linguae Latinae* (1532). He was a Protestant, and in 1551 was exiled to Geneva. His son Henri Estienne (1531–98) spent most of his life at Geneva, where he printed for the Republic, but also visited France, Italy, Flanders, and England: an ardent Hellenist, he printed works of Greek authors and compiled a *Thesaurus Graecae Linguae* (1572).

Esto Perpetua Club, founded in 1784, consisted of supporters of Fox against Pitt, including Dr French Laurence, G. *Ellis, the antiquary General Richard Fitzpatrick, and Lord John Townshend. The idea of *The Rolliad* originated with this club.

Estrildis, a German princess captured and brought to England by King *Humber according to *Geoffrey of Monmouth's *History*, ii. 2–5. *Locrine, king of Britain, fell in love with her and they had a daughter Habren (*Sabrina). Locrine put aside his wife Gwendolen for her, but she exacted vengeance on him by pursuing and slaying him in battle and having Estrildis and her daughter drowned in the river Severn, thereafter named from the daughter. Geoffrey says: 'It thus comes about that right down to our own times this river is called Habren in the British language, although by a corruption of speech it is called Sabrina in the other tongue' (ii. 5; Penguin trans. Lewis Thorpe, 1966, p. 77). In *Wace and *Laȝamon the river is called 'Auren' which Madden, in his edition of Laȝamon, identifies as the Dorsetshire Avon. The story is treated in *Lodge's 'The Complaynt of Elstred' (1593), in Spenser's *Faerie Queene* (II. x), and in *Swinburne's drama *Locrine* (1887). See *Comus* in which *Milton makes Thyrsis invoke Sabrina as the goddess of the river Severn.

Ethan Frome, see WHARTON, E..

ETHEREGE, or **ETHEREDGE,** Sir George (?1634–91), seems to have spent part of his early years in France, and was a man about town in London when his first comedy, *The Comical Revenge, or Love in a Tub*, was performed in 1664. The serious portions are in rhymed heroics, setting a fashion that was followed for some years, while the lively and realistic comic underplot, in prose, was the foundation of the English comedy of manners of *Congreve and *Goldsmith; Etherege drew his inspiration in part from *Molière's farces and from Italian mime, styles which were to have important influence on the lighter modes of English drama for the rest of the century. In 1668 *She wou'd if she cou'd was performed, and in the same year Etherege travelled to Turkey as secretary to the ambassador, returning in 1671. His best play, *The Man of Mode, was performed in 1676. He married a wealthy widow and was knighted, c.1680, and was an envoy of James II in Ratisbon, 1685-9; his Letterbook recording his stay and his nonchalant attitude to his duties was edited in 1928 by S. Rosenfeld. He died in Paris, a Jacobite exile. His polished and fashionable comedies were savagely attacked as immoral and coarse by the more genteel generation of *Steele and the 19th cent. found them formless and plotless, but they now enjoy a high reputation.

Etherington, earl of, a character in Scott's *St Ronan's Well.

Eton College, near Windsor, was founded by Henry VI, as a preparatory school for King's College, Cambridge, the charter of foundation being dated 1440 and followed by various charters of endowment. The College included, in addition to some 300 sons of noblemen and gentlemen, 70 king's scholars on the foundation, who passed by seniority to King's College, Cambridge. In 1443 Waynflete, headmaster of Winchester, was induced by the king to migrate to Eton, and was accompanied by five fellows and thirty-five scholars of Winchester.

Among the many names eminent in literature connected with Eton may be mentioned *Wotton, *Waller, *Fielding, T. *Gray, *Shelley, *Swinburne, *Bridges, *Orwell, and *Connolly.

Ettrick Shepherd, The, a name given to James *Hogg.

Eugene Aram, a novel by *Bulwer-Lytton, published 1832. It is the story of a schoolmaster, driven to crime by poverty, who is later tormented by remorse. The same subject suggested T. *Hood's poem 'The Dream of Eugene Aram'.

Eugenius, a minor character in *Tristram Shandy, and *A Sentimental Journey, by L. Sterne, thought to be based on Sterne's friend, *Hall-Stevenson.

EUHEMERUS, a Sicilian in the service of Cassander of Macedonia (311–298 BC). He wrote a 'Sacred History' in which he advanced the theory that the Greek gods were human kings or heroes, deified after their death by those whom they had ruled over or benefited. This method of explaining mythological stories was called after him 'Euhemerism'.

EULENSPIEGEL, Till, a German born according to tradition about 1300, the son of a peasant, and the subject of a collection of satirical tales, German or Flemish in origin, published in 1519 (Flemish version 1520–1). He is a scapegrace whose knaveries and escapades are carried on under a pretence of simplicity and stupidity, and are directed against noblemen, priests, tradesmen, and innkeepers. One of these incidents figures in Chaucer's 'Summoner's Tale' (see CANTERBURY TALES, 8). The book was translated into many languages, among others into English in an abridged form by William Copland, under the title of A merye jest of a man that was called Howleglas (?1555, ?1560). See The Marvellous Adventures . . . of Master Tyll Owlglass, trans. K. R. H. Mackenzie (1860).

Euphorion, in Pt II of Goethe's *Faust represents, at one stage of the drama, Lord *Byron, whom Goethe laments in a dirge.

Euphues, a prose romance by *Lyly, of which the first part, Euphues. The Anatomy of Wit, was published 1578, and the second, Euphues and his England, 1580. The plot of each is very slender and little but a peg on which to hang discourses, conversations, and letters, mainly on the subject of love. The work is largely based on North's *Diall of Princes.

In the first part Euphues, a young Athenian, visits Naples, where he makes the acquaintance of Philautus, an Italian, and a friendship develops between them. None the less Euphues proceeds to oust Philautus from the affections of Lucilla, to be in turn ejected by one Curio. Euphues and Philautus, after upbraiding one another, unite in holding Lucilla 'as most abhominable', and part friends, Euphues returning to Greece and leaving behind him a pamphlet of advice to lovers, which he terms 'A cooling Carde for Philautus'.

In Pt II Euphues and Philautus travel to England, where their adventures are even less entertaining than at Naples. They are largely concerned with the love affairs on which Philautus embarks, in spite of the advice of Euphues to use circumspection in his dealings with English ladies; and much space is occupied by a discussion on such questions as 'whether in love be more required secrecie or constancie'. Finally Euphues is recalled to Greece. From Athens Euphues addresses a letter to the ladies of Italy, 'Euphues' Glasse for Europe', in which he describes England, its institutions, its ladies, its gentlemen, and its queen; and a final letter of general advice from Euphues to Philautus completes the work.

Euphues is famous for its peculiar style, to which it has given the name 'Euphuism'. Its principal characteristics are the excessive use of antithesis, which is pursued regardless of sense, and emphasized by alliteration and other devices; and of allusions to historical and mythological personages and to natural history drawn from such writers as *Plutarch, *Pliny, and *Erasmus. Sir W. *Scott satirized Euphuism in the character of Sir Piercie Shafton in *The Monastery and C. *Kingsley defended Euphues in *Westward Ho!

Euphues Golden Legacie, see ROSALYNDE.

Euphuism, see EUPHUES.

EURIPIDES (480–406 BC), the youngest and during his life the least successful of the great Attic tragedians. Even at that time some admired him much, mainly, it seems, because of the beauty of his choral odes, but conventional people distrusted a man who called into question the morality of the legends which gave objective reality to their religious beliefs. The strength of Euripides lay, however, in his ability to represent ordinary human beings, especially women, with impassioned sympathy, and thanks to this his popularity increased in the Roman and the Byzantine age, so that 19 of his plays have survived as against 7 each by *Aeschylus and *Sophocles. *Petrarch ranked him next to *Homer, and G. *Buchanan took him as a model for his two Latin plays. Milton's *Samson Agonistes was the first English tragedy to show his influence. *Dryden praised his depiction of human behaviour, and *Shelley translated his satyr play Cyclops. But it was at the end of the 19th cent. that Euripides truly made his mark. W. *Morris sentimentalized the Medea in The Life and Death of Jason (1867) and the Alcestis in *The Earthly Paradise (1868–70). R. *Browning, commenting on the Alcestis, arraigned Admetus in *Balaustion's Adventure (1871) and defended Euripides in *Aristophanes' Apology (1875). T. S. *Moore tried his hand at the Phaedra story and G. *Murray's translations (1904–8) scored a remarkable theatrical success.

Europe: A Prophecy, a poem by W. *Blake, printed 1794 at Lambeth, in which Blake portrays the oppression of Albion during the 1,800-year sleep of *Enitharmon, the female principle, and the approach of the French revolution, symbolized by her son, the terrible *Orc, spirit of revolt. The frontispiece of Europe portrays *Urizen as the Creator with his measuring instruments, and I. *Newton appears in the poem as an ambiguous herald of change.

EUSDEN, Laurence (1688–1730), poet laureate from 1718 until his death. He had celebrated the marriage of the duke of Newcastle, who gave him the laureateship. Pope refers to his notorious drinking habits in *The Dunciad, (Bk i. 293):

> Know, Eusden thirsts no more for sack or praise;
> He sleeps among the dull of ancient days.

EUSEBIUS of Caesarea, in Palestine (AD 265–340), bishop of Caesarea, and a celebrated historian and theologian. His Chronicle in Greek (known in a Latin version by *Jerome) contains an epitome of universal history and chronological tables, the foundation of much of our knowledge of the dates of events in Greek and Roman history. He was involved in the *Arian controversy, was one of the leaders at the Council of Nicaea, and voted for the 'Nicene formula'. He was a voluminous writer and a valuable authority on the early church, showing diligence and sincerity. His Ecclesiastical History, which earned him the title of 'Father of Church history', was completed c.325. His De Vita Constantini, often tacked on to the History but evidently written earlier, is of especial interest; the question whether Constantine was ever actually baptized rests upon Eusebius.

Eustace, Father, a character in Scott's *The Monastery, the energetic sub-prior of Kennaquhair.

Eustace, Lizzie, heroine of A. Trollope's novel *The Eustace Diamonds.

Eustace Diamonds, The, a novel by A. *Trollope, published 1873, the third in the *'Palliser' series.

Lizzie Eustace marries for money and, when Sir Florian Eustace dies, she not only inherits the family estates at Portray, but pockets the family diamonds as well, despite the demands of the Eustace lawyers that they be returned. She looks for support to her cousin and legal adviser Frank Greystock, but when his engagement to the demure governess Lucy Morris proves too durable, she sets her cap at the stuffy Lord Fawn. Fawn proposes, but stipulates that the necklace must be returned to the Eustace estate. Lizzie retires to Portray, and assembles a curious collection of house–guests, including dashing Lord George de Bruce Carruthers, who becomes her third suitor, and the fashionable preacher Mr Emilius, who becomes her fourth. When Lizzie and her entourage set off southwards, Lizzie's bedroom is robbed at Carlisle. The thieves get away with the casket but not the jewels, which Lizzie has extracted for safe keeping. The police begin to be suspicious, and when Lizzie is robbed a second time she is unable to conceal her trickery. Lord Fawn drops her immediately, Frank Greystock stops procrastinating and marries Lucy Morris, Lord George disappears, and Lizzie has no alternative but to marry Mr Emilius—without, as it will turn out, sufficiently enquiring into his shady past.

Eva, Little, see LITTLE EVA.

Evadne, a character in Beaumont and Fletcher's *The Maid's Tragedy.

Evandale, Lord, a character in Scott's *Old Mortality.

Evangelical, a term applied from the 18th cent. to that school of Protestants which maintains that the essence of 'the Gospel' consists in the doctrine of salvation by faith in the atoning death of Christ, lays more stress on faith than on works or on sacramental grace, and upholds the verbal inspiration of the Bible. As a distinct party designation, the term came into general use, in England, at the time of the Methodist revival; and it may be said, with substantial accuracy, to denote the school of theology which that movement represents.

Evangeline, a narrative poem by *Longfellow.

Evan Harrington, a novel by G. *Meredith, published 1861.

In its earlier chapters this novel has many elements of autobiography, for both Meredith's grandfather (known as the 'Great Mel') and his father were tailors. Evan is the son of Melchizedek Harrington, the handsome, dashing tailor of Lymport. Evan's sisters have married, one an officer of the marines, one a rich brewer, and one a Portuguese nobleman, the Count de Saldar. The sisters are all anxious to forget their connection with tailoring, and to establish Evan in a grand marriage. Staying with the countess in Lisbon, where he is temporary secretary to the British envoy, Evan has fallen in love with the envoy's niece, Rose Jocelyn. His father has just died, leaving heavy debts, and the novel, which is much (and often comically) concerned with the problems of social class, describes the determined fight made by the countess to launch Evan in high society and to conceal the humiliating origins of the family; while his mother, equally determined, wishes him to carry on the family business. Eventually the countess overreaches herself, and involves Evan in assuming blame for a forgery of which he knew nothing. He is dismissed and his engagement to Rose broken off. But meanwhile Juliana Bonner, the ailing cousin of Rose, and heiress to the Jocelyn property, discovers Evan's innocence; on her deathbed she makes the truth known to Rose and bequeaths the whole Jocelyn estate to Evan. His renunciation of this in favour of the Jocelyns, and the clearing of his character, leads to his happy re-engagement to Rose.

Meredith wished the book to be a popular success, and wrote it without the 'lumen purpureum' which he usually liked his prose to cast.

EVANS, Sir Arthur John (1851–1941), son of the archaeologist Sir John Evans, was educated at Harrow and Brasenose College, Oxford. As curator of the Ashmolean Museum from 1885, he devoted much energy to transforming the museum into the centre of archaeology in Oxford in the face of opposition from *Jowett and other classicists. From 1893 his archaeological investigations in Crete, which centred on the excavations of the palace at Knossos, resulted in the discovery of the pre-Phoenician script and an entire new Bronze Age civilization which he named 'Minoan'. His most important publications were *Scripta Minoa* (1909–52) and *The Palace of Minos at Knossos* (1922–35).

Evans, Sir Hugh, Welsh parson in Shakespeare's *The Merry Wives of Windsor.*

EVANS, Mary Ann, see ELIOT, G.

Evans's, in the NW corner of the Piazza, Covent Garden, originally the residence of the earl of Orford (d. 1727), converted into a hotel in 1774. In 1844 it passed under the management of one Paddy Green and became famous for its musical parties and suppers. *Thackeray's 'Cave of Harmony' is partly drawn from it. It was subsequently, for a time, the home of the National Sporting Club.

Evelina, or a Young Lady's Entrance into the World, an *epistolary novel by F. Burney, published anonymously 1778.

Sir John Belmont, disappointed of the fortune he expected to receive with his wife, abandons her and their child Evelina, who is brought up in seclusion by a guardian, Mr Villars. Evelina, who has grown up a beautiful and intelligent girl, goes to visit a friend, Mrs Mirvan, in London, where she is introduced into society and falls in love with the handsome and noble Lord Orville. But she is much mortified by her vulgar grandmother, Mme Duval, her ill-bred relatives, and the pursuit of her bold and persistent lover, Sir Clement Willoughby. Sir John Belmont is asked to recognize Evelina as his daughter, but he insists that his daughter has been in his care since infancy. It is now discovered that Lady Belmont's nurse had passed her own child off on Sir John. Evelina is recognized as his heir, and joyfully marries Lord Orville.

The novel enjoyed huge success, numbering among its admirers Dr *Johnson (who preferred it to the work of *Fielding), *Burke, *Gibbon, *Reynolds, *Sheridan, and many others from both fashionable and literary circles. The young author's mastery of character, speech, pathos, and satire, was, and still is, much admired. The *Critical Review* wrote, 'Readers will weep . . . will laugh, and grow wiser.'

EVELYN, John (1620–1706), born at Wotton House, Surrey, and educated at Balliol College, Oxford. After his father's death in 1640 he spent much time on the Continent, settling in England with his wife in 1652. He was a member of the *Royal Society, a royalist in sympathy, and a man of varied cultural interests, including gardening; among his friends were Jeremy *Taylor and *Pepys. He published in 1661 *Fumifugium or The Inconvenience of the Air and Smoke or London dissipated;* in 1662 *Sculptura,* on engraving; and in 1664 his influential work

Sylva, a book on practical arboriculture; *Navigation and Commerce* in 1674; and a number of translations from the French on architecture, gardening, etc. He is remembered principally for his *Memoirs* or *Diary,* first published in 1818 and in a full and authoritative edition by E. S. de Beer in 1955 (6 vols). It covers most of his life, describing his travels abroad, his contemporaries, and his public and domestic concerns, and is an invaluable record of the period. He appears not to have composed regularly day by day, but on occasion some time after the event; he also added to and began to transcribe his own work. His diary is thus less spontaneous and personal than that of Pepys, though its more sober and religious tone is due more to his character than to its method of composition. His *Life of Mrs Godolphin* was first printed in 1847, and various other minor works have been published in recent times.

'Evening, Ode to, see COLLINS, W.

Evening's Love, An, or *The Mock Astrologer,* a comedy by *Dryden, produced 1668, published 1671.

The Preface to this play is among the most attractive of Dryden's critical essays. It represents his views when he was least sympathetic to *Jonson and is therefore of importance in the dispute with *Shadwell which culminated in *Mac-Flecknoe.

'Eve of St Agnes, The, a narrative poem in Spenserian stanzas by *Keats, written 1819, published 1820.

The poem is set in a remote period of time, in the depths of winter. Madeline has been told the legend that on St Agnes's Eve maidens may have visions of their lovers. Madeline's love, Porphyro, comes from a family hostile to her own, and she is herself surrounded by 'hyena foemen, and hot-blooded lords'. Yet he contrives to steal into the house during a ball on St Agnes's Eve, and with the aid of old Angela is secreted in Madeline's room, where he watches his love prepare for sleep. When she wakes from dreams of him, aroused by his soft singing, she finds him by her bedside. Silently they escape from the house, and fly 'away into the storm'. With its rich and vivid imagery, its heightened atmosphere of excitement and passion, the poem is generally regarded as among Keats's most effective and successful works.

Everard, Colonel Markham, a character in Scott's *Woodstock.

Everdene, Bathsheba, a character in Hardy's *Far from the Madding Crowd.

Ever Green, The, see RAMSAY, A.

Evergreen Review (1957–73), an avant-garde American literary periodical, edited by Barney Rossett (1922–), famed for its radical politics and uncensored writings on sex; contributors included *Beckett, W. *Burroughs, *Cummings, *Nabokov, *Kerouac, *Ginsberg, and Che Guevara.

'Everlasting Gospel, The', see BLAKE, W.

Everyman, the title of a popular morality play of *c.*1509–19, in 921 lines, almost certainly derived from its Dutch close counterpart *Elckerlijc* (see below). Everyman is summoned by death and, in the last hour of his life, he discovers that his friends Fellowship, Kindred, Cousin, and Goods will not go with him. He is dependent on the support of Good Deeds whom he has previously neglected. It is the most admired of the English *Morality Plays and it has had a revival of popularity in the 20th cent. The lines of Knowledge have become legendary;

Everyman, I will go with thee and be thy guide,
In thy most need to go by thy side.

See ed. A. C. Cawley, *Everyman and Medieval Miracle Plays* (1956); E. R. Tigg, 'The Dutch *Elckerlijc* is prior to the English *Everyman*' (1981).

Everyman, a literary weekly of 'Books, Drama, Music, Travel', which ran from 1929 to 1935, becoming more political than literary in its later years; the first series (1929–32) was edited by C. B. Purdom (1883–1965). Contributors included D. H. *Lawrence, G. B. *Shaw, W. *Lewis, G. D. H. *Cole, and G. *Greene.

Every Man in his Humour, a comedy by *Jonson, performed by the Lord Chamberlain's Men 1598, with Shakespeare in the cast, printed 1601. In his folio of 1616 Jonson published an extensively revised version, with the setting changed from Florence to London and the characters given English names.

In the latter version Kitely, a merchant, is the husband of a young wife, and his 'humour' is irrational jealousy. His house is resorted to by his brother-in-law Wellbred with a crowd of riotous but harmless gallants, and these he suspects of designs both on his wife and on his sister Bridget. One of these young men is Edward Knowell, whose father's 'humour' is excessive concern for his son's morals. Bobadill, one of Jonson's greatest creations, a 'Paul's man', is a boastful cowardly soldier, who associates with the young men and is admired by Matthew, a 'town gull' and poetaster, and Edward's cousin Stephen, a 'country gull'. Out of these elements, by the aid of the devices and disguises of the mischievous Brainworm, Knowell's servant, an imbroglio is produced in which Kitely and his wife are brought face to face at the house of a water-bearer to which each thinks the other has gone for an amorous assignation; Bobadill is exposed and beaten; Edward Knowell is married to Bridget; and Matthew and Stephen are held up to ridicule. The misunderstandings are cleared up by the shrewd and kindly Justice Clement.

To the folio version Jonson added a prologue giving an exposition of his dramatic theory.

Every Man out of his Humour, a comedy by *Jonson, acted by the Lord Chamberlain's Men at the newly built Globe theatre 1599, printed 1600.

The play parades a variety of characters dominated by particular 'humours', or obsessive quirks of disposition; Macilente, a venomous malcontent; Carlo Buffone, a cynical jester; the uxorious Deliro and his domineering wife Fallace; Fastidious Brisk, an affected courtier devoted to fashion; Sordido, a miserly farmer, and his son Fungoso, who longs to be a courtier; Sogliardo, 'an essential clown, enamoured of the name of a gentleman'; and Puntarvolo, a fantastic, vainglorious knight, who wagers that he, his dog, and his cat can travel to Constantinople and back. By means of various episodes, such as Macilente's poisoning of Puntarvolo's dog and Brisk's imprisonment for debt, each character is eventually driven 'out of his humour'. Two judicious onlookers, Mitis and Cordatus, oversee the action throughout, and provide a moral commentary. Their opening debate with their friend Asper, who represents Jonson, contains an exposition of Jonson's theory of humours.

Everyman's Library, a series of reprints of the world's masterpieces in literature founded in 1906 by publisher Joseph Malaby Dent (1849–1926) and first edited by Ernest Rhys (1859–1946); the series also includes some original works of reference.

Evidences of Christianity, see PALEY, W.

EWART, Gavin Buchanan (1916–   ), poet, contributed to G. Grigson's *New Verse* when he was seventeen; his first volume, *Poems and Songs*, appeared in 1939. After the war he worked for many years as an advertising copywriter before becoming, in 1971, a full-time freelance writer. His second volume, *Londoners*, followed his first after a long interval, in 1964, and since then he has published several volumes of poetry, mainly of light, comic, satiric, and erotic verse, which shows the influence of *Auden: these include *Pleasures of the Flesh* (1966), *Or Where a Young Penguin Lies Screaming* (1977), *All my Little Ones* (1978), *More Little Ones* (1982). *The Collected Ewart 1933–1980* (1980) was followed by *The new Ewart: Poems 1980–1982* (1982). He has also edited the *Penguin Book of Light Verse* (1980) and *Other People's Clerihews* (1983), and is himself a master of the *limerick, the *clerihew, and the occasional verse.

Ewart, Nanty, captain of the smuggler's brig in Scott's *Redgauntlet*.

EWING, Mrs (Juliana Horatia) (1841–85), writer of children's stories, whose inventive and unsentimental tales brought her much success and admiration. Her first volume was *Melchior's Dream* (1862), and after that most of her work first appeared in *Aunt Judy's Magazine*, edited by her mother Mrs Gatty. Of her many publications the most enduring were probably *The Land of the Lost Toys* (1869), *Jackanapes* (1879), a touching soldier-story illustrated by Randolph Caldecott; *A Flat Iron for a Farthing* (1872); and *Lob-lie-by-the-Fire* (1873).

Examination of Sir William Hamilton's Philosophy, a treatise by J. S. *Mill, in which he attacks *Hamilton's epistemology and his logic, published 1865, amplified in subsequent editions.

The most important part of the work is the doctrine developed by Mill in regard to the external world (expressed in the famous phrase 'permanent possibility of sensation') and the mind or self. 'If we speak of the Mind as a series of feelings, we are obliged to complete the statement by calling it a series of feelings which is aware of itself as past and future; and we are reduced to the alternative of believing that the Mind, or Ego, is something different from any series of feelings, or possibilities of them, or of accepting the paradox, that something which *ex hypothesi* is but a series of feelings, can be aware of itself as a series.' 'I ascribe a reality to the Ego—to my own Mind—different from that real existence as a Permanent Possibility, which is the only reality I acknowledge in Matter.'

Examiner, The, (1) a Tory periodical started by *Bolingbroke in Aug. 1710; *Swift briefly took charge in Oct. (Nos 14–46), and was succeeded by Mrs *Manley in 1711. It engaged in controversy with Steele's *Guardian and *Addison's *Whig Examiner*. It lasted with interruptions until 1716. (2) (1808–81), a Radical weekly periodical, established by John and Leigh *Hunt. It remained independent and individual until its end, but its first 20 years were of particular interest because of Leigh Hunt's support, as editor, for the work of his friends, in particular of *Shelley, *Keats, *Lamb, and *Hazlitt, whose writing was often bitterly attacked, in particular by the *Quarterly and *Blackwood's (see also COCKNEY SCHOOL). The political section of the journal ardently supported reform, and frequently derided the prince of Wales. Both the Hunts were fined £500 and sentenced to two years' imprisonment for a libel on the prince.

Excalibur, a corrupt form of 'Caliburn' (the name used in *Geoffrey of Monmouth), was King Arthur's sword, which he drew out of a stone when no one else could move it or which was given to him by the Lady of the Lake (*Malory, Bk I). Malory says that the name means 'cut-steel', but the Welsh form in the *Mabinogion* is related to the Irish *Caladbolg* (battle-sword), a famous legendary sword. According to Malory, when Arthur was mortally wounded in the last battle, he ordered Sir Bedevere to throw Excalibur into the lake. A hand rose from the water, took the sword, and vanished.

Excursion, The, a poem in nine books by W. *Wordsworth, published 1814. This is the middle section of a projected three-part poem 'on man, on nature and on human life', of which this part alone was completed. The whole work was to have been entitled 'The Recluse', 'as having for its principal subject the sensations and opinions of a poet living in retirement'. It was planned in 1798, when Wordsworth was living near *Coleridge at Alfoxden. *.*The Prelude* was originally intended to be the introduction to the first part of 'The Recluse'.

The story is very slight. The poet, travelling with the Wanderer, a philosophic pedlar, meets with the pedlar's friend, the sad and pessimistic Solitary. The source of the Solitary's despondency is found in his want of religious faith and of confidence in the virtue of man, and he is reproved with gentle and persuasive argument. The Pastor is then introduced, who illustrates the harmonizing effects of virtue and religion through narratives of people interred in his churchyard. They visit the Pastor's house, and the Wanderer draws his general and philosophic conclusions from the discussions that have passed. The last two books deal in particular with the industrial expansion of the early part of the century, and the degradation that followed in its train. The poem ends with the Pastor's prayer that man may be given grace to conquer guilt and sin, and with praise for the beauty of the world about them. Bk I contains 'The Story of Margaret' or *'The Ruined Cottage', originally written as a separate poem.

Exequy, An, see KING, H.

Exeter Book, The, one of the most important manuscripts containing Old English poetry, copied about 940, given by Bishop Leofric (d. 1072) to Exeter Cathedral, where it still remains. It contains many of the most admired shorter poems, such as *The Wanderer, *The Seafarer, *Deor, *Widsith, *The Ruin, *'Wulf and Eadwacer', The Wife's Lament, *The Husband's Message, and Resignation, more or less all of which are grouped together as 'The Exeter Book Elegies', as well as a famous collection of Riddles (excellently translated by K. Crossley-Holland, 1978; ed. C. Williamson, 1977) and some longer poems of a religious nature, notably *Guthlac, Christ, *The Phoenix, and *Cynewulf's Juliana. Also of interest are the Physiologus and Maxims.

Anglo-Saxon Poetic Records, vol. III (in ASPR, 6 vols, ed. G. V. Krapp and E. V. K. Dobbie,

1931–53); ed. I. Gollancz and W. S. Mackie, EETS 104 and 194 (1895, 1934).

Existentialism, the name commonly given to a group of somewhat loosely associated philosophical doctrines and ideas which have found contemporary expression in the work of such men as *Sartre, Heidegger, *Marcel, *Camus, and Jaspers. Though the theories advanced by different existentialist writers diverge widely in many important respects, so that it would be misleading to speak of a philosophical 'school' or 'movement', certain underlying themes can be singled out as characteristic. Existentialists tend, for example, to emphasize the unique and particular in human experience; they place the individual person at the centre of their pictures of the world, and are suspicious of philosophical or psychological doctrines that obscure this essential individuality by speaking as if there were some abstract 'human nature', some set of general laws or principles, to which men are determined or required, by their common humanity, to conform. Each man is what he chooses to be or make himself; he cannot escape responsibility for his character or his deeds by claiming that they are the pre-determined consequence of factors beyond his power to control or resist, nor can he justify what he does in terms of external or 'objective' standards imposed upon him from without. Sartre, in particular, insists upon the notion of the individual as the source of all value, and as being obliged to choose for himself what to do and what standards to adopt or reject: consciousness of such freedom is a condition of 'authentic' existence, as opposed to the type of behaviour stigmatized as springing from 'bad faith' (*mauvaise foi*), whereby people deceive themselves into thinking that they are bound to act in certain ways, play certain roles. Thus existentialists typically give priority to sincerity and creativity in the moral life, and sometimes appear to regard any decision as justified if it is made in perfect honesty and with absolute inner conviction. Critics have pointed out that existentialist ethics seem to provide little guidance to practical choices; the bare reference to 'authenticity' is hardly helpful in the assessment of the relative merits of alternative courses of action. Again, it has been argued that, through their romantic preference for 'extreme situations', existentialists have been led to overlook or distort the character of more everyday moral perplexities and problems. Even so, in their psychological explorations they have often shown an impressive insight and introduced interpretative concepts which have greatly extended the area of moral self-knowledge and self-awareness. This, perhaps more than anything, explains the wide appeal of their writings.

Exodus, a 590-line poem in Old English, based

on the biblical story, contained in the *Junius manuscript and probably dating from the early 8th cent. It used to be attributed to *Caedmon, and it contains a vigorous description of the destruction of the Egyptians in the Red Sea. The narrative departs considerably from the letter of the biblical narrative, and discussion of the poem has centred mostly on possible explanations for its allusive structure and the fact that it draws material from various parts of the Bible. It has been edited by E. B. Irving (1953).

Exoteric, see ESOTERIC.

Experience, Songs of, see SONGS OF INNOCENCE.

Expressionism, a term coined in the early 20th cent. to describe a movement in art, then in literature, the theatre, and the cinema, characterized by boldness, distortion, and forceful representation of the emotions. One of its earliest manifestations was in the group of German painters, *Die Brücke* ('the Bridge'), formed in Dresden in 1905 and influenced by Van Gogh and Munch: a later group was *Der blaue Reiter* ('the Blue Rider', from the title of a painting by Kandinsky), formed in 1911, which was more concerned with the evocative qualities of colour and pattern, unrelated to content. In the theatre the term has been associated with the works of *Toller, *Strindberg, *Wedekind, and early *Brecht, and embraces a wide variety of moods—satirical, grotesque, visionary, exclamatory, violent, but always anti-naturalistic. The epitome of Expressionism in German cinema was Robert Wiene's *The Cabinet of Dr Caligari* (1919). Expressionism flourished principally in Germany, and took little root in Britain, though W. *Lewis and *Vorticism have some affinities with it, and traces of its influence can be found in the verse dramas of *Auden and *Isherwood, and later in the cinema (e.g. G. *Greene's *The Third Man*, directed by Carol Reed, 1949).

Eyeless in Gaza, a novel by A. *Huxley, published 1936. The title is a quotation from Milton's *Samson Agonistes*.

It traces the career of Anthony Beavis from the death of his mother in his early boyhood in 1902, through various emotional entanglements and intellectual quests, to his involvement with a pacifist movement in 1935; it uses a complicated but clearly demarcated system of sections in non-chronological flashback. At preparatory school Beavis is acquainted with three characters whose lives deeply affect his own: his closest friend, the sensitive intellectual Brian Foxe (modelled on Huxley's brother Trevenen) who later, like Trevenen, commits suicide; Hugh Ledwidge, pompous victim, with whose wife Helen he has an affair; and Mark Staithes, who becomes a Marxist and leads Beavis to a revolution in Mexico where he loses a leg and Beavis finds a faith. The main theatre of the novel is a sophisticated, iconoclastic, intellectual, middle-class English world, rich in references to Pavlov and Krafft-Ebing, anthropology and sociology, masturbation and Proust, where the great sport is 'sticking pins in large, highly inflated balloons'. In a characteristically shocking and memorable Huxlean image, a dead dog at one point drops arbitrarily from an aeroplane on to a flat roof where Beavis and Helen are making love; it explodes, splattering them with blood. The real and the ideal, the physical and the intellectual, attraction and nausea are sharply contrasted throughout, and Beavis's search for a mystical wholeness is brought to what some have seen as a satisfactory conclusion, others a vague and wordy evasion. Much of the novel, written over a period of four years, is clearly autobiographical: the loss of his mother, the death of his brother, the father's remarriage, his involvement with the Peace Pledge Union, all find their fictional counterparts. It is rich in portraits, ranging from that of Beavis's pedantic and uxorious philologist father, to Mary Amberley, Helen's mother, who turns from lovers to morphia, and the possessive, high-minded, destructive Mrs Foxe.

EYRE, Simon (d. 1459), according to *Stow, a draper who became mayor of London, was a generous benefactor of the city, and built Leadenhall as a public granary and market. He figures in Dekker's *The Shoemaker's Holiday*.

F

FABER, Frederick William (1814–63), was educated at Balliol College, Oxford, and came under the influence of *Newman. He was appointed rector of Elton in 1842; was received into the Roman Catholic Church in 1845; and became head of the London Oratory (now the Brompton Oratory) in 1849. He was author of many devotional books, and hymns including 'My God, how wonderful Thou art'.

Faber Book of Modern Verse, The, an anthology published in 1936, edited by M. *Roberts, which did much to influence taste and establish the reputations of a rising generation of poets, including *Auden, *MacNeice, *Empson, *Graves, Dylan *Thomas. In his introduction, Roberts traces the influences of *Clough, G. M. *Hopkins (himself well represented), the French *Symbolists, etc. on modern poetry, defines the 'European' sensibility of such writers as T. S. *Eliot, *Pound, and *Yeats, and offers a persuasive apologia for various aspects of *Modernism which the reading public had resisted, identifying them as an apparent obscurity compounded of condensed metaphor, allusion, intricacy and difficulty of ideas, and verbal play. The poet, he declared, 'must charge each word to its maximum poetic value': 'primarily poetry is an exploration of the possibilities of language.'

FABIAN, Robert, see FABYAN.

Fabian Society, The, a society founded in 1884 consisting of Socialists who advocate a 'Fabian' policy, as opposed to immediate revolutionary action, and named after Quintus Fabius Maximus, nicknamed 'Cunctator' or 'the Delayer' (see below). One of its instigators was Thomas Davidson (1840–1900), the illegitimate son of a Scottish shepherd, a charismatic figure with many disciples who was also responsible for founding in 1883 the Fellowship of the New Life, a body which at first attracted some of the same membership, although its aims were mystical and philosophical rather than political. The Fabians aimed to influence government and affect policy by permeation rather than by direct power, and to provide the research and analysis to support their own views and introduce them to others. One of their methods was the publishing of tracts, or *pamphleteering: the first two Fabian tracts were *Why are the Many Poor* (1884) by W. L. Phillips, a house painter and one of the few working-class members, and *A Manifesto* (1884) by G. B. *Shaw.

Shaw wrote many other important tracts, as did S. *Webb: *Fabian Essays in Socialism* (1889), edited by Shaw, and with contributions by Webb, Sydney Olivier, and A. *Besant sold well and attracted much attention. The Society itself continued to attract a distinguished membership of politicians, intellectuals, artists, and writers, ranging from Keir Hardie, Ramsay Macdonald, and G. D. H. *Cole to E. *Carpenter, E. *Nesbit, R. *Brooke, and W. *Crane. See Margaret Cole, *The Story of Fabian Socialism* (1961) and N. and J. Mackenzie, *The First Fabians* (1977).

FABIUS (Quintus Fabius Maximus) (d. 203 BC), nicknamed *Cunctator* (the man who delays taking action), was appointed dictator after Hannibal's crushing victory at Trasimene (217 BC). He carried on a defensive campaign, avoiding direct engagements and harassing the enemy. Hence the expression 'Fabian tactics' and the name of the *Fabian Society (1884), dedicated to the gradual introduction of Socialism.

Fable, a term most commonly used in the sense of a short story devised to convey some useful moral lesson, but often carrying with it associations of the marvellous or the mythical, and frequently employing animals as characters. *Aesop's fables and the *'Reynard the Fox' series were well known and imitated in Britain by *Chaucer, *Henryson, and others, and *La Fontaine, the greatest of modern fable writers, was imitated by *Gay. *Mandeville's *The Fable of the Bees,* Swift's *Gulliver's Travels* and Orwell's *Animal Farm* may be described as satirical fables. The form enjoyed something of a vogue in the 1920s and 1930s, in works by T. F. *Powys, D. *Garnett, John *Collier, and others, and has always been popular in children's literature.

Fable of the Bees, The, see MANDEVILLE, B. DE.

Fables, Ancient and Modern, by *Dryden, published 1700.

Verse paraphrases of tales by *Ovid, *Boccaccio, and *Chaucer are interspersed with poems of Dryden's own, and together with the Preface, in itself one of the most important examples of Dryden's criticism, they compose themselves into an Ovidian and Catholic meditation on the place of nature, sex, and violence in the flux of history.

Fabliau, a short tale in verse, almost invariably in octosyllabic couplets, dealing for the most part from a comic point of view with incidents of ordinary life (*Saintsbury). The fabliau was an important element in French poetry in the 12th–13th cents, and was imitated by Chaucer, in e.g. 'The Miller's Tale' (*Canterbury Tales, 2).

FABYAN, Robert (d. 1513), chronicler, was sheriff of London in 1493. He reworked various sources into The Concordance of Chronicles, a compilation extending from the arrival of Brutus in England (see BRUT) to the death of Richard III (first printed 1516; ed. Ellis, 1811). His chronicles are of importance with respect to the history of London, and were several times brought up to date.

Face, one of the rogues in Jonson's *The Alchemist.

Faction, a term coined c.1970 to describe fiction based on and mingled with fact, applied particularly to American works of fiction such as In Cold Blood (1966) by *Capote and The Armies of the Night (1968) by *Mailer.

Factotum, see JOHANNES FACTOTUM.

Faerie Queene, The, the greatest work of *Spenser, of which the first three books were published 1590, and the second three 1596.

The general scheme of the work is proposed in the author's introductory letter addressed to *Ralegh. By the Faerie Queene the poet signifies Glory in the abstract and *Elizabeth I in particular (who also figures under the names of *Britomart, *Belphoebe, *Mercilla, and *Gloriana). Twelve of her knights, the 'patrons' or examples of twelve different virtues, each undertake an adventure, on the twelve successive days of the queen's annual festival, and an account of their origins was to have been given in the last of twelve books. Prince Arthur symbolizes 'magnificence', in the Aristotelian sense (says the author) of the perfection of all the other virtues (he must have meant not 'magnificence' but 'magnanimity', or 'gentlemanliness'). Arthur has a vision of the Faerie Queene and, determining to seek her out, is brought into the adventures of the several knights and carries them to a successful issue. This explanation, given in the introduction, does not appear from the poem itself, for the author starts at once with the adventures of the knights; as we have it the poem does not conform to his scheme. Of the six books Spenser published, the subjects are:

I, the adventures of the *Redcrosse Knight of Holiness (the Anglican Church), the protector of the Virgin *Una (truth, or the true religion), and the wiles of *Archimago and *Duessa;

II, the adventures of Sir *Guyon, the Knight of Temperance, his encounters with *Pyrochles and *Cymochles, his visit to the cave of *Mammon and the House of Temperance, and his de-struction of *Acrasia and her *Bower of Bliss. Canto x of this Book contains a chronicle of British rulers from *Brut to Elizabeth;

III, the legend of Chastity, exemplified by *Britomart and *Belphoebe;

IV, the legend of *Triamond and *Cambell, exemplifying Friendship; together with the story of *Scudamour and *Amoret;

V, the adventures of *Artegall, the Knight of Justice, in which allegorical reference is made to various historical events of the reign of Queen Elizabeth: the defeat of the Spaniards in the Netherlands, the recantation of Henry IV of France, the execution of *Mary Queen of Scots, and the administration of Ireland by Lord Grey de Wilton;

VI, the adventures of Sir *Calidore, exemplifying Courtesy.

There is also a fragment on *Mutabilitie, being the sixth and seventh cantos of the legend of Constancie, which was to have formed the seventh Book. This fragment contains a charming description of the seasons and the months.

The work as a whole, modelled to some extent on the *Orlando Furioso of Ariosto, suffers from a certain monotony, and its chief beauties lie in the particular episodes with which the allegory is varied and in descriptions, such as those of the Cave of Mammon and the temptation of Sir Guyon by the Lady of the Idle Lake, in Bk II. The meaning of many of the allusions, which must have added to the interest of the work for contemporaries, is now lost. The poem is written in the stanza invented by Spenser (and since utilized by James *Thomson, *Keats, *Shelley, and *Byron), in which a ninth line of twelve syllables is added to eight lines of ten syllables, rhyming a b a b b c b c c.

Fagin, a character in Dickens's *Oliver Twist.

Fainall and Mrs Fainall, characters in Congreve's *The Way of the World.

Fairchild Family, The, see SHERWOOD, M.

FAIRFAX, Edward (d. 1635), Yorkshire scholar and gentleman, remembered for his translation of Tasso's *Jerusalem Delivered as Godfrey of Bulloigne done into English Heroicall verse (1600). A new edition by K. M. Lea was published in 1980.

Fairford, Alan, a character in Scott's *Redgauntlet.

Fair Maid of Perth, Saint Valentine's Day, the, a novel by Sir W. *Scott, published 1828, as the second of the *Chronicles of the Canongate.

The scene is Perth in the turbulent times at the close of the 14th cent. when the mild Robert III was king of Scotland; and the story opens with an attempt by the profligate young duke of Rothsay, the king's son, aided by his villainous Master of the Horse Sir John Ramorny, to break into the house of an honest burgher, Simon Glover, and carry off his daughter Catharine, the Fair Maid of Perth. The attempt is defeated by the sturdy armourer, Henry Smith or Gow, who in the affray hacks off the hand of Ramorny. Henry is as strong and skilful in the use of weapons as in their forging, and his addiction to fighting mars his prospect of winning the hand of the gentle Catharine, though he has a vigorous advocate in her father. This incident is followed by the endeavours of Ramorny to wreak his vengeance, first on the armourer, in which he is unsuccessful, then on his patron Rothsay, by whom he considers himself betrayed. At the instigation of the crafty duke of Albany, the king's ambitious brother, the unfortunate Rothsay is lured by Ramorny, with Catharine as bait, to the Castle of Falkland, where he is murdered. Meanwhile a Highland apprentice of Simon Glover, the fiery youth Conachar, has become, by the death of his father, chief of the clan Quhele. He passionately loves Catharine, and bitter enmity has arisen between him and the armourer. A feud between the clan Quhele and the clan Chattan is to be settled by mortal combat between 30 representatives of each clan, among whom the chiefs are necessarily included. But here enters a tragic element; for Conachar's hot temper is strangely blended with constitutional cowardice, of which the youth is grievously conscious. One of the champions of the clan Chattan having at the last moment defaulted, his place is taken by the armourer, who eagerly grasps the opportunity of finding himself face to face with Conachar. After a fearful battle during which Conachar has been protected by the devotion of his foster-father, Torquil of the Oak, and his eight sturdy sons, most of the combatants lie dead or wounded on the field, and Conachar is finally confronted by Henry Smith. His courage, hitherto painfully maintained, now gives way, and he turns and flees, to hide his disgrace in suicide. Henry, sickened with the carnage, vows to hang up his broadsword for ever, and is accepted by Catharine.

Fair Maid of the West, The, or *A Girl worth Gold,* a comedy of adventure by *Heywood, in two parts, Pt I c.1600, Pt II c.1630, both printed 1631.

The first part opens with a vivid scene at Plymouth, where Essex's expedition is on the point of sailing for the Azores (1597), and gallant Master Spencer has the misfortune to kill a man while protecting Bess Bridges, 'the flower of Plymouth', from insult. He has to fly the country, but first makes provision for Bess by handing over to her the Windmill Tavern at Fowey, which she subsequently conducts with equal spirit and decorum. Meanwhile Spencer, who has sailed to the Azores, is wounded to the point of death in trying to stop a quarrel. He sends a message to Bess, bidding her adieu and

making over all his property to her. Bess employs part of this to fit out a privateer, in which she sets sail to bring home his body. Instead she rescues Spencer himself, who has recovered and been captured by Spaniards. After many adventures, leading as far as Morocco, Bess is finally united to her lover. The first part makes a breezy and entertaining melodrama, but Pt II, a less effective sequel, contains more extreme coincidences and intrigues, including a 'bedtrick' and supposed deaths.

Fair Penitent, The, a tragedy in blank verse by N. *Rowe, produced 1703.

The plot of the play is that of Massinger and Field's *The Fatal Dowry, shortened and somewhat modified at the end. Charalois becomes Altamont; Beaumelle, Calista; Rochford, Sciolto; Romont, Horatio; and Novall, Lothario. The play was extremely successful and was constantly revived until the early 19th cent. The 'haughty, gallant, gay Lothario' has become proverbial, and was the model on which Richardson drew Lovelace in *Clarissa. In revivals of the play *Garrick acted Lothario, and subsequently Mrs *Siddons, Calista. Dr *Johnson said of it that 'there is scarcely any work of any poet at once so interesting by the fable, and so delightful by the language.' He observes, however, with reference to the title of the play, that Calista 'may be reasonably suspected of feeling pain from detection rather than from guilt'.

Fair Quarrel, A, a comedy by J. *Middleton and W. *Rowley, published 1617.

Captain Ager receives from a fellow officer an insult which reflects on his mother's virtue. A duel is arranged, but Ager is too conscientious to fight unless he is satisfied that his cause is a just one. He tells his mother of the accusation, which she at first indignantly denies, but presently, in order to prevent the duel, admits to be true. Ager then declines to fight, and is branded by his adversary as a coward. Having now what he considers an adequate reason, he fights and defeats his enemy. They are reconciled and all ends well.

Fair Rosamond, see ROSAMOND.

Fairservice, Andrew, in Scott's *Rob Roy, a gardener at Osbaldistone Hall, employed as servant by Francis Osbaldistone. He is a sanctimonious, self-important, cowardly rascal, who by his loquacity and disloyalty adds to his master's difficulties.

'Fair Star', see CHERRY.

Faithful, in Bunyan's *Pilgrim's Progress, the companion of *Christian; he is put to death at *Vanity Fair.

Faithful Shepherdess, The, a pastoral tragicomedy by J. *Fletcher, printed not later than 1610.

The action takes place at night in the woods of Thessaly, and revolves around the central figure of the faithful shepherdess herself, Clorin, who has dedicated herself to a life of chastity in memory of her dead love. Thenot is in love with her, or rather with the image of her fidelity, for when she pretends to accept him, he spurns her. Other characters in the amorous round include Amarillis, who loves Thenot, who in turn loves Amoret; the wanton Cloe and the coy Daphnis; and the Sullen Shepherd, who intervenes by transforming Amarillis into the form of Amoret. With the aid of various magic herbs, a satyr, and the God of the River, all is happily resolved. Though without much dramatic interest, the play is full of passages of poetic beauty, and ranks as a pastoral with Jonson's *Sad Shepherd and Milton's *Comus.

Fakredeen, in *Tancred by B. Disraeli.

FALCONER, William (1732–69), son of a barber and himself a seaman, author of The Shipwreck (1762, rev. 1764, 1769), a poem in three cantos recounting the wreck of a ship on the coast of Greece, which had considerable vogue in its day. Falconer was drowned at sea.

Falconet, an incomplete novel by B. *Disraeli, broken off by his death; left without a title, the fragment was first published in *The Times in 1905, then included in Moneypenny and Buckle's Life of Disraeli (1910–20) and published under the name 'Falconet' in the 1927 Bradenham edition of the novels.

Joseph Falconet, a brilliant but humourless young MP, whose power of oratory is like 'a cataract in the Alps', comes from a worthy Clapham background, and was intended to develop as a satirical portrait of *Gladstone. The introduction of a Buddhist philosopher, and intimations of *Nihilism, suggest that the novel might have developed along philosophical lines. The hero of *Lothair, and others from that novel, appear in the fragment, which also contains endearing portraits of the Palmerstons as Lord and Lady Bertram.

Falkland, a novel by *Bulwer-Lytton.

Falkland, one of the principal characters in Godwin's *Caleb Williams.

FALKLAND, Lucius Cary, second Viscount (1610–43), a famous royalist, 'a man learned and accomplished, the centre of a circle [at Great Tew, near Oxford] which embraced the most liberal thinkers of his day, a keen reasoner and an able speaker, whose convictions still went with the Parliament, while his wavering and impulsive temper, his love of the Church, his passionate longings for peace, led him to struggle for a king whom he distrusted, and to die for a cause that was not his own' (J. R. *Green). He fell at Newbury. The circle at Great Tew included *Jonson, *Suckling, *Sandys, *Earle, *Godolphin, and *Chillingworth; also *Clarendon, who draws a memorable portrait of him. Falkland wrote verses and theological works (Discourses of Infallibility and a Reply, 1660).

FALKNER, J(ohn) Meade (1858–1932), novelist, antiquarian, and topographical writer, who rose to a senior position with a firm of Newcastle armaments manufacturers, and later became honorary librarian to the dean and chapter of Durham. He is remembered for his three novels: The Lost Stradivarius (1895), a tale of the supernatural set largely in Oxford and Naples; Moonfleet (1898), a romance involving smuggling; and The Nebuly Coat (1903), an antiquarian romance dealing with a church threatened by collapse, in which Falkner was able to display his love and knowledge of ecclesiastical history and architecture, heraldry, etc. He also wrote poetry, a volume of which was published as Poems (c.1933); three of his poems appear in *Larkin's The Oxford Book of Twentieth Century English Verse (1973).

Fall of Robespierre, The, a drama written in 1794 by *Coleridge, who wrote Act I, and R. *Southey, who wrote Acts II and III.

'Fall of the House of Usher, The', see POE, E. A.

False One, The, a drama attributed to J. *Fletcher, in which *Massinger may also have had a share, performed ? c.1620, printed 1647.

The play deals with the joint occupation of the throne of Egypt by Ptolemy and his young sister Cleopatra; the treacherous murder of Ptolemy by Septimius, 'the False One'; and the entanglement of Caesar by the charms of Cleopatra.

Falstaff, Sir John, a character in Shakespeare's 1 and 2 *Henry IV and *The Merry Wives of Windsor. To Dr *Johnson 'unimitated, unimitable' a 'compound of sense and vice'; the subject of *Morgann's important early critical essay. His remote historical original seems to have been the Wycliffite Sir John *Oldcastle, but his more important literary foundations lie in the stock figure of the *Vice, together with some elements of the Plautine *Miles gloriosus. He is fat, witty, a lover of sack and of jests, and skilful at turning jokes on him to his own advantage—'I am not only witty in myself, but the cause that wit is in other men' (2 Henry IV, I. ii. 8–9). In 1 Henry IV he is shown as the drinking companion of Prince *Hal, and anticipates great advancement when Hal becomes king. Hal humours him, allowing him to give his own version of the *Gadshill encounter with the men 'in buckram', to mimic his father, Henry IV, and even to take credit for the death of *Hotspur at the battle of Shrewsbury. In 2 Henry IV he is seen little with Hal, but is portrayed as old, ill, and unscrupulous in his financial dealings with Mistress *Quickly and with his old friend Master Justice *Shallow, from whom he borrows £1,000. His embodiment of anarchy is suggested in his confrontation with the Lord Chief Justice (I. ii). On succeeding to the throne Hal/Henry V rejects him in the speech beginning 'I know thee not, old man. Fall to thy prayers', which Falstaff throws off by assuring his friends that he will be sent for privately. In *Henry V, however, Mistress Quickly tells us that 'the King has kill'd his heart' (II. i), and she later describes his death, in a tavern, in a speech which includes the famous line (as emended by *Theobald) 'his nose was as sharp as a pen, and 'a babbl'd of green fields'. The Falstaff of The Merry Wives of Windsor is a diminished figure, whose attempts to mend his fortunes by wooing two citizens' wives simultaneously end in his discomfiture in Windsor Forest. It is this Falstaff, however, who is the subject of at least nine operas, including *Verdi's Falstaff (1893), and *Vaughan Williams's Sir John in Love (1929). *Elgar's symphonic study Falstaff (1913) is based on the Henry plays. Falstaff is also the eponymous hero of a highly praised Rabelaisian novel (1976) by Robert Nye.

Family Reunion, The, a play by T. S. *Eliot.

Fancyfull, Lady, a character in Vanbrugh's *The Provok'd Wife.

Fanny, a character in Fielding's *Joseph Andrews.

Fanny, Lord, see HERVEY, J.

Fanny Hill, see MEMOIRS OF A WOMAN OF PLEASURE.

Fanny Price, a character in J. Austen's *Mansfield Park.

FANSHAWE, Anne, Lady (1625–80), wife of Sir Richard Fanshawe, a supporter of the royalist cause who after the Restoration was ambassador to Portugal, then to Spain. She shared her husband's travels and her interesting Memoirs were first printed in 1829. Sir Richard (1608–66) translated *Horace, some *Virgil, *Guarini's Il pastor fido (1647), and *Camoëns' Lusiads (1655).

FARADAY, Michael (1791–1867), the son of a blacksmith, was apprenticed as a bookbinder. He attracted the attention of Sir H. *Davy and was engaged as his assistant in 1812. He made contributions to nearly all branches of physical science, but his greatest achievement was the discovery of magneto-electricity. He propounded the theory of 'lines of force', developed electro-chemistry, and originated the theory of the atom as a 'centre of force',

influenced probably by Kantian Idealism. (See KANT.)

Farewell to Arms, A, a novel by E. *Hemingway.

Farfrae, Donald, a character in Hardy's *The Mayor of Casterbridge.

Far from the Madding Crowd, a novel by T. *Hardy, published 1874. The title is a quotation from Gray's *Elegy . . . in a Country Churchyard.

The theme, which occurs in others of Hardy's novels, is the contrast of a patient and generous love with unscrupulous passion. The shepherd Gabriel Oak serves the young and spirited Bathsheba Everdene, owner of the farm, with unselfish devotion. She depends greatly on his support, but cannot regard him as a suitor. Another of her admirers is a neighbouring farmer, Boldwood. The dashing Sergeant Troy loves one of Bathsheba's servants, Fanny Robin, but after a fatal misunderstanding deserts her and she eventually dies in childbirth in the workhouse. Troy has meanwhile captivated and married Bathsheba, but soon begins to neglect and illtreat her. When he hears of Fanny's death he leaves the farm, disappears, and is deemed to have been drowned. Farmer Boldwood, now obsessed with Bathsheba, gives a party at which he pledges Bathsheba to marry him some time in the future. Troy reappears at the party and Boldwood, driven to madness by his reappearance, shoots him. Boldwood is tried and pronounced insane. Gabriel and Bathsheba are at last married.

Hardy made a stage version of the novel, which was eventually produced by the Hardy Players in Dorchester in 1924.

FARJEON, Eleanor (1881–1965), born in London into a highly literary Hampstead family, became well known as a children's writer after the success of Martin Pippin in the Apple-Orchard (1921, not originally written for children); she followed it with many volumes of poems, fantasies, stories, etc., and A Nursery in the Nineties (1935), reminiscences of her childhood. She was a close friend of E. *Thomas: see her Edward Thomas: The Last Four Years (1958).

FARMER, Richard, see ESSAY ON THE LEARNING OF SHAKESPEARE.

Farmer's Boy, The, see BLOOMFIELD, R.

FARNOL, (John) Jeffery (1878–1952), historical novelist, whose tales of adventure and the open road, many of them set in the Regency period (The Broad Highway, 1910; The Amateur Gentleman, 1913; and many others) were immensely popular; they show a debt both to *Borrow and to *Weyman.

FARQUHAR, George (1678–1707), born in Londonderry, was a sizar at Trinity College,

Dublin, and became an actor, but gave up the stage in consequence of accidentally wounding a fellow player. He took to writing comedies, and produced *Love and a Bottle* in 1698, *The Constant Couple, or a Trip to the Jubilee* in 1699, *Sir Harry Wildair* in 1701, *The Inconstant* and *The Twin Rivals* in 1702, *The Stage Coach* (with *Motteux) in 1704, *The Recruiting Officer* in 1706, and *The Beaux' Stratagem* in 1707. The last two are the best of his plays and are still regularly performed; *The Recruiting Officer* was used by *Brecht as the basis of his *Pauken und Trompeten* (1955). They are marked by an atmosphere of reality and good humour, revealing the easy-going character of the author, though his satire is sometimes pungent. He is said to have been deceived by his wife, from love of him, about her fortune, but to have always treated her with tenderness and indulgence. He died in poverty. A present of 20 guineas from the actor Robert Wilks gave him the means of writing his last play, *The Beaux' Stratagem*, and he lived just long enough to hear of its success. (See RESTORATION.)

FARRAR, F(rederic) W(illiam) (1831–1903), philosopher and theologian, eventually dean of Canterbury, who, when a master at Harrow, published *Eric, or, Little by Little* (1858), an edifying story of school life, partly autobiographical, which achieved enormous success. As well as many works of theology, he also wrote *Julian Home; a tale of College life* (1859) and *St Winifred's, or the World of School* (1862). (See also CHILDREN'S LITERATURE.)

FARRELL, J(ames) G(ordon) (1935–79), novelist. Born in Liverpool, the son of an accountant, he was educated at Rossall School and Brasenose College, Oxford, where, in his first term, he contracted poliomyelitis. He later travelled widely in America, Europe, and the East. His first novel, *A Man from Elsewhere* (1963), was set in France, his second, *The Lung* (1965), describes the experiences of a polio victim, and *A Girl in the Head* (1967) the desultory adventures of Count Boris Slattery in an English seaside town called Maidenhair. His first substantial novel, *Troubles* (1970), is set in Ireland, in the decaying Majestic Hotel, just after the First World War, against a background of Sinn Fein violence. *The Siege of Krishnapur* (1973, *Booker Prize) deals with the events of the Indian Mutiny, in a characteristically ironic and comic vein. *The Singapore Grip* (1978) moves closer to the epic, blending real and fictitious characters and describing the fall of Singapore to the Japanese, an event which Farrell portrays as a death-blow to the British Empire. His last three novels involved considerable historical research, and all reflect a sense of the end of the Empire and the stubborn, at times heroic, at times stupid, refusal of his characters to

recognize the course of history. His most vivid creation is Major Brendan Archer, courteous, faithful, and chivalrous, holding fast to his own code of civilized conduct in increasingly violent circumstances: he appears in *Troubles* and again in *The Singapore Grip*. Similarly the sardonic kindly rationalist Dr McNab from *The Siege* reappears in *The Hill Station* (1981), which was left unfinished when Farrell was accidentally drowned, shortly after moving from London to Ireland.

FARRELL, J(ames) T(homas) (1904–79), American naturalist novelist, Chicago-born, and best known in Britain for his trilogy about Studs Lonigan, a young Chicago Catholic of Irish descent. *Young Lonigan* (1932) describes his boyhood, *The Young Manhood of Studs Lonigan* (1934) his desultory career as housepainter, small time crook, etc., and *Judgement Day* (1935) his unemployment during the depression and early death from a heart condition aggravated by poverty and poor living.

Fashion, Sir Novelty and Young, characters in Vanbrugh's *The Relapse*, who reappear in Sheridan's adaptation *A Trip to Scarborough*.

Fashionable novel, or 'silver-fork school', a class of novel, popular *c*. 1825–50, which held up for admiration the lives of the wealthy and fashionable. *Hook was one of the leaders of this highly successful school of writing. *Hazlitt, in his essay on 'The Dandy School' (*The Examiner*, 1827), castigates the narrow superficiality of such novels which encourage the reader, he feels, only to 'the admiration of the folly, caprice, insolence, and affectation of a certain class'. *Bulwer-Lytton (whose own *Pelham* was a celebrated example) held that the genre was influential in the paradoxical sense that its effect was ultimately to expose 'the falsehood, the hypocrisy, the arrogant and vulgar insolence of patrician life'. M. W. Rosa, in *The Silver-Fork School* (1936), discusses the work of S. *Ferrier, T. H. *Lister, *Disraeli, P. *Ward, Mrs *Gore, and others, and argues that the school 'culminated in a single great book—*Vanity Fair*'. (See also NOVEL, RISE OF THE.)

FASTOLF, Sir John (1380–1459), a successful soldier in the French wars of Henry IV and Henry V, who contributed towards the building of philosophy schools at Cambridge and bequeathed money towards the foundation of Magdalen College, Oxford. He figures prominently in the *Paston Letters. In Shakespeare's 1 *Henry VI, however, he is presented as a coward who repeatedly betrays the heroic *Talbot, is stripped of his Garter, and banished by the king. The *Folio text calls him *'Falstaffe', but from *Theobald onwards it has become traditional to call him 'Fastolfe' to distinguish him from his similar but more purely fictitious namesake. To Shakespeare's audiences, however, the figures probably appeared identical, despite historical and chronological difficulties.

Fatal Curiosity, The, a tragedy in blank verse by *Lillo, first produced by *Fielding in 1736. It is based on an old story of a Cornish murder, but its plot is archetypal and appears in many literatures; Lillo's version influenced the German 'fate-drama', and *Camus used it in *Le Malentendu* (1945).

Old Wilmot, under stress of poverty and urged by his wife, murders a stranger who has deposited a casket with them, only to find the victim is his son, supposed lost in a shipwreck.

Fatal Dowry, The, a tragedy by *Massinger and *Field, acted c.1617–19, printed 1632. The play is based on one of the *controversiae* (or imaginary legal disputes) of Seneca the elder.

Charalois's father, the distinguished marshal of the duke of Burgundy, has died in debt, and his creditors refuse to allow his body to be buried. Charalois offers to go to prison if the creditors will release the body. The offer is accepted; Charalois goes to prison with his friend, the blunt soldier Romont. Rochfort, ex-president of the parliament, touched by the piety of Charalois and the honesty of Romont, procures their release, and moreover gives Charalois his daughter Beaumelle to wife. She is presently found by Romont exchanging kisses with her former suitor, the mean-spirited fop Novall. Charalois, at first incredulous, presently himself finds Beaumelle and Novall together, and forcing a duel on the latter kills him. He calls upon Rochfort to judge his daughter. The father himself condemns her, and Charalois stabs her. But the father immediately turns on Charalois and upbraids him for his lack of mercy. Charalois is tried for the murder of Novall and Beaumelle and acquitted, but is killed by a friend of Novall, who in turn is killed by Romont.

Rowe's *The Fair Penitent* is founded on this play.

Fatal Marriage, The, or the Innocent Adultery, a tragedy by *Southerne, performed 1694.

Biron, having married Isabella against his father's wish, is sent by him to the siege of Candy and reported killed. His widow is repudiated by the father and brought to misery. During seven years she is courted by Villeroy, and finally, from gratitude for his devotion and urged by Carlos, Biron's younger brother, she marries him. Biron, who has all this time been a captive, now returns and reveals himself to Isabella. Carlos, it now appears, had known that Biron was alive, but had concealed his knowledge, wishing to oust him from the succession. For the same reason he had urged the marriage of Isabella, in order finally to ruin her and her son in his father's estimation. Carlos waylays and mortally wounds Biron. Isabella, already distracted by the situation in which she finds herself, takes her own life. The guilt of Carlos is exposed.

The play is founded on A. *Behn's novel *The Nun or the Perjur'd Beauty* but, unlike Mrs Behn's heroine, Southerne's Isabella is portrayed as a helpless victim, 'born to suffer' and condemned by fate to 'a long line of woe'. The role was originally played by Mrs *Barry with great effect, and was subsequently played by many leading actresses, including Mrs *Cibber, Mrs *Siddons, and Fanny *Kemble. The play was revived by *Garrick in 1757 as *Isabella, or the Fatal Marriage*; he cut out the comic sub-plot and made other minor alterations.

Fata Morgana, see MORGAN LE FAY.

Fat Boy, The, Joe, Mr Wardle's servant, in Dickens's *Pickwick Papers*.

Father and Son, see GOSSE, E.

Father Brown, see BROWN, FATHER.

'Father O'Flynn', a popular Irish song by A. P. *Graves.

Fathers of the Church, the early Christian writers, a term usually applied to those of the first five cents. Sometimes the Greek and Latin fathers are distinguished, the former including *Clement of Alexandria, *Origen, Cyprian, *Athanasius, Basil the Great, Gregory Nazianzen, and *Chrysostom; the latter *Tertullian, *Jerome, *Ambrose, *Augustine, *Gregory (Pope Gregory I), and *Bernard.

Fathom, see FERDINAND COUNT FATHOM.

Faulconbridge, Robert and Philip, the legitimate and illegitimate sons of Sir Robert Faulconbridge in Shakespeare's *King John*. Philip's true father is *Richard I (Coeur de Lion). See also under BASTARD.

Faulkland, a character in Sheridan's *The Rivals*.

FAULKNER (originally Falkner), William Harrison (1897–1962), American novelist, born in Mississippi, where his family had long been settled; he spent most of his life there, in the town of Oxford, and the history and legends of the South, and of his own family, were the material of his greater books. After a desultory education and working at various odd jobs, he met S. *Anderson while working as a journalist in New Orleans, who encouraged him to write his first novel, *Soldier's Pay* (1926). This was followed by others, including *Sartoris* (1929), the first of the series in which he describes the decline of the Compson and Sartoris families, representative of the Old South, and the rise of the crude and unscrupulous Snopes family. The principal setting of these novels is 'Jefferson'—a composite picture of several Mississippi towns—

in the mythical Yoknapatawpha County. *The Sound and the Fury* (1929) is a narrative *tour de force* in which Faulkner views the decline of the South through several eyes, most remarkably those of Benjy Compson, a 33-year-old 'idiot'. The work is an astonishing display of technical brilliance written in a sombre and lyrical mood. *As I Lay Dying* (1930) is equally distinguished, and demonstrates Faulkner's comic as well as his tragic vision, in his account of the death of poor white Addie Bundren, and of her children's grotesque attempts to fulfil her wish to be buried in Jefferson. He made his name, however, not with these but with *Sanctuary* (1931) a more sensational work written to attract sales. *Light in August* (1932) and *Absalom, Absalom!* (1936) confirmed his reputation as one of the finest of modern novelists. Other important works include *The Hamlet* (1940), *Intruder in the Dust* (1948), and several volumes of short stories, collected in 1950. He was awarded the *Nobel Prize in 1949. In England he found an early champion in Arnold *Bennett, who wrote warmly of his work in the *Evening Standard*, having been introduced to it by R. *Hughes, who wrote a preface for the 1930 English edition of *Soldier's Pay*.

FAURÉ, Gabriel (1845–1924), French composer. Apart from his work in instrumental and choral music, Fauré was one of the greatest of all French song-writers. The standard collection of his works in this form contains two songs with a Shakespearean tinge, the charming 'Chanson (Shylock)' and the madrigal that follows it: both of these originated in 1889 with incidental music for the play *Shylock*, a translation and adaptation (with altered sequence of events) of *The Merchant of Venice* by Edmond Haraucourt. An orchestral suite, including both songs, was later made from the music and contains much that is admirable, though Fauré's accent in Shakespeare remains distinctly French. The beautiful little 'Nocturne' was among the music played at Fauré's funeral.

Faust, the subject of the great dramas of *Marlowe and *Goethe, was a wandering conjuror, who lived in Germany about 1488–1541 (H. G. Meed, *Johann Faust*, 1930) and is mentioned in various documents of the period. (He is not to be confused with Johann *Fust or Faust, the printer.) For Marlowe's play see DR FAUSTUS. *Faust*, the drama by Goethe, was begun by him about the year 1770 and not completed till just before his death in 1832. It consists of two parts, the first published 1808, the second 1832.

It begins with a Prologue in Heaven, in which Mephistopheles obtains permission to try to effect the ruin of the soul of Faust, the Lord being confident that he will fail and predicting the ultimately positive conclusion at the end of Pt II. The play itself opens with a soliloquy by

Faust, disillusioned with the world and despairing. Mephistopheles having presented himself, Faust enters into a compact to become his servant if Faust should exclaim, of any moment of delight procured for him, 'Stay, thou art so fair.' Then follow the attempts of Mephistopheles to satisfy Faust, culminating in the incident of Gretchen (Margaret), whom Faust, at the Devil's instigation, though not without some rebellion by his better self, seduces, bringing about her miserable death. This is the end of Pt I, Faust being left remorseful and dissatisfied.

The story of Pt II is extremely complex and its symbolism obscure. It consists in the main of two portions, of which the first is the incident of Helen, originally written as a separate and complete poem. Helen, symbolizing perfect beauty as produced by Greek art, is recalled from Hades and ardently pursued by Faust, but finally reft from him. Euphorion, their son, personifying poetry and the union of the classical and the romantic, and at the end representing Lord *Byron, vanishes in a flame. In the second portion (Acts IV and V) the purified Faust, pursuing the service of man, reclaims from the sea, with the help of Mephistopheles, a stretch of submerged land. But Care attacks and blinds him. Finally satisfied in the consciousness of good work done, he cries to the fleeting moment, 'Ah, stay, thou art so fair', and falls dead. Hell tries to seize his soul, but it is borne away by angels.

Faustus, Doctor, see DR FAUSTUS.

Fauves, Les (wild beasts), a group of French painters, so called by a critic of the Paris Salon d'Automne of 1905, on account of the violent colours in their paintings. They reduced landscape and other subjects to flat patterns, suggesting form by outline rather than by perspective and chiaroscuro. Henri Matisse (1869–1954) was the principal painter of the group.

FAWCETT, Millicent Garrett, see WOMEN'S SUFFRAGE.

Fawn, The, see PARASITASTER.

Feast of Fools, a medieval festival originally of the sub-deacons of the cathedral, held about the time of the Feast of the Circumcision (1 Jan.), in which the humbler cathedral officials burlesqued the sacred ceremonies. A lord of the feast was elected, styled bishop, cardinal, abbot, etc., according to the locality (cf. BOY BISHOP). The Feast of Fools had its chief vogue in the French cathedrals, but there are a few English records of it, notably in Lincoln cathedral and Beverley Minster. See E. K. *Chambers, *The Medieval Stage* (1903).

Feathernest, Mr, in Peacock's **Melincourt,* a caricature of *Southey.

Feeble, in Shakespeare's 2 **Henry IV* (III. ii), one of the recruits brought before *Falstaff, who is a 'woman's tailor', a phrase with bawdy connotations.

Feenix, Cousin, a character in Dickens's **Dombey and Son,* the nephew of Mrs Skewton, and cousin of Edith, Dombey's second wife.

FEINSTEIN, Elaine (1930–), novelist, poet, and translator, born in Bootle and educated at Newnham College, Cambridge. Her novels, which include *The Circle* (1970), *Children of the Rose* (1975), and *The Shadow Master* (1979), show a development from the experimental towards the naturalistic; *The Survivors* (1982) is a saga about a Jewish immigrant family in Liverpool. A selection of her poems, *Some Unease and Angels* (1977), contains new work and work from earlier collections, and a selection of her notable translations (pub. 1971) of the poetry of *Tsvetayeva.

Félibrige, a literary movement founded in 1854 by seven Provençal poets under the leadership of Frédéric Mistral (1830–1914) to foster a renaissance of Provençal writing. Its most memorable products are Mistral's vernacular epics *Mireio* (1859) and *Calendau* (1867). It has served as an inspiration to a number of more recent movements favouring dispossessed languages and cultures.

Felix Holt, The Radical, a novel by G. *Eliot, published 1866.

Set in 1832 in Loamshire, it vividly evokes the political ferment and corrupt electioneering tactics of the times. Harold Transome arrives home after many years in the East to inherit the family estate on his elder brother's death, and startles his family by standing as a Radical candidate. Although good-natured and intelligent, his political convictions are not incompatible with 'treating' the local workers, and his character is strongly contrasted with that of Felix Holt, austere, idealistic, and passionate, who although educated has deliberately chosen the life of an artisan, and who aims to stir his fellow workers to a sense of their own worth and destiny. The heroine, Esther, who supposes herself to be the daughter of old Lyon, the Independent minister, has an innate love of refinement, and when Felix chastises her for her frivolity she gains a new consciousness, and gradually falls in love with him. A complex and somewhat implausible chain of events reveals that Esther is in fact the heir to the Transome estate; Harold woos her, from motives not entirely mercenary, and Esther is forced to choose between his worldly attractions, and poverty with Felix, who has been imprisoned for his rash but innocent involvement in a riot. She renounces her claim to the estate and chooses Felix. It is revealed to Harold at the end of the novel (the reader having known from the beginning) that he is not his father's son, but the son of the hated lawyer Jermyn; the account of the years of suffering of the proud and lonely Mrs Transome, subjected in secrecy to a man she no longer respects, ever fearful of her son's discovery, befriended only by her faithful servant Denner, forms, in the view of *Leavis, the most successful part of the book, though H. *James (who found the whole plot clumsily artificial) declared that, although intensely drawn, she was dramatically superfluous.

FELL, Dr John (1625–86), dean of Christ Church, Oxford, and bishop of Oxford, is chiefly to be remembered in a literary connection as the promoter of the *Oxford University Press, to the development of which he greatly contributed, procuring for it the matrices and punches of the best types that could be found, undertaking with three other University men the financial responsibility for the printing work (previously done by craft printers), and arranging every year for the publication of some classical author. Fell was author of a valuable critical edition of Cyprian (1682), and edited with many arbitrary alterations the *Historia Universitatis Oxoniensis* of A. *Wood. He is the subject of the well-known epigram beginning 'I do not love you, Dr Fell', a translation by T. *Brown of *Martial, *Epigrams,* i. 32.

FELLTHAM, Owen (?1602–68), published a series of moral essays, *Resolves* (*c.*1620), and also contributed to *Jonsonus Virbius* (see JONSON).

Female Quixote, The, or *The Adventures of Arabella,* a novel by C. *Lennox, published 1752.

This vivacious and ironical work was probably the most consistent of the various attempts to reproduce the spirit of *Cervantes in English. Arabella, the daughter of a marquis, grows up in a remote castle into a beautiful young woman with a passion for reading romance and a determination to live herself in such a world. A naïve delight in her own beauty leads her to assume that all men are her slaves, and potential abductors and ravishers; so that innocent men, who find themselves in her company, are constantly thrown into confusion by her impassioned accusations. Nevertheless she is benevolent and virtuous, and sharply contrasted with her envious, worldly female cousin. After many ludicrous events at home, she travels, with her devoted cousin Mr Glanville and other friends, to Bath and London, where her beauty and singularity lead to dreadful confusions, a duel, illness, and expected death. But the ferment subsides, and Arabella marries the patient, sensible Mr Glanville. The novel was successful and praised by *Fielding.

Female, or **Feminine, Rhymes,** see RHYMES.

Feminist Criticism, a critical approach to be detected retrospectively in e.g. the early reviewing of Rebecca *West and V. Woolf's *A Room of One's Own* (1929), but which acquired a distinct identity in the late 1960s and 1970s with the publication of such works as Mary Ellmann's *Thinking about Women* (1968), Eva *Figes's *Patriarchal Attitudes* (1970), Elizabeth Hardwick's *Seduction and Betrayal* (1974), *Literary Women* (1976) by Ellen Moers, *A Literature of their Own* (1977) by Elaine Showalter, and *The Mad Women in the Attic* (1978) by Sandra Gilbert and Susan Gubar. The influence of S. de *Beauvoir's *The Second Sex* (1949, translated) is evident in many of these studies. Feminist criticism, which ranges from the scholarly to the political and prescriptive, seeks to re-examine women's literature of the past and present with the aid of a new feminist awareness ('raised consciousness') of female and male stereotypes, women's economic situation as authors, the supposed prejudice of male critics and publishers, the relationship between writing and gender, etc. Women's Studies as a separate subject grew in popularity greatly during the 1970s, particularly in the United States; the same period also saw the founding in Britain of feminist publishing houses, notably Virago (which published its first independent title in 1977) and The Women's Press (1978). Feminist criticism may thus be associated with the rediscovery and reprinting of many works by women writers of the past, ranging from H. *Martineau to E. B. *Browning and M. *Sinclair; with re-examinations of the achievements of writers whose reputation has been consistently high; with a continuing process of enquiry into sexist attitudes, in male and female literature; and with the encouragement of new feminist writing, both scholarly and creative.

Fenella, or Zarah, a character in Scott's *Peveril of the Peak,* suggested to the author by Mignon in *Goethe's *Wilhelm Meister.*

FÉNELON, François de Salignac de la Mothe (1651–1715), French theologian and educator. Appointed archbishop of Cambrai, he wielded considerable influence at court until his political independence and his quietism—which earned the censure of *Bossuet—relegated him to his diocese. His best-known works were written for his pupil, the duc de Bourgogne, grandson of Louis XIV: *Télémaque* (1699), a didactic romance modelled on Telemachus' voyage in the *Odyssey,* teaching the skills and virtues of the enlightened monarch, and *Dialogues des morts* (1712–30), presenting the lives of the heroes and statesmen of history for the edification of the prince. The seductive distinction of his style raised French prose to a new level.

Fenians, originally a semi-mythical, semi-historical military body said to have been raised for the defence of Ireland against Norse raids. *Finn, in his day, was its chief. The force was exterminated by King Cairbré, it is said, at the end of the 3rd cent. The Fenians of modern times were an association formed among the Irish in the United States and in Ireland in the middle of the 19th cent. for promoting the overthrow of the English government in Ireland. Their activity was greatest between 1865 and 1870, when they attempted invasions of Canada and caused a disastrous explosion at Clerkenwell, but it continued to the end of the century and a Fenian plot to blow up public buildings in London was discovered in 1883.

Fenton, a spendthrift young gentleman in love with Anne Page in Shakespeare's *The Merry Wives of Windsor.*

Ferdinand, (1) in Shakespeare's *Love's Labour's Lost,* the king of Navarre; (2) in his *The Tempest,* son of *Alonso, king of Naples, and lover of *Miranda; (3) in Webster's *The Duchess of Malfi,* the brother of the duchess.

Ferdinand Count Fathom, *The Adventures of,* a novel by T. *Smollett, published 1753.

In his Dedication Smollett outlines his ideas on form in the novel. It should create, 'a large diffused picture' dominated by a central figure to which various groups and episodes are subordinated; within this framework digression may be permitted. In these *Adventures* the figure of Count Fathom, a deliberately created monster 'from the purlieus of treachery and fraud', is starkly contrasted with the noble Count de Melvil and his son Renaldo. Fate and coincidence play a decisive part in the story, much of which is written in a mock-heroic style. The character of the book changes considerably in the last quarter, which becomes self-consciously *'romantic', in many ways anticipating the later *Gothic novel.

Far from being a count, Ferdinand is the son of a camp-follower of Marlborough's army. While she is robbing the dead on the field of Petervarad she saves Count de Melvil, who becomes Ferdinand's benefactor and brings the boy up with his own son. At 16 Ferdinand plans to seduce Melvil's daughter, and by the time he is 18 he is established in Vienna with his friend the evil Ratchcali, as womanizer, cheat, and social success. In London, again with Ratchcali, he conquers fashionable society with his talents and charm, organizes a swindle in fake antiques, and continues with his seductions, driving Elenor to Bedlam and Celinda to drink. After further successes in Bristol he is exposed cheating at cards, betrayed, and thrown into the debtor's prison. Freed by young Melvil, he shows his gratitude by creating bitterness between Melvil and his love Monimia, but fails in his attempt to rape her. As he cannot now return to high society, he takes up medicine, but his scandalous life and a legal action brought by a cleric ruin his repute. A rapid series of events bear down on him. In an attempt to escape he marries a wealthy widow, but he is again indicted and again imprisoned, when at last signs of remorse begin to appear. He now almost disappears from the story, the rest of which relates, with lachrymose sentiment and many *frissons* of horror (including a hint of necrophilia), the misfortunes and eventual joys of young Melvil and Monimia.

FERGUSON, Adam (1723–1816), one-time chaplain to the Black Watch, succeeded *Hume as Advocates' Librarian in 1757, was professor in turn of natural philosophy, moral philosophy, and mathematics at Edinburgh after 1764, and was a member of the *Select Society and co-founder of the *Royal Society of Edinburgh. His writings include *The Morality of Stage-Plays Seriously Considered* (1757), written in defence of J. Home's *Douglas, performed the previous year; *An Essay on the History of Civil Society* (1767), a pioneer work in political sociology; *The History of the Progress and Termination of the Roman Republic* (3 vols, 1783); and *Principles of Moral and Political Science* (2 vols, 1792). This last work carries further the analysis of human character begun in the *Essay,* and offers a more teleological ethic than is found in other moralists of the period. Ferguson is also more explicit in the development of the sharp contrast between questions of fact and questions of value. In the *Essay* he has a discussion 'Of the History of Literature', in which he argues that poetry is a more original and natural form of literary expression than prose, and that all literature develops better in periods and contexts of great social activity than in leisure and solitude.

FERGUSON, Sir Samuel (1810–86), an important figure in the *Irish revival, was educated at Trinity College, Dublin, and became the deputy keeper of the records of Ireland. Among many translations and works based on Gaelic legend, he published a widely praised elegy on Thomas Davis, a nationalist leader, in 1845; *Lays of the Western Gael* (1865); and an epic, *Congal* (1872), on the last stand of Irish paganism against Christianity. A long narrative poem, 'Conary', based on a bardic story, and a retelling of the legend of *Deirdre both appeared in 1880. *Ogham Inscriptions in Ireland, Wales, and Scotland,* his most important antiquarian work, was published in 1887. A biography, *Ascendency of the Heart,* by R. O'Driscoll, appeared in 1976.

FERGUSSON, Robert (1750–74), was obliged by poverty to leave St Andrews on his father's death, and subsequently worked as a clerk in the Commissary Office. His first poems were published in Ruddiman's *Weekly Magazine* (1771), in imitation of English models, and his first *Scots poem, 'The Daft Days', appeared in 1772. A volume appeared in 1773 which was

to have a profound influence on *Burns, who found himself inspired to 'emulating vigour': Fergusson's 'The Farmer's Ingle', a vernacular description of homely rustic life, is a clear foreshadowing of Burns's *'The Cotter's Saturday Night'. Fergusson vividly evokes the street life, taverns, and amusements of Edinburgh, and mocks the established literary world in satirical attacks on Dr *Johnson and *Mackenzie ('The Sow of Feeling'). In 1773 he developed manic-depressive symptoms, and died not long after being shut up in the local Bedlam. An edition of his works in two volumes with a life by M. P. McDiarmid appeared in 1954–6.

Ferishtah's Fancies, a volume of poems by R. *Browning, published 1884. The main part of the collection consists of twelve poems focused on the sayings of an imaginary Persian sage, Ferishtah, on various moral and religious topics. The device of a non-Christian speaker to suggest Christian teaching (Ferishtah with his parables recalls Jesus) had been used before by Browning, in such poems as 'Cleon' (see MEN AND WOMEN), but not in so systematic a format. The poems, with their intercalated lyrics, are in general the weakest that Browning ever wrote.

FERLINGHETTI, Lawrence, see BEAT GENERATION.

FERRAR, Nicholas (1592–1637), educated at and fellow of Clare College, Cambridge, was a Member of Parliament and active in the affairs of the Virginia Company. In 1625 he retired to *Little Gidding, an estate belonging to his mother, and established there with his brother, his brother-in-law John Collett, and their families a religious community based on Anglican principles. Ferrar wrote little himself, but was a close friend of G. *Herbert, who on his deathbed entrusted to him the manuscript of his poems *The Temple,* published 1633.

Ferrars, (1) Mrs, and her sons Edward and Robert, in *Sense and Sensibility* by J. Austen; (2) William, and his children Endymion and Myra, in *Endymion* by B. Disraeli.

Ferrau, or Ferragus, in *Orlando Innamorato and *Orlando Furioso, a Moorish knight of Spain, one of the suitors for the hand of *Angelica, and the slayer of her brother *Argalia.

FERRERS, George, see MIRROR FOR MAGISTRATES, A.

Ferret, a character in Smollett's *Sir *Launcelot Greaves.*

Ferrex and Porrex, see GORBODUC.

FERRIER, James Frederick (1808–64), nephew of Susan *Ferrier, educated at Edinburgh University and Magdalen College, Oxford, studied German philosophy at Heidelberg and was successively professor of civil history at Edinburgh

(1842–5) and of moral philosophy and political economy at St Andrews (1845–64).

His idealistic philosophy, connected with that of *Berkeley, is set forth in *The Institutes of Metaphysic* (1854) and *Lectures on Greek Philosophy and other Philosophical Remains* (mostly published in *Blackwood's*, 1838–43, and in volume form 1866). The principal positions of his philosophy are two: first, that 'Along with whatever any intelligence knows, it must, as the ground or condition of its knowledge, have some cognisance of itself.' Nor can it know itself except in relation with objects. Mind and matter, *per se*, are unknowable. Secondly, that we can be ignorant only of what is capable of being known. From these positions he argues that it is necessary to 'conceive a supreme intelligence as the ground and essence of the Universal whole'. In substance, Ferrier's conclusions closely resemble those of *Hegel, though reached independently and from a different starting-point; *De Quincey said that Ferrier produced 'German philosophy reflected through a Scottish medium'.

FERRIER, Susan Edmonstone (1782–1854), the daughter of an Edinburgh lawyer who was a friend of Sir W. *Scott, was the successful authoress of three good novels of Scottish life: *Marriage* (1818), *The Inheritance* (1824), and *Destiny* (1831). Her object was avowedly to instruct, particularly on the subject of marriage, but her method lies in shrewd observation and comedy.

Ferumbras (or **Firumbras**), **Sir,** a Middle English metrical romance of 10,540 short lines related to the French Charlemagne romances *Fierabras* and the *Destruccion de Rome*. It is one of the more artistic of the English romances of 'The Matter of France', and more distinguished than the version known from its 19th-cent. owner as the 'Fillingham Firumbras' (ed. M. I. O'Sullivan, EETS os 198, 1935). The story tells of the capture by Ferumbras, the son of the Sultan of Babylon, of Rome and the Holy Relics, of his combat and later friendship with Oliver, and of the conversion to Christianity of Ferumbras and his sister Floripas. The two become friends of Roland, Oliver, and Charlemagne, and Floripas marries Guy of Burgundy. The same story is told in *The Sowdone of Babylon*, a version from about 1400 of a lost French romance. Ed. S. J. Herrtage (EETS es 34, 1879; reprinted 1966).

Feste, in Shakespear's *Twelfth Night*, *Olivia's jester, who is the prime mover in the plot to gull *Malvolio. His name, which indicates mirthfulness, occurs only once. He concludes the play with his song, 'When that I was and a little tiny boy'.

Festin de pierre, Le, see DON JUAN.

Festus, see BAILEY, P. J.

FET, Afanasy Afanasevich (A. A. Shenshin) (1820–92), Russian lyric poet, and a close friend of *Turgenev. His first volume of verse appeared in 1850, but by the late 1850s Fet's concern for 'pure art' and his themes from nature, which he describes with startling freshness, went out of fashion. In his last years four collections entitled *Evening Lights* were published and he found a new fame with the younger generation of Russian Symbolist poets. The first selection of his poetry in English, *I Have Come to You to Greet You* (trans. James Greene), appeared in 1982.

FEUCHTWANGER, Lion (1884–1958), German Jewish novelist, best known as the author of *Die hässliche Herzogin* (1923, *The Ugly Duchess*) and *Jud Süss* (1925, *Jew Süss*). He lived as an expatriate in France, was interned by the Vichy government, then escaped to the USA, where he settled in Hollywood. *Jew Süss*, in a translation by W. and E. *Muir (1927) was highly praised by Arnold *Bennett in his *Evening Standard* column ('a complete picture of a complex social organism'), and became a best-seller. Feuchtwanger appears as a character in Christopher Hampton's play *Tales from Hollywood* (1983).

FEUERBACH, Ludwig (1804–72), German philosopher and critic of the Bible, a disciple of *Hegel. Feuerbach's most influential work was *Das Wesen des Christentums* (*The Essence of Christianity*, 1841), in which he asserted that Christianity is a man-created myth, satisfying man's need to imagine perfection: 'Man, by means of the imagination, involuntarily contemplates his inner nature; he represents it as out of himself. The nature of man, of the species . . . is God.' G. *Eliot, who translated the work into English in 1854, wrote that she agreed with Feuerbach's religion of humanity, and her novels show the influence not only of Feuerbach's thought but also of his application of religious terms to a secular philosophy.

Fezziwig, Mr and Mrs, characters in Dickens's *A Christmas Carol.*

Fiammetta, the name given by *Boccaccio to the lady he loved, and the title of one of his works.

FICHTE, Johann Gottlieb (1762–1814), German philosopher, a pupil of *Kant, from whose dualism he subsequently dissented. He became professor of philosophy at Jena in 1794, but was accused of atheism and dismissed. He subsequently taught at the universities of Erlangen and Berlin. Fichte's philosophy is pure idealism. Though his philosophical system grew out of Kant's, it has the distinguishing feature that the thinking self, or *ego*, is seen as the only reality.

This *ego*, in defining and limiting itself, creates the *non-ego*, the world of experience, as its opposite, the medium through which it asserts its freedom. He expounded this doctrine in his principal work, *Wissenschaftslehre* (*Doctrine of Knowledge*, 1794). Influenced by the humiliation of Prussia in 1806–7, he became increasingly interested in the idea of nationhood, and sought reality, not in the *ego* but in the notion of a divine idea lying at the base of all experience, of which the world of the senses is the manifestation. His *Reden an die deutsche Nation* (*Speeches to the German Nation*, 1814) helped to arouse the patriotism of his contemporaries under the Napoleonic occupation. His view of history as the biography of its heroes greatly influenced *Carlyle, particularly in the latter's lectures On *Heroes and Hero-Worship* (1841), as did his idealism. See *Sartor Resartus* (1833–4) for Carlyle's use of Fichte's idea of the world of Appearances as a vesture under which lies the essence or Divine Idea.

FICINO, Marsilio (1433–99), Italian humanist and philosopher, and a highly influential exponent of Platonism. He translated into Latin many important works of *Plato and the *Neoplatonists (e.g. *Porphyry, *Plotinus, and *Dionysius the Areopagite), sought to establish an essential harmony between Platonism and Christianity, and under the patronage of Cosimo de'Medici was the leader of a 'Platonic Academy' at Florence. His views influenced *Reuchlin and *Colet and were an inspiration to many English poets, including *Sidney and *Milton.

Fidele, in Shakespeare's *Cymbeline*, the name assumed by *Imogen when disguised as a boy, suggesting her faithfulness.

Fidessa, in Spenser's *Faerie Queene* (I. ii), the name assumed by the fair companion of *Sansfoy, whom the *Redcrosse Knight takes under his protection after slaying that 'faithlesse Sarazin'. She turns out to be the false *Duessa.

FIELD, Eugene (1850–95), American journalist, poet, and bibliophile, born in Missouri. He wrote light verse for adults and children, and his collection *A Little Book of Western Verse* (1889), which contains 'Little Boy Blue' and 'Dutch Lullaby' (better known later as 'Wynken, Blynken and Nod') had a considerable vogue in England.

FIELD, Michael, the pseudonym of Katharine Bradley (1846–1914) and her niece Edith Cooper (1862–1913), who together published many verse dramas, including *Callirrhoe* (1884) and *Canute the Great* (1887).

FIELD, Nathan (1587–1619/20), actor and dramatist, sometimes called Nathaniel by confusion with his brother, a printer. Educated at St Paul's, he was impressed into the company of the Children of the Chapel, and probably succeeded to Shakespeare's place as actor and shareholder in the King's Men, *c.*1616. He wrote two comedies, *A Woman is a Weathercock* (1609), which shows the influence of *Jonson and includes a parody of a speech in *The Spanish Tragedy*, and *Amends for Ladies* (1610). He later collaborated with a number of other dramatists, including *Fletcher and *Massinger, and is best known for his share of Massinger's *The Fatal Dowry*.

FIELDING, Henry (1707–54), the son of a lieutenant (who later became lieutenant-general), was born at Sharpham Park, the house of his maternal grandfather in Somerset. His mother died when he was eleven, and when his father remarried Henry was sent to Eton. There he was happy, enjoyed his studies, and made lifelong friends of *Lyttleton, who was to become a generous future patron, and of *Pitt the elder. At 19 he attempted to elope with a beautiful heiress, but failing in this he settled in London, determined to earn his living as a dramatist. Lady M. W. *Montagu, a distant cousin, encouraged him, and in 1728 at Drury Lane his play *Love in Several Masques* was successfully performed. In the same year he became a student of letters at Leyden, where he remained about 18 months, greatly enlarging his knowledge of classical literature. On his return to London he continued his energetic but precarious life as a dramatist, and between 1729 and 1737 wrote some 25 assorted dramas, largely in the form of farce and satire, and including two adaptations of *Molière, *The Mock Doctor* and *The Miser*. In 1730 three of his plays were performed: *The Author's Farce*; *Rape upon Rape*, a savage satire on the practices of the law, embodied in Justice Squeezum; and the most successful of all his dramas, *Tom Thumb* (which was published in a revised form the following year as *The Tragedy of Tragedies, or The Life and Death of Tom Thumb the Great*), one of several extravagant burlesques modelled on Buckingham's *The Rehearsal*, of the turgid fashionable tragedies of the day. *Hogarth designed the frontispiece, and a long and close friendship began. *Don Quixote*, a satire which is part a tribute to *Cervantes, appeared in 1734. In the same year Fielding married Charlotte Cradock, who became his model for Sophia in *Tom Jones* and for the heroine of *Amelia*, and with whom he enjoyed ten years of great happiness until her death. His improvidence led to long periods of considerable poverty, but he was greatly assisted at various periods of his life by his close and wealthy friend R. *Allen, who became, with Lyttleton, the model for Allworthy in *Tom Jones*. In 1736 Fielding took over the management of the New Theatre, for the opening of which he wrote the highly successful satirical comedy *Pasquin*, which aimed at various religious and political targets, including electioneering abuses. But *The Historical Register for 1736* was fiercer political satire than *Walpole's government would tolerate, and the Licensing Act of 1737, introducing censorship by the Lord Chamberlain, brought Fielding's career in the theatre to an end. (See App. I, section 2.)

He entered the Middle Temple and began to read for the bar. In 1739–40 he wrote most of the columns of *The Champion*, a satirical and anti-Jacobite journal. In 1740 he was called to the bar but his health began to fail and he suffered acutely from gout. In the same year Richardson's *Pamela* appeared and enjoyed tremendous popular success; in 1741 Fielding expressed his contempt in his pseudonymous parody, *An apology for the life of Mrs *Shamela Andrews*. Meanwhile, because of increasing illness, he was unable to pursue his legal career with any consistency. Instead, in 1742, he produced *The Adventures of *Joseph Andrews and his Friend, Mr Abraham Adams*, for which he received from his publisher £185 11s. In 1743 his old friend *Garrick put on Fielding's *The Wedding Day*, and in the same year Fielding published three volumes of *Miscellanies*, which included *A Journey from this World to the Next* and a ferocious satire, *The Life and Death of *Jonathan Wild the Great*. In 1744 he suffered a terrible blow in the death of his wife, and for a year or so he wrote little except a Preface to his sister Sarah's novel *David Simple*, and some journalism, particularly *The True Patriot* and *The Jacobite's Journal*. In 1746 he probably began *The History of Tom Jones, a Foundling*, and in 1747 caused some scandal by marrying his wife's maid and friend Mary Daniel. With the aid of Lyttleton, he was appointed JP for Westminster in 1748 and once again joined battle, now from the inside, with legal corruption and the 'trading justices' who imposed and embezzled fines. In 1749 *Tom Jones* was enthusiastically received by the general public, if not by *Richardson, *Smollett, Dr *Johnson, and other literary figures. In the same year his legal jurisdiction was extended to the whole county of Middlesex, and he was made chairman of the quarter sessions of Westminster. From his court in Bow Street he continued his struggle against corruption and lawlessness and, with his blind half-brother and fellow magistrate Sir John Fielding, strove to establish new standards of honesty and competence on the bench. He wrote various influential legal enquiries and pamphlets, including a proposal for the abolition of public hangings. In 1751 he published *Amelia*, which sold the best of all his novels. He returned to journalism in 1752 with *The Covent-Garden Journal*, and published in 1753 a humane and exhaustive *Proposal for making effective provision for the Poor*. He organized and saw successfully implemented a plan for breaking up the criminal gangs who

were then flourishing in London. But his gout, asthma, and other afflictions were now so far advanced that he had to use crutches, and in 1754, in hope of improvement, he set off with his wife and one of his daughters for Portugal. *The Journal of a Voyage to Lisbon*, published posthumously in 1755, describes in lively and observant detail the departure and journey. He had prepared it for the press ('a novel without a Plot') before he died in Lisbon in October.

Fielding is generally agreed to be an innovating master of the highest originality. He himself believed he was 'the founder of a new province of writing' and Sir W. *Scott commended him for his 'high notions of the dignity of an art which he may be considered as having founded'. His three acknowledged masters were *Lucian, *Swift, and Cervantes. In breaking away from the epistolary method of his contemporary Richardson, and others, he devised what he described as 'comic epics in prose', which are in effect the first modern novels in English, leading straight to the works of *Dickens and *Thackeray.

There are biographies by W. L. Cross (3 vols, 1918) and F. H. Duddon (2 vols, 1952); see also *Henry Fielding: The Critical Heritage* (1969), ed. R. Paulson and T. Lockwood).

FIELDING, Sarah (1710–68), sister of H. *Fielding. For much of her life she lived quietly near London, where she became part of S. *Richardson's circle, and later near Bath. In 1744 she published her best-known work, *The Adventures of *David Simple*, a 'Moral Romance', with (in its second edition of that year) a Preface by her brother Henry. The book was only moderately successful, but sold well in France. *Familiar Letters between the Principal Characters in David Simple* followed in 1747, and in 1753 the sombre *Volume the Last*, completing the story of Simple. With Jane Collier she published *The Cry* (1754), a clever dialogue between Portia (the Solo) representing integrity, and an audience (the Chorus) representing malice and ignorance. The parallel of author against critic is implied throughout. There followed *The Lives of Cleopatra and Octavia* (1757), a series of dramatic monologues in which the subtle self-seeking of Cleopatra is contrasted with the honesty of Octavia. In 1749 appeared *The History of the Countess of Dellwyn*, tracing the disastrous relationship of an old husband and a young wife. The light-hearted *History of Ophelia* (1760), relates the adventures of an ingenuous young woman constantly astonished by the unquestioned conventions of society. Translations of *Xenophon's *Memorabilia* and *Apologia* appeared in 1762.

Sarah Fielding was one of the earliest of the English novelists to explore with close attention varying states of feeling and the roots of motive. Like her brother Henry, she seems to have been particularly interested in self-deception, but her gift was in following what her friend Richardson described as 'the finer springs and movements' of the heart. She may have been the author of *Remarks on Clarissa* (1749).

FIENNES, Celia (1662–1741), granddaughter of the first viscount Saye and Sele, was probably born at Newton Toney near Salisbury. Nearly all that is known about her life is to be found in her Journal, of which an incomplete version was published in 1888 under the title *Through England on a Side Saddle in the Time of William and Mary*. A definitive edition, *The Journeys of Celia Fiennes*, ed. Christopher Morris, was published in 1947. Between 1685 and 1703 Celia Fiennes travelled into every county of England, and her Journal provided the first comprehensive survey of the country since *Harrison and *Camden. She recorded throughout what interested her: enclosures, mining, cloth manufacture, gardens, and domestic architecture; and while living in London she described in detail the coronations of James II, William and Mary, and Anne. Her style is breathless and her spelling erratic, but she communicates a lively enthusiasm.

Fierabras, or **Fierebras,** see FERUMBRAS.

Fifine at the Fair, a poem in alexandrine couplets by R. *Browning, published 1872.

The speaker in Don Juan, who is strolling with his wife Elvire near Pornic in Brittany, where a fair is being held. Don Juan, attracted by the gipsy dancer Fifine, dissertates to Elvire on the nature of his feelings, contrasting the intense ephemerality of desire with the dull permanence of love, this initial theme then giving rise to a series of brilliant variations on the interconnected topics of knowledge, identity, and truth in life and art. The poem's interest in the casuistry of an over-wrought self-consciousness has been attributed in part to Browning's bitterness in the aftermath of his quarrel with Lady Ashburton, which began in 1869 with a failed proposal of marriage (whether from him to her or vice versa is uncertain) and was still going on in 1871; Fifine would stand for Lady Ashburton in the interpretation, and Elvire for Elizabeth Barrett (*Browning). But this background is not essential to a reading of the poem. Browning told his friend *Domett that the poem was 'the most metaphysical and boldest he had written since Sordello, and [he] was very doubtful as to its reception by the public'. The comparison with *Sordello* is illuminating: the poem may be regarded as Browning's mature return to the difficulty and splendour of the earlier work. The poem indeed proved baffling to the public and critics, though its modern critical standing is high.

Figaro, the barber in *Beaumarchais's *Le Barbier*

de Séville and hero of his *Le Mariage de Figaro*, a witty resourceful fellow, and a rebel against the abuses of the *ancien régime*.

FIGES, Eva (1932–), novelist and feminist, born in Berlin; she came to England in 1939 and was educated at Queen Mary College, University of London. Her novels, which are distinguished by a poetic use of language and an exploration of the uncertainties and fragmentation of identity, often through interior monologue, include *Winter Journey* (1967), *B* (1972), *Days* (1974), *Nelly's Version* (1977), and *Waking* (1981). Her non-fiction works include *Patriarchal Attitudes* (1970), a seminal work of *Feminist social and literary criticism, and *Sex and Subterfuge: Women Writers to 1850* (1982).

FILMER, Sir Robert (*c.*1590–1653), was an extreme defender of the divine right of kings, and his *Patriarcha, or the Natural Power of Kings*, written ?1638, published 1680, was attacked and ridiculed in his first *Treatise of Government* (1690). He also opposed the witch-hunting mania.

Filostrato, a poem in *ottava rima* on the story of Troilus and Cressida, by *Boccaccio, of special interest as the source of Chaucer's *Troilus and Criseyde*.

FINCH, Anne, see WINCHILSEA.

Fingal, an Ancient Epic Poem, in Six Books: together with several other Poems, composed by Ossian, the Son of Fingal. Translated from the Galic language, 1762, and *Temora, an ancient epic poem, in Eight Books* (1763).

These epics, which purported to be translated from an ancient Gaelic original were in fact largely the work of J. *Macpherson; the first was based loosely on various old ballads and fragments, the second was entirely invented. Macpherson transforms the legendary Irish hero *Finn or Fionn into the Scottish Fingal, ignores various episodes and characters in the original Fenian and Ossianic stories (including *Grainne, Finn's faithless wife, and her lover Diarmid, who do not appear at all) and brings together Fingal and Cuthullin (the Irish Cuchulain) who according to legend were divided by centuries. Morven, Fingal's kingdom in the north-west of Scotland, is Macpherson's invention. The original Finn MacCoul, whether historical or mythical, is usually assigned to the 3rd cent. AD; he was the son of Comhal, and father of Ossian the warrior bard; he was also leader of the Fianna or *Fenians, a semi-mythical military body said to have been raised for the defence of Ireland against the Norse. Fingal is pictured by Macpherson as fighting both the Norwegians and the Romans under Caracalla—'Caracul, King of the World'. The astonishing sway of Macpherson's version is indicated by the fact that even *Gibbon took the trouble to discuss it; he writes (though with some irony) of 'the tenderness, the elegant genius of Ossian', and contrasts the 'untutored Caledonians, glowing with the warm virtues of nature' with 'the degenerate Romans, polluted with the mean vices of wealth and slavery'. The appeal of *Fingal* lay in its *primitivism, its qualities of the *sublime, and its sentiment. H. *Blair found that it conformed to the rules of *Aristotle, and bestowed upon it such epithets as 'grand . . . pathetic . . . serious . . . grave . . . wild and romantic . . . sublime and tender'. In fact Macpherson conformed a little too closely to the rules, and the Homeric, biblical, and Miltonic echoes in his work helped to draw attention to its lack of authenticity.

FINLAY, Ian Hamilton (1925–), Scottish poet and artist, renowned for his highly experimental poems and sculptures: see CONCRETE POETRY.

Finn, or **Fionn,** the principal hero of the southern or later cycle of Irish legends, also called the Fenian or Ossianic cycle. Finn MacCoul has been thought a historical personage by some modern authorities; others regard him as mythical. He was the son of Cumal (Comhal) and father of Ossian, and is supposed to have lived in the 3rd cent. AD, a contemporary of King Cormac. The king appointed him chief of the Fianna (pron. Fēna) or *Fenians, a military body composed of men of exceptional strength and prowess, of whose heroic or romantic deeds there are endless tales. Finn was chosen their leader not for surpassing physical qualities, but on account of his truth, wisdom, and generosity. He is said to have perished in an affray with mutinous Fenians in AD 283.

For the story of Finn, Grainne, and Diarmid see GRAINNE; see also FINGAL.

Finn, Phineas, hero of A. Trollope's novels *Phineas Finn* and *Phineas Redux*.

Finnegans Wake, a prose work by J. *Joyce, published 1939. It is written in a unique and extremely difficult style, making use of puns and portmanteau words, and a very wide range of allusion. The central theme of the work is a cyclical pattern of fall and resurrection.

This is presented in the story of Humphrey Chimpden Earwicker, a Dublin tavern-keeper, and the book is apparently a dream-sequence representing the stream of his unconscious mind through the course of one night. Other characters are his wife Anna Livia Plurabelle, their sons Shem and Shaun, and their daughter Isabel. In the relationships of these characters all human experience, mythical and historical, is seen to be historically subsumed. In spite of its obscurity it contains passages of great lyrical beauty, and also much humour.

Finnsburh, The Fight at (known as 'The Finnsburh Fragment', to distinguish it from the 'Finnsburh Episode' in *Beowulf*), a 48-line fragmentary poem in Old English dealing with part of the tragic tale of Finn and Hildeburh, a later part of which is sung by the scôp in Beowulf, ll. 1,063–1,159. An attempt is made to heal the long-standing feud between the Danes and the Frisians by the marriage of the Frisian king Finn to Hildeburh, the sister of Hnaef who is king of the Half-Danes. Apparently after a period of peace, the feud breaks out again in a bloody battle at Finn's court and Hnaef is killed, as is his nephew, the son of Finn and Hildeburh. The beginning of this battle is the subject of the Fragment; the *Beowulf* episode seems to begin almost immediately after its end as Hildeburh laments the tragedy. After an uneasy winter truce, during which the Danes have to remain as guests of Finn, the slayer of their leader, the Danes gain vengeance by killing Finn when the spring comes. The fragment is included by F. Klaeber in his edition of *Beowulf* (1922, etc.) and in other editions such as Wrenn's; see also interpretation in Part III of R. W. *Chambers's *Beowulf: an Introduction* (rev. C. L. Wrenn, 1959, pp. 245–89).

FIONA MACLEOD, see SHARP, W.

Fiordespina, in *Orlando Furioso*, a princess who falls in love with *Bradamante, being led by her armour to take her for a man.

FIRBANK, (Arthur Annesley) Ronald (1886–1926), novelist, son of Sir Thomas Firbank, MP (1850–1910), and grandson of Joseph Firbank (1819–86), a wealthy self-made railway contractor; he derived from the latter an income which enabled him to travel extensively and to pay for the publication of most of his own work. His education was largely private until he went to Trinity Hall, Cambridge, where he took no examinations, but met R. H. *Benson, who received him in 1907 into the Roman Catholic church. He had already published in 1905 a volume of two stories, *Odette d'Antrevernes* (revised version, 1916) and *A Study in Temperament*; this was followed by several novels: *Vainglory* (1915); *Inclinations* (1916); *Caprice* (1917, the story of the spectacularly brief and dazzling theatrical career of the daughter of a rural dean); *Valmouth* (1919, set in a watering place dominated by the erotic and manipulative black masseuse Mrs Yajñavalkya); *Santal* (1921, set in North Africa); and *The Flower beneath the Foot* (1923). A play, *The Princess Zoubaroff*, was published in 1920. The first of his novels to be financed by a publisher, not by himself, was *Prancing Nigger* (1924), which appeared under that title in America, and under his own preferred title, *Sorrow in Sunlight*, in Britain; set in the West Indies, 'with a brilliant background of sunlight, sea, and as tropical', it describes the social aspirations and adventures of a Negro family, the Mouths. (In this novel he himself appears, characteristically, as the name of an orchid, 'a dingy lilac blossom of rarity untold'.) His last finished work, *Concerning the eccentricities of Cardinal Pirelli* (1926), appeared shortly after his death, from a disease of the lungs, in Rome; other posthumous publications include *The Artificial Princess* (1934) and *The New Rhythum and Other Pieces* (1962); the latter includes a very early work, *Lady Appledore's Mésalliance*, and chapters from an unfinished novel, set in New York, on which he was working when he died.

Dandy, aesthete, exotic, homosexual, and habitué of the *Café Royal, Firbank received little encouragement as a writer during his lifetime (except from such pro-modernists as the *Sitwells), but nevertheless succeeded in creating a distinctive 'Firbankian' style, in both life and works. His use of dialogue, his oblique narration, his highly coloured fantasies, and his intense concentration of language and image are now seen as truly innovative, and some writers have claimed that he did more to liberate the novel from 19th-cent. concepts of realism than *Joyce himself. Those who show traces of his influence include E. *Waugh, I. *Compton-Burnett, *Gerhardi, and M. *Spark. See *Ronald Firbank: A Memoir* (1930) by I. K. Fletcher, and Brigid *Brophy's appreciative critical biography *Prancing Novelist* (1973).

Fir Bolgs, legendary early invaders of Ireland, according to tradition of an Iberian tribe, who were driven into Arran, Islay, and the Hebrides by the *Milesians.

FIRDAUSI, Abul Kasim Mansur (c.950–1020), Persian poet, and author of the *Shah-nama* (or *Shanameh*), the great epic which recounts the legendary history of the ancient kings and heroes of Persia. It is known to English readers principally through M. *Arnold's version of one of its main incidents, *'Sohrab and Rustum'.

Firmilian, see AYTOUN, W. E.

Firmin, Dr George Brand and Philip, characters in Thackeray's *The Adventures of Philip*.

Firumbras, Sir, see FERUMBRAS.

FISHER, St John (1469–1535), was educated at Michaelhouse (absorbed in Trinity College, 1546), Cambridge, of which he was appointed master in 1497. He became chancellor of the university and bishop of Rochester, 1504, and was president of Queens' College, Cambridge, from 1505 to 1508. He was a patron of *Erasmus and induced him to lecture on Greek at Cambridge from 1511 to 1514. He wrote three treatises against the Lutheran reformation and was fined for denying the validity of the divorce of Queen Catherine, 1534. He was committed to the Tower for refusing to swear

to the Act of Succession, and the pope did not improve his chances of escape from death by sending him a cardinal's hat while he was in prison. Fisher was deprived, attainted, and beheaded for refusing to acknowledge *Henry VIII as supreme head of the Church. His Latin theological works were issued in 1597 (republished 1967); his English works, edited by J. E. B. Mayor, appeared in 1876. His English prose style showed a great advance, in point of rhetorical artifice and effect, on that of his predecessors. He was canonized in 1935 and is commemorated on 22 June.

FISHER, Roy, see JAZZ POETRY.

FitzBoodle, George Savage, one of *Thackeray's pseudonyms. As the narrator of the *Fitz-Boodle Papers*, published in *Fraser's Magazine* 1842–3, FitzBoodle, a bachelor clubman, tells the story of his own amorous misadventures.

FITZGERALD, Edward (1809–83), whose parents owned estates in England and Ireland, was the third son in a family of eight and was born in Suffolk, where he spent most of his life. He was educated at the King Edward VI Grammar School, Bury St Edmunds, and Trinity College, Cambridge. He never engaged in any profession or made any extended travels, but often visited London. His quirky but engaging personality made him much beloved by many close friends, who included *Thackeray, Alfred and Frederick *Tennyson, and *Carlyle. He lived for 16 years in a cottage on his family's estate at Boulge, and for the last 23 years of his life he was based in Woodbridge. In these years he spent much time sailing with Lowestoft fishermen off the Suffolk coast. His first published book (1849) was a biography of the Quaker poet Bernard Barton, whose daughter he afterwards married; the middle-aged couple were incompatible and separated after a few months. In 1851 he published *Euphranor, a Dialogue on Youth* and later he produced translations of plays by *Calderón, *Aeschylus, and *Sophocles, a collection of aphorisms, and a selection of *Crabbe's poetry. His only celebrated work is his free translation of *The Rubáiyát of *Omar Khayyám* (1859). His other translations from Persian included Attar's *Bird Parliament* and Jami's *Salaman and Absal*. He was a prolific and delightful letter-writer, whose anecdotes of his literary friends have been a gold-mine to biographers. His Collected Letters, which had previously appeared in selected versions, was published in 1980, ed. A. M. and A. B. Terhune.

FITZGERALD, F(rancis) Scott (Key) (1896–1940), American novelist and short story writer, born in Minnesota and educated at Princeton, where, as a friend and contemporary of E. *Wilson, he aimed for stardom in the social, athletic, and literary fields. His first novel, *This Side of Paradise* (1920), made him instantly famous; shortly after its publication he married the glamorous Zelda Sayre, and together they embarked on a life of high living, big spending, and party going, fortified by a view of themselves as representative figures of the 'Jazz Age'. He published stories in fashionable periodicals such as the *Saturday Evening Post, Vanity Fair*, and *The Smart Set*, in which he chronicled the mood and manners of the times; these were collected as *Flappers and Philosophers* (1920) and *Tales of the Jazz Age* (1922), the latter including his child's-eye fantasy of extravagance, 'The Diamond as Big as the Ritz'. *The Beautiful and Damned* (1922), a novel about a wealthy, doomed, and dissipated marriage, was followed by *The Great Gatsby* (1925), widely considered his finest work. This is the story of shady, mysterious financier Jay Gatsby's romantic and destructive passion for Daisy Buchanan, played against a backdrop of Long Island glamour and New York squalor; the story is narrated by the innocent outsider Nick Carraway, Gatsby's neighbour and Daisy's distant cousin, who observes from a distance as adultery, hard drinking, fast driving, and finally murder take their toll, as the age of 'miracles, art and excess' turns to ashes. More short stories followed (*All the Sad Young Men*, 1926; *Taps at Reveille*, 1935), but by this time Zelda was suffering from mental breakdown, Scott from the effects of their violent lives, and *Tender is the Night* (1934, but later in various revised versions) records, through the story of American psychiatrist Dick Diver and his schizophrenic wife Nicole, his own sense of impending disaster. This novel, with its Riviera setting and cast of predominantly idle, wealthy expatriates, was not well received in the America of the depression, and Fitzgerald's own 'crack-up' accelerated, as Zelda failed to recover: he died in Hollywood, of a heart attack, after working as a screenwriter, leaving his last novel, *The Last Tycoon*, unfinished. It appeared in 1941, edited by E. Wilson, and was followed by a posthumous collection (1945), in which he records that 'ten years this side of forty-nine, I suddenly realised that I had prematurely cracked', and analyses his own deterioration. See *The Far Side of Paradise* (1951, rev. 1965), a biography by A. Mizener.

Fitzpiers, Edred, a character in Hardy's *The Woodlanders*.

FITZRALPH, Richard (d. 1360), frequently referred to as 'Armachanus', was chancellor of Oxford (1333) and archbishop of Armagh (1347). He was greatly admired as a preacher, attacked the friars, and was arraigned before the pope at Avignon in 1357 to defend his opinions, which he did in his *Defensio Curatorum*. He was regarded as the official spokesman of the secular clergy against the friars, and he wrote a treatise against the friars' doctrine of obligatory poverty, *De Pauperie Salvatoris*, in which he discussed 'dominion' or 'lordship', taking a view on the subject similar to that later adopted by *Wyclif. See K. Walsh, *A Fourteenth-Century Scholar and Primate: Richard Fitzralph in Oxford, Avignon and Armagh* (1981).

Fitzrovia, a term coined to describe the area north of Oxford Street, London, which centred first on the Fitzroy Tavern, 'a largish pub on the corner of Charlotte Street', and which was, in the words of A. *John (*Finishing Touches*, 1964) 'the Artist's Quarter, its only rival being Chelsea'; its focus then moved, according to John Maclaren-Ross (*Memoirs of the Forties*, 1965) to the Wheatsheaf. Dylan *Thomas, W. *Empson, Tambimuttu of *Poetry London*, W. *Lewis, G. *Orwell, and many of the characters observed by A. *Powell were among its habitués.

FITZROY, Vice-Admiral Robert (1805–65), commanded the *Beagle* in the surveying expedition to Patagonia and the Straits of Magellan (1823–36), having C. *Darwin as naturalist for the last five years; like Darwin, he wrote a narrative of the voyage. He was governor of New Zealand 1843–5. He became chief of the new meteorological department of the Board of Trade in 1854, suggested the plan of the Fitzroy barometer, and instituted a system of storm warnings, the first British weather forecasts. He died by his own hand.

FITZSTEPHEN, William, author of a Latin life of *Becket (c.1180), which contains a valuable account of early London first printed in *Stow's *Survey of London* (1598). It was translated by H. E. Butler in F. M. Stenton, *Norman London: an Essay* (1934).

Five Towns, The, in the novels of A. *Bennett, Tunstall, Burslem, Hanley, Stoke-on-Trent, and Longton, now forming the federated borough of Stoke-on-Trent. These are represented in the novels by Turnhill, Bursley, Hanbridge, Knype, and Longshaw.

Fizkin, Horatio, in Dickens's *Pickwick Papers*, the Buff candidate in the Eatanswill election.

F.J., *The pleasant Fable of Ferdinando Jeronimi and Leonora de Valasco*, normally referred to, from its running headline, as *The Adventures of Master F.J.*; a novella by G. *Gascoigne, supposedly translated 'out of the Italian riding tales of *Bartello*', but probably his own invention.

It concerns the love affair between F.J., a Venetian, and the lady of the house where he is staying in Lombardy. The love affair is pursued and discussed in a large number of letters and poems; after enjoying Leonora's favours for a time, F.J. is supplanted by her secretary, and returns to Venice, 'spending there the rest of his dayes in a dissolute kind of lyfe'. The novella exists in two versions: the first, printed in *A Hundreth Sundrie Flowres* in 1573, is set in the north of England, is frankly erotic, and has every appearance of being a *roman à clef*. The second, printed in *The Posies of George Gascoigne* (1575), is more fully Italianate and has been to some extent expurgated.

FLACCUS, see HORACE.

Flagellant, The (1792), a magazine produced while at Westminster School by the young *Southey, for which he was expelled.

Flamineo, a character in Webster's *The White Devil*.

Flaming Tinman, The, a character in Borrow's *Lavengro*.

Flanders, Moll, see MOLL FLANDERS.

Flashman, a character in *Tom Brown's Schooldays* by T. *Hughes and revived in a series of humorous novels by George Macdonald Fraser.

FLATMAN, Thomas (1637–88), educated at Winchester and New College, Oxford, was much esteemed as a painter of miniatures and also wrote poetry. *Poems and Songs* (1674) contains 'A Thought of Death', 'Death, a Song', and 'The Dying Christian to his Soul', the last of which was imitated by *Pope.

FLAUBERT, Gustave (1821–80), French novelist, one of the masters of 19th-cent. fiction, was born in Rouen, the second son of a noted physician. His first published novel, *Madame Bovary* (1857), the story of the adulteries and suicide of a doctor's wife in provincial Normandy, is notable for its rigorous psychological development, and manifests the qualities that mark all of his mature work: authenticity of detail, an impersonal narrative method, a precise and harmonious style. Certain passages in *Madame Bovary* having been judged to be offensive to public morals, Flaubert, his publisher, and his printer were tried but acquitted. Ancient Carthage is re-created amply and minutely in his next novel, *Salammbô* (1862), for which he undertook detailed researches. *L'Education sentimentale* (1869), Flaubert's 'moral history of the men of my generation', charts the progress and decline of the successive amours, enthusiasms, and ambitions of Frédéric Moreau and his circle of friends, against the background of Paris in the 1840s. The unfinished and posthumously published *Bouvard et Pécuchet* (1881), relating the various projects and experiments of two retired copying clerks, was to form 'a sort of farcical critical encyclopaedia'. Each of the stories of *Trois Contes* (1877, 'Un coeur simple', 'La légende de Saint-Julien l'Hospitalier', 'Hérodias' is an accomplished example of a different narrative

mode. The fantastic visions of *La Tentation de Saint-Antoine* (1874) had exercised him intermittently over more than 25 years. Flaubert's *Correspondance*, which contains searching reflections on the art of fiction and the life of the novelist, has earned him the reputation of the exemplary artist.

Flavius, the faithful steward of *Timon of Athens in Shakespeare's play.

FLAXMAN, John (1755–1826), English neoclassical sculptor and draughtsman. Flaxman was steeped in the writings of Winckelmann, and his linear style is influenced by Greek vases and classical reliefs. He designed very many funerary sculptures, of which the most famous is the monument to the earl of Mansfield (1793–1801, London, Westminster Abbey). From 1787 to 1794 he studied in Rome, and here created a series of illustrations to the *Iliad* and the *Odyssey* (*Pope's translation, published 1793) which won him—unusually for an English artist—an immense reputation throughout Europe. His illustrations to Dante's *Divina Commedia* (1793) were commissioned by T. *Hope and praised by *Goethe (1799). Flaxman maintained a lifelong friendship with *Blake; the two artists influenced one another, and Blake engraved Flaxman's illustrations to Hesiod in 1817. He was created professor of sculpture at the Royal Academy in 1810, and his lectures were published posthumously in 1829.

Fleance, son of *Banquo in Shakespeare's *Macbeth*, who escapes (III. iii) from Macbeth's hired killers in fulfilment of the witches' prophecy that Banquo's issue will be kings.

FLECKER, James (Herman) Elroy (1884–1915), was educated at Uppingham and Trinity College, Oxford, where he was influenced by the last flowering of the *Aesthetic movement. In the course of a career in the consular service (which further emphasized his love of the East), he produced several volumes of lyrical romantic verse, some of which was included in *Georgian Poetry*: his collections include *The Bridge of Fire* (1907), *Forty-Two Poems* (1911), and his best-known collection, *The Golden Journey to Samarkand* (1913). He also published *The Grecians* (1910), a dialogue on education, and an experimental, highly individual novel, *The King of Alsander* (1914). Flecker died of tuberculosis. The work for which he is best remembered, the poetic Eastern play *Hassan*, was published posthumously in 1922, and his other play, *Don Juan*, in 1925.

FLECKNOE, Richard (d. ?1678), a lay brother, said to have been a Roman Catholic priest, a writer with an interest in experimental forms, many of whose works were published privately. His *Miscellanea* (1653) includes a defence of the stage (in his 'Discourse upon

Languages') and a lament for the theatres silenced under the Commonwealth. His *Ariadne* (1654) is probably the first English opera, though the music (which he composed himself) is lost; its preface, which discusses the use of recitative and the art of writing words for music, shows that he was familiar with current developments in Italy. His *Love's Dominion* (1654), a pastoral with songs, was performed privately on the Continent, and acted after the Restoration under the title *Love's Kingdom*. Its reputation for insipidity, and *Marvell's earlier satire ('Flecknoe, an English priest at Rome', ?1645) suggested to Dryden his attack on *Shadwell, *MacFlecknoe*.

Fledgeby, in Dickens's *Our Mutual Friend*, a cowardly villain, who conceals his money-lending business under the description 'Pubsey and Co.'

Fleet Prison, in the neighbourhood of the present Farringdon Street, London, alongside the Fleet river. It was built in the time of Richard I, and long afterwards served as a place of imprisonment for persons condemned by the Star Chamber. After the abolition of the latter in 1640, it served mainly as a debtors' prison, until demolished in 1848, and it figures as such in Dickens's novels, notably *Pickwick Papers*.

Fleet Street, now the headquarters of London journalism, takes its name from the old Fleet river, which, running south from Hampstead, along the line of the Farringdon Road, flowed into the Thames at Blackfriars, passing under the Fleet Bridge at what is now Ludgate Circus. In its upper course it appears to have been known as the Hole Bourne (Holborn), or the Turnmill Brook. Boats could ascend the Fleet as far as the Holborn Bridge as late as the 16th cent. (*Stow). *Wren in his plan for rebuilding London after the Great Fire proposed to canalize it as far as Holborn Bridge.

Fleet Street Eclogues, see DAVIDSON, J.

FLEMING, Ian Lancaster (1908–64), journalist and thriller writer, was educated at Eton and Sandhurst; he subsequently worked for Reuters and as foreign manager of Kemsley newspapers. His first novel, *Casino Royale* (1953), introduced his handsome, tough, romantic hero James Bond, who subsequently appeared in many other adventures with exotic settings, including *Live and Let Die* (1954), *Diamonds are Forever* (1956), and *On Her Majesty's Secret Service* (1963). Bond also appeared in many highly popular films, which mingle sex and violence with a wit that, for some, renders them intellectually respectable: these include *Dr No* (1962), *From Russia With Love* (1963), and *Goldfinger* (1964).

FLEMING, (Robert) Peter (1907–71),

journalist and travel writer, brother of Ian *Fleming, was educated at Eton and Christ Church, Oxford. He wrote regularly for the *Spectator* (in later years as 'Strix') and *The Times*, but is remembered largely for his travel books, which include *Brazilian Adventure* (1933), a characteristically light-hearted and debonair account of a search party in the Matto Grosso, and *News from Tartary* (1936), an account of an overland journey from Peking to Kashmir.

Fleming, (1) Rose and Agnes, characters in Dickens's *Oliver Twist*; (2) Archdeacon, in Scott's *The Heart of Midlothian*; (3) Lady Mary, in his *The Abbot*; (4) Sir Malcolm, in his *Castle Dangerous*; (5) Paul, in *Longfellow's *Hyperion*; (6) Farmer, Rhoda, and Dahlia, in Meredith's *Rhoda Fleming*.

Flemish painting. Flanders roughly corresponds to modern Belgium and Luxembourg. In the 15th cent. religious subjects and portraits were painted with minute finish and realistic detail by Jan van Eyck, Rogier van der Weyden, and other artists of the Flemish school. In the following century Patenier and *Bruegel developed landscape painting and in the 17th cent. *Rubens's religious subjects served the Counter-Reformation and his secular paintings the Court, while the genre painters, such as Brouwer and *Teniers, appealed to the middle classes.

Fleshly School of Poetry, see ROSSETTI, D. G., and BUCHANAN, R.

FLETCHER, Giles, the elder (1546–1611), educated at Eton and King's College, Cambridge, of which he became a fellow, 1568, was sent as envoy to Russia in 1588. He published *Of the Russe Commonwealth*, a pioneering account of Russian government, in 1591. His *Licia, or Poemes of Love* (1593), is notable both for being one of the first sonnet sequences to follow the publication of *Astrophel and Stella* (1591) and for having a dedication in which he sets out his belief that 'a man may write of love, and not bee in love, as well as of husbandrie, and not goe to plough.' He was the uncle of John *Fletcher and father of Giles and Phineas *Fletcher. His English works were edited by Lloyd E. Berry (1964).

FLETCHER, Giles, the younger (?1585–1623), the younger son of Giles *Fletcher the elder, was educated at Trinity College, Cambridge. He was rector of Alderton, Suffolk, and a poet of the Spenserian school whose allegorical treatment of religious themes is said to have influenced *Milton. His principal work was *Christs Victorie and Triumph in Heaven and Earth* (1610). His works and those of his brother Phineas (below) were edited by Boas in 2 vols, 1908; he is generally considered the better poet.

FLETCHER, John (1579–1625), was born at Rye in Sussex, where his father (subsequently chaplain at the execution of *Mary Queen of Scots and bishop of Bristol and of London) was then minister. John Fletcher was nephew of Giles *Fletcher the elder and cousin of Giles the younger and Phineas *Fletcher. He was educated at Corpus Christi College, Cambridge, and, his father dying (in debt and under royal displeasure) in 1596, he was left to make his own way in the world. Little is known of his early life; about 1605 he began to write plays in collaboration with Sir F. *Beaumont, and, before his death of the plague, he produced some 15 plays with Beaumont, some 16 of which he was sole author, and collaborated with *Massinger, *Rowley, *Middleton, *Jonson, *Chapman, and others in the writing of many other works. The principal plays of which Fletcher was probably sole author are: * The Faithful Shepherdess (printed not later than 1610); Wit Without Money, a comedy, printed 1639; *Valentinian, perf. 1610–14; The Loyal Subject, acted 1618; The Mad Lover, acted ?1616; * The Humorous Lieutenant, acted 1619; Women Pleased, a comedy, perf. c.1620; *The Wilde Goose Chase, perf. 1621; The Pilgrim, a comedy, perf. 1621; The Island Princess, a romantic comedy, perf. 1621; Monsieur Thomas, a comedy, perf. 1619, printed 1639; * The Woman's Prize, written 1604–17; A Wife for a Month, a romantic drama, perf. 1624; *Rule a Wife and Have a Wife, perf. 1624; * The Chances, written c.1617.

Plays certainly or probably by Beaumont and Fletcher are: Four Plays in One, four short plays (two founded on *Boccaccio, one on *Bandello, one an allegory about false and true friends) probably acted c.1608 (possibly with collaboration from N. *Field); The Scornful Lady, perf. 1610, printed 1616; *Philaster, written 1609; * The Maid's Tragedy, written 1610–11; *A King and No King, perf. 1611; The Coxcomb, a romantic comedy, perf. 1612; Cupid's Revenge, a tragedy based on material in the second book of Sidney's *Arcadia, perf. 1612, printed 1615; The Captain, a comedy, perf. 1612–13; The Honest Man's Fortune, printed 1647; *Bonduca, perf. 1613–14; The Knight of Malta, a tragi-comedy performed before March 1619, printed 1647; * Thierry King of France, printed 1621 (with Beaumont and *Massinger); Love's Cure (later rewritten by Massinger, printed 1647).

Probably by Fletcher and some other dramatists: Love's Pilgrimage and The Double Marriage, comedies, printed 1647; Sir John Van Olden *Barnavelt, perf. 1619; * The False One, perf. c.1620; The Little French Lawyer, * The Custom of the Country, and The Laws of Candy, all printed 1647; * The Spanish Curate and * The Beggar's Bush, both perf. 1622. In all the above Fletcher certainly or probably collaborated with Massinger. The romantic drama, * The Lover's Pro-

gress, perf. 1623, was later revised by Massinger. The Maid in the Mill was written by Fletcher and Rowley (licensed 1623). * The Elder Brother, printed 1637, is thought to have been written by Fletcher and revised by Massinger. The Fair Maid of the Inn was probably the result of a collaboration between Fletcher and Massinger, possibly with assistance from Jonson, *Webster, and Rowley. The Nice Valour, a comedy, printed 1647 (which contains the lyric 'Hence all you vain delights', which suggested *'Il Penseroso'), was probably by Fletcher and Middleton. * The Bloody Brother, or Rollo, Duke of Normandy (perf. c.1616) is by Fletcher, Jonson, Chapman, and Massinger. The Noble Gentleman, a comedy, acted 1626, is probably by Fletcher, possibly with Beaumont or Rowley. Fletcher also collaborated with Shakespeare in * The Two Noble Kinsmen and *Henry VIII.

The attribution of various plays in the Beaumont and Fletcher canon by use of versification and idiom tests was pioneered by F. G. Fleay, in On Metrical Tests as Applied to Dramatic Poetry (1874), and his successors in the field include E. H. C. Oliphant (The Plays of Beaumont and Fletcher, 1927); C. Hoy (The Shares of Fletcher and his Collaborators in the Beaumont and Fletcher Canon, in Studies in Bibliography, 1956–7, 1958–62); and B. Hensman, The Shares of Fletcher, Field, and Massinger in Twelve Plays of the Beaumont and Fletcher Canon (1974). An edition of the works under the general editorship of F. *Bowers is in preparation, five volumes having appeared, 1966–82. Meanwhile the standard edition remains that of A. Glover and A. R. Waller (10 vols, 1905–12), and various works have been edited separately (see under individual entries).

FLETCHER, Phineas (1582–1650), the elder son of Giles *Fletcher the elder, was educated at King's College, Cambridge, and was rector of Higay, Norfolk. Like his brother Giles (above), he was a poet of the Spenserian school. His chief work, The Purple Island (1633), is an allegory of the human body and mind; The Locusts of Apollyonists (1627) is a violently anti-Catholic piece with a conclave in hell thought by some to have influenced *Milton. Britain's Ida (1628), attributed to *Spenser, appears to be his. The works of Giles and Phineas were edited in 2 vols, 1908, by Boas.

Flintwinch, a character in Dickens's *Little Dorrit. His wife was known as Affery.

Flippanta, a character in Vanbrugh's * The Confederacy.

Flite, Miss, a character in Dickens's *Bleak House.

Flodden, or **Floddon Field,** the battle of Flodden, in Northumberland, fought on 9 Sept. 1513, when the earl of Surrey on behalf of

Henry VIII (then in France) defeated James IV of Scotland, the latter being killed on the field. It was made the subject of poems, of rejoicing or lament, on both sides of the border. *Skelton's 'Agaynst the Scottes' is a rude song of exultation of the English victory, and several English ballads appeared. On the Scottish side there is the beautiful lament 'The Flowers o' the Forest', of which the most popular version is by J. *Elliot. The battle is described in the 6th canto of Scott's *Marmion: A Tale of Flodden Field.

Florac, comte de, his wife, son, and daughter-in-law, characters in Thackeray's *The Newcomes*. The comte also appears as a young French officer in *The Virginians.*

FLORENCE OF WORCESTER (d. 1118), a monk of Worcester, traditionally regarded as the author of the *Chronicon ex Chronicis* (based on the work of Marianus, an Irish monk, as well as on a lost version of the *Anglo-Saxon Chronicle* up to 1130) from its beginning to 1117, when it was continued by other hands to its end in 1295. A modern view regards the *Chronicon* as the work of John of Worcester, the claims of the name of Florence being on the material of the Chronicle up to 1117, not on its writing. For all matters relating to the medieval chronicles, see A. Gransden, *Historical Writing in England c.550–c.1307* (1974).

Florent, see GOWER, J., and CANTERBURY TALES, 6.

Flores and Blancheflour, see FLORIS AND BLANCHEFLOUR.

Florestan (also known as Albert and Otranto), in *Endymion* by B. Disraeli.

Flore et Zephyr, a series of ballet caricatures drawn by *Thackeray, published 1836.

Florimell, in Spenser's *Faerie Queene*, Bks III and IV, the type of chastity and virtue in woman. She is in love with the knight Marinell, who 'sets nought' by her. She takes refuge from her pursuers in the sea and is imprisoned by Proteus. Finally the heart of Marinell is touched by her complaint, and Neptune orders Proteus to release her.

FLORIO, John (c.1553–1625), son of an Italian Protestant refugee, was born in London and educated at Magdalen College, Oxford. After a spell as tutor to the earl of Southampton he was reader in Italian to Anne of Denmark, wife of James I (1603), and groom of the privy chamber from 1604. His interesting collections of Italian–English dialogues, *Firste* and *Second Frutes*, were followed in 1598 by an Italian dictionary entitled *A Worlde of Wordes*; it was revised and augmented as *Queen Anna's New World of Words* (1611). His most important work was his translation from *Montaigne:

Essayes, Or Morall, Politike and Millitarie Discourses (1603, 1613). Not only did Florio make Montaigne's work available in English, but he displayed great resourcefulness and ingenuity in the process of translation. Florio's friends included *Daniel and *Jonson, and some have thought that Shakespeare ridiculed him in *Love's Labour's Lost.* Certainly Shakespeare drew on Florio's version of Montaigne, in *The Tempest* and elsewhere. Florio has also been suggested as the earliest translator of the *Decameron.* There is a book on him by F. A. *Yates (1934).

Floris and Blancheflour, a Middle English metrical romance in 1,083 lines from the first half of the 13th cent., based on a 12th-cent. French original and surviving in four later manuscripts, all of which lack the opening lines.

Floris and Blancheflour are brought up together: he is the son of a Saracen king and she the daughter of a Christian lady who has been captured and brought to the king's court. They fall in love and Blancheflour is banished. Floris sets off to find her, equipped with a precious cup and a magic ring which prove instrumental in his finding her and their ultimate marriage by consent of the Emir. The story, which has analogues in the *Arabian Nights* and elsewhere, is the subject of *Boccaccio's *Filocolo*. The English romance is one of the most popular and 'romantic' of its genre. See editions by A. B. Taylor (1927) and in D. B. Sands, *Middle English Verse Romances* (1966), pp. 279–309.

Florisando, see AMADIS OF GAUL.

Florizel, in Shakespeare's *The Winter's Tale*, the prince of Bohemia who falls in love with the rustic *Perdita. 'Florizel' was the name adopted by George IV, when prince of Wales, in his correspondence with Mary Robinson, the actress, with whose performance as Perdita he had been captivated.

Flosky, Mr, a character in Peacock's *Nightmare Abbey*, who illustrates the transcendentalism of *Coleridge.

Floure and the Leaf, The, a 15th-cent. allegory in 595 lines of rhyme-royal, formerly attributed to *Chaucer and included by Skeat in *Chaucerian and Other Pieces*, appended as vol. 7 to his edition of Chaucer. The votives of the flower and the leaf were the two parties in the mannered, courtly debates on love in the French poetry of writers such as *Deschamps. In the English poem, the poet wandering in a grove sees the white company of knights and ladies of the leaf (Diana, goddess of chastity) and the green company of the flower (Flora), 'folk that loved idleness' and had delight 'of no businesse but for to hunt and hauke and pley in medes'. It has the rather limited charm of its tradition, and it was modernized by *Dryden in his *Fables*

Ancient and Modern. There is an edition by D. A. Pearsall (1962).

FLOWER, Sir Newman Walter (1879–1964), publisher and author, who started work for Cassell's publishing company in 1906 and became the proprietor of the business in 1927. He published biographies of *Handel (1923), *Sullivan (1927), and *Schubert (1928), and edited the journals of Arnold *Bennett.

'Flowers of the Forest, The', see ELLIOT, J., and COCKBURN, A.

FLUDD, Robert (1574–1637), educated at St John's College, Oxford, and on the Continent, became a fellow of the Royal College of Physicians in 1609, and had a successful practice. He entered the debate on the authenticity of the *Rosicrucian texts with his defence, *Apologia*, in 1616, and was deeply interested in Hermeticism and Neoplatonism, which he held to be of greater authority than *Aristotle and *Galen. His views on the universe as macrocosm–microcosm attracted much controversy, but despite his own mystical views on the circulation of the blood, he was the first to defend W. *Harvey's *De Motu Cordis.* The standard biography is by J. B. Craven, 1902; see also *The English Paracelsians* (1965) by A. G. Debus and *The Rosicrucian Enlightenment* (1972) by F. *Yates.

Fluellen, a pedantic but courageous Welsh captain in Shakespeare's *Henry V.*

Flute, in Shakespeare's *A Midsummer Night's Dream,* a bellows-mender, who takes the part of Thisbe in the play of 'Pyramus and Thisbe'.

Flyting, derived from the Old English word *flitan,* to quarrel or dispute, was a verse contest in obloquy, practised in particular by the Scottish poets of the early 16th cent. The most famous example is the *Flyting of Dunbar and Kennedy.*

FO, Dario (1926–), leftist Italian playwright and actor. His best known play is *Morte accidentale di un anarchico* (*Accidental death of an Anarchist,* 1970).

Foedera, Conventiones et Cujuscunque generis Acta Publica, a collection of public records in 20 vols, by *Rymer and Robert Sanderson, published 1704–35. The documents (treaties, letters, etc. between kings of England and foreign states and sovereigns) extend down to 1654, and provide for the first time a scientific basis for the writing of history.

FOGAZZARO, Antonio (1842–1911), Italian novelist and essayist. His humour and powers of characterization are at their best in *Piccolo mondo antico* (*The Little World of the Past,* 1895), set north of Lake Lugano during the last ten years of Austrian rule, and reflecting the author's Catholic preoccupations. Owing to his unorthodoxy two of his novels, *Il santo* (*The Saint,* 1905) and *Leila* (1910), were placed on the *Index Expurgatorius.

Fogg, Phileas, the hero of J. *Verne's *Around the World in Eighty Days.*

Foible, in Congreve's *The Way of the World,* Lady Wishfort's woman.

Foker, Harry, a character in Thackeray's *Pendennis.*

FOLENGO, Teophilo (1491–1544), an Italian monk, who under the pseudonym 'Merlin Coccai' wrote a long burlesque-heroic poem, *Opus Macaronicum,* in *macaronic verse. Its hero is Baldus, who has for followers the giant Fracassus and the cunning Cingar. Rabelais's *Panurge is partly modelled on the latter.

Folios and Quartos, Shakespearian. *Shakespeare's earliest published plays are referred to as folios or quartos according to the folding of the printed sheets and therefore the size of the book: folios being large, tall volumes and the quartos smaller and squarer.

Of about 1,200 copies of the First Folio printed between Feb. 1622 and Nov. 1623 and sold, probably for £1 each, by the *Jaggards, some 230 survive, 80 or so in the Folger Shakespeare Library and 5, the next largest collection, in the British Library. A second Folio was issued in 1632, containing 'An Epitaph on . . . Shakespeare' by *Milton, which was his first published poem. A third Folio was issued in 1663, whose second impression of 1664 contained *Pericles* and six apocryphal plays; the fourth and last Folio was published in 1685. Except for the text of *Pericles* none of the Folios later than the first has any textual integrity.

Thirty-six plays, eighteen printed for the first time, were arranged by *Heming and Condell into sections of comedies, histories, and tragedies for F1. It was dedicated to William Herbert, earl of Pembroke, and Philip Herbert, earl of Montgomery, and contains the *Droeshout portrait and a list of 'the Principall Actors in all these Playes', together with commendatory verses by contemporaries including *Jonson.

During his lifetime 18 of Shakespeare's plays were published in quartos: *Othello* appeared in 1622. Following A. W. *Pollard's analysis, it is now established that over half of those quartos are 'bad' ones. Their texts are extremely corrupt as a result of their reconstruction from memory by a member, or members, of their cast. Thus, Q1 of *The Merry Wives of Windsor* (1604) is probably based on the recollections of the actor who played the part of the Host. Some 'bad' quartos, for example *The First Part of the Contention* (1594) and *The True Tragedy of Richard Duke of York* (1595), were once thought of as source plays (for 2 and 3 *Henry VI*); similarly the quarto *The Taming of a Shrew* (1594) is probably 'bad' and the Folio text, *The Taming of the Shrew*, is 'good'. In two cases, *Romeo and Juliet* (1597) and *Hamlet* (1603), 'good' second quartos were soon issued (in 1599 and 1604–5 respectively) to correct the 'bad' first quartos.

Textual criticism and bibliography have largely been concerned with establishing relationships between the 'good' quartos (and in some cases the 'bad' ones as well) and their versions in the Folio, to determine on which text an editor is to base his edition. In trying to establish this relationship scholars have mainly sought to determine the nature of the copy of which the printers made use. The chief types of copy which have been distinguished are: (1) foul papers, that is an original authorial draft, as in Q1 of *A Midsummer Night's Dream* (1600); (2) a fair scribal copy, as in F's text of *The Tempest*; (3) a prompt copy from the theatre, as in F's text of *As You Like It*; (4) a memorial text, as discussed above; and (5) a reconstructed text, that is one based on an early quarto but where some kind of manuscript copy has also been used as in the case of F's *Richard III*. There is still much disagreement about the nature of these categories and into which ones the plays in their various quarto and Folio versions belong.

The fullest accounts of F1 are W. W. *Greg's *The Shakespeare First Folio* (1955) and C. *Hinman's *The Printing and Proof-reading of the First Folio of Shakespeare* (1963); see also his Norton Facsimile of F (1968). Sixteen facsimiles of quartos were issued in the Oxford Shakespeare Quarto Facsimiles series, ed. W. W. Greg and C. Hinman (1939–75).

Folklore, the traditional beliefs, legends, and customs current among the common people; and the study of them. The term was first introduced by J. W. *Thoms in the *Athenaeum* (1846).

Folk-song, a song, origin usually unknown, that is handed down orally from generation to generation, evolving as it does so at the whim of individual performers, and often existing in different forms in different parts of the country. In England the first person to make any systematic attempt at recording the material in this field was *Percy in the middle of the 18th cent.; he was concerned only with the poetry, but interest in the music followed naturally enough. The end of the 19th and the beginning of the 20th cents saw an immense increase of activity in the collection, transcription, and publication of folk-songs, before the rapidly increasing industrialization and urbanization of the whole country effectively wiped them out for ever. See also SHARP, C.; GRAINGER, P.; HOLST; VAUGHAN WILLIAMS.

Folliott, The Revd Doctor, a character in Peacock's *Crotchet Castle*.

Fomors, the sea-giants of Gaelic mythology. They are represented as more ancient than the gods (the *Tuatha Dé Danann), and as having been ousted by them and destroyed at the battle of Moytura (C. Squire, *Mythology of the British Islands*). See also BALOR.

Fondlewife, one of the characters in Congreve's *The Old Bachelor*.

FONTANE, Theodor (1819–98), German novelist who lived in England during the years 1855–9, when he wrote reports for German newspapers on British political affairs. He is best known for the novels *Frau Jenny Treibel* (1892), an ironic criticism of middle-class hypocrisy and small-mindedness, and *Effi Briest* (1895), the story of a spoilt but charming girl who marries an older man on the advice of her parents and because she is infatuated with the idea of marriage and social status. Effi's adultery, discovered by her stiff husband several years later, is punished by his banishing her and indoctrinating their child against her. Fontane has been compared to *Flaubert and *Tolstoy in his human handling of the theme of adultery.

FONTENELLE, Bernard le Bovier (1667–1757), French man of letters. The nephew of *Corneille, he was a man of wide curiosity and learning. His varied output is notable for his *Dialogues des morts* (1683), a deceptively light-hearted attack on received ideas, and for his *Entretiens sur la pluralité des mondes* (1686), a graceful introduction to contemporary astronomical ideas and speculations, which represented the first true case of scientific popularization. His demystifying influence strongly marked the early phase of the *Enlightenment.

Fonthill Abbey, see BECKFORD, W.

Fool of Quality, The, a novel in 5 vols by H. *Brooke, published in Dublin 1765–70 and in London 1766–70.

In this unusual and impassioned work, which was highly influential in its day, Harry Clinton, the Fool of Quality, born in the later 17th cent., is the second son of the earl of Moreland; the narrative follows his education, growth, and manhood. The most important adult in his world is not his decadent father but his merchant uncle, Mr Clinton (sometimes Fenton), whose enlightened views on Harry's education (much influenced by *Rousseau's *Émile* and *Locke's *On Education*) guide the boy's growth into a wise and generous adult. Clinton is more than a merchant, for he carries a hint of kingly or even divine power. Harry is protected from calamity largely by his innocence, but Clinton possesses an omnipotence which enables him to rescue the unfortunate, such as Hammel Clement and his family, from terrible misfortune and destitution; and a philosophy which reconciles human wretchedness with divine providence. The various episodes, which are interrupted by much literary and philosophical digression (as well as by curious discussions between the author and a 'friend' on passages in the book itself) fluctuate between extremes of the euphoric and the despairing, and the tone of the narration is held at a high level of tearful, ecstatic, or nostalgic sensibility.

The book appealed greatly to *Wesley and to *Kingsley (who found it 'more pure, sacred and eternal than anything since the *Faerie Queene*', and who drew on it for his own novel *Yeast*); both produced new editions of it. (See also SENTIMENTAL NOVEL and BILDUNGSROMAN.)

FOOTE, Samuel (1720–77), actor and dramatist, spent three years at Oxford, where he dissipated a fortune. He then turned to the stage, and as an actor was particularly successful in comic mimicry; acting in his own plays, he caricatured his fellow actors and other well-known persons, often savagely. He wrote a number of dramatic sketches, depending for their success on topical allusions, of which *Taste* (1752) was the first. *The Minor* (1760), a satire directed against the Methodists in which Foote mimicked *Whitefield as 'Dr Squintum', was his most powerful work. Other works include *The Liar* (1762), *The Patron* (1764, depicting *Dodington), and *The Mayor of Garret* (1764). In *The Maid of Bath* (1771) Foote pilloried Squire Long, the unscrupulous sexagenarian lover of Miss Elizabeth Linley, who was to marry *Sheridan. *The Nabob* (1772) was aimed at the directors of the East India Company and *Piety in Patterns* (1773) ridiculed *sentimental comedy and Richardson's *Pamela. Foote had a leg amputated in 1766, after some ducal horseplay, but this did not quell his spirit; he received as compensation a patent for a theatre and built the new Haymarket in 1767. He was known to his contemporaries as 'the English Aristophanes'. His works were collected in 4 vols, 1770–86.

Fopling Flutter, Sir, a character in Etherege's *The Man of Mode.

Foppington, Lord, a character in Vanbrugh's comedy *The Relapse and Sheridan's *A Trip to Scarborough; also in C. Cibber's *The Careless Husband.

FORD, Ford Madox (formerly Ford Hermann Hueffer) (1873–1939), was the son of Dr Francis Hueffer, a music critic of *The Times, and grandson of Ford Madox Brown; much of his childhood was spent in *Pre-Raphaelite circles, an inheritance which deeply affected him and towards which he expressed ambiguous feelings in both critical and fictional works. His first published works were fairy-stories (*The Brown Owl*, 1892, etc.). In 1894 he eloped with and married Elsie Martindale, an act which was pre-lude to a turbulent emotional life. In 1898 he met *Conrad and they collaborated in various works including the novels *The Inheritors* (1901) and *Romance* (1903); for some years they worked in happy intimacy, united by their faith in 'the novel as a work of Art', although from 1901 their relationship deteriorated: Ford's own published recollections of it are revealing but not reliable. During a diverse and productive literary career Ford published over 80 books, both fiction and non-fiction, and developed his own theory of 'Impressionism' in the novel. His *Fifth Queen* trilogy (1907, 1907, 1908), described by Conrad as 'a noble conception'—the swan song of Historical Romance' describes in ornate and colourful prose, the fate of Catherine Howard, wife of *Henry VIII, portrayed as an earnest, innocent Catholic idealist. In 1908 Ford embarked on two significant enterprises, an affair with the glamorous and emancipated novelist Violet *Hunt, which was to involve him in scandal and in complex, unsuccessful divorce proceedings; and the founding of the *English Review*, which he edited for 15 months, with much éclat but also with much financial and personal stress.

In 1915 Ford published what he himself regarded as his finest achievement, his 'one novel', *The Good Soldier, and in the same year enlisted in the army: he was invalided home from France in 1917 and changed his name from Hueffer to Ford in 1919. The war inspired a volume of poems (1918), sketches, and propaganda pieces written for his friend *Masterman; also, more significantly, his other major work of fiction, now known as *Parade's End* (or sometimes, after its hero, as the 'Tietjens' tetralogy), which was published in four parts between 1924 and 1928. Ford began writing it in Paris, whither he moved in 1922 and where he founded in 1924 the *Transatlantic Review*, in which he published work by *Joyce, *Pound, G. *Stein, E. E. *Cummings, and others. During his last years, which were spent in France and America, he published several volumes of autobiography and reminiscence (including *Return to Yesterday*, 1931, and *It was the nightingale*, 1933) and a final characteristically personal and ambitious volume of criticism, *The March of Literature* (1938). He died in Deauville. As a writer he has been more studied than read, a neglect due partly, perhaps, to the diversity of his output, and partly to his own unsettled emotional and eccentric personality, which has somehow obscured the outlines of his achievements; as an editor he has long been regarded as a highly influential figure whose devotion to literature and ready appreciation of originality and quality in others (see MODERNISM) did much to shape the course of 20th-cent. writing. See *The Saddest Story* (1971), a biography by A. Mizener.

FORD, John (1586–after 1639), was born in

Devonshire, and admitted to the Middle Temple in 1602. He probably spent many years there, since he is called 'Master John Ford, of the Middle Temple' as late as 1638. His earliest work was non-dramatic (1606–20), but he wrote all or a substantial part of 18 plays, of which seven have been lost. Between 1621 and 1625 he collaborated with *Dekker and others in at least five plays including *The Witch of Edmonton. After 1625 Ford probably worked alone. His chief plays are *The Lover's Melancholy (1629), *Love's Sacrifice (1633), *'Tis Pity She's a Whore (1633), *The Broken Heart (1633), *Perkin Warbeck (1634), The Lady's Trial (1639). Ford's plays are predominantly concerned with human dignity, courage, and endurance in suffering. He explores melancholy, torture, incest, delusion, but always seriously and objectively, through 'the distinct personal rhythm in blank verse which could be no one's but his alone' (T. S. *Eliot). He is described in William Heminges's 'Elegy on Randolph's Finger':

> Deep in a dump Jack Ford alone was got
> With folded arms and melancholy hat.

The standard edition is still *The Works of John Ford*, ed. Gifford, rev. Dyce (1869), but there are modern editions of *'Tis Pity She's a Whore* (ed. Bawcutt, 1966, Morris, 1968, Roper 1975), *The Broken Heart* (ed. Morris, 1965), *Perkin Warbeck* (ed. Anderson, 1965).

FORD, Richard (1796–1858), educated at Winchester and Trinity College, Oxford. He contributed to various periodicals; in articles published in the *Quarterly Review* and *Penny Magazine* he was largely responsible for introducing English readers to Velázquez. He is remembered as author of the remarkable *A Handbook for Travellers in Spain* (1845) which owes its survival to his unrivalled knowledge of the Spain of his day, acquired through travels, often on horseback, between 1830 and 1834, and to its individual style, rich with anecdote and local idiom, with frequent allusions to the Peninsular War. His *Gatherings in Spain* (1846) was also popular. Ford was a friend of *Borrow, encouraged him with *The Bible in Spain and Zincali, and recommended Murray to publish these works. His Letters edited by Lord Ernle appeared in 1905.

Ford, and Mrs Ford, characters in Shakespeare's *The Merry Wives of Windsor*.

Foresight, the foolish old astrologer in Congreve's *Love for Love*.

Forest, The, a collection of miscellaneous short poems, odes, epistles, and songs, by *Jonson, printed in the folio of 1616, including 'To Penshurst' and the songs 'Drink to me only with thine eyes' and, from *Volpone, 'Come, my Celia, let us prove'. The title was suggested by

Latin *silva*, which can mean both 'collection' and 'wood'.

FORESTER, C(ecil) S(cott) (Cecil Lewis Troughton Smith) (1899–1966), is principally remembered for his seafaring novels set during the Napoleonic wars, featuring Horatio Hornblower, introduced in 1937 in *The Happy Return*, and rising by degrees over subsequent volumes to the rank of admiral. Forester gives an account of his own creation in *The Hornblower Companion* (1964). His other works include *Brown on Resolution* (1929) and *The African Queen* (1935).

Forester, Sylvan, a character in Peacock's *Melincourt*, partly based on Peacock's friend *Shelley.

Forget-me-not, see ACKERMANN, R.

FORMAN, Simon (1552–1611), physician and astrologer, who in his *Booke of Plaies* (preserved in a manuscript in the Bodleian Library, Oxford) records and comments on visits to performances of Shakespeare's *Macbeth and *The Winter's Tale at the Globe theatre in 1611 and to an unspecified *Cymbeline. See also ROWSE, A. L.

Fors Clavigera; Letters to the Workmen and Labourers of Great Britain, by *Ruskin, was issued monthly from Jan. 1871 to March 1878, then at irregular intervals: two numbers appeared in 1880, four in 1883, the last three in 1884.

Fors Clavigera was a continual challenge, deliberate and serious, to the supporters of and apologists for a capitalist economy. The obscurity of the title suggests how little he wished to ingratiate himself with the working classes; he analyses the letters of 'clerks, manufacturers and other' in the 'Notes and Correspondence' section as mercilessly as the writings and speeches of his more famous enemies; only *Whistler sued for libel. Ruskin's tactics were demonstrative rather than discursive. He delivers lessons in 'the principles and plans of political economy' by setting events from contemporary history and his own immediate experience against the nobler human possibilities expressed in literature and art. *Fors Clavigera* became the mouthpiece of Ruskin's Guild of St George.

FORSTER, E(dward) M(organ) (1879–1970), was the only child of Edward Morgan Forster, architect, who died in 1880, and of Alice 'Lily' Whichelo (1855–1945). His boyhood was dominated by women, among them his influential great-aunt and benefactress Marianne Thornton, whose father had been a leading member of the *'Clapham Sect'; on her death in 1887 she left him £8,000 in trust. His happiest childhood years (1883–93) were spent at Rooksnest, Stevenage, a house he evokes in *Howards End*. In 1893 he and his mother moved to Tonbridge, and Forster attended Tonbridge School, where he was deeply unhappy and developed a lasting dislike of public-school values. In 1897 he went to King's College, Cambridge, where he found congenial friends; the atmosphere of free intellectual discussion, and a stress on the importance of personal relationships inspired partly by G. E. *Moore was to have a profound influence on his work. In 1901 he was elected to the *Apostles and largely through them was later drawn into closer contact with *Bloomsbury. A year of travel in Italy with his mother and a cruise to Greece followed, providing material for his early novels, which satirize the attitudes of English tourists abroad, Baedeker in hand, clinging to English *pensioni*, and suspicious of anything foreign. On his return from Greece he began to write for the new *Independent Review*, launched in 1903 by a group of Cambridge friends, led by G. M. *Trevelyan; in 1904 it published his first short story, 'The Story of a Panic'. In 1905 he completed *Where Angels Fear to Tread*, which was published the same year, and spent some months in Germany as tutor to the children of the Countess *von Arnim. In 1906, now established with his mother in Weybridge, he became tutor to Syed Ross Masood, a striking and colourful Indian Muslim patriot, for whom Forster developed an intense affection. *The Longest Journey* appeared in 1907, *A Room with a View* in 1908, and *Howards End*, which established Forster as a writer of importance, in 1910. In 1911 he published a collection of short stories, mostly pastoral and whimsical in tone and subject matter, *The Celestial Omnibus*. In 1912–13 he visited India for some months, meeting Masood in Aligarh and travelling with him. In 1913 another significant visit to the home of E. *Carpenter near Chesterfield resulted in his writing *Maurice*, a novel with a homosexual theme which he circulated privately; it was published posthumously in 1971. It did not as he had hoped open a new vein of creativity, and the outbreak of war further impeded his career. He worked for a while at the National Gallery, then went to Alexandria in 1915 for the Red Cross; his *Alexandria: A History and a Guide* was published somewhat abortively in 1922 (almost the entire stock was burned) and reprinted in revised form in 1938. In Alexandria he met *Cavafy, whose works, on his return to England in 1919, he helped to introduce; an essay on Cavafy appears in *Pharos and Pharillon* (1923). In 1921–2 he revisited India, working as personal secretary for the maharajah of the native state of Dewas Senior for several months. The completion of *A Passage to India* (1922–4) which he had begun before the war, was overshadowed by the death of his closest Egyptian friend Mohammed, but when the novel appeared in June 1924 it was highly acclaimed. Forster's fears that this would be his last novel proved

correct, and the remainder of his life was devoted to a wide range of literary activities; over many years he took a firm stand against censorship, involving himself in the work of PEN and the NCCL, of which he became the first president, campaigning in 1928 against the suppression of *The Well of Loneliness*, and appearing in 1960 as witness for the defence in the trial of the publishers of *Lady Chatterley's Lover*. In 1927 he delivered the Clark lectures at Cambridge, printed the same year as *Aspects of the Novel*; his tone in these was in his own words 'informal, indeed talkative', and they contain the celebrated comment, 'Yes—oh dear yes—the novel tells a story.' *Leavis, representing the new school of Cambridge criticism, found the lectures 'intellectually null', but they were a popular success, and King's offered him a 3-year fellowship, and, in 1946, an honorary fellowship and a permanent home. In 1928 *The Eternal Moment*, a volume of pre-1914 short stories, whimsical and dealing with the supernatural, appeared. He wrote two biographies, *Goldsworthy Lowes Dickinson* (1934) and *Marianne Thornton* (1956). *Abinger Harvest*, essays named after the village in Surrey in which Forster inherited a house in 1924, appeared in 1936, *Two Cheers for Democracy* in 1951, *The Hill of Devi*, a portrait of India through letters and commentary, in 1953. Between 1949 and 1951 he worked with Eric Crozier on the libretto for *Britten's opera *Billy Budd*. He spent his last years in Kings College, and was awarded the OM in 1969. *Maurice* was followed by another posthumous publication, *The Life to Come* (1972), a collection of short stories, many with homosexual themes, including the tragic story 'The Other Boat' written 1957–8. See biography by P. N. Furbank (2 vols, 1977–8); *Selected Letters*, ed. M. Lago and P. N. Furbank, 1983, 1985.

FORSTER, John (1812–76), educated at Newcastle Grammar School, University College London, and the Inner Temple, was called to the bar in 1843. His career in journalism began as editor of the short-lived *Reflector* owned by E. *Moxon and he became drama critic for *True Sun* in 1832, eventually leading to editorship of *Foreign Quarterly Review*, 1842–3, *Daily News*, 1846, and *Examiner*, 1847–55. He was engaged for a short time in 1835 to Letitia *Landon, but married Eliza Colburn, the wealthy widow of the publisher Henry Colburn, in 1856. He was the literary associate and close friend of Leigh *Hunt, C. *Lamb, W. S. *Landor, *Bulwer-Lytton, and *Dickens: from 1837 on he read in MS or proof everything Dickens wrote. His earliest biographical work, *Lives of Eminent British Statesmen* (1836–9) in Lardner's *Cyclopedia*, was followed by various political lives partly reprinted as *Historical and Biographical Essays* (1858). His popular literary biographies include *Life and Adventures of Oliver Goldsmith* (1848; rev. 2 vols, 1854), *Landor* (2 vols, 1869), *Dickens* (3 vols, 1872–4), and the first volume of a scholarly life of *Swift (1875). He is recognized as the first professional biographer of 19th-cent. England. His business acumen plus activities as a man of letters made his assistance valued by many. Landor, Dickens, and *Carlyle appointed him their literary executor.

Forsyte Saga, The, a sequence by J. *Galsworthy, published 1922.

The three novels containing the story, *The Man of Property* (1906), *In Chancery* (1920), and *To Let* (1921, with two interludes, 'Indian Summer of a Forsyte', 1918, and *Awakening*, 1920), appeared together in 1922 as *The Forsyte Saga*, tracing the fortunes of three generations of the Forsyte family. The Forsyte sequence *A Modern Comedy* (1929) is often (but incorrectly) included under the title of the *Saga*. In his Preface Galsworthy describes his use of the word 'saga' as ironic, yet at the same time indicates that he is exposing a primal tribal and acquisitive urge.

Soames Forsyte, a successful solicitor, the son of 'old Jolyon', lives in London surrounded by his prosperous old uncles and their families. He marries the penniless Irene and builds a country house for her, Robin Hill; when she falls in love with its architect, Bosinney, Soames asserts his rights over his property and rapes her. Bosinney is killed in a street accident and Irene returns to Soames. *In Chancery* describes the growing love of young Jolyon, Soames's cousin, for Irene; Irene's divorce from Soames and her happy marriage with Jolyon; and the birth of their son Jon. Meanwhile Soames marries Annette Lamotte and they have a daughter, Fleur. In *To Let* Fleur and Jon fall in love; Jon's father feels compelled to reveal the past of Irene and Soames, and the agonized Jon, in spite of Fleur's Forsyte determination, rejects her. She marries Michael Mont, the heir to a barony, and when young Jolyon dies Irene leaves to join Jon in America. The desolate Soames learns that his wife is having an affair with a Frenchman, and discovers that Irene's house, Robin Hill, is empty and to let. *The Forsyte Saga* was successfully serialized for television in 1967.

FORTESCUE, Sir John (?1394–?1476), chief justice of the king's bench under Henry VI, and the earliest English constitutional lawyer. He was a Lancastrian during the Wars of the Roses but, having been captured at Tewkesbury in 1471, was pardoned and made a member of the council on recognizing Edward IV (1471). His principal works were a Latin treatise, *De Natura Legis Naturae* (1461–3), distinguishing absolute from constitutional monarchy; an English treatise on the same subject (*Monarchia* or *The Difference between an Absolute and a Limited Monarchy*); a Latin treatise, *De Laudibus Legum*

Angliae (1471); and an English work, *On the Governance of England*. His recantation of his Lancastrian views is contained in *A Declaration upon Certain Wrytinges* (1471–3). See *Works* ed. Lord Clermont (2 vols, 1869), containing a short biography.

Fortinbras, prince of Norway in Shakespeare's *Hamlet*, whose name, 'strong-in-arm', suits his military temperament.

FORTINI, Franco, pseudonym of Franco Lattes (1917–), Italian poet and modernist critic. His poems have been translated by M. *Hamburger; the best are in *Foglio di via* (*Expulsion Order*, 1946), *Poesia ed errore* (*Poetry and Error*, 1959), *Una volta per sempre* (*Once and for All*, 1963), and *Questo muro* (*This Wall*, 1973). His essays and his left-wing critique of Communism, and especially of *socialist realism, have posed the problem of poetry and political commitment.

Fortnightly Review, The (1865–1934), an influential and respected literary periodical, which retained its high standard throughout its existence. G. H. *Lewes, the first editor, required that all articles be signed, thus breaking a long tradition of anonymity in reviews. The contents were miscellaneous, but the *Review* is largely remembered for its literary value. Almost all numbers ran a serialized novel; the first contained a chapter of Trollope's *The Belton Estate* and a part of *Bagehot's *The English Constitution*. Positivist and anti-orthodox, Lewes and his successor John *Morley published work by *Thackeray, G. *Eliot, M. *Arnold, T. H. *Huxley, *Meredith, D. G. *Rossetti, L. *Stephen, *Pater, and *Hardy, among others. In this century work published included that of H. *James, *Gissing, *Kipling, H. G. *Wells, *Joyce, and *Pound. In 1934 it changed its name to *The Fortnightly*, under which title it survived until 1954. It was then incorporated in the *Contemporary Review*.

Fortunate Mistress, The, see ROXANA.

Fortunatus's purse, the subject of a European 15th-cent. romance, translated into many languages and dramatized by *Dekker. For the story see OLD FORTUNATUS.

Fortunes of Nigel, The, a novel by Sir W. *Scott, published 1822.

The young Nigel Olifaunt, Lord Glenvarloch, threatened with the loss of his ancestral estate if he is unable promptly to redeem a heavy mortgage, comes to London to endeavour to recover from James I a sum of 40,000 marks lent to him at a crisis in his fortunes by Nigel's father. The king is induced to sign an order on the Scottish treasury for the amount in favour of Nigel. But the estate is coveted by Prince Charles and the duke of Buckingham, and Nigel finds great difficulties opposed to his recovery of the money. Lord Dalgarno, the favourite of Charles and Buckingham, a dissembling villain, lures Nigel into evil ways, keeps him from the court, and spreads false rumours about him. Nigel, discovering his treachery, challenges him in St James's Park and strikes him, an offence for which he is liable to lose his right hand. He takes sanctuary in Alsatia, the strange and lawless society of which is vividly described. He is subsequently imprisoned in the Tower. Meanwhile Margaret Ramsey, pretty, petulant daughter of an old clockmaker in the City, has fallen deeply in love with Nigel. She takes steps to rescue him, and even seeks, disguised as a page, an interview with James himself, to advance Nigel's cause and at the same time to secure reparation for her patroness, Lady Hermione, who has been grievously wronged by her husband Lord Dalgarno. She is successful in her endeavours. Nigel is released and, touched by the devotion of Margaret, marries her. He recovers his estate, and Lord Dalgarno is killed by robbers as he proceeds to Scotland in a last attempt to seize the property.

The novel contains a number of interesting characters, including the pedantic freakish James I; Richard Moniplies, Nigel's conceited servant; Dame Ursula Suddlechop, milliner and secret agent; the miser Trapbois and his austere daughter; the rattling Templar Lowestoffe; and the embittered courtier Sir Mungo Malagrowther.

For Whom the Bell Tolls, a novel by E. *Hemingway.

Foscari, The Two, see TWO FOSCARI, THE.

Fosco, Count, a character in Wilkie Collins's *The Woman in White.

FOSCOLO, Ugo (1778–1827), Italian poet, tragedian, and critic. He was the first modern Italian poet of exile, and the writer of his generation who was most sensitive to the crisis of his age. In 1797 he wrote an ode to Bonaparte as Liberator, but when later that year Napoleon's Treaty of Campoformio handed over Venetian independence to the Austrians, Foscolo was bitter at the betrayal. Nevertheless he fought with the French throughout Napoleon's occupation of northern Italy. In 1804, with the plan to invade England, he was stationed in northern France where he fell in love with an Englishwoman by whom he had a daughter, 'Floriana'. After Napoleon's defeat and the reoccupation of northern Italy by the Austrians in 1814, Foscolo went into exile, first in Switzerland; then, from 1816, in London where, tended by his daughter, he was to die in poverty. He wrote tragedies in imitation of *Alfieri and intensely lyrical neoclassical sonnets (1802). In the first Romantic Italian novel, *Ultime lettere di Jacopo Ortis (Last*

Letters of Jacopo Ortis, 1802, rev. 1814), inspired by Goethe's *Werther* (see WERTHERISM), the hero chooses suicide, having lost both his love and his political hopes after the Treaty of Campoformio. His greatest work is *Dei Sepolcri (Of Sepulchres*, 1807), a 295-line poem influenced by T. *Gray. This poem deals with the tension between the modern poet's prophetic 'interrogation' of history and his exile from society with which he is at odds. In his last years he contributed critical essays—notably on *Dante, *Petrarch, and *Tasso—to the *Edinburgh Review, *Quarterly Review, and *New Monthly Review. He died in Turnham Green, London.

Foster, Anthony, a character in Scott's *Kenilworth.

Fotheringay, Miss, the stage name of Emily Costigan, a character in Thackeray's *Pendennis.

FOUCAULT, Michel, see MARXIST LITERARY CRITICISM.

FOULIS, Robert (1707–76), originally Faulls, was a barber's apprentice in Glasgow. With his brother Andrew he visited Oxford and France in 1738–40, collecting rare books, and started as bookseller and printer in Glasgow. He printed for the university their first Greek book (1743) and the 'immaculate' *Horace (1744). He issued a number of other remarkable books, the fine folio *Iliad of 1756, the *Odyssey (1758), the Olivet *Cicero (1749), the small folio *Callimachus (1755), the quarto edition of *Gray (1768), and *Paradise Lost (1770). (See James MacLehose, *The Glasgow University Press,* 1931.)

Foul Play, a novel by C. *Reade.

FOUQUÉ, De La Motte, see UNDINE.

'Four Ages of Poetry, The', a literary essay by *Peacock, published 1820. It makes ironic use of the argument advanced by 18th-cent. cultural historians such as *Winckelmann, that as society progresses, poetry deteriorates in inevitable stages. Shelley's reply, *A Defence of Poetry, takes Peacock's charges seriously, and argues that poetry in modern times continues to play an important social role, through advocating the ideal and stimulating the life of the mind.

Four Feathers, The, see MASON, A. E. W.

FOURIER, Charles (1772–1837), French social reformer. Persuaded that the competitive principles of civilization had created unhappiness by establishing inequality of wealth and repressing human passions, Fourier advocated a system of social reorganization, generally known as *Fouriérisme,* which was to ensure the maximum of co-operation in the interests of personal and collective harmony. To this end he proposed the regrouping of society into communities, or *phalanges,* of about 1,600 persons. Each *phalange* was to be a co-operative enterprise providing for the subsistence of all its members, and dividing its remaining revenues among them according to capital invested, labour, and talent. The internal organization of the community would allow for variety of occupation and a large measure of sexual freedom. Fourier's major works are *Théorie des quatre mouvements* (1808), *Traité de l'association domestique agricole* (1822), *Le nouveau monde industriel* (1829–30).

Fouriérisme, see FOURIER.

Four Quartets, a poem in four parts by T. S. *Eliot, published as a whole in 1943. The first part, 'Burnt Norton', was the final poem in *Collected Poems 1909–35* (1936); 'East Coker', 'The Dry Salvages', and 'Little Gidding' first appeared in the *New English Weekly* in 1940, 1941, and 1942 respectively, and were then published separately in pamphlet form by Faber and Faber.

The four quartets represent the four seasons and the four elements; the imagery of the first centres on a Cotswold garden, that of the second round a Somerset village (whence Eliot's own ancestor had departed in 1669 for the New World), the third mingles the landscapes of Missouri and New England, the landscapes of Eliot's youth; and the fourth uses as symbol *Little Gidding, the home of N. *Ferrar. But all are concerned with time past and time present, with the wartime London of the blitz as well as the England of *Julian of Norwich and Sir T. *Elyot. These were the first of Eliot's poems to reach a wide public (they were seen as a unifying force in the war years), and they succeeded in communicating in modern idiom the fundamentals of Christian faith and experience. For a discussion of their sources and composition, see H. *Gardner, *The Composition of Four Quartets* (1978), in which she describes the whole work as an 'austere and rigorously philosophic poem on time and time's losses and gains'.

Four Sons of Aymon, see AYMON.

Fourth Estate, The, the Press. The use of the expression in this sense is attributed by *Carlyle (*On *Heroes and Hero-Worship*) to *Burke, but not traced in his speeches. A correspondent to *N. & Q.* (1st series, xi. 452) attributes it to *Brougham.

Four Zoas, The, a symbolic poem by *Blake, originally entitled *Vala,* written and revised 1795–1804, described by John Beer (*Blake's Humanism,* 1968) as 'a heroic attempt to write the first psychological epic'. It presents characters familiar from Blake's earlier symbolic works (*Urizen, *Los, *Enitharmon, *Orc, and others), elaborating his cosmic mythology in a framework of a 'Dream of Nine Nights'; this frame-

work was possibly suggested by Young's *Night Thoughts,* which Blake was illustrating at the same period. The Four Zoas appear to represent the four human faculties, once united, but then at war with one another until the final radiant vision of joy and peace when the eyes of the Eternal Man 'behold the depths of wondrous worlds' and around his tent 'the little children play among the wooly flocks'.

FOWLER, Henry Watson (1858–1933), and Francis George (1870–1918), lexicographers and grammarians; joint authors of *The King's English* (1906), *The Concise Oxford Dictionary* (1911), and *The Pocket Oxford Dictionary* (1924). *A Dictionary of Modern English Usage* (1926; 2nd edn. 1965, ed. Sir E. Gowers) is the work of H. W. Fowler.

FOWLES, John Robert (1926–), novelist, was educated at Bedford School and New College, Oxford, where he read French. He worked as a schoolteacher before embarking on a career as a full-time writer. His first novel, *The Collector* (1963), a psychological thriller, consists largely of the laconic first-person narration of a repressed clerk and butterfly collector who spends a fortune won on the football pools on the kidnapping of an art student, Miranda; the novel ends with her death and his plans to add another specimen to his collection. This was followed by *The Aristos* (1965), an idiosyncratic collection of notes and aphorisms aimed at a 'personal philosophy', and *The Magus* (1966, revised version 1977), a novel set largely on the Greek island of 'Phraxos', where British schoolmaster Nicholas D'Urfe, half guest and half victim, is subjected to a series of mysterious apparitions and tableaux which, despite their naturalistic explanations, give the novel a narrative complexity and mythological dimension faintly suggestive of *Magic Realism. *The French Lieutenant's Woman* (1969) is a semi-historical novel, set largely in Lyme Regis in 1867; wealthy amateur palaeontologist Charles Smithson, engaged to conventional Ernestina Freeman, falls under the spell of eccentric, sensual, apparently 'fallen' Sarah Woodruff, a lady's companion, who is believed to have been deserted by the French lover of the title. His pursuit of Sarah breaks his engagement, but Sarah eludes him, and when he finds her again (in the protection of D. G. *Rossetti) she has become a *New Woman. The novel is notable for the author's intrusive commentary and suggestion of alternative endings, an aspect represented in *Pinter's screenplay by a double action of film-within-film. *The Ebony Tower* (1974) is a collection of novellas; *Daniel Martin* (1977) is a long, self-searching, semi-naturalistic, semi-experimental account of screenwriter Daniel and his relationships with Hollywood, capitalism, art, and his sister-in-law, set in a wide variety of locations, ranging from opening sequences in Devon and Oxford to a closing sequence in the ruins of Palmyra; *Mantissa* (1982) consists largely of extended erotic fantasy on the subject of *la femme inspiratrice*, with mythological undertones.

FOX, Charles James (1749–1806), a great Whig statesman and orator, who first made his mark by speeches against *Wilkes in 1769. He was one of the managers of the proceedings against *Hastings, and a constant opponent of the policy of *Pitt. Sir G. *Trevelyan described him as 'our first great statesman of the modern school' (*The Early History of Charles James Fox*, 1880). He was a man of great personal charm, noted for his scholarship but also for his gambling and drinking and the bad influence he exercised over the prince of Wales. He was elected a member of Dr Johnson's *Club (1774).

FOX, George (1624–91), son of a Leicestershire weaver and founder of the Society of *Friends, or Quakers, who left home in 1643 in search of enlightenment, and after many struggles and wanderings began to preach the doctrine of the Inner Light of Christ. He was a magnetic preacher and attracted a large following; he travelled widely in the British Isles and to the New World and Holland. His *Journal*, revised by a committee under the superintendence of *Penn and published in 1694, describes in simple, direct but powerful prose his visions, his teaching, and the frequent imprisonments and persecutions to which he and other Friends were exposed.

FOXE, John (1516–87), the martyrologist, was born at Boston, Lincolnshire, and was educated at Oxford, where he became a fellow of Magdalen College but resigned his fellowship in 1545, being unwilling to conform to the statutes in religious matters. In 1554 he retired to the Continent, and issued at Strasburg his *Commentarii* (the earliest draft of his *Actes and Monuments*). From 1555 to 1559 he was employed at Basle as reader of the press by Oporinus (Herbst), who published Foxe's verse drama *Christus Triumphans* in 1556, his appeal to the English nobility on toleration in 1557, and the first issue of his *Rerum in ecclesia gestarum . . . commentarii* in 1559. On his return to England he was ordained priest by Grindal in 1560, and in 1564 joined John *Day, the printer, who in 1563 had issued the English version of the *Rerum in ecclesia gestarum . . . commentarii* as *Actes and Monuments*, popularly known as the *Book of Martyrs*. He became a canon of Salisbury in 1563, but objected to the use of the surplice and to contributing to the repairs of the cathedral. He preached at Paul's Cross a famous sermon, 'Of Christ Crucified', in 1570. His edition of the canon laws *Reformatio Legum* appeared in 1571. He was buried in St Giles' Church, Cripplegate. Four editions of the *Actes and*

Monuments (1563, 1570, 1576, and 1583) appeared in the author's lifetime; of the posthumous issues, that of 1641 contains a memoir of Foxe, attributed to his son.

Fradubio, in Spenser's *Faerie Queene* (I. ii. 32 *et seq.*), 'the doubter', the lover of Fraelissa; he doubts whether her beauty is equal to that of *Duessa. Duessa transforms Fraelissa into a tree, obtains Fradubio's love, and when he discovers her deformity, turns him also into a tree.

Frail, Mrs, a character in Congreve's *Love for Love*.

'Fra Lippo Lippi', a poem by R. Browning, included in *Men and Women*.

Framley Parsonage, a novel by A. *Trollope first published 1861, the fourth in the *'Barsetshire' series.

Mark Robarts is an ambitious young clergyman. At the age of 26 Lady Lufton helped him to the comfortable living at Framley, but he has now become involved with the unreliable Mr Sowerby and hopes for further preferment from the duke of Omnium. Sowerby promises Robarts a prebendal stall at Barchester and Robarts rashly guarantees some bills in return. When the bills fall due, Sowerby makes no attempt to pay them. He is by this time in considerable financial difficulty and, after an abortive attempt to marry the money of the patent-medicine heiress Miss Dunstable, his career ends in ruin. Mark Robarts becomes liable for the full amount of the debts and has to appeal to his original patron, Lady Lufton.

This is doubly embarrassing for the Luftons, as young Lord Lufton has fallen in love with Robarts's sister, Lucy. At first Lady Lufton vehemently opposes the match, and hopes to interest her son in Griselda Grantly, daughter of the archdeacon. Griselda, however, marries the wealthy Lord Dumbello, and Lady Lufton and Lucy are thrown together by the illness of Mrs Crawley, wife of a neighbouring clergyman. In nursing her Lucy shows her true worth, and Lady Lufton removes her opposition to the match; Mark Robarts's debts are paid as a gesture of goodwill. The novel is remarkable for the first appearance of the proud, impoverished curate Mr Crawley.

FRANCE, Anatole, the pseudonym of Jacques-Anatole-François Thibault (1844–1922), French novelist and man of letters, the son of a Parisian bookseller. As writer, journalist, and editor he became a leading figure in French literary life from about 1890. His first successful novel, *Le Crime de Sylvestre Bonnard* (1881), was followed by *La Rôtisserie de la reine Pédauque* (1893) which, with its companion volume *Les Opinions de M. Jérôme Coignard* (1893) attempts a fictionalized revival of the mind and sensibility of 18th-cent. France. Social and political satire dominate the four novels which introduce the observant and disenchanted provincial professor M. Bergeret and which together form the *Histoire contemporaine* (1897–1901). *L'Île des pingouins* (1908) gives a fanciful and satirical version of the evolution of human society and institutions. Many consider *Les Dieux ont soif* (1912), a study of fanaticism during the French revolution, to be his finest novel. His numerous tales, variously exotic, philosophical, and satirical, were collected in, notably: *L'Étui de nacre* (1892), *Crainquebille* (1901), and *Sur la pierre blanche* (1905). Anatole France provided a somewhat fictionalized account of his childhood and early years in *Le Livre de mon ami* (1885), *Pierre Nozière* (1899), *Le Petit Pierre* (1918), and *La Vie en fleur* (1922). He was awarded the *Nobel Prize for literature in 1921.

Francesca da Rimini, see PAOLO AND FRANCESCA.

FRANCIS, Sir Philip (1740–1818), the son of the Philip Francis who was *Gibbon's schoolmaster, was educated at St Paul's School with Woodfall, subsequently publisher of the letters of *Junius. From 1762 to 1772 he was a clerk in the War Office, and became one of the four newly-appointed councillors of the governor-general of India in 1774. He left India in 1780 and assisted *Burke in preparing the charges against *Hastings.

Recent research tends to confirm the long-standing identification of Francis as the author of the letters of Junius, although Woodfall always denied it, and the letters themselves show some malignity towards Francis's friends and benefactors.

FRANCIS OF ASSIS, St, Giovanni Francesco Bernardone (1181/2–1226), experienced as a young man two serious illnesses and a spiritual crisis on a military expedition, in consequence of which he lived for a time in solitude and prayer and devoted himself to the relief of the poor, the sick, and the lepers. He was joined by disciples, the first members of the Franciscan order for which he drew up the rule in 1209, the principal characteristic of which was humility, in token of which they called themselves 'Friari Minori'. He preached in Italy, and went to the Holy Land and Spain. The special notes of his teaching were poverty and love of nature (St Francis preaching to the birds is a favourite painter's subject). Two years before his death, after a period of fasting on Mount Alverno, he is said to have discovered on his body the stigmata, the marks made by the nails of Christ's Crucifixion. Two 13th-cent. biographies of him were written, by Bonaventura and by Thomas of Celano. The *Fioretti de San Francisco* (*Little flowers of St Francis*) is a 14th-cent. Italian narrative, partly legendary, of the doings of St Francis and his first disciples. See *Penguin Book of Italian Verse* (ed. G. Kay, 1958) for his 'Cantico delle creature'. He occurs with St Dominic, the founder of the Dominicans, in *Dante's *Paradiso*, xii. See A. Fortini, *Francis of Assisi*, trans. H. Moak (1981); *Little Flowers of St Francis*, trans. H. E. Manning (1864), rev. R. Huddleston (1926, 1953).

Frankenstein, *or the Modern Prometheus*, a *Gothic tale of terror by M. *Shelley, published 1818. In her preface she records that she, *Shelley, and *Byron had spent the wet summer of 1816 in Switzerland reading German ghost stories; all three agreed to write tales of the supernatural, of which hers was the only one to be completed. She also records that the original concept came to her in a half-waking nightmare.

Technically an *epistolary novel, told through the letters of Walton, an English explorer in the Arctic, the tale relates the exploits of Frankenstein, an idealistic Genevan student of natural philosophy, who discovers at the university of Ingolstadt the secret of imparting life to inanimate matter. Collecting bones from charnel-houses, he constructs the semblance of a human being and gives it life. The creature, endowed with supernatural strength and size and terrible in appearance, inspires loathing in whoever sees it. Lonely and miserable (and educated in human emotion by studies of *Goethe, *Plutarch, and *Paradise Lost*), it turns upon its creator, and, failing to persuade him to provide a female counterpart, eventually murders his brother, his friend Clerval, and his bride Elizabeth. Frankenstein pursues it to the Arctic to destroy it, but dies in the pursuit, after relating his story to Walton. The monster declares that Frankenstein will be his last victim, and disappears to end its own life. This tale inspired many film versions, and has been regarded as the origin of modern *science fiction, though it is also a version of the myth of the *Noble Savage, in which a nature essentially good is corrupted by ill treatment. It is also remarkable for its description of nature, which owes much to the Shelleys' admiration for *Wordsworth, *Coleridge, and in particular the *Ancient Mariner*.

'Frankie and Johnny', or Frankie and Albert, the most popular specimen of modern American balladry. It is said to be of Negro origin and is known to exist in more than 200 variants. The refrain is of the type:

He was her man, but he done her wrong.

Frankie revenged her wrong by shooting her lover. (See BALLAD.)

FRANKLIN, Benjamin (1706–90), born in Boston, Massachusetts, the son of a tallow chandler, was largely self-educated. He was apprenticed at the age of 12 to his half-brother, a printer, to whose *New England Courant* he contributed, but they later quarrelled and he went off to seek independence in Philadelphia. In 1724 he travelled to England, hoping to buy equipment for his own printing press, and worked in a London printing house for some months, returning to Philadelphia in 1726. Four years later he set up his own press, from which he issued *The Pennsylvania Gazette*, and, by thrift and hard work, became prosperous. He acquired a wide reputation by his occasional writings, especially *Poor Richard's Almanack* (1733–58), the best-known of American *almanacs, which followed the British pattern of mixing practical information with satiric prognostications, aphorisms, proverbs, etc. He was active as a public figure, founding the American Philosophical Society and the academy that became the University of Pennsylvania, and he also became well known for his practical interest in natural philosophy; his experiment with lightning and electricity, using a kite to demonstrate their identity, was famous, and he also invented the Franklin stove and a new kind of clock. In 1757 he travelled to England as agent for the colonies, where he mixed widely in intellectual society (his friends including *Burke, *Hume, Adam *Smith, *Strachan, and J. *Priestley) and contributed greatly to the controversies that caused the breach with England; he returned home in 1774 and, after helping to draft the Declaration of Independence, travelled to France as ambassador, where he was enthusiastically welcomed. Upon his return in 1785 he continued to be active in public affairs, and signed the Constitution as a member of the Federal Constitutional Convention. His *Autobiography*, which he began to write in England, at Twyford, in 1771, and which breaks off with an account of his return to England in 1757, was published in England in 1793 (translated from the French), in America in 1818. Franklin's prose was much admired in England; *Jeffery (1806, *Edinburgh Review*) praised its 'force and clearness', and *Lecky (*History of England in the Eighteenth Century*) described it as 'always terse, luminous, simple, pregnant with meaning, eminently persuasive'. D. H. *Lawrence, however, deplored 'middle-sized, sturdy, snuff-coloured Doctor Franklin' and his thrift and orderliness: 'He tries to take away my wholeness and my dark forest, my freedom' (*Studies in Classic American Literature*, 1923).

FRANKLIN, Sir John (1786–1847), Arctic explorer, was author of two *Narratives* (1823 and 1828) of voyages to the Polar Sea. His final voyage of discovery in *Erebus* and *Terror* in search of the North-West Passage, began in 1845, and resulted in disaster. Numerous relief expeditions were sent out including one organized by his widow which found a record of the expedition proving that Franklin had discovered the North-West Passage.

'Franklin's Tale, The', see CANTERBURY TALES, 12.

FRASER, Lady Antonia, *née* Pakenham (1932–), biographer, broadcaster, and writer of mystery stories, educated at Lady Margaret Hall, Oxford. She married H. *Pinter in 1980. Her biographies include lives of *Mary Queen of Scots (1969), *Cromwell (1973), and King James I of England (1974). Her female detective Jemima Shore was introduced in *Quiet as a Nun* (1977), and has since appeared in several mystery novels and in a television series.

FRASER, George Sutherland, see NEW APOCALYPSE.

Fraser's Magazine (1830–82), a general and literary Tory journal of high standing, founded by *Maginn and Hugh Fraser, which provided some competition for *Blackwood's*. Unlike *Blackwood's*, the *Edinburgh*, or the *Quarterly* it was not owned by a publisher of books, and prided itself that it could not therefore be accused of partisanship in its reviews. Among notable contributors were J. *Hogg, *Coleridge, *Southey, *Peacock, *Carlyle, *Ainsworth, *Thackeray, and *Ruskin. J. A. *Froude was editor from 1860 to 1874, but the journal had by then declined in influence and repute.

Fraternitie of Vacabondes, a tract printed by John Awdely (*fl.* 1559–75), published in 1565 in two parts, the first dealing with thieves' cant and the devices of beggars to excite compassion; the second with the methods employed by well-dressed impostors.

FRAUNCE, Abraham (?1558–93), was educated at Shrewsbury School. Under the patronage of P. *Sidney he involved himself in contemporary movements, such as Ramism (see RAMUS), in logic, rhetoric, and metrics. His most interesting work, *The Arcadian Rhetorike* (1588), illustrates rhetorical tropes with examples from Sidney's *Arcadia*, side by side with *Tasso, *Du Bartas, and *Boscan. Other works include *The Lawiers Logike* (1588), *The Countesse of Pembrokes Emanuel* (1591), and *The Countesse of Pembrokes Yvychurch* (1591).

FRAYN, Michael (1933–), novelist and playwright, was educated at Kingston Grammar School and Emmanuel College, Cambridge, and worked for some years as a humorous columnist for the *Manchester Guardian*, then for the *Observer*. His novels include *The Russian Interpreter* (1966), *Towards the End of the Morning* (1967, a comedy of Fleet Street life and London middle-class domestic *mores*), and *A Very Private Life* (1968, a satiric anti-Utopian fantasy). His stage comedies include *Alphabetical Order* (1975, pub. 1976), again with a background of journalism; *Donkeys' Years* (1976, pub. 1977) based on a college reunion; and *Noises Off* (1982), a farce of theatre life.

FRAZER, Sir James George (1854–1941), was appointed to the first named chair of social anthropology in Liverpool, in 1907, but spent most of his life in Cambridge, where he was fellow of Trinity from 1879. Often regarded as one of the founders of modern anthropology, he did much to popularize his own field of study and to make its agnostic tendencies acceptable, although his methods (he relied on secondary sources) and many of his conclusions are now unacceptable. *The Golden Bough* (of which the first volume appeared in 1890, and the twelfth and last in 1915, followed by *Aftermath, a supplement* in 1936) is a vast and enterprising comparative study of the beliefs and institutions of mankind, offering the thesis that man progresses from magical through religious to scientific thought. Its discussion of fertility rites, the sacrificial killing of kings, the dying god, the scapegoat, etc., and its analysis of the primitive mind, caught the literary imagination, and its influence may perhaps be seen more lastingly in the works of D. H. *Lawrence, T. S. *Eliot, *Pound and others than in works of scholarly anthropology. Frazer's many other works include *Totemism and Exogamy* (1910) and *Folklore in the Old Testament* (1918), and he also published translations with commentary of Pausanias (1898) and the *Fasti* of *Ovid (1929).

Frederick, the usurping duke in Shakespeare's *As You Like It.*

FREDERICK THE GREAT, of Prussia (1712–86), military genius, able administrator, and a man of considerable culture, who established the nationhood of Prussia; he was the subject of a biography by T. *Carlyle, entitled *The History of Frederick II of Prussia called Frederick the Great* (6 vols, 1858–65), in which he is described as 'a questionable hero' who nevertheless was able to emerge from a 'century opulent in accumulated falsities'. The work was a labour of many years of what Carlyle himself described as 'horrid struggles'; after finishing it, characteristically, he says he 'sank into new depths of stupefaction and dull misery of body and mind'.

FREEMAN, E(dward) A(ugustus) (1823–92), historian and controversialist. Endowed with private means, which he supplemented by regular writing for the *Saturday Review, he spent much of his life in the study of medieval and ancient history, but he was handicapped by an uncontrollable prolixity, an inability to handle MS material, and a marked aversion to public libraries, a trait shared by many Victorian scholars (e.g. *Carlyle, *Buckle). His best-known work is his gigantic *History of the Norman Conquest* (5 vols, 1867–79), and its sequel on

The Reign of William Rufus (2 vols, 1882). Here his firm Whig belief in the excellence of the British Constitution as it had developed from the Conquest was at odds with his deep affection and respect for Anglo-Saxon culture, which also led him to write in a curiously archaic style, eschewing Latin derivations wherever possible. In his hands, therefore, the events of 1066 emerge as a happy tragedy. Those with the patience to dig will unearth some gems of characterization and description, particularly of battles, but the selectivity of his sources and his eccentric handling of them meant that his work was already being superseded when he died, leaving unfinished a *History of Sicily* (4 vols, 1891–4) and a *History of Federal Government* (1863). He was a man of violent temperament and warm emotions, capable of close friendships (for instance with W. *Stubbs and J. R. *Green), but guilty of almost paranoid hatreds which are not rationally explicable, particularly for C. *Kingsley and J. H. *Froude, whom he pursued with unexampled venom. His aversion to blood sports also involved him in public controversy with A. *Trollope, and all his work is infected with anti-Semitism and a violent though selective xenophobia. Appointed Regius professor of modern history at Oxford, in 1884, he soon alienated his colleagues by his open contempt for their teaching methods and for the new honours degree in modern history. His boorishness inflicted long-lasting damage on the professorial image.

W. R. W. Stephens's *Life and Letters* (1895) is a tactful piece of bowdlerization. See also *A Liberal Descent* by J. W. Burrow (1981), who also edited a drastically abridged version of *The Norman Conquest* (1974).

FREEMAN, Mary E. Wilkins (1852–1930), American author, born in Massachusetts, distinguished for her realistic stories of New England life. Her best-known books are *A Humble Romance and Other Stories* (1887) and *A New England Nun and Other Stories* (1891).

French Lieutenant's Woman, The, see FOWLES, J.

French Revolution, The: *A History*, the work by which T. *Carlyle established his reputation, written in London 1834–7, published 1837. ·

It is in three volumes, 'The Bastille', 'The Constitution', and 'The Guillotine'; it opens with the death of Louis XV in 1774, covers the reign of Louis XVI, the period which included the assembly of the States General, the fall of the Bastille, the Constituent and Legislative Assemblies, the flight of the king to Varennes, the Convention, the trial and execution of the king and queen, the reign of terror, the fall of Robespierre, and extends to 5 Oct. 1795, when Bonaparte quelled the insurrection of the Vendémiaire, the title of the last chapter being

'The Whiff of Grapeshot'. It is a work of great narrative and descriptive power, with a notable gallery of portraits (Mirabeau, Lafayette, Danton, Robespierre), and impressive set pieces; it was greatly admired by *Dickens, and was in part the inspiration of *A Tale of Two Cities.

French Revolution, Reflections on the, by E. Burke, see REVOLUTION IN FRANCE.

FRENEAU, Philip Morin (1752–1832), the 'poet of the American Revolution', and miscellaneous writer, editor, and journalist, was born in New York and educated at the College of New Jersey (later Princeton). He lived for a while (1775–8) in the West Indies, where he wrote poems inspired by the tropical atmosphere and landscape, and in 1780 during the Revolutionary War was captured by the British, an experience which prompted the bitter satire of his poem The British Prison-Ship (1781), one of his many attacks on the British. His not wholly prosperous career as a writer was interspersed with periods at sea as a ship's master (1784–90 and 1803–7). His first collection of verse, Poems (1786), was followed by various volumes of essays, poems, etc., and he wrote widely for newspapers and periodicals, some of which he also edited. His verse ranged from the satirical and patriotic to works such as 'The Wild Honey Suckle' (1786), a nature poem of delicacy and sensitivity which heralds *Romanticism.

FRERE, John Hookham (1769–1846), educated at Eton and Caius College, Cambridge, was a friend of *Canning, an MP, and an official of the Foreign Office, who occupied many important positions at home and abroad. While at Eton Frere wrote a translation of *Brunanburh, and was one of the founders of The Microcosm periodical (1786–7). He contributed some accomplished humorous verse to *The Anti-Jacobin, including most of 'The Loves of the Triangles' (a parody of E. *Darwin). He collaborated in *Ellis's Specimens of the Early English Poets (1801), and in *Southey's Chronicle of the Cid; his translations from the Poema del Cid were said by *Coleridge to be 'incomparable'. He was one of the founders of *The Quarterly Review in 1809, and an adviser to John *Murray the publisher. He is, however, chiefly remembered as the inspirer of the style, stanza, and idiom of Byron's *Beppo and *Don Juan. In the Italian verses of *Pulci he found a verse-form and a colloquial voice which he felt could be adapted to English, and in 1817 he published the first two cantos of his mock-epic Prospectus and Specimen of an Intended National Work . . . by William and Robert Whistlecraft . . . relating to King Arthur and his Round Table. It gave *Byron what he wanted, and he describes Beppo as 'in or after the excellent manner of Mr Whistlecraft'. Frere also published lively metrical versions of *Aristo-

phanes: Frogs (1839); Archarnians, Knights, and Birds in 1840; and Theognis Restitutus (1842).

FREUD, Sigmund (1856–1939), born at Freiberg in Moravia, and known as the creator of psychoanalysis, a science (or, as some claim, a mythology) which has had an incalculable effect both on literature and on literary theory. Freud, after studying with the neurologist Charcot in Paris, practised for many years in Vienna, until Hitler's invasion of Austria drove him to London, where he died. His theories of the normal and abnormal mind were evolved originally from his study of neurotic ailments. His many contributions to knowledge include his studies of the development of the sexual instinct in children, his descriptions of the workings of the unconscious mind and of the nature of repression, and his examinations and interpretations of dreams. Many of his concepts have become universally familiar in a vulgarized form, e.g. the Oedipus complex, the death wish, the family romance, penis envy, *phallic symbolism, and the formulation of the divisions between the 'Id, the Ego and the Superego'. Such phrases rapidly acquired a currency even among those who had not read the works of Freud, and direct or indirect influence is frequently hard to ascertain. A characteristic case is that of D. H. Lawrence's *Sons and Lovers (1913), considered by many a classic example of a novel about the Oedipus complex; Lawrence himself claimed not to have read Freud, and dismissed the theory of complexes as 'vicious half-statements of the Freudians' (1916, on a review in the Psychoanalytic Review), but his wife Frieda was greatly interested in psychoanalysis and claimed that they discussed Freud's theories together. L. *Strachey, in Elizabeth and Essex (1928), produced what is possibly the first consciously Freud-oriented biography; its many successors include Leon Edel's life of H. *James. (See also under ERIKSON for psychobiography.) The significance for both biographers and novelists of Freud's stress on the formative experiences of childhood is obvious; equally obvious is the importance to poets and prose-writers such as *Joyce of Freud's theories of word association, although Joyce (possibly for Freudian reasons) always indignantly repudiated the influence of Freud, whose work he certainly knew. Freud's works were made available in English by James Strachey, Lytton's brother, who was responsible for the Standard Edition of the Complete Psychological Works of Sigmund Freud (24 vols, 1953–73). The works reveal Freud himself as a writer of great distincton: D. M. *Thomas, in his foreword to The White Hotel (1981, in which Freud appears as a character), reminds us that the case histories are themselves 'masterly works of literature', and Freud was also highly perceptive as a critic. (See below, under FREUDIAN CRITICISM.) See also Ernest Jones, The Life and Works of *Sigmund Freud* (1953-7) and R. Clark, *Freud: The Man and the Cause* (1980).

Freudian Criticism and Artistic Theory. The connection between psychoanalytic theory and the arts has been much discussed, one widely-held assumption being that, in Freudian terms, artistic creativity is a form of sublimation, and that both art and the artist are pathological phenomena. This is the view suggested by E. *Wilson in *The Wound and the Bow* (1941), a study of the biographical relationship between painful childhood experience and artistic creation, which *Trilling (a great admirer of Freud) summarized as the view that 'the poet is a poet by reason of his sickness as well as by reason of his power' ('Neurosis and the Health of the Artist', 1947). Freud's own views on this, according to the philosopher Richard Wollheim, would seem to be agnostic. The use of works of art and literature as subjects of analysis is a separate issue: Freud himself did this, writing with great brilliance on the characters of *Hamlet and Oedipus (*The Interpretation of Dreams*, 1900); on the 'Theme of the Three Caskets', (1913, a discussion of *The Merchant of Venice* and *King Lear*, which identifies the choice of the leaden casket and the reconciliation with Cordelia with the acceptance of death); on the *Moses* of *Michelangelo (1914) and on *Richard III, Lady Macbeth, and *Ibsen's Rebecca West in 'Some Character-Types met with in Psycho-analytic Work' (1915). Thus what may broadly describe itself as Freudian criticism may direct itself to detecting connections between the biography of the artist and its product in art or artefact, or to the analysis of fictional characters; it may also direct itself to the analysis of 'Freudian' imagery, either deliberate or unintentional, within a work. The spread of these various lines of approach has been so pervasive that they are widely employed by many who would reject the label of Freudian, although the label itself has been more acceptable in America than in England. In sum, the influence of Freud, both on literature and its interpretation, has been vast: *Auden, who saw it as a liberation, wrote in his eloquent elegy 'In Memory of Sigmund Freud' (1939): 'to us he is no more a person | now but a whole climate of opinion | under whom we conduct our different lives . . . the child . . . feels calmer now and somehow assured of escape'; whereas other writers have submitted to what could be described as a bleak Freudian determinism.

Friar Bacon and Friar Bungay, see FRIAR BACON AND FRIER BONGAY.

FRIAR BUNGAY, see BUNGAY, T.

'Friar's Tale, The', see CANTERBURY TALES, 7.

Friar Tuck, one of the principal characters in the legend of *Robin Hood; the fat, jovial, and pugnacious father confessor of the outlaw chief. He figures in Scott's *Ivanhoe* and in Peacock's *Maid Marian*. See *Ritson's *Robin Hood* (2 vols, 1795, a collection of songs, ballads, etc., with a full introduction) and *The Outlaws of Medieval England* (1961) by M. Keen. (See also BALLAD.)

Friday, Man, see ROBINSON CRUSOE.

Friend, The, a weekly periodical edited and largely written by S. T. *Coleridge in the Lake District, 1809-10.

It was the first to publish early sections of Wordsworth's *Prelude*. In its final 3-vol. book form of 1818, Coleridge transformed it into a substantial series of interlinked essays 'to aid in the formation of fixed principles in politics, morals, and religion, with literary amusements interspersed'. Vol. I contains a notable defence of 'free communication' in the press; Vol. II attacks Jacobin theories of the 'Rights of Man'; Vol. III expounds the 'Principles of Method'.

Friends, Society of, a religious society founded in 1648-50 by G. *Fox, distinguished by pacifist principles, plainness of dress and manners, refusal to take oaths, faith in the Inner Light, and the absence of clergy or ministers; the Society is also now noted for its involvement with social and educational reform. Members of the Society are also known as Quakers; according to Fox, the name was first given to himself and his followers by Justice Bennet at Derby in 1650 'because I bid them, Tremble at the word of the Lord'. The name had, however, been previously applied to a foreign religious sect. See also PENN; NAYLOR; BARCLAY, R.

Friendship's Garland, a collection of essays in letter form by M. *Arnold, originally printed in the *Pall Mall Gazette*, published 1871.

The principal imaginary correspondent is a Prussian, Arminius, Baron von Thunder-ten-Tronckh (a descendant of a character in *Voltaire's *Candide*), and through him Arnold expresses his mockery of the English *Philistine as represented by Bottles, a wealthy manufacturer; of narrow Liberal reform as represented by the 'deceased-wife's-sister' Act; of the *Daily Telegraph* and its naïve patriotism, and of English foreign and educational policy. Arminius believes in the application of 'Geist' or 'Intelligence', which the English persistently undervalue, and teases 'poor Arnold' for his supposed 'infatuation about everything English'.

Frier Bacon, and Frier Bongay, The Honorable Historie of, a comedy in verse and prose by R. *Greene, acted 1594. The play is partially based on a prose pamphlet *The famous historie of Fryar Bacon*, embodying legends relating to R. *Bacon and T. *Bungay.

Bacon with the help of Friar Bungay makes a head of brass, and, conjuring up the Devil, learns how to give it speech. It is to speak within a month, but 'if they heard it not before it had done speaking, all their labour should be lost.' After watching day and night for three weeks, Bacon hands over the duty to his servant Miles and falls asleep. The head speaks two words, 'Time is'. Miles, thinking his master would be angry if waked for so little, lets him sleep. The head presently speaks again, 'Time was'; and finally, 'Time is past', when it falls down and breaks. Bacon awakes, and heaps curses on Miles's head. The tale is diversified with the pleasant story of the loves of Edward prince of Wales (afterwards Edward I) and Lord Lacy for the fair Margaret, the keeper's daughter of Fressingfield, and the prince's surrender of her to Lacy. There is also an amusing scene where Bacon, Bungay, and a German rival display their respective powers before the German emperor and the kings of England and Castile.

FRISCH, Max (1911–), Swiss playwright and novelist, also a qualified architect. His best-known play (written for radio) is *Biedermann und die Brandstifter* (*The Fire-Raisers*, 1958), a satire on the passivity of the middle class as represented by the man who tolerates, even abets, criminal arson in his own home. The novel *Homo Faber* (1957) concerns the helplessness of a technologist to control the events of his life. Coincidences which defy statistical analysis pursue him like the Furies in a Greek tragedy. Since the 1960s Frisch has published several short stories and essays of an autobiographical nature.

FROISSART, Jean (*c*.1337–*c*.1410), French chronicler and poet. He travelled widely in Western Europe, collecting material for his future histories. In 1361 he was received in England by Edward III, and visited Scotland. In 1366 he accompanied the *Black Prince to Bordeaux, and in 1368 the duke of Clarence to Milan. He revisited England in 1394–5. His chronicles record the chivalric exploits of the nobles of England and France from 1325 to 1400. They were translated into English by John Bourchier in 1523–5. As author of lively personal *lais* and *ballades* he had some influence on *Chaucer.

FROST, Robert Lee (1874–1963), American poet, born in San Francisco of New England stock. He was taken at the age of ten to the New England farm country of which his poetry was to be so deeply expressive. He spent some time at both Dartmouth College and Harvard, but left to teach, edit a country paper, learn to make shoes, and to farm. In 1912 he came to England with his wife and family, where he published his first volumes of poems, *A Boy's Will* (1913) and *North of Boston* (1914), which contains 'Mending Wall' and 'The Death of the Hired Man'; he met the *Georgian poets, and formed a particularly close and fruitful friendship with E. *Thomas, whom he was to describe as 'the only brother I ever had'. Upon his return to New England in 1915 he settled in New Hampshire and continued to write poetry, supporting himself by successive teaching appointments in several colleges. His volumes include *Mountain Interval* (1916), which contains 'Birches' and 'The Road Not Taken'; *New Hampshire* (1923); *Collected Poems* (1930); *A Witness Tree* (1942); and *In The Clearing* (1962). He established himself as one of the most popular of 20th-cent. American poets, admired for the blend of colloquial and traditional in his verse, and hailed as a fitting heir, in his response to the natural world, of *Wordsworth and *Emerson; his dramatic monologues and pastorals have been particularly popular. But beneath the country lore and wisdom hailed in a 1913 review of his first book by N. *Douglas as his 'simple woodland philosophy' lay a more troubled, combative, at times destructive spirit, both in his life and work, expressed in such poems as 'Fire and Ice' (1923) and 'Bereft' (1928), which led to *Trilling's praise of him, on the occasion of his 85th birthday, as a 'poet of terror'. His *Selected Letters*, ed. L. Thompson, were published in 1965.

'Frost at Midnight', a blank verse poem by S. T. *Coleridge written at Stowey, Somerset, in Feb. 1798. Addressed to his sleeping child Hartley *Coleridge, it meditates on the poet's own boyhood, and magically evokes the countryside, ending on a note of rare and thrilling happiness. It is possibly the finest of Coleridge's series of 'conversation' poems.

Froth, Lord and Lady, characters in Congreve's *The Double Dealer*.

FROUDE, J(ames) A(nthony) (1818–94), historian. Educated at Westminster and Oriel College, Oxford, he was an early casualty of the *Oxford Movement. Surrendering to the charismatic leadership of J. H. *Newman, he lost his faith when Newman reneged on the Church of England in 1845. Out of his religious agonies and his sexual frustrations he wrote a bad but spectacular novel, *The Nemesis of Faith* (1849), which obliged him to resign his fellowship at Exeter College and leave for London, where he maintained himself by journalism; he wrote for several of the reviews, and edited *Fraser's Magazine* 1860–74. He now fell under the influence of *Carlyle, and became one of his most faithful companions, though with no apparent effect on his own work; he was also a friend of A. H. *Clough and C. *Kingsley (later his brother-in-law). His *History of England from the Death of Cardinal Wolsey to the defeat of the Spanish Armada* (12 vols, 1856–70), was a distinguished work of scholarship on which all subsequent Tudor studies rest, and he was the first English historian to make a thorough and systematic use of archive material in the manner laid down by *Ranke. He was also the first to publicize and glorify the deeds of the Elizabethan seamen, a topic to which he returned in his Oxford lectures on English Seamen in the Sixteenth Century (1892–4, published 1895). All his books were highly successful, even his collected essays, Short Studies in Great Subjects (4 vols, 1867–83); but he was criticized for his partisan treatment of the English Reformation and his attempt to rehabilitate Henry VIII, and the accuracy of his scholarship was unjustly impugned by E. A. *Freeman, whose charges seem to have been accepted by the profession, especially when Froude went on to publish a slipshod history of 18th-cent. Ireland (2 vols, 1872–4). Latterly he seemed to attract public controversy; his American lecture tour in 1872 was cut short by Irish nationalist agitation, his attempt to intervene in South African politics in 1874–5 provoked a storm, and even his visit to the West Indies in 1886–7 had political repercussions. But this was nothing to the uproar which greeted his Reminiscences of Carlyle (1881) and his Letters and Memorials of Jane Welsh *Carlyle (1883), which were distinguished by their shattering frankness. Nevertheless, in 1892 Lord Salisbury offered him the Regius chair of modern history at Oxford, an appointment which met with a distinctly mixed reception. He was a brilliant public speaker and his lectures attracted large audiences, but he died after only two years in office.

See Herbert Paul's Life of Froude (1907) and Waldo Hilary Dunn's biography (1961–3).

FROUDE, R(ichard) H(urrell) (1803–36), Tractarian, brother of J. A. *Froude, educated at Oriel College, Oxford, where he became a fellow. He was intimate with *Newman with whom he collaborated in the early stages of the *Oxford Movement. He contributed three of the Tracts for the Times and wrote poems contained in *Lyra Apostolica. His Remains (1838–9), including strictures on the Reformers, aroused public hostility against the Movement.

Frugal, Sir John and Luke, characters in Massinger's *The City Madam.

FRY, Christopher (Harris) (1907–), born in Bristol of Quaker stock, worked as schoolmaster, actor, and theatre director before making his name as a playwright with works that were hailed in the late 1940s as a sign of a new renaissance of poetic drama; his mystical and religious plays (The Boy with a Cart, 1939; The Firstborn, 1946; Thor with Angels, 1949; A Sleep of Prisoners, 1951) were frequently compared to those of T. S. *Eliot, though the theatre-going public tended to prefer the ebullient optimism and exuberant word-play of his comedies, e.g. A Phoenix too Frequent (1946, based on *Petronius), The Lady's not for Burning (1949, set in the Middle Ages), and Venus Observed (1950, a romantic château comedy). The Dark is Light Enough (1954) was less successful; the vogue for poetic drama proved short-lived, giving way to the *kitchen sink school, and Curtmantle (1962), about *Becket, struck critics as dated. Fry also wrote several screenplays, and successful translations and adaptations of *Anouilh (Ring round the Moon, 1950; The Lark, 1955) and *Giraudoux (Tiger at the Gates, 1955; Duel of Angels, 1958).

FRY, Roger Eliot (1866–1934), art critic and painter, born in London of a Quaker family, was educated at Clifton and King's College, Cambridge, where he read natural sciences and became a member of the *Apostles. He became art critic of the *Athenaeum in 1901, helped to establish the Burlington Magazine in 1903, and from 1905 to 1910 was director at the Metropolitan Museum of Art in New York. On his return to England he organized two highly influential and controversial exhibitions of *Post-Impressionist paintings (a term he coined himself) at the Grafton Galleries in 1910 and 1912, and his collected essays (Vision and Design, 1920; Transformations, 1926) were also instrumental in spreading his enthusiasm for modern French painting. He was closely associated with the *Bloomsbury Group, and his biography was written by V. *Woolf (1940).

Fudge Family in Paris, The, verses by T. *Moore published 1818.

In these light verses the author endeavoured to collect 'the concentrated essence of the various forms of cockneyism and nonsense of those groups of ridiculous English who were at that time swarming in all directions throughout Paris'. They take the form of letters written by or to various members of the Fudge family when visiting Paris in 1817, shortly after the restoration of the Bourbons. They include inane descriptions by the mindless Fudges, and pompous, sycophantic letters from Mr Fudge to *Castlereagh.

FUGARD, Athol (1932–), South African playwright, born in Middlesburg, the son of a small shopowner; he was brought up in Port Elizabeth and educated there and at Cape Town University. After various jobs, some connected with the theatre, he moved in 1958 with his actress wife to Johannesburg, where he worked for some time as clerk to the Native Commissioner's Court, an experience which greatly sharpened his awareness of racial tension and inequality, the subject of much of his drama. His plays include The Blood Knot (1961, pub. 1963), about the fraught relationship of two coloured brothers; Boesman and Lena (1968, pub. 1969), a sombre work figuring a derelict, middle-aged couple of Coloured migrant workers, whose presence as they set up their shelter on the open stage has a symbolic quality akin to that of the characters of *Beckett; Sizwe

Bansi is Dead (1972, pub. 1974, written with John Kani and Winston Ntshona), based on the problems created by the pass laws; *A Lesson from Aloes* (1980, pub. 1981), which contrasts the political attitudes, ranging from stoicism to defeat, of an Afrikaner, his wife, and their Coloured friends; and '*Master Harold*' ... *and the boys* (1982, pub. 1983), portraying the relationship between a white South African teenager and two black family servants, 'the boys'.

Fugard's career has been greatly complicated by the politics of racialism; he was in 1962 active in encouraging a boycott of South African theatre by overseas English-speaking playwrights, insisting that plays should be performed before non-segregated audiences, but has since modified this attitude in view of the complexities and necessities of a situation which his own works vividly evoke.

Fulgens and Lucrece, a late 15th-cent. *interlude by Henry Medwall (fl.1486), regarded as the earliest known purely secular play in English. It has been edited by G. Wickham in *English Moral Interludes* (1976).

FULGENTIUS, Fabius Planciadis (fl. late 5th cent. AD), Latin grammarian who lived in North Africa. His *Mythologiae* and his 'explanation' of *Virgil's *Aeneid* provided ancient legends with spiritualizing interpretations that found great favour with later Christian moralizers. His works were extensively used by *Boccaccio and by other mythographers and poets during the Renaissance.

FULLER, John Leopold (1937–), poet and novelist, son of Roy *Fuller. His several volumes of poetry include *Fairground Music* (1961), *Cannibals and Missionaries* (1972), *Lies and Secrets* (1979, which contains one of his most sustained works, 'The Most Difficult Position', about the non-confrontation of two 19th-cent. chess masters), and *The Illusionists* (1980), a satiric narrative in stanza form of contemporary life. His poems range from lyrics to pastiche verse epistles, from sonnets to long unrhymed monologues, and his subjects are also diverse. His novel *Flying to Nowhere* (1983), set on a Welsh island, is a fantasy about a 16th-cent. abbot who thinks he has discovered, through surgical dissection, the seat of the soul.

FULLER, (Sarah) Margaret (1810–50), American author and feminist, born in Massachusetts, whose name is associated with the New England Transcendentalists; she helped to found *The Dial, which she edited for two years from 1840 to 1842, and at the same period (1839–44) conducted a series of conversations or seminars for educated women in Boston. One of the products of these discussions was her influential feminist tract *Women in the Nineteenth Century* (1845). In 1844 she moved to New York, where she wrote for *Greeley's *New York Tribune, and in 1846 she went to Europe and settled in Italy, where she married one of Mazzini's followers, the Marquis Ossoli. Sailing from Leghorn to America in 1850, she and her husband were drowned when their ship was wrecked just short of its destination. Her *Memoirs* (1852) were edited by *Emerson, W. H. Channing, and J. F. Clarke. She is said to have suggested the character of the magnetic and passionate Zenobia in Hawthorne's *The Blithedale Romance*.

FULLER, Roy Broadbent (1912–), poet and novelist, born near and brought up in Oldham, the son of a director of a rubber-proofing company. He was educated at Blackpool High School, and then became a solicitor, working for many years for a building society. During the 1930s he contributed to left-wing literary magazines, including *New Verse, and his first volume, *Poems* (1939), shows the influence of *Auden and *Spender. This was followed by several collections of poetry: *Collected Poems 1936–1961* (1962), with work from several previous volumes, forms a link between the poets of the thirties and the poets of the *Movement, in its lucid, ironic, detached tone, and its formal accomplishment. His later volumes, which include *From the Joke Shop* (1975) and *The Reign of Sparrows* (1980), while displaying an equal interest in technique, frequently strike a more personal note, particularly in the many sardonic reflections on old age and the ageing process. Fuller has also published several novels, including, notably, *Image of a Society* (1956), which is a portrait of personal and professional conflicts in a northern provincial building society, narrated in a low-key, naturalistic, yet ironic manner. He was professor of poetry at Oxford, 1968–73, and *Owls and Artificers* (1971) and *Professors and Gods* (1973) are collections of his Oxford lectures. He has also published three volumes of memoirs, *Souvenirs* (1980), *Vamp till ready* (1982), and *Home and Dry* (1984).

FULLER, Thomas (1608–61), born at Aldwinkle St Peter's in Northamptonshire and educated at Queens' and Sidney Sussex Colleges, Cambridge, became rector of Broadwindsor, Dorset, in 1634, and shortly before the Civil War was made a preacher at the Savoy. A moderate royalist, he followed the war as chaplain to Sir Ralph Hopton and during his travels conceived the idea of 'a more exact collection' of the worthies of England. After the Restoration he became 'chaplain in extraordinary' to the king. He published *The History of the Holy Warre* (i.e. of the crusades) in 1639; *The Holy State and The Profane State* in 1642; *Good Thoughts in Bad Times* in 1645 (followed by two sequels); *A Pisgah of Palestine*, a *topographical and historical work, in 1650. His *The church-history of Britain; with the history of the University of Cambridge* (1655), which covers from the birth of Christ to the execution of Charles I, was criticized (by *Heylyn, among others) for its 'puns and quibbles' and its 'trencher-jests', but was widely read and enjoyed. *The History of the *Worthies of England*, his best-known and most characteristic work, appeared after his death in 1622, and was the fruit of much research; in his own words, 'My pains have been scattered all over the land, by riding, writing, going, sending, chiding, begging, praying, and sometimes paying too, to procure manuscript material.' *Lamb referred to him as 'the dear, fine, silly, old angel', and he was much admired by *Coleridge. His writings are marked by a lively and eccentric curiosity, by 'fantastic caprices' (L. *Stephen), and by a fondness for aphorisms.

Funeral, The, or *Grief à-la-Mode*, a comedy by R. *Steele, produced 1701.

Lord Brumpton has disinherited his son Lord Hardy, owing to the misrepresentations of his wife, the young man's stepmother; he has left her all his property, as well as two wards, the ladies Sharlot and Harriot. When the play opens Lord Brumpton has, as is generally believed, just died. He has in fact, however, recovered from a 'lethargic slumber', a fact known only to himself and his steward Trusty (and the audience). At Trusty's instance he remains in concealment, and thus discovers his supposed widow's unseemly rejoicing at her release, her machinations against her stepson, and her unscrupulous design to dispose profitably of Sharlot and Harriot. The widow is exposed, Lord Hardy reinstated, and the ladies bestowed on their true lovers, Lord Hardy and his friend. The devices by which these results are effected are somewhat clumsy; but the play is notable as marking a change of moral tone in the drama after the licentiousness of the *Restoration.

Fungoso, a foolish law student in Jonson's *Every Man out of his Humour*, obsessed with courtly fashion.

FURNIVALL, Frederick James (1825–1910), educated at University College London and Trinity College, Cambridge, began his career as a barrister, but soon devoted his great energy to educational, philological, and literary pursuits. He was from 1847 a member of the *Philological Society, and became its secretary; in 1861 he became editor of the proposed New English Dictionary which developed into the *Oxford English Dictionary. He founded the *Early English Texts Society (1864), the Chaucer Society (1868), the Ballad Society (1869), the New Shakspere Society (1873), the Wyclif Society (1881), the Browning Society (1881), and the Shelley Society (1886), and himself edited many texts. He was also a leader in the move for popular education, and taught grammar at the Working Men's College founded in 1854.

FUSELI, Henry (1741–1825), Swiss artist who came to England in 1764; after studying in Rome (1770–8) he settled in London. Fuseli's works show the powerful attraction that Burke's *sublime of terror held for early Romantic artists. He was fascinated by the supernatural and by the darkest of human passions; the disturbing intensity of his works depends on sudden contrasts of scale, and on the frenzied expressions and muscular energy of his stylized figures. Fuseli drew his subjects from Shakespeare, *Milton, *Dante, *Ossian, and other poets. He were the most brilliant contributions to *Boydell's Shakespeare Gallery; a monumental series of illustrations to Milton reflect the Romantic conception of Satan as hero. The fame of the *Nightmare* (1782; the earliest version is in Detroit, Institute of Arts), a work full of Gothic horror, spread throughout Europe. Fuseli, who began his career as a translator, was a learned artist who shone in literary and artistic society in London. His extravagant wit is recorded by many of his contemporaries and his lectures and essays illumine the intellectual life of his times. Both *Hazlitt and *Coleridge despised his nightmare fantasy, but *Blake, a constant friend, wrote: 'The only man that e'er I knew | Who did not make me almost spew | was Fuseli.' The two artists admired each other and worked together: Blake engraved some of Fuseli's designs and Fuseli wrote the preface to Blake's edition of *Blair's *The Grave*. Mary *Wollstonecraft suffered from an obsessive passion for Fuseli.

FUST, Johann (d. 1467), German goldsmith. He financed *Gutenberg's experiments in printing, but the partnership between them was dissolved probably in 1455 and Fust carried on with his son-in-law Peter Schöffer. Their Latin Psalter of 1457 is the first to bear a printer's imprint and date. R. *Browning wrote a dialogue, 'Fust and his Friends' (in *Parleyings with certain People*).

Futhorc, the runic alphabet, named from its first six letters (th = þ, 'thorn'). (See RUNE.)

Futurism, a 20th-cent. avant-garde movement in Italian art, literature, and music, promoted by *Marinetti and others. Its programme, outlined in the *Futurist Manifesto* (1909), was to break with the past and its academic culture and to celebrate technology, dynamism, and power. In language and in poetry it advocated the destruction of traditional syntax, metre, and punctuation in the name of the 'free word'. The *Manifesto of Futurist painting* (1910), by Boccioni, Carrà, Balla, Russolo, and Severini, advocated a new art which represented nature in a dynamic state and in simultaneous movements. The movement petered out during the 1930s after Marinetti's incorporation into Fascist academic culture. (For Russian Futurism, see MAYAKOVSKY.)

G

GABORIAU, Émile (1832–73), French writer of crime fiction, considered to be the first practitioner in France of the *roman policier*. He created two famous characters, the professional detective Monsieur Lecoq and the amateur Le Père Tabaret. Gaboriau's best-known works are: *L'Affaire Lerouge* (1866), *Le crime d'Orcival* (1867), *Le Dossier No. 113* (1867), *Monsieur Lecoq* (1869), *Les Esclaves de Paris* (1869).

Gabriel, the name of one of the archangels (Dan. 9: 21 and Luke 1: 19, 26). Also in the Muslim religion one of the four principal angels. Milton makes him 'Chief of the angelic guards' (**Paradise Lost*, iv. 550).

GADBURY, John, see ALMANACS.

GADDA, Carlo Emilio (1893–1973), Italian novelist. His most important novels are *Il castello di Udine* (*The Castle of Udine*, 1934), a memoir of his experience in the Second World War; *Adalgisa* (1944), a critique of contemporary Milanese society; and the unfinished *Cognizione del dolore* (*The Cognizance of Sorrow*, 1963, written 1938–41). Also unfinished is *Quer pasticciaccio brutto de via Merulana* (*That dreadful mess on the Via Merulana*, 1957), which uses the conventions of the thriller to dissect Roman society under Fascism. That his two major works are incomplete is not accidental: in *Cognizione* the relationship between the protagonist and his mother is irresoluble, and *Pasticciaccio* stops short of revealing the murderer. His style is remarkable for its grotesquerie, its implicit use of European philosophy, and its pastiches of different languages and dialects.

Gadshill, near Rochester, the scene of Prince **Hal's joke robbery of *Falstaff in Shakespeare's *1 *Henry IV* (II. ii); confusingly, one of Falstaff's companions also has the name Gadshill. Gadshill was the home of **Dickens in his later years.

Gahagan, Major, see TREMENDOUS ADVENTURES OF MAJOR GAHAGAN, THE.

Gaheris, in **Malory, the fourth and youngest son of King Lot of Orkney and Arthur's sister Morgawse. He killed his mother when he found her in bed with Lamorak. He was accidentally killed by Launcelot, an event which led to the implacable hatred of his brother Gawain for Launcelot. Variant forms of his name are confusable with variants of Gareth (Gaheret) his brother, so the two may be archetypally identical.

GAIMAR, Geoffrei (*fl.* c.1140), author of *L'Estoire des Engleis,* an Anglo-Norman romance history in octosyllabic rhymed couplets covering the period from the Anglo-Saxon settlements to the death of William Rufus. An earlier section, beginning (like **Geoffrey of Monmouth's contemporary *History*) with the fall of Troy, has been lost, probably as a consequence of being replaced in the manuscripts by the more fashionable account by **Wace. It contains the Lincolnshire story of Havelok, corresponding to the Anglo-Norman *Le Lai d'Haveloc.* Gaimar was probably a secular clerk of Norman blood; his work has no great historical authority. His patron was Ralph FitzGilbert of Lincolnshire and Hampshire, areas in which Gaimar displays particular interest. See *L'Estoire des Engleis,* ed. A. Bell (Anglo-Norman Texts Soc., 1960); English trans. by T. D. Hardy and C. T. Martin (Rolls Series, 1888–9).

GAINSBOROUGH, Thomas (1727–88), British portrait and landscape painter; after training in London he returned to his native Suffolk (1748). He painted landscapes whose fresh, detailed naturalism is close to 17th-cent. Dutch pictures, and small portrait groups in landscape settings, of which the most famous is *Mr and Mrs Andrews* (c.1748, London, National Gallery). Gainsborough moved to Bath in 1759, where his style aspired to a new Van Dyckian elegance (*The Blue Boy,* c.1770) and his landscapes became broader and richer. From 1774 he worked in London. He became a fashionable portrait painter, and his varied landscapes included decorative rococo idylls, seascapes, and pictures of mountain grandeur—in 1783 he planned a visit to the Lakes 'to show you that your Grays and Dr Brownes were tawdry fan-Painters'. The 'fancy pictures', Arcadian rustic themes like the *Peasant Girl gathering sticks* (Fredericton, New Brunswick), with their sense of the purity and simplicity of the peasant's life, lead on to the sentiment of early **Romanticism. Gainsborough, in both style and temperament is quite unlike his rival **Reynolds, although Reynolds's *Fourteenth discourse* is the most brilliant appreciation of his art. Gainsborough's biographer and friend William Jackson wrote that he 'avoided the company of literary men, who were his aversion . . . he detested reading . . .' Yet

Jackson compared the style of Gainsborough's letters to that of *Sterne and the letters—spontaneous, vivid, and intimate—create a strong sense of character. See E. Waterhouse, *Gainsborough* (1958).

Gai saber, the title of a 13th-cent. society in Toulouse which devoted itself to a consideration and cultivation of the courtly troubadour idea of 'jois', 'exaltation'.

Galafron, or **Galaphron,** in *Orlando Innamorato* and *Orlando Furioso*, the king of Cathay and father of *Angelica.

Galahad (The Haute Prince), in *Malory, is (by enchantment) the son of *Launcelot and *Elaine, daughter of King *Pelles. He is predestined by his immaculate purity to achieve the Siege Perilous (see ROUND TABLE) and the *Grail, after the vision of which he dies in ecstasy.

Galehaut (or **Galehault**) of Surluse and the Long Isles, a highly significant character in the story of the love of Launcelot and Guinevere as described in the early 13th-cent. French prose 'Vulgate' cycle. He was a close friend of Launcelot who demanded tribute from Arthur; he first introduced the lovers but later became jealous of the queen's influence over Launcelot. He is most famous as the Galeotto in *Dante's reference to this story in the episode of Paolo and Francesca (*Inferno*, v. 137). *Malory wrongly calls him 'the Haute Prince' through a confusion with the similar name *Galahad. See J. Frappier, 'The Vulgate Cycle' in R. S. Loomis ed., *Arthurian Literature in the Middle Ages* (1959), p. 299.

GALEN (Claudius Galenus) (*c.* AD 129–99), perhaps the most influential of ancient physicians. He is reputed to have written some 500 treatises in Greek, a number of which have survived. Translated into Latin during the 11th and 12th cents, his writings dominated the development of medieval medicine, and in the 16th cent. he was greatly esteemed also as an exponent of scientific method. *Linacre translated six of his works and there are references to him in *Chaucer, F. *Bacon, and Sir T. *Browne.

Galeotti, Martius, in Scott's *Quentin Durward*, the astrologer of Louis XI.

Galeotto, see GALEHAUT.

GALIGNANI, Giovanni Antonio (1757–1821), with his English wife Anne Parsons, set up an English bookshop and circulating library in Paris *c.*1799, and in 1814 founded a newspaper, *Galignani's Messenger*, which had a wide circulation among English residents on the Continent. The paper was carried on by his sons, John Anthony (1796–1873) and William (1798–1882), who were born in London. As publishers in Paris they issued reprints of English books, and guides to Paris, Switzerland, etc. There is a bookshop of this name on the rue de Rivoli in Paris.

GALILEO GALILEI (1564–1642), Italian astronomer and physicist, was born at Pisa of a Florentine family. He made important discoveries (the isochronism of the pendulum, Jupiter's satellites, the libration of the moon) and experiments, proving, e.g., that unequal weights drop with equal velocity, by, it is said, making the experiment from the leaning tower of Pisa. His observations brought him into conflict with the Inquisition, and in 1633 he was compelled to repudiate the Copernican theory ('eppur si muove', he is said to have muttered after his recantation, 'all the same it [the earth] *does* move'), and was sent to prison. His principal works were the dialogues *Delle nuove scienze* and *Ai due massimi sistemi.* *Milton records his conversation with Galileo on his visit to Florence in *Areopagitica.*

Gallathea, a play by *Lyly.

Galliambic, the metre of the *Attis* of *Catullus, so called because it was the metre used by the Galli, or priests of Cybele, in their songs. It was imitated by *Tennyson in his 'Boadicea':

So the Queen Boädicéa, standing loftily charioted,
Brandishing in her hand a dart and rolling glances
lioness-like,
Yell'd and shriek'd between her daughters in her fierce
volubility.

GALSWORTHY, John (1867–1933), was educated at Harrow and New College, Oxford, and trained for the law. But a chance meeting with *Conrad, and the strong influence of his future wife, turned him to writing, in which career he was greatly assisted by a long association, beginning in 1900, with E. *Garnett. His first volume of stories, *From the Four Winds*, appeared in 1897 and in 1898 his first novel, *Jocelyn*, which he never republished. The first appearance of the Forsyte family was in one of the stories in *Man of Devon* (1901). In 1902 he married Ada, his cousin's wife, with whom he had been living for ten years. *The Island Pharisee* (1904), a novel revealing his abiding interest in the effects of poverty and the constraints of convention, was much praised and other novels followed including *Fraternity* (1909), which attacked the artificial veneer of urban life, and *The Dark Flower* (1913), about the creative and disruptive effects of love. The first of the Forsyte novels, *A Man of Property*, appeared in 1906, followed by *In Chancery* (1920) and *To Let* (1921) which, together with two interludes, appeared collectively as *The Forsyte Saga* in 1922. The second part of the Forsyte chronicles, containing *The White Monkey* (1924), *The Silver Spoon* (1926), *Swan Song* (1928), and the two interludes 'A Silent Wooing' and 'Passers By' was published as *A Modern Comedy* in 1929. In 1931 Galsworthy followed the immense success of the Forsyte books with a further collection of stories, *On Forsyte Change*.

Galsworthy began his playwriting career in 1906 with *The Silver Box*—a play about theft in which he employed a favourite device of 'parallel' families, one rich and one poor. This was the first of a long line of plays on social and moral themes. His reputation as a dramatist became firmly established with *Strife* (1909), an examination of men and managers in industry, which was followed by *Justice* (1910), in which a minor felon is ground down by the cruel majesty of the law; the play was part of Galsworthy's long campaign against the practice of solitary confinement, a campaign which strongly influenced the Home Office. His later plays include *The Skin Game* (1920), tracing the rivalry between a *nouveau-riche* manufacturer and an aristocrat; *Loyalties* (1922); and *Old English* (1924).

Posthumous publications included *Collected Poems* (1934) and in 1935 *The End of the Chapter*, consisting of *Maid in Waiting* (1931), *The Flowering Wilderness* (1932), and *Over the River* (1933), relating the family history of the Charwells, cousins of the younger Forsytes. Galsworthy received the *Nobel Prize for literature in 1932; he was already an OM, and received several honorary degrees and many other literary honours (but had refused a knighthood). Yet (although the Forsyte stories have had a history of continuing popularity) his work has never received high critical acclaim. His detached stance has tended to provoke the suspicion that some part of him respected the qualities he professed to satirize and that his satire lacked gall. There is a life by C. Dupré (1976).

GALT, John (1779–1839), born in Ayrshire, was employed for some time in the customs-house at Greenock. While travelling on the Continent he made the acquaintance of *Byron (of whom he published a life in 1830) and later of *Carlyle, who admired his work. From 1824 to 1827 he was secretary of the Canada Company, and between 1825 and 1829 he visited Canada as a member of a Government commission to evaluate the price of land, but these enterprises proved unprofitable and he returned to England to meet heavy debts and to make his living by his pen. Galt produced a good deal of miscellaneous writing, including poems, dramas, historical novels, and travel books, but is chiefly remembered for his studies of country life in Scotland: *The Ayrshire Legatees* (1821), *Annals of the Parish* (1821), *The Entail* (1823), *The Provost* (1822), and *The Member* (1832). The last two were reprinted in 1973 and 1975 respectively, edited by Ian A. Gordon, who also published *John Galt, The Life of a Writer* (1972).

Galt was not greatly admired in his own time, but he made a unique contribution to fiction with the subtlety and irony of his writing in the first person, and he was an acute observer of social change. He wished his most important fiction to be regarded not as 'novels' but as 'theoretical histories'.

Gama, King, the father of Princess Ida in Tennyson's *The Princess*.

GAMA, Vasco Da (*c*.1469–1524), the great Portuguese navigator, who was the first to double the Cape of Good Hope (1497) and to sail to India. He died at Cochin on 24 December. His exploits are celebrated in the *Lusiads* of *Camoëns.

Game and Playe of the Chesse, The, a translation by *Caxton from Vignay's French version of the *Liber de ludo scacchorum* of Jacobus de Cessolis, probably the second book printed at Caxton's press in Bruges, *c*.1475.

Game at Chesse, A, a comedy by T. *Middleton, produced 1624, when it successfully ran for nine nights at the Globe until suppressed by the authorities.

It deals allegorically with the rivalry of England and Spain (the White House and the Black House) and the project of the 'Spanish Marriage' (1623). It places on the stage the sovereigns of the two countries, Charles, prince of Wales, Buckingham, and the Spanish ambassador *Gondomar, and represents the discomfiture of the Black House. The play, reflecting the popular aversion to the Spanish match, was enthusiastically received, but gave great offence to the Spanish ambassador and to King James.

Gamelyn, *The Tale of*, a verse romance of the mid-14th cent. from the East Midlands, in 902 lines of long couplets. It is found in a number of manuscripts of *The Canterbury Tales*, usually assigned to the Cook, and it is possible that Chaucer did intend to write a version of it for use as the Cook's tale. It is included in *Skeat's *Chaucerian and Other Pieces*, appended as vol. 7 to his edition of Chaucer.

Gamelyn is the youngest of three brothers whose father leaves them his property in equal shares but whose eldest brother cheats him of his entitlement. Like Orlando in *As You Like It* (which is clearly related to it), Gamelyn overthrows the court wrestler and flees to the forest, from where he wages a campaign to recover his birthright, ultimately with success. The story also has striking affinities with the legends of *Robin Hood. It has been edited by D. B. Sands in *Middle English Verse Romances* (1966).

Gamesmanship, see POTTER, S. M.

Gamester, The, a comedy by J. *Shirley, acted 1633, printed 1637.

This was one of Shirley's most popular plays,

adapted (and sentimentalized) by C. *Johnson in 1712 as *The Wife's Relief* and by *Garrick in 1758 as *The Gamesters*. Its main plot is taken from the *Heptameron* of Marguerite of Navarre.

Wilding, the title character, tells his wife of his intention to make love to his ward, her relation Penelope, and makes an assignation with the girl. Mrs Wilding takes Penelope's place; Wilding, who has just lost heavily to his friend Hazard, sends him in his place as a way of paying his debt. Naturally, when husband and wife compare notes, he is appalled at the revelation of the double bed-trick. To save his honour and conceal his own cuckolding, he arranges for Hazard to marry Penelope; it then turns out that everyone's honour has been preserved anyway, so he has cheated himself twice. There is a romantic sub-plot, and a comic one featuring young Barnacle, a citizen's son who wants to learn the art of being a 'roaring boy'.

The Gamester is also the title of a play by Mrs *Centlivre and of a tragedy by E. *Moore.

Gammer Gurtons Nedle, the second English comedy in verse (the first being *Ralph Roister Doister*), published 1575, having been acted 1566, at Christ's College, Cambridge. Its authorship has been attributed either to J. Still, fellow of Christ's College, or to William Stevenson, a fellow of the College and one of its leading spirits in dramatic activities.

It is written in rhymed long doggerel, and deals farcically with the losing and finding of the needle used to mend the garments of Hodge, Gammer Gurton's man. The other characters, besides Hodge and the Gammer, are Tib and Cock, their maid and boy; Diccon the Bedlem; Dame Chatte and Doll, her maid; Master Baylye and his servant Scapethryft; Doctor Rat the curate; and Gyb the cat. The mischievous Diccon persuades the Gammer that Dame Chatte has taken the needle; a quarrel ensues and Doctor Rat is called in, but gets his head broken. Finally Hodge becomes acutely aware that the needle is in the seat of his breeches. The play includes the famous old drinking song with the refrain:

> Back and syde go bare, go bare,
> booth foote and hande go colde:
> But Bellye god sende thee good ale ynoughe,
> whether it be newe or olde.

Gamp, Sarah, a character in Dickens's *Martin Chuzzlewit*. Her large cotton umbrella has given rise to the expression 'a gamp' for an umbrella, especially an untidy one; also for a midwife.

Gandalin, in *Amadis of Gaul*, the son of a knight of Scotland and squire of Amadis. In *Don Quixote* (I. xx) the Don reminds Sancho that Gandalin 'always spoke to his master cap in hand, his head inclined and his body bent, in the Turkish fashion'.

Gandercleugh, the imaginary place of residence of Jedediah *Cleishbotham in Scott's *Tales of my Landlord*.

GANDHI, Mohandas Karamchand (1869–1948), was born in Rajkot, in western India, of Banya (merchant caste) parents. After studying law in England he practised in South Africa, where he devoted himself to the welfare of the Indian settlers and led them in passive resistance campaigns against discriminatory legislation. He returned to India in 1915 and quickly established his ascendancy over the Indian National Congress party, which he persuaded in 1920 to adopt a policy of non-violent non-co-operation to secure *swaraj* (independence) from Britain. He also devised tactics of civil disobedience, which involved the public breach of unpopular laws and the acceptance of the consequent penalties. These methods won much support for the nationalist movement, though they occasionally led to popular violence, much to his distress. He claimed that they were in harmony with Hindu doctrines of *ahimsa* (non-violence), and that they would have a moral effect both on those who practised them and on those against whom they were directed. He lived an austere life in an *ashram*, or religious community, devoted to truth, non-violence, chastity, and vegetarianism. In his search for spiritual development he was willing to learn from western writers like *Tolstoy and *Thoreau, as well as from the teachings of Hinduism and other religions—a pragmatic approach indicated by the title of his autobiography, *The Story of My Experiments with Truth*. The government soon found that imprisonment only added to his prestige as a *mahatma* (great soul) suffering for his ideals. The last months of his life were saddened by the partition of the subcontinent and the communal violence that followed. His pleas for tolerance towards Muslims living in India aroused hostility among certain fanatical groups, and in Jan. 1948 he was assassinated by a Hindu extremist.

Ganelon, or **Gano,** in the *Charlemagne romances and the *Morgante maggiori* of *Pulci, the count of Mayence, the villain and traitor who schemes for the defeat of the rearguard at Roncesvalles (see ROLAND). He figures among the traitors in *Dante's *Inferno* (xxxii. 122) and in *Chaucer's 'Nun's Priest's Tale' (see CANTERBURY TALES, 20).

Ganlesse, in Scott's *Peveril of the Peak*, a name taken by Edward Christian.

Gann, Mr, Mrs, and Caroline, characters in Thackeray's *A Shabby Genteel Story*.

GARAMOND, Claude (d. 1561), French typefounder, noted for his elegant roman types, inspired by one cut for *Aldus in 1495, and for his 'Grecs du roi', the Greek type he cut for François I for use by R. *Estienne, the king's printer.

GARCÍA LORCA, Federico (1898–1936), Spanish poet and dramatist, also gifted as a painter and pianist, born in Andalusia, and educated (although without much academic commitment on his part) at the universities of Granada and Madrid. In Madrid he at once became deeply involved in literary and artistic life; his first volume of poems, *Libro de poemas* (1921), was followed by others, including his extremely popular collection of gypsy ballads, *Romancero gitano* (1928). A reaction against the label of 'poet of the gypsies' took him to New York in 1929; his response is expressed in his collection of surreal poems (some of which appeared earlier in *Ortega y Gasset's Revista de Occidente*), *Poeta en Nueva York* (1940). On his return to Spain in 1930 he increasingly turned his attention to the theatre, setting up a government-sponsored travelling company with which he visited remote villages, playing classic works and new plays for peasant audiences. His own plays include the lyrical, intense, poetic tragedies *Bodas de sangre* (*Blood Wedding*, perf. 1933); *Yerma* (perf. 1934), and *La casa de Bernarda Alba* (*The House of Bernarda Alba*, perf. and pub. posthumously, 1945). He also wrote several comedies and tragi-comedies but is best known in England for his evocation of the profound and primitive passions of Spanish peasant life. He continued to write poetry: one of the finest of his later works is his elegy for his friend, a bullfighter, *Llanto per la muerte de Ignacio Sánchez Mejías* (1934). Lorca was murdered by Nationalist partisans in July 1936, shortly after the outbreak of Civil War. His body was never found.

GARCÍA MÁRQUEZ, Gabriel (1928–), Colombian novelist, born in Aracataca, and educated at a Jesuit college in Bogotá. He became a journalist at the age of eighteen, came to Europe in 1954 for the liberal *El Heraldo*, and began to write novels during this period. His works include *La hojarasca* (1955, English trans. as *Leaf Storm*, 1972), a novella which introduces the village of Macondo, the setting for his most famous novel *Cien años de soledad* (1967; *A Hundred Years of Solitude*, 1970). This is an account of small, remote, decaying Macondo, seen through the eyes of seven generations of the much intermarried and incestuous Buendía family; a classic work of *Magic Realism, it mingles the ordinary and the miraculous, the semi-supernatural and the concrete detail, in a kaleidoscopic survey in which time, numbers, repetition, superstitions, magic, and natural phenomena are all charged with a curiously heightened power and colour. García Márquez's other works include *La mala hora* (1968; *In Evil Hour*, 1980), *Le otoño del patriarca* (1975; *The Autumn of the Patriarch*, 1977), and various collections of short stories. He was awarded the *Nobel Prize for literature in 1982.

GARCILASO DE LA VEGA (?1501–36), Spanish poet and friend of *Boscán; the names of the two poets are coupled in Byron's *Don Juan* (i. 95). With Boscán he brought about the renaissance of poetry in Spain, writing in his short and active life (he was a soldier in the armies of Charles V and was killed in battle) sonnets, eclogues, and odes, which won the praise of Cervantes (*Don Quixote*, II. lviii).

'Garden, The', a poem by *Marvell.

Garden of Cyrus, The, by Sir T. *Browne, the companion piece to *Hydriotaphia, published 1658, treats of the occurrence of the quincunx (:.:) or lozenge and the number five in man-made objects, primarily the plantations of the ancients, and then their buildings, other artefacts, and customs, in plants, in animals, and in traditional philosophy and theology. He chooses his 'bye and barren theme' partly to please the dedicatee, an ardent horticulturist, partly because 'Paradise succeeds the Grave'. By intertwining many heterogeneous observations he playfully demonstrates his ability to elaborate and digress.

Gardiner, Colonel James, a character in Scott's *Waverley. For the original of the character see DODDRIDGE. He was also commemorated in a song by Sir Gilbert Elliot (1722–77).

GARDINER, Samuel Rawson (1829–1902), educated at Winchester and Christ Church, Oxford. He settled in London to study the history of the Puritan revolution, supporting himself meanwhile by teaching. In 1872 he became lecturer and subsequently professor of modern history at King's College, London. He was elected a fellow of All Souls in 1884, and of Merton in 1892. As Ford lecturer in 1896 he lectured on 'Cromwell's place in history'. The first instalment of his great *History* of the first Stuarts and Cromwell appeared in 1863; successive instalments followed, and in 1883–4 appeared a second edition of all these, entitled a *History of England from the Accession of James I to the Outbreak of the Civil War, 1603–42. The History of the Great Civil War* (1886–91) and the *History of the Commonwealth and Protectorate* (1894–1901) carried the record down to the year 1656 (an additional chapter was published posthumously). Gardiner's historical writing shows minute accuracy and impartiality, but is, perhaps necessarily, lacking in picturesque quality. He was very proud of his descent from Bridget, daughter of Oliver Cromwell and wife of Henry Ireton.

GARDNER, Dame Helen Louise (1908–), scholar and critic, educated at North London Collegiate School and St Hilda's College, Oxford. Her works include an important edition of *The Divine Poems of John Donne* (1952, 2nd edn 1978), other editions of the *Metaphysical poets, and a revealing study of T. S. *Eliot's work, *The Composition of Four Quartets* (1978). She also edited *The Faber Book of Religious Verse* (1972) and *The New Oxford Book of English Verse 1250–1950* (1972).

'Gareth and Lynette', one of Tennyson's *Idylls of the King*, published 1872. It describes Gareth's disguise as a scullion at court, and his winning of Lynette through his rescue of her besieged sister Lyonors.

Gareth of Orkney (or **Gaheret**), Sir, the third son of King Lot of Orkney and Arthur's sister Morgawse who, on his arrival at Camelot, is made to work in the kitchen and nicknamed by Kay 'Beaumains'. The fourth of *Malory's eight Works* as edited by Vinaver is named *Sir Gareth of Orkney* and the book (VII in *Caxton) is largely concerned with his rescue of the lady Lyonesse from Ironsyde and his being brought there by the haughty Lynette. Malory's exact source for this book is not known. See GARETH AND LYNETTE.

Gargantua, *Pantagruel*, etc., by F. *Rabelais, the first two volumes published under the pseudonym Alcofribas Nasier.
   Gargantua (1534) introduces Pantagruel's father: his birth, early education, and attendance at the University of Paris, his successful defence of the paternal territories against military invasion, his foundation of a commemorative abbey. The book evokes the province of Rabelais' birth, parodies and criticizes various kinds of education, attacks aggressive war, commends the virtues of the *vita activa*, and defines ecclesiastical and communal ideals (the abbey of Thélème).
   Pantagruel (1532 or 1533), the first of the sequence to be written, celebrates the prodigious strength and appetite of a popular giant. It describes his fantastic birth and childhood, his tour of the French universities, his experience of Paris, his employment of the rascally Panurge, and his military exploits in the remote Utopia. These events become opportunities for parading Renaissance exuberance, burlesquing medieval learning and literature, mocking classical and ecclesiastical authority, and affirming humanist values.
   The *Tiers Livre* (1546) turns Pantagruel into a sensible and humorous prince and Panurge into a voluble buffoon. The action centres on a variety of attempts by the latter, who is now the spendthrift governor of an independent province, to discover whether he should marry. This produces a highly inventive, anti-feminist contribution to a current debate on women and marriage. The *Quart Livre* (ch. 1–11, 1548, the remainder 1552) relates Pantagruel's journey to the oracle of the 'Dive Bouteille' (or 'divine bottle') in Cathay in quest of a solution for Panurge's dilemma. Drawing on narratives of voyages to the North-West Passage and on the satirical possibilities of travel literature in general, it mocks a whole variety of contemporary abuses, including the worship of Rome and the greed and idleness of monks. The *Cinquième Livre* (published posthumously, ch. 1–16 as *L'Isle Sonnante*, 1562, the whole 1564), conducts the travellers to their destination. This book, the authenticity of which has been questioned, shows evidence of decline, the satire of the administration of justice never rising above crudity and the material of the second part consisting for the most part of mere translations and imitations.

Gargery, Joe, a character in Dickens's *Great Expectations*.

GARIOCH, Robert, the pen-name of Robert Garioch Sutherland (1909–81), Scottish poet, born and educated in Edinburgh, who worked for many years in England as a schoolmaster. He is known principally for his witty and satiric poems in *Scots. His first volume, published in 1940 in collaboration with S. *Maclean (*17 poems for 6d. In Gaelic, Lowland Scots and English*) was followed by several other volumes, including *The Masque of Edinburgh* (1954), and his *Collected Poems* appeared in 1977. He also translated into Scots *Pindar, G. *Buchanan, Belli, *Apollinaire, and others. *Two Men and a blanket* (1975) is a prose work describing his experiences as a prisoner of war in Italy and Germany. His *Complete Poetical Works*, ed. R. Fulton, was published in 1983.

Garland, (1) Mr and Mrs, characters in Dickens's *The Old Curiosity Shop*; (2) Anne, a character in Hardy's *The Trumpet Major*.

GARNER, Alan, see CHILDREN'S LITERATURE.

GARNETT, Constance (1862–1946), wife of E. *Garnett, educated at Newnham College, Cambridge, began to study Russian while awaiting the birth of her son David (below), and became a distinguished translator, responsible for introducing many of the great Russian classics to English readers. She translated *Turgenev, *Tolstoy, *Dostoevsky, *Chekhov, *Gogol, and *Herzen, and although her versions have in many cases been superseded (and criticized in some quarters as banal or prudish) they had enormous impact and influence in their day; K. *Mansfield wrote to her in 1921 that 'the younger generation owe you more than we ourselves are able to realise. These books have changed our lives, no less.'

GARNETT, David (1892–1981), novelist and critic, son of E. and C. *Garnett, and friend and associate of the *Bloomsbury Group. He studied botany for some years at the Royal College of Science, was a conscientious objector and farm labourer during the First World War, then opened a bookshop in Soho in association with Francis Birrell, son of A. *Birrell. His first short novel, *Lady into Fox* (1922), an enigmatic fable about a young wife transformed into a vixen, had a considerable success, and was followed by another fable, *A man in the zoo* (1924), about a thwarted lover who donates himself as a specimen of *homo sapiens* for exhibition in the zoo. *The sailor's return* (1925) describes the conflict between a sailor and his black African wife and the Dorset villagers among whom they settle. Other works include a biography, *Pocahontas: or the nonpareil of Virginia* (1933), the semifictional *Beany-eye* (1935), and three volumes of autobiography, *The Golden Echo* (1953), *The Flowers of the Forest* (1955), and *The Familiar Faces* (1962). Garnett also edited the letters of T. E. *Lawrence (1938), the novels of *Peacock (1948), and his own correspondence with T. H. *White (1968). His early works were memorably illustrated by his first wife, Rachel Alice ('Ray' Marshall, d. 1940). His second wife, Angelica, was the daughter of V. *Bell.

GARNETT, Edward (1868–1936), son of R. *Garnett and husband of C. *Garnett, published several volumes, including novels, plays, and critical works, but is chiefly remembered as publisher's reader for several successive firms, the last of which was Jonathan Cape. In this role he encouraged and advised many of the most important writers of the period, amongst them *Conrad, D. H. *Lawrence, D. *Richardson, E. M. *Forster, and W. H. *Hudson.

GARNETT, Richard (1835–1906), was the son of Richard Garnett (1789–1850), linguist, philologist, and from 1838 assistant keeper of printed books at the British Museum. The younger Richard also worked at the British Museum, where his erudition became legendary; he was superintendent of the Reading Room from 1875, a post from which he resigned in 1884 to become chief editor of the library's first printed catalogue. He published several volumes of original and translated verse, several biographies, and edited many works, including *Relics of Shelley* (1862). He is best remembered as a writer for his collection of pagan tales, *The Twilight of the Gods* (1888), some of which originally appeared in *The Yellow Book. See also GARNETT, E.

Garraway's, a celebrated coffee-house in Change Alley, Cornhill, founded by one Thomas Garway, a tea, coffee, and tobacco merchant, in the 17th cent. It was a meeting-place of dealers in stocks and shares, notably in the days of the *South Sea Company and contained an auction-room (referred to in *The Tatler, No. 147). It is mentioned in the works of *Addison, *Pope, *Swift, and *Gay: see e.g. Swift's 'Ballad on the South Sea Scheme'.

GARRICK, David (1717–79), of Huguenot descent, was born in Hereford, the son of a recruiting officer, and educated in Lichfield, where

he became a pupil of Dr *Johnson at Edial. He accompanied Johnson to London, and set up briefly with his brother in the wine trade before turning to the stage. His mythological burlesque *Lethe* was performed at Drury Lane in 1740, and in 1741 he appeared as an actor at Ipswich in Southerne's *Oroonoko. Later that year he made his London début as Richard III at Goodman's Fields, with great success, and subsequently proved his versatility by many successes in both comic and tragic parts, ranging from Abel Drugger and Sir John Brute to Lear (in the version by Nahum *Tate). He wrote a number of lively farces, including *The Lying Valet* (1741), *Miss in her Teens* (1747), *A Peep behind the Curtain* (1767), and *Bon Ton, or High Life above Stairs* (1775), and collaborated with *Colman in writing *The Clandestine Marriage (1766). He also wrote many prologues and epilogues. In 1747 he joined Lacy in the management of Drury Lane, where he produced many of Shakespeare's dramas; he made his last appearance in 1776, when he sold his share of the patent to *Sheridan and two others for £35,000. In 1773 he was elected a member of Johnson's *Club; his interesting correspondence with many of the most distinguished men of his day was published in 1831–2 and in a greatly enlarged collection, edited by D. M. Little and G. M. Kahrl, in 1963. Garrick's fame as an actor was unsurpassed, and there are many contemporary tributes and descriptions, including those by *Boswell, *Lichtenberg, F. *Burney, H. *More, and *Burke. He was also painted by many of his celebrated contemporaries, including *Reynolds, *Hogarth, *Gainsborough, and Zoffany. A life by T. *Davies appeared in 1780, shortly after Garrick's sudden death, and another in 1801 by A. *Murphy. His widow, the dancer Eva-Maria Violetti, long outlived him, dying in 1822; they were childless. There is a critical biography (1979) by G. W. Stone.

Garrick Club, founded in 1831 as a club in which 'actors and men of education and refinement might meet on equal terms'. Its original premises were at 35 King Street. *Barham, *D'Orsay, and S. *Rogers were among its first members. It was much frequented by *Thackeray, and possesses a famous collection of portraits of actors and actresses and theatrical memorabilia.

Garsington Manor, the Oxfordshire home of Ottoline *Morrell from 1915 to 1927, where she and her husband entertained many distinguished guests from the political and artistic worlds.

GARTH, Sir Samuel (1661–1719), a physician, free-thinker, and member of the *Kit-Cat club, is remembered as the author of *The Dispensary* (1699), a burlesque poem in which he ridiculed the opposition of apothecaries to the supply of medicines to out-patients' dispensaries. He also wrote a prospect poem, *Claremont* (1715), in the vein of his friend Pope's *Windsor Forest*. *Pope described him as 'the best good Christian without knowing it'. See TOPO-GRAPHICAL POETRY.

GASCOIGNE, George (*c.*1534–77), soldier and poet, came from a good Bedfordshire family. He was educated at Trinity College, Cambridge, entered Gray's Inn in 1555, and spent more than ten years there. In 1561 his marriage to the already-married Elizabeth Boyes, mother of the poet N. *Breton, initiated a series of legal and financial difficulties, culminating in a spell in debtors' gaol in Bedford in 1570. From 1572 to 1574 he was a soldier in the Netherlands, spending four months as a prisoner of the Spanish. His poems and plays were published during his absence, supposedly without his authority, as *A Hundreth Sundrie Flowres* (1573); on his return he brought out a corrected and augmented edition under the title of *The Posies of George Gascoigne*. In the last two years of his life he achieved some success as a court poet.

Many of Gascoigne's works were contained in *The Posies*: a variety of secular and devotional verse, including 'The delectable history of Dan Bartholmew of Bathe'; a verse account of his adventures in the Netherlands, 'The fruites of Warre', dedicated to Lord Grey de Wilton; two plays written for performance at Gray's Inn in 1566, *Supposes, a prose comedy based on *Ariosto's *I Suppositi*, and *Jocasta*, a blank verse tragedy supposedly based on *Euripides but actually translated from Lodovico Dolce; a strange Chaucerian novella, *The Adventures of Master *F.J.*, whose Italian source, if it existed, has never been found; and *Certayne notes of Instruction concerning the making of verse or ryme in English*, a pithy but pioneering account of English versification. Gascoigne's other works include *The Glasse of Governement. A tragicall Comedie* (1575), *The Droomme of Doomes day* (1576), and *The Steele Glas. A Satyre* (1576). His posthumously published *Tale of Hemetes the Heremyte* had been written for Queen Elizabeth's entertainment at Woodstock in 1575. Gascoigne's achievement has been overshadowed by the later Elizabethan poets who were to tread hard on his heels, such as *Spenser, *Marlowe, and *Sidney, but he was an innovator in a wide variety of literary forms. His novel of sexual intrigue *The Adventures of Master F.J.* is the only one of his works to have commanded much interest in the 20th cent. His works were edited by J. W. Cunliffe (1907–10), and there is a book on him by C. T. Prouty (1942).

GASCOIGNE, Sir William (?1350–1419), appointed lord chief justice of the king's bench in 1400 by Henry IV, he figures in that capacity in Shakespeare's *Henry IV*. Shakespeare follows *Holinshed's apparently apocryphal story (told in *Elyot's *Governour*) that Prince Hal struck Gascoigne when he was chief justice for attempting to arrest one of the prince's unruly followers, whereupon Gascoigne arrested the prince himself. Hal, when Henry V, praises Gascoigne when confirming him in office for this fearless and even-handed administration of justice. See *1 Henry IV*, III. ii. 32–33 and *2 Henry IV*, v. ii. 65ff.

GASCOYNE, David (1916–), poet, published his first volume, *Roman Balcony* (1932), when only 16, and in 1935 *A Short Survey of Surrealism*, which established him as a champion of *surrealism and a writer unusually aware of European literature. He translated many of the French surrealists, and his own work shows the influence of and pays tribute to artists and writers such as Max Ernst, Magritte, *Éluard, *Apollinaire, Tzara, and Djuna *Barnes. His work includes *Man's Life is His Meat* (1936), *Hölderlin's Madness* (1938), *Poems 1937–1942* (1943, illustrated by Graham Sutherland), and *Night Thoughts*, a long poem commissioned by the BBC, broadcast 1955, published 1956.

Gashford, a character in Dickens's *Barnaby Rudge*.

GASKELL, Mrs Elizabeth Cleghorn (1810–65), daughter of William Stevenson, a Unitarian minister and later a treasury official and journalist, was brought up by her aunt in Knutsford, Cheshire (the original of 'Cranford' and of 'Hollingford' in *Wives and Daughters*). In 1932 she married William Gaskell, minister at the Cross Street Unitarian Chapel in Manchester; they had four daughters and a son who died in infancy. As a distraction from her sorrow at his death she wrote her first novel, *Mary Barton* (1848). It won the attention of *Dickens, at whose invitation most of her work was first published in *Household Words* and *All the Year Round*. Her other full-length novels were *Cranford* (1853), *Ruth* (1853), *North and South* (1855), *Sylvia's Lovers* (1863), and *Wives and Daughters* (1866), which was left unfinished when Mrs Gaskell died suddenly of heart failure at the Hampshire house she had just bought for her husband's retirement. She also wrote the first and most celebrated biography of C. *Brontë—which caused a furore because it contained some allegedly libellous statements which had to be withdrawn—and many vivid and warm-hearted short stories and novellas, of which the finest was *Cousin Phyllis* (1864).

Mrs Gaskell was an active humanitarian and the message of several of her novels was the need for social reconciliation, for better understanding between employers and workers, between the respectable and the outcasts of society. She was a keen observer of human behaviour and speech, among both industrial workers in

Manchester and farming and country-town communities, and a careful researcher of the background and technicalities of her novels. She had a natural gift for story-telling, although she was at first rather uncertain in plot creation and given to melodramatic devices. She was a beautiful and much-liked woman, at ease in any company and a devoted wife and mother, with many friends who included (besides Charlotte Brontë) *Ruskin, *Milnes, the *Carlyles, *Kingsley, C. E. *Norton, the Howitts, Mme Mohl, and Florence Nightingale. Her relations with Dickens were chiefly professional, as their characters were not congenial: on one occasion, exasperated by her waywardness as a contributor, he exclaimed to his sub-editor: 'If I were Mr G. Oh Heaven how I would beat her!' Her contemporaries classed her as a novelist with the Brontës and G. *Eliot, but although Cranford has always remained a favourite with the general reader her other novels were underrated in critical esteem for a full century after her death. See Winifred Gérin, Elizabeth Gaskell (1976).

GATTO, Alfonso (1909–76), Italian poet, Communist, and Resistance fighter. Like many other writers of his generation he left the Party shortly after the Second World War. His poetry is highly lyrical, condensing hermetic symbolism with autobiographical, political, and social motifs. His best poems are in Isola (Island, 1930), Il capo sulla neve (Head down on the snow, 1949; first published clandestinely); his Resistance poems Storia delle vittime (History of victims, 1960); and Poesie d'amore (Love poems, 1973).

GAUDEN, Dr J., see EIKON BASILIKE.

GAUDIER-BRZESKA, Henri (1891–1915), French sculptor and draughtsman, who came to London in 1910, where he became associated with the most avant-garde artists and writers. His most brilliantly accomplished works are his pen and pencil line drawings, some of which were published in *Rhythm. Gaudier, with W. *Lewis and *Pound, founded the Vorticist group in 1914 (see VORTICISM), and contributed a Vorticist history of sculpture to Blast No. 1 which exalts the energy and intensity of primitive art and condemns the ideals of the Greeks and the Renaissance. In 1914 Gaudier enlisted in the French army and he was killed in action. In 1916 Pound's Gaudier-Brzeska: A Memoir republished several of his writings. Pound stressed that Gaudier had given him 'a new sense of form' and of 'planes in relation': Gaudier's immense marble head of Pound is on loan to the Tate Gallery, London, which also houses his celebrated Red Stone Dancer.

GAUNT, John of, see JOHN OF GAUNT.

Gautier, Marguerite, heroine of La Dame aux camélias by A. *Dumas fils.

GAUTIER, Théophile (1811–72), French poet, novelist, critic, and journalist. He was an admirer of *Hugo, and played a prominent role in the Romantic movement in the 1830s (his Histoire du romantisme appeared in 1874). He was closely associated with the doctrine of l'art pour l'art (*'art for art's sake'), expounded in the preface to his novel Mademoiselle de Maupin (1835). His best-known collection of poems is Émaux et camées (1852), which exercised considerable influence on the *Parnassians. He had a long career in journalism, and wrote widely on travel, art, ballet, and the theatre.

Gavroche, a character in Les Misérables by V. *Hugo, whose name has been adopted as typifying the Parisian street-arab.

Gawain (Walwain), the eldest of the four sons of King Lot of Orkney and Arthur's sister Morgawse. His wife, in some stories, was Dame Ragnell and their son was Ginglain, the Fair Unknown (*Libeaus Desconsus); he also had two natural sons. In the Arthurian legends he is prominent from the first 12th-cent. stories in which he is the leading knight, courageous, pure, and courteous. In later versions his excellence was surpassed by that of Launcelot and his character becomes harsher, more ruthless, and often philandering. In *Geoffrey of Monmouth he is Arthur's ambassador to Rome; in *Malory he becomes at the end the bitter enemy of Launcelot who has accidentally killed Gawain's beloved youngest brother Gaheris and who also killed Gareth (who tries to avenge Gaheris) and Agravain, the witness and betrayer of the affair between Launcelot and Guinevere. Gawain is killed when Arthur lands at Dover before the final battle with Mordred. He is related to Gwalchmei, the sun-god of Welsh mythology, and elements of this relation surface in many stories about Gawain (possibly including the most admired, Sir *Gawain and the Green Knight: see essay by John Speirs in Medieval English Poetry, 1957); in Malory too there is allusion to Gawain's strength waxing and waning with the sun (see R. S. Loomis, Arthurian Tradition and Chrétien de Troyes, 1949, pp. 146–55). The most celebrated single adventure of Gawain is the one described in Sir Gawain and the Green Knight. In Malory his characterization varies according to the source being followed; for example his status is not very high in The Book of Sir Tristram de Lyones (the fourth of the eight Works in Vinaver), but he is great again in the eighth, the Morte Arthur Saunz Guerdon.

J. L. Weston, The Legend of Sir Gawain (1897); B. J. Whiting, 'Gawain: his reputation, his courtesy and his appearance in Chaucer's Squire's Tale' (Medieval Studies 9, 1947); The Wedding of Sir Gawain and Dame Ragnell (15th-cent. East Midland) and Sir Gawain and the Carl of Carlisle (late 15th-cent. Northern), ed. in

D. B. Sands, *Middle English Verse Romances* (1966).

Gawain and the Green Knight, Sir, a greatly admired alliterative poem from the north-west midlands, dating from the second half of the 14th cent. (some authorities date it around 1375), the only manuscript of which is the famous Cotton Nero A x which is also the sole manuscript of **Pearl*, **Patience*, and **Cleanness*. The poem is in 2,530 lines in long-lined alliterative stanzas of varying length, each ending with a **'bob and wheel'*. Most modern critics regard the four poems in the manuscript as the work of a single poet; but as far as the interpretation of this poem is concerned, the question of single authorship is largely irrelevant, so different is its subject from the three doctrinal pieces.

The story of the poem is as follows (under the headings of its four 'fitts', narrative divisions). *Fitt 1*: Arthur and his court are seated at a New Year's feast in Camelot waiting for a marvel when a huge green man enters, bearing an axe and a holly bough. He challenges a knight to cut his head off on condition that the knight agrees to have his head cut off a year hence. Gawain accepts the challenge and cuts the green knight's head off; the knight picks it up and rides away. *Fitt 2*: A year later Gawain sets off to keep his side of the bargain. After riding through grim landscapes in wintry weather, on Christmas Eve Gawain comes upon a beautiful castle where he is graciously received. The lord of the castle makes an agreement with Gawain that each day he himself will hunt in the fields and Gawain in the castle; at the end of the day they will exchange spoils. *Fitt 3*: For three consecutive days, the lord hunts and Gawain, famous for his skill and prowess in love, is amorously approached by the beautiful lady of the castle, who gives him one kiss on the first day, two on the second, and on the third day three kisses and a girdle which has magic properties that will save his life. Each evening Gawain exchanges the kisses with his host for the animals slain in the hunt; but on the third evening he keeps the girdle (thus breaking his bargain), to protect him in the imminent meeting with the green knight. *Fitt 4*: Gawain is directed to the green knight's chapel where he kneels to receive his blow. Twice the knight feints at him, and the third time he makes a slight cut in Gawain's neck. Then he explains that he is the knight of the castle in a different form, and that the cut in the neck was sustained because of Gawain's infidelity in keeping the girdle. Gawain bitterly curses his failing and the snares of women; but the green knight applauds him and, on Gawain's return to Arthur's court, they declare that they will all wear a green girdle in honour of his achievement. The poem may be connected with the founding of the Order of the Garter. The elegance of the construction of the narrative, as well as the vivid language of the poem, are universally admired, and this is agreed to be one of the greatest poems in Middle English. Interpretation of its somewhat enigmatic *raison d'être* has been more varying; Speirs stressed its connection with some unexpressed archetypal story of seasons and vegetation; John Burrow concentrates on the moral seriousness underlying its colourful romantic exterior; modern critics, such as E. Wilson, see it in relation to the other Christian poems in the manuscript.

Ed. J. R. R. **Tolkien*, E. V. Gordon, and N. Davis (2nd edn, 1967); J. A. Burrow, *A Reading of Sir Gawain and the Green Knight* (1965); J. Speirs, *Medieval English Poetry* (1957), pp. 215–51; A. C. Spearing, *The Gawain Poet* (1970), ch. 5; E. Wilson, *The Gawain-Poet* (1976); W. R. J. Barron, *Trawthe and Treason* (1980); D. R. Howard and C. K. Zacher ed. *Critical Studies of Sir Gawain and the Green Knight* (1968).

GAY, John (1685–1732), born at Barnstaple, was apprenticed for a time to a London mercer. In 1708 he published a burlesque poem, *Wine*, and in 1713 *Rural Sports*, on the model of his friend Pope's **Windsor Forest*, and *The Fan*, which is in the mock-heroic style of **The Rape of the Lock*. **The Shepherd's Week* (1714) was the first poem to show his real ability. His first play, *The What d'ye Call it*, a satirical farce, was produced in 1715, and **Trivia* appeared in 1716. With **Pope* and **Arbuthnot* he wrote a comedy, *Three Hours after Marriage*, which was acted in 1717. He speculated disastrously in **South Sea* funds with the proceeds of his *Poems* (1720) and his hopes of advancement under the new king were disappointed; he was intermittently helped in his early career by various patrons, and eventually became an inmate of the household of the duke of Queensberry, who was to be his literary executor. The first series of his popular *Fables* appeared in 1727, but real success came in 1728 with **The Beggar's Opera* and its sequel **Polly*, which was banned from the stage but earned a considerable sum on publication in 1729. These two plays contain many of Gay's best-known ballads, but 'Sweet William's Farewell to Black-Eyed Susan' was published in *Poems* (1720) and 'Twas when the seas were roaring' is from his first play. He also wrote, c.1718, the librettos of **Handel's Acis and Galatea* (pub. 1732) and *Achilles*, an opera produced at Covent Garden in 1733. His poem in *ottava rima*, 'Mr Pope's Welcome from Greece', first published in 1776, was written to celebrate his friend's finishing his translation of *The Iliad*; it gives a vivid picture of the members of the **Scriblerus Club* (Pope, **Swift*, Arbuthnot, and **Parnell*) and of many other contemporary figures. Gay was a genial and much-loved man, but his health appears to have been undermined by financial anxieties and he died of an old intestinal disorder; he was buried in Westminster Abbey, accompanied by his own epitaph:

Life is a jest, and all things show it;
I thought so once, and now I know it.

The duke of Queensberry attended to various posthumous publications, including the second series of *Fables* (1738). Gay's *Poetry and Prose*, ed. V. A. Dearing and C. E. Beckwith, was published in 2 vols (1974).

Gay, Walter, a character in Dickens's *Dombey and Son.*

Gayferos, Don, in Spanish romance, a kinsman of *Roland and husband of Charlemagne's daughter Melisenda, who is carried off by the Moors and rescued by Gayferos. In *Don Quixote* (II. xxvi) the story is the subject of a puppet play.

Gazette, from It. *gazzetta*, apparently so called from the coin of that name, which may have been the sum paid either for the paper itself or for the privilege of reading it [*OED*]. The *gazzetta* was a news-sheet first published in Venice about the middle of the 16th cent., and similar news-sheets (see CORANTO, and NEWSPAPERS, ORIGINS OF) appeared in England from the 17th cent., giving news from foreign parts.

Gazetteer, a geographical index or dictionary. A work of this kind by L. Echard (2nd edn, 1693) bore the title *The Gazetteer's or Newsman's Interpreter; Being a Geographical Index*, intended for the use of 'gazetteers' or journalists.

Gebir, an epic poem by W. S. *Landor in seven books, published 1798.

Gebir, an Iberian prince, invades Egypt, but his conquest is arrested by his love for its young queen Charoba. Because of treachery by the queen's nurse Dalica, he is slain during the marriage feast, and the city that he is founding is destroyed by magic. Tamat, his shepherd-brother, who hopes to win the love of a sea-nymph, is carried away by her beyond the world of mortals. Parts of the poem were first written in Latin, and the author subsequently published a Latin version, *Gebirus.*

GEDDES, Alexander (1737–1802), Catholic priest, linguist, and biblical scholar, wrote a 'Dissertation on the Scoto-Saxon Dialect' which appeared in the *Transactions of the Society of Antiquaries of Scotland* (1792), in which he discusses the theory and practice of the *Scots language, and complains of the new vogue for introducing 'low words and trite proverbial phrases' instead of seeking the 'genuine Scottish idiom'.

Gellatley, Davie, in Scott's *Waverley*, the 'innocent' dependant of the Baron Bradwardine, in whose mouth the author places some of his finest lyrics.

GELLIUS, Aulus (2nd cent. AD), Roman man of letters, the author of a miscellany, *Noctes Atticae*, which contains extracts from many authors, anecdotes, and short discussions on a variety of topics. Twelve of the stories in Painter's *Palace of Pleasure* are taken from Gellius.

Gem, The, (1) a literary annual, edited by T. *Hood, 1829–32; (2) a weekly paper for boys, largely written by C. *Hamilton under the pen-name Martin Clifford, 1907–39.

General, Mrs, in Dickens's *Little Dorrit*, the lady companion to Mr Dorrit's daughters, and inventor of the formula 'prunes and prism'.

Generydes, a late Middle English romance surviving in two forms: 10,000 short rhyming lines and 7,000 lines of rhyme-royal, perhaps from the first part of the 15th cent. It tells of the love of Generydes and Clarionas who, after his exile, cures and marries him.

Genesis, meaning 'origin', 'creation', is the first in order of the books of the Bible, containing the account of the creation of the world. The name was given to it by the Greek translators.

Genesis, an Old English poem of 2,396 lines in the *Junius manuscript and previously attributed hypothetically to *Caedmon. Lines 235–851 are an interpolated section (usually called 'Genesis B') translated from a continental Saxon original which deals in a dramatic and vivid manner with the Fall of the Angels (the title of this excerpt in Sweet's *Anglo-Saxon Reader*). It has often been suggested that this section may have been the Old English poem on the subject that *Milton knew and that it may therefore have been a seminal influence on *Paradise Lost*. There are also some echoes of it in the early poems of *Auden. Ed. ASPR 1 (1931); see also *The Later Genesis*, ed. B. J. Timmer (1948).

Genesis and Exodus, a Middle English poem in just over 4,000 lines of rhyming couplets, written about the middle of the 13th cent. in Norfolk. It relates scriptural history from the Creation to the death of Moses in popular form, based partly on the Bible but mostly on the *Historia Scholastica* of *Comestor. The poem, particularly in its early sections, has a lively vigour. It has been edited by O. Arngart (Lund Studies in English 36), 1968.

GENEST, John (1764–1839), educated at Westminster and Cambridge, cleric, and author of *Some Account of the English Stage from the Restoration in 1660 to 1830* (10 vols, 1832), an accurate and comprehensive work of reference.

GENET, Jean (1910–), French novelist and dramatist. Much of the earlier part of his life was spent in reformatories or in prison, and his literary work is clearly marked by those experiences. He has published the autobiographical *Journal du voleur* (1949; English trans., *The*

Thief's Journal, 1954), and novels such as *Notre-Dame des fleurs* (1944; *Our Lady of the Flowers*, 1949), and *Miracle de la rose* (1946; *Miracle of the Rose*, 1965). His plays include *Les Bonnes* (1948; *The Maids*, 1954), *Le Balcon* (1956; *The Balcony*, 1957), and *Les Nègres* (1958; *The Blacks*, 1960). He is the subject of *Sartre's *Saint Genet, comédien et martyr* (1952; *Saint Genet, Actor and Martyr*, 1964).

Geneva Bible, see BIBLE, THE ENGLISH.

Genevieve, the heroine of S. T. *Coleridge's poem 'Love', first published in the *Morning Star* (1799) and included in the second edition of *Lyrical Ballads*.

Gentle Art of Making Enemies, The, see WHISTLER, J. M.

Gentleman Dancing-Master, The, a comedy by *Wycherley, probably performed 1671, published 1673. It is loosely based on *Calderón's *El maestro de danzar*.

Hippolita, who has been closely confined from the world by her aunt Mrs Caution, at the instigation of her father Mr Formal, is wooed by her cousin, the affected, Frenchified Monsieur de Paris. She prefers young Gerrard, and persuades him to present himself as her dancing-master, with Monsieur's gullible connivance. Gerrard's incompetence in this role is at many times on the point of betraying him, and in the final confusion he and Hippolita contrive to get themselves married by the parson who had intended to marry her to Monsieur. The moral of the play appears to be contained in the final verse of Act II:

> Our Parents who restrain our liberty
> But take the course to make us sooner free,
> Though all we gain be but new slavery;
> We leave our Fathers, and to Husbands fly.

Gentleman's Journal, The, a periodical edited by *Motteux from 1692 to 1694, containing the news of the month and miscellaneous prose and poetry. It was the germ of the modern magazine.

Gentleman's Magazine, The (1731–1914), a periodical founded by *Cave under the pseudonym Sylvanus Urban.

Its original aim was to produce monthly, from the innumerable daily and weekly news-sheets and journals, interesting news, essays, anecdotes, and information. Cave's appears to be the first use of the word 'magazine' to describe a journal. By about 1739 original contributions had largely replaced news-digests; the magazine, while remaining general in scope, began to include serious works of criticism, essays, a record of publications, and parliamentary reports. Dr *Johnson, a friend of Cave, was a regular contributor and had a great influence on the management of the *Magazine*; with Cave he devised

a means of evading the official ban on parliamentary reporting by pretending his reports were from 'Lilliput'. J. *Nichols was an effective editor from 1792 to 1826, but although he published some work of *Lamb and other young contemporaries the *Magazine* seemed antiquated to the young writers of the day, and *Hazlitt's comments on it, written in 1823, sound a valedictory note. However, as a journal of general interest the *Gentleman's* lasted nearly another century.

Gentleman Usher, The, a tragi-comedy, by *Chapman, probably acted *c.*1602, printed 1606.

The duke Alphonso and his son Vincentio are both in love with Margaret, daughter of Earl Lasso. The daughter loves Vincentio, who is ordered into exile. Margaret in despair disfigures herself with a poisonous unguent. The remorseful duke surrenders Margaret, who on account of her disfigurement refuses to marry Vincentio. The doctor provides a remedy and solves the difficulty. The name of the play is taken from the usher, Bassiolo, a conceited major-domo, possibly based on *Malvolio, who acts as go-between for the lovers and is fooled and made ridiculous.

Gentle Shepherd, The, see RAMSAY, A.

GEOFFREY CRAYON, pseudonym of W. *Irving.

GEOFFREY DE VINSAUF (*fl.* *c.*1200), an English rhetorician, author of *Nova Poetria* and *Summa de Coloribus Rhetoricis*, which were the standard and much-cited textbooks of poetic rhetoric in the later Middle Ages. Chaucer (in 'The Nun's Priest's Tale', *Canterbury Tales*, 20; VII. 3,347) laments his lack of the skill to apostrophize the downfall of the cock Chauntecleer with which Geoffrey in the *Nova Poetria* addressed the Friday on which Richard I died (in 1199): 'O Veneris lacrimosa dies!' His works have usually been dismissed as tedious catalogues of figures; recently they have begun to be taken more seriously as poetic aesthetics. (See also ANGLO-LATIN LITERATURE.)

GEOFFREY OF MONMOUTH (Gaufridus Monemutensis) (d. 1155), probably a Benedictine monk of Monmouth, studied and worked at Oxford and was attached to *Robert, earl of Gloucester. He is said to have been archdeacon of Llandaff, and he was appointed bishop of St Asaph in 1152. In his *Historia Regum Britanniae* (*c.*1136) he purports to give an account of the kings who dwelt in Britain since before the Incarnation of Christ, extending over a period of 1,900 years, from Brutus (see BRUT), the great-grandson of Aeneas, to Cadwallader (AD 689), 'and especially of Arthur and the many others who succeeded him'. For this purpose he states that he drew upon a 'most ancient book in the British tongue' (presumably early

Welsh), handed to him by Walter, archdeacon of Oxford (also known as *Calenius); but this book is unknown to any chronicler of the time. It is possible that this alleged work is an invention; *William of Newburgh condemns it as such in strong terms, in about 1198, and Geoffrey's veracity was also questioned by *Higden in *Polychronicon*. He drew on *Bede and *Nennius, on British traditions, perhaps on Welsh documents now lost, and probably for the rest on a romantic imagination. The life and clarity of his writing contributed substantially to the popularity of the Arthurian legends. The *Historia* was translated into Anglo-Norman by *Gaimar and *Wace, and into English verse by *Laȝamon and by *Robert of Gloucester; its translation into French was a major factor in the dissemination of the Arthurian legend because of the hegemony of French courtly literature. Geoffrey's Section Five is *The Prophecies of Merlin*, originally printed separately (1603). (See also ANGLO-LATIN LITERATURE.) There is a translation by Lewis Thorpe (1966) and a discussion by J. J. Parry and R. A. Caldwell in *Arthurian Literature in the Middle Ages*, ed. R. S. Loomis (1959), ch. 8.

GEORGE, Henry (1839–87), American writer on political economy, who advocated the nationalization of land and a 'single tax' on its increment value. Although not himself a Socialist, he considerably influenced the British socialist movement and the *Fabian Society. G. B. *Shaw heard him speak in 1882, and claimed that at that point 'the importance of the economic basis dawned' on him; he was led on to *Marx and *Proudhon. H. G. *Wells bought a sixpenny paperback copy of George's bestselling *Progress and Poverty* (1879) when a young man in Midhurst and records its 'fermenting influence' upon his mind. Marx himself described George's proposals as 'the capitalist's last ditch'.

George-a'-Green, the merry pinner or pinder (pound-keeper) of Wakefield. The story is given in W. C. *Hazlitt's *Tales and Legends*. George-a'-Green wins the pindership by defeating all competitors at quarterstaff, defies the messenger who comes from Prince John (during Richard I's absence) demanding a contribution from Wakefield, and elopes with Justice Grymes's daughter. *Maid Marian provokes *Robin Hood to challenge him, but George-a'-Green defeats both Robin and his companions. He is the subject of a play (licensed for publication, 1595; the earliest known edition appears to be that of 1599, in the Bodleian) probably by R. *Greene.

George Barnwell, The History of, or The London Merchant, a domestic tragedy in prose by *Lillo, produced 1731. In this play, for the first time, everyday commercial life is made the theme of tragedy. The play was a great success, was translated into French, German, and Dutch, and was highly commended by G. E. *Lessing and *Diderot, who used it as a model for *Miss Sara Sampson* (1755) and *Le Fils naturel* (1757) respectively. *Goldsmith mocked it as a 'Tradesman's Tragedy' but *Pope admired it greatly. Based on an old ballad, it tells the story of an innocent young apprentice, Barnwell, who is seduced by a heartless courtesan, Millwood. She encourages him to rob his employer, Thorowgood, and to murder his uncle, for which crime both are brought to execution, he profoundly penitent and she defiant. It was frequently performed at holidays for apprentices as a moral warning.

Georgian, a term applied in a literary sense to the writers of the reign of George V (1910–36), and usually indicating poetry of a pastoral or, as later critics asserted, an escapist nature. (See GEORGIAN POETRY.) When applied to architecture, the term suggests the earlier period of the reigns of George I (1714–27), George II (1727–60), and George III (1760–1820), when *Palladian principles of classical proportions were adapted to an unpretentious, refined, and discreet style suited to the needs of the rising middle classes.

Georgian Poetry, a series of volumes of verse planned by R. *Brooke, H. *Monro, and E. *Marsh. The series appeared in 5 vols between 1912 and 1922, edited by Marsh and published by Monro at the Poetry Bookshop. The early volumes were widely influential and successful bringing a fresh vision and manner into the tired poetry of the time. Writers represented in the first volume included Brooke, W. H. *Davies, *Masefield, D. H. *Lawrence, *de la Mare, *Abercrombie, *Bottomley, and *Drinkwater; R. *Hodgson and others were added for the second volume. Later volumes contained the work of *Blunden, *Sassoon, Robert *Graves, and *Rosenberg. However, the poems of quality were fewer in the volumes of 1919 and 1922; several poets (including Graves, Sassoon, and Blunden) objected to being identified as 'Georgian', in the company of J. C. *Squire, *Baring, and other traditionalists; and the term began to acquire its present strong pejorative sense. *Pound, T. S. *Eliot, and the *Sitwells attacked the entire series, though about half of the poets represented are now of high repute.

Georgics, The, see VIRGIL.

'Geraint and Enid', one of Tennyson's *Idylls of the King*, first published under this title 1886. It originally formed with 'The Marriage of Geraint' a single idyll, published in 1859 as 'Enid' and divided in 1873. Geraint, suspecting his wife's virtue, subjects her to various trials, from which she emerges patient and triumphant.

Geraldine, (1) the hero of T. Heywood's *The English Traveller*; (2) the name under which Elizabeth, daughter of the 9th earl of Kildare, is traditionally held to have been courted by *Surrey: the connection is extremely tenuous; (3) the beautiful but malignant enchantress in Coleridge's *'Christabel'.

Gerard, (1) the hero of Reade's *The Cloister and the Hearth*; (2) Brigadier Gerard, the hero of historical romances by A. C. *Doyle.

GERARD, Alexander (1728–95), theological and philosophical writer, was professor of moral philosophy and logic in Marischal College, and later professor of divinity in King's College, Aberdeen. He published two analytical studies which contributed to the development of aesthetics in Britain: 'An Essay on Taste' (1759, augmented 1780) and 'An Essay on Genius' (1774).

GERARD, John (1545–1612), a herbalist and superintendent of Burghley's gardens, was author of the celebrated *Herball or Generall Historie of Plantes* (1597), in a large measure adapted from the *Pemptades* of Rembert Dodoens. A revised edition of the *Herball* was issued by Thomas Johnson in 1633. The work gives a description of each plant, the localities in which it is found, and its medical virtues (correcting superstitions, e.g. about the mandrake); discusses nomenclature; and contains a large number of beautiful woodcuts, many of which had appeared in an earlier work.

Gerard, Walter, the heroine's father in B. Disraeli's novel *Sybil*.

GERHARDIE (originally GERHARDI), William Alexander (1895–1977), was born of English parents in St Petersburg. During the First World War he served in the British embassy at Petrograd, then with the British military mission in Siberia. He then attended Worcester College, Oxford, where he wrote the first English book on *Chekhov, *Anton Chehov* (1923) and his first novel, *Futility: A Novel on Russian Themes* (1922). During the next 15 years he produced many other novels admired by, among others, H. G. *Wells, E. *Waugh, *Beaverbrook, and O. *Manning. They include *The Polyglots* (1925), perhaps his best-known work, the bizarre narrative of a wildly egocentric young officer, George Hamlet Alexander Diabologh, who on a military mission in the Far East comes into contact with a highly eccentric Belgian family, the Vanderflints; the intermingling of comedy and tragedy, of events of historical significance and the utmost human triviality, of Belgians, British, Russians, and Japanese, of love and war, create an oblique, lyrical, inconsequential world which is characteristic of Gerhardie, and largely autobiographical in content. Other novels include *Pending Heaven* (1930), *Resurrection* (1934), and *Of Mortal Love* (1936). His autobiography *Memoirs of a Polyglot* appeared in 1931, and in 1940 a historical study, *The Romanovs*. For the rest of his life he lived increasingly as a recluse, planning novels, but, it seems, not writing them. *God's Fifth Column*, a biography of the age 1890–1940, ed. Michael *Holroyd and Robert Skidelsky, was published in 1981. His name was spelt Gerhardie for the first time on the revised Collected Edition of his works, published in 10 vols in the early 1970s.

Germ, The, *Thoughts towards Nature in Poetry, Literature and Art*, a periodical of which the first issue appeared on 1 Jan. 1850. Edited by W. M. *Rossetti, it was the organ of the *Pre-Raphaelite Brotherhood, and ran for only four issues, the last appearing on 30 April 1850; the last two were renamed *Art and Poetry, being Thoughts towards Nature*. It contained work by D. G. *Rossetti (including 'The Blessed Damozel'), C. *Rossetti, *Patmore, F. M. Brown, W. B. *Scott, and others and although short-lived, was credited by W. M. Rossetti as the inspiration behind W. *Morris's *Oxford and Cambridge Magazine* (1856) which continued the Pre-Raphaelite impetus.

Géronte, in *Molière's comedies, the typical old man whose absurdities are held up to ridicule. In *Les Fourberies de Scapin* he is a miser, outwitted by Scapin. In *Le Médecin malgré lui* he is a credulous fool, imposed upon by Sganarelle.

Gerontius, *The Dream of*, see NEWMAN, J. H.

Gertrude, in Shakespeare's *Hamlet*, mother of Hamlet and married to her late husband's brother *Claudius. It is she who describes *Ophelia's death in the speech beginning 'There is a willow grows aslant the brook' (IV. vii).

Gertrude of Wyoming, a poem by T. *Campbell, in Spenserian stanzas, published 1809.

The poem, which was immensely popular, centres on a historical event. It describes the destruction of the settlement of Wyoming in Pennsylvania by a force of Indians under the Mohawk Brandt, and the destruction of the happiness of a home by the death of Gertrude, the newly-married wife of Sir Henry Waldegrave, and of her father Albert. Campbell later withdrew the charge of cruelty against Brandt.

Gerusalemme Liberata, see JERUSALEM DELIVERED.

Geryoneo, in Spenser's *Faerie Queene* (V. x and xi), a three-bodied giant who represents Philip II's power which controlled Spain, Portugal, and the Low Countries.

Gesta Francorum, a chronicle in medieval Latin, the first known to have been written by a layman. It gives the story of the First Crusade. Its actual author is unknown. It has been edited with a translation by Rosalind Hill (Nelson's Medieval Texts), 1962.

Gesta Romanorum, a collection of fictitious stories in Latin, probably compiled in England in the late 13th cent. The stories and fables have an attached moralization, like the *bestiaries and *allegories. Some of the stories are of oriental origin. There are about 165 manuscripts of the Latin versions, and the immense popularity of the work is shown by the existence of 15th-cent. versions in many European languages and by its influence on later medieval writers such as *Boccaccio, *Chaucer, *Hoccleve, and *Lydgate. See ed. S. J. Herrtage, *Early English Versions of the Gesta Romanorum* (EETS ES 33, 1879; reprinted 1962).

Ghost-words, a term used by *Skeat to signify words which have no real existence, 'coinages due to the blunders of printers or scribes, or to the perfervid imaginations of ignorant or blundering editors' (*Trans. Philol. Soc.*, 1885–7, ii. 350).

Giafar, see JAFFAR.

Giaffir, in Byron's *Bride of Abydos,* the father of Zuleika.

Giant Pope, in Bunyan's *Pilgrim's Progress,* a giant by whose power and tyranny many men were cruelly put to death in the past, but who is 'grown so crazy and stiff in his joints that he can now do little more than sit in his cave's mouth, grinning at pilgrims as they go by, and biting his nails, because he cannot come at them'.

Giaour, The, a poem by Lord *Byron, published 1813. Eight editions of the work appeared in the last seven months of that year, and the length was increased from 685 to 1,334 lines.

The story is of a female slave, Leila, who loves the Giaour, a true *'Byronic' hero, and is in consequence bound and thrown in a sack into the sea by her Turkish lord, Hassan. The Giaour avenges her by killing Hassan, then in grief and remorse banishes himself to a monastery.

An indication of the romantic passions aroused by the poem may be found in the response of Captain Benwick in *Persuasion* (ch. 11) whose interest in 'hopeless agony' and broken hearts leads Anne to say, 'that she thought it was the misfortune of poetry, to be seldom safely enjoyed by those who enjoyed it completely'.

Gibbie, Guse, in Scott's *Old Mortality,* a half-witted lad of very small stature who kept Lady Margaret Bellenden's poultry.

GIBBINGS, Robert, see GOLDEN COCKEREL PRESS.

GIBBON, Edward (1737–94), born in Putney of a good family, was a sickly child and his education at Westminster and at Magdalen College, Oxford, was irregular; in his posthumously published *Memoirs* he paints a vivid portrait of the 'narrow, lazy and oppressive' spirit of Oxford, and of the 'idle and unprofitable' time he spent there. He became a Catholic convert at the age of 16, partly through reading C. *Middleton and *Bossuet, and was sent off to Lausanne by his father, where he was reconverted to Protestantism. There he continued to read voraciously, as he had done since boyhood, his 'blind and boyish taste' for exotic history maturing into serious study of French and Latin classics; he also became attached to Suzanne Curchod (later Mme *Necker, mother of Mme de *Staël), but his father persuaded him to break off the engagement and he returned to England in 1758 after an absence of nearly 5 years. In 1761 he published his *Essai sur l'étude de la littérature,* of which an English version appeared in 1764. From 1759 he served as a captain in the Hampshire Militia until he left again for the Continent in 1763; it was in Italy, while 'musing amid the ruins of the Capitol' that he formed the plan of his *The History of the *Decline and Fall of the Roman Empire.* His improvident father's death left him in some difficulties, but he was able to settle in London in 1772 to proceed with his great work.

He entered Parliament in 1774, voted steadily for Lord North, and was made a commissioner of trade and plantations, but his parliamentary career added nothing to his reputation. He was also elected to Dr Johnson's *Club in 1774. In 1776 appeared the first volume of the *History* which was very favourably received, although his chapters on the growth of Christianity provoked criticisms, of which the most weighty were those of *Dalrymple and *Porson. To his theological critics Gibbon replied in 1779 in *A Vindication of some Passages in the XVth and XVIth Chapters.* The second and third volumes appeared in 1781, but were less warmly received; he himself suspected he had become prolix through 'superfluous diligence'. He retired to Lausanne in 1783 to share the home of his old friend Deyverdun, who died not long afterwards. There Gibbon completed the work; he wrote as memorably of its completion as of its inception, describing his sense of freedom followed by a sober melancholy at taking 'an everlasting leave of an old and agreeable companion'. The last three volumes were published in 1788. He returned to England and spent most of his remaining days in the home of his friend the earl of Sheffield (John Baker Holroyd), who put together his remarkable *Memoirs* from various drafts and fragments, publishing them in 1796 with his *Miscellaneous Works.* The memoirs reveal Gibbon's sense of vocation as a historian, and record on several occasions his gratitude at having been born 'in a free and enlightened country'; he was in many ways a representative product of the *Enlightenment, anticlerical, rational, and one of the last of the great Augustans. The standard edition of the *History* is by J. B. Bury (7 vols, 1896–1900, rev. 1909–14, 1926–9), and the standard biography is by D. M. Low (1937).

GIBBON, Lewis Grassic, the pen-name of James Leslie Mitchell (1901–35), born on his father's farm near Auchterless, Aberdeenshire; he was educated at Arbuthnott School and (stormily and briefly) at Mackie Academy, Stonehaven. He then worked as a journalist in Glasgow, and in 1919 joined the Royal Army Service Corps; from 1923 to 1929 he was a clerk in the RAF. The army offered him opportunities to travel which resulted in various works written under his own name, including *The Calends of Cairo* (1931), and he also published fiction under the same name, including *Stained Radiance* (1930), his first novel, and *Spartacus* (1933). He worked productively but not with great financial success in his last years, with the encouragement of H. G. *Wells, *MacDiarmid, and others, and published works on exploration, archaeology, etc., but is now remembered principally for his trilogy *A Scots Quair*, published under this collective title in 1946. It consists of *Sunset Song* (1932), *Cloud Howe* (1933), and *Grey Granite* (1934), novels which relate the life of Chris Guthrie from girlhood on her father's farm, through three marriages, the First World War, the Depression, her son's commitment to the Communist Party, etc. All three were published under the name of Grassic Gibbon, taken from his mother's maiden name, and written in a powerful, idiosyncratic, lyrical prose, with a highly personal use of Scottish dialect and archaisms; the narrator shares his heroine's mixture of love and hatred for their ancestral land, 'the red clay of the Mearns', and the plot abounds in lurid and violent incident, as well as in impassioned description. *Sunset Song* was hailed as the first really Scottish novel since *Galt, though many objected to its rawness and frankness. Mitchell died of a perforated ulcer in Welwyn Garden City, where he had been living since 1931. There is a life by I. S. Munro (1966).

GIBBONS, Orlando (1583–1625), English composer. After some early years as a chorister at Cambridge, Gibbons became a gentleman of the Chapel Royal and later its senior organist, as well as organist of Westminster Abbey. As a composer by far the largest part of his output is either instrumental or sacred vocal music, but he published one book of secular vocal works, *The First Set of Madrigals and Mottets, apt for Viols and Voyces* (1612), one of the best of the later *madrigal collections. Unlike many of the ear-lier ones, the tone here is predominantly serious, and poems like *Ralegh's 'What is our life?', or 'Ah! deare heart' (attributed to *Donne), are typical of the set and indicative of the temperament of the composer. 'The Silver Swan', one of the best-known of all English madrigals, is in this collection.

GIBBONS, Stella, see COLD COMFORT FARM.

GIBSON, Dr, Mrs, and Molly, characters in Mrs Gaskell's *Wives and Daughters*.

GIBSON, Wilfrid Wilson (1878–1962), poet, born in Hexham, Northumberland, moved to London in 1912, where he met E. *Marsh (to whose *Georgian Poetry he contributed) and R. *Brooke, who made him one of his heirs. Gibson published many volumes of verse and verse drama, much of it dealing somewhat conventionally with Northern rural themes; his experiences in the First World War inspired several shorter, sharper battle pieces, such as 'Breakfast'. His *Collected Poems 1905–25* appeared in 1926.

GIDE, André (1860–1951), French novelist, essayist, critic, and dramatist. He published a number of short novels, including *L'Immoraliste* (1902; English trans., *The Immoralist*, 1930), *La Porte étroite* (1909; *Strait is the Gate*, 1924), and *La Symphonie pastorale* (1919; *The Pastoral Symphony*, 1931); two longer novels, *Les Caves du Vatican* (1914; translated under various titles: *The Vatican Swindle*, 1925; *Lafcadio's Adventures*, 1928; *The Vatican Cellars*, 1952) and *Les Faux-monnayeurs* (1925; *The Counterfeiters*, 1927); and a number of autobiographical works, including *Si le grain ne meurt . . .* (1926; *If it Die . . .* , 1935), which describes his revolt against his Protestant upbringing, and his *Journal* for the years 1889 to 1949 (*The Journals of André Gide*, 1947–51). He was awarded the *Nobel Prize for literature in 1947.

GIFFORD, William (1756–1826), the son of a glazier and himself a shoemaker's apprentice, was sent with the help of a friendly surgeon to Oxford, after which he became tutor to the son of Lord Grosvenor. He published in 1791 and 1795 two satires, *The Baviad* and *The Maeviad*, the first directed against the *Della Cruscan school of poetry, and the second divided between the Della Cruscans and the contemporary drama. In 1797–8 he was editor of *The Anti-Jacobin*, where he made his mark as an industrious and caustic writer. In 1809 he was appointed to a position far beyond his abilities as the first editor of the *Quarterly Review*, a post he held until 1824. He bitterly attacked most of the young innovating writers of his time; among many instances, he wholly altered the warm tone of *Lamb's essay on Wordsworth's *The Excursion and published J. W. *Croker's virulent attack on Keats's *Endymion. His character and inadequacies are mercilessly exposed by Hazlitt in *The Spirit of the Age. He translated the satires of *Juvenal (1802) and of *Persius (1821), and edited the works of *Massinger, *Jonson, *Ford, and *Shirley. A short autobiography is prefixed to the 1827 edition of Juvenal.

GIFFORD LECTURES, on natural theology without reference to creeds, founded in the universities of Edinburgh, Glasgow, Aberdeen, and St Andrews by the bequest of £80,000 by Adam, Lord Gifford (1820–87), a Scottish judge.

GILBERT, William (1540–1603), physician to *Elizabeth I and James I. He delared the earth to be a magnet in his *De Magnete* (1600), the first great scientific book to be published in England.

GILBERT, Sir William Schwenck (1836–1911), was educated at King's College, London, and afterwards was employed as a clerk at the Privy Council office, but resigned after four years to study law; he practised as a barrister for several years, without success. In 1861 he began contributing regular columns of comic verse, with his own illustrations, to the magazine *Fun*; this was the beginning of the *Bab Ballads* (collected under this title in 1869), which laid the foundation of his fame on the stage and which became the source of some of his operatic plots. Here he showed his ingenious metrical skill and sketched out his fantasy world, turning the odd into the ordinary, calling it 'Topsy-Turvydom'. The ballads became the favourite literature of sailors, soldiers, lawyers, doctors, and other non-literary people, though Gilbert had a low opinion of his own work: 'I am a doggerel bard', runs the refrain in one of them. Encouraged by T. W. *Robertson he produced his first dramatic work, *Dulcamara* (1866), a burlesque based on *Donizetti's opera *L'elisir d'amore*, followed by several other light stage works. His second period, which began with *The Palace of Truth* (1870), a poetical fantasy based on a novel by Mme de Genlis and influenced by the fairy work of *Planché, included the verse plays *Pygmalion and Galatea* (1871); *The Wicked World* (1873) and a burlesque version, *The Happy Land* (1873), in collaboration with Gilbert Arthur *A Becket; and *The Princess* (1870), a 'respectful perversion' of *Tennyson's poem.

Gilbert was a great verbal rhythmist; his true province was satirical light verse, frequently topical and absurdly funny; and in his third period he found his true genius in comic opera. He met *Sullivan in 1869 and their first collaboration was *Thespis* (1871), but it was not until 1874 that Gilbert met D'Oyly Carte. For him they wrote *Trial by Jury* (1875), which began the series of light operas which was permanently to link the names of Gilbert and Sullivan (see

GILBERT AND SULLIVAN OPERAS). D'Oyly Carte leased the old Opéra Comique for their productions and in 1881 built the Savoy Theatre especially for the D'Oyly Carte company. The collaboration lasted for over 20 years, though after *The Gondoliers* (1889) there was a rift resulting from a business transaction in which Sullivan sided with D'Oyly Carte. *Utopia Limited* (1893) healed the breach. *The Grand Duke* (1896), the only unsuccessful Savoy opera, was the last. Gilbert continued writing plays and operas without Sullivan; among them *Rosencrantz and Guildenstern* (1891), *Fallen Fairies* (1909), with music by E. German, and *The Hooligans* (1911), his last play. He was knighted in 1907, and died of a heart attack while attempting to rescue a young woman who had fallen into a lake. He used the profits from his plays to build the Garrick Theatre.

Gilbert was an outstanding figure in a period which had witnessed a decline in the literary quality of drama; 'and it may be that in the remote future that laughter will still be heard, when all the voices of that age are silent' (G. K. *Chesterton, in his introduction to A. H. Godwin's *Gilbert and Sullivan*, 1926; see also *W. S. Gilbert: A Century of Scholarship and Commentary*, ed. J. B. Jones, 1970).

GILBERT AND SULLIVAN OPERAS, comic operas containing much social satire, the librettos of which were written by Sir W. S. *Gilbert, and the music by Sir A. *Sullivan, for D'Oyly Carte. The operas are: *Trial by Jury* (1875); *The Sorcerer* (1877); *H.M.S. Pinafore* (1878); *The Pirates of Penzance* (1879, NY; 1880, London); *Patience* (1881); *Iolanthe* (1882), probably the cleverest; *Princess Ida* (1884), a satire on feminism suggested by Tennyson's *The Princess; The Mikado* (1885); *Ruddigore* (1887); *The Yeomen of the Guard* (1888); *The Gondoliers* (1889); *Utopia, Limited* (1893); and *The Grand Duke* (1896). They are sometimes known as the 'Savoy Operas' because from *Iolanthe* onwards they were produced at the Savoy Theatre.

GILBERT MARKHAM, in A. Brontë's *The Tenant of Wildfell Hall*, the narrator.

GIL BLAS, see LESAGE, A.-R.

GILCHRIST, Anne, née Burrow (1828–85), was the wife of Alexander Gilchrist (1828–61), author of a *Life of Etty* (1855) and a life of the then largely unrecognized *Blake, on which he was working when he died. She finished it, and it was published in 1863; it made a considerable contribution to the awakening of interest in Blake's work in the late 19th cent. Mrs Gilchrist was friendly with the *Carlyles, and with W. M. *Rossetti (also an admirer of Blake), who imparted to her his admiration for *Whitman. She corresponded passionately with Whitman (who occasionally replied), wrote appreciations of his work, and visited him in America in 1876–9. She also wrote a life of Mary *Lamb (1883) and various articles, sketches, etc. See *Anne Gilchrist, her life and writings*, ed. H. H. Gilchrist (1887).

GILDAS (d. 570), a British historian who lived in the west of England and wrote shortly before 547 a Latin sketch of the history of Britain, *De Excidio et Conquestu Britanniae*, followed by a castigation of the degraded rulers and priests of his day. In the historical section he says nothing of Arthur, but he does refer to the victory of Mount *Badon. He is the first writer of history in Britain; his work is impoverished by insufficiency of dating and by ignorance of the Anglo-Saxons, against whose invasions he shows the 5th-cent. Britons appealing. But he was an important source for later historians from *Bede onwards. *Geoffrey of Monmouth mentions his 'excellent book' in the first sentence of his *Historia Regum Britanniae*.

Gilfil, The Revd Maynard, see SCENES OF CLERICAL LIFE.

GILFILLAN, George (1813–78), a Scottish Dissenting minister, literary critic, and editor, who for a brief period in the mid-19th cent. exercised considerable influence, particularly as the champion of the *Spasmodic school. He was befriended by *Carlyle, who found his prose 'full of fervour, and crude, gloomy fire—a kind of opium style'. His *A Gallery of Literary Portraits* ran to three series, 1845, 1850, 1854, with essays on the Spasmodics, *Macaulay, Carlyle, etc., and he also edited many useful volumes of minor British poets, with notes and memoirs.

GILL, (Arthur) Eric (Rowton) (1882–1940), stone-carver, engraver, and typographer, who cut lettering and designed types, among them Perpetua and Gill Sans-serif. He settled in Ditchling in 1907, where a community of craftsmen and artists began to gather round him; D. *Jones was there for four years from 1921. In 1913 Gill became a Roman Catholic, and he worked for some years from 1914 on a commission to carve the Stations of the Cross for Westminster Cathedral. From 1924 he was associated with the *Golden Cockerel Press, for which he illustrated many books, including *The Four Gospels* and Chaucer's *Troilus and Criseyde*. Gill wrote many essays, pamphlets, and books on art, sculpture, typography, etc., proclaiming the religious basis of art, the validity of craftsmanship in the machine age, and the holiness of the body (many of his early works were erotic); his works include *Art-Nonsense and other essays* (1929), *The Necessity of Belief* (1936), and an *Autobiography* (1940).

GILLRAY, James (1757–1815), caricaturist. He used his mordant wit and political independence to show up the abuses and vices of Parliament and the royal family, and his often vicious caricatures of Napoleon helped to rouse the patriotism of the country to the threat of invasion.

Gills, Solomon, a character in Dickens's *Dombey and Son*.

Gil Morrice, the subject of an old Scottish ballad, included in Percy's *Reliques*. He is the natural son of an earl and Lady Barnard. A message he sends to his mother leads Lord Barnard to think that he is his wife's lover, and to kill him. The ballad is the same as that of *Child Maurice* in the *Oxford Book of Ballads*, where 'Lord Barnard' is 'John Steward'.

Gilpin, John, see JOHN GILPIN.

GILPIN, William (1724–1804), educated at The Queen's College, Oxford, and subsequently a schoolmaster and vicar of Boldre, is remembered for his extremely influential writings on the *Picturesque, which did much to form the taste in landscape, art, and the literary treatment of nature in the later 18th cent. and which some have seen as heralds of *Romanticism. From 1768 onwards he embarked on various travels in search of the picturesque, visiting many parts of the British Isles, and produced the series of illustrated tours parodied by *Combe in his *Dr Syntax*. These include accounts of Wye and South Wales (1782), the Lake District (1789), and the Highlands (1800). His theoretical principles are set out in his *Three Essays: On Picturesque Beauty; On Picturesque Travel; and on Sketching Landscape* (1792), in which he defines the characteristics of the picturesque. See W. D. Templeman, *The Life and Work of William Gilpin* (1939).

Ginevra, (1) a character in *Orlando Furioso*, whose story is that of Hero in *Much Ado about Nothing*; (2) the subject of a section of S. *Rogers's poem *Italy*, in which a young bride on her wedding-day in playful mood hides herself inside a trunk, of which the lid is closed with a spring lock. Fifty years later her skeleton is discovered there. Rogers notes, 'The story is, I believe, founded on fact; though the time and the place are uncertain. Many old houses lay claim to it.' It is retold by *Bayly in his ballad 'The Mistletoe Bough'; (3) Ginevra Fanshawe, in *Villette* by C. Brontë.

'Gioconda Smile, The', see LEONARDO DA VINCI and HUXLEY, A.

GIORGIONE DA CASTELFRANCO (1476/8–1510), Venetian painter, of whom very little is known, and to whom only three pictures—the Castelfranco altarpiece, the *Three Philosophers*, and the *Tempest* (c.1504) are universally attributed. Yet, since *Vasari, his importance has been recognized; he introduced a new kind of painting in his small oils of pastoral subjects, where the figures and soft, hazy landscape together create a poignant, dreamy mood. Ruskin in *Modern Painters* ('The Two Boyhoods') compared him with *Turner. In the later 19th cent. literary interest in Giorgione was intense, although it centred on a picture, the *Fête Champêtre* (c.1510), which most scholars now give to *Titian. It shows young men making music with naked girls in an idyllically sunny landscape, and was introduced to aesthetic writers by D. G. *Rossetti's sonnet 'For a Venetian Pastoral by Giorgione' (1850, rev. 1870); thereafter it inspired the suggestive prose of *Pater's 'The School of Giorgione' (1877) with its celebrated dictum, 'All art constantly aspires to the condition of music.'

GIOTTO DI BONDONE (c.1267–1337), the most celebrated of the early Italian painters, whose art marks a turning away from the flat patterns and symbols of the Byzantine tradition to the clear space and dignified human figures of Renaissance art; his undisputed works are frescoes in the Arena Chapel at Padua (1303–13) and in the Peruzzi and Bardi chapels in Sta Croce, Florence. Giotto was the first artist to be celebrated by literary men in his own day; praised by *Dante, *Boccaccio, and *Petrarch, and his epitaph written by *Poliziano, he was seen as the start of a new artistic era and rapidly became a legendary figure. Yet there followed a long period of neglect, until the late 19th cent. when he was admired by *Ruskin, followed by R. *Fry and *Berenson. E. M. Forster, in *A Room with a View*, wittily describes a scene in Sta Croce, where his heroine looks for Giotto's 'tactile values'—a phrase made famous by Berenson's essay *The Florentine Painters*.

Gipsies Metamorphosed, The, a masque by *Jonson, performed before James I 1621, printed 1640. It is the most elaborate of his masques, and unique in its assigning of speaking parts to members of the court. The chief event is the telling of the king's fortune by the gypsy captain, a part taken by the duke of *Buckingham.

GIRALDUS CAMBRENSIS (de Barri) (?1146–?1220), a native of Pembrokeshire and son of Nesta, a Welsh princess. He studied at Paris before 1176 and again 1177–80. As a churchman he had a stormy career. He was archdeacon of Brecon, and twice (1176 and 1198) a nominee for the see of St David's, but was rejected, as a Welshman, first by Henry II, then by Archbishop Hubert. He appealed to Rome, sought the support of the Welsh, was outlawed, fled abroad, and was imprisoned at Châtillon. He was finally reconciled to the king and archbishop and was buried at St David's. In 1184 he accompanied Prince John to Ireland. From 1196 to 1198 he led a student's life at Lincoln.

His works (ed. J. S. Brewer and J. F. Dimock, 1861–77) include *Topographia Hibernica*, *Expugnatio Hibernica*, *Itinerarium Cambriae*, *Gemma Ecclesiastica*, *De Rebus a se gestis*, and lives of St *Hugh of Lincoln, St David, and others. The *Topographia*, which he read aloud to the assembled masters at Oxford in 1184 or 1185, is an account of the geography, fauna, marvels, and early history of Ireland; the *Expugnatio* a narrative of the partial conquest of Ireland (1169–85); the *Itinerarium* (the most important of his works) a description of the topography of Wales; the *Gemma* a charge to the clergy of his district, affording interesting information as to the conditions then prevailing. (See also ANGLO-LATIN LITERATURE.)

Ed. T. Wright, *The Historical Works of Giraldus Cambrensis* (1905); H. E. Butler, ed. and trans., *The Autobiography of Giraldus Cambrensis* (1937); R. Bartlett, *Gerald of Wales* (1982).

GIRAUDOUX, Jean (1882–1944), French diplomat, novelist, and playwright; his first novel, *Suzanne et le Pacifique*, was published in 1921. In 1928 the novel *Siegfried et le Limousin* (1922) was successfully adapted for the stage. Thereafter the drama became the most suitable medium for Giraudoux's gifts of irony and paradox; his plots are frequently stylized and modernized versions of biblical or classical legend. His plays include *Amphitryon 38* (1929), *Judith* (1931), *La Guerre de Troie n'aura pas lieu* (1935; trans. 1955 by C. *Fry as *Tiger at the Gates*), *Ondine* (1939; see UNDINE), and *Pour Lucrèce* (1953, trans. by Fry as *Duel of Angels*, 1958).

Girton College, a college for women, which owes its existence mainly to the energy of Sarah Emily Davies (1830–1921), a pioneer in the cause of the higher education of women. The college was opened at Hitchin in 1869 and transferred to Cambridge in 1873. Men were admitted at undergraduate level in 1979.

GISBORNE, Maria, *née* James (1770–1836). She refused *Godwin, and married John Gisborne in 1800. Both she and her husband were close friends of *Shelley. They lent him their Italian villa when they were in London, and in 1820 he published his buoyant 'Letter to Maria Gisborne', written to London from the workshop of the villa.

Gismond of Salerne, see TANCRED AND GISMUND.

GISSING, George Robert (1857–1903), educated at a Quaker boarding school, Alderley Edge, Cheshire, and Owen's College, Manchester (now the University). Caught stealing, he was expelled and went to prison for a month. In 1876 he went to America, wandering for a year, and in 1877 moved to London, coaching in Latin and Greek at four shillings for three hours' tuition. Obsessed with his vocation as a writer, self-absorbed and secretive, he had few friends apart from H. G. *Wells, who came from a similar background. Gissing was twice married, unhappily, to proletarian girls. In Wells's words: 'He felt that to make love to any woman he could regard as a social equal would be too elaborate . . . so he flung himself at a social inferior whom he expected to be eager and grateful.' Although Gissing wrote about poverty and failure, he was a successful writer though not a rich one. He published his first novel, *Workers in the Dawn* (1880), at the age of 23; followed by *The Unclassed* (1884); *Isabel Clarendon and Demos* (1886); *Thyrza* (1887); *A Life's Morning* (1888); *The Nether World* (1889); *The Emancipated* (1890); and his best-known work, *New Grub Street* (1891). His other famous novel, *Born in Exile*, was published in 1892. *The Odd Women* appeared in 1893; then *Sleeping Fires* (1895); *The Whirlpool* (1897); *Human Odds and Ends* (short stories, 1897); a critique, *Charles Dickens* (1898); *The Town Traveller* (1898); *The Crown of Life* (1899); *Our Friend the Charlatan* (1901). In 1900 Gissing published *By the Ionian Sea*, impressions of Italy. He had become successful, comparatively prosperous, and, at last, sociable. *The Private Papers of Henry Ryecroft*, which reflects in part the time Gissing spent in seclusion in Devon, was published in the year of his death. The narrator has been released from financial worry by a legacy. In the preface, Gissing writes: 'Naturally a man of independent and rather scornful outlook, he had suffered much from defeated ambition, from disillusions of many kinds, from subjection to grim necessity; but the result of it . . . was, certainly, not a broken spirit, but a mind and temper . . . sternly disciplined.' Posthumous publications were *Veranilda* (1904), a historical romance of 6th-cent. Italy; *Will Warburton* (1905); *The House of Cobwebs* (short stories, 1906); *The Immortal Dickens* (1925); *The Sins of the Fathers* (1924); *A Victim of Circumstances* (1927); *Brownie* (1931); *Notes on Social Democracy* (1968). Respected in his own time as a naturalistic novelist in the continental style, Gissing went out of fashion for half a century, but interest in England and America steadily revived from the 1960s onwards, manifesting itself in many new editions of his works and in the publication of previously unpublished works, including volumes of correspondence, *George Gissing's Commonplace Book* (1962, ed. J. Korg), *The Diary of George Gissing, Novelist* (1978, ed. P. Coustillas), and other items. The same period saw many critical and biographical studies, including lives by J. Korg (1963) and J. Halperin (1982).

GITTINGS, Robert William Victor (1911–), poet and biographer, born in Portsmouth, the son of a naval surgeon, and educated at Jesus College, Cambridge. His first volume of poetry,

The Roman Road and other poems (1932), was followed by several volumes of poems and plays, and a *Collected Poems* (1976). His biographical works include *John Keats* (1968) and a 2-vol. life of *Hardy (1975, 1978); and a study (based on lectures delivered at the University of Washington), *The Nature of Biography* (1978).

GIULIO ROMANO (?1499–1546), Italian Mannerist painter and architect, and the most important of *Raphael's pupils; his most famous works were created for Federigo Gonzaga at Mantua and include the Palazzo del Te (begun 1526)—where the frescoes in the Sala dei Giganti and the witty, erotic decoration of the Sala de Psiche are most notable—and decorations in the Ducal Palace. Giulio is the only Renaissance artist mentioned by Shakespeare, who thought that he was a sculptor: in *The Winter's Tale* (v. ii) he mentions 'that rare Italian master, Julio Romano'. *Aretino wrote obscene verses to accompany engravings made after pornographic drawings by Giulio; 'Aretine's pictures' are mentioned by *Jonson, *Donne, and *Pope, who perhaps knew them by repute.

GLADSTONE, William Ewart (1809–98), the great Liberal statesman, was born in Liverpool, the son of a prosperous tradesman; he was educated at Eton (where one of his close friends was A. H. *Hallam) and at Oxford, where he distinguished himself as an orator, although it took him some time to determine on a career as politician rather than churchman. He is remembered in literary history for his *Studies on Homer and the Homeric Age* (1858), a subject further dealt with in his *Juventus Mundi* (1869) and *Homeric Synchronism* (1876). He firmly maintained his belief in a personal *Homer and 'a solid nucleus of fact in his account of the Trojan war', and sought to justify classical studies as the basis of a Christian education. (For an account of Gladstone as classical scholar, see J. L. Myers, *Homer and His Critics*, 1958.) His political writings include *The State in its Relations with the Church* (1838), in which he defended the principle of a single state religion (a principle that he was later to abandon), and his impassioned *Bulgarian Horrors and the Question of the East* (1876). His minor political writings and contributions to periodicals were republished as *Gleanings of Past Years* (7 vols, 1879, with a supplementary vol. 1890). J. *Morley's *The Life of Gladstone*, 3 vols, was published in 1903; see also a life by R. Shannon (vol. 1, 1982). *The Gladstone Diaries* (1968– ; vol. 8, 1982), ed. M. R. D. Foot and H. C. G. Matthew, shed new light on his complex personality, particularly on his interest in prostitutes, which expressed itself in a zeal for 'rescuing' them and was associated with bouts of self-flagellation, dutifully recorded in what Matthew describes as 'a classic of mid-Victorian self-analysis of guilt'. The diaries (which are for the most part restrained and factual) also illustrate Gladstone's literary tastes; he read *Marmion*, *Lalla Rookh*, and his own verses to his wife immediately after their marriage, was given to reading Tennyson's *The Princess* and *Guinevere* to his rescue cases, found *Ainsworth's *Jack Shepherd* 'dangerous' reading for the masses, and G. Eliot's *Felix Holt* 'a most inharmonious book'. The journalistic nickname 'G.O.M.' ('Grand Old Man'), current from 1882, is said to have been coined by Lord Rosebery.

GLANVILL, Joseph (1636–80), educated at Exeter College and Lincoln College, Oxford, was rector of the Abbey Church at Bath, and held other benefices. He attacked the scholastic philosophy in *The Vanity of Dogmatizing* (1661), a work that contains the story of *"The Scholar-Gipsy'. He defended belief in the pre-existence of souls in *Lux Orientalis* (1662) and belief in witchcraft in *Saducismus Triumphatus* (1681).

GLANVILLE, Ranulf de (d. 1190), chief justiciar of England. The authorship of the first great treatise on the laws of England, *Tractatus de Legibus et Consuetudinibus Angliae*, has been doubtfully ascribed to him on the evidence of *Hoveden.

Glasgerion, an old English ballad of a king's son who is a harper and wins the favour of the king's daughter of Normandy. By a trick his page takes his place at an assignation. When the lady learns the deceit she takes her own life, and Glasgerion cuts off the lad's head and kills himself. The ballad is included in Percy's *Reliques*.

GLASGOW, Ellen Anderson Gholson (1873–1945), American novelist, born in Richmond, Virginia, where she spent most of her life, and which formed the setting of much of her work. In 1896 she took the first of many trips to Europe, and in 1897 published (anonymously) her first novel, *The Descendant*, which was followed by many other works; most critics agree with her own judgement that she began to write her best books in the 1920s, despite ill health, increasing deafness, and much domestic and emotional trouble. She was a woman of advanced views, a supporter of *Women's Suffrage, attracted by *Fabianism; in her fiction she attempted to show realistically the social and political conflicts of her native region, perceived through a sharp, informed, at times lyrical, and somewhat isolated sensibility. Her novels include *The Voice of the People* (1900); *Virginia* (1913); *Barren Ground* (1925; the story of farmer's daughter Dorinda Oakley, a tough survivor of misfortune); *The Romantic Comedians* (1926); *They Stooped to Folly* (1929); and *The Sheltered Life* (1932), a tragi-comedy set in quiet Queensborough, where beautiful Eva Birdsong clings to past romance and elegance through straitened circumstances, ill health, and the philanderings of her husband George, observed by her neighbours, the dangerously awakening adolescent Jenny Blair and Jenny's grandfather, old General Archbald, symbol of a dying chivalry. *Vein of Iron* (1935) is the story of another survivor, the spirited Ada Fincastle of Shut-In Valley, Virginia, who lives through the First World War, an illegitimate baby, a difficult marriage, and the Depression. *In This Our Life* (1941) describes an aristocratic Virginian family in decline, and *The Woman Within* (1954) is a posthumously published autobiography.

Glass Menagerie, The, a play by T. *Williams.

Glastonbury, in Somerset, the abbey of which was said to have been founded by Joseph of Arimathea, according to the *Grail legends (for example in the *Joseph d'Arimathie* of Robert de *Boron, c.1200). The abbey certainly predates the 10th cent. *William of Malmesbury, in his *De Antiquitate Glastoniensis Ecclesiae* (c.1140), suggests that it may have been one of the first Christianized areas in England, founded by French monks. *Giraldus Cambrensis tells the story of the discovery there by the monks of the bodies of Arthur and Guinevere in the 1180s, confirming the story of 'a certain Breton poet' who, according to Henry II, said they were buried there. This led to the identification of Glastonbury with *Avalon. It has been suggested that Henry II arranged the finding of Arthur's body to scotch the tradition that the British king would return to claim his throne. The tradition of the foundation by Joseph of Arimathea advanced to the point in the late 14th cent. where it was claimed by John of Glastonbury that his bones had been found there. See J. A. Robinson, *Two Glastonbury Legends* (1926); R. S. Loomis, *The Grail from Celtic Myth to Christian Symbol* (1963), ch. 15, 250–70.

Glastonbury Romance, A, a novel by J. C. *Powys.

Glatysaunt Beast, The, the creature in Malory's *Morte D'Arthur* which is the original of *Spenser's 'blatant beast'. The word is from an Old French term meaning 'baying', 'barking'. In Malory it is pursued by Palomydes the Saracen. See BLATANT BEAST; QUESTING BEAST.

Glaucé, in Spenser's *Faerie Queene* (III. ii. 30, etc.), the nurse of *Britomart.

Glegg, Mr and Mrs, characters in G. Eliot's *The Mill on the Floss.

Glenallan, earl of, a character in Scott's *The Antiquary.

Glendinning, Halbert and Edward, characters in Scott's *The Monastery* and *The Abbot.

GLENDOWER, Owen (?1359–?1416), Welsh

rebel leader who in Shakespeare's 1 *Henry IV* allies himself with *Hotspur and *Mortimer to divide the kingdom between them. The chroniclers associate him with wizardry and prophecy, which Shakespeare presents sympathetically. His failure to appear at the battle of Shrewsbury contributes to Hotspur's defeat.

Glennaquoich, the seat of Fergus Mac-Ivor, in Scott's *Waverley.*

Glenvarloch, Lord, the title borne by Nigel Olifaunt in Scott's *The Fortunes of Nigel.*

Globe Theatre, the *Burbages' theatre on Bankside in Southwark, erected in 1599 with materials from the old Theatre on the north side of the river. It was a large circular building, thatched, with the centre open to the sky. The thatch caught fire in 1613, owing to the discharge of a peal of ordnance at an entry of the king in *Henry VIII*, and the whole building was destroyed. It was rebuilt in 1614 and demolished in 1644. Shakespeare had a share in the theatre and acted there.

Gloriana, one of the names under which Queen *Elizabeth I is indicated in Spenser's *Faerie Queene*, and the title of the opera composed by *Britten for the coronation of Elizabeth II (1953), with a libretto by *Plomer.

Glossin, Gilbert, a character in Scott's *Guy Mannering.*

Gloucester, earl of, in Shakespeare's *King Lear*, father of *Edgar and the bastard *Edmund. *Regan and *Cornwall blind him (on stage) because they suspect him of supporting *Cordelia's French troops.

GLOVER, Richard (1712–85), was MP for Weymouth, 1761–85, and an opponent of R. *Walpole. He published much blank verse including *Leonidas* (9 books, 1737) and *The Athenaid* (30 books, 1788), but is remembered as the author of the ballad 'Admiral Hosier's Ghost' (1740) which was included in Percy's *Reliques*. This was a party song, contrasting the fate of Admiral Hosier (sent in 1726 with a fleet to the Spanish West Indies but obliged to remain there inactive till most of his men perished and he himself died of a broken heart) with the successful attack of Admiral Vernon on Portobello in 1739.

Glover, Simon and Catharine, two of the principal characters in Scott's *The Fair Maid of Perth.*

Glowry, Scythrop, see SCYTHROP.

Glumdalclitch, in *Gulliver's Travels*, the farmer's daughter who attended on Gulliver during his visit to Brobdingnag.

GLYN, Elinor, *née* Sutherland (1864–1943), author of many sensational and romantic novels, of which the best known is *Three Weeks* (1907), a *succès de scandale*, which features illicit passion in Venice on a tiger skin. As exotic as her characters in appearance, she and adaptations of her works achieved great success in Hollywood during the silent movie era.

Gnomes, see PARACELSUS.

Gnomic, from Gr. γνῶσις, consisting of gnomes or general maxims, sententious.

Gnosticism, a Christian heresy which flourished under the Roman Empire, first documented in the 2nd cent. but possibly much older; some scholars have suggested that there may have been a pre-Christian Gnostic religion, and some of its individual beliefs may be traced back to the *Dead Sea Scrolls and even earlier. For a long period, Gnosticism was known to the modern world only from patristic sources. It influenced many early Christians (including *Clement of Alexandria and *Origen), and was described from a hostile standpoint by chroniclers of contemporary heresies, including *Irenaeus and Hippolytus. If later writers such as *Comenius, Henry More (see CAMBRIDGE PLATONISTS), and *Blake were, as has been claimed, familiar with Gnosticism, their information must have come, directly or indirectly, from these patristic works. At the end of the 19th cent. some genuine Gnostic treatises were translated from the Coptic, but as they reflected the system in its decline they did little to advance knowledge. A breakthough came in the 1950s when a Berlin manuscript containing earlier writings was translated and work began on the publication of a Gnostic library of some 40 separate documents that had been discovered in 1945 at Nag Hammadi in Egypt.

This new material demonstrated that there was no single unified Gnostic faith, but numerous sects with distinct, if vaguely related, beliefs. All, however, were preoccupied with the problem of evil and rejected the concept of a Supreme Being who had created suffering. They opted for a dualism that set a 'good' spiritual world of Light against a 'bad' material world of Darkness. To explain Man, they posited a succession of emanations (*aeons*), the first of which derived directly from the Godhead and each further one from the one above it. On the lowest rung of the ladder stood the Demiurge, identified with Jehovah the Creator. Primal Man, a direct emanation from the Godhead, descended into Darkness, was captured by the forces of evil, and, when rescued, left some of his divine substances behind him; this the Demiurge mixed with Matter to create Man. The purpose of Man's life is to escape his material integument and return to the Godhead, an enterprise in which he is aided by Christ the Saviour (sometimes identified with Primal Man). Christ was supposed to have imparted to his disciples a fund of secret knowledge (Gnosis) with which to ward off the attacks of the Demiurge as the soul ascends to God.

Perhaps the most important feature of Gnosticism is its insistence that behind the Creator and his Law stands a higher divinity with whom the Son is closely allied. This led to a certain antinomianism, the individual aspiring to a state superior to the Creator and Lawgiver. Other features were an extreme asceticism (coupled sometimes with licentiousness among those who did not yet aspire to perfection, since no distinction was made between legitimate and illegitimate carnal desires) and also a marked elitism: outsiders of Gnosis were doomed to extinction and there was a hierarchy among initiates.

Gnosticism declined during the 3rd and 4th cents and was replaced eventually by another dualist sect, *Manicheism.

Gobbo, Launcelot, the 'clown' and servant to *Shylock in Shakespeare's *The Merchant of Venice*; he teases his father, Old Gobbo, who is 'sand-blind' (II. ii).

Go-Between, The, a novel by L. P. *Hartley.

Goblin Market, a poem by C. *Rossetti, published 1862. It is a fairy-tale which has been subjected to many interpretations, some seeing it as religious allegory, others as sexual symbolism.

The story tells, in short, irregularly rhymed verses, of two sisters, Lizzie and Laura, both tempted by goblins selling forbidden fruit. Laura yields, eats, and pines for more; she falls sick, unable to hear the song of the goblins, which still haunts Lizzie. Lizzie, for Laura's sake, braves their temptations, while refusing to eat herself, and redeems her sister by carrying back the juices of the fruits which the goblins have crushed upon her in vain.

GODFREY OF BOUILLON, see BOUILLON, GODEFROI DE; FAIRFAX, E.

GODIVA, the wife of Leofric, ealdorman of Mercia, one of Edward the Confessor's great earls. According to legend, her husband having imposed a tax on the inhabitants of Coventry, she begged him to remit it, which he jestingly promised to do if she would ride naked through the streets at noonday. She took him at his word, directed the people to stay indoors and shut their windows, and complied with his condition. Peeping Tom, who looked out, was struck blind.

The story is told by Drayton in his *Poly-Olbion*, xiii; by Leigh *Hunt; and by *Tennyson in 'Godiva'. Lady Godiva figures as the mother of Hereward in C. *Kingsley's *Hereward the Wake* and in one of Landor's *Imaginary Conversations*.

GODLEY, A(lfred) D(enis) (1856–1925), classical scholar and writer of light verse, was public orator of Oxford, 1910–25, and joint editor of the *Classical Review*, 1910–20. He translated *Horace's Odes (1898) and *Herodotus' Works (Loeb Series, 1921–3). His volumes of verse, much of which deals with university life, include *Verses to Order* (1892), *Lyra Frivola* (1899), and *Reliquiae A. D. Godley* (1926).

Godolphin, a novel by *Bulwer-Lytton.

GODOLPHIN, Sidney (1610–43), poet and Royalist, a friend of *Falkland and described by *Suckling as 'little Sid'. He was killed at Chagford. His poems, not collected during his life, were edited by W. Dighton (1931). Hobbes dedicated *Leviathan to his brother Francis.

God That Failed, The: *Six Studies in Communism*, a volume published in 1950, edited by R. H. S. Crossman, which marked a significant point in the reaction against the pro-Communist mood of the 1930s. It contained contributions by three ex-Communists, *Koestler, *Silone, and R. *Wright, and by three sympathizers, *Gide (presented by Enid Starkie), Louis Fischer, and *Spender (who had been a party member for a matter of weeks only).

GODWIN, William (1756–1836), educated at Hoxton Academy, was at first a Dissenting minister, but became an atheist and philosopher of anarchical view. He believed that men acted according to reason, that it was impossible to be rationally persuaded and not to act accordingly, that reason taught benevolence, and that therefore rational creatures could live in harmony without laws and institutions. He married Mary *Wollstonecraft in 1797; she died at the birth of their daughter Mary, the future wife of *Shelley, and Godwin subsequently married Mrs Clairmont, whose daughter by her first marriage, Claire *Clairmont bore a daughter, Allegra, to Lord *Byron.

Godwin produced in 1793 his *Enquiry concerning Political Justice*, in which he proclaimed that 'Truth is omnipotent . . . Man is perfectible, or in other words susceptible of perpetual improvement.' In 1794 he published *The Adventures of *Caleb Williams* and *Cursory Strictures*, a pamphlet defending twelve Radicals, including his friends *Tooke and *Holcroft, against the charge of high treason. His life of Mary Wollstonecraft, *Memoirs of the author of a Vindication of the Rights of Woman*, appeared in 1798; and there is a portrait of her in his novel *St Leon* (1799). He wrote several other novels (*Fleetwood*, 1805; *Mandeville*, 1817; *Cloudesley*, 1830; *Deloraine*, 1833) and a life of *Chaucer (1803–4).

Göemot, the name under which *Gogmagog figures in Spenser's *Faerie Queene*.

Goesler, Madame Marie Max, a character of importance in the *'Palliser' novels of A. Trollope.

GOETHE, Johann Wolfgang von (1749–1832), born at Frankfurt am Main, the son of an Imperial Councillor, was trained for the law against his inclination. In 1775 he was invited by the duke of Weimar, Karl August, to his court, and thereafter spent most of his life in Weimar, occupying positions of increasing importance in the government until 1786. He was raised to the nobility in 1782. In 1791 he was appointed director of the Weimar court theatre, a post he held for many years. Throughout his life he was interested in a variety of studies and pursuits, including painting, for which he had only a mediocre gift, though his scattered critical remarks on the visual arts are of great interest. In the field of scientific research he evolved a new theory of the character of light, which he expounded and defended in the *Farbenlehre* (*Treatise on Colour*, 1810). He also made important discoveries in connection with plant and animal life.

In the field of literature his most famous work was the poetic drama in two parts, *Faust. His first important work was *Götz von Berlichingen mit der eisernen Hand* (1773), a drama written under the influence of his friend and critic *Herder, who had called for a German Shakespeare to emerge and begin a new flourishing period of German literature. This rough, exuberant play excited Sir W. *Scott, who translated it (inaccurately) in 1799, and it was adapted for the English stage by J. *Arden under the title *Iron Hand* (1965). *Die Leiden des jungen Werthers* (*The Sorrows of Young Werther*, 1774) is a semi-autobiographical *epistolary novel. Werther is a sensitive artist, ill at ease in society and hopelessly in love with Charlotte, who is engaged to someone else. This novel, with the eventual suicide of the hero, caused a sensation throughout Europe (see WERTHERISM). In 1786 Goethe made the first of two important visits to Italy, which he recorded in *Italienische Reise* (*Italian Journey*, 1816–17), translated by W. H. *Auden and Elizabeth Mayer in 1962. He returned with his ideas about art radically changed in favour of 'classicism' and cured of the *Sturm und Drang tendencies of his early works. In 1787 there appeared his drama *Iphigenie auf Tauris* (*Iphigenia in Tauris*) based on *Euripides, but differing in many respects from the Greek play, particularly in its more humane conception of man. *Tasso* (1790) dramatizes the problems of the artist in society and is based, like all Goethe's works, partly on his own experience as resident poet in Weimar. In 1795 Goethe published the *Römische Elegien* (*Roman Elegies*), sensuous poems relating partly to Christiane Vulpius, who became Goethe's mistress in 1789 and whom he married in 1806. *Hermann und*

Dorothea (1797) is a pastoral epic founded on the expulsion of the Protestants by the archbishop of Salzburg in 1732, but with the scene shifted to France under the revolution.

Die Wahlverwandtschaften (*Elective Affinities*) appeared in 1809, a novel dealing in a strikingly unmoralistic way with the mutual attraction of a married couple for two other persons. Goethe modelled his collection of poems, *Der west-östliche Divan* (*East-west Divan*, 1819) on the *Divan* of the Persian poet *Hafiz. In the successive volumes of *Dichtung und Wahrheit* (*Poetry and Truth*), which were published between 1811 and 1832, Goethe recalled and reshaped those experiences in his life which had most influenced his artistic development. Along with the *Conversations with Goethe* published by his secretary Eckermann, these were the source of much interest in Goethe's life in England as well as Germany. The famous 'Wilhelm Meister' novels, written at intervals between 1777 and 1829, are the prototype of the German *Bildungsroman. The first part deals with the disillusioning experiences of the stage-struck youth as he travels the country with a theatrical company, among whose members are the mysterious *Mignon and the Harper, whose songs, particularly 'Kennst du das Land' ('Know'st thou the land'), are well known in settings by *Schubert and *Wolf. In this first part, *Wilhelm Meister's Apprenticeship* (1795–6), translated into English by *Carlyle in 1824, Goethe plays ironically with the forces of fate and chance, and the novel includes a debate on the modes appropriate to the novel as opposed to the drama and some interesting criticism (not unlike *Coleridge's) of *Hamlet. In the sequel, *Wilhelm Meisters Wanderjahre* (*Wilhelm Meister's Travels*), also translated by Carlyle (in a volume of stories translated from the German, *German Romance*, 1827), Wilhelm's education for life is completed. Though Goethe is most celebrated, particularly outside Germany, for *Faust* and the novels, he was also a lyric poet of great genius. Many of his poems, as well as the songs from 'Wilhelm Meister', were set to music by German Romantic composers.

Goethe's achievement in literature covers an astonishing range of forms, though all his works stand in a close relation to the social and emotional events of his life; as he said, they are 'Bruchstücke einer grossen Konfession' ('fragments of a great confession'). The most decisive influences in his life were Herder, who introduced him to Shakespeare and encouraged him in his early works, the visits to classical Italy, and *Schiller, with whom he began a close friendship in 1794. The correspondence of the two poets shows how mutually helpful they were as critics of one another's work in progress. In Britain, Goethe exercised an enormous influence on Carlyle, who translated him, wrote proselytizing essays on his works, and elevated

Goethe to the status of 'the Wisest of our Time' (*Sartor Resartus*). Through Carlyle a whole generation of Victorians turned their attention to Goethe, and eminent authors like G. *Eliot and M. *Arnold paid tribute to his genius both in essays on Goethe and in their creative works (for example, the dénouement of *The Mill on the Floss* may owe something to that of *Elective Affinities*, and the chapter mottoes of *Middlemarch* and *Daniel Deronda* are frequently quotations from Goethe). G. H. *Lewes wrote the first full biography of Goethe in any language (*The Life and Works of Goethe*, 1855), a book he researched, with George Eliot's help, in Weimar in 1854. This biography is still one of the best introductions to Goethe for English readers.

GOGARTY, Oliver Joseph St John (1878–1957), poet, surgeon, and for some time a close friend of *Joyce who portrayed him in *Ulysses* as 'stately, plump Buck Mulligan'. He published several novels and volumes of verse, and *Yeats, who included 17 of his poems in *The Oxford Book of Modern Verse* (1936), rated his work highly.

Gogmagog, according to *Geoffrey of Monmouth's *History* (i. 16), a twelve-foot member of the tribe of giants who occupied Britain before the coming of Brutus (*Brut*). He attacked Brutus and the settlers, killing many of them. Brutus told the avenging Britons to spare Gogmagog so that he could wrestle with Brutus's ally Corineus (a companion of Antenor who joined Brutus at the Pillars of Hercules. Geoffrey, i. 12). Corineus defeats the giant, throwing him to his death far out in the sea. See Spenser, *Faerie Queene* (III. ix. 50). The hills near Cambridge are called the Gogmagog Hills.

The name was divided between two giant figures of wicker and plaster, Gog and Magog, which were carried in the Lord Mayor's procession through the City of London from the 15th cent. Carved wooden copies 14 ft 6 in high were placed flanking the Guildhall's council chamber door in 1708: these were destroyed in the Second World War, and modern copies now stand in the west gallery.

GOGOL, Nikolai Vasilevich (1809–52), Russian prose writer and dramatist. Born in the Ukraine, which he used as a setting for his early writings, he left for St Petersburg in 1828. His first collection of stories, *Evenings on a Farm near Dikanka*, appeared in 1831–2. He was appointed adjunct professor of history at St Petersburg University in 1834, but was dismissed in 1835. His collections *Mirgorod* and *Arabesques* (1835) were followed by the play *The Government Inspector* (or *The Inspector-General*) (1836), a savagely satirical picture of life in a provincial Russian town. His brilliant St Petersburg stories, 'Nevsky Prospekt' (1835), 'Notes of a Madman' (1835), 'The Portrait' (1835), 'The

Nose' (1836), and 'The Greatcoat' (1842), are set in a mad city where nothing is what it seems. From 1836 to 1848 Gogol lived mainly abroad, spending most of his time in Rome. During this period he was at work on his masterpiece, the comic epic *Dead Souls*; the first part was published in 1842, but in 1845, during a developing spiritual crisis, he burnt the drafts of the second part. In 1847 he published an intended moral testament, the *Selected Passages from Correspondence with Friends*, to almost universal rebuke, especially from *Belinsky and *Aksakov. In 1848 he made a pilgrimage to Jerusalem. On his return he continued with *Dead Souls*, but by now he had fallen under the influence of Father Matvei Konstantinovsky, who encouraged him to renounce literature. In Feb. 1852, during a régime of fasting and prayer, Gogol burnt the manuscript of part two of *Dead Souls* and ten days later he died.

Gogol's prose is characterized by extraordinary imaginative power and linguistic originality. His fictional world is unique and fantastic. Among English writers, he was an admirer of Shakespeare, *Fielding, *De Quincey, Sir W. *Scott, and particularly *Sterne, who may have influenced him. He was himself much admired by the young *Dostoevsky, and has been claimed as precursor by many significant writers. 'The Portrait' was translated into English in 1847, in *Blackwood's*. The most complete early translation is by C. *Garnett (1922–8).

Golagros and Gawain, a 15th-cent Scottish poem of 1,362 lines in 13-line alliterative stanzas, printed in a pamphlet in Edinburgh in 1508, and having some similarities to *The Awntyrs of Arthure*. It is loosely based on the French prose *Perceval* and is concerned with a journey of Arthur and his knights to the Holy Land. There are two episodes, both demonstrating the courtesy of Gawain: in the first, Kay churlishly and Gawain courteously ask for hospitality; in the second Arthur unwisely lays siege to the stronghold of Golagros and Gawain fights in single combat against the latter, ending with Golagros's defeat and reflections on the vagaries of fortune. But the stress throughout is on chivalry, especially that of Gawain. See edition by F. J. Amours, *Scottish Alliterative Poems* (STS, 1897).

Golden, a term used by C. S. *Lewis (*English Literature in the Sixteenth Century*, Introduction) to distinguish the literature of the later Elizabethan period from its predecessors in the *'Drab' age. According to Lewis, 'for a few years nothing more is needed than to play out again and again the strong, simple music of the uncontorted line and to load one's poem with all that is naturally delightful.' The 'Golden' period may be seen as running roughly from Lyly's

Euphues (1579) to the death of Queen *Elizabeth in 1603. All the major works of *Spenser, *Sidney, and *Marlowe fall within this period, as does two-thirds of the work of Shakespeare. The term suggests a certain bright, innocent, repetitive beauty, which one might see exemplified in such poems as T. *Campion's:

> There is a Garden in her face,
> Where Roses and white Lillies grow;
> A heav'nly paradice is that place,
> Wherein all pleasant fruits doe flow.

But the limited applicability of the term will be realized when we remember that *Hamlet*, *Dr Faustus*, and much of the poetry of *Donne were among the works written within the period of so-called 'Golden' poetry.

Golden Age, The, see GRAHAME, K.

Golden Ass, The, see APULEIUS.

Golden Bough, The, see FRAZER, J. G.

Golden Bowl, The, the last completed novel of H. *James, published 1904.

The widowed American Adam Verver is in Europe with his daughter Maggie. They are rich, finely appreciative of European art and culture, and deeply attached to each other. Maggie has all the innocent charm of so many of James's young American heroines. She is engaged to Amerigo, an impoverished Italian prince; he must marry money and, as his name suggests, an American heiress is the perfect solution. The golden bowl, first seen in a London curio shop, is used emblematically throughout the novel. Not solid gold but gilded crystal, the perfect surface conceals a flaw; it is symbolic of the relationship between the main characters and of the world in which they move.

Also in Europe is an old friend of Maggie's, Charlotte Stant, a girl of great charm and independence, and Maggie is blindly ignorant of the fact that she and the prince are lovers. Maggie and Amerigo are married and have a son, but Maggie remains dependent for real intimacy on her father, and she and Amerigo grow increasingly apart. Feeling that her father has suffered a loss through her marriage Maggie decides to find him a wife, and her choice falls on Charlotte. The affair with the prince continues and Adam Verver seems to Charlotte to be a suitable and convenient match. When Maggie herself finally comes into possession of the golden bowl the flaw is revealed to her, and, inadvertently, the truth about Amerigo and Charlotte. Fanny Ashingham (an older woman, aware of the truth from the beginning) deliberately breaks the bowl, and this marks the end of Maggie's 'innocence'. She is no pathetic heroine-victim. Abstaining from outcry and outrage, she takes the reins and manœuvres people and events. She still wants Amerigo but he must continue to be worth having and they must all be saved further humiliations and indignities. To be a wife she must cease to be a daughter; Adam Verver and the unhappy Charlotte are banished forever to America, and the new Maggie will establish a real marriage with Amerigo.

Golden Cockerel Press, a *private press founded in 1920 at Waltham St Lawrence, Berkshire, by Harold Taylor, and taken over in 1924 by Robert Gibbings (1889–1958), wood-engraver, illustrator, and writer of travel books. The Golden Cockerel type was designed by *Gill, who was associated with the press from 1924 and designed one of its most celebrated productions, *The Four Gospels* (1941).

Golden Grove, The, see TAYLOR, JEREMY.

Golden Legend, The, a medieval manual of ecclesiastical lore: lives of saints, commentary on church services, homilies for saints' days, and so on. A version in English of this compilation from various sources was published by *Caxton in 1483 and was his most popular production, often reprinted. One of its most important sources was the *Legenda Aurea* in Latin by Jacobus de Voragine (1230–98), an Italian Dominican friar who became archbishop of Genoa. Caxton's version was edited by F. S. Ellis, 3 vols, 1892 (Temple Classics 1900); selections ed. G. V. O'Neill (1914).

Golden Notebook, The, a novel by D. *Lessing.

Golden Treasury, see PALGRAVE, F. T.

GOLDING, Arthur (?1536–?1605), translator of Latin and French works, including *Ovid's *Metamorphoses* (1565–7), *Caesar's *Gallic War* (1565), Justin's abbreviation of Trogus Pompeius (1564), and Philippe de Mornay's *A Woorke concerning the trewnesse of the Christian Religion* (1587), which had originally been undertaken by Sir P. *Sidney. His translations are clear, faithful, and fluent, and his Ovid was known to Shakespeare.

GOLDING, William (1911–), was born in Cornwall and educated at Marlborough Grammar School and Brasenose College, Oxford. He worked as a writer, actor, and producer with small theatre companies and then as a teacher; during the war he served in the Royal Navy and was lieutenant in command of a rocket ship. After the war he returned to writing and teaching. He had published a volume, *Poems*, in 1935 but his first novel, *Lord of the Flies*, did not appear until 1954 when it was an immediate success. *The Inheritors* (1955) tells of man's brutal extermination of his gentler ancestors; the intrinsic cruelty of man is at the heart of many of Golding's novels. *Pincher Martin* (1956), *The Brass Butterfly* (a play, 1958), *Free Fall* (1959), *The Spire* (1964), were followed by a collection of essays, *The Hot Gates* (1965). His other novels are *The Pyramid* (1967), *The Scorpion God* (three novellas, 1971), *Darkness Visible* (1979), and *Rites of Passage* (1980, *Booker Prize). Golding often presents isolated individuals or small groups in extreme situations dealing with man in his basic condition stripped of trappings, creating a quality of a fable. His novels are remarkable for their strikingly varied settings, several of them historical.

Golding was awarded the *Nobel Prize in 1983, and his novel *The Paper Men* (1984), which describes the pursuit of world famous English novelist Wilfred Barclay by American academic Rick L. Turner, echoes some of the author's previously expressed irritation at finding himself 'the raw material of an academic light industry'. (See the title lecture, delivered in 1976, of a collection of lectures and essays, *A Moving Target*, 1982.)

GOLDMANN, Lucien, see MARXIST LITERARY CRITICISM.

GOLDONI, Carlo (1707–93), Italian dramatist, whose comedy is based on the society of his native Venice. He renewed stage comedy, which had been dominated by the *commedia dell'arte*. He wrote 250 plays, of which 150 are comedies. In 1762 he settled in Paris, where after writing two successful plays, *Il ventaglio* (*The Fan*) and *Le Bourru bienfaisant* (*The Beneficent Grumbler*), he died a pauper. The majority of his plays, many of which satirize the aristocracy, fall into three categories: comedies retaining the masked characters of the *commedia dell'arte*, who speak in their traditional dialects, e.g. *La vedova scaltra* (*The Clever Widow*); Italian comedies of manners without masks, e.g. *La locandiera* (*The Mistress of the Inn*), *La bottega del caffè* (*The Coffee-shop*); and comedies in Venetian dialect, generally considered his best, e.g. *I rusteghi* (*The Tyrants*).

GOLDSMITH, Oliver (?1730–74), the second son of an Anglo-Irish clergyman, was born probably at Pallas, Co. Longford, or perhaps at Elphin, Roscommon. He spent much of his childhood at Lissoy, and is thought to have drawn on his memories of it when writing *The Deserted Village*. He was educated at Trinity College, Dublin, and graduated after some upheavals in 1750; he then presented himself for ordination, was rejected, and went to Edinburgh, where he studied medicine but took no degree. He studied in Leyden, and during 1755–6 wandered about France, Switzerland, and Italy, reaching London destitute in 1756, where he supported himself with difficulty as a physician in Southwark and as an usher in Peckham; he may at this period have received a medical degree from Trinity, though this remains unclear. He applied for a medical post in India, but failed to obtain it; meanwhile he had embarked on a literary career as reviewer and hack-writer for Griffith's *Monthly Review*, one of his early pieces being a favourable review of Burke's *Philosophical Enquiry . . . into the *Sublime and Beautiful*; *Burke was to become a close friend. In 1758 he published, under the pseudonym 'James Willington', his translation of *The Memoirs of a Protestant, condemned to the Galleys of France for his Religion* (by Jean Marteilhe of Bergerac, a victim of the Edict of Nantes), and in 1759 his first substantial work, *An Enquiry into the Present State of Polite Learning in Europe*. It was at this period he met *Percy, later bishop of Dromore, who was to become a loyal friend and also his biographer. He was by now contributing to many periodicals (*The Busy Body*, *The Monthly Review*, *The Critical Review*, *The Ladies Magazine*, etc.), and during Oct. and Nov. 1759 published his own little periodical, *The Bee*, in which appeared his 'Elegy on Mrs Mary Blaize' (a pawnbroker) and 'A City Night-Piece'. He contributed to *Smollett's *British Magazine*, started in 1760, and was also employed by *Newbery, for whose new *Public Ledger* he wrote his 'Chinese Letters', subsequently republished as *The Citizen of the World* in 1762; he is also said to have written the nursery tale *Goody Two-Shoes*. In 1761 he met Dr *Johnson, who admired his work; he became one of the original members of Johnson's *Club. Johnson remained his friend and champion, and in 1762 sold for him the (possibly unfinished) manuscript of *The Vicar of Wakefield* to Newbery, thereby saving him from arrest for debt. Goldsmith was still struggling as a writer, and making his living with a variety of hack-work in the form of biographies, compilations, translations, abridgements, etc.: these include lives of *Voltaire (1761) and Beau *Nash (1762), an abridgement of *Plutarch (1762), a *History of England in a series of letters from a nobleman to his son* (1764), a *Roman History* (1769), a *Grecian History* (1774), lives of T. *Parnell and *Bolingbroke (1770), etc.—in all more than 40 volumes. But he first achieved literary distinction with his poem *The Traveller* (1764) which also introduced him to his only patron, Lord Clare; it was his first signed work, and was much admired by Johnson and *Fox among others. *The Vicar of Wakefield* (1764), which was to become one of the most popular works of fiction in the language, was slower to find its audience, possibly because it was, as *The Monthly Review* commented, 'difficult to characterize'.

Goldsmith's first comedy, *The Good-Natur'd Man*, was rejected by *Garrick but produced at Covent Garden in 1768 with moderate success; *She Stoops to Conquer* followed in 1773 with immense success. Goldsmith had criticized the vogue for *sentimental comedy and the prejudice against laughter (see CHESTERFIELD) in an essay in *The Westminster Magazine* entitled 'A

Comparison between Laughing and Sentimental Comedy' (1773); his own play's lasting popularity justified his comments.

His best-known poem, *The Deserted Village*, was published in 1770; his lighter verses include *Retaliation* (1774) and the posthumously-published *The Haunch of Venison* (1776), written to thank Lord Clare for a gift of game from his estate. His *An History of the Earth and Animated Nature* (1774), also published posthumously, in 8 vols adapted from *Buffon, *Linnaeus, *Ray, and others, inventively portrays 'tygers' in Canada, and squirrels migrating on bark boats in Lapland, fanning themselves along with their tails.

There are many anecdotes about Goldsmith in Boswell's *Life of *Johnson*, which represent him as ridiculous, vain, extravagantly dressed, improvident, and naïve, but also as tender-hearted, simple, and generous, with flashes of brilliance in conversation (despite Garrick's gibe that he 'wrote like an angel, but talked like poor Poll'). He was regarded with much affection; Johnson, in his Latin epitaph, stated that he adorned whatever he touched. He never married, and his relationship with Mary Horneck, his 'Jessamy bride', remains mysterious. He was introduced to the Horneck family by *Reynolds in 1766, when Mary was 14, and accompanied Mrs Horneck, Mary, and her other daughter Catherine ('Little Comedy', who married H. W. *Bunbury) to Paris in 1770; in 1773 he attacked Thomas Evans for publishing in *The London Packet* a letter from 'Tom Tickler' mocking his feelings for 'the lovely H——k'. She long outlived him, and provided material for J. Prior's life (1837); another biographer, W. *Irving (1844) concluded that Goldsmith had suffered from unrequited love, but this has been much disputed.

The 1801 *Miscellaneous Works* contain Percy's memoir, and there are other lives by J. *Forster (1848) and Ralph M. Wardle (1957). *The Collected Works* (5 vols, 1966) were edited by A. Friedman, and the correspondence by K. C. Balderstone (1928).

Goliard, Goliardic, see GOLIAS.

Golias, or **Goliardus,** the name found attached in English MSS of the 12th and 13th cents to Latin poems of a satirical and profane kind, the most famous of these being the so-called 'Apocalypse of Golias', for which no certain evidence of authorship can be claimed. According to F. J. E. Raby (*A History of Secular Latin Poetry in the Middle Ages*), the conception of Golias as 'Bishop' or 'Arch-poet' is a myth, largely of English creation. The 'Goliards' are, it seems, to be linked with Golias, Goliath of Gath, the symbol of lawlessness and of evil, though the original derivation may have been from 'gula', on account of their gluttony. The famous

'Goliardic' measure or 'Vagantenstrophe' appears to have passed from secular into religious verse. See CARMINA BURANA.

GOLLANCZ, Israel (1864–1930), after lecturing at University College London, 1892–6, was appointed in 1896 as the first lecturer in English at Cambridge. In 1905 he became professor of English at King's College, London, a post he held until his death. He followed *Furnivall as director of the Early English Texts Society, and he was one of the founders and original fellows of the *British Academy (1902). He was an outstanding medieval and Shakespearean scholar and editor. As well as editing several texts in Old and Middle English, he was the general editor of the Temple Shakespeare and of Temple Classics. A British Academy lectureship and prize were founded in his memory. He was one of the most active and distinguished members of the British Jewish community, promoting Jewish cultural causes.

GOLLANCZ, Sir Victor (1893–1967), nephew of Sir I. *Gollancz, publisher; he founded his own firm in 1928, and in 1936 the *Left Book Club. He was well known for his progressive views, his resistance to Fascism, his 'Save Europe Now' movement in 1945 to relieve starving Germany, and his opposition to capital punishment; these were reflected in his firm's publications.

G.O.M., see GLADSTONE.

GOMBRICH, Sir Ernst (1909–   ), distinguished British art historian, who was long associated with the Warburg Institute in the University of London, as director and as professor of the history of the classical tradition. His immensely popular work *The Story of Art* (1950) is now widely used as a textbook by many schools and universities. He has written extensively on the theory of art and on the psychology of pictorial representation; three volumes of essays, *Studies in the Art of the Renaissance* (1966, 1972, 1976), discuss the style of Renaissance painting, its symbolism, and its relationship to the classical tradition.

GONCHAROV, Ivan Aleksandrovich (1812–91), Russian prose writer. From 1834 to 1867 he worked in the Russian bureaucracy, serving from 1855 as an official censor. In 1852–4 he journeyed round the world as secretary to an admiral. The book he wrote about his travels, *The Frigate Pallas*, contains impressions of England and of English colonialism. Goncharov's most important works are the novels *An Ordinary Story* (1847, trans. C. *Garnett, 1894), *The Ravine* (1869, trans. 1915), and his masterpiece *Oblomov* (1859, trans. 1915), where in the portrait of a man who disdains to get out of bed he created a literary archetype admired the world over.

GONCOURT, Edmond and Jules de (1822–96 and 1830–70), French authors, brothers, who wrote in close collaboration. Their earliest interests were art criticism, in which field they published several works (including the important *L'Art du dix-huitième siècle*, 1859–75), and French social history. From 1851 they wrote novels, painstakingly documented studies which they regarded as a form of contemporary social history. *Soeur Philomène* (1861), *Germinie Lacerteux* (1864), and *Madam Gervaisais* (1869) are among the best known. Their *écriture artiste*, an impressionistic, highly mannered style, elaborate in syntax and vocabulary, is well exemplified in *Manette Salomon* (1867), a novel of artist life. Some years after Jules's death Edmond returned to novel-writing with, for example, *Les Frères Zemganno* (1879). The famous *Journal des Goncourt* is a richly detailed record of literary life in Paris between 1851 and 1896. Several volumes were published, omitting many passages likely to shock or give offence, during Edmond de Goncourt's lifetime. An integral edition appeared between 1956 and 1959. The Académie Goncourt, founded under the will of Edmond de Goncourt, is a body of ten men or women of letters which awards an annual money prize (*Prix Goncourt*) for imaginative prose. (See also NATURALISM.)

Gondal, see ANGRIA AND GONDAL.

Gondibert, an uncompleted romantic epic by *D'Avenant, published 1651, consisting of some 1,700 quatrains.

It is a tale of chivalry, set in Lombardy; Duke Gondibert loves Birtha, and is therefore impervious to the love of Rhodalind, the king's daughter, who is in turn loved by Oswald, but before these issues are resolved the author declares himself bored with the poem. D. F. Gladish in his 1971 edition describes it as 'a poetic museum of seventeenth century literature and theory'.

GONDOMAR, Don Diego Sarmiento de Acuña, marquis de, the Spanish ambassador in the reign of James I. He was the enemy of *Ralegh, and caused *Middleton to be imprisoned for his play *A Game at Chesse*.

Goneril, in Shakespeare's *King Lear*, the king's eldest daughter, who marries *Albany.

Gone with the Wind, see MITCHELL, M.

Gongorism, an affected type of diction and style introduced into Spanish literature in the 16th cent. by the poet Luis de Góngora y Argote (1561–1627), a style akin to Euphuism in England and Marinism in Italy (see EUPHUES and MARINO). Góngora was none the less a poet of genius, and both his earlier and his latest verses were simple and unaffected.

Gonzalo, 'an honest old Councellor' loyal to *Prospero and part of Antonio's company in Shakespeare's *The Tempest*.

Goodbye to Berlin, see ISHERWOOD, C.

Good Companions, The, a novel by J. B. *Priestley.

Good-Natur'd Man, The, a comedy by *Goldsmith, produced 1768.

Mr Honeywood is an open-hearted but foolishly good-natured and credulous young man, who gives away to the importunate what he owes to his creditors. His uncle, Sir William Honeywood, decides to teach him a lesson by having him arrested for debt and letting him see who are his true friends. Young Honeywood is in love with Miss Richland, a lady of fortune, and she with him, but he is too diffident to propose to her. He even recommends to her the suit of Lofty, a government official to whom he believes himself indebted for release from arrest. In fact it is Miss Richland who has secured the release, and Lofty is exposed; Honeywood, cured from his folly, is united with Miss Richland. There is a sub-plot turning on a love affair between Leontine, the son of Croaker, Miss Richland's doleful guardian, and Olivia; these two are also united through the intervention of Sir William. The character of Croaker, 'always lamenting misfortunes he never knew' (T. *Davies), was taken from Suspirius, in *The Rambler* No. 59, according to *Boswell. The theme of excessive generosity was treated several times by Goldsmith and, according to Davies, he himself, 'rather than not relieve the distressed, would borrow'. (See also CITIZEN OF THE WORLD, 'The Man in Black'.) In a Preface Goldsmith attacks 'genteel comedy' and praises the comedy of 'nature and humour'.

Good Soldier, The: *A Tale of Passion*, a novel by F. M. *Ford, published 1915; an earlier version of the first part of the novel appeared in *Blast*, 20 June 1914, as 'The saddest story'.

Generally considered Ford's finest technical achievement, as well as his most readable novel, it consists of the first-person narration of American John Dowell (an archetypally ambiguous 'unreliable narrator'), who relates the history of relationships that begin in 1904, when he and his wife Florence meet Edward and Leonora Ashburnham in a hotel in Nauheim. The two couples form a foursome, a 'round table', and meet regularly. In August 1913 the Ashburnhams take their young ward Nancy Rufford to Nauheim with them, and Florence commits suicide. Later that year the Ashburnhams send Nancy to India (where she goes mad) and Edward also commits suicide, although we do not learn the manner of his death until the last page. Dowell becomes Nancy's 'male sick nurse'; Leonora remarries. The substance of the novel lies in Dowell's growing understanding of the intrigues and passions that lay behind the orderly Edwardian façade both couples had presented to the world; the carefully-plotted time-scheme (orchestrated round the fatal date of 4 August, Florence's wedding day and death day) introduces the 'facts' (that Edward and Florence had been lovers, that both Edward and Dowell were in love with Nancy and Nancy with Edward) in an apparently casual, haphazard way that lends plausibility to an essentially melodramatic tale. The frequent time-shifts show an affinity with Ford's one-time collaborator, *Conrad, and the constellation of relationships owes something to H. *James. The novel remains, through its ironies, ambiguities, and inconsistencies, an interpreter's delight.

Good Thoughts in Bad Times, a collection of reflections by T. *Fuller, published 1645 at Exeter, where Fuller was living as chaplain to Sir Ralph Hopton. It was followed in 1647 by *Good Thoughts in Worse Times,* and in 1660, at the Restoration, by *Mixt Contemplations in Better Times.* The work consists of meditations on his own shortcomings, observations of passages of scripture, and applications of historical incidents and anecdotes to current events, and is marked by his usual good humour.

Goody Two-Shoes, a moralistic nursery tale, said to have been written by *Goldsmith, published by *Newbery.

GOOGE, Barnabe (1540–94), a member of both universities, was a kinsman of Sir William Cecil, who employed him in Ireland, 1547–85. He published *Eglogs, Epytaphes, and Sonnetes* (1563, reprinted 1871), and translations, including Heresbachius's *Foure Bookes of Husbandrie* (1577). His eclogues are of interest as being, with those of *Barclay, the earliest examples of pastorals in English.

Gorboduc, or *Ferrex and Porrex,* one of the earliest of English tragedies, of which the first three acts are by Thomas Norton (1532–84) and the last two by T. *Sackville. It was acted in the Inner Temple Hall on Twelfth Night 1561. The play is constructed on the model of a Senecan tragedy, and the subject is taken from the legendary chronicles of Britain.

Gorboduc and Videna are king and queen, Ferrex and Porrex are their two sons, and the dukes of Cornwall, Albany, Logres, and Cumberland are the other chief characters. Ferrex and Porrex quarrel over the division of the kingdom. Ferrex is killed by Porrex, and Porrex is murdered in revenge by his mother. The duke of Albany tries to seize the kingdom and civil war breaks out. There is no action on the stage, the events being narrated in blank verse. Sidney praised the play in his *Defence of Poetry* as being 'full of stately speeches and well-sounding phrases'.

The legend of Gorboduc is told by *Geoffrey of Monmouth, and figures in Spenser's *Faerie Queene* (II. x. 34 and 35), where Gorboduc is called Gorbogud.

GORDIMER, Nadine (1923–   ), South African novelist and short story writer, most of whose work is concerned with the political situation in her native land; her protests against apartheid and censorship have been outspoken. Her collections of stories include *The Soft Voice of the Serpent* (1953), *Friday's Footprint* (1960), and *Livingstone's Companions* (1972); her novels include *A Guest of Honour* (1970), in which an English colonial administrator returns to the complexities of a newly independent African country from which he had been previously expelled for his sympathies with the black population; *The Conservationist* (1974, joint winner of the *Booker Prize); *Burger's Daughter* (1979), which describes the personal and political heritage of Rosa Burger, whose Communist father had died in prison; and *July's People* (1981), a novella set in the future, in which a white family on the run from civil war find themselves dependent on their black servant.

GORE, Mrs Catherine Grace Frances, née Moody (1799–1861), a novelist of the *Silver Fork school, who published about 70 novels between 1824 and 1862, many anonymously; they include *Mothers and Daughters* (1830) and *Mrs Armytage: or female domination* (1836), generally considered her best; *Cecil, or the adventures of a coxcomb* (1841); and *The banker's wife, or court and city* (1843). She also wrote several plays and many short stories. Her novels, with their marked predilection for titled ladies and fashionable life, were parodied by *Thackeray in 'Lords and Liveries', one of *Mr Punch's Prize Novelists.

GORE, Charles (1853–1932), bishop of Oxford 1911–19, wrote a number of works on religious subjects and edited and contributed to *Lux Mundi* (1889), a collection of essays on the Christian faith written by various hands which attempted 'to put the Catholic faith into its right relation to modern intellectual and moral problems'; the book caused some distress among the older and more conservative school of High Churchmen.

GORGES, Sir Arthur (1557–1625), courtier and poet, was educated at Oxford, and from 1580 was a gentleman pensioner at court. He was a close friend of *Ralegh. His grief for the death of his young wife Douglas Howard was depicted by *Spenser in *Daphnaïda* (1591). His love poems *Vannetyes and toyes of yowth* were not published until 1953; other works include *The Olympian Catastrophe* (1612), an elegy on

Prince Henry; *Lucans Pharsalia* (1614), a powerful rendering of *Lucan's epic into rhyming tetrameters; and a translation of F. *Bacon's *Wisedome of the Ancients* in 1619. His English poems were edited by H. E. Sandison (1953).

GORKY, Maxim (Aleksei Maksimovich Peshkov) (1868–1936), Russian prose writer and playwright. Obliged to work for his living from the age of eight, Gorky roamed all over Russia. He was self-educated and read voraciously. He suffered for his radical views and after taking part in the 1905 revolution he went abroad to collect funds for the revolutionary movement. After the 1917 revolution his independent views and increasing ill-health led, in 1921, to his leaving Russia for Italy. In 1928 he returned to the Soviet Union as an enthusiastic supporter of the government. The position of Gorky in the last years of his life is paradoxical and obscure. Officially lionized as the father of the new Socialist art, he was partly responsible for the formulation of the doctrine of *Socialist Realism, and in 1934 he became first president of the Union of Soviet Writers. Yet he is also said to have intervened to protect writers who came under attack. The circumstances of his death, too, remain shrouded in mystery.

His first story was 'Makar Chudra' (1892), but it was 'Chelkash' (1895) which established his reputation. His best-known works are *Twenty-six Men and a Girl* (1899), *Foma Gordeev* (1899), *The Mother* (1906–7), the story of the radicalization of an uneducated woman that was later taken as a model for the Socialist Realist novel, and his autobiographical masterpiece *Childhood* (1913), *Among People* (1915), *My Universities* (1923). Then came *The Artamonov Business* (1925) and the unfinished cycle of novels *The Life of Klim Samgin* (1925–36). Gorky also wrote plays, of which the most famous are *Philistines* and *The Lower Depths* (both 1902). Two stories, 'The Orlov Couple' and 'Malva', appeared in translation by E. Jakowleff and D. Montefiore in 1901, since when most of Gorky's work has been translated into English. His plays have recently enjoyed success on the London stage, with productions of *Enemies* (1971), *The Lower Depths* (1972), *Summerfolk* (1975), *The Zykovs* (1976), and *Children of the Sun* (1979).

Gorlois, in the Arthurian legend, duke of Cornwall and husband of *Igraine.

Gormenghast, see PEAKE, M. L.

GOSSE, Sir Edmund William (1849–1928), the son of Philip Henry Gosse (1810–88), eminent zoologist and fanatical fundamentalist Christian, his relations with whom he describes in *Father and Son* (1907), his masterpiece. This is in Gosse's own words 'the record of a struggle between two temperaments, two consciences

and almost two epochs', as well as a moving and amusing study of an individual childhood.

Gosse came to London from Devon in 1867 to work as a transcriber at the British Museum. In 1875, the year of his marriage, he became a translator at the Board of Trade. He saw himself as a poet and made early acquaintance with the *Pre-Raphaelites. *Swinburne became a close friend. When Gosse applied for the post of Clark lecturer at Cambridge in 1883, he was able to give *Tennyson, R. *Browning, and M. *Arnold as references. A great deal of his early critical work was devoted to Scandinavian literature and he was the first to introduce *Ibsen's name to England. A successful lecture tour of America in 1884–5 was followed by Churton *Collins's attack on his published lectures *From Shakespeare to Pope*, an indictment of his carelessness which shadowed the rest of his life.

His books include lives of *Gray (1882), *Congreve (1888), P. H. Gosse (1890), *Donne (1899), Jeremy *Taylor (1904), *Patmore (1905), Ibsen (1907), and Swinburne (1917), as well as collections of poems and critical essays. He introduced *Gide to England and was honoured by the *Académie française for his services to the literature of France. His close friends included R. L. *Stevenson, H. *James, and *Hardy. From 1904 he was librarian of the House of Lords and exercised considerable power and influence: H. G. *Wells dubbed him the 'official British man of letters'. He was writing regularly for the *Sunday Times* until his death. A biography by Ann Thwaite appeared in 1984.

GOSSON, Stephen (1554–1624), was educated at Corpus Christi College, Oxford. His plays are not now extant, but were ranked by *Meres among 'the best for pastorall': however, he soon became a leader of the Puritan attacks on plays and players. His *Schoole of Abuse* (1579) was dedicated to *Sidney, as was a romance, *The Ephemerides of Phialo*, to which he appended *An Apologie of the Schoole of Abuse*. Whether or not he was 'scorned' by Sidney as *Spenser claimed in a letter to *Harvey, his *Schoole of Abuse* helped to stimulate Sidney to write his *Defence of Poetry*. T. *Lodge replied more directly to Gosson in *A Defence of Stage Plays*, provoking a reply from Gosson in *Playes confuted in Five Actions* (1582). Gosson's attacks on the stage were edited by A. F. Kinney under the title *Markets of Bawdrie* (1974).

Gotha, Almanach de, see ALMANACH DE GOTHA.

Gotham, see CHURCHILL, CHARLES.

Gothic Novel, tales of the macabre, fantastic, and supernatural, usually set amid haunted castles, graveyards, ruins, and wild *picturesque landscapes. They reached the height of their considerable fashion in the 1790s and the early years of the 19th cent. The word 'Gothic' originally implied 'medieval', as in Walpole's *The Castle of Otranto: A Gothic Story* but in the later 18th cent. its meaning altered until its emphasis lay on the macabre, and the original medieval element was sometimes wholly disregarded. The first of the true Gothic novels is generally accepted to be The Castle of Otranto (1764). Many of the best of its successors (e.g. by M. G. *Lewis, C. R. *Maturin, W. *Beckford, and Mrs *Radcliffe) show a rich exuberance of invention, and produce moments of horror far greater than the mere *frisson* conveyed by less skilful imitators. *Peacock mocks the form vigorously, notably in *Nightmare Abbey* and *Gryll Grange*, as does J. *Austen, who comments in *Northanger Abbey* that it is not in the works of Mrs Radcliffe that 'human nature, at least in the midland counties of England, is to be looked for'. The leading American exponent of the early period was Charles Brockden *Brown. Later practitioners include Mary *Shelley, *Pope, and *Le Fanu, and there is a strong Gothic strain in many mainstream 19th-cent. works, including the works of the *Brontës (notably *Villette) and many of the novels of *Dickens. In the 20th cent. the genre flourishes notably in popular horror fiction and films, but critics have also detected Gothic elements in *Faulkner, *McCullers, *Plath, John Gardner (1935–   ), Joyce Carol *Oates, Diane Johnson (1934–   ), E. *Tennant, and Angela Carter (1940–   ).

Gothic Revival, a revival of the Gothic style of architecture which began in the late 18th cent. with a new romantic interest in the medieval, and produced Walpole's *Strawberry Hill and *Beckford's Fonthill. This was followed in the 19th cent. by a more scholarly study of Gothic, expressed in the works of *Pugin and the writings of *Ruskin. The widespread adoption of the Gothic style transformed the appearance of English towns and cities, not always, it was long thought, for the better; its leading architects (William Butterfield, 1814–1900; G. E. Street, 1824–81; Gilbert Scott, 1811–78) had many less successful imitators. See K. *Clark, *The Gothic Revival*, first published 1928, reprinted 1950 with a foreword by the author crediting *Betjeman with initiating a change of taste and a new respect for Victorian architecture.

Götz von Berlichingen, see GOETHE.

GOULD, Nat(haniel) (1857–1919), journalist and novelist, born in Manchester; from 1884 he spent 11 years in Australia, and his first book, The Double Event (1891), was published while he was there. Most of his novels (about 130) were concerned with horse-racing, and he also wrote two books of Australian life, On and Off

the Turf in Australia (1895) and Town and Bush (1896).

GOUNOD, Charles François (1818–93), French composer. Gounod's four-year stay in London, 1870–4, produced a considerable number of settings of English poetry, from *Byron and *Shelley via *Longfellow and *Kingsley to *Palgrave, Weatherley, and Mrs C. F. Alexander: Gounod was not proof against the Victorian taste for sentimental ballades, particularly of the more pious variety. His later oratorios for the English market catered to a similar taste. In his earlier manner, however, the opera Roméo et Juliette (1867) is one of the more successful Shakespearian adaptions: the libretto (by Barbier and Carré, who eight years before had provided the composer with the much more questionable libretto for Faust) stays reasonably close to Shakespeare in letter if not in spirit, and though there is inevitably a high proportion of love music, it is attractively written and handled with delicacy and a sense of character.

Governour, The, a treatise on politics and education by *Elyot.

Gow, Henry, or Henry Smith, a character in Scott's *The Fair Maid of Perth.

Gower, in Shakespeare: (1) a Welsh captain, friend of Fluellen, in *Henry V; (2) the poet Gower (below), who acts as Chorus and narrator in *Pericles.

GOWER, John (?1330–1408), of a family of gentry who owned land in Kent and Yorkshire, probably lived in Kent throughout the first half of his life. He may have been trained in the law, but from about 1377 to his death he lived at the priory of St Mary Overie's in Southwark, devoted to his writing. He was married (perhaps for the second time) in 1398 when he was probably nearly 70; he went blind about 1400. He was a friend of Chaucer and (jointly with *Strode) the dedicatee of *Troilus and Criseyde (see V. 1856); it is possible that the two authors became estranged, because a tribute to Chaucer in the first version of Confessio Amantis is removed in a later one. In his revision of the Confessio (in the early 1390s, while Richard II was still on the throne) he removed the praises of King Richard at its conclusion and dedicated the final version to Henry of Lancaster (later Henry IV).

Gower's considerable learning is attested by his writing with accomplishment in three languages. In French he wrote his Cinkante Balades (written in *Anglo-Norman before 1374, and presented to Henry IV in 1400) and, his first large-scale work, the Mirour de l'Omme (Speculum Meditantis), an allegory written c.1376–8 in about 32,000 lines of octosyllabics in twelve-line stanzas, concerned with fallen man, his virtues and vices. His second major work was the much more considerable Latin *Vox Clamantis* (c.1379–81), an apocalyptic poem of seven books in 10,265 lines of elegiac couplets, dealing with politics and kingship and containing reflections on the disturbances of the early years of Richard II and the Peasants' Revolt of 1381. In English he wrote the late poem 'In Praise of Peace' (which influenced the closing section of *Hoccleve's *Regiment of Princes*, 5,020–5,439) in 55 stanzas of rhyme-royal, as well as his principal work, the *Confessio Amantis*.

The *Confessio* exists in three manuscript versions from the 1390s, the first of which, published in 1390, is the most commonly attested amongst the 49 manuscripts. It is over 33,000 lines long, containing 141 stories in octosyllabic couplets which are handled with a metrical sophistication and skill unsurpassed in English. The framework of the poem is the confession of a lover, Amans, to Genius, a priest of Venus; the confessor helps to examine the lover's conscience and tells him exemplary stories of behaviour and fortune in love, organized under the headings of the *Seven Deadly Sins and drawing widely on classical story (most prominently *Ovid) and medieval romance. There are eight books: one for each of the sins, and one (Book VII) which gives an encyclopedic account of philosophy and morals. Although the framework is a container for stories (like *The Canterbury Tales* or *Decameron*), it is as interesting for its Prologue and admirable Epilogue, and for its exchanges between the priest and lover, as it is for the narratives themselves. At the end, when the lover has been entirely shriven of his sins and his grasp of the ethics of love is complete, the confessor tells him that he is too old for love and disappears. After pondering his abandonment, the lover sees the reason in this and

Homward a softe pas y wente (VIII. 2,967):

a conclusion which has been seen as a comment on the longueurs of the lover's apprenticeship in the self-perfecting of courtly love. Several of the exemplary tales are paralleled by stories in The Canterbury Tales and other works of Chaucer: for example, the story of Florent (I. 1,407–1,861) corresponds to 'The Wife of Bath's Tale' (CT, 6); Constance (II. 587–1,612) to 'The Man of Law's Tale' (CT, 5); Phebus and Cornide (III. 768–835) to 'The Manciple's Tale' (CT, 23); Pyramus and Thisbe (III. 1,331–1,494) to Chaucer's 'Legend of Thisbe' (*The Legend of Good Women*, II. 706–923); Ceix and Alceone (IV. 2,927–3,123) to *The Book of the Duchess* (62–220); Tarquin and his son Aruns (VII. 4,593–5,123) to the 'Legend of Lucrece' (LGW, V. 1,680–1,885). The pairs of narrative are usually compared to Gower's disadvantage, because his stories lack the development and dramatic scope of Chaucer's; but the lucidity and pointedness, as well as the stylistic

accomplishment, of Gower are admirable too. Moreover the stories in common with Chaucer are not, in general, Gower's best; 'Jason and Medea' (V. 3,247–4,222) and some of the shorter stories ('Narcissus', I. 2,275–2,358; 'Canace and Machaire', III. 143–336; 'Rosinphilee', IV. 1,245–1,446) are slight masterpieces of the classical narrative. Up to the 17th cent. almost every writer who praised Chaucer coupled his name with Gower's (see C. F. E. Spurgeon, *500 Years of Chaucer Criticism and Allusion*, 1925, vol. I); he has more examples than any other writer in *Jonson's *Grammar*, and he speaks the Prologue to Shakespeare's *Pericles*, part of the story of which is taken from Gower's 'Apollonius of Tyre' (CA, VIII. 271–2,008). Perhaps his significance as an English writer is to have brought into the mainstream of the canon of the literature the disparate narratives of the classics and the popular romances. (See also ANGLO-LATIN LITERATURE.)

Works (French, Latin, and English), ed. G. C. Macaulay (1899–1902); trans. of *Vox Clamantis* in E. W. Stockton, *The Major Latin Works of John Gower* (1962); selections from *Confessio Amantis* by J. A. W. Bennett (1968) and R. A. Peck (1968). For criticism and discussion see introduction to Macaulay's edition of the *Confessio*; W. P. Ker, *Essays on Medieval Literature* (1905) ch. 5; J. H. Fisher, *John Gower: moral philosopher and friend of Chaucer* (1964); D. A. Pearsall, 'Gower's Narrative Art' (PMLA 81, 1966, 475–84).

Graal, Holy, see GRAIL.

Grace Abounding to the Chief of Sinners, *or the brief Relation of the exceeding Mercy of God in Christ to his poor Servant John Bunyan,* a homiletic narrative by *Bunyan, published 1666.

The author relates his spiritual history, his mean birth, his wicked childhood and youth, his escapes from death by various accidents and the perils of military service, and his gradual awakening to religion as a result of reading two works of devotion owned by his wife. He tells how he went to Bedford and there entered the small Bedford Separated Church (which still exists as Bunyan Meeting), and recounts his spiritual experiences, temptations, and final call to the ministry. The book is written with intense fervour and sincerity.

Gradasso, in *Orlando Innamorato* and *Orlando Furioso*, the king of Sericane, who invades Spain, overcomes its king Marsilio, and presses Charlemagne back to Paris. His object is to secure *Bayard and *Durindana, which he succeeds in doing, but not by his prowess. He is killed with *Agramant by Orlando, in the great fight at Lipadusa.

Gradgrind, Mr, Louisa, and Tom, leading characters in Dickens's *Hard Times*.

Graeme, or Avenel, Roland, the hero of Scott's *The Abbot.*

GRAEVIUS (Latinized form of GREFFE), Johann Georg (1632–1703), Dutch scholar and antiquary, professor at Utrecht, the foremost Latinist of his day, a friend of Richard *Bentley.

GRAHAM, James, see MONTROSE.

GRAHAM, R. B. Cunninghame, see CUN-NINGHAME GRAHAM, R. B.

GRAHAM, William Sydney (1918–   ), Scottish poet, born in Greenock, and brought up on Clydeside; he was educated at Greenock High School, and worked as an engineer as a young man. He later settled in Cornwall, which provides the landscape for many of his later poems. His first volume, *Cage without Grievance* (1942), shows considerable verbal energy and a debt to Dylan *Thomas; his own voice emerges more clearly by *The White Threshold* (1949), through which the image of drowning and the seascapes of his youth resound. The poems in *The Nightfishing* (1955) range from its long and complex title poem, which uses the metaphor of a herring fishing expedition to explore the poet's struggle with language and vocation, to the grim but lively ballad 'The Broad Close' (which evokes his grandfather, 'the rude oak of his day'). Later collections, *Malcolm Mooney's Land* (1970) and *Implements in Their Places* (1977), continue the same preoccupations with the metaphors of sea and language, and the embattled struggle of artistic creation, often with a sense that the language itself is alive, hostile, independently animate, or else 'a frozen tundra of the lexicon and the dictionary'. Graham's *Collected Poems 1942–1977* were published in 1979.

GRAHAME, Kenneth (1859–1932), was born in Edinburgh, and after school in Oxford entered the Bank of England, where he became Secretary in 1898. As a young man he contributed to *The Yellow Book* and was encouraged by W. E. *Henley, who published many of the essays which later appeared in *Pagan Papers* in 1893. Six of the 'papers' described the life of a family of five orphans, whose activities then filled the chapters of *The Golden Age* (1895) and its continuation, *Dream Days* (1898). The sharp, authentic vision of childhood, and the shrewd observation of the child narrator, were widely praised, not least by *Swinburne, and brought Grahame great success both in England and the US. *The Wind in the Willows*, based largely on bedtime stories and letters to his son, was never intended by Grahame to become a published work; the MS was given reluctantly to an importunate American publisher, who then rejected it. Published in England in 1908, its reception was muted, and it was not for some years that the story of Rat, Mole, Badger, and Toad, and their life by the river, became established as a children's classic. The book was dramatized by A. A. *Milne in 1929, and has been performed widely since.

GRAHAM OF CLAVERHOUSE, John (?1649–89), first viscount Dundee, a royalist officer employed by the Scottish Privy Council in executing the severities of the government in Scotland during the reigns of Charles II and James II. In 1688, when James 'forsook his own cause', Graham's life was in danger even in Scotland; he determined to raise the Highlands for James (after the manner of his collateral, Montrose, in 1644) and was killed at the battle of Killiecrankie. He figures prominently in Scott's *Old Mortality*; see also *Wordsworth's sonnet 'In the Pass of Killiecranky' (written 1803, published 1807).

Grail, The Holy, in Arthurian legend, a symbol of perfection sought by the knights of the Round Table. In the latest development of the legend it is identified as the cup of the Last Supper in which Joseph of Arimathea caught the blood of the crucified Christ and which, in some versions, he brought to north Wales at the end of his lengthy wanderings. The legend has a long history, drawing on Celtic elements as well as middle-eastern ones, and it is most familiar in English in the version of *Malory which is mostly an abridgement of the stories contained in three of the romances of the early 13th-cent. French prose 'Vulgate' cycle. R. S. Loomis notes that, in spite of its long history, the ten principal versions of the legend were written in a period of about 50 years, between 1180 (*Chrétien de Troyes) and 1230 (Gerbert). As well as Chrétien's *Perceval* or *Conte del Graal* and the Vulgate versions, there is a third major version in that period, the *Parzival* of *Wolfram von Eschenbach (c.1205) which was the inspiration for *Wagner's *Parsifal. Von Eschenbach's and Chrétien's story, in which Perceval is the successful quester, may be regarded as related to the original and more 'authentic' Grail myth which was joined by accretions and euhemerization of a Christian kind until, by Malory's time, it was very far removed from its archetype.

  In Malory's *Tale of the Sankgreal* (the sixth of Vinaver's eight *Works*) Launcelot fathers Galahad on *Elaine, the daughter of the Grail King *Pelles. On the feast of Pentecost Galahad is brought to the Round Table and seated at the *Siege Perilous; the Grail appears, accompanied by lightning, but the knights cannot see it. Led by Gawain they set off in search of it. Launcelot fails in the Quest, despite several glimpses, because of the sin of his amour with Guinevere; Gawain gives up the quest. Three knights distinguished by great purity, Galahad, Bors, and Perceval, come to the castle of *Corbenic where they have a vision of Christ and receive the Eucharist from him; they take the Grail from him and carry it to Sarras. Galahad dies in ecstasy; Perceval becomes a monk and dies two months later; Bors returns to Logrus and reports their adventures in Camelot, in particular telling Launcelot of the eminence of his son Galahad.

The origins and motivation of the Grail have been explained in three principal ways: (1) as a Christian legend from the first, which altered only in detail through its history (J. D. Bruce, *The Evolution of Arthurian Romance*, 1923); (2) as a pagan fertility ritual, 'the horn of plenty', related to the devastation of the land of King Pellam and its redemption—a connection made briefly by Malory (see DOLOROUS STROKE; J. L. Weston, *From Ritual to Romance*, 1920; and the essays on Arthurian romances in J. Speirs, *Medieval English Poetry*, 1957); (3) as a Celtic story, already mythological in its origins in Irish, transmitted through Welsh (see MABINOGION) and Breton to the French romance tradition and gradually christianized (Loomis). There is disagreement too as to whether a fairly coherent myth has been constructed out of a series of originally disparate elements (Vinaver), or an originally coherent myth has been obscured by misunderstandings and mistranslations of elements in it (Loomis). Loomis believes, for example, that the horn of plenty (*cor*) of Celtic myth has been misinterpreted as the body (*cors*) of Christ, and that the phrase *San Grael* (Holy Grail, derived possibly from the Latin word for dish) has been wrongly divided *Sang real* (royal blood, for the Eucharist). It is likely that the symbol was effective, in the Middle Ages as now, precisely as a 'heap of broken images' (T. S. *Eliot) whose crypticism made it particularly apt as the object of a romance quest, a genre whose creators were constantly in search of difficult tasks. See R. S. Loomis, *The Grail from Celtic Myth to Christian Symbol* (1963); C. L. Brown, *The Origin of the Grail Legend* (1943).

GRAINGER, James (?1721–66), physician and man of letters, emigrated to the West Indies in 1759. His didactic poem *Sugar-Cane* (1764) pleased many, but not Dr *Johnson, who said to Boswell, 'One might as well write "The Parsley-bed, a Poem", or "The Cabbage-garden, a Poem".'

GRAINGER, Percy (1882–1961), Australian composer, pianist, and folk-song collector. He settled in London in 1901 as a concert pianist and in 1905 became a member of the English Folk-Song Society, in which capacity he was active as a collector of folk-songs, working alongside figures like *Vaughan Williams and C. *Sharp in this field and being the first to introduce the wax cylinder phonograph as a means of recording his discoveries. He later made many very original and very beautiful folk-song settings, although his most famous work *Country Gardens*, based on a morris dance

sent to him by C. *Sharp, is simply a variant of the well-known tune of *'The Vicar of Bray'. He also made, at various periods of his life, a great many settings of *Kipling.

Grainne, in the legends relating to the Irish hero *Finn, the daughter of King Cormac. Finn, though a great warrior and hunter, was unfortunate in love. He sought to marry Grainne, but she fell in love with Finn's nephew Diarmait O'Duibhne and eloped with him. The long story of their flight and Finn's unsuccessful pursuit ends in Finn's temporary acceptance of the situation; but Finn finally caused the death of Diarmait.

Grammar of Assent, The, a work by J. H. *Newman.

Gramont, *Mémoires de la Vie du Comte de*, published anonymously at Cologne 1713, was written by Anthony Hamilton (?1646–1720), third son of Sir George Hamilton and grandson of the earl of Abercorn. Anthony Hamilton was the brother-in-law of the Comte de Gramont, who married Elizabeth Hamilton in 1663. The memoirs were edited (in French) by Horace *Walpole and translated into English (with many errors) by *Boyer in 1714; and this translation, revised and annotated by Sir W. *Scott, was reissued in 1811. A new translation was made in 1930 by *Quennell, with an introduction and commentary by C. H. Hartmann.

The first part of the memoirs, dealing with Gramont's life on the Continent down to the time of his banishment from the French court, was probably dictated by Gramont to Hamilton. The second part, relating to the English court, appears to be Hamilton's own work. It is an important source of information, but its trustworthiness on details is doubtful.

GRAMSCI, Antonio (1891–1937), founder of the Italian Communist Party (1921) and, through his ideas on culture, an important factor in its appeal. Born in Sardinia, son of a minor civil servant, he read literature and philology at Turin University. Elected to Parliament in 1924, he was arrested in 1926, sentenced to 20 years in jail by the Fascist Special Tribunal, and died from illnesses contracted in prison. His *Quaderni del carcere* (*Prison Notebooks*, 1948–56) deal with philosophy, history, culture, folklore, literature, language, and the role of the intellectuals. They include his theatre criticism, and journalism for *Ordine Nuovo* (*New Order*) which he founded. His letters from prison are a classic of Italian prose.

GRAND, Sarah (1854–1943), the pseudonym of novelist Frances Elizabeth Bellenden McFall, *née* Clarke, adopted in 1893 after she had left her surgeon husband and published several volumes anonymously. She achieved sensational success with *The Heavenly Twins* (1893), which attacked the sexual double standard in marriage and dealt frankly with the dangers of syphilis and the immorality of the Contagious Diseases Act. This novel launched her on a public career as a *New Woman (a phrase she is said to have coined in 1894); she lectured and wrote extensively, and was for six years (1922–9) mayoress of Bath. *The Beth Book* (1897), a semi-autobiographical novel, describes with much spirit (and occasional lapses into melodramatic absurdity) the girlhood, disillusioning marriage, literary aspirations, and eventual independence of its heroine. See G. Kersley, *Darling Madame: Sarah Grand and Devoted Friend* (1983).

Grandison, (1) Cardinal, in *Lothair*, (2) Katherine, in *Henrietta Temple*, both by B. Disraeli.

***Grandison,** Sir Charles,* see SIR CHARLES GRANDISON.

Grand Tour, The, which began in the 16th cent. and became a fashion in 18th-cent. England, was a leisurely journey through Europe, perhaps of two or three years, during which the sons of the aristocracy enriched their knowledge of the classical past and developed the socially desirable skills of the connoisseur. By the mid-1760s the educated middle classes were also travelling, and a colony of British painters and architects was studying in Rome. Travellers followed a well-established route, musing—more enthusiastically as the century wore on—on the sublime landscape of the Alps, with the glories of ancient Rome and Naples as their main aim; Herculaneum was excavated from 1711 onwards, and Pompeii from 1733. Travellers admired the works of the great Venetians and of 17th-cent. Bolognese painters; they sat to Pompeo Batoni or Rosalba Carriera, and were caricatured by Thomas Patch; *Canaletto, Panini, and Piranesi satisfied a taste for souvenir cityscapes. Celebrated collections of antiquities, among them those of Charles Townley, Sir W. *Hamilton, and T. *Hope, were made in this period; back in England the Palladian villa and Claudian garden suggest an English nostalgia for Italian grace. Guide-book writing flourished; *Addison's *Remarks on several parts of Italy* (1705) was a frequent companion in the first half of the century; J. *Richardson's (father and son) *An Account of the Statues, Bas-reliefs, Drawings and Pictures in Italy, France, etc.* (1722) is the first English guide book to the works of art in Italy; the exclamatory *Letters from Italy* of Mariana Starke (?1762–1838; written in 1797 and 1815) is a forerunner of *Baedeker and the *Guide Bleu*. The letters of *Gray and Horace *Walpole describe the Grand Tour that they made together in 1739–41; among very many repetitive travel writings, accounts by *Boswell, *Gibbon, and *Beckford stand out. *Smollett's

Travels through France and Italy (1766) is a cross, original account (his dislike of the Medici Venus was notorious) which was satirized in Sterne's *A Sentimental Journey through France and Italy* (1768).

GRANGE, John (*c.*1557–1611), was educated at The Queen's College, Oxford, and the Inns of Court and wrote *The Golden Aphroditis* (1577). This novel of romantic intrigue, comparable to G. Gascoigne's *Adventures of Master *F.J.*, is largely made up of speeches, moral discourses, letters, and poems and concerns the courting of Lady A.O. (who turns out to be the daughter of Diana and Endymion) by Sir N.O.

Granger, Edith, in Dickens's *Dombey and Son*, the daughter of the Hon. Mrs Skewton, and Dombey's second wife.

Grangerize, to, to illustrate a book by the addition of prints, engravings, etc., especially such as have been cut out of other books. In 1769 James Granger (1723–76) published a *Biographical History of England*, with blank pages for the reception of engraved portraits or other pictorial illustrations of the text. The filling up of the 'Granger' became a favourite hobby, and afterwards other books were treated in the same manner [*OED*].

Grania, see GRAINNE.

GRANT, James (1822–87), served in the 62nd regiment and wrote prolifically on military and historical subjects. His novels include *The Romance of War* (1845) and *Adventures of an Aide-de-Camp* (1848). Among his other works are memoirs of Kirkcaldy of Grange (1849), Sir J. Hepburn (1851), and *Montrose (1858). He was a distant cousin of Sir W. *Scott.

Granta, The, a Cambridge University undergraduate periodical started in 1889 by Murray Guthrie to replace the *Gadfly*, which came to an end owing to an article of a personal character. The name 'Granta' was appropriated by Guthrie from O. *Browning, who intended it for a paper that he was about to edit. Guthrie, the first editor, was succeeded by R. C. Lehmann, and the last editor before the First World War was John Norman of Emmanuel College, who was killed at the Dardanelles in 1915. It subsequently went through various transformations, looking at times like a boy's school magazine, at other times like an amateur *Punch, and in the 1950s and 60s was edited as a literary magazine devoted to publishing poetry and fiction by promising young students (who included S. *Plath and Ted *Hughes). After some years' disappearance it re-emerged in 1979 as an avant-garde literary periodical, publishing work by G. *Steiner, A. *Sillitoe, Angela Carter, E. *Tennant, Salman Rushdie, and others; its editor Bill Buford described it in 1983 as 'an international paperback magazine of contemporary fiction and cultural journalism'. In 1983 appeared Granta No. 7, *Best of Young British Novelists*, its first in association with *Penguin Books, with work by Martin Amis, Ian McEwan, A. N. Wilson, and others.

Grantly, The Revd Theophilus, Mrs, and their daughter Griselda, in the *'Barsetshire' novels of A. Trollope.

Grantorto, in Spenser's *Faerie Queene* (v. xii), the tyrant from whom Sir *Artegall rescues *Irena (Ireland). He probably represents the spirit of rebellion.

GRANVILLE-BARKER, Harley (1877–1946), was born in London, where his mother taught elocution. He became an actor at the age of 14, and quickly gained recognition. From 1904 to 1907 he directed with brilliant success at the Royal Court Theatre, producing Shakespeare, many classics, the work of moderns (such as *Galsworthy, and his own *The Voysey Inheritance*, 1905), and above all establishing the reputation of G. B. *Shaw. At the Savoy (where his own play *Waste* was banned by the Lord Chamberlain) he produced in 1910 his *The Madras House* and Galsworthy's *Justice*; then in 1912 two productions, *A Winter's Tale* and *Twelfth Night*, which revolutionized the presentation of Shakespeare. An apron stage, simple settings, an authentic text, and swift continuity of action were new to critics and public, and not until a similar production of *A Midsummer Night's Dream* in 1914 did Barker meet with any general acclaim. In the same year he produced a version of Hardy's *The Dynasts*, which was a failure, and he spent much of the years 1914–18 producing in New York. After the war he retired from the stage (and hyphenated his name), but in 1919 became president of the new British Drama League, and in 1923 began his Prefaces to the new *Players' Shakespeare*. The project was abandoned, but Barker continued with his Prefaces, of which he eventually published five series between 1927 and 1947, covering twelve plays. These studies, which broke new ground in presenting the producer's rather than the scholar's point of view, are generally held to be the best of his written work. Among much other writing, lectures, and broadcasts he published *On Dramatic Method* (1931), *On Poetry in Drama* (1937), and *The Use of Drama* (1946).

Grapes of Wrath, The, a novel by J. *Steinbeck.

GRASS, Günter (1927–), German novelist, born in Danzig. His long, humorous, experimental novels (sometimes called 'Rabelaisian' by critics) include *Die Blechtrommel* (*The Tin Drum*, 1959), *Hundejahre* (*Dog Years*, 1963), *Der Butt* (*The Flounder*, 1977), and *Das Treffen in Telgte* (*The Meeting at Telgte*, 1979). Grass, a committed and outspoken socialist, lives in West Berlin.

Gratiano, in Shakespeare's *The Merchant of Venice*, one of Antonio's friends, who marries *Portia's servant Nerissa.

Grave, The, see BLAIR, R.

GRAVES, Alfred Perceval (1846–1931), born in Dublin, an inspector of schools, 1875–1910, published many volumes of Irish songs and ballads, and an autobiography, *To Return to All That* (1930). He composed the popular 'Father O'Flynn', written in 1875, first published in the *Spectator.

GRAVES, Richard (1715–1804), a highly educated and cultivated West Country cleric, who was a close friend of *Shenstone and R. *Allen, taught the young *Malthus at his rectory school and wrote successful novels, verses, and articles. He is now chiefly remembered for his lively novel *The Spiritual Quixote, or the Summer's Ramble of Mr Geoffry Wildgoose* (1773), which ran into several editions. The eccentric Methodist Wildgoose travels, with many ludicrous adventures, through the West Country and to the Peak District, encountering (and refuting) everywhere the 'enthusiasm' of the new Methodists, whose intrusion into religious life Graves greatly resented. Graves's old acquaintance, the Methodist *Whitefield, is satirized in the book. His other chief novels, *Columella* (1779), based on the life of Shenstone, and *Eugenius* (1785), are illuminating on social manners and conditions of the time. He published *Recollections of William Shenstone* in 1788.

GRAVES, Robert von Ranke (1895–), son of A. P. *Graves, was born in London and educated at Charterhouse; he joined the army in 1914 and his first poetry appeared (with the encouragement of E. *Marsh) while he was serving in the First World War (*Over the Brazier*, 1916; *Fairies and Fusiliers*, 1917); his poems also appeared in *Georgian Poetry. In 1918 he married, and in 1919 went to St John's College, Oxford, to read English, though he left without taking a degree, later successfully submitting a critical work, *Poetic Unreason and other studies* (1925), as a thesis for a B.Litt. In 1926, accompanied by his wife and a new acquaintance, Laura *Riding, he went briefly to Egypt as professor of literature. He was to live and work with Laura Riding in Majorca, then Brittany, until 1939, publishing various works in collaboration with her, including *A Survey of Modernist Poetry* (1927). He spent the Second World War in England, then returned to Majorca in 1946 with his second wife Beryl Hodge, and settled there permanently.

Graves's output was prodigious; he wrote many volumes of poetry, essays, fiction, biography, and works for children, and published many free translations from various languages. He saw himself primarily as a poet, and wrote some of his prose reluctantly, for financial reasons, but much of it is of lasting quality. His powerful autobiography, *Goodbye to all that* (1929), which describes his unhappy schooldays and the horrors of the trenches, and gives a frank account of the breakdown of his first marriage, is an outstanding example of the new freedom and passionate disillusion of the post-war generation. He wrote many novels, most of them with a historical basis; they include *I, Claudius* and *Claudius the God* (both 1934), narrated in the imaginatively and idiosyncratically conceived persona of the Emperor Claudius (10 BC–AD 54); *Antigua, Penny, Puce* (1936), a barbed tale of sibling rivalry; and the controversial *The story of Mary Powell, Wife to Mr Milton* (1943). Notable amongst his non-fiction works is *The White Goddess: a historical grammar of poetic myth* (1948), which argues that true poets derive their gifts from the Muse, the primitive, matriarchal Moon Goddess the female principle, once dominant but now disastrously dispossessed by male values of reason and logic. Graves's often unorthodox interpretation of myth may also be seen in his *The Greek Myths* (1955), *The Hebrew Myths* (1963, with R. Patei), and other works.

A personal mythology also manifests itself, although not to the point of obscurity, in much of his poetry. His volumes of verse appeared regularly over the years, and his *Collected Poems* of 1955 confirmed a world-wide reputation; the most recent volume of *Collected Poems* appeared in 1975. Since his early days, when he rid himself of tendencies towards Georgian poetic diction, Graves (partly through voluntary exile) avoided identification with any school or movement, speaking increasingly with a highly individual yet ordered voice in which lucidity and intensity combine to a remarkable degree. His love poetry, some of his best-known and most distinctive work, is at once cynical and passionate, romantic and erotic, personal and universal. He has also written ballads, songs for children, dramatic monologues, narratives, and poetic anecdotes; his technique is not experimental, but the classical precision of his verse is rarely archaic.

Graves received many honours, and refused many. He was professor of poetry at Oxford from 1961 to 1966, and various of his essays and lectures have been published in *Poetic craft and principle* (1967), *The Crane Bag and other disputed subjects* (1969), and other works. There is a life by M. Seymour-Smith (1982), and a volume of letters, *In Broken Images: Selected Letters 1914–1946* (1982, ed. P. O'Prey).

Graveyard poets, a term applied to 18th-cent. poets who wrote melancholy, reflective works, often set in graveyards, on the theme of human mortality. Examples include T. *Parnell's 'Night-Piece on Death' (1721), E. Young's *Night Thoughts* (1742), and R. *Blair's *The Grave* (1743). See also Gray's *Elegy written in a Country Church-Yard* (1751), the best-known product of this kind of sensibility.

GRAY, David (1838–61), Scottish poet, born in Duntiblae, the son of a handloom weaver, and educated at the University of Glasgow. Befriended by R. *Buchanan and *Milnes, he aspired to be a poet, but was struck by consumption; he lived just long enough to see the proofs of *The Luggie and other poems* (1862), the title poem of which is a blank verse celebration of the River Luggie. The sonnets which he wrote while approaching death have many echoes of *Keats, whom he greatly admired.

Gray, Gideon, the surgeon in Scott's *The Surgeon's Daughter. His daughter is Janet.

GRAY, John Henry (1866–1934), poet, born in Woolwich of a Nonconformist background, became a Roman Catholic, was ordained in 1901, and spent many years as rector of St Peter's in Edinburgh. He was a friend of *Wilde, who paid for the publication of his first volume of poetry, *Silverpoints* (1893), which contained translations from *Verlaine and *Mallarmé. He published other volumes of poetry, booklets of devotional verse, and a surreal novel, *Park: A Fantastic Story* (1932), set in the future. His best long poem, 'The Flying Fish', first appeared in *The Dial* in 1896, and was republished in *The Long Road* (1926). A life by B. Sewell, *In the Dorian Mode*, was published in 1983.

GRAY, Simon James Holliday (1936–), playwright and lecturer in English, educated at Trinity College, Cambridge. He is best known for his plays about the problems and contradictions of middle-class and academic life: these include *Butley* (1971) and *Otherwise Engaged* (1975).

GRAY, Thomas (1716–71), was born in London, the son of a scrivener; his mother and aunt kept a milliner's shop. He was educated at Eton, with Horace *Walpole, and at Peterhouse, Cambridge. He accompanied Walpole on a tour of France and Italy in 1739–41, but they quarrelled and returned home separately. Also in 1741 his father died, leaving the family financially insecure. In 1742 Gray moved to Cambridge, where he was to live, apart from travels and visits, for the rest of his life, first at Peterhouse, then from 1756 at Pembroke; in 1741–2 he began to write English rather than Latin poetry, producing a fragment of a Racinian tragedy, *Agrippina* (first published 1775), and his first odes, including *Ode on a Distant Prospect of Eton College* (1747), the first of his works to appear in print. In June 1742 his other Etonian friend Richard *West died, just after Gray had sent him his 'Ode on the

Spring' (1748); Gray paid tribute in 'Sonnet on the Death of West' (1775) and in some lines of his Latin poem, *De Principiis Cogitandi*. He was reconciled with Walpole in 1745, and the following year showed him some of his earlier poetry, including probably the beginning of his *Elegy written in a Country Church-Yard* (1751); in 1750 he completed the elegy at Stoke Poges, where his mother and aunt had lived since 1742. He sent Walpole in 1747 his 'Ode on the Death of a Favourite Cat' (1748).

In 1754 Gray finished his Pindaric ode on *The Progress of Poesy*, and in 1757 a second Pindaric ode, *The Bard*, both remarkably ambitious and intense, and marking a clear shift from *neo-classical lucidity towards the obscure and the *Sublime; both were published by Walpole in 1757, the first works printed by the *Strawberry Hill Press. These were his last major poems, but by this time, owing largely to the *Elegy*, his poetry was extremely popular, and on the death of *Cibber (1757) he was offered the laureateship, which he declined. His remaining years were devoted largely to antiquarian and botanical studies and to travels to Scotland and the Lake District in search of the *picturesque; he was deeply interested in new discoveries of Old Norse and Welsh poetry (including *Macpherson's) and produced various imitations, including 'The Fatal Sisters' and 'The Descent of Odin' (written 1761, published 1768). One of the best of his later poems is the satiric 'On Lord Holland's Seat near Margate, Kent' (1769). His *Journal* (published 1775) is an account of his visit to the Lakes, kept for Dr Thomas Wharton, who had hoped to accompany him, and his letters (3 vols, ed. P. Toynbee and L. Whibley) are an interesting mixture of erudition, affectionate informality, and enthusiasm for nature and literature. The standard editions of the poems are by H. W. Starr and J. R. Hendrickson (1966) and R. Lonsdale (with W. *Collins, 1977).

Great Expectations, a novel by *Dickens, which first appeared in *All the Year Round* 1860–1, published in book form in the latter year.

It recounts the development of the character of the narrator, Philip Pirrip, commonly known as 'Pip', a village boy brought up by his termagant sister, the wife of the gentle, humorous, kindly blacksmith Joe Gargery. He is introduced to the house of Miss Havisham, a lady half-crazed by the desertion of her lover on her bridal night, who, in a spirit of revenge, has brought up the girl Estella to use her beauty as a means of torturing men. Pip falls in love with Estella, and aspires to become a gentleman. Money and expectations of more wealth come to him from a mysterious source, which he believes to be Miss Havisham. He goes to London, and in his new mode of life meanly abandons the devoted

Joe Gargery, a humble connection of whom he is now ashamed. Misfortunes come upon him. His benefactor proves to be an escaped convict, Abel Magwitch, whom he, as a boy, had helped; his great expectations fade away and he is penniless. Estella marries his sulky enemy Bentley Drummle, by whom she is cruelly ill-treated. Taught by adversity, Pip returns to Joe Gargery and honest labour, and is finally reunited to Estella who has also learnt her lesson. Other notable characters in the book are Joe's uncle, the impudent old impostor Pumblechook; Jaggers, the skilful Old Bailey lawyer, and his good-hearted clerk Wemmick; and Pip's friend in London, Herbert Pocket.

It appears from *Forster's life of Dickens that the author originally devised a less happy ending to the story, which he altered in deference to the advice of *Bulwer-Lytton.

Great Gatsby, The, a novel by F. S. *Fitzgerald.

Great-heart, in the second part of Bunyan's *Pilgrim's Progress*, the escort of Christiana and her children on their pilgrimage.

Great Hoggarty Diamond, The, a story by *Thackeray, published in *Fraser's Magazine* in 1841.

The Hoggarty diamond, given to an obscure young clerk, Samuel Titmarsh, by his aunt, at first brings him prosperity. But he falls into the hands of swindlers, his child dies, and he is sent to prison for debt. Only when he gets rid of the diamond, pawning it to pay for his child's funeral, do his fortunes begin to take a turn for the better.

Great Tew, see FALKLAND.

Grecian Coffee-House stood in Devereux Court, Essex Street, Strand, and was frequented by *Addison, *Steele and *Goldsmith, and by many fellows of the *Royal Society, which gave it a reputation for learning. It was announced in No. 1 of *The Tatler* that all learned articles would proceed from the Grecian.

'Grecian Urn', see ODE ON A GRECIAN URN.

Greek Anthology, The, see ANTHOLOGY, THE GREEK.

GREELEY, Horace (1811–72), founder of the *New York Tribune* (1841), and one of the prominent figures in the history of American journalism, who did much to raise its political and literary standards.

GREEN, Henry (1905–73), novelist and industrialist, was born Henry Vincent Yorke, the son of a wealthy and well-connected Midlands industrialist, and educated at Eton and Magdalen College, Oxford. His first novel, *Blindness* (1926), was published while he was still an undergraduate, when, in his aesthete phase, he was a contemporary of E. *Waugh and H. *Acton. His second novel, *Living* (1929), in marked contrast, describes life on the factory floor in Birmingham, and is based on his own experiences working for the family firm, H. Pontifex and Sons; he himself rose from the shop floor to become managing director, and the novel vividly records working-class dialogue, as well as the reactions of the manager's son, Dupret. It also manifests the idiosyncracies of prose—dropped articles, sentences without verbs, a highly individual use of colloquial language in both narrative and dialogue—which contribute to his work's distinctive quality. *Party Going* (1939), describing a group of rich, idle young people, delayed at a railway station in fog on the brink of departure for a winter holiday, has strong symbolic suggestions in an apparently trivial narrative. This was followed by his autobiographical *Pack my Bag: A Self-Portrait* (1940) and several other novels: *Caught* (1943); *Loving* (1945), one of his most admired works, which describes life above and below stairs in an Irish country house during wartime, with a notable portrait of the butler, Raunce; *Back* (1946); *Concluding* (1948); *Nothing* (1950); and *Doting* (1952), the latter two written almost wholly in dialogue. His wartime service in the ranks of the NFS provided him with new social experiences and further widened his range. Although he liked to describe himself as 'a business man whose pastime was romancing over a bottle to a good band', he was a highly conscious and original artist, who commanded more admiration from fellow writers (including E. *Bowen, A. *Wilson, and W. H. *Auden) than from the common reader; J. *Updike, in an introduction to a 1979 Picador reprint, praises his rich content and intricate formal design, and comments, 'With upper-class obliquity he champions the demotic in language and in everything.'

GREEN, John Richard (1837–83), was educated at Magdalen College School and at Jesus College, Oxford, where he was unhappy and did badly. After a spell as a curate in the East End of London he took to journalism, contributing frequently to the *Saturday Review*. He is best known for his *Short History of the English People*, dedicated to *Stubbs and *Freeman, who encouraged his career as a historian. This work, which was immensely popular, was remarkable for its broad approach, simple style, generosity of outlook, and attention to the social, economic, and intellectual aspects of national history; Green aimed to chart 'the growth . . . of the people itself' and to produce an account in which 'Aidan and Bede would claim more space than the wars of the Anglo-Saxon kingdoms.' It was enlarged in *The History of the English People* (1877–80).

GREEN, Matthew (1697–1737), poet. Little is known of his life; he appears to have been of Quaker background, and was employed at the Customs House; his only literary friend was *Glover, to whom he left his MSS. He is remembered for his poem *The Spleen* (1737), which praises in fluent octosyllabics the simple life and describes his dream of 'a farm some twenty miles from town' where he could live (with occasional visits to London) on 'two hundred pounds half-yearly paid'.

GREEN, Thomas Hill (1836–82), educated at Rugby and Balliol College, Oxford, was fellow of Balliol, 1866–78 (the first fellow not in orders), and was appointed White's professor of moral philosophy in 1878. Green's philosophical publications began with a criticism of *Locke, *Hume, and *Berkeley in the form of two very full introductions to a new edition of Hume's *Treatise*. His philosophical views as set forth in his *Prolegomena to ethics* (1883) and his collected *Works* (1885–8) show a qualified acceptance of the doctrines of *Hegel as speculatively true but requiring to be supplemented for practical purposes.

Mrs H. *Ward pays tribute to his moral influence in her sympathetic portrait of him as Henry Grey in *Robert Elsmere* (1888); she quotes from his *The Witness of God, and faith: two lay sermons* (1883) and describes him as one who held 'a special place in the hearts of men who can neither accept fairy tales, nor reconcile themselves to a world without faith'.

GREENAWAY, Kate (1846–1901), writer and illustrator of children's picture books who worked in London. Her drawings suggest an idyllic world, where demure, quaintly dressed children sweetly play and sing amid flowery meadows and trim gardens. Her first success was *Under the Window* (1878), a collection of rhymes for children which she both wrote and illustrated. Her many later works include *Marigold Garden* (1885)—another collection of verses and pictures—and her illustrated edition of *The Pied Piper of Hamelin* (1888) by R. *Browning. She was encouraged by *Ruskin, whom she met in 1882 and with whom she corresponded. Ruskin lectured on her art at Oxford in 1883; he praised the innocence of her vision of childhood—'no gasworks! no waterworks, no mowing machines, no sewing machines, no telegraph poles . . .' Her books and watercolour drawings were immensely popular and widely influenced contemporary design and children's dress. She nursed ambitions as a poet and wrote many sonnets which remained unpublished.

GREENE, (Henry) Graham (1904–), novelist and playwright, was educated at Berkhamsted School, where his father was headmaster, then at Balliol College; a book of verse, *Babbling April* (1925), was published while he was still at Oxford. He joined the Roman Catholic church in

1926, married in 1927, and was from 1926 to 1930 on the staff of *The Times, which he left in order to attempt to make a living as a writer. His first three novels (1929–31), which he later disclaimed, made little impression, but *Stamboul Train* (1932) sold well and was followed by many increasingly successful novels, short stories, books of reportage and travel, plays, children's books, etc. Greene describes his own early years in *A Sort of Life* (1971), which gives a vivid impression of a manic-depressive temperament tempted by deadly nightshade and Russian roulette, and a literary imagination nourished by influences as diverse as *Weyman, M. *Bowen, and R. *Browning: Greene states, 'if I were to choose an epigraph for all the novels I have written, it would be from *Bishop Blougram's Apology*:

"Our interest's on the dangerous edge of things,
The honest thief, the tender murderer,
The superstitious atheist . . ." '

His pursuit of danger (despite quieter interludes, e.g. as literary editor on the *Spectator and *Night and Day) dominated much of his life and travels, as described in his second volume of autobiography, *Ways of Escape* (1980). His novels include *England Made Me* (1935); *The Power and the Glory* (1940); *The Heart of the Matter* (1948); *The End of the Affair* (1951; a wartime love affair with strong religious-supernatural touches modified by Greene himself in a later version); *The Quiet American* (1955, set in Vietnam); *A Burnt-Out Case* (1961, set in a leper colony in the Congo); *The Honorary Consul* (1973, set in Argentina); and *The Human Factor* (1978, a Secret Service novel). Other works of fiction he classed as 'entertainments': these include *Brighton Rock* (1938, paradoxically the first novel in which critics detected a strong Catholic message, not surprisingly, in view of the fact that it introduces what was to be his central concept of 'the appalling strangeness of the mercy of God'); *The Confidential Agent* (1939); *Loser Takes All* (1955); and *Our Man in Havana* (1958). *The Third Man* (1950), also described as an entertainment, was originally written as a screenplay and filmed (1949) by Carol Reed (see EXPRESSIONISM). Greene's plays include *The Living Room* (1953), *The Potting Shed* (1957), and *The Complaisant Lover* (1959). He also published travel books, describing journeys in Liberia (*Journey without Maps*, 1936), Mexico (*The Lawless Roads* 1939), and Africa (*In search of a character: two African journals*, 1961). His *Collected Essays* appeared in 1969. His range as a writer is wide, both geographically and in variations of tone, but his preoccupations with moral dilemma (personal, religious, and political), his attempts to distinguish 'good-or-evil' from 'right-or-wrong', and his persistent choice of 'seedy' (a word which he was to regret popu-larizing) locations give his work a highly distinctive and recognizable quality, while his skilful variations of popular forms (the thriller, the detective story) have brought him a rare combination of critical and popular admiration.

GREENE, Robert (1558–92), born in Norwich, was educated at St John's College and Clare Hall, Cambridge, from 1575 until 1583, and was incorporated at Oxford in 1588. From about 1585 he lived mainly in London. Although he liked to stress his connections with both universities, his later literary persona was that of a feckless drunkard, who abandoned his wife and children to throw himself on the mercies of tavern hostesses and courtesans; writing pamphlets and plays was supposedly a last resort when his credit failed. He is said to have died of a surfeit of Rhenish wine and pickled herrings, though it may more likely have been plague, of which there was a severe outbreak in 1592. Greene was attacked at length by G. *Harvey in *Foure Letters* (1592) as the 'Ape of Euphues' and 'Patriarch of shifters'; *Nashe defended him in *Strange Newes* in the same year, acknowledging Greene to have been a drunkard and a debtor, but claiming that 'Hee inherited more vertues than vices.' Greene's 37 publications, progressing from moral dialogues to prose romances, romantic plays, and finally realistic accounts of underworld life, bear out Nashe's assertion that printers were only too glad 'to pay him deare for the very dregs of his wit'. The sententious moral tone of his works suggests that his personal fecklessness and death-bed repentance may have been partly a pose.

Among the more attractive of his romances are the Lylyan sequel *Euphues his Censure to Philautus* (1587); *Pandosto. The Triumph of Time* and *Perimedes the Blacke-Smith* (1588); *Menaphon* (1589). Among his 'repentance' pamphlets are *Greenes Mourning Garment* and *Greenes Never too late* (1590) and *Greenes Groats-Worth of Witte* (1592). *Greenes Vision* (1592) is a fictionalized account of his death-bed repentance in which he receives advice from *Chaucer, *Gower, and King Solomon. The low-life pamphlets include *A Notable Discovery of Coosnage* (1592) and three 'conny-catching' pamphlets in the same year. His eight plays were all published posthumously. The best-known are *Orlando Furioso* (1594), *Frier Bacon, and Frier Bongay* (1594), and *James the Fourth* (1598). The last two have been edited in recent times by J. A. Lavin and N. Sanders.

Greene is now best known for his connections with Shakespeare. His attack on him in the *Groats-Worth of Witte* (below) as an 'upstart Crow, beautified with our feathers' is the first reference to Shakespeare as a London dramatist; and his *Pandosto* provided Shakespeare with the source for *The Winter's Tale*. The voluminousness of Greene's works and the supposed profligacy of his life have caused him to be identified with the typical Elizabethan hack-writer; he probably provided a name and a model for the swaggering Nick Greene in V. *Woolf's *Orlando* (1928). Greene's works were edited in 15 vols by *Grosart (1881–6).

Greenes Groats-Worth of Witte, *bought with a Million of Repentance,* an autobiographical prose tract by R. *Greene, published 1592.

It begins with the death of the miser Gorinius, who leaves the bulk of his large fortune to his elder son, Lucanio, and only 'an old groat' to the younger, Roberto (i.e. the author), 'wherewith I wish him to buy a groats-worth of wit'. Roberto conspires with a courtesan to fleece his brother, but the courtesan betrays him, subsequently ruining Lucanio for her sole profit. The gradual degradation of Roberto is then narrated, and the tract ends with the curious 'Address' to his fellow playwrights *Marlowe, *Lodge, and *Peele, urging them to spend their wits to better purpose than the making of plays. It contains the well-known passage about the 'upstart Crow, beautified with our feathers', the *'Johannes *fac totum*', who 'is in his owne conceit the onely Shake-scene in a countrey', which probably refers to Shakespeare as a non-graduate dramatist newly arrived in London.

Green Knight, see GAWAIN AND THE GREEN KNIGHT, SIR.

Green Mansions, a novel by W. H. *Hudson, published 1904.

The young hero, Abel, fleeing from persecution in Venezuela, travels into the vast jungle (the 'green mansions'). Eventually he settles with the tribe of Runi, an Indian friend. Finding that one part of the forest is mysteriously forbidden, he investigates and becomes haunted by the recurring cry, half bird, half human, which terrifies the Indians. He finds the caller, Rima, a wild and beautiful girl of the woods, and meets her grandfather, Nuflo. Abel and Rima fall in love, and the three of them set out on a long journey to find her mother. They fail, and impetuously Rima returns home first; when Nuflo and Abel arrive they discover that the Indians have burned her on a great pyre built round a forest tree. In anguish Abel kills Runi and his friends, and makes a long, desolate journey, carrying Rima's ashes, back to the coast. The animistic overtones of the book, and its intimations of love and death, made a deep impression.

The sculpture of Rima in London's Hyde Park is by Sir Jacob Epstein (1880–1959).

Green-sleeves, the name of an inconstant lady-love, who is the subject of a ballad published in 1580. This, and the tune to which it was sung, became and remain very popular; both are mentioned by Shakespeare (*The Merry Wives of Windsor*, II. i and v. v).

GREENWOOD, Walter (1903–74), novelist,

born in Salford of radical working-class parents, who is remembered for his classic novel of life in a northern town during the depression, *Love on the Dole* (1933; dramatized 1934; filmed 1941). He wrote several other novels and a volume of autobiography, *There was a Time* (1967).

GREG, Sir Walter Wilson (1875–1959), scholar and bibliographer, educated at Harrow and Trinity College, Cambridge, where he came to know *McKerrow. His first publication (1900) was a finding list of English plays written before 1700 which was the beginning of his more important work, *A Bibliography of the English Printed Drama to the Restoration* (1939–59). In 1906 he founded, and was general editor of (1906–39), the *Malone Society, for the exact reproduction of English plays and dramatic documents before 1640. His edition of *Henslowe's Diary and Papers (1904–8) is an outstanding example of his skill in palaeography and his knowledge of Elizabethan theatrical history, which he further developed in later works. Greg raised the standards of bibliography and textual criticism in his constructive reviews, and in editions of manuscript plays, notably *Sir Thomas *More (1911), and in his works, including *Dramatic Documents from the Elizabethan Playhouses* (1931) and *English Literary Autographs 1550–1650* (1925–32). In his last and most fruitful years he published, in addition to his *Bibliography*, a remarkable edition of '*Doctor Faustus*' *1604–1616* (1950), *The Editorial Problem in Shakespeare* (1942), *The Shakespeare First Folio* (1955), and *Some Aspects and Problems of London Publishing 1550–1650* (1956).

Gregorian Calendar, see CALENDAR.

GREGORY I, St (Gregory the Great) (540–604), one of the greatest of the early popes (from 590), a reformer of monastic discipline and a prolific writer whose works include the *Cura Pastoralis* (see ALFRED), the *Dialogues*, and famous collections of letters and sermons. He sent *Augustine to England. *Bede (*Ecclesiastical History*, II. i) tells the story of him that, seeing Anglo-Saxon boys for sale in the slave-market at Rome, he remarked: 'Not *Angli* but *Angeli*, if they were Christians.' The story that he delivered the emperor Trajan from Hell by his prayers, touched by his humility and justice, is mentioned by *Aquinas, by *Dante more than once, and by Langland (*Piers Plowman*, B XI. 140ff.). See *Dialogues*, trans. O. J. Zimmerman (1959); P. Batiffol, *Saint Gregory the Great*, trans. J. L. Stoddard (1929).

GREGORY, (Isabella) Augusta, Lady, *née* Persse (1852–1932), was born at Roxborough, Co. Galway. She married the former MP and governor of Ceylon, Sir William Gregory of nearby *Coole Park, in 1880, and was widowed in 1892. They had one child (see below). A leading figure in the *Irish Revival, she assisted *Yeats and *Martyn in the foundation of the *Irish Literary Theatre, forerunner of the *Abbey Theatre, for which she became playwright, director, and patent holder. She helped popularize Irish legends with her translations *Cuchulain of Muirthemne* (1902) and *Gods and Fighting Men* (1904), and Irish folklore with *Poets and Dreamers* (1903), *A Book of Saints and Wonders* (1906, enl. 1907), and *Visions and Beliefs in the West of Ireland* (1920). Lady Gregory's idiomatic style (often called 'Kiltartanese') and knowledge of folklore were assets in her collaboration with Yeats on several plays including *Cathleen ni Houlihan* (1902) and *The Unicorn from the Stars* (1908). Excelling in the one-act form, with plays such as *Spreading the News*, *The Workhouse Ward*, *The Rising of the Moon*, and *The Gaol Gate*, Lady Gregory wrote or translated over 40 plays, mostly published in *Seven Short Plays* (1909), *The Kiltartan Molière* (1910), *Irish Folk History Plays* (1912), *New Comedies* (1913), *Three Wonder Plays* (1922), *The Image and Other Plays* (1922), and *Three Last Plays* (1928). Her *Our Irish Theatre* (1913) is a somewhat biased account of the Abbey's early years, but her defence of Synge's *Playboy of the Western World*, G. B. *Shaw's *The Shewing up of Blanco Posnet*, and *O'Casey's *The Plough and the Stars* typify her tenacious work. Lady Gregory's stance as a cultural nationalist culminated in her fight for the return to Ireland of 39 French Impressionist pictures collected by her nephew Sir Hugh Lane, who drowned in the sinking of the *Lusitania* in 1915 leaving an unwitnessed codicil to his will, a campaign she partly recorded in Hugh Lane's *Life and Achievement* (1921). Her collected works are published in the Coole Edition (1970–82), ed. Colin Smythe.

GREGORY, (William) Robert (1881–1918), artist. The son of Sir William and Lady *Gregory, he designed sets for early *Abbey Theatre productions. In 1916 he joined the RFC and was killed in action. *Yeats wrote several commemorative poems about him, including 'An Irish Airman Foresees his Death' and 'In Memory of Major Robert Gregory'.

GREGORY OF TOURS (c.540–94), bishop of Tours, whose *Historia Francorum* is the chief authority for the early Merovingian period of French history. He places in 520 the raid against the Frisian territory of the Franks by a Scandinavian leader 'Chochilaicus' (in Latin) who has been identified with the Geatish king Hygelac in *Beowulf*; the raid is mentioned in *Beowulf* at lines 1207, 2357, 2503, and 2912. Gregory's identification provides the only historical corroboration for any character or event in the poem. The *Historia* has been translated by O. M. Dalton (1927).

Gregynog Press, a *private press founded in 1922 at Gregynog Hall, near Newtown, Monmouthshire, and endowed by Miss Gwendolen and Miss Margaret Davies as part of their plan to establish an arts and crafts centre. It excelled in the fineness of its bindings, and survived until 1940.

Grendel, see BEOWULF.

GRENFELL, Julian (1888–1915), educated at Eton, where he began to publish, and at Balliol College, Oxford; he joined the regular army in 1910 and in 1914 was sent to France, where he won the DSO and was killed at Ypres. His celebrated poem, 'Into Battle', appeared in *The Times* in 1915 and has been much anthologized. There is a life by N. *Mosley (1976).

GRESHAM, Sir Thomas (?1519–79), a celebrated financier and financial agent of the Crown, and an intimate friend of Cecil. He was the son of Sir Richard Gresham (?1485–1549), lord mayor of London, who initiated the design of the Royal Exchange. This was built at the expense of Sir Thomas Gresham, who also founded Gresham College. Gresham's School, Holt, which was founded by his uncle John, has produced such distinguished figures as *Britten and *Auden.

Gretchen, diminutive in German of Margaret, the principal female character in Part I of Goethe's *Faust*.

GREVILLE, Charles Cavendish Fulke, see GREVILLE MEMOIRS.

GREVILLE, Sir Fulke, first Baron Brooke (1554–1628), was educated at Shrewsbury School, where he was an exact contemporary of P. *Sidney, and at Jesus College, Cambridge. From the mid-1560s he was at court, where he had a long and moderately successful career, culminating in his peerage in 1621, when he was granted Warwick Castle and Knowle Park by James I. It was in Warwick Castle that he died, mysteriously stabbed by a servant who went on to stab himself. The servant died at once, the 74-year-old master four weeks later.

Greville began to write poetry during Sidney's lifetime and was intimately concerned with the first plans for posthumous publication of his friend's works. Poems written after Sidney's death, gathered together with earlier ones in his sequence *Caelica*, show him moving away from secular love towards broader political and religious themes. His neo-Stoic *Letter to an Honourable Lady* belongs to 1589; his two Senecan tragedies *Mustapha* (published 1609) and *Alaham* in their earliest versions, before the fall of *Essex in February 1601; the verse *Treatise of Monarchy* about 1600; and his major prose work, the *Life of Sir Philip Sidney*, was probably begun in 1610. Greville was a compulsive reviser of his own work, however, and many of his works survive in versions which reflect different stages of revision. Often he seems to change his mind about his central theme or purpose. The *Life of Sir Philip Sidney* is as much about Greville's own political ideals and disappointments as about his friend's career, and in its published version (1652) it incorporates judgements of *Elizabeth I and her reign which he had originally hoped to include in a life of that monarch.

Type-casting of the poetry of this period as either 'Elizabethan' or 'Metaphysical' has not helped Greville's literary reputation, but a movement led by *Winters, characterizing Greville as a master of the 'plain style', has stimulated admiration among a sizeable minority of critics. C. S. *Lewis saw him as a writer of 'genuinely didactic verse, verse utterly unadorned and dependent for interest almost exclusively on its intellectual content'. These qualities are well reflected in Greville's best-known lines, from the 'Chorus Sacerdotum' in *Mustapha*:

Oh wearisome Condition of Humanity!
Borne under one Law, to another bound.
Vainely begot, and yet forbidden vanity,
Created sicke, commanded to be sound.

His *Poems and Dramas* have been edited by G. *Bullough (1939); *The Remains* by G. Wilkes (1965); the *Life of Sir Philip Sidney* by D. Nowell Smith (1907). There is a *Life* by R. A. Rebholz (1971).

Greville Memoirs, The, the memoirs of Charles Greville (1794–1865), politician and man of public affairs, who was for many years clerk to the Privy Council. From 1820 to 1860 he kept a detailed diary of his life in the inner circles of politics and power. He was the friend and trusted confidant of both Whigs and Tories, and includes in his work many lively portraits of friends and colleagues, such as the duke of *Wellington and Lord Palmerston. His *Memoirs* were first edited and published in 1874–87.

Grewgious, Mr, a character in Dickens's *Edwin Drood*.

Gride, Arthur, a character in Dickens's *Nicholas Nickleby*.

GRIERSON, Sir Herbert John Clifford (1866–1960), scholar, was first professor of English literature at Aberdeen University, 1894–1915, and succeeded *Saintsbury as professor of rhetoric and English literature at Edinburgh University, 1915–35. He advanced the study of *Donne and the *Metaphysical poets in his pioneering, well annotated edition of Donne's poems (1912) and in *Metaphysical Lyrics and Poems of the Seventeenth Century* (1921). He also edited (with G. *Bullough) *The Oxford Book of Seventeenth Century Verse* (1934), was co-editor of a 12-vol. edition of Sir W.

*Scott's letters (1932–37), and published a biography of Scott (1938).

Grieux, Chevalier des, the hero of the Abbé *Prévost's *Manon Lescaut*.

GRIEVE, C. M., see MACDIARMID, H.

GRIFFIN, Gerald (1803–40), Irish dramatist, novelist, and poet, remembered chiefly for his impressive social novel *The Collegians* (1829), in which young Cregan, allured by wealth and beauty, permits the murder of his humble country wife. *Boucicault made it the basis of a very successful play, *The Colleen Bawn*, in 1860. Griffin's play *Gisippus*, a blank verse drama of classical times, was produced at Drury Lane in 1842. A biography by J. Cronin was published in 1978.

Griffith Gaunt, or *Jealousy*, a novel by C. *Reade, published 1866.

The story is set in the 18th cent. Griffith Gaunt, an impoverished gentleman of Cumberland, wishes to marry Kate Payton, a spirited and ardent young Roman Catholic, who dreams of taking the veil but feels at the same time bound to the world. She prefers her other suitor, George Neville, but when Griffith loses his inheritance for her sake she accepts him, hoping for a contented marriage without undue submission. After some happy years, in which children are born, Griffith begins to drink heavily, and does not perceive Kate's disguised but growing passion for her new spiritual director, the exalted Father Leonard. She cannot eat after listening to his sermons, she finds her glove secreted in his room, and begins to understand that their religious ardours stem from human love. The envious housekeeper goads Griffith into a jealous fury, and he drags Leonard through a horse-pond. When he finds Kate and the priest walking together in a grove, at a time when Kate is supposed to be ill in her room, he attacks Leonard with demonic violence and the terrified Kate renounces her love. Griffith gallops away, and in his fever is nursed by Mercy Vint, an innkeeper's daughter, whom he eventually bigamously marries. When he briefly returns home to fetch some money the frenzied Kate tries to stab him, and although he escapes a disfigured body is later found in a mere and Kate is tried for murder. Mercy Vint walks miles alone with her child to save Kate. Eventually Kate and Griffith are happily reconciled, Mercy marries Kate's old suitor Neville, and the four live as neighbours, ostracized but happy in their good works.

The novel, based on a story by Wilkie *Collins, was unusually frank for its time and Reade was prosecuted in a case in which *Dickens ('as a husband and father') refused to help defend him. Reade's interest lay clearly not only in the theme of jealousy, both male and female, but in the sexual nature of Kate. Reade himself thought it a better novel than *The Cloister and the Hearth*, and many modern critics would agree with him.

GRIGSON, Geoffrey Edward Harvey (1905–), poet, critic, and editor of many publications, including the influential *New Verse* (1933–9) which he founded. His first volume of poetry, *Several Observations* (1939), was followed by many others, including *Under the Cliff* (1943), *The Isles of Scilly* (1946), *Collected Poems 1924–1962* (1963), *Angles and Circles* (1974), and *History of Him* (1980). Much of his prose and verse celebrates his native Cornwall, and his collections of essays, which, with his other journalism, earned him a reputation as a fierce polemicist and controversialist, include *The Harp of Aeolus* (1947) and *The Contrary View* (1974). He has also edited selections of work by W. *Barnes (1950), J. *Clare (1950), W. S. *Landor (1964), C. *Cotton (1975), and others, and his eclectic reading is expressed in several Faber anthologies. His wife Jane Grigson (*née* McIntire, 1928–) is a distinguished writer on food and cookery.

Grim, see HAVELOK THE DANE.

GRIMALD, Nicholas (*c*.1519–*c*.1562), of Christ's College, Cambridge, chaplain to Bishop *Ridley, contributed 40 poems to *Tottel's *Miscellany* and assisted in its compilation. He made translations from *Virgil (a Latin paraphrase of the *Eclogues*) and *Cicero (*De Officiis*), and wrote two Latin plays. He was admiringly commemorated in an elegy by *Googe.

GRIMALDI, Joseph (1779–1837), a celebrated clown and pantomimist, who first appeared as an infant dancer at Sadler's Wells, and acted there and at Drury Lane for many years. He had a son of the same name who succeeded him as pantomimist and died in 1863. Grimaldi's *Memoirs* were edited (without much enthusiasm) by *Dickens, with illustrations by *Cruikshank (2 vols, 1838).

GRIMBALD, or GRIMBOLD (?820–903), a native of Flanders and a monk of St Bertin's at St Omer. King *Alfred summoned him to England for the promotion of learning and appointed him abbot of the new minster at Winchester. Alfred mentions him as one of his teachers in the Preface to the *Cura Pastoralis*. A hagiographical *Life of Grimbald* survives in the 13th-cent. breviary of Hyde Abbey; but the events of his life are notoriously confused.

Grimes, (1) Peter, see PETER GRIMES; (2) Thomas, chimney-sweep, Tom's employer in C. Kingsley's *The Water-Babies*.

GRIMM, Jacob Ludwig Carl (1785–1863), and Wilhelm Carl (1786–1859), German brothers who pioneered the study of German philology, law, mythology, and folklore. They are chiefly known in England for their collection of fairy-tales, *Kinder- und Hausmärchen* (1812–15), of which an English translation by Edgar Taylor, illustrated by *Cruikshank, was published in 1823 under the title *German Popular Stories*. The brothers also began the German etymological dictionary, *Deutsches Wörterbuch*, the German equivalent of the *OED*, in 1852. The work was continued by later scholars, and brought to completion in 1960. Jacob Grimm formulated 'Grimm's Law' of the mutations of the consonants in the several Aryan languages.

GRIMMELSHAUSEN, Johannes Jacob Christoffel von (*c*.1621–76), German writer, author of the picaresque novel *Simplicissimus* and, among other things, of a novel from which *Brecht took the story of his *Mother Courage*.

Grimwig, Mr, a character in Dickens's *Oliver Twist*.

Gringolet, or **Gryngolet,** Gawain's horse, in *Chrétien (*Erec et Énide*, 3,935), *Le Chevalier à l'Épée* (226), *Sir *Gawain and the Green Knight* (597), etc. Speght, in his 1598 edition of Chaucer, gives it as the name of *Wade's infamous boat.

Grip, in Dickens's *Barnaby Rudge*, Barnaby's raven.

Gripe, one of the chief characters in Vanbrugh's *The Confederacy*.

Griselda, the type of long-suffering fortitude; see PATIENT GRISELDA.

Groatsettar, The Misses, characters in Scott's *The Pirate*.

Groats-Worth of Witte, see GREENES GROATSWORTH OF WITTE.

Grobian (German *Grobheit*, rudeness), an imaginary personage often referred to by writers of the 15th and 16th cents in Germany as a type of boorishness. Sebastian Brant in his *Narrenschiff* (see SHIP OF FOOLS) invented St Grobianus as typical of ill-mannered and indecent behaviour. In 1549 F. Dedekind, a German student, wrote a poem in Latin elegiacs, *Grobianus, de morum simplicitate*, a burlesque of the generally uncivilized social conditions then prevailing in Germany, in the form of ironical advice on conduct given to a gallant. This was translated into German by Kaspar Scheidt, and into English, and suggested to Dekker his *Guls Hornebooke*.

GROCYN, William (1449–1519), educated at Winchester and New College, Oxford, held various ecclesiastical preferments. He studied in Italy with *Linacre under *Poliziano and Chalcondyles, and was instrumental in introducing the study of Greek at Oxford.

Grongar Hill, see DYER, J.

GRONOVIUS, Johann Friedrich (1611–71),

a Dutch scholar and editor of Greek and Roman classics. His son, Jakob Gronovius (1645–1716), was professor of Greek at Leyden, and, like his father, an editor of classical authors.

GROSART, Alexander Balloch (1827–99), editor remembered for his reprints of rare Elizabethan and Jacobean literature; between 1868 and 1896 he edited more than 130 volumes.

GROSSETESTE, Robert (1175–1253), bishop of Lincoln and the first chancellor of Oxford University. He was the author of translations from the Greek, including *Aristotle's Ethics* and the works of Pseudo-Dionysius (see DIONYSIUS THE AREOPAGITE). Though closely connected with the Franciscans in thought, he remained a secular throughout his life. He was a major figure in the development of the Augustinian philosophical tradition, and he was largely responsible for the Oxford emphasis on the development of the natural sciences; it is likely that he passed on to his pupil R. *Bacon his knowledge of and interest in experimental science, especially optics and mathematics. Influenced by the Platonic tradition of the Arabs, he developed his light-metaphysic in his work *De Luce*, which identifies a form of corporaneity as the most important of forms and makes the individual the essence of the form. See S. H. Thompson, ed., *Writings* (1940); James McEvoy, *The Philosophy of Robert Grosseteste* (1983).

GROSSMITH, George (1847–1912) and Weedon (1852–1919), brothers whose father was a friend of H. *Irving, the *Terry family and other theatrical people. Both pursued successful theatrical careers. In 1852 *The Diary of a Nobody* began to appear in *Punch*, with text by both brothers and illustrations by Weedon. Its popularity with a wide range of readership was immediate, and has not faltered.

Grosvenor Gallery, The, Bond Street, London, for the exhibition of pictures of the modern school, erected by Sir Coutts Lindsay in 1876. It was especially associated for a time with the *aesthetic movement. Bunthorne in *Gilbert and Sullivan's *Patience* describes himself as:

A pallid and thin young man,
A haggard and lank young man,
A greenery-yallery, Grosvenor Gallery,
Foot-in-the-grave young man.

The Gallery closed in 1890. See H. Hubbard, *A Hundred Years of British Painting* (1951).

GROTE, George (1794–1871), banker, educated at Charterhouse, was MP for the City of London, 1832–41, and took an active part in favour of the reform movement, publishing a pamphlet on the subject in 1820 and another in 1831. His outlook was much influenced by James *Mill and *Utilitarianism. He retired from Parliament in order to devote himself to historical work. His famous *History of Greece*, in eight vols, on which he had been intermittently at work since 1823, was published in 1846–56, and achieved immediate success. Grote's other works include studies of *Plato (1865) and *Aristotle (1872), and various papers and essays on philosophical and ethical subjects.

GROTIUS, Hugo (1583–1645), Dutch statesman and jurist, was born at Delft, studied law at Orleans and Leyden, and became the leader of the bar at The Hague. He wrote in 1601 a sacred drama in Latin, *Adamus Exsul*, with which Milton was probably familiar when he wrote *Paradise Lost*. Grotius was Dutch ambassador in London in 1613, but his intimacy with Barnavelt (who was executed in 1619 for conspiracy against the State) led to his condemnation to imprisonment for life. From this he escaped in a large box in which books were sent to him for the purpose of study, and took refuge in Paris. He became the ambassador of Queen Christina of Sweden at the French Court, and died, after shipwreck, in her service. He wrote a large number of works, including a Latin history of the revolt of the Netherlands. But his principal title to fame is his great treatise of international law, the *De jure Belli ac Pacis*, published in 1625. In the midst of the Thirty Years War (1618–48) he asserted in this work the principle of a rule of law binding upon nations in their relations with one another.

Group, The, an informal association of writers, mostly poets, set up in London by Philip *Hobsbaum in 1955. A number of poems or a chapter of a novel (which had been previously distributed to other participants) would be read aloud by the author and discussed by all present. Membership was by invitation of the chairman, and during the formative years, 1956–7, most of the key figures were recruited: these included *Redgrove, P. *Porter, *Lucie-Smith, and G. *MacBeth. Lucie-Smith took over as chairman in 1959, and the group expanded to include F. *Adcock, B. S. *Johnson, and others. An anthology of the Group's writings, edited by Hobsbaum and Lucie-Smith, appeared in 1963 (*A Group Anthology*). In 1965 the Group was restructured into a more formal organization called the Writers' Workshop, but its basic purpose, to expose the work of young writers to their peers, remained constant: it would be considered, not as a movement in poetry, but as a critical approach.

GROVE, George, see MUSIC, LITERATURE OF.

Grubbinol, a shepherd in Gay's *The Shepherd's Week*.

Grub Street, London, according to Dr *Johnson was 'originally the name of a street near

Moorfields in London, much inhabited by writers of small histories, dictionaries, and temporary poems, whence any mean production is called *grubstreet*' (*Dictionary*). The name of the street was changed in the 19th cent. to Milton Street (Cripplegate). 'Grub Street' is current in modern usage as an epithet meaning 'of the nature of literary hack-work'.

Grub Street Journal, The, a weekly literary newspaper, highly satirical in tone, which ran from Jan. 1730 to Dec. 1737; its targets included the **Gentleman's Magazine* and *The Bee*, *Theobald, *Cibber, *Eusden, and *Curll. *Pope (whose enemies were reviled as 'Knights of the Bathos') is thought to have had a hand in it, although the connection has not been established. See James T. Hillhouse, *The Grub Street Journal* (1928).

Grueby, John, a character in Dickens's **Barnaby Rudge*, servant to Lord George Gordon.

Grundy, Mrs, the symbol of rigid conventional propriety. For the origin of the name see MORTON, T.

Gryll, in Spenser's **Faerie Queene* (II. xii. 86), the hog in the Bower of *Acrasia who repined greatly at being changed back into a man. The incident is based on a dialogue of *Plutarch, in which Gryllus is one of the Greeks transformed into swine by Circe.

Gryll Grange, the last satirical novel of T. L. *Peacock, serialized 1860, issued as a book 1861.

The main plot concerns Mr Falconer, idealist, ascetic, and classicist, who lives in a tower attended by seven virgins, but is persuaded to join a convivial house party at Gryll Grange, where he woos and wins its presiding genius, Morgana Gryll. A second plot concerns the courtship of the scientific, outgoing Lord Curryfin, and the musical, meditative Alice Niphet. The characters debate many mid-Victorian issues, often criticizing the misuse of science. As part of the Christmas festivities they act an Aristophanic play which parodies the competitive examinations newly introduced into the Civil Service: Hannibal, Richard Coeur de Lion, and Oliver Cromwell are all failed. Notable characters include the Revd Dr Opimian, an agreeable gourmet with conservative views, and Miss Ilex, a wise and cheerful spinster. Perhaps the most urbane and polished of Peacock's books, *Gryll Grange* upholds civilization, harmony, and completeness against both technology and religious asceticism, two dominant strands of mid-Victorian thought.

Guardian, The, (1) a periodical started by *Steele in March 1713. It professed at the outset to abstain from political questions, and *Addison contributed 51 papers to it. It included also among its contributors *Berkeley, *Pope, and *Gay. But Steele soon launched into political controversy, falling foul of the Tory **Examiner*. Owing to some disagreement with Tonson, the publisher, *The Guardian* came to an abrupt end in Oct. 1713 and was succeeded by *The Englishman*; there is an edition by J. C. Stephens (1983). (2) a national daily paper originally published as **The Manchester Guardian*.

GUARINI, Giovanni Battista (1538–1612), born at Ferrara, author of the pastoral drama *Il pastor fido* (1589), written in emulation of *Tasso's *Aminta*. It had a considerable vogue in England in the 17th cent., where it was translated many times; notably by Sir Richard *Fanshawe in 1647 as *The Faithfull Shepherd* (ed. W. F. Staton and W. E. Simeone, 1964). Guarini also wrote an influential defence of tragi-comedy, the *Compendio della poesia tragicomica* (1601).

Gudrun, (1) in the **Vǫlsunga saga* and in W. Morris's **Sigurd the Volsung*, the daughter of the king of the Niblungs; (2) the heroine of the *Laxdaela saga* (see SAGA), who appears in Morris's version, 'The Lovers of Gudrun', in **The Earthly Paradise*; (3) Gudrun Brangwen, one of the two sisters in D. H. Lawrence's **Women in Love*.

GUEDALLA, Philip (1889–1944), historian and biographer, often compared (for his irreverence, epigrammatic wit, etc.) to L. *Strachey, who claimed him as 'an imitator'. His works include *Supers and Supermen* (1920), *Palmerston* (1926), *The Duke* (1931, biography of *Wellington), and *Mr Churchill* (1941).

Guendolen, in Scott's **The Bridal of Triermain*, a fay who beguiles King Arthur into loving her, and becomes the mother of Gyneth.

Guest, Stephen, a character in G. Eliot's **The Mill on the Floss*.

GUICCIARDINI, Francesco (1483–1540), Florentine historian and statesman, employed by the Medici and the papacy. He was commissioner general for the papal army at the time of the sack of Rome (1527). His *Storia d'Italia*, a history of Italy from 1492 to 1534, was translated into English (from a French version) by Fenton, and is of lasting significance; passages from it were inserted in the second edition of *Holinshed's Chronicles. Both *Ralegh and F. *Bacon knew the work well. The *Ricordi*, a collection of aphorisms, also had a wide diffusion.

Guiderius, in Shakespeare's **Cymbeline*, elder son of the king, who in mountain exile bears the name Polydore. The supplements to **A Mirror for Magistrates* contained two 'tragedies' of Guiderius, presenting him as a powerful opponent of the Romans.

GUIDO DELLE COLONNE, a 13th-cent. Sicilian writer of Latin romances, author of the *Historia Destructionis Troiae* which was in fact a prose version of a poem by *Benoît de Sainte-Maure, though Guido did not acknowledge this. His romance was used as a source in poems attributed to *Barbour and *Huchown, and by *Lydgate in his *Troy Book*. The story of Troilus and Cressida, taken by Guido from Benoît, was in turn developed by *Boccaccio, *Chaucer, *Henryson, and Shakespeare. Muriel Bowden, in *A Commentary on the General Prologue to the Canterbury Tales* (1948, p.20), shows that the famous opening of the *Prologue* corresponds very closely to a passage in Guido.

Guignol, the chief character in the popular French puppet-show of that name, similar to the English Punch and Judy show. The word is also used for the theatre where the show is performed. Grand Guignol is a term applied to a theatre presenting plays of a gruesome character (resembling in this respect the play of *Punch and Judy*).

Guildenstern, see ROSENCRANTZ.

Guild of St George, see RUSKIN, J.

GUILLAUME DE LORRIS, see ROMAN DE LA ROSE.

GUILLAUME DE MACHAUT (*c.*1300–77), French musician and poet. He was prominent in the development of the *ballade* and the *rondeau*, and one of the most widely celebrated composers in the field of polyphonic songwriting. His poetry influenced Chaucer, particularly in *The Book of the Duchess*.

GUILPIN, Everard (b. ?1572), is presumed to be the author of *Skialetheia. Or, A shadowe of Truth, in certaine Epigrams and Satyres* (1598), which has interesting affinities with the satires of *Marston and *Donne. It has been edited by D. Allen Carroll (1974).

Guinea, Chrysal, or the Adventures of a, see JOHNSTONE, C.

Guinevere, the wife of King *Arthur in the Arthurian legend. The name figures in various forms: in *Geoffrey of Monmouth she is 'Guanhamara', of a noble Roman family, brought up in the household of Cador, duke of Cornwall. In the *Brut* of *Laȝamon she is 'Wenhaver', a relative of Cador; in *Sir *Gawain and the Green Knight* she is Wenore, Guenore, Gwenore, and Gaynor (the form also in *The Awntyrs of Arthure*). The most prevailing form both of her name and her story developed in the French tradition, in *Chrétien's *Lancelot* (1170s) and the related early 13th-cent. prose *Lancelot* of the Vulgate cycle, where the queen Guénièvre is the lover of Lancelot, with disastrous consequences: Lancelot fails to achieve the *Grail, and in the final confrontation with Modred he arrives too late to save Arthur, finding that the queen has become a nun. This traces only the main tradition of Guinevere, from Chrétien to Malory; there is also a more disreputable version of her as unfaithful and vengeful, reflected in such poems as *Sir Launfal*. But in this main tradition, the tragic love of Guinevere and Lancelot is one of the classics of *Courtly Love.

'Guinevere', one of Tennyson's *Idylls of the King*, published 1859. It describes Guinevere's growing repentance, her parting with Launcelot, her last meeting with Arthur, and her death as abbess of the nunnery of Almesbury.

Gulley Jimson, in *The Horse's Mouth* by J. *Cary.

Gulliver's Travels, a satire by *Swift, published 1726.

Swift probably got the idea of a satire in the form of a narrative of travels at the meetings of the *Scriblerus Club, and intended it to form part of the 'Memoirs of Scriblerus'; indeed Scriblerus is described in the 'Memoirs' as visiting the same countries as Gulliver. Swift appears to have worked at the book from as early as 1720.

In the first part Lemuel Gulliver, a surgeon on a merchant ship, relates his shipwreck on the island of Lilliput, the inhabitants of which are six inches high, everything on the island being in the proportion of an inch to a foot as compared with things as we know them. Owing to this diminutive scale, the pomp of the emperor, the civil feuds of the inhabitants, the war with their neighbours across the channel, are made to look ridiculous. The English political parties and religious dissensions are satirized in the description of the wearers of high heels and low heels, and of the controversy on the question whether eggs should be broken at the big or small end.

In the second part Gulliver is accidentally left ashore on Brobdingnag, where the inhabitants are as tall as steeples, and everything else is in proportion. Here the king, after inquiring into the manners, government, and learning of Europe, sums up his impression of what Gulliver tells him as follows: 'By what I have gathered from your own relation . . . I cannot but conclude the bulk of your natives to be the most pernicious race of little odious vermin that nature ever suffered to crawl upon the surface of the earth.'

The third part (which was written last) is occupied with a visit to the flying island of Laputa, and its neighbouring continent and capital Lagado. Here the satire is directed against philosophers, men of science, historians, and projectors, with special reference to the *South Sea Company. In Laputa Gulliver finds the wise men so wrapped up in their speculations as to be utter dotards in practical affairs. At Lagado he visits the Academy of Projectors, where professors are engaged in extracting sunshine from cucumbers and similar absurd enterprises. In the Island of Sorcerers he is enabled to call up the great men of old, and discovers, from their answers to his questions, the deceptions of history. The Struldbrugs, a race endowed with immortality, so far from finding this a boon, turn out to be the most miserable of mankind.

In the fourth part Swift describes the country of the Houyhnhnms, who are horses endowed with reason; their rational, clean, and simple society is contrasted with the filthiness and brutality of the Yahoos, beasts in human shape whose human vices Gulliver is reluctantly forced to recognize. So alienated is he from his own species that when he finally returns home he recoils from his own family in disgust.

Gulliver's Travels was an immediate success and was read (in the words of *Pope and *Gay) from the cabinet council to the nursery'; it continues to appeal to readers of all ages, both as a travel book and as a powerful satire, although many find themselves repelled or disturbed by the darkness of Swift's vision, particularly in the last book, which *Thackeray described as furious, raging, obscene', and L. *Stephen found 'painful and repulsive'.

Guls Hornebooke, The, a satirical book of manners by *Dekker, published 1609.

It is an attack on the fops and gallants of the day under the guise of ironical instructions how they may make themselves conspicuous in places of public resort by their offensive conduct. The occupations of a young man of leisure are described; his dressing, his walk in 'Paul's', his meal at the 'ordinary', the visit to the playhouse, etc. It is a parody of the *courtesy-books of the period, and was suggested by a German original (see GROBIAN).

GUMILEV, Nikolai Stepanovich (1886–1921), Russian poet and critic. The son of a naval doctor, he was born at Kronstadt and educated at Tsarskoe Selo, where in 1903 he met *Akhmatova, whom he was to marry in 1910. His first book of poetry, *The Path of the Conquistadors*, was published in 1905. In 1911 he founded the Guild of Poets, which brought together the members of the school of Russian *Acmeism, whose poetic ideals were clarity and precision, and whose 'teachers' were *Shakespeare, *Rabelais, *Villon, and *Gautier. After serving with the Uhlans from 1914 he visited England in June 1917 and again in Jan.–April 1918. He met R. *Fry and A. *Huxley, and visited *Garsington in June 1917. He also met G. K. *Chesterton and during an air raid made a 'mad' speech suggesting that countries should be ruled by poets and offering Chesterton the crown of England. He made the acquaintance of most of the writers and artists associated with

*Orage's *The New Age*, which frequently published translations from the Russian and articles about Russian writers. From England he returned to Russia; he was divorced from Akhmatova in 1918. On 3 Aug. 1921 he was arrested for alleged participation in the so-called 'Tagantsev conspiracy', a pro-monarchist plot, and he was executed later that month. The whole affair remains shrouded in mystery. Gumilev has never been re-published in the Soviet Union, but his poetry of love and the romantic cult of spiritual and physical endeavour is increasingly valued abroad. The major English edition is *Selected Works of Nikolai S. Gumilev* (trans. Burton Raffel and Alla Burago, 1972).

Gummidge, Mrs, a character in Dickens's *David Copperfield*, a 'lone lorn creetur'.

GUNN, Thom(son William) (1929–), poet, born in Gravesend, the son of a journalist, and educated at University College School and Trinity College, Cambridge, where he was a contemporary (though not at that time, despite the frequent linking of their names, a friend) of Ted *Hughes. His first volume of poems, *Fighting Terms*, was published in 1954; shortly afterwards he took up a fellowship at Stanford University, California (where he came under the influence of *Winters), and in 1960 he settled permanently in San Francisco, gradually relinquishing the academic life for a full-time career as a writer. His collections include *The Sense of Movement* (1959), *My Sad Captains* (1961), *Moly* (1971), and *Jack Straw's Castle* (1976). His celebration of men of action (soldiers, motor-cyclists, tough boys), his fascination with violence, his gallery of heroes (who range from Elvis Presley to Caravaggio), together with his predominantly low-key, rational, laconic, colloquial manner provide an interesting synthesis of the English *Movement and the romantic elements of American *Beat poetry.

GUNNING, Susannah (?1740–1800), lived a difficult life, largely in high London society, with a turbulent Army husband, a beautiful high-spirited daughter, and a countess and a duchess for sisters-in-law. *Walpole referred to the notorious family as 'the Gunningiad'. She wrote some poetry, and from 1763 onwards produced almost a dozen unmemorable novels, many of them successful, including *Barford Abbey* (1768) and *The Heir Apparent* (1802).

Guppy, a character in Dickens's *Bleak House*.

GURDJIEFF, Georgei Ivanovitch (?1874–1949), esoteric thinker and teacher, son of a Greek father and Armenian mother, was born at Alexandrople, just inside Russia on the Turkish frontier. He claimed to have spent his youth travelling in Central Asia, India, and Tibet with a company of fellow seekers acquiring occult knowledge. In 1910 he appeared in St

Petersburg practising as a healer with theosophical leanings, and in 1914 met *Ouspensky who became his principal disciple and recorded his teaching in *In Search of the Miraculous* (1950). He moved to the Caucasus during the revolution, then via Constantinople and Berlin to France, where in 1922, from mysterious funds, he set up the Institute for the Harmonious Development of Man at Fontainebleau, where K. *Mansfield died in 1923. His ideas influenced A. *Huxley (see *After Many a Summer*, 1939, and *The Doors of Perception*, 1954) and *Isherwood. *Orage, editor of *The New Age*, was a disciple, followed him to Fontainebleau in 1922, and spent some years teaching the doctrine, raising funds, and organizing groups. A powerful and hypnotic personality, often labelled as a charlatan, Gurdjieff insisted that his knowledge was more a method than a doctrine, and could only be acquired by initiates through long discipline and a technique of self-observation.

GURNEY, Ivor (Bertie) (1890–1937), poet and composer, born in Gloucester, the son of a tailor. He was awarded a scholarship in composition at the Royal College of Music, which he attended from 1911. He volunteered at the outbreak of the First World War, served on the Western Front as a private from 1915 to 1917, and was wounded and gassed. He published two volumes of verse, *Severn and Somme* (1917) and *War's Embers* (1919). After the war he became increasingly unsettled, and worked at various jobs, at times sleeping rough, and taking night-walks back to Gloucestershire from London. He was committed to a mental institution in 1922, and spent the rest of his life in care, dying in the City of London Mental Hospital. He continued in these later years to compose and to write poetry of growing individuality. He set few of his own poems to music, but produced two A. E. *Housman cycles (*Ludlow and Teme* and *The Western Playland*, both 1919) and a set of six E. *Thomas songs, *Lights Out* (1918–25). In the short time at his disposal he produced altogether nearly 300 songs. *Blunden made a selection of his post-1919 poems, published 1954, and Leonard Clark published a larger selection in 1973. Interest in his verse—with its memories of the war, its evocations of Gloucestershire, and descriptions of his own mental state—continued to grow, and his *Collected Poems*, edited and with an introduction by P. J. Kavanagh, appeared in 1982. See also M. Hurd's biography, *The Ordeal of Ivor Gurney* (1978).

GURNEY, Thomas (1705–70), shorthand-writer at the Old Bailey, the first shorthand-writer to hold an official appointment. His *Brachygraphy* (1750), originally an improvement of W. Mason's *Shorthand*, has been frequently reissued and improved. His grandson, William Brodie Gurney, shorthand-writer to the Houses of Parliament (1813), is referred to by Byron in *Don Juan* (i. 189).

Gurth, the Saxon swineherd in Scott's *Ivanhoe*.

Guster, a character in Dickens's *Bleak House*.

GUTENBERG, Johann (c.1400–?68), traditionally considered the inventor of printing with movable types. Born at Mainz, he went to Strasbourg c.1428 and there began experimenting with the use of cast letters and a press for printing. He went back to Mainz c.1445, and developed his invention in partnership with *Fust, who provided the capital. Fust dissolved the partnership in 1455 and took possession of the implements and stock. Gutenberg died in 1467 or 1468, leaving 'sundry forms, letters, instruments, tools, and other things pertaining to the work of printing' which had been loaned to him by a Dr Konrad Hummery of Mainz. No work printed by him can be identified, though the 42-line Bible (sometimes called the 'Gutenberg Bible', printed at Mainz 1453–5) and other of the earliest books have been attributed to him on grounds of probability.

GUTHLAC, St (d. 714/15), a young nobleman of Mercia who reacted against his military life and became a hermit at Crowland (or Croyland) in Lincolnshire. Æthelbald, king of Mercia, had a church built over his tomb, which later became the abbey of Crowland. Not long after his death was written the Latin *Vita Sancti Guthlaci* (c.740) by Felix of Croyland, which is in the tradition of Latin saints' lives such as Evagrius's *Vita Sancti Antonii*, and of which there is a late Old English prose version from Mercia. Two adjacent poems in Old English, found in the *Exeter Book known as *Guthlac A* and *Guthlac B*, are distinguished from each other in style and in the degree of their dependence on Felix: B is much more closely copied from him and is written in a more elaborate, Cynewulfian style than A. The poems used to be attributed to *Cynewulf and they are thought to date originally from the late 9th cent. See W. de G. Birch ed., *Memorials of St Guthlac* (Wisbech, 1881).

GUY, Thomas (?1645–1724), the founder of Guy's Hospital, set up as a bookseller in London in 1668 and was one of the Oxford University printers, 1679–92. He greatly increased his fortune by selling his *South Sea Company stock. He lived a penurious life but was liberal in benefactions, erecting the hospital that bears his name at a cost of some £18,000 and leaving £200,000 for its endowment, besides other charitable bequests.

Guy Livingston, see LAWRENCE, G. A.

Guy Mannering, a novel by Sir W. *Scott, published 1815.

The story, laid in the 18th cent., centres in the fortunes of young Harry Bertram, son of the laird of Ellangowan in the county of Dumfries, who is kidnapped by smugglers when a child, and carried to Holland. This is done at the instigation of a rascally lawyer, Glossin, who has hopes of acquiring on easy terms the Ellangowan estate, in default of an heir male. Bertram, ignorant of his parentage and bearing the name of Brown, goes to India, joins the army, and serves with distinction under Colonel Guy Mannering. Bertram (or Brown) is suspected by Mannering of paying attentions to his wife, and is wounded by him in a duel and left for dead. In reality Bertram is in love with Julia, Mannering's daughter. Recovering from his wound, he follows her to England and the neighbourhood of Ellangowan. Glossin, now in possession of the Ellangowan estate, is alarmed by the return of Bertram and the possibility that he may learn the secret of his parentage. He plots with Dirk Hatteraick, the smuggler who had originally kidnapped the child, to carry him off once more and make away with him. But an old gypsy, Meg Merrilies, also recognizes Harry and devotes all her energies to secure his restoration. She frustrates the plot with the help of Bertram and Dandie Dinmont, a sturdy Lowland farmer, but at the sacrifice of her own life. Hatteraick and Glossin are captured, and Hatteraick, after murdering Glossin in prison as the author of his misfortunes, takes his own life. Bertram is acknowledged and restored to his property and to Mannering's favour, and marries Julia. The novel includes the notable character of Dominie Sampson, the uncouth simple-minded tutor of the little Harry Bertram.

Guy of Gisborne, see ROBIN HOOD AND GUY OF GISBORNE.

Guy of Warwick, a very popular verse romance of about 1300, based on an Anglo-Norman original (of which there are 13 manuscripts), occurring in four manuscripts ranging from 7,000 to 12,000 lines.

Guy is the son of Siward, steward of Rohand, earl of Warwick, and the romance tells of the exploits he performs in order to win the hand of the earl's daughter Fenice. He rescues the daughter of the emperor of Germany, fights the Saracens, and slays the Soldan. He returns to England where he is honourably received by King Athelstan and marries Fenice, but soon returns to the Holy Land where he performs more great exploits. He comes back again to England and fights the Danish giant Colbrand in a famous combat, slays the Dun Cow of Dunsmore, and vanquishes a winged dragon in Northumberland. He becomes a hermit and is fed by Fenice who does not recognize him until he sends her his ring from his deathbed.

The romance served as a patriotic rallying-poem because of its celebration of Athelstan's resistance to the Danes, and its popularity was enhanced by its nature as saint's life combined with violent adventure story. The legend was accepted as authentic by chroniclers and versified by *Lydgate (c.1450); the Beauchamp earls claimed descent from Guy. The story of the encounter between Guy and Colbrand is told in Drayton's *Poly-Olbion, xii. 130 ff., which describes other feats of Guy in xiii. 327 ff. See edition by J. Zupitza (3 vols EETS ES, 42, 49, 59, 1883–91).

Guyon, Sir, in Spenser's *Faerie Queene, the knight of Temperance. His various exploits, the conquest of *Pyrochles, the visit to the cave of *Mammon, the capture of *Acrasia, and the destruction of her *Bower of Bliss, are related in Bk. II. v–xii.

Guzman de Alfarache, a Spanish *picaresque romance, the second of its kind (the successor of *Lazarillo de Tormes) by Mateo Alemán (1547–c.1614). It was translated into English (as The Rogue) in 1622 and published with an introductory poem by *Jonson.

Guzman is by turns scullion, thief, gentleman, beggar, soldier, page to a cardinal and to a French ambassador, and his career gives occasion for 'sketches of character and humorous descriptions to which it would be difficult to produce anything superior' (*Hazlitt).

Gwendolen, in *Geoffrey of Monmouth's History, the daughter of Corineus and wife of King *Locrine who threw *Estrildis and Sabrina (Habren) into the Severn.

GWYN, Nell (1650–87), orange-seller, actress, and mistress of Charles II; her best role seems to have been the 'breeches part' of Florimel in *Dryden's Secret Love. One of her sons was created duke of St Albans in 1684.

Gyneth, in Scott's *The Bridal of Triermain, the daughter of King Arthur and *Guendolen.

H

Habbakkuk Hilding, the name given to *Fielding in a scurrilous pamphlet of 1752, possibly by *Smollett.

HABINGTON, William (1605–54), of an old Catholic family, educated at St Omer and Paris, married Lucy Herbert, daughter of the first baron Powis, and celebrated her in *Castara* (1634, anon.), a collection of love poems. A later edition (1635) contained in addition some elegies on a friend, and the edition of 1640 a number of sacred poems. He also wrote a tragi-comedy, *The Queene of Arragon* (1640). His poems were edited by Kenneth Allott, 1948, with a life.

Hadrian the Seventh, see ROLFE, F. W.

HĀFIZ, Shams ud-din Muhammad (d. c.1390), a famous Persian poet and philosopher, born at Shiraz, whose poems sing of love and flowers and wine and nightingales. His principal work is the *Divan*, a collection of short lyrics called *ghazals*, or *ghasels*, in which some commentators see a mystical meaning. Translations of his works include *Odes of Hafez* (1774) by J. Richardson, and versions by Sir W. *Jones, G. *Bell (*Poems from the Divan of Hafiz*, 1897), and R. *Le Gallienne (1905). See also *Persian Poems* (1954), ed. A. J. Arberry. Hāfiz and *Sa'dī were buried near one another at Shiraz.

Hafnia, in imprints, Copenhagen.

Haga Comitum, in imprints, The Hague.

Hagenback, Archibald of, a character in Scott's *Anne of Geierstein*.

HAGGARD, Sir H(enry) Rider (1856–1925), sixth son of a Norfolk squire, spent six years in South Africa as a young man, and later served on official commissions concerned with agriculture, forestry, and emigration, and wrote books on South African history and on farming; but it was his 34 adventure novels that made him famous. These were notable chiefly for weird invention and spell-binding narrative, and were diversely set in Iceland, Mexico, Constantinople, and Ancient Egypt; but his best novels—of which *King Solomon's Mines* (1886) and *She* (1887) are the most celebrated—were set in Africa, and vividly conveyed the fascination he found in its landscape, wild-life, tribal society, and mysterious past. *Kipling and *Lang were close friends of his, and he had a world-wide readership which included *Jung,

who used *She* as a striking example of the anima concept. Haggard's novels have remained continuously popular, and several of them have been filmed. *The Days of My Life: an Autobiography* appeared in 1926, and there is a biography by Morton Cohen (1960).

Haidée, a character in Byron's *Don Juan*.

Haiku, a Japanese lyric form of 17 syllables in lines of 5, 7, 5 syllables. It emerged in the 16th cent. and flourished from the 17th to the 19th cent., and dealt traditionally with images of the natural world; in this century it has been much imitated in Western literature.

HAILES, see DALRYMPLE.

Hajji Baba of Ispahan, The Adventures of, see MORIER, J. J.

HAKLUYT (pron. Haklit), Richard (1552–1616), of a Herefordshire family, was educated at Westminster and Christ Church, Oxford. He was chaplain to Sir Edward Stafford, ambassador at Paris, 1583–8. Here he learnt much of the maritime enterprises of other nations, and found that the English were reputed for 'their sluggish security'. He accordingly decided to devote himself to collecting and publishing the accounts of English explorations, and to this purpose he gave the remainder of his life. He had already been amassing material, for in 1582 he published *Divers voyages touching the discoverie of America*. In 1587 he published in Paris a revised edition of the *De Orbe Novo* of Peter Martyr of Anghiera (subsequently translated into English by Peter Lok), and in the same year appeared his *A notable historie, containing four Voyages made by certain French Captains into Florida*, a translation of Réné de Laudonnière. His *Principall Navigations, Voiages, and Discoveries of the English Nation* was issued in 1589, and, much enlarged, in three vols, 1598–1600. It contained some account of the voyages of the *Cabots, and narratives of Sir Hugh Willoughby's voyage to the NE in search of Cathay, Sir John *Hawkins's voyages to Guinea and the West Indies, *Drake's voyages of 1570–2 and his circumnavigation, Sir Humphrey Gilbert's last voyage in which he perished, Martin Frobisher's search for the North-West Passage, John Davys's Arctic voyages, and the voyages of *Ralegh, James Lancaster, and others. He thus brought to light the hitherto obscure achievements of English navigators, and gave a great impetus to discovery and colonization. He was closely associated with *Sidney in the last years of his life, and from 1582 with Ralegh (particularly between 1583 and 1590). He is referred to by many contemporary scholars and writers, some of whom were his personal friends, including *Camden, Gabriel and Richard *Harvey, *Mulcaster, *Nashe, and *Drayton. He was a pluralist, holding pre-bendaryships at Bristol and Westminster; he was rector of Wetheringsett, 1590–1616, and of Gedney, 1612–16. He left unpublished a number of papers which came into the hands of *Purchas.

The Hakluyt Society was founded in 1846 as an offshoot of the (Royal) Geographical Society to publish voyages and travels, which it has done at the rate of at least two volumes a year since then. Its publications include reissues and re-editions of Hakluyt's writings, and very many original narratives. Its history and that of its founder are succinctly set out in D. B. Quinn, ed., *The Hakluyt Handbook* (2 vols, 1974).

Hal, Prince, in Shakespeare's *1* and *2* *Henry IV*, the prince of Wales who later becomes Henry V.

Halcro, Claud, a character in Scott's *The Pirate*.

HALDANE, J(ohn) B(urdon) S(anderson) (1892–1964), geneticist and brother of N. *Mitchison, was professor of genetics, then of biometry, at University College London, and, 1940–9, chairman of the editorial board of the Communist *Daily Worker*, to which he contributed hundreds of articles. He became known to a large public as a witty popularizer of science with such works as *Daedalus* (1924), *Possible Worlds* (1927, in the forewords of which he stresses the public's 'right to know'), *Animal Biology* (with J. *Huxley, 1927), and a collection of children's stories, *My Friend Mr Leakey* (1937). His scientific but imaginative speculations about the future have much in common with those in *Brave New World*, and Haldane himself appears as Shearwater, a biologist with a flighty wife, in A. *Huxley's *Antic Hay*. A Marxist from the 1930s, Haldane resigned from the Communist Party c.1950 on the issue of Lysenko's claims to have manipulated the genetic structure of plants and '*Stalin's interference with science'. See a life by R. Clark (1968).

Hale, Mr, Mrs, Margaret, and Frederick, characters in E. Gaskell's *North and South*.

HALE, Sir Matthew (1609–76), educated at Oxford, became lord chief justice and was a voluminous writer on many subjects, but much of his best work was left in manuscript and published long after his death. His works include a *History of the Common Law* (1713) and an unfinished *History of the Pleas of the Crown* (1736). He was a friend and admirer of *Selden and G. *Burnet wrote his biography.

HALES, Alexander of, see ALEXANDER OF HALES.

HALÉVY, Élie (1870–1937), French social and political historian, author of *Histoire du peuple anglais au XIXᵉ siècle*, a study of political, economic, and religious change in England after 1815. Having dealt with the period 1815–41 in three volumes (1913–23), Halévy went on to write a further two (1926–32) on the years 1895–1915 before turning his attention to the middle of the century. His last work (1946), on the years 1841–52, was published after his death. The English translation (2nd edn, rev. 1949–52) by E. I. Watkin and D. A. Barker, which contains additional material on the period 1852–95 by R. B. McCallum, comprises six parts: I. *England in 1815*; II. *The Liberal Awakening*; III. *The Triumph of Reform*; IV. *Victorian Years* (1841–95); V. *Imperialism and the Rise of Labour* (1895–1905); VI. *The Rule of Democracy* (1905–14).

HALIBURTON, Thomas Chandler (1796–1865), born at Windsor, Nova Scotia, became a judge of the supreme court of the province. As a writer he became known for his *The Clockmaker; or, the Sayings and Doings of Samuel Slick, of Slickville* (1836; London, 1837), a satirical and humorous work of fiction published anonymously which had a great vogue in England. It was followed by other works in the same series, including *The Attaché or Sam Slick in England* (1843–4), designed to stimulate political reform through the satirical observations of the character Sam Slick, a Yankee from Ohio. See V. L. O. Chittick, *Thomas Chandler Haliburton: A Study in Provincial Toryism* (1924).

HALIFAX, George Savile, marquess of (1633–95), a powerful influence in the court of Charles II, and a noted anti-Catholic, is chiefly remembered for his *Character of a Trimmer*, published 1688 but previously circulated in manuscript, in which he urged the king to free himself from his brother's influence and advocated compromise and moderation. His political tracts (which include his subtle piece of argument *The Anatomy of an Equivalent*, 1688) were reprinted in 1898. He also wrote some much-reprinted essays, *A Lady's New Year's Gift, or Advice to a Daughter* (1688). His other works include *A Letter to a Dissenter upon Occasion of his Majesties late Gracious Declaration of Indulgence* (1687) and *A Character of King Charles II* (printed with *Political, Moral, and Miscellaneous Reflexions* in 1750). He saved the throne by his resolute opposition to the Exclusion Bill. He is the 'Jotham' of Dryden's *Absalom and Achitophel*.

Hali Meiohad (Holy Maidenhood), a prose treatise on virginity from the West Midlands, written in the period 1190–1225. It occurs in two manuscripts which also contain *Sawles Warde* and one or more members of the group of saints' lives known as the *Katherine Group. It is vigorously written in an accomplished style, very reminiscent of that of *Ancrene Wisse*, but it takes an extreme, dualist position on its subject. There is an edition by B. Millett (EETS 284, 1982).

HALL, Edward (d. 1547), educated at Eton and King's College, Cambridge, was the author of a chronicle glorifying the House of Tudor entitled *The Union of the two Noble and Illustre Families of Lancastre and York*, which was prohibited by Queen Mary and which is interesting for the account it gives of the times of Henry VIII and the vivid description of his court and of the Field of the Cloth of Gold. It was used by Shakespeare as a source in his early history plays.

HALL, Joseph (1574–1656), was educated at Ashby de la Zouch and Emmanuel College, Cambridge. He was successively bishop of Exeter (1627) and Norwich (1641). He was imprisoned in 1641 in the course of the attack on episcopacy, and released after five months. In 1643 he was sequestered at Norwich, his revenues and bishop's palace seized, his cathedral desecrated. As a student at Cambridge he published two volumes of satires, *Virgidemiarum Sex Libri*; a semi-bawdy satirical novel in Latin, *Mundus Alter et Idem*; and, very probably, the last play in the St John's College *Parnassus Plays*. He is responsible for initiating several literary genres: the first to publish his epistles in English (1608–10); the beginner of the mode of *character-writing (1608); the introducer of Juvenalian satire; the first to mine his own sermons for his great meditations written for Protestants to counter the popular Ignatian mode of meditation on the Continent. A favourite of King James, he was sent three times on royal embassies abroad; and he was employed as a controversialist by the king and later by *Laud against *Smectymnuus. His collected works fill ten volumes, and he is famous for his plain, Senecan prose style. *A Biographical and Critical Study* by F. Huntley was published in 1979.

HALL, (Marguerite) Radclyffe (1883–1943), published four volumes of verse and eight novels, but is chiefly remembered for her novel *The Well of Loneliness* (1928). Its open treatment of lesbianism occasioned a trial for obscenity; it was banned and an appeal refused, despite the support of many eminent writers including E. M. *Forster, L. and V. *Woolf, and Arnold *Bennett. It was republished in 1949.

HALL, Willis (1929–), playwright, born and educated in Leeds. His successful play *The Long and the Short and the Tall* (1958, pub. 1959), set in 1942 in the Malayan jungle during the Japanese advance on Singapore, was followed by many other works for stage, screen, and television, many written in collaboration with K. *Waterhouse.

HALLAM, Arthur Henry (1811–33), educated at Eton and Trinity College, Cambridge, where he became a close friend of *Tennyson, and after his early death the subject of Tennyson's poem *In Memoriam. He was a young man of great promise, an Italian scholar, and an ardent admirer of the Romantic poets. His *Remains*, edited by his father Henry *Hallam in 1834, contain work of distinction in poetry, philosophy, and criticism.

HALLAM, Henry (1777–1859), historian, and the father of *Tennyson's friend Arthur *Hallam, was educated at Eton and Christ Church, Oxford. He became a barrister and a commissioner of stamps. He spent some ten years on the preparation of his first published work, *A View of the State of Europe during the Middle Ages* (1818), in which he attempts 'a comprehensive survey of the chief circumstances that can interest a philosophical enquirer'. Hallam's best-known work, his *Constitutional History of England* (1827), to the death of George II, became a work of great and prolonged influence. The work was continued by Sir T. E. May. In 1834 he edited, with a Memoir, verse and prose of his son Arthur. His last great work was *An Introduction to the Literature of Europe during the Fifteenth, Sixteenth, and Seventeenth Centuries* (1837–9), the sweep of which covers not only creative literature but the literature of the classics, mathematics, theology, science, and, most notably, of philosophy and thought.

HALLIWELL, afterwards HALLIWELL-PHILLIPPS, James Orchard (1820–89), a noted Shakespearian scholar, entered Trinity College, Cambridge, in 1837 where he had unlimited access to the locked-up manuscripts. After it was discovered that 17 volumes were missing, he transferred to Jesus College. He was elected a fellow of the *Royal Society before he was 19 and was a founder member of the Shakespeare Society. In 1842 he married Henrietta, daughter of Sir T. *Phillipps. His published works include *The Life of William Shakespeare* (1848), *Observations on the Shakespearean Forgeries at Bridgewater House* (1853), on the J. P. *Collier controversy, *A Dictionary of Old English Plays* (1860), *Outlines of the Life of Shakespeare* (1881–87), which became a primary source for subsequent 19th-cent. Shakespeare biographies. He edited the *Works* of Shakespeare (16 vols, 1853–65) and some 150 volumes, mainly of 17th-cent. literature (some in collaboration with T. *Wright), and did much work for the *Percy Society, notably *The Nursery Rhymes of England*

(1842–46), a pioneering study which remained standard until that of the *Opies, and for the *Camden Society.

HALL-STEVENSON, John (1718–85), the friend of *Sterne, traditionally said to be the original of Eugenius in *Tristram Shandy* and *A Sentimental Journey*. He was squire of Skelton Castle, near Saltburn-by-the-Sea, Yorkshire, where he was host to a circle of literary friends, 'the Demoniacs', which included Sterne. He published *Fables for Grown Gentlemen* (1761), *Crazy Tales* (1762), and other coarse, sometimes indecent, verse satires done in what he conceived to be imitations of French *fabliaux. He was not, as has been said, the author of *A Sentimental Journey Continued* (1769). His *Works*, edited carefully though anonymously, appeared in 1795.

Hamartia, see POETICS, THE.

Hambledon Club, a famous cricket club of the early days of the game. It flourished about 1750–91, being supported by wealthy patrons of cricket, and played its matches on Broadhalfpenny and Windmill Downs in Hampshire. Its historian was John *Nyren.

HAMBURGER, Michael Peter Leopold (1924–), poet and translator, born in Berlin of a German family which emigrated to England in 1933. His own collections of poetry include *Flowering Cactus* (1950), *Weather and Season* (1963), and *Ownerless Earth: New and Selected Poems* (1973), and his many distinguished translations include versions of *Hofmannsthal (1961), *Grass (1966), and, notably, the *Poems and Fragments* of *Hölderlin (1966), a collection on which he worked for many years. His *Collected Poems* appeared in 1984.

Hamet Ben Engeli, Cid, see CID HAMET BEN ENGELI.

HAMILTON, Anthony, see GRAMONT.

HAMILTON, Charles Harold St John (1876–1961), born in Ealing, the son of a journalist. His first boys' story was published when he was 17, and he was to become for half a century the world's most prolific author for boys. He wrote under many different pen-names, but was most renowned as 'Frank Richards' of the *Magnet* (1908–40) and 'Martin Clifford' of the *Gem* (1907–39). The *Magnet*'s Greyfriars School included, among other household names, Billy Bunter, who survived with his friends, after the *Magnet*'s closure, in book form, on television, and in the theatre. *Orwell, writing in *Horizon* in 1939, objected to the snobbery, insularity, dated slang, and tedious style of this exclusively male world, but Hamilton's game reply conceded nothing.

HAMILTON, Cicely, see WOMEN'S SUFFRAGE.

HAMILTON, Ian, see REVIEW, THE (2).

HAMILTON, (Anthony Walter) Patrick (1904–62), the son of an eccentric clergyman, worked for a time as a repertory actor and wrote several successful plays, including *Rope* (1929) and *Gas Light* (1939), both thrillers, and *The Duke in Darkness* (1943), a historical drama. He also wrote radio plays. His novels include *Craven House* (1926), the story of the inmates of a boarding-house; *The Midnight Bell* (1929), *The Siege of Pleasure* (1932), and *The Plains of Cement* (1934), a trilogy published in 1935 as *Twenty Thousand Streets Under the Sky*, which deals respectively with the interlocking lives of Bob, a waiter, Jenny, a prostitute, and Ella, a barmaid; *Hangover Square* (1941), a thriller set in Earls Court dealing with George Harvey Bone's fatal passion for destructive Netta; and *The Slaves of Solitude* (1947), also set in a boarding-house, which centres on the wartime experiences of the quiet spinster Miss Roach. Hamilton's particular gift is for describing, in the words of J. B. *Priestley, 'a kind of No-Man's-Land of shabby hotels, dingy boarding-houses and all those saloon bars where the homeless can meet' (1972); *Holroyd praises his 'invention of the monster-bore—that terrible mixture of the banal and the sinister who entertains the reader by driving the other characters in the book to distraction' (*Unreceived Opinions*, 1973). All the novels show a preoccupation with the perils and pleasures of drinking, and Hamilton's Marxism is expressed in his compassion for the hopelessness of his characters' lives.

HAMILTON, Sir William (1730–1803), diplomat, archaeologist, and collector, and British envoy and plenipotentiary at Naples from 1764, where his embassy became a cultural and musical centre; he entertained many travellers on the *Grand Tour, studied Vesuvius (recording his observations in *Campi Phlegraei: Observations on the Volcanos of the Two Sicilies*, 1776), collected so-called Etruscan vases and paintings, and in 1791 married, as his second wife, Emma Hart (born Amy Lyon) who was to achieve notoriety as the mistress of Nelson. The Hamiltons were recalled to England in 1800, where Sir William died, with both Emma and Nelson attending his deathbed. His friends and correspondents included *Beckford and Horace *Walpole, and his collections exerted a wide influence on *neo-classicism in Britain; one of his most important collections of vases, terracottas, coins, etc., sold to the British Museum in 1771, laid the foundation for its department of classical antiquities.

HAMILTON, Sir William (1788–1856), was educated at Glasgow and Balliol College, Oxford. His philosophical reputation was made by a number of articles which appeared in the

Edinburgh Review, 1829–36 (republished in 1852 as *Discussions on Philosophy and Literature, Education and University Reform*), of which the most important were those on 'the Philosophy of the Unconditioned', 'the Philosophy of Perfection', and 'Logic'. He was elected to the chair of logic and metaphysics at Edinburgh in 1836. His *Lectures on Metaphysics and Logic* appeared in 1859–60, after his death.

A man of great philosophical erudition rather than a great philosophical thinker, Hamilton represents the influence of *Kant upon the commonsense philosophy of the Scottish school set forth by *Reid. He maintained that we have immediate perception of external objects, or rather of their primary and real qualities; he also expounded the doctrine of the phenomenal and relative quality of all knowledge, according to which we must remain ignorant of ultimate reality, since knowledge, whether of mind or matter, must be conditioned by the knowing mind, and cannot therefore be knowledge of the thing-in-itself. If we attempt to think of things not so conditioned, we are faced by two contradictory propositions, both inconceivable, and one of which must be true; for example, time must be either finite or infinite, but we cannot conceive of it as either.

In logic, Hamilton introduced a modification of the traditional doctrine, known as the 'Quantification of the Predicate'. His philosophical views were vigorously attacked by J. S. *Mill in his *Examination of Sir William Hamilton's Philosophy*.

HAMILTON, William Gerard (1729–96), known as 'Single-Speech Hamilton' from his celebrated 3-hour maiden speech in 1755 as MP for Petersfield. His friend Dr *Johnson was for a time his unofficial adviser and *Burke was his private assistant from 1759 to 1765. Some of his contemporaries claimed he was *'Junius'. His works were published after his death by *Malone under the title *Parliamentary Logick*.

HAMILTON, Sir William Rowan (1805–65), a distinguished mathematician whose fame rests principally on his discovery of the science of quaternions, a higher branch of calculus. He was also an amateur poet, and friend and correspondent of *Wordsworth, *Coleridge, M. *Edgeworth, and other literary figures.

HAMILTON, William, of Bangour (1704–54), Scottish Jacobite patriot and poet, who commemorated the battle of Gladsmuir in an ode and fought at Culloden. He is chiefly remembered for his song 'The Braes of Yarrow' ('Busk ye, busk ye, my bony bony bride'), published in *Ramsay's *Miscellany*.

Hamlet, a tragedy by *Shakespeare, written perhaps, in its first version, in mid-1599, probably completed by 1601: it was registered as 'latelie Acted' in July 1602. A short, 'bad' Quarto was published 1603 and another text, almost twice as long, 1604–5. The *Folio text (1623) adds some passages not in the Second Quarto, and omits others. References by *Nashe, *Lodge, and others show that a play on the same subject (now lost) preceded Shakespeare's; it was presumably a source. His chief nondramatic source was *Saxo Grammaticus's narrative in his *Historiae Danicae*, as retold by Belleforest in his *Histoires Tragiques*.

Old Hamlet, king of Denmark, is recently dead, and his brother Claudius has assumed the throne and married his widow Gertrude. Young Hamlet, returning from university at Wittenberg, learns from the ghost of his father that Claudius murdered him by pouring poison into his ear, and is commanded to avenge the murder without injuring Gertrude. Hamlet tells his friend Horatio and the two guards Barnardo and Marcellus of this revelation, swearing them to secrecy and warning them that he intends to feign madness. Immediately after his famous speech of deliberation beginning 'To be, or not to be' (III. i) he repudiates Ophelia, whom he has loved, while spied on by Claudius and by Ophelia's father Polonius. He welcomes a troupe of visiting players, and arranges a performance of a play ('the Mouse-trap') about fratricide, which Claudius breaks off, in apparently guilty and fearful fury, when the player Lucianus appears to murder his uncle by pouring poison into his ear. Hamlet refrains from killing Claudius while he is at prayer, but stabs through the arras in his mother's bedroom, killing the old counsellor Polonius, before reprimanding his mother for her affection for Claudius. Claudius sends Hamlet to England with sealed orders that he should be killed on arrival. Hamlet outwits him, however, returning to Denmark, having arranged the deaths of his old friends Rosencrantz and Guildenstern, who were his uncle's agents. During Hamlet's absence Ophelia has gone mad with grief from Hamlet's rejection of her and her father's death, and is found drowned. Her brother Laertes returns from France intent on avenging his sister's death. Hamlet and Laertes meet in the graveyard where Ophelia is to be buried, and fight in her grave. Claudius arranges a fencing match between Hamlet and Laertes, giving the latter a poisoned foil; an exchange of weapons results in the deaths of both combatants, not before Gertrude has drunk a poisoned cup intended for her son, and the dying Hamlet has succeeded in killing Claudius. Fortinbras, prince of Norway, whose resolute military heroism has been alluded to throughout the play, appears fresh from wars with Poland and gives Hamlet a military funeral. (See also OBJECTIVE CORRELATIVE.)

Hamley, Squire, Mrs, and their sons Osborne and Roger, in *Wives and Daughters* by E. Gaskell.

HAMMETT, (Samuel) Dashiell (1894–1961), American writer of detective fiction, whose tough, realistic works (*Red Harvest*, 1929; *The Maltese Falcon*, 1930; *The Glass Key*, 1931; *The Thin Man*, 1932; etc.), based in part on his own experiences as a detective in San Francisco, created a vogue for a new kind of hard-boiled hero and seedy locale. Many of his stories were filmed, and he himself worked as a screen-writer in Hollywood, where he was imprisoned in the McCarthy era for 'un-American activities'. He was for many years the friend and companion of the playwright Lillian Hellman (1905–84), whom he met in 1930. See a life by Diane Johnson, the American novelist, published in 1983.

HAMPDEN, John (1594–1643), a much respected leader of the parliamentary opposition and later of the Long Parliament, is famous for his historic refusal in 1636 to pay the ship money exacted by Charles I. His attempted seizure in 1642 was one of the events that led to the Civil War. He was mortally wounded at Chalgrove Field, near Oxford.

HAMPTON, Christopher James (1946–   ), see under ENGLISH STAGE COMPANY.

Hampton Court Conference, held in 1604 to settle points of dispute between the Church party and the Puritans, out of which arose the preparation of the Authorized Version of the Bible. See BIBLE, THE ENGLISH.

HAMSUN, Knut (1859–1952), Norwegian novelist, poet, and dramatist, born Knut Petersen in central Norway. He is best known for his novel *Hunger* (1890), set in Christiania (now Oslo), in which his narrator suffers the state of semi-starvation which Hamsun himself had endured during ten years of hardship and work as a labourer in Norway and the US; its nervous, hallucinatory quality and abrupt, vivid prose made a considerable impact, and he followed its success with many other works of fiction, including *Mysteries* (1892), *Pan* (1894), *Victoria* (1898), and *Growth of the Soil* (1917). He was awarded the *Nobel Prize for literature in 1920, and continued to write almost to the end of his life, although his work lost its original subjective, fragmentary lyric power, and he further alienated his followers by his support of Hitler during the Second World War. The influence of his early work was, however, great; I. B. *Singer has stated that 'the whole modern school of fiction in the twentieth century stems from Hamsun' ('Knut Hamsun, Artist of Skepticism', 1967). *Hunger* was originally translated by G. *Egerton, and has subsequently appeared in other English versions.

HANDEL, George Frideric (1685–1759), composer of German birth who settled in London at the age of 27 and became a natural-ized Englishman 15 years later. He scored an immediate triumph with his first London production in 1711; but *Rinaldo*, like the 35 operas that followed it during the next 30 years, was written to an Italian text and in the prevailing manner of Italian *opera seria*, a convention with which he never really broke in his works for the secular stage.

Handel's great contribution to English music was the English oratorio. His earliest setting of English words, a little cantata by John Hughes, dates from the same period as *Rinaldo*, at a time when he was still only learning the language; but a more substantial, notably successful, treatment of an English text came with the masque *Acis and Galatea* (1718), written for performance at Cannons, the seat of Lord Carnarvon (later duke of Chandos). The libretto of *Acis* was written by *Gay, and it seems probable that several members of the literary circle with which Gay was associated, *Pope, *Arbuthnot, *Swift (with all of whom Handel was already acquainted), had a hand in the text of Handel's last work for Cannons, the masque of *Esther* (?1720).

In 1732 a revised version of *Esther* was given in London. The intention had been to stage the work at the King's Theatre, with the Children of the Chapel Royal as performers; but, the bishop of London objecting to the representation of a sacred subject within the immoral precincts of an opera house, Handel was obliged to adapt the piece for concert performance, without stage action and with the children replaced by professional adult singers. Its success encouraged him to produce *Deborah* and *Athalia* in the following year, and from this almost accidental beginning grew the whole series of 'oratorios or sacred dramas' which, when he finally turned his back on the Italian operatic scene, became the chief glory of Handel's later years. *Saul* (1739), and immediately after it the choral epic *Israel in Egypt*, both had texts (the former written, the latter arranged from biblical sources) by the wealthy amateur Charles Jennens, who also provided the composer with the brilliantly constructed anthology from the Old and New Testaments to which he had given the title *Messiah*. This, the most famous of all Handel's oratorios (1742), must be regarded as one of the greatest and most consistently inspired of all musical works written to English words. In its essentially spiritual rather than narrative or dramatic intention, however, it stands a little apart from the other oratorios: its successor *Samson* (1743), with a text from Milton's *Samson Agonistes* and other poems, is very much at the opposite pole, a strongly dramatic work that has proved particularly effective in stage performances. Jennens was again the librettist for *Belshazzar* (1745), but was then succeeded as Handel's main collaborator by Thomas Morell, who was responsible for most of the remaining oratorio texts, starting with *Judas Maccabaeus* (1747) and ending with the two masterpieces of Handel's old age, *Theodora* (1750) and *Jephtha* (1752).

Comparable to the sacred dramas are the secular odes and oratorios: *Semele* (1743), 'after the manner of an oratorio', is a setting of a *Congreve text originally designed for music (1707) and now adapted for Handel by Pope which, though not intended for the stage, has very much the feel of a successor to the operas and semi-operas of *Purcell; *Alexander's Feast* (1736), an adaptation of *Dryden's Cecilian ode, is one of Handel's most successful works, and was followed by the rather smaller scale *Ode for St Cecilia's Day* (1739) with words by the same author. The only other substantial setting of an English poet is *L'Allegro, il Penseroso ed il Moderato* (1741), in which an adaptation of *Milton's two poems is followed by a third section by Jennens in praise of moderation, which Handel later dropped.

Handful of Dust, A, a novel by E. *Waugh, published 1934.

It describes the infatuation of Lady Brenda Last with an idle, parasitic young man-about-town, John Beaver, which leads her to neglect her 'madly feudal' husband Tony, her son, and her country home of Hetton. When her son is killed in a hunting accident, Brenda leaves Tony, expecting him to grant her a divorce, but after an 'arranged' visit to Brighton to acquire evidence of adultery Tony realizes that he will lose Hetton if he meets Brenda's alimony demands. He departs instead up the Amazon, where he is rescued from the brink of death by the old mad recluse Mr Todd, and consigned to a fate of reading Dickens aloud forever to his host, who keeps him captive. Hetton passes to cousins and Brenda is remarried, but not to Beaver. The epigraph and title are from *The Waste Land*, and although the novel resembles Waugh's earlier comic works, it has also been seen as a serious comment on the empty morality and shifting values of the 1930s.

Handlyng Synne, by *Mannyng of Brunne, a verse treatise on sin, written in rough octo-syllabics in lively narrative and begun in 1303. It is based on the French *Manuel des Pechez*, written in the north of England by William of Wadington. It deals with sin under various headings: the Ten Commandments, the Seven Deadly Sins, Sacrilege and the Sacraments, culminating with Penance. Each sin is illustrated by a story, rather in the manner of *Gower's *Confessio Amantis*, and the value of the work lies in Mannyng's narrative vigour. His most familiar and often anthologized story is 'The Dancers of Colbek' (item one, for example, in Sisam's *Fourteenth Century Verse and Prose*) which tells of some churchyard revellers, including the priest's daughter, who would not stop dancing when the priest bade them do so and whom he

cursed, condemning them to dance incessantly for a year. They do this, and at the end of the year the priest's daughter drops dead. There is an edition by F. J. *Furnivall (EETS os 119 and 123, 1901 and 1903).

Hand of Ethelberta, The, a novel by T. *Hardy, published 1876.

As the author states in his preface, this is 'a somewhat frivolous narrative'. Ethelberta is one of the numerous family of Chickerel, a butler. She marries the son of the house where she is governess, and is soon left a widow at 21. Her spirited efforts to maintain her social position, while concealing her relationship to the butler (and yet helping her brothers and sisters), account for most of the story. She finally secures a wicked old peer for a husband, while her faithful admirer, the musician Christopher Julian, is left to marry her sister Picotee.

Hansard, the official reports of the proceedings of the Houses of Parliament, colloquially so called because they were for a long period compiled by Messrs Hansard. Luke Hansard (1752–1828) commenced printing the *Journal of the House of Commons* in 1774. *Hansard* is now no more than an established familiar title. The name disappeared from the title-page of the Reports from 1892 onwards; the Reports were published by Reuter's Telegram Company in 1892, Eyre & Spottiswoode, 1893–4, and subsequently by a number of other firms in succession; they are now a regular publication of HM Stationery Office.

Harapha, in Milton's *Samson Agonistes*, the giant of Gath who comes to mock the blind Samson in prison.

Hard Cash, a novel by C. *Reade.

Hardcastle, Squire, Mrs, and Miss, characters in Goldsmith's *She Stoops to Conquer*.

HARDENBERG, Friedrich Leopold von (1772–1801), known as 'Novalis', German Romantic poet and novelist, author of poems religious, mystic, and secular, including *Hymnen an die Nacht* (*Hymns to the Night*, 1800), laments on the death of his young fiancée Sophie von Kuhn, and the unfinished novels *Heinrich von Ofterdingen* (1802) and *Die Lehrlinge zu Sais* (*The Disciples at Sais*, 1802). Novalis was influenced by the idealism of *Fichte, and was the subject of an enthusiastic essay by *Carlyle in the *Foreign Review*, 1829.

Harding, The Revd Septimus, a character in the *'Barsetshire' novels of A. Trollope. He is most prominent in *The Warden* and *Barchester Towers*.

Hard Times, a novel by *Dickens, published 1854.

Thomas Gradgrind, a citizen of Coketown, a

northern industrial city (based on impressions of Preston, which Dickens visited in 1854), is a misguided exponent of *Utilitarianism, an 'eminently practical man', who believes in facts and statistics and brings up his children Louisa and Tom accordingly, ruthlessly suppressing the imaginative sides of their nature. He marries Louisa to Josiah Bounderby, a manufacturer 30 years older than herself. Louisa consents partly from the indifference and cynicism engendered by her father's treatment, partly from a desire to help her brother, who is employed by Bounderby and who is the only person she loves. James Harthouse, a young politician without heart or principles, comes to Coketown and, taking advantage of her unhappy life with Bounderby, attempts to seduce her. The better side of her nature is awakened at this experience, and at the crisis she flees for protection to her father, who in turn is awakened to the folly of his system. He shelters her from Bounderby and the couple are permanently separated. But further trouble is in store for Gradgrind. Tom has robbed the bank of his employer, and though he contrives for a time to throw suspicion on a blameless artisan, Stephen Blackpool, is finally detected and hustled out of the country. Among the notable minor characters are Sleary, the proprietor of a circus, and Cissy Jupe, whose father had been a performer in his troupe, whose generous hearts are contrasted with the harshness of Gradgrind's régime; also Mrs Sparsit, Bounderby's venomous and intriguing housekeeper.

Condemned by *Macaulay for its 'sullen socialism', the novel was not in its day greatly popular, but gained a considerable reputation in this century partly through the admiration of G. B. *Shaw (who published a Preface, 1912) and *Leavis (The Great Tradition, 1947), who saw Dickens in this work 'for once possessed by a comprehensive vision'.

HARDY, Thomas (1840–1928), born at Upper Bockhampton, near Dorchester in Dorset, son of a stonemason, whose family had known better days. His father taught Hardy the violin and his mother greatly encouraged his early interest in books. He attended school in Dorchester and at 16 was articled to John Hicks, a local architect. At the age of 22 he went to London, where he worked for the architect Arthur Blomfield, pursued a hectic London life, and also found time for extensive reading. During this time he lost the religious faith which had once led him to consider taking Holy Orders. He returned home in 1867 to continue architectural work in Dorchester, and began his first (unpublished) novel, The Poor Man and the Lady. At this time he probably fell in love with Tryphena Sparks, a girl of 16 who was regarded as his cousin but may have been his niece. The history of his relationship with her, and of her relationship with Hardy's great friend Horace

Moule, continues to be the subject of considerable speculation. In 1868 he was sent on an architectural mission to St Juliot, Cornwall, where he met the rector's sister-in-law, Emma Gifford. His first published novel, *Desperate Remedies, appeared in 1871, to be followed by *Under the Greenwood Tree (1872), *A Pair of Blue Eyes (1873), and *Far from the Madding Crowd (1874). The success of the last enabled him, in 1874, to give up architecture for writing, and to marry Emma Gifford. The marriage soon produced intolerable strains, but it also produced, after Emma's death in 1912, some of Hardy's most moving poems. Between 1874 and the publication of *Jude the Obscure in 1895 Hardy wrote twelve other novels (see below), as well as many short stories and poems. He and his wife travelled in Europe and Hardy spent several months of nearly every year in London. In 1887 they moved into Max Gate, near Dorchester, a forbidding house, shrouded by trees and shrubberies, to Hardy's own design. During this time Hardy became both famous and infamous. He greatly enjoyed the admiration of London's literary and aristocratic society; what he did not enjoy was the constant carping of reviewers on his 'pessimism' and 'immorality', culminating in the bitterly hostile reception of *Tess of the D'Urbervilles in 1891 and Jude the Obscure in 1895. He gave up the writing of fiction (which he had always regarded as inferior to poetry) and began to assemble his first volume of verse, Wessex Poems (1898). His successive collections, ending with Winter Words in 1928, were received without enthusiasm, except by a discerning few. In 1912 Emma died and in 1914 Hardy married Florence Dugdale. She, together with the terrier Wessex, did much to protect Hardy from the adulation of his admirers. Public honours fell upon him, among them the OM, honorary degrees from Cambridge and Oxford, a visit from the prince of Wales, the gold medal of the *Royal Society of Literature. Among the pall-bearers at his funeral in Westminster Abbey were *Barrie, *Galsworthy, *Gosse, A. E. *Housman, *Kipling, and G. B. *Shaw.

The underlying theme of many of the novels, the short poems, and the epic drama *The Dynasts is, in *Binyon's words, 'the implanted crookedness of things'; the struggle of man against the indifferent force that rules the world and inflicts on him the sufferings and ironies of life and love. Hardy's sharp sense of the humorous and absurd finds expression largely in the affectionate presentation of the rustic characters in the novels. Most of the poems and novels reveal Hardy's love and observation of the natural world, often with strong symbolic effect.

Hardy's novels and short stories, according to his own classification, fall into three groups; most of them are described separately under their titles:

Novels of Character and Environment: *Under the Greenwood Tree* (1872); *Far from the Madding Crowd* (1874); *The Return of the Native* (1878); *The Mayor of Casterbridge* (1886); *The Woodlanders* (1887); *Wessex Tales* (1888); *Tess of the D'Urbervilles* (1891); *Life's Little Ironies* (1894); *Jude the Obscure* (1896, in the edition of the *Works* of that year).

Romances and Fantasies: *A Pair of Blue Eyes* (1873); *The Trumpet Major* (1880); *Two on a Tower* (1882); *A Group of Noble Dames* (1891); *The Well-Beloved*, (published serially 1892, revised and reissued 1897.)

Novels of Ingenuity: *Desperate Remedies* (1891); *The Hand of Ethelberta* (1876); *A Laodicean* (1881).

A Changed Man, The Waiting Supper, and other Tales (1913) is a reprint of 'a dozen minor novels' belonging to the various groups.

Hardy published eight volumes of poetry: *Wessex Poems* (1898); *Poems of the Past and Present* (1899); *Time's Laughingstocks* (1909); *Satires of Circumstance* (1914); *Moments of Vision* (1917); *Late Lyrics and Earlier* (1922); *Human Shows* (1925); *Winter Words* (1928). The *Collected Poems* (1930), published posthumously, contain over 900 poems of great variety and individuality, yet consistent over more than 60 years in their attitudes to life and fate. Probably the most remarkable are in the group of poems written in recollection of his first wife ('Poems of 1912–13' in *Satires of Circumstance*). Hardy followed *Wordsworth and R. *Browning in his endeavour to write in a language close to that of speech, and he abhorred, to use his own words, 'the jewelled line'. He experimented constantly with rhythms and stresses and verse forms, disliking and avoiding any facile flow. Gosse, *Blunden, and *Strachey were of the small band who greatly admired his poetry, but not until long after his death did it begin to receive general critical acclaim.

He published over 40 short stories, most of which were collected in *Wessex Tales* (1888); *A Group of Noble Dames* (1891); *Life's Little Ironies* (1894); and *A Changed Man* (1913). The stories vary considerably in content, form, and style, and in many cases demonstrate a high degree of skill, but Hardy's reputation in this field has never approached his reputation as a novelist or poet.

The Dynasts, a vast work in blank verse and prose, occupied him for many years, and was published in three volumes, 1904, 1906, and 1908. He wrote one other poetic drama, *The Famous Tragedy of The *Queen of Cornwall* (1923).

Hardy continues to attract a great deal of biographical and critical attention: recent works include a critical biography by J. I. M. *Stewart (1971); a two-vol. life by R. *Gittings (*Young Thomas Hardy*, 1975; *The Older Hardy*, 1980); *An Essay on Thomas Hardy* by J. Bayley; and *Thomas Hardy* (1982) by M. Millgate.

HARDYNG, John (1378–*c*.1465), author of *The Chronicle of John Hardyng* in verse which was written between the years 1440 and 1457. The Chronicle covers the period from Brutus (see BRUT) to 1437 and argues the claims of English kings (in the interests of Henry V and Henry VI) to overlordship of Scotland. A second version revises the work in the Yorkist interest, expunging the earlier eulogy of Henry V and declaring Henry VI to be 'of small intelligence'; it is perhaps the (dubious) authority for that prevailing view of him. It was edited by H. Ellis (1812, reprinted New York, 1974); see A. Gransden, *Historical Writing in England II* (1982), pp. 274 ff.

HARE, Julius Charles (1795–1855), educated at Trinity College, Cambridge, was elected fellow in 1818 and became an intimate companion of *Whewell. He was ordained in 1826 and in 1832 appointed rector of Hurstmonceaux. Through travel in Germany he became influenced by German scholars and theologians. He was author, with his brother Augustus William Hare (1792–1834, biographer and compiler of travel books), of the popular *Guesses at Truth* (1827), a collection of observations on philosophy, religion, literature, language, and related subjects. He translated with *Thirlwell *Niebuhr's *History of Rome* (1828–42), which was vehemently attacked for its scepticism in the *Quarterly Review*, prompting the translators to publish a *Vindication of Niebuhr's History* (1829). Also with Thirlwell he was joint editor of the *Philological Museum* (1832–3), which made some effort to introduce the much neglected new continental philology of *Grimm. He edited *Sterling's *Essays and Tales* (1848) with a memoir which treated Sterling chiefly as a cleric who deserted his vocation; *Carlyle replied with his *Life of John Sterling* (1851).

Haredale, Geoffrey and Emma, characters in Dickens's *Barnaby Rudge*.

HARINGTON, James, see HARRINGTON.

HARINGTON, Sir John (*c*.1561–1612), godson of Queen *Elizabeth I, was educated at Eton and King's College, Cambridge. Supposedly at the command of the queen, he translated Ariosto's *Orlando Furioso* (1591), retaining the *ottava rima* of the original and providing *A Preface or Briefe Apologie of Poetrie*, closely modelled on Sidney's *Defence of Poetry*, and interesting, often gossipy notes referring to such stray figures as his own pet dog Bungy, who is also depicted on the title-page. Though *Jonson claimed 'that John Harington's *Ariosto*, under all translations, was the worst', it has been read and enjoyed by many generations of readers including, in modern times, A. *Powell. Harington's next work, *A new Discourse of a Stale Subject, called the Metamorphosis of Ajax* (1596) (a proposal for the introduction of water closets), was an ill-judged bid for royal favour; together with other satires and epigrams it led to a period of exile from court. In 1599 Harington accompanied *Essex to Ireland, and was deputed by him to appease the queen's anger on his return, without success. His letters and miscellaneous writings were collected in Henry Harington's *Nugae Antiquae* (1769–75); N. E. McClure edited his letters and epigrams (1930); Robert McNulty edited the *Orlando Furioso* (1972) and E. S. Donno *The Metamorphosis of Ajax* (1962). The lasting interest of Harington's writings lies in his lively personality and ability to record detailed impressions of his world. He gives, for instance, an account of a visit to the queen a few weeks before her death, in which she said to him, 'When thou doste feele creepinge tyme at thye gate, these fooleries will please thee lesse.'

HARLAND, Henry (1861–1905), American author born in New York, who wrote several novels about Jewish immigrant life under the pseudonym of Sidney Luska. In 1889 he moved to Paris, and in 1890 to London, where he became editor of *The Yellow Book*. He published several romances during his London period, including the popular *The Cardinal's Snuff-Box* (1900).

Harleian Miscellany, The, a reprint of a selection of tracts from the Harleian MSS, edited by *Oldys and Dr *Johnson, published 1744–6 by T. *Osborne.

Harleian MSS, The, a collection of manuscripts made by R. *Harley, first earl of Oxford, and augmented by his son Edward, the second earl (1689–1741). It consisted of some 50,000 books, 350,000 pamphlets, and over 7,000 volumes of manuscripts, including early biblical texts in Greek, Latin, and Hebrew, texts of classical authors and church fathers, papal bulls and registers, deeds, charters, state papers, etc. The manuscripts were bought by Parliament in 1753 after Edward's death and placed in the British Museum.

Harleian Society, The, was founded in 1869 for the publication of heraldic visitations, pedigrees, etc.

Harlequin, from the Italian *arlecchino*, via French Arlequin, originally a character in Italian comedy (*commedia dell'arte*), a mixture of childlike ignorance, wit, and grace, always in love, always in trouble, easily despairing, easily consoled; in English pantomime a mute character supposed to be invisible to the clown and the pantaloon, the rival of the clown in the affections of Columbine. The Italian word is possibly the same as the old French *Hellequin, Hennequin,* one

of a troop of demon horsemen riding by night [OED].

Harleth, Gwendoline, the heroine of G. Eliot's *Daniel Deronda.*

Harley, (1) the principal character in *The Man of Feeling* by H. Mackenzie; (2) Adrian Harley, in Meredith's *The Ordeal of Richard Feverel*, the cynical 'wise youth' and tutor of Richard, drawn from Meredith's friend Maurice Fitz-Gerald.

HARLEY, Robert, first earl of Oxford (1661–1724), Tory statesman and bibliophile. He frequented the *Scriblerus Club, and several verse invitations to him composed by *Pope, *Swift, and others survive. He acquired a great library of books and manuscripts, which his son inherited: see HARLEIAN MSS.

Harley Lyrics, a collection of 32 Middle English lyrics occurring with other material in the manuscript Harley 2253, from the West Midlands, dated c.1314–25 (though the poems are thought to be originally from various parts of the country). W. P. Ker says the manuscript contains 'everything best worth remembering in the old lyrical poetry' and, although we might add other individual poems, his high assessment of them finds general assent. Among the most celebrated poems in the collection are 'Alysoun', 'Lenten ys come with love to toune', 'Blow, Northerne Wynd', 'Wynter wakeneth al my care', and 'The Man in the Moon'. In spite of their liveliness the poems are highly sophisticated in themes, diction, and literary forms. They have been edited by G. L. Brook (1956).

Harlot's Progress, The, see HOGARTH, W.

Harlowe, Clarissa, see CLARISSA.

Harmon, John, alias John Rokesmith, alias Julius Handford, the hero of Dickens's *Our Mutual Friend.*

HARMSWORTH, Alfred Charles William, 1st viscount Northcliffe (1865–1922), born in Dublin, the oldest of five brothers who were distinguished as newspaper magnates and politicians. He was largely self-educated, rejecting Cambridge and the bar for journalism, and in 1887 formed, with his brother Harold, a publishing business which issued a growing number of periodicals including the popular *Answers* (1888), which laid the foundations of his career. In 1894 the brothers acquired the *Evening News* and in 1896 Alfred started the *Daily Mail*, which changed the course of English journalism. In 1903 he added to his empire the *Daily Mirror*, the first newspaper devoted exclusively to women's interests, and in 1908 he became chief proprietor of *The Times*. The period of the First World War saw his (not conspicuously successful) emergence from journalism to public affairs; but in 1917 Lloyd George appointed him to lead a war mission to the USA and in 1918 he directed British propaganda in enemy countries. He was created baronet in 1903, baron in 1905, and viscount in 1917.

Harold, a historical drama by *Tennyson, published 1876, based on the brief reign of Harold II who died in 1066.

Harold, Childe, see CHILDE HAROLD'S PILGRIMAGE.

Harold the Dauntless, a poem by Sir W. *Scott, published 1817. Harold is the son of Witikind, a Danish Viking, converted to Christianity by St Cuthbert and granted lands between the Wear and the Tyne. Harold, like his father a fierce warrior, comes to England to claim these lands, which have been resumed at his father's death. A probation is imposed on him, that he shall spend a night in a lonely castle. In the course of this he sees visions, which lead to his conversion.

Harold, the Last of the Saxon Kings, a historical romance by *Bulwer-Lytton.

HAROUN-AL-RASCHID, see HĀRŪN AR-RASHĪD.

Harpagon, in Molière's L'*Avare, the typical miser, whose avarice causes him to be surrounded by persons who deceive him.

Harper's Monthly Magazine, founded in 1850 by Messrs Harper & Brothers of New York, originally for the avowed purpose of reproducing in America the work of distinguished English contributors to magazines (including *Dickens, *Thackeray, and *Bulwer-Lytton). It subsequently became more American in character, publishing work by *Melville, *Howells, S. O. *Jewett, and many others. From 1900 to 1925 it was known as Harper's New Monthly Magazine, and subsequently as Harper's Magazine.

Harper's Weekly (1857–1916), an illustrated political and literary journal, published in New York, best known for its engravings and woodcuts. It also serialized novels by *Dickens, Mrs *Gaskell, and others, and later published work by *Kipling, H. *James, A. C. *Doyle, etc.

HARPSFIELD, Nicholas (c.1519–75), educated at Winchester and New College, Oxford. A lawyer by training, he attached himself to Cardinal Pole, but was imprisoned in the Fleet, 1562–74. As well as controversial works and a history of the English church, he wrote (c.1557) an important life of Sir T. *More, first published in full in 1932.

Harriet Smith, a character in J. Austen's *Emma.

HARRINGTON, or **HARINGTON,** James

(1611–77), born in Northampton of an ancient family, and educated at Trinity College, Oxford, where he took no degree; he subsequently travelled on the Continent, and attended the court of the Elector Palatine. During the Civil War he attended Charles I in his captivity (1647–8), and a tradition (through *Aubrey and *Wood) was established that his deep personal devotion to the monarch plunged him into years of profound melancholy on his execution; some have seen this as one of the impulses behind his great republican work, *The Commonwealth of Oceana (1656). Harrington also wrote several tracts in defence of this work, and other political works (The Prerogative of Popular Government, 1657–8; The Art of Law-giving, 1659; Aphorisms Political, 1659) in all of which he expounds his concept of a republic or commonwealth, advocates the ballot, rotation of officers, indirect elections, etc. He was the founder of the *Rota, which met for political discussion. In 1661 he was arrested and imprisoned on a charge of treason, defended himself ably, and was later released, but by this time his health was in decline, and little is known of the remaining years of his life. Harrington has never been considered a great stylist (*Hume described his prose as 'altogether stiff and pedantic') but he had many admirers, including *Wordsworth and *Coleridge, and his shrewd historical analysis and political projections have increasingly attracted attention. See The Political Works of James Harrington (1977), ed. J. G. A. Pocock.

HARRINGTON, John, see HARINGTON.

HARRIOT, or **HARIOT,** Thomas (1560–1621), mathematician and astronomer, was taken into the household of *Ralegh, c.1580, as mathematical tutor, and in 1585 went on Ralegh's expedition to Virginia, where he stayed for a year. His A Brief and True Report of the new found land of Virginia, one of the earliest examples of a large-scale economic and statistical survey, was published in 1588 and printed by *Hakluyt. He corresponded with Kepler and is thought to have influenced *Descartes. His name was popularly associated with atheism and necromancy; the judge at Ralegh's trial in 1603 referred to him as 'that devil Harriot' and *Kyd, while himself attempting to evade an accusation of atheism, claimed that *Marlowe had been one of his intimates. He was thought by some to have been the leading spirit of the so-called *'School of Night', but appears to have been a faithful believer.

HARRIS, Frank (really James Thomas) (1856–1931), born in Galway, went to America at the age of 14, then travelled on the Continent before settling in London, where he soon made his mark in the literary world. He edited the Evening News (1882–6), the *Fortnightly Review (1886–94), and, most significantly, the

Saturday Review (1894–8), in which he published, among others, G. B. *Shaw (as dramatic critic), H. G. *Wells, and *Beerbohm, all of whom left vivid recollections of him. As an editor he had great flair, though his extrovert arrogance made him as many enemies as friends; Wells described him as 'too loud and vain . . . to be a proper scoundrel', but a scandalous reputation gathered round him, occasioned by his fight against Victorian prudery, by his decreasingly respectable role as editor (of such periodicals as *The Candid Friend, Vanity Fair,* and *Hearth and Home*), by his championship of Germany while in America during the First World War, and by his sexually boastful, explicit (and unreliable) memoirs, *My Life and Loves* (4 vols, 1922–7). His other publications include volumes of short stories, a novel (*The Bomb*, 1908, set in Chicago), two plays, one of them (*Mr and Mrs Daventry*, 1900, pub. 1956) based on a scenario by his friend *Wilde, and lives of Shakespeare, Wilde (1916), and Shaw (1931). He advertised himself with characteristic bravado as the greatest Shakespearian of his day, and his *The man Shakespeare and his tragic life story* (1909), though derided by scholars, had a considerable impact; like his other biographies, it reveals more about its author than its subject. Harris remains an enigmatic and controversial figure, whose personality continues to attract attention and whose real achievements tend to be obscured by his persistent and self-destructive self-aggrandisement. There is a lively biography by his one-time admirer and employee *Kingsmill, published 1932. See also Philippa Pullar, *Frank Harris* (1975).

HARRIS, Joel Chandler (1848–1908), American author, was born at Eatonton, Georgia, and devoted from childhood to English literature. To this taste he added an extraordinary knowledge of Negro myth and custom and of Negro dialect and idiom, which he reproduced in his famous 'Uncle Remus' series. These contain a great number of folklore tales, relating to a variety of animals, with the rabbit as hero and the fox next in importance, told by a Negro to a little boy and interspersed with comments on many other subjects. The principal volumes of this series were *Uncle Remus, his Songs and Sayings* (1881), *Uncle Remus and his Friends* (1892), *Mr. Rabbit at Home* (1895), *The Tar-Baby* (1904), *Told by Uncle Remus* (1905), *Uncle Remus and Brer Rabbit* (1906), *Uncle Remus and the Little Boy* (1910).

HARRIS, John (1820–84), Cornish poet and miner, born at Bollenowe, near Camborne, who published several volumes of poetry celebrating his native landscapes, including *Lays from the Mine, the Moor and the Mountains* (1853) and *A Story of Carn Brea* (1863). *Songs from the Earth,* a selection (1977), has an introduction by D. M.

*Thomas which praises his 'Romantic visionary quality which breathes life into an Augustan vocabulary'.

HARRIS, (Theodore) Wilson (1921–), Guyanese-born novelist, educated at Queen's College, Georgetown, British Guiana, where he qualified and subsequently worked as a land surveyor before coming to England in 1959. His 'Guiana Quartet' consists of *Palace of the Peacock* (1960), *The Far Journey of Oudin* (1961), *The Whole Armour* (1962), and *The Secret Ladder* (1963), and his later works include *The Waiting Room* (1967), *The Age of the Rainmakers* (1971), and *The Tree of the Sun* (1978). His fiction is experimental in form, built on a complex, poetic structure, interweaving history, mythology, and the contemporary world.

Harrison, Dr, a character in Fielding's *Amelia.

HARRISON, Frederic (1831–1923), educated at King's College School, London, and Wadham College, Oxford, was professor of jurisprudence and international law to the Inns of Court (1877–89), and from 1880 to 1905 president of the English Positivist Committee, formed to disseminate the doctrines of *Comte. He was the author of many works on historical, political, and literary subjects, and attracted the censure of M. Arnold in *Culture and Anarchy* for his challenging remarks on culture: 'The man of culture is in politics one of the poorest mortals alive. For simple pedantry and want of good sense no man is his equal . . .', a view which roused Arnold to his own defence of the meaning of culture.

HARRISON, G(eorge) B(agshawe) (1894–), author of a wide range of scholarly publications on Shakespeare and his world. His *Elizabethan* and *Jacobean Journals* gather up in chronological sequence much primary material from the years 1591–1610. He was general editor of the Penguin Shakespeare (1937–59), producing extremely useful old-spelling texts. With *Granville-Barker he edited *A Companion to Shakespeare Studies* (1934).

HARRISON, Tony (1937–), poet and translator, born in Leeds, and educated at Leeds Grammar School and Leeds University; memories of his working-class childhood and family life provide the material for much of his poetry, although he has travelled widely and his works also reflect experiences of Africa, the Soviet Union, and America. His volumes include *The Loiners* (1970), *From 'The School of Eloquence' and other poems* (1978), and *Continuous* (1981), and he has also written theatrically effective verse translations of *Molière's *The Misanthrope* (1973), *Racine's *Phèdre* (*Phaedra Britannica*, 1975), and the *Oresteia* (1981). Both his original works and his translations show a great facility in rhyme and a skilful adaptation of colloquial speech.

HARRISON, William (1535–93), born in London and educated at St Paul's and Westminster Schools and Christ Church, Oxford, was rector of Radwinter and canon of Windsor. He was the author of the admirable *Description of England* and translator of *Bellenden's Scottish version of *Boece's *Description of Scotland*, both included in the *Chronicles* of *Holinshed.

Harrowing of Hell, a semi-dramatic poem of 250 lines in octosyllabic couplets from about 1250, based on the legend (very popular in the Middle Ages) that Christ descended into Hell to lead out the souls of the just condemned there by the closing of the gates of Heaven by Adam's sin. The legend derives from the account in the Apocryphal Gospel of Nicodemus (2nd–3rd cents AD). There are also versions in Old and Middle English prose and in *Piers Plowman*, as well as recurrent appearances as one of the most popular scenarios in the *Mystery Plays. In the poem a narrative introduction is followed by speeches assigned to Christ, Satan, the Doorkeeper of Hell, and some of the souls in Hell: Adam, Eve, Abraham, David, John, and Moses. Christ reproves Satan and claims Adam; Satan replies that he will win one of mankind on Earth for every soul released. But Christ breaks down the door, binds Satan, and frees his servants. See, ed. W. H. Hulme, *The Middle English Harrowing of Hell and Gospel of Nicodemus* (EETS ES 100, 1907); A. W. Pollard, *English Miracle Plays* (1927, 8th edn).

Harrow School, at Harrow-on-the-Hill, Middlesex, founded and endowed by John Lyon (*c.*1514–91) of Preston, under letters patent and a charter granted by Queen *Elizabeth I. The most distinguished literary figure connected with the school was *Byron; it also produced several prime ministers, including Sir Robert Peel, Lord Palmerston, and Sir W. *Churchill.

Harry Richmond, The Adventures of, a novel by G. *Meredith, published 1871.

This, the longest of Meredith's novels, began as 'an autobiographical study', and that element is strong in the early part of the book, which describes his schooldays near Petersfield in some detail. More deeply autobiographical, however, is the father–son relationship portrayed. Richmond Roy, the father of Harry, is the son of an actress and a mysterious royal personage. Although a flamboyant and romantic figure, he is in fact only an indigent teacher of singing, once employed by Squire Beltham, one of whose daughters he carried off and married. She shortly dies, and young Harry, their son, is dramatically captured by his father from his grandfather's house. At this point the narrative adroitly switches to the first person, and the rest of the

story is related by Harry. The conflict between his father and grandfather, and his father's obsessive determination to marry him well, are important comic themes in the book. Harry loves his tempestuous father, but as he matures he realizes that he must escape the 'dreadful devotion' of his parent. Richmond Roy lives a life of splendour in the courts of petty German princes, interrupted by periods in a debtors' prison. At one of these courts Harry and the beautiful Princess Ottilia fall in love; the determined and outrageous manœuvres of Harry's father to settle the unlikely match, and the many humiliations to which Harry is exposed, are related with much humorous detail. Harry also encounters the fascinating gypsy Kioni, but in the end marries an English girl, Janet Ilchester, whom his grandfather had long wished to see as Harry's wife.

HARRY THE MINSTREL, see HENRY THE MINSTREL.

HARTE, (Francis) Bret (1836–1902), born at Albany, New York, was taken to California at 18, where he saw something of mining life. He worked on various newspapers and periodicals in San Francisco, to which he contributed some excellent writing including the short stories which made him famous. Notable among these were 'The Luck of Roaring Camp' (1868), and 'Tennessee's Partner' and 'The Outcasts of Poker Flat', which were included in *The Luck of Roaring Camp and Other Sketches* (1870). His humorous–pathetic verse includes 'Plain Language from Truthful James' (1870), often referred to as 'The Heathen Chinee'. Bret Harte was American consul at Crefeld in Germany (1878–80) and at Glasgow (1880–5), after which he lived in England, where his repetitive and inferior later work was more readily accepted by literary editors than in his own country, where his popularity had declined.

Hartford (or **Connecticut**) **Wits,** a group of writers who flourished during the last two decades of the 18th cent. at Hartford and New Haven, Connecticut, USA, now chiefly remembered for their vigorous political verse satires. Chief among them were Timothy Dwight, J. *Barlow, John Trumbull, David Humphreys, Richard Alsop, Lemuel Hopkins, and Theodore Dwight. They were all either graduates of Yale or associated with that college.

Harthouse, James, a character in Dickens's *Hard Times*.

Hartley, Adam, a character in Scott's *The Surgeon's Daughter*.

HARTLEY, David (1705–57), was educated at Bradford Grammar School and Jesus College, Cambridge, and practised as a physician. In his *Observations on Man, his Frame, his Duty, and his*

Expectations, published 1749, he repudiated the view of *Shaftesbury and *Hutcheson that the 'moral sense' is instinctively innate in us, and attributed it to the association of ideas, i.e. the tendency of ideas which have occurred together, or in immediate succession, to recall one another. From this association of the ideas of pain and pleasure with certain actions, he traces the evolution of the higher pleasures out of the lower, until the mind is carried to 'the pure love of God, as our highest and ultimate perfection'. With this psychological doctrine he combined a physical theory of 'vibrations' or 'vibratiuncles' in the 'medullary substance' of the brain. This mechanistic theory of the processes of the imagination was popularized by Joseph *Priestley in *Lectures on Oratory and Criticism* and influenced the development of critical theory up to the time of *Coleridge. It replaced the psychology of 'animal spirits' and 'traces' found in Cartesian philosophers and in *Mandeville and *Hume. Coleridge named his first son Hartley in honour of the philosopher, and many of his poems (e.g. 'The Nightingale' and *'Frost at Midnight') show that he took the theory of association in a touchingly literal sense; indeed, it considerably influenced the Romantic view of man's relationship with the natural world. (See ROMANTICISM.)

HARTLEY, L(eslie) P(oles) (1895–1972), novelist, was the son of a solicitor who became the director of a brickworks, and he spent his childhood at the family home, Fletton Towers, near Peterborough. He was educated at Harrow and Balliol College, Oxford. He began his literary career as a writer of short stories and as a fiction reviewer; his stories were published as *Night Fears* (1924) and *The Killing Bottle* (1932); *Simonetta Perkins*, a novella set in Venice (where Hartley spent much of his time) describing a young Bostonian's adventure with a gondolier, appeared in 1925. His first full-length novel, *The Shrimp and the Anemone* (1944), was followed by *The Sixth Heaven* (1946) and *Eustace and Hilda* (1947), the last being the title by which the trilogy is known: the first volume is a powerfully evocative account of a childhood summer by the sea in Norfolk, at the end of which Eustace unexpectedly inherits a small fortune, and the two subsequent volumes take him through fashionable Oxford undergraduate life to Venice and the Continent, as he struggles with his complex, intense relationship with his elder sister Hilda. Hartley's best-known novel is *The Go-Between* (1953), narrated in the first person by an elderly man recalling in 1952 the events of the hot summer of 1900, when, staying with a schoolfriend in a Norfolk country house for the holidays, he innocently carried letters between the friend's sister and the local farmer with whom she was having an affair. As the story progresses, it becomes clear that this

distant holiday has marked him for life. The portrayal of leisurely Edwardian England, with its cricket matches, bathing parties, and lurking social embarrassments, is masterly. Hartley's other novels include *A Perfect Woman* (1955); *The Hireling* (1957), which takes up the recurrent theme of dangerous inter-class sexual relationships in its story of the widowed Lady Franklin and her friendship with her driver; *The Brickfield* (1964); and *The Love-adept* (1969).

HARTLIB, Samuel (d. 1662), born in Prussia and educated in Silesia; he studied at Cambridge from 1621 to 1626, and settled in England in 1628. In 1637 he made contact with *Comenius whom he published. He was a promoter of useful inventions, interested in science and educational reform, a patron of Robert *Boyle, and a friend of *Milton, who addressed his *Of Education* (1644) to him. His *A Description of the Famous Kingdom of Macaria* (1641) is a Utopian vision of a reformed society.

Hārūn ar-Rashīd (763–809), caliph of Baghdad, who figures in many tales of the *Arabian Nights*, together with *Jaffar, his vizier, and *Mesrour, his executioner. He was the most powerful and vigorous of the Abbasid Caliphs, his rule extending from India to Africa. He entertained friendly relations with *Charlemagne, who was almost his exact contemporary.

HARVARD, John (1607–38), of humble origin, MA of Emmanuel College, Cambridge, settled in Charlestown, Massachusetts, and bequeathed half his estate and all his books to the newly founded educational institution at Cambridge, Massachusetts, known in memory of him as Harvard College.

HARVEY, Gabriel (c.1550–1631), son of a Saffron Walden rope-maker, was educated at Christ's College, Cambridge. Elected a fellow of Pembroke Hall, he became the friend of *Spenser and was probably his tutor. The poet remembered him in his sonnet 'Harvey, the happy above happiest men'. He benefited from the patronage of Sir Thomas Smith, whom he commemorated in a series of Latin elegies *Smithus* (1578), which may have influenced the form of Spenser's 'Tears of the Muses'. After a brilliant but troubled academic career, mainly concerned with rhetoric, Ramism (see RAMUS), civil law, and Latin poetry, he turned his interests towards the court and the vernacular. In his exchange of *Letters* with Spenser (1580) he sensibly indicated the difficulties and limitations of writing English verse in classical metres, but also delivered his famous judgement of *The Faerie Queene*, as it then existed, as 'Hobgoblin runne away with the Garland from *Apollo*'. He was in trouble with the University and the government for these *Letters*, which included satirical verses on the earl of *Oxford, but was protected by the earl of

*Leicester, for whom he worked for a time. His attack on the dying *Greene in *Foure Letters* (1592) provoked *Nashe's stinging replies which Harvey's *Pierces Supererogation* (1593) did not mitigate. With his old-fashioned humanist values and often awkward prose style Harvey came off worse in the controversy, and spent the last 30 years of his life in retirement at Saffron Walden, probably practising medicine.

Harvey's extraordinarily wide range of interests is reflected in the marginalia beautifully written in the books he owned. Many of these survive and record penetrating comments and notes on rhetoric, mathematics and navigation, astrology, medicine, his contemporaries, and literature, including references to Shakespeare and his friends *Sidney and Spenser. His English works were edited by A. B. *Grosart in 1884–5 and there is a life and an account of his library by V. F. Stern (1979).

HARVEY, Sir (Henry) Paul (1869–1948), scholar and diplomat, educated at Rugby and New College, Oxford. He was orphaned at an early age, and the first stages of his distinguished career were watched over with interest by H. *James and Lady *Gregory, both friends who had known him since boyhood. He was the compiler of *The Oxford Companion to English Literature* (1932), the first of the *Oxford Companions*, the idea for which originated in a suggestion from Kenneth Sisam at the *Oxford University Press in 1927–8. It was conceived as a reference book on the lines of *Brewer's *Dictionary of Phrase and Fable*, to contain English authors, plots of their works, and characters; foreign authors commonly quoted; legendary characters; a little classical background; and allusions, such as 'The Wise Men of Gotham'. Somewhat to Harvey's dismay, the project grew to include literary terms, periodicals, social clubs, etc., and the pressure of work obliged him to concede that he could not on the average deal with more than three five-act plays a day 'and to do this is a burden; the shorter the article, the greater the labour of condensation'. The result of his labours was a much-loved and idiosyncratic volume, with a very wide range of reference and some masterly plot summaries, which went through four editions. After his death, the volume was updated by Dorothy Eagle. Harvey went on to compile the *Oxford Companions* to *Classical Literature* (1937) and *French Literature*, completed by Janet E. Heseltine (1959).

HARVEY, William (1578–1657), was the eldest son in a large family from Folkestone, which enjoyed ever-growing prosperity owing to involvement in Levant trade. Educated at King's School, Canterbury, and Caius College, Cambridge, he obtained his MD at Padua, then at the height of its reputation as a centre for medical research. He practised in London, be-

came influential in the College of Physicians, and acted as physician to James I and Charles I. His career and researches were completely disrupted by the Civil War; when the court moved to Oxford the king presented him with the wardenship of Merton College; but he was compelled to retire to London under the Commonwealth.

Harvey's discovery of the circulation of blood was announced in *De motu cordis* (1628; English trans. 1653). He then worked on a major embryological treatise which was left incomplete, but a fragment, *De generatione* (1651; trans. 1653), was published by his disciple George Ent. Despite its innovatory nature, Harvey's work was rapidly accepted by the medical establishment. Harvey drew on circle symbolism, and metaphysical poets such as H. *Vaughan and Henry More made use of the imagery of Harveian circulation. Harvey's work was also actively exploited by his fellow physician Sir T. *Browne. Harvey, like the *Cambridge Platonists, resisted trends towards mechanization of the world view.

HASSALL, Christopher Vernon (1912–63), poet, song-writer, and biographer, born in London, the son of painter and illustrator John Hassall, and educated at Wadham College, Oxford. He was encouraged when young by E. *Marsh, published his first of several books of verse in 1935 (*Poems of Two Years*) and wrote the lyrics for several musicals for Ivor Novello in the 1930s. He also wrote librettos for W. *Walton (*Troilus and Cressida*, 1954) and *Bliss. His biography *Edward Marsh, patron of the arts* (1959) was followed by a biography of R. *Brooke (1964).

Hastings, a character in Goldsmith's *She Stoops to Conquer*.

HASTINGS, Warren (1732–1818), the first governor-general of British India, who left India in 1785, was impeached on the ground of cruelty and corruption in his administration, and acquitted after a trial of 145 days, extending, with long intervals, from 1788 to 1795. *Burke and C. J. *Fox were among the prosecutors.

Hatchway, Lieutenant, a character in Smollett's *Peregrine Pickle*.

HATHAWAY, Anne (1555/6–1623), married *Shakespeare in Nov. 1582. Her family home, 'Anne Hathaway's cottage', is still to be seen in Shottery, on the edge of Stratford-upon-Avon.

Hatteraick, Dirk, the smuggler captain in Scott's *Guy Mannering*.

HATTON, Sir Christopher (1540–91), is said to have attracted the attention of Queen *Elizabeth I by his graceful dancing (alluded to by Sheridan, *The Critic*, II. ii), became her favourite, and received grants of offices and estates (including Ely Place, now the site of Hatton Garden). Hatton was lord chancellor, 1587–91, and chancellor of Oxford University, 1588. He was the friend and patron of *Spenser and *Churchyard, and wrote Act IV of *Tancred and Gismund*.

Haunch of Venison, The, a poetical epistle to Lord Clare by *Goldsmith, written about 1770, published 1776.

Haunted Man and the Ghost's Bargain, The, a Christmas book by *Dickens, published 1848.

Redlaw, a learned man in chemistry, is haunted by the memories of a life blighted by sorrow and wrong. His Evil Genius tempts him to think that these memories are his curse, and makes a bargain with him by which he shall forget them; but on condition that he communicates this power of oblivion to all with whom he comes in contact. He discovers with horror that with remembrance of the past he blots out from his own life and the lives of those about him (in particular the delightful Tetterbys) gratitude, repentance, compassion, and forebearance. He prays to be released from his bargain, which is effected by the influence of the good angel Milly Swidger.

HAUPTMANN, Gerhart (1862–1946), German dramatist. His early plays, e.g. *Vor Sonnenaufgang* (*Before Sunrise*, 1889) and *Die Weber* (*The Weavers*, 1892), are important documents of German *Naturalism. With *Hanneles Himmelfahrt* (*The Ascension of Joan*, 1893) he began to move towards a new symbolism, returning from time to time to more realistic drama. His narrative works, such as the story *Bahnwärter Thiel* (*Signalman Thiel*, 1888), are skilful. On the whole his output is characterized by its variety of styles. He won the *Nobel Prize for literature in 1912. Hauptmann was much admired by *Joyce, who translated two of his plays and described *The Weavers* as a masterpiece: 'a little immortal thing'.

Haut-ton, Sir Oran, the orang-utan in Peacock's *Melincourt*, in which Peacock makes satiric use of *Monboddo's claim that the higher primates have most of the essential qualities of human beings, except speech.

Havelok the Dane, The Lay of, a 13th-cent. romance (before 1272) from Lincolnshire, in 3,000 lines of rhyming octosyllables. There is an Anglo-Norman version from c.1130–40 which has resemblances to the 800-line account in Anglo-Norman at the beginning of *Gaimar's *Histoire des Engles* (c.1150). The story tells of the dispossessed Havelok, prince of Denmark, and his marriage to Goldborough, the dispossessed daughter of King Athelwold of England. Havelok is brought up at Grimsby by the eponymous fisherman Grim and becomes kitchen-boy in the household of Godrich, the treacherous guardian of Goldborough. His noble origins are twice declared, once to Grim and once to Goldborough, by a mystical light that shines over his head. At the end all three return to Denmark, defeat and hang Havelok's usurping guardian Godard, and reclaim the throne. The story has parallels with events in English and Norwegian history: Havelok has been etymologically identified with Anlaf Cuaran, the son of a Viking chief Sihtric, king of Northumberland in 925, who was defeated with King Constantine of Scotland in 937 at *Brunanburh; but most of its material and themes are legendary. It is one of the most admired of all Middle English romances nowadays, because of its narrative coherence and life and the sustained interest of its action. The loss of the story was lamented by *Tyrwhitt in the 1770s and by *Ritson just afterwards; the manuscript was discovered only by a happy accident in the Bodleian Library. It was edited by W. W. *Skeat, rev. K. Sisam (1967).

Havisham, Miss, a character in Dickens's *Great Expectations*.

HAWES, Stephen (c.1475–1511), a poet of the school of *Chaucer and *Lydgate, was groom of the chamber to Henry VII. His *Passetyme of Pleasure* or *The Historie of Graunde Amoure and La Bell Pucel* was first printed by *Wynkyn de Worde, 1509. His *Example of Vertu*, a poem in rhyme-royal, an allegory of life spent in the pursuit of purity, much after the manner of the *Passetyme of Pleasure*, was also printed by Wynkyn, in 1512.

Hawk, Sir Mulberry, a character in Dickens's *Nicholas Nickleby*.

HAWKER, R(obert) S(tephen) (1803–75), educated at Pembroke College, Oxford, was from 1834 vicar of Morwenstow in Cornwall; much of his poetry was inspired by Cornish landscape and legend, and by the frequent shipwrecks off the dangerous coast of his parish. He was an isolated and eccentric figure, though the portrait drawn in *Baring-Gould's *The Vicar of Morwenstow* (1875) has been modified by Piers Brendon's *Hawker of Morwenstow* (1975). He was the author of 'The Song of the Western Men', first published anonymously in 1825; based on an old Cornish ballad, it has the refrain: 'And shall Trelawney die?' He published various volumes of poetry, including in 1864 part of a projected long blank verse Arthurian poem, *The Quest of the Sangraal*, which has passages of visionary power attributed by some to his opium addiction.

HAWKES, Jacquetta, née Hopkins (1910–), studied archaeology at Newnham College, Cambridge, and subsequently took part in many excavations. Her first work, *The Archaeology of Jersey* (1939), was followed by many others, written in a style which successfully conveys her enthusiasm to a lay reader; the best-known is *A Land* (1951), with drawings by H. *Moore, a personal evocation of the geological shaping of Britain. She collaborated with her first husband, Christopher Hawkes, in *Prehistoric Britain* (1944), and with her second husband, J. B. *Priestley, in *Journey Down a Rainbow* (1955), an account of travels in New Mexico and Texas.

HAWKESWORTH, John (1715–73), was a schoolmaster and writer of miscellaneous essays, plays, stories, and general journalism. With the considerable assistance of his friend Dr *Johnson, and of J. *Warton, he successfully conducted the *Adventurer*, a bi-weekly successor to the *Rambler*, 1752–4. He produced a reliable edition of *Swift, with a biography, in 1754–5, and in 1766 an edition of Swift's letters. His highly successful *Almoran and Hamet* (1761) is an exotic *Oriental tale. Untrammelled by space or time, Almoran can change into any shape to pursue his strange, and often supernatural, adventures among magnificent heroes and base villains. Hawkesworth edited and annotated various journals, including *Cook's and Carteret's, for his *Account of the Voyages . . . in the Southern Hemisphere* (1773). His sympathy with the native inhabitants of the Pacific Islands led him to convey a picture of innocent indulgence which was widely condemned as indecent. There is a biography by J. L. Abbott (1983).

Hawkeye, the name used by Natty *Bumppo in J. F. Cooper's *The Last of the Mohicans*.

HAWKINS, Sir Anthony Hope (1863–1933), barrister and author, who gave up the law after the success of *The Prisoner of Zenda* (1894), published under the pseudonym 'Anthony Hope'. A sequel, *Rupert of Hentzau*, followed in 1898. Hawkins also published several other novels and plays, and *The Dolly Dialogues* (1894), reprinted from the *Westminster Gazette*, which is a series of light-hearted conversations featuring a flirtation between Samuel Carter, a bachelor, and Dolly Foster, who in ch. 5 marries Lord Mickleham.

Hawkins, Jim, the narrator and hero of R. L. Stevenson's *Treasure Island*.

HAWKINS, Sir John (1532–95), naval commander, who led expeditions in 1562, 1564, and 1567 to the West African and Spanish-American coasts, slave-trading and fighting the Spaniards, and published an account of his voyages in 1569.

HAWKINS, Sir John (1719–89), a lawyer and magistrate who devoted much of his life to music and literature. He was a friend of Dr *Johnson, who, however, found him 'a most

unclubable man', an opinion endorsed by most of his contemporaries. Johnson made him an executor, and Hawkins wrote a life (later overshadowed by *Boswell's), published 1787: he also edited Johnson's works in 15 vols, 1787–8. His scholarly *General History of the Science and Practice of Music* (5 vols, 1776), based on 16 years of research, had a similar misfortune in that it appeared in the same year as, and was seen as the rival of, Dr *Burney's history: these were the first two histories of music in England of their kind. There is a life by B. H. Davis (1973). (See MUSIC, LITERATURE OF.)

HAWKWOOD, Sir John (d. 1394), the famous *condottiere*, figures in *Froissart as 'Haccoude'. *Machiavelli calls him 'Giovanni Acuto'. He was the leader of the body of English mercenaries known as the White Company and fought for one Italian city or another, and for pope or prince, from 1360 to 1390. He was finally commander-in-chief of the Florentine forces, died at Florence, and was buried in the Duomo (his body was subsequently removed to England). He is said to have started life as a tailor's apprentice.

HAWTHORNE, Nathaniel (1804–64), American novelist and short story writer, born at Salem, Massachusetts. He was a descendant of Major William Hathorne (1607–81), one of the Puritan settlers in America, the 'grave, bearded, sable-cloaked and steeple-crowned progenitor' whose portrait is drawn in the introductory chapter of *The Scarlet Letter*: he was remembered for his persecution of the Quakers, as his son, John Hathorne, also a magistrate, was remembered for his persecution of the so-called Witches of Salem. Hawthorne (who adopted this spelling of the family name) spent a solitary childhood with his mother, a widowed recluse, during which he read widely; he was educated at Bowdoin College, Brunswick (with *Longfellow), then returned to Salem, where he began to write stories and sketches and published a novel, *Fanshawe* (1828), at his own expense. His stories began to appear in periodicals (notably in S. G. Goodrich's *The Token*) and were collected in *Twice-Told Tales* (1837) and later volumes, including *Mosses from an Old Manse* (1846) and *The Snow-Image and Other Twice-Told Tales* (1851); he also did a considerable amount of hack-work as writer and editor, and wrote some lasting works for children, including *A Wonder Book* and *Tanglewood Tales* (1852 and 1853, stories from Greek mythology).

He was, however, slow to earn his living as a writer; he was employed for some time as measurer at the Boston Custom House (1839–41), then spent in 1841 several months at Brook Farm, an experience on which he based *The Blithedale Romance* (1852), a novel which conveys his mixed response to the *Transcendentalists. He married in 1842 and settled in Concord; from 1846 to 1849 he was Surveyor of the port of Salem. He lost his post through a change of administration, and then wrote *The Scarlet Letter* (1850), a classic enquiry into the nature of American Puritanism and the New England conscience, and *The House of the Seven Gables* (1851), a study in ancestral guilt and expiation, also deeply rooted in New England and his own family history. In 1850 he met *Melville, who admired Hawthorne's work enormously, and indeed wrote an enthusiastic review comparing him to the Shakespeare of the tragedies. From 1853 to 1857 Hawthorne was in England, as American consul at Liverpool; he then spent two years in Italy, which provided the setting and inspiration for *The Marble Faun* (1860), returning in 1860 to Concord, where he spent his last years, which were marked by declining creative powers. *Our Old Home*, sketches of his life in England, appeared in 1863.

Hawthorne has long been recognized as one of the greatest of American writers, a moralist and allegorist much preoccupied with the mystery of sin, the paradox of its occasionally regenerative power, and the compensation for unmerited suffering and crime. The optimistic answers of *Emerson to these questions left him unconvinced, and the 'darkness' of his genius, first noted by Melville, has found a ready response in the 20th cent. A study of his life and work by H. *James, published in 1879 in the 'English Men of Letters' series, is remarkable for the light that it sheds on both author and subject; James's comments on Hawthorne's 'exaggerated, painful, morbid national consciousness' clearly relate to James's own relation to his American and European experiences, and sense of national identity; he wrote of *The Scarlet Letter*: 'Something might at last be sent to Europe as exquisite in quality as anything that had been received, and the best of it was that the thing was absolutely American . . . it came out of the very heart of New England.'

HAYDN, (Franz) Joseph (1732–1809), Austrian composer. Haydn's early years in Vienna, followed by his long involvement with the court of Esterhazy, kept his interests predominantly local for most of his life, and this was perfectly in accord with the modesty and essential simplicity of his disposition. But his two triumphant visits to London, in 1791–2 and 1794–5, undertaken at the invitation of the concert manager Johann Peter Salomon, provided him with a new stimulus and resulted not only in the twelve last and most famous symphonies, but also in two works directly inspired by the English experience. The oratorio *Die Schöpfung* (1798), better known by its English title *The Creation*, was written to a text compiled from the 1st chapter of Genesis and the 7th and 8th books of *Paradise Lost*, translated into German

by Baron van Swieten. It is said that the original version of this text had been intended for *Handel, and in the event there is a strongly Handelian feel about this unexpected masterpiece of Haydn's old age. (The English version to which it is now normally sung outside the German-speaking countries, however, is a retranslation by van Swieten and not without its absurdities.) The enormous success of *The Creation* encouraged Haydn to produce a second oratorio, *Die Jahreszeiten* (1801), with a text (again by van Swieten) drawn from Thomson's *The Seasons*, though with a less consistently fine result. Two sets of six *Original Canzonettas* (1794/5) were published at the time of the London visits, and 125 arrangements with instrumental accompaniment of Scottish and Welsh folk-songs. After his return to Vienna Haydn made another 250 of these for the Scottish publishers Whyte and Thomson (the latter in a series continued by *Beethoven after Haydn's death).

HAYDON, Benjamin Robert (1786–1846), a historical painter but best known for his posthumously published *Autobiography and Journals* (selections ed. Tom *Taylor, 1853; complete text in 5 vols, ed. W. B. Pope, 1960, 1963). Haydon, son of a Plymouth bookseller, at first had some success with his large paintings of biblical and classical subjects, but quarrelled with most of his patrons, fell deeply in debt, and finally committed suicide. His vigorous advocacy helped to secure the Elgin Marbles for the British Museum, and his pioneering theories on art education, industrial design, and state patronage of the arts, expressed in his *Lectures on Painting and Design* (1846), had much influence. He was a friend of *Keats, *Wordsworth, *Hazlitt, Leigh *Hunt, M. R. *Mitford, and Elizabeth Barrett (*Browning), and his vivid and vehement journals contain many interesting anecdotes and pen-portraits of his contemporaries. His outrageous personality has interested many novelists, notably Dickens who used him (combined with Leigh Hunt) as the model for Harold Skimpole in *Bleak House*, and A. *Huxley, whose Casimir Lypiatt in *Antic Hay* is based on Haydon. See *A Sultry Month: Scenes of London Literary Life in 1846* (1965) by Alethea Hayter, which gives a vivid portrait of his last days.

HAYLEY, William (1745–1820), a prolific poet, whose most ambitious works, *The Triumphs of Temper* (1781) and *The Triumphs of Music* (1804), were ridiculed by *Byron as 'For-ever feeble and for ever tame', but were nevertheless popular. In 1805 his *Ballads on . . . Animals* was illustrated by *Blake, who was at that time his friend and protégé, although the two were not always in sympathy. He was a close friend of *Cowper, whose *Life* he published in 1803; he also published lives of *Milton (1804) and *Romney (1809). His friend *Southey commented that, 'Everything about that man is good except his poetry.' He was nevertheless offered the laureateship in 1790, but declined it.

Haymarket, The, London, so called from the Hay Market established there in 1664, and maintained until 1830. Her Majesty's Theatre, Haymarket (called also the Opera House), was the first opera house in London (1705). The first performances in England of *Handel's operas were given there. The Haymarket Theatre, on the opposite side of the street, also built at the beginning of the 18th cent., was *Foote's theatre from 1747, and later that of the Bancrofts.

Hayraddin, the Maugrabin or gypsy, a character in Scott's *Quentin Durward.

Hayston, Frank, the laird of Bucklaw, a character in Scott's *The Bride of Lammermoor.

HAYWARD, Abraham (1801–84), essayist, called to the bar in 1832, was author of The Art of Dining (1852); his gastronomic dinners in his chambers were famous for their distinguished company which included *Lockhart and *Macaulay. Some of his essays and reviews including More about Junius (1868), a vigorous attack on the Franciscan theory of *'Junius', and an account of the life and work of J. S. *Mill (1873) provoked acute controversy. His articles appeared in the leading periodicals of his day and many were collected in 5 vols of Biographical and Critical Essays (1858–74). He also published biographical and legal works and a translation of Goethe's *Faust.

HAYWARD, Sir John (?1564–1627), educated at Pembroke College, Cambridge, was the author of various historical works, in which he emulated the style of the great Roman historians. His First Part of the Life and Raigne of Henrie the IIII (1599), dedicated to *Essex, gave offence to *Elizabeth I and led to his imprisonment. His other chief works were the Lives of the III Normans, Kings of England (1613), the Life and Raigne of King Edward the Sixt (1630), and The Beginning of the Reign of Elizabeth (1636).

HAYWOOD, Eliza (?1693–1756), an actress and author of several plays and many novels. She conducted a periodical, The Female Spectator, 1744–6, and in 1751 published the most memorable of her novels, The History of Miss Betty Thoughtless, followed in 1753 by Jenny and Jemmy Jessamy. Her writing has vivacity, particularly in situations of high emotion, but her licentiousness and her habit of thinly disguising figures of society, brought denunciations by *Swift, Horace *Walpole, and others. *Pope

cited her in the *Dunciad, and in a note described her as 'a shameless scribbler'.

HAZLITT, William (1778–1830), born at Maidstone, the son of a Unitarian minister, whose strong liberal views he inherited. Most of his youth was spent in the village of Wem, near Shrewsbury. He began to train for the ministry, relinquished his training in the hope of becoming a painter, then (under the powerful influence of *Coleridge), decided on writing as his career. In London he became the friend of C. *Lamb, who introduced him to other literary men, and he began a long career as a prolific journalist, parliamentary reporter, dramatic and literary critic, essayist, and lecturer. He was an ardent supporter of the French revolution and of Napoleon, and was deeply concerned about the social ills of his own country. In 1807 he published A Reply to *Malthus's Essay on Population and The Eloquence of the British Senate which contained, among other 'characters', studies of *Burke, *Chatham, C. J. *Fox, and the younger *Pitt. In 1808 he married Sarah Stoddard. From about 1812 he wrote abundantly for various periodicals, including the *Edinburgh Review, and began to turn from political journalism to the writing of literary criticism and essays. His Lectures on English Philosophy appeared in 1812; in 1817 *Characters of Shakespeare's Plays and a book of essays, The Round Table, written with Leigh *Hunt; in 1818 A View of the English Stage and *Lectures on the English Poets. In this year he was violently attacked by *Lockhart, the editor of *Blackwood's Magazine, who called him a 'mere quack', and derided him as one of the members of the *'Cockney school of poetry'. In 1819 he produced Lectures on the *English Comic Writers and his Political Essays concerning the distresses of the poor. In that year he met Sarah Walker, with whom he fell so obsessively in love that for more than three years his sanity was frequently under threat. Essays entitled Table Talk appeared in 1821–2, and in 1822 he obtained a divorce from his wife.

By 1823 his fortunes had fallen so low he was arrested for debt, and he became the subject of public obloquy with the publication of *Liber Amoris, an agonized account of his love for Sarah Walker. Characteristics, a calmer reflection on love, appeared in the same year, and he contributed to *The Liberal, a short-lived joint venture of *Byron and Leigh Hunt. In 1824 he married Isabella Bridgewater and travelled in Europe, where he began collecting material for a life of his great hero Napoleon. In 1825 he published *The Spirit of the Age, a collection of studies of famous men of his own time and of the previous 50 years; and in 1826 The Plain Speaker and Notes of a Journey through France and Italy. His second wife left him in 1827, in which year he published Boswell Redivivus, a conversational portrait of the painter Northcote. In 1828 appeared the first two volumes of his *Life of Napoleon*, and in 1820 volumes three and four: he believed it was his highest achievement, but it has never been greatly esteemed. *Winterslow*, a series of reflections and essays, and *Sketches and Essays* were published posthumously.

Hazlitt was the first English writer to make a large part of his livelihood from descriptive criticism. In his essays on literature he despised 'formulas of criticism', hoping 'to feel what was good'. His merits as a critic are not always agreed, yet even his detractors concede the great range of his reading and his achievement as a critical historian at a time when no history of English literature existed. See P. P. Howe, *Life of William Hazlitt* (1922, rev. 1928); Howe also edited his *Complete Works* (21 vols, 1930–4). See also H. Baker, *William Hazlitt* (1962).

HAZLITT, William Carew (1834–1913), bibliographer, grandson of William *Hazlitt. Among his works are a *Hand-book to the popular poetical and dramatic literature of Great Britain, from the invention of printing to the Restoration* (1867), *Bibliographical Collections and Notes* (1876–89, 3 series), and memoirs of his grandfather (1867). His editorial work included *English Proverbs and Proverbial phrases collected from the most authentic sources* (1869, for which H. G. *Bohn accused him of plagiarism), *Letters of Charles Lamb* (1886), reprints of Hazlitt, *Herrick, *Suckling, and a translation of *Montaigne. His *Confessions of a Collector* appeared in 1897. *Schoenbaum describes him as 'unreliable' and 'an antiquarian bumbler'.

H.D., see DOOLITTLE, H.

Headlong Hall, a satire by T. L. *Peacock, published 1816, the first of the series of books in which Peacock adapts the Socratic dialogue as a tool for satirizing contemporary culture.

Mr Foster the optimist, Mr Escot the pessimist, Mr Jenkinson the status-quo-ite, Dr Gaster, a gluttonous cleric, Mr Milestone, a landscape gardener, and many others gather at the Welsh country house of Squire Headlong to eat, drink, and discuss the arts. In the central comic episode, Mr Milestone blows up part of the grounds in order to achieve the smooth effect preferred by his real-life prototype, Repton. The debates of the philosophers enact the clash between the optimism of Condorcet and *Godwin and the pessimism of *Malthus. See also PICTURESQUE.

Headrigg, Cuddie, in Scott's *Old Mortality*, ploughman to Lady Margaret Bellenden, and Mause, his old Covenanting mother.

Headstone, Bradley, a character in Dickens's *Nicholas Nickleby*.

HEANEY, Seamus Justin (1939–), Irish poet, educated at St Columb's College, Derry, and Queen's University, Belfast. In the 1960s he belonged to a group of poets in Belfast, who, he said, 'used to talk poetry day after day with an intensity and prejudice that cannot but have left a mark on all of us'. After lecturing on poetry at Queen's for six years he moved in 1972 to the Republic of Ireland, living first in Co. Wicklow and then in Dublin. His early poetry is rooted in the farmland of his youth, and communicates a strong physical sense of environment with subtlety and economy of words, as in *Eleven Poems* (1965), *Death of a Naturalist* (1966), and *Door into the Dark* (1969). His later work, densely written and often poignant, as in *Wintering Out* (1972), *North* (1975), and *Field Work* (1979), broods on the cultural and historical implications of words and explores their use in wider social and political contexts. *Selected Poems, 1965–1975* was published in 1980. *Preoccupations* (1980), a collection of essays and lectures from 1968 to 1978, includes 'The Fire i' the Flint: Reflections on the Poetry of Gerard Manley Hopkins' (Chatterton Lecture, 1975).

HEARD, Gerald, see HUXLEY, A.

HEARN, Lafcadio (1850–1904), born in Santa Maura (Levkas), one of the Ionian Islands, of Irish-Greek parentage, was educated in England, where he lost through an accident the sight of one eye. In 1869 he left penniless for America, where he worked as a journalist in Cincinnati and incurred scandal by living openly with a mulatto woman; he also translated from the French, and his own works show the influence of the exoticism of Pierre Loti, *Baudelaire, and *Gautier. He then lived in Martinique, an experience which produced *Two Years in the French West Indies* (1890) and a novel, *Youma* (1890). In 1890 he went to Japan, where he spent the rest of his life. He married a Japanese wife, took the name of Yakumo Koizumi, and adopted Japanese dress, though he never mastered the language. He taught at a school in Matsue, and from 1896 to 1903 lectured on English literature at the Imperial University, Tokyo. He published several works which affectionately and vividly evoke the landscapes, mythology, and customs of his adopted country, including *Glimpses of Unfamiliar Japan* (1894), *Out of the East* (1895), and *Japan: an attempt at interpretation* (1904). See lives by E. Bisland (1906) and E. Stevenson (1961).

HEARNE, Thomas (1678–1735), historical antiquary, author of *Reliquiae Bodleianae* (1703) and editor of a valuable collection of early English chronicles, of *Leland's *Itinerary*, *Camden's *Annales*, and other works. He was the 'Wormius' of Pope's *Dunciad*. He might have held high office in Oxford University but for his staunch Jacobitism: he refused to take the oath of allegiance to George I.

Heartbreak House: *A Fantasia in the Russian manner on English themes*, a play by Bernard *Shaw, first performed in New York 1920, published there 1919; probably written 1916–17, despite Shaw's claims that he began it before the war.

It describes the impact of Ellie Dunn, daughter of the idealistic and unworldly Mazzini Dunn, upon the eccentric, complacent, and 'horribly Bohemian' household of 88-year-old Captain Shotover, with whom she strikes up an alliance: the inmates include energetic, beautiful, dominating Hesione Hushabye (determined Ellie shall not marry the ageing business magnate Boss Mangan); her husband, the romantic liar and fantasist Hector Hushabye; her sister, the apparently conventional, newly-returned Lady Utterword; and Lady Utterword's devoted brother-in-law Randall, prototype of the useless artist. Shaw appears to be portraying, in 'this silly house, this strangely happy house, this agonizing house, this house without foundations', an aspect of British (or European) civilization (suggested in part by the *Bloomsbury Group, in part by the society portrayed by *Chekhov), about to run on the rocks or blow itself up through lack of direction and lack of grasp of economic reality, but, after various Shavian debates on money, marriage, and morality, the play ends in deep ambiguity: an air raid destroys Boss Mangan, the practical man, who takes refuge in a gravel pit where the Captain stores dynamite, and is greeted with exhilarated rapture by Hesione and Ellie ('It's splendid: it's like an orchestra: it's like Beethoven'), who with the rest of the household refuse to take shelter, and survive.

Heartfree, (1) a character in Vanbrugh's *The Provok'd Wife*; (2) Heartfree and Mrs Heartfree, characters in Fielding's *Jonathan Wild*.

'Heart of Darkness', a tale by J. *Conrad, published 1902. On board a boat anchored peacefully in the Thames the narrator, Marlow, tells the story of his journey on another river.

Travelling in Africa to join a cargo boat, Marlow grows disgusted by what he sees of the greed of the ivory traders and their brutal exploitation of the natives. At a company station he hears of the remarkable Mr Kurtz who is stationed in the very heart of the ivory country and is the company's most successful agent. Leaving the river, Marlow makes a long and arduous cross-country trek to join the steamboat which he will command on an ivory collecting journey into the interior, but at the Central Station he finds that his boat has been mysteriously wrecked. He learns that Kurtz has dismissed his assistant and is seriously ill. The other agents, jealous of Kurtz's success and possible promotion, hope that he will not recover and it becomes clear that Marlow's arrival at the Inner Station is being deliberately delayed. With repairs finally completed Marlow sets off on the two-month journey towards Kurtz. The river passage through the heavy motionless forest fills Marlow with a growing sense of dread. The journey is 'like travelling back to the earliest beginnings of the world'. Ominous drumming is heard and dark forms glimpsed among the trees. Nearing its destination the boat is attacked by tribesmen and a helmsman is killed. At the Inner Station Marlow is met by a naïve young Russian sailor who tells Marlow of Kurtz's brilliance and the semi-divine power he exercises over the natives. A row of severed heads on stakes round the hut give an intimation of the barbaric rites by which Kurtz has achieved his ascendancy. Ritual dancing has been followed with human sacrifice and, without the restraints imposed by his society, Kurtz, an educated and civilized man, has used his knowledge and his gun to reign over this dark kingdom. While Marlow attempts to get Kurtz back down the river Kurtz tries to justify his actions and his motives: he has seen into the very heart of things. But dying his last words are: 'The horror! The horror!' Marlow is left with two packages to deliver, Kurtz's report for the Society for Suppression of Savage Customs, and some letters for his girlfriend. Faced with the girl's grief Marlow tells her simply that Kurtz died with her name on his lips.

Heart of Midlothian, The, a novel by Sir W. *Scott, published 1818, as the 2nd series of *Tales of My Landlord*.

The novel takes its name from the old Edinburgh Tolbooth, or prison, known as the 'Heart of Midlothian, and opens with the Porteous riot of 1736. Captain John Porteous, commander of the City Guard, had, without sufficient justification, caused the death of a number of citizens by ordering his force to fire, and had himself fired, on the crowd on the occasion of the hanging of a convicted robber, Wilson. He had been sentenced to death but reprieved; whereupon a body of the incensed citizens, headed by Robertson, the associate of Wilson, broke into the Tolbooth, carried Porteous out, and hanged him. With these substantially historical events, Scott links the story of Jeanie and Effie Deans, which also has some basis in fact. Robertson, whose real name is George Staunton, a reckless young man of good family, is the lover of Effie Deans, who is imprisoned in the Tolbooth on a charge of child-murder, and the attack on the Tolbooth is partly designed by him to free Effie. But Effie refuses to escape. She is tried, and as her devoted half-sister Jeanie, in a poignant scene, refuses to give the false evidence which would secure her acquittal, is sentenced to death. Jeanie sets out on foot for London, through the influence of the duke of Argyle obtains an interview with Queen Caroline, and by her moving and dignified pleading obtains her sister's pardon. By the duke's favour she is also enabled to marry her lover, the Presbyterian minister Reuben Butler; and her stern Cameronian father, 'Douce Davie Deans', is placed on a comfortable farm on the duke's estate, under the rule of the duke's agent, the Captain of Knockdunder. Effie marries her lover, and becomes Lady Staunton, and it comes to light that her child, whom she was accused of having murdered, is in fact alive. He had been sold to a vagrant woman by Meg Murdockson (who had charge of Effie during her confinement) presumably in revenge against Robertson (alias Staunton) for having seduced her daughter 'Madge Wildfire'. Staunton, in his efforts to recover his son, encounters a band of ruffians and is killed by a boy who turns out to be his own son.

Among the notable minor characters are the officious Bartoline Saddletree, the law-loving harness-maker; and the Laird of Dumbiedikes, Jeanie's taciturn suitor. Beautiful lyrics are placed in the mouth of Madge Wildfire, in particular 'Proud Maisie', which she sings on her deathbed.

In recent decades this has been perhaps the most highly praised of Scott's novels; T. Crawford (*Walter Scott*, 1982) summarizes various critical accounts and concludes that it is 'a domestic ballad-epic in prose that explores the heroism of everyday life in relation to a series of concretely presented, historically conceived conflicts of conscience'.

Heart of the Matter, The, a novel by G. *Greene, published 1948.

Set in West Africa, 'the white man's grave', during the Second World War, it describes how the deputy commissioner of police, Scobie, a just and honourable man, is led to make various false moves, initially by pity for his unhappy, hysterical, 'literary' wife Louise, then through a mixture of pity and love for a 19-year-old widow, Helen, with whom he has an affair. He borrows money, compromises himself, is indirectly responsible for the death of his faithful servant Ali, and finally, with much deliberation, commits suicide, a mortal sin which, as a Catholic, he attempts to conceal from his wife by laying a false trail in his diary. The deceit is posthumously exposed by the young intelligence agent Wilson, who has been watching his every move, motivated partly through his own love for Scobie's wife. The novel vividly evokes an area of 'Greeneland' characterized by intense heat, vultures, cockroaches, rats, heavy drinking, corruption, and a painful struggle to maintain faith, in a hostile environment, with concepts of justice and religion.

Heartwell, the title role in Congreve's comedy *The Old Bachelor.

Heathcliff, the central figure in E. Brontë's *Wuthering Heights.

HEATH-STUBBS, John Francis Alexander (1918–), poet and critic, educated at The Queen's College, Oxford, where his first published poems appeared in *Eight Oxford Poets* (1941, ed. S. *Keyes and M. Meyer). He describes himself as a traditionalist in literature, who believes that traditional values can only be maintained at the price of continual change and flexibility. His inspiration comes chiefly from Ancient Greece, Rome, Alexandria, classical myth, Christian legend, and works of art and scholarship, and his poetry includes translations from *Hāfiz and *Leopardi. But he is also a poet of contemporary urban society, and in *A Charm Against the Toothache* (1954) the megalopolis is modern London. His principal works include poetry: *Wounded Thammuz* (1942), *Beauty and the Beast* (1943), *The Divided Ways* (1946), *The Swarming of the Bees* (1950), *The Blue-Fly in his Head* (1962), *Artorius* (an epic poem on Arthurian legend, 1972), and *Naming the Beasts* (a collection, 1982); and criticism: *The Darkling Plain* (a study of Victorian romantic poetry, 1950) and *Charles Williams* (a monograph, 1955).

Heaven and Earth, a poetic drama by Lord *Byron, published in *The Liberal*, 1822.

Like *Cain it is subtitled 'A Mystery' and, as in *Cain*, the Almighty is accused of creating only to destroy. The story, on a recurrent theme of Byron's, tells of the marriage of angels and mortal women, and the creation of an intermediate race. The principal characters are the seraph Samiasa and Aholibamah, the grand-daughter of Cain.

Heavenly Twins, The, see GRAND, S.

HEBER, Reginald (1773–1833), educated at Oxford, became in 1822 bishop of Calcutta. He published various works, including *Poems and Translations* (1812); an edition of the works of Jeremy *Taylor (1822), and his *Life* (1824); various hymns of his own authorship, including 'Hark, the herald angels sing', 'From Greenland's icy mountains', and 'Holy, holy, holy' in 1827; a *Narrative of a Journey through India* (1828); and his *Poetical Works* (1841).

HEBER, Richard (1773–1833), half-brother of Reginald *Heber, a devoted bibliophile, travelled widely to collect his library of 150,000 volumes, and edited *Persius and other classical authors. He is the 'Atticus' of T. F. *Dibdin's *Bibliomania*.

Hebrew Melodies, a collection of short poems by Lord *Byron, published 1815.

Most of the poems are on scriptural subjects, and some were arranged to traditional Hebrew melodies by I. Nathan. The collection also contains love-songs, including 'She walks in beauty'; and also the much anthologized 'The

Destruction of Sennacherib' ('The Assyrian came down like the wolf on the fold . . .').

Hebrides, *The Journal of a Tour to the,* see JOURNAL OF A TOUR TO THE HEBRIDES. See also JOURNEY TO THE WESTERN ISLANDS OF SCOTLAND.

Hector, Sir, see ECTOR.

Heep, Uriah, a character in Dickens's *David Copperfield.*

HEGEL, Georg Wilhelm Friedrich (1770–1831), German philosopher. His first important work was *Phänomenologie des Geistes (Phenomenology of Spirit,* 1807), followed by his *Logik* (1812–16), and later by the *Philosophie des Rechts (Philosophy of Right,* 1820), embodying his political views.

*Kant had left an essential dualism in his philosophy, nature opposed to spirit, object opposed to subject, the outer world composed of isolated unrelated substances whose nature is beyond the reach of knowledge. Hegel endeavours to bridge the gulf and reduce duality to unity. He shows that all difference presupposes a unity, that a definite thought cannot be separated from its opposite, that the idea of fullness, e.g., cannot be separated from that of emptiness, that they are identical in difference. Duality and unity are blended in consciousness and the boundaries between mind and matter set aside. Hegel's central idea is the dialectic of thesis–antithesis–synthesis, which he applied to the problem of historical evolution as represented by the *Weltgeist* or World Spirit. His dialectical method was adopted by political thinkers of both right and left, those who supported authoritarian rule in Prussia in the 19th cent. and those, like *Feuerbach, *Marx, and *Engels, who advocated reform and revolution. As Engels said, his doctrine was large enough to give shelter to the ideas of the most varied groups. Hegel enjoyed a vogue in philosophical circles in England, particularly at Oxford, in the 1880s and 1890s.

Heidelberg, Mrs, a character in Colman and Garrick's *The Clandestine Marriage.* Her illiteracy and mispronunciation of words bring her into some sort of kinship with Mrs *Malaprop.

Heimskringla, a series of short sagas making up a history of the kings of Norway from mythical times to the year 1177, written by Snorri *Sturluson. It is of more value for its high literary quality than for its historicity, although it is basically reliable and its political analyses are illuminating. It has a bearing on English history, covering as it does the reign of the Danish king *Canute (Knútr) and describing Viking expeditions to England. Its title is taken from its opening words, 'Kringla heimsins'—'orb of the world'. See S. Laing trans., *The Olaf Sagas from Heimskringla* (1914, etc).

HEINE, Heinrich (1797–1856), German poet, was born of Jewish parents in Düsseldorf. Disappointed in his hopes of a liberal régime in Germany after the expulsion of Napoleon, he emigrated in 1830 to Paris, where he remained for the rest of his life. His political works show him a Radical and a cosmopolitan (he wrote both in German and in French), but he was most famous as a lyric poet, many of whose songs were set to music by German composers in the 19th cent. He called himself 'the last Romantic', and his lyrics are characterized by a combination of self-indulgent emotion and sharp self-criticism and deflating irony. His chief works include the *Buch der Lieder (Book of Songs,* 1827), one of the most widely read and influential books of poetry in Germany, combining *Romanticism with irony; the satirical travel sketches in his *Reisebilder (Travel Pictures,* 1826–31); and his savage and witty attacks on German thought and literature in *Zur Geschichte der Religion und Philosophie in Deutschland (On the History of Religion and Philosophy in Germany,* 1834) and *Die romantische Schule (The Romantic School,* 1836). G. *Eliot and M. *Arnold wrote critical essays on his works. Both appreciated the paradoxes in his writings; as Arnold wrote in 1865, Heine 'unites so much wit with so much pathos' (*Essays in Criticism,* 1st Series).

HEINSIUS, Daniel (1580–1655), Dutch scholar, editor of Aristotle's *Poetics* and author of a Latin work on tragedy. His son Nicolaas Heinsius (1620–81), also a famous scholar, published critical editions of Roman poets and travelled in England; his *Virgil is his most famous work.

Heir-at-Law, The, a comedy by G. *Colman the younger.

Heiress, The, a comedy by *Burgoyne.

Heir of Redclyffe, The, a novel by C. M. *Yonge, published 1853.

This novel, illustrating the contrast between real and apparent goodness of character, is the story of the cousins Guy and Philip Morville; the former—who is the heir of a baronetcy and an ancient house—is hot-tempered but generous, the latter a much-admired prig. Philip, by passing on ill-founded suspicions about Guy, at first succeeds in thwarting Guy's marriage to his guardian's daughter Amy, but Guy's character is eventually vindicated and he marries Amy. On their honeymoon they find Philip severely ill with fever; Guy nurses him through the fever, catches it himself, and dies, whereby the now repentant Philip inherits Redclyffe.

He Knew He Was Right, a novel by A. *Trollope, published 1869.

Louis Trevelyan, on a visit to the Mandarin Islands, marries Emily Rowley, daughter of the governor. The couple return to England, where

Trevelyan begins to be troubled by visits from the governor's old friend, the aging philanderer Colonel Osborne. Osborne enjoys the sensation he creates, and continues to call; Emily's pride gives her husband further fuel for his jealousy. Partly as a result of misunderstanding, partly as a result of Trevelyan's morbid instability of temperament, a separation ensues, and Bozzle, a private detective, becomes the only mediator between the couple. Trevelyan abducts his son and takes him off to Italy. In time Emily pursues them, only to find her husband in a state of complete mental breakdown. There is a partial reconciliation between husband and wife, but Trevelyan dies soon after his return to England.

The Italian scenes allow Trollope time to caricature the transatlantic feminism of Miss Wallachia Petrie and to marry off the English aristocrat Mr Glascock to the charming American Caroline Spalding. The novel also contains the story of old Aunt Stanbury at the cathedral close at Exeter, with her protégés, particularly her nephew Hugh, whose engagement to Emily's sister Nora temporarily angers her.

Helena, (1) the taller of the two young heroines in Shakespeare's *A Midsummer Night's Dream* and lover of Demetrius; (2) the heroine of his *All's Well that Ends Well*, whose name may derive from the Queen Helen in Sidney's *Arcadia*, who is unhappily in love and skilled in surgery; (3) Helen of Troy in Goethe's *Faust*.

Helen of Kirkconnell, the subject of an old ballad (included in Sir W. Scott's *Minstrelsy of the Scottish Border* and F. T. *Palgrave's Golden Treasury*), who throws herself before her lover when his rival fires at him, and dies to save him. The story is also the subject of *Wordsworth's* 'Ellen Irwin'.

Heliand, The, an Old Saxon paraphrase in alliterative verse of the NT, dating from the 9th cent.

HELIODORUS, see AETHIOPICA.

Hellas, a lyrical drama by P. B. *Shelley written at Pisa in late 1821, the last work to be published in his lifetime, 1822. Based in form on the *Persians* of *Aeschylus, it was inspired by news of the Greek War of Independence against the Turkish empire, and dedicated to their national leader, Prince Mavrocordato, whom Shelley had known at Pisa.

The action, 'a series of lyric pictures', is set at Constantinople, where the Turkish Sultan Mahmud receives a number of messengers reporting the insurrection, and prophesying Greek victory. Shelley uses visionary figures—Christ, Mahomet, Ahasuerus the Wandering Jew, and the phantom of Mahomet II—to explore a cyclical philosophy of history. But the main interest lies in the choruses, composed like songs for opera, and concluding with the celebrated poem,

'The world's great age begins anew'. Shelley's Preface, his last great appeal for political liberty in Europe, remains a classic statement of English philhellenism: 'We are all Greeks.'

Hellenistic, a term that has come to replace during the present century the earlier adjective 'Alexandrian', applied to the civilization, language, art, and literature of the Graecized lands of the eastern Mediterranean from the death of *Alexander (323 BC) to that of Cleopatra (31 BC). In the creative arts Hellenism was distinguished by a preference for small, delicate, and highly decorated products intended to please a public of connoisseurs. Hellenistic literature displayed (sometimes in one and the same work) a mandarin artificiality full of recondite, learned allusions and a lively, realistic interest in everyday life. Its treatment of the gods of Greece showed at times genuine religious feeling, but was often playful and mocking, marked by a preoccupation with the excitements of sex that bordered on the pornographic. Subtly ironic, highly polished, it seems in spite of its sincerities to hold life at arm's length. Much of this literature has perished, and what we possess of it today is, thanks to papyrus discoveries, far more than was available during the *Renaissance. But the Hellenistic tradition had a marked influence on the Latin poets of the late Republic and the *Augustan age and so exercised a far-reaching, if indirect, influence.

Hellenore, in Spenser's *Faerie Queene* (III. x), the wife of *Malbecco, who elopes with *Paridell.

HELLER, Joseph (1923–), novelist, born in New York. He served as a bombardier in the air force during the Second World War, an experience which resurfaced in his first novel, *Catch-22 (1961), which took him eight years to write and brought him instant fame. His second novel, *Something Happened* (1974), is the domestic tragi-comedy of a middle-aged New York executive, and *Good as Gold* (1979) a surreal and comic satire about Jewish New York and Washington politics.

Hell-fire Clubs, associations of reckless and profligate young ruffians who were a nuisance to London chiefly in the early 18th cent. There was a later and more famous Hell-fire Club, founded about 1745, at *Medmenham Abbey.

Héloïse, or Eloisa, see ABELARD.

HELVÉTIUS, Claude Arien (1715–71), see PHILOSOPHES.

HEMANS, Mrs Felicia Dorothea, *née* Browne (1793–1835), a precocious and copious poet of intermittent but often considerable skill, published her first volume of *Poems* when she was 15. From the publication of *Domestic Affections* in 1812 she produced further fluent and innocuous volumes, exhibiting a wide range of subject and style, almost every year until her death. She made many translations from *Camoëns and other Portuguese or Spanish poets, including *Translations from Camoens and other Poets* (1818). Her works were very popular, especially in America. The most famous of her poems, 'Casabianca', beginning 'The boy stood on the burning deck', appeared in *The Forest Sanctuary* (1829).

HEMING, or **HEMINGES,** John (1556–1630), and CONDELL, Henry (d. 1627), were fellow actors of Shakespeare and joint editors of the First *Folio of his plays (1623). Heming is said to have been the first player of *Falstaff.

HEMINGWAY, Ernest Miller (1899–1961), American short story writer and novelist, born in Illinois, the son of a doctor. After working as a Kansas City reporter he served in 1918 as a volunteer with an ambulance unit on the Italian front, where he was wounded, then worked as a reporter for the Toronto *Star* before settling in Paris among the American expatriate literary group, where he met *Pound, G. *Stein, F. M. *Ford, and others described in his posthumously published *A Moveable Feast* (1964). His *Three Stories and Ten Poems* (1923), was followed by *In Our Time* (1925; stories) and two novels, the satirical *The Torrents of Spring* (1926) and the more characteristic *The Sun Also Rises* (1926; in England, as *Fiesta*, 1927), with which he made his name. It catches the post-war mood of disillusion of the so-called 'lost generation' through its portrayal of the wanderings of Lady Brett Ashley and her entourage, which includes the war-wounded, impotent American reporter Jake Barnes; its economy of style and characterization and its 'toughness' of attitude made a great impression. *A Farewell to Arms* (1929), the story of a love affair between an American lieutenant and an English nurse during the war on the Italian front, confirmed his position as one of the most influential writers of the time. He has been considered a finer writer of short stories than of novels, and his collections *Men without Women* (1927) and *Winner Take Nothing* (1933) are especially notable. His growing dissatisfaction with contemporary culture was shown by his deliberate cultivation of the brutal and the primitive; he celebrated bullfighting in *Death in the Afternoon* (1932) and big-game hunting in *The Green Hills of Africa* (1935). He actively supported the Republicans during the Spanish Civil War, and *For Whom the Bell Tolls* (1940) is set against its background. He was a war correspondent in Europe in the Second World War. In his later years he lived mostly in Cuba, where his passion for deep-sea fishing provided the setting for his most successful later work, *The Old Man and the Sea* (1952), a parable-novella about man's struggle against na-

ture. He was awarded the *Nobel Prize in 1954 and wrote little thereafter; he shot himself in July 1961, having been seriously ill for some time. Various posthumous publications followed, including volumes of selected journalism and his *Selected Letters* (1981).

Hemlock and After, a novel by Sir A. *Wilson.

Henchard, Michael, the mayor in Hardy's *The Mayor of Casterbridge*.

Hendecasyllabic, a verse line of eleven syllables (- - - ∪ ∪ - ∪ - ∪ - -), used by *Catullus and imitated by *Tennyson:

> O you chorus of indolent reviewers.

(See METRE.)

Hendiadys, from the Greek words meaning 'one by means of two', a figure of speech by which a single complex idea is expressed by two words joined by a conjunction, e.g. 'Such as sit in darkness and in the shadow of death, being fast bound in misery and iron' (Ps. 107: 10).

HENDRY, James Findlay, see NEW APOCALYPSE.

HENGIST and **HORSA,** the traditional leaders of the Jutes who, according to *Bede (*Ecclesiastical History*, I. 15), landed at Ebbsfleet in 449 and were given by *Vortigern the Isle of Thanet for a dwelling-place. Horsa was killed in battle against Vortigern in 455, but Hengist was the progenitor of a line of Kentish kings through his son Aesc.

HENLEY, John (1692–1756), an eccentric preacher, generally known as 'Orator' Henley, who published works on oratory, theology, and grammar. He was caricatured by *Hogarth and ridiculed by *Pope:

> Still break the benches, Henley! with thy strain,
> While Sherlock, Hare and Gibson preach in vain.
>
> (*Dunciad*, iii. 203)

HENLEY, W(illiam) E(rnest) (1849–1903), son of a Gloucester bookseller, and pupil there of T. E. *Brown, suffered from boyhood from tubercular arthritis and had a foot amputated; to save the other he went in 1873 to Edinburgh where he spent a year in the Infirmary under the care of Lister. His 'Hospital Sketches', a sequence of poems first published in the *Cornhill* in 1875 and subsequently revised, are a striking record of this grim ordeal, and his best-known poem, the defiant and stoic 'Invictus' ('Out of the night that covers me') was written in 1875. While in hospital he was introduced by L. *Stephen to R. L. *Stevenson, who became a close friend and with whom he collaborated in the plays *Deacon Brodie* (1880), *Admiral Guinea* (1884), *Beau Austin* (1884), and *Macaire* (1885), none of which had much success. He did a great deal of miscellaneous literary work, much of it as editor of the *Magazine of Art* (1881–6), *The Scots Observer*, continued as the *National Observer* (1888–94), and the *New Review* (1895–8); he was a courageous and independent editor, publishing important work by *Hardy, *Kipling, Stevenson, *Yeats, H. *James, and H. G. *Wells, among many others. He also compiled anthologies, and edited *Slang and its Analogues* (7 vols, 1890–1904). A powerful and flamboyant personality, described by Stevenson (in his portrait of him as 'Burly' in his essay 'Talk and Talkers') as 'boisterous and piratic', he had considerable influence on his contemporaries, particularly in his defence of realism and activism, although his literary judgements were not always dictated by his strong Tory imperial views. His volumes of poetry include *A Book of Verses* (1888), *The Song of the Sword and other verses* (1892), *London Voluntaries* (1893), and *For England's Sake* (1900), some of which, notably the last, expound his jingoistic patriotism. But he also wrote ballads, lyrics, and impressionistic free verse; he dedicated an evocation of the Thames ('Under a stagnant sky') to *Whistler, whose work he had consistently championed. Stevenson acknowledged him as the inspiration behind the creation of Long John Silver in *Treasure Island*. There are lives by L. C. Cornford (1913), K. Williamson (1930), and J. H. Buckley (1945).

HENRI, Adrian Maurice (1932–), poet and painter, born in Birkenhead and educated at the University of Durham, where he studied fine art. He settled in Liverpool in 1957, and during the 1960s was known (with Roger McGough and Brian Patten) as one of the *'Liverpool Poets'; from 1967 to 1970 he led the poetry/rock group 'Liverpool Scene'. His own collections of poetry include *Tonight at Noon* (1968), *City* (1969), and *From the Loveless Motel* (1980).

Henrietta Temple: *a Love Story*, a novel by B. *Disraeli, published 1837. The novel was begun in 1834, during Disraeli's open love affair with Lady Henrietta Sykes, then resumed in seclusion to escape arrest for debt in 1836.

The dashing Ferdinand Armine, of an old but impoverished family, enters the army, and in a world of horses, gambling, and women gets heavily into debt. His grandfather's estate, upon which he was counting, does not come to him, so he becomes engaged to his wealthy cousin Katherine Grandison, a kind and clever young woman. During the year of mourning for his grandfather Ferdinand falls deeply in love with the penniless Henrietta Temple and becomes engaged to her as well as to Katherine; but Henrietta, hearing of his treachery through gossip, falls desperately ill and is taken to Italy, leaving Ferdinand in despair. In Italy Henrietta meets the noble, gentle Lord Montfort, to whom she

becomes engaged. Ferdinand, ill and pressed by creditors, reads of her engagement in the paper. Katherine, who has meanwhile forgiven and released him, encounters Montfort and Henrietta in London and, together with the spirited Count Mirabel, arranges that the four lovers shall meet. Eventually Ferdinand and Henrietta are reunited, and Katherine and Montfort find happiness together. *Tennyson thought that 'the "silly sooth" of love was given perfectly there.'

HENRY II, king of England 1154–89. His literary occurrences tend to be related to his order (traditionally regarded as misinterpreted) to kill *Becket.

Henry IV, *Parts 1* and *2*, historical plays by *Shakespeare, written and performed about 1597. Part 1 was printed in quarto 1598, Part 2 1600. The chief sources are the chronicles of *Hall and *Holinshed, and *Daniel's historical poem *The Civil Wars*. The contemporary popularity of the plays on the stage was recorded by Leonard Digges (1640):

let but *Falstaffe* come,
Hall, *Poines*, the rest you scarce shall have a roome
All is so pester'd.

They have been popular fairly continuously ever since.

The subject of Pt 1 is the rebellion of the Percys, assisted by Douglas and in concert with Mortimer and Glendower; and its defeat by the king and Prince Hal, the prince of Wales, at Shrewsbury (1403). *Falstaff first appears in this play. The prince of Wales associates with him and his boon companions, Poins, Bardolph, and Peto, in their riotous life. Poins and the prince contrive that the others shall set on some travellers at Gadshill and rob them, and be robbed in their turn by themselves. The plot succeeds, and leads to Falstaff's well-known fabrication to explain the loss of the booty, and his exposure. At the battle of Shrewsbury, Prince Hal kills *Hotspur in a heroic single combat, and then discovers Falstaff feigning death, whom he mourns with the words, 'I could have better spar'd a better man.' After Hal's exit Falstaff resourcefully claims credit for having slain Hotspur.

Pt 2 deals with the rebellion of Archbishop Scroop, Mowbray, and Hastings; while in the comic under-plot the story of Falstaff's doings is continued, with those of the prince, *Pistol, Poins, Mistress *Quickly, and Doll Tearsheet. Falstaff, summoned to the army for the repression of the rebellion, falls in with Justices *Shallow and *Silence in the course of his recruiting, makes a butt of them, and extracts £1,000 from the former. Henry IV dies, reconciled to his son, and Falstaff hastens from Gloucestershire to London to greet the newly crowned king, who rejects him in the speech beginning 'I know thee not, old man. Fall to thy prayers', banishing him from his presence but allowing him 'competence of life'.

Henry V, King, a historical drama by *Shakespeare, written, as the reference to *Essex in Ireland (v. Chorus, 30–2) indicates, in the spring or summer of 1599. It was printed in 1600 from a memorial reconstruction; the First *Folio text (1623) is based on Shakespeare's own papers. Its chief sources are the chronicles of *Hall and *Holinshed. The play, with its strongly patriotic theme, has most often been popular in time of national crisis, as in the film version made in 1944 with Laurence Olivier as Henry.

The play opens with the newly ascended Henry astonishing clergy and courtiers by his piety and statecraft (cf. Prince *Hal). The archbishop of Canterbury demonstrates, in the long 'Salic Law' speech, Henry's claim to the throne of France, and the Dauphin's jesting gift of tennis balls gives him an immediate pretext for invasion. Henry unmasks the three traitors, Scrope, Grey, and Cambridge, and sets out for France; he besieges and captures Harfleur, and achieves a resounding victory at Agincourt (1415), a battle for which he prepares his soldiers in the 'Crispin Crispian' speech. Comic relief is provided by the old tavern companions of *Falstaff, who have fallen on hard times, and by some of Henry's soldiers, especially the pedantic but courageous Welsh captain Fluellen. The new, patriotic, comic characters symbolically defeat the old when Fluellen compels the braggart Pistol to eat a leek (v. i). The last act is given to Henry's wooing of Katherine of France.

Henry VI, King, Parts 1, 2, and 3, sections of a historical tetralogy (completed by *Richard III) by *Shakespeare written between 1590 and the summer of 1592. Part 1 was not published until the First *Folio (1623), but Part 2 was published anonymously in 1594 under the title 'The First part of the Contention betwixt the two famous Houses of Yorke and Lancaster . . .', and Part 3 in 1595 as 'The true Tragedie of Richard Duke of Yorke, and the death of good King Henrie the Sixt'. Shakespeare's authorship of the plays, especially of Part 1, was doubted throughout the 18th and 19th cents, on the grounds that the plays were artistically unworthy of him. In the 20th cent., however, scholars have made increasingly confident claims for his sole authorship. Reference to 'an upstart Crow' in *Greenes Groats-Worth of Witte used to be taken as evidence of plagiarism, but is now generally read as merely the malice of a rival dramatist. The plays' chief sources are the chronicles of *Hall and *Holinshed.

Pt 1, opening with the funeral of Henry V, deals with wars in France in which the gallant Talbot is a powerful leader on the English side, and the witch-like *Joan of Arc, 'La Pucelle', on the French. After a series of encounters Talbot, together with his valiant son John Talbot, are killed near Bordeaux (IV. vii). A crucial scene (II. iv) is that in the Temple garden, in which the plucking of red and white roses establishes the opposition of Plantagenet and York in the subsequent wars. In the fifth act the earl of Suffolk arranges a marriage between the young Henry VI and *Margaret of Anjou, daughter of the king of Naples, vowing ominously to rule both king, queen, and kingdom.

Pt 2 shows Henry's marriage to Margaret. The giving of Anjou and Maine to her father as a price for her marriage angers *Humphrey, duke of Gloucester, the Lord Protector; his wife Eleanor is banished as a witch (II. iii) and he is arrested on a charge of high treason, against the king's better judgement, and murdered. Suffolk is banished and, after a touching farewell to Queen Margaret, murdered by pirates on the Kent coast. Richard, duke of York, pretender to the throne, stirs up Jack Cade to rebellion (IV): after considerable success, Cade is eventually killed by Alexander Iden, a Kentish gentleman. The final act concerns the battle of St Albans (1455), in which Somerset is killed, a victory for the Yorkists.

Pt 3 opens with Henry's attempt to buy peace by making the duke of York his heir, thus disinheriting his son by Margaret. Savagery and strife proliferate, however; Margaret, enraged and eloquent, instigates the murder of the boy Rutland, York's youngest son, by Clifford, and the mock-coronation and murder of York himself, who addresses to her the line that *Greene was to parody, 'O tiger's heart wrapp'd in a woman's hide!' Clifford is killed at the battle of Towton, which also includes a scene symbolic of the horrors of civil war in which a son who has killed his father encounters a father who has killed his son. Henry VI is captured and Edward (IV) declared king; he marries the dowerless widow Elizabeth Grey, though previously promised to Bona, the French king's sister. Richard, duke of Gloucester (later Richard III), emerges as an ambitious *Machiavelli. Warwick, a powerful contriver on the Lancastrian side, is killed at Barnet by King Edward; the battle of Tewkesbury is a decisive victory for Edward, and Margaret's young son (also an Edward) is killed in cold blood by Edward, Richard, duke of Gloucester, and George, duke of Clarence. King Henry, imprisoned in the Tower, is murdered by Richard.

HENRY VIII (1491–1547), king of England, from 1509. His life was written by Lord *Herbert of Cherbury. His book A defence of the Seven Sacraments, directed against *Luther's teaching, was printed in 1521 and presented to *Leo X, who thereupon conferred on Henry the title

'Defender of the Faith'. Henry was also an accomplished musician and poet, and several of his compositions survive, including 'Pastyme with good companye', 'Alas, what shall I do for love?', and 'O my hart and O my hart'. His lyrics deal with courtly and chivalric themes, with one known exception, the sacred composition 'Quam pulcra es'. (See J. Stevens, *Music and Poetry in the Early Tudor Court*, 1961.) *Holbein was painter at Henry's court, and drew and painted many of his circle, as well as the king himself. Henry's private life became the subject of many dramas and works of fiction, including a work by Shakespeare and *Fletcher (below), and he remains legendary on account of his six wives, who were, successively, Catherine of Aragon (m. 1509), Anne Boleyn, mother of *Elizabeth I (m. 1533), Jane Seymour (m. 1536), Anne of Cleves (m. 1539), Catherine Howard (m. 1540), and Catherine Parr (m. 1543).

Henry VIII, a historical drama also known to contemporaries as 'All is True'. Shakespeare has been claimed as its sole author, but it is usually held that he was responsible for less than half of the play, the remainder being written by J. *Fletcher, whose hand in it was originally suggested by *Tennyson. Its early production may have been connected with the marriage in February 1613 of Frederick, the Elector Palatine, and Princess Elizabeth, daughter of James I and Anne of Denmark. Its performance in June 1613 resulted in the burning down of the *Globe Theatre.

It deals with the fall and execution of the duke of Buckingham; the question of the royal divorce (vividly depicting the dignity and resignation of Queen Catherine); the pride and fall of Cardinal Wolsey and his death; the advancement and coronation of Anne Boleyn; the triumph of Cranmer over his enemies; and the christening of the Princess Elizabeth.

The chief sources of the play are *Holinshed's *Chronicles* and Foxe's *Actes and Monuments* (or *Book of Martyrs*).

HENRY, O., pseudonym of William Sydney Porter (1862–1910), American short story writer, born in North Carolina. He had a chequered early career, which included a term in prison for embezzlement (1896). He began to write short stories in prison, based on his observations of life, and published the first of his many collections, *Cabbages and Kings*, in 1904. He was prolific, humorous, and highly ingenious, especially in his use of coincidence, and became the most famous writer of his kind of the day.

HENRY OF HUNTINGDON (?1084–1155), archdeacon of Huntingdon, compiled at the request of bishop Alexander of Lincoln a *Historia Anglorum*, which in its latest form extends to 1154.

HENRYSON, Robert (?1424–?1506), a Scottish poet of the school known until recently as 'Scottish *Chaucerians', and, along with *Dunbar, its most prominent member. His dependence on Chaucer is not now much stressed. His most important poems are *The Testament of Cresseid*, written as a moralizing but sympathetic sequel to Chaucer's *Troilus and Criseyde* and printed with editions of Chaucer as its Book VI until the 18th cent., and his *Morall Fabillis of Esope*. Henryson was a schoolteacher from Dunfermline; his distinctive virtue is the combination of stern morality with humane sympathy.

Ed. H. Harvey Wood (Edinburgh, 1933; rev. 1958); J. Speirs, *The Scots Literary Tradition* (1940); M. W. Stearns, *Robert Henryson* (1949); Douglas Gray, *Robert Henryson* (1979).

HENRY THE MINSTREL, or BLIND HARRY or HARY (?1440–?92), a half-legendary Scottish poet, perhaps a native of Lothian, who wrote in about 1460 The Wallace, one of the most famous of all *Scots poems. This vigorous poem consists of about 12,000 lines in heroic couplets concerning the martial feats of Wallace, who was executed by the English in 1305. It claims to be based on a work of John Blair, Wallace's chaplain. The earliest text is a manuscript (in the Scottish National Library) written in 1488 by John Ramsay, the scribe of Barbour's *Bruce*. A popular version of the poem was a rewriting in 1722 by William Hamilton of Gilbertfield, which inflamed *Burns. See ed. M. P. McDiarmid, *Hary's Wallace* (STS, 2 vols, 1968–9).

HENSLOWE, Philip (d. *c*.1616), built the Rose Theatre on Bankside in 1587, and thereafter was involved in theatrical affairs as financier, manager, and owner until his death. With his stepson-in-law *Alleyn he was involved in the affairs of several important companies of actors, notably the Lord Admiral's Men, and in the building of the Fortune and Hope theatres. Most of the dramatists of the period, apart from Shakespeare, at some time wrote for his companies. His *Diary* (ed. R. A. Foakes and R. T. Rickert, 1961) contains a mass of information about theatrical life, and about dramatists and their methods of writing plays.

HENTY, G(eorge) A(lfred) (1832–1902), enlisted as a soldier in the Crimea, where he became a war correspondent, a career he followed subsequently in Italy, Abyssinia, Ashanti, Spain, India, and in Paris during the Commune. He wrote without success some dozen novels for adults, including *Colonel Thorndyke's Secret* (1898), but was very successful for many years as the author of stories for boys, mainly based on military history. *Out in the Pampas* (1868) was followed by some 35 other books, sometimes at the rate of three or four a year. Most ran to several editions, and some are still available. Among the best-remembered are *The Young Buglers* (1880), *Under Drake's Flag* (1883), *With Clive in India* (1884), and *The Lion of St Mark's* (1889). The didactic influence, conveyed largely through the manly characters of the heroes, is supported by strong narrative and an appearance of historical fidelity.

HENZE, Hans Werner (1926–   ), German composer. His very substantial list of works includes two operas to librettos by W. H. *Auden and Chester Kallman, *Elegy for Young Lovers* (1961) and *The Bassarids* (1966), and *Moralities* (1968), a set of three scenic cantatas with texts by Auden after *Aesop. There is an early *Whitman cantata and one unusual Shakespearian work, *Royal Winter Music* (1976), a sonata for guitar in which each movement is concerned with a character from one of the plays. Henze's large-scale stage work *We Come to the River*, described as 'actions for music' with a text by E. *Bond, was written for the Royal Opera House, Covent Garden (1976).

Heorot, see BEOWULF.

Heptameron, The, a collection of tales of love (depicted as a serious and sometimes tragic passion) linked by the fiction that the narrators are travellers detained in an inn by a flood. It was composed by Marguerite, sister of Francis I and queen of Navarre (1492–1549). Only 72 of the intended 100 tales were completed. The name 'Heptameron', 'seven days', was first given to the collection in 1559, on the analogy of Boccaccio's *Decameron*.

HERACLITUS of Ephesus (*fl. c.*500 BC), a philosopher who maintained that all things are in a state of flux, coming into existence and passing away. He condemned thinkers who sought for permanence in the universe. F. *Bacon calls him 'the profound', but more generally he was called 'the weeping philosopher' because of his conviction that nothing lasts.

Herball or Generall Historie of Plantes, see GERARD, J.

HERBERT, A(lan) P(atrick) (1890–1971), a writer of great versatility and humour, contributed to *Punch* for many years. His works include *The Secret Battle* (1919), a stirring account of the horrors of war; *Misleading Cases in the Common Law* (1929), which ridiculed some absurdities in court procedure; *A Book of Ballads* (1949); and *Independent Member* (1950), describing his experiences as MP for Oxford University (1935–50). Herbert campaigned for several causes, such as reform in the divorce laws (a theme treated in *Holy Deadlock*, 1934), re-

form in English spelling (in *What a Word*, 1935), improving author's rights, changes in the obscenity laws, and water-buses on the Thames. *Riverside Nights* (1926; a revue) and his best-known novel *The Water Gipsies* (1930) reflect his affection for the Thames. He was knighted in 1945. His autobiography, *My Life and Times*, appeared in 1970.

HERBERT, George (1593–1633), fifth son of Richard and Magdalen Herbert and younger brother of Lord *Herbert of Cherbury, was born in Montgomery into an old and prominent family. His father died when he was three, and in 1608 his mother, the friend and patron of *Donne, remarried Sir John Danvers, who was 20 years her junior. Educated at *Westminster School (?1604–9: he was elected a scholar in 1605), and Trinity College, Cambridge, where he was named King's Scholar in 1609, George published his first poems (two sets of memorial verses in Latin) in a volume mourning prince Henry's death in 1612. But he had already, according to his earliest biographer, I. *Walton, sent his mother at the start of 1610 a New Year's letter dedicating his poetic powers to God and enclosing two sonnets ('My God, where is that ancient heat towards thee?' and 'Sure, Lord, there is enough in thee to dry'). In 1616 he was elected a major fellow of Trinity, and in 1618 appointed reader in rhetoric. In 1620 he managed, after some lobbying, to procure election to the highly-regarded post of public orator at the university (holding it until his resignation in 1628). He seems at this period to have been rather proud and pushing, keen on making the acquaintance of the great and conscious of his distinction of birth. F. *Bacon and Donne were among his friends, and the public oratorship introduced him to men of influence at court. Although he was obliged, by the terms of his fellowship, to take orders within seven years, he seems to have gravitated towards a secular career, leaving his university duties to be performed by proxies. In 1624, and again in 1625, he represented Montgomery in Parliament. This fairly brief experience of worldly ambition seems, however, to have disillusioned him. He was ordained deacon, probably before the end of 1624, and installed in 1626 as a canon of Lincoln cathedral and prebendary of Leighton Bromswold in Huntingdonshire, near *Little Gidding, where *Ferrar, whom Herbert had known at Cambridge, had recently settled and established a religious community. Once installed, Herbert set about restoring the ruined church at Leighton, largely from his own resources. His mother, whom he greatly loved, died in 1627, and his *Memoriae matris sacrum* was published in the volume containing Donne's commemoration sermon. In March 1629 Herbert married his stepfather's cousin, Jane Danvers, and they adopted two orphaned nieces of

Herbert's. He became rector of Bemerton, near Salisbury, in April 1630, being ordained priest the following September. In his short priesthood he gained a reputation for humility, energy, and charity. He was also a keen musician, and would go twice a week to hear the singing in Salisbury cathedral which was, he said, 'Heaven upon earth'. He died of consumption shortly before his fortieth birthday. When he realized he was dying he sent his English poems to his friend Ferrar with instructions to publish them, if he thought they might 'turn to the advantage of any dejected soul', and otherwise to burn them. *The Temple*, containing nearly all his surviving English poems, was published in 1633, *Outlandish Proverbs* (a collection of foreign proverbs in translation), in 1640 (enlarged as *Jacula prudentum*, 1651), and Herbert's prose picture of the model country parson, *A Priest to the Temple*, in 1652, as part of *Herbert's Remains*. His translation of Luigi Cornaro's *Trattato de la vita sobria* appeared in 1634, and his 'Brief Notes' on Juan de Valdés's *Hundred and Ten Considerations* in 1638. He told Ferrar that his poems represented 'a picture of the many spiritual conflicts that have passed betwixt God and my soul, before I could subject mine to the will of Jesus my Master'. Their simple piety was much admired in the 17th cent., not least by Puritans, and 13 editions of *The Temple* came out between 1633 and 1679. In the 18th cent. Herbert went out of fashion, though J. *Wesley adapted some of his poems. The Romantic age saw a revival, and the appreciative notice in Coleridge's *Biographia Literaria* (1817) enhanced Herbert's reputation. Modern critics have noted the subtlety rather than the simplicity of his poems, seeing them as an attempt to express the ultimately ineffable complications of the spiritual life. The precise nature of Herbert's relationship to Calvinism has also generated debate. See *Works* (ed. F. E. Hutchinson, 1941); Amy M. Charles, *Life* (1977).

Herbert, Marmion, in *Venetia* by B. Disraeli.

HERBERT, Mary, see PEMBROKE.

HERBERT, Zbigniew (1924–   ), Polish poet, born in Lvov, whose predominantly political poetry has appeared in English as *Selected Poems* (1968, translated by *Milosz and Peter Dale Scott) and in another selection by John and Bogdana Carpenter, published 1977.

HERBERT of Cherbury, Edward, Lord (1582–1648), elder brother of G. *Herbert, was born in his maternal grandmother's house at Eyton-on-Severn, Shropshire, into one of the foremost families of the Welsh border. In 1596, aged 14, he was enrolled as gentleman commoner at University College, Oxford. In October of that year his father died, and Herbert became ward of Sir George Moore (later

*Donne's father-in-law). At 16 he was married to his cousin Mary, daughter of Sir William Herbert of St Julians, five years Edward's senior and heiress to her father's estates in England, Wales, and Ireland. By the time he was 21 the couple had had, he reports, 'divers children', of whom none survived him. He was created knight of the Bath in 1603. His adventures, from birth to 1624, are recounted by Herbert in his *Life*, a remarkable document, not least for its unabashed presentation of its author's martial valour, success with women, truthfulness, sweetness of breath, and other virtues. His family pride, fiery sense of honour, and readiness to fight duels also appear. Herbert aspired to a career in public service and spent much of the time from 1608 to 1618 in France, getting to know the French aristocracy and court. He also travelled in Italy and the Low Countries, fighting at the siege of Juliers (1610) where, as he recounts, he gallantly exposed himself to the enemy's fire when dared to do so by a French gentleman.

In 1619 he became ambassador to France, on *Buckingham's recommendation. His most famous philosophical work, *De Veritate*, was finished by 1623. Much to his chagrin he was recalled to London in 1624. Deeply in debt, he petitioned unsuccessfully for £3,000 expended in his public duties, for an English baronetcy, and for a seat on the Privy Council: all he got was the title of Lord Herbert of Castle Island in the Irish peerage. Although he joined Charles's council of war in 1629, becoming Baron Herbert of Cherbury, the recognition he felt he deserved still eluded him. To attract royal notice he wrote, in 1630, *The Expedition to the Isle of Rhé*, which tries to justify Buckingham's calamitous generalship, and in 1632 he began a detailed 'official' history of *Henry VIII's reign, assisted by Thomas Masters, which was published in 1649. At the outbreak of the civil war he retired to Montgomery Castle and declined to become involved. The castle was threatened by royalists in 1644, and he admitted a parliamentary garrison, under Sir Thomas Myddleton, in exchange for the return of his books, which had been seized. He moved to his London house in Queen Street, St Giles, and dedicated himself to the study of philosophy, supplementing his *De Veritate* with *De Causis Errorum* and *De Religione Laici*, both published in 1645, and writing besides *De Religione Gentilum* and his autobiography (begun in 1643). In 1647 he visited Gassendi in Paris. When archbishop *Ussher offered him the last sacrament Herbert replied, according to *Aubrey, 'If it did no good 'twould doe no hurt', whereupon Ussher refused it.

Herbert's *De Veritate* postulates that religion is common to all men and that, stripped of superfluous priestly accretions, it can be reduced to five universal innate ideas: that there is a God;

that he should be worshipped; that virtue and piety are essential to worship; that man should repent of his sins; and that there are rewards and punishments after this life. According to his autobiography Herbert, having completed this work, knelt and asked for a sign from heaven to instruct him whether to publish it or not, whereupon 'a Loud though yet Gentle noise' from a clear blue sky assured him that he should. *De Veritate* gained Herbert the title of father of English *Deism. It was widely read in the 17th cent., earning the attention and disagreement of Mersenne, Gassendi, *Descartes, and *Locke. Herbert also wrote poetry which is obscure and metrically contorted, evidently influenced by his friend Donne. According to *Jonson, Donne said that he wrote his epitaph on prince Henry ('Look to me, Faith; and look to my Faith, God') 'to match Sir Ed: Herbert in obscurenesse'. (See also METAPHYSICAL POETS.)

Life (ed. S. Lee, 1886, rev. 1906; and ed. J. M. Shuttleworth, 1976); *Poems English and Latin* (ed. G. C. Moore Smith, 1923); *De Veritate* (ed. and trans. M. H. Carré, 1937); *De Religione Laici* (ed. and trans. H. R. Hutcheson, 1944); R. D. Bedford, *The Defence of Truth* (1979).

HERD, David (1732–1810), a learned and modest Edinburgh clerk and antiquary, who produced in 1769 a collection of *Scots songs, which appeared in a two-volume revised version in 1776 as *Ancient and Modern Scottish Songs*. Unlike many of his contemporaries, Herd was faithful to the texts as he found them, and his section of 'fragments of comic and humorous songs' provided *Burns with many suggestions.

HERDER, Johann Gottfried (1744–1803), German philosopher and critic, who decisively influenced *Goethe during the latter's early *Sturm und Drang* period. He was an ardent collector of folk-song, publishing two volumes of *Volkslieder* (1778–9); an investigator of problems of language, *Über den Ursprung der Sprache* (*On the Origin of Language*, 1772); an enthusiastic critic of Shakespeare, essay in *Von deutscher Art und Kunst* (*Of German Art*, 1773); and a philosopher of history, *Ideen zur Philosophie der Geschichte der Menschheit* (*Ideas towards the Philosophy of Mankind*, 1784–91). As a philosopher Herder's chief contribution lay in his recognition of historical evolution.

HEREWARD THE WAKE (*fl.* 1070), a Lincolnshire outlaw, a legendary account of whose exploits is given by the 15th-cent. forger who calls himself Ingulf of Croyland in his *Gesta Herewardi*. He headed a rising of the English, aided by a Danish fleet, against William the Conqueror in 1070. He is said to have been pardoned by William and (according to *Gaimar) killed by Normans at Maine. C. *Kingsley tells a legendary version of the story of Hereward

and his wife Torfrida (1866). His mare was Swallow.

Hergest, *Red Book of,* see MABINOGION.

Hermengyld, in Chaucer's 'Man of Law's Tale' (see CANTERBURY TALES, 5), the wife of the constable of Northumberland, to the coast of which Constance is borne when set adrift on the sea.

Hermes Trismegistus, the 'thrice great Hermes' of Milton's *'Il Penseroso', the name given by the *Neoplatonists and the devotees of mysticism and alchemy to the Egyptian god Thoth, regarded as more or less identical with the Grecian Hermes, and as the author of all mystical doctrines. From the 3rd cent. onwards the name was applied to the author of various Neoplatonic writings, some of which have survived, notably the Ποιμάνδρης, a word of uncertain derivation used to signify the Divine Intelligence. This work, translated by *Ficino (*c.*1490) into Latin and by John Everard (1650) into English, made a notable impact on 16th- and 17th-cent. minds. Its influence cannot, however, be isolated from the general one exercised by the Neoplatonist, cabbalistic, and occultist tradition which had such a marked effect on writers like G. *Chapman (*The Teares of Peace*, 1609), H. *Vaughan, Sir T. *Browne, *Comenius, and the *Cambridge Platonists.

Hermeticism, a *Modernist trend in Italian poetry, practised by *Ungaretti, *Quasimodo and, later, *Gatto, Sereni, and Luzi. Influenced by French *Symbolism and the ideal of *la poésie pure*, it concentrated on extreme precision and intensity of language. This tended to obscurity and to drastic concision, focusing on a single image, isolating phrases or even simple words (compare *Imagism). Uneasily related to the poetics of *Marinetti, the formalism of the hermeticists allowed them to work through the Fascist period unscathed by political censorship; but this was later held against them by writers associating themselves with the Resistance.

Hermia, one of the two young heroines, the lover of Lysander, in Shakespeare's *A Midsummer Night's Dream*, the smaller in stature.

Hermione, (1) daughter of Menelaus and Helen, the wife first of Neoptolemus, then of Orestes; (2) in Shakespeare's *The Winter's Tale*, the wife of Leontes.

'Hermit, The, or Edwin and Angelina', a ballad by *Goldsmith, written 1764 and included in *The Vicar of Wakefield*. Angelina, benighted in the wilderness, and sorrowing for her lost Edwin, whom she believes dead, is welcomed to the Hermit's cell and in answer to his question reveals the cause of her sorrow. Whereupon the Hermit acknowledges himself to be Edwin. (See BALLAD.)

'The Hermit' is also the title of a poem by T. *Parnell.

Hermit of Hampole, see ROLLE, R.

Hermit of Warkworth, The, a Northumberland *ballad by T. *Percy.

Hermsprong, or Man as He is not, a novel by R. *Bage, published 1796.

Hermsprong, who as a boy and youth has been brought up among American Indians, finds himself in England in the conventional and wealthy circle of Lord Grondale. The originality of his views on, for instance, the equality of women or the class divisions of society shock the company in which he moves, and lead him into much trouble. He does not drink, play cards, or eat more than he strictly needs, and he fervently hopes that these indulgences, and the horrors of disease, will be kept away from the land of his boyhood. In the end his engaging manner and his manly, benevolent nature win him the hand of Lord Grondale's daughter. (See PRIMITIVISM.) There is a critical edition by S. Tave (1981).

Hernani (1830), a tragedy by V. *Hugo, one of the landmarks of French *Romanticism and the source of *Verdi's opera *Ernani*.

Herne the Hunter, a spectral hunter said to have been in medieval times a keeper in Windsor Forest, who hanged himself from the tree known as Herne's (or, later, Falstaff's) oak, and thereafter haunted the forest; the origins of the story are uncertain, though it bears some resemblance to the tale of the *Wild Huntsman, and a version of it is related by Mrs Page in *The Merry Wives of Windsor* (IV. iv). Falstaff dresses as Herne, for the denouement at Herne's oak. Herne also appears in *Ainsworth's historical romance *Windsor Castle* (1843), with vivid illustrations by *Cruikshank.

Hero, the beloved of Claudio in Shakespeare's *Much Ado about Nothing.*

Hero and Leander, the tragic story of Leander's love for Hero, the priestess of Aphrodite: he is drowned while swimming to her at night across the Hellespont, and she then in despair throws herself into the sea. This story has been made the subject of poems by *Marlowe and T. *Hood, and of a burlesque by T. *Nashe in his *Lenten Stuffe.*

HERODOTUS (*c*.480–*c*.425 BC), a Greek historian, often referred to as the 'father of history' since he was the first to collect his materials systematically, test their accuracy as far as he was able, and arrange them agreeably. His work, the first masterpiece of Greek prose, takes as its main theme the struggle between Asia and Europe which culminated in the Persian invasions of Greece. His 'fabulosities', as Sir T. *Browne called them, provided material for miscellanists

like *Painter (1567–8) and Thomas Miller (1613–19) and later for *Landor in some early works, for Beddoes in *Death's Jest Book* and for M. *Arnold's 'Mycerinus' (1849).

Heroes, Hero-worship and the Heroic in History, On, a course of six lectures by T. *Carlyle, delivered 1840, published 1841. In this series Carlyle elaborates his view that 'Universal History, the history of what man has accomplished in this world, is at bottom the History of . . . Great Men', and chooses for his examples The Hero as Divinity (e.g. Odin, the 'Type Norseman'); The Hero as Prophet (e.g. *Muhammad); The Hero as Poet (e.g. *Dante, Shakespeare); the Hero as Priest (e.g. *Luther, *Knox); The Hero as Man of Letters (e.g. Dr *Johnson, *Rousseau, *Burns); and The Hero as King (e.g. *Cromwell, Napoleon).

Heroic Couplet, a pair of rhymed lines of iambic pentameter. The form was introduced into English by *Chaucer, and widely used subsequently, reaching a height of popularity and sophistication in the works of *Dryden and *Pope.

Heroic Poetry, the same as *Epic.

Heroic Verse, that used in *epic poetry: in Greek and Latin poetry, the hexameter; in English, the iambic of five feet or ten syllables; in French, the alexandrine of twelve syllables.

HERRICK, Robert (1591–1674), seventh child of Nicholas Herrick, a prosperous goldsmith who migrated to London from Leicester, and of Julian, daughter of a London mercer, William Stone, whom Nicholas married in 1582. In Nov. 1592, 16 months after Robert's birth, and two days after making his will, Herrick's father fell to his death from a fourth-floor window in his London house. Suicide was suspected, but being 'moved with charity' the Queen's Almoner did not confiscate the Herrick estate for the crown, as was usual with suicides. There is no record of Robert attending school, but the family was wealthy and the classical bent of his poetry makes it likely he had a grammar-school education. In 1607 he was apprenticed to his uncle Sir William Herrick, goldsmith, a man of mark who was MP for Leicester, owned land in 13 counties, and had been knighted in 1605. Herrick's earliest datable poem was written about 1610 to his brother Thomas on his leaving London to farm in Leicestershire ('A Country Life: To his Brother M. Tho. Herrick'). 'To my dearest Sister M. Mercie Herrick' must also have been written before 1612.

In 1613, having obtained release from his apprenticeship, he entered St John's College, Cambridge, as a fellow commoner, a status reserved for sons of wealthy families, which entailed double fees and privileges such as dining at high table. He lived lavishly at university and, despite his private income, frequently sent to his uncle William for additional funds. College friends included Clipsby Crew (knighted 1620) to whom he addressed several poems including the outstanding 'Nuptiall Song'. Herrick moved to Trinity Hall, perhaps to cut down expenses, graduating BA in 1617, MA in 1620. In 1623 he was ordained priest. He evidently mixed with literary circles in London, particularly the group around *Jonson, and was well known as a poet by 1625 when Richard James in 'The Muses' Dirge' ranked him beside Jonson and *Drayton. Friends included *Fletcher, W. *Browne, *Selden, *Corbett, Mildmay Fane (second earl of Westmorland), and W. and H. *Lawes. In 1627 he was one of the army chaplains on the duke of *Buckingham's disastrous expedition to the Isle of Rhé, in aid of the Protestants of La Rochelle. In reward for his services he received the living of Dean Prior, a village deep in the south Devonshire countryside, taking up the living in Sept. 1630.

Repelled by the barren isolation of rural life at first, he developed, as his poems show, a feeling for folk customs and festivals like May Day and Harvest Home, which appealed partly because the Puritans tried to suppress them. He also made friends among the country gentry, writing poems to their daughters. He left Dean Prior for a period, without permission from his bishop, and lived in Westminster with Tomasin Parsons, daughter of a musician and 27 years younger than Herrick, by whom he may have had an illegitimate daughter. An ardent loyalist, Herrick was ejected from his living by Parliament in 1647 and returned to London, where the following year his poems Hesperides, together with his religious poems Noble Numbers, were published. During the Commonwealth he probably subsisted on the charity of his relations, and in 1660 was reinstated at Dean Prior where he remained for the rest of his life, writing, apparently, no more poems, and being buried in an unmarked grave in the churchyard. As late as 1810 villagers there could repeat some of his verses. According to local tradition, he kept a pet pig, which he taught to drink from a tankard, and one day threw his sermon at the congregation with a curse for their inattention.

Herrick's secular poems are mostly exercises in miniature, very highly polished (as comparison with surviving earlier versions shows) and employing meticulous displacements of syntax and word order so as to give diminutive, aesthetic grace to the great chaotic subjects—sex, transience, death—that obsess him. He is one of the finest English lyric poets, and has a faultless ear. *Swinburne, with little exaggeration, called him 'the greatest song-writer ever born of English race'. His religious poems have generally been derided as childish, but more recent scholarship has seen them as part of a calculated 17th-cent.

Anglican attempt to idealize childhood in face of the Puritan emphasis on the deadly corruption of the child, lost in original sin. See Works (ed. L. C. Martin, 1956); Complete Poetry (ed. J. Max Patrick, 1963); G. W. Scott, Robert Herrick (1974).

HERRICK, Robert (1868–1938), American novelist, born in Massachusetts. Among his best-known novels are The Master of the Inn (1908), Together (1908), One Woman's Life (1913), and Clark's Field (1914).

HERVEY, James (1714–58), rector of Collingtree and Weston Favell in Northamptonshire, was prominent in the early Methodist movement. His prose poems Meditations among the Tombs, Reflections on a Flower Garden, Contemplations on the Night, etc. (1746–7) were extremely popular, and bear some affinity to the works of the *Graveyard school.

HERVEY, John, Baron Hervey of Ickworth (1696–1743), as vice-chamberlain exercised great influence over Queen Caroline. He was a close friend of Lady M. W. *Montagu and collaborated with her in response to attacks from *Pope. He was satirized by Pope in various works from 1732 onwards, at first with mildness, as 'Lord Fanny', an idle versifier, and then with increasing bitterness in *The Dunciad and as *'Sporus' in the Epistle to Dr Arbuthnot ('this painted child of dirt, that stinks and stings'). He also appears in other works under the names Narcissus and Adonis; his effeminacy was a particular target. His Memoirs of the Reign of George II, first published in 1848, edited by J. W. *Croker, give a vivid satirical picture of the court. A new edition in 3 vols by R. Sedgwick was published in 1931.

HERZEN, Alexander Ivanovich (1812–70), leading Russian revolutionary thinker, born in Moscow, the son of a wealthy Russian nobleman. His early involvement in Radical politics led to two periods of exile in Russia. He emigrated to the west in 1847, at first to Italy, France, and Switzerland, and to London in 1852. The Romantic and idealist philosophy of *Goethe and *Schelling and the French Utopian socialism of *Proudhon were early influences on Herzen's thought. However, the failure of the revolutions of 1848 and the tragedies and turbulence of his private life deeply affected his political outlook. His disillusionment (described in From the Other Shore, 1850) led him to embrace a more nationalistic and agrarian kind of socialism. In London he established the first Free Russian Press (1853) and in 1857, with Ogarev, published The Polar Star and The Bell which were smuggled into Russia, where they became a major influence on Radical opinion towards the establishment of reform and emancipation of the serfs. His major work was his classic autobiography, *My Past and Thoughts* (1885), in which his personal life is interwoven with the development of his political ideology. Herzen also wrote an important critique of *Hegel from a Russian left standpoint; *Who is to Blame* (1847, one of two novels); numerous essays on historical, philosophical, and political subjects; and short stories.

HESIOD (8th cent. BC), an early Greek epic poet, the reputed author of three surviving poems, which may however be by different hands, the products of a school rather than of a single author living in Boeotia. The *Theogony* contains an account of the origins of the world and the genealogy of the gods. *Works and Days* gives an account of a farmer's life that was to serve *Virgil for a model in the *Georgics*. The *Shield of Heracles*, modelled on *Homer's *Shield of Achilles*, is a poor piece of work. There are references to Hesiod in *Sidney, *Chapman, and *Dryden, and both *Spenser and *Milton made use of him.

Hesperides, see HERRICK, R.

HESSE, Hermann (1877–1962), German author of several novels of a more or less mystical nature which attracted a revival of interest in Germany and Britain in the 1960s. *Siddhartha* (1922) is a novel of oriental mysticism, describing the spiritual quest of two Hindu friends, and *Der Steppenwolf* (1927) came into vogue with the cult of 'the outsider' initiated in part by C. *Wilson. The latter reflects Hesse's interest in double personalities (a legacy of *Romanticism also connected with Hesse's interest in psychoanalysis). *Narziss und Goldmund* (1930) is a surrealist work set in the Middle Ages and *Das Glasperlenspiel* (*The Glass Bead Game*, 1943), Hesse's last novel, envisages a philosophical Utopia under the control of a quasi-monastic élite. Hesse was awarded the *Nobel Prize for literature in 1946.

Hetty Sorrel, a character in G. Eliot's *Adam Bede*.

HEWLETT, Maurice Henry (1861–1923), novelist, poet, and essayist, became known for his romantic novel of the Middle Ages, *The Forest Lovers* (1898), which was followed by other historical novels, including *The Queen's Quair* (1904); three books, *Halfway House* (1908), *The Open Country* (1909), and *Rest Harrow* (1910), of which the imaginary gypsy scholar John Maxwell Senhouse is the central figure; and various volumes of poetry, including *The Song of the Plow* (1916), a long poem which recounts the history of the 'governed race' in England and particularly of Hodge, the agricultural labourer, from the Norman conquest. He joined the *Fabian Society in 1917, and worked on a report on wages for the Board of Agriculture. Many of his essays (*In a green shade*, 1920; *Wiltshire Essays*, 1921; etc.) describe country life in Wiltshire, where he spent much of his life.

Hexameter, a verse of six metrical feet, which in the typical form consists of five dactyls and a trochee or spondee; for any of the dactyls a spondee may be substituted, except in the fifth foot, where a spondee is rare. It is not frequently used in English, but has sometimes been employed, as in *Clough's *The Bothie of Toberna-Vuolich*, to considerable effect. (See METRE.)

Hexapla, see BIBLE.

HEYER, Georgette (1902–74), writer of detective stories and *historical novels; she was best known for her Regency romances, which included *Devil's Cub* (1934), *Regency Buck* (1935), and *Faro's Daughter* (1941).

Hey for Honesty, Down with Knavery, a comedy by T. *Randolph, printed 1651.

'Chremylus, an honest decayed gentleman, willing to become rich, repaireth to the oracle of Apollo, to inquire how he might compass his design. The oracle enjoineth him to follow that man whom he first met with, and never part from his company. The man whom he met is the old blind God of Wealth disguised. After this Chremylus calleth his poor (but honest) neighbours to partake of his happiness. The honest party rejoice at the news; rascals only and vicious persons are discontented. Plutus is led to the temple of Esculapius and recovers his eyesight. At this knaves are even mad, they murmur and complain exceedingly. Nay the pope himself is even starved. Lastly to vex them more, the God of Wealth is introduced, married to Honesty' (Argument prefixed to the play). The play is a free adaptation of *Aristophanes' *Plutus*, and contains interesting allusions to current events and recent plays, including mentions of *Falstaff, *Hamlet's ghost, and Shakespeare himself.

HEYLYN, Peter (1600–62), was an Anglican controversialist and writer of ecclesiastical history, whose works include a defence of *Laud (*Cyprianus Anglicus*, 1668), histories of the Reformation (1661) and Presbyterianism (1670), and a *Cosmographie* (1652).

HEYWOOD, John (?1497–?1580), was probably born in London. He married Elizabeth Rastell, niece of Sir T. *More. Under *Henry VIII he was a singer and player on the virginals. He was much favoured by Queen Mary, and on her death withdrew to Malines, and afterwards to Antwerp and Louvain. He published *interludes, substituting the human comedy of contemporary types for the allegory and instructive purpose of the *morality; but he did this in the form of narrative and debate rather than of plot and action. His principal works were *The Four P's*, first printed ?1545, *The*

Play of the Wether (1533), in which Jupiter takes the conflicting opinions of various persons regarding the kind of weather to be supplied, and *A Play of Love* (1533). He may also have been the author of *The Pardoner and the Frere* and *Johan Johan the husbande, Tyb his wyfe & syr Jhān the preest*, comedies of a wider scope. Heywood also wrote a dialogue called *Witty and Witless*, collections of proverbs and epigrams, and a long satirical poem, *The Spider and the Flie* (1556).

HEYWOOD, Thomas (?1574–1641), dramatist, a Lincolnshire man, and a student at Cambridge. He was writing for *Henslowe's Admiral's Men in 1596, and later became a leading dramatist of Queen Anne's and Lady Elizabeth's Men at the Red Bull and Cockpit theatres. He claimed to have written over 200 plays, many of which are lost; his chief strength lay in domestic drama. His best plays are *A Woman Killed with Kindness* (acted 1603, printed 1607), *The Fair Maid of the West* (printed 1631), and *The English Traveller* (printed 1633). His other chief plays were *The Four Prentices of London* (produced *c*.1600, printed 1615), ridiculed in Beaumont's *Knight of the Burning Pestle* (?1607); *Edward IV* (two parts, 1599); *The Rape of Lucrece* (1608); *The Royal King and the Loyal Subject* (printed 1637); *The Wise Woman of Hogsdon* (*c*.1604, printed 1638); and perhaps the *Fair Maid of the Exchange* (printed 1607), whose attribution is questioned. *The Golden Age* (1611), *The Brazen Age* and *The Silver Age* (1613), and *The Iron Age* (two parts, 1632) are a panoramic dramatization of classical mythology. His *An Apology for Actors* (1612) is the best Jacobean summary of traditional arguments in defence of the stage, and has some good anecdotes. He also published poems (including *The Hierarchy of the Blessed Angels*, 1635), translations, and pageants for seven Lord Mayor's shows. Two plays, *The Captives* (1624) and *The Escapes of Jupiter* (a mildly erotic cut version of the golden and silver *Ages*), survive in his own hand.

Hiawatha, *The Song of*, a narrative poem in unrhymed trochaic tetrameter, by *Longfellow, published 1855, reproducing American Indian stories which centre in the life and death of Hiawatha, reared by his grandmother Nokomis on the shores of Lake Superior. He marries Minnehaha ('laughing water'), the Dacotah maiden, and after various adventures departs for the Isles of the Blest to rule the kingdom of the Northwest Wind. Longfellow took nothing but the name from the historical figure of Hiawatha (*fl. c*.1570), an Indian statesman, probably a Mohawk. The poem's incantatory metre and novel subject matter made it immensely popular, and attracted many parodies and imitations.

Hibernia, one of the Latin names for Ireland,

*Ptolemy's Ἰουερνία, a corruption of 'Iverna', the equivalent of an old Celtic word, whence 'Erin' is derived. *Claudian used the form 'Ierne'.

HICHENS, Robert Smythe (1864–1950), novelist, short story writer, and music critic, remembered for *The Green Carnation* (1894), a sub-Wildean novel of fashionable London society, and for the best-selling *The Garden of Allah* (1904), a romance of the desert set in North Africa.

HICKES, George (1642–1715), Anglo-Saxon scholar and non-juring divine, and a passionate controversialist. He was the acknowledged leader of the first great generation of Anglo-Saxon scholars which included the *Elstobs, *Wanley, William Nicholson (1655–1727), and Edmund Gibson (1669–1748). He published the first Anglo-Saxon grammar in 1689. The climax of his work was the *Linguarum Veterum Septentrionalium Thesaurus*—the Treasury of the Northern Tongues (1703–5), a comparative grammar of Old English and the related Germanic tongues, for which he acquainted himself with almost every Teutonic manuscript of northern Europe. Its examination of the manuscript sources of Anglo-Saxon history had a deep influence upon the study of the whole Old English past. See D. C. Douglas, *English Scholars* (1939).

HICKEY, William (?1749–1830), son of the Joseph Hickey who figures in Goldsmith's *Retaliation, was the author of entertaining *Memoirs*, 1749–1809 (first published 1913–25), in which he describes his numerous voyages to India and other parts of the world, his chequered career as an attorney, and, with great frankness, his weakness for women and claret.

Hieroglyphics, the characters used in writing by the ancient Egyptians, consisting of figures of objects representing (directly or figuratively) words or parts of words. They were first interpreted by Jean François Champollion (1790–1832). The term is also used of the picture-writing of other peoples.

Hieronimo, the principal character in Kyd's *The Spanish Tragedy*.

HIERONYMUS, see JEROME, ST.

Higden, Mrs Betty, a character in Dickens's *Our Mutual Friend*.

HIGDEN, Ranulf (d. 1364), a Benedictine of St Werburg's, Chester, credited by popular tradition with the composition of the Chester Cycle of *Mystery Plays. He wrote in Latin prose *Polychronicon*, a universal history extending down to 1327, which was translated by John of *Trevisa in 1387 and printed by *Caxton in 1482. It was very popular in the 14th cent. and influenced such works as the *Stanzaic Life of Christ.

HIGGINS, Frederick Robert (1896–1941), Irish lyric poet, whose volumes of poetry include *Island Blood* (1925, with a foreword by 'Æ', G. W. *Russell), *The Dark Breed* (1927), and *Arable Holdings* (1933); most of his poems deal with rural life, landscape, and legend.

Higgins, Henry, the phonetician in Shaw's *Pygmalion*, modelled on H. *Sweet.

HIGGINS, Matthew James (1810–68), known as 'Jacob Omnium', a prominent journalist who contributed to *The Times*, *Punch*, and the *Cornhill Magazine*; his articles, which often exposed abuses of social and public life, brought him into contact with *Thackeray, who dedicated his *Adventures of Philip* to Higgins. His *Essays on Social Subjects* was published in 1875.

Highland Widow, The, a short, tragic tale by Sir W. *Scott, one of the stories in *The Chronicles of the Canongate*, published 1827.

The story, told by Mrs Bethune Baliol to Chrystal Croftangry, is that of the widow of MacTavish Mhor, one of the last of the Highland caterans, killed by 'red soldiers' after the '45. She lives a lonely life in the mountains with her infant son, and when he grows to manhood expects to see him revive the feats and mode of life of his cateran father. The son, who adds common sense and some knowledge of the world to a brave heart, enlists instead for active service in a regiment going to America. At first incredulous, then indignant at what she considers a base surrender, the widow contrives by a sleeping potion to make him outstay his leave, and then taunts him into killing the Cameron sergeant who comes to arrest him. He is shot as a deserter and a murderer, and the mother spends her remaining years in misery and remorse, and disappears to die, like a wild beast, where none may see her.

High Life above Stairs, the subtitle of *Bon Ton*, a farce by *Garrick.

High Life below Stairs, a comedy by the Revd J. *Townley, produced 1759.

Lovel, a rich young West Indian merchant, receives warning that he is being outrageously robbed by his servants. He pretends to go to Devonshire, but returns, assumes the character of a country lad who seeks to be trained as a servant, and obtains employment under his own butler. We are presented with the gay doings below stairs, in which the servants ape the vices and follies of their masters until, the iniquities of most of his staff having been revealed to him, Lovel reveals himself and packs them off. *Wordsworth, who saw the play performed in London in 1812, wrote to his wife describing

it as 'very entertaining; it is an excellent Piece' (*The Love Letters of William and Mary Wordsworth*, 1982).

HIGHSMITH, Patricia (1921–), writer of mixed German and English–Scots parentage, educated at Barnard College and Columbia University, New York. Her stylish crime novels have a distinctively black humour: the best-known (*The Talented Mr Ripley*, 1956; *Ripley Under Ground*, 1971; *Ripley's Game*, 1974, etc.) feature her amoral anti-hero, the leisure-loving amateur villain Tom Ripley, like the author resident in France.

Hildebrandslied, a 68-line fragment of an alliterative poem in Old High German, thought to date from about 800, consisting of a dialogue between Hildebrand, a follower of Theodoric, who is returning home after many years' absence, and a young knight who challenges him. Hildebrand tries to avert a fight but fails; and, just as it transpires that the young knight is Hadubrand, the son of Hildebrand, the poem breaks off. The text is in Klaeber's *Beowulf* (App. 4, pp. 290–2).

HILL, Aaron (1685–1750), poet, dramatist, theatre-manager, and projector, wrote a much criticized history of the Ottoman Empire (1709), the libretto for *Handel's *Rinaldo* (1711), and an unfinished epic poem, *Gideon* (1749). He was satirized by Pope in *The Dunciad* and elsewhere, and responded in *The Progress of Wit* (1730). He was responsible for launching *The Plain Dealer* (1724), a bi-weekly, and also dabbled in various commercial concerns, such as clearing the river Spey of rocks and manufacturing potash at Plaistow. He had a wide circle of literary friends, including *Dyer, Charles *Churchill, and James *Thomson, and *A Collection of letters between Mr Aaron Hill, Pope and Others* (1751) is an interesting record of the period. He also edited with *Popple a bi-weekly theatrical periodical *The Prompter* (1734–6; selection ed. W. Appleton and K. A. Burnim, 1966).

HILL, (John Edward) Christopher (1912–), Marxist historian, educated at St Peter's School, York, and Balliol College, Oxford; he was for many years a fellow, then (1965–78) master of Balliol. His many works on the period of the Civil War include *The World Turned Upside Down; Radical Ideas during the English Revolution* (1972), which provides a lively introduction to the prose of many of the lesser known and radical writers of the period, including *Clarkson, *Coppe, *Walwyn, *Winstanley, and the anonymous author of *Tyranipocrit Discovered*. He also edited the works of Winstanley, and has written studies of *Cromwell (*God's Englishman*, 1970) and *Milton (*Milton and the English Revolution*, 1978).

HILL, Geoffrey (1932–   ), poet and lecturer, born in Bromsgrove and educated there and at Keble College, Oxford. His first volume of poetry was *For the Unfallen* (1959), followed by *King Log* (1968), *Mercian Hymns* (1971), which consists of prose poems celebrating Offa, 'a presiding genius of the West Midlands', and *Tenebrae* (1978). His early works show the influence of *Blake and A. E. *Housman; his language is rich and complex, and his themes predominantly historical and religious, many of the poems brooding over the violence of the near and distant past. His long poem *The Mystery of the Charity of Charles Péguy* (1983) is a densely allusive meditation on the life, faith, and death of the French poet *Péguy.

HILL, G(eorge) B(irkbeck Norman) (1835–1903), educated at Pembroke College, Oxford, is chiefly remembered as the editor of Dr *Johnson. After his resignation as a headmaster in 1869 he wrote for the *Saturday Review* and began work on Johnson and other 18th-cent. writers. *Dr Johnson, his Friends and Critics* appeared in 1878, and a *Life of Rowland Hill* in 1880. *Jowett's encouragement led to a six-vol. edition in 1887 of Boswell's *Life of *Johnson*, generally regarded as a masterpiece of editing. This was followed by editions of *Johnson's Letters* (1892), *Miscellanies* (1897), and *Lives of the Poets* (1905). He also edited the letters of *Swift, wrote a memoir of *Gibbon, and produced editions of the works of *Goldsmith and *Chesterfield.

HILLIARD, Nicholas (*c.*1547–1619), miniaturist, patronized by *Elizabeth I from the early 1570s and later by James I. His gorgeously patterned portraits of the queen and of courtiers perfectly evoke the poetic mythology that surrounded the Virgin Queen. His miniatures, which often bear inscriptions and emblems, played a part in the ceremonies of love at the Elizabethan court; his famous *An unknown youth leaning against a tree amongst roses* (London, Victoria and Albert Museum) suggests the fresh, delicate beauty of the Elizabethan lyric. Hilliard was the first British painter who won widespread fame and was accepted as an equal by a cultivated society; he was eulogized by contemporary poets, including *Constable and *Donne. Between 1589 and 1603 he wrote a treatise, the *Art of Limning*, influenced by *Alberti, Lomazzo, and *Castiglione's *Book of the Courtier*; Hilliard argues that limning is a noble art, 'fittest for gentlemen'. The treatise mentions an artistic discussion with Sir P. *Sidney, and a conversation about shadow with Elizabeth I. The subtlety of expression he sought is apparent in a beautiful passage where he describes how carefully the miniaturist must watch the delicate movements of the eyes, mouth, and nostrils, and how the 'curious drawer' must capture 'these

lovely graces, witty smilings, and these stolen glances which suddenly, like lightning, pass and another countenance taketh place'. Hilliard found the more prosaic court of James I less stimulating, and his art declines after 1600.

HILTON, James (1900–54), novelist, remembered principally for *Lost Horizon* (1933), set in the Tibetan lamasery of Shangri-La where the inmates enjoy perpetual youth, and *Good-bye Mr Chips* (1934), a novella about an ageing schoolmaster. Hilton became a Hollywood scriptwriter and died in California.

HILTON, Walter (d. 1396), an Augustinian canon of Trurgarton, near Newark, in Nottinghamshire, the mystical author of *The Scale of Perfection* and perhaps of a number of lesser works (see D. Jones, *Minor Works of Walter Hilton*, 1929). The *Scale*, which is addressed to a single woman recluse, has some things in common with *Rolle and *The Cloud of Unknowing* (Hilton used to be considered as a possible author of the latter), but it is the most approachable and least esoteric of the celebrated 14th-cent. English mystical texts. It was edited by E. Guy (1869) and translated by G. Sitwell (1953).

Hind and the Panther, The, a poem by *Dryden, published 1687.

Dryden became a Catholic in 1685, and the poem represents an attempt to reconcile Anglican and Catholic political interests, while at the same time defending Catholic doctrine. The first part describes various religious sects under the guise of different beasts, and in particular the Catholic Church and the Church of England as the Hind and the Panther respectively. The second part is occupied with arguments about Church authority and transubstantiation, issues full of political as well as ecclesiological implications. This leads into the third part, which constitutes half the poem, and is designed to recommend a political alliance between both Churches and the Crown against Whigs and Dissenters. It contains two celebrated fables, that of the swallows and that of the doves. However the balance of the latter, and so of the whole poem, may have been upset by James II's Second Declaration of Indulgence which appealed to dissenting Protestant sects over the heads of the Anglican establishment.

HINMAN, Charlton (1911–77), a modern pioneer in the study of Shakespeare's texts. His two-vol. *The Printing and Proof-reading of the First Folio* (1963) offers a detailed analysis of how the *Folio was printed, based on a close comparison of 80 copies of the First Folio in the Folger Library aided by a machine of his own invention, the Hinman Collator. In particular, his work has shown how the shares of individual compositors who set up the type in different sections may be distinguished and characterized.

HIPPOCRATES (*c*.460–357 BC), born in the island of Cos, one of the Cyclades, the most celebrated physician of antiquity. Of the *Corpus Hippocraticum*, or collection of Greek medical works of various dates which have come down to us, only a small portion can be attributed to Hippocrates himself. One of the most interesting parts of it is the ethical doctrine of the medical profession, the 'Hippocratic Oath'. It is given on p. 213 of *The Legacy of Greece* (ed. R. Livingstone, 1921).

Hippolyta, a queen of the Amazons given in marriage to *Theseus by Hercules, who had conquered her and taken away her girdle, the achievement being one of his twelve labours. She had a son by Theseus called *Hippolytus. According to another version she was slain by Hercules, and it was her sister Antiope that was the wife of Theseus. She and Theseus frame the action in Shakespeare's *A Midsummer Night's Dream.*

Hippolytus, a son of *Theseus and *Hippolyta. The fatal passion of Phaedra for her stepson Hippolytus is the subject of one of *Racine's dramas, *Phèdre.*

Hispalis, in imprints, Seville.

Historia Britonum, see NENNIUS.

Historia Ecclesiastica Gentis Anglorum, the most famous work of *Bede, was finished in 731. It is a Latin history of the English people, in five books, from the invasion of Julius Caesar, beginning with a description of Britain and ending with an account of the state of the country in 731. The author draws on *Pliny and other Latin authors, and on *Gildas and probably the *Historia Britonum* of *Nennius. In the second book, in connection with the consultation between Edwin of Northumbria and his nobles whether they shall accept the gospel as preached by Paulinus, occurs the famous simile of the life of man as a sparrow flying out of the night into the lighted hall, and out again into the night. There is a version of this in *Wordsworth's *Ecclesiastical Sonnets*, entitled 'Persuasion'. The *Historia* was translated into Old English in the 890s, in the course of the programme of translations inaugurated by *Alfred. There is a modern trans. by L. Sherley-Price (1955).

Historical Novel, a novel set in a period before the birth of the author, and often containing not only fictional but historical people and/or events. In serious work there is a real attempt at accuracy and credibility. In England the form developed largely from *La Fayette's *Princesse de Clèves* (1678) through the *Gothic novel to M. Edgeworth's *Castle Rackrent* (1800) and *Adelaide* (1806), and J. Porter's *The Scottish Chiefs* (1810), culminating in *Waverley* (1814) by Sir W. Scott. *Scott, who acknowledged his

debt to *Edgeworth, established the form so emphatically that its influence spread throughout Europe, and it continued to flourish for the rest of the century in England, in the works of *Thackeray, *Dickens, *Bulwer-Lytton, *Reade, *Kingsley, G. *Eliot, *Hardy, and many others. (See *Lukács, *The Historical Novel*, English trans. 1962, for a discussion of the changes in historical awareness that created the historical novel of Scott, and an account of its evolution through *Pushkin, *Balzac, *Stendhal, F. *Cooper, *Tolstoy, T. *Mann, etc.) The attraction of the form has now greatly declined, except in the popular market, where G. *Heyer succeeded such writers as *Orczy, *Weyman, and *Hewlett; but the form has also been successfully used by writers as diverse as M. *Renault, N. *Mitchison, W. *Golding, and J. G. *Farrell. Documentary fiction which mingles fact and fiction (see FACTION) may be seen as an extension of the historical novel.

Historical Society, see ROYAL HISTORICAL SOCIETY.

Historic Doubts on . . . Richard III, see WALPOLE, HORACE.

History Man, The, see BRADBURY, M.

History of Henry Esmond, Esquire, The, a novel by *Thackeray, published 1852.
   Henry Esmond, who narrates his own story, mainly in the third person, is the (supposed illegitimate) son of the third Viscount Castlewood, who dies at the battle of the Boyne. Henry, a serious, lonely boy, continues to live at Castlewood House under the protection of the fourth viscount, his father's cousin, and his young wife Rachel. The couple have two children, Frank, the heir, and Beatrix, a beautiful but wilful girl. Henry is devoted to Lady Castlewood, who treats him with much kindness. The Castlewoods become estranged after Lady Castlewood catches smallpox, inadvertently brought to the household by Henry, and loses much of her beauty. The wicked Lord Mohun takes advantage of Castlewood's neglect of his wife to attempt to seduce her. There is a duel and Castlewood is killed. On his deathbed he reveals to Henry that he is in fact legitimate and the rightful heir, but Henry keeps silent for the sake of Lady Castlewood and her son. He is imprisoned for a year for having acted as Castlewood's second in the duel, for which Lady Castlewood bitterly reproaches him, and on his release joins the army and fights in the war of the Spanish Succession. On a visit to England he is reconciled to Lady Castlewood, who is secretly in love with him, and falls in love with Beatrix, now grown up. But Beatrix is too ambitious to consider a man who has no fortune or position in society. Henry goes back to the wars and fights in Marlborough's Flemish campaign.

The wayward Beatrix becomes engaged, first to Lord Ashburnham, then to the much older duke of Hamilton, who fights a duel with Lord Mohun, in which both are killed. Beatrix and her brother Frank, now the fifth viscount, are ardent Jacobites, and Esmond becomes involved with them in a plot to restore James Edward Stuart, the Old Pretender, to the throne on the death of Queen Anne. The plot fails because Beatrix is carrying on an intrigue with the Pretender, and at the moment when he should be in London he is at Castlewood, 'dangling after Trix'. Esmond, disillusioned with Beatrix and the Jacobite cause, marries her mother Rachel and they emigrate to Virginia. The later history of the family in America and England is told in *The Virginians.

History of the Decline and Fall of the Roman Empire, The, see DECLINE AND FALL OF THE ROMAN EMPIRE.

History of the Rebellion and Civil Wars, see CLARENDON.

History Today, a historical magazine with illustrations, aimed at the general reader, launched in 1951, and edited from 1951 to 1979 by P. *Quennell and Alan Hodge (1915–79). Contributors have included A. L. *Rowse, G. D. H. *Cole, J. *Hawkes, L. B. *Namier, K. *Clark, and many others.

Histriomastix, see PRYNNE, W.

HITLER, Adolf (1889–1945), an Austrian by birth. He became leader of the German National Socialist (Nazi) Party after the First World War, was appointed chancellor of the Reich by Hindenburg in 1933, and succeeded him as president the following year. As dictator (Führer) of Germany he pursued the policy outlined in his political manifesto *Mein Kampf* (2 vols, 1925, 1926; English trans. 1939, by J. Murphy) of flouting the Versailles Treaty and rearming, of national economic self-sufficiency, suppression of trade unions, and persecution of the Jews.

He seized Austria by force in 1938 and Czechoslovakia in March 1939, and finally, by attacking Poland on 1 Sept. 1939, caused the outbreak of the war with Britain and France. After overrunning France in 1940 and Greece in 1941, he attacked Russia. He took over the supreme military command in 1942, escaped a plot to kill him in 1944, and is believed to have perished during the Russian attack on Berlin of 30 April 1945.

See Alan Bullock, *Hitler: A Study in Tyranny* (1952, rev. 1962).

HOADLY, Benjamin (1676–1761), bishop successively of Bangor, Hereford, Salisbury, and Winchester, a Low Church divine much in favour with the Whigs and Queen Caroline, whose famous sermon 'The Nature of the Kingdom or

Church of Christ' (1717) initiated the *Bangorian Controversy.

HOADLY, Dr Benjamin (1706–57), son of Bishop Hoadly (above). He was a physician and (with his brother) the author of one comedy, *The Suspicious Husband* (1747).

HOBBES, John Oliver (1867–1906), the pseudonym of Mrs Pearl Mary Teresa Craigie, began writing articles and criticisms for various journals. After an unhappy marriage she turned to Roman Catholicism, adding 'Mary Teresa' to her name. Her first novel, *Some Emotions and a Moral* (1891), established her reputation as a serious novelist. Others followed including *The Sinner's Comedy* (1892), *Robert Orange* (1899), *The Serious Wooing* (1901), and several plays, the most successful of which was *The Ambassador* (1898). She also wrote critical essays on G. *Eliot (1901, for the 10th edn of *EB*) and G. *Sand (1902).

HOBBES, Thomas (1588–1679), philosopher, was born at Malmesbury and educated at Magdalen Hall, Oxford. For a great part of his life he was in the service of the Cavendish family, and in 1647 was appointed mathematical tutor to the prince of Wales. At some time (probably between 1621 and 1626) he was in contact with F. *Bacon, translated some of his essays into Latin, and took down his thoughts from his dictation. On three occasions he travelled on the Continent with a pupil, and met *Galileo, Gassendi, *Descartes, and the French mathematician Mersenne. On his return to England he submitted to the Council of State in 1652, and was pensioned after the Restoration. He was intimate with G. *Harvey, *Jonson, *Cowley, and *Godolphin.

As a philosopher Hobbes resembles Bacon in the practical or utilitarian importance that he attaches to knowledge. Nature and man are the objects of his enquiry. But he does not share Bacon's enthusiasm for the inductive method; he regards science as essentially deductive, and the geometrical method of demonstration as the true scientific method. Hobbes has been generally described as a nominalist, owing to the importance he attaches to the definition of the meaning of terms. But he does not deny the reality of the common element entitling things to the same name. The basis of all knowledge, according to him, is sensation, and the causes of all sensations are the 'several motions of matter, by which it presseth on our various organs diversely'. Motion is the one universal cause, and our appetites are our reactions, in the direction of self-preservation, to external motions. Accordingly man is essentially a selfish unit. Upon this theory Hobbes bases the political philosophy expounded in *De Corpore Politico* (1650, originally *Elements of Law*), *De Cive* (Latin 1642, English 1651), and *Leviathan*

(English 1651, definitive Latin text 1668). This brought him into general disfavour on both political and religious grounds; and, indeed, the royalists had some reason to regard *Leviathan* as designed to induce *Cromwell to take the crown.

Hobbes's philosophical works, founded on a comprehensive plan in which matter, human nature, and society were successively to be dealt with, include *Human Nature* (1650), *De Corpore* (Latin 1655, English 1656), and *De Homine* (1658). (See J. W. N. Watkins, *Hobbes's System of Ideas*, 1965, and M. M. Goldsmith, *Hobbes's Science of Politics*, 1966.) He published a translation of *Thucydides in 1629, and of *Homer in quatrains (1674–5); also a sketch of the Civil Wars, *Behemoth, or the Long Parliament* (1680), which was suppressed. His reply to *D'Avenant's dedication of *Gondibert, published in 1650, expresses his literary theory; he believes poetry 'should avert men from vice and incline them to virtuous and honourable actions', holds that 'Judgement begets the strength and structure, and Fancy . . . the ornaments of a Poem', and wittily applauds D'Avenant for neglecting the customary and in his view meaningless invocation of a Muse. His prose is masterly, distinguished by economy, directness, a highly effective use of metaphor, and passages of sustained and inventive irony, such as that in *Leviathan*, ch. 27, which compares the papacy with the kingdom of the fairies. The aphorism which expresses a central tenet of his philosophy, that the life of man in a state of nature is 'solitary, poore, nasty, brutish and short', has had an incalculable influence on later writers.

His complete works were edited by Sir William Molesworth (1839–45).

Hobbinol, in *Spenser's writings, the poet's friend G. *Harvey.

Hobbit, The, see TOLKIEN, J. R. R.

HOBHOUSE, John Cam (1786–1869), a politician, and close friend of Lord *Byron, one of whose executors he became. His *Imitations and Translations from the Ancient and Modern Classics* (1809) contains nine poems by Byron, with whom he travelled in Europe; his *Journey through Albania* (1813) describes the same journey that appears in Byron's *Childe Harold*. In 1818 he produced the 'Historical Illustrations' to Canto IV of that poem, and the Canto is dedicated to him. He was an adviser to John *Murray, who published most of Byron's work, and he ensured that Byron's *Memoirs* were burnt immediately after the poet's death. In 1865 appeared his *Recollections of a Long Life*, which contains much material relating to Byron.

HOBSBAUM, Philip Dennis (1932–   ), poet and lecturer, educated at Downing College, Cambridge. He was the founder of the *Group;

a poem by M. *Bell, 'Mr Hobsbaum's Monday Evening Meeting' celebrates its gatherings, over which: 'Below the ceiling, guardian of the Grail | The ghost of Dr Leavis floats.'

HOBSON, a Cambridge carrier, who 'sickened in the time of his vacancy, being forbidden to go to London by reason of the plague'. He died in Jan. 1630–1. *Milton wrote two epitaphs on him, and his name survives in the phrase 'Hobson's choice', which refers to his custom of letting out his horses in rotation, and not allowing his customers to choose among them. (See *Spectator, No. 509.)

HOBSON, Harold, see SUNDAY TIMES, THE.

Hobson's Choice (1916), by Harold Brighouse (1882–1958), the most successful and often revived play of the *Manchester School.

HOBY, Sir Thomas (1530–66), was educated at St John's College, Cambridge; from 1547 to 1555 he made frequent visits to the Continent and his notebook covering the years 1547–64, with interesting accounts of Italy, was published by the *Camden Society (1902). In 1552–3, while staying in Paris, he translated *Castiglione's *Il Cortegiano*, though his *The Courtyer* was not published until 1561. It became immediately popular, even being translated into Latin in 1577, and was an important influence on such writers as *Spenser, *Jonson, and Shakespeare. It was edited by W. *Raleigh (1900).

HOCCLEVE, or OCCLEVE, Thomas (?1369–1426), apart from *Lydgate the most significant named English poet of the 15th cent. He was a clerk in the office of the Privy Seal and, although most of his small corpus is taken up with moral writings, a significant part of his output describes (ostensibly at least) the events of his own life, in 'La Male Regle de Thomas Hoccleve', the prologue to *The Regiment of Princes* (1411–12), and in a number of his 'Series Poems', such as 'The Complaint' and 'The Dialogue with a Friend' (linked into a series by the device of an interchange with a friend who discusses the poems). Of his 'autobiographical' writings, the most interesting deal with his mental breakdown. Traditionally he has been regarded as a poor imitator of *Chaucer; more sympathetic recent accounts (such as that of Mitchell) examine him in his own right and find him less wanting.

Ed. in two EETS volumes (ES Nos. 61 and 73, by F. J. *Furnivall and I. *Gollancz, rev. A. I. Doyle and J. Mitchell 1970, and ES No. 72, 'The Regiment of Princes', etc. by F. J. Furnivall, 1897); convenient selections by M. C. Seymour (1981) and B. O'Donoghue (1982); J. Mitchell, *Thomas Hoccleve. A Study in Early Fifteenth-Century English Poetic* (1968).

Hock-Tuesday Play, an early English mimetic

performance, perhaps of ritual origin, representing the defeat of the Danes by the English. It was revived during the festival given to *Elizabeth I at Kenilworth in 1575, and knowledge of it is chiefly based on descriptions of this. Hock Tuesday, or Hocktide, is the third Tuesday after Easter Sunday.

Hodge, a familiar adaptation of Roger, used as a typical name for the English rustic. Also the name of Dr *Johnson's cat.

HODGSON, Ralph Edwin (1871–1962), born in Co. Durham, the son of a coalmerchant, was brought up in the south, where his lifelong love and observation of the natural world took root. He worked in the theatre in New York, then as an artist in London in the 1890s. His first collection of poems, *The Last Blackbird*, appeared in 1907, but his reputation was not established until 1917, when he published *Poems*, a volume which contains one of his most ambitious, visionary works, 'A Song of Honour'. In 1913 he founded a publishing house, 'The Sign of the Flying Fame', which had some influence on contemporary typography. Hodgson was much encouraged by friends such as *de la Mare, *Sassoon, and T. S. *Eliot, as well as by E. *Marsh who published some of his work in *Georgian Poetry*. He lectured in Japan, 1924–38, and spent the rest of his life in the US. *The Skylark and Other Poems*, which appeared in 1958, contained, among many shorter works, two important long poems; 'To Deck a Woman' (a new version of 'The Last Blackbird'), a passionate protest against man's cruelty to the animal world, and 'The Muse and the Mastiff'. The *Collected Poems* were published in 1961. The widely anthologized poems, which include 'Stupidity Street' and 'The Bells of Heaven', are not generally thought to do justice to the author of such poems as 'To vegetate', 'The Moor', 'Of Nature, write', and the longer poems.

HODGSON, Shadworth Holloway (1832–1912), educated at Rugby and Corpus Christi College, Oxford, devoted his life, after the death of his wife and child in 1858, to the study of philosophy. He regarded himself as continuing and improving on the work of *Hume and *Kant, and was the first president and leading spirit of the Aristotelian Society, whose proceedings contain many addresses by him.

HOFF, Harry Summerfield, see COOPER, W.

HOFFMANN, Ernst Theodor Amadeus (originally Wilhelm) (1776–1822), German Romantic writer and music critic. His works include the extravagantly fantastic *Phantasiestücke* (1814–15) and *Elixire des Teufels* (*The Devil's Elixir*, 1815–16). His stories and his wild unhappy life provided the inspiration for Offenbach's *Tales of Hoffmann*.

HOFFMANN, Heinrich (1809–74), German physician, author of the immortal *Struwwelpeter* (*Shock-head Peter*, 1847), written for the amusement of his children, and translated into several languages.

HOFMANNSTHAL, Hugo von (1874–1929), Austrian poet, dramatist, and essayist. Among his earlier plays are *Gestern* (*Yesterday*, 1891), *Der Tod des Tizian* (*The Death of Titian*, 1892), *Oedipus und die Sphinx* (*Oedipus and the Sphinx*, 1906). *Jedermann* (*Everyman*, 1912), a modernization of the old morality play destined to become a regular feature (originally in Max Reinhardt's production) of the Salzburg Festival (which Hofmannsthal helped to found), prefigures *Das Salzburger grosse Welttheater* (*The Great Salzburg World Theatre*, 1922) and inaugurated Hofmannsthal's increasing tendency towards a religious art with strongly Roman Catholic associations. He wrote the librettos for six of R. *Strauss's operas, including *Der Rosenkavalier* (1911), *Ariadne auf Naxos* (1912), and *Arabella* (1933), and his correspondence with Strauss is of both literary and musical interest. His last play *Der Turm* (*The Tower*, 1925), influenced (like some of his other works) by *Calderón, completed Hofmannsthal's development away from *fin-de-siècle* aestheticism to the idea of literature as carrying a social and religious message.

HOGARTH, David George (1862–1927), archaeologist and authority on Near Eastern affairs. From 1908 until his death he was keeper of the Ashmolean Museum at Oxford. His publications include *A Wandering Scholar in the Levant* (1896), *The Penetration of Arabia* (1904), and *The Life of C. M. Doughty* (1928). One of his disciples at Oxford was T. E. *Lawrence, who came very much under his influence and who was later to write of him, 'He is the man to whom I owe everything I have had since I was seventeen.' See P. Knightley and C. Simpson, *The Secret Lives of Lawrence of Arabia* (1969).

HOGARTH, William (1697–1764), British painter and engraver. He was apprenticed to a goldsmith and began engraving c.1720. In 1726 he designed 12 large engravings for Butler's *Hudibras*; his earliest paintings were conversation pieces, and he also painted portraits. In 1732 *The Harlot's Progress* introduced his 'modern moral subjects'; it was followed by *The Rake's Progress* (1733–5) and *Marriage à la Mode* (1743–5; London, National Gallery). This highly original genre consisted of a series of paintings, popularized through engravings, which tell a story that is topical, erotic, spiced with contemporary portraits, and yet comments with humanity and passion on social and political vices and corruption. Hogarth's later engravings, the *Industry and Idleness* series (1747) and the prints *Beer Street* and *Gin Lane* (1750–1), are coarser, and their harsher morality is aimed at a mass market. Hogarth also published a work on aesthetics, *The Analysis of Beauty* (1753).

His series of engravings were immensely successful and immediately inspired numerous plays and novels; his success was such that his work was pirated and he was instrumental in obtaining the passage of 'Hogarth's Act' (1735) protecting the copyright of engravers. *Fielding became Hogarth's friend and collaborator in the early 1730s; in his preface to *Joseph Andrews* (1742) he describes Hogarth as a 'Comic History-Painter', defending him against critics who attacked his work as mere caricature or burlesque. Fielding, and later *Smollett, compared characters and scenes in their novels to the prints of Hogarth. The artist aroused less interest in the late 18th cent. but his popularity soared in the early 19th cent., with essays by *Hazlitt and *Lamb that emphasized his literary qualities. Both *Dickens and *Thackeray admired and were influenced by him; Dickens, in the preface to *Oliver Twist*, writes that he had never met 'the miserable reality' of low-life London except in Hogarth. No other British painter has had such close connections with literature; Hogarth's *Portrait of the Painter and his Pug* (1745, London, Tate Gallery) shows his aggressive image resting on volumes of Shakespeare, *Milton, and *Swift and lays claim to his place within a British artistic tradition. See R. E. Moore, *Hogarth's Literary Relationships* (1948).

Hogarth Press, The, was founded in 1917 by L. and V. *Woolf at their home, Hogarth House, Richmond, and their earliest publications included K. *Mansfield's *Prelude* (1918), V. Woolf's *Kew Gardens* (1919, illustrated with woodcuts by V. *Bell), and T. S. *Eliot's *Poems* (1919). Their policy was to publish new and experimental work; they also published translations of *Gorky, *Chekhov, *Tolstoy, *Dostoevsky, *Bunin, *Rilke, and *Svevo. They were the first to introduce the work of *Jeffers, J. C. *Ransom, and E. A. *Robinson in England. Until 1923 they operated on a subscription basis. In 1924 they moved to Tavistock Square, where J. *Lehmann became assistant (1931–2), and then part-owner (1938–46). The press also published papers and pamphlets on psychoanalysis, politics, aesthetics, economics, and disarmament, and with its outstanding list of authors made a major contribution to the literary and intellectual life of the nation. The present Hogarth Press has been an allied company of Chatto and Windus since 1947.

HOGG, James (1770–1835), was born in Ettrick Forest and became a shepherd: after he began to write he became known as the 'Ettrick Shepherd'. His poetic gift was discovered by Sir W. *Scott, to whom he had sent poems for *The Minstrelsy of the Scottish Border* and who remained his friend. His early ballads were published as *The Mountain Bard* (1807). He came to Edinburgh in 1810, and in 1813 made his reputation as a poet with *The Queen's Wake. He became the friend of *Byron, *Wordsworth, *Southey, John *Murray, and other literary figures. He was on the editorial board of *Blackwood's Edinburgh Magazine*, to which he frequently contributed, notably to the 'Noctes Ambrosianae'; and he conceived the idea of the notorious *'Chaldee MS' of 1817. In 1816 he was granted a farm in Yarrow and here he mainly lived for the rest of his life, combining farming with writing. He published *Pilgrims of the Sun* in 1815 and *The Jacobite Relics of Scotland* (with music) in 1819. His chief prose works are *The Three Perils of Man* (1822), *The Private Memoirs and Confessions of a Justified Sinner* (1824; now considered his most important work), and *The Domestic Manners and Private Life of Sir Walter Scott* (1834). With *Motherwell he published an edition of *Burns (1834–5). He was well thought of by his contemporaries, and Wordsworth wrote a poem 'Upon the Death of James Hogg'. See E. C. Batho, *The Ettrick Shepherd* (1927); L. Simpson, *James Hogg: A Critical Study* (1962).

HOGG, Thomas Jefferson (1792–1862), educated at Oxford with *Shelley and sent down with his friend on the publication of the latter's *Necessity of *Atheism. He was one of the circle of Shelley, *Peacock, and other friends who about 1820 referred to themselves as 'The Athenians'. In 1832 he contributed reminiscences of Shelley at Oxford to *The New Monthly Magazine*, and these later formed a part of his *Life of Shelley* (1858). Peacock, in his *Memorials of Shelley*, felt obliged to question and revise many of Hogg's observations.

HOGGART, Richard (1918–), scholar and writer, brought up in Leeds and educated at Leeds University. He has held many academic and public appointments, and was warden of Goldsmith's College, London, 1976–84. His interest in literature, education, and the means of communication was expressed in his influential work *The Uses of Literacy* (1957), which has been followed by many other works of literary criticism and sociology.

HOLBACH, Paul Henri, baron d' (1723–89), see PHILOSOPHES.

HOLBEIN, Hans, the younger (1497/8–1543), German painter, born in Augsburg; by 1515 he was in Basle, where he designed woodcuts for the publisher Johannes Froben and met *Erasmus. In 1516 he made a remarkable series of marginal drawings in Erasmus' *The Praise of Folly* (edn 1515; Basle, Print Room) and painted Erasmus several times. His religious paintings include the unflinchingly realistic *Dead

Christ (1521); *c*.1525 he designed a series of woodcuts, *The Dance of Death*. Erasmus recommended Holbein to Sir T. *More, and he spent the years 1526–8 in England, probably staying at More's house in Chelsea; he painted the friends and patrons of Erasmus, including Archbishop Warham (1527) and Sir Henry Guildford (1527), and More and his family. After four years back in Basle, Holbein settled in England in 1532, when Thomas *Cromwell seized on his potential as a court painter. His brilliant drawings and paintings of the period include many literary figures—Sir T. *Wyatt, *Surrey, Sir Thomas and Lady *Elyot, and Sir Philip Hoby, friend of Titian and Aretino. Stylistically these works move away from the warmth and solidity of the heroic paintings of his first English period towards a greater emphasis on linear pattern and a hair-by-hair precision. Holbein created the massive, overpowering image of *Henry VIII; contemporaries were 'abashed and annihilated' before the mural painting of the king and his parents at Whitehall Palace (1537; destroyed; part of the cartoon is in the National Portrait Gallery). Holbein's verisimilitude startled an English public little used to the new art of the Renaissance. The 19th cent. was fascinated by his *Dance of Death*: *Dickens bought a set in 1841; and W. *Cather took from it the title of *Death comes for the Archbishop*. The painter Hans Meyrick in *Daniel Deronda* is named after Holbein, and F. M. *Ford's fascination with both Holbein and Henry VIII inspired his historical novel *The Fifth Queen*.

HOLCOT, Robert (d. 1349, probably young), a Dominican, perhaps born at Northampton where he spent the last seven years of his life, studied and taught at Oxford from *c*.1326 to 1334. Theologically, he was a follower of *Ockham in his insistence on human free will, in opposition to his contemporary *Bradwardine (Holcot may have been one of his 'New Pelagians'). The canon of his works is large but uncertain; his most important work is his *Moralitates Historiarum*, a series of metaphorical stories (corresponding to Ridevall's *Fulgentius Metaforalis*, but much more vivid) which were very influential on the *Gesta Romanorum*. Throughout his work he alluded to and used 'pictures', metaphorical representations of abstract phenomena, in a lively and literary way. See Beryl Smalley, *English Friars and Antiquity in the Early Fourteenth Century* (1960), ch. 7, pp. 133–202.

HOLCROFT, Thomas (1745–1809), successively stable-boy, shoemaker, actor, and author. He was largely self-educated, a militant atheist, and believed fervently in man's capacity for self-improvement. His varied and energetic life is described in his *Memoirs* (edited and completed by his friend *Hazlitt), which contain early reminiscences of *Foote and the aged *Macklin, and later accounts of radical associates such as *Godwin and *Tooke. He was tried with Tooke for high treason in 1794, and acquitted. He wrote a number of sentimental plays, of which the best-known was *The Road to Ruin* (1792): also several novels, including *Anna St Ives* (1792) and *The Adventures of Hugh Trevor* (1794), both of them influenced by Godwin's radical philosophy, but less successful as literature than *Caleb Williams*. After the hostile reception of his play *Knave or Not?* in 1798, Holcroft, plagued by debt, moved to Hamburg, then Paris, returning to England in 1802; he died in London after a long illness, during which he dictated a large part of his *Memoirs*. *Anna St Ives* (ed. P. Faulkner) and *Hugh Trevor* (ed. S. Deane) were reissued in 1970 and 1973 respectively.

HÖLDERLIN, Friedrich (1770–1843), German poet and friend of *Hegel and *Schelling. He suffered from insanity from 1802. He wrote novels (e.g. *Hyperion*, 1797–9) and poems on classical subjects, in which he expressed a hopeless, romantic yearning for ancient Greek harmony with nature and beauty in classical verse forms. His works have been translated by M. *Hamburger (1966).

HOLINSHED, Raphael (d. ?1580), was of a Cheshire family and is said by Anthony *Wood to have been a 'minister of God's word'. He came to London early in the reign of *Elizabeth I, and was employed as a translator by Reyner *Wolfe, the printer and publisher. While in his employ he planned the *Chronicles* (1577) which are known by his name and are by several hands. They form the first authoritative vernacular and continuous account of the whole of English history. The *Historie of England* was written by Holinshed himself. The *Description of England*, a vivid account, not devoid of humour, of English towns, villages, crops, customs, etc., of the day, was written by W. *Harrison. The *History and Description of Scotland* and the *History of Ireland* were translations or adaptations, and the *Description of Ireland* was written by Richard Stanyhurst and E. *Campion. A few passages in the *History of Ireland* offended the queen and her ministers, and were expunged. The *Chronicle* was reissued, with continuation, edited by John Hooker, alias Vowell, in 1587, and politically offensive passages again taken out. This edition was widely used by Shakespeare and other dramatists.

HOLLAND, Philemon (1552–1637), master of the free school at Coventry from 1628, is celebrated for his translations of *Livy (1600), *Pliny's *Natural History* (1601), *Plutarch's *Moralia* (1603), *Suetonius (1606), Ammianus Marcellinus (1609), Camden's *Britannia

(1610), and *Xenophon's *Cyropaedia* (1632). His knowledge of Greek and Latin was accurate and profound, and his renderings are made in a vivid, familiar, and somewhat ornamented English.

Holland House, Kensington, London, built at the beginning of the 17th cent. for Sir Walter Cope, passed by marriage into the possession of Henry Rich (son of Penelope *Rich), 1st earl of Holland, who took his title from the 'parts of Holland' in Lincolnshire; he was executed in 1649. In 1767 it was acquired by Henry Fox, 1st baron Holland, who entertained Horace *Walpole and George Selwyn there. In the time of his grandson, the 3rd baron (1773–1840), Holland House became a great political, literary, and artistic centre, and many eminent authors, such as *Sheridan, T. *Moore, T. *Campbell, S. *Rogers, *Macaulay, *Grote, *Dickens, and *Thackeray, were received there. *Addison, who had married the widow of one of the earls of Warwick and Holland, died at Holland House in 1719.

'Hollow Men, The', a poem by T. S. *Eliot.

HOLME, Constance (1881–1955), novelist, born in Westmorland, where her successful *Regional novels were set; they include *The Lonely Plough* (1914), *The Splendid Fairing* (1919), and *The Trumpet in the Dust* (1921), written in the genre satirized by Stella Gibbons in *Cold Comfort Farm*.

HOLMES, J. C., see BEAT GENERATION.

HOLMES, Oliver Wendell (1809–94), born at Cambridge, Massachusetts, was professor of anatomy and physiology at Harvard University from 1847 to 1882. His *Autocrat of the Breakfast-Table* appeared in the *Atlantic Monthly* in 1857–8, *The Professor at the Breakfast-Table* in 1860, *The Poet at the Breakfast-Table* in 1872, and *Over the Tea-Cups* in 1891. He also wrote novels, *Elsie Venner* (1861) and *The Guardian Angel* (1867), some volumes of poems and essays, and memoirs of *Emerson and *Motley. His essays in the *Breakfast-Table* series are notable for their kindly humour and width of erudition; they take the form of discourses by the author, the other characters being listeners, who interpose occasional remarks. He also wrote a considerable quantity of mainly light and occasional verse, collected in many volumes; among the best-known are 'The Last Leaf' (1831), on an aged survivor of the Boston Tea Party; 'The Deacon's Masterpiece; Or, The Wonderful "One-Hoss Shay" ' (1857), a comic tale; and 'Dorothy Q' (1871), inspired by a family portrait.

Holmes, Sherlock, the private detective who appears in *The Adventures of Sherlock Holmes* and other books by A. C. *Doyle.

Holofernes, (1) Nebuchadnezzar's general, who was decapitated by Judith (Judith, ch. 4), a subject often treated by Renaissance painters; (2) the great doctor in theology (Tubal Holofernes) who instructed the youthful Gargantua (*Rabelais, I. xiv); (3) the pedantic schoolmaster in Shakespeare's *Love's Labour's Lost*.

HOLROYD, Michael de Courcy Fraser (1935–   ), author and biographer, born in London and educated at Eton. His first book was a critical biography of *Kingsmill, which was followed by a two-vol. life of L. *Strachey (*The Unknown Years*, 1967; *The Years of Achievement*, 1968), a work which greatly contributed to a revival of interest in the *Bloomsbury Group and to a new interest in the art of *biography, and which incidentally achieved a remarkable recovery of the personality of Strachey's friend and companion, the painter Dora Carrington (1893–1932). Other works followed, including a major two-volume biography of Augustus *John (1974, 1975).

HOLST, Gustav (1874–1934), English composer, who, with his friend *Vaughan Williams, was involved in the folk-song movement and was attracted to the Elizabethan composers and *Purcell, influences which guided him in his search for what he called 'the musical idiom of the English language'. He was a slow developer: his earlier works, including a first *Whitman setting, *The Mystic Trumpeter* (1904), show traces of *Wagner-worship, and even *The Planets* (1917) is not musically one of his best pieces. But from the same year *The Hymn of Jesus*, a setting from the apocryphal Acts of St John, is a masterpiece, and at the other end of the scale the *Four Songs for voice and violin* on medieval texts show that he could already produce a masterly fusion of language and melodic line. Later choral works include a setting of Whitman's *Ode to Death* (1919) and the *First Choral Symphony* (1924) to poems of *Keats. The last of the big choral works was the *Choral Fantasia* (1930) with words by his friend *Bridges, who also provided the words for one of the best of Holst's smaller compositions, the *Seven Partsongs* (1926) for soprano, female chorus, and strings.

Holst's next purely orchestral composition after *The Planets* was *Egdon Heath* (1927), a spare but tensely evocative score headed with a quotation from his friend Hardy's *The Return of the Native*, describing the heath's 'swarthy monotony'. Holst wrote the librettos for three of his operas: *Savitri* (1909), a one-act chamber opera of great originality; *The Perfect Fool* (1923); and *At the Boar's Head* (1925), in which the tavern scenes from both parts of *Henry IV* were strung together and set to traditional country dances and folk tunes with great ingenuity but little theatrical appeal. His last opera, *The Wandering

Scholar (1930), has a libretto by Clifford Bax after H. *Waddell: in this one-act comedy the economy of the musical presentation serves to drive home the wit and brevity of the text.

Holt, Father, a character in Thackeray's *The History of Henry Esmond*, a Jesuit priest and Jacobite spy, tutor to the young Henry Esmond.

HOLTBY, Winifred (1898–1935), writer, born in the East Riding of Yorkshire, broke off her studies at Oxford to serve in France with the WAAC, an experience which led her to devote much time to lecturing on international questions. She was also a vocal feminist. She published several novels, the best-known of which is her last, *South Riding* (1936), set in Yorkshire, which is at once the story of enterprising headmistress Sarah Burton and a portrait of a whole community. Her other novels include *Anderby Wold* (1923), *The Crowded Street* (1924), *The Land of Green Ginger* (1927), and *Mandoa, Mandoa!* (1933). She was a prolific journalist, contributing to the *Manchester Guardian*, *Time and Tide*, and many other periodicals. For an account of her life and early death after a long illness, see V. *Brittain, *Testament of Friendship* (1940).

'Holy Fair, The', a satirical poem by *Burns, published 1786, in which the poet contrasts the conviviality of the young parishioners assembled for a prayer-meeting with the exhortations of the ministers and elders, preaching of damnation and hell-fire.

Holy Grail, see GRAIL.

'Holy Grail, The' one of Tennyson's *Idylls of the King*, published 1869, in which Sir Percivale, now a monk, describes the quest of the Holy Grail, and the differing degrees of failure of himself, Bors, Gawain, and Launcelot.

Holy Living and *Holy Dying*, see TAYLOR, JEREMY.

Holy State and the Profane State, The, by T. *Fuller, published 1642, was the most popular of his works during his life, a mixture of *character-writing, essays, and 30 short biographies; the characters include, for example, 'The Good Widow', 'The Good Merchant', and 'The True Gentleman'.

Holy War, The, an allegory by *Bunyan, published 1682.

The author narrates how Diabolus gets possession by his wiles of the city Mansoul (i.e. soul of man), the metropolis of the universe. Thereupon King Shaddai, the builder of the city, sends Boanerges and three other captains to recover it, and finally his own son Emmanuel to lead the besieging army. The vicissitudes of the siege are recounted with much spirit. The city falls to the assault conducted by Emmanuel, after much

parley between the defenders ('Diabolonians') and the besiegers. But when the power of the king has been re-established, the city presently relapses into evil ways. Diabolus recaptures the city but cannot take the citadel, and is presently defeated by Emmanuel. Bunyan in this allegory evidently drew upon his experience as a soldier in the parliamentary war. It is an allegory both of the progress of the Christian soul and of the history of the Christian church.

'Holy Willie's Prayer', a satirical poem by *Burns, published 1799, takes the form of a dramatic monologue by an elder in Burns's parish of Mauchline. In the course of his musings Holy Willie unconsciously reveals his selfish hypocrisy. The poem was not included in the Kilmarnock edition of 1786 for fear of giving offence.

Homage to Catalonia, see ORWELL, G.

'Homage to Sextus Propertius', see POUND, E.

HOME, Daniel Dunglas (1833–86), a spiritualistic medium, whose seances in England in 1855 and subsequent years were attended by well-known people including R. *Browning, who, unlike his wife, remained sceptical (see his 'Mr Sludge, "The Medium" '). He published *Incidents of my Life* (1863, 1872).

HOME, Henry, Lord Kames (1696–1782), Scottish judge and landowner, keenly interested in agricultural improvement and philosophy. A representative figure of the *Scottish Enlightenment, he wrote on law, history, natural religion, and farming; his works, much read in his day, include *Elements of Criticism* (1762) and *Sketches of the History of Man* (1774). He was a member of the *Select Society.

HOME, John (1722–1808), succeeded R. *Blair as minister of Athelstaneford, and later became secretary to Bute and tutor to the prince of Wales. His friends included *Hume, Adam *Smith, W. *Collins, and W. *Robertson. His first tragedy, *Agis*, was initially rejected by *Garrick, but *Douglas* was performed with much success at Edinburgh in 1756, and at Covent Garden in 1757. His later tragedies were less successful. He was a friend of *Macpherson and a firm believer in the authenticity of 'Ossian'.

Homecoming, The, a play by H. *Pinter, performed and published 1965.

A black Freudian family drama, the play presents the return to his North London home and ostentatiously womanless family of Teddy, an academic, and his wife of six years, Ruth, once a photographic model. The patriarch, Mac, a butcher, is alternately violent and cringing in manner, and the other two sons, Lenny and Joey, in a very short time make sexual overtures to Ruth, who calmly accepts them; by the end of the play Teddy has decided to leave her with the family, who intend to establish her as a professional prostitute. The tone is dark, erotic, and threatening; the shocking and the banal are sharply juxtaposed throughout. Ruth's acceptance of her role as mother, mistress, and possibly breadwinner for her new family, and her rejection of her husband, are intricately connected with the enigmatic figure of the long-dead mother, Jessie, who is both reviled and idolized by her survivors.

HOMER, the supposed author of two famous early Greek epics, *The Iliad and *The Odyssey. Nothing is known about him for certain, not his birthplace, nor his date. It is now considered unlikely that the same man wrote both epics, or indeed that either, as now known, is the work of a single poet. U. von Wilamowitz's theory (1916) that a poet, 'Homer', living in the 8th cent. BC combined and remodelled earlier poems, and that his work was in its turn enlarged and remodelled by others, seems the most plausible account of the genesis of *The Iliad*, while *The Odyssey*, which has a much closer structural unity, is generally held to consist of a substantial kernel poem with some later additions. Homer occupied in the culture of ancient Greece a position even more central than Shakespeare's in England, since his works provided everyone's elementary education. No one in antiquity questioned his claim to be the greatest of poets, and his reputation survived in the Middle Ages even in the Latin West where his works were unknown. When the humanists began to learn Greek in the 14th cent. they turned eagerly to *The Iliad*, but found its directness and realism disappointing. The study of Homer stagnated, and a serious interest in his work did not show itself, in spite of G. *Chapman's heroic versions (*Il.* 1611, *Od.* 1614–15), until *Hobbes's and *Dryden's attempts at translation towards the end of the century. The 18th-cent. interest in Homer had a number of different causes. There was the natural wish to make an ancient masterpiece available to contemporary readers which produced *Pope's *Iliad* (1715–20); there was the new view of poetic inspiration fostered by *'Longinus', which justified the 'fire' Pope found in Homer; there was the cult of *Primitivism as an alternative to the corruptions of civilization, which was to lead to the foolish veneration of 'Ossian', and which prepared the ground for F. A. Wolf's theory (1795) that *The Iliad* consisted of bardic lays woven roughly together, a theory that produced a long (and still undecided) struggle between 'analysts' and 'unitarians'. In the 19th cent. some poets like *Tennyson (in 'The Lotos-Eaters') made use of a Homeric story for unhomeric purposes, others, like M. *Arnold or *Kingsley, attempted (unsuccessfully) to write in a Homeric manner; but it is Arnold's lectures 'On Translating Homer' that indicate most forcefully the almost ex-

travagant worship that the poet inspired in cultivated Englishmen of the Victorian age, including *Gladstone, who wrote several works on Homer.

In the 20th cent. the most widely read English translations are those of E. V. Rieu, whose prose version of the *Odyssey* was the first *Penguin Classic in 1946, but there have also been several attempts at verse, including those of Richmond Lattimore (1965–7) and C. *Logue, and a 'plain prose' adaptation by I. A. *Richards (1950).

Homeric Hymns, of unknown authorship and various dates, are preludes to epic poems, addressed to various deities and recounting legends relating to them. They do not figure seriously in English literature until the 19th cent., when *Shelley, *Peacock, *Tennyson, *Swinburne, and *Bridges are all indebted to them in particular poems.

'Home, Sweet Home', a song by J. H. *Payne. It formed part originally of the opera *Clari* (1823). The music is by Sir H. R. *Bishop.

Homilies, Books of, a title applied in the Church of England to two books of Homilies, published 1547 and 1563, appointed to be read in the churches. The second Book of Homilies is mentioned in Article 35 of the Thirty-nine Articles in the Book of *Common Prayer.

HONE, William (1780–1842), author and bookseller, who published numerous political satires, parodies, and pamphlets, some illustrated by *Cruikshank. He was prosecuted for his *Political Litany* (1817). He published his *Every-Day Book*, which was dedicated to *Lamb and praised by Sir W. *Scott and *Southey, in 1826–7; his *Table-Book* in 1827–8; and *The Early Life* in 1841.

Honest Whore, The, a play by *Dekker in two parts, both written c.1604/5, of which the first was printed 1604, the second 1630. It appears from *Henslowe's diary that *Middleton collaborated in writing the first part.

In Pt I Count Hippolito, making the acquaintance of Bellafront, and discovering that she is a harlot, upbraids her bitterly for her mode of life and converts her to honesty. She falls in love with Hippolito, who repels her and marries Infelice, daughter of the duke of Milan. Bellafront is married to Matheo, who had caused her downfall.

In Pt II we find the converted Bellafront as the devoted wife of the worthless Matheo, who, to get money for his vices, is prepared to see her return to her old way of life. Hippolito, now falling in love with her, tries to seduce her. She stoutly resists temptation and is finally rescued from misery by her father, Orlando Friscobaldo. The painful character of the play, one of the great dramas of the age, heightened by Dekker's powerful treatment and by scenes in Bedlam and Bridewell, is somewhat alleviated by the admirable character Orlando Friscobaldo, and by the comic underplot, dealing with the eccentricities of the patient husband Candido, the linen-draper.

Honeychurch, Lucy, a character in E. M. Forster's *A Room with a View*.

Honeycomb, Will, in *The Spectator*, introduced in No. 2 as an expert in 'the female world' of fashion and conversation.

Honeyman, the Revd Charles and Miss Martha, characters in Thackeray's *The Newcomes*.

Honeythunder, Lure, a character in Dickens's *Edwin Drood*.

Honeywood, Mr and Sir William, characters in Goldsmith's *The Good-Natur'd Man*.

Honorificabilitudinitatibus, the long word in Shakespeare's *Love's Labour's Lost* (v. i), in which Baconians see a cryptogram indicating that Bacon was the author of the works attributed to Shakespeare. (See BACONIAN THEORY.)

HOOD, Thomas (1799–1845), born in London, the son of a bookseller, was assistant editor of the *London Magazine*, 1821–3, and the friend of *Lamb, *Hazlitt, *de Quincey, and other literary men. He edited various periodicals: *The Gem* (1829), the *Comic Annual* (1830), *The New Monthly Magazine* (1841–3), and *Hood's Magazine* (1843). He and J. H. *Reynolds published *Odes and Addresses to Great People* (1825), a series of satires and parodies which sold well. He wrote much humorous and satirical verse, often making use of his remarkable skill with puns, but his satire lacked bite. Lamb, recognizing this lack, and referring to Hood's attempts to do in verse for London what W. *Hogarth had done with engraving, called him 'our half-Hogarth'. His serious poems include *'The Song of the Shirt', which was immensely successful; *'The Bridge of Sighs', and 'The Dream of Eugene Aram', the first about a suicide by drowning, the second about a murder; 'The Last Man'; 'The Plea of the Mid-summer Fairies' (which includes 'I remember, I remember'); and shorter pieces, such as 'The Death-bed'. He wrote a comedy, *York and Lancaster*, and in *Hood's Own* (1839) published a lively account of an assembly at the Lambs' house. He received a civil list pension not long before his death.

HOOD, Thomas, the younger (1835–74), a talented humorous writer and artist, known as Tom Hood, was the son of Thomas *Hood. The first of his illustrated books, *Pen and Pencil Pictures*, was published in 1857. He became editor of *Fun* in 1865, in which year he published the most successful of his six novels, *Captain Master's Children*. In 1867 he founded *Tom Hood's Comic Annual*, which continued after his death. He wrote and illustrated many children's books; his collected verse, *Favourite Poems*, was published in 1877.

Hood, Robin, see ROBIN HOOD.

Hook, Captain, the pirate captain in J. M. *Barrie's *Peter Pan*.

HOOK, Theodore Edward (1788–1841), is remembered as a wit, a writer of light verses and dramas, a successful editor of the Tory *John Bull*, and a prolific and popular novelist. He was the most successful of the writers of the *'Fashionable Novel'. As a friend of the prince of Wales Hook knew the fashionable world, and he described it admiringly in his novels, which were read in large numbers by those aspiring to social fashion. Among his various novels *Sayings and Doings* (1824–8), *Maxwell* (1830), *Gilbert Gurney* (1836), *Jack Brag* (1837), and *Gurney Married* (1838) were all popular; but their interest is now chiefly for the social historian.

HOOKER, Sir Joseph, see DARWIN, C.

HOOKER, Richard (?1554–1600), theologian, was born at Exeter of poor parents, and by Bishop Jewel's patronage sent to Corpus Christi College, Oxford, where he remained till 1584, becoming a fellow and deputy professor of Hebrew. He was appointed to the living of Drayton-Beauchamp in 1584, master of the Temple 1585, rector of Boscombe in Wiltshire, and of Bishopsbourne in Kent, where he died and where the inscription on his monument first called him 'Judicious'. Of his great prose classic, the defence of the Church of England as established in Queen Elizabeth's reign entitled *Of the Laws of Ecclesiastical Politie*, four books appeared in 1593, the fifth in 1597. Other works by Hooker were issued at Oxford in 1612–14. A pleasant biography of Hooker was written by I. *Walton and published with the 1666 edition of his *Works*. There is some reason to credit Hooker with the first steps towards making known in England the theory of 'original contract' as a basis of sovereignty.

Hoosier Schoolmaster, The, see EGGLESTON, E.

HOPE, Anthony, see HAWKINS, A. H.

HOPE, Thomas (?1770–1831), a man of great wealth, architect, art historian, and traveller, was the author of the once popular novel *Anastasius*, published in 1819 and at first attributed to Lord *Byron, who wished he had written it. It tells, at considerable length, the story of a brave but unscrupulous Greek who, in the 18th cent., travels in the Middle East and becomes involved in a variety of escapades. It is possible that the story influenced the later cantos of *Don Juan*.

Hope Theatre, on Bankside, Southwark, built

in 1613 by *Henslowe as a bear-garden, with a movable stage on which plays could be performed. Jonson's *Bartholomew Fair* was acted there in 1614.

HOPKINS, Gerard Manley (1844–89), born in Stratford, Essex, the eldest son of middle-class parents who combined strong High Anglican principles with a deep interest in literature, art, and music. He attended Highgate School, where he showed great academic and artistic promise, and won a prize for his first surviving poem, 'The Escorial'. In 1863 he went to Balliol College, Oxford, as an exhibitioner, and in the same year published 'Winter with the Gulf Stream'. At Oxford he made many friends, including *Bridges, wrote much poetry, including 'Heaven-Haven' and 'The Habit of Perfection', and obtained a First Class degree; he came under the influence of the *Oxford Movement and *Newman, and in 1866 was received into the Roman Catholic Church. In 1868 he resolved to become a Jesuit and symbolically burned his poems, though he sent some copies to Bridges for safekeeping. For the next few years he wrote little, devoting himself to the life of a novice at Roehampton (1868–70) and to study at Stoneyhurst (1870–3); he was professor of rhetoric at Roehampton 1873–4, then studied theology at St Beuno's in North Wales (1874–7), where he also learned Welsh. During this period he was developing his theories of instress, inscape, and sprung rhythm.

A new phase of creativity began in 1876. Inspired by the loss of the *Deutschland* in December 1875, which had among its passengers five Franciscan nuns exiled for their faith, Hopkins, encouraged by his rector, wrote his most ambitious poem, 'The Wreck of the Deutschland'. It was rejected by the Jesuit journal, *The Month*, as too difficult for its readers, but Hopkins, revived by the sympathetic interest of his spiritual directors, continued to write, and in 1877, while studying for ordination, composed some of his best-known poems, including 'The Windhover' and 'Pied Beauty'. After ordination he was sent to Chesterfield, then London, then Oxford, where he wrote 'Henry Purcell' ('one of my very best pieces'). Work in various industrial parishes followed, including an exhausting spell in Liverpool (1880–1) where he was oppressed by 'vice and horrors' and a sense of his own failure as a preacher. 'Felix Randal' and 'Spring and Fall' belong to this period.

In 1881 R. W. *Dixon (a devoted admirer, who had taught Hopkins briefly at Highgate) persuaded Hopkins to submit some sonnets to an anthology which *Caine was preparing, but they were rejected; Dixon had for some time tried to persuade Hopkins, without success, to alter his conviction that he should publish only if encouraged by his superiors. Hopkins worked briefly in Glasgow (where a visit to Loch Lo-

mond produced 'Inversnaid'), returned again to Roehampton and Stoneyhurst (1881–4), then in 1884 was appointed to the chair of Greek and Latin at University College, Dublin. There he found himself overwhelmed with administrative and academic work, became ill and deeply depressed, and wrote (mainly in 1885) a number of 'Dark Sonnets', powerfully expressing his sense of exile and frustration; these include 'Carrion Comfort' and 'No worst, there is none'. He wrote to Bridges describing his weakness and desolation, but managed to produce in these last years less desperate poems, including 'Harry Ploughman' and 'That Nature is a Heraclitean Fire'. 'Thou art indeed just, Lord' was written in March 1889; he died in June, of typhoid.

Many of his poems and papers went to Bridges. Apart from work in anthologies (including *Poets . . . of the Century*, 1893, and Bridges's own *The Spirit of Man*, 1916), nothing was published until 1918, when Bridges produced his *Poems*; Bridges had judged the public not ready to receive Hopkins's 'oddity', but initial bewilderment was followed by steadily rising admiration, and Hopkins is now recognized as a major poet. His poems, letters, and journals reflect his whole-hearted involvement in all aspects of his life—his sense of vocation (sometimes conflicting) as priest and poet, his love of beauty in nature and man, his technical interest in prosody, and his search for a unifying sacramental view of creation. His concepts of 'inscape', 'instress', and 'sprung rhythm' have been much discussed, and although they have given rise to a large body of aesthetic theory, they evade rigorous definition. By 'inscape' he seems to have meant 'the individual or essential quality of the thing'; 'instress' refers to the energy which sustains an inscape, and flows into the mind of the observer. Both words were coined by Hopkins. *'Sprung rhythm' he considered less an innovation than a return to the rhythms of speech and of earlier forms of verse; it involves scanning by accent (or stress), rather than by the counting of syllables. But the great (though delayed) impact of Hopkins's work may be seen less in terms of technical innovation than as a renewal of poetic energy, seriousness, and originality, after a period marked by much undistinguished and derivative verse.

Poems (4th edn, 1967), ed. W. H. Gardner and N. H. Mackenzie; *Letters of Hopkins to Robert Bridges; Correspondence of Hopkins and Richard Watson Dixon*, ed. C. C. Abbott (2 vols, 1935); *Further Letters*, ed. C. C. Abbott (1938, rev. 1956); *Note-books and papers of Hopkins*, ed. H. House (1937; rev. and enlarged as *Journals and Papers*, 2 vols, 1959, ed. H. House and G. Storey); Fr A. Thomas, *Hopkins the Jesuit* (1969); Bernard Bergonzi, *Gerard Manley Hopkins* (1977).

HOPKINS, Matthew (d. 1647), the witchfinder, said to have been a lawyer at Ipswich and Manningtree. He initiated many prosecutions, and procured a special judicial commission under which 60 women were hanged in Essex in one year, and many in Norfolk and Huntingdonshire. His *The Discovery of Witches* was published in 1647. See C. L'Estrange Ewen, *Witch Hunting and Witch Trials* (1929) and Keith Thomas, *Religion and the Decline of Magic* (1971).

Hop o' my Thumb, *Little Thumb,* a fairy-tale, from the French of *Perrault, translated by Robert Samber (?1729).

Hop o' my Thumb (*petit Poucet*) is the youngest of seven children of a woodman and his wife, who are forced by poverty to abandon them in the forest. Hop o' my Thumb, having overheard the plan, fills his pocket with white pebbles, which he drops along the way, and by means of these leads his brothers home again. The parents once more lose them, Hop o' my Thumb this time using breadcrumbs to mark the way. But the birds eat up the breadcrumbs, and the children arrive at the house of an ogre, who is deluded by Hop o' my Thumb into killing his own children instead of the woodman's. Hop o' my Thumb moreover steals his seven-league boots, and with the help of these obtains enough wealth to set his parents at ease. *Lang, in *Perrault's Popular Tales* (1888), discusses the origins of this story.

HORACE (Quintus Horatius Flaccus) (65–8 BC), Latin poet, a member of the literary circle round Augustus' minister Maecenas. Like his friend *Virgil, he joined in celebrating the restoration of order after the civil wars and worked to lift Latin literature to the level of Greek. In his *Odes* he imitated the lyric poets of early Greece. His *Satires* and *Epistles* were characterized by perceptive realism and by an ironical approach, novel at the time, in that the persona of the satirist was mocked as well as his ostensible victims. His critical works, notably the *Ars Poetica,* supplemented and in some cases distorted the teachings of *Aristotle. English satire from *Wyatt to Dr *Johnson derives much of its manner and aims from Horace. The writers of formal odes, *Marvell and *Dryden in particular, are also indebted to him and the critical writings of Dryden and the *Augustans plainly reveal the influence of his *Ars Poetica.* Horace's poems, taught with great thoroughness in every school, formed during the 17th and 18th cents an essential element in the pattern of English culture.

Horatio, in Shakespeare's *Hamlet,* the university friend of Hamlet who is left alive 'To tell my story' at the end of the play. For another version of this narrative, see Alethea Hayter's novel *Horatio's Version* (1972).

Horizon, a literary magazine founded in 1939 by *Connolly, *Spender, and Peter Watson, which ran from 1940 to 1950. It was edited throughout by Connolly, and published works by *Orwell, *Waugh, Angus *Wilson, L. *Lee, *Auden, and *Grigson, amongst others. Spender (*World Within World,* 1951) attributed its success to Connolly's eclecticism, vitality, and idiosyncrasy.

HORMAN, William (*c.*1458–1535), fellow of New College, Oxford, and headmaster of Winchester and Eton, of which he became vice-provost, author of *Vulgaria,* Latin aphorisms for boys to learn. It was printed by Pynson (1519), *Wynkyn de Worde (1530), and for the Roxburghe Club (ed. M. R. *James, 1926); a most remarkable book.

Hornblower, Horatio, see FORESTER, C. S.

Horn-book, a leaf of paper containing the alphabet (often with the addition of the ten digits, some elements of spelling, and the Lord's Prayer) protected by a thin plate of translucent horn, and mounted on a tablet of wood with a projecting piece for a handle, used for teaching children to read. A simpler and later form of this, consisting of the tablet without the horn covering, or a piece of stiff cardboard varnished, was also called a battledore. For an exhaustive account see A. W. Tuer, *History of the Hornbook* (1896).

Horn Childe, a northern verse-romance from the period 1290–1340 of 1,136 lines in tail-rhyme stanza. The plot is broadly similar to that of *King Horn though different in some details. Horn is a prince in the north of England who flees with his teacher and companions to the south where a king's daughter, Rimnild, falls in love with him. Two of Horn's companions betray the lovers to the king, and Horn flees to Wales and Ireland, taking Rimnild's magic ring with him. After ridding Ireland of the pagans, he returns to England where he is revenged on his treacherous companions and marries Rimnild. There is a ballad of 'Hind Horn', and it is believed that *Horn Childe* is the version of the romance referred to in 'Sir Thopas' (*Canterbury Tales,* 17); it is certainly the kind of romance that Chaucer's satire was aimed at. Ed. in *King Horn* by J. Hall (1901).

HORNE, John, see TOOKE, J. H.

HORNE, Richard Henry or Hengist (1802–84), educated at Sandhurst, served in the Mexican navy, and, in his own words, 'took up scribbling' when he was thirty. He made his name with *Orion,* an allegorical epic which he published in 1843 at a farthing 'to mark the public contempt into which epic poetry had fallen', and also no doubt through a desire for notoriety. The poem deals with the myth of Orion, portrayed as 'a Worker and a Builder for his fellow men', and contrasted with Akinetos, the 'Great Unmoved', or Apathy. It was much praised by *Carlyle, *Lewes, and *Poe, who found it 'one of the noblest, if not the very noblest poetical work of the age'; contemporary reviewers compared it not unfavourably with Keats's *Hyperion and *Endymion. Horne wrote several blank verse tragedies, influenced by *Webster, and adapted various plays for the stage, including *The Duchess of Malfi. He contributed many articles to Dickens's *Daily News and *Household Words, published other volumes of verse, and in 1852, in the midst of the gold fever, went to Australia (leaving his wife behind) where he stayed until 1869. His varied adventures there are described in the autobiographical preface to his Australian Facts and Prospects (1859). From 1839 he corresponded with E. B. *Browning (whom he first met in 1851), and he published two volumes of her letters to him (1877). She collaborated with him in his A New Spirit of the Age (1844). There is a life by C. Pearl (1960).

HORNECK, see GOLDSMITH, O.

Horner, a character in Wycherley's *The Country Wife.

HORNIMAN, Annie Elizabeth Fredericka (1860–1937), a pioneer supporter of the modern English drama, founder of Miss Horniman's Company of Actors, and of the Manchester Repertory Theatre, for the purposes of which she acquired the Gaiety Theatre in that town in 1908. By her generous assistance the Irish National Theatre Society was provided with a permanent home in the *Abbey Theatre, Dublin.

HORNUNG, E(rnest) W(illiam) (1866–1921), novelist, is remembered as the creator of Raffles, the gentleman burglar, public-school man, and cricketer, who first appeared in The Amateur Cracksman (1899), narrated by his admiring assistant and ex-fag Bunny. See 'Raffles and Miss Blandish' (1944) by G. *Orwell.

HOROVITZ, Frances, née Hooker (1938–83), poet, actress, and broadcaster, whose volumes of poetry Water Over Stone (1980) and Snow Light, Water Light (1983) provide intense, lyrical evocations of the landscapes of Gloucestershire, where she lived for some years, and of Northumberland, where she lived shortly before her death from cancer. Her work also appeared in New Departures, edited by her husband Michael Horovitz. (See UNDERGROUND POETRY.)

HOROVITZ, Michael, see JAZZ POETRY.

Hortensio, friend to Petruchio and suitor of Bianca in Shakespeare's *The Taming of the Shrew.

'Hosier's Ghost, Admiral', see GLOVER, R.

HOSKYNS, John (1566–1638), born in Monmouthshire and educated at Winchester and New College, Oxford, was a lawyer who enjoyed a high reputation for wit and learning. He is best known for his Directions for Speech and Style, drawn on by *Jonson in his *Timber, or Discoveries, but not published in full until 1935 (ed. H. H. Hudson). The Directions were written in 1599; most of Hoskyns's examples are drawn from Sidney's *Arcadia, but he also makes interesting use of other authors of the previous 20 years.

HOTSON, Leslie (1897–), Canadian scholar and literary detective who has specialized in the minute examination of Shakespeare's life and times. He has made some notable discoveries (including vital material relating to *Marlowe's death), but many of his theories and conclusions about Shakespeare's works have not gained widespread acceptance.

HOTSPUR, nickname of Sir Henry Percy (1364–1403), eldest son of the first earl of Northumberland. He figures in Shakespeare's *Richard II and 1 *Henry IV. Shakespeare changes his age (following *Daniel) to make him as young as Prince *Hal, and stresses his fiery, impetuous valour as contrasted with Hal's apparent idleness.

HOUGHTON, Baron, see MILNES, R. M.

HOUGHTON, William Stanley (1881–1913), was born in Manchester, where he worked in the cotton trade while pursuing his passion for the drama. He did much dramatic criticism in Manchester, then in 1908 had his play The Dear Departed performed by Miss *Horniman's Repertory Theatre. Independent Means (1909), The Younger Generation (1910), Master of the House (1910), and Fancy-Free (1911) led up to the great and lasting success of Hindle Wakes in 1912. Most of Houghton's plays centre, with sympathy and insight, on problems of homely Lancashire life, and are strongly influenced by *Ibsen, both in theme and manner. (See MANCHESTER SCHOOL.)

'Hound of Heaven, The', a poem by Francis *Thompson.

Hours of Idleness, a collection of poems by Lord *Byron, published 1807.
   The first of Byron's published works, these poems show a wide variety of attitudes and skills, and it is possible to see in them hints of his mature work. The collection was in general well received, but it was bitterly attacked by *Brougham in *The Edinburgh Review as 'so much stagnant water', an attack which led to Byron's reply *English Bards and Scotch Reviewers.

House for Mr Biswas, A, see NAIPAUL, V. S.

HOUSEHOLD, Geoffrey (Edward West) (1900–), novelist, educated at Clifton and Magdalen College, Oxford, and the author of many successful adventure stories in the tradition of *Buchan. The most characteristic (including his best-known, *Rogue Male,* 1939, and its sequel *Rogue Justice,* 1982) pit a sporting, well-bred, lonely adventurer against the forces of darkness in the modern world (e.g. Nazis and Nazi agents), and depend on the suspense of pursuit and revenge. Other titles include *Watcher in the Shadows* (1960), and *Dance of the Dwarfs* (1968).

Household Words, a weekly periodical started in 1850 by *Dickens, and incorporated in 1859 into *All the Year Round,* which he edited until his death. It was aimed at a large audience, carried contributions from well known writers such as Mrs *Gaskell, *Reade, and *Bulwer-Lytton, established the reputation of Wilkie *Collins, and published poems by the young *Meredith and *Patmore, as well as much of Dickens's own work. Although its attacks on the abuses of the day (poor sanitation, slums, factory accidents) were radical and persistent, its subject matter was varied and entertaining, and it captivated a vast readership.

House of Fame, The, an unfinished dream-poem by *Chaucer, composed at some time between 1374 and 1385. There are three books, in 2,158 lines of octosyllabics; it is believed to be Chaucer's last poem in that French form. The poem remains cryptic, and it is uncertain what its purpose or extent would have been (though the poem says that the third book will, in fact, be the final one).

After the Prologue on Dreams and the Invocation to the god of sleep, Bk I says the poet fell asleep and dreamt that he was in a Temple of Glass where he saw depicted Aeneas and Dido (based on *Aeneid,* IV); the dream moves on to deal more briefly with other parts of the *Aeneid.* At the end of Bk I the poet sees an eagle who alights by him and is his guide through the House of Fame in Bk II (initially suggested, perhaps, by *Fama,* Rumour, in *Aeneid,* IV. 173 ff.). The eagle explains, philosophically and at length, how Fame works in its arbitrary ways and the book ends with a vision of the world (thought by some to be amongst Chaucer's most inspired writing: 896–1,045). The eagle departs and at the beginning of Bk III Chaucer enters the Palace of Fame (Rumour) where he sees the famous of both classical and biblical lore. Eolus blows a trumpet to summon up the various celebrities who introduce themselves in categories reminiscent of the souls in Dante's *Divina Commedia.* Towards the end of the poem comes a vision of bearers of false tidings: shipmen, pilgrims, pardoners, and messengers, whose confusion seems to be about to be re-solved by the appearance of 'A man of gret auctorite . . .'; but there the poem ends. The identity of this figure has been much discussed; *Boethius seems the most plausible suggestion. Versions of the poem were made by *Lydgate (in *The Temple of Glas*), *Douglas, and *Skelton.

J. A. W. Bennett, *Chaucer's Book of Fame: an Exposition of the House of Fame* (1968); P. G. Ruggiers, 'The Unity of Chaucer's *House of Fame*' (1953; reprinted in R. J. Schoeck and J. Taylor, *Chaucer Criticism,* II); for interpretations, see Robinson's edition (1957), 778–9.

'House of Life, The', a sonnet sequence by D. G. *Rossetti, written over a long period, and published in two parts in *Poems* (1870) and *Ballads and Sonnets* (1881).

Rossetti described these sonnets as an evocation of 'life representative, as associated with love and death, with aspiration and foreboding, or with ideal art and beauty'. They have been seen both as a record of his love for his dead wife and sorrow over her death, and as a record of his passion for W. *Morris's wife Jane. Their emphasis on secrecy, delayed union, and 'regenerate rapture' would seem to support the latter view, though both Rossetti and his brother William were at pains to avoid a biographical interpretation.

House of Mirth, The, see WHARTON, E.

House of the Seven Gables, The, a novel by N. *Hawthorne, published 1851.

It deals with the problem of hereditary guilt, unmerited misfortune, and unexpiated crime, through the story of the Pyncheon family, suffering from generation to generation from the curse of old Maule, the dispossessed owner of the Pyncheon property; persecuted as a wizard, Maule on the scaffold curses Colonel Pyncheon, with the words 'God will give him blood to drink!' Pyncheon's descendant Hepzibah Pyncheon is a poor, grotesque old spinster inhabiting the decayed paternal mansion of the title; under stress of poverty, she is obliged to do violence to family pride by opening a small shop. At this moment, to add to her anxieties, her brother Clifford Pyncheon, an amiable, epicurean, weak-minded bachelor, who has spent long years in prison for a crime of which he has been unjustly convicted by the machinations of his cousin Judge Pyncheon, returns home. On the other hand, a young country cousin, Phoebe, arrives to lighten the gloom of the old house. Judge Pyncheon, a bland, prosperous hypocrite, diffusing a 'sultry' benevolence, continues his persecution of Clifford; but this is arrested by the judge's sudden death. With the help of Holgrave, a young daguerreotypist, a descendant of 'old Wizard Maule', Clifford is rehabilitated; Holgrave, who has fallen in love with Phoebe, marries her, and the curse appears to be lifted. The semi-allegorical treatment of the theme of the 'transmitted vices of society' is characteristic of Hawthorne, and manifests his acute sensitivity about his own Puritan ancestry.

House that Jack Built, The, a nursery accumulative tale of great antiquity, possibly based on an old Hebrew original, a hymn in Sepher Haggadah, beginning 'A kid my father bought for two pieces of money'; 'then came the cat and ate the kid, etc.'; 'then came the dog and bit the cat, etc.'; ending with the Angel of Death who killed the butcher who slew the ox, etc.; and the Holy One who slew the Angel of Death. That the English version is an early one is indicated by the reference to the 'priest, all shaven and shorn'. There is also a Danish version (*Halliwell).

House with the Green Shutters, The, see DOUGLAS, G.

HOUSMAN, A(lfred) E(dward) (1859– 1936), was educated at Bromsgrove and St John's College, Oxford. While at university he formed a passionate attachment to his contemporary Moses Jackson, who became an important inspiration of his later verse. For unexplained reasons the brilliant Housman failed his Finals and became for ten years a clerk in the Patent Office in London, during which time he worked on *Propertius, *Ovid, *Juvenal, and other classical authors, publishing articles when he could. In 1897 Jackson married and emigrated to India, and soon afterwards the anguished Housman (who had not written verse since his schooldays) began to experiment, composing poems which he wrote, rewrote, and completed in notebooks which have been preserved, and which he continued until Jackson's death in 1923. In 1892 he was appointed a professor of Latin in London University, where he began to produce his definitive edition of Manilius, which appeared in five vols, 1902– 30. In 1896 he published, at his own expense, *A Shropshire Lad*, a series of 63 spare and nostalgic verses, based largely on ballad-forms, and mainly set in a half-imaginary Shropshire, a 'land of lost content', and often addressed to, or spoken by, a farm-boy or a soldier. Housman met with little encouragement, and made the barest profit from the publication. However, *Le Gallienne found the verse of 'exquisite simplicity', and another reviewer noted its 'heart-penetrating quality'; public indifference slowly gave way to interest, and sales mounted steadily. In 1911 Housman was appointed professor of Latin at Cambridge, and during the years of the First World War *A Shropshire Lad* became hugely popular. The notebooks then yielded *Last Poems* (1922), whose 41 poems met with great acclaim. In 1931 Housman published, in Germany, *Praefanda*, a collection of bawdy and obscene passages from Latin authors, with a learned Preface of solemn irony. His lecture 'The Name and Nature of Poetry', given in 1933, was partly based on observations in his notebooks, which provide illuminating comments on the process of poetic creation. In 1936 *More Poems* appeared, from work in the notebooks, 18 further poems were printed in L. *Housman's *Memoir* of his brother (1937), and *Collected Poems* appeared in 1939. A volume of letters, ed. H. Maas, was published in 1971; see also R. P. Graves, *A. E. Housman: The Scholar Poet* (1979).

HOUSMAN, Laurence (1865–1959), brother of A. E. *Housman, trained as an artist, wrote art criticism, and illustrated books throughout his life, but is remembered chiefly as a writer and dramatist. He published many stories, for both children and adults, and wrote much on feminism and on socialist and pacifist themes. Among his works were volumes of somewhat derivative poems, including *Green Arras* (1896) and *Spikenard* (1898); *An Englishwoman's Loveletters* (1900), which enjoyed some notoriety and was widely parodied; and several successful novels, among them a political satire, *Trimblerigg* (1924), directed against Lloyd George, and *The Duke of Flamborough* (1928). His first play, *Bethlehem*, was banned in 1902, as were many later plays on religious or royal figures. *The Little Plays of St Francis* (1922), together with further plays on the same theme and on St Clare, were well received and much performed for many years. *Angels and Ministers* (1921), consisting of gently mocking scenes laid in the court of Queen Victoria, were collected with further royal playlets into *Victoria Regina* (1934); when the Lord Chamberlain's ban on the impersonation of members of the royal family was lifted in 1937 the play enjoyed great success. In 1937 Housman published an autobiography, *The Unexpected Years*, and in the same year produced *A. E. Housman*, a volume which contained some new poems, some letters, and a valuable *Memoir* of his brother.

Houyhnhnms, the talking horses in *Gulliver's Travels* by Swift.

HOVEDON, or **HOWDEN,** Roger of (d. ?1201), a Yorkshireman and a chronicler who lived in the reign of Henry II. He was the author of both the main chronicles of the reigns of Henry II and Richard I, the *Gesta Regis Henrici*, that long went under the name of Benedict of Peterborough, and the *Chronica*.

HOWARD, Henry, see SURREY.

HOWARD, John (1726–90), philanthropist and prison reformer, was born in London, the son of a prosperous upholsterer, and was educated in Dissenting circles. In 1773 he became sheriff of Bedford, where an inspection of the local gaol quickened his interest in the sufferings of prisoners. He devoted the rest of his life to visiting prisons both in England and on the Continent; his great work *The State of the Prisons in England and Wales, and an account of some foreign prisons and hospitals* was published in 1777; a subsequent work on lazarettos appeared in 1789. He died of typhoid at Kherson in the Ukraine. A Howard Association was formed in 1866, which merged in 1921 with the Penal Reform League to become the Howard League for Penal Reform, which concerns itself with many aspects of criminal justice.

Howards End, a novel by E. M. *Forster, published 1910, deals with personal relationships and conflicting values.

On the one hand are the Schlegel sisters, Margaret and Helen, and their brother Tibby, who care about civilized living, music, literature, and conversation with their friends; on the other, the Wilcoxes, Henry and his children Charles, Paul, and Evie, who are concerned with the business side of life and distrust emotions and imagination. Helen Schlegel is drawn to the Wilcox family, falls briefly in and out of love with Paul Wilcox, and thereafter reacts away from them. Margaret becomes more deeply involved. She is stimulated by the very differences of their way of life and acknowledges the debt of intellectuals to the men of affairs who guarantee stability, whose virtues of 'neatness, decision and obedience . . . keep the soul from becoming sloppy'. She marries Henry Wilcox, to the consternation of both families, and her love and steadiness of purpose are tested by the ensuing strains and misunderstandings. Her marriage cracks but does not break. In the end, torn between her sister and her husband, she succeeds in bridging the mistrust that divides them. Howards End, where the story begins and ends, is the house that belonged to Henry Wilcox's first wife, and is a symbol of human dignity and endurance.

Howe, Anna, the heroine's principal correspondent in Richardson's *Clarissa.*

HOWE, Julia Ward, see BATTLE HYMN OF THE REPUBLIC, THE.

HOWELL, James (?1593–1666), of Welsh descent held diplomatic and administrative posts under Charles I and was imprisoned in the Fleet as a royalist, 1643–51; at the Restoration he became Historiographer Royal. His *Dodona's Grove* (1640) is a political allegory, and in 1642 he published his entertaining *Instructions for Forreine Travell.* A violently anti-Scots pamphlet, *A Perfect Description of the Country of Scotland,* reprinted in *The North Briton,* no. 31, was attributed to him, but its authorship is disputed. Howell wrote many other works, including poems and historical pamphlets, but is chiefly remembered for his *Epistolae Ho-Elianae: familiar letters domestic and forren* (1645–55, reprinted

many times, ed. J. Jacobs 1890–2). These letters to correspondents, most of whom are imaginary, were written largely during his imprisonment; their intimate 'back-stairs' view of history had a lasting appeal, and *Thackeray wrote of them, 'Montaigne and Howell's *Letters* are my bedside books . . . I like to hear them tell their old stories over and over again.'

HOWELL, Thomas (*fl.* 1568–81), was a minor Tudor poet patronized by the Herbert family. His *Devises* (1581) contains the earliest printed reference to P. Sidney's *Arcadia.*

HOWELLS, William Dean (1837–1920), American novelist, was born in Ohio, and began life as a printer and journalist. He was American consul at Venice, 1861–5, an experience reflected in his *Venetian Life* (1866) and *Italian Journeys* (1867). He was sub-editor of the *Atlantic Monthly,* 1866–71, and chief editor, 1871–81, and was associate editor of *Harper's Magazine,* 1886–91, to which periodicals he contributed many articles on literary subjects. His numerous romances include *Their Wedding Journey* (1872), *The Lady of the Aroostook* (1879), *The Undiscovered Country* (1880), *A Modern Instance* (1882), *The Rise of Silas Lapham* (1885; his greatest work), *Indian Summer* (1886; another charming book), and *A Hazard of New Fortunes* (1890), which shows the effect of his political and critical moves towards socialism and social realism. His works of criticism and reminiscence include *Criticism and Fiction* (1891), *My Literary Passions* (1895), *Literary Friends and Acquaintances* (1900), *Literature and Life* (1902). He also wrote several dramas. His industry and his influence made him the leading American man of letters of his age, and he did much to encourage H. *James and other writers.

Howleglass, see EULENSPIEGEL.

'How many children had Lady Macbeth?', see BRADLEY, A. C., and KNIGHTS, L. C.

Hoyden, Miss, a character in Vanbrugh's *The Relapse* and in Sheridan's *A Trip to Scarborough.*

Hrothgar, see BEOWULF.

HROTSVITHA, or ROSWITHA (*fl.* 10th cent.), a Benedictine abbess of Gandersheim in Saxony, who adapted the comedies of *Terence for the use of her convent, an example of the survival of classical influence in the Middle Ages.

Hubbard, Mother, see MOTHER HUBBARD and MOTHER HUBBERDS TALE.

Hubris, see POETICS, THE.

HUCHOWN (*fl.* 14th cent.), apparently a northern alliterative poet. 'Huchown of the Awle Ryale' is mentioned by Andrew of *Wyntoun, *c.*1400, who claims that, 'He made the gret Gest of Arthure | And the Anteris of

Gawane, | The Epistill als of Suete Susane.' These poems have been tentatively identified as respectively the alliterative *Morte Arthure, *The Awntyrs of Arthure, and *The Pistyll of Susan. Huchown was declared by G. Neilson (1902) to be the Scot Sir Hew of Eglinton, famous from the reference to him in *Dunbar's 'Lament for the Makaris' (53); but there is little advantage in postulating a particular poet since so little is known of him. It has been argued that the named poems are unlikely to be the work of the same writer; on the other hand, it is hard to see why Andrew of Wyntoun should invent a poetic canon more or less contemporary with himself. In the past other works were, with little justification, added to the canon, of which the most distinguished were the four poems in the manuscript containing *Pearl.

Huckleberry Finn, The Adventures of, a novel by Mark *Twain, published 1884, as a sequel to *Tom Sawyer, and generally accepted as his masterpiece and one of the great works of American fiction.

Huck Finn, the narrator, recounts his adventures after being taken away from the Widow Douglas's by his drunken and brutal father. He escapes from his father, faking his own death, and joins up with a runaway slave, Jim, and together they make their way down the Mississippi on a raft. The picaresque device of a journey serves to introduce a number of events and a variety of characters: Huck becomes a witness of the blood feud between the Granger and Shepherdson families; he and Jim are joined by two villainous confidence men, the 'Duke' and the 'Dauphin', who sell Jim into captivity again, but at the end of the book Tom reappears in time to help Huck to rescue him in a characteristically romantic and quixotic manner (unnecessarily, as it turns out, for Jim had earlier and unknowingly been given his freedom). Perennially popular as an adventure story, the novel is also a profound moral commentary on the nature of the 'American experience' and the institution of slavery, and a vital contribution to the myth of the frontier, told with a freshness and raciness that shocked some of its readers, and has given rise to many theses on the subject of 'Southern Humour'. Twain's use of the innocent narrator to present oblique moral judgement is masterly, and his use of the vernacular extremely sensitive; he claimed in a preface to have used 'the Missouri Negro dialect; the extremest form of the backwoods South-Western dialect; and four modified varieties of this last', and the flexibility and power of his narrative is in no way impeded by this adherence to realistic speech. Among many tributes to the novel's imaginative power might be mentioned Jonathan Raban's Old Glory (1981), an account of a boyhood passion that resulted in a lone Mississippi voyage.

Hudibras, a satire in three parts, each containing three cantos, written by Samuel *Butler (1613–80). Part I, dated 1663, appeared in Dec. 1662, Part II, dated 1664, was published 1663, and a revised version of both parts came out in 1674. Part III was published 1680.

Its narrative form is that of a mock romance, derived from *Don Quixote, in which a grotesque Presbyterian knight, Sir Hudibras, and his sectarian squire Ralpho set out on horseback and encounter a bear-baiting mob who, after a comic skirmish, imprison them in the stocks. In the second part a widow, whom Hudibras hopes to marry for the sake of her jointure, agrees to release them on condition that the knight undergoes a whipping for her sake. They visit Sidrophel, a charlatan posing as an astrologer, whom Hudibras assaults and leaves for dead. In Part III Hudibras returns to the widow and claims that he has fulfilled his promise to whip himself, but is interrupted by a gang which he mistakes for Sidrophel's supernatural agents. They cudgel him and force him to confess to his iniquities. He consults a lawyer, who advises him to write love-letters to the widow in order to inveigle her in her replies. The second canto of Part III has no connection with the rest of the poem but consists of an account of political events between the death of *Cromwell and the restoration of Charles II and a dialogue between two politicians, one of them modelled on *Shaftesbury.

The loose narrative framework of the poem allows Butler ample opportunity to digress; in fact the digressions form the substance of the poem. They deal with academic pedantry, the theological differences between the Presbyterians and independent sectarians, Aristotelian logic, the hermetic philosophy, the politics of the civil war period, the ethics of oath-breaking, witchcraft, alchemy, astrology, and the nature of marriage. Hudibras is the most learnedly allusive poem in English but Butler treats all erudition with contempt. His most powerful satirical weapon is his style, the deliberately cumbersome octosyllabic metre and comic rhymes of which render absurd every subject to which they are applied.

Hudibras, or **Huddibras,** in Spenser's *Faerie Queene (II. ii. 17), the lover of *Elissa,

> an hardy man;
> Yet not so good of deedes, as great of name,
> Which he by many rash adventures wan.

Another Huddibras, in II. x. 25 of the same poem, is a legendary king of Britain.

Hudibrastic, in the style of Butler's *Hudibras; in octosyllabic couplets and with comic rhymes.

HUDSON, W(illiam) H(enry) (1841–1922), was born near Buenos Aires, the son of poor American parents of English descent who had moved to the Argentine to farm. His education was haphazard and he ran wild on the family ranch. Rheumatic fever at 15 disabled him for the outdoor life he had intended, and his lifelong interest in birds intensified. He began to publish stories and articles on natural history in both English and Argentine journals, then in 1874 came to London, where he remained, often in poverty, for the rest of his life. He wrote prolifically, but until his last decade his work was little regarded. In 1885 he published *The Purple Land*, a series of strange and vivid stories set in South America, and *Belloc expressed great admiration for *The Crystal Age* (1887), an account of a Utopian land where the sex impulse has burned out and society is therefore at last stable and at peace. In 1888 a standard work, *Argentine Ornithology*, of which Hudson was part-author, appeared. A. R. *Wallace praised *The Naturalist in La Plata* (1892), the first of Hudson's books to enjoy some success. In 1895 his *British Birds* appeared. In 1901 he met R. *Garnett, who henceforth greatly encouraged him, and in the same year he was awarded a civil list pension of £150. *Idle Days in Patagonia*, an engaging work of travel and natural lore, appeared in 1893, and in 1900 *Nature in Downland*. His novel *Green Mansions* (probably the best-known of his books) was published in 1904; success came slowly, but in the course of the next ten years the book made huge sales in both England and America. *A Shepherd's Life* (1910), which some hold to be his finest book, describes Caleb Bawcombe, a Wiltshire shepherd, who lives night and day, through all seasons, with his sheep and dogs among the people and the wild life of the downs. By now E. *Thomas, *Galsworthy, and others were ensuring that Hudson's work was widely noticed; *Adventures among Birds* (1913) was much praised, and the joyful account of his boyhood, *Far Away and Long Ago* (1918), received great acclaim. Another standard work, *Birds of La Plata*, appeared in 1920. New editions of Hudson's earlier books now began to appear, and by the time of his death he was generally recognized as a masterly writer on the natural world.

Hugh, in Dickens's *Barnaby Rudge*, the ostler of the Maypole Inn.

HUGH OF LINCOLN, St (?1246–55), a child supposed to have been crucified by a Jew named Copin or Joppin at Lincoln, after having been starved and tortured. The body is said to have been discovered in a well and buried near that of *Grosseteste in the cathedral, and to have been the cause of several miracles. The story, a frequent theme for poets, is referred to by Chaucer ('The Prioress's Tale', *Canterbury Tales*, 16) and by Marlowe in *The Jew of Malta*. See also the ballad of 'The Jew's Daughter' in Percy's *Reliques*.

HUGHES, Langston, see JAZZ POETRY.

HUGHES, Richard Arthur Warren (1900–76), writer of Welsh descent, was born in Surrey and educated at Charterhouse and Oriel College, Oxford. He began writing at an early age and while at Oxford published a volume of poems, *Gipsy Night* (1922). In the same year his one-act play *The Sister's Tragedy*, sponsored by *Masefield, was performed at the Royal Court, London. He travelled widely in Canada, the West Indies, and America before settling in 1934 in Wales. His first ambition was to be a dramatist and he was commissioned by the BBC to write the first original radio play, *Danger*, produced by Nigel Playfair in 1924; in the same year a full-length play, *A Comedy of Good and Evil*, appeared at the Royal Court. *Confessio Juvenis* (collected poems) appeared in 1926. He gained fame with his first novel, *A High Wind in Jamaica* (1929), the story of the adventures of a family of children bound for England and captured by pirates. His unconventional and unsentimental treatment of childhood in this novel is said to have ended the Victorian myth of childhood, and paved the way for works such as Golding's *Lord of the Flies. In Hazard* (1938), a seafaring novel, contains a brilliant description of a hurricane which prompted comparisons with *Conrad. He produced three volumes of short stories, *A Moment of Time* (1926), *The Spider's Palace* (1931), and *Don't Blame Me* (1940), the last two for children. He worked for the Admiralty during the war, and in 1961 broke a long silence with *The Fox in the Attic*, the first volume of an ambitious new project, 'The Human Predicament', a long historical sequence which was to cover the rise of Nazism and end with the Second World War. Opening in Wales just after the First World War, it mingles real and fictional characters, both German and British, ending with Hitler's Munich *putsch*. The second volume, *The Wooden Shepherdess* (1973), ends with the murder of Röhm, and was less well received. Hughes was a highly original and idiosyncratic writer, and his influence can be traced in the novels of J. G. *Farrell.

HUGHES, Ted (Edward James) (1930–), poet, born in West Yorkshire, and educated at Mexborough Grammar School, then at Pembroke College, Cambridge, where he met Sylvia *Plath, whom he married in 1956. As a boy he spent much time on shooting and fishing expeditions with his brother, and his obsession with animals and his sense of the beauty and violence of the natural world appear in his first volume, *The Hawk in the Rain* (1957). This was followed by *Lupercal* (1960), *Wodwo* (1967, prose and verse), and several books of children's verse. *Crow* (1970) is a sequence of poems introducing the central symbol of the crow (partly inspired by a meeting with the American artist Leonard Baskin who has illustrated much of Hughes's work), which recurs frequently in subsequent volumes. Hughes retells the legends of creation and birth through the dark vision of predatory, mocking, indestructible crow, 'screaming for blood' amidst 'the horror of creation'. Later volumes include *Cave Birds* (1975), *Season Songs* (1976), and *Moortown* (1979), the last of these containing the sequence 'Prometheus on his crag', written in Iran in 1971, on his expedition with the stage director Peter Brook, during which he also wrote *Orghast*, a play in an invented language. He has also published plays for children, a version of *Seneca's Oedipus (1968), and edited various anthologies. *Remains of Elmet* (1979), with photographs by Fay Godwin, celebrates the landscapes of his youth in the Calder valley, which he describes as 'the last ditch of Elmet, the last British kingdom to fall to the Angles'; *River* (1983), with photographs by P. Keen, is a sequence of poems invoking riverside and river life. Together these volumes constitute interesting examples of the renewed vogue for *topographical poetry (with illustrations) that arose in the environment-conscious second half of the 20th cent. Hughes's stress on the physical, animal, and subconscious is in marked contrast to the urbane tone of the *Movement, and his poetry, hailed as vital and original, has also been described as excessively brutal and violent. He was appointed poet laureate in 1984.

HUGHES, Thomas (1822–96), educated at Rugby and Oriel College, Oxford, was a barrister and Liberal MP, and, under the influence of F. D. *Maurice, devoted much energy to Working Men's Education, the Co-operative movement, etc. He is remembered as the author of *Tom Brown's Schooldays* (1857, by 'An Old Boy'), which evokes the Rugby of his youth and his veneration for its headmaster, Dr T. *Arnold. Hughes condemned, in the character of the tyrannical Flashman, the bullying prevalent in public schools of the day, and advocated a form of what came to be known as 'muscular Christianity', which attempted to combine Christian principles with physical courage, self-reliance, love of sport, school loyalty, and patriotism, a mixture that had much impact on the public school ethos. Its detractors found it Philistine, and indeed there are few mentions in the novel of any intellectual pursuits. The sequel, *Tom Brown at Oxford* (1861), is less interesting. Hughes wrote several biographies and memoirs, one other novel (*The Scouring of the White Horse*, 1859), and published various sermons and addresses, including *The Manliness of Christ* (1879), which attacks the view that Christianity is a religion for the timid and fearful. There is a life by E. C. Mack and W. H. G. Armytage (1953).

Hugh Selwyn Mauberley, see POUND, E.

HUGO, Victor(-Marie) (1802–85), poet, novelist, and dramatist, the central figure of the Romantic movement in France. Coming late to active political life, he was elected to the Assembly in 1848, but spent the years 1851–70 in exile, the greater part of the time in Guernsey. He returned to Paris in 1870 and was again chosen as a deputy, later becoming a senator of the Third Republic. He had been elected to the *Académie française in 1841. Hugo is one of the masters of French poetry, to which he brought a new freedom of subject, diction, and versification. His many collections include: *Odes* (1822), *Odes et Ballades* (1826), *Les Orientales* (1829), *Les Feuilles d'automne* (1831), *Les Chants du crépuscule* (1835), *Les Voix intérieures* (1837), *Les Rayons et les ombres* (1840), followed after a long interval by *Les Châtiments* (1853, a violent satire against Louis Napoleon, written in exile). Spiritual and cosmic themes come to the fore in *Les Contemplations* (1856). The poems of *La Légende des siècles* (1859, 1877, 1883) compose an epic and prophetic treatment of history, of which the posthumously-published *La Fin de Satan* (1886) and *Dieu* (1891) were intended to form the final parts. Of Hugo's plays, *Cromwell* (1827), *Hernani* (1830), and *Ruy Blas* (1838) are variously important; the first because of its Preface, which became a manifesto of the French Romantic movement. The first two performances of *Hernani*, taking place amidst the vociferous manifestations of the partisans and opponents of the new drama, mark an epoch in the French theatre and have entered its mythology. *Ruy Blas* continued his success in verse drama. Besides his well-known *Notre Dame de Paris* (1831) and *Les Misérables* (1862), Hugo wrote a number of other novels, e.g., *Les Travailleurs de la mer* (1866, set in Guernsey) and *Quatre-vingt-treize* (1873, Royalist insurrections in Brittany and the Vendée during the French revolution).

HUIZINGA, Johan (1872–1945), Dutch historian, is chiefly known in Britain for four books, *Homo Ludens* (1938, trans. 1949), *Erasmus of Rotterdam* (1924, trans. 1924), *In the Shadow of Tomorrow* (1935, trans. 1936), and *The Waning of the Middle Ages* (1919, trans. 1924), and perhaps principally for the last of these, a cultural history which has been compared to a vast canvas, which 'like the great altarpieces of the brothers Van Eyck, contains a prodigious variety of detail, and yet does not detract from the main central theme of the picture' (B. F. Hoselitz, Introduction to *Men and Ideas*, 1960, by J. Huizinga).

HULL, E. M., see SHEIK, THE.

HULME, T(homas) E(rnest) (1883–1917), poet, essayist, and (in his own phrase) 'philosophic amateur', whose reaction against *Romanticism and advocacy of the 'hard dry image' influenced *Imagism. His essay 'Romanticism and Classicism' defines Romanticism as 'spilt religion', and predicts a new 'cheerful, dry and sophisticated' poetry; similarly, in the visual arts, he predicted the triumph of precise, abstract geometric form. (His friends included Jacob Epstein and *Gaudier-Brzeska.) His own poems (of which only six were published in his lifetime, five in *Orage's *The New Age*, 1912, as 'The Complete Poetical Works of T. E. Hulme') largely bear out his thesis; several of the handful that survive are short, provocative treatments of the subject of 'Sunset'. Hulme also contributed regularly to the *New Age*, notably in his essays on *Bergson, whom he also translated. He was killed in action, and much of his work survived only in notebooks. *Speculations: essays on humanism and the philosophy of art* (1924) and *Notes on language and style* (1929) were edited by *Read. Hulme's double role as conservative and Modernist had considerable influence on the development of 20th-cent. taste; T. S. *Eliot described him in 1924 as 'classical, reactionary and revolutionary . . . the antipodes of the eccentric, tolerant and democratic mind of the end of the century', and Hulme's stress on Original Sin and man's 'extraordinarily fixed and limited nature' finds echoes in Eliot's own work. See A. R. Jones, *The Life and Opinions of T. E. Hulme* (1960).

Human Understanding, *Enquiry concerning*, see HUME, D.

Humber, in *Geoffrey of Monmouth's *History* (ii. 1–2), a king of the Huns who invaded northern Britain in the reign of *Locrine, who defeated him and drowned him in the river Albus which afterwards bore his name. He brought to England *Estrildis with whom Locrine fell in love. The story is told in Spenser's *Faerie Queene* (II. x. 15–16).

HUMBOLDT, (Friedrich Heinrich) Alexander von (1769–1859), German traveller and scientist, published a series of works embodying the results of a scientific expedition to South America and Mexico, which were translated into English (1814–21). His greatest work was the *Cosmos* (published in German, 1845–62), a physical description of the universe, passing from celestial phenomena to the earth and its atmosphere, and finally to organic life.

HUMBOLDT, Wilhelm von (1767–1835), German writer, philologist, and educationalist. He introduced educational reforms in Prussia in the early 19th cent., his particular achievement being the founding of the University of Berlin on the principle of 'akademische Freiheit' ('academic freedom'). Students were to be educated on a humanist model, based on the study of the classical languages; universities were to be autonomous; and students were to be free to migrate from one university to another to complete their degrees. This was the basis of higher education in modern Germany.

HUME, David (1711–76), born and educated at Edinburgh, developed early in life a passion for philosophy. He spent three years (1734–7) in private study in France, and in 1739 published anonymously his *Treatise of Human Nature* in two volumes, a third volume and a promotional *Abstract* appearing in 1740. During his lifetime it sold poorly and was generally received with hostility, but its doctrines had an important impact on H. *Home and Adam *Smith. Hume's *Essays Moral and Political* (1741–2) was more successful. *A Letter from a Gentleman to his Friend in Edinburgh* (1745) includes Hume's defence of his *Treatise* when he contended unsuccessfully for the moral philosophy chair at Edinburgh, against the opposition of *Hutcheson and *Wishart. He accompanied General St Clair as judge-advocate in the expedition to Port L'Orient in 1747 and on a mission to Vienna and Turin in 1748. His *Enquiry concerning Human Understanding* (originally entitled *Philosophical Essays*) appeared in 1748 and his *Enquiry concerning the Principles of Morals* in 1751. In 1752 he published his *Political Discourses*, which was translated into French and made Hume famous on the Continent. In the same year he was appointed Advocates' Librarian in Edinburgh, subsequently surrendering the stipend to the poet *Blacklock. In 1754 appeared the first volume of his *History of Great Britain*, devoted to the early Stuarts, followed by further volumes in 1757, 1759, and 1762; publication was initially obstructed by the London book trade, but the work became immensely popular both in Britain and abroad, was extolled by *Gibbon and *Voltaire, and appeared in nearly 200 lifetime and posthumous editions. *Four Dissertations*, dedicated to J. *Home, was published in 1757, after the prudential suppression of controversial essays on suicide and immortality. From 1763 to 1765 Hume was secretary to the embassy in Paris, where he was well received by the court and by literary society. He brought back *Rousseau to England and befriended him, but Rousseau's suspicious nature presently led to a quarrel, Hume's account of which was published in 1766. Hume was under-secretary of state in 1767–8, and after this finally settled in Edinburgh. After his death, his friend Adam Smith published his autobiography with a eulogy (1777). Hume's *Dialogues concerning Natural Religion* was published in 1779 by his nephew. A collection of letters to him was published by J. H. Burton in 1849, and collections of letters from him by J. Y. T. Greig in 1932 and R. Klibansky and E. C. Mossner in 1954.

For Hume's philosophical views, see TREATISE OF HUMAN NATURE. His views on religion are contained, (a) in sections X–XI of *An Enquiry* concerning *Human Understanding*, in which he argues that the evidence for miracles is necessarily inferior to the evidence for the 'laws of nature' established by uniform experience of which they purport to be a violation, and that our belief in a supreme intelligence is founded not in the rational but in the imaginative faculty; (b) in the dissertation entitled *The Natural History of Religion*, in which he investigates its origin in human nature and traces its development from polytheism to monotheism and its inevitable degeneration; (c) in the *Dialogues concerning Natural Religion*, of which the cautious and ambiguous conclusion is 'that the cause or causes of order in the universe probably bear some remote analogy to human intelligence'.

Hume's writings on politics and history show a strong interest in human character and motivation. Though a believer in civil liberties (except freedom of divorce), and an opponent of 'divine right', he also defended the characters of the Stuart kings; and he rejected the social contract theory of society and social obligation as historically unrealistic, tracing these instead to custom and convenience. By deliberately steering between the extremes of prevailing Whig and Tory philosophies he incurred the complaints of both sides. As a political economist Hume attacked the mercantile system, and in general anticipated the views of later economists in the tradition of Adam Smith.

Hume was an early friend of James *Thomson and of the family of *Ramsay. He was a consummate stylist, but personal partialities made him an erratic judge of others. His high opinion of the writing of John Home and *Wilkie, and low opinion of A. *Ferguson, have not been supported by later critics. He preferred the classical style of *Milton, *Racine, and *Pope, to what he saw as the linguistic liberties of Shakespeare. In aesthetic theory he followed *Dubos.

Humgudgeon, Corporal Grace-be-here, a character in Scott's *Woodstock*.

Humorous Lieutenant, The, a comedy by J. *Fletcher, produced about 1619.

Prince Demetrius is in love with Celia, a captive. His father Antigonus, king of Syria, also falls in love with her, and during his son's absence at the wars, tries to seduce her, but she remains faithful to her younger lover. On Demetrius's return from victory, Antigonus informs him that Celia is dead, and while Demetrius shuts himself up in despair, tries to obtain her affection by a love-philtre. But the plot miscarries, and finally Celia's virtue and loyalty prevail on the king to surrender her to his son.

The title is taken from an eccentric lieutenant, suffering from an infirmity which stimulates him to wonderful deeds of courage in war. When cured, his courage fails him; and it comes again when he is deluded into thinking himself sick once more. By accident he drinks the love-philtre intended for Celia, and in consequence falls grotesquely in love with the king.

Humours, Comedy of, a term applied especially to the type of comic drama written by *Jonson, where a 'humour' is the embodiment in one of the characters of some dominating individual passion or propensity. The cardinal humours, whose balance was thought to determine a man's nature, were blood, phlegm, choler, and melancholy or black choler.

HUMPHREY, duke of Gloucester (1391–1447), youngest son of Henry IV, 'the Good Duke Humphrey', was, according to *Bale, educated at Balliol College, Oxford. He was appointed Protector on the death of Henry V in 1422 and acted as regent, 1420–1 and periodically until 1431, in place of his brother, the duke of Bedford, who was abroad in the French wars much of the time. Politically he was naïvely ambitious and factious; he owes the epithet 'Good' only to his patronage of men of letters, including *Lydgate and *Capgrave. He read Latin and Italian literature, and he promoted Renaissance humanism in England. He collected books from his youth and gave the first books for a library at Oxford; still named after him is the oldest part of the Bodleian which was built to house his bequest in the 15th cent. He married the luckless Jacqueline of Bavaria late in 1422 (Lydgate wrote a ballad in celebration of the wedding), but he abandoned her in Burgundy in 1425 in favour of Eleanor Cobham, and the marriage was annulled in 1428. He married Eleanor before 1431; in the 1440s she was repeatedly tried for witchcraft (it seems that she did experiment with black magic), and she was finally imprisoned on the Isle of Man in 1446.

Humphry Clinker, *The Expedition of*, a novel by T. *Smollett, published 1771.

The mellowest and most accomplished of Smollett's works, the novel achieves its effects by a new and pointed economy. It is *epistolary in form, describing, in the words of Sir W. *Scott (who published a Memoir in 1821), 'the various effects produced upon different members of the same family by the same objects'. Nearly two-thirds of the letters are either from Matthew Bramble to his friend and doctor Lewis, or from young squire Jery Melford (Bramble's nephew) to his friend Phillips at Oxford; the rest are from Bramble's sister Tabitha to her housekeeper Mrs Gwyllim at Brambleton-hall; from Bramble's niece Lydia to her school-friend Letty; and from the wildly illiterate Winifred Jenkins, Tabitha's servant, to Molly, a maid at the hall. The two principal non-letter-writers are Clinker himself and the Scot Lismahago. The narrative is simple, covering a round trip from Wales to London, to Scotland and back again, and its principal interest lies in the interplay of characters, whose mutual hostility is resolved by the end of the journey into general amity, or, as Winifred puts it, 'a family of love'.

The letters begin in Gloucester, whence the party proceeds to Clifton. Here Lydia first meets Wilson, apparently a mere strolling player, whom the outraged Jery challenges to a duel. After a stay at Bristol the party travels to Bath, which enchants Lydia and where the husband-hunting Tabitha fastens on Sir Ulic MacKilligut, but which is castigated by Bramble as 'a sink of profligacy and extortion'. On the journey to London the carriage overturns, Thomas the postilion is bitten by Tabitha's ferocious and much-loved cur Chowder, and the destitute Humphry is engaged in Thomas's place. In London Humphry is detected by Bramble preaching Methodism among servants at court, on the streets, and later (when he has been mistaken for a felon) in prison; he is outraged, but Lydia, Tabitha, and Win are moved, and Bramble is reconciled to Humphry's simple sincerity. The party then leaves for the north. At Harrogate they encounter the de Melvils and a reformed Count Fathom (see FERDINAND COUNT FATHOM) and at Scarborough Humphry 'rescues' his master from an enjoyable sea-bathe. At Durham they meet the disputatious Lismahago, his face 'half a yard in length', and hear of his exotic history, during which he was scalped by Red Indians. Tabitha scents a husband and prepares her pursuit. Once in Scotland Bramble recovers his health and Lydia becomes the toast of Edinburgh, a city which, however, disgusts them by its filth. Praise for Glasgow is followed by an Arcadian interlude by Loch Lomond. Returning by Carlisle, they meet Lismahago again and he and Tabitha become engaged. Various tumultuous and ludicrous events interrupt the journey south; Lydia catches sight of her beloved Wilson, but Jery will not permit them to meet. The carriage in which the party is travelling overturns in a river, and Humphry saves the life of the drowning Bramble. Shortly afterwards, through a chance encounter with Bramble's old friend Dennison, Humphry is revealed as Bramble's natural son, and Wilson as the son of Dennison. At the end of the story Bramble, filled with new vigour and magnanimity, is delighted to be on the way back to Brambleton-hall; Lydia is united with Wilson, Tabitha with Lismahago, and Humphry with Winifred. While none have been improbably transformed, all have advanced considerably in understanding of themselves and of the world.

Huncamunca, a character in Fielding's *Tom Thumb*. (See also SOPHONISBA.)

Hundreth Good Pointes of Husbandrie, see TUSSER, T.

Hungarian Brothers, The, a novel by A. M. *Porter.

Hunger, a novel by K. *Hamsun.

HUNT, (William) Holman (1827–1910), painter, and founder member of the *Pre-Raphaelite Brotherhood. Many of his most famous paintings (*The Scapegoat, The Light of the World*), have a strong religious inspiration, though he also painted many literary and historical subjects from Shakespeare, *Tennyson, *Keats, *Bulwer-Lytton, etc. His autobiographical *Pre-Raphaelitism and the Pre-Raphaelite Brotherhood* (1905) is a full but personal history of the movement.

HUNT, John (1775–1848), the brother of Leigh *Hunt, was a courageous and enterprising publisher who was prosecuted, threatened with legal actions, and fined many times. In 1805 he founded a short-lived paper, *The News*, then in 1808 he and Leigh established the very successful *Examiner, a general weekly independent paper devoted to liberal and reforming causes, which ran for many years and was frequently threatened with actions for libel. In 1810 he started a quarterly, *The Reflector* (with Leigh as editor), in which several essays by *Lamb appeared, but it ran for only four numbers. He was prosecuted in 1811 for an article against military flogging and was successfully defended by *Brougham. But in 1813 he and Leigh were both sentenced to two years' imprisonment in separate gaols and fined £500 apiece for a libel on the prince regent. Both men refused a guarantee to abstain from further attacks on the prince. In 1815–17 John published those essays of his brother and of *Hazlitt which were collected as *The Round Table* (1817). Hazlitt, in dedicating his *Political Essays* of 1819 to John Hunt, described him as 'the tried, steady, zealous and conscientious advocate of the liberty of his country'. He was the publisher and Leigh the editor of the short-lived but brilliant *Liberal, founded in 1822, in which *Byron published *The Vision of Judgement*, a work which had been refused by Byron's publisher, John *Murray. John was prosecuted for 'a seditious libel' on the late king, but Byron's executors settled the costs and the fine of £100. In the same year John published in the *Liberal* all the later cantos of *Don Juan (from Canto VI), which Murray had again refused. The *Literary Examiner*, founded in 1823, was short-lived, and in the same year John's long collaboration with his unbusinesslike brother, who owed him large sums, ended in unhappy litigation.

HUNT, (James Henry) Leigh (1784–1859), was born at Southgate, the son of a poor clergyman. Hunt received his schooling as a charity boy at Christ's Hospital. His first collection of poems appeared in 1807. In 1808 he founded and edited, with his brother John (above), the *Examiner, the first of many journals he was to initiate. He was to write poetry and drama, but he bulk of his large output was in the form of essays on a wide variety of subjects, many of which were published in his journals. The *Reflector, in which he published *Lamb's essays on Shakespeare and *Hogarth, appeared in 1810. In 1813 he and his brother were fined £500 and sentenced to two years' imprisonment for a libel in the *Examiner* on the prince regent. While in jail he was allowed to have his family with him, to continue to write and edit the *Examiner*, and to receive visits from friends, who included *Byron, *Moore, the *Lambs, *Bentham, James *Mill, and *Brougham. In 1816 he printed *Keats's early sonnet 'O Solitude' in the *Examiner*, and began his vigorous and lifelong support of Keats, *Shelley, and the *Romantic poets; his name was linked with that of Keats and Hazlitt in attacks on the so-called *Cockney school. He published his influential poem *The Story of Rimini* in the same year. His verses appeared in a volume, *Foliage* (1818), and in 1819 he published his poems *Hero and Leander* and *Bacchus and Ariadne*. In his journal the *Indicator* he published in 1821 Keats's *'La Belle Dame sans Merci', and in a journal founded jointly with Byron, the *Liberal*, appeared in 1822 *The Vision of Judgement*, and in the three subsequent numbers work by Byron, Shelley, *Hazlitt, Hunt, *Hogg, and others. The *Companion*, a magazine which contains some of Hunt's best work, appeared in 1828, his *Tatler* in 1830–2, and his *London Journal* in 1834–5. *Captain Sword and Captain Pen* (1835) is an effective poem describing the horrors of war. 'Abou Ben Adhem' (probably, with 'Jenny kissed me', Hunt's best-known poem) was published in an anthology, the *Book of Gems* (1838). Hunt's play *A Legend of Florence* (1840), a semi-Elizabethan tragedy, was produced at Covent Garden and was well received: he wrote many others without success. In the same year he published an edition of Restoration dramatists. In 1844 appeared his *Poetical Works* and *Imagination and Fancy*, in which he usefully compares painting and poetry; in 1846 an anthology, *Wit and Humour*, and *Stories from Italian Poets*; in 1847 (the year in which he received a civil list pension) appeared *Men, Women, and Books*; in 1848 *A Jar of Honey from Mount Hybla* and *The Town*, an evocation of London; in 1850 a lively *Autobiography*, much admired by *Carlyle and others; in 1851 *Table Talk*; in 1853 *The Religion of the Heart*; in 1855 *The Old Court Suburb*, essays on Kensington, and a bowdlerized edition of *Beaumont and *Fletcher.

Hunt's essays, although much influenced by the essayists of the previous century, were not moral in intent. His aim was to convey appreciation and enjoyment ('to reap pleasure from every object in creation'), and, although he is not considered a great critic, his pleasure in literature, drama, music, and friendship is agreeably infectious. His gift for detecting talent,

from Keats to *Tennyson, and his determined support for it, made him an invaluable editor. His sunny, optimistic nature is sketched in the early character of Skimpole in *Bleak House*; *Dickens denied the later knavery of Skimpole had anything to do with Hunt.

HUNT, Thornton Leigh (1810–73), journalist and editor, was the eldest son of Leigh *Hunt. He was, with G. H. *Lewes, joint founder of *The Leader*, and in 1855 joined the staff of the new *Daily Telegraph*, of which he became the virtual editor. His prolonged relationship with Lewes's wife Agnes, who bore him four children, was the indirect cause of the unorthodoxy of the union of Lewes with George *Eliot.

HUNT, (Isobel) Violet (1866–1942), novelist, born in Durham, the daughter of artist Alfred Hunt and novelist Margaret Hunt. She was for some years the companion of F. M. *Ford. A flamboyant feminist, a supporter of *Women's Suffrage, and a friend of H. G. *Wells, H. *James, and many others in the literary world, she published several novels (including *The Maiden's Progress*, 1894, and *White Rose of Weary Leaf*, 1908) and an autobiography, *The Flurried Years* (1926). M. *Sinclair, in *The English Review* (1922), attempts to qualify the novels' reputation for 'a merely hard yet superficial cleverness', praises her 'gallery of *demivierges*', and singles out her macabre *Tales of the Uneasy* (1911).

HUNTER, Sir William Wilson (1840–1900), born in Glasgow, educated there and in Paris and Bonn. He entered the Indian civil service in 1862. He was a man of broad cultural interests and was author of several notable volumes mainly on Indian historical subjects including *Annals of Rural Bengal* (1868), *Orissa* (1872), *The Imperial Gazetteer of India* (1881), *The Old Missionary* (1895), and *The Thackerays in India* (1897). He had completed only two volumes of his *History of British India* (1899–1900) at his death.

Huntingdon, Arthur and Helen (Graham), leading characters in A. Brontë's *The Tenant of Wildfell Hall*.

HUNTINGDON, Robert, Earl of, see ROBIN HOOD.

HUNTINGDON, Selina Hastings, countess of (1707–91), founder of the group of Calvinistic Methodists known as 'Lady Huntingdon's Connection', and warm supporter of *Whitefield. She was largely responsible for introducing Methodism to the upper classes.

Huntingdon's Connection, Lady, see HUNTINGDON.

Huntinglen, earl of, a character in Scott's *The Fortunes of Nigel*.

Hunting of the Snark, The, a mock-heroic nonsense poem by Lewis Carroll (C. L. *Dodgson), published 1867. Dodgson said that the poem sprang from 'one line of verse—one solitary line—"For the Snark *was* a Boojum, you see" ', that came to him one day in 1874 while he was out walking: to questions asking whether the poem was an allegory, or a political satire, or contained some hidden moral, he claimed to have 'but one answer, "I don't know!" ' (*The Theatre*, April 1887).

Huon of Bordeaux, the hero of a French 13th-cent. *chanson de geste*. He has the misfortune to kill Charlot, son of *Charlemagne, in an affray, not knowing who his assailant is. He is thereupon condemned to death by the emperor, but reprieved on condition that he will go to the court of Gaudisse, amir of Babylon, bring back a handful of his hair and four of his teeth, kill his doughtiest knight, and kiss Esclarmonde his daughter. By the help of the fairy Oberon, Huon achieves the adventure. The work was translated by Lord *Berners and printed by *Wynkyn de Worde in 1534. Huon's adventure is the theme of *Weber's opera *Oberon*.

HURD, Richard (1720–1808), son of a Staffordshire farmer, was bishop successively of Lichfield and Worcester. He produced an edition of *Horace's *Ars Poetica* (1749) and *Epistola ad Augustum* (1751), adding to the second his 'A Discourse concerning Poetical Imitation'. His *Moral and Political Dialogues* appeared in 1759, with dialogues between, e.g., A. *Cowley and *Sprat. *Letters on Chivalry and Romance* (1762) is an important reassessment of Elizabethan literature: Hurd was notably sympathetic to *Spenser, argued that the 'Gothic' was more poetic than the 'Grecian', and that *neo-classical rules were inappropriately applied to chivalric romances, which were composed on different but no less artistic principles. The 'revolution' in taste of the *Augustan age had produced 'a great deal of good sense', but, 'What we have lost is a world of fine fabling.' His ideas on the classic and the romantic were developed by T. *Warton. Hurd was a friend and correspondent of W. *Mason and T. *Gray; the letters were edited by E. H. Pearce and L. Whibley (1932).

HURDIS, James (1763–1801), minor poet, and friend and correspondent of *Cowper. He was professor of poetry at Oxford in 1793. His best-known work is *The Village Curate. A Poem* (1788). See A. P. Whitaker, *James Hurdis, His Life and Writings* (1960).

Hurlothrumbo (1729), a popular burlesque by Samuel Johnson (1691–1773) a Manchester dancing master; it was described by his fellow Mancunian *Byrom (who also wrote an epilogue for it) as full of 'oddities, out-of-the-waynesses, flights, madness, comicalities etc.'

Husbandrie, *Hundreth Good Pointes of,* see TUSSER, T.

Husband's Message, The, an Old English poem of 53 lines in the *Exeter Book*, one of the group usually called 'elegies'. Its ostensible form is a message to a woman from her husband who has had to leave his own country because of a feud, telling her of his prosperity in another land and asking her to join him. The speaker of the poem is the inscription itself which bears the message, and it is sometimes thought to be the continuation of the riddle (no. 60, the Reed) which it follows in the *Exeter Book*. It has also, not too implausibly, been interpreted in a religious sense, perhaps as an address from Christ to the Church.

Ed. and translated by R. Hamer, *A Choice of Anglo-Saxon Verse* (1970); ed R. F. Leslie in *Three Old English Elegies* (1961).

HUTCHESON, Francis (1694–1746), an Ulsterman, educated at Glasgow University, was professor of moral philosophy at Glasgow from 1729 until his death. Before this he had published aesthetic, moral, and political essays in the Dublin and London press, and two books, *An Inquiry into the Original of our Ideas of Beauty and Virtue* (1725) and *An Essay on the Nature and Conduct of the Passions and Affections with Illustrations on the Moral Sense* (1728), both subsequently revised. His posthumous *System of Moral Philosophy* was published in 1755 with a biography by William Leechman.

A protégé of *Molesworth, Hutcheson introduced the civic humanist tradition into higher education: he trained a whole generation of students, among them Adam *Smith, in the Whig philosophy of personal liberty and government restraint, and his progressive views on social justice, representative government, colonial autonomy, and the rejection of slavery, were influential among Scots émigrés to America. In ethics he developed the ideas of *Shaftesbury on the moral sense into a fully-fledged system. He saw a close relation between aesthetic and moral perception, by which we come to be aware of providentially designed order. We have a 'moral sense of beauty in actions and affections' which is stimulated by contemplating benevolence directed at another person. Virtue is identical with benevolence insofar as it gives disinterested pleasure, that action being best which aims at the greatest happiness of the greatest number. This view anticipates *Utilitarianism.

Hutcheson was instrumental in helping to establish the publishing and printing business of the *Foulis brothers.

HUTCHINSON, R(ay) C(oryton) (1907–

5), novelist, educated at Oriel College, Oxford; he worked for some years in the advertising department of Colman's at Norwich before becoming a full-time writer. His works include *The Unforgotten Prisoner* (1933), a powerful portrayal of revenge and conciliation in the aftermath of the First World War, seen partly through the sufferings of young Klaus, half English and half German, a victim of the conflicts of his parents and of his country; *Testament* (1938), set in Russia at the time of the Revolution; *The Stepmother* (1955); and *Rising* (1976), a historical novel set in South America.

HUTCHINSON, Mrs Lucy (b. 1620), daughter of Sir Allen Apsley, and wife of John Hutchinson (1615–64). She was the author of *Memoirs of the Life of Colonel Hutchinson*, which she wrote after his death to preserve his memory for her children; it is a vivid and valuable account of the state of the country at the outbreak of civil war and of the conflict in the vicinity of Nottingham, told from the Puritan point of view. John Hutchinson held Nottingham for Parliament as governor, signed the king's death warrant, was imprisoned at the Restoration, and saved from execution partly through his wife's intervention. Her narrative was first published in 1806, ed J. Hutchinson, with a brief 'Fragment' of her own life, in which she records with some satisfaction that she 'outstripped' her brothers in intellectual achievement; her work as a whole shows an interesting mixture of strength, shrewdness, religious devotion, and personal vanity.

Hutchinsonians, (1) the followers of Mrs Anne Hutchinson (1591–1643), who emigrated from England to Massachusetts, where she founded an Antinomian sect, was banished from the colony, and eventually massacred by Indians at Hell Gate, New York county, with all but one of her family; (2) the followers of John Hutchinson (1674–1737), whose chief work, *Moses's Principia* (1724), maintained that Hebrew was the primitive language of mankind and the key to all knowledge. It was written as an attack on I. *Newton's Principia*, and is thought to have influenced *Smart.

HUTH, Henry (1815–78), merchant banker and bibliophile. His library contained narratives of voyages, Shakespearian and early English literature, early Spanish and German books, and valuable editions of the Bible.

HUTTEN, Ulrich von, see EPISTOLAE OB-SCURORUM VIRORUM.

HUTTON, Richard Holt (1826–97), educated at University College London, prepared for the Unitarian ministry at Manchester New College, and became joint editor with his friend Bagehot of the *National Review* (1855–64). From 1861 until his death he was joint editor of

the *Spectator*, and under his control the journal wielded great influence. His works, most of which show his theological inclinations, include *Essays, Theological and Literary* (1871), a volume on *Newman (1891), *Criticisms on Contemporary Thought* (1894), and *Aspects of Religious and Scientific Thought* (1899).

HUXLEY, Aldous Leonard (1894–1963), grandson of T. H. *Huxley and brother of Julian *Huxley; his mother died when he was 14, and when he was 16 at Eton he developed serious eye trouble which made him nearly blind and prevented any possibility of a scientific career, though he recovered sufficiently to read English at Balliol College, Oxford. During the war he met Lady O. *Morrell and visited Garsington frequently; she and other literary figures that he met there were to appear, not always to their own satisfaction, in his early satirical novels. By 1919, when he began to write for *Murry in *The Athenaeum*, he had already published three volumes of verse; a volume of stories, *Limbo* (1920), was followed by *Crome Yellow* (1921), a country-house satire which earned him a reputation for precocious brilliance and cynicism, and much offended Lady Ottoline. During the 1920s and 1930s Huxley and his wife Maria lived in Italy, then France; during this period he wrote much fiction, including *Mortal Coils* (1922, stories; includes 'The Gioconda Smile'); *Antic Hay* (1923), set in post-war London's nihilistic Bohemia); *Those Barren Leaves* (1925, set in Italy); and *Point Counter Point* (1928), in which were recognized portraits of his friend D. H. *Lawrence as Rampion and Murry as Burlap. *Brave New World* (1932), his most enduringly popular work, was followed by *Eyeless in Gaza* (1936). Huxley's literary reputation deteriorated when he left in 1937 for California, partly for the sake of his eyes, partly in disillusion with the failure of the peace movements of Europe, partly in search (with his friend Gerald Heard, 1899–   ) of new spiritual direction. He continued to write in many genres: novels include *After Many A Summer* (1939), in which Heard appears as the mystic Propter, and *Island* (1962), an optimistic Utopia; and other works include essays, historical studies, travel works, and *The Devils of Loudun* (1952), a study in sexual hysteria which became the basis of *Whiting's play *The Devils*. He became deeply interested in mysticism and parapsychology; *The Doors of Perception* (1954) and *Heaven and Hell* (1956) describe his experiments with mescalin and LSD.

   Although *Brave New World* has an assured place as a popular classic, Huxley's other novels have proved difficult to 'place' as literature. Their mixture of satire and earnestness, of apparent brutality and humanity, have led some to dismiss them as smart and superficial, a symptom rather than an interpretation of a hollow age; others have seen them as brilliant and provocative 'novels of ideas' written by a man who was not by nature a novelist, but who (according to *Berlin) helped to liberate a generation by shedding light 'in dark places'. A biography by S. *Bedford (2 vols) was published 1973–4.

HUXLEY, Sir Julian Sorell (1887–1975), biologist and writer, brother of Aldous *Huxley, educated at Eton and Balliol College, Oxford. He won the Newdigate Prize for poetry in 1908, and published a small collection of verse, *The Captive Shrew and other poems of a biologist* (1932), which shows, though less vividly than some of his scientific works, his keen interest in and love of the natural world, particularly of birds. He held many important appointments, was professor of zoology at King's College, London, 1925–7, professor of physiology in the Royal Institution, 1926–9, and secretary of the Zoological Society, 1935–42. He was well known as a writer and broadcaster, and, like his grandfather T. H. *Huxley, had a gift for popular exposition which did not impede the rigours of his scientific work. His writings include *Essays of a Biologist* (1923), *Animal Biology* (with J. B. S. *Haldane, 1927), *The Science of Life* (with H. G. and G. P. *Wells, 1929) and *Soviet genetics and world science* (on the Lysenko controversy, 1949). See R. W. Clark, *The Huxleys* (1968).

HUXLEY, T(homas) H(enry) (1825–95), studied at Charing Cross Hospital and was assistant surgeon on HMS *Rattlesnake*, 1846–50. His surveys of marine life on the Australian Barrier Reef appeared as papers for the *Royal and *Linnean Societies, he was elected FRS in 1851, and in 1854 became professor of Natural History at the Royal School of Mines. He wrote extensively on specialist subjects, but also became widely known and admired as a lecturer to lay audiences, often of working men; he aimed to avoid 'technical dialect' and had a gift for explaining complicated scientific points in language that was generally intelligible. His views on religion, education, philosophy and evolution, and on man's newly conceived place in the universe (e.g. in *Evidence as to man's place in nature*, 1863, *Evolution and Ethics*, 1893, and other essays) had a profound impact on 19th-cent. thought. He was a friend of *Darwin, and an influential though discriminating supporter of his theories. He coined the word 'agnostic' to describe his own philosophical position, which he expounded at the *Metaphysical Society and in the *Nineteenth Century. A vigorous though courteous disputant, he engaged in controversy with *Owen, *Gladstone, and other critics of evolutionary theory. His *Collected Essays* were published in 1893–4, his *Scientific Memoirs* in

1898–1903, and his *Life and Letters*, edited by his son Leonard, in 1900–3.

HUYSMANS, Joris-Karl (1848–1907), French novelist. After a number of early novels in a Naturalistic vein (e.g., *Marthe, histoire d'une fille*, 1876; *En ménage*, 1881), he adopted another mode in *A rebours* (1884; English trans. *Against Nature*, 1959), the work for which he is now chiefly remembered. Introducing the neuraesthenic aristocrat Des Esseintes, who turns his back on the world as he finds it to create a world of sensuousness and artifice within which to cultivate extremes of self-awareness, *A rebours* has been regarded as a manual of the extravagant aestheticism of the *fin de siècle*. It was much admired by *Wilde, who introduces it into *The Picture of Dorian Gray* as the 'yellow book' given to Dorian by Lord Henry Wotton. Huysmans' later work includes four novels which follow the spiritual progress of the central character Durtal towards Roman Catholicism: *Là-bas* (1891), *En route* (1895), *La Cathédrale* (1898), *L'Oblat* (1903).

HYDE, Douglas (1860–1949), Irish writer and ardent pioneer in the *Irish Revival, became the first professor of Irish at the National University in 1908. He founded the Gaelic League in 1893 and was its president until 1915. Several of his writings, including in particular *Love Songs of Connacht* (1893) and *A Literary History of Ireland* (1892), together with several volumes of verse translations from the Gaelic, were highly influential. In 1901 the *Irish Literary Theatre produced Hyde's Gaelic *Casadh*, and he later became one of the vice-presidents of the *Abbey Theatre company. He was the first president of Eire, holding office from 1938 to 1945. A biography by G. W. Dunleavy appeared in 1974.

HYDE, Edward, see CLARENDON.

Hyde Park, a comedy by J. *Shirley, acted 1632, printed 1637.

This comedy seems to have been written for performance at the time of the annual opening of the park, and it exploits the topical appeal of the subject. The fourth act features horse-racing: when *Pepys saw a revival of the play after the Restoration, horses were actually led across the stage. Apart from the local colour, there is a plot about the return of a long-lost husband in disguise; another plot, sometimes seen as a foreshadowing of *Restoration comedy, is the courtship of the witty Carol and her no less witty suitor Fairfield, culminating in what is probably the earliest example of a 'proviso scene' such as Congreve was to develop more fully in *The Way of the World*.

Hydriotaphia, or *Urn Burial,* by Sir T. *Browne, the companion piece to *The Garden of Cyrus*, published 1658, has been called the first archaeological treatise in English. He takes the discovery of some burial urns in a Norfolk field as the occasion for a wide-ranging meditation on the funeral procedures of many nations. The fragility of all relics and monuments prompts him to turn to the Christian doctrine of resurrection as the only lasting hope. From the first words of the 'Epistle Dedicatory', 'When the Funerall pyre was out, and the last valediction over', to the solemn splendour of the closing pages, beginning, 'But the iniquity of oblivion blindely scattereth her poppy', Browne achieves the 'high style' demanded by his subject with a richness of diction and rhythmical power seldom if ever equalled in English prose.

Hye Way to the Spyttel House, The, a tract printed and probably composed by Robert Copland (*fl.* 1508–48), describing the beggars and other types of the poorer classes who visit the hospital, in the form of a dialogue between the author and the porter of the hospital. It throws a vivid light on the poverty prevailing in the early 16th cent.

HYGINUS, Gaius Julius, an immensely erudite freedman whom the Emperor Augustus (d. AD 14) put in charge of the Palatine Library. He was a prolific author, but the astronomical treatise with stellar myths and the book of legends that now bear his name are probably no more than incompetent summaries of two of his works. They remain, however, our sole authorities for a number of legends and were widely used by later mythographers.

Hymenaei, a marriage masque by *Jonson, performed at Whitehall on Twelfth Night 1606, and printed in that year, with the theme of union. The marriage was that of the earl of Essex and Lady Frances Howard, the murderer of *Overbury. It ended in scandal and divorce.

Hymns Ancient and Modern, a collection promoted and edited by the Revd Sir H. W. Baker (1821–77), vicar of Monkland, near Leominster, who contributed to it many original hymns and translations from the Latin. The collection first appeared in 1861 and various supplements and revised editions have since been published.

'Hymn to the Naiads', see AKENSIDE, M.

Hypallage, from a Greek word meaning 'exchange', a transference of epithet, as 'Sansfoy's dead dowry' for 'dead Sansfoy's dowry' (*Spenser).

Hypatia, a novel by C. *Kingsley.

Hyperbole, the use of exaggerated terms not in order to deceive but to emphasize the importance or extent of something. *Puttenham translated it as 'the over reacher', which in turn provides the title of H. Levin's study of *Marlowe, *The Overreacher* (1952), Marlowe having been particularly addicted to this figure of speech: e.g. 'Was this the face that launched a thousand ships? | And burnt the topless towers of Ilium?' (*Dr Faustus*).

Hyperion: *a fragment* and *The Fall of Hyperion*, fragments of epic poems by *Keats, written 1818–19. *Hyperion* was published 1820, *The Fall of Hyperion* not until 1856. In 1818 Keats gave up the effort to finish *Hyperion*, then began to rewrite and recast it as *The Fall of Hyperion*, but once again the effort was abandoned.

In the first version, written as direct narrative, the tremendous figure of the fallen Saturn, conquered by Jove, mourns the loss of his kingdom and debates with his fallen fellow-Titans, in their craggy lair, how he may regain his kingdom. They conclude that only the magnificent Hyperion, who is still unfallen, will be able to help them. In Bk III the golden Apollo, god of music, poetry, and knowledge, speaks to the goddess Mnemosyne of his inexplicable anguish; then, at the moment of his deification, the fragment ends. In the second version, the poet is in a luxuriant garden, where he drinks an elixir which induces a vision. He finds himself in a vast domed monument, then proceeds with pain and difficulty to climb the stair to the shrine of the priestess Moneta. Together they find the agonized fallen Saturn, and with Mnemosyne and Thea they speak to him of his pain and loss. In despair he leaves with Thea to comfort his fellow-Titans, while the poet and Moneta watch the magnificent, but much troubled, Hyperion blaze into the west. The precise meaning of the allegory is not always clear, but both poems have as their general theme the nature of poetry and the nature and development of the poet. It is not known why Keats abandoned what was to have been his great work, but one of his fears, expressed in a letter to his friend *Reynolds, was that his writing was too Miltonic.

Hysteron Proteron, in grammar and rhetoric, a figure of speech in which the word or phrase that should properly come last is put first; in general, 'putting the cart before the horse'.

Hythloday, Raphael, in More's *Utopia*, the traveller in whose mouth the author places the criticisms of English institutions, and the description of the 'wise and godly ordinances' of the Utopians.

I

Iachimo, the villain in Shakespeare's *Cymbeline*, whose name, a diminutive of Iago, may recall the villain in *Othello*.

Iago, the villainous ensign in Shakespeare's *Othello*. The equivalent character in the source was nameless. His character has often been seen as problematic, *Coleridge speaking in a famous phrase of the 'motive-hunting of motiveless malignity'.

Iamb, Iambic trimeter, Iambic pentameter, see METRE.

IBSEN, Henrik (1828–1906), Norwegian dramatist, generally acknowledged as the founder of modern prose drama. His first successes, *Brand* (1866) and *Peer Gynt* (1867), created his name in Scandinavia, but it was over 20 years before the work of *Gosse and *Archer (and later the support of *Hardy, W. *James, G. B. *Shaw, and others) established him as a major dramatist in England. In 1871 Gosse wrote a review of *Poems* of the unknown Ibsen, translated an early play (*Love's Comedy*), and in 1873 published an enthusiastic account of Ibsen's work. In the same year Archer read Ibsen's *Emperor and Galilean*, and his translation of *The Pillars of Society* was used for the first performance of Ibsen in England in 1880, which was largely ignored. Archer introduced and read Ibsen to the young Shaw, who became deeply interested. By the end of the 1880s Archer's few translations were selling well, and in 1889 a long review of Ibsen's work by Gosse was followed by a highly successful production of *A Doll's House* (1879). In 1890 Shaw gave a lecture which he published in 1891 as *The Quintessence of Ibsenism*, and the first volumes of Archer's translation of Ibsen's collected works were well received. In 1891 a single performance of *Ghosts* (1881) and a commercial production of *Hedda Gabler* (1890) both caused a storm of outrage; in 1892 a production of *The Master Builder* (1892) was reviled by critics but supported by the public. In the course of the next ten years Ibsen became established in England as a major dramatist and an important influence, both through Archer's continuing translations and through productions of many of the plays. In 1890 the *Fortnightly Review* contained an enthusiastic review of *When We Dead Awaken* (1900) by the 18-year-old *Joyce, who became a lifelong admirer.

Ibsen's earlier plays (such as *Ghosts* and *An Enemy of the People*, 1882) were concerned largely with social and political themes, but the last six (which include *Rosmersholm*, 1886; *The Lady from the Sea*, 1888; *The Master Builder*; and *Little Eyolf*, 1896) are more deeply concerned with the forces of the unconscious, and were greatly admired by *Freud. At the end of his life Ibsen commented that he was 'more of a poet and less of a social philosopher than people . . . suppose', and also declared that his interest was not so much in women's rights as in human rights. Ibsen created new attitudes to drama, and is credited with being the first major dramatist to write tragedy about ordinary people in prose. The quality of his dialogue, and his discarding of traditional theatrical effects, demanded and achieved a new style of performance. All his great prose dramas are now in the standard English-language repertoire, and *Peer Gynt* (written in verse) is frequently revived; there have been many translations since Archer's, including versions by Una Ellis-Fermor, M. Meyer, R. Farquharson Sharp, J. W. McFarlane, and Peter Watts, and recent stage adaptations include those by A. *Miller, J. *Osborne, C. *Fry, A. *Jellicoe, G. *Hill, and Christopher Hampton. There is a life by M. Meyer (3 vols, 1967–71).

Iceman Cometh, The, see O'NEILL, E.

Icon Basilike, see EIKON BASILIKE.

Ida, Princess, the heroine of Tennyson's *The Princess*, which is the basis of the *Gilbert and Sullivan opera *Princess Ida*.

Idea, a sonnet sequence by M. *Drayton, first published as *Ideas Mirrour* in 1594, much revised and expanded, reaching its final form of 63 sonnets in 1619.

Idealism, in philosophy, the view that minds or spirits are the only, or the fundamental, entities in the world, material things being unreal or in some way parasitical upon the mental. There are several varieties of idealist philosophy, and their most notable exponents include *Berkeley, *Kant, and *Hegel.

Idea of a University, The, see NEWMAN, J. H.

Ideas Mirrour, see IDEA.

Idea, the Shepheards Garland, see DRAYTON, M.

'Idiot Boy, The', a ballad by *Wordsworth,

first published in *Lyrical Ballads* (1798). One of the most characteristic and controversial of the poet's early works, it takes as hero the idiot son of a poor countrywoman, Betty Foy, who is sent off on horseback by night to fetch the doctor for a sick neighbour. He is so long gone that his mother sets out to seek him, and finds him at last by a waterfall, whither the pony has wandered freely through the moonlight, to the boy's delight. The neighbour recovers and sets out to meet mother and son, and all three are happily reunited; the boy's description of his adventures,

'The cocks did crow to-whoo, to-whoo,
And the sun did shine so cold',

fittingly illustrate Wordsworth's intention of 'giving the charm of novelty to things of every-day'. Wordsworth ably defended his choice of subject matter (which offended many) in a letter to John *Wilson, June 1802, attacking the 'false delicacy' of his detractors, and praising the natural humanity of the poor: 'I have indeed, often looked upon the conduct of fathers and mothers of the lower classes of society towards idiots as the great triumph of the human heart.'

Idler, The, (1) a series of papers contributed by Dr *Johnson to the *Universal Chronicle: or Weekly Gazette* between 15 April 1758 and 5 April 1760. These papers are shorter and lighter than those of *The Rambler*, but their general character is the same. They include the well-known sketches of Dick Minim, the critic, of Mr Sober (the author himself), Jack Whirler (*Newbery the publisher), and Tom Restless. Twelve were by other contributors, including three by *Reynolds and three by T. *Warton the younger. (2) a monthly journal edited by J. K. *Jerome and Robert Barr, 1892–1911.

Idylls, see ECLOGUE.

Idylls of the King, The, a series of 12 connected poems by *Tennyson, of which *'Morte d'Arthur', subsequently incorporated in 'The Passing of Arthur', was composed in 1833 after A. H. *Hallam's death and published in 1842. It was a project that preoccupied Tennyson over many years, during which he studied *Malory, *The Mabinogion, *Laȝamon, and other sources of Arthurian legend. In 1855–6 he began writing the first Idyll, which was to become 'Merlin and Vivien', which he followed with 'Enid', later divided into 'The Marriage of Geraint' and 'Geraint and Enid'. The first four were published in 1859 as 'Enid', 'Vivien', 'Elaine', and 'Guinevere' and constituted, though with many revisions, roughly half of the final version. They were extremely successful, selling 10,000 copies in six weeks. In 1869 followed 'The Coming of Arthur', 'The Holy Grail', 'Pelleas and Ettarre', and 'The Passing of Arthur'. 'The Last

Tournament' was published in the *Contemporary Review* in 1871, then, with 'Gareth and Lynette', in 1872. 'Balin and Balan', written 1872–4, did not appear until 1885. The sequence as now printed first appeared in 1891.

The poems present the story of *Arthur, from his first meeting with Guinevere to the ruin of his kingdom and his death in the 'last, dim, weird battle of the west'. The protagonists are Arthur and Guinevere, Launcelot and Elaine, but the design embraces the fates of various minor characters. The adultery of Guinevere and Launcelot is seen as one of the forces that destroys the idealism and bright hopes of the Round Table, and the scene in which the guilty Guinevere 'grovelled with her face against the floor' before Arthur to listen to his long denunciatory speech was received with great enthusiasm; his forgiveness of her ('Lo! I forgive thee, as Eternal God | Forgives') moved the poet himself to tears. But even in his day some critics found the poems abstract, shadowy, and defective in dramatic power, the scenes of violence false, and the medieval costume trappings absurd; *Swinburne commented ironically on the fact that 'our Laureate should find in the ideal cuckold his type of the ideal man'. These doubts have been endorsed by most subsequent criticism, though some, following Tennyson's own hint that 'there is an allegorical or perhaps rather a parabolic drift in the poem', have argued in favour of the *Idylls* as 'a dramatic parable of enormous variety, richness and complexity' (F. E. L. Priestley, 1973) or as a new and therefore perplexing genre, a symbolist vision of apocalyptic doom (Rosenberg, *The Fall of Camelot*, 1973).

Ignatius His Conclave, see DONNE, J.

IGNATIUS LOYOLA, St (1491–1556), a page to Ferdinand V of Aragon, and subsequently an officer in the Spanish army, was wounded at the siege of Pampeluna (1521), and thereafter devoted himself to religion. He constituted himself the Knight of the Blessed Virgin, went on a pilgrimage to the Holy Land, and on his return in 1534 founded in Paris the Society of Jesus (Jesuits), bound by vows of chastity, poverty, obedience, and submission to the holy see, and authorized by papal bull in 1540. Its principal activities were preaching, instruction, and confession, and it formed a spiritual army bound to obedience. The object of the society was to support the Roman church in its conflict with the 16th-cent. reformers and to propagate its faith among the heathen. Francis *Xavier and other missionaries carried on the latter work in the most distant parts of the world. The secret power of the organization brought it into collision with the civil authorities even in Roman Catholic countries, whence its members have at times been expelled. Loyola's *Exercitia* (*Spiritual Exercises*), a manual of devotion and of rules for meditation and prayer, was finished in 1548.

Ignoge, in *Geoffrey of Monmouth's *History* (i. 11), the daughter of the Greek king Pandrasus, abducted and married by Brutus (*Brut). She was the mother of *Locrine, *Camber, and Albanactus. Spenser (*Faerie Queene*, II. x. 14) calls her Inogene of Italy.

Ignoramus, a famous university farcical play by George Ruggle (1575–1622), a fellow of Clare College, Cambridge, produced in 1615 before James I, an adaptation of an Italian comedy by Della Porta. The title part is a burlesque of the recorder of Cambridge, Brackyn, who is subjected to various humiliations; he falls in love with the heroine Rosabella, but is fobbed off with the virago Polla, belaboured, thought to be possessed by evil spirits, subjected to exorcism, and finally carried off to a monastery for treatment. Brackyn had already been held up to ridicule in the last part of *The Parnassus Plays*.

Igraine, in Arthurian legend, the wife of *Gorlois of Cornwall, taken as his wife by Uther *Pendragon who assumed the likeness of Gorlois by Merlin's magic. *Arthur was the child of this union.

Iliad, The, a Greek epic poem attributed to *Homer, describing the war waged by Achaean princes against Troy for the purpose of recovering Helen, wife of Menelaus, whom Paris, son of King Priam of Troy, had carried off. In particular it deals with the wrath of Achilles, the special hero of the poem, at the slight put upon him by Agamemnon, leader of the host, and his final return to the field and slaying of Hector.

'Il Penseroso', a poem in rhymed octosyllabics (with a ten-line prelude) by *Milton, written ?1631, printed 1645. The title (which in correct Italian should read 'pensieroso') means 'the contemplative man'. The poem is an invocation to Leisure and Contemplation. It describes the pleasures of the studious, meditative life, of tragedy, epic poetry, and music. It had a considerable influence on the meditative *graveyard poems of the 18th cent., and there are echoes in Pope's *Eloisa to Abelard*, and later *Gothic works. It is a companion piece to *'L'Allegro'.

Imaginary Conversations of Literary Men and Statesmen, by W. S. *Landor, published 1824–9, followed by *Imaginary Conversations of Greeks and Romans*, published 1853.

If *Pericles and Aspasia* and *The Pentameron are included, these represent the bulk of Landor's prose work. The conversations are between characters from classical times to the 19th cent.; some are dramatic, some idyllic, some satirical. Many concern political matters, but social and literary questions are also considered. Action and incidents are occasionally interposed. There are some 150 dialogues and the quality is very uneven, for Landor's own passionate and often prejudiced views tend to obtrude. *Wordsworth

observed that the dialogues between classical characters, such as between Cicero and his brother, were often the best. The dialogues between the following are generally considered to be among the most successful: Dante and Beatrice; Princess Mary and Princess Elizabeth; Louis XIV and Père La Chaise; Aesop and Rhodope; Romilly and Wilberforce; Fra Filippo Lippi and Pope Eugenius IV; Calvin and Melanchthon; Bacon and Hooker; Leonora d'Este and Father Parigarola; Leofric and Lady Godiva.

Imagism, a movement of English and American poets in revolt from *Romanticism, which flourished *c.*1910–17, and derived in part from the aesthetic philosophy of T. E. *Hulme. Its first anthology, *Des Imagistes* (1914), edited by *Pound, had eleven contributors; R. *Aldington, H. *Doolittle, F. S. Flint, Skipwith Cannell, A. *Lowell, W. C. *Williams, *Joyce, Pound, F. M. Hueffer (*Ford), Allen Upward, and John Cournos. Some of D. H. *Lawrence's poems of this period may also be described as Imagist. The characteristic products of the movement are more easily recognized than its theories defined: they tend to be short, composed of short lines of musical cadence rather than metrical regularity, to avoid abstraction, and to treat the image with a hard, clear precision rather than with overt symbolic intent. (Pound: 'the natural object is always the adequate symbol.') The influence of Japanese forms (tanka and *haiku) is obvious in many. Amy Lowell succeeded Pound as spokesperson of the group, and was responsible for several Imagist anthologies.

Imitation of Christ, or *De Imitatione Christi*, see THOMAS À KEMPIS.

Imitations of Horace, see POPE, A.

Imlac, a character in Dr Johnson's *Rasselas.

Immortals, The (*Les Immortels*), the 40 members of the *Académie française, so called because of their enduring fame, with side reference to the fact that their number is always filled up. The name was also given in ancient times to a body of 10,000 Persian infantry, the flower of the army, whose number was kept constantly full.

Imogen, the heroine of Shakespeare's *Cymbeline*. Her name may be the result of a typographical error by the printers of the First *Folio; *A Mirror for Magistrates*, *Holinshed, and *Forman all give the name as 'Innogen', which is also that of *Leonato's silent wife in *Much ado About Nothing*.

Imoinda, see OROONOKO.

Impertinent, The Curious, see CURIOUS IMPERTINENT, THE.

Importance of Being Earnest, The: *A Trivial*

Comedy for Serious People, a play by O. *Wilde, first performed at the St James's Theatre, London, on 14 Feb. 1895.

Wilde's most dazzling and epigrammatic work, it describes the courtships and betrothals of two young men-about-town, John Worthing (Jack) and Algernon (Algy) Moncrieff, who are in pursuit respectively of Gwendolen Fairfax (Algy's cousin) and Jack's ward, Cecily Cardew. Both young men lead double lives, in that Jack is known in town under the name of Ernest, while representing to his ward Cecily in the country that he has a wicked brother Ernest; Algy, to cover his own diversions, has created a fictitious character, the sickly Bunbury, whose ill health requires a visit whenever engagements in town (particularly those with his formidable aunt Lady Bracknell) render his absence desirable. After many confusions of identity, during which it transpires that Cecily's governess, Miss Prism, had once mislaid Jack as a baby in a handbag at Victoria Station, it is revealed that Jack and Algy are in fact brothers, and that Jack's name is indeed Ernest. All objections, both financial and genealogical, to both matches, are thus overcome, and Gwendolen's addiction to the very name of 'Ernest' is satisfied, so all ends happily.

Impressionism, the name given in derision (from a painting by Monet called *Impression, soleil levant*) to the work of a group of French painters who held their first exhibition in 1874. Their aim was to render the effects of light on objects rather than the objects themselves. They painted out of doors, using a high key and bright colours. Claude Monet (1840-1926), Alfred Sisley (1839-99), and Camille Pissarro (1831-1903) carried out their aims most completely. Among artists associated with the movement, Auguste Renoir (1841-1919) reacted against its spontaneity in the early 1880s, while *Cézanne became increasingly interested in an analysis of form that led on to *Cubism. Eduard Manet (1832-83) did not exhibit with the Impressionists, but many of his aims were similar; he and Edgar Degas (1834-1917) were concerned to create a new style that should capture the rapid tempo of modern urban life. The term is used by transference in literature and music.

Impressions of Theophrastus Such, The, a volume of essays by G. *Eliot, published 1879. Most of the 18 essays are character studies loosely based on the model of *Theophrastus; the author writes in the character of the bachelor son of a Tory Midlands country parson, himself a Londoner, and reflects on various contemporary types, such as the carping and arrogant Lentulus and the ever-youthful though ageing Ganymede. The last chapter echoes *Daniel Deronda* in its defence of Jewish nationalism and its attack on various manifestations of anti-Semitism.

Imprimatur, 'let it be printed', the formula signed by an official licenser authorizing the printing of a book.

I'm Talking about Jerusalem, see WESKER TRILOGY.

In a Glass Darkly, a collection of stories by J. S. *Le Fanu, published 1872. They purport to be cases from the papers of 'Dr Martin Hesselins, the German Physician'—the first of a long line of psychic investigators in English literature. Of the five stories the best-known are 'Green Tea', featuring an apparition in the form of a malignant monkey, and 'Carmilla', an extremely powerful tale of a female vampire which antedates Stoker's *Dracula* by 25 years and was adapted by Carl Dreyer in his film *Vampyr* (1932).

INCHBALD, Mrs Elizabeth, *née* Simpson (1753-1821), was a novelist, dramatist, and actress, and a close friend of *Godwin until his marriage with Mary *Wollstonecraft. She is chiefly remembered for her two prose romances, *A Simple Story* (1791) and *Nature and Art* (1796), both of which display some skill in character and narration and illustrate her faith in natural upbringing (see PRIMITIVISM); and her play *Lovers' Vows* (1798), which retains its fame as the drama enacted by the Bertram family in J. Austen's *Mansfield Park.* Her most successful play was *I'll Tell You What,* produced in 1795. She edited *The British Theatre,* a large collection of plays, both old and new, in 1806-9.

'Inchcape Rock, The', a ballad by R. *Southey, written 1796-8, published 1802. Because the rock, off the Firth of Tay, was dangerous to mariners, the abbot of Arbroath, or Aberbrothock, fixed a warning bell upon it. A piratical character, Sir Ralph the Rover, in order to plague the abbot, cuts the bell from its float and later, on his homeward way, is wrecked upon the rock.

Incunabula, Incunables, books printed before the 16th cent., from the Latin word for 'swaddling clothes', hence 'infancy'.

Index Expurgatorius, strictly, an authoritative specification of the passages to be expunged or altered in works otherwise permitted to be read by Roman Catholics. The term is frequently used in England to cover the 'Index Librorum Prohibitorum', or list of forbidden books (not authors, as sometimes thought). Rules for the formation of this list and of the 'Index Expurgatorius' were drawn up by the Council of Trent, and successive editions of the former have been published from time to time [*OED*]. The 'Index Expurgatorius' and the 'Index Librorum Prohibitorum' were abrogated in 1966.

Index on Censorship, a periodical founded in

1972 by Writers and Scholars International, a group of writers, scholars, artists, and intellectuals concerned with the promotion of intellectual freedom, formed largely at the instigation of the Soviet dissident Pavel Litvinov and S. *Spender. Its editors have been Michael Scammell (1972–80), Hugh Lunghi (1980–2), and George Theiner (1982–   ). It contains reports on cases of censorship and imprisonment of writers throughout the world, and also publishes original poetry and prose by authors many of whom are suppressed in their own countries.

Indicator, The (1819–21), established and edited by Leigh *Hunt. It was non-political and entirely devoted to literary matters. Hunt and his friends, notably *Hazlitt and *Lamb, thought it Hunt's happiest venture in periodical publishing. It published the work of the young poets, including Keats's *'La Belle Dame sans Merci', and introduced much foreign literature. Although short-lived, it sold well.

Indo-European, the name applied to the great family of cognate languages (formerly called Indo-Germanic and Aryan) spoken over most of Europe and extending into Asia as far as northern India. Much of the energy of the 19th-cent. Comparative Philologists was devoted to illustrating the cognations between these groups of languages of which fourteen are distinguished by W. B. Lockwood in *A Panorama of Indo-European Languages* (1972).

Iñez, a character in Byron's *Don Juan*.

IÑEZ DE CASTRO, the daughter of a Castilian nobleman attached to the court of Alphonso IV of Portugal. Prince Pedro married her secretly, and lived with her in happy seclusion. When the marriage was discovered, the king authorized the murder of Iñez. On the accession (1357) of Pedro, who had been reduced to despair by the death of his wife, his first measure was to take vengeance on her murderers. The subject has been treated by various poets and dramatists, including *Camoëns, *Landor, and, more recently, *Montherlant.

Infernal Marriage, The, a burlesque by B. *Disraeli, published 1834, describing the abduction of Proserpine by Pluto. Elysium represents the London of 1834, Pluto is *Brougham, Jupiter is Louis-Philippe, Enceladus is *Wellington, and so on, with much (now incomprehensible) political banter.

Inferno, The, of Dante, see DIVINA COMMEDIA.

INGE, William Ralph (1860–1954), dean of St Paul's, 1911–34, dubbed 'the gloomy dean' by the *Daily Mail* in 1911 for his pessimistic views on democracy, progress, education, etc. He became a well known public figure, partly through his journalism (principally for the

Evening Standard), and he also published diaries, memoirs, and many volumes on religion, politics, and philosophy.

INGELOW, Jean (1820–97), poet, born in Boston, Lincolnshire. She published several volumes of verse and some stories for children; her best-known poems are 'Divided' and 'The High Tide on the Coast of Lincolnshire, 1571', both in *Poems* (1863).

Ingoldsby Legends, The, see BARHAM, R. H.

Inheritance, The, a novel by S. *Ferrier, published 1824.

The novel relates, in an improbably complex plot, but with much humour, the fortunes of Gertrude St Clair, grand-daughter of the earl of Rossville and heiress presumptive to his estate. On the death of her father (who had been repudiated by the earl) she and her mother are admitted to Rossville Castle and encounter the earl, a conceited tyrant. Gertrude falls in love with her fascinating cousin Colonel Delmour and after the earl's death becomes engaged to him, to the despair of all who care for her, and in particular of another cousin, Edward Lyndsay, who loves Gertrude with self-effacing humility. A vulgar American now comes forward and claims to be Gertrude's father. It is revealed that the ambitious Mrs St Clair, despairing of children, has adopted the daughter of a servant and passed her off as her own. Gertrude, having lost title and fortune, is abandoned by Colonel Delmour, and the faithful Edward Lyndsay gradually wins her love. Miss Pratt, a garrulous and eccentric spinster, is a memorable character.

Inkhorn, a term originating in the 16th cent., applied to excessively literary, bookish, or pedantic language: see WILSON, T., for an example.

Inkle and Yarico, a romantic musical comedy by G. *Colman the younger, performed 1787.

The young Londoner, Inkle, saved from cannibals on a voyage to Barbados by the beautiful native girl Yarico, has to decide between fidelity to her and a wealthy marriage to Narcissa, the Governor's daughter; he chooses the latter and is punished for his ingratitude. *Burns, on seeing Fanny *Kemble as Yarico in Dumfries in 1794, wrote, 'At Yarico's sweet notes of grief | The rocks with tears had flowed.' (See PRIMITIVISM.)

'Inklings, The', a group of friends who gathered round C. S. *Lewis at Oxford from the 1930s to the 1960s, and read aloud their original compositions. Members included J. R. R. *Tolkien and C. *Williams.

In Memoriam A.H.H., a poem by *Tennyson, written between 1833 and 1850 and published anonymously in the latter year. The poem was written in memory of A. H. *Hallam, the son of H. *Hallam, a young man of great promise and an intimate friend of Tennyson, who died at Vienna aged 22. It is written in stanzas of four octosyllabic lines rhyming a b b a, and is divided into 132 sections of varying length.

It is not so much a single elegy as a series of poems written over a considerable period, inspired by the changing moods of the author's regret for his lost friend, and expressing his own anxieties about change, evolution, and immortality, the last a subject which continued to perturb him deeply. The epilogue is a marriage-song on the occasion of the wedding of the poet's sister Cecilia to Edward Lushington; Hallam had himself been engaged to his sister Emily. A critical and popular success (G. H. *Lewes referred to it as 'the solace and delight of every house where poetry is loved') it was widely regarded as a message of hope and an affirmation of faith; but T. S. *Eliot commented in 1936: 'It is not religious because of the quality of its faith, but because of the quality of its doubt. Its faith is a poor thing, but its doubt is a very intense experience. In Memoriam is a poem of despair, but of despair of a religious kind.'

Inn Album, The, a poem of approximately 3,000 lines, in blank verse, by R. *Browning, published 1875. Browning originally intended to write a play on the subject, but changed his mind to avoid competing with Tennyson's forthcoming *Queen Mary. The poem has affinities with drama in its use of long passages of dialogue, but the whole is more like a short novel.

The story is based on the career of a famous Regency rake, Lord de Ros, but was influenced by the trial of the Tichborne Claimant which had just ended, and has a contemporary setting. It is an intricate melodrama, involving a spend-thrift aristocrat, his cast-off mistress, his wealthy young protégé and dupe, and the pure young girl to whom the younger man has cynically become engaged; it concludes with blackmail, suicide, and murder. At another level this sensational tale of social and psychological corruption, treated with the satirical realism of *Red Cotton Night-Cap Country, may be read as a bleak fable of the dualism of human art, its self-destructive combination of ideal and material elements.

INNES, Michael, the pseudonym of J. I. M. *Stewart.

Innisfail, a poetic name for Ireland.

Innocence, Songs of, see SONGS OF INNO-CENCE.

Innocents Abroad, The, a satirical account by Mark *Twain, published 1869 (in England, 1870, as The New Pilgrim's Progress), of a cruise on the Quaker City to the Mediterranean with a company of Americans in 1867. The comedy lies in seeing Europe, its scenes, customs, and religious rites and attitudes, through the irreverent and chauvinist eyes of an American 'innocent', and is at the expense both of the Old World and the New. The work, originally published as travel letters in New York and Californian newspapers, was a great success on both sides of the Atlantic, despite some reviews which took its satire at face value, the *Saturday Review describing Twain as 'a very offensive specimen of the vulgarest kind of Yankee'.

Inogene, see IGNOGE and IMOGEN.

Inscape, Instress, see HOPKINS, G. M.

Intelligencer, The, see L'ESTRANGE.

Intelligent Woman's Guide to Socialism and Capitalism, The (1928), was G. B. *Shaw's answer, 200,000 words long, to a request for 'a few ideas on socialism' from his sister-in-law, to whom the book is dedicated. This closely-argued and passionately-felt political testament treats women as the have-nots of a male culture and traces specific social evils to inequality of income. A new edition, with two additional chapters and retitled The Intelligent Woman's Guide to Socialism, Capitalism, Sovietism and Fascism, was published in 1937 as the first two Pelican Books (see PENGUIN).

Interior Monologue, see STREAM OF CON-SCIOUSNESS.

Interludes were plays performed at Court, in the halls of the nobles, at the Inns of Court, and in colleges, generally but not exclusively by professional actors, dealing with a short episode and involving a limited number of characters. That interludes were sometimes performed by villagers we know from 'Pyramus and Thisbe' in *A Midsummer Night's Dream. Their vogue was chiefly in the 15th and 16th cents. They succeeded *Morality Plays in the history of the drama, and are not always clearly distinguishable from them. The characters are still frequently allegorical, but the comic or farcical element is more prevalent, the versification tends to doggerel, and they are shorter than the moralities. There are good examples by *Heywood, *Rastell, and *Medwall. The origin of the name is obscure. The OED speaks of interludes as 'commonly introduced between the acts of long mystery-plays or moralities'; Ward finds the probable origin in the fact that interludes were 'occasionally performed in the intervals of banquets and entertainments'. E. K. *Chambers gives reasons for questioning both these explanations. He is inclined to interpret interludium not as a ludus in the intervals of something else, but as a ludus carried on between two or more performers, and as primarily applicable to any kind of dramatic performance. See ed. G. Wickham, English Moral Interludes (1976).

'Intimations of Immortality from Recollections of Early Childhood', an ode by *Wordsworth, composed 1802–4/6, published 1807.

It is Wordsworth's most profound and memorable exploration of the significance of the intensity of childhood experience of the natural world (which suggests to him a state of pre-existence), of its gradual fading into 'the light of common day', and of the consolations of maturity, where man can still retain 'shadowy recollections' of former glory, and can still have sight, if only by glimpses, 'of that immortal sea which brought us hither'. The poem ends with a moving affirmation of the poet's faith in the powers of the philosophic mind and the human heart. The tone throughout is tentative rather than dogmatic, and Wordsworth was later to insist that he used the concept of pre-existence (which had both a popular and a Platonic basis) not as a philosopher but as a poet, using his own peculiarly vivid childhood recollections of 'a splendour in the objects of sense' and his conviction of personal immortality.

Invisible Man, The, (1) a science fiction romance by H. G. *Wells, published 1897, about a scientist who fatally stumbles upon the secret of invisibility; (2) *Invisible Man,* a Kafkaesque and claustrophobic novel by the American writer Ralph Waldo Ellison (1914–), published 1952, which describes the life of a young black man in New York City.

IONESCO, Eugène, see ABSURD, THEATRE OF THE.

Ionic a Minore, see METRE.

Ipomadon, a Middle English romance, taken from the French of Huon de Rotelande (c.1190). There are three English versions: one in prose which seems to be early 14th cent.; the most famous, in 8,890 lines of twelve-line, tail-rhyme stanzas, thought to be from Lancashire of the mid-14th cent.; and a more condensed version in rhyming couplets from a 15th-cent. manuscript. Ipomadon is a prince of Apulia who wins by his exploits (mostly in disguise) the love of La Fière, the disdainful duchess of Calabria.

Ed. H. Weber, *Metrical Romances of the xiii, xiv and xv Centuries* (1810); selections in W. E. French and C. B. Hale, *Middle English Metrical Romances* (1930), in *Medieval English Romances,* Part Two, ed. A. V. C. Schmidt and N. Jacobs (1980).

IQBAL, Sir Muhammad (1875–1938), poet and philosopher, was born in the Punjab, where his education began. He continued his studies in England, where he was called to the bar, and in Germany, before returning home to practise as a lawyer. As a poet, he worked primarily in two veins, the first in the tradition of the Farsi-derived lyric poem, often with metaphysical or allegorical content, and the second in a more directly political mode, as in his poem *Lenin's Interview with God* (1935). Writing in both Persian and Urdu, he soon became a leader of Islamic modernism not only in India but elsewhere in the Islamic world. He emphasized the international character of Islam but eventually concluded that it could only find expression, in the modern world, in the free association of Muslim states. As president of the Muslim League in 1930 he advocated the creation of a separate Muslim state in NW India.

Iras, in Shakespeare's *Antony and Cleopatra,* one of Cleopatra's attendants. Her name is in *Plutarch's *Life of Antony.*

IRELAND, John (1761–1842), the son of an Ashburton butcher, bible-clerk at Oriel College, Oxford, became dean of Westminster, and founded a professorship of exegesis and the Ireland Scholarship for classics at Oxford.

IRELAND, William Henry (1777–1835), is remembered chiefly as a forger of Shakespeare manuscripts. He began his audacious series of deceptions at the age of 17, when he was working in a lawyer's office with easy access to old parchment, deeds, and antiquated forms of writing. An exhibition of his forgeries of poems and deeds, arranged in 1794 by his innocent and excited father, wholly deceived the general public, and *Boswell kissed the parchments. A facsimile edition of the 'works' was published in 1795, and other works, including the plays *Vortigern and Rowena* and *Henry II,* made their appearance. However, strong doubts were expressed, *Kemble's production of *Vortigern* was jeered, and in 1796 *Malone published *An Inquiry into the Authenticity* . . . In the same year Ireland admitted to the forgeries, and embarked on a more conventional literary career. He published two volumes of poems, then in 1808 *The Fisher Boy,* which, like *Bloomfield's earlier *Farmer's Boy,* satisfied the fashion for tales of rural life. *The Sailor Boy* (1809) relates the rise of humble Dick to be a captain at Trafalgar. In 1815 he published *Scribbleomania,* a doggerel collection of entertaining but frequently inaccurate descriptions of his contemporaries.

'I remember, I remember', the first line of a well known work by T. *Hood.

Irena, in Spenser's *Faerie Queene* (Bk V), personifies Ireland, oppressed by *Grantorto and righted by Sir *Artegall.

Irene, a blank verse tragedy by Dr *Johnson, written 1736, performed 1749, without much success.

The story, taken from *Knolles's history of the Turks, concerns the fate of Irene, a Greek slave loved by the emperor Mahomet, but in Knolles's account a helpless victim, but in Johnson's the victim of her own weakness. It cost its author much effort, but remained frigid and static.

Irish Literary Theatre was founded by W. B. *Yeats, Lady *Gregory, and E. *Martyn in 1899 to encourage Irish drama. It eventually became the Irish National Theatre Society in 1903, with Yeats as president, and moved into the new *Abbey Theatre in 1904.

Irish Revival, a resurgence of Irish nationalism and culture which began in the last quarter of the 19th cent. and flourished until the 1920s. Among the books which fostered the revival were translations and re-tellings of Irish legend, folklore, and poetry, such as S. *Ferguson's *Lays of the Western Gael* (1865) and D. *Hyde's *Love Songs of Connacht* (1893). Histories, such as Standish O'Grady's bardic *History of Ireland* (1880) and Hyde's *Literary History of Ireland* (1892), were also highly influential. The *Irish Literary Theatre, founded by W. B. *Yeats and others in 1899, developed eventually into the important *Abbey Theatre company. Plays by Yeats, *Synge, G. B. *Shaw, and *O'Casey made the Abbey renowned. Meanwhile the poetry of Yeats and the prose work of G. *Moore, *Joyce, and many others established the new literary stature of Irish writing.

Irish R.M., see SOME EXPERIENCE OF AN IRISH R.M.

Irish Sketch Book, The, a personal and impressionistic account by *Thackeray of a journey through Ireland, published 1843.

IRON, Ralph, pseudonym of O. *Schreiner.

IRVING, Edward, see IRVINGITES.

IRVING, Sir Henry (1838–1905), originally John Henry Brodribb, achieved fame as an actor for his performance in *The Bells* (1871–2), and afterwards scored successes in a large number of Shakespearian and other parts, his impersonation of *Tennyson's Becket being one of his chief triumphs. His management of the Lyceum Theatre in association with Ellen *Terry, 1878–1902, was distinguished, and he revived popular interest in Shakespeare. He was a romantic actor, highly intellectual, of magnetic personality and originality of conception, but of mannered elocution and gait.

IRVING, Washington (1783–1859), born in New York, the son of a wealthy British merchant who had sided with the rebels in the Revolution. After training as a lawyer, Irving turned to a literary career, writing for various newspapers, and publishing (1807–8), with his brother William Irving and friend J. K. Paulding, a series of whimsical and satirical essays and poems, collected in book form as *Salmagundi: or, the Whim-Whams and Opinions of Launcelot Langstaff, Esq. and others* (1808). This was followed by his highly successful burlesque *A History of New York from the Beginning of the World to the End of the Dutch Dynasty*, by 'Diedrich Knickerbocker', a pseudonym chosen to represent the solid, phlegmatic Dutch burgher created by Irving; the name became synonymous with the descendants of the original Dutch settlers of the New Netherlands in America. Over the next years Irving struggled (unsuccessfully) to save the family business from bankruptcy, visiting England and making the acquaintance of Sir W. *Scott, T. *Moore, T. *Campbell, John *Murray, and others during the process; on his return, encouraged by Scott, he wrote *The Sketch Book*, essays and tales under the pseudonym 'Geoffrey Crayon, Gent.', published serially in the US (1819–20) and in book form in England (1820). This work, which contains sketches of English life ('The Christmas Dinner', 'Westminster Abbey', etc.), essays on American subjects, and American adaptations of German folk-tales (including *'Rip Van Winkle' and *'The Legend of Sleepy Hollow'), made him a celebrity in both continents. It was followed by other popular works, including *Bracebridge Hall* (1822), which features Squire Bracebridge, a sort of 19th-cent. de *Coverley. Some of his subsequent works were inspired by his period as diplomatic attaché in Spain (1826–9), including a life of Columbus (1828) and *Legends of the Alhambra* (1832). He then rejoined the literary world of London as secretary to the US legation (1829–32), and returned to America in 1832 on an enthusiastic welcome as the first American author to have achieved international fame. His later works include *The Crayon Miscellany* (1835), *Astoria* (1836; an account of John Jacob Astor's development of the fur trade), various biographies, and his monumental 5-vol. life of George Washington (1855–9).

Irvingites, members of the Catholic Apostolic Church, a religious body founded about 1835, which developed from a revivalist circle which had gathered round H. Drummond (1851–97), and was partly inspired by the teachings of Edward Irving (1792–1834), a Scottish minister, who was a friend and encourager of *Carlyle. They believed in the near approach of the second coming of Christ and sought the re-establishment of the primitive offices of the Church (viz. the apostles, prophets, evangelists, etc.).

Isaac of York, in Scott's *Ivanhoe*, the father of Rebecca.

Isabella, (1) in *Orlando Furioso*, daughter of a Saracen king of Spain, with whom the Scottish prince *Zerbino fell in love. After his death she fell into the power of *Rodomont, and to protect her honour caused him by guile to slay her. (2) in Kyd's *Spanish Tragedy*, wife to

Hieronymo; (3) queen to Marlowe's *Edward II*; (4) the heroine of Shakespeare's *Measure for Measure*.

'Isabella, or The Pot of Basil', a narrative poem by *Keats, written 1818, published 1820.

The poem is based on a story in Boccaccio's *Decameron*. The worldly, ambitious brothers of Isabella intend that she shall marry a nobleman. When they discover her love for the humble Lorenzo they lure him away, murder him, and bury his body in a forest. His ghost then appears to Isabella and tells her where he is buried. With the help of her old nurse she finds his body, severs the head, and places it in a pot with a plant of basil over it. Her brothers, observing how she cherishes the plant, steal the pot, discover the mouldering head, and fly, conscience-stricken, into banishment. Pathetically Isabella mourns her loss, pines away, and dies. The poem reflects a contemporary fashion for the macabre, and *Lamb pronounced it the best work in the volume of poems of 1820, but Keats himself very soon came to dislike it.

Isengrym, or **Isengrin**, the wolf in *Reynard the Fox*.

Iseult the Fair (also Isolde, Isoud, Isode, Ysoude), the daughter of the king of Ireland in Arthurian legend. She is the lover of *Tristram (Tristan) who has been sent by his uncle King Mark of Cornwall to bring Iseult as his wife. The story of Tristram and Iseult is the great classic of doomed love; Tristram is the slayer of her uncle Marhaus and they are fated to love each other by drinking in error the potion which was meant to have been shared by Mark and Iseult on their wedding night, binding them in everlasting love. Her mother is also called Iseult (even sometimes Iseult the Fair), and in some versions of the story it is she, the sister of Marhaus, who becomes Tristram's lover. No doubt the two, as well as their rival *Iseult of the White Hands, are archetypally related.

Iseult of the White Hands, in Arthurian legend, daughter of the ruler of Brittany, with whom *Tristram falls in love and marries after his banishment by King Mark. But Iseult of Brittany does not succeed in erasing the memory of *Iseult the Fair; when Tristram is dying, he sends for his first Iseult by ship; if she is on the ship on its return from Ireland she is to fly a white flag: if not a black one. The white flag is flown; but Iseult of the White Hands tells Tristram it is black, whereupon he dies.

ISHERWOOD, Christopher William Bradshaw (1904–), novelist, born in Cheshire, the son of an army captain who was killed in the First World War. He made the acquaintance of *Auden at preparatory school, and of *Upward at Repton; he and Upward were at Cambridge together, where both began to write. His first novels, *All the Conspirators* (1928) and *The Memorial* (1932), show the influence (as he acknowledged) of E. M. *Forster and V. *Woolf; his own voice appears distinctly in *Mr Norris Changes Trains* (1935) and *Goodbye to Berlin* (1939), works which reflect his experiences of living in Berlin, 1929–33, where he supported himself by giving English lessons. They were planned as part of a long novel, to be entitled *The Lost*, which was never written, and are largely autobiographical in manner and content, although the narrator appears as Bradshaw in the first and as Isherwood in the second, and the overlapping cast of characters shows a certain fictional inconsistency. The first is a novel about a con-man and double agent, the corrupt, seedy, emotional, and engaging Arthur Norris, and his adventures in the criminal and political underworld; the second is a series of sketches, some of which were originally published in *New Writing*, and of which the best-known is the section 'Sally Bowles' (published independently in 1937). Sally is a cabaret artist of more beauty, eccentricity, and wit than talent, and her Bohemian enterprises were later successfully dramatized in 1951 by John Van Druten as *I am a Camera*, and turned into a stage musical in 1968 as *Cabaret*. Both novels give a vivid portrait of Germany of the eve of Hitler's rise to power. Isherwood travelled widely in Europe after leaving Berlin, went to China with Auden in 1938, and in 1939 went with him to America; he became an American citizen in 1946.

During the 1930s he collaborated with Auden in the writing of *The Ascent of F6* and several other works (see under AUDEN), translated some of *Brecht, and wrote the semi-autobiographical *Lions and Shadows* (1938), in which his friends (Auden, *Spender, Upward, V. *Watkins, and others) appear under fictitious names. After settling near Hollywood, he became interested in Hindu philosophy and Vedanta, influenced partly by A. *Huxley and Gerald Heard, and edited various works on the subject (*Vedanta for the Western World*, 1945, etc.) and translated the *Bhagavad-gītā* (1944, with Swami Prabhavananda) and other Hindu classics. Novels written in America include *Down there on a Visit* (1962) and *A Single Man* (1964); *Kathleen and Frank* (1972) is an account of his parents, and *Christopher and His Kind* (1976) is a frank account of the homosexual affairs of his young manhood.

ISIDORE OF SEVILLE (570–636), archbishop of Seville, an encyclopaedic writer much admired in the Middle Ages, author of *Origines* or *Etymologiae* in 20 books (ed. W. M. Lindsay, 2 vols, 1910). This work argues that the natures of all things can be derived etymologically from their names. Much of it is fantastic, but it remained popular down to the 14th cent. and can be seen as one of the first texts in the encyclopaedic tradition in medieval literature.

Island, The, a poem by Lord *Byron, published 1823. The poem, a mixture of romance and humour, is based on the story of the mutiny on HMS *Bounty,* and idolizes nature at the expense of society. The mutineers' island is depicted as an earthly paradise, which forms the background to the idyllic love of Torquil and Neuha, children of nature. Byron himself did not think well of the poem.

Island in the Moon, An, an untitled burlesque fragment by W. *Blake, written *c.*1784–5, first printed (though inaccurately) in 1907 by E. J. Ellis in *The Real Blake.* It is a satirical portrait of scientific and cultural dilettantism and pretension, interspersed with songs (some of them bawdy) including the fragment with the lines 'Winking and blinking | Like Doctor Johnson'; its characters include 'Sipsop the Pythagorean' and 'Inflammable Gas', the latter probably inspired by J. *Priestley.

Island of Dr Moreau, The, a *science fiction tale by H. G. *Wells, published 1896. It is an evolutionary fantasy about a shipwrecked naturalist who becomes involved in an experiment to 'humanize' animals by surgery. The theme was developed by *Aldiss.

'Isles of Greece, The', a lyric by *Byron from Canto III of *Don Juan.*

Isumbras, Sir, a verse-romance in 804 lines of twelve-line tail-rhyme stanzas, from the North-East Midlands, popular before 1320 and mentioned in *Cursor Mundi.* Its theme is that of 'the man tried by fate' of which the model is St Eustace, of Eastern origin. Isumbras is strong, handsome, and prosperous, but also proud and arrogant. A bird sent by God offers him the choice of suffering in youth or old age, and he chooses the former. He loses his wife, children, and possessions, and suffers for 21 years among the Saracens. But he bears all patiently, and at the end of that period an angel tells him that his sins are expiated and he is restored to his family and possessions. Its moral theme is typical of the concern of the 14th-cent. tail-rhyme romances. Ed. M. Mills in *Six Middle English Romances* (1973); discussion by A. McI. Trounce, 'The English Tail-Rhyme Romances' (*Medium Aevum* 1, 2, and 3, 1932–4).

Itala, the name given to an old Latin version of the Bible on which, after St *Jerome's recension of it, the *Vulgate came to be founded.

It is Never too Late to Mend, a novel by C. *Reade.

Iuliene, St, see KATHERINE GROUP, THE.

Ivanhoe, a novel by Sir W. *Scott, published 1819. This was the first of the author's novels in which he adopted a purely English subject. *Freeman (*Hist. of the Norman Conquest,* vol. v, app.) criticized, as unsupported by the evidence of contemporary records, the enmity of Saxon and Norman, represented as persisting in the days of Richard I, which forms the basis of the story.

Wilfred of Ivanhoe, son of Cedric, of noble Saxon birth, loves his father's ward, the lady Rowena, who traces her descent to King Alfred, and who returns his love. Cedric, who is passionately devoted to the restoration of the Saxon line to the throne of England and sees the best chance of effecting this in the marriage of Rowena to Athelstane of Coningsburgh, also of the Saxon blood royal, has in anger banished his son. Ivanhoe has joined Richard Cœur de Lion at the crusade and there won the king's affection. In Richard's absence, his brother John has found support among the lawless and dissolute Norman nobles for his plan to depose Richard, a design favoured by Richard's imprisonment in Austria on his return from Palestine.

The story centres in two chief events: a great tournament at Ashby de la Zouch, where Ivanhoe aided by Richard, who unknown to all has returned to England with Ivanhoe, defeats all the knights of John's party, including the fierce Templar Sir Brian de Bois-Guilbert and Sir Reginald Front-de-Bœuf; and the siege of Front-de-Bœuf's castle of Torquilstone, whither Cedric and Rowena, with the wounded Ivanhoe, Athelstane, the Jew Isaac, and his beautiful and courageous daughter Rebecca, have been carried captives by the Norman nobles. After an exciting fight, the castle is carried by a force of outlaws and Saxons, led by Locksley (otherwise *Robin Hood) and King Richard himself. The prisoners are rescued, with the exception of Rebecca, of whom the Templar has become passionately enamoured, and whom he carries off to the Preceptory of Templestowe. Here the unexpected arrival of the Grand Master of the order, while relieving Rebecca from the dishonourable advances of Bois-Guilbert, exposes her to the charge of witchcraft, and she escapes sentence of death only by demanding trial by combat. Ivanhoe, whose gratitude she has earned by nursing him when wounded at the tournament of Ashby, appears as her champion, and in the encounter between him and Bois-Guilbert (on whom has been thrust the unwelcome duty of appearing as the accuser), the latter falls dead, untouched by his opponent's lance, the victim of his own contending passions. Ivanhoe and Rowena, by the intervention of Richard, are united; the more interesting Rebecca, suppressing her love for Ivanhoe, leaves England with her father.

Among the many characters in the story, besides Robin Hood and Friar Tuck, are the poor fool Wamba, who imperils his life to save that of his master Cedric; Gurth, the swineherd; and Isaac the Jew, divided between love of his shekels and love of his daughter. Thackeray's *Rebecca and Rowena* is an amusing sequel to, and critical reinterpretation of, Scott's tale.

'Ixion in Heaven', a story by B. *Disraeli which appeared in the *New Monthly* in 1833. A Jove reminiscent of George IV, a *Byronic Apollo, an amorous Juno, and King Ixion himself are the chief characters in the frolic. On discovering the passion of Ixion and Juno, Jove binds the king to a wheel and hurls him down to Hades.

J

Jabberwock, a fictitious monster, the subject of the poem 'Jabberwocky' in Lewis Carroll's *Through the Looking-Glass*. The story, told in an invented vocabulary, begins: ' 'Twas brillig and the slithy toves'. *Tenniel's drawing of the Jabberwock, originally intended as a frontispiece, was considered so terrifying by *Dodgson that it was printed by the ballad in the volume; the White Knight became the frontispiece.

Jack, Colonel, see COLONEL JACK.

'Jack and Jill', a nursery rhyme, involving perhaps originally some political allusion now lost. Lord Houghton is quoted by Sir M. Grant Duff ('Notes from a Diary', 7 June 1878) as thinking that Jack and Jill were Empson and Dudley, notorious for their fiscal exactions in Henry VII's reign and executed for constructive treason soon after Henry VIII came to the throne, to the great satisfaction of the Londoners. *Baring-Gould (*Curious Myths*) finds the origin of Jack and Jill in the Hjuki and Bil of Scandinavian mythology, two children who had been drawing water and were stolen by the moon.

Jack and the Bean-stalk, a nursery tale based on a world-wide myth, found e.g. among the North American Indians and the native tribes of S. Africa. The bean-stalk is said to be derived from the ash tree Yggdrasil, the world-tree of northern mythology.

Jack, the son of a poor widow, exchanges his mother's cow for a hatful of beans. His mother in anger throws the beans out of the window. The next morning a bean-stalk has grown up into the clouds. Jack climbs up and finds himself in a strange country, where a fairy directs him to the house of a giant who has killed his father. He robs the giant of a hen that lays golden eggs, a self-playing harp, and bags of diamonds, and is finally discovered by the giant and pursued down the bean-stalk. Jack, reaching the ground first, cuts the bean-stalk with an axe, and the giant falls and is killed.

'Jackdaw of Rheims, The', see BARHAM, R. H.

Jacke Wilton, *The Life of*, see UNFORTUNATE TRAVELLER, THE.

Jack Horner, the subject of a nursery rhyme ('Little Jack Horner sat in a corner', etc.), which occurs in an 18th-cent. chapbook, *The Pleasant History of Jack Horner, containing his witty Tricks,* etc. The rhyme is also referred to by H. *Carey in 1725. The origin of the rhyme is dubiously attributed to a Jack Horner who was steward to the abbot of Glastonbury in the reign of Henry VIII and by a trick acquired the deeds of the manor of Mells at the dissolution of the monasteries, took them to the king, and was handsomely rewarded: the Horner family still holds the manor.

Jack of Dover, in Prologue to Chaucer's 'Cook's Tale' (*Canterbury Tales*, 4; l. 4,347–8), refers probably to a pie (or, less probably, fish) that has been reheated. In 'Jack of Dover, his quest of Inquirie' given in W. C. *Hazlitt's *Shakespeare Jest Books*, Jack travels in search of a greater fool than himself, and fails to find one.

Jack of Newbery, or **Newbury,** John Winchcombe, alias Smallwood (d. 1520), a clothier of Newbury, whose wealth inspired the authors of numerous chapbook stories. According to legend he led 100 or 250 men, equipped at his own expense, at the battle of *Flodden Field and entertained *Henry VIII and Catherine of Aragon in his house. (See DELONEY.)

Jack Straw, the leader of a party of insurgents from Essex in the Peasants' Revolt of 1381. A *macaronic poem on him is included in *Medieval English*, ed. R. Kaiser (3rd edn, 1958), p 386.

Jack the Giant-Killer, a nursery tale of Northern origin, known in England from very early times.

Jack was the son of a Cornish farmer, and lived in the days of King Arthur. His first achievement was the destruction of the giant of Mount Cornwall, which he effected by digging a pit, covering it with branches and earth, and luring the giant into it. He subsequently acquired from another giant by his ingenuity a coat that made him invisible, shoes that gave him extraordinary speed, and a sword of magic potency. With the help of these, he destroyed all the giants in the land.

Jack the Ripper, the name given to a murderer who, between 1888 and 1891, killed and eviscerated several prostitutes (at least five, possibly more) in the Whitechapel area of London. Attempts to guess his identity have included a Harley Street surgeon, a mad midwife, a Russian anarchist, the duke of Clarence (1864–92), and F. K. *Stephen. He has been the subject of many novels and films, including Mrs Belloc

Lowndes's *The Lodger* (1913) and C. *Wilson's *Ritual in the Dark* (1960), in which he appears as a homosexual sadist. See also C. Wilson, *A Casebook of Murder* (1962).

Jacobin, originally a name of the French friars of the order of St Dominic, so called because the church of St Jacques in Paris was given to them and they built their first convent near it. From them the name was transferred to the members of a French political club established in 1789, in Paris, in the old convent of the Jacobins, to maintain the principles of extreme democracy and absolute equality. It was applied in a transferred sense to sympathizers with their principles, and about 1800 was a nickname for any political reformer.

Jacob Omnium, see HIGGINS, M. J.

JACOBS, W(illiam) W(ymark) (1863–1943), born in Wapping, the son of a wharfinger, became a clerk in the Civil Service. He began to publish stories in J. K. *Jerome's *Idler* and the *Strand Magazine* in the 1890s, and in 1896 published his first collection, *Many Cargoes,* the success of which led to his resignation from his clerkship. He wrote several novels, including *At Sunwich Port* (1902) and *Dialstone Lane* (1904), but it was chiefly his short stories which established his popularity. These fall roughly into two groups: those dealing humorously with the escapades of sailors on shore (as well as at sea) and of country characters and rogues, as in the highly successful 'Claybury' stories; and tales of the macabre, such as the celebrated 'The Monkey's Paw', which was dramatized with great success. *Light Freights,* often held to be the best of his collections, appeared in 1901; *The Lady of the Barge* in 1902; and *Night Watches* in 1914.

Jacob's Room, see WOOLF, V.

Jacobus de Voragine, see GOLDEN LEGEND, THE.

Jaffar the Barmecide (Ja'far al-Barmeki), in the *Arabian Nights,* the vizier of *Hārūn ar-Rashīd, who, with the executioner Mesrour, accompanied him when, disguised as a merchant, he walked at night about the streets of Baghdad. (See BARMECIDE.)

Jaffeir, one of the principal characters in Otway's *Venice Preserv'd.*

JAGGARD, William (*fl.* 1594–1623), and Isaac (*fl.* 1613–27), London printers and principal publishers of the Shakespeare First Folio (see FOLIOS AND QUARTOS, SHAKESPEARIAN).

Jaggers, Mr, a character in Dickens's *Great Expectations.*

JAGO, Richard (1715–81), of Cornish descent, born in Warwickshire, and holder of three livings in that county. He was the author of

Edge-hill (1767), a *topographical poem in four books describing, with many digressions, the views seen at morning, noon, afternoon, and evening, as he looks from that famous spot over his favourite county.

Jakin, Bob, a character in G. Eliot's *The Mill on the Floss.*

JAKOBSON, Roman (1896–), a Russian-born linguist who was one of the most celebrated members of the school of criticism known as 'Russian formalism' and principal member of the 'Prague School' of linguistics; in 1939 he settled in America. His principal linguistic contribution was to apply to phonetics the idea of *Saussure that linguistic systems are characterized by *oppositions* which define various units, developing the notion of 'distinctive features' in phonology. Latterly he has become more celebrated for his influence on literary criticism, partly through the medium of Roland Barthes; his work laid the foundation for a *Structuralist approach to literary theory.

JAMES I (1394–1437), king of Scotland, was captured while on his way to France by an English ship, probably in 1406. He was detained in England for 19 years and well educated; he was a captive at the court at the same time as another famous literary hostage, *Charles d'Orléans. In 1424 he married Lady Jane Beaufort, daughter of the earl of Somerset and granddaughter of *John of Gaunt, who is the heroine of James's famous poem *The Kingis Quair,* which he composed in England. He was assassinated at Perth by Sir Robert Graham (see SHIRLEY, JOHN). The authorship of *The Kingis Quair* has been doubted, but there seems no good reason to deny it to James. One or two other poems have been doubtfully attributed to him: 'The Ballad of Good Counsel', *'Christis Kirk on the Green', and 'Peblis to the Play'. *Skeat attributed to him the 'B' section of the Middle English *Romaunt of the Rose* (ll. 1,706–5,810), but this is very unlikely to be his. See E. W. M. Balfour-Melville, *James I, King of Scots 1406–37* (1936).

JAMES I (James VI of Scotland) (1566–1625), king of England 1603–25. He is reputedly the author of *True Law of Free Monarchies* (1598), a reply to the argument of G. *Buchanan in his *De Jure Regni* that the king is elected by and responsible to the people. He wrote *Basilikon Doron* (1599, precepts on the art of government, addressed to his son); *A Counterblaste to Tobacco* (1604), a good many theological works, and poetry in Scots, Latin, and English. His works include metrical versions of 30 psalms, translations of *Du Bartas and *Lucan, a long poem on the battle of Lepanto, numerous occasional songs and sonnets, and a short treatise on the rules for writing *Scots poetry.

James the Fourth, *The Scottish Historie of,* a play by R. *Greene, published posthumously 1598. In spite of the title, this is a fictionalized romantic comedy, framed by the comments of Oberon, king of fairies. James, king of Scots, marries the English princess Dorothea, but is in love with Ida, daughter of the countess of Arran. Dorothea remains constant in her love for the king, disguising herself as a man when she learns that he seeks her life; she is wounded, but survives to be reconciled to the king after Ida has married the English lord Eustace. Notable among the minor characters are the *Machiavellian counsellor Ateukin and the affectionate dwarf Nano.

JAMES, George Payne Rainsford (1799–1860), travelled widely, served in the Napoleonic wars, held various diplomatic posts, and was appointed historiographer royal by William IV. Influenced by Sir W. *Scott he wrote numerous romantic novels, biographies, and popular historical works, including *Richelieu* (1829), *Darnley* (1830), *Life of Edward the Black Prince* (1836). *Thackeray parodied him as 'the solitary horseman' in his burlesque *Barbazure, by G. P. R. Jeames, esq.* for the two horsemen who were a frequent beginning to his romances.

JAMES, Henry (1843–1916), was born in New York of ancestry originally both Irish and Scottish. His father, Henry James senior, was a remarkable writer on questions of theology and a follower of *Swedenborg. His elder brother William (below) was a distinguished philosopher. After a desultory education in New York, London, Paris, and Geneva, Henry James entered the law school at Harvard in 1862. He settled in Europe in 1875. From 1865 he was a regular contributor of reviews and short stories to American periodicals and owed much to his friendship with W. D. *Howells. His first considerable piece of fiction, *Watch and Ward,* appeared serially in 1871, followed by *Transatlantic Sketches* and *A Passionate Pilgrim* in 1875, and his first important novel *Roderick Hudson* in 1876 (in the *Atlantic Monthly,* 1875). For more than 20 years he lived in London, and in 1898 moved to Lamb House, Rye, where his later novels were written. He at first chiefly concerned himself with the impact of the older civilization of Europe upon American life, and to this period belong his novels *Roderick Hudson, The American* (1877), *Daisy Miller* (1879), and *Portrait of a Lady* (1881). He next turned to a more exclusively English stage in *The Tragic Muse* (1890), *The Spoils of Poynton* (1897), and *The Awkward Age* (1899), in which he analysed English character with extreme subtlety, verging at times on obscurity. *What Maisie Knew* appeared in 1897. In his last three great novels,

The Wings of the Dove (1902), *The Ambassadors* (1903), and *The Golden Bowl* (1904), he returned to the 'international' theme of the contrast of American and European character. In 1914 he began work on two novels, *The Ivory Tower* and *The Sense of the Past,* which remained unfinished at his death and were published in fragments in 1917. For the revised collection of his fiction, of which the issue began in 1907, James wrote a series of prefaces of high interest. In his critical essays James concentrated on the 19th-cent. novel. He felt that *Dickens was limited by his failure to see below the surface of things; he was a firm admirer of G. *Eliot; but his hero was *Balzac whom he called 'the master of us all'.

Besides nearly 100 short stories (including the well-known ghost story *The Turn of the Screw,* 1898), James wrote several volumes of sketches of travel (*Portraits of Places,* 1883; *A Little Tour in France,* 1884). He wrote a number of plays, of which the few that were acted were not successful. At the opening of *Guy Domville* in 1895 James was booed by the audience and although the play was praised by some critics, including G. B. *Shaw, its failure plunged James into a severe depression. For the English Men of Letters series he wrote a life of *Hawthorne; and in *The American Scene* (1906) a record of the impressions produced on him by a visit to America after an absence of nearly 20 years. *A Small Boy and Others* (1913) and *Notes of a Son and a Brother* (1914) are evocations of his early days in New York and Europe. A short story called 'The Middle Years' appeared in the volume *Terminations* in 1895. The autobiographical work of the same title is a fragment (published posthumously, 1917) 'representing all that James lived to write of a volume of autobiographical reminiscences to which he had given the name of one of his own short stories' (from the prefatory note to the autobiographical fragment).

In addition to the works referred to above, the following may be mentioned: *Madonna of the Future* (1879), *Washington Square* (1881), *The Siege of London* (1883), *The Bostonians* (1886), *The Princess Casamassima* (1886), *The Reverberator* (1888), *The Aspern Papers* (1888), *The Real Thing* (1893), *Embarrassments* (1896), *The Other House* (1896), *In the Cage* (1898), *The Two Magics* (1898), *The Better Sort* (1903).

In 1915 James became a British subject, and in 1916 was awarded the OM. Two volumes of his letters were published in 1920, and re-edited by Leon Edel, 1975 and 1980; Edel's comprehensive biography in four volumes (1953–72) is of the *Freudian school.

JAMES, M(ontague) R(hodes) (1862–1936), born near Bury St Edmunds, a brilliant linguist, palaeographer, medievalist, and biblical scholar, was successively provost of King's College,

Cambridge, and (from 1918) of Eton. His memoirs, *Eton and King's*, were published in 1926. He edited works by *Le Fanu, whom he greatly admired, and himself wrote several volumes of distinguished ghost stories, many with East Anglian settings, including 'Oh, Whistle, and I'll Come to You, My Lad', which appeared in *Ghost Stories of an Antiquary* (1904). *More Ghost Stories of an Antiquary* appeared in 1911, and his collected stories in 1931. The masterly combination of scholarly control and antiquarian detail with suggestions of underlying supernatural horror have made them lastingly popular.

JAMES, William (1842–1910), American philosopher, the son of Henry James senior (a Swedenborgian philosopher), and elder brother of Henry *James, was at first a student of art and then a teacher of physiology, but turned his attention to psychology. His views are embodied in his *Principles of Psychology* (1890), and show a tendency to subordinate logical proof to intuitive conviction. He was a vigorous antagonist of the idealistic school of *Kant and *Hegel, and an empiricist who made empiricism more radical by treating pure experience as the very substance of the world. Yet he was not a monist but a pluralist, 'willing to believe that there may ultimately never be an all-form at all, that the substance of reality may never get totally collected . . . and that a distributive form of reality, the each-form, is as acceptable as the all-form' (*Pluralistic Universe*, p. 34). Pragmatism, for which he is best remembered by philosophers, was his method of approach to metaphysics: abstract ideas are true if 'they work', if they harmonize with our other experience and accepted ideas. James's principal works were, besides the *Principles of Psychology*, *Varieties of Religious Experience* (1902), *Pragmatism* (1907), *The Meaning of Truth* (1909), *A Pluralistic Universe* (1909), *Essays in Radical Empiricism* (1912). The conclusions of his *Varieties of Religious Experience* are notable: 'the visible world is part of a more spiritual universe from which it draws its chief significance; union with the higher universe is our true end; spiritual energy flows in and produces effects within the phenomenal world.' He coined the phrase *'stream of consciousness' now widely used as a literary term.

JAMESON, Anna Brownell (1794–1860), began adult life as a governess. Friendship with the *Kembles, and a long visit to Germany, brought her into contact with literary society, and she became a close friend of the *Brownings, M. R. *Mitford, and eventually of the *Carlyles. She first attracted attention in 1826 with *A Lady's Diary* (later re-titled *The Diary of an Ennuyée*), describing a visit to Italy. From that time on she produced many highly respected works of art history and criticism, biography, theology, history, travel, social comment, and general essays, some of which exhibited a strong interest in the position and education of women. The work for which she is now chiefly remembered is *Characteristics of Women* (1832, later known as *Shakespeare's Heroines*), dedicated to Fanny *Kemble, and illustrated with her own etchings. Shakespeare she saw as 'the Poet of Womankind', whose heroines display all the aspects and complexities of womanhood. She divides the 25 heroines of her book into four groups: the characters of intellect, such as Portia; those of passion and imagination, such as Viola; those of the affections, such as Desdemona; and those from history, such as Cleopatra and Lady Macbeth. In preparation Mrs Jameson read Dr *Johnson, *Hazlitt, *Coleridge, *Lamb, and other major critics, as well as relevant European and Greek drama, and thoroughly investigated the sources of the histories. Although she makes little attempt to relate character to context, her interpretations, many of which are very detailed, were considered illuminating, and the work was received with considerable respect, G. M. *Hopkins placing her among the most eminent of Shakespeare's critics.

JAMESON, (Margaret) Storm (1891–   ), was born in Whitby, the daughter of a sea captain, and educated at Leeds University; her first novel, *The Pot Boils* (1919), was followed by many other works of fiction, including *Women Against Men* (1933, stories), *Company Parade* (1934), *Love in Winter* (1935), and *None turn Back* (1936), the last three forming a trilogy. She also published poems, essays, and biographies, and several volumes of autobiography, including *Journey from the North* (1969), describing her time during the Second World War as president of *PEN. Her second husband was the historian and author Guy Chapman (1889–1972), remembered for his vivid personal account of trench warfare in France, *A Passionate Prodigality* (1933).

JAMIESON, John (1759–1838), lexicographer and antiquary, a friend of Sir W. *Scott. His chief work was the *Etymological Dictionary of the Scottish Language*, which first appeared in 1808.

Jane Eyre, a novel by C. *Brontë, published 1847.

The heroine, a penniless orphan, has been left to the care of her aunt Mrs Reed. Harsh and unsympathetic treatment rouses her defiant spirit, and a passionate outbreak leads to her consignment to Lowood Institution (based on Cowan Bridge, which the author herself briefly attended). There, consoled for the severity of the régime by the kindness of the superintendent Miss Temple and a fellow orphan, Helen Burns, who dies in Jane's arms of consumption, she spends some miserable years, eventually becoming a teacher. On Miss Temple's marriage she obtains a post as governess at Thornfield Hall to Adèle, the illegitimate daughter of Mr Rochester, a *Byronic hero of grim aspect and sardonic temper. Rochester, despite Jane's plainness, is fascinated by her sharp wit and independence, and they fall in love. After much resistance she agrees to marry him, but on the eve of their wedding her wedding veil is rent by an intruder who Rochester assures her is a servant, Grace Poole, but who is the next day revealed to be his mad Creole wife Bertha, confined to the upper regions of the Hall for years, whose unseen presence has long disturbed Jane. The marriage ceremony is interrupted by Mrs Rochester's brother from the West Indies and, despite Rochester's full confession and pleadings with Jane to stay with him, she flees. After nearly perishing on the moors, she is taken in and cared for by the Revd St John Rivers and his sisters Mary and Diana. It emerges that they are her cousins, and that Jane has inherited money from an uncle; the legacy is equally divided between the four. Under pressure from the earnest appeals and strong personality of the dedicated Rivers, she nearly consents to marry him and share his missionary vocation in India, but is prevented by a telepathic appeal from Rochester. She returns to Thornfield Hall to find the building burned, and Rochester blinded and maimed from his attempt to save his wife from the flames. She marries him, and in the last chapter we learn that his sight is partially restored.

From its first publication, the novel's exceptional emotional and narrative power made it a success, though, despite its strict adherence to conventional moral standards, it was considered by many to be unsuitable for young ladies; more recently its strong sexual undercurrents have subjected it to many *Freudian interpretations encouraged by the author's frequent use of dream imagery. Additional scandal attended the publication of the second edition, which Charlotte dedicated to *Thackeray, unaware that he too had a wife certified as insane. The story of the first Mrs Rochester was told by J. *Rhys in *Wide Sargasso Sea*.

JANE SHORE, see SHORE.

'Janet's Repentance', see SCENES OF CLERICAL LIFE.

Jansenism, the doctrine developed by Cornelius Jansen (1585–1638), bishop of Ypres in Flanders, who maintained after St *Augustine the perverseness and inability for good of the natural human will. The capacity for the love of God, he held, could be obtained only by 'conversion', and God converts whom he pleases. His doctrine thus approximated to that of predestination, and was closely analogous to Calvinism, but Jansen repudiated justification by faith and maintained that the personal relation

of the human soul with God was possible only through the Roman Church. These austere views were introduced at *Port-Royal and powerfully influenced the society and literature of 17th-cent. France (see PASCAL and RACINE), but were strongly opposed by the Jesuits and condemned by successive popes; Port-Royal was finally destroyed after much persecution in 1710, and many French Jansenists took refuge in the Netherlands.

'January and May', a version by *Pope of Chaucer's 'Merchant's Tale' (see CANTERBURY TALES, 10).

Jaquenetta, a country wench loved by *Armado in Shakespeare's *Love's Labour's Lost*.

Jaques, a discontented lord attending the banished duke in Shakespeare's *As You Like It*. Many of the play's most memorable lines are his, including the speech beginning 'All the world's a stage' (II. vii). His name is clearly to be pronounced as two syllables: 'Jake-is' or 'Jack-is'. A second Jaques, 'the second son of old Sir Rowland', appears in the final scene of the play.

Jarley, Mrs, in Dickens's *The Old Curiosity Shop*, the proprietor of a travelling waxworks show.

Jarndyce, John, a character in Dickens's *Bleak House*.

JARRELL, Randall (1914–65), American poet and critic, born in Nashville, Tennessee; he taught for many years in various colleges, and his one novel, *Pictures from an Institution* (1954), is a satire on life in a progressive women's college and an early example of a *campus novel. He published several volumes of poetry, from his first, *Blood for a Stranger* (1942), to *The Lost World*, published posthumously in 1966 with a memoir by his friend R. *Lowell.

JARRY, Alfred, see ABSURD, THEATRE OF THE.

Jarvie, Bailie Nicol, a character in Scott's *Rob Roy*.

Jazz Poetry, a genre presaged in the US by (Nicholas) Vachel Lindsay (1879–1931) with his incantatory ballads, 'General William Booth' (1913), 'The Congo' (1914), *The Daniel Jazz* (1920), etc.; and then by (James) Langston Hughes (1902–67), who was probably the first to pitch his verse in conjunction with musicians in the late 1930s. The fusion was developed in the 1950s by Kenneth Patchen (1911–72), Kenneth Rexroth (1905–82), Amiri Baraka (adopted name of black militant writer Everett Le Roi Jones, 1934–), Ted Joans (1928–), and the poets of the American *Beat Generation; and in Britain from the mid-1950s to the 1980s by C. *Logue, Roy Fisher (1930–), Michael Horovitz (1935–), Pete Brown (1940–), Spike Hawkins (1942–), and others. Various permutations of primarily non-academic, often regional, entertainers and singer-songwriters have proliferated since, with the punk-rock, post-punk, and 'new wave' voices of John Cooper Clarke, Paul Weller of The Jam, and the Rastafarian and reggae-cadenced contributions of Anglo-Jamaican poets such as James *Berry, E. K. *Brathwaite, Linton Kwesi Johnson, and Benjamin Zephaniah. See also UNDERGROUND POETRY.

Jean de Meun, see ROMAN DE LA ROSE.

Jean Jacques, a current abbreviation of the name of Jean-Jacques *Rousseau.

Jean Paul, a frequent abbreviation of the name of J. P. F. *Richter.

JEBB, Richard Claverhouse (1841–1905), professor of Greek at Glasgow University 1874, regius professor at Cambridge 1889. Unfriendly reviewers of his first major work, The Attic Orators (1876), saw no merit in it beyond diligence and a certain elegance, and in a way this verdict holds good for all his writings. The critical editions familiar to generations of students show that his knowledge of ancient Greece and its language was voluminous and exact. His style reflected the fastidiousness which we know from his wife's witty letters to have characterized him as a man. But when there was need for literary criticism or for an understanding of human nature, he could produce nothing but generalities. That his career was markedly successful in spite of these shortcomings—he became MP for his university (1891) and received the OM and a knighthood in 1900—sheds an interesting light on the character of late Victorian scholarship.

Jeeves, in many of P. G. *Wodehouse's stories, the omniscient and resourceful valet.

JEFFERIES, Richard (1848–87), writer and naturalist, the son of a Wiltshire farmer. As a boy of 16 he attempted to run away to Moscow or perhaps America, but only got as far as Liverpool. He began his literary career as a local reporter in Wiltshire, and from then on he wrote much, including novels (which had no success), works of natural history and country life, and essays in journals and magazines. The books for which he is remembered combine his love of the natural world with a poetic apprehension and individuality of thought which blur the usual literary distinctions. He first attracted attention with The Gamekeeper at Home: Sketches of Natural History and Rural Life (1878), published first in the *Pall Mall Gazette. This, together with Hodge and his Masters (1880), appears to have influenced *Hardy's article of 1883 on 'The Dorsetshire Labourer'. For these books, as for most of his others, Jefferies relied greatly on 'field notebooks', where he entered his meticu-

lous observations on the life of the countryside. Wild Life in a Southern County, in which the author, sitting on a Wiltshire down, observes in ever widening circles the fields, woods, animals, and human inhabitants below him, was published with success in 1879, as was The Amateur Poacher. Wood Magic (1881), in which a solitary boy lives in a magical world of speaking wild animals, was followed in 1882 by *Bevis, The Story of a Boy, an evocation (for both adults and children) of his country childhood (see CHILDREN'S LITERATURE). The book for which he is probably best known, *The Story of my Heart, tracing the growth of his unorthodox beliefs, caused some scandal on its publication in 1883. After London, a savage vision of the future, in which London is a poisonous swamp inhabited by cruel dwarfs, followed in 1885, as did a collection of essays much reprinted, The Open Air. Published in the year of his death, Amaryllis at the Fair, though lacking narrative, contains in Iden an impressive portrait of Jefferies's father. See Richard Jefferies (1965) by S. J. Looker and C. Porteous; there is also a life (1909) by E. *Thomas.

JEFFERS, (John) Robinson (1887–1962), American poet, born in Pittsburgh, the son of a professor of biblical languages. He travelled widely with his parents as a boy until they settled in California, then studied at Occidental College and other universities before himself settling, with his wife Una, at Carmel on the Californian coast, where they lived in seclusion, in a granite house on the cliffs facing the sea. The scenery of the redwood and seashore inspires much of his works, and one of his dominant themes is what he called 'Inhumanism'—the insignificance of man, contrasted with the vast, merciless, enduring processes of nature and the animal kingdom; the hawk provides one of his most strikingly recurrent symbols. After two minor volumes he made his name with Tamar and Other Poems (1924), of which the title poem is a tragic narrative of family passion and incest in a wild Californian setting; this was followed by other volumes, many of them of a similar pattern—a long narrative, together with shorter lyrics. These include The Women at Point Sur (1927), Cawdor and Other Poems (1928), Thurso's Landing and Other poems (1932), and, in 1938, Selected Poetry. He suffered a certain lapse in popularity due to his wartime espousal of an attitude of isolationism, expressed in 'The Eye', written during the war; the eye is the Pacific, to which 'our ships, planes, wars are perfectly irrelevant'. He had a stage success with his adaption of *Euripides' Medea in 1947, and his last volume of poetry, Hungerfield and Other Poems, appeared in 1954.

JEFFREY, Francis, Lord (1773–1850), educated at Edinburgh and Glasgow Universities, a

Whig who became a Scottish judge and an MP. He is remembered in a literary connection as the founder, with Sydney *Smith, of *The Edinburgh Review* in 1802, as its editor until 1829, and as a stern but judicious critic of the writers of his day. Although he was often severe (and was challenged to a duel by T. *Moore), he nevertheless wrote appreciatively of many writers, including *Crabbe, Sir W. *Scott, *Byron, and, most notably *Keats, in whose *Poems* of 1820 he discerned genius. *Hazlitt thought him an admirable editor, perceptive and just, with 'a great range of knowledge, an incessant activity of mind'. His inability to understand Wordsworth—his review of *The Excursion* in 1814 begins: 'This will never do'—led to a series of attacks on 'a *sect* of poets' designated as *"The Lake Poets'. Smith complained, 'The whole effect of your mind is to destroy', but this seems no more just than Byron's lampoons in *English Bards and Scotch Reviewers* on 'the self-constituted judge of poesy'.

JEFFREYS, George, first Baron Jeffreys (1648–89), was lord chief justice, 1682, and is notorious as the judge who held the 'Bloody Assizes' in 1685 after the defeat of Monmouth's rebellion. He was arrested in 1688 and died in the Tower.

Jekyll and Mr Hyde, *The Strange Case of Dr,* a novel by R. L. *Stevenson, published 1886.

Dr Jekyll, a physician conscious of the duality, the mixed good and evil, in his own nature, and fascinated by the idea of the advantage that would arise if these two elements could be clothed in different personalities, discovers a drug by means of which he can create for himself a separate personality that absorbs all his evil instincts. This personality, repulsive in appearance, he assumes from time to time and calls Mr Hyde, and in it he gives rein to his evil impulses. The personality of Hyde is pure evil. It gradually gains the greater ascendancy, and Hyde commits a horrible murder. Jekyll now finds himself from time to time involuntarily transformed into Hyde, while the drug loses its efficacy in restoring his original form and character. On the point of discovery and arrest he takes his own life.

JELLICOE, (Patricia) Ann (1927–), playwright and director, trained as an actress at the Central School of Speech and Drama. She was associated for some years with the *English Stage Company, which in 1958 put on the play which made her name, *The Sport of My Mad Mother,* an experimental drama about a London street gang described by *Tynan as a '*tour de force*'. This was followed by *The Knack* (1962) and *Shelley* (1965). She has also written plays for children, drama-documentaries on historical themes performed by the local West Country community, and several translations.

Jellyby, Mrs, a character in Dickens's *Bleak House.*

Jenkins, (1) Nicholas, the narrator of A. *Powell's *A Dance to the Music of Time;* (2) Mrs Winifred, a character in Smollett's *Humphry Clinker.*

Jenkyns, Deborah, Matilda, and Peter, characters in Mrs Gaskell's *Cranford.*

Jennings, Mrs, (1) a character in J. Austen's *Sense and Sensibility;* (2) the mother of *Keats, as she became by her second marriage.

JENNINGS, Elizabeth (1926–), poet, born in Boston, Lincolnshire, of a Roman Catholic family, and educated at St Anne's College, Oxford. She worked as a library assistant, in advertising, and in publishing, while publishing her early collections of poetry, *Poems* (1953), *A Way of Looking* (1955), and *A Sense of the World* (1958). She was somewhat arbitrarily associated with the *Movement, through Robert Conquest's inclusion of some of her work in *New Lines* (1956), but her subsequent volumes of verse (e.g. *Recoveries,* 1964; *The Mind has Mountains,* 1966) are highly personal and confessional accounts of mental breakdown and hospital treatment, very far removed in tone from the laconic detachment of the more representative Movement poets. Her *Collected Poems* were published in 1967 and she has since published several more volumes, including *Lucidities* (1970) and *Moments of Grace* (1979), which manifest her quiet and sensitive control of, and openness towards, experiences of suffering, loneliness, friendship, and religious faith.

'Jenny', a poem by D. G. *Rossetti, first published 1870, although he had been working on it for many years, and was further to revise it. It was one of the poems buried with his wife Lizzie in 1862. The poet describes a night spent in the chamber of a prostitute, golden-haired Jenny; she falls asleep against his knees and at dawn he leaves her, after much meditation on her thoughtless gaiety, shame, and beauty, and on the toad Lust which has ruined her. Fallen women and prostitutes were favourite subjects with the Pre-Raphaelites: e.g. Rossetti's painting *Found* and H. *Hunt's *The Awakening Conscience.* This poem roused the indignation of those like R. W. *Buchanan who thought Rossetti's work too sensual, and *Ruskin greatly disliked it.

Jenny Wren, see WREN.

JENYNS, Soame (1704–87), MP and minor poet, is chiefly remembered for his *A Free Enquiry into the Nature and Origin of Evil* (1757), which elicited a brilliant and scathing attack from Dr *Johnson in *The Literary Magazine.* Jenyns's work is a classic statement of the more facile elements of 18th-cent. optimism, justifying evil and suffering by their place in the 'scale of Being' and ignorance as the 'opiate' of the poor: 'the sufferings of individuals are absolutely necessary to universal happiness.' Johnson poured scorn on a philosophy which envisaged superior beings laughing at human misery, and links Jenyns's view with that of *Pope (see ESSAY ON MAN): 'This author and Pope perhaps never saw the miseries which they imagine thus easily to be borne.'

Jeremiad, a doleful complaint, in allusion to the *Lamentations of Jeremiah* in the OT.

Jeremy, a character in Congreve's *Love for Love*.

JEROME, St (Hieronymus) (c.342–420), one of the four 'Doctors of the Church', was born at Strido near Dalmatia, educated at Rome, and baptized in 360. He visited Gaul and Asia Minor, and after a period of dissipation (perhaps conventional) he practised asceticism. He lived as a hermit near Chalcis (south-east of Antioch), spent the years 382–5 at Rome, where he was the spiritual counsellor of some noble Roman ladies, and in 386 settled at Bethlehem, where he died in 420 after 25 years of writing and translation. His principal works were a translation and continuation of the chronicles of *Eusebius and the Latin version of the scriptures which came to be known as the *Vulgate, afterwards the standard Latin version up to the Renaissance.
Dogmatic and Political Works (including *Against Rufinus* and *Against the Pelagians*), trans. J. N. Hritzu (1965); J. Steinmann, *Saint Jerome*, trans. R. Matthews (1959).

JEROME, Jerome K(lapka) (1859–1927), brought up in east London, the son of an unsuccessful ironmonger, became an actor and published a volume of humorous pieces about the theatre, *On The Stage and Off* (1885), and another collection of light essays, *Idle Thoughts of an Idle Fellow* (1886). He achieved lasting fame with *Three Men in a Boat* (1889), the story of three young men and their dog who take a rowing holiday on the Thames. In 1892 Jerome and some friends founded *The Idler*, a humorous magazine which published work by *Harte, *Twain, and W. W. *Jacobs, among others. *Three Men on the Bummel*, describing a tour in Germany, appeared in 1900, and in 1902 *Paul Klever*, an autobiographical novel. Jerome also wrote many plays, in the manner of his friend *Barrie, including the most memorable, *The Passing of the Third Floor Back* (1907). There is a life by J. Connolly (1982).

Jeronimo, or Hieronimo, the chief character in Kyd's *The Spanish Tragedy*.

JERROLD, Douglas William (1803–57), the son of an actor-manager, served in the navy, was apprenticed to a printer, and became dramatic author of the Surrey Theatre before making his name in the theatre with *Black-Ey'd Susan* (1829), founded on *Gay's ballad; other successful plays included *Fifteen Years of a Drunken's Life* (1828), *The Rent Day* (1832), and *The Prisoner of War* (1842). He was a friend of *Dickens. In his later years Jerrold turned to journalism; he was associated with *Punch from its beginnings and became a regular contributor, writing several serial works, including social political articles signed 'Q' which gave Punch a liberal trend in politics and *Mrs Caudle's Curtain Lectures* (issued as a book in 1846), which greatly added to the journal's popularity. From 1845 he ran *Douglas Jerrold's Shilling Magazine* and from 1846 *Douglas Jerrold's Weekly Newspaper*. He wrote several novels and his studies of *Men of Character* (1838) were illustrated by *Thackeray.

JERROLD, William Blanchard (1826–84), son of D. *Jerrold; journalist, playwright, biographer, and writer of miscellaneous works on food, travel, etc. He wrote the text of *London* (1872), illustrated by *Doré, and wrote a life of Doré (1891).

Jerry Hawthorn, a character in Pierce *Egan's *Life in London*.

Jerusalem: The Emanation of the Giant Albion, a prophetic poem by *Blake, written and etched, with 100 plates, 1804–20. (It is not to be confused with the short poem beginning 'And did those feet . . .', commonly known as 'Jerusalem', which appears at the beginning of Blake's *Milton*.) After a Preface in which he defends his use of free verse ('Poetry Fetter'd Fetters the Human Race') Blake proceeds to personify England as the fallen giant *Albion, and to summon him to the 'awakening of Eternal Life' which lies beyond the Vegetable Universe, and to reunion with his banished emanation, the lovely Jerusalem. Blake mingles prophecy with social criticism, biblical legend with legends of druids and of Gog and Magog (see GOGMAGOG), and references to 'Hampstead, Highgate, Finchley, Hendon, Muswell Hill' with descriptions of *Los labouring in his furnace to build the city of Golgonooza. The long poem ends with a 'fourfold vision' of regeneration, 'rejoicing in Unity in the Four Senses' and in the 'Forgiveness of Sins which is Self-Annihilation'.

Jerusalem Delivered (*Gerusalemme Liberata*), a poem by *Tasso, published without his consent 1580, in authorized form 1581. (Tasso later rewrote the poem, giving it a more 'regular' structure and a more austere moral tone, and changing the title to *Gerusalemme Conquistata*. The new work, published 1593, was inferior to the original.)
    The poem is an epic of the First Crusade, with

the addition of romantic and fabulous elements. By the side of Godfrey of Bouillon, the leader of the Christian host besieging Jerusalem, and other historical characters, we have the romantic figures of Sofronia and her lover Olindo, who are prepared to face martyrdom to save the Christians in the beleaguered city; the warlike Clorinda, who is beloved by Tancred the Norman, and killed by him unwittingly; and Armida, the niece of the king of Damascus, who lures away the Christians to her enchanted gardens. Rinaldo, prince of Este (an imaginary personage, introduced as a way of extolling the author's patron), rescues the prisoners of Armida, and Armida falls in love with him. By her enchantments they live happily together until Rinaldo is summoned away to help the army by slaying the devil-enchanted wood. He takes part in the capture of Jerusalem, and at last marries a repentant Armida.

The poem was translated into English in 1594 by R. Carew (1555–1620), and in 1600 by *Fairfax as Godfrey of Bulloigne. Spenser's description of Acrasia's Bower of Bliss (*Faerie Queene, II. xii) was modelled on the gardens of Armida, and the poem considerably influenced *Milton and others (see TASSO).

Jervis, Mrs, a character in Richardson's *Pamela.

JESPERSEN, Jens Otto Harry (1860–1943), Danish philologist, educated at Copenhagen, where he became professor of English in 1893. He wrote many philological books, the most important perhaps being A Modern English Grammar on Historical Principles (Parts 1–7, 1909–49, Heidelberg); The Growth and Structure of the English Language (1909; 9th edn. 1938); Essentials of English Grammar (1933). But he also wrote works more concerned with the theoretical analysis of language, the principal ones being The Philosophy of Grammar (1929), Analytic Syntax (1937), and, most importantly, Language, its Nature, Development and Origin (1922).

Jessamy Bride, The, the name given by *Goldsmith to the younger Miss Horneck, with whom he is supposed to have been in love.

Jessica, Shylock's daughter in Shakespeare's *The Merchant of Venice.

Jessica's First Prayer, see STRETTON, H.

Jest Book Literature, collections of 'merie Tales', 'quicke answeres', and 'pleasant conceites' popular throughout the 16th and 17th cents and later. Their authorship was often ascribed to witty writers such as *Skelton and *Peele or to famous jesters such as J. *Scogan and R. Armin. The genre is related to the apophthegm and adage, popularized by *Erasmus, and to *rogue literature, and can be detected in some early fiction, for example in the opening of T. Nashe's

*The Unfortunate Traveller. (See also JOE MILLER'S JESTS.)

Jesuits, see IGNATIUS LOYOLA.

Jew, The Wandering, see WANDERING JEW.

Jewel in the Crown, The, see SCOTT, P.

JEWETT, Sarah Orne (1849–1909), American novelist and short story writer, born in Maine, the daughter of a doctor. She was inspired when young by H. B. *Stowe's novel set in Maine, The Pearl of Orris Island, to write about her native region of New England, and began her career by publishing short stories in *The Atlantic Monthly. Her volumes include Deephaven (1877), A Country Doctor (1884), A White Heron (1886; short stories), and The Country of the Pointed Firs (1896), which describes daily life in a decaying Maine seaport town. Her precise, realistic, subdued portraits of ordinary people and her sense of community and place bear witness to her admiration for *Flaubert as an artist, and won her an enduring reputation; W. *Cather records her debt to her in Not Under Forty.

Jewkes, Mrs, a character in Richardson's *Pamela.

Jew of Malta, The, a drama in blank verse by *Marlowe, performed about 1592, not published until 1633.

The Grand Seignior of Turkey having demanded the tribute of Malta, the governor of Malta decides that it shall be paid by the Jews of the island. Barabas, a rich Jew who resists the edict, has all his wealth impounded and his house turned into a nunnery. In revenge he indulges in an orgy of slaughter, procuring the death of his daughter Abigail's lover among others, and poisoning Abigail herself. Malta being besieged by the Turks, he betrays the fortress to them and, as a reward, is made its governor. He now plots the destruction of the Turkish commander and his force at a banquet by means of a collapsible floor; but is himself betrayed and hurled through this same floor into a cauldron, where he dies. The Prologue to the play is spoken by 'Machevil', and Barabas is one of the prototypes for unscrupulous *Machiavellian villains in later Elizabethan and Jacobean drama. His praise of gold and precious stones as 'Infinite riches in a little roome' is often quoted.

JEWSBURY, Geraldine Endsor (1812–80), an intimate friend of the *Carlyles. Her brilliant wit and conversation made her house in Manchester, and later in London, a centre for such eminent visitors as the Carlyles, J. A. *Froude, T. H. *Huxley, *Ruskin, D. G. *Rossetti, and *Thirlwall. Besides contributing articles and reviews to the *Athenaeum, the *Westminster Review, and other journals, she wrote six novels, including Zöe (1845), The Half Sisters (1848), and *Marian Withers* (1851), and two stories for children. *A Selection from the Letters of Geraldine Jewsbury to Jane Carlyle* (1892, edited with a memoir by Mrs A. Ireland), gave undue emphasis to the emotional element of the friendship between the two women and was the subject of an interesting article by V. *Woolf ('Geraldine and Jane', *TLS*, 28 Feb. 1929). Miss Jewsbury had destroyed all the letters to her from Jane Carlyle, except for one which was published in Mrs Ireland's *Life of Jane Welsh Carlyle* (1891); it was the wish of both women that their letters be destroyed.

JHABVALA, Ruth Prawer (1927–), novelist, born in Germany, the daughter of a Polish Jewish solicitor; she came to England in 1939 as a refugee and was educated in London. In 1951 she married an Indian architect, and subsequently lived for 24 years in India, where she wrote several novels including *Esmond in India* (1958), *A New Dominion* (1973), and *Heat and Dust* (1975, *Booker Prize), all of which reflect her mingled affection for and impatience with her adopted country and show intimate knowledge of the lives of both Indian and European families. She published volumes of short stories and wrote several original screenplays, including *Shakespeare-Wallah* (1965), the story of a troupe of travelling actors. In 1975 she moved to New York, where her novel *In Search of Love and Beauty* (1983) is set.

Jig, 'an afterpiece in the form of a brief farce which was sung and accompanied by dancing', popular in the Elizabethan and Jacobean theatre. Few have survived, but there are numerous references to them in contemporary literature and both W. *Kemp and *Tarlton performed them with great success. Cf. *Hamlet's comment on Polonius: 'he's for a jig, or a tale of bawdry, or he sleeps' (II. ii. 494).

Jimson, Gulley, the Bohemian artist hero of J. *Cary's novel *The Horse's Mouth.* Although popularly supposed to be based on the painter Stanley Spencer (1891–1959), he also contains some of the characteristics of Augustus *John, including the urge to paint large murals.

Jingle, Alfred, a character in Dickens's *Pickwick Papers.*

Jiniwin, Mrs, in Dickens's *The Old Curiosity Shop,* the mother of Mrs Quilp.

Jo, the crossing-sweeper in Dickens's *Bleak House.*

JOAN OF ARC, St (1412–31), Jeanne D'Arc, or more correctly Jeanne Darc, as it was spelt in all contemporary documents (Littré), the daughter of Jacques Darc, a farmer of Domrémy in the valley of the Meuse, an illiterate girl who contributed powerfully to liberate France from the English in the reign of Charles VII. Inspired,

she claimed, by the voices of Sts Michael, Catherine, and Margaret, her mission was a double one, to raise the siege of Orléans, and to conduct Charles to his coronation at Rheims. She accomplished both these tasks and then wished to return home; but she yielded to the demands of the French patriots and was taken prisoner by the Burgundians, who handed her over to the English. But it was a French court of ecclesiastics (with the help of the Inquisition) who sentenced her as a witch, and the English who burned her at Rouen. She was canonized in 1920. She is the subject of Voltaire's *La *Pucelle,* of a tragedy by *Schiller, of a poem by *Southey, and of dramas by G. B. *Shaw and *Anouilh. See also Marina Warner's *Joan of Arc: The Image of Female Heroism* (1981) for a discussion of St Joan's changing function as national and political symbol.

Job Trotter, a character in Dickens's *Pickwick Papers.*

Jocasta, a tragedy in blank verse, translated from an Italian adaptation of the *Phoenissae* of *Euripides, by G. *Gascoigne and F. Kinwelmarshe, included in Gascoigne's *Posies* (1575).

JOCELIN DE BRAKELOND (*fl.* 1200), a monk of Bury St Edmunds, whose chronicle of his abbey (1173–1202) inspired *Carlyle's *Past and Present.*

Jocoseria, a volume of ten poems of various lengths and metres by R. *Browning, published 1883. The collection is consciously a miscellany; Browning borrowed the title from Otto Melander's book of jokes and stories (1597) to suggest its lightweight character, though several of the poems ('Donald', 'Cristina and Monaldeschi', 'Ixion') do not bear out this judgement. The volume contains the much-parodied lyric 'Wanting is—what?', an exquisite miniature of Browning's whole philosophy of art as a mode of desire.

'Jock o' Hazeldean', a ballad, of which one stanza is ancient, the rest by Sir W. *Scott. The lady is to marry young Frank, chief of Errington, but she weeps for Jock. On her wedding-day she is found to have eloped with him over the border.

Joe, 'the fat boy' in Dickens's *Pickwick Papers.*

Joe Gargery, a character in Dickens's *Great Expectations.*

Joe Miller's Jests: *or the wit's vade-mecum* (1739), a *jest-book by J. *Mottley. The name is taken from Joseph Miller (1684–1738), an actor in the Drury Lane company, and a reputed humorist. It was a childhood favourite of G. *Eliot.

Johannes Factotum, 'John Do-everything', a Jack of all trades, a would-be universal genius. The phrase, as also *Dominus Factotum, Magister*

Factotum, and the corresponding Italian *fa il tutto*, is found in the 16th cent. It occurs in **Greenes Groats-Worth of Witte, bought with a Million of Repentance*, attacking Shakespeare:

... beeing an absolute *Johannes fac totum*, is in his owne conceit the onely Shake-scene in a countrey.

JOHN, Augustus (Edwin), OM (1878–1961), painter, born at Tenby, the son of a solicitor, and trained at the Slade School. His autobiography, *Chiaroscuro* (1952), contains many good anecdotes about writers whom he met or knew as friends (including **Wilde, G. B. *Shaw, *Joyce, and W. *Lewis), and he also painted some remarkable portraits of literary figures, including **Yeats, Shaw, Dylan *Thomas, T. E. *Lawrence, *Firbank, and Joyce. M. *Holroyd's two-volume biography (1974–5) gives a full and entertaining account of John's flamboyant personality and unorthodox domestic life, and suggests various fictitious characters who were partly based on John, including Struthers in D. H. *Lawrence's **Aaron's Rod*, Albert Sanger in M. *Kennedy's *The Constant Nymph*, Gulley Jimson in **Cary's *The Horse's Mouth*, and the younger Strickland in **Maugham's *The Moon and Sixpence*. His sister, Gwen John (1876–1939), was also a painter of distinction.

John, Little, one of the companions of **Robin Hood.

'John Anderson, my Jo', a lyric by **Burns, suggested to him by an older song.

John Bull, The History of, a collection of pamphlets by **Arbuthnot, issued 1712, rearranged and republished in **Pope and **Swift's *Miscellanies* of 1727.

The pamphlets (of which the first, *Law is a Bottomless Pit*, appeared on 6 March 1712) were designed to advocate the cessation of war with France, and introduced the allegorical character John Bull, who represents England; he is 'an honest plain-dealing fellow, choleric, bold, and of a very inconstant temper . . . very apt to quarrel with his best friends, especially if they pretend to govern him . . . a boon companion, loving his bottle and his diversion'. Other characters are Nicholas Frog (the Dutch), Lord Strutt (Philip of Spain), Lewis Baboon (Louis XIV of France), and Humphrey Hocus, an attorney (the duke of Marlborough). Ed. A. W. Bower and R. A. Erickson (1976).

John Bull is also the title of a play by G. **Colman the younger.

John Bull's Other Island, an ironic description of Ireland deriving from Leon Paul Blouet's *John Bull and His Island* (1884) and used by G. B. **Shaw as the title of a play (1904) written at the request of **Yeats 'as a patriotic contribution to the repertory of the Irish Literary Theatre'.

John Buncle Esq, The Life and Opinions of, a novel by T. **Amory, published in two volumes, 1756, 1766.

Buncle, a man of passionate temperament and a highly original turn of mind, sets out on a journey through the more magnificent and dangerous landscapes of northern England. Among the moors and mountains he comes upon small centres of civilized elegance and culture, in many of which he encounters beautiful and learned women, seven of whom (with the intervention of successive deaths) he marries. Miss Spence, with 'the head of Aristotle, the heart of a primitive Christian, and the form of Venus de Medicis', who discusses differential calculus after dinner, is typical of his wives. But the bulk of the book is taken up with eloquent discussion and digression on religious, scientific, and literary subjects, descriptions of awesome scenery, and much eating and drinking. How far the author is in humorous command of his material, and how far subject to his own fantasy, is difficult to establish. **Hazlitt, who enjoyed the book, found 'the soul of Rabelais' in it.

'John Gilpin, The Diverting History of', a poem by **Cowper, first published anonymously in ** The Public Advertiser*, reprinted in chapbook form, and included in the same volume as ** The Task* (1785). The story of John Gilpin was told to Cowper by Lady Austen to divert him from melancholy. He laughed over it during the night and next day had turned it into a ballad.

John Gilpin, a 'linen-draper bold' of Cheapside, and his wife, decide to celebrate their 20th wedding anniversary by a trip to the Bell at Edmonton, he on a borrowed horse, she, her sister, and the children in a chaise and pair. But John loses control of his horse, and the poem describes his headlong career to Edmonton, ten miles beyond it to Ware, and then back again.

John Halifax, Gentleman, a novel by Mrs **Craik published 1856.

The story, set between the Bredon hills and Tewkesbury, tells of the poor honest orphan John, who finds employment with the tanner Abel Fletcher and is befriended by Abel's weakling son Phineas, improves his position, and marries the book's heroine, Ursula March. John's status as 'gentleman' is earned not by birth and wealth but by his own integrity and worth. The book was immensely successful both in England and America, and ran into numerous editions over many years. Long after Mrs Craik's death American tourists would visit the 'Halifax country' of Tewkesbury.

John Inglesant, see SHORTHOUSE, J. H.

JOHN OF AUSTRIA, Don (1547–78), a natural son of Charles V. He defeated the Turkish fleet at Lepanto (1571), a victory celebrated in **Chesterton's poem 'Lepanto'.

JOHN OF GAUNT (1340–99), duke of Lancaster, the fourth and longest-lived son of Edward III and the father of Henry IV, named from his birthplace Ghent (Gaunt). He was first the regent, in effect, during the early years of the reign of the young Richard II and afterwards his bitter enemy. He was the dominant figure in English politics during much of Richard's reign, and his oppressive rule was repeatedly but unsuccessfully opposed, first by his eldest brother the *Black Prince in the year of his death and of the 'Good Parliament' (1376). He was the employer of *Wyclif and the patron of Chaucer whose *Book of the Duchess is commonly believed to be an elegy for the death of Gaunt's duchess Philippa in 1369. He is a major figure in Shakespeare's *Richard II.

JOHN OF HOVEDEN, see ANGLO-LATIN LITERATURE.

JOHN OF SALISBURY (fl. 1120–80), was born at Salisbury and studied at Paris under *Abelard and at Chartres. He returned to England in 1154, remaining mostly at Canterbury where he was secretary to archbishop Theobald and was sent on missions to Rome. He was also secretary to *Becket with whom he was exiled when he fell into disfavour with Henry II. John retired to Rheims where he composed his *Historia Pontificalis.* He is said to have been present in Canterbury Cathedral when Becket was assassinated; he wrote a life of Becket (and of *Anselm), arguing for the canonization of both. He became bishop of Chartres in 1176. He was the most learned classical writer of his time, often seen as the principal humanist inspiration in 'the twelfth-century Renaissance'. Among his many works, the principal items are the *Polycraticus* (or *De nugis Curialium*), on the vanities of the court and miscellaneous questions on philosophy, and the *Metalogicon*, a treatise on logic and an account of Aristotle's treatment of the subject. (See also ANGLO-LATIN LITERATURE.)
    Ed. C. C. J. Webb, *Polycraticus* (1909) and *Metalogicon* (1929); C. C. J. Webb, *John of Salisbury* (1932).

JOHN OF THE CROSS, St (Juan de la Cruz) (1542–91), a friar of the Carmelite order, and, with St *Theresa's encouragement, a joint founder of the Discalced Carmelites. A major figure of the Counter-Reformation, he was imprisoned in Toledo in 1577 for his reformist views, an experience which inspired some of his finest mystical writing. Less than a thousand lines of his poetry survive, but they are regarded as some of the greatest in the Spanish language; particularly well known are his *Cantico espiritual* (Spiritual Canticle), most of which was composed in prison; his *En una noche oscura* (The Dark Night), composed shortly afterwards; and *Llama de amor viva* (The Living Flame of Love), written c.1583–4. He writes of the stages of union of the soul with God, and of the ecstasy of that union, in a language both erotic and spiritual, and of an exceptional power, grace, and intensity. His work has been translated by E. Allison Peers (1934–5), and a selection of his poems by R. *Campbell (1951).

JOHNSON, B(ryan) S(tanley) William) (1933–73), London-born novelist whose works include *Albert Angelo* (1964), *Trawl* (1966), *The Unfortunates* (1969, consisting of 27 unbound sections in a box), *House Mother Normal* (1971), and *Christy Malry's Own Double-Entry* (1973). Johnson was an experimental novelist, an admirer of *Joyce and *Beckett, and his works combine verbal inventiveness with typographical innovations that resemble the techniques of *concrete poetry (holes in the page, blank pages, black pages, diagrammatic type, etc.). He died by suicide.

JOHNSON, Charles (1679–1748), dramatist, was the author of 18 plays, including *The Wife's Relief* (1712), adapted from Shirley's *The Gamester, and *The Country Lasses* (1715), his most successful comedy. He was ridiculed by Pope in the early version of *The Dunciad for the fatness of his person, his prolific output, and his plagiaries.

JOHNSON, Joseph (1738–1809), a radical bookseller and publisher of St Paul's Churchyard, who encouraged and published many writers, including *Wordsworth (*Descriptive Sketches*, 1793), *Cowper, E. *Darwin, and M. *Wollstonecraft. He held literary dinners over the shop, where his guests included *Blake, *Fuseli, *Godwin, J. *Priestley, and *Paine. From 1788 to 1799 he published the scientific and literary monthly *The Analytical Review. Although his shop served as an important meeting-place, he himself had the reputation of a retiring and self-effacing man.

JOHNSON, Linton Kwesi, see JAZZ POETRY.

JOHNSON, Lionel Pigot (1867–1902), educated at Winchester and New College, Oxford, became an influential man of letters, and one of the notable Catholic converts of his day. A perceptive supporter of *Hardy, his *The Art of Thomas Hardy* (1894) was one of the first full-length studies to appear. His *Poems* appeared in 1895, *Ireland and other poems* in 1897, and *Post liminium*, a posthumous collection of essays, in 1911. He was a member of the *Rhymers' Club and a friend of *Yeats, who much admired his poetry; there is an account of his personality and decline into alcoholism in Yeats's *Autobiographies.* See also ART FOR ART'S SAKE.

JOHNSON, Pamela Hansford (1912–81), critic and novelist, the daughter of H. *Irving's manager, was brought up in Clapham, a district evoked in several of her many works, from her first novel, *This Bed thy Centre* (1935), to her last, *The Bonfire* (1981). In 1950 she married C. P. *Snow. She is perhaps most widely known for her comic 'Dorothy Merlin' trilogy, a satire on the pretensions of literary life, which consists of *The Unspeakable Skipton* (1959), *Night and Silence, Who is Here* (1962), and *Cork Street, Next to the Hatter's* (1965).

JOHNSON, Paul (Bede) (1928–), journalist and historian, educated at Magdalen College, Oxford. He was editor of the *New Statesman* from 1965 to 1970, since which period his political views have moved to the independent Right. His publications include *Merrie England* (1964, a novel); *The Offshore Islanders* (1972); *Elizabeth I* (1974); *Pope John XXIII* (1975); and his idiosyncratic and polemic *A History of the Modern World, from 1917 to the 1980s* (1983).

JOHNSON, Richard (1573–?1659), was the author of *The Famous History of the Seven Champions of Christendom* (*c.*1597), a widely read romance of chivalric legend, which influenced *Spenser; *The Nine Worthies of London* (1592); *The Crowne Garland of Golden Roses* (ballads, 1612, reprinted by the *Percy Society); *Tom a Lincoln*, a romance of Arthurian times (1599–1607); and *Pleasant Conceites of Old Hobson* (1607, reprinted 1843).

JOHNSON, Samuel (1709–84), born at Lichfield of elderly parents; his father was a bookseller. When three years old he was brought to London to be touched for the king's evil (scrofula) by Queen Anne; the illness seriously affected his sight, but he was from an early age an avid reader. He was educated at Lichfield Grammar School and Pembroke College, Oxford, where he spent 14 months, 1728–9, but took no degree, despite evidence of creative and scholastic powers; his college days were marred by poverty, and during the scantily documented period between leaving Oxford and his father's death in 1731 he appears to have suffered acute mental stress; bouts of melancholia were to recur in later life and gave him much sympathy with those similarly afflicted, such as W. *Collins and *Smart. He worked briefly and unhappily as an under-master at Market Bosworth, then moved to Birmingham, where he contributed essays (none of which survive) to the *Birmingham Journal*, and translated and abridged from the French an account (originally in Portuguese) of Father Lobo's *Voyage to Abyssinia*; his version appeared anonymously in 1735. In the same year he married Mrs Elizabeth Porter, a widow considerably older than himself, and started a private school at Edial, near Lichfield. This was not a success; Johnson's lack of a degree and convulsive mannerisms hindered his prospects as a teacher, and in 1737 he set off with one of his few pupils, *Garrick, to try his fortune in London, where his wife shortly joined him. He entered the service of Edward Cave (whom he had already

approached in Birmingham), the founder of *The Gentleman's Magazine*, to which he contributed regularly for years; he did editorial work and prefaces, and wrote essays, poems, Latin verses, biographies, and, most notably, his *Parliamentary Debates*, which were widely accepted as authentic speeches by the great politicians of the day. In 1738 he published his poem *London*, which may record his friendship with the poet *Savage, whose nocturnal wanderings he often shared during this period of poverty and hack-work; his *Life of Mr Richard Savage* (1744) is a vivid evocation of *Grub Street and a notable stage in the evolution of the art of biography. It was subsequently included in his *The Lives of the English Poets*. In 1747 he issued the 'Plan' of his Dictionary (see JOHNSON's DICTIONARY), on which he had already started work at his new home in Gough Square; he dedicated it to *Chesterfield, with results recorded under the latter's name. In 1749 he published *The Vanity of Human Wishes*, the first work to bear his own name, and in the same year Garrick produced his tragedy *Irene*, written in 1736 at Edial; it brought him almost £300. In 1750 he started *The Rambler*, a periodical written almost entirely by himself, partly for money and partly for 'relief' from the *Dictionary*. His wife died in 1752, a loss which caused him great and prolonged grief, bequeathing to his care her blind friend Anna Williams, who became an inmate of his home; another dependant was Robert Levet, an obscure physician and friend of the poor, on whose death in 1783 Johnson was to write the elegy beginning, 'His virtues walked their narrow round'. From March 1753 to March 1754 Johnson contributed regularly to *Hawkesworth's *The Adventurer*; in 1754 his biography of his old employer Cave appeared in *The Gentleman's Magazine*. His *Dictionary* was published in 1755, after nine years of labour; it firmly established his reputation, and also brought him, just before publication and through the support of Francis Wise and T. *Warton, the Oxford degree he had failed to achieve earlier. He continued to write essays, reviews, and political articles for various periodicals, and during 1758–60 contributed the *Idler* series of papers to the *Universal Chronicle*. In 1759 appeared *Rasselas, Prince of Abyssinia*. In 1762 Johnson was relieved of much of the drudgery of hack-work by the receipt of a crown pension of £300 a year, and the following year he met his biographer, *Boswell, in the bookshop of his friend T. *Davies.

From this period onwards we have Boswell's account of Johnson's life as one of the most eminent literary figures of his day, and also vivid portraits of his contemporaries, notably of the members of the *Club (later known as the 'Literary Club'), founded in 1764. These include *Reynolds, *Burke, and *Goldsmith; Garrick,

*C. J. Fox, *Gibbon, and Boswell were later added. Although Johnson himself was a fervent Tory, it is interesting to note that he was on friendly and intimate terms with several well known Whigs. In January 1765 he met the *Thrales, in whose town and country houses he found much comfort and companionship. Later that year appeared his edition of Shakespeare, on which he had been at work for some years; in the last months he received help from *Steevens. Although superseded by later scholarship, it contained valuable notes and emendations, and its Preface is regarded as one of his finest works of critical prose. In 1773 he travelled with Boswell to Scotland and the Hebrides, a journey recorded in his *A Journey to the Western Islands of Scotland (1775) and Boswell's *Journal of a Tour to the Hebrides (1785); in 1774 he visited North Wales with the Thrales, and in 1775 went with them to Paris, his only visit to the Continent. In 1777 he undertook, at the request of a number of booksellers, to write The Lives of the English Poets, the crowning work of his old age (1779–81). In 1784, saddened by the deaths of Levet and Thrale and by his estrangement from Mrs Thrale, he died at his house in Bolt Court and was buried in Westminster Abbey.

Johnson's reputation rests not only on his works but also on Boswell's evocation of his brilliant conversation, his eccentricities and opinionated outbursts (against Scots, Whigs, Americans, players, etc.), his interest in the supernatural (see COCK LANE GHOST), his generosity and humanity, and many other aspects of his large personality. His profound but melancholy religious faith is revealed also in his diaries and meditations, and in his attacks on the facile optimism of mid-18th-cent. thought (see JENYNS, S.). Two useful accounts appeared before Boswell's: Anecdotes of the Late Samuel Johnson (1768) by Mrs Piozzi, formerly Mrs Thrale, and a Life by Sir John *Hawkins (1787). For a 20th-cent. assessment of Johnson, see T. S. *Eliot's essay, 'Johnson as Critic and Poet' (1944).

Johnson's other works include: Marmor Norfolciense (1739), an ironical political pamphlet attacking Horace *Walpole; The Compleat Vindication of the Licensers of the Stage (1739), an ironic 'defence' of the Stage Licensing Act of 1737 by which Walpole's government in 1739 banned H. *Brooke's Gustavus Vasa; his work with *Oldys in 1743–4 on the *Harleian Miscellany; Miscellaneous Observations on the Tragedy of Macbeth (1745), praised by *Warburton; 'The Vision of Theodore, Hermit of Teneriffe', contributed in 1748 to *Dodsley's The Preceptor, an allegory about the power of habit, which he described to *Percy, somewhat misleadingly, as the best thing he ever wrote; a dedication to C. Lennox's *The Female Quixote and many other prologues, dedications, etc.; and four political pamphlets, The False Alarm (1770), against

*Wilkes; Thoughts . . . Respecting Falkland's Islands (1771); The Patriot (1774); and Taxation No Tyranny (1775), on the question of American taxation and representation: Johnson supported taxation as warmly as he opposed slavery. His remarkable Prayers and Meditations were published in 1785, his diaries of his visits to Wales and France in 1816. His correspondence was edited by R. W. Chapman (3 vols, 1952) and the Yale edition of his works (Vol. i, 1958–Vol. xiv, 1978, continuing) is under the editorship of A. T. Hazen and J. H. Middendorf. There are biographies by J. *Wain (1974) and W. J. Bate (1978).

Johnson, The Life of Samuel, by *Boswell, published 1791.

Boswell informed Dr *Johnson in 1772 of his intention to write his life, and had been collecting materials for this purpose since their first meeting in 1763. After Johnson's death in 1784 he set to work arranging and adding to the 'prodigious multiplicity of materials', a task which, he writes in 1789, involved him in great labour, perplexity, and vexation. The result was the most celebrated biography in the English language. Boswell learned much from his master's own love of the art of biography, and brought to the task boundless curiosity, persistence, and zest. His portrait is vivid and intimate, in his own words a 'Flemish picture' made up of trifling incidents as well as significant events, and Boswell's skill in stage-managing encounters (as with *Wilkes or, in contrast, Johnson's old fellow-collegian, the modest Mr Edwards) adds greatly to the liveliness of the whole. The final edition, after Boswell's death, was revised by *Malone. The standard edition (G. B. *Hill, 6 vols, 1887) has been revised by L. F. Powell (1934–50). (See also BIOGRAPHY.)

'Johnson's Dictionary', A Dictionary of the English Language, by S. *Johnson, published 1755.

Johnson entered into an agreement in 1746 with *Dodsley and others to write a dictionary, the first of its kind in English, and started work with six humble assistants in newly rented premises in Gough Square. A Plan and dedication to *Chesterfield followed in 1747. Johnson said his object was to produce 'a dictionary by which the pronunciation of our language may be fixed, and its attainment facilitated; by which its purity may be preserved, its use ascertained, and its duration lengthened'. He wrote the definitions of over 40,000 words, illustrating them with about 114,000 quotations drawn from every field of learning and literature from the time of *Sidney onwards; his derivations suffer from the scantiness of etymological knowledge in his day, but the work as a whole remained without rival until the creation of the *Oxford English Dictionary. Five editions were published in his own lifetime. His well-known playful definitions (e.g. *lexicographer*, 'a writer of dictionaries, a harmless drudge') represent a mere handful in the body of this enormous achievement. (See also DICTIONARIES.)

JOHNSTON, (William) Denis (1901–84), playwright, critic, director of the Dublin Gate Theatre, and mystical philosopher. He is best known for his plays, which include *The Old Lady Says 'No!'* (1929), *A Bridge for the Unicorn* (1925), *The Moon in the Yellow River* (1935), his adaptation of *Toller's *Die blinde Göttin* as *Blind Man's Buff* (1938) and *The Scythe and the Sunset* (1958). He wrote many plays for radio and television, and his non-dramatic writings include *In Search of Swift* (1959) and *The Brazen Horn* (1976). His daughter Jennifer Johnston (1930–) is well known as a novelist.

JOHNSTONE, Charles (?1719–1800), was educated in Dublin and became a lawyer. He travelled in 1782 to Calcutta, where he remained as a journalist and later as a prosperous newspaper proprietor. His best-known work is *Chrysal, or the Adventures of a Guinea* (1760–5). 'Chrysal' is the articulate spirit of gold in the guinea, whose progress from hand to hand, through some six different countries, serves to link various inventive and satirical episodes, including a section on the *Hell-fire Club at *Medmenham Abbey. Various characters, good and bad, from high life and low (many of whom were libellously identified with characters of the day), covet and become corrupted by the golden coin. *The History of Arsaces, Prince of Betlis* (1774) is an *Oriental tale, in which thinly disguised comment on the struggle between Great Britain and her American colonies leans strongly towards sympathy with the latter. *The Pilgrim* followed in 1775 and *John Juniper* in 1781.

'Jolly Beggars, The', a poem by *Burns, written 1786. A company of vagrants meet and carouse, with their female companions, in an alehouse kept by Poosie Nancy, in Burns's parish of Mauchline. A maimed soldier, his girl, a strolling player, a thief, a fiddler, and a ballad singer each sing a song in character, and the songs are connected by descriptions of the various rogues. Burns thought poorly of the work and it was not printed in his lifetime. However, both *Carlyle and M. *Arnold regarded it as the most original of his works.

Jonathan Wild the Great, *The Life of*, a short novel by H. *Fielding, published as the third volume of his *Miscellanies*, 1743, based on the life of a notorious thief-taker, Jonathan *Wild.

It is a satire on the figure of the 'Great Man', in low life or in high, who is held up to our admiration for his clever practice of avarice, corruption, and cruelty, which so often achieve success at the expense of the simple and the good. Fielding's hatred of hypocrisy here finds its most mordant expression. The quality Wild most

values in himself and in others is 'that of hypocrisy'. His own position as the Great Man among thieves, cheats, and bullies is constantly compared, directly and by implication, with that of the Great Man among public figures of power (with Sir Robert *Walpole as a particular target), whose palaces are no more than 'Newgate with the mask on'. The name and something of the history of Jonathan Wild are borrowed from a thief and thief-taker who was hanged in 1725. The life of Fielding's Wild is traced from his birth to his death on the gallows, through a series of episodes involving thieves, highwaymen, whores, cheats, murderers, and the corrupt and brutal officers of Newgate.

As a young man Wild enters a career of professional crime under the direction of the corrupt Mr Snap, a sheriff's officer, thief-taker, and receiver of stolen goods, whose shrewish daughter Wild eventually marries. After becoming an expert pickpocket Wild organizes a gang of thieves, whose goods he receives and sells at huge profit to himself. Fireblood, Blueskin, Count la Ruse, and his own unfeeling daughters Tishy and Doshy are a few of the people he dominates and whose criminal activities he directs. He begins to live in style, dressing finely as a gentleman, and cunningly keeping himself beyond the reach of the law. If any of his men defy him, as Blueskin does, Wild denounces him and sees him hanged. He determines to ensnare an old schoolfellow, Heartfree, an innocent and gullible jeweller, who lives happily with his wife and children and his amiable apprentice Friendly. He arranges that Heartfree shall be robbed, then ensures that he is imprisoned as a bankrupt. Once the Heartfrees are ruined, Wild plans for the attractive and innocent Mrs Heartfree to become entangled in the underworld of vice, and has her abducted to Holland. Heartfree escapes Wild's malevolence, only to be implicated by Wild in a robbery, which means he is convicted and likely to be hanged. Only at this point, when he has apparently entirely destroyed the Heartfrees, does Wild feel a glimmer of remorse. By this time his embittered gang are turning on him, and eventually, in a foolish confusion over a piece of lace, he is committed to Newgate. Heartfree is pardoned and his wife returns unharmed, but Wild is condemned and meets his end with the same bravura with which he has lived his destructive life.

Jonathan's, a coffee-house in Change Alley, Cornhill, referred to in *The Tatler*, No. 38, and *The Spectator*, No. 1, as a mart for stockjobbers.

JONES, David Michael (1895–1974), poet and artist, born in Kent; his Welsh father gave him his strong sense of identity with Wales, although he lived there only from 1924 to 1927. After art school he served in the trenches throughout the First World War, an experience which produced one of his major works and left him with a lifelong interest in warfare and soldiers. In 1921 he became a Roman Catholic and in 1922 began a long association with *Gill. He preferred that his work in engraving, watercolour, and drawing should be intimately combined with his own writing, or the writing of others. The Welsh *Mabinogion, the *'matter of Britain' (centring on King *Arthur), and the Bible provided much of the material and the background for his poetry. In 1927 he began In Parenthesis, an epic work of mixed poetry and prose on the subject of the war, which was published in 1937. The personal story and terrible sufferings of Private John Ball are related to the long history of war, and embedded in Welsh legend and the work of *Malory. A few, including T. S. *Eliot and H. *Read, admired it greatly. In 1952 Jones published The Anathemata, a long, complex work of poetry and prose, part chronicle, part incantation, celebrating in richly allusive language the ancient 'matter of Britain'. The small circle of admirers, including K. *Raine and E. *Muir, grew considerably. The Sleeping Lord (1974) is a collection of complete fragments of a projected work centred on the Crucifixion, and the lives of Roman soldiers at the time. Jones received the CH in 1974. The Dying Gaul, a selection of his writing, was published posthumously in 1978. There is a life by D. Blamires (1971).

JONES, Henry Arthur (1851–1929), left school at twelve, and worked as a draper's assistant and warehouseman before his first play was produced in 1878. His first London production, in 1882, was The Silver King, which met with instant success. A friend and contemporary of *Pinero, Jones also was a prolific playwright, who did much to re-establish serious themes in the theatre. As a young man he was greatly encouraged by G. B. *Shaw and *Beerbohm. Although he wrote many comedies (including The Liars, 1897; Dolly Reforming Herself, 1908; Mary Goes First, 1913), his most influential plays treated social themes, often the double standards of behaviour expected of men and of women; The Dancing Girl (1891), The Case of Rebellious Susan (1894), Mrs Dane's Defence (1900), and The Lie (1923) were considered among the most effective. *Archer judged Jones the most popular playwright of the 1890s, but his popularity, like that of Pinero, faded. As well as writing plays, pamphleteering, lecturing, and managing a theatre, Jones fought for the abolition of censorship, for the publication of plays, and for a new dignity for the theatre.

JONES, Inigo (1573–1652), architect, stage designer, painter, mathematician, and man of letters, whose depth of knowledge of Roman and Italian art and of Renaissance theory was new in England, and whose revolutionary buildings brought the classical style to this country. Little is known of his early career; he travelled abroad some time between 1598 and 1604, and again in 1613–14, when he developed a deep admiration for *Palladio, met Scamozzi, and copied ancient Roman monuments. In 1615 he became surveyor of the King's Works; his most famous buildings are the Queen's House, Greenwich (1616–18 and 1629–35), and the Banqueting Hall, Whitehall (1619–22), both lucid, classic, harmonious buildings with crisp detail which mark a turning point in English architecture. Jones's career as a designer of *masques opened in 1605, and many of his drawings for costume and scenery—influenced by his European counterparts, among them Buontalenti and Callot—survive. A stormy but fruitful collaboration with *Jonson began in 1605 with The Masque of Blacknesse, and lasted until 1630/1; their quarrel about the rival claims of the visual arts and literature was also long standing, and became notorious. Later Jones worked with other poets, producing with T. *Carew, in Coelum Britannicum (1634), perhaps the most brilliant of later Caroline masques. Jones's fame in England soared between 1710 and 1760, when, with Palladio, he became one of the heroes of the Palladian movement, revered by Lord Burlington and *Pope. Many of his designs were published in two folio volumes, edited by William Kent (1727). See Inigo Jones: The Theatre of the Stuart Court (1973) by S. Orgel and R. Strong.

JONES, Sir William (1746–94), a distinguished orientalist and brilliant jurist, and a friend of Dr *Johnson, *Gibbon, and *Burke, was judge of the high court at Calcutta from 1783 till his death. A master of Sanskrit and a pioneer in the science of comparative philology, he did much to make Indian literature and learning known in Europe, and is remembered for his translations (including The Moallakat, 1782, from the Arabic, and Sacontala, or the Fatal Ring: an Indian Drama, 1789), and for the well-known 'A Persian Song of Hafiz' (Poems consisting chiefly of translations from the Asiatic languages, 1772). He had considerable influence on the Oriental themes of the Romantic poets such as *Byron, *Southey, and T. *Moore. His collected works were edited by Lord Teignmouth (6 vols, 1799) and his letters by G. H. Cannon (2 vols, 1970). There is a life, Oriental Jones, by G. H. Cannon (1964).

JONSON, Ben(jamin) (1572/3–1637), dramatist, poet, scholar, and writer of court *masques. He was of Border descent, but was born in or near London, the posthumous son of a clergyman. He was educated at *Westminster School under *Camden. During the early 1590s he worked as a bricklayer in his stepfather's employ, saw military service in Flanders, where he killed an enemy champion in single combat, and joined a strolling company of players for whom he acted the part of Hieronimo in *The Spanish Tragedy*, a play for which he wrote additional scenes in 1601–2. In 1597 he began to work for *Henslowe's companies as player and playwright, and was imprisoned for his share in The Isle of Dogs, a satire now lost 'containing very seditious and slandrous matter'. In 1598 he killed a fellow actor in a duel, but escaped hanging by pleading benefit of clergy, being branded instead as a felon. He became a Roman Catholic during imprisonment, but returned to Anglicanism twelve years later. His first important play, *Every Man in his Humour, with Shakespeare in the cast, was performed by the Lord Chamberlain's company at the Curtain in 1598, and *Every Man out of his Humour at the Globe in 1599. *Cynthia's Revels (1600) and *Poetaster (1600–1, attacking *Dekker and *Marston), were performed by the Children of the Queen's Chapel. His first extant tragedy, *Sejanus, was given at the Globe by Shakespeare's company, 1603; his first court masque, The Masque of Blackness, written to accommodate Queen Anne's desire to appear as a Negress, was given on Twelfth Night, 1605. In that year he was imprisoned, and in danger of having his nose and ears slit, for his share in *Eastward Hoe, and gave evidence to the Privy Council concerning the Gunpowder Plot. Then followed the period of his major plays: *Volpone, acted at both the Globe and the two universities, 1605–6; *Epicene, or The Silent Woman, 1609–10; *The Alchemist, 1610; and *Bartholomew Fair, 1614. In 1612–13 he was in France as tutor to *Ralegh's son, and in 1618–19 journeyed on foot to Scotland, where he stayed with *Drummond of Hawthornden, who recorded their conversation.

Though not formally appointed the first poet laureate, the essentials of the position were conferred on Jonson in 1616, when a pension was granted to him by James I. In the same year he published a folio edition of his Works, which raised the drama to a new level of literary respectability, received an honorary MA from the University of Oxford, and about this date became lecturer in rhetoric at Gresham College in London. He was elected chronologer of London in 1628. After *The Devil is an Ass (1616) he abandoned the public stage for ten years, and his later plays, *The Staple of News (1626), *The New Inn (1629), *The Magnetic Lady (1631), and *A Tale of a Tub (1633), show a relatively unsuccessful reliance on allegory and symbolism; *Dryden called them his 'dotages'. From 1605 onwards Jonson was constantly producing masques for the court, with scenery by I. *Jones. This form of entertainment reached its highest elaboration in Jonson's hands. He introduced

into it the 'antimasque', an antithetical, usually disorderly, prelude to the main action which served to highlight by contrast the central theme of political and social harmony. There are examples of this in The Masque of Queens (1609), Love Restored (1612), Mercury Vindicated from the Alchemists at Court (1616), Pleasure Reconciled to Virtue (1618, which gave Milton his idea for *Comus), and Neptune's Triumph for the Return of Albion (1624). After Chloridia (1631), his collaboration with Jones ended with a famous quarrel, which Jonson treated in several vituperative poems, concerning the relative priority of verbal and thematic content and spectacle. His last masques were produced in 1633–4. His non-dramatic verse includes Epigrams and *The Forest, printed in the folio of 1616, and *The Underwood and a translation of *Horace's Ars Poetica, printed in 1640. His chief prose works are The English Grammar and *Timber, or Discoveries, printed in 1640.

During the reign of James I Jonson's literary prestige and influence were unrivalled. He presided over a literary circle which met at the *Mermaid Tavern, and later in the Apollo Room of the Devil and St Dunstan Tavern, where his leges convivales or 'social rules' were inscribed over the mantelpiece. His friends included Shakespeare, whom he loved 'on this side idolatry', *Donne, F. *Bacon, George *Chapman, *Beaumont, *Fletcher, *Cotton, and *Selden, and among the younger writers (who styled themselves the 'sons' or 'tribe of Ben') R. *Brome, *Carew, *Cartwright, Sir K. *Digby, Lord *Falkland, *Herrick, Nabbes, *Randolph, and *Suckling. His chief patrons were the *Sidney family, the earl of Pembroke, the countess of Bedford, and the duke and duchess of Newcastle. Jonson suffered a stroke in 1628, after which he was perhaps permanently bedridden until his death in August 1637. He was buried in Westminster Abbey under a tombstone bearing the inscription 'O rare Ben Jonson', and celebrated in a collection of elegies entitled Jonsonus Virbius (1638). As a man Jonson was arrogant and quarrelsome, but fearless, warm-hearted, and intellectually honest. His reputation declined sharply from about 1700, as Shakespeare's, with whom he was inevitably compared, increased, but in this century it has revived, thanks partly to the comprehensive edition of C. H. Herford and P. and E. Simpson (11 vols., 1925–52), vols 1 and 2 of which contain the standard biography.

Jonsonus Virbius, see JONSON, B.

JORDAN, Dorothy, née Phillips (1761–1816), actress, made her first stage appearance in 1779 in Dublin under the name of Miss Francis. She came to England and adopted the name of Mrs Jordan, under which she appeared as Calista in *The Fair Penitent at Leeds in 1782.

She made her début at Drury Lane as Peggy in *Garrick's *The Country Girl* in 1785, and took many parts there, at the Haymarket, and at Covent Garden, Lady Teazle in *The School for Scandal* being one of her finest roles. Her last London performance was in 1814 and her final stage appearance at Margate in 1815. She was much praised by *Hazlitt, *Lamb, Leigh *Hunt, etc. She was for long mistress of the duke of Clarence (William IV), and bore him ten children. She went to France in 1815 and died at St Cloud.

Jorkins, see SPENLOW AND JORKINS.

Jorrocks, Mr, see SURTEES, R. S.

José, Don, the father of the hero in Byron's *Don Juan*.

Joseph Andrews, The History of the Adventures of, and of his Friend Mr Abraham Adams, a novel by H. *Fielding, published 1742.

In an important Preface Fielding relates his book to classical forms; he describes it as a 'comic romance', and outlines his purpose in devising 'this kind of writing, which I do not remember to have seen hitherto attempted in our language'. His declared object is to defend what is good by displaying the Ridiculous, which he believes arises from Affectation, and ultimately from Vanity and Hypocrisy.

The work begins as a parody of Richardson's *Pamela*, with Joseph as Pamela's brother and 'Mr B.' appearing as young Booby. But it soon outgrows its origins in parody, and its deepest roots lie in *Cervantes and in *Marivaux. The son of the humble Gaffer and Gammer Andrews, Joseph becomes at ten years old stable-boy to Sir Thomas Booby. His supposed sister Pamela lives at the home of young Squire Booby, nephew to Sir Thomas. Parson Adams, poor, learned, and innocently certain that everyone is as good as himself, takes an interest in the boy. Eventually Joseph falls in love with Fanny, a milkmaid, becomes footman to Sir Thomas and Lady Booby, and, together with Mrs Slipslop the chambermaid, attends them for their season in London. After Sir Thomas's death Lady Booby makes amorous advances to Joseph, and when he stoutly rejects them he is thrown out. He sets off on foot to return to the seat of the Boobys in Somerset. After he has been robbed and stripped naked he is taken to an inn kept by the Towwouses, where he encounters Parson Adams, now on his way to London in the hope of having his sermons published. However, finding he has forgotten to bring them, Adams turns back with Joseph towards Somerset. Adams rescues a girl from an attack in a wood, only to find that she is Fanny, on her way to look for Joseph, and both become embroiled in a farcical scene before a JP. The three travellers, Joseph, Fanny, and Adams, constantly in trouble and short of

money, are on almost every occasion rescued by some fellow traveller equally poor, such as a poacher or a coachman; their application for assistance from the prosperous Parson Trulliber is sanctimoniously refused. When almost destitute they are given hospitality by Mr Wilson, a country gentleman who tells them the story of his life. This tale, with its recollections of poverty, the iniquities of London life, the vanities of the playhouse, and a brief scene of idyllic marriage, clearly echoes much of Fielding's own experience. Mr Wilson describes how his baby son was stolen by gypsies, and hopes to re-encounter Joseph and Adams when he is next in Somerset. After further adventures the party returns at last to Booby Hall, where Lady Booby, in a desperate attempt to secure Joseph, tries to have Fanny committed to Bridewell. Eventually both Fanny and Joseph are arraigned and convicted for cutting and bearing off a hazel twig. But Parson Adams calls their banns, young Squire Booby appears with Pamela, now his wife, and a series of events reveals that Joseph is the son of Wilson and Fanny is Pamela's sister. Joseph and Fanny are joyfully married, and Adams is given a handsome living.

The novel, a major innovation in form and style, was only moderately successful, and was considerably less popular than *Pamela* which it set out to mock. However, a few discerning critics, including E. *Carter, privately gave it high praise, and the greater success of *Tom Jones* in 1749 probably owed much to the establishment of the form in *Joseph Andrews*.

Joseph of Arimathea. For the legend of Joseph and the Holy Grail, see GRAIL and GLASTONBURY. According to fable, St Philip sent twelve disciples into Britain to preach Christianity, of whom Joseph of Arimathea was the leader. They founded at Glastonbury the first primitive church, which subsequently was developed into Glastonbury Abbey. Here Joseph was buried. His staff, planted in the ground, became the famous Glastonbury Thorn, which flowered at Christmas (*William of Malmesbury, *De Antiquitate Glastoniensis Ecclesiae*). The fullest version of the Joseph Grail story is Robert de *Boron's *Joseph d'Arimathie* (Burgundy, *c*.1200), for which see ch. 19 in R. S. Loomis ed., *Arthurian Literature in the Middle Ages* (1959), pp. 251–62.

JOSEPHUS, Flavius (AD 37–*c*.98), a celebrated Jew, who proved his military abilities by supporting against Vespasian a siege of 47 days in a small town of Judaea. He obtained the esteem of Vespasian by foretelling that he would one day become ruler of the Roman Empire. He was present at the siege of Jerusalem by Titus, and received from the conqueror the gift of certain sacred books that it contained, besides an estate in Judaea. He came to Rome with Titus, was honoured with Roman citizenship, and devoted himself to study. He wrote in Greek a *History of the Jewish War* and *Jewish Antiquities*, which is a history of the Jews down to AD 66.

Joseph Vance, see DE MORGAN, W.

JOSH BILLINGS, see SHAW, H. W.

Jourdain, Monsieur, in *Molière's *Le Bourgeois Gentilhomme*, a wealthy bourgeois obsessed with the desire to pass for a perfect gentleman. He apes people of quality, and is exploited in consequence. His surprise at learning, in the course of his education, that he has been talking prose all his life is proverbial.

Journal of a Disappointed Man, The, see CUMMINGS, B. F.

Journal of a Tour to the Hebrides, The, by *Boswell, published 1785. It is a narrative of the journey taken by Boswell and Dr *Johnson in Scotland and the Hebrides in 1773, recording Johnson's encounters with Boswell's family and eminent Scottish literati, including W. *Robertson, *Dalrymple, *Monboddo, and *Blacklock. It also describes Johnson's responses to Scottish landscape and traditions, his sceptical enquiries about Ossian (see MACPHERSON), and his remarkable physical fortitude. Boswell's manuscript, which Johnson and others read, was discovered at Malahide Castle with other private papers and published in 1936, ed. F. A. Pottle and C. H. Bennett; it is longer by about a third than the earlier publication.

Journal of a Voyage to Lisbon, The, a work by H. *Fielding, published posthumously 1755.

When he set out for Portugal in 1754, in the vain hope of recovering his health, Fielding was suffering so greatly from gout, dropsy, asthma, and other complications, that he had to be carried aboard the *Queen of Portugal*. In his Preface to the *Journal*, which he then began, he declares that he is once again attempting something that has not been done before, in that he proposes to write a work of travel which leaves out all fabulous adventures, monsters, and tedious detail. He writes of the daily events of the difficult voyage, the eccentricities of Captain Veal, the abuses suffered by the sailors, the devotion of his wife and daughter, the terror of storms, a sunset and moonrise at sea, and the details of his food and drink. The most personal and most painful of his works, the *Journal*, which he describes as 'possibly the production of the most disagreeable hours which ever haunted the author', reflects his shifting moods of stoicism, good humour, irritability, and the deep despondency of patience stretched beyond endurance. He described it as 'a novel without a Plot', and had prepared it for the press before he died in Lisbon in October.

Journal of the Plague Year, A, see PLAGUE YEAR.

Journey from this World to the Next, A, the second volume of *Miscellanies* by H. *Fielding, published 1743.

The author purports to have found an almost indecipherable manuscript, consisting of a series of 'Epistles', which was left in an attic by someone now departed to the West Indies. The soul leaves the body in its lodgings in Cheapside and finds itself, guided by Mercury, in a stage-coach with other departing souls. They pass through the City of Diseases and past the black marble Palace of Death, on to the Wheel of Fortune. At the door of Elysium Minos dictates who shall be permitted to enter; the generous and the honest are favoured, whatever their station, while the cruel and hypocritical are rejected. In the Elysian Fields heroes and writers of antiquity converse animatedly with Shakespeare, *Milton, *Dryden, *Addison, Fielding's own *Tom Thumb, and many others. The spirit of Julian the Apostate appears and, for the major part of the book, discourses in several guises as slave, Jew, courtier, and statesman. The tale (the last part of which, about Anne Boleyn, may have been by Sarah *Fielding) comes to a somewhat haphazard end with the excuse that the rest of the 'manuscript' has been unfortunately burned. It was edited by C. Rawson, 1973.

'Journey of the Magi, The', a poem by T. S. *Eliot.

Journey's End, see SHERRIFF, R. C.

Journey to London, The, see PROVOK'D HUSBAND, THE.

Journey to the Western Islands of Scotland, A, by Dr *Johnson, published 1775. It is a narrative of the tour undertaken by *Boswell and Johnson in 1773 in Scotland and the Hebrides. (For Boswell's account, see JOURNAL OF A TOUR TO THE HEBRIDES.) It describes Johnson's response to Scottish history, culture, and landscape, and on publication aroused the wrath of *Macpherson because of its sceptical comments on the authenticity of 'Ossian'. Macpherson demanded, unsuccessfully, a cancellation or a revision, and received instead a letter from Johnson saying, 'What shall I retract? I thought your book an imposture from the beginning, I think it upon yet surer reasons an imposture still.'

Joviall Crew, A, or *The Merry Beggars*, a romantic comedy by R. *Brome, produced 1641.

Oldrents, a rich and kindly country squire, has been thrown into melancholy by a gypsy's prediction that his two daughters must be beggars. Springlove, an honest vagabond whom Oldrents has tried to reclaim to a settled life by making him his steward, is seized each spring with a desire to return to his wandering life, and rejoins a party of beggars, whom Oldrents from kindness of heart entertains in his barn.

Oldrents's daughters, wearied by their father's melancholy, decide to join the beggars for a frolic, with their two lovers. They thus give effect to the gypsy's prediction, but their begging exposes them to unforeseen dangers. Meanwhile Justice Clack's niece has run away with the Justice's clerk, and they too fall in with the beggars. The search for the runaways, and the apprehension of the beggars, give occasion for amusing scenes, and all ends well.

The play, Brome's masterpiece, is highly original in its picture of Oldrents's compassion for the poor and Springlove's longing for a vagabond life and response to the call of the spring.

JOWETT, Benjamin (1817–93), one of the legendary figures of late Victorian Oxford, famed for his 'cherubic chirp', long silences, and occasional devastating rudeness, was professor of Greek from 1855 and master of Balliol College from 1870. A Broad Churchman in the tradition of T. *Arnold, he outraged the Tractarians with the common sense of his *Epistles of Paul* (1855), came near to being charged with heresy before the vice-chancellor because of his contribution to *Essays and Reviews* (1860), and was successful in promoting the Act that abolished religious tests for university degrees (1871). His translations of *Plato (1871), *Thucydides (1881), and Aristotle's *Poetics* (1885), criticized by scholars, charmed the public. But he was primarily a teacher of genius. He held that the purpose of university education was the personal development of each student and hoped more particularly to form future statesmen. As Asquith, Milner, Grey, and *Curzon were among his pupils, he may be fairly regarded as a founding father of Edwardian England.

JOYCE, James Augustine Aloysius (1882–1941), novelist, born at Rathgar, Dublin, and educated at the Jesuit schools Clongowes Wood College and Belvedere College, and at University College, Dublin, where *Gogarty was a fellow student. A good linguist, from an early age he read and studied widely, and in 1901 wrote a letter of profound admiration in Dano-Norwegian to *Ibsen. Other early influences included *Hauptmann, *Dante, G. *Moore, and *Yeats; Yeats was to treat him with considerable personal kindness. Dissatisfied with the narrowness and bigotry of Irish Catholicism, as he saw it, Joyce went to Paris for a year in 1902, where he lived in poverty, wrote verse, and discovered Dujardin's novel *Les Lauriers sont coupés* (1888), which he was later to credit as the source of his own use of interior monologue (see STREAM OF CONSCIOUSNESS). He returned to Dublin for his mother's death, stayed briefly in the Martello tower of *Ulysses* with Gogarty, then left Ireland more or less for good with Nora Barnacle, the woman with whom he spent the rest of his life,

and who bore him a son and a daughter. They lived at Trieste for some years, where Joyce taught English at the Berlitz school and made the acquaintance of *Svevo, whose writing he encouraged; they moved in 1915 to Zurich, and settled finally after the war in Paris. His first published work was a volume of verse, *Chamber Music* (1907), followed by *Dubliners* (1914), a volume of short stories published after great delays and difficulties, culminating in his final visit to Ireland in 1912, when the sheets were destroyed through the prospective publisher's fear of libel. When the stories at last appeared they were greeted with enthusiasm by *Pound, in a review in *The Egoist*. Pound's friendship and support greatly encouraged Joyce's career and reputation. Another important ally gained at this period was Harriet Shaw Weaver, business manager and then editor of *The Egoist*, and a lifelong benefactress of Joyce. Difficulties also attended the performance and publication of Joyce's play *Exiles*: it was published in 1918 and staged unsuccessfully the same year in Munich, then first performed in London by the Stage Society in 1926 after years of hesitation. It was revived and directed by *Pinter in 1970. *A Portrait of the Artist as a Young Man*, a largely autobiographical work, was published serially in the *Egoist*, 1914–15: (part of a first draft, *Stephen Hero*, appeared in 1944). With strong backing from Yeats and Pound, Joyce received a grant from the *Royal Literary Fund in 1915, and shortly after a grant from the civil list. Despite growing recognition, he continued to struggle against poverty, and also suffered from increasing eye trouble; a severe attack of glaucoma in 1917 led to years of pain and several operations. He was also much troubled in later years by his daughter's mental illness.

His famous novel *Ulysses* was first published in Paris on 2 February 1922, his 40th birthday, and was received as a work of genius by writers as varied as T. S. *Eliot, *Hemingway, and Arnold. *Bennett: others (*Claudel, V. *Woolf, G. *Stein) were less admiring. The first UK edition appeared in 1936. Another small volume of verse, *Pomes Penyeach*, appeared in 1927, and his second great work, *Finnegans Wake*, extracts of which had already appeared as 'Work in Progress', was published in its complete form in 1939. *Ulysses* and *Finnegans Wake* revolutionized the form and structure of the novel, decisively influenced the development of the 'stream of consciousness' or 'interior monologue' (see also RICHARDSON, D.), and pushed language and linguistic experiment (particularly in the latter work) to the extreme limits of communication. (See MODERNISM.) They have also produced a mass of critical commentary in many languages, covering Joyce's use of Homeric myth, puns, Catholicism, Irish folklore, Scholastic philosophy, etc. There is a full life by R. *Ellmann (1959, 2nd edn 1982).

JOYCE, Patrick Weston (1827–1914), was author, among other works, of *Irish Names of Places* (1869–1913), *A Grammar of the Irish Language* (1878), *Old Celtic Romances* (1879, 1894, from which *Tennyson drew his 'Voyage of Maeldune'), and a *Social History of Ireland* (1903–20), all highly influential in the *Irish revival. He also published *Irish Peasant Songs* (1906) and contributed folk-songs to Petrie's *Ancient Music of Ireland*.

Joyous Gard, the castle of Launcelot in Arthurian legend. It is situated somewhere in the north, and *Malory says it has been variously identified as Alnwick or Bamburgh (near Berwick-on-Tweed). Tristram once keeps Isoud there for three years (see TRISTRAM AND ISOUD); after Launcelot has to surrender Guinevere it is renamed 'Dolorus Gard'.

Juan, Don, see DON JUAN.

Jubilate Agno, see SMART, C.

'Judas', the oldest *ballad in *Child's collection, recorded in a manuscript of *c.*1300, deals with the betrayal of Christ.

Jude the Obscure, a novel by T. *Hardy, originally printed in abridged form in *Harper's New Monthly Magazine* (1894–5, as *Hearts Insurgent*), then in the 1895 edition of his works.

In the author's words, it is a story 'of a deadly war waged between flesh and spirit'. Jude Fawley, a young Wessex villager of exceptional intellectual promise, is encouraged by the schoolmaster Phillotson, and conceives the ambition of studying at Christminster (which represents Oxford). But he is trapped into marriage by the coarse, handsome barmaid Arabella Donn, who feigns pregnancy to win him, and shortly afterwards deserts him. He moves to Christminster, earning his living as a stonemason and continuing his studies, hoping one day to be admitted to the university, the vision of which still dominates him. He meets his cousin, Sue Bridehead, an unconventional, hypersensitive, *Swinburne-quoting young woman who works in a shop selling ecclesiastical ornaments: they fall in love, despite efforts on both sides to avoid one another, and Sue, in what appears to be a fit of desperate masochism, suddenly marries Phillotson, who had long been interested in her. She is driven from him by physical revulsion, and flies to Jude; they begin to live together in Christminster, but do not consummate their love until Arabella reappears on the scene. Jude, who had been planning to enter the priesthood as a licentiate, as a substitute for his thwarted intellectual ambitions, is now doubly defeated. He and Sue become free to marry, but Sue shrinks from the step, partly because of her apprehension that a conventional union will destroy love, and partly from a superstitious fear that the Fawley family is doomed to marry un-

happily: she at one point compares the family to the house of Atreus, and Jude compares it to the house of Jeroboam, an interchange which reflects the theme of Hellenism and Hebraism prominent throughout the novel.

Under the pressure of poverty and social disapproval their relationship deteriorates, and tragedy overtakes them in the death of their children: the eldest, 'Old Father Time', son of Jude and Arabella, hangs the two babies and himself, leaving a note saying, 'Done because we are too menny.' In an agony of remorse and self-abasement, Sue returns to Phillotson and the church, and Jude, deeply shocked by her abandoning of her free-thinking principles, begins drinking heavily (a weakness to which he had always been susceptible) and is inveigled back by Arabella. He dies wretchedly, not yet thirty, and his last words are: 'Wherefore is light given to him that is in misery, and life unto the bitter in soul?'

The novel caused an uproar, and the *Pall Mall Gazette* set the tone by castigating it as 'dirt, drivel and damnation'; even Hardy's friend *Gosse found it 'grimy' and 'indecent'. Hardy describes in the Preface to the 1912 edition how the work was 'burnt by a bishop—probably in his despair at not being able to burn me'. The reception of the book was no doubt one of the several reasons why Hardy wrote no more fiction.

Judith, a 350-line poem in Old English, fragmentary at the beginning, found in the *Beowulf* manuscript (ASPR 4), probably dating from the late 9th cent. The poem tells the story of the Apocryphal Book of Judith, and the surviving sections (numbered in divisions x, xi, and xii, presumably preceded by the last part of ix) correspond to about the last quarter of the biblical book. It describes the banquet in the Assyrian camp, the bringing of Judith to the drunken Holofernes, her beheading of him and escape, and the defeat and flight of the Assyrians. The language of the poem is opulent and its battle description is celebrated; critical discussion of it has largely been confined to deliberations about what proportion of the original the surviving fragment is. There is an edition by B. J. Timmer (1952).

Julia, the faithful lover of Proteus in Shakespeare's *The Two Gentlemen of Verona*.

Julia, Donna, in Byron's *Don Juan*, a lady of Seville, whose love for the hero is the first incident in his career.

Julia de Roubigné, a novel by H. *Mackenzie.

Julia Melville, a character in Sheridan's *The Rivals*.

Julian, Count, a character in Southey's *Roderick, the Last of the Goths*.

'Julian and Maddalo, A Conversation', a poem partly in dialogue form by P. B. *Shelley, written at Venice and Este in 1818, published 1824. It is the most naturalistic of Shelley's long poems, deliberately opposed to the 'idealism' of his dramas.

Julian (Shelley) and Count Maddalo (*Byron) ride and boat through 'bright Venice', discussing problems of free will, progress, and religious belief. They visit a 'Maniac', confined in elegant rooms in an island asylum in the Venetian lagoon, whose tortured and confused monologue shows how superficial their arguments have been. The Maniac, partly based on *Tasso and partly on Shelley himself, has suffered some profound 'wrong' in love. His presence, like the uncensored outpourings of the Freudian unconscious, deepens and darkens the terms of the debate: he provides 'the text of every heart'. A little child, based on Claire Clairmont's baby Allegra, is also introduced to show the powers of innocence and good: though the outcome of the 'conversation' is not entirely optimistic. This is one of Shelley's most subtle studies of human affections and hopes. It is composed in fluent, almost chatty couplets, with marvellous evocations of the deserted Venetian lido and twinkling lagoon: 'I love all waste | And solitary places; where we taste | The pleasure of believing what we see | Is boundless, as we wish our souls to be.' It powerfully influenced Browning's *dramatic monologues.

JULIAN OF NORWICH (*c.*1342–after 1416), a recluse in a cell attached to the church of St Julian at Norwich. She wrote, 20 years after the events they describe, her *Sixteen Revelations of Divine Love* which describes visions revealed to her during her illness in 1373 and her reflections on them. She is well known now because of the quotation of a sentence from the *Revelations* in T. S. *Eliot's 'Little Gidding': 'Sin is behovely; but all shall be well and all shall be well and all manner of thing shall be well'; but in general she is not in fact the most appealing of the 14th-cent. English prose mystics. See *Julian's Showings*, Parts 1 and 2 (Short and Long Texts), ed. E. Colledge and J. Walsh (1978); P. Molinari, *Julian of Norwich* (1958, trans. C. Wolters, 1966).

Julie, the heroine of *La Nouvelle Héloïse* of *Rousseau, loved by Saint-Preux.

Juliet, (1) the heroine of Shakespeare's *Romeo and Juliet*; (2) the lover of *Claudio in his *Measure for Measure*.

Julius Caesar, a Roman tragedy by *Shakespeare, probably written and performed 1599, not printed until the First *Folio (1623). Its major source is *North's translation of *Plutarch's *Lives*. The play seems to have been a popular one.

It begins with the events of the year 44 BC, after Caesar, already endowed with the dictatorship, had returned to Rome from a successful campaign in Spain, and when there are fears that he will allow himself to be crowned king. Distrust of Caesar's ambition gives rise to a conspiracy against him among Roman lovers of freedom, notably Cassius and Casca; they win over to their cause Brutus, who reluctantly joins them from a sense of duty to the republic. Caesar is slain by the conspirators in the Senate house. Antony, Caesar's friend, stirs the people to fury against the conspirators by a skilful speech at Caesar's funeral. Octavius, nephew of Julius Caesar, Antony, and Lepidus, united as triumvirs, oppose the forces raised by Brutus and Cassius. The quarrel and reconciliation of Brutus and Cassius, with the news of the death of Portia, wife of Brutus, provide one of the finest scenes in the play. Brutus and Cassius are defeated at the battle of Philippi (42 BC), and kill themselves.

Jumpers, a comedy by T. *Stoppard performed and published 1972.

The play's central character is a professor of moral philosophy, George Moore, who shares with G. E. *Moore not only his name but also his intuitionist ethics. The physical acrobatics of the jumpers of the title parallel the 'verbal gymnastics' of Moore's lengthy speeches, which are brilliantly witty parodies of academic philosophy.

Jumping Frog of Calvaleras County, The Celebrated, one of the best-known stories of Mark *Twain.

JUNG, Carl Gustav (1875–1961), Swiss psychiatrist, whose professional career began at the Burghölzli mental hospital in Zurich, where he was the first to apply psychoanalytic ideas to the study of schizophrenia. He collaborated with *Freud 1907–13, but then parted with him to found his own school of 'Analytical Psychology'. Jung introduced into psychology the terms 'complex', 'collective unconscious', 'extrovert'–'introvert', *'archetype', and 'individuation', and his concept of psychological types has been taken over by the experimental psychologists. His notion of the mind as a self-regulating system is in line with modern ideas on cybernetics. In emphasizing the importance of man's search for meaning in life, he anticipated *Existentialism. Jung specialized in the treatment of older patients, and his main contribution to psychotherapy was to the study of adult development. The central theme of his work is the idea that mental illness is characterized by disunity of the personality, while mental health is manifested by unity, towards which the personality is striving.

Jung's influence has been felt in many fields outside psychiatry. The physicist Wolfgang Pauli, the art historian H. *Read, and the composer M. *Tippett have all acknowledged their debt to Jung. J. B. *Priestley made use of his ideas in *Literature and Western Man*; the title of Maud Bodkin's *Archetypal Patterns in Poetry* (1934) is directly derived from Jung; and his influence pervades the criticism of the Canadian critic Northrop Frye (1912–). Alex Aronson's *Psyche and Symbol in Shakespeare* (1972) is an interpretation of Shakespearian drama in terms of Jungian psychology. *Hesse made use of Jung's concepts in his novels, and Jung himself wrote an essay on Joyce's *Ulysses*.

Jungle, The, a novel by U. *Sinclair.

Jungle Book, The (1894), and *The Second Jungle Book* (1895), stories by *Kipling, which tell how the child Mowgli was brought up by wolves and was taught by Baloo, the bear, and Bagheera, the black panther, the law and business of the jungle.

JUNIUS, the pseudonymous author of a series of letters that appeared in the *Public Advertiser*, Jan. 1769–Jan. 1772, attacking, with bitter scorn and invective, among others, the duke of Grafton, Lord Mansfield, and George III himself. Junius also takes an active part on behalf of *Wilkes. Both before 1769 and after 1771 political letters under other pseudonyms, which have been traced to the same hand, appeared in the public press. Though personal invective is the cheap weapon of Junius, his political arguments, written from the Whig standpoint, are shrewd and lucidly expressed, and he shows himself well read in *Hobbes and *Locke. The identity of Junius, which he concealed with great skill, has never been definitely established, and many candidates were offered during his life time and later, including Lord *Temple, *Lyttleton, *Gibbon, *Burke, W. *Hamilton (1729–96), and Wilkes himself. He is now generally thought to have been Sir Philip *Francis. There is a full discussion in Alvar Ellegård's *Who Was Junius?* (1962), which argues conclusively for Francis on the basis of statistico-linguistic tests.

JUNIUS, Francis, or DU JON, François (1589–1677), philologist and antiquary, born at Heidelberg, a friend of *Milton, and librarian and tutor in the household of Thomas Howard, earl of Arundel. His *Etymologicum Anglicanum* (1743) was used by Dr *Johnson. He gave Anglo-Saxon manuscripts, including the so-called *Caedmon manuscript (see below), to the Bodleian Library (see LIBRARIES), and to the *Oxford University Press materials for printing in Gothic, Runic, Anglo-Saxon, and Roman founts. He published an edition of Caedmon in 1655.

Junius Manuscript, The, one of the four major manuscripts containing Old English poetry, named after the editor (above) who first printed it at Amsterdam in 1655, calling it 'Caedmon the monk's poetical paraphrase of Genesis, etc.' The biblical poetry in the manuscript (*Genesis A and B, Exodus, Daniel*, and *Christ and Satan*) continued to be associated with the name of *Caedmon for some time, but it is clear that they are unconnected with him; the title 'The Caedmon Manuscript' has proved tenacious however. See editions by G. V. Krapp and E. V. Dobbie, *Anglo-Saxon Poetic Records*, Vol. I (1931), and in facsimile by I. *Gollancz (British Academy, 1927).

Juno and the Paycock, see O'CASEY, S.

Jupe, Cissy, a character in Dickens's *Hard Times*.

JUVENAL (Decimus Junius Juvenalis) (*c.* AD 60–*c.*136), Roman satirist, whose 16 satires lack *Horace's urbanity, being exercises in rhetorical indignation against the vices of his age. Juvenal's great merit as a poet is his ability to depict with unusual vividness scenes that arouse his anger. Imitations of his work are found in J. *Hall, *Jonson, *Oldham, and Dr *Johnson. *Dryden edited and wrote in part a translation of Juvenal's Satires to which he prefixed his long discourse on Satire (1693). The references to 'the English Juvenal' in Scott's *Waverley* and to 'the British Juvenal' in *The Heart of Midlothian* are to *Crabbe. The former title has also been applied to Oldham.

K

Kabbalah, The, see CABBALA.

KAFKA, Franz (1883–1924), German-speaking Jewish novelist, born in Prague. He is the author of three novels, *Der Prozess* (*The Trial*, 1925), *Das Schloss* (*The Castle*, 1926), and the unfinished *Amerika* (1927), and also a large number of short stories, of which 'Die Verwandlung' ('The Metamorphosis', 1915) and 'Das Urteil' ('The Judgement', 1913) are among the best known. His novels were first published after his death, by his friend Max Brod, and were translated into English by E. and W. *Muir, beginning with *The Trial* in 1930. Kafka's letters and diaries contain interesting insights into his complex relationship with his father and with Felice Bauer, to whom he was twice briefly engaged. Characteristic of Kafka's work is the portrayal of an enigmatic reality, in which the individual is seen as lonely, perplexed, and threatened, and guilt is one of his major themes. The opening sentence of *The Trial* gives a sense of the combination of the ordinary and the sinister in his works: 'Someone must have slandered Joseph K., because one morning, without his having done anything wrong, he was arrested.' The word 'Kafkaesque' is frequently used to describe work which employs similar narrative techniques, and evokes a similarly uneasy response.

Kafkaesque, see KAFKA.

Kailyard School, from 'Kail-yard' (cabbage patch), a term applied to a group of Scottish writers who exploited a sentimental and romantic image of small town life in Scotland, with much use of the vernacular; the vogue lasted from about 1888 to 1896. Leading writers in this vein were J. M. *Barrie, 'Ian Maclaren' (John Watson, 1850–1907), and S. R. Crockett (1860–1914). These false notions of Scottish life were shattered by G. *Douglas in *The House with the Green Shutters* (1909); in J. B. *Priestley's words, 'into this cosy chamber of fiction Brown let in the East wind.' See G. Blake, *Barrie and the Kailyard School* (1951).

KAISER, Georg (1878–1945), German dramatist, who died in exile, author of *Die Bürger von Calais* (*The Burghers of Calais*, 1914) and *Gas* (1918–20), leading examples of the German Expressionist theatre (see EXPRESSIONISM). He was a prolific and inventive writer, author of some 60 plays.

Kalevala, 'Land of Heroes', the national epic poem of Finland, transmitted orally until 1822, when a collection was published by Zacharius Topelius. The myths it contains are of great antiquity, possibly dating from the time when the Finns and Hungarians were still one people. It was translated into English by W. M. Crawford in 1887, and tone-poems have been composed around some of the myths by Sibelius.

KĀLIDĀSA, a great Indian poet and dramatist, best known for his play *Shakūntalā*, which was translated from the Sanskrit by Sir W. *Jones (1789). Kālidāsa probably lived in the 3rd cent. AD, but there is a diversity of opinion on this point.

Kama Sutra, see BURTON, SIR R.

KAMES, Lord, see HOME, H.

Kangaroo (1925), a novel by D. H. *Lawrence, based on the Lawrences' visit to Australia in 1922.

Richard Lovat Somers, a writer, and his wife Harriet are in Sydney for an indefinite period. Through their neighbour Jack Calcott, Somers makes the acquaintance of 'Kangaroo' Ben Cooley, a Jewish barrister involved in radical politics. He tries to enlist Somers's sympathy for his programme, but fails, and the novel ends with his death after a violent Labour meeting at Canberra Hall (at which Calcott claimed to have killed a demonstrator) and the departure of the Somers for America. The book mingles political outbursts and meditations with observant evocation of Australian life and landscape. Chapter 10, 'The Nightmare', describes Lawrence's own wartime confrontations with authority in Cornwall and his humiliating examinations, in Bodmin and Derby, for military service. Like Somers, he was rejected as unfit.

KANT, Immanuel (1724–1804), second son of a leather-worker (of Scottish descent), of Königsberg in Prussia, was educated at the university of that town, and supported himself as a tutor. He published his first considerable work, *A General Natural History of the Heavens*, in 1755, and in that year became a lecturer at Königsberg, an unsalaried post in which he remained for 15 years, during which he published a number of minor philosophical treatises. In 1770 he became professor of logic and metaphysics at Königsberg, retaining the appointment until his death. He remained unmarried. His *Critique of Pure Reason* appeared in 1781, *Prolegomena to any future Metaphysics* in 1783, *Fundamental Principles of the Metaphysic of Ethics* in 1785, *Metaphysical Rudiments of Natural Philosophy* in 1786, the second edition of the *Critique of Pure Reason* in 1787, the *Critique of Practical Reason* in 1788, and the *Critique of Judgement* in 1790. His *Religion within the Boundaries of Pure Reason* (1793) called down on him the censure of the government.

In Kant's philosophy, knowledge is the outcome of two factors, the senses and the understanding. Sensations are the starting point of knowledge. Space and time are essential conditions of our sensuous perception, the forms under which our sensations are translated into consciousness. Therefore space and time are essential conditions of knowledge, although they exist only as forms of our consciousness. These forms, continuous and infinite, provide the possibility of unifying our individual perceptions, and the unification is effected by the understanding. This act of synthesis Kant analyses into twelve principles or 'categories', or laws of thought. The categories are to the understanding very much what time and space are to the consciousness. They include such notions as quality, quantity, and, notably, causation. The external world is thus the product of sensations conditioned by the forms of consciousness and linked by thought according to its own laws. It consists of appearances, 'phenomena'; but the causes of these appearances, 'noumena', things in themselves, lie beyond the limits of knowledge, nor can we, by the aid of reason alone, apart from appearances, arrive at absolute truth, for reason leads to certain insoluble contradictions, or 'antinomies', such as the impossibility of conceiving either limited or unlimited space.

Where metaphysics fails us, practical reason comes to our aid. The moral consciousness assents to certain 'categorical imperatives', such as 'do not lie'. From this follow the conviction that man is in a certain sense free, the belief in immortality (because self-realization within any finite period is impossible), and the belief in God. We are driven by the nature of our minds to see design in nature, and man as the centre of that design. Though the advantages resulting from obedience to particular moral laws can be shown, the moral obligation itself is a categorical imperative, something that we feel but cannot explain. Interpreted as a practical rule of conduct, the moral law bids you 'act as if the principle by which you act were about to be turned into a universal law of nature', and do all in your power to promote the highest good of all human beings. This highest good is not realizable unless the course of the world is itself guided by moral law, that is to say by a moral Master of the universe, whose existence we are driven to assume. But metaphysics places religion and morality outside the province of knowledge, and in the region of faith.

Kant's philosophy was developed and profoundly modified by *Fichte, *Schelling, and *Hegel. In Britain, *Coleridge and *Carlyle valued Kant's criticism of the empirical philosophy (and the atheism) of the 18th cent., particularly that of *Hume.

KARAMZIN, Nikolai Mikhailovich (1766–1826), Russian prose writer and historian. Born into the provincial gentry, Karamzin studied in Moscow and spent most of his life in that city. In his writings he is associated with the reform of the Russian language under French influence, and with the growth of Sentimentalism, particularly in his most famous stories *Poor Liza* and *Natalya, the Boyar's Daughter* (both 1792, first English trans. John Battersby Elrington, 1803). Later he turned to writing history and his *History of the Russian State* appeared in twelve volumes (1818–29). Karamzin's enthusiasm for England and English literature was immense. His first published book was a translation of *Julius Caesar* (1787) and his consistent admiration for Shakespeare as psychologist, particularly in *Othello*, *King Lear*, *A Midsummer Night's Dream*, and *The Tempest*, did much to advance Shakespeare's reputation in Russia. He also from his early years admired *Milton, *Young, *Thomson (whose *The Seasons* he translated in 1787), and *Macpherson's Ossian. In 1789–90 he travelled to western Europe, including England, and his *Letters of a Russian Traveller* (1801, trans. Florence Jonas, 1957) describe his disillusionment with the English and their 'sluggish blood', but his fascination with English eccentricity.

Kaspar, the old man in *'The Battle of Blenheim' by Southey, who relates to his grandson Peterkin the events of the battle.

Kastril, the rustic lad in Jonson's *The Alchemist*, who comes to London to learn the speech of the roaring boys.

Katharina, the 'shrew', or self-willed girl, in Shakespeare's *The Taming of the Shrew*.

Katharine, (1) a character in Shakespeare's *Love's Labour's Lost*; (2) in his *Henry V*, the daughter of the king of France.

KATHARINE OF ARAGON, Queen, the wife of Henry VIII, whose divorce is one of the principal incidents in Shakespeare's *Henry VIII*.

Katherine, St, see KATHERINE GROUP, THE.

Katherine Group, The, the name given to five Middle English works of devotional prose found together in the manuscript Bodley 34, dating from *c.*1190–1225: *Seinte Marherete*, *Seinte Iuliene*, *Seinte Katerine*, *Sawles Warde*, and *Hali Meiohad*. They come from Herefordshire, and their common language is also, for the most part, shared with *Ancrene Wisse* and therefore called 'Language AB' from the first letter of that text combined with that of Bodley 34. It is a distinctive and interesting language from a transitional period of English; but the interest of the works in the group is not only philological: they are all written in a lively, often colloquial style, with vivid details of illustration. They use alliteration and rhythmic art in a way that has been compared to the prose of *Ælfric. The three saints' lives are all concerned with heroic virgins who were frequently exalted in medieval writings: St Katherine of Alexandria, St Juliana of Nicomedia, and St Margaret of Antioch, who were all believed to have suffered from the persecutions of Diocletian in the first decade of the 4th cent. The most celebrated English life of one of them is the Old English *Juliana* by *Cynewulf.

See N. R. Ker, *Facsimile of Ms Bodley 34* (EETS 247, 1960); S. R. T. O. d'Ardenne and E. J. Dobson, *Seinte Katerine* (EETS ss 7, 1981); S. R. T. O. d'Ardenne, *The Liflade and te Passiun of Seinte Iuliene* (EETS 248, 1961); F. M. Mack, *Seinte Marherete* (EETS 193, 1934).

KAUFFER, E(dward) McKnight (1890–1954), American-born artist and illustrator, who settled in England in 1914, and won great praise for his posters and commercial designs, notably for the London Transport Board and the Great Western Railway: Arnold *Bennett (*Evening Standard*, 1928) wrote that he had 'changed the face of London streets' and that his success 'proves that popular taste is on the up-grade'.

KAVANAGH, Julia (1824–77), born in Thurles, educated at home, spent much of her youth in France, which gave her an insight into French life and character which she conveyed faithfully in her novels and tales. Of the novels the best-known were *Madeleine* (1848), *Nathalie* (1850), and *Adèle* (1858). Then followed *French Women of Letters* (1862) and *English Women of Letters* (1863), biographical sketches, both of which received high praise. *Forget-me-nots* (1878) is a collection of short stories.

KAVANAGH, Patrick (1905–67), Irish poet, born in Co. Monaghan, the son of a small farmer and shoemaker; after some years of farming he went to Dublin in 1939 and embarked on a literary career as journalist and poet. His works include *Ploughman and other Poems* (1936), *A Soul for Sale* (1947), *Terry Flynn* (1948, a novel set on a small farm in his home county), and *Collected Poems* (1964). His best-known work is probably *The Great Hunger* (1942), a long poem contrasting the realities of life for an archetypal peasant, Patrick Maguire (figuratively 'locked in a stable with pigs and cows forever', and in fact dominated by an elderly mother, and suffering from sexual and intellectual hunger, as well as a

humdrum poverty), with the more conventional idealized peasant of the *Irish revival, with his 'little lyrical fields'. Much of Kavanagh's work is concerned with the relationship between Irish archetype and stereotype; he rejected the 'stage-Irish' of some of his early work, but nevertheless turned himself into a kind of caricature of the hard-drinking Irish poet. His *Collected Pruse* (1967, *sic*) includes autobiographical essays and articles from the periodical *Kavanagh's Weekly*, which he produced with his brother Peter in 1952.

Kay, Sir, in the Arthurian legend (as in *Malory), Arthur's steward, a brave but churlish knight. He was the son of Sir *Ector and therefore the foster-brother of Arthur. His churlishness is accounted for in the Merlin legends by the fact that he was supplanted by Arthur at his mother's breast and brought up by a rough-speaking nurse. His most famous churlish greetings are those accorded to Sir *Gareth and Sir *Perceval.

KAYE-SMITH, Sheila (1887–1956), born in Sussex, where she spent all her life; her successful *Regional novels are precisely located, principally on the Kent–Sussex border, and include *Starbrace* (1909) and *Joanna Godden* (1921). Hers was the genre of novel satirized by Stella Gibbons in *Cold Comfort Farm.

KEAN, Edmund (1787/90–1833), actor of uncertain parentage, whose adventurous childhood gave rise to innumerable legends. He was befriended by various guardians, including Moses Kean, a mimic and ventriloquist, and worked on stage as infant prodigy and strolling player before achieving fame in 1814 as Shylock in *The Merchant of Venice*, a performance recorded by *Hazlitt. He was a great tragic actor, whose numerous successes included Richard III, Hamlet, Othello, Iago, Macbeth, Lear, and *Marlowe's Jew of Malta. *Dumas *père* wrote a play based on his colourful life which was subsequently adapted by *Sartre (1954). His son, Charles John Kean (1811–68), was also an actor, and manager of the Princess's Theatre, 1851–9.

KEATS, John (1795–1821), the son of the manager of a livery stables in Moorfields, who died when he was eight; his mother remarried, but died of tuberculosis when he was 14. The oldest of the family, he remained deeply attached to his brothers George and Tom and to his sister Fanny. He was well educated at Clarke's school, Enfield, where he began a translation of the *Aeneid*, and in 1810 was apprenticed to an apothecary-surgeon. His first efforts at writing poetry appear to date from 1814, and include an 'Imitation of Spenser'; his school friend Cowden-*Clarke recorded the profound effect of early reading of *Spenser. In 1815 Keats cancelled his fifth year of apprenticeship and became a student at Guy's Hospital; to the same year belong 'Ode to Apollo' and 'Hymn to Apollo'. In 1816 he was licensed to practise as an apothecary, but in spite of precarious finances abandoned the profession for poetry. In 1816 he also met Leigh *Hunt, who published in the same year in *The Examiner* Keats's poem, 'O Solitude', and in the course of a survey of young poets in the same journal he included Keats's sonnet 'On First Looking into Chapman's Homer'. Keats met *Shelley and *Haydon, began to plan *Endymion*, and wrote 'I stood tiptoe upon a little hill' as a first effort towards that poem. His first volume of poems was published in March 1817. It included, among sonnets, epistles, and miscellaneous poems, 'I stood tiptoe upon a little hill' and 'Sleep and Poetry'. There were at first some pleasing reviews, but public interest was not aroused and sales were meagre; and in the autumn came the first of *Lockhart's harsh attacks in *Blackwood's*, labelling Keats and his associates as members of the so-called *Cockney school. He finished the first draft of *Endymion* and during the winter of 1817–18 saw something of *Wordsworth and *Hazlitt, both of whom much influenced his thought and practice. In December Haydon gave his 'immortal dinner', whose guests included Wordsworth, *Lamb, and Keats. *Endymion*, dedicated to *Chatterton, whom Keats greatly admired, was published in the spring of 1818, and *'Isabella, or the Pot of Basil' finished in May. With his friend Charles Armitage Brown (1786–1842) Keats then toured the Lakes, spent July and August in Scotland, and included a brief visit to Northern Ireland. He had travelled frequently in southern England but he had never before seen scenery of rugged grandeur. It moved him deeply and he made full use of it when he came to write *Hyperion*. Bitter attacks on *Endymion* came in the autumn from Lockhart in *Blackwood's* and from *The Quarterly Review*. For the time being Keats concealed his pain and wrote to his brother George that, in spite of the reviews, 'I think I shall be among the English poets after my death', but his friends believed the wound was very deep. Meanwhile his brother Tom was very ill and Keats spent much time with him. When Tom died in December Keats moved into his friend Brown's house in Hampstead, now known as Keats House. There, in the early winter, he met Fanny *Brawne, with whom he fell deeply in love, and with whom he remained in love until his death. During the course of the summer and autumn of 1818 his sore throats had become more frequent and persistent. Nevertheless September 1818 marked the beginning of what is sometimes referred to as the Great Year; he began *Hyperion* in its first version, abandoning it a year later; he wrote, consecutively, *'The Eve of St Agnes', 'The Eve of St Mark', the 'Ode to Psyche', *'La Belle Dame sans Merci', *'Ode to a Nightingale', and probably at about the same time the *'Ode on a Grecian Urn', *'Ode on Melancholy', and 'Ode on Indolence'; *'Lamia Part I', *'Otho the Great' (in collaboration with Brown); the second version of *Hyperion*, called *The Fall of Hyperion*, *'To Autumn', and 'Lamia Part II'. During this year he was beset with financial problems, both his own and those of his friends and relations, and intensely preoccupied with his love for Fanny, to whom he became engaged. In the winter of 1819 he began the unfinished 'The Cap and Bells', but he became increasingly ill with tuberculosis and his great creative work was now over. His second volume of poems, *Lamia, Isabella, The Eve of St Agnes, and other Poems*, was published in July 1820, and included, as well as the title poems, five odes, *Hyperion*, 'Fancy', and other works. The volume was generally well received, gaining much praise in some quarters, with criticism from *Blackwood's* much muted, but the sales were very slow. Shelley invited Keats to Italy and in September, after sorting out his copyrights and financial affairs, Keats set off with his friend *Severn. They did not go to the Shelleys but settled in Rome, where Keats died the following February.

Keats has always been regarded as one of the principal figures in the *Romantic movement, and his stature as a poet has grown steadily through all changes of fashion. *Tennyson considered him the greatest poet of the 19th cent., and M. *Arnold commended his 'intellectual and spiritual passion' for beauty; in the 20th cent. he has been discussed and reconsidered by critics from T. S. *Eliot and *Leavis to *Trilling (*The Opposing Self*, 1955) and Christopher Ricks (*Keats and Embarrassment*, 1974).

His letters, published in 1848 and 1878, have come to be regarded with almost the admiration given to his poetry, to which many of them act as a valuable commentary. He wrote fully and revealingly to Fanny Brawne, to his brothers and sister, to Shelley, Leigh Hunt, Haydon, Severn, and many others, mixing the everyday events of his own life with a lively and delicate interest in that of his correspondents, and displaying wit and high spirits as well as his profoundest thoughts on love, poetry, and the nature of man. T. S. Eliot described the letters as 'certainly the most notable and most important ever written by any English poet' (*The Use of Poetry and the Use of Criticism*, 1933). The major biographies are by W. J. Bate (1963) and R. *Gittings (1968).

KEBLE, John (1792–1866), educated at Corpus Christi College, Oxford, became fellow and tutor at Oriel College (where *Newman and *Pusey were also fellows) and professor of poetry at Oxford, 1831–41. His sermon on national apostasy in 1833 was considered the start of the *Oxford Movement, which he also supported by nine of the *Tracts for the Times*. Although a leading figure in Oxford intellectual life, he was personally unambitious, and from 1836 until his death was vicar of the country parish of Hursley. His volume of sacred verse *The Christian Year*, published anonymously in 1827, had an immense success, and was widely admired, not only by those with Tractarian leanings, but also by *Evangelical and *Broad Church readers; intended as a guide to devotion and a commentary on the Book of Common Prayer, it shows the influence of G. *Herbert and, in its feeling for the natural world, of *Wordsworth, and combines Keble's considerable scholarship with deep personal feeling. A second volume, *Lyra Innocentium* (1846), was less popular, and was criticized by some for its undue reverence for the Virgin Mary. C. M. *Yonge was a pupil of his, and drew a vivid character sketch in *Musings over the Christian Year . . . with a few gleanings of recollections of Keble* (1871). Keble also edited *Hooker (1836), helped Newman with *Froude's *Remains*, contributed to *Lyra Apostolica*, and published a life of Bishop Thomas Wilson. Keble College, Oxford, was founded in his memory in 1870. There are lives by W. Lock (1893) and G. Battiscombe (1963).

Keep the Aspidistra Flying, see ORWELL, G.

Kehama, The Curse of, see CURSE OF KEHAMA, THE.

Kells, Book of, an 8th- to 9th-cent. manuscript of the four Gospels, with Prefaces, Summaries, and Canon Tables; seven charters of the abbey of Kells have been added on blank pages. It is written in Irish majuscule and has magnificent illustrations consisting of intricate patterns made up of abstract and animal forms. It was probably written at Kells in Co. Meath, the headquarters of the Columban community after the sack of Iona in 806. It was collated by *Ussher in 1621 and presented to Trinity College, Dublin, after the Restoration.

KELLY, Hugh (1739–77), an Irishman who came to London in 1760, edited the *Court Magazine* and the *Lady's Museum*, and afterwards the *Public Ledger*. His *False Delicacy*, produced by *Garrick in 1768, is a *sentimental comedy with a triple plot in which the mistakes arise from excessive tact or delicacy, which keeps the three couples apart until the misunderstandings are resolved through the intervention of the down-to-earth Mrs Harley: 'Your people of refined sentiments are the most troublesome creatures in the world to deal with', she declares. Kelly also wrote *A Word to the Wise* (1770) and *The School for Wives* (1773). In 1774 he was called to the bar and gave up literature.

Kelmscott Press, see MORRIS, W.

KELVIN, Lord, see THOMSON, SIR W.

KEMBLE, Charles (1775–1854), son of a strolling actor-manager, Roger Kemble (1721–1802) and brother of Sarah *Siddons, J. P. *Kemble, Stephen, and other theatrical siblings; father of Fanny *Kemble and the scholar J. M. *Kemble. A leading actor for some 25 years, he was a respected member of London society. His voice was light, and his most successful roles were of young men, such as Mirabell in *The Way of the World*, Mercutio, Orlando, Benedick, and, most especially, Romeo. His range was considerable in comedy and romance, but he did not often attempt tragedy.

KEMBLE, Fanny (Frances Anne) (1809–93), daughter of Charles *Kemble, was a very beautiful and accomplished actress. She first appeared under her father's management at Covent Garden in 1829, when she played Juliet to his Mercutio. She played comedy and tragedy with equal success, and added most of the great roles to her repertoire, including Portia, Lady Macbeth, Beatrice, Lady Teazle in *The Way of the World*, Belvidera in *Venice Preserv'd*, and many others. She published a volume of poems in 1844 and *Records of a Later Life* in 1882.

KEMBLE, John Mitchell (1807–57), historian and philologist, elder son of Charles *Kemble, was educated at Trinity College, Cambridge, where he was a member of the *Apostles and a friend of R. C. *Trench, *Milnes, and *Tennyson. He later studied in Germany, where he became a close friend of *Grimm and was converted to the new continental philology, which he warmly supported on his return. His text of *Beowulf* (1833), dedicated to Grimm, aroused much controversy, and he did useful work on the early history of England.

KEMBLE, John Philip (1757–1823), eldest brother of Charles *Kemble. He achieved success as a formal tragic actor, and was particularly renowned in the roles of Coriolanus and Hamlet, in which part *Hazlitt particularly admired him.

KEMBLE, Sarah, see SIDDONS, S.

KEMP, William (fl. 1600), a comic actor and dancer, who acted in plays by Shakespeare and *Jonson. He danced a morris-dance from London to Norwich, in *Rowley's words a 'wild morrige to Norridge'; his own account, *Kemps Nine Daies Wonder*, was published in 1600.

KEMPE, Margery (c.1373–c.1439), a mystic, daughter of John Brunham who was once mayor of King's Lynn in Norfolk, married John Kempe of Lynn c.1393. She gave up married life to devote herself to religion and she travelled widely on pilgrimage: to Jerusalem, Rome, Compostella, and Wilsnack in Poland. She dictated, probably in the 1420s, her *Book of*

Margery Kempe which recounts with great vividness her visions and experiences of a more general kind: her temptations to lechery, her travels, and her trial for heresy. Though the work is not a strictly mystical text (like *The Cloud of Unknowing*), it is a vigorous and readable piece of early autobiography with considerable appeal. Ed. S. B. Meech and E. H. Allen (EETS OS 212, 1940).

KEMPIS, Thomas À, see THOMAS À KEMPIS.

Kemp Owyne, an old ballad in *Child's collection, from an Icelandic source. Isabel, who has been transformed into a monster by a wicked stepmother, is released from the enchantment by three kisses of her lover, Kemp Owyne. In modern versions of the ballad he is 'Kempion'.

KEN, Thomas (1637–1711), fellow of Winchester and New College, Oxford, became bishop of Bath and Wells. He was a writer of devotional prose and verse; his works include *The Practice of Divine Love* (1685), the extremely popular *A Manual of Prayers for the use of Scolars of Winchester College* (1674), and some well known hymns, including 'Awake, my soul, and with the sun'. His works were collected by W. Hawkins in 1721.

Kenilworth, a novel by Sir W. *Scott, published 1821.

The novel is based on the tradition of the tragic fate of the beautiful Amy Robsart, daughter of Sir John Robsart (called Sir Hugh in the novel). She has been enticed, by the designs of the villainous Richard Varney, into a secret marriage with his patron the earl of Leicester, Queen Elizabeth's favourite, rejecting the worthy Edmund Tressilian, a Cornish gentleman and an adherent of Leicester's rival, the earl of Sussex. This marriage Leicester is forced to conceal from the jealous queen. Amy is accordingly mewed up in Cumnor Place, an old country house near Oxford, and is believed by Tressilian to be living there as the paramour of Varney. After vainly attempting to induce her to return to her father, he lays before the queen a charge of seduction against Varney, who, to shield Leicester, declares Amy to be his wife. Elizabeth thereupon orders that Amy shall appear before her at Kenilworth, whither the queen is shortly going as the guest of Leicester. Varney, who has evil designs on Amy, persuades Leicester to direct Amy to present herself at Kenilworth in the character of Varney's wife. Amy, indignant at the order, goes secretly to Kenilworth, aided by Tressilian, determined to demand recognition as Leicester's countess. She obtains admission to the castle, unknown to Leicester, and is discovered by the queen. Amy's strange behaviour arouses Elizabeth's jealous suspicions and she finally extorts from Leicester a confession of his marriage. Varney, by mis-

representing the relations of Amy and Tressilian, has already induced Leicester to believe her guilty of infidelity to him and Leicester has ordered Varney to remove Amy to Cumnor Place and kill her. Leicester learns too late that Varney's accusations are false and Tressilian arrives at Cumnor only to find that Amy, by Varney's machinations, has fallen through a trap-door and perished.

Among the many interesting features in the novel are the glimpses of the court of Elizabeth, where the young Ralegh is just coming into favour; the descriptions of the revels at Kenilworth (see under LANEHAM); and the adaptations of the legend of Wayland Smith, the skilful farrier and physician, who aids Tressilian in his attempts to recover Amy. Dickie Sludge, or Flibbertigibbet, the impish friend of Wayland Smith, also deserves mention.

KENNEDY, John Pendleton (1795–1870), American author and statesman, born in Baltimore, Maryland; his writing was much influenced by W. *Irving, whose friend and admirer he was. His best-known books are *Swallow Barn* (1832) and *Horse-Shoe Robinson* (1835), a tale of the American Revolution, set in the Carolinas.

Kennedy, Lady Laura, a character in A. Trollope's novels *Phineas Finn* and *Phineas Redux*.

KENNEDY, Margaret Moore (1896–1967), novelist, is remembered principally for her highly-praised best-seller *The Constant Nymph* (1924), which was dramatized (1926) and filmed several times.

KENNEDY, Walter (?1460–?1508), a Scottish poet, the rival (ostensibly at least, and probably in reality) of *Dunbar in 'The Flyting of Dunbar and Kennedy' (1508) and mentioned by him in his 'Lament for the Makaris' (ll. 89–91) as being on the point of death. The few poems by him that survive were edited by J. Schipper in *Denkschriften der kaiserlichen Akademie der Wissenschaften*, 48 (Vienna, 1902).

Kenneth, Sir, or the Knight of the Leopard, the hero of Scott's *The Talisman*.

Kent, earl of, loyal follower of the king in Shakespeare's *King Lear*; he is banished in the opening scene, but continues to attend him in disguise.

KENTIGERN, St (St MUNGO) (?518–603), brought up in the monastic school of Culross in Scotland, where he received the name 'Mungo', a corruption of the Gaelic for 'my love'. He was a missionary to the Strathclyde Britons, from whom he proceeded to evangelize in Cumberland and Wales. He founded the monastery of Llanelwy, later named St *Asaph's after its first abbot. He was recalled to Strathclyde and settled at Glasgow where he is buried in the crypt of the cathedral, named St Mungo's after him.

Kenwigs, Mr and Mrs, a genteel couple in Dickens's *Nicholas Nickleby*.

Kenyon Review, see RANSOM, J. C.

KER, William Paton (1855–1923), born in Glasgow, a fellow of All Souls College, Oxford, from 1879 to his death. He was professor of literature at Cardiff from 1883 to 1889 when he became Quain professor at London. In 1917 he became director of the Scandinavian Studies School and in 1920 Oxford professor of poetry. He is buried in Italy where he died on holiday. He is celebrated for the width of his humane criticism in English, Norse, and Scottish literature. His *Collected Essays* were edited by C. Whibley and published in 1925. His other most admired works are *Epic and Romance* (1897) and *The Dark Ages* (1904), both often republished.

KEROUAC, Jack (1922–69), American novelist, born in Massachusetts of French-Canadian parents, and educated at Columbia University. He became a spokesman for the *Beat generation, and is best known in Britain for his semi-autobiographical novel *On the Road* (1957), which describes the wanderings across America, casual friendships, labours, and affairs of Sal Paradise, a young writer, and his friend and hero, Dean Moriarty. Episodic, fast-moving, unstructured, it produced a mythology of its own and many imitators. Kerouac's other works include *The Dharma Bums* (1958) and *The Subterraneans* (1958).

Kettledrummle, The Revd Mr, in Scott's *Old Mortality*, a fanatical Covenanting divine.

Kew, countess of, a character in Thackeray's *The Newcomes*.

KEYES, Sidney Arthur Kilworth (1922–43), poet, born in Dartford, the son of an army officer. He was brought up largely by his grandfather, whom he commemorates in several poems, and was educated at Tonbridge School, where he began to write poetry, and at Oxford, where he became friendly with *Heath-Stubbs, and edited, with Michael Meyer, *Eight Oxford Poets* (1941) which contains some of his own work. His first collection, *The Iron Laurel*, appeared in 1942; in the same year he joined the army. His second, *The Cruel Solstice*, appeared in 1943, after his presumed death in Tunisia. He was awarded the Hawthornden Prize posthumously in 1944, and his *Collected Poems*, with a Memoir by M. Meyer, appeared in 1945. He himself claimed as his major influences *Wordsworth, *Yeats, *Rilke, and *Jung; H.

*Read described his characteristic note as 'elegiac'.

KEYNES, Sir Geoffrey Langdon (1887–1982), surgeon, scholar, and bibliographer, born in Cambridge, the brother of J. M. *Keynes, and educated at Rugby and Pembroke College, Cambridge. His works include bibliographies of *Donne, *Evelyn, and notably *Blake (1921, 1953); his editions of Blake (1925–1966, and various studies) were a major contribution towards the 20th-cent. reappraisal of Blake's work. His autobiography *The Gates of Memory* was published in 1981.

KEYNES, John Maynard, first baron Keynes of Tilton (1883–1946), a distinguished economist, whose book *A General Theory of Employment, Interest, and Money* (1936) revolutionized economic theory by showing how unemployment could occur 'involuntarily'. For 30 years after the Second World War governments of western nations pursued 'Keynesian' full-employment policies. He regarded economists as the 'trustees . . . of the possibility of civilisation', and in his essay 'The Future Possibilities for Our Grandchildren' wrote that with the coming of economic abundance man would for the first time be faced with his 'real, his permanent problem . . . how to occupy the leisure, which science and compound interest will have won for him, to live wisely and agreeably and well'. Keynes was a member of the *Bloomsbury Group and a noted patron of the arts. He founded and endowed the Arts Theatre at Cambridge, and was chairman of CEMA (Council for the Encouragement of Music and the Arts) in 1942 and the first chairman when it became the *Arts Council of Great Britain in 1945. At its best Keynes's writing had a strong visual sense, and he was a fine phrase-maker. His portraits of President Woodrow Wilson, Georges Clemenceau, and Lloyd George (the first two of which appeared in his book *The Economic Consequences of the Peace*, 1919) are justly famous; V. *Woolf was much impressed by his 'method of character drawing' in his essay 'Dr Melchior: A Defeated Enemy' which he read to Bloomsbury's Memoir Club in 1921. The latter, together with 'My Early Beliefs', was published posthumously in 1949. Keynes's *Collected Writings* have been issued by the Royal Economic Society. A biography, *The Life of John Maynard Keynes* by Sir Roy Harrod, was published in 1951; see also *John Maynard Keynes: Hopes Betrayed 1883–1920* (1983) by Robert Skidelsky.

Keynotes, see EGERTON, G.

KID, Thomas, see KYD.

Kidnapped and *Catriona* (Gaelic for Catherine and pronounced Catreena), a novel and its sequel by R. L. *Stevenson, published in 1886 and 1893.

The central incident in the story is the murder of Colin Campbell, the 'Red Fox' of Glenure, the king's factor on the forfeited estate of Ardshiel: this is a historical event. The young David Balfour, left in poverty on the death of his father, goes for assistance to his uncle Ebenezer, a miserly old villain who has illegally taken control of the Balfour estate. Having failed to effect the death of David, Ebenezer has him kidnapped on a ship to be carried off to the Carolinas. On the voyage Alan Breck is picked up from a sinking boat. He is 'one of those honest gentlemen that were in trouble about the years forty-five and six', a Jacobite who 'wearies for the heather and the deer'. The ship is wrecked on the coast of Mull, and David and Alan journey together. They are witnesses of the murder of Colin Campbell, and suspicion falls on them. After a perilous journey across the Highlands they escape across the Forth, and the first novel ends with the discomfiture of Ebenezer and David's recovery of his rights.

Catriona is principally occupied with the unsuccessful attempt of David Balfour to secure, at the risk of his own life and freedom, the acquittal of James Stewart of the Glens, who is falsely accused, from political motives, of the murder of Colin Campbell; with the escape of Alan Breck to the Continent; and with David's love affair with Catriona Drummond, the daughter of the renegade James More.

KIERKEGAARD, Søren Aabye (1813–55), Danish philosopher and theologian. His life was tortured and unhappy, but within its short span he managed to write a very large number of books on a wide variety of topics. Thus, although he is now chiefly remembered and referred to as having initiated much that is characteristic of existentialist trends in modern philosophy (e.g. *Concluding Unscientific Postscript*, trans. W. Lowrie and D. F. Swenson, 1941), he was also the author of works whose themes were primarily religious, psychological, or literary (e.g. *The Concept of Dread* and *Fear and Trembling*, both trans. W. Lowrie, 1944); moreover, his satirical gifts made him a formidable social critic, witness his essay on *The Present Age* (trans. A. Dru, 1962), reminiscent in some respects of *Carlyle's polemics. Yet, for all their diversity of subject, his writings have certain distinctive common features: a distrust of abstract dogma and a correlative emphasis upon the particular case or concrete example; an acute and imaginative concern with the forms under which human character and motivation may manifest themselves; and a passionate belief in the value of individual choice and judgement as contrasted with tame acquiescence in established opinions and norms. It was precisely his insistence upon the importance of personal

decision, direct and unmediated by artificial ratiocination, that lay at the root of his rejection of *Hegel. For he saw in Hegelianism a philosophy which tended to obliterate, in the name of pretended metaphysical demonstrations, the element of subjective commitment and 'risk' implicit in every valid act of faith, and which sought to submerge the unique and unassimilable consciousness of the individual beneath a welter of universal categories. To all such speculative attempts to conceal or explain away what is central to human existence as genuinely understood and known, Kierkegaard opposed the conception of authentic choice, the explicit self-commitment of a person who stakes his whole being and future upon a belief which he cannot prove but which he maintains in the face of all intellectual doubt and uncertainty. This idea finds forceful exemplification in the religious sphere, but it also applies within other domains of experience, e.g. the ethical. Some of Kierkegaard's most penetrating psychological observations occur in his descriptions of the 'leap of faith' and in his analyses of the state of 'dread' (*Angst*) which precedes and accompanies it; in such passages, too, one is made aware of the peculiar significance he attached to the notion of freedom. The stress upon freedom in his sense, as an inescapable condition of life and action and as something which both fascinates and repels the choosing individual, represents perhaps the clearest link between his philosophical ideas and the doctrines of his existentialist successors. (See EXISTENTIALISM.)

KILLIGREW, Henry (1613–1700), brother of T. *Killigrew the elder, educated at Christ Church, Oxford, master of the Savoy in 1663, was the author of one play, *The Conspiracy* (1638). He was the father of Anne Killigrew (1660–85; see DRYDEN).

KILLIGREW, Thomas, the elder (1612–83), was page to Charles I and groom of the bedchamber and a favourite companion of Charles II. With *D'Avenant he held the monopoly of acting in Restoration London. He built a playhouse on the site of the present Drury Lane Theatre, in 1663, and was master of the revels in 1679. His most popular play, *The Parson's Wedding*, a bawdy farcical comedy, was first performed 1640/1 and printed in 1664 with his other plays, which include *The Princess*, *The Prisoners*, *Claracilla*, and *Thomaso, or the Wanderer* (in two parts), on the last of which A. *Behn based her successful adaptation *The Rover*. *Cecilia and Clorinda*, a tragi-comedy in two parts, is based on a subject from *The Grand Cyrus* by *Scudéry.

KILLIGREW, Thomas, the younger (1657–1719), son of T. *Killigrew the elder, and gentleman of the bedchamber to George II when prince of Wales. He was the author of *Chit Chat*, a comedy acted in 1719.

KILLIGREW, Sir William (?1606–95), brother of T. *Killigrew the elder and author of *Selindra* and *Ormasdes, or Love and Friendship*, tragi-comedies, and *Pandora*, a comedy, published in 1664; and of *The Siege of Urbin*, a tragi-comedy, published in 1666. *Pandora* and *Selindra* were acted, and there is reason to think (*TLS* 18 Oct. 1928) that *The Siege of Urbin* was also acted.

Killigrew, Mrs Anne, *To the pious Memory of,* see DRYDEN.

Killing No Murder, a pamphlet ironically dedicated to *Cromwell, 'the true father of your country; for while you live we can call nothing ours, and it is from your death that we hope for our inheritances'; it advocates his assassination. It was written by the Leveller Edward Sexby (d. 1658) and printed in 1657 in Holland. The name on the title-page is that of William Allen, who had been one of Cromwell's Ironsides. See *Des Révolutions d'Angleterre à la révolution française: le tyrannicide et Killing No Murder* (1973) by O. Lutaud.

Kilmeny, the subject of the thirteenth bard's haunting supernatural song in *The Queen's Wake* by J. Hogg. The girl Kilmeny goes up the glen, does not return, and is mourned for dead. At last she comes back. She had been carried away from the troubles of men to 'ane land of love, and ane land of lychte', from which she had a vision of war and sin in the world below. She asked to return to tell her friends what she had seen, and she returns transformed and sanctified; but after a month and a day she disappears and passes again to another world.

KILVERT, (Robert) Francis (1840–79), curate at Langley Burrell, Clyro, and St Harmon's, became vicar of Bredwardine in 1877. He is remembered for his diary, kept with no thought of publication, from 1870 until his death; it was first published in a three-volume selection edited by W. *Plomer, 1938–40, and has become established as a classic of its kind. His wife, whom he married only five weeks before his death of peritonitis, destroyed large portions of it, but enough is left to provide a full portrait of the author and the remote and beautiful region of the Welsh borders where he lived and worked. He records the landscape which he loved and through which he indefatigably walked; the distresses of his parishioners; the life of the gentry, with their balls and conversaziones; and the beauty of girls, from early childhood to young womanhood, in clear and vivid prose, with much sensitivity and memorable detail. Two encounters of great importance to him were with the niece of

*Wordsworth, who told him that her uncle 'could not bear the act of writing', and with W. *Barnes, 'the great idyllic Poet of England'.

Kim, a novel by *Kipling, published 1901.
   Kimball O'Hara, the orphaned son of a sergeant in an Irish regiment, spends his childhood as a vagabond in Lahore, until he meets an old lama from Tibet and accompanies him in his travels. He falls into the hands of his father's old regiment, is adopted, and sent to school, resuming his wanderings in his holidays. Colonel Creighton of the Ethnological Survey remarks his aptitude for secret service ('the Great Game'), and on this he embarks under the directions of the native agent Hurree Babu. While still a lad he distinguishes himself by capturing the papers of a couple of Russian spies in the Himalayas. The book presents a vivid picture of India, its teeming populations, religions and superstitions, and the life of the bazaars and the road.

Kind Harts Dreame, a pamphlet by *Chettle, licensed ?1592, noteworthy for its allusion to Shakespeare.

Kind of Loving, A, a novel by S. *Barstow.

KING, Edward (1612–37), a contemporary of Milton at Cambridge and commemorated by him in *Lycidas. There is no evidence that they were close friends.

KING, Francis Henry (1923–), novelist, short story writer, and critic, born in Switzerland, and brought up partly in Switzerland and India. He was educated at Shrewsbury School and Balliol College, Oxford, and for some years (1949–63) worked abroad for the British Council; several of his novels have foreign settings, notably Japan and Greece. They include *To the Dark Tower* (1946), *The Dividing Stream* (1951), *The Widow* (1957), *The Custom House* (1961), *Flights* (1973), and *The Action* (1979), and are marked by a cool and ironic detachment, close analysis of human motivation (particularly in some of its less admirable aspects), and an unobtrusive technical elegance. *Act of Darkness* (1983) is a psychological thriller, set largely in India; it describes, with considerable narrative power and an insight into perverse and pathological behaviour, the murder of a small boy, and the implication in his death of father, sister, and governess. Volumes of short stories, which show the influence of *Chekhov and K. *Mansfield, include *The Brighton Belle and other stories* (1968) and *Hard Feelings and other stories* (1976). He has also written travel books, and a study of E. M. *Forster (*E. M. Forster and His World*, 1978), to whose work, in terms of social comedy and nuance and narrative lucidity his own bears some similarity.

KING, Henry (1592–1669), educated at

Westminster and Christ Church, Oxford, became bishop of Chichester and was the friend of *Donne and I. *Walton. He published poems sacred and profane, an unauthorized volume appearing in 1657. His best-known poem is 'An Exequy to his Matchless never to be forgotten Friend', written for his wife Anne who died in 1624. An edition of his poems, with a life, ed. Margaret Crum, appeared in 1965.

KING, Jessie, see ART NOUVEAU.

KING, William (1650–1729), archbishop of Dublin, author of *State of the Protestants in Ireland under the late King James's Government* (1691) and *De Origine Mali* (1702).

KING, William (1663–1712), educated at Westminster and Christ Church, Oxford, an advocate at Doctors' Commons, a high church Tory and a writer of burlesques, satires, and light verse, much of which was published anonymously. In his *Dialogues of the Dead* (1699) he joined Charles Boyle in the attack on *Bentley. (See BATTLE OF THE BOOKS.) Other works include *The Furmetary* (1699), *The Transactioneer* (1700, a satire on Sir H. *Sloane), and *The Art of Cookery, in imitation of Horace's Art of Poetry* (1708).

King Alisaunder, an early 14th-cent. romance, probably from London, in 8,034 lines of short couplets, based on the late 12th-cent. Anglo-Norman *Roman de toute chevalerie* (which is unpublished). Passing remarks suggest that it was composed for oral delivery, though it also suggests wide literary range. It is based on a legend according to which Alexander was not the son of Philip of Macedon but of the Egyptian king Nectanabus who tricked Philip's wife by magic into sleeping with him. The poem deals with the birth and youth of Alexander, his succession to Philip's throne, his conquest of Carthage and other cities, and his wars with Darius. The latter parts of the poem deal with his perils and conquests in the Far East (describing the geography and wonders of those regions), his seduction by Candace, and his death by poison. Though somewhat rambling in structure, the work is written in a lively verse and flexible metre that make it more compelling than most English romances of its period. Ed. G. V. Smithers (EETS os 227, 1952, and 237, 1957).

King and No King, A, a tragi-comedy by *Beaumont and *Fletcher (probably largely by Beaumont), performed 1611, printed 1619; it was one of their most successful dramas.

The emotional and erratic Arbaces, king of Iberia, has defeated Tigranes, king of Armenia, in single combat, thus bringing to an end a long war. Arbaces offers his prisoner freedom if he will marry his sister Panthea, who has grown up to womanhood during his long absence, but

Tigranes loves Spaconia, an Armenian lady, declines the offer, and sends Spaconia to engage Panthea to oppose the match. However, when Tigranes and Arbaces meet Panthea, they are both so smitten by her beauty that they both fall violently in love with her. Arbaces encourages his own incestuous passion, and Panthea appears to return it; all seems set for sin, retribution, and tragedy when, in the last act, the Lord Protector of the kingdom, Gobrias, confesses that Arbaces is in fact his own son, therefore 'no king', and Panthea the true queen of Iberia. Arbaces and Panthea react to this news with joy and are united; Tigranes repents of his infidelity, takes Spaconia as his queen, and is released from captivity. Comic relief throughout is provided by Bessus, a cowardly braggart captain in Arbaces' army, who brings to mind *Parolles in *All's Well that Ends Well, a play which has other similarities of plot and tone.

Dryden, in *Of Dramatick Poesy, praises the play warmly for its skilful and theatrically effective denouement, and for the complex character of Arbaces ('that strange mixture of a man', derived, he supposes, from the extravagances of Alexander the Great); he writes, 'I find it moving when it is read', and concludes that the 'lively touches' of passion overcome the faults of the plot.

There is a modern edition by R. K. Turner (1964).

King Charles's head, a phrase taken from Mr Dick's obsession in *David Copperfield, and thence used to describe any recurrent and irrational obsession.

King Horn, the earliest surviving English verse romance, of about 1,500 lines, dating from about 1225. The story is substantially the same as that of the later *Horn Childe, concerning Horn, the son of the king and queen of Suddene, who is turned adrift by invading Saracens and falls in love with Rymenhild, the daughter of the king of Westernesse. Horn's companion Fikenhild betrays the lovers, has Horn banished to Ireland, and marries Rymenhild. After spectacular deeds of prowess in Ireland, Horn returns to Westernesse in disguise and makes himself known to Rymenhild. Then, having recovered his land of Suddene, he kills Fikenhild and marries Rymenhild who becomes his queen. The plot is over-elaborate and the style is rudimentary, but the romance is full of life and traditional motifs. Ed. in W. H. French, *Essays on King Horn* (1940); the three manuscripts are edited together in J. Hall's edition, *King Horn* (1901).

Kingis Quair, The, 'The King's Book', a poem of 379 lines of rhyme-royal (so called because of its employment in this king's poem but previously used in Chaucer's *Troilus and Criseyde* and elsewhere), by *James I of Scotland while he was a prisoner in England and about the time of his marriage (*c*.1424) to Lady Jane Beaufort, the poem's heroine. It was discovered and printed by Lord Woodhouselee in 1783. It is one of the works traditionally described as 'Scottish *Chaucerian', and it does show the influence of Chaucer. C. S. *Lewis calls it the first poem in celebration of married love (though there are German poems of this kind about 1200, including a famous one by *Wolfram von Eschenbach, 'Der helden Minne'). The royal prisoner, lamenting his fortune, sees (like the noble prisoners in 'The Knight's Tale', *Canterbury Tales, 1) a beautiful lady walking in the garden below, and is smitten with love. He visits the empire of Venus and the palace of Minerva, goddess of wisdom; he speaks with the goddess Fortuna, and finally is assured by Venus of the ultimate success of his suit. *Rossetti quotes from the poem in The King's Tragedy. Ed. J. Norton-Smith (1971); W. A. Craigie, 'The language of the King's Quhair' (Essays and Studies xxv, 1940).

King John, a historical drama written in a first version before 1536, by *Bale.

King John, The Life and Death of, a historical play by *Shakespeare, probably largely based on an earlier anonymous play, The Troublesome Raigne of John King of England (1591). Its date is uncertain, but must be some time between 1591 and 1598. It was first printed in the *Folio of 1623.

The play, with some departures from historical accuracy, deals with various events in King John's reign, and principally with the tragedy of young Arthur. It ends with the death of John at Swinstead abbey. It is striking that no mention of Magna Carta appears in it. The tragic quality of the play, the poignant grief of Constance, Arthur's mother, and the political complications depicted, are relieved by the wit, humour, and gallantry of the Bastard, supposed son of Faulconbridge, actually the son of Richard Cœur de Lion.

KINGLAKE, Alexander William (1809–91), educated at Eton and Trinity College, Cambridge, published anonymously in 1844 Eōthen: or traces of travel brought home from the East, an account of a journey taken some ten years earlier which achieved instant success and is regarded as a classic of its genre. In his preface Kinglake explains that after several false starts he decided to cast his account in the form of a personal communication to a friend, which would aim at intimacy and avoid antiquarian research, statistics, and all display of 'sound learning, and religious knowledge'. The result is a lively description of his travels, giving his own reactions to, for example, the desert, the relics of the Holy Land, an encounter with Lady Hester *Stanhope, and the plague in Cairo; his friend

B. E. G. *Warburton said it evoked 'the East itself in vital actual reality', and critics have often compared its familiar tone with that of Sterne's *Sentimental Journey. He followed the British expedition to the Crimea in 1854, and devoted many years to an exhaustive history of the Crimean war (1863–87) which shows his great admiration for Lord Raglan.

King Lear, a tragedy by Shakespeare, dating from 1604–5, performed at Court 1606. The play appeared in quarto in 1608 (reprinted 1619), and, in a different form, in the First *Folio (1623). Traditionally the two versions have been held to represent a common original and have been conflated editorially, but recent scholarship suggests that the quarto prints a text which was performed but later revised to create the version printed in the Folio. The play's sources include a chronicle play, King Leir (performed 1594, printed 1605), the chronicles of *Holinshed, and the *Mirror for Magistrates. The Gloucester sub-plot derives from Sidney's *Arcadia.

Lear, king of Britain, a petulant and unwise old man, has three daughters: Goneril, wife of the duke of Albany; Regan, wife of the duke of Cornwall; and Cordelia, for whom the king of France and duke of Burgundy are suitors. Intending to divide his kingdom among his daughters according to their affection for him, he bids them say which loves him most. Goneril and Regan make profession of extreme affection, and each receives one-third of the kingdom. Cordelia, self-willed, and disgusted with their hollow flattery, says she loves him according to her duty, not more nor less. Infuriated with this reply, Lear divides her portion between his other daughters, with the condition that himself with 100 knights shall be maintained by each daughter in turn. Burgundy withdraws his suit for Cordelia, and the king of France accepts her without dowry. The earl of Kent, taking her part, is banished. Goneril and Regan reveal their heartless character by grudging their father the maintenance that he had stipulated for, and finally turning him out of doors in a storm. The earl of Gloucester shows pity for the old king, and is suspected of complicity with the French, who have landed in England. His eyes are put out by Cornwall, who receives a death-wound in the affray. Gloucester's son Edgar, who has been traduced to his father by his bastard brother Edmund, takes the disguise of a lunatic beggar, and tends his father till the latter's death. Lear, whom rage and ill-treatment have deprived of his wits, is conveyed to Dover by the faithful Kent in disguise, where Cordelia receives him. Meanwhile Goneril and Regan have both turned their affections to Edmund. Embittered by this rivalry, Goneril poisons Regan, and takes her own life. The English forces under Edmund and Albany defeat the French, and Lear and Cordelia are imprisoned; by Edmund's order Cordelia is hanged, and Lear dies from grief. The treachery of Edmund is proved by his brother Edgar. Gloucester's heart has ' 'Twixt two extremes of passion, joy and grief, | Burst smilingly'. Albany, who has not abetted Goneril in her cruel treatment of Lear, takes over the kingdom.

King's College, Cambridge, founded in 1441 by Henry VI and completed by Henry VII and Henry VIII. Its great Chapel is famous as a fine example of ornate Perpendicular. Giles *Fletcher, Sir W. *Temple, E. *Waller, and Horace *Walpole were educated at this college and one of its most eminent literary connections this century was E. M. *Forster, who was educated there and spent many of his later years in residence as honorary fellow.

KINGSLEY, Charles (1819–75), born at Holme in Devonshire, where his father was curate-in-charge, was educated at Helston Grammar School (where Derwent Coleridge was headmaster), at King's College, London, and at Magdalene College, Cambridge. He became curate and subsequently, in 1844 (the year of his marriage to Frances Grenfell), rector of Eversley in Hampshire. During his engagement to her he had been working on a version of the life of St Elizabeth of Hungary which finally appeared as a blank verse drama, *The Saint's Tragedy*, in 1848; it deals with the conflict between natural affections and asceticism, and in a characteristically militant introduction Kingsley attacks 'those miserable dilettanti, who in books and sermons are whimpering meagre second-hand praises of celibacy', thus striking early in his career an anti-*Tractarian note that recurs throughout his work. At this period he was much influenced by F. D. *Maurice and the writings of *Carlyle; he took a vigorous interest in the movement for social reform, while condemning the violent policies of the *Chartists. He contributed, over the signature 'Parson Lot', to *Politics for the People* in 1848, and to its successor, *The Christian Socialist*, in 1850–1.

His first novel, *Yeast*, was serialized in *Fraser's Magazine* in 1848, and published in book form in 1850; *Alton Locke* also appeared in 1850. Both are reforming novels, showing his concern with the sufferings of the working classes. A visit to Germany in 1851 inspired his first historical novel, *Hypatia, or New Foes with Old Faces*, published in *Fraser's* in 1851 and in book form in 1853; set in 5th-cent. Alexandria, it exalts the Greek Neoplatonic philosopher Hypatia who was torn to pieces in AD 415 by a mob of infuriated Christians, and condemns the ignorant fanaticism of the Alexandrian monks. It had a mixed reception; many complained of its violence, its anachronisms, and its emphasis on Hypatia's nakedness at death; and *Newman's *Callista* was written in part to correct its hostile portrait of the early Church. His next novel, *Westward Ho!* (1855), was inspired by an upsurge of patriotism with which he greeted the Crimean War; set in the Elizabethan period, its hero, Devonshire seaman Amyas Leigh, wages war against the Armada and the Spanish captain Don Guzman, his rival in love. Its violent anti-Catholicism and bloodthirsty narrative shocked some readers, but delighted more; G. *Eliot's judgement in the *Westminster Review* was that Kingsley 'sees, feels and paints vividly, but he theorizes illogically and moralizes absurdly'. *Two Years Ago* (1857) returns to the theme of social reform and *Hereward the Wake* (1866) is a historical novel based on the exploits of the legendary outlaw, in Kingsley's version the son of Leofric of Mercia and Lady Godiva, who attempts to save England from the Normans.

Kingsley's other works include *The Heroes* (1856), in which he tells for young readers the stories of Perseus, Theseus, and the Argonauts, and *The Water-Babies* (1863), also for the young. The latter displays his profound and sympathetic interest in underwater and seashore life, as does his earlier work (which contains several tributes to his friend and fellow-naturalist P. H. Gosse, father of E. *Gosse) *Glaucus: or the Wonders of the Shore* (1855). Of his poetry, the hexameters of 'Andromeda' (1858) and the dying monologue in blank verse of Saint Maura (1858), though psychologically revealing, are forgotten, whereas many of his songs and ballads remain popular; these include 'Airly Beacon' and 'The Sands of Dee', and many of his lines, such as 'Be Good, sweet maid, and let who will be clever' (quoted in *Two Years Ago*) and 'For men must work and women must weep', from 'The Three Fishers', have become proverbial. Kingsley also wrote tracts on many topics, published lectures and sermons, and his *At Last* (1871) is a record of a long-desired visit to the West Indies.

Kingsley in his lifetime was a celebrated and revered figure, who gained towards the end of his life (as professor of modern history at Cambridge, 1860–9, and as canon of Chester and Westminster) a high degree of public and indeed royal approval, but he remained the centre of controversy. His leanings towards polemics were most damagingly displayed in his celebrated confrontation with Newman, which was initiated by Kingsley's review in *Macmillan's Magazine* (Jan. 1864) of *Froude's *History of England*, Vols VII and VIII; in this he misrepresented Newman's sermon on 'Wisdom and Innocence' in support of his own statement that 'Truth for its own sake has never been a virtue of the Roman clergy.' After some correspondence, Newman's crushing rejoinder appeared in the form of his *Apologia*, and he was widely considered the victor of the exchange.

Although Kingsley's works are now read largely for their social interest and admired for their brilliantly evocative descriptive passages, his complex personality continues to interest biographers, and he seems to represent some of the central paradoxes of his age. A keen sportsman who was tender to animals, a champion of the working man who despised Negroes, a muscular Christian who wrote much (like his friend T. *Hughes) of the virtues of 'manliness' and who nevertheless held an unusually explicit physical passion for his wife, an admirer of physical prowess who himself suffered from an acute stammer and occasional nervous breakdowns, he was both Philistine and artist; his strong didacticism, while it mars many of his works, is inseparable from them. See R. B. Martin, *The Dust of Combat* (1959); Susan Chitty, *The Beast and the Monk* (1974); Brenda Collom, *Charles Kingsley* (1975).

KINGSLEY, Henry (1830–76), younger brother of C. *Kingsley, was born at Barnack, Northamptonshire, where his father was rector. He spent his childhood at Clovelly, in Devonshire, and in Chelsea. He was educated at King's College School, London, and at Worcester College, Oxford, which he left without taking a degree. From 1853 to 1858 he was in Australia, at the gold-diggings and as a trooper in the Sydney Mounted Police. His Australian experiences provided the basis for two of his best novels, *Geoffrey Hamlyn* (1859) and *The Hillyers and the Burtons* (1865), which have been influential in Australian literary history. After his return to England in 1858 he married his cousin Sarah Haselwood and lived at Wargrave, Berkshire, making a precarious living as a novelist and journalist (after his first four novels his popularity waned). For a time he was editor of the *Edinburgh Daily Review*, and was its correspondent at the Franco-Prussian War.

Ravenshoe (1862), the best-known of his 21 books, is a story of inheritance intrigues in a Roman Catholic landed family in Devonshire, and includes Crimean War scenes. Kingsley's best novels are distinguished for admirable descriptions of landscape in England and Australia, for engrossing accounts of storms and cyclones, attacks and alarms, and for humorous and well-observed character sketches. He was less skilled at sustained narration and at devising convincing plots, and was somewhat obsessed by his ideal of the virile and athletic 'English gentleman'. He was himself a keen athlete who once at Oxford, for a bet, ran a mile, rowed a mile, and trotted a mile, all within 15 minutes. His premature departure from Oxford, where he was a founder-member of an extremely misogynist club, has sometimes been attributed to homosexual tendencies, and he was also rumoured to have been an alcoholic in his later years, but there is no firm evidence on either of these points. Kingsley, an impulsive, convivial but insecure man, was a friend of M. *Arnold, *Swinburne, *Dodgson (Lewis Carroll), and Anne Thackeray (*Ritchie). His relations with his brother Charles in later life were soured by his frequent requests for money loans. See S. M. Ellis, *Henry Kingsley. Towards a Vindication* (1931); W. H. Scheuerle, *The Neglected Brother: A Study of Henry Kingsley* (1971).

KINGSLEY, Mary Henrietta (1862–1900), niece of C. *Kingsley, was largely self-educated, and until the death of her parents in 1892 devoted herself to caring for them. In 1893 she made her first journey to West Africa, returning in 1894. *Travels in West Africa* (1897) is an account of her travels and ethnological researches, written in a lively, witty, and informal style, expressing her admiration for the peoples and landscape of the country, and recommending a closer understanding of African culture to its British rulers. She went to South Africa in 1900 to nurse Boer prisoners of war, and died at Simonstown of enteric fever.

KINGSMILL, Hugh (Hugh Kingsmill Lunn) (1889–1949), anthologist, biographer, literary critic, novelist, and parodist, whose lives of M. *Arnold (1928), *Dickens (1935), and D. H. *Lawrence (1938) gave him a reputation for iconoclasm. He also wrote a life of F. *Harris (1932), with whom he had worked in 1912 on *Hearth and Home*. His other works include *The Return of William Shakespeare* (1929, a fictional fantasy with some perceptive literary criticism), and *The Progress of a Biography* (1949, collected literary criticism). See M. *Holroyd, *Hugh Kingsmill: a critical biography* (1964); *The Best of Kingsmill*, ed. Holroyd (1970).

King's, or **Queen's, Printer,** the printer of royal proclamations, etc., appointed under royal patent. The earliest known patent was granted to Thomas Berthelet (or Bartlet) in 1530. At the present day the controller of the Stationery Office (under Letters Patent) is the Queen's Printer of Acts of Parliament, and in him is vested the copyright in all government publications. Messrs Eyre & Spottiswoode are also termed the Queen's Printers; their privilege is the printing of the Bible and Prayer Book, a privilege shared with the University Presses of Oxford and Cambridge.

KINGSTON, W(illiam) H(enry) G(iles) (1814–80), an extremely prolific and successful writer of stories for boys, covering adventures in all continents, at sea, in history, at school, and elsewhere. Much of his work was published by the *SPCK, and a strong patriotic and didactic message is evident.

Kinmont Willie, see ARMSTRONG, W.

KIPLING, Rudyard (1865–1936), born in Bombay, son of John Lockwood Kipling, author and illustrator of *Beast and Man in India* (1891), and Alice Kipling, sister-in-law of *Burne-Jones. He was brought to England in 1871, where he spent five years as a boarder in Southsea with his younger sister, separated from his parents, a period recalled with bitterness in his short story 'Baa, Baa, Black Sheep' (1888) and his novel *The Light that Failed* (1890). From 1878 to 1882 he attended the United Services College, Westward Ho!, later depicted in his schoolboy tales *Stalky & Co.* (1899). From 1882 to 1889 he worked as a journalist in India; many of his early poems and stories were originally published in newspapers or for the Indian Railway Library, and were later collected under various titles, which include *Departmental Ditties* (1886), *Plain Tales from the Hills* (1888), *Soldiers Three* (1890, in which the three soldiers are the three privates Learoyd, Mulvaney, and Ortheris), and *Wee Willie Winkie* (1890). In 1889 he came to London, where he achieved instant literary celebrity, aided by *Henley's publication in his *Scots Observer* of many of the poems ('Danny Deever', 'Mandalay', etc.) later collected as *Barrack-Room Ballads* (1892). In 1892 he married Caroline Balestier, sister of his American agent *Balestier (with whom he had written *The Naulahka*, 1892); from 1892 to 1896 the Kiplings lived on Balestier home-ground at Brattleboro, Vermont. In 1896 they returned to England, settling finally at 'Bateman's' in Sussex in 1902, though Kipling continued to travel extensively, spending much time in South Africa, which he first visited in 1900 during the Boer War, where he had his first sight of warfare. Widely regarded as unofficial poet laureate, he refused many honours; in 1907 he was the first English writer to receive the *Nobel Prize.

Kipling's output was vast and varied, and has been variously judged. His early tales of the Raj, praised for their cynical realism, were compared to those of *Maupassant, but his growing reputation as the poet of Empire cut both ways. His poem 'Recessional', written for Jubilee Day 1897, was acclaimed for catching the mood of the moment, but the mood changed. Kipling retained his popularity with the common soldier and reader, and his verse has added many phrases to the language (including, significantly, 'the white man's burden'), but he was increasingly accused of vulgarity and jingoism in aesthetic and anti-imperialist circles. His fluent versification, with its powerful echoes of hymns and ballads, and his use in both prose and verse of colloquial speech, impressed many but alienated others; even such admirers as H. *James, *Yeats, and T. S. *Eliot were uneasy about the nature of his art. His most uncontroversial and durable achievements are perhaps his tales for children (principally *The Jungle Book*, 1894; *Just So*

Stories, 1902; *Puck of Pook's Hill*, 1906; and *Rewards and Fairies*, 1910) and his picaresque novel of India *Kim*, generally considered his masterpiece. His autobiographical fragment *Something of Myself* was published in 1937, and there are biographies by C. Carrington (1955), Angus *Wilson (1977), and Lord Birkenhead (1978).

Kipps, a novel by H. G. *Wells.

KIRK, Robert, see SECRET COMMONWEALTH OF ELVES, FAUNS AND FAIRIES.

KIRKE, Edward (1553–1613), a friend of *Spenser, educated at Pembroke Hall and Caius College, Cambridge. He probably wrote the preface, the arguments, and a verbal commentary to Spenser's *Shepheardes Calender*, under the initials 'E.K.' (1579). Modern critics have, on insufficient grounds, sought to prove that 'E.K.' was Spenser himself.

Kirkrapine, in Spenser's *Faerie Queene* (I. iii), 'a stout and sturdie thiefe' of the church, who is destroyed by *Una's lion.

KIRKUP, James (1923–), poet, translator, and travel writer, born in Sunderland and educated at South Shields High School and Durham University; he has held many academic posts in England and abroad, notably in Japan and Malaya. His volumes of poetry include *A Correct Compassion* (1952, of which the title poem celebrates the precision of a surgical operation), *The Descent into the Cave* (1957), *Paper Windows* (1968), and *A Bewick Bestiary* (1971). In 1977 his poem 'The love that dares to speak its name' (which deals with the homosexual love of one of the Roman centurions for Christ) became the subject of the first prosecution for blasphemous libel for over 50 years, and as a result the editor of *Gay News*, the periodical which published the poem, was fined and given a suspended prison sentence. (See Appendix II: Censorship.) Kirkup's autobiographical *The Only Child* (1957) is an evocative account of a working-class northern childhood, and he has also published many books on Japan, and translated works by *Dürrenmatt, *Ibsen (with C. *Fry), *Valéry, and others.

Kit-Cat Club, founded in the early part of the 18th cent. by leading Whigs, including (according to *Pope) *Steele, *Addison, *Congreve, *Garth, and *Vanbrugh. *Tonson, the publisher, was for many years its secretary and moving spirit. It met at the house of Christopher Cat (or Kat), a pastrycook, in Shire Lane (which ran north from Temple Bar). Cat's mutton-pies were called Kit-cats, hence the name of the club (*Spectator*, No. 9). The club subsequently met at Tonson's house at Barn Elms. The portraits of the members (painted by *Kneller and now in the possession of the National Portrait Gallery) had to be less than half-length because the dining-room was too low for half-size portraits. The term 'kit-cat' is in consequence still used for portraits of this size.

KITCHIN, Clifford Henry Benn (1895–1967), novelist and barrister, educated at Exeter College, Oxford, whose great gifts as a chess-player, bridge-player, pianist, author, and investor of an inherited fortune led his close friend L. P. *Hartley to describe him as 'the most talented man I have ever known'. His early novels, *Streamers Waving* (1925) and *Mr Balcony* (1927), were witty and allusive, with a strong element of fantasy; the later ones, such as *The Birthday Party* (1938) and *The Secret River* (1956), were works of settled accomplishment. He also wrote several detective stories, including the well known *Death of My Aunt* (1929).

Kitchen Sink Drama, a term applied in the late 1950s to the plays of writers such as *Wesker, S. *Delaney, and J. *Osborne, which portrayed working-class or lower-middle-class life, with an emphasis on domestic realism. These plays were written in part as a reaction against the drawing-room comedies and middle-class dramas of *Coward and *Rattigan, and also undermined the popularity of the verse drama of T. S. *Eliot and C. *Fry. *Tynan was a principal advocate of this new group of writers.

Kite, Sergeant, one of the chief characters in Farquhar's *The Recruiting Officer*. One of his songs is the well known 'Over the hills and far away'.

Kitely, the jealous husband of Jonson's *Every Man in his Humour*.

Kit Nubbles, a character in Dickens's *The Old Curiosity Shop*.

KLOPSTOCK, Friedrich Gottlieb (1724–1803), German poet, famous for his patriotic odes and his great religious epic *Messias* (*The Messiah*), inspired by Milton's *Paradise Lost*, of which the first three cantos were published in 1748 and the last in 1773, and which is characterized by its pietistic delight in sentiment and its disregard for action.

Knag, Miss, in Dickens's *Nicholas Nickleby*, Madame Mantalini's forewoman.

KNELLER, Godfrey (1646 or 1649–1723), born in Lübeck, trained in Holland and Italy, and arrived in England in 1676. His immensely successful career at the English court spans the reigns of five monarchs; he was knighted in 1692 and made a baronet in 1715. *Addison's poem on his picture of George I looks back at his portraits of earlier rulers, and is a witty résumé of the entire era somewhat drably recorded by the

artist. Kneller painted many hundreds of portraits, of royalty, of the 'beauties' of the court, of admirals and generals, and of men eminent in the world of affairs and in literary life. Frequently his pictures—especially the official full lengths, which often seem tired derivations from the *Lely–Van Dyck tradition—suffer from their heavy dependence on studio assistants. Kneller's finest achievements are the *Kit-Cat series (1702–17; London, National Portrait Gallery) and several related portraits of scholars and poets. At their best, these works, sharp and direct in their portrayal of individual personality, reflect the sophisticated urbanity and rational temper of the 18th-cent. man of letters; outstanding are the portraits of *Dryden (*c.* 1698) and *Prior (1700) (both Trinity College, Cambridge). Kneller, who lived in a grand house at Whitton, a neighbour of *Pope at Twickenham, knew most of the leading literary figures of the day. He was constantly flattered by poets, among them Dryden, Prior, and *Gay. Pope later told many amusing stories of Kneller's immense conceit and vulgarity. Pope also wrote his epitaph, which he adapted from Raphael's, commenting that it was 'the worst thing I ever wrote in my life'.

KNICKERBOCKER, Diedrich, the pseudonym under which W. *Irving wrote his *History of New York*, and other sketches. The word as used for loose-fitting breeches is said to have been given to these because of their resemblance to the knee-breeches of the Dutchmen in *Cruikshank's illustrations to the *History of New York* [OED].

Knickerbocker Magazine, The, founded in New York City, 1 Jan. 1833, under the editorship of Charles Fenno Hoffman (1806–84). From that date until it was discontinued in 1865 the *Knickerbocker* numbered many of the foremost American writers among its contributors, including W. *Irving, H. W. *Longfellow, W. C. *Bryant, O. W. *Holmes, J. R. *Lowell, H. *Greeley, and J. F. *Cooper.

KNIGHT, Charles (1791–1873), son of a bookseller, an industrious and influential publisher who did much to introduce the sale of cheap books. He worked diligently to make knowledge available to the poor; and greatly assisted in creating, from the 1820s onwards, an entirely new class of reader. He was publisher to the 'Society for the Diffusion of Useful Knowledge', for whom he produced *The Penny Magazine*, *The Penny Cyclopaedia*, and other works, including 'The Library of Useful Knowledge'. Christopher Thomson, who in 1847 published his *Autobiography of an Artisan*, described how he went without sugar in his tea in order to afford *The Penny Magazine*. In 1825 Knight published his *Library of Entertaining Knowledge* and in 1842 his *Store of Knowledge*. His popular illustrated history of London appeared between

1841 and 1844, when his series 'Weekly Volumes', containing contributions from H. *Martineau, was published; in 1842 and 1844 his biographies of Shakespeare, of whose works he had produced a popular pictorial edition (1839–41), and *Caxton; and in 1856–62 The Popular History of England. His admirable Passages of a Working Life (1864–5) contains valuable information about the writers and the publishing trade of his time.

KNIGHT, G(eorge Richard) Wilson (1897–), Shakespeare scholar and critic. His poetic and symbolic approach to Shakespeare is perhaps seen at its best in The Wheel of Fire (1930), The Starlit Dome (1941), and The Crown of Life (1947), among many other publications. He also exercised considerable influence on Shakespearian production, himself giving memorable solo performances as *Timon and *Caliban.

KNIGHT, William Payne, see PICTURESQUE.

Knightley, George, and John, his brother, characters in J. Austen's *Emma.

Knight of the Burning Pestle, The, a comedy now thought to be the unaided work of *Beaumont, but formerly generally attributed to Beaumont and *Fletcher; it was probably performed 1607–8, and was printed (anonymously) 1613. The most successful of Beaumont's plays, it is a high-spirited comedy of manners, and a burlesque of knight-errantry and of such fabulous and patriotic plays as *Heywood's The Four Prentices of London and The Travels of the Three English Brothers by *Day, *Rowley, and George Wilkins. It has clear echoes of *Don Quixote, both in attitude and incident, and satirizes the middle-class taste for such popular and improbable romances as *Palmerin of England.

It takes the form of a play-within-a-play: a grocer and his wife, members of an audience about to watch a drama called 'The London Merchant', interrupt the prologue to insist that their apprentice, Rafe, have a part. He therefore becomes a Grocer Errant, with a Burning Pestle portrayed on his shield, and undertakes various absurd adventures, including the release of patients held captive by a barber, Barbarossa. These are interspersed with the real plot, in which Jasper, a merchant's apprentice, woos, and after much opposition wins, his master's daughter Luce.

There are several modern editions, including those by A. Gurr (1968) and M. Hattaway (1969).

Knight of the Leopard, Sir Kenneth of Scotland, the earl of Huntingdon, hero of Scott's *The Talisman.

Knight of the Rueful (or **Sad,** or **Woeful,** or **Sorrowful**) **Countenance,** *Don Quixote.

Knight of the Swan, see LOHENGRIN.

KNIGHTS, L(ionel) C(harles) (1906–), Shakespeare critic, and for 22 years member of the editorial board of *Scrutiny. His longer books include Drama and Society in the Age of Jonson (1937) and Some Shakespearean Themes (1959). One of his best-known essays is 'How many children had Lady Macbeth?' (1933), a celebrated attack on the style of criticism represented by A. C. *Bradley.

Knights of the Round Table, see ROUND TABLE.

'Knight's Tale, The,' see CANTERBURY TALES, I.

Knockdunder, The Captain of, in Scott's *The Heart of Midlothian, the duke of Argyle's agent.

KNOLLES, Richard (?1550–1610), author of The Generall Historie of the Turkes (1603), which was much admired by Dr *Johnson (who took from it the plot of his *Irene), and also by *Byron, who credited it with inspiring the 'oriental colouring' of his poetry.

Knowell, in Jonson's *Every Man in his Humour, Edward's over-solicitous father.

KNOWLES, James Sheridan (1784–1862), after trying the army, medicine, and teaching, became an actor and verse dramatist, and was described by the *Edinburgh Review in 1833 as 'the most successful dramatist of the day'. His Virginius was produced at Covent Garden with C. *Kemble and *Macready in 1820; Caius Gracchus in 1823 (1815, Belfast); William Tell in 1825. His greatest success was The Hunchback, produced in 1832; The Wife, with Prologue and Epilogue by *Lamb, followed in 1833, and in 1837 his highly successful The Love Chase. His friend *Hazlitt described Knowles as 'the first tragic writer of his time', and he was the recipient of many of the letters in Hazlitt's *Liber Amoris.

KNOWLES, Sir James Thomas (1831–1908), editor, architect, and a friend of *Tennyson, published in 1862 The Story of King Arthur and his Knights from Malory's *Morte D'Arthur. He founded the *Metaphysical Society, became editor of the *Contemporary Review in 1870 and in 1877 founded the *Nineteenth Century.

KNOX, Edmund George Valpy ('Evoe') (1881–1971), essayist, humorist, and parodist, brother of R. A. *Knox. He contributed to *Punch as 'Evoe', and was editor 1932–49.

Knox, Flurry, the MFH in *Some Experiences of an Irish R.M. by Somerville and Ross.

KNOX, John (c.1513–72), was educated at

Haddington School and Glasgow University. He was called to the ministry and began preaching for the reformed religion in 1547. In 1551 he became chaplain to Edward VI. He went abroad at the accession of Mary Tudor, wrote his 'Epistle on Justification by Faith' in 1548, met *Calvin at Geneva in 1554, was pastor of the English congregation at Frankfurt am Main, 1554–5, and from 1556 to 1558 lived at Geneva. Thence he addressed epistles to his brethren in England suffering under the rule of Mary Tudor, and in Scotland under the regency of Mary of Lorraine. It was this situation which led to the publication of his *First Blast of the Trumpet against the Monstrous Regiment of Women* (1558), of which the title, *Saintsbury remarks, was the best part. (The phrase is often now misapplied: 'Regiment' here has its old sense of 'rule, magisterial authority', and has no connection with the later sense of 'large body of troops'.) In 1559 appeared the *First Book of Discipline*, of which Knox was part-author, advocating a national system of education ranging from a school in every parish to the three universities. His *Treatise on Predestination* was published in 1560. In 1572 he was appointed minister at Edinburgh, where he died. His *History of the Reformation of Religioun within the realme of Scotland* was first printed in 1587 (the best edition of this is in the first two vols of Laing's edition of Knox's *Works*, 1846–8). It contains, in its fourth book, the notable account of the return of Mary Stuart to Scotland, of Knox's interviews with her, and his fierce denunciations from the pulpit of St Giles.

KNOX, the Rt Revd Monsignor Ronald Arbuthnott (1888–1957), educated at Eton and Balliol College, Oxford, where he acquired a reputation as a writer of witty light verse, was fellow of Trinity, 1910–17, when he was received into the church of Rome. His autobiographical *A Spiritual Aeneid* (1918) describes his conversion. Knox wrote many theological works, published a new translation of the Bible, based on the *Vulgate (1945–9), and acquired a wide reputation as journalist and broadcaster. He also wrote six detective stories. *Let Dons Delight* (1939), a work for which he himself had a particular affection, uses a dream framework to describe, through conversations in an Oxford senior common room at 50-year intervals, the process of specialization and fragmentation that leads to the loss of a common culture. After the Second World War he became a close friend of E. *Waugh, who wrote his official biography (1959); see also *The Knox Brothers* (1977) by Penelope Fitzgerald, daughter of E. G. V. *Knox.

KNOX, Vicesimus (1752–1821), educated at St John's College, Oxford, is remembered as the compiler of *Elegant Extracts* (1784), an anthology of passages from H. *Blair, *Hurd, *Sterne, *Smollett, etc. He was author of *Essays, Moral and Literary* (1778).

KNYVETT, Thomas (1596–1658), born at Ashwellthorpe in Norfolk, and educated at Emmanuel College, Cambridge, was a landowner in the eastern counties, and a royalist in sympathy during the Civil War. His letters to his wife, which have been preserved, throw an interesting light on the life of the period. They have been edited by B. Schofield (1949).

KOESTLER, Arthur (1905–83), author, born in Budapest and educated at the University of Vienna. He worked as foreign correspondent in the Middle East, Paris, and Berlin. In 1932 he joined the Communist Party and travelled in the USSR; he was imprisoned under Franco during the Spanish Civil War and broke from the Party in 1938. In 1940 he came to England, adopting the language with his first book written in English, *Scum of the Earth* (1941). His publications manifest a wide range of political, scientific, and literary interests, and include *Darkness at Noon* (1940), *Arrival and Departure* (1943), and *Thieves in the Night* (1946), novels concerned with the ethics of revolution and survival. Non-fiction includes *The Yogi and the Commissar and Other Essays* (1945), *The Trail of the Dinosaur and Other Essays* (1955), and *The Act of Creation* (1964). *The Roots of Coincidence* (1972) reflects his interest in parapsychology. He was one of the contributors to *The God that Failed: six studies in communism* (1950). He died by suicide, having frequently expressed a belief in the right to euthanasia.

Koran, or Qur'ān, the sacred book of the Muslims, consisting of revelations orally delivered from time to time by *Muhammad, some at Mecca, others at Medina, and first committed to memory by professional remembrancers, then inscribed, and collected and put in order after his death during the caliphate of Omar, the second Caliph. An authorized version was established during the caliphate of Omar's successor Othman (644–56). It is written in a pure classical Arabic, and consists of 114 chapters, or 'suras'. There is a *Penguin translation by N. J. Dawood (1956, rev. 1974).

KOTZEBUE, August von (1761–1819), a German dramatist, author of a large number of sentimental plays which had considerable vogue in their day and influenced the English stage. His *Menschenhass und Reue* enjoyed great popularity as *The Stranger*, brought out by *Sheridan in 1798, the story of a wife duped and erring, her husband in consequence turned misanthropical, the wife's repentance, the reconciliation, and the husband's return to sanity. *Lovers' Vows*, made famous by J. Austen's *Mansfield Park*, was adapted by Mrs *Inchbald from Kotzebue's

Das Kind der Liebe. Sheridan adapted *Die Spanier in Peru* as *Pizarro.*

'Kraken, The', a short poem by *Tennyson, published in *Poems, Chiefly Lyrical* (1830). It describes the mythical sea-monster mentioned by *Pontoppidan, sleeping in the depths of the sea 'his ancient, dreamless, uninvaded sleep', and waiting only to rise and die; Christopher Ricks (*Tennyson*, 1972) describes it as an example of the poet's 'pained fascination with the thought of a life which somehow is not life at all'.

Krook, a character in Dickens's *Bleak House.*

KRYLOV, Ivan Andreevich (1769–1844), Russian writer of fables. He entered the civil service at an early age, but soon turned to satirical journalism. When the journal he edited, the *St Petersburg Mercury*, was closed down, he abandoned literature until 1805, when he translated his first fable by *La Fontaine. In 1809 a book of 23 fables, some still based on La Fontaine, met with enormous success. He wrote nine books of fables in all, and their common sense, universality, and linguistic vigour has secured their continuing popularity. Many of their conclusions and morals have become proverbial in Russia. The fables were first translated by W. R. S. Ralston in 1869, and are now most accessible in the translations of Sir Bernard Pares (1926, etc.).

'Kubla Khan; a Vision in a Dream', a poem by S. T. *Coleridge, published 1816.

In 1797, while living near the *Wordsworths in Somerset, Coleridge took opium and fell asleep when reading a passage in *Purchas his Pilgrimage* (see PURCHAS), relating to the Khan Kubla and the palace that he commanded to be built. On awaking he was conscious of having composed in his sleep two or three hundred lines on this theme, and eagerly began to set down the lines that form this fragment. He was then unfortunately interrupted by 'a person . . . from Porlock', and, on returning to his task an hour later, found that almost the entire remainder of the poem had slipped from his memory. The poem has no narrative line, but consists of a series of potent visionary images, suggesting themes of eternity and change. Alph, the sacred river, flung up in a tremendous fountain, connects Khan's 'stately pleasure-dome', great caverns, and the 'sunless sea'. Within the gardens of the pleasure-dome is growth and sunlight and colour. There are hints of death and war, the vision of a damsel with a dulcimer, and of the frenzy of the poet who has drunk 'the milk of Paradise'. Coleridge thought the poem 'a psychological curiosity', but later in his work on literary criticism vigorously defended poetic images 'just on the vestibule of Consciousness'. *Lowes, in *The Road

to Xanadu* (1927), traces the varied sources of Coleridge's imagery. See also Alethea Hayter, *Opium and the Romantic Imagination* (1968).

KUNDERA, Milan (1929–), Czech novelist, born in Brno, and educated in Prague, where he later taught at the Institute for Advanced Cinematographic Studies. He lost his post after the Russian invasion in 1968, and in 1975 settled in Paris. His first novel, *Zert*, was published in 1967 (English trans., *The Joke*, 1969). His other novels (which have not been published in his own country) include *The Farewell Party* (1976) and *The Book of Laughter and Forgetting* (French, 1979; English, 1980), a semi-fictional, semi-autobiographical evocation of the cultural, political, and sexual life of post-war Europe, seen partly through Kundera's own eyes, partly through those of several of the 'two or three new fictional characters baptized on earth every second'.

Kurtz, a character in Conrad's *'Heart of Darkness' whose epitaph, 'Mistah Kurtz—he dead', provides the epigraph for T. S. *Eliot's 'The Hollow Men'.

KYD, or **KID**, Thomas (1558–94), dramatist, was educated at *Merchant Taylors' School, London, whose headmaster was *Mulcaster; he may have worked for a time as a scrivener. He seems to have been closely associated with *Marlowe, with whom he shared lodgings in 1591, and whose 'atheistical' writings led to Kyd's suffering a period of torture and imprisonment. His *Spanish Tragedy* was published anonymously in 1592; the only work published under his name was a translation from Robert Garnier, *Cornelia* (1594), re-issued in 1595 as *Pompey the Great, his faire Corneliaes Tragedie. The First Part of Jeronimo* (1605) is a fore-piece to *The Spanish Tragedy*, but probably not the work of Kyd, though some other such fore-piece by him may have existed. Other works Kyd may have written are *The Tragedye of Solyman and Perseda* (1592) and a lost pre-Shakespearian play on the subject of Hamlet. *The Spanish Tragedy* was an exceptionally popular play on the Elizabethan stage, and it passed through ten printed editions by 1633.

KYRLE, John, The Man of Ross (1637–1724), lived very simply upon his estates at Ross and devoted his surplus income to charity. *Pope's portrait of him in his *Epistle to Bathurst* (see MORAL ESSAYS) was based on information supplied by the elder *Tonson, who had an estate in Ledbury. There is a later account in *The Gentleman's Magazine* (1786) by 'Viator'.

L

'La Belle Dame sans Merci', a ballad by *Keats, written 1819, published 1820, which describes a knight fatally enthralled by an elfin woman. Although Keats himself spoke of it lightly, critics and biographers have written of it at length, many concurring with Robert *Graves (*The White Goddess*, 1948) that 'the Belle Dame represented Love, Death by Consumption . . . and Poetry all at once.' It was much admired by the *Pre-Raphaelites and W. *Morris asserted that 'it was the germ from which all the poetry of his group had sprung.' *La Belle Dame sans mercy* is also the title of a poem translated from *Chartier, attributed at one time to *Chaucer, but now thought to be the work of Sir Richard Ros.

LA BRUYÈRE, Jean de (1645–96), French satiric moralist, author of *Les Caractères ou les mœurs de ce siècle* (1688; English trans., *The Characters, or the Manners of the Age*, 1699). The work, consisting of short portrait sketches revelatory of the vanity and corruption in human behaviour, was published as an appendage to La Bruyère's translation of the *Characters* of *Theophrastus from which it derives its method. It was immediately successful on publication, and has been widely admired by such writers as *Flaubert, *Gide, and *Proust.

LA CALPRENÈDE, Gauthier de Costes de (1614–63), French novelist. His heroic romances achieved an immense international vogue, and had a marked effect on the heroic drama of high classicism in France and of the English Restoration. They divide into three cycles: *Cassandre* (10 vols, 1644–50), trans. Sir Charles Cotterell (1667), centred on the life of the daughter of Darius, wife of Alexander the Great; *Cléopâtre* (10 vols, 1647–56), trans. R. Loveday and others (1652–9), describing the adventures of the daughter of Antony and Cleopatra; and *Pharamond* (12 vols, 1661–70), trans. John Davies (1662), narrating the loves of the first French kings for the Cambrian princess Rosemonde.

LACAN, Jacques, see STRUCTURALISM and MARXIST LITERARY CRITICISM.

LACLOS, Pierre Choderlos de (1741–1803), French novelist. His masterpiece, *Les Liaisons dangereuses* (1782), influenced by *Richardson's epistolary novels, brings neo-classical fiction to a pitch of perverse perfection. In depicting the moral and sexual raids of a cynical aristocratic couple on an unsuspecting society, it remarkably combines searching psychological analysis in the manner of 17th-cent. drama, the assumptions of 18th-cent. philosophical sensationalism, and intimations of demonic Romantic revolt.

La Creevy, Miss, the cheerful little miniature-painter in Dickens's *Nicholas Nickleby*.

Ladislaw, Will, a character in G. Eliot's *Middlemarch*.

Lady Audley's Secret, see BRADDON, M. E.

Lady Chatterley's Lover, a novel by *D. H. Lawrence (privately printed, Florence 1928; expurgated version, London 1932; full text, London 1960).

Constance Chatterley is married to Sir Clifford, writer, intellectual, and landowner, of Wragby Hall in the Midlands. He is confined to a wheelchair through injuries from the First World War. She has an unsatisfying affair with a successful playwright, Michaelis, followed by a passionate love relationship with gamekeeper Oliver Mellors, son of a miner and ex-officer from the Indian army. She becomes pregnant by him, goes to Venice with her sister Hilda partly to obscure the baby's parentage, but returns and tells her husband the truth, spurred on by the knowledge that Mellors's estranged wife Bertha has been stirring scandal in an effort to reclaim him. The novel ends with the temporary separation of the lovers, as they hopefully await divorce and a new life together.

Lawrence's detailed and poetic descriptions of sexual union, and his uncompromising use of four-letter words, caused the book (long available in foreign editions) to be unpublishable in full in England until 1960 when *Penguin Books took the risk of producing a complete text. They were prosecuted under the Obscene Publications Act 1959, and acquitted after a celebrated trial during which many eminent authors (including E. M. *Forster, R. *Hoggart, H. *Gardner) appeared as witnesses for the defence, a victory which had a profound effect on both writing and publishing in subsequent decades.

Lady Margaret Professorships were chairs of divinity at Oxford and Cambridge Universities founded in 1502 by Margaret, Lady Beaufort (1443–1509), countess of Richmond and mother of Henry VII. She also established a preachership at Cambridge to which her chaplain *Fisher was appointed in 1504: with him she helped found St John's College. She also contributed to the endowment of Christ's College and patronized *Caxton and his successor *Wynkyn de Worde.

Lady of Lyons, The, a romantic comedy by *Bulwer-Lytton.

Lady of May, The, a short pastoral entertainment by P. *Sidney. It consists of a dispute between a shepherd and a forester for the hand of the rustic May Lady, and was performed under the aegis of the earl of *Leicester for *Elizabeth I when she visited him at Wanstead in 1578 or 1579. The character of the pedantic schoolmaster Rombus may have suggested that of Holofernes in *Love's Labour's Lost.

Lady of Pleasure, The, a comedy by J. *Shirley, acted 1635, printed 1637.

In the central plot Lady Bornwell is cured of her desire to live a life of thoughtless pleasure, partly by the discovery of the worthlessness of her foppish suitors and partly by her husband's pretence that he too means to live extravagantly. The play's scenes of fashionable conversation, the contrast between the manners of the true gentleman and lady of the sub-plot and the affected main-plot characters, and the rapid transformation of the scholarly bashfulness of Lady Bornwell's nephew Frederick into town debauchery, are a cross between *Jonson's comedy of humours and *Restoration comedy of manners; the moral tone of the ending, in which Lady Bornwell decides to return to the country, contrasts with the largely amoral tone of much that has gone before. G. E. Bentley has suggested (*Jacobean and Caroline Stage*, V. p. 1127) that the relationship between Sir Thomas and Lady Bornwell may have influenced that of Sheridan's Sir Peter and Lady Teazle in *The School for Scandal.

'Lady of Shalott, The', a poem by *Tennyson, published 1832, much revised for the 1842 *Poems*. Tennyson said of it 'I met the story first in some Italian novelle: but the web, mirror, island etc. were my own. Indeed, I doubt whether I should ever have put it into that shape if I had then been aware of the Maid of Astolat in Mort Arthur.' (Quoted by F. J. *Furnivall, 1868.) The story bears little resemblance to his subsequent treatment of it in 'Lancelot and Elaine' of the *Idylls of the King. The Lady, like *Mariana, was one of several enchanted or imprisoned maidens to capture the Victorian imagination, and was the subject of many illustrations, including a notable one by Holman *Hunt.

Lady of the Idle Lake, see PHAEDRIA.

Lady of the Lake, in the Arthurian legends, a rather shifting supernatural character. In *Malory she gives Arthur the sword Excalibur, but when she asks for the head of Balyn as payment Balyn strikes off her head, for which deed he is banished from the court. Also called the Lady of the Lake (in Malory 'chief' lady, suggesting more than one) is *Nimiane (Nymus and probably by scribal misreading, Vivien), the wife of Pelleas, who loves Merlin whom she tricks into revealing his magic arts and then imprisons in a tower of air in the forest of *Broceliande from which he never escapes. In Malory she is said to have accompanied the three queens who bore Arthur away by ship after his death. In Celtic origin she may derive from Morgan, the archetypal lake lady.

Lady of the Lake, The, a poem in six cantos by Sir W. *Scott, published 1810.

A knight, who gives his name as James Fitz-James, receives hospitality in the home on Loch Katrine of Roderick Dhu, the fierce Highland chief, where he falls in love with Ellen, daughter of the outlawed Lord James of Douglas. Roderick himself and the young Malcolm Graeme are also suitors for her hand, and Ellen loves Malcolm. Under threat of an attack by the royal forces, Roderick summons his clans. Douglas, regarding himself as the cause of the attack, sets out for Stirling to surrender himself to the king. Meanwhile James Fitz-James returns and proposes to carry Ellen off to safety. She refuses, confessing her love for another. Fitz-James generously withdraws, giving her a signet ring which will enable her to obtain from the king any boon. On his way back to Stirling he falls in with Roderick. A fierce quarrel springs up between them and they fight. Fitz-James's skill prevails, and the wounded Roderick is carried prisoner to Stirling. Ellen appears at the king's court, presents her signet ring, asks for her father's pardon, and discovers that Fitz-James is the king himself. The king and Douglas are reconciled, Roderick dies of his wounds, and Ellen marries Malcolm Graeme. The poem includes the beautiful *coronach* 'He is gone on the mountain', and Ellen's song 'Soldier, rest, thy warfare o'er'. The king is as much drawn from James V as from anyone.

Lady of the Lamp, see NIGHTINGALE, F.

Lady Susan, a novel by J. *Austen, written probably 1793–4, published 1871, from an untitled manuscript dated 1805: the manuscript is a fair copy, and the date of composition is discussed by B. C. Southam, *Jane Austen's Literary Manuscripts* (1964). It is Jane Austen's only *epistolary novel, although her first version of *Sense and Sensibility*, called *Elinor and Marianne*, was also in letter form.

The story consists of letters, written chiefly between the kindly Mrs Vernon and her mother Lady de Courcy, and between Lady Susan and her London friend Mrs Johnson. The events occur mainly at Churchill, the country house of the Vernons. Lady Susan, the widow of Mr Vernon's brother, is beautiful, selfish, and unscrupulous. She has had to leave the house of the Mainwarings, where both Mr Mainwaring and his sister's suitor Sir James Martin have fallen in love with her. At Churchill she meets Reginald de Courcy, Mrs Vernon's brother, young and gullible, who also succumbs to her superficial charms. Lady Susan's 16-year-old daughter Frederica is terrorized by her mother, and becomes so distraught when learning of her mother's plan to marry her off to Sir James Martin that she begs Reginald de Courcy to intercede for her. The story then breaks off and the author appends a 'Conclusion', informing the reader that Lady Susan herself married Sir James Martin; that Frederica went to live at Churchill and would in time marry Reginald; and that 'this correspondence [i.e. the novel] . . . could not, to the great detriment of the Post Office revenue, be continued any longer.'

Laertes, in Shakespeare's *Hamlet*, the brother of Ophelia.

LA FAYETTE, Marie-Madeleine de la Vergne, comtesse de (1634–93), French novelist. The centre of a select circle in Paris which included Mme de *Sévigné and *La Rochefoucauld, she published three novels, the third of which, *La Princesse de Clèves* (1678), ensured her place in French literature. It is concerned with its heroine's overwhelming passion for an outsider from the point of view of its effects on her otherwise successful marriage. Written with harmonious sobriety and unaffected sympathy, *La Princesse* transformed the novel of romance, as practised by Mme de *Scudéry and *La Calprenède, into the novel of character. It was translated into English in 1679.

Lafeu, an old lord in Shakespeare's *All's Well that Ends Well.*

La Fleur, Yorick's French servant in Sterne's *A Sentimental Journey.*

LA FONTAINE, Jean de (1621–95), French poet, author of the *Fables,* a collection of some 240 poems, published in twelve books between 1668 and 1694 (English trans., 1734). The material for the fables is drawn from Eastern, classical, and modern sources, and a number of them, such as 'La Cigale et la fourmi' ('The Grasshopper and the Ant') or 'Le Corbeau et le renard' ('The Crow and the Fox'), have long enjoyed widespread popularity in France.

La Foole, Sir Amorous, in Jonson's *Epicene,* a foolish, chattering courtier.

LAFORGUE, Jules (1860–87), French poet, prominent in the development of *vers libre,* author of *Les Complaintes* (1885), *L'Imitation de Notre-Dame la Lune* (1886), and the posthumously published *Derniers vers* (1890). The characteristic tone of his poetry is one of ironic self-deprecation. He was an important influence on the early work of T. S. *Eliot, and on the poetry of *Pound (see *Canto* CXVI). Three of his poems were translated by H. *Crane (1922). He also published a collection of short stories, *Moralités légendaires* (1887).

Lagado, see GULLIVER'S TRAVELS.

Lake Poets, Lake School, terms applied to *Coleridge, *Southey, *Wordsworth, and sometimes to *De Quincey, who lived in the Lake District. The expression 'Lake School' seems first to appear in the *Edinburgh Review* of August 1817. *Byron makes play with the term, and in the Dedication to *Don Juan* (1819) refers slightingly to 'all the Lakers'. In his *Recollections of the Lake Poets* De Quincey denies the existence of any such 'school'.

Lallans, see SCOTS.

Lalla Rookh, a series of *oriental tales in verse connected by a story in prose, by T. *Moore, published 1817.

The frame story tells of the journey of Lalla Rookh, the daughter of the emperor, from Delhi to Kashmir, to be married to the king of Bucharia. On the way she and her train are diverted by four verse tales told by Feramorz, a young Kashmiri poet, with whom she falls in love and who turns out, on her arrival, to be the king of Bucharia himself. A series of accidents on the way throws the pompous chamberlain Fadladeen into a bad temper, which he vents in pungent criticisms of the young man's verse, in the style of the *Edinburgh Review. The four tales are:

'The Veiled Prophet of Khorassan.' The beautiful Zelica is lured into the harem of Mokanna, on the promise of admission to Paradise. Her lover Azim, supposed dead, returns from the wars to find Zelica wedded to Mokanna, and joins the army of the Caliph in order to overthrow his rival. Mokanna kills himself, and a fatal mistake by Azim leads to the death of Zelica.

'Paradise and the Peri.' A Peri, one of the offspring of fallen angels, is promised admission to Paradise if she will bring to the gate the gift that is most dear to Heaven. She brings first a drop of the blood of a youthful warrior; then the expiring sigh of an Egyptian maiden; finally, she brings a repentant tear wrung from a criminal, and this opens the gate.

'The Fire-Worshippers', a tale of the Ghebers, who maintained their resistance against the conquering Muslims. Hafed, a young Gheber, falls in love with Hinda, daughter of the Emir al Hassan, and wins her love. Presently Hinda is captured by the Ghebers and discovers that her lover is their chief; but the Ghebers are betrayed to al Hassan, and Hafed and Hinda die.

'The Light of the Haram.' Nourmahal, the beloved wife of Selim, has quarrelled with her husband. Namouna, the enchantress, teaches her a magic song, which Nourmahal sings at Selim's banquet, and thus wins back her husband's love.

The first of the tales is written in heroic couplets, the others in stanzas of varied metre. The work enjoyed immense popularity, and went into 20 editions by 1840. Lady Holland said to Moore at her own table: 'Mr Moore, I have not read your Larry O'Rourke; I don't like Irish stories.'

'L'Allegro', a poem in rhymed octosyllabics with a ten-line prelude by *Milton, written ?1631, printed 1645. The Italian title means 'the cheerful man', and this idyll is an invocation to the goddess Mirth to allow the poet to live with her, first amid the delights of pastoral scenes, then amid those of 'towered cities' and the 'busy hum of men'. It is a companion piece to *'Il Penseroso'.

La Mancha, an ancient province of Spain from which *Don Quixote took his title.

LAMARCK, Jean Baptiste de Monet, chevalier de (1744–1829), French naturalist. He advanced the view that species were not unalterable, and that the higher and more complex forms of life were derived from lower and simpler forms; that environment and new needs led to new actions and hence to organic modifications or the creation of new organs, and that these were transmitted to descendants. C. *Darwin adopted from Lamarck the theory of the transmissibility of acquired characteristics, but in other respects their views were not in harmony.

LAMARTINE, Alphonse de (1790–1869), French poet and politician. In addition to the poetry which, from the *Méditations poétiques* of 1820, established him as one of the leading figures in the French Romantic movement, he produced many volumes of biography, memoirs, political and historical works, novels, and travel writing. His work, both literary and historical, was widely translated into English from the late 1820s. His other collections of poetry include the *Nouvelles méditations poétiques* (1823), the *Harmonies poétiques et religieuses* (1830), and the *Recueillements poétiques* (1839); he also published two fragments of a projected epic poem, *Jocelyn* (1836) and *La Chute d'un ange* (1838), while in 1835 he published his account of a journey to Syria, Lebanon, and the Holy Land. In the provisional government of 1848 he served as minister of foreign affairs (*Trois mois au pouvoir*, 1848), withdrawing from public life in 1851. His historical works include the *Histoire des Girondins* (1847) and the *Histoire de la Révolution de 1848* (1849).

LAMB, Lady Caroline (1785–1828), daughter of the third earl of Bessborough, married William Lamb, afterwards second Viscount Melbourne. In 1812, shortly after her marriage, she became infatuated with *Byron, and about the same time began to show signs of serious mental instability. Her first novel, *Glenarvon*, published anonymously in 1816 after Byron had broken with her, is a wild *Gothic extravaganza, in which she herself is cast as the dashing Calantha and Byron as the fated, fascinating Glenarvon. The novel enjoyed a tremendous but brief *succès de scandale*. Neither *Graham Hamilton* (1822) nor *Ada Reis* (1823) is remembered. Her accidental meeting with Byron's funeral procession on its way to Hucknall Torkhard further provoked the disintegration of her mind.

LAMB, Charles (1775–1834), was born in London. His father, the Lovel of 'The Old Benchers of the Inner Temple' in *Essays of Elia*, was the clerk to Samuel Salt, a lawyer, whose house in Crown Office Row was Lamb's birthplace and his home during his youth. He was educated at Christ's Hospital, where he formed an enduring admiration for S. T. *Coleridge. After a few months at the South Sea House (see ESSAYS OF ELIA), he obtained at 17 an appointment in the East India House, where he remained until his retirement in 1825. For a short time in 1795–6 he was mentally deranged, and the threat of madness became a shadow on his life. In 1796 his sister Mary, in a fit of insanity, killed their mother. Lamb undertook the charge of his sister, who remained liable to periodic breakdowns, and she repaid him with great sympathy and affection. They lived in London, which Lamb loved, then from 1823 in Islington, Enfield, and Edmonton, where Lamb died. Four sonnets of Lamb's appeared in 1796 in a volume of poems by Coleridge, who became a lifelong friend. In 1798 appeared *Blank Verse* by Charles Lloyd and Charles Lamb, which included the poem 'The Old Familiar Faces'. In the same year appeared the *Tale of Rosamund Gray and Old Blind Margaret*, a melodramatic, sentimental village tragedy, in which Rosamund meets a fate worse than death, then death itself. In 1802 Lamb published *John Woodvil* (at first called *Pride's Cure*), an ineffective tragedy in the Elizabethan style; and in 1806 his farce *Mr H* proved a failure at Drury Lane. With his sister he wrote *Tales from Shakespear* (1807), designed to make the stories of Shakespeare's plays familiar to the young; and also *Mrs Leicester's School* (1809), a collection of stories. *The Adventures of Ulysses* (1808) was an attempt to do for the *Odyssey* what they had done for Shakespeare. In 1808 he published *Specimens of English Dramatic Poets who lived about the time of Shakespeare*. Between 1810 and 1820 his literary output was not great. It includes the essays 'On the

Tragedies of Shakespeare', which presents the characters of the tragedies as individual 'objects of meditation', stripped of their dramatic function; and an admiring analysis 'On the Genius and Character of Hogarth' in 1811. He wrote for Leigh Hunt's *Reflector and for the *Examiner, and in 1814 contributed to the *Quarterly Review an article (much altered by *Gifford, the editor) on Wordsworth's *The Excursion, commending the originality of Wordsworth's genius, as well as his high seriousness. A collection of his miscellaneous writings in prose and verse appeared in 1818. From 1820 to 1823 Lamb was a regular contributor to the *London Magazine, in which appeared the first series of essays known as *Essays of Elia, published in a collected volume in 1823. The second series was published in 1833. Of his poems the best known are 'The Old Familiar Faces', the lyrical ballad 'Hester' (1803), and an elegy 'On an Infant dying as soon as born' (1827), probably his finest poem. Album Verses (1830) includes many other lyrics and sonnets.

A. C. *Bradley regarded Lamb as the greatest critic of his century, but few would follow Bradley quite so far. Lamb's literary criticism is scattered and small in volume. He had no interest in critical theory, and a poor sense of structure; as he wrote to *Godwin: 'I cannot grasp at a whole.' But his sympathies were wide and his sensitivity acute; while careful always to approve moral worth he also enjoys 'an airing beyond the diocese of strict conscience', as into the then little read Jacobean or Restoration drama. His habit of brief but accurate characterization, and of generalized but perceptive comment (such as he employs in his Specimens) results in original and illuminating work. He was a prolific letter-writer of great charm and quality, and many of his observations on literature are scattered throughout the letters. He was much loved, and his various homes were a meeting-place for Coleridge, *Wordsworth, Leigh *Hunt, *Hazlitt, *Southey, and other literary men. His Letters have been edited by E. W. Marrs (3 vols., 1975–8); see also D. *Cecil, A Portrait of Charles Lamb (1983) and the standard life by E. V. *Lucas (1905).

LAMB, Mary Ann (1764–1847), the sister of Charles *Lamb, under whose name the facts of her life will be found. She collaborated with her brother in writing for children the prose Tales from Shakespear (1807), and she wrote the greater part of Mrs Leicester's School (1809), a book of stories for children containing many autobiographical details, to which her brother contributed three tales.

Lambert, General, Mrs, Theo, and Hetty, characters in Thackeray's *The Virginians.

LAMBERT, Constant (1905–51), English composer, conductor, and writer on music. Like W. *Walton, Lambert was a member of the *Sitwell circle, and his best-known work, The Rio Grande (1928), is a brilliant and jazzy setting for piano solo, chorus, contralto, and orchestra of a poem by Sacheverell Sitwell. In a different but equally characteristic vein is the masque to words from *Nashe's 'pleasant comedy' Summer's Last Will and Testament (1936), and there is a deeply nostalgic version of the dirge from Cymbeline, 'Fear no more the heat of the sun' (1940). Only marginally connected with Shakespeare, however, is the ballet Romeo and Juliet (written for Diaghilev in 1926), in which an actor and actress, rehearsing Shakespeare's play, themselves fall in love and eventually elope in an aeroplane.

As a writer Lambert's stimulating but controversial book Music Ho! (1934), subtitled 'A Study of Music in Decline', was enthusiastically acclaimed in its day: it has since come in for a good deal of criticism on grounds of prejudice, but still retains its status as a classic of its period and a testimony of an exceptional musical and critical intelligence. (See also MUSIC, LITERATURE OF.)

Lambeth Books, a name sometimes given to the symbolic poems which *Blake wrote and etched while living at Lambeth (1790–1800). They include America, *Europe, and The Song of Los.

Lament of Tasso, The, a poem by Lord *Byron, published 1817.

The poem tells the story of the tragic love of the imprisoned *Tasso for Leonora d'Este, and of the writing of his *Jerusalem Delivered.

'Lamia', a narrative poem by *Keats, written 1819, published 1820.

The story was taken from Burton's *Anatomy of Melancholy, there quoted from Philostratus. Lamia, a sorceress, is transformed by Hermes from a serpent into a beautiful woman. She loves the serious young Corinthian Lycius, and he, spellbound by her beauty and believing her human, falls in love with her. They retire to her secret and sumptuous palace in Corinth. Here, not content with his happiness and against Lamia's wishes, Lycius orders a magnificent bridal feast and summons his friends. Among them, though uninvited, comes his old guide and mentor, the sage Apollonius, who pierces Lamia's disguise and calls her by her name. Her beauty withers, with a frightful scream she vanishes, and Lycius dies in a frenzy of grief. Keats wrote to his brother George that he believed the poem had 'a sort of fire in it' and that it would please a sensation-loving public. Interpretations of the work vary considerably, but it is clearly connected with Keats's persistent theme of the relationship between the real and the ideal.

LAMMING, George Eric (1927–   ), novelist

and poet, born in Barbados. His first novel, *In the Castle of the Skin* (1953), is the story of a boy's adolescence in a small peasant village in Barbados, and of his growing awareness of the colonial situation; this was followed by *The Emigrants* (1954), which describes the voyage to and arrival in Britain of a group of West Indians. *Of Age and Innocence* (1958) and *Season of Adventure* (1960) are more optimistic works, set on the imaginary island of San Cristobal. Other works include *Water with Berries* (1971) and *Natives of my Person* (1972). *Thiong'o commented (*Homecomings*, 1972) that Lamming's novels are dominated by the theme of 'exile as a universal experience'.

Lammle, Alfred and Sophronia, in Dickens's *Our Mutual Friend*, unscrupulous social adventurers.

Lamorak de Galis (of Wales), Sir, in *Malory, the brother of Perceval and son of Pellinore. Just as his father kills King Lot of Orkney and is killed by Lot's son Gawain, he is slain by the four sons of King Lot because of his adultery with Arthur's sister Morgawse, the wife of King Lot. In some versions he is treacherously stabbed in the back by Mordred; in others he is slain without ignobility by Gawain.

LA MOTTE FOUQUÉ, see UNDINE.

LAMPEDUSA, Giuseppe Tomasi Di (1896–1957), Sicilian aristocrat, author of a remarkable novel, *Il gattopardo* (*The Leopard*, 1955–6), which describes the reactions of a noble Sicilian family to the political and social changes following Garibaldi's annexation of Sicily in 1860.

LANCASTER, Joseph (1778–1838), the founder of a system of education, based 'on general Christian principles' (i.e. undenominational), in schools organized 'on the monitorial or mutual system', described in *Improvements in Education* (1803). The proposal gave rise to heated controversy, of which the outcome was the 'voluntary system' of elementary schools that endured until 1870.

Lancelot, see LAUNCELOT OF THE LAKE.

Lancelot du Lake, Sir, a ballad included in Percy's *Reliques*, recounting the adventure of Lancelot with Tarquin, who had in prison three-score of Arthur's knights. Lancelot kills him and liberates the knights. Falstaff sings a snatch from this ballad in Shakespeare's 2 *Henry IV* (II. iv).

Land, A, see HAWKES, J.

Landeval, Sir, see SIR LAUNFAL.

Landfall, the most important of New Zealand's literary periodicals, founded in 1947 as a quarterly.

Landless, Neville and Helena, characters in Dickens's *Edwin Drood*.

LANDON, Letitia Elizabeth (1802–38), wrote under the initials L.E.L., and supported herself from an early age by her writing. She published between 1824 and her death a number of volumes of poetry, contributed to periodicals, and wrote several novels, of which the best is *Ethel Churchill* (1837). Her unprotected position as a woman in the literary world gave rise to various vague scandals linking her name to *Maginn and, less certainly, to *Bulwer-Lytton, who appears with his wife Rosina in her novel *Romance and Reality* (1831). Such rumours caused her to break off her engagement to J. *Forster, and she later married George Maclean, with whom she travelled to West Africa, where she died shortly afterwards in mysterious circumstances, probably from an overdose of prussic acid.

LANDOR, Robert Eyres (1781–1869), a cleric, youngest brother of W. S. *Landor, was the author of five tragedies, including *The Count of Arezzi* (1823), which was attributed to *Byron and enjoyed a brief success for that reason. He also published a poem, *The Impious Feast* (1828); a fantastic prose story, *The Fawn of Sertorius* (1846); and *The Fountain of Arethusa* (1848), dialogues between a certain Anthony Lugwardine and famous men of classical times.

LANDOR, Walter Savage (1775–1864), was educated at Rugby and at Trinity College, Oxford, where he was rusticated. An intractable temper involved him in trouble throughout his life. As a young man he fought as a volunteer in Spain against the French. In 1795 he published a miscellany of verses, *Poems*, and in 1798 an epic poem in seven books, *Gebir*. In 1802 followed *Poetry by the author of Gebir*, and in 1806 another collection of poems, *Simonidea*, which included *'Rose Aylmer'. In 1811 he married Julia Thuillier. A dramatic tragedy, *Count Julian*, followed in 1812, but was never staged. In the same year Landor's intemperate 'Commentary on the Memoirs of Mr Fox' had to be suppressed. In 1815 he began a long residence in Italy, which did not end until 1835, when he separated from his wife. The *Imaginary Conversations of literary men and statesmen* appeared 1824–9, and a volume containing *Count Julian, Gebir*, and new poems, came out in 1831. In 1834 he published the light-hearted *Citation and Examination of William Shakespeare touching Deer-Stealing*. *Pericles and Aspasia*, a full-length work which grew out of an imaginary conversation, appeared in 1836, and in 1837 *The Pentameron*, in which *Boccaccio and *Petrarch discuss the poetry of *Dante. The trilogy *Andrea of Hungary, Giovanna of Naples*, and *Fra Rupert* was published in 1839–40, and *The Hellenics*, a re-telling in verse of various Greek myths, completed in 1847. In 1853 appeared *Imaginary Conversations of Greeks and Romans*. His work was much admired by R. *Browning and many others, but has not recently enjoyed any great esteem. Boythorn in Dickens's *Bleak House* is a genial caricature of Landor. See *Landor: a Replevin* (1958) by M. Elwin.

'Land o' the Leal, The' (the land of the blessed departed), the title of a song by Lady *Nairne.

LANDSEER, Sir Edwin Henry (1802–73), painter, the son of an engraver. A visit to Sir W. *Scott in 1824 introduced him to the landscapes of Scotland, which featured prominently in his work. Professional and social success came rapidly to him; he enjoyed the favour of Queen Victoria, and his friends included *Dickens, *Thackeray, *Macready, and *D'Orsay. Although he painted portraits, historical scenes (mostly from Scott), and, in his late days, some strange allegorical works, he is best remembered for his animal paintings, such as *The Monarch of the Glen* and *Dignity and Impudence*.

LANE, Allen (1902–70), publisher, was born Allen Lane Williams, in Bristol, and took the name Allen Lane when he went to London to work at the Bodley Head for his distant cousin, 'Uncle John' *Lane. With the foundation in 1935 of the *Penguin series, he became a pioneer in the paperback revolution in publishing.

LANE, Edward William (1801–76), Arabic scholar, published in 1836 *An Account of the Manners and Customs of the Modern Egyptians* and in 1838–40 a translation of *The Thousand and One Nights* (see ARABIAN NIGHTS ENTERTAINMENTS), an expurgated but scholarly version with copious notes illustrating his profound knowledge of Egyptian customs and beliefs. His publishers resisted his attempts to reproduce authentic Arabic names and spellings, preferring the more familiar anglicized versions. Sir R. *Burton attacked his and other early translations as 'garbled and mutilated, unsexed and unsouled'.

LANE, John (1854–1925), *fin-de-siècle* publisher who, with Charles Elkin Mathews, established The Bodley Head in 1887. Authors who appeared under its imprint included *Davidson, *Dowson, *Le Gallienne, J. A. *Symonds, and *Wilde. The firm gained a high reputation for the quality of its publications, and as publishers of *The Yellow Book* it became the centre of ferment in art and letters in the 'nineties'.

LANEHAM, or **LANGHAM,** Robert, the name attributed to the author of the letter describing some of the entertainments put on by the earl of *Leicester for the queen's visit to Kenilworth in 1575. The pamphlet is probably in fact by William Patten. Shakespeare may have remembered the shows in *A Midsummer Night's Dream* (II. i. 148–68) and Scott used the description in *Kenilworth*. The list of Captain Cox's books which 'Laneham' gives is an important source for the titles of ballads, romances, and other popular literature still read at this time. The ghost of Captain Cox appears again in *Jonson's *Masque of Owles* (1624).

LANFRANC (*c*.1015–89), born in Pavia, archbishop of Canterbury from 1070 to his death, whereupon William Rufus left the see vacant until the appointment of *Anselm in 1093. He was a man of wide secular and classical learning (including Greek) who worked successfully with William the Conqueror and rebuilt the cathedral at Canterbury which had been burnt down in 1067. He was a celebrated teacher who had preceded Anselm as prior of Bec, from 1045 to 1070. See A. J. Macdonald, *Lanfranc* (1926).

LANG, Andrew (1844–1912), born at Selkirk, was educated at St Andrews University and at Oxford, where he became a fellow of Merton. In 1875 he settled down in London to a life of journalism and letters, becoming one of the most prolific and versatile writers of his day as poet, essayist, reviewer, biographer, bibliographer, historian, translator, editor, and anthropologist.

His first book of verse, *Ballads and Lyrics of Old France* (1872), was followed by several others, including *Ballades in Blue China* (1880, 1881), *Rhymes à la Mode* (1884), and *Grass of Parnassus* (1888). Many of his poems were written in the old French forms of *rondeau, *triolet, etc. The poor reception of his ambitious narrative poem *Helen of Troy* (1882) discouraged him from serious poetry, and his verse became increasingly lightweight. His *Collected Poems* (4 vols) was published in 1923.

Lang appears to have valued himself most as an anthropologist. His first book on folklore, *Custom and Myth*, did not appear until 1884, but contained papers written and printed much earlier. *Myth, Ritual and Religion*, dealing chiefly with totemism, was published in 1887, and *The Making of Religion* in 1898, the second edition of *Myth, Ritual and Religion* in 1899 being drastically rehandled to harmonize with his more developed views. *Freud's *Totem and Taboo* refers to Lang's work in this field.

As a Greek scholar Lang devoted himself largely to *Homer. He was one of the joint authors (with S. H. Butcher) of prose versions of the *Odyssey* (1879, preceded by his well known sonnet, 'The Odyssey'), and (with W. Leaf and E. Myers) of the *Iliad* (1883). He wrote three books on the Homeric question, arguing the unity of Homer. He also took part in the *Baconian controversy, arguing in favour of Shakespearian authorship, in *Shakespeare, Bacon and the Great Unknown* (1912).

His many works of *belles-lettres*, imaginary letters and dialogues, literary reminiscences, historical monographs, etc., are now largely forgotten (e.g. *The Library*, 1881; *Letters to Dead Authors*, 1886; *Old Friends*, 1890; *Pickle Spy*, 1897), as are his melodramatic novels, which include *The Mark of Cain* (1886) and *The Disentanglers* (1902). He collaborated with H. R. *Haggard in *The World's Desire* (1891) and with A. E. W. *Mason in *Parson Kelly* (1899). As a critic he showed a distinct preference for romantic and adventurous works such as those of Haggard, A. Hope (*Hawkins), and A. C. *Doyle, while he disliked *Hardy and the later H. *James; James in turn in a letter to *Gosse attacked Lang for cultivating 'the puerile imagination and the fourth-rate opinion'.

Ironically or appropriately, he is now perhaps best remembered for his own fairy-tales, which include *The Gold of Fairnilee* (1888, set in Scotland) and *Prince Prigio* (1889, set in Pantouflia), and for his collections of fairy-tales, each volume named after a different colour; the first was *The Blue Fairy Book* (1889). The series did much to revive an interest in fairy-tales, which had been for some time out of fashion; in its compilation Lang was greatly aided by his wife Leonora (*née* Alleyne). In this connection, see also Lang's introduction to *Perrault's Popular Tales* (1888, see PERRAULT) in which he discusses the origins of many nursery stories. There is a critical biography of Lang by R. L. Green (1946).

LANGHORNE, John (1735–79), worked first as a tutor near Ripon, in 1768 became rector of Blagdon, Somerset, and was from 1772 a justice of the peace. He published several volumes of poetry, an *Oriental tale, and a reply to Charles *Churchill's *Prophecy of Famine* entitled *Genius and Valour: a Scotch pastoral* (1764). He edited the works of W. *Collins (1765) and, with his brother William (1721–72), translated *Plutarch's *Lives* (1770). His best-remembered poem is *The Country Justice* (1774), which was praised by *Wordsworth for bringing 'the Muse into the Company of Common Life', and by *Davie in the introduction to his anthology *The Late Augustans* (1958) for its earnest and informed response to 'the strain of historical change'.

LANGLAND, William (perhaps *c*.1330–*c*.1386), the author of *Piers Plowman*, of whose identity and life very little is known for certain. That the 'lives' of Langland reconstructed from internal evidence in the poem were highly dubious was demonstrated by George Kane in *Piers Plowman: The Evidence for Authorship* (1965). It seems that Langland lived in London, but that he had lived in the Malvern district of the West Midlands. Kane takes seriously the evidence of a note in the Trinity College, Dublin,

manuscript of the C-Text, that Langland was the son of Stacy de Rokayle of Shipton-under-Wychwood in Oxfordshire. He was probably in minor orders. No other poem is now attributed to him; *Skeat's parallel-text edition of the poem is still printed with *Richard the Redeless* which Skeat believed was by Langland but cannot be his, being part of *Mum and the Sothsegger*, which dates from the very early 15th cent.

Langue d'oïl, the language of the north of France during the medieval period, so called to distinguish it from the *langue d'oc* (see PROVENÇAL), the distinction being based on the particle of affirmation: late Latin 'hoc ille' for 'yes' became 'o'il' in the North and 'oc' in the South. The distinction of language corresponded to a difference of culture and literature, the *langue d'oïl* being the literary medium of the *trouvères, the *langue d'oc*, or Provençal, that of the *troubadours. The dialects of the *langue d'oïl*, particularly Norman, Picard, and Francien (the language of the Paris region), each had some literary independence during the 12th and 13th cents, but Francien gradually became the standard language, and is the ancestor of modern standard French.

Languish, Lydia, the heroine of Sheridan's *The Rivals*.

LANIER, Emilia, *née* Bassano (1569–1645), was a member of a large Italian family of musicians living in London. *Rowse has edited her collection of religious poems *Salve Deus Rex Iudaeorum* (1611) under the title *The Poems of Shakespeare's Dark Lady* (1978). There is, however, no documentary proof that she and Shakespeare knew each other.

LANIER, Sidney (1842–81), American poet and critic, born in Georgia. After serving in the Confederate army during the Civil War, he devoted himself to poetry, in spite of ill health and poverty. He published his *Poems* in 1877; a complete *Poems* appeared in 1884, with further additions in subsequent editions. His lyrical and metrically experimental verse is strongly influenced by his knowledge and practice of music. He became a lecturer in English at Johns Hopkins University in 1879, and his critical writings include *The Science of English Verse* (1880).

Laodicean, A, a novel by T. *Hardy, published 1881.

Paula Power is a vacillating young woman, the Laodicean of the title. Faced with the ordeal of total immersion, according to her father's Baptist faith, she cannot take the plunge. She wavers between her love for George Somerset, a young architect, and Captain de Stancy, the heir of an ancient family which once owned the castle in which she now lives. She accepts the more romantic Captain, but discovers in time a plot hatched by Willy Dare, his illegitimate son, to blacken the character of George Somerset. She finally marries Somerset, her ancient castle is burned to the ground, and she remains a Laodicean to the end.

Laokoon, an essay in literary and artistic criticism by G. E. *Lessing, published 1766. It takes its title from the celebrated group of statuary disinterred at Rome in the 16th cent. representing Laocoön and his sons in the coils of a serpent. Adopting this group and the Horatian formula 'ut pictura poesis' ('poetry resembles painting') as the initial subject of discussion, Lessing examines the grounds for the divergence in the treatment of the scene by the artist and by *Virgil who described it, and develops the essential differences between the art of poetry and the plastic arts. The work was left unfinished.

'Laon and Cythna', see REVOLT OF ISLAM, THE.

Laputa, see GULLIVER'S TRAVELS.

Lara, a poem by Lord *Byron, published 1814.
Lara is in fact Conrad of * The Corsair returned to his domains in Spain accompanied by his page Kaled, who is his love, the slave Gulnare, in disguise. Lara lives, like other *'Byronic' heroes, aloof and alien, shrouded in mystery. He is, however, recognized as Conrad, and becomes involved in a feud in which he is finally killed, dying in the arms of Kaled.

LARKIN, Philip Arthur (1922–   ), poet and novelist, was born in Coventry and educated at King Henry VIII School, Coventry, and at St John's College, Oxford, where he was a contemporary of K. *Amis and developed an interest in jazz which was later to produce a volume of essays, All What Jazz (1970). From 1943 he worked in various libraries before becoming librarian of the Brynmor Jones Library in Hull. Larkin's early poems appeared in an anthology, Poetry from Oxford in Wartime (1944), and a collection, The North Ship (1945), and were, by his own account, much influenced by *Yeats. He then published Jill (1946), set in wartime Oxford, a novel which describes the undergraduate career of John Kemp, a working-class boy from Lancashire, and his encounters with the world of traditional privilege; 'Jill' is the fantasy sister he creates, who is transformed into a teasing reality. A second novel, A Girl in Winter (1947), relates a day in the life of refugee librarian Katherine Lind, working in a drab English provincial town, with a lengthy flashback to an abortive adolescent romance with a pen-friend. Larkin's own poetic voice (with a new allegiance to *Hardy rather than Yeats) became distinct in The Less Deceived (1955), where the colloquial bravura of a poem like 'Toads' is offset by the half-tones and somewhat bitter lyricism of other pieces; his name was at this time associated with the *Movement,

and his work appeared in *New Lines (1956) The Whitsun Weddings (1964) adds a range o melancholy urban and suburban provincial land scapes, a satiric sociological commentary, an more stoic wit, manifested in 'Toads Revisited' with its characteristic Larkin conclusion: 'Giv me your arm, old toad; | Help me down Ceme tery Road.' Many of the poems in High Win dows (1974), notably 'The Old Fools', show a preoccupation with death and transience; i 'Annus Mirabilis' and 'Posterity' the poet ironi cally places himself as somewhat defiantly ou of date; in the words of his fictitious America biographer: 'One of those old-type natura fouled-up guys.' Throughout his work, th adaptation of contemporary speech rhythms an vocabulary to an unobtrusive metrical elegance is highly distinctive. Larkin edited The Oxfor Book of Twentieth Century English Verse (1973) a wide-ranging selection which includes wor by many little known or unfashionable poets. volume of essays, Required Writing, was pub lished in 1983.

Lark Rise to Candleford, see THOMPSON FLORA.

LA ROCHEFOUCAULD, François de Mar sillac, duc de (1613–80), French courtier soldier and moralist, author of Réflexions ou sen tences et maximes morales (1665), usually know as Maximes. By the 5th (1678) edition, the Max imes consisted of 504 brief reflections of extrem concision and finish which range widely ove human nature and society, investigating and ex tending the sense of such traditional moral con cepts as love, friendship, wit and folly, virtue an vice, happiness and misfortune. The epigraph t the collection, 'Our virtues are mostly vices i disguise', expresses one of its leading themes another is the discovery of the springs of men' actions in their vanity, self-interest, desire fo praise, and readiness to deceive themselves. Th possibility of noble conduct and genuine wort is admitted, but most men and women ar judged to be ruled by circumstances and thei passions. There are several English translation of the Maximes in the 17th and 18th cents including one by A. *Behn: Reflections o morality or Seneca unmasqued (1685).

LAROUSSE, Pierre (1817–75), Frenc grammarian, lexicographer, and encyclopaedist he edited and (in part) compiled the Grand Dic tionnaire universel du XIXe siècle (1866–76), vast encyclopaedia which aimed to comprehen every department of human knowledge. I 1852 he founded, together with Augustin Boyer, the publishing house of Larousse, whic continues to issue the dictionaries and referenc works that bear its name.

La Saisiaz and The Two Poets of Croisic, tw long poems by R. *Browning, published 1878 the third and final such pairing in his work.

La Saisiaz is a philosophical elegy prompted by the sudden death of a close friend of Browning's, with whom he had been holidaying in a chalet called 'La Saisiaz' (the sun) near Geneva. It deals with the central religious question 'Does the soul survive the body? Is there God's self, no or yes?', though the terms are equally applicable to the creative imagination; the poem, like *In Memoriam*, is as much a self-scrutiny as a tribute to the dead. *The Two Poets of Croisic* is much less solemn in tone than *La Saisiaz*: it tells the stories of two obscure poets associated with the small village of Croisic in Brittany, each of the stories illustrating, in comic and grotesque vein, the folly of human (and specifically poetic) aspiration. Coming immediately after *La Saisiaz*, in which Browning had asserted (however equivocally) his own status as a visionary poet, *The Two Poets of Croisic* makes a strong and effective contrast.

LAS CASAS, Bartolomé de (?1474–1566), Spanish historian and bishop of Chaipa (Mexico), famous for his protest against the ill treatment by his countrymen of the Indians of South America, in his *Very Brief Account of the Ruin of the Indies* (1542). He also wrote an unfinished general *History of the Indies*.

Lassalle, Ferdinand, see TRAGIC COMEDIANS, THE.

Last Chronicle of Barset, The, a novel by A. *Trollope, published 1867, the last of the *'Barsetshire' series.

The Revd Josiah Crawley is accused of fraudulently acquiring a cheque for £20, and using it to pay off the debts he inevitably incurs in an attempt to subsist on his meagre curate's income. As ever, Crawley broods deeply over his wrongs, but he cannot remember the exact origin of the cheque and is thus committed for trial. Even before the sessions come on the autocratic Mrs Proudie pre-judges his case, and attempts to oust Crawley from his church. Matters are not finally cleared up in Crawley's favour until Dean Arabin's family are recalled from the Continent, whereupon Mrs Arabin explains her part in the muddle. At the close of the novel the Crawley fortunes brighten decidedly: Mr Crawley is presented with the fatter living of St Ewold's, and the archdeacon finally removes his opposition to the marriage of Grace Crawley and his son, Major Grantly.

Interleaved with the theme of Crawley's cheque is the London life of Johnny Eames and his continuing love for Lily Dale despite his unfortunate flirtation with Madalina Demolines; and the deaths of Mrs Proudie and Mr Harding, once warden of Hiram's Hospital.

Last Days of Pompeii, The, a novel by *Bulwer-Lytton.

Last Man, The, (1) a collection of poems by T. *Campbell and T. *Hood; (2) a novel by M. *Shelley.

Last of the Barons, The, a historical novel by *Bulwer-Lytton.

Last of the Mohicans, The, a novel by J. F. *Cooper.

Last Tycoon, The, a novel by F. S. *Fitzgerald.

Latimer, Darsie, in Scott's *Redgauntlet*, the name borne by the hero, Sir Arthur Darsie Redgauntlet.

LATIMER, Hugh (?1492–1555), was educated at Cambridge, took priest's orders, and became known as a preacher. He was accused of heresy, brought before convocation, and absolved on making a complete submission, 1532. He was appointed bishop of Worcester in 1535, but resigned his bishopric and was kept in custody for a year because he could not support the Act of the Six Articles, 1539. His famous sermon 'of the plough' was preached in 1548. Latimer was committed to the Tower on Mary's accession, 1553; was sent to Oxford with *Ridley and *Cranmer to defend his views before the leading divines of the University, 1554; and was condemned as a heretic and burnt at Oxford with Ridley on 16 Oct. 1555. His extant writings were edited for the Parker Society in 1844–5. They are notable for a simple vernacular style and for their graphic and vivid illustrations.

Latter-Day Pamphlets, see CARLYLE, T.

LAUD, William (1573–1645), educated at St John's College, Oxford, became predominant in the Church of England at Charles I's accession, being at the time bishop of St David's. He was promoted successively to the sees of Bath and Wells and London, and became archbishop of Canterbury (1633). He supported the king in his struggle with the Commons and adopted the policy of enforcing uniformity in the Church of England. He was impeached of high treason by the Long Parliament in 1640, committed to the Tower in 1641, tried in 1644, condemned, and beheaded. A few of his sermons were published in 1651, and a collected edition of his works in 1696–1700. In these he shows himself a sturdy defender of the Anglican Church as a national institution, resisting the claim of the Church of Rome to universality and infallibility, and equally resisting the claims of Puritanism. Laud gave some 1,300 manuscripts in 18 different languages, and his collection of coins, to the Bodleian Library.

LAUDER, William (d. 1771), literary forger, a good classical scholar, was proved to have interpolated in the works of Masenius and Staphorstius (17th-cent. Latin poets) extracts from a Latin verse rendering of *Paradise Lost.* Incidentally he proved that *Milton had deeply studied the works of modern Latin poets.

Launce, clownish servant to *Proteus in Shakespeare's *Two Gentlemen of Verona.*

Launcelot Gobbo, see GOBBO, LAUNCELOT.

Launcelot Greaves, see SIR LAUNCELOT GREAVES.

Launcelot of the Lake, Sir, the greatest and most romantic of the knights of the Round Table, son of King *Ban of Benwick in Brittany, father of *Galahad by *Elaine Sans Pere (daughter of King *Pelleas) and the lover of Guinevere. He is a relatively late development in the English Arthurian tradition, not appearing at length before the 14th cent., although the story of his love for Guinevere is the subject of *Chrétien de Troyes' *Lancelot* (c.1170s) and of the early 13th-cent. French prose 'Vulgate' *Lancelot* (and there is a lost Anglo-Norman story earlier than these). His name, which probably has Welsh etymological connections, refers to a tradition that he was abducted at birth and brought up by a lake-lady, before being brought by a hermit to Arthur's court. Chrétien's romance *Lancelot, or Le Chevalier de la Charrette,* is concerned exclusively with the love of Lancelot and Guinevere, presented faithfully as a *Courtly Love affair, to an extent that has been thought to be self-parodying by some critics. The main elements of the Launcelot story are found in the three romances of the French prose cycle: *Lancelot*; the *Queste del Saint Graal*; and the *Mort Artu* (for these, see ch. 22, 'The Vulgate Cycle', by Jean Frappier in R. S. Loomis, *Arthurian Literature in the Middle Ages,* 1959). *Malory's treatment of Launcelot is closely based on this: Launcelot's love for the queen is again central; it is strained by his relations with Elaine the Fair Maid of Astolat whose death ends Guinevere's jealousy. Their love is betrayed by *Agravain; the lovers flee to Launcelot's castle of *Joyous Gard and, after a siege, the queen is restored to Arthur. Launcelot withdraws to Brittany where he is pursued by Arthur and Gawain; in the ensuing clash Launcelot injures Gawain. Arthur returns to Dover to fight the usurping *Modred and Gawain is killed. Launcelot comes back to help the king, but arrives too late for the final battle in Cornwall in which both Arthur and Modred die. He finds that Guinevere has become a nun, so he becomes a priest. On his death he is carried to Joyous Gard where visions suggest that he is taken to heaven. He is very prominent in Malory who stresses the tragedy of his imperfection (his courtly amour with the queen) which prevents his full achievement of the *Grail, though he has glimpses of it. Malory also makes much of his later bitter hatred by Gawain because of his killing of

Gawain's brothers; the implacability of Gawain's hatred prevents Arthur from making a peace with Launcelot which might have enabled them to ally to defeat Modred. See T. P. Cross and W. A. Nitze, *Lancelot and Guenevere* (1930).

Launfal, Sir, see SIR LAUNFAL.

Laura, (1) see PETRARCH; (2) the wife of Beppo in Byron's poem *Beppo.*

Laurence, Friar, in Shakespeare's *Romeo and Juliet,* counsellor and confessor to the lovers, who performs their marriage at the end of Act II.

Laurentian Library, The, had its origin in the private collections of Cosimo and Lorenzo de' *Medici in the 15th cent. On the expulsion of the Medici from Florence the collection passed to the monks of S. Marco in Florence and was subsequently purchased from them by *Leo X, taken to Rome, and enlarged by him, with the intention that it should ultimately be returned to Florence. This intention was carried out by Clement VII (also a Medici).

LAURIE, Annie (1682–1764), the subject of the famous Scottish song that bears her name. She was the daughter of Sir Robert Laurie of Maxwelton, Dumfriesshire, and married Alexander Ferguson. The song was written by her rejected lover William Douglas. It was revised and set to music by Lady John Scott in 1835.

LAUTRÉAMONT, comte de, the pseudonym of Isidore-Lucien Ducasse (1846–70), French writer of prose poems. Little is known of his life, and his reputation depends largely on the prominence given to his work by the *Surrealists. *Les Chants de Maldoror,* a work of violent and anguished inspiration, appeared in 1868, and his *Poésies* in 1870.

LAVATER, Johann Kaspar (1741–1801), Swiss theologian and poet, and a close friend of *Fuseli. He is chiefly remembered as the inventor of the so-called science of phrenology (or Physiognomy, as he called it), which had many adherents, including the young G. *Eliot and her friend Charles Bray.

Lavengro, The Scholar—The Gypsy—The Priest, a narrative by G. *Borrow, published 1851. 'Lavengro', in gypsy language, means 'philologist'. The name was supplied to Borrow in his youth by Ambrose Smith, who figures in this work as Jasper Petulengro.

This work purports to be the story of Borrow's own wandering, restless life, but in it, as in his other works, fact is mingled with fiction. The son of a professional soldier, he had followed his parents while they moved from station to station around England, Scotland, and Ireland, visiting strange places and striking up unusual friendships on his travels—he became attached to a family of gypsies and met tinkers, including the Flaming Tinman, with whom he had a memorable fight, horse-copers, an old apple-woman (also a receiver of stolen goods), and a brace of future murderers. He tells the reader much of his comparative study of languages (though his scholarship is often suspect); he had violent prejudices, including a savage hatred of the Roman Catholic Church, that frequently overflow into his books. The book closes in the midst of the romantic episode with Belle Berners, an Amazonian vagrant, which is resumed in *The Romany Rye*.

Lavinia, Titus's daughter, who is raped and mutilated in Shakespeare's *Titus Andronicus*.

LAW, William (1686–1761), born at King's Cliffe near Stamford, the son of a grocer, was elected a fellow of Emmanuel College, Cambridge, but, declining to take the oath of allegiance to George I, lost his fellowship. Edward Gibbon made him the tutor of his son, the father of the historian *Gibbon, in c.1727, and he remained as an honoured friend of the family in their Putney home until 1740, when he returned to King's Cliffe and became the centre of a small spiritual community which included the historian's aunt Hester.

Law's earlier writings are of a controversial nature; he replied to Bishop *Hoadly's latitudinarian doctrine in *Three Letters to the Bishop of Bangor* (1717–19, see BANGORIAN CONTROVERSY); attacked *Mandeville in *Remarks upon the Fable of the Bees* (1723); outdid *Collier in his condemnation of the theatre in *Absolute Unlawfulness of the Stage-Entertainment* (1726); and attacked the *Deists and particularly Tindal in *The Case for Reason* (1731). But he is chiefly remembered for his treatises of practical morality, *A Practical Treatise on Christian Perfection* (1726), and more particularly *A Serious Call to a Devout and Holy Life* (1728). This work greatly influenced Law's friend J. *Wesley, who said it 'will hardly be excelled, if it be equalled, in the English tongue, either for beauty of expression or for justice and depth of thought'. It had an equally profound effect on Dr *Johnson, who read it while at Oxford and told *Boswell that it was 'the first occasion of my thinking in earnest of religion'. It is addressed to believers, and urges them to a simple and pious way of life, with emphasis on private rather than public prayer; it is enlivened with many satiric character portraits of, for example, Calidus the business man, forced to live, eat, drink, pray, and take his pleasures at a great pace, and of Flavia, worldly, vain, but with 'an expensive collection of all our English poets'. Gibbon, whose *Autobiography* contains some interesting comments on Law, thought his Characters as good as those of *La Bruyère. See also BYROM for other aspects of his personality.

In later life Law became increasingly interested in mysticism and in the writings of *Boehme; some critics have seen in *The Spirit of Prayer* (1749–50) and *The Spirit of Love* (1752–4) a foreshadowing of *Blake's attacks on materialism and reason.

LAWES, Henry (1596–1662), and William (1602–1645), English composers. Of the two brothers, Henry was widely recognized in his day as the most important English song-writer of the period after *Dowland: his 430-odd songs include settings of *Carew (38), *Waller (16), *Herrick (14), *Suckling, *Lovelace, and *Milton, the best of them probably written after his entry into court circles as one of Charles I's musicians in 1631. As a particular friend of Milton, he arranged the original performances of *Arcades (c.1630) and *Comus (1634), for both of which he wrote the songs.

William was a more versatile composer, writing a great deal of instrumental music and contributing, in varying degrees, to the music of many stage works during the period immediately before the establishment of opera in England. He wrote a large part of the music for the most sumptuous of all English *masques, Shirley's *The Triumph of Peace* (1634), and composed incidental music for several of the masques and plays of *D'Avenant. In his vocal writing, like his brother, he experimented with a declamatory style on the lines of the new Italian 'stile recitativo', and in so doing paved the way for the later operatic developments of *Locke, *Blow, and *Purcell.

LAWLESS, Emily (1845–1913), daughter of an Irish peer, was author of the successful Irish novels *Hurrish* (1886), a peasant story set in Clare, and *Grania* (1892), set on the Aran Islands. She also wrote *With Essex in Ireland* (1890); a collection of poems, *With the Wild Geese* (1902); and a *Life of Maria Edgeworth* (1904).

LAWRENCE, D(avid) H(erbert) (1885–1930), was born at Eastwood, Nottinghamshire, one of five children of a miner and an ex-schoolteacher. He was often ill as a child (he was later to develop tuberculosis) and grew up in considerable poverty. His ill-suited parents quarrelled continually, and a passionate bond grew between Lawrence and his mother; she was determined to keep him out of the mines and encouraged him at school. This love for his mother had a crucial effect on his early life and work. With the help of a scholarship he attended Nottingham High School for three years, but at 15 was forced to give up his education and take a job for a short time as a clerk in a surgical goods factory and then became a pupil teacher. At this time he formed a close friendship with Jessie Chambers, a local farmer's daughter, the Miriam of *Sons and Lovers*. In 1906, having worked to save the necessary £20 fee, he took up a scholarship at Nottingham University College to study for a teacher's certificate.

He was already writing poetry and short stories and he now began his first novel *The White Peacock* (1911), which was followed by *The Trespasser* (1912). He taught for two years at an elementary school in Croydon but after the death of his mother he became seriously ill and was advised to give up teaching. His first major novel, *Sons and Lovers* (1913), is a faithful autobiographical account of these early years, though he was later to think he had been unjustly harsh about his father. In 1912 he met Frieda Weekley (*neé* von Richthofen), wife of his old professor at Nottingham. Six years older than Lawrence and mother of three children, she was dissatisfied with her marriage and suffocated by life in Nottingham. They fell in love and eloped to Germany. They were always on the move, always short of money, and their life together was passionate and stormy. Lawrence's nomadic life supplied him with material for much of his writing and he wrote four travel books of a very personal kind. He spent the war years in England and began to form friendships in literary and intellectual circles: A. *Huxley and his wife Maria, D. *Garnett, Lady O. *Morrell, J. M. Murry and K. *Mansfield, *Aldington, and B. *Russell (with whom he was later to quarrel bitterly). His next novel, *The Rainbow* (1915), was seized by the police and declared obscene; his frankness about sex, and his use of four-letter words, was to keep him in constant trouble with the law. He was outspoken in his criticism of the war (he was unfit for service); while living in Cornwall he and his German-born wife were persecuted as suspected German agents and he felt life in England to be intolerable. In 1917 he published a volume of poems, *Look! We Have Come Through!* and in 1919 he and Frieda left for Italy. He had finished his novel *Women in Love* in 1916 but was unable to find a publisher until 1920 in New York, where an action against it failed, and 1921 in London. In 1920 *The Lost Girl* (begun before the war) won the James Tait Black Memorial Prize, the only official honour he was to receive during his lifetime. *Aaron's Rod*, which shows the influence of *Nietzsche, followed in 1922 and the same year he began his serious travels, to Ceylon and Australia and finally to America and Mexico. While in Australia he wrote *Kangaroo, which appeared in 1923, the same year as a critical book, *Studies in Classic American Literature*.

Lawrence's output was remarkable considering his unsettled life, his poor health, and his now increasingly fraught relationship with his wife. He lived in constant anxiety about money, struggling to publish a few stories and articles in various periodicals, and was sometimes helped by well-to-do friends or admirers. While in Mexico he began work on *The Plumed Serpent* (1926) and wrote many short stories and poems. In 1923 Frieda returned to Europe alone, and after an exchange of tug-of-war letters Lawrence joined her in England. But he was miserable there and early the next year they were back in New Mexico at the Kiowa Ranch, where Lawrence had hoped to found Rananim, his ideal community. While on a visit to Old Mexico he fell desperately ill and was told that he was in an advanced state of tuberculosis, with two years to live. They returned to Italy, via England and Germany, settling first at the Villa Bernardo at Spotorno and finally near Florence at the Villa Mirenda. He became seriously interested in painting: in 1929, at an exhibition in London, 13 pictures were removed by the police and pronounced obscene. At the Villa Mirenda he also finished *Lady Chatterley's Lover, his last novel and the one that was to cause more furore than any other. It was privately printed in Florence in 1928 by his good friend Pino Orioli and was finally published in unexpurgated editions in the United States and England over 30 years later, after unsuccessful prosecutions for obscenity. It had become clear that he was dying and Frieda took him first to Germany and along to the south of France in search of what could only have been a miraculous cure. He died in Vence on 2 March 1930.

It is difficult now to understand the outrage occasioned by Lawrence's work which blinded many readers to its lasting value. He was a moralist (and at his worst a preacher); he believed that modern man was in danger of losing his ability to experience the quality of life. Passionately involved with his characters and the physical world of nature, he wrote of them with a fresh immediacy and vividness. His reputation as a short story writer has always been high, many stories appearing first in small collections (*The Prussian Officer*, 1914; *England, My England*, 1922; *The Woman Who Rode Away*, 1928 and in a complete edition in 3 vols, 1955). His travel books, containing a great deal of personal narrative, are *Twilight in Italy* (1916), *Sea and Sardinia* (1921), *Mornings in Mexico* (1927) and *Etruscan Places* (1932).

In his poems Lawrence wanted to be free of the weight of formalism but not, as he said, to 'dish up the fragments as a new substance'. At times uneven, his poetry always has the immediate and personal quality of his prose. His volumes include *Love Poems* (1913), *Amores* (1916), *Look! We Have Come Through!* (1917) *Birds, Beasts and Flowers* (1923), *Pansies* (1929) *Complete Poems* (3 vols, 1957).

Other non-fiction works include *Movement in European History* (1921), *Psychoanalysis and the Unconscious* (1921), *Fantasia of the Unconscious* (1922), *Studies in Classic American Literature* (1923), and *Apocalypse* (1931). *The Boy in the Bush* (1924) is a novel he wrote in conjunction with M. L. Skinner. A first collection of *The*

Letters of D. H. Lawrence (1932) was edited by A. *Huxley. A new edition, ed. J. T. Boulton, began to appear in 1979 (vol. I; vol. II, 1982).

LAWRENCE, George Alfred (1827–76), educated at Rugby and Balliol College, Oxford, was called to the bar but abandoned law for a literary career. His first and best-known novel, *Guy Livingstone* (1857), was an immediate and lasting success; its glorification of brute strength and questionable morality provoked criticism from those who objected to endowing the immoral, blood-lusting Livingstone with 'heroic qualities and social aplomb', but won applause from others for its lack of hypocrisy. As an example of 'muscular blackguardism', the novel showed a revolt against the 'muscular Christianity' of the time, and set a fashion not only in literature (*'Ouida' was a notable disciple) but even in the mode of dress and behaviour of the young men of the period. *Sword and Gown* followed in 1859, and *Border and Bastille* in 1863, which describes Lawrence's adventures when he attempted to join the Confederate forces during the American Civil War, was captured by Northern authorities, and sent back to England. He continued producing successful novels almost every other year. *Guy Livingstone* was parodied by *Harte in his 'Guy Heaveystone'.

LAWRENCE, Sir Thomas (1769–1830), painter. His portraits are distinguished for their courtliness and social elegance. He painted portraits for the Waterloo Chamber at Windsor of persons who took part in the defeat of Napoleon.

LAWRENCE, T(homas) E(dward) (1888–1935), the illegitimate son of an Anglo-Irish landowner, was educated at Jesus College, Oxford, where, under the guidance of D. G. *Hogarth, he became deeply interested in both archaeology and the Middle East. He studied Arabic, read *Doughty, travelled to Syria in 1909, and from 1910 to 1914 worked on the excavation of Carchemish, on the banks of the Euphrates. During this period he became involved with British Intelligence, and his daring exploits during the First World War won him the confidence and admiration of the Arabs, and later made him, as 'Lawrence of Arabia', a mythical figure in his own country. He entered Damascus in 1918 with the Arab forces after the defeat of the Turks, and after the war spent some time as adviser to the Colonial Office, resigning in 1922. His subsequent career was marked by mental breakdown, self-accusation, and anxiety about his own legend; he enlisted in the RAF in 1922 as an aircraft hand under the name of John Hume Ross, and a year later joined the tank corps as T. E. Shaw, a name he adopted by deed poll in 1927. He later returned to the RAF, retiring from it shortly before he was killed in a motor-cycle accident near his home at Clouds Hill, Dorset.

He began writing *The Seven Pillars of Wisdom*, his account of the Arab Revolt and his own part in it, shortly after the war (losing much of the text, which he later rewrote, while changing trains at Reading in 1919); he sought literary advice from E. M. *Forster (who found his style 'granular') and G. B. *Shaw, both of whom encouraged him greatly, and became close friends. (He formed an even closer friendship with Shaw's wife Charlotte, to whom he confided his most intimate anxieties.) It was printed for private circulation in a limited edition in 1926 (published 1935); a shortened version, *Revolt in the Desert*, was published in 1927. It has been described as the last great romantic war book, and W. S. *Churchill declared it one of 'the greatest books ever written in the English language'. Meanwhile Lawrence was working on a documentary account of army life, sketches of which he showed to Forster who found in them 'a world of infinite suffering, but of limited cruelty' (1928); these were published posthumously in 1936 (NY) and 1955 (England) as *The Mint*, by '352087 A/C Ross'.

Lawrence's complex personality and multiple roles as man of action, poet, ascetic, neurotic, and leader of men fascinated friends, writers, and the general public, and his many biographers have suggested various explanations for both his masochism and his heroism. *Auden (who based *The Ascent of F6* in part on the Lawrence legend) described his life in a review of Liddell Hart's biography in *Now and Then* (1934) as 'an allegory of the transformation of the Truly Weak Man into the Truly Strong Man'. He appeared, complete with motor cycle, as Private Meek in Shaw's *Too True to be Good* (performed 1932); in *Rattigan's play *Ross* (1960); and as the hero of the popular film *Lawrence of Arabia* (1962). His friend Henry *Williamson imagined him as a leader who might have formed with Hitler an Anglo-German alliance. It has been suggested that he was all things to all men, a character who acted as a mirror to those who wrote of him. Robert *Graves wrote the first authorized life (1927); *Aldington's in 1955 caused outrage by its iconoclastic portrayal of him as a hysterical homosexual. More recent attempts (e.g. *The Secret Lives of Lawrence of Arabia*, 1969, by P. Knightley and Simpson) have attempted to present a more balanced picture. See also his *Letters* (1938), ed. D. *Garnett, his introductions to *Doughty (1921) and R. *Garnett (1924), and his essay on *Flecker (1937).

Laws of Ecclesiastical Politie, Of the, by R. *Hooker, a philosophical and theological treatise of which four books appeared in 1593, the fifth in 1597. The sixth and eighth appeared in 1648, the seventh was first included in Gauden's edition of 1661–2. These last three books, as we have them, not published until after Hooker's death, do not represent work prepared by him for the press. The whole was reissued with a life of Hooker by I. *Walton in 1666.

The work is a defence, written in a dignified and harmonious prose, of the position of the Anglican Church against the attacks of the Puritans. The first book is a philosophical discussion of the origin and nature of law in general, as governing the universe and human society, and of the distinction between laws of a permanent and of a temporary character. The second, third, and fourth books deal with the assertion of the Puritan party that Scripture is the sole guide in determining the actions of a Christian and the form of Church polity, and that the Anglican Church is corrupted with popish rites and ceremonies. The fifth book is a defence of the Book of Common Prayer. According to Hooker's scheme, the last three books were to deal with Church discipline, the power of jurisdiction (whether of the bishops or lay elders), and the nature of the king's supreme authority. The principal characteristics of the work are its breadth of outlook and tolerant spirit, and its advocacy of intellectual liberty against the dogmatism of *Calvin and the ecclesiastical despotism recommended in the *Admonition to Parliament*, a statement of the Puritan case by John Field and Thomas Wilcox (1572).

Lay, a short lyric or narrative poem intended to be sung; originally applied specifically to the poems, usually dealing with matter of history or romantic adventure, which were sung by minstrels.

Lay of the Last Minstrel, The, a poem in six cantos by Sir W. *Scott, published 1805. It is in irregular stanzas of lines of four accents and seven to twelve syllables. This was Scott's first important original work. It is a metrical romance, put in the mouth of an ancient minstrel, the last of his race. It is based on an old Border legend of the goblin Gilpin Horner. The period of the tale is the middle of the 16th cent.

The lady of Branksome Hall, the seat of the Buccleuchs, has lost her husband in an affray in which Lord Cranstoun was one of his opponents. Lord Cranstoun and Margaret, the lady's daughter, are in love, but the feud renders their passion hopeless. The lady commissions Sir William Deloraine to recover from the tomb of the wizard Michael Scott in Melrose Abbey the magic book which is to help her in her vengeance. As Deloraine returns, he encounters Lord Cranstoun and is wounded by him. At Lord Cranstoun's bidding, his elfin page carries the wounded man to Branksome Hall, and, impelled by the spirit of mischief, lures away the lady's little son, the heir of the house, who falls into the hands of her English enemy, Lord Dacre. The latter, with Lord William Howard, intends to storm Branksome, alleging Deloraine's misdeeds as a Border thief. The Scots army is on its way to relieve Branksome. A single combat is suggested between Sir William Deloraine, now lying wounded, and Sir Richard Musgrave, whose lands Deloraine has harried; the lady's little son to be the prize. The challenge is accepted and Musgrave defeated. It is discovered that the victor is Lord Cranstoun, who with his page's assistance has assumed the form and arms of Deloraine. The service rendered to the house of Buccleuch heals the feud, and Lord Cranstoun marries Margaret. The poem includes some notable ballads, such as that of Albert Graeme and the touching 'Rosabelle'; also a version of the *'Dies Irae'.

Lays of Ancient Rome, a collection of poems by *Macaulay, published 1842, in which Macaulay deals with episodes from traditional Roman history (some taken from *Livy), such as the defence of the bridge leading to Rome against the Tuscans ('Horatius'); 'The Battle of Lake Regillus'; and 'Virginia' (see VIRGINIA).

LAȝAMON (*fl.* late 12th cent.), according to his own testimony a priest of Ernley (Arley Regis in Worcestershire), he wrote the *Brut*, a history of England from the arrival of the legendary Brutus to Cadwallader (AD 689), based mostly on Wace's French version of *Geoffrey of Monmouth's *Historia Regum Britanniae* (1155). There are additions from other sources which are uncertain; they are not from *Bede and St *Alban and St *Augustine, as he claims himself. The *Brut* gives for the first time in English not only the story of Arthur but also those of Lear, Cymbeline, and other figures prominent in later English literature. The poem is in 32,241 short lines, corresponding broadly to the later, debased Old English alliterating half-line with occasional rhyme; it also employs some of the epic formulas and other stylistic features of Old English, which contribute to the poem's energy and vigour. It is in some ways a transitional work, and one of the earliest major works in Middle English. (See BRUT.) There are two 13th-cent. manuscripts, both of which are in the edition by F. Madden (3 vols, 1847); see ed. G. L. Brook and R. F. Leslie, EETS OS 250, 277 (1963, 1978).

Lazarillo de Tormes, the first of the Spanish *picaresque romances, of uncertain authorship, printed 1553. It is the autobiography of the son of a miller, who lived on the banks of the Tormes, near Salamanca. The boy begins his career of wit and fraud as a blind man's guide, whose money and victuals he steals. He passes into the service of various poverty-stricken or rascally employers, and ultimately reaches the position of town-crier of Toledo. His career provides occasion for many satirical portraits of Spanish types.

LEACOCK, Stephen Butler (1869–1944), political economist and humorist, was born in Britain but brought up and educated in Canada, where he was for many years lecturer, then professor, at McGill University, Montreal. His many volumes of collected humorous essays and stories include *Literary Lapses* (1910), *Nonsense Novels* (1911), *Sunshine Sketches of a Little Town* (1912), *Arcadian Adventures with the Idle Rich* (1914), and *Frenzied Fiction* (1918). J. B. *Priestley described his best work as 'balanced between cutting satire and sheer absurdity' (introduction to *The Bodley Head Leacock*, 1957).

Leader, The, a weekly periodical started in 1850 by *Lewes and T. L. *Hunt, to which Lewes contributed satirical pieces and lively theatre reviews under the pseudonym of 'Vivian'. The staff included *Spencer and *Kinglake. It ran until 1866, in its later issues as *Saturday Analyst and Leader*.

Leander, see HERO AND LEANDER.

LEAR, Edward (1812–88), artist, traveller, and writer, was born in Holloway, the 20th child of a stockbroker, and was brought up largely by his elder sister Ann. He worked as a zoological draughtsman until he came under the patronage of the earl of Derby, for whose grandchildren he wrote *A Book of Nonsense* (1845), with his own *limericks and illustrations. He travelled widely, and published accounts of Italy (1846), Albania and Illyria (1851), Calabria (1852), and Corsica (1870); he also visited and sketched Egypt, the Holy Land, Greece, and India. He settled in 1871 in San Remo and died there. His posthumous reputation as a watercolourist has risen steadily and as a writer he is remembered for his nonsense verses, with their linguistic fantasies and inventiveness and their occasional touches of underlying melancholy; Lear suffered from epilepsy and depression, and despite many close friends (including *Tennyson's wife Emily) from loneliness. Later nonsense volumes were *Nonsense Songs, Stories, Botany and Alphabets* (1871), which contains 'The Owl and the Pussy-Cat' and 'The Jumblies'; *More Nonsense, Pictures, Rhymes, Botany etc.* (1871); and *Laughable Lyrics* (1877), with the Dong, the Yonghy-Bonghy-Bò, and the Pobble who has no toes. There are lives by Angus Davidson (1938) and Vivien Noakes (1968).

Lear, King, see KING LEAR.

Leasowes, see SHENSTONE, W.

Leatherstocking, nickname of Natty Bumppo, the hero of the five novels of American frontier life by J. F. *Cooper, which are in consequence called the 'Leatherstocking' novels.

Leaves of Grass, see WHITMAN, W.

LEAVIS, F(rank) R(aymond) (1895–1978), critic, was Cambridge born, bred, and educated. He read history, then English, at Emmanuel College, was appointed probationary lecturer 1927–31, and a college lecturer at Downing in 1935. He continued to teach in Cambridge until 1964, establishing a new critical approach that largely superseded the historical and narrative type of literary history favoured by Émile Legouis, Oliver Elton, and *Saintsbury. As a young man he attended and contributed to the Practical Criticism courses of I. A. *Richards, which encouraged close attention to the text. In 1929 he married Q. D. Leavis (1906–81), whose study of the relationship between literature and literacy, *Fiction and the Reading Public* (1932), originated as a thesis under Richards's supervision. From 1932 to 1953 he was chief editor of the quarterly *Scrutiny*, a periodical which was a vehicle for the new Cambridge criticism, upholding rigorous intellectual standards and attacking the dilettante élitism which he believed to characterize the *Bloomsbury Group. *For Continuity* (1933), *Culture and Environment* (1933, with Denys Thompson), followed by *Education and the University* (1943) stress the importance of creating within universities, and particularly within English departments, an informed, discriminating, and highly-trained intellectual élite whose task it would be to preserve the cultural continuity of English life and literature, a continuity he believed to be threatened by mass media, technology, and advertising. *New Bearings in English Poetry* (1932) attacked Tennysonian and Swinburnian 'late Victorian poetastry' and Georgian verse, presenting in their place the claims of E. *Thomas, T. S. *Eliot, *Pound, and (with qualifications) *Yeats: he also made an important reassessment of G. M. *Hopkins. *Revaluation* (1936) continued to reshape the main line of English poetry, tracing it through *Donne, *Pope, and Dr *Johnson to Hopkins and Eliot, and producing iconoclastic attacks on *Spenser, *Milton, and *Shelley. In 1948 he turned his attention to fiction in *The Great Tradition*, possibly his finest work; he traced this tradition through J. *Austen, G. *Eliot, H. *James, and *Conrad, dismissing other major authors (e.g. *Sterne and *Hardy) in a somewhat summary fashion. In later years he changed his position on *Dickens, whose *Hard Times* was the only novel to win unqualified admiration in this volume. (See *Dickens the Novelist*, with Q. D. Leavis, 1970.) *D. H. Lawrence: Novelist* (1955) presented the claims of *Lawrence, then much underrated, as a great English writer and moralist.

Leavis in his writing thus radically altered the literary map of the past and laid out new patterns for the future; but perhaps his most vital contribution lay not in his assessment of individual authors, but in his introduction of a new seriousness into English studies. As a teacher he was admired and revered, and his influence spread throughout the educational world. His vehement dismissal of opposing views earned him much hostility, notably on the occasion of his response to C. P. Snow's Rede Lecture on *'The Two Cultures': *Two Cultures?: The Significance of C. P. Snow* (1962). He was a controversial figure who inspired both deep devotion and profound antagonism, and occasionally a mixture of the two. Despite the impact of his career, he and his followers continued to believe that his achievements remained largely unrecognized; his presence in 20th-cent. literature and criticism is in fact inescapable. See also NEW CRITICISM.

LE CARRÉ, John, pseudonym of David John Moore Cornwell (1931–   ), who was educated at Oxford, taught briefly at Eton, then joined the Foreign Office. His earliest novels were conventional thrillers; the first, *Call for the Dead* (1961), introduced the mild-mannered mastermind and secret agent George Smiley, who appears in many of his later books. *The Spy Who Came in from the Cold* (1963), a cold-war thriller inspired by the Berlin Wall (described by G. *Greene as the best spy story he has ever read) brought Le Carré immediate fame. Its successors, *The Looking Glass War* (1965), *A Small Town in Germany* (1968), *Tinker, Tailor, Soldier, Spy* (1974), *The Honourable Schoolboy* (1977), and *Smiley's People* (1980), confirmed his reputation as a story-teller who mixes grim and realistic detail with Byzantine elaboration of plot. (Le Carré has described the spy stories of I. *Fleming as 'candyfloss'.) *The Little Drummer Girl* (1983) moves its scene from the Soviet-European theatre to the Middle East.

LECKY, William Edward Hartpole (1838–1903), historian, born in Co. Dublin and educated at Trinity College, Dublin, published anonymously in 1860 *The Religious Tendencies of the Age* and in 1861 *Leaders of Public Opinion in Ireland*, which at the time met with little success. His *History of the Rise and Influence of Rationalism in Europe*, published in 1865 after visits to Spain and Italy, attracted much attention; in it he traced the progress of the spirit of rationalism from religious dogmatism and persecution to tolerance. His *History of European Morals from Augustus to Charlemagne* (1869) discussed the relationship of morality and theology, and was also widely read. His *History of England in the Eighteenth Century* (1878–92) was concerned primarily with the history of political ideas and institutions, and social and economic history; the last volumes are devoted to the history of Ireland, and designed to refute *Froude's misstatements. He published several other historical studies, but devoted his last years to politics, as MP for Dublin University from 1895 to 1902.

LECONTE DE LISLE, Charles-Marie-René (1818–94), French poet and leader of the *Parnassians. He published a number of collections, including *Poèmes antiques* (1852), *Poèmes barbares* (1862), and *Poèmes tragiques* (1884).

Lectures on the English Poets, by W. *Hazlitt, published 1818.

Half the lectures are devoted to *Pope and the poets of the 18th cent., but there are essays on others from *Spenser onwards, and on a number of the poets of Hazlitt's own time, including an attack on the work of the popular Samuel *Rogers (in which 'the decomposition of prose is substituted for the composition of poetry'), and an appreciative assessment of *Wordsworth.

LEDGWIDGE, Francis (1891–1917), Irish poet, born in Slane, Co. Meath. He was encouraged and befriended by *Dunsany, who saw in his work promise of the authentic Irish rural voice, and wrote introductions for his three volumes of poetry, *Songs of the Fields* (1916), *Songs of the Peace* (1917), and *Last Songs* (1918). The poems are chiefly lyrics of the countryside, although there are some that deal with Irish mythology and folklore, in a manner reminiscent of the *Celtic Twilight period of *Yeats. Ledgwidge was killed in action in Flanders.

LEE, Harriet (1757–1851), daughter of an actor, ran a private school in Bath with her sister Sophia *Lee. She became both dramatist and novelist, but succeeded only as the latter. An *epistolary novel, *Errors of Innocence*, appeared in 1786; *Clare Lennox* in 1797; and her very successful *Canterbury Tales* (in part a collaboration with Sophia) in 1798, with three further volumes in 1805. The twelve stories of the *Tales*, told by travellers accidentally thrown together, include 'Kruitzner', on which Byron based *Werner*, with acknowledgement. Her own adaptation of the story for the stage was briefly performed. She was a friend of Jane and Anna *Porter; of Sir T. *Lawrence, who presented the sisters with several important portraits of actors; and of *Godwin, who proposed to her in 1798.

LEE, Sir Henry (1531–1611), was master of the armoury and ranger of Woodstock. Lee was closely involved in much Elizabethan pageantry and probably initiated around 1570 the celebration of the queen's accession day (17 Nov.) with tilts and allegorical devices: some of these are reflected in Sidney's revised *Arcadia. He played a part in the Woodstock entertainments of 1575 and 1592, and his own retirement as queen's champion in 1590, when what has been claimed as his own poem, 'His Golden lockes, | Time hath to Silver turn'd', was sung, was commemorated by G. Peele in his *Polyhymnia. He appears in Scott's *Woodstock.

LEE, Laurie (1914–   ), writer, born in Gloucestershire and educated at Slad Village

School and Stroud Central School. He worked for some time in an office in Stroud before travelling in Europe from 1935 to 1939, and then worked in various film units, for the Ministry of Information, the Festival of Britain, etc. His volumes of poetry (*The Sun my Monument*, 1944; *The Bloom of Candles*, 1947; *My Many-Coated Man*, 1955) show a rich sensuous apprehension of the natural world, as does his best-known work, the widely popular *Cider with Rosie* (1959), a highly evocative and nostalgic account of his country boyhood in a secluded Cotswold valley. It describes a vanished rural world of home-made wine, village school, church outings, 'a world of silence . . . of hard work and necessary patience . . . of white roads, rutted by hooves and cartwheels, innocent of oil and petrol'; Lee describes himself as a chance witness of 'the end of a thousand years' life'. The 'Rosie' of the title is a village girl who 'baptized [him] with her cidrous kisses' behind a haycock. A second autobiographical volume, *As I Walked Out One Midsummer Morning* (1969), describes his departure from Stroud, his walk to London, and his months in Spain on the eve of the Spanish Civil War. His other works include screenplays, travel books, and an essay on the birth of his daughter, *The Firstborn* (1964).

LEE, Nathaniel (?1649–92), educated at Westminster School and Trinity College, Cambridge, was a failed actor turned playwright, whose tragedies, marked by extravagance and passion, were long popular. They include *Nero* (1675), *Sophonisba* and *Gloriana* (1676), all in heroics; his best-known tragedy, *The Rival Queens* (1677), in blank verse; *Theodosius* (1680); and one of his most serious dramas, *Lucius Junius Brutus*, which was banned for its anti-monarchical speeches after only three performances. He collaborated with *Dryden in *Oedipus* (1679) and *The Duke of Guise* (1682), and wrote one comedy, *The Princess of Cleve* (?1681), which is nearly as extreme as his tragedies. He lost his reason, was confined to Bedlam 1684–9, and died after a drinking bout. Several editions of his collected plays appeared in the 18th cent., and an edition in 2 vols, ed. T. B. Stroup and A. L. Cooke, in 1954–5.

LEE, Sir Sidney (1859–1926), born Solomon Lazarus Levi, educated at City of London School and Balliol College, Oxford, a member of the editorial staff of the *DNB* from the beginning, joint editor in 1890, and sole editor from 1891. His publications include *Stratford-on-Avon from the Earliest Times to the Death of Shakespeare* (1885, new edn 1906), *Life of William Shakespeare* (1898, rev. edn 1925), *Life of Queen Victoria* (1902), *Great Englishmen of the 16th Century* (1904), *Elizabethan Sonnets* (1904), *Shakespeare and the Modern Stage* (1906), *The French Renaissance in England* (1910), *Principles of Biography* (1911), *Shakespeare and the Italian Renaissance* (1915), *Life of King Edward VII* (1925–7).

LEE, Sophia (1750–1824), daughter of an actor, ran a private school in Bath with her sister Harriet *Lee. She had some success as both dramatist and novelist. Her play *The Chapter of Accidents* (1780) was frequently staged; and her first novel, *The Recess* (1783–5), a form of early historical novel, sold well and was translated into French. A long ballad, *The Hermit's Tale*, followed in 1787, and a verse tragedy, *Almeyda, Queen of Grenada*, with *Kemble and Mrs *Siddons, was staged in 1796. She contributed to her sister's *Canterbury Tales* (1798), and published an epistolary autobiographical novel, *The Life of a Lover* (1804).

LEE, Vernon, pseudonym of Violet Paget (1856–1935), essayist and novelist, who spent most of her life in Italy. She published some 45 volumes, including essays on Italian history, art, aesthetics, and travel; her travel writings (*Genius Loci*, 1899; *The Sentimental Traveller*, 1908; etc.) were much admired by A. *Huxley, whereas H. *James described her novel *Miss Brown* (1884) as 'a deplorable mistake'. A biography by P. Gunn was published in 1964.

LEECH, John (1817–64), caricaturist and illustrator, who formed a lifelong friendship with *Thackeray at Charterhouse; he was also a close friend of *Dickens, whose *A Christmas Carol* and other Christmas books he illustrated. From 1841 until his death he contributed to *Punch* political cartoons and scenes of everyday middle-class life. He drew for a number of other magazines, and illustrated the works of *Surtees.

LE FANU (pron. Léff-anew), J(oseph) S(heridan) (1814–73), journalist, newspaper proprietor, and writer of novels and tales of mystery and the supernatural, came of a well-educated Dublin family of Huguenot origins, connected by marriage with the Sheridans; Joseph's paternal grandmother was the sister of R. B. *Sheridan. After graduating at Trinity College, Dublin, Le Fanu was called to the bar, but never practised. By 1840 he had published a dozen or so stories (including 'A Strange Event in the Life of Schalken the Painter', rated by M. R. *James as 'one of the best of Le Fanu's good things') in the *Dublin University Magazine*, which had been founded in 1833 by a group of young Trinity College men with strong literary interests. From 1840 onwards he became increasingly involved in Irish journalism as editor of *The Warden* and owner or part-owner of that and other papers. His first two novels, *The Cock and Anchor* (1845) and *Torlogh O'Brien* (1847), were in the tradition of Sir W. *Scott and *Ainsworth; and it was not until 1861, three years after his wife's death, that his main output began with the serialization in the *Dublin University Magazine*, which he acquired in that year, of *The House by the Churchyard*. There followed *Wylder's Hand* (issued in book form in 1864), *Uncle Silas* (1864), *Guy Deverell* (1865), *The Tenants of Malory* (1867), *A Lost Name* (1868), *The Wyvern Mystery* (1869), *Checkmate* (1871), *The Rose and the Key* (1871), and *Willing to Die* (1873). In 1872 appeared the remarkable collection of stories entitled *In a Glass Darkly*.

Le Fanu was one of the best-sellers of the 1860s–80s, and in a story published in 1888 H. *James wrote: 'There was the customary novel of Mr Le Fanu for the bedside; the ideal reading in a country house for the hours after midnight.' But thereafter he entered a period of what has been called 'unmitigated famelessness'. This century's revival of interest dates from the publication in 1923 of *Madam Crowl's Ghost and Other Tales of Mystery*, a collection of forgotten tales by Le Fanu edited by M. R. James, who considered that Le Fanu 'stands absolutely in the first rank as a writer of ghost stories'. Since then Le Fanu's reputation has steadily risen, and he is now recognized as the equal of Wilkie *Collins as a writer of mysteries, and as occupying a place all of his own in the field of the sinister and the supernatural.

Le Fever, and his son, the subjects of a story related in Sterne's *Tristram Shandy*.

Left Book Club, a publishing venture founded by V. *Gollancz in association with John Strachey and Harold Laski; modelled on commercial book club lines, its educational aim was to resist the rise of Fascism and Nazism by providing, as Gollancz wrote in the first issue of *Left Book Club News*, 'the indispensable basis of *knowledge* without which a really effective United Front of all men and women cannot be built'. It flourished as a movement, circulating political books to some 50,000 members; the vast majority were factual (though three novels and one play, *Waiting for Lefty*, 1937, by *Odets, were included). The best-known title today is *Orwell's *The Road to Wigan Pier* (1937), which appeared with an introduction by Gollancz warning readers against the provocative second half of the book in which Orwell, he claimed, appeared as 'devil's advocate for the case against Socialism'. The Club defended *Stalin over the Moscow show trials, but was divided on the Nazi-Soviet pact of 1939, and was dissolved in 1948.

LE GALLIENNE, Richard (1866–1947), of Channel Islands descent, born in Liverpool where he was an apprentice accountant for seven years. His first volume, *My Ladies Sonnets and other poems*, was printed privately in 1887 and in 1888 he left for London with the ambition of becoming a man of letters. There he became attached to the *fin-de-siècle* group which centred

on *Beardsley; he was an original member of the *Rhymers' Club with *Yeats, *Wilde, L. *Johnson, and others. He contributed to *The Yellow Book*, throughout the nineties wrote verse and literary criticism, and published a romantic novel, *The Quest for the Golden Girl* (1896). This period he later described in his *The Romantic '90s* (1926). In 1901 he settled in the United States, returning to Europe in 1927 to spend his last years in the south of France.

Legend, Valentine, the hero of Congreve's *Love for Love*, and Sir Sampson, his father.

Legenda Aurea, see GOLDEN LEGEND.

Legend of Good Women, The, written by *Chaucer between 1372 and 1386, is based on such works as *Ovid's *Heroides*, and *Boccaccio's *De Claris Mulieribus* and *Vitae Virorum et Feminarum Illustrium*. The Prologue is more admired than the stories which make up the body of the poem. This Prologue occurs in two forms, the dates and order of precedence of which have been disputed; the prevailing modern view is that the one known as 'F' dates from 1385–6 and 'G' from 1394. It opens with some famous lines in praise of the daisy (conforming to the tradition of 'Marguerite' poems in French) and continues with a description of the rebuking of the sleeping narrator by the god of love because of the things he had written in dispraise of women (another commonplace convention). Chaucer vows to make amends by composing this work in praise of women celebrated for their fidelity in love, as directed by the queen of love, Alceste (who has been identified as Anne of Bohemia). The poem (which is unfinished) contains nine stories of famous women (the narratives lacking the expansiveness and wit of the best of the *Canterbury Tales*): Cleopatra, Thisbe, Dido, Hypsipyle and Medea, Lucrece, Ariadne, Philomela, Phyllis, and Hypermnestra. The poem is significant, as well as for the charm of its Prologue, for the fact that it is the first attested use of the heroic couplet in Chaucer (and, as far as is known, in English poetry). *Tennyson refers to it in his 'A Dream of Fair Women'. There is an interesting brief discussion of the Prologue in A. C. Spearing, *Medieval Dream-Poetry* (1976), pp. 101–10; see also R. W. Frank, *Chaucer and the Legend of Good Women* (1972).

Legend of Montrose, A, a novel by Sir W. *Scott, published 1819, in *Tales of My Landlord*, 3rd series.

It is the story of the campaign of 1644, in which the Highland clans, having risen in favour of Charles I and against the Scottish Covenanters, inflicted a succession of defeats on their opponents, thanks in great measure to the skilful generalship of their great commander, the earl of *Montrose, whose character the author strongly contrasts with that of his rival, the marquess of *Argyle.

With this for historical background, the author tells the tale, which also has some basis of fact, of a barbarous murder committed by a small clan of Highland bandits, the Children of the Mist, and of the tragic events following thereon. Allan M'Aulay, the nephew of the murdered man, obsessed with the thirst for vengeance, grows up moody and violent, and passionately loves Annot Lyle, a young girl whom in one of his forays against his uncle's murderers he has rescued from them. She, however, returns the love of the gallant young earl of Menteith. Both Allan and Menteith are prevented from pressing their suit by the obscurity in which the birth of Annot Lyle is involved. When the leader of the caterans reveals on his deathbed that Annot is the daughter of Sir Duncan Campbell, her marriage to Menteith becomes possible, but is interrupted by Allan, who furiously attacks and stabs his rival, and then disappears.

The gloom of the story is relieved by the character of Captain Dugald Dalgetty, a mixture of the loquacious pedant, who makes great show of the knowledge gained at the Marischal College of Aberdeen, and the brave but self-seeking soldier of fortune; he has served indifferently under Gustavus and Wallenstein, and is prepared to do so under King Charles or the Covenanters according to the prospects offered by each.

Legree, Simon, see SIMON LEGREE.

LEHMANN, (Rudolph) John (Frederick) (1907–), poet, publisher, and editor, brother of Rosamond *Lehmann, educated at Eton and Trinity College, Cambridge, where he became friendly with Julian Bell, nephew of V. *Woolf; from 1931 he was associated with the *Hogarth Press, of which he became a partner in 1938. It published his first book of poems, *A Garden Revisited* (1931), and several others. His *Collected Poems 1930–63* appeared in 1963. Lehmann is probably best known as the editor of *New Writing* and of the *London Magazine*. His three volumes of autobiography, *The Whispering Gallery* (1951), *I am my Brother* (1960), and *The Ample Proposition* (1966), record a life rich in literary friendships and activity, as do his several volumes of reminiscence and biography, which include works on the *Sitwells (1969), the Woolfs, and R. *Brooke (1980).

LEHMANN, Rosamond Nina (1901–), novelist, sister of John *Lehmann, was born in Buckinghamshire, the second daughter of a Liberal MP and contributor to *Punch. She was educated privately and at Girton College, Cambridge, and shortly after her first marriage achieved a *succès de scandale* with her first novel, *Dusty Answer* (1927), which describes the awakening into womanhood of 18-year-old Judith Earle, through Cambridge and through her emotional entanglements with a neighbouring family of cousins. In 1928 she married the painter Wogan Philipps. Her second novel, *A Note in Music* (1930), also created a stir with its frank treatment of homosexuality. *Invitation to the Waltz* (1932) describes the impact on innocent 17-year-old Olivia Curtis of her first dance; its sequel, *The Weather in the Streets* (1936), shocked some of its readers by taking Olivia through a failed marriage, an adulterous love affair, and an abortion. *The Ballad and the Source* (1944) is a child's eye view of adult passion: ten-year-old Rebecca Landon listens entranced to the experienced and enigmatic Sybil Jardine. (Both characters reappear in R. Lehmann's later novel *A Sea-Grape Tree*, 1976.) *The Echoing Grove* (1953), a novel about the relationship of two sisters, one of whom had had an affair with the other's husband, was followed by a long silence, then by *The Swan in the Evening: Fragments of an Inner Life* (1967). This short autobiographical testament opens by recalling her own childhood, then describes her reactions to the sudden death from poliomyelitis of her daughter Sally in Java in 1958; her spiritual experiences (she quotes *Jung and F. W. H. *Myers in support) convinced her of her daughter's survival after death, and of their continuing relationship.

Rosamond Lehmann's novels, in their insistence on the emotional and sensuous aspects of life, have fairly been described as romantic and female, by both admirers and critics, qualifications that led in part to their neglect; the new wave of *feminist criticism which inspired many reprints in the 1980s prefers to point to their pioneering frankness and their confident assumption that women's lives are essentially as interesting and important as men's lives.

LEIBNIZ, Gottfried Wilhelm (1646–1716), German philosopher and mathematician, born at Leipzig, was the founder of the Society (later Academy) of Sciences at Berlin. He discovered the infinitesimal calculus at about the same time as I. *Newton, but by a different method. As a philosopher he was inspired by *Descartes, *Spinoza, and *Hobbes, but broke away from Descartes's mechanical conception of the universe. Matter he regarded as a multitude of monads, each a nucleus of force and a microcosm or concentration of the universe. Admitting that the interaction of spirit and matter is inexplicable, he assumed a 'pre-established harmony' between them: the spirit is modified by final causes, bodies by efficient causes; the two series are brought together, like two clocks ticking in unison (the simile is *Voltaire's), by a harmony established from all time by God, the supreme monad and perfect exemplar of the human soul. His system is embodied in his *Theodicée* (1710) and *Monadologie* (1714), written in

French. Leibniz was one of the chief forces in the German *Enlightenment.

Leicester, Robert Dudley, earl of (?1532–88), the favourite of *Elizabeth I, figures in Scott's *Kenilworth as the husband of the unfortunate Amy Robsart.

Leigh, Amyas, the hero of C. *Kingsley's *Westward Ho!*

LEIGH, Augusta (1784–1851), half-sister of Lord *Byron, daughter of his father by the latter's earlier marriage to Lady Carmarthen. Augusta's relations with Byron have been the subject of much speculation, and it is probable that he was the father of her daughter, Elizabeth Medora, born in 1814.

LEIGHTON, Frederic, Lord (1830–96), Victorian classical artist, born at Scarborough, but educated on the Continent, at Florence, Frankfurt, and Rome. In 1855 his *Cimabue's celebrated Madonna carried in procession through the streets of Florence* (1855) was shown at the *Royal Academy; his first exhibit, it was immensely successful, and was bought by Queen Victoria and praised by *Ruskin. Thereafter the handsome, cultivated, and utterly respectable Leighton rose to occupy a privileged position in the art establishment; he became president of the Royal Academy in 1878, a peer in 1896. His interest in Florentine Renaissance subjects led to his commission to illustrate *Romola. Throughout his life Leighton's personality captured the imagination of writers. In Rome in the early 1850s he moved in the circle of A. *Sartoris, and was to appear as the exuberant Mr Kiowski in her *A Week in a French Country House* (1867); he also met there R. *Browning and *Thackeray, and suggested aspects of Clive Newcome, 'the cock of the whole painting school, the favourite of all', in *The Newcomes*. He appeared as Gaston Phoebus in Disraeli's *Lothair, and less sympathetically as the public artist, Lord Mellifont, in H. *James's story, 'The Private Life' (1892). The parties at his exotic Moorish house in Holland Park are recalled in many memoirs of the period. See L. and R. Ormond, *Lord Leighton* (1975).

Leila, (1) in Byron's *Don Juan*, the Muslim child whom Juan rescues at the siege of Ismail; (2) in his *The Giaour*, the unfortunate heroine.

Leinster, Book of, an Irish MS of the 12th cent., containing stories of Gaelic mythology, in particular the feats of *Cuchulain.

L.E.L., see LANDON, L. E.

LELAND, John (c.1503–52), the earliest of modern English antiquaries, was educated at St Paul's School and Christ's College, Cambridge. He studied at Paris, took holy orders, and by 1530 was involved with the royal libraries, and

said he received a commission in 1533 to search monastic and collegiate libraries for old authors. He made a tour through England in 1535–43, intending his researches to be the basis of a great work on the 'History and Antiquities of this Nation', but he left merely a mass of undigested notes. In *A Newe Yeares Gyfte* (1549) he described to the king the manner and aims of his researches. He became insane in 1550. *Leland's Itinerary* was first published at Oxford, in nine volumes, by *Hearne in 1710–12; and his *Collectanea* in six (1715). Leland claimed to have 'conservid many good autors, the which other wise had beene like to have perischid', in the dissolution of the religious houses. There is an edition of the *Itinerary* by Lucy Toulmin Smith (1906–10).

LELY, Sir Peter (1618–80), British portrait painter, of Dutch origin, who is best known as the painter of the voluptuous beauties who graced the court of Charles II. He became principal painter to the king in 1661 and his style is a vulgarized version of *Van Dyck's. Lely was a friend of *Lovelace, who eulogized him in verse. Lely's poignant double portrait of *Charles I and the Duke of York* (1647; His Grace the Duke of Northumberland) inspired Lovelace's poem 'See what a clouded majesty', which contains the somewhat unexpected praise: 'None but my Lilly ever drew a mind.' His most characteristic works are the *Windsor Beauties* (Hampton Court). To *Pope, Lely epitomized the Restoration world:

> Lely on animated canvas stole
> The sleepy eye, that spoke the melting soul.

See O. Millar, *Sir Peter Lely* (1978).

LEMON, Mark (1809–70), a founder, first joint-editor, then editor of *Punch, from 1841 until his death, and contributor to other periodicals. He wrote prolifically for the stage, and performed in *Dickens's private theatricals. He collaborated with Dickens in *Mr Nightingale's Diary* (1851), a one-act farce with both authors in the cast.

LEMPRIÈRE, John (d. 1824), classical scholar; author of a standard classical dictionary, *Bibliotheca Classica*, which has frequently been enlarged and revised and is still in use.

LENCLOS, Anne, known as Ninon de Lenclos (1620–1705), a Frenchwoman noted for her beauty and wit, which she retained to a very advanced age, depicted by Mlle *Scudéry as 'Clarisse' in her *Clélie*. She had many celebrities for her lovers, and her *salon* was frequented by *St Évremond, *Molière, *Voltaire, etc.

LENIN, Vladimir Ilich (V. I. Ulyanov) (1870–1924), born in the Volga area, son of a schools inspector. A lawyer by training, he soon stopped practising and in 1893 became a professional revolutionary. He was active for the Marxists in polemics against the Populists, rivals in the socialist movement, and in 1895 led the St Petersburg Union of Struggle for the Liberation of the Working Class. Arrested that year, he spent two years in prison and three in Siberia, publishing *The Development of Capitalism in Russia* (1899). Upon release Lenin set out, with the help of an informal organization inside the party called 'The Spark', to gain control of the Social-Democratic Labour Party (founded in 1898). In the pamphlet 'What Is To Be Done?' (1902) he laid down his views on political strategy, tactics, and organization, the basis of Communist practice ever since. From 1900 to 1917 (except during the 1905–7 revolution) he was an émigré in Western Europe, whence he tried to direct the activities in Russia of the Social-Democratic Party, which was torn by factional strife, largely due to his uncompromising attitude towards opponents. He constantly insisted on Marxist orthodoxy (though his interpretation of Marxism was challenged by other leaders) and on the priority of the political struggle against the government over the workers' struggle against the employers for better conditions.

During the First World War Lenin took up a 'defeatist' stand, and argued that workers in each country should aim at a defeat of their own government so as to facilitate a proletarian revolution. After the fall of the monarchy in March 1917, he returned and led his supporters, now organized in a separate Bolshevik Party (later renamed Communist), towards the seizure of power from the democratically minded, half-socialist Provisional Government, arguing (in *Imperialism as the Last Stage of Capitalism*) that Russia was ripe for a socialist revolution and (in *State and Revolution*) that such a revolution should bring about a 'dictatorship of the proletariat'. The régime established after the coup in Nov. 1917 was in fact a dictatorship of the Party, which was regarded as the avant-garde of the working class but actually remained a self-perpetuating body. The Communist government headed by Lenin confiscated privately owned land, distributing it among the peasants, and most industry, dispersed the Constituent Assembly (where the Communists were a minority), concluded a separate peace treaty with Germany and won the Civil War (1918–20), during which a policy of 'War Communism' included nationalization of all industry, suppression of private trade, wages in kind, compulsory food deliveries by the peasants, and labour service. In 1921 Lenin inaugurated the 'New Economic Policy' of concessions to the peasants and the permitting of some private trade and industry, though at the same time he suppressed the socialist parties and rival factions within the Communist party. Lenin became paralysed in 1922 and thereafter took a much less active part in public affairs.

LENNOX, Charlotte (1720–1804), was the daughter of a lieutenant-governor of New York, where she was born. When she came to England she failed as an actress and turned to writing, largely novels. The *Life of Harriot Stuart* appeared in 1750, and in 1752 her most important work, *The Female Quixote*, which established her name and was praised by *Fielding. Her collection and translation of the sources of Shakespeare's plays appeared as *Shakespear Illustrated* (1753–4), and *Henrietta* (1758), a novel concerned with female dependence, was dramatized. Her comedy *The Sister* was performed in 1769. Dr *Johnson, a friend and admirer of her work, cited her under 'Talent' in his *Dictionary*. She was skilled in discerning and describing fleeting moments of emotion, and may be grouped with practitioners of the Novel of *Sentiment.

'Lenore' (1774), a celebrated ballad by the German poet Gottfried August Bürger (1747–94), based on the Scottish ballad 'Sweet William's Ghost'. Lenore is carried off on horseback by the spectre of her lover after his death and married by him at the graveside. it was translated first by W. *Taylor, whose version circulated in manuscript and was published in 1797 in the *Monthly Magazine*; Mrs *Barbauld said Sir W. *Scott told her that he had been inspired by a reading of Taylor's translation, and his own version (with the borrowing of two lines from Taylor acknowledged) appeared also in 1797, anonymously, as 'William and Helen' in *The Chase and William and Helen*. The two poets corresponded about their versions: see J. W. Robberds's *Memoir* of Taylor (1843). Other imitations of 'Lenore' appeared almost simultaneously, and a parody, 'Miss Kitty' (1797). As late as 1872 the ballad provided the programme for Joachim Raff's 5th ('Lenore') Symphony, very popular in its time. (See also WILD HUNTSMAN, THE.)

LEO X, Giovanni de' Medici (1475–1521), Pope 1513–21, a patron of literature and art, notably of *Raphael. It fell to him to deal with the theses of *Luther, whom he excommunicated in 1520. It was he who gave *Henry VIII the title of 'Defender of the Faith'. See also LAURENTIAN LIBRARY. There is a life by W. *Roscoe.

Leodegrance ('Leodegan' elsewhere in the Arthurian cycles), in *Malory, king of Cameliard and father of *Guinevere.

Leo Hunter, Mrs, a character in Dickens's *Pickwick Papers*.

LEÓN, Fray Luis Ponce de (?1527–91), a Spanish Augustinian monk, and professor for nearly 30 years at the university of Salamanca; like his near contemporary *John of the Cross, he endured imprisonment for his beliefs. Known as a scholar in his lifetime, he subsequently became known as a mystic poet. See a life by A. F. G. Bell (1925).

LEONARDO DA VINCI (1452–1519), Florentine painter, sculptor, musician, scientist, and thinker, who developed in his painting greater significance and complexity in composition, chiaroscuro, and psychological insight than had ever been achieved before; his *sfumato* technique was deeply influential. *The Last Supper* (c.1495) and the *Mona Lisa* (c.1503) are perhaps the two most celebrated pictures in the western tradition. In 1481/2 Leonardo went to Milan, and remained in the employ of Ludovico Sforza until 1499; he was then in Florence, Rome, and Milan again, and he finally went to Paris c.1516/17, where he died. In the 19th cent. the enigmatic charm of Leonardo's women mesmerized writers; *Gautier and the *Goncourt brothers pondered over the subtle smile of the *Mona Lisa*, the 'Gioconda smile'; in the second half of the century her beauty was seen as darker and tinged with evil, and was most powerfully evoked in a famous passage by *Pater, in an essay which owes something to D. G. *Rossetti's early sonnet 'Our Lady of the Rocks' and to *Swinburne's descriptions of Fatal Women. Pater's 'Lady Lisa' popularized the Fatal Women whose development has been outlined by *Praz, and echoes of her fascination recur through decadent poetry until she is parodied by A. *Huxley in 'The Gioconda Smile'.

Leonato, in Shakespeare's *Much Ado about Nothing,* the father of Hero and uncle of Beatrice.

Leonatus, Posthumus, see POSTHUMUS LEONATUS.

Leonine verse, a kind of Latin verse much used in the Middle Ages, consisting of hexameters, or alternate hexameters and pentameters, in which the last word rhymes with that preceding the caesura; for instance:

His replicans clare tres causas explico quare
More Leonino dicere metra sino.

The term is applied to English verse of which the middle and last syllables rhyme. It is derived, according to Du Cange, from the name of a certain poet Leo, who lived about the time of Louis VII of France (1137–80) or his successor Philippe-Auguste (1180–1223).

LEONORA D'ESTE, sister of Alfonso II, duke of Ferrara, with whom (according to a story now declared untrue) the poet *Tasso fell in love, and was in consequence imprisoned in a madhouse. The legend is the foundation of Byron's *The Lament of Tasso.*

LEONOV, Leonid Maksimovich (1899–   ),

Russian novelist. His first two novels, *The Badgers* (1924), a Dostoevskian study of a counter-revolutionary, and *The Thief* (1927), which tells the story of an anti-Soviet band of criminals, are suffused with the experimentalism of 1920s Russian prose and brought him great prestige. With his third novel, *The River Sot* (1929), he wrote one of the best examples of the so-called 'five-year plan novel' about the building of a paper-mill on a northern river, but in the early 1930s the novel came under attack, as did his next novels, *Skutarevsky* (1932) and *The Road to the Ocean* (1935). *The Russian Forest* (1953), combining the story of the first year of the Russo-German war, 1941–2, with a description of the hero's life stretching back before the revolution, is held by many to be his best work. English translations of *The Thief* (by H. Butler) and *The River Sot* (by Ivor Montagu and S. S. Nolbandov) appeared in 1931.

Leontes, in Shakespeare's *The Winter's Tale,* the husband of Hermione.

LEOPARDI, Giacamo (1798–1837), the greatest Italian Romantic poet. His richly suggestive lyrics (*Canti,* 1845) were written between 1816 and 1837. In 1824 he turned his attention to philosophical prose, notably the ironical dialogues *Operette morali* (*Moral Tales,* 1827). The 'cosmic pessimism' of his poems is often attributed to chronic illness, but it was also an intensely intellectual and even scholarly development. In his early thought, based on *Vico and the classics, poetry is given the task of recovering the freshness of the Greek response to nature. Later he was to see nature as purposeless, indifferent, or even cruel—the 'stepmother' of humanity; and he elaborated a Romantic poetics based on the tension between past and present, childhood innocence and adult awareness of insignificance, illusions and their loss. This gave rise to a wistful poetry of images he called 'vague', in that they evoke memory: the present is too precise to be beautiful. Both *Pound and R. *Lowell produced versions of his poems.

'Lepanto', see JOHN OF AUSTRIA, DON.

Lêr, or Lir, in Gaelic mythology, the sea-god, one of the *Tuatha Dé Danann; perhaps to be identified with the British sea-god Llyr. He was the father of *Manannán.

According to the story of 'The Children of Lêr', one of the 'three sorrowful tales of Erin', Lêr had one daughter, Fionnuala, and three sons. These were changed into swans by their jealous stepmother Aoife, and condemned to spend 900 years on the seas and lakes of Ireland. Before the end of this period St Patrick arrived, the old gods were swept away, and the swans were able to return to their home. They were converted to Christianity and restored to human shape; but were now old people and soon died.

LERMONTOV, Mikhail Yurevich (1814–41), Russian Romantic poet and novelist. Descended from a Scottish officer and adventurer, Captain George Learmont, who entered the Russian service in the early 17th cent., Lermontov was himself an army officer. Strongly influenced by *Byron, he wrote lyric and narrative poetry on the themes of disillusionment, rebellion, and personal freedom. He was killed in a duel. His best-known poems are 'A Wish' (1831), in which he expresses nostalgia for Scotland, 'The Sail' and 'No, I am not Byron' (both 1832), 'The Death of a Poet' (1837), which bemoans the death of *Pushkin, the bitter 'Gratitude' (1840), and the romantic narratives 'Mtsyri' ('The Novice', 1840) and 'The Demon' (1829–41). His prose masterpiece, the novel *A Hero of Our Times*, first translated in 1854, is his lasting monument.

LESAGE, Alain-René (1668–1747), French novelist and playwright. Generally regarded as the first major writer in France to live entirely by his pen, he produced over 60 farces and librettos. He specialized in picaresque narratives: *Le Diable boiteux* (1707) and his masterpiece *Gil Blas* (1715–35) are notable for their narrative brio and their shrewd, good-humoured presentation of human nature. *Gil Blas* was translated by *Smollett in 1749: with *Don Quixote* and *Rabelais, it can be considered the greatest foreign influence on 18th-cent. English comic fiction.

LESKOV, Nikolai Semenovich (1831–95), Russian prose writer, born near Orel in central Russia. His maternal uncle, Alexander Scott, was a Russianized British Protestant, and between 1857 and 1860 Leskov travelled widely in provincial Russia for the agricultural firm of Scott and Wilkins. After this he turned to journalism, his first work appearing in 1860 and his first story in 1862. Leskov's major themes, provincial Russia and Russian religion, expressed with an uncanny ear for the speech of ordinary people, are perhaps best seen in his stories 'The Musk-Ox' (1863), 'Lady Macbeth of the Mtsensk District' (1865), 'The Sealed Angel' and 'The Enchanted Wanderer' (both 1874), and his major long work, the 'chronicle' *Cathedral Folk* (1872). In his most famous story 'Lefty' (1881) the eponymous Russian craftsman is sent by Tsar Alexander I to England to match his skills against English rivals. The first translations of Leskov into English, by A. E. Chamot, appeared in 1922.

Lesly, Ludovic, 'Le Balafré', a character in Scott's *Quentin Durward*.

LESSING, Doris May, *née* Taylor (1919–), novelist and short story writer, born in Persia of British parents who moved when she was five to a farm in Southern Rhodesia. She left school at 15 and worked as a nursemaid, then as a shorthand-typist and telephone operator in Salisbury. After the break-up of her first marriage she became involved in radical politics. She remarried in 1945, but in 1949 left for England with her youngest child and the manuscript of her first novel to be published, *The Grass is Singing* (1950), the story of the complex relationship between a white farmer's wife and her black servant, and its violent conclusion. From this period she supported herself and her son by her writing. Her quintet *Children of Violence* is a *Bildungsroman, tracing the history of Martha Quest from her childhood in Rhodesia, through post-war Britain, to an apocalyptic ending in AD 2000 (*Martha Quest*, 1952; *A Proper Marriage*, 1954; *A Ripple From the Storm*, 1958; *Landlocked*, 1965; and *The Four-Gated City*, 1969). Perhaps her best-known book, *The Golden Notebook* (1962) is a lengthy and ambitious novel which was hailed as a landmark by the Women's Movement: sections of conventional narrative ironically entitled 'Free Women' enclose and intersperse the four experimental notebooks of writer Anna Wulf who is struggling with crises in her domestic and political life, and with a writer's block. In each notebook she approaches experience from a different angle (through fiction, parody, political documentation, realistic recording of daily events), a method that reflects her sense of fragmentation and need to keep aspects of life in separate compartments. The novel ends, after a period of breakdown, with release, union, and renewed creativity. Anna gives the 'golden notebook' to her American lover with a suggestion for the first sentence of his new novel: he in turn suggests the first sentence of hers, which is the first of the 'Free Women' section. The conventional narrative ends more prosaically with Anna's declaration that she is about to join the Labour Party. Later novels, *Briefing for a Descent into Hell* (1971) and *Memoirs of a Survivor* (1975), enter the realm of 'inner space fiction', exploring mental breakdown and the breakdown of society. The sequence collectively entitled *Canopus in Argus Archives* (Re: Colonised Planet 5, Shikasta, 1979; *The Marriages Between Zones Three, Four and Five*, 1980; *The Sirian Experiments*, 1981; *The Making of the Representative for Planet 8*, 1982; *Documents Relating to the Sentimental Agents in the Volyen Empire*, 1983) marks a complete break with traditional realism, describing the epic and mythic events of a fictional universe with a remarkable freedom of invention. She has written many other works of fiction and non-fiction, displaying her concern with politics, with the changing destiny of women, with a fear of technological disaster, and has also written of her interest in Sufi thought and the works of I. *Shah. Her *Collected*

Stories (2 vols, 1978) show a similarly broad range of interests, from the feminism of 'One off the Short List' to meditations on the material and spiritual life in 'The Temptation of Jack Orkney'; they include her much-anthologized evocation of childhood bravado, 'Through the Tunnel'.

LESSING, Gotthold Ephraim (1729–81), German critic and dramatist. He was educated at Leipzig University, was the literary adviser of the National Theatre at Hamburg (1765–9), and in 1770 became librarian to the duke of Brunswick at Wolfenbüttel, where he died. As a dramatist his principal works were: the serious comedy *Minna von Barnhelm* (1767); *Emilia Galotti* (1772), a tragedy on a social theme; and *Nathan der Weise* (1779), a plea for religious tolerance. *Miss Sara Sampson* (1755), the first significant domestic tragedy in German, was· modelled on Lillo's **George Barnwell* (1731). Lessing was, in the words of *Macaulay, 'beyond all dispute, the first critic in Europe', who emancipated German literature from the narrow conventions of the French classical school, suggesting that German writers look instead to Shakespeare and English literature as more congenial models. His chief critical works were the *Briefe die neueste Litteratur betreffend* (*Letters relating to Recent Literature*, 1759–65), the **Laokoon* (1766), on the limits of the several arts, and the *Hamburgische Dramaturgie* (1767–9). In England, Lessing was much admired not only by Macaulay, but also by *Coleridge, G. *Eliot, and G. H. *Lewes, both for his humane and liberal beliefs and for the clarity of his prose style.

L'ESTRANGE, Sir Roger (1616–1704), journalist and pamphleteer, and an active royalist, was obliged to flee to the Continent in 1648. After the Restoration he was appointed surveyor of printing presses and licenser of the press. He issued *The News* and *The Intelligencer* (1663–6) which were ousted by *The London Gazette* of *Muddiman; also many political pamphlets, one of the earliest being a reply to *Milton, *No Blind Guides* (1660). In his periodical *The Observator* (1681–7) he attacked the Whigs, *Oates, and Dissenters, often employing a lively dialogue form of question and answer; his prose is colloquial, forceful, and conversational. He was knighted by James II in 1685, but after the revolution was regarded by the Whigs as a grave threat to liberty, and was several times imprisoned; he thereafter supported himself by translations which include *The Visions of Quevedo* (1667), **Aesop's Fables* (1692), and the works of *Josephus (1702).

Letter on the Spirit of Patriotism, A, see BOLINGBROKE, H. ST J.

Letters on a Regicide Peace, see REGICIDE PEACE.

Letters on the Study and Use of History, see BOLINGBROKE, H. ST J.

Letters . . . To and For Particular Friends, a collection by S. *Richardson.

Letter to a Friend, A, see BROWNE, SIR T.

Letter to a Noble Lord *on the attacks made upon him and his pension in the House of Lords by the Duke of Bedford and the Earl of Lauderdale,* by E. *Burke, published 1796.

Burke retired from Parliament in 1794 and received a pension from the government of *Pitt. This grant was criticized in the House of Lords, principally by the peers above named, as excessive in amount and inconsistent with Burke's own principles of economical reform. Burke replied in one of the greatest masterpieces of irony and feeling in the English language, comparing his own services to the State with those rendered by the duke of Bedford and his house, which had been the recipient of enormous grants from the Crown.

Letter to Sir William Wyndham, A, see BOLINGBROKE, H. ST J.

Letter to the Sheriffs of Bristol, A, by E. *Burke, published 1777.

The American war had at this time followed its disastrous course for two years. The letter begins with a protest against certain Acts of Parliament subjecting the rebels to exceptional legal disabilities, treating them in fact as traitors, and passes to a review of the current humiliating situation. Burke goes on to defend the course that he has taken. Asserting his zeal for the supremacy of Parliament, he defines the problem which the exercise of this supremacy involves: 'to conform our government to the character and circumstances of the several people who compose this mighty and strangely diversified' empire. The scheme of taxing America is incompatible with this conception of imperial policy, and Burke has consequently voted for the pacification of 1766, and even for the surrender of the whole right of taxation.

LEVER, Charles (1806–72), born and educated in Dublin, qualified as an MD and practised in Ireland. He became a prolific and successful novelist, writing chiefly of military and Irish life. His first novels, *Harry Lorrequer* (1839), *Charles O'Malley* (1841), and *Jack Hinton the Guardsman* (1843), were extremely popular, and in 1842 he gave up medicine for the editorship of the *Dublin University Magazine*. *Tom Burke of Ours* (1844) and a historical novel, *The Knight of Gwynne* (1847), were notable among the stream of his racy, anecdotal works. In 1845 he left Ireland and eventually settled in Italy. *The Martins of Cro'Martin* (1847) provides a spirited portrait of life in the west of Ireland, and *The Dodd Family Abroad* (1852–4) an account of an English family's vicissitudes on the Continent. His later novels were more carefully constructed; *Sir Jasper Carew* (1855), *The Fortunes of Glencore* (1857), and *Lord Kilgobbin* (1872) are considered among the best of this period. Lever received much encouragement and advice from *Thackeray, and was admired by G. *Eliot and A. *Trollope.

LEVERSON, Ada (1862–1933), whose novels enjoyed a belated vogue in the 1960s, is chiefly remembered for her association with *Wilde, who named her 'The Sphinx'. She sheltered him during his trials, and his letters to her were published in a limited edition in 1930. For some years she held a salon frequented by the *Sitwells, *Beerbohm, the novelist G. *Moore, and H. *Acton. Her novels, set in fashionable London society, include *Love's Shadow* (1908), *Tenterhooks* (1912) and *Love at Second Sight* (1916), all of which feature Edith Ottley as protagonist; they were published in one volume in 1962 as *The Little Ottleys*, with a foreword by C. *MacInnes, praising her as 'the classic author of the comedy of manners'.

LEVI, Peter Chad Tigar (1931–), poet, translator, classical scholar, travel writer, and archaeologist, born in Ruislip, near London, and educated at Campion Hall, Oxford, where he was tutor and lecturer, 1965–77: he was a Jesuit priest from 1964 to 1977, when he resigned the priesthood. His first volume of poetry, *The Gravel Ponds* (1960), was followed by several others, including a *Collected Poems 1955–1975* (1976); his poems mingle imagery and themes from classical antiquity, British history and prehistory, Christianity, and domestic life. A volume of autobiography, *The Flutes of Autumn* (1983), concludes with an eloquent tribute to David *Jones. Levi was elected professor of poetry at Oxford in 1984.

LEVI, Primo (1919–), Italian writer in several genres; his most important works are his poignant yet humane memoirs of his experience in Auschwitz: *Se questo è un uomo* (*If this is a man*, 1947) and *La tregua* (*The Ceasefire*, 1963).

Leviathan, The, or the Matter, Form, and Power of a Commonwealth, Ecclesiastical and Civil, a treatise of political philosophy by *Hobbes, published 1651, Latin text 1668.

By 'The Leviathan' the author signified sovereign power. The basis of his political philosophy is that man is not, as *Aristotle held, naturally a social being, recognizing the claims of the community upon him and sharing in its prosperity, but a purely selfish creature, seeking only his own advantage. The state of nature is one of general war, and 'the notions of Right and Wrong, Justice and Injustice, have there no place.' There is 'continuall feare . . . And the life of man [is] solitary, poore, nasty, brutish and

short.' To escape these conditions man has adopted certain 'articles of peace', those 'Laws of Nature', by which a man is forbidden to do 'that which is destructive of his life' and of which the science is 'true moral philosophy'. Virtue is the means of 'peaceful, sociable and comfortable living'. The first law of nature is, 'that every man ought to endeavour Peace'. The second is, 'That a man be willing, when others are so too . . . to lay down his right to all things; and be contented with so much liberty against other men, as he would allow other men against himselfe.' The third is, 'that men performe their Covenants made'.

To enforce these covenants it is necessary to establish an external power, which shall punish their infraction; accordingly all individuals must enter into a contract 'to conferre all their power and strength upon one Man, or upon one Assembly of men'. 'This done, the Multitude so united in one Person, is called a Common-Wealth.' This representative person is sovereign, and his power is inalienable. The contract is not between the subjects and the sovereign, but only between the subjects. The sovereign power is indivisible; it cannot for instance be divided between king and parliament. Hobbes is careful to repudiate the rival claim of the Church to control over the citizen, which involves either a division of sovereign power, or the absorption of the State in the Church. He accordingly makes the Church subordinate to the State.

The absolute power thus given to the sovereign is, however, subject to certain limits. There is liberty to refuse obedience if the command of the sovereign frustrates the end for which the sovereignty was ordained, i.e. the preservation of the life of the individual. Moreover, the obligation of subjects to the sovereign is understood to last so long as, and no longer than, 'the power lasteth, by which he is able to protect them'. The sovereign finally is responsible to God, if not to his subjects, for the proper discharge of his office.

LÉVI-STRAUSS, see STRUCTURALISM.

LEWES, G(eorge) H(enry) (1817–78), a writer of extraordinarily varied interests and talents, is best known in his secondary role as 'husband' and encourager of the diffident George *Eliot. When he met her in 1851, however, he already had behind him a varied career as comic dramatist, actor, essayist on subjects ranging from *Hegel's aesthetics (his was the first proselytizing article on the subject in England) to Spanish drama, and author of a novel in imitation of *Goethe, *Ranthorpe* (1847). He wrote one of the first books in English on *Comte's positivist philosophy (1853), and a popular history of philosophy from F. *Bacon to Comte (*Biographical History of Philosophy*, 1845–6). His liaison with George Eliot, dating from 1854, could not be regularized because he had condoned the adultery of his wife Agnes with T. L. *Hunt; admirers of *Shelley, the Leweses believed in free love, and when Agnes bore the first of her four children by Hunt in 1850 Lewes registered the boy as his own. By the time he met George Eliot, he was estranged from Agnes, but unable to obtain a divorce.

Lewes's most distinguished work is his still valuable *Life of Goethe* (1855), which he researched, with George Eliot's help, in Weimar and Berlin in 1854–5. Lewes turned his attention increasingly to science: his later works range from biological works like *Seaside Studies* (1858) and *The Physiology of Common Life* (1859) to his ambitious attempt at psychology, *Problems of Life and Mind* (1873–9), the last volume of which was completed by George Eliot after his death. That George Eliot benefited not only from his encouragement of her talents but also from his studies, is evident from the scientific metaphors which inform her works.

Lewesdon Hill, a *topographical poem by William Crowe (1745–1829), published 1788, in the style of James *Thomson.

LEWIS, Alun (1915–44), born in a Welsh mining village, went to university at Aberystwyth and trained as a teacher before joining the army (after much hesitation) in 1940. His first volume of poems, *Raiders' Dawn*, appeared in 1942, and in 1943 a volume of stories, *The Last Inspection*, most of which deal with army life in England, 'the rootless life of soldiers having no enemy', as does his most anthologized poem, 'All Day it has Rained . . .', first published in 1941. Lewis was killed in Burma. Letters and stories were collected in *In the Green Tree* (1948); *Selected Poetry and Prose*, with a biographical introduction by Ian Hamilton, appeared in 1966, and a paperback selection by J. Hooker and G. Lewis in 1981. Many of Lewis's poems show a recurring obsession with the themes of isolation and death, and a debt to E. *Thomas, to whom one of his best poems is addressed.

LEWIS, Cecil Day, see DAY-LEWIS, C.

LEWIS, C(live) S(taples) (1898–1963), literary scholar, critic, and novelist, fellow of Magdalen College, Oxford, 1925–54, and afterwards professor of Medieval and Renaissance English at Cambridge. His critical works include *The Allegory of Love* (1936) and *English Literature in the Sixteenth Century* (vol. 3 in the *Oxford History of English Literature*, 1954). He is more widely known for his popular religious and moral writings, such as *The Problem of Pain* (1940), *The Screwtape Letters* (1940), and *The Four Loves* (1960). *Out of the Silent Planet* (1938) is the first of three science fiction novels with a strong Christian flavour, influenced by his friendship with *Tolkien and C.

*Williams. With *The Lion, The Witch, and The Wardrobe* (1950) he began a series of seven 'Narnia' stories for children. *Surprised by Joy* (1955) is his spiritual autobiography. 'The Inklings', a group of his friends, met in his Oxford rooms for many years to talk and read aloud their compositions.

LEWIS, Sir George Cornewall (1806–63), Liberal statesman and author, educated at Eton and Christ Church, Oxford. He contributed to the *Edinburgh Review* (of which he was editor, 1852–8), *Fraser's Magazine*, and *Notes and Queries*. Among his many works are *An Essay on the Influence of Authority in Matters of Opinion* (1849), an *Enquiry into the Credibility of Early Roman History* (1855), and *An Historical Survey on the Astronomy of the Ancients* (1862).

LEWIS, M(atthew) G(regory) (1775–1818), educated at Westminster and Christ Church, Oxford, is remembered as the author of *The Monk* (1796), a representative *Gothic novel, from which his nickname 'Monk' Lewis was derived. Lewis was greatly influenced by German Romanticism, and wrote numerous dramas. His verses (of which 'Alonzo the Brave and the Fair Imogine', which appears in *The Monk*, is probably the best-known) had some influence on Sir W. *Scott's early poetry.

LEWIS, (Harry) Sinclair (1885–1951), American novelist, born in Minnesota. After graduating from Yale he spent some years in journalism and published several novels, but none was of much importance until *Main Street* which scored an enormous success upon its appearance in 1920. In it he described with realism and satire the dullness of life in a small midwestern town called Gopher Prairie. He strengthened his reputation as the most widely read and controversial of American writers with *Babbitt* (1922), the story of George Babbitt, a prosperous and self-satisfied house-agent in the mid-western town of Zenith, who comes to doubt the conventions of middle-class society, but who is eventually re-absorbed after a period of defiance and ostracism; *Arrowsmith* (1925), which describes the career of a bacteriologist and, like many of Lewis's works, is based on considerable research; *Elmer Gantry* (1927), a satiric view of mid-western religious evangelism; and *Dodsworth* (1929), which describes the marital relations of a middle-aged American industrialist and his adventures in Europe. Lewis was awarded the *Nobel Prize in 1930. His later novels lack the strength and originality of those that made his reputation. See Mark Schorer, *Sinclair Lewis: An American Life* (1961).

LEWIS, (Percy) Wyndham (1882–1957), artist, novelist, and critic. He was born in the US but came to England as a child and studied at the Slade School of Art, then, from 1901 to 1908, on the Continent, based in Paris. He was a leader of the *Vorticist movement and, with *Pound, edited *Blast, the Review of the Great English Vortex* (1914–15). His novels include *Tarr* (1918), *The Apes of God* (1930), *The Revenge for Love* (1937), and *Self Condemned* (1957); his projected four-part work *The Human Age* (*The Childermass*, 1928; *Monstre Gai* and *Malign Fiesta*, both 1955) remained unfinished. Essays and criticism include *Time and Western Man* (1927), *The Lion and the Fox: the Role of Hero in the Plays of Shakespeare* (1927), and *The Writer and the Absolute* (1952). *Blasting and Bombardiering* (1937) and *Rude Assignment* (1950) are autobiographies. Although his criticism of the increasing hollowness and mechanization of 20th-cent. civilization has affinities with the ideas of Pound, T. S. *Eliot and D. H. *Lawrence, his savage satirical attacks on his contemporaries (particularly the *Bloomsbury Group), his association with the British Fascist party, and his praise of Hitler alienated him from the literary world, and his biographer Jeffrey Myers (*The Enemy*, 1980) describes him as 'one of the loneliest figures in the intellectual history of the thirties'. The title of the biography is taken from Lewis's own little magazine *The Enemy*, which appeared in three book-length issues, 1927–9, written largely by himself (with poems by L. *Riding and R. *Campbell): it contained the text of the volume published as *Time and Western Man* and three of his most important essays, 'Paleface', 'The Diabolical Principle' and 'The Revolutionary Simpleton'. (He is not to be confused with D. B. Wyndham Lewis, 1894–1969, the Catholic biographer.)

Lewis and Short, Latin–English dictionary, by Charlton T. Lewis and Charles Short, first published in 1879, and frequently revised.

Lewis Baboon, see JOHN BULL.

LEYDEN, John (1775–1811), Scottish antiquarian, physician, poet, and orientalist, who was equally inspired by Border ballads and the travels of Mungo *Park. He assisted Sir W. *Scott in *Minstrelsy of the Scottish Border*, contributed to M. G. *Lewis's *Tales of Wonder* (1801), and in 1803 set off for India and the Far East; he died at Batavia, Java, having mastered many oriental languages and having set himself up somewhat prematurely as the rival of Sir W. *Jones. Scott mourned his 'bright and brief career' in *The Lord of the Isles* (Canto IV. xi), and contributed a Memoir to the *Edinburgh Annual Register*, 1811, dwelling on his friend's colourful eccentricities. This was reproduced with Leyden's *Poems and Ballads* (1858, 1875). He published several treatises on oriental languages, and translated the Malay Annals (1821) and the *Commentaries of Baber* (1826).

Libeaus Desconsus (a corruption of *le bel inconnu*, the fair unknown), a late 14th-cent. romance in 2,250 lines of 12-line, tail-rhyme stanzas, surviving in six manuscripts, and previously attributed to Thomas Chestre (see SIR LAUNFAL). Gingelein, the illegitimate son of Gawain, asks Arthur for knighthood and, since his name is unknown, he is knighted as *Li Beaus Desconsus*. The poem is concerned with his adventures in rescuing the imprisoned Lady of Sinadoune. In *Chaucer's 'Sir Thopas' the knight's name, whether satirically or not, is given simply as 'Sir Lybeux' (see CANTERBURY TALES, 17) and it has been argued that this romance is the closest in form to 'Thopas'. See edition by M. Mills, EETS os 261, 1969); W. H. Schofield, *Studies on the Libeaus Desconsus* (1895).

Libelle of Englyshe Polycye, The ('the Little Book of English Policy'), a political poem of about 2,250 lines written c.1436, in which the author exhorts his countrymen to regard the sea as the source of national strength, discusses commercial relations with other countries, and urges the importance of retaining Ireland, Calais, and Wales. The poem was included by *Hakluyt, and it has been doubtfully attributed to Adam Moleyns or Molyneaux (d. 1450), clerk of the king's council. See T. Wright, *Political Poems and Songs . . . Edward III to Richard III* (Rolls Series Vol. II, 1861); best edn by F. G. Warner (1926).

Liberal, The (1822–4), a magazine of four issues only but of great brilliance. Conceived by *Shelley, the plan was carried out after his death by *Byron and Leigh *Hunt from Pisa. Byron's *The Vision of Judgement* first appeared in its pages, as did his *Heaven and Earth*, and much other work by Shelley, Hunt, *Hazlitt, J. *Hogg, and others. Libel problems with *The Vision of Judgement* and the incompatibility of Byron and Hunt, brought the magazine to an untimely close.

Liber Albus, see CARPENTER, J.

Liber Amoris, by W. *Hazlitt, published 1823.
    This fevered piece of autobiography describes the author's obsessive and almost insane love for a simple girl, Sarah Walker, who appears to have been in turn flirtatious, frightened, and finally bored. The book takes the form of letters and conversations between Hazlitt and Sarah, and of intimate letters to two friends, J. S. *Knowles and P. *Patmore. *De Quincey described the book as 'an explosion of frenzy'. It does not read as if it were intended for publication; yet although it is often dismissed as an embarrassing failure, it has some power as a raw record of suffering.

Liberty, On, an essay by *J. S. Mill, published 1859. In this work Mill examines the proper relations of society to the individual. In his view, 'the sole end for which mankind are warranted, individually or collectively, in interfering with liberty of action of any of their number, is self-protection.' The only part of the conduct of anyone, for which he is amenable to society, is that which concerns others. A man's own good, either physical or moral, is not a sufficient warrant for the interference of society. 'Mankind are greater gainers by suffering each other to live as seems good to themselves, than by compelling each to live as seems good to the rest.'

Liberty of Prophesying, The, see TAYLOR, JEREMY.

Libraries: a listing of major university libraries and national collections in England, Ireland, Scotland, and Wales, with some details of holdings.

Aberdeen University Library. A 12th-cent. bestiary, Jacobite literature, extensive minor literature of the 18th and 19th cents.

Ashley Library. Private library collected by *Wise. First editions from *Jonson onwards. Acquired by the British Museum in 1937.

Bodleian Library, Oxford. Founded by Sir T. *Bodley. In 1610 the *Stationer's Company undertook to give the library a copy of every book printed in England. It received also important gifts of books and MSS from *Laud, *Cromwell, F. *Junius, and Robert *Burton. Other considerable accessions included *Selden's library, in 1659, the Tanner, Rawlinson, Gough, Malone, and Douce collections of MSS, and John Nichols's collection of newspapers in more recent times. Many of the MSS of *Locke were acquired in 1947, and the collections of manuscripts, both oriental and western, are being continually extended. Copyright library.

British Library. The national library for the United Kingdom. It was established in 1973 under Act of Parliament by the amalgamation of the library departments of the *British Museum and other organizations, as the national centre for reference, lending, bibliographical, and other information services based on its vast collections of books, MSS, maps, music, periodicals, and other material. Copyright library.

Cambridge University Library. The Royal (Bishop Moore's) Library, presented by King George I; the Bradshaw Collection of Irish Books; Taylor-Schechter collection of Hebraica; papers of C. *Darwin. Incunables include a *Gutenberg Bible and unique *Caxton items; *Codex Bezae Cantabrigiensis*, a 5th-cent. manuscript of the Gospels and Acts in Greek and Latin. Copyright library.

Durham University Library. Middle English MSS; letters of G. M. *Hopkins, the *Rossettis, E. *Thomas; MSS of *Plomer, and letters to him from *Britten, E. M. *Forster, etc. Printed books 16th–18th cent.

Glasgow University Library. 1.3 million volumes, including 350 medieval MSS, 1,100 incunabula. Research collections include: *emblem literature, Sir T. *Browne's works, broadside ballads, Scottish theatre archives, 19th-cent. art and literature.

National Library of Scotland, Edinburgh. Founded by Sir George Mackenzie of Rosehaugh (1636–91) as library of the Faculty of Advocates, opened in 1689. Became the National Library of Scotland in 1925. Four million printed items, one million maps, and 34,000 MSS, mainly of Scottish interest. Also modern foreign literature. Copyright library.

National Library of Wales, Aberystwyth. Manuscripts, books, maps, prints, and drawings relating to Wales and the Celtic peoples. Copyright library.

Queen's University of Belfast, The. University library. Hibernica Collection (Irish literature and history), Macdouall Collection (philology), Hamilton Harty Collection (music), and Thomas Percy Library.

St Andrews University Library, Scotland. First four Shakespeare Folios on permanent loan from the Folgar Library; Bibles; first editions of Galileo.

Trinity College Library, University of Dublin. Largest research library in Ireland. Important collection of manuscripts, including Book of *Kells.

Libraries, Circulating, libraries from which, for a fee, books were borrowed by the public. The first appears to have been A. *Ramsay's, founded in Edinburgh in 1726, and the system flourished for over two centuries, at its most dominant in the second half of the 18th and the latter part of the 19th cents. It greatly stimulated the production of books, particularly of novels, though not all approved of this development; the light romantic novels provided by such successful libraries as those of William Lane in the mid-18th cent. were often considered improper, and Sir Anthony Absolute declared, in Sheridan's *The Rivals*, 'A circulating library . . . is an evergreen tree of diabolical knowledge.' But there was also a strong link between Dissent, the self-education of the lower classes, and the circulating library, as J. *Priestley noted. The great new libraries of the 19th cent., *Mudie's, W. H. *Smith's, and *Boots, exercised a powerful censorship; Smith's refused Moore's *Esther Waters* in 1894, and in this century most circulating libraries banned some of the works of H. G. *Wells, *Caine, D. H. *Lawrence, and others. The three-volume novel of the middle and late 19th cent. was largely supported by these libraries, and died out at the end of the century when they no longer wanted it. The chief circulating libraries of this century (Boots, the Times Book Club, the Army and Navy, Mills and Boon, Harrods, etc.) enjoyed great success in the 1920s and 30s, but all were closed by 1970, and replaced by the system of Book Clubs. (See VIZETELLY, H.)

Libraries, Copyright, see LIBRARIES (above) and Appendix II.

Libraries, Public. The first British public libraries were established under the Museum Act, in Canterbury (1847), Warrington (1848), and Salford (1850). A library service was begun in Brighton in 1850 by a private Act. The 1850 Public Libraries Act, piloted by William Ewart against stiff opposition, empowered borough councils in England and Wales (extended to Scotland in 1853, where growth followed a parallel but different course) with a population of 10,000 plus to spend a halfpenny rate on libraries and museums, thus establishing a principle though imposing severe restrictions in practice. In 1855 this was raised to a penny rate and the population limit was lowered to 5,000; in 1866 the population limit was removed. Norwich was the first authority to adopt the 1850 Act, but provided no services until 1857. Winchester was the first library opened under the Act, in 1851, succeeded the following year by Manchester, then Liverpool (by a special Act), Sheffield, and Birmingham. St Margaret and St John's at Westminster was London's only public library from 1857 until 1885, when another was opened in Wandsworth. Growth was slow at first, only 48 libraries being established before 1870, chiefly in England, but also in Wales and Scotland. Thereafter growth was faster, and by the turn of the century some 400 libraries had been set up. The supporters of the Public Libraries Acts hoped that they would encourage working people in refinement, thrift, and sobriety; opponents objected to the burden on the rates and expected the libraries to lead to idleness and discontent.

Public meanness was shamed by private generosity. By 1913 the American philanthropist *Carnegie had given £2m for public libraries and, through the Carnegie UK Trust set up in that year, he continued to give important and influential support. John Passmore Edwards supported 24 libraries, chiefly in and around London and his native Cornwall. After the First World War, the Public Libraries Act of 1919 removed the rate limitation and extended library powers to the counties. By 1928, with the help of the Carnegie Trust, most counties had started a library service. The Mitchell Report of 1924 and the Kenyon Report of 1927 reflected an increasing interest in library development, and marked a stage in the development of libraries for all. Village reading rooms were set up, and library provisions were made for children. The Public Library service continued to grow despite being set back by the depression of 1931–3, helped by the overall increase of local government spending on libraries between 1928 and 1939 (£1.8m to £3.2m). The growth of the county library service was a notable feature of the post-war years, until it was arrested by the recession of the early 1980s. Attempts (some of them controversial) were also made from the 1960s onwards to make libraries attractive as community centres, and to extend their activities to include exhibitions of art and photography, schemes for loaning both reproductions of and original works of art, poetry readings, book order points, etc.; also to attract a larger readership of children through story-telling sessions, school visits, etc.

Library, The, a magazine of bibliography and literature, published from 1889 to 1898 as the organ of the Library Association, and from 1899 to 1918 as an independent journal. In 1920 it was merged with the *Transactions* of the *Bibliographical Society, though retaining its original title.

Libretto, the Italian word for the 'little book' in which the text of an opera (or oratorio) was printed, and hence the text itself. A few composers (*Berlioz, *Wagner, *Tippett) have written their own librettos, one or two have set stage plays more or less as they stood (*Debussy, R. *Strauss), but the majority have used a poet or professional librettist.

A libretto must provide the composer with three elements: a core of character, situation, and plot; a framework of words laid out for musical treatment; and language that will stimulate the creative imagination. Few writers have succeeded in satisfying all the requirements of this difficult and inevitably self-effacing métier. The fact that a libretto possesses beauty of language—as with, e.g., *Hofmannsthal's librettos for Strauss, *Boito's for *Verdi's *Falstaff*, or *Auden's for *Stravinsky's *The Rake's Progress*—is a bonus, but the other elements must also be present. Nor is the language necessarily to be evaluated in terms of conventional literary criticism: *Tate's libretto for *Purcell's *Dido and Aeneas*, which has been much attacked on literary grounds, nevertheless succeeded in firing Purcell's imagination, and its naïvely florid imagery is transmuted by his setting.

Tate was not the first English librettist: he is generally held to have been preceded by *D'Avenant with *The Siege of Rhodes*. Other early English librettists include *Shadwell, whose *Psyche* (1675, music by M. *Locke) was an adaptation from *Molière, and *Dryden, whose *Albion and Albanius* (1685) ended up as a tedious political allegory set to feeble music by Louis Grabu.

In the 18th cent. the taste for Italian music gained ground in England, and the future of the English libretto was threatened. *Addison's single attempt, *Rosamond*, met with a disastrous failure in Clayton's setting in 1707, and with *Handel's arrival in London in 1710 the fate of English opera was sealed. Only in the lighter field did the English libretto survive; the *ballad operas which followed Gay's *The Beggar's Opera* were effectively straight plays interspersed with music, and nearer to the true libretto were the many comic opera texts produced by I. *Bickerstaffe in the 1760s and 1770s, set mainly by *Arne and *Dibdin, often, as was the custom, at least partly as *pasticcios*. In the same vein is Sheridan's *The Duenna* (1775).

Handel's oratorios gave rise to an English libretto of a different character, and the arrangements of biblical and other words by Charles Jennens and Thomas Morell established a precedent that was eagerly taken up by the purveyors of Victorian oratorio, with dreary results: the operatic texts for works by Balfe, Benedict, and Vincent Wallace of librettists like Alfred Bunn and Edward Fitzball have become bywords for absurdity. It was not until 1871 that the first of the *Gilbert and Sullivan operas introduced a new and invigorating talent. Many 20th-cent. composers have taken an active part in the preparation of their own librettos, perhaps motivated by the dire example of 19th-cent. failures, and the professional librettist has disappeared: in his place names like *Hardy, *Synge, A. P. *Herbert, Clifford Bax, J. B. *Priestley, and *Plomer have been found in the opera programmes of the last sixty years, and Auden, in his librettos for *Britten, Stravinsky, and *Henze established himself as the most important writer in this form in the last few decades.

LICHTENBERG, Georg Christoph (1742–99), born in Hessen, was educated and later a professor at Göttingen, thus becoming a subject of George III, of whose Hanoverian dominions Göttingen formed part. A distinguished scientist, but interested also in philosophy (a disciple of *Kant), he twice visited England, in 1770 and 1774–5, and was a guest at Kew of George III. He was an ardent admirer of English institutions and literature and a keen dramatic critic. His letters from England to his friends in Germany (*Lichtenberg's Visits to England*, 1938) contain shrewd comments on the acting of *Garrick, *Macklin, etc., and throw an interesting light on contemporary English manners. He also published (1794–9) in Germany explanations of W. *Hogarth's engravings.

Licia, or *Poemes of Love*, see FLETCHER, G. (the elder).

LIDDELL, Henry George (1811–98), born into a family with substantial aristocratic connections, became successively headmaster of *Westminster School (1846) and dean of Christ Church, Oxford (1855). A lifelong friend of *Ruskin, he did much to reform both these institutions. Earlier he had compiled with Robert Scott (1811–87) the famous Greek lexicon, which, repeatedly revised, is still in use today. Held in the highest esteem by his contemporaries, he is chiefly remembered now as the father of the little girl who served Lewis Carroll (C. L. *Dodgson) as a model for Alice.

Life and Adventures of Sir Launcelot Greaves, The, see SIR LAUNCELOT GREAVES, THE LIFE AND ADVENTURES OF.

Life and Death of Jason, The, a poem in heroic couplets by W. *Morris.

Life and Labour of the People in London, see BOOTH, C.

Life and Letters, a literary monthly periodical founded and edited from 1928 to 1933 by D. *MacCarthy. It subsequently continued as *Life and Letters Today*, and in 1939 absorbed the *London Mercury and Bookman*, reverting from 1945 to 1950 to its original title. The final issue appeared in June 1950. Early issues contained essays, reviews, fiction, passages of autobiography, etc., from many distinguished contributors, including *Beerbohm, A. *Huxley, C. *Bell, V. *Woolf, and C. *Connolly; poetry was better represented in its later years by G. *Barker, V. *Watkins, and others.

Life in London, see EGAN, P.

Life of Samuel Johnson, The, see JOHNSON, THE LIFE OF SAMUEL.

Life on the Mississippi, an autobiographical account by Mark *Twain.

Light, Christina, a character in H. James's *Roderick Hudson* and *The Princess Casamassima*.

LIGHTFOOT, John (1602–75), biblical and rabbinic scholar, and from 1643 master of Catherine Hall, Cambridge. His best-known work is his series of *Horae Hebraicae et Talmudicae* (1658–78), which relates Jewish studies to the interpretation of the New Testament. He assisted Brian Walton with the *Polyglot Bible.

Light of Asia, The, see ARNOLD, SIR E.

Light Shining in Buckinghamshire, (1) the title of an anonymous pamphlet issued by the Levellers in 1648, attacking monarchy and calling for equality of property; it was followed by a sequel, *More Light Shining in Buckinghamshire* (1649) (see PAMPHLETEERING, ORIGINS OF); (2) the title of a play by Caryl *Churchill, staged in 1976 by Joint Stock at the Theatre Upstairs at the Royal Court Theatre for the *English Stage Company.

Light That Failed, The, a novel by R. *Kipling.

LILBURNE, John (c.1614–57), pamphleteer,

political agitator, and Leveller, was brought before the Star Chamber in 1638 for printing an unlicensed book, and imprisoned; *The Work of the Beast* (1638) gives an account of his barbarous treatment. He fought with distinction in the parliamentary army, but repeatedly criticized the army officers and was repeatedly imprisoned; he was banished in 1652 but returned the following year. In 1655 he became a Quaker. In his many pamphlets he speaks for the rights of the common man, describing his followers as 'clubs and clouted shoon', for God 'doth not choose many rich, nor many wise . . . but the fools, idiots, base and contemptible poor men and women in the esteem of the world', but he never advocated Communism. He published pamphlets jointly with *Overton and *Walwyn. A life by P. Gregg was published in 1961.

'Lilli-Burlero Bullen-a-la!' 'said to have been the words of distinction used among the Irish Papists in their massacre of the Protestants in 1641' (*Percy). They were made the refrain of a song, attributed to Lord Wharton, satirizing the earl of Tyrconnel on the occasion of his going to Ireland in Jan. 1686-7 as James II's papist lieutenant. The song is given in Percy's *Reliques* where Percy quotes *Burnet's account:

A foolish ballad was made at that time, treating the Papists, and chiefly the Irish, in a very ridiculous manner, which had a burden said to be Irish words, 'Lero, lero, lilliburlero', that made an impression on the army, that cannot be imagined by those that saw it not. The whole army, and at last the people, both in city and country, were singing it perpetually. And perhaps never had so slight a thing so great an effect.

According to Chappell's *Popular Music of the Olden Time*, the tune of 'Lilliburlero' was included, in 1689, in the second part of *Music's Handmaid* as 'a new Irish Tune' by 'Mr Purcell', but it occurs in *The Delightful Companion* of 1686.

Lilliput, see GULLIVER'S TRAVELS.

Lilliput Levee, see RANDS, W. B.

LILLO, George (1693–1739), was the author of the famous prose domestic tragedy *The London Merchant, or the History of *George Barnwell*, produced in 1731. Little is known of his life; he is said to have been a jeweller of Flemish descent, praised by *Fielding as 'content with his little state of life'. His other plays include *The Christian Hero*, produced in 1735, *The Fatal Curiosity* (1736), and a tragedy on the subject of *Arden of Feversham (also 1736). Lillo's introduction of middle-class domestic tragedy had an influence which extended beyond English literature: see LESSING, G. E., and DIDEROT.

LILLY, William (1602–81), a noted astrologer, patronized by *Ashmole, who built up a highly successful London practice, and managed to survive the political upheavals of the period despite several arrests; he supported Parliament during the 1640s and was favoured by the Protectorate, but wrote with some sympathy of Charles I as 'not the worst, but the most unfortunate, of Kings' (*Monarchy or no monarchy in England*, 1651) and from 1660 protested loyalty to the crown. He published almanacs yearly from 1644 until his death (issued from 1647 under the title *Merlini Anglici Aphemeris*) and by 1659 these were selling in vast quantities of *c.*300,000 a year. His *Christian Astrology* (1647) was the standard guide to the subject for those who could read only English. He is thought to have been in part the model for Sidrophel in *Hudibras*. The case-books recording his consultations survive in the Ashmole MSS of the Bodleian library, and his autobiography appears with Ashmole's *Memoirs*, in the 1774 edition. (See ALMANACS.)

Lillyvick, Mr, a character in Dickens's *Nicholas Nickleby*.

LILY, William (*c.*1468–1522), friend of *Colet and Sir T. *More, grandfather of J. *Lyly, and a leader of the revival of Greek studies in England. Though married and a layman, he was made first high master of St *Paul's School. He contributed a short Latin syntax, with the rules in English, to the Latin grammar by Colet and *Erasmus, *c.*1509. This, with another grammar, was the basis of the work known as *Lily's Grammar* which was long familiar to English schoolboys; cf. the Latin lesson in *The Merry Wives of Windsor*, IV. i. On the complete history of his grammatical writings, see C. G. Allen in *The Library* (June 1954).

Limberham, central character in Dryden's *Mr Limberham*.

Limerick, a form of facetious jingle, of which the first instances occur in *The History of Sixteen Wonderful Old Women* (1820) and *Anecdotes and Adventures of Fifteen Gentlemen* (*c.*1821), subsequently popularized by *Lear in his *Book of Nonsense*. The name is said to be derived from a custom at convivial parties, according to which each member sang an extemporized 'nonsense-verse', which was followed by a chorus containing the words 'Will you come up to Limerick?' [OED]. Limericks have been composed on a great variety of subjects from philosophic doctrines to jokes of extreme obscenity.

In the older form of limerick, as written by Lear, D. G. *Rossetti, and others, the first and last lines usually ended with the same word, but in more recent examples, such as the following comment on G. *Berkeley's philosophy by R. *Knox, and those written by W. H. *Auden, G. *Ewart, O. *Nash, N. *Douglas, R. *Conquest, and others, a third rhyming word is supplied:

There once was a man who said: 'God
Must think it exceedingly odd
　　If he finds that this tree
　　Continues to be
When there's no-one about in the Quad.

A great number of the best-known limericks are, for obvious reasons, anonymous.

LINACRE, Thomas (?1460–1524), physician and classical scholar, was educated at Oxford and was a fellow of *All Souls College. He was MD of Padua, and became one of *Henry VIII's physicians. Later he was Latin tutor to the Princess Mary, for whom he composed a Latin grammar, *Rudimenta Grammatices*. He was mainly instrumental in founding the College of Physicians in 1518. He wrote grammatical and medical works, and translated from the Greek, mainly from *Galen.

LINCOLN, Abraham (1809–65), was president of the United States, 1861–5, and political leader of the Northern States in the Civil War. He was assassinated by the actor John Wilkes Booth. His great inaugural and other speeches show a direct, pregnant, non-rhetorical style, a gift for political aphorism, and a strong sense of rhythm. Notable among them was the Gettysburg Address, given at the dedication of the national cemetery at Gettysburg on 19 Nov. 1863, four months after the battle there.

Lindisfarne Gospels, a manuscript of the four Gospels in the *Vulgate text, probably written in honour of the canonization of St *Cuthbert (698). The script is Anglo-Saxon majuscule and there are magnificent illuminations and decorative capitals. An Anglo-Saxon gloss was added in the late 10th cent. in Northumbrian dialect with a colophon stating that the text was written by Eadfrith, bishop of Lindisfarne 698–721, and naming the binder, the goldsmith who ornamented the binding, and the translator, Aldred of Chester-le-Street. The manuscript is in the Cottonian collection in the *British Museum. See Janet Backhouse, *The Lindisfarne Gospels* (1981).

LINDSAY, Lady Anne (1750–1825), daughter of the fifth earl of Balcarres, wrote in 1771 the immensely popular ballad 'Auld Robin Gray', but did not acknowledge authorship until two years before her death. She became by marriage Lady Anne Barnard, and accompanied her husband to South Africa, where she wrote the journals *Lady Anne Barnard at the Cape, 1797–1802*, which provide important authority for events during the first British occupation of Cape Town. After the death of her husband she returned home, and with her sister established a literary salon in London.

LINDSAY, or LYNDSAY, Sir David (*c.* 1486–1555), Scottish poet and Lyon king-of-arms; usher to Prince James (afterwards James V). His first poem, 'The Dreme', written in 1528 but not printed till after his death, is an allegorical lament on the misgovernment of the realm, followed by a vigorous exhortation to the king. In 1529 he wrote the *Complaynt to the King*, in octosyllabic couplets, commenting on the improved social condition of the realm except as regards the Church, lamenting that others have been preferred before him at court, and requesting the king that he 'wyll uther geve or len me' 'off gold ane thousand pound, or tway'. The *Testament, and Complaynt, of our Soverane Lordis Papyngo* (finished 1530, printed 1538) combines advice to the king, put in the mouth of his parrot, with a warning to courtiers drawn from the examples of Scottish history, and with a satire on ecclesiastics in the form of a conference between the dying parrot and its 'Holye Executouris'. Lindsay's principal poem, *Ane *Pleasant Satyre of the Thrie Estaitis*, a morality, was produced in 1540 before the king and court. Other poems by Lindsay include *The Monarchie (Ane dialog betwix Experience and ane Courteour, off the miserabyll estait of the Warld)* (1554) and the *Historie of Squyer Meldrum* (first extant edition of 1582), a spirited verse romance on the career and exploits of a Scottish laird.

Works, ed. D. Hamar (STS, 3rd series, 1, 2, 6, 8, 1931–6); selection ed. M. Lindsay (Saltire Society Classics, 1948); *The Thrie Estaitis* ed. J. Kinsley (1954) and by P. Happé in *Four Morality Plays* (1979).

LINDSAY, Robert (?1500–?65), of Pitscottie, author of *The Historie and Croniclis of Scotland* from the reign of James II, one of Sir W. *Scott's principal sources for the period.

LINDSAY, Vachel, see JAZZ POETRY.

LINGARD, John (1771–1851), a Roman Catholic priest, was the author of *The Antiquities of the Anglo-Saxon Church* (1806); and, more importantly, of a *History of England* (1819–30), the principal object of which is to emphasize the disastrous effects of the Reformation. His idealized portrait of the Middle Ages had considerable influence on writers and thinkers as diverse as W. *Morris and the founders of the *Oxford Movement.

Linguistics (also 'Theoretical' or 'General' linguistics), a term used to characterize the study of language in the 20th cent. owing much to the Swiss linguist *Saussure; it distinguishes itself from earlier language study by concentrating on the language at a particular time ('synchronic') rather than the history of language and languages ('diachronic'). It claims to be the principal new science, and its method has been influential in several other areas (anthropology, sociology, mathematics, and literary criticism, for example). For major practitioners, see SAUSSURE; BLOOMFIELD, L.; CHOMSKY; and JAKOBSON.

Linkinwater, Tim, in Dickens's *Nicholas Nickleby*, clerk to the brothers Cheeryble.

LINKLATER, Eric (1899–1974), born in Orkney, served in the First World War, and after graduating from Aberdeen University became assistant editor to *The Times of Bombay*. During 1928–30, he was in the US as Commonwealth fellow, where he gathered material for *Juan in America* (1930), a satirical novel which brought him immediate fame. *Ben Jonson and King James* appeared in the same year. His other works include *Juan in China* (1937); *Private Angelo* (1946), describing the campaign in Italy and one of his best-known works; *Husband of Delilah* (1962); *The Voyage of the Challenger* (1972); and *The Corpse on Clapham Common* (1971). *The Man on My Back* (1941) and *A Year of Space* (1953) were autobiographical.

LINNAEUS, Latinized form of LINNÉ, Carl (1707–78), Swedish naturalist and founder of the internationally used binomial system for scientifically naming animals and plants. He was from 1741 professor of medicine and botany at Uppsala. His most important publications were *Species Plantarum* (1753) and *Systema Naturae*, 10th edn, vol. 1 (1758), both in Latin, but in Sweden he is more esteemed for the accounts of his travels in Lapland, Oland, and Gotland, written in simple and vivid Swedish. In 1783 James Edward Smith bought his collections and in 1788 was one of the founders of the Linnean Society of London, still active, Britain's oldest biological society.

Linnean Society, see LINNAEUS.

Linton, Edgar, Isabella, and Catherine, characters in E. Brontë's *Wuthering Heights*.

LINTON, Eliza Lynn, *née* Lynn (1822–98), English novelist and journalist, born in Keswick, who launched herself on a London literary career with two historical novels (*Azeth the Egyptian*, 1846; *Amymone*, 1848), which she followed with many more successful novels of contemporary life, such as *Rebel of the Family* (1880). She offended many of her female contemporaries by her essays attacking feminism and the *New Woman, some of which were collected from the *Saturday Review* as *The Girl of the Period* (1883). Her posthumously published memoir *My Literary Life* (1899) contains a notably hostile portrait of G. *Eliot.

LINTOT, or **LINTOTT,** Barnaby Bernard (1675–1736), bookseller and printer, published a *Miscellaneous Poems and Translations by several hands* (1712), which contained the first version of *The Rape of the Lock*. He published other works by *Pope (who compared his uncouth appearance to that of a dabchick in the *Dunciad*, ii. 63), and poems and plays by *Gay, *Farquhar, *Steele, *Rowe, and others.

Lipsia, in imprints, Leipzig.

LIPSIUS, Justus, or Joest LIPS (1547–1606), a Flemish humanist, who adopted the Protestant faith and was professor at Jena and subsequently at the University of Leyden, where he was succeeded by J. J. *Scaliger. His principal work was a learned edition of *Tacitus.

Lir, see LÊR.

Lisle Letters, a collection of some 3,000 letters written to and from Arthur Plantagenet, Viscount Lisle (an illegitimate son of Edward IV), his family and household, while he was lord deputy of Calais from 1533 to 1540. They give a vivid picture of the political and domestic life of the time; the originals are in the Public Record Office and have been edited by Muriel St Clare Byrne (6 vols, 1981), with a one-volume abridgement by B. Boland (1983).

Lismahago, Obadiah, a character in Smollett's *Humphry Clinker*.

Listener, The, a BBC weekly magazine, of which the first number appeared on 16 Jan. 1929; it publishes reviews, broadcasts, essays, poetry, etc. Its literary editor from 1935 to 1959 was J. R. *Ackerley, who attracted work from many distinguished writers. *The Music of What Happens: Poems from the Listener* (1981), edited by Derwent May, poet and novelist, and literary editor from 1965, contains work by Stevie *Smith, P. *Larkin, P. *Porter, Ted *Hughes, S. *Heaney, and others.

LISTER, Thomas Henry (1800–42), the first registrar-general of England and Wales, was a neglected but very accomplished novelist, much influenced by J. *Austen, whose tone he noticeably adopts and the names of whose characters he sometimes uses. Although they contain certain overdramatic incidents, *Granby* (1826), *Herbert Lacy* (1828), and *Arlington* (1832) are all shrewd and animated works, which describe with an ironic eye the aristocratic and upper-middle-class society of the time.

Lisuarte, see AMADIS OF GAUL.

LISZT, Franz (1811–86), Hungarian composer and pianist, one of the greatest of all performers on a solo instrument and a central figure of the musical Romantic movement. In both capacities he created a legend, not always kind to himself, and it is perhaps worth recalling G. B. *Shaw's summing up at the time of his death: 'a man who loved his art, despised money, attracted everybody worth knowing in the nineteenth century, lived through the worst of it, and got away from it at last with his hands unstained'.

About Liszt's qualities as a composer opinion has differed, though it is generally conceded that he was a figure of importance and often of striking originality. The series of 12 'symphonic poems' (his own term, and a form of which he is credited with the invention) that he wrote between 1848 and 1858 ends with a *Hamlet, originally planned as an overture to Shakespeare's play and providing, characteristically, a well thought out psychological study of the prince himself, rather than any attempt to describe the action of the play in music. It is one of Liszt's best orchestral works. Other English literary influences, however, are hard to find. *Byron hovers, predictably, but an early operatic project adapted from *Sardanapalus got no further than 111 sheets of sketches and, among the symphonic poems, Tasso is based on *Goethe, Mazeppa on *Hugo; three pieces in the first book of the Années de pèlerinage are prefaced by quotations from *Childe Harold's Pilgrimage, though not apparently with any very precise descriptive intention.There is a single, delicate, English setting, *Tennyson's 'Go not, happy day', and more surprisingly a late choral work, Die Glocken des Strassburger Münsters (1875), based on an episode from *Longfellow's Golden Legend preceded by an orchestral prelude entitled Excelsior—the whole dedicated to Longfellow himself.

Literary Anecdotes of the Eighteenth Century, see NICHOLS, J.

Literary Club, see CLUB, THE.

Literary Gazette, The (1817–62), a very successful journal founded by *Colburn, with William Jerdan as editor. It aimed at a very wide coverage of books, fine arts, and sciences, but most of the space was given to book reviews and long extracts from the works reviewed. Early contributors, in the days of its greatest success, included *Crabbe, M. R. *Mitford, *Cornwall, and L. E. *Landon.

Literary Magazine, The: or Universal Review, a periodical started in 1756, nominally edited by the printer William Faden, but in practice conducted largely by Dr *Johnson, who contributed many articles, including, notably, his review of *Jenyns's A Free Enquiry into the Nature and Origin of Evil (1757). The magazine was discontinued in 1758.

Literati, a term introduced by Robert *Burton to refer to the literate class in China, and later applied to the writers and readers of fashionable literature in other communities, often by contrast with the practical scientists, or virtuosi. The term is now frequently used to identify those who frequented the literary clubs of 18th-cent. Edinburgh, and the bookshops of *Ramsay, Creech, and Kincaid. They included resident literary figures like R. *Fergusson, A. *Cockburn, *Boswell, and H. *Mackenzie, and temporary residents like *Gay, *Defoe, *Goldsmith, and *Smollett. But it is more particularly applied to a group of professional men, mostly lawyers and clergy, and mostly supporters of or supported by the Moderate party in the Scottish church; at a time when vernacular writing was in decline, they self-consciously cultivated an English writing style, both to make a cultural impact on London society and to cement the political union with England. They included the lawyers H. *Home and *Monboddo, the philosophers *Hume and Adam *Smith, and the clerical coterie of H. *Blair, A. *Carlyle, A. *Ferguson, J. *Home, W. *Robertson, and *Wilkie, several of whom were associated with the abortive first *Edinburgh Review. Although their writings were primarily on history, philosophy, and the theory of criticism, many of them also supported the legalization and revival of the legitimate theatre, against fierce Calvinist opposition. Hume in 1752 and *Beattie in 1779 assisted the movement for stylistic improvement by publishing collections of unacceptable 'Scotticisms'; and Thomas Sheridan, father of the dramatist, lectured to men's and women's classes on English elocution in 1761 under the auspices of the *Select Society. (See also SCOTTISH ENLIGHTENMENT.)

Litotes, a figure of speech in which an affirmative is expressed by the negative of the contrary, e.g. 'a citizen of no mean city'; an ironical understatement.

Littimer, in Dickens's *David Copperfield, Steerforth's hypocritical valet.

Little, Thomas, see MOORE, T.

Little Billee, a humorous ballad of three sailors of Bristol, of whom Little Billee is the youngest. When provisions fail he narrowly escapes being eaten by the other two. *Thackeray wrote a version of the ballad. 'Little Billee' was the nickname of the hero of Du Maurier's *Trilby.

Little Dorrit, a novel by *Dickens, published in monthly parts, 1855–7.

William Dorrit has been so long in the Marshalsea prison for debtors that he has become the 'Father of the Marshalsea'. He has had the misfortune to be responsible for an uncompleted contract with the Circumlocution Office (a satirical portrait of the government departments of the day, with their incompetent and obstructive officials typified in the Barnacles). His lot is alleviated by the devotion of Amy, his youngest daughter, 'Little Dorrit', born in the Marshalsea, whose diminutive stature is compensated by the greatness of her heart. Amy has a snobbish sister Fanny, a theatrical dancer, and a scapegrace brother, Tip. Old Dorrit and Amy are befriended by Arthur Clennam, the middle-aged hero, for whom Little Dorrit conceives a deep passion, at first unrequited. The unexpected discovery that William Dorrit is heir to a fortune raises the family to affluence. Except Little Dorrit, they become arrogant and purse-proud. Clennam, on the other hand, owing to an unfortunate speculation, is brought in turn to the debtor's prison, and is found in the Marshalsea, sick and despairing, by Little Dorrit, who tenderly nurses him and consoles him. He has meanwhile learnt the value of her love, but her fortune stands in the way of his asking her to marry him. The loss of it makes their union possible, on Clennam's release.

With this main theme is wound the thread of an elaborate mystery. Clennam has long suspected that his mother, a grim old puritanical paralysed woman, living in a gloomy house with a former attendant and present partner, Flintwinch, has done some wrong to Little Dorrit. Through the agency of a stagy villain, Rigaud, alias Blandois, this is brought to light, and it appears that Mrs Clennam is not Arthur's mother, and that her religious principles have not prevented her from suppressing a codicil in a will that benefited the Dorrit family.

There are a host of minor characters in the work, of whom the most notable are the worthy Pancks, rent-collector to the humbug Casby; Casby's voluble daughter Flora Finching, the early love of Arthur Clennam; her eccentric relative 'Mr F's Aunt'; Merdle, the swindling financier, and Mrs Merdle, who 'piques herself on being society'; Affery, the villain Flintwinch's wife; 'Young John' Chivery, the son of the Marshalsea warder; and the Meagles and Gowan households.

Little Dorrit was heavily criticized on publication, largely for its sombre tone and complex plot, but later critics such as G. B. *Shaw (his 'masterpiece among many masterpieces'), *Trilling, and Angus *Wilson have done much to reverse this judgement.

Little Eva, the saintly child Evangeline St Clair in H. B. *Stowe's *Uncle Tom's Cabin* whose deathbed scene rivals in sentiment the death of Little Nell in *The Old Curiosity Shop.

Little Gidding, a manor in Huntingdonshire where N. *Ferrar and his family established, 1625–46, a religious community of some forty members, following a systematic rule of private devotion, public charity, and study. The house was visited by Charles I, *Crashaw, and G. *Herbert, and *Shorthouse's novel *John Inglesant* (1881) portrays its life vividly. It was raided by Cromwell's soldiers in 1646, and the community dispersed. T. S. Eliot celebrates it in 'Little Gidding', one of the *Four Quartets (1944), and a record of its activities survives in *The Little Gidding Story Books*, five manuscript volumes bound by Mary Collett, part of which was printed in 1899, ed. E. C. Sharland.

Little John, one of the companions of *Robin Hood in the legends relating to that outlaw. He was a sturdy yeoman and a skilled archer, originally called John Little. He figures in Sir W. Scott's *Ivanhoe.

Littlejohn, Hugh, John Hugh Lockhart, the grandson of Sir W. *Scott, to whom *The Tales of a Grandfather* are dedicated.

Little Lord Fauntleroy, see BURNETT, F. H.

Little Magazines, a term used to describe minority literary and artistic periodicals, possibly derived, as G. *Grigson suggests in an issue of the *Times Literary Supplement* devoted to the subject (25 April 1968) from one of the better known of such publications, the *Little Review*. English 'little magazines' include *The Savoy, *Rhythm, Blast, *New Verse, *The Review and its successor The New Review, *Stand, *Ambit, and *Agenda.

Little Musgrave and Lady Barnard, an ancient ballad, given in Percy's *Reliques, which tells how Lady Barnard, loving Little Musgrave, invited him to pass the night with her in her bower at Bucklesford-Bury. A little foot-page overhears the assignation and tells Lord Barnard. He finds the lovers together, fights with Musgrave and kills him, then kills his wife and is afterwards filled with remorse.

Musgrave is referred to in Beaumont and Fletcher's *The Knight of the Burning Pestle, Act V, and in D'Avenant's *The Wits, III. iii.

Little Nell (Trent), the heroine of Dickens's *The Old Curiosity Shop.

Little Review, The, an American monthly magazine founded in Chicago in 1914 by Margaret Anderson. In 1916 it came under the influence of *Pound, who was foreign editor from 1917 to 1919; it published *Yeats, W. *Lewis, T. S. *Eliot, F. M. *Ford, and, notably, from 1918, chapters of Joyce's *Ulysses. It later became a quarterly published from Paris (1924–9), edited principally by Jane Heap and including work by *Hemingway, *Cummings, H. *Crane, etc. It folded in 1929 with Jane Heap's statement: 'For years we offered the *Little Review* as a trial-track for racers . . . But you can't get race horses from mules. We have given space in the *Little Review* to 23 new systems of art (all now dead), representing 19 countries. In all of this we have not brought forward anything approaching a masterpiece except the *Ulysses* of Mr Joyce.'

Little Women, by L. M. *Alcott, one of the most popular juvenile books ever written, published 1868–9, and based on the author's memories of her childhood home. The story concerns the daily lives of four girls—Jo March, who aspires to be a writer, and her sisters Meg, Beth, and Amy—in a New England family in the mid-19th cent. Their mother is cheerful and uncomplaining, their father an improvident army chaplain in the Civil War.

LITTRÉ, Émile (1801–81), French scholar, philosopher, and lexicographer, began work on his great dictionary of the French language in 1846. It was published in four volumes (1863–73), with a supplementary volume in 1877. The whole work was reprinted in 1950. Littré was a follower of *Comte, after whose death he became the leading exponent of the positive philosophy, publishing *Auguste Comte et la philosophie positive* in 1863. In 1867 he founded with G. N. Wyrouboff, the Russian positivist, the *Revue de Philosophie Positive*. Littré also edited and translated the works of *Hippocrates (1839–61) and wrote an *Histoire de la langue française* (1862).

Liverpool Poets, the name given to a group of three poets, Adrian *Henri, Roger McGough (1937–), and Brian Patten (1946–), who came together in the 1960s in the period of the Liverpool euphoria generated partly by the success of the *Beatles. They performed together, and published together in various periodicals and anthologies including *The Mersey Sound* (1967), *The Liverpool Scene* (1967), and *New Volume* (1983). The combined tone of their work was pop, 'underground', urban, anti-academic, good-humoured, and vocal: poetry was conceived by them as a medium for public rather than private consumption, a performance art.

Lives of the English Poets, The, a work by Dr *Johnson, originally entitled *Prefaces biographical and critical to the Works of the English Poets,* published 1779–81.

Johnson was invited in 1777 by a deputation of London booksellers to provide biographical prefaces for an edition of the works of various English poets, from the period of *Milton onwards; the selection was made by them, and includes poets of very differing merit. The final total was 52, including 4 minor poets suggested by Johnson himself. When the work was completed the prefaces were issued without the texts as *Lives of the Poets.* The *Lives* contain much interesting biographical matter, but are not always trustworthy. The criticism has been considered unequal, particularly in respect of its strictures on Milton's *Lycidas*, *Gray's Odes, and its evident prejudice against *Swift; Johnson's hostile analysis of the *metaphysical style, in his life of *Cowley, became notorious. But the work remains a classic, important both as a landmark in the history of critical taste and judgement, and for its own insights; T. S. *Eliot ('Johnson as Critic and Poet', 1944) credited it 'with a coherence, as well as an amplitude, which no other English criticism can claim'.

Lives of the Poets, see LIVES OF THE ENGLISH POETS, THE.

Living, a novel by H. *Green.

LIVINGSTONE, David (1813–73), Scottish missionary and explorer. From the age of 10 he worked in a cotton factory, while educating himself. He took his medical degree in 1840 and in the same year was ordained under the London Missionary Society and embarked for the Cape of Good Hope. In the following 30 years he travelled across more than one-third of the African continent gathering important information about the country, it products, its native tribes, and the slave trade. His many geographical discoveries included Lake Ngami, Lake Nyasa, and the Victoria Falls. His expeditions are described in *Missionary Travels and Researches in South Africa* (1857) and *Narrative of an Expedition to the Zambesi and its Tributaries and the discovery of the Lakes of Shirwa and Nyassa* (1865, in collaboration with his brother Charles). During his final expedition, to discover the sources of the Nile, he was rescued, almost dying, by H. M. *Stanley in Ujiji in 1871; he resumed his explorations but never recovered his health. He was buried in Westminster Abbey. His *Last Journals of David Livingstone in Central Africa from 1865 to his death* appeared posthumously in 1874.

LIVY (Titus Livius) (59 BC–?AD 17), the most attractive of Roman historians. His great work related the history of Rome from its beginnings to 9 BC. Of its 142 books only 35 have survived, the best-known of which give us the legendary history of early Rome and the second Punic War. Livy had no great influence on English historians, who seem to have passed straight from the writing of chronicles to *Machiavellian analyses of statecraft. But his stories of Rome's beginnings provided material for Painter's *Palace of Pleasure* (1566–7) and *Pettie's similar work of 1576, for Shakespeare's *Rape of Lucrece* (1594), and later for Macaulay's *Lays of Ancient Rome* (1842).

Lizzie Hexam, a character in Dickens's *Our Mutual Friend.*

LLANDAFF, bishop of, see WATSON, R.

Llangollen, The Ladies of, were Lady Eleanor Butler (?1739–1829) and Miss Sarah Ponsonby (?1735–1831), two devoted friends who left their families (against strong opposition) to set up a lifelong residence together in Plas Newydd in Llangollen Vale. Their house, adorned in the *Gothic style, became a place of admiration and curiosity far beyond its neighbourhood, visited by distinguished guests, including *Wordsworth (who wrote them a sonnet), A. *Seward (who commemorated them in her poem 'Llangollen Vale', 1795), *Burke, and Mme de Genlis. See *The Hamwood Papers of the Ladies of Llangollen and Caroline Hamilton* (1930), ed. Mrs. G. H. Bell, and 'Living the Gothic Pastoral Romance' (1949, *Modern Language Review*; reprinted in *Women and Literature,* 1982) by M. C. *Bradbrook.

Llyr, see MABINOGION. Perhaps to be identified with Lir (see LÊR).

Lochinvar, the hero of a ballad included in the fifth canto of Scott's *Marmion*. His fair Ellen is about to be married to 'a laggard in love and a dastard in war', when the brave Lochinvar arrives at the bridal feast, claims a dance with her, and, as they reach the hall door, swings the lady on to his horse, and rides off with her.

LOCKE, John (1632–1704), born at Wrington, Somerset, was educated at Westminster and Christ Church, Oxford. He held various academic posts at that university, and became physician to the household of the first earl of *Shaftesbury in 1667. He held official positions and subsequently lived at Oxford, then fled to Holland in 1683 as a consequence of Shaftesbury's plotting for Monmouth; how far he was himself involved is not certain. In 1687 he joined William of Orange at Rotterdam; on his return to England he became commissioner of appeals and member of the council of trade. His last years were spent in Essex in the home of Sir Francis and Lady Masham, the latter being the daughter of Ralph Cudworth, one of the *Cambridge Platonists.

Locke's principal philosophical work is the *Essay concerning Human Understanding* (1690), a work which led J. S. *Mill to call him the 'unquestioned founder of the analytic philosophy of mind'. Always critical of 'enthusiasm', he was originally opposed to freedom of religion, and never supported Catholic emancipation; but in his maturity he defended the rights of the Dissenters on both moral and economic grounds. He published three *Letters* on Toleration between 1689 and 1692; a fourth was left unfinished at his death. His defence of simple biblical religion in *The Reasonableness of Christianity* (1695), without resort to creed or tradition, led to a charge of *Socinianism, which Locke replied to in two *Vindications* (1695, 1697). He was also involved in an extensive pamphlet war with *Stillingfleet (1696–8) over the alleged compatibility of his *Essay* with Socinianism and *Deism.

Locke published in 1690 two *Treatises of Government* designed to combat the theory of the divine right of kings. He finds the origin of the civil state in a contract. The 'legislative', or government, 'being only a fiduciary power to act for certain ends, there remains still in the people the supreme power to remove or alter the legislative when they find the legislative act contrary to the trust reposed in them.' Throughout, Locke in his theory of the 'Original Contract' opposes absolutism; the first *Treatise* is specifically an attack on Sir Robert Filmer's *Patriarcha*. Although Locke in his early manuscripts was closer to *Hobbes's authoritarianism and continues to share with Hobbes the view that civil obligations are founded in contract, he strongly rejected Hobbes's view that the sovereign is above the law and no party to the contract. He published a volume on education in 1693, and on the rate of interest and the value of money in 1692 and 1695. The first edition of his collected works appeared in 1714. A full critical edition of his works, including eight volumes of correspondence, was launched in 1975.

Locke's writings had an immense influence on the literature of succeeding generations, and he was very widely read; his *Thoughts concerning Education*, which are concerned with practical advice on the upbringing of 'sons of gentlemen' were given to *Richardson's Pamela by Mr B—, and to his son by *Chesterfield, and their influence is seen in *Rousseau's Émile; his view of the child's mind as a *tabula rasa*, and his distinctions between wit and judgement, were the subject of much discussion in the *Augustan age. The anti-philosophy jokes of the *Scriblerus Club demonstrate the currency of his ideas; *Addison was his champion in many essays. But perhaps his greatest impact was on *Sterne, who quotes him frequently in *Tristram Shandy*, and who was deeply interested in his theories of the random association of ideas, of the measuring of time, of the nature of sensation, etc. On this subject, see Kenneth MacLean, *John Locke and English Literature of the Eighteenth Century* (1936). (See also RESTORATION.)

LOCKE, Matthew (1621–77), the most eminent composer of the early Restoration, prolific in many forms and of the first importance as a producer of music for the stage during the period when opera was on the verge of being introduced into England. His earliest work of this type was the music for *Shirley's masque *Cupid and Death* (1653), written in collaboration with Christopher Gibbons (Orlando's son): this is the only work of its kind of which the complete score has survived, and is particularly interesting for its use of the declamatory, recitative style of word setting, the essential feature upon which the future development of opera was to depend. The music he wrote, with four other composers, for what is generally regarded as the first English opera, *D'Avenant's *The Siege of Rhodes* (1656), is all lost; and what was for years considered as one of the classics of Shakespearian incidental music, for D'Avenant's version of *Macbeth, is now known not to have been by Locke. But he made another contribution to the development of opera in his music for *Shadwell's *Psyche* (1675), grandly entitled in the libretto 'The English Opera . . . ', though it is in fact clearly based on a *tragédie-ballet* by *Molière of four years earlier and does not step over the borderline that divides the courtly *masque from its operatic successors.

LOCKER-LAMPSON, Frederick (1821–

95), born Locker, is remembered for his light verse, included in *London Lyrics* (1857), *Lyra Elegantiarum* (1867, an anthology, which, in its preface, offers a description of *vers de société*, in which 'sentiment never surges into passion, and where humour never overflows into boisterous merriment'), and *Patchwork* (1879), a miscellany of prose and verse.

Locket's, a fashionable ordinary, or tavern, in Charing Cross, frequently alluded to in the drama of the 17th–18th cents, so named from Adam Locket, the landlord.

LOCKHART, John Gibson (1794–1854), born at Cambusnethan, was educated at Glasgow and Balliol College, Oxford. He was called to the Scottish bar, and became one of the principal contributors to *Blackwood's Magazine*. In 1817 he began a long series of attacks on, in particular, Leigh *Hunt, *Keats, and *Hazlitt, castigating them as the low-born *'Cockney School of Poetry' and treating their work with great harshness. He did, however, support *Wordsworth and *Coleridge. In 1818 he translated *Schlegel's *Geschichte der alten und neuen Literatur* as *Lectures on the History of Literature, Ancient and Modern*, and he contributed several important articles on German literature to *Blackwood's* during the 1820s. From 1825 to 1853 he was editor of *The Quarterly Review*, and his ferocity as a critic was well reflected in his chosen nickname, 'The Scorpion'. He published a wide range of books. *Peter's Letters to his Kinsfolk* (1819) contains spirited sketches of life in Edinburgh and Glasgow. In 1821 he published *Valerius*, a simple tale of Rome under Trajan; in 1822 came his novel *Some Passages in the Life of Adam Blair*, a dark and disquieting story of a Scots minister. This was followed in 1823 by a conventional and popular romance, *Reginald Dalton*, and by his translations of *Ancient Spanish Ballads*. In 1824 he published another arresting novel, *Matthew Wald*, about the love of cousins. His *Life of Burns* appeared in 1828, and in 1837–8 his *Memoirs of the Life of Sir Walter Scott* (his father-in-law), which is comprehensive, methodical, and full of personal detail.

Lockit, and his daughter Lucy, characters in Gay's *The Beggar's Opera*.

Locksley, the name under which *Robin Hood figures in Scott's *Ivanhoe*. *Ritson states that Robin Hood was born at Locksley in Nottinghamshire.

Locksley Hall, a poem in trochaics by *Tennyson, published 1842, probably written 1837–8. It consists of a monologue spoken by a disappointed lover, revisiting the desolate moorland home by the sea where he had been brought up by an unsympathetic uncle, and where he fell in love with his cousin Amy; she returned his love, but, through family pressure, accepted another suitor. The narrator proceeds to rail against the modern world of steamship and railway, and ends with an ambiguous acceptance of 'the ringing grooves of change'—a phrase that the notoriously poor-sighted Tennyson wrote while under the impression that the new railways ran in grooves, not on rails.

Lockwood, the narrator of E. Brontë's *Wuthering Heights*.

Locrine, or **Logrin,** according to *Geoffrey of Monmouth's *History* (ii. 1–5), the eldest son of Brutus (*Brut) and *Ignoge. He rules over Loegria (*Logres) which is named after him, as his inherited third of his father's kingdom. He married Gwendolen but abandoned her for *Estrildis and was the father of her daughter Sabrina. He is mentioned by Spenser in *The Faerie Queene* (II. x. 13–18). T. *Lodge's 'The Complaynt of Elstred' (1593) tells the story of his unhappy mistress Estrildis, and *Swinburne wrote a play on the subject (*Locrine*, 1887).

Locrine, *The Lamentable Tragedie of,* a play published in 1595, and included in the third Shakespeare folio. The authorship is unknown. The play deals with the legend of *Locrine, king of England, his queen Gwendolen, and *Estrildis.

LODGE, David John (1935–), critic and novelist, born in London and educated at University College London; he has held several academic appointments and in 1976 became professor of modern English literature at the University of Birmingham. His critical works (*Language of Fiction*, 1966; *The Novelist at the Crossroads*, 1971; *The Modes of Modern Writing*, 1977; *Working with Structuralism*, 1981) display his gift for lucid exposition, and he has done much to introduce and explain continental literary theory in Britain, while maintaining for himself 'a modest affirmation of faith in the future of realistic fiction'. His novels include *The British Museum is Falling Down* (1965); *Changing Places* (1975, a satirical 'two-*campus novel' about a transatlantic academic exchange); and *How Far Can You Go?* (1980), a novel which charts the response over two decades of an interconnected group of Roman Catholics to moral and sociological change both inside and outside the church. *Small World* (1984) reintroduces the American academic Morris Zapp and the English professor Philip Swallow from *Changing Places*, in a jet-set world of international conferences, academic gamesmanship, and romantic pursuits. The novels' relationship to traditional realism is ironic and oblique, as Lodge employs an intrusive narrator, jokes about omniscience, film techniques, and other fictive devices to establish a tone of detachment that serves to intensify an underlying seriousness of intention.

LODGE, Sir Oliver, see SOCIETY FOR PSYCHICAL RESEARCH.

LODGE, Thomas (1558–1625), son of Sir Thomas Lodge, lord mayor of London, was educated at *Merchant Taylors' School, London, and Trinity College, Oxford. He was a student of Lincoln's Inn in 1578. In 1579–80 he published an anonymous *Defence of Poetry, Music and Stage Plays*, a reply to Gosson's *Schoole of Abuse*, and in 1584 *An Alarum against Usurers* (dedicated to Sir P. *Sidney), depicting the dangers that moneylenders present to young spendthrifts. Appended to it was a prose romance *Forbonius and Prisceria*. *Scillaes Metamorphosis*, an Ovidian verse fable, was published in 1589. In about 1586 Lodge sailed on a privateering expedition to the Terceras and the Canaries, and in 1591–3 to South America. On the earlier voyage he wrote his best-known romance *Rosalynde* (1590), 'hatcht in the stormes of the Ocean, and feathered in the surges of many perillous seas'. After four more minor prose romances he published *Phillis: Honoured with Pastorall Sonnets, Elegies, and amorous delights* (1593), including many poems adapted from Italian and French models, to which was appended 'The complaynt of Elstred', the story of the unhappy mistress of King *Locrine. His play *The Wounds of Civill War* (1594), about Marius and Sulla, had been performed by the Lord Admiral's Men; he also wrote *A Looking Glasse for London and England* (1594), in collaboration with R. *Greene. It is not clear whether he wrote any other plays. *A fig for Momus* (1595) was a miscellaneous collection of satirical poems including epistles addressed to S. *Daniel and M. *Drayton. *Wits Miserie and the Worlds Madnesse: Discovering the Devils Incarnat of this Age* was published in 1596, as was a remarkable romance, *A Margarite of America*, written during his second voyage, under Thomas Cavendish, while they were near the Magellan Straits. Lodge soon after this became a Roman Catholic, and studied medicine at Avignon; he was incorporated MD at Oxford in 1602, and in the next year published *A Treatise of the Plague*. He completed two major works of translation: *The Famous and Memorable Workes of Josephus* (1602), which was frequently reprinted, and *The Workes of Lucius Annaeus Seneca* (1614). His last work was a translation of Goulart's commentary on *Du Bartas (1621). Lodge is now mainly remembered for *Rosalynde* and for the lyrics scattered throughout his romances. His works were edited by E. *Gosse (4 vols, 1883).

LOEB, James (1867–1933), an American banker, educated at Harvard, a member until 1900 of the firm of Kuhn, Loeb & Co. He founded in 1912 the well-known Loeb Classical Library of Greek and Latin authors, which gives the original text with parallel translation.

Loegria, see LOGRES.

LOFFT, Capel (1751–1824), barrister, reformer, and eccentric, who lived on his family estate near Bury St Edmunds and corresponded with many eminent literary figures. He published poems, essays, etc., but is perhaps best remembered for his support of R. *Bloomfield, whose poem *The Farmer's Boy* (1800) he edited (claiming to have made only 'occasional corrections . . . with respect to orthography and sometimes in the grammatical construction'). His son, also Capel Lofft (1806–73) and also somewhat eccentric, complained that his father's 'love of literature was excessive' in his own 'mental autobiography', *Self-formation* (1837); he also wrote an epic on *Chartism called *Ernest* (1839).

LOFTING, Hugh, see CHILDREN'S LITERATURE.

Logic, *A System of, ratiocinative and inductive*, a treatise by J. S. *Mill, published 1843, revised and enlarged in the editions of 1850 and 1872.

The importance of Mill's *Logic* lies in the fact that it supplied, to use the author's own words (*Autobiography*), 'a text-book of the opposite doctrine [to the *a priori* view of human knowledge put forward by the German school]—that which derives all knowledge from experience, and all moral and intellectual qualities principally from the direction given to the associations'. In this work Mill stressed the importance of inductive methods, while, unlike F. *Bacon, giving its proper share to deduction. He lays down methods for investigating the causal relations of phenomena, assuming the causal principle, in defence of which he can only say that 'the belief we entertain in the universality, throughout nature, of the law of cause and effect, is itself an instance of induction', constantly verified by experience; if there were an exception to this law, we should probably have discovered it.

In attributing to experience and association our belief in mathematical and physical laws, he came into conflict with the intuitional philosophers, and gave his own explanation 'of that peculiar character of what are called necessary truths, which is adduced as proof that their evidence must come from a deeper source than experience'. This peculiar certainty, he holds, is 'an illusion, in order to sustain which it is necessary to suppose that those truths relate to, and express the properties of purely imaginary objects' as in the laws of geometry, which are only approximately true in the real world. Geometry being built on hypotheses, 'it owes to this alone the peculiar certainty supposed to distinguish it'. This conflict with the intuitional school is further developed in Mill's *Examination of Sir William Hamilton's Philosophy*.

Logistilla, in *Orlando Furioso*, a beneficent

witch who defends *Rogero against her wicked sisters *Alcina and Morgana, and gives *Astolfo his magic horn and book.

Logres, according to *Geoffrey of Monmouth's *History* (where it is called Loegria), the part of Brutus's kingdom assigned to his eldest son *Locrine, i.e. England. It is the usual term for Arthur's kingdom in medieval romance from *Chrétien de Troyes onwards. Spenser calls it 'Logris' (*Faerie Queene*, II. x. 14).

Logrin, see LOCRINE.

Logris, or Loegria, see LOGRES.

LOGUE, Christopher (1926–), poet, playwright, journalist, and actor, associated with the early years of the *English Stage Company, which put on several of his plays, including the Brechtian musical, *The Lily White Boys* (1960, with H. Cookson). He was a pioneer in the *Jazz Poetry movement, and experimented with publishing his poems as Verse Posters. His volumes of poetry include *Wand and Quartet* (1953), *Songs* (1959), *New Numbers* (1969), and *Ode to the Dodo: Poems from 1953–1978* (1981); he has also adapted Books 16–19 of the *Iliad*, collected in *War Music* (1981), and written several screenplays.

Lohengrin, the son of *Perceval, first mentioned in the *Parzival* (c.1205) of *Wolfram von Eschenbach, and in Wolfram's incomplete epic *Titurel*. According to legend he is summoned from the temple of the *Grail at Montsalvatsch (possibly Montserrat in Catalonia) and borne in a swan-boat to Antwerp. He saves Princess Elsa of Brabant from Frederick of Telramund who wants to marry her against her wishes. Lohengrin will marry Elsa if she does not ask what his race is; but she does, and the swan-boat carries him back to the Grail castle. The story is the subject of *Wagner's opera (1850). In early forms of the legend the Knight of the Swan is called Helias (Helis in Icelandic).

Lolita, a novel by V. *Nabokov.

Lollards, from Dutch *lollaerd*, 'mumbler', applied to a heretical sect devoted to piety, implying pretentions to great virtue; it was borrowed in late 14-cent. English to apply with the same connotations to the Wyclifites, but originally with a commoner variant form 'loller' which *Skeat says (in his note to *Piers Plowman* C, X. 213) was deliberately confused in writers such as *Langland and *Chaucer with an earlier English sense 'one who lolls around'. But the verb 'to loll around' was new in English of that period, and the entries in the OED leave the question open. See WYCLIF and OLDCASTLE.

LOLLIUS, an unknown author mentioned three times by Chaucer in connection with the Trojan War (*Troilus and Criseyde*, I. 394, V.

1,653, and *The House of Fame*, 1,468), once regarded as a great puzzle, but no doubt correctly explained (by R. G. Latham in 1868) as a misreading of *Horace, *Epistles*, I. ii. 1: 'Troiani belli scriptorem, Maxime Lolli, . . . relegi', where 'Lolli' is the vocative for the addressee of the letter, not the *scriptor*. Lollius came by this misreading to be regarded as a writer on the Trojan War whose work, naturally, was missing and he thus provided a useful fiction as Chaucer's source. The *scriptor* in Horace is Homer, and *Maxime* is a cognomen.

LOMBARD, Peter, see PETER LOMBARD.

LOMONOSOV, Mikhailo Vasilevich (1711–65), Russian poet, historian, chemist, physicist, mathematician, mining engineer: he has been described as the founder of modern Russian literature and of modern Russian culture. The son of a fisherman from the distant north, he entered the Slavo-Graeco-Latin Academy in Moscow in 1730. In 1736 he left for Germany, where he studied philosophy, physics, and chemistry at Marburg and practical mining at Freiburg in Saxony. In 1741 he returned to Russia and was made assistant professor at the Academy of science in St Petersburg. He remained at the Academy until his death, virtually in charge of it from 1758. Lomonosov was a passionate patriot and lover of science, whose aim in life was to create a Russian science and a Russian literature. In literature he fixed the standard of the literary language and introduced a new syllabo-tonic prosody (see his 'Letter on the Rules of Russian Versification', 1778). His greatest literary achievements are in the ode, both sacred and panegyrical: 'Ode on the Taking of Khotin' (1739), 'Ode on the Ascension of the Empress Elizaveta Petrovna' (1747), 'Evening Meditation on the Majesty of God' (1743), 'Morning Meditation on the Majesty of God' (1751), 'Ode, Selected from Job, Chapters XXXVIII–XLI' (1750). His poetry was first translated by John Bowring in 1821.

London, a poem by Dr *Johnson, published anonymously 1738, in imitation of the Third Satire of *Juvenal. *Pope predicted its unknown author would soon be 'déterré'. Thales (perhaps *Savage), disgusted with London, and about to leave for Wales, reflects on London's vices and affectations, and on the oppression of the poor— 'All crimes are safe, but hated poverty.' Johnson attacks Sir R. *Walpole's administration in his allusions to excise, the abuse of pensions, and the new stage licensing laws; the poem's success was in part political.

LONDON, Jack (John) Griffith (1876–1916), American novelist, born in San Francisco, the son of an itinerant astrologer and a spiritualist mother; he took the name of his stepfather, John London. He grew up in poverty, scratching a living in various legal and illegal ways—robbing the oyster beds, working in a canning factory and a jute mill, serving aged 17 as a common sailor, and taking part in the Klondike gold rush of 1897. These various experiences provided the material for his works, and made him a socialist; as he was later to write, he had seen as a youth 'the cellar of society . . . the pit, the abyss, the human cess-pool', and he was to attack capitalism and exploitation with great vigour, while maintaining, to the embarrassment of some of his comrades, some markedly chauvinist and racist attitudes. *The Son of the Wolf* (1900), the first of his many collections of tales, is based upon life in the Far North, as is the book that brought him recognition, *The Call of the Wild* (1903), which tells the story of the dog Buck, who, after his master's death, is lured back to the primitive world to lead a wolf pack. In the same year appeared *The People of the Abyss*, an emotive documentary based on some weeks spent in the slums of London's East End. Many other tales of struggle, travel, and adventure followed, including *The Sea-Wolf* (1904), *White Fang* (1906, another tale with dog as hero), *South Sea Tales* (1911), and *Jerry of the South Seas* (1917). *The Iron Heel* (1908) is a novel about the class struggle, which prophesies a Fascist revolution; *The Valley of the Moon* (1913) advocates a return to the land in an ideal community. One of London's most interesting novels is the semi-autobiographical *Martin Eden* (1909), which describes the struggles of the protagonist, a sailor and labourer, to acquire education and to become a writer, inspired partly by his love for Ruth Morse, a girl of education and what appears to him to be refinement; he succeeds, spectacularly, only to find himself disillusioned with her and the world he has entered, and he drowns himself on the way to the South Seas. *John Barleycorn* (1913), also semi-autobiographical, is a record of London's own struggle against alcohol. He also wrote socialist treatises, autobiographical essays, and a good deal of journalism in his short but intensely active life, and was remembered by his friend U. *Sinclair as 'one of the great revolutionary figures' of America's history.

London, *Survey of*, see STOW.

London Assurance, see BOUCICAULT, D.

London Cuckolds, The, a rollicking farce by Edward Ravenscroft (*fl.* 1671–97), which was produced in 1682 and annually revived on Lord Mayor's Day for nearly a century.

London Gazette, see under OXFORD GAZETTE.

London Labour and the London Poor, see MAYHEW, H.

London Library, The, was founded in 1840, largely at the instance of *Carlyle, with the sup-

port and encouragement of many eminent men of letters of the day, including *Gladstone, *Grote, H. *Hallam, and Mazzini; the manifesto, published on 15 Feb. 1841, deplored the dearth of libraries in London, and carried a quotation from *Gibbon stating that: 'The greatest city in the world is destitute of that useful institution, a public library.' It opened on 3 May 1841, in two rooms in Pall Mall, with a stock of 3,000 volumes and with John George Cochrane (1761–1852) as its first librarian. Its initial subscribers included *Dickens, *Macaulay, and *Macready. It moved to its present premises in St James's Square in 1845, and continues to be much valued by its many members. See *The London Library* by Miron Grindea, first published in 1977 as Nos 387–400 of *Adam International Review*, which contains tributes from A. *Wilson, R. *Fuller, S. *O'Faolain, and many others.

London Magazine, The, (1) a periodical which ran from 1732 to 1785, founded in opposition to the *Gentleman's Magazine*; (2) a magazine of great brilliance (1820–9), established under the editorship of John *Scott on roughly the same miscellany plan as *Blackwood's*, except that it was non-political and gave a large proportion of its space to writers and books. Scott championed the work of the younger writers, including *Wordsworth, *Lamb, *De Quincey, *Clare, *Hood, *Carlyle, and in particular the *'Cockney School', *Keats, Leigh *Hunt, and *Hazlitt. But he was soon provoked into attacks on *Blackwood's*, which bitterly derided most of his writers, and he was killed in a duel by a representative of that magazine. John *Taylor then took over the editorship with the assistance of Hood; but, although the magazine continued successfully for another eight years, Taylor's habit of textual interference angered his writers, and many, including Lamb and Hazlitt, withdrew their work; see J. Bauer, *The London Magazine 1820–29* (1953). (3) a monthly literary magazine founded in 1954 by J. *Lehmann, and edited by him until 1961. It was welcomed in its first issue by T. S. *Eliot as a non-university-based periodical that would 'boldly assume the existence of a public interested in serious literature'. It aimed to avoid being 'narrowly British' or political in content; Lehmann (*The Ample Proposition*, 1966) writes that he aimed to create 'the *London* magazine, and not the Magazine of Oxford, or Cambridge, or Redbrick' and to reach Dr *Johnson's 'common reader'. He was succeeded as editor by the poet, journalist, and cricket enthusiast Alan Ross (1922–), who enlarged the magazine's range to cover other arts, including photography. Its distinguished contributors have included *MacNeice, E. *Waugh, R. *Fuller, *Auden, C. *Causley, D. *Walcott, G. *Ewart, John Horder, and many others.

London Merchant, The, or *The History of George Barnwell*, see GEORGE BARNWELL.

London Mercury, The, a monthly literary periodical founded in 1919 by J. C. *Squire, who edited it until 1934, and used it in its early days as a vehicle to condemn *Modernism and what he described as 'anarchical cleverness'; it published fiction, poetry, reviews, etc., and contributors included *de la Mare, *Chesterton, *Belloc, W. H. *Davies, *Yeats, and D. H. *Lawrence. In 1939 it was incorporated in *Life and Letters.

London Prodigal, The, a comedy published in 1605, attributed to Shakespeare in the title of the quarto edition of that year and included in the 3rd and 4th folios, but undoubtedly by some other hand.

The play is a comedy of London manners, and deals with the reclaiming of the prodigal young Flowerdale by the fidelity of his wife.

London Review of Books, a literary and cultural review founded in 1979 and edited by Karl Miller (1931–), professor of modern English literature at University College London, in conscious emulation of the *New York Review of Books* (founded 1963) in both design and editorial approach. It has published critical essays and articles by many of the most prominent critics and scholars of the day, including Christopher Ricks, John Bayley, Frank Kermode, A. J. P. *Taylor, D. *Lodge, Sir Peter Medawar, and Dan Jacobson, and has published poems and fiction by S. *Heaney, N. *Gordimer, G. *Ewart, Douglas Dunn, Tom Paulin, Ted *Hughes, P. *Redgrove, D. *Walcott, and many others.

Loneliness of the Long Distance Runner, The, a novel by A. *Sillitoe.

Longaville, in Shakespeare's *Love's Labour's Lost*, one of the three lords attending on the king of Navarre.

Long Day's Journey into Night, see O'NEILL, E.

Longest Journey, The (1907), a novel by E. M. *Forster.

Rickie Elliot, a sensitive and congenitally lame young man, orphaned at the age of 15, escapes from the misery of suburban life and the bullying of public school to Cambridge, where, like Forster himself, he finds sympathetic friends, chief amongst them Ansell, a grocer's son. He has literary aspirations (his short stories, Arcadian pastoral fantasies, are remarkably like Forster's own), but is also attracted by Agnes Pembroke, the conventional but beautiful sister of a schoolmaster friend and protector, and by her handsome, athletic, ex-bully fiancé Gerald. After Gerald's sudden death in a football match, Rickie idealizes Agnes, through whom he imagines that he has glimpsed true passion. Despite Ansell's faintly misogynist warnings, he becomes en-

gaged to her. On a visit to his aunt Mrs Failing in Wiltshire he discovers that he has a half-brother, the healthy and 'pagan' Stephen Wonham, who lives with her at Cadover; Stephen himself is unaware of the relationship, and Agnes, horrified by the potential scandal, prevents Rickie or Mrs Failing from telling him. Rickie suffers 'a curious breakdown', his stories, a collection called 'Pan Pipes', are rejected by various publishers, one of whom advises him 'to see life', but instead, discouraged, Rickie marries Agnes and becomes a schoolmaster at his brother-in-law's school, Sawston. He sinks into a world of petty jealousy and domesticity, cut off from his old Cambridge friends, increasingly aware of Agnes's failings. Their only child, a daughter, is born crippled and dies. Stephen Wonham, having discovered his relationship to Rickie, turns up at Sawston, and Agnes tries to buy him off with money, thinking he has come to blackmail them. Offended, Stephen vanishes penniless, and it emerges that he has been thrown out of Cadover by Mrs Failing, largely through Agnes's machinations; also that he is the son of Rickie's mother, not of his disliked father, as he had supposed. A reconciliation follows, and although Rickie is killed while rescuing the drunken Stephen, the novel ends with the information that his stories achieved posthumous recognition.

*Trilling described the novel 'as perhaps the most brilliant, the most dramatic, and the most passionate of his works' (E. M. Forster, 1944), and it is almost certainly the most autobiographical, but its construction has puzzled many, and the number of sudden deaths is high even by Forsterian standards. It was his own favourite of his works; he admitted its faults, but felt that in Stephen, although 'a theoretic figure', he had created a living being, and expressed some of his feelings for the English landscape.

LONGFELLOW, Henry Wadsworth (1807–82), American poet, born in Maine and educated at Bowdoin, where he was the classmate of *Hawthorne. The offer of a professorship of modern languages at Bowdoin took him to Europe to study, 1826–9; after lecturing at Bowdoin he returned to Europe again to prepare for the post of professor at Harvard. His wife, travelling with him, died in Holland in 1835. In 1836 he began his many influential years of teaching at Harvard.

His prose romance *Hyperion* (1839), a product of his bereavement, is the tale of a young man who seeks to forget sorrow in travel, a thread on which are hung philosophical discourses, poems, and legends. In the same year was published *Voices of the Night*, which includes his didactic pieces 'A Psalm of Life', 'Footsteps of Angels', and 'The Reaper and the Flowers'. In 1841 appeared *Ballads and other Poems*, with such well known pieces as 'The Wreck of the

Hesperus' and 'The Village Blacksmith'. In 1842 he met *Dickens in America, and visited him in London later in the same year; on his voyage home he wrote his *Poems on Slavery* (1842). In 1843 he married Frances Appleton, an event foreshadowed in *Hyperion*. By this time he was already one of the most widely read poets in America, and subsequent volumes confirmed his reputation in the English-speaking world as second only to that of *Tennyson in popularity; these include *The Belfry of Bruges and other Poems* (1847); *Evangeline* (1849; a narrative poem in hexameters, set in Acadia, now Nova Scotia, with some fine evocations of 'the forest primeval' to balance the sentimentality of the tale); *The Song of *Hiawatha* (1858); and *The Courtship of Miles Standish* (1858; another long hexameter narrative, based on a New England legend. In 1854 he had resigned his professorship, but his peaceful creative life was tragically interrupted in 1861 by the death of his wife, who was burned to death in a domestic accident. *Tales of a Wayside Inn* (1863, first series; with the rousing 'Paul Revere's Ride' and 'The Song of King Olaf') follows the form of the *Canterbury Tales* and the *Decameron*; a group of travellers, in the 'old-fashioned, quaint abode' of the inn pass the evening by telling tales, directed by the landlord. Much of this was written before his wife's death, and an increased sombreness may be seen in his translation of *Dante (1867) and his trilogy *Christus* (1872; incorporating the earlier *Golden Legend* of 1851), which he considered his masterpiece. Other 'Tales of a Wayside Inn' followed in 1872 (in *Three Books of Song*) and in 1874 (in *Aftermath*). His last volumes, *The Masque of Pandora* (1875), *Ultima Thule* (1880), and *In the Harbor* (1882) contain some poignant autumnal reflections on old age, including his 'Morituri Salutamus' (1875), written for the 50th anniversary of the class of 1825 at Bowdoin, in which he urges his one-time classmates to remember that 'Cato learned Greek at eighty; Sophocles | Wrote his grand Oedipus . . . '

LONGINUS, the name bestowed by a scribe's error on the author of the Greek critical treatise περι υψους (On the Sublime) written probably in the 1st cent. AD. It locates the sources of poetic excellence in the profundity of the writer's emotions and the seriousness of his thought. The first English translation, by John Hall, appeared in 1652, but it was not until the appearance of *Boileau's French version (1674) and its influence on *Dryden that the concept of creative fire became popular. 'Longinus' had a marked effect on 18th-cent. critics and aestheticians. *Dennis, *Shaftesbury, and even *Pope were influenced by him, while the later Primitivists like John Brown and William Duff, as well as mediocrities like J. *Warton, fell wholly under his spell. The cult of the *Sublime did much to prepare the way for *Romanticism.

Longinus ('Longeus' in *Malory), the traditional name of the Roman soldier who pierced with his spear the side of Christ at the Crucifixion. The lance in the *Grail legend is sometimes identified as his spear, as by Malory (Vinaver, *Works*, p. 54). See ch. 21 in R. S. Loomis ed., *Arthurian Literature in the Middle Ages* (1959).

Long John Silver, a character in Stevenson's *Treasure Island.

LONGMAN, Thomas (1699–1755), established the family firm of publishers still in existence as the Longman Group. The original Thomas published various important works of reference, including a share in *Johnson's Dictionary*. Thomas III (1771–1842) published, among other work, that of *Wordsworth, *Coleridge, T. *Moore, *Southey, and Sir W. *Scott, and became the proprietor of the *Edinburgh Review.

Longman's Magazine, a family magazine, a successor to *Fraser's, which ran from 1882 to 1905. It published short stories, serialized novels, poetry, and reviews, and contributors included A. *Dobson, G. *Allen, *Kipling, Mrs *Oliphant, *Newbolt, and *Hardy.

LONSDALE, Frederick (1881–1954), playwright, born Lionel Frederick Leonard, in St Helier, Jersey, the son of a seaman. His many successful, worldly, witty, and light-hearted drawing-room comedies include *Aren't We All?* (perf. 1923), *The Last of Mrs Cheyney* (1925), and *On Approval* (1927). He also wrote musical comedies. See *Freddy Lonsdale* (1957) by his daughter, Frances Donaldson.

Look Back in Anger, a play by J. *Osborne, first produced by the *English Stage Company at the Royal Court Theatre on 8 May 1956, published 1957. It proved a landmark in the history of the theatre, a focus for reaction against a previous generation (see KITCHEN SINK DRAMA), and a decisive contribution to the corporate image of the *Angry Young Man.

The action takes place in a midlands town, in the one-room flat of Jimmy and Alison Porter, and centres on their marital conflicts, which appear to arise largely from Jimmy's sense of their social incompatibility: he is a jazz-playing ex-student from a 'white tile' university, working on a market sweet stall, she is a colonel's daughter. He is by turns violent, sentimental, maudlin, self-pitying, and sadistic, and has a fine line in rhetoric. The first act opens as Alison stands ironing the clothes of Jimmy and their lodger Cliff, as Jimmy reads the Sunday papers and abuses her and the 'Edwardian brigade' which her parents represent. In the second act the battle intensifies, as Alison's friend Helena attempts to rescue her from her disastrous marriage; Alison departs with her father, and Helena falls into Jimmy's arms. The third act opens with Helena at the ironing board; Alison returns, having lost the baby she was expecting, and she and Jimmy find a manner of reconciliation through humiliation and games-playing fantasy. In its use of social milieu, its iconoclastic social attitudes, and its exploration of sado-masochistic relationships, the play was highly influential.

Looking Backward, a novel by E. *Bellamy.

LOPE DE VEGA, see VEGA CARPIO.

LORCA, Frederico García, see GARCÍA LORCA, F.

Lord, My, a character in Fielding's *Amelia.

Lord Jim, a novel by J. *Conrad, published 1900.

Jim is chief mate on board the Patna, an ill-manned ship carrying a party of pilgrims in Eastern waters. He is young, idealistic, and a dreamer of heroic deeds. When the Patna threatens to sink and the cowardly officers decide to save their own skins and escape in the few lifeboats, Jim despises them, but at the last moment, dazed by the horror and confusion of the moment, he joins them. He acts without conscious decision and his last-minute jump into the boat is almost involuntary. The Patna does not sink and the pilgrims are rescued. What happens to Jim thereafter is related by an observer, Marlow. Jim, alone among the crew, remains to face the court of enquiry, deeply disturbed at his defection from a code of conduct dear to him. Condemned by the court and stripped of his papers, he tries to disappear, moving from place to place whenever his past threatens to catch up with him. He searches for anonymity and the chance to redeem himself. Through Marlow's intervention Jim is sent to a remote trading station in Patusan. His efforts create order and well-being in a previously chaotic community and he wins the respect and affection of the people for whom he becomes Tuan—or Lord Jim. He has achieved some sense of peace, but the memory of his jump is still with him. When Gentleman Brown and his gang of thieves arrive to disrupt and plunder the village Jim begs the chiefs to spare them, pledging his own life against their departure. But Brown behaves treacherously and a massacre takes place. Jim feels he has only one course of action; rejecting the idea of flight he delivers himself up to Chief Doramin whose son was a victim of the massacre. Doramin shoots him and Jim willingly accepts this honourable death.

Lord of the Flies (1954), a novel by W. *Golding.

An aeroplane carrying a party of schoolboys crashes on a desert island. The boys' attempts, led by Ralph and Piggy, to set up a democratically run society quickly fail and the savagery which in Golding's work underlies man's true nature takes over. Terror rules under the dictator Jack, and two boys are killed; it is only with the arrival of a shocked rescue officer that a mask of civilization returns. It is a savage reply to the naïve optimism of *Ballantyne's The Coral Island. (See also BEELZEBUB.)

Lord of the Isles, The, a poem in six cantos by Sir W. *Scott, published 1815.

The poem, founded on the chronicles of the Bruce, deals with the return of Robert Bruce in 1307 to Scotland, whence he had been driven after the murder of the Red Comyn, and the period of his subsequent struggle against the English, culminating in the battle of Bannockburn. With this is woven the story of the love of Edith of Lorn for Lord Ronald, the Lord of the Isles. She is his affianced bride, but his heart is given to Isabel, Bruce's sister. His marriage to Edith is prevented by the return of Bruce. Edith, in the disguise of a mute page, follows Bruce and Ronald, and, at the risk of her life, saves them from destruction. Her devotion finally wins Lord Ronald's heart.

Lord of the Rings, The, see TOLKIEN, J. R. R.

Lord Ormont and his Aminta, a novel by G. *Meredith, published 1894.

The earl of Ormont, a distinguished cavalry commander, has met the young and beautiful Aminta Farrell on a trip to Spain, and in spite of her lowly birth and her vulgar aunt, Mrs Pagnell, he responds to her youthful worship and marries her. But when they eventually return to London he becomes ashamed of her set. Matthew Weyburn is appointed Ormont's secretary, and discovers in the countess the 'Browny' whom he loved as a youth. In spite of restraint on both sides, they find themselves much in love. Lord Ormont finally repents his cruelty and prepares to give Aminta her proper position, but Matthew and Browny decide to live together. Defying convention, they leave to run a school in Switzerland.

Lord Strutt, see JOHN BULL.

'Lord Ullin's Daughter', a ballad by T. *Campbell.

Lorel, the swineherd in Jonson's *The Sad Shepherd.

Lorenzo, (1) son of the duke of Castile in Kyd's *The Spanish Tragedy; (2) the lover of *Jessica in Shakespeare's *The Merchant of Venice.

Lorna Doone, a novel by R. D. *Blackmore, published 1869.

This celebrated and continuously popular story is set in the later 17th cent. on Exmoor, where an outlawed family, the Doones, and their retainers terrorize the surrounding countryside. They murder a farmer, father of the novel's hero, John Ridd, a boy of twelve when the story starts. He secretly discovers the child Lorna, who has been kidnapped by the Doones, and they grow up to love each other. John Ridd, by now a giant in height and strength, is involved in adventures with the highwayman Tom Faggus, who marries his sister Annie, in the events leading up to Monmouth's rebellion, and in a rivalry with the villainous Carver Doone, from whom he rescues Lorna during a superbly described blizzard. The Doones are eventually destroyed, Lorna turns out not to be a Doone but an heiress of noble family, and she and John are married; but Carver Doone shoots her at the altar. John avenges her, she recovers, and the story ends happily. The infamous Judge *Jeffreys plays a part in the action, and John Ridd and Tom Faggus are also based on historical characters.

LORRIS, Guillaume de, see ROMAN DE LA ROSE.

Lorry, Jarvis, a character in Dickens's *A Tale of Two Cities.

Los, one of the principal characters in the symbolic books of *Blake, a complex and ambiguous figure, described in the opening of The Song of Los (1795) as 'the Eternal Prophet'. He is usually portrayed as the antagonist of *Urizen; in his role as blacksmith (which links him with the Loki of northern mythology, and the Roman Vulcan) he is portrayed in The Book of Los (1795) binding Urizen in iron links forged in his glowing furnace, and in earlier poems of the cycle (and also in *The Four Zoas) he binds his own son, the rebellious *Orc. He represents the artist, and also Time; his female counterpart is *Enitharmon (Inspiration, and Space); his periods of estrangement from her spell disaster for the universe. His character changes during the evolution of Blake's mythology, and he finally becomes in *Jerusalem a great heroic force of energy, while remaining morally ambiguous. An insight into the nature of Blake's vision is offered in his verse epistle to his friend Butts (dated 22 Nov. 1802) in which he describes Los descending before his face 'in fierce flames; in my double sight | 'Twas outward a Sun: inward Los in his might'.

'Lost Leader, The', a poem by R. *Browning (1845) deploring *Wordsworth's political change of heart, and suggesting that he abandoned his radical views 'just for a handful of silver' and 'just for a riband to stick in his coat'.

Lot, king of Orkney in the Arthurian legends, is the husband of Arthur's sister or half-sister *Morgawse. Their sons are *Gawain, *Agravain, *Gareth, and *Gaheris, as well as *Modred in the earlier versions (before Arthur was made his unwitting, incestuous father). The feud between his family and *Pellinore's is one of the running themes in *Malory.

Lot, Parson, the pseudonym of C. *Kingsley.

Lothair, a novel by B. *Disraeli, published 1870.

Like the hero of *Tancred, Lothair is a young man determined to seek the true path. He is a wealthy nobleman, left, when his parents died, in the joint guardianship of Lord Culloden, a member of the Scottish kirk, and the brilliant cleric Grandison, who adopts the Catholic faith and rapidly becomes a cardinal. A deep interest in the merits of the Anglican and Catholic faiths, and their shared background in Judaism, pervades the book. At about the time of Lothair's coming of age in 1866 the forces of Garibaldi were confronting the Papacy, and for most of the rest of the book both the Catholics and the Italian patriots struggle and manœuvre for control of the wealthy and influential Lothair. Like *Endymion (in the novel of that name), Lothair is reflective rather than active and is much influenced by three women, the beautiful Catholic Clare Arundel, the charming Lady Corisande, and the stormy Italian patriot Theodora. Lothair joins Theodora in Italy, but she is killed at Viterbo and he is himself wounded at Mentana. Lothair continues his search for the first 'cradle' of Christianity, and in Jerusalem the mystic Paraclete gives him a revelation of the origins of Christianity. The cardinal and fellow prelates struggle to convince and convert Lothair, but he resists, realizing that the fanaticism of both the Catholics and the Italian patriots is corrupting. After further travels he returns home, confirmed in his Anglicanism, and marries Lady Corisande.

The wit and irony of the scenes of high social life are thought by some to foreshadow *Wilde. Various memorable incidental characters include the radiant artist Mr Phoebus, modelled on *Leighton, and Lord St Aldegonde, the aristocratic republican opposed to all privileges except those of dukes, and in favour of the equal division of all property except land. 'Lothair-mania' swept England, the US, and Europe; although the book was poorly reviewed (and said to lack gravitas), the first edition sold out in two days and there were eight editions in 1870 alone. The book, according to its author, was more widely read than any other work published in the previous half century.

Lothario, (1) the heartless libertine (proverbial as 'the Gay Lothario') in Rowe's *The Fair Penitent; (2) a character in the episode of *The Curious Impertinent in Don Quixote; (3) a character in *Goethe's Wilhelm Meister.

Lotte, the heroine of *Goethe's The Sorrows of Werther. She was drawn from Lotte Buff, with whom Goethe fell in love at Wetzlar and who married Goethe's friend Kestner.

Lousiad, The, a heroic-comic poem by J. *Wolcot (Peter Pindar), published 1785-95.

The subject of this exuberant mockery is the appearance of a louse in a dish of peas served to George II, the king's feelings on the discovery, and his subsequent order that all the servants in the kitchen should have their heads shaved.

LOVE, Nicholas (*fl.* 1410), prior of the Carthusian House of Mount Grace near Middlesbrough, author before 1410 of *The Mirrour of the Blessed Lyf of Iesu Christ*, an accomplished prose translation of the *Meditationes Vitae Christi* attributed to Bonaventura. It has been edited by L. F. Powell (1908).

Love à la Mode, a comedy by *Macklin, produced 1759.

Four suitors, an Englishman, an Irishman, a Scot, and a Jew, are rivals for the hand of the heroine. Their quality is tested by the pretence that she has lost her fortune. The play is famous for the characters of Sir Archy MacSarcasm and Sir Callaghan O'Brallaghan.

Loveday, John and Bob, brothers in Hardy's *The Trumpet Major.*

Loved One, The, a novel by E. *Waugh.

Love for Love, a comedy by *Congreve, performed 1695.

Valentine has fallen under the displeasure of his father by his extravagance, and is besieged by duns. His father, Sir Sampson Legend, offers him £4,000 (only enough to pay his debts) if he will sign a bond engaging to make over his inheritance to his younger brother Ben. Valentine, to escape from his embarrassment, signs the bond. He is in love with Angelica, who possesses a fortune of her own, but she has hitherto not yielded to his suit. Sir Sampson has arranged a match between Ben, who is at sea, and Miss Prue, an awkward country girl, the daughter of Foresight, a superstitious old fool who claims to be an astrologer. Valentine, realizing the ruin entailed by the signature of the bond, tries to move his father by submission, and fails; then pretends to be mad and unable to sign the final deed of conveyance to his brother. Finally Angelica intervenes. She induces Sir Sampson to propose marriage to her, pretends to accept, and gets possession of Valentine's bond. Valentine, finding that Angelica is about to marry his father, generously declares himself ready to sign the conveyance in order to make her happy. She reveals the plot, tears up the bond, and declares her love for Valentine.

The comedy is enlivened by its witty dialogue and its humorous characters. Among these are Jeremy, Valentine's resourceful servant; Sir Sampson, with his 'blunt vivacity'; Ben, the rough and stupid young sailor, who intends to marry whom he chooses; Miss Prue, only too ready to learn the lessons in love given her by Tattle, the vain, half-witted beau, who finds himself married to Mrs Frail, the lady of easy

virtue, when he thinks he has captured Angelica; and Foresight, the gullible old astrologer.

Love in a Tub, see COMICAL REVENGE, THE.

Lovel, (1) the name assumed by the hero in Scott's *The Antiquary*; (2) the principal character in Townley's *High Life below Stairs*.

Lovel the Widower, a story by *Thackeray, published in the *Cornhill Magazine*, 1860.

The story is told by Lovel's friend Mr Batchelor, who is more than half in love with the young governess Bessy Prior, who copes tactfully with Lovel's spoiled children, his interfering mother-in-law Lady Baker, her own greedy relatives, and her other suitors, who include the highly educated butler Bedford. Lady Baker discovers that Miss Prior once earned her living as a dancer in the theatre and orders her out of the house, but Lovel finally asserts himself and asks Bessy to marry him.

LOVELACE, Richard (1618–57/8), educated at Charterhouse School and Gloucester Hall, Oxford, was the heir to great estates in Kent. Wealthy, handsome, and elegant, he was a courtier, and served in the Scottish expeditions of 1639. Having presented a 'Kentish Petition' to the House of Commons in 1642, he was thrown into the Gatehouse prison, where he is supposed to have written the song 'To Althea'. He rejoined Charles I in 1645, and served with the French king in 1646. According to A. *Wood, his betrothed Lucy Sacheverell married another on a false report of his death. He was imprisoned again in 1648 and in prison prepared for the press his *Lucasta; Epodes, Odes, Sonnets, Songs etc.* which includes the well-known lyric 'On going to the wars'. He died in extreme poverty. After his death his brother published his remaining verses, *Lucasta: Posthume Poems.* He wrote two plays, now lost. During the earlier part of the 18th cent. his work was entirely neglected, until Percy reprinted two of his lyrics in his *Reliques* (1765), since when his reputation as a *Cavalier poet has steadily increased. His works were edited by C. H. Wilkinson (2 vols, 1925).

Lovelace, Robert, a character in Richardson's *Clarissa.

Loveless, a character in Vanbrugh's *The Relapse and Sheridan's *A Trip to Scarborough.

Lovell, Lord, a character in Massinger's *A New Way to pay Old Debts.

Love on the Dole, a novel by W. *Greenwood.

LOVER, Samuel (1797–1868), Irish painter, novelist, song-writer, and founder of the *Dublin University Magazine*. He is chiefly remembered for his ballad 'Rory O'More' and the novel developed from it in 1837 (later dramatized), which relates the tragic events in Ireland in 1798; for his *Songs and Ballads* (1839); his comic novel *Handy Andy* (1842); and *Lyrics of Ireland* (1858).

'Lover's Complaint, A', a poem in rhyme-royal appended to Shakespeare's *Sonnets (1609). In it a nameless maiden complains, in a rustic setting, of her seduction by a charming but untrustworthy young man.

Lover's Melancholy, The, a romantic comedy by J. *Ford, printed 1629.

Palador, prince of Cyprus, has been betrothed to Eroclea, daughter of Meleander, an old lord; but, to escape the evil designs of Palador's father, she has been conveyed away to Greece, where she has remained disguised as a boy. Meleander has been accused of treason, imprisoned, and driven to madness. Palador, after his father's death, is left in a state of hopeless melancholy. Eroclea returns to Cyprus as the page of Menaphon. Thamasta, cousin of the prince, falls in love with her in this disguise, and to escape her attentions Eroclea is obliged to reveal her identity. She is then restored to Palador; Meleander is released and cured; Thamasta marries Menaphon; and all ends happily. The play contains a version of Strada's contest of the lute-player and the nightingale, which is also dealt with by *Crashaw.

The conventional romantic plot is the framework for Ford's analysis of love melancholy, strongly influenced by Burton's *Anatomy of Melancholy*. The scene in which Eroclea is recognized by Palador contains some of Ford's purest poetry ('Minutes are numbered by the fall of sands, | As by an hourglass').

Lovers' Progress, The, a romantic drama by J. *Fletcher, produced 1623, revised 1634 as *The Wandering Lovers* by *Massinger, printed 1647.

Lidian and Clarangè, devoted friends, are both in love with Olinda. Clarangè lets it be believed that he is dead, and finally turns friar, in order to surrender Olinda to Lidian. The plot is complicated with another illustration of the conflict of love and friendship. Lisander loves the virtuous Calista, wife of his friend Cleander. Cleander is killed by a servant. The imprudent but not criminal conduct of Lisander and Calista throws grave suspicion on them, and they narrowly escape condemnation for the murder.

Lovers' Vows, a play by Mrs *Inchbald, adapted from *Das Kind der Liebe* by *Kotzbue, acted 1798. The play is chiefly of interest because of the place it occupies in the story of J. Austen's *Mansfield Park*.

Baron Wildenhaim has in his youth seduced and deserted Agatha and married another woman. When the play opens Agatha is reduced to destitution, in which state she is found by her son Frederic, who now for the first time learns the story of his birth. To assist his mother's needs he goes out to beg, chances upon his unknown father, and attempts to rob him. He is arrested, discovers who the baron is, reveals his own identity and his mother's, and finally, with the aid of the pastor Anhalt, persuades the baron to marry Agatha. The baron consents also to the marriage of his daughter Amelia to Anhalt, instead of the wealthy Count Cassell.

Love's Labour's Lost, a comedy by *Shakespeare, probably written and performed about 1595, printed in quarto 1598. No major sources for it have been identified. It has often been felt to contain topical references (see SCHOOL OF NIGHT), but none of these has been firmly established.

The king of Navarre and three of his lords have sworn for three years to keep from the sight of woman and to live studying and fasting. The arrival of the princess of France on an embassy, with her attendant ladies, obliges them 'of mere necessity' to disregard their vows. The king is soon in love with the princess, his lords with her ladies, and the courting proceeds amidst disguises and merriment, to which the other characters contribute: Don Adriano de Armado, the Spaniard, a master of extravagant language, Holofernes the schoolmaster, Dull the constable, Sir Nathaniel the curate, and Costard the clown. News of the death of the princess's father interrupts the wooing, and the ladies impose a year's ordeal on their lovers. The play ends with the beautiful owl and cuckoo song, 'When icicles hang by the wall'.

Loves of the Angels, The, a poem by T. *Moore, published 1823.

The poem, founded on the *oriental tale of Harût and Marût and certain rabbinical fictions, recounts the loves of three fallen angels for mortal women, and illustrates the decline of the soul from purity. The first angel loved Lea, and taught her the spell which opens the gate of heaven. At once she uttered it and rose to the stars. The second angel loved Lilis; he came to her in his full celestial glory and she was burned to death. The third, Zaraph, loved Nama; they were condemned to live in imperfect happiness among mortals, but would ultimately be admitted to immortality.

This was Moore's last long poem, and it enjoyed great popularity as well as provoking much stricture.

Loves of the Plants, The, see DARWIN, E.

'Loves of the Triangles, The', a clever parody by G. *Canning and J. H. *Frere in *The Anti-Jacobin* in 1798 of E. *Darwin's *The Loves of the Plants*. Darwin good-humouredly acknowledged its skill.

Love's Sacrifice, a tragedy by J. *Ford, printed 1633.

Fernando, favourite of the duke of Pavia, falls in love with Bianca, the duchess. He declares his love, but is repulsed. Presently, however, the duchess, in whom he has awakened a strong passion, comes to his room and offers herself to him, but warns him that she will not survive her shame, but take her own life before morning. Fernando masters his passion and determines to remain her distant lover. Fiormonda, the duke's sister, who has vainly importuned Fernando with her love for him, discovers his affection for Bianca, and pursues her vengeance. With the help of D'Avolos, the duke's base secretary, she stirs up the duke's jealousy, and a trap is laid for Fernando and Bianca. The duke finds them together, and kills Bianca. Convinced too late, by Fernando's declarations and Bianca's manner of meeting her death, of her innocence, he stabs himself, and Fernando takes poison in Bianca's tomb.

Less wide-ranging than *'*Tis Pity She's a Whore*, the play's main theme is the folly of love, including the Platonic love cult, fashionable at the Caroline court. Its tone has aroused critical perplexity: 'In the beginning of it everyone knows what is decent; in the middle Fernando and Bianca grow sceptical as to what is decent; in the end no one knows what is decent—not even the author' (Stuart Sherman).

Loving, a novel by H. *Green.

LOWELL, Amy Lawrence (1874–1925), American poet, born in Massachusetts. Her first volume of poetry, *A Dome of Many-Coloured Glass* (1912), was relatively conventional; shortly thereafter she took up *Imagism and in 1913 and 1914 visited England, where she met *Pound, D. H. *Lawrence, 'H.D.' (Hilda *Doolittle), and other writers active in or on the fringes of the movement, becoming so active in it herself that Pound spoke of 'Amy-gism'. Her subsequent volumes, which include *Sword Blades and Poppy Seed* (1914), *Men, Women and Ghosts* (1916; which contains 'Patterns'), and *Can Grande's Castle* (1918), show her experiments in what she called 'polyphonic prose' as well as her allegiance to Imagism; her love of New England is expressed in two of her own favourite pieces, 'Lilacs' and 'Purple Grackles', published in *What's O'Clock* (1925). She became well known as a public figure, vast and cigar-smoking, through her lectures and readings in America.

LOWELL, James Russell (1819–91), born in Cambridge, Massachusetts, and educated at Harvard, succeeded *Longfellow as professor of French and Spanish in 1855, and was American minister in Spain, 1877–80, and in England, 1880–5. He was editor of the *Atlantic Monthly* in 1857, and subsequently (1864), with C. E. *Norton, of the *North American Review*. His works include several volumes of verse, the satirical *Biglow Papers* (1848 and 1867, prose and verse), and memorial odes after the Civil War; and various volumes of essays, including *Among my books* (1870) and *My Study Window* (1871). His *Letters*, ed. C. E. Norton, appeared in 1894.

LOWELL, Robert Traill Spence (1917–77), American poet, born in Boston, of ancient New England families on both his father's and his mother's side. He was educated at Kenyon College, where he became friendly with R. *Jarrell and J. C. *Ransom, of whose influence he later wrote (*Kenyon Collegian*, 1974), 'The kind of poet I am was largely determined by the fact that I grew up in the heyday of the New Criticism. From the beginning, I was preoccupied with technique, fascinated by the past, tempted by other languages.' In 1940 he married his first wife, the novelist Jean Stafford, and became a fanatical convert to Roman Catholicism: his first volume of verse, *Land of Unlikeness* (1944), betrays the conflict of Catholicism and his Boston ancestry. He was jailed for six months during the Second World War as, in effect, a conscientious objector. His second volume, *Lord Weary's Castle* (1946), which contains 'The Quaker Graveyard in Nantucket' and 'Mr Edwards and the Spider', was hailed in extravagant terms. In 1949, having divorced, he married the writer Elizabeth Hardwick. *The Mills of the Kavanaughs* (1951) has as its title poem a meditation by a Catholic widow, Anne Kavanaugh, reflecting on the past in her ancestral home in Maine; this was followed by *Life Studies* (1959), *For the Union Dead* (1964), *Near the Ocean* (1967), and volumes of translation, plays, etc. He reached the height of his public fame during his opposition to the Vietnam war and support of Senator Eugene McCarthy, as his *Notebook 1967–1968* (1968) records; but he had long been suffering bouts of manic illness and heavy drinking, and a visit to Britain (at the invitation of All Souls, Oxford, and Essex University) in 1970 increased the disorder of his private life. His highly personal, confessional volume of poetry *The Dolphin* (1973) caused scandal with its revelations of marital anguish and discord. He married the writer Caroline Blackwood in 1973, but later returned to America, where he died: *Day by Day*, a last collection, was published just before his death. A legendary figure in his lifetime, both *poète maudit* and aristocrat, both classic and romantic, he suffered from the claims made on his behalf as the greatest American poet of his time, a heroic myth-maker whose work was compared favourably with that of *Yeats, an ironic intellectual whose ambiguous, complex imagery satisfied the demands of the *New Criticism; the response to Ian Hamilton's frank biography, published in 1982, bore witness to a sense of the need for reassessment.

LOWES, J(ohn) L(ivingstone) (1867–1945), professor of English in several American universities and at Harvard from 1918. He is best known for three of his books: *Convention and Revolt in Poetry* (1919); his brilliant study of *Coleridge, The Road to Xanadu* (1927); and *The Art of Geoffrey Chaucer* (1931). He is a greatly admired critic of 14th-cent. English, especially *Chaucer.

LOWNDES, William Thomas (d. 1843), author of *The Bibliographer's Manual of English Literature* (1838) and *The British Librarian* (1839), early bibliographical works of importance. The former was revised and enlarged (1857–8) by H. G. *Bohn.

LOWRY, (Clarence) Malcolm (1909–57), novelist, born in Cheshire, the fourth son of a wealthy cotton broker. Under the influence of *Melville, *O'Neill, *Conrad, and Jack *London he went to sea on leaving school, travelling to the Far East, then returned to take a degree at Cambridge. In 1933 he published *Ultramarine*, which shows a considerable debt to *Blue Voyage* by his friend *Aiken, in whose autobiography *Ushant* (1952) he was to appear as Hambro. He travelled widely in Europe and the US, settling in Mexico with his first wife Jan from 1936 to 1938, where he worked on *Under the Volcano*, published 1947. Various manuscripts were meanwhile rejected. In 1940 he settled in Dollarton, British Columbia, with his second wife ex-starlet Margerie. His last years were spent in England, and he died 'by misadventure' in Sussex. He was a chronic alcoholic, as are many of his characters, and had severe problems in disciplining his work, which went through innumerable revisions, many with Margerie's help. His posthumous publications include: *Hear Us O Lord from Heaven Thy Dwelling Place* (1961), *Selected Poems*, ed. Earle Birney and M. B. Lowry (1962), *Dark as the Grave Wherein my Friend is Laid* (1968), and *October Ferry to Gabriola* (1970). There is a biography by Douglas Day (1974) and a selection of his letters (ed. Harvey Breit and M. B. Lowry, 1965, London 1967).

Loyal Subject, The, a drama by J. *Fletcher, produced 1618.

The subject is the jealousy shown by the duke of Muscovy of his late father's loyal general, Archas, whom he dismisses and replaces by an incompetent flatterer, Boroskie. The young Archas, son of the general, disguised as a girl (Alinda) is placed in the service of Olympia, the duke's sister, wins her affection, and attracts the duke's love. On an invasion of the Tartars, Boroskie feigns sickness, Archas is recalled and conquers. But Boroskie inflames the duke's suspicion of Archas. On signs of the disaffection of the troops, who are devoted to him, Archas is carried off to torture. The infuriated troops attack the palace, and then march away to join the Tartars, but are brought back to submission by Archas, fresh from the rack. The repentant duke marries Honora, daughter of Archas. The identity of Alinda, who has been dismissed by Olympia on suspicion of yielding to the duke's advances, is now declared, and the young Archas is married to Olympia.

LOYOLA, St Ignatius, see IGNATIUS LOYOLA, ST.

LUBBOCK, Percy (1879–1965), critic and biographer, whose works include *Earlham* (1922), an account of his own Norfolk childhood holidays; *Roman Pictures* (1923), which describes an English tourist's responses to Rome; *Shades of Eton* (1923), recollections of his schooldays; and *Portrait of Edith Wharton* (1947). He was a friend of H. *James, and edited a selection of his letters (1920); also of A. C. *Benson, a selection from whose diary he edited (1926). His *The Craft of Fiction* (1921), which analyses the techniques of *Tolstoy, *Flaubert, James, etc., appears to have been closely studied by G. *Greene, who describes it as an 'admirable primer' in *Ways of Escape* (1980).

LUCAN (Marcus Annaeus Lucanus) (AD 39–65), a Roman poet of Spanish origin, the nephew of *Seneca. Favoured by Nero, then estranged from him, Lucan joined Piso's conspiracy and was forced on its discovery to commit suicide. The only one of his works to have survived is a historical epic in 10 books about the Civil Wars called the *Pharsalia* or the *Bellum Civile*. This work shows he had a remarkable skill in the depiction of character, a mastery of epigram, and a passionate love of freedom, but he set no limits on his unruly imagination and liking for bombast. The worst features of his style had an influence on the so-called Senecan drama of the 16th cent. *Dryden thought him lacking in artistic judgement, but *Shelley and *Macaulay were firm admirers. There are important translations by A. *Gorges, T. *May, and N. *Rowe.

LUCAS, E(dward) V(errall) (1868–1938), journalist and essayist, acquired much of his education working in a Brighton bookshop, and thereafter wrote prolifically on a great variety of subjects, including art, literature, and travel. His works include biographies, novels, and romances (such as *Over Bemerton's*, 1908, set over an antiquarian bookshop); he edited the works and letters of Charles and Mary *Lamb (1903–35) and many popular anthologies, contributed to *Punch, and was a member of its staff for some time. His autobiographical *Reading, Writing and Remembering* (1932) describes some odd corners of the book world, and a life which combined hard work and amateur inaccuracy.

LUCAS, F(rank) L(aurence) (1894–1967), scholar, critic, and poet, was educated at Colfe's

Grammar School, Lewisham, and at Trinity College, Cambridge; he became a fellow of King's, Cambridge. His critical works include *Tragedy in Relation to Aristotle's Poetics* (1927) and *The Decline and Fall of the Romantic Ideal* (1936), and he edited an edition of J. *Webster (4 vols, 1927). He also published several volumes of verse and translations from the classics, and edited various anthologies.

Lucasta, see LOVELACE, R.

Lucentio, successful suitor of *Bianca in Shakespeare's *The Taming of the Shrew*.

LUCIAN OF SAMOSATA (AD *c.*125–*c.*200), Greek writer of prose satires. Many of his works are dialogues where mythical or historical figures are placed in ridiculous situations, and the contrast between their traditional dignity and what they are made to say or do becomes a fruitful source of irony. Lucian was popular with the humanists. Sir T. *More put some of his dialogues into Latin, and *Erasmus's mock encomium the *Praise of Folly* made his irony familiar to the whole of Europe. But the piece by Lucian that had perhaps the most influence was *The True History* which claimed to describe a visit to the moon and inspired a long series of imaginary voyages from J. *Hall's *Mundus alter et idem* (1605) to S. Butler's *Erewhon* (1872), Swift's *Gulliver's Travels* being the most eminent example of the genre.

LUCIE-SMITH, (John) Edward Mackenzie (1935–), poet and art critic, born in Jamaica. *A Tropical Childhood and other Poems* appeared in 1961, and in the early 1960s Lucie-Smith was associated with the *Group, but since then has moved more towards literary journalism; his works include various editions of contemporary poetry, works of art history and criticism, a life of *Joan of Arc (1976), *The Burnt Child* (autobiography, 1975), etc.

Lucifera, in Spenser's *Faerie Queene* (I. iv. 12), the symbol of baseless pride and worldliness.

Lucina, in *Orlando Innamorato* and *Orlando Furioso*, a lady in the power of a cruel monster called an orc, released by *Mandricardo and *Gradasso.

Lucinda, see CARDENIO.

Lucius, (1) a mythical king of Britain, supposed to have been the first to receive Christianity: see Spenser, *The Faerie Queene* (II. x. 53); (2) Lucius (Iberius) is the Roman Emperor who demands tribute from King Arthur who makes war on Rome (in e.g. Malory's Second Romance in Vinaver's edition); in *Malory he is slain by Arthur, in other versions by Gawain. In *Geoffrey of Monmouth's *History* he is slain by an unknown hand when on the territorial offensive against Arthur. (3) Brutus's page in Shake-

speare's *Julius Caesar*; (4) a character in his *Timon of Athens*; (5) a character in his *Titus Andronicus*; (6) in his *Cymbeline*, Caius Lucius is 'General of the Roman Forces'.

Luck of Barry Lyndon, The, a satirical novel by *Thackeray, published in *Fraser's Magazine* 1844, republished under the title *The Memoirs of Barry Lyndon, Esquire, by Himself* (1852, New York).

It is the story of an Irish adventurer who unconsciously reveals his villainy while attempting self-justification. Redmond Barry flees from Ireland after a duel, wrongly believing he has killed his opponent. He serves in the Seven Years War, first in the English, then in the Prussian, army. He is set to spy upon the Chevalier de Balibari, who turns out to be his uncle Cornelius Barry. The two set up as card-sharpers, and Barry becomes a successful gambler and man of fashion. He marries a wealthy, foolish widow, the countess of Lyndon, and takes her name. He spends her fortune and ill-treats her and her son, showing affection only to his old mother and his own son Bryan, whom he indulges until the boy is killed in a riding accident. Finally the countess, with the help of her son Viscount Bullingdon, now grown up and no longer susceptible to his stepfather's bullying, is released from Barry's hold over her. Barry is forced to live abroad on a pension, and when left penniless after the countess's death ends his life miserably in the Fleet Prison, prematurely senile and cared for by his devoted old mother.

Lucky Jim, a novel by K. *Amis.

Lucrece, *The Rape of*, see RAPE OF LUCRECE, THE.

Lucretia, or **Lucrece,** a celebrated Roman lady, daughter of Lucretius and wife of Tarquinius Collatinus, whose beauty inflamed the passion of Sextus (son of Tarquin, king of Rome), which he used threats and violence to satisfy. Lucretia, after informing her father and husband of what had passed and entreating them to avenge her indignities, took her own life. The outrage committed by Sextus, coupled with the oppression of the king, led to the expulsion of the Tarquins from Rome, and the introduction of republican government. See also RAPE OF LUCRECE.

LUCRETIUS, Titus Lucretius Carus (probably *c.*99–55 BC), Roman poet. His chief work is a philosophical poem in hexameters, in six books, *De Rerum Naturâ*. He adopts the atomic theory of the universe of *Epicurus, and seeks to show that the course of the world can be explained without resorting to divine intervention, his object being to free mankind from terror of the gods. The work is marked by passages of great poetical beauty. Echoes of Lucretius can be found in *Spenser, *Hobbes, *Dryden, who produced some vigorous translations, and *Shelley; but the only major poem inspired by his work is *Tennyson's 'Lucretius' (1869).

Lucy and Colin, a *ballad by T. *Tickell.

Lucy Poems, The, name given to a group of poems by *Wordsworth, most of which were written in Germany in the exceptionally cold winter of 1798–9. 'She dwelt among the untrodden ways' and 'Strange fits of passion have I known' were sent to *Coleridge in a letter, as was 'A slumber did my spirit seal'; 'Three years she grew in sun and shower' was written a little later, in the spring. All four were published in the *Lyrical Ballads of 1800. A fifth poem, 'I travelled among unknown men', was sent in a letter in 1801 to Mary Hutchinson, and published in 1807. The poems are remarkable for their lyric intensity and purity, and the identity of Lucy has aroused much speculation; in 'Strange Fits of Passion' she appears to be identified with Dorothy *Wordsworth (who was with him in Germany), but in other poems she is presented as having died. Coleridge reflected that, 'Most probably, in some gloomier moment he had fancied the moment in which his sister might die' (Letter to T. Poole, 1799). The name Lucy is used in the ballad 'Lucy Gray' also written in Germany and published in 1800, where it is also associated with death and solitude. See also H. W. Garrod's essay on 'Wordsworth's Lucy' in *Wordsworth* (1927).

Lucy Snowe, the narrator of *Villette*.

Lud, a mythical king of Britain, according to *Geoffrey of Monmouth's *History* (i. 17) the eldest brother of *Cassivelaunus. He built walls around the city of Brutus (Trinovantum) and renamed it Caerlud (Lud's city) from which derives its modern name London. Geoffrey says that Gildas recounts at length the quarrel that ensued between Lud and his brother Nennius because of the impiety of renaming their father's city.

Luddites, a band of English craftsmen and labourers, organized 1811–16, who felt their livelihoods threatened by machinery and set about its destruction. The name is said to have come from Ned Ludd, who lived about 1779, and who in a rage smashed two frames of a 'stockinger'. Luddites appear in *Shirley* by C. Brontë, and *Byron wrote 'A Song for the Luddites', published 1830. The term is now commonly applied to any person who resists technological change.

LUDLOW, Edmund (?1617–92), Puritan general and regicide, author of *Memoirs*, first printed 1698–9, which cover the course of the Civil War and the Protectorate, and his own flight to Geneva in 1660. He died at Vevey.

Ludus Coventriae, see MYSTERY PLAYS.

Lugdunum, in imprints, Lyons.

Lugdunum Batavorum, in imprints, Leyden.

Lugh, see TUATHA DÉ DANANN.

LUKÁCS, Georg (1885–1971), Hungarian Marxist philosopher and literary critic, born in Budapest, the son of a wealthy banker; his cultural background and education were dominated by German influences (notably that of *Hegel) and he wrote largely in German. In 1918 he joined the Hungarian Communist Party, and fled to Austria after the overthrow of Communist Béla Kun's coalition government. He settled in Vienna, where he wrote his major Marxist theoretical work, *History and Class Consciousness* (1923; English trans. 1971). In 1931 he moved to Berlin, then, when Hitler came to power, to Moscow; he returned to Hungary in 1945, became minister of culture under the Nagy government, was deported to Romania for a period after the Russian invasion, and later allowed to return.

Lukács's critical works (which had a delayed impact in Britain, owing partly to the unavailability of translations) include the early, pre-Marxist *The Theory of the Novel* (1920, trans. 1971), in which, after Hegel, he describes the novel as a 'bourgeois epic' in which the alienated, solitary hero is in constant conflict with his environment; *The Historical Novel* (written 1936–7, first published in Russian, English trans. 1962), a major work which analyses the growth of historical awareness in the novelist, relating it to the change in European consciousness that followed the French revolution (with particular emphasis on Sir W. *Scott, the only British novelist treated in depth, whom Lukács sees as giving 'perfect artistic expression to . . . the historical defence of progress'); and *The Meaning of Contemporary Realism* (1958, trans. 1969) in which Lukács attempts to account for the Modernists (*Joyce, *Kafka, *Beckett, etc.) and argues that the artist has a duty to do more than mirror the despair and futility of bourgeois society. His large output also includes works on Hegel, *Goethe, Russian and German Realism, aesthetics, etc. Despite ideological shifts (which perplexed both Soviet and Western admirers), Lukács's emphasis is throughout on the ethical rather than the formal properties of literature; his admiration for the great 19th-cent. masters (*Balzac, *Stendahl, *Tolstoy) leads him to see them as writers who transcend their class bias to produce works of art which are a harmonious totality, reconciling all contradictions. It also leads him to reject experimentalism, in conformity with the doctrine of *socialist realism. He was much criticized for this in the 1930s by his fellow Marxist *Brecht, who saw his position as essentially reactionary, academic, and nostalgic: T. *Mann (perceived by Lukács as the tragic bourgeois artist exiled from history) stressed Lukács's strong sense of the German humanist tradition. See G. Steiner, *Language* *and Silence* (1967) and T. Eagleton, *Marxism and Literary Criticism* (1976).

LULLY, Raymond (Raimon Lull) (*c*.1235–1315), a Catalan born in Majorca, who, after visions of Christ crucified, became a Franciscan, a mystic, a philosopher, a missionary to the Arabs, an author of controversial treatises, and a poet. He urged on the Council of Vienne the establishment of schools for missionary languages and obtained a decree for the foundation of chairs of Hebrew, Greek, Chaldee, and Arabic at various universities (including Oxford; *Rashdall, ii. 459). He died of wounds received in a missionary crusade in North Africa, undertaken in his 80th year, after he had been twice expelled from Barbary.

Lumpkin, Tony, a character in Goldsmith's *She Stoops to Conquer*.

Luria, a tragedy in blank verse by R. *Browning, published 1846, together with *A Soul's Tragedy*, as no. VIII of *Bells and Pomegranates*. It was written, Browning told Elizabeth Barrett (see BROWNING, E. B.), 'for a purely imaginary stage', and is set in the 15th cent. during the conflict between Florence and Pisa, though the actual episode is unhistorical. The plot concerns the fall of the noble-hearted Florentine commander Luria, a Moorish mercenary (Browning acknowledged the influence of *Othello*) who, at the height of his triumph, is falsely accused of plotting a coup against the Republic. The failure of political idealism, consummated and transcended by a heroic death, relates the play to the earlier *Sordello*.

LURIE, Alison (1926–   ), American novelist, born in Chicago, and for some years a member of the English department at Cornell. Her sharply satiric and observant novels include *Love and Friendship* (1962), *Imaginary Friends* (1967), and *The War Between the Tates* (1974), a *campus novel involving student politics, teenage revolt, and marital anguish and infidelity. Her ironic detachment and sense of social nuance have led to a warm reception in Britain.

Lusiads, The, see CAMOËNS, L.

Lussurioso, a character in *The Revenger's Tragedy*.

Lutetia, or **Lutetia Parisiorum,** (1) the modern Paris, on an island in the Sequana (Seine), was the capital of the Parisii, a Gallic tribe. Two wooden bridges connected it with the banks of the river, and it became a place of importance during the Roman Empire. (2) in imprints, Paris.

LUTHER, Martin (1483–1546), the leader of the Reformation in Germany, was born of humble parents at Eisleben, and entered the Augustinian order. As a monk he visited Rome, and his experience of the corruption in high ecclesiastical places influenced his future career. He attacked the principle of papal indulgences by nailing his famous *Theses* to the door of the church at Wittenberg, and as a consequence the papal ban was pronounced on him (1521) at the Diet of Worms. He left the monastic order and married, and devoted himself to forming the League of Protestantism. His chief literary work, apart from polemical treatises, was his translation into German of the Old and New Testaments, known as the Lutheran Bible (1534; portions had appeared earlier). He also composed hymns of great popularity in Germany, notably 'Ein' feste Burg'.

Luther's power lay in these hymns of joy and strength and in his revival of the doctrine of justification by the faith of the individual, implying religious liberty and attacking the scandal of indulgences.

He is the subject of a play by J. *Osborne, *Luther* (1961), which traces his career from 1506, when he is received into the Augustinian Order of Eremites, to 1530, when, married, he has settled into 'the tired pain of middle age'. There is a psychoanalytical biography by *Erikson.

LUTTRELL, Henry (?1765–1851), wit and member of the *Holland House circle, was author of clever and lively verses, including *Advice to Julia*, admired by *Byron.

LUTTRELL, Narcissus (1657–1732), annalist and bibliographer, compiled *A Brief Historical Relation of State Affairs from September 1678 to April 1714*, published in 1857 (6 vols), after *Macaulay had drawn attention to the manuscript in *All Souls College, Oxford.

Luve Ron, or 'the Love Song', traditionally but wrongly called 'the Love Rune', a mystical love-poem in 210 lines by the Franciscan Thomas de Hales, written probably in the early part of the reign of Henry III (between 1216 and 1250). It describes to a young woman novice the love of Christ and the joy of mystical union with him. Ed. in *An Old English Miscellany* by R. Morris (1872), EETS OS 49, pp. 93–9.

Lux Mundi, see GORE, CHARLES.

LYALL, Sir Alfred Comyn (1835–1911), had a distinguished career with the Indian Civil Service, and published several volumes on Indian history, religion, and folklore, as well as literary studies and a volume of poetry, *Verses written in India* (1889).

LYALL, Edna, the pseudonym of Ada Ellen Bayly (1857–1903), novelist and supporter of political liberal causes including women's emancipation. Her convictions were expounded in many of her novels. She admired *Bradlaugh, whose life is vaguely reflected in her first success, *We Two* (1884), the sequel to *Donovan* (1882). Her other novels include *In the Golden Days* (1885), which was the last book to be read to *Ruskin on his deathbed, and *Doreen* (1895), which strongly states the case for Home Rule for Ireland, and won praise from *Gladstone.

Lycidas, a poem by *Milton, written 1637, at Horton, published the following year. It is a pastoral elegy on the death of Edward *King, a fellow of Christ's College, Cambridge, who had been a student there at the same time as Milton, though not, it would appear, a close friend. Like Milton himself, he had aspirations as a poet and as a clergyman. He was drowned while crossing from Chester Bay to Dublin, his ship having struck a rock and foundered in calm weather. Milton, in lamenting his premature death and the uncertainty of life, suggests deep anxieties about his own ambitions and unfulfilled promise; his apparent digression when, in the voice of St Peter, he violently attacks the unworthy clergy whose 'hungry Sheep look up, and are not fed' (a passage which unites the Christian pastoral tradition with the pagan) may refer to his mixed feelings about and delay in entering the ministry. The poem ends with a moving expression of faith in resurrection and redemption. It has been subjected to innumerable conflicting interpretations, but most critics agree that it is one of the finest elegies in the English language, and a work of great originality.

LYDGATE, John (?1370–1449), born in Lydgate, Suffolk, and admitted to the monastery of Bury St Edmunds in about 1385. He was in Paris in about 1426, and was briefly abbot of Hatfield Broadoak in Essex shortly before that; otherwise he spent nearly all his life in the monastery at Bury. He is one of the most voluminous of all English poets, with a corpus of well over 100,000 lines. Of his more readable poems, most were written in the first decade of the 15th cent. in a Chaucerian vein: *The Complaint of the Black Knight* (originally called *A Complaynt of a Loveres Lyfe* and modelled on Chaucer's *The Book of the Duchess); The Temple of Glas* (indebted to *The House of Fame); The Floure of Curtesy* (like *The Parliament of Fowls,* a Valentine's Day poem); and the allegorical *Reason and Sensuality.* His short poems tend to be the best; as he got older, his poems grew progressively longer, and it is on the later poetry that *Ritson's harsh characterization of him is based: 'a voluminous, prosaick and drivelling monk'. His bulkiest works are his *Troy Book* (1412–20), a 30,000-line translation of *Guido delle Colonne; The Siege of Thebes* (1420–2), translated from a French prose redaction of the *Roman de Thebes; The Pilgrimage of Man* (1426–30), translated from Deguileville, which comprises 24,000 lines of octosyllabic couplets; and,

last and longest, *The Fall of Princes* (1431–8) which is a translation in 36,000 lines of a French version of *Boccaccio's *De Casibus Virorum Illustrium.* There have been some recent attempts, notably by D. A. Pearsall, to re-elevate the reputation of Lydgate to the stature he enjoyed up to the 17th cent., until which time he was almost invariably coupled for praise with *Chaucer and *Gower.

For editions of the various poems and discussion, see D. A. Pearsall, *John Lydgate* (1970), p. 301; see also A. Renoir, *The Poetry of John Lydgate* (1967); W. F. Schirmer, *John Lydgate: a Study in the Culture of the XVth Century* (in German 1952; trans. A. E. Keep, 1961); convenient selections ed. J. Norton Smith (1966).

Lydgate, Tertius, a character in G. Eliot's *Middlemarch.*

LYELL, Sir Charles, see DARWIN, C.

Lyle, Annot, a character in Scott's *A Legend of Montrose.*

LYLY, John (?1554–1606), was the grandson of W. *Lily. He was educated possibly at the King's School, Canterbury, then at Magdalen College, Oxford; he studied also at Cambridge. He was MP successively for Hindon, Aylesbury, and Appleby (1598–1601), and supported the cause of the bishops in the *Martin Marprelate controversy in a satirical pamphlet, *Pappe with an Hatchet* (1589). The first part of his *Euphues. The Anatomy of Wit* appeared in 1578, and the second part, *Euphues and his England,* in 1580. Its peculiar style came to be known as 'Euphuism'. Among Lyly's plays, all of which were written for performance by boy actors to courtly audiences, are *Alexander, Campaspe and Diogenes* (see under CAMPASPE, its later title); *Sapho and Phao* (1584); *Endimion* (1591); *Midas* (1592); *Mother Bombie* (1594, see under BUMBY). The attractive songs in the plays, including such well known lyrics as 'Cupid and my Campaspe played', were first printed in Blount's collected edition of 1632: it is doubtful to what extent they are the work of Lyly. Although *Euphues* was Lyly's most popular and influential work in the Elizabethan period, his plays are now admired for their flexible use of dramatic prose and the elegant patterning of their construction. R. W. Bond edited Lyly's works in 1902, and there is a good study of him by G. K. Hunter, *John Lyly: the Humanist as Courtier* (1962).

LYND, Robert Wilson (1879–1949), journalist and essayist, described by L. *Woolf as 'one of those impeccable journalists who every week for 30 or 40 years turn out an impeccable essay (called in the technical jargon of journalism a "middle") like an impeccable sausage, about anything or everything or nothing' (*Beginning Again,* 1964). Born in Belfast, and educated there at Queen's College, Lynd came to England in 1901, and worked as a freelance journalist before joining the *Daily News* in 1908 to which he contributed until 1947. He was best known for his weekly articles in the *Nation*, then in the *New Statesman*, signed 'Y.Y.', which were collected in various volumes with titles such as *The pleasures of ignorance* (1921), *The Green Man* (1928), and *In defence of pink* (1937).

LYNDSAY, Sir David, see LINDSAY, SIR D.

Lynet (also Linet, Lunet, or the *Saveage Damsel*), in *Malory, is the sister of the lady *Lyones who brings Gareth to fight Ironsyde, liberating Lyones who marries Gareth. Another lady of the same name (also called the Saveage Damsel once) is the Lunete in *Chrétien's *Yvain* (and in the English *Iwain and Gawain*) who is also an intermediary; she commends Ywain to Laudine (Alundyne) whom he marries. Chrétien explains her name by reference to the moon. See GARETH AND LYNETTE.

Lyones (also Liones and, in *Malory, Lyonesse), (1) the sister of *Lynet, imprisoned by Ironsyde in the Castle Perilous and freed by *Gareth whom she marries; (2) in Malory, the region of origin of Tristram; the name is also geographical in *Tennyson who makes it the place of the last battle between Arthur and Mordred. It is traditionally said to be a tract of land between the Isles of Scilly and Land's End, now submerged.

Lyonesse, see LYONES.

Lyra Apostolica, a collection of sacred poems contributed originally to the *British Magazine* and reprinted in a separate volume in 1836. The poems, 179 in all, appeared anonymously, the six authors each being designated by a Greek letter: J. W. Bowden (α) contributed six, R. H. *Froude (β) eight, *Keble (γ) forty-six, *Newman (δ) 109, R. I. Wilberforce (ϵ) one, and I. *Williams (ζ) nine. All the writers were associated with the *Oxford Movement.

Lyric, Lyric Poetry, derived from the Greek adjective 'lurikos' ('for the lyre'), was the name given in ancient Greece to verses sung to a lyre, whether as a solo performance (*Sappho) or by a choir (*Pindar). The Greek lyrists were then imitated in Latin at an artistic level by *Catullus and *Horace, but what appears to have been more important for the development of the genre was the tradition of popular song which existed both in Rome and among the German tribes. This continued to flourish in spite of the Church's disapproval and produced in all the medieval literatures of Western Europe a lyric harvest that ranged from hymns to bawdy drinking songs and drew its authors from every social category. In England lyric poems flourished in the Middle English period (in such manuscript collections as the *Harley Lyrics),

and in the 16th-cent. heyday of humanism this already quite sophisticated lyric tradition was enriched by the direct imitation of ancient models and reached perfection in the song-books and plays of the Elizabethan age. During the next 200 years the link between poetry and music was gradually broken, and the term 'lyric' came to be applied to short poems expressive of a poet's thoughts or feelings, and which could not be classed under another heading. The convention that a poem communicates its author's feelings to a reader reached the high point of its popularity in the Romantic period, but soon after *Baudelaire introduced the modern form of lyric poetry in which the poet seems to struggle to express for his own satisfaction psychic experiences whose nature he at times only half understands: the lyric of *Mallarmé, *Rilke, *Yeats, and T. S. *Eliot.

Lyrical Ballads, *with a few other Poems,* a collection of poems by *Wordsworth and *Coleridge, of which the first edition appeared 1798, the second with new poems and a preface (known as the 1800 edition) Jan. 1801, and a third 1802.

The book was a landmark of English *Romanticism and the beginning of a new age. The poems were written largely in Somerset, and Coleridge, in the *Biographia Literaria* (ch. xiv) describes the nature of their collaboration: 'it was agreed that my endeavours should be directed to persons and characters supernatural or at least romantic . . . Mr Wordsworth, on the other hand, was to propose to himself as his object, to give the charm of novelty to things of everyday.' Coleridge's contributions to the first edition were *The Rime of the *Ancient Mariner*, 'The Foster-Mother's Tale', 'The Nightingale', and 'The Dungeon'; Wordsworth's include ballads and narratives such as 'The Thorn', *'The Idiot Boy', and 'Simon Lee, the old Huntsman', and more personal poems such as 'Lines written in early spring' and 'Lines written a few miles above *Tintern Abbey'. They appeared with a brief 'Advertisement' by Wordsworth, stating his theory of *poetic diction and attacking the 'gaudy and inane phraseology of many modern writers'; his views were much expanded in his important Preface to the second edition, and enlarged again in 1802. The poems themselves, with their 'low' subjects and language and their alleged banality and repetitions, were subjected to much ridicule, as was Wordsworth's confident and unperturbed maintaining of his own position, which had little of the defensive in its attitude. The second volume of the second edition added many of Wordsworth's most characteristic works, including the so-called *'Lucy poems', 'The Old Cumberland Beggar', and *'Michael, a Pastoral'.

Lysander, a character in Shakespeare's *A Midsummer Night's Dream*.

LYTTLETON, George, first baron Lyttleton (1709–73), a prominent politician, and an opponent of Sir R. *Walpole, was also a friend of *Pope, *Shenstone, and *Fielding, and a liberal patron of literature. It is he whom Thomson addresses in *The Seasons* and who procured the poet a pension; he also contributed a stanza to *The Castle of Indolence*. He published, among numerous works, poems in *Dodsley's *Collection* (1748, vol. 2), *Dialogues of the Dead* (1760), and a history of Henry II (1767–71). Of the *Dialogues*, the last three were by Mrs *Montagu. He was caricatured by Smollett as Scragg in *Peregrine Pickle*.

LYTTON, Edward Earle Lytton Bulwer-, see BULWER-LYTTON.

LYTTON, Edward Robert Bulwer, first earl of Lytton (1831–91), son of E. *Bulwer-Lytton, was educated at Harrow and Bonn; his childhood was overshadowed by the quarrels of his parents, and he relied much on the protective interest of his father's friend J. *Forster, who encouraged his literary efforts. After a successful career in the diplomatic service he became viceroy of India (1876–80), where his 'Forward' policy aroused much opposition. He published several volumes of verse, at first under the pseudonym 'Owen Meredith'. *Clytemnestra, The Earl's Return, The Artist and other Poems* (1855) was followed by *The Wanderer* (1858); both show talent, and the Wanderer's mildly *Byronic and lyrical continental adventures had some success. His later volumes, which include two long verse-romances, are marred by prolixity and facile versification. His own favourite, *King Poppy: a story without end*, an obscure, fanciful, and lengthy blank verse allegory, was circulated privately to his friends in 1875, constantly revised over many years, and published in 1892. Lytton seems to have found his dual career as statesman and poet problematic, and to have sensed his own failure in the latter role: in 'Last Words of a Sensitive Second-Rate Poet', published in *Chronicles and Characters* (1868), the poor reception of which much distressed him, he writes, 'Talk not of genius baffled. Genius is master of man. | Genius does what it must, and Talent does what it can.' There is a critical biography by A. B. Harlan (1946).

M

Mab, Queen, see QUEEN MAB.

MABBE, James (1572–?1642), educated at, and fellow of, Magdalen College, Oxford, became a lay prebendary of Wells. He is remembered for his translations of Fernando de Rojas's *Celestina and of The Spanish Ladye, one of *Cervantes's 'Exemplary Novels'. Mabbe Hispanicized his name as 'Puedeser' (may-be).

Mabinogion, The, strictly, the first four Welsh tales contained in the collection of Lady Charlotte Guest, made in 1838–49. The four are preserved in two Welsh manuscripts: The White Book of Rhydderch (1300–25) and The Red Book of Hergyst (1375–1425). 'Mab' is the word for 'youth', but, even by the time of the medieval title, it is· likely that the word meant nothing much more precise than 'story'. In the four stories it is likely that the original common element was the hero Pryderi; as they survive their subjects are (1) Pwyll, the father of Pryderi; (2) Branwen, the daughter of Llyr and her marriage to the Irish king Matholwch; (3) Manawyddan, the son of Llyr and his association with Pryderi; (4) the death of Pryderi in battle with the nephews of Math who had cheated him. There is no mention of *Arthur in these four branches of the Mabinogion proper; but five of the other seven tales published by Guest from The Red Book of Hergyst deal indirectly with him: 'The Lady of the Fountain'; 'Peredur'; 'Gereint', three romances from French originals; 'Culhwch and Olwen'; and 'The Dream of Rhonabwy'; the latter two native tales are perhaps the most appealing of the collection. The other two tales in Guest's collection are 'The Dream of Macsen Wledig' and 'Lludd and Llefelys'.

Trans. by Gwyn Jones and Thomas Jones (1949). *Math vab Mathonwy* by W. J. Gruffydd (1928); I. L. Foster, chapters 4 and 16 in R. S. Loomis ed., *Arthurian Literature in the Middle Ages* (1959).

Macabre, Dance, see DANCE OF DEATH.

Macaronic verse, a term used to designate a burlesque form of verse in which vernacular words are introduced into a Latin context with Latin terminations and in Latin constructions ... and *loosely* to any form of verse in which two or more languages are mingled together [*OED*]. The chief writer of macaronic verse was *Folengo.

M'Aulay, Angus and Allan, characters in Scott's *A Legend of Montrose.

MACAULAY, Catherine, afterwards Graham (1731–91), republican historian, whose *History of England* in 8 volumes appeared 1763–83, and in a French translation 1791–2. Dr *Johnson mocked her radical views, but she was much admired in France. Mary *Wollstonecraft praised her highly, and *Lecky was to write with respect of her ability.

MACAULAY, Dame (Emilie) Rose (1881–1958), novelist, essayist, and travel writer, whose many works include *Potterism* (1920), *They were Defeated* (1932), both fiction, and *Pleasures of Ruins* (1953). Her best-known novels, *The World my Wilderness* (1950) and *The Towers of Trebizond* (1956), appeared after a decade in which she wrote no fiction, and followed her return to the Anglican faith, from which she had been long estranged through her love for a married man who died in 1942. Her religious revival was inspired partly by the Revd J. H. C. Johnson, and her correspondence with him was published after her death in two volumes, 1961–2, as *Letters to a Friend.*

MACAULAY, Thomas Babington (1800–59), politician and historian, son of the noted philanthropist and reformer Zachary Macaulay. After graduating at Trinity College, Cambridge, he was called to the bar, but his essay on *Milton for the *Edinburgh Review* in August 1825 brought him instant fame, and for the next 20 years he wrote article after article on historical and literary topics for the *Review*, becoming one of the acknowledged intellectual pundits of the age (see ESSAYS CONTRIBUTED TO THE EDINBURGH REVIEW). In 1830 he entered Parliament on the Whig ticket, first for Calne (Wilts), then for Leeds, and he took an ardent and active part in the passing of the Reform Bill. But in 1834, in order to achieve financial independence, he accepted a place on the Supreme Council of India, where his famous Minutes on Law and Education had a decisive influence on the development of the sub-continent. On his return in 1838 he began to write a detailed history of England from the revolution of 1688, though he still flirted with a political career; he was elected MP for Edinburgh in 1839 and again in 1852; he was a secretary at war 1839–41 and paymaster-general 1846–7. But by now his literary fame was such that everything he published was a dazzling success, beginning in 1842 with *Lays of Ancient Rome*. Their rocking-horse rhythms and naïvety of expression are now decidedly out of fashion, but they retained their popularity in schools into the 1930s, when there were few children who had not re-fought 'The Battle of Lake Regillus' or stood shoulder to shoulder with Horatius at the bridge. Similarly, his collected *Essays Critical and Historical* (1834) sold steadily down the century. They are dogmatic and overbearing, and irredeemably shallow; Lord Acton called them 'A key to half the prejudices of our age'; but their urgent, declamatory style, their bustling self-confidence and biting wit, endeared them to the reading public all over the world. His *History of England* (vols 1–2, 1849; vols 3–4, 1855) had some of the same qualities, but it was more restrained and more deeply researched, as befits its purpose. That purpose is not so clear as it once was, and it will no longer do to classify Macaulay as a simple, out-and-out Whig. He took an immense pride in the English constitution, and shared with many Victorians a rather immature exaltation at the material advances of the 19th cent., under the shadow of the French revolution, and the purpose of the *History* was strictly defensive—to demonstrate that revolution on the continental model was unnecessary in England because of the statesmanlike precautions taken in 1688. He used a wide range of manuscript sources with great skill, and modern historians neglect his reconstruction of events at their peril; his is still the most detailed factual account, for instance, of the reign of James II. He also affected an interest in social history, though this was focused on his superficial and discredited Chapter III, on 'The Condition of England in 1685'. He acknowledged a great debt to Sir W. *Scott, which is evident in his habit of exploring on the ground all the places in which his narrative was set. His descriptive power was one of his great assets; another was the narrative momentum he was able to achieve. He is one of the few writers to whom the reviewer's cliché 'compulsively readable' is entirely appropriate. The *History* was one of the best-sellers of the century, and it has never since gone out of print. It brought him great wealth, and a peerage (as Lord Macaulay of Rothbury Temple, 1857). He at first intended to take the *History* up to 1830, then he lowered his sights to 1714, but when he died in 1859 he had only reached 1697. Macaulay was always criticized for his philistinism and his overweening self-confidence; Lord Melbourne once said, 'I wish I was as cocksure of anything as Tom Macaulay is of everything.' He came to wealth and fame as a young man, he never married, and he lived a very sheltered domestic life, which betrays itself in an evident emotional immaturity and a fallibility in the judgement of character. From the beginning he was accused of glamorizing history and in some sense diminishing it—even of killing the market for any other kind of history, however worthwhile, which was not as attractively packaged. On the other hand, it can be argued that he created a market for history which did not previously exist. Certainly his literary brilliance has always been such as to disarm criticism, which explains Lord Acton's paradoxical judgement: 'He remains to me one of the greatest of all writers and masters, although I think him base, contemptible and odious.'

Appropriately enough, he was the subject of one of the best Victorian biographies, by his nephew, Sir G. O. *Trevelyan (1876). See also John Clive, *Thomas Babington Macaulay: The Shaping of the Historian* (1976). The best literary study is by Jane Millgate (1973). His letters have been edited by Thomas Pinney (5 vols, 1974–80) and his journal is also being edited for publication.

Macaulay's History of England, see under MACAULAY, T. B.

Macbeth, a tragedy by *Shakespeare, probably written and first performed at the Globe in 1606, but not printed until the First *Folio (1623). The text is an unusually brief one, and has often been thought to contain some non-Shakespearian material, possibly by *Middleton. Two songs certainly by him were added to the play. It may have been performed before James I, who had a strong interest in witches and was supposedly a descendant of Banquo.

Macbeth and Banquo, generals of Duncan, king of Scotland, returning from a victorious campaign against rebels, encounter three weird sisters, or witches, upon a heath, who prophesy that Macbeth shall be thane of Cawdor, and king hereafter, and that Banquo shall beget kings though he be none. Immediately afterwards comes the news that the king has created Macbeth thane of Cawdor. Stimulated by the prophecy, and spurred on by Lady Macbeth, Macbeth murders Duncan, who is on a visit to his castle. Duncan's sons, Malcolm and Donalbain, escape, and Macbeth assumes the crown. To defeat the prophecy of the witches regarding Banquo, he orders the murder of Banquo and his son Fleance, but the latter escapes. Haunted by the ghost of Banquo, Macbeth consults the weird sisters, and is told to beware of Macduff, the thane of Fife; that none born of woman has power to harm Macbeth; and that he never will be vanquished till Birnam Wood shall come to Dunsinane. Learning that Macduff has joined Malcolm, who is gathering an army in England, he surprises the castle of Macduff and causes Lady Macduff and her children to be slaughtered. Lady Macbeth goes mad and dies. The army of Malcolm and Macduff attacks Macbeth; passing through Birnam Wood every man cuts a bough and under these 'leavy screens' marches on Dunsinane. Macduff, who was 'from his mother's womb | Untimely ripp'd', kills Macbeth. Malcolm is hailed king of Scotland.

Macbeth, Lady, ambitious wife of Macbeth in Shakespeare's play; a favourite role among 18th- and 19th-cent. actresses, for example Mrs *Siddons. L. C. *Knights's essay 'How many children had Lady Macbeth?' (1933) is a teasing riposte to the sort of biographical speculation favoured by A. C. *Bradley.

MacBETH, George Mann (1932–), poet, born in Lanarkshire, but educated in England. From 1955 to 1976 he produced programmes on poetry and the arts for the BBC, and he has also edited various anthologies. He was a member of the *Group during the 1950s, and in the 1960s was associated with the vogue for poetry in performance. His early work was experimental, and at times macabre and violent in its preoccupations; later collections show (in his own words) fewer 'comic and performance and experimental elements' (foreword to *Poems from Oby*, 1982). His works include *A Form of Words* (1954), *The Colour of Blood* (1967), and *Collected Poems 1958–1970* (1971). He has also published novels.

MacCAIG, Norman Alexander (1910–), Scottish poet, born and educated in Edinburgh, who worked for many years as a schoolmaster, and afterwards as a lecturer at the University of Stirling. His first volume of poetry, *Far Cry* (1943), was followed by many others which (notably in the 1960s), showed an increasing discipline and sensitivity; they include *Measures* (1965), *Rings on a Tree* (1968), and *A Man in my Position* (1969). His *Selected Poems* appeared in 1971, and he also edited two anthologies of Scottish poetry, *Honour'd Shade* (1959) and (with Alexander Scott) *Contemporary Scottish Verse 1959–1969* (1970). Much of his own poetry is inspired by the landscapes of the West Highlands and the life of Edinburgh, but his inspiration is less exclusively Scottish than that of many of his contemporaries.

MacCARTHY, Sir (Charles Otto) Desmond (1877–1952), educated at Cambridge, where he was an *Apostle, and later on friendly terms with the *Bloomsbury Group, is remembered largely for his perceptive theatre criticism, some of it collected in *The Court Theatre, 1904–7* (1907), *Drama* (1940), and *Shaw* (1951). He described himself as a 'literary journalist', was dramatic critic then literary editor of the *New Statesman* (1913–27), and from 1928 to 1952 wrote weekly for the *Sunday Times*. He also edited *Life and Letters* from 1928 to 1933.

McCARTHY, Justin (1830–1912), Irish journalist, historian, and novelist, author of a *History of our own Times* (1879–80) and of the novels *Dear Lady Disdain* (1875) and *Miss Misanthrope* (1878), among other works.

McCARTHY, Mary (1912–), novelist, short story writer, and critic, born in Seattle and orphaned at the age of six. She was raised by an aunt and uncle and two sets of grandparents of Catholic, Jewish, and Protestant backgrounds, a mixture that she describes in *Memoirs of a Catholic Girlhood* (1957). After graduating from Vassar she worked as a drama critic, then taught for some years at Bard College and Sarah Lawrence College, experiences she used in her satirical *campus novel *The Groves of Academe* (New York 1952, London 1953), which describes the political persecutions of the McCarthy period. Her first novel, *The Company she Keeps* (1942), is a portrait of a Bohemian intellectual, and *The Oasis* (1949, London 1950, as *A Source of Embarrassment*) describes the failure of a New England Utopia. *Cast a Cold Eye* (1950, short stories) and *A Charmed Life* (1955, novel) were followed by *The Group* (1963), a study of the lives and careers of eight Vassar girls, which caused some stir when published in England because of its frank and amusing descriptions of contraception, breastfeeding, and other gynaecological matters. She published two volumes of reportage, *Vietnam* (1967) and *Hanoi* (1968), protesting against American involvement in Vietnam. *Birds of America* (1971) is a novel written from the point of view of an idealistic, ecology-conscious young American boy living in Paris and Rome, deploring the effects of the growing tourist industry. *Cannibals and Missionaries* (1980) deals with a hijacking in Holland, in which a group of art-collectors and would-be philanthropists are held hostage by terrorists; it explores the conflicting values of art, élitism, and democracy. She has also published several volumes of essays and criticism. Her second husband was Edmund *Wilson.

McCULLERS, Carson Smith (1917–67), American novelist and short-story writer, born in Georgia, where most of her works are set. These include *The Heart is a Lonely Hunter* (1940), *Reflections in a Golden Eye* (1941), *The Member of the Wedding* (1946, dramatized by the author, 1950), and a collection, *The Ballad of the Sad Café* (1951), of which the title story was dramatized by *Albee, 1963. Critics have detected *Gothic elements in her work, which is frequently tinged with the macabre; she herself wrote that her central theme was 'spiritual isolation'.

MacDIARMID, Hugh, the pseudonym of Christopher Murray Grieve (1892–1978), poet and critic, was a founder (in 1928) of the

National Party of Scotland. In 1922, influenced by the prose experimentation of *Ulysses, he adopted the pseudonym and began to write lyrics in a Synthetic Scots that drew on various dialects and fortified the oral idiom with words preserved in *Jamieson's etymological dictionary. MacDiarmid deplored the sentimentality of post-Burnsian verse and wanted to renew the poetic tradition once carried by makars like *Dunbar: 'Not Burns—Dunbar!' was one of his many mottoes. His masterpiece, A Drunk Man Looks at the Thistle (1926), presents a vision that remakes Scotland in the MacDiarmidian image; a drunk man comes to consciousness on a hillside and has to contend with the huge thistle that confronts him symbolically in the moonlight before he can resume his odyssey to the arms of his wife Jean. In the process the alcoholic spirit wears off and is replaced by a spiritual awareness of what Scotland can be: 'The thistle rises and forever will, | Getherin' the generations under't. | This is the monument o' a' they were, | And a' they hoped and wondered.' MacDiarmid's Scots literary renaissance of the 1920s was followed by his political poetry of the 1930s; in 1931 he published his First Hymn to Lenin and thereby initiated the leftist verse of the decade. Expelled from the National Party in 1933, he joined the Communist Party the following year: in 1938 he was expelled from the Communist Party, which he rejoined in 1956. A powerful polemicist, MacDiarmid delighted in causing controversy: his autobiography Lucky Poet (1943) offended the officials of his native Langholm, so he was never offered the freedom of the burgh, despite his achievements. MacDiarmid scored some of his greatest poetic triumphs in English, albeit a Synthetic English. His long meditative poem 'On a Raised Beach', from Stony Limits (1934), is a subtle statement of the MacDiarmidian metaphysic: 'I will have nothing interposed | Between my sensitiveness and the barren but beautiful reality.' His later work comprises a series of long, linguistically dense, poems amounting to a modern epic of the Celtic consciousness. MacDiarmid's Complete Poems 1920–1976, edited by Michael Grieve and W. R. Aitken, appeared (posthumously) in 1978. See Alan Bold, MacDiarmid: The Terrible Crystal (1983) and The Letters of Hugh Mac-Diarmid (1984, ed. A. Bold). (See also SCOTS.)

MacDONALD, George (1824–1905), son of a Scottish miller, was briefly a Congregationalist minister, but was rejected by his congregation, and thereafter struggled to support his family of eleven children by writing. In his own day he was celebrated chiefly as poet, preacher, and lecturer, and as the author of numerous novels, including David Elginbrod (1863), Alec Forbes of Howglen (1865), and Robert Falconer (1868), often with banal melodramatic plots and card-board villains, but illuminated by compassionate affection for humanity and nature. The Scottish setting of his best novels helped to found the *'Kailyard School' of fiction. MacDonald is now best known for his children's stories, including At the Back of the North Wind (1871) and The Princess and the Goblin (1872), memorably illustrated by Arthur Hughes, and for his two allegorical fantasies for adults, Phantastes (1858) and Lilith (1895), in which he creates dream worlds of power and vivid strangeness, influenced by his study of *Novalis and E. T. A. *Hoffmann, and in turn strongly influencing G. K. *Chesterton, W. H. *Auden, and C. S. *Lewis. There are biographies by Greville MacDonald (George MacDonald and His Wife, 1924) and R. H. Reis (1972).

Macduff and Lady Macduff, characters in Shakespeare's *Macbeth. Macbeth's murder of Lady Macduff and her children ('What, all my pretty chickens and their dam | At one fell swoop?') precipitates the play's denouement.

MacFlecknoe, or A Satyr upon the True-Blew-Protestant Poet, T. S., a poem by *Dryden published 1682, and in a definitive edition, 1684.
   The outcome of a series of disagreements, personal, professional, and critical, between Dryden and *Shadwell, the poem represents the latter as heir to the kingdom of poetic dullness, currently governed by the minor writer *Flecknoe. It brilliantly exploits the crudity of Shadwell's farces (notably The Virtuoso) and critical writings; while the range of its allusions to 17th-cent. theatre demonstrates the complexity of Dryden's critical thought and, since he satirizes his own work (notably *Tyrannick Love) as well as Shadwell's, his humility towards the tradition in which he was working.

McGill University, The, Canada, commemorates James McGill (1744–1813), who left £30,000 for the foundation of a university. A charter was granted in 1821, but it was not until the middle of the century that the institution became prosperous. It has its headquarters at Montreal, with affiliated colleges in certain other centres.

McGONAGALL, William (1825 or 1830–1902), the son of an Irish weaver, attracted a certain following in Edinburgh with his readings in public houses and his broadsheets of topical verse. His naïve and unscanned doggerel continues to entertain, and he now enjoys a reputation as the world's worst poet.

McGOUGH, Roger, see LIVERPOOL POETS.

Macgregor, Rob Roy and Helen, see ROB ROY.

MACHAUT, Guillaume de, see GUILLAUME DE MACHAUT.

Macheath, Captain, the hero of Gay's *The Beggar's Opera*.

MACHEN, Arthur Llewellyn (1863–1947), son of a Welsh clergyman, was deeply influenced by his lonely childhood, the Welsh landscape, and local folklore. He left for London in 1880 and a period of employment as a cataloguer of diabolistic and occult books introduced him to various secret sects and societies (he later joined the Order of the Golden Dawn of which *Yeats and *Crowley became members). He translated *The Heptameron* (1886) and *The Memoirs of Casanova* (1894) and began writing the mystic, supernatural tales of evil and horror for which he is best remembered. The most successful of these were written in the 1890s (some were published later), including *The Great God Pan* (1894), *The Hill of Dreams* (1907), and *The Three Impostors* (1895). He spent several years from 1901 as an actor in Sir Frank Benson's Shakespeare Repertory Company and in 1910 joined the London *Evening News*, which led to his rediscovery and the publication in 1923 of the Caerleon Edition of his works. His belated recognition came when his creative powers had waned and his later works were less successful. Other works include *Hieroglyphics* (1902, criticism); and *Far off Things* (1922) and *Things Near and Far* (1923), both autobiographical.

MACHEREY, Pierre, see MARXIST LITERARY CRITICISM.

MACHIAVELLI, Niccolò (1469–1527), a Florentine statesman and political theorist. After holding office in the restored Florentine republic and discharging various missions abroad, he was exiled on suspicion of conspiracy against the Medici, but was subsequently restored to some degree of favour. He turned his experience to advantage in his writings, which include *Arte della guerra* (*The art of war*, written 1517–20, English trans. 1560–2) and a history of Florence (*Storie Fiorentine*, 1520–5, trans. 1595). His comedy *Mandragola*, probably written in 1518, is a powerful satire. His best-known work was *Il Principe* (*The Prince*, written in 1513), a treatise on statecraft by an acute observer of the contemporary political scene with an idealistic vision of an Italian saviour who should expel all foreign usurpers. He teaches that the lessons of the past (of Roman history in particular) should be applied to the present, and that the acquisition and effective use of power may necessitate unethical methods not in themselves desirable. Although manuscript versions of the work were circulating earlier, the first public translation was that of Edward Dacres in 1640. *Il Principe* is none the less repeatedly referred to in Elizabethan drama, and influenced the policy of Thomas *Cromwell, Cecil, and Leicester. It was appreciated critically by F. *Bacon; exploited intelligently by *Marlowe; used guardedly in

the Maxims of State attributed to *Ralegh, and published posthumously in 1658 as *The Cabinet-Council*. Selected maxims from *Il Principe* were translated into French and refuted by Gentillet, a French Huguenot, in 1576; there was an English translation, by Paterick, in 1602. It was formerly argued that Gentillet was the main source for the hostile English attitude to Machiavelli, but the case was modified by *Praz in his British Academy lecture in 1928 (reprinted in *The Flaming Heart*, 1958). Valuable critical studies are by F. Chabod (*Machiavelli and the Renaissance*, 1958); F. Raab (*The English Face of Machiavelli*, 1964); and F. K. McConica and Christopher Morris (*Rivista di Storia delle Idee Politiche e Sociale*, Anno II. IV. 3, 1970).

In Elizabethan and Jacobean drama, Machiavellian villains and anti-heroes (descended, Praz argues, from Senecan tyrants) abound, appearing in many guises, as pandar, atheist, poisoner, politician, miser, and revenger, and the name of Machiavelli himself is frequently invoked: for example by Gloucester, who resolved in *3 *Henry VI* 'to set the murtherous Machiavel to school' (III. iii. 193), by Flamineo in *The White Devil*, who rejoices in 'the rare trickes of a Machivillian' (v. iii. 196), and in the prologue to *The Jew of Malta* by the spirit of Machiavelli himself. There is a sketch of his character in G. Eliot's *Romola*. *The New Machiavelli* (1911) is a novel by H. G. *Wells.

M'Ian, Ian Eachin, otherwise Conachar, in Scott's *The Fair Maid of Perth*, Simon Glover's Highland apprentice.

MacINNES, Colin (1914–76), novelist, son of the novelist Angela Thirkell (1890–1961), was brought up partly in Australia; on his return to England, after a period in art school and (during the war) the army, he embarked on a career as writer and journalist. He is best remembered for his novels of teenage and black immigrant culture *City of Spades* (1957) and *Absolute Beginners* (1957), which described the new Bohemian underworld of Notting Hill, coffee bars, jazz clubs, drugs, drink, and homosexuality: see *Inside Outsider* (1983), a biography by T. Gould.

M'Intyre, Captain Hector and Maria, in Scott's *The Antiquary*, nephew and niece of Jonathan Oldbuck.

Mac-Ivor, Fergus, of Glennaquoich, otherwise known as Vich Ian Vohr, a character in Scott's *Waverley*.

MACKENZIE, Sir (Edward Morgan) Compton (1883–1972), was educated at St Paul's and Magdalen College, Oxford, and became a prolific writer, who produced books of travel, biography, essays, poems, and much journalism, as well as the novels for which he is best remembered. He lived at various times on

Capri, in the Channel Islands, and in Scotland, all of which provided settings for his work. The most notable of the novels include *Carnival* (1912), a grim story of Jenny, an actress and singer, who settles for the chorus-line and makes a disastrous marriage; then in 1913 and 1914 Mackenzie published *Sinister Street* (2 vols) which presents a semi-autobiographical figure, Michael Fane, 'handicapped by a public school and university education', passing through school, Oxford, and low life in London. For many years the book was widely popular; F. M. Ford found it 'the history of a whole class . . . during a whole period of life'; and Scott *Fitzgerald acknowledged its deep influence on his early work. In 1915 Mackenzie fought at Gallipoli and after the war continued to write prolifically in all genres. In 1927 he published *Vestal Fire*, a story based on real events, of two cousins, Maimie and Virginia, who take up residence on the Mediterranean island of Sirene, find their Anglo-Saxon attitudes loosening delightfully, and become disastrously devoted to the scandalous Count Marsac. Mackenzie came near to prosecution for *Extraordinary Women* (1928), again set on Sirene, in which various absurd lesbian entanglements are set against a brittle hedonistic society. In 1929 and 1932 he published two volumes of war memoirs, *Gallipoli Memories* and *Greek Memories*. During 1937–5 appeared the six volumes of *The Four Winds of Love*, his most ambitious work, tracing the life of John Ogilvie, a pensive and individualistic Scot, from the time of the Boer War to the emergence of Scottish nationalism in 1945. *Whisky Galore* (1947), a fictional account of an actual wreck of a ship loaded with whisky on Eriskay, was made into a highly successful film. *Thin Ice*, a perceptive story of two homosexuals and their fate, appeared in 1956, and in 1963–1 the ten 'Octaves' of *My Life and Times*, a rambling, entertaining autobiography which met with much popular and critical success. Mackenzie was knighted and became a CH, as well as receiving many honorary degrees.

His remarkable powers of recall made his selection of material difficult, and he is often thought to have written too much, too indiscriminately; but after a long period of neglect the best of his work is receiving increasing attention.

MACKENZIE, Henry (1745–1831), a lawyer, educated in Edinburgh, held the position of Comptroller of the Taxes for Scotland. He was the author of a highly influential novel, *The Man of Feeling* (1771), in which the refined and gentle hero is presented in a series of sketches loosely woven together, somewhat in the manner of *Addison's essays on Sir Roger de *Coverley. Mackenzie's book was greatly admired by the young C. *Lamb and was one of *Burns's 'bosom favourites'. In 1773 he

published *The Man of the World*, in which the protagonist is a villain; and in 1777 *Julia de Roubigné*, a novel in the manner of Richardson's *Clarissa. Mackenzie also wrote a play, *The Prince of Tunis* (1773); was chairman of the committee that investigated *Macpherson's 'Ossian'; and edited two periodicals, *The Mirror* and *The Lounger*, to both of which he also frequently contributed. He has been referred to as 'the Addison of the North'. (See SENTIMENT, NOVEL OF.) See H. W. Thompson, *A Scottish Man of Feeling* (1931).

McKERROW, Ronald Brunlees (1872–1940), bibliographer and editor, co-founder of the *Malone Society, 1906, became joint secretary of the *Bibliographical Society, 1912, and in 1925 founded the *Review of English Studies*. His best-known works were an important edition of the works of T. *Nashe (1904–10) and *An Introduction to Bibliography for Literary Students* (1927).

MACKINTOSH, Sir James (1765–1832), educated at Aberdeen University, a doctor, philosopher, disputant, and barrister, was the author of the highly successful *Vindiciae Gallicae* (1791), a reasoned defence of the French revolution. Mackintosh later recanted his views, in a lecture attended by a disapproving *Hazlitt. He published a *Dissertation on the Progress of Ethical Philosophy* (1830) and wrote the first three volumes of a *History of England* (1830–1) for Lardner's *Cabinet Cyclopaedia*, as well as an unfinished *History of the Revolution in England in 1688* (1834).

MACKLIN, Charles (MacLaughlin) (?1699–1797), an Irish-born actor who made his reputation by his impersonation of Shylock, a role he first played in 1741. He wrote several plays, of which the most successful were *Love à la Mode*, performed 1759, and *The Man of the World*, performed 1781, with himself in the leading role. He continued to act until a failing memory drove him from the stage in 1789. A life by W. W. Appleton was published in 1961.

McKNIGHT KAUFFER, E., see KAUFFER, E. M.

MACLAREN, Ian, see KAILYARD SCHOOL.

MACLEAN, Sorley (Somhairle Macgill-Eain) (1911–   ), Gaelic poet, born on the island of Raasay and educated at the University of Edinburgh. He is one of the leading writers in Gaelic of the 20th-cent. Scottish Renaissance.

MacLEISH, Archibald (1892–1982), American poet and dramatist, born in Illinois and educated at Yale and Harvard. He was one of the American expatriates in Paris in the 1920s, and was strongly influenced by *Pound and T. S. *Eliot. His volumes of verse include *The Pot of Earth* (1924); *The Hamlet of A. MacLeish* (1928); *New Found Land* (1930); the narrative poem

Conquistador (1932); and his *Collected Poems, 1917–1933* (1933). Among his verse dramas are *Panic* (1935), the anti-totalitarian *The Fall of the City* (1937), and the successfully staged *J.B.* (1958), an updating of the trials of Job. After his return to America at the end of the 1920s, MacLeish became an increasingly public figure, holding many important posts; he was Librarian of Congress (1939–44), assistant secretary of state (1944–5), and Boylston professor at Harvard (1949–62).

MACLEOD, Fiona, see SHARP, W.

MACLISE, Daniel (1806–70), Irish portrait and history painter; he sketched Sir W. *Scott in 1825, when Scott was visiting Cork with Maria *Edgeworth. In 1827 he settled in London where he moved in literary circles and became a close friend of *Dickens and of J. *Forster; his well known portrait of Dickens is in the National Portrait Gallery, London (1839). He contributed a brilliant series of caricatures of celebrated authors to *Fraser's Magazine*. Later Maclise became more interested in history painting; he painted subjects from Shakespeare; in his last years he was involved with a disastrous scheme for redecorating the Houses of Parliament.

Macmillan's Magazine, a periodical founded in 1859, and edited successively by D. *Masson (1859–68), G. *Grove (1868–83), J. *Morley (1883–85), and Mowbray Morris (1885–1907). It was one of the first magazines to use signed articles only, and published a wide variety of material, including poetry, serialized fiction, articles on politics, travel, etc. Contributors included *Tennyson, Thomas *Hughes, *Milnes, and F. D. *Maurice.

Macmorris, Captain, in Shakespeare's *Henry V*, the only Irishman presented in Shakespeare's plays.

MACK MURDO, A. H., see ART NOUVEAU.

MacNEICE, (Frederick) Louis (1907–63), poet, born in Belfast, the son of the rector of Holy Trinity, later bishop of Down, Connor, and Dromore. He left Ulster for Sherborne preparatory school, Marlborough, and Merton College, Oxford, where he took a first in Greats, made the acquaintance of *Auden and *Spender, and published a book of poems, *Blind Fireworks* (1929). After lecturing in Classics at Birmingham University and Bedford College he joined the BBC Features Department in 1941 as writer-producer. Meanwhile he had made several unsuccessful attempts at writing for the theatre, including *Station Bell* (1935) and *Out of the Picture* (1937); produced a fine verse translation of the *Agamemnon* (1936); and was becoming known as a poet through his contributions to *New Verse* and his *Poems*

(1935). *Letters from Iceland* (1937) was written in collaboration with Auden. Subsequent volumes of poetry include *The Earth Compels* (1938); *Autumn Journal* (1938), a long personal and political meditation on the events leading up to Munich; *Plant and Phantom* (1941); *Springboard* (1944); *Holes in the Sky* (1948); *Autumn Sequel* (1954); and *The Burning Perch* (1963).

His early work revealed a technical virtuosity, a painter's eye for an image, humour, and an impulse towards making sense of what he later called the 'drunkenness of things being various'; suspicious of all rigid systems, whether political or philosophical, he worked to establish some pattern from life's flux. He used most of the classic verse forms, but his distinctive contribution was his deployment of assonance, internal rhymes, and half rhymes, and ballad-like repetitions that he had absorbed from the Irishry of his childhood. He was also renowned as an outstanding writer of radio documentaries and radio parable plays; these include *Christopher Columbus* (1944) and his most powerful dramatic work, *The Dark Tower* (1947). He also published a pseudonymous novel (*Roundabout Way*, 1932, by 'Louis Malone'), various pot-boilers, a book on *Yeats (1941), and a translation of an abridged version of *Goethe's *Faust* (1951); *Varieties of Parable* (from the 1963 Clark lectures) and a volume of autobiography, *The Strings are False*, both appeared posthumously in 1965. Although overshadowed in the 1930s and 40s by Auden, and later by critical fashion, his reputation was revived by the publication in 1966 of his *Collected Poems*, edited by E. R. Dodds.

MACPHERSON, James (1736–96), born near Kingussie, the son of a farmer, was educated at Aberdeen and Edinburgh Universities. In 1758 he published *The Highlander*, a heroic poem in 6 cantos. In 1759 he met John *Home, for whom he produced his first 'Ossianic' fragment 'The Death of Oscar'; encouraged by Home and Hugh *Blair he then produced *Fragments of Ancient Poetry, Collected in the Highlands of Scotland, and Translated from the Galic or Erse Language* (1760). Interest in *Primitivism was at this period considerable, and rumours that a Gaelic epic existed aroused much curiosity and enthusiasm; pressed on by his admirers, Macpherson travelled round Scotland collecting the materials for *Fingal, an Ancient Epic Poem, in Six Books*, which appeared in 1762. It purported to be Macpherson's faithful translation of an epic by Ossian, the son of Finn (or, in this version, Fingal), dating from some vague but remote period of early Scottish history. A second epic, *Temora* (1763), followed with suspicious speed. These works created a great sensation; patriotic Scots, delighted at the revelation of so rich a national treasure, praised them highly. *Hume and Adam *Smith were at first convinced by them: Home and Blair remained so. Ossian's fame spread to the Continent, where *Klopstock, *Schiller, and *Goethe joined in the chorus of praise: Goethe quoted Ossian at length in *The Sorrows of Young Werther*, which, with Ossian, was to be one of the favourite works of Napoleon. But at home doubts of the poems' authenticity sprang up almost at once, with Dr *Johnson as the most formidable of sceptics; his enquiries during his tour of Scotland and remarks published in his *Journey to the Western Islands* (1775) were highly critical. Macpherson, when called upon to produce his originals, was obliged to fabricate them. A committee appointed after his death, chaired by Henry *Mackenzie, investigated the mystery and reported in 1805 that Macpherson had liberally edited Gaelic poems and inserted passages of his own; subsequent investigation supports this view. The immense popularity of the poetry survived the exposure of its origins; as late as 1866 M. *Arnold in his lectures on Celtic literature was defending its 'vein of piercing regret and sadness'; 'Choose any of the better passages in Macpherson's *Ossian* and you can see even at this time of day what an apparition of newness and power such a strain must have been to the eighteenth century.'

Macpherson's other works include a prose translation of the *Iliad* (1773) and a *History of Great Britain* (1775). He wrote in defence of Lord North's ministry, was MP for Camelford from 1780, and was buried in Westminster Abbey at his own expense.

MACREADY, William Charles (1793–1873). son of a provincial actor-manager, educated at Rugby under T. *Arnold. He achieved a considerable reputation in the provinces before appearing at Covent Garden in 1816. By 1819 he was an established rival of *Kean, appearing regularly at both Covent Garden and Drury Lane; he was manager of both theatres at various times where he sought to improve standards of production and made many reforms in both acting and the texts. In 1837 he appeared in *Strafford*, which *Browning had written for him, and in 1838 in *Byron's *Two Foscari*; but it was in the roles of Lear, Hamlet, and Macbeth that he gained eminence as a tragic actor. He enjoyed the society of some of the most important writers of his day and was a friend of *Dickens. His last performance was as Macbeth in 1851 and *Tennyson wrote a sonnet to mark the occasion.

Macro, in Jonson's *Sejanus*, the evil agent of Tiberius, who supplants the protagonist.

Macro Plays, The, three Morality plays (*The Castle of Perseverance*, *Mankind*, and *Wisdom*), named after their 18th-cent. owner. Ed. Mark Eccles in *The Macro Plays* (EETS 262, 1969).

MacSarcasm, Sir Archy, a character in Macklin's *Love à la Mode*.

MacStinger, Mrs, in Dickens's *Dombey and Son*, Captain Cuttle's termagant landlady.

MacSycophant, Sir Pertinax, a character in Macklin's *The Man of the World*.

McTAGGART, John McTaggart Ellis (1866–1925), philosopher, fellow of Trinity College, Cambridge, and lecturer in moral sciences 1897–1923. He was an exponent of *Hegel's *Logic*, and published several studies of Hegel. His massive treatise *The Nature of Existence* was published in 2 vols, 1921–7. He is now chiefly remembered, perhaps, for his arguments about the nature of time, which issued in the conclusion that it did not exist.

MacTurk, Captain, a character in Scott's *St Ronan's Well*.

Macwheeble, Bailie Duncan, a character in Scott's *Waverley*.

Madame Bovary, the chief work of G. *Flaubert.

MADGE, Charles Henry (1912–   ), poet and sociologist, whose left-wing sympathies were manifested in his poetry (his first volume was *The Disappearing Castle*, 1937) and other work and writings. In 1937 with H. Jennings and T. Harrisson he founded Mass Observation. His first wife was Kathleen *Raine.

Madge Wildfire, see MURDOCKSON.

Madoc, a narrative poem by *Southey, published 1805.

Madoc is the youngest son of Owen Gwyneth, king of Wales (d. 1169). He has left Wales and sailed to a western land across the ocean where he has founded a settlement and defeated the Aztecas. He returns to Wales for a fresh supply of adventurers and tells his tale. After his return to the settlement in Aztlan, war breaks out again with the Aztecas. Madoc is ambushed and captured, chained by the foot to the stone of human sacrifice, and required to fight in succession six Azteca champions. He slays the first, Ocellopan, and engages Tlalala 'the Tiger'. Then Cadwallon comes to the rescue, and after much fighting the Aztecas are finally defeated and migrate to another country. Among the Aztecas figures Coatel, daughter of the priest Aculhua; she assists the white men, and thus brings herself, her husband, and her father to a tragic end.

Madrigal, originally a short lyrical poem of amatory character, but used in musical terminology to describe a type of part-song, or short polyphonic composition, to secular words and usually without instrumental accompaniment, designed on the whole for amateur performance. The madrigal originated in Italy; it reached England from Europe in the 1530s but developed its own native style in the 1580s with the poetic experiments of the *'Golden Age'. It was first widely disseminated in this country in *Musica Transalpina* (1588), an anthology of 57 Italian madrigals with English texts and the most influential of the five such volumes which appeared in England between 1588 and 1598. Native composers rapidly took over the form, some (like *Morley, the first in the field, or Farnaby, Farmer, and Bennet) staying fairly close to the Italian model, others (like *Weelkes and *Wilbye) adapting it to a more serious and specifically English manner. By the beginning of the 17th cent. practically all English composers (with the exception of the rather older *Byrd) were producing works in the new form, and when Morley brought out the famous madrigal collection *The Triumphes of Oriana* as a tribute to *Elizabeth I in 1601 he was able to include contributions by no less than 21 musicians. The marvellous flowering of the English madrigal was of short duration, however, and the quality of many individual pieces in later collections by masters like *Gibbons (1612), Ward (1613), or *Tomkins (1622) does not alter the fact that by this time there was much in them that was old-fashioned; by the third decade of the 17th cent. the madrigal as the Elizabethans understood it was effectively dead. See *English Madrigal Verse* (1967, 3rd edn), ed. E. H. Fellowes.

Mad World, My Masters, A, a comedy by T. *Middleton, written 1604–7, printed 1608.

In a complex plot of deceits and disguises, the impecunious young Follywit seeks to pre-empt his inheritance by robbing his wealthy old grandfather, Sir Bounteous Progress; and Penitent Brothel seeks to seduce the wife of the jealous and suspicious citizen Hairbrain. A courtesan, Gullman, the mistress of Sir Bounteous, plays a part in both actions, and in the last act Follywit (who has married her, believing her to be a virgin) finds himself the gull, married to his grandfather's whore. But she protests reform, Sir Bounteous generously endows the young couple, and all ends reasonably happily. There is an edition by S. Henning (1965).

MAETERLINCK, Maurice (1862–1949), Belgian poetic dramatist and essayist. He wrote in French, establishing himself as one of the leading figures in the *Symbolist movement with his play *La Princesse Maleine* (1889, English trans. 1892). In 1892 *Pelléas et Mélisande* appeared (trans. 1894), the work for which he is now chiefly remembered and the source of *Debussy's opera of the same name (1902). He also achieved great contemporary popularity with *L'Oiseau bleu* (1908, *The Blue Bird*, 1909). He drew heavily on traditions of romance and fairy-tale, and the characteristic tone of much of his drama is one of doom-laden mystery and timeless melancholy. He also produced a number of essays of a philosophical nature, including *La*

Vie des abeilles (1901, *The Life of the Bee*, 1901) and *L'Intelligence des fleurs* (1907, *The Intelligence of Flowers*, 1907).

Maeve, or **Medb** (pron. Maeve), in the Ulster cycle, queen of Connaught. See under CUCHULAIN and TAIN-BO-CUAILGNE.

Maeviad, The, see GIFFORD, W.

'Maga, The', see BLACKWOOD'S MAGAZINE.

Magazine, originally a place where goods are stored, now also a periodical publication containing articles by different authors. Thus the *Gentleman's Magazine* in the introduction to its first number (1731) described itself as 'a Monthly Collection to store up, as in a Magazine, the most remarkable Pieces on the Subjects above-mentioned'. The word had been used before this for a storehouse of information.

Magdalen (pron. Maudlen) **College,** Oxford, was founded in 1458 by William Waynflete (1395–1486), provost of *Eton, bishop of Winchester, and lord chancellor of England. It is celebrated for its beautiful tower, on which the Magdalen choristers sing a hymn on the morning of 1 May at 5 a.m. (6 a.m. BST).

Magdalene (pron. Maudlen) **College,** Cambridge, is renowned in a literary context as the home of the *Pepys library, Pepys having left to his old college his invaluable collection of books, manuscripts, and diaries.

Magic Realism, a term coined by Franz Roh (*Nach-expressionismus, magischer Realismus: Probleme der neuesten europäischer Malerei*, 1925), to describe tendencies in the work of certain German artists of the *neue Sachlichkeit* (new objectivity), characterized by clear, cool, static, thinly-painted, sharp-focus images, frequently portraying the imaginary, the improbable, or the fantastic in a realistic or rational manner. The term was adopted in the United States with the 1943 exhibition (containing work by Charles Sheeler, 1883–1965, and Edward Hopper, 1882–1967) at the New York Museum of Modern Art, entitled 'American Realists and Magic Realists'. The term has subsequently been used to describe the works of such Latin American authors as *Borges, *García Márquez, and Alejo Carpentier (1904–), and elements of it have been noted in *Grass, *Calvino, *Fowles, and other European writers. In the 1970s and 1980s it was adopted in Britain by several of the most original of younger fiction writers, including, notably, Emma *Tennant; Angela Carter (1940– ; titles include *The Infernal Desire Machines of Doctor Hoffman*, 1972, and the remarkable *Nights at the Circus*, 1984); and Salman Rushdie (1947– ; *Midnight's Children*, 1981; *Shame*, 1983). Magic realist novels and stories have, typically, a strong narrative drive, in which the recognizably realistic mingles with the unexpected and the inexplicable, and in which elements of dream, fairy-story, or mythology combine with the everyday, often in a mosaic or kaleidoscopic pattern of refraction and recurrence. English Magic Realism also has some affinity with the neo-*Gothic.

MAGINN, William (1793–1842), an immensely precocious Irish boy who graduated from Dublin at the age of fourteen. He came to London, where he wrote under various pseudonyms including 'Ensign Morgan O'Doherty', in whose persona he produced memoirs, anecdotes, and verses in English, Latin, and Greek for the *Literary Gazette and other journals. He was an important and prolific contributor to *Blackwood's, notably to the *Noctes Ambrosianae, in the devising of which he seems to have had some part. He became assistant editor of the Evening Standard, and in 1830 helped in the establishing of *Frasers' Magazine, in which much of his best work, including Homeric Ballads and A Gallery of Literary Characters, appeared. His wit and learning are evident in his parodies of Sir W. *Scott, *Coleridge, T. *Moore, *La Rochefoucauld, *Disraeli, *Carlyle, and many others. He wrote seriously and well on Shakespeare and others, and his 'A Story without a Tail' is still admired; but he never fulfilled his early promise. He was the original of Captain Shandon in Thackeray's *Pendennis.

Magnano (meaning 'locksmith'), one of the characters in the bear-baiting episode in Butler's *Hudibras.

Magnet, The, see HAMILTON, C.

Magnetic Lady, The, or Humours Reconciled, a comedy by *Jonson, performed 1632, printed 1641.

Lady Loadstone, the 'Magnetic Lady', who 'draws unto her guests of all sorts', has a niece Placentia, of age to be married. The girl is pursued by various suitors until, after an argument between two of them, she goes into labour and gives birth. Her uncle, the usurer Sir Moth Interest, uses this as an excuse to take possession of her dowry. However, Compass, the play's hero, learns that Lady Loadstone's real niece is her waiting-woman Pleasance, who had been exchanged with Placentia when the two were infants. He marries Pleasance, whom he loves, reveals her true identity, and receives her dowry. Placentia is married to the father of her child, Lady Loadstone's steward Needle, and Lady Loadstone marries Compass's brother Captain Ironside. Between the acts there is an interlude of debate about the theatre between a boy actor and two scoffing gallants, Probee and Damplay.

Magnus, Mr Peter, a character in Dickens's *Pickwick Papers.

Magnyfycence, a morality play by *Skelton.

Magnyfycence, symbolizing a generous prince, is ruined by mistaken liberality and bad counsellors, but restored by Good-hope, Perseverance, and other similar figures. The play was edited by Paula Neuss (1980).

Magus, The, see FOWLES, J.

Magwitch, Abel, a character in Dickens's *Great Expectations.

MAHOMET, see MUHAMMAD.

MAHONY, Francis Sylvester (1804–66), born in Cork, best known by his pseudonym Father Prout, a Jesuit priest who admitted he had mistaken his vocation and left the order for a career as a journalist and poet. He contributed many lively papers and poems to *Fraser's Magazine and *Bentley's Miscellany. These included translations from *Horace, *Béranger, *Hugo, etc., and, interspersed amongst them, mystifications in the form of invented 'originals' in French, Latin, and Greek for well known poems by T. *Moore, C. *Wolfe, and others. He travelled much abroad, and was Paris correspondent for the Globe, 1858–66. The contributions to Fraser's were collected in 1836 as The Reliques of Father Prout.

Maid Marian, a female personage in the May-game (see MAY DAY) and *Morris dance. In the later forms of the story of *Robin Hood she appears as the companion of the outlaw, the association having probably been suggested by the fact that the two were both represented in the May-day pageants [OED]. According to one version of the legend she was Matilda, the daughter of Lord Fitzwater.

Maid Marian, a medieval romance by *Peacock largely written 1819, published 1822. It features *Robin Hood, *Maid Marian, *Friar Tuck, and Prince John, while lampooning institutions such as the monarchy and the church in the post-Napoleonic era. The irreverent treatment of Prince John's government also mocks the idealized medievalism newly fashionable among conservative propagandists, artists, and historians. Peacock wrote Maid Marian at a time when he had fallen under the spell of the new Italian opera of *Rossini, *Bellini, and *Donizetti. Many scenes already seem cast as duets or quartets, and the book was later adapted as a popular operetta.

'Maid of Athens', a poem by Lord *Byron, written 1810.

The 'Maid' is said to have been the 12-year-old daughter of Mrs Macri, a widow whose husband had been vice-consul in Athens.

Maid of Honour, The, a romantic drama by *Massinger, acted about 1621–2, published 1632. It is based on a story by *Boccaccio.

Bertoldo, natural brother of the king of Sicily

and a knight of Malta, is in love with Camiola. Departing on an expedition to aid the duke of Urbino against the duchess of Siena, he asks for her hand, but she refuses on the ground of the disparity of their station and his oath as a knight of Malta not to marry. Bertoldo is taken prisoner by the Sienese, cast into prison, and held to ransom for a large sum, which the king of Sicily, being incensed against Bertoldo, forbids anyone to pay. Camiola directs her follower Adorni, who is passionately devoted to her, to carry the ransom (which she provides from her own estate) to Bertoldo, and to require of him a contract to marry her. Adorni, though it means the defeat of his own hopes, faithfully discharges his mission; Bertoldo is released and signs the contract. But the duchess of Siena falls in love with him, and he yields to her wooing. They are on the point of being married when Camiola interposes and pleads her cause with spirit, so that all, including the duchess, condemn the ingratitude of Bertoldo and the marriage is broken off. Camiola, 'the Maid of Honour', takes the veil, and the humiliated and repentant Bertoldo resumes his vocation as a knight of Malta. Camiola is Massinger's best female character, and the play contains some of his finest scenes.

Maid of Norway, see SIR PATRICK SPENS.

Maid's Tragedy, The, a tragedy by *Beaumont and *Fletcher, written ?1610–11, published 1619, generally considered one of their best works.

Amintor, a gentleman of Rhodes, breaks his engagement to Aspatia at the king's request and in her stead marries Evadne, sister to his friend Melantius. On their wedding night, in a powerful confrontation, Evadne reveals that she is the king's mistress and refuses to sleep with him. Amintor initially agrees to conceal the position and present a mock marriage to the world; but later he reveals the truth to Melantius, who passionately reproaches the by now penitent Evadne, and persuades her to murder the king. Meanwhile the desolate Aspatia laments her loss in some of the finest verse in the play (II. ii); her lines 'And the trees about me, | Let them be dry and leafless; let the rocks | Groan with continual surges; and behind me | Make all a desolation. Look, look, wenches!' were used by T. S. *Eliot as an epigraph to 'Sweeney Erect'; the speech is also quoted by Emily *Eden in *The Semi-Detached House* (ch. 20). Aspatia later takes action by disguising herself as her brother and provoking the reluctant Amintor to a duel. He wounds her; as she lies dying Evadne arrives, fresh from the king's murder, hoping to be pardoned by Amintor. He rejects her; she commits suicide; Aspatia reveals herself and dies; Amintor takes his own life. There are modern editions by A. Gurr (1969) and H. Norland (1968). The last act of the play was rewritten by E. *Waller,

with a happy ending in which Amintor marries Aspatia.

Maigret, le Commissaire, the detective-superintendent in the crime stories of G. *Simenon.

MAILER, Norman (1923–), American novelist and essayist, educated at Harvard, whose naturalistic first novel *The Naked and the Dead* (1948) was based on his experiences with the army in the Pacific. It was followed by other novels, including *Barbary Shore* (1951), *The Deer Park* (1955), and *An American Dream* (1965). Most of his work is of a more unorthodox genre, mixing journalism, autobiography, political commentary, and fictional passages in a wide range of styles. (See *Advertisements for Myself*, 1959; *The Presidential Papers*, 1963; *The Armies of the Night*, 1968; and many other titles.) *The Executioner's Song* (1979), a lengthy non-fiction account of a murderer, bears some resemblance to *In Cold Blood* by *Capote. (See also FACTION.) His lengthy and ambitious novel, *Ancient Evenings* (1983; described by A. *Burgess as possibly 'one of the great works of contemporary mythopoesis') is set in ancient Egypt (1290–1100 BC).

MAIMONIDES (1135–1204), a Jew of Cordoba who went to Fez and Cairo when the Jews were expelled from Spain. His chief work was *The Guide for the Perplexed* of which there are English, French, and German translations. This work influenced *Aquinas (who drew on it in the course of his proofs of the existence of God) and other *Scholastic theologians; its endeavour was to reconcile Talmudic scripture with the philosophy of *Aristotle.

Main Street, a novel by S. *Lewis.

MAINTENON, Françoise d'Aubigné, marquise de (1635–1719), the wife of the French burlesque poet *Scarron. After her husband's death she was charged with the education of the children of Louis XIV and Mme de Montespan. She obtained a great ascendancy over the king, who secretly married her in 1684.

MAITLAND, Frederic William (1850–1906), legal historian and founder of the *Selden Society, was educated at Eton and Trinity College, Cambridge. After eight years' practice at the bar he was elected reader in English law at Cambridge, and in 1888 Downing professor. His first important work was *Bracton's Note-Book* (1887), followed by *The History of English Law before the time of Edward I* (with Sir F. Pollock, 1895) and *Roman Canon Law in the Church of England* (1898), both tracing the Roman influence on English law, essays on *Domesday Book and Beyond* (1897), his Ford lectures on *Township and Borough* (1898), his Rede lecture on *English Law and the Renaissance*

(1901), *Year Books of Edward II* (1903–5), and his 1887 lectures on *The Constitutional History of England* (posthumously, 1908). H. A. L. Fisher edited his collected papers (1911) and *The Letters of F. W. Maitland*, ed. C. H. S. Fifoot, was published in 1965.

Maitland Club, a club founded at Glasgow in 1828 for the publication of works on the literature and antiquities of Scotland.

MAJOR, or **MAIR,** John (*c*.1467–1550), born near Berwick, has been called 'the last of the schoolmen'. He studied at Cambridge and Paris, where he became doctor of theology. He lectured on scholastic logic and theology at Glasgow and St Andrews from 1518 to 1525, and then returned to Paris, where he was regarded as the most eminent exponent of medieval learning. He published between 1509 and 1517 a Latin *Commentary on the Sentences of Peter Lombard* and in 1521 a Latin *History of Greater Britain, both England and Scotland*, in which he showed himself in advance of his times by advocating the union of the two kingdoms.

According to *Rabelais (II. vii), among the books found by Pantagruel in the library of St Victor was a treatise by Major, *De modo faciendi puddinos* ('On the art of making black-puddings').

Major Barbara, a play by Bernard *Shaw, performed 1905, published 1907.

It portrays the conflict between spiritual and worldly power embodied in Barbara, a major in the Salvation Army, and her Machiavellian father, millionaire armaments manufacturer Andrew Undershaft. While visiting her East End shelter for the poor, as part of a bargain struck between them, he reveals that the shelter's benefactor, Lord Saxmundham, made his money through 'Bodgers' whisky', and she suffers a crisis of faith as she glimpses the possibility that all salvation and philanthropy are tainted at the source: the next day, visiting his factory with her mother Lady Britomart and her fiancé, classical scholar Adolphus Cusins, she is further shaken to discover her father is a model employer. Cusins enters the debate, reveals that he is technically a foundling and therefore eligible to inherit the Undershaft empire (as Undershaft's own children are not), strikes a hard bargain with his prospective father-in-law, and agrees to enter the business, partly persuaded by Undershaft's quoting of *Plato to the effect that 'society cannot be saved until either the Professors of Greek take to making gunpowder, or else the makers of gunpowder become Professors of Greek.' Barbara, recovering her spirits, embraces this synthesis as a possibility of hope for the future. The portrait of Cusins is based on G. *Murray.

Malagigi, in *Orlando Innamorato*, a cousin of *Rinaldo, possessed of magic lore, who detects

the wiles of *Angelica and attempts to slay her, but is taken prisoner and carried to Cathay. He is released on condition that he shall lure Rinaldo to her.

Malagrowther, (1) Malachi, the pseudonym under which Sir W. *Scott addressed three letters in 1826, on the question of the Scottish paper currency, to the *Edinburgh Weekly Journal*; (2) Sir Mungo, a character in Scott's *The Fortunes of Nigel*.

Malambruno, in *Don Quixote* (II. xxxix), the giant necromancer who transforms Antonomasia into a monkey of brass and Don Clavijo into a metal crocodile, and is appeased by Don Quixote.

MALAMUD, Bernard (1914–), American novelist, born in Brooklyn, best known for his novel *The Fixer* (1967), the story of a Jewish handyman or 'fixer' in Tsarist Russia just before the First World War, who is falsely accused of murder and turned into the scapegoat for anti-Semitic feeling in his neighbourhood. Other works include *A New Life* (1961), *The Tenants* (1971), *Dubin's Lives* (1979), and *God's Grace* (1982). He has also published volumes of short stories.

Malaprop, Mrs, in Sheridan's *The Rivals*, the aunt and guardian of Lydia Languish, noted for her aptitude in misapplying words; for instance (among many brilliant inventions of Sheridan's) 'as headstrong as an allegory on the banks of the Nile' or 'He is the very pineapple of politeness.' Her solecisms have given the word 'Malapropism' to the language.

Malbecco, in Spenser's *Faerie Queene* (III. ix, x), a 'cancred crabbed Carle', jealous and avaricious, married to the lovely *Hellenore. *Paridell elopes with her, and Malbecco, unable to escape from his jealous thoughts, throws himself from a rock. But his 'aery Spright' lives for ever, under the name of Jealousy.

Malcontent, The, a tragi-comedy by *Marston, and generally considered his best play, published 1604 (with additions by *Webster), written not earlier than 1602.

The central character is Altofronto, banished Duke of Genoa, disguised as the malcontent Malevole; in this role he reveals to his successor Pietro that he is being deceived by his wife Aurelia, and watches over the attempts of the Machiavellian Mendoza to supplant Pietro, to banish Aurelia, and to marry Altofronto's own wife, Maria. After much intrigue Altofronto reveals himself to the by now penitent Pietro, and the two expose Mendoza's villainy and regain their own wives. The plot resembles that of *Measure for Measure* in several respects, but the exposure of court corruption, lust, and greed is more harshly satiric, reflecting (in *Swinburne's view) 'the poet's own ambitions and dissatisfied intelligence'.

Maldon, *Battle of,* a 325-line poem in Old English, incomplete at the beginning and the end, probably written *c*.1000, dealing with the battle fought in 991 at Maldon in Essex against Danish raiders. The Danes are drawn up on the shore of the river Pant (Blackwater), opposed by Byrhtnoth (*c*.926–91), ealdorman of Essex since 956, who rejects the demand for tribute by the Danes. In the fight Byrhtnoth is killed and the English are defeated, partly because some of his men flee but partly too because of Byrhtnoth's 'ofermod', his excessive pride, in yielding ground to the Danes as a gesture of magnanimity. The second half of the poem, concerned with the loyalty of the followers of Byrhtnoth to their dead leader, is a powerful statement of fidelity and determination to avenge his death. The poem survives only in a transcript, fortunately made by John Elphinston, under-keeper of the Cotton Library (1677–1729), because the manuscript was destroyed in the fire at the Cotton Library in 1731. Ed. E. V. Gordon (1937, etc.).

Maldon, Jack, in Dickens's *David Copperfield,* the scapegrace cousin of Mrs Strong.

Malecasta, 'unchaste', in Spenser's *Faerie Queene* (III. i), the lady of Castle Joyeous.

Maleger, in Spenser's *Faerie Queene* (II. xi), the captain of twelve troops, the seven deadly sins and the evil passions that assail the five senses. He is lean and ghostlike, and Prince *Arthur's sword has no effect on him. Finally, remembering that earth is his mother and that he draws his strength from her, Arthur lifts him up and squeezes the life out of him.

Malengin, in Spenser's *Faerie Queene* (V. ix), the personification of guile. Sought out by Prince *Arthur and *Artegall, he runs away assuming various disguises, but is destroyed by *Talus.

Male Règle, La, see HOCCLEVE.

MALLARMÉ, Stéphane (1842–98), French poet, one of the founders of modern European poetry, and more recently one of the heroes of *structuralism. He spent the years 1862–3 in London; thereafter he taught English in various lycées, mostly in Paris. The hermetic preciousness of his later verse made him the object of a cult. Two of his longer pieces, the icily poised 'Hérodiade' (*c*.1864) and the sensuously textured 'Prélude à l'après-midi d'un faune' (*c*.1865), celebrate the hidden virtues of deferment and absence against the vulgarity of possession and plenitude. His pursuit of a perfection realizable only through renunciation of the actual demanded a new effort of language: the rare, intensely-wrought lyrics, sonnets, and

elegies gathered in *Poésies* (1887) and *Vers et Prose* (1893) attempt a science of suggestion through the exploitation of syntactical and metaphoric ambiguities and of the formal and aural properties of verse. These tendencies reach their culmination in 'Un coup de dès jamais n'abolira le hasard' (1897), a poem which makes revolutionary use of typographical possibilities to suggest a musical score and to indicate what he called the 'prismatic subdivisions of the idea'.

MALLET, or **MALLOCH,** David (?1705–65), Scottish author, who anglicized his name, to the disapproval of *Boswell. He wrote the well known ballad *'William and Margaret', *The Excursion* (1728, a poem), and various tragedies, including *Elvira* (1763) which was admired by his friend *Gibbon but criticized in *Critical Strictures* by Boswell and others. He collaborated with *Thomson in the masque of *Alfred* (1740), wrote a *Life of Francis Bacon* (1740), and edited *Bolingbroke's *Works* (5 vols, 1754).

Malleus Maleficarum, or *Hexenhammer,* the 'Hammer of Witches', published in 1484 by Jakob Sprenger, the Dominican inquisitor of Cologne, and Heinrich Krämer, prior of Cologne. It was the textbook of the day on witchcraft, setting out how it may be discovered and how it should be punished.

MALLOCH, David, see MALLET, D.

MALLOCK, William Hurrell (1849–1923), nephew of R. H. and J. A. *Froude, educated at Balliol College, Oxford, is best known as author of *The New Republic: or culture, faith and philosophy in an English country house* (1877), a lively satire on English society and ideas, in which *Ruskin figures as Mr Herbert, and *Jowett, M. *Arnold, *Pater, T. H. *Huxley, and *Tyndall appear under thin disguises among the other characters. He published various other works, including poems, novels, and memoirs; a High Anglican Tory, he attacked socialism and the *Fabian society in several studies of social and economic science, and was himself attacked for his views by G. B. *Shaw in the *Fortnightly Review,* April 1894.

MALMESBURY, William of, see WILLIAM OF MALMESBURY.

MALONE, Edmond (1741–1812), literary critic and Shakespearian scholar, educated at Trinity College, Dublin, who came to London in 1777 and established himself as a writer and as a friend of Dr *Johnson, Sir J. *Reynolds, *Burke, and many others. He published in 1778 his *An attempt to ascertain the order in which the plays attributed to Shakespeare were written,* and edited the works of *Goldsmith (1780), Reynolds (1791), and the prose works of *Dryden (1800). A friend of *Boswell, and a member of the *Club, he revised the *Journal of a Tour to the Hebrides (1785) while it was going through the press, and gave great assistance with Boswell's Life of Samuel *Johnson (1791), of which he edited the third to sixth editions. He exposed the forgeries of *Chatterton and *Ireland. His new edition of Shakespeare was issued posthumously in 1821 in 21 vols by James Boswell the younger.

Malone Society, The, was founded by *Greg in 1906 for the purpose of making accessible materials for the study of early English drama, by printing dramatic texts and documents. Its name is taken from E. *Malone.

MALORY, Sir Thomas (d. 1471), author of Le *Morte D'Arthur, although his exact identity is uncertain, is identified by his editor Vinaver as Sir Thomas Malory of Newbold Revel, Warwickshire, who was a knight before 1442. The Morte D'Arthur was written in prison and we know that Malory of Newbolt Revel was charged with crimes of violence, theft, and rape after 1450. For a Yorkshire identification see W. M. Matthews, The Ill-Framed Knight (1966). The fact that much of the work was translated from a 'French book' has led to a proposed identification as a hostage held in France during the French wars. But the identity remains a matter of conjecture.

MALRAUX, André (1901–76), French novelist, essayist, and art critic. Out of his experiences as a political activist, in China in the 1920s and in Spain during the Civil War, he wrote a number of novels on revolutionary themes, including Les Conquérants (1928, English trans. The Conquerors, 1929), La Condition humaine (1933, trans. under various titles: Storm in Shanghai, 1934, Man's Fate, 1934, Man's Estate, 1948), and L'Espoir (1937, Days of Hope, 1938, Man's Hope, 1938). His writings on art include Les Voix du silence (1951, The Voices of Silence, 1953). In 1967 his Antimémoires appeared (Anti-memoirs, 1968).

MALTHUS, Thomas Robert (1766–1834), educated at Cambridge, where he had a brilliant student career, became curate of Albury in Surrey in 1798. In that year, provoked by *Godwin's Political Justice of 1793, he published An Essay on the Principle of Population, in which he argued that population (growing geometrically) would soon increase beyond the means of subsistence (which grew only arithmetically), and that checks in the form of poverty, disease, and starvation were necessary. After he had collected a great deal of further information from travels in northern Europe, the Essay was heavily recast in a second edition of 1803; in this Malthus modified his conclusions, suggesting that the regulation of greed and sexual activity would act as more acceptable checks on population

growth. His work was vigorously attacked by Godwin, *Cobbett, *Hazlitt, and others, but it exerted a powerful influence on social thought in the 19th cent. C. *Darwin declared in his Life that Malthus's Essay helped to point him towards his own theory of evolution.

Malvolio, in Shakespeare's *Twelfth Night, the joyless steward whose gulling forms the play's secondary plot. His name, which denotes 'ill will', has on occasion (e.g. at court, 1623) been used as the play's title.

Mambrino, in *Orlando Furioso, a pagan king whose magic helmet is acquired by *Rinaldo. In *Don Quixote (Part I) there is frequent mention of Mambrino's helmet. Don Quixote, seeing a barber riding with his brass basin upon his head, takes this for the golden helmet of Mambrino, and gets possession of it.

Mammon, Sir Epicure, in Jonson's *The Alchemist, a voluptuous, gourmandizing knight, one of Jonson's greatest characters.

Mammon, The Cave of, described in Spenser's *Faerie Queene (II. vii), is the treasure-house of the god of wealth, visited by Sir Guyon. Milton in his *Areopagitica uses the example of Spenser making Guyon visit the cave of Mammon 'that he might see and know, and yet abstain'.

Man and Superman: A Comedy and a Philosophy, a play by Bernard *Shaw, first published 1903, first performed (without Act 3) in 1905 by the Stage Society at the Court Theatre.

The play is Shaw's paradoxical version of the *Don Juan story, in which his hero, John Tanner (Don Juan Tenorio), provocative, eloquent, and witty ideologue and author of the Revolutionist's Handbook (a work which appears in full as an appendix to the play), is relentlessly if obliquely pursued by Ann Whitefield, who is more interested in him as a potential husband than she is in his political theories. Ann has been entrusted as ward by her dead father jointly to Tanner and to the elderly respectable Ramsden, who expects her to marry the devoted and poetic Octavius. Tanner is made aware of Ann's intentions by his chauffeur, Straker (the New Man of the polytechnic revolution), and flees to Spain whither he is pursued by Ann and her entourage, which includes her mother and Octavius's sister Violet, who demonstrates, through a matrimonial subplot, the superior force of women. Act Three consists of a dream sequence set in hell in which Tanner, captured by the brigand Mendoza, becomes his ancestor Don Juan, Mendoza the Devil, Ramsden 'the Statue', and Ann becomes Ana: in one of Shaw's most characteristic 'Shavio-Socratic' debates, the four characters discuss the nature of progress, evolution, and the Life Force, the Devil arguing powerfully that man is essentially destructive, and Don Juan arguing for the saving power of ideas and rational effort, for the philosopher as 'nature's pilot'. In the last act Ann achieves her object, despite Tanner's struggles; the play ends with the announcement of their impending marriage and Tanner's submission to the Life Force.

The concept of the Life Force bears some similarity to *Bergson's 'élan vital', although Shaw was not at the time familiar with Bergson's work: the echo in his 'Superman' of *Nietzsche's 'Übermensch' (*Also sprach Zarathustra*) is, however, deliberate.

Manannán, the son of *Lêr, a highly popular god of the old Gaelic pantheon, the subject of many legends and the patron of sailors and merchants. The Isle of Man was his favourite abode, and is said to take its name from him. There he has degenerated into a legendary giant, with three legs (seen revolving in the coat of arms of the island).

Manawyddan, see MABINOGION.

Manchester Guardian, The, founded in 1821 as a weekly, and in 1855 as a daily paper; the principal Liberal organ outside London, edited 1872–1929 by Charles Prestwich Scott (1846–1932). Its title was changed to *The Guardian* in 1959; since 1961 it has been published from London.

Manchester School, the name first applied by *Disraeli to the political party, led by *Cobden and *Bright, who advocated the principles of free trade. It was afterwards extended to the party who supported those leaders on other questions of policy. 'Manchester policy' was used derisively to signify a policy of laissez-faire and self-interest. The 'Manchester School' of drama refers loosely to the playwrights associated with Miss *Horniman's repertory seasons at the Gaiety Theatre, Manchester, 1907–14, including Harold Brighouse (1882–1958), W. S. *Houghton, and Allan Monkhouse (1858–1936).

'Manciple's Tale, The', see CANTERBURY TALES, 23.

Mandarin, used as an adjective to describe esoteric, highly decorative, or highbrow prose. According to C. *Connolly, those favouring it included *Donne, *Addison, and *De Quincey, and its last great exponents were *Pater and H. *James (*Enemies of Promise*, 1938).

MANDELSTAM, Osip Emilevich (1891–?1938), Russian poet, born into the family of a Jewish leather merchant in Warsaw and brought up in St Petersburg. He spent most of 1907–10 in Western Europe, particularly Paris, and then studied at St Petersburg University. His first poems appeared in 1910. In 1911 he joined the Acmeist 'Guild of Poets' with *Akhmatova and *Gumilev, and the poems of his first collection, *Stone* (1913), are marked by Acmeist brevity and clarity. He met Nadezhda Yakovlevna

Khazina in Kiev in 1919 and married her in 1922. His second collection, *Tristia* (1922), confirmed his status while considerably widening his range. During the 1920s Mandelstam came under increasing attack for being 'out of step' with the new Soviet age, and his ruminations on the subject produced such important poems as 'The Age' and 'The Slate Ode'. His third volume, *Poems*, and collections of prose and criticism appeared in 1928. In 1930 he made a long visit to Armenia, from which emerged *The Journey to Armenia*, a major prose piece (trans. Clarence Brown, 1980), his last work to be published in the Soviet Union for 30 years. His first arrest, in 1934, resulted from his recitation of his famous poem denouncing *Stalin. Prison was followed by internal exile and attempted suicide. In exile he wrote his important late poetry the 'Voronezh Notebooks'. Arrested again in 1938, he was sentenced to five years' hard labour and died of a heart attack on the way to the camps (the exact date of his death has not been established). His collected works have only been published abroad, though an edition of his poetry appeared in Leningrad in 1973. The two volumes of memoirs by Nadezhda Mandelstam, *Hope against Hope* (1971) and *Hope Abandoned* (1974), are not only the main source of information on the poet but also a powerful and harrowing description of the experience of 20th-cent. totalitarianism. Mandelstam's reputation continues to grow, and he is now regarded as one of the major poets of the 20th cent. He has been widely translated into English, notably by Clarence Brown and W. S. Merwin (*Selected Poems*, 1973) and by David McDuff (*Selected Poems*, 1973).

MANDEVILLE, Bernard de (1670–1733), born in Holland, trained as a physician at Leyden, settled in London, and published *A Treatise of the Hypochondriack and Hysterick Passions* (1711, expanded into three dialogues, 1730). His other prose works include *The Virgin Unmasked* (1709, 1714), arguing for a better status and better education for women; *Free Thoughts on Religion, the Church and National Happiness* (1720), a defence of *Deism and an attack on clericalism; *A Modest Defence of Public Stews* (1724), recommending governmental regulation of bawdy-houses; and *An Enquiry into the Origin of Honour* (1732), distinguishing self-esteem from self-love. Of his moral and satirical verse the best known is 'The Grumbling Hive, or Knaves turn'd Honest' (1705), which was incorporated with various prose supplements into *The Fable of the Bees, or Private Vices, Public Benefits* (1714, 1723). Mandeville here rejects the optimistic view of benevolent human nature put forward by *Shaftesbury, and argues that the mutual help on which society thrives like a colony of bees is due to personal acquisitiveness and the love of luxury: a 'virtuous' society, where only subsistence needs are satisfied, would lack both culture and trade and would collapse from want of employment. Mandeville's writing was admired by *Defoe, and later by Dr *Johnson and *Hume, but his ironic use of the language of 'vice' and 'virtue' was widely misconstrued. He was attacked by W. *Law (*Remarks upon a Late Book*, 1723), *Dennis (*Vice and Luxury Public Mischiefs*, 1724), *Hutcheson (letters in the *Dublin Journal*, 1726), *Watts (*An Essay towards the Encouragement of Charity Schools*, 1728), and G. *Berkeley (*Alciphron*, 1732), Mandeville himself responding to the last in *A Letter to Dion* (1732). Mandeville was a literary target in Pope's *Dunciad* and Fielding's *Amelia*, but is favourably portrayed in R. *Browning's *Parleyings with certain People of Importance*.

MANDEVILLE, Sir John, the ostensible author of the famous travel book which is found in many European languages after its first appearance in Anglo-Norman French in 1356–7. There are a number of English manuscripts, one of a metrical version from Coventry, and the first probably coming from Lincolnshire c.1375. Jean d'Outremeuse, a historian from Liège, tells us that he knew the writer, who left his native St Albans in 1322 and died in Liège in 1372. Until J. W. Bennett's *The Rediscovery of Sir John Mandeville* (1954), Jean d'Outremeuse himself was believed to be the writer of the work. The book purports to be an account of the author's journeys in the East, but it is really a compilation, drawn especially from William of Boldensele and Friar Odoric of Pordenone, and from the *Speculum Majus* of *Vincent of Beauvais. It claims to be a guide, both geographical and ethical, for pilgrims to the Holy Land, but it carries the reader far off course, to Turkey, Tartary, Persia, Egypt, and India. It is a highly entertaining work, combining geography and natural history with romance and marvels, such as the fountain of youth and the ant-hills of gold-dust. It was an important influence on subsequent English writers from *Chaucer to Shakespeare, and was the prototype in English of the popular genre of the fabulous travel book.

Ed. C. W. R. D. Moseley (1983); metrical version ed. M. C. Seymour (EETS os 269, 1973).

Mandricardo, in *Orlando Furioso*, the son of *Agrican, king of Tartary. He wears the armour of Hector, and comes to Europe to secure Hector's sword *Durindana, now in the possession of Orlando, and to avenge his father's death. He carries off Doralis, who is betrothed to *Rodomont, meets Orlando and fights with him (but the fight is broken off), gets Durindana after Orlando in his madness has thrown it away, and is finally killed by *Rogero.

Manette, Dr and Lucie, characters in Dickens's *A Tale of Two Cities*.

Manfred, a poetic drama by Lord *Byron, published 1817.

Manfred, a Faustian figure, 'half-dust, half deity', lives alone as an outcast in a castle in the Alps, and is tortured by guilt for 'some half-maddening sin'. He summons the spirits of the universe, who offer him everything except the oblivion he seeks. Eventually, overcoming his terror of death, he tries to hurl himself from an alpine crag, but is dragged back by a hunter. He invokes the Witch of the Alps and reveals his sin—his incestuous love for his sister Astarte. He descends to the underworld, the Hall of Arimanes, and encounters a vision of Astarte, who promises him death on the morrow. Back in his castle an abbot begs him to repent, but he cannot. He denies the power of the demons who summon him, and when they vanish he dies.

Byron was deeply interested in the idea of supermen, half way between gods and mortals, and was to return to the theme in *Heaven and Earth*. But he was dissatisfied with *Manfred* and did not wish it ever to be performed, a wish which was ignored after his death. Aspects of the drama were satirized in *Nightmare Abbey* by T. L. Peacock.

MANGAN, James Clarence (1803–49), Irish poet, born in Dublin, whose life was plagued by poverty and alcohol, despite the efforts of friends who found him occasional employment in the library of Trinity College, Dublin. Under various pseudonyms he published prose and verse in newspapers and periodicals and is chiefly remembered for a few powerful ballads and songs including 'Dark Rosaleen' and 'The Nameless One' ('Roll forth, my song, like the rushing river'). He died of malnutrition in extreme destitution. His tragic career suggested part of the theme of B. *Moore's *The Mangan Inheritance* (1979).

Manichaeism, a religion of Persian origin, spread to China in the east and to North Africa in the west. Its founder, Mani, began preaching in Ctesiphon, AD 242. His success provoked persecution and led to his martyrdom AD c.276. Mani made use of a mythology borrowed from *Gnosticism. He pictured a universe divided initially between the kingdoms of Light and Darkness, between the Spiritual and the Material. The powers of Darkness wantonly invaded their neighbours' territory, overthrew its defender, the Primal Man, and captured some elements of the Light. Our world was then made out of these captured elements imprisoned in Matter, and Man's purpose in life is to achieve their liberation by rejecting everything material. The Manichaeans had, like the Gnostics, their Initiates and their Catachumens and seem to have differed from the Gnostics more in the rigour of their practice than in doctrine. They advocated complete simplicity of life, were vegetarians, and were bound to abstain from harming man or beast. They did not care to acquire wealth and, since they despised ceremony and luxury, had little respect for authorities of Church and State. Their 'Elect' or initiates renounced marriage, owned no property and lived as beggars on alms. The ordinary 'Hearers' were also encouraged to refrain from having children and had to support the Elect. In the West Manichaeism adapted itself to Christianity. Manichaeans worshipped Jesus as a spirit: they denied his humanity, however, and the reality of the Crucifixion.

The writings of St *Augustine, polemics by Greek and Syrian Christians, and a couple of Arabic accounts all show the Manichaeans through the eyes of their opponents. Some of their own records have been found recently in Turkestan, but they are fragmentary and have still to be properly assembled. Manichaean proselytizing lost its impetus after the 6th cent., but the Paulicians who flourished in Asia Minor during the next 300 years retained many of their tenets and exported them to Europe, where they had close connections with the Bogomils and Cathars. The fascination of Manichaeism, which persisted in its various modes for over a thousand years, as well as the savagery of its persecutors, are matters that have still to be explained.

Mankind, a Morality play in 914 lines from East Anglia, dating from *c*.1465, one of the group called *Macro plays after their 18th-cent. owner (the others are *Wisdom and *The Castle of Perseverance). Its principal theme is Sloth (Accidia), and it is written in the Low Style with much employment of obscenity. Earlier critics and editors regarded the play with some primness, declaring it to be 'unprintable' in parts; more recently it has been admired for its dramatic vigour and for its ingenious structure. Ed. G. Wickham in *English Moral Interludes* (1976); it is discussed briefly by Richard Axton in 'The Morality Tradition' (*Pelican Guide to English Literature* 1, pp. 340–52, 2nd edn, 1982).

MANLEY, Mrs (Mary?) Delarivière (1663–1724), had a colourful life, which included a bigamous marriage with her cousin John Manley and some years as mistress of the warden of the Fleet Prison, John Tilly. She published several novels and memoirs, including *The New Atalantis* (1709), a *roman à clef (published with a Key to its characters) in which she attacked various Whigs and people of note. Her *The Adventures of Rivella* (1714) is largely autobiographical. She also wrote several plays. In 1711 she succeeded *Swift as editor of *The Examiner*: Swift wrote of her (*Journal to Stella*, Jan. 1711/12), 'she has very generous principles, for one of her sort; and a great deal of sense and invention.' Her novels, with an introduction by P. Koster, were reproduced in facsimile in 1971.

Manly, (1) a character in Wycherley's *The Plain Dealer*; (2) a character in Vanbrugh and Cibber's *The Provok'd Husband*.

MANN, Heinrich (1871–1950), German novelist, brother of Thomas *Mann. His early work includes some notable satirical novels directed against life and institutions in Wilhelmine Germany: *Professor Unrat* (1905) and *Der Untertan* (*The Subject*, 1918), for example. More politically engaged than his brother in the period before 1918, and standing more to the left, he provided the model for the type of 'Zivilisationsliterat' with whom his brother took issue in his *Betrachtungen eines Unpolitischen* (*Observations of an Unpolitical Man*, 1918). Like his brother, he emigrated from Nazi Germany.

MANN, Sir Horace (1701–86), British envoy at Florence, where the Young Pretender was residing. Horace *Walpole made his acquaintance there in 1739, and they became correspondents for 45 years, although they never met again. Walpole requested the return of his letters and used them in his historical works, as well as retouching them for publication.

MANN, Thomas (1875–1955), German novelist and essayist. Born in Lübeck, he went into emigration (most of the time in the United States) in the Nazi period. *Buddenbrooks*, a novel on the theme of the decay of a family, with strongly autobiographical features, appeared in 1901 and quickly made him famous. *Tonio Kröger* (1903), one of his most celebrated novellas, is, like so many of his works, about the nature of the artist. *Der Tod in Venedig* (*Death in Venice*, 1912), influenced particularly by the thought of *Schopenhauer and *Nietzsche, presents the artist and artistic creation in a highly ironic light. Originally a man of rather conservative sympathies, as expressed in *Betrachtungen eines Unpolitischen* (*Observations of an Unpolitical Man* 1918), he caused surprise by quickly lending his public support to the Weimar Republic. *Der Zauberberg* (*The Magic Mountain*), appeared in 1924, the 'Joseph' novels (in four parts) in 1933–43, during which time he also published his novel *Lotte in Weimar*, expanding on a brief episode in the life of *Goethe, the writer whom Mann most admired and whom he resembled in the ironic detachment of his writing. Constantly concerned with the character and role of the artist, particularly in what Mann saw as his culpable, even criminal, relation to society, he linked this theme with the problem of Nazism in *Dr Faustus* (1947), also elaborating the subject in a book about this novel, *Die Entstehung des Dr Faustus* (*The Genesis of Dr Faustus*, 1949). His last full-length novel derived from the picaresque tradition: *Die Bekenntnisse des Hochstaplers Felix Krull* (*The Confessions of the Confidence Trickster Felix Krull*,

1954). He was awarded the *Nobel Prize in 1929.

Mannerism, a term used to describe any stylistic habit that becomes exaggerated or is carried to excess, but more specifically applied to the style of Italian art of *c.*1520–*c.*1600, between the High Renaissance and the Baroque. A powerful and disturbing effect is achieved by distorted or elongated figures, violent perspective, and unexpected colour harmonies. The beginning of the style can be seen in the late work of *Michelangelo and *Raphael; it was developed by Tintoretto, El Greco, Bronzino, *Vasari, and others.

MANNING, Henry Edward (1808–92), educated at Balliol College, Oxford, became archdeacon of Chichester (1840) and succeeded *Newman as one of the leaders of the *Oxford Movement. He joined the Roman Catholic Church in 1851, and became archbishop of Westminster in 1865 and cardinal in 1875. He published many religious and polemical works, was a great preacher and ecclesiastical statesman, and a subtle controversialist. He is one of the subjects of L. *Strachey's *Eminent Victorians*.

MANNING, Olivia (1908–80), novelist, was brought up in Portsmouth, the daughter of a naval officer of small means. Her first novel, *The Wind Changes* (1937), was set in Dublin. In 1939 she married R. D. Smith, then a British Council lecturer, subsequently a BBC producer, and at the outbreak of war travelled with him to Bucharest. Her experiences there, and later in Greece, Egypt, and Jerusalem, inspired the works for which she is best remembered, *The Balkan Trilogy* (*The Great Fortune*, 1960; *The Spoilt City*, 1962; *Friends and Heroes*, 1965) and *The Levant Trilogy* (*The Danger Tree*, 1977; *The Battle Lost and Won*, 1978; and *The Sum of Things*, 1980). This sequence opens with the experiences of the newly-married Guy and Harriet Pringle in rumour-filled Roumania, surrounded by a crowd of vividly drawn minor characters and hangers-on, most memorable among them an amiable scrounger, the Russian émigré Prince Yakimov, now down-at-heel but trailing dubious memories of a glorious past. Harriet spends much of her time trying to protect Guy and herself from Guy's impulsive generosity. As the German army advances the couple flee to Athens, and the second trilogy finds them in Egypt. The novels are a fine portrait of the tragi-comedy of war and of its effects on civilian life, and give a vivid sense of place and period; *The Battle Lost and Won* also contains a striking account of the battle of Alamein seen through the eyes of Simon Boulderstone, a young British officer. Olivia Manning wrote five other novels and two volumes of short stories (*Growing Up*, 1948; *A Romantic Hero*, 1966).

MANNINGHAM, John (d. 1622), a barrister whose diary or commonplace book (among the Harleian manuscripts in the British Library) records a performance at the Middle Temple in 1602 of Shakespeare's *Twelfth Night*, which he compares to *The Comedy of Errors*, and the only known and probably authentic contemporary anecdote about Shakespeare.

MANNYNG, Robert, of Brunne (Bourne) in Lincolnshire (*fl.* 1288–1338), is known only from what he tells us of himself in the Prologues to his two works, his verse *Chronicle of England* (finished 1338) and *Handlyng Synne*. He was a member of the Gilbertine Order. Part I of *Chronicles*, ed. F. J. *Furnival (Rolls Series), 2 vols, 1887.

Man of Feeling, The, a novel by H. *Mackenzie, published 1771.

The work is generally considered to have been the most influential 'Novel of *Sentiment'. The author deliberately fragments the story, with the explanation that the MS has been mutilated, so that the effect is of a series of abrupt but concentrated episodes. Harley, the hero, is the man of feeling, whose unwavering benevolence and acute, often tearful, sensibility are demonstrated through various scenes in which he assists the down-trodden, loses his love, and fails to achieve worldly success.

'Man of Law's Tale, The', see CANTERBURY TALES, 5.

Man of Mode, The, the last and finest comedy of *Etherege, first performed at court 1676. It was an immediate success, and remains a classic of the *Restoration period. *Steele singled it out for attack in *The Spectator*, 65, and *Dennis provided a spirited defence.

There are two main plots, neatly interwoven. Dorimant rids himself of his mistress Mrs Loveit, with the aid of faint-hearted Bellinda whom he seduces in the process. In doing so he meets the heiress Harriet Woodvil, with whom he appears to fall in love. She is wise enough to keep him at arm's length until he proposes marriage, and even then requires him to follow her into the country, there to receive her answer after the play is ended. In counterpoint, Young Bellair has been ordered by his father to marry Harriet; but he loves Emilia, who with the help of his aunt Lady Towneley enables him to outwit the old man, who has fallen for Emilia. The revelation of his own dotage induces Old Bellair to give his blessing to his son's marriage.

Slight though the action is, it is natural and easy, and Etherege sustains interest through his unsentimental views, eloquent dialogue, and telling social detail. Dorimant was said to be drawn after *Rochester, and Dennis considered that the comedy 'so burnished his vices that they appeared as virtues', though a modern reader might find the play's values more ambiguous, and the satire directed not only at Sir Fopling Flutter, 'the prince of fops' who gives the drama its name.

Man of Ross, The, see KYRLE, J.

Man of the World, The, (1) a novel by H. *Mackenzie; (2) a comedy by *Macklin, performed 1781, and adapted from his own earlier unpublished work *The True Born Scotchman*, performed 1764. It had long been refused a licence because of its satire on the Scots, though Macklin claimed in a preface that his intention was only to 'explode the reciprocal national prejudices that equally soured and disgraced the minds of both English and Scots men'.

A Scottish politician, Sir Pertinax Mac-Sycophant (originally played by the author), has risen to parliamentary eminence through pliability and flattery, and now seeks to gain control of three parliamentary boroughs by marrying his eldest son, Egerton, to Lady Rodolpha, the daughter of another servile but needy politician, Lord Lambercourt. The young couple, at their parents' insistence, reluctantly embark on a scene of courtship, to find to their mutual relief that both have affections otherwise engaged, and they combine to defeat their parents' purposes. Rodolpha, who secretly loves Egerton's younger brother, is ordered to marry him, which suits all concerned; Egerton marries his own choice, his father's ward Constantia.

Manon Lescaut, see PRÉVOST, A.-F.

MANSFIELD, Katherine, pseudonym of Kathleen Mansfield Beauchamp (1888–1923), was born in Wellington, New Zealand, educated at Queen's College, London, 1903–6, returned to New Zealand to study music for two years, then came back to London in 1908. In 1909 she married, but left her husband after a few days; she became pregnant by another man and gave birth to a stillborn child in Bavaria, an experience that formed the background to her first collection of stories *In a German Pension* (1911), most of which were previously published in *Orage's *New Age*. In 1911 she met John Middleton *Murry, whom she was to marry in 1918; he was editing *Rhythm*, to which, and to its successor *The Blue Review*, she also contributed stories, many based on her New Zealand childhood. In 1915 she and Murry spent some weeks in Zennor, Cornwall, in close and sometimes strained proximity to their friends D. H. *Lawrence and Frieda; in 1916 she, Murry, and Lawrence founded a magazine, *Signature*, which survived for only three issues. From this period she knew that she was suffering from tuberculosis, and spent part of every year abroad in the South of France and Switzerland. In 1918 'Prelude' was published by the *Hogarth Press, and later in a collection, *Bliss, and other stories* (1920). She was increasingly

recognized as an original and experimental writer, whose stories were the first in English to show the influence of *Chekhov, whom she greatly admired. Her success aroused the jealousy of V. *Woolf, who began to describe her work as 'hard' and 'shallow'. *The Garden Party, and other stories* (1922) was the third and last collection to be published in her lifetime: in that year she entered the institute run by *Gurdjieff near Fontainebleau, hoping to regain spiritual and physical health, and died the following January. Her stories vary greatly in length and tone, from long, impressionistic, delicate evocations of family life ('At the Bay', 'Prelude') to short, sharp sketches such as 'Miss Brill'. Two collections were published posthumously (*The Dove's Nest*, 1923; *Something Childish*, 1924) as well as various collections of letters, extracts from her journal, etc.; a biography by A. Alpers appeared in 1980, superseding his own earlier version of 1954. Her *Collected Letters*, vol. i, ed. V. O'Sullivan and M. Scott, appeared in 1984.

Mansfield Park, a novel by J. Austen, begun 1811, published 1814.

Sir Thomas Bertram of Mansfield Park, a stern but kind-hearted man, has two sons, Tom and Edmund, and two daughters, Maria and Julia. His wife, a charming, indolent woman, has two sisters: Mrs Norris, a near neighbour, who is spiteful and selfish, and Mrs Price, the wife of an impecunious officer of marines, with a large family of young children. In order to assist the Prices, Sir Thomas undertakes the charge of their eldest daugher Fanny, a timid child of nine. In spite of her humble situation and the cruelty of Mrs Norris, Fanny, by her gentle and modest disposition, gradually becomes an indispensable part of the household. The strength and earnestness of her character is particularly shown during Sir Thomas's absence in the West Indies, when family discipline is considerably relaxed, forbidden private theatricals are mounted, and an unseemly flirtation begins between Maria Bertram, who is already engaged to marry Mr Rushworth, and Henry Crawford, the attractive, worldly brother-in-law of the parson of Mansfield. Against all this Fanny resolutely sets her face. Loving her cousin Edmund, she grieves greatly to see him fascinated by the frivolous Mary Crawford, sister of Henry. Maria having become Mrs Rushworth, Henry turns his attention to Fanny, to his own and her astonishment falls in love with her, and proposes marriage. Fanny unhesitatingly rejects him, incurring the grave displeasure of Sir Thomas for what he regards as a piece of ungrateful perversity. During a visit paid by Fanny to her own home in Portsmouth matters come to a crisis. Henry, accidentally encountering Maria Rushworth again, runs away with her; and Julia elopes with a foolish and unsuitable suitor, Mr Yates. Mary Crawford's failure to condemn her brother's conduct, together with her aversion to marrying a clergyman (for Edmund has by now taken orders) finally opens Edmund's eyes to her true character. He turns for comfort to Fanny, falls in love, and they are married.

Mansoul, (1) see HOLY WAR; (2) a poem by *Doughty.

Mantalini, Madame, in Dickens's *Nicholas Nickleby,* a fashionable dressmaker. Her husband, Mr Mantalini, a selfish, affected fop, lives on her earnings and ruins her.

Man that Corrupted Hadleyburg, The, a story by Mark *Twain.

Mantua Carpetanorum, in imprints, Madrid.

MANTUAN, or **MANTUANUS** (1448–1516), Johannes Baptista Spagnolo, a Carmelite of Mantua who wrote Latin eclogues. These had a considerable vogue in England and influenced the pastorals of *Barclay and *Spenser. He is the 'good old Mantuan' quoted by Holofernes in *Love's Labour's Lost (IV. ii).

MANUTIUS, Aldus, see ALDUS MANUTIUS.

MANZONI, Alessandro (1785–1873), Italian novelist, author of I promessi sposi (The Betrothed), a work of unique historical significance. In a long series of painstaking revisions from its first published version (1825–7) to its final form (1840–2), it forged from Tuscan the literary Italian which, after the unification of Italy (1870), became standard Italian. It is also remarkable for its powerfully characterized historical reconstruction of 17th-cent. Lombardy, under Spanish domination and ravaged by plague. The simple attempts of two poor silk-weavers to marry is used to explore the corrupt and oppressive rule of the Spaniards and, by implication, of the later Austrians. Manzoni also wrote two historical tragedies in verse, Il conte di Carmagnola (The Count of Carmagnola, 1820) and Adelchi (1822), which deal with the relationship between oppressed and oppressors, and the role of divine providence in history. He was greatly admired by Sir W. *Scott, and was the subject of a great Requiem Mass by *Verdi.

MAP, Walter (c.1140–c.1209), a Welshman who was archdeacon of Oxford in the time of Henry II and the author between 1181 and 1192 of a satirical and entertaining miscellany De Nugis Curialium, 'Courtiers' Trifles', which contains the disquisition formerly attributed to St *Augustine, 'Dissuasio Valerii ad Rufinum de non ducenda uxore', referred to by Chaucer in the 'Prologue to the Wife of Bath's Tale' (*Canterbury Tales, III. 671). Some goliardic poems have been doubtfully attributed to him, as well as a lost Latin original of the prose Lancelot. He was highly regarded as a poet in his own day and he used to be identified as *Golias and hence

the author of all the goliardic poems; this is certainly not right, though he must have been the composer of more works than the small certain œuvre that survives. (See also ANGLO-LATIN LITERATURE.)

De Nugis Curialium, trans. F. Tupper and M. B. Ogle (1924). Ed. T. Wright, The Latin Poems commonly attributed to Walter Mapes (Camden Soc. 1841: inauthentic works).

MARANA, Giovanni Paolo, see TURKISH SPY.

Marble Faun, The, a novel by *Hawthorne, published 1860 (in England as Transformation). It is the product of Hawthorne's two years in Italy; the scene is laid in Rome, and the title is taken from the resemblance of one of the principal characters, Count Donatello, to the Marble Faun of Praxiteles.

Donatello is in love with the liberated young American art student Miriam, who is being persecuted by a mysterious stranger—a 'dusty, death-scented apparition', with whom she has some guilty connection. Roused to sudden fury when encountering her with him on a moonlight expedition, Donatello murders him, with her unspoken assent, thus binding them together in a relationship 'cemented by blood'. A sub-plot describes the relationship of a sculptor, Kenyon, and Miriam's art student friend Hilda, 'the Dove'; Hilda, although herself totally innocent, feels herself under a 'mysterious shadow of guilt', by connection with Miriam. Hawthorne uses the image of Beatrice Cenci, in the painting attributed to *Reni, which Hilda is engaged in copying, as a symbol for the mystery of sin, which, in the character of Donatello, has a purifying power. He surrenders himself to justice, and Kenyon's reflection is, 'Sin has educated Donatello, and elevated him. Is sin, then . . . merely an element in human education?'

MARCEL, Gabriel (1889–1973), French Catholic existentialist. Following *Kierkegaard and Jaspers, he repudiated abstraction, generalization, categorization, in favour of individual authenticity. From Être et Avoir (1935) to Le Mystère de l'Être (1951), he argued that being is a concept that cannot be analysed, only recognized, and that man has to confront it not as a problem to be posed or conceived, but as an experience to be lived and explored.

Marcelia, the heroine of Massinger's *The Duke of Milan.

Marchioness, The, a character in Dickens's *The Old Curiosity Shop.

Marcia, a character in Addison's *Cato.

MARCIAN, see MARTIANUS CAPELLA.

MARCO POLO, see POLO, M.

MARCUS AURELIUS ANTONINUS (AD 121–80), Roman emperor 161–80 and

Stoic philosopher, was the author of twelve books of 'Meditations'. The *Meditations* were not printed till 1555, but a Spanish counterfeit by Antonio da Guevara purporting to be a life of Marcus Aurelius was translated by J. *Berners as *The Golden Book* (1535) and by T. *North as the *Dial of Princes* (1557), and enjoyed great public favour. But so did Jeremy *Collier's translation (1701) of the authentic *Meditations* which saw 58 editions before the end of the century. They were highly valued also by M. *Arnold and had a further spell of popularity in the decades preceding the First World War. For his philosophy, see STOICISM.

Marfisa, in *Orlando Innamorato* and *Orlando Furioso*, the warrior sister of *Rogero. Brought up by an African magician, she becomes queen of India, and leads an army to the relief of *Angelica besieged in *Albracca. Later, discovering her own Christian parentage, Marfisa joins Charlemagne and is baptized. She falls in love with Rogero before discovering that he is her brother.

Marforio, see PASQUIL.

Margaret, (1) in Shakespeare's *Much Ado about Nothing*, a gentlewoman attendant on *Hero; (2) in Goethe's *Faust*, the principal female character ('Gretchen') of Pt I, a girl of humble station, simple, confiding, and affectionate.

Margarete, St, see KATHERINE GROUP, THE.

MARGARET OF ANJOU (1430–82), the 'She-wolf of France', daughter of Reignier, king of Naples, who is a dominant character in Shakespeare's *1, 2,* and *3 *Henry VI* and *Richard III*. In *1* and *2 Henry VI* she is the mistress of Suffolk, though married to Henry; in *3 Henry VI* her role as a termagant develops, with her mocking and murder of York, and in *Richard III* she is a powerful prophetess of doom. The historical Margaret remained in France after her defeat at the battle of Tewkesbury. Peggy Ashcroft played the role memorably in John Barton's adaptation of the four plays as *The Wars of the Roses* (1963). She figures also in Scott's *Anne of Geierstein*.

Margarite of America, A, a prose romance by T. *Lodge published 1596, but written during his voyage to South America under Thomas Cavendish in 1591–3. It describes the tragic love of Margarite, daughter of the king of Muscovy, for the treacherous and violent Arsadachus, son of the emperor of Cusco, who eventually kills her, together with his wife Diana and their child. It is notable for its variety of visual spectacle and pageantry, its highly patterned poems and songs, and the unsparing savagery of many of the incidents. It was edited by G. B. *Harrison (1927).

Marguerite of Navarre, see HEPTAMERON.

Maria, (1) one of the ladies attending the princess in Shakespeare's *Love's Labour's Lost*; (2) Olivia's waiting woman in his *Twelfth Night*; (3) a character in Sterne's *Tristram Shandy* (vol. vii) and *A Sentimental Journey*; (4) a character in Sheridan's *The School for Scandal*.

Marian, Maid, see MAID MARIAN.

Mariana, (1) Diana's friend in Shakespeare's *All's Well that Ends Well*; (2) in his *Measure for Measure*, a lady betrothed to *Angelo, but cast off by him. The duke describes her as living 'dejected' 'at the moated grange' (III. i. 255), the phrase which suggested *Tennyson's poems (below).

'Mariana' (1830) and **'Mariana in the South'** (1832), two poems by *Tennyson, suggested by Shakespeare's Mariana of 'the moated grange' in *Measure for Measure*. Both describe women waiting hopelessly and in desolate loneliness for their lovers; the first inspired *Millais' painting of 1851, and the landscape of the second was drawn from Tennyson's journey with A. H. *Hallam in 1832. Tennyson appears to have invented the stanza form.

MARIANA, Juan de (1535–1624), a Spanish Jesuit who taught theology at Rome and Paris, and then settled at Toledo, and wrote a long and remarkable history of Spain. He also wrote a notable Latin treatise *De rege et regis institutione* (Toledo, 1599), in which he spoke with approval of the assassination of Henri III of France by Jacques Clément and defined the circumstances in which it was legitimate to get rid, even by violence, of a tyrannical prince. This book was condemned in Paris to be burnt by the public executioner immediately after the assassination of Henri IV by Ravaillac in 1610, and encouraged the belief in England that the Jesuits were responsible for the Gunpowder Plot of 1605.

MARIE DE CHAMPAGNE, daughter of *Eleanor of Aquitaine and her first husband, Louis VII of France, became Countess of Champagne in 1164 on her marriage to Count Henry, and regent there on his death in 1181. She set up at Troyes from the 1160s onwards a cultural centre modelled on that of her mother at Poitiers. Her most famous protégé was *Chrétien de Troyes who attributes to her the *sen* and *matière* of his *Lancelot* in the first lines of the poem. *Andreas Capellanus also claims to be a courtier of hers.

MARIE DE FRANCE (*fl.* 1160–90), a French poet of whom little certain is known, the author of twelve *Lais*, a series of apparently Celtic stories told in Anglo-Norman couplets. She appears to have been born in France and to have done much or all of her literary work in England. She knew Latin and English as well as

French, and she wrote a French version of the Latin *St *Patrick's Purgatory*. As well as her famous *Lais*, some of which were copied in English (see BRETON LAYS), she wrote a collection of *Aesop's Fables which she called *Isopet* and which she says she translated from English. See *Lais*, ed. A. Ewert (1944); E. Rickert, *Marie de France: Seven of her Lays done into English* (1901).

Marina, in Shakespeare's *Pericles*, the daughter of Pericles, whose name alludes to her being born at sea. She inspired T. S. *Eliot's poem 'Marina' (1930).

Marinell, see FLORIMELL.

MARINETTI, Filippo Tommaso (1876–1944), Italian dramatist, novelist, and poet, who launched *Futurism in 1909. In his poems he anticipated the *Dada technique of juxtaposing words without syntactical links. In his plays he abandoned verisimilitude and traditional methods of characterization and plot development. His innovations include: the use of automatons; the simultaneous staging of unrelated actions; the 'drama of objects', in which human interlocutors play no significant part. He shared with Fascism the glorification of virility, nationalism, and war.

MARINO, Giambattista (1569–1625), Neapolitan poet, best known for his *Adone* (1623), a long poem on the love of Venus and Adonis. The term *marinismo* (or sometimes *secentismo*) denotes the flamboyant style of Marino and his 17th-cent. imitators, with its extravagant imagery, excessive ornamentation, and verbal conceits. *Crashaw was profoundly influenced by Marino. See *Secentismo e Marinismo* (1925) by M. *Praz.

Marino Faliero, Doge of Venice, a poetic drama by Lord *Byron, published 1821, produced in the same year at Drury Lane, against Byron's wish.
   Marino Faliero was elected doge of Venice in 1354 and the events of Byron's play, based on historical facts, occur in 1355. Michael Steno, affronted by the doge, an aristocratic and passionate man, writes on the doge's chair of state a gross lampoon on the dignitary and his wife. Steno is tried and given a punishment the doge considers utterly inadequate. In his desire for vengeance the doge enters into a conspiracy with a discontented mob to overthrow the Venetian constitution. The plot is revealed, and Faliero is executed.
   The conspiracy of the doge was also the subject of a tragedy by *Swinburne, *Marino Faliero* (1885).

Maritornes, the chambermaid at the inn that *Don Quixote took for a castle.

Marius the Epicurean, a philosophical romance by *Pater, published 1885.

Pater describes the boyhood, education, and young manhood of Marius, a serious young Roman imbued with a 'morbid religious idealism'. With his friend Flavian (who, like so many of Pater's characters, dies young) he discovers the 'jewelled' delights of *Apuleius, in particular of the story of *Cupid and Psyche*, then progresses through the philosophies of *Heraclitus, Aristippus, and *Marcus Aurelius to Christianity. He dies more or less a martyr to save a Christian friend. The work is a vehicle for Pater's own reflections on pagan and Christian art and religion; T. S. *Eliot in his essay 'Arnold and Pater' (1930) quotes with approval A. C. *Benson's view that Pater's true interest was in the sensuous appeal and liturgical solemnities of religion, and concludes that the book documents an important historical moment in the process whereby 'religion became morals, religion became art, religion became science and philosophy'.

MARIVAUX, Pierre (1688–1763), French playwright. After the loss of his provincial inheritance he lived by his pen and frequented the literary salons of Paris. In 1722 he founded a *Spectateur français* in imitation of Addison's *Spectator*. In all he produced about 30 comedies, the intrigues of which are motivated by social and psychological obstacles to the union of lovers. The refined and subtle analysis of sentiment known as *marivaudage* which is his trademark as a dramatist is best revealed in *Le Jeu de l'amour et du hasard* (1730) and *Les Fausses Confidences* (1737). His plays have held the French stage ever since.

Mark, King, in Arthurian legend, the king of Cornwall and the husband of Isoud of Ireland, who is brought to Mark by her lover *Tristram; in some versions Tristram is the son of Mark's sister Elizabeth. Various Tristram stories represent the king as nobly trusting, or as a treacherous coward. See TRISTRAM AND ISOUD.

MARKANDAYA, Kamala (1923–), British novelist, born and educated in India. *Nectar in a Sieve* (1954) established her as the first notable woman novelist from the Indian subcontinent. The impact of new economic and political ideas on traditional Indian society is Markandaya's main theme in *A Silence of Desire* (1960), *Possession* (1963), *A Handful of Rice* (1966), and *The Coffer Dams* (1969). *The Nowhere Man* (1972) transports the clash of cultures to England, where Markandaya settled in the early 1960s. *Two Virgins* (1973) marks a radical change, showing a much more experimental style and a more positive view of modernization. Her most ambitious novel is *The Golden Honeycomb* (1977)—a historical look at how the coming of Indian independence affected a native or princely state. *Pleasure City* (1982) provides a subtle and ironic view of a friendship between Rikki, a local fisherboy, and Tully, a representative of the multi-national company which builds a modern holiday resort next to Rikki's village.

MARKHAM, Mrs, pseudonym of Mrs Elizabeth Penrose (1780–1837), who wrote for children, and published two very popular school histories, of England (1823) and of France (1828), from which she carefully omitted all instances of cruelty and deception.

MARKHAM, Gervase (1568–1637), wrote on country pursuits, the art of war, and horsemanship; also plays and poems. His principal works are *A Discourse of Horsemanshippe* (1593), *Cavelarice, or the English Horseman* (1607), *Markham's Method, or Epitome* (1616), and *The Faithful Farrier* (1635). His chief work on country occupations, *A Way to get Wealth* (1631–8), contains treatises on 'Cheap and Good Husbandry' (the management of domestic animals); 'Country Contentments' (hunting, hawking, fishing), with a section on the 'English Huswife' (cooking, dairying, physic); and agriculture and horticulture. (These treatises had been separately published earlier.) Other works include a poem about Sir Richard Grenville (1595) and *The English Arcadia* (prose, 1607). R. *Gittings in *Shakespeare's Rival* (1960) argues (after Fleay: see *DNB*) that he was the rival poet of the sonnets, and that Armado in *Love's Labours Lost* was based on him.

Markleham, Mrs, in Dickens's *David Copperfield*, familiarly known as the 'Old Soldier', was the mother-in-law of Copperfield's old schoolmaster at Canterbury, Dr Strong. Her nickname was due to the 'skill with which she marshalled great forces of relations against the Doctor'.

Mark Tapley, in Dickens's *Martin Chuzzlewit*, servant at the Dragon Inn, who leaves it to find some position in which it will be a credit to show his indomitable good humour. He becomes the devoted attendant of Martin during his American tour, and finally marries the hostess of the Dragon.

MARK TWAIN, see TWAIN, M.

Marley, Jacob, in Dickens's *A Christmas Carol*, Scrooge's late partner, whose ghost appears.

Marlow, (1) a character in and part-narrator of several of the works of J. *Conrad, including *Lord Jim*, *Heart of Darkness*, *Youth*, and *Chance*; (2) Sir Charles and his son, characters in Goldsmith's *She Stoops to Conquer*.

MARLOWE, Christopher (1564–93), son of a Canterbury shoemaker, was educated at the King's School, Canterbury, and Corpus Christi College, Cambridge. He became a BA in 1584, and MA, after some difficulty, in 1587. Though of excellent classical attainments, as his writings make clear, he seems to have been of a violent and at times criminal temperament. It is not clear whether visits he made to the Continent related to espionage. In 1589 he was involved in a street fight in which the poet T. *Watson killed a man; an injunction was brought against him by the constable of Shoreditch three years later. Early in 1592 he was deported from the Netherlands for attempting to issue forged gold coins. On 30 May 1593 he was killed by one Ingram Frizer (as *Hotson discovered) in a Deptford tavern after a quarrel over the bill; Marlowe was at the time under warrant to appear before the Privy Council on unknown charges. *Kyd and another friend, Richard Baines, testified after his death to his blasphemy and outrageous beliefs.

*The Tragedie of *Dido, Queene of Carthage*, published in 1594, may have been written while Marlowe was still at Cambridge, and in collaboration with *Nashe. Part I of *Tamburlaine* was written not later than 1587, and Part II in the following year; it was published in 1590. The next plays may have been *The Jew of Malta*, not published until 1633, and *Edward II*, published in 1594. The highly topical *Massacre at Paris*, which survives only in a fragmentary and undated text, and *Dr Faustus*, published 1604, may both belong to the last year of Marlowe's life. At various times he translated *Ovid's *Amores*, published without date as *All Ovids Elegies*, together with some of Sir John *Davies's 'Epigrammes'; wrote two books of an erotic narrative poem *Hero and Leander*, which was completed by G. *Chapman and published in 1598; made a fine blank verse rendering of *Lucans First Booke*, Book I of *Lucan's *Pharsalia*; and wrote the song 'Come live with me and be my love', published in *The Passionate Pilgrim* (1599) and *England's Helicon* (1600), with a reply by *Ralegh. In spite of his violent life Marlowe was an admired and highly influential figure: within weeks of his death *Peele paid tribute to him as 'Marley, the Muses darling for thy verse'. Shakespeare's early histories are strongly influenced by Marlowe, and he paid tribute to him in *As You Like It* as the 'dead shepherd'. *Jonson referred to 'Marlowes mighty line', and among others who praised him were Nashe, Chapman, G. *Harvey, and *Drayton. There are many modern editions of his plays and poems: the Revels Plays editions of the plays are to be recommended, and in the same series, Millar Maclure's edition of the *Poems* (1968).

MARMION, Shackerley (1603–39), educated at Wadham College, Oxford, served in the Netherlands, and joined *Suckling's expedition to Scotland in 1638, though he became ill en route and returned to London. He wrote three plays, *Hollands Leaguer* (1632), *A Fine Companion* (1633), and, his best, *The Antiquary* (performed ?1635, printed 1641). He also wrote a long verse narrative in heroic couplets, *Cupid and Psyche* (1637), and contributed verse to the

Annalia Dubrensia (see COTSWOLD OLIMPICK GAMES).

Marmion: *A Tale of Flodden Field*, a poem by Sir W. *Scott, published 1808.

The story is set in 1513. Lord Marmion, a fictitious character, a favourite of Henry VIII and a mixture of villainy and nobility, has tired of Constance de Beverley, a perjured nun who has followed him disguised as a page, and seeks to marry the wealthy Lady Clare, who is betrothed to Sir Ralph de Wilton. He accuses de Wilton of treason, proving it by a forged letter; he is helped by Constance, who hopes to regain her hold over him. She, however, is betrayed to her convent and walled up alive. Meanwhile, Marmion and de Wilton have fought in the lists, and the latter has been left for dead. Lady Clare goes to a convent to escape Marmion. He, while in Scotland, unknowingly encounters de Wilton, who has survived and is disguised as a palmer. The abbess of St Hilda, who has received from Constance the proofs of Marmion's crime, entrusts them to the palmer; having revealed himself to Clare, who is in attendance on the abbess, he escapes to the English camp. Marmion, with Clare in his train, joins the English forces at *Flodden, where he is killed. De Wilton and Clare are finally united.

The poem contains the two well-known songs 'Where shall the lover rest' and 'Lochinvar', and a beautiful introduction to each canto.

Marney, Lord, in *Sybil* by B. Disraeli.

Maro, see VIRGIL.

MAROT, Clément (1496–1544), French poet. He spent the greater part of his life in court service, and from 1527 was *valet de chambre* to Francis I. His Protestant sympathies led to arrest or exile on several occasions, and he spent some time in Italy and Geneva. He enjoyed great popularity in the 16th cent., developed the *rondeau* and *ballade*, and introduced a number of new forms into French poetry, including the elegy, the eclogue, the epigram, the epithalamium, and (probably) the Petrarchan sonnet. His translations of the Psalms were much admired by *Calvin, and were very frequently reprinted for some 200 years after his death.

Marplot, a character in Mrs Centlivre's *The Busie Body*.

Marprelate Controversy, see MARTIN MARPRELATE.

MÁRQUEZ, Gabriel García, see GARCÍA MÁRQUEZ, G.

Marriage, a novel by S. *Ferrier, published 1818.

Lady Juliana, the foolish and romantic daughter of the earl of Courtland, elopes with a penniless young officer, Henry Douglas, who takes her to his Highland home, a gaunt, lonely house, where she is greeted by 'three long-chinned spinsters' and 'five awkward purple girls'. The dismay of the worldly Juliana, and the characters of the household and of the neighbouring gentry, are presented with liveliness and wit. Lady Juliana gives birth to twin daughters, the climax of her misfortunes. The couple move to London, and Henry eventually joins a regiment in India, permanently separating from his wife. Of the twins, Mary is brought up in Scotland, and grows into a plain but a wise and sensible girl. She rejects her mother's choice of a wealthy husband for her, marries happily, and settles in Scotland. Adelaide, her sister, marries an ageing duke, and eventually elopes with a man as heartless as herself. The novel, which Sir W. *Scott greatly admired, is clearly intended to commend prudent marriage.

Marriage-à-la-Mode, a tragi-comedy by *Dryden produced 1672, published 1673.

The main plot concerns a usurper's discovery that his daughter and his (lawful) predecessor's son have been secretly reared together in rural seclusion, and have fallen idealistically in love. The comic plot is a double intrigue involving two friends and their pursuit respectively of the wife of the one and the betrothed of the other. The counterpointing of these contrasting plots is particularly striking, especially as each ends anti-climactically, the lawful heir being restored to his throne in an overtly stagey manner, and the adulterous lovers failing to consummate their affairs. The play contains some of Dryden's finest songs, and embodies the principles of comic writing outlined in his Preface to *An Evening's Love.

Marriage of Heaven and Hell, The, a prose work by W. *Blake, etched *c.*1790–3, introduced by a short poem ('Rintrah roars and shakes his fires in the burden'd air'). It consists of a sequence of paradoxical aphorisms in which Blake turns conventional morality on its head, claiming that man does not consist of the duality of Soul = Reason and Body = Evil, but that 'Man has no Body distinct from his Soul . . . Energy is the only life, and is from the Body . . . Energy is Eternal Delight.' He proceeds to claim that *Milton's Satan was truly his Messiah, and that Milton 'was a true Poet and of the Devil's party without knowing it', and to produce a series of 'Proverbs of Hell' ('Sooner murder an infant in its cradle than nurse unacted desires' being one of the most notorious), which also celebrate the holiness of the natural world. He then moves to a sequence of visionary encounters with angels and prophets, in the course of which he dismisses the writings of *Swedenborg (whom he had greatly admired) as 'a recapitulation of all superficial opinions', accuses him of not having conversed sufficiently with Devils but only with

Angels, and ends with an evocation of an Angel turned Devil 'who is my particular friend; we often read the Bible together in its infernal or diabolical sense . . .' The aphorisms, both in form and content, resemble the paradoxes of G. B. *Shaw, who greatly admired Blake and was much influenced by his doctrine of contraries; they were also adopted by those active in the counter-culture movement of the 1960s: see under UNDERGROUND POETRY.

Marrow of Modern Divinity, The, a book advocating Calvinistic views, written by E.F. (unidentified) in 1645, the condemnation of which in 1720 by the general assembly of the church of Scotland gave rise to the prolonged 'Marrow Controversy'.

MARRYAT, Captain Frederick (1792–1848), author, naval captain, and FRS. His first novel, *The Naval Officer: or Scenes and Adventures in the Life of Frank Mildmay* (1829), a partly autobiographical story of adventure at sea, was a success, and he resigned his commission in 1830, after which he wrote another 15 novels as well as many miscellaneous essays and articles. Among his most successful works, *Peter Simple* (1834), *Jacob Faithful* (1834), and *Mr *Midshipman Easy* (1836), all sea stories, were followed in 1836 by *Japhet in Search of a Father*, the story of the struggles of a foundling. In 1837 came *Snarleyyow*, the tale of an indestructible dog, in 1839 *The Phantom Ship*, and in 1840 *Poor Jack*. Between writing his novels he travelled widely in Europe, America, and Canada. With *Masterman Ready* (1841) he turned his attention to children's books, and it is chiefly for these he is remembered. *The Settlers in Canada* (1844) was followed by *Children of the New Forest* (1847), the popularity of which lasted well into this century.

MARSH, Sir Edward Howard (1872–1953), classicist, scholar, patron of modern poetry and painting, was a lifelong and eminent civil servant. An early champion of *Ibsen, he became a friend and executor of Rupert *Brooke, and between 1912 and 1922 edited five highly influential volumes of *Georgian Poetry. He edited Brooke's *Collected Poems*, with a long Memoir, in 1918; made many translations of classical and French authors, including *La Fontaine; and in 1939 published *A Number of People*, reminiscences of his many friends in the literary and political worlds. See C. Hassall, *Edward Marsh, patron of the arts* (1959).

MARSH, Dame Ngaio (pron. Ny-o) Edith (1899–1982), writer of *detective fiction, born at Christchurch, New Zealand. When young she worked as an actress and devoted much time in later life to theatre in New Zealand, an interest reflected in many of her novels. Her hero, Chief Detective Inspector Roderick Alleyn, first

appears in *A Man Lay Dead* (1934); other titles include *Vintage Murder* (1937), *Surfeit of Lampreys* (1941), *Died in the Wool* (1945), and *Final Curtain* (1947).

MARSTON, John (?1575–1634), dramatist, whose mother was Italian, graduated from Oxford in 1594, and joined his father, a lawyer, in the Middle Temple, where he maintained rooms until 1606. There he began to write satirical verse and plays for the new professional children's companies, playing at private indoor theatres. He took orders in 1609 and was incumbent of Christchurch, Hampshire, 1616–31. His *The Metamorphosis of Pigmalion's Image and certaine satyres* and *The Scourge of Villanie* (both 1598) were published under the pseudonym Kinsayder, under which name he figures in *The Returne from Parnassus* (see PARNASSUS PLAYS). Some of these satires were directed against literary rivals, including Bishop J. *Hall, and were burned by order of the archbishop of Canterbury in 1599. Marston's quarrel with *Jonson resulted in his portrayal as Crispinus in *The Poetaster*, but the two became friends again. His dramatic works were printed as follows: *The History of *Antonio and Mellida* (1602), of which *Antonio's Revenge* is the second part; *The Malcontent* (1604), with additions by *Webster; *Eastward Hoe* (1605), a comedy, written with Jonson and *Chapman; *The Dutch Courtezan* in the same year; *The Parasitaster*, a comedy, and *Sophonisba*, a tragedy (both 1606); *What you Will* (1607), a comedy; and *The Insatiate Countess* (1613), a tragedy (possibly completed by William Barksted). The plays were edited by H. H. Wood, 1934–9 (including the doubtfully assigned *Histriomastix*, 1610), the poems by A. Davenport, 1961. Wood, in line with most current critical opinion, gave highest praise to *The Malcontent* as 'one of the most original plays of its period', but T. S. *Eliot ('John Marston', 1934) somewhat eccentrically singled out *Sophonisba* for its 'exceptional consistency of texture' and 'underlying serenity'.

MARSTON, John Westland (1819–90), dramatic poet and critic, who contributed to the *Athenaeum, wrote several critical works, and more than a dozen plays, including the successful *The Patrician's Daughter*, which was performed at Drury Lane in 1842. His son, Philip Bourke Marston (1850–87), blinded in infancy, published several volumes of poems and short stories (*Collected Poems*, 1892). Their London home was a meeting place for many eminent friends in the theatrical and literary world, including *Kean, *Macready, *Dickens, *Swinburne, and D. G. *Rossetti.

Martext, Sir Oliver, vicar of a country parish in Shakespeare's *As You Like It*.

MARTIAL (Marcus Valerius Martialis) (c. AD

40–104) Roman epigrammatist of Spanish origin. His 1,500 epigrams, mostly satirical and often coarse, are very witty and have a great formal perfection. He found a translator in *May (1613) and was popular throughout the 17th cent. He influenced T. *Campion, *Jonson, *Herrick, and *Cowley. *Dryden thought him much inferior to *Virgil and *Lucan, but nevertheless quoted him a good deal. More recently he has been translated by P. *Porter (*After Martial*, 1972).

MARTIANUS CAPELLA (Marcian) (*fl.* 410–39), a North African writer, celebrated in the Middle Ages. He was the author of *De Nuptiis Philologiae et Mercurii* in nine books of prose and verse. The first two deal with the wooing (in a wide, metaphorical sense) of Philology by Mercury, and the last seven are an allegorical encyclopaedia of the *Seven Liberal Arts. This allegorization, together with that of the contemporary Prudentius, remained popular up to the Renaissance. Marcian is referred to by Chaucer in 'The Merchant's Tale' (*Canterbury Tales*, 10; IV. 1,732 ff.) and in *The House of Fame* (985). *Mulcaster is still using Martianus' method in his allegorizing of Philology in *The First Part of the Elementarie* (1582).

Martin, (1) in Dryden's *The Hind and the Panther*, symbolizes the Lutheran party; (2) in Swift's *A Tale of a Tub*, the Anglican Church, the allusion being to Martin Luther.

MARTIN, John (1789–1854), painter, came to London from Northumberland in 1806. He specialized in apocalyptic visions of landscapes torn apart by fire and flood, where man is reduced to a tiny struggling figure. From the 1820s date a succession of pictures showing the sensational destruction of the legendary cities of antiquity—of Babylon, Nineveh, Sodom and Gomorrah; these are vast paintings, where nightmare is made concrete by elaborate and often exotic architectural detail. Martin's relationship with literature was close; he illustrated Milton's *Paradise Lost* (1823–7); he drew subjects from *Gray, *Byron, and Mary *Shelley; he was extravagantly admired by poets and writers. It has been suggested that his *Sadak in search of the waters of Oblivion* (1812, Southampton Art Gallery) may have inspired a passage in Keats's *Hyperion*; Shelley wrote a poem to accompany the engraving, published in 1828. *Beckford took Martin to Fonthill (1823); the descriptions of gloom and grandeur in *Vathek* (1782) are close to the vision of the painter. *Bulwer-Lytton enthused over his works, and his *Last Days of Pompeii* (1834) is indebted to Martin. Through his prints Martin became a widely popular artist; they were copied by both Branwell and Charlotte *Brontë, and Martin's fantastic cities influenced the imagery of their juvenilia: Martin himself plays a role as Edward

de Lisle of Verdopolis, painter of Babylon. He was widely acclaimed in France; *Hugo drew images from him; Romantic writers use the world 'Martinien' to describe the spectacular and grandiose. Martin's paintings are the astonishing swan-song of the taste for the Burkeian *sublime; he was vigorously attacked by *Ruskin, and by the end of the century his reputation had fallen dramatically. None the less something of his magnificence lingered on in the lavish productions of Cecil B. de Mille.

MARTIN, Sir Theodore (1816–1909), educated at Edinburgh University, practised as a solicitor in Edinburgh and moved to London in 1846. He contributed, under the pseudonym *'Bon Gaultier', to *Tait's Magazine* and *Fraser's Magazine*, and collaborated with W. E. *Aytoun in the writing of the 'Bon Gaultier ballads', published in 1845. He also translated many works from German, Latin, Danish, and Italian, wrote a life of Prince Albert (5 vols, 1875–80), reminiscences of Queen *Victoria (*Queen Victoria as I knew her*, 1902), and other memoirs and monographs.

Martin Chuzzlewit, The Life and Adventures of, a novel by *Dickens, published 1843–4.

Martin, the hero, is the grandson of old Martin Chuzzlewit, a wealthy gentleman made misanthropical by the greed of his family. The old man has reared Mary Graham, a young orphan, to look after him, and regards her as his daughter. Young Martin is in love with Mary; but the grandfather, mistrusting his selfish character, repudiates him and gets him dismissed from his position as pupil to his cousin Mr Pecksniff, architect and arch-hypocrite. Martin, accompanied by the indomitably cheerful Mark Tapley as his servant, sails for America to seek his fortune. He goes as an architect to the fraudulent Eden Land Corporation, where he loses his money and nearly dies of fever. (This part gave great offence in the US.) He then returns to England, his experiences having reformed his selfish attitudes. His grandfather has meanwhile established himself and Mary in Pecksniff's household and pretended to place himself under his direction, thus satisfying himself of Pecksniff's meanness and treachery. (Pecksniff tries to inveigle and bully Mary into marrying him.) He exposes the hypocrite, restores his grandson to favour, and gives him Mary's hand.

A sub-plot concerns Jonas Chuzzlewit, the son of old Martin's brother, a character of almost incredible villainy. He murders his father (in intention if not in fact); marries Mercy Pecksniff and treats her with the utmost brutality; murders the director of a bogus insurance company, by whom he has been taken in and blackmailed; is detected; and finally poisons himself.

The book contains many pleasant minor characters: Tom Pinch, Pecksniff's gentle loyal assistant, and his sister Ruth; Pecksniff's daughters Charity and Mercy (Cherry and Merry); and Mrs Gamp, the disreputable old nurse; while 'Todgers's' is an eccentric London boarding-house.

MARTIN DU GARD, Roger, see ROMAN FLEUVE.

MARTINEAU, Harriet (1802–76), was born in Norwich; her childhood and youth were dogged by illness and poverty. A devout Unitarian in youth, her first published work was *Devotional Exercises* (1823), from which time she wrote indefatigably for the rest of her life. She began to review for the *Monthly Repository*, then in 1830 won all three prizes in an essay competition set by the Unitarians. Between 1832 and 1834 she published a series of stories, *Illustrations of Political Economy*, revealing both her passion for social reform and the influence of *Bentham and J. S. *Mill. The stories were immensely successful, as were her tales for *Brougham's Society for the Diffusion of Useful Knowledge, and she became a literary celebrity, including among her friends *Malthus, Sydney *Smith, and *Milnes, as well as politicians who consulted her on economic and social matters. In 1834 she travelled in America, and supported the abolitionists at some personal risk. *Society in America* appeared in 1837, and her first novel, *Deerbrook* (always her favourite among her works), in 1839. *The Hour and the Man*, a biography of *Toussaint L'Ouverture, came out in 1840, and a book of children's stories, *The Playfellow*, in 1841. In 1845 she settled in the Lake District and became a friend of the *Wordsworths. She had by now repudiated her Unitarian faith, and indeed all religious belief. Her radical *History of the Thirty Years' Peace* was published in 1849, and her anti-theological *Laws of Man's Social Nature* in 1851. Her translation and condensation of *Comte, *The Philosophy of Comte*, appeared in 1853. For most of the rest of her life she continued energetically with her journalism, and wrote a book which appeared posthumously as *An Autobiographical Memoir*, containing many observations on public and literary figures of her day. On several occasions she refused the offer of a civil list pension, feeling it would compromise her independence.

MARTINEAU, James (1805–1900), brother of Harriet *Martineau, was educated at Norwich Grammar School and Manchester New College, where, after working as a Unitarian minister at Dublin and Liverpool, he was appointed professor of moral philosophy in 1840; he was principal of the college from 1869 to 1885. He was an ardent upholder of the theist position, a powerful critic of materialism and naturalism, and was prompt to recognize the claims of the Darwinian philosophy of evolution. His chief books, mainly philosophical religious works,

were mostly published after his 80th year. These include *Types of Ethical Theory* (1885), *A Study in Religion* (1887), and *The Seat of Authority in Religion* (1890). He also wrote a *Study of Spinoza* (1882), contributed to the *National Review* and was joint editor of the *Prospective Review* (1845–54). (See UNITARIANISM.)

Martin Eden, a novel by J. *London.

MARTIN MARPRELATE, the name assumed by the authors of a number of anonymous pamphlets (seven are extant) issued in 1588–9 from a secret press, containing attacks in a railing, rollicking style on the bishops, and defending the Presbyterian system of discipline. They were stimulated by Archbishop *Whitgift's attempts to impose uniformity in liturgical practice and to promote royal supremacy and the authority of the Articles.

The Marprelate tracts are among the best prose satires of the Elizabethan age. Their titles (in abbreviated form) are: *The Epistle, The Epitome, Minerall and Metaphisicall Schoolpoints, Hay any worke for Cooper* (a familiar street cry, here alluding to Thomas Cooper, bishop of Westminster), *Martin Junior, Martin Senior,* and *The Protestatyon*. As well as ballads, rhymes, and plays, they provoked replies from such noted writers as *Lyly and *Nashe; Gabriel and Richard *Harvey later became involved in the controversy. But the replies are on the whole less entertaining than the original pamphlets. *Hooker's work eventually settled the matter for the Church. The suspected authors, a Welshman named Penry and a clergyman named Udall, were arrested. The latter died in prison, the former was executed. Their collaborator, Job Throckmorton, denied his complicity at the trial of Penry, and escaped punishment.

Martinus Scriblerus, Memoirs of, a satirical work, directed against 'false tastes in learning', initiated by the *Scriblerus Club and written mainly by *Arbuthnot. It was printed in the second volume of *Pope's prose works in 1741. Martinus is the son of Cornelius, an antiquary of Munster, and the description of his birth, christening, education, and travels is a burlesque on various forms of contemporary pedantry.

The name 'Martin Scriblerus' was occasionally used by Pope as a pseudonym, and by *Crabbe in some of his earlier poems.

MARTYN, Edward (1859–1923), born in the west of Ireland and educated in England; he was one of the founders of the *Irish Literary Theatre in 1899, as well as an ardent supporter of Irish educational and musical activities. His best-known plays are *The Heather Field* (chosen as one of the plays to open the Literary Theatre in 1899) and *Maeve* (1899), a drama of Anglo-Irish antagonism. He is caricatured as 'dead Edward' in G. A. *Moore's *Hail and Farewell*.

MARVELL, Andrew (1621–78), son of the Revd Andrew Marvell, was born at Winstead in Holderness, Yorks. In 1624 the family (Andrew, his parents, and three older sisters) moved to Hull on his father's appointment as lecturer at Holy Trinity Church. Marvell attended Hull Grammar School. He matriculated at Trinity College, Cambridge, as a sizar in Dec. 1633, being elected to a scholarship in April 1638 and graduating BA in 1639. In 1637 he had contributed Greek and Latin verses to a Cambridge volume congratulating Charles I on the birth of a daughter. His mother died in April 1638, his father remarrying in November. Around 1639 Marvell may have come under the influence of Roman Catholic proselytizers: according to one story he went to London with them and was fetched back by his father. In January 1641 his father was drowned while crossing the Humber, and soon after Marvell left Cambridge for London. Between 1643 and 1647 he travelled for four years in Holland, France, Italy, and Spain, learning languages and fencing, and perhaps deliberately avoiding the civil war (he said later that 'the Cause was too good to have been fought for'). On his return from the Continent he apparently moved in London literary circles and had friends among Royalists. His poems to *Lovelace ('his Noble Friend') and on the death of Lord Hastings were published in 1649. In the early summer of 1650 he wrote 'An Horatian Ode upon Cromwell's Return from Ireland', perhaps the greatest political poem in English.

From 1650 to 1652 Marvell tutored young Mary Fairfax, daughter of the parliamentarian general, at Nun Appleton in Yorkshire. In this period, it is usually assumed, he wrote 'Upon Appleton House' and lyrics such as 'The Garden' and the Mower poems. In 1653 he was appointed tutor to Cromwell's ward William Dutton, and moved to John Oxenbridge's house at Eton, where he probably wrote 'Bermudas'. In 1654 with 'The First Anniversary' (published 1655) he began his career as unofficial laureate to *Cromwell, and was appointed in 1657 Latin secretary to the Council of State (a post previously occupied by his friend and sponsor *Milton, now blind). For eight months during 1656 Marvell was in Saumur with Dutton, where he was described as 'a notable English Italo-Machiavellian'. He mourned Cromwell in 'Upon the Death of His late Highness the Lord Protector' (1658) and took part in the funeral procession. The following year (January) he was elected MP for Hull, and remained one of the Hull members until his death. At the Restoration his influence secured Milton's release from prison.

From June 1662 to April 1663 Marvell was in Holland on unknown political business, possibly espionage, and in July 1663 he travelled with the earl of Carlisle as private secretary on his embassy to Russia, Sweden, and Denmark, returning in January 1665. His satires against *Clarendon were written and published in 1667. Later that year he composed his finest satire 'Last Instructions to a Painter', attacking financial and sexual corruption at Court and in Parliament, and took part in the impeachment of Clarendon. *The Rehearsal Transpros'd*, a controversial prose work advocating toleration for Dissenters, which set new standards of irony and urbanity, appeared in 1672 (Part II, 1673). Gilbert *Burnet called these 'the wittiest books that have appeared in this age', and Charles II apparently read them 'over and over again'. According to the report of government spies, Marvell (under the codename 'Mr Thomas') was during 1674 a member of a fifth column promoting Dutch interests in England, and in touch with Dutch secret agents. The second edition of *Paradise Lost* contained a commendatory poem by Marvell, and in his prose works he continued to wage war against arbitrary royal power. *Mr Smirk, Or the Divine in Mode* and *A Short Historical Essay Concerning General Councils* (both 1676), and *An Account of the Growth of Popery and Arbitrary Government in England* (1677), were all Marvell's though prudently published anonymously. The *London Gazette* offered a reward, in March 1678, for information about the author or printer of *An Account*. That August, however, Marvell died in his house in Great Russell Street from medical treatment prescribed for a tertian ague. His *Miscellaneous Poems* appeared in 1681, printed from papers found in his rooms by his housekeeper Mary Palmer, who gave herself out to be his widow and signed the Preface 'Mary Marvell' in order to get her hands on £500 which Marvell had been keeping for two bankrupt friends. This volume did not contain the satires (the authorship of some of which is still disputed): these appeared in *Poems on Affairs of State* (1689–97).

The history of Marvell's reputation is extraordinary. Famed in his day as patriot, satirist, and foe to tyranny, he was virtually unknown as a lyric poet. Even when his poems were published in 1681, they were greeted by two centuries of neglect. C. *Lamb started a gradual revival, but Marvell's poems were more appreciated in 19th-cent. America than in England. It was not until after the First World War, with *Grierson's *Metaphysical Lyrics* and T. S. *Eliot's 'Andrew Marvell', that the modern high estimation of his poetry began to prevail. In the second half of the 20th cent. his small body of lyrics has been subjected to more exegetical effort than the work of any other *metaphysical poet. His oblique, ironic, and finally enigmatic way of treating what are often quite conventional poetic materials (as in 'The Nymph Complaining for the death of her Faun' or 'To his Coy Mistress') has especially intrigued the modern mind.

Poems and Letters, ed. H. M. Margoliouth, 3rd edn rev. P. Legouis and E. E. Duncan-Jones (2 vols, 1971); *Latin Poems*, ed. and trans. W. A. McQueen and K. A. Rockwell (1964); *The Rehearsal Transpros'd*, ed. D. E. B. Smith (1971); P. Legouis, *Andrew Marvell: poet, Puritan, patriot* (2nd edn, 1968); H. Kelliher, *Andrew Marvell: Poet and Politician* (1978).

Marwood, Mrs, a character in Congreve's *The Way of the World*.

MARX, Karl (1818–83), born in Rhenish Prussia, of Jewish descent, was editor of the *Rheinische Zeitung* at Cologne in 1842. His extreme radical views led to the suppression of the paper, and Marx went to Paris, where he met *Engels and collaborated with him in works of political philosophy. He was expelled from Paris, moved to Brussels, and at the time of the revolutionary movement of 1848 returned to Cologne, where, with Engels, he again conducted a newspaper, the *Neue Rheinische Zeitung*. His revolutionary and communistic views caused him to be once more expelled, and he finally settled in London. He and Engels wrote about contemporary politics and society in England, finding in *Carlyle's works, particularly *Latter-Day Pamphlets* (1850), the only example of proper concern on the part of a British writer for the social condition of workers. They adopted Carlyle's rhetoric about the 'cash nexus' connecting worker, product, and manufacturer, but they differed radically from Carlyle's proposed solution to the misery of the working class in a return to a feudal system of government.

In 1867 appeared the first volume of Marx's treatise *Das Kapital*, in which he propounded his theory of political economy. After the death of Marx this was completed from his papers by Engels. It is a criticism of the capitalistic system under which, according to Marx, a diminishing number of capitalists appropriate the benefits of improved industrial methods, while the labouring class are left in increasing dependency and misery. Marx holds the view that the price of a commodity should be the remuneration of the labour required to produce it, and that it fails to be this because capital exacts a share of the price, while competition among the workers obliges them to accept less than their proper due. The remedy for this state of things Marx finds in the total abolition of private property, to be effected by the class war. When the community has acquired possession of all property and the means of production, it will distribute work to each individual and provide him with the means of sustenance: 'From everyone according to his faculties, to everyone according to his needs.'

Marx was the principal creator of the First International Working Men's Council.

Marxist Literary Criticism, a term used to cover a wide variety of interpretations of and attitudes towards literature, but always involving the recognition that literature, in both form and content, is profoundly influenced by historical, economic, and social forces. *Marx and *Engels themselves did not develop a systematic aesthetic theory, and their many observations on literature and art are found in essentially philosophical, economic, or political works and in their letters. Subsequently a large and varied body of work has arisen which seeks to develop a Marxist aesthetic, and which uses the work of later Marxist writers (*Lenin, *Trotsky, *Gramsci, the French philosopher Louis Althusser, 1918–) and related intellectual influences (*Freudian criticism, *Structuralism). The dominant figure is *Lukács, whose concept of 'critical realism' argued that the work of avowedly non-Socialist writers (e.g. *Balzac, Sir W. *Scott) could transcend the writers' own ideological limitations and reveal the fundamental tensions of their times. Since Lukács, nearly all Marxist criticism has been West European rather than British in origin (e.g. Walter Benjamin, 1892–1940; Lucien Goldmann, 1913–70; Pierre Macherey). Eastern European critics have been prescriptive rather than analytic, concerned to foster *Socialist Realism. The first English Marxist critic of note is C. *Caudwell. In post-war years the most significant figure is R. *Williams, whose work has moved from a general 'left Leavisite' concern with the social and cultural context of writers to an increasing engagement with problems in Marxist cultural theory. Terry Eagleton (1943–), originally a student of Williams at Cambridge, has assimilated influences from continental writers and critics (e.g. Macherey; Michel Foucault, 1926– ; Jacques Lacan, 1901– ; Jacques Derrida, 1930–) to a greater extent than Williams.

Many other critics have absorbed or intermittently utilized the insights of Marxist theory. *Steiner says, 'The Marxist sensibility has contributed a sociological awareness to the best of modern criticism', and notes in support the illumination shed by *Trilling on *Dostoevsky, by L. C. *Knights on Elizabethan drama, and by Q. D. *Leavis on the reading public ('Marxism and the Literary Critic', *Language and Silence*, 1967). The work of *Hoggart also shows a marked awareness of cultural influences on writers and readers.

Mary, in Dickens's *Pickwick Papers*, Mr Nupkins's pretty housemaid, who marries Sam Weller.

Mary Barton, *A Tale of Manchester Life*, a novel by Mrs *Gaskell, published 1848.

The entirely working-class cast of characters in this novel was then an innovation. The background of the story is Manchester in the 'hungry forties' and the acute poverty of the unemployed mill-hands. Mary Barton is the daughter of an active and embittered worker and trade unionist, John Barton. She has attracted Henry Carson, son of one of the employers, and, flattered by his attentions and the hope of a grand marriage, has repulsed in his favour her faithful admirer Jem Wilson, a young engineering worker. A group of workmen, exasperated by the failure of the employers to consider their grievances, decide to kill young Carson (who has mocked their attempts to reach an understanding), as a warning to his class, and the lot falls on Barton to do the deed. When Carson is shot dead suspicion falls on Jem Wilson as his rival with Mary, and she, who has by now realized that it is Jem whom she loves, discovers that her father is the real murderer. Jem is tried for his life, and is saved by Mary's frantic and finally successful efforts to prove his innocence without betraying her father. Made desperate by his guilt, John Barton confesses to the fiercely vindictive old father of Henry Carson, and wins his forgiveness as he dies.

The book was violently attacked by Manchester mill-owners and the Tory press as being biased against the employers, but it was admired by *Carlyle and *Dickens and was translated into many languages, including Finnish and Hungarian.

Mary Graham, a character in Dickens's *Martin Chuzzlewit*.

Mary Magdalene, *Play of,* the only surviving play in late medieval English drama which is based on the legend of a saint, presenting events in the saint's life both before the Resurrection and during her subsequent legendary residence in Provence. It is a very long play, in the Digby set, in two parts, 52 scenes and 2,144 lines. It has some claims to sophistication and is dedicated to 'Miles Blomefylde' whose name appears as *Poeta* in the Digby 'The Conversion of St Paul'.

Digby Plays, ed. F. J. *Furnivall (EETS ES 70, 1896, reprinted 1967, pp. 55–136); D. L. Jeffrey, 'English Saints' Plays' in *Medieval Drama,* ed. N. Denny (1973).

'Mary Morison', a lyric by *Burns, published 1786, possibly addressed to Alison Begbie, one of his youthful loves.

MARY QUEEN OF SCOTS (Mary Stuart) (1542–87), daughter of James V of Scotland, married Francis II of France (1558), Lord Darnley (1565), and *Bothwell (1567). She was imprisoned by *Elizabeth I and finally beheaded on a charge of conspiring against the latter's life. She figures in Scott's *The Abbot,* and is the subject of a tragedy by *Schiller, of a trilogy of plays by *Swinburne, and of the novel *The Queen's Quair* by M. *Hewlett; she also figures in *Baring's *In My End is My Beginning* (1931).

Mascarille, a type of clever impudent valet, occurring in three of *Molière's comedies, *L'Étourdi, Le Dépit amoureux,* and *Les Précieuses ridicules.* In this last it is he who, in the character of a marquis and in the clothes of his master, makes love to the *précieuses,* in order to render them ridiculous.

MASEFIELD, John Edward (1878–1967), born in Herefordshire; his idyllic early childhood was vital to his later work, but in 1884 his mother died and he was brought up by relatives. School in Warwick was followed at the age of 13 by training for the merchant navy. In 1894 Masefield sailed for Chile, suffered acutely from sea-sickness, endured some kind of breakdown, and was returned home. He sailed again across the Atlantic, but at the age of 17 deserted ship and became a vagrant in America, taking what jobs he could find, reading voraciously, and writing verse. Back in England he began his prolific writing career, which was eventually to compass some 50 volumes of verse, over 20 novels, eight plays, and much miscellaneous work. His first published book, *Salt-Water Ballads* (which included 'I must go down to the sea again'), was received with interest in 1902. Masefield joined the *Manchester Guardian* in 1907. *Ballads and Poems* (1910), which contained 'Cargoes', was followed by the first of many narrative poems, *The Everlasting Mercy,* which in its account of the conversion of the rough Saul Kane, provoked some indignation. *The Widow in the bye street* (1912) was similarly pungent, and *Reynard the Fox* (1919) was a rattling verse tale set in the rural world of Masefield's childhood. Meanwhile he had produced collections of shorter verse, as well as stories, novels, and plays: his *Collected Poems* (1923) sold in great numbers, as did the novels *Sard Harker* (1924), *Odtaa* (1926), *The Bird of Dawning* (1933), and his story for children *The Midnight Folk* (1927). In 1930 Masefield became poet laureate and in 1935 received the OM. He continued to write with energy, producing more volumes of poetry, the sea-novels *Dead Ned* (1938) and *Live and Kicking Ned* (1939) and the autobiographical *So Long to Learn* (1952). A final luminous fragment of autobiography, describing his country childhood up to his mother's death, appeared in 1966 as *Grace before Ploughing*.

Masefield's great reputation sank rapidly in the 1930s, but his major narrative verse, many of his lyrics, and some of his prose are once again highly regarded. There is a life by C. Babington Smith, published 1978.

Mask of Anarchy, The, a poem of political protest by P. B. *Shelley, written in response to the 'Peterloo Massacre' at Manchester in August 1819, published 1832.

Composed at speed and in anger, the poem

uses the popular ballad form with immense power and sometimes surreal effect. The 'mask' is a pageant, or masquerade, of British political leaders—Castlereagh, Eldon, Sidmouth—whom Shelley blames not only for the killing and wounding of some 500 people at a public demonstration for parliamentary reform, but also for the general conditions of harshness and oppression in England: what he calls the 'triumph of Anarchy' (compare *'The Triumph of Life'). Anarchy rides on a horse: 'He was pale even to the lips, | Like Death in the Apocalypse.' His bloody progress is only prevented by Hope, 'a Maniac maid', who throws herself under the trampling hooves. The poem ends with a celebration of freedom, and Shelley's historic appeal for non-violent mass political protest in a great assembly of working people: 'Rise like lions after slumber | In unvanquishable number.'

Masks, see MASQUES.

Maskwell, the *'Double Dealer' in Congreve's comedy of that name, 'a sedate, thinking villain, whose black blood runs temperately bad'.

MASON, A(lfred) E(dward) W(oodley) (1865–1948), failed actor turned successful novelist, is best remembered for *The Four Feathers* (1902, film version, 1939), the story of Harry Feversham's heroism in redeeming himself from the accusation of cowardice in the eyes of three fellow officers and his beloved, Ethne Eustace. His many other popular works include the series featuring Inspector Hanaud, which began with *At the Villa Rose* (1910).

Mason, Mary, Lady, the principal character in A. Trollope's novel *Orley Farm*.

MASON, William (1725–97), poet, and friend of T. *Gray and Horace *Walpole, with both of whom he corresponded; he became Gray's executor, edited his poems and letters, and wrote his life. His own work includes the tragedies *Elfrida* (1751) and *Caractacus* (1759); the latter clearly shows the influence of Gray's interest in *primitivism in its subject, its *Pindaric odes, and its chorus of bards. He also wrote a long blank verse poem on landscape gardening, *The English Garden* (4 books, 1771–81), which expresses his enthusiasm for the *picturesque.

Masora(h), or **Massora(h),** the body of traditional information relating to the text of the Hebrew Bible, compiled by Jewish scholars in the 10th and preceding cents; or the collection of critical notes in which this information is preserved. Also occasionally used as a collective name for the scholars (*Masoretes*) whose opinions are embodied in the *Masora*, and to whom is ascribed the constitution of the present Hebrew text and the addition of the vowel points, etc.

Masques, or **Masks,** dramatic entertainments involving dances and disguises, in which the spectacular and musical elements predominated over plot and character. They were acted indoors by amateurs, and were designed to include their spectators in the action, sometimes simply by a concluding dance. As they were usually performed at court, often at very great expense, many have political overtones. They were perhaps of Italian origin, but assumed a distinctive character in England in the 16th and 17th cents. Many of the great poets and dramatists, S. *Daniel, T. *Campion, G. *Chapman, and T. *Middleton, wrote masques, and they reached their highest degree of elaboration in the hands of *Jonson who introduced the 'anti-masque' as a comic and grotesque foil to the main spectacle. The great architect Inigo *Jones designed the machinery or decoration (the 'Painting and carpentry' as Jonson scathingly dismissed them) for some of them. Jonson's *The Sad Shepherd*, Milton's *A Maske*, better known as *Comus*, and other such works often called masques, can only be loosely assigned to the genre, and are closer to *pastoral dramas.

Massacre at Paris, The, a play by *Marlowe written c.1592. The undated first edition (c.1593/4) describes it as having been acted by the Admiral's Men. It is a short and poor text, probably representing a mangled version of what Marlowe wrote. A single leaf surviving in manuscript used to be thought to be a forgery by J. P. *Collier, but is now believed to be a fragment of an authentic acting version.

The play deals with the massacre of Protestants in Paris on St Bartholomew's day, 24 August, 1572 (an event witnessed by P. *Sidney, who was staying in Paris at the time). Its most memorable character is the Machiavellian duke of Guise, whose high aspiring language seems to have influenced Shakespeare in his early history plays. The massacre is depicted in a series of short episodes, a notable one being that in which the rhetorician *Ramus is killed after a verbal onslaught by the Guise on his emendations of Aristotle. The Guise himself is eventually murdered at the behest of Henry III, dying on the lines:

> Vive la messe! Perish Huguenots!
> Thus Caesar did go forth, and thus he died.

whose relationship to Shakespeare's *Julius Caesar* (II. ii. 10, 28, 48) has not been satisfactorily explained. Leaping over 17 years, the play concludes with the murder of Henry III and the succession of the (then) Protestant Henry of Navarre. It is difficult to tell whether the frequent comic effect of the play is authorially intended or is the result of the incompleteness of the text. Ed. H. J. Oliver (1968).

Massacre of St Bartholomew, see BARTHOLOMEW, MASSACRE OF ST.

MASSINGER, Philip (1583–1640), was

born at Salisbury, and educated at St Alban Hall, Oxford. His father was the trusted agent of the Herbert family, to members of which the playwright addressed various dedications and poems. He became the chief collaborator of J. *Fletcher after the withdrawal of *Beaumont, and on Fletcher's death in 1625 he became the principal dramatist of the King's Men. He was buried in Fletcher's grave at St Saviour's, Southwark (now Southwark Cathedral).

He is known to have written or shared in the writing of 55 plays. Of these 22 are lost. Of the extant plays 15 are of his sole composition, 16 were written in collaboration with Fletcher, and two in collaboration with others. Massinger's share in the Fletcher plays was given no acknowledgement in the Beaumont and Fletcher folios, but has been identified with reasonable accuracy by modern scholars. He shared with Fletcher the writing of such plays as *The Custom of the Country (?1619–22), Sir John Van Olden *Barnavelt (1619), The Double Marriage (?1621), *The Beggars' Bush (?1622) and A Very Woman (?1625) and with Fletcher and others collaborated in *The Bloody Brother (c.1616). With *Dekker he shared the writing of a religious play, *The Virgin Martyr, a work uncharacteristic of both men. With N. *Field he wrote *The Fatal Dowry, in which his high romantic seriousness blends strikingly with Field's satire.

He wrote only two social comedies, *A New Way to Pay Old Debts and *The City Madam. A New Way was a mainstay of the English stage in the late 18th and early 19th cents, with the villainous Sir Giles Overreach providing a vehicle for the talents of a long line of actors including *Kemble and *Kean. Both plays are inspired by his patrician contempt for the ambitions and affectations of the rising mercantile classes in the city. Two amusing and sophisticated but much more romantic comedies are The Guardian (1633) and his feminist play The Picture (1629).

He wrote several excellent tragedies. The early *Duke of Milan, a tragedy of jealousy, was followed by *The Roman Actor, which was his favourite play. It makes remarkable use of plays-within-the-play, and in the person of Paris the actor he was able to show something of his own prolonged difficulties with political censorship. Because of this censorship he was forced to do a complete rewriting of *Believe As You List, perhaps his greatest tragedy. It is a powerful story of a returned nationalist leader failing to get support and being hounded by the imperial authorities.

The remainder of his plays are in the Fletcherian vein of tragi-comedy. These include *The Maid of Honour, *The Bondman, The Renegado, and The Great Duke of Florence (perf. 1627, printed 1636).

The equable and lucid verse of Massinger's plays, once a big point in their favour, went out of fashion when *Webster and *Tourneur became better known, and it may well be that a lack of interest in the linguistic texture of his plays is the reason for the present comparative neglect of one of the most serious professional dramatists of the post-Shakespearian period.

The standard edition of Massinger's plays is by Philip Edwards and Colin Gibson (5 vols, 1976). The most recent biographical and critical study is T. A. Dunn, Philip Massinger (1957).

MASSINGHAM, H(arold) J(ohn) (1888–1952), eldest son of H. W. *Massingham, published many works reflecting a deep appreciation of many aspects of the English countryside and natural history; they include The English Countryman (1942).

MASSINGHAM, H(enry) W(illiam) (1860–1924), described by his friend G. B. *Shaw as 'the perfect master journalist' was the influential editor of The Nation from 1907 to 1923, when he resigned in response to a change in its political intentions.

MASSON, David (1822–1907), biographer, critic, journalist, was successively professor of English literature at University College London (1853) and Edinburgh University (1865). He is remembered for his standard Life of Milton (7 vols, 1859–94), now superseded. He was a disciple of *Carlyle, and became the founder and editor of *Macmillan's Magazine (1859). His other works include biographies of *Drummond of Hawthornden (1873) and *De Quincey (1881), editions of *Milton, *Goldsmith, and De Quincey, and Essays Biographical and Critical (1856). His Edinburgh Sketches and Memories (1892), Memories of London in the Forties (1908), and Memories of Two Cities (1911) are accounts of literary circles in mid-century London and Scotland.

Massora(h), Masorete, see MASORA(H).

Master Humphrey's Clock, a weekly founded by *Dickens in 1840, originally intended as a miscellany which would contain a continuous narrative (*The Old Curiosity Shop) linked by the reminiscences of the narrator, Master Humphrey. This device was soon dropped, as was the periodical's title after the publication in weekly numbers of *Barnaby Rudge (1841).

MASTERMAN, C(harles) F(rederick) G(urney) (1874–1927), Liberal politician, author, and journalist, whose writings describe, with a mixture of Christian Socialist sympathy, Edwardian–Georgian nostalgia, and apprehension, the changing social conditions of England. From the Abyss (1902) is an impressionistic collection of essays about slum life; In Peril of Change (1905) collects essays on literary and social topics, including the telling piece 'In

Dejection near Tooting', in which he reflects on the ravaged landscape and hideous architecture of London's dumping ground; *The Condition of England* (1909) laments a 'land of radiant beauty' and expresses fears for a nation acquiring social improvements without spiritual renewal. Samuel Hynes, in *The Edwardian Turn of Mind* (1968), suggests that part of Masterman's weakness as a practical politician lay in his dependence on imaginative literature rather than politics or economics. He was a friend of F. M. *Ford, and inspired the portrait of the Liberal minister Waterhouse in *Parade's End.

Masterman Ready, see MARRYAT, F.

Master of Ballantrae, The: *A Winter's Tale*, a novel by R. L. *Stevenson, published 1889.

It is the story of the lifelong feud between the Master of Ballantrae, violent, unscrupulous, elegant, and courageous, and his younger brother Henry, at the outset a quiet, dull, honest fellow. The Master joins Prince Charles Edward in the '45 rebellion, disappears after Culloden, and is believed dead. After many adventures the Master returns, with a price on his head, to find that Henry has succeeded to his place and the woman whom he was to have married. Embittered by misfortune, he embarks on a course of persecution, first in Scotland then in America, which brings both brothers to an untimely grave in the Adirondacks, where Stevenson first conceived the story. The extravagant action and the hints of the supernatural are rendered more plausible by the character of the dour narrator, the unimaginative but loyal Ephraim Mackellar.

MASTERS, Edgar Lee (?1868–1950), American poet and novelist, born in Kansas, who is best known for his collection of poems *Spoon River Anthology* (1915), which consists of dramatic monologues spoken from beyond the grave by the inhabitants of a Midwestern cemetery.

MATHER, Cotton (1663–1728), Presbyterian divine of Boston, Massachusetts, a narrow, self-righteous minister and voluminous writer, one of the best-known examples of the tyrannical Puritan ministers of his time in New England. He was noted for the part he played in the Salem witchcraft trials of 1692, on which he commented in his best-known work, *Magnalia Christi Americana* (1702).

MATHIAS, Thomas James (?1754–1835), published anonymously in 1794 the first part of *The Pursuits of Literature*, a work which went through 16 editions, in which he satirizes many contemporary authors, most of them radicals; other parts followed in 1797. He became librarian at Buckingham Palace in 1812. In 1817, pursuing an ardent love of Italy and Italian literature, he moved to the Continent, and spent his last years at Naples.

MATISSE, Henri, see FAUVES, LES.

'Matter of Britain, The', the term used by Jean Bodel (late 12th–early 13th cent.) in a French verse romance about *Charlemagne (dating from the late 12th cent.) to describe the subject-matter of the romances concerned with the Arthurian legends, as distinct from those concerned with classical stories (the *matter of Rome), or with Charlemagne and his circle (the *matter of France). The 'matter of Britain' was a source of inspiration in the 20th cent. for D. *Jones and C. *Williams.

'Matter of England, The', a term sometimes used by 20th-cent. scholars to refer to romances concerned with English heroes or localized in England (such as *King Horn or *Havelok the Dane), which therefore fall outside the three subject-matters said by Jean Bodel to be the only ones: the matters of Britain (above), Rome, and France (below).

'Matter of France, The', the term used by Jean Bodel, a late 12th-cent. romance writer, to refer to the romances based on stories about *Charlemagne and his circle, as distinct from those based on Arthurian (the *matter of Britain) or classical (the *matter of Rome) legend.

'Matter of Rome, The', the term used by Jean Bodel, a late 12th-cent. French romance writer, to refer to those romances concerned with classical stories, as distinct from Arthurian (the *matter of Britain) or *Charlemagne legends (the *matter of France).

MATTHEW PARIS, see PARIS, M.

Matthews, Miss, a character in Fielding's *Amelia.

Matthew's Bible, see BIBLE, THE ENGLISH.

Matty, Miss (Matilda Jenkyns), the principal character in Mrs Gaskell's *Cranford.

MATURIN, Charles Robert (1782–1824), educated at Trinity College, Dublin, took orders and for a time kept a school. He was one of the most important writers of the *'Gothic' novel. He published *The Fatal Revenge* in 1807; *The Wild Irish Boy* in 1808; and *The Milesian Chief* in 1811. In 1816 his tragedy *Bertram was produced by *Kean at Drury Lane, on the recommendation of Sir W. *Scott and *Byron, with great success. His next two tragedies, *Manuel* (1817) and *Fredolfo* (1819), were failures. He then returned to novels, publishing *Women, or Pour et Contre* (1818) and his most memorable work *Melmoth the Wanderer* (1820). His last novel, *The Albigenses*, appeared in 1824.

Maud, a poem by *Tennyson, published 1855, composed 1854, but springing from the germ of the lyric 'Oh! that 'twere possible', composed 1833–4.

The poem is a monodrama in sections of different metres, in which the narrator, a man of morbid temperament, describes the progress of his emotions: first describing his father's death and his family's ruin, both contrived by the old lord of the Hall; then expressing his growing love for Maud, the old lord's daughter, and the scorn of her brother, who wishes her to marry a vapid 'new-made' lord; his triumph at winning Maud; their surprisal and her brother's death in a duel; his own flight abroad and ensuing madness; and his final re-awakening to hope in the service of his country. The poem contains several of Tennyson's best lyrics ('I have led her home', 'Come into the garden, Maud'), but some contemporary critics found it obscure or morbid; G. *Eliot protested against its 'faith in war as the unique social regenerator', and *Gladstone disliked the emphasis on bloodshedding as a cure for disappointed love, writing, 'We do not recollect that 1855 was a season of serious danger from a mania for peace and its pursuits.'

MAUGHAM, W(illiam) Somerset (1874–1965), was born in Paris, the fourth surviving son of a lawyer attached to the British embassy. His mother died when he was eight, shortly after the birth of a baby who lived only a day; stillbirths and fatal pregnancies were to feature prominently in Maugham's fiction. His father died of cancer in 1884, and William was sent to Whitstable to live with a childless middle-aged aunt and clergyman uncle. Educated at the King's School, Canterbury, and at Heidelberg University, he then trained as a doctor at St Thomas's Hospital in London. His first novel *Liza of Lambeth* (1897), which belonged to the 'new realist' school of G. A. *Moore, drew on his experiences of slums and Cockney life as an obstetric clerk. It was the beginning of a long and prolific career. Success was not instant, but he achieved fame in 1907 with the production of *Lady Frederick*, a comedy of marriage and money which had been previously rejected by many managements. In 1908 he had four plays running simultaneously in London.

In 1911 he met Syrie Wellcome, daughter of Dr Barnardo (of Barnardo Homes) and wife of an American businessman. Their only child Liza was born in 1915 and he married Syrie in 1917. The marriage was unorthodox, and they spent most of their time apart; Syrie made a name for herself as an interior decorator, and was famed for her 'white-on-white' colour schemes. In 1914 Maugham met Gerald Haxton in Flanders, where both were working for an ambulance unit. Haxton, 18 years younger than Maugham, became his secretary and companion, and in 1916 they set out on the first of many journeys together, this time to the South Seas. Further travels to China, south-east Asia, and

Mexico followed; the extrovert Haxton made many useful contacts for the more reserved Maugham, and the stories they heard appeared almost verbatim in Maugham's fiction and plays. In 1926 Maugham bought a house, the Mauresque, at Cap Ferrat on the French Riviera, which became a meeting place for a wide variety of writers, personalities, and politicians, including, in later years, W. S. *Churchill and *Beaverbrook. It was Maugham's home until his death, although he continued to travel widely. In 1954 he was created a Companion of Honour.

Among Maugham's plays should be mentioned *The Circle* (1921), the story of a young wife who falls in love with a rubber planter from Malaya and elopes with him, despite many warnings about the inevitable death of romance; *Our Betters* (1917), a satire on title-hunting Americans; *East of Suez*, which impressed audiences on its opening in 1922 by its spectacular evocation of street scenes in Peking; *The Constant Wife* (1926), in which a woman takes revenge on her unfaithful husband by gaining financial and emotional independence and departing for Italy with an old admirer; and *For Services Rendered* (1932), an anti-war play bitterly attacking 'this muddle of a post-war world'. His best-known novel is a thinly-disguised autobiography, *Of Human Bondage* (1915), which describes Philip Carey's lonely boyhood in Whitstable (which becomes Blackstable, as Canterbury becomes Tercanbury) and his subsequent adventures. Carey is handicapped by a club foot, as Maugham was handicapped by a severe stammer. *The Moon and Sixpence* (1919), in which Maugham used the first-hand knowledge of Tahiti acquired in 1917, recounts the life of Charles Strickland, a Gauginesque artist who neglects duty for art. *Cakes and Ale* (1930), his most genial book, is a comedy about the good-natured Rosie Driffield, the wife of a Grand Old Man of Letters, whom most took to be based on *Hardy; Alroy Kear, a self-promoting writer, was recognized as Hugh *Walpole. Maugham's last important novel, *The Razor's Edge* (1944), the title of which comes from the Katha-Upanishad, takes a mystical turn; its American hero Larry Darrell goes to India, stays in an ashram, and learns the value of non-attachment. In 1949 *A Writer's Notebook* appeared; it consisted of extracts from the 15 large volumes of notes that Maugham had kept from the age of 18 and shows him at his best, as detached, observant, and affecting a pose of worldliness even in his apparently private thoughts.

Of his short stories, particular mention should be made of 'Rain' (in *The Trembling of a Leaf*, 1921). Based on a real encounter, it tells of the conflict between a life-affirming American prostitute, Sadie Thompson, and a repressed Scottish missionary, Davidson. It ends with Davidson's suicide. It is characteristic of

Maugham's work in its remarkable and economical evocation of the atmosphere of hot, wet,
tropical Samoa, and its neat twist of plot. Like
many of his works it was staged successfully and
it has been filmed three times. 'The Alien Corn',
a story which appeared in *Six Stories in the First
Person Singular* (1931), about an aspiring pianist
who commits suicide when told he will never
be better than second rate, has also remained
popular. Other works include *Home and Beauty*
(play, 1919), *The Painted Veil* (novel, 1925),
The Sacred Flame (play, 1928), *Ashenden* (short
stories, 1928), and *The Narrow Corner* (novel,
1932).

Despite his worldly success and great popularity as a writer, Maugham throughout his
career seemed conscious of a lack of serious recognition, and the view expressed in his autobiography *The Summing Up* (1938), that he
stood 'in the very first row of the second-raters',
has been largely endorsed by literary critics. A
full but anecdotal biography, *Maugham* by Ted
Morgan, was published in 1980.

Maugrabin, Hayraddin, a character in Scott's
Quentin Durward. Maugrabin is an Arabic word
meaning 'man of the West', an African Moor.

Maule, Matthew, a character in Hawthorne's
The House of the Seven Gables, whose curse at
the point of execution condemns the house of
Pyncheon for its persecution of him.

MAUPASSANT, Guy de (1850–93), French
short story writer and novelist, a literary
disciple of *Flaubert and one of the group of
young *Naturalistic writers that formed around
*Zola. To their collection of tales *Les soirées de
Médan*, he contributed 'Boule de suif', a story
of the Franco-Prussian war that many regard as
his finest. The hundreds of stories, simply and
directly told, that he published in a brief creative
life typically deal with country folk or urban
employees and civil servants, though other social
groups (aristocrats, prostitutes, soldiers) also
appear regularly. *La Maison Tellier* (1881), *Clair
de Lune* (1884), *Miss Harriet* (1884), *Le Horla*
(1887), *L'Inutile Beauté* (1890) are among his
many collections. Besides his stories he wrote six
novels, of which the best known are *Une vie*
(1883), *Bel-Ami* (1885), and *Pierre et Jean*
(1888).

MAURIAC, François (1885–1970), French
novelist, dramatist, and critic, author of *Thérèse
Desqueyroux* (1927) and other short psychological tales set usually in the 'Landes' country
round Bordeaux; *Le Nœud de vipères* (1932) and
Le Mystère Frontenac (1933), longer studies of
family life; *Asmodée* (1938) and *Les Mal Aimés*
(1945), dramas; etc. His characters are fettered
by prosperous bourgeois convention and by religion and human frailty. He was awarded the
*Nobel Prize in 1952.

MAURICE, (John) F(rederick) D(enison)
(1805–72), educated at Trinity Hall, Cambridge. He joined the Church of England in
1830 and was ordained in 1834. His most
enduring book, *The Kingdom of Christ* (1838),
was a plea for Christian unity. In 1840 he became professor of English literature and history
at King's College, London. His belief in the
application of Christian principles to social reform gained him many followers; he became a
leader of the Christian Socialist movement
which brought him into close contact with C.
*Kingsley. His *Theological Essays* (1835) presented his unorthodox views on Eternal Punishment and caused his dismissal from King's
College. In 1854 he founded a Working Men's
College, and was its first principal. In 1866 he
became professor of moral philosophy at Cambridge. There is considerable literature on
Maurice's views and *Tennyson's lyric inviting
him to visit the Isle of Wight ('Come, when no
graver cares employ') is well known.

MAUROIS, André (1885–1967), French
author of biography: *Ariel* (1923, *Shelley; the
first *Penguin paperback, 1935) *Disraëli*
(1927), *Byron* (1930), *A la recherche de Marcel
Proust* (1949), *Lélia* (i.e. George *Sand, 1952),
etc.; histories of England (1937) and the United
States (1948); novels: *Climats* (1928), *Le Cercle
de famille* (1932), etc.; also of the early *Les
Silences du Colonel Bramble* (1918), sketches of
an English officers' mess.

Mause Headrigg, in Scott's *Old Mortality*, the
zealous covenanting mother of Cuddie, the
ploughman.

Maw-worm, see BICKERSTAFFE.

Maximin, a character in Dryden's *Tyrannick
Love*.

MAX MÜLLER, Friedrich (1823–1900), son
of the German poet Wilhelm Müller. He came
to England in 1846 and became a British subject. He was commissioned by the East India
Company to bring out an edition of the Sanskrit
Rigveda which was published in 1849–73. He
settled in Oxford in 1848 and was Taylorian
professor of modern European languages from
1854 to 1868, and one of the curators of the
Bodleian Library, 1856–63 and 1881–94.
Max Müller delivered two remarkable courses
of lectures on 'The Science of Languages' at the
Royal Institution in 1861–4, and was professor
of comparative philology at Oxford from 1868
until his death. He devoted much attention to
comparative mythology and the comparative
study of religions. A full edition of his works
was published in 1903.

MAXWELL, Gavin (1914–69), writer, traveller, and conservationist, educated at Stowe and
Hertford College, Oxford, where he studied

estate management. He is best remembered for *Ring of Bright Water* (1960), a poignant evocation of life on the remote Scottish coast and of his relationship with two semi-tame otters; his other works include travel writings and the autobiographical *The House of Elrig* (1965).

MAY, Thomas (1595–1650), educated at Sidney Sussex College, Cambridge, adopted the parliamentary cause and was secretary for the Parliament (1646). He was author of two narrative poems on the reigns of Edward III and Henry II and of a history of the Long Parliament (1647). He also wrote translations of *Virgil's *The Georgics* and *Lucan's *Pharsalia* (which were praised by *Jonson), two comedies, *The Heir* and *The Old Couple* (c.1620), and three tragedies on classical subjects. It appears that he had hoped to succeed Jonson as laureate in 1637, and transferred his allegiance from court to Parliament when *D'Avenant obtained the post; it is for this reason that *Marvell in his poem 'Tom May's Death' (1681) writes of his 'Most servile wit and Mercenary Pen'.

MAYAKOVSKY, Vladimir Vladimirovich (1893–1930), Russian Futurist poet. Born in Georgia, he grew up in Moscow, where in 1908 he joined the Bolshevik Party, which he later left. He was arrested three times in 1908–9, but in prison he read widely and began to write poetry. In 1911 he entered the Moscow Institute of Painting, Sculpture, and Architecture, where he met other painter-poets with whom he published the first Russian Futurist collection *A Trap for Judges* (1910) and signed the Futurist manifesto 'A Slap in the Face for Public Taste' in 1912. Mayakovsky's early poetry is difficult and inventive ('But could you have?', 'Urban Megahell'). His first long poem, *A Cloud in Trousers* (1914–15), began a series of masterpieces on his main theme, impossible fate and impossible love. In July 1915 he met Lili Brik, the great love of his life, and her husband, the Formalist critic Osip Brik, with whom he was also to have a fruitful friendship. From then on his long love and fate poems, *The Backbone-Flute* (1915), *Man* (1916–17), *About That* (1923), are dedicated to Lili Brik. He also wrote a powerful long poem on the First World War, *War and the Universe* (1916). Mayakovsky greeted the revolution and expected the Futurists to provide the vanguard of the new state's art, but the Futurists found little favour with the Communist authorities, *Lenin in particular finding Mayakovsky's *150,000,000,* a narrative of a boxing match between the 150,000,000 Russian Ivans and the American President Woodrow Wilson, 'incomprehensible rubbish'. In 1923 Mayakovsky was one of the founders of LEF (the Left Front of the Arts), but this was forced to disband in 1925 (to re-emerge briefly as 'New Lef ', 1927–8). On the death of Lenin in

1924 he wrote the long narrative poem *Vladimir Ilich Lenin.* His work in the 1920s shows a constant tension between the personal and the civic, between his hopes from the revolution and his awareness that nothing has changed, that his mortal enemy *byt,* routine, dull ordinary life, remains. By the end of the decade Mayakovsky was in a state of crisis. His relationship with the Briks had soured, he had fallen in love with an émigrée, Tatyana Yakovleva, who refused to return to Russia, his plays *The Bedbug* and *The Bath-House* (both 1929) had failed. As a final act of compromise, he joined the Russian Association of Proletarian Writers in 1930, but his work was still boycotted. He shot himself on 14 April 1930, leaving an unfinished poem, 'At the top of my voice', in which he speaks of having 'trodden on the neck of my own song'. The suicide cast a shadow over his official reputation, but when in 1935 Lili Brik wrote to *Stalin drawing attention to Mayakovsky's 'enormous revolutionary heritage', Stalin's response was to declare that 'Mayakovsky was and remains the best and most talented poet of our Soviet epoch.' From then on he became (in a suitably 'politicized' reading) official laureate. As *Pasternak put it, he was 'propagated compulsorily like potatoes in the reign of Catherine the Great. This was his second death. He had no hand in it.' Mayakovsky has been widely translated into English: the best versions are those by Herbert Marshall (*Mayakovsky,* 1965, etc.) and G. Reavey and M. Hayward (*The Bedbug and Selected Poetry,* 1960).

May Day, 1 May, celebrated with garlands and dancing, the choice of a queen of the May (gaily dressed and crowned with flowers), the erection of a Maypole (painted with spiral stripes and decked with flowers) to dance round, and so forth. Perhaps derived from the Roman *Floralia.* The May-game was a set performance in the May-day festivities, in which *Robin Hood and *Maid Marian figured. May Day was adopted in 1889 as the international Labour holiday.

MAYHEW, Henry (1812–87), the son of a London solicitor, was educated at Westminster School, from which he ran away. He was briefly articled to his father before becoming a dramatist and journalist. The first of his many plays and farces (some very successful) was *The Wandering Minstrel* (1834). In 1841 he was a co-founder and briefly a joint editor of *Punch.* He wrote many novels and stories, as well as books on science, religion, education, and travel, including works on Germany and the Rhine (where he briefly lived), and *The Boyhood of Martin Luther* (1865). But he is chiefly remembered for the philanthropic journalism to which he turned at the end of the 1840s; his remarkable series of 82 articles, couched as lengthy 'letters', in the *Morning Chronicle* were published with some alterations as *London Labour and the London Poor* (1851). His painstaking and compassionate investigations into the plight of the London poor revealed the extent to which starvation, disease, and transportation were daily horrors. He performed similar work on the subject of prisons, publishing *The Criminal Prisons of London* (1862) and *London Children* (1874), illustrated by W. S. *Gilbert. His plain but harrowing descriptions, often told in the words of those he spoke with, did much to stir the public conscience towards reform.

Maylie, Mrs and Harry, characters in Dickens's *Oliver Twist.*

Mayor of Casterbridge, The, a *Story of Character*, a novel by T. *Hardy, published 1886.

Michael Henchard, a hay-trusser, gets drunk at a fair and sells his wife and child for five guineas to a sailor, Newson. When sober again he takes a solemn vow not to touch alcohol for 20 years. By his energy and acumen he becomes rich, respected, and eventually the mayor of Casterbridge. After 18 years his wife returns, supposing Newson dead, and is reunited with her husband. She brings with her her daughter Elizabeth-Jane, and Henchard is led to believe that she is his child, whereas she is in fact Newson's. Through a combination of unhappy circumstances, and the impulsive obstinacy of Henchard, troubles accumulate. He quarrels with his capable young assistant in his corn business, Donald Farfrae. Mrs Henchard dies and Henchard learns the truth about the girl. Farfrae becomes his successful rival, both in business and in love, and marries Lucetta, whom Henchard had hoped to win. Soon Henchard's business is ruined, the story of the sale of his wife is revealed, and he takes again to heavy drinking. Farfrae now has Henchard's business, his house, and Lucetta, while Henchard works as a labourer in his yard. Eventually Farfrae becomes mayor, the office Henchard once held. His stepdaughter is his only comfort, then Newson returns and claims her and after Lucetta's death Farfrae marries her. Thus he possesses all that was once Henchard's. Henchard becomes lonelier and more desolate, and dies wretchedly in a hut on Egdon Heath.

MAZARIN, Jules (1602–61), of an ancient Sicilian family, was sent as papal legate to Paris in 1634, attracted the notice of Richelieu, entered the French service, and was made a cardinal in 1641. He succeeded Richelieu as prime minister, was retained in that office by the queen regent (Anne of Austria) on the death of Louis XIII, and governed France during the minority of Louis XIV. His internal administration provoked the civil wars of the Fronde. He founded a splendid library in Paris, the Bibliothèque Mazarine.

Mazarin Bible, The, the first printed bible, and probably the first book to be printed with movable type, c.1455, probably by *Gutenberg in association with *Fust and Schöffer. The first known copy was discovered in the Mazarine Library (see above) in Paris. It is also known as the 'forty-two line Bible' from the number of lines to the column.

Mazeppa, a poem by Lord *Byron, published 1819.

The poem, which forms an interesting transition between Byron's romantic and colloquial styles, is founded on a passage in *Voltaire's *Charles XII*. While Charles, the king of Sweden, and his men rest after their defeat at Pultowa, one of the king's officers, Mazeppa, tells a tale of his early life. Being detected in an intrigue, he had been bound naked onto the back of a wild horse from the Ukraine, which was then loosed and lashed into madness. The horse galloped off, through forest and river, carrying its fainting rider, and never stopped until it reached the plains of the Ukraine, where it fell dead. Mazeppa, at the point of death, was rescued by Cossack peasants.

Meagles, Mr, Mrs, and their daughter Pet, characters in Dickens's *Little Dorrit.*

Meaning of Meaning, The, see RICHARDS, I. A.

Meanjin (pron. Me-an-jin) *Quarterly,* a review of literature and art in Australia, founded in 1940 and edited by C. B. Christesen. The title is taken from the aboriginal name for Brisbane, where the magazine was first published.

Measure for Measure, a tragi-comedy by *Shakespeare, written probably in the summer of 1604, but not printed until the First *Folio (1623). Its chief source is *Whetstone's play *Promos and Cassandra*, itself based on a story in *Cinthio's *Hecatommithi*. It has often been categorized as a 'problem play' because of the unpleasantness of its subject matter and the complexity of its plot and themes.

The duke of Vienna, on the pretext of a journey to Poland, hands over the government to his virtuous-seeming deputy Angelo, who enforces strict laws against sexual licence which for the past 14 years had been neglected. Angelo at once sentences to death Claudio, a young gentleman who has got his betrothed Julietta with child. Claudio's sister Isabella, who is a novice in a sisterhood of nuns, pleads with Angelo for her brother's life, urged on by Claudio's friend Lucio. In response to her repeated pleas, Angelo offers to spare Claudio's life if she will consent to be his mistress. Isabella refuses, and will not be persuaded even by the desperate entreaties of Claudio in prison. The duke, disguised as a friar, has made a visit of spiritual comfort to Claudio, and now devises a way of saving his life. Isabella is to agree to a midnight assignation with

Angelo, but her place is to be taken by Mariana, who was betrothed to Angelo and still loves him. Mariana is first seen (IV. i) listening to the song 'Take, O, take those lips away'. This scheme is successful, but Angelo still proceeds with the order for Claudio's execution, though unknown to Isabella Claudio is saved by the substitution of the head of Ragozine, a pirate, who has died that night in the same prison. The duke lays by his disguise, simulates a return to Vienna, and pretends to disbelieve the complaints of Isabella and suit of Mariana, in favour of Angelo's hypocritical denial. When Angelo is forced to confess, both Mariana and Isabella plead for his life; Mariana is married to Angelo, Lucio to a whore, and at the end of a baffling final speech the duke appears to propose marriage to the novice Isabella.

Medall, The, a poem by *Dryden, published 1682.

The earl of *Shaftesbury, who is represented in *Absalom and Achitophel and possibly in *Mr Limberham*, was acquitted of charges of high treason in 1681, and a medal was struck to commemorate the event. Dryden's response includes savage attacks on Shaftesbury himself, the City, and the Commons. It predicts with some accuracy the constitutional instability which was to beset the country in the ensuing 30 years. *Shadwell and Samuel Pordage (1633–?91) both wrote replies.

MEDICI, the, the family that were rulers of Florence from 1434 and grand dukes of Tuscany from 1569 to 1737. The earlier Medici were great patrons of art and literature, chief among them Cosimo (1389–1464) and Lorenzo 'the Magnificent' (c.1449–92), founders of the Medicean or *Laurentian Library. The latter, himself a poet, was father of Pope *Leo X. Cathérine de Médicis, as she is known in France (1519–89), daughter of the grandson of Lorenzo the Magnificent, was consort of Henry II of France, and regent during the minority of Charles IX; her rule there was the source of much of the anti-Italian feeling embodied in the myth of the *Machiavellian politician. Marie de Médicis (1573–1642), niece of the grand duke of Tuscany, was consort of Henry IV of France from 1600 and regent 1610–17. There is a life of Lorenzo by W. *Roscoe (1795).

Medina, in Spenser's *Faerie Queene (II. ii), represents the golden mean of sensibility, her sisters *Elissa and Perissa representing its extremes.

Mediolanum, in imprints, Milan.

Medmenham Abbey, a ruined Cistercian abbey on the Thames near Marlow, rebuilt in the 18th cent. as a residence and notorious in the 18th cent. as the meeting-place of a convivial club known as the Franciscans or the Hell-fire Club. This was founded by Sir Francis Dashwood, and *Wilkes

and *Dodington were among its members. Its motto 'Fay ce que voudras' was adopted from that of Rabelais's abbey of *Thelema. There is a good deal about it in *Johnstone's Chrysal, or the Adventures of a Guinea (III. ii, chs 17 et seq.).

Medoro, in *Orlando Furioso, a young Moor of humble birth, with whom *Angelica falls in love and whom she marries, thereby causing the despair and madness of Orlando.

MEDWALL, Henry, see FULGENS AND LUCRECE.

Megatherium, The, a club mentioned in several of Thackeray's novels, e.g. *The Newcomes (V), *The Adventures of Philip (V. ix).

Meg Dods, see DODS.

Meg Merrilies, see MERRILIES.

Meg Murdockson, see MURDOCKSON.

MEHTA, Ved Parkash (1934–), Indian writer and journalist (now an American citizen), born near Lahore, and educated at Balliol College, Oxford, and at Harvard. His works include several studies of Indian life and autobiographical and biographical memoirs, including Face to Face (1957); Daddyji (1972); Mamaji (1979); and Vedi; My early education in an Indian orphanage for the blind (1982). Fly and the Fly-Bottle (1963) is a personal account of meetings with various British intellectuals, including I. *Berlin, A. J. *Ayer, A. J. P. *Taylor, and I. *Murdoch, originally published in the *New Yorker, to which he is a regular contributor.

Meiosis, an understatement, sometimes ironical or humorous and intended to emphasize the size, importance, etc., of what is belittled. Except in *litotes, which is a form of meiosis, the use of meiosis is chiefly colloquial; e.g. 'He's doing all right out of it'; 'That must be worth a few bob.'

Meistersinger, a title taken in the 15th cent. by certain professional German poets of high skill and culture, to distinguish themselves from the wandering gleemen. They were often craftsmen in their ordinary avocations—smiths, weavers, and the like. They represent a phase of the development of German verse from the minnesang (see MINNESINGERS). The Meistersang and singer were governed by an elaborate set of rules and organization, which are depicted in *Wagner's opera Die Meistersinger von Nürnberg, produced in 1868.

MELANCHTHON, the graecized name of Philip Schwartzerd (1497–1560), German humanist who was professor of Greek at Wittenberg University; one of the principal advocates of the *Reformation.

Melantius, a character in Beaumont and Fletcher's *The Maid's Tragedy*.

Melbury, Grace, a character in Hardy's *The Woodlanders*.

Meleagant (Mellyagaunce, Mellygaunt, etc., in *Malory), in the Arthurian legends, the evil son of the good king Bademagus (Baudemagus) of Gorre. He abducts Guinevere after winning her by a trick at Arthur's court and is pursued by Arthur's knights, most significantly by Launcelot. Their conflict is the central story in the *Lancelot* of *Chrétien de Troyes.

Melford, Jery and Lydia, characters in Smollett's *Humphry Clinker*.

'Melibeus, The Tale of ', see CANTERBURY TALES, 18.

Melincourt, or *Sir Oran Haut-ton*, a satire by *Peacock, published 1817.

One of the longest and most ambitious of Peacock's books, it has a more novelistic plot than the others, which features the wooing by various suitors of a rich young heiress, Anthelia Melincourt, her abduction by a villainous peer, Lord Anophel Achthar, and his friend, the Revd Mr Grovelgrub, and her rescue when she is about to be raped by Lord Anophel. The plot, which is indebted to Richardson's *Clarissa* and to *Holcroft's *Anna St Ives*, has strong feminist connotations. Anthelia is ultimately rescued by a humorous variant on the Noble Savage, Sir Oran *Haut-ton (see MONBODDO), an orangutan whom the hero, Mr Sylvan Forester, has educated to everything except speech, and for whom he has bought a seat in Parliament. Sir Oran is affectionate and chivalrous and plays delightfully on the flute. His virtues show up the corruptions of 'advanced' society, as Forester, an idealistic primitivist, intends. Forester, whose views resemble *Shelley's literary brand of radicalism, debates with Mr Fax, a Malthusian economist, such causes as rotten boroughs, paper currency, slavery, and the recent conservatism of the Lake Poets. Provoked by an article by *Southey in the *Quarterly Review*, vol. xvi (1816), Peacock censures Southey himself (Mr Feathernest), *Coleridge (Mr Mystic), *Wordsworth (Mr Paperstamp), and *Gifford, the editor of the *Quarterly* (Mr Vamp), as a group of political renegades. The central set piece is the election in the borough of One-Vote, in which Sir Oran Haut-ton is returned to Parliament by the single, bought vote of Mr Christopher Corporate.

Melissa, in *Orlando Furioso*, the beneficent witch who releases *Rogero from the power of *Alcina.

Mell, Mr, in Dickens's *David Copperfield*, the poor usher at Creakle's school.

Mellefont, a character in Congreve's *The Double Dealer*.

Melmoth, Courtney, see PRATT, S. J.

Melmoth the Wanderer, a novel by C. R. *Maturin, published 1820.

This novel, which was praised by writers as diverse as *Thackeray, D. G. *Rossetti, and *Baudelaire, was in effect the last, and also one of the most effective, of the *'Gothic' school. The tale rushes energetically through every kind of horror and iniquity, and has moments of genuine power. Melmoth, who has sold his soul for the promise of prolonged life, offers relief from suffering to each of the characters, whose terrible stories succeed one another, if they will take over his bargain with the Devil. But Stanton, imprisoned in the cell of a raving lunatic; Moncada in the hands of the Inquisition; Walberg, who sees his children dying of hunger; and many other sufferers, all reject the proposed bargain.

After his trial *Wilde adopted the name Sebastian Melmoth.

Melmotte, Augustus, a financial speculator, one of the principal characters in A. Trollope's novel *The Way We Live Now*.

Melodrama, in early 19th-cent. use, a stage play (usually romantic and sensational in plot and incident) in which songs and music were interspersed. In later use the musical element gradually ceased to be an essential feature, and the name now denotes a dramatic piece characterized by sensational incident and violent appeals to the emotions, but with a happy ending [OED].

Melvil, Count de, and his son Renaldo, in Smollett's *Ferdinand Count Fathom*.

MELVILLE, Herman (1819–91), American novelist and poet, born in New York City, a product of the American mercantile gentry. After his father's business failure and death in 1832, however, Melville left school and was largely an autodidact, devouring Shakespeare, the Authorized Version of the Bible, and 17th-cent. meditative writers such as Sir T. *Browne, as well as the numerous historical, anthropological, and technical works which he used to supplement his experiences when he wrote. After sailing as a 'boy' on a packet to Liverpool in 1839, Melville shipped in 1841 on the whaler *Acushnet* for the South Seas, where he jumped ship, joined the US Navy, and finally returned three years later to begin writing.

The fictionalized travel narrative of *Typee or a Peep at Polynesian Life* (1846), was Melville's most popular book during his lifetime. Like most of his works, *Typee* was published first in Britain, for prestige and to guard against piracy, and throughout his career Melville enjoyed a rather higher estimation in Britain than in America. After a well-received sequel, *Omoo: A Narrative of Adventures in the South Seas* (1847), the perfunctorily plotted *Mardi and a Voyage Thither* (1849), an allegorical romance with philosophical meditations, fared less well.

Having married Elizabeth Shaw, daughter of the chief justice of Massachusetts, in 1847, and with a mother, sisters, and eventually four children to support, Melville wrote the realistic sea stories *Redburn: His First Voyage* (1849) and *White-Jacket; or The World in a Man-of-War* (1850), which he considered pot-boilers. Inspired by the achievement of *Hawthorne, Melville changed his next sea tale into *Moby-Dick, or, The Whale* (1851), whose brilliance was noted by some critics and very few readers.

After the critical disaster of *Pierre, or the Ambiguities* (1852), a *Gothic romance with Shelleyan overtones and a satire on the literary profession, Melville wrote anonymous magazine stories, among them *'Bartleby the Scrivener' and *'Benito Cereno', which were collected in *The Piazza Tales* (1856), and the historical novel *Israel Potter: His Fifty Years of Exile* (1855) about a neglected hero of the American revolution. To recover from a breakdown he undertook a long journey to Europe and the Holy Land (depicted in the narrative poem *Clarel*, 1876). Sceptical and tormented, but unable to discard his Manichean view of God, Melville remarked while visiting Hawthorne in Liverpool in 1856, 'I have just about made up my mind to be annihilated.'

The Confidence-Man: His Masquerade (1857), a mordantly nihilistic satire of human gullibility, was Melville's last novel. After unsuccessful lecture tours, he worked as customs officer in New York harbour, where he wrote *Battle-Pieces and Aspects of the War* (1865), trenchant poems of disillusion with civil-war era America. *John Marr and Other Sailors* (1888) and *Timoleon* (1891) were privately printed. Despite some revival of interest in Britain, Melville died virtually forgotten, with *Billy Budd, Foretopman* still in manuscript: contemporary misunderstanding, censorship, and neglect, and the subsequent revision of Melville's reputation since the 1920s, have made him a classic case of the artist as reviled Titan. He enlarged the stylistic range and metaphysical concerns of fiction while helping to create the characteristically American mixed-genre, symbolic novel which Hawthorne called 'romance'; and *Moby-Dick* is the closest approach the United States has had to a national prose epic.

Melyodas, in *Malory, king of Lyones, the father of Tristram by his first wife Elizabeth, the daughter of King Mark.

Memoir-novel, an early form of the novel, purporting to be true autobiographical history, often including diaries and journals, but in fact largely or wholly fictitious. The author appears, if at all, merely as 'editor' of another's memoirs. The form arose in 17th-cent. France, and *Defoe, with *Robinson Crusoe* (1719) and *Moll Flanders* (1722), was the first English master. During the 18th cent. the author's claim to be presenting a genuine (as opposed to a fictional) memoir dwindled to a literary convention; Smollett's *Roderick Random*, Goldsmith's *The Vicar of Wakefield*, Mackenzie's *The Man of Feeling*, M. Edgeworth's *Castle Rackrent*, and many others were presented as memoirs under only the thinnest disguise. The popularity of the form declined sharply in the 19th cent., but Hogg's *Private Memoirs and Confessions of a Justified Sinner*, Dickens's *David Copperfield*, Melville's *Moby-Dick*, C. Brontë's *Jane Eyre*, and several novels of Thackeray (notably *Henry Esmond*) are outstanding examples. (See also NOVEL, RISE OF THE.)

Memoirs of a Cavalier, a historical romance attributed with good reason to *Defoe, published 1724.

The pretended author, 'Col. Andrew Newport', a young English gentleman born in 1608, travels on the Continent, starting in 1630, goes to Vienna, and accompanies the army of the emperor, being present at the siege and sack of Magdeburg, which is vividly presented. He then joins the army of Gustavus Adolphus, remaining with it until the death of that king and taking part in a number of engagements which he describes in detail. After his return to England he joins the king's army, first against the Scots, then against the forces of Parliament, being present at the battle of Edgehill, which he fully describes, the relief of York, and the battle of Naseby.

Memoirs of a Woman of Pleasure (1748–9), often known as *Fanny Hill*, a work by J. *Cleland, published 1748–9.

Unlike, for instance, her predecessor *Moll Flanders, Fanny Hill is only narrowly developed as a character. However, Cleland employs her cleverly, in breathless epistle and journal, as a vehicle for his absorbed examination of sexuality, in both men and women, in its many varieties and in minute physiological detail. His occasional pretence of moral indignation, and use of euphemistic language, add an ironic and spurious respectability to his work.

Memoirs of Captain Carleton, a narrative published 1728 as *The Memoirs of an English Officer*, by Capt. George Carleton. Its authorship has been contested and, although it is now almost universally agreed to be by *Defoe, it was at one time, with no serious grounds, attributed to *Swift. Captain Carleton, who unquestionably existed, is the subject of an attractive tale of soldierly adventure. Sir W. *Scott, who regarded the Memoirs as Carleton's own work, brought out a new edition in 1808.

Carleton volunteers on board the *London* on the declaration of war with the Dutch in 1672. In 1674 he enters the service of the prince of Orange, remaining there until the peace of Nijmegen. Returning to England, he receives a commission from James II and serves in Scotland and then in Flanders until the peace of Ryswick. The most interesting part of the memoirs follows. Carleton embarks with Lord Peterborough for Spain in 1705, and gives a stirring narrative of the siege, capture, and subsequent relief of Barcelona and of the campaign by which Peterborough, with scanty resources, temporarily placed the Archduke Charles on the throne of Spain. This is followed by some account of various parts of Spain visited by the author as a prisoner of war.

Menaechmi, see PLAUTUS.

MENANDER (*c*.342–292 BC), an Athenian dramatic poet, was the most distinguished writer of New Comedy, which, with its trend towards realistic fiction based on contemporary life, gave a pattern for much light drama from the Renaissance onwards, making its influence felt through Latin adaptations by *Plautus and *Terence, at least eight from Menander himself. No play survived the Dark Ages; but *Dyskolos* (or *Misanthrope*), a lighthearted early play, and large parts of others have been recovered from papyri in the 20th cent.; they show at first hand something of the blend of amusement and perceptive human sympathy which earned Menander his reputation.

Men and Women, a collection of 51 poems by R. *Browning, published in two vols, 1855. The poems date from the period after Browning's marriage in 1846, and express a new-found energy and confidence—'poems of all sorts and sizes and styles and subjects', as he said, adding, 'I hope to be listened to, this time.' But the volumes made their way slowly. The poems show Browning's mind at its most multitudinous and eclectic, ranging over history, art, philosophy, and religion; they include many of his finest dramatic monologues, such as 'Fra Lippo Lippi', 'Bishop Blougram's Apology', 'Andrea del Sarto', and 'Cleon', whose effect is based on the fusion of an intensely realized situation with an unsurpassed feeling for the cadences of the speaking voice. The collection also includes Browning's most famous love-poem, 'Love Among the Ruins', and the problematic *'Childe Roland to the Dark Tower Came'. The collection closes with an address to Elizabeth Barrett (*Browning), 'One Word More' (a phrase picked up during their correspondence in 1845–6).

Menaphon, a prose romance with interludes of verse by R. *Greene, published 1589. *Nashe's preface to the first edition offered a satirical survey of contemporary literature.

The romance tells the adventures of the princess Sephestia, shipwrecked on the coast of Arcadia. The convention of impenetrable disguise is taken to ridiculous lengths as Sephestia, disguised as Samela, is wooed simultaneously by her father and her teenage son, while herself carrying on a love affair with her (disguised) husband. Her fourth lover is the shepherd Menaphon of the title. Some charming lyrics, including the cradle-song 'Weepe not my wanton, smile upon my knee', diversify the intricate narrative.

MENCKEN, H(enry) L(ouis) (1880–1956), American journalist and critic, born in Baltimore, who, as literary editor from 1908, then as co-editor, 1914–23 (with G. J. *Nathan), of *The Smart Set* exercized a great influence on American taste, upholding the inconoclasm of writers as diverse as G. B. *Shaw, *Ibsen, *Nietzsche, *Zola, and Mark *Twain, and attacking the 'ferocious intolerance', 'snouting Puritanism', and 'literary standards derived from the *Ladies' Home Journal* which prevailed in America. Nevertheless he strongly opposed European 'patronage' of America, and supported such native writers as *Dreiser and S. *Anderson. In 1924 he founded with Nathan the *American Mercury*, which he edited until 1933, and in which he continued to satirize and goad his countrymen. His many books include *The American Language* (1919), in which he defends the developing vigour and versatility of colloquial American usage. There is a life by D. C. Stenerson (1971).

MENDELSSOHN (-BARTHOLDY), Felix (1809–47), German composer. Mendelssohn's most popular work is also one of the most famous of all compositions inspired by Shakespeare, the incidental music to *A Midsummer Night's Dream*. The overture was written when the composer was only 17, originally for piano duet performance within his own family though it was orchestrated immediately afterwards; he had known the *Schlegel translations of Shakespeare from an early age, and the score proclaims his delight in matching every musical idea to some character or incident in the play. The remaining 13 numbers of the incidental music, some of them short interludes based on themes from the overture, a few, like the Scherzo, the Nocturne, and the ubiquitous Wedding March, on a more extended scale, were added for a stage performance in Berlin in 1843. The whole set is still one of the most successful of all musical accompaniments to a stage play. It remained, however, Mendelssohn's only contribution to Shakespeare music: another early project, an opera on *The Tempest*, got as far as a libretto which the composer rejected in 1831, and was taken up again in 1846 (this time with two librettists, Scribe in France and Romani in Italy) with the same result.

Mendelssohn made many visits to England, the first of them including a trip to Scotland which later bore fruit in the overture *The Hebrides* and the 'Scottish' Symphony; the latter, not finished until 1842, was dedicated to Queen *Victoria, who had twice received the composer during his visit to London in that year. Another outcome of his English connection was the oratorio *Elijah*, a deliberate essay in the Handelian tradition which was commissioned by the Birmingham Festival and first performed there in 1846, though it was originally written to a German text (from the Lutheran Bible) and only translated into English after the music had been composed. There are a number of anthems and psalms to English (biblical) words, of which 'Hear My Prayer' (containing the immensely popular 'O for the wings of a dove') is the best known; but the most widely sung of all his music associated with English sacred texts is the tune, originally part of a *Festgesang* for the Gutenberg Festival, now irrevocably united with the words 'Hark! the herald-angels sing'. There are surprisingly few songs to English texts, but the eight books of *Songs without Words* for piano solo were staple piano fodder in the Victorian drawing-room, and over-popularity has made it difficult, until recently, to see them for the distinguished compositions that the best of them are.

MENEGHELLO, Luigi (1927–), Italian novelist, emeritus professor at the University of Reading. His novels *Libera nos a malo* (*Free us from evil*, 1963) and *I piccoli maestri* (*The Outlaws*, 1964), and *Pomo pero* (*Eeny Meeny*, 1974, a commentary on *Libera nos a malo*), deal with memories, including the Resistance against Fascism. His extreme linguistic self-consciousness draws on a variety of stylistic registers and language (including English), making him one of the most original writers to have emerged from post-war Italy.

Ménippée, Satire, see SATIRE MÉNIPPÉE.

Men's Wives, stories by *Thackeray, which appeared in *Fraser's Magazine*, 1843.

They are concerned with different kinds of unhappy marriage, and the exploitation of one partner by the other. The longest and most fully developed story, 'The Ravenswing', concerns Morgiana Crump ('The Ravenswing'), who possesses beautiful hair and a beautiful singing voice, marries the profligate Captain Walker, and supports him by singing.

Menteith, earl of, a character in Scott's *A Legend of Montrose*.

Mephistopheles, a word of unknown origin, which appears first in the German *Faustbuch* of

1587 as 'Mephostophiles'. It is the name of the evil spirit to whom *Faust was said in the German legend to have sold his soul. Shakespeare, in *The Merry Wives of Windsor* (I. i), mentions 'Mephostophilus'.

Mercator, a trade journal edited by *Defoe. It succeeded *The Review* in 1713 and continued till the following year.

MERCATOR, Gerardus, the Latinized form of the name of Gerhard Kremer (1512–94), a Flemish geographer who devised the form of map known as 'Mercator's Projection', in which the meridians of longitude are shown at right angles to the parallels of latitude, enabling the navigator to plot the correct compass bearing for a direct course from one point to another.

MERCER, David (1928–80), playwright, born in Wakefield, the son of an engine-driver. After attempts at various careers he achieved recognition with his trilogy of television plays *Where the Difference Begins* (1961), *A Climate of Fear* (1962), and *The Birth of a Private Man* (1963), published together as *The Generations* in 1964. The trilogy is primarily concerned with problems of left-wing political commitment; it opens in a Yorkshire working-class home, and ends with death on the Berlin Wall. Mental disturbance, alienation, class conflict, generation conflict (particularly between working-class father and educated son), and the meaning of Marxism, both British and continental, are recurrent themes in many subsequent works for stage, screen, and television, which include *A Suitable Case for Treatment* (TV 1962, published in *Three TV Comedies*, 1966, filmed as *Morgan*, 1965); *After Haggerty*, staged and published in 1970, which has as protagonist a Marxist theatre critic; and *Shooting the Chandelier* (TV 1977, pub. 1978). Mercer was one of the first playwrights to appreciate the possibilities of television as a writer's medium.

Merchant of Venice, The, a comedy by Shakespeare written between 1596 and 1598. It was printed in 1600, and this text was reprinted in the First *Folio (1623). Its chief source is the first story of the fourth day in *Il Pecorone*, Giovanni Fiorentino's collection of *novelle*. Other sources include *Munday's *Zelauto* and the *Gesta Romanorum*. In performance *Shylock, treated sometimes comically, sometimes tragically, has often been made into the central character. An adaptation by George Granville, *The Jew of Venice*, was the normal stage version from 1701 to 1741.

Bassanio, a noble but poor Venetian, asks his friend Antonio, a rich merchant, for 3,000 ducats to enable him to prosecute fittingly his suit of the rich heiress Portia at Belmont. Antonio, whose money is all employed in foreign ventures, undertakes to borrow the sum from

Shylock, a Jewish usurer, whom he has been wont to upbraid for his extortions. Shylock consents to lend the money against a bond by which, if the sum is not repaid at the appointed day, Antonio shall forfeit a pound of flesh. By her father's will Portia is to marry that suitor who selects of three caskets (one of gold, one of silver, one of lead) that which contains her portrait. Bassanio makes the right choice—the leaden casket—and is wedded to Portia, and his friend Gratiano to her maid Nerissa. News comes that Antonio's ships have been wrecked, that the debt has not been repaid when due, and that Shylock claims his pound of flesh. The matter is brought before the duke. Portia disguises herself as an advocate, Balthazar, and Nerissa as her clerk, and they come to the court to defend Antonio, unknown to their husbands. Failing in her appeal to Shylock for mercy, Portia admits the validity of his claim, but warns him that his life is forfeit if he spills one drop of blood, since his bond gives him right to nothing beyond the flesh. Pursuing her advantage, she argues that Shylock's life is forfeit for having conspired against the life of a Venetian citizen. The duke grants Shylock his life, but gives half his wealth to Antonio, half to the State. Antonio surrenders his claim if Shylock will turn Christian and make over his property on his death to his daughter Jessica, who has run away and married a Christian and been disinherited; to which Shylock agrees. Portia and Nerissa ask as rewards from Bassanio and Gratiano the rings that their wives have given them, which they have promised never to part with. Reluctantly they give them up, and are taken to task accordingly on their return home. The play ends with news of the safe arrival of Antonio's ships.

'Merchant's Tale, The', see CANTERBURY TALES, 10.

Merchant Taylors' School was founded in 1561, in the parish of St Lawrence Poultney, on Suffolk Lane (near what is now Cannon St). It was a middle-class school catering largely for the children of tradesmen, and its first headmaster, *Mulcaster, held enlightened views on education; during his time it became the largest school in England, with 250 students. Pupils included *Spenser, *Kyd, *Andrewes, and T. *Lodge.

Mercilla, in Spenser's *Faerie Queene (v. viii), 'a mayden Queene of high renowne' (Queen Elizabeth), whose crown the *Soldan seeks to subvert.

Mercurius Aulicus, see BERKENHEAD.

Mercurius Librarius: or A Catalogue of Books, a booksellers' trade journal founded in 1668 by two stationers, John Starkey and Robert Clavell, described by Walter Graham (*The Beginnings of English Literary Periodicals*, 1926) as 'in a very limited sense . . . entitled to be regarded as the first literary periodical published in England'. It survived until 1709, and a reprint (as *Term Catalogue*), edited by *Arber, was published in 1903. A second *Mercurius Librarius: or a faithful account of all books and pamphlets* began as a weekly in 1680, but does not appear to have lasted long.

Mercutio, in Shakespeare's *Romeo and Juliet, the lively, cynical friend of Romeo who is killed in a brawl by Juliet's cousin Tybalt. It is he who speaks the famous 'Queen Mab' speech (I. iv. 53–94).

Mercy, in the second part of Bunyan's *Pilgrim's Progress, a companion of Christiana.

Merdle and Mrs Merdle, characters in Dickens's *Little Dorrit.

MEREDITH, George (1828–1909), had a precarious childhood in Portsmouth as the son of an indigent, but flamboyant and extravagant, tailor who was early a widower—a background which Meredith was later at pains to conceal, although he made use of it in several of his novels. He was intermittently educated in Portsmouth and Southsea, and then with much success at the unusual school of the Moravians at Neuwied in Germany. In London, after a period with a solicitor, he began his long literary career with 'Chillianwallah', a poem published in 1849. In the same year he married Mary Ellen Nicholls, the widowed daughter of T. L. *Peacock, and in 1851 paid for the publication of his own *Poems*, a volume he later disowned but which was praised by *Tennyson and C. *Kingsley. *The Shaving of Shagpat (1856) was well received by the critics and acclaimed by G. *Eliot as 'a work of genius', but it did not sell well and was soon remaindered. In the same year he sat as the model for Henry Wallis's painting *The Death of Chatterton*. In 1857 his wife left him for Wallis, and *Farina*, a German burlesque reminiscent of *Shagpat*, appeared with little success. His first major novel, *The Ordeal of Richard Feverel*, was published in 1859; it sold poorly, caused much scandal, and *Mudie's cancelled its order of 300 copies, but it brought praise in *The Times and the *Athenaeum, as well as the friendship of *Carlyle and the *Pre-Raphaelites.

Meredith was now contributing to many periodicals, including the *Fortnightly Review, in which *Evan Harrington began to appear in 1860; in the same year he became reader for *Chapman and Hall (a post he retained until 1894) and also became a regular compiler of news for the *Ipswich Chronicle*, a task he endured for eight years. *Modern Love and Poems of the Roadside appeared in 1862. In 1864 he published *Emilia in England* (retitled *Sandra Belloni* in 1886) and married his second wife, Marie Vulliamy. *Rhoda Fleming appeared in 1865, and *Vittoria (a sequel to Sandra Belloni) began to appear in 1866, but was enlarged, after Meredith had spent a brief inactive period as a war correspondent in Italy, before its publication in book form in 1867. Few of these works had brought much profit, but Meredith's reputation was growing steadily with the discerning public. The Adventures of *Harry Richmond (1871) brought some success, and also the friendship of the influential *Milnes. A political novel, *Beauchamp's Career, followed in 1876, and in 1877 Meredith delivered a lecture on 'The Idea of Comedy', which was published in 1897 and enjoyed a long reputation. The novel for which he is chiefly celebrated, *The Egoist, appeared in 1879. *The Tragic Comedians was published in 1880 and Poems and Lyrics of the Joy of Earth, often held to contain his best poetry, including the final version of 'Love in a Valley', in 1883. The only novel to meet with general popularity, although exhibiting the growing preciosity of Meredith's style, was *Diana of the Crossways, which ran to three editions in 1885 alone. Among other volumes of verse were Ballads . . . of Tragic Life (1887) and A Reading of Earth (containing the 'Hymn to Colour', 1888); then came three more novels, *One of our Conquerors (1891), *Lord Ormont and his Aminta (1894), and *The Amazing Marriage (1895). A collection of short stories, including the celebrated 'The Case of General Ople and Lady Camper', appeared in 1898, as did Odes . . . of French History; A Reading of Life followed in 1901 and Last Poems in 1909. Celt and Saxon, an unfinished story, was published posthumously in 1910, and a conversational comedy, The Sentimentalists, was produced in the same year.

By the time he died Meredith had written steadily for 50 years, had received the OM and an Oxford DCL, was president of the *Society of Authors, and had become a greatly revered man of letters, sought out by many younger poets and novelists, such as H. *James, *Hardy, and R. L. *Stevenson, as well as by the rich and famous. He himself felt he was a poet first and a novelist after, but that has not been the verdict of his readers. His reputation stood very high well into this century, with his perceptive portrayal of women, his narrative skill, and his incisive dialogue receiving most praise; but the deliberate intricacy of much of his prose (twisted, as *Trollope wrote, 'into curl-papers') defeats many modern readers, and for the last 50 years or so neither his poetry nor his novels have received any great popular or critical acclaim. See L. Stevenson, The Ordeal of George Meredith (1954) and G. Beer, Meredith: a change of masks (1970).

MEREDITH, Owen, see LYTTON, E. R. B.

MERES, Francis (1565–1647), educated at Pembroke College, Cambridge, and rector and schoolmaster at Wing, was author of Palladis Tamia, Wits Treasury (1598), containing quotations and maxims from various writers. In this Meres reviewed all literary effort from the time of *Chaucer to his own day, contrasting each English author with a writer of like character in Latin, Greek, or Italian. He thus commemorates 125 Englishmen; his list of Shakespeare's works with his commendation of the dramatist's 'fine filed phrase' and his account of *Marlowe's death are notable elements in English literary history. The section on 'Poetrie' was edited by D. C. Allen (1933).

MÉRIMÉE, Prosper (1803–70), French novelist, playwright, and writer of short fiction. One of the earliest of the French Romantic dramatists, he successfully passed off the six short plays of Le Théâtre de Clara Gazul (1825) as having been written by the imaginary Spanish actress of the title. Another hoax was La Guzla, a collection of supposed translations of Illyrian poetry, in reality his own inventions. La Jacquerie (1828) was a series of dramatic scenes of medieval life; La chronique du règne de Charles IX (1829) a historical novel of the religious wars of the 16th cent. Mérimée's short stories—he is a recognized master of the form—include 'Matteo Falcone' (1829), 'La vision de Charles XI' (1829), 'La Vénus d'Ille' (1837), 'Colomba' (1840), 'Carmen' (1845), which inspired *Bizet's opera, and 'Lokis' (1869). His Lettres à une inconnue (written to Mlle 'Jenny' Dacquin) display his critical and ironic temperament.

Merion, Diana, the heroine of Meredith's *Diana of the Crossways.

Merle, Madame, a character in H. James's *The Portrait of a Lady.

MERLEAU-PONTY, Maurice (1908–61), French philosopher. With *Sartre, co-editor of Les Temps modernes, he dominated French intellectual life during the post-war period. Reacting against Cartesian idealism, he based his epistemology on the relationship between consciousness and the world. His main work Phénoménologie de la perception (1945, English trans. C. Smith, 1962), attempts to do equal justice to the mind's constructive powers in perception and to the independence of the object of perception, arguing that the structure of consciousness is neither discernible from first principles nor dependent on causal mechanisms, but exhibited in the mind's actual encounters with the world.

Merlin, the magician who guides the destinies of *Arthur and his predecessor *Uther, though the range of his activities extends beyond this feature of him for which he is most celebrated now. His story is first set out by *Geoffrey of Monmouth in his Vita Merlini (c.1150), which draws on the story of Ambrosius told by

*Nennius. Merlin is born of a devil and a virtuous maiden and is named after his maternal grandfather. He is superhumanly precocious and hairy but, although wilful, not malevolent as his diabolical father intended. He grows infatuated with Nimiane (Nimue or Vivien: see LADY OF THE LAKE), who imprisons him in a forest of air in Broceliande where he dies. He is also linked to the Welsh bard Myrddhin and is credited, like him, with a series of prophecies. He predicts to *Vortigern (as Ambrosius did in Nennius) the triumph of the Britons over the Saxons, as a gloss on the killing of a white dragon by a red one after the two creatures are released by the digging of the foundations of a citadel from which Vortigern is to fight the Saxons. In Geoffrey of Monmouth's *Historia Regum Britanniae* (Book 8) he aids Uther in the deceit by which he marries Igraine (Ygerna) and fathers Arthur, and he helps by magic to bring the great stones of Stonehenge from Naas in Ireland. The Arthurian stories connected with him form a very important part of the whole tradition in French in the Middle Ages, particularly as transmitted by the (fragmentary) stories of Merlin by Robert de *Boron, c.1200, the prose Vulgate *Merlin* and the *Suite du Merlin* (*Huth Merlin*); the latter two are related to de Boron. See R. S. Loomis ed., *Arthurian Literature in the Middle Ages* (1959), chapters 8, 19, 23, and 24, for a series of detailed accounts.

'Merlin and Vivien', one of Tennyson's *Idylls of the King*, published 1859 as 'Vivien', retitled 1870. The wily Vivien, filled with hatred for Arthur and his court, seduces the aged Merlin and imprisons him forever in an old oak.

Mermaid Series, The, a series of unexpurgated reprints of early English dramatists, published originally by *Vizetelly, at the suggestion of Havelock *Ellis, who edited the series from 1887 to 1889. It continued through various transformations, and became in 1964 the New Mermaid Series, under the general editorship of Philip Brockbank, later with Brian Morris. The series now includes English plays from the late medieval period up to the time of *Synge and *Wilde.

Mermaid Tavern, a tavern that stood in Bread Street (with an entrance in Friday Street), London. One of the earliest of English clubs, the Friday Street Club, started by Sir W. *Ralegh, met there and was frequented by Shakespeare, *Selden, *Donne, *Beaumont, and J. *Fletcher. It is celebrated by Beaumont in the fine lines ('Master Francis Beaumont to Ben Jonson'):

What things have we seen
Done at the Mermaid! heard words that have been
So nimble, and so full of subtle flame,
As if that every one from whence they came
Had meant to put his whole wit in a jest,
And had resolved to live a fool the rest
Of his dull life.

*Keats also wrote 'Lines on the Mermaid Tavern' beginning: 'Souls of poets dead and gone'.

Merrilies, Meg, the old gypsy woman in Scott's *Guy Mannering*. She is the subject of a poem by *Keats, 'Old Meg she was a gipsy'.

MERRY, Robert, see DELLA CRUSCANS.

Merry Devil of Edmonton, The, a romantic comedy published 1608, authorship unknown. C. *Lamb, who praised it highly, suggested *Drayton as the possible author. It was included in a volume in Charles II's library entitled 'Shakespeare' but there is no evidence in support of this attribution.

The prologue presents Peter Fabel of Edmonton, a magician, who has made a compact with the devil. The period of it has run out, and the fiend comes to claim Fabel. He is, however, tricked into sitting down in a necromantic chair, where he is held fast and is obliged to give a respite. The play itself, in which the magical element is practically absent, deals with the attempt of Sir Arthur Clare and his wife to break off the match between their daughter Millicent and Raymond Mounchensey, and its defeat by the elopement of the young couple, aided by the kindly magician Fabel.

Merry Wives of Windsor, The, a comedy by *Shakespeare, possibly written or adapted for the occasion of George Carey, Lord Hunsdon's installation as a knight of the Garter on 23 April 1597. Various topical allusions have been discerned in the play, but the tradition that it was written at the request of *Elizabeth I for a play showing *Falstaff in love is documented no earlier than 1702 (by J. *Dennis). The passage alluding to the Garter Feast is found only in the *Folio text (1623), which is twice the length of the 'bad' quarto (1602); the latter appears to be based on a report of a less courtly performance.

Falstaff, who is 'out at heels', determines to make love to the wives of Ford and Page, two gentlemen dwelling at Windsor, because they have the rule of their husband's purses. Nym and Pistol, the discarded followers of Falstaff, warn the husbands. Falstaff sends identical love-letters to Mrs Ford and Mrs Page, who contrive the discomfiture of the knight. At a first assignation at Ford's house, on the arrival of the husband, they hide Falstaff in a basket, cover him with foul linen, and have him tipped into a muddy ditch. At a second assignation, they disguise him as the 'fat woman of Brainford', in which character he is soundly beaten by Ford. The jealous husband having also been twice fooled, the plot is now revealed to him, and a final assignation is given to Falstaff in Windsor Forest at Herne's oak (see HERNE THE HUNTER), where he is beset and pinched by mock fairies and finally seized and exposed by Ford and Page.

The sub-plot is concerned with the wooing of Anne, the daughter of Page, by three suitors: Doctor Caius, a French physician, Slender, the foolish cousin of Justice Shallow, and Fenton, a wild young gentleman, whom Anne loves. Mistress Quickly, servant to Dr Caius, acts as go-between for all three suitors, and encourages them all impartially. Sir Hugh Evans, a Welsh parson, interferes on behalf of Slender and receives a challenge from the irascible Dr Caius, but hostilities are confined to the 'hacking' of the English tongue. At the final assignation with Falstaff in the forest, Page, who favours Slender, arranges that the latter shall carry off his daughter, who is to be dressed in white; while Mrs Page, who favours Dr Caius, arranges that he shall carry her off dressed in green. In the event both of these find themselves fobbed off with a boy in disguise, while Fenton has run away with and married the true Anne.

Merton College, Oxford, was founded in 1264 by Walter de Merton (d. 1277), chancellor of England and bishop of Rochester. It is generally regarded as the first society on the present collegiate model. R. *Bacon, *Duns Scotus, and *Wyclif are traditionally connected with it. A. *Wood was educated there.

Mertoun, Basil and Mordaunt, characters in Scott's *The Pirate.

Merygreeke, Mathewe, a character in Udall's *Ralph Roister Doister.

Mesrour, in the *Arabian Nights, the executioner of the Caliph *Hārūn ar-Rashīd, who with the vizier Jaffar used to accompany him when he walked at night disguised about the streets of Baghdad.

Messiah, (1) a famous oratorio by *Handel; (2) a religious epic (Messias) by *Klopstock; (3) a sacred eclogue by *Pope published in *The Spectator in May 1712, embodying in verse the Messianic prophecies of Isaiah.

Messianic Eclogue, see VIRGIL'S FOURTH OR MESSIANIC ECLOGUE.

Metamorphoses, see APULEIUS and OVID.

Metaphor, the transfer of a name or descriptive term to an object different from, but analogous to, that to which it is properly applicable, e.g. 'abysmal ignorance'. Mixed Metaphor is the application of two inconsistent metaphors to one object.
*Empson defines metaphor as the first of his *Seven Types of Ambiguity.

Metaphysical Poets. Poets generally grouped under this label include *Donne (who is regarded as founder of the 'school'), G. *Herbert, *Crashaw, H. *Vaughan, *Marvell, and *Traherne, together with lesser figures like *Benlowes, *Herbert of Cherbury, H. *King, A.

*Cowley, and *Cleveland. The label was first used (disparagingly) by Dr *Johnson in his 'Life of Cowley' (witten in 1777), where he identifies them as a 'race of writers' who display their learning, use far-fetched comparisons, and lack feeling. But *Pope partly anticipated Johnson when he spoke (Spence's Anecdotes) of Cowley borrowing his 'metaphysical' style from Donne, and earlier *Dryden had complained that Donne 'affects the metaphysics', perplexing the minds of the fair sex with 'nice speculations of philosophy'. Earlier still W. *Drummond, probably with Donne in mind, censured poetic innovators who employed 'Metaphysical Ideas and Scholastical Quiddities'. The label is misleading, since none of these poets is seriously interested in metaphysics (except Herbert of Cherbury, and even he excludes the interest from his poetry). Further, these poets have in reality little in common: the features their work is generally taken to display are sustained dialectic, paradox, novelty, incongruity, 'muscular' rhythms, giving the effect of a 'speaking voice', and the use of 'conceits', or comparisons in which tenor and vehicle can be related only by ingenious pseudo-logic.

With the new taste for clarity and the impatience with figurative language that prevailed after the *Restoration, their reputation dwindled and, though their 'quaintness' earned some recognition from critics, their revival was delayed until after the First World War. When it came, however, it was dramatic: indeed, the revaluation of metaphysical poetry, and the related down-grading of the *Romantics and *Milton, was the major feature of the rewriting of English literary history in the first half of the 20th cent. Key documents in the revival were H. J. C. *Grierson's Metaphysical Lyrics and Poems of the Seventeenth Century (1921) and T. S. *Eliot's essay 'Metaphysical Poets', which first appeared as a review of Grierson's collection (TLS, 20 Oct. 1921). According to Eliot these poets had the advantage of writing at a time when thought and feeling were closely fused, before the *'dissociation of sensibility' set in about the time of Milton. Their virtues of difficulty and tough newness were felt to relate them closely to the modernists—*Pound, *Yeats, and Eliot himself. Some more recent critics, notably Tuve, have questioned this. Modern scholarship has also followed Johnson's hint and related the English metaphysicals to *Marino, *Gongorism, and the European baroque generally.

Rosemond Tuve, Elizabethan and Metaphysical Imagery (1947); J. E. Duncan, The Revival of Metaphysical Poetry (1959); F. J. Warnke, European Metaphysical Poetry (1961); L. Nelson, Baroque Lyric Poetry (1961); J. M. Cohen, The Baroque Lyric (1963).

Metaphysical Society, The, was founded in 1869 by Sir J. T. *Knowles. It lasted until 1880 and brought together for discussion meetings most of the leaders of English thought of the period, of all shades of opinion, including T. H. *Huxley, *Tyndall, *Manning, *Gladstone, and *Tennyson.

METASTASIO (Pietro Trapassi) (1698–1782), the most important poet of the Arcadian school—members of an academy founded in 1690 in Rome by Queen Christina of Sweden: they represented a post-baroque search for simpler, pastoral forms. His importance lies in the development of opera: he invented melodrama and his *Didone abbandonata* (1724) was set by Scarlatti, his *Clemenza di Tito* (1734) by Scarlatti, *Mozart, and Gluck.

Metathesis, the transposition of letters or sounds in a word. When the transposition is between the letters or sounds of two words, it is popularly known as a 'Spoonerism', of which a well-known specimen, attributed to the Revd W. A. Spooner (1844–1930), warden of New College, Oxford, is 'Kinquering congs their titles take'.

Metre. The sound patterns on whose recurrence rhythm depends were formed in antiquity by arrangements of long and short syllables. Lines of verse consisted of 'feet', the commonest being the iambus (◡–), trochee (–◡), anapaest (◡◡–), dactyl (–◡◡), spondee (––). The pyrrhic (◡◡), tribrach (◡◡◡), amphibrach (◡–◡) (–◡), paeon (–◡◡◡), bacchius (◡–––), ionic a minore (◡◡––), and choriamb (–◡◡–) featured mainly in lyric poems. The most popular ancient measure was the *hexameter. Made up of four dactyls (replaceable by spondees) and then an invariable dactyl and spondee, it was divided by a *caesura (a break where a word ends before a foot is finished) usually in the third foot. Elegiac couplets linked the hexameter with a pentameter which, never found alone, consisted of two feet (dactyls or spondees) and a single long syllable before the caesura followed by two dactyls and a single syllable, always end-stopped. Dramatists used the iambic trimeter because of its closeness to common speech. This comprised six feet arranged in pairs (hence 'trimeter') where the iamb could be replaced by other feet according to strict rules. There were also numerous lyric metres. Alcaics, Sapphics, and Asclepiads organized trochees, dactyls, and spondees in various patterns, and trochaic *hendecasyllabics flourished in satire.

The 5th cent. AD brought, however, the beginnings of a radical change. The shape of the classical feet was retained, but stress became their determining feature, so that a trochee was an accented followed by an unaccented syllable. The trochaic tetrameter catalectic, which was divided by a caesura after the fourth trochee, the second half consisting of three trochees and a single syllable, provided the basis for most medieval hymns.

English prosody is similarly based on stress. The earliest measures to develop were trochaic, but soon iambic couplets of four or five feet linked by rhyme became more popular. In the four-foot couplet we find extensive modulation: often the first foot has only one syllable, and the final syllable in the fifth foot is dropped. The five-foot couplet had a strict form, end-stopped with a marked middle break, but also a form that allowed overflow from one line to the next and substitution of different two- or even three-syllable feet for the iamb. But it is not in the couplet that the five-foot iambic line (iambic pentameter) attained greatest importance. Introduced into poetic drama in 1562, it had a distinguished history as *'blank verse', with more modulations than in the couplet and the final foot often replaced by an amphibrach. When blank verse was used later in epic by *Milton, the modulations, if more controlled, were also more frequent and the use of overflow developed into paragraph construction. Five-foot lines were also built into stanzas with a variety of rhyme schemes: *rhyme-royal (or rime royal; seven lines rhymed ababbcc), used for narrative from *Chaucer to W. *Morris; the nine-line *Spenserian stanza, ababbcbcc; and, principally, the *sonnet introduced by *Wyatt and used since by every major English poet. (Wyatt copied *Petrarch, dividing the sonnet into an octave rhymed abba, abba, and a sestet ccd, ccd or cde, cde; but Shakespeare preferred three quatrains ending with a couplet.) Other popular iambic metres include in Tudor times the awkward *Poulter's Measure, a rhymed couplet where the first line had twelve, the second fourteen syllables. Broken by pause and internal rhyme, this makes a stanza 3343 which has been widely used by hymn writers. Fourteeners appear unresolved in *Chapman's *Homer*, but provide, when divided 4343 and rhymed, the buoyant and well-known ballad stanza. Trochaic, anapaestic, and dactylic metres, though they figure in many poems, have not been as popular as the iambic.

Verse in the 20th cent. has largely escaped the straitjacket of traditional metrics.

Metroland, Margot (originally Margot Beste-Chetwynde), a character in E. Waugh's *Decline and Fall*, *Vile Bodies*, *Scoop*, and other novels.

MEUN, Jean de, see ROMAN DE LA ROSE.

MEW, Charlotte Mary (1869–1928), poet and short story writer, was the daughter of a prosperous London architect and was born in Bloomsbury where she spent most of her life. Although stubborn and reserved in temperament, she accepted a civil list pension procured for her by *Hardy, but, beset by increasing family and financial problems that stifled her literary output, she eventually committed suicide. Her short story 'Passed' appeared in *The Yellow Book* in 1894, but she did not become well known until her first volume of poetry, *The Farmer's Bride* (1915). Her second volume, *The Rambling Sailor*, appeared posthumously in 1929. Her poems are notable for a restraint of expression combined with a powerful and passionate content which distinguish her from many of her Georgian contemporaries. Her collected poems and prose was edited by V. Warner, 1981; see also P. Fitzgerald, *Charlotte Mew and her Friends* (1984).

MEYNELL, Alice, *née* Thompson (1847–1922), became a Roman Catholic in 1868, and in 1875 published her first volume of poetry, *Preludes*, which attracted the attention of Wilfrid Meynell (1852–1948), author and editor, whom she married in 1877. She had many friends in the literary world, including F. *Thompson, *Meredith, and *Patmore, and a busy domestic life. Her poetic inspiration was intermittent, but her several volumes of verse, which include *Poems* (1893), *Later Poems* (1902), and *Last Poems* (1923), won her a considerable reputation; many of her most successful poems deal with the theme of religious mystery. She is perhaps now more admired for her essays, introductions, and anthologies, which, despite her prolific output, manifest independence and sensitivity of critical judgement; her essays, published in the *National Observer*, the *Pall Mall Gazette*, *The Tablet*, and other periodicals were collected under various titles, which include *The Rhythm of Life* (1893), *The Colour of Life* (1896), and *The Spirit of Place* (1899). There is a life by J. Badeni (1981).

MEYNELL, Sir Francis Meredith Wilfrid (1891–1975), book designer, publisher, and journalist, and son of Wilfrid and Alice *Meynell. He was founder and director of the *Nonesuch Press, and his autobiography *My Lives* was published in 1971.

Micawber, Wilkins and Mrs, characters in Dickens's *David Copperfield*.

'Michael', a pastoral poem by *Wordsworth, written and published 1800. The poem is a narrative in blank verse, describing, with a moving strength and simplicity, the lonely life in Grasmere of the old shepherd Michael, his wife, and his beloved son Luke. Because of family misfortune Luke is sent away to a dissolute city, where he disgraces himself; he eventually disappears abroad. Michael dies in grief and the cottage and pasture become a ruin.

Michael Angelo Titmarsh, see TITMARSH, M. A.

Michaelmas Terme, see MIDDLETON, T.

MICHELANGELO **BUONARROTI** (1475–1564), Florentine painter, sculptor, architect, and poet. His first patron was Lorenzo de' Medici. On Lorenzo's death in 1492 he left Florence; by 1496 he was in Rome, where he established his reputation with the *Pietà* (completed 1499; St Peter's, Rome). He returned to Florence in 1501; his two major early works, the *David* (1501–4, Florence, Accademia) and the *Bathers*, a cartoon for a battle scene to decorate the Palazzo Vecchio, express the humanistic ideals of the High Renaissance through the portrayal of the nude, depicting the beauty, strength, and rich diversity of movement and expression of which the human body is capable. From 1505 he was in Rome where Julius II first commissioned him to carve his vast tomb and then interrupted the work by requiring him to paint the ceiling of the Sistine chapel (1508–12). A very reduced version of the tomb, with his statue of *Moses*, was later set up in S. Pietro in Vincoli. Michelangelo's later works, the Medici chapel (1519–34) in S. Lorenzo, Florence, and especially the *Last Judgement* (Sistine chapel, Vatican; 1536–41), reveal a disillusionment which echoes the instability of church and state after the Reformation and the sack of Rome. In 1546 he became chief architect to St Peter's and designed the dome.

Michelangelo left around 300 poems and many letters. Amongst them are many love poems, full of Platonic imagery, to the beautiful Tommaso de' Cavalieri, whom Michelangelo met in 1532. Others, intensely spiritual, are addressed to Vittoria *Colonna; his latest poems express the fears of age over sin and salvation.

Michelangelo's contemporaries idolized 'il divino Michelangelo'; and yet feared his passionate, melancholy character. His biography was written in his lifetime; *Vasari described him as towering over the Greeks and Romans and bringing to perfection the great artistic tradition that had opened with Cimabue. Michelangelo's pupil Ascanio Condivi, spurred on by Michelangelo, brought out a life in 1553. Yet by the 1540s Michelangelo's piety had come under attack; *Aretino, in a famous letter of 1545, poured scurrilous abuse on his character and on the nudes of the *Last Judgement*. Throughout the 17th and 18th cents classicist writers, while accepting his greatness, felt uneasy with his individuality and favoured *Raphael. A change may first be sensed in the late 18th cent., when Sir J. *Reynolds, in his last discourse, declared his wish that 'the last words which I should pronounce in this Academy, and from this place, might be the name of Michael Angelo' (1790). The change is associated with new concepts of the *Sublime and with the cult of Romantic genius, and finds increasingly passionate expression in writings and drawings of *Fuseli, West, and *Blake and, in Europe, in the writings of *Goethe, *Delacroix, and *Stendhal. In the late 19th cent. scholarly editions of the poems and letters were published for the first time and a lavishly documented, albeit romantic, biography was written by J. A. *Symonds (1893). In the 20th cent. scholars concentrate on analysing the works in an art historical context but the legend lingers on, as in Irving Stone's novel *The Agony and the Ecstasy* (1961).

MICHELET, Jules (1798–1874), French historian, keeper of National Historical Archives (1831–52), professor at the Collège de France (1838–51). His principal work, *L'Histoire de France* (vols I–VI, 1833–43; vols VII–XVII, 1855–67), is remarkable for its luminous and eloquent style, its aim to re-create the past in its complex fullness, and for the part that the author attributes to geographical and racial factors in forming the men who were the agents of historical change. Michelet's fervent republicanism is evident in his other major work, *La Révolution française* (7 vols, 1847–53). He also wrote a number of monographs and shorter studies on subjects allied to history in his broad conception of it: e.g, *Les Jésuites* (1843, with Edgar Quinet), *Du prêtre, de la femme, de la famille* (1845), *Le Peuple* (1846), *La Femme* (1860).

MICKIEWICZ, Adam (1798–1855), Polish poet, born near Nowogrodek, and educated at the University of Wilno, where he became involved in nationalist politics, was imprisoned, and then exiled in 1824 to Russia for five years by the Russian authorities. He subsequently lived in Dresden, Paris, and Rome, and died in Constantinople. His first collection of poems, published 1822, contained his poetic manifesto, an essay 'On Romantic Poetry'; in the same year he studied English and became a devoted admirer of *Byron, whose struggles for freedom strongly influenced him. His passionately patriotic works include *Konrad Wallenrod* (1828), a narrative poem presenting in historical guise the enduring hostility between Russia and Poland, and *Dziady* (*Forefathers' Eve*), an extremely complex and baffling work, of which the first part appeared in 1823, and the third and greatest in 1832. Part 3 is a poetic drama (unfinished), in which the central character, Gustav, awakens to political and prophetic consciousness; it is based on Mickiewicz's own political experiences at Wilno. *Pan Tadeusz* (1834) is an epic poem set in Lithuania on the eve of Napoleon's expedition to Russia in 1812: it has been adapted by D. *Davie.

Microcosm of London, The, see ACKERMANN, R.

Microcosmographie, see EARLE, J.

Midas, a prose play by *Lyly, published 1592, on the legend of Midas, king of Phrygia.

Middle Ages, the period from the Roman decadence (AD 5th cent.) to the Renaissance (about 1500), to designate the period between the end of classical culture proper and its revival at the Renaissance. The high point of its culture is the 12th and 13th cents, with the growth of vernacular literature around 1200 and the Scholastic compendia of theology and philosophy in the 13th cent. The earliest use of 'Middle Age' in this sense yet discovered is in one of *Donne's sermons (1621), but the corresponding Latin terms, *medium aevum, media aetas,* etc., are found in the 16th cent. The term is sometimes restricted to the 11th–15th cents, the earlier part of the period being called the Dark Ages.

Middle English, see ENGLISH.

Middlemarch, *A Study of Provincial Life,* a novel by G. *Eliot, published 1871–2.

The scene is laid in the provincial town of Middlemarch, Loamshire, during the years of the agitation immediately preceding the first *Reform Bill. It has a multiple plot, with several interlocking sets of characters. Dorothea Brooke, an ardent, intelligent, idealistic young woman, under the negligent though affable care of her eccentric uncle, marries the elderly pedant Mr Casaubon, despite the doubts of her sister Celia, her neighbour and suitor Sir James Chettam (who later marries Celia), and Mrs Cadwallader, the rector's outspoken wife. The marriage proves intensely unhappy; Dorothea realizes during a disastrous honeymoon in Rome that Casaubon's scholarly plans to write a great work, a 'Key to all Mythologies', are doomed, as are her own aspirations to share and aid her husband's intellectual life, and her respect for him gradually turns to pity. She is sustained by the friendship of Casaubon's young cousin, Will Ladislaw, a lively, light-hearted, good-natured young man, detested by Casaubon, who begins to suspect that Dorothea's feelings for Ladislaw are questionable; his irritation is increased by the fact that he fears he has acted justly but not generously by his impoverished kinsman. Shortly before he dies, with characteristic meanness, he adds a codicil to his will by which Dorothea forfeits her fortune if she marries Ladislaw.

Meanwhile other threads have been added to the remarkably broad canvas of the novel. We follow the fortunes of Fred and Rosamund Vincy, son and daughter of the mayor of Middlemarch; the extrovert Fred, unsuitably destined to be a clergyman, is in love with his childhood sweetheart Mary Garth, a practical, shrewd young woman, daughter of Caleb Garth, a land agent. Mary, who at the opening of the novel is nursing her disagreeable and aged relative Mr Featherstone, will not pledge herself to Fred unless he abandons his father's plan for him to enter the church and proves himself stable and self-sufficient. Rosamund, the town's beauty, sets herself to capture the ambitious, idealistic, and well-connected doctor Tertius Lydgate; she succeeds, and their marriage, wrecked by her selfishness, insensitivity, and materialism, proves as unhappy as the Casaubons'. Lydgate finds himself heavily in debt, and against his better judgement borrows money from Mr Bulstrode, the mayor's brother-in-law, a religious hypocrite; Lydgate's career is ruined when he finds himself involved in a scandal concerning the death of Raffles, an unwelcome visitor from Bulstrode's shady past. Only Dorothea, now widowed, maintains faith in him, but she is severely shocked to find Ladislaw and Rosamund together in what seem to be compromising circumstances. Rosamund finally rises above self-interest to reveal that Ladislaw has remained faithful to the memory of Dorothea, though with no prospect of any happy outcome. Dorothea and Ladislaw at last confess their love to one another; she renounces Casaubon's fortune and marries him. Fred, partly sobered by the spectacle of Lydgate's decline, and encouraged by Caleb Garth to enter his own profession, marries Mary. Lydgate is condemned to a successful and fashionable practice and dies at 50, his ambitions frustrated.

Through the histories of these characters, George Eliot analyses and comments upon the social and political upheavals of the period, contrasting the staunch Tory attitudes of Chettam and the Cadwalladers with the growing demand for Reform, somewhat unsatisfactorily espoused by Mr Brooke, more satisfactorily by Ladislaw, who in the last chapter becomes 'an ardent public man' and a member of Parliament, with Dorothea's support. The importance of marital loyalty is also widely illustrated, not least in Mrs Bulstrode's support of her husband in his disgrace.

George Eliot's reputation reached its height with *Middlemarch*, despite some complaints that the action was slow or the tone didactic; H. *James found faults in its organization, but concluded, 'It sets a limit . . . to the development of the old-fashioned English novel' (1874). Its status as one of the greatest works of English fiction was confirmed by *Leavis (*The Great Tradition*, 1948), despite his doubts about the indulgent portrayal of Dorothea.

Middlemas, Richard, a character in Scott's *The Surgeon's Daughter*.

Middleton, Clara and Dr, characters in Meredith's *The Egoist*.

MIDDLETON, Conyers (1683–1750), was a fellow of Trinity College, Cambridge, and protobibliothecarius of the University Library. His *Letter from Rome* was published in 1729, and his life of Cicero in 1741. His *A Free Inquiry into the Miraculous Powers which are supposed to have subsisted in the Christian Church* (1749), which attacked the authenticity of post-apostolic miracles, caused much controversy; ironically, it was partly responsible for *Gibbon's temporary

conversion to Catholicism, but is quoted to very different effect in Chapter XV of *The Decline and Fall of the Roman Empire*.

MIDDLETON, Thomas (1580–1627), the son of a prosperous London bricklayer, matriculated at Oxford but probably did not take a degree. His first published work was a long and undistinguished poem, *The Wisdome of Solomon Paraphrased* (1597), which was followed by other verses and prose pamphlets. By 1600 he was in London, 'daylie accompaninge the players', one of whose sisters he married, and by 1603 he was writing for *Henslowe, collaborating with J. *Webster, *Dekker, *Rowley, *Munday, and others; many of these works are now lost. He collaborated with Dekker in writing the first part of *The Honest Whore* (1604) and wrote many successful comedies of city life, including *The Familie of Love* (with Dekker?, written 1602, published 1608), *The Roaring Girle* (with Dekker, written 1604–8?, published 1611), *Michaelmas Terme* (written 1604–6, published 1607), *A Trick to Catch the Old-One* (written 1604–7, published 1608), *A Mad World, My Masters* (written 1604–7, published 1608), *A Chaste mayd in Cheap-side* (written 1613, published 1630), and *The Mayor of Quinborough* (written 1615–20, published 1661). *A Fair Quarrel*, a tragi-comedy written with Rowley (c.1615–16, published 1617), a play in a very different genre, discusses the ethics of duelling: *The Spanish Gipsy*, also with Rowley (and possibly *Ford, written 1623, published 1625) is a romantic comedy based on two plots from *Cervantes. Other plays include *The Witch* (written 1609–16, not published until 1778); *The Widow* (with *Jonson? and *Fletcher?, written 1615–17, published 1652), and *Anything for a Quiet Life* (with Webster?, written c.1620–2, published 1662).

A writer of great versatility, Middleton also wrote many pageants and masques for city occasions, and was appointed city chronologer in 1620. His political satire *A Game at Chesse* (written 1624, published 1625) created a furore, and caused him and the actors to be summoned before the Privy Council: it was described by T. S. *Eliot as 'a perfect piece of literary political art'. But Middleton is now best known for his two great tragedies, *The Changeling* (with Rowley, written 1622, published 1653) and *Women beware Women* (written 1620–7, published 1657), both of which were highly praised by Eliot in his influential essay on Middleton (1927). Both have been successfully revived on stage in recent years. Many scholars now also consider that *The Revenger's Tragedy* (1607) is certainly by Middleton (see D. J. Lake, *The Canon of Thomas Middleton's Plays*, 1975), but this and many other suggested attributions are still disputed. The works were edited by A. H. Bullen in 8 vols, 1885–6, and there are several recent single editions in the New *Mermaid series. For an account of the life see R. H. Barker, *Thomas Middleton* (1958).

Midshipman Easy, Mr, a novel by F. *Marryat, published 1836.

Jack Easy is the son of a wealthy gentleman who brings his boy up to believe that all men are equal, a notion which causes considerable problems to Jack as a midshipman. But he is heir to a fortune and this, together with his cheerful honesty and the help of his Ashanti friend Mesty, help him through many clashes, encounters, and adventures. Hawkins, the bellicose chaplain, Mr Biggs the boatswain, and Mr Pottyfar, the lieutenant who kills himself with his own universal medicine, are notable among the ship's company.

Midsummer Night's Dream, A, a comedy by *Shakespeare, written probably about 1595 or 1596. It was printed in quarto in 1600 and 1619. The play has often been thought to be associated with a courtly marriage but scholarly opinion is undecided as to which of several possible weddings it may celebrate. It has no single major source, but Shakespeare drew, among other authors, on *Chaucer, *Golding's translation of *Ovid, and *Apuleius's *Golden Ass*.

Hermia, ordered by her father Egeus to marry Demetrius, refuses, because she loves Lysander, while Demetrius has formerly professed love for her friend Helena, and Helena loves Demetrius. Under the law of Athens, Theseus, the duke, gives Hermia four days in which to obey her father; else she must suffer death or enter a nunnery. Hermia and Lysander agree to leave Athens secretly in order to be married where the Athenian law cannot pursue them, and to meet in a wood a few miles from the city. Hermia tells Helena of the project, and the latter tells Demetrius. Demetrius pursues Hermia to the wood, and Helena Demetrius, so that all four are that night in the wood. This wood is the favourite haunt of the fairies.

Oberon and Titania, king and queen of the fairies, have quarrelled, because Titania refuses to give up to him a little changeling boy for a page. Oberon tells Puck, a mischievous sprite, to fetch him a certain magic flower, of which he will press the juice on the eyes of Titania while she sleeps, so that she may fall in love with what she first sees when she wakes. Overhearing Demetrius in the wood reproaching Helena for following him, and desirous to reconcile them, Oberon orders Puck to place some of the love-juice on Demetrius' eyes, but so that Helena shall be near him when he does it. Puck, mistaking Lysander for Demetrius, applies the charm to him, and as Helena is the first person Lysander sees he at once woos her, enraging her because she thinks she is being made a jest of. Oberon, discovering Puck's mistake, now places some of the juice on Demetrius' eyes; he on waking also first sees Helena, so that both Lysander and Demetrius are now wooing her. The ladies begin to abuse one another and the men go off to fight for Helena.

Meanwhile Oberon has placed the love-juice on Titania's eyelids, who wakes to find Bottom the weaver near her, wearing an ass's head (Bottom and a company of Athenian tradesmen are in the wood to rehearse a play for the duke's wedding, and Puck has put an ass's head on Bottom); Titania at once becomes enamoured of him, and toys with his 'amiable cheeks' and 'fair large ears'. Oberon, finding them together, reproaches Titania for bestowing her love on an ass, and again demands the changeling boy, whom she in her confusion surrenders; whereupon Oberon releases her from the charm. Puck at Oberon's orders throws a thick fog about the human lovers, and brings them all together, unknown to one another, and they fall asleep. He applies a remedy to their eyes, so that when they awake they return to their former loves. Theseus and Egeus appear on the scene, the runaways are forgiven, and the couples married. The play ends with the 'play' of 'Pyramus and Thisbe', comically acted by Bottom and his fellow tradesmen, to grace these nuptials and those of Theseus and Hippolyta.

Miggs, Miss, in Dickens's *Barnaby Rudge*, the shrewish maidservant of Mrs Varden.

MIGNE, Jacques-Paul (1800–75), French priest and publisher. He founded a printing house to make theological works available at moderate prices. His most famous publication was the *Patrologiae Cursus Completus* ('Complete Course of the Teachings of the Church Fathers'), comprising the *Patrologia Latina* ('Collection of the Latin Fathers', 221 vols, 1844–64), the works of Latin ecclesiastical writers from the earliest known to Innocent III (d. 1216), and the *Patrologia Graeca* ('Collection of the Greek Fathers', 161 vols, 1857–66), the writings of Christian Greeks down to the time of the Council of Florence (1438–9).

Mignon, in the *Wilhelm Meister's Apprenticeship* of *Goethe, a fairy-like child rescued by Wilhelm from a troupe of rope-dancers. She becomes passionately attached to him, and from hopeless love and longing for her Italian home pines away and dies. She is the prototype of Fenella in Scott's *Peveril of the Peak*. Goethe puts in her mouth the famous song 'Kennst du das Land' ('Know'st thou the land'), which is well known in settings by *Schubert and *Wolf.

Miles gloriosus, the braggart soldier, a stock character in Greek and Roman comedy, and also the title of a play by *Plautus, which contains a prototype of the role in its protagonist, Pyrgopolynices. Elements of the miles gloriosus may be found in Shakespeare's *Parolles, *Pistol, and *Falstaff, in Jonson's Captain *Bobadill, and in Beaumont and Fletcher's *Bessus.

Milesians, the people of Miledh, a fabulous Spanish king, whose sons are said to have invaded Ireland about 1300 BC. They represent probably the first Gaelic invaders of the country. See FIR BOLGS.

Milesian Tales, a collection, now lost, of short Greek stories of love and adventure, of a generally licentious character, by Aristides of Miletus of the 2nd cent. BC.

MILL, James (1773–1836), born near Forfar, the son of a shoemaker, was educated for the ministry, but came to London in 1802 and took up journalism. He published in 1817 a *History of British India* which obtained him a high post in the East India Company's service. He was closely associated with *Bentham and *Ricardo, whose views in philosophy and political economy, respectively, he adopted. He published his *Elements of Political Economy* in 1821, *Analysis of the Phenomena of the Human Mind* in 1829, and *Fragment on Mackintosh* in 1835. In the *Analysis* he provided, by an elaboration of *Hartley's theory of association, a psychological basis for Bentham's utilitarianism: associations may become inseparable and transform what had merely been means into ends sought on their account, thus explaining disinterested conduct by the egoistic individual. He also endeavoured to found on the association of ultimate sensations a theory of knowledge and reality. The *Fragment on Mackintosh* is a rejoinder to the attack on the utilitarians contained in the *Dissertation on the Progress of Ethical Philosophy* of *Mackintosh. Mill helped to found and contributed to the *Westminster Review*. An interesting picture of his austere personality is given in the *Autobiography* (1873) of his son J. S. *Mill.

MILL, John Stuart (1806–73), son of James *Mill, by whom he was rigorously educated from a very early age, and by whose influence he obtained a clerkship in the India House. He formed the Utilitarian Society which met during 1823–6 to read essays and discuss them, and in 1825 edited *Bentham's *Treatise upon Evidence*. In 1826 an acute mental crisis caused him to reconsider his own aims and those of the Benthamite school; he found a new will to live in poetry, particularly in that of *Wordsworth, who brought him 'a greatly increased interest in the common feelings and common destiny of human beings'. In 1831 he met Harriet Taylor, whom he saw constantly for the next 20 years and who was, in his view, the chief inspiration of his philosophy; after her husband's death they married in 1851. His divergence from strict Benthamite doctrine is shown in his essays on

'Bentham' and 'Coleridge' (1838, 1840, *London and Westminster Review*) whom he describes as 'the two great seminal minds of England in this age'; and, later, in *Utilitarianism* (1861). In 1843 he published his *System of *Logic* and in 1848 *Principles of Political Economy*. In 1859 appeared his essay on *Liberty* and two volumes of *Dissertations and Discussions*, and in 1865 his *Examination of Sir William Hamilton's Philosophy*. Among other works may be mentioned *Thoughts on Parliamentary Reform* (1859), *Representative Government* (1861), *Auguste Comte and Positivism* (1865), his *Inaugural Address* on being installed rector of the University of St Andrews in 1867, and *The Subjection of Women* (1869). His *Autobiography* (1873), a classic of its genre, describes his intellectual and moral development from his earliest years to his maturity.

On the dissolution of the East India Company in 1858 he retired with a pension, and was independent MP for Westminster 1865–8. He passed most of the remainder of his life in France, and died at Avignon.

MILLAIS, Sir John Everett (1829–96), who began his spectacular career as child prodigy and finished as president of the *Royal Academy (1896), is best known as a founder member of the *Pre-Raphaelite Brotherhood. His *Lorenzo and Isabella* (1848–9; Liverpool, Walker Art Gallery), from *Keats's poem, is one of the earliest pre-Raphaelite works; the startling realism of his *Christ in the House of his Parents* (1849–50) was brutally attacked by *Dickens in *Household Words* in 1850. His loveliest pictures—*Ophelia* (1851–2), *Mariana* (1851; collection of Lord Sherfield) which was exhibited with lines from *Tennyson's poem, and the poignant, melancholy *Autumn Leaves* (1856; Manchester, City Art Gallery)—display his brilliant technique and fresh, precise detail. His portrait of his champion *Ruskin was painted in Scotland in 1853; Millais fell in love with Effie Ruskin on this holiday and married her in 1855. Millais made a distinguished contribution to the revival of book illustration in the 1860s; he had contributed to E. *Moxon's edition of Tennyson in 1857; he illustrated several of *Trollope's novels with sharply-observed scenes from contemporary Victorian life and became a close friend of Trollope. He also became a friend of Dickens and drew him the day after the novelist's death. Millais' later paintings are less interesting; *Bubbles* (1886; A. and F. Pears Ltd) became celebrated as a soap advertisement.

Millamant, the heroine of Congreve's *The Way of the World*, a witty coquette, who is at the same time a lady of fashion, the author's most vivid creation.

MILLAY, Edna St Vincent (1892–1950), American poet, born in Maine and educated at Vassar. Her first volume, *Renascence and other*

poems (1917), was followed by *A Few Figs from Thistles* (1920), which established her persona as a reckless, romantic, cynical, 'naughty' New Woman with such poems as 'The Penitent' and 'My Candle Burns at Both Ends'. This was followed by many other volumes, including dramatic pieces; her *Collected Poems* were published in 1956. Her impact on a whole generation was recorded by D. *Parker, who wrote, 'We all wandered in after Miss Millay. We were all being dashing and gallant, declaring that we weren't virgins, whether we were or not. Beautiful as she was, Miss Millay did a great deal of harm with her double-burning candles . . . made poetry seem so easy that we could all do it. But, of course, we couldn't.'

Millbank, Oswald and Edith, in *Coningsby* by B. Disraeli.

MILLER, Arthur (1915–), American playwright, born in New York and educated at the University of Michigan, where he began to write plays. He made his name with *All My Sons* (1947), an Ibsenesque drama about a manufacturer of defective aeroplane parts, and established himself as a leading dramatist with *Death of a Salesman* (1949), in which a travelling salesman, Willie Loman, is brought to disaster by accepting the false values of contemporary society. This was followed by *The Crucible* (1952), in which the Salem witchcraft trials of 1692 are used as a parable for McCarthyism in America in the 1950s. *A View from the Bridge* (1955) is a tragedy of family honour and revenge, sparked by the presence in longshoreman Eddie's apartment of two illegal Italian immigrants; the lawyer Alfieri comments as chorus on the inevitability of the action. *The Misfits* (1961) is a screenplay written for his then wife, Marilyn Monroe. *After the Fall* (1964) presents the semi-autobiographical figure of Quentin, seeking to comprehend the meaning of his own past relationships, and *The Price* (1968) contrasts the lives and opinions of two long-estranged brothers, who meet to dispose of the old family house. Miller has also published short stories and essays, and adapted *Ibsen's *An Enemy of the People* (1951). Although most of Miller's plays are set in contemporary America, and on the whole offer a realistic portrayal of life and society, the overtones from Ibsen and Greek tragedy are frequently conspicuous, and the theme of self-knowledge and self-realization is recurrent; in some of the works, symbolism and naturalism are unobtrusively combined.

MILLER, Henry Valentine (1891–1980), American novelist and essayist, born in New York, the son of a middle-class tailor of German origin. He was brought up in Brooklyn, early acquiring the intensely individualistic and rebellious spirit that led him to reject university in favour of a sequence of odd jobs and intellectual,

sexual, and literary enterprises. He left America for Europe in 1930, and his autobiographical novel *Tropic of Cancer* was published in Paris in 1934 by the Obelisk Press; it is a frank and lively account of an American artist's adventures in Paris, and was banned for decades (as were many of his works) in Britain and the US. This was followed by many other works which mingled metaphysical speculation (he was interested in both theosophy and astrology) with sexually explicit scenes, surreal passages, and scenes of grotesque comedy; they include *Tropic of Capricorn* (France, 1939; US 1962), *The Colossus of Maroussi* (1941), *The Air-Conditioned Nightmare* (1945, reflections on a return to America), and a sequence of three works, *Sexus* (1949), *Plexus* (1953), and *Nexus* (1960), known together as *The Rosy Crucifixion*. In 1944 he settled in Big Sur, near Carmel, California, and despite continuing attacks from censors in various countries, including his own, he gradually became accepted as a major figure in the fight for literary and personal freedom, a spiritual sage who greatly influenced the *Beat generation in its search for salvation through extremes of experience. Works which had been previously condemned as pornographic are now widely described as works of 'innocent eroticism', although modern *feminist criticism (while recognizing his importance) has strongly attacked the sexism of his obsession with male potency and female masochism.

MILLER, Hugh (1802–56), born in Cromarty, began to write poetry while working as a stonemason (*Poems written in the Leisure Hours of a Journeyman Mason*, 1829), but made a more lasting mark as journalist and as self-educated palaeontologist. From 1840 he was editor of *The Witness*, a radical and evangelical twice-weekly for which he wrote on many subjects, including rural poverty, geology, and foreign affairs. His books include *The Old Red Sandstone, or New Walks in an Old Field* (1841), a vivid account of his sense of excitement and discovery when, as a young man, he learned to look for fossils in the sandstone quarries; it became a Victorian classic, highly regarded both for its learning and its lucidity of expression. His autobiographical *My Schools and Schoolmasters* (1854) also enjoyed a considerable success. In *The Footprints of the Creator* (1849), which was an attack on R. *Chambers's *The Vestiges of Creation*, Miller expounded his own God-centred and pre-Darwinian views of evolution, and argued that evolutionary change took place not slowly but suddenly. He shot himself on Christmas Eve 1856, after recording 'a fearful dream'. See George Rosie, *Hugh Miller: Outrage and Order* (1981).

'Miller of Dee, The', see BICKERSTAFFE.

'Miller's Tale, The', see CANTERBURY TALES, 2.

Mill on the Floss, The, a novel by G. *Eliot, published 1860.

Tom and Maggie, the principal characters, are the children of the honest but ignorant and obstinate Mr Tulliver, the miller of Dorlcote Mill on the Floss. Tom is a prosaic youth, narrow of imagination and intellect, animated by conscious rectitude and a disposition to control others. Maggie in contrast is highly strung, intelligent, emotional, and, as a child, rebellious. From this conflict of temperaments, and from Maggie's frustrated sense of purpose, spring much of her unhappiness and the ultimate tragedy. Her deep love of her brother is thwarted by his lack of understanding, and she turns to Philip Wakem, the deformed son of a neighbouring lawyer, for intellectual and emotional companionship. Unfortunately lawyer Wakem is the object of Mr Tulliver's suspicion and dislike, which develop into hatred when Tulliver is made bankrupt as a result of litigation in which Wakem is on the other side. Tom, loyal to his father, discovers the secret friendship of Maggie and Philip, and forbids their meetings: Maggie reluctantly complies. After Mr Tulliver's death, accelerated by a scene of violence in which he thrashes the lawyer, Maggie leaves the mill for a visit at St Ogg's to her cousin Lucy Deane, who is to marry the handsome and agreeable Stephen Guest. Stephen, though loyal in intention to Lucy, is attracted by Maggie, and she by him. A boating expedition on the river leads, partly by Stephen's design, partly by accident, to Maggie's being irremediably compromised; Stephen implores her to marry him, but she refuses. Her brother turns her out of the house, and the society of St Ogg's ostracizes her. She and her mother take refuge with the loyal friend of her childhood, the packman Bob Jakins. Only Lucy, Philip, and the clergyman Dr Kenn show sympathy. The situation seems without issue, but in the last chapter a great flood descends upon the town, and Maggie, whose first thought is of her brother's safety, courageously rescues him from the mill. There is a moment of recognition and reconciliation before the boat overturns, and both, locked in a final embrace, are drowned.

The portrayal of childhood, of rural life, and the subsidiary characters of Mrs Tulliver's sisters, the strong-minded Mrs Glegg and the melancholy Mrs Pullett, with their respective spouses, delighted most critics, though the book was felt to lack the charm of *Adam Bede; Maggie's lapse into passion, the character of the lightweight Stephen, and the arbitrary tragedy of the denouement enraged others. It remains, however, one of the most widely read of her works.

Mills, Miss, in Dickens's *David Copperfield, Dora's friend.

Mills and Boon, a publishing company founded in 1908; its early authors included P. G. *Wodehouse and Jack *London, and it launched the career of Georgette *Heyer. Its name has since become almost synonymous with popular romantic fiction; as the circulating *libraries declined in the 1950s and paperback fiction became more popular, Mills and Boon (in association with a Canadian company, Harlequin) published increasing quantities of light romances, doctor/nurse romances, and historical fiction, selling not only in bookshops, but also in supermarkets, newsagents, etc.

MILMAN, Henry Hart (1791–1868), educated at Eton and Brasenose College, Oxford, became incumbent of St Mary's, Reading, then professor of poetry at Oxford (1821–31) and dean of St Paul's (1849). He wrote a number of verse dramas, of which Fazio (1815), a neo-Jacobean tragedy set in Italy, proved successful on the stage; also a Miltonic epic, Samor (1818), set in 5th-cent. Britain. His historical writings include The History of the Jews (1829) and History of Latin Christianity (1854–5).

MILNE, A(lan) A(lexander) (1882–1956), educated at Westminster School and Trinity College, Cambridge, became a prolific author of plays, novels, poetry, short stories, biography, and essays, all of which have been overshadowed by his children's books. After freelance work in London he became from 1906 to 1914 assistant editor of *Punch; and after the First World War began a successful career as playwright with Mr Pim Passes By (1919; pub. 1921), The Truth about Blayds (1921; pub. 1922), The Dover Road (1921; pub. 1922), and Toad of Toad Hall (1929; a dramatization of *Grahame's The Wind in the Willows). In 1924 his book of verses for children When We Were Very Young was immediately successful, outdone only by the phenomenal and abiding success of Winnie-the-Pooh (1926). Further popular verses, Now We Are Six (1927), were followed in 1928 by The House at Pooh Corner, no less successful than its predecessor. (See CHILDREN'S LITERATURE.)

MILNES, (Richard) Monckton (1809–85), later Baron Houghton, was educated at Trinity College, Cambridge, where he became the friend of *Tennyson, A. H. *Hallam, and *Thackeray, the first of many close literary friendships, which included, most notably, *Swinburne (whom he greatly assisted), *Burton, the *Brownings, *Patmore, W. S. *Landor, and many others. In 1837 he became an MP and worked for various reforming causes, including the Copyright Act and the establishment of Mechanics' Institutes. He published his first volume of verse in 1838 and Palm Leaves in 1844, following these with works of biography, history, sociology, and Boswelliana. His major work was probably his Life and Letters of Keats (1848), a poet whom he consistently championed. He also did much to enhance the reputation of *Blake, and in 1875 edited the works of T. L. *Peacock. His own collected *Poetical Works* appeared in 1876. His large collection of erotic books included the first serious collection of de *Sade. See J. Pope-Hennessy, *Monckton Milnes* (2 vols, 1950–2).

MILOSZ, Czesław (1911–   ), Polish poet and writer, born on the Polish–Lithuanian borderland of Wilno. He was a leader of the Polish literary avant-garde in the 1930s, and prominent in the Resistance movement. After some years in the diplomatic service, he emigrated to America, settling in California, and teaching at Berkeley. His works include novels, volumes of essays, and poetry, and *The Captive Mind* (1951), an apologia for his withdrawal from Poland. He has also translated Shakespeare, *Milton, and T. S. *Eliot into Polish. He was awarded the *Nobel Prize for literature in 1980.

Milton, a poem in two books by W. *Blake, written and etched 1804–8, one of his longest and most complex mythological works, which is prefaced by his well-known lines 'And did those feet in ancient time', commonly known as 'Jerusalem'. It uses the mythological and allegorical framework of his earlier poems and also develops Blake's own extremely powerful and personal response to *Paradise Lost* and its author, which had affected and perplexed his imagination for years (see also under MARRIAGE OF HEAVEN AND HELL, THE). Blake appears to suggest that he himself becomes imbued with the spirit of *Milton, who descends to earth in order to save Albion through the power of Imagination: the bizarre and the sublime mingle, as Blake describes the spirit of Milton entering his foot—'and all this Vegetable World appear'd on my left Foot | As a bright sandal form'd immortal of precious stones and gold. | I stooped down and bound it to walk forward through eternity' (Bk 1, Pt 21, ll. 12–14). Blake imagines himself carried from Lambeth to Felpham by *Los, where, walking in his cottage garden, he is visited by the Virgin Ololon (Bk 2, Pt 36), in search of Milton, and the poem draws to an end with Milton's address to Ololon, in which he proclaims his mission of regeneration, 'To cast off the rotten rags of Memory by Inspiration | To cast off Bacon, Locke and Newton from Albion's covering', and prophesies the purging away by Jesus of the 'sexual garments' which hide 'the human lineaments'. The final section is an apocalyptic vision, in which Jesus 'wept and walked forth | From Felpham's Vale clothed in Clouds of blood', from which Blake returns to his 'mortal state' to hear the mounting lark. The mythology of the poem is obscure, but much of it clearly relates to the experiences of his time at Felpham, and some of the descriptive passages (notably of *Beulah, at the opening of Bk 2) show a magnificent combination of mystic vision and natural observation.

MILTON, John (1608–74), was born in Bread Street, Cheapside, at the Sign of the Spread Eagle, the house of his father, John Milton the elder, a scrivener and composer of music. He was educated at St *Paul's School, where he became friendly with *Diodati, then at Christ's College, Cambridge, where he acquired the nickname 'the Lady of Christ's', and may have alienated his fellow students by, in his own words, 'a certain niceness of nature, an honest haughtiness'. He was briefly rusticated in 1626, became BA in 1629, and MA in 1632. During his Cambridge period, while considering himself destined for the ministry, he began to write poetry in Latin and Italian, and also in English, on both sacred and secular themes. His first known attempt at English verse, 'On the Death of a Fair Infant' (in a complex stanza repeated in the opening of the 'Nativity Ode'), was probably written in 1628 on the death of his niece Anne Phillips (although P. *Levi, *TLS*, 25 March 1983, suggests an earlier date and a different occasion), and 'At a Vacation Exercise' probably belongs to the same year. His first distinctively Miltonic work, 'On the Morning of Christs Nativity', written at Christmas 1629, shows a growing mastery of stanza and structure, an exuberant and at times baroque use of imagery, and the love of resounding proper names so marked in his later work. His fragmentary 'The Passion' was probably written at Easter 1630, and the *'Arcades' possibly in the same year. 'On Shakespeare', his two epitaphs for *Hobson, the university carrier, and 'An Epitaph on the Marchioness of Winchester' belong to 1631. His twin poems, *'L'Allegro' and *'Il Penseroso', may have been written at Cambridge, or possibly at Hammersmith, whither Milton the elder moved 1631/2: Milton himself on leaving Cambridge adopted no profession, but embarked on an ambitious course of private study at his father's home in preparation for a future as poet or clergyman; his Latin poem 'Ad Patrem' (?1634) appears to be an attempt to persuade his father that the two pursuits were reconcilable. His 'masque' *Comus, published anonymously in 1637, was written, and performed at Ludlow, in 1634. In 1635 the Miltons moved to Horton, Buckinghamshire, where John pursued his studies in Greek, Latin, and Italian, devoting much time to the Church Fathers. In 1637 he wrote *Lycidas, an elegy, which dwells on fears of premature death, unfulfilled ambition, and wasted dedication; during the 20 years that elapsed between this and his composition of *Paradise Lost* Milton wrote no poetry, apart from some Latin and Italian pieces, and some sonnets, of which the most notable are those 'On the late Massacre in Piedmont', on his blindness, on his deceased wife (whether the first or second wife is disputed), his addresses to *Cromwell, Fairfax, and Vane, and those to *Lawes (with whom he had collaborated on the 'Arcades' and *Comus*) and to his young friends and students Edward Lawrence and Cyriack *Skinner. From 1637 to 1639 Milton travelled abroad, chiefly in Italy; he met *Grotius in Paris and *Galileo, still under official condemnation, at his villa just outside Florence. On his return he established himself in London and became tutor to his nephews Edward and John *Phillips; he appears at this time to have been contemplating an epic on an Arthurian theme, which he mentions in his Latin epitaph on his friend Diodati, *Epitaphium Damonis*; Diodati died while Milton was abroad. The epitaph was written in 1639, and privately printed and distributed.

His attentions were now diverted by historical events to many years of pamphleteering and political activity, and to a tireless defence of religious, civil, and domestic liberties. In 1641 he published a series of five pamphlets against episcopacy, engaging in controversy with bishops *Hall and *Ussher, and displaying from the first (*Of Reformation in England and the Causes that Hitherto Have Hindered it*) a vigorous, colourful Ciceronian prose, and a keenly polemic spirit which could yet rise to visions of apocalyptic grandeur. *The Reason of Church Government* (1642) was the first to which he put his name; it was followed in the same year by *An Apology against a Pamphlet . . . against *Smectymnuus*, which contains interesting autobiographical details. In June 1642 Milton married Mary Powell, daughter of royalist parents; he was 33, she 17. Within six weeks he consented to her going home to her parents at Forest Hill, near Oxford (the royalist stronghold), on condition that she returned by Michaelmas. She did not do so, for reasons perhaps connected with the outbreak of the Civil War. Milton published in 1643 *The Doctrine and Discipline of Divorce*, arguing among other points that a true marriage was of mind as well as of body, and that the chaste and modest were more likely to find themselves 'chained unnaturally together' in unsuitable unions than those who had in youth lived loosely and enjoyed more varied experience. This pamphlet made him notorious, but he pursued his arguments in three more on the subject of divorce in 1644–5, including *Tetrachordon*, and also published in his own support a translation of Martin Bucer's views on the same theme. *Of Education*, addressed to his friend *Hartlib, appeared in 1644, as did his great defence of the liberty of the press, *Areopagitica*. It was at this period that he became aware of his growing blindness; by 1651 he was to be totally blind. His wife rejoined him in 1645, and their first daughter Anne was born a year later: a second daughter Mary was born in

1648 and Deborah in 1652. A son, John, born 1651, died in infancy.

After the execution of Charles I, Milton published *The Tenure of Kings and Magistrates* (1649), arguing in general terms that a people 'free by nature' had a right to depose and punish tyrants, and attacking the Presbyterians, who were in his view a growing threat to freedom. He was appointed Latin secretary to the newly formed Council of State. He replied officially to *Eikon Basilike* in *Eikonoklastes* (i.e. Image-breaker, 1649), and to *Salmasius in *Pro Populo Anglicano Defensio* (1651), a work which created a furore on the Continent and was publicly burned in Paris and Toulouse; also to Du Moulin's *Clamor* (which he attributed to Alexander More, or Morus) in *Defensio Secunda* (1654), which contains some self-defensive autobiographical passages and reflections on his blindness. He was now assisted in his secretarial duties successively by G. R. Weckherlin, Philip Meadows, and *Marvell. His first wife died in 1652, three days after the birth of their third daughter, and in 1656 he married Katherine Woodcock, then aged 28, who died in 1658, having given birth to a daughter who survived only a few months. He retained his post as Latin secretary until the Restoration, having lived during most of this period at Petty France, Westminster. On the eve of the Restoration, he boldly published *The Ready and Easy Way to Establish a Free Commonwealth* (1660), a last-minute attempt to defend the 'Good old Cause' of republicanism and to halt the growing tide of royalism and the 'defection of the misguided and abused multitude'. At the Restoration he went into hiding briefly, then was arrested, fined, and released: *D'Avenant and Marvell are said to have interceded on his behalf. He now returned to poetry and set about the composition of *Paradise Lost*; he had shown his nephews a sketch of lines from Book 4 as early as 1642, and his notebooks show that he had earlier contemplated a drama on a similar theme. In 1663 he married his third wife, Elizabeth Minshull (who survived him), and moved to what is now Bunhill Row, where he spent the remaining years of his life, apart from a brief visit to Chalfont St Giles in 1665, to avoid the plague, organized by his Quaker friend *Ellwood. *Paradise Lost* is said by *Aubrey to have been finished in 1663, but the agreement for his copyright was not signed until 1667. *Paradise Regained* was published in 1671 with *Samson Agonistes*: the composition dates of the latter have been much discussed, and the assumption that it was his last, or even one of his latest poems has been strongly challenged. In these late years he also published various works written earlier in his life, including a *History of Britain* (1670), from legendary times to the Norman Conquest, and a compendium of *Ramus's *Logic* (1672). In 1673 appeared a second edition of his *Poems*, originally published in 1645, including most of his minor verse. His *A Brief History of Moscovia*, drawn from the *Hakluyt and *Purchas collections, appeared posthumously in 1682.

Of Milton's Latin poems, the finest is his epitaph to Diodati, but his epistle 'Ad Patrem' and his address to 'Mansus' (Giovanni Battista Manso, intimate friend of *Tasso and *Marini) also have great interest: the latter was probably written in 1639.

The State Papers that he wrote as Latin secretary (discovered in 1743) are mostly concerned with the routine work of diplomacy, but include an interesting series of dispatches, 1655–8, on the subject of the expulsion and massacre of the Protestant Vaudois by the orders of the Prince of Savoy, who had commanded them to abandon their faith. These breathe the same indignation that found more impassioned expression in his sonnet 'Avenge O Lord thy slaughter'd Saints'. The Latin prose writings include his *De Doctrina Christiana*, printed in 1825, which for many confirms the suspicions raised by *Paradise Lost* that Milton was theologically unorthodox, with strong *Arian leanings. His *Commonplace Book*, with interesting insights into his studies and plans for composition, came to light in 1874.

Milton died from 'gout struck in' and was buried beside his father in St Giles', Cripplegate. There are full biographies by D. *Masson (1859–94) and W. R. Parker (1968). His personality continues to arouse as much discussion as his works; as a man he has been variously presented as sociable, good-natured, and increasingly serene, as a domestic tyrant who bullied his daughters, as a strict Puritan, a misogynist, a libertine, and, recently, as a radical heretic. (See C. *Hill, *Milton and the English Revolution*, 1977.) As a writer, his towering stature was recognized early. Although appreciated as a master of polemical prose as well as of subtle lyric harmony, his reputation rests largely on *Paradise Lost*, which *Dryden (who made a rhymed version of it) was describing by 1677 as 'one of the greatest, most noble and sublime poems which either this age or nation has produced'. Poets and critics in the 18th cent. were profoundly influenced by Milton's use of blank verse (previously confined largely to drama) and his treatment of the *Sublime, and he inspired many serious and burlesque imitations and adaptations. (See THOMSON, J. 1700–48; COWPER; PHILLIPS, J.; SOMERVILE.) But even at this period there were murmurs of dissent: Dr *Johnson complained that Milton used 'English words with a foreign idiom', and found *Lycidas* 'harsh': *Addison, although greatly admiring, felt that 'our language sunk under him', and *Bentley's revisions were notorious for their insensitivity. Blake's famous dictum from *The Marriage of Heaven and Hell* (1790) that Milton was 'a true Poet, and of the Devil's party without knowing it'

preceded the Romantic version, disseminated principally by *Shelley, which represented Satan the Arch-Rebel as the true hero of *Paradise Lost* and its God as either dull or wicked; critics (and notably C. S. *Lewis, *A Preface to Paradise Lost*, 1942) have endeavoured in vain to dismiss this notion, which continues to attract students and creative writers, including *Empson (*Milton's God*, 1961). A different controversy, echoing the older complaints of Johnson and Addison, was brought into focus by T. S. *Eliot's attack, in 1936, in which he described Milton as one whose sensuousness had been 'withered by book-learning' and further impaired by blindness, who wrote English 'like a dead language'. He claimed that Milton's poetry 'could *only* be an influence for the worse'. He modified these views later, but they were endorsed by *Leavis, who condemned the rhythmic deadness, mechanical externality, and Latinate syntax of the later works, praising in contrast the sensuous Spenserian richness of the earlier. The debate continues in e.g. *Milton's Grand Style* by C. Ricks (1963), which claims that Milton's verse, although powerful, is also subtle and suggestive. See also E. M. W. *Tillyard, *The Miltonic Setting* (1938); *The Living Milton*, ed. F. Kermode (1960).

MILWARD, Richard (1609–80), amanuensis to *Selden, whose *Table Talk* he compiled.

Mime, in modern usage, a term used to describe a kind of theatrical performance without words in which meaning is conveyed by gesture and movement. As an art form it flourishes more on the Continent, in the work of such performers and writer-performers as Marcel Marceau (1923–   ) and Dario *Fo, than in England.

The earliest form of mimes were the dramatic scenes from middle-class life, realistic and often though not invariably, obscene, first composed in the 5th cent. BC by the Athenian Sophron, who is said to have served *Plato as a model for the writing of dialogue. His works have not survived, and the only known Greek mimes (by *Theocritus and Herodas) date from two centuries later. How they were presented is not known, but it seems probable that they were declaimed to a musical accompaniment by a single actor with appropriate gestures. Later still in Rome, sketches of low life performed by several actors with masks and scenic effects became so popular that they drove both tragedy and comedy from the stage. After an interlude in the Middle Ages, the genre flourished again in the 16th cent. with the *commedia dell'arte* in which the actors relied mainly on dumb-show though they did extemporize snatches of dialogue. Divertissements with music, dancing, and mime were also much in fashion from the Renaissance onwards and contributed to the development of ballet, opera, and the English *pantomime.

Mimesis, see POETICS, THE. See also under AUER-BACH, E.

Mind: *A Quarterly Review of Psychology and Philosophy,* was founded in 1876 and edited until 1891 by G. Croom Robertson; from 1891 to 1920 by G. F. Stout; from 1921 to 1948 by G. E. *Moore; from 1948 to 1971 by G. *Ryle, and from 1972 to 1984 by D. W. Hamlyn.

Minnehaha, see HIAWATHA.

Minnesingers, German lyric poets of the late 12th to the 14th cent., so called because love (*Minne*) was the principal subject of their poetry. They correspond to the Provençal troubadours (who influenced them) and the Northern French *trouvères.* The *Minnesang* flourished at its best in the period called the Blütezeit, *c.*1200; after the first quarter of the 13th cent. it degenerated (as did the contemporary French lyric poetry), and the later *Meistergesang* lacks the inspiration of the earlier singers (the theme of *Wagner's Die Meistersinger von Nürnberg). Some of the greatest Minnesingers were also writers of epic: Hart-mann von Aue, *Wolfram von Eschenbach, and Gottlieb von Strassburg. The other most ad-mired exponents of the *Minne* lyric are Reinmar von Hagenau, Heinrich von Morungen, and Walther von der Vogelweide. See ed. Olive Sayce, *Poets of the Minnesang* (1967).

MINOT, Laurence, probably a soldier, the au-thor (of whom nothing is known) of a series of spirited and patriotic war-songs, written about 1352, concerning events of the period 1333–52 in the English wars against the Scots and French. There are poems on Crécy, Halidon Hill, the sieges of Berwick and Calais, and such victorious topics. The poems give some sugges-tion of what medieval warfare was like, but they have little claim to literary distinction. They were edited by J. Hall (1897; 3rd edn rev. 1914).

Minstrel, The, see BEATTIE, J.

Minstrelsy of the Scottish Border (3 vols, 1802–3), a collection of *ballads compiled by Sir W. *Scott, who divided them into three sections, Historical Ballads, Romantic Ballads, and Imitations of the Ancient Ballad. He was aided by various friends and advisers, who in-cluded *Leyden, J. *Hogg, R. *Surtees, and many old women (including Hogg's mother) who kept alive the oral traditions. The extent to which Scott himself altered and improved on the texts has been much discussed; it appears to vary from minor adjustments to the insertion of whole lines and stanzas. In his introduction Scott stated a patriotic intention: 'By such efforts, feeble as they are, I may contribute somewhat to the history of my native country; the peculiar features of whose manners and character are

daily melting and dissolving into those of her sister and ally.' According to *Motherwell, Scott later in life regretted the extent of his editorial work; 'In fact, I think I did wrong myself in endeavouring to make the best possible set of an ancient ballad out of several copies obtained spects, if I improved the poetry, I spoiled the simplicity of the old song.' The volumes contain many well known ballads, including 'The Wife of Usher's Well' (its first printing) and 'The Twa Corbies', in a version that M. J. C. Hodgart (*The Ballads,* 1950) claims is 'largely of Scott's making'.

Mirabell, (1) the hero of J. Fletcher's *Wilde Goose Chase; (2) in Congreve's *The Way of the World,* the lover of Millamant.

Mirabilia Urbis Romae, a medieval guide-book to Rome. Its first form probably dates from the 12th cent., and it was perhaps 'kept up to date' till the 15th. There is a translation by F. Nichols (1889).

Miracle Plays, see MYSTERY PLAYS.

Miranda, in Shakespeare's *The Tempest,* the daughter of *Prospero. Her name means 'To be wondered at'.

Mirobolant, Monsieur, a character in Thack-eray's *Pendennis,* a temperamental French chef who falls in love with Blanche Amory.

Mirour de l'Omme (*Speculum Meditantis*), see GOWER, J.

Mirror (mirour), as a literary term, based on the Medieval Latin use of the word *speculum* (e.g. *Speculum Historiale* of *Vincent of Beauvais or *Speculum Meditantis* of *Gower, translated into French as *Mirour de l'Omme*) to mean a true reflection or description of a particular subject, hence compendium. Thus there are titles such as *Mirrour of the Blessed Lyf of Iesu Christ* by N. *Love, the *Mirrour of the World* (translated by *Caxton from French), the *Mirror of Fools* (trans-lation of the late 12th-cent. *Speculum Stultorum* by *Wireker), and, in the Renaissance, *A Mirror for Magistrates.*

Mirror for Magistrates, A, a work planned by George Ferrers, Master of the King's Pastimes in the reign of Henry VIII, and William Baldwin of Oxford. In it various famous men and women, most of them characters in English his-tory, recount their downfall in verse. The book was originally begun as a continuation of Lydgate's *Fall of Princes,* itself based on *Boccaccio's De Casibus. After a suppressed edition of 1555 it first appeared in 1559, con-taining 20 tragedies by various authors. In the enlarged edition of 1563 T. *Sackville con-tributed the 'Induction', set in deep winter, in which Sorrow leads the poet to the realms of the dead, and the *'Complaint of Buckingham'. Further editions, with more tragedies added, were published in 1574, 1575, 1578, 1587, and 1609. John Higgins, compiler of the 1574–87 additions, added complaints by figures from early or mythical British history, such as Locrinus, Elstride, and Cordila, as well as Roman history, e.g. Julius Caesar, Nero.

Though the *Mirror* may not seem to offer much to a modern reader, it was one of the major achievements of what C. S. Lewis called the *'Drab Age', and provided source material for many major writers, including *Spenser, Shakespeare, *Daniel, and *Drayton. The *Mirror* and its continuations were edited by L. B. Campbell (1938–46).

Mirror of Fools (*Speculum Stultorum*), see WIREKER.

MIRSKY, D. S. (Prince Dmitry Petrovich Svyatopolk-Mirsky) (1890–1939), prolific literary historian and critic, the most influential interpreter of Russian literature to the English. He studied both Chinese and Classics at St Petersburg University and served in the First World War and, on the side of the Whites, in the Civil War, before leaving Russia in 1920. From Oct. 1920 he became a contributor to the *London Mercury*, and in 1921 he arrived in England. In spring 1922 he was appointed lecturer in Russian literature and literary criticism at King's College, London, and in October he took up a post at the School of Slavonic Studies. In 1926 he published two books, *Contemporary Russian Literature* and *Pushkin*, and in 1927 his pioneering *A History of Russian Literature*. In exile he moved steadily to the left, joining the Communist Party of Great Britain in 1931. In March 1932 he was dismissed from London University, and in September he returned to the USSR. There he continued to publish on Russian and English literature, and to engage in literary polemics. His *The Intelligentsia of Great Britain*, including estimates of G. B. *Shaw, *Wells, B. *Russell, D. H. *Lawrence, A. *Huxley, V. *Woolf, W. *Lewis, and others, caused a scandal on its London publication in 1935. In 1937 he was arrested and sent to Siberia, where he died in a prison hospital. His activities as journalist and critic, and as teacher at the University of London, were posthumously crowned by the appearance in 1949 of *A History of Russian Literature*, edited from his books of 1926 and 1927 by Francis Whitfield. This book, in its many reprints and translations, remains the best and most widely-read 'beginners' guide' to Russian literature.

'Mirzah, The Vision of ', see VISION OF MIRZAH, THE.

Misanthrope, Le, one of the greatest comedies of *Molière, produced in 1666, in which he represents the conflict between the noble but cross-grained Alceste, exasperated by the corruption of society, and the worldly, coquettish Célimène whom he loves.

Misfortunes of Elphin, The, a satirical romance by *Peacock, published 1829.

It is an ingenious blend of Welsh Arthurian legend, in which Peacock was learned, and current political debate about reform. Elphin is king of Ceredigion in western Wales, but the bulk of his territory has been engulfed by the sea, owing to the drunkenness of Seithenyn, who was in charge of the embankment to keep out the waves. The 'inundation of Gwaelod', in the generation before the main action, becomes an allegory for the French revolution. Elphin succeeds to the diminished kingdom and is imprisoned by a powerful neighbour, whereupon his bard Taliesin sets out to rescue him through the poetic gifts of divination, or, since Peacock remains a sceptic, truth-telling. In Seithenyn the book contains what is perhaps Peacock's finest political parody, the celebrated drunken speech about the wall ('the parts that are rotten give elasticity to those that are sound'), which imitates a speech made by *Canning in 1822 in defence of the existing Constitution. The book contains the celebrated 'War Song of Dinas Vawr', in context a sly comment on political opportunism, and a clever bardic contest in which the current Romantic fashion for escapist themes is gently mocked.

Misrule, King, Lord, or **Abbot of,** at the end of the 15th and beginning of the 16th cents, an officer appointed at court to superintend the Christmas revels. At the Scottish court he was called the 'Abbot of Unreason'. Lords of Misrule were also appointed in some of the university colleges and inns of court.

'Mistletoe Bough, The', see GINEVRA.

MISTRAL, Frédéric, see FÉLIBRIGE.

MITCHEL, John (1815–75), Irish nationalist and solicitor, was editor of the influential *Nation*, and later of the *United Irishman*. He was tried for sedition for his part in the rising of 1848, and transported to Tasmania to serve a 14-year sentence. In his *Jail Journal, or Five Years in British Prisons* (1854) he left a vivid account of his experiences. He escaped to America, where he again became editor of various journals. His work also includes a *Life and Times of Aodh O'Neill, earl of Tyrone* (1845) and *The History of Ireland* (1869).

MITCHELL, Adrian (1932–), poet, novelist and playwright, born in London and educated at Christ Church, Oxford. He was associated with the pacifism, social protest and free verse forms of *Underground poetry; his collections of verse include *Out Loud* (1969), *Ride the Night-*

mare (1971), and *For Beauty Douglas; Collected Poems and Songs* (1981). His novels include *If You See Me Comin'* (1962) and *Wartime* (1973), and his many plays and stage adaptations, which make considerable use of songs and lyrics, an adaptation of Peter Weiss's *Marat/Sade* (1966), *Tyger* (1971), based on the life and work of *Blake, and *Man Friday* (1973).

MITCHELL, James Leslie, see GIBBON, L. G.

MITCHELL, Julian (1935–), novelist and playwright, educated at Winchester and Wadham College, Oxford. His novels include *Imaginary Toys* (1961), *The White Father* (1964, set in Africa), and the more experimental *The Undiscovered Country* (1968), in which a narrator, 'Julian Mitchell', in an apparently straight autobiographical mode, tells the story of his school and university days, and describes his relationship with 'Charles Humphries', a boyhood friend who, on his suicide, leaves Julian the manuscript of his novel *A New Satyricon*, which he proceeds to transcribe. Mitchell then turned to the theatre and television, adapting the novels of I. *Compton-Burnett for the stage and achieving West End success with *Half-Life* (1977), a play about an ageing archaeologist, and *Another Country* (1981, pub. 1982), set in a public school, which examines the pressures and conflicts that turned some of the young intellectuals of the 1930s towards Marxism, and made one of them a potential spy.

MITCHELL, Margaret (1900–49), American novelist, whose one novel, the best-selling and Pulitzer-prize-winning *Gone with the Wind* was published in 1936; the equally popular film was released in 1939. Set in Georgia at the time of the Civil War, it is the story of headstrong Scarlett O'Hara, her three marriages, and her determination to keep her father's property of Tara, despite the vicissitudes of war and passion.

MITCHISON, Naomi Mary Margaret (1897–), novelist, and sister of J. B. S. *Haldane, was born in Edinburgh and brought up in Oxford. In 1916 she married the barrister and future Labour politician G. R. Mitchison. She early began to write both prose and verse, and her many works of fiction include *The Corn King and the Spring Queen* (1931), a historical novel set in Greece and the Eastern Mediterranean countries in 228–187 BC, *The Blood of the Martyrs* (1939), and *The Big House* (1950). Her non-fiction works, including three volumes of autobiography (*Small Talk*, 1973; *All Change Here*, 1975; *You May Well Ask*, 1979), illustrate her own commitment to the progressive political and social causes of the intellectual circles in which she moved.

MITFORD, Mary Russell (1787–1855), was born of a father whose extravagance and gambling compelled her to try to earn a living as a writer. She published a volume of verse in 1810, and was encouraged to continue writing by *Coleridge. Further volumes of poems appeared, and various essays in magazines, then in 1823 her drama *Julian*, with *Macready in the title role, was produced successfully at Covent Garden, and was followed by the even more successful *Foscari* in 1826 and *Rienzi* in 1828. She wrote other historical dramas, but meanwhile, in 1824, she had begun a series of sketches and stories which made up *Our Village* (1832), the work by which she is justly remembered. This was followed by *Belford Regis* (1835), a portrait of Reading; *Country Stories* (1837); and *Recollections of a Literary Life* (1852); a novel, *Atherton, and other Tales*, was published in 1854, but, as the author confessed, prose fiction was not her métier. Her fluent letters, to *Lamb, *Haydon, *Horne, *Ruskin, Elizabeth Barrett (*Browning), W. S. *Landor, and many others reveal an intense enjoyment of people and places and a sunny, affectionate nature: they were published in a selection ed. A. G. L'Estrange (*Life of M. R. Mitford in a selection from her Letters to Her Friends*, 3 vols, 1870) and in *Letters of M. R. Mitford, 2nd Series*, ed. H. Chorley (2 vols, 1872). See also a life by V. Watson (1949).

MITFORD, Nancy Freeman (1904–73), writer, daughter of the second Lord Redesdale, who appears in many of her novels as the eccentric 'Uncle Matthew'. She published three novels before her first popular success, *The Pursuit of Love* (1945), in which the sensible Fanny, daughter of the irresponsible Bolter, describes the affairs of her six Radlett cousins, and in particular the progress of the lovely Linda through several marriages and passions to a premature death. Subsequent works (*Love in a Cold Climate*, 1949; *The Blessing*, 1951; *Don't Tell Alfred*, 1960) accompany the family and its associates through various social and amatory trials and triumphs; the appeal of the novels lies in the reckless upper-class Bohemianism of many of the characters, determined to find life 'amusing' at all costs, and in Nancy Mitford's sharp ear for dialogue. *Noblesse Oblige: an enquiry into the identifiable characteristics of the English aristocracy* (1956, with A. S. C. Ross et al.), also a manifestation of her sense of social nuance, provoked a debate on 'U' and 'Non-U' vocabulary, terms she had herself promoted in *Encounter* (1955). She also wrote several historical biographies (chiefly French), and edited two volumes of family correspondence (*The Ladies of Alderley*, 1938; *The Stanleys of Alderley*, 1939). Her sister, Jessica Mitford (1917–), has written a vivid account of Mitford family life, *Hons and Rebels* (1960), as well as commentaries on social and political life in the US, where she settled.

MITFORD, William (1744–1827), educated at The Queen's College, Oxford, was the author of a *History of Greece* (1785–1810) down to the death of Alexander, written at the suggestion of *Gibbon, which enjoyed great popularity. It was the work of a pioneer and was superseded by the histories of *Grote and *Thirlwall.

Moby-Dick, *or, The Whale* (1851), a novel by H. *Melville, first published in Britain, as *The Whale,* and slightly later in New York. It is made up of 135 chapters, written in an extraordinary variety of styles, from sailors' slang to biblical prophecy and Shakespearian rant.

Inspired by his friend *Hawthorne to say 'NO! in thunder' to Christianity, Melville fused his original *Bildungsroman* with the tragic quest narrative of 'stricken' Captain Ahab seeking revenge on the white whale that has bitten off his leg. 'Call me Ishmael', is the striking opening phrase of a story that takes the young narrator to sea on the doomed whaler *Pequod.* Both Ahab and Ishmael seek knowledge, but while Ishmael learns love and humanity 'monomaniacal Ahab' pursues a demonic God behind the 'hooded phantom' or 'unreasoning mask' of the symbolic whale. The *Pequod* is a male microcosm with, among others, the 'soothing savage' harpooner Queequeg, 'right-minded' first mate Starbuck, jolly Stubb, and Pip the cabin boy, driven prophetically mad, all involved in the whale fishery whose adventures and rituals Melville energetically describes. He interrupts the narrative with facts, tales, and soliloquies, including Father Mapple's sermon on the Leviathan, the Town-ho's story, a dissertation on whales ('Cetology'), and a metaphysical dissertation on the ambiguous 'whiteness of the whale'. After a fierce three-day chase Moby-Dick destroys the *Pequod.* Ishmael survives the vortex, buoyed up on Queequeg's coffin: 'And only I am escaped alone to tell thee', begins his epilogue, citing the Book of Job.

Moby-Dick had some initial critical appreciation, particularly in Britain, but only since the 1920s has it been recognized as a masterpiece, an epic tragedy of tremendous dramatic power and narrative drive.

Modern Comedy, A, see GALSWORTHY, J.

Modernism, an omnibus term for a number of tendencies in the arts which were prominent in the first half of the 20th cent.; in English literature it is particularly associated with the writings of T. S. *Eliot, *Pound, *Joyce, V. *Woolf, W. B. *Yeats, F. M. *Ford, and *Conrad. Broadly, Modernism reflects the impact upon literature of the psychology of *Freud and the anthropology of Sir J. *Frazer, as expressed in *The Golden Bough* (1890–1915). A sense of cultural relativism is pervasive in much modernist writing, as is an awareness of the irrational and the workings of the unconscious mind. Technically it was marked by a persistent experimentalism; it is 'the tradition of the new',

in Harold Rosenberg's phrase. It rejected the traditional (Victorian and Edwardian) framework of narrative, description, and rational exposition in poetry and prose, in favour of a *stream-of-consciousness presentation of personality, a dependence on the poetic image as the essential vehicle of aesthetic communication, and upon myth (see ULYSSES) as a characteristic structural principle. Modernist literature is a literature of discontinuity, both historically, being based upon a sharp rejection of the procedures and values of the immediate past, to which it adopts an adversary stance; and aesthetically. Although so diverse in its manifestation, it was recognized as representing, as H. *Read wrote (*Art Now,* 1933), 'an abrupt break with all tradition . . . The aim of five centuries of European effort is openly abandoned.' Modernist works (for instance, the poetry of Eliot and Pound) may have to the unfamiliar reader a tendency to dissolve into chaos of sharp atomistic impressions, and some critics (e.g. *Ortega y Gasset) have deplored their drift towards what he describes as 'dehumanization', away from the 'human, all too human elements predominant in romantic and naturalistic production'.

A comprehensive anthology of Modernist documents is *The Modern Tradition: Background of Modern Literature* (1965, ed. R. *Ellmann and C. Feidelson, Jr). See also *The Tradition of the New* (1959) by Harold Rosenberg; 'Modernisms' in *Modern Essays* (1971) by F. Kermode *Innovations: Essays on Art and Ideas* (1968, ed B. Bergonzi); and *Modernism 1890–1930* (1976 ed. M. *Bradbury and J. McFarlane). Harry Levin's essay 'What was Modernism?', originally published 1960, is reprinted in *Refraction* (1966).

Modern Love, a poem by G. *Meredith, published 1862.

An innovative work of fifty verses, or poems each of sixteen lines; spoken by a narrator who painfully discovers how unreal and idealistic are his ideas of women, the verses are connected a much by theme as by direct sequence of events They unfold the disillusionment of passionate married love slowly giving place to discord, jealousy, and intense unhappiness, ending in the separation and wreck of two ill-assorted lives, and the death by poison of the wife, the 'Madam who has given way to the narrator's mistress the 'Lady'.

Modern Painters, by *Ruskin, a work of encyclopaedic range which filled five volumes I, 1843; II, 1846; III and IV, 1856; V, 1860.

It began as a defence of contemporary landscape artists, especially *Turner. Ruskin's plan was to show his artists' 'Superiority in the Art of Landscape Painting to all the Ancient Masters Proved by Examples of the True, the Beautiful and the Intellectual'. Volume I deals with the true. Turner had been accused of defying nature. For Ruskin he was the first painter in history to have given 'an entire transcript of the whole system of nature'. Knowledge is to be attained not from the traditions of 17th-cent. landscape but from direct observation of the facts of nature.

In vol. II the logical framework of ideas was rapidly constructed. Beauty is perceived by the 'theoretic', i.e. contemplative faculty (as opposed to the aesthetic, which is sensual and base). It consists of the varied manifestations, in natural forms, of the attributes of God. But Ruskin now wanted to write, not of 'party or person' but of the functions of all art. Two years' study of old art brought revelations: Tuscan painting and sculpture of the 13th and 14th cents, Venetian Gothic architecture, and oil painting of the Renaissance. The outcome was that *Modern Painters* II belies its title and exalts the 'great men of old time'.

In the third and subsequent volumes the earlier systematic treatment gives way to a looser structure. An unrelentingly detailed analysis of mountain beauty takes up most of *Modern Painters* IV, to Ruskin 'the beginning and the end of all natural scenery'. Part of Turner's greatness lies in his representation of the gloom and glory of mountains to express the wrath of God. *Modern Painters* V is the work of a man embarking on a vital old age, not a little eccentric. He concludes his investigation of natural beauty. The volume reflects a new interest in myth as a source of wisdom and instrument of interpretation. A history of *Invention Spiritual* from ancient Greece to the present ends in the defeat of man's spiritual and intellectual powers by the 'deathful selfishness' of modern Europe. Turner's greatness is finally revealed in his mythological paintings, which express despair at the triumph of mortifying labour over beauty.

Modest Proposal, A, *for preventing the Children of poor People in Ireland, from being a Burden to their Parents or Country; and for making them beneficial to the Publick* (1729), a pamphlet by *Swift in which he suggests that the children of the poor should be fattened to feed the rich, an offer he describes as 'innocent, cheap, easy and effectual'. It is one of his most savage and powerful tracts, a masterpiece of ironic logic.

Modred, in the Arthurian legends, the nephew of King *Arthur, the son of King Lot of Orkney and Arthur's sister *Morgawse or Morcades (sometimes Anna; see PENDRAGON). *Geoffrey of Monmouth makes him the son of Arthur and his sister by an illicit union; he is accordingly the brother or half-brother of Gawain and his brothers. During Arthur's absence on a Roman war he treacherously seizes the queen (with her compliance, according to Geoffrey of Monmouth and his followers, such as *Laȝamon and

*Wace) and the kingdom. In the final battle in Cornwall he is slain by Arthur but deals the king his death blow. He is alluded to as a definitive traitor in the *Divina Commedia* (*Inferno*, xxxii. 61–2). The form of his name from *Malory to *Tennyson is Mordred.

Moguntia, or **Moguntiacum,** in imprints, Mainz.

MOIR, David Macbeth (1798–1851), a Scottish doctor, who signed himself Δ, Delta, published a number of volumes of poems, and contributed much prose and verse to *Blackwood's Magazine* and to many other periodicals. He is chiefly remembered as the author of *Mansie Wauch, Tailor in Dalkeith* (1828), which is an imaginary autobiography, in the manner of Moir's friend, *Galt, revealing a comically parochial view of the world, and satirizing the rising fashion for autobiography. Moir also published works on medicine, and in 1851 *Lectures on Poetical Literature*.

Molesworth, Helen, the heroine of *A Year at Hartlebury* by S. and B. *Disraeli.

MOLESWORTH, Mary Louisa, *née* Stewart (1839–1921), wrote novels under the pseudonym Ennis Graham, but is known for her much-loved children's books, fairy-tales, including *The Cuckoo Clock* (1877) and *The Tapestry Room* (1879), and realistic studies of child psychology in everyday life such as *Carrots* (1876) and *Two Little Waifs* (1883). The effect of her stories was much enhanced by illustrations by W. *Crane. See Roger Lancelyn Green, *Mrs Molesworth* (1961).

MOLESWORTH, Robert, first viscount (1656–1725), diplomatist and political writer, born and died in Dublin. His publication in 1694 of *An Account of Denmark as it was in the Year 1692*, extolling the liberty of postrevolution England in comparison with political and clerical 'tyranny' in Denmark, brought him to the notice of *Locke, led to a lifelong friendship with *Shaftesbury, and caused a diplomatic storm. He was answered by W. *King (1663–1712) in *Animadversions upon the Pretended Account of Denmark*. In a subsequent controversy in 1713 *Steele wrote in his defence in *The Crisis* and *Swift responded in *The Public Spirit of the Whigs*. Swift nevertheless admired him as an Irish patriot and later dedicated to him the fifth of *The Drapier's Letters*. As leading spokesman for the 'Old Whigs' or 'Commonwealth Men', Molesworth was the common patron of the different groups of Shaftesbury's followers among the English *Deists (Anthony *Collins, *Toland), the Irish Presbyterians (*Arbuckle, *Hutcheson), and the Edinburgh *Rankenian club (*Turnbull, *Wishart).

MOLIÈRE, pseudonym of Jean-Baptiste

Poquelin (1622–73), French comic playwright and actor. Son of the court furnisher, he was educated at the Jesuit Collège de Clermont, but at the age of 21 abandoned his commercial prospects in order to found a professional theatre. From 1645 to 1685 he toured the provinces. Returning to Paris he was granted by royal favour the use of the Théâtre du Petit-Bourbon. For the next 15 years he played regularly before city and court audiences, his troupe being adopted by the king in 1665. He was at once enormously popular and the object of professional and ecclesiastical malice. Equally gifted as actor, director, and playwright, he was the creator of French classical comedy, bringing to a new synthesis the major comic traditions at his disposal: the high comedy of *Corneille and Rotrou, the Latin comedy of *Plautus and *Terence, and the improvisatory farce of the *commedia dell'arte. The 30 comedies that he composed after his return to Paris reveal an art capable of admitting serious and even tragic experience without sacrificing the laughter, gaiety, and exuberance proper to comedy. He has a profound understanding of the incongruities of human life. Whether dealing with the conflicts between husbands and wives (L'École des maris, 1661, and L'École des femmes, 1662), between youth and age (L'Avare, 1669), between artifice and nature (Les Précieuses ridicules, 1659, and Les Femmes savantes, 1672), between professional and domestic life (Le Tartuffe, 1664, and Le Malade imaginaire, 1673), between master and servant (Sganarelle, 1660, and Le Bourgeois Gentilhomme, 1660), between nobleman and peasant (Don Juan, 1665), or even between moral principle and relativism (Le Misanthrope, 1666), he shows an unwavering insight into human falsity and an equally undeviating delight in the generous virtues. He possessed an unrivalled knowledge of French society in the second half of the 17th cent. and has left a comprehensive gallery of portraits and types. He possessed an equally unrivalled ear for the rhythms of dialogue, the flavours of patois, and the extravagances of jargon. His major plays show that he was saturated in *Montaigne; and although he is less sceptical than Montaigne and more confident in man's powers of renewal, he has a similar capacity for reconciling the comic and the intellectual. His influence on English *Restoration comedy exceeded that of *Jonson: dramatists like *D'Avenant, *Dryden, *Wycherley, *Vanbrugh, and *Shadwell quarried his plays for characters and situations.

MOLINA, Tirso da, see TÉLLEZ.

MOLINOS, Miguel (1628–96), priest, founder of *Quietism. His Guía Espiritual (Spiritual Guide) was published in 1675.

Moll Flanders, The Fortunes and Misfortunes of the famous, a romance by *Defoe, published 1722.

This purports to be the autobiography of the daughter of a woman who had been transported to Virginia for theft soon after her child's birth. The child, abandoned in England, is brought up in the house of the compassionate mayor of Colchester. The story relates her seduction, her subsequent marriages and liaisons, and her visit to Virginia, where she finds her mother and discovers that she has unwittingly married her own brother. After leaving him and returning to England, she is presently reduced to destitution. She becomes an extremely successful pickpocket and thief, but is presently detected and transported to Virginia in company with one of her former husbands, a highwayman. With the funds that each has amassed they set up as planters, and Moll moreover finds that she has inherited a plantation from her mother. She and her husband spend their declining years in an atmosphere of penitence and prosperity.

Molly Mog, or the Fair Maid of the Inn, a *crambo ballad probably by *Gay, with *Pope and *Swift possibly as part authors. It first appeared in Mist's Weekly Journal in 1726, with a note to the effect that 'it was writ by two or three Men of Wit . . . upon the Occasion of their lying at a certain Inn at Ockingham, where the Daughter of the House was remarkably pretty, and whose Name is Molly Mog.'

Moloch, or **Molech,** the name of a Canaanite idol, to whom children were sacrificed as burnt offerings (Lev. 18: 21 and 2 Kings 23: 10), represented by Milton (*Paradise Lost, i. 392) as one of the chief of the fallen angels. Hence applied to an object to which horrible sacrifices are made.

Mona Lisa, see LEONARDO DA VINCI.

Monastery, The, a novel by Sir W. *Scott, published 1820.

The story centres in the monastery of Kennaquhair, of which the prototype is Melrose Abbey on the Tweed, in the reign of Elizabeth, when the reformed doctrines were first making their way in Scotland and raising troubles for the religious community that gives its title to the work. The plot is slight. Halbert and Edward, sons of a tenant of the monastery, Simon Glendinning, are brought up with Mary Avenel, orphan daughter of a noble house, whose misfortunes have brought her to the hospitable roof of the Glendinnings. Both lads fall in love with Mary, on whose affections the gallant Halbert gains a stronger hold than the more studious and contemplative Edward. An English knight, Sir Piercie Shafton, takes refuge in Scotland from the pursuit to which his intrigues in the Catholic interest have exposed him, and is lodged by the abbot of Kennaquhair at the home of the Glendinnings. His arrogance, vanity, and ridiculous euphuistic manner of speech incense Halbert, and a duel ensues in which the knight is left for dead. Halbert flees, enters the service of the earl of Murray, whose favour he wins by his gallant demeanour, and who finally bestows on him the hand of Mary Avenel. Edward, disappointed of Mary, becomes a monk.

The author makes use in this novel of supernatural machinery, in the form of the White Lady of Avenel, a spirit or sylph, to restore Sir Piercie Shafton to life after being mortally wounded, and to work other marvels. More interesting are the characters of the easy-going abbot Boniface; his energetic subprior, Father Eustace; and the stern reformer, Henry Warden. See also ABBOT, THE.

MONBODDO, James Burnett, Lord (1714–99), a Scottish judge and pioneer in anthropology, who published *Of the Origin and Progress of Language* (1773–92) and *Antient Metaphysics* (1779–99). An admirer of *Rousseau, he was deeply interested in primitive societies; he himself lived an eccentrically austere life, believing civilization caused corruption and degeneracy. The orang-utan for which he is remembered figures in both these works as an example of 'the infantine state of our species', who was gentle, sociable, and intelligent, could play the flute, but never learned to speak; he suggested to *Peacock the character of Sir Oran Haut-ton in *Melincourt*. Some writers consider Monboddo a precursor of C. *Darwin, and although he was mocked in his day for his gullibility and his keen interest in whether or not primitive men possessed vestigial tails, he was a prominent member of Scottish literary and intellectual life, and a member of the *Select Society. (See also PRIMITIVISM.)

Money, a comedy by *Bulwer-Lytton, produced 1840.

Alfred Evelyn, private secretary to the worldly-wise Sir John Vesey, loves Clara Douglas, as poor as himself. She refuses him, not wishing to involve him in her own poverty. Evelyn comes into a large fortune, and, stung by Clara's refusal, which he attributes to the wrong motive, proposes to the worldly Georgina, daughter of Sir John; but soon has reason to regret the step. To test her affection and her father's loyalty, he pretends to be ruined by gambling and the breaking of a bank. Thereupon Georgina promptly transfers the promise of her hand to a rival suitor, while Clara comes forward to help Evelyn. Thus released, and earlier misconceptions removed, Evelyn marries Clara.

Monimia, (1) the heroine of Otway's *The Orphan*; (2) a character in Smollett's *Ferdinand Count Fathom*.

Moniplies, Richie, a character in Scott's *The Fortunes of Nigel*.

Monitor, The, a short-lived thrice-weekly folio half-sheet, which appeared in 1713, written entirely in verse (much of it by N. *Tate) of a morally uplifting intent, on themes such as 'The Upright Man', 'The Gamester', etc. The name was adopted by several equally short-lived successors. *The Monitor: or British freeholder*, a weekly political paper founded in 1755 by Richard Beckford, a London merchant, and edited by John Entick, in the Whig interest, lasted for ten years; *Wilkes contributed to it, and it was prosecuted for its attacks on Lord Bute's government.

Monk, The, a novel by M. G. *Lewis, published 1796.

Ambrosio, the worthy superior of the Capuchins of Madrid, falls to the temptations of Matilda, a fiend-inspired wanton who, disguised as a boy, has entered his monastery as a novice. Now utterly depraved, Ambrosio falls in love with one of his penitents, pursues the girl with the help of magic and murder, and finally kills her in an effort to escape detection. But he is discovered, tortured by the Inquisition, and sentenced to death, finally compounding with the Devil for escape from burning, only to be hurled by him to destruction and damnation. Although extravagant in its mixture of the supernatural, the terrible, and the indecent, the book contains scenes of great effect. It enjoyed a considerable contemporary vogue.

Monkbarns, Laird of, Jonathan Oldbuck, the principal character in Scott's *The Antiquary*.

'Monk' Lewis, the soubriquet of M. G. *Lewis, author of *The Monk*.

Monks, a character in Dickens's *Oliver Twist*.

'Monk's Tale, The', see CANTERBURY TALES, 19.

Monmouth, marquis of, in *Coningsby* by B. Disraeli.

MONRO, H(arold) E(dward) (1879–1932), is chiefly remembered for his Poetry Bookshop which he founded in 1913 to publish poetry, to encourage its sale, and to promote poetry-readings; and for publishing the series *Georgian Poetry*, edited by E. *Marsh. He founded and edited the *Poetry Review*, among other journals and broadsheets, and wrote poetry himself; his *Collected Poems*, introduced by T. S. *Eliot, appeared in 1933. His poems 'Bitter Sanctuary' and 'Milk for the Cat' appear in many anthologies.

MONROE, Harriet, see POETRY: A MAGAZINE OF VERSE.

MONSARRAT, Nicholas John Turney (1910–79), novelist, best remembered for his highly successful novel *The Cruel Sea* (1951), based on his wartime experiences at sea; his other works include *The Tribe that Lost Its Head*

(1956), about the struggle for independence in an African state, and two volumes of auto-biography (1966–70).

Monsieur D'Olive, a comedy by *Chapman, published 1606, acted a few years before. The plot is of little interest, but the play is enlivened by the remarkable character D'Olive, 'the perfect model of an impudent upstart', fluent, self-confident, good-humoured, witty, 'a mongrel of a gull and a villain'.

MONTAGU, Basil (1770–1851), the natural son of John, fourth earl of Sandwich, and his mistress Martha Ray, the singer. He met *Wordsworth in 1795, and became friendly with him, *Coleridge, and *Godwin, sharing their youthful radical views; his young son, also Basil Montagu, lived with William and Dorothy Wordsworth during their West Country period, and inspired William's poem, 'Anecdote for Fathers'. Montagu became a successful barrister and author, published many legal and political works on such subjects as bankruptcy, copyright, the death penalty, etc.; edited F. *Bacon (1825–37); and in 1846 published a little volume of mock-heroic couplets, *Railroad Eclogues*, in which he describes the advent of the railways in rural England, the effects of speculation, and so on.

MONTAGU, Mrs (Elizabeth) (1720–1800), was a celebrated member of the *Blue Stocking Circle. She was an impressive woman, married to the wealthy grandson of the earl of Sandwich. After a markedly precocious childhood, she became a woman of great learning and wit. Dr *Johnson was amazed by her 'radiations of intellectual excellence' and dubbed her 'Queen of the Blues'. Her receptions, begun in the early 1750s, were more formal than Mrs *Vesey's, with the guests ranged in a half-circle around their hostess. She told *Garrick that, whatever their birth, wealth, or fame, 'I never invite idiots.' F. *Burney, a younger member of the circle, writing late in the century, found Mrs Montagu 'brilliant in diamonds, solid in judgement, and critical in talk'. She was generous and charitable, and deeply interested in literature; many young authors, such as *Beattie and R. *Price, were befriended with hospitality, encouragement, and gifts of money. Hannah *More described her as 'the female Maecenas of Hill St'. She wrote the first three of George Lyttleton's *Dialogues of the Dead* (1760), but only one, between Mercury and Mrs Modish, reflects anything of her learning and wit. In 1769 appeared her *Essay on the Writings and Genius of Shakespeare*, refuting the strictures of *Voltaire. It was received with general acclaim, Dr Johnson being apparently the only critic to perceive its weakness, and it made her a celebrity when she visited Paris in 1776. She retained her position as 'Queen of the Blues' for almost 50 years.

MONTAGU, Lady Mary Wortley, *née* Pierrepont (1689–1762), daughter of the fifth earl and first duke of Kingston. Her mother died in 1694, and she early became acquainted with social and literary life; she wrote verses while young and taught herself Latin. In 1712 she secretly married Edward Wortley Montagu, and accompanied him in 1716 when he went to Constantinople as ambassador. She wrote there her celebrated 'Turkish Letters' (published in 1763 after her death), and introduced into England on her return in 1718 the practice of inoculation against smallpox, an illness by which she herself had been badly marked in 1715. For the next two decades she was a leading member of society, famed for her wit. In 1716 *Curll piratically published some of her *Town Eclogues* and *Court Poems*; the *Eclogues* with other poems were republished in 1747. In 1737–8 she wrote an anonymous periodical, *The Nonsense of Common-Sense* (ed. R. Halsband, 1947), and in 1739 left England and her husband to live abroad for nearly 23 years in France and Italy, spending ten years near Brescia; during this period she wrote many letters, mostly to her daughter, Lady Bute. She returned to England shortly before her death. She is remembered principally for her letters, which are erudite as well as entertaining (though she disliked the label of *Blue Stocking attached to Mrs E. *Montagu and others); *Voltaire praised them above those of Mme de *Sévigné. But she is also known for her quarrels with *Pope, with whom she was on terms of close friendship before her visit to Turkey, and for some time after. The reasons for their rupture are not clear, but in later works he was to attack her viciously, and she unwisely joined with Pope's enemy *Hervey in *Verses addressed to the Imitator of Horace* (1733) which understandably increased Pope's animosity. Her *Letters and Works*, ed. Lord Wharncliffe, appeared in 1837; R. Halsband published a *Life* (1956) and edited the *Complete Letters* (1965–6).

MONTAGUE, C(harles) E(dward) (1867–1928), educated at Balliol College, Oxford, joined the staff of the *Manchester Guardian* in 1890 and later became assistant editor. He earned a considerable reputation as a reviewer and dramatic critic, and wrote several novels, including *A Hind Let Loose* (1910), *Rough Justice* (1926), and *Right off the Map* (1927). *Disenchantment* (1922) is his bitter account of the First World War in which he served as a private soldier.

MONTAGUE, John Patrick (1929–), Irish poet, born in New York, and educated at St Patrick's College, Armagh, and University College, Dublin. His volumes of poetry include

Forms of Exile (1958), *Poisoned Lands* (1961), *Tides* (1970), *The Great Cloak* (1978), and *Selected Poems* (1982). Many of his short, intense lyrics evoke the landscapes and heritage of rural Ireland, in a fine, spare diction; other poems recall periods spent in France and America and personal moments of family history. He has also edited various anthologies of Irish literature, and published short stories and a play.

Montagues, the, in Shakespeare's *Romeo and Juliet*, see under CAPULETS.

MONTAIGNE, Michel Eyquem de (1533–92), French moralist and essayist. He is generally regarded as the inventor of the modern 'essay', a genre which he fashioned out of the late medieval 'compilation', transforming it into a personal test of ideas and experience. The first two books of his *Essais* appeared in 1580, the fifth edition, containing the third book, in 1588, and a posthumous edition in 1595, each successive version containing extensive additions to the existing material. The first English translator was *Florio (1603). Traditionally the *Essais* are held to exhibit three stages of development, leading from an early Stoicism, under the influence of *Seneca, to a philosophical scepticism (*Apologie de Raimond Sebond*, II. 12), and finally to a moderate Epicureanism, but such an outline does only partial justice to a complex process. The *Apologie*, his most sustained piece, is a comprehensive attack on reason as a source of presumption in man, and its challenge was taken up by a number of later thinkers, including *Descartes, *Pascal, and F. *Bacon. Other notable readers of his work have been Robert *Burton, Sir T. *Browne, *Swift, and *Peacock. His essay 'Des Cannibales' (I. 31) was a source, via Florio, of Shakespeare's *The Tempest*.

Montalban, in *Orlando Innamorato*, the home of *Rinaldo, and the scene of a great battle, in which the Christians under Charlemagne are driven back by the Saracens under Marsilio. See *Paradise Lost*, Bk I. 583.

MONTALE, Eugenio (1896–1981), the greatest Italian poet of the 20th cent., recipient of the *Nobel Prize (1971). He draws on an extreme range of language from the prosaic to the lyrical—from naval and biological terminology to the dialect of Genoa, his native city—and on all the strains in Italian literary tradition, recovering 'dead' words, coining new ones, and subjecting every word to intense multiplicity of meaning. This linguistic engagement means that he rejected the aloof 'Petrarchan' role for the poet, although his wariness of moral keys has often attracted the accusation of apoliticality. His main books of poems (now all included in the critical edn approved by him shortly before his death, *E. M.: L'opera in versi*, ed. F. Contini, 1980) are: *Ossi di seppia* (*Cuttle-fish Bones*,

1925), *Le occasioni* (*Occasions*, 1932), *La bufera e altro* (*The Storm and Others*, 1943–54), *Satura* (1962), *Diario del '71 e del '72* (*Diary of 1971 and 1972*, 1973). His translations of Shakespeare, G. M. *Hopkins, *Yeats, and T. S. *Eliot are in *Quaderno di traduzioni* (*Translator's Notebook*, 1975). He has been translated by R. *Lowell and by E. *Morgan.

Monte Cristo, *Count of* (*Le Comte de Monte Cristo*), a novel by *Dumas *père*, published 1844–5.

Edmond Dantès, falsely denounced by a personal enemy as a Bonapartist conspirator in 1815, is imprisoned in the Château d'If for many years, escapes, recovers a concealed treasure in the Island of Monte Cristo, and devotes years to the pursuit of his revenge under various names, including that of Count of Monte Cristo.

MONTEMAYOR, Jorge de (1519–61), a Portuguese poet and author who wrote in Spanish. His chief work is *Diana* (?1559), a prose pastoral interspersed with verses, in which he transferred Arcadia to the heart of Spain. It was extremely popular and was translated into French, German, and English. The English translation was by B. *Yonge (1598); the episode of Felix and Felismena in Yonge's version is almost certainly the direct source of much of the plot of Shakespeare's *The Two Gentlemen of Verona*. The scene is laid at the foot of the mountains of Leon and the pastoral is occupied with the misfortunes of Sereno and Sylvanus, two shepherd lovers of the fair Diana, a shepherdess; and the loves, transfers of affection, and disguises of various other shepherds and shepherdesses. Happiness is finally restored by the agency of enchanted potions. A continuation (or, as has recently been argued, a rejoinder), *Diana enamorada* by Gaspar Gil Polo (*c*.1519–85), appeared in 1564, and was also very popular.

MONTESQUIEU, Charles-Louis de Secondat (1689–1755), French social and political philosopher. A member of the lesser nobility of Guyenne, he trained as a lawyer and served as president of the Bordeaux *Parlement*. He made his name as a writer with the publication of *Lettres Persanes* (1721, English trans. Ozell, 1722), in which the correspondence of a Persian visitor to Paris occasions a satirical review of French legal and political institutions. His masterpiece, *De l'esprit des lois* (1748), is the first European work to employ a recognizable sociological method. It analyses a variety of political constitutions, and advocates a liberal constitutional monarchy on the English model. He lived in England during 1729–31, and he travelled in Western Europe in the company of Lord *Chesterfield.

MONTEZUMA (1466–1520), the ruler of

Mexico at the time of the Spanish conquest. He was seized by *Cortès and held as a hostage. The Aztecs rose and attacked the Spaniards' quarters, and Montezuma, who at the request of Cortès attempted to dissuade them, was mortally wounded. See W. H. *Prescott's *Conquest of Mexico* (1843). *Dryden's play *The Indian Emperour* (1665) has Montezuma as subject.

Montfort, Lord and Lady, in *Endymion* by B. Disraeli.

MONTGOMERIE, Alexander (*c.*1545–*c.*1598), a Scottish poet, who held office in the Scottish court in 1578 and received a pension from James VI in 1583. He left to travel abroad in 1586, having got into trouble. His principal work is *The Cherry and the Slae,* a long allegorical poem on the contrast between the cherry growing high up and valued, and the sloe growing close at hand and despised, in which Hope, Experience, Cupid, etc., take part in the conversation. It was published twice in 1597, the first edition being unfinished and corrupt. He also wrote a *Flyting of Montgomerie and Polwart* (published 1621), sonnets, and miscellaneous poems.

MONTHERLANT, Henri de (1896–1972), French novelist and dramatist. Born of an aristocratic and Roman Catholic family, he showed himself receptive to the ideas of *Barrès, *D'Annunzio, and *Gide, evolving in his early novels—notably *Les Célibataires* (1934)—an ideology of chivalric ardour and masculine disdain. His major plays, which include *La Reine morte* (1942), *Le Maître de Santiago* (1947), *La Ville dont le prince est un enfant* (1951), and *Port-Royal* (1954), exhibit his gifts for mordant writing and heroic intensity. His culminating work, the novel *Le Chaos et la nuit* (1963), evokes the proud and austere isolation of an exiled Spanish anarchist. He travelled widely and sometimes dangerously during his early life. An extreme right-winger in politics, he consistently rejected modern French democracy. His work has been translated into English variously by T. Kilmartin and J. Griffin.

Monthly Magazine, The, an influential radical publication founded in 1796 by Richard Phillips, a Jacobin and a supporter of *Paine. Contributors included *Godwin, *Malthus, *Hazlitt, *Southey, and W. *Taylor. The magazine had an encyclopaedic range, covering literature (including German, Spanish, and oriental literature), science, politics, philosophy, etc. Its first editor was Dr J. *Aikin (to whom *Coleridge originally intended to send the *Ancient Mariner*); its last (in 1825) was *Thelwall. Both the *Anti-Jacobin* and the *New Monthly Magazine* were founded to oppose the views of the *Monthly*.

Monthly Review, The (1749–1845),

founded by the bookseller Ralph Griffiths, began as a series of digests of miscellaneous matters, but about 1780 became the first of the influential literary reviews. It was liberal in outlook, and its standard of contributions, from *Sheridan, Dr C. *Burney, *Goldsmith, and others, was very high. Its attempt, by 1790, to review all publications in each month gives it considerable bibliographical interest. The term 'autobiography' seems first to have appeared in its columns, in Dec. 1797.

MONTROSE, James Graham, fifth earl and first marquis of (1612–50), royalist and general, is remembered as a poet for a few songs and epigrams (printed in Mark Napier's *Memoirs of Montrose,* 1856, and since much anthologized), including 'My dear and only love' and lines said to have been written on his prison window the night before his execution in Edinburgh.

Montsurry, see BUSSY D'AMBOIS.

Moody and Sankey, Dwight Lyman Moody (1837–99) and Ira David Sankey (1840–1908), American evangelists. After undergoing 'conversion' as a young man, Moody began his evangelizing activities by starting a Sunday-school in Chicago. He devoted himself to missionary work there and among soldiers during the American Civil War. With Sankey as singer and organist, they carried on a revival campaign in America and England. The compilation of the *Sankey and Moody Hymn Book* (1873) and its many subsequent editions (as *Sacred Songs and Solos,* etc.) was due to Sankey.

Moonstone, The, a novel by Wilkie *Collins, published 1868.

The moonstone, an enormous diamond originally stolen from an Indian shrine, is given to an English girl, Rachel Verrinder, on her eighteenth birthday, but disappears the same night. Under suspicion of stealing it are Rosanna Spearman, a hunchbacked housemaid, formerly a thief; a troop of Indian jugglers; Franklin Blake, Rachel's cousin; and Rachel herself. A detective, Sergeant Cuff, is called in to solve the mystery, and is aided by the house steward Gabriel Betteredge, principal narrator of the story, but thwarted by Rachel's reticence and by the tragic suicide of Rosanna. It is eventually discovered that Franklin Blake was seen by Rachel to take the diamond, that at the time he was sleep-walking under the influence of opium, that it was taken from him by Rachel's other suitor, Godfrey Ablewhite, a sanctimonious hypocrite, and finally secured (by the murder of Ablewhite) and returned to the shrine by the Indian jugglers, who were high-caste Brahmins in disguise.

MOORCOCK, Michael (1939–   ), one of the most prominent of the 'New Wave' *Science Fiction writers of the 1960s, part of whose aim was to invest the genre with literary merit. He edited *New Worlds* from 1964 to 1971, and has also edited many collections of short stories, etc.; his own works include the novels *The Final Programme* (1968), *A Cure for Cancer* (1971), and *The English Assassin* (1972), featuring Jerry Cornelius and described by *Aldiss as the meeting point of 'the worlds of Ronald Firbank and Ian Fleming'.

MOORE, Brian (1921–   ), novelist, born and educated in Belfast, who emigrated in 1948 to Canada and subsequently moved to the USA. His first novels were published pseudonymously under the name of Michael Bryan; the first under his own name was *Judith Hearne* (1955; published in the US as *The Lonely Passion of Judith Hearne*, 1956), a poignant story of a lonely Belfast spinster who takes refuge in alcohol. His subsequent works, many of which deal with transatlantic migrations, include *The Luck of Ginger Coffey* (1960, describing the misfortunes and daydreams of an Irish immigrant in Canada), *I am Mary Dunne* (1968, a first-person female narration set in America), *Catholics* (1972, a papal representative visiting an Irish religious community some time in the future), and *The Mangan Inheritance* (1979, an American journalist in search of his Irish heritage and the *poète maudit* J. C. *Mangan). Critics have praised both the versatility of his subject matter and the economy and understatement of his style.

MOORE, Edward (1712–57), a linen draper turned author, contributed to the *Gentleman's Magazine* and other periodicals, wrote poems and fables which show a debt to *Gay, and edited *The World*, 1753–6, which included *Walpole and *Chesterfield amongst its contributors. He is best remembered as a dramatist. His first comedy, *The Foundling* (1748), may owe something to Richardson's *Pamela*, and was warmly praised by *Fielding. *Gil Blas* (1751) is a lively comedy of intrigue, the plot of which is taken from *Lesage's *Gil Blas of Santillane* (IV. iii *et seq.*), where a lady masquerades as a student in order to get acquainted with a young man who has taken her fancy, maintains by a series of quick changes the dual role of lady and student, and achieves her object of winning the young man's heart. His most successful play, however, was a domestic prose tragedy, *The Gamester* (1753), an exposure of the vice of gambling, through which the weak creature Beverley is lured to ruin and death by the villain Stukeley; this play was widely translated, and was described by Moore's biographer J. H. Caskey (*The Life and Works of Moore*, 1927) as 'the most modern English tragedy written in the eighteenth century'. It was adapted by *Diderot.

MOORE, Francis, see OLD MOORE.

MOORE, George Augustus (1852–1933),

Anglo-Irish novelist, born at Moore Hall in Co. Mayo; his father's racing stables provided background for his most successful novel, *Esther Waters*. He studied painting in Paris for some years and the knowledge of French writing he gained there stood him in good stead when, returning to England c.1880, he set about revitalizing the Victorian novel with naturalistic and, later, realistic techniques borrowed from *Balzac, *Zola, and the *Goncourts. His first novel, *A Modern Lover* (1883), set in artistic Bohemian society, was banned by the circulating *libraries, a circumstance which confirmed Moore in his outspoken battle against prudery and censorship. It was followed by *A Mummer's Wife* (1885, set in the Potteries, which influenced Arnold *Bennett); *Esther Waters* (1894); *Evelyn Innes* (1898) and its sequel *Sister Teresa* (1901). *The Untilled Field* (1903) is a collection of short stories strongly influenced by *Turgenev and *Dostoevsky. In his later novels, e.g. *The Brook Kerith* (1916), which unfolds the interwoven lives of Christ (who survives the Cross), St Paul, and *Joseph of Arimathea, and *Héloïse and Abélard* (1921), he aimed at epic effect. *Confessions of a Young Man* (1888), *Memoirs of my dead life* (1906), and *Hail and Farewell* (3 vols, 1911–14) are all autobiographical; the last is an important though unreliable source for the history of the *Irish revival. Moore collaborated in the planning of the Irish National Theatre (see ABBEY THEATRE), a work which, in the words of *Yeats, 'could not have been done at all without Moore's knowledge of the stage'. His collection of short stories *Celibate Lives* (1927) shows the influence of *Flaubert, not only in subject (all five tales deal with the state of celibacy) but also in their careful reworking and publishing of earlier material. The Ebury edition of Moore's works (20 vols, 1936–8) owes its name to 121 Ebury Street ('that long, lack-lustre street', in his own words), where he lived from 1911 until his death, an object of pilgrimage for many younger writers and admirers. See J. M. Hone, *The Life of Moore* (1936). (See VIZETELLY, H.)

MOORE, G(eorge) E(dward) (1873–1958), brother of T. Sturge *Moore, was educated at Dulwich College and Trinity College, Cambridge. He was professor of philosophy in the University of Cambridge, 1925–39. His *Principia Ethica* (1903) inaugurated a new era in British moral philosophy, and also had great influence outside academic philosophy, particularly on the *Bloomsbury Group, who adopted its emphasis on 'the pleasures of human intercourse and the enjoyment of beautiful objects'. His other writings, which include *Philosophical Studies* (1922) and *Some Main Problems of Philosophy* (1953), have had a great, but more narrowly confined, influence. For an account of his personal influence (which, despite his modest nature, was profound) see P. Levy, *G. E. Moore and the Cambridge Apostles* (1979).

MOORE, Henry (1898–   ), sculptor, son of a Yorkshire miner. His figures and groups show, on the one hand, a deep humanity and, on the other, an interest in the forms and rhythms of natural objects.

MOORE, John (1729–1802), studied medicine at Glasgow, and practised in the army and in London as a surgeon until 1772. He then travelled in Europe for several years, publishing accounts of his journeys in 1779, 1781, and 1793. In 1786 he published a successful novel, *Zeluco*, the history of a wicked man; *Edward* (1796), in sharp contrast, redressed the balance by telling the story of a thoroughly good one, and was clearly influenced by *Marivaux's *Vie de Marianne*. In 1797 he produced a collected edition of *Smollett, who had been a friend and patient, and provided a brief biography. *Mordaunt*, an *epistolary novel of some quality, was published in 1800. Moore was the father of Sir John *Moore of Corunna.

MOORE, Sir John (1761–1809), lieutenant-general, son of the above, became commander-in-chief in the Peninsula on the recall of Sir Harry Burrard (1808). He led the historic retreat to Corunna during the winter of 1808–9 and began the embarkation of the British force on 13 Jan. The French, who now appeared, were repulsed, but Moore was mortally wounded, and buried at midnight of 16 Jan. 1809, in the citadel of Corunna. He is the subject of the famous elegy by C. *Wolfe.

MOORE, Marianne Craig (1887–1972), American poet, born in Missouri. From 1925 to 1929 she was editor of *The Dial*, and contributed greatly to its distinction. Her first volume, *Poems* (1921), was followed by *Observations* (1924), *Selected Poems* (1935, with an introduction by T. S. *Eliot), *The Pangolin, and Other Verse* (1936), and other collections; her *Collected Poems* appeared in 1951. Her early work was well known in Britain, admired by I. A. *Richards, and anthologized by M. *Roberts. Her tone is characteristically urbane, sophisticated, and conversational, her observations detailed and precise, and her poems are composed for the page with a strong sense of visual effect. Her subject matter—animals, both homely and exotic, baseball matches, art galleries, catalogues, etc.—is idiosyncratic and has been described as 'incontrovertibly American'.

MOORE, Thomas (1779–1852), born in Dublin, the son of a grocer, was educated at Trinity College, Dublin, and entered at the Middle Temple. In 1801 he published a collection of indifferent poems, *The Poetical Works of the late Thomas Little*, under which pseudonym Byron refers to him in *English Bards and Scotch

Reviewers. In 1803 he was appointed admiralty registrar in Bermuda, a post which he briefly occupied before transferring it to a deputy. In 1806 appeared *Epistles, Odes, and other Poems* which *Jeffrey brought to general notice by his strictures in the *Edinburgh Review*. From 1801 to 1834 Moore continued to add to his *Irish Melodies*, which established him as the national bard of Ireland. He was a good musician and a skilful writer of patriotic and often nostalgic songs, which he set to Irish tunes, mainly of the 18th cent. He himself felt he had 'an instinctive turn for rhyme and song'. Among his more famous songs are 'The Harp that once through Tara's Halls', 'The Minstrel Boy', and 'The Last Rose of Summer'. In 1813 he issued *The Twopenny Post Bag*, a collection of satires directed against the prince regent. He acquired fame and a European reputation with the publication of *Lalla Rookh* (1817), In 1818 appeared the satirical and entertaining *The Fudge Family in Paris*. His deputy in Bermuda then defaulted, leaving Moore to meet a debt of £6,000. He left England for Italy, returning in 1822 when the debt had been paid. *The Loves of the Angels* (1823) enjoyed a considerable vogue and caused some scandal. In 1824 he was prevailed upon to permit the burning of *Byron's *Memoirs*, which Byron (a close friend) had given to him. In 1825 there appeared a life of Sheridan; in 1827 *The Epicurean*, a novel about a Greek philosopher; in 1830 a life of Byron; and in 1831 a *Life of Lord Edward Fitzgerald*. He was awarded a literary pension in 1835, and in the same year published *The Fudges in England*, a light satire on an Irish priest turned Protestant evangelist and on the sentimental literary absurdities of the day. His *History of Ireland* (1835–46) was not a success. He was awarded a civil list pension in 1850.

Moore's *Letters* were edited by W. S. Dowden (2 vols, 1964); see also *The Journal of Thomas Moore* (1964), ed. P. *Quennell.

MOORE, T(homas) Sturge (1870–1944), poet, wood-engraver, and illustrator, and brother of G. E. *Moore; he was a friend of *Ricketts and Shannon, and also of *Yeats, his correspondence with whom was published in 1953, and for whom he designed several books. His first volume of verse, *The Vinedresser and other poems* (1899), was followed by several others, and by various verse dramas, including *Tragic Mothers: Medea, Niobe, Tyrfing* (1920).

Mopsa, a character in Sidney's *Arcadia*.

Moral and Political Philosophy, *Principles of,* see PALEY, W.

Moral Essays, four ethical poems by *Pope, published 1731–5; the collective title was added later by Pope's editor *Warburton.

They were inspired by *Bolingbroke and take the form of four Epistles. Epistle I, addressed to

Viscount Cobham, deals with the knowledge and characters of men; it sets forth the difficulties in judging a man's character and finds their solution in the discovery of the ruling passion, which 'clue once found unravels all the rest'. Epistle II, addressed to Martha *Blount, deals with the characters of women. Atossa was intended either for Sarah, duchess of Marlborough, or for Katherine, duchess of Buckinghamshire; *Chloe for Lady Suffolk; Philomodé for Henrietta, duchess of Marlborough. These three portraits were suppressed at the last moment, and withheld until 1744; it was rumoured that Pope received £1,000 for the suppression. Epistle III, to Lord Bathurst, deals with the use of riches, which is understood by few, neither the avaricious nor the prodigal deriving happiness from them. The Epistle contains the famous characters of the 'Man of Ross' (see KYRLE) and 'Sir *Balaam'. Epistle IV, to Lord Burlington, deals with the same subject as Epistle III, giving instances of the tasteless use of wealth, particularly in architecture and gardening, where nature should be followed, and ending with advice on the proper use of wealth.

Morality Plays, medieval allegorical plays in which personified human qualities acted and disputed, mostly coming from the 15th cent. They developed into the *Interludes, from which it is not always possible to distinguish them, and hence had a considerable influence on the development of Elizabethan drama. They lost popularity with the development of naturalistic drama, but interest in them has revived in the 20th cent., prompted by a new interest in more mannered, pageant-like theatre, such as the Japanese *Nōh theatre and the plays of *Yeats and *Brecht. Among the most celebrated English examples are *Everyman; *Ane Pleasant Satyre of the Thrie Estaitis by Sir D. Lindsay; *Magnyfycence by Skelton; King John by *Bale; *Mankind; *The Castle of Perseverance. See P. Happé ed., Four Morality Plays (1979); G. Wickham ed., English Moral Interludes (1976).

Moral Ode, The, see POEMA MORALE.

Moral Sentiments, The Theory of, see THEORY OF MORAL SENTIMENTS, THE.

MORAVIA, Alberto, pseudonym of Alberto Pincherle (1907–), Italian novelist. He played a major part in shaping *neo-realism in Italian fiction after the Second World War. His first novel Gli indifferenti (The Time of Indifference, 1929), portrayed a middle-class society sick with a moral inertia which favoured the rise of Fascism. La ciociara (Two Women, 1957), the most lyrical and complex of his novels, deals with the close of the war, when Italy was occupied by both Germans and Allies. La romana (The Woman of Rome, 1947) and Racconti romani (Roman Tales, 1957) draw on the language and

culture of Roman plebeians in order to criticize middle-class values. Other full-length novels, notably Il conformista (The Conformist, 1951) and 1934 (1983), explore the psycho-sexual basis of politics.

Mordaunt, a novel by J. *Moore, published 1800.
This *epistolary novel, of considerable quality, falls uneasily into three parts; in the first the cool but kindly Mordaunt describes his travels through Europe; in the second a French marquise relates her fearful experiences during the Terror; and in the third various friends and acquaintances of Mordaunt reveal their lives and characters in correspondence. The hypocrite Mrs Demure and her friend the spiteful countess, the charming spinster Lady Franklin and her young friend Horatia Clifford, together with Mordaunt himself, are the chief letter-writers. To his own amused surprise, Mordaunt falls in love with Miss Clifford and the novel ends with their betrothal.

Morddure, in Spenser's Faerie Queene (II. viii. 20–1), the name of the sword made by Merlin for Prince Arthur. Its more general name is *Excalibur.

Mordern, Colonel, a character in Richardson's *Clarissa.

Mordred, see MODRED.

MORE, Hannah (1745–1833), was an eminent member of the *Blue Stocking Circle. She was educated at her sister's boarding school in Bristol; there, and at home, she acquired French, Italian, Spanish, Latin, and mathematics. In 1773 she published The Search for Happiness, a pastoral play for schools. She came to London in 1774, where she became very friendly with *Garrick and his wife, who in 1776 offered her a suite of rooms in their house. She became the friend of *Burke, Dr *Johnson, S. *Richardson, J. *Reynolds, *Percy, Mrs *Montagu, and all the Blue Stocking ladies. She was greatly esteemed by Horace *Walpole, who honoured her in 1781 by printing her Bishop Bonner's Ghost on his press at *Strawberry Hill. Her tragedy Percy was produced by Garrick in 1777, and established her as a social as well as a literary success. It was followed by another tragedy, The Fatal Falsehood (1779). Her poem Bas Bleu, written some years earlier, was published in 1786, and vividly describes the charm of Blue Stocking society. Meanwhile she had begun to write tracts directed towards the reform of the conditions of the poor; Village Politics appeared in 1793, and in 1795–8 Cheap Repository Tracts (of which the best-known is The Shepherd of Salisbury Plain), which sold two million copies in four years and led to the formation of the Religious Tract Society in 1799. Her Thoughts on the Importance of the Manners of the Great (1788) also went into many large editions. In 1809 she published an immensely successful novel, *Coelebs in Search of a Wife*, the sale of which was not apparently affected by the strictures of Sydney *Smith in the *Edinburgh Review*. She was a lively letter-writer, and her letters give a full and entertaining picture of the intellectual and social world she frequented. See M. G. Jones, *Hannah More* (1952).

MORE, Henry, see CAMBRIDGE PLATONISTS.

MORE, Sir Thomas (St) (?1477–1535), son of Sir John More, a judge, was educated at St Antony's School, Threadneedle Street, London, and at Canterbury College, Oxford. He was for a time in youth in the household of Cardinal Morton, and it was probably from Morton's information that he derived his account of Richard III's murder of the princes, etc. He was called to the bar, where he was brilliantly successful. He devoted his leisure to literature, becoming intimate with *Colet, *Lily, and, in 1499, *Erasmus, who afterwards stayed frequently at his house. He entered Parliament in 1504. During an absence as envoy to Flanders he sketched his description (in Latin) of the imaginary island of *Utopia*, which he completed and published in 1516. He became Master of Requests and privy councillor in 1517, being treated by *Henry VIII with exceptional courtesy during his residence at court. He was present at the Field of the Cloth of Gold, 1520, where he met *Budé, the greatest Greek scholar of the age. He completed his *Dialogue*, his first controversial book in English (directed mainly against *Tyndale's writings), in 1528. He succeeded Wolsey as lord chancellor in 1529, but resigned the post in 1532 and lived for some time in retirement, mainly engaged in controversy with Tyndale and Frith.

Although willing to swear fidelity to the new Act of Succession, More refused to take any oath that should impugn the pope's authority, or assume the justice of the king's divorce from Queen Catherine, 1534; he was therefore committed to the Tower of London with John *Fisher, bishop of Rochester, who had assumed a like attitude. During the first days of his imprisonment he prepared a *Dialoge of Comfort agaynst Trybulacion* and treatises on Christ's passion. He was indicted of high treason, found guilty, and beheaded in 1535. His body was buried in St Peter's in the Tower and, according to Stapleton, his head exhibited on London Bridge. The head was later buried in the *Roper vault in St Dunstan's, Canterbury.

More was a critic and a patron of art, and *Holbein is said to have stayed in his house at Chelsea, and painted portraits of More and his family during his first English visit in 1526–8. More's other chief English works are his *Lyfe of Johan Picus erle of Mirandula* (printed by John

*Rastell, c.1510), his *History of Richard III* (printed imperfectly in Grafton's *Chronicle*, 1543, used by *Hall, and printed fully by William Rastell in 1557), *Supplycacyon of Soulys* (1529), *Confutacyon of Tyndales Answere* (1532), and *The Apology of Syr Thomas More* (1533). His English works were collected in 1557. His Latin publications (collected 1563, etc.) included, besides the *Utopia*, four dialogues of *Lucian, epigrams, and controversial tracts in divinity. There is a pleasant description of More in his Chelsea home in the epistle of Erasmus to Ulrich Hutten, 23 July 1519. He was beatified by the Church of Rome in 1886, and canonized in 1935. *Bolt's play about More, *A Man for All Seasons* (1960), was also made into a successful film.

More, Sir Thomas, a play based on *Hall's Chronicle and biographies of *More, surviving in an incomplete transcript with additions in various hands (British Library, MS Harley 7368) which was submitted to Sir Edmund Tilney, Master of the Revels, probably about 1593. The scribe, *Munday, is likely to have been at least part-author of the original play. Tilney required major changes before granting permission to perform. The revisions (which may date from 1593–5 or 1601–3) are in five different hands, probably including those of *Chettle, *Heywood, *Dekker, and a playhouse scribe known to have worked for the Admiral's Men. The fifth ('Hand D') has been claimed, with strong support, as Shakespeare's. If so, this is his only surviving literary manuscript. A scene of three pages, it depicts More, as sheriff of London, pacifying apprentices in a May-Day rebellion against foreigners. *More* was first printed in 1844; there is a scholarly transcript in the *Malone Society reprints (1911, repr. 1961) and a reliable edition, by Harold Jenkins, in C. J. Sisson's edition of Shakespeare (1954). The first known professional performance was at Nottingham in 1964, with Ian McKellen as More.

Morgan, (1) a character in Thackeray's *Pendennis*, Major Pendennis's valet; (2) a character in Smollett's *Roderick Random*.

MORGAN, Lady, née Sydney Owenson (1776–1859), a prolific and popular writer, who published ten novels, as well as volumes of poetry, biography, and memoirs. She made her name in 1806 with *The Wild Irish Girl*, and was paid £1,200 (a huge sum) by her publisher for *Florence Macarthy* in 1818. *France* (1817) and *Italy* (1821) were both highly successful.

MORGAN, Charles Langbridge (1894–1958), novelist and dramatist, and from 1926 to 1939 dramatic critic of *The Times. His novels include *The Fountain* (1932), *Sparkenbroke* (1936), *The Judge's Story* (1947), and *The River*

Line (1949, dramatized 1952). The last is set against a background of the French resistance; Morgan's status as a writer has been and remains significantly higher in France than in Britain.

MORGAN, Edwin George (1920–   ), Scottish poet and translator, educated at the University of Glasgow and professor of English there from 1975. He has published several volumes of poetry, from *The Vision of Cathkin Braes* (1952) onwards, in which he mingles traditional forms with experimental and *concrete poems such as 'The Computer's First Christmas Card, December 1963'; many of his poems, such as *Glasgow Sonnets* (1972), evoke Scottish urban landscape. He has also translated the poetry of *Montale, *Belli, *Neruda, and others.

MORGAN, William De, see DE MORGAN, W.

Morgan le Fay, queen of *Avalon, the daughter of Arthur's mother Igerne and therefore his half-sister; she is derived from a figure in Welsh and Irish (the Morrigan) mythology, and has a curiously ambivalent attitude to Arthur. In *Malory she attempts to kill Arthur through the agency of her lover Sir Accolon, but she is also the leader of the queens who carries him away to cure his wounds. She is sometimes represented as the bitter enemy of Guinevere (a tradition indicated by the end of *Sir *Gawain and the Green Knight*, where it is said that she instigated the beheading game to frighten Guinevere to death). *Geoffrey of Monmouth calls the fairy lady who takes Arthur off to Avalon Argante, but all later accounts (such as *Giraldus Cambrensis and the prose Vulgate cycles) call her Morgan. A related figure occurs in the *Orlando Innamorato and *Orlando Furioso, called 'Morgana' there and being a *Lady of the Lake. The term *Fata Morgana* (*fata* means 'fairy' in Italian) is given in Sicily to a vision traditionally seen at sea from the Calabrian coast. See MORGAWSE.

MORGANN, Maurice (1726–1802), secretary to the embassy for peace with America in 1782, and author of various political pamphlets, is remembered chiefly as the author of an *Essay on the Dramatic Character of Sir John Falstaff* (1777) in which he defends *Falstaff from the charge of cowardice, and points to 'a certain roundness and integrity in the forms of Shakespeare, which gives them an independence . . .' A. C. *Bradley said of it: 'There is no better piece of Shakespeare criticism in the world.'

Morgante Maggiore, a poem by *Pulci which recast, with humorous additions and alterations, the popular epic *Orlando* (see ROLAND). Orlando (Roland) encounters three giants. He slays two and subdues the third, Morgante, converts him, and makes him his brother in arms. *Byron translated the first canto.

Morgawse, or **Morcades,** half-sister of Arthur, the wife of King Lot of Orkney, and mother of *Modred, Gawain, Agravain, Gareth, and Gaheris. She seems to be in some ways identical in origin with *Morgan le Fay; in later versions Arthur sleeps with her in disguise, thus begetting Modred. She is called 'Anna' in *Geoffrey of Monmouth, though Anna is otherwise attested as Arthur's full sister.

Morgiana, a character in the story of *Ali Baba and the Forty Thieves*.

Morglay, the name of the sword of *Bevis of Hampton, sometimes used allusively for a sword in general.

Moriarty, Professor, the enemy of Sherlock *Holmes, a character created by A. C. *Doyle.

MORIER, James Justinian (?1780–1849), born in Smyrna, educated at Harrow, joined the diplomatic service in 1807. He became attached to Sir Harford Jones's mission to Persia, during which he collected valuable information about a country little known at that time. His account of these travels appeared in *A Journey through Persia, Armenia and Asia Minor to Constantinople in the years 1808–1809* (1812); *A Second Journey through Persia* appeared in 1818. He retired from the foreign office in 1817 to devote his time to literature. He published a number of *oriental romances including the popular *The Adventures of Hajji Baba of Ispahan* (1824), a picaresque tale (the hero undergoes amusing vicissitudes, becoming successively barber, doctor, and assistant executioner) which gives a colourful and accurate presentation of life in Persia during the early 19th cent. Its sequel *The Adventures of Hajji Baba in England* (1828) was less successful. His later works, including *Ayesha* (1834) which introduced the Turkish word 'bosh' into the English language, did not reach the level of his earlier ones.

Morland, Catherine, a character in J. Austen's *Northanger Abbey*.

MORLAND, George (1763–1804), genre painter, son of a painter, Henry Robert Morland (1716–97). He first exhibited at the Royal Academy at the age of 10. His vast output of country scenes, popular but superficial, failed to keep him out of debt and he died in a sponging-house, his own epitaph on himself being, 'Here lies a drunken dog'.

MORLEY, Henry (1822–94), turned from medicine to journalism, joined the staff of *Household Words* at Dickens's invitation, edited *The Examiner*, and devoted his long academic career to the development of English literature as an academic subject. He published biographies of Palissy the Potter (1852), Cardano (1854), and Agrippa (1856), wrote *A First Sketch of English Literature* (1873), 11 volumes of *English*

Writers (1887–95), and edited cheap editions of English classics in Morley's Universal Library (1883–8) and Cassell's National Library (1886–92).

MORLEY, Henry Parker, Lord (1476–1556), was a successful courtier and diplomat under Henry VIII. His *Exposition and Declaration* of Psalm 94 was really a defence of Henry's position as head of the Church of England; better known now is his other published work, a translation of *Petrarch's *Trionfi* (c.1553), which has been edited by D. Carnicelli (1971).

MORLEY, John, first viscount Morley of Blackburn (1838–1923), educated at Cheltenham College and Lincoln College, Oxford. He began his literary career as a journalist, writing chiefly for the *Fortnightly Review*, of which he was editor (1867–82), and became a friend of *Meredith and J. S. *Mill; he was editor of the *Pall Mall Gazette*, 1881–3. Many of his essays on historical and literary subjects are collected in *Critical Miscellanies* (1871–7). His literary achievements, chiefly biographical, include *Edmund Burke; an historical study* (1867), *Voltaire* (1872), *Rousseau* (1873), *On Compromise* (1874), *Burke* (1879), *The Life of Richard Cobden* (1881), *Oliver Cromwell* (1900), *Life of Gladstone* (1903), and he edited the English Men of Letters series. He was a Liberal MP (1883–1908) and a close supporter of *Gladstone; he was chief secretary for Ireland (1886 and 1892–5) and secretary of state for India (1905–10). From 1910 he was lord president of the Council but resigned at the outbreak of war.

Morley, Stephen, in *Sybil* by B. Disraeli.

MORLEY, Thomas (1557/8–1602), English composer, organist, and writer. He studied music under *Byrd, to whom in later life he dedicated his extremely successful treatise *A Plaine and Easie Introduction to Practicall Musicke* (1597), the first work of its kind in the English language and still one of the most famous. He became organist of St Paul's and a gentleman of the Chapel Royal, and in his later years was much involved in the printing and publishing of music.

Morley produced music in many forms, but his peculiar historical importance as a composer stemmed from his championship of the Italian *madrigal, and his consequently influential position in the development of its English counterpart. His first two publications, the *Canzonets, or Little Short Songs to Three Voyces* (1594) and the first book of *Madrigalls to Foure Voyces* (1594), contain the best of his own work in this form, brightly Italianate in style yet finished with the seriousness proper to a pupil of Byrd. The famous 'Aprill is in my mistris face', in the 1594 collection, is perfectly characteristic. The two volumes of *Balletts* and *Canzonets*

which followed in 1595 were largely free transcriptions of pieces by contemporary Italian composers, and were in fact printed in both English and Italian—'Now is the month of maying', for example, appearing also as 'Se ben mi c'ha bon tempo' (after Orazio Vecchi). As publisher he later produced two straight 'anthologies' of Italian works, and he was the moving spirit behind *The Triumphes of Oriana* (1601), a collection of madrigals by 21 English composers in honour of *Elizabeth I. Most of Morley's madrigal texts are either from Italian originals or from anonymous sources. His one book of *Ayres . . . to the Lute* (1600), however, contains a setting of 'It was a lover and his lass' which is apparently the earliest Shakespeare setting to survive, though it is not known whether it was ever used in a production of *As You Like It*. Shakespeare and Morley lived for some time in the same London parish, and the possibility of a connection between the two men has been debated, though with little result.

Morning Advertiser, The, established in 1794, and therefore one of the oldest of London newspapers with a continuous history. It was devoted primarily to the defence of trade interests, having been founded by the Society of Licensed Victuallers of London, whose organ it remains.

Morning Chronicle, The, a Whig journal founded by the printer William Woodfall (1746–1803) in 1769, and successfully conducted by him for 20 years. It rose to importance when James Perry became chief proprietor and editor in 1789. Its staff then included *Sheridan, *Lamb, T. *Campbell, Sir J. *Mackintosh, *Brougham, T. *Moore, and *Ricardo. Perry was succeeded by John Black (1783–1855), scholar, Scotsman, and friend of James *Mill; J. S. *Mill described Black as 'the first journalist who carried criticism and the Spirit of Reform into the details of English institutions . . . Black was the writer who carried the warfare into those subjects, and by doing so he broke the spell.' Both Mills were among his contributors, *Dickens was one of his reporters, and *Thackeray his art critic. The *Morning Chronicle* came to an end in 1862.

Morning Herald and Public Advertiser, The, a London newspaper that ran from 1780 to 1869; it published the mock criticisms of the mock epic *The Rolliad* in 1784. One of its special features for a time was a selection of reports of police cases, illustrated by *Cruikshank.

Morning Post, The, a London daily newspaper founded in 1772. Under the management of D. *Stuart, Sir J. *Mackintosh and S. T. *Coleridge were enlisted in its service, and *Southey, *Wordsworth, and A. *Young were also contributors. After a period of decline, it recovered its position under the direction of Peter Borthwick and his son Algernon Borthwick (Lord Glenesk, 1830–1908). It was amalgamated with the *Daily Telegraph* in 1937.

Morose, in Jonson's *Epicene*, a crabbed old bachelor who hates noise.

MORRELL, Lady Ottoline (1873–1938), daughter of Lieutenant-General Arthur Bentinck and half-sister of the duke of Portland, married Philip Morrell, shortly to become a Liberal MP, in 1902. From 1908 she entertained a wide circle of political and literary celebrities at her Thursday evening gatherings at 44 Bedford Square, and continued her career as hostess and patron of the arts at Garsington Manor, Oxfordshire, between 1915 and 1927. Her friends and guests included *Asquith, H. *James, L. *Strachey, B. *Russell, V. *Woolf, T. S. *Eliot, *Yeats, D. H. *Lawrence, and A. *Huxley. Tall, striking, and eccentric, she appeared as a character in several works of fiction by her protégés, most memorably in Lawrence's *Women in Love* and Huxley's *Crome Yellow*. Both portraits caused considerable offence. Her Memoirs, edited by Robert Gathorne-Hardy, appeared in 2 volumes in 1963 and 1974.

Morrice, Gil, see GIL MORRICE.

Morris, Dinah, a character in G. Eliot's *Adam Bede*.

MORRIS, Sir Lewis (1833–1907), born at Carmarthen and educated at Oxford, contributed actively to the establishment of the University of Wales. He published several volumes of mediocre verse, imitative of *Tennyson; the most popular were *Songs of Two Worlds* (1871) and *The Epic of Hades* (1876–7). The latter, which consists of monologues by various characters from Greek mythology, owes much to Tennyson's *A Dream of Fair Women*.

MORRIS, William (1834–96), the son of a successful business man, was educated at Marlborough School and Exeter College, Oxford. He was articled to the architect G. E. Street, and in 1858 worked with *Rossetti, *Burne-Jones, and others on the frescoes in the Oxford Union. He was one of the originators of the *Oxford and Cambridge Magazine* (1856), to which he contributed poems, essays, and tales. In 1858 he published *The Defence of Guenevere and other poems*, which contains much of his best work, including 'The Haystack in the Floods', 'Concerning Geffray Teste Noire', 'Shameful Death', and 'Golden Wings', poems marked by a striking mixture of beauty and brutality, all with medieval settings. In 1859 he married Jane Burden, one of the most painted Pre-Raphaelite 'stunners'; their home, Red House at Bexley, was designed by Philip Webb, and was an important

landmark in domestic architecture, adapting late Gothic methods to 19th-cent. needs; it was described as 'grand and severely simple'. The failure to find suitable furniture for it strengthened Morris's growing hatred of industrial 'shoddy', and led to the founding, together with Rossetti, Burne-Jones, Webb, Madox Brown, and others, of the firm of Morris, Marshall, Faulkener and Co. This firm produced furniture, printed textiles, tapestries, wallpapers, and stained glass; its designs brought about a complete revolution in public taste, though Morris was well aware of the irony that only the rich could afford its products. In 1867 he published *The Life and Death of Jason*, a poem in heroic couplets based on the story of Jason, Medea, and the Argonauts; in 1868–70 appeared *The Earthly Paradise*, which established him as one of the most popular poets of the day, though critics now condemn its verse as archaic and escapist, compared with the freshness of his early work. In 1871 he took a joint tenancy of Kelmscott Manor with Rossetti, wrote the poem *Love is Enough* (1872), and visited Iceland, which stimulated his interest in the heroic themes of Icelandic literature. His epic *Sigurd the Volsung* appeared in 1876. In 1877 he founded the Society for the Protection of Ancient Buildings (the 'Antiscrape Society') in protest against the destruction being caused by the restorers. From this time on he turned increasingly towards political activity; in 1883 he joined the Social Democratic Federation, the doctrine of which, largely under his leadership, developed into Socialism. On its disruption in 1884 he became head of the seceders, who organized themselves as the Socialist League, and was to lecture and write for the cause with great energy. The verse tale 'The Pilgrims of Hope' appeared in the League's magazine *Commonweal* in 1885. His later works, with the exception of *Poems by the Way* (1891) and *Chants for Socialists* (1884–5), were mainly in prose, and most remarkable among them were *A Dream of John Ball* (1888) and *News from Nowhere* (1891), both socialist fantasies cast in a dream setting. He also wrote several historical romances set in the distant past of northern Europe. These include *The House of the Wolfings* (1889), which he said was 'meant to illustrate the melting of the individual into the society of the tribes', *The Roots of the Mountains* (1890), *The Story of the Glittering Plain* (1890), *The Wood beyond the World* (1894), and the work which he completed just before his death, *The Sundering Flood* (1898). All were published by the Kelmscott Press, which he had founded at Hammersmith in 1890, and for which he designed founts of type and ornamental letters and borders. The Press also published other works by Morris, reprints of English classics (including *Caxton's *The Golden Legend* and the Kelmscott *Chaucer), and various smaller books by other authors, including poems by *Blunt. Morris's later romances were described by G. B. *Shaw as 'a startling relapse into literary Pre-Raphaelitism', but they were admired by *Yeats, who was much influenced in his early years by Morris. On his death Morris was widely mourned as 'our best man' by his fellow socialists, by whom he was deeply revered; his view that 'the true incentive to useful and happy labour is, and must be, pleasure in the work itself' links his political and artistic aspirations, both of which have remained profoundly influential. Morris published many other works, including lectures on art, architecture, and politics, and various translations, including the *Aeneid* (1875) and the *Odyssey* (1887); he collaborated with E. Magnusson in translations from the Icelandic. The standard life is by J. W. Mackail (1899), and E. P. *Thompson's *Morris; Romantic to Revolutionary* (1961) gives a detailed appraisal of his political development. His letters were edited by P. Henderson (1950).

Morris Dance, a series of folk-dance pageants, performed at various seasons of the year since the 15th cent. at least, and found in many places throughout England. The most important recurrent subjects are the characters of the *Robin Hood legends in the Spring play (especially Friar Tuck and Maid Marian, who often appears as Queen of the May), 'harvest home', dances in the autumn, and year-ending plays for Christmas, emblematic of the ending of the old year. For an example see REVESBY PLAY. See *The Morris Book* by Cecil J. Sharp and H. C. MacIlwaine (1907).

MORRISON, Arthur (1863–1945), novelist, whose 'realist' tales of East End life in London were first published in *Macmillan's Magazine* and later collected as *Tales of Mean Streets* (1894). He is chiefly remembered for his novel *A Child of the Jago* (1896). He devoted the latter part of his life to the study and collection of oriental art.

Morte Arthure, The Alliterative, a 14th-cent. poem of 'The *Alliterative Revival' in 4,346 alliterative long lines, used as a source by *Malory in his Book I, the story of Arthur and Lucius. It used to be identified wrongly as 'the gret Gest off Arthure' by *Huchown. Correspondences with the *Roman de Brut* by *Wace suggest that, directly or indirectly (perhaps mediated through *Mannyng), this may have been the poet's principal source. The poem has claims to be regarded (as it was by R. W. *Chambers) as the most powerful epic narrative in Middle English. Its material corresponds roughly to Malory's first, second, and eighth romances (in Vinaver's numbering): the early exploits of Arthur, his European ventures, and the final battle with Modred. The obscurity of its dialect makes it somewhat forbidding (though it is less difficult than the popular Sir *Gawain and

the Green Knight). At any rate it is one of the most important and influential Middle English poems, the influence of which has been detected in Malory, *Cleanness, *The Awntyrs of Arthur, *Henry the Minstrel's *Wallace*, and elsewhere.

Selections ed. J. Finlayson (1967); ed. L. D. Benson in *King Arthur's Death* (1976). For discussion, see J. L. N. O'Loughlin in R. S. Loomis ed., *Arthurian Literature in the Middle Ages* (1959), pp. 522–6 and T. Turville-Petre, *The Alliterative Revival* (1977).

Morte Arthur, Le (The Stanzaic Morte Arthur), a late 14th-cent. poem from the North-West Midlands in 3,834 lines of eight-lined rhyming stanzas, surviving in one manuscript, and the source (directly or indirectly) for the sections in *Malory leading up to and dealing with the death of Arthur (i.e. the last two 'works' in the Vinaver's edition; though in these it is clear that Malory was also using a French text). It deals with Launcelot's love affairs with Guinevere and the Maid of Astolat, with Arthur's last battles, and with the king's being borne away to Avalon.

Ed. L. D. Benson in *King Arthur's Death* (1976); J. D. Bruce, EETS ES 88 (1903).

Morte D'Arthur, Le, the title generally given to the lengthy cycle of Arthurian legends by *Malory, finished in 1470 and printed by *Caxton in 1485, divided into 21 books. But in 1934 W. F. Oakeshott discovered in Winchester College Library a manuscript of the same period as Caxton's but without his division into 21 books and without several of his colophons. This superior manuscript, dividing the whole into eight parts, was used by Vinaver as the basis of his new standard edition of Malory. Though Malory refers throughout to a 'French book' as his source, it is clear that his sources were more various than this implies. Vinaver divides the cycle into eight *Works* which he wishes to treat as separate romances: (1) The Tale of Arthur and Lucius, based principally on the Alliterative English *Morte Arthure*; (2) The Book of King Arthur, based largely on the *Suite du Merlin* (Huth Merlin) (see MERLIN). The *Suite* is believed to be a later rewriting of part of the 13th-cent. prose Vulgate cycle; (3) The Tale of Sir Launcelot du Lake, mostly from two sections of the prose *Lancelot* in the Vulgate cycle; (4) Sir Gareth of Orkney, the precise source of which is not known; (5) Tristram de Lyones, thought to be a translation of part of a lost 13th-cent. prose *Tristan* in French; (6) The quest of the Holy Grail, principally from the prose Vulgate *Queste del Saint Graal* (see GRAIL); (7) Launcelot and Guinevere; and (8) The Morte Arthur, both based to a considerable degree on the French Vulgate *Mort Artu*, and the 15th-cent. English stanzaic *Le Morte Arthur* (above). Since the publication of Vinaver's 3-vol. edition in 1947 criticism of Malory has concentrated on the rather terminological matter of whether his work is to be regarded as a single 'whole Book' (see Lumiansky and Moorman below) or as eight Works (Vinaver), a middle position being taken by C. S. *Lewis and by D. S. Brewer (see Bennett below). Although Vinaver's edition is now regarded as authoritative, the traditional view of Malory as a single whole, compounded of disparate parts, is the prevailing one.

E. Vinaver ed., *The Works of Sir Thomas Malory* (2nd edn 1968); in one volume as *Malory: Works* (2nd edn 1971). Caxton's edition, ed. J. Cowen (Penguin, 2 vols, 1969); J. A. W. Bennett ed., *Essays on Malory* (1963); R. M. Lumiansky ed., *Malory's Originality* (1964); C. Moorman, *The Book of Kyng Arthur* (1965); T. Takimaya and D. S. Brewer eds, *Aspects of Malory* (1982).

'Morte d'Arthur', a poem by *Tennyson, written 1833–4, published 1842, subsequently incorporated in 'The Passing of Arthur' (1869), preceded by 169 lines and followed by 29, where it formed one of the *Idylls of the King*, though it continued to be published separately as well. Tennyson's first major Arthurian work, it describes the last moments of Arthur after the battle with Mordred's forces, and includes his elegy on the Round Table, delivered to Sir Bedivere: 'The old order changeth, yielding place to new . . .'

Mortimer, a character in Marlowe's *Edward the Second.*

MORTIMER, John Clifford (1923–), novelist, barrister, and playwright, was formerly married to Penelope *Mortimer. He is well known in the legal and literary worlds for his stand against censorship, and known to a wide public as the author of many successful television plays, including his series about an eccentric QC, Rumpole of the Bailey. His plays include *The Dock Brief* (produced for both radio and television in 1957, pub. 1958) and the autobiographical *A Voyage Round my Father* (perf. 1970, pub. 1971), a portrait of his blind and histrionic barrister father. A volume of autobiography, *Clinging to the Wreckage*, appeared in 1982.

MORTIMER, Penelope Ruth, née Fletcher (1918–), novelist, whose works, with their emphasis on frankness about female experience, contributed to the development of the woman's novel in the 1960s. They include *The Pumpkin Eater* (1962), *The House* (1971), and *Long Distance* (1974). A volume of autobiography, *About Time*, appeared in 1979.

Mortimer his Fall, fragments of a tragedy by *Jonson, printed in 1640, concerning the earl of Mortimer, the murderer of Edward II. Only the Argument and two speeches survive.

Morton, Henry, of Milnwood, the hero of Scott's *Old Mortality.*

MORTON, John Maddison (1811–91), son of the dramatist T. *Morton, educated in France, wrote farces and showed a special gift for adaptations from the French. His most successful piece was *Box and Cox* (1847); *Done on Both Sides* appeared in the same year.

MORTON, Thomas (?1764–1838), entered Lincoln's Inn in 1784, and was the author of three successful comedies, *The Way to get Married* (1796), *A Cure for Heartache* (1797), and *Speed the Plough* (1798). The last of these introduced the name and character of 'Mrs Grundy', and the conception of Grundyism as the extreme of moral rigidity.

Mosca, Volpone's parasite in Jonson's *Volpone.*

MOSCHUS (*fl. c.*150 BC), a pastoral poet of Syracuse. The beautiful *Lament for Bion*, doubtfully attributed to Moschus, is a dirge for the author's friend and teacher. There is an echo of it in *Milton's Latin *Epitaphium Damonis*, in his *Lycidas*, in Shelley's *Adonais*, and in M. Arnold's *'Thyrsis'.

MOSELEY, Humphrey (d. 1661), a London bookseller and the chief literary publisher of his time, who published the first collected edition of *Milton's *Poems* (1645) which contains the unflattering portrait engraved by William Marshall. Moseley also published the 1647 folio of *Beaumont and *Fletcher, and work by *Crashaw, *D'Avenant, *Denham, *Donne, *Waller, and many others.

MOSLEY, Nicholas, 3rd Baron Ravensdale (1923–), novelist and biographer, educated at Eton and Balliol College, Oxford. His highly intellectual, experimental, and metaphysical novels include *Accident* (1964) and *Impossible Object* (1968), both of which were filmed; *Natalie Natalia* (1971); and *Catastrophe Practice* (1979), a complex network of three plays with prefaces and a short novel, built on the mathematical 'catastrophe theory' of the 1970s, applied here to human relationships and identity. His biographies include a life of J. *Grenfell (1976) and a two-volume study of his father, *Rules of the Game: Sir Oswald and Lady Cynthia Mosley 1896–1933* (1982) and *Beyond the Pale: Sir Oswald Mosley 1933–1980* (1983).

Mosses from an Old Manse, published 1846, a collection of tales and sketches by N. *Hawthorne. The Old Manse itself is the author's Concord home, and best-known among the book's contents are 'Young Goodman Brown', 'Rappaccini's Daughter', and 'Roger Malvin's Burial'.

Moth, (1) in Shakespeare's *Love's Labour's Lost*, *Armado's page; (2) in his *A Midsummer Night's Dream*, one of the fairies. The name, interchangeable aurally with 'mote', suggested diminutive size.

Mother Hubbard, the subject of a nursery rhyme attributed to Sarah Catherine Martin (1768–1826) and published in 1805, but probably based on oral tradition.

'Mother Hubberds Tale', or *'Prosopopoia'*, a satire in rhymed couplets, by *Spenser, included in the volume of *Complaints* published in 1591. The ape and the fox, 'disliking of their evill | And hard estate', determine to seek their fortunes abroad, and assume the disguises first of an old soldier and his dog, then of a parish priest and his clerk, then of a courtier and his groom; their knaveries in these characters are recounted. Finally they steal the lion's crown and sceptre and abuse the regal power, until Jove intervenes and exposes them. The poem is a satire on the abuses of the church and the evils of the court.

MOTHERWELL, William (1797–1835), a native of Glasgow, became editor of the *Paisley Advertiser* and *Glasgow Courier*. In 1827 he published a collection of ballads, *Minstrelsy ancient and modern*, and in 1832 *Poems narrative and lyrical*, of which the best-known and least characteristic is 'Jeanie Morrison', addressed to a childhood sweetheart. With *Hogg he issued an edition of *Burns's works in 1834–5.

Motion, the name given to puppet-plays in the 16th and 17th cents. These dealt originally with scriptural subjects, but their scope was afterwards extended. Shakespeare in *The Winter's Tale* (IV. iii) refers to a 'motion of the Prodigal Son', and there are references to 'motions' in Jonson's *Bartholomew Fair*, *A Tale of a Tub*, and *Every Man out of his Humour*.

MOTLEY, John Lothrop (1814–77), born in Massachusetts, educated at Harvard, Göttingen, and Berlin (where he formed a lifelong friendship with Bismarck). He was American minister to Austria, 1861–7, and to Great Britain, 1869–70. He is chiefly remembered as a historian and author of *The Rise of the Dutch Republic* (1855). This was followed by the *History of the United Netherlands* (1860–7) and *The Life and Death of John Barneveld* (1874).

MOTTEUX, Peter Anthony (1660–1718), was born at Rouen and came to England after the revocation of the Edict of Nantes (1685). He edited and wrote much of *The Gentleman's Journal*, completed Sir T. *Urquhart's translation of Rabelais (1693–4), and published a free translation of *Don Quixote* (1700–3).

MOTTLEY, John (1692–1750), author of several plays and lives of Peter the Great and Catherine I, is remembered as having published *Joe Miller's jests: or the wit's vade-mecum* (1739).

MOTTRAM, R(alph) H(ale) (1883–1971),

novelist, born in Norwich, where his family had long worked for Gurney's Bank; he himself worked as a bank clerk before establishing himself as a novelist with, principally, *The Spanish Farm Trilogy* (1927), a sequence of novels based on his own experiences in France and Flanders while serving in the First World War. It consists of *The Spanish Farm* (1924), *Sixty-four, Ninety-four* (1925), and *The Crime at Vanderlynden's* (1926), and is set in northern France on the 'Ferme Espagnole' of Flemish-speaking, French-writing farmer Jerome Vanderlynden and his daughter Madeleine.

Mouldy, Ralph, in Shakespeare's 2 *Henry IV* (III. ii), one of Falstaff's recruits.

Mourning Becomes Electra, see O'NEILL, E.

Mourning Bride, The, a tragedy by *Congreve, produced 1697. This was the author's only attempt at tragedy, and was received with enthusiasm.

Almeria, daughter of Manuel, king of Granada, has secretly married Alphonso, prince of the enemy state of Valencia. He becomes a captive of Manuel. The discovery of his marriage to Almeria infuriates the king, who orders the immediate murder of Alphonso and, further to punish his daughter, decides to impersonate the captive in his cell, so that when she comes to save him he may mock her disappointment. As a result he is by mistake killed instead, and decapitated. Zara, a Moorish queen, a fellow captive in love with Alphonso but repulsed by him, finding the headless body, takes poison in despair. A revolt against Manuel releases the true Alphonso, and he and Almeria are reunited.

The play contains lines that are widely known, such as the first in the play:

> Music has charms to soothe a savage breast,

and those which close the third act:

> Heaven has no rage, like love to hatred turned,
> Nor hell a fury, like a woman scorned.

'Mouse, To a' ('Wee, sleekit, cow'rin', tim'rous beastie . . .'), a poem by *Burns, published in 1786; one of a small group of tender, unsentimental poems about animals, which include 'Poor Mailie's Elegy', *'The Twa Dogs', and 'The Auld Farmer's . . . Salutation to his . . . Mare, Maggie'.

Movement, The, a term coined by J. D. Scott, literary editor of the *Spectator*, in 1954 to describe a group of writers including *Amis, *Larkin, *Davie, *Enright, *Wain, E. *Jennings, and *Conquest. Two anthologies (Enright's *Poets of the 1950s*, 1955, and Conquest's *New Lines*, 1956) illustrate the Movement's predominantly anti-romantic, witty, rational, sardonic tone; its fictional heroes (e.g.: Larkin's John Kemp in *Jill*, 1946, and Amis's Dixon in *Lucky Jim*, 1954) tended to be lower-middle-class scholarship boys. Definitions of its aims were negative (Conquest: 'a negative determination to avoid bad principles') and by 1957 its members began to disown it, claiming, in Wain's words, 'its work is done.' See Blake Morrison, *The Movement* (1980).

Mowbray, Clara, and her brother John, characters in Scott's *St Ronan's Well*.

Mowcher, Miss, in Dickens's *David Copperfield*, a humorous and good-hearted dwarf, a hairdresser and manicurist.

Mowgli, the child in R. Kipling's *The Jungle Book*.

MOXON, Edward (1801–58), became a distinguished London publisher and bookseller, and a less distinguished poet: Leigh *Hunt described him as 'a bookseller among poets, and a poet among booksellers'. Various volumes of his poems were published between 1826 and 1835, and his chief interest in publishing was in poetry. He became a close friend of *Lamb, who introduced him to many of the writers of his day and whose 'adopted' daughter, Emma Isola, he married. He set up his own business in 1830, when he proceeded to build a remarkable list which included *Shelley, *Clare, *Wordsworth, *Coleridge, Lamb, Hunt, *Keats, *Southey, R. *Browning, *Patmore, and *Longfellow, as well as *Tennyson, whose close friend he became and whose work he continued to champion and publish until his death. Hunt wrote that 'Moxon has no connection but with the select of the earth.' In 1831 he established the *Englishman's Magazine*, in which he published much of the work of the writers he supported, and in which he defended them against the attacks of *Blackwood's, and the *Edinburgh and *Quarterly Reviews. Apart from their literary qualities, his publications were famed for a high standard of typography and binding.

MOXON, Joseph (1627–91), maker of globes and mathematical instruments, printer and typefounder, born in Wakefield, the son of a printer. He wrote *Mechanick Exercises; Or, the Doctrine of Hand-Works applied to the Art of Printing* (1683–4; ed. Herbert Davis and Harry Carter, 1958), the first manual of printing and typefounding in any language, and probably the first book to be published serially.

MOZART, Wolfgang Amadeus (1756–91), Austrian composer. He visited London with his parents and sister when he was eight years old: he was received three times by George III, who put him through his paces at the keyboard, and was later systematically 'tested' by *Barrington, whose 'Account of a Very Remarkable Young Musician' first appeared in the *Philosophical Transactions* of the *Royal Society for the year 1770. The first two Mozart symphonies were written in Ebury Street (then Ebury Row), and before he left London in July 1765 he composed and presented to the British Museum his first vocal work, the unaccompanied motet 'God is our refuge'.

Mozart never came to England again, and never again set any music to English words or wrote any work with English literary associations. In 1786, encouraged by his friends Stephen and Nancy Storace, his pupil Thomas Attwood, and the Irish tenor Michael Kelly, he did plan a visit, but it fell through and he went instead to Prague where he received the commission that was to result in *Don Giovanni*.

He certainly knew some Shakespeare, for in a letter to his father about the speech of the oracle in *Idomeneo* he observed: 'if the speech of the ghost in *Hamlet* were not so long, it would be far more effective.' Yet he seems not to have considered him as an operatic source until right at the end of his life, when he is said to have accepted a libretto based on *The Tempest by F. H. von Einsiedel, with revisions (probably for Mozart) by F. W. Gotter. The text, which *Goethe called a masterpiece, was eventually set by no less than four composers in 1798. It is an odd, and not very Shakespearian, piece of work, but when one considers what Mozart created, at just this time, out of Schikaneder's text for *Die Zauberflöte* (with which the new libretto had affinities—the comparison has, indeed, been made between Pamina and Sarastro, and Shakespeare's Miranda and Prospero) it is difficult not to regret Mozart's *Die Geisterinsel* as one of the most tantalizing of the operas that might have been. Mozart and his contemporary Salieri were the principal characters in P. *Shaffer's successful play *Amadeus*.

Mr B, the hero of Richardson's *Pamela*.

'Mr Gilfil's Love-Story', see SCENES OF CLERICAL LIFE.

Mr Limberham, *or the Kind Keeper*, a comedy by *Dryden, produced 1679, published 1680.

The play was banned by royal decree after three performances and execrated since, but Dryden none the less thought highly of it. The title role is possibly based on *Shaftesbury. Limberham is an impotent masochist, who is cuckolded by the over-sexed hero Woodall, to whom every woman in the play succumbs. In this Woodall (who has been brought up abroad and is under an assumed name) is enthusiastically abetted by his unknowing father, Aldo. By implication the play attacks the patriarchism of a sexually corrupt court, the blind hedonism of the nobility, and the hypocrisy of Dissenters.

Mr Norris Changes Trains, a novel by C. *Isherwood.

Mr Polly, *The History of*, a novel by H. G. *Wells.

Mr Scarborough's Family, a novel by A. *Trollope, published 1883.

John Scarborough has gone through two marriage ceremonies, and by producing the certificate of either earlier or later date can pronounce his eldest son and heir Mountjoy legitimate or illegitimate as he pleases. When he hears that Mountjoy has been passing post-obits on his estate, Scarborough takes a summary revenge: Mountjoy is declared illegitimate and his younger brother Augustus is named as heir. Augustus, however, begins to show an ill-concealed impatience to inherit, and, by now on his deathbed, Scarborough again alters the will. At first Augustus is to keep the entail, the moveable property reverting to Mountjoy; then the fatal first marriage certificate is produced, and Augustus is completely disinherited. In the last pages of the novel Mountjoy returns to the money-lenders, and sets about mortgaging the property to the hilt.

Mrs Caudle's Curtain Lectures, see JERROLD, D. W.

Mrs Dalloway, a novel by V. *Woolf, published 1925.

The action is restricted to the events of one day in central London, punctuated by the chimes of Big Ben; it opens on a June morning in Westminster as Clarissa Dalloway, wife of Richard Dalloway MP (both had appeared briefly and enigmatically in an earlier novel, The Voyage Out), sets off to buy flowers for her party that evening, the party which provides the culmination and ending of the book. Her interior monologue (see STREAM OF CONSCIOUSNESS), interwoven with the sights and sounds of the urban scene, is handled with a technical confidence and bravura that herald a new phase in Woolf's mastery of the novel. Clarissa herself—51 years old, fashionable, worldly, wealthy, the 'perfect hostess' who possesses a 'virginity preserved through childbirth'—is captured in her many shifting moods and recollections, and contrasted with and seen through the eyes of many other characters, including her one-time suitor Peter Walsh, returned after five years in India; her girlhood friend Sally Seton; her daughter Elizabeth and her dowdy and envious spinster tutor, Miss Kilman; the political hostess, Lady Bruton. Her day is also contrasted with that of the shell-shocked Septimus Warren Smith, who hears the sparrows sing in Greek in Regent's Park, and who at the end of the day commits suicide by hurling himself from a window; news of his death intrudes upon Clarissa's party, brought by the Harley Street doctor whom he had uselessly consulted. Woolf insisted upon the mutual dependence of these two characters, noting in her workbook, 'Mrs D. seeing the truth. SS seeing the insane truth.' The novel was accused by some (including *Strachey) of triviality, but was generally well received, and sold well; it succeeds as a richly textured impression of the cross-currents of sophisticated social life, as a celebration of the mysterious growth and change of human relationship and personality (for so brief a work its sense of the passage of time is remarkable), and as a portrait of a type of society woman who both fascinated and alarmed her creator. Her doubts that she was making Clarissa 'too stiff, too glittering and tinsely' have not been reflected in its popularity as one of her most accessible works.

Mrs Lirriper's Lodgings and **Mrs Lirriper's Legacy,** Christmas stories by *Dickens, which appeared in All the Year Round, 1863 and 1864. Mrs Lirriper lets lodgings in Norfolk Street, Strand, and her lodgers and past lodgers tell their stories.

'Mr Sludge, the "Medium"', a poem by R. *Browning, included in *Dramatis Personae.

Mr Weston's Good Wine, see POWYS, T. F.

Mucedorus, A Comedie of, a play of uncertain authorship, published 1598, and included in the Shakespeare apocrypha.

Mucedorus, prince of Valencia, in order to discover the virtues of Amadine, the daughter of the king of Arragon, assumes the disguise of a shepherd, saves her from a bear, and falls in love with her. Banished from her father's court, he next appears as a hermit, saves Amadine from a 'wild man', reveals his identity to her father, and is now successful in his suit.

Much, in the Robin Hood legend, a miller's son, one of the outlaw's companions. He figures in A Lytell Geste of Robyn Hode (*Ritson's collection of ballads).

Much Ado About Nothing, a comedy by *Shakespeare, written probably 1598-9, first printed 1600. Its chief sources are a novella by *Bandello and an episode in Ariosto's *Orlando Furioso. The play has always been a popular one in performance.

The prince of Arragon, with Claudio and Benedick in his suite, visits Lorenzo, duke of Messina, father of Hero and uncle of Beatrice. The sprightly Beatrice has a teasing relationship with the sworn bachelor Benedick. Beatrice and Benedick are each tricked into believing the other in love, and this brings about a genuine sympathy between them. Meanwhile Don John, the malcontented brother of the prince, thwarts Claudio's marriage by arranging for him to see Hero apparently wooed by his friend Borachio on her balcony—it is really her maidservant Margaret in disguise. Hero is publicly denounced by Claudio on her wedding day, falls into a swoon, and apparently dies. Benedick proves his love for Beatrice by challenging Claudio to a duel. The plot by Don John and

Borachio is unmasked by the 'shallow fools' Dogberry and Verges, the local constables. Claudio promises to make Leonato amends for his daughter's death, and is asked to marry a cousin of Hero's; the veiled lady turns out to be Hero herself. Benedick asks to be married at the same time; Beatrice, 'upon great persuasion; and partly to save your life, for I was told you were in a consumption', agrees, and the play ends with a dance.

Mucklebackit, Elspeth, Steenie, etc., characters in Scott's *The Antiquary.*

Mucklewrath, Habakkuk, a fanatical preacher in Scott's *Old Mortality.*

MUDDIMAN, Henry (b. 1629), a pensioner at St John's College, Cambridge, was authorized as a journalist by the Rump Parliament, at the request of General Monck, in 1659, in which year he started *The Parliamentary Intelligencer* and *Mercurius Publicus.* He became the most famous of the 17th-cent. journalists, and his *newsletters in manuscript, sent twice a week to subscribers all over the kingdom, were an important political feature of the day. One of his principal rivals was *L'Estrange, whose papers, however, he drove from the field. In 1665, under the direction of his patron, Sir J. Williamson (1633–1701), he started *The Oxford Gazette* (the predecessor of *The London Gazette*), the court being then at Oxford on account of the great plague. (See also GAZETTE and NEWSPAPERS, ORIGINS OF.)

MUDIE, Charles Edward (1818–90), the founder of Mudie's Lending Library (see LIBRARIES, CIRCULATING), was the son of a bookseller, and embarked on a career as bookseller, stationer, and lender of books in Bloomsbury; the lending proved so successful that he opened premises in Oxford Street in 1852, where the business prospered for many years, despite frequent complaints about Mudie's moral scruples in selecting his stock, which amounted, some claimed, to a form of censorship. G. A. *Moore was a particularly outspoken adversary.

Muggletonians, a sect founded c.1651 by Lodowicke Muggleton, a tailor (1609–98), and his cousin John Reeve (1608–58), who claimed to be the 'two witnesses' of Rev. 11: 3–6. They denied the doctrine of the Trinity, and taught that matter was eternal and reason the creation of the devil.

MUHAMMAD, or Mahomet (c.570–632), the founder of the Muslim religion, who was born at Mecca, and, according to Muslim tradition, called by the Angel Gabriel c.610 to his role as prophet. He imparted from time to time to his disciples the revelations that he received, which became known as the *Koran. He believed himself to be the messenger of God, sent to confirm the previous scriptures of the Jews, which had been corrupted by their own dis-

sensions and misinterpreted by the Christians. He preached faith in the submission to the will of God, and the importance of prayer, almsgiving, fasting, and pilgrimage to the Sacred House at Mecca.

Muiopotmos, or *The Fate of the Butterflie*, a mythological poem by *Spenser published among his *Complaints* (1591). It describes the destruction of the butterfly Clarion by the jealous spider Aragnoll, and contains the lines:

> What more felicitie can fall to creature,
> Than to enjoy delight with libertie?

MUIR, Edwin (1887–1959), poet, son of a tenant farmer, born in Orkney, where he spent his childhood. His family moved to Glasgow when he was fourteen, and within five years both parents and two of his brothers were dead; he himself suffered poor physical and mental health, and while working as office boy and clerk he turned to Socialism (through the writings of *Blatchford) and to the works of *Nietzsche. He began to write, contributing to *Orage's *New Age*, and in 1919 married Willa Anderson (1890–1970); they moved to London, where Muir became assistant to Orage, and underwent a course of psychoanalysis which profoundly affected his writing. In 1921 the Muirs went to Prague, and remained in Europe for four years, a period that later produced their collaborative translations from the German (notably of *Kafka, 1930–49). More importantly, it freed Muir's imagination as a poet. *First Poems* (1925) was followed by several other collections, including *Chorus of the newly dead* (1926), *The Labyrinth* (1949), and *Collected Poems 1921–1951* (1952). Muir's poetry is traditional rather than experimental in form, and much of his imagery is rooted in the landscapes of his childhood; a recurrent theme is the dream journey through time and place, and the narrative of the poet's own life lends itself naturally to the myth of an Eden threatened by various forms of catastrophe or expulsion. A sense of subdued menace lies beneath many of his quiet and orderly poems, which sometimes (as in his well known piece 'The Horses') achieve the *apocalyptic. Muir also published three novels, a number of critical works, and a highly evocative autobiography (again with much emphasis on the significance of dreams), published in 1940 as *The Story and the Fable* and revised as *An Autobiography* in 1954. See also P. H. Butter, *Edwin Muir: Man and Poet* (1966) and *Belonging: A Memoir* (1968) by Willa Muir.

MUIR, Kenneth (1907–), professor of English literature at Liverpool University (1951–74). As well as *Wyatt's poems and letters, he has edited many of Shakespeare's plays and done much work on their sources.

MULCASTER, Richard (*c.*1530–1611), educated at Eton, King's College, Cambridge, and Christ Church, Oxford, was the first head-master of *Merchant Taylors' School, London, where his pupils included *Spenser, *Kyd, *Lodge, and *Andrewes, and he was later high master of St *Paul's. He wrote two books on education, *Positions* (1581), dedicated to *Elizabeth I, and *The Elementarie* (1582). Both books show his humanist interests and ideals, such as his suggestion that gentlewomen should be educated in school, though only up to the age of thirteen or fourteen, and his stress on physical exercise, music, and vernacular literature, in-cluding the writing of English verse. Presumably the future poets who attended his school benefited from this last. He also published Latin and English verses on the queen's death (1603), and helped devise City shows and pageants.

Muley Moloch, a character in Dryden's *Don Sebastian*.

MULGRAVE, earl of, see SHEFFIELD, J.

Mulla, frequently referred to in *Spenser's poems, is the river Mulla or Awbeg, a tributary of the Blackwater in Ireland, near which stood Kilcolman Castle, his residence when he com-posed much of *The Faerie Queene*.

MÜLLER, Friedrich Max, see MAX MÜLLER, F.

Mulliner, Mr, (1) in Mrs Gaskell's *Cranford*, the Hon. Mrs Jamieson's butler; (2) the teller of some of the stories by P. G. *Wodehouse.

MULOCK, Dinah Maria, see CRAIK, MRS.

Mum and the Sothsegger, an alliterative poem of *c.*1403–6, bewailing the follies of Richard II and offering advice to Henry IV. Two sections survive with a gap between them: the first of 857 lines (the Cambridge manuscript) was previously called *Richard the Redeless* and edited by *Skeat with *Piers Plowman* which it resembles in language and in its division into Prologue and four *passus*; the second of 1,751 lines (in a British Museum manuscript). Skeat and Jusserand believed, probably wrongly, that the poem was by *Langland. Mum (as in 'keep mum') remains silent in evil days, such as those of Richard II, while the Truth-teller is ignored as he speaks the unwelcome truth. Ed. M. Day and R. Steele (EETS os 199, 1936; reprinted Kraus 1971).

MUMBY, Frank A. (1872–1954), journalist and historian of the British book trade, whose *Romance of Bookselling* (1910) was the basis of *Publishing and Bookselling: A History from the Earliest Times to the Present Day* (1930). This be-came a standard work and was revised extensively by Ian Norrie, who wrote a com-pletely new second section, 1870–1970, which was itself revised as *Mumby's Publishing and Book-selling in the Twentieth Century*. Mumby, who also wrote a history of Routledge and Kegan Paul and other volumes of publishing history, was on the staff of the *Times Literary Supplement* from 1923 to 1940.

Mummers' Play, or St George Play, a folk-play evolved from the *sword-dance, wide-spread through England, Scotland, Ireland, and Wales. The play, in its characters and detailed action, varies in different localities, but the main lines are as follows. The principal characters are St George (Sir George, King George, Prince George), the Turkish knight, Captain Slasher, and the Doctor. Minor personages bear, according to the different versions, a great var-iety of names. After a brief prologue, the fight-ing characters advance and introduce themselves, or are introduced, in vaunting rhymes. A duel or several duels follow, and one or other of the combatants is killed. The Doctor then enters, boasts his skill, and resuscitates the slain. Supernumerary grotesque characters are then presented, and a collection is made. The central incident of the play is doubtless con-nected with the celebration of the death of the year and its resurrection in the spring. See E. K. *Chambers, *The English Folk-Play* (1933).

A celebrated description of mumming occurs in Bk 2, ch. 4–6 of Hardy's *The Return of the Native*, in which Eustacia Vye disguises herself as the Turkish knight, in the place of the young lad Charley, in order to engineer a meeting with Clym Yeobright.

MUNBY, Arthur Joseph (1828–1910), edu-cated at Trinity College, Cambridge, published various volumes of verse, including *Verses New and Old* (1865) and *Relicta* (1909), but is now chiefly remembered for his diaries and note-books, used by Derek Hudson as the basis of his *Munby: Man of Two Worlds* (1972). These give an interesting picture of Victorian literary and social life; they also reveal Munby's obsession with working women and the story of his secret marriage to a maidservant, Hannah, which ex-plain some of the allusions in his poems.

Munchausen, Baron, *Narrative of his Mar-vellous Travels*, by Rudolph Erich Raspe, pub-lished 1785.

The original Baron Münchhausen is said to have lived in 1720–97, to have served in the Russian army against the Turks, and to have been in the habit of grossly exaggerating his experiences. Raspe (1737–94) was a Hano-verian who, when librarian at Cassel, stole gems from the Landgraf's collection, fled to England to escape the consequences, and added to his resources by publishing in English a version of the Baron's narratives. They include such stories as that of the horse who was cut in two, drank of a fountain, and was sewn up again; of the stag that the Baron shot with a cherry-stone, and afterwards found with a cherry-tree growing out of its forehead; and so forth.

MUNDAY, Anthony (1560–1633), hack-writer, wrote or collaborated in a number of plays, and was ridiculed by Jonson as Antonio Balladino in *The Case is Altered*. Among his plays are *John a Kent and John a Cumber* (acted *c.*1594, dealing with a conflict between two wizards of those names) and *The Downfall of Robert, Earle of Huntington* (printed 1601), followed by *The Death* of the same, of which the subject is the legend of *Robin Hood, with whom the earl is identified. Munday wrote ballads, which are lost, and as 'Shepheard Tonie' contributed several poems to *Englands Helicon* (1600). He also translated popular romances, including the *Palmerin cycle (1581–95), *Palladine of England* (1588), and *Amadis of Gaul* (?1590), and wrote City pageants from 1605.

Mundungus, the ill-tempered author (possibly Dr Sharp) of a travel-book satirized by Sterne in *A Sentimental Journey*.

Munera, The Lady, in Spenser's *Faerie Queene* (v. ii), the daughter of the Saracen Pollente, the personification of ill-gotten wealth, whom Sir *Artegall besieges and whom *Talus drowns in the moat of her castle after chopping off her golden hands and feet.

Munera Pulveris, see RUSKIN, J.

Mungo, see Bickerstaffe's PADLOCK, THE.

MUNGO, St, see KENTIGERN.

MUNRO, H(ector) H(ugh), see SAKI.

MUNTHE, Axel Martin Fredrik (1857–1949), Swedish-born doctor, whose memoir *The Story of San Michele* (1929) was an international best-seller; it is an account of his fashionable practice in Paris and Rome, and of the building of a dream villa on Capri.

Murder in the Cathedral, a play by T. S. *Eliot.

Murder on the Orient Express, a detective story by A. *Christie.

'Murders in the Rue Morgue, The', see POE, E. A.

MURDOCH, Iris Jean (1919–), novelist and philosopher, was born in Dublin of Anglo-Irish parents, and educated at Badminton School and Somerville College, Oxford. She worked for some time in the Civil Service, then lectured in philosophy in Oxford and London; her works on philosophy include *Sartre, Romantic Rationalist* (1953) and *The Sovereignty of Good* (1970). In 1956 she married the literary critic John Bayley. Her first novel, *Under the Net* (1954), a first-person male narration, was followed by many other successful works, including *The Bell*

(1958, set in a lay community in a country house); *A Severed Head* (1961, dramatized 1963 by J. B. *Priestley); *The Red and the Green* (1965, set in Ireland); *The Time of the Angels* (1968, set in a murky vicarage in the City, dominated by a satanic priest); *Bruno's Dream* (1969); *The Black Prince* (1973, another first-person male narration); *A Word Child* (1975); *The Sea, The Sea* (1978, a novel about a theatre director and his childhood love, with strong echoes of *The Tempest*, which won the *Booker Prize); and *The Philosopher's Pupil* (1983, her 21st novel). She has also written three plays. Her novels, which have been described as psychological detective stories, portray complicated and sophisticated sexual relationships (usually, but not exclusively, amongst the professional classes), and her plots have an operatic quality, combining comic, bizarre, and macabre incidents in a highly patterned symbolic structure. Though clearly not intended as strictly realistic, her portrayal of 20th-cent. middle-class and intellectual life shows acute observation as well as a wealth of invention, and has baffled critics by its evasion of recognized fictional genres. Her narrative skill conceals (or effortlessly conveys) the seriousness and abstraction of her preoccupations—with the nature of good and evil, the religious life, the sacred and the taboo, the nature of sexuality and Freudian determinism—and has brought her a wide readership. She has herself several times declared her allegiance to the large, realistic tradition of the Anglo-Russian novel; in 'Against Dryness' (*Encounter, Jan. 1961) she distinguished between the 'crystalline' novels which exhibit 'smallness, clearness, self-containedness', and the 'large, shapeless, quasi-documentary' novel, and her own works may be seen as an attempt to resolve the contradictions between the 'fantasy-myths' of the one form, and the 'unfashionable naturalistic idea of character', which brings vitality to the other.

Murdockson, Meg, and her daughter Magdalen, called 'Madge Wildfire', characters in Scott's *The Heart of Midlothian*.

Murdstone, Edward and Jane, characters in Dickens's *David Copperfield*.

MURPHY, Arthur (1727–1805), barrister, journalist, actor, and playwright, wrote over 20 farces, comedies, and tragedies, including adaptations of *Molière and *Voltaire; his better-known pieces include *The Way to Keep Him* (1760), *Three Weeks after Marriage* (1764), and *Know Your Own Mind* (1777). He also wrote lives of *Fielding (1762), Dr *Johnson (1792), and *Garrick (1801). He and Johnson became lifelong friends after their first meeting in 1754, which arose from Murphy's inadvertent borrowing of a tale from *The

Rambler, and Murphy was later responsible for introducing Johnson to the *Thrales.

MURPHY, Richard (1927–   ), Irish poet, born in Co. Mayo, who spent his early childhood in Ceylon, and was educated at Magdalen College, Oxford, and the Sorbonne. Much of his poetry portrays the landscapes, and more particularly the seascapes, of Ireland; his publications include *The Archeology of Love* (1955), *Sailing to an Island* (1963, which contains his long narrative poem about a fishing tragedy, 'The Gleggan Disaster', and other sea tales), *The Battle of Aughrim* (1968), a poetic non-partisan evocation, interweaving past and present, of the battle of 1691, first broadcast in 1968 with Ted *Hughes and *Day-Lewis among its readers; and *Selected Poems* (1979).

MURRAY, (George) Gilbert (Aimé) (1866–1957), perhaps the most brilliant Greek scholar of his generation in England and the model for Adolphus Cusins in Shaw's *Major Barbara*. Born in Sydney, New South Wales, he became professor of Greek at Glasgow in 1889 and was Regius professor of Greek at Oxford 1908–36. Although he possessed a thorough mastery of the techniques of Greek scholarship fashionable in his day, his claim to brilliance lay rather in his ability to make the ancient world sensitively real to his contemporaries; and while he produced influential studies in Greek epic and drama, he is best remembered for his translations of *Euripides, which, by romanticizing their originals, appealed to a wide, if unacademic, public. Murray had, however, many interests beyond scholarship and the stage. Always an eloquent champion of women's rights and other liberal causes, he devoted his energies after 1918 to the furtherance of peace, and as chairman of the League of Nations Union (1922–38) he struggled without much hope to save Europe from war.

MURRAY, Sir James Augustus Henry (1837–1915), the son of a clothier from Hawick, was educated at Cavers school, near his native village of Denholm, and at Minto school, but his great philological and antiquarian knowledge was acquired largely through his own studies. He became a schoolmaster and moved to London in 1864, where he worked for some years as a bank clerk before returning to his earlier profession at Mill Hill. Throughout these years he pursued his philological interests and made the acquaintance of many scholars with similar preoccupations, including *Skeat, *Sweet, and *Furnivall; he became a member of the *Philological Society, to which he delivered in 1868 papers later printed as *The Dialect of the Southern Counties of Scotland* (1873) which were received with much respect. In 1879, after lengthy negotiation and much hesitation, he was appointed editor of the *Oxford English Dictionary*, a monumental work which was to occupy the rest of his life. He laid down the lines on which the work was to be compiled, and persevered through many difficulties (some financial), resisting suggestions that the work be completed more rapidly. There is a detailed account of the dictionary's composition in *Caught in the Web of Words* (1977) by his granddaughter, K. M. E. Murray, which also gives a vivid portrait of his industrious personality, his high moral standards and sense of responsibility, and his happy family life. He was the father of eleven children, several of whom aided him considerably in the great work that dominated their early lives.

MURRAY, John (1778–1843), the son of John Murray I (1745–93), who founded the publishing house still in existence. The second John Murray was one of those who, together with the reviews such as the *Edinburgh and the *Quarterly, began to substitute for the dying system of personal patronage his own personal encouragement and commercial expertise. He was one of the first publishers, according to T. *Dibdin, who treated authors 'with the respect due to gentlemen'. His publishing house became a social meeting-place for many of the literary figures of his time, and it is probable that the plan for the founding of the *Athenaeum club was devised in his rooms. With the help and encouragement of Sir W. *Scott he established the Tory *Quarterly Review* in 1809, and took a close interest in its management. He gave up the London agency of *Blackwood's in protest at its attacks on the *Cockney school. He was the friend and publisher of *Byron, who was his single most important author. *Childe Harold appeared under his imprint, as did most of Byron's other work (*The Corsair sold 10,000 copies on its day of publication). But he was so apprehensive of the public reception of *Don Juan that he published only the early cantos, and those without his imprint; the later cantos were published by the intrepid John *Hunt, who also produced *The Vision of Judgement*, which Murray had refused. Murray bought Byron's memoirs of 1818–21 from T. *Moore, and reluctantly consented to having them burned in his grate at Albemarle Street. His other authors included J. *Austen, *Crabbe, *Coleridge, *Southey, Leigh *Hunt, and *Borrow. Mariana Starke's *Guide for Travellers on the Continent* (1820) led to a long and profitable series of guide-books, several of which were written by John Murray III (1808–92). In the publishing slump of the late 1820s and 1830s Murray noted, 'the taste for literature is ebbing' and he sold his copyright of Jane Austen's novels. He disliked the new fashion for cheap books but recognized their necessity, and published, amongst others, the Family Library and Cabinet Cyclopaedia.

The John Murray succession, and the firm's independence, has continued to the present day.

MURRAY, Lindley (1745–1826), Quaker grammarian, born in Pennsylvania, who came to England in 1784 and settled in York. He published an English Grammar in 1795, a Reader in 1799, and a Spelling Book in 1804, which were widely used in schools and earned him the title of 'the father of English grammar'. He wrote many other educational works, and his *Memoirs*, in epistolary form, were published in 1826.

MURRY, John Middleton (1889–1957), born in Peckham of ambitious lower-middle-class parents, made his mark while still an Oxford undergraduate as editor of the *modernist periodical *Rhythm* (1911–13), through which he met in 1912 Katherine *Mansfield, whom he was later (in 1918) to marry. In 1914 he met D. H. *Lawrence, who greatly influenced him; the relationship of the Lawrences and the Murrys was intense and tempestuous, particularly during the war years, and is reflected in *Women in Love*. From 1919 to 1921 Murry was editor of the *Athenaeum*, in which he published an impressive range of writers, including V. *Woolf, T. S. *Eliot, and *Valéry, and in which he himself attacked *Georgian poetry. In 1923, the year of his wife's death, he founded *The Adelphi*; although he was to marry again three times, he continued to dwell on her memory, editing her works, publishing reminiscences, letters, etc. His many critical works include *Dostoevsky* (1916), *The Problem of Style* (1922), *Countries of the Mind* (1922, 1931), *Keats and Shakespeare* (1925), and *Son of Woman, the Story of D. H. Lawrence* (1931). He also wrote many works of a semi-mystical nature, became deeply interested in the concept of an ideal community (a concern dating back to the days when he and Lawrence had planned the Utopian community of 'Rananim') and in pacifism. Throughout his turbulent emotional and professional life he was attracted to the extreme and the romantic, seeing life as a spiritual search; his reputation as a critic declined in a new age of specialization and professionalism, but he remains an important figure in literary history. See his autobiography, *Between Two Worlds* (1935) and the standard life by F. A. Lea (1959).

MUSAEUS, (1) a legendary Greek poet, said to have been a pupil of *Orpheus; (2) a Greek poet, who perhaps lived about AD 500, the author of a poem on the story of *Hero and Leander which provided the groundwork for *Marlowe's poem.

Muse's Looking-Glasse, The, a defence of the drama, in the form of a play, by *Randolph, printed 1638.

'The scene lies in the play-house at Blackfriars. Bird and Mistress Flowerdew, two Puritans, who serve the theatre with feathers and other small wares, enter; they express their abhorrence of play-houses; Roscius joins them; he prevails on them to see the representation of the play; Roscius explains the drift of it to them as it proceeds. This play has no plot; the object of it is to show that all virtues, and every commendable passion, proceed from mediocrity or a just medium between two extremes. At the conclusion [Bird and Mistress Flowerdew] agree that a play may be productive of moral good' (*Genest).

Musgrave, (1) Little, see LITTLE MUSGRAVE AND LADY BARNARD; (2) Sir Richard, a character in Scott's *The Lay of the Last Minstrel*.

Musgrove, Mr and Mrs, their son Charles and his wife Mary (*née* Elliot), and their daughters Henrietta and Louisa, characters in J. Austen's *Persuasion*.

Music, Literature of. The first English contribution to musical literature of any importance is T. *Morley's *Plaine and Easie Introduction to Practicall Musicke, set downe in forme of a Dialogue* (1597), probably the most famous musical treatise in the language and for many years the standard didactic work in its field. There is a chapter on music in *Peacham's *Compleat Gentleman* (1622), but on the whole the musical writings of the 17th cent. were mainly technical or instructional rather than literary, as in the various publications of John Playford, whose *Breefe Introduction to the Skill of Musicke* (1654) continued to appear, in new and enlarged editions, until well into the 18th cent. An exception, of somewhat idiosyncratic literary charm, is Thomas Mace's *Musick's Monument; or, a Remembreancer of the Best Practical Musick, both Divine, and Civil, that has ever been known, to have been in the World* (1676).

An interesting figure in the early 18th cent. is R. *North, whose treatises *The Musicall Grammarian* and *Memoires of Musick* remained in manuscript at his death in 1734 and have been collected in a modern edition (1959): his very personal approach to the theory and aesthetics of music was carried on, almost to excess, by Charles Avison in *An Essay on Musical Expression* (1752), an early example of musical criticism which raised much controversy in its own day. The later 18th cent. produced the two great histories of music by Dr C. *Burney and Sir J. *Hawkins. Burney published the first volume of *A General History of Music from the Earliest Ages to the Present Period* in 1776, only to see it followed some nine months later by Hawkins's *A General History of the Science and Practice of Music* complete in five volumes; Burney's remaining three volumes came out in 1782 and 1789. Of the rival works, Hawkins's is stronger on the earlier periods, while Burney's is the more personal, readable, and accomplished in its literary style; it was preceded by much travelling to collect material, recounted with characteristic perspicacity and humour in *The Present State of Music in France and Italy* (1771) and *The Present State of music in Germany, the Netherlands and the United Provinces* (1773). On the subject of opera, *Addison's critical essays in the early issues of the *Spectator* are among the first of interest in any language, but the theorizing and polemics that flourished in Italy and France later in the century had little counterpart in England, where the best writing in this field was of a more personal nature: the *Musical Reminiscences* of Lord Mouth-Edgcumbe (1825), the *Reminiscences* of the Irish tenor Michael Kelly (1826), George Hogarth's *Memoirs of the Opera* (1838), or the chronicles of theatrical managers like Ebers, Lumley, Mapleson, etc.

The first monograph devoted to a single composer was by an Englishman, John Mainwaring's *Memoirs of the Life of the Late George Frederic Handel* (1760). Hawkins and Burney also made contributions in this field, the former on *Corelli* (1777) and the latter on *Handel* (1785, in connection with the great *Handel Commemoration in Westminster Abbey in the previous year). Occasional works of this kind appear during the next half-century, like Edward Holmes's still valuable *Life of Mozart* (1845) and the monumental *Life of Beethoven* by the American Alexander Wheelock Thayer, begun in 1849 but not finally published in English until 1921. Most of the important biographical work in the 19th cent. was done outside England and introduced into this country in translation, but the growing interest in musical scholarship and history produced, between 1879 and 1889, a major English reference work in the four volumes of George Grove's *Dictionary of Music and Musicians*, not the first compilation of its kind in the language but by far the most comprehensive and authoritative—as, in the 20 vols of the 6th edn (*The New Grove*, 1980), it still is today. The same stimulus inspired the publication of *The Oxford History of Music* (6 vols, 1901–5), an important undertaking in its day which has now been superseded by *The New Oxford History of Music* (designed in 11 vols, of which 8 appeared 1954–74). Both these works are collections of writings by a variety of distinguished authors: as a monument to the efforts of a single man, Percy Scholes's *Oxford Companion to Music* (1938; 11th edn, *The New Oxford Companion to Music*, ed. Denis Arnold, 1983) remains an unrivalled lexicographical *tour de force*.

The years that saw the conclusion of Grove's great enterprise saw also the beginning of G. B. *Shaw's activities as a music critic. His work in this field was brought together under the titles *London Music in 1888–89 as heard by Corno di Bassetto* (1937) and *Music in London* (3 vols, 1932), and provides some of the liveliest and most stimulating reading in all musical literature; his major critical essay *The Perfect

Wagnerite came out in 1898. Another landmark in English Wagnerian writing appeared in the following year, *A Study of Wagner* by a young music critic writing under the pseudonym Ernest Newman (William Roberts, 1868–1959): this was the first of several treatments of this subject which culminated in the 4-vol. *Life of Richard Wagner* (1933–47), the most important of many excellently written books and critical notices produced by Newman in the course of an exceptionally long and active career. The 20th cent. has seen a vast increase in books on every aspect of musical activity, from which one might select as samples Edward Dent's critical study *Mozart's Operas* (1913), and his study of the life and works of Scarlatti (1905); Edmund Fellowes's pioneering biographies of native composers, *Orlando Gibbons* (1925), *William Byrd* (1936), *The English Madrigal Composers* (1921); Scholes's *The Great Dr Burney* (1948); Frank Walker's *Hugo Wolf* (1951) and *The Man Verdi* (1962); the seven volumes of Donald Tovey's *Essays in Musical Analysis* (1933–9); and even such an occasional squib as *Music Ho!* (1934) by C. *Lambert. In recent years the scholarly and technical aspects of musical writing have sometimes tended to elbow out the more aesthetic qualities of presentation, producing a type of book more valuable for its scientific accuracy than for any persuasiveness of literary style.

Musidorus ('gifted by the Muses'), the young duke of Thessalia in Sidney's *Arcadia*.

MUSIL, Robert Elder von (1880–1942), born in Klagenfurt of Austrian and partly Czech descent, is best known for his massive (and unfinished) novel, *Der Mann ohne Eigenschaften* (1930–2), which appeared in an English translation by E. Wilkins and E. Kaiser as *The Man without Qualities* (1953–60). He had previously published various short works of fiction and two plays, but devoted the rest of his life (including exile, from 1938, in Switzerland) to his great work, which has been variously described as Expressionistic, satirical, and the last work of the classical tradition.

'Musophilus, or A Generall defence of learning', a verse dialogue in six- and eight-lined stanzas by S. *Daniel, dedicated to his friend Fulke *Greville, published 1599.

Musophilus defends the claims of culture against the worldly arts practised by Philocosmus, the unlettered man of action. The poem shows at its best Daniel's gift for moral reflection in dignified but plain language, and his faith in a poetic vocation independent of worldly recognition: neglect cannot undo 'The love I beare unto this holy skill; | This is the thing that I was borne to do, | This is my Scene, this part must I fulfill' (ll. 576–9). The poem also contains a notable description of Stonehenge

(l. 337 ff.) and ends with a fine invocation of 'heavenly Eloquence' and the prophetic lines:

> And who in time knowes whither we may vent
> The treasure of our tongue, to what strange shores
> This gaine of our best glorie shal be sent,
> T'inrich unknowing Nations with our stores?
> What worlds in th'yet unformed Occident
> May come refin'd with th'accents that are ours?

MUSSET, Alfred de (1810–57), French poet and playwright. His first published work was a free translation of *De Quincey's *Opium Eater* (1828). His career as a littérateur was interrupted by a notorious liaison with G. *Sand (1833–5). His most famous poems, *Le Souvenir* (1841) and *Les Nuits* (1835–7), rehearse the central Romantic motif of lost love. His most original achievements are his plays, in particular *Fantasio*, *On ne badine pas avec l'amour*, and *Lorenzaccio* (all 1834), which blend irony, fantasy, and psychological penetration. Even his liveliest work is seldom free from the melancholy and anxiety known as the *mal du siècle*.

MUSSOLINI, Benito (1883–1945), was the leader (*Il Duce*) of Fascism in Italy. After the 'march on Rome' in October 1922 Mussolini became prime minister of a coalition government and, in 1925, dictator, with the Fascist party as the sole official instrument of political power. He pursued a policy of economic self-sufficiency and rearmament together with colonial aggrandizement as manifested in the Italian conquest of Abyssinia, 1935–6. He allied himself with Hitler in 1936 in the 'Berlin–Rome Axis'. After the fall of France in 1940 he entered the war as Germany's ally, but was forced to resign in 1943 and was executed by Italian partisans.

Mustapha, (1) a tragedy (1609) by Sir F. *Greville; (2) a heroic play (1665) by R. *Boyle, based on *Ibrahim* by Mlle de Scudéry.

'Mutabilitie Cantos', name given to the fragmentary 'Book VII' of Spenser's *Faerie Queene*: two cantos only, first published with the folio edition of The Faerie Queene in 1609. They describe the challenge of the Titaness Mutabilitie to the cosmic government of Jove. (The first canto includes the charming topographical fable of Faunus and Molanna, which reflects Spenser's affection for his Irish home.) The goddess Nature vindicates Jove's rule, displaying its orderly beauty in a procession of Seasons and Months, asserting finally that natural things 'are not changed from their first estate | But by their change their being doe dilate'. The Cantos can be seen as an epilogue to The Faerie Queene, ending with the poet's prayer:

> O! that great Sabaoth God, grant me that
> Sabaoths sight.

My Antonía, a novel by W. *Cather.

MYERS, F(rederic) W(illiam) H(enry) (1843–1901), poet and inspector of schools, educated at Cambridge, where he spent much of his life. He published several volumes of poetry and critical essays; his essay on G. *Eliot, first published in the *Century Magazine* in 1881 (and reprinted in *Essays Classical and Modern*, 1883), describes the celebrated incident in which she spoke to him of 'God, Immortality, Duty', and declared 'how inconceivable was the *first*, how unbelievable the *second*, and yet how peremptory and absolute the *third*'. Myers's own childhood obsession with the possibility of survival after death led to his involvement with the *Society for Psychical Research, of which he was a founder; he was joint author (with E. Gurney and F. Podmore) of *Phantasms of the Living* (1886), a two-volume work dealing largely with telepathy, which embodied the first considerable results of the society's labours.

MYERS, L(eopold) H(amilton) (1881–1944), novelist, the son of F. W. H. *Myers. His novels are concerned with the problem of how human beings can live rightly in society if they exclude spirituality, which, to his mind, was an activity as natural as sex. In his troubled personal life he failed to reconcile the flesh and the spirit, but he believed deeply that society would find a way to transcend itself. Here he was in violent opposition to humanism and to the values of the *Bloomsbury group, which he thought were a denial of life. After trying several political solutions he became a Communist. Apart from the *Orissers* (1922), The 'Clio' (1925), and *Strange Glory* (1936), the novels are set in an imaginary 16th-cent. India: *The Near and the Far* (1929), *Prince Jali* (1931), *The Root and the Flower* (1935), and *The Pool of Vishnu* (1940); all collected under the title *The Near and the Far* (1943). He died from an overdose of veronal.

'My Mind to me a Kingdom is', the first line of a poem on contentment which was first printed in *Byrd's *Psalmes, Sonets, & Songs* (1588). It was frequently referred to in the 16th and 17th cents, and often attributed to Sir E. *Dyer. It is more probably by the earl of *Oxford.

Mysie Happer, the miller's daughter in Scott's *The Monastery*, who marries Sir Piercie Shafton.

Mysteries of Udolpho, The, a novel by A. *Radcliffe, published 1794.

The orphaned Emily St Aubert is carried off by her aunt's villainous husband Montoni to a remote castle in the Apennines, where her life, honour, and fortune are threatened and she is surrounded by apparently supernatural terrors. These are later explained as due to human agency and Emily escapes, returns to France and, after further mysteries and misunderstandings, is reunited with her lover Valancourt. The book plays an important part in J. Austen's *Northanger Abbey.

Mysterious Mother, The, a tragedy in blank verse by Horace *Walpole, printed at *Strawberry Hill in 1768.

It deals with the remorse of a mother (the countess of Narbonne) for an act of incest committed many years before. Under the calamity of the marriage of her son Edmund, who had been the unwitting partner of her crime, with the girl Adeliza (brought up as her ward, but in fact the fruit of their union) she takes her own life. The theme of incest shocked many of his admirers but greatly interested *Byron, who described the play as 'a tragedy of the highest order, and not a puling love-play'.

Mysterious Stranger, The, a story by Mark *Twain.

Mystery Plays, biblical dramas popular in England from the 13th to the later 16th cent., take their name from the *mestier* (métier or trade) of their performers; they were previously called 'Miracle Plays' which, strictly, are enactments of the miracles performed by the saints. The Mysteries enact the events of the Bible from the Creation to the Ascension (and in some cases later). Their origin is much disputed; one of the earliest is the Anglo-Norman *Jeu d'Adam* (see ADAM), and there were cycles in many countries: France, Italy, Ireland, and Germany (surviving in the *Oberammergau Passion Play). Though it is clear from their archives that many English towns had them, only four complete cycles survive: York, Chester, Wakefield (also called Towneley from the owners of the manuscript), and the *Ludus Coventriae*, also called the Hegge cycle, and N-town because it is not known where it comes from. The argument over their origins is whether they were derived from Latin liturgical pageants or developed as new vernacular drama. They are connected with the feast day of Corpus Christi (29 June) which was declared in 1264 and first observed as a Holy Day in 1311. The various pageants (whose number varies from 25 in Chester to nearly 50 in York) were each assigned to a particular trade-guild, often with a humorous or macabre connection between the métier and the play: the York Shipwrights enact the story of Noah, for instance. Their great popularity in England from the time of *Chaucer to Shakespeare is repeatedly attested by those writers, among others. Their end was no doubt mainly caused by Reformation distaste for idols and religious pageantry (an attitude occasionally manifested earlier), though there are some signs of decadence, in the later Digby plays, for example (see MARY MAGDALENE). Their great interest is as an early, popular form of theatre, manifesting energy, humour, and seriousness; it is not accurate to think of their composers as unlearned, as is clear from the group of six plays in the Towneley cycle assigned to a presumed author known as 'the Wakefield Master'. The latter's most celebrated play is the Second Shepherd's Play in which the Nativity is parodied by and collocated with a contemporary case of sheep stealing. It was not these plays, so much as the Moralities and *Interludes, which affected the development of Elizabethan drama. But they have had a considerable vogue in the 20th cent., with its interest in popular, less articulated forms of drama (such as *Nōh plays from Japan); evidence of this is *Britten's *Noye's Fludde*, and revivals of performances of the cycles, most notably at York.

There are editions of the Cycles in EETS ES Chester, nos. 62 and 115, ed. H. Deimling and J. Matthews (1892 and 1914); Wakefield, no. 71 (1897, reprinted 1973), ed. G. England and A. W. Pollard; *Ludus Coventriae*, no. 120 (1917), ed. K. S. Block. L. Toulmin Smith ed., *The York Plays* (1885, reprinted 1963). See also E. K. *Chambers, *The Medieval Stage* (2 vols, 1903); V. A. Kolve, *The Play Called Corpus Christi* (1966); R. E. Woolf, *The English Mystery Plays* (1972). For a very useful selected edition, see P. Happé, *The English Mystery Plays* (1975).

Mystic, Mr, a character in Peacock's *Melincourt*, a caricature of *Coleridge.

N

NABOKOV, Vladimir Vladimirovich (1899–1977), Russian novelist, poet, and literary scholar. The son of a leading member of the Cadet party and of the Kerensky Government, Nabokov had published only a small volume of poetry when his family left Russia for Germany in 1919. After studying French and Russian literature at Trinity College, Cambridge (1919–23), Nabokov lived in Berlin (1923–37) and Paris (1937–40), writing mainly in Russian, under the pseudonym 'Sirin'. In 1940 he moved to the USA, working as a lecturer at Wellesley College (1941–8) and as professor of Russian literature at Cornell University (1948–59). From then on all his novels were written in English. The outstanding success of his novel *Lolita* (US, 1958) enabled him to give up teaching and devote himself fully to writing. From 1959 he lived in Montreux, in Switzerland, where he died.

Nabokov's reputation as one of the major, most original prose writers of the 20th cent., a stylist with extraordinary narrative and descriptive skill and a wonderful linguistic inventiveness in two languages, is based on his achievement in the novels *Mary* (1926), *King, Queen, Knave* (1928), *The Eye* (1930), *The Defence* (1930), *Glory* (1932), *Laughter in the Dark* (1932), *Despair* (1936), *Invitation to a Beheading* (1938), *The Gift* (1938), *The Real Life of Sebastian Knight* (1941), *Bend Sinister* (1947), *Lolita* (1955), *Pnin* (1957), *Pale Fire* (1962), *Ada* (1969), *Transparent Things* (1972), and *Look at the Harlequins!* (1974), and on several volumes of short stories. All his works first written in Russian were translated into English with his own collaboration, and the English novels into Russian. Nabokov's admiration for *Dickens, R. L. *Stevenson, and *Joyce, among English writing, and his unease with J. *Austen, can be seen in his *Lectures on Literature* (1980).

NAIPAUL, V(idiadhar) S(urajprasad) (1932–), novelist, born in Trinidad of a Brahmin family, the son of a journalist. He was educated at Queen's Royal College, Port of Spain, and University College, Oxford. He settled in England, married in 1955, and embarked on a career of literary journalism. His first three books, *The Mystic Masseur* (1957), *The Suffrage of Elvira* (1958), and *Miguel Street* (short stories, 1959), are comedies of manners, all set in Trinidad. His next novel, *A House for Mr Biswas* (1961), also set in Trinidad, traces the fortunes of its mild hero (a portrait inspired by Naipaul's father) from birth to death; he progresses from the job of sign-writer to that of journalist, is trapped into marriage and almost absorbed by his wife's vast family, the Tulsis, but continues to bid for independence, symbolized by the house which he acquires shortly before his death. The novel describes the dissolution of a whole way of life, as the younger members of the family depart for new educational opportunities in Europe. *Mr Stone and the Knights Companion* (1963), his only novel set in London, was followed by *The Mimic Men* (1967), set on a fictitious Caribbean island and narrated by failed politician and visionary Ralph Singh. From this time Naipaul's work becomes more overtly political and pessimistic. *In a Free State* (1971, *Booker Prize) explores problems of nationality and identity through three linked narratives, all describing displaced characters—a servant from Bombay transported to Washington, a lost and angry West Indian youth in London, two whites in a hostile African state. *Guerrillas* (1975) is a portrait of political and sexual violence in the Caribbean, ending with a sado-masochistic murder; *A Bend in the River* (1979) is an equally horrifying portrait of emergent Africa. Naipaul's intense, broad, and predominantly melancholy experience of human nature in the modern world may also be seen in the travel books and works of political journalism which have provided a background for his fiction; these include *The Middle Passage* (1962), on the Caribbean; *An Area of Darkness* (1964), his highly controversial and critical account of India; *The Return of Eva Peron; with The Killings in Trinidad* (1980); and *Among the Believers: an Islamic Journey* (1981). *The Overcrowded Barracoon* (1972) is a collection of personal and political articles. Naipaul's recurrent themes of political violence, innate homelessness, and alienation inevitably give rise to comparisons with *Conrad.

NAIRNE, Carolina, Baroness, *née* Oliphant (1766–1845), was the author of many spirited and well-known Jacobite songs, including 'Will ye no come back again?' and 'Charlie is my darling'; also of humorous and pathetic ballads, such as 'The Laird of Cockpen' (suggested by an older song) and 'The Land o' the Leal'. She concealed her authorship during her lifetime, and her poems were collected and published as *Lays from Strathearn* in 1846.

Namancos, in Milton's *Lycidas*, 'Where the great vision of the guarded mount | Looks toward Namancos and Bayona's hold', is a place in Galicia, near Cape Finisterre, shown in *Mercator's Atlas of 1623. The castle of Bayona is shown near it. A line from the 'guarded mount' (St Michael's Mount in Cornwall) to Finisterre passes clear of Ushant.

Namby-Pamby, see PHILIPS, A.

NAMIER, Sir Lewis Bernstein (1888–1960), historian, born in Poland of a Jewish family; his father was a Roman Catholic convert. Namier came to England and was educated at the London School of Economics and Balliol College, Oxford; in 1913 he became a British subject and in 1931 professor of modern history at Manchester. His major works include *The Structure of Politics at the Accession of George III* (1929) and *England in the Age of the American Revolution* (1930). During the 1930s he became deeply involved with the plight of Jewish refugees and with Zionism, to which he devoted much energy. He was an admirer of *Freud, and stressed Freud's importance in historical and biographical science; *Berlin, in *Personal Impressions* (1980), gives a vivid account of his personality, explains his twofold reputation as a dazzling talker and a bore, and contrasts his 'desire to reduce both the general propositions and the impressions of historians to pellet-like "facts" ' with the romantic, nationalist elements in his character.

Nancy, in Dickens's *Oliver Twist*, the fancy woman of Bill Sikes.

Nandy, John Edward, in Dickens's *Little Dorrit*, the father of Mrs Plornish.

Nannetae, in imprints, Nantes.

NAPIER, John (1550–1617), laird of Merchiston, near Edinburgh, was educated at St Andrews. A mathematician and inventor, he devised logarithms, the nature of which he explained in his *Mirifici Logarithmorum Canonis Descriptio* (1614). His *Rabdologia* (1615) explains the use of numerating rods ('Napier's bones') and metal plates for effecting multiplications and divisions—the earliest form of calculating machine. He also invented the present notation of decimal fractions.

NAPIER, Sir William Francis Patrick (1785–1860), military historian, served in Sir J. *Moore's campaign in Spain (1808) and in the subsequent war in the Peninsula; these events are recounted in his *History of the War in the Peninsula* (1828–40), which has placed him high among historical writers. The work earned commendation from *Wellington in spite of the author's Radical outlook. This was followed by *The Conquest of Scinde* (1845), a defence of his brother Charles's conduct. He received a knighthood in 1848 and was promoted to general in 1859.

NARAYAN, R(asipuram) K(rishnaswami) (1906–), Indian novelist writing in English; he was born in Madras, and educated at the Collegiate High School in Mysore, where his father was headmaster, then at Maharaja's College, Mysore. He worked (very briefly) as a teacher, then as a journalist, before publishing his first novel, *Swami and Friends* (1935), in which he created the imaginary small town of Malgudi, which he was to map out and populate in several succeeding novels, including *The Bachelor of Arts* (1937), *The English Teacher* (1945), *Mr Sampath* (1949), *The Financial Expert* (1952), *The Vendor of Sweets* (1967), and *The Painter of Signs* (1977). His fictional world is peopled with characters—journalists, printers, professors, financial experts, lawyers, dreamers—portrayed with a gentle irony as they struggle to accommodate tradition with Western attitudes inherited from the British. G. *Greene, who recommended his first novel for publication, compared the tragi-comedy, pathos, and frequently disappointed aspirations of his characters to those of *Chekhov's, and commented that Narayan's particular comic gift flourished in 'the strong framework of social convention'. Narayan's other publications include short stories (*An Astrologer's Day and other stories*, 1947; *Lawley Road*, 1956; *A Horse and Two Goats*, 1970; *Malgudi Days*, 1982) and a memoir, *My Days* (1975).

Narcissa, (1) in Pope's *Moral Essays* is Anne *Oldfield; (2) Roderick's love in Smollett's *Roderick Random*; (3) one of the persons mourned in Young's *Night Thoughts*.

Narrenschiff, see SHIP OF FOOLS.

NASH, Ogden (1902–71), American writer of sophisticated light verse, renowned for his puns, epigrams, elaborate rhymes, elaborate lack of rhymes, wildly asymmetrical lines, and other verbal fancies. His verse appeared in many collections from 1931 onwards.

NASH, Richard, 'Beau', (1674–1761), born at Swansea, was educated at Carmarthen Grammar School and for a time at Jesus College, Oxford. He supported himself in London as a gamester, and went to Bath in 1705, where he established the Assembly Rooms, drew up a code of etiquette and dress, and became unquestioned autocrat of society. The gambling laws of 1740–5 deprived him of his source of income, and his popularity waned after 1745. In 1758 he was allowed ten guineas a month by the corporation of Bath. *Goldsmith's life of Nash, published 1762, was probably written without personal knowledge of its subject, despite Goldsmith's hints to the contrary.

NASHE, Thomas (1567–1601), was a sizar of St John's College, Cambridge. By 1588 he had settled in London. His first publication was a preface to Greene's *Menaphon*, 1589, surveying the follies of contemporary literature; he expanded this theme in *The Anatomie of Absurditie* later in the same year. His hatred of Puritanism drew him into the *Martin Marprelate controversy, but it is not clear which of the seven or more unascribed anti-Martinist pamphlets were his work. In 1592 Nashe replied to the savage denunciations of Richard Harvey, astrologer and brother of Gabriel *Harvey, with *Pierce Pennilesse his Supplication to the Divell*, which he claimed was translated into French. In the same year he avenged Gabriel Harvey's attack on R. *Greene with *Strange Newes, of the Intercepting certaine Letters*. A florid religious meditation, *Christs Teares over Jerusalem*, dedicated to Lady Elizabeth Carey, was published in 1593, and in the following year *The Terrors of the Night*, a discourse on dreams and nightmares, was dedicated to her daughter, to whom he may have acted as tutor for a time. *The Unfortunate Traveller. Or The life of Jacke Wilton* also appeared in 1594, described in the dedication to the earl of Southampton as 'being a cleane different vaine from other my former courses of writing'. It is a medley of picaresque narrative, literary parody, and mock-historical fantasy. Nashe returned to satire with *Have with you to Saffron-walden. Or, Gabriell Harveys Hunt is up* (1596), to which Harvey replied; in 1599 Archbishop *Whitgift ordered that the works of both writers should be suppressed. Nashe's lost satirical comedy *The Isle of Dogs* also led to trouble with the authorities, and though it is not clear whether Nashe, like his collaborator *Jonson, had a spell in prison, he was forced to flee London. *Nashes Lenten Stuffe* (1599), a mock encomium of the red herring (or kipper), includes a burlesque version of the story of *Hero and Leander. In 1600 *Summers Last Will and Testament* was published, though it had probably been written in the plague year of 1592–3, when the archbishop's household was removed to Croydon. Nashe had a share in Marlowe's *Dido, Queene of Carthage*, and probably other plays now lost. He was amusingly satirized as 'Ingenioso', a Cambridge graduate who lost favour with his patrons and turned to satire, in the three *Parnassus Plays (1598–1606). In this century *The Unfortunate Traveller* and the satirical works have been much admired. The entire works were definitively edited by R. B. *McKerrow in 1904–10 and revised with corrections and additions by F. P. Wilson in 1958; see also a Life by C. Nicholl, *A Cup of News* (1984).

NASO, see OVID. The word means 'nose', to which Holofernes alludes in Shakespeare's *Love's Labour's Lost* (IV. ii).

Nasrudin, a semi-legendary Turkish sage and folk-hero, around whose name has gathered a body of jokes, stories, and anecdotes. They have been collected and translated many times: for recent versions, see *The Pleasantries of the Incredible Mulla Nasrudin* (1968) and *The Subtleties of the Inimitable Mulla Nasrudin* (1973) by I. *Shah.

NATHAN, George Jean (1882–1958), American essayist, drama critic, and polemicist, co-founder in 1924 with H. L. *Mencken of *The American Mercury*, a lively monthly cultural magazine, of which he remained an editor until 1930. He published many collections of theatrical reviews and essays, including *The Popular Theatre* (1918), *The Critic and the Drama* (1922), and *Art of the Night* (1938), which show him as an early supporter of the works of *O'Neill.

Nathaniel, Sir, in Shakespeare's *Love's Labour's Lost*, a curate and friend to Holofernes.

Nathan the Wise, see LESSING, G. E.

National Anthem, The. The first recorded public performance of 'God Save the King' took place at Drury Lane Theatre on 28 Sept. 1745, during the excitement and alarm caused by the Jacobite invasion of that year. It was an unannounced addition by the actors to the ordinary programme of the day and a manifestation of their loyal zeal. The score used on this occasion was prepared by *Arne, leader of the orchestra at the theatre and composer of *'Rule, Britannia'. The example set at Drury Lane was followed at other theatres and the song was soon very popular. It became customary about 1747 or 1748 to greet the king with it when he entered a place of public entertainment. In George III's reign it figured as a political battle-song in connection with the regency troubles and later during the dissensions aroused by the French revolution. It was sung at the coronation banquet of George IV and the description of it as 'National Anthem' appears to have been adopted early in the 19th cent. Variant versions, imitations, and parodies have been very numerous; among the imitations may be mentioned the 'New National Anthem' written by *Shelley in 1819 after Peterloo, and the 'New National Anthem' of E. *Elliott, the Corn-Law Rhymer (1830).

The remoter origin of 'God save the King' is obscure. Before being sung at Drury Lane in 1745, words and tune, with slight differences, had appeared in *Thesaurus Musicus*, a song collection published in 1744. The opening words in the Drury Lane version were

> God bless our noble King,
> God save great George our King,
> God save the King.

In the *Thesaurus Musicus* they were

> God save our Lord the King,
> Long live our noble King,

which might apply equally to a Stuart or a Hanoverian monarch. There is good evidence that the song was originally written in favour of James II in 1688 (when the invasion by the prince of Orange was threatening) or possibly of Charles II in 1681; but the author is unknown. As regards the melody, various 17th-cent. tunes of the same rhythm more or less resemble that of 'God save the King'. The closest resemblance is that of a galliard composed by Dr *Bull in the early 17th cent. But this may be the keyboard setting of some folk-tune or other well-known air of the time, and the tune of 'God save the King' may have been drawn directly from that original. The tune has been adopted by a number of continental countries for their national anthems.

For a fuller treatment of the subject see Percy Scholes, *God save the King* (1942), on which the above article is based.

National Biography, *Dictionary of,* see DICTIONARY OF NATIONAL BIOGRAPHY.

National Book League, an independent charitable organization founded in 1925 as the National Book Council by the Society of Bookmen (Harold Macmillan, *Galsworthy, Stanley Unwin, Maurice Marston, and others); its function is to promote the use and enjoyment of books by working with all branches of the book world (booksellers, publishers, authors, printers, librarians, teachers, etc.). The Council was renamed The National Book League in 1945, and moved in 1980 from its central London premises at 7 Albemarle Street to Book House, Wandsworth. Its services include the Mark Longman Library of Books about Books, a Centre for Children's Books, a Book Information Service, and the administration of literary prizes, including the *Booker McConnell: it also acts as a pressure group in fighting cuts in expenditure on the provision of books, etc.

National Library of Scotland, see under LIBRARIES.

Natty Bumppo, the hero of the 'Leatherstocking' novels of J. F. *Cooper.

Naturalism, as a term of literary history, primarily a French movement in prose fiction and (to a lesser extent) the drama during the final third of the 19th cent., although it is also applied to similar movements or groups of writers in other countries (e.g. Germany, the USA) in the latter decades of the 19th and early years of the 20th cents. In France *Zola was the dominant practitioner of Naturalism in prose fiction and the chief exponent of its doctrines. His novel *Thérèse Raquin* (1867), together with the *Gon-

courts' *Germinie Lacerteux* (1865), are considered as marking the beginnings of the movement; its most substantial and important achievement in fiction is the series of twenty novels written by Zola between 1871 and 1893 under the general title of *Les Rougon-Macquart.* Other writers who shared, in a greater or lesser degree, the ideas and aims of Naturalism are *Daudet, *Maupassant and, in his early fiction, *Huysmans.

Broadly speaking, Naturalism is characterized by a refusal to idealize experience and by the persuasion that human life is strictly subject to natural laws. The Naturalists shared with the earlier Realists the conviction that the everyday life of the middle and lower classes of their own day provided subjects worthy of serious literary treatment. These were to be rendered so far as possible without artificiality of plot and with scrupulous care for *documentation,* i.e. for the authenticity and accuracy of detail, thus investing the novel with the value of social history. Emphasis was laid on the influence of the material and economic environment on behaviour, and, especially in Zola, on the determining effects of physical and hereditary factors in forming the individual temperament.

Many of the Naturalists wrote for the theatre, sometimes adapting their own fiction for stage presentation; these plays, and more especially those of the dramatist Henri Becque (1837–99), enlarged the scope of the movement, which was promoted in the Théâtre Libre (1887–94) of André Antoine. In Germany, the movement flourished from *c.*1885 until the 1890s, largely in the theatre, influenced both by *Ibsen (whose interest in heredity was easily explicable in naturalist terms) and by the Théâtre Libre, which visited Berlin in 1889; one of its principal exponents was *Hauptmann. See also REALISM.

Nature, a periodical founded in 1869, with Norman Lockyer as editor, for the purpose of providing the public with information on scientific matters. C. *Darwin, T. H. *Huxley, *Tyndall, and Sir John Lubbock (1834–1913) were among its distinguished early supporters. It still continues.

Nature and Art, a romance by Mrs *Inchbald, published 1796, the story of two contrasted brothers, William and Henry, and their equally contrasting sons. The story illustrates the wholesome effects of a natural and simple upbringing compared with the warping effects of civilization.

NAYLER, James (1616/17–60), a Quaker from near Wakefield, regarded by R. *Baxter as a leader. He attracted a following of fervent devotees who encouraged him to ride in triumph on a donkey into Bristol in 1656; he was charged with blasphemy, cruelly punished, and imprisoned. He subsequently repented of his xcesses and wrote movingly of his new spirit of humility and endurance. He was a brilliant preacher, and his writings, particularly the later ones, were described by W. C. Braithwaite in *The First Period of Quakerism* (1912) as possessing 'great force and beauty'.

NEALE, J(ohn) M(ason) (1818–66), educated at Trinity College, Cambridge, was founder of the Cambridge *Camden Society. He was author of *The History of the Holy Eastern Church* (1847–73), and many hymns (some of them translations from Greek, medieval Latin, and Eastern sources) including 'O happy band of pilgrims', 'Art thou weary', and 'Jerusalem the Golden'; *Hymns Ancient and Modern* owes much to his inspiration.

NECKER, Mme, *née* Suzanne Curchod (1739–94), a Swiss woman, at one time engaged to *Gibbon; she became the wife of Jacques Necker, the French financier and statesman. She was prominent in French literary circles of the period preceding the revolution. Her daughter became Mme de *Staël.

Neckett, Mr, the sheriff's officer in Dickens's *Bleak House*, generally referred to as Coavinses, the name of the sponging-house which he keeps. He has three children, Tom, Emma, and Charlotte (known as 'Charley'), who becomes Esther Summerson's maid.

Nectabanus, the dwarf in Scott's *The Talisman.*

NED, the 'New English Dictionary', now called the *Oxford English Dictionary.*

NEDHAM, or **NEEDHAM,** Marchamont (1620–78), journalist, and chief author of *Mercurius Britanicus* (1643–6), the arch enemy of the royalist *Mercurius Aulicus* of *Berkenhead. His subsequent professional career showed shifting loyalties, and he was several times imprisoned. In 1660, after some years of considerable power as editor of *Mercurius Politicus*, he fled to Holland, obtained a pardon, and returned to England, where he practised medicine and continued to write pamphlets. He was also the author of verses and a translation of *Selden's *Mare Clausum* (1652). His prose was powerful, and *Milton was not implausibly credited with some of his anonymous works. (See also NEWSPAPERS, ORIGINS OF.)

Negative capability, a phrase coined by *Keats to describe his conception of the receptivity necessary to the process of poetic creativity. In a letter to Benjamin Bailey (22 Nov. 1817) he wrote, 'If a Sparrow come before my Window I take part in its existence and pick about the Gravel', and a month later (22 Dec. 1817) he wrote to his brothers George and Thomas. defining his new concept: '*Negative Capability*, that is when man is capable of being in uncertainties,

Mysteries, doubts, without any irritable reaching after fact and reason—'. Keats regarded Shakespeare as the prime example of negative capability, attributing to him the ability to identify completely with his characters, and to write about them with empathy and understanding; he contrasts this with the partisan approach of *Milton and the 'wordsworthian or egotistical sublime' (Letter to Woodhouse, 27 Oct. 1818) of *Wordsworth. However, he was ambivalent about his own attitude, and sometimes expressed admiration for the Miltonic approach; Douglas Bush ('Keats and his Ideas', *English Romantic Poets*, ed. M. H. Abrams, 1960) writes, 'As artist he fluctuates—and is aware of his fluctuations—between belief in the poetic efficacy of a wise passiveness, and belief in the active pursuit of rational knowledge and philosophy.'

Négritude, a term used to denote a movement in literature that dates from the 1930s, and which derived its impetus from French-speaking African and Caribbean writers. It was a movement that sought to recover and define the richness of black cultural values in the face of the dominant values of European colonialism, and it emerged specifically as a protest against French colonial rule and the French policy of assimilation. Prominent amongst its members were the poet and essayist Léopold Sédar Senghor (1906–), who became, in 1960, the first president of the Republic of Senegal; Aimé Césaire (1913–), poet and dramatist from Martinique (*Cahier d'un retour au pays natal*, 1939; English trans., *Return to My Native Land*, 1968); and Léon Damas (1912–), from French Guiana.

NEHRU, Jawaharlal, Pandit (1889–1964), Indian statesman, was born at Allahabad, the son of Motilal Nehru, an eminent lawyer. He was educated in England, at Harrow and Trinity College, Cambridge, and was called to the bar before returning to Allahabad to practise there. He joined the non-co-operation movement under Gandhi in 1920, was imprisoned several times, and soon attained a leading position in the Indian National Congress party. He became the first prime minister of independent India, remaining in office until his death. He wanted India to be a secular state, based on parliamentary government and a socialist economy, with a foreign policy of 'neutralism', or independence of both the Western and Communist blocs. His policy of friendship with China was discredited by the Chinese invasion of India in 1962. His *Autobiography* (1936) gives some insight into the development of his ideas. His *Glimpses of World History* (1939) paid more attention to Asia than was usual in universal histories, and his *Discovery of India* (1946) revealed his sympathy with India's traditions.

His daughter Indira Gandhi was prime

minister of India, 1966–77 and again from 1980 until she was assassinated in 1984.

Nekayah, in Johnson's *Rasselas*, the sister of the hero.

NEKRASOV, Nikolai Alekseevich (1821–77), Russian poet and editor. His first poems were published in 1838. In 1840 his first collection *Dreams and Sounds* appeared, with little success, and he began work as a journalist. As an editor he showed extraordinary discernment. In 1846 he edited the *Petersburg Collection*, which included 'Poor Folk', the first work by *Dostoevsky to be published. From 1847 to 1866 he was editor of the leading review of the day, *The Contemporary*, which in 1852 contained the first published work by *Tolstoy, *Childhood*, and also published *Turgenev, *Ostrovsky, and other major figures. His second collection. *The Poems of Nikolai Nekrasov* (1856), brought him great success, despite heavy censorship. In 1857 he visited London in an attempt to see *Herzen. After the closure of *The Contemporary* he was editor, from 1868 until his death, of the radical review *Notes of the Fatherland*, jointly with *Shchedrin. Nekrasov is considered the greatest of Russia's 'civic' poets: in his 1856 poetic dialogue, 'The Poet and the Citizen', the Citizen famously contends that 'You do not have to be a poet, | But you must be a citizen'; but Turgenev considered that 'poetry never so much as spent a night in his [Nekrasov's] verse'. In poetry his main theme is the life of the Russian peasant. His major works are the narrative poems *The Peddlers* (1861), *Red-nosed Frost* (1862–3), *The Railway* (1864), *Who is Happy in Russia?* (1865–77), and *Russian Women* (1871–2). *Red-nosed Frost* appeared in a translation by J. Sumner Smith in 1886.

Nelly Dean, a character in E. Brontë's *Wuthering Heights*.

Nemesis of Faith, The, a novel by J. A. *Froude.

Nemo (1) the law-writer in Dickens's *Bleak House*; (2) Captain Nemo, in *Verne's *Twenty Thousand Leagues under the Sea*, commander of the submarine *Nautilus*.

NENNIUS (*fl. c.830*), the author or reviser of the *Historia Britonum*, lived on the borders of Mercia in Brecknock or Radnor and was a pupil of Elfodd, bishop of Bangor (d. *c.*811). The 33 surviving manuscripts enshrine several versions: the North-West, the South-West, the Irish, and the English. It is a collection of notes, drawn from various sources including *Gildas and (perhaps indirectly) *Bede, on the history and geography of Britain, and is interesting for the account it purports to give of the historical *Arthur who, as *dux bellorum*, after Hengist's death led the Britons against the Saxons in twelve battles (including Mount Badon) which Nennius enumerates. It is one of the sources on which *Geoffrey of Monmouth drew for his *Historia Regum Britanniae*. A mixture of legend and history, it is characterized by pride in the Celtic people of Britain and interest in its topography. See A. Gransden, *Historical Writing in England c.550–c.1307* (1974), pp. 5–12.

Neo-classicism, in literature, the habit of imitating the great authors of antiquity (notably its poets and dramatists) as a matter of aesthetic principle; and the acceptance of the critical precepts which emerged to guide that imitation. Medieval writers had often used classical works for models, but *Petrarch in the 14th cent. was the first to do so because he considered it the only way to produce great literature; and where he led a host of later authors followed. The epic, eclogue, elegy, ode, satire, tragedy, comedy, and epigram of ancient times all found imitators, first in Latin, then in the vernaculars, and eventually practice was succeeded by precept. At the beginning of the 16th cent. the recovery of the previously neglected *Poetics* of Aristotle provoked an attempt to establish rules for the use of the ancient genres. The *Poetics* itself was repeatedly edited, translated, and supplied with commentaries, the most popular being the one by *Castelvetro (1570), and there also appeared a number of treatises on poetry, culminating in J. C. *Scaliger's controversial *Poëtice* (1561). These theoreticians imprisoned imitation within a rigid framework of rules, for which the flexibility of ancient practice offered little precedent. The most famous of their inventions was the observance of the dramatic *unities of time, place, and action, which won great support in France where a new generation of playwrights in the 1620s and 1630s was eager to attract a more educated public. A noisy battle over *Corneille's popular tragi-comedy *Le Cid* (1637), which was blamed for breaking the rules, ended in an acceptance of the unities, and during the next 30 years a succession of critics, the best-known of whom was *Boileau, extended the scope of their prescriptions from drama to all other major genres.

Up to the last quarter of the 17th cent. neo-classicism had little influence in England. The imitation of classical models was less common than on the Continent and, except for *Jonson, no important writer paid strict attention to the rules humanist critics had formulated. But at that point, unsettled perhaps by the successes of their colleagues in France, playwrights responded to the urgings of *Rymer and began to take neo-classical theories more seriously. Translations and adaptations of Corneille and *Racine enjoyed some popularity. Dryden produced *All for Love* (1677) and Addison his *Cato* (1713), which has been called the only correct neo-classical tragedy in English; but the fashion was not to last.

The usual excuse for the rules was that they helped writers to be true to nature. *Pope wrote,

Those RULES of old *discover'd*, not *devis'd*,
Are *Nature* still, but *Nature methodiz'd*,

and implicit in his view was the assumption that 'nature' consisted in what was generally true. But this assumption, advanced first by Scaliger and echoed much later by Dr *Johnson, had never commanded unquestioning support. As early as the beginning of the 17th cent. *Cervantes had argued for the representation of true acts of an exceptional nature, even though they were implausible, and a hundred years later it had become clear to everybody that extraordinary phenomena furnished literary material of considerable value. The scope of what could be regarded as natural was steadily growing, and simultaneously the difficulty *Homer's readers experienced in appreciating his poems made them aware of the fact that behaviour usual in one age could prove unacceptable in another. What is natural came to be seen no longer as an absolute, but as historically conditioned. What undermined neo-classicism most decisively however in the 18th cent. was the changing view of the goal of literary creation provoked by Boileau's translation (1674) of the pseudo-Longinian treatise of the *Sublime. A cult of sublimity—greatness of conception and emotion—replaced the wish to produce a just representation of general Reality, and the way to Romanticism lay open.

In the context of art history, the term 'neo-classical' generally refers to the style and aesthetics of a somewhat later period (mid- to late 18th cent.), when an emphasis on the 'antique' ideals of harmony and grandeur (see WINCKELMANN) emerged in part as a reaction against the excesses of *baroque and the triviality of rococo.

Neo-Impressionism, the style of painting developed by Georges Seurat (1869–91), who tried to work out a scientific basis to the Impressionists' ideas on the rendering of light. The technique is sometimes called pointillism or divisionism, for the pigment was applied in dots of pure colour which appear to fuse when viewed from a distance, giving the effect of blended colour without loss of brilliance.

Neoplatonism, a philosophical and religious system, combining Platonic ideas with oriental mysticism, which originated at Alexandria in the 3rd cent. and is especially represented in the writings of *Plotinus, Porphyry, and Proclus. This system of thought, which thanks to Augustine left a deep mark on Christianity, combined in the 5th and 6th cents AD with survivals of *Gnosticism and persisted in this form through the Middle Ages. It experienced a notable revival in the 15th cent., associated with Ficino, *Pico della Mirandola, *Agrippa, and

*Paracelsus. The conglomeration of ideas found in the works of these writers extends well beyond Neoplatonism, but is often given that name, and it influenced literature in a number of distinct ways. (1) The 'Neoplatonic' theory of love rested on the beliefs that earthly beauty was an image of absolute beauty and that spiritual graces in a beloved were even more important than bodily ones. These beliefs find frequent expression in the poetry of the Renaissance and recur in *Shelley. (2) Belief in the existence of airy creatures that could be invisible, and that served or crossed mankind, appears in Dr *Dee's familiar, Prospero's Ariel in *The Tempest, or on a humorous level the sylphs of *The Rape of the Lock. (3) The attempt to bring together all systems of belief—Christian, Neoplatonist, Cabbalistic—that maintained the power of spirit over matter appears in poets like T. *Vaughan and in the writings of the *Cambridge Platonists. (4) There was the view that both Art and Nature are copies of the same supersensuous reality and that Art could be the better copy, a view that appealed to *Sidney and *Spenser.

Neo-realism, a movement in the post-war Italian novel and film which may be seen as a continuation of *Verismo. While its narratives were naturalistic on the surface, the works were imbued with a lyrical populism that was occasionally sentimental and even owed something to the style of films made under Fascism. As Fascism collapsed, the Resistance emerged as the theme of neo-realist novels by Beppe Fenoglio (1922–63), Elio Vittorini (1908–66), and the young *Calvino, and of films by Rossellini, whose *Roma città aperta* (*Rome Open City*, 1945) is a classic of this genre. At the same time, neo-realism documented the lives of poor people in the underdeveloped south or struggling in northern cities: this strand is represented by the novels of Carlo Levi (1902–75) and *Pavese, and by the films of De Sica (e.g. *Bicycle Thieves*, 1948), Olmi, Rosi, and the young Visconti.

Nerissa, in Shakespeare's *The Merchant of Venice*, Portia's waiting-woman, who marries Gratiano.

NERUDA, Pablo (1904–73), the pen-name (adopted by deed poll in 1946, after the Czech poet Jan Neruda, 1834–91), of Chilean poet and diplomat Ricard Eliecer Neftali Reyes, born in Parral, Chile, the son of a railwayman. He travelled widely in the diplomatic service from 1927 to 1938 (in south-east Asia and Spain), and after the Second World War (having joined the Communist party in 1939) he visited the USSR, China, and Eastern Europe. His poetry, which ranges from short, intense personal lyrics to odes, political meditations, and various autobiographical works, both in prose and verse, won him an international reputation, and, in

1971, the *Nobel Prize for literature. A political activist and in many ways the prototype of the committed poet, he supported the Communist president Allende, and was Chilean ambassador to Paris in 1970. He died in Santiago shortly after Allende's own death.

NERVAL, Gérard de (1808–55), French poet and prose-writer, best known for his sonnet sequence *Les Chimères* (1854). He also produced a number of short stories, including 'Sylvie' (1853), a considerable amount of journalism, and an account of a journey to the Middle East, *Le Voyage en Orient* (1851). Much of his later life was dominated by his struggle against mental instability, of which he gives an account in *Aurélia* (1855). The deeply private, elusive, and visionary quality of much of his work exercized an influence over the adherents of both *Symbolism and *Surrealism.

NESBIT, E(dith) (1858–1924), enjoyed as a girl the society of her sister Mary's friends, who included *Swinburne, the *Rossettis, and W. *Morris. Her husband Hubert Bland was a founder member of the *Fabian Society and a noted philanderer; after the failure of his health and business she was obliged to abandon her aspirations as a poet and write pot-boilers in order to support her family. She is remembered, however, for her children's books, tales of everyday family life sometimes mingled with magic. In 1898 her first stories about the young Bastables appeared with such success that she published three 'Bastable' novels in quick succession: *The Story of the Treasure-Seekers* (1899), *The Wouldbegoods* (1901), and *The New Treasure-Seekers* (1904). Other well known titles with a lasting appeal include *Five Children and It* (1902), *The Phoenix and the Carpet* (1904), *The Railway Children* (1906), and *The Enchanted Castle* (1907). There is a life by D. K. Moore, published 1933.

Neuchatel, Mr and Adriana, in *Endymion* by B. Disraeli.

Neville, Miss, a character in Goldsmith's *She Stoops to Conquer*.

New Age, The, see ORAGE, A. R.

New Apocalypse, The, a group of writers who flourished briefly as a movement in the 1940s, united by a romantic reaction against what they saw as the 'classicism' of *Auden; it expressed itself in wild, turbulent, and at times surreal imagery. Their work appeared in three anthologies, *The New Apocalypse: an anthology of criticism, poems and stories* (1940), edited by James Findlay Hendry (1912–); *The White Horseman: prose and verse of the New Apocalypse* (1941), edited by Hendry and Henry Treece (1911–66), with an introduction by George Sutherland Fraser (1915–80), and *The Crown*

and the Sickle (1945), also edited by Hendry and Treece. They described themselves as 'anti-cerebral', claimed a 'large, accepting attitude to life', invoked the name of D. H. *Lawrence, and approved of Dylan *Thomas; G. *Barker and V. *Watkins also were associated with the movement.

New Atalantis, The, see MANLEY, MRS.

New Atlantis, The, a treatise of political philosophy in the form of a fable, by F. *Bacon. The work, which was left unfinished, was published in 1626.

It is an account of a visit to an imaginary island of Bensalem in the Pacific and of the social conditions prevailing there; and also of 'Solomon's House', a college of natural philosophy 'dedicated to the study of the works and creatures of God'.

NEWBERY, John (1713–67), publisher and bookseller, who established himself in 1744 in St Paul's Churchyard, and was one of the earliest and best-known publishers of children's books. He produced and partly wrote many books of riddles, fables, stories, etc. *Goldsmith was one of his authors, and may have written the much-imitated *Goody Two-Shoes* for him: he contributed his *Chinese Letters* (later *The Citizen of the World*) to Newbery's *The Public Ledger* (1760). Newbery also published *Smart, who married one of his stepdaughters. He was a friend of Dr *Johnson, and appears as 'Jack Whirler' in *The Idler*; he features as 'the philanthropic bookseller' in *The Vicar of Wakefield*. He also ran a profitable business in patent medicines.

NEWBOLT, Sir Henry John (1862–1938), barrister, poet, and man of letters, educated at Clifton and Corpus Christi College, Oxford, is remembered principally for his rousing patriotic nautical ballads, which include 'Drake's Drum', published in *Admirals All and Other Verses* (1897). His other collections include lyrics and satires, and he also published novels, short stories, and *A Naval History of the War, 1914–18* (1920). He was benevolent and active in public life, and served on many committees, including that of the *Royal Literary Fund.

NEWCASTLE, Margaret, duchess of (1623–73), daughter of Sir Thomas Lucas, was the second wife of William Cavendish (below), whom she met in Paris during his exile. Her first volume of verse, *Poems and Fancies* (1653), which displays her interest in chemistry and natural philosophy, was followed by many other works, including plays, letters, and an affectionate, vivid, and informal biography of her husband (1667). Dismissed as 'mad, conceited and ridiculous' by *Pepys and as 'airy, empty, whimsical and rambling' by *Evelyn's wife, she was nevertheless praised (and influenced) by

*Hobbes, and both *Lamb and V. *Woolf wrote of her with sympathy. Although she appears deliberately to have espoused singularity in dress and manners, much of her prose has an engaging and honest directness, notably in her apologies for her own audacity in writing at all, being a woman.

NEWCASTLE, William Cavendish, 1st duke of (1592–1676), husband of Margaret Cavendish (above), supported the king generously during the Civil War, and from 1644 lived abroad, often in much poverty, until the Restoration. He was the author of several poems and plays, collaborating in the latter with *Shirley, whose patron he was, and with *Dryden and *Shadwell.

Newcomes, The, a novel by *Thackeray, published in numbers 1853–5.

The story, told by Arthur Pendennis, is concerned with the descendants of a self-made man, Thomas Newcome. His eldest son, Colonel Thomas Newcome, is a simple, unworldly soldier, who has lived most of his life in India. In contrast, his half-brothers Hobson and Brian are wealthy and pretentious. Colonel Newcome is a widower, and his only son Clive is sent home to England to be educated. When Clive is almost grown up, his father returns from India, and indulgently allows him to become an art student. Clive loves his cousin Ethel, daughter of Sir Brian Newcome, but Ethel's brother Barnes and her grandmother Lady Kew intend her to make a grand marriage. Ethel is intelligent and independent-minded, but finds it difficult to fight the pressures of the marriage-market; she allows herself to become engaged first to her cousin, Lord Kew, and, after that match is broken off, to Lord Farintosh. The disastrously unhappy marriage of Barnes, who treats his wife so badly that she runs away with a former admirer, Jack Belsize, makes Ethel decide that she will not marry at all, but will devote herself to her brother's children. Meanwhile Clive has been manœuvred into marriage to a pretty, superficial girl, Rosey Mackenzie. When Colonel Newcome's fortune is lost with the failure of the Bundelcund Bank, he and Clive and Rosey are reduced to extreme poverty, and Rosey's mother makes life so intolerable for the Colonel with her accusations and reproaches that he finally takes refuge from her by becoming a pensioner in the Grey Friars almshouse, where he dies. Rosey has also died, and Thackeray allows the reader to assume that Clive and Ethel will get married. Certain aspects of Clive's character were suggested by *Leighton, whom Thackeray met in Rome.

New Country, an anthology of prose and verse published 1933, edited by M. *Roberts, with contributions by *Auden, *Spender, *Day-Lewis, *Empson, *Isherwood, *Upward, and R.

*Warner. Its tone was highly political, verging on the revolutionary: Roberts wrote in his preface, 'It is time that those who would conserve something which is still valuable in England began to see that only a revolution can save their standards.' A collection with many of the same contributors, *New Signatures,* also edited by Roberts, had appeared in 1932.

New Criticism, a term which was widely adopted after the publication of *Ransom's *The New Criticism* (1941), and applied not always very precisely to various tendencies in modern critical practice and theory. Ransom's book was a discussion (not wholly adulatory, but respectful) of I. A. *Richards, T. S. *Eliot, *Empson, *Winters, and others, and the term (despite Ransom's many qualifications) stuck to them as a description; other practitioners (some of whom resisted the label) included Cleanth Brooks, R. P. *Warren, A. *Tate, and R. P. *Blackmur (all, significantly, Americans) and, in England, in some respects, F. R. *Leavis. These critics differ so much one from another that it is impossible to generalize about their aims, but it might be safely claimed that the New Criticism insisted on close reading of the text and awareness of verbal nuance and thematic (rather than narrative) organization, and was not concerned with the biographical or social backgrounds of works of art. The text existed as a text on a page, an object in itself, with its own structure, which should be explored in its own terms; inquiries into the writer's personality or motivation were considered largely illegitimate or irrelevant. The New Criticism thus did much to weaken the tradition of old-fashioned 'literary history', in which literature was seen as a succession of dates and influences, accompanied by broad generalizations; and schools of criticism which diverge sharply in theory (see MARXIST LITERARY CRITICISM, FREUDIAN CRITICISM) nevertheless owe much to its techniques.

New Departures, see UNDERGROUND POETRY.

NEWDIGATE, Sir Roger (1719–1806), educated at Westminster School and University College, Oxford, MP successively for Middlesex and Oxford University, was founder of the Newdigate Prize at Oxford for English verse (1805).

New English Dictionary, The, now called the *Oxford English Dictionary.*

Newgate Calendar, The, was published about 1773 in 5 vols, and recorded notorious crimes from 1700 to that date. Similar compilations appeared in the next 50 years under varying titles, including *The Malefactor's Register* (1779); Andrew Knapp and William Baldwin, attorneys-at-law, issued *Criminal Chronology* (1809), *The Newgate Calendar* (1824–6), and *The New Newgate Calendar* (1826), All the

Newgate Calendars began in 1700 and they continued until before or a little after 1820. Plots derived from Newgate Calendars appear in novels by *Ainsworth (*Jack Sheppard* and *Rookwood*), *Bulwer-Lytton (*Pelham* and *Eugene Aram*), *Fielding (*Jonathan Wild*), *Godwin (*Caleb Williams*), and in *Hood's poem 'The Dream of Eugene Aram'. See also Thackeray's *Catherine* and Dickens's *Oliver Twist*. *Celebrated Trials*, attributed to *Borrow, is a selection of trials from about 1413 to 1825. See Rayner Heppenstall, *Reflections on the Newgate Calendar* (1975).

New Grub Street, a novel by *Gissing, published 1891.

In this work Gissing depicts the struggle for life, the jealousies, and intrigues of the literary world of his time, and the blighting effect of poverty on artistic endeavour. The main theme is the contrast of the career of Jasper Milvain, the facile, clever, selfish, and unscrupulous writer of reviews (who accepts the materialistic conditions of literary success), with those of more artistic temperaments. Among these are Edwin Reardon, the author of two fine works, who is hampered by poverty and by the lack of sympathy of his worldly wife, and the generous Harold Biffen, a poor scholar, the author of a work of 'absolute realism in the sphere of the ignobly decent'. The literary world is presented in a multitude of characters, of which one of the best is the learned pedant Alfred Yule, rendered rancorous and sardonic by constant disappointment. Jasper is attracted to Yule's daughter and assistant Marian, who passionately loves him; but he proposes to her only when she inherits a legacy of £5,000. When this legacy proves not to be forthcoming, he shabbily withdraws, and marries Amy Reardon, the young widow of Edwin, whom failure and his wife's desertion have driven to an early grave. The sombre story ends with Jasper's success, the triumph of self-advertisement over artistic conscience.

New Inn, The, or *The Light Heart*, a comedy by *Jonson, performed in 1629 by the King's Men, printed 1631.

Frances, the young Lady Frampul, invites some lords and gentlemen to make merry at the New Inn at Barnet. One of the guests, Lord Beaufort, falls in love with, and is promptly married to, the son of the innkeeper, who has been dressed up as a girl, while Frances falls in love with Lovel, a melancholy gentleman staying at the inn. In a succession of discovered identities it is learnt that the innkeeper's son really is a girl and, moreover, Frances's sister Laetitia; that the innkeeper is Frances's long-lost father; and that the son's old Irish nurse is the father's long-lost wife and Frances's mother. Jonson records in his dedication that the play was hissed at its first performance.

New Lines (1956), an anthology edited by R. *Conquest, containing work by himself, E. *Jennings, John Holloway (1920–), *Larkin, *Gunn, *Amis, *Enright, *Davie, and J. *Wain, poets associated with the *Movement. In his introduction Conquest attacked obscure and over-metaphorical poetry, presenting the claims of 'rational structure and comprehensible language'. *New Lines Volume II* (1963) added other poets including *Thwaite, *Scannell, and G. *Macbeth.

NEWMAN, Ernest, see MUSIC, LITERATURE OF.

NEWMAN, John Henry (1801–90), educated privately at Ealing and at Trinity College, Oxford, became a fellow of Oriel, where he came in contact with *Keble and *Pusey and later with R. H. *Froude. In 1828 he was presented to the vicarage of St Mary's, Oxford, where his 4 o'clock Sunday sermons attracted much attention. In 1832 he went to the south of Europe with Froude, and with him in Rome wrote much of the *Lyra Apostolica*; 'Lead, kindly Light', which appeared in this collection, was composed during a passage from Palermo to Marseilles in 1833. In the same year he resolved with William Palmer (1803–85), Froude, and A. P. Perceval (1799–1853) to fight for the doctrine of apostolic succession and the integrity of the Prayer Book, and began *Tracts for the Times* (see OXFORD MOVEMENT). He was moving slowly towards the Roman Catholic Church, and in 1841 his celebrated *Tract XC*, on the compatibility of the Articles with Catholic theology, roused great opposition and brought the Tractarians under official ban. He retired to Littlemore in 1842, where he adopted a semi-monastic way of life; he had always favoured celibacy and argued in its defence. In 1843 he resigned the living of St Mary's, preaching his last sermon there in September of that year, and in 1845 he joined the Church of Rome, a move which profoundly shocked many of his fellow Tractarians, caused a rift with Keble and Pusey, and isolated him from his old Oxford life. He went to Rome in 1846 and was ordained; on his return in 1847 he established the Oratory in Birmingham. He was in Ireland as rector of the new Catholic University in Dublin, 1854–8; his lectures and essays on university education appeared in various forms from 1852, and finally as *The Idea of a University Defined and Illustrated* (1873). In these he maintained that the duty of a university is instruction rather than research, and to train the mind rather than to diffuse useful knowledge; he also defended theological teaching and the tutorial system. In 1864 appeared his *Apologia pro Vita Sua*, in answer to C. *Kingsley, who had remarked in *Macmillan's Magazine*, misrepresenting Newman, that Newman did not consider truth a necessary virtue. The *Apologia* came out serially, and was not so entitled until it appeared in volume form. It is an exposition of his spiritual history, written with much sincerity and feeling, which also displays his formidable powers of argument. It made a profound impression on many who did not share his religious convictions, including G. *Eliot (who said it had 'breathed much life' into her), and is now recognized as a literary masterpiece. His poem *The Dream of Gerontius* (later set to music by *Elgar) appeared in *The Month* in 1865, and in book form in 1866; it is a vision of a just soul leaving the body at death, with choruses of angels, demons, etc., and includes the well known hymn 'Praise to the Holiest in the height'. In 1870 Newman published *The Grammar of Assent*, an examination of the nature of belief, which argues that we reach certainties not through logic but through intuitive perception; the real universe is not logical, and the premises of logic are not realities but assumptions. In 1879 Newman was created a cardinal.

Newman also published two novels, both anonymously. *Loss and Gain* (1848) gives a vivid portrait of the religious ferment of Oxford at the period of the Oxford Movement; his protagonist, Charles Reding, undergraduate son of a clergyman, is gradually drawn towards the Roman Catholic Church, despite the efforts of friends, teachers, and advisers, many of whom are drawn with satiric wit; the absurdities and weaknesses of the opposition are set against the loneliness and sacrifice involved in Reding's conversion. *Callista* (1856), a less interesting work, describes the persecution and martyrdom of a Christian convert, the sculptor Callista, in the 3rd cent. Newman also published many volumes of sermons, lectures, lives of saints, etc. Although he himself argued that most of his writing was prompted by occasion and duty, and that he found the process of writing painful 'like gestation or childbirth', many of his works have long outlived the occasions that prompted them, and remain a powerful intellectual and emotional influence.

New Monthly Magazine, The (1814–84), a periodical founded by *Colburn in opposition to the *Jacobin *Monthly Magazine*, whose 'political poison' it attacked over many years. Under T. *Campbell, who took over the editorship in 1821, it became more literary in interest. Colburn's tendency to promote his own publications became less apparent, and much literary work of distinction appeared. *Talfourd wrote well on *Wordsworth, *Lamb, *Keats, and others; and among other distinguished editors were *Bulwer-Lytton (for three stormy years), *Hood, and *Ainsworth.

NEWNES, Sir George (1851–1910), publisher and magazine proprietor, who founded *Tit-Bits* in 1881, and in 1890, with his old school friend W. T. *Stead, *The Review of Reviews*. Stead took over the latter, and Newnes proceeded to found the *Strand Magazine* and other publications, including the liberal daily the *Westminster Gazette* (1893).

Newnham College, a college for women at Cambridge, opened in 1876, developed from an earlier house of residence for women students, of which *Sidgwick was one of the chief promoters, and Anne Jemima Clough (1820–92) the first principal.

New Republic, The, see MALLOCK, W. H.

New Review, The, (1) a literary review edited by Archibald Grove from 1889 to 1894, and then, with much *éclat*, by W. E. *Henley, from 1895 to 1897, who serialized H. G. *Wells's *The Time Machine* (1895), A. Morrison's *A Child of the Jago* (1896), and H. James's *What Maisie Knew* (1897), and published poetry by *Verlaine, *Kipling, R. L. *Stevenson, and others. (2) the successor to the *Review*, edited from 1974 to 1979 by Ian Hamilton.

News, The, see L'ESTRANGE, R.

Newsbooks, or Diurnalls, the successors of the *corantos in the evolution of the newspaper. Newsbooks consisting of one printed sheet (8 pages) and later of two printed sheets (16 pages), were issued during the period 1641–54, then gave place to the *Oxford* (later *London*) *Gazette*. (See also GAZETTE; NEWSPAPERS, ORIGINS OF; BERKENHEAD; MUDDIMAN; and NEDHAM.)

News Chronicle, see DAILY NEWS, THE.

News from Nowhere, a Utopian socialist fantasy by W. *Morris, first published in *Commonweal*, Jan.–Oct. 1890, in volume form 1891.

The narrator falls asleep in the 'shabby London suburb' of Chiswick, after an evening at the Socialist League spent discussing the Morrow of the Revolution, and wakes in the future, to find London and its surroundings transformed into a communist paradise where men and women are free, healthy, and equal, the countryside reclaimed from industrial squalor, and money, prisons, formal education, and central government abolished. In a lengthy conversation with the old historian Hammond, he learns of the struggles and bloodshed (which took place in 1952) that achieved this happy state. There is a characteristic Morris stress on the beauty of the new craftsmanship in comparison with the shoddiness of the 19th cent., and a powerful poetic evocation of a journey up the Thames through the restored landscape. At the close he fades back into the past, inspired by the vision of what he has seen and the need to work for its fulfilment. *News from Nowhere* was in part a critical response to *Bellamy's *Looking Backward*, a Utopian portrait of a state socialist future dominated by machinery.

Newsletters, a term specially applied to the manuscript records of parliamentary and court news, sent twice a week to subscribers from the London office of *Muddiman in the second half of the 17th cent.

New Society, a weekly periodical founded in 1962, edited by Timothy Raison, 1962–8, and Paul Barker, 1968– . It covers the social sciences, social policy, documentary reportage, and the arts, and reviews books of a wide range of interest.

Newsome, Chad, a leading character in H. James's * The Ambassadors.

Newspapers, origins of. The direct ancestors of newspapers devoted to English news were the Dutch *corantos, newsbooks dealing with foreign events. The first to appear in English was a single-sheet publication, known as the *Corrant out of Italy, Germany &c*, printed in 1620 in Amsterdam by a Dutch map-engraver, Van den Keere. The first English weekly of home news appeared in Nov. 1641 (*The Heads of Severall Proceedings In This Present Parliament*), shortly followed by various other publications, mostly eight pages, e.g. Samuel Pecke's *A Perfect Diurnall*, Colling's *The Kingdomes Weekly Intelligencer*, *Berkenhead's *Mercurius Aulicus* edited from the royalist headquarters in Oxford, *Mercurius Civicus*, which was the first to be illustrated with woodcuts, and, perhaps the most popular, *Mercurius Britanicus*, edited by Thomas Audley and the most professional journalist of the period, *Nedham. Decreasingly efficient censorship and the stirring political climate stimulated demand for news, and by 1645 fourteen papers were on sale in English in London, including Dillingham's *Moderate Intelligencer*. In 1647 appeared the pro-royalist *Mercurius Pragmaticus*, edited by Nedham, *Cleveland, and the minor poet Samuel Sheppard: in 1648 *The Moderate*, edited by chief censor Gilbert Mabbott, became the first paper consistently to preach a radical programme. This period of rapid journalistic expansion also saw the birth of many unlicensed, short-lived, and counterfeit newsbooks, as well as the publication of literally thousands of pamphlets (see PAMPHLETEERING). The style of the newsbooks ranges from the baldly informative, through attempts at non-controversial objectivity, to the colourful, scurrilous, and highly polemical; Colling's prose was perhaps the most consciously literary, and his paper contains the only interregnum newspaper reference to *Chaucer yet discovered. The thirst for information introduced many new readers to familiarity with the printed word and created a new class of professional journalist: the newsbooks introduced many of the ingredients of

modern journalism, such as features, fillers, advertising, human-interest items, as well as news and political argument. This vigorous proliferation came to a sudden end in Sept. 1649 when Parliament, irritated by the onslaughts of both radical pamphleteers and royalist mercuries, and anxious about public reaction to the massacre at Drogheda, passed a stringent printing law with heavy fines which effectively silenced all the licensed weeklies, while authorizing two new papers, one to deal with army news, the other with news from Westminster. Both were predictably cautious, as were other new publications that slowly surfaced, and a period of press docility followed, leaving Nedham with a virtual monopoly of information in his official 16-page *Mercurius Politicus* and its close relation *The Publick Intelligencer* (1650–60): Nedham, having offended various shades of political opinion, fled to Holland in 1660. His place was taken by *Muddiman, who started his career as spokesman for the revived monarchy in 1659 with the *Parliamentary Intelligencer*, later *Kingdomes Intelligencer*. In 1665 he founded the *Oxford Gazette*, the first real newspaper. (See GAZETTE, also L'ESTRANGE.) See J. Frank, *The Beginnings of the English Newspaper 1620–1660* (1961).

New Statesman, The, a weekly journal of politics, art, and letters, originally planned as an organ of the *Fabian Society, Socialist in standing but independent in party. It was first published in 1913 with Clifford Sharp as editor, J. C. *Squire as literary editor, and the *Webbs and G. B. *Shaw as regular contributors. From that time and under the editorships of Kingsley Martin (1931–60), John Freeman (1961–5), P. *Johnson (1965–70), R. H. S. Crossman (1970–2), Anthony Howard (1972–8), and Bruce Page (1978–) it has maintained its policy of 'dissent, of scepticism, of inquiry, of nonconformity'. Among other writers connected with the journal have been J. M. *Keynes, L. *Woolf, G. D. H. *Cole, Raymond Mortimer, J. B. *Priestley, and V. S. *Pritchett.

New Timon, The, a satirical poem by *Bulwer-Lytton, published 1846, in which he sketches various celebrities of the day.

NEWTON, Sir Isaac (1642–1727), was the only child of a humble family from Woolsthorpe, near Grantham. His career was uneventful; he was attached to Trinity College, Cambridge, from 1661 to 1696; the rest of his life was spent in London as master of the mint and president of the *Royal Society, being knighted in 1705. Newton was unmarried and averse to luxury. He had few friends, but was not intellectually isolated; his vast correspondence kept together a band of dedicated disciples, some of whom were used as intermediaries in his debates with philosophical adversaries such as *Leibniz. Newton's intellect was quite as formidable as his flatterers maintained. Modern scholarship has not seriously affected his stature in the fields of mathematics, dynamics, celestial mechanics, astronomy, optics, natural philosophy, or cosmology. We now appreciate more fully the extent of his dedication to theology, biblical chronology, prophecy, and alchemy. In these latter spheres, Newton relates to the *Cambridge Platonists, especially More and Cudworth. Newtonianism was based on just three major works by Newton: *Philosophiae naturalis principia mathematica* (1687), the *Opticks* (1704), and *Arithmetica universalis* (1707). Newton's ideas were diffused through popularizations such as Henry Pemberton's *View of Sir Isaac Newton's Philosophy* (1728). Newtonianism was the dominant philosophy of the *Enlightenment, influencing all fields of science, and finding its way into the poetry of *Pope, J. *Thomson, and E. *Young, but eventually producing a reaction from *Goethe and *Blake. The latter could not have known from his public reputation that Newton had written more than two million words on alchemy; he was as steeped in the hermetic tradition as themselves. F. *Bacon and Newton were fused together to become the twin deity of English science in the 19th cent. under the banner 'inductive philosophy'.

NEWTON, John (1725–1807), an evangelical minister who went to sea as a boy and worked in the slave trade. His *An Authentic Narrative* (1764) gives a vivid picture of his ordeals and slowly growing doubts about the morality of his occupation. He became curate of Olney in 1764 and with *Cowper (on whom his powerful faith and at times overbearing personality had a profound influence) wrote *Olney Hymns* (1779). His *Journal* for 1750–4 was edited by B. Martin and M. Spurrell (1962).

New Verse, a little magazine edited 1933–9 by its founder G. *Grigson. It included work by *Auden, *MacNeice, G. *Barker, *Empson, R. *Fuller, and the young *Ewart, among others, and attacked, among other objects, the drowsy poeticism of the preceding century and the 'self-righteous' *Scrutiny.

New Way to pay Old Debts, A, a comedy by *Massinger, acted probably in 1625–6, published 1633, perhaps the best known of his works.

The play deals with the discomfiture of Sir Giles Overreach, a character based in part on the notorious extortioner Sir Giles Mompesson (1584–?1651). The cruel and rapacious Overreach, having got possession of the property of his prodigal nephew Frank Wellborn and reduced him to utter poverty, treats him contemptuously. Lady Allworth, a rich widow, to whose husband Wellborn had rendered important services, agrees to help him by pretending she is about to marry him. Overreach, deceived, changes his attitude and helps Wellborn. Tom Allworth, Lady Allworth's stepson and page to Lord Lovell, is in love with Overreach's daughter Margaret, who returns his love. Overreach is determined that his daughter shall marry Lord Lovell and become 'right honourable'. Lovell consents to help Allworth to win Margaret, and a trick is played on Overreach by which he helps the marriage along, thinking that Lord Lovell is to be the bridegroom. Overreach goes mad on discovering the deceit and on finding that his claim to Wellborn's property cannot be maintained; he is sent to Bedlam. Wellborn receives a company in Lord Lovell's regiment, and Lovell marries Lady Allworth.

New Woman, a phrase said to have been coined by Sarah *Grand in 1894 in the *North American Review* to describe a new generation of women, influenced by J. S. *Mill and other campaigners for women's rights, who believed in *Women's Suffrage, abolition of the double standard in sexual matters, Rational Dress, educational opportunities for women, etc. New Women appear in the works of *Ibsen, G. B. *Shaw, *Wells, O. *Schreiner, Rebecca *West, *Gissing, G. *Allen, and G. *Egerton, among many others.

New Writing, a book-periodical edited by J. *Lehmann, first published in 1936 and afterwards at approximately half-yearly intervals until 1940. It published imaginative writing, mainly by young authors (including *Spender, *Auden, *Isherwood, *Upward, *Anand, *Pritchett), and particularly those whose work was too unorthodox for the established magazines. New contributors were recruited from many parts of Europe, India, New Zealand, South Africa, China, and Russia. In 1940 it came out as *Folios of New Writing*; it became *New Writing and Daylight* in 1942 and this lasted until 1946. Meanwhile *Penguin New Writing* appeared in 1940, first as a monthly paperback and then in 1942 as a quarterly. It reprinted some work from *New Writing*, but relied more and more on new material. A series of 11 articles based on personal experience of the upheavals of war, all published in 1941, was especially notable.

New Yorker, The, an American weekly magazine founded in 1925 by Harold Ross (1892–1951). It is sophisticated, satirical, and urbane, and although famed for its humour has also published distinguished articles of reportage, such as, notably, 'Hiroshima' by John Hersey (1914–), which occupied an entire issue in 1946. Writers and cartoonists associated with the magazine include *Thurber, O. *Nash, Charles Addams, Saul Steinberg, *O'Hara,

S. J. Perelman (1904–79), and *Updike. See Brendan Gill, *Here at the New Yorker* (1975).

NGUGI, James, see THIONG'O, NGUGI WA.

Niamh, in the second or southern cycle of Irish mythology, the daughter of *Manannán, the sea-god. She fell in love with *Oisin, the son of *Finn, carried him off over the sea, and kept him with her for 300 years. She then let him return to his own country, mounted on a magic steed, but on condition that he should not set foot on earth. Oisin disregarded the caution, immediately lost his youth, and became a blind, decrepit old man.

Nibelung, Niblung, or **Niebelung,** in the Norse *sagas and German *Nibelungenlied, a mythical king of a race of dwarfs, the Nibelungs, who dwelt in Norway. The Nibelung kings and people also figure in W. Morris's *Sigurd the Volsung*.

Nibelungenlied, a German poem of the 13th cent. embodying a story found in primitive shape in both forms of the *Edda. In these the story is substantially as told by W. Morris in *Sigurd the Volsung*, Sigurd being the Siegfried of the German poem.

In the *Nibelungenlied* the story is somewhat different. Siegfried, son of Siegmund and Sieglind, king and queen of the Netherlands, having got possession of the Nibelung hoard guarded by Alberich, rides to woo Kriemhild, a Burgundian princess, sister of Gunther, Gernot, and Giselher. Hagen, their grim retainer, warns them against Siegfried, but the match is arranged, and the hoard is given to Kriemhild as marriage portion. Siegfried undertakes to help Gunther to win Brunhild, queen of Issland, by defeating her in trials of skill and strength, which he succeeds in doing. The double marriage takes place, but Brunhild remains suspicious and ill-humoured, and Siegfried, called in by Gunther to subdue her, does so in Gunther's semblance and takes away her ring and girdle, which he gives to Kriemhild. The two queens quarrel, and Kriemhild reveals to Brunhild the trick that has been played on her. Hagen, who thinks his master's honour injured by Siegfried, treacherously kills the latter at a hunt.

Kriemhild later marries Etzel (Attila), king of the Huns, and in order to avenge her husband and secure the hoard, which her brothers have seized and sunk in the Rhine, persuades them to visit Etzel's court. There they are set upon and overcome, but refuse to betray the hiding-place of the hoard, and are slain. Hagen, the last survivor of the party who knows the secret, is killed by Kriemhild with Siegfried's sword; and Kriemhild herself is slain by Hildebrand, a knight of *Dietrich of Bern. See RING DES NIBELUNGEN for *Wagner's version.

Nice, Sir Courtly, see SIR COURTLY NICE.

Nicholas Nickleby, a novel by *Dickens, published 1838–9.

Nicholas, a generous, high-spirited lad of nineteen, his mother, and his gentle sister Kate are left penniless on the death of his father. They appeal for assistance to his uncle, Ralph Nickleby, a griping usurer, of whom Nicholas at once makes an enemy by his independent bearing. He is sent as usher to Dotheboys Hall, where Wackford Squeers starves and maltreats forty urchins under pretence of education. His special cruelty is expended on Smike, a half-witted lad left on his hands and employed as a drudge. Nicholas, infuriated by what he witnesses, thrashes Squeers and escapes with Smike, who becomes his devoted friend. For a time he supports himself and Smike as an actor in the provincial company of Vincent Crummles; he then enters the service of the brothers Cheeryble, whose benevolence and good humour spread happiness around them. Meanwhile Kate, apprenticed to Madame Mantalini, dressmaker, is by her uncle's designs exposed to the gross insults of Sir Mulberry Hawk, one of his associates. From this persecution she is released by Nicholas, who breaks Sir Mulberry's head and makes a home for his mother and sister. Nicholas himself falls in love with Madeline Bray, the support of a selfish father and the object of a conspiracy of Ralph Nickleby and another revolting old usurer, Gride, to marry her to the latter. Ralph, whose hatred for Nicholas has been intensified by the failure of his plans, knowing Nicholas's affection for Smike, conspires to remove the latter from him; his plots are thwarted with the help of Newman Noggs, his eccentric clerk, but nevertheless Smike falls a victim to consumption, and eventually dies in the arms of Nicholas. Confronted with ruin and exposure, and finally shattered by the discovery that Smike was his own son, Ralph hangs himself. Nicholas, befriended by the Cheerybles, marries Madeline, and Kate marries the Cheerybles' nephew, Frank. Squeers is transported, and Gride is murdered.

NICHOLS, John (1745–1826), printer, author, and devoted antiquarian, joined in the management of the *Gentleman's Magazine* in 1778 and became its manager and editor from 1792 until his death. In the pages of the *Magazine* he built up his digressive, disordered, but invaluable work, *Literary Anecdotes of the Eighteenth Century* (published as a collection 1812–16); and his *Illustrations of the Literary History of the Eighteenth Century* which was published 1817–58, having been continued after his death by his son. He also collected *The Progresses and Public Processions of Queen Elizabeth* (which was used by Scott for *Kenilworth); published *Anecdotes of Mr Hogarth* (1780); an edition of *Swift (1801); and a massive *History and Antiquities of the County of Leicester* (1795–1815).

His valuable collection of newspapers is in the Bodleian Library, Oxford.

NICHOLS, Peter Richard (1927–), playwright, educated in Bristol. He worked as an actor and teacher before making his name with both stage and television plays. His works include *A Day in the Death of Joe Egg* (1967), in which schoolteacher Bri and his wife Sheila struggle to share the burden of their handicapped daughter, Joe; *The National Health* (1969, pub. 1970), a satirical hospital comedy which contrasts reality with soap opera; *Forget-me-not-Lane* (1971), a family drama set during the Second World War; and *Passion Play* (1980, pub. 1981), a marital tragi-comedy.

NICHOLS, Robert Malise Bowyer (1893–1944), educated at Winchester and Oxford, fought in France in the First World War; his volumes of poems, *Invocation* (1915) and *Ardours and Endurances* (1917), were highly regarded; he appeared in **Georgian Poetry*, and was thought by some to be another R. **Brooke. But *Aurelia* (1920) was his last volume of lyrics, after which he taught for many years in Tokyo and concentrated on writing plays, where he believed his talent lay. However, *Guilty Souls* (1922), *Wings Over Europe* (1930), and other dramas met with little success. *Such was my Singing* (1942) contained fragments from two vast projected works, *Don Juan Tenorio the Great*, on the subject of **Don Juan, and *The Solitudes of the Sun*, a series of vigorous poems and monologues by the romantic Prince Axel. Neither work was ever finished.

NICOLAI, Otto (1810–49), German composer. *Il Templario* (1840), the second of Nicolai's five operas, is based on **Ivanhoe* and had considerable success in Italy and Germany, but the work for which he remains famous is his last opera *Die lustigen Weiber von Windsor*, produced in Berlin in 1849. In spite of the formidable competition of **Verdi's *Falstaff* on the same subject, Nicolai's comic masterpiece has remained in the repertory in Germany and is still occasionally revived elsewhere: the text, sketched by the composer and versified by S. H. Mosenthal, is carefully worked out with due respect for Shakespeare, and the music, though not profound, has charm, vitality, and lyrical appeal. The overture is deservedly popular as a concert piece.

Nicolette, see AUCASSIN AND NICOLETTE.

NICOLSON, Sir Harold George (1886–1968), born in Teheran, the son of a diplomat, himself became a diplomat and, less successfully, a politician. He published critical and biographical works (on **Verlaine, 1921; **Swinburne, 1926; **Constant, 1945; King George V, 1952; and others), travel books, books on diplomacy, essays, etc., and some fiction: *Some People* (1927), a series of nine closely observed, semi-fictitious, semi-autobiographical sketches, is perhaps his most memorable work. He married V. **Sackville-West in 1913, and his diaries were edited (3 vols, 1966–8) by his son Nigel Nicolson.

Niebelung, see NIBELUNG.

NIEBUHR, Barthold Georg (1776–1831), the son of a distinguished German traveller, was educated at Kiel, and studied physical science at Edinburgh in 1798. His great *History of Rome*, which originally took the form of lectures delivered at Berlin in 1810–12, appeared in 1827–8. Niebuhr was the first historian to deal with the subject in a scientific spirit, discussing critically the early Roman legends and paying more attention to the development of institutions and to social characteristics than to individuals and incidents. The *History* was translated into English by J. C. **Hare and **Thirlwall in 1828–42.

NIETZSCHE, Friedrich Wilhelm (1844–1900), German philosopher and poet, educated at the ancient grammar school of Schulpforta and appointed very young to a professorship of classical philology at Basle. He resigned because of ill health and in 1889 suffered a mental breakdown from which he never properly recovered. His first work, *Die Geburt der Tragödie* (*The Birth of Tragedy*, 1872), was of revolutionary importance, challenging the accepted tradition of classical scholarship; it argued against the 'Apollonian' views associated with **Winckelmann in favour of a 'Dionysiac' interpretation which allowed for pessimism and passion as central features of Greek literature. In *Unzeitgemässe Betrachtungen* (*Thoughts out of Season*, 1873–6) he heavily criticized the complacency of German culture in the age of Bismarck. For his general philosophical position, his most important works were *Also sprach Zarathustra* (*Thus Spake Zarathustra*, 1883–92), *Jenseits von Gut und Böse* (*Beyond Good and Evil*, 1886), and *Der Wille zur Macht* (*The Will to Power*) (published posthumously from fragments). His basic ideas are the affirmation of the Superman, the rejection of Christian morality as the morality of the slave, the doctrine of power, and the 'revision of all values'. Nietzsche began as a disciple of **Schopenhauer, but later rejected his pessimism and quietism. For some time he was an admirer of **Wagner, but was eventually unable to accept the Christian and nationalist elements in Wagner's outlook, and a breach between the two men took place. T. **Mann's works show the influence of Nietzsche's thought, as do D. H. **Lawrence's (see, for example, the repudiation of Christianity and the doctrine of power, particularly in **Aaron's Rod*, 1922, and *Apocalypse*, 1931). A version of Nietzsche's 'Übermensch' (from *Also sprach Zarathustra*) appears in Shaw's **Man and Superman*.

Nigger of the 'Narcissus', The, a novel by J. *Conrad, published 1897.

The voyage of the *Narcissus* from Bombay to London is disrupted by two new hands, James Wait, the 'nigger' of the title, and Donkin, a compulsive troublemaker. During a ferocious gale Wait has to be rescued from his sickbed; and in the ensuing calm Donkin tries unsuccessfully to incite the crew to mutiny. Finally, as predicted by Singleton, 'the oldest able seaman in the ship', Wait dies, the wind rises, and the *Narcissus* is able to dock in London.

Described by H. *James as 'the very finest and strongest picture of the sea and sea life that our language possesses', the novel is generally regarded as Conrad's first masterpiece. Its preface contains perhaps the clearest expression of the author's artistic aims and beliefs.

Night and Day, (1) a novel by V. *Woolf; (2) a weekly periodical which ran from July to Dec. 1937, edited by John Marks and G. *Greene, with contributions by *Betjeman, E. *Bowen, *Kingsmill, E. *Waugh, H. *Read, and others. It folded as the result of a libel action rising from a review written by Greene of a film adaptation of *Kipling's story *Wee Willie Winkie*, in which he was alleged to have insulted Shirley Temple. See Greene, *Ways of Escape* (1980, ch. 2). (3) a play by T. *Stoppard.

NIGHTINGALE, Florence (1820–1910), known as the 'Lady of the Lamp', the founder of the modern nursing profession, famous for her services during the Crimean War and the reforms that she brought about in army hospitals.

Nightmare Abbey, a satire by *Peacock, published 1818.

The most literary of Peacock's satires, it mocks the modish gloom infecting contemporary literature: *Coleridge's German transcendentalism is the prime example, but *Byron's self-dramatizing and *Shelley's esotericism are also ridiculed. In imitation of the opening of *Godwin's novel *Mandeville* (1817), Mr Glowry's isolated house is staffed by servants with long faces and names like Diggory Deathshead. He gives a house party attended by Mr Toobad, the millenarian pessimist, Mr Flosky (Coleridge), Mr Cypress (Byron), and Mr Listless, the common reader, who is currently immersed in the blue devils. Two guests remain unfashionably cheerful, Mr Asterias the scientist and Mr Hilary, whose literary tastes come from the Greeks. Scythrop Glowry, the son of the house, a young writer who resembles Shelley, cannot decide between his frivolous cousin Marionetta and Mr Toobad's sybilline daughter Stella. Peacock seems to have intended to present, in amusing contemporary terms, the dilemma facing the young Milton in *'L'Allegro' and *'Il Penseroso'. In a classic comic denouement, in which the ladies are discovered to one another, Scythrop loses both. He briefly contemplates suicide in Werther's manner (see WERTHERISM), but calls instead for a bottle of Madeira.

'Night-Piece on Death', see PARNELL, T.

Night Thoughts on Life, Death, and Immortality, *The Complaint or*, a didactic and reflective poem of some 10,000 lines of blank verse, in nine books, by E. *Young, published 1742–5.

This work was extremely popular and had considerable influence in Europe, where it was admired by *Klopstock, *Diderot, and Robespierre, among others. It is a long and somewhat rambling meditation on life's vicissitudes, death, and immortality, and includes lines which have become proverbial, such as 'Procrastination is the thief of time' (Bk 1, l. 393). The poet deplores the deaths of Lucia, Narcissa, and Philander, loosely indentified as his wife, his stepdaughter, and her husband; he also addresses much reproof and exhortation to the worldly and infidel young Lorenzo, a character unlikely to be based on his own son, as many supposed, for the boy was only eight when the poem was begun. Thus a certain narrative and autobiographical interest is added to his evocations of 'delightful gloom' and the 'populous grave'.

Nihilism (Latin *nihil*, nothing), originally a movement in Russia repudiating the customary social institutions, such as marriage and parental authority. The term was introduced by *Turgenev. It was extended to a secret revolutionary movement, social and political, which developed in the middle of the 19th cent.

Nimphidia, a fairy poem by *Drayton which appeared in 1627.

Nimphidia, a fairy attendant on Queen Mab, reports to the poet the doings at the fairy court. It appears that Pigwiggin has fallen in love with Mab and made an assignation to meet her in a cowslip. The queen in her snail-shell coach, and the maids of honour hurrying after her on a grasshopper and shrouded with a spider's web, set off for the cowslip. King Oberon, roused to frenzy by the loss of his queen, and armed with an acorn cup, goes in pursuit, belabouring whomsoever he finds and meeting with mortifying adventures. He comes upon the faithful Puck (or Hobgoblin) and sends him to continue the search. Meanwhile Pigwiggin sends a challenge to Oberon, and a combat ensues between the two, mounted on earwigs. Proserpina, goddess of fairyland, intervenes, with mist and Lethe water, and restores harmony.

Nimue (Nimiane or Vivien), see LADY OF THE LAKE.

Nineteen Eighty-four, a novel by G. *Orwell, published 1949.

It is a nightmare story of totalitarianism of the future and one man's hopeless struggle against it and final defeat by acceptance. Winston Smith, the hero, has no heroic qualities, only a wistful longing for truth and decency. But in a social system where there is no privacy and to have unorthodox ideas incurs the death penalty he knows that there is no hope for him. His brief love affair ends in arrest by the Thought Police, and when, after months of torture and brainwashing, he is released, he makes his final submission of his own accord. The book is a warning of the possibilities of the police state brought to perfection, where power is the only thing that counts, where the past is constantly being modified to fit the present, where the official language, 'Newspeak', progressively narrows the range of ideas and independent thought, and where Doublethink becomes a necessary habit of mind. It is a society dominated by slogans—'War is Peace, Freedom is Slavery, Ignorance is Strength'—and controlled by compulsory worship of the head of the Party, *Big Brother. The novel had an extraordinary impact, and many of its phrases and coinages (including its title) passed into the common language, although the precise implications of Orwell's warning (and it was a warning, rather than a prophecy) have been subjected to many different political interpretations.

Nineteenth Century, The, a monthly review founded in 1877 by J. T. *Knowles, who was its first editor. It was more impartial in its attitude than the *Fortnightly, bringing together in its pages the most eminent advocates of conflicting views; one of its celebrated controversies (1890–1) was that between *Gladstone and T. H. *Huxley on the subject of the miracle of the Gadarene Swine. Other contributors included *Ruskin, B. *Webb, W. *Morris, *Ouida, and *Wilde. *Tennyson, a friend of Knowles, provided a prefatory sonnet for the first issue, welcoming contributions from the faithful and from 'wilder comrades' seeking a harbour 'In seas of Death and sunless Gulfs of Doubt'. When the century of the title ended, the review added to its old title 'And After', and changed the whole title to *The Twentieth Century* in 1951. See *Nineteenth Century Opinion* (1951), a selection from the years 1877–1901, edited by Michael Goodwin.

Nine Worthies, The, see WORTHIES OF THE WORLD.

NINON DE LENCLOS, see LENCLOS.

Nipper, Susan, a character in Dickens's *Dombey and Son.*

Nobel Prizes were established under the will of Alfred Bernhard Nobel (1833–96), a Swedish chemist distinguished in the development of explosives, by which the interest on the greater part of his large fortune is distributed in annual prizes for the most important discoveries in physics, chemistry, and physiology or medicine respectively, to the person who shall have most promoted 'the fraternity of nations' (the Nobel Peace Prize), and to the 'person who shall have produced in the field of literature the most outstanding work of an idealistic tendency'. The winners of the Nobel Prize for literature are as follows:

1901 René-François-Armand Sully-Prudhomme
1902 Theodor Mommsen
1903 Bjørnstjerne Bjørnson
1904 José Echegaray/Frédéric Mistral
1905 Henryk Sienkiewicz
1906 Giosué Carducci
1907 Rudyard *Kipling
1908 Rudolf Eucken
1909 Selma Lagerlöf
1910 Paul Heyse
1911 Maurice *Maeterlinck
1912 Gerhart *Hauptmann
1913 Rabindranath *Tagore
1914 No award
1915 Romain *Rolland
1916 Verner von Heidenstam
1917 Karl Kjellerup/Henrik Pontoppidan
1918 No award
1919 Carl Spitteler
1920 Knut *Hamsun
1921 Anatole *France
1922 Jacinto *Benavente y Martínez
1923 W. B. *Yeats
1924 Wladyslaw Reymont
1925 G. B. *Shaw
1926 Grazia *Deledda
1927 Henri *Bergson
1928 Sigrid Undset
1929 Thomas *Mann
1930 Sinclair *Lewis
1931 Erik Axel Karlfeldt
1932 John *Galsworthy
1933 Ivan *Bunin
1934 Luigi *Pirandello
1935 No award
1936 Eugene *O'Neill
1937 Roger Martin du Gard
1938 Pearl S. Buck
1939 F. E. Sillanpää
1940–3 No awards
1944 Johannes V. Jensen
1945 Gabriela Mistral
1946 Herman *Hesse
1947 André *Gide
1948 T. S. *Eliot
1949 William *Faulkner
1950 Bertrand *Russell
1951 Pär Lagerkvist
1952 François *Mauriac
1953 Winston S. *Churchill
1954 Ernest *Hemingway
1955 Halldór Laxness

1956 Juan Ramón Jiménez
1957 Albert *Camus
1958 Boris *Pasternak
1959 Salvatore *Quasimodo
1960 *Saint-John Perse
1961 Ivo Andrić
1962 John *Steinbeck
1963 George *Seferis
1964 Jean-Paul *Sartre
1965 Mikhail *Sholokhov
1966 S. Y. Agnon/Nelly Sachs
1967 Miguel Ángel Asturias
1968 Yasunari Kawabata
1969 Samuel *Beckett
1970 Alexander *Solzhenitsyn
1971 Pablo *Neruda
1972 Heinrich *Boll
1973 Patrick *White
1974 Eyvind Johnson/Harry Martinson
1975 Eugenio *Montale
1976 Saul *Bellow
1977 Vicente Aleixandre
1978 Isaac Bashevis *Singer
1979 Odysseus Elytis
1980 Czesław *Milosz
1981 Elias *Canetti
1982 Gabriel *Garcia Márquez
1983 William *Golding
1984 ·Jaroslav Seifert

Noble Savage, see PRIMITIVISM.

Noctes Ambrosianae, a series of dialogues, which appeared ih *Blackwood's Edinburgh Magazine* from 1822 to 1835. The series was devised by J. G. *Lockhart, and bears some resemblance to his own *Peter's Letters to his Kinsfolk*, in which the scene of the *Noctes*, *Ambrose's Tavern, first appears. The conversations take place between various friends, largely based on real people, such as the 'Shepherd' (J. *Hogg) and 'Christopher North' (John *Wilson). Wilson wrote more than half the 71 dialogues, but Lockhart, Hogg, and *Maginn also contributed. The conversations, which cover a wide range of subjects, and present a romanticized and whimsical view of Scotland, were extremely popular.

NOEL, Roden Berkely Wriothesley (1834–94), was the author of several volumes of verse, including *A Little Child's Monument* (1881), inspired by the death of his son Eric, and *Songs of the Heights and Deeps* (1885). His collected works were issued in 1902.

Noetics, The, a group of fellows of Oriel College, Oxford, who in the first quarter of the 19th cent. were noted for their free criticism of current theology. Chief among them was *Whately. The name is derived from Gr. νόησις, intelligence.

Noggs, Newman, in Dickens's *Nicholas Nickleby*, Ralph Nickleby's clerk, who has seen better days.

Nōh Plays, form of traditional, ceremonial, or ritualistic drama peculiar to Japan, symbolical and spiritual in character. It was evolved from religious rites of Shinto worship, was perfected in the 15th cent., and flourished during the Tokugawa period (1652–1868). It has since been revived. The plays are short (one or two acts), in prose and verse, and a chorus contributes poetical comments. They were formerly acted as a rule only at the Shōgun's court, five or six in succession, presenting a complete life drama, beginning with a play of the divine age, then a battle piece, a 'play of women', a psychological piece (dealing with the sins and struggles of mortals), a morality, and finally a congratulatory piece, praising the lords and the reign. The text was helped out by symbolic gestures and chanting. About 200 Nōh plays are extant. Of these the most interesting are the psychological pieces, in which some type of human character or some intense emotion is taken as the subject. In various respects the Nōh plays are comparable with the early Greek drama (see 'Noh, or Accomplishment', by Ernest Fenollosa and Ezra Pound).

Both *Pound and *Yeats were much influenced by the Nōh theatre: Yeats in his essay 'Certain Noble Plays of Japan' (1916) describes the impact of its ritual, simplicity, and stylization on his own plays, and compared its treatment of the supernatural with that of Lady *Gregory.

No Laughing Matter, a novel by A. *Wilson.

Nominalism (as opposed to *Realism), the view of those Scholastics and later philosophers who regarded universals or abstract conceptions as a 'flatus vocis', mere names without any corresponding reality. The founder of the school of thought is usually said to be Roscelin (c.1050–1125) whose view (as well as its extreme opposite Realist view) was opposed by *Abelard. Its anti-Platonic emphasis on Individuals has some affinity with later Empiricist philosophy.

Nonesuch Press, a publishing firm established in 1923 by F. *Meynell, Vera Mendel, and D. *Garnett, for the production of books of high quality of content and presentation, at a moderate price. Not strictly a *private press, it shared many of the aims of the private presses. See *The Nonesuch Century* (1936), by A. J. A. *Symons, Desmond Flower, and F. Meynell, which describes the first 100 books and 12 years of the press's life.

NOONAN, Robert, see under TRESSELL, R.

Norimberga, in imprints, Nuremberg.

Norna of the Fitful-head, Ulla Troil, a character in Scott's *The Pirate*.

Norris, Mrs, a character in J. Austen's *Mansfield Park*.

NORRIS, Frank (Benjamin Franklin Norris) (1870–1902), American novelist, born in Chicago, the son of a wholesale jeweller, but brought up partly in San Francisco, and educated at the University of California and in Paris, where he studied art. The influence of *Zola and *Naturalism is seen in his best works, which includes *McTeague* (1899), a tragic account of violence, greed, and treachery in San Francisco, in which McTeague, an unlicensed dentist, becomes both thief and murderer; and in his unfinished trilogy *The Epic of the Wheat*: the masterly first two volumes, *The Octopus* (1901) and *The Pit* (1903), describe the raising of wheat in California and speculation on the Chicago wheat exchange. A projected third volume, *The Wolf*, to be set in famine-stricken Europe, was never written.

NORRIS, John (1657–1711), poet, philosopher, and from 1691 rector of Bemerton; he is considered as the last of the *Cambridge Platonists, and is remembered for his *An Essay towards the Theory of the Ideal or Intelligible World* (1701–4), in which he shows himself a supporter of Malebranche's development of the theories of *Descartes. His poems were edited by A. B. *Grosart, 1871.

NORTH, Christopher, a pseudonym used by John *Wilson (1785–1854).

NORTH, Roger (1653–1734), youngest son of Dudley, fourth Baron North, and great-great nephew of Sir T. *North. Educated at Jesus College, Cambridge, he had a successful career as a lawyer which came to an end with the accession of William of Orange. He is remembered as the author of interesting biographies, published in 1742–4, of three of his brothers, Francis North, Lord Guildford, keeper of the Great Seal; Dudley North, the great Turkey merchant; and John North, master of Trinity College, Cambridge. They are enriched by much affectionate personal detail. His own *Autobiography* was published in 1887. For an account of his posthumously published musical treatises, see under MUSIC, LITERATURE OF.

NORTH, Sir Thomas (?1535–?1601), son of Edward North, first Baron North, perhaps studied at Peterhouse, Cambridge. He entered Lincoln's Inn, was knighted in 1591, and pensioned by *Elizabeth I in 1601. He is famous for his translations, which include the *Diall of Princes* from Guevara's *El Relox de Principes* with *The Famous Booke of Marcus Aurelius*, *The Morall Philosophie of Doni*, from the Italian (1570, see BIDPAI), and *Plutarch's *Lives* from the French of *Amyot (1579), to which he made additions from other authors in 1595 and 1603. His Plutarch, written in a noble and vivid English, formed Shakespeare's chief storehouse of classical history and exerted a powerful influence on Elizabethan prose.

North American Review, The (1815–1939), a Boston quarterly, later monthly, review of the old solid type, and one of the most distinguished of American periodicals. Its editors included C. E. *Norton, J. R. *Lowell, and H. *Adams, and its contributors ranged from *Emerson, W. *Irving, *Parkman, and *Longfellow in its earlier days, to H. *James, *Wells, and *Twain towards the end of the century. It then declined, and was revived again as a quarterly in 1963 by the University of Northern Iowa.

North and South, a novel by Mrs *Gaskell, published serially in *Household Words* 1854–5, in volume form 1855.

This novel is a study of the contrast between the values and habits of rural southern England and industrial northern England. The heroine, Margaret Hale, is the daughter of a parson whose religious doubts force him to resign his Hampshire living and to move with his family to a sooty cotton-spinning northern city. Here, at a moment of conflict between workers and employers, Margaret meets the grim intolerant Mrs Thornton and her son, an able, stubborn manufacturer, whose lack of sympathy for the workers Margaret at first finds unattractive. When she endangers herself to protect him from a mob of strikers he misunderstands her motives and offers marriage, which she refuses. But when he suspects her of an intrigue with another man (in fact her brother, whom she has to shield as he is in danger of arrest), and shows his suspicion, her unhappiness reveals to her that she really loves him. It is not till after a series of deaths and other misfortunes that Margaret and Thornton are finally united. The theme in the title is gradually worked out as Margaret—at first aristocratically repelled by 'trade' and its practitioners—comes to know and respect the ideas and the family life of both mill-hands and mill-owners.

Northanger Abbey, a novel by J. Austen, begun 1798, sold to a publisher 1803, but not published until 1818, when it appeared posthumously with *Persuasion. It is probably the earliest of her completed works.

The purpose of the novel is to ridicule the popular tales of romance and terror, such as Mrs Radcliffe's *Mysteries of Udolpho*, and to contrast with these the normal realities of life. Catherine Morland, the daughter of a well-to-do clergyman, is taken to Bath for the season by her friends, Mr and Mrs Allen. Here she makes the acquaintance of Henry Tilney (son of the eccentric General Tilney) and his pleasant sister, Eleanor. Catherine falls in love with Henry, and has the good fortune to gain his father's approval, which is founded upon the exaggerated report of her parents' wealth given him by the foolish young John Thorpe, brother of Catherine's friend Isabella. Catherine is invited to Northanger Abbey, the medieval seat of the Tilneys. Somewhat unbalanced by a too assiduous reading of Mrs Radcliffe's novels, Catherine imagines a mystery in which General Tilney is criminally involved, and suffers severe mortification when her suspicions are discovered. General Tilney, having now received a second report from John Thorpe as misleading as the first, representing Catherine's parents as extremely humble, packs her off back to her family and forbids Henry to have any further thoughts of her. Henry, disobeying his father, follows Catherine to her home, proposes, and is accepted. General Tilney's consent is obtained at a time when his humour has been greatly improved by the marriage of his daughter Eleanor to a peer, and his discovery of the true financial position of Catherine's family.

Interwoven with the main plot is the flirtation of Captain Tilney, Henry's elder brother, and the vulgar Isabella Thorpe, who is engaged to Catherine's brother; the consequent breaking of the engagement, and the rupture of the friendship between Catherine and Isabella; and Isabella's failure to secure Captain Tilney.

North Briton, The, a weekly political periodical founded in 1762 by *Wilkes, in opposition to The Briton, which *Smollett was conducting in the interests of Lord Bute. In this venture Wilkes was assisted by Charles *Churchill, the author of The Rosciad. The North Briton purports ironically to be edited by a Scotsman, who rejoices in Lord Bute's success and the ousting of the English from power. Wilkes's attacks on the government grew bolder, and in No. 45, in an article on the speech from the throne, he exposed himself to prosecution for libel. Though Wilkes was discharged on the ground of privilege, The North Briton was suppressed. See The North Briton: A Study in Political Propaganda (1939) by G. Nobbe.

NORTHCLIFFE, Viscount, see HARMSWORTH, A. C. W.

Northern Lass, The, a comedy by *Brome, printed 1632.

This is the earliest of Brome's extant plays, and was very popular. Sir Philip Luckless is about to marry the rich city widow Fitchow, when he receives a letter from Constance, the 'northern lass', reminding him of her love for him. Mistaking the writer for another Constance of a less reputable character, he disregards the letter and marries the widow, only to discover his mistake too late. The play is occupied with the devices by which the widow is induced to agree to a divorce, while her foolish brother, whom she tries to marry to Constance, is fobbed

off with an inferior substitute, and Luckless and the true Constance are united.

Northward Hoe, a comedy by *Webster and *Dekker, written 1605, printed 1607.

Greenshield, having failed to seduce Mayberry's wife, but having obtained by force her ring, to avenge himself produces the ring to her husband as evidence of her infidelity. The husband, assisted by the little old poet Bellamont, a genial caricature of *Chapman, becomes convinced of her innocence, and obtains an appropriate revenge on Greenshield and his confederate Featherstone.

The play was a good-humoured retort to the *Eastward Hoe of Chapman, Jonson, and Marston. Like *Westward Hoe it presents a curious picture of the manners of the day.

Norton, The Hon. Mrs, see DIANA OF THE CROSSWAYS.

NORTON, Charles Eliot (1827–1908), born in Cambridge, Massachusetts, and educated at Harvard, where he was professor of fine arts from 1873 to 1898. Although his direct contributions to literature were small, he was an intellectual leader of great influence beyond the confines of the university. His aim was, in his own words, to arouse in his countrymen 'the sense of connection with the past and gratitude for the efforts and labours of other nations and former generations'. He was a frequent contributor to the *Atlantic Monthly, joint editor of the *North American Review (1864–8), and founder and co-editor of The Nation (1865). His many friendships with English writers and artists (including *Clough, Mrs *Gaskell, the *Brownings, *Carlisle, and L. *Stephen) are recorded in his Letters (1913), ed. S. Norton and M. A. D. Howe.

Norval, see DOUGLAS (the tragedy).

NOSTRADAMUS (1503–66), French astrologer and physician, whose enigmatic prophecies, cast in the form of rhymed quatrains grouped in sets of 100 and published under the title Centuries (1556, English trans. 1672), enjoyed widespread popularity during the Renaissance.

Nostromo, a novel by J. *Conrad, published 1904.

In an imaginary South American country, Costaguana, Charles Gould runs a silver mine of national importance in the province of Sulaco. He is married to Emilia, a woman of charm and intelligence, whose arrival has been of great benefit to the local people. In a time of political unrest and revolution the dictator President Ribiera is forced to flee the country and the opposing factions struggle for control. Nostromo ('our man' or 'boatswain') is an Italian sailor, now Capataz de Cargadores, handsome, courageous, strong, and a hero to all. When the silver from the mine is in danger of being seized by the rebel forces, Gould becomes obsessed with the idea of saving it. He enlists the help of Decoud, the cynical, Paris-influenced journalist suitor of Antonia Avellanos (daughter of Don José Avellanos, the 'hereditary friend' of the Gould family), and of an older man, Dr Monygham, who was tortured under the previous régime and is a fond admirer of Emilia, and together they appeal to Nostromo. With great daring Decoud and Nostromo sail off with the treasure. Their silent journey through the night, their collision with an enemy boat, and their eventual arrival at a nearby island where they bury the treasure are vividly described. Decoud is left on guard while Nostromo returns to Sulaco. Alone on the deserted island Decoud loses his mind and, after shooting himself, drowns, his body weighted with silver. Nostromo learns that the woman to whom he has refused the offices of a priest has died, and is filled with a superstitious dread that this offence will threaten the whole venture and his own future. The common assumption is that the silver was lost at sea and the temptation proves too much for Nostromo, who decides to steal it. His old friend Viola, an ex-Garibaldino, is appointed lighthouse keeper on the island and, unwittingly, guard for the silver. Nostromo trifles with Viola's two infatuated daughters, grows rich as he gradually pilfers the silver, and is finally shot when mistaken for an intruder. Mortally wounded, he sends for Emilia, and confesses his crime in the hope of absolution, but dies without revealing the whereabouts of the treasure; as the 'incorruptible' Emilia, appalled by the destruction it has caused and by Nostromo's miserable subjection to his obsession, declares: 'No one misses it now. Let it be lost forever.'

Notebooks, The, a modern edition of the personal notebooks and journals of S. T. *Coleridge, edited by Kathleen Coburn 1956– . So far three volumes, 1794–1819, consisting of separate Text and Notes, have been published: they supersede the *Anima Poetae* edited by E. H. Coleridge in 1895. They consist of Coleridge's sometimes daily comments on his life, travels, writing, and dreams: full of his anxiety and self-consciousness, they throw remarkable light on the raw materials of his thought and art. Biographically, they reveal his struggle with opium, and the tortuous side of his relations with the *Wordsworths and his beloved Sara Hutchinson ('Asra').

Notes and Queries, a periodical founded in 1849 by *Thoms, designed to furnish a means for the interchange of thought and information among those engaged in literature, art, and science, and a medium of communication with

each other. Its motto was (until 1923) Captain Cuttle's 'When found, make a note of' (see DOMBEY AND SON).

Notes of a Journey from Cornhill to Grand Cairo, a travel book by *Thackeray, first published in 1846, which is principally concerned with the author's reactions to the places he visits.

Notre Dame des Amours, a name given by Horace *Walpole to Ninon de *Lenclos.

Nouveau Roman ('New Novel'), a term applied to the work of a wide range of modern French novelists, including Nathalie Sarraute (1902–), Claude Simon (1913–), Marguerite Duras (1914–), Robert Pinget (1919–), Alain Robbe-Grillet (1922–), and *Butor. What distinguishes these novelists is primarily a shared conviction as to the inadequacies of the traditional novel. Thus Robbe-Grillet (*Pour un nouveau roman*, 1963; English trans., *Snapshots, and, Towards a New Novel*, 1965) argues that the traditional novel, with its dependence on an omniscient narrator, creates an illusion of order and significance which is denied by the reality of experience. The task of the new novel is therefore to foster change by dispensing with any technique which imposes a particular interpretation on events, or which organizes events in such a way as to endow them with a collective significance.

Nouvelle Héloïse, La, see ROUSSEAU.

Nouvelle Revue Française, La, a monthly review of literature, drama, and the other arts, founded in 1909 by a group that included *Gide, the novelist Jean Schlumberger, and the actor and theatre director Jacques Copeau. A publishing enterprise associated with the review, the 'maison d'éditions de la nrf', was started soon afterwards. The *NRF* published a number of little-known writers later to bacome famous, including *Valéry, *Giraudoux, *Claudel, *Montherlant, and *Mauriac, and made efforts to introduce German, Russian, and English authors to French readers. Valéry Larbaud's celebrated lecture on Joyce's *Ulysses*, delivered in Adrienne Monnier's bookshop, La Maison des Amis des Livres, on 7 Dec. 1921, appeared in the *NRF* in April 1922. Publication was interrupted during the First World War and ceased in 1943, to recommence in 1953 as *La Nouvelle Nouvelle Revue Française*. In 1959 the original title was re-adopted, under which it continues to appear.

NOVALIS, pseudonym of *Hardenberg.

Nova Solyma, *the ideal city; or Jerusalem Regained*: an anonymous Latin romance written in the time of Charles I, probably by Samuel Gott. It contains a notable scheme of education.

Novel, rise of the. The word 'novellae' was

employed in the 16th cent. to describe the short tales of the *Decameron and the *Heptameron, and others like them. Used in a recognizably modern sense, the word 'novel' appears in England in the mid-17th cent., when it was chiefly associated with romances of illicit love. For this reason the word 'history' was more often favoured to describe the long prose fictions of the 18th cent. which were the precursors of the modern novel. The novel form developed slowly, through the memoir-novel and the epistolary novel of the 16th and 17th cents to the novel of the omniscient third-person narrator, which has dominated from the late 18th cent. to the present time. The chief novelists of the 18th cent. (*Defoe, *Richardson, *Fielding, *Smollett, and *Sterne) so greatly and rapidly developed the form that by the early 19th cent. J. *Austen could write (albeit with a hint of irony) in *Northanger Abbey, that in the novel 'the greatest powers of the mind are displayed'. Form, style, and subject matter varied considerably, but by 1824 Sir W. *Scott could confidently define the novel as 'a fictitious narrative . . . accommodated to the ordinary train of human events', a definition which may be allowed to stand today. (See also EPISTOLARY NOVEL; FASHIONABLE NOVEL; HISTORICAL NOVEL; MEMOIR-NOVEL; ORIENTAL NOVEL; SENTIMENT, NOVEL OF.)

Novum Organum, a philosophical treatise in Latin by F. *Bacon, published 1620. It consists of two books: the first is a carefully constructed series of highly polished aphorisms; the second, though nominally in aphoristic form, is much more loosely organized, and is evidently merely a fragment of a much larger treatise. The title *Novum Organum* means literally 'new instrument', *organon* being the Greek word which had become used as the name for Aristotle's treatise on logic and the theory of science.

Bacon's ambition was to extend to the utmost the dominion of man over nature. The *Novum Organum* was written to outline the method by which the new science was to be discovered. The purpose of the first book was both to destroy men's confidence in the methods of enquiry which had hitherto been used, and at the same time to encourage the hope that some better procedure lay ready to be discovered and put to use. The received view of science was that it proceeded by syllogistic deduction, but syllogisms cannot bring certainty when the words of which they are composed are the marks of confused and hastily abstracted concepts. The remedy is to employ induction and to rise by a gradual ascent to axioms of successively greater generality. First, however, the mind must be cleansed as far as possible from its intellectual defects. Under the name of 'Idols of the Mind' Bacon distinguished four distinct types of inducement to error: (1) 'Idols of the Tribe'

(*Idola tribus*), which have their origin in human nature, and are common to all men; (2) 'Idols of the Cave' (*Idola specus*), which arise from the peculiar constitution and circumstances of each individual; (3) 'Idols of the Market Place' (*Idola fori*), which result from the association of men together and their need to communicate by the treacherous medium of language; (4) 'Idols of the Theatre' (*Idola theatri*), which arise from the hold on men's minds of false philosophical systems, these systems being in Bacon's view like so many stage plays, representing imaginary worlds of their own manufacture.

The second book contains an exposition of Bacon's new method and an illustration of its use in practice in an investigation of the nature (in Bacon's words the 'form') of heat. The procedure is to prepare a natural and experimental history of the phenomenon, and then to draw up three tables, or lists: (1) of instances when the phenomenon under investigation is present; (2) of instances as similar as possible to those in the first list where the phenomenon is absent; and (3) of instances where the phenomenon is observed to increase or decrease in intensity, or vary in some other way. From these tables, in a manner never made adequately clear, the nature of the phenomenon is discovered by a procedure of eliminative induction.

Now and Then, a house periodical published from 1921 till 1944 by Jonathan Cape, the publishing company, which contained poems, essays, and reviews by W. H. *Davies, *Auden, *Spender, D. H. *Lawrence, H. *Read, and many others. A selection taken from its first 50 issues was published in 1935 as *Then and Now*.

NOYES, Alfred (1880–1959), poet, playwright, novelist, and anthologist, who held violently anti-*Modernist views on literature; his own collections of verse (many of them about seafaring) include *Drake* (1908), an epic, and *Tales of the Mermaid Tavern* (1913). His anecdotal autobiography, *Two Worlds for Memory*, appeared in 1953.

Nubbles, Mrs and Kit, characters in Dickens's *The Old Curiosity Shop*.

Number of the Beast, see BEAST.

'Nun's Priest's Tale, The', see CANTERBURY TALES, 20.

Nupkins, Mr, a character in Dickens's *Pickwick Papers*.

Nurse, the loquacious and humorous attendant of *Juliet in Shakespeare's *Romeo and Juliet*. She acts as a go-between for the lovers. Her name may have been Angelica (IV. iv. 5).

'Nut-Brown Maid, The', a 15th-cent. poem in praise of woman's fidelity. The lover, to prove the Maid, tells her that he must to the greenwood go, 'alone, a banyshed man' and live the life of an outlaw. She declares her intention of accompanying him, nor can be dissuaded by the prospect of hardships and humiliations. The lover finally reveals his deceit and that he is an earl's son 'and not a banyshed man'. The poem is included in Percy's *Reliques*. It is the foundation of *Prior's 'Henry and Emma'.

NUTTALL, Jeff, see UNDERGROUND POETRY.

Nym, Corporal, appears in Shakespeare's *Merry Wives of Windsor* and *Henry V* as a follower of *Falstaff, a rogue and thief, obsessed with 'Humours'. To 'nim' was slang for to steal.

Nymphidia, see NIMPHIDIA.

Nymphs, see PARACELSUS.

NYREN, John (1764–1837), a famous early cricketer and cricket chronicler. He belonged to the *Hambledon Club, and was a left-handed batsman of average ability and a fine field at point and mid-wicket. His recollections were published in *The Young Cricketer's Tutor* (1833, edited by C. C. *Clarke), which includes some history of the game, reminiscences of great games and 'cricketers I have known', advice on tactics, etc.

O

Oak, Gabriel, a character in Hardy's *Far from the Madding Crowd.*

OATES, Joyce Carol (1938–), American novelist and short story writer, educated at the universities of Syracuse and Wisconsin, and for some years professor of English literature at Detroit, a city which provides the setting for much of her work. Her novels, many of which portray extremes of human passion and violence, are predominantly naturalistic, with suggestions of the neo-*Gothic; they include *A Garden of Earthly Delights* (1967), *them* (1969), *Wonderland* (1971), and *A Bloodsmoor Romance* (1982). She has also published many collections of short stories, and with her husband Raymond J. Smith edits the *Ontario Review* (1974–).

OATES, Titus (1649–1705), the fabricator of the *Popish Plot (1678), is the 'Corah' of Dryden's *Absalom and Achitophel.*

Obadiah, the manservant of the Shandy family in Sterne's *Tristram Shandy.*

Oberammergau, a village in Upper Bavaria, noted for the performances there, every tenth year, of a Passion Play. These performances are said to have had their origin in a vow taken by the villagers in 1633 in order to stay an epidemic of the plague. The text of the play was probably written by the monks of the neighbouring monastery of Ettal.

Obermann, see SENANCOUR.

Oberon, in Shakespeare's *A Midsummer Night's Dream, the king of the fairies and husband of *Titania. He also appears in R. Greene's play *James the Fourth* and is the eponymous hero of *Weber's opera.

Objective correlative, a term used by T. S. *Eliot in his essay 'Hamlet and his Problems' (1919; included in *The Sacred Wood*, 1920). Eliot ascribes the alleged 'artistic failure' of the play *Hamlet* to the fact that Hamlet himself is 'dominated by an emotion which is inexpressible, because it is in *excess* of the facts as they appear ... The only way of expressing emotion in the form of art is by finding an "objective correlative"; in other words, a set of objects, a situation, a chain of events which shall be the formula of that *particular* emotion.' This phrase, like *'dissociation of sensibility', became very fashionable, and was doubtless one of those to which Eliot referred in a lecture in 1956

('The Frontiers of Criticism') when he spoke of 'a few notorious phrases which have had a truly embarrassing success in the world'.

O'Brallaghan, Sir Callaghan, a character in *Love à la Mode by Macklin.

O'BRIEN, Edna (1932–), Irish novelist and short story writer, born in the west of Ireland. Her first novel *The Country Girls* (1960) describes the girlhood of Caithleen Brady (Kate) and Bridget Brennan (Baba), who escape from their country homes and convent education to the addictive 'crowds and lights and noise' of Dublin. They continue their search for experience through *The Lonely Girl* (1962, in which Kate falls in love with film director Eugene Gaillard) and *Girls in their Married Bliss* (1963, in which both have moved to London). Her subsequent novels include *August is a Wicked Month* (1964), *A Pagan Place* (1971, an evocation of rural Ireland), *Night* (1972, the sombre, impassioned, night-time monologue of middle-aged Mary Hooligan), and *Johnny I hardly knew you* (1977, a tale of *crime passionel*). Her themes are female sensuality, male treachery, Irish nostalgia, and celebration of the intermittent 'good times' which even her much abused and self-abusing heroines enjoy, and her lyrical descriptive powers and lack of inhibition have led to comparisons with *Colette.

O'BRIEN, Flann, pseudonym of Brian O'Nolan or O Nuallain (1911–66), born at Strabane, Co. Tyrone, and educated at University College, Dublin. He worked for the Irish Civil Service until his retirement through ill health in 1953, and also for many years contributed a satiric weekly column under the name 'Myles na Gopaleen' to the *Irish Times*. His first novel, *At Swim-Two-Birds* (1939), is an exuberant work, operating on several levels of invention: the narrator, a young Dublin student living with his uncle, offers variants of reality which include a naturalistic portrayal of student and lower-middle-class life; a 'novel-within-a-novel' written by 'eccentric author Dermot Trellis' which deals with the legendary Irish hero *Finn Mac Cool; and a layer of Irish folklore rendered in terms of farce, featuring the Pooka, the Good Fairy, etc. The effect is a multi-dimensional exploration of Irish culture and of the nature of fiction, much influenced by *Joyce. O'Brien's second novel, *An Béal Bocht* (1941), was written in Gaelic, translated into

English in 1973 as *The Poor Mouth*. The best-known of his other works is *The Third Policeman* (written 1940, published 1967) which *Wain (*Encounter*, 1967) found 'tense, grim and threatening', closer in tone to *Beckett than his 'hilarious, elegiac, sarcastic, relaxed and genial' first novel.

Obscurorum Virorum, *Epistolae*, see EPISTOLAE OBSCURORUM VIRORUM.

Observations on the Present State of the Nation, see PRESENT STATE OF THE NATION.

Observator, The, see L'ESTRANGE, R.

Observer, The, a Sunday paper founded in 1791 by W. S. Bourne, and now Britain's oldest national Sunday paper. In 1814 it passed into the control of William Innell Clement (1770–1852), a powerful newspaper proprietor, under whose charge it flourished, partly through its pioneering use of woodcut illustrations to report sensational incidents (e.g. notably, the Cato Street conspiracy in 1820). It declined after Clement's death, reviving in the last decades of the century with Julius Beer (1837–80) as proprietor and Edward Dicey (1832–1911) as editor. It was bought by *Harmsworth in 1905, and edited from 1905 to 1908 by Austin Harrison (1873–1928), then from 1908 to 1942 by James Louis Garvin (1868–1947), who impressed his own personality and professional judgement deeply on the paper during his lengthy period as editor. The paper was bought in 1911 by William Waldorf Astor (1848–1919), and edited from 1948 to 1975 by David Astor (1912–   ). In 1977 control of the paper passed to a multi-national oil company, Atlantic Richfield.

O'CASEY, Sean (John Casey) (1880–1964), Irish playwright, born in Dublin of Protestant parents, was educated, according to his own autobiographies, in the streets of Dublin. He worked from the age of 14 at a variety of jobs, spending nine years from 1903 as a labourer on the Great Northern Railway of Ireland, meanwhile learning Irish, joining the Gaelic League and the Irish Republican League, and developing an enthusiasm for the theatre through amateur dramatics and the plays of *Boucicault. He began to publish articles, songs, and broadsheets under the name of Sean O Cathasaigh; his first plays were rejected by the *Abbey Theatre, but he received encouragement from Lady *Gregory and Lennox *Robinson, and *The Shadow of a Gunman* was performed in 1923, followed by *Juno and the Paycock* in 1924; they were published together as *Two Plays* (1925). *The Plough and the Stars* provoked nationalist riots at the Abbey in 1926. All three plays deal realistically with the rhetoric and dangers of Irish patriotism, with tenement life, self-deception, and survival; they are tragi-comedies in which

violent death throws into relief the blustering masculine bravado of e.g. Jack Boyle and Joxer Daly in *Juno*, and the heroic resilience of Juno herself, or of Bessie Burgess in *The Plough*. O'Casey moved to England in 1926, and settled there permanently; his alienation from Ireland was confirmed by a rift with *Yeats and the Abbey over its rejection of *The Silver Tassie* (1928), an experimental anti-war play about an injured footballer, which introduced the symbolic *Expressionist techniques employed in his later works. These include *Within the Gates* (1933), *Red Roses for Me* (1942), *Cock-a-Doodle Dandy* (1949), and *The Bishop's Bonfire* (1955); although none achieved the popularity of his 'Abbey' plays, O'Casey continued to arouse both controversy and admiration, on stage and off. He also published a much-praised series of autobiographies, in six volumes, beginning with *I Knock at the Door* (1939) and ending with *Sunset and Evening Star* (1954). See David Krause, *Sean O'Casey: The Man and his Work* (1960); Eileen O'Casey, *Sean* (1971); and his *Letters* (ed. D. Krause; Vol. I, 1975–   ).

OCCAM, and **Occam's Razor,** see OCKHAM.

OCCLEVE, see HOCCLEVE.

Oceana, see COMMONWEALTH OF OCEANA, THE.

Ochiltree, Edie, a character in Scott's *The Antiquary*.

OCKHAM, William of (*c.*1300–49), born at Ockham in Surrey, he joined the Franciscans and studied at Oxford where he wrote a Commentary on the *Sentences* of *Peter Lombard, Book 1. In 1324 he was summoned by the pope to Avignon to answer charges of unorthodoxy, and several of his writings were condemned in 1326. In 1328 he fled from Avignon along with the Franciscan General, Michael of Cesena, having taken the side of the Spiritual Franciscans in their dispute with Pope John XXII. Thereafter he remained with the emperor, Louis of Bavaria, concerned with the question of papal power until his death (possibly of the plague) in 1349 or 1350. His importance is as a theologian with a strongly developed interest in logical method, and whose approach (characteristic of his century, perhaps) was critical rather than system-building. He is usually said to have been the most important figure in the breakdown of the Thomist synthesis between Aristotelian philosophy and Christian theology, though he always shied away from the radicalism of this division. The logical axiom associated with him is Ockham's 'Razor', that 'entities (*entia*) must not be unnecessarily multiplied', an attack on the postulation of Universals by the *Realists. The logical precision of his theory of language has been much admired (and, to some extent, copied) by 20th-cent. theoretical linguists and linguistic philosophers. His importance for literature in the century of *Langland lies in his stress on the Augustinian/Franciscan pre-eminence of Faith and the relative relegation of philosophical 'Reason', founded on Aristotle. See P. Boehner ed., *Ockham: Philosophical Writings; a Selection* (1957); G. Leff, *William of Ockham* (1975).

O'CONNOR, Flannery (1925–64), American novelist and short story writer, born in Georgia, whose works may be described as examples of Southern *Gothic. *Wise Blood* (1952) is a novel about a violent young religious extremist and *The Violent Bear It Away* (1960) also deals with fanaticism, as do many of her short stories, collected as *The Complete Stories* (1971). E. *Bishop described her work as 'clear, hard, vivid, and full of . . . more real poetry than a dozen books of poems'.

O'CONNOR, Frank, pseudonym of Michael Francis O'Donovan (1903–66), born in Cork, the son of a soldier; his work includes two novels, a life of Michael Collins (1937), trans-lations from the Irish, literary criticism, and dramatizations, but he is best known for his short stories, many of them much revised and re-written. Collections include *Bones of Contention* (1936), *Crab Apple Jelly* (1944), *Traveller's Samples* (1951), and *Domestic Relations* (1957). Realistic and closely observed, they offer a full portrait of the middle and lower classes of Ire-land, and of the 'warm dim odorous feckless evasive southern quality' of his native Cork, which as a young man he had shocked by his productions of plays by *Ibsen and *Chekhov, and by his support of *Joyce (whose art, how-ever, he was later to conclude, was too removed from life). He also wrote two volumes of auto-biography, *An Only Child* (1961) and *My Father's Son* (1969), and his critical works in-clude *The Lonely Voice: A Study of the Short Story* (1962).

O'CONNOR, Thomas Power (1848–1929), journalist and politician, supporter of *Parnell. His first book, *Lord Beaconsfield* (1879, first appeared in serial form anonymously, 1876) attracted much attention for its unsparing attack on *Disraeli. He was founder of the *Star* (1887), the *Sun* (1893), and *T.P.'s Weekly* (1902–16), a penny literary paper of some merit.

Octavia, the sister of Octavian (Augustus) and Mark Antony's wife, figures in Shakespeare's *Antony and Cleopatra* and Dryden's *All for Love*.

October Club, The, a club of Tory MPs of Queen Anne's time, who met at the Bell (afterwards the Crown) in King Street, West-minster, to drink October ale, 'consult affairs and drive things on to extremes against the Whigs' (*Swift, letter of 10 Feb. 1710/11).

Octosyllabics, consisting of eight syllables, usually applied to the eight-syllabled rhyming iambic metre of, e.g. Milton's *'Il Penseroso'.

Odd Women, The, see GISSING, G.

Ode, in ancient literature, a poem intended or adapted to be sung; in modern use, a rhymed (rarely unrhymed) lyric, often in the form of an address, generally dignified or exalted in subject, feeling, and style, but sometimes (in earlier use) simple and familiar (though less so than a song) [*OED*].

'Ode on a Grecian Urn', a poem by *Keats, written 1819, published 1820.

While he describes the various pastoral scenes of love, beauty, and joy illustrated on the urn, the poet reflects on the eternal quality of art and the fleeting nature of human love and happiness. The last two lines are particularly well known and their meaning much debated:

> 'Beauty is truth, truth beauty,' — that is all
> Ye know on earth, and all ye need to know.

'Ode to a Nightingale', a poem by *Keats, written 1819, published 1820.

Keats's friend Charles Brown relates that a nightingale had nested near his house in Hamp-stead (now known as Keats House), and that one morning Keats sat under a plum-tree in the garden composing his Ode on 'some scraps of paper'. Briefly, the poem is a meditation on the immortal beauty of the nightingale's song and the sadness of the observer, who must in the end accept sorrow and mortality.

'Ode to Autumn', see TO AUTUMN.

'Ode to the West Wind', a poem by P. B. *Shelley, 'chiefly written in a wood that skirts the Arno, near Florence' in Oct. 1819, published 1820.

The Ode is a passionate invocation to the spirit of the West Wind, both 'Destroyer and Pre-server'. It is composed in five sweeping stanzaic movements, each taking the form of a sonnet, but with complex musical patterns of internal rhyme and run-on lines, culminating in a breath-less series of cries or questions. The symbolism is rich. The Wind is the seasonal force of renewal in Nature; it is also the power that produces self-sacrifice (even self-destruction) in personal life; the 'unextinguished' political hopes that drive continually over the 'unawakened Earth'; and the very passion of the ideal—aspiration, creativity—itself. Shelley's minute observations of wind, water, wood, cloud, and sky, combine imagery which is simultaneously scientific, mythical, and even biblical. The total effect is one of transcendent hope and energy, achieved through suffering and despair.

ODETS, Clifford (1906–63), American dramatist, born in Philadelphia. He was a foun-der member in 1931 of the Group Theatre, which followed the naturalistic methods of the Moscow Art Theatre, and his reputation was made when it performed his short play *Waiting for Lefty* (1935), about a taxi-drivers' strike. This was followed in the same year by two other dramas of social conflict, *Till the Day I Die*, about the German Communists and the rise of the Nazis, and *Awake and Sing!*, portraying struggle and tragedy in a poor Jewish family in the Bronx. Later works include *Clash by Night* (1941), *The Big Knife* (1948, an attack on the corruptions of Hollywood), and *The Country Girl* (1950, first known in Britain as *Winter Journey*) about an alcoholic actor's marriage.

O'Dowd, Major and Mrs, characters in Thackeray's *Vanity Fair*.

Odyssey, The, a Greek epic poem attributed to *Homer describing the adventures of Odysseus in the course of his return from the Trojan War to his kingdom of Ithaca.

OED, see OXFORD ENGLISH DICTIONARY, THE.

Oedipus, see SOPHOCLES.

OEXMELIN, see ESQUEMELING.

O'FAOLAIN, Sean (1900–), Irish novelist and short story writer, born in Cork, the son of a police constable. He was educated at the National University of Ireland, was a member of the Irish Republican Army during the Troubles, studied at Harvard for three years from 1926, then taught at Strawberry Hill Training College before returning to Ireland in 1933, where, with the encouragement of E. *Garnett, and a subsidy from Jonathan Cape, he settled as a writer, having already published his first collection, *Midsummer Night Madness and other stories* (1932). This was followed by other collections, by three novels (*A Nest of Simple Folk*, 1934; *Bird Alone*, 1936; and *Come back to Erin*, 1940; all of which deal with the frustrations of Irish society and the doomed aspirations of Irish nationalists), biographies of Constance Markiewicz (1934), Daniel O'Connell (1938), De Valera (1939), and Hugh O'Neill (1942), and a study of the Irish people, *The Irish* (1947). His autobiography *Vive-moi!* was published in 1964, and his *Collected Stories* in 1981. He is best known for his short stories, many of which evoke frustrated lives, missed opportunities, characters limited by their environment (as he had felt himself to be by provincial Cork), and which clearly demonstrate O'Faolain's allegiance to *Chekhov; later stories (*The Heat of the Sun; stories and tales*, 1966; *The Talking Trees*, 1971) tend to be dryer, more amusing, and more resilient in tone.

Of Dramatick Poesy: *an Essay* by *Dryden, published 1668.
The essay is in the form of a dialogue between Eugenius (C. *Sackville), Crites (Sir Robert Howard), Lisideius (*Sedley), and Neander (Dryden himself), who take a boat on the Thames on the day of the battle between the English and Dutch navies in June 1665, and subsequently discuss the comparative merits of English and French drama, and of the old and new in English drama. The essay is largely concerned with justifying Dryden's current practice as a playwright. It also contains admirable appreciations of Shakespeare, J. *Fletcher, and *Jonson.

O'FLAHERTY, Liam (1897–1984), Irish nationalist, novelist, and short story writer, was born in the Aran Islands. His first novel, *The Neighbour's Wife* (1923), was published with the encouragement of E. *Garnett, and followed by several others, notably *The Informer* (1925), *The Puritan* (1931), and *Famine* (1937). But he is best known for his short stories, published in many periodicals and several volumes including *Spring Sowing* (1924), *The Tent* (1926), *Two Lovely Beasts* (1948), etc. Characteristic stories are those which deal unsentimentally with life, or more often death, from an animal's point of view, e.g. 'The Cow's Death' (1923), 'The Wounded Cormorant' (1925), and 'The Seal' (1948). O'Flaherty published three volumes of flamboyant and inventive memoirs of his restless life: *Two Years* (1930), *I Went to Russia* (1931), and *Shame the Devil* (1934). He was described by *O'Faolain as 'an inverted romantic'. A life by P. A. Doyle was published in 1971.

Of Mice and Men, a novel by J. *Steinbeck.

Og, Dryden's name for *Shadwell in *The Second Part of *Absalom and Achitophel*.

Ogham, or **Ogam,** an alphabet of twenty characters used by the ancient British and Irish, consisting of conjunctions of upright and sloping strokes, and dots. It is found in inscriptions on stone and wood.

Ogier the Dane, a hero of the *Charlemagne romances, identified with a Frankish warrior, Autgarius, who fought against Charlemagne and then submitted to him. According to the romances, he is hostage for his father Gaufrey of Dannemarch at Charlemagne's court, and there are a number of legends about him, some of them including him as one of the *Paladins. It is doubtful if he had anything to do with Denmark; 'Dannemarch' perhaps signifies the marches of the Ardennes. Nevertheless, as Holger Danske he became the subject of Danish folk-song, identified as a national hero who fought with the Ostrogoth *Dietrich of Bern (c.500).

OGILBY, John (1600–76), Scottish author, topographer, and printer, published verse translations of *Virgil, *Aesop, and *Homer; also maps, atlases, and *Road Books of England and*

Wales, the last of which were constantly revised until they faded into Mogg's *Road Books*.

O'HARA, John (Henry) (1905–70), American writer, born in Pennsylvania, the son of a doctor. More than 200 of his sharp, satiric short stories were published in the **New Yorker*, and contributed to its characteristic tone; they were later collected under many different titles, from *The Doctor's Son* (1935) onwards. His novels, which gained wide popularity with their toughness, frankness, and sophistication, include *Appointment in Samarra* (1934), set in the country club and cocktail belt; *BUtterfield 8* (1935), which evokes the promiscuity, violence, and hard drinking of Manhattan under prohibition; *Pal Joey* (1940; later a musical), told in the form of letters from a nightclub singer; *A Rage to Live* (1949), presenting the torments of a faithless wife; and many others, of generally decreasing interest and increasing prolixity.

O. HENRY, see HENRY, O.

Oisin, a legendary Gaelic warrior and bard, known also as Ossian (see MACPHERSON and FINGAL). In *The Wanderings of Oisin* (1889), a narrative poem by *Yeats, the bard tells Saint Patrick the story of his love for *Niamh, the daughter of the sea-god Manannán.

O'KEEFFE, John (1747–1833), Irish actor and dramatist, wrote his first play at the age of fifteen. He produced his *Tony Lumpkin in Town* in 1778, after which he wrote some 50 farces and musical pieces. Of these the best known are *The Castle of Andalusia* (1782); *The Poor Soldier* (1783), which had great success in America; and *Wild Oats*, a romp of much skill and wit, produced at Covent Garden in 1791, and successfully revived in London in the late 1970s. O'Keeffe was the author of the song 'I am a friar of orders grey' (from his opera *Merry Sherwood*). *Hazlitt described him as 'the English Molière', but the compliment seems excessive.

OLCOTT, Colonel H. S., see THEOSOPHY.

Old Bachelor, The, the first comedy of *Congreve, produced 1693.

The 'Old Bachelor' is Heartwell, a 'surly old pretended woman-hater', who falls in love with Silvia, not knowing her to be the forsaken mistress of Vainlove, and is inveigled into marrying her, only discovering her true character afterwards from the gibes of his acquaintances. The parson who has been brought in to marry them, however, is in fact Vainlove's friend Bellmour, who has assumed the disguise for the purpose of an intrigue with Laetitia, the young wife of an uxorious old banker, Fondlewife; and Heartwell is relieved to find the marriage is only a pretence. The comedy includes the amusing characters of Sir Joseph Wittol, a foolish knight, who allows himself to be really married to Silvia, under the impression that she is the wealthy Araminta; and his companion, the cowardly bully Captain Bluffe, who under the same delusion is married to Silvia's maid. Bellmour in the end marries Belinda, whom he has been courting, in spite of her affectations, but Vainlove, who loves women only as long as they refuse him, finds that Araminta will not yet agree to marry him.

Oldbuck, Jonathan, Laird of Monkbarns, the principal character in Scott's **The Antiquary*. Miss Griselda ('Grizzy') Oldbuck is his sister.

Oldcastle, The First Part of Sir John, a play published in 1619 as Shakespeare's, and included in the Third and Fourth Folios of his plays. It is certainly not by him, though the historical John Oldcastle seems to have been Shakespeare's original model for *Falstaff.

The play deals with the proceedings in Henry V's reign against Oldcastle as the chief supporter of the Lollards. Its true authorship is unknown.

Old Curiosity Shop, The, a novel by *Dickens, published as a separate volume in 1841. It was originally intended to be fitted into the framework of **Master Humphrey's Clock* (1840–1), and Master Humphrey is, in fact, the narrator of the first few chapters, but this idea was soon abandoned.

Little Nell Trent lives in the gloomy atmosphere of the old curiosity shop kept by her grandfather, whom she tends with devotion. Reduced to poverty by a spendthrift son-in-law, and his remaining means drained by Nell's profligate brother Fred, he has borrowed money from Daniel Quilp, a hideous dwarf and a monster of iniquity, and this money he secretly expends in gambling, in the vain hope of retrieving his fortunes, for Little Nell's sake. Quilp, who believes him a rich miser, at last discovers where the borrowed money has gone, and seizes the shop. The old man and the child flee and wander about the country, suffering great hardships and haunted by the fear of being discovered by Quilp, who pursues them with unremitting hatred. They at last find a haven in a cottage by a country church, which they are appointed to look after. The grandfather's brother, returning from abroad, and anxious to relieve their needs, has great difficulty in tracing them. At last he finds them, but Nell, worn out with her troubles, has just died, and the grandfather soon follows her.

The novel contains a number of well known characters. Besides the loathsome and grotesque Quilp (who is drowned when on the point of being arrested for felony), there are his associates, the attorney Sampson Brass and his grim sister Sally; the honest lad Kit Nubbles, devoted to Little Nell, who incurs the hatred of Quilp and is nearly transported through his machinations; Mr and Mrs Garland, the kindly old couple who befriend Kit; Dick Swiveller, the disreputable facetious friend of Fred Trent, placed by Quilp for his own purposes as clerk to Brass; 'the Marchioness', the half-starved drudge in the Brass household (she marries Dick in the end); Codlin and Short, the Punch and Judy men, whom Little Nell and her grandfather accompany for a time in their wanderings; and Mrs Jarley, of the waxworks.

The death of Little Nell, in its day one of the most celebrated scenes in fiction, later became the focus of much of the reaction against Dickens's use of pathos. See G. H. Ford, *Dickens and his Readers* (1955), ch. iv.

Old English, see ENGLISH.

Old English Baron, The, see REEVE, C.

OLDFIELD, Anne (1683–1730), an actress who excelled in both tragedy and comedy. She first made her mark as Lady Betty Modish in Cibber's *The Careless Husband*, but her best parts are said to have been Calista (in Rowe's *The Fair Penitent*), and Lady Townly (in Cibber's *The Provok'd Husband*). She was buried in Westminster Abbey, beneath *Congreve's monument. She is the 'Narcissa' of Pope's *Moral Essays*.

Old Fortunatus, a comedy by *Dekker, published 1600, based on a story contained in a German 'Volksbuch' of 1509 and dramatized by *Sachs in 1553.

The beggar Fortunatus, encountering Fortune, is offered the choice between wisdom, strength, health, beauty, long life, and riches, and chooses the last. He receives a purse from which he can at any time draw ten pieces of gold. He goes on his travels, in the course of which he secures the marvellous hat of the Soldan of Turkey, which transports the wearer wherever he wishes to go. But at the height of his success Fortune steps in and puts an end to his life. His son Andelocia, refusing to take warning by his father's fate and equipped with the purse and hat, goes through a series of adventures at the court of Athelstane, is finally deprived of his talismans, and meets a miserable death.

The character of Orléans, the 'frantic lover' of Athelstane's daughter, was much praised by C. *Lamb.

OLDHAM, John (1653–83), educated at St Edmund Hall, Oxford, published several Pindaric odes, but is chiefly remembered for his ironical *Satire against Virtue* (1679) and *Satires upon the Jesuits* (1681). He also translated and wrote imitations of *Juvenal, *Horace, *Bion, *Moschus, and *Boileau. His *Poems and Translations* were collected in 1683. He died young of smallpox, and *Dryden commemorated him and his verse in the well known lines beginning 'Farewell, too little and too lately known'.

Old Man and the Sea, The, a parable-novella by E. *Hemingway.

Old Men at the Zoo, The, a novel by Angus *Wilson.

OLDMIXON, John (?1673–1742), Whig historian and pamphleteer, who also wrote plays, poems, and pastorals. He published *The British Empire in America* (1708), *The Secret History of Europe* (1712–15, anonymously), and histories of England during the Stuart reigns (1729) and those of William III, Anne, and George I (1735–9). By his 'Essay on Criticism', prefixed to the third edition (1728) of his *Critical History of England* (1724–6) he incurred the hostility of *Pope, who pilloried him in *The Dunciad and *Peri Bathous*.

OLD MOORE, Francis Moore (1657–1714), astrologer, licensed physician, and Whig partisan, who had an astrological practice in Lambeth, later in Southwark. His *Vox Stellarum, an Almanac for 1701 with astrological observations* appeared in 1700. *Old Moore's Almanac* long outlived its creator, and sold extremely well throughout the 18th and 19th cents, and it still thrives thanks to its reputation for sensationalism and prophecy; its print-order in 1975 ran to one and three quarter millions. (See also ALMANACS.)

Old Mortality, a novel by Sir W. *Scott, published in 1816 in *Tales of my Landlord*, 1st series.

The title is taken from the nickname of a certain Robert Paterson, who towards the end of the 18th cent. wandered about Scotland cleaning and repairing the tombs of the Cameronians, a sect of strict Covenanters who took up arms for their religious opinions in the reign of Charles II. The story is supposed to be based on the anecdotes told by this supporter of their cause, and covers the period from the military operations undertaken against them in 1679, under the command of John Grahame of Claverhouse, to the more peaceful days of religious toleration introduced by William III. It is particularly concerned with the fortunes of Henry Morton of Milnwood, a young man of courage and high character and a moderate Presbyterian, who, at the outset of the tale, is arrested by the dragoons of Claverhouse for having harboured an old friend of his father, the fanatical Covenanter, John Balfour of Burley, not knowing that this man had just taken part in the assassination of the archbishop of St Andrews. Morton narrowly escapes immediate execution, and this act of oppression, coupled with a sense of his countrymen's sufferings, induces him to throw in his lot with the Covenanters, who have taken up arms for the cause of religious freedom, little as he shares their extreme religious opinions. He accordingly becomes one of their leaders. This brings him into violent antagonism with Lady Margaret Bellenden, the Royalist owner of Tillietudlem Castle, with whose granddaughter Edith he is in love. Her intervention with Lord Evandale, one of Claverhouse's officers and Morton's rival for her hand, saves Morton's life when he is first brought before Claverhouse. This act of generosity on Evandale's part is repaid by Morton at the skirmish of Drumclog, and again when the rebel forces under Burley have almost reduced Tillietudlem to surrender and have captured Evandale himself. Morton thus retains his place in Edith's heart. But the final defeat of the Covenanters at Bothwell Bridge, and his own capture and banishment, sever him for years from Edith, who believes him dead; and she is on the point of yielding to the patient suit of Evandale, when Morton, after the accession of William III, returns to England, and his arrival puts an end to the preparations for Edith's marriage. Evandale, in spite of Morton's efforts to save him, is killed in a skirmish with a few fanatics, and Morton marries Edith. The story includes an interesting study of the character of Claverhouse and a vivid picture of the follies to which religious enthusiasm carried the Covenanters.

Old Possum's Book of Practical Cats, a volume of verse for children, by T. S. *Eliot.

Old Q, the nickname of William Douglas, third earl of March and fourth duke of Queensberry (1724–1810), a friend of the prince of Wales, notorious for his escapades and dissolute life, much interested in horse-racing. He was satirized by *Burns, and is the 'degenerate Douglas' of *Wordsworth's sonnet.

Old Uncle Tom Cobbleigh, and all, see WIDDICOMBE FAIR.

Old Vic Theatre (previously the Royal Victoria), a theatre in the Waterloo Road, London, famous for its notable productions of Shakespeare's plays under the management of Lilian Baylis (1874–1937), who took it over in 1912.

Old Wives' Tale, The, a play in prose by *Peele, published 1595.

The play is a satire on the romantic dramas of the time, the first English work of this kind. Two brothers are searching for their sister Delia, who is held captive by the magician Sacrapant. The brothers also fall into his hands. They are all rescued by the knight Eumenides aided by Jack's ghost, who is impelled by motives of gratitude, because the knight had borne the expense of Jack's funeral. The play is rich in songs and magical invocations such as: 'Gently dippe, but not too deepe, | For feare thou make the goulden beard to weep.'

Old Wives' Tale, The, a novel by Arnold *Bennett, published 1908.

It is the long chronicle of the lives of two sisters, Constance and Sophia Baines, daughters of a draper of Bursley (Burslem, one of the *Five Towns) from their ardent girlhood, through disillusionment, to death. The drab life of the draper's shop, its trivial incidents, are made interesting and important. Constance, a staid and sensible young woman, marries the estimable and superficially insignificant Samuel Povey, the chief assistant in the shop, and spends all her life in Bursley. The more passionate and imaginative Sophia elopes with the fascinating Gerald Scales, a commercial traveller who has come into a fortune. He is an unprincipled blackguard, has to be forced to marry her, carries her to Paris, where she is exposed to indignities, and finally deserts her. She struggles to success as a lodging-house keeper in Paris, where she lives through the siege of 1870. The sisters are reunited, and spend their last years together in Bursley.

OLDYS, William (1696–1761), antiquary, and editor of the *Harleian Miscellany. His principal interest was biography, and his *Life of Sir Walter Raleigh* was prefixed to the 1736 edition of *Ralegh's *History of the World*. He contributed many biographies to and was general editor of the *Biographia Britannica* (6 vols, 1747–66). He also wrote the poem 'Busy, curious, thirsty fly', first published in 1732. He was relieved from poverty and the Fleet prison by being appointed Norroy king-of-arms.

Olindo, the lover of Sofronia in Tasso's *Jerusalem Delivered.

OLIPHANT, Laurence (1829–88), born at Cape Town of Scottish descent; after a desultory education and extensive travel with his parents, he became a barrister in Ceylon, where his father was chief justice. *A Journey to Khatmandu* (1852) and *The Russian Shores of the Black Sea* (1853–4) are accounts of some of his early adventures. He was secretary to Lord Elgin in Washington, Canada, and China; the latter is described in *A Narrative of the Earl of Elgin's Mission to China 1857–9* (1859). He acted as *The Times correspondent in Circassia during the war and again during the Franco-Prussian war. He is then heard of as plotting with Garibaldi in Italy, as secretary of a legation in Japan, and in other parts of the world. His novel *Piccadilly* (1870) is a satirical exposure of the venal side of London society. He was an MP during 1865–7 and high office appeared within his grasp, but by 1867 he had come under the influence of the spurious American 'prophet' Thomas Lake Harris, joined his Brotherhood of New Life in New York State, and surrendered to him most of his property. His allegiance with Harris ended in 1882 and in that year Oliphant and his wife founded a community for Jewish immigrants in Haifa. There he wrote his second novel, *Altiora Peto* (1883), and the strange *Sympneumata* (1885) which was dictated by his wife as if possessed by a spirit. M. *Oliphant (no relation) published his biography in 1891. A recent biography by Anne Taylor (1982) suggests that Oliphant's crazed behaviour was attributable to inherited syphilis.

OLIPHANT, Margaret (M.O.W.), *née* Wilson (1828–97), a prolific Scots writer, author of well over 100 books and innumerable articles. Early widowed, she was compelled to write for an income, both for her own and for her brother's families. In 1849 she published *Passages in the Life of Mrs Margaret Maitland*, a tale of Scotland which had an encouraging reception; *Caleb Field*, a historical novel, appeared in 1851; and among her many domestic romances *The Athelings* (1857) was probably the most interesting. In 1862 appeared her biography of the brilliant heretical preacher Edward Irving and in 1891 a life of Laurence *Oliphant. But it is for her 'Chronicles of Carlingford' series that she is best remembered. Carlingford is a quiet country town near London, and this series of novels (the most notable of which are *Salem Chapel*, 1863; *The Perpetual Curate*, 1864; *Miss Marjoribanks*, 1866; and *Phoebe Junior*, 1876) is set among the aristocracy, professional families, and tradesmen of the town. Religious themes predominate, but the books are sharp and humorous. In 1868 Mrs Oliphant was awarded a civil list pension of £100 a year. Her other most interesting group of books, *Stories of the Seen and Unseen*, all connected in some way with death and the experience of the soul, began with *A Beleaguered City* (1880) which was followed by *A Little Pilgrim* (1882) and others. Her astute *Literary History of England* (1882) earned much praise, but the continuing stream of undemanding romances and novels of domestic life brought little further success. Her long association with *Blackwood's* was commemorated in the posthumous *Annals of a Publishing House* (1897). Her autobiography (1899) poignantly describes the destructive necessity of having to write so much.

Olivant, the ivory horn (from *Oliphaunt*) of *Roland.

Oliver, in the *Charlemagne cycle of legends, one of Charlemagne's *Paladins. He is the close friend of *Roland, with whom he has a prolonged and undecided single combat (the origin of their comradeship), and is his equal in bravery, but more prudent. At the battle of Roncesvalles he urges Roland to summon help by sounding his horn, but Roland postpones doing so till too late. Oliver's sister Aude, is betrothed to Roland.

Oliver de Boys, Orlando's elder brother in Shakespeare's *As You Like It*, who marries *Celia.

Oliver Twist, a novel by *Dickens, published 1837–8.

Oliver Twist is the name given to a child of unknown parentage born in a workhouse and brought up under the cruel conditions to which pauper children were formerly exposed, the tyrant at whose hands he especially suffers being Bumble, the parish beadle. After experience of an unhappy apprenticeship, he runs away, reaches London, and falls into the hands of a gang of thieves, at the head of which is the old Jew Fagin, and whose other chief members are the burglar Bill Sikes, his mistress Nancy, and 'the Artful Dodger', an impudent young pickpocket. Every effort is made to convert Oliver into a thief. He is temporarily rescued by the benevolent Mr Brownlow, but kidnapped by the gang, whose interest in his retention has been increased by the offers of a sinister person named Monks, who has a special interest in Oliver's perversion. Oliver is now made to accompany Bill Sikes on a burgling expedition, in the course of which he receives a gun-shot wound, and comes into the hands of Mrs Maylie and her protégée Rose, by whom he is kindly treated and brought up. After a time, Nancy, who develops some redeeming traits, reveals to Rose that Monks is aware of Oliver's parentage, and wishes all proof of it destroyed; also that there is some relationship between Oliver and Rose herself. Inquiry is set on foot. In the course of it Nancy's action is discovered by the gang, and she is brutally murdered by Bill Sikes. A hue and cry is raised; Sikes, trying to escape, accidentally hangs himself, and the rest of the gang are secured and Fagin executed. Monks, found and threatened with exposure, confesses what remains unknown. He is the half-brother of Oliver, and has pursued his ruin, animated by hatred and the desire to retain the whole of his father's property. Rose is the sister of Oliver's unfortunate mother. Oliver is adopted by Mr Brownlow. Monks emigates and dies in prison. Bumble ends his career in the workhouse over which he formerly ruled.

Dickens resented the implication that this work made crime glamorous, and in a Preface to the third edition (April 1841) tactfully dissociated it from the popular *'Newgate novels' of the period, by *Ainsworth, *Bulwer-Lytton, and others.

Olivia, (1) the wealthy Illyrian countess in Shakespeare's *Twelfth Night*; (2) a character in Wycherley's *The Plain Dealer*; (3) the elder daughter of Dr Primrose, in Goldsmith's *The Vicar of Wakefield*.

Olney Hymns, see COWPER, W., and NEWTON, J.

OLSEN, Charles, see BLACK MOUNTAIN POETS.

Olympian Odes, The, see PINDAR.

Olyssipo, in imprints, Lisbon.

Omar Khayyám, *The Rubáiyát of,* a translation by E. *Fitzgerald of the *rubais* or quatrains of the 12th-cent. Persian poet. The translation was first published anonymously in 1859; Fitzgerald produced further editions, revised and with added quatrains, in 1868, 1872, and 1879. Fitzgerald's translation preserved the stanza form of the original, but adapted the quatrains into a connected theme, sceptical of divine providence, mocking the transience of human grandeur, and concentrating on the pleasures of the fleeting moment. The felicitously phrased aphorisms of this cynical yet genial poetic sequence are among the most frequently quoted lines in English poetry.

Omnium, duke and duchess of (Plantagenet Palliser and Lady Glencora), leading characters in the *****'Palliser' novels of A. Trollope; in his view Plantagenet was 'a perfect gentleman'.

Omnium, Jacob, see HIGGINS, M. J.

Omoo (1847), a romance by H. *Melville, a sequel to *Typee.

'O my luve's like a red, red rose', a lyric by *Burns, published in *The Scots Musical Museum* (1787–1803).

O'NEILL, Eugene (1888–1953), American dramatist, born in New York. The son of a well known romantic actor, he had a varied career (as seaman, gold prospector, journalist, and actor) before associating himself (1916) with the experimental theatre group the Provincetown Players, which staged several of his early one-act plays, including *Bound East for Cardiff* (1916) and *The Moon of the Caribbees* (1918). His first big success was the full-length naturalistic drama *Beyond the Horizon* (1920), which was followed in the same year by his expressionistic *The Emperor Jones,* a tragedy which describes the rise and fall of the Negro 'emperor' of a West Indian island, and *Anna Christie* (1921), a naturalistic study of a prostitute on the New York waterfront and her redemption. Among other important plays of this period were *The Hairy Ape* (1922), *All God's Chillun Got Wings* (1924), and *Desire under the Elms* (1924). O'Neill's criticism of contemporary materialistic values was powerfully and poetically expressed in *The Fountain* (1925), *The Great God Brown* (1926), *Lazarus Laughed* (1927), and *Marco Millions* (1927). He experimented with a *stream-of-consciousness technique in *Strange Interlude* (1928), and adapted the theme of the *Oresteia to the aftermath of the American Civil War in his trilogy *Mourning Becomes Electra* (1931). *Ah! Wilderness* (1932) and *Days without End* (1934) were followed by a long absence from the stage, during which he was awarded the *Nobel Prize (1936) and worked on several plays, including

The Iceman Cometh (1946), a lengthy naturalistic tragedy set in Harry Hope's Bowery saloon, where a collection of down-and-out alcoholics nourish their illusions ('pipe dreams') with the aid of an extrovert, apparently cheerful salesman, Hickey. His masterpiece, *Long Day's Journey into Night,* was written in 1940–1, and posthumously produced and published in 1956; it is a semi-autobiographical family tragedy, portraying the mutually destructive relationships of drug-addicted Mary Tyrone, her ex-actor husband James, and their two sons, hard-drinking Jamie and intellectual Edmund. His last play, *A Moon for the Misbegotten,* was written by 1943 and produced in 1947; it portrays, with humour and lyricism, the relationship of Phil Hogan, tenant farmer, with his spirited and allegedly promiscuous daughter Josie, and Josie's chaste and compassionate love for their self-tormenting, haunted, dissolute landlord, James Tyrone. Despite occasional lapses into melodrama and rhetoric, O'Neill's plays remain powerfully theatrical and original; he transcends his debt to *Ibsen and *Strindberg, producing an œuvre in which the struggle between self-destruction, self-deception, and redemption is presented as essentially dramatic in nature.

One of our Conquerors, a novel by G. *Meredith, published 1891.

Victor Radnor has married a rich elderly widow and then fallen in love with her young companion, Natalia Dreighton. Victor and Natalia have defied convention and decided to live together. They have a daughter, Nesta Victoria, attractive and courageous, who eventually becomes aware of her illegitimacy. The novel closely follows the complexities of the dilemmas involved. Victor remains energetic and hopeful, but Natalia becomes overwhelmed with the problems of their lives. Nesta, now grown up, finds herself faced with several suitors, the most eligible being Dudley Sowerby, heir to an earldom. Victor, misguidedly attempting to make amends to Natalia, struggles hard to bring about the match, but the discovery of Nesta's illegitimacy causes Dudley to retreat. Harassed beyond bearing, Natalia dies, and Victor, driven almost insane with grief, lives only a few years longer. Nesta marries a worthy suitor, Dartrey Fenellan. The preciosity which increasingly overtook Meredith's prose is often evident, but the book earned considerable respect, and H. G. *Wells later described it as 'one of the books that have made me'.

ONIONS, C(harles) T(albut) (1873–1965), grammarian and lexicographer, co-editor of the *Oxford English Dictionary* and its original *Supplement,* 1914–33; editor of *A Shakespeare Glossary* (1911), *The Shorter Oxford English Dictionary* (1932), *The Oxford Dictionary of English*

Etymology (1966); author of *An Advanced English Syntax* (1904: rev. edn, *Modern English Syntax*, 1971).

ONIONS, George Oliver (1873–1961), novelist and short story writer born in Bradford, whose works include *The Compleat Bachelor* (1900), *Widdershins* (1911, tales of the uncanny), and *The Story of Ragged Robyn* (1945). He changed his name by deed poll in 1918 to George Oliver. He was married to the romantic novelist Berta Ruck (1878–1928), whose name appeared inadvertently in V. *Woolf's *Jacob's Room*, thus occasioning first a dispute, then an acquaintance between the two women.

Onomatopoeia, the formation of a word by an imitation of the sound associated with the object or action designated: as 'hurlyburly', 'buzz', 'creak'. The term is also applied to the use of a combination of words to evoke by sound a certain image or mood, the most frequently quoted example being *Tennyson's 'murmuring of innumerable bees'.

Opera, a dramatic performance in which music forms an essential part, consisting of recitatives, arias, and choruses, with orchestral accompaniment and scenery; also, a dramatic or musical composition intended for this, a libretto or score [*OED*]. The most important word in this definition is 'essential', for it is precisely the integration of music into the substance of the drama that differentiates opera from the *masque (in which the music is generally episodic and accompanimental) or the straight play with incidental music. This integration, and hence the first operas, developed out of the experiments in the *stile recitativo* (the 'reciting style') made by a group of cultured intellectuals at the Medici court in Florence towards the end of the 16th cent.: the distinctive combination of elements in which it results has been differently balanced at different times and in different countries, though usually with music in a dominant role.

In England, in spite of a continuous and often passionate interest in imported foreign examples, opera never established itself as an indigenous form in the way that it did in Italy, France, and Germany—a comment on the way the English feel about music which isolated exceptions like *Purcell in the 17th cent. or *Britten in the 20th do not really disprove. The first attempts at opera in English were somewhat obstructed by the 'Puritan interregnum' and the closing of the public theatres under *Cromwell. It is difficult at this stage to distinguish between opera and masque, but the first English work that is normally regarded as an opera is *The Siege of Rhodes* (1656), of which the text was by *D'Avenant: the music is lost, and was anyhow a collective effort by a number of different composers. The first English example of which the

music has survived is John *Blow's *Venus and Adonis* (*c*.1684), a genuine opera in miniature which preceded Purcell's *Dido and Aeneas* by some five years. See also LIBRETTO.

Ophelia, in Shakespeare's *Hamlet*, the daughter of Polonius.

OPIE, Mrs Amelia (1769–1853), wife of John Opie the painter, and friend of Sydney *Smith, *Sheridan, Mme de *Staël, and many other members of literary society. She was a copious novelist and poet, and was satirized by T. L. Peacock in *Headlong Hall* as Miss Poppyseed, 'an indefatigable compounder of novels'. Her works include: *Poems* (1802); *Adeline Mowbray* (suggested by the story of Mary *Wollstonecraft) in 1804; *Simple Tales* (1806); a *Memoir* of her husband in 1809; and *Lays for the Dead* in 1833.

OPIE, Peter Mason (1918–82), author and folklorist, and his wife Iona Margaret Balfour Opie (1923–), produced, after many years of research together, such distinguished works as the *Oxford Dictionary of Nursery Rhymes* (1951), *The Lore and Language of Schoolchildren* (1959), and *Children's Games in Street and Playground* (1969). They also edited various anthologies, including *The Oxford Book of Children's Verse* (1973).

Opimian, The Revd Dr Theophilus, a character in Peacock's *Gryll Grange*. (*Opimianum* was a celebrated wine of the vintage of AUC 633 = 121 BC, when Opimius was consul. Lewis and Short.)

***Opium Eater,** Confessions of an English*, see CONFESSIONS OF AN ENGLISH OPIUM EATER.

ORAGE, Alfred Richard (1875–1934), born in Yorkshire, the son of a schoolmaster, became himself a schoolmaster in Leeds, where he joined the *Fabian Society, and was active in a wide range of artistic, political, and intellectual activities. He came to London in 1906, and from 1907 till 1922, partly financed by G. B. *Shaw and assisted initially by Holbrook Jackson (1874–1948), edited *The New Age*, a periodical which acquired during this period much political and literary prestige. His contributors include both the established (Shaw, Arnold *Bennett, *Wells, and others) and the as yet unknown (including *Pound, K. *Mansfield, *Aldington, and T. E. *Hulme). He was an advocate of Social Credit, and in later years came under the influence of *Gurdjieff; after leaving the *New Age* in 1922 he went to Fontainebleau, then New York, as a Gurdjieff disciple, returning to England in 1931 to found a new paper, the *New English Weekly*, which he edited until his death. See the life by Philip Mairet (1936) and '*The New Age*' under *Orage* (1967) by W. Martin.

Oran Haut-ton, see HAUT-TON.

Orc, (1) a mythical sea-monster mentioned by
*Ariosto, *Drayton, *Milton, and others, from
the Latin 'orca', a kind of whale; (2) in the
Prophetic Books of *Blake, the symbol of rebellion and anarchy, the son of *Los and *Enitharmon, who is chained, like *Prometheus, to
a rock in *The Book of *Urizen*, and who bursts
his bonds in *America: A Prophecy* to fight and
defeat Albion's Angel; (3) in the personal mythology of J. R. R. *Tolkien, Orcs are the evil and
hideous creations of the rebellious Vala, Melkor.

Orcades, the Orkney Islands.

***Orchestra** Or a Poeme of Dauncing*, see DAVIES,
SIR J.

ORCZY, Baroness (Mrs Montague Barstow)
(1865–1947), Hungarian-born novelist who
lived from the age of 15 in London. She achieved
fame with her romantic novel *The Scarlet Pimpernel* (1905), the story of the League of the
Scarlet Pimpernel, a band of Englishmen
pledged to rescue the innocent victims of the
Reign of Terror in Paris. Its leader, Sir Percy
Blakeney, outwits his opponents—in particular
the wily Chauvelin—by means of his courage
and ingenious disguises, at the same time concealing his identity from his friends in England.
The success of the novel followed its success in a
dramatized version, written in collaboration
with her husband, in which Fred Terry took the
leading part. It was performed first in Nottingham in 1903, then, to great acclaim, in London
in 1905. She wrote many other historical and
romantic novels, including several sequels to *The
Scarlet Pimpernel*.

Ordeal of Gilbert Pinfold, The, see WAUGH, E.

Ordeal of Richard Feverel, The, a novel by
G. *Meredith, published 1859.

This book, in which Meredith found his
strength as a novelist, was written just after the
painful collapse of his first marriage; it exhibits
clearly for the first time his theory of 'comedy',
and the growing luxuriance of his style. Sir
Austin Feverel's wife has run off with a poet,
leaving him with their son Richard. Sir Austin,
arrogant and obtuse, devises a 'System' for
Richard's education, which consists in keeping
the boy at home (for schools are corrupting) and
in trusting to authoritarian parental vigilance.
The slow collapse of the 'System', and Richard's
struggle for freedom and knowledge, form the
underlying theme of the book. Richard and
Lucy Desborough, a neighbouring farmer's
niece, fall in love at first sight, and an idyllic
courtship ends in the discovery of their
attachment. Lucy has every natural charm, but
not the birth Sir Austin requires for his son. His
attempts to break their relationship result in their
secret marriage and the fury of the possessive Sir
Austin, who cruelly ensures the separation of the
young couple by playing on Richard's love and

duty. Ordered to await his father in London,
Richard earnestly sets about the redemption of
ladies of pleasure, succeeding only in falling a
temporary victim to the beautiful Bella Mount,
who falls equally in love with him. Initially Bella
has acted at the instigation of the predatory Lord
Mountfalcon, who has plans to ensnare Lucy.
Richard becomes increasingly overwhelmed
with shame at his treatment of his wife, then
hears that he is a father and that Lucy and Sir
Austin are reconciled. But as soon as he returns
to her he learns of the designs of Lord Mountfalcon; he furiously challenges him to a duel and
is seriously wounded. In the succeeding fever his
confusions are stripped away and he is finally
freed of his devouring father. But the shock of
events proves overwhelming for Lucy, who
loses her mind and eventually dies.

ORDERICUS   VITALIS   (1075–1142/3),
born near Shrewsbury of a Norman father and
probably English mother, a monk of St Évroul
in Normandy. He wrote between 1114 and
1141 his *Ecclesiastical History of England and Normandy* in Latin, covering events from the beginning of the Christian era down to 1141,
which is one of the standard authorities for the
Norman period. His accounts of the Conquest
and other events show a lively sympathy with
the English and a predominant interest in English
matters.

Oresteia, The, a trilogy of plays by *Aeschylus.
Agamemnon describes the return to Argos after
the Trojan war of the victorious Agamemnon,
brother of Helen's husband Menelaus, and his
murder by his wife Clytemnestra foretold by
his captive, the prophet Cassandra, daughter of
King Priam of Troy. The *Choephoroe* (or *The
Libation Bearers*) portrays the vengeance of the
son and daughter of Agamemnon, Orestes and
Electra: Orestes murders Clytemnestra and her
lover Aegisthus, and is himself pursued by the
Eumenides, or Furies. The *Eumenides* shows the
Furies in pursuit of Orestes, who is protected
by the younger god Apollo. Orestes is tried,
Athena, goddess of wisdom, delivers her casting
vote on his behalf, and he goes free, released
from the ancient blood vengeance: Athena
reconciles the Furies to the new Law, and they
are transformed into the Kindly Ones, who bless
the city of Athens and the land.

Other versions of the story appear in the
works of *Sophocles (who wrote *Electra*) and
*Euripides, and it reappears in many forms
throughout Western literature; there are notable
20th-cent. dramatic versions by T. S. *Eliot
(*The Family Reunion*, 1939), *O'Neill (*Mourning Becomes Electra*, 1931), and *Sartre (*Les
Mouches*, 1942).

Orfeo, Sir, a metrical romance of the early
14th cent. in about 600 lines (the poem varies
considerably in its three manuscript versions),

identified in its prologue as a *Breton lay. It represents the story of Orpheus and Eurydice (see ORPHEUS) in a Celtic guise: Queen Heurodys is carried off to fairyland and pursued by King Orfeo whose melodious playing of his harp succeeds in bringing her back to the world of men. The Middle English version (to which *Child's ballad 'King Orfeo' is related) ends happily: the queen's return is permanent, and the steward left in charge of the kingdom by Orfeo during his absence passes the romance test of his fidelity. The poem is much admired as one of the most charming and interesting of Middle English romances. Ed. A. J. Bliss (1954; rev. 1966).

Orgilus, a character in Ford's *The Broken Heart.

Orgoglio (Ital., signifying haughtiness), in Spenser's *Faerie Queene (I. vii, viii), captures the *Redcrosse Knight, and is slain by Prince *Arthur.

Orgon, the credulous dupe in Molière's Le *Tartuffe.

Oriana, (1) see under AMADIS OF GAUL; (2) a name frequently applied by poets to *Elizabeth I, as in T. *Morley's collection of madrigals The Triumphes of Oriana (1601); (3) the heroine of Fletcher's *The Wild-Goose Chase; (4) the subject of an early ballad by *Tennyson.

Oriental (or Eastern) **novel** (or tale), a class of story exotically set in the Middle or Far East, and varying greatly in tone, from Johnson's *Rasselas to Beckford's *Vathek and Byron's *The Corsair and *The Giaour. Many of the tales (such as those of *Dow, *Hawkesworth, *Ridley, and F. *Sheridan) relate the flamboyant adventures of well-defined heroes and villains, often with the intervention of the supernatural; others (such as Southey's poem *The Curse of Kehama or Moore's *Lalla Rookh) are more complex. These tales enjoyed great popularity in the second half of the 18th and the early part of the 19th cents. Public interest in the Orient was no doubt greatly stimulated by the translation into English in 1705–8 of the *Arabian Nights; by *Knolles's history of the Turks (much admired by both Dr Johnson and *Byron); and by the translations of Sir W. *Jones. (See also NOVEL, RISE OF THE.)

ORIGEN (c.185–c.253), a great Christian thinker and scholar in the Alexandrian school, the author of many theological works and compiler of the famous Hexapla versions of the Old Testament (see BIBLE). He studied under Ammonius, sometimes regarded as the founder of *Neoplatonism, and he is of great importance as the introducer of Neoplatonic elements into Christianity. His Principles, which were rejected by Church orthodoxy, were translated by *Jerome and quoted by St *Bernard, and he

influenced the allegorical method of literary criticism developed by *Augustine. See J. Daniélou, Origen, trans. W. Mitchell (1955).

Origin of Species, On the, the great work of C. *Darwin, published 1859. Its full title was On the Origin of Species by means of Natural Selection, or the Preservation of Favoured Races in the Struggle for Life.

Orinda, The Matchless, see PHILIPS, K.

Orion, see HORNE, R. H.

Orlando, (1) the Italian form of *Roland, a hero of the *Charlemagne romances (see also ORLANDO FURIOSO and ORLANDO INNAMORATO); (2) in Shakespeare's *As You Like It, the lover of Rosalind; (3) the title of a novel by V. *Woolf.

Orlando Furioso, a poem by *Ariosto, published in its complete form in 1532, designed to exalt the house of Este and its legendary ancestor *Rogero (Ruggiero) and to continue the story of Orlando's love for *Angelica begun by Boiardo in *Orlando Innamorato.

The main theme of the poem is this: Saracens and Christians, in the days of *Charlemagne, are at war for the possession of Europe. The Saracens under *Agramant, king of Africa, are besieging Charlemagne in Paris with the help of Marsilio, the Moorish king of Spain, and two mighty warriors, *Rodomont and *Mandricardo. Christendom is imperilled. Angelica, who at the end of Boiardo's poem had been consigned by Charlemagne to the care of Namo, escapes. Orlando, chief of the Paladins, a perfect knight, invincible and invulnerable, is lured by her beauty to forget his duty and pursue her. Angelica meets with various adventures, finally coming upon the wounded Moorish youth *Medoro, whom she tends, falls in love with, and marries. A charming description follows of their honeymoon in the woods. Orlando, arriving there by chance and learning their story, is seized with a furious and grotesque madness, runs naked through the country, destroying everything in his path, and at last returns to Charlemagne's camp, where he is finally cured of his madness and his love and in a great conclusive battle kills Agramant.

Although the madness of Orlando gives the poem its name, a not less important theme in it is the love of Rogero for *Bradamante, a maiden warrior, sister of *Rinaldo, and the many adventures and vicissitudes that interrupt the course of true love. Other notable episodes in the work are the voyage of *Astolfo on the hippogriff to the moon, whence he brings back the lost wits of Orlando; and the self-immolation of *Isabella, the widow of the Scottish prince *Zerbino, to escape the attentions of the pagan king, Rodomont. Orlando's horse is Brigliandoro; his sword Durindana.

Spenser, in *The Faerie Queene, aimed to

'overgo' Ariosto's epic, and owes much to it for his characters and form of narration. The first complete English version 'in English Heroical Verse' is that of Sir J. Harington (1591; ed. R. McNulty, 1972). John Hoole's translation (1783) was read and enjoyed by *Scott and *Southey. A version by W. S. Rose (8 vols, 1823–31) in ottava rima, though less amusing than Harington's, is more faithful, and was highly praised by Rose's friend *Foscolo. Recent versions are by G. Waldman (1974) and B. Reynolds (1975).

Orlando Innamorato, a poem by *Boiardo published 1487, on the subject of the falling in love of *Orlando (the Roland of the *Charlemagne cycle) with *Angelica, daughter of *Galafron, king of Cathay. She arrives at the court of Charlemagne, with her brother *Argalia, under false pretences, to carry off the Christian knights to her father's country. Several knights attempt to win her, the chief among them being *Astolfo, *Ferrau, *Rinaldo, and Orlando. Argalia is slain and Angelica flees, but, drinking of an enchanted fountain, falls in love with Rinaldo, who, drinking of another enchanted fountain, conceives a violent aversion to her. He runs away, pursued by her, and they reach her father's country, where she is besieged in the capital, *Albracca, by *Agrican, king of Tartary, to whom her hand had been promised (an incident to which Milton refers in *Paradise Regained*, iii. 337 ff.). Orlando comes to Angelica's rescue, slays Agrican, and carries Angelica off to France whither he has been summoned to assist Charlemagne against *Agramant, king of the Moors. Owing once more to enchanted waters, Rinaldo this time falls in love with Angelica, and Angelica into hatred of him. A fierce combat ensues between Orlando and Rinaldo, suppressed by Charlemagne, who entrusts Angelica to Namo, duke of Bavaria.

The poem, which was left unfinished, was refashioned by *Berni, and translated into English by W. S. Rose (1823). There is some slight evidence that *Spenser knew Boiardo's poem as well as Ariosto's sequel, *Orlando Furioso*. See M. Murrin, *The Allegorical Epic* (1980).

Orley Farm, a novel by A. *Trollope, published 1862.

While Joseph Mason of Groby Park inherits the bulk of his father's property, the small estate at Orley Farm goes unexpectedly to Lucius Mason, the old man's son by his second marriage. The will is unsuccessfully contested, and matters hang fire for many years until discontented Samuel Dockwrath, formerly a tenant at Orley Farm, discovers important irregularities in the evidence brought before the court. The suspicion grows that the codicil attached to Sir Joseph's will was forged by Lucius's mother,

Lady Mason, still living at Orley Farm. The case is re-opened, and though the verdict is in Lady Mason's favour, this is largely due to the professional skill of the lawyers who represent her, including the indefatigable Chaffanbrass. Lady Mason confesses her guilt to her aged lover Sir Peregrine Orme and to his daughter Edith, her closest friend, and surrenders the property. Mother and son embrace voluntary exile in Germany.

Ormond, a novel by M. *Edgeworth, published 1817.

This is largely a tale of life in Ireland, but also of fashionable Paris society in the 18th cent. The main characters are Harry Ormond, an orphan; his fascinating but unprincipled guardian, Sir Ulick O'Shane; the kind-hearted eccentric Cornelius O'Shane, the 'king of the Black Islands'; and his daughter Dora, who has been plighted before her birth to one or other of the twin sons of Cornelius's companion Connal, with disastrous results.

Ormulum, The, a Middle English poem of which about 20,000 short lines survive, written in the East Midlands in the late 12th cent. by an Augustinian canon called Orm. It purports to consist of paraphrases of the gospels for the year as arranged in the Mass book, supplemented by a homily on each; but in fact it is a series of sermons arranged chronologically around the Gospel versions of the life of Christ. In any case what we have is only about an eighth of the writer's ambitious scheme. Its literary merit is inconsiderable, but it is of great linguistic interest, particularly for the semi-phonetic spelling system devised by the writer (largely a matter of doubling consonants after short vowels). Ed. R. M. White and R. Holt (1878).

Oroonoko, or the History of the Royal Slave, a novel by A. *Behn, published c.1688, adapted for the stage by *Southerne, 1695.

Oroonoko, grandson and heir of an African king, loves and wins Imoinda, daughter of the king's general. The king, who also loves her, is enraged and orders her to be sold as a slave. Oroonoko himself is trapped by the captain of an English slave-trading ship and carried off to Surinam, then an English colony, where he is reunited with Imoinda and renamed Caesar by his owners. He rouses his fellow slaves to revolt, is deceived into surrender by deputy-governor Byam (a historical figure), and brutally whipped. Oroonoko, determined on revenge but not hoping for victory, kills Imoinda, who dies willingly. He is discovered by her dead body and cruelly executed.

The novel is remarkable as an early protest against the slave-trade, and as a description of primitive people in 'the first state of innocence, before men knew how to sin'; the author comments on the superior simplicity and morality of both African slaves and the indigenous Indians, whose Christian oppressors are shown as treacherous and hypocritical. Afra Behn's memories of her own visit to Surinam in 1663 provide a vivid background, and much of the story is narrated as by a personal witness. Southerne's tragedy follows the broad lines of the novel, but the deputy-governor's passion for Imoinda is made a chief motive of action, Imoinda herself is presented as the daughter of a white European, and Oroonoko dies by his own hand, alterations which decrease the violence of the story and increase its intended pathos.

OROSIUS (*fl.* early 5th cent.), a priest of Tarragona in Spain, disciple of St *Augustine and friend of St *Jerome, author of the *Historia Adversus Paganos*, a universal history and geography which was translated by the circle of King *Alfred in the 890s. See *Seven Books of History Against the Pagans*, trans. I. W. Raymond (1936).

Orphan, The, a tragedy in blank verse by *Otway, produced 1680.

Castalio and Polydore are the twin sons of Acasto. Monimia, the orphan daughter of a friend of Acasto's, has been brought up with them. Castalio and Polydore, loyally devoted to one another, have both fallen in love with Monimia, who returns the love of Castalio. But the latter, out of mistaken consideration for his brother, feigns indifference for Monimia. Chamont, an honest but rough and tactless soldier, brother of Monimia, comes as a guest to Acasto's house; he suspects that Monimia has been wronged by one of the young men, and annoys her with his questions. Castalio and Monimia thereupon are secretly married. Polydore, ignorant of this and overhearing them arranging for a meeting in the night, takes Castalio's place in the darkness, and is not detected. Castalio, coming later, is shut out, and curses his wife for what he supposes to be her heartless and tactless conduct. The truth being discovered through Chamont, the brothers fall into despair. Both kill themselves, and Monimia takes poison.

The play proved a great success, and was frequently revived. Monimia was one of Mrs *Barry's most celebrated parts.

Orpheus, a legendary Greek hero, son of Apollo (or according to some authorities of a Thracian king Oeagrus) by the Muse Callipe, was renowned as a musician, a religious leader, and a seer. He was reputed to have made trees and rocks follow his singing, been one of the Argonauts, visited Egypt, and founded mystery cults in several parts of Greece. He was eventually torn to pieces by Maenads (frenzied votaresses of Dionysus); and his head and lyre, thrown into the river Hebrus, drifted to Lesbos where the head became an oracle, while Apollo

placed the lyre among the stars. The relationship of Orpheus to Dionysus remains puzzling. The Maenads are said to have attacked him because as a priest of Apollo he censured their orgiastic rites. Orphic beliefs seem however to have been rooted in the assumption that 'the body is the tomb of the soul', so that one's aim in life must be to free oneself from an endless series of reincarnations, not only by moral and physical purity, but also through certain rites which involved eating the flesh of a sacrifice that represented the god; and on such occasions the god in question was always Dionysus.

Orphism had a decisive influence on Pythagoreanism and through this on Platonism and *Neoplatonism. There existed many writings ascribed to Orpheus and his son Musaeus, which are quoted by ancient writers; but the Orphic literature that survives belongs probably to the 5th cent. AD, though this was not established until Gottfried Hermann's edition of 1805.

The legend which found most favour in later literature was, oddly, one of which there is no early record: the story of Orpheus going down into hell, persuading Hades to let him have back his wife, Eurydice, and then losing her because he disregarded the instruction not to look back before they reached the light of day. The popularity of this legend was due perhaps to its presence in poems that were widely read in the Middle Ages: *Virgil, *Georgics*, IV. 454–527, *Ovid, *Metamorphoses*, X. 1–85, and especially *Boethius, *De Consolatione Philosophiae*, III. 12, so that it appears in the English *Sir *Orfeo*, in the 14th-cent. *King Orfew*, and, in Italy, *Politian chose it as the subject of his pastoral play *Orfeo* (1480). Robert *Burton cites it as evidence that beasts respond to music, and it inspired one of *Poussin's finest paintings. But appropriately enough opera has been the genre that has made most use of the Orpheus story in modern times. The first opera of which the complete music exists is an *Euridice* that Peri based on an Italian poem by Ottavio Rinuccini (1600). This was followed by Monteverdi's more competent *Orfeo* (1607). Gluck's opera with the same title appeared in 1762, and in a lighter vein there is Crémieux and Offenbach's *Orpheus in the Underworld* (1858). The best-known modern version is *Cocteau's tragedy *Orphée* (1927), filmed in 1950. The legend has exercised a spell that is not immediately easy to explain.

Orpheus Caledonius: *or a collection of the best Scotch songs* (1725), the first printed collection of Scots airs for the voice, collected by William Thomson, which contains many of the songs first printed by *Ramsay.

ORRERY, earls of, see BOYLE.

Orsin, the bear-warden who appears in Butler's

Hudibras. His name is derived from Italian *orso*, a bear.

Orsino, the duke of Illyria in Shakespeare's *Twelfth Night*, whose words 'If music be the food of love, play on' begin the play.

Orson, see VALENTINE AND ORSON.

ORTEGA Y GASSET, José (1883–1955), Spanish writer and philosopher, born in Madrid. He studied philosophy in Germany and was professor of metaphysics in Madrid University 1910–36. He was a bitter opponent of the dictator Primo de Rivera, and was elected to the Constituent Cortes of the Second Republic. During the Civil War he went into voluntary exile, finally returning to Spain in 1945. He was a prolific and versatile writer of essays on philosophy, literature, and politics; his newspaper articles and his journal, *Revista de Occidente* (1923–35), were influential in introducing European writers to Spain. His publications include *España invertebrada* (1921; *Invertebrate Spain*, 1937); *El tema de nuestra tiempo* (1923; *The Modern Theme*, 1933); *La deshumanización del arte* (1925), which discusses the nature of *Modernism and the hostility it inspires; and his most widely-read work, *La rebelión de las masas* (1929; *The Revolt of the Masses*, 1932), which continues the socio-historical arguments of *España invertebrada*, deploring the lack of intellectual leadership in Spain, and advocating a United States of Europe.

ORTELIUS, Abraham (1527–98), a geographer and scholar of Antwerp, who visited England and became familiar with *Camden. He published his atlas, *Theatrum Orbis Terrarum*, in 1570.

ORTON, Joe (1933–67), playwright, born in Leicester, left school at 16 to train as an actor. His comedies, which include *Entertaining Mr Sloane* (1964), *Loot* (1965), and the posthumously performed *What the Butler Saw* (1969), are black, stylish, and violent, and their emphasis on corruption and sexual perversion made them a *succès de scandale*. Orton was battered to death by his friend and companion, who then committed suicide.

Orville, Lord, the hero of F. Burney's *Evelina*.

ORWELL, George, the pen-name of Eric Arthur Blair (1903–50), who was born in Bengal, brought to England at an early age, and educated at St Cyprian's (of which his account, 'Such, such were the joys', was considered too libellous to print in this country until 1968) and then at Eton, at both with C. *Connolly. His first patriotic poem appeared in a local Henley paper in 1914. He served with the Indian Imperial Police in Burma, 1922–7, and his experiences are reflected in his first novel, *Burmese Days* (1934); he resigned 'to escape not merely

from imperialism but from every form of man's dominion over man', as he later put it, and returned to Europe where he worked in Paris and London in a series of ill-paid jobs in a state of 'fairly severe poverty' (see *Down and Out in Paris and London*, 1933), struggling with rejection of his work. His second novel, *A Clergyman's Daughter* (1935), describes the adventures of Dorothy, who through loss of memory briefly escapes from her narrow spinster's life to join the tramps and hop-pickers; in style it somewhat uneasily mixes realism with Joycean experiment. *Keep the Aspidistra Flying* (1936), which he wrote while working in a Hampstead bookshop, recounts the literary aspirations, financial humiliations, and shotgun wedding of Gordon Comstock, bookseller's assistant. A journey north in 1936, commissioned by *Gollancz, produced his vivid and impassioned documentary of unemployment and proletarian life *The Road to Wigan Pier* (1937, published by the *Left Book Club), and the Spanish Civil War (in which he fought for the Republicans and was wounded) intensified his political preoccupations and produced *Homage to Catalonia* (1939). The threat of the coming war hung over his next novel, *Coming up for Air* (1939), which deals with suburban frustration and Georgian nostalgia in the person of insurance man George Bowling. By this stage Orwell saw himself primarily as a political writer, a democratic socialist who avoided party labels, hated totalitarianism, and was to become more and more disillusioned with the methods of Communism; his plain, colloquial style made him highly effective as pamphleteer and journalist (he was literary editor of *Tribune*, 1943–5, and contributed regularly to it and other papers). V. S. *Pritchett, reviewing his *The Lion and the Unicorn: socialism and the English genius* (1941), compared him to *Defoe and *Cobbett both for his 'subversive, non-conforming brand of patriotism' and for his 'lucid conversational style'. His collections of essays include *Inside the Whale* (1940), *Critical Essays* (1946), and *Shooting an Elephant* (1950). But his most popular works were undoubtedly his political satires *Animal Farm* (1945) and *Nineteen Eighty-four* (1949), which brought inevitable comparisons with *Swift. His first wife, Eileen, died in 1945, and he married Sonia Mary Brownwell in 1949, shortly before his death from tuberculosis, an illness from which he had suffered for many years. His *Collected Essays, Journalism and Letters* (4 vols, ed. S. Orwell and I. Angus) appeared in 1968; see also *George Orwell: A Life* (1980) by Bernard Crick.

Osbaldistone, Mr, Francis, Rashleigh, and Sir Hildebrand, characters in Scott's *Rob Roy*.

Osborne, Mr, his son George, and Maria and Jane, his daughters, characters in Thackeray's *Vanity Fair*.

OSBORNE, Dorothy (1627–95), met William *Temple on the Isle of Wight in 1648, when she was 21, he 20. After considerable family opposition they married in 1654. Her letters to him during the period 1652–4, most of them written from her family home of Chicksands, came to light when T. P. Courtenay published some in an appendix to his life of Temple in 1836; *Macaulay singled them out for praise and Parry's edition (1888) was followed by G. C. Moore's more scholarly edition in 1928. The letters are lively and witty, though occasionally solemn in their reflections; she believed that letters 'should be as free and easy as one's discourse'. They provide an intimate picture of the life, manners, and reading habits of the times, of the relations between the sexes, and particularly of a woman's attitudes to marriage and filial duty.

OSBORNE, John James (1929–), playwright, born in Fulham, London, the son of a commercial artist who died in 1940; the first volume of his autobiography, *A Better Class of Person* (1981), describes his childhood in suburbia, his brief spell as a journalist, and his years as an actor in provincial repertory, during which he began to write plays, the first of which was performed in 1950. He made his name with *Look Back in Anger (1956, pub. 1957), which was followed by Epitaph for George Dillon (1957, pub. 1958; written in the mid-1950s in collaboration with Anthony Creighton); The Entertainer (1957, which starred Laurence Olivier as Archie Rice, a faded survivor of the great days of music hall); Luther (1961, based on the life of Martin *Luther, with much emphasis on his physical as well as his spiritual problems); Inadmissible Evidence (1964, the tragedy of a down-at-heel solicitor, Bill Maitland, plunging rhetorically towards self-destruction); and A Patriot for Me (1965, a highly theatrical piece set in Vienna, based on the rise and fall of Redl, a homosexual officer in the Austro-Hungarian army, ruined by blackmail). Iconoclastic, energetic, and impassioned, Osborne's works at their most positive praise the qualities of loyalty, tolerance, and friendship, but his later works (which include West of Suez, 1971; A Sense of Detachment, 1972; Watch it Come Down, 1976) have become increasingly vituperative in tone, and the objects of his invective have become apparently more arbitrary; his outbursts of rage against contemporary society are frequently exhilarating, for the anger that made him known as an *'Angry Young Man' remains one of his strongest theatrical weapons, but he also expresses from time to time an ambivalent nostalgia for the past that his own work did so much to alter. (See also KITCHEN SINK.)

OSBORNE, Thomas (d. 1767), bookseller, remembered as having issued Richardson's

*Pamela, and published the *Harleian Miscellany. He was beaten by Dr *Johnson for impertinence and ridiculed by *Pope.

O'SHAUGHNESSY, Arthur William Edgar (1844–81), poet and friend of D. G. *Rossetti, worked at the British Museum in the department of printed books and the natural history department. He published several volumes of poetry, his best known, 'Ode' ('We are the music-makers'), appeared in *Music and Moonlight* (1874) and has been noted as a characteristic example of Victorian escapist verse.

OSLER, Sir William (1849–1919), distinguished physician, born in Canada, was professor of medicine at McGill, Pennsylvania, and Johns Hopkins universities and Regius professor of medicine at Oxford (1905–11). His many published works include the notable *Principles of Practice of Medicine* (1892) and his valuable medical library is now at McGill University, Montreal.

OSORIO DA FONSECA, Jeronimo (1506–80), Portuguese historian, born in Lisbon, and educated at the universities of Salamanca, Paris, and Bologna. He was for a time professor of theology at Coimbra and, from 1564, bishop of Silves. He wrote in Latin (and was dubbed the 'Portuguese Cicero'); his *De Rebus Emmanuelis Regis Lusitaniae* (1571) was much admired. In 1562 he wrote an attack on the English Reformation, which was answered by Haddon, master of requests to Elizabeth, and by *Foxe (1577, English translation 1581). His library was seized on the occasion of Essex's expedition of 1596 and subsequently given to the newly founded Bodleian (see LIBRARIES).

Osric, an affected courtier in Shakespeare's *Hamlet, referred to as 'a Braggart Gentleman' in the first Quarto.

Ossian, the name commonly given to *Oisin, a legendary Gaelic warrior and bard. See MACPHERSON and FINGAL.

OSTROVSKY, Alexander Nikolaevich (1823–86), Russian playwright, was born into a merchant family in Moscow. The first of his plays to be staged was *The Poor Bride* (1853), and by the time of his death he had produced about forty prose plays and eight in blank verse. He translated * The Taming of the Shrew (1865) and was working on a translation of *Antony and Cleopatra when he died. His main subject matter is the life of Muscovite and provincial merchants and lower officialdom. Among his best plays are *It's a Family Affair—We'll Settle it Ourselves* (1850), *The Poor Bride* (pub. 1852), *The Dowerless Girl* (1879), and his two acknowledged masterpieces, *The Storm* (1860, an intensely poetical work) and *The Forest* (1871). Ostrovsky remains to this day extremely popular in Russia. *A Domestic Picture* (1847) and *Incompatibility of Temper* (1858) appeared in English translation by E. *Voynich in 1895, and C. *Garnett's translation of *The Storm* in 1898. Since then a number of his plays have appeared in English. He has recently enjoyed some success on the London stage, with productions of *The Storm* (1964), *The Forest* (1981), and his 1881 play *Artistes and Admirers* (1982).

OSWALD, St (d. 992), one of the three leading figures (along with *Dunstan and *Æthelwold) in the 10th-cent. Benedictine Revival in England, became a Benedictine monk at Fleury and accompanied Oskitel, archbishop of York, to Rome. On Dunstan's initiative he was appointed bishop of Worcester in 961. He founded monasteries at Westbury, Worcester, Winchcombe, and on the Isle of Ramsey. In 972 he was made archbishop of York, but (like his successor *Wulfstan) retained the see of Worcester as well, for which he had a special affection and where he is buried in the church of St Mary.

Othello, *The Moor of Venice*, a tragedy by *Shakespeare, written between 1602 and 1604 when it was performed before James I at Whitehall. It was first printed in quarto in 1622, and again in a different version in the *Folio of 1623. The story is taken from *Cinthio, which Shakespeare could have read in Italian or French.

The play's first act (which *Verdi's opera *Otello* omits) is set in Venice. Desdemona, the daughter of Brabantio, a Venetian senator, has secretly married Othello, a Moor in the service of the state. Accused before the duke and senators of having stolen Brabantio's daughter, Othello explains and justifies his conduct, and is asked by the Senate to lead the Venetian forces against the Turks who are about to attack Cyprus.

In the middle of a storm which disperses the Turkish fleet, Othello lands on Cyprus with Desdemona, Cassio, a young Florentine, who helped him court his wife and whom he has now promoted to be his lieutenant, and Iago, an older soldier, bitterly resentful of being passed over for promotion, who now plans his revenge. Iago uses Roderigo, 'a gull'd Gentleman' in love with Desdemona, to fight with Cassio after he has got him drunk, so that Othello deprives him of his new rank. He then persuades Cassio to ask Desdemona to plead in his favour with Othello, which she warmly does. At the same time he suggests to Othello that Cassio is, and has been, Desdemona's lover, finally arranging through his wife Emilia, who is Desdemona's waiting-woman, that Othello should see Cassio in possession of a handkerchief which he had given to his bride. Othello is taken in by Iago's promptings and in frenzied jealousy smothers Desdemona in her bed. Iago sets Roderigo to murder Cassio, but when Roderigo fails to do

this Iago kills him and Emilia as well, after she has proved Desdemona's innocence to Othello. Emilia's evidence and letters found on Roderigo prove Iago's guilt; he is arrested, and Othello, having tried to stab him, kills himself.

According to *Rymer one of the play's morals was 'a warning to all good wives that they look well to their linen'. *Coleridge in a famous phrase described Iago's soliloquy at the end of I. iii as 'the motive-hunting of motiveless malignity'.

Otho the Great: *A Tragedy in Five Acts*, a play written by *Keats in 1819, in collaboration with his friend Charles Brown, who planned its construction. The plot is based on the history of the rebellion against Otho, during his Hungarian wars, by his son Ludolf and the Red Duke Conrad of Lorraine. For both artistic and financial reasons Keats had hoped that *Kean would undertake the part of Ludolf, but the hope was not fulfilled.

O'Trigger, Sir Lucius, a character in Sheridan's *The Rivals.*

Ottava rima, an Italian stanza of eight 11-syllabled lines, rhyming a b a b a b c c, employed by *Tasso, *Ariosto, etc. It was introduced into England by *Wyatt, and used to great effect by Byron in *Don Juan, with a 10-syllable iambic line.

Otter, Captain Thomas and Mistress, the ill-matched husband and wife in Jonson's *Epicene. Charles II, joking about the henpecked state of his brother the duke of York, christened him Tom Otter.

Otterbourne, *The Battle of,* one of the earliest of English ballads, included in Percy's *Reliques.

The Scots in 1388, returning from a raid into England, attacked the castle of Otterburn in Northumberland, and after an unsuccessful assault were surprised in their camp by Henry *Hotspur, Lord Percy. In the ensuing engagement James, earl of Douglas, commanding the Scottish force, was killed, and Percy taken prisoner. These events are the subject of the ballad.

Otuel, Sir, a pagan knight, miraculously converted, who became one of *Charlemagne's *Paladins. He is the nephew of Vernagu, killed in combat by *Roland as recounted in the English romance *Roland and Vernagu*. The Otuel story is told in three English Romances: *Otuel,* in four-stress couplets in the Auchinlech Manuscript (EETS ES 39, ed. S. J. Herrtage, 1882); *Duke Rowland and Sir Otuell of Spayne* (EETS ES 35, ed. S. J. Herrtage, 1880); the Fillingham *Otuel and Roland* (EETS OS 198, ed. M. O'Sullivan, 1934).

OTWAY, Thomas (1652–85), born at Milland near Trotton in Sussex, was educated at

Winchester and Christ Church, Oxford. He appeared unsuccessfully on the stage, being given a part by the kindness of A. *Behn. In 1678 he enlisted in the army in Holland and received a commission, but soon returned. He died in destitution at the early age of 33.

Of his three great tragedies, *Don Carlos, in rhymed verse, was produced in 1676; *The Orphan, in blank verse, in 1680; and *Venice Preserv'd, also in blank verse, in 1682. Of his other plays Alcibiades, a tragedy, was produced in 1675 (and provided Mrs *Barry, for whom Otway cherished an unrequited passion, with her first successful part); Titus and Berenice, adapted from a tragedy by *Racine, and The Cheats of Scapin, from a comedy by *Molière, in 1676; The History and Fall of Caius Marius, an adaptation of *Romeo and Juliet, in 1679; Friendship in Fashion, a comedy, in 1681; The Atheist, also a comedy, in 1683. He also wrote prologues, epilogues, and a few poems. The standard edition of Otway, ed. J. C. Ghosh, was published in 1932.

OUIDA, pen-name of Marie Louise de la Ramée (1839–1908), born in Bury St Edmunds; her mother was English and her father, Louis Ramée, a teacher of French. Her pseudonym is a childish mispronunciation of 'Louise'. She began her career contributing stories to *Bentley's Miscellany (1859–60) encouraged by its editor *Ainsworth. Her first real success was Held in Bondage (1863), which was followed by Strathmore (1865). By this time her reputation was established. She spent much time in Italy from 1860 and in 1874 settled in Florence where she pursued her work as a novelist while living in lavish style. Her other popular novels included Under Two Flags (1867), perhaps her most famous, Folle-Farine (1871), which *Bulwer-Lytton considered 'a triumph of modern English fiction', Two Little Wooden Shoes (1874), Moths (1880), A Village Commune (1881), and In Maremma (1882). Her 45 novels, often set in a fashionable world far removed from reality, show a spirit of rebellion against the moral ideals reflected in much of the fiction of the time. She suffered frequent ridicule for her extravagantly portrayed heroes, often languid guardsmen, miracles of strength, courage, and beauty, and for her inaccuracies in matters of men's sports and occupations; but her faults were redeemed by her narrative power and emotional energy. She wrote several animal stories, including A Dog of Flanders (1872) and Bimbi, Stories for Children (1882). After 1890 her popularity waned and she wrote chiefly critical and social articles for magazines. When her literary profits declined, she fell into debt, moved to Lucca in 1894, and from 1904 lived in destitution in Viareggio.

Our Man in Havana, see GREENE, G.

Our Mutual Friend, a novel by *Dickens, published in monthly parts between May 1864 and Nov. 1865.

John Harmon returns from the exile to which he has been sent by a harsh father, a rich dust-contractor; he expects to receive the inheritance to which his father has attached the condition that he shall marry a certain girl, Bella Wilfer. Bella is unknown to him, and he confides to a mate of the ship which is bringing him home his intention of concealing his identity until he has formed some judgement of his allotted wife. The mate lures him to a riverside haunt, attempts to murder him, throws his body into the river, and is in turn murdered and his body likewise thrown into the river. Harmon recovers and escapes; the mate's body is found after some days, and, owing to Harmon's papers found upon it, it is taken to be that of Harmon. Harmon's intention of remaining unknown is thus facilitated; he assumes the name of John Rokesmith and becomes the secretary of the kindly, disinterested Mr Boffin, old Harmon's foreman, who, in default of young Harmon, inherits the property. He is thrown into close contact with Bella, a flighty minx, who is adopted by Boffin and who is turned by her first taste of wealth into an arrogant, mercenary jade. Rokesmith nevertheless falls in love with her and is contemptuously rejected. Harmon's identity is now discovered by the amiable Mrs Boffin, and the Boffins, devoted to their old master's son and convinced of Bella's soundness of heart, contrive a plot to prove her. Boffin pretends to be transformed by his wealth into a hard and griping miser, and heaps indignities on Harmon, who is finally dismissed with contumely. Bella, awakened to the evils of wealth and to the merits of Rokesmith, flies from the Boffins and marries her suitor. His identity presently comes to light, and with his assistance the scheme of a one-legged old villain, Silas Wegg, to blackmail Boffin is exposed.

Concurrently with this main theme runs the story of the love of Eugene Wrayburn, a careless, insolent young barrister, for Lizzy Hexam, daughter of a disreputable boatman. His rival for her affections, Bradley Headstone, a schoolmaster, attempts to murder Wrayburn. The latter is saved by Lizzy and marries her. Among the notable characters in the book are the Veneerings, types of social parvenus; the good Jew Riah; the blackmailing waterside villain Rogue Riderhood; Jenny Wren, the dolls' dressmaker; Bella Wilfer's grotesque father, mother, and sister; and the spirited Betty Higden, an old woman with a haunting dread of the workhouse.

Many early reviewers agreed with H. *James, who found the novel 'forced' and 'wanting in inspiration', but later critics (including Humphry House and E. *Wilson) have praised it highly, stressing in particular the complex use of the dirt–money symbolism.

Our Village: sketches of rural life, character, and scenery, by M. R. *Mitford, published 1832.

The sketches, episodes, and descriptions which make up the book were written between 1824 and 1832, most of them appearing in the *Lady's Magazine*. The *Sketch Book* of W. *Irving provided her with the original idea. The village is based on Three Mile Cross, near Reading, where she and her father lived for 30 years, but other locations and memories are also used. The author declared, before beginning the series, that it was to describe 'country scenery and country manners', and that she abhorred sentimentality and pathos. Seasons, places, events, and people are sharply observed and precisely described, with affection and humour. Her lucid, unpretentious prose was evidently the result of diligence, for she wrote that 'what looks like ease in my style is labour'.

OUSPENSKY (1878–1947), journalist and unorthodox philosopher, was born in Moscow, and, although a brilliant student, refused to take regular courses, though he attended the university as a 'free listener'. He met *Gurdjieff in 1914 and became a disciple, devoted to disseminating his doctrines.

Outsider, The, (1) a novel by American author R. *Wright, published 1953; (2) a study by C. *Wilson published 1956.

OVERBURY, Sir Thomas (1581–1613), was educated at The Queen's College, Oxford, and went to the Middle Temple. He opposed the marriage of his patron Robert Carr (afterwards earl of Somerset) with the divorced countess of Essex, and on the pretext of his refusal of diplomatic employment was sent to the Tower, where he was slowly poisoned by the agents of Lady Essex. Four of these were hanged; Somerset and his wife were convicted and pardoned. The prosecution was conducted by F. *Bacon. The whole business remains a historical mystery. Overbury's poem *A Wife* appeared in 1614, and with its second edition the Theophrastian 'Characters' by which he is chiefly remembered. Later editions added new characters, some by J. *Webster and some by *Dekker (see W. J. Taylor's edition, *The Overburian Characters*, 1936). The types include 'A Roaring Boy', 'A Puny Clerk', 'A Mere Scholar', and few are as benign as the portrait of a milkmaid; *Earle responded to their harsh and anti-scholastic tone in his own *Microcosmographie*. (See CHARACTER-WRITING.)

Overdo, Justice Adam, the busy seeker-out of 'enormities' in Jonson's *Bartholomew Fair*.

Overreach, Sir Giles, a character in Massinger's *A New Way to pay Old Debts*.

OVERTON, Richard (*fl.* 1646), printer and leader of the Leveller movement, was a prolific, forceful, and versatile pamphleteer, much of whose work was published anonymously, and some under the pseudonym of Martin Marpriest, in the tradition of *Martin Marprelate. A tract on the immortality of the soul, *Man's Mortality* (1643), aroused much controversy, and he was imprisoned many times for his unorthodox religious and radical political views. He adopted *Lilburne's cause and was imprisoned in 1649 with him, Prince, and *Walwyn. His writing displays a firm faith in human reason, a colourful and often caustic prose (Walwyn praised his 'comic' and 'satiric' pen), and some powerful arguments for religious tolerance.

OVID (Publius Ovidius Naso) (43 BC–AD 18), Roman writer of love elegies (*Amores*), who then experimented with the imaginary letter (*Heroides*), mock didactic verse (*Ars Amatoria*), 'collective' narrative relating disconnected stories inside a large historical (*Metamorphoses*) or chronological (*Fasti*) frame, and finally with elegies of nostalgic complaint (*Tristia, Epistulae ex Ponto*), when Augustus had exiled him in AD 8 to the Black Sea for some mysterious indiscretion. Ovid continued in favour with writers and public so long as Rome was pagan, but the Christian Church disapproved of his immorality, so that little is heard of him during the six centuries that followed the conversion of Constantine. It is likely however that he was read surreptitiously. His works were certainly copied, and interest in them revived with the 11th cent. Poets in the cathedral schools took him for a model. The *Metamorphoses*, rendered edifying by moralization, were widely read (see, e.g. OVIDE MORALISÉ). During the Renaissance Ovid enjoyed great favour with writers and painters alike. *Chaucer and *Gower both borrowed his stories. But the late 16th and early 17th cents were England's Ovidian Age when *Lodge, *Marlowe, *Spenser, *Shakespeare, *G. *Chapman, *Drayton, T. *Heywood, were all indebted to him directly or through A. *Golding's translation of the *Metamorphoses* (1565–7). By the middle of the 17th cent. his popularity was in decline, although echoes of his lines can be found in *Milton. With the growth of Puritan seriousness, the mixture of wit and sensuality that Ovid offered no longer had an immediate appeal. Themes from the *Metamorphoses* were handled by W. *King ('Orpheus and Eurydice', 1704), Swift (*Baucis and Philemon*), *Prior ('Daphne and Apollo', 1740), *Shelley (*Arethusa*, 1820), Morris ('Pygmalion' in *The Earthly Paradise*, 1868–70), Swinburne (*Atalanta in Calydon*, 1865), and Shaw (*Pygmalion*, 1916), but they stray very far from their originals.

Ovide Moralisé, a French work influential on

*Chaucer and on the *Ovidius Moralizatus* by Pierre Bersuire (d. 1362) which is Book XV of his huge *Reductorium Morale*, completed in 1340. It moralizes 15 books of the *Metamorphoses* and is highly significant in the development of late medieval and Renaissance literature by bringing secular literature into the official canon. Cf. *Fulgentius Metaforalis* by Ridewall (*c*.1330) for the practice of allegorizing the stories of classical authors.

OWEN, John (?1563–1622), educated at Winchester and New College, Oxford, was the author of several volumes of Latin epigrams, mostly in elegiac couplets, which were translated into several languages and frequently reprinted down to the 19th cent.

OWEN, Sir Richard (1804–92), educated at Lancaster School with *Whewell, became conservator of the Hunterian museum and first Hunterian professor of comparative anatomy and physiology. He opposed C. *Darwin's views on evolution, and was a fierce controversialist.

OWEN, Robert (1771–1858), socialist and philanthropist, was born in Wales, the son of a shopkeeper, and became the wealthy owner of cotton-spinning mills in Manchester. In 1799 he purchased the New Lanark mills in Scotland, and proceeded to set up there his model community and model village, organized on principles of mutual co-operation, as well as infant schools and other educational institutions. His example was largely instrumental in bringing about the Factory Act of 1819, although, disappointed with the slow rate of reform, he left Britain in 1821 for some years to set up another model community, New Harmony, in America. Owen was the pioneer of co-operation between workers and consumers, and his ideas strengthened the growing co-operative movement. He published *A New View of Society* in 1813 and *The Revolution in Mind and Practice of the Human Race* in 1849. There is a life by G. D. H. *Cole, published 1925. (See also SOCIALISM.)

OWEN, Wilfrid (1893–1918), born in Shropshire, where his father was a railway-worker, was educated in Liverpool and at Shrewsbury Technical College. He began to experiment with verse from an early age, and read widely. After a period assisting in a poor country parish, he left in 1913 to teach English in Bordeaux, then returned in 1915 to join the army, in which he was soon commissioned. After concussion and trench-fever on the Somme he was invalided to hospital in Edinburgh, where he was greatly encouraged in his writing by *Sassoon. He returned to France in 1918, won the MC, and was killed on the Sambre Canal a week before the Armistice. He found his own voice as a poet in the trenches, and most of the poems for which he is remembered were written in a creative burst between the summer of 1917 and the autumn of the next year. Only five of his poems were published in his lifetime, and they made little mark on a public revering Rupert *Brooke. However, his reputation slowly grew, greatly assisted by *Blunden's edition of his poems, with a Memoir, in 1931, and he is now generally regarded as a war poet of the first rank. His bleak realism, his energy and indignation, his compassion, and his high technical skills (he was a master of metrical variety and of assonance) are evident in most of his work. His poems were chosen by *Britten for the *War Requiem*. The poems were collected again in 1963, edited by *Day-Lewis, and a biography by Jon Stallworthy appeared in 1974.

Owl and the Nightingale, The, an early Middle English poem of 1,794 lines of octosyllabic couplets, probably from the beginning of the 13th cent., two of the three known manuscripts of which survive. It is a debate between the grave owl and the gay nightingale as to the benefits each confers on mankind, the symbolic implications of which have been much disputed; they have been said, for example, to represent the religious poet and the love poet. It is a very learned work which touches with light, scholastic legalism on many matters of serious contemporary interest: foreknowledge, music, Confession, papal missions, and so on. It is a virtuoso poem, highly accomplished in its style and in its humorous tone, which reaches no definite conclusion. The debate is to be submitted at the end to the judgement of one Nicholas of Guildford who is likely to be the author; a certain John of Guildford, who is known to have written *c*.1225, has also been proposed. See editions by E. G. Stanley (1960), J. W. Atkins (1922, with translation); see also K. Hume, *The Owl and the Nightingale: the Poem and its Critics* (1975).

Owlglass, see EULENSPIEGEL.

OXFORD, Edward De Vere, 17th earl of (1550–1604), was educated at Cambridge. A. *Golding, the translator of Ovid, was his uncle. He married Lord Burleigh's daughter, and high hopes were placed on him as a courtier and patron, but they were dissipated as his capricious and quarrelsome temperament became apparent. His most famous quarrel was with *Sidney, whom, according to *Greville, he addressed as 'puppy' in a dispute at the tennis court in 1579; there is also some evidence that he planned to kill him. It is perhaps appropriate that one of the 15 or so surviving poems attributed to him is entitled 'Love compared to a tennis playe'. By some his literary capacities have been highly regarded: T. J. Looney identified him in 1920 as the author of Shakespeare's plays, and a sizeable body of 'Oxfordians' have since built on this claim.

Oxford, John, earl of, disguised as the merchant Philipson, a character in Scott's *Anne of Geierstein.*

OXFORD, Robert, 1st earl of, see HARLEY, R.

Oxford and Cambridge Magazine, The, a periodical of the year 1856, of which twelve monthly numbers appeared, financed mainly by W. *Morris. Among its (anonymous) contributors were Morris and *Burne-Jones (of Oxford), and Henry Lushington (1812–55) of Cambridge, and by invitation D. G. *Rossetti, whose 'Burden of Nineveh' appeared in its pages. The contents were predominantly literary, and included poems, tales, fairy-stories, essays, and reviews.

Oxford English Dictionary, The. The scheme of 'a completely new English Dictionary' was conceived in 1858, chiefly as the result of the reading of two papers 'On some Deficiencies in our English Dictionaries' by Dr R. C. *Trench to the *Philological Society in 1857. Herbert Coleridge (1830–61), and after him Dr F. J. *Furnivall, were the first editors. Their work, which covered twenty years, consisted mainly in the collection of materials, and it was not until Dr J. A. H. *Murray took the matter up in 1878 that the preparation of the Dictionary began to take active form. The first part (A–Ant) was published in 1884, at which time Murray estimated that the whole might be completed in another twelve years. It was not in fact finished until 1928, seventy years from the inception of the undertaking. Murray, who laid down the lines of the work, did not live to see it completed (at his death, T had been reached); but more than half was produced under his personal editorship. His co-editors were Dr H. *Bradley (from 1888), Dr W. A. *Craigie (from 1901), and Dr C. T. *Onions (from 1914).

The essential feature of the Dictionary is its historical method, by which the meaning and form of the words are traced from their earliest appearance on the basis of an immense number of quotations, collected by more than 800 voluntary workers. The Dictionary contains a record of 414,825 words, whose history is illustrated by 1,827,306 quotations. A supplement of 867 pages appeared in 1933. In 1957 work began, under the editorship of R. W. *Burchfield, on the new supplement, superseding that of 1933, and treating all the vocabulary which came into use while the main Dictionary was being published or after its completion. The outcome of this work, entitled *A Supplement to the Oxford English Dictionary*, contains a record of approximately 120,000 words and is about one-third of the length of the main

Dictionary. Of its four volumes, the first three (covering the letters A–Scz) appeared in 1972, 1976, and 1982, and the fourth is due for publication in 1986. The original title of the main work was 'A New English Dictionary on Historical Principles' (abbreviated as *NED*). The title *The Oxford English Dictionary* first appeared in the reprint of 1933.

Oxford Gazette, The, was the first real newspaper, other than a newsletter, to be published in England. It appeared in Nov. 1665, the court being then at Oxford owing to the great plague, and was started by H. *Muddiman under the direction of his patron Sir Joseph Williamson. It became the *London Gazette* in 1666. It still survives, not now a newspaper, but a record of official appointments, notices of bankruptcy, etc., having passed in 1923 into the keeping of the Stationery Office. See P. M. Handover, *A History of the London Gazette 1665–1965* (1965), in which she describes its slow evolution to its present form, and describes its anomalies and eccentricities as 'relics of ancient pride and state'.

Oxford Movement, or Tractarian Movement, a movement of thought and doctrine within the Church of England, centred at Oxford, the impulse of which was the Assize Sermon on National Apostasy preached by *Keble in 1833. This criticized the prevalent Erastian and latitudinarian tendencies of the Anglican church, and generated an investigation into the nature of the church. The movement aimed to defend the Church of England as a divine institution with an independent spiritual status, and to revive the High Church traditions of the 17th cent.; the Reform Act of 1832, and the views of *Broad Church supporters such as T. *Arnold, had led many to believe that the church was in danger of increasing subordination to the state. Keble's sermon inspired *Newman, R. H. *Froude, and others to launch their series *Tracts for the Times* in 1833 (which gave the Tractarian movement its name); the series attracted the influential support of *Pusey, who gave the movement cohesion and authority. The tracts varied from short leaflets to learned treatises, and covered a wide range of theological issues; it was Newman's famous Tract XC (1841) on the compatibility of the Thirty-nine Articles with Roman Catholic theology that brought the Tractarians under official ban, but hostility had already been aroused by the publication of the first volumes of Froude's *Literary Remains* in 1838, with its strictures on the Reformation. W. G. *Ward's *The Ideal of a Christian Church* (1844), with its praise of the Roman Catholic church, intensified hostility, and led to suspicions that the Tractarians (and principally Newman) were subversively leading their followers towards Rome. Newman himself became a Roman Catholic in 1845, a decision which dealt a severe blow to the unity of the movement. There is a remarkable history of the movement by R. W. *Church (1891); see also Newman's *Apologia pro Vita Sua* (1864) and the autobiography of I. *Williams. Other leaders of the movement included J. W. Bowden, W. Palmer, and A. P. Perceval.

The impact of the Tractarians on intellectual, religious, and cultural life was immense. In literary terms, the revival of interest in the medieval and 17th-cent. church influenced *Tennyson, W. *Morris and the *Pre-Raphaelites, C. *Rossetti and C. M. *Yonge, among others; it also added strength to the revival of *Gothic architecture associated with *Pugin.

Oxford University Press, a publishing and printing business owned by the University and directed by its Delegates of the Press, of whom the Vice-Chancellor is *ex officio* chairman. Its aims are to produce books of religious, scholarly, and educational value, and, its surplus profits being devoted to financing the editing and production of unremunerative works of this kind, its status is that of a charity.

Printing in Oxford by independent craftsmen began in the 15th cent. (see UNIVERSITY PRESSES), and in 1584 one of these was appointed 'Printer to the University'. This title was borne by a succession of printers in the 17th cent. and was revived in 1925 for the head of the printing department of the Press. One press at Oxford was excepted from the prohibition of printing outside London by a decree of the Star Chamber in 1586, and in 1632 a royal charter allowed the University three presses and to print and sell 'all manner of books'. *Laud in 1634 bound the University to provide itself with a printing house; but a press under its immediate control did not come into being until 1690. In the meantime *Fell had won an international reputation for Oxford books by his exercise of the University's privilege of printing, let to him in 1672. By his bequest his unsold books and printing equipment became the property of the University in 1690.

Under the management of the Delegates since then the Press has produced such famous books as *Clarendon's *History* (1702), *Blackstone's *Commentaries* (1769), Kennicott's Hebrew Bible (1780), Clerk Maxwell's *Treatise on Electricity and Magnetism* (1873), the Revised Version of the English Bible (1885), and *The Oxford English Dictionary*, completed in 1928, besides many millions of Bibles and prayer-books and, in recent times, of standard classical and modern texts, school books, and English and bilingual dictionaries.

The copyright in Clarendon's works, once very profitable, is secured to the University in perpetuity, and in his honour the building to which the Press moved in 1829 was named 'The Clarendon Press'. This is the imprint given to learned books published under the supervision of the Secretary to the Delegates at Oxford. Books of more general appeal, including verse anthologies and reference books covering a wide range of topics, were published between 1880 and 1976 from the Press's London offices, subsequently from Oxford.

Oxford Sausage, The, see WARTON, T.

Oxymoron, from two Greek words meaning 'sharp', 'dull', a rhetorical figure by which two incongruous or contradictory terms are united in an expression so as to give it point; e.g. 'Faith unfaithful kept him falsely true' (Tennyson, *Idylls of the King*).

P

Pacchiarotto and *How He Worked in Distemper: with other poems,* a collection of 19 poems, in various metres, by R. *Browning, published 1876. The title poem, the three which follow it, and the epilogue, were directed at Browning's critics, in satirical or serious vein; the remaining poems are a miscellany on topics of religion, love, and art. 'Numpholeptos', 'St Martin's Summer', and 'A Forgiveness' deserve particular mention. The most unusual poem in the volume is, however, the ballad 'Hervé Riel', about the heroic exploit of a French sailor in a fight against the British.

Padlock, The, a comic opera by *Bickerstaffe, with music by *Dibdin, performed with much success in 1768.

The elderly Don Diego is the temporary guardian of the young Leonora and is about to make her his wife. But, in spite of a large padlock on the door, Leander, a young lover, presents himself during Diego's absence, cajoles the duenna and Mungo, the Negro servant, and gains admission to the lady. Diego returns unexpectedly, but sensibly accepts the situation and handsomely endows Leonora. The story is taken from one of *Cervantes's novels.

The part of Mungo (taken in the original production by Dibdin himself) provided the London stage with its first black-faced comedian, and created a sensation: for a while his lines 'Mungo here, Mungo dere, Mungo every where' were a catch-phrase. As feeling for the oppressed Negro grew, the role appears to have been played with increasing stress on sentiment.

*Prior wrote a short poem called 'An English Padlock', containing advice to the jealous husband of a young wife. It contains the well-known lines:

> Be to her virtues very kind;
> Be to her faults a little blind;
> Let all her ways be unconfin'd
> And clasp a padlock on her mind.

Paean, a song of thanksgiving for deliverance from evil or danger, addressed usually to Apollo who, as god of healing, was given the name Paean. Later the word is used for a shout or song of triumph.

Paeon, see METRE.

PAGANINI, Nicolò (1782–1840), Italian violinist and composer. The most famous of all violin virtuosi, his playing produced an extraordinary effect on his hearers, with a daemonic quality that gave rise to romantic talk about supernatural powers. Paganini's influence on *Liszt and other virtuoso composers of the 19th cent. was of the greatest importance. At a more practical level, it was Paganini who commissioned *Berlioz to write a work for viola and orchestra (the *Byronic *Harold en Italie*) and, though he did not like the result and never played it, later made the generous gift of 20,000 francs which enabled Berlioz to compose the greatest of all his Shakespearian works, the dramatic symphony *Roméo et Juliette*.

Page, Mrs Page, and Anne Page, their daughter, characters in Shakespeare's *The Merry Wives of Windsor*.

PAGET, Violet, see LEE, V.

PAINE, Thomas (1737–1809), son of a Quaker staymaker of Thetford, followed various pursuits before being dismissed as an exciseman in 1774 for agitating for an increase in excisemen's pay. At the suggestion of his friend Benjamin *Franklin he sailed for America, where he published in 1776 his pamphlet *Common Sense* and in 1776–83 a series of pamphlets, *The Crisis,* encouraging American independence and resistance to England; he also wrote against slavery and in favour of the emancipation of women. In 1787 he returned to England (via France), and published in 1791 the first part of *The Rights of Man* in reply to Burke's *Reflections on the *Revolution in France.* The second part appeared in 1792, when, alerted by *Blake of an impending arrest, Paine left for France, where he was warmly received and elected a member of the Convention. However, he opposed the execution of Louis XVI, was imprisoned for nearly a year, and narrowly escaped the guillotine. *The Age of Reason* (1793), an attack on Christianity and the Bible from a Deist point of view, greatly increased the violent hatred with which he was regarded in England, where his effigy and books were repeatedly burned; he was attacked in print by R. *Watson, bishop of Llandaff, and many others. He returned to America in 1802, where his views on religion and his opposition to Washington had made him unpopular, and his last years were saddened by ill health and neglect. He was buried at his farm in New Rochelle; ten years later *Cobbett, who had once vehemently opposed Paine, exhumed his bones and brought them back to England, planning some kind of memorial as reparation, but they were eventually mislaid.

Paine's early biographers did their best to denigrate him, but his writings became a textbook for the Radical party in England and were extremely influential; his connection with the American struggle and the French revolution gave him a unique position as an upholder of the politics of the *Enlightenment. His prose is plainer, more colloquial, and less rhetorical than that of *Burke, whose 'high-toned exclamation' he despised. He gave away most of the considerable earnings from his pen, in part to the Society of Constitutional Information, founded in 1780.

PAINTER, George, see BIOGRAPHY.

PAINTER, William, see PALACE OF PLEASURE.

Pair of Blue Eyes, A, a novel by T. *Hardy, published 1873.

The scene is the northern coast of Cornwall. Stephen Smith, a young architect, comes to Endelstow to restore the church tower and falls in love with Elfride Swancourt, the blue-eyed daughter of the vicar. Her father is incensed that someone of Stephen's humble origin should claim his daughter. Elfride and Stephen run away together, but Elfride vacillates over marriage, and Stephen, hoping to better himself, accepts a post in India. Henry Knight, Stephen's friend and patron, then meets Elfride, and after she has saved his life on a cliff they become engaged. However, Knight is horrified to hear of Elfride's truancy with Stephen and is convinced that they must have been lovers. He harshly breaks off the engagement leaving Elfride heart-broken. Eventually he and Stephen meet; Stephen learns that Elfride is still unmarried and Knight learns the innocent facts of her past escapade with Stephen. But the train which carries them both to Cornwall is also carrying Elfride's dead body. They learn when they arrive at Endelstow that she has died, and that she had recently married Lord Luxellian.

Palace of Pleasure, a collection of translations into English of 'Pleasant Histories and excellent Novelles . . . out of divers good and commendable Authors', made by William Painter (c.1525–95), Clerk of the Ordnance, and published in 1566, 1567, and 1575. Many of the translations are from *Boccaccio, *Bandello, and Marguerite of Navarre (see HEPTAMERON), but Painter also drew on *Herodotus, *Livy, and *Gellius. The book provided a storehouse of plots for Elizabethan writers, especially dramatists; Shakespeare probably used it for *The Rape of Lucrece and *All's Well that Ends Well, and Webster certainly drew the plot of *The Duchess of Malfi from it. It was edited by Joseph Jacobs (1890).

Paladins, The, in the cycle of *Charlemagne legends, the twelve peers who accompanied the king. The origin of the conception is seen in the *Chanson de Roland* (see ROLAND), where the twelve peers are merely an association of particularly brave warriors, under the leadership of Roland and *Oliver, who all perish at Roncesvalles. From the Spanish war the idea was transported by later writers to other parts of the cycle, and Charlemagne is found always surrounded by twelve peers. The names of the twelve are differently stated by different authors, most of the original names given by the *Chanson de Roland* being forgotten by them; but Roland and Oliver figure in all the enumerations. Among the best known are *Otuel, Fierabras or *Ferumbras, *Ogier the Dane, and the Count Palatine. In the early 13th cent. there was a French court, comprising six ecclesiastics and six laymen, known as 'The Twelve Peers of France'; this court in 1202 declared King John deprived of his fiefs in France. Since the 16th cent. the word is applied to any great knightly champion (cf. word 'Peer').

Palamon and Arcite, the two Theban princes whose love for Emelye is the subject of Chaucer's 'The Knight's Tale' (see CANTERBURY TALES, 1), following the *Teseida* of *Boccaccio. The tale was paraphrased in heroic couplets by *Dryden under the title 'Palamon and Arcite'. It is also the subject of *The Two Noble Kinsmen.

PALEY, William (1743–1805), educated at Christ's College, Cambridge, of which he became fellow. He was one of the principal exponents of theological utilitarianism of which his *Moral and Political Philosophy* (1785), based largely on the doctrine of *Tucker, is the textbook; an attack on private property in Book III, drawing an analogy between human greed and the behaviour of a flock of pigeons, gave him his nickname 'Pigeon' Paley. In *Evidences of Christianity* (1794) and *Natural Theology* (1802) he finds proof of the existence of God in the design apparent in natural phenomena, and particularly in the mechanisms of the human body; the opening pages of *Natural Theology* introduce the celebrated analogy of an abandoned watch found upon a heath, from which he argues the existence of God as designer, for as 'the watch must have had a maker', so must the natural world.

PALGRAVE, Sir Francis (1788–1861), barrister, historian, and antiquarian, changed his name from Cohen on his marriage and conversion to Christianity in 1823. He wrote various historical works, was deputy-keeper of the records, 1838–61, and did much to promote the critical study of medieval history.

PALGRAVE, Francis Turner (1824–97), son of Sir F. *Palgrave, was educated at Balliol College, Oxford, was an official in the education department 1855–84, and professor of poetry at Oxford, 1885–95. He is chiefly remembered for his anthology *The Golden Treasury of best songs and Lyrical poems in the English language* (1861, and much reprinted; second series, 1897). In the selection for the first edition Palgrave was advised by his close friend *Tennyson; it contained no work by living poets, and is a reflection of the taste of the age (e.g. no *Donne and no *Blake, though work by these poets was added to subsequent editions). New and enlarged editions with poems by later writers have since appeared; the most recent in 1965, with a fifth book selected by John Press. Palgrave compiled other anthologies and selections, and published several volumes of his own verse.

PALGRAVE, William Gifford (1826–88), son of Sir F. *Palgrave, educated at Trinity College, Oxford, became a Jesuit missionary in Syria and Arabia. After undertaking a daring journey through Arabia for Napoleon III, in the guise of a doctor, he wrote *Narrative of a Year's Journey through Central and Eastern Arabia* (1865), his interesting but somewhat unreliable reminiscences of this expedition. He then left the Jesuits to join the diplomatic service in which he held various posts from 1865. Shortly before his death he became reconciled to the Church.

Palimpsest, from πάλιν 'again', and ψηστός 'rubbed smooth', a manuscript in which a later writing is superimposed on an effaced earlier writing. Of frequent occurrence in the early Middle Ages because of the cost of parchment.

Palindrome, from παλίνδρομος, 'running back again', a word, verse, or sentence that reads the same forwards or backwards, e.g.:

> Lewd did I live & evil I did dwel
> (Phillips, 1706)

and the Latin line descriptive of moths:

> In girum imus noctes et consumimur igni.

Palinode, from παλινωδία 'singing over again', a recantation. 'Palinode' is the name of the Catholic shepherd in the fifth eclogue of Spenser's *The Shepheardes Calender.*

Palinurus, see CONNOLLY, C.

Palladianism, a revival of the style and ideas of *Palladio and of his English follower I. *Jones, dominated English architectural theory from *c.*1720 to 1770. The Whig aristocrat and man of taste admired the rationality and the mathematical proportions of Palladio's buildings; the movement marks a turning away from the panache of Hawksmoor and *Vanbrugh towards a purer form of classicism. Palladianism opened with two publications; Colen Campbell's *Vitruvius Britannicus* (1st vol. 1715), a collection of engravings of English buildings inspired by antiquity, and Giacomo Leoni's English version of Palladio's *I Quattro libri dell'architettura* (1st

vol. 1715). In the 1720s the architect-earl Lord Burlington dominated; his Chiswick House (1725–9), deeply influenced by Palladio's Villa Rotonda and by Inigo Jones, epitomizes the Palladian movement in England. *Pope was a Palladian enthusiast; his *Epistle to Burlington* (1731), both satirizes its excesses and sums up its aspirations; he invites the earl to:

> Erect new wonders, and the old repair
> Jones and Palladio to themselves restore,
> And be whate'er Vitruvius was before.
> (192–4)

PALLADIO, Andrea (1508–80), highly influential Italian architect of the late Renaissance, whose elegant style was formed by his passion for the buildings of antiquity, by his knowledge of *Vitruvius, and by his response to High Renaissance and Mannerist architects. The symmetry and harmonious proportions of his buildings epitomize one aspect of Renaissance thought; the name Palladio (from Pallas Athena) was given him by the humanist Giangiorgio Trissino of Vicenza, who sensed in him a renewal of Greek wisdom and beauty. Palladio was unrivalled in his ability to express the ideas of antiquity in a modern idiom, yet he was a sophisticated Mannerist architect, and as his career progressed his treatment of classical themes became increasingly imaginative. Palladio designed the churches of San Giorgio Maggiore (1566–80) and Il Redentore (begun 1577) in Venice, but most of his works are in and around Vicenza; they include many town palaces, the Teatro Olimpico (begun 1580; finished by Scamozzi), and many country houses and villas which were to affect English architecture in the early 18th cent. The characteristic Palladian villa has a symmetrically planned central block, with a portico deriving from a classical temple front and low wings. The most famous is the untypical Villa Rotonda (1550–1). Palladio's buildings became widely known through his *Quattro libri dell'architettura* (1570). (See also PALLADIANISM.)

Palladis Tamia, see MERES, F.

Palliser Novels, The, a term used to describe the political novels of A. *Trollope, which are: *Can You Forgive Her?, *Phineas Finn, *The Eustace Diamonds, *Phineas Redux, *The Prime Minister,* and * The Duke's Children.*

Pall Mall Gazette, The, was an evening paper founded in 1865 by Frederick Greenwood (1830–1909) and George *Smith to combine the features of a newspaper with the literary features of the *Spectator and the *Saturday Review. Its name was taken from Thackeray's *Pendennis,* where Captain Shandon in the Marshalsea prepares the prospectus of 'The Pall Mall Gazette', 'written by gentlemen for gentlemen'. Its early contributors included Sir Henry

Maine (1822–88), *Trollope, Sir F. J. *Stephen, L. *Stephen, and M. *Arnold (whose *Friendship's Garland* first appeared in it); in 1880 Smith parted with it to his Liberal son-in-law, and J. *Morley took over as editor, to be succeeded (1883–9) by W. T. *Stead, whose sensational journalism altered the character of the paper. Greenwood produced instead the newly founded Conservative *St James's Gazette*.

Palmerin of England (*Palmerin de Inglaterra*), a chivalric romance attributed to the 16th-cent. Portuguese writer Francisco de Moraes.

The 'Palmerins' consist of eight books dealing with the exploits and loves of Palmerin d'Oliva, emperor of Constantinople, and his various descendants, of which Palmerin of England is the subject of the sixth. The daughter of Palmerin d'Oliva, Flerida by name, married Don Duardos, son of Fadrique, king of Great Britain, and became the mother of Palmerin of England and his brother, Floriano of the Desert. Duardos having been imprisoned in the castle of the giant Dramusiando by Eutropa, a magician, a savage carries off Palmerin and Floriano intending them as food for his hunting lions, but his wife insists on bringing them up. Palmerin is taken to Constantinople and appointed to wait on his cousin Polinarda, with whom he falls in love; while Floriano is taken to London and appointed to wait on Flerida. Palmerin and Floriano undertake the quest of Don Duardos, and the former is successful. Thereafter the identity of the brothers is revealed and Palmerin marries Polinarda. Then the Soldan advances against the Christians and demands the surrender of Polinarda as a condition of peace. Finally the Turks attack Constantinople; all the Turks and most of the Christians perish, but Palmerin survives.

*Munday translated the Palmerin cycle into English (through a French intermediary), 1581–95. It was highly popular with the Elizabethan middle classes, and there are many references to Palmerin in the plays of the time (e.g. *The Knight of the Burning Pestle*, where the vogue for such chivalric fantasies is mocked). A revised translation by *Southey appeared in 1807, in which Southey suggests debts to Palmerin from Shakespeare, *Spenser, and *Sidney. See *The Palmerin Romances in Elizabethan Prose Fiction* (1947) by M. Tatchell.

Palmerin of England and *Amadis of Gaul* were two romances of chivalry specially excepted from the holocaust of such works carried out by the curate and the barber in *Don Quixote*.

Palomydes the Saracen, in *Malory, a prominent knight and great fighter who follows the *Questing Beast and who once abducts *Iseult, for whom he entertains an unrequited and mostly selfless passion. He is the great friend of Tristram who has him christened at the end.

The French prose romance *Palamedes* seems to have been written as an addition to the Vulgate *Tristan* and *Lancelot* in the early 13th cent.; it achieved enormous popularity in the later Middle Ages and influenced *Boiardo and *Ariosto, who said it was his favourite among the Arthurian romances.

PALTOCK, Robert (1697–1767), author of *Peter Wilkins*. He was an attorney of Clement's Inn.

Pamela, the heir to the dukedom of Arcadia in the romance of *Sidney. Richardson took her name for the heroine of his first novel (below).

Pamela, or *Virtue Rewarded*, a novel by S. *Richardson, published 1740–1.

The first of Richardson's three novels, *Pamela* consists, like them, entirely of letters and journals, of which Richardson presents himself as the 'editor'. He believed he had hit upon 'a new species of writing' but he was not the inventor of the *epistolary novel, several of which already existed in English and French. He did however raise the form to a level hitherto unknown, and transformed it to display his own particular skills.

There are six correspondents in *Pamela*, most with their own particular style and point of view, but Pamela herself provides most of the letters and journals, with the 'hero', Mr B., having only two. Pamela Andrews is a handsome, intelligent girl of fifteen when her kind employer Lady B. dies. Penniless and without protection, Pamela is pursued by Mr B., Lady B.'s son, but she repulses him and remains determined to retain her chastity and her unsullied conscience. Letters reveal Mr B.'s cruel dominance and pride, but also Pamela's half-acknowledged tenderness for him, as well as her vanity, prudence, and calculation. Angrily Mr B. separates her from her friends, Mrs Jervis the housekeeper and Mr Longman the steward, and dispatches her to B— Hall, his remote house in Lincolnshire, where she is imprisoned, guarded, and threatened by the cruel Mrs Jewkes. Only the chaplain, Mr Williams, is her friend, but is powerless to help. For forty days, allowed no visits or correspondence, she keeps a detailed Journal, analysing her situation and her feelings, and at the same time revealing her faults of prudence and pride. She despairs, and begins to think of suicide. Mr B., supposing her spirit must now be broken, arrives at B— Hall, and, thinking himself generous, offers to make her his mistress and keep her in style. She refuses indignantly, and he later attempts to rape her and then to arrange a mock-marriage. Two scenes by the pond mark a turning-point in their relationship. Both begin to be aware of their faults, and of the genuine nature of their affection. However, Pamela again retreats and refuses his proposal of marriage. She is sent away from

B— Hall, but a message gives her a last chance. Overcoming her pride and caution, she decides to trust him, accepts his offer, and they are married. In the remaining third of the book Pamela's goodness wins over even Lady Davers, Mr B.'s supercilious sister, and becomes a model of virtue to her circle of admiring friends; but (as in *Pamela, Part II*) the author's creative drive becomes overwhelmed by his urge to moralize.

The book was highly successful and fashionable, and further editions were soon called for. Richardson felt obliged to continue his story, not only because of the success of *Pamela* but because of the number of forged continuations that began to appear. *Pamela, Part II* appeared in 1741. Here Pamela is exhibited, through various small and separate instances, as the perfect wife, patiently leading her profligate husband to reform; a mother who adores (and breast-feeds) her children; and a friend who is at the disposal of all, and who brings about the penitence of the wicked. Much space is given over to discussion of moral, domestic, and general subjects.

*Shamela (1741, almost certainly by *Fielding) vigorously mocked what the author regarded as the hypocritical morality of *Pamela*; and Fielding's **Joseph Andrews*, which begins as a parody of *Pamela*, appeared in 1742.

Pamphleteering, origins of. The word 'pamphlet' appears to derive, curiously, from the generalized use of the title of a popular 12th-cent. Latin love poem called *Pamphilus, seu de Amore*, which was adapted to 'Pamphilet'. *Orwell, in his introduction to British *Pamphleteers* (Vol. I, 1948), describes a pamphlet as 'a short piece of Polemical writing, printed in the form of a booklet and aimed at a large public', usually of 5,000–10,000 words, and without hard covers. Pamphleteering may be said to have started with the Reformation, and during the 16th cent. became widespread (see NASHE, DEKKER, and MARTIN MARPRELATE); J. *Knox's *First Blast of the Trumpet against the Monstrous Regiment* (i.e. 'government') *of Women* (1588) was perhaps the first British political pamphlet. In the 17th cent. the religious and political ferment that gave rise to the Civil War produced many thousands of pamphlets, some of high literary quality; *Milton's are perhaps the best known, but see also WINSTANLEY, OVERTON, WALWYN, CLARKSON, COPPE, LILBURNE, NEDHAM, and BERKENHEAD. **Tyranipocrit Discovered* and **Light Shining in Buckinghamshire* (1648) were both anonymous, as were many others. These writers played an important part in the transition from the learned, allusive prose of men like *Donne, *Andrewes, and Sir T. *Browne to the plain, clear, and colloquial style recommended by the *Royal Society. (See C. *Hill, *The World Turned Upside Down*, 1972.) In the 18th cent., though important works in pamphlet form were produced by writers as considerable as *Defoe

and *Swift, the rise of weekly periodicals tended to reduce the demand for this form of communication. The form was revived in the 19th cent. by two important intellectual movements, the *Oxford Movement, and the *Fabian Society, both of which used the pamphlet (or tract) extensively and to much effect.

Pancks, a character in Dickens's **Little Dorrit*.

Pandarus, in classical legend, a son of Lycaon who assisted the Trojans in their war against the Greeks. The role that he plays in *Chaucer's and Shakespeare's stories of Troilus and Criseyde (Cressida) was the invention of *Boccaccio in his *Filostrato* (where he is called Pandaro; see N. R. Havely, *Chaucer's Boccaccio*, 1980). In Boccaccio he is the cousin of Cressida, presumably much the same age as her and Troilus; Chaucer strikingly changes him from her cousin to her uncle and guardian, for reasons that are not entirely clear but whose effect is to increase the sense of irresponsibility towards her in arranging their love affair. His role plays a striking part in the atmosphere of sourness in which the events of Shakespeare's play occur. The word 'pander' (as Shakespeare says: v. x. 34) derives from his role as go-between for Troilus and Criseyde.

Pandemonium, a word coined by *Milton, the abode of all the demons; a place represented by Milton (**Paradise Lost*, i. 756) as the capital of Hell, containing the council-chamber of the Evil Spirits.

Pandosto, or *The triumph of time*, a prose romance by R. *Greene published 1588. It went through nine editions up to 1632, but is now best known as the source for **The Winter's Tale*. Shakespeare followed Greene's romance closely, except that he preserved the life of Hermione (Bellaria in *Pandosto*), and made Leontes, not Hermione/Bellaria, appeal to the oracle. Pandosto, the Leontes figure, is killed at the end of the romance, 'to close up the Comedie with a Tragicall stratageme'. *Pandosto* is one of Greene's best narratives, and of understandable popularity in its time.

Pandulph, Cardinal, the papal legate in Shakespeare's **King John*.

Pangloss, Dr, (1) in *Candide* by *Voltaire, an optimistic philosopher who holds that all is for the best in the best of all possible worlds, in spite of a series of most distressing adventures (including unsuccessful hanging by the Inquisition and subsequent dissection). He is brought, however, to recognize that, to be happy, man must work and must 'cultivate his garden'. The intended object of the satire was *Leibniz. (2) in *The Heir-at-Law* by G. *Colman the younger, a pompous pedant.

PANIZZI, Antonio (later Sir Anthony)

(1797–1879), born in Italy, fled to England as a political exile in 1823, where he was befriended by *Foscolo, W. *Roscoe, and Lord *Brougham. He taught Italian before obtaining a post in the British Museum, where he eventually became (in 1856) principal librarian. He had a great talent for administration, and among many achievements was responsible for the preparation of a new catalogue and for the plans of the celebrated circular domed Reading Room which he opened personally in 1857.

PANKHURST, Emmeline and Christabel, see WOMEN'S SUFFRAGE.

Pantagruel, see GARGANTUA.

Pantaloon, adapted from the Italian *Pantalone*, 'a kind of mask on the Italian stage, representing the Venetian', supposed to be derived from *San Pantaleone*, formerly a favourite saint of the Venetians. The Venetian character in the *commedia dell'arte* was represented as a lean and foolish old man, wearing slippers, pantaloons, and spectacles. In the Victorian pantomime or harlequinade he was represented as a foolish and vicious old man, the butt of the clown's jokes, and his abettor in his tricks [OED].

Panthea, the heroine of Beaumont and Fletcher's *A King and no King*, who is revealed in the last act as the rightful queen of Iberia.

Pantisocracy, a Utopian scheme invented by *Coleridge and *Southey in 1794–5, to set up an egalitarian commune of six families 'on the banks of the Susquehanna' in New England, based on a joint-stock farm.

Pantomime, (1) originally a Roman actor, who performed in dumb show, representing by mimicry various characters and scenes; (2) an English dramatic performance, originally consisting of action without speech, but in its further development consisting of a dramatized traditional fairy-tale, with singing, dancing, acrobatics, clowning, topical jokes, a transformation scene, and certain stock roles, especially the 'principal boy' (i.e. hero) acted by a woman and the 'dame' acted by a man. (See MIME.)

Panurge, one of the principal characters in Rabelais's *Pantagruel* (see GARGANTUA), a cunning, voluble, witty, and in the later books cowardly buffoon, 'and a very dissolute and debauched fellow, if there were any in Paris: otherwise and in all matters else, the best and most virtuous man in the world; and he was still contriving some plot, and devising mischief against the serjeants and the watch'.

Panza, Sancho, see DON QUIXOTE.

Paolo and Francesca. Francesca, daughter of Giovanni da Polenta, count of Ravenna, was given in marriage by him to Giovanni (Sciancato, the Lame) Malatesta, of Rimini, an ill-favoured man, in return for his military services. She fell in love with Paolo, her husband's brother, and, their relations being discovered, the two lovers were put to death in 1289. *Dante, at the end of the fifth canto of the *Inferno*, relates his conversation with Francesca, who told him how her fall was occasioned by the reading of the tale of Lancelot and Guinevere. The 'Galeotto' mentioned by Dante is Galahault, the prince who, in the story of the early loves of Lancelot and Guinevere, not included in *Malory, introduces Lancelot to the queen. The story of Paolo and Francesca was the subject of the poem *The Story of Rimini* by Leigh *Hunt, and it remained popular throughout the 19th cent., most famously in *Tchaikovsky's symphonic fantasy *Francesca da Rimini*.

Paper Money Lyrics, burlesque poems by *Peacock, ridiculing political economists and bankers. They were written in the late 1820s, but not published until 1837, after the death of J. *Mill, Peacock's immediate superior at the India Office.

Pappe with an hatchet, the title of a tract contributed in 1589 by *Lyly to the Marprelate controversy (see MARTIN MARPRELATE) on the side of the bishops. The sense of the expression appears to be 'the administration of punishment under the ironical style of a kindness or benefit' [OED]. Lyly's pamphlet is a mixture of abuse and ribaldry.

PARACELSUS (Theophrast Bombast Von Hohenheim) (1493–1541), Swiss-born physician, lectured in medicine (in German) in Basle in 1527–8, but quarrelled with the faculty and thereafter led a wandering life. He was attracted to alchemy, astrology, and mysticism, and flouted the traditional methods of *Avicenna and *Galen, but was nevertheless credited with remarkable cures, had a genuinely original and enquiring mind, and initiated improvements in pharmacy and therapeutics. His arrogance, unconventionality, and ambiguous philosophy won him many enemies, and led to his being pronounced a charlatan, but he also had many followers and exerted considerable influence, particularly through the *Rosicrucian movement. He believed in the divine alchemy of the Creation, in which God (the Divine Artificer) separated by chemical process the elements from the primal matter, the Mysterium Magnum: he supported the notion of the four Aristotelian elements (earth, air, fire, water), and added the concept of the 'three principles' of sulphur, mercury, and salt. The elements were inhabited by spirits—the air by sylphs, the water by nymphs or undines (see UNDINE), the earth by gnomes, the fire by salamanders—and by many other spiritual or supernatural beings, such as syrens, nenuphar, lorins, etc. (Paracelsus: *De Nymphis,*

Pygmiis, Salamandris, De Homonculis et Monstris, etc., *Works,* 1658). This mythological machinery was borrowed by Pope, via the Rosicrucians, in * *The Rape of the Lock.* Paracelsus died shortly after being offered a permanent post in Salzburg in 1541. He was the subject of a poem by *Browning (below). See also A. Debus, *The English Paracelsians* (1965); F. *Yates, *The Rosicrucian Enlightenment* (1972).

Paracelsus, a dramatic poem in blank verse by R. *Browning, published 1835. The career of the historical *Paracelsus serves Browning, despite his claim to the contrary, as a stalking-horse for his own exploration of the processes of the creative imagination, in particular the conflict between 'Love' (self-forgetting) and 'Knowledge' (self-assertion) in the mind of the artist. The poem's critical success introduced Browning to literary London and launched his career, at first in the (unhappy) direction of the theatre. Browning's works up to the end of *Bells and Pomegranates* were published as by 'Robert Browning, author of Paracelsus'.

Parade's End, a tetralogy by F. M. *Ford, now known under this collective title, but originally published as *Some Do Not . . .* (1924), *No More Parades* (1925), *A Man Could Stand Up* (1926), and *Last Post* (1928).

The hero is Christopher Tietjens of Groby, a Tory Yorkshire squire and younger son, heavy, idealistic, at first rooted in tradition; he is married to the neurotic, beautiful, tormenting, unfaithful Catholic, Sylvia. In the first volume Christopher agrees to take back his wife and to conceal her adultery; meanwhile he himself falls in love with a young suffragette schoolteacher, Valentine Wannop, but the affair is not consummated. The next two volumes cover his wartime experiences and his resolution, on Armistice Day, to leave Sylvia and make Valentine his mistress. In *Last Post* Valentine is pregnant, Christopher is making his living by restoring antiques, and his older brother Mark is dying; Sylvia eventually agrees to divorce Christopher. Other major characters include the Pre-Raphaelite hostess Edith Ethel Duchemin, both elegant and vulgar, who has an affair with and later marries Christopher's friend, critic and writer Vincent Macmaster; their attitudes to sexual morality are contrasted with Christopher's own. The subject of the novel appears to be the breakdown of the accepted standards of the old world and the necessary emergence of a new order; the breadth of Ford's canvas, his impressionistic and highly idiosyncratic narrative technique, and his creation of the deeply English 'saintly mealsack' Tietjens have been admired by many (including G. *Greene), although others are made uneasy by a sense of unresolved conflict, narrative inconsistency, and emotional posturing.

Paradise Lost, an epic poem by *Milton, originally in ten books, subsequently rearranged in twelve, first printed 1667.

Milton formed the intention of writing a great epic poem, as he tells us, as early as 1639. A list of possible subjects, some of them scriptural, some from British history, written in his own hand about 1640–1, still exists, with drafts of the scheme of a poem on 'Paradise Lost'. The work was not, however, begun in earnest until 1658, and it was finished according to *Aubrey, in 1663. It was licensed for publication by the Revd Thomas Tomkyns, chaplain to the archbishop of Canterbury. Milton entered into an agreement for the copyright with Samuel Simmons by which he received £5 down, and a further £5 when the first impression of 1,300 copies was exhausted. His widow subsequently parted with all further claims for the sum of £8.

Milton added to later copies of the first edition not only an 'Argument', summarizing the contents of each of the books, but also a spirited defence of his choice of blank verse, 'Rime being no necessary Adjunct or true Ornament of Poem or good Verse, in longer works especially, but the Invention of a barbarous Age, to set off wretched matter and lame Meeter'.

Book I. The poet, invoking the 'Heav'nly Muse', states his theme, the Fall of Man through disobedience, and his aim, which is no less than to 'justifie the wayes of God to men'. He then presents the defeated archangel Satan, with *Beelzebub, his second-in-command, and his rebellious angels, lying on the burning lake of hell. Satan awakens his legions, rouses their spirits, and summons a council. The palace of Satan, Pandemonium (a word coined by Milton), is built.

Book II. The council debates whether another battle for the recovery of Heaven be hazarded, *Moloc recommending open war, *Belial and Mammon recommending peace in order to avoid worse torments. Beelzebub announces the creation of 'another World, the happy seat | Of som new Race call'd *Man*', which may prove a means of revenge. Satan undertakes to visit it alone, and passes through Hell-gates, guarded by Sin and Death, and passes upward through the realm of Chaos.

Book III. Milton invokes celestial light to illumine the 'ever-during dark' of his own blindness, then describes God, who sees Satan's flight towards our world, and foretells his success and the fall and punishment of man, emphasizing that man will fall not through predestination but through free will. The Son of God offers himself as a ransom, is accepted, and exalted as the Saviour. Satan alights on the outer convex of our universe, 'a Limbo large and broad, since call'd | The Paradise of Fools'. He finds the stairs leading up to Heaven, descends to the Sun, disguises himself as 'a stripling Cherube', and in this shape is directed to Earth by Uriel, where he alights on Mount Niphates in Armenia.

Book IV. Satan, at first tormented by doubts, resolves 'Evil be thou my Good' and journeys on towards the Garden of Eden, where he first sees Adam and Eve 'in naked Majestie', and overhears their discourse about the forbidden Tree of Knowledge. He resolved to tempt them to disobey the prohibition but is discovered by the guardian angels Ithuriel and Zephon as he squats like a toad near the ear of Eve, and expelled from the garden by their commander, *Gabriel.

Book V. Eve relates to Adam the disquieting dream of temptation which Satan had inspired. He comforts her, and they set about their daily tasks. Raphael, sent by God, comes to Paradise, warns Adam, and enjoins obedience. They discourse of reason, free will, and predestination, and Raphael, at Adam's request, relates how Satan, inspired by hatred and envy of the newly anointed Messiah, inspired his legions to revolt, resisted only by Abdiel—'Among the faithless, faithful only hee'.

Book VI. Raphael continues his narrative, telling how Michael and Gabriel were sent to fight against Satan. After indecisive battles the Son of God himself, alone, attacked the hosts of Satan, and, driving them to the verge of Heaven, forced them to leap down through Chaos into the deep.

Book VII. Milton evokes Urania (in classical times the Muse of Astronomy, but perhaps here the Christian Muse: a much disputed passage), and requests her to aid him to 'fit audience find, though few', in the evil days on which he has fallen; then continues Raphael's narrative, with an account of God's decision to send his Son to create another world from the vast abyss. He describes the six days of creation, ending with the creation of man, and a renewed warning to Adam that Death will be the penalty for eating of the fruit of the tree of knowledge.

Book VIII. Adam inquires concerning the motions of the heavenly bodies, and is answered 'doubtfully'. (The controversy regarding the Ptolemaic and Copernican systems was at its height when *Paradise Lost* was written, and Milton was unable to decide between them, as seen in Bk X, 668 ff.) Adam relates what he remembers since his own creation, notably his own need for rational fellowship, and his plea to his Maker for a companion, which is answered by the creation of Eve. Adam and Raphael talk of the relations between the sexes, then, with a final warning to 'take heed least Passion sway | Thy Judgement', Raphael departs.

Book IX. Insisting that his argument is 'not less but more Heroic' than the themes of *Homer and *Virgil, Milton describes Satan's entry into the body of the serpent, in which form he finds Eve, she having insisted, despite Adam's warnings, on pursuing her labours alone. He persuades her to eat of the Tree of Knowledge. Eve relates to Adam what has passed and brings him of the fruit. Adam, recognizing that she is doomed, resolves to perish with her: 'If Death | Consort with thee, Death is to mee as Life; | So forcible within my heart I feel | The Bond of Nature draw me to my owne.' He also eats of the fruit, and after initial intoxication in their lost innocence, they cover their nakedness and fall to mutual accusation.

Book X. God sends his Son to judge the transgressors. They greet him with guilt and shame, and confess, and he pronounces his sentence. Sin and Death resolve to come to this world, and make a broad highway thither from Hell. Satan returns to Hell and announces his victory, whereupon he and his angels are temporarily transformed into serpents. Adam, recognizing that in him 'all Posteritie stands curst', at first reproaches Eve, but then, reconciled, they together resolve to seek mercy from the Son of God.

Book XI. The Son of God, seeing their penitence, intercedes. God decrees that they must leave Paradise, and sends down Michael to carry out his command. Eve laments; Adam pleads not to be banished from the 'bright appearances' of God, but Michael reassures him that God is omnipresent, then unfolds to him the future, revealing to him the consequences of his original sin in the death of Abel and the future miseries of mankind, ending with the Flood and the new Covenant.

Book XII. Michael relates the subsequent history of the Old Testament, then describes the coming of the Messiah, his incarnation, death, resurrection, and ascension, which leads Adam to rejoice over so much good sprung from his own sin. Michael also foretells the corrupt state of the Church until the Second Coming. Eve meanwhile, during these revelations, has been comforted by a dream presaging 'some great good'. Resolved on obedience and submission, and assured that they may possess 'a Paradise within', they are led out of the Garden.

Paradise Lost has inspired a mass of critical commentary and histories of critical commentary, theological discussion, imitations and adaptations, and illustrations. (For Bibliography, see under MILTON.) Illustrators include *Fuseli, 1802; *Blake, 1806; J. *Martin, 1827, 1846, 1847, etc.; *Turner, 1835; and *Doré, 1866.

Paradise Regained, an epic poem in four books by *Milton, published 1671. (See ELLWOOD.)

It is a sequel to *Paradise Lost*, and deals exclusively with the temptation of Christ in the wilderness. According to the poet's conception, whereas Paradise was lost by the yielding of Adam and Eve to Satan's temptation, so it was regained by the resistance of the Son of God to the temptation of the same spirit. Satan is here represented not in the majestic lineaments of *Paradise Lost*, but as a cunning, smooth, and dissembling creature, a 'Spirit unfortunate', as he describes himself. There is a comparative scarcity of similes and ornament, and only a vivid and ingenious expansion of the biblical texts.

Book I relates the baptism of Christ by John at Bethabara, and the proclamation from Heaven that he is the Son of God. Satan, alarmed, summons a council of his peers, and undertakes his temptation. Christ is led into the wilderness, where, after forty days, Satan in the guise of 'an aged man in rural weeds' approaches him and suggests that he, being now hungry, should prove his divine character by turning the stones around him into bread. Christ, seeing through his guile, sternly replies. Night falls on the desert.

Books II and III. Meanwhile Andrew and Simon seek Christ, and Mary is troubled at his absence. Satan confers again with his council. He once more tries the hunger temptation, placing before the eyes of Christ a 'table richly spread', which is contemptuously rejected. He then appeals to the higher appetites for wealth and power, and a disputation follows as to the real value of earthly glory. Satan, confuted, next reminds Christ that the kingdom of David is now under the Roman yoke, and suggests that he should free it. He takes Christ to a high mountain and shows him the kingdoms of the earth. A description follows (iii. 251–346) of the contemporary state of the eastern world, divided between the powers of Rome and of the Parthians, as seen in this vision. Satan offers an alliance with, or conquest of, the Parthians, and the liberation of the Jews then in captivity.

Book IV. Christ remaining unmoved by Satan's 'politic maxims', the tempter, turning to the western side, draws his attention to Rome and proposes the expulsion of the wicked emperor Tiberius; and finally, pointing out Athens, urges the attractions of her poets, orators, and philosophers. All these failing, Satan brings Christ back to the wilderness, and the second night falls. On the third morning, confessing Christ proof against all temptation, Satan carries him to the highest pinnacle of the temple and bids him cast himself down, 'to know what more he is than man', only to receive the well-known answer, 'Tempt not the Lord thy God'. Satan falls dismayed, and angels bear Christ away.

Paradiso, of Dante, see DIVINA COMMEDIA.

Paradyse of Dainty Devises, The, a collection of works by minor poets of the 1560s and 70s: they include Lord *Vaux, the earl of *Oxford, *Churchyard, and William Hunnis. The volume was compiled by R. *Edwards, published after his death (1576), and frequently reprinted. It was edited by H. E. Rollins (1927).

Parasitaster, The, or *The Fawn*, a comedy by J. *Marston, published 1606.

Hercules, the widowed duke of Ferrara, wishes his son Tiberio to marry Dulcimel, daughter of a neighbouring prince, and, in order to defeat his unwillingness, declares that he will marry Dulcimel himself. He sends Tiberio to negotiate the marriage, and under the name of Faunus follows in disguise to see how matters develop. Dulcimel falls in love with Tiberio and, being a woman of wit and resource, manages to win him.

Pardiggle, Mrs, in Dickens's *Bleak House*, a lady 'distinguished for rapacious benevolence'.

'Pardoner's Tale, The', see CANTERBURY TALES, 14.

Paridell, in Spenser's *Faerie Queene*, a false and libertine knight (Bks III. viii, ix, x, and IV. i, ii) who consorts with *Duessa and elopes with *Hellenore, the wife of *Malbecco.

Paris, Count, a Capulet and suitor of *Juliet in Shakespeare's *Romeo and Juliet*.

PARIS, Matthew (d. 1259), monk and historian, entered the monastery of St Albans in 1217, succeeding *Roger of Wendover as chronicler, and compiling the *Chronica Majora*, his greatest work, there from 1235 to 1259. He extends the range of the chronicle to include foreign events; as well as its great historical value, the work is outstanding for its expressive liveliness. He also wrote the *Historia Minor* (or *Historia Anglorum*), a summary of events in England from 1200 to 1250, and the *Vitae Abbatum S. Albani*, the lives of the first 23 abbots up to 1255, the last two or three of which were composed by him. It is unlikely that the *Vitae Duorum Offarum*, which are found with manuscripts of the *Chronica*, are by him. He went to Norway on a papal visit in 1248 and he knew French, which has been taken by some to suggest a period spent in Paris to explain his name. But Paris was an English surname in the 13th cent., especially in Lincolnshire.

'Parish Register, The', a poem by *Crabbe, published 1807.

Developing the form of *The Village*, 'The Parish Register' relates the memories of a country parson, as he looks through the entries in his registers of births, marriages, and deaths. The work first revealed Crabbe's gift for narrative, and reaffirmed his determination to present the truth, however sordid. The tales include the story of Phoebe Dawson, which pleased Sir W. *Scott and C. J. *Fox; and the terrible account, written in stanzas (and possibly under the effect of opium) in 'Sir Eustace Grey', of a patient in a madhouse.

Parisina, a poem by *Byron, published 1816,

founded on a passage in *Gibbon's *Antiquities of the House of Brunswick.*

When his beloved wife Parisina murmurs the name of Hugo in her sleep, Prince Azo learns of her incestuous love for his bastard son. Hugo is a noble youth, loved by his father, but he must suffer death for his sin. Wild with grief, Parisina leaves the court for ever, and Azo is left alone with his sorrow.

Paris Sketch Book, The, *Thackeray's first full-length book, published 1840, a collection of articles and stories.

PARK, Mungo (1771–1806), born near Selkirk, was educated at Edinburgh and became a surgeon in the mercantile marine. He explored the course of the Niger and became famous by his vivid account of his travels, *Travels in the Interior Districts of Africa . . . in the Years 1795, 1796 and 1797*, published on his return in 1799. He went back to the Niger in 1805, and perished at Boussa in a conflict with the natives. He was a friend of Sir W. *Scott. See K. Lupton, *Mungo Park, the African Traveler* (1979).

PARKER, Dorothy (Rothschild) (1893–1967), New York-born American humorist and journalist, legendary for her instant wit and for her satirical verses; she also wrote sketches and short stories, many of them published in the *New Yorker* and various collections.

PARKER, Matthew (1504–75), educated at St Mary's Hostel and Corpus Christi College, Cambridge. He was in 1544 elected master of the college, where he reformed the library, to which he was to bequeath his fine manuscripts. He fled to Frankfurt-on-Main during Queen Mary's reign, reluctantly accepted the archbishopric of Canterbury on Elizabeth's accession, and was consecrated at Lambeth in 1559. He identified himself with the party (afterwards known as the Anglican party) which sought to establish a *via media* between Romanism and Puritanism. From 1563 to 1568 he was occupied with the production of the Bishop's Bible (see BIBLE, THE ENGLISH), his most distinguished service to the theological studies of the day. In his later years he retired more and more from society, being conscious of the strength of the opposing current, headed by Leicester. He was buried in his private chapel at Lambeth. In 1648 his remains were disinterred and buried under a dunghill, but after the Restoration they were restored to their original resting-place. He was a great benefactor to his college and to the University of Cambridge, where he constructed a handsome new street, which he named University Street, leading from the schools to Great St Mary's. To his efforts we are indebted for the earliest editions of *Asser, *Ælfric, the *Flores Historiarum* of Matthew of Westminster, *Paris, and other early chroniclers

(an important manuscript of the *Anglo-Saxon Chronicle*, given by him to Corpus Christi College, is known as the 'Parker Chronicle'). In spite of Queen Elizabeth's dislike of clerical matrimony, he was married, and left one son. His *De Antiquitate Britannicae Ecclesiae et Privilegiis Ecclesiae Cantuariensis cum Archiepiscopis eiusdem 70* (1572–4) is said to be the first book privately printed in England.

PARKINSON, John (1567–1650), king's herbalist, author of *Paradisi in sole Paradisus terrestris, or a garden of all sorts of pleasant flowers which our English ayre will permitt to be noursed up . . .* (1629), with woodcuts; also of a great herbal, *Theatrum botanicum* (1640).

PARKMAN, Francis (1823–93), American historian, born in Boston. After graduation from Harvard he travelled in Europe, then journeyed out to Wyoming to study Indian life, giving an account of his journey in *The Oregon Trail* (1849), which was dictated, owing to his own ill health, to his cousin and companion Quincy A. Shaw. His history of the struggle of the English and French for dominion in North America was published in a series of studies, beginning with his *History of the Conspiracy of the Pontiac* (1851) and continuing through several volumes, concluding with *A Half-Century of Conflict* (1892). D. *Davie pays tribute to Parkman's distinguished prose in *A Sequence for Francis Parkman* (1961), inspired by Parkman's vivid evocation of Lasalle, Frontenac, Montcalm, Wolfe, Pontiac, and others.

Parleyings With Certain People of Importance in Their Day, a volume of poems in blank verse by R. *Browning, published 1887. The phrase 'certain people of importance' derive from a passage in *Dante's *Vita Nuova*. Browning refers to a number of obscure historical figures whose works he had studied in his youth, and who had contributed to the formation of his mind. Each of these figures is matched by a contemporary of Browning's, and Browning 'parleys' with them in a renewed consideration of the central topics of art and life that had preoccupied him since the beginning of his career. The collection therefore constitutes an oblique autobiography and personal testament, and is of unique value to an understanding both of the sources of Browning's art and of the mature processes of that art. Perhaps the finest of the 'Parleyings' are the two concluding ones, with 'Gérard de Lairesse' and 'Charles Avison'.

Parliament of Bees, The, see DAY, J.

Parliament of Fowls, The, a dream-poem by *Chaucer in 699 lines of rhyme-royal, centring on a conference of birds to choose their mates on St Valentine's Day; it has accordingly been thought to be a poem in celebration of a marriage, perhaps the marriage of the young Richard II to Anne of Bohemia in 1382. This date would accord with the Italian influences on the poem, which otherwise cannot be dated more closely than between 1372 and 1386.

The poet falls asleep after a prologue in which he makes the Boethian lament that he has not what he wants, and has what he does not want (this usually refers to unrequited love in medieval writing). He then has a vision of a garden of the kind which is the setting for the *Roman de la Rose and in which the goddess Nature presides over the choosing of mates. Three tercel eagles pay court to a beautiful 'formel' (female) and there follows a long dispute about the criteria for success in a love suit, the argument of which centres on the opposition between the courtly love approach of the noble eagles and the pragmatism of the duck (whose worldly advice has been called 'bourgeois'): 'But she will love him, let him take another.' The debate is unresolved, and the birds agree to assemble again a year later to decide. Although the argument is inconclusive, the poem itself has a rounded completeness which makes it almost unique in Chaucer's works; it has rightly been called one of the finest occasional poems in the language.

Ed. D. S. Brewer (1960); J. A. W. Bennett, *The Parlement of Fowles* (1957); R. O. Payne, *The Key of Remembrance: A Study of Chaucer's Poetics* (1963); D. C. Baker in B. Rowland, *Companion to Chaucer Studies* (rev. edn 1979, pp. 428–45).

Parnassians, a group of French poets, headed by *Leconte de Lisle, who sought restraint, precision, and objectivity in poetry, in reaction to the emotional extravagances of Romanticism. Their name derives from the three collections of their work published under the title *Le Parnasse contemporain*, in 1866, 1871, and 1876. Associated with the group, besides Leconte de Lisle, were José-Maria de Hérédia (1842–1905), whose collection *Les Trophées* appeared in 1893, Catulle Mendès (1841–1909), and René-François-Armand Sully-Prudhomme (1839–1907).

Parnassus Plays, The, the name given to a trilogy produced between 1598 and 1602 by students of St John's College, Cambridge, consisting of *The Pilgrimage to Parnassus* and *The Returne from Parnassus*, the latter apparently in two parts. Authorship has not been established, but they seem to be the work of two dramatists, unusually writing academic drama in the vernacular; they have been attributed to J. *Day and, more recently, to John Weever of Queen's and J. *Hall. They treat amusingly of the attempts of a group of young men (one apparently modelled on *Nashe) to resist temptation and to gain preferment or at least a livelihood, and are full of allusions to contemporary literature. In the third more satirical section the students are shown on their way to London, learning how to catch a patron or cheat a trades-man, and following menial occupations, which they finally abandon in discouragement and 'returne' to Cambridge. They were not published as a whole until the edition by J. B. Leishman (1949).

PARNELL, Charles Stewart (1846–91), born at Avondale, Co. Wicklow, educated at Magdalene College, Cambridge. He became MP for Meath in 1875 and was elected chairman of the Home Rule party in its fight for Irish self-government, in spite of being a Protestant himself, and exerted enormous influence outside the House. In 1878 he was elected president of the Irish National Land League. Parnell formulated the tactic of 'boycotting' in 1880. He was imprisoned in Kilmainham jail in 1881 for his incendiary speeches, and gained the title of 'uncrowned king of Ireland'. He converted *Gladstone and the Liberal Party to the idea of Home Rule and overthrew the Tory Government in 1886. In an article published by *The Times, 'Parnellism and Crime' (1887), he was accused of connivance with outrage and crime, but he vindicated himself of the charges in 1888–9. His career was ruined by his appearance as co-respondent in a divorce case brought by Capt. O'Shea against his wife; the scandal turned the Irish Catholics against him and contributed to a split amongst the Irish Nationalists. He died five months after his marriage to Mrs O'Shea.

PARNELL, Thomas (1679–1718), born in Dublin and educated at Trinity College, Dublin, was archdeacon of Clogher and a friend of *Swift and *Pope (to whose *Iliad* he contributed an introductory essay). He was a member of the *Scriblerus Club. His 'Hymn to Contentment' was published in *Steele's *Poetical Miscellanies* (1714) and his mock-heroic *Homer's Battle of the Frogs and Mice with the Remarks of Zoilus* in 1717 (see BATRACHOMYOMACHIA), but most of his work was published posthumously by Pope in 1721. His poems include 'The Hermit', a moral narrative in heroic couplets, in which the mysterious ways of God are revealed to the hermit by the apparently ruthless and amoral actions of a disguised angel, and 'Night-Piece on Death', in fluent octosyllabics, perhaps the first of the 18th-cent. *graveyard poems (though reminiscent of *'Il Penseroso') which in *Goldsmith's view inspired 'all those night-pieces and church-yard scenes that have since appeared' (Goldsmith's *Life of Parnell*, 1770). Dr *Johnson praised 'the easy sweetness of his diction'. The first complete edition of his poems, ed. C. Rawson and F. P. Lock, was published in 1985.

Parolles, the cowardly follower of Bertram in Shakespeare's *All's Well That Ends Well*; his name means 'words' and suggests that he promises more talk than action.

Paronomasia, a play on words, a kind of *pun,

in which the repeated words are similar but not identical; e.g. Lady Macbeth: 'I'll gild the faces of the grooms withal, | For it must seem their guilt.'

PARR, Samuel (1747–1825), a fine Latin scholar, excelled as a writer of Latin epitaphs, and wrote that on Dr *Johnson in St Paul's. He was regarded as 'the Whig Johnson' (*DNB*), but his conversation was apparently far inferior to that of his model, and his works (collected in 8 vols, 1828) are marked by verbosity and mannerism.

PARRY, Sir Hubert (1848–1918), English composer and teacher. He and *Stanford were the two composers who first began to put new life and new standards into English music after the doldrums of the Victorian period. The year 1880, which saw the first performance of Parry's Piano Concerto and of the cantata *Scenes from 'Prometheus Unbound'* (*Shelley), is usually taken to represent the starting point of the English musical renascence, and the two choral settings of *Milton which followed, *Blest Pair of Sirens* (1887) and *L'Allegro ed il penseroso* (1890), confirmed Parry's position as its figure-head: the former, in particular, is generally considered his masterpiece, and is one of his few works that is still heard today. The later choral works tend to sound more conventional, though there is a nice vein of humour in *The Pied Piper of Hamelin* (1905), and the six short *Songs of Farewell* (1916, with words by *Vaughan, John *Davies, *Campion, *Lockhart, and *Donne) are outstanding. On a smaller scale, from the early 1880s until the last years of his life, he produced 12 sets of *English Lyrics* for solo voice and piano (74 songs in all), settings of many of the greatest poems in the language that are too little remembered today. For most people, indeed, Parry is by now remembered almost exclusively for one musical inspiration of undying popularity, the unison setting, made in the hardest days of the First World War, of *Blake's short poem 'Jerusalem'.

PARRY, Sir William Edward (1790-1855), Arctic explorer, whose expeditions are described in his three *Journals* of voyages for the discovery of a North-West Passage, undertaken between 1819 and 1825 (published 1821, 1824, 1826) and in his *Narrative of an attempt to reach the North Pole, 1827* (1828).

Parsifal, see PERCEVAL.

Parson Lot, see KINGSLEY, C.

'Parson's Tale, The', see CANTERBURY TALES, 24.

Parthenissa, see BOYLE, R.

Parthenophil and Parthenope, a collection of sonnets by B. *Barnes, issued in 1593, notable as one of the first of such collections to appear after Sidney's *Astrophel and Stella*.

PARTINGTON, Mrs, referred to by Sydney *Smith in his speech on the rejection of the *Reform Bill. He compares the attempts of the House of Lords to stop the progress of reform to the efforts of a Mrs Partington to keep out the Atlantic with a mop, during a great storm at Sidmouth in 1824.

B. P. Shillaber (1814–90), American humorist, published in 1854 the *Life and Sayings of Mrs Partington*, a benevolent village gossip reminiscent of an American Mrs *Malaprop.

Partlet, the hen in the tale of *Reynard the Fox and in Chaucer's 'The Nun's Priest's Tale' (*Canterbury Tales*, 20) as Pertelote. 'Sister Partlet with her hooded head' in Dryden's *The Hind and the Panther* stands for Catholic nuns.

Partridge, a character in Fielding's *Tom Jones*.

PARTRIDGE, John (1644–1715), the victim of a mystification by *Swift. See BICKERSTAFF and ALMANACS.

Party Going, a novel by Henry *Green.

Parzifal, an epic by *Wolfram von Eschenbach, composed early in the 13th cent. on the subject of the legend of *Perceval and the Holy *Grail. (See also TITUREL.)

PASCAL, Blaise (1623–62), French mathematician, physicist, and moralist. As gifted in science as in letters, he did important work in geometry, hydrodynamics, and atmospheric pressure, and invented a calculating machine, a syringe, and a hydraulic press. He came under the influence of Jansenism from around 1646, and entered the convent of *Port-Royal in 1655. His literary fame rests on two works, *Les Provinciales* (1656–7, English trans., 1657), polemical letters directed against the casuistry of the Jesuits, and the posthumously published *Pensées* (1670, trans., 1688), fragments of an uncompleted defence of the Christian religion. These form a survey of the contradictions of human existence, pursued with an intensity of logic and passion characteristic of all his work, and encompassing all the major branches of knowledge, from history and ethics to rhetoric and psychology. He exercised an influence on a number of later thinkers, notably *Rousseau, *Bergson, and the *Existentialists.

PASCOLI, Giovanni (1855–1912), the major precursor of *modernism in Italian poetry. A socialist sympathizer, he was imprisoned for some months after demonstrations in 1879. Nature and simple things often provide his themes, but he draws from symbolism the suggestion of enigma and evanescence. His language spans the range from pure sound (animal- and baby-talk) to the literary conventions of lyric tradition. He translated from the classics and English Romantic poets. The essential

Pascoli is in *Myricae* (1891–1905) and *Canti di Castelvecchio* (1903).

PASOLINI, Pier Paolo (1922–75), Italian poet, novelist, critic, and film director. Much of his work deals with the theme of innocence corrupted by capitalism. In his films he challenged *neo-realism with its conventions of sentimentalism and linear narrative. His main films are: *Accattone* (1961), *Mamma Roma* (1962), *The Gospel according to Saint Matthew* (1964), *Oedipus Rex* (1967), *Theorem* (1968), *Pigsty* (1969), *Medea* (1970), *Decameron* (1971), *Canterbury Tales* (1973), *Arabian Nights* (1974), *Salò* (1975). In Italy he was also known for his novels *Ragazzi di vita* (*The Regazzi*, 1955) and *Una vita violenta* (*A Violent Life*, 1958), in which he explores the culture and language of outcast plebeians of the Roman shanty suburbs (he was murdered in such a setting); and for his anti-establishment polemics, as in *Scritti corsari* (*Pirate Writings*, 1975). His best critical essays are in *Passione e ideologia* (*Passion and Ideology*, 1960) and his best poetry is in *Le ceneri di Gramsci* (*Gramsci's Ashes*, 1957).

Pasquil, Pasquin. 'Pasquino' or 'Pasquillo' was the name popularly given to a mutilated statue disinterred at Rome in 1501, and set up by Cardinal Caraffa at the corner of his palace near the Piazza Navona. It became the custom to salute Pasquin on St Mark's day in Latin verses. In process of time these *pasquinate* or pasquinades tended to become satirical, and the term began to be applied, not only in Rome but in other countries, to satirical compositions and lampoons, political, ecclesiastical, or personal. According to Mazocchi, the name Pasquino originated in that of a schoolmaster who lived opposite the spot where the statue was found; a later tradition made Pasquino a caustic tailor or shoemaker; another calls him a barber [*OED*]. Replies to the pasquinades used to be attached to the *Marforio*, an ancient statue of a river-god, thought to be of Mars.

PASQUIN, Anthony, see WILLIAMS, J.

Passage to India, A, a novel by E. M. *Forster, published 1924. It is a picture of society in India under the British Raj, of the clash between East and West, and of the prejudices and misunderstandings that foredoomed goodwill. Criticized at first for anti-British and possibly inaccurate bias, it has been praised as a superb character study of the people of one race by a writer of another.

The story is told in three parts, I, *Mosque*, II, *Caves*, III, *Temple*, and concerns Aziz, a young Muslim doctor, whose friendliness and enthusiasm for the British turn to bitterness and disillusionment when his pride is injured. A sympathy springs up between him and the elderly Mrs Moore, who has come to visit her son,

the City Magistrate. Accompanying her is Adela Quested, young, earnest, and charmless, who longs to know the 'real' India and tries to disregard the taboos and snobberies of the British circle. Aziz organizes an expedition for the visitors to the famous Caves of Marabar, where an unforeseen development plunges him into disgrace and rouses deep antagonism between the two races. Adela accuses him of insulting her in the Caves, he is committed to prison and stands trial. Adela withdraws her charge, but Aziz turns furiously away from the British, towards a Hindu–Muslim *entente*. In the third part of the book he has moved to a post in a native state, and is bringing up his family in peace, writing poetry and reading Persian. He is visited by his friend Mr Fielding, the former Principal of the Government College, an intelligent, hard-bitten man. They discuss the future of India and Aziz prophesies that only when the British are driven out can he and Fielding really be friends. Among the many characters is Professor Godbole, the detached and saintly Brahmin who is the innocent cause of the contretemps, and who makes his final appearance in supreme tranquillity at the festival of the Hindu temple.

Passetyme of Pleasure, or *The Historie of Graunde Amoure and La Bell Pucel,* an allegorical poem in rhyme-royal and decasyllabic couplets by *Hawes, written about 1506 and first printed by *Wynkyn de Worde in 1509 (edited by *Southey, 1831, and by *Wright for the Percy Society, 1845). It describes the education of a certain Graunde Amour in the accomplishments required to make a knight perfect and worthy of the love of La Bell Pucell, and narrates his encounters with giants (representing the vices), his marriage, and his death; the whole constituting an allegory of life in the form of a romance of chivalry. It contains a well known couplet in perhaps its original form:

> For though the day be never so longe,
> At last the belles ryngeth to evensonge.

'Passing of Arthur, The', see MORTE D'ARTHUR.

Passionate Pilgrim, The, an unauthorized anthology of poems by various authors, published by *Jaggard in 1599, and attributed on the title-page to Shakespeare, but containing only a few authentic poems by him.

Past and Present, see CARLYLE, T.

PASTERNAK, Boris Leonidovich (1890–1960), Russian poet and prose writer. He was born in Moscow, the son of the painter Leonid Pasternak and the pianist Rozaliya Kaufman. He originally studied music, but gave it up at the age of 18 for poetry. At this stage he was greatly influenced by the work of *Rilke, *Blok, and *Bely. In 1912 he studied philosophy at Marburg University under Hermann Cohen. On his return to Russia he became involved with the Russian Futurist poets and published his first verse collection *A Twin in the Clouds* (1914). A second volume, *Above the Barriers*, appeared in 1917, but it was his third collection, *My Sister Life* (the poems of 1917, published 1922), which established his reputation. It was followed by a number of important publications, the collection *Themes and Variations* (1923), a collection of *Stories* (1925), the long poems *The Year 1905* and *Lieutenant Shmidt* (both 1927), and *Spektorsky* (1931). In 1931 he also published his first autobiography *A Safe Conduct*, followed by another major verse collection *Second Birth* (1932), associated with his meeting with his second wife, Zinaida Neigauz. In the 1930s Pasternak's position became increasingly difficult. After a doomed effort to become a 'Soviet writer', he began what he described as his 'long silent duel' with *Stalin. After 1933 no original work by Pasternak could be published for ten years, when two further poetry collections, *On Early Trains* (1943) and *The Breadth of the Earth* (1945), appeared. During this time he earned his living by translating, notably Goethe's *Faust*, the poetry of *Ralegh, *Jonson, *Shelley, *Byron, and *Keats, and Shakespeare. His excellent translations of *Hamlet*, *Othello*, *Romeo and Juliet*, *King Lear*, *Macbeth*, *Antony and Cleopatra*, and *1* and *2 *Henry IV* are extremely highly valued in the USSR. His main literary concern in the final decades of his life, however, was feverish activity, despite declining health, on the work he intended to be his testament, a witness to the experience of the Russian intelligentsia before, during and after the Revolution, the novel *Doctor Zhivago*. In October 1946 he met Olga Ivinskaya, who was to become the companion of his last years and on whom Lara, the heroine of *Doctor Zhivago*, is largely based. Eventually despairing of publication in the USSR, he gave permission for publication in Italy, where the novel appeared in 1957. In 1958 he wrote a second 'Autobiographical sketch', and was awarded the *Nobel Prize for literature. This led to a vehement and shameful campaign against him, the so-called 'Pasternak affair', and he declined the prize. Ivinskaya was arrested and imprisoned. Publication of Pasternak's poetry resumed in the USSR soon after his death, and a volume of his short prose appeared in 1982. But *Doctor Zhivago*, on which his world-wide fame is based, has never been published in the USSR, where his reputation depends on the poetic achievement of *My Sister Life* and *Second Birth*.

Pastiche, a literary composition made up from various authors or sources, or in imitation of the style of another author; or a picture made up of fragments pieced together or copied with modification from an original, or in professed imitation of the style of another artist: the imitative intention is now the most usual meaning.

Paston Letters, The, a collection of letters preserved by the Pastons, a well-to-do Norfolk family, written between *c.*1420 and 1504. They are of great value for the evidence they give of the language of their time, but even more for the general historical, political, and social interest they provide. They concern three generations of the family, and most were written in the reigns of Henry VI, Edward IV, and Richard III. They are unique as historical material, showing the violence and anarchy of 15th-cent. England and the domestic conditions in which a family of this class lived. The letters were published in three volumes, in 1787, 1789, and 1823. The originals were recovered in the second half of the 19th cent.
  Ed. Norman Davis (1971, 1976, vol. 3 forthcoming); *Selections* (1958); *Selections* (modernized) (1963).

Pastoral, a form of escape literature concerned with country pleasures, which is found in poetry, drama, and prose fiction. Its earliest examples appear in the *Idylls* of *Theocritus in which shepherds lead a sunlit, idealized existence of love and song. The eclogues of *Virgil and Longus' romance *Daphnis and Chloe* blended the idealization with a more authentic picture of country life, and Virgil added an important new feature to the tradition in making his poems a vehicle for social comment. Neglected during the Middle Ages, the pastoral reappeared during the Renaissance when *Petrarch and his imitators composed eclogues in Latin and in the vernaculars. These were often more realistic and richer in contemporary references than their Virgilian models; but it was with drama (*Tasso, *Guarini, *Fletcher) and the prose romance (*Sannazar, *Cervantes, *Sidney, *D'Urfé) that pastoral attained the peak of its popularity. In the 17th cent., however, the Theocritean vision which had so far satisfied men's desire to escape from the pressures of urban life gave place to a more realistic dream of enjoying a rural retreat. Poets like James *Thomson extolled country pleasures and represented rural trades as enjoyable, until *Crabbe showed that their descriptions were divorced from reality, and *Wordsworth taught men to seek comfort in a Nature endowed with visionary power. The pastoral in its traditional form died with the rise of *Romanticism.

Pastorella, in Spenser's *Faerie Queene* (VI. ix–xii), a shepherdess, loved by Coridon the shepherd and by Sir *Calidore, believed to be the daughter of Meliboe. She is carried off by brigands, rescued by Sir Calidore, and discovered to be the daughter of Sir Bellamour and the Lady Claribell.

Pastor Fido, Il, see GUARINI.

Patavium, in imprints, Padua.

Patelin, see PATHELIN.

PATER, Walter Horatio (1839–94), born in Stepney, the son of a surgeon who died in 1842. Educated at King's School, Canterbury, and The Queen's College, Oxford, he became a fellow of Brasenose in 1864, and from 1869 lived with his unmarried sisters Hester and Clara, first at Oxford, then in London, in a style much influenced by the *Pre-Raphaelites: among his friends were *Swinburne, *Rossetti, the Humphry *Wards, and the Mark *Pattisons. He first became known through *Studies in the History of the Renaissance* (1873), which included essays on *Winckelmann and the then neglected *Botticelli, and his celebrated evocation of the Mona Lisa in his essay on *Leonardo da Vinci (previously published 1869) describing her as one 'who has learned the secrets of the grave'. This volume (which concludes, 'To burn always with this hard gem-like flame, to maintain this ecstasy, is success in life'), though attacked by some as unscholarly and morbid, had a profound influence on the undergraduates of the day and was acclaimed by *Wilde as 'the holy writ of beauty'. 'The Child in the House' (**Macmillan's Magazine,* 1878) indirectly revealed much of Pater's own childhood, and **Marius the Epicurean* (1885), a fictional biography set in the days of Marcus Aurelius, was also highly personal, reflecting his responses to paganism, Christianity, and Rome (which he had visited in 1882): Mrs H. Ward commented, 'No one can fail to catch the autobiographical note.' *Imaginary Portraits,* historical fantasies on a favourite theme of early promise and early death, appeared in 1887, and with *Appreciations: with an Essay on Style* (1889) Pater was widely acknowledged as a master of English prose. *Plato and Platonism* (1893) collected his earlier lectures and is said to have occasioned a reconciliation with *Jowett, who had disapproved of his influence in the university. But his predilection for morbid violence was still much apparent in a lecture on *Mérimée (1890), in two short historical romances, 'Emerald Uthwart' (**The New Review,* 1892) and 'Apollo in Picardy' (*Harper's New Monthly,* 1893), and in his posthumous and unfinished *Gaston de Latour* (1896), which clearly reveal a preoccupation with the cruelty, beauty, and religious sensibility of a largely imaginary 'impassioned past'. (See also ART FOR ART'S SAKE.)

Pathelin, *La Farce de Maistre Pierre,* the most celebrated of the medieval French farces, dating from before 1470, of uncertain authorship, and written in octosyllabic couplets. Its central figure is the duplicitous lawyer Pathelin, who is himself finally duped by the shepherd Aignelet.

Pathetic fallacy, a phrase coined by *Ruskin in 'Of the Pathetic Fallacy' (**Modern Painters,* III, 1856, ch. 12), indicating the tendency of writers and artists to ascribe human emotions and sympathies to nature. Ruskin sees in it morbidity and 'a falseness in all our impressions of external things', preferring the 'very plain and leafy fact' of a primrose to those poets (e.g. Wordsworth in **Peter Bell*) 'to whom the primrose is anything else than a primrose'. The technique was extensively used in the late 18th and 19th cents by *Goethe, *Gray, *Collins, *Cowper, *Wordsworth, *Shelley, and *Tennyson: Shelley's **Adonais* and Tennyson's **In Memoriam* contain notable examples, and Wordsworth's faith that 'every flower enjoys the air it breathes' was tellingly mocked in an anonymous parody (*The Simpliciad,* 1808):

> See, with impassioned flowers each bank
>   is teeming;
> See, with blue sparrow's eggs each hedge
>   is gleaming;
> Ecstatic birds, whose thought no bard
>   can measure,
> Blossoms that breathe, and twigs that pant
>   with pleasure.

Nevertheless Wordsworth used the pathetic fallacy with great seriousness, as did other Romantic poets, not as a decorative device (Wordsworth in particular claimed to 'look steadily at my subject' in an attempt to avoid 'falseness of description' in the Preface of 1800 to *Lyrical Ballads) but as an expression of a sense of communion with the natural world, and of the unity of creation. Its use declined after Ruskin's formulation, but it is still widely though perhaps not so conspicuously employed. See J. Miles, *Pathetic Fallacy in the Nineteenth Century* (1942); J. D. Thomas, 'Poetic Truth and Pathetic Fallacy', in *Texas Studies in Literature and Language,* III (1961).

Pathfinder, The, one of the 'Leatherstocking' novels of J. F. *Cooper, and a nickname of the hero, Natty Bumppo.

Path to Rome, The, see BELLOC, H.

Patience, an alliterative poem in 531 lines from the second half of the 14th cent., the only manuscript of which is the famous Cotton Nero A x which is also the sole manuscript of **Pearl, *Cleanness,* and *Sir *Gawain and the Green Knight.* It tells in a vigorous and humorous way the story of Jonah and his trials sent by God. Modern critical practice usually treats the four poems in the manuscript as the work of a single author, and there are some affinities between them (particularly between *Patience* and *Pearl*) which make this not implausible. Ed. J. J. Anderson (1969).

Patience, an opera by *Gilbert and *Sullivan produced in 1881, a deliberate satire on the *Aesthetic Movement, in which *Bunthorne is said to be modelled on *Wilde and Grosvenor on *Swinburne.

Patient Grissil, a comedy by *Dekker in collaboration with *Chettle and Haughton, written 1600, printed 1603.

The marquess of Salucia, smitten with the beauty of Grissil, the virtuous daughter of a poor basket-maker, makes her his bride. Wishing to try her patience, he subjects her to a series of humiliations and cruelties, robbing her of her children and making her believe them dead, and finally pretending to take another wife and making her attend upon the new bride. All these trials she bears submissively. The new bride is revealed to be Grissil's daughter, and Grissil is restored to honour. The play contains the well-known songs 'Art thou poore yet hast thou golden slumbers, | O sweet content' and 'Golden slumbers kisse your eyes'.

The same subject is treated in Chaucer's 'Clerk's Tale' (see CANTERBURY TALES, 9). It was taken originally from the *Decameron (Day 10, Tale 10).

PATMORE, Coventry Kersey Dighton (1823–96), son of P. G. *Patmore, published his first volume of *Poems* (including 'The Woodman's Daughter', later subject of a well known painting by *Millais) in 1844. In 1846, after his father's financial collapse, he became assistant in the printed book department of the British Museum, on the recommendation of *Milnes. His work was much admired by the *Pre-Raphaelites, with whom he became acquainted, and he contributed to *The Germ*. In 1847 he married his first wife, Emily, who inspired his long and popular sequence of poems in praise of married love, *The Angel in the House* (1854–63); together the Patmores represented an image of the ideal Victorian couple, and in this role entertained many eminent literary figures, including *Tennyson, *Ruskin, and R. *Browning, who wrote a poem to Emily. Emily died in 1862, leaving him with six children. In 1864 he travelled to Rome, where he met his second wife Marianne, a Roman Catholic, and was himself converted to Catholicism, factors which may have contributed to his decline in popularity as a poet; *The Unknown Eros* (1877) was received with much less enthusiasm than his previous work. It contains odes marked by an erotic mysticism, but also some more autobiographical pieces (now the most anthologized), including 'The Azalea', 'Departure', 'A Farewell', directly inspired by Emily's illness and death, and 'The Toys', inspired by a moment of anger and grief aroused by one of his sons. *Amelia, Tamerton church-tower*, etc., with a preface on English metrical law, appeared in 1878. His second wife died in 1880 and he married Harriet, the governess of his children, who survived him. In his later years he formed new friendships, predominantly with other Catholic writers including G. M *Hopkins, F. *Thompson, and A. *Meynell, who helped to revive interest in his poetry. His *The Rod, The Root and The Flower* (1895) is chiefly meditations on religious subjects.

PATMORE, Peter George (1786–1855), the father of C. *Patmore, a close friend of *Lamb and *Hazlitt, and an active journalist. He was editor of the *New Monthly Magazine*, 1841–53, and among other varied works published in 1854 *My Friends and Acquaintances*, a lively but unreliable account of Lamb, Hazlitt, *Campbell, *Sheridan, and others. Many of the intimate letters in Hazlitt's *Liber Amoris* are addressed to him.

PATON, Alan, the author of *Cry, the Beloved Country*.

PATRICK, St (*c*.389–*c*.461), the patron saint of Ireland, the son of a Roman centurion, was probably born in Scotland (or Wales). He was taken captive to Ireland when he was a child, and returned there voluntarily to preach the Gospel in 432, after years of study in Gaul, directed by Martin of Tours. He journeyed first through Ulster and then, it is said, through the whole of Ireland. Many stories, legends, and purported writings of his are current in Ireland. See J. T. McNeill, *The Celtic Churches, A History A.D. 200 to 1200* (1974), ch. 4; R. P. C. Hanson, *St Patrick, His Origins and Career* (1968).

Patrick's Purgatory, St, a cave on an island on Lough Derg in the west of Ireland, where, according to legend, an entrance to purgatory was revealed to St Patrick, that he might overcome the obstinacy of those whom he was trying to convert. Henry of Saltrey (*fl.* 1150), a Cistercian of Saltrey in Huntingdonshire, who had the story from Gilbert of Louth, wrote an account of the visit of Sir Owain, a knight of King Stephen, to St Patrick's Purgatory, undertaken by way of penance for his sins. This was translated into other languages, and the cave has been a place of pilgrimage since at least the 13th cent. *Calderón wrote a play on this subject, translated (1853, and again 1873) by D. F. MacCarthy.

Patriotic Gore, see WILSON, E.

Patriot King, The Idea of a, see BOLINGBROKE, H. ST J.

Patrologiae, see MIGNE, J.-P.

Patronage, Literary, traditionally, individual patronage, in the form of financial help, payment in kind, or more indirect assistance, exercised by royalty and the wealthy in return for dedications, entertainment, and prestige (as well as sometimes for more altruistic motives). Among innumerable examples, *Chaucer was assisted by *John of Gaunt, *Shakespeare by the earl of Southampton, *Donne by Sir Robert Drury, Dr *Johnson (belatedly) by the earl of *Chesterfield, *Wordsworth by Sir G. *Beaumont. The relationship was not always happy, as Johnson's definition of a patron as 'a wretch who supports with insolence and is paid with flattery' suggests, but it also directly inspired many fine works, such as *Jonson's tribute to the *Sidneys in his 'country house poem', 'To Penshurst' (see PENSHURST PLACE).

Patronage was also exercised through the gift of clerical livings; *Crabbe, befriended by the duke of Rutland, wrote of the possible misfortunes of such an experience in 'The Patron' (1812). Another indirect form of patronage was through *subscription publishing.

Early in the 18th cent. new sources of support for authors began to develop. The circulating *libraries offered new openings for sales, and the rising success of *periodicals provided more work until well into the 20th cent. So in the course of the 18th cent. patronage passed largely from men of individual wealth to men of professional power or commercial interest, such as literary editors and library owners and suppliers. *Goldsmith commented that 'the few poets of England no longer depend on the great for subsistence; they have now no other patrons than the public.'

In 1790 David Williams founded the *Royal Literary Fund, and in 1837 the Civil List Act permitted the Treasury to assist authors by the grant of pensions (and by the occasional gift of a 'bounty'), provided they could demonstrate 'desert and distress'. Over 750 authors (and their dependants) have benefited, including *Wordsworth, *Tennyson, M. *Arnold, W. H. *Hudson, W. B. *Yeats, and T. F. *Powys. *Conrad eventually returned his pension; Mrs *Craik set hers aside for less fortunate authors, and H. *Martineau refused several offers, fearing they would compromise her independence. The proportion of the civil list monies awarded to authors has declined from over 40 per cent in the last century, to around 35 per cent, and the pension is now worth on average only £600 p.a. It is awarded on the recommendation of the Royal Literary Fund, the *Society of Authors, the *Poetry Society, and other bodies. The *Arts Council also has provided grants to individual writers, as well as assisting literature in more indirect ways through grants to bodies, support for schemes such as 'Writers in Schools', 'Writers in Residence', etc., support for periodicals, and other projects.

PATTEN, Brian, see LIVERPOOL POETS.

Patterne, Sir Willoughby, Eleanor and Isabel, Lieutenant, and Crossjay, characters in Meredith's *The Egoist.

Pattieson, Peter, a schoolmaster, the imaginary author of *Tales of My Landlord by Sir W. Scott.

PATTISON, Mark (1813–84), educated at Oriel College, Oxford, a supporter of Newman and the *Oxford Movement until Newman's departure for Rome. He was ordained priest in 1843 and became successively fellow and tutor (1843–55) of Lincoln College, Oxford; he would have been elected rector in 1851 but for an intrigue among the reactionary fellows of the college. He was an influential tutor, keenly interested in university reform, and travelled to Germany to study continental systems of education. His ideas on education can be found in *Oxford Studies* (1855) and *Suggestions on Academical Organisation* (1868); his life work—a history of European learning surrounding a biography of *Scaliger—was never completed. His best-known work was his classic life of *Isaac Casaubon 1559–1614* (1875). His other published works included a contribution to *Essays and Reviews* on the *Tendencies of Religious Thought in England, 1688–1750* (1860), a short life of *Milton (1875), editions of certain of *Pope's and Milton's poems, and, contributions to the *Encyclopaedia Britannica, articles on *Erasmus, Sir T. *More, and *Grotius. In 1861, still embittered from his earlier rejection, he was finally elected rector of Lincoln. In the same year he married Emilia Francis Strong (later Lady *Dilke) who was 27 years his junior; this and the fact that both parties remained apart as far as convention would allow gave rise to the famous theory that Mr and Mrs Pattison were the originals of Casaubon and Dorothea in G. Eliot's *Middlemarch*. The question has been often debated and produced many differences of learned opinion. His *Memoirs* (1885) are an important study of 19th-cent. Oxford.

Paul Emmanuel, a character in *Villette* by C. Brontë.

Paul and Virginie, see SAINT-PIERRE, J.-H. B.

Paul Ferroll, see CLIVE, MRS C. A.

Paulina, the wife of *Antigonus and loyal defender of *Hermione in Shakespeare's *The Winter's Tale*.

Pauline, a poem in blank verse, the first poem to be published by R. *Browning; it appeared anonymously in 1833. Subtitled 'A Fragment of a Confession', it is marked by the influence of Browning's Romantic predecessors, notably *Shelley; but its form and theme already declare Browning's independence. The 'confession' is addressed to Pauline by the first in a long series of 'fallen' speakers whose ambivalent rhetoric combines self-reproach and self-justification. The poem was barely noticed, but an important commentary by J. S. *Mill, in the form of an annotated copy, reached Browning through their common friend W. J. Fox. Mill assumed the speaker of the poem to be the author, and severely criticized his morbidity and self-regard.

Partly in response to this misunderstanding of the poem's 'dramatic' form, Browning suppressed it for over 30 years, finally acknowledging it 'with extreme repugnance' in the collected edition of 1867, to avoid the threat of pirate publication.

Paul's, Children of, a company of boy actors, recruited from the choristers of St Paul's Cathedral, whose performances enjoyed great popularity at the end of the 16th and beginning of the 17th cents. They performed among others the plays of *Lyly. The Children of the Chapel, recruited from the choristers of the Chapel Royal, was another company enjoying popular favour at the same time. Their rivalry with men actors is alluded to in *Hamlet (II. ii).

Paul's Letters to his Kinsfolk, a series of letters by Sir W. *Scott, published in 1816, describing a visit by the author to Brussels, Waterloo, and Paris a few weeks after the battle of Waterloo. The account of the battle is interesting for the details it contains, some of them obtained from Napoleon's Belgian guide.

Paul's School, St, was founded between 1509 and 1512 by *Colet. *Lily was its first High Master. The school was removed from St Paul's Churchyard to Hammersmith in 1884, and to Barnes in 1968. Among its many distinguished scholars may be mentioned *Milton, *Pepys, Sir P. Francis, *Camden, G. K. *Chesterton, and E. *Thomas.

PAUL THE DEACON (Paulus Diaconus) (*c*.725–97), a Lombard who was at one time an inmate of the Benedictine house of Monte Cassino, where he met *Charlemagne. He is one of the best chroniclers of the Dark Ages, author of the *Historia Lombardorum*, and an important figure in the Carolingian Renaissance.

PAVESE, Cesare (1908–50), Italian novelist and poet, whose last novel, *La luna e i falò* (*The Moon and the Bonfires*, 1950), is his finest. Realism and myth, lyrical memoir and contemporary reality, combine in the highly individual texture of his prose, which expresses the heart-searchings of a solitary man with a restless social conscience. Other main novels are: *Il compagno* (*The Comrade*, 1947), *Prima che il gallo canti* (*Before Cock-Crow*, 1949), *La bella estate* (*The Beautiful Summer*, 1949). His best poems are in *Lavorare stanca* (*Work Wearies*, 1936). He made many translations from English and American authors (*Joyce, *Faulkner, etc.) who influenced him; his translation of Melville's *Moby-Dick* is definitive. His suicide was seen as representative of intellectuals broken by the tensions of post-war Europe.

PAYN, James (1830–98), educated at Trinity College, Cambridge, was a regular contributor to *Household Words* and became editor of *Chambers's Journal* (1859–74) and *The Cornhill Magazine* (1882–96). He published a volume of poems in 1853 and several volumes of essays, including *Some Private Views* (1894), *Some Literary Recollections* (1884), *Gleams of Memory* (1894), and *The Backwater of Life* (1899), with an introduction by Sir L. *Stephen. He wrote 100 novels of which *Lost Sir Massinberd* (1864) and *By Proxy* (1878) were the most popular.

PAYNE, John Howard (1791–1852), American actor, playwright, and song-writer, born in New York City, famous as author of the popular song *'Home, Sweet Home'.

PEACHAM, Henry (?1576–?1643), educated at Trinity College, Cambridge, an author and a man of very varied talents. He published in 1606 *Graphice*, a practical treatise on art, issued in many subsequent editions under the title *The Gentleman's Exercise*. He published *The Compleat Gentleman*, the work by which he is best known, in 1622. From the last edition of this (1661) Dr *Johnson drew all the heraldic definitions in his dictionary.

Peachum, and his daughter Polly, characters in Gay's *The Beggar's Opera.

PEACOCK, Thomas Love (1785–1866), satirist, essayist, and poet, was the son of a London glass merchant, though brought up by his mother. He inherited private means just sufficient to enable him to live as a man of letters. He had published two volumes of verse when, in 1812, he met *Shelley, whose close friend he afterwards remained. Peacock's prose satires, *Headlong Hall (1816), *Melincourt (1817), and *Nightmare Abbey (1818), survey the contemporary political and cultural scene from a Radical viewpoint. Formally they owe much to two classical genres: the 'Anatomy', or miscellaneous prose satire, and the Socratic dialogue, especially perhaps Plato's *Symposium which, like many of Peacock's convivial arguments, takes place over a dinner table. The satiric debate is diversified by a romantic love-plot, increasingly important in *Crotchet Castle (1831) and *Gryll Grange (1860–1), and by amusing, clever songs. Peacock's fictional world is an exceptionally pleasant one, for he assembles his characters in English country houses, and sends them on excursions into mountain and forest scenery. In *Maid Marian (1822) and *The Misfortunes of Elphin (1829) he varies his format by employing a historical setting, 12th-cent. England and 6th-cent. Wales, but the topical satirical reference remains unmistakable. Peacock's early volumes of poetry are of antiquarian interest, but *Rhododaphne (1818) is a fine and historically important poem, in the mythological manner of Keats's *'Lamia'; Peacock also wrote some touching lyrics, especially 'Long Night Succeeds thy little Day' (1826) and 'Newark Abbey' (1842). Of his satirical poems and squibs, *The Paper Money Lyrics (1837) lampoon the dogmas of political economists and the malpractices of bankers. Peacock's sceptical attitude to the fashionable cult of the arts is apparent in his two most sustained critical essays, 'Essay on Fashionable Literature' (a fragment, written 1818) and *'The Four Ages of Poetry' (1820), to which Shelley's *A Defence of Poetry is a reply. In 1819 Peacock married Jane Gryffydh, the 'White Snowdonian antelope' of Shelley's 'Letter to Maria Gisborne'; she suffered a breakdown at the death of their third daughter in 1826, though she lived on until 1851. His favourite child was his eldest daughter Mary Ellen, who became the first wife of G. *Meredith, and features in Meredith's sonnet sequence *Modern Love. Peacock entered the East India Company's service in 1819 and worked immediately under J. *Mill until the latter's death in 1836, when he succeeded to the responsible position of examiner.

The standard books on Peacock are the Life by C. van Doren (1911), and M. Butler's Peacock Displayed (1979). The best editions are H. F. B. Brett-Smith and C. E. Jones (eds), Halliford Edition of the Works of T. L. Peacock (10 vols, 1924–34) and D. *Garnett, The Novels (2 vols, 1948).

PEAKE, Mervyn Laurence (1911–68), novelist, poet, and artist, born at Kuling in China, the son of a medical missionary; he came to England aged eleven, was educated at Eltham College, Kent, then attended the Royal Academy Schools. He spent three years from 1934 with a group of artists on the island of Sark, then returned to London, where he taught art, exhibited his own work and illustrated books, published verse and stories for children, etc. He was invalided out of the army in 1943 after a nervous breakdown, but was later commissioned as a war artist, and also visited Belsen in 1945 on a journalistic expedition for The Leader, an experience which profoundly affected him. Meanwhile he was working on a novel, Titus Groan, which was published in 1946; it was followed by Gormenghast (1950) and Titus Alone (1959), which as a trilogy form the work for which Peake is best remembered, a creation of grotesque yet precise Gothic fantasy, recounting the life of Titus, 77th earl of Groan, in his crumbling castle of Gormenghast, surrounded by a cast of characters which includes the colourful Fuchsia, Dr Prunesquallor, and the melancholy Muzzlehatch. Peake's poetry includes The Glassblowers (1950) and The Rhyme of the Flying Bomb (1962), a ballad of the blitz; he illustrated most of his own work, and also produced memorable drawings for The Rime of the *Ancient Mariner (1943), *Treasure Island (1949), and other works. A lighter side of his prolific imagination is seen in his posthumous A Book of Nonsense (1972). The last years of his life were overshadowed by Parkinson's disease, as described by his widow Maeve Gilmore in her memoir A World Away (1970). For an account of the relationship between his drawings and his prose, see Hilary Spurling's introduction to The Drawings of Mervyn Peake (1974).

PEARCE, Philippa A., see CHILDREN'S LITERATURE.

Pearl, an alliterative poem in 1,212 lines of twelve-lined octosyllabic stanzas from the second half of the 14th cent., the only manuscript of which is the famous Cotton Nero A x which is also the sole manuscript of *Patience, *Cleanness, and Sir *Gawain and the Green Knight and which comes from the North-West Midlands. Pearl was the author's daughter and only child who has died before she was two years old. Wandering in misery in the garden where she is buried, he has a vision of a river beyond which lies Paradise. Here he sees a maiden seated whom he recognizes as his daughter. She chides him for his excessive grief and describes her blessed state. He argues with her about the justice that makes her queen of Heaven when she died so young. Convinced by her, he plunges into the river in an attempt to join her, and awakes, comforted and reassured of his faith in God. Discussion of the poem has centred on the extent to which it is to be interpreted literally, as elegy, or allegorically. The form and language of the poem are extremely brilliant, and its literary relations apparently not confined to England: *Boccaccio's Olympia and the Earthly Paradise sections of *Dante's Purgatorio (from Canto xxviii to the end) seem to be parallels to the poem. Ed. E. V. Gordon (1953); P. M. Kean, The Pearl: an interpretation (1967).

PEARSON, Sir (Cyril) Arthur (1866–1921), newspaper magnate, educated at Winchester, who embarked on a career in journalism with *Tit-Bits, inspired by his own passion for quizzes and puzzles. He soon set up a successful rival to Tit-Bits in the form of Pearson's Weekly, in 1890, and in 1900 founded the Daily Express. He went blind, and was more widely honoured for his work for the blind than for his journalistic talents.

PEARSON, (Edward) Hesketh (Gibbons) (1887–1964), actor and biographer, who joined the company of Beerbohm Tree as a young man, and whose first book, Modern Men and Mummers (1921), contained portraits of many of the theatre personalities of the time. The Whispering Gallery (1926), an anonymous work purporting to be 'leaves from the diary of an ex-diplomat', occasioned a scandal, a court case, and an acquittal for Pearson, who went on to write many lively and widely-read biographies, of (for example) *Hazlitt (1934), Sydney *Smith (*The Smith of Smiths*, 1934), G. B. *Shaw (1942), *Wilde (1946), Beerbohm Tree (1956), and several others. He also wrote literary travel books in collaboration with *Kingsmill, and his autobiography, *Hesketh Pearson by himself*, appeared posthumously in 1965.

PEARSON, John (1613–86), educated at Eton and Cambridge, a royalist chaplain during the Civil War, and after the Restoration master of Jesus College, then of Trinity, Cambridge. He became bishop of Chester in 1673. From 1654 he preached at St Clement's, Eastcheap, the series of lectures which he published in 1659 as his classic *Exposition of the Creed*, the notes of which are a rich mine of patristic learning. He was one of the most erudite theologians of his age.

Peasants' Revolt, the popular insurrection of the labourers of Essex and Kent which began in May 1381, provoked in part by the tyrannies of *John of Gaunt. While the Kentish leader Wat Tyler was treating with the king, the 14-year-old Richard II, was pulled from his horse and killed by Walworth, the mayor of London. The rebels dispersed and by the end of June the revolt had been repressed with ferocity everywhere. Its principal motivation—the wish of tenants to end repressive feudal rights—is reflected in literature, most famously in the couplet of the preacher John Ball (who was condemned after the revolt):

> When Adam delved and Eve span
> Who was then a gentleman?

The introduction of the fable of Belling the Cat into the later B and C texts of *Piers Plowman* is thought to be a response to the revolt and accordingly to date those later texts after 1381. See R. B. Dobson, *The Peasants' Revolt of 1381* (1970).

Pecksniff, Mr, a character in Dickens's *Martin Chuzzlewit*.

PECOCK, Reginald (1395–c.1460), a Welshman who became bishop successively of St Asaph and Chichester. Most of his writings employ the syllogistic logic of the Scholastics (in a somewhat debased form), and many were directed against the *Lollards, notably his *Repressor of over much Blaming of the Clergy* (1455), a monument of 15th-cent. English prose of considerable eloquence and lexical variety. His *Book of Faith*, also in English, was issued in 1456, and in his *Donet* and the *Folewer to the Donet* he sought to define a body of faith acceptable to all. He alienated by his writings all sections of theological opinion in England, was arraigned before the archbishop of Canterbury, and obliged to resign his bishopric and

recant his opinions (1458), whereupon he was sent to Thornley Abbey where he probably lived in seclusion. His work has considerable importance from a literary viewpoint for its development of the English vocabulary, which he added to, both by loan-translations such as 'untobethoughtupon' (*imponderabile*) and by borrowings such as 'anagogy' and 'tropology'.

EETS os editions: *The Donet*, ed. E. V. Hitchcock (No. 156, 1918); *The Folewer to the Donet*, ed. E. V. Hitchcock (No. 164, 1923); *The Reule of Christen Religioun*, ed. W. C. Greet (No. 171, 1926). See also *The Repressor*, ed. C. Babington (2 vols, 1860); V. H. H. Green, *Bishop Reginald Pecock* (1945).

Pecunia, Lady, the rich heiress in Jonson's *The Staple of News*.

Pedro, Don, the prince of Aragon who defeated his illegitimate brother *Don John and who woos *Hero on Claudio's behalf in Shakespeare's *Much Ado About Nothing*.

Peebles, Peter, a character in Scott's *Redgauntlet*.

Peel, John (1776–1854), the hero of the well known hunting song 'D'ye ken John Peel?', was born at Caldbeck, Cumberland, and for over 40 years ran the famous pack of hounds that bore his name. The words of the song were composed by his friend John Woodcock Graves.

PEELE, George (1556–96), was the son of James Peele, Clerk of Christ's Hospital and author of city pageants and books on accountancy. He was educated at Christ's Hospital, Broadgates Hall (Pembroke College), and Christ Church, Oxford. From about 1581 he was mainly resident in London, and pursuing an active and varied literary career. He was an associate of many other writers of the period, such as T. *Watson and R. *Greene. His works fall into three main categories: plays, pageants, and 'gratulatory' and miscellaneous verse. His surviving plays are *The Araygnement of Paris (1584); *Edward I* (1593); *The Battle of Alcazar (1594); *The Old Wives' Tale (1595); and *David and Fair Bethsabe (1599). His miscellaneous verse includes *Polyhymnia (1590) and *The Honour of the Garter* (1593), a gratulatory poem to the Earl of Northumberland. Peele's work is dominated by courtly and patriotic themes, and his technical achievements include extending the range of non-dramatic blank verse. The jest-book *The Merrie Conceited Jests of George Peele* (1607) seems to bear little relation to Peele's actual personality. His *Life and Works* were edited by C. T. Prouty (3 vols, 1952–70).

Peggotty, Daniel, Clara, and Ham, characters in Dickens's *David Copperfield*.

Pegler, Mrs, in Dickens's *Hard Times*, Bounderby's mother.

PÉGUY, Charles (1875–1914), French poet and essayist. Profoundly responsive to traditional French forms of life, he expressed his non-conformist Catholic faith in such poems as the biblical *Le Porche du mystère de la deuxième vertu* (1911) and the fresco-like stanzas of *Sainte Geneviève* (1912) and *Ève* (1913). His death on the Marne only served to deepen the effect of his almost mystical vision of France on his contemporaries. He is the subject of a long poem by G. *Hill, published 1983, *The Mystery of the Charity of Charles Péguy*.

Peg Woffington, a novel by C. *Reade, based on an episode in the life of Peg *Woffington, and adapted from his play *Masks and Faces*.

PELAGIAN, derived from **PELAGIUS,** the latinized form of the name of a British monk, Morgan, of the 4th and 5th cents whose doctrines were fiercely combated by Germanus, bishop of Auxerre, and by St *Augustine, and condemned by Pope Zosimus in 418. The Pelagians denied the doctrine of Original Sin, asserting that Adam's fall did not involve his posterity, and maintained that the human will is itself capable of good without the assistance of divine grace. In spite of their condemnation, their beliefs died slowly and were only finally defeated by the Augustinian view that grace is God-given at the Council of Orange (529). Even so, the voluntarist tendency of Pelagianism revived in the Middle Ages; many of the thinkers opposed by *Bradwardine (d. 1349) he called 'modern Pelagians' in their attempts to qualify the immanence of God's grace by their views of Free Will. See R. E. Evans, *Pelagius, Inquiries and Appraisals* (1968).

Pelham: or *The Adventures of a Gentleman*, a novel by *Bulwer-Lytton, published 1828. This was his second novel, and is generally considered his best.

It recounts the adventures of Henry Pelham, a young dandy, wit, and aspiring politician, who falls in love with Ellen, sister of his old friend from Eton days, Reginald Glanville. The latter is falsely suspected of a murder, and tells his story to Pelham, who unearths the real murderer, Thornton, a character drawn from the well known murderer Thurtell. But the interest of the novel lies in its lively portrayal of fashionable society, in English country houses, in Paris, in Cheltenham, in London, etc., and in such minor characters as Lady Frances, Pelham's worldly mother, and Lord Vincent, whose conversation is laced with puns, largely in Latin. Bulwer-Lytton mocks the genre of the *Fashionable novel even while employing it, which adds to the tone of sparkling cynicism

which captivated contemporary readers and made his hero's name a catch-phrase.

Pell, Solomon, in Dickens's *Pickwick Papers*, an attorney in the Insolvent Court.

Pellam, King, 'The Maimed King', in Arthurian legend, father of the Grail King, *Pelles. Wounded by Balyn's *'Dolorous Stroke', he is healed by his great-grandson Galahad in the Grail quest.

Pelleas, Sir, 'The Noble Knight', in Arthurian legend the lover of Ettarde. After her death he marries *Nimue, the Lady of the Lake.

'Pelleas and Ettarre', one of Tennyson's *Idylls of the King*, published 1869. Pelleas woos the heartless Ettarre, is tricked by Gawain, learns of the adultery of Lancelot and Guinevere, and vows to avenge the treasons of the Round Table.

Pelléas et Mélisande, see MAETERLINCK, M.

Pelles, King, 'The Grail King', in *Malory, one of the Fisher Kings and said to be 'cousin nigh unto Joseph of Arimathie'. He is maimed for drawing the sword of David on the mysterious ship. Founded perhaps on *Pwyll of Welsh mythology, he was the father of Elaine who was the mother of Galahad by Launcelot.

Pellinore, King, 'The King of the Waste Lands', in *Malory the father of Sir Lamorak, Sir Perceval, and Sir Torre, and the brother of King *Pelles. He follows the *Questing Beast and kills King Lot of Orkney, because of which ten years later he is killed by Lot's son Gawain. Charles Moorman (in *The Book of Kyng Arthur*, 1965) believes that the rivalry between the houses of King Lot and King Pellinore is one of the three principal running themes in Malory.

PEMBROKE, Mary Herbert, countess of (1561–1621), was the younger sister of P. *Sidney, whose first version of the *Arcadia was written for her at Wilton early in her married life. After her brother's death in 1586 she became in effect his literary executrix, overseeing the publication of the *Arcadia* and the rest of his works for the editions of 1593 and 1598 and undertaking literary projects of which he would have approved. She completed the *Psalms*, of which Sidney had translated only the first forty-two, rendering them in a very wide variety of English verse forms; they were not published as a whole until the edition of J. C. A. Rathmell (1963), but *Ruskin, who much admired them, made a selection from them under the title of *Rock Honeycomb* (1877). She translated Du Plessis Mornay's *Discourse of Life and Death* and R. Garnier's Senecan tragedy *Antonius* (both published in 1592; the latter also published as *Antonie*, 1595), and at an unknown date she translated *Petrarch's *Trionfo della morte*.

Her reputation as a patroness perhaps outstripped her specific achievements (T. S. *Eliot's essay 'Apology for the Countess of Pembroke', 1932, implies a deliberate control of a literary clique which she probably never had); but she certainly had links with such writers as S. *Daniel, N. *Breton, and Sir J. Harington. A letter from her once seen at Wilton by *Cory said 'we have the man Shakespeare with us'; it has since disappeared, and her connection with Shakespeare, if any, cannot be proved. The epitaph on her by W. *Browne was popular throughout the 17th cent.:

> Underneath this sable herse
> Lies the subject of all verse:
> Sidney's sister, Pembroke's mother:
> Death, ere thou hast slain another,
> Fair, and learn'd, and good as she,
> Time shall throw a dart at thee.

PEN, an international association of Poets, Playwrights, Editors, Essayists, and Novelists founded in 1921 by Mrs Dawson-Scott, under the presidency of J. *Galsworthy, to promote co-operation between writers all over the world in the interests of literature, freedom of expression, and international goodwill.

***Pendennis,** The History of,* a novel by *Thackeray, published in numbers 1848–50.

A *Bildungsroman in which the main character, Arthur Pendennis, is the only son of a devoted and unworldly widow, Helen. As a very young man he falls in love with an actress, Emily Costigan ('Miss Fotheringay'), and is only rescued from an unsuitable marriage by the tactful intervention of his uncle, Major Pendennis, who persuades her disreputable old father, Captain Costigan, that Arthur has no money of his own. Pendennis then goes to the university of Oxbridge, where he runs up bills and has to be rescued by a loan from Helen's adopted daughter, Laura Bell. Helen hopes that Laura and her son will marry, but Pendennis's next entanglement is with Blanche Amory, an affected and hard-hearted girl, the daughter of the rich, vulgar Lady Clavering by her first husband. Major Pendennis encourages a match between his nephew and Blanche, although he is secretly aware that Blanche's father is an escaped convict who is still alive and is blackmailing Sir Francis Clavering.

Pendennis goes to London and is supposed to be reading for the bar. He shares chambers with George Warrington, who starts him on a literary career by introducing him to Captain Shandon, a debt-ridden Irish journalist who is editing a new magazine, the 'Pall Mall Gazette', from prison. Pendennis has a mild flirtation with a working-class girl, Fanny Bolton, and, when he falls ill, Fanny nurses him devotedly. Helen Pendennis jumps to the false conclusion that Fanny is Pendennis's mistress, and treats the girl very

unkindly. Pendennis is so indignant when he discovers this, that he threatens to marry Fanny, but is dissuaded by Warrington, who tells the story of his own unfortunate early marriage. Fanny soon finds consolation with Sam Huxter, a medical student, but Blanche is harder to shake off. After the exposure of the existence of her villainous father, Pendennis feels obliged to go through with an engagement to her, although he does not really care for her. Fortunately Blanche decides in favour of Harry Foker, heir to a brewing fortune, and Pendennis and Laura finally marry, after Helen's death.

Pendragon, a title given to an ancient British or Welsh chief holding or claiming supreme power. In English chiefly known as the title of Uther Pendragon, father of *Arthur. The word means 'chief dragon', the dragon being the war standard.

Penefeather, Lady Penelope, a character in Scott's *St Ronan's Well.*

Penguin Books, the name first given to a series of paperback books published in 1935 by A. *Lane, and established in its own right as a publishing company in 1936. The first ten titles, which sold for sixpence each, included *Ariel* by *Maurois (No. 1). and fiction by A .*Christie, *Hemingway, D. L. *Sayers and M. *Webb. In 1937 the non-fiction Pelican series was launched with the publication, in two parts, of Shaw's *Intelligent Woman's Guide to Socialism,* and Puffin Picture Books for children followed in 1940. Other notable ventures include the Penguin Classics, edited for many years by E. V. Rieu (1887–1972), whose own translation of the *Odyssey* (1946) was its first and best-selling volume; *Pevsner's series *The Buildings of England* (1951–74); and the first unexpurgated edition of *Lady Chatterley's Lover* (1960), which led to a celebrated trial and acquittal at the Old Bailey.

PENN, William (1644–1718), a Quaker and founder of Pennsylvania, son of the admiral Sir William Penn. He was committed to the Tower in 1668 for publishing *The Sandy Foundation Shaken* (an attack on orthodox doctrines of the Trinity and the Atonement, and on the Calvinist theory of justification) and there wrote *No Cross, No Crown* (1669), an eloquent and learned dissertation on Christian duty and a Quaker classic. He suffered frequent persecutions, turned his thoughts to America as a refuge for his faith, and in 1682 obtained grants of East New Jersey and Pennsylvania, and framed, possibly in concert with A. *Sidney, a new constitution for the colony by which religious toleration would be secured. He travelled twice to America, returning in 1701 to spend the rest of his life in England. *Some Fruits of Solitude,* a collection of aphorisms praised by R. L. *Stevenson, was published anonymously in 1693. Most of his many writings were occasional pieces.

PENNANT, Thomas (1726–98), naturalist, antiquarian, and traveller, published *A Tour in Scotland* in 1771, *A Tour in Wales* in 1778–81, *A Tour in Scotland and Voyage to the Hebrides* in 1774–6, and *The Journey from Chester to London* in 1782. His travel writings were admired by Dr *Johnson, though *Boswell disapproved of his portrait of Scotland. He was also a distinguished zoologist, and figures in G. *White's *Selborne* as one of the author's correspondents. *Literary Life of the late Thomas Pennant, Esq., By himself* appeared in 1793.

Penny Magazine, The, see KNIGHT, C.

'Penseroso, Il', see IL PENSEROSO.

Penshurst Place, in Kent, has been in the possession of the Sidney family since 1552, and was the birthplace of Sir P. *Sidney. Many writers enjoyed its hospitality, including *Jonson, who paid a graceful tribute in 'To Penshurst' (*The Forest*, 1616), praising the fruitfulness of the landscape and the gardens, the 'high huswifery' of its lady, the generosity of its lord, and the virtues of the whole household, who learned there 'the mysteries of manners, armes and arts'. (See also PATRONAGE.)

Pentameron, The, a prose work by W. S. *Landor, published 1837, is an expression of Landor's admiration of *Boccaccio. The book consists of imaginary conversations between *Petrarch and Boccaccio, while the latter lies ill at his village near Certaldo, and Petrarch visits him on five successive days. They speak mainly of Dante's *Divina Commedia*; but Petrarch also reproves Boccaccio for the licentious character of some of his tales. The work provides a pleasing picture of two old friends, and of several attractive minor characters.

Pentameter, see METRE and BLANK VERSE.

Pentapolin, see ALIFANFARON.

Penthea, a character in Ford's *The Broken Heart*.

PEPYS (pron. peeps or peppis), Samuel (1633–1703), son of John Pepys, a London tailor, was educated at St Paul's School, London, and at Trinity Hall and Magdalene College, Cambridge. In 1655, when 22, he married Elizabeth St Michel, a girl of 15, the daughter of a French father and English mother. He entered the household of Sir Edward Montagu (afterwards first earl of Sandwich), his father's first cousin, in 1656; and his subsequent successful career was largely due to Montagu's patronage. His famous *Diary* opens on 1 Jan. 1660, when Pepys was living in Axe Yard, Westminster, and was very poor. Soon after this

he was appointed 'clerk of the King's ships' and clerk of the privy seal, with a salary of £350 (supplemented by fees). In 1665 he became surveyor-general of the victualling office, in which capacity he showed himself an energetic official and a zealous reformer of abuses. Owing to an unfounded fear of failing eyesight he closed his diary on 31 May 1669, and in the same year his wife died. In 1672 he was appointed secretary to the Admiralty. He was committed to the Tower on a charge of complicity in the *'Popish Plot' in 1679 and deprived of his office, but was soon set free. In 1683 he was sent to Tangier with Lord Dartmouth and wrote an interesting diary while there. In 1684 he was reappointed secretary to the Admiralty, a post which he held until the revolution, labouring hard to provide the country with an efficient fleet. At the revolution he was deprived of his appointment and afterwards lived in retirement, principally at Clapham. His *Diary* remained in cipher (a system of shorthand) at Magdalene College, Cambridge, until 1825, when it was deciphered by John Smith and edited by Lord Braybrooke. An enlarged edition by Mynors Bright appeared in 1875–9, and an edition in 10 vols (1893–9) by Henry B. Wheatley remained the standard text until the appearance of a new and unbowdlerized transcription by R. Latham and W. Matthews (11 vols, 1970–83). On his death his friend and fellow-diarist *Evelyn remembered him as 'a very worthy, industrious and curious person, none in England exceeding him in knowledge of the navy . . . universally beloved, hospitable, generous, learned in many things, skilled in music, a very great cherisher of learned men'. Pepys's *Memoirs of the Navy, 1690* were edited by J. R. Tanner, 1906. (See also RESTORATION.)

Perceforest, a vast French prose romance of the 14th cent., in which the author seeks to link the legends of *Alexander and *Arthur. Alexander, after the conquest of India, is driven by a storm on the coast of England, and makes one of his followers (called Perceforest because he has killed a magician in an impenetrable forest) king of the land. Under the latter's grandson the *Grail is brought to England.

Perceval, Sir, probably to be identified with Peredur of the *Mabinogion*, is a legendary figure of great antiquity, first found in European poetry in the 9,000-line, incomplete *Perceval, ou Le Conte du Graal* of *Chrétien de Troyes (c.1182) and the German *Parzival* (c.1205) of *Wolfram von Eschenbach (which was the inspiration for *Wagner's opera). In English he appears in *Sir Perceval of Galles*, a 2,288-line romance, in 16-line stanzas in tail-rhyme from the 15th cent. (ed. W. H. French and C. B. Hale, *Middle English Metrical Romances*, 1930) and in *Malory. The former tells of the childhood of Perceval and his being knighted by Arthur, without any allusion to the *Grail. Malory makes him a son of King *Pellinore, describing his success in the Quest for the Grail with Galahad and Bors. In the French prose Vulgate *La Queste del Saint Graal*, the three successful questers are joined on Solomon's ship by Perceval's sister who dies by giving her blood to heal a lady suffering from a great illness, and is committed to the waves in a boat; her body is found and buried in the Grail land of Sarras where the three are borne in Solomon's boat.

Percy, a tragedy by Hannah *More.

PERCY, Thomas, born Piercy (1729–1811), son of a Bridgnorth grocer, was educated at Oxford and became bishop of Dromore in 1782. He was a man of varied intellectual and antiquarian interests; in 1761 he published a translation (from the Portuguese) of the first Chinese novel to appear in English, *Hau Kiou Choaan*, and in 1763 his *Five Pieces of Runic Poetry Translated from the Islandic Language*, including the 'Incantation of Hervor' and the 'Death-Song of Ragnar Lodbrog'. The latter had a considerable influence on the study of ancient Norse in England. Percy also published poetry (including his ballad *The Hermit of Warkworth*, 1771), translated from the Hebrew and Spanish, and wrote a *Memoir of Goldsmith* (1801). He is best known for his celebrated collection *Reliques of Ancient English Poetry* (3 vols, 1765), which was attacked by later writers (see RITSON) as unscholarly, but which nevertheless contributed greatly to the understanding of and enthusiasm for the older English poetry, reached a fourth edition by 1794, and has since been several times re-edited. (See also PERCY FOLIO and BALLAD.)

Percy Folio, The, a manuscript in mid-17th-cent. handwriting, which belonged to Humphrey Pitt of Shifnal, the most important source of our *ballad literature and the basis of *Child's collection. From it T. *Percy drew the ballads included in his *Reliques*. It also contains the 14th-cent. alliterative allegorical poem 'Death and Liffe' (modelled on *Piers Plowman*) and 'Scottish Feilde' (mainly on the battle of *Flodden). The Percy Folio was printed in its entirety by Hales and *Furnivall in 1867–8. It is now in the British Museum.

Percy Society, The, was founded in 1840 by T. C. *Croker, *Dyce, *Halliwell-Phillipps, and J. P. *Collier, for the purpose of publishing old English lyrics and ballads. It was named in honour of T. *Percy.

Percy's Reliques, see RELIQUES OF ANCIENT ENGLISH POETRY.

Perdita, the daughter of *Hermione and *Leontes, brought up in Bohemia, in Shakespeare's *The Winter's Tale*; her name means 'the lost one'.

Peredur, the Arthurian subject of one of the seven tales added by Lady Charlotte Guest to the *Mabinogion* proper and now, accordingly, normally included in it. The Welsh *Peredur* is found most completely in the White Book, rather than the Red Book used by Guest (see MABINOGION), and it is found in two additional manuscripts. The story corresponds closely to the *Perceval* of *Chrétien de Troyes, from which however it departs in a number of ways, and it corresponds too to a number of other Arthurian texts, such as *Perlesvaus* (ed. F. Nitze et al., 1932).

Peregrine Pickle, *The Adventures of*, a novel by T. *Smollett, published 1751.

Unlike *Roderick Random*, this lengthy novel is told by an omniscient narrator, and its principal target appears to be Pride, in all its manifestations. Peregrine's circle is introduced, principally his apathetic father Gamaliel, his fanciful mother, and his parents' friends, the Trunnions. Commodore Hawser Trunnion, one of Smollett's happiest creations, lives in a house known as 'the garrison', and has as his comrades the boatswain Pipes and Lieutenant Hatchway, who become friends of Peregrine. Even as a boy Peregrine shows 'a certain oddity of disposition' which manifests itself in arrogant behaviour and ferocious practical jokes. At Winchester and at Oxford Peregrine plunges into hectic living, and develops further his violent vein of humour. He meets Emilia, with whom he falls abruptly in love, and who remains throughout the book, and through all his wanderings, a fixed point to which he always returns. But she is beneath him in fortune and in rank, and pride forbids him to court her. He meets Godfrey, Emilia's brother, and together they share a long series of wild japes and adventures.

Peregrine's *Grand Tour provides opportunity for heavy satire on foreign lands. Peregrine, a 'professed enemy to all oppression' (by which he means all authority), behaves with violent aggression and suffers imprisonment in the Bastille. Affectation and ignorance are ridiculed in the figures of the tutor, Jolter, the artist Pallet, and the didactic Doctor, all of whom are involved with Peregrine in a gross feast in the style of the ancients. His tempestuous and often frustrated adventures with women, such as Mrs Hornbeck and a high-born Flemish lady, succeed each other pell-mell, and his brief repentances are always overcome by the next violent passion.

Far gone in degradation, Peregrine returns to England. He allies himself in Bath with the misanthrope Crabtree, but demonstrates that he has not yet lost all generous feeling when Trunnion is ill. He nurses the old man lovingly and is filled with grief at his death. But with the money Trunnion has left him he reverts to profligacy and becomes obsessed with his object of seducing Emilia. When perjury and drugging fail he becomes almost mad, and develops a dangerous fever.

At this point, the lengthy, scandalous, and erotic memoirs of Lady *Vane are inserted into the narrative. The story is broken, but the tale of a life of pleasure is not irrelevant to Peregrine's own. Debauchery now takes almost complete hold on Peregrine. Emilia again rejects him, he loses a vast sum in an attempt to enter politics, and is eventually sent to prison for a gross libel. Another long story, of the unfortunate poet Mackercher, whose generous character contrasts strongly with those of both Peregrine and Lady Vane, is interpolated at this point. In prison Peregrine becomes morose and withdrawn, quarrels with the faithful Pipes and Hatchway, and begins to long for death. But this is the beginning of repentance. He is rescued by Godfrey, Emilia returns to him, and he inherits his father's fortune. When he and Emilia marry he rejects the fashionable urban world, pays his debts, and retires with her to the country.

The novel which contained many savage caricatures of, for instance, *Fielding as Mr Spondy, *Garrick as Marmozet, and *Akenside as the Doctor, was only moderately successful, and was modified both in form and tone for the second edition of 1758.

Perfectibilism, the doctrine that man, individual and social, is capable of progressing indefinitely towards physical, mental, and moral perfection. Mr Foster, in Peacock's *Headlong Hall*, was a 'perfectibilian'.

Perfumed Garden, The, see BURTON, SIR R.

Peri-Banou, The Fairy, see AHMED.

Peri Bathous, or the Art of Sinking in Poetry (1727), a treatise by *Pope.

Pericles and Aspasia, a prose work by W. S. *Landor, published 1836.

The book consists of imaginary letters, the bulk of them from Aspasia to her friend Cleone, together with Cleone's replies. Others are addressed by Pericles to Aspasia, or by her to him; while others again are from or to prominent figures of the time, such as Anaxagoras and Alcibiades. The letters, which end with the death of Pericles, include discussions of artistic, literary, religious, philosophical, and political subjects.

Pericles, Prince of Tyre, a romantic drama by *Shakespeare, the first two acts probably written with a collaborator. It was composed between 1606 and 1608, when it was registered and when George Wilkins's prose narrative *The Painfull Adventures of Pericles Prince of Tyre*, which was based on a performance of the play,

was published. A textually corrupt quarto of *Pericles* appeared in 1609 and was reprinted five times; the play was omitted from the First *Folio of 1623, but was included in the second issue of the third Folio of 1664. The play is based on the story of Apollonius of Tyre in *Gower's *Confessio Amantis* and a prose version (itself derived from the *Gesta Romanorum), *The Patterne of Painefull Adventures*, registered 1576 and reprinted 1607, by Laurence Twine.

The play is presented by Gower, who acts as Chorus throughout, and tells how having solved the riddle set by King Antiochus and discovered his incestuous relationship with his daughter, Pericles, prince of Tyre, finds his life in danger. He leaves his government in the hands of his honest minister, Helicanus, and sails from Tyre to Tarsus where he relieves a famine. Off the coast of Pentapolis Pericles alone survives the wreck of his ship, and in a tournament defeats the suitors for the hand of Thaisa, daughter of King Simonides, whom he marries.

Hearing that Antiochus has died, Pericles sets sail for Tyre, and during a storm on the voyage Thaisa gives birth to a daughter, Marina, and faints. Apparently dead, Thaisa is buried at sea in a chest, which is cast ashore at Ephesus, where Cerimon, a physician, opens it and restores Thaisa to life. She, thinking her husband drowned, becomes a priestess in the temple of Diana. Pericles takes Marina to Tarsus, where he leaves her with its Governor Cleon and his wife Dionyza.

When the child grows up Dionyza, jealous of her being more favoured than her own daughter, seeks to kill her; but Marina is carried off by pirates and sold in Mytilene to a brothel, where her purity and piety win the admiration of Lysimachus, the governor of the city, and the respect of the brothel-keeper's servant, Boult, and secure her release. In a vision Pericles is shown Marina's tomb, deceivingly erected by Cleon and Dionyza. He puts to sea again and lands at Mytilene, where through Lysimachus and to his intense joy Pericles discovers his daughter. In a second vision, Diana directs him to go to her temple at Ephesus and there recount the story of his life. In doing this, the priestess Thaisa, his lost wife, recognizes him, and is reunited with her husband and daughter. At the end of the play the Chorus tells how Cleon and Dionyza are burnt by the citizens of Tarsus as a penalty for their wickedness.

Perilous Chair, the 'Siege Perilous' at the *Round Table.

Periodical, Literary, a term here taken to describe any repeating series of literary journal, magazine, or review. From the beginning of the 18th cent. until the beginning of the Second World War the literary periodical flourished, and contributed greatly to the development of creative writing and criticism. It stemmed from 17th-cent. abstracts of books and comments on publishers' puffs. The *Mercurius Librarius* of 1668 was the first periodical to catalogue books, and the *Universal Historical Bibliotheque* of 1687 the first publication to invite contributions and include rudimentary comments on essays and other recent writings. At about this time periodical publications began to divide into two main types; the first to become established was the magazine miscellany, whose contents were partly but not exclusively literary. *The Gentleman's Journal* of 1692 is generally held to be the first established ancestor of this abiding form which developed (to take only a few notable examples) through the *Tatler* (1709–11) of *Addison and *Steele, *Cave's influential *Gentleman's Magazine*, and the *Analytical Review* (1788–99); to the 19th-cent. *Blackwood's Magazine* (1817–1980), the *London Magazine* (1820–9), and *Bentley's Miscellany* (1837–69); and on to the 20th-cent. *Monthly Review* (1900–7), *John O'London's* (1919–54), the *London Mercury* (1919–39), and many others.

The second type of periodical was the review, with which may be grouped the weekly journal of original, critical, and general literary work. The *Monthly Review* (1749–1845), Smollett's *Critical Review* (1756–90), and the *Analytical Review* established a form which culminated in the magisterial and influential reviews of the 19th cent.—the *Edinburgh Review* (1802–1929), the *Quarterly Review* (1809–1967), the *Examiner* (1808–81), the *Westminster Review* (1824–1914), the *Athenaeum* (1828–1921), the *Cornhill Magazine* (1860–1975), the *Fortnightly Review* (1865–1934), and others, including the notorious *Yellow Book* (1894–7). Although by this time the distinction between miscellany and review was blurring, these led directly to the significant periodicals of this century, such as the *Bookman* (1891–1934), the *English Review* (1908–37), the *Times Literary Supplement* (1902–), the *Criterion* (1922–39), and many others, including in particular *Horizon* (1940–50) and the post-war *Encounter* (1953–) and *London Magazine* (1954–). Specialist reviews, such as *Scrutiny* (1932–53), designed for the more academic reader, have exerted great critical influence.

The single-essay (or serial-essay) publication, best represented by the most celebrated of all periodicals, Steele's *Spectator* (1711–12, 1714) and Johnson's *Rambler* (1750–2), had immeasurable literary influence and reputation, but the form did not last beyond the end of the 18th cent.

Although for almost a century before 1800 the periodical had encouraged many talents, including those of *Defoe, *Swift, *Fielding, *Smollett, and *Goldsmith, by the beginning of the 19th cent. the dying system of personal *patronage was largely replaced by the support of the literary periodicals and their editors (such as Leigh *Hunt and John *Scott). The work of the *Romantics, and of the Victorian poets and novelists, was greatly encouraged and widely published. For the first part of the 20th cent. new weeklies and periodicals joined others living on from the 19th cent. in supporting a wide range of new writers. But economic problems have compelled the closure of many periodicals, and its seems likely that their three centuries of influence and support has largely come to an end.

(See also ANTI-JACOBIN; CHAMPION; ENGLISHMAN'S MAGAZINE; FLAGELLANT; FRASER'S MAGAZINE; FRIEND; INDICATOR; LIBERAL; LITERARY GAZETTE; MONTHLY MAGAZINE; NEW MONTHLY MAGAZINE; POLITICAL REGISTER; RETROSPECTIVE REVIEW; WATCHMAN.)

Peripeteia, see POETICS, THE.

Perissa, in Spenser's *Faerie Queene*, see MEDINA.

Perker, Mr, in Dickens's *Pickwick Papers*.

Perkin Warbeck, a historical play by J. *Ford, printed 1634.

The play deals with the arrival of Warbeck at the court of King James IV of Scotland and his marriage, at the king's instance and against her father's wish, to Lady Katherine Gordon; the treason of Sir William Stanley and his execution; the expedition of James IV with Warbeck into England; the desertion of Warbeck's cause by James; Warbeck's landing in Cornwall, his defeat, capture, and execution.

Ford takes up, in a new key, the much earlier fashion for plays in English history, but departs from his sources in making Perkin convinced that he actually is duke of York, not an impostor. Thus Perkin is a victim, not a villain, and the play is a study of delusion rather than ambition.

PERRAULT, Charles (1628–1703), French raconteur. Although known in his lifetime for his participation in the quarrel between the ancients and the moderns (see CORNEILLE), he is remembered today for a collection of fairy-tales published under the name of his son Pierre: *Histoires et contes du temps passé* (1697), subtitled 'Contes de ma Mère l'Oye'. These tales, based on French popular tradition and told with simplicity and charm, were translated into English as 'Mother Goose Tales' by Robert Samber in 1729.

PERSIUS (Aulus Persius Flaccus) (AD 34–62), Roman satirist, author of six satires, which show the influence of *Horace and of *Stoicism and which were all translated by *Dryden (1692).

Persuasion, a novel by J. *Austen, written 1815–16, published posthumously 1818.

Sir Walter Elliot, a spendthrift baronet and widower, with a swollen sense of his social importance and personal elegance, is obliged to retrench and let his seat, Kellynch Hall. His eldest daughter, Elizabeth, haughty and unmarried, is now twenty-nine; the second, Anne, who is pretty, intelligent, and amiable, had some years before been engaged to a young naval officer, Frederick Wentworth, but had been persuaded by her trusted friend Lady Russell to break off the engagement, because of his lack of fortune and a misunderstanding of his easy nature. The breach had brought great unhappiness to Anne, and caused angry indignation in Wentworth. When the story opens Anne is twenty-seven, and the bloom of her youth is gone. Captain Wentworth, who has had a successful career and is now prosperous, is thrown again into Anne's society by the letting of Kellynch to Admiral and Mrs Croft, his sister and brother-in-law. Sir Walter's youngest daughter, Mary, is married to Charles Musgrove, the heir of a neighbouring landowner. Wentworth is attracted by Charles's sisters, Louisa and Henrietta, and in time becomes involved with Louisa. During a visit of the party to Lyme Regis, Louisa, being 'jumped down' from the Cobb by Wentworth, falls and is badly injured. Wentworth's partial responsibility for the accident makes him feel an increased obligation to Louisa at the very time that his feelings are being drawn back to Anne. However, during her convalescence Louisa becomes engaged to Captain Benwick, another naval officer, and Wentworth is free to proceed with his courtship. He goes to Bath, where Sir Walter is now established with his two elder daughters and Elizabeth's companion, Mrs Clay, an artful woman with matrimonial designs on Sir Walter. There Wentworth finds another suitor for Anne's hand, her cousin William Elliot, the heir to the Kellynch estate, who is also indulging in an intrigue with Mrs Clay, in order to detach her from Sir Walter. Anne has remained unshaken in her love for Wentworth and moreover learns about the duplicity of William Elliot. Accidentally made aware of Anne's constancy, Wentworth renews his offer of marriage and is accepted.

In this, Jane Austen's last completed work, satire and ridicule take a milder form, and the tone is more grave and tender. There is a tradition—poorly substantiated—that a love-story of her own life is reflected in Anne Elliot's, although she wrote to her niece Fanny, 'You may *perhaps* like the heroine, as she is almost too good for me.'

Pertelote, the hen in Chaucer's 'Nun's Priest's Tale' (see CANTERBURY TALES, 20); also the wife of Chanticleer in *Reynard the Fox* (see PARTLET). The word in Old French was a female proper name. Its later equivalent, used as the proper name of a hen, is Partlet.

Peter Bell, a poem by *Wordsworth, written 1798, published with a dedication to *Southey 1819.

Peter Bell is a potter, a lawless, roving man, insensible to the beauty of nature. Coming to the edge of the Swale he sees a solitary ass and hopes to steal it. The ass is gazing into the water at some object, which turns out to be the dead body of its owner. After a series of supernatural events Peter mounts the ass, which eventually leads him to the cottage of the drowned man's widow. Peter's spiritual and supernatural experiences on this ride make him a reformed man. The ludicrous nature of part of the poem diverted attention from its merits, and it was made the subject of many parodies, including one by Shelley, *Peter Bell The Third.

Peter Bell The Third, a satirical poem by P. B. *Shelley written at Florence 1819, published 1839.

It is a demonic parody of *Wordsworth's poem of the same title (above). A second 'Peter Bell' had already been published by *Keats's friend J. H. *Reynolds. Shelley uses inventive doggerel, outrageous rhymes, and effervescent social satire to mock Wordsworth's 'defection' from the radical cause—'a solemn and unsexual man'. He follows Peter's progress through a black, comic underworld, described in seven sections: 'Death', 'The Devil', 'Hell', 'Sin', 'Grace', 'Damnation', and 'Double Damnation'. Part III begins with the celebrated, 'Hell is a city much like London'; while Part V draws a surprisingly sympathetic cartoon of Peter the poet, who remembered 'Many a ditch and quick-set fence; | Of Lakes he had intelligence'.

Peterborough Chronicle, The, the last part of the Laud manuscript of the *Anglo-Saxon Chronicle, written in Peterborough at various times between 1121 and 1154, the date of its last annal. It is the only part of the Chronicle to extend beyond 1080, and is of great linguistic interest in exemplifying the developments between Old and Middle English. The 12th-cent. entries, in particular, as they describe the disasters and hardships of Stephen's reign, have a vigour and circumstantiality far beyond the earlier parts of the Chronicle. See C. Clark, *The Peterborough Chronicle 1070–1154* (1958); facsimile edn D. Whitelock (1954); trans. G. N. Garmonsway (1953).

'Peter Grimes', one of the tales in Crabbe's *The Borough*. Grimes is a fisherman who 'fish'd by water and who filch'd by land' and killed his apprentices by ill-treatment, until, becoming suspect and forbidden to keep apprentices, he lived and worked in solitude. Under the pressure of guilt and remorse he became insane, and died after enduring terrible imagined terrors. He is the principal figure in *Britten's opera *Peter Grimes*.

Peterkin, old Kaspar's grandson in 'The Battle of *Blenheim' by R. Southey.

PETER LOMBARD (*c*.1100–60), *Magister Sententiarum*, or Master of the Sentences, born at Novara and educated at Bologna. He came to Paris where he became professor of theology and, in 1159, bishop. The *Sententiae* were written between 1145 and 1150. They are a collection of opinions on the Church Fathers, dealing with God, the Creation, the Redemption, and (most importantly) the nature of the Sacraments. It was very popular and became the standard theological textbook of the 13th cent., upon which all those with aspirations to theological authority had to write a Commentary: see COMESTOR; ALEXANDER OF HALES; SCOTUS; OCKHAM.

Peterloo, see CASTLEREAGH.

PETER MARTYR (1500–62), Pietro Vermigli, born in Florence, an Augustinian monk, who accepted the Reformed faith, fled from Italy in 1542 to Switzerland, and subsequently to England, and became Regius professor of divinity at Oxford (1548). He helped *Cranmer in the preparation of the second *Book of *Common Prayer* and was responsible for an important collection of *Loci Communes*. In 1553 he escaped to Strasburg and died at Zurich. His wife is buried in Christ Church Cathedral, Oxford.

PETER OF BLOIS, see ANGLO–LATIN LITERATURE.

Peter Pan, see BARRIE, J. M.

Peter Peebles, a character in Scott's *Redgauntlet*.

PETER PINDAR, see WOLCOT, J.

Peter Porcupine, see COBBETT, W.

Peter Wilkins, A Cornishman, *The Life and Adventures of* (1751), a romance by *Paltock.

This is the tale of a shipwrecked mariner, in the manner of but more fantastic than *Robinson Crusoe*. Wilkins is shipwrecked in the Antarctic region and reaches a land where the inhabitants can fly. One of them, the beautiful Youwarkee, falls outside his hut, and he takes her up, tends her, and eventually marries her. This work was much admired in the Romantic period by *Southey, *Coleridge, *Shelley, *Lamb, and Sir W. *Scott.

PETHICK-LAWRENCE, E., see WOMEN'S SUFFRAGE.

Peto, a crony of *Falstaff's in Shakespeare's *1* and *2* *Henry IV*.

Petowker, Henrietta, a character in Dickens's *Nicholas Nickleby*. She marries Mr Lillyvick.

'Petra', see BURGON, J. W.

PETRARCH (Francesco Petrarca) (1304–74), Italian poet and humanist, and the most popular Italian poet of the English Renaissance. He was born at Arezzo, the son of a notary who was expelled from Florence (in the same year as *Dante) by the Black Guelfs and migrated to Avignon in 1312. Here in 1327 Petrarch first saw the woman who inspired his love poetry. He calls her Laura; her true identity is unknown. Until 1353 Petrarch's life was centred in Provence (Avignon and his beloved retreat at Vaucluse), but he made extended visits to Italy, on the first of which, in 1341, he was crowned poet laureate in Rome, for him the most memorable episode of his life. From 1353 onwards he resided in Italy, though he travelled widely, both on his own account and at the instance of his patrons. He died in Arquà in the Euganean Hills.

Today Petrarch is best known for his 'Rime Sparse', the collection of Italian lyrics which includes the long series of poems in praise of Laura; but to his contemporaries and the generations that immediately succeeded him he was best known as a devoted student of classical antiquity. This enthusiasm he shared with his friend *Boccaccio. The encouragement which Petrarch gave to Cola di Rienzo in 1347, at the time of the restitution of the Roman republic, may be seen as an expression of the humanist spirit with which he was imbued, and in accordance with which he wrote the majority of his works in Latin. These include: a large number of letters and treatises (*De vita solitaria, De remediis utriusque fortuna*, etc.); a Latin epic, *Africa*, on the struggle between Rome and Carthage; and the *Secretum*, a self-analysis in the form of a dialogue between himself and St *Augustine.

Petrarch is justly regarded as the father of Italian humanism and the initiator of the revived study of Greek and Latin literature, but for English writers his chief inspiration was to the early sonnetteers; he was imitated and translated by *Surrey, *Wyatt, T. *Watson, and, later, by *Drummond of Hawthornden. *Sidney, while mocking the poets who slavishly echoed 'poor Petrarch's long deceased woes', yet bears witness to his powerful and pervasive influence. (See George Watson, *The English Petrarchans*, 1967.) Henry Parker, Lord Morley (1476–1556), translated at some point before 1546 his *Trionfi* as *The Tryumphes of Fraunces Petrarcke* (?1555; ed. D. D. Carnicelli, 1971), and the countess of *Pembroke translated the *Trionfo della Morte* into *terza rima*. The Petrarchan vogue declined in the 17th cent. with the waning popularity of the sonnet sequence, and in 1756 J. *Warton in his essay on *Pope dismissed Petrarch as 'metaphysical and far fetched'. *Gray, in a note on the last stanza of his *Elegy*, credits Petrarch with his phrase 'trembling hope' (*paventosa speme*), which indicates a renewal of interest in the later 18th cent.

PETRONIUS, the author of the *Satyricon*, a realistic novel of low life, pornographic, but written in a pure and elegant Latin, interspersed with verses and containing a great deal of parody. He is traditionally identified with the Gaius Petronius Arbiter who having been one of Nero's favourites was forced to commit suicide AD 65. Internal evidence certainly suggests that the novel was written in Nero's reign. The pornographic nature of the text occasioned unusual mortality among the manuscripts which were often hidden from the public eye; only excerpts have survived, the most striking of which are the description of a dinner given by a rich freedman (*Cena Trimalchionis*), a poem on the Civil War covering the same ground as *Lucan, and a story, The Matron of Ephesus. After a long period of obscurity during the Middle Ages, the *Cena* was discovered by the Florentine collector Poggio, copied in 1423, and promptly lost again, and until its rediscovery and its publication in 1660, only the smaller excerpts were known. Petronius is not an important influence on English literature. He is mentioned by religious writers like John Hales and Jeremy *Taylor in the first half of the 17th cent. and by *Dryden in his critical works. The first English translation was William Burnaby's in 1694. A passage about death was imitated by Peacock in *Rhododaphne* (1818). But the piece which aroused most interest was *The Matron of Ephesus* which inspired Walter Charleton's *Ephesian Matron* (1639) and *Fry's one-act play *A Phoenix too Frequent* (1946).

Petruchio, a gentleman of Verona and suitor to *Katharina in Shakespeare's *The Taming of the Shrew*.

PETTIE, George (*c*.1548–89), was educated at Christ Church, Oxford. His *A petite Pallace of Pettie his pleasure*, first published in 1576, often reprinted. This collection of twelve 'pretie Hystories' concerns lovers, and all but one derive from classical sources. They are mainly made up of long speeches with little action, and their style to some extent anticipates *Lyly's euphuism. Writing about a hundred years after their first publication, Pettie's grand-nephew A. *Wood calls them 'more fit to be read by a schoolboy, or rustical amoratto, than by a gent. of mode or language'. Pettie's work follows on from Painter's *Palace of Pleasure* from which he derived his title, and his translation of most of Guazzo's *Civile Conversation* (1581) contributed to the Elizabethan vogue for *courtesy literature and fiction.

PETTY, Sir William (1623–76), a political economist, studied on the Continent and became the friend of *Hobbes. He executed for the Commonwealth the 'Down Survey' of forfeited lands in Ireland, the first attempt on a large scale at carrying out a survey scientifically. Petty acquiesced in the Restoration, and was knighted and made an original member of the *Royal Society in 1662. He published economic treatises, the principal of which was entitled *Political Arithmetic* (1690), a term signifying that which we now call statistics. In this he examined, by the quantitative method, the current allegations of national decay. He rejected the old 'prohibitory' system, and showed the error of the supporters of the 'mercantile' system in regarding the abundance of the precious metals as the standard of prosperity. He traced the sources of wealth to labour and land.

Petulengro, Jasper, the principal gypsy character in Borrow's *Lavengro* and *The Romany Rye*, founded upon the Norfolk gypsy Ambrose Smith, with whom Borrow was acquainted in his youth. 'Petulengro' means 'shoeing smith'.

Peveril of the Peak, a novel by Sir W. *Scott, published 1823.

Sir Geoffrey Peveril, an old Cavalier, and Major Bridgenorth, a fanatical Puritan, are neighbouring landowners in Derbyshire, and though of widely different opinions and modes of life, have been connected by ties of reciprocal kindness in the days of the Civil War. Julian, son of Sir Geoffrey, and Alice, the daughter of Bridgenorth, are deeply in love. The recrudescence of bitter political feeling during the period of the *'Popish Plot' brings the parents into acute conflict. Julian, who has spent some years in the household of the countess of Derby, goes to England on her service. He arrives at the moment when popular suspicion of the Catholics has reached its greatest intensity, finds his father under arrest by Bridgenorth as a suspected Papist, attempts to liberate him, is himself arrested, is rescued by tenants and friends, and finally reaches London. Meanwhile Edward Christian, Bridgenorth's brother-in-law, to whom Alice has been entrusted by her father, contrives with Chiffinch, the minister of Charles II's pleasures, to bring her to the king's notice, with a view to her becoming his mistress. In order to avenge his brother, the victim of a judicial murder carried out in the Isle of Man under Lady Derby's authority, he has, moreover, placed in the latter's service Fenella, his daughter by a Moorish woman. This creature, gifted with strange beauty and grace, has maintained for years the character of a deaf-mute, in order to worm herself into her employer's secrets. Alice falls into the hands of the licentious Buckingham, and is rescued by Fenella's agency. Julian, with whom Fenella has fallen in love, is by her action brought to the notice of the king and Buckingham, incurs the hostility of the latter, and is imprisoned and involved, with his father, in an accusation of participating in the 'Plot'. They are acquitted on trial, thanks to the intervention of the king, who shows some sense of obligation to the old Cavalier; and all ends well.

The author draws elaborate portraits of Charles II and Buckingham, and gives glimpses of such historical characters as Titus Oates, Colonel Blood (the impudent revolutionary who tried to steal the crown jewels from the Tower), and Sir Geoffrey Hudson (Henrietta Maria's dwarf).

PEVSNER, Sir Nikolaus Bernhard Leon (1902–83), art historian, born in Germany and educated at the universities of Leipzig, Munich, Berlin, and Frankfurt. He lectured for four years at Göttingen before the rise of Hitler brought him to England, where he became in 1941 associated with *Penguin Books, as editor of King Penguins and of his celebrated county-by-county series *The Buildings of England* (1951–74). He was professor of fine art successively at Cambridge (1949–55) and at Oxford (1968–9). His many works on art, design, and architecture include *Pioneers of the Modern Movement, from William Morris to Walter Gropius* (1936), *High Victorian Design* (1951), and *The Englishness of English Art* (1956).

Pew, the blind buccaneer in Stevenson's *Treasure Island*.

PFEFFERKORN, Johannes (c.1469–c.1522), a Jewish-born Christian convert, the associate of the Dominicans in their controversy with *Reuchlin regarding the proposed destruction of works of Jewish literature and philosophy. See EPISTOLAE OBSCURORUM VIRORUM.

Phaedria, in Spenser's *Faerie Queene* (II. vi), the Lady of the Idle Lake, symbolizing immodest mirth.

Phalaris, *Epistles of,* were letters attributed to Phalaris, a tyrant of Acragas in Sicily (6th cent. BC), with a reputation for extreme cruelty. They were edited by Charles Boyle, fourth earl of Orrery (1676–1731) in 1695, and praised by Sir W. *Temple. R. *Bentley proved that they were spurious and dated from perhaps the 2nd cent. AD. There is an echo of the controversy in Swift's *The Battle of the Books*.

Phallic Symbols, objects used, in Freudian theory, to represent the phallus, which itself is in its original sense a representation or image of the penis, symbolizing male or regenerative power. Any erect and pointed object may be a phallic symbol: Freud himself in case histories cites swords, knives, pens, flames, closed umbrellas, screwdrivers, and even powder puffs. *Freudian literary criticism frequently applies itself to the detection of such symbols, whether consciously or unconsciously deployed, as an aid to interpretations (see D. H. *Lawrence's poem 'Snap-Dragon'), whereas *Hardy, who in *Tess of the D'Urbevilles* speaks of 'myriads of loose white flints in bulbous, cusped and phallic shapes', would seem to be using the term in an archaeological sense. It is interesting to note that no similar term exists for the female regenerative symbol, although *Feminist Criticism has recently begun to employ such phrases as 'Uterine symbolism' and 'Vaginal symbolism'.

Phaon, (1) in Spenser's *Faerie Queene* (II. iv), is the unfortunate squire who, deceived by Philemon and under the influence of Furor (mad rage), slays Claribel and poisons Philemon; (2) in classical mythology, the boatman with whom *Sappho is said to have fallen in love. *Lyly wrote a play on the subject (*Sapho and Phao*).

Pharonnida, see CHAMBERLAYNE, W.

Pharsalia, see LUCAN.

Phebe, a shepherdess in Shakespeare's *As You Like It* who marries Silvius.

Phèdre, see RACINE and HIPPOLYTUS.

Philander, to, to play the trifling and even promiscuous lover. Philander, in an old ballad, was the lover of Phillis; and in *Beaumont and *Fletcher's *Laws of Candy* the lover of Erota.

Philaster, or *Love lies a-Bleeding,* a romantic tragi-comedy by *Beaumont and *Fletcher (see FLETCHER, J.), written ?1609, printed 1620. One of the most successful of the Beaumont and Fletcher collaborations, the play draws on the conventions of the prose romances, notably on *Montemayor's *Diana* and Sidney's *Arcadia*.

The king of Calabria has usurped the crown of Sicily. The rightful heir, Philaster, loves and is loved by Arethusa, daughter of the usurper, but the latter intends to marry her to Pharamond, prince of Spain. To maintain contact with her, Philaster places his page, Bellario, in her service. Arethusa reveals to the king that Pharamond (made impatient by her own frigid reception of him) has embarked on an affair with Megra, a lady of the court; Megra in turn accuses Arethusa of misconduct with the handsome young Bellario. After various pastoral pursuits and disasters, during which Bellario touchingly and constantly demonstrates devotion to Philaster, and Philaster himself manifests a marked lack of chivalry, it is revealed that Bellario is in fact Euphrasia, daughter of a Sicilian lord, in love with Philaster. Reassured thus of Arethusa's virtue, Philaster regains both his loved one and his kingdom, whereas Bellario is left with their gratitude, to devote herself to a life of chastity.

An edition in the Revels series by Andrew Gurr was published in 1969.

Philip, see ADVENTURES OF PHILIP, THE.

Philippics, see CICERO and DEMOSTHENES.

Philip Quarll, *The Adventures of,* an adventure story originally published as *The Hermit* (1727) by 'Edward Dorrington', but generally attributed to Peter Longueville, though some authorities ascribe it to Alexander Bicknell. A derivative of *Robinson Crusoe*, it describes Quarll's fifty years of solitude and suffering on a South Sea island. It went through many editions, and was much adapted for children.

PHILIPS, Ambrose (1674–1749), poet, and fellow of St John's College, Cambridge, was a member of *Addison's circle. He wrote *The Distrest Mother* (1712), a successful adaptation of *Racine's *Andromaque*, but is remembered chiefly for his quarrel with *Pope over the relative merits of their pastorals. Pope drew, in the *Guardian* (No. 40, 1713), 'a comparison of Philips's performance with his own, in which, with an unexampled and unequalled artifice of irony, though 'he has himself always the advantage, he gives the preference to Philips' (Johnson, *Lives of the English Poets*). Philips's 'Epistle to the Earl of Dorset' (1709) memorably evokes the frozen landscape of Denmark. His infantile trochaics addressed to children ('Dimply damsel, sweetly smiling', etc.) earned him the nickname of 'Namby Pamby', though Johnson described them as his pleasantest pieces. For the 'pastoral war', see also Gay's *The Shepherd's Week*.

PHILIPS, John (1676–1709), educated at Christ Church, Oxford, was the author of *The Splendid Shilling* (unauthorized 1701, authorized 1705), a burlesque in Miltonic blank verse, in which Philips contrasts the happy possessor of the splendid shilling, who 'nor hears with pain | New oysters cry'd, nor sighs for chearful ale', with the poor poet in his garret, hungry and thirsty, and beset by creditors. In 1705 he published *Blenheim*, written at the suggestion of *Harley and *Bolingbroke, as a Tory counterpart to *The Campaign* of *Addison. *Cyder* (1708), a poem in blank verse written in imitation of *Virgil's *Georgics*, celebrates the cultivation, manufacture, and virtues of cider; it provided a model for later blank verse georgics, such as *Smart's *The Hop-Garden* and parts of Thomson's *The Seasons*. Thomson, in 'Autumn', salutes 'Philips, Pomona's bard' both for his 'native theme' and for his 'rhyme-unfetter'd verse' (ll. 640–50), and later critics have endorsed this view of his place in literary tradition. There is an edition by M. G. L. Thomas (1927).

PHILIPS, Katherine (1631–64), known as the 'Matchless Orinda', was the daughter of John Fowler, a London merchant. In 1648 she married James Philips of Cardigan. Her earliest verses were prefixed (1651) to the *Poems* of H. *Vaughan. Her translation of *Corneille's *Pompée* was acted in Dublin with great success in 1663, and her version of *Horace*, completed by *Denham, in 1668. Her collected poems appeared unauthorized in 1664 (a fact about which she protested in a letter to Dorothy *Osborne). She died of smallpox, and was mourned

in elegies by *Cowley and Sir W. *Temple; her collected poems were published in 1667. They indicate the existence of some kind of Platonic 'Society of Friendship', but the only known member is Mrs Anne Owen, 'Lucasia', to whom she addressed almost half her verses, and the notion of a literary salon appears to have been given currency by *Gosse. She was, however, on friendly terms with a circle including *Cartwright, *Berkenhead, and Jeremy *Taylor, and was given to addressing them by poetic names. Her biographer P. W. Souers (*The Matchless Orinda*, 1931) claims her as one of the few poets to carry the tradition of the *cavalier lyric through to the Restoration. She was much admired in her day, and also by *Keats, who copied out one of her poems in a letter to his friend Reynolds.

Philip Sparrow, see PHYLLYP SPAROWE.

Philistine, the name of an alien warlike people who in early biblical times constantly harassed the Israelites. The name is applied, (1) humorously or otherwise to persons regarded as 'the enemy' into whose hands one may fall, bailiffs, literary critics, etc.; (2) to persons deficient in liberal culture and enlightenment, from *philister*, the term applied by German students to one who is not a student at the university, but a townsman. In sense (2) the word was introduced into English by M. *Arnold ('Heine', *Essays in Criticism*); he describes *Heine as a progressive, a lover of ideas and hater of Philistinism, and the English as a nation dominated by 'inveterate inaccessibility to ideas'. In other works, notably *Culture and Anarchy*, he develops the concept; the English middle classes are predominantly Philistine, whereas the aristocracy, with its love of field sports, physical prowess, and external graces, is described as 'Barbarian'. The working classes are described as the 'Populace'.

PHILLIPPS, Sir Thomas (1792–1872), educated at Rugby and University College, Oxford, early developed a passion for collecting books and, more particularly, manuscripts (he described himself as 'a perfect vello-maniac'), and assembled an extremely valuable library at his home in Broadway, Worcestershire. He also established there a private printing press, where he printed visitations, extracts from registers, cartularies, etc. In 1863 he moved his library to Thirlestaine House, Cheltenham, and on his death left it to his daughter, Mrs Fenwick: it has been gradually dispersed in sales to public institutions at home and abroad and to private collectors. Some unique items (such as *Herrick's commonplace book and the manuscript of part of a translation of *Ovid's *Metamorphoses* associated with *Caxton) came to light as late as 1964: the Caxton manuscript is now reunited with its other half, which had been in the possession of *Pepys, in the Pepys Library at *Magdalene College, Cambridge. See A. N. L. *Munby, *Phillipps Studies* (1951–60); N. J. Barker, *Portrait of an Obsession* (1967).

PHILLIPS, Edward (1630–?96), brother of John *Phillips and nephew of *Milton, by whom he was educated. He was tutor to the son of *Evelyn, and then to Philip Herbert, afterwards 7th earl of Pembroke. His various literary works include an edition of the poems of *Drummond of Hawthornden (1656); a popular philological dictionary called *The New World of English Words* (1658); and *Theatrum Poetarum* (1675), a collection of literary biographies in the preface to which some have seen the hand of Milton. He also wrote a short life of his uncle, published 1694. *Lives of Edward and John Philips* by W. *Godwin was published in 1815.

PHILLIPS, John (1631–1706), younger brother of Edward *Phillips and nephew of *Milton, by whom he was educated. He wrote a scathing attack on Puritanism in his poem, *A Satyr against Hypocrites* (1655), supported Charles II and *Oates, and worked as translator and hack-writer; he translated *La Calprenède's *Pharamond*, *Scudéry's *Almahide*, and wrote a travesty of *Don Quixote* (1687) in which he mentions *Paradise Lost*, but his biographer *Godwin (who much prefers his elder brother Edward) was unable to determine whether the reference was 'intended as a compliment or a slur'.

PHILLIPS, Stephen (1864–1915), actor and poet, who resolved, after the success of his *Poems* (1898), to revive poetic drama; his *Paolo and Francesca* (pub. 1900, perf. 1902) was received with great enthusiasm and compared by serious critics to Sophocles and Shakespeare. *Herod* (1901), *Ulysses* (1902), and *Nero* (1906) were also well received, but his later plays were failures.

Phillotson, Richard, a character in Hardy's *Jude the Obscure*.

PHILLPOTTS, Eden (1862–1960), prolific and popular novelist, playwright, and poet, most of whose many novels are set in Dartmoor. He collaborated as playwright with Arnold *Bennett and J. K. *Jerome.

Philoclea, younger sister of Pamela in Sidney's *Arcadia*.

Philological Society, The, was founded in its present form in 1842 to investigate and to promote the study and knowledge of the structure, the affinities, and the history of language. Active in its formation were *Thirlwall, A. P. *Stanley, and T. *Arnold; prominent members were to include *Furnivall, *Trench, and James *Murray, all of whom were involved in the creation of the *Oxford English Dictionary. See

H. Aarsleff, *The Study of Language in England 1780–1860* (1967).

Philosophes, the collective name of a group of 18th-cent. writers and thinkers united by their faith in the efficacy of reason and their dislike of repressive traditions. Its most significant representatives included *Montesquieu, *Voltaire, *Diderot, *Rousseau, *Buffon, *Condillac, Condorcet, d'Alembert, d'Holbach, and Helvétius. They inclined to scepticism in religion, materialism in philosophy, and hedonism in ethics.

***Philosophical Enquiry** into the Origin of our Ideas of the Sublime and Beautiful*, see SUBLIME AND BEAUTIFUL.

Philosophical View of Reform, A, a political essay by P. B. *Shelley, written at Pisa 1820, not published until 1920.

Intended as an 'instructive and readable' octavo booklet, this was Shelley's most mature political statement about Liberty, Revolution, and Reform: it confirms his position as a Radical (rather than a liberal)—but not a revolutionary. Chapter 1 is a historical sketch of the continuous overthrow of Imperial powers in Europe; it argues that periods of great literary creativity have always coincided with libertarian movements. Chapter 2 describes conditions of political and economic oppression in contemporary Britain and proposes specific measures of radical change, including parliamentary reform and alteration of laws regarding marriage, property inheritance, capital investment, and working hours. Chapter 3 (unfinished) suggests actual means of enforcing political change, including non-violent protest, the intervention of 'poets and philosophers', and the 'last resort' of resistance which is 'undoubtedly insurrection'. The essay illuminates the thinking behind Shelley's political poems of 1817–20, and provided much material for the *Defence of Poetry*, such as the concept of 'unacknowledged legislators'.

Philotas, a Senecan tragedy in blank verse by S. *Daniel, published 1605.

Philotas, a gallant and bountiful soldier held in high estimation among the Macedonians, incurs the suspicion of Alexander by his boasts. He is accused of concealing his knowledge of a conspiracy against the king, is tortured, and, having confessed, is stoned to death.

The author had subsequently to defend himself against the charge of covertly defending, by this play, the rebellion of Essex. Performance of the play was suppressed in 1604.

***Phineas Finn,** The Irish Member*, a novel by A. *Trollope, published 1869, the second of the *'Palliser' series.

Phineas Finn, a young Irish barrister, catches the eye of Lord Tulla and is elected to Parliament for the family seat of Loughshane. In London

Phineas wins friends on all sides, is admitted to high society, and falls in love with the politically-minded Lady Laura Standish. Lady Laura's personal fortune is considerably diminished after paying the debts of her brother Lord Chiltern, and she feels she must marry money, in the person of the chilly but wealthy Mr Kennedy. Phineas is at first disappointed, and is later deeply grieved at the unhappiness and finally the collapse of the Kennedy marriage, but turns for consolation elsewhere. He first pursues Violet Effingham, Lord Chiltern's childhood sweetheart, but after a brief quarrel between the two suitors (featuring a duel fought in Belgium), Violet settles for Chiltern, and they are married. Madame Max Goesler, the rich widow of a Viennese banker, is Phineas's next favourite. Phineas has lost his government salary by sticking to his principles over the issue of Irish Tenant Right, and has no money to cover the cost of re-election. Madam Max offers to help him out, and when Phineas refuses she offers him her hand in marriage and her fortune to finance a fresh political career. This he is too scrupulous to accept in view of his prior engagement to a pretty Irish girl, Mary Flood-Jones, and he returns to Ireland.

Phineas Redux, a novel by A. *Trollope, published 1874, the fourth in the *'Palliser' series.

Phineas Finn returns to politics in time for the fall of Mr Daubeny's government, and earnestly hopes for office under Mr Gresham. Unhappily a series of quarrels makes his progress anything but smooth. First Mr Kennedy, outraged at Phineas's visit to his wife Lady Laura in her Dresden exile, unsuccessfully tries to shoot him. Then Phineas exchanges heated words with the president of the Board of Trade, Mr Bonteen, and when, later that night, Bonteen is murdered, the burden of circumstantial evidence against Phineas is very strong. He is arrested and remanded for trial, and only the spirited efforts of Madam Max in discovering the true culprit, and a brilliant courtroom performance by Chaffanbrass in presenting her findings, succeed in getting him off. For a time Phineas is shattered by his experiences, but towards the end of the novel he rallies, returns to politics, and marries Madame Max.

In this novel the old duke of Omnium dies, and Plantagenet and Lady Glencora become duke and duchess. Madame Max, the old duke's favourite, is left some valuable jewellery in his will, but refuses to accept it. Instead the legacy is made over to Plantagenet's cousin Adelaide Palliser, who is thus able to marry the impoverished Gerard Maule.

Bonteen's murderer turns out to have been the Revd Mr Emilius, the converted Jew who married Lizzie Eustace. Emilius, who has a previous wife still living at Prague, is convicted of bigamy and imprisoned, but there is insufficient evidence to hang him.

Phiz, see BROWNE, H. K.

Phoenix, The, an Old English poem of 677 lines, found in the *Exeter Book and possibly written in the later 9th cent. It is a beast allegory of the kind found in the *bestiaries but developed over a greater length than usual. The descriptive part of the poem is closely based on *Carmen de ave phoenice,* probably by Lactantius (d. c.340), and the later allegorizing section has not been attributed to any certain source. The poem is admired for the vividness of its imagery and the accomplishment of its syntax. Ed. N. F. Blake (1964).

'Phoenix and the Turtle, The', an allegorical elegy ascribed to *Shakespeare which was included in Robert Chester's collection *Love's Martyr* (1601).

Phoenix Nest, The, a poetic miscellany published in 1593 and compiled by one R.S., who has never been identified. It includes poems by *Ralegh, *Lodge, and *Breton, and opens with three elegies on *Sidney, the 'Phoenix' of the title. It was edited by H. E. Rollins (1931).

Phunky, Mr, in Dickens's *Pickwick Papers,* Serjeant Snubbin's junior in the case of Bardell v. Pickwick.

Phyllyp Sparowe, a poem by *Skelton.

'Physician's Tale, The', see CANTERBURY TALES, 13.

Physiocrat, one of a school of political economists founded by François Quesnay (1694–1774) in France in the 18th cent. They maintained that society should be governed according to an inherent natural order, that the soil is the sole source of wealth and the only proper object of taxation, and that security of property and freedom of industry and exchange are essential [OED]. The other principal exponents of the physiocrat doctrines were Jacques Turgot (1727–81), an able financier, whose dismissal in 1776 from the post of controller-general of the finances was the prelude of the French national bankruptcy; and Victor de Riquetti, marquis de Mirabeau (1715–89), the author of *L'Ami des hommes* and father of the revolutionary statesman. Adam *Smith, though no physiocrat in the technical sense of the word, was strongly influenced by the sounder doctrines of the school.

Physiologus, see BESTIARIES.

Picaresque, from the Spanish *pícaro,* a wily trickster; the form of novel accurately described as 'picaresque' first appeared in 16th-cent. Spain with the anonymous *Lazarillo de Tormes* (1553) and Alemán's *Guzmán de Alfarache* (1599–1604), which relate the histories of ingenious rogues, the servants of several masters, who eventually repent the error of their ways;

examples of their descendants in English would be *Moll Flanders*, *Roderick Random*, and *Tom Jones*. The term was apparently first used in England in the 19th cent.; Sir W. *Scott, for example, writing in 1829, describes the *Memoirs of Vidoq* as 'a pickaresque tale . . . a romance of roguery', and *The Bookman* in 1895 defined a picaresque tale as that of a 'trickster'. Nowadays the term is commonly, and loosely, applied to episodic novels, especially those of *Fielding, *Smollett, and others of the 18th cent. which describe the adventures of a lively and resourceful hero on a journey. *The Golden Ass* of *Apuleius is regarded as a forerunner of the picaresque novel.

PICASSO, Pablo Ruiz y (1881–1973), Spanish painter. He settled in Paris in 1901 and first painted the characters of the Paris slums with a predominantly blue palette, then actors and clowns in warmer colours. In 1907 Picasso and Braque developed *Cubism. In 1917 he designed ballets for Diaghilev; then came the period of monumental nudes which developed in the 1930s into terrifyingly distorted forms (*Guernica*, 1936). In his later years he designed ceramics. A brilliant draughtsman, Picasso produced an enormous number of etchings and lithographs, and illustrated books.

PICCOLOMINI, Aeneas Silvius (1405–64), Pope Pius II from 1458, was a patron of letters and author of a romance, *Eurialus and Lucretia*, of treatises on many subjects, and of commentaries on his times. His secular works include the *Miseriae Curialium*, which provided one of the models for the *Eclogues* of A. *Barclay. He visited Scotland in 1435, and wrote a somewhat hostile report of its poverty-stricken condition.

PICKARD, Tom, see UNDERGROUND POETRY.

PICKERING, William (1796–1854), publisher, commenced business in London in 1820, and did much to raise the standard of design in printing. He published the 'Diamond Classics' 1821–31, and in 1830 adopted the trade-mark of the Aldine Press (see ALDUS MANUTIUS). He increased his reputation by his Aldine edition of the English poets in 53 vols.

Pickwick Papers (*The Posthumous Papers of the Pickwick Club*), a novel by *Dickens, first issued in 20 monthly parts April 1836–Nov. 1837, and as a volume in 1837 (when Dickens was only 25 years old).

Mr Samuel Pickwick, general chairman of the Pickwick Club which he has founded, Messrs Tracy Tupman, Augustus Snodgrass, and Nathaniel Winkle, members of the club, are constituted a Corresponding Society of the Club to report to it their journeys and adventures, and observations of characters and manners. This is the basis on which the novel is constructed, and the Club serves to link a series of detached incidents and changing characters, without elaborate plot. The entertaining adventures with which Mr Pickwick and his associates meet are interspersed with incidental tales contributed by various characters. The principal elements in the story are: (1) the visit of Pickwick and his friends to Rochester and their falling in with the specious rascal Jingle, who gets Winkle involved in the prospect of a duel (fortunately averted). (2) The visit to Dingley Dell, the home of the hospitable Mr Wardle; the elopement of Jingle with Wardle's sister, their pursuit by Wardle and Pickwick, and the recovery of the lady; followed by the engagement of Sam Weller as Pickwick's servant. (3) The visit to Eatanswill, where a parliamentary election is in progress, and Mr Pickwick makes the acquaintance of Pott, editor of a political newspaper, and Mrs Leo Hunter. (4) The visit to Bury St Edmunds, where Mr Pickwick and Sam Weller are fooled by Jingle and his servant, Job Trotter. (5) The pursuit of Jingle to Ipswich, where Mr Pickwick inadvertently enters the bedroom of a middle-aged lady at night; is in consequence involved in a quarrel with Mr Peter Magnus, her admirer; is brought before Mr Nupkins, the magistrate, on a charge of intending to fight a duel; and obtains his release on exposing the nefarious designs of Jingle on Nupkins's daughter. (6) The Christmas festivities at Dingley Dell. (7) The misapprehension of Mrs Bardell, Mr Pickwick's landlady, regarding her lodger's intentions, which leads to the famous action of Bardell v. Pickwick for breach of promise of marriage, in which judgement is given for the plaintiff, with damages £750. (8) The visit to Bath, in which Winkle figures prominently, first in the adventure with the blustering Dowler, and secondly in his courtship of Arabella Allen. (9) The period of Mr Pickwick's imprisonment in the Fleet in consequence of his refusal to pay the damages and costs of his action; and the discovery of Jingle and Job Trotter in that prison, and their relief by Mr Pickwick. (10) The affairs of Tony Weller (Sam's father) and the second Mrs Weller, ending in the death of the latter and the discomfiture of the pious humbug and greedy drunkard Stiggins, deputy shepherd in the Ebenezer Temperance Association. (11) The affairs of Bob Sawyer and Benjamin Allen, medical students and subsequently struggling practitioners. The novel ends with the happy marriage of Emily Wardle and Augustus Snodgrass.

PICO DELLA MIRANDOLA, Giovanni (1463–94), an Italian humanist and philosopher, born at Mirandola, of which his family were the lords. He spent part of his short life at Florence in the circle of Lorenzo de' *Medici. In 1486 he published 900 theses, offering to maintain them at Rome, but some of his propositions were pronounced heretical and the public debate did not take place. The famous oration *De dignitate hominis*, with which he intended to introduce the debate, is one of the most important philosophical works of the 15th cent. Pico was a daring syncretist, who vainly tried to make a synthesis of Christianity, Platonism, Aristotelianism, and the Jewish Cabbala. As a pioneer in the study of Hebrew philosophy he influenced *Reuchlin. His life (*Lyfe of Johan Picus, erle of Myrandula, Greate Lorde of Italy*) and some of his pious writings were translated by Sir T. *More. *Colet was influenced by Pico.

Picturesque, a term which came into fashion in the late 18th cent., principally to describe a certain kind of scenery. Writers on the picturesque include W. *Gilpin, W. *Mason, William Payne Knight (1750–1824, who published *The Landscape* in 1794), Uvedale Price (1747–1829, who published *Essays on the Picturesque*, 1794), and the landscape gardener Humphry Repton (1752–1818). The impact of these writers on the sensibility and vocabulary of writers of the 19th cent. was considerable. The 'picturesque', as defined by Price, was a new aesthetic category, to be added to *Burke's recently established categories of the *Sublime and the Beautiful; its attributes were roughness and irregularity, and its most complete exponent in terms of painting was *Rosa, whose works enjoyed much popularity at this period; Constable described him as 'a great favourite with novel writers, particularly the ladies'. Mrs *Radcliffe's works dwell frequently on the picturesque, and J. *Austen and many of her characters were familiar with the works of Gilpin; in *Mansfield Park* she mocks the spirit of 'improvement' in the character of the foolish Mr Rushworth. The entertaining aesthetic disputes of Price and Knight, both of whom owned estates near the Welsh borders, are satirized in Peacock's *Headlong Hall*, and *Combe's adventures of Dr Syntax are aimed at the movement in general and Gilpin in particular. Although the excesses of picturesque theory became a popular target for satire, these writers made a lasting contribution to our vision, and writers as diverse as *Dickens, G. *Eliot, and H. *James found the term useful. The development of the picturesque movement into *Romanticism is a subject of much complexity and literary interest. See C. Hussey, *The Picturesque* (1927, 1967).

'Pied Piper of Hamelin, The, A Child's Story', a poem by R. Browning, included in *Dramatic Lyrics*.

Pierce the Ploughman's Crede, an alliterative poem dating from the last decade of the 14th cent., influenced by *Langland, to whom it pays tribute, and attacking the friars. It is as evocative and forceful as Langland himself, and it contains the most effective piece of social criticism in Middle English, in its lines describing the hardships of the ploughman and his wife (ll. 420–42). Ed. W. W. *Skeat (EETS 30, 1867: reprinted 1973).

Pierce Penniless, *His Supplication to the Divell*, a fantastic prose satire by T. *Nashe, published 1592. The author, in the form of a humorous complaint to the Devil, discourses on the vices of the day, throwing interesting light on the customs of his time. One of the best passages is that relating to the recently developed practice of excessive drinking, 'a sinne, that ever since we have mixt our selves with the Low-countries, is counted honourable', and containing a description of the various types of drunkards, drawn with a coarse Rabelaisian humour and vigour. The work is directed in part against Richard Harvey the astrologer (brother of Gabriel *Harvey) and the Martinists (see MARTIN MARPRELATE). It ends with a discussion of hell and devils.

PIERO DELLA FRANCESCA (?1416–92), Italian painter, whose most celebrated works, *The History of the True Cross* (1452–64; San Francesco, Arezzo), *The Resurrection* (Borgo, San Sepolcro), and the *Madonna del Parto* (Monterchi, Chapel of the Cemetery), are now perhaps the most revered of all Renaissance frescoes. Yet Piero was almost ignored until the 20th cent.; *Ruskin scarcely mentions him, and it was left to the generation that followed *Cézanne to rediscover the formal beauties of his works. A. *Huxley, in *Along the Road*, describes the *Resurrection* as 'The greatest picture in the world': in *Ape and Essence* he imagines a composition by Piero—'luminously explicit, an equation in balanced voids and solids, in harmonising and contrasting hues'.

Pierre, a character in Otway's *Venice Preserv'd*.

Piers Plowman, the greatest poem of the Middle English *Alliterative Revival, by *Langland. It survives in about 50 manuscripts, in three widely varying versions, known as the A, B, and C texts. The A-text, totalling 2,567 lines in its longest version, was probably written about 1367–70; the B-text, a very considerable extension of the A-text which both rewrites the parts of the poem that occur in the A-text and adds more than as much again to the end of it, extends to 7,277 lines (or more) and probably dates from about 1377–9; and the C-text is a substantial revision of the B-text, about the same length, dating from about 1385–6. It is now generally agreed (following Kane, *Piers Plowman: The Evidence for Authorship*, 1965, and Donaldson, *Piers Plowman: The C-Text and its Poet*, 1949) that the three versions were all the work of Langland, who would, therefore, have been occupied with the work and its revisions for at least the last twenty years of his life. Structurally, the poem is divided in a number of ways which are also problematical because the evidence of the manuscripts is conflicting. The principal division of the poem has been into two parts, the 'Visio' and the 'Vita', the 'Visio' comprising the Prologue and the first seven *Passus* ('step': the term used in the poem for the section divisions, varying from 129 to 642 lines in length) in the B-text (Prologue and the first eight in A; the first ten *Passus* in C which sometimes does not have a Prologue). This 'Visio'–'Vita' distinction has been seen to be of such importance by some critics that they have argued that they are properly to be regarded as two distinct poems (see T. P. Dunning, *Piers Plowman: An Interpretation of the A-Text*, rev. T. P. Dolan, 1980); but the distinction is not found in B manuscripts at all (see Schmidt's edition, 1978, p. xx). There has been argument too whether B or C is to be taken as the more authoritative text; C is the latest and in many places clarifies points which remained obscure in B, but its revisions have damaged the shape of the poem at some points so that it no longer divides into coherent visions, describing falling asleep—vision—awakening. B has the advantage of being complete and coherent in this way (and it can also be claimed that some of the very obscurities that C clarifies, such as the tearing of the pardon in *Passus* VII, display great imaginative power). A, though some claims have been made for its integrity as a poem, may be regarded as superseded by the other versions. The following account follows the B-text (where there is any divergence in plot), in its division into eight separate visions.

Vision 1. While wandering on the Malvern Hills, the narrator (who, it transpires later, is called Will) falls asleep and has a vision of a Tower where Truth dwells, a deep Dungeon, and between them 'a fair feeld ful of folk' (*Prologue* 17) where all the order of human society can be seen about their business. The worldly values thus raised are expounded by Lady Holy Church in *Passus* 1; the theme is sustained by the analytical trial of Lady Meed in *Passus* 2–4 which considers whether Meed (Reward or payment) is to be given to Wrong or according to Conscience and Reason.

Vision 2. The narrator observes what J. A. Burrow has shown to be an established sequence of events: Sermon (preached here by Reason); Confession (by the Seven Deadly Sins, colourfully personified in *Passus* 5, the longest in the poem); Pilgrimage (to Truth, led by Piers the Plowman who first appears as the just leader on the road to Salvation); and Pardon (a paper pardon sent to Piers by Truth, but torn up by him when its validity is questioned by a priest, who rejects it as a moral statement rather than a papal document). The conflict with the priest awakens the dreamer; this is the end of the 'Visio'

as distinct from 'Vita', if such a distinction is indicated (as in A and C manuscripts).

Vision 3 shows Will turning to the faculties and sources of knowledge and understanding, as the search for Truth (now referred to as 'Dowel') becomes individualized. In *Passus* 8–12 Will progressively consults Thought, Wit, Study, Clergy, Scripture, Ymagynatyf (Imagination—linked with Nature in an inner dream containing an inspired description of the workings of nature, ll. 326–67), and Reason.

Visions 4 and 5. The theme of these visions is Charity, and *Passus* 13–17 attempt to show in action the ideas concerning doing well which were offered in Vision 3. Piers Plowman reappears, in a transfigured form in which his action is indistinguishable from that of Christ.

Vision 6. The Passion of Christ is described as the culmination of doing well in *Passus* 18, where the death of Christ is evoked with great power (ll. 57–63), and after his death the *harrowing of Hell.

Visions 7 and 8. These *Passus* (19 and 20) continue with the liturgical cycle begun in Lent in *Passus* 16 (l. 172) and show the attempts to put into practice the lessons gained from observing the saving actions of Christ. The attempts to perfect the Church are still frustrated by evildoers, as Piers Plowman had first been in *Passus* 6 as he set out on his first pilgrimage, and the poem ends with Conscience setting out to find Piers, to lead the perfected search for salvation.

The strength of *Piers Plowman* does not lie in its structure or argument, both of which are often confusing and uncertain. The same crypticism that often results in sublimely imaginative poetry often blocks a literal understanding (as Rosemary Woolf says). But the passages of greatest imaginative power (such as those mentioned in *Passus* 11 and 18, or the metaphor of 'the plant of peace' 1, 148–57) have a sublimity beyond the reach of any other medieval English writer.

The 'official' editions, based on all the manuscripts, of A and B have appeared, and C is in preparation: *Piers Plowman: the A Version*, ed. G. Kane (1960), and *Piers Plowman: the B Version*, ed. G. Kane and E. T. Donaldson (1975). The most useful editions are *The Vision of Piers Plowman: A Complete Edition of the B-Text*, ed. A. V. C. Schmidt (1978) and *Piers Plowman: An Edition of the C-Text*, ed. D. A. Pearsall (1978). Translation by Terence Tiller (1981).

Pierston, Jocelyn, a character in Hardy's *The Well-Beloved*.

Pigwiggin, a character in Drayton's *Nimphidia*.

Pilgrim's Progress, The, *from this World to that which is to come*, an allegory by *Bunyan, Part I published 1678 (a second edition with additions appeared in the same year, and a third in 1679), Part II 1684.

The allegory takes the form of a dream by the author. In this he sees *Christian, with a burden on his back and reading in a book, from which he learns that the city in which he and his family dwell will be burned with fire. On the advice of Evangelist, Christian flees from the *City of Destruction, having failed to persuade his wife and children to accompany him. Pt I describes his pilgrimage through the *Slough of Despond, the Interpreter's House, the House Beautiful, the *Valley of Humiliation, the *Valley of the Shadow of Death, *Vanity Fair, *Doubting Castle, the *Delectable Mountains, the country of *Beulah, to the *Celestial City. On the way he encounters various allegorical personages, among them Mr *Worldly Wiseman, *Faithful (who accompanies Christian on his way but is put to death in Vanity Fair), Hopeful (who next joins Christian), Giant *Despair, the foul fiend *Apollyon, and many others.

Pt II relates how Christian's wife Christiana, moved by a vision, sets out with her children on the same pilgrimage, accompanied by her neighbour Mercy, despite the objections of Mrs Timorous and others. They are escorted by *Great-heart, who overcomes Giant Despair and other monsters and brings them to their destination.

The work is remarkable for the beauty and simplicity of its language (Bunyan was permeated with the English of the Bible, though he was also a master of the colloquial English of his own time), the vividness and reality of the characterization, and the author's sense of humour and feeling for the world of nature. It circulated at first mainly in uneducated circles, and its wide appeal is shown by the fact that it has been translated into well over 100 languages.

Pills to Purge Melancholy, see D'URFEY, T.

Pimlyco, or Runne Red-Cap, a satirical pamphlet, published 1609, of unknown authorship, in which the poet describes a crowd of persons of all classes of society, from courtiers to 'greasie lownes', pressing towards Hogsden to drink Pimlico ale.

Pinch, Tom and Ruth, characters in Dickens's *Martin Chuzzlewit.

Pinchwife, a character in Wycherley's *The Country Wife.

PINDAR (c.522–443 BC), Greek lyric poet, the majority of whose surviving works are odes celebrating victories in the games at Olympia and elsewhere. Antiquity's most notable exponent of the Greater Ode, he served as an inspiration to all subsequent poets attempting this difficult genre. His compositions were elevated and formal, distinguished by the boldness of their metaphors and a marked reliance on myth and gnomic utterance. He used a framework of strophe, antistrophe, and epode which his imi-

tators sought to copy, but in Pindar this framework rested on an elaborate prosodic structure that remained unknown until it was worked out by August Boeckh in his edition of the Odes (1811). The 17th- and 18th-cent. writers of Pindarics—*Cowley, *Dryden, *Pope, *Gray—employed a much looser prosodic system, so that their odes, although elevated and rich in metaphor, lack Pindar's architectural quality.

PINDAR, Peter, see WOLCOT, J.

Pindaric, see PINDAR.

PINERO, Sir Arthur Wing (1855–1934), left school at ten to work in his father's solicitor's practice, but stage-struck from youth, became an actor, and was noticed by H. *Irving who later produced some of his plays. His first one-act play, Two Hundred a Year, performed in 1877, heralded a successful and prolific career. The first of his farces, The Magistrate (perf. 1885), involves a series of ludicrous confusions between Mr Posket, the magistrate, and his family; it brought Pinero both fame and wealth. Later farces, The Schoolmistress (1887) and Sweet Lavender (1888), did nearly as well. His first serious play, on what was to be the recurrent theme of double standards for men and women, was The Profligate (1889); it was praised by *Archer, and noted not only for its frankness but also for its absence of the standard devices of soliloquy and aside. Lady Bountiful (1891) was the first of the 'social' plays in which Pinero was deemed to display his understanding of women. *The Second Mrs Tanqueray (1893), returning to the theme of double standards, was a lasting success. The Notorious Mrs Ebbsmith (1895) again dealt with a woman's dubious past. Trelawny of the 'Wells' (1898), a sentimental comedy nostalgically recalling his own passion for the theatre he had haunted as a boy, also had great success. He continued to write, but, although knighted in 1909, lived through many years of dwindling reputation and disillusion, eclipsed by the rising popularity of the new theatre of *Ibsen and G. B. *Shaw.

PINKER, J. B., see AGENTS, LITERARY.

Pinkerton, the Misses, characters in Thackeray's *Vanity Fair.

Pinner of Wakefield, The, see GEORGE-A'-GREEN.

PINTER, Harold (1930–), poet and playwright, born in East London, the son of a Jewish tailor, and educated at Hackney Downs Grammar School. He began to publish poetry in periodicals before he was twenty, then became a professional actor, working mainly in repertory. His first play, The Room, was performed in Bristol in 1957, followed in 1958 by a London production of The Birthday Party, in which Stanley, an out-of-work pianist in a seaside boarding house, is mysteriously threatened and taken over by two intruders, an Irishman and a Jew, who present him with a Kafkaesque indictment of unexplained crimes. Pinter's distinctive voice was soon recognized, and many critical and commercial successes followed, including *The Caretaker* (1960), *The Lover* (1963), *The Homecoming* (1965), *Old Times* (1971), *No Man's Land* (1975), and *Betrayal* (1978). Pinter's gift for portraying, by means of dialogue which realistically produces the nuances of colloquial speech, the difficulties of communication and the many layers of meaning in language, pause, and silence, have created a style labelled by the popular imagination as 'Pinteresque', and his themes—nameless menace, erotic fantasy, obsession and jealousy, family hatreds and mental disturbance—are equally recognizable. Pinter has also written extensively for radio and television, directed plays, and written several screenplays, which include versions of L. P. *Hartley's The Go-Between* (1969), *A la recherche du temps perdu* (1978) and J. *Fowles's The French Lieutenant's Woman* (1982). *Poems and Prose, 1947–1977* was published in 1978.

PINTO, Fernão Mendes (?1509–83), a Portuguese traveller in the East, who left a narrative of his voyages (*Peregrinação*, 1614), marked by a vivid imagination. *Cervantes calls him the 'Prince of Liars', and Congreve in *Love for Love* (II. i) couples his name with that of *Mandeville when describing a 'Lyar of the first Magnitude'.

Piozzi, Mrs, see THRALE, H.

Pip, in Dickens's *Great Expectations*, the name by which the hero, Philip Pirrip, is commonly known.

Pipchin, Mrs, in Dickens's *Dombey and Son*, a boarding-house keeper in Brighton.

Pipe Rolls, see ROLLS.

Pippa Passes, by R. *Browning, published 1841 as no. I of the series *Bells and Pomegranates*. Although subtitled 'A Drama', it was not written for the stage. In its final version it consists of an 'Introduction', in verse and four parts, entitled 'Morning', 'Noon', 'Evening', and 'Night'. The first two parts have a verse section followed by one in prose; the third part has two verse sections; the fourth part has a prose section followed by one in verse. (This combination of verse and prose was influenced by Browning's study of Elizabethan and Jacobean drama; see also SOUL'S TRAGEDY, A.)

The play is set in and around Asolo, a small town near Venice which Browning visited in 1838 (see ASOLANDO). The plot is a web of dramatic ironies. The Introduction shows Pippa, a young silk-worker, waking up on the morning of her annual holiday. She contrasts the life of 'Asolo's Four Happiest Ones' with her own, and decides to 'pass' by them all in the course of the day. These four constitute an ascending scale of value, from carnal love (Ottima, wife of a rich silk-merchant, and her lover Sebald), through married love (Jules, a sculptor, and his bride), filial love (the young patriot Luigi and his mother), reaching at last the love of God (the good bishop). Each life turns out to be different from Pippa's imagining of it, though she herself does not realize this. Ottima and Sebald are quarrelling after their murder of Ottima's husband; Jules's bride turns out not to be the cultivated patrician he thought her, but an ignorant peasant girl; Luigi and his mother are disputing over his intention to carry out a political assassination; and the bishop is negotiating with a corrupt official about the destruction of Pippa herself, who turns out to be his own lost niece, heiress to a fortune he might otherwise appropriate. Pippa 'passes' by each of the four main scenes in turn, singing as she goes; each song, ironically juxtaposed with the action, effects a moral revolution in the characters concerned. (The famous concluding lines of Pippa's first song, 'God's in his heaven—All's right with the world!', are often quoted out of context as evidence of Browning's own naïve optimism.) At the end of the drama we see Pippa back in her room at nightfall, unaware of the day's events. The focus of modern criticism is the ambivalent moral and aesthetic value of Pippa's 'innocence', a theme repeated in the figure of Pompilia in *The Ring and the Book*.

PIRANDELLO, Luigi (1867–1936), Italian dramatist, short story writer, and novelist, was awarded the *Nobel Prize in 1934. He exercised a pervasive influence on European drama by challenging the conventions of *Naturalism. Among his plays, ten of which he published as *Maschere nude (Naked Masks*, 1918–22), the best known are: *Così è (se vi pare) (Right You are, If You Think You are*, 1917), *Sei personaggi in cerca di autore (Six Characters in Search of an Author*, 1921), and *Enrico IV (Henry IV*, 1922). In these plays he anticipated the anti-illusionist theatre of *Brecht, *Wilder, and Peter Weiss; his exploration of the disintegration of personality foreshadowed *Beckett; his probing of the conflict between reality and appearance has echoes in the work of *O'Neill; and his examination of the relationship between self and persona, actor and character, face and mask, is a precursor of the work of *Anouilh, *Giraudoux, and *Genet. Yet much of Pirandello's best work is to be found in his very short stories (28 of which were dramatized), where themes in common with his plays are more deeply explored. His main full-length novels are: *L'esclusa (The Outcast*, 1901), which deals with a woman's desire for independence within patriarchal Sicilian society; *Il* *fu Mattia Pascal* (*The Late Mattia Pascal*, 1904), where Pascal goes home to discover it is impossible to alter his status as 'deceased'; and *I vecchi e i giovani* (*The Old and The Young*, 1909), dealing with the effects of the unification of Italy on Sicily at the turn of the century.

PIRANESI, Giovanni Battista (1720–78), an Italian architect, who published many dramatic etchings of the ruins of classical Rome. In literary circles Piranesi is most famous for the *Carceri d'Invenzione* (*c*.1745; rev. edn *c*.1761), dark visions of Roman prisons where chains, ropes, and instruments of torture swing before massive arches, and where isolated figures wander aimlessly along stairs, ladders, and bridges that lead nowhere. Before his death his works were already popular in England, where their vast scale and obscurity were associated with the Burkeian *Sublime; Horace *Walpole wrote of 'the sublime dreams of Piranesi . . . He piles palaces on bridges, and temples on palaces, and scales Heaven with mountains of edifices'; *The Castle of Otranto* perhaps shows this influence. *Beckford, in Venice in 1780, associated Piranesi's gloomy horrors with the ducal prisons. Piranesi's deepest influence was on the Romantics. In *Confessions of an English Opium Eater* (1821) De Quincey compared Piranesi's prisons with the illusions induced by opium: 'With the same power of endless growth and self-reproduction did my architecture proceed in dreams.' Curiously, he had not seen the etchings but had listened to *Coleridge's description of a print showing Piranesi feverishly groping up endless flights of stairs. This passage became famous in France, where *Musset, *Gautier, and *Hugo were fascinated by Piranesi: Gautier wanted to produce *Hamlet* with scenery drawn from his prints. Later Piranesi appealed to writers who saw the *Carceri* as symbolizing metaphysical despair; A. *Huxley, who likened them to *Kafka, wrote of their 'colossal pointlessness'. To him they expressed 'obscure and terrible states of spiritual confusion and acedia'.

Pirate, The, a novel by Sir W. *Scott, published 1821. *Lockhart refers to 'the wild freshness' of its atmosphere. Scott absorbed the 'local colour' on a voyage of the Scottish Lighthouse Commissioners (on which he was an invited guest) with R. L. *Stevenson's grandfather.

The scene is Zetland (Shetland) in the 17th cent. In a remote part of the island live a misanthropical recluse, Basil Mertoun, of whose antecedents nothing is known, and his son Mordaunt, a gallant attractive youth. Mertoun is tenant of Magnus Troil, a rich Zetlander of noble Norse ancestry with two daughters, Minna, high-minded and imaginative, and Brenda, of a cheerful and more homely temperament. Mordaunt is their constant guest, and friend of the girls. Their pleasant relations are interrupted

by the arrival of Clement Cleveland, a buccaneer captain, shipwrecked on the coast and rescued from the sea by Mordaunt. Between these two a bitter enmity springs up. Minna, ignorant of the true character of a pirate's life, falls in love with Cleveland and he with her. Mordaunt, on the other hand, finds himself excluded from the friendship of the Troils, owing to false reports about him which have reached Magnus, but Brenda remains faithful to him and so attracts his love. A half-crazy relative of Magnus, Ulla Troil, known as Norna of the Fitful-head, who believes herself endowed with supernatural powers, believes she is Mordaunt's mother. She contrives to bring them all to Orkney, and in Kirkwall Cleveland is recognized by his old comrades and compelled to rejoin them. The pirates are eventually captured by a government frigate on information supplied by Norna, who discovers too late that Cleveland is her son by Basil Mertoun and Mordaunt his son by another woman. Minna and Cleveland are separated for ever; Brenda and Mordaunt are united.

There are some entertaining minor characters, in the persons of Triptolemus Yellowley, a farmer in the Mearns, sent to introduce improved agriculture among the backward islanders, and his shrewish sister, Barbara; Claud Halcro, poet and bard, and worshipper of *Dryden; Bryce Snailsfoot, the pedlar; and Jack Bunce, the actor-pirate.

Pisanio, in Shakespeare's *Cymbeline*, the servant *Posthumus leaves to *Imogen's service when he is banished.

Pistol, Ancient or Ensign, in Shakespeare's *2 *Henry IV*, *Henry V*, and *The Merry Wives of Windsor*, one of Falstaff's associates, a braggart with a fine command of bombastic language.

Pistyl of Susan (or *The Pistel of Swete Susan*), meaning 'the epistle of Susanna', a northern alliterative poem, *c*.1350–60, in 364 lines of 13-line tail-rhyme stanzas, telling the story of Susanna and the Elders (Daniel, 13). Up to recently, though no longer, scholars accepted the attribution of the work to *Huchown made in the *Orygynale Cronykil* (*c*.1420) of Andrew of *Wyntoun. Ed. H. Koster, *Huchown's Pistel of Swete Susan* (*Quellen und Forschungen* LXXVI, Strasburg, 1895).

PITMAN, Sir Isaac (1813–97), the inventor of phonography. He published at fourpence in 1837 *Stenographic Sound-Hand*, substituting phonographic for the mainly orthographic methods adopted by former shorthand authors.

PITT, William, first earl of Chatham (1708–78), a great Whig statesman and orator, who entered Parliament in 1735. He was secretary of state in 1765–7, but his fame as a great administrator rests on the period that immediately followed, when Pitt and Newcastle were the chief ministers in the coalition. He strenuously opposed from 1774 onwards the harsh measures taken against the American colonies, though unwilling to recognize their independence. His speeches were marked by lofty and impassioned eloquence and, judged by their effect on their hearers, place him among the greatest orators, but only fragments have survived.

PITT, William, 'the Younger' (1759–1806), second son of the first earl of Chatham, became chancellor of the exchequer in his 22nd and prime minister in 1783 in his 25th year, and retained the position until 1801. He returned to office in 1804, formed the third coalition, and died shortly after the battle of Austerlitz.

Pizarro, a tragedy adapted by *Sheridan from a German play by *Kotzebue, on the Spanish conqueror of Peru (1471–1541).

Place-Name Society, The, see ENGLISH PLACE-NAME SOCIETY.

Plagiary, Sir Fretful, a character in Sheridan's *The Critic, a caricature of R. *Cumberland.

Plague Year, *A Journal of the*, a historical fiction by *Defoe, published 1722.

It purports to be the narrative of a resident in London during 1664–5, the year of the Great Plague; the initials 'H. F.' which conclude it have been taken to refer to Defoe's uncle Henry Foe, a saddler, from whom the author may have heard some of the details he describes. It tells of the gradual spread of the plague, the terror of the inhabitants, and the steps taken by the authorities, such as the shutting up of infected houses and the prohibition of public gatherings. The symptoms of the disease, the circulation of the dead-carts, the burials in mass graves, and the terrible scenes witnessed by the supposed narrator are described with extraordinary vividness. The general effects of the epidemic, notably in the closing down of trading and the flight from the city, are also related, and an estimate of the total number of deaths is made. The *Journal* embodied information from various sources, including official documents; some scenes appear to have been borrowed from *Dekker's *The Wonderfull Yeare* (1603). Defoe's subject was suggested by fears of another outbreak, following the one in Marseilles in 1721 which occasioned Sir R. *Walpole's unpopular Quarantine Act. *Hazlitt ascribed to the work 'an epic grandeur, as well as heart-breaking familiarity'.

Plain-Dealer, The, a comedy by *Wycherley, probably performed 1676, published 1677. It disputes the honour of being his best play with *The Country Wife*, and was highly praised by *Dryden and *Dennis, though from the start it was criticized for obscenity, and in the 18th cent. was performed in a version bowdlerized by *Bickerstaffe.

It is loosely based on *Molière's *Le Misanthrope*; Wycherley's hero Manly, an honest misanthropic sea-captain (from whom the playwright took the nickname 'Manly' Wycherley) corresponds to Molière's Alceste, and his treacherous, worldly beloved Olivia to Célimène. Manly, returned from the Dutch wars, has lost faith in all but Olivia, to whom he has confided his money, and his friend Vernish: he finds Olivia married to Vernish, and faithless even to him. Manly is beloved by Fidelia, a young woman who has followed him to sea in man's clothes; she intercedes with Olivia on his behalf, in a scene reminiscent of the Olivia–Viola scene in *Twelfth Night*, is discovered by Vernish, who attempts to rape her, and is finally wounded in an attempt to defend Manly from Vernish. Manly forswears Olivia and pledges himself to Fidelia. There is a subplot in which the litigious widow Blackacre, who has a passion for legal jargon, trains up her son Jerry (a literary ancestor of Tony Lumpkin in *She Stoops to Conquer*) in her footsteps, and thereby overreaches herself.

The *Plain Dealer* is also the name of a periodical established by A. *Hill.

PLANCHÉ, James Robinson (1796–1880), prolific dramatist of Huguenot descent. Besides his many original pieces for the stage, mainly burlesques and extravaganzas, he made translations and adaptations from French, Spanish, and Italian authors, including fairy-tales by the Countess d'Aulnoy (1855) and by *Perrault (1858). His stage works include *The Vampyre; or the Bride of the Isles* (1820), an adaptation of a French melodrama which introduced the 'vampire' trap to the English stage, and *The Island of Jewels* (1849). He wrote several opera librettos including *Maid Marian* (1822) adapted from a tale by *Peacock, *Weber's *Oberon* (1826), and English versions of *William Tell* and *The Magic Flute*. Planché also made a reputation as an antiquary and a scholar of heraldry and costume; his *History of British Costumes* (1834) long remained a standard work; he also published an edition of Strutt's *Regal and Ecclesiastical Antiquities of England* (1842). He was appointed Somerset Herald in 1866.

Plantagenet Palliser, see OMNIUM, DUKE OF.

PLATH, Sylvia (1932–63), poet and novelist, born in Boston, Massachusetts, the daughter of a German immigrant professor and entomologist, who died when she was eight. She was educated at Smith College, Massachusetts, and Newnham College, Cambridge. She married Ted *Hughes in 1956. After teaching for a while in America, she and Hughes returned to England in 1959, where they lived in London before moving to Devon in 1961. Her first volume of poetry, *The Colossus*, appeared in 1960, and in 1963 her only novel *The Bell Jar*. Less than a month after its publication, in the coldest February for many years, she committed suicide in London. In 1965 appeared her best-known collection, *Ariel*, which established her reputation with its courageous and controlled treatment of extreme and painful states of mind. Much of her symbolism was deeply rooted in actuality; the poems on bee-keeping ('The Bee Meeting', 'The Arrival of the Bee Box', etc.) are based on her own attempts to keep bees in Devon, and other poems—'Elm', 'Letter in November', 'The Moon and the Yew Tree'—describe the physical surroundings of the house and the views from it. Other poems refer directly to her own experiences: 'Lady Lazarus' is based on her two previous suicide attempts, 'Daddy' on the early loss of her father, 'Tulips' on a week spent in hospital undergoing an appendectomy. Other posthumous volumes include *Crossing the Water* and *Winter Trees* (both 1971); *Johnny Panic and the Bible of Dreams* (1977, collected prose pieces); and *Collected Poems* (1981, with an introduction by T. Hughes). A volume of letters, *Letters Home*, edited by her mother, A. S. Plath, with a commentary, appeared in 1975. Although her best-known poems deal with illness, suffering, and death, others (particularly those addressed to her two children, such as 'Morning Song' and 'You're') are exhilarating, tender, and affectionate, and her tone is frequently witty as well as disturbing.

PLATO (*c*.428/7–*c*.348/7 BC), Greek philosopher, eminent for the profundity of his thought, the number of his surviving writings, and the extent of his influence. Born in Athens of an aristocratic family, he was a friend and admirer of *Socrates, after whose death in 399 BC he went into exile; he returned to Athens in the 380s and set up a school which was then or at a later stage known as the Academy. The majority of his works are in dialogue form and may have been intended for public performance or for performance to a select audience of pupils. The principal speaker is nearly always Socrates, but it is impossible to say how close Plato's 'Socrates' stands to the real man either in character or in his teaching. The dialogues fall roughly into three groups. About a dozen demonstrate what has been called the Socratic Method. Socrates plies his interlocutors with a chain of questions, and their replies trap them into self-contradiction. These dialogues, the best-known of which are the *Ion, Euthyphro, Protagoras*, and *Gorgias*, are considered Plato's earliest work. The second group includes the *Crito, Apology, Phaedo,* *Symposium; these do not employ the Socratic Method and are considered to have been written between 371 and 367 BC. Finally, the profound and technically subtle dialogues such as the *Theaetetus, Parmenides, Timaeus, Sophistes, Philebus* are the products of Plato's old age. There are also two monumental treatises, *The Republic and *The Laws*, which were probably compiled over a period, *The Laws* being the later.

Plato's ideas have had a lasting appeal for philosophers, and some of them also caught the popular imagination. Notable among these were; (1) the Theory of Forms which is best illustrated by an example. The concept 'cat' is derived from our knowledge of particular cats. Plato held that concepts of this nature have a real existence outside the world of sense, and this belief served to reinforce men's hope that there existed an eternal order. (2) The project of establishing philosopher-kings which produced a multitude of schemes for the education of princes. (3) *Platonic Love, a devotion inspired by the best qualities of the beloved and aiming at their further development, was formulated originally by Plato in the context of a homosexual relationship, but by the 16th cent. it was applied to a heterosexual love that could rise above sexual desire.

Plato has played a markedly vitalizing role in the history of European thought. Through *Augustine he came to exercise a formative influence on Christianity. Through the Florentine Platonists of the 15th cent. he made a manifold impact on art and ideas in the major countries of Europe. It is impossible, however, to separate Plato's direct from his indirect influence. Platonic themes appear in many writers—*Spenser, *Chapman, *Donne, *Marvell, and later *Wordsworth, *Bridges—the extent of whose reading of Plato must remain in doubt, as well as in the work of his attested students such as the *Cambridge Platonists, *Milton, *Gray, *Shelley, E. B. *Browning, M. *Arnold, and *Pater. But what we find in all these cases are just generalities that could have issued from a Christian or *Neoplatonist source as surely as from a reading of Plato himself.

Platonic Love, now used to mean love of a purely spiritual character, free from sensual desire. *Amor Platonicus* was used by *Ficino synonymously with *Amor Socraticus* to denote the kind of interest in young men which was imputed to Socrates; cf. the last few pages of Plato's *Symposium. As thus originally used it had no reference to women, but by the 16th cent. it was extended to include heterosexual love that rose above sensual desire (see e.g. CASTIGLIONE). The ennobling and idealizing aspects of the homosexual Platonic concept appear in many English writers, however, particularly towards the end of the 19th and the beginning of the 20th cents; the 'love that dared not speak its name' appeared frequently in a pagan-Hellenic context, consciously or subconsciously, in the works of *Pater, J. A. *Symonds, F. *Reid, E. M. *Forster, and many others.

Platonists, Cambridge, see CAMBRIDGE PLATONISTS.

PLATONOV, Andrei Platonovich (A. P. Klimentov) (1899–1951), Russian prose writer. He was born, the son of a railway electrician, in Voronezh in central Russia and from the age of 13 had various manual jobs. He fought for the Bolsheviks in the Civil War and then qualified as an engineer. In 1927 he gave up his job to devote himself to literature. His first collection of stories, *The Locks of Yepifan*, appeared in 1927. During 1928–30 he wrote his most important works, *Chevengur*, which relates with bitter irony the tale of a group of proletarians who dream of building a Communist Utopia and choose the steppe town of Chevengur for their experiment, and *Kotlovan* (*The Pit*), in which the inhabitants of a village plan to build a house for communal living but get no further than the enormous foundation pit. Both these works have now been published abroad (1972, 1968) and translated into English (1978, 1973), but they have not appeared in the Soviet Union. The publication of his story 'For Future Use: A Poor Farmhand's Chronicle' (1931) led to accusations of 'kulak tendencies' and a ban on his work till 1936, and he was again in disfavour from 1946 until his death. He began to be published again in 1958. Among works published only posthumously is the story 'Dzhan', a nightmarish tale of desert searchings. He is now extremely highly regarded in the USSR despite his only partial publication.

PLAUTUS, Titus Maccius (*c.*254–184 BC), early Roman dramatist who adapted the Greek New Comedy for the Roman stage. The extent of his originality remains uncertain. He does not seem to have translated exactly, but he certainly worked within the Greek convention using the same stock characters—miserly fathers, spendthrift sons, boastful soldiers, resourceful parasites, courtesans, and slaves—and often borrowing the plots of his Greek models. Twenty of his plays have survived, and it was from him and from his successor *Terence that Europe learned about ancient comedy. His direct influence on English literature is slight, though Udall was indebted to him in *Ralph Roister Doister*, Shakespeare adapted his *Menaechmi* in *The Comedy of Errors*, Jonson conflated the *Captivi* and the *Aulularia* in *The Case is Altered*, and Dryden adapted his *Amphitryon*; but the tradition he represented is responsible for the form taken by English comedy up to the 19th cent.

Playboy of the Western World, The, a comedy by *Synge, performed and published 1907.
Christy Mahon, 'a slight young man, very tired and frightened', arrives at a village in Mayo. He gives out that he is a fugitive from justice, who in a quarrel has killed his bullying father, splitting him to the chine with a single blow. He is hospitably entertained, and his character as a dare-devil gives him a great advantage with the women (notably Pegeen Mike and Widow Quin) over the milder-spirited lads of the place. But admiration gives place to angry contempt when the father himself arrives in pursuit of the fugitive, who has merely given him a crack on the head and run away. The implication that Irish peasants would condone a murder and the frankness of some of the language (Christy speaks of 'all the girls in Mayo . . . standing before me in their shifts') caused outrage and riots when the play was first performed at the *Abbey Theatre. In his Preface, Synge compares the 'joyless and pallid' language of the naturalistic theatre of *Ibsen with the 'rich and living' imagination and language of the Irish people, and this play is his best-known effort to fuse the language of ordinary people with a dramatic rhetoric of his own making.

Pleasant Satyre of the Thrie Estaitis, Ane, in Commendatioun of Vertew and Vituperatioun of Vyce, a morality play by Sir D. *Lindsay, produced 1540.
Pt I represents the temptation of Rex Humanitas by Sensuality, Wantonness, Solace, and other evil companions, while Good Counsel is hustled away, Verity is put in the stocks, and Chastity is warned off. An interlude follows in which are described the adventures of Chastity among humbler folks, a tailor, a soutar, and their wives. Then Chastity is put in the stocks. But the arrival of Correction alters the situation. Verity, Good Counsel, and Chastity are admitted to the king, and Sensuality is banished.
After an interlude in which an impoverished farmer exposes his sufferings at the hands of the ecclesiastics and a pardoner's trade is ridiculed, Pt II presents the Three Estates summoned before the king, and their misdeeds denounced by John the Common Weal. The Lords and Commons repent, but the clergy remain impenitent, are exposed, and the malefactors brought to the scaffold.
The play, which is extremely long and exists in three different versions, is written in various metres, eight- and six-lined stanzas and couplets. It is, as a dramatic representation, in advance of all contemporary English plays, and gives an interesting picture of the Scottish life of the time.

Pleasures of Hope, The, a poem by T. *Campbell published 1799.
In Pt I the poet considers the consolation and inspiration of Hope and by contrast the hard fate of a people deprived of it, described in a passage on the downfall of Poland. In Pt II he reflects upon Love in combination with Hope, and on the belief in a future life.

Pleasures of Imagination, The, a philosophical poem by *Akenside, published 1744; it was completely rewritten and issued as *The Pleasures of the Imagination* in 1757.

The poem is based on the philosophical and aesthetic doctrines and distinctions of *Addison, *Shaftesbury, and *Hutcheson; *Gray found it 'too much infected with the Hutchesonian jargon'. It examines the primary and secondary pleasures of the imagination, the first connected with the *Sublime, the wonderful, and the beautiful, the second with passion and sense. Akenside's speculations, which many found obscure (and Dr *Johnson 'loquacious'), range from Platonic theories of form and essence to I. *Newton's account of the rainbow. Mrs *Barbauld in her 1794 edition gives a sympathetic and useful interpretation.

Pleasures of Memory, The, see ROGERS, S.

Pléiade, La, a group of seven French writers of the 16th cent., led by *Ronsard. The name, deriving ultimately from the seven stars of the constellation of the Pleiades, had originally been applied by Alexandrian critics to a group of seven poets from the reign of Ptolemy II. Ronsard's use of the term dates from 1556. The other members of the group were *du Bellay, Pontus de Tyard, Baïf, Jodelle, Belleau, and either Peletier or, according to some authorities, Dorat. The group, inspired by a common interest in the literatures of antiquity and of the Italian Renaissance, sought to promote the claims of the French language to a comparably dignified status as a medium for literary expression, and their aims were set forth in du Bellay's *Deffence et illustration de la langue françoyse* of 1549. The Pléiade were largely responsible for the acclimatization of the sonnet form in France, and for the establishment of the alexandrine as the dominant metrical form for much later French poetry. Indeed, the group did much, in ways both formal and intuitive, to create the conditions for the emergence of modern poetry in France.

Pleydell, Mr Counsellor Paulus, a character in Scott's *Guy Mannering*.

Pliable, in Bunyan's *Pilgrim's Progress*, one of *Christian's companions, who turns back at the *Slough of Despond.

Pliant, (1) Dame, the rich widow in Jonson's *The Alchemist*; (2) Sir Paul, see PLYANT.

PLINY THE ELDER (Gaius Plinius Secundus) (AD 23–79), Roman compiler of a Natural History, which is an encyclopaedic rag-bag of popular science. Widely read in the Middle Ages, it provided a cosmology for *Du Bartas's *La Semaine, ou la création du monde* (1578), which *Sylvester's translation established for the 17th cent. as an English classic. But Pliny's direct influence in England was small. Sir T. *Browne made use of him, and so occasionally did *Milton. D. G. *Rossetti borrowed an anecdote for

'Troy Town', but generally the growth of scientific knowledge led to his being neglected.

PLINY THE YOUNGER (Gaius Plinius Caecilius Secundus) (AD 62–c.112), Roman letter-writer, nephew of the above. The vogue for letter-writing in the 1690s led to the translation of some of his correspondence, and William Melmoth produced a full but inaccurate version in 1746. Pliny was a more formal writer than *Cicero, and is remembered mainly for his description of the eruption of Vesuvius and his official correspondence with Trajan.

PLOMER, William Charles Franklyn (1903–73), poet and novelist, was born in Pietersberg of British parents, and several of his works, including his first novel, the savagely satirical *Turbott Wolfe*, published in 1926 by the *Hogarth Press, are portraits of South African life. In 1926, with R. *Campbell, he founded a magazine, *Voorslag* ('Whiplash'); they were joined in the enterprise by L. *van der Post. Plomer then spent some two years teaching in Japan, an experience reflected in his poems, in *Paper Houses* (1929, stories), and *Sado* (a novel, 1931). He came to England in 1929 and settled in Bloomsbury, where he was befriended by L. and V. *Woolf, and in 1937 succeeded E. *Garnett as principal reader to Jonathan Cape. His first volume of poetry, *The Fivefold Screen* (1932), was followed by several others, and his *Collected Poems* appeared in 1973. His poems are largely satirical and urbane, with a sharp eye for character and social setting; many of them, like the title piece of *The Dorking Thigh* (1945), are modern ballads with a macabre touch. His edition of *Kilvert's *Diary* appeared in 3 vols, 1938–44. He wrote the librettos for several of *Britten's operas, including *Gloriana*, which is based on L. *Strachey's *Elizabeth and Essex*.

Plornish, Mr and Mrs, in Dickens's *Little Dorrit*, a plasterer and his wife who lived in Bleeding Heart Yard. Mrs Plornish was a notable interpreter of the Italian language.

PLOTINUS (AD c.203–62), Greek philosopher, the chief exponent of *Neoplatonism. His *Enneads* did much to shape Christian theology in the 4th cent. and also exercised a wide influence on Renaissance thought through *Ficino's translation (1492). They were studied by the *Cambridge Platonists. The concept of the Chain of Being which Plotinus elaborated was generally accepted until the end of the 18th cent., as was the principle, which *Sidney learnt from *Scaliger, that a poet is a second creator, Art re-ascending to the Ideas from which Nature is derived. Plotinus' influence on Christianity was ably discussed by Dean *Inge in his Gifford Lectures of 1918.

Plough and the Stars, The, see O'CASEY, S.

Plough Monday Play, a folk-drama of the East Midlands, surviving in versions from Cropwell in Nottinghamshire and from Lincolnshire. Like the St George Play, the Plough Monday Play probably symbolizes in its central incident the death and resurrection of the year. See E. K. *Chambers, *The Medieval Stage* (1903) and *The English Folk Play* (1933).

Plumdamas, Peter, a character in Scott's *The Heart of Midlothian.*

Plume, Captain, a character in Farquhar's *The Recruiting Officer.*

Plumed Serpent, The, a novel by D. H. *Lawrence, published 1926.

Kate Leslie, an Irish widow of 40, weary of Europe, arrives in Mexico at a turning-point in her life. She has had lovers and children, and loved her husband Joachim 'to the bounds of human love'. The theme of the novel is Kate's struggle for deliverance, for a mystical rebirth. She meets and is drawn to General Don Cipriano Viedma, who introduces her to Don Ramón Carrasco, a mystic and revolutionary leader, reviver of the cult of the ancient god Quetzalcoatl, the plumed serpent. The book contains scenes of violent Aztec 'blood-lust' (Cipriano ceremoniously stabbing half-naked prisoners, the drinking of the victims' blood); Kate, though repelled, is fascinated by the darkness and elemental power of Mexico and its people, and herself enters the cult as the fertility goddess Malintzi and the bride of Cipriano. The novel ends with her acceptance of the subjugation and loss-of-self demanded of her by Cipriano and her hopes for fulfilment. This is the Lawrence of 'dark gods' and 'phallic power', containing besides much of his usual vivid descriptive writing.

Plurabelle, Anna Livia, a character in Joyce's *Finnegans Wake*, and also the title of a section of the novel published as 'Work in Progress' (1928), with an introduction by P. *Colum.

PLUTARCH (AD *c*.50–*c*.125), biographer and moralist, the most popular of Greek authors at the time of the Renaissance. His *Parallel Lives* exemplified the tradition of biography associated with the Peripatetic school, illustrating the moral character of his subjects through a series of anecdotes. Translated by T. *North (1579), they served as a source-book for Shakespeare's Roman plays and later for *Otway's *Caius Marius* and Addison's *Cato*. They also served as a model for I. *Walton's *Lives* (1670). Sir T. *Browne gave them to his sons to read, *Dryden gave a pioneer analysis of their style and structure in his *Life of Plutarch* (1683), and in America the Founding Fathers turned to them for models of republican virtue.

The *Moral Essays* provide a compendium of ancient wisdom on a variety of topics: moral philosophy, religious belief, education, health, literary criticism, and social customs. Individual essays were translated into English during the 16th cent., including the probably pseudonymous love stories (by James Sanford, 1572), and material from Plutarch's Morals can be found in a number of Elizabethan authors: *Elyot, *Painter, *Lyly, Fennes, *Meres, Cornwallis, *Chapman. The first complete version in English, by *Holland appeared in 1603, when its popularity was enhanced by the almost simultaneous publication of *Florio's translation of *Montaigne, for the latter cites Plutarch on nearly every page. After the middle years of the 17th cent., when they were read by Jeremy *Taylor and *Milton, the popularity of the *Moral Essays* declined. By then there were more recent examples of the genre with which they could not compete. (See also BIOGRAPHY.)

Plyant, Sir Paul, in Congreve's *The Double Dealer*, 'an uxorious foolish old knight'.

Plymley, Letters of Peter, by Sydney *Smith, published 1807–8.

The letters purport to be written by Peter Plymley to his brother in the country, the Revd Abraham Plymley ('a bit of a goose') in favour of Catholic emancipation. The arguments, both serious and absurd, of the Revd Abraham for maintaining the disabilities of the Catholics are taken one by one, and demolished with sense, wit, and humour; while at the same time the author makes his own Anglican position plain, and ridicules the 'nonsense' of the Roman Catholic Church.

POCAHONTAS, or Matoaka (1595–1617), an American-Indian princess, the daughter of Powhattan, an Indian chief in Virginia. According to Capt. John *Smith, one of the Virginia colonists who had been taken prisoner by the Indians, he was rescued by her when her father was about to kill him in 1607 (she was then only 12). In 1612 she was seized as a hostage by the colonists for the good behaviour of the Indian tribes (or for the restitution of English captives), became a Christian, was named Rebecca, and married a colonist, John Rolfe. She was brought to England in 1616, where she at first attracted considerable attention, but died neglected. Those who claim descent from her are legion. She is introduced by Jonson in his *The Staple of News*, II. i. George Warrington in Thackeray's *The Virginians* composes a tragedy on her, and she becomes a national symbol in H. *Crane's *The Bridge* (1930).

Pocket, Herbert, a character in Dickens's *Great Expectations.*

Podsnap, Mr, a character in Dickens's *Our Mutual Friend*, a type of self-satisfaction and self-importance.

POE, Edgar Allan (1809–49), born in Boston, Massachusetts, the son of itinerant actors, became an orphan in early childhood, and was taken into the household of John Allan, a tobacco exporter of Richmond; he took his foster-father's name as his middle name from 1824 onwards. He came to England with the Allans (1815–20) and attended Manor House school at Stoke Newington (which he describes, in an imaginative manner but with some accurate detail, in his *Doppelgänger* story 'William Wilson', 1839); he spent a year at the University of Virginia, which he left after incurring debts and gambling to relieve them. He published his first volume of verse, *Tamerlane and other poems* (1827), anonymously and at his own expense; then enlisted in the US army under the name of Edgar A. Perry. He was sent to Sullivan's Island, South Carolina, which provided settings for 'The Gold Bug' (1843) and 'The Balloon Hoax' (1844). Allan (from whom he had been estranged) procured his discharge from the army, and he entered West Point in 1830, having published a second volume of verse, *Al Aaraaf* (1829); he was dishonourably discharged in 1831, for intentional neglect of his duties, and published a third volume of *Poems* (containing 'To Helen') in the same year. He now turned to journalism, living from 1831 to 1835 with a relative, Mrs Clemm, in Baltimore, whose 13-year-old daughter, his cousin Virginia, he married in 1836. He worked as editor on various papers, including the *Southern Literary Messenger*, and began to publish his stories in magazines. His first collection, *Tales of the Grotesque and Arabesque* (1839, for 1840), contains one of his most famous works, 'The Fall of the House of Usher', a *Gothic romance in which the narrator visits the crumbling mansion of his childhood companion, Roderick Usher, to find both Usher and his twin sister Madeline in the last stages of mental and physical weakness; Madeline is buried alive while in a trance, arises, and carries her brother to death 'in her violent and now final death agonies', whereupon the house itself splits asunder and sinks into the tarn. In 1845 his poem 'The Raven', published in a New York paper and then as the title poem of *The Raven and other Poems* (1845), brought him fame, but not security; he and his ménage continued to suffer poverty and ill health, his wife dying in 1847 and he himself struggling with alcohol addiction and nervous instability. His end was characteristically tragic; he died in Baltimore, five days after having been found semi-conscious and delirious, from alcohol, heart failure, epilepsy, or a combination of these. His posthumous reputation and influence have been great; he was much admired by *Baudelaire, who translated many of his works, and in Britain by *Swinburne, *Wilde, *Rossetti, and *Yeats. *Freudian critics (and Freud himself) have been intrigued by the macabre and pathological

elements in his work, ranging from hints of necrophilia in his poem 'Annabel Lee' (1849) to the indulgent sadism of 'The Pit and the Pendulum' (1843); *Existentialism has been detected in the motiveless obsession in such stories as 'The Cask of Amontillado' (1846). *Borges, R. L. *Stevenson, and a vast general readership have been impressed by the cryptograms and mysteries of the stories which feature Poe's detective, Dupin ('The Murders in the Rue Morgue', 1841; 'The Purloined Letter', 1845) and the morbid metaphysical speculation of 'The Facts in the Case of M. Waldemar' (1845). His critical writings include 'The Philosophy of Composition' (1846, which includes the statement: 'The death of a beautiful woman is, unquestionably, the most poetical topic in the world') and 'The Poetic Principle' (1850, originally a lecture) which preaches a form of *Art for Art's Sake.

Poema Morale (or 'The Moral Ode'), a Southern poem in early Middle English of about 400 lines, surviving in seven manuscripts, and dating from *c*.1175. It is a vigorous work on the themes of transience and repentance, and is very early in the Middle English period after the transition from Old English. Ed. in J. Hall, *Selections from Early Middle English* (1920).

Poetaster, a comedy by *Jonson, performed by the Children of the Queen's Chapel 1601, printed 1602.

Set in the court of the Emperor Augustus, the main plot concerns the conspiracy of the poetaster Crispinus and his friend Demetrius (who represent Jonson's contemporaries *Marston and *Dekker) and a swaggering captain, Pantilius Tucca, to defame Horace, who represents Jonson. The matter is tried before Augustus, with Virgil as judge. Horace is acquitted, the 'dresser of plays' Demetrius is made to wear a fool's coat and cap, and Crispinus is given a purge of hellebore and made to vomit up his windy rhetoric. A secondary plot concerns Ovid's love for the daughter of Augustus, and his subsequent banishment. Marston and Dekker replied to the attack in *Satiromastix*, where the main characters of this play reappear.

Poetical Rhapsody, A, a collection of Elizabethan verse published by Francis Davison (?1575–?1619) and his brother Walter in 1602, 'containing divers sonnets, odes, elegies, madrigals and other Poesies', 2nd edn 1611, 3rd 1621, and edited by H. E. Rollins in 2 vols, 1931–2. It includes 'The Lie', attributed to *Ralegh; the song 'In praise of a Beggar's Life' quoted in *The Compleat Angler*; and poems by *Greene, *Wotton, *Sidney, *Spenser, *Donne, and others.

Poetic Diction, a term used to mean language and usage peculiar to poetry, which came into prominence with *Wordsworth's discussion in his Preface (1800) to the *Lyrical Ballads, in which he claims to have taken pains to avoid 'what is usually called poetic diction', and asserts that there is and should be no essential difference between the language of prose and the language of metrical composition. Wordsworth thus implies that there should be no such thing as 'language and usage peculiar to poetry', and illustrates his point by attacking a sonnet of *Gray (who had, he said, attempted to widen the gap between poetry and prose); Gray himself had declared (1742, letter to West) that 'the language of the age is never the language of poetry.' Wordsworth's attack on *Neo-classicism, archaisms, abstractions, personifications, etc., was both forceful and revolutionary, although it is noticeable that he himself did not always consider it necessary to use 'the real language of men', and his views were later repudiated by *Coleridge; moreover, although poetry became less stilted in its language, its vocabulary remained on the whole distinctive throughout the Romantic and Victorian periods, and few followed Wordsworth in his faith that the language of low and rustic life is plainer, more emphatic, and more philosophical than the 'gaudiness and inane phraseology' which he condemned. *Clare is a rare and isolated example of a poet capable of resisting conventional notions of 'poetic diction' and writing in his own idiom; it was not until the 20th cent. and the advent of *Modernism in the works of *Yeats, T. S. *Eliot, *Pound, and others that another major attempt to enlarge the poetic vocabulary and bring it closer to ordinary speech was made.

Poetics, The, a fragment of a treatise by *Aristotle which greatly influenced the theory of *Neo-classicism. It is the source of the principles elaborated by later critics as the *Unities, and it also introduced many much-discussed concepts related to the theory of tragedy, such as *mimesis* (imitation); *catharsis* (purification or purgation); *peripeteia* (reversal); and *hamartia* (either 'tragic flaw' or, more accurately, 'error of judgement'). *Hubris* (overweening pride or confidence) was a form of *hamartia*.

Poet Laureate, the title given to a poet who receives a stipend as an officer of the Royal Household, his duty (no longer enforced) being to write court-odes, etc. The title was sometimes conferred by certain universities.

The first poet laureate in the modern sense was *Jonson, followed by *D'Avenant, whose successor *Dryden was the first to be given the title officially. The other laureates in chronological order are: *Shadwell, *Tate, *Rowe, *Eusden, *Cibber, *Whitehead, T. *Warton, *Pye, *Southey, *Wordsworth, *Tennyson, A. *Austin, *Bridges, *Masefield, *Day-Lewis, *Betjeman, Ted *Hughes. See E. K. Broadus, *The Laureateship* (1921).

Poetry: A Magazine of Verse (1912–), founded at Chicago by the American poet and critic Harriet Monroe (1860–1936), who edited it until her death. In its early days it published work by E. *Pound, A. *Lowell, T. S. *Eliot, *Frost, H.D. (Hilda *Doolittle), F. M. *Ford, and others, and has continued to flourish, publishing work by nearly every major American poet of the 20th cent.

Poetry Bookshop, see MONRO, H. E.

Poetry London, a bi-monthly which became the leading poetry magazine of the 1940s. It was conceived by a group of four, Dylan *Thomas, James Meary Tambimuttu (1915–83), Anthony Dickins, and Keidrych Rhys, and edited by Tambimuttu, who had arrived in 1938 from Ceylon, almost penniless, and entered the literary London of Soho and *Fitzrovia. The first issue appeared in Feb. 1939; Tambimuttu produced 15 numbers, and it was subsequently edited by Richard Marsh and Nicholas Moore. It published work by G. *Barker, V. *Watkins, G. *Ewart, H. *Pinter, C. *Tomlinson, D. *Gascoyne, L. *Durrell, and many others.

Poetry Nation, a twice-yearly poetry magazine edited by C. B. Cox and Michael Schmidt (6 issues, 1973–6), founded in sympathy with what its first editorial described as 'a renewed popularity and practice of clearly formal writing, a common bridling at vacuous public and private rhetoric'. Contributors included C. *Tomlinson, P. *Porter, E. *Jennings, G. *Hill, and Douglas Dunn; D. *Davie and C. H. *Sisson became co-editors of its thrice-yearly successor, *PN Review* (1976–).

Poetry Review, see MONRO, H. E., and POETRY SOCIETY.

Poetry Society, The, a society founded in 1909 (as the Poetry Recital Society) for the promotion of poetry and the art of speaking verse, and sponsored by many figures in the literary world, including G. *Murray, A. P. *Graves, Sturge *Moore, *Gosse, *Newbolt, Arnold *Bennett, E. V. *Lucas, and A. C. *Benson. Its many activities now include the organization of poetry competitions, workshop sessions, and examinations in and awards for the speaking of verse and prose. Its journal is *Poetry Review*, founded 1912, which succeeded the earlier *Poetry Gazette*; its first editor was H. E. *Monro, and its contributors have included most of the notable British 20th-cent. poets.

Poets' Corner, part of the south transept of Westminster Abbey containing the tombs or monuments of *Chaucer, *Spenser, Shakespeare, *Jonson, *Milton, *Drayton, Samuel *Butler, A. *Behn, *Gay, and many later distinguished poets and authors. Many of the monuments are by *Rysbrack.

Poins, in Shakespeare's *1* and *2* *Henry IV, one of Prince Henry's companions.

Point Counter Point, see HUXLEY, A.

Poirot, Hercule, the Belgian detective in A. *Christie's murder mysteries.

Polite Learning, *An Enquiry into the Present State of,* see ENQUIRY INTO THE PRESENT STATE OF POLITE LEARNING.

POLITIAN, see POLIZIANO.

Political Register, The (1802–35), a weekly newspaper founded by *Cobbett. It began as a Tory paper but by 1809 was thoroughly Radical. He continued to issue it even when committed to prison for an article condemning military flogging. His new version of the paper produced in 1816 at 2*d.* reached a remarkable circulation of 40,000–50,000 a week. In 1821 *Rural Rides began to appear serially. Cobbett continued the paper until his death.

Politic Would-be, Sir and Lady, the foolish traveller and his loquacious wife in Jonson's **Volpone.*

Polixines, the king of Bohemia in Shakespeare's **The Winter's Tale.*

POLIZIANO, in English POLITIAN, Angelo (1454–94), the name assumed from his birth place, Montepulciano, by Angelo Ambrogini, Italian humanist and friend of Lorenzo the Magnificent. He was professor of Greek and Latin at the University of Florence, and wrote poetry in both these languages. His Italian works include *Stanze per la giostra* and *Orfeo* (1480), the first secular drama in Italian. His philological acumen, seen at its best in two collections of studies of textual problems (the first and second *Miscellaneorum centuria*), made him one of the founders of modern textual criticism. *Linacre was one of his students, and G. *Chapman translated and imitated his verse.

POLLARD, A(lfred) W(illiam) (1859–1944), honorary secretary of the *Bibliographical Society, was keeper of the Department of Printed Books at the British Museum, 1919–24. He was an authority on Chaucer and Shakespeare, edited several volumes of Chaucer's *Canterbury Tales (1886–7) and the 'Globe' Chaucer (1898), and published other pioneering works which influenced the study of medieval literature. His important contributions to Shakespearian criticism included *Shakespeare's Folios and Quartos 1594–1685* (1909) and *Shakespeare's Fight with the Pirates* (1917). He was largely responsible for the completion of the *Short-title Catalogue of Books printed in England, Scotland and Ireland . . . 1475–1640* (1926).

Pollente, in Spenser's *Faerie Queene (v. ii), the 'cruell Sarazin' who holds a bridge and despoils those who pass over it, the father of *Munera. He is slain by Sir *Artegall.

Pollexfen, Sir Hargreve, a character in Richardson's **Sir Charles Grandison.*

Polly, a musical play by J. *Gay, published 1729, the sequel to **The Beggar's Opera.* Its performance on stage was prohibited by the Lord Chamberlain.

Macheath has been transported to the West Indies, and has escaped from the plantation; he is disguised as Morano, chief of the pirates. Polly comes to seek him, but is trapped in the household of an amorous planter, whose advances she escapes owing to an attack by the pirates. Disguised as a man, she joins the loyal Indians, helps to beat off the attack, takes Morano prisoner, discovers his identity too late to save him from execution, and marries an Indian prince. *Polly* brought Gay nearly £1,200 in subscriptions.

Polly, The History of Mr, a novel by H. G. *Wells.

POLO, Marco (1254–1324), a member of a patrician family of Venice, accompanied his father and uncle in 1271 on an embassy from the pope to Kublai, Grand Khan of Tartary. They travelled through Armenia, Iraq, Khorasan, and the Pamir, to Kashgar; thence to Khoten, across the desert of Lop, and into Chinese territory, where they were well received by the emperor and where Marco was employed on services of importance. After 17 years in the territories of the Grand Khan, the Polos obtained permission to return home, which they did by sea to the Persian Gulf, eventually reaching Venice after an absence of 24 years. Marco Polo's account of his travels was written while imprisoned by the Genoese, by whom he had been captured in a sea-fight with the Venetians. The original text appears to have been in French. The existence of other and wilder romances of Eastern travel (such as *Mandeville, etc.) tended to make Polo 'suspect', at least in places; but there is no reason for any such suspicion. The work became very popular and was translated into many languages. It was Englished by John Frampton in 1579; but the first serious English translation was by W. Marsden early in the 19th cent. The classic one is by Sir Henry Yule, with full notes, which first appeared in 1871 (there are subsequent editions). A standard edition of the Italian text, with new materials, by L. F. Benedetto was published in Florence in 1928.

Polonius, the lord chamberlain, father of *Ophelia and *Laertes in Shakespeare's **Hamlet.* Dr *Johnson described him as 'a man bred in courts, exercised in business, stored with observation, confident of his knowledge, proud of his eloquence, and declining into dotage'.

Polychronicon, The, see HIGDEN, R.

Polydore, (1) in Shakespeare's *Cymbeline,* the name borne by Guiderius while in the Welsh forest; (2) a character in Otway's *The Orphan;* (3) a character in J. *Fletcher's *The Mad Lover.*

POLYDORE VERGIL, see VERGIL, P.

Polyglot Bible, The, edited in 1653–7 by Brian Walton (?1600–61), bishop of Chester, with the help of many scholars. It contains various oriental texts of the Bible with Latin translations, and a critical apparatus.

Polyglots, The, a novel by W. *Gerhardie.

Polyhymnia, a poem by *Peele written in 1590 commemorating the retirement of Sir H. *Lee from the office of queen's champion, and describing the ceremonies that took place on this occasion. It contains at the end the beautiful song 'His Golden lockes, | Time hath to Silver turn'd' made widely known by Thackeray's quotation of part of it in *The Newcomes,* ch. 76.

Poly-Olbion, The (this is the spelling of the 1st edn), the most ambitious work of *Drayton. It was written between 1598 and 1622 and consists of thirty 'Songs' each of 300–500 lines, in hexameter couplets, in which the author endeavours to awaken his readers to the beauties and glories of their country.

Travelling from the south-west to Chester, down through the Midlands to London, up the eastern counties to Lincoln, and then through Lancashire and Yorkshire to Northumberland and Westmorland, he describes, or at least enumerates, the principal topographical features of the country, but chiefly the rivers and rivulets, interspersing in the appropriate places, legends, fragments of history, catalogues of British saints and hermits, of great discoverers, of birds, fishes, and plants with their properties. The first part, published 1612–13, was annotated by *Selden. The word 'poly-olbion' (from the Greek) means 'having many blessings'.

POMFRET, John (1667–1702), a Bedfordshire vicar remembered for his poem *The Choice* (1700), derived from *Horace, *Satire VI,* which describes the pleasures of a quiet country estate where the author 'might live genteelly, but not great'. It enjoyed considerable success, and secured its author inclusion in Johnson's *Lives of the English Poets,* where Pomfret's choice was described as 'such a state as affords plenty and tranquillity, without exclusion of intellectual pleasures'.

POMPADOUR, Antoinette Poisson, marquise de (1721–64), mistress of Louis XV of France, an intelligent patroness of art and literature, but her political influence was less fortunate. It was she who said, 'Après nous le déluge!' The name 'pompadour' is applied to fashions, colours, etc., popular in her day.

Pompey the Great, his faire Corneliaes Tragedie, see CORNELIA.

Pompey the Little, The History of, see COVENTRY, F.

PONSONBY, Sarah, see LLANGOLLEN, THE LADIES OF.

PONTOPPIDAN, Erik (1698–1764), a Danish author and bishop of Bergen in Norway. His principal works are the *Gesta et vestigia Danorum extra Daniam* (1740), and a *Natural History of Norway* (1755), frequently mentioned on account of its description of the *kraken.

POOLE, John (?1786–1872), a dramatist of great success, who also produced poems and essays and wrote for many years for the *New Monthly Magazine.* His comedies and farces were produced at Drury Lane, Covent Garden, and the Haymarket, with C. *Kemble and other well-known actors. There were few years between 1813 and 1829 when no play of his was produced. The most successful were *Paul Pry* (1825), *'Twixt the Cup and the Lip* (1826), and *Lodgings for a Single Gentleman* (1829). Later in his life *Dickens obtained him a state pension of £100 p.a.

POOLE, Thomas (1765–1837), farmer and tanner, born at Nether Stowey; he became a close friend of *Coleridge and *Wordsworth, and assisted them both in finding homes to rent in his neighbourhood in 1796–7. Coleridge wrote 'This lime tree bower my prison' in Poole's garden, and Sara Coleridge corresponded with him for many years. Another of his friends was Sir H. *Davy. He was a man of progressive and generous spirit; Wordsworth said of him, 'he felt for all men as his brothers.'

Poor Richard's Almanack, see FRANKLIN, B.

Poor Tom, a name assumed by one who feigns madness in the *Fraternitie of Vacabondes,* and by *Edgar in Shakespeare's *King Lear* (II. iii).

Pooter, the archetypally suburban protagonist of *The Diary of a Nobody* by G. and W. Grossmith.

Popanilla (first issued as *The Voyage of Captain Popanilla*), a tale by B. *Disraeli, published 1827.

The imitative Swiftian satire follows the adventures of Popanilla from an island paradise to 'the railroad state of Vraibleusia' (i.e. England), and its capital Hubbabub (London). The social and political life of the 'aboriginal inhabitants', with their Debt, their currency debates, their pompous Economists, their greed for colonies, and their leaders (in particular *Canning and *Wellington), is derisively described.

POPE, Alexander (1688–1744), was the son of a Roman Catholic linen-draper of London. His health was ruined and his growth stunted by a severe illness at the age of 12 (probably Pott's disease, a tubercular affection of the spine.) He lived with his parents at Binfield in Windsor Forest and was largely self-educated. He showed his precocious metrical skill in his 'Pastorals' written, according to himself, when he was 16, and published in *Tonson's *Miscellany* (vol. vi) in 1709. (For Pope's quarrel with Ambrose Philips on this subject see under PHILIPS, A.) He became intimate with *Wycherley, who introduced him to London life. His *Essay on Criticism* (1711) made him known to *Addison's circle, and his *'Messiah' was published in *The Spectator* in 1712. *The Rape of the Lock* appeared in *Lintot's *Miscellanies* in the same year and was republished, enlarged, in 1714. His *Ode for Music on St Cecilia's Day* (1713), one of his rare attempts at lyric, shows that his gifts did not lie in this direction. In 1713 he also published *Windsor Forest*, which appealed to the Tories by its references to the Peace of Utrecht, and won him the friendship of *Swift. He drifted away from Addison's 'little senate' and became a member of the *Scriblerus Club, an association that included Swift, *Gay, *Arbuthnot, and others. He issued in 1715 the first volume of his translation in heroic couplets of Homer's *Iliad. This work, completed in 1720, is more *Augustan than Homeric in spirit and diction, but has nevertheless been much admired; *Coleridge thought it an 'astonishing product of matchless talent and ingenuity'. It was supplemented in 1725–6 by a translation of the *Odyssey, in which he was assisted by William Broome and Elijah Fenton. The two translations brought him financial independence. He moved in 1718 with his mother to Twickenham, where he spent the rest of his life, devoting much time to his garden and grotto; he was keenly interested in landscape gardening and the growing cult of the *picturesque.

In 1717 had appeared a collection of his works containing two poems dealing, alone among his works, with the passion of love. They are 'Verses to the Memory of an Unfortunate Lady', an elegy on a fictitious lady who had killed herself through hopeless love, and *'Eloisa to Abelard', in which Eloisa describes her inner conflicts after the loss of her lover. About this time he became strongly attached to Martha *Blount, with whom his friendship continued throughout his life, and to Lady M. W. *Montagu, whom in later years he assailed with bitterness; Lady Mary left for Turkey in July 1716 and Pope sent her 'Eloisa to Abelard' with a letter suggesting that he was passionately grieved by her absence.

Pope assisted Gay in writing the comedy *Three Hours after Marriage* (1717), but made no other attempt at drama. In 1723, four years

after Addison's death, appeared (in a miscellany called *Cytherea*) Pope's portrait of *Atticus, a satire on Addison written in 1715. An extended version appeared as 'A Fragment of a Satire' in a 1727 volume of *Miscellanies* (by Pope, Swift, Arbuthnot, and Gay), and took its final form in *An Epistle to Dr Arbuthnot* (1735). In the same *Miscellanies* volume Pope published his prose treatise *Peri Bathous, or the Art of Sinking in Poetry*, ridiculing among others Ambrose Philips, *Theobald, and J. *Dennis. In 1725 Pope published an edition of Shakespeare, the errors in which were pointed out in a pamphlet by Theobald, *Shakespeare Restored* (1726). This led to the selection of Theobald by Pope as hero of his *Dunciad, a satire on Dullness in three books, on which he had been at work for some time and of which the first volume appeared anonymously in 1728. Swift, who spent some months with Pope in Twickenham in 1726, provided much encouragement for this work, of which a further enlarged edition was published in 1729. An additional book, *The New Dunciad*, was published in 1742, prompted this time, it appears, by *Warburton. The complete *Dunciad* in four books, in which C. *Cibber replaces Theobald as hero, appeared in 1743. Influenced in part by the philosophy of his friend *Bolingbroke, Pope published a series of moral and philosophical poems, *An Essay on Man* (1733–4), consisting of four Epistles; and *Moral Essays* (1731–5), four in number; *Of the knowledge and Characters of Men*, *Of the Characters of Women*, and two on the subject *Of the Use of Riches*. A fifth epistle was added, addressed to Addison, occasioned by his dialogue on Medals. This was originally written in Addison's lifetime, c.1716. In 1733 Pope published the first of his miscellaneous satires, *Imitations of Horace*, entitled 'Satire I', a paraphrase of the first satire of the second book of Horace, in the form of a dialogue between the poet and William Fortescue, the lawyer. In it Pope defends himself against the charge of Malignity, and professes to be inspired only by love of virtue. He inserts, however, a gross attack on his former friend Lady Mary Wortley Montagu as 'Sappho'. He followed this up with his *Imitations* of Horace's Satires II, ii and I, ii ('Sober Advice from Horace'), in 1734, and of Epistles I, vi; II, ii; II, i; and I, i, in 1737. Horace's Epistle I, vii and the latter part of Satire II, vi, 'imitated in the manner of Dr Swift', appeared in 1738. The year 1735 saw the appearance of the *Epistle to Dr Arbuthnot*, the prologue to the above Satires, one of Pope's most brilliant pieces of irony and invective, mingled with autobiography. It contains the famous portraits of Addison (ll. 193–214) and Lord *Hervey, and lashes his minor critics, Dennis, Cibber, *Curll, Theobald, etc. In 1738 appeared *One Thousand Seven Hundred and Thirty Eight*, two satirical dialogues. These satires, and the 'Satires (II and IV) of Dr Donne Versified' (1735), with the New Dunciad, closed his literary career.

He was partly occupied during his later years with the publication of his earlier correspondence, which he edited and amended in such a manner as to misrepresent the literary history of the time. He also employed discreditable artifices to make it appear that it was published against his wish. Thus he procured the publication by Curll of his 'Literary Correspondence' in 1735, and then endeavoured to disavow him. He appears to have taken advantage of Swift's failing powers to saddle him with the responsibility for a similar publication in 1741.

With the growth of *Romanticism Pope's poetry was increasingly seen as artificial; *Coleridge commented that Pope's thoughts were 'translated into the language of poetry', *Hazlitt called him 'the poet not of nature but of art', and W. L. *Bowles compared his work to 'a game of cards'. M. *Arnold's famous comment, 'Dryden and Pope are not classics of our poetry, they are classics of our prose' (Essays in Criticism, 1880), summed up much 19th-cent. opinion, and it was not until *Leavis and *Empson that a serious attempt was made to rediscover Pope's richness, variety, and complexity.

Minor works by Pope that deserve mention are:

Verse: the Epistles 'To a Young Lady [Miss Blount] with the works of Voiture' (1712), to the same 'On her leaving the Town after the Coronation' (1717); 'To Mr Jervas with Dryden's translation of Fresnoy's Art of Painting' (1716) and 'To Robert, Earl of Oxford and Earl Mortimer' (1721); 'Vertumnus and Pomona', 'Sappho to Phaon', and 'The Fable of Dryope', translations from *Ovid (1712); *'January and May', 'The Wife of Bath, her Prologue', and The Temple of Fame, from *Chaucer (1709, 1714, 1715).

Prose: The Narrative of Dr Robert Norris (1713), a satirical attack on Dennis; A full and true Account of a horrid and barbarous Revenge by poison, on . . . Mr Edmund Curll (1716), an attack on Curll (to whom he had secretly administered an emetic).

The standard edn of Pope's poetry is the Twickenham Edition, under the general editorship of J. Butt (11 vols plus Index, 1940–69); see also E. *Sitwell, Alexander Pope (1930); G. Sherburn, The Early Career of Alexander Pope (1934); N. Ault, New Light on Pope (1949); P. *Quennell, Alexander Pope: the education of a Genius (1968).

Popish Plot, a plot fabricated in 1678 by Titus *Oates. He deposed at the end of September before the Middlesex magistrate Sir Edmond Berry Godfrey that it was intended to murder Charles II, place James on the throne, and suppress Protestantism. Godfrey disappeared on 12 Oct. and was found murdered on 17 Oct. The existence of the plot was widely believed and great excitement prevailed. Many persons were falsely accused and executed.

POPPER, Sir Karl Raimund (1902–), Austrian philosopher of science, born in Vienna, and originally connected with the Vienna circle, the source of logical positivism. He left Vienna for New Zealand on Hitler's rise to power, and came to England in 1946, where, in 1949, he was appointed professor of logic and scientific method at the London School of Economics. Popper asserts that a statement, if it is to count as scientific rather than merely metaphysical, must be falsifiable: such that the conditions that would make it false are clearly known. His philosophy of science claims to solve the problem of induction: the problem of extrapolating from past to future, or, more precisely, from limited evidence to a general conclusion. This work has appealed greatly to many scientists. He has also contributed to political philosophy and a defence of free will and the 'self-conscious mind'. His works include The Logic of Scientific Discovery (Logik der Forschung, 1934); The Open Society and Its Enemies (1945), and The Self and Its Brain (1977, with John C. Eccles).

POPPLE, William (1701–64), dramatist, and friend of A. *Hill, with whom he edited The Prompter (1734–6), a bi-weekly theatrical periodical (selection ed. W. Appleton and K. A. Burnim, 1966). He wrote two comedies, The Lady's Revenge (1734) and The Double Deceit: or a cure for Jealousy (1735), in which two young men, intended to marry two heiresses, conspire to avoid their fate by exchanging places with their valets. The ladies, apprised of the trick, exchange places with their maids, the pseudo-valets fall in love with the pseudo-maids, and all ends well.

Porretta, Clementina, a character in Richardson's *Sir Charles Grandison.

PORSON, Richard (1759–1808), the distinguished classical scholar, was elected Regius professor of Greek at Cambridge in 1792. He edited four plays of *Euripides (most notably Hecuba), and advanced Greek scholarship by his elucidation of Greek idiom and usage, by his study of Greek metres, and by his emendation of texts. He is also remembered for various witticisms and for contributions to *The Gentleman's Magazine, in which appeared in 1787 letters ironically praising *Hawkins's Life of Johnson and in 1788–9 his Letters to Mr Archdeacon Travis (reprinted separately 1790) on the authenticity of the text of 1 John 5: 7, 'For there are three that bear record in heaven.' There is a life by M. L. Clarke (1937).

Porteous, Captain John, see HEART OF MID-LOTHIAN, THE.

Porter, in Shakespeare's *Macbeth*; he lets *Macduff* and *Lennox* into Macbeth's castle (II. iii), and is the subject of *De Quincey's essay 'On the Knocking at the Gate'.

PORTER, Anna Maria (1780–1832), poet and novelist, whose martial tale of the French revolution, *The Hungarian Brothers* (1807), was a considerable success and went into several editions. She published *Don Sebastian* in 1809, and several other novels, as well as ballads and poems.

PORTER, Endymion (1587–1649), was groom of the bedchamber to Charles I, and the friend and patron of painters and poets. He was painted by *Van Dyck, and *Jonson, *Herrick, *D'Avenant, and *Dekker, among others, celebrated him in verse. He sat in the Long Parliament but was expelled, lived abroad in poverty, and compounded with the Parliament for a small fine in 1649.

PORTER, Jane (1776–1850), sister of A. M. *Porter, published in 1803 *Thaddeus of Warsaw*, which was immensely successful and led to friendship with one of its heroes, the Polish General Kosciuszko. In 1810 she published *The Scottish Chiefs*, a story of William Wallace, which was also successful, and was translated into German and Russian. *The Pastor's Fireside* (1815) is a story of the later Stuarts. Her tragedy *Switzerland*, produced in 1819 with *Kean and C. *Kemble, was a disastrous failure. Among several other volumes she produced *Sir Edward Seaward's Narrative*, on Caribbean exploration, a work which purported to be a genuine diary but which was almost certainly largely fictitious. (See HISTORICAL NOVEL.)

PORTER, Katherine Ann (1890–1980), Texan-born short story writer and novelist whose collection of short stories include *Flowering Judas* (1930), *Pale Horse, Pale Rider* (1939), and *The Leaning Tower* (1944). Her novel *Ship of Fools* (1962) is a heavily allegorical treatment of a voyage from Mexico to Germany on the eve of Hitler's rise to power.

PORTER, Peter Neville Frederick (1929–   ), poet, born and educated in Brisbane, where he worked as a journalist before coming to England in 1951. Since then he has worked as clerk, bookseller, and as copywriter in an advertising agency (in the company of G. *Ewart, P. *Redgrove, and other poets), before becoming a full-time writer, broadcaster, and critic in 1968. He was briefly associated with the *Group in the 1960s, and the work in his early collections (*Once Bitten, Twice Bitten*, 1961; *Poems, Ancient and Modern*, 1964; *The Last of England*, 1970) provides a sharply satiric portrait of London in the 'swinging sixties', with a gallery of fops, publishers, concrete poets, film-makers, etc. In the 1970s, his work became more meditative, complex, and allusive, though no less colloquial and urbane; its learned references to a vast range of subjects, from Italian baroque to classical mythology, opera, and German Romanticism, add both richness and obscurity. *The Cost of Seriousness* (1978) and *English Subtitles* (1981) introduce a new and sombre exploration of the poet's conflicting responsibilities to his art and to others. *After Martial* (1972) is a volume of translations. His *Collected Poems* were published in 1983.

PORTER, William Sydney, see HENRY, O.

Porthos, see THREE MUSKETEERS, THE.

Portia, (1) the heroine of Shakespeare's *The Merchant of Venice*; (2) in his *Julius Caesar*, the wife of Brutus.

Portrait of a Lady, The, a novel by H. *James, published 1881.

This is one of the best of James's early works, in which he presents various types of American character transplanted into a European environment. The story centres in Isabel Archer, the 'Lady', an attractive American girl. Around her we have the placid old American banker, Mr Touchett; his hard repellent wife; his ugly, invalid, witty, charming son Ralph, whom England has thoroughly assimilated; and the crude, brilliant, indomitably American journalist Henrietta Stackpole. Isabel refuses the offer of marriage of a typical English peer, the excellent Lord Warburton, and of a bulldog-like New Englander, Caspar Goodwood, to fall a victim, under the influence of the slightly sinister Madame Merle (another cosmopolitan American), to a worthless and spiteful dilettante, Gilbert Osmond, who marries her for her fortune and ruins her life; but to whom she remains loyal in spite of her realization of his vileness.

Portrait of the Artist as a Young Dog (1940), a collection of stories by Dylan *Thomas.

Portrait of the Artist as a Young Man, A, an autobiographical novel by J. *Joyce, first published in *The Egoist*, 1914–15.

It describes the development of Stephen Dedalus (who reappears in *Ulysses* in a slightly different incarnation) from his early boyhood, through bullying at school and an adolescent crisis of faith inspired partly by the famous 'hellfire sermon' preached by Father Arnall (ch. 3) and partly by the guilt of his own precocious sexual adventures, to student days and a gradual sense of his own destiny as poet, patriot, and unbeliever, who paradoxically must leave his own land in order to 'encounter . . . the reality of experience and to forge in the smithy of my soul the uncreated conscience of my race'. Relatively conventional in form, the novel foreshadows many of the themes and verbal complexities of *Ulysses*.

Port-Royal, originally a Cistercian nunnery near Chevreuse (Seine-et-Oise, France), became in 1636 a place of retreat for pious and learned men holding the *Jansenist doctrine, where they devoted themselves to prayer, study, and manual employments. It became the headquarters of Jansenism and the centre of a system of education, and exercised a wide influence, notably on *Pascal and *Racine. The institution was persecuted by the Jesuits, and finally destroyed by Louis XIV in 1710. A history of Port-Royal was published by *Sainte-Beuve in 1840–59.

Positivist Philosophy, see COMTE.

Posthumus Leonatus, the hero of Shakespeare's *Cymbeline* and husband of *Imogen; 'The fit and apt construction' of his name, as the Soothsayer partially explains, is that he was the last-born of his father Sicilius Leonatus and his mother, who died in labour.

Post-Impressionism, a term invented by R. *Fry to cover the work of painters, particularly *Cézanne, Gauguin, and Van Gogh, who were opposed to the aims of *Impressionism.

'Pot of Basil, The', see ISABELLA.

Pott, Mr, in Dickens's *Pickwick Papers*, the editor of the 'Eatanswill Gazette'.

POTTER, (Helen) Beatrix (1866–1943), born in Kensington to wealthy parents and never sent to school, grew up a lonely child. She taught herself to draw and paint small natural objects and as a young woman did serious work dissecting, drawing, and classifying fungi. She invented a cipher so elaborate that the half-million words she wrote in it were not deciphered until Leslie Linder broke the code and published *The Journal of Beatrix Potter* (1966). In a letter to the son of her former governess in 1893 she began *The Tale of Peter Rabbit*, and other books began in the same way. Copied out and more fully illustrated, *Peter Rabbit* was published at her own expense in 1901 and *The Tailor of Gloucester* in 1902. Warne then took over publication and in 1903 *Squirrel Nutkin* was her first great success. Her farm at Sawrey in the Lake District, which she bought in 1905, became the background for six of her books. In 1913 she married William Heelis, a Lakeland solicitor, and for the rest of her life devoted herself almost entirely to her farms and the new National Trust. *Johnny Town-Mouse* (1918) was the last of her books in the old style; those later written for the US, such as *The Fairy Caravan* (1928), are of little interest. A biography by Margaret Lane appeared in 1968.

POTTER, Dennis Christopher George (1935–), playwright, born in the Forest of Dean, the son of a miner. He was educated at Oxford, where he became involved in left-wing politics, and subsequently worked as journalist and critic; *The Glittering Coffin* (1960) is an analysis of the Labour Party and the political climate of the time. He has written fiction, stage plays, screenplays, and adapted works for television (notably Angus *Wilson's *Late Call*, 1975), but is best known for his own television plays, which show an original and inventive use of the medium. These include two plays dealing with the career of an aspiring working-class, Oxford-educated politician, *Vote, Vote, Vote for Nigel Barton* (1965) and *Stand up, Nigel Barton* (1965), published together in 1968; *Pennies from Heaven*, a six-part serial (1978, pub. 1981); and *Blue Remembered Hills* (1979, a tragic evocation of childhood). *Brimstone and Treacle* (1978) was first performed on stage after being banned for television performance.

POTTER, Stephen Meredith (1900–69), writer, editor, and radio producer, whose book *The Theory and Practice of Gamesmanship; or the Art of Winning Games without Actually Cheating* (1947) had a great vogue and added a new word and concept to the language; he followed it with *Some Notes on Lifemanship* (1950), *One-Upmanship* (1952), and *Supermanship* (1958). His other works include an edition of Sara *Coleridge's letters to T. *Poole, published as *Minnow among Tritons* (1934).

Poulter's measure, a fanciful name for a metre consisting of lines of 12 and 14 syllables alternately. Poulter = poulterer.
'Poulter's measure, which giveth xii for one dozen, and xiiij for another.'
(*Gascoigne, *The Steele Glas*)

POUND, Ezra Weston Loomis (1885–1972), American poet born in Idaho, of Quaker parents; he studied at Hamilton College, Pennsylvania, where he met Hilda *Doolittle. He taught briefly in Indiana, but was asked to resign, and in 1908 came to Europe and published his first volume of poems, *A Lume Spento* (1908), at his own expense in Italy; he then moved to London, where he lectured for a time in medieval Romance literature at the Regent Street Polytechnic and soon became prominent in literary circles. He published several other volumes of verse, including *Personae* (1909), *Canzoni* (1911), *Ripostes* (1912), and *Lustra* (1916). Together with F. S. Flint, R. *Aldington, and Hilda Doolittle he founded the *Imagist school of poets, advocating the use of free rhythms, concreteness, and concision of language and imagery; in 1914 he edited *Des Imagistes: An Anthology*. Pound also championed the *Modernist work of avant-garde writers and artists like *Joyce, W. *Lewis, *Gaudier-Brzeska, and T. S. *Eliot, whom he was always ready to assist critically and materially; Eliot, who described him as 'more responsible for the XXth Century revolution in poetry than any other individual', greatly valued his advice, as may be seen from the history of the composition of *The Waste Land*. Further volumes of poetry include *Quia Pauper Amavi* (1919, which contains 'Homage to Sextus Propertius') and *Hugh Selwyn Mauberley* (1920). Pound was now increasingly turning away from the constrictions of Imagism, and finding freedom partly through translations; his early volumes had contained adaptations from Provençal and early Italian, a version of the Old English *The Seafarer*, and in 1915 *Cathay*, translations from the Chinese of Li Po, via a transliteration. Pound was thus moving towards the rich, grandly allusive, multi-cultural world of the *Cantos*, his most ambitious achievement; the first three Cantos appeared in 1917 in *Poetry*. In 1920 Pound left London for Paris with his English wife Dorothy Shakespear, where he lived until 1924, finding a new literary scene figuring Gertrude *Stein, *Hemingway, etc.; in 1925 he settled permanently in Rapallo, where he continued to work on the Cantos, which appeared intermittently over the next decades until the appearance of the final *Drafts and Fragments of Cantos CX to XCVII* (1970).

In Italy Pound became increasingly preoccupied with economics, embraced Social Credit theories, and was persuaded that 'Usura', or credit capitalism, lay at the root of all social and spiritual evils. (See Canto XLV for his violent attack on usury.) His own interpretations of these theories led him into anti-Semitism and at least partial support for Mussolini's social programme. During the Second World War he broadcast over the Italian radio: in 1945 he was arrested at Genoa, then sent to a US Army Disciplinary Training Centre near Pisa, a period which produced the much-admired *Pisan Cantos* (1948). He was then moved to Washington, found unfit to plead, and confined to a mental institution; he was released in 1958 and returned to Italy, where he died.

Inevitably, Pound's literary reputation was obscured by the tragedy of his last decades, and also by the difficulty of the work itself, which resides principally in its astonishingly wide range of reference and assimilation of cultures; *Hugh Selwyn Mauberley*, despite the advocacy of Eliot and *Leavis (who described it as 'the summit of Mr Pound's superbly supple and varied art'), never quite reached the 'popular classic' status of *The Waste Land*, and the *Cantos* remain formidable both in style and content. As Eliot has said, Pound suffers from being seen as 'objectionably modern' and 'objectionably antiquarian' at the same time. Nevertheless, he is widely accepted both as a great master of traditional verse forms and as the man who regenerated the poetic idiom of his day.

See *Literary Essays of Ezra Pound* (1954; collected critical writings, with an introduction by T. S. Eliot); *Letters of Ezra Pound 1907–1941* (1950, ed. D. D. Paige); N. Stock, *The Life of Ezra Pound* (1970).

Poundtext, the Revd Peter, in Scott's *Old Mortality*, a Presbyterian divine, the 'indulged' pastor of Milnwood's parish.

POUSSIN, Nicolas (1593/4–1665), French painter, who worked mainly in Rome. His early works are romantic treatments of subjects from *Ovid and *Tasso; later he developed an austerely classical style. In the early 18th cent. Poussin, an unusually learned artist, was already deeply admired by English men of letters, and many of his greatest works were in English collections. *Dryden compared the nobility of a picture by Poussin with the unity of classical tragedy (1695). Sir J. *Reynolds wrote movingly of the artist: 'A mind thrown back 2000 years and, as it were, naturalized in Antiquity'. James *Thomson's descriptions of landscape are indebted to Poussin and, in the second half of the century, poets, travellers, and landscape gardeners frequently contrast the nobility of Poussin's landscapes with the wildness of *Rosa and the beauty of *Claude. In the late 18th cent. Poussin's most severe works were most admired. *Hazlitt wrote many passionate descriptions of his painting; *Keats was inspired by the lyrical Ovidian pictures; *Ruskin described the *Triumph of Flora* (Paris, Louvre) as 'a Keats-like revel of body and soul of most heavenly creatures'. The picture most admired by literary men was Poussin's second treatment of the theme 'Et in Arcadia Ego', *The Shepherds of Arcady*, c.1650–5 (Paris, Louvre), a picture which fascinated later writers and painters. It has been suggested that *Gray thought of it when he wrote his *Elegy* (1751); *The Monument in Arcadia: a Dramatic Poem* (1773) by the minor poet and dilettante George Keate (1729–97) derives from it. English admiration paused with *Ruskin, who loathed Poussin, but revived in the late 19th cent. when he was most admired for his formal brilliance. *Powell's image of *A Dance to the Music of Time* was inspired by Poussin's picture in the Wallace Collection, London.

Povey, Samuel, a character in Bennett's *The Old Wives' Tale*.

POWELL, Anthony Dymoke (1905–), novelist, whose initial reputation as a satirist and light comedian rests on five pre-war books, beginning with *Afternoon Men* (1931) which maps a characteristically seedy section of pleasure-loving, party-going London: a territory contiguous with E. *Waugh's, bounded at opposite extremes by N. *Mitford and by Powell's Oxford contemporary and friend, Henry *Green.

After the war he embarked on a more

ambitious sequence of twelve novels, *A Dance to the Music of Time* (named after *Poussin's painting, with which the sequence shares a certain classical severity as well as an architectural command of structural rhythm). Starting with *A Question of Upbringing* (1951) and ending with *Hearing Secret Harmonies* (1975), the whole is framed and distanced through the eyes of a narrator, Nicholas Jenkins, whose generation grew up in the shadow of the First World War to find their lives dislocated by the Second. Jenkins's canvas, following the perspectives of time rather than space, is hospitable and broad, especially rich in literary and artistic hangers-on, stiffened by a solid contingent from society, politics, and the City, enlivened and sometimes convulsed by eccentrics, derelicts, and drop-outs of all classes and conditions from the socialist peer Erridge to a shifty crew of baleful, semi-fraudulent gurus and seers. Against these looms Kenneth Widmerpool, one of the most memorable characters of 20th-cent. fiction, whose ruthless pursuit of power, which carries him from innately ludicrous beginnings to a position of increasingly formidable, eventually sinister, authority, is the chief of many threads binding this higgledy-piggledy, jampacked, panoramic view of England.

The narrative is part humorous, part melancholy, and at times so funny that readers have tended if anything to underrate its sombre, even tragic, sweep and range. Powell's naturalism takes on the almost surrealistic overtones implicit in Jenkins's rule of thumb: 'All human beings, driven as they are at different speeds by the same Furies, are at close range equally extraordinary.' Powell's memoirs, which shed considerable light on the creation of the characters of his fictional world, were published in four vols, 1976–82, under the general title *To Keep the Ball Rolling*.

Power, Paula, a character in Hardy's *A Laodicean*.

Power and the Glory, The, a novel by G. *Greene, published 1940.

Set in Mexico (which Greene had visited in 1938) at a time of religious persecution in the name of revolution, it describes the desperate last wanderings of a whisky priest as outlaw in his own state, who, despite a sense of his own worthlessness (he drinks, and has fathered a bastard daughter), is determined to continue to function as priest until captured. He is contrasted with Padre Jose, a priest who has accepted marriage and humiliation; with 'the gringo', bank robber, murderer, and materialist, also on the run; and with the lieutenant, portrayed as an angry idealist and 'a good man', who pursues the priest and corners him when he is drawn back (by the Judas-figure of a half-caste) to offer the last rites to the dying gringo, just as he has

reached safety over the border. His execution (and martyrdom?) is witnessed by the grotesque expatriate dentist Mr Tench, and the final episode indicates that the church will survive its persecution. Greene describes it as his only novel 'written to a thesis'; it was condemned as 'paradoxical' by the Holy Office, but not publicly. Like many of Greene's works, it combines a conspicuous Christian theme and symbolism with the elements of a thriller.

POWYS, John Cowper (1872–1963), the son of a country parson, brother of Llewelyn and Theodore *Powys, was brought up in the Dorset–Somerset countryside which was to become of great importance in his later writing, even though he spent much of his life in the US. Educated at Sherborne and Corpus Christi College, Cambridge, he became a prolific writer, including poetry and many essays on philosophy, religion, literature, and the arts of living among his publications, as well as a remarkable *Autobiography* (1934). It is, however, for his highly individual novels that he is chiefly remembered; the first, *Wood and Stone* (1915, NY; 1917, London) contains many hints of the powerful characters and intense relationships, the attachment to place, and the arresting oddity of personal names which were more fully developed in later works. *Rodmoor* (1916) was followed by *Ducdame* (1925), one of the simplest of his novels, with a single plot, relating a hapless Dorset love story. His first major novel, and major success, was *Wolf Solent* (1929), a crowded work, set again in the West Country, of many interweaving stories, but chiefly concerning Wolf and Gerda, and the destructive pull of opposites. *A Glastonbury Romance* (1932, NY; 1933, London), probably the best-known of Powys's novels, is a work on a huge scale, in which *Glastonbury and its legends, both Christian and pagan, exert a supernatural influence on the life of the town—on the religious revival led by Johnny Geard, on the hard commercial interests of Phil Crow, on the Communist workers, and on the complex loves, both sacred and sexual, of the town's inhabitants. *Weymouth Sands* (1934, NY) had, because of a libel action, to be recast as *Jobber Skald* (1935), but was restored and republished as *Weymouth Sands* in 1963. Against a sombre background of Portland and the sea, the human struggle centres on Jobber, his love for Perdita and his hatred of Dog Cattistock, and on the final relinquishing of dream in favour of the possible. *Maiden Castle* (1936, NY; 1937, London), set in Dorchester and among the excavations of the fort, follows the interlocking loves of several couples, no longer young; dominated by Dud No-man, and the girl Wizzie, the lives of the protagonists move towards disillusion and endurance. Most of the later novels, written after Powys had settled in Wales, share an extravagance of subject and style and strong elements of the supernatural. In *Morwyn* (1937), cast as a letter from the narrator to his son, the theme of man's cruelty, to his fellows and to animals, is carried through various meetings with characters from history. *The Inmates* (1952), a story on the theme of madness, was followed by the most successful of the historical novels, *Owen Glendower* (1940, NY; 1941, London), describing the confused events and passions surrounding Owen and his cousin Rhisiart. Set in the dark ages of Wales, *Porius* (1951) presents a fraught world of giants, Mithraic cults, and Arthurian legend filling the void the Romans have left. *The Bronze Head* (1956), on the subject of Roger *Bacon, was followed in 1954 by *Atlantis*, containing Powys's most extreme flights of imagination, in which Odysseus, returned from Troy, sets out again through a world of talking giants, heroes, animals, and inanimate objects, to discover the continent of America, where he settles.

Much controversy centres on Powys's stature as a writer. Some regard him as unjustly neglected, an arresting and major novelist, while others find his talent spurious and verbose. See *The Brothers Powys* (1983), a life of all three brothers by R. P. Graves.

POWYS, Llewelyn (1884–1939), brother of John Cowper and Theodore *Powys was educated at Sherborne and Corpus Christi College, Cambridge, and shared his brothers' individuality of temperament. He was a prolific essayist and journalist: the best of his many books and collections are generally thought to be *Skin for Skin* (1925), a sombre account of the course of his tuberculosis and the idyllic Dorset interludes when it seemed to be cured; *Impassioned Clay* (1931), an intensely personal account of the human predicament, the Epicurean ethic, and the confrontation with death; and *Love and Death* (1939), an eloquent 'imaginary autobiography', on the theme of his lost first love and his approaching death. Apart from these works, and among many others, was a novel, *Apples be Ripe* (1930), and two volumes, *Earth Memories* (1934) and *Dorset Essays* (1935), the essays in which had originally achieved wide circulation in London newspapers. *Damnable Opinions* (1935) presented many of the radical, iconoclastic views he shared with his brothers.

POWYS, T(heodore) F(rancis) (1875–1953), brother of John Cowper and Llewelyn *Powys, was sent away from the West Country to school in East Anglia, where he later farmed. But in 1902 he returned to Dorset and settled in East Chaldon, whose local landscape became the significant background to almost all his novels and stories. His first book, *Soliloquies of a Hermit* (1916), a series of brief meditations, gave notice of a highly original, idiosyncratic mind.

Volumes of short stories, including *The Left Leg* and *Black Bryony* (both 1923) and *Mr Tasker's Gods* and *Mark Only* (both 1924), introduced the characters of Tinker Jar and Mr Dottery (who were to reappear many times), as well as many grotesque individuals, and dealt in Powys's recurring themes of cruelty, innocence, and the supernatural. *Innocent Birds* (1926), stories of eccentric village simpletons, was followed in 1927 by the novel for which Powys is best remembered, *Mr Weston's Good Wine*. In this vivid allegory Mr Weston (or God) comes to the worldly village of Folly Down, selling from his old van his vintages of Love and Death; after his departure he leaves no paradise, but the good are happier, and the evil (such as Mrs Vosper, the procuress) are vanquished. *Fables* (1929), in which Powys's beliefs are most clearly exposed, was followed by his other major novel, *Unclay* (1931), in which John Death (or the archangel Michael) arrives in Dodder with instructions from God to 'unclay', or kill, various people; however, he loses his instructions, is unsettled by the mysterious Tinker Jar, and falls in love with a village girl. The most complex of Powys's works, it interlocks the stories of several bizarre characters, innocent, evil, and mad, whose lives and loves are altered by Death's arrival. Other volumes of short stories, including the melancholy *Bottle's Path* (1946) and the sunnier *God's Eyes A-Twinkle* (1947), followed, but Powys almost stopped writing about 1940.

Poyser, Martin and Mrs, characters in G. Eliot's *Adam Bede*.

Practical Criticism, a term given currency by I. A. *Richards's experiment in *Practical Criticism: A Study in Literary Judgement* (1929) and thence spread through the academic literary world to describe a certain method of literary criticism, which was to form a quasi-scientific foundation for the *New Criticism; for an account of the experiment, see under RICHARDS, I. A. The term 'practical' was clearly chosen deliberately to distinguish this approach from the theoretical; in his Introduction Richards describes his book as 'a piece of field work in comparative ideology', but he moves on from the purely descriptive to the prescriptive, and his work became a textbook for the sharpening of critical appreciation and attention.

PRAED, Winthrop Mackworth (1802–39), was educated at Eton, where he founded the *Etonian*, and at Trinity College, Cambridge. He was called to the bar, then went into Parliament, and was appointed secretary to the Board of Control in 1834. He is remembered principally as a humorous poet and composer of elegant *vers de société*; 'The County Ball', 'A Letter of Advice', 'Stanzas on seeing the Speaker Asleep', and 'The Vicar' are characteristic examples of his light verse. Like *Hood, with whom he is often compared, he sometimes uses humour to clothe a grim subject, as in 'The Red Fisherman'. He also wrote verse epistles, some to his sister, and historical ballads similar to those of his Cambridge friend *Macaulay, e.g. 'Sir Nicholas at Marston Moor'. His verse was published largely in periodicals and annuals, and his early death from consumption prevented him from taking an interest in more formal publication, but his inoffensive satire, gentle wit, and fluent metrical variations assured him a more lasting readership; his *Poems*, with a memoir by his friend Derwent Coleridge, appeared in 1864. See also D. Hudson, *A Poet in Parliament* (1939).

Praeterita, see RUSKIN, J.

Pragmatism, in philosophy, the doctrine that the test of the value of any assertion lies in its practical consequences, i.e. in its practical bearing upon human interests and purposes. See JAMES, W.

Prancing Nigger, see FIRBANK, R.

PRATT, Samuel Jackson (1749–1814), who wrote as 'Courtney Melmoth', was a failed actor who became a voluminous and popular writer of poetry, essays, biography, travel, letters, plays, and anthologies. A play, *The Fair Circassian* (1781, based on *Hawkesworth's *Almoran and Hamet*), was a success, but his novel *Shenstone-Green* (1779), together with his many other novels of *Sentiment, made no permanent mark, and his work in general was much criticized, by *Byron and *Lamb among others.

Prayer, The Book of Common, see COMMON PRAYER.

PRAZ, Mario (1896–1982), Italian critic and scholar, born in Rome, who spent ten years in England, in Liverpool and Manchester (1924–34), as senior lecturer, then professor, of Italian studies, before returning to Rome as professor of English literature. He wrote on many aspects of English literature and the connections between the English and Italian traditions; his best-known work is *La Carne, La Morte e Il Diavolo nella Letteratura Romantica* (1930; published in a translation by Angus Davidson as *The Romantic Agony*, 1933) in which he explores the legacy of de *Sade, the perverse and pathological elements in *Poe, *Swinburne, *Wilde, etc., and the cult of the Fatal Woman. His other works include *The Flaming Heart* (1958; essays on *Crashaw, *Machiavelli, T. S. *Eliot, and others) and *La Casa della fama* (1952; as *The House of Life*, 1958).

Précieuse, the French equivalent of the English *Blue Stocking. The circle of the Marquise de *Rambouillet was mocked by *Molière in *Les Précieuses ridicules*.

Precious Bane, see WEBB, M.

Prelude, The: or, *Growth of a Poet's Mind*, an autobiographical poem in blank verse by *Wordsworth, addressed to *Coleridge, and begun in 1798–9; a complete draft in 13 books was finished in 1805, but it was several times remodelled, and published posthumously in its final version in 1850, with its present title, suggested by Mary Wordsworth. The full text, showing the work of Wordsworth on it in his later years (which increased the number of books to 14, toned down some of the earlier political views, tidied up structure, syntax, etc.) was published by de *Selincourt in 1926. The poem was originally intended as an introduction to 'The Recluse', a vast work which Wordsworth planned but never completed (see EXCURSION, THE).

The Prelude is thus composed of passages written at various periods, and sometimes with another purpose; in the first book Wordsworth describes his search for a conventional epic theme, and moves from this to an evocation of his own childhood which leads him less by logic than by imaginative association to his central subject, his own development as a poet and the forces that shaped his imagination. Although profoundly autobiographical, the poem does not proceed in terms of strict chronology; it deals with infancy, school days, Cambridge, his walking tour through the Alps, his political awakening in France, and consequent horrors, etc., but (for example) the passage describing the 'visionary dreariness' of a highly charged moment in his early boyhood is delayed until Book XI ('Imagination, How Impaired and Restored') and the landscape there described is immediately linked in the immediate past with his sister Dorothy and Coleridge, both of whom are intermittently addressed throughout the work. The tone is similarly flexible and variable; conversational and informal in some passages, narrative and naturalistic in others, it rises at points to an impassioned loftiness. A constant theme throughout is Wordsworth's sense of himself as a chosen being, with an overriding duty to his poetic vocation. Wordsworth was aware that his choice of subject (highly original in its day, when the confessional mode in poetry was little developed) might be construed as 'self-conceit', but he insisted that he wrote thus through 'real humility' and 'diffidence'. Apart from its poetic quality, the work is remarkable for its psychological insight into the significance of childhood experience, a theme dear to *Romanticism, but rarely treated with such power and precision.

Premium, Mr, the name taken by Sir Oliver Surface in Sheridan's *The School for Scandal*.

Pre-Raphaelite Brotherhood, a group of artists, poets, and critics—J. E. *Millais, D. G. *Rossetti, W. Holman *Hunt, W. M. *Rossetti, T. *Woolner, Frederick George Stephens (1828–1907), and James Collinson (?1825–81)

—who first met as a group, led by the first three, in 1848. Various derivations have been assigned to the term 'Pre-Raphaelite', which indicated the group's admiration for the Italian quattrocento and its defiance of the authority both of *Raphael as a master and of 19th-cent. academic painting. The initials 'P.R.B.' first appeared on their work in the RA exhibition of 1849. As its periodical *The Germ* (1850) suggests, the movement was strongly literary, and some of its most striking paintings were inspired by *Keats (see Millais's *Isabella*), *Dante, Shakespeare, and *Tennyson. Common aspirations of the group included fidelity to nature (manifested in clarity, brightness, detailed first-hand observation of flora, etc.), and moral seriousness, in some expressed in religious themes or symbolic mystical iconography. Many of the subjects were medieval as well as literary, and the movement (much influenced by *Ruskin, who became its champion) saw itself in part as a revolt against the ugliness of modern life and dress. Its revolutionary aims thus became in some of its products inextricably mingled with nostalgia. Artists connected with the PRB include Ford Madox Brown, W. B. *Scott, William Dyce, Henry Wallis, Arthur Hughes, *Burne-Jones, and *De Morgan. In literary terms, the movement's most important recruits were perhaps W. *Morris and, more indirectly, *Pater. The brotherhood dissolved in the 1850s, and the original members went their different ways, some achieving considerable commercial success, but its influence was enduring, and the term 'Pre-Raphaelite' has come to denote a distinctive style of appearance, décor, design, etc.

PRESCOTT, William Hickling (1796–1859), born at Salem, Massachusetts, and educated at Harvard, had his sight affected by an accident while at college, but nevertheless devoted himself, with the help of a reader, to the study of ancient and modern literature. His first work, *The History of Ferdinand and Isabella*, appeared in 1838. It was followed by the *History of the Conquest of Mexico* (1843) and the *History of the Conquest of Peru* (1847). The first two volumes of his unfinished *History of Philip II, King of Spain* appeared in 1855, the third in 1858.

Present Discontents, *Thoughts on the cause of the*, a political treatise by E. *Burke, published 1770.

The occasion of this work was the turbulence that had attended and followed the expulsion of *Wilkes from Parliament after his election for Middlesex, and in it Burke expounds for the first time his constitutional creed. He attributes the convulsions in the country to the control of Parliament by the cabal known as the 'King's friends', a system of favouritism essentially at variance with the constitution. Burke considers

in detail the Wilkes case, of which the importance lies in its being a test whether the favour of the people or of the court is the surer road to positions of trust. He dismisses various remedies that have been proposed, as endangering the constitution, which 'stands on a nice equipoise'. He thinks the first requirement is the restoration of the right of free election, and looks for further safeguards in the 'interposition of the body of the people itself' to secure decent attention to public interests, and in the restoration of party government.

Present State of the Nation, *Observations on a late publication intituled the*, a political treatise by E. *Burke, published 1769.

This was Burke's first controversial publication on political matters. It is a reply to an anonymous pamphlet attributed to George Grenville, in which the decision of the Grenville administration to tax America was defended on the ground that the charges left by the war had made this course necessary. Burke reviews the economic condition of England and France, and defends the repeal of the Stamp Act by the Rockingham administration for the reason that 'politics should be adjusted, not to human reasonings, but to human nature', and that 'people must be governed in a manner agreeable to their temper and disposition'.

PRESTON, Thomas (1537–98), was a fellow of King's College, Cambridge, master of Trinity Hall, and vice-chancellor of Cambridge, 1589–90. He is thought to have been the Thomas Preston who wrote *A lamentable Tragedie, mixed full of plesant mirth, containing the life of Cambises king of Percia* (1569, see CAMBYSES).

Pretty-man, Prince, in Buckingham's *The Rehearsal*, 'sometimes a fisher's son, sometimes a prince', falls asleep while making love to Cloris, his mistress.

PRÉVOST, Antoine-François, l'Abbé (1696–1763), French novelist. Successively Jesuit novice, professional soldier, Benedictine priest, Protestant convert, and literary hack, he is remembered today for one novel, *Manon Lescaut* (1731), the story of a mutually destructive passion between a refined but weak nobleman (des Grieux) and a bewitching demi-mondaine. Although classical in form, the novel was already romantic in substance, and acquired a huge readership. Prévost translated *Richardson's *Pamela* (1742), *Clarissa* (1751), and *Grandison* (1755–8).

Price, Fanny, a character in J. Austen's *Mansfield Park*.

PRICE, Richard (1723–91), a Dissenting minister who became, with his friend Joseph *Priestley, one of the original members of the Unitarian Society in 1791; he was from 1758 minister at Newington Green, which had been a centre of Dissent for many years, where he influenced many younger writers, including S. *Rogers and M. *Wollstonecraft. He published in 1756 his best-known work, *A Review of the Principal Questions in Morals*, in which he questions *Hutcheson's doctrine of 'moral sense', and argues that the rightness and wrongness of an action belong to it intrinsically. (See BUTLER, J., with whose natural theology and views on conscience he was in sympathy.) He was a close friend of *Franklin, and supported the cause of American independence; he also supported the French revolution, and his sermon delivered on 4 Nov. 1789, celebrating 'the ardour for liberty' of the French, provoked Burke to write his *Reflections on the *Revolution in France*.

PRICE, Uvedale, see Picturesque.

Pride and Prejudice, a novel by J. *Austen, published 1813. It was originally a youthful work entitled 'First Impressions' and was refused by Cadell, a London publisher, in 1797.

Mr and Mrs Bennet live with their five daughters at Longbourn in Hertfordshire. In the absence of a male heir, the property is due to pass by entail to a cousin, William Collins. Through the patronage of the haughty Lady Catherine de Bourgh, Collins has been presented with a living near Rosings, the Kentish seat of Lady Catherine. Charles Bingley, a rich young bachelor, takes Netherfield, a house near Longbourn, bringing with him his two sisters and his friend Fitzwilliam Darcy, nephew of Lady Catherine. Bingley and Jane, the eldest of the Bennet girls, very soon fall in love. Darcy, though attracted to the next sister, the lively and spirited Elizabeth, greatly offends her by his supercilious behaviour at a ball. This dislike is increased by the account given her by George Wickham, a dashing young militia officer (and son of the late steward of the Darcy property), of the unjust treatment he has met with at Darcy's hands. The aversion is further intensified when Darcy and Bingley's two sisters, disgusted with the vulgarity of Mrs Bennet and her two youngest daughters, effectively separate Bingley from Jane.

Meanwhile the fatuous Mr Collins, urged to marry by Lady Catherine (for whom he shows the most grovelling and obsequious respect), and thinking to remedy the hardship caused to the Bennet girls by the entail, proposes to Elizabeth. When firmly rejected he promptly transfers his affections to Charlotte Lucas, a friend of Elizabeth's, who accepts him. Staying with the newly married couple in their parsonage, Elizabeth again encounters Darcy, who is visiting Lady Catherine. Captivated by her in spite of himself, Darcy proposes to her in terms which do not conceal the violence the proposal does to his self-esteem. Elizabeth indignantly rejects him, on the grounds of his overweening pride,

the part he has played in separating Jane from Bingley, and his alleged treatment of Wickham. Greatly mortified, Darcy in a letter justifies the separation of his friend and Jane, and makes it clear that Wickham is, in fact, an unprincipled adventurer.

On an expedition to the north of England with her uncle and aunt, Mr and Mrs Gardiner, Elizabeth visits Pemberley, Darcy's seat in Derbyshire, believing Darcy to be absent. However, Darcy appears, welcomes the visitors, and introduces them to his sister. His manner, though still grave, is now gentle and attentive. At this point news reaches Elizabeth that her youngest sister Lydia has eloped with Wickham. With considerable help from Darcy, the fugitives are traced, their marriage is arranged, and (again through Darcy) they are suitably provided for. Bingley and Jane are reunited and become engaged. In spite, and indeed in consequence, of the insolent intervention of Lady Catherine, Darcy and Elizabeth also become engaged. The story ends with both their marriages, an indication of their subsequent happiness, and an eventual reconciliation with Lady Catherine.

Jane Austen regarded Elizabeth Bennet as her favourite among all her heroines.

PRIESTLEY, J(ohn) B(oynton) (1894–1984), was born in Bradford, the son of a schoolmaster, and worked as junior clerk in a wool office before serving in the infantry in the First World War; he then took a degree at Trinity Hall, Cambridge, and in 1922 settled in London, where he quickly made a name as journalist and critic. His first major popular success as a novelist was with the high-spirited, rambling *The Good Companions* (1929), an account of theatrical adventures on the road, which was followed by the grimmer, somewhat self-consciously *'Realist' novel of London life, *Angel Pavement* (1930). His many other novels, which vary greatly in scope, include *Bright Day* (1946), *Festival at Farbridge* (1951), *Lost Empires* (1965), and *The Image Men* (1968). Priestley also wrote some 50 plays and dramatic adaptations; amongst the best known are his 'Time' plays, influenced by the theories of J. W. *Dunne (*Dangerous Corner*, 1932; *I have been here before*, 1937; *Time and the Conways*, 1937), his psychological mystery drama *An Inspector Calls* (1947), and his West Riding farce *When We Are Married* (1938). He also published dozens of miscellaneous works, ranging from *English Journey* (1934), an account of his own travels through England, to collections of his popular and influential wartime broadcasts (*Britain Speaks*, 1940; *All England Listened*, 1968); from the ambitious, *Jungian *Literature and Western Man* (1960) to informal social histories and commentaries, many of which attempt to define the Englishness of the English, such as *The*

Edwardians (1970) and *The English* (1973). He also wrote *Journey Down a Rainbow* (1955) with his wife, Jacquetta *Hawkes, describing travels in New Mexico; and several volumes of auto-biography, including *Margin Released* (1962) and *Instead of the Trees* (1977). He was awarded the Order of Merit in 1977.

Priestley's output was so vast and varied that it is hard to single out his unique qualities. He consciously cultivated various poses—of grumbling patriot, cosmopolitan Yorkshireman, professional amateur, cultured Philistine, reactionary Radical, etc. He much admired H. G. *Wells (whose spirited disregard of the 'mandarin conventions' of the literary novel he applauded), and in a sense inherited his role as Man of Letters, who remained nevertheless a spokesman for the common sense of the common man.

PRIESTLEY, Joseph (1733–1804), the son of a Yorkshire cloth-dresser, became Presbyterian minister at Nantwich and other places, but his views grew increasingly unorthodox and he became with his friend R. *Price one of the original members of the Unitarian Society in 1791. In politics he was a Radical, labelled 'Gunpowder' Priestley for his remarks about laying gunpowder 'under the old building of error and superstition'; on 14 July 1791 his Birmingham house was wrecked by a mob outraged by his public support of the French revolution and his attacks on *Burke. Finding life in England uncomfortable, he emigrated to America in 1794, and died there.

He wrote on theology, grammar, education, government, psychology, and other subjects; his *Essay on the First Principles of Government* (1768) considerably influenced *Bentham's development of the principle of Utilitarianism. He was himself influenced by *Hartley. His work as a chemist was of the first importance; he was the discoverer of oxygen and the author of various valuable scientific works. *Coleridge, in describing him as 'Patriot, and Saint, and Sage' ('Religious Musings', 1796), expresses the esteem in which he was held by radical Dissenters.

Prig, Betsey, a character in Dickens's *Martin Chuzzlewit*, who nurses in partnership with Mrs Gamp, until her remark concerning the apocryphal Mrs Harris, 'I don't believe there's no sich person', causes a difference between them.

Primas, the name (meaning 'first', 'chief') given to Hugh of Orleans, a canon of Orleans c.1140 and a *Goliardic poet who excelled in Latin lyrics which reveal both scholarship and a libertine disposition. Although he taught in Paris and Orleans and was admired by his contemporaries, his career was erratic and he died in the *Hospitium* amongst the destitute. See K. Langosch, *Hymnen und Vagantenlieder* (Basle, 1954), pp. 170 ff.

Prime Minister, The, a novel by A. *Trollope, published 1876, the fifth in the *'Palliser' series.

Ferdinand Lopez is disappointed in his marriage to Emily Wharton. He had hoped it would bring him money and social position, but Emily's father ties up her fortune, and Lopez is revealed as an improvident adventurer. The duchess of Omnium promises Lopez support in the Silverbridge by-election, but the duke, who is now prime minister, refuses to exert his influence. Lopez claims he has been cheated, and presses the duke to pay his election expenses, to the duke's political embarrassment. But even this effrontery does not save Lopez from financial ruin. Briefly flirting with the idea of managing a Guatemalan mine, he prefers death to exile, and walks in front of an express train.

The novel also records the history of the duke of Omnium's ministry. He is appointed head of a rickety coalition, which few observers believe will last long, but which he holds together for three years, while the duchess makes a determined attempt to support the ministry by a programme of lavish entertainment.

Primer, a term in English from the 14th cent. (used by both *Chaucer and *Langland) for a first reading-book of prayers. Because it was used as the basic instruction in reading for children, the term gradually came to be applied to a book containing the rudiments of instruction in reading or any language, an elementary schoolbook. This sense survived up to the 20th cent. (archaically pronounced 'primmer'), in the titles of works such as the *Anglo-Saxon Primer* of *Sweet.

Prime of Miss Jean Brodie, The, a novel by M. *Spark, published 1961.

Set in Edinburgh during the 1930s, it describes the career of eccentric and egotistical Miss Brodie, teacher at the Marcia Blaines School for Girls, and her domination of her 'set' of 16-year-olds, Monica Douglas ('famous mostly for mathematics'), Rose Stanley ('famous for sex'), Eunice Gardiner ('spritely gymnastics and glamorous swimming'), Jenny Gray (an intended actress), Mary Macgregor (famed as 'silent lump' and scapegoat), and Sandy Stewart, who becomes Miss Brodie's betrayer. With many flashes back and forward, it describes the manner in which Miss Brodie fascinates her disciples, who are particularly intrigued by her relationships with two male teachers, the married and Catholic art master, Mr Lloyd, and the bachelor Church of Scotland singing-master, Mr Lowther, who, rejected after much dalliance by Miss Brodie, in despair marries the science mistress. Sandy (rather than Rose, as Miss Brodie plans) has an affair with Mr Lloyd while Miss Brodie is away in the summer of 1938 touring Hitler's Germany; the results of this are that Sandy becomes a Catholic and arranges the dismissal of Miss Brodie on the grounds of her sympathy with Fascism, manifested not only in her enthusiasm for Hitler but also in her indirect responsibility for the death of another schoolgirl, not one of 'the set', who had died on a journey to Spain in the Spanish Civil War, encouraged by Miss Brodie to support Franco. Miss Brodie herself, dangerous but compelling, 'an Edinburgh Festival all on her own', is the centre of the novel's considerable moral ambiguity and complexity; she is seen most clearly through the 'treacherous' little eyes of Sandy, who, we are told in the second chapter, in a characteristic omniscient narrative leap, becomes a nun and writes a 'psychological treatise on the nature of moral perception, called "The Transfiguration of the Commonplace" '. The theme of the novel, *Lodge suggests (*Critical Quarterly*, 1970), is 'the loss of primal innocence'.

Primitivism, and the cult of 'the noble savage', are associated predominantly with the 18th cent., though they are clearly in some aspects descended from the classical concept of the Golden Age, and preceded by individual works like A. Behn's *Oroonoko* (which was extremely successful during the 18th cent. in *Southerne's stage version). Primitivism took the form of a revolt against luxury (see Goldsmith's *The Deserted Village*), against sophistication (see Colman's *Inkle and Yarico*, Cumberland's *The West Indian*, Mrs *Inchbald's *The Child of Nature*, Bage's *Hermsprong*, all works which stress the superiority of a simple education), and, in terms of critical theory, against *Neoclassicism. (See HURD, T. GRAY, HERDER.) Primitivism proposed a belief in man's natural goodness, and in the inevitable corruptions of civilization. Interest in the educational and philosophic theories of *Rousseau was accompanied by great enthusiasm for travel writings and for real-life South Sea Islanders, Eskimos, Lapplanders, Negroes, etc.; the South Sea Islander Omai from Tahiti received a warm welcome in London in 1776 from men of the world like *Boswell, who found him 'elegant'. There was also much curiosity about the phenomenon of the 'wild child' (which found recent versions in *Kipling's Mowgli, *Burroughs's Tarzan, and Truffaut's film *L'Enfant sauvage*); *Monboddo, a keen disciple of Rousseau, wrote a preface to a French case history of a 'savage girl' in 1768. Home-grown primitives were also in demand, and 'peasant' poets such as S. *Duck and A. *Yearsley were taken up by eager patrons: the notorious fake primitives *Macpherson and *Chatterton enjoyed a considerable vogue. They in turn were stimulated by the scholarly researches of *Percy and *Ritson, who revived an interest in early English poetry. One of the most important figures in the movement was Gray, whose poems *The Bard* and *The Progress of Poesy* reflect his own interest in and feelings for

the non-classical past: a note on the latter insisted on the 'extensive influence of poetic genius over the remotest and most uncivilized nations; its connection with liberty, and the virtues that naturally attend on it' (see also STUKELEY). It was in the cause of liberty that writers such as *Cowper and T. *Day defended the Noble Savage and attacked the slave trade. The ideas embodied in Primitivism were in many ways continued in the *Romantic movement, with its stress on Nature, freedom (both political and artistic), and the natural man. See C. B. Tinker, *Nature's Simple Plan* (1922); H. N. Fairchild, *The Noble Savage* (1928); L. Whitney, *Primitivism and the Idea of Progress* (1934).

Primrose, Dr, the vicar of Wakefield in *Goldsmith's novel of that name. His family consists of his wife Deborah; daughters Olivia and Sophia; sons George and Moses; and two younger boys.

Prince, The, see MACHIAVELLI, N.

PRINCE, F(rank) T(empleton) (1912–), poet, born in South Africa, and educated there and at Balliol College, Oxford, and Princeton. From 1957 to 1974 he was professor of English at Southampton University. His collections of poetry include *Poems* (1938), *Soldiers Bathing and other poems* (1954), and *The Doors of Stone: Poems 1938–62* (1963); his *Collected Poems* appeared in 1979. His poems range from dramatic monologues ('The Old Age of Michelangelo') to long meditations on R. *Brooke (*Afterword on Rupert Brooke*, 1977) and on *Sterne's *Eliza* ('A Last Attachment', 1979); from technical experiments with little-used verse forms (e.g. the Italian *strambotto*) to the wartime immediacy and pictorial qualities of the title poem of *Soldiers Bathing*.

Prince Hohenstiel-Schwangau, Saviour of Society, a poem in blank verse by R. *Browning, written and published 1871. The Prince is based on the Emperor Napoleon III.

The title 'saviour of society' was often used of Napoleon by his adherents; Browning makes ironic use of it in his depiction of a statesman who reviews his long career of compromise and tergiversation, ostensibly addressing himself to his mistress in a hotel in Leicester Square, where he is living in exile and disgrace, and justifying his conduct by appeal to a pragmatism which he believes is inherent in the relation between humanity and God. But the last lines of the poem reveal that the prince has been fantasizing the whole episode; that he has been meditating, on the brink of an important political decision, what he *would* say if his plans failed and he were forced into exile. Thus, while the poem alludes in detail to Napoleon III's career, its form also raises questions about truth and imagination which are central to Browning's aesthetics: political and poetic idealism, opposed to and yet dependent on the materialism of action and language, mirror one another.

Princes in the Tower, Edward V and Richard, duke of York, his brother. They were lodged in the Tower of London in 1483 and were there secretly murdered in the same year, when Edward was 13 years old. It was traditionally believed that they were killed by order of their uncle the king, Richard III, and so it is reported by T. *More in his *History of King Richard III*. But Richard's responsibility has recently been questioned, on the grounds that the survival of the princes posed more of a threat to his successor Henry VII.

Princess, The, *A Medley*, a poem by *Tennyson, published 1847. Some of the well-known lyrics ('The splendour falls', 'Ask me no more: the moon may draw the sea') were added in the third edition of 1850, but others, including 'Tears, idle tears' (composed in 1834 at Tintern) and 'Now sleeps the crimson petal, now the white' were included in the first. The poem, which opens with a description of a summer fête based on an event at the Lushingtons' home Park House, near Maidstone, purports to be a tale of fancy composed in turn by some young people, based on an old chronicle.

A prince has been betrothed since childhood to Princess Ida, daughter of neighbouring King Gama. She becomes a devotee of women's rights, abjures marriage, and founds a university. The prince and two companions, Cyril and Florian, gain admission to the university dressed as women, and are detected by the two tutors, Lady Psyche and Lady Blanche, who from different motives conceal their knowledge. The deceit is presently detected by Ida, but not before the prince has had occasion to rescue her from drowning. Her determination is unshaken, and a combat ensues, between fifty warriors led by the prince and fifty led by Gama's son, during which the three comrades are wounded. The university is turned into a hospital, the prince urges his suit, and he wins Ida, envisaging a future in which 'The man [may] be more of woman, she of man'; the epilogue is a plea for gradual social reform: 'Maybe wildest dreams | Are but the needful prelude of the truth.' The work was well received on the whole, though Tennyson wrote of it to his friend E. *Fitzgerald 'I hate it and so will you', and subjected it to considerable revision. It formed the basis of the satirical *Gilbert and Sullivan opera *Princess Ida*.

Princesse de Clèves, La, see LA FAYETTE, M.-M.

Princeton University, founded as a college for the middle American colonies (corresponding to Harvard and Yale for New England) under a charter of 1746, first at Elizabeth NJ, transferred to Princeton in 1754.

Principe, Il, see MACHIAVELLI, N.

Principia Ethica, see MOORE, G. E.

Principia Mathematica, see NEWTON, I., and RUSSELL, B.

Principles of Moral and Political Philosophy, see PALEY, W.

Principles of Morals and Legislation, An *Introduction to the*, see BENTHAM, J.

Pringle, Guy and Harriet, the principal characters of O. *Manning's *Balkan Trilogy* and *Levant Trilogy*.

PRINGLE, Thomas (1789–1834), studied at Edinburgh University, became a friend of Sir W. *Scott, and was for a short time editor of the *Edinburgh Monthly Magazine*, the first of several editorships of various journals. In 1809 he published his first volume of poems, which included 'The Emigrant's Farewell', and emigrated to South Africa. He is remembered chiefly as a poet of that country. His *Ephemerides* (1828) and *African Sketches* (1834) reveal his sympathetic interest in the native races and the wild life of Africa, and contain some poems of quality, such as 'The Hottentot' and 'Afar in the Desert', which was highly praised by *Coleridge.

PRIOR, Matthew (1664–1721), the son of a joiner of Wimborne, Dorset, was educated at Westminster School and St John's College, Cambridge. He began writing early, and joined with Charles Montagu (later earl of Halifax) in *The Hind and the Panther Transvers'd to the Story of the Country Mouse and the City Mouse* (1687, see TOWN MOUSE AND COUNTRY MOUSE), a satire on Dryden's *The Hind and the Panther*. He was appointed secretary to the ambassador ·at The Hague and employed in the negotiations for the treaty of Ryswick; his poem 'The Secretary' (1696) gives a lively picture of this period of his life. He joined the Tories and in 1711 was sent to Paris as a secret agent at the time of the peace negotiations, the subsequent treaty of Utrecht (1713) being popularly known as 'Matt's Peace'. He was recalled on Queen Anne's death and imprisoned for over a year. A handsome folio edition of his poems was brought out in 1718 after his release, by which he gained 4,000 guineas in subscriptions; *Harley gave him £4,000 for the purchase of Down Hall in Essex. Prior is best remembered for his brilliant occasional verses, epigrams and familiar pieces ('My noble, lovely, little Peggy' and 'Jinny and Just', for example, in which he combines lightness of touch with mock seriousness), but also wrote longer works in various styles. *Carmen Seculare* (1700) is an ode celebrating the arrival of William III; 'Alma; or the Progress of the Mind' (1718) is a *Hudibrastic dialogue ridiculing various systems of philosophy; and 'Solomon on the Vanity of the World' (1718) is a long soliloquy in heroic couplets on the same theme. 'Hans Carvel' (1701) and 'The Ladle' (1718) are narratives ending with coarse jests, in a genre popular at the time, whereas 'Henry and Emma' (1709) (described by *Cowper as 'enchanting') is a sentimental burlesque of the old ballad *'The Nut-Brown Maid'. *Down-Hall, a Ballad* (1723), a lively account of a trip to Essex, also deserves mention. His prose works include an *Essay upon Learning*, an *Essay upon Opinion*, and *Four *Dialogues of the Dead*, which were not published until A. R. Waller's 2-vol. edition of 1905–7. His *Literary Works*, ed. H. B. Wright and M. K. Spears, were published in 2 vols, 1959.

'Prioress's Tale, The', see CANTERBURY TALES, 16.

Prisoner of Chillon, The, a poem by *Byron, published 1816.

The poem describes the imprisonment of a historical character, the patriot François de Bonnivard (1496–?1570), in the castle of Chillon, on the lake of Geneva. Defying tyranny, he endures his chains and his imprisonment for many years. One by one he watches his beloved brothers die. Eventually he is rescued from madness by the song of a bird, and he longs again to see the lake and mountains. But, ironically, when he is at last released he has lost his longing for liberty, finds prison has become his home, and regains his freedom 'with a sigh'. The narrative is cast as a monologue, in a style simple and controlled, revealing a credible and un-*'Byronic' man.

Prisoner of Zenda, The, and its sequel *Rupert of Hentzau*, novels by Anthony Hope (*Hawkins), published 1894 and 1898.

They deal with the perilous and romantic adventures of Rudolf Rassendyll, an English gentleman, in Ruritania, where, by impersonating the king (to whom he bears a marked physical resemblance), he defeats a plot to oust him from the throne. He falls in love with the king's betrothed, Princess Flavia, and she with him, but gallantly relinquishes her to the restored king. In the sequel he defeats a plot of the villain Rupert of Hentzau against Flavia, now the unhappy wife of the king, and has another chance of taking the throne and of marrying Flavia. But he is assassinated before his decision is known.

PRITCHETT, Sir V(ictor) S(awdon) (1900–), novelist, critic, and short story writer, was born in Ipswich, the son of a travelling salesman, and spent a peripatetic childhood in the provinces and various London suburbs before attending Alleyn's School, Dulwich, which he left at 15 to work in the leather trade. He went to Paris at the age of 21, where he worked in the photographic trade; he then became a journalist, writing for the *Christian Science Monitor* in Ireland, then Spain, before settling to a literary life in London. His first novel, *Clare Drummer* (1929), was followed by several others, but Pritchett is principally known for his short stories, the first of which appeared in the *Cornhill, the *New Statesman, etc., in the 1920s; his first collection, *The Spanish Virgin and other stories* (1930), was followed by many others, including *You Make Your Own Life* (1938), *When my Girl Comes Home* (1961), and *The Camberwell Beauty* (1974). Two volumes of *Collected Stories* appeared, 1982, 1983. They are distinguished by their wide social range, shrewd observation of the quirks of human nature, and humane irony. Pritchett's other works include *The Living Novel* (1946), studies of *Balzac (1973) and *Turgenev (1977), and two volumes of much-praised autobiography, *The Cab at the Door: Early Years* (1968, of which the title refers to his household's frequent removals, which he claimed gave him a lifelong love of travel) and *Midnight Oil* (1971), which ends with the Second World War. He also edited the *Oxford Book of Short Stories* (1981). As critic he has contributed most regularly to the *New Statesman*, of which he became a director in 1946.

Private Memoirs and Confessions of a Justified Sinner, The, a novel by J. *Hogg, published 1824, a macabre and highly original tale, inviting psychological as well as literary interpretation.

In the first part of the book Colwan, believing himself to be one of the 'saved' (according to the Calvinist doctrine of predestination), and under the influence of a malign stranger who may be interpreted as his evil alter-ego, commits a series of horrifying crimes, including the murder of his half-brother. The second section of the book purports to be a memoir written by Colwan, and discovered when his grave was opened a century after his suicide. This reveals that he also murdered his mother, a girl, and a preacher, all under the supposed auspices of divine justice, before coming eventually to believe that the stranger who haunts him is in fact the Devil. His skull, on exhumation, is found to have two horn-like protuberances.

Private Presses are distinguished by aims that are aesthetic rather than commercial and by printing for the gratification of their owners rather than to order. Many such have been set up since the 17th cent. by amateurs of books or printing: that of Horace *Walpole at *Strawberry Hill (1757–97) is a well-known example. At the end of the 19th cent. presses of this kind were intended as a protest against the low artistic standards and degradation of labour in the printing trade. W. *Morris set up the Kelmscott Press (1891–8) with this object; and others, notably C. H. St John Hornby (the Ashendene Press,

1895), *Ricketts (the Vale Press, 1896), and T. J. Cobden-Sanderson and Emery Walker (the Doves Press, 1900), followed him. The *Cuala Press was founded in Ireland in 1902. The 1920s saw the foundation of the *Golden Cockerel Press, the *Gregynog Press, and the *Nonesuch Press, and a considerable revival of interest in the art of wood engraving. The term 'private press' is sometimes applied, perhaps unjustifiably, to such publishing companies as the Nonesuch, which used commercial printers and called itself 'architects rather than builders' of books. See W. Ransom, *Private Presses and their Books* (1929) and Roderick Cave, *The Private Press* (1971).

PROCTOR, Adelaide Anne (1825–64), daughter of B. W. Proctor (Barry *Cornwall), contributed to Dickens's *Household Words* under the pseudonym 'Mary Berwick'. She was the author of much popular sentimental (and often morbid) verse, including 'A Lost Chord' (*Legends and Lyrics*, 1858–61). Her complete works were issued in 1905 with a foreword by Dickens.

PROCTOR, Brian Waller, see CORNWALL, B.

Prodigal Son, The, the general subject of a group of plays written about 1540–75, showing the influence of the continental neo-classic writers of the period, particularly Gnaphaeus in his *Acolastus*, on the early Tudor dramatists and novelists. The chief of these are *Misogonus*, dating from about 1560 (author unknown), *Jacke Jugeller* (1563), and *Gascoigne's *Glasse of Government* (1575). The parable of the Prodigal Son is in Luke 15: 11–32.

Professor, The, a novel by C. *Brontë, written 1846 (before *Jane Eyre*), but not published until 1857.

The story is based, like *Villette*, on the author's experiences in Brussels, and uses much of the same material, though the two principal characters are transposed. William Crimsworth, an orphan, after trying his hand at trade in the north of England, goes to seek his fortune in Brussels. At the girls' school where he teaches English he falls in love with Frances Henri, an Anglo-Swiss pupil teacher and lace mender, whose Protestant honesty and modesty are contrasted with the manipulating duplicity of the Catholic headmistress, Zoraide Reuter. Crimsworth resists Mlle Reuter's overtures; she marries the headmaster of the neighbouring boys' school, M. Pelet, Crimsworth resigns his post, and, after finding a new and better one, is able to marry Frances.

Professor's House, The, a novel by W. *Cather.

Progress of Poesy, The, a Pindaric ode by T. *Gray, published 1757. Gray describes the different kinds of poetry, its varying powers, its primitive origins, and its connections with political liberty. He recounts its progress from Greece, to Italy, to Britain, paying homage to Shakespeare, *Milton, and *Dryden—a footnote singling out Dryden's *'Sublime' 'Ode on St Cecilia's Day'—and concludes that no one in his day can equal them. Dr *Johnson found the poem obscure. (See also BARD, THE.)

PROKOFIEV, Sergei (1891–1953), Russian composer. His first composition with English literary connections was a Soviet commission towards the end of his time abroad (1918–36), the music for a strange theatrical experiment combining excerpts from G. B. *Shaw's *Caesar and Cleopatra*, Shakespeare's *Antony and Cleopatra*, and *Pushkin's *Egyptian Nights*, given in Moscow in 1935 with little success.

In the same year the first version of Prokofiev's ballet *Romeo and Juliet* was heard by the directors of the Bolshoi Theatre and turned down as unsuitable for dancing: the composer revised and improved his score (incidentally restoring the original tragic ending to the drama, which he had originally altered precisely because of the difficulty of dancing it), but even so he had to wait until 1940 for the first performance in his own country of this classically beautiful score. Another Shakespearian enterprise, from about the same period, was the incidental music for *Hamlet (1939), but more important was the opera *Betrothal in a Monastery*, based on Sheridan's *The Duenna*. Here Prokofiev laid aside the well-meaning *socialist realism of some of his more recent compositions and produced a brightly lyrical score which perfectly matches the wit and romance of Sheridan's play. It was completed by 1941, but not performed until 1946, actually after the première of the composer's next and greatest opera, the huge epic adaptation of *Tolstoy's *War and Peace*.

PROMETHEUS (the name means 'Forethought') appears in Greek myth as a divine being, one of the Titans, descended from the original union of the Sky God with the Earth Mother. In some stories he is the creator of mankind, and he is always their champion. He is supposed to have stolen fire for them from Heaven when they were denied it by Zeus, and to have been punished by being fastened to a cliff in the Caucasus where an eagle tore daily at his liver. *Hesiod explains Zeus' enmity to Prometheus and his human dependants by stating that Prometheus had played a trick on him over a sacrifice, but this story, like so many in Hesiod, has the air of a rationalization. It is certainly possible that behind the rebellious Titan of *Aeschylus there lurks an early Greek or Indo-European divinity, a benevolent demiurge, whom the Olympians supplanted. But even if we allow for a measure of distortion in the story as we know it, this primitive deity must have been an ambivalent figure. The fire and the skills which were his gifts to mankind were not an unmixed blessing, since they were also the source of work and war. It is interesting that Prometheus seems as a god to have been firmly rooted in the real world of effort, danger, and pain, while the Olympians who successfully supplanted him were the products of an idealizing daydream, beautiful, potent, happy, and free from suffering and death.

The modern popularity of the Promethean myth dates from the 1770s when *Goethe came to see in the Titan a symbol of man's creative striving and of his revolt against the restraints of society and life. Goethe set the pattern which the 19th cent. followed. Shelley's *Prometheus Unbound* (1820) glorified the virtues of revolt, representing authority as responsible for man's sufferings. *Coleridge wrote an essay on the *Prometheus* of Aeschylus (1825), Elizabeth Barrett (*Browning) translated the play (1833) and *Bridges wrote a version called *Prometheus the Firegiver* (1883). Finally, in the present century, *Gide's enigmatic *Prométhée mal enchaîné* has a hero who is still a symbol of mankind's quest to transcend the obvious.

Prometheus the Firegiver, a poem by *Bridges.

Prometheus Unbound, a lyrical drama in four acts by P. B. *Shelley, written in Italy 1818–19, published 1820.

A great but uneven work that orchestrates all Shelley's aspirations, and contradictions, as a poet and radical, it is partly mythical drama (or 'psychodrama') and partly political allegory. Shelley began with the idea of completing the Aeschylian story of *Prometheus the firebringer and champion of mankind, who is bound to his rock for all eternity by a jealous Jupiter. He combined this with his view of Satan as the hero of *Paradise Lost*, and of God as the Oppressor. Boldly re-writing or updating these two myths, he presents a Prometheus–Lucifer figure of moral perfection and 'truest motives', who is liberated by 'alternative' and benign forces in the universe and triumphs over Tyranny in the name of all mankind. The work is executed in a bewildering variety of verse forms, some more successful than others: rhetorical soliloquies, dramatic dialogues, love-songs, dream visions, lyric choruses, and prophecies.

Act I shows Prometheus chained in agony, 'in a ravine of Icy rocks in the Indian Caucasus', comforted by his mother Earth, but tempted to yield to Jupiter's tyranny by Mercury and the Furies. Act II introduces Asia and Panthea, the lovely daughters of Ocean, who determine to release Prometheus by confronting the ultimate source of power, *Demogorgon, a volcanic force dwelling in a shadowy underworld. Act III abruptly presents Jupiter vanquished by the eruption of Demogorgon, and Prometheus released and united with his beloved Asia. Their child, the Spirit of the Hour, prophesies the liberation of mankind. Act IV is a cosmic coda, or epithalamium, sung by a chorus of Hours, Spirits, Earth, and Moon.

The sexual, scientific, and political symbolism of the drama have been variously interpreted: but the concept of liberation is central. Act II sc. 4 in which Asia (the Spirit of Love) confronts and questions Demogorgon (Fate, Historical Necessity, or perhaps 'the People-Monster') must count among Shelley's poetic masterpieces. The work has an important Preface on the role of poetry in reforming society, which links with the *Defence of Poetry*.

Promos and Cassandra, see WHETSTONE, G.

PROPERTIUS, Sextus (*c*.50–*c*.16 BC), the most obscure and abrupt of the three surviving Roman elegiac poets, though some of his obscurity may be due to imperfections in his text. The sophisticated chronicler of a sophisticated love, he employed an allusive style full of mythological references in a Hellenistic manner, but conveyed great intensity and variety of feeling. Echoes of his verse can be found in B. *Barnes and T. *Campion and more recently he has been brought to public notice by *Pound's 'Homage to Sextus Propertius' (1919).

Prophecy of Famine, The, see CHURCHILL, CHARLES.

Prophetic Books, the name sometimes given to the symbolic and prophetic poems of *Blake, e.g. *The Book of *Urizen*, *The Book of *Los*, *Milton*, and *Jerusalem*.

Prose Brut, The, see BRUT, THE PROSE.

'Prosopopoia', the subtitle of Spenser's *'Mother Hubberds Tale'.

Prospero, (1) in Shakespeare's *The Tempest*, the usurped duke of Milan and father of *Miranda; (2) a character in Jonson's *Every Man in his Humour*, a play in which Shakespeare himself acted.

Proteus, one of *The Two Gentlemen of Verona* in Shakespeare's play; his name suggests his fickle and changing nature.

Prothalamion, a 'Spousall Verse' written by *Spenser, published 1596, in celebration of the double marriage of the Lady Elizabeth and the Lady Katherine Somerset, daughters of the earl of Worcester. The name was invented by Spenser on the model of his *Epithalamion*.

Proudfute, Oliver, the bonnet-maker in Scott's *The Fair Maid of Perth*.

PROUDHON, Pierre-Joseph (1809–65),

French social philosopher and political activist. His writings laid the basis for the organized anarchist movement in France, and exercised considerable influence on the thought and practice of anarchist and socialist movements throughout Europe. He published a large number of works, including *Quest-ce que la propriété?* (1840; English trans., *What is Property?*, 1876), *Idée générale de la révolution au XIXe siècle* (1851), *De la justice dans la révolution et dans l'église* (1858), and *De la capacité politique des classes ouvrières* (1865). His prose style was admired by *Baudelaire and *Flaubert, and his influence extended to such figures as Courbet and *Tolstoy, as well as to large numbers of political activists in Italy, Spain, Russia, and elsewhere.

Proudie, Mrs, the violently Evangelical wife of the bishop of Barchester, and a leading character in the *'Barsetshire' novels of A. Trollope.

PROUST, Marcel (1871–1922), French novelist, essayist, and critic, author of *A la recherche du temps perdu* (1913–27; English trans., *Remembrance of Things Past*, 1922–31). In the 1890s Proust moved in the most fashionable Parisian circles, but in later years became a virtual recluse, dedicating himself to the completion of *A la recherche*, which occupied him till the end of his life. In 1896 he published a collection of essays, poems, and short stories, *Les Plaisirs et les jours* (*Pleasures and Regrets*, 1948), and in the period c.1895–1900 worked on an early version of *A la recherche* which was published posthumously, as *Jean Santeuil*, in 1952 (English trans. 1955). He was actively involved, on the side of *Dreyfus, in the Dreyfus case of 1897–9. Around 1899 he discovered *Ruskin's art criticism, and subsequently translated Ruskin's *The Bible of Amiens* and *Sesame and Lilies* into French. In 1919 he published a collection of literary parodies, *Pastiches et mélanges*. He explored his own literary aesthetic in *Contre Sainte-Beuve* (1954; *By Way of Sainte-Beuve*, 1958), where he defines the artist's task as the releasing of the creative energies of past experience from the hidden store of the unconscious, an aesthetic which found its most developed literary expression in *A la recherche*.

Prout, Father, see MAHONY, F. S.

Provençal, or *langue d'oc* (as distinct from the *langue d'oïl*), the language of the southern part of France, and the literary medium of the *troubadours. Their language was a *koiné*, a class language avoiding marked regional features; it was known as *lemosi* (Limousin), probably because some of the most famous troubadours came from that region. Provençal declined as a literary language after the defeat of the south in the Albigensian War. The language is now generally called *occitan*, though the terms Provençal and *langue d'oc* are still in use.

Provençal literature in the medieval period consisted chiefly of the lyric poetry composed by the troubadours for the feudal courts of the Midi, northern Italy, and Spain. The *canso*, the love song in the courtly style which was the troubadours' special achievement, was known all over western Europe, and inspired the courtly poetry of northern France, the Minnesang of Germany, and the Petrarchan poetry of Italy. The *sirventes*, the satirical poem mostly on political or moral themes, was also much cultivated by the troubadours. There is little literature of an epic kind, or literature in prose, extant in Old Provençal, and Provençal was considered the language *par excellence* of lyric poetry, courtly in content and very elaborate in style. This poetic flowering came to an end with the decline, after the Albigensian crusade, of the aristocratic society which had produced it.

Proverbial Philosophy, see TUPPER, M.

Proverbs of Alfred, The, an early Middle English poem, dating, in the form in which it has reached us, from the 13th cent., though probably composed about 1150–80. The poem's 600 lines begin by giving an account of Alfred and proceed to a series of 35 sayings, each beginning 'Thus quath Alfred', containing proverbial instructions. The attribution of the proverbs to Alfred is no more than traditional: many different proverbs are attributed to him in *The Owl and the Nightingale*: see H. P. South's edition (1931), pp. 43–63.

'Proverbs of Hell', see MARRIAGE OF HEAVEN AND HELL, THE.

Provok'd Husband, The, or *a Journey to London*, a comedy by *Vanbrugh, finished by C. *Cibber, produced 1728.

The 'provok'd husband' is Lord Townly, who, driven to desperation by the extravagance of his wife, decides to separate from her and to make his reasons public. The sentence (according to Cibber's ending) brings Lady Townly to her senses, and a reconciliation is promoted by Manly, Lord Townly's sensible friend and the successful suitor of Lady Grace, Lord Townly's exemplary sister. A second element in the plot is the visit to London of Sir Francis Wronghead, a simple country gentleman, with his wife, a foolish, extravagant woman who wants to be a fine lady, and their son and daughter. Count Basset, an unprincipled gamester, under cover of making love to Lady Wronghead, plans to entice her daughter into a secret marriage, and to effect a match between her son and his own cast-off mistress. The plot nearly succeeds, but is frustrated by Manly.

Provok'd Wife, The, a comedy by *Vanbrugh, produced 1697, but possibly written before *The Relapse*.

Sir John Brute, a debauched man of quality,

married his wife for love, but is now disillusioned with her and with matrimony, and rails against both. Lady Brute married for money, but has remained technically faithful; she is courted by Constant, whose cynical friend Heartfree falls in love with her niece Belinda. The two ladies, for a frolic, invite Constant and Heartfree to meet them in Spring Garden. Here Lady Brute is on the point of yielding to Constant when they are interrupted by the jealous and affected Lady Fancyfull. The two couples return to Lady Brute's house and sit down to cards, confident that Sir John will not return from a drinking bout for some hours. Sir John, however, having been arrested by the watch for brawling in the streets disguised in a parson's gown, has been dismissed by the magistrate. (Vanbrugh rewrote scenes i and iii of Act IV for the 1725/6 revival and had Sir John put on 'a light lady's short cloak and wrapping goun' and call himself 'Bonduca, Queen of the Welchmen' when arrested, but 'Lady Brute' before the justice.) He comes home unexpectedly, finds the two men hidden in a closet, but declines the duel offered by Constant. The presence of the men is attributed to the proposed marriage of Heartfree and Belinda, and in spite of Lady Fancyfull's attempts to make mischief all ends relatively well, though the problems of the Brutes clearly remain unresolved.

Provost, The, a novel by J. *Galt, published 1822, a book in which Galt's particular skills are at their best.

The Provost, Mr Pawkie, reflects on the arts of authority and rule, and his own successful manipulation of them throughout his life. The ironic revelation of his self-righteous, contriving character is of more importance in this work than the Scottish social scene he describes.

PRUDENTIUS (Aurelius Prudentius Clemens) (348–post 405), a Christian Latin poet born in Spain, the composer of many hymns and of the *Psychomachia* (*The Battle for the Soul of Man*), written in 405. The *Psychomachia* was a very important influence on the development of medieval and Renaissance allegorical works, and it is given extended attention in *The Allegory of Love* (pp. 66–73) by C. S. *Lewis, who had little admiration for the work. It is translated (along with some of the hymns) in H. Isbell's *The Last Poets of Imperial Rome* (1971).

Prue, Miss, a character in Congreve's *Love for Love.*

'Prufrock, The Love Song of J. Alfred', a poem by T. S. *Eliot.

Pryderi, see MABINOGION.

Prynne, Hester, the heroine of Hawthorne's *The Scarlet Letter.*

PRYNNE, William (1600–69), Puritan pamphleteer, was educated at Bath grammar school and Oriel College, Oxford, and was a barrister of Lincoln's Inn. He wrote against *Arminianism from 1627, and endeavoured to reform the manners of his age. He published *Histriomastix,* an enormous work attacking stage-plays, in 1632. For a supposed aspersion on Charles I and his queen in it he was sentenced by the Star Chamber, in 1634, to be imprisoned during life, to be fined £5,000, and to lose both his ears in the pillory. He continued to write in the Tower of London, and in 1637 was again fined £5,000, deprived of the remainder of his ears, and branded on the cheeks with the letters S.L. ('seditious libeller') which Prynne humorously asserted to mean 'Stigmata Laudis' (i.e. of Archbishop *Laud). He was released by the Long Parliament, and his sentences declared illegal in Nov. 1640. He continued an active paper warfare, attacking Laud, then the independents, then the army (1647), then, after being arrested by Pride, the government. In 1660 he asserted the rights of Charles II, and was thanked by him. He was MP for Bath in the Convention Parliament and was appointed keeper of the records in the Tower of London. He published his most valuable work, *Brevia Parliamentaria Rediviva,* in 1662. He published altogether about 200 books and pamphlets.

PSALMANAZAR, George (?1679–1763), a literary impostor, was a native of the south of France. His real name is unknown: he adapted his pseudonym from the biblical character Shalmaneser. He was educated at a Dominican convent and commenced life as a mendicant in the character of a native Japanese Christian, but afterwards represented himself as still a pagan, living on raw flesh, roots, and herbs, and invented an elaborate alphabet and grammar and a worship of his own. He enlisted in a regiment of the duke of Mecklenburg, and attracted the attention of William Innes, chaplain to the Scottish regiment at Sluys, who became a confederate in the imposture, baptized Psalmanazar as a Protestant convert, and for security persuaded him to alter his birthplace to the obscurity of Formosa. He came to London at the end of 1703 and became a centre of interest, presenting Bishop Compton with the catechism in 'Formosan' (his invented language), and talking volubly in Latin to Archbishop Tillotson. He published in 1704 a *Description* of Formosa, with an introductory autobiography. After the withdrawal of his mentor Innes, who was rewarded for his zeal in converting Psalmanazar by being appointed chaplain-general to the forces in Portugal (*c.*1707), he was unable to sustain the imposture unaided, and passed from ridicule to obscurity, although he still found patrons. He renounced his past life after a serious illness in 1728, became an accomplished Hebraist, wrote *A General History of Printing,* and contributed to the *Universal History*. Psalmanazar was regarded with veneration by Dr *Johnson, who used to sit with him at an alehouse in Old Street, London. In 1764 appeared posthumously his autobiographical *Memoirs*, containing an account of the imposture.

Psalms, The, the Book of Psalms, one of the books of the Old Testament, often called the Psalms of David, in accordance with the belief that they, or part of them, were composed by David, king of Israel. This belief, maintained by many of the Latin fathers (e.g. St *Ambrose and St *Augustine), was largely dismissed in the 19th cent., although modern scholars assign some to him and date many from the early years of the Monarchy. The Psalms were the basis of the medieval church services, probably the only book in the Bible on the use of which, by the laity, the medieval church imposed no veto at all. The Prayer Book version of them, attributed to *Coverdale, is one of our greatest literary inheritances. A *Metrical Version* of the Psalms was begun by *Sternhold and Hopkins (2nd edn, 1551), and continued at Geneva during Mary's reign by Protestant refugees. The complete *Old Version* (metrical) was published in 1562. The *New Version* by *Tate and Brady appeared in 1696. The Psalms have been translated and adapted by many English poets, including *Wyatt, G. *Herbert, *Addison, *Smart (whose *A Song to David* celebrates their supposed author), and *Watts.

PSEUDO-DIONYSIUS, see DIONYSIUS THE AREOPAGITE.

Pseudodoxia Epidemica: or, Enquiries into Very many received Tenents, And commonly presumed Truths, often referred to as *Vulgar Errors,* by Sir T. *Browne, first published 1646, revised and augmented 1650, 1658, and 1672.

Whereas *Religio Medici* made him famous for wit, this, his longest work, established him as a man of learning. Fulfilling Bacon's desire in *The Advancement of Learning* for a 'Calendar of Dubitations, or Problemes' and a 'Calendar of Falshoods, and of popular Errors', it comprises one general book, treating of the sources and propagation of error—original sin, popular gullibility, logical fallacy, learned credulity and laziness, reverence for antiquity and authority, influential authors, and Satan—and six particular books, three on natural history—mineralogy, botany, zoology, physiology—and three on civil, ecclesiastical, and literary history—iconography, magic and folklore, chronology, historical geography, and biblical, classical, and medieval history. Browne examines more than 100 problems in the light of his extensive learning, the verdicts of reasoned argument, and the results of his own experiments and observations. The standard edition, comprising a critical text

with introduction and full commentary, is by Robin Robbins (1981).

Pseudo-Martyr, see DONNE, J.

Psychobiography, see ERIKSON, E. H.

PTOLEMY (Claudius Ptolemaeus), who lived at Alexandria in the 2nd cent. AD, was a celebrated mathematician, astronomer, and geographer. He devised the system of astronomy (according to which the sun, planets, and stars revolved round the earth) which was generally accepted until displaced by that of *Copernicus. Combined with *Aristotle's natural philosophy, which saw Nature as orderly, hierarchical, and teleological, Ptolemaic astronomy when suitably Christianized formed the core of the medieval world picture. Ptolemy's work on this subject is generally known by its Arabic name of *Almagest*. His great geographical treatise remained a textbook until superseded by the discoveries of the 15th cent. Ptolemy compiled a map of the world in which both the parallels and the meridians are curved.

Public Advertiser, The, originally *The London Daily Post and General Advertiser,* was started in 1752 and expired in 1798. From 1758 to 1793 it was edited by Henry Sampson Woodfall (1739–1805), who published the famous letters of *'Junius'. It contained home and foreign intelligence, and correspondence, mainly political, from writers of all shades of opinion. *Wilkes and *Tooke carried on a dispute in its columns. The notable pamphlets of 'Candor' against Lord Mansfield (1764) also appeared originally as letters to the *Public Advertiser*. The author of these is unknown.

Public Lending Right, a right achieved by Act of Parliament in 1979. The idea that the author of a book (in copyright) should be paid for its use by a public, commercial, or other kind of lending library was conceived by the novelist John Brophy in 1951, then formally adopted by the *Society of Authors which conducted a prolonged campaign—later reinforced by the Writers' Action Group—for 'Public Lending Right' (PLR). The campaign was opposed by most librarians, and bedevilled by confused thinking: in essence, the argument was that public lending constituted an ancillary use of the author's property which, for historical reasons, had been omitted from copyright legislation, but which in natural justice copyright had been designed to protect.

PLR was finally secured, not by amendment to the Copyright Act, but by a separate statute, because of the need for reciprocal agreements with other countries, e.g. West Germany, operating comparable schemes. The Registrar of PLR operates from an office in Stockton-on-Tees, and the scheme is financed by a central grant from the Treasury. Qualifying authors received their first cheques in 1984. (See Appendix II, for Copyright.)

Publishing, subscription, a system by which the author (sometimes with his publishers' help) collected a pre-publication list of buyers prepared to pay for his book in advance and usually at a reduced rate. The first book known to be published by a fully developed form of this system was John Minsheu's lexicographical *Guide into Tongues* of 1617, but it is known that *Caxton, in the late 15th cent., acquired promises of sales before producing his major works. The system flourished most widely in the 18th cent. when authors frequently issued 'Proposals' for future works and collected subscribers; for instance, *Pope enlisted *Swift's help in obtaining subscribers for his *Iliad*; Dr *Johnson, who had great trouble with the list for his edition of Shakespeare, said, 'he that asks subscriptions soon finds that he has enemies'; *Burns, proposing to. issue the Kilmarnock second edition of his poems, was delighted to obtain a list of over 300 subscribers; and the name of the young J. *Austen appears in 1796 on a subscription list for F. *Burney's forthcoming *Camilla*. Subscription publishing was still flourishing at the end of the 19th cent. and survives in a modified form in certain areas of scholarly and technical publishing.

PUCCINI, Giacomo (1858–1924), Italian composer, almost exclusively of opera. Of Puccini's twelve completed operas only two have any remote connection with English literature: both *Madama Butterfly* (1904) and *La Fanciulla del West* (1910, from *The Girl of the Golden West*) are based on stage plays by the American actor-manager and playwright David Belasco, the former taken in its turn from a magazine story by John Luther Long. The uncompleted operas, however, present a different picture. Puccini once described himself as 'a passionate hunter of women, wild duck and libretti', and his quarry in the third category included, at various stages of his career, *Enoch Arden, *Oliver Twist, Two Little Wooden Shoes* (*Ouida), *A Florentine Tragedy* and *The Duchess of Padua* (*Wilde), *Henry IV* and *V, *King Lear*, *The Last Days of Pompeii* (*Bulwer-Lytton), *The Light That Failed* (*Kipling), *Lorna Doone*, *Trilby*, and *Rip van Winkle*.

Pucelle, La (*The Maid*), a burlesque epic by *Voltaire on the subject of *Joan of Arc, published 1755. Joan is called 'la Pucelle' in Shakespeare's 1 *Henry VI*.

Puck, originally an evil or malicious spirit or demon of popular superstition; from the 16th cent. the name of a mischievous or tricksy goblin or sprite, called also Robin Goodfellow and Hobgoblin. In this character he figures in Shakespeare's *A Midsummer Night's Dream* (II. i. 40) and Drayton's *Nimphidia* (xxxvi).

Puff, Mr, a character in Sheridan's *The Critic*.

PUGIN, Augustus Welby Northmore (1812–52), architect, son of the French artist Auguste-Charles Pugin (1762–1832). He was the protagonist and theorist of the *Gothic Revival, and developed his thesis that Gothic was the only proper Christian architecture in *Contrasts: or, a parallel between the noble edifices of the fourteenth and fifteenth centuries and similar buildings of the present day, shewing the present decay of taste* (1836), an important work that foreshadowed *Ruskin and *Carlyle's *Past and Present*. He wrote various other works on architectural and ecclesiastical matters, including *An apology for the revival of Christian architecture in England* (1843), and was also responsible for designing the decorations and furniture for Barry's Houses of Parliament.

PULCI, Luigi (1432–84), Florentine poet of the circle of Lorenzo de' *Medici. His poem *Morgante Maggiore* was the first romantic epic to be written by an Italian *letterato*, and was a major source for *Rabelais.

Pulitzer Prizes, annual prizes established under the will of Joseph Pulitzer (1847–1911), an American newspaper-proprietor of Hungarian birth, who used sensational journalism for the correction of social abuses. The prizes, which are confined to American citizens, are offered in the interest of letters (American history and biography, poetry, drama, and novel-writing), music, and good newspaper work. A fund of $500,000 was set aside for the prizes, which are controlled by the School of Journalism (also founded under the terms of Pulitzer's will) at Columbia University.

Pullet, Mr and Mrs, characters in G. Eliot's *The Mill on the Floss*.

Pumblechook, Mr, a character in Dickens's *Great Expectations*.

Pun, a play on words, depending on similarity of sound and difference in meaning. Shakespeare was greatly given to punning, both in comic and in serious contexts: for an example of the latter, see Sonnet 135, 'Therefore I lie with her, and she with me, | And in our faults by lies we flattered be.' The pun fell in to disrepute in the 18th and 19th cents, but was somewhat reinstated as a form of ambiguity in W. Empson's *Seven Types of Ambiguity* (See also PARONOMASIA.)

Punch, or *The London Charivari*, an illustrated weekly comic periodical, founded 1841; at first a rather strongly Radical paper, gradually becoming more bland and less political.

Various accounts have been given of the birth

of this famous paper. One or two illustrated comic papers had already appeared in London, notably Gilbert Abbott *à Beckett's *Figaro in London* (1831) and *Punchinello* (1832), illustrated by *Cruikshank. It appears that the idea of starting in London a comic paper somewhat on the lines of Philippon's Paris *Charivari* first occurred to Ebenezer Landells, draughtsman and wood-engraver, who submitted it to *Mayhew. Mayhew took up the proposal and enlisted the support of *Lemon and Joseph Stirling Coyne (1803–68), who became the first joint-editors. The first number was issued on 17 July 1841. Joseph Last was the first printer, and Landells the first engraver. A Beckett and *Jerrold were among the original staff, soon joined by *Thackeray, *Hood, *Leech, and *Tenniel, among others. Shirley Brooks (1816–74) became editor in 1870, Tom *Taylor in 1874, and *Burnand in 1880. Sir Owen Seaman was editor from 1906 to 1932; he was succeeded by E. V. *Knox, 1932–49. Kenneth Bird (better known as the cartoonist 'Fougasse'), was editor from 1949 to 1952; Malcolm Muggeridge 1953–7; Bernard Hollowood 1958–68; William Davis 1969–78; and Alan Coren (who introduced full colour cartoon covers, mainly topical) from 1978. Recent regular contributors have included M. *Bragg, Hunter Davis, Benny Green, and Alan Brien.

Among other famous draughtsmen of the past may be mentioned Charles Keene (1823–91), whose first drawing in *Punch* appeared in 1851 and who joined the staff in 1860; and *Du Maurier, who contributed drawings from 1860 and joined the staff in 1864. The most famous drawing for the cover, by R. *Doyle, was used from 1849 to 1956, when it was replaced by a full-colour design, different each week. The Punch figure and the dog Toby usually appeared in the design on the front cover until 1969, and the last vestige of the original Doyle frieze disappeared from the inside pages in 1978. Amongst the many eminent cartoonists of later years, mention may be made of Ronald Searle, Bill Tidy, Michael Heath, Norman Thelwell, and Gerald Scarfe.

Puntarvolo, in Jonson's *Every Man out of his Humour*, a boastful, quixotic knight.

Puppet-play, see MOTION.

PURCELL, Henry (1659–95), English composer, who began his musical career as a chorister and later organist of the Chapel Royal, and at the age of 20 succeeded *Blow as organist at Westminster Abbey. A considerable part of his output consisted of anthems and other sacred works, the former to texts from the Bible or Book of Common Prayer, the latter with words by *Cowley, *Tate, *Quarles, *Flatman and others. Comparable to these in the secular field are the various Odes and Welcome songs, written mainly for royal occasions to texts in courtly language, which drew from the composer music that was often splendid but generally uncomplicated in style.

The mixture of instrumental, choral, and vocal styles in works like these is complex and varied, yet throughout it is the solo vocal line, idiomatic, flexible, and richly coloured by a vivid harmonic sense, that most profoundly influenced later composers. His 250 solo songs range from simple, almost folk-song-like tunes to elaborate sequences of recitative and aria that develop and improve on the declamatory style introduced from Italy by *Lawes and M. *Locke; some of these were independent compositions, but many more were written for the 49 stage works (by *Dryden, *Shadwell, *D'Urfey, *Southerne, and others) for which Purcell is known to have provided music. 'The Author's extraordinary Talent in all sorts of Musick is sufficiently known', wrote musician John Playford in 1698, 'but he was especially admir'd for the *Vocal*, having a peculiar Genius to express the Energy of *English* Words, whereby he mov'd the Passions of all his Auditors.'

It was this distinctive gift that assured the position of Purcell's one opera *Dido and Aeneas* (modelled in part on Blow's *Venus and Adonis*) in the history of music. It was written to a libretto by Tate for performance by the young gentlewomen of Josias Priest's boarding-school at Chelsea in 1689. Though short and restricted in theatrical scope, *Dido* achieves an astonishing range of dramatic expression: from the ribald vitality of the sailors to the fiery exchanges between Dido and Aeneas and the noble resignation of Dido's lament, 'When I am laid in earth', there is a sureness of characterization and depth of human understanding that justifies the work's place as the most famous of English operas.

It was Purcell's only opera in the strict sense of the word, but he also provided music for five 'semi-operas' in the last five years of his life. Of these, only *King Arthur* (by Dryden, 1691) was written with Purcell's music in mind, and it is therefore perhaps the most satisfactory whole; the song 'Fairest Isle' comes in the fifth act. The music for *The Prophetess, or the History of Dioclesian* (1690), adapted from *Beaumont and *Fletcher by *Betterton, includes a much admired masque that is complete in itself, and *The Fairy Queen* (1692), an elaboration of *A Midsummer Night's Dream*, consists almost entirely of masques, to the virtual exclusion of Shakespeare's play. (This is the longest of Purcell's dramatic works, but it contains no setting of Shakespeare's words.) The two last stage works, *The Indian Queen* and a final Shakespearian adaptation, Shadwell's arrangement of Dryden and *D'Avenant's version of *The Tempest*, were both written in the last year of Purcell's life. They exhibit the composer's dramatic and musical gifts at their highest, yet they remain obstinately hybrid period pieces. (See also LIBRETTO; OPERA.)

PURCHAS, Samuel (?1577–1626), educated at St John's College, Cambridge, and rector of St Martin's, Ludgate, published in 1613 *Purchas his Pilgrimage, or Relations of the World and the Religions observed in all Ages*; in 1619 *Purchas his Pilgrim*; and in 1625 *Hakluytus Posthumus, or Purchas his Pilgrimes, contayning a History of the World in Sea Voyages and Land Travell by Englishmen and others*. This last is in part based on manuscripts left by *Hakluyt, and consists of two sections, each of ten books. The first section, after an introductory book, contains accounts of voyages to India, China, Japan, Africa, and the Mediterranean. The second part deals with attempts to discover the North-West Passage, the Muscovy expeditions, and explorations of the West Indies and Florida. Among the best narratives are William Adams's description of his voyage to Japan and residence there and William Hawkins's account of his visit to the court of the Great Mogul at Agra. *Coleridge, according to his own account, was reading about Kubla Khan in Purchas when he fell into the trance that produced his own poem on the subject, and J. L. *Lowes in *The Road to Xanadu* (1927) further traces his debt. (See also ROMANTICISM.)

Purgatorio, The, of Dante, see DIVINA COMMEDIA.

Puritan, The, or *the Widow of Watling-Street*, a comedy published in 1607 as 'written by W.S.' and included in the 3rd and 4th Shakespeare folios, but by some other hand, almost certainly *Middleton's.

The play is a farcical comedy of London manners, and sets forth the tricks played on the widow and her daughter by Capt. Idle and George Pye-boord in order to win their hands, with scenes in the Marshalsea.

Purley, The Diversions of, see TOOKE, J. H.

Purple Island, The, see FLETCHER, P.

Pursuits of Literature, The, see MATHIAS, T. J.

PUSEY, Edward Bouverie (1800–82), educated at Christ Church, Oxford, was elected a fellow of Oriel College in 1823. In 1828 he was ordained deacon and priest, and appointed Regius professor of Hebrew. He became attached to the *Oxford Movement in 1833 and joined *Keble and *Newman in contributing, in 1834, No. 18 for *Tracts for the Times* and Nos. 67–9, in 1836, on 'Scriptural Views of Holy Baptism'; Pusey gave the Movement cohesion and prestige by his erudition, and in 1841 when Newman withdrew he became its leader. His most influential activity was preaching and his sermon on 'The Holy Eucharist, a Comfort

to the Penitent' (1843) caused his suspension for heresy from the office of university preacher for two years. The condemnation drew him wide publicity and attracted attention to the doctrine of the Real Presence of which he was a devoted defender. He was a principal defender of the doctrines of the High Church Movement, a passionate believer in the union of the English and Roman Churches, and endeavoured to hinder secessions to the Roman Catholic Church which prevailed at that time.

PUSHKIN, Alexander Sergeevich (1799–1837), Russia's greatest poet. Born in Moscow into an ancient gentry family, he attended the Lyceum at Tsarskoe Selo, outside St Petersburg, where he began to write poetry. He worked in government service, but was expelled from St Petersburg in 1820 for writing revolutionary epigrams. From 1820 to 1823 he served in Kishinev. In August 1824 he was dismissed from the civil service for atheistic writings, and his seclusion at his mother's estate prevented him from taking part in the revolt of the Decembrists, with whom he sympathized. In 1832 he married a young beauty, Natalia Goncharova. The attentions paid to his wife by Baron Georges D'Anthès, a French royalist in the Russian Service, caused him to challenge D'Anthès to a duel, in which Pushkin was fatally wounded.

Pushkin wrote prolifically in a variety of genres: lyric poems, among the most important of which are 'Winter Evening' (1825), 'The Prophet' (1826), 'I remember a wondrous moment' (1827), 'The Poet' (1827), 'The Upas-tree' (1828), and 'I loved you' (1829); narrative poems in various styles, including *Ruslan and Ludmilla* (1820), a Romantic epic, *The Prisoner of the Caucasus* (1820–1) and *The Fountain of Bakhchisarai* (1822), which examine Romantic and *Byronic themes, *The Gypsies* (1824), in which Romantic influences are discarded, the comic *Count Nulin* (1825) and *The Little House in Kolomna* (1830), the historical *Poltava* (1829), and *The Bronze Horseman* (1833), in which the statue of Peter the Great chases the clerk Evgeny through St Petersburg during the flood of 1824; the novel in verse *Eugene Onegin* (1823–31), his greatest and most sophisticated work; plays, including the blank verse historical drama *Boris Godunov* (1825) and the four 'Little Tragedies': 'Mozart and Salieri', 'The Covetous Knight', 'The Stone Guest', and 'The Feast during the Plague' (all 1830); and prose, on which he concentrated after 1830, *The Tales of Belkin* (1830), *The Queen of Spades* (1834), and *The Captain's Daughter* (1836). No Russian writer of note since his time escaped his influence.

Pushkin was extremely widely read in English literature, and particularly interested, at different times, in Shakespeare, *Sterne, *Richardson, *Byron, and Sir W. *Scott. Allusions to these and other English writers are common in his writings. The first English translation, by G. *Borrow, was *The Talisman: from the Russian of Alexander Pushkin. With other pieces* (St Petersburg, 1835). Recent translations include those by John Fennell (1964), Gillon Aitken (*The Complete Prose Tales*, 1962, etc.), Antony Wood (1982), and D. M. *Thomas (1982). *Nabokov's controversial but scholarly translation (in unrhymed iambics) of *Eugene Onegin* appeared in 1964 (rev. edn 1977, when it was described by R. *Lowell as a work of 'fascinating eccentricity'); it was followed by Sir Charles Johnston's stanzaic version, which also appeared in 1977.

Puss in Boots, a popular tale, from the French of *Perrault, translated by Robert Samber (?1729). A version is also found in *Straparola's *Piacevoli Notti*.
A miller bequeaths to his three sons respectively, his mill, his ass, and his cat. The youngest, who inherits the cat, laments his ill-fortune. But the resourceful cat, by a series of unscrupulous ruses, in which he represents his master to the king as the wealthy marquis of Carabas, secures for him the hand of the king's daughter.
*Lang, in *Perrault's Popular Tales* (1888), discusses the origin of the story, which is found, in various forms, in several countries.

PUTTENHAM, George (*c*.1529–91), was a nephew of Sir T. *Elyot, and almost certainly author of *The Arte of English Poesie*, sometimes ascribed to his brother Richard. It appeared anonymously in 1589, but is thought to have been in manuscript in some form perhaps 20 years earlier. It is a critical treatise in three books, *Of Poets and Poesie*, *Of Proportion*, and *Of Ornament*, important as a record of Elizabethan taste and theory, and lively in its own right. The author's tone is personal, and he mingles anecdotes with serious appraisal, illustrating the view that epitaphs should be brief by telling us that he was locked up in a cathedral by the sexton while reading a long one. He condemns *Gower for 'false orthographie', finds *Skelton 'a rude rayling rimer and in all his doings ridiculous', and praises *Wyatt and *Surrey as the stars of a 'new company of courtly makers'. In the second book he discusses 'courtly trifles' such as anagrams, *emblems, and posies, showing a fondness for 'ocular representations'—in particular for poems shaped liked eggs and pillars. The third book defines and illustrates various figures of speech and suggests vulgar names for Greek and Latin originals, e.g. 'single supply, ringleader and middlemarcher' (zeugma, prozeugma, and mezozeugma), 'the drie mock' (irony), 'the bitter taunt' (sarcasm), and 'the over reacher' (hyperbole). He attacks excessive use of foreign words, but was aware of the rapidly changing vernacular. The *Arte* was edited by

G. D. Willcock and Alice Walker (1936). George Puttenham may also be the author of a royal panegyric, *Partheniades*.

Pwyll, in Welsh mythology, prince of Dyfed and 'Head of Hades', the subject of the first story in the *Mabinogion*. The stories of Sir *Pelleas and King *Pelles in *Malory are perhaps connected with his myth. See J. Rhys, *Studies in the Arthurian Legend* (1891).

PYE, Henry James (1745–1813), became poet laureate in 1790, and was the constant butt of contemporary ridicule.

Pyke and Pluck, in Dickens's *Nicholas Nickleby*, the toadies of Sir Mulberry Hawk.

Pygmalion, one of the most popular plays of Bernard *Shaw, first performed 1913 in Vienna, published and performed in London, 1916.
It describes the transformation of a Cockney flower-seller, Eliza Doolittle, into a passable imitation of a duchess by the phonetician Professor Henry Higgins (modelled in part on H. *Sweet), who undertakes this task in order to win a bet and to prove his own points about English speech and the class system: he teaches her to speak standard English and introduces her successfully to social life, thus winning his bet, but she rebels against his dictatorial and thoughtless behaviour, and 'bolts' from his tyranny. The play ends with a truce between the two of them, as Higgins acknowledges that she has achieved freedom and independence, and emerged from his treatment as a 'tower of strength: a consort battleship': in his postscript Shaw tells us that she marries the docile and devoted Freddy Eynsford Hill. *My Fair Lady*, the 1957 musical version, makes the relationship between Eliza and Higgins significantly more romantic.
Pygmalion, in classical legend, was the king of Cyprus, who fell in love with his own sculpture; Aphrodite endowed the statue with life and transformed it into the flesh-and-blood of Galatea.

Pylon School, a nickname for the group of younger left-wing poets of the 1930s, chiefly *Auden, *Day-Lewis, *MacNeice, and *Spender, alluding to the rather self-conscious use of industrial imagery in their work. Spender's poem 'The Pylons' was published in 1933, and pylons and skyscrapers appear in Day-Lewis's poem to Auden ('Look west, Wystan, lone flyers') in *The Magnetic Mountain* (1933); Auden's own verse features power stations ('Out on the lawn I lie in bed', 1933), and landscapes of arterial roads and filling stations are evoked in, e.g., Auden and *Isherwood's *The Dog beneath the Skin* (1935), whereas MacNeice's early work has a high preponderance of poems about trains and trams.

PYM, Barbara Mary Crampton (1913–80), novelist, the daughter of a Shropshire solicitor. She was educated at St Hilda's College, Oxford, and later worked at the International African Institute in London. Her novels include *Excellent Women* (1952), *Less than Angels* (1955), *A Glass of Blessings* (1958, described by *Larkin as 'the subtlest of her books'), and *Quartet in Autumn* (1977). They are satirical tragicomedies of middle-class life, and contain some distinctive portraits of church-going spinsters and charismatic priests; many of the relationships described consist of a kind of celibate flirtation.

Pyncheon, Hepzibah, a character in Hawthorne's *The House of the Seven Gables*.

PYNCHON, Thomas (1937–), American novelist, born on Long Island, and educated at Cornell. His first novel, *V* (1963), a complex philosophical allegory featuring, among other characters, the mythical albino alligators that inhabit the sewers of New York, was followed by the shorter fable *The Crying of Lot 49* (1966), a surreal comedy satirizing Californian life, and the lengthy *Gravity's Rainbow* (1973), set in the closing years of the Second World War. His work, which offers a fantastic survey of the contemporary scene, has affinities with *Magic Realism.

Pyrochles, in Spenser's *Faerie Queene*, symbolizes rage. He is the brother of *Cymochles, the son of 'old *Acrates* and *Despight*' (II. iv. 41). On his shield is a flaming fire, with the words '*Burnt I do burne*'. He is overcome by Sir *Guyon (II. v), and tries to drown himself in a lake to quench his flames. He is rescued and healed by *Archimago (II. vi. 42–51), and finally killed by Prince *Arthur (II. viii).

Pyrocles, the young prince of Macedon in Sidney's *Arcadia*, who adopts a disguise as an Amazon in order to woo Philoclea.

Pyrrhic, see METRE.

Pyrrho, see SCEPTICISM.

PYTHAGORAS, the Greek philosopher, native of Samos, who lived in the second half of the 6th cent. BC. He settled in Cortona in Italy where he founded a brotherhood who combined ascetic practices and mystical beliefs with the study of mathematics. Pythagoras is credited with the discovery of the proof of the proposition that the square on the hypotenuse of a right-angled triangle is equal to the sum of the squares on the other two sides, which is called therefore the Pythagorean Theorem. He worked out a mathematical basis for music and supposed the heavenly bodies to be divided by intervals according to the laws of musical harmony, whence arose the idea of the harmony of the spheres. He discovered the rotation of the earth on its axis and found in this the causes of day and night. His religious teaching centred on the doctrine of metempsychosis, or the transmigration of souls from man to man, man to animal, or animal to man in a process of purification or punishment. There are references to this Pythagorean doctrine in the dialogue between Feste and Malvolio (*Twelfth Night*, IV. ii), in *The Merchant of Venice* (IV. i), and in *As you Like It* (III. ii); and Faustus, in *Marlowe's tragedy, cries in his last moments of anguish, 'Ah, Pythagoras' *metempsychosis*, were that true This soul should fly from me' (*Dr Faustus*, V. ii). The *Pythagorean Letter* is the Greek Y used as symbol of the divergent paths of vice and virtue. None of Pythagoras' writings have survived, but his teachings exerted a marked influence on later Greek philosophers and notably on *Plato.

Pythias, see DAMON AND PITHIAS.

Q

Q, the initial of German *Quelle*, 'source', is the symbol used, in the comparative study of the synoptic Gospels, to designate a supposed Greek translation of a collection attributed to Matthew of the *logia* of Christ, from which the parts common to the Gospels of Matthew and Luke, but omitted from Mark, are derived. It is supposed to have contained certain narrative parts, but not the Passion.

'Q', see JERROLD, D. W., and QUILLER-COUCH.

Quackleben, Dr, a character in Scott's *St Ronan's Well.*

Quadrivium, the higher division of the Seven Liberal Arts, comprising the sciences, arithmetic, geometry, astronomy, and music (as distinct from the methodological subjects of the *Trivium*, grammar, rhetoric, and logic). Although the Liberal Arts in groupings of this kind were a staple of Greek and Roman education, the Quadrivium as such originates with *Martianus Capella (early 5th cent.), followed by *Boethius and his pupil Cassiodorus whose 6th-cent. *On the Arts and Disciplines of the Liberal Letters* was the definitive text for the Middle Ages. The Quadrivium had great importance for the writers of Chartres in the 11th–12th cents; it was neglected by the metaphysical synthesists of the 13th cent., and became associated thereafter with Oxford rather than with the Schools of continental Europe which were less interested in the material sciences. (See BACON, R.) See G. Leff, *Medieval Thought: St Augustine to Ockham* (1958), *passim.*

Quakers, members of the Society of *Friends.

QUARITCH, Bernard (1819–99), bookseller, at first employed by *Bohn, started his own firm in 1847. He was the first to publish Fitzgerald's *The Rubáiyát of *Omar Khayyám* (1859). He was the author of the valuable bibliographical work *A General Catalogue* (1887–97). His interests were wide and above all he was known as a collector of incunabula, fine manuscripts, Bibles, Shakespeariana, early English literature, and cartography.

QUARLES, Francis (1592–1644), born near Romford in Essex, was educated at Christ's College, Cambridge, and at Lincoln's Inn. He went abroad in the suite of the Princess Elizabeth on her marriage with the Elector Palatine. He made his reputation in the 1620s by a series of biblical paraphrases (e.g. *A Feast for Worms*, 1620), and in 1629 published a 'vain amatory poem', *Argalus and Parthenia*, based on an episode in Sidney's *Arcadia*. He is chiefly remembered for his extremely successful and popular *Emblems* (1635) and *Hieroglyphikes of the Life of Man* (1638). In 1639 he was appointed chronologer to the City of London. From 1640 he turned to prose, publishing pamphlets, some anonymous, holding a constitutionalist–royalist position. A petition circulated against him in 1644 accused him of popery, but A. *Wood declared that he was a Puritan. *Eclogues* (1646) and a comedy, *The Virgin Widow* (1649), were published posthumously. A nearly complete collection of his works was edited by *Grosart (3 vols, 1880–1) and additional poems by J. Hordern (1960).

Quarterly Review, The (1809–1967), was founded by John *Murray as a Tory rival to the Whig *Edinburgh Review*. Sir W. *Scott, who had been harshly reviewed in the *Edinburgh*, became an ardent supporter of the venture and offered much guidance, but refused the editorship. The journal stood, politically, for the defence of the established order, Church, and Crown; its unwavering adherence to the bishops and the Church was satirized by Peacock in *Melincourt*. Its tone was magisterial from the beginning, and its influence, both literary and political, was for the best part of the century matched only by that of the *Edinburgh*. The first editor, *Gifford, brought with him several clever writers from *The Anti-Jacobin*, including *Canning and *Frere, but the quality of his chief writers (largely Scott and *Southey) could not match that of the *Edinburgh*, who had *Hazlitt, *Macaulay, *Carlyle, and *Jeffrey, among many others. The *Quarterly's* enemies averred that its political bias strongly affected its literary criticism. However, unlike the *Edinburgh*, it supported the *'Lake School' and *Byron, although it fiercely condemned *Keats, *Hunt, Hazlitt, *Lamb, *Shelley, and later *Tennyson, Macaulay, *Dickens, and C. *Brontë. Two of its more famous early articles were those of Scott in praise of J. Austen's *Emma*; and Croker's review of Keats's *'Endymion', a review which, according to the poet's friends, hastened Keats's death (but see CROKER, J. H.). Gifford was succeeded as editor in 1825 by *Lockhart, who was in his turn followed by a distinguished line, including members of the Murray family. In the second half of the 19th cent. the *Quarterly* published the work of many notable writers and critics, including *Bulwer-Lytton, *Thackeray, *Martineau, *Borrow, M. *Arnold, and *Swinburne.

QUASIMODO, Salvatore (1901–68), Italian poet associated with *hermeticism, was awarded the *Nobel Prize (1959). His main collections are *Acque e terre* (*Water and Land*, 1930), *Oboe sommerso* (*Sunken Oboe*, 1932), and *Ed è subito sera* (*And it's suddenly evening*, 1942). After the Second World War his hermeticism yielded to a more extrovert poetry of social conscience, as in *Con il piede straniero sopra il cuore* (*With the alien foot on our heart*, 1946), *La vita non è sogno* (*Life is not dream*, 1949), and *Dare e avere* (*Giving and having*, 1966). He has been translated by R. *Wilbur.

Quasimodo Sunday, the first Sunday after Easter, so called from the first two words of the introit of the mass of that day.

Quasimodo is the name of the deformed bell-ringer of Notre Dame in *Hugo's *Notre Dame de Paris*.

Queen Mab, a visionary and ideological poem by P. B. *Shelley, written in England and Wales during his early period of political activism, published privately 1813, when he was 21.

The poem is in nine cantos, using 'didactic and descriptive' blank verse greatly indebted to *Milton and to Southey's *Thalaba*. Despite its lyrical opening, invoking 'Death and his brother Sleep' and Mab the Fairy Queen in her time-chariot (Cantos I and II), the poem largely consists of attacks on Monarchy (III), War (IV), Commerce (V), and Religion (VI and VII). In place of these Shelley celebrates a future of Republicanism, Free Love, Atheism, and Vegetarianism. The verse is furious and polemical in style, with occasional passages of grandiloquent beauty, such as Canto VIII, presaging Asia's speeches in *Prometheus Unbound*. Seventeen remarkable prose *Notes* are attached as Appendices, many of them substantial essays, 'against Jesus Christ, & God the Father, & the King, & the Bishops, & Marriage, & the Devil knows what', as Shelley himself later put it. They are often better than the poetry: Note 9 on Free Love is especially striking, showing the influence of *Hume, *Godwin, *Wollstonecraft, and *Rousseau. The work was extremely popular among working-class radicals, and ran to 14 cheap editions by 1840.

Queen Mary, a historical drama by *Tennyson published 1875, a lengthy treatment of the reign of Mary Tudor in 23 scenes.

Queen of Cornwall, *The Famous Tragedy of the,* a poetic drama by T. *Hardy, published 1923.

The play is a re-telling of the old story of King Mark, the two Iseults, and Tristram. The events are conjured up by Merlin, and the Chanters perform as Chorus. Queen Iseult has been to seek her love Tristram in Brittany, but is told that he is dead. Tristram discovers that his wife, Iseult of Brittany, had deceived him in telling him that the queen would not come to him. Disguised as a harper, he travels to Cornwall, followed by his wife. King Mark, the jealous husband of Queen Iseult, discovers his wife with Tristram and kills him. The queen then stabs Mark and leaps over a cliff to her death. The play was first produced in 1923 by the Hardy Players in Dorchester.

Queen of the May, see MAY DAY.

Queen's Maries (or **Marys**), **The,** the four ladies named Mary attendant on *Mary Queen of Scots. The list is variously given, including: Mary Seton, Mary Beaton, Mary Livingstone, Mary Fleming, Mary Hamilton, and Mary Carmichael. They are frequently mentioned in Scottish ballads.

Queen's Wake, The, a poem by J. *Hogg, published 1813. Queen Mary of Scotland holds her 'wake' at Holyrood, during which seventeen bards, including Rizzio, sing their songs in competition. These are verse-tales in various styles: martial, comic, horrible, or mystical. The most memorable is the tale of *Kilmeny, but 'The Witch of Fife' is also an effective work.

QUENNELL, Peter (1905–), poet, historian, biographer, and editor, and the son of social historians Marjorie and C. H. B. Quennell, was educated at Berkhamsted Grammar School and Balliol College, Oxford. He was editor of the *Cornhill Magazine* (1944–51) and of *History Today* (1951–79). His first volume, *Poems* (1926), was followed by many other works, including *Four Portraits* (1945; studies of *Boswell, *Gibbon, *Sterne, and *Wilkes) and works on *Pope, *Byron, *Ruskin, and Dr *Johnson. *The Marble Foot* (1976) is a volume of autobiography.

Quentin Durward, a novel by Sir W. *Scott, published 1823.

The scene is laid in the 15th cent. and the principal character is Louis XI of France, crafty, cruel, and superstitious, yet prudent and capable, in contrast to his vassal and enemy, the violent and impetuous Charles the Bold of Burgundy. The story is concerned with the intrigues by which Louis attempts to procure, with the assistance of William de la Marck, the Wild Boar of the Ardennes, the revolt of Liège against Charles; with the murder of the bishop of Liège; and with the famous visit of Louis to Charles at Peronne and their temporary reconciliation. Quentin Durward is a young Scot of good family who engages himself in the corps of the Scottish Archers of the Guard of Louis. He is sent to conduct the young Countess Isabelle de Croye, a Burgundian heiress who has fled from a threatened marriage with the odious Campo-Basso, to the protection of the bishop of Liège; saves her from many perils; and finally wins her hand by compassing the destruction of William de la Marck. Among the interesting secondary characters may be mentioned: Tristan l'Hermite, Louis's provost marshal; Oliver le Dain, his counsellor and one-time barber; Martius Galeotti, his astrologer; the Cardinal La Balue, and Philippe de *Commines (called Philip des Comines in the novel) whose *Mémoires* provided the background for the plot. The well known lyric 'County Guy' occurs in ch. iv.

Querno, in Pope's **Dunciad* (ii. 15), was an Apulian poet to whom the author compares C. *Cibber. According to Paulus Jovius, Querno, hearing that Pope Leo X patronized literature, set out for Rome where he recited some 20,000 lines of his *Alexias* and was made poet laureate as a joke.

Questing Beast, The, in *Malory, pursued by *Palomydes the Saracen. See GLATYSAUNT BEAST.

QUEVEDO VILLEGAS, Francisco de (1580–1645), the great Spanish satirist, was author of the picaresque novel *La Vida del Buscón* (1626), translated into English (through a French intermediary) by John Davies of Kidwelly, as *The life and adventures of Buscan* (1657), and later by J. Stevens as *The Life of Paul the Spanish sharper* (1707). His *Sueños* (1627), which are biting satiric portraits of members of all classes of society, were translated by *Crashaw (from the French) as *Visions or hels kingdom* (1640), and later by *L'Estrange (1667). Quevedo also wrote political works, satirical poetry, etc.

Quickly, Mistress, in Shakespeare's *1* and *2* **Henry IV*, hostess of the Boar's Head Tavern in Eastcheap; *Falstaff is betrothed and in debt to her. In **The Merry Wives of Windsor* she is housekeeper to Dr Caius. In **Henry V* she is married to *Pistol and describes Falstaff's death (II. iii).

Quietism, a form of religious mysticism (originated before 1675 by *Molinos), consisting in passive devotional contemplation, with extinction of the will and withdrawal from all things of the senses [*OED*]. One of the best-known exponents of Quietist doctrines was *Fénelon, whose *Maximes des Saints*, embodying his opinions, was condemned by Rome. Another noted Quietist was Mme Guyon (1648–1717).

QUILLER-COUCH, Sir Arthur Thomas (1863–1944), son of a Cornish doctor, was educated at Clifton and Oxford, where he began writing parodies under the pseudonym 'Q', which he used all his life. His prolific literary career opened with the publication of a novel of adventure, *Dead Man's Rock* (1887), after which followed a vast output of criticism, fiction, verse, anthologies, and literary journalism. In 1900 he edited the first *Oxford Book of English Verse*, which had considerable influence and large international sales. A knighthood in 1910 was followed in 1912 by the chair of English at Cambridge, where in 1917 he established the Final Honours School in that subject. Two influential volumes of lectures, *On the Art of Writing* and *On the Art of Reading*, appeared in 1916 and 1920, and his edition of the *New Cambridge Shakespeare* began to appear in 1921. In 1928 his collected novels and stories appeared in 30 volumes. The first volume of his unfinished autobiography, *Memories and Opinions* (1944), covers his early years. See a life by F. Brittain (1947).

Quilp, Daniel and Mrs, characters in Dickens's **The Old Curiosity Shop*.

QUILTER, Roger (1877–1953), English composer, remembered chiefly for his many songs, which enjoyed considerable popularity in their day and were fluently and sensitively written, if not touching any very profound level of emotion. He made many Shakespeare settings, among which the *Three Shakespeare Songs* of 1905 are outstanding, but took texts from most periods of English literature: songs like 'Love's Philosophy' (*Shelley) and 'Now sleeps the crimson petal' (Tennyson, **The Princess*) were staple recital diet during the first half of the 20th cent.

QUIN, James (1693–1766), an actor who first made his name playing Bajazet in Rowe's **Tamerlane*. He took leading parts in tragedy at Drury Lane, Lincoln's Inn Fields, and Covent Garden. He was the last of the old school of actors, which gave place to that of *Garrick. Smollett introduces him in **Humphry Clinker*.

Quinbus Flestrin, 'the Great Man-Mountain', the name by which Gulliver was known in Lilliput (**Gulliver's Travels*, ch. 2), and sometimes used as a pseudonym in magazines of the period.

Quince, Peter, in Shakespeare's **A Midsummer Night's Dream*, a carpenter, the stage-manager of the interlude 'Pyramus and Thisbe'.

QUINE, Willard Van Orman (1908–), American mathematical logician and philosopher, born in Ohio and educated at Harvard, where he became Edgar Pierce professor of philosophy. He has defended a system of logic, inspired by B. *Russell, where singular terms are eliminated in favour of general terms. He has argued against the existence of a sharp distinction between analytic truths (e.g. 'All bachelors are unmarried') and synthetic truths (e.g. 'Hume was a bachelor'). He has also doubted the extent to which translation is possible between languages. His slogan, 'To be is to be the value of a variable', is a logician's criterion of what it is for something to exist. Quine's works include *Methods of Logic* (1950), *From a Logical Point of View* (1953), and *Word and Object* (1960).

QUINTILIAN (Marcus Fabius Quintilianus) (AD *c.*35–*c.*100), Roman rhetorician, educationist, and literary critic. His monumental *De Institutione Oratoria* is not only a treatise on rhetoric, but discusses also the training of an ideal orator for whom Quintilian like Cicero advocates a wide general education; Book X contains a critical history of Greek and Roman literature. This work was known in a mutilated form only until Poggio unearthed a complete text in 1416, after which it served the humanists as a guide on all literary and educational matters. Jonson excerpted it in *Timber, Milton referred to it in the *Tetrachordon sonnet, and *Dryden cited it on a number of points.

Quinze Joyes de Mariage, Les, a French anti-feminist satire, of doubtful authorship, dating from the early 15th cent. Several English versions of the work were made in the 17th and 18th cents, including one by *Dekker entitled *The Batchelars Banquet* (1603).

Quirk, Gammon, and Snap, see WARREN, S.

Quixote, see DON QUIXOTE.

R

'**Rabbi Ben Ezra**', a poem by R. Browning, included in *Dramatis Personae*.

RABELAIS, François (c.1494–c.1553), French physician, humanist, and satirist. The son of a Touraine lawyer, he became successively a Franciscan monk, the secretary of the bishop of Maillezais (c.1524), and a Bachelor of Medicine from Montpellier (1530). He published various works on archaeology and medicine in Latin, and in French the satirical entertainments with the popular giants *Gargantua and *Pantagruel for which he is remembered. He travelled regularly in France and Italy, and acquired a widespread reputation for his erudition and medical skill. For much of his life he enjoyed the patronage of Cardinal Jean du Bellay and the protection of François I, but he was subject to frequent proscriptions and condemnations. Rabelais' great prose work is a unique expression of Renaissance energy and plenitude. His comic inventiveness, ranging from obscenity, wit, and jokes to parody, invective, and fantasy, is inexhaustible. His intellectual curiosity, which encompasses virtually all the sciences and techniques of his age—theology, law, medicine, natural science, politics, military art, navigation, botany, Hebrew, Basque, etc.—is insatiable. His knowledge of contemporary life and society, from rustics, artisans, and monks to merchants, landowners, and academics, is without rival. His command of the vernacular, sustained by an encyclopaedic vocabulary and a virtuoso's rhetorical repertoire, and extending beyond French and its dialects to a dozen contemporary languages, remains unique in French literature. His work as a whole seems to rest on a moderate, progressive Protestantism opposed to tyranny, dogmatism, and war. His realism recognizes the physical functions of mankind, affirms its uncorrupted origins, trusts in the effectiveness of virtuous action, and urges gaiety of mind as a supreme good. Although he was known to G. *Harvey and F. *Bacon, he was not translated into English until *Urquhart's magisterial version of 1653 (Books I and II) and 1693–4 (Book III together with *Motteux's translation of Books IV and V). Thereafter his influence on English literature was widespread, though particularly marked on S. *Butler, *Swift, *Sterne, *Peacock, and *Joyce.

RACHMANINOV, Sergei Vasilyevich (1873–1943), Russian composer and pianist. His long choral symphony *Kolokola* (1913) is a setting of an adaptation, by the Russian symbolist poet Konstantin Balmont, of *The Bells* by *Poe. One of the best of Rachmaninov's large-scale works, and his own favourite, it is skilfully orchestrated to convey Poe's symbolical interpretation of the different types of bell. Poe's text was peculiarly suited to Rachmaninov's temperament; apart from an unfinished (and lost) orchestral work on *Manfred, and a single early setting of *Shelley, it remained his only composition inspired by an English-language writer.

RACINE, Jean (1639–99), French tragic dramatist. He was informally educated by the Jansenists of *Port-Royal, but was estranged from them between 1666 and 1677, during which time he wrote the majority of his plays. His tragedies derive from various sources: from Greek and Roman literature, *Andromaque* (1667), *Iphigénie* (1674), and *Phèdre* (1677); from Roman history, *Britannicus* (1669), *Bérénice* (1670), and *Mithridate* (1673); from contemporary Turkish history, *Bajazet* (1672); and from the Bible, *Esther* (1689) and *Athalie* (1691). He also wrote one comedy, *Les Plaideurs* (1668), drawn from *Aristophanes. Central to the majority of the tragedies is a perception of the blind folly of human passion, continually enslaved to the pursuit of its object and destined always to be unsatisfied. The plays were extensively translated into English from the 1670s, but differences in national tastes and dramatic conventions have rendered most English versions wildly unfaithful to their originals. The most famous of these versions was *The Distrest Mother*, an adaptation of *Andromaque* by A. *Philips, which ran to many editions between 1712 and the 1820s. There are modern versions of *Phèdre* by R. *Lowell (1961) and T. *Harrison (1975).

RACKHAM, Arthur (1867–1939), children's book illustrator. Amongst his most successful works are *Fairy Tales of the Brothers Grimm* (1900), *Rip van Winkle* (1905), which established him as the fashionable illustrator of his time, and *Peter Pan in Kensington Gardens* (1906). Rackham's vein of fantasy is Nordic—he created a sinister, enchanted world, full of the twisting roots and tendrils of gnarled trees with gnome-like faces, and peopled by spiky goblins, fairies, weird birds, mice, and monsters. Rackham believed passionately in 'the greatest stimulating and educative power of imaginative, fantastic and playful pictures and writings for children in their most impressionable years'.

RADCLIFFE, Mrs Ann (1764–1823), daughter of a London tradesman, William Ward, married in 1786 William Radcliffe, manager of *The English Chronicle*. In the next twelve years she published five novels, *The Castles of Athlin and Dunbayne* (1789), *A Sicilian Romance* (1790), *The Romance of the Forest* (1791), **The Mysteries of Udolpho* (1794), and *The Italian* (1797), and a description of journeys to Holland, Germany, and the Lake District. A further romance, *Gaston de Blondeville*, and her journals of travels in southern England were published after her death. She and her husband led such a retired life that unfounded rumours that she was already dead or insane circulated towards the end of her life. She suffered much from asthma, and died of pneumonia.

She was the leading exponent of the **Gothic novel*, which relates terrifying adventures in lonely castles. On human relationships she was unconvincing, but her portrayals of the raptures and terrors of her characters' imagination in solitude are compelling, and she was one of the first novelists to include vivid descriptions of landscape, weather, and effects of light. Her plots were wild and improbable, but she was expert at maintaining suspense and devising striking incidents. Her novels were immensely popular throughout Europe, and were much imitated. The £500 advance which she received for *Udolpho* was then unprecedented for a novel. See *Memoir* by T. N. *Talfourd, in *Posthumous Works of Ann Radcliffe* (1833); Aline Grant, *Ann Radcliffe* (1951).

Radigund, in Spenser's **Faerie Queene* (v. iv–vii), a queen of the Amazons, who subdues *Artegall and forces him to spin flax and tow until he is rescued by *Britomart.

Raffles, see HORNUNG, E. W.

Ragged Trousered Philanthropists, The, see TRESSELL, R.

Rainbow, The, a novel by D. H. *Lawrence, published 1915.

It opens as a family chronicle relating the history of the long-established Brangwen family of March Farm, on the Derbyshire–Nottinghamshire border. Tom Brangwen marries the vicar's housekeeper, a Polish widow who already has a daughter, Anna, by her first marriage. Tom takes the child to his heart. Anna marries Will Brangwen, Tom's nephew, a craftsman and draughtsman at a lace factory; they move into Yew Tree Cottage, Cossethay, and produce over the succeeding years a large family, of which the two oldest are Ursula and Gudrun of **Women in Love*. Ursula becomes the

'child of her father's heart', and the interest of the novel gradually shifts to her developing consciousness. When she is about eight her grandfather is drowned one night when the canal embankment bursts, and Ursula grows close to her grandmother Lydia at the March, intrigued by her Polish heritage; her interest is reinforced when she meets Anton, son of a Polish émigré friend of Lydia's, Baron Skrebensky, who had married an English girl late in life. Ursula and Anton fall in love, but he, a subaltern, departs for the Boer war, leaving her to finish school. She has a brief but intense relationship with a schoolmistress (Winifred, who marries her uncle, colliery manager Tom Brangwen), then matriculates, and resolves to earn her living as a teacher, somewhat against her parents' wishes. Her struggles at a poor school in Ilkeston are based on Lawrence's own teaching experience there (1902–6). Will Brangwen is appointed Art and Handwork Instructor for the County of Nottingham, and the whole family move to Beldover, Ursula embarking on a three-year BA course and Gudrun on studies at the Art School. Anton returns, and they renew their relationship, become engaged, and plan to go out to India together, but Ursula breaks away, and Anton abruptly marries his colonel's daughter. The novel ends with Ursula emerging from a spell of illness and suffering (and an implied miscarriage) to contemplate a rainbow arching symbolically over the ugly industrial landscape. The book is remarkable for its study of the 'recurrence of love and conflict' within the marriages it describes; for its attempt to capture the flux of human personality; and for its sense of a mystic procreative continuity within the 'rhythm of eternity' both of the seasons and the Christian year.

RAINE, Kathleen Jesse (1908–), poet and critic, the daughter of a Scottish mother and a Northumbrian farmer. She was formerly married to Charles *Madge. She published many collections of poetry, from her first, *Stone and Flower* (1943), to her *Collected Poems* of 1981, and also three volumes of autobiography, *Farewell Happy Fields* (1973), *The Land Unknown* (1975), and *The Lion's Mouth* (1977). Much of her poetry is inspired by the landscapes of Scotland, particularly of Wester Ross, and has what she describes as 'a sense of the sacred', an intense and mystic vision of the vitality of the natural world which also informs her critical work on *Blake and the *Neoplatonic tradition.

RAINOLDS, John (1549–1607), an Oxford academic among whose pupils was R. *Hooker. As well as composing Latin lectures on Aristotle which contributed to the development of euphuism (see EUPHUES), and controversial works and Protestant apologetics, including his *De Romanae Ecclesiae Idolatria* (1596), he also took part in a controversy over the lawfulness of acting plays. His contributions to this were published in Th'Overthrow of Stage-Playes (1599).

Raj Quartet, The, see SCOTT, P.

Rake's Progress, The, a series of engravings by *Hogarth which inspired an opera by *Stravinsky of the same title with a libretto by W. H. *Auden in collaboration with Chester Kallman.

RALEGH, Sir Walter (?1554–1618), was born at Hayes Barton in South Devon; the sailor Sir Humfrey Gilbert was his half-brother. After little more than a year at Oriel College, Oxford, he spent four years as a volunteer with the Huguenot forces in France, being present at the battle of Montcontour in 1569. After a period in London loosely attached to the Middle Temple, Ralegh began his long career as an explorer and colonizer. In Ireland in 1580 he became acquainted with *Spenser, who approved of Ralegh's commanding role in the massacre of Smerwick, in which 600 Spanish mercenaries were killed. Throughout the 1580s he seems to have enjoyed royal favour, though *Fuller's story of his throwing a plush cloak over a puddle for the queen to tread on is most unlikely to be true. His marriage to Elizabeth Throckmorton, one of the maids of honour, led to a period of imprisonment in the summer of 1592. The journey to Guiana (now Venezuela) in 1595 in search of gold was in part a bid for royal favour; his leadership of the expedition to sack Cadiz harbour in June 1596 was a more successful one, and by adroitly dissociating himself from the earl of *Essex he maintained a strong position until the queen's death. Ralegh's trial, on largely trumped-up charges of high treason, was one of the first events of James I's reign, and from 1603 to 1616 he was imprisoned in the Tower with his wife and family, a dead man in the eyes of the law. He was released to search out the gold mine he claimed to have discovered in Guiana 20 years before. On returning from this disastrous expedition, in which his eldest son was killed and his chief lieutenant, Keymis, committed suicide, a commission of inquiry set up under Spanish pressure determined that the gold mine was a fabrication, the old charge of treason was renewed, and on 29 Oct. 1618 Ralegh was executed.

His poems are beset by uncertainties as to date and authenticity, though a few of them, including the fragmentary '21th: and last booke of the Ocean to Scinthia', survive in his own handwriting. Two well known poems formerly attributed to him, 'The Lie' and 'The Pilgrimage', are not now thought to be his work. Among the authentic poems are his 'Epitaph of Sir Philip Sidney' and the prefatory sonnet to *The Faerie Queene which begins, 'Methought I saw the grave, where Laura lay'. There are

numerous prose works. His 'Report of the Truth of the Fight about the Isles of Açores' (1591) was a source of *Tennyson's 'The Revenge' (1878). His Discoverie of Guiana (1596) includes a description of 'Eldorado', and describes the plainlands as a natural Eden:

still as we rowed, the deer came down feeding by the water's side, as if they had been used to a keeper's call.

The History of the World (1614), written during Ralegh's long imprisonment, was originally intended for Henry, prince of Wales (d. 1612). This ambitious book, which Ralegh worked on with the help of several assistants, deals with Greek, Egyptian, and biblical history up to 168 BC. The Preface, at the beginning of which he affirms his 'fidelity towardes Her, whom I must still honor in the dust', summarizes modern European history, demonstrating the unchangeableness of God's judgement. The History contains many reflective passages, most characteristically elegiac in tone:

For this tide of mans life, after it once turneth and declineth, ever runneth, with a perpetuall ebbe and falling streame, but never floweth againe: our leafe once fallen, springeth no more, neither doth the Sunne or the Summer adorne us againe, with the garments of new leaves and flowers.

The best-known such passage comes on the final page:

O eloquent, just and mightie Death! whom none could advise, thou hast perswaded; what none hath dared, thou hast done; and whom all the world hath flattered, thou only hast cast out of the world and despised: thou hast drawne together all the farre stretched greatnesse, all the pride, crueltie, and ambition of man, and covered it all over with these two narrow words, Hic iacet.

The poems have been edited by A. Latham (1951); Pierre Lefranc's Sir Walter Ralegh, Écrivain (1968) offers detailed theories about the relationship of the poems to the life; C. A. Patrides has edited selections from The History of the World (1971).

RALEIGH, Sir Walter Alexander (1861–1922), after holding chairs at Liverpool and Glasgow, became in 1904 the first holder of the chair of English literature at Oxford. Among his works are Style (1897), Milton (1900), and Shakespeare (1907), but in his day he was renowned more as a stimulating if informal lecturer than as a critic. He wrote the first volume of the official The War in the Air (1922), and his selected letters were published in 1926.

Ralpho, the squire in Butler's *Hudibras. (See VAUGHAN, T.)

Ralph Roister Doister, the earliest known English comedy, by *Udall, probably performed about 1552 and printed about 1566, and perhaps played by *Westminster boys while Udall was headmaster of that school. The play, in short rhymed doggerel, represents the courting of the widow Christian Custance, who is betrothed to Gawin Goodlucke, an absent merchant, by Roister, a swaggering simpleton, instigated thereto by the mischievous Mathewe Mery-greeke. Roister is repulsed and beaten by Custance and her maids; and Goodlucke, after being deceived by false reports, is reconciled to her. The play shows similarity to the comedies of *Plautus and *Terence.

Ralph the Rover, see INCHCAPE ROCK.

Rambler, The, a twice-weekly periodical in 208 numbers issued by Dr *Johnson from 20 March 1750 to 14 March 1752.

The contents are essays on all kinds of subjects, character studies, allegories, eastern fables, criticisms, etc., and were, with the exception of five, written by Johnson himself. The moral seriousness of his enterprise is indicated by the fact that he wrote a prayer on beginning the work, and in the last paper he claimed never to have exploited 'the topic of the day'. The other contributors were *Richardson, E. *Carter, Mrs *Chapone, and Catherine Talbot (1720–70). Despite initial protests against its 'solemn' tone, The Rambler was pirated and imitated, and went through ten numbered reprintings in Johnson's lifetime.

Rambouillet, Hotel de, town house of Catherine de Vivonne, marquise de Rambouillet (1588–1665), near the site of the Palais-Royal, and the intellectual centre of fashionable Paris in the first half of the 17th cent. Mme de Rambouillet exerted a refining influence on French language and literature. Although *Molière, *Boileau, and *Racine reacted against her salon, it was the inaugurating example of what became a French cultural institution for over two centuries.

Ramorny, Sir John, a character in Scott's *The Fair Maid of Perth.

RAMSAY, Allan (1686–1758), Scottish poet, born in Lanarkshire, came to Edinburgh where he spent most of his life. He was a wig-maker, then a bookseller, and an important figure in Edinburgh literary society; he opened the first circulating library in Edinburgh in 1726 (see LIBRARIES, CIRCULATING). In 1718 he brought out anonymously several editions of *Christis Kirk on the Green, with supplementary verses of his own in fake antique *Scots, and also various vernacular mock elegies. A collection of his elegies and satires appeared in 1721. In 1724–37 he issued The Tea-Table Miscellany, the first of many 18th-cent. collections of songs and ballads, and in 1724 The Ever Green, which contained work by the great poets of late medieval Scotland, notably *Dunbar and *Henryson, though with revisions and additions of his own. These contributed much to the revival of vernacular Scottish poetry, and in his preface to the latter Ramsay makes clear his patriotic in-

tentions: 'When these good old Bards wrote, we had not yet made Use of imported Trimming.' Ramsay's pastoral comedy The Gentle Shepherd (1725), with its Scots songs, was very successful and much admired by *Boswell among others for its 'beautiful rural imagery' and its 'real picture of manners'. His son, also Allan (1713–84) became a well known portrait painter; *Hume and *Rousseau were among his subjects.

Ramsay, Margaret, a character in Scott's *The Fortunes of Nigel.

RAMUS, Petrus, Latin form of Pierre de la Ramée (1515–72), French philosopher and grammarian. A supporter of the Protestant faith, he perished in the Massacre of St *Bartholomew, an event portrayed by Marlowe in *The Massacre at Paris. His Dialectique of 1555, the first work of its kind to be written in French, systematically challenged and refuted Aristotelian and *Scholastic logic. It was introduced into England in the late 16th cent. by Andrew Melville and William Temple, and obtained wide academic currency, especially at Cambridge. His followers were known as Ramists and his anti-Scholastic system of logic as Ramism.

RANDOLPH, Thomas (1605–35), was educated at Westminster School and Trinity College, Cambridge, where he became known as a writer in English and Latin verse. He returned to London in 1632. His principal plays are Amyntas, a pastoral comedy, and *The Muse's Looking Glass, printed 1638; and *Hey for Honesty, printed 1651. He wrote an eclogue included in Annalia Dubrensia, verses in celebration of the *Cotswold Games. His plays and poems were edited by W. C. *Hazlitt (1875).

Ranelagh Gardens, Chelsea, a place of public amusement opened in 1742 in the grounds of the earl of Ranelagh. It had a famous Rotunda, 150 feet in diameter, with an orchestra in the centre, and boxes round it, where people promenaded. The gardens were closed in 1804. They now form part of Chelsea Hospital Gardens.

RANDS, William Brighty (1823–82), the 'laureate of the nursery', who wrote sometimes under the pseudonyms Henry Holbeach and Matthew Browne. His best-known work was Lilliput Levee (1864), a book of verse for children with illustrations by *Millais and G. J. Pinwell, which was followed by Lilliput Lectures (1871, mostly prose) and Lilliput Legends (1872). All three were published anonymously. He was a reporter in the House of Commons, and also wrote a good deal of miscellaneous journalism.

Ranger, (1) a rakish man of fashion in Love in a Wood by *Wycherley; (2) a character in Hoadley's *The Suspicious Husband.

RANKE, Leopold von (1795–1886), German

historian. His history of *The Popes of Rome* (1834–6) is, among his numerous works, that best known in England. He began writing a *History of the World* when he was over 80 and reached the 12th cent. AD.

Rankenian Club, one of the most influential 18th-cent. Edinburgh clubs, founded *c.*1717 by a group of radical divinity students who were admirers of the moral and political writings of the third earl of *Shaftesbury. Its leading members rose to prominence in the universities, the church, medicine, and the law, and were influential in the improvement of literary style in Edinburgh. Lord Auchinleck, father of *Boswell, was a member.

RANSOM, John Crowe (1888–1974), American poet and critic, born in Tennessee, the son of a Methodist minister, and educated there and at Oxford. From 1937 to 1958 he was a professor at Kenyon College, Ohio, where he founded and edited the important *Kenyon Review*, a scholarly publication committed to the close textual analysis associated with the *New Criticism. His critical works include *God without Thunder* (1930) and *The New Criticism* (1941), the latter an independent survey of the works of I. A. *Richards, Y. *Winters, and others. His period of activity as a poet was relatively brief, but his output, notably in *Chills and Fever* (1924) and *Two Gentlemen in Bonds* (1927), impressive, and he is particularly remembered for his formal, subtle, taut ballad-portraits and elegies, which include 'Captain Carpenter' and 'Bells for John Whiteside's Daughter'.

RANSOME, Arthur Michell (1884–1967), journalist and author, born in Leeds, the son of a professor of history, and educated at Rugby. He started work in London as office boy for Grant *Richards, then graduated to ghost-writing, reviewing, and short story writing, and eventually became a reporter, first for the *Daily News*, then (in 1919) for the *Manchester Guardian*. He went to Russia in 1913 to learn the language, and covered the revolution at first hand for the *Daily News*; his collection of Russian legends and fairy stories, *Old Peter's Russian Tales* (1916), had a considerable success. In 1924 he married, as his second wife, Evgenia Shelepin, who had been *Trotsky's secretary. He is best remembered for his classic sequence of novels for children, which reflect his keen interest in sailing, fishing, and the countryside: beginning with *Swallows and Amazons* (1930) and ending with *Great Northern?* (1947), it describes the adventures of the Walker (Swallow) and Blackett (Amazon) families, and various of their friends, in the Lake District, the Norfolk Broads, and other vividly drawn locations. See *The Autobiography of Arthur Ransome* (1976), ed. Rupert Hart-Davis, and a biography by Hugh Brogan (1984).

RAO, Raja (1909–   ), Indian writer, born at Hassan, Karnataka, and educated at Nizam College, Hyderabad, and the universities of Montpellier and the Sorbonne. His first novel, *Kanthapura* (1938), an account of the Independence movement seen from the perspective of a small South Indian village, attempts to forge an Indian idiom and tempo through the medium of the English language. This was followed by the more sophisticated *The Serpent and the Rope* (1960), the story of a young Indian Brahmin intellectual, Rama, and his French wife Madeleine in their search for spiritual truth in India, France, and England. Rao's stories have been collected in *The Cow of the Barricades* (1947) and *The Policeman and the Rose* (1978).

Rape of Lucrece, The, a poem in rhyme-royal by Shakespeare, published 1594 and dedicated to Henry Wriothesley, earl of Southampton. It is presumably the 'graver labour' which he promised to the earl in the dedication of *Venus and Adonis* the previous year. It is a highly rhetorical expansion of the story as told by *Livy. See LUCRETIA.

Rape of the Lock, The, a poem by *Pope, in two cantos, published in *Lintot's *Miscellany* 1712; subsequently enlarged to five cantos and thus published 1714.

Lord Petre having forcibly cut off a lock of Miss Arabella Fermor's hair, the incident gave rise to a quarrel between the families. With the idea of allaying this, Pope treated the subject in a playful mock-heroic poem, on the model of *Boileau's *Le Lutrin*. He presents Belinda at her toilet, a game of ombre, the snipping of the lock while Belinda sips her coffee, the wrath of Belinda and her demand that the lock be restored, the final wafting of the lock, as a new star, to adorn the skies. The poem was published in its original form with Miss Fermor's permission. Pope then expanded the sketch by introducing the machinery of sylphs and gnomes, adapted from a light erotic French work, *Le Comte de Gabalis*, a series of five discourses by the Abbé de Montfaucon de Villars, which appeared in English in 1680; in his dedication he credits both *Gabalis* and the *Rosicrucians. (See also PARACELSUS.) One of Pope's most brilliant performances, it has also been one of his most popular; Dr *Johnson called it 'the most attractive of all ludicrous compositions', in which 'New things are made familiar and familiar things are made new.'

RAPHAEL (Raffaello Sanzio) (1483–1520), Italian painter, son of the painter Giovanni Santi, was born at Urbino. He worked in Perugino's studio and then in Florence. In 1509 he was painting the Stanze in the Vatican; the *School of Athens* and the *Disputà* in the Stanza della Segnatura exemplify to perfection the art of the High Renaissance. He succeeded Bramante as architect of St Peter's. Seven of his cartoons for tapestries for the Sistine Chapel were bought by Charles I (now on loan to the Victoria and Albert Museum). He employed assistants to cope with the great number of commissions he received, among them the decoration of the Farnesina, Rome, and many portraits and Madonnas.

Throughout the 17th, 18th, and 19th cents Raphael was generally revered as the greatest of all painters; his supremacy was challenged by Romantic admirers of *Michelangelo, and in the 19th cent. the *Pre-Raphaelites revolted—somewhat vaguely—against his authority.

RASHDALL, Hastings (1858–1924), philosopher and theologian, was educated at New College, Oxford. His most important work, *The Theory of Good and Evil* (1907), expounds his own version of what he called 'ideal utilitarianism'. *The Universities of Europe in the Middle Ages* (1895; new edn, ed. Powicke and Emden, 1936) is a standard work.

RASPE, Rudolph Erich, see MUNCHAUSEN.

Rasselas, Prince of Abyssinia, The History of, a didactic romance by Dr *Johnson, published 1759, and composed during the evenings of a week to pay for his mother's funeral and to settle her debts. It is an essay on the 'choice of life', a phrase repeated throughout the work, usually in italics.

Rasselas, a son of the emperor of Abyssinia, weary of the joys of the 'happy valley' where the inhabitants know only 'the soft vicissitudes of pleasure and repose', escapes to Egypt, accompanied by his sister Nekayah, her attendant Pekuah, and the much-travelled old philosopher Imlac. Here they study the various conditions of men's lives, and after a few incidents of no great importance resolve to return to Abyssinia, in a 'conclusion, in which nothing is concluded'. The charm of the work lies not in its plot, which is minimal, but in its wise and humane melancholy; in many ways it echoes the theme of *The Vanity of Human Wishes*, stressing that happiness in unobtainable, and demonstrating that philosophers, hermits, and the wealthy all fail to achieve it. 'Harmless pleasures', Imlac concludes, are very rare. Imlac also produces Johnson's celebrated definition of the 'business of a poet', which is to 'examine not the individual, but the species . . . he does not number the streaks of the tulip'; and to write 'as the interpreter of nature, and the legislator of mankind . . . presiding over the thoughts and manners of future generations' (ch. x)—a phrase that anticipated Shelley's arguments in *The Defence of Poetry*. *Rasselas,* though much milder in tone, bears some resemblance in plan to *Voltaire's Candide*, published in the same year but not read by Johnson until later, when he himself commented on the similarity.

RASTELL, John (c.1475–1536) was a printer, barrister, playwright, and brother-in-law of Sir T. *More. He wrote and published an interlude called *Four Elements* (c.1520), and two comedies of c.1525, *Calisto and Melebea* and *Gentleness and Nobility*. The latter has been attributed to Rastell's son-in-law J. *Heywood.

Rastignac, Eugène de, one of the principal characters drawn by *Balzac. He figures intermittently throughout the series of the *Scènes de la Vie Parisienne*, but is especially analysed in *Le Père Goriot*. He starts as a humble student, and with the help of his female admirers, achieves success in the corrupt society of the Paris of the day.

Ratcliffe, James, a character in Scott's *The Heart of Midlothian*; a notorious thief who ingratiates himself with the magistrates and becomes a warder in the Tolbooth.

Rat, the Cat, and Lovel the dog, in the political rhyme:

> The Rat, the Cat, and Lovel the dog
> Rule all England under the Hog,

refers to three adherents of Richard III: Sir Richard Ratcliffe (killed at Bosworth, 1485), Sir John Catesby (d. 1486), and Francis, first Viscount Lovell (1454–?88; his skeleton was found in a vault, where he had evidently starved to death). The Hog is a reference to the boar that figured as one of the supporters of the royal arms.

RATTIGAN, Sir Terence Mervyn (1911–77), the son of a diplomat, was educated at Harrow and Trinity College, Oxford, and early embarked on a career as a playwright. His first West End success was a comedy, *French Without Tears* (1936, pub. 1937). This was followed by many other works, including *The Winslow Boy* (1946), a drama in which a father fights to clear his naval-cadet son of the accusation of petty theft; *The Browning Version* (1948), about Crocker Harris, a repressed and unpopular schoolmaster with a faithless wife; *The Deep Blue Sea* (1952), of which the heroine is a judge's wife suffering from passion for a test pilot; *Separate Tables* (1954, pub. 1955), two one-act plays set in a hotel, both studies of emotional failure and inadequacy; *Ross* (1960), based on the life of T. E. *Lawrence; and *Cause Célèbre* (1977, pub. 1978), based on an actual murder trial. When Rattigan's *Collected Works* were published in 1953, he wrote a preface to the second volume in which he created the character of 'Aunt Edna', the average middle-brow matinée attender whom playwrights must take into account, and critics were later to use this light-hearted invention as a focus for their complaints about the middle-class, middle-brow nature of his own plays; the so-called *kitchen-sink dramatists of the 1950s and 1960s reacted against Rattigan (expressly, in the case of S. *Delaney), but his works are still much performed, and *Rudkin in a BBC Radio 3 programme in 1976 stressed not his celebrated 'craftsmanship' but his sense of 'existential bleakness and irresoluble carnal solitude'. A biography by M. Darlow and G. Hodson (1979) gives an interesting account of his troubled personal life and successful career.

Rauf Coilyear, a rhymed poem of the *Charlemagne cycle, in stanzas of 13 lines, of which a copy survives, printed in Scotland in 1572 (written probably c.1475). This humorous poem tells how Charlemagne loses his way and takes refuge in the hut of Rauf, a plain-spoken and self-willed charcoal-burner who treats him hospitably but with excessive freedom. Ed. S. J. Herrtage (EETS ES 39, 1882).

'Raven, The', a poem by E. A. *Poe.

Ravenshoe, a novel by H. *Kingsley.

Ravenswing, The, a character in Thackeray's *Men's Wives.

Ravenswood, Edgar, Master of, the hero of Scott's *The Bride of Lammermoor.

RAVERAT, Gwen(dolen Mary), née Darwin (1885–1957), wood-engraver and granddaughter of C. *Darwin, born in Cambridge; her childhood is described in her autobiographical Period Piece (1952). Works illustrated by her include Spring Morning (1915) by her cousin F. *Cornford, and various anthologies in association with K. *Grahame. Her husband Jacques Raverat (d. 1925) was a correspondent of V. *Woolf.

RAWLINSON, Thomas (1681–1725), educated at Eton and St John's College, Oxford, a book-collector, whose manuscripts are in the Bodleian Library. He was satirized by Addison in *The Tatler (No. 158) as 'Tom Folio'.

RAY, John (1627–1705), the son of a blacksmith, became one of England's greatest naturalists. He was pre-eminently a botanist (he originated the division of plants into monocotyledons and dicotyledons), but also took up the unfinished zoological work of his friend Francis Willughby. His Historia Plantarum was published 1686–1704, and his Wisdom of God manifested in the Works of Creation (1691) went through many editions. He also published A Collection of English Proverbs (1670) and was keenly interested in philology.

READ, Sir Herbert Edward (1893–1968), born in Yorkshire, and educated at Leeds University, served in France throughout the First World War. He worked in the Victoria and Albert Museum, 1922–31, as professor of fine art in Edinburgh, 1931–3, and as editor of the Burlington Magazine, 1933–9. The first volumes of his spare, taut poems (much influenced by *Imagism) were Songs of Chaos (1915) and Naked Warriors (1919), largely based on the war; these were followed by various volumes of collected poems, a long poem, The End of a War (1933), and the final Collected Poems of 1966. His critical work includes studies of *Wordsworth, *Malory, *Sterne, and others; Form in Modern Poetry (1932), The True Voice of Feeling (1953), and Essays in Literary Criticism (1969) contain much of his most valuable work. Many publications on art include Art and Industry (1934) and Education through Art (1943). His personal prose writing includes two records of trench life, In Retreat (1925) and Ambush (1930); The Innocent Eye (1933), a brief autobiography of his Yorkshire childhood, and a full autobiography in 1963, The Contrary Experience; and his only novel, The Green Child (1935), an allegorical fantasy, based on a folktale, of the return to innocence. He also edited works by T. E. *Hulme, *Orage, Kropotkin, and *Jung, and various anthologies. His son Piers Paul Read (1941–) is well known as a novelist.

READE, Charles (1814–84), was born at Ipsden, in Oxfordshire, the son of a solidly respectable country squire. In 1831 he won a demyship to Magdalen College, Oxford, beginning a long association which brought him a fellowship and various important college offices over the years. The effects of enforced celibacy (as required by college life) provided an important theme in several of his novels. He travelled abroad, then in 1842 began to study for the bar; in 1846 he tried studying medicine in Edinburgh; and in 1847, the year in which he obtained a DCL, he began to deal in violins, on which he was an expert. He began his literary career publishing a stage version of Smollett's *Peregrine Pickle in 1851, and in 1852 entered on his long career as theatre manager and dramatist. Masks and Faces, successfully produced in that year, became a novel, Peg Woffington, in 1853. In that year he also published Christie Johnstone, the first of his 'reforming' novels, urging the reform of prisons and the treatment of criminals, which was followed in 1856 by It is Never Too Late to Mend, a highly successful work in the same genre, which was later dramatized. Gold!, a play converted in 1869 into the novel Foul Play, also appeared in this prolific year. At the same time Reade was also writing short stories, working as a journalist, and writing plays. In 1854 he met the actress Mrs Seymour, with whom he lived until her death in 1879. The Autobiography of a Thief and Jack of all Trades (both greatly admired by *Orwell) appeared in 1858; Love Me Little, Love Me Long in 1859; and in 1861 the work for which he is chiefly remembered, *The Cloister and the Hearth. Hard Cash, a novel exposing the scandal of lunatic asylums (which Reade considered 'my best production'), appeared in 1863, and in 1866 *Griffith Gaunt*, which some judge superior to *The Cloister and the Hearth*. The frankness of its attitude to sexual problems provoked scandal and considerable litigation, in which Reade pugnaciously defended himself against 'the Prurient Prudes'. For much of the rest of his life he was engaged in various personal and legal controversies. A long collaboration with *Boucicault, a highly successful adapter of plays and novels, began in 1867, and the last of Reade's major novels, *Put Yourself in his Place*, attacking the trade union practice of 'rattening' or enforcing membership, appeared in 1870. In 1871 he published another novel, *A Terrible Temptation*, and in 1872 quarrelled with *Trollope over the adaptation of one of Trollope's novels, following this with a libel action in 1873 over his own new novel, *The Simpleton*. The *Wandering Heir* (1873), suggested by the Tichborne trial, was again both novel and play; Reade persuaded Ellen *Terry to emerge from retirement to perform in the stage version. He continued to produce short stories, journalistic work, and plays for his touring company, and to be embroiled in disputes and legal actions. By the time he published *A Woman Hater* (1877) he had lost his determination to present honestly the problems of sex in society, and meekly agreed to all *Blackwood's objections. After the death of Mrs Seymour in 1879 he wrote little, turned to religion, and in 1882 gave up theatrical management. *A Perilous Secret* appeared posthumously in 1884.

Reade enjoyed great fame and success, and was accepted by the public as the natural successor of *Dickens (whose novels had considerably influenced him). Among critics, both the young H. *James and *Swinburne regarded him as a novelist of genius, and placed his work above that of G. *Eliot (a view which at the time did not apparently seem eccentric). But his reputation has considerably dimmed, and he is now remembered only for *The Cloister and the Hearth* and *Griffith Gaunt*. The 'realism' of his novels was based on immense research, recorded in intricate detail in his mass of notebooks; for *The Cloister and the Hearth*, he read *Erasmus, *Froissart, *Luther, *chronicles, *jest-books, and all the records he could find. He wished by this method to impart an authentic reality to his work, and also to discipline the 'inner consciousness', which he distrusted; but the detail of information is often thought to overwhelm his considerable narrative power. His expression of sexual frustration and fantasy (celibacy, he wrote, is 'an invention wholly devilish'), and its place in religious feeling, was much stifled by the proprieties of the time. See M. Elwin, *Charles Reade* (1931); W. Burns, *Charles Reade: a Study in Victorian authorship* (1961).

READE, William Winwood (1838–75), explorer, novelist, and nephew of C. *Reade. His explorations in West and South-West Africa are described in *Savage Africa* (1863), *The African Sketchbook* (1873), and *The Story of the Ashanti Campaign* (1874). His fictional works, which aroused some controversy for their criticism of religion, included the notable *The Martyrdom of Man* (1872), which exposes the author's atheistical views and influenced H. G. *Wells who described it as 'an extraordinarily inspiring presentation of human history as one consistent process'.

Ready-to-Halt, Mr, in Bunyan's *Pilgrim's Progress*, a pilgrim who follows Mr *Greatheart, though upon crutches. When he comes to the land of *Beulah and is about to cross the river, he bequeaths his crutches to his son, for he sees chariots and horses ready to carry him into the City.

Real Charlotte, The, see SOMERVILLE AND ROSS.

Realism, in *Scholastic philosophy, the doctrine that attributes objective or absolute existence to universals, the principal exponent of which was St Thomas *Aquinas. The opposite view is *Nominalism which regards universals simply as words, a *flatus vocis*.

Realism, a literary term so widely used as to be more or less meaningless except when used in contradistinction to some other movement, e.g. *Naturalism, *Expressionism, *Surrealism. Sir P. *Harvey's original definition was 'a loosely used term meaning truth to the observed facts of life (especially when they are gloomy)', which would seem to indicate that he had in mind such post-French-realist works as those of *Gissing, A. *Morrison, G. A. *Moore, *Maugham's *Liza of Lambeth*, etc., most of which have proletarian or lower-middle-class settings. The French realist school of the mid-19th cent. (for which the novelist Champfleury, 1821–89, produced a manifesto, *Le Réalisme*, 1857) stressed 'sincerity' as opposed to the 'liberty' proclaimed by the Romantics; it insisted on accurate documentation, sociological insight, an accumulation of the details of material fact, an avoidance of poetic diction, idealization, exaggeration, melodrama, etc.; and subjects were to be taken from everyday life, preferably from lower-class life. This emphasis clearly reflected the interests of an increasingly positivist and scientific age. *Balzac and *Stendhal were seen as the great precursors of Realism; *Flaubert (though he disliked the label, and was also claimed by the Naturalists) and the *Goncourts as among its practitioners. French Realism developed into Naturalism, an associated but more scientifically applied and elaborated doctrine, seen by some later critics (notably *Marxist critics) as degenerate. In England, the French realists were imitated consciously and notably by

Moore and Arnold *Bennett, but the English novel from the time of *Defoe had had its own unlabelled strain of realism, and the term is thus applied to English literature in varying senses and contexts, sometimes qualified as 'social' or 'psychological' realism etc. (See also SOCIALIST REALISM.)

Reasonableness of Christianity, see Locke's ESSAY CONCERNING HUMAN UNDERSTANDING.

Rebecca, (1) the name given (in allusion to Gen. 24: 60) to the leader, in woman's attire, of the rioters who demolished tollgates in S. Wales in 1843–4; (2) a character in Scott's *Ivanhoe*; (3) a novel by D. *Du Maurier.

Rebecca and Rowena, a humorous sequel by *Thackeray to Scott's *Ivanhoe*, in which Ivanhoe tires of domestic life with Rowena, and after various comic vicissitudes is reunited with Rebecca.

RÉCAMIER, Jeanne-Françoise, Mme (1777–1849), a Frenchwoman renowned for her beauty and wit, whose salon during the Napoleonic years and the Restoration was frequented by the most brilliant society of the day, including *Chateaubriand.

'Recluse, The', see EXCURSION, THE.

Records of Shelley, Byron, and the Author, reminiscences by E. J. *Trelawny, published 1858. The recollections provide a lively and entertaining, but often inaccurate, account of Trelawny's friendships with *Shelley and *Byron.

Recruiting Officer, The, a comedy by *Farquhar, produced 1706.

It deals with the humours of recruiting in a country town, with a vividness suggesting that the author drew on his own experience. The plot is slender; it presents Capt. Plume making love to the women in order to secure their followers as recruits; Kite, his resourceful sergeant, employing his wiles and assuming the character of an astrologer, for the same purpose; while Sylvia, daughter of Justice Ballance, who is in love with Plume but has promised not to marry him without her father's consent, runs away from home disguised as a man, gets herself arrested for scandalous conduct, is brought before her father, and delivered over by him to Capt. Plume, as a recruit. Capt. Brazen, a rival recruiting officer, who boasts of battles and friends in every quarter of the globe, endeavours to marry the rich Melinda, but finds himself fobbed off with her maid.

Recusant, a term used to describe those who from Elizabeth's reign to about the end of the 18th cent. refused to attend the services of the Church of England. It was especially applied to Roman Catholics.

Red Badge of Courage, The, see CRANE, S.

Red Book of Hergest, see MABINOGION.

Red Cotton Night-Cap Country or *Turf and Towers,* a poem in blank verse by R. *Browning, published 1873. The title refers ironically to the description by Browning's friend Anne Thackeray (*Ritchie) of a district in Normandy as 'white cotton night-cap country'; Browning undertakes to show that the 'red' of passion and violence should replace the 'white'.

The story is based on a contemporary *cause célèbre*, involving the wealthy heir to a Paris jewellery business, Antoine Mellerio (in the poem, Léonce Miranda). As Browning tells it, Miranda's life was dominated by the opposed principles of sensual indulgence and religious fanaticism, symbolized by the 'turf' and 'towers' of the subtitle. He lived with his mistress Anna (in the poem, Clara) at a luxurious estate in Normandy, to which he had added a grandiose belvedere. His mother's death in Paris occasioned a fit of violent remorse, in which he renounced Clara and mutilated himself by burning off both his hands. However, he soon resumed his relationship with Clara and, in the period before his death, made extravagant donations to a convent near his estate, which housed a famous statue of the Virgin. He died by a fall from the top of his belvedere, leaving his fortune to the convent, with a life-interest for Clara. The will was challenged by his family, but their suit was comprehensively rejected by the courts, who upheld the will and declared Miranda's death to be due to an accident. Browning, however, maintains that Miranda leapt from the tower in a deliberate test of the power of the Virgin to save him, and thus resolve the struggle in his spirit between idealism and materialism. This struggle is the real topic of the poem: Miranda, weak-headed victim of a self-imposed dualism, is a nightmare parody of the figure of the artist in Browning. The poem has never been popular, because of its sordid plot and harsh, sardonic style; but contains, in Miranda's long interior monologue before he jumps, one of the most powerful single passages of Browning's late work.

Redcrosse Knight, The, in Bk I of Spenser's *Faerie Queene,* is St George, the patron saint of England. He is the 'patron' or champion of Holiness, and represents the Anglican Church. He is separated from *Una (the true religion) by the wiles of *Archimago (hypocrisy), and is led away by *Duessa (the Roman Catholic religion) to the House of Pride. He drinks of an enchanted stream, loses his strength, and is made captive by the giant *Orgoglio (pride). Orgoglio is slain by Prince *Arthur, and Una leads her knight to the House of Holiness, to learn repentance and be healed. The Knight and Una are finally betrothed, after he has killed the dragon which besieged her parents' castle.

Redgauntlet, a novel by Sir W. *Scott, published 1824.

Prince Charles Edward returns to England some years after 1745, to try once more his fortunes, an attempt that meets with inglorious failure. Mr Redgauntlet, otherwise known as Herries of Birrenswork, a fanatical Jacobite, is the leader of the movement, and, to promote its success, kidnaps his young nephew Darsie Latimer (whose true name is Sir Arthur Darsie Redgauntlet), the head of his house, to get the support of his followers. Darsie's young friend Alan Fairford sets out to rescue him. The novel also contains the notable characters of Joshua Geddes, the Quaker, the hypocrite Thomas Trumbull, Nanty Ewart the sea-captain, and the blind fiddler 'Wandering Willie'; together with some amusing pictures of old legal Edinburgh (including the grotesque-pathetic figure of Peter Peebles, the crazy litigant). Though not generally accounted one of the three or four greatest *Waverley novels, *Redgauntlet* (written in the last years of Scott's prosperity) contains some of his finest writing, notably in 'Wandering Willie's Tale', a perfect example of the short story.

REDGROVE, Peter William (1932–), poet and novelist, educated at Taunton School, Somerset, and at Queens' College, Cambridge, where he read Natural Sciences. He worked for some years as a scientific journalist, and has written some *Science Fiction. In 1966 he became resident author at Falmouth School of Art, Cornwall, a county that appears in many of his landscapes and seascapes. He was a founder-member of the *Group, and his first volume of poetry, *The Collector and Other Poems* (1960), was followed by many others, including *The Force and Other Poems* (1966), *Sons of my Skin: Selected Poems 1954–74* (1975), and *The Weddings at Nether Powers* (1979). His poetry is marked by a richness of visual imagery, a sense of physical immediacy, and a deep preoccupation with religious and sexual mysteries. His novels, which include *In the Country of the Skin* (1973) and *The Beekeepers* (1980), are also rich in imagery, written in a highly poetic prose. He has written several works in collaboration with the poet and novelist Penelope Shuttle; these include *The Terrors of Dr Treviles* (1974), a novel of the occult and the psychic, of dream and identity, based on the relationship of psychologist Gregory Treviles and his witch-wife Robyn; and *The Wise Wound* (1978), a study of the mythology and reality of menstruation. Although Redgrove's work has some affinity with that of the *Magic Realists, it appears to spring from a different, possibly less cerebral source; with him, the artist as magician is less of a conjurer, more of a mystic.

REDI, Francesco (1626–98), physician to the grand duke of Tuscany and author of a spirited dithyrambic poem, *Bacco in Toscana (Bacchus in Tuscany,* 1685), which Leigh *Hunt translated. It may have helped to inspire *Dryden's *Alexander's Feast.*

Redmond O'Neale, a character in Scott's *Rokeby.*

Red Riding Hood, Little, a popular tale translated from the French of *Perrault by Robert Samber (?1729).

Little Red Riding Hood is sent by her mother to take a cake and a pot of butter to her sick grandmother. She loiters on the way, and gets into conversation with a wolf, who learns her errand. He hurries on, eats up the grandmother, takes her place in the bed, and impersonates her when Red Riding Hood arrives, finally devouring her. In the German variant the child is resuscitated. *Lang in *Perrault's Popular Tales* (1888), discusses the analogies of the story in other legends.

Redworth, Thomas, a character in G. Meredith's *Diana of the Crossways.*

REED, Henry (1914–), poet, translator, and radio dramatist, educated at the University of Birmingham. He is best known for his book of verse *A Map of Verona* (1946), which contained his much-anthologized poem, inspired by his wartime experiences in the army, 'Naming of Parts'. His plays made a notable contribution to radio drama in the 1950s, and two collections have been published: *The Streets of Pompeii* (1971), which contains five verse plays, and *Hilda Tablet and others* (1971), which contains his four prose comedies of contemporary cultural life, based on the central character of composer Hilda Tablet.

REED, Isaac (1742–1807), biographer, editor, and bibliophile, was born in London, the son of a baker, and practised, reluctantly, as a conveyancer, devoting the greatest part of his energy to literature: his works include a new edition of *Dodsley's *Select Collection of Old Plays* (1780); *Biographica Dramatica* (2 vols, 1782, biographies of English dramatists); contributions to Dr Johnson's *The Lives of the English Poets*; and a 'first variorum' edition of Shakespeare (21 vols, 1803). He was a modest and good-natured man, generous with his large library and much liked by his contemporaries; the only scholar to find fault with him was the irritable *Ritson. See *The Reed Diaries 1762–1804* (1946), ed. C. E. Jones.

REEVE, Clara (1729–1807), was born and died in Ipswich. *The Champion of Virtue; a Gothic Story,* published 1777, was reprinted in 1778 as *The Old English Baron,* and met with tremendous success. The author acknowledged her debt to

Walpole's *The Castle of Otranto*, but found its machinery so violent that it destroyed its own effect; to which Walpole replied that he found her novel 'insipid'. Her hero, the virtuous and noble Edmund, moves resolutely through many adventures of romantic horror in order to obtain his rightful heritage, but the ghost of the murdered baron provides the only element of the supernatural. The story concludes with a dramatic day of retribution. Clara Reeve wrote several other novels, and a critical dialogue on *The Progress of Romance* (1785).

'Reeve's Tale, The', see CANTERBURY TALES, 3.

Reflections on the Revolution in France, see REVOLUTION IN FRANCE.

Reflector, The (1810–11), founded and edited by Leigh *Hunt, a literary and political quarterly consisting of 'a collection of essays'. Hunt and *Lamb were the principal contributors, and in its pages Lamb's essays on *Hogarth and on the plays of Shakespeare first appeared.

Reformation, The, the great religious movement of the 16th cent., aiming to reform the doctrines and practices of the Church of Rome, and ending in the establishment of the various Reformed or Protestant churches of central and north-western Europe. Its principal leaders were *Luther in Germany, *Calvin in Geneva, *Zwingli in Zurich, and J. *Knox in Scotland. The principal points contended for by the reformers were the general use and authority of the Scriptures and the need of justification by faith; they repudiated the doctrine of transubstantiation, the worship of the Virgin Mary, and the supremacy of the pope.

Reformation, History of the, see KNOX, J.

Reform Bills. The Reform Bill of 1832 widened the parliamentary franchise by extending the vote to include the rich middle classes, and removed some of the inequalities in the system of representation by redistributing members of Parliament to correspond with the great centres of population. The Bill was introduced by Lord J. *Russell in 1831, and carried in 1832. The Reform Bill of 1867, which more than doubled the electorate, extended the franchise to include many male members of the industrial working class, and the Bill of 1884 took in (with the exception of certain categories, i.e. lunatics, convicted criminals, and peers) all males over 21. In 1872 voting by ballot was introduced. Women over 30 were enfranchised in 1918; and women over 21 received the vote in 1928. (See also WOMEN'S SUFFRAGE.) In 1969 an Act was passed which lowered the age of all voters to 18. The question of Reform is a principal theme in many Victorian novels, notably in G. Eliot's *Middlemarch* and *Felix Holt*.

Regan, in Shakespeare's *King Lear*, the second of Lear's daughters, who marries Cornwall.

Regicide Peace, Letters on a, by E. *Burke, the first two published 1796, the third 1797, the fourth posthumously in the collected works.

The theme of these letters, which purport to be addressed to a Member of Parliament, is the necessity for stamping out the Jacobin government of France, that 'vast tremendous unformed spectre'; and the ability of England from an economic standpoint to carry on the struggle. Burke describes Jacobinism as 'the spirit of ambition' which had overtaken the swelling middle classes, and which caused them to assert their pretensions against the propertied classes, impatient of 'the places which settled society prescribes to them', in an attempt to destroy pre-existing laws and institutions.

Regiomontium, in imprints, Königsberg (now Kaliningrad).

Regional Novel, a novel set in a real and well-defined locality, which is in some degree strange to the reader. The first English regional novel, set in a specific and little-known locality, appears to have been M. Edgeworth's *Castle Rackrent* (1800), set in Ireland. It was rapidly followed by the Irish novels of Lady *Morgan and by the Scottish novels of *Galt and Sir W. *Scott (who later acknowledged his debt to Miss Edgeworth). From about 1839 the localities described in regional novels were often smaller and more exact, as in the works of Mrs *Gaskell and G. *Eliot (set in the Midlands) and of the *Brontës (set in Yorkshire). Later novelists became ever more interested in precise regional attachment and description, as is shown in much of the work of C. *Kingsley and R. D. *Blackmore (Devon); *Hardy (Dorset and 'Wessex'); R. *Jefferies (Hampshire); R. L. *Stevenson (Highlands and Lowlands); J. M. *Barrie (Angus); Arnold *Bennett (Staffordshire); and D. H. *Lawrence (Nottinghamshire). The industrial or urban novel, set in a specific town or city, flourished in the mid-19th cent., with *Disraeli's *Sybil*, Mrs Gaskell's *Mary Barton*, Dickens's *Hard Times*, and G. Eliot's *Middlemarch*, and the tradition continued into this century, notably in the work of *Joyce. (See also NOVEL, RISE OF THE.)

Register, Stationer's, see STATIONER'S COMPANY.

Regius professorships were first founded by Henry VIII in 1540 at Cambridge (divinity, civil law, physic, Hebrew, and Greek). In 1546 five further Regius professorships were founded at Oxford (theology, medicine, civil law, Hebrew, and Greek). Regius professorships of modern history at Cambridge, and of ecclesiastical history, modern history, and moral and pastoral theology at Oxford, have since been added.

Rehearsal, The, a farcical comedy attributed to George Villiers, 2nd duke of *Buckingham, but probably written by him in collaboration with others, among whom are mentioned S. *Butler and Martin Clifford, master of the Charterhouse; printed 1672.

The play satirizes the heroic tragedies of the day, and consists of a series of parodies of passages from these, strung together in an absurd heroic plot. The author of the mock play is evidently a laureate (hence his name 'Bayes'), and *D'Avenant was probably intended; but there are also hits at *Dryden (particularly his *Conquest of Granada) and his brothers-in-law, Edward and Robert Howard. Bayes takes two friends, Smith and Johnson, to see the rehearsal of his play, and the absurdity of this work (which includes the two kings of Brentford, entering hand in hand), coupled with the comments of Bayes, his instructions to the actors, and the remarks of Smith and Johnson, remains highly entertaining. Prince Pretty-man, Prince Volscius, and *Drawcansir are among the characters. It was one of the earliest of English dramatic *burlesques, and was much performed during the 18th cent., during which period the genre developed to one of its highest points in Sheridan's *The Critic.

REID, Forrest (1875–1947), Ulster novelist, whose uneventful life was spent in and near Belfast. His fiction includes The Kingdom of Twilight (1904), The Garden God: a Tale of two boys (1905), Following Darkness (1912), and a trilogy, Uncle Stephen (1931), The Retreat (1934), and Young Tom (1944); the last three were published in one volume in 1955 as Tom Barber, with an introduction by Reid's friend E. M. *Forster. Reid's dominant subject is boyhood and the longing for an ideal dream playmate; he evokes a pagan, lyrical world of 'lonely garden and sombre grove', in which hints of the supernatural are contrasted with the realities of everyday. His autobiographies, Apostate (1926) and Private Road (1940), vividly describe his sense of the numinous in nature. See The Green Avenue (1980), a critical biography by B. Taylor.

REID, Thomas (1710–96), graduated from Marischal College, Aberdeen, in 1726. He was elected regent in philosophy at King's College, Aberdeen, in 1751, and he succeeded Adam *Smith as professor of moral philosophy at Glasgow in 1764, largely through the influence of his patron Henry *Home, Lord Kames. While at King's he composed his first major work, An Inquiry into the Human Mind, on the Principles of Common Sense (1764), and after retiring from active teaching at Glasgow in 1780 he published his Essays on the Intellectual Powers of Man (1785) and Essays on the Active Powers of Man (1788). His lectures on the fine arts were first published in 1973. Reid was perhaps the most notable 18th-cent. exponent of the philosophy of common sense, by which phrase he meant both a faculty of the mind, and a set of incontrovertible beliefs implanted in the human mind by God. He also questioned the widely-held theory that the immediate objects of perception are 'ideas', arguing that we directly perceive external objects rather than mental representations of them. Aesthetic qualities he conceived either as intrinsic qualities of mind, or, derivatively, as the qualities of objects of design. He was a vigorous critic of the writings of *Hume, and, later in life, J. *Priestley, and he championed the inductive methods of F. *Bacon and I. *Newton. Reid was an accomplished mathematician and scientist as well as a philosopher, contributing 'An Essay on Quantity' to the Philosophical Transactions of the Royal Society of London in 1748. The Scottish poet Thomas *Campbell was named after him.

Rejected Addresses, by James and Horatio *Smith, published 1812.

A competition was held to find a suitable address to celebrate the opening of the new *Drury Lane Theatre in 1812. James and Horatio Smith produced a large batch of bogus entries, purporting to be by *Wordsworth, *Byron, T. *Moore, *Southey, *Coleridge, *Crabbe, Sir W. *Scott, *Cobbett, and others. The parodies are mixed in quality, but the brilliance of some made the Smiths famous, and caused T. *Campbell to feel annoyed that he had been left out.

Relapse, The, or Virtue in Danger, the highly successful first play of *Vanbrugh, produced 1696.

It is an avowed continuation of Love's Last Shift by C. *Cibber, some of the characters being retained, though more effectively presented. It contains two plots, very slenderly related to each other. Loveless, a reformed libertine, living happily in the country with his wife Amanda, is obliged to go with her to London, where he suffers a relapse under the temptation of Berinthia, an unscrupulous young widow. Worthy, a former lover of Berinthia, prevails on her to favour Loveless's suit and to persuade Amanda of the infidelity of her husband, in order to promote his own chances of seducing Amanda. But Amanda, though bitterly resenting her husband's faithlessness, remains firm in her virtue.

The second plot is more entertaining. Sir Novelty Fashion, the perfect beau, who has just become (by purchase) Lord Foppington, is about to marry Miss Hoyden, daughter of Sir Tunbelly Clumsey, a country squire, neither father nor daughter having yet seen him. Foppington's younger brother, Young Fashion, having overspent his allowance, vainly appeals to Foppington for help. To revenge himself and rehabilitate his fortunes, he decides to go down to Sir Tunbelly's house, impersonate his brother, and marry the heiress. The plot is at first successful. Sir Tunbelly welcomes him unsuspectingly, and Miss Hoyden is only too ready to marry him next morning; but Sir Tunbelly will not hear of the marriage for a week, so Fashion bribes the nurse and parson, and a secret marriage is at once celebrated. Foppington arrives, is treated as an impostor, and subjected to indignities, until a neighbour vouches for his identity. Meanwhile young Fashion escapes. Hoyden, the parson, and the nurse decide to say nothing of the former marriage, and Hoyden is married to Foppington, who immediately brings his wife to London. Here young Fashion claims his bride, the nurse and parson are bullied and cajoled into admitting the earlier marriage, and Hoyden is reconciled to her lot on learning that Fashion is Lord Foppington's brother.

The play was adapted by Sheridan as *A Trip to Scarborough.

Religio Laici, a poem by *Dryden, published 1682.

Written in defence of Anglicanism against Deist, Catholic, and Dissenting arguments, *Religio Laici* combines an exalted recognition of religious sublimity with a defence of a 'layman's' reasonable and straightforward religious attitudes. The poem may have implicit political significance, and its opening lines, beginning 'Dim as the borrow'd Beams of Moon and Stars', are among the finest Dryden wrote.

Religio Medici, a self-directed stocktaking by Sir T. *Browne of his attitudes as a Christian and a doctor towards God and the Church, faith and reason, the classical tradition, private friendship, and national prejudice, first published in an unauthorized edition 1642, reprinted 1643 with some authorial corrections, revisions, and additions.

Written in about 1635, after experience of life in Ireland, France, Italy, and Holland, the work is divided into two parts, relating broadly to God and to man. The first treats of matters of faith, the hostilities among rival sects and religions, and man as microcosm. Its breadth of vision and tolerance are matched in the second part, where he expresses love for all sorts and conditions of men, English or foreign, rich or poor, learned or ignorant, friend or foe, good or bad. While based on biblical teaching, the arguments are reinforced and widened with citations of classical philosophers, historians, and poets. Often reprinted, and translated into many languages, *Religio Medici* quickly made the author famous as much by its wit and style as by its piety.

Reliques of Ancient English Poetry, a collection of *ballads, sonnets, historical songs, and metrical romances published in 1765 by T. *Percy. The majority of them were extracted from the *Percy Folio and edited and 'restored' by Percy. They were of very different periods, some of great antiquity, some as recent as the reign of Charles I. Ancient poems drawn from other sources and a few of more modern date (including works by *Wither, *Dryden, *Lovelace, *Shenstone, and *Glover) were added by the editor. The editions of 1767, 1775, and 1794 each contained new matter.

REMARQUE, Erich Maria (1898–1970), German novelist, author of *Im Westen nichts Neues* (*All Quiet on the Western Front*, 1929) and *Der Weg zurück* (*The Road Back*, 1931), a sequel.

Remorse, a tragedy by S. T. *Coleridge, written in 1797 as *Osorio*, produced at Drury Lane 1813.

The story, set in Granada at the time of the Spanish Inquisition, tells of the slow corruption of the character of Osorio, a man who supposed himself strong but who is gradually led by temptations and events into guilt and evil.

Renaissance, the great flowering of art, architecture, politics, and the study of literature, usually seen as the end of the Middle Ages and the beginning of the modern world, which came about under the influence of Greek and Roman models. It began in Italy in the late 14th cent., culminated in the High Renaissance in the early 16th cent. (the period of *Michelangelo and *Machiavelli), and spread to the rest of Europe in the 15th cent. and afterwards. Its emphasis was humanist: that is, on regarding the human figure and reason without a necessary relating of it to the superhuman; but much of its energy also came from the *Neoplatonic tradition in writers such as *Pico della Mirandola. The word Renaissance has been applied in the 20th cent. to earlier periods which manifested a new interest in and study of the classics, such as the 12th cent. and the period of *Charlemagne. But the Italian Renaissance is still seen as a watershed in the development of civilization, both because of its extent and because of its emphasis on the human, whether independent of or in association with the divine. See J. A. *Symonds, *History of the Renaissance in Italy* (1875–86); W. *Pater, *Studies in the History of the Renaissance* (1873); J. *Burckhardt, *The Civilisation of the Renaissance in Italy* (English trans., S. G. C. Middlemore, 1929).

RENAN, Ernest (1823–92), French philologist, historian, and essayist. After a childhood spent in his native Brittany he went to Paris to continue his training for the priesthood, but abandoned it after his understanding of biblical criticism had shaken his faith. The application of a scientific historical method to the birth and spread of Christianity was the aim of his *Histoire des origines du Christianisme*, the first part of which, *Vie de Jésus* (1863), combines a critical examination of the Gospel narratives with an imaginative presentation of the figure of Christ. It earned him both fame and persecution. The remaining volumes are: *Les Apôtres* (1866), *La vie de Saint Paul* (1869), *L'Antéchrist* (1873), *Les Évangiles* (1877), *L'Église Chrétienne* (1879), and *Marc-Aurèle* (1881). He also wrote an *Histoire du peuple d'Israël* (5 vols, 1887–93). Besides his historical and philological works, Renan published a number of critical, reflective, and prophetic essays, among them: *Essais de morale et de critique* (1859), *La réforme intellectuelle et morale* (1871), *Examen de conscience philosophique* (1888), *L'Avenir de la science* (written 1848–9, published 1890). His early years are recalled in *Souvenirs d'enfance et de jeunesse* (1883).

'Renascence of Wonder in English Poetry, The', see WATTS-DUNTON, T.

Renaud, in the *chansons de geste* a rebel against *Charlemagne, better known under the Italian name of *Rinaldo.

Renault, a character in Otway's *Venice Preserv'd*.

RENAULT, Mary, pseudonym of Mary Challans (1905–83), novelist, known principally for her *historical novels, most of which are lively first-person narratives set in Ancient Greece or Asia Minor, incorporating the new anthropological and historical insights of the 20th cent. They include *The King must Die* (1958) and *The Bull from the Sea* (1962), both retelling the legend of Theseus, and *The Persian Boy* (1972), set in the time of Alexander the Great.

RENÉ OF PROVENCE, duc d'Anjou and comte de Provence (1408–80), known as 'le bon Roi René', son of Louis II, duke of Anjou, was titular king of Naples, the two Sicilies, and Jerusalem, 'whose large style agrees not with the leanness of his purse' (Shakespeare, 2 *Henry VI*, I. i). His daughter *Margaret of Anjou was wife of Henry VI. As count of Provence, he gave free play to his love of music and poetry, tilting and hunting, minstrels and knight-errants, and showed indifference to political affairs, There is a picture of his court in Scott's *Anne of Geierstein*. He figures in *Henry VI* as 'Reignier'. He left some prose and verse romances, pastorals, and allegories.

RENI, Guido (1575–1642), Bolognese painter, whose classicizing style was formed in the Carracci Academy at Bologna. He was particularly admired in England in the 18th and early 19th cents, when he was ranked second only to *Raphael; Horace *Walpole's comment in *Aedes Walpolianae* (1747)—'all the qualities of a perfect painter never met but in Raphael, Guido and Carracci'—typifies the response of this period. *Shelley, in Bologna in 1818, wrote

rapturously to *Peacock describing the Guidos in the Pinacoteca, and from Rome (1819) exclaimed that only Raphael, Guido, and *Rosa could sustain comparison with antiquity. A painting traditionally described as a portrait of the ill-famed Beatrice Cenci, loosely derived from a figure in Reni's *St Andrew led to Martyrdom* (1608) and almost certainly not by Reni himself, cast a spell over the Romantics; Shelley describes it in the preface to *The Cenci*, and later it fascinated *De Quincey, *Dickens, *Swinburne, *Melville, and many others. In *The Marble Faun* Hawthorne uses the *Beatrice Cenci* and Reni's *Archangel Michael* to symbolize various aspects of his central characters. Yet in 1818 *Keats had written disparagingly of the 'canting, solemn melodramatic mawkishness' of Reni; his reputation plunged with *Ruskin, whose scorn for the entire Bolognese school was inherited by G. *Eliot, who satirizes Reni in *Middlemarch*. The highly charged baroque pathos that characterizes such a work as the *Ecce Homo* (c.1640, Fitzwilliam Museum, Cambridge) has since been found unpleasantly theatrical in this country; only very recently has Guido's true stature again been recognized, and his works praised for the grace and beauty of their line and for their daring and ravishing combinations of mauves, oranges, and pinks.

Representative, The, a daily paper founded by B. *Disraeli and John *Murray.

Repressor of over much Blaming of the Clergy, see PECOCK, R.

REPTON, Humphry, see PICTURESQUE.

Republic, The, one of the dialogues of *Plato, in which *Socrates is represented as eliciting, in the course of a discussion on justice, the ideal type of state. In this the perfect forms of goodness, truth, and beauty are cultivated, and everything repugnant to them excluded. The famous apologue of the men who live bound in a cavern, so that they can see only the shadows of real objects projected by a bright fire on its inner wall, occurs in Book VII.

Republic of Letters, The, the collective body of those engaged in literary pursuits. The expression occurs first in *Addison's *Dialogues upon Ancient Medals* (i. 19).

RERESBY, Sir John (1634–89), a Yorkshire baronet and Member of Parliament, travelled during the Commonwealth on the Continent, and his *Memoirs* (1734, as *Travels and Memoirs*, 1813, and standard edition, ed. A. Browning, 1936) give an interesting picture of political life.

RESTIF DE LA BRETONNE, Nicolas (1734–1806), French novelist. His vast, rambling output reflects the dissipations of his life as a peasant adrift in Paris. Long forgotten, he has recently been restored to critical favour for his knowledge of the life of the humble classes (*Le Paysan perverti*, 1775, and *Monsieur Nicholas*, 1794), and by his understanding of rural values (*La Vie de mon père*, 1779).

'Resolution and Independence', a poem by *Wordsworth, written 1802, published 1807, sometimes known as 'The Leech Gatherer'.

The poet describes his own elation as he walks over the moors on a fine spring morning after a storm, and his sudden descent into apprehension and dejection, as he ponders the fate of earlier poets, such as *Chatterton: 'We Poets in our youth begin in gladness; | But thereof come in the end despondency and madness.' At this stage he comes upon the aged leech gatherer, whom he cross-questions in characteristically Wordsworthian manner about his way of life: the old man responds with cheerful dignity, and the poet resolves to remember him as an admonishment. The poem was based on a meeting recorded in Dorothy *Wordsworth's *Journal*, 3 Oct. 1800, with an 'old man almost double', whose trade was to gather leeches. Its mixture of elevated language and sentiment with prosaic detail is peculiarly Wordsworthian, and led *Coleridge to comment on its 'inconstancy of style'. Wordsworth's own comments on his use of imagery in the poem and 'the conferring, the abstracting, and the modifying powers of the Imagination' in his 1815 Preface are of great interest.

Restoration, the re-establishment of monarchy in England, with the return of Charles II (1660); also the period marked by this event of which the chief literary figures are *Dryden, *Rochester, *Bunyan, *Pepys, *Locke, and the Restoration dramatists. One of the characteristic genres of the period is Restoration comedy, or the comedy of manners, which developed upon the re-opening of the theatres. Its principal writers were *Congreve, *Etherege, *Farquhar, *Vanbrugh, and *Wycherley, and its predominant tone was witty, bawdy, cynical, and amoral. The plays were mainly in prose, with passages of verse for the more romantic moments; the plots were complex and usually double, sometimes triple, though repartee and discussions of marital behaviour provide much of the interest, reflecting the fashionable manners of the day. Standard characters include fops, bawds, scheming valets, country squires, and sexually voracious young widows and older women; the principal theme is sexual intrigue, either for its own sake or for money. Respectable citizens avoided the theatres, which they saw as a source of corruption, and the playwrights came under heavy attack for frivolity, blasphemy, and immorality (see COLLIER, JEREMY): they and their subsequent admirers defended their works as serious social criticism, and mirrors to the age. During the 18th cent. the plays were presented in more 'genteel' versions, and in the 19th cent. hardly at all: the 20th cent. saw a considerable revival of interest, with such notable productions as *The Way of the World*, one of the masterpieces of the period, in 1924 with Edith Evans as Millamant.

Retaliation, an unfinished poem by *Goldsmith, published 1774, consisting of a string of humorous and critical epitaphs on *Garrick, Sir J. *Reynolds, *Burke, and other friends, in reply to their similar efforts directed against himself. Of the latter Garrick's is the best known:

Here lies Nolly Goldsmith, for shortness called Noll,
Who wrote like an angel, but talked like poor Poll.

Retrospective Review, The (1820–8), founded by Henry Southern (1799–1853), its first editor, as a 'Review of past literature', the object of which was 'to exhibit a bird's-eye view of the rise and progress of our literature' and to rouse interest 'in the old and venerable literature of the country'. Extracts from poetry, essays, drama, and other prose, chiefly drawn from the 16th and 17th cents, included the work of Sir T. *Browne, F. *Bacon, G. *Herbert, *Vaughan, *Jonson, G. *Chapman, and many others. Some three-quarters of the work was English; the rest consisted of translations from past European literature. Another of the founder's objects was to question the deference accorded to contemporary critics, such as those of the *Quarterly and the *Edinburgh, and to expose their substitution of prejudice for true critical principles. The method of the *Review* was to consider each piece or extract as if it were just from the press, and sometimes to compare the quality of the old with some work of the 'moderns'. The *Review* was briefly revived in 1853–4.

Return of the Druses, The, a tragedy in blank verse by R. *Browning, published 1843 as no. IV of *Bells and Pomegranates*. It was written for the stage, but was rejected by *Macready, although Browning had created the role of Djabal with him in mind.

The action of the play is unhistorical. Browning places the religious sect of the Druses in exile and subjection on a small Aegean island, and the plot concerns the downfall of the impostor Djabal, who claims to be the incarnation of Hakeem, divine founder of the sect, in order both to liberate his people from their oppressors and to gain the love of Anael. Djabal and Anael both perish in the end, but the 'return of the Druses' to their homeland, the Lebanon, is assured.

Return of the Native, The, a novel by T. *Hardy, published 1878.

The scene is the sombre Egdon Heath, powerfully and symbolically present throughout the novel. Damon Wildeve, once an engineer but now a publican, dallies between the two women by whom he is loved—the gentle Thomasin Yeobright and the wild, capricious Eustacia Vye. Thomasin rejects her humble suitor Diggory Venn, a reddleman, and is eventually married to Wildeve, who takes her less for love than from a wish to hurt Eustacia. Thomasin's cousin Clym Yeobright, a diamond merchant in Paris, disgusted with the worthlessness of his occupation, returns to Egdon intending to become a schoolmaster in his native heath. He falls in love with Eustacia, and she in a brief infatuation marries him, hoping to induce him to return to Paris, thus escaping from Egdon, which she detests. But to her despair he will not return; his sight fails and he becomes a furze-cutter on the heath. She becomes the cause of estrangement between Clym and his beloved mother, and unintentionally causes the mother's death. This, together with the discovery that Eustacia's relationship with Wildeve has not ceased, leads to a violent scene between Clym and his wife, and ultimately to Eustacia's flight with Wildeve, in the course of which both are drowned. Clym, blaming himself for the death of his mother and his wife, becomes an itinerant preacher, and the widowed Thomasin marries Diggory Venn.

RETZ, Paul de Gondi, cardinal de (1613–79), French memorialist. Churchman and political adventurer under Louis XIV, he wrote his *Mémoires* late in life, probably at the suggestion of Mme de *Sévigné. They were published posthumously in 1715 and quickly acquired the status of a classic. Composed in a passionate and turbulent style, and expressing attitudes inspired by the moral realism of *Machiavelli, they document the manners, conduct, and motives of the Fronde generation with penetration and panache.

REUCHLIN, Johann (1455–1522), born at Pforzheim, a celebrated humanist and the foremost oriental scholar of his day. Braving the powerful Dominicans, he published in 1494 his *De Verbo Mirifico*, defending Jewish literature and philosophy, and became the centre of an acute controversy in which he was opposed by *Pfefferkorn and which was the occasion of the publication of the *Epistolae Obscurorum Virorum*. Reuchlin was author of the first Hebrew grammar.

Revelation, Book of, see APOCALYPSE.

Revels, Master of the, an officer appointed to superintend *masques and other entertainments at court. He is first mentioned in the reign of Henry VII. The first permanent master of the revels was Sir Thomas Cawarden, appointed in 1545. Holders of the office in Shakespeare's day were Edmund Tilney, 1579–1610, and Sir George Buc, 1610–22 (he had been deputy master since 1603).

Revenge of Bussy D'Ambois, The, a tragedy by G. *Chapman, written 1610/11, printed 1613, a sequel to *Bussy D'Ambois.*

Clermont D'Ambois, brother of Bussy, described by his close friend the duc de Guise as the ideal 'Senecal man', gentle, noble, generous, and 'fix'd in himself', is urged by his brother's ghost to avenge his murder, but will only do so by the honourable method of a duel. He sends a challenge to Montsurry, who evades it; urged again by the ghost, he introduces himself to Montsurry's house, forces him to fight, and kills him. He then learns of the assassination of the Guise, and, refusing to live amid 'all the horrors of the vicious time' as 'the slave of power', he kills himself. The hero's reluctance to exact revenge recalls certain aspects of *Hamlet. (See also REVENGE TRAGEDY.)

Revenger's Tragedy, The, a tragedy published anonymously in 1607, and from 1656 ascribed to *Tourneur; modern scholarship attributes the play to *Middleton, though its authorship is still disputed.

The central character is Vendice (or Vindice), intent on revenging the death of his mistress, poisoned by the lecherous old duke. The court is a centre of vice and intrigue; the duchess's youngest son is convicted of rape, she herself seduces Spurio, the duke's bastard, and her two older sons, the duke's stepsons, plot against each other and against Lussurioso, the duke's heir. Vendice, disguised as Piato, appears to attempt to procure his own sister Castiza for Lussurioso; she resists, but their mother Gratiana temporarily succumbs to his bribes and agrees to play the bawd. Vendice murders the duke by tricking him into kissing the poisoned skull of his mistress, and most of the remaining characters kill one another or are killed in a final masque of revengers and murderers; Vendice, who survives the bloodbath, owns up to the murder of the duke, and is promptly condemned to death with his brother and accomplice Hippolite by the duke's successor, old Antonio. He is led off to execution, content to 'die after a nest of dukes'. The play is marked by a tragic intensity of feeling, a powerfully satiric wit, and passages of great poetic richness, all combined, for example, in Vendice's address to 'the bony lady', his dead mistress: 'Does the silkworm expend her yellow labours | For thee?' (III. v. 71 ff.) (See also REVENGE TRAGEDY.)

Revenge Tragedy, a dramatic genre that flourished in the late Elizabethan and Jacobean period, sometimes known as 'the tragedy of blood'. Kyd's *The Spanish Tragedy* (1592), a much-quoted prototype, helped to establish a demand for this popular form; later examples are Marlowe's *The Jew of Malta*, Shakespeare's *Titus Andronicus*, *The Revenger's Tragedy*, and, most notably, *Hamlet*; there are also strong revenge elements in *Webster. Common ingredients include: the hero's quest for vengeance, often at the prompting of the ghost of a murdered kinsman or loved one; scenes of real or feigned insanity; a play-within-a-play; scenes in graveyards, severed limbs, scenes of carnage and mutilation, etc. Many of these items were inherited from Senecan drama, with the difference that in revenge tragedy violence was not reported but took place on stage: as Vendice in *The Revenger's Tragedy* rather baldly puts it, while in the process of slowly murdering the duke, 'When the bad bleeds, then is the tragedy good.' The revenge code also produced counterattacks, as in *The Atheist's Tragedy*, in Chapman's *The Revenge of Bussy D'Ambois*, and again in *Hamlet*, in which the heroes refuse or hesitate to follow the convention.

Revesby Play, The, a folk-drama acted by morris-dancers at Revesby in Lincolnshire at the end of the 18th cent. The characters are the Fool and his sons—Pickle Herring, Blue Breeches, Pepper Breeches, Ginger Breeches—and Mr Allspice and Cicely. The Fool fights with a hobbyhorse and a dragon. The sons decide to kill the Fool; he kneels down, the swords of the dancers are locked around his neck, and he is slain. He revives when Pickle Herring stamps his foot. Sword-dances and the wooing of Cicely by the Fool and his sons conclude the play. The central incident no doubt symbolizes the death of the year and its resuscitation in the spring. The text is given by T. F. Ordish in the *Folk-Lore Journal*, vii. 338. See also E. K. *Chambers, *The Mediaeval Stage* (1903).

Review, The, (1) a periodical started by *Defoe in 1704, under the title of *A Weekly Review of the Affairs of France*, which after various transformations became *A Review of the State of the British Nation* in 1707; it lasted until 1713. It was a non-partisan paper, an organ of the commercial interests of the nation; it appeared thrice weekly and was written, practically in its entirety, by Defoe himself, who expressed in it his opinions on all current political topics, thus initiating the political leading article. It also had lighter articles on love, marriage, gambling, etc.; Defoe's attitude to his readers was that he strove to '*wheedle them in* (if it may be allowed that expression) to the knowledge of the world; who, rather than take more pains, would be content with their ignorance, and search into nothing'. (2) a quarterly magazine of poetry and criticism, founded in 1962 and edited by Ian Hamilton (1938–), poet, biographer, and critic. It ran for 30 issues, and was succeeded by *The New Review*, also edited by Hamilton, which ran from 1974 to 1979. Contributors included R. *Lowell, E. *O'Brien, P. *Porter, R. *Fuller, J. *Fuller, S. *Heaney, and Douglas Dunn.

Review of English Studies, a scholarly quarterly devoted to 'research in all departments of its subject', founded by R. B. *McKerrow, with an advisory panel including A. C. *Bradley, E. K. and R. W. *Chambers, W. W. *Greg, J. D. *Wilson and others. The first issue appeared in Jan. 1925, and the present New Series began in 1950.

Revised Version, The, see BIBLE, THE ENGLISH.

Revolt of Islam, The, an epic political poem by P. B. *Shelley, written at Great Marlow in 1817 (under the title 'Laon and Cythna: or The Revolution in the Golden City, A Vision of the Nineteenth Century'), published 1818.

The poem is Shelley's idealized and highly idiosyncratic version of the French revolution, transposed to an Oriental setting. It is composed in Spenserian stanzas (too ornate for effective narrative), forming twelve Cantos. The revolt is organized by a brother and sister, Laon and Cythna, whose temporary success is celebrated in incestuous love-making (Canto VI). But the tyrants recover power, and Islam is subject to plague and famine, vividly described (Canto X). Brother and sister are burnt at the stake, but sail together with an illegitimate child to a visionary Hesperides (Canto XII). Though cumbersome, diffuse, and obsessive (there is much disguised autobiography), the poem contains powerful images of struggle and renewal which are brilliantly clarified in Shelley's poems of 1819. The figure of Cythna, the revolutionary feminist, is of historical interest; and the prose Preface, concerning reactions to the French revolution, is impressively argued.

Revolutionary Epic, The, the first three books of a historical epic by B. *Disraeli, published 1834.

The poem, conceived in Greece, was to be a celebration of the French revolution and a companion to the *Iliad*, the *Divina Commedia*, and *Paradise Lost*. Written in Miltonic blank verse, and strongly influenced by Shelley's *The Revolt of Islam*, the poem opens with a debate between Magros, the Genius of Feudalism, and Lyridon, the Genius of Federalism. Beginning with the Greeks, the narrative proceeds (with many digressions on themes such as Nobility, Power, and other abstractions) through the history of the West to the French revolution. These first three books of the poem were then published, but they were poorly received and Disraeli did not continue.

Revolution in France, *Reflections on the,* by E. *Burke, published 1790.

This treatise was provoked by a sermon preached by R. *Price in Nov. 1789, in which he exulted in the French revolution and asserted that the king of England owes his throne to the choice of the people, who are at liberty to cashier him for misconduct. Burke repudiates this constitutional doctrine, and contrasts the inherited rights of which the English are tenacious with the 'rights of man' of the French revolutionaries, based on 'extravagant and presumptuous speculations', inconsistent with an ordered society and leading to poverty and chaos. He examines the character of the men who made the French revolution, and the proceedings of their National Assembly, a 'profane burlesque of that sacred institute'. The well-known eloquent passage on the downfall of Marie Antoinette leads to the lament that 'the age of chivalry is gone . . . All the decent drapery of life is to be rudely torn off' in deference to 'the new conquering empire of light and reason'. His general conclusion is that the defective institutions of the old régime should have been reformed, not destroyed.

Revue des deux mondes, La, a celebrated French review which first appeared in 1829 and which continues to be published today. Under the editorship (1831–77) of François Buloz it became one of the leading periodicals of its kind in Europe, dealing with foreign and domestic politics as well as literature, philosophy, and the fine arts, and attracting contributions from such writers as *Balzac, *Sainte-Beuve, *Dumas *père*, *Hugo, *Vigny, and G. *Sand.

Reynard the Fox, the central character in the *Roman de Renart,* a series of popular satirical fables, related to the *Bestiaries and the tradition from *Aesop's Fables, written in France at various times c.1175–1250. The first known cycle is the Latin one by Nivard of Ghent, *Ysengrimus* (c.1148), and this was followed by the Middle High German *Reinhard Fuchs* (c.1180). There is a Flemish version from c.1250; another Flemish version (now lost) was translated into English and printed by *Caxton in 1481. In these anthropomorphic stories, the fox is the man who preys on society, is brought to justice, but escapes by his cunning. The popularity of the series was most marked in French (which took from it the German word *Regin-hart,* 'strong in counsel', for 'fox' in place of its etymological *goupil* which is found in some of the earlier stories), but there are some derived and related English works. The most important of these is the Middle English 'The Fox and the Wolf' (in *Early Middle English Verse and Prose,* ed. J. A. W. Bennett and G. V. Smithers, 2nd edn 1968, pp. 67–76). Other related works in English are Chaucer's 'The Nun's Priest's Tale' (*Canterbury Tales,* 20), some of *Henryson's 'Morall Fabillis of Esope' (where the fox is called Lowrence), and J. C. *Harris's Uncle Remus stories (where the role of the fox is taken by *Brer Rabbit). The principal characters in Caxton's version are: Reynard the Fox, King Noble the Lion, Isengrym the Wolf, Courtoys the Hound, Bruin the Bear, Tybert the Cat, Grymbert the Badger, Coart (or Cuwaert) the Hare, Bellyn the Ram,

Martin and Dame Rukenawe the Apes, Chanticleer the Cock, Partlet the Hen. Ermeline is Reynard's wife and Malperdy (*Malpertuis*) his castle.

Le Roman de Renart, Branche II (ed. M. Roques, Classiques Française du Moyen Âge, 79, Paris, 1951); L. Flinn, *Le Roman de Renart dans la littérature française et dans les littératures étrangères au moyen âge* (Paris, 1963); *The History of Reynard the Fox translated from the Dutch Original by William Caxton,* ed. N. F. Blake (EETS os 263, 1970).

REYNOLDS, John Hamilton (1796–1852), poet, and a close friend and correspondent of *Keats. (Keats's letter to Reynolds of May 1818 on *The Fall of *Hyperion is particularly important.) In 1814 Reynolds published *Safie,* an *oriental novel reminiscent of *Byron, and *The Eden of the Imagination,* which echoes late 18th-cent. verse. *The Garden of Florence* (1821) contains his most effective serious work, and includes two verse tales from *Boccaccio, as part of a Boccaccio volume he and Keats intended to write together, and for which Keats originally produced *'Isabella'. He had great skill in parody and comic verse; his parody of Wordsworth's *Peter Bell* appeared in 1819, *The Fancy* in 1820, and *Odes and Addresses* (with T. *Hood) in 1825.

REYNOLDS, Sir Joshua (1723–92), born in Devon, was apprenticed in London (1740–4) and studied in Italy (1750–2); on his return to London (1753) he swiftly became the most successful portrait painter of his age, who painted most of the celebrated men and women of the day. Reynolds sought to give new dignity to British portraiture by relating it to the Grand Style of European art. His portraits are immensely varied and enriched by allusions to the antique and to Renaissance and 17th-cent. Italian art. He was furthermore a distinguished man of letters; it was he who suggested the idea of the *Club to his friend Dr *Johnson. He painted Johnson at least five times and wrote a Memoir of him and two Johnsonian dialogues; *Boswell dedicated his *Life of Johnson* to the painter. Goldsmith dedicated *The Deserted Village* to him in 1770. Reynolds's first literary works were three essays published in the *Idler* (1759). In 1768 he was made first president of the Royal Academy and his *Discourses,* delivered to the students (1769–90), are his most significant achievement as a writer. With clarity and elegance he supported the traditional values of academic art, and stressed the importance to young painters of a thorough study of the great masters of the past. Yet the *Discourses* also reveal that he was sensitive to the new ideals of Romantic art; the last is a moving tribute to *Michelangelo, whose sublimity Reynolds had come to value above the perfection of *Raphael. *Hazlitt pointed out the contradictions in the *Discourses* and *Blake, in a series of annotations to his copy of the *Works*, attacked Reynolds for hypocrisy and for his lack of faith in the inspiration of genius—on the title page he wrote, 'This man was hired to depress art.' Yet he was admired by *Constable, *Turner, and *Ruskin, and *Wordsworth paid tribute to him in lines on Sir G. *Beaumont's cenotaph to his memory at Coleorton.

Rhetoric, in Greek, the art of speaking so as to persuade, was from the first tied up with ethics (persuasion of what is true) and literature (use of language in order to please). It was a branch of the medieval *Trivium and therefore an important part of the school syllabus up to the 17th cent. Literary rhetoric is concerned with the organization (*inventio* and *dispositio*) and embellishment (*elecutio*) of works. The first of these is prominent in many 18th-cent. works (*Tristram Shandy* and *A Tale of a Tub, for instance), and the second is important in its provision of poetic 'devices' (figures and tropes) in poets from *Chaucer to the present day. See B. Vickers, *Classical Rhetoric in English* (1970).

Rhoda Fleming, a novel by G. *Meredith, published 1865.

One of Meredith's shorter novels, regarded by the author as 'a plain story'. Rhoda and Dahlia Fleming are the daughters of a Kentish yeoman farmer. His assistant, Robert Eccles, is a stalwart man, also of the yeoman class. The gentle Dahlia is seduced by the smooth and cynical Edward Blancove, who soon deserts her. Robert, who loves the proud and fiery Rhoda, determines to see Dahlia properly treated. But Edward hires a blackguard, Sedgett, who waylays Robert and strikes him violently down. Recovered, Robert at last succeeds in discovering the pregnant Dahlia's hiding-place. But Edward has meanwhile bribed the vile Sedgett to marry her, and the sick and broken-hearted Dahlia has consented, for her family's sake. Robert is too late to prevent the marriage, but he eventually succeeds in discovering that Sedgett is already married. Edward has by now repented and wishes to marry Dahlia, but she, terrified at the thought of returning to Sedgett, has taken poison. Though her life is saved she is broken in spirit, and finds marriage with Edward now impossible. Rhoda, tamed at last by these violent events, marries the steadfast Robert.

RHODES, Cecil John (1853–1902), born in Bishop's Stortford, gained a degree at Oriel College, Oxford, after some delay, and made a fortune at the diamond fields of Kimberley. He became a statesman of South Africa and was instrumental in securing part of Bechuanaland for the Cape government (1884) and later (1887) the charter for the British South Africa Co. whose territory became known as Rhodesia. He was prime minister of Cape Colony from 1890, but resigned after being pronounced guilty of grave breaches of duty arising from the unauthorized raid into the Transvaal of Dr Jameson. In his will he endowed 170 scholarships at Oxford, for students from the colonies, America, and Germany.

RHODES, William Barnes (1772–1826), a bank teller, who translated the *Satires* of *Juvenal in 1801 and the *Epigrams* in 1803. He did not acknowledge his authorship of his highly successful farce *Bombastes Furioso* (1810) until 1822. Rhodes collected volumes of plays, old and new, and bought heavily at the *Roxburghe sale in 1812.

Rhodes Scholars, see RHODES, C. J.

Rhododaphne, a narrative poem in octosyllabics by *Peacock, published 1818.

In ancient Thessaly, the shepherd boy Anthemion is torn between the mortal girl Calliroë and the nymph Rhododaphne. Calliroë appears to die, and Rhododaphne takes Anthemion to an enchanted palace (anticipating the one built by Keats's *Lamia), but Rhododaphne is struck down by the spirit of Heavenly Love, and Calliroë is restored.

RHONDDA, Viscountess, see TIME AND TIDE.

Rhyme: 'male' or 'masculine' rhymes or endings are those having a final accented syllable, as distinguished from 'female' or 'feminine' rhymes or endings in which the last syllable is unaccented.

Rhyme-royal, or Rime royal, see METRE.

Rhymers Club, a group of poets that met at the *Cheshire Cheese in Fleet Street for two or three years, from 1891, to read poetry. Members and associates included *Yeats, Ernest Rhys (1859–1946, poet and editor of the *Everyman's Library), *Le Gallienne, *Dowson, L. *Johnson, Arthur *Symons, and J. *Davidson. It published two collections of verse, 1892 and 1894.

Rhyming Poem, The, an Old English poem from the *Exeter Book and therefore not later than the 10th cent., striking for the fact that the two halves of its alliterating lines rhyme (as happens sporadically in later Old English poetry). It is a loose discussion of the vicissitudes of life, contrasting the misfortunes of a fallen king with his past glory, a common Boethian, elegiac theme in Old English. The form is autobiographical but the speaker is not individuated to any extent; it has been suggested that the poem is a paraphrase of Job 29 and 30. See ASPR 4.

RHYS, Ernest, see RHYMERS CLUB and EVERYMAN'S LIBRARY.

RHYS, Jean (Ella Gwendolen Rees Williams)

?1890–1979), novelist, was born in Dominica, he daughter of a doctor of Welsh descent, and ame to England in 1907. She briefly attended he Perse School, Cambridge, and the Academy of Dramatic Art, then worked as chorus girl and ilm extra, and, during the First World War, as volunteer cook. In 1919 she left England to marry the first of three husbands, Jean Lenglet, and remained abroad for many years, living mainly in Paris, where she began to write and where much of her early work is set. *The Left Bank: Sketches and Studies of Present-Day Bohemian Paris* appeared in 1927 with an introduction by F. M. *Ford, followed by *Postures* (1928, reprinted 1969 as *Quartet*) and *After Leaving Mr Mackenzie* (1930). *Voyage in the Dark* (1934) is a first-person account of 19-year-old Anna Morgan's experiences as a chorus girl in London and on tour, and *Good Morning, Midnight* (1939) is the story, also told in the first person, of middle-aged Sasha Jensen, lonely and adrift in Paris, with a dead marriage and a dead baby behind her, seeking ambiguous consolation in a relationship with a gigolo. A long silence followed, during which Jean Rhys returned to England, living quietly in the West Country, until a radio adaptation of *Good Morning, Midnight* in 1958 brought her back to public attention. *Wide Sargasso Sea* (1966), set in Dominica and Jamaica during the 1830s, presents the life of the mad Mrs Rochester from **Jane Eyre*, a Creole heiress here called Antoinette Cosway; in the brief last section she is imprisoned in the attic in Thornfield Hall. This book was very well received and reprints of earlier novels were issued, to much praise of their 'bitter poetry', and were followed by two collections of short stories, *Tigers are Better Looking* (1968) and *Sleep It Off, Lady* (1976), and an unfinished autobiography, *Smile Please* (1979). Her *Letters 1931–66*, ed. F. Wyndham and D. Melly, was published in 1984.

Rhythm (1911–13, superseded 1913 by *The Blue Review*), a periodical edited by J. M. *Murry, with M. *Sadleir and K. *Mansfield. Murry conceived it as '*The Yellow Book* of the modern movement', and in it appeared work by D. H. *Lawrence, Mansfield, F. M. *Ford, *Picasso, *Gaudier-Brzeska, and others.

Riah, the Jew in Dickens's **Our Mutual Friend*.

RICARDO, David (1772–1823), English economist, of Dutch-Jewish family, who made a fortune on the London stock exchange, and then, under the influence of Adam *Smith, devoted himself to the study of political economy. In 1811 he met James *Mill, who became a close friend, and encouraged him in the composition and publication of his chief work, *On the Principles of Political Economy and Taxation* (1817), in which he sets forward his views on prices, wages, and profits, and his theory of rent.

Again with Mill's encouragement, he became a Member of Parliament for Pontarlington in 1819. J. S. *Mill, who was as a boy obliged by his father to learn the rudiments of political economy from Ricardo's works, described him as 'the most modest of men' (*Autobiography*, ch. 1), but his personal and social interests and sympathies appear to have been narrow, and in many ways he represents the archetypal 'Dryasdust' economist, concerned only with facts and statistics, of *Carlyle's diatribes.

RICE, Elmer (1892–1967), American dramatist, born Elmer Reizenstein in New York. His first major play was the expressionist drama *The Adding Machine* (1923), which satirized increasing regimentation and mechanization through the posthumous adventures of Mr Zero, a bookkeeper. His plays of the 1930s (*We, the People*, 1933; *Judgment Day*, 1934; *Between Two Worlds*, 1934) are a response to the Depression and international ideological conflict. Rice was a campaigner for social justice and an outspoken critic of censorship. He wrote many other plays, some of them farces and melodramas, four novels, and a memoir, *Minority Report* (1963).

RICE, James (1843–82), novelist and journalist, educated at Queens' College, Cambridge. While editing the failing periodical *Once a Week* he made the acquaintance of Walter *Besant, and proposed to him that they should collaborate in writing a novel: the result was *Ready-Money Mortiboy* (1872), the tale of a Prodigal Son who returns home 'ten times worse than when he went away' and proceeds to ruin his father. Their successful association produced several novels and volumes of short stories.

RICH, Barnaby (1542–1617), fought at Le Havre, in Ireland, and in the Netherlands, rising to the rank of captain; from 1574 he turned to literature, writing romances in the style of Lyly's **Euphues*, pamphlets, and reminiscences. From 1587 he received a pension. His best-known romance is *Farewell to Militarie Profession* (1581), which includes 'Apolonius and Silla', the source of Shakespeare's **Twelfth Night*. It was edited by T. M. Cranfill (1959).

RICH, John (?1692–1761), theatrical producer, and son of the notoriously mean manager of Drury Lane, Christopher Rich (d. 1714). John opened the New Theatre in Lincoln's Inn Fields in 1714, where he had much success with pantomime. In 1728 he produced Gay's **Beggar's Opera* which was popularly said to have 'made Rich gay and Gay rich'. He became manager of Covent Garden in 1732, and in 1735 founded the Sublime Society of *Beef Steaks, a club with many eminent members which met and dined in a room at the theatre.

RICH, Penelope (c.1562–1607), was the sister of Robert Devereux, earl of *Essex, *Elizabeth I's last favourite. Her father's dying wish, when she was only 13 or 14, that she should marry *Sidney, came to nothing; in 1581 she was unhappily married to Lord Rich, and soon after provided the model for Sidney's 'Stella'. The exact nature of their relationship can never be known, but details in some sonnets, e.g. the comment that Stella 'Hath no misfortune, but that Rich she is', make it clear that she is the lady in question. After bearing Lord Rich seven children she became the mistress of Charles Blount, Lord Mountjoy (later earl of Devonshire), bearing him five or six children: they were married, after she had been legally separated from Lord Rich, by *Laud, but the legality of the match was not accepted, and both died soon after. She was a famous beauty and a good linguist, especially in Spanish; took part in masques by *Jonson and *Daniel, and was addressed by other poets besides Sidney, e.g. *Constable. According to Fr John Gerrard, she died in the Roman Catholic faith.

RICHARD I, 'Cœur de Lion', king of England 1189–99, was one of the leaders of the Third Crusade and became a figure of romantic admiration in England (in the *Robin Hood legends, for instance, and in Scott's *The Talisman* and *Ivanhoe*), in spite of the fact that only six months of his ten-year reign were spent in England. For the Middle English verse romance see RICHARD COEUR DE LION.

Richard II, King, a historical tragedy by *Shakespeare, probably written and acted 1595. It was an immediate success and the first quarto of 1597 was followed by two more in 1598. After the death of *Elizabeth I a fourth quarto was issued in 1608, which contained the first appearance in print of the deposition scene (IV. i. 155–320), probably previously suppressed because of the politically contentious subject of the queen's succession, upon which it could be taken to reflect. The scene was included in the text of the play printed in the First *Folio of 1623. Shakespeare's main source was the *Chronicles* of *Holinshed, but he appears possibly to have known the anonymous play about Richard II called *Woodstock*, and to have drawn on S. Daniel's narrative poem *The Civil Wars*.

The play begins with the quarrel between Henry Bolingbroke, son of John of Gaunt, and Thomas Mowbray, duke of Norfolk, which King Richard resolves arbitrarily by exiling Mowbray for life and Bolingbroke for ten years. When 'time-honoured' John of Gaunt dies Richard confiscates his property to pay for his Irish wars, for which he leaves the country. Bolingbroke returns to claim his inheritance and takes Berkeley Castle, which the duke of York has as regent to yield him. The king returns to Wales, hears that his Welsh supporters have deserted him and that Bolingbroke has executed

the king's favourites Bushy and Green; accompanied by York's son Aumerle, he withdraws to Flint Castle, where Bolingbroke accepts his surrender. The first half of the play ends with a discussion between a gardener and Richard's Queen Isabel about the government of the garden-state and the possibility of the king's deposition (III. iv).

In London Richard relinquishes his crown to Bolingbroke, who sends him to the Tower. The earl of Carlisle's and Aumerle's plot to kill Bolingbroke, who has now proclaimed himself Henry IV, is foiled by York. Richard is transferred to Pomfret Castle, where he hears of Henry's coronation and is murdered by Sir Pierce of Exton.

Richard II, like 1 *Henry VI* and *King John*, is written entirely in verse and it contains some of Shakespeare's most famous speeches, including John of Gaunt's evocation of England as 'This royal throne of kings, this scept'rd isle'. Its telling 'the sad stories of the death of kings' contributed to its potent appeal. On the day before the earl of *Essex's planned revolt in 1601 his supporters paid for a performance of a play about Richard II, which was almost certainly Shakespeare's.

Richard III, King, a historical tragedy by *Shakespeare probably written and performed 1591. It was first published in a quarto in 1597, which was reprinted five times before it appeared again, in a fuller and more reliable text in the First *Folio of 1623. The play's chief sources are the chronicles of R. *Holinshed and E. *Hall which contained material from *Vergil's *Anglicae Historiae* and Sir T. More's *The History of King *Richard the Thirde*.

The play completes the tetralogy whose first three parts are the *Henry VI* plays. It centres on the character of Richard of Gloucester, afterwards King Richard III, ambitious and bloody, bold and subtle, treacherous, yet brave in battle, a murderer, and usurper of the crown. The play begins with the deformed Richard's announcement: 'Now is the winter of our discontent | Made glorious summer by this sun of York', that is the king, Edward IV, who is dying. Richard is determined that he shall succeed to the crown and sets out to eliminate any opposition to this and to secure his position. He has his brother the duke of Clarence, who has been imprisoned in the Tower, murdered. As she accompanies the corpse of her dead father-in-law Henry VI, Anne, the widow of Edward, prince of Wales, is wooed by Richard, and they are later married.

When the king dies Richard begins his attack on Queen Elizabeth's family and supporters, with the help of the duke of Buckingham. Hastings, Rivers, and Grey are all executed, and Buckingham persuades the citizens of London to proclaim Richard king. After his coronation e murders his nephews, the *princes in the 'ower, and following the death of his wife anne, which he encourages, tries to marry his iece, Elizabeth of York. However, Buckngham rebels and goes to join Henry Tudor, arl of Richmond, who has landed in Wales at Milford Haven to claim the crown. Buckngham is captured and Richard has him excuted, but he now has to face Richmond's army t Bosworth. On the night before the battle the hosts of those whom Richard has killed appear ɔ him and foretell his defeat. In the battle the ext day he loses his horse and is killed by Richnond, who is then proclaimed Henry VII, the rst of the Tudor monarchs.

Richard Coeur de Lion, a verse romance in ,136 lines of short couplets dating from the arly 14th cent., which some scholars suggest nay be by the same writer as two other long ɔmances of the same period, Of *Arthour and of Merlin and *King Alisaunder (see introduction to ne latter by G. V. Smithers for discussion of authorship). The writer says he is taking his ɔem from a French source, but it is marked by ɔirited English patriotism and contempt for the rench King Philip. It is assumed that the source Anglo-Norman, dating from about 1230– o. The poem describes the discomfiture of the aracens in the course of the Third Crusade and reaks off, unfinished, when a three-year truce arranged. There are several manuscripts and ragments. Quotations from it are found in the ɔtes to Scott's *The Talisman, referring to the ɔoking and eating of the Saracen's head, and of ne heads served to the Paynim ambassadors. 'he edition by K. Brunner (Vienna, 1913) is a ritical edition of the seven manuscripts then nown.

RICHARD DE BURY, see BURY, RICHARD ɔE.

Richard Feverel, see ORDEAL OF RICHARD EVEREL, THE.

RICHARDS, Frank, see HAMILTON, C.

RICHARDS, (Thomas Franklin) Grant 1872–1948), publisher and author, son of an Oxford don; he worked for W. T. *Stead on the *eview of Reviews before setting up as a publisher imself. His Memories of a Misspent Youth (1932) nd Author Hunting (1934) describe a life devoted to literature, and to the support of authors s diverse as A. E. *Housman, *Firbank, *Tresll, and *Dreiser; he was more adventurous and nthusiastic than financially prudent, and *Shaw wrote to him (23 May 1934), 'You should call our book The Tragedy of a Publisher who Allowed Himself to Fall in Love with Literaure.' He was the founder, in 1901, of the World's Classics series.

RICHARDS, I(vor) A(rmstrong) (1893–

1979), critic and poet, educated at Clifton and Magdalene College, Cambridge, where he became a fellow; in 1929 he travelled to China, then in 1931 moved to Harvard, where he devoted many years to the study of linguistics and education. He was the founder, with Charles Kay Ogden (1889–1957), of Basic English, 'an auxiliary international language comprising 850 words arranged in a system in which everything may be said for all the purposes of everyday language'; Richards and Ogden published two works together, The Foundations of Aesthetics (1922, with J. Wood) and The Meaning of Meaning (1923). In a literary context Richards is best known for his Principles of Literary Criticism (1924), Science and Poetry (1926), and above all Practical Criticism: a study of literary judgement (1929), a work which revolutionized the teaching and study of English. It was based on an experiment conducted by Richards in Cambridge in which he issued unsigned poems to students and asked for their written comments; the results were both entertaining and alarming, revealing that a majority of readers condemned poems by *Donne, D. H. *Lawrence, and G. M. *Hopkins, while praising highly the work of G. A. Studdert Kennedy ('Woodbine Willie') and J. D. C. Pellew. In his commentary, Richards analyses the stock responses, preconceptions, metrical insensitivities, lack of attentive reading, etc., of his guinea-pigs, and, while he refrains from concluding that 'a man who is stupid with poetry *must* be stupid with life', he does assert that 'a general insensitivity to poetry does witness a low level of general imaginative life.' Richards's attacks on vagueness, sentimentality, and laziness in poets and readers, his praise of irony ('a characteristic of poetry of the highest order'), ambiguity, complexity, and allusiveness, did much to create the climate which accepted *Modernism, and greatly influenced *Empson (his student from 1928 to 1929) and *Leavis; but perhaps his greatest contribution lay in his emphasis on the importance of close textual study and the danger of random generalization. His methods have now become standard classroom procedure in many schools and universities (see NEW CRITICISM and PRACTICAL CRITICISM). Richards's views on scientific and emotive language, and on the nature of the status of statements (or pseudo-statements) in poetry have been less widely accepted. Richards also published several volumes of poetry; a collection, Internal Colloquies: Poems and Plays, appeared in 1972.

RICHARDSON, Dorothy Miller (1873– 1957), novelist, was the third of four daughters of an impoverished gentleman, obliged to earn her living from an early age, first as governess, then as secretary, translator, and journalist. She became an intimate friend of H. G. *Wells and other avant-garde thinkers of the day who encouraged her to write. In 1915 appeared *Pointed Roofs*, the first of a sequence of highly autobiographical novels entitled *Pilgrimage*, of which the last volume, *March Moonlight*, first appeared posthumously in 1967. She was a pioneer of the *stream-of-consciousness technique, narrating the action through the mind of her heroine Miriam. She believed in 'unpunctuated' female prose (citing *Joyce in support), and V. *Woolf credited her with inventing 'the psychological sentence of the feminine gender'.

The formidable length of her great work deterred many readers, but interest revived in the 1960s and 1970s with the growth of *feminist criticism: Angus *Wilson ('Sexual Revolution', *The Listener*, Oct. 1968) acclaimed her as a defiant writer who 'enters more fully than any novelist I know into the material and spiritual struggles of a young, very gifted, but at the same time utterly underprivileged woman in a world made by men for men'. *Pilgrimage* was reissued in 1979 in four volumes by the Virago Press, and a critical biography by John Rosenberg appeared in 1973.

RICHARDSON, Henry Handel, the pen-name of Ethel Florence Lindesay Richardson (1870–1946), novelist, born in Melbourne, Australia; her father, an Edinburgh-educated Irish doctor, and her English mother married after emigrating during the gold rushes. Her mother worked as postmistress after her father's death in 1879. Ethel was educated at the Presbyterian Ladies College in Melbourne, then, from 1888, in Leipzig, where she studied music. In 1895 she married John George Robertson, a philologist, and from 1904 (with one brief return visit to Australia in 1912) she lived in England. Her first novel, *Maurice Guest* (1908), is a tale of *grande passion* set in Leipzig, with an English provincial schoolmaster, studying music, as protagonist. Her second, and most economical, *The Getting of Wisdom* (1910), describes her Australian schooldays in the person of Laura Rambotham, an intelligent child caught between rebellion and the desire to please, between ambition and reality, who makes the discovery that the art of fiction is the art of lying plausibly. Her most ambitious work, the trilogy *The Fortunes of Richard Mahony*, consists of *Australia Felix* (1917), *The Way Home* (1925), and *Ultima Thule* (1929), of which the last was the most successful. Clearly rooted in the biography of her own parents, it traces the fluctuating progress of Mahony, from storekeeper in a rough mining settlement, through a prosperous medical career and even more prosperous financial speculation, to bankruptcy, madness, and death; throughout he is loyally supported by his wife Mary, who is finally obliged to work as a postmistress to support her small children. In its epic sweep it is at once the history of a man, a marriage, and a continent, capturing with imaginative recollection the landscapes, developing social attitudes, and growing prosperity and respectability of Australia. Her last novel, *The Young Cosima* (1939), returns to a musical theme, and is based on a life of Cosima Wagner; her autobiography, *Myself when young* (1948), was unfinished at her death.

RICHARDSON, Jonathan, the elder (1665–1745), British portrait painter, who was highly successful in his own day. Yet his stiff, dull portraits are less interesting than his writings on art, and on the newly fashionable science of connoisseurship. His *Theory of Painting* (1715) was the first significant work on aesthetic theory by an English author; in the second edition, 1725, he added an influential essay on the *Sublime. He was himself a brilliant connoisseur with a superlative collection of drawings; he had a wide circle of literary friends, amongst them *Pope, *Gay, and *Prior, and himself wrote a book on *Milton. He drew and painted Pope and his family many times. His son did the research for a guidebook to Italy which was a popular companion on the *Grand Tour.

RICHARDSON, Samuel (1689–1761), the son of a joiner, was born near Derby, where his parents lived briefly before returning to London. Little is known of his boyhood, but because of his father's comparative poverty he appears to have received (in his own words) 'only common School-learning'. The tradition that he attended either Merchant Taylors' or Christ's Hospital cannot be substantiated. As a boy he read widely, told stories to his friends, and by the age of 13 was employed writing letters for young lovers. In 1706 he was apprenticed to a printer (as his father could not afford to enter him for the church), and in 1715 he was admitted a freeman of the *Stationers' Company. He set up in business on his own in 1721, in which year he married Martha Wilde, the daughter of his former master. All his working life he was extremely industrious, and his business prospered and expanded steadily. Like all printers of his time, he combined printing and publishing, producing books, journals, advertisement posters, and much miscellaneous work. In 1723 he took over the printing of an influential Tory journal, the *True Briton*, and by 1727 was sufficiently established in his profession to be appointed Renter Warden of the Stationers' Company. In the 1720s and early 1730s he suffered the early deaths of all his six children, and in 1731 that of his wife. He attributed the nervous disorders of his later life to the shock of these deaths. In 1733 he married Elizabeth Leake, the daughter of a fellow printer, and four of the daughters of their marriage survived. In the same year he published his *The Apprentice's Vade Mecum*, a book of advice on morals and conduct. In 1738 he purchased in Fulham a weekend 'country house, which he always referred to as 'North End', and which later became famous for his readings and literary parties. He published in 1739 his own version, pointedly moral, of *Aesop's Fables*, and, more importantly, he began *Pamela*.

The novel started as a series of 'familiar letters' which fellow printers had encouraged him to write on the problems and concerns of everyday life. While these eventually grew into *Pamela*, they were also published separately as *Letters . . . to and for Particular Friends* (1741). *Pamela* was written in two months, between November 1739 and January 1740, and was published later in that year, to very considerable acclaim. The morality and realism of the work were particularly praised, as Richardson had hoped. However, complaints of its impropriety persuaded him to revise his second edition considerably. The work had a great vogue abroad, and was soon adapted for the stage in France. Imitations and forged 'continuations' persuaded Richardson to go on with the story, and volumes 3 and 4 (*Pamela II*) were published in 1741. that year there appeared a stinging parody called *An Apology for the Life of Mrs *Shamela Andrews*, which Richardson believed to be by *Fielding (as it almost certainly was) and which he never forgave. Fielding's *Joseph Andrews*, which begins as a parody of *Pamela*, was published in 1742 but did not affect the popularity of *Pamela II*.

Richardson's business continued to prosper, although his health was beginning to cause him great concern, and he extended his publications in religion, history, biography, and literature. In 1733 he had begun printing for the House of Commons and in 1742 he secured the lucrative post of printer of its Journals. His circle of friends had by now vastly increased, and included many admiring young ladies, known as his 'songbirds' or 'honorary daughters'.

During the writing of *Clarissa*, which was probably begun in 1744, he endlessly asked his friends for comments and advice, and read passages aloud to them in his 'grotto' (or summer house) at North End. The first two volumes of *Clarissa* appeared in 1747 and were very favourably received. After heavy revision, and determined efforts to prune, a further five volumes appeared in 1748. Correspondents and the circle of friends continued to grow and now included the *Bluestocking ladies Mrs *Delany, Mrs *Carter, and later Mrs *Chapone. *Clarissa* was an undoubted success but there were complaints about both its length and its indecency, and it was not reprinted as often as *Pamela*. However, it also became very popular abroad and was translated into French, Dutch, and German.

Urged by friends, Richardson began thinking, in about 1750, of the portrayal of a 'Good Man'. He asked for the views of his extensive acquaintance and began experimenting with the 'letters' of Harriet, who was to become one of the heroines of his next novel. His illnesses and general malaise, which appear to have included a form of Parkinson's disease, increased steadily but he persevered strenuously both with his business and his writing. His authors in the 1750s included C. *Lennox, S. *Fielding, E. *Young, and G. *Lyttleton. He had by now become friendly with Dr *Johnson, to whose *Rambler* he contributed in 1750 and whom he helped with money in 1751. In 1752 Johnson (together with many of Richardson's other friends) read the draft of *Sir Charles Grandison*, and Richardson printed the fourth volume of the *Rambler*. In 1753 he travelled to Bath and Cheltenham, which was as far as he had ever gone, and in 1753–4 he published the seven volumes of *Sir Charles Grandison*. The book sold well and rapidly became fashionable, but was assailed in various critical pamphlets for length, tedium, and doubtful morality.

In 1754–5 Richardson was master of the Stationers' Company. He published in 1755 *A Collection of the Moral and Instructive Sentiments . . . in the Histories of Pamela, Clarissa, and Sir Charles Grandison*, a book which he considered contained the pith of all his work. In the same year Dr Johnson published the *Dictionary*, which contained 97 citations from *Clarissa*, almost double the number from any other single work. In 1756 Richardson was asked by *Blackstone for advice on the reform of the *Oxford University Press. Towards the end of his life Richardson wrote a few 'letters' to, from, and about Mrs Beaumont, a minor character from *Sir Charles Grandison*, who had been someone of mysterious importance in his early life. He continued to revise his novels heavily, and remained active in his business until his death.

Richardson is generally agreed to be one of the chief founders of the modern novel. All his novels were *epistolary, a form he took from earlier works in English and French, which he appreciated for its immediacy ('writing to the moment' as he called it), and which he raised to a level not attained by any of his predecessors. The 'letters', of which his novels consist, contain many long transcriptions of conversations, and the kinship with drama seems very strong. He was acutely aware of the problems of prolixity ('Length, is my principle Disgust') and worked hard to prune his original drafts, but his interest in minute analysis led inevitably to an expansive style.

A selection of his letters (6 vols, 1804) was edited by Mrs *Barbauld: see also *Selected Letters of Samuel Richardson* (1964), ed. J. Carroll. There is a life by T. C. D. Eaves and B. D. Kimpel (1971); see also M. Kinkead-Weekes, *Samuel Richardson, Dramatic Novelist* (1971); M. A. Doody, *A Natural Passion* (1974).

Richard the Redeless (now known to be part

of *Mum and the Sothsegger*), a fragmentary alliterative poem dealing with the incompetences of Richard II, with similarities to *Langland that led *Skeat to attribute it to him provisionally and to include it in his edition of *Piers Plowman*.

Richard the Thirde, The History of King, by Sir T. *More, written in English and Latin and included in his Workes (1557) and the Latina Opera (1565). It is distinguished from earlier English chronicles by its unity of scheme and dramatic effectiveness. Shakespeare probably used More's work only as filtered through *Hall and *Holinshed; it was More, however, who was ultimately responsible for the image of Richard as a *Machiavellian tyrant which Shakespeare transmits in *Richard III*. (See also BIOGRAPHY.)

RICHELIEU, Armand Jean du Plessis, Cardinal and duc de (1585–1642), one of the greatest of French statesmen, first came into prominence as bishop of Luçon, and became prime minister of Louis XIII in 1624. He disciplined the nobles by a series of executions, destroyed the political importance of the Protestants by the siege and capture of La Rochelle (1628), and intervened successfully in the Thirty Years War. He was the founder of the *Académie française, and built the Palais-Royal in Paris (originally called Palais-Cardinal). He figures in *The Three Musketeers* of Dumas, and is the anti-hero of a blank verse drama by *Bulwer-Lytton.

Richland, Miss, the heroine of Goldsmith's *The Good-Natur'd Man*.

RICHMOND, Sir Bruce (1871–1964), educated at Winchester and New College, Oxford, joined The Times in 1899, and for 35 years was editor of the *Times Literary Supplement* from its first production in 1902.

RICHMOND, Legh (1772–1827), an evangelical divine who lived in the Isle of Wight, where he collected the material for his immensely successful pious tales of country life, published between 1809 and 1814, *The Dairyman's Daughter*, The Young Cottager, and The Negro Slave. He gave money for the establishment of a library, which still exists, on the island of Iona.

RICHTER, Johann Paul Friedrich (1763–1825), German Romantic novelist, who wrote under the name 'Jean Paul'. Reared in humble village surroundings, he was at his best in idyllic representations of the life he knew. His combination of humour with mystic idealism appealed to *Carlyle and *De Quincey, both of whom translated stories by Jean Paul and wrote appreciations of his works. His best-known works are: Hesperus (1795), Quintus Fixlein (1796), Siebenkäs (1796), and Vorschule der Ästhetik (Introduction to Aesthetics, 1804).

RICKETTS, Charles (1866–1931), English aesthete, illustrator, designer, and painter. His brilliant conversation and rarefied tastes attracted many writers to his house in the Vale, Chelsea, and later to Townshend House; among his friends were *Wilde, J. H. *Gray, *Yeats, G. B. *Shaw, 'Michael *Field' (Edith Cooper and Katherine Bradley), and *Binyon. Ricketts illustrated and designed many of Wilde's books; most beautiful are A House of Pomegranates (1891) and The Sphinx (1894). After Wilde's death he wrote a memoir to him, Recollections of Oscar Wilde (1932). With Charles Shannon, Ricketts edited *The Dial (1889–97), a lavishly illustrated literary magazine deeply influenced by the then little known works of French and Belgian Symbolists. His Vale Press, founded in 1896, was one of the most important of the *private presses; it printed great works of literature with woodcut borders. Later Ricketts worked as a stage designer; Shaw's Saint Joan (1924) was his most successful production. Ricketts was a distinguished collector, connoisseur, and writer on art, and in his last years designed and illustrated two of his own prose works, Beyond the Threshold (1929) and Unrecorded Histories (1933).

RICKWORD, Edgell (1898–1982), poet, critic, and radical, edited from 1925 to 1927 *The Calendar of Modern Letters, an influential literary periodical which helped to form the critical attitudes of *Leavis. He also edited two volumes of *Scrutiny (1928–32), the Left Review (1936–8), and Our Time (1944–7), and edited the essays of *Caudwell (1949). Essays and Opinions (1921–51), edited by A. Young, appeared in 1974.

Ridd, John, see LORNA DOONE.

Riddle of the Sands, The, see CHILDERS, E.

Riderhood, Rogue, a character in Dickens's *Our Mutual Friend*.

RIDING, Laura (1901–), American poet and critic, who lived and worked with Robert *Graves from 1927 until 1939. She was well represented in the *Faber Book of Modern Verse (1936) and her elliptical verses were brought together in Collected Poems (1938). Critical works include (with Graves) A Survey of Modernist Poetry (1927) and Contemporaries and Snobs (1928). A novel, A Trojan Ending, appeared in 1937, and Lives of Wives, on various marriages in history, in 1939.

RIDLEY, James (1736–65), a cleric, is remembered for his Tales of the Genii, published in 1764. As often with *Oriental novels, the author purports to be merely the discoverer and translator, in this case 'Sir Charles Morell', ambassador to the Great Mogul. Many of these curious and exotic tales are modelled on those of the *Arabian Nights. The book enjoyed a great and abiding success; it was later bowdlerized, and read by several generations of children, including the young *Dickens, who founded his youthful tragedy *Misnar* on one of the tales.

RIDLEY, Nicholas (?1500–55), successively bishop of Rochester and London, was a fellow of Pembroke Hall, Cambridge. He became one of *Cranmer's chaplains and began gradually to reject many Roman doctrines. If any hand beside that of Cranmer can be detected in the two Prayer Books of Edward VI, it is believed to be Ridley's. As bishop of London he exerted himself to propagate reformed opinions. On Edward VI's death he denounced Queen Mary and Elizabeth as illegitimate at St Paul's Cross, London. He was sent to the Tower in June 1553 and deprived of his bishopric. In September 1555 he was condemned on the charge of heresy and burnt alive with *Latimer at Oxford, 16 Oct. He wrote several theological treatises, which appeared after his death. In 1841 the *Works of Nicholas Ridley* were edited for the Parker Society by Henry Christmas.

Rience, see RYENCE.

Rienzi, a novel by *Bulwer-Lytton.

RIEU, E(mile) V(ictor), see PENGUIN BOOKS.

Rigaud, a character in Dickens's *Little Dorrit.*

Rigby, in *Coningsby* by B. Disraeli.

Rigdum-Funnidos, see CHRONONHOTONTHO-LOGOS.

Rights of Man, The, a political treatise by T. *Paine in two parts, published 1791 and 1792.

Pt I is in the main a reply to Burke's *Reflections on the *Revolution in France*. Paine accuses *Burke of 'rancour, prejudice and ignorance', of seeking theatrical effects at the expense of truth, and of disorderly arguments: 'Mr Burke should recollect that he is writing history, and not *plays*.' He denies that one generation can bind another as regards the form of government, and argues that the constitution of a country is an act of the people constituting the government. He traces the incidents of the French revolution up to the adoption of the Declaration of the Rights of Man by the National Assembly, and criticizes Burke's account of these incidents as over-emotional and inaccurate; he alleges that Burke cares only for the forms of chivalry, and not for the nation. 'He pities the plumage, and forgets the dying bird.'

Pt II touches on Burke's *Appeal from the New to the Old Whigs*, then passes to a comparison of the new French and American constitutions with those of British institutions, to the disadvantage of the latter. The work also contains Paine's far-sighted proposals for reform of taxation, family allowances, maternity grants, etc.

Rights of Woman, Vindication of the, see WOLL-STONECRAFT, M.

RILKE, Rainer Maria (1875–1926), German lyric poet. His early collections were not particularly interesting or distinguished. Of decisive importance were his two visits to Russia which, deepening his religious experience, led to *Das Stundenbuch* (*The Book of Hours*, 1905), in which death is the central theme, handled in a highly individual way. The subjective emotionalism of the early work began to give way to poetry of a more objective type, the transition to which is seen in *Das Buch der Bilder* (*The Book of Pictures*, 1902) and which finds its mature expression in the *Neue Gedichte* (*New Poems*, 1907–8). The latter was greatly influenced by the French sculptor Rodin, whose secretary Rilke was for a time. In 1910 appeared a full-scale prose work, *Die Aufzeichnungen des Malte Laurids Brigge* (*Sketches of Malte Laurids Brigge*), in which Rilke explored the relationship between a sensitive poet and a threatening environment. The *Duineser Elegien* (*Duino Elegies*), begun shortly before the First World War and completed not long afterwards, arose from Rilke's endeavour to discover for himself as a poet a satisfactory spiritual position amid the decay of reality; and the *Die Sonette an Orpheus* (*Sonnets to Orpheus*, 1923), written in a sudden frenzy of inspiration, are the jubilant outcome of that endeavour. His extensive correspondence is of great literary interest. He is the most important lyric poet of 20th-cent. Germany, and his poetry has been translated into many languages—various collections have appeared in English translated by J. B. Leishmann, sometimes in collaboration with *Spender.

RIMBAUD, Arthur (1854–91), French poet. One of the most revolutionary figures in 19th-cent. literature, he was by the age of 16 in full revolt against every form of authority. Expressing the exhilaration of his regular escapes from maternal discipline and his fascination with cabbalistic and alchemical imagery, his verse was already fiercely independent of religious, political, and literary orthodoxy. By the age of 17 he had written his most famous poem, 'Le Bateau ivre', a hymn to the quest of unknown realities, which became a sacred text for the next two generations of writers. By the time he was 19 his poetic career was over. Between 1871 and 1873—the period of his association with *Verlaine and his sojourns in England—he undertook a programme of 'disorientation of the senses' in order to try to turn himself into a voyant or seer. This resulted in his most original work, two collections of prose poems, *Les Illuminations*, which explored the visionary possibilities of this experiment, and *Une Saison en enfer*, recording its moral and psychological failure. The remainder of his life has been described as a prolonged act of passive resistance. Having repudiated poetry, he gave himself up to vagabondage, first in Europe, and later in the northeastern regions of Africa.

'Rime of the Ancient Mariner, The', see ANCIENT MARINER, THE RIME OF THE.

Rime royal, or Rhyme-royal, see METRE.

Rimini, The Story of, see STORY OF RIMINI, THE.

Rinaldo, or **Renaud**, first figures under the latter name in the *Charlemagne cycle of legends as the eldest of the Four Sons of *Aymon, who were first the enemies of Charlemagne but later pardoned on condition that Renaud goes to Palestine to fight the Saracens and surrenders his horse Bayard. Renaud complies and becomes a hermit in Palestine; but Bayard will allow no one else to mount him. As Rinaldo, he figures in Boiardo's *Orlando Innamorato, Ariosto's *Orlando Furioso, and Tasso's *Gerusalemme Liberata: in the first two as the cousin of Orlando and the suitor of Angelica; in the third as a prince of Este, the lover of Armida and the victor in the battle for Jerusalem.

Ring and the Book, The, a poem in blank verse, in twelve books, totalling over 21,000 lines, by R. *Browning, published in four monthly instalments Nov. 1868–Feb. 1869. The poem was a critical and popular success, and established Browning's contemporary reputation.

The 'Ring' of the title is a figure for the process by which the artist transmutes the 'pure crude fact' of historical events into living forms; the 'Book' is a collection of documents relating to the Italian murder trial of the late 17th cent. on which the poem is based. Browning found the volume on a market stall in Florence, and offered it to several of his acquaintances (including *Tennyson and *Trollope) before finally deciding to use it himself.

The story in bare outline is as follows. Pietre and Violante Comparini were a middle-aged childless couple living in Rome. Their income could only be secured after Pietre's death if they had a child; so Violante bought the child of a prostitute and passed it off as her own. This child, Pompilia, was eventually married to Count Guido Franceschini, an impoverished nobleman from Arezzo. The marriage was unhappy, and the Comparini, disappointed by life in Arezzo, returned to Rome, where they sued Guido for the restoration of Pompilia's dowry on the grounds of her illegitimacy, which Violante now revealed. Pompilia herself eventually fled from Arezzo in the company of a young priest, Giuseppe Caponsacchi. Guido pursued them and had them arrested on the outskirts of Rome; as a result, Caponsacchi was exiled to Civita Vecchia for three years, and Pompilia

was sent to a convent while the lawsuits were decided. But then, because she was pregnant, she was released into the custody of the Comparini. A fortnight after the birth of her child, Guido and four accomplices murdered her and her putative parents. They were arrested and tried for the murder, Guido claiming justification on the grounds of his wife's adultery with Caponsacchi; nevertheless he and his accomplices were convicted and sentenced to death. Guido then pleaded exemption for himself, but his appeal was rejected and the five were executed.

In Browning's poem, the story is told by a succession of speakers—citizens of Rome, the participants themselves, the lawyers, and the pope—each of whose single, insufficient perceptions combines with the others to form the 'ring' of the truth. This design represents Browning's response to a number of pressing concerns in his own creative life and in contemporary philosophies of art and religion. He saw 'truth' as both absolute (in its divine essence) and relative (in its human manifestation); the artist partakes of either quality, all means of expression (such as language) being an inadequate 'witness' to the true life of the imagination, just as historical witnesses give a partial and inadequate account of 'real' events.

In its immense but ordered size and scope; in the vitality of its characters and the rich evocation of time and place; and in its magnificently troubled exposition of the relation between sign and significance, the poem stands at the centre of Browning's achievement.

Ring des Nibelungen, Der, a series of four music dramas by *Wagner, based on the *Nibelungenlied, composed 1853–70, produced 1869–76.

Das Rheingold tells the story of the stealing of the gold of the Rhine maidens by Alberich, king of the Nibelungs, and the forging and theft (by Wotan) of the magic ring. *Die Walküre (The Valkyries)* deals with the love of Sieglinde and Siegmund, and of the laying to sleep of Brynhilde the Valkyrie by Wotan, who surrounds her with a ring of fire. In *Siegfried* the son of Siegmund and Sieglinde obtains the magic ring and passes through the flames to awaken Brynhilde. In *Gotterdämmerung (The Twilight of the Gods)* Siegfried betrays Brynhilde for Gutrune, under the influence of a magic potion, and is slain: Brynhilde places the ring on her finger and throws herself on Siegfried's pyre, whereupon the ring is recovered by the Rhine maidens.

Rintherout, Jenny, in Scott's *The Antiquary,* servant to Jonathan Oldbuck.

'Rip Van Winkle', a story by W. *Irving attributed to 'Diedrich *Knickerbocker' and included in *The Sketch Book* (1820).

Rip Van Winkle, taking refuge from a termagant wife in a solitary ramble in the Catskill mountains, falls asleep, and awakens after twenty years, to find his wife dead, his house in ruins, and the world completely changed.

Rise of Silas Lapham, The, the best-known of W. D. *Howells's novels, published 1885.

Lapham, who has risen from a Vermont farm to fortune, is typical of the self-made New Englander. The story is mainly concerned with his and his family's adaptation to the Boston society in which they find themselves.

Risingham, Bertram, a character in Scott's *Rokeby.

Risorgimento, 'resurrection', a name given to the movement for the union and liberation of Italy which took place in the middle of the 19th cent. The principal names associated with it are those of Mazzini, Cavour, Victor Emmanuel (king of Sardinia), and Garibaldi. In 1847 Cavour founded a newspaper called *Risorgimento.* An insurrection in Lombardy and Venice, in 1848, supported by the king of Sardinia (Charles Albert, Victor Emmanuel's father), was suppressed by Austria in 1849, the king being defeated at Novara and abdicating in favour of his son. The movement gathered force in 1859, in which year Napoleon III in alliance with the Italians defeated the Austrians at Magenta. Victor Emmanuel was declared king of Italy in 1860, and the kingdom of Italy, with Florence as its first capital, was recognized by foreign States in 1861. Venetia was ceded to Victor Emmanuel in 1866, and the union of Italy was completed when Italian troops entered Rome in 1870 and the temporal power of the papacy came to an end.

RITCHIE, Anne Isabella Thackeray, Lady (1837–1919), elder daughter of *Thackeray. She wrote novels of an impressionistic kind which influenced her step-niece V. *Woolf, who drew a portrait of her in *Night and Day as 'Mrs Hilbery'. *Old Kensington* (1873) and *Mrs Dymond* (1885) are probably the best remembered of her novels today. She also wrote reminiscences of the literary figures she had known in her youth: *Records of Tennyson, Ruskin and Robert and Elizabeth Browning* (1892) and *Chapters from some Memoirs* (1894), among others. A biography of her by Winifred Gérin was published in 1981.

Ritho, see RYENCE.

RITSON, Joseph (1752–1803), literary antiquarian, vegetarian, republican, and eccentric, and a friend of Sir W. *Scott, who consulted him while working on his *Border Minstrelsy.* Ritson was a man of an irritable and bitter nature, exacerbated by ill health, which expressed itself in his attacks (often justified) on the works of fellow scholars: he challenged

T. *Warton's *History of English Poetry* (1782) and also Dr *Johnson's and *Steevens's edition of Shakespeare. In 1783 he published *A Select Collection of English Songs* containing strictures on Percy's *Reliques, accusing *Percy of corrupting texts 'to give the quotations an air of antiquity, which it was not intitl'd to', and of other 'monstrous lies' and misrepresentations. In 1795 he published *Robin Hood: a collection of all the ancient poems, songs and ballads now extant relative to that outlaw*, with illustrations by *Bewick: Scott attributed a 'superstitious scrupulosity' to this work, which he thought excessively comprehensive. His *Ancient English Metrical Romances* appeared in 1802. Ritson also published several popular collections and anthologies of songs, children's verses, fairy-stories, etc. He became increasingly odd in later life, more and more fanatically vegetarian (his diet was originally inspired by reading *Mandeville), and finally insane. (See also PRIMITIVISM and BALLAD.)

Rival Queens, The: or the Death of Alexander the Great, a tragedy by N. *Lee, founded on the *Cassandre* of *La Calprenède, produced 1677. C. *Cibber attributed its success to the performance of *Betterton, but it held the stage for 100 years.

Statira, daughter of Darius and wife of Alexander, learning that Alexander has again fallen a victim to the charms of his first wife Roxana, whom he had promised to discard, vows never to see him again. Alexander, returning from his campaign and passionately loving Statira, is deeply distressed. Roxana goads Statira to fury, Statira revokes her vow, and Alexander banishes Roxana, who later stabs her rival to death. Alexander is poisoned by the conspirator Cassander.

Rivals, The, a comedy by R. B. *Sheridan, produced 1775.

This was Sheridan's first play, written rapidly when he was only 23, yet it is generally agreed to be one of the most engaging and accomplished of English comedies. It is set in Bath, where Sheridan lived from 1770 to 1772. Captain Absolute, son of Sir Anthony Absolute, a warm-hearted but demanding old gentleman who requires absolute obedience from his son, is in love with Lydia Languish, the niece of Mrs Malaprop. As he knows the romantic Lydia prefers a poor half-pay lieutenant to the heir of a baronet with £3,000 a year, he has assumed for the purposes of courtship the character of Ensign Beverley, and in this guise he is favourably received. But Lydia will lose half her fortune if she marries without her aunt's consent, and Mrs Malaprop will not approve of an indigent ensign. Sir Anthony arrives in Bath to propose a match between his son and Lydia Languish, a proposal welcomed by Mrs Malaprop. Captain Absolute is now afraid of revealing his deception to Lydia in case he loses her; while Bob Acres, who is also Lydia's suitor and has heard of Beverley's courtship, is provoked by the fiery Irishman Sir Lucius O'Trigger to ask Captain Absolute to carry a challenge to Beverley. Sir Lucius himself, who has been deluded into thinking that some love-letters received by him from Mrs Malaprop are really from Lydia, likewise finds Captain Absolute in his path, and challenges him. But when Acres finds that Beverley is in fact his friend Absolute, he declines his duel with relief and resigns all claim to Lydia. Sir Lucius's misapprehension is removed by the arrival of Mrs Malaprop, and Lydia, after a pretty quarrel with her lover for shattering her hopes of a romantic elopement, finally forgives him. Another plot, neatly interwoven with the rest, concerns the love-affair of the perverse and jealous Faulkland with Lydia's friend Julia Melville.

'Rizpah', a poem by *Tennyson, published in *Ballads and other poems* (1880), the monologue of a mother who collects the unhallowed bones of her son night by night from the foot of the gallows and buries them secretly in the churchyard. Her claim that the bones are hers because 'they had moved in my side' gave to *Swinburne 'perfect proof once more of the deep truth that great poets are bisexual'.

Road to Oxiana, The, see BYRON, R.

Road to Ruin, The, see HOLCROFT, T.

Road to Wigan Pier, The, see ORWELL, G., and LEFT BOOK CLUB.

Road to Xanadu, The, see LOWES, J. L.

Roaring Girle, The, or *Moll Cut-Purse,* a comedy by T. *Middleton and *Dekker, written ?1604–8, published 1611.
In this play Moll Cutpurse, a notorious thief in real life, takes on for once the character of an honest girl, who helps lovers in distress and defends her virtue with her sword. Sebastian Wentgrave is in love with and betrothed to Mary Fitz-allard, but his covetous father forbids the match. Sebastian pretends he has fallen desperately in love with Moll Cutpurse and is about to marry her; and Moll good-naturedly lends herself to the deception. Old Wentgrave, distracted at the prospect, is only too glad to give his blessing when the real bride turns out to be Mary Fitz-allard. There are some pleasant bustling scenes in which the life of the London streets is vividly presented, shop-keepers selling tobacco and feathers, their wives intriguing with gallants, and Moll talking thieves' cant and discomfiting overbold admirers. The play was highly praised by T. S. *Eliot.

Robene and Makyne, a pastoral by *Henryson, on the model of the French *pastourelle* rather than the classical *eclogue, included in Percy's *Reliques*. Robene is a shepherd, and Makyne (a form of Malkin, a diminutive of Matilda which seems to have been a stereotypical name for an unattractive woman: see *Piers Plowman* B, I. 184) loves him. He rejects her advances and she goes away. Robene changes his mind and appeals to her, whereupon she delivers the Henrysonian moral:

> Robene, thow hes hard soung and say
> In gestis and storeis auld:
> The man that will nocht quhen he may
> Sall haif nocht quhen he wald   (ll. 89–92).

Robert Elsmere, see WARD, M. A.

ROBERT, earl of Gloucester (d. 1147), a natural son of Henry I, and the chief supporter of Matilda against Stephen. He was a patron of literature, in particular of *William of Malmesbury, *Henry of Huntingdon, and *Geoffrey of Monmouth. Geoffrey's *History* is dedicated to him.

ROBERT OF GLOUCESTER (*fl.* 1260–1300), the reputed author of a metrical Chronicle of England from Brutus to Henry III, for much of which he drew upon *Laȝamon. It is written in long lines, running to fourteen syllables and more, and is not the work of a single hand, though probably the whole was composed in the abbey of Gloucester. It contains among passages of special interest a famous description of the death of Simon de Montfort at the battle of Evesham and a section in praise of England beginning: 'Engelond his a wel god lond.' Ed. W. A. Wright, Rolls Series 86, 1887.

ROBERTS, Michael William Edward (1902–48), poet, critic, editor, and teacher of mathematics, whose anthologies *New Signatures* (1932) and *New Country* (1933), containing work by *Auden, *Day-Lewis, *Empson, *Spender, and others established him, in T. S. *Eliot's phrase, as 'expositor and interpreter of the poetry of his generation'. *The Recovery of the West* (1941) is a study of the ills of Western civilization and *The Estate of Man* (1951), written in 1947–8, shows him as a pioneer ecologist, issuing a then unfashionable warning about the devastation of the earth's resources. He also edited the influential *Faber Book of Modern Verse* (1936). See *Michael Roberts: Selected Poems and Prose,* ed. F. Grubb (1980).

ROBERTSON, T(homas) W(illiam) (1829–71), began life as an actor, but retired from the stage and became a dramatist. His plays *Society* (1865), *Ours* (1866), *Caste* (1867), *Play* (1868), *School* (1869), and *M.P.* (1870), introduced a new and more natural type of comedy to the English stage than had been seen during the first half of the century. His earlier drama *David Garrick* (1864) was also well received. Marie Wilton (Lady Bancroft) was the great exponent of Robertson's best female characters.

ROBERTSON, William (1721–93), was educated at Edinburgh University, of which, after some time as a Presbyterian parish minister, he became principal in 1762. He achieved fame on the publication of his *History of Scotland during the Reign of Queen Mary and of King James VI* (1759), which was followed by his history of the reign of Charles V (1769), *The History of America* (1777), and a *Disquisition concerning the knowledge which the Ancients had of India* (1791). Both in style and in scholarship his work is comparable with that of *Hume. (Dr. *Johnson found it had too much 'painting' and verbiage.) Robertson was a member of the *Select Society, and an account of his life and writings was published in 1801 by D. *Stewart.

Robert the Devil, 6th duke of Normandy and father of William the Conqueror, a personage about whom many legends gathered in consequence of his violence and cruelty. In *The Life of Robert the Devil*, Robert is represented as having been devoted soul and body to Satan by his mother, who had long been childless and prayed to the Devil to give her a son; but as finally repenting of his misdeeds and marrying the emperor's daughter (he in fact died on a pilgrimage to Palestine). This verse-tale is a translation from the French and was printed in 1496 by *Wynkyn de Worde. T. *Lodge wrote a drama on the same subject.

'Robin Gray, Auld', see LINDSAY, LADY A.

Robin Hood, a legendary outlaw. The name is part of the designation of places and plants in every part of England. The facts behind the legend are uncertain. In the portion of the Pipe *Roll of 1230 relating to Yorkshire there is mention of a 'Robertus Hood fugitivus'. Robin Hood is referred to in *Piers Plowman. As a historical character he appears in *Wyntoun's The Orygynale Cronykil (c.1420), and is referred to as a ballad hero by Abbot Bower (d. 1449), *Major, and *Stow. The first detailed history, *Lytell Geste of Robyn Hode* (printed c.1495), locates him in south-west Yorkshire; later writers place him in Sherwood and Plumpton Park (Cumberland), and finally make him earl of Huntingdon. *Ritson, who collected all the ancient songs and ballads about Robin Hood, says definitely that he was born at Locksley in Nottinghamshire about 1160, that his true name was Robert Fitz-Ooth, and that he was commonly reputed to have been earl of Huntingdon. There is a pleasant account of the activities of his band in Drayton's *Poly-Olbion, song 26. According to Stow, there were about the year 1190 many robbers and outlaws, among whom were Robin Hood and Little John, who lived in the woods, robbing the rich,

but killing only in self-defence, allowing no woman to be molested, and sparing poor men's goods. A date for his death (18 Nov. 1247) was given by Martin Parker (*True Tale*, c.1632) and by the antiquarian Ralph Thoresby (1658–1725), and his pedigree was supplied by *Stukeley. Legend says that he was bled to death by a treacherous nun at Kirklees in Yorkshire. According to Joseph Hunter (antiquary, 1783–1861), with support from the court rolls of the manor of Wakefield in Yorkshire, he was a contemporary of Edward II (1307–27) and adherent of Thomas of Lancaster. He is the centre of a whole cycle of ballads, one of the best of which is *Robin Hood and Guy of Gisborne, printed in Percy's *Reliques, and his legend shows affinity with Chaucer's 'Cook's Tale of Gamelyn' (see GAMELYN) and with the tales of other legendary outlaws such as Clym of the Clough and *Adam Bell. Popular plays embodying the legend appear to have been developed out of the village *May Day game, the king and queen of May giving place to Robin and Maid Marian. Works dealing with the same theme were written by *Munday, *Chettle, *Tennyson, and others. The *True Tale of Robin Hood* was published in 1632, *Robin Hood's Garland* in 1670, and a prose narrative in 1678. He figures in Scott's *Ivanhoe as Locksley.

Robin Hood, *A Tale of*, sub-title of Jonson's *The Sad Shepherd.

Robin Hood and Guy of Gisborne, one of the best known of the ballads of the *Robin Hood cycle. Robin Hood and Little John having gone on their separate ways in the forest, the latter is arrested by the sheriff of Nottingham and tied to a tree. Meanwhile Robin Hood meets with Guy of Gisborne, who has sworn to take Robin; they fight and Guy is slain. Robin puts on the horse-hide with which Guy was clad, takes his arms, and blows a blast on his horn. The sheriff mistakes him for Guy, thinks he has killed Robin, and gives him permission, as a reward, to kill Little John. Robin releases Little John, gives him Guy's bow, and the sheriff and his company take to their heels.

Robin Oig M'Combich, the Highland drover in Scott's *The Two Drovers.

ROBINS, Elizabeth, see WOMEN'S SUFFRAGE.

ROBINSON, E(dwin) A(rlington) (1869–1935), American poet, born at Head Tide, Maine, the son of a general merchant and lumber dealer. He records that at the age of 17 he became 'violently excited over the structure and music of English blank verse', and his admiration for *Hardy, *Crabbe, and R. *Browning is manifest in his many volumes of poetry about New England life, beginning with *The Torrent and the Night Before* (1896) and *The Children of the Night* (1897), which introduce, often through dramatic monologues, the population of his fictitious and representative Tilbury Town. His predominantly dry, restrained, ironic tone continues through most of his prolific output, in which he employs traditional forms with a delicate and original skill. As well as the New England character sketches for which he is best remembered in Britain, he also wrote several long blank-verse narratives, including an Arthurian trilogy (*Merlin*, 1917; *Lancelot*, 1920; *Tristram*, 1927) and *The Man who Died Twice* (1924), a tale of genius destroyed. He was introduced in England by a *Collected Poems* (1922) with an introduction by *Drinkwater.

ROBINSON, Henry Crabb (1775–1867), was a solicitor and later a barrister, but is chiefly remembered for his diaries, reading-lists, and letters, first collected in 1869, which provide valuable information about the writers and events of his time. He was the friend of *Wordsworth, *Coleridge, *Lamb, *Hazlitt, and later *Carlyle, and because of his indefatigable attendance at public lectures was able to provide useful descriptions of the lecturing of Coleridge (with his 'immethodical rhapsody'), Hazlitt, and others. He was an admirer of the German writers, of *Goethe in particular, travelled in Germany, and did much to popularize German culture in England. For many years he wrote for *The Times*, at home and abroad, and he was one of the founders of both University College London, and the *Athenaeum club.

ROBINSON, (Esmé Stuart) Lennox (1886–1958), prolific Irish dramatist, who was also manager of the *Abbey Theatre, 1910–14 and 1919–23, when he became the director until his death. Among his best-known plays are *The Clancy Name* (1911); the patriotic *Harvest* (1911) and *Patriots* (1912); *The Whiteheaded Boy*, a comedy (1920); *Crabbed Youth and Age* (1924); the ambitious *The Big House* (1928), on the changing state of Ireland; and two successful later comedies, *The Far-off Hills* (1931) and *Church Street* (1955). He also edited the *Oxford Book of Irish Verse* (with D. MacDonagh, 1958) and other anthologies; and wrote *The Irish Theatre* (1939) and *Ireland's Abbey Theatre. A History* (1951).

Robinson Crusoe, The Life and strange and surprising Adventures of, a romance by *Defoe, published 1719.

In 1704 Alexander *Selkirk, who had run away to sea and joined a privateering expedition under *Dampier, was at his own request put ashore on the uninhabited island of Juan Fernandez. He was rescued in 1709 by Woodes *Rogers. Defoe was probably familiar with several versions of this tale, and added many incidents from his own imagination to his account of Crusoe, presenting it as a true story. The extraordinarily convincing account of the ship-wrecked Crusoe's successful efforts to make himself a tolerable existence in his solitude first revealed Defoe's genius for vivid fiction; it has a claim to be the first English novel. Defoe was nearly sixty when he wrote it.

The author tells how, with the help of a few stores and utensils saved from the wreck and the exercise of infinite ingenuity, Crusoe built himself a house, domesticated goats, and made himself a boat. He describes the perturbation of his mind caused by a visit of cannibals, his rescue from death of an indigenous native he later names Friday, and finally the coming of an English ship whose crew are in a state of mutiny, the subduing of the mutineers, and Crusoe's rescue.

The book had immediate and permanent success, was translated into many languages, and inspired many imitations, known generically as 'Robinsonnades', including *Philip Quarll, *Peter Wilkins, and *The Swiss Family Robinson. Defoe followed it with *The Farther Adventures of Robinson Crusoe* (1719), in which with Friday he revisits his island, is attacked by a fleet of canoes on his departure, and loses Friday in the encounter. *Serious Reflections . . . of Robinson Crusoe . . . with his vision of the Angelick World*, which is more a manual of piety than a work of fiction, appeared in 1720, and was never as popular. The influence of *Robinson Crusoe* has been very great. *Rousseau in *Émile* recommended it as the first book that should be studied by a growing boy, *Coleridge praised its evocation of 'the universal man', and *Marx in *Das Kapital* used it to illustrate economic theory in action. In recent years 'Man (later Girl) Friday' came to describe a lowly assistant performing a multiplicity of tasks.

In *The Rise of the Novel* (1957) and other essays Ian Watt provides one of the most controversial modern interpretations, relating Crusoe's predicament to the rise of bourgeois individualism, division of labour, and social and spiritual alienation.

Robot, see ČAPEK, K.

Rob Roy, a novel by Sir W. *Scott, published 1817.

The story takes place just before the Jacobite rising of 1715. Francis Osbaldistone, the son of a rich London merchant, on refusing to adopt his father's profession, is banished to Osbaldistone Hall in the north of England, the home of his fox-hunting, hard-drinking uncle, Sir Hildebrand Osbaldistone. Here he is brought into contact with Sir Hildebrand's six boorish sons, one of whom, Rashleigh, is a malignant plotter who has been selected to occupy the place of Francis in the London counting-house, and Sir Hildebrand's niece, the high-spirited Diana Vernon. Rashleigh is deeply involved in Jacobite intrigues, has evil designs on Diana, and becomes the bitter enemy of Francis, who falls in love with Diana and is received by her with favour. The story is occupied with the attempts of Rashleigh to destroy Francis and to rob and ruin Francis's father, attempts that are defeated partly by Diana, and partly by the singular Scotsman Rob Roy Macgregor. This historical character, member of a proscribed clan, was once an honest drover; embittered by misfortune and injustice, he is now an outlaw, the ruthless and cunning opponent of the government's agents, but capable of justice and even generosity. At the instance of Diana, he supports Francis against Rashleigh. To avert the ruin which threatens his father as a result of Rashleigh's machinations, Francis, accompanied by a delightful character, Bailie Nicol Jarvie of Glasgow, goes to seek Rob Roy in the Highlands, and is the unwilling witness of an encounter between the clansmen and the royal troops and the extraordinary escape of Rob Roy from their hands. Rashleigh is forced to surrender the funds that he has misappropriated, and is killed by Rob Roy after having betrayed his Jacobite associates to the government. Francis is restored to his father's favour, becomes the owner of Osbaldistone Hall, and marries Diana. His rascally servant Andrew *Fairservice is one of Scott's great characters.

Robsart, Amy, daughter of Sir John Robsart, married to Sir R. *Dudley, afterwards earl of Leicester, in 1549; she figures in Scott's *Kenilworth.*

ROCHESTER, John Wilmot, second earl of (1647–80), lyric poet, satirist, and a leading member of the group of 'court wits' surrounding Charles II. He was born at Ditchley in Oxfordshire, his father a Cavalier hero and his mother a deeply religious woman related to many prominent Puritans. In his early teens he was sent to Wadham College, Oxford, the home of the *Royal Society, and then went on a European tour, returning to the court late in 1664. At the age of 18 he romantically abducted the sought-after heiress Elizabeth Malet in a coach-and-six. Despite the resistance of her family, and after a delay of 18 months (during which Rochester fought with conspicuous gallantry in the naval wars against the Dutch), she married him. Subsequently his time was divided between periods of domesticity with Elizabeth at his mother's home in the country (the couple had four children), and fashionable life in London with, among several mistresses, the brilliant actress Elizabeth *Barry, and his riotous male friends, who included the earl of Dorset (C. *Sackville) and the duke of *Buckingham. Wherever he was staying he tried to keep up the other side of his life through letters, many of which survive.

Although Dr *Johnson dismissed Rochester's lyrics, their wit and emotional complexity give him a good claim to be considered one of the last important *Metaphysical poets of the 17th cent., and he was one of the first of the *Augustans, with his social and literary verse satires. He wrote scurrilous lampoons—some of them impromptu—dramatic prologues and epilogues, 'imitations' and translations of classical authors, and several other brilliant poems which are hard to categorize, such as his tough self-dramatization 'The Maimed Debauchee' and the grimly funny 'Upon Nothing'. He wrote more frankly about sex than anyone in English before the 20th cent., and is one of the most witty poets in the language. Although his output was small (he died young), it was very varied. *Marvell admired him, *Dryden, *Swift, and *Pope were all influenced by him (he was Dryden's patron for a time), and he has made an impression on many subsequent poets—*Goethe and *Tennyson, for example, and in modern Britain, *Empson and P. *Porter.

Rochester is famous for having, in Johnson's words, 'blazed out his youth and health in lavish voluptuousness'. He became very ill in his early thirties and engaged in discussions and correspondence with a number of theologians, particularly the deist Charles Blount and the rising Anglican churchman G. *Burnet, an outspoken royal chaplain who superintended and subsequently wrote up the poet's death-bed conversion. It was the final contradiction in a personality whose many oppositions—often elegantly or comically half-concealed—produced an important body of poems. See *Complete Poems* (1968), ed. D. M. Vieth; *Poems* (1984), ed. K. Walker; *Letters* (1980), ed. J. Treglown. There is a life by V. de Sola Pinto (1953, 2nd edn 1964); see also *Lord Rochester's Monkey* (1974) by G. *Greene.

Rochester, Edward Fairfax, the hero of C. Brontë's *Jane Eyre.*

Rock, The, a play by T. S. *Eliot.

Roderick, *Vision of Don,* a poem by Sir W. *Scott, published 1811. Roderick, the last Gothic king of Spain, in order to learn the future, dares to enter a magic vault which has been denounced as fatal to the Spanish monarchy. He there sees a vision of his own defeat by the Moors and their occupation of the country; next, of the peninsula when Spanish and Portuguese conquests have raised it to the height of its power, sullied, however, by superstition; lastly, of the usurpation of the Spanish crown by Bonaparte, and the arrival of British succour.

Roderick Dhu, a character in Scott's *The Lady of the Lake.*

Roderick Hudson, the first novel of H. *James, published in book form 1876. It is the story of a young man transplanted from a lawyer's office in a Massachusetts town to a sculptor's studio in Rome. Incapable of adjustment to his environment, he fails both in art and love, and meets a tragic end in Switzerland. The leading female character, Christina Light, was taken up again by the author in a later novel, *The Princess Casamassima*.

Roderick Random, *The Adventures of,* by T. *Smollett, published 1748.

Smollett's first novel, narrated with rampant, youthful vigour in the first person, is strongly influenced by *Lesage's *Gil Blas*. In his Preface the author declares his wish to arouse 'generous indignation . . . against the vicious disposition of the world'. Roderick is combative, often violent, but capable of great affection and generosity. His father had been disinherited and has left Scotland, leaving his young son penniless with a neglectful grandfather. Roderick is befriended and rescued by his uncle, Lt Tom Bowling of the navy. After a brief apprenticeship to a surgeon, and accompanied by an old school-fellow, Strap, the innocent Roderick travels to London, where he encounters various rogues. Eventually, after struggling against assault, deception, and other tribulations, he qualifies as a surgeon's mate. He is then pressed as a common sailor aboard a man-of-war, the *Thunderer*, where he eventually becomes mate to the ebullient Welsh surgeon Morgan. They are present at the siege of Cartagena, and after much suffering and ill-treatment (which he does not accept supinely) Roderick returns to England. Here he lives under a false name as a footman, falls in love with Narcissa, and is once again kidnapped, this time by smugglers, who bear him off to France. He finds and helps his uncle, Tom Bowling, joins the French army, and fights at Dettingen. He again encounters his generous friend Strap, who arranges his release from the army and undertakes to serve Roderick as his valet. The two return to England, where Roderick intends to marry a lady of fortune. Again in London, he becomes embroiled in riotous life, amatory adventures, and fiery debates on a great range of subjects. He courts, among others, Miss Melinda Goosetrap, but does not succeed in deceiving her mother; other matrimonial enterprises are no more successful. Again he meets Narcissa, but he is shortly in prison for debt, and on his release, when he cannot find her, he sinks into despair. He is rescued by Tom Bowling, and embarks as surgeon on a ship under Bowling's command; in the course of the voyage he meets Don Roderigo, who turns out to be his long-lost father, now a wealthy merchant. When they return to England Roderick marries Narcissa, and Strap marries her maid, Miss Williams. Two long digressive stories are inserted into the narrative, the history of Miss Williams, who had earlier been a prostitute; and the story of Melopoyn, based on Smollett's own experience in trying to get his *The Regicide* accepted for the stage.

Roderick, *the last of the Goths,* a narrative poem by *Southey, published 1814.

Roderick, the last king of the Visigoths, has dishonoured Florinda, daughter of Count Julian. The latter, in revenge, calls the Moors into Spain, and Roderick is driven from his throne. In penitence he assumes the garb of a monk and, under the name of Father Maccabbee, persuades his cousin Pelayo to lead the Christian forces against the infidel at the battle of Covadonga. In the heat of battle Roderick throws off his disguise, reveals himself to the Christian army, and leads it to victory. He then disappears, and it is only generations later that, in a hermitage, a tomb bearing his name is discovered. Pelayo becomes the founder of the Spanish royal line.

The subject is also treated by W. S. Landor in his *Count Julian*.

Roderigo, *Iago's gull in Shakespeare's *Othello*.

Rodomont, in *Orlando Innamorato* and *Orlando Furioso*, the king of Sarza, arrogant and valiant, the doughtiest of the followers of *Agramant. His boastfulness gave rise to the word 'rodomontade'. He leads the first Saracen invasion into France. Doralis, princess of Granada, is betrothed to him, but falls into the power of *Mandricardo. After an indecisive duel between the two Saracen heroes, the conflict is referred to the princess herself, who, to Rodomont's surprise, expresses her preference for Mandricardo. Rodomont retires in disgust to the south of France. Here *Isabella falls into his power and, preferring death, by guile causes him to slay her. In remorse, in order to commemorate her, he builds a bridge and takes toll of all who pass that way. Orlando, coming in his madness to the bridge, throws Rodomont into the river. Rodomont is also defeated by *Bradamante. Thus humiliated he temporarily retires from arms, emerges once more, and 'is finally killed by *Rogero.

Roehampton, Lord, in *Endymion* by B. Disraeli.

ROETHKE, Theodore (1908–63), American poet born in Michigan, who taught from 1947 at the University of Washington. His first book of poems, *Open House* (1941), already displays characteristic imagery of vegetable growth and decay, rooted in childhood memories of the greenhouses of his father, who was a keen horticulturalist. It was followed by various volumes including *The Lost Son* (1948), *Praise to the End* (1951), a book of light verse (divided into 'Nonsense' and 'Greenhouse' poems) called *I Am! Says the Lamb* (1961), and a posthumous collection, *The Far Field* (1964). His work has affinity with both *Yeats and *Blake, and influenced the early poetry of S. *Plath.

Roger, the name of the London cook (from

Ware) in Chaucer's *Canterbury Tales*. His name may have been Roger Knight; see note ix, 50 in Robinson's edition, pp. 763–4.

Roger de Coverley, Sir, see COVERLEY.

Rogero, or **Ruggiero,** the legendary ancestor of the house of Este, extolled in *Orlando Furioso*. He is the son of a Christian knight and a Saracen lady of royal birth, brought up in Africa, and taken by *Agramant on the expedition against Charlemagne, where he falls in love with the warrior maiden *Bradamante and she with him. He falls into the power of *Alcina and is released by *Melissa. He then, mounted on the hippogriff, rescues *Angelica from the Orc. Bradamante has also an active rival in *Marfisa, a lady fighting on the Moorish side, who is smitten with love for Rogero, but eventually turns out to be his sister. Finally, after the retreat of Agramant, Rogero joins Charlemagne and is baptized. He now hopes to marry Bradamante, but her ambitious parents vigorously oppose the match. Bradamante, to secure her lover without openly opposing her parents, declares, with Charlemagne's approval, that she will marry no one who has not withstood her in battle for a whole day. This Rogero alone does, and after many vicissitudes the lovers are united. In a final duel Rogero slays *Rodomont. Some elements of the Bradamante/Rogero romance can be discerned in the relationship between *Spenser's Britomart and Artegall.

ROGER OF WENDOVER (d. 1236), monk and chronicler at St Albans; his *Flores Historiarum* was a history of the world from the creation to AD 1235, compiled from many different sources. He was succeeded as chronicler by M. *Paris.

ROGERS, James Edwin Thorold (1825–90), educated at King's College, London, and Oxford, was professor of political economy at Oxford in 1862–7 and again in 1888. He had been a strong *Tractarian until about 1860, but put off his orders and swung right round, being the first clergyman to take advantage of the Clerical Disabilities Relief Act of 1870. He was Radical MP for Southwark, 1880–6, and a father figure of economic history; all subsequent studies of inflation rest on his *A History of Agriculture and Prices in England . . . from 1259–1793* (1866–87).

ROGERS, Samuel (1763–1855), the son of a banker and himself a banker for some years, was in his lifetime a highly successful poet, and well known as an art collector and for the celebrated 'breakfasts' which he held for over 40 years. In 1792 he published *The Pleasures of Memory*, in which the author wanders reflectively round the villages of his childhood. The work went into four editions in its first year, and by 1816 over 23,000 copies had been sold. In 1810 he published a fragmentary epic, *Columbus*; in 1814 *Jacqueline*; in 1822–8 *Italy*, a collection of verse tales; and in 1832 *Poems*. His work was praised by *Jeffrey and admired by *Byron, who came to believe that only Rogers and *Crabbe were free from 'a wrong revolutionary system'. But *Hazlitt spoke for many younger writers when he declared in a lecture in 1818 that in Rogers's work 'the decomposition of prose is substituted for the composition of poetry.'

ROGERS, Woodes (d. 1732), commander of a privateering expedition (1708–11) in which *Dampier was pilot, and in the course of which *Selkirk was discovered on the island of Juan Fernandez and rescued, the town of Guayaquil was taken and held to ransom, and a Manila ship captured. These incidents are described in Rogers's entertaining journal, *A Cruizing Voyage round the world*.

Roget's Thesaurus of *English Words and Phrases*, by Dr Peter Mark Roget (1779–1879), English physician and scholar, is a compilation of words classified in groups according to the ideas they express, the purpose of which is to supply a word, or words, which most aptly express a given idea; conversely, a dictionary explains the meaning of words by supplying the ideas they are meant to convey. The volume, first published in 1852, has been followed by many successive revised editions: by Roget's son, John Lewis Roget (from 1879), and his grandson, Samuel Romilly Roget (from 1933). The family connection came to an end with the death of Samuel Roget in 1953. Updated editions have since been published under the editorship of Robert A. Dutch (from 1962) and Susan M. Lloyd (1982).

Rogue Literature, a very popular type of underworld writing in the 16th and 17th cents. Its practitioners include the Kentish magistrate Thomas Harman, whose a *Caveat for Commen Cursetors* appeared in 1567; R. Copland (see under HYE WAY TO THE SPYTTEL HOUSE); R. *Greene, whose pamphlets describe 'coney-catching', that is, the deception of innocents; and T. *Dekker. Rogue literature is generally vividly descriptive and often confessional, providing an important source for our knowledge of everyday common life and its language, as well as for the canting terms of thieves and beggars. It can be related to stories about *Robin Hood, *jest-book literature, and early attempts at writing fiction and autobiography. A large collection of such tracts was edited by A. V. Judges in 1930.

ROJAS, Fernando de (*c*.1465–1541), a Spanish author born at Puebla de Montalbán, near Toledo, his family being *conversos*, or Jews converted to Christianity. He studied law at the

University of Salamanca and, in spite of difficulties owing to his racial origin, rose to the position of *alcalde* (mayor) of Talavera. He is remembered for his masterpiece **Celestina*, but there is no record of any other work by his hand.

Rokeby, a poem in six cantos by Sir W. *Scott, published 1813.

The scene is Rokeby, near Greta Bridge in Yorkshire, immediately after the battle of Marston Moor (1644). The complicated plot concerns the conspiracy of Oswald Wycliffe, lord of Barnard Castle, with the sturdy ruffian Bertram Risingham, to murder the latter's patron Philip of Mortham, in order to obtain his lands and the treasure he brought back from the Spanish main. Mortham is shot and left for dead, but recovers. An attack on Rokeby Castle to secure the treasure is defeated, largely by the prowess of young Redmond O'Neale, Lord Rokeby's page. Meanwhile Oswald, to whom Rokeby has been entrusted as a prisoner after Marston Moor, threatens to execute him unless Rokeby's daughter Matilda, agrees to marry Oswald's son, Wilfred, a gentle poetic youth, who refuses to take advantage of Matilda's reluctant consent. Just as Rokeby is about to be executed, Bertram, struck with remorse, rides in and kills Oswald, and is himself slain. Redmond O'Neale is discovered to be the lost son of Mortham, and marries Matilda.

The poem includes the beautiful songs 'A weary lot is thine, fair maid' and 'Brignal Banks'. Scott (in spite of the good first reception of the poem) recognized his own comparative failure as a poet, and thereupon turned to his true vocation as a novelist.

Rokesmith, John, in Dickens's **Our Mutual Friend*, the name assumed by John Harmon.

Roland, the most famous of the **Paladins of Charlemagne. According to the chronicler **Einhard, his legend has the following basis of fact. In August 778 the rearguard of the French army of Charlemagne was returning through the Pyrenees from a successful expedition in the north of Spain, when it was surprised in the valley of Roncevaux by the Basque inhabitants of the mountains; the baggage was looted and all the rearguard killed, including Hrodland, count of the Breton marches. The story of this disaster was developed by the imagination of numerous poets. For the Basques were substituted the Saracens. Roland becomes the commander of the rearguard, appointed to the post at the instance of the traitor Ganelon, who is in league with the Saracen king Marsile. Oliver is introduced, Roland's companion in arms and the brother of Aude, Roland's betrothed. Oliver thrice urges Roland to summon aid by sounding his horn, but Roland from excess of pride defers doing so until too late. Charlemagne returns and destroys the pagan army. Ganelon is tried and executed.

The legend has been handed down in three principal forms: in the fabricated Latin chronicle of the 12th cent. erroneously attributed to Archbishop Turpin (d. *c.*800); in the *Carmen de proditione Guenonis* of the same epoch; and in the *Chanson de Roland*, in medieval French, also of the early 12th cent. It is a well known tradition that Taillefer, a *jongleur* in the army of William the Conqueror, sang a poem on Roncesvalles at the battle of Hastings (1066), possibly an earlier version of the extant *Chanson*. Roland, as Orlando, is the hero of Boiardo's **Orlando Innamorato* and Ariosto's **Orlando Furioso*. Roland's sword was called 'Durandal' or 'Durindana', and his horn 'Olivant'. (See also OLIVER.)

Roland, Childe, see CHILDE ROLAND.

Roland de Vaux, (1) the baron of Triermain, in Scott's **The Bridal of Triermain*; (2) in Coleridge's **'Christabel'*, the estranged friend of Christabel's father.

ROLFE, Frederick William (1860–1913), who liked to call himself 'Baron Corvo', or, equally misleadingly, Fr Rolfe, was by turns schoolmaster, painter, and writer. From a Dissenting background, he was a convert to Roman Catholicism and an unsuccessful candidate for the priesthood; his most outstanding novel, *Hadrian the Seventh* (1904), appears to be a dramatized autobiography—a self-justification and a dream of wish-fulfilment, in which Rolfe's protagonist, George Arthur Rose, is rescued from a life of literary poverty and elected pope. His other writings include *Stories Toto Told Me* (published in 1898, after first appearing in the **Yellow Book*), *Chronicles of the House of Borgia* (1901, an eccentric historical study), *Don Tarquinio: A Kataleptic Phantasmatic Romance* (1905, a novel relating 24 hours in the life of a young nobleman in the company of the Borgia in 1495), and *The Desire and Pursuit of the Whole: a romance of modern Venice* (1934). This last work was written largely in 1909; Rolfe moved to Venice (where he died) in 1908, and he here describes his own poverty, his homosexual fantasies, and the beauties of Venice, as well as abusing in characteristic vein many of those who had previously befriended him, including R. H. *Benson; *Auden in a 1961 foreword describes him as 'one of the great masters of vituperation'. Two other novels (*Nicholas Crabbe: or the one and the many*, 1958; *Don Renato: an ideal content*, 1963) and several fragments were published posthumously. Rolfe's style is highly ornate and idiosyncratic; his vocabulary is arcane, his allusions erudite, and although he had admirers during his lifetime, he alienated most of them by his persistent paranoia and requests for financial support. The story of his unhappy life is told by A. J. A. *Symons in

The Quest for Corvo: An Experiment in Biography (1934). See also D. Weeks, *Corvo* (1971).

Roll, Ragman, a set of rolls in the Public Record Office, in which are recorded the instruments of homage made to Edward I by the Scottish king (Balliol), nobles, etc., at the Parliament of Berwick in 1296; so called apparently from the pendent seals attached.

ROLLAND, Romain, see ROMAN FLEUVE.

ROLLE, Richard, of Hampole (*c.*1300–49), one of the principal 14th-cent. English mystical writers, in prose and poetry. He was born at Thornton in North Yorkshire and is said to have left Oxford in his 19th year to become a hermit. He lived at various places in Yorkshire, finally at Hampole where he died, near a Cistercian nunnery where he had disciples. Among these was Margaret Kirkeby who became an anchoress in his neighbourhood and to whom a number of his major English works (notably *The Forme of Perfect Living*) are addressed. He wrote in the Yorkshire dialect, in a somewhat mannered, rhetorical language which makes much use of alliteration. The essential element in his mysticism is personal enthusiasm, rather than the rationalism of the more classical mystical writings; the echoing words he returns to are *calor, canor, dulcor*: warmth, melodiousness, sweetness. One of his earliest English writings is the *Meditations on the Passion*, and among the most familiar, later works are *Ego Dormio* and *The Commandment of Love*. The canon of his works, in Latin as well as English, is very large. (See also ANGLO-LATIN LITERATURE.) See H. E. Allen, *Writings Ascribed to Richard Rolle* (1927); ed. H. E. Allen, *The English Writings of Richard Rolle* (1931); ed. C. T. Horstman, *Yorkshire writers: Rolle and his followers* (2 vols, 1895–6).

Rolliad, *Criticism on the,* a collection of Whig political satires directed against the younger *Pitt and his followers after their success at the election of 1784, first published in the *Morning Herald and Daily Advertiser* during that year. The authors, members of the *'Esto Perpetua' club, are not known with certainty, but among them were Dr French Laurence, who became Regius professor of civil law at Oxford; G. *Ellis; General Richard Fitzpatrick; and Lord John Townshend. The satires originally took the form of reviews of an imaginary epic, 'The Rolliad', which took its name from John Rolle, MP, one of Pitt's supporters, and dealt with the adventures of a mythical Norman duke, Rollo, his ancestor. These were followed by 'Political Eclogues', 'Probationary Odes' for the vacant laureateship, and 'Political Miscellanies', all directed to the same purpose, the ridicule of the Tories. A complete collection was published in 1791.

Rollo Duke of Normandy, see BLOODY BROTHER, THE.

Rolls, Pipe, the Great Rolls of the Exchequer, comprising the various 'pipes', or enrolled accounts, of sheriffs and others for a financial year. The complete series of Pipe Rolls dates from the reign of Henry II (1155–89), but there is an isolated one (of the highest importance) of the year 1130.

Rolls Series, otherwise *Chronicles and Memorials of Great Britain and Ireland from the Invasion of the Romans to the Reign of Henry VIII*. Their publication was authorized by governments in 1847 on the suggestion of Joseph Stevenson, the archivist, and the recommendation of Sir John Romilly, master of the rolls, and it produced texts of many of the most important literary and historical writings of the Middle Ages and Renaissance. Among its most celebrated editors were the historians James Gairdner (1828–1912) and J. H. Round (1854–1928).

ROMAINS, Jules, see ROMAN FLEUVE.

Roman à clef, i.e. a 'novel with a key', in which the reader (or some readers) are intended to identify real characters under fictitious names. The key is sometimes literal, sometimes figurative, and sometimes provided by the author, as in the case of Mrs *Manley's *The New Atalantis*, sometimes published separately by others, as in the case of Disraeli's *Coningsby*.

Roman Actor, The, a tragedy by *Massinger, acted 1626, printed 1629. The play is based on the life of the Emperor Domitian as told by *Suetonius and Dio Cassius.

The cruel and licentious Domitian forcibly takes from Aelius Lamia, a Roman senator, his wife Domitia. He executes Lamia and makes her his empress. He dotes on her, but she falls in love with the actor Paris. So well does he act before her a scene in which, as Iphis scorned by Anaxarete, he threatens to take his life, that she betrays her feelings to her enemies, who warn Domitian. The emperor finds her wooing Paris, and kills the actor with his own hand in the course of a play in which he takes the part of an injured husband and Paris the part of a false servant. Domitia escapes punishment but, incensed at the death of Paris and presuming on her power over the emperor, she rails at and taunts him. At last he writes down her name in a list of those marked for death. Domitia finds the list while he sleeps, and joins others whose names are there in a conspiracy. Domitian is lured from the protection of his guards and assassinated.

Romance, derived from the Medieval Latin word *romanice*, 'in the Roman language'. The word *roman* in Old French was applied to the popular courtly stories in verse which dealt with three traditional subjects: the legends about Arthur, Charlemagne and his knights, and stories of classical heroes especially Alexander (see MATTER). English correspondents, almost always translations, are found from the 13th cent. onwards. Some of the most distinguished include *King Horn*, *Havelok*, Sir *Gawain and the Green Knight*, Sir *Orfeo* (see also BRETON LAYS). Defining them by theme is very difficult; they usually involve the suspension of the circumstances normally attendant on human actions (often through magic) in order to illustrate a moral point. From the 15th cent. onwards English romances are mostly in prose, and some 16th-cent. examples were the inspiration for *Spenser and Shakespeare (as, for instance, *Pandosto* by R. Greene was used by Shakespeare in *The Winter's Tale*). A new interest in the medieval romance (in writers such as Sir W. *Scott and *Keats) contributed to the naming of 19th-cent. *Romanticism, though the term was also used to embrace some sentimental novels from the 18th cent. onwards, as in the *Mills and Boon romances of the modern era. See John Stevens, *Medieval Romance* (1973); G. Beer, *Romance* (1970).

Romance languages, the group of modern languages descended from Latin (which itself joins with them to form the branch of *Indo-European known as Italic), the chief of which are French, Italian, Spanish, Portuguese, and Romanian (and, of literary-historical importance, *Provençal).

Roman d'Alexandre, see ALEXANDER THE GREAT.

Roman de Brut and **Roman de Rou**, see WACE.

Roman de la Rose. The first 4,058 lines of this allegorical romance were written c.1230 by Guillaume de Lorris (d. 1237) to expound 'the whole art of love'; the remaining 17,622 lines were composed c.1275 by Jean de Meun as a more wide-ranging anatomy of love within a social and philosophical framework. The story in de Lorris's part of the poem is an allegorical presentation of *courtly love; the allegorical figures mostly embody various aspects of the lady whom the lover-narrator meets in his endeavours to reach the rose which symbolizes the lady's love. The story is set in the walled garden of the god of love, the unpleasant realities of life being depicted on the walls outside. In the second part Jean de Meun shows love in a wider context of scholarship, philosophy, and morals, shifting the work from the courtly to the encyclopaedic literary tradition, in line with the rationalist and compendious spirit of the 13th cent. The poem, in its allegorical dream form and in its presentation of both the courtly and the philosophical discussions of love, remained

an immense literary influence all through the later Middle Ages, both inside and outside France. About one-third of the whole (ll. 1–5,154 and 10,679–12,360) is translated in the Middle English *The Romaunt of the Rose*, the first part of which may be by *Chaucer. The *Roman* was much the most important literary influence on writings in English in the 14th cent.
Ed. D. Poiriou (Paris, 1974); trans. C. Dahlberg (1971); A. M. F. Gunn, *The Mirror of Love: a Reinterpretation of the Romance of the Rose* (1952).

Roman de Renart, see REYNARD THE FOX.

Romanes Lectures, founded at Oxford in 1891 by scientist George John Romanes (1848–94), professor at Edinburgh and the Royal Institution, author of *Darwin and after Darwin* (1892–7) and works on physiology, psychology, and zoology. The lectures are on subjects related to science, art, and literature.

Roman fleuve, the French term for a novel sequence. The practice of pursuing a family story through a number of related novels in order to render a comprehensive account of a social period ultimately derives from *Balzac and *Zola, but it reached its culmination between 1900 and 1940. Its major exemplars were: Romain Rolland (1866–1944), whose *Jean Christophe* (10 vols, 1905–12) describes the career of a musical genius; Roger Martin du Gard (1881–1958), whose *Les Thibault* (10 vols, 1922–40) explores the reaction of two brothers against their bourgeois inheritance; Georges Duhamel (1884–1966), whose *Chronique des Pasquiers* (10 vols, 1933–41) traces the moral and cultural development of a Parisian family; and Jules Romains (1885–1972), whose *Les Hommes de bonne volonté* (27 vols, 1932–47) offers a panorama of French society between 1910 and 1940. Translations of these works have been popular in England, but the English version of the phenomenon, descending from *Trollope and including such novelists as *Galsworthy and C. P. *Snow, did not have the same conviction and consistency.

Romanticism (the Romantic Movement), a literary movement, and profound shift in sensibility, which took place in Britain and throughout Europe roughly between 1770 and 1848. Intellectually it marked a violent reaction to the *Enlightenment. Politically it was inspired by the revolutions in America and France and popular wars of independence in Poland, Spain, Greece, and elsewhere. Emotionally it expressed an extreme assertion of the self and the value of individual experience (the *'egotistical sublime'), together with the sense of the infinite and the transcendental. Socially it championed progressive causes, though when these were frustrated it often produced a bitter, gloomy, and despairing outlook. The stylistic keynote of Romanticism is intensity, and its watchword is 'Imagination'. In Britain, Romantic writers of the first generation included *Wordsworth and *Coleridge (*Lyrical Ballads, 1798), *Burns, and *Blake; though introspective 18th-cent. poets such as *Gray and *Cowper show pre-Romantic tendencies, as well as *Gothic novelists such as Horace *Walpole and 'Monk' *Lewis. Terror, passion, and the *Sublime are essential concepts in early Romanticism; as is the sense of primitive mystery rediscovered in the Celtic bardic verse of *Macpherson's 'Ossian', the folk ballads collected by *Percy, and the medieval poetry forged by *Chatterton (whom *Southey edited) (see PRIMITIVISM). Foreign sources were also vital: *Goethe's The Sorrows of Young Werther (1774); the ghostly ballads of Bürger (*Lenore, 1773); the verse dramas of *Schiller (The Robbers, 1781); and the philosophical criticism of A. W. *Schlegel. The tone of Romanticism was shaped by the naked emotionalism of *Rousseau's Julie, ou la nouvelle Héloïse (1761), and the exotic legends and mythology found in Oriental and Homeric literatures and 17th-cent. travel writers (see PURCHAS). The second generation of British Romantics—*Byron, *Shelley, and *Keats—absorbed these tumultuous influences, wrote swiftly, travelled widely (Greece, Switzerland, Italy), and died prematurely: their life-stories and letters became almost as important for Romanticism as their poetry. They in turn inspired autobiographical prose-writers such as *Hazlitt, *De Quincey, and *Lamb; while the historical imagination found a champion in Sir W. *Scott. The Romantics saw and felt things brilliantly afresh. They virtually invented certain landscapes—the Lakes, the Alps, the bays of Italy. They were strenuous walkers, hill-climbers, sea-bathers, or river-lovers. They had a new intuition for the primal power of the wild landscape, the spiritual correspondence between Man and Nature, and the aesthetic principle of 'organic' form (seen at their noblest in Wordsworth's *Prelude or J. M. W. *Turner's paintings). In their critical writings and lectures (see COLERIDGE, HAZLITT, DE QUINCEY) they described poetry and drama with new psychological appreciation (the character of Hamlet, for example); they discussed dreams, dramatic illusion, Romantic sensibility, the process of creativity, the limits of Classicism and Reason, and the dynamic nature of the Imagination. Remembered childhood, unrequited love, and the exiled hero were constant themes. The Romantics' sense of Liberty also helped the emergence of an influential generation of women writers, including M. *Wollstonecraft, D. *Wordsworth, M. *Shelley, and later the *Brontë sisters. Romanticism expressed an unending revolt against classical form, conservative morality, authoritarian government, personal insincerity, and human moderation. The British Romantics had a powerful influence in France after the Napoleonic wars, especially remarkable in *Chateaubriand, *Hugo, De *Vigny, the paintings of *Delacroix, and the music of *Berlioz.

Romany Rye, The, a novel by *Borrow, published 1857. 'Romany Rye' in gypsy language means 'Gypsy Gentleman', a name applied to Borrow from his youth by Ambrose Smith, the Norfolk gypsy. This book is a sequel to *Lavengro, and continues in a less accomplished style the story of the author's wanderings and adventures.

Romaunt of the Rose, The, a translation into Middle English octosyllabics of about one-third of the *Roman de la Rose, lines 1–5,154 and 10,679–12,360, made in the time of *Chaucer and usually included in editions of his Works (such as Robinson's) because previously attributed to him. *Skeat (in The Chaucer Canon, 1900) argued that only Part A (1–1,705, corresponding to 1–1,672 in De Lorris's French) is by Chaucer, and that B (1,706–5,810, being the remainder of De Lorris, up to 4,432, and Jean de Meun as far as 5,154 of the French) and C (5,811–7,696, corresponding to De Meun 10,679–12,360) are not his. A. Brusendorff in The Chaucer Tradition (1925) argued against Skeat that all the parts were by Chaucer, but almost all modern authorities follow Skeat; his findings were strongly corroborated in 1967 by Ronald Sutherland who showed that A is descended from a different manuscript tradition from B and C.

In this dream poem the narrator enters the Garden of Mirth where he sees various allegorized figures and falls in love with a rosebud. Parts A and B describe the dreamer's instructions by the god of love, his being befriended by Bialacoil who is imprisoned, the opposition of Daunger and other adverse figures, and (in the Jean de Meun section) the discourse of Resoun; Part C is a fragment of Jean de Meun, satirizing the hypocrisy (represented by Fals-Semblant) of religion, women, and the social order. Part A is a closer translation than the other sections. See R. A. Sutherland ed., The Romaunt of the Rose and Le Roman de la Rose: a Parallel-Text Edition (1967).

Romeo and Juliet, Shakespeare's first romantic tragedy, based on Arthur Brooke's poem The Tragicall Historye of Romeus and Juliet (1562), a translation from the French of Boaistuau of one of *Bandello's Novelle. Shakespeare's play was probably written about 1595 and first printed in a bad quarto in 1597; a good quarto published in 1599 and reprinted in 1609 served as the copy for the play's text in the First *Folio of 1623.

The Montagues and Capulets, the two chief families of Verona, are bitter enemies; Escalus, the prince, threatens anyone who disturbs the peace with death. Romeo, son of old Lord Montague, is in love with Lord Capulet's niece Rosaline. But at a feast given by Capulet, which Romeo attends disguised by a mask, he sees and falls in love with Juliet, Capulet's daughter, and she with him. After the feast he overhears, under her window, Juliet's confession of her love for him, and wins her consent to a secret marriage. With the help of Friar Laurence, they are wedded next day. Mercutio, a friend of Romeo, meets Tybalt, of the Capulet family, who is infuriated by his discovery of Romeo's presence at the feast, and they quarrel. Romeo comes on the scene, and attempts to reason with Tybalt, but Tybalt and Mercutio fight, and Mercutio falls. Then Romeo draws and Tybalt is killed. The prince, Montague, and Capulet come up, and Romeo is sentenced to banishment. Early next day, after spending the night with Juliet, he leaves Verona for Mantua, counselled by the friar, who intends to reveal Romeo's marriage at an opportune moment. Capulet proposes to marry Juliet to Count Paris, and when she seeks excuses to avoid this, peremptorily insists. Juliet consults the friar, who bids her consent to the match, but on the night before the wedding drink a potion which will render her apparently lifeless for 42 hours. He will warn Romeo, who will rescue her from the vault on her awakening and carry her to Mantua. The friar's message to Romeo miscarries, and Romeo hears that Juliet is dead. Buying poison, he comes to the vault to have a last sight of Juliet. He chances upon Count Paris outside the vault; they fight and Paris is killed. Then Romeo, after a last kiss on Juliet's lips, drinks the poison and dies. Juliet awakes and finds Romeo dead by her side, and the cup still in his hand. Guessing what has happened, she stabs herself and dies. The story is unfolded by the friar and Count Paris's page, and Montague and Capulet, faced by the tragic results of their enmity, are reconciled. The play begins with a sonnet spoken by the chorus and in its poetry, language, and plot reflects the sonnet craze of the 1590s, from which period Shakespeare's own sequence dates.

Romford, Mr Facey, see SURTEES, R. S.

ROMNEY, George (1734–1802), successful and fashionable portrait painter, born in Dalton-in-Furness, the son of a builder. He spent two years in Italy (1773–5) and the pose and graceful rhythms of his most distinguished works (e.g. *The Gower Family*, 1776–7; Kendal, Abbots Hall Museum) suggest his love of *Raphael and the antique. Yet Romney (who was a friend of *Hayley, who later wrote Romney's life, and of *Flaxman) felt trapped by the demands of portraiture. His many drawings of literary and historical subjects suggest an intensely romantic temperament. They develop from a precise, neo-classical treatment towards a wilder, more violent style; and his increasing obsession with *Sublime and horrific subject matter from *Aeschylus, *Milton, and Shakespeare links him to *Fuseli and J. H. Mortimer (c.1741–79). Romney, after 1781, became obsessed with Emma Hart, later Lady Hamilton; he painted her very many times in different guises.

Romola, a novel by G. *Eliot, published 1863.

The background of the novel is Florence at the end of the 15th cent., the troubled period, following the expulsion of the Medici, of the expedition of Charles VIII, distracted counsels in the city, the excitement caused by the preaching of Savonarola, and acute division between the popular party and the supporters of the Medici. The various historical figures, including Charles VIII, Machiavelli, and Savonarola himself, are drawn with great care, as well as the whole picturesque complexion of the city, though the novel is generally held to be overloaded with detail, and has never been one of her most admired. The story is that of the purification by trials of the noble-natured Romola, devoted daughter of an old blind scholar. Into their lives comes a clever, adaptable young Greek, Tito Melema, whose self-indulgence develops into utter perfidy. He robs, and abandons in imprisonment, the benefactor of his childhood, Baldassare. He cruelly goes through a mock marriage ceremony with the innocent little contadina Tessa. After marrying Romola he wounds her deepest feelings by betraying her father's solemn trust. He plays a double game in the political intrigues of the day. Nemesis pursues and at last overtakes him in the person of old Baldassare, who escapes from imprisonment crazed with sorrow and suffering. Romola, with her love for her husband turned to contempt, and her trust in Savonarola destroyed by his falling away from his high prophetic mission, is left in isolation, from which she is rescued by the discovery of her duty in self-sacrifice. The novel was illustrated by *Leighton, much to George Eliot's satisfaction.

Roncesvalles or **Roncevaux,** a valley in the western Pyrenees, celebrated as the scene of the defeat of the rearguard of *Charlemagne's army and the death of *Roland in 778.

Rondeau, a French verse form consisting of ten (or, in stricter sense, thirteen) lines, having only two rhymes throughout, and with the opening words used twice as a refrain. It became popular in England in the late 19th cent. and was much used by *Dobson, *Swinburne, and others. The rondel is a form of rondeau, again using two rhymes and a refrain, usually of three stanzas.

Rondel, see RONDEAU.

RONSARD, Pierre de (1524–85), French poet, leader of the *Pléiade. He won early success with the publication of the *Odes* of 1550, and the first of a series of love sequences, *Les Amours* of 1552–3. The latter collection (the 'Cassandre' cycle) contains the famous 'Mignonne, allons voir si la rose'; there followed the *Continuation des Amours* of 1555 and the *Nouvelle Continuation des Amours* of 1556, forming the basis of the 'Marie' cycle. His last important love sequence, the *Sonets pour Hélène* of 1578, contains the sonnet 'Quand vous serez bien vieille, au soir à la chandelle'. Besides the collections of love poetry, Ronsard wrote on a wide variety of themes, political, philosophical, pastoral, and religious, his works including *Les Hymnes* (1555–6), the *Discours des misères de ce temps* (1562), written at the beginning of the religious wars, and the unfinished epic *La Franciade* (1572). He exercised considerable influence on the English sonnet-writers of the 16th cent.

Room at the Top, see BRAINE, J.

Room of One's Own, A, a feminist essay by V. *Woolf, published 1929 and based on two lectures on 'Women and Fiction' delivered in Oct. 1928 to Newnham College and Girton College, Cambridge.

The author describes the educational, social, and financial disadvantages and prejudices against which women have struggled throughout history (using the hypothetical fate of a talented sister of Shakespeare as an illustration; her literary aspirations end in suicide), arguing that women will not be able to write well and freely until they have the privacy and independence implied by 'a room of one's own' and 'five hundred a year'. She pays tribute to women writers of the past (including A. *Behn, D. *Osborne and J. *Austen, the *Brontës); to woman's achievements in the form of the novel, which suited her because, unlike older forms of literature, it was 'young enough to be soft in her hands'; and projects a future in which increasing equality would enable women to become not only novelists but poets. In the last chapter she discusses the concept of 'androgyny', pleading for unity and harmony rather than a rigid separation into 'male' and 'female' qualities: 'Perhaps a mind that is purely masculine cannot create, any more than a mind that is purely feminine.'

Room with a View, A, a novel by E. M. *Forster, published 1908.

It opens in an English pensione in Florence with a confrontation between Lucy Honeychurch's chaperone Miss Bartlett and the upstart Mr Emerson and his son George; the two men generously, but in Miss Bartlett's view indecorously, offer to exchange rooms, in order to give the ladies the benefit of a room with a view, a favour which they reluctantly accept. The novel describes the inmates of the Pensione Bertolini, among them the clergyman Mr Beebe

and the 'original' lady novelist Miss Lavish, and their reactions to Italy and to one another. Lucy, an impressionable and artistic but immature girl, is disturbed first by witnessing a street murder, and then by an impulsive embrace from George Emerson during an excursion to Fiesole. Miss Bartlett removes her charge from these dangers, and the two return to Summer Street, in Surrey, where Lucy becomes engaged to a cultured dilettante, Cecil Vyse, whom Mr Beebe, who has reappeared as the local vicar, ominously describes as 'an ideal bachelor'. The Bertolini cast continues to reassemble as the Emersons take a villa in the neighbourhood. Lucy comes to realize that she loves George, not Cecil, but it takes her some time to extricate herself (helped, unexpectedly, by Miss Bartlett) from what she describes as 'the muddle'. The second half of the drama is played against a sharply and intimately observed background of tennis and tea parties and amateur piano recitals; it ends in the Pensione Bertolini, with George and Lucy on their honeymoon.

As in *Where Angels Fear to Tread*, Forster satirizes the English abroad, criticizes the sterility, snobbery, and 'witty weariness' of the self-consciously cultured, and describes Italy itself as a liberating vision. Summer Street, however, is seen with much more affection than Sawston, and the easy-going Mrs Honeychurch (based on Forster's maternal grandmother) and Lucy's brother Freddy are portrayed with sympathy. The moments of abandon—George's embrace in a field of violets, the naked bathing party in a pool in the Surrey woods (ch. 12)—are handled with a light touch that does not disturb the comedy of manners.

Roots, see WESKER TRILOGY.

ROPER, Margaret (1505–44), daughter of Sir T. *More. According to Stapleton (1535–98), she purchased the head of her dead father nearly a month after it had been exposed on London Bridge and preserved it in spices until her death. It is believed that it was buried with her. *Tennyson alludes to this:

> her, who clasped in her last trance
> Her murdered father's head.
> ('A Dream of Fair Women')

ROPER, William (1498–1578), of Lincoln's Inn, married Sir T. *More's daughter Margaret (above) and wrote an early life of his father-in-law first published at Paris (1626).

ROS, Amanda McKittrick, *née* Anna Margaret McKittrick (1860–1939), Irish writer, known as 'the World's Worst Novelist', wrote *Irene Iddesleigh* (1897), *Delina Delaney* (1898), and other works, remarkable for their extraordinary and unselfconsciously colourful prose, to which A. *Huxley devoted an essay, 'Euphues Redivivus' (1923).

ROSA, Salvator (1615–73), Neapolitan painter, etcher, satirical poet, and actor, who worked in Florence and Rome. He painted genre scenes, battles, marines, and ambitious figure compositions, but has remained most famous for his macabre subjects (witches, monsters, and meditations on death) and for his wild landscapes. In these, remote valleys, craggy cliffs, and jagged, moss-laden trees create a sense of desolation that contrasts sharply with the serenity of *Claude. In England his reputation rose steadily throughout the 18th cent. Horace *Walpole, crossing the Alps in 1739, exclaimed: 'Precipices, mountains, torrents, wolves, rumblings—Salvator Rosa', and this sentiment neatly suggests how spontaneously the 18th-cent. traveller associated the *Sublime in natural scenery with the landscapes of Rosa. His popularity was at its height in the 1770s and 1780s; writers on the *picturesque frequently invoked his name and his horrific subjects influenced early Romantic painters, especially Barry, *Fuseli, and Mortimer. Rosa's stormy personality fascinated artists, and with the publication of Lady *Morgan's *The Life and Times of Salvator Rosa* (1824), the legends associated with him—that he had lived with bandits, and fought in a popular uprising in Naples—became more important than his pictures. He came to represent the perfect Romantic artist, outlawed by a corrupt society, whose untrammelled genius bore comparison with Shakespeare. The roughness and bravura of Rosa's handling of paint was admired as evidence of a passionate temperament that could not be contained by the conventions of academic art. Rosa's reputation fell with *Ruskin, who, while responding powerfully to the artist's darkness and despair, condemned his artificial rendering of trees and rocks.

Rosa Bud, a character in Dickens's *Edwin Drood*.

Rosalind, in Spenser's *Shepheardes Calender* and *Colin Clouts come home againe*, an unknown lady celebrated by the poet as his love; (2) the heroine of Shakespeare's *As You Like It*, whose chief source was Lodge's *Rosalynde*.

Rosaline, (1) in Shakespeare's *Love's Labour's Lost*, a lady attendant on the princess of France, and loved by *Berowne; (2) in his *Romeo and Juliet*, Capulet's niece, with whom Romeo is in love before he sees *Juliet. She is mentioned, but does not appear in the play. Both Rosalines are, like the lady of the *Sonnets, described as being dark.

Rosalynde, *Euphues Golden Legacie*, a pastoral romance in the style of Lyly's *Euphues*, diversified with sonnets and eclogues, written by *Lodge during his voyage to the Canaries

('everie line was wet with a surge'), published 1590.

The story is borrowed in part from *The Tale of *Gamelyn* and was dramatized by Shakespeare in *As You Like It*. Lodge's Rosader is Shakespeare's Orlando; Saladyne is Oliver; Alinda, Celia; and Rosalind is common to both. Jaques and Touchstone have no equivalents. The ill-treatment of Rosader (Orlando) is more developed by Lodge, and the restoration of the rightful duke to his dukedom is effected by arms instead of persuasion. Lodge's romance, which includes such well known lyrics as 'Love in my bosome like a Bee | Doth sucke his sweete', is also diversified by a variety of rhetorical speeches and descriptions.

ROSAMOND, Fair, Rosamond Clifford (d. ?1176), probably mistress of Henry II in 1174. She was buried in the choir of Godstow Abbey near Oxford, and her remains were removed to the Chapter House there c.1191. A legend transmitted by *Stow following *Higden declares that Henry kept her in a maze-like house in Woodstock where only he could find her, but the queen, *Eleanor of Aquitaine, traced her whereabouts by following a thread and 'so dealt with her that she lived not long after'. The story is told in a ballad by *Deloney included in Percy's *Reliques*; *Daniel published in 1592 'The Complaint of Rosamond', a poem in rhyme-royal; and *Addison wrote an opera, *Rosamond*, in 1707.

Rosciad, The (1761), a satire by Charles *Churchill in heroic couplets, originally 730 lines, but expanded in later editions to 1,090.

It describes the attempt to find a worthy successor to Roscius, the celebrated Roman comic actor who died c.62 BC. It provides satiric sketches of many famous theatrical personalities of the day, both actors and critics (including *Quin, *Foote, and *Colman the elder). It caused a great sensation, and T. *Davies in his *Life of Garrick* wrote that 'the players . . . ran about like so many stricken deer.' But Churchill's criticism is not all negative, and his praise of *Garrick, chosen to succeed Roscius, is high.

ROSCOE, William (1753–1831), lawyer and banker, book-collector, writer, scholar, and botanist, published his early verses in 1777, and from then until the end of his life, a considerable number of works of poetry, biography, jurisprudence, botany, and arguments against the slave-trade. His principal work was his *Life of Lorenzo de' Medici* (1795), which was much commended in England, Italy, and Germany. In 1805 (having now acquired Greek) he published the *Life of Leo the Tenth*, and in 1806 *The Butterfly's Ball and the Grasshopper's Feast*, which became a children's classic. His edition of *Pope appeared in 1824. He did much to stimulate an interest in Italy and Italian literature in England.

ROSCOMMON, earl of, see DILLON, W.

Rose and the Ring, The, a fairy-story written and illustrated by *Thackeray, first published 1855.

The magic rose and ring have the property of making those who have possession of them seem irresistibly attractive, which introduces comic complications into the story of Prince Giglio and Princess Rosalba, who have been ousted from their proper positions as a result of the Fairy Blackstick's wish that they shall suffer 'a little misfortune'. Thackeray makes gentle fun both of fairy-story conventions, and of 'improving' children's books in this 'Fireside Pantomime for Great and Small Children'.

'Rose Aylmer', a short poem by W. S. *Landor, published 1806, on the daughter of Lord Aylmer. She was an early love of Landor's, but on her mother's second marriage she was sent out to her aunt at Calcutta, where she died at the age of twenty.

ROSENBERG, Isaac (1890–1918), was born in Bristol, but moved with his family to Whitechapel in 1897; his parents were émigrés from western Russia, and his father, a scholarly Jew, worked as a pedlar and market-dealer. During his irregular East End schooling Isaac learned to paint, and began to experiment with poetry. He became an apprentice engraver at 14, but in 1911 another Jewish family paid for him to attend the Slade School of Art; in 1912 he published at his own expense a collection of poems, *Night and Day,* and was encouraged by *Bottomley, *Pound, and others. In 1915 he published another volume of verse, *Youth,* which passed largely unregarded. In the same year he defied his family's pacifist views and joined the army, arriving as a private in the trenches in 1916. He was killed in action. His poetry is forceful, rich in its vocabulary, and starkly realistic in its attitudes to war; Rosenberg greatly disliked *Brooke's 'begloried sonnets'. His poor Jewish urban background gives the poems a note not found in the work of his fellow war-poets. His reputation was slow to grow with the public; Bottomley edited a selection of his poems and letters, introduced by *Binyon, in 1922, but it was not until his *Collected Works* appeared in 1937 that his importance became generally accepted. A biography by Jean Liddiard appeared in 1975.

Rosencrantz and Guildenstern, courtiers who serve the king in Shakespeare's *Hamlet;* both of their names were current in Denmark at the time of the play's writing. In *Hamlet* the two men always appear together; their view of the play is interpreted in Stoppard's *Rosencrantz and Guildenstern are Dead.*

Rosencrantz and Guildenstern are Dead, a comedy by T. *Stoppard, performed and pub-lished 1966, which places the peripheral 'attendant lords' from *Hamlet* at the centre of a drama in which they appear as bewildered witnesses and predestined victims. This device is used to serious as well as to comic effect, for underlying the verbal wit and Shakespearian parody there is a pervasive sense of man's solitude and lack of mastery over his own life reminiscent of *Beckett, whom Stoppard greatly admires.

Rose Tavern, in Russell Street, Covent Garden, was a favourite place of resort in the later part of the 17th and early 18th cents. It is frequently referred to in the literature of the period, e.g. by *Pepys (18 May 1668), and by Farquhar (*The Recruiting Officer).

Rose Theatre, on Bankside, Southwark, opened in 1592 and was managed by *Henslowe. Shakespeare acted there.

Rosicrucian, a member of a supposed society or order, 'the brethren of the Rosy Cross', reputedly founded by one Christian Rosenkreuz in 1484, but first mentioned in 1614. Its manifestos were the *Fama Fraternitatis* (1614) and the *Confessio Fraternitatis* (1615), which aroused intense interest on the Continent and in Britain. Its members were said to claim various forms of secret and magic knowledge, such as the transmutation of metals, the prolongation of life, and power over the elements and elemental spirits, and to derive much of their alchemy and mystical preoccupations from *Paracelsus. No Rosicrucian society appears to have actually existed, and the Rosicrucian movement seems to have been rooted in some kind of anti-Jesuit Protestant alliance, with deep religious interests, as well as interests in alchemy, medicine, and the *Cabbala. F. *Yates, in her study *The Rosicrucian Enlightenment* (1972), describes the term as representing 'in the purely historical sense . . . a phase . . . intermediate between the Renaissance and the so-called scientific revolution of the 17th cent.', 'a historical label for a style of thinking', and names as major figures in the English Rosicrucian movement *Dee, *Fludd, and *Ashmole; she also discusses the Rosicrucian connections of F. *Bacon, *Comenius, I. *Newton, *Leibniz, and many others.

Rosinante, or **Rozinante,** the horse of *Don Quixote.

ROSS, Alan, see LONDON MAGAZINE (3).

ROSS, Alexander (1699–1784), a Forfarshire schoolmaster, and an early follower of *Ramsay, published a lengthy pastoral in *Scots entitled *The Fortunate Shepherdess* (1768); several editions are called *Helenore, or the fortunate shepherdess.* But he is best remembered as the author of various spirited songs, including 'Woo'd and Married and a'.

ROSS, Sir James Clark (1800–62), Arctic and Antarctic explorer, accompanied his uncle Sir John *Ross on his first two polar voyages, and in 1831 discovered the north magnetic pole. He was author of *A Voyage of Discovery and Research in the Southern Antarctic Regions during the years 1839–43* (1847). He commanded the first relief expedition in search of *Franklin in 1848–9.

ROSS, Sir John (1777–1856), Arctic explorer, uncle of Sir James Clark *Ross, was author of *A Voyage of Discovery inquiring into the Probability of a North-West Passage* (1819) and a *Narrative of a Second Voyage of Discovery . . . 1829–1833* (1833). He failed in his expedition to find *Franklin in 1850.

ROSS, Martin, see SOMERVILLE AND ROSS.

Ross, The Man of, see KYRLE, J.

ROSSETER, Philip (?1567–1623), court musician, composer, and lutanist, was a friend of T. *Campion, and wrote half the songs in Campion's first *Book of Ayres* (1601). He was appointed a lutanist at the court of James I in 1603.

ROSSETTI, Christina Georgina (1830–94), sister of D. G. and W. M. *Rossetti, was educated at home, shared her brothers' intellectual interests, and contributed to their childhood family journals. Ill-health (possibly strategic when young, but later severe) ended her attempts to work as a governess, and confined her to a quiet life. Her engagement to the painter James Collinson, an original member of the *Pre-Raphaelite Brotherhood, was broken off in 1850 when he rejoined the Roman Catholic church; Christina, like her mother and sister Maria, was a devout High Anglican, much influenced by the Tractarians (see OXFORD MOVE-MENT). She contributed to *The Germ* (1850), where five of her poems appeared under the pseudonym 'Ellen Alleyn'. In 1861 *Macmillan's Magazine* published 'Up-hill' and 'A Birthday', two of her best-known poems. *Goblin market and other poems* appeared in 1862, *The prince's progress and other poems* in 1866, *Sing-Song, a nursery rhyme book* (with illustrations by Arthur Hughes) in 1872, and *A Pageant and other poems* in 1881. *Time Flies: a reading diary* (1885) consists of short passages and prose, one for each day of the year. She also published much prose and poetry in periodicals and anthologies, and many prose devotional works. Her *Poetical Works*, ed. W. M. Rossetti, with a memoir, was published in 1904. Her work ranges from poems of fantasy and verses for the young to ballads, love lyrics, sonnets, and religious poetry. Much of it is pervaded by a sense of melancholy, verging at times on the morbid. The recurrent themes of unhappy, delayed, or frustrated love and of premature resignation ('Grown old be-

fore my time') led her biographer L. M. Packer (1963) to suppose an unsatisfied passion for W. B. *Scott, who was already married when she met him in 1847; G. Battiscombe (*A Divided Life*, 1981) questions this, stressing the close connection in her work of the spiritual and the erotic. Her work has often been compared with that of E. *Brontë, but, while both share a sense of mystical yearning, Rossetti's is more subdued, more hopeless, less fulfilled. Her technical virtuosity was considerable, and her use of short, irregularly rhymed lines is distinctive.

ROSSETTI, Dante Gabriel (1828–82), whose full Christian names were Gabriel Charles Dante (but the form which he give it has become inveterate), the son of Gabriele Rossetti (1783–1854), an Italian patriot who came to England in 1824, was brought up in an atmosphere of keen cultural and political activity which contributed more to his artistic development than his formal education at King's College School, London. He studied painting with *Millais and H. *Hunt, and in 1848, with them and four others, founded the *Pre-Raphaelite Brotherhood. For many years he was known only as a painter, though he began to write poetry early. Several of his poems, including *'The Blessed Damozel' and 'My Sister's Sleep', and a prose piece, 'Hand and Soul', were published in *The Germ* (1850), the year in which he met Elizabeth (Lizzie) Siddal (or Siddall), whose own writing and painting he encouraged and who modelled for him and many of his circle; she appears as the drowned Ophelia in the well known painting by Millais. In 1854 he met *Ruskin, who did much to establish the reputation of the Pre-Raphaelite painters, and in 1856 W. *Morris whom he greatly influenced; he was to paint Morris's wife Jane many times. In 1860 Rossetti and Lizzie married, after a long and at times vexed liaison; she was by this time an invalid, and after a brief recovery of health and spirits she gave birth to a still-born child. She died in 1862, from an overdose of laudanum, which may have been taken deliberately. Rossetti buried with her the manuscript of a number of his poems. Later that year he moved to 16 Cheyne Walk, Chelsea, where *Swinburne and *Meredith were briefly joint tenants; he filled the house with antiques, bric-à-brac, and a curious selection of animals, including a wombat. In 1868 he showed a renewed interest in poetry, possibly inspired by renewed contact with Jane Morris; sixteen sonnets, including the 'Willowwood' sequence, were published in March 1869 in *The Fortnightly Review*. That summer he wrote many more, and also arranged the exhumation of the poems buried with his wife. *Poems* (1870) contained 'Sister Helen', 'Troy Town', 'Eden Bower', *'Jenny', and the first part of his sonnet sequence *'The House of Life'; it was well received, partly because Rossetti took care that his

ROSSINI 849

friends should review it. In 1871 Morris and Rossetti took a joint lease of Kelmscott Manor, where Rossetti continued his intimacy with Jane, with Morris's apparent approval, and continued to paint her; there also he wrote the ballad 'Rose Mary' and further sonnets for the 'House of Life' sequence. In Oct. 1871 appeared R. *Buchanan's notorious attack 'The Fleshly School of Poetry' (under the pseudonym Thomas Maitland) in *The Contemporary Review. This accused Rossetti and his associates of impurity and obscenity; the sonnet 'Nuptial Sleep' was singled out for particular criticism, and was not reprinted in the 1881 edition, though the prolonged and bitter controversy which Buchanan aroused ended with the Pre-Raphaelites on the whole victorious. Rossetti's reply, 'The Stealthy School of Criticism' appeared in *The Athenaeum, Dec. 1872. Rossetti's later years were overshadowed by ill-health and chloral, though he continued to paint and to write and was recognized by a new generation of aesthetes, including *Pater and *Wilde, as a source of inspiration; the admiration was not wholly mutual. Poems and Ballads and Sonnets both appeared in 1881; the first was largely rearrangements of earlier works, and the second completed 'The House of Life' with 47 new sonnets, and also contained other new work, including 'The King's Tragedy' and 'The White Ship', both historical 'ballads'.

Rossetti's poetry is marred for many readers by its vast and cloudy generalities about Life, Love, and Death, though some of his work shows in contrast a Pre-Raphaelite sharpness of detail, and much of it has an undeniable emotional and erotic power. His letters (ed. O. Doughty and J. R. Wahl, 4 vols, 1965–7) reveal another side of his colourful and extravagant personality; they are witty, irreverent, at times coarse, and demonstrate the wide range of his artistic interests. Mention should also be made of his translations from the Italian (The Early Italian Poets together with Dante's Vita Nuova, 1861, known later as Dante and his Circle, 1874), and of *Villon. Many of his poems were written as commentaries on his own and other paintings.

The standard edition of his collected works, edited by W. M. *Rossetti, appeared in 1911. Oswald Doughty's life, A Victorian Romantic, was published in 1960.

ROSSETTI, William Michael (1829–1919), brother of D. G. *Rossetti, educated at King's College School, London, worked as an official of the Inland Revenue, and is remembered as a man of letters and art critic. He was a member of the *Pre-Raphaelite Brotherhood, edited *The Germ, and wrote the sonnet that was printed on its cover. His reviews of art exhibitions for the *Spectator were published as Fine Art: Chiefly Contemporary (1867). He

edited 15 volumes of *Moxon's Popular Poets, and was responsible for important editions of *Blake and *Shelley. He edited *Whitman in 1868, introducing him to a British public, and the two corresponded frequently. He translated *Dante, and was responsible for encouraging James *Thomson ('B.V.'). He also edited many of his family's papers, letters, and diaries, and wrote memoirs of his brother and his sister Christina (above). Ruskin: Rossetti: Preraphaelitism (1899); Preraphaelite Diaries and Letters (1900); Rossetti Papers, 1862–70 (1903); D. G. Rossetti, his family letters, with a memoir (1895); Family Letters of Christina Rossetti (1908). His Some Reminiscences (1906) is a valuable biographical source. His diary for 1870–3 was edited with notes by O. Bornand, 1977.

ROSSINI, Gioacchino (1792–1868), Italian composer and, with *Donizetti and *Bellini, one of the creators of the Italian operatic style of the 19th cent. On the whole Rossini's early success was based on opera buffa, with Il Barbiere di Siviglia (1816) the culminating masterpiece. Nevertheless, Tancredi (1813), an opera seria, had given him one of his most resounding early triumphs and, when, after The Barber, he returned to Naples and devoted himself to serious drama, he began with Otello. Unfortunately the text was adapted for him by a wealthy literary dilettante, Francesco Berio di Salsa, whose treatment has become a locus classicus of operatic trivialization. 'They have been crucifying Othello into an opera', wrote Lord *Byron after seeing it; 'the music is good, but lugubrious; but as for the words, all the real scenes with Iago cut out, and the greatest nonsense inserted; the handkerchief turned into a billet-doux, and the first singer would not black his face, for some exquisite reasons.' Nevertheless Otello is not without its qualities, particularly in the last act, where the librettist keeps closest to Shakespeare and the composer responds instinctively with music of real expressive power; it has been well said that in this act Rossini 'came of age as a musical dramatist'. The opera continued to be played through most of the 19th cent., but it was no match for *Boito and *Verdi's version in 1887 and has subsequently fallen into oblivion.

The only other English author drawn on by Rossini was Sir W. *Scott, whose poem *The Lady of the Lake supplied the libretto of La donna del lago (1819). Two later Scott works Ivanhoé (1826) and Robert Bruce (1846), are both pasticcios, the former with music strung together, with the composer's permission, from half a dozen of his operas, the latter adapted, with the composer's assistance, mostly but not entirely from a French version of La donna del lago, and therefore only very loosely connected with Scott. Also put together from pre-existing music was the Pianto delle muse in morte di Lord Byron which Rossini produced, shortly after the news of Byron's death had reached London, at the second of his London concerts in 1824.

ROSTAND, Edmond (1868–1918), French playwright, author of *Les Romanesques* (1894), *La Princesse lointaine* (1895), *La Samaritaine* (1897), *L'Aiglon* (1900, based on the life of Napoleon's son), and *Chantecler* (1910). The poetic drama *Cyrano de Bergerac* (1897), his most popular and successful work, revives in romantic guise the 17th-cent. soldier and duellist *Cyrano.

Rosy Cross, see ROSICRUCIAN.

Rota, The, a coffee-house academy for political discussion, one of the first of its kind in England, founded in 1659 by James *Harrington. It was attended by a wide variety of people, including *Aubrey (who left an account of it), *Pepys, Cyriack *Skinner, soldiers, peers of the realm, etc; Harrington encouraged free-ranging, balanced debate, but the club's aim was to defend the concept of a commonwealth or republic, to advocate rotation in the offices of government, election by ballot, etc. See H. F. Russell Smith, *Harrington and his Oceana* (1914).

ROTA, Bertram (1903–66), bookseller, entered the book trade in 1918 in the bookshop conducted by his uncles Percy and Arthur Dobell. In 1923, at the age of 19, he began his own business with £100 borrowed from his mother's savings. The firm has continued its tradition of specializing in first editions of literature of the last 100 years.

ROTH, Philip (1933–), novelist, born in New Jersey and brought up in an orthodox Jewish family. His writing career has been combined with various teaching posts in America. His complex relationship with his Jewish background is reflected in most of his works, and his portrayal of contemporary Jewish life has aroused much controversy. His works include *Goodbye, Columbus* (1959, a novella with five short stories), *Letting Go* (1962), and a sequence of novels featuring Nathan Zuckerman, a Jewish novelist who has to learn to contend with success: *My Life as a Man* (1974), *The Ghost Writer* (1979), *Zuckerman Unbound* (1981), and *The Anatomy Lesson* (1983). He remains best known for *Portnoy's Complaint* (1969), a *succès de scandale* which records the intimate confessions of Alexander Portnoy to his psychiatrist.

Rothomagus, in imprints, Rouen.

Rothsay, duke of, eldest son of Robert III of Scotland, figures in Scott's *The Fair Maid of Perth*.

ROUBILIAC, Louis François (1702 or 1705–62), French rococo sculptor, who settled in London *c.*1732. His first triumph was the statue of *Handel* (1738; London, Victoria and Albert Museum) commissioned for Vauxhall Gardens, which introduced a new informality and lively rhythm into English sculpture. Later Roubiliac was successful as a tomb sculptor; the monuments to *General Hargrave* (1757) and to *Lady Elizabeth Nightingale* (1761; both Westminster Abbey) are his most famous works; both are strikingly original and sensationally baroque; J. *Wesley thought they were the finest monuments in the abbey. As a portrait sculptor Roubiliac attracted a very wide circle of patrons, amongst them many poets and writers; his image of *Pope (there are four surviving marble busts dating from 1738, 1740, and 1741, all inscribed *ad vivum*; and one terracotta model) is unflinchingly realistic yet deeply poignant. Roubiliac also executed a series of vivid historical busts of famous scientists, writers, and men of letters for the library of Trinity College, Cambridge. Amongst his few free-standing statues is one of *Shakespeare* (1756; London, British Museum) intended for the Shakespeare Temple that stood in *Garrick's Hampton garden.

Rouge et le Noir, Le, a novel by *Stendhal.

ROUGEMONT, Louis De, assumed name of Swiss-born Louis Grin (1847–1921), an adventurer who decided at the age of 16 to see the world. He began as footman to Fanny *Kemble, touring through Europe and America, and eventually became butler to the governor of Australia. After spending many years there he contributed to *Wide World Magazine* in 1898 sensational articles relating to his extraordinary, mostly bogus, voyages and adventures in search of pearls and gold, where he encountered an octopus with tentacles 75 feet long and rode turtles in the water.

Roundabout Papers, The, a series of discursive essays by *Thackeray, published in the *Cornhill Magazine*, 1860–3.

Round Table, The, in the Arthurian legend, the symbol of the common purpose of Arthur's court and knights. According to *Malory (in Vinaver's Tale 1) it was made for *Uther Pendragon who gave it to King Lodegran (see LEODEGRANCE) of Camelerde (Cornwall). The latter gave it as a wedding gift, with 100 knights, to Arthur when he married Guinevere, his daughter. It would seat 150 knights, and all places round it were equal. The 'Siege Perilous' was reserved for the knight who should achieve the quest of the *Grail. In *Laʒamon's *Brut*, however, the table was made for Arthur by a crafty workman. It is first mentioned by *Wace.

ROUSSEAU, Jean-Jacques (1712–78), was born into a Protestant artisan family at Geneva. His mother having died soon after his birth, Jean-Jacques was cared for in childhood by an aunt, by his father, a watchmaker of unstable temperament, and (after the latter's departure or France) by a maternal uncle. He was apprenticed to an engraver when, at the age of 15, he decided to leave his master and Geneva. Thus began the movement of residence which was to become habitual and which took him to many parts of Switzerland, France, and Italy, and (in 1766–7) to England. During these peregrinations he owed much to the generosity of friends and patrons; otherwise he maintained himself by a succession of clerical, secretarial, and tutorial posts and by teaching and copying music. Rousseau's emotional nature, his often tempestuous personal relations, extreme sensitivity, and penchant for controversy fill his career with striking and dramatic episodes; while his critical and enquiring intellect, his life-long interest in music and excursions into opera and drama, a voluminous correspondence, and important and influential contributions to social and political philosophy, the novel, autobiography, moral theology, and educational theory mark him out as one of the dominant writers and thinkers of the age.

Rousseau was 38 years old when his essay on a subject proposed by the Academy of Dijon, *Discours sur les sciences et les arts* (1750) was awarded first prize and published. In the *Discours*, the first of many works in which the natural man is preferred to his civilized counterpart, Rousseau argued that the development and spread of knowledge and culture, far from improving human behaviour, had corrupted it by promoting inequality, idleness, and luxury. The *Discours sur l'origine de l'inégalité* (1755) contrasts the innocence and contentment of primitive man in a 'state of nature', his mode of existence determined by none but genuine needs, with the dissatisfaction and perpetual agitation of modern social man, the majority of whom are condemned to the legally sanctioned servitude necessary to preserve the institution of private property. The suggestion by d'Alembert that a theatre should be established at Geneva prompted the *Lettre sur les spectacles* (1758), in which the passive nature of playgoing, the preoccupation of modern plays with love, and the consequent unnatural bringing forward of women are seen as dangerous symptoms of the ills of society.

A return to primitive innocence being impossible, these ills were only to be remedied, Rousseau held, by reducing the gap separating modern man from his natural archetype and by modifying existing institutions in the interest of equality and happiness. *Émile* (1762) lays down the principles for a new scheme of education in which the child is to be allowed full scope for individual development in natural surroundings, shielded from the harmful influences of civilization, in order to form an independent judgement and a stable character. The 'Profession de foi du vicaire savoyard', contained in the 4th book of *Émile*, sets against institutional

Christianity a form of Deism grounded in religious sentiment and guided by the divine instinct of conscience. The year 1762 also saw the publication of *Du contrat social*, his theory of politics, in which he advocated universal justice through equality before the law, a more equitable distribution of wealth, and defined government as fundamentally a matter of contract providing for the exercise of power in accordance with the 'general will' and for the common good, by consent of the citizens as a whole, in whom sovereignty ultimately resides.

In the novel *Julie, ou la Nouvelle Héloïse* (1761), Rousseau's greatest popular success, a critical account of contemporary manners and ideas is interwoven with the story of the passionate love of the tutor St Preux and his pupil Julie, their separation, Julie's marriage to the Baron Wolmar and the dutiful, virtuous life shared by all three on the Baron's country estate.

The posthumously published autobiographical works *Les Confessions* (1781–8) and *Les Rêveries du promeneur solitaire* (1782) were written towards the end of Rousseau's life as exercises in self-justification and self-analysis. As expressions of the complex individuality of a personality and a sensibility, unexampled in their time for candour, detail, and subtlety, they remain landmarks of the literature of personal revelation and reminiscence.

Roussillon, countess of, *Bertram's mother and *Helena's guardian in Shakespeare's *All's Well that Ends Well*. Roussillon was a province in the south-west of France near Spain.

ROUTH, Martin Joseph (1755–1854), president of Magdalen College, Oxford, for 63 years, edited the *Gorgias* and *Eutheydemus* of *Plato, and *Reliquiae Sacrae* (1814–43), a collection of writings of ecclesiastical authors of the 2nd and 3rd cents. Routh was a man of immense learning, and a strong, old-fashioned 'High Churchman'. He was also, perhaps, the last man in England who always wore a wig. His long life (he died in his 100th year) and literary experience lend weight to his famous utterance: 'I think, Sir, you will find it a very good practice *always to verify your references.*' A life of Routh by R. D. Middleton was published in 1938.

Rover, The, see BEHN, A.

ROWE, Nicholas (1674–1718), was educated at Westminster School and became a barrister of the Middle Temple; but abandoned the legal profession for that of a playwright, and made the acquaintance of *Pope and *Addison. He produced at Lincoln's Inn Fields his tragedies *The Ambitious Stepmother* (1700), *Tamerlane* (1701), and *The Fair Penitent* (1703). His *Ulysses* was staged in 1705, *The Royal Convert* in 1707, *Jane Shore* in 1714, and *Lady Jane Grey* in 1715. He also produced one unsuccessful comedy, *The Biter* (1704). He became poet laureate in 1715, and was buried in Westminster Abbey. His poetical works include a famous translation of *Lucan (1718), 'one of the greatest productions of English poetry', according to Dr *Johnson. Rowe also did useful work as editor of Shakespeare's plays, dividing them into acts and scenes, supplying stage directions, and generally making the text more intelligible. As a writer he is best remembered for his 'She-Tragedies' (his own phrase), which provided Mrs *Siddons, as Calista and Jane Shore, with two of her most famous roles: their tone is moral, their stress is on the suffering and penitence of victimized women, and their intention is to arouse 'pity; a sort of regret proceeding from good-nature'. Rowe saw himself as the heir of *Otway, who had also been renowned for tenderness and pathos. See *Three plays*, ed. J. R. Sutherland (1929), with a life and bibliography.

Rowena (1) the legendary daughter of Hengist, who married the British chief *Vortigern; (2) a character in Scott's *Ivanhoe*.

Rowland, Childe, see CHILDE ROLAND.

ROWLANDS, Samuel (?1570–?1630), a writer of satirical tracts, epigrams, jests, etc., mainly in verse. His works include a satire on the manners of Londoners, *The Letting of Humors Blood in the Head-Vaine* (1600); '*Tis Merrie when Gossips Meete* (1602), a vivid and dramatic character sketch of a widow, a wife, and a maid who meet in a tavern and converse; *Greene's Ghost* (1602), on the subject of 'coney-catchers' (see GREENE, R.); *Democritus, or Doctor Merryman his Medicines against Melancholy Humors* (1607); and *The Melancholie Knight* (1615). His *Complete Works*, including *Martin Mark-all* (1610), now considered spurious, were edited with an essay by *Gosse in 1880.

ROWLANDSON, Thomas (1756–1827), caricaturist and painter of humorous low life scenes. Among his illustrations were those for the 'Dr Syntax' series of *Combe, which like many of his other works, were published by *Ackermann.

ROWLEY, Samuel (d. ?1624), an actor in the Admiral's Company and a playwright employed by *Henslowe; he is believed to be responsible for the comic additions to Marlowe's *Dr Faustus*. His only extant play is a chronicle drama about Henry VIII, *When you see me, You know me*, acted 1603.

ROWLEY, Thomas, a fictitious 15th-cent. poet invented by *Chatterton.

ROWLEY, William (?1585–1626), dramatist and actor. Nothing is known about his birth and his early life. His first compositions were episodic adventure-plays for Queen Anne's Men, *The Travels of the Three English Brothers*

(1607), written with *Day and Wilkins, *Fortune by Land and Sea* (1607–9, printed 1655), with *Heywood, and, unassisted, *A Shoemaker, a Gentleman* (1607–9, printed 1638). Collaborations, in which he usually contributed comic subplot, account for nearly all of his surviving dramatic work. His most notable partnership was with *Middleton with whom he wrote *Wit at Several Weapons* (1613, printed 1647), *A Fair Quarrel* (1615–16, printed 1617), *The Old Law* (c.1618, printed 1656), *The World Tossed at Tennis* (1619–20, printed 1620), and *The Changeling* (1622, printed 1653). He also assisted in *The Witch of Edmonton* (1621, printed 1658), with *Dekker and *Ford; *The Maid in the Mill* (1623, printed 1647), with *Fletcher; *A Cure for a Cuckold* (1624–5, printed 1661), with *Webster; and *A New Wonder, a Woman Never Vexed* (1624–6, printed 1632), with an unknown collaborator. His non-dramatic work includes a satirical pamphlet, *A Search for Money* (1609), and elegies on Prince Henry and a fellow actor, Hugh Attwell. From 1609 he was a member of the Duke of York's (later Prince Charles's) Men, and by 1616 had become leader of the company. His speciality as an actor was the role of a fat clown, and he took the part of Jacques in his own *All's Lost by Lust* (c.1619). In 1625 he was cited in a legal action over *Keep the Widow Waking*, a sensational dramatization, now lost, of two contemporary scandals which he had written with Dekker, Ford, and Webster. He died before he could testify, and was buried at St James's, Clerkenwell.

Rowley Poems, see CHATTERTON, T.

ROWSE, A(lfred) L(eslie) (1903–), poet, biographer, and Tudor historian, born at St Austell, Cornwall, and educated at St Austell Grammar School and Christ Church, Oxford. Cornwall forms the setting for many of his poems and works of history and autobiography, including *A Cornish Childhood* (1942). He has published several books on Shakespeare (1963, 1973, and 1977), and argued that Emilia *Lanier was the 'dark lady' of Shakespeare's *Sonnets.

Roxana, a character in N. Lee's *The Rival Queens*.

Roxana, or the Fortunate Mistress, a romance by *Defoe, published 1724.
This purports to be the autobiography of Mlle Beleau, the beautiful daughter of French Protestant refugees, brought up in England and married to a London brewer, who, having squandered his property, deserts her and her five children. She enters upon a career of prosperous wickedness, passing from one protector to another in England, France, and Holland, amassing much wealth, and receiving the name Roxana

by accident, in consequence of a dance that she performs. She is accompanied in her adventures by a faithful maid, Amy, a very human figure. She finally marries a Dutch merchant and lives as a person of consequence in Holland, until he discovers her deceit. He shortly afterwards dies, leaving her only a small sum of money. She is imprisoned for debt, and dies in a state of penitence.

ROXBURGHE, John Ker, 3rd duke of (1740–1804), an ardent bibliophile, who secured an unrivalled collection of books from *Caxton's press. His splendid library, housed in St James's Square, was dispersed in 1812. Valdarfer's edition of *Boccaccio (1471), for which the 2nd duke had paid 100 guineas, was then sold to the marquis of Blandford for £2,260. To celebrate this event the chief bibliophiles of the day dined together at St Alban's Tavern, St Alban's Street, under the presidency of Lord Spencer, and there inaugurated the Roxburghe Club, the first of the 'book-clubs', consisting of 25 members, with T. F. *Dibdin as its first secretary. The Club, at first rather convivial in character, began its valuable literary work with the printing of the metrical romance of *Havelok the Dane (1828). Each member is expected once in his career to present (and pay for a limited edition of) a volume of some rarity. See N. Barker, The Publications of the Roxburghe Club 1814–1962 (1964).

Roxburghe Club, see ROXBURGHE, J. K.

Royal Academy of Arts was founded under the patronage of George III in 1768, for the annual exhibition of works of contemporary artists and for the establishment of a school of art. It was first housed in Pall Mall, moved in 1780 to Somerset House, then to the National Gallery, and finally to Burlington House, Piccadilly, in 1869. Sir Joshua *Reynolds was its first president. Since 1870 the Academy has also held important loan exhibitions.

Royal Court Theatre, see ENGLISH STAGE COMPANY.

Royal Historical Society was founded in 1868 and took the title 'Royal' in 1887. Its aim is to promote the study of history by publishing documentary material and, from time to time, bibliographical and reference works; its papers are published annually as Transactions. In 1897 the *Camden Society was amalgamated with the Royal Historical Society, which now publishes the Camden Series.

Royal Literary Fund, a benevolent society to aid authors and their dependants in distress, founded in 1790 as the Literary Fund Society at the instigation of the Revd David Williams, a Dissenting minister. In 1818 it was granted a Royal Charter, and was permitted to add 'Royal'

to its title in 1845. Beneficiaries have included *Coleridge, *Peacock, *Hogg, *Clare, D. H. *Lawrence, E. *Nesbit, *Joyce, and Dylan *Thomas. It has also made grants to literary refugees, including *Chateaubriand. The Fund receives no government subsidy and depends on gifts, subscriptions, and legacies—including authors' royalties.

Royal Society, The, more correctly The Royal Society of London for the Improving of Natural Knowledge, obtained its Royal charters in 1662 and 1663. The prehistory of the Society extends back to a variety of scientific meetings held in London and Oxford from 1645 onwards. Traditionally, the originator of these meetings is identified as Theodore Haak, known also as the first to translate Milton into German. F. *Bacon provided the major philosophical inspiration for the Society; Solomon's House in *New Atlantis has been taken as its model. No scientific society has made a more conspicuous début—its founders and early members included *Boyle, Hooke, *Petty, *Ray, Wilkins, and *Wren. Among more literary figures, *Ashmole, *Aubrey, *Cowley, *Dryden, *Evelyn, and *Waller were members. The Society featured prominently in Dryden's *Annus Mirabilis. Its Philosophical Transactions (1665–), first edited by Henry Oldenburg, is the first permanent scientific journal. Individual members of the Royal Society made an outstanding scientific contribution, but the Society itself was not entirely successful. It was attacked and ridiculed by a bizarre coalition of interests, including Henry Stubbe, S. *Butler, and *Shadwell; the latter's The Virtuoso threatened the stature of the latitudinarian 'Christian Virtuosi' of the Society. The Society was also drawn into the ancients versus moderns controversy (see BATTLE OF THE BOOKS). In replies to attacks by the ancients, the modernism of the Society was defended by J. *Glanvill and *Sprat. The latter's History of the Royal Society (1667) is known for its defence of the 'close, naked, natural way' of style. The Society risked degenerating into a squabbling London club. Its decline was temporarily arrested under I. *Newton. Its fortunes revived in the later 19th cent., but in the modern period the Royal Society has played a less active part in the nation's cultural life.

Royal Society of Edinburgh, The, was established in 1783 for 'the cultivation of every branch of science, erudition, and taste'. The membership was originally divided into the Physical Class and a larger Literary Class, the latter including A. *Alison, *Beattie, H. *Blair, *Burke (elected 1784), A. *Carlyle, A. *Ferguson, A. *Gerard, J. *Home, *Jamieson (1803), H. *Mackenzie, T. *Reid, W. *Robertson (who was instrumental in the society's creation), and Sir W. *Scott (elected 1800, president 1820–32). D. *Stewart was a member of the Physical Class. *Tennyson (1864) and T. *Carlyle (1866) had honorary membership. Scientific proceedings and publications have been predominant in the society's work since the early 19th cent., but the Literary Class was revived in 1976. The society is the successor of the Philosophical Society of Edinburgh (1737), of which *Hume was once joint secretary, and its library is the principal repository for Hume's correspondence and surviving manuscripts.

Royal Society of Literature, The, was founded in 1823 at the suggestion of Thomas Burgess, bishop of St David's, and under the patronage of George IV, who assigned the sum of 1,100 guineas to be applied in pensions of 100 guineas to each of ten Royal Associates, and in a premium of 100 guineas for a prize dissertation. The Associates were elected by the council of the Society (*Malthus and S. T. *Coleridge were among the first ten). The Society published papers read to it under the title *Transactions*; publication was suspended during the First World War and was resumed in 1921 as a new series under the title *Essays by Divers Hands*. The Society has Members, Fellows, and since 1961, Companions; recipients of the title of Companion have included *Betjeman, *Koestler, E. M. *Forster, Angus *Wilson, and many others.

Royns, see RYENCE.

Rubáiyát of Omar Khayyám, The, see OMAR KHAYYÁM.

RUBENS, Peter Paul (1577–1640), Flemish painter, the chief northern exponent of the baroque. Studying first under Flemish masters, he went to Italy in 1600 and became court painter to the duke of Mantua. He returned to Antwerp in 1608, became court painter to the Spanish ruler of Flanders, and set up a large workshop with numerous assistants, from which poured religious, decorative, historical, and mythological paintings, as well as portraits and landscapes. His control and organization of the work ensured its quality. In addition, he served on various diplomatic missions, visiting Spain in 1628 and England in 1629, where he was knighted and commissioned to paint the ceiling of the Banqueting House, Whitehall, a building designed by I. *Jones. During his visit to England Rubens stayed with his friend the Zeeland-born painter, courtier, and architect Sir Balthazar Gerbier (?1591–1667), whose children appear in his magnificent *Allegory of Peace and War* (1629, National Gallery, London).

Rubens was an enormously prolific and vital painter, robust and rich. His style was based on the great Italian masters, but in later life he painted for his own pleasure landscapes with a new feeling for the country. His first wife, Isa-

bella Brant, who died in 1626, and his second wife, Hélène Fourment, whom he married in 1630 when she was sixteen, also inspired some fine personal portraits. One of the few English writers to appreciate his full stature as an artist was G. *Eliot, who wrote from Munich (1858, in a letter), 'His are such real, breathing men and women—men and women moved by passions, not mincing and grimacing and posing in mere apery of passion! What a grand, glowing, forceful thing life looks in his pictures—'.

RUCK, Berta, see under ONIONS, G. O.

RUDKIN, David (1936–   ), playwright, born in London, the son of a Nonconformist minister, and educated at King Edward School, Birmingham, and Oxford; he then became a schoolteacher. He made his name with a powerful drama set in a rural district of the Black Country, *Afore Night Come* (1962, published in Penguin's *New English Dramatists 7*, 1963); subsequent works include *Ashes* (1974, pub. 1977), and *Penda's Fen* (TV 1974, pub. 1975).

'Rugby Chapel', a poem by M. *Arnold.

Rugby School, founded by Laurence Sheriff in 1567. T. *Arnold was its headmaster from 1828 to 1842. A vivid picture of school life at Rugby in his time is given in *Tom Brown's Schooldays* by Thomas *Hughes. The game of Rugby football originated there: a tablet in the school commemorates William Webb Ellis, 'who, with a fine disregard of the rules of football as played in his time, first took the ball in his arms and ran with it' in 1823.

Ruggiero, see ROGERO.

RUGGLE, George, see IGNORAMUS.

'Ruin, The', a 45-line poem in Old English in the *Exeter Book*, one of the group known as 'elegies'. The poem describes the result of the devastation of a city, and it is thought likely that the reference is to the Roman city of Bath which was a ruin in Anglo-Saxon times. There are two references to hot baths in the poem, the second of them extensive. Ed. R. F. Leslie, *Three Old English Elegies* (1961).

'Ruined Cottage, The', or 'The Story of Margaret', a poem by *Wordsworth, written in 1797, and subsequently embodied in Bk I of *The Excursion*.

It is a harrowing tale of misfortune befalling a cottager and his wife. The husband leaves his home and joins a troop of soldiers going to a distant land. The wife stays on, pining for his return in increasing wretchedness, until she dies and the cottage falls into ruin.

'Ruines of Time, The', a poem by *Spenser, included in the *Complaints* published in 1591. It is an allegorical elegy on the death of Sir P. *Sidney, which had also been the occasion of his earlier elegy '*Astrophel'. The poet passes to a lament on the decline of patronage and neglect of literature, with allusion to his own case. The poem is dedicated to the countess of *Pembroke, Sidney's sister.

Rule a Wife and Have a Wife, a comedy by J. *Fletcher, performed 1624.

Margarita, a rich heiress of Seville, plans to marry, but only in order to provide a cover for her own pleasures; she must therefore choose a husband 'of easy faith', who will allow her to dominate and deceive him, and serve as 'a shadow, an umbrella, | To keep the scorching world's opinion' from her good name. Altea, her companion, plots to win her for her brother Leon; he assumes the character of a fool, but, once married, abandons docility, asserts his authority, and finally wins her affection.

'Rule, Britannia'; for the words see THOMSON, J. The air was composed by *Arne for Thomson and *Mallet's masque *Alfred*.

Rune, a letter or character of the earliest surviving Germanic script, most extensively used in inscriptions on wood or stone by the Scandinavians and Anglo-Saxons. The earliest runic alphabet seems to date from about the 3rd cent. AD, and is formed by modifying the letters of the Greek and Roman alphabets. Magical and mysterious powers were associated with runes from the Anglo-Saxon period, perhaps because of their employment in riddles, as in the *Rune Poem*, a 94-line piece illustrating the runes of the Anglo-Saxon Runic alphabet, the *Futhorc (see ASPR, VI, pp. 28–30 for edition). The other important occurrence of runes in Old English literature is in the runic signature to the poems of *Cynewulf. See R. W. V. Elliott, *Runes, an Introduction* (1959).

Rupert of Hentzau, a novel by Anthony Hope (*Hawkins), a sequel to *The Prisoner of Zenda*.

Rural Rides, a collection of essays by W. *Cobbett, published 1830, which had originally appeared in the *Political Register*. A committee in 1821 had proposed certain remedies for the agricultural distress that followed the war. Cobbett disapproved of these and 'made up his mind to see for himself, and to enforce, by actual observation of rural conditions, the statements he had made in answer to the arguments of the landlords before the Agricultural Committee'. The result was this series of lively, opinionated accounts of his travels on horseback between Sept. 1822 and Oct. 1826, largely in the south and east of England. (Later journeys, in the midlands and the north, were added in subsequent editions.) He rails against tax-collectors, 'tax-eaters', landlords, gamekeepers, stock-jobbers, and excisemen, and against the monstrous swelling of the 'Great Wen' of London; but the whole work is also informed with

his own knowledge of and love of the land in all its minutely observed variety, and he breaks occasionally into rapturous praise for a land-scape, a hedgerow, a hanging wood, or, less characteristically, the ruins of Malmesbury Abbey. The standard edition is by G. D. H. and M. *Cole (3 vols, 1930).

Ruritania, an imaginary kingdom in central Europe, the scene of *The Prisoner of Zenda* by Anthony Hope (*Hawkins). The name connotes more generally a world of make-believe romance, chivalry, and intrigue.

RUSHDIE, Salman, see MAGIC REALISM.

RUSKIN, John (1819–1900), the only child of John James and Margaret Ruskin, grew up in Surrey. His father paid off family debts and built up the wine business of which he was a founding partner; he was able to pass on to his son a large fortune, of which Ruskin gave much away. To his parents Ruskin also owed a reliance on the Bible, a strong affection for romantic literature, stern political views, and an early attraction to contemporary landscape painting. Much of his schooling was given at home, and from 1836 to 1842 he was at Christ Church, Oxford, where he won the Newdigate Prize but did not find the curriculum profitable. Travel was a more important part of his education. The family took regular tours through the picturesque areas of Britain, and, from 1833, on the Continent. These helped fix Ruskin's lifelong preference for French cathedral towns, the Alps, and certain cities of northern Italy, and gave scope to what he spoke of as his main passion, the study of the facts of nature. Among his earliest publications were essays in Loudon's *Magazine of Natural History* (1834 and 1836). Others were 'The Poetry of Architecture' (*Architectural Magazine*, 1837–8) and numerous Byronesque poems and stories written for Christmas annuals. He contributed regularly from 1835 to 1846, mainly to *Friendship's Offering*, whose editor, W. H. Harrison, acted as his personal literary adviser. He also devoted time to drawing; he admired the work of Copley Fielding, J. D. Harding, Clarkson Stanfield, James Holland, David Roberts, Samuel Prout, and, above all, *Turner. He took lessons from two of these artists (Fielding and Harding), made friends of several, and bought the work of all. With the first of the five volumes of *Modern Painters* (1834) he became their public champion.

Seven months' work in Italy in preparation for *Modern Painters II* (1846) confirmed Ruskin in his 'function as interpreter'. They also compelled him to write of the medieval buildings of Europe before they should be destroyed by neglect, restoration, industrialization, and revolutions. He postponed further enquiry into natural beauty and its representation: *Modern Painters III* and *IV* did not appear until 1856.

The interval produced *The Seven Lamps of Architecture* (1849) and *The Stones of Venice* (1851–3), both written during the period of his marriage to Euphemia Chalmers Gray, for whom the lastingly popular *The King of the Golden River* had been a gift (written 1841, published 1851). In 1854, after seven years of marriage, she divorced him on grounds of impotence, and soon afterwards married *Millais. Ruskin had defended Millais and the *Pre-Raphaelites in letters to *The Times* and the pamphlet *Pre-Raphaelitism* (1851). He continued to notice their work in *Notes on the Royal Academy* (1855–9 and 1875), guides intended to influence public taste and to intervene in the production and distribution of a national art.

Ruskin wrote for the Arundel Society (*Giotto and his Works in Padua*, 1853–4, 1860), taught at the Working Men's College in Red Lion Square, produced drawing manuals, helped with plans for the Oxford Museum of Natural History building, arranged for the National Gallery the drawings of the Turner bequest, tried to guide the work of individual artists (D. G. *Rossetti, J. Inchbold, J. W. Brett), gave evidence before parliamentary committees, and lectured extensively throughout the country. Some of these addresses appeared in *Lectures on Architecture and Painting* (1854) and *The Two Paths* (1859). But Ruskin's was a critical, not a collaborative intervention, and his judgements often offended. Speaking in Manchester on *The Political Economy of Art* (1857), Ruskin challenged economic laws affecting matters in which he had a standing. In the final volume of *Modern Painters* (1860) he denounced greed as the deadly principle guiding English life. In attacking the 'pseudo-science' of J. S. *Mill and *Ricardo in *Unto this Last* (1860) and *Essays on Political Economy* (1862–3; later *Munera Pulveris*, 1872), Ruskin entered new territory and declared open warfare against the spirit and science of his times.

This fight, against competition and self-interest, for the recovery of heroic, feudal, and Christian social ideals was to occupy Ruskin for the rest of his life. It is expressed in considerations of engraving or Greek myth (*The Cestus of Aglaia*, 1865–6; *The Queen of the Air*, 1869), geology lectures for children (*The Ethics of the Dust*, 1866), as essays on the respective duties of men and women (*Sesame and Lilies*, 1865, 1871), lectures on war, work, and trade (*The Crown of Wild Olives*, 1866, 1873), or letters to a workman (*Time and Tide, by Weare and Tyne*, 1867). The letter was a favourite mode with Ruskin. In *Fors Clavigera* (1871–8) he found a serial form well suited to his public teaching and to the diversity of his interests, which also expressed themselves during the 1870s and 1880s in a multitude of writings on natural history, travel, painting, etc., and in practical projects, many associated with the

Guild of St George, a Utopian society founded by Ruskin under his own mastership in 1871.

In 1870 Ruskin was elected first Slade professor of art at Oxford. He started a drawing school, arranged art collections of his own gift, and drew crowds to his eleven courses of lectures. Seven volumes of them were published shortly after delivery: *Lectures on Art* (1870), *Aratra Pentelici*, *The Relation between Michael Angelo and Tintoret*, *The Eagle's Nest* (all 1872), *Love's Meinie* (1873, 1881), and *Ariadne Fiorentina* (1873–6). But, despite caution, Ruskin did not keep his 'own peculiar opinions' out of his lectures. Senior members of the University were alarmed, Ruskin offended: he resigned in 1878. Although Ruskin returned to Oxford in 1883 and gave two more courses of lectures, some of his statements were even more startling than before, and he resigned once more in 1885.

The isolation of his later years was barely mitigated by the loyalty of his disciples, who included J. W. Bunney and George Allen, both students of the Working Men's College, and W. G. Collingwood, who acted as Ruskin's secretary at Brantwood, the home in the Lake District which was his home after 1870. Older friends, such as Sir Henry Acland and *Carlyle, remained doubtful about the schemes, the vehemence and the frequent obscurity of his later pronouncements. They were also disturbed by Ruskin's private dreams of Rose La Touche. In middle and old age he made many young girls the objects of his affection. Rose, an Anglo-Irish girl, was 11 when Ruskin came across her in 1858, 18 when he proposed in 1866. But she could not share her Evangelical religious views, her parents were also opposed, and she died, mad, in 1875. Four years later Ruskin himself went through the first of a series of delirious illnesses. He often wrote for her and, indirectly, of her, in later life, and in *Praeterita*, the autobiography on which he worked sporadically between 1885 and 1889, he would have spoken of her directly; but he did not complete it. After 1889 Ruskin wrote nothing and spoke rarely, but was cared for by his cousin, John Severn, at his house on Coniston Water.

Russell, Lady, a character in J. Austen's *Persuasion*.

RUSSELL, Bertrand Arthur William, 3rd Earl Russell (1872–1970), educated privately and at Trinity College, Cambridge, of which he became a fellow. He wrote voluminously on philosophy, logic, education, economics, and politics, and throughout his life was the champion of advanced political and social causes. While much of his writing was relatively practical and ephemeral in intent, and successfully aimed at a wide audience, he also contributed work of lasting importance in some of the most technical fields of philosophy and logic. He was the inventor of the Theory of Descriptions. *The Principles of Mathematics* (1903) and *Principia Mathematica* (the latter in collaboration with A. N. *Whitehead, 1910) quickly became classics of mathematical logic. Other important philosophical works include *The Analysis of Mind* (1921), *An Inquiry into Meaning and Truth* (1940), and *Human Knowledge, its Scope and Limits* (1948). Russell was awarded the *Nobel Prize for literature in 1950. For an account of his relationships with Ottoline *Morrell, D. H. *Lawrence, G. *Murray, G. E. *Moore, *Wittgenstein, and many other figures in the literary and intellectual world, see a life by R. W. Clark (1975).

RUSSELL, George William (Æ) (1867–1935), born in Ireland, became an art student in Dublin, and in 1894 published *Homeward*, his first volume of mystical verses, with the encouragement of *Yeats. His poetic drama *Deirdre* was performed in 1902 at the Irish National Theatre (later the *Abbey), which he helped to found. From 1905 to 1923 he edited *The Irish Homestead*, a journal which encouraged interest in Irish crafts, arts, writing, agriculture, and home economics, and achieved large sales in Ireland and the US; meanwhile he continued to publish poetry, including *The Divine Vision* (1904), *Gods of War* (1915), *The Interpreters* (1922), and *Midsummer Eve* (1928). From 1923 until 1930 he edited *The Irish Statesman*, a literary and political journal supporting the Free State. *The Avatars*, a fantasy of the future, aroused much interest in 1933. In 1934 he published an ambitious poem of Celtic mythology, *The House of the Titans*, and in 1935 his *Selected Poems*. He published many political essays, and did much to support young Irish writers, such as *Colum and *Stephens. His pseudonym 'Æ' was a contraction of the word 'æon', which he had once used as a signature. See H. Summerfield, *That Myriad-Minded Man* (1975).

RUSSELL, Lord John, 1st Earl Russell (1792–1878), educated at Westminster and Edinburgh University. He entered Parliament as member for Tavistock in 1813 and strenuously supported parliamentary reform; he proposed the *Reform Bill of 1832. In 1845 he announced his support for the repeal of the Corn Laws, which led to Peel's resignation and Russell's elevation to prime minister (1846–52); he was prime minister again under Palmerston (1865–6); and foreign secretary in 1852–3 under Aberdeen and in 1859–65 under Palmerston, in which capacity he did much for Italian unity. He published a *Life of William Lord Russell* (1819), Memoirs of C. J. *Fox and of T. *Moore, and other works. He was often caricatured in *Punch*.

RUSSELL, Countess Mary Annette, see VON ARNIM, E.

Ruth, a novel by Mrs *Gaskell, published 1853.

Ruth Hilton, a 15-year-old orphan apprenticed to a dressmaker, is seduced and then deserted by the wealthy young Henry Bellingham. She is rescued from suicide by Thurston Benson, a Dissenting minister, who with the connivance of his sister and of his outspoken old servant Sally takes her into his own house under an assumed name as a widow. She bears Bellingham's son, and is redeemed by her love for her child and by the guidance of Benson. Later she is employed as a governess in the family of the tyrannical and pharisaical Mr Bradshaw, where she is discovered by Bellingham, whose offer of marriage she rejects. Bradshaw, learning the truth about her past, brutally dismisses her and quarrels with Benson. Ruth regains esteem by becoming a heroic hospital nurse during a cholera epidemic, and dies after nursing Bellingham to recovery. Mrs Gaskell's purpose in this novel was to arouse more sympathy for 'fallen women' who had been unprotected victims of seduction, but she shocked many contemporary readers.

RUTHERFORD, Mark, see WHITE, W. H.

Ruthwell Cross, a stone monument in the parish church at Ruthwell, Dumfriesshire, dating perhaps from the 8th cent., on which are inscribed in *runes some alliterating phrases closely corresponding to parts of the Old English poem *The Dream of the Rood*. It was thrown down by the Presbyterians in 1642 and the inscriptions partly effaced. See *The Dream of the Rood*, ed. B. Dickins and A. S. C. Ross (1934), pp. 1–13; J. L. Dinwiddie, *The Ruthwell Cross and its Story* (1927).

Ryecroft, *The Private Papers of Henry*, see GISSING, G.

Ryence (Rion, Rience or **Royns),** King, a British or Celtic king (usually of Ireland but of North Wales in *Malory) who sent an arrogant message to Arthur demanding his beard to make up a set of twelve taken from his vanquished enemies. He was overcome and taken prisoner by *Balyn and *Balan who delivered him to Arthur's court (in the first of Vinaver's eight Works of Malory). He is usually represented as a pagan giant, the same as the 'Ritho' mentioned by *Geoffrey of Monmouth and *Wace as a challenger of *Arthur.

RYLE, Gilbert (1900–76), educated at Brighton College and The Queen's College, Oxford; Waynflete professor of metaphysical philosophy in the University of Oxford (1945–68). The author of numerous articles on a wide variety of philosophical topics, he is best known for his attack on the traditional metaphysical dualism of mind and body, which he calls the 'dogma of the ghost in the machine'. His best-known book is *The Concept of Mind* (1949). A general account of his view of philosophical problems is contained in *Dilemmas* (1954).

RYMER, Thomas (1641–1713), educated at Sidney Sussex College, Cambridge, is chiefly remembered for his valuable collection of historical records, *Foedera* (1704–35). He wrote a play in rhymed verse, *Edgar, or the English Monarch* (1678, unperformed), but is better known as a critic of considerable learning but dogmatic views, who supported the ancients in the battle between them and the moderns (see BATTLE OF THE BOOKS) and upheld French *neoclassical principles. *The Tragedies of the Last Age Considered* (1678) was a critical attack on Elizabethan drama, continued in his *A Short View of Tragedy* (1692) which contains his famous condemnation of *Othello* as 'a bloody farce'.

RYSBRACK, Michael (1694–1770), Flemish sculptor, trained in Antwerp, who settled in England; the classicism of his style (albeit attractively modified by a baroque vitality) made him popular with the virtuosi in the circle of Lord Burlington. The moral gravity of Rysbrack's Roman reliefs at Houghton and Clandon Park satisfied the taste of an era formed by the writings of *Shaftesbury, and his bust of Daniel Finch, earl of Nottingham (1723), with its short hair and classical drapery, introduced the fashion for the portrait bust into English sculpture. *Pope (of whom he made a noble and idealized bust, 1730) admired him, and collaborated with him on some of his many monuments in Westminster Abbey, where his most famous work is the monument to Sir I. *Newton; his contributions to *Poets' Corner include memorials to *Jonson (c.1737), *Gay (1736), *Prior, and N. *Rowe. The national pride that inspired Poets' Corner found its most striking expression in the cult of British Worthies; William Kent's Temple of British Worthies (1733) at Stowe is decorated with many busts by Rysbrack, including Shakespeare, F. *Bacon, *Milton, *Locke, and Newton.

S

SABA, Umberto (1883–1957), Italian poet. Born Umberto Poli in Trieste of a Jewish mother, he adopted the name Saba (Heb.: bread) from his nurse, his father having deserted him before his birth. He draws on different strands of Italian literary tradition, *Petrarch, *Pascoli, *D'Annunzio, and from Freudian ideas; but on the surface he remains a simple poet of nature and domestic affections. His main poems are in his *Canzoniere*, of which there are three different collections (1921, 1945, 1948). He has been translated by R. *Lowell.

Sabrina, a poetic name for the river Severn (see under ESTRILDIS). In Milton's *Comus, Sabrina is the nymph of the Severn.

Miss Sabrina is the new schoolmistress in Galt's *Annals of the Parish*. 'Old Mr Hookie, her father, had, from the time he read his Virgil, maintained a sort of intromission with the Nine Muses, by which he was led to baptize her Sabrina, after a name mentioned by John Milton in one of his works.'

Sacharissa, see WALLER, E.

SACHS, Hans (1491–1576), shoemaker of Nuremberg, and author of a vast quantity of verse, including meistersongs and some 200 plays. He figures in *Wagner's opera *Die Meistersinger von Nürnberg*.

SACKVILLE, Charles, Lord Buckhurst, and later 6th earl of Dorset (1638–1706), a favourite of Charles II and noted for dissipation, who later became a loyal supporter of William. He was a friend and patron of poets, was praised as a poet by *Prior and *Dryden, and has been identified with the Eugenius of the latter's *Of Dramatick Poesy*. His poems, which appeared with those of *Sedley in 1701, include some biting satires and the ballad 'To all you Ladies now at Land'.

SACKVILLE, Thomas, 1st earl of Dorset and Baron Buckhurst (1536–1608), was son of Sir Richard Sackville. He was probably educated at Oxford. He was a barrister of the Inner Temple. He entered Parliament in 1557, was raised to the peerage in 1567, and held a number of high official positions, including those of lord treasurer and chancellor of Oxford University. He wrote the Induction and *'The Complaint of Buckingham' for *A Mirror for Magistrates*, and collaborated (probably writing only the last two acts) with Thomas Norton in the tragedy of *Gorboduc. He was an ancestor of V. *Sackville-West and is discussed in her *Knole and the Sackvilles* (1922).

SACKVILLE-WEST, Hon. Victoria Mary ('Vita'), CH (1892–1962), poet and novelist, was born at Knole, Kent, about which she wrote *Knole and the Sackvilles* (1922) and which provided the setting for her novel *The Edwardians* (1930). In 1913 she married Harold *Nicolson, with whom she travelled widely during his diplomatic career before settling at Sissinghurst, Kent, where she devoted much time to gardening. In 1922 she met Virginia *Woolf, whose *Orlando* (1928) was inspired by their close friendship. Her other works include a pastoral poem, *The Land* (1926, Hawthornden Prize), *All Passion Spent* (1931, novel), *Collected Poems* (1933), and many works on travel, gardening, and literary topics. Her unorthodox marriage was described by her son Nigel Nicolson in *Portrait of a Marriage* (1973). A biography by Victoria Glendinning was published in 1983.

Sacripant, (1) in *Orlando Innamorato and *Orlando Furioso*, the king of Circassia and a lover of *Angelica. He catches *Rinaldo's horse *Bayard, and rides away on it, and Rinaldo calls him a horse-thief. (2) in Tassoni's *Seccia Rapita (The Rape of the Bucket)*, he is a hectoring braggart. (3) Sacrapant, a magician in Peele's *The Old Wives' Tale*. In modern French *sacripant* is a rascal or blackguard.

Saddletree, Bartoline, a character in Scott's *The Heart of Midlothian*.

SADE, Donatien Alphonse, Comte, known as marquis de (1740–1814), French novelist and pornographer. His career as a cavalry officer was destroyed by the disorder of his life. During prolonged periods of imprisonment he wrote a number of licentious novels, including *Justine ou les malheurs de la vertu* (1791), *La philosophie dans le boudoir* (1795), and *Nouvelle Justine* (1797). Their obsession with the minutiae of sexual pathology and their extreme hedonistic nihilism have persuaded recent critics that they anticipate *Nietzsche and *Freud.

SADI (d. ?1292), a celebrated Persian poet, whose principal works were the collections of verse known as the 'Gulistan' or Rose Garden, and the 'Bustan' or Tree Garden.

SADLEIR, Michael (formerly Sadler) (1888–1957), bibliographer and novelist, educated at Rugby and Balliol College, Oxford, joined the publishing house of Constable of which he became director in 1920. He amassed an outstanding collection of 19th-cent. books, often of less-known authors, and wrote important bibliographical works, including *Excursions in Victorian Bibliography* (1922) and *Nineteenth Century Fiction* (2 vols, 1951). His best-known novel, *Fanny by Gaslight* (1940), has been made into a film.

Sad Shepherd, The, or *A Tale of Robin Hood*, the last and unfinished play of *Jonson, a pastoral tragi-comedy written c.1635, printed 1641.

Robin Hood invites the shepherds and shepherdesses of the Vale of Belvoir to a feast in Sherwood Forest, but the feast is marred by the arts of the witch Maudlin, aided by her familiar, Puck-Hairy. Aeglamour, the Sad Shepherd, relates the loss of his beloved Earine, whom he believes drowned in the Trent. In reality Maudlin has stripped her of her garments to adorn her daughter and shut her up in an oak as a prey for her son, the uncouth swineherd Lorel. The witch assumes the form of Maid Marian, sends away the venison prepared for the feast, abuses Robin Hood, and throws his guests into confusion. Lorel tries to win Earine but fails. The wiles of Maudlin are detected, and Robin's huntsmen pursue her. Only the first three acts of the play exist.

Saga, an Old Norse word meaning 'story', applied to narrative compositions from Iceland and Norway in the Middle Ages. There are three main types of saga: family sagas, dealing with the first settlers of Iceland and their descendants; kings' sagas, historical works about the kings of Norway; and legendary or heroic sagas, fantastic adventure stories about legendary heroes. The family sagas and the kings' sagas share an elegant, laconic style, notable for its air of detached objectivity. This led early scholars to suppose that the family sagas were reliably historical, being based almost wholly on oral traditions from an earlier period; but modern critics see these works as literary fictions with some historical basis. The most celebrated of the family sagas is *Njáls saga*, a long but tightly structured narrative about Gunnarr, a brave and worthy man who marries the beautiful but morally flawed Hallgerðr; she sets in motion a series of feuds which culminates first in her husband's heroic last stand and death, and then in the burning of Gunnarr's friend Njall, a wise and peaceable lawyer who accepts his fate with Christian resignation. The main concerns of the saga (the growth of social stability, legal and political, among the settlers of a new community, and the part played by human emotions, especially rivalry, loyalty, and sexual jealousy, in the course of this development) are characteristic of the other family sagas too, though *Njáls saga* stands out because of its scope and breadth of characterization. *Eyrbyggja saga* is especially concerned with the emergence of a politically stable community, though it also recounts some bizarre supernatural incidents. *Laxdaela saga* deals with the theme of a tragic love triangle and the fortunes of one of Iceland's most powerful families at that time. *Grettis saga* tells, with remarkable psychological depth and subtlety, the story of a famous Icelandic outlaw; Grettir's fights with the monstrous walking corpse Glámr and with a troll woman are analogous to Beowulf's fight with Grendel and Grendel's mother (see BEOWULF). Snorri Sturluson's *Heimskringla* comprises a history of the kings of Norway; *Vǫlsunga saga* is notable amongst the legendary ones and recounts the legends of the Goths and Burgundians which underlie *Wagner's *Ring* cycle. *Sturlunga saga* is unique in being a compilation of sagas about figures almost contemporary with their 13th-cent. authors. W. *Morris did much to popularize Icelandic literature in England. (See SIGURD THE VOLSUNG.)

Njáls saga, trans. M. Magnusson and H. Pálsson (1960); *Eyrbyggja saga*, trans. H. Pálsson and P. Edwards (1973); *Laxdaela saga*, trans. M. Magnusson and H. Pálsson (1969); *The Saga of Grettir the Strong*, trans. G. A. Hight (1965).

St Barbe, in *Endymion* by B. Disraeli.

SAINTE-BEUVE, Charles-Augustin (1804–69), French critic. His famous articles in periodicals such as *La Revue de Paris* and *La *Revue des deux mondes* were collected as *Critiques et portraits littéraires* (1832, 1836–9). Between 1849 and 1869 he contributed weekly critical essays to Paris newspapers; these were the celebrated 'Causeries du lundi', appearing on Mondays and collected in book form as *Causeries du lundi* (15 vols, 1851–62) and *Nouveaux lundis* (13 vols, 1863–70). His two long studies, each of which began life as a course of lectures, *Port-Royal* (6 bks, 1840–59), are classics of literary and biographical criticism. To the care and method of the professional critic Sainte-Beuve joined a subtle and enquiring curiosity about books and authors, wide-ranging interests and a humane and tolerant spirit. He is generally regarded as one of the founders of modern criticism. Some of his early essays, and notably his *Tableau historique . . . de la poésie française . . . au XVIe siècle* (1828), helped to promote the poetry of the Romantic movement in France by tracing its affinities with 16th-cent. poetry. He later revised his opinion of the Romantics.

St Cleeve, Swithin, a character in Hardy's *Two on a Tower*.

SAINT-EVRÉMOND, Charles de Saint-Denis (1613–1703), French critic. He spent the latter part of his life in exile in England, where he acted as arbiter of taste from the reign of Charles II to that of William III. In his sceptical epicureanism he was a representative *libertin* who wrote with witty sobriety on a variety of subjects, including English Comedy. His works were translated in 1714, some of his essays having previously appeared in English in 1693, with a preface by *Dryden.

SAINT-EXUPÉRY, Antoine de (1900–44), French novelist. He was actively involved in the early years of commercial aviation, and his novels are intimately linked with his flying experiences: *Courrier Sud* (1928; English trans., *Southern Mail*, 1933), *Vol de Nuit* (1931; *Night Flight*, 1932), *Terre des hommes* (1939; *Wind, Sand and Stars*, 1939), and *Pilote de guerre* (1942; *Flight to Arras*, 1942). He also wrote a book for children, *Le Petit Prince* (1943; *The Little Prince*, 1944).

St James, duke of, hero of *The Young Duke* by B. Disraeli.

ST JOHN, Henry, see BOLINGBROKE, H. ST J.

SAINT-JOHN PERSE, pseudonym of Alexis Saint-Léger Léger (1887–1975), French poet and diplomat. His early poems, *Éloges* (1911), evoked his childhood in the West Indies. He travelled widely for most of his life, his career in the French foreign service taking him as far afield as Peking. He first became known to the English-speaking world through T. S. *Eliot's translation of his epic poem *Anabase* (1924), a sumptuous chronicle of Asiatic tribal migrations. Exiled to the United States after 1940, he produced a succession of highly wrought prose poems of rare rhythmic subtlety: *Exil* (1942), *Pluies* (1943), *Neiges* (1944), and *Vents* (1946). These transcended his predicament as a Frenchman and more generally as a human being through celebrations of the powers and rituals of nature. His work as a whole displays an extraordinary command of the rhetorical possibilities of the French language. He was awarded the *Nobel Prize in 1960.

ST JOHN SPRIGG, Christopher, see CAUDWELL, C.

St Patrick's Day, a play in two acts by R. B. *Sheridan, produced 1785.
In this brief skit a wily lieutenant, in love with the daughter of a Justice, impersonates a German quack and, when the Justice is convinced he is poisoned, extracts the promise of the daughter's hand, as the price for a cure.

SAINT-PIERRE, Jacques-Henri Bernardin de (1737–1814), French natural philosopher and novelist, a friend and follower of *Rousseau

of whom he left an account in *La vie et les ouvrages de Jean-Jacques Rousseau* (1820). His *Études de la Nature*, a series of essays in natural history and philosophy discovering the operations of Divine Providence in the order and harmony of Nature, appeared in 1784; in the 3rd edn of the *Études* (1788) he included the work of fiction now regarded as his masterpiece and which was to achieve phenomenal popularity, *Paul et Virginie*. This pastoral romance tells the story of the idyllic childhood of two children of French parentage, Paul and Virginia, who are brought up as brother and sister by their mothers on a tropical island, the Île de France (Mauritius). The two mothers, refugees from social disgrace in France, determine that their children shall be reared in conformity with Nature's laws, and accordingly accustom them to a simple, frugal, and hard-working existence free from social prejudice, religious superstition, or fear of authority. In these conditions Paul and Virginia grow to adolescence, healthy, humane, pious, and benevolent, actively supporting their less fortunate neighbours. But Virginia is sent to Paris at the behest of a rich maiden aunt who desires to educate her to receive her fortune. On her return, after two years and more, her vessel is caught in a hurricane and thrown on to the reefs within sight of shore; Virginia refuses to undress to save herself, and is drowned when the ship founders. Paul and the two mothers die soon after of shock and grief.

Saint-Preux, the lover of Julie in *La Nouvelle Héloïse* of *Rousseau.

St Ronan's Well, a novel by Sir W. *Scott, published 1823.
In this work the author for once chose a contemporary scene, in the Scottish spa of St Ronan's Well, whose idle fashionable society is satirically described: Lady Penelope Penfeather, Sir Bingo Binks, Capt. MacTurk, and so on. It is the story of two half-brothers, sons of the late earl of Etherington, who had married, first secretly abroad, and then publicly at home. The younger son bears the title, though not entitled to it, and is at bitter enmity with his half-brother, Francis Tyrrel: he had intervened in a love-affair between Francis and Clara Mowbray, the daughter of the laird of St Ronan's, and actually impersonated his brother at a midnight marriage with Clara, so that Clara finds herself wedded to a man whom she fears and detests. (Scott had intended that Francis should seduce Clara, but altered the plot in deference to James *Ballantyne.) The brothers make a compact to leave Clara undisturbed and still bearing her maiden name, both undertaking never to return to Scotland; and the whole affair remains a secret. But Etherington, fearing that Francis will claim the earldom and discovering that by his marriage to Clara he will come into a fortune,

breaks his word and comes to St Ronan's to demand her hand in a more regular fashion. He uses the gambling of Clara's brother, now the laird, to blackmail him, so that Mowbray actually threatens to kill his sister if she does not accept Etherington. Meanwhile Francis has been at work on Clara's behalf, and the plotter is counterplotted and finally exposed by the intrigue-loving old nabob Mr Touchwood, but too late. Clara, already unhinged by her misfortunes, succumbs to her fresh terrors before they can be resolved.

One of the best characters in the book is Meg Dods, the sturdy refractory landlady of the old inn at St Ronan's.

SAINTSBURY, George Edward Bateman (1845–1933), educated at King's College School, London, and Merton College, Oxford. Having failed to obtain a fellowship at Oxford, he became a schoolmaster, spending six years in Guernsey, and began contributing articles on French literature to the *Academy. In 1876 he came to London to become a professional writer and made his name, at first, as a reviewer of French literature. He contributed numerous articles to the *Fortnightly Review, *Pall Mall Gazette, and other journals. He was an industrious journalist for the *Daily News and the *Manchester Guardian, and was introduced by his friend *Lang to the *Saturday Review, of which he became assistant editor (1883–94). His first book, A Primer of French Literature, was published in 1880, and thereafter he published voluminously; his works include a volume on Dryden (EML, 1881), a re-edition of Sir W. *Scott's Works of Dryden (1882–93), A Short History of French Literature (1882), A History of Elizabethan Literature (1887), as well as introductions to editions of prose and poetry, and 36 articles for the *Encyclopaedia Britannica. In 1895 he was appointed to the chair of rhetoric and English literature at Edinburgh, which he held for 20 years, during which he published some of his largest works, including A History of Nineteenth Century Literature (1896), A Short History of English Literature (1898, reprinted 1960), The History of Criticism and Literary Taste in Europe (1900–4), A History of English Prosody (1906–10), and books on Sir Walter Scott (1897) and Matthew Arnold (1898). He retired to Bath and published A History of the French Novel (1917–19). Saintsbury was a connoisseur of wine and the success of his Notes on a Cellarbook (1920) led to the founding of the Saintsbury Club. He left instructions in his Will that no biography be written, but his three Scrap-Books (1922–4) are collections of reminiscences and observations. He remains a doyen of Victorian taste in literature, but his hedonistic approach to literary criticism, based on style rather than on content, is no longer in favour.

Saint's Everlasting Rest, The, see BAXTER, R.

SAINT-SIMON, Claude-Henri de Rouvroy, comte de (1760–1825), French social philosopher and political economist, whose father was a cousin of the duc de *Saint-Simon. In his various writings Saint-Simon laid down a set of principles for the reorganization of European society after the French revolution in conformity with current scientific and economic notions. Conceiving of a nation as a vast productive enterprise, he proposed that industrialists should hold political power and that spiritual authority should be vested in scientists and artists in order to secure the physical and moral improvement of all classes. After his death his followers formed a religious association and elaborated his ideas along broadly socialist lines into the doctrine known as *Saint-Simonisme*. They advocated the abolition of the right of private inheritance and its transfer to the state, the institution of a hierarchy of merit, and the enfranchisement of women. The association was declared illegal in 1832.

SAINT-SIMON, Louis de Rouvroy, duc de (1675–1755), French chronicler and memorialist. After a period of reluctant army service, he sought advancement at court until 1723, when the death of his protector, the duc d'Orléans, put an end to his participation in public affairs. His great work, the *Mémoires* (first authentic edition in 21 vols, 1829–30), composed during the 20 years of his retirement, offer an incomparable record of life at court in the latter part of Louis XIV's reign. The verve of his writing, the liveliness of his observation, and the penetration of his portraits have made this work a classic of the genre. It was among *Proust's favourite reading. A new translation in 3 vols by Lucy Norton was published 1967–72.

Saint Valentine's Day, see FAIR MAID OF PERTH, THE.

SAKI, pseudonym of Hector Hugh Munro (1870–1916), known principally for his short stories; he was born in Burma, the youngest of three children: his mother died when he was an infant, and he was brought up in North Devon by two aunts. In 1893 he joined the military police in Burma, but was invalided home and went to London to earn his living as a writer. In 1899 he published The Rise of the Russian Empire, in 1900 wrote political satire for the Westminster Gazette, and between 1902 and 1908 was correspondent for the *Morning Post in Poland, Russia, and Paris. His first characteristic volume of short stories, Reginald, was published under the pseudonym Saki (of uncertain origin) in 1904, followed by Reginald in Russia (1910), The Chronicles of Clovis (1911), Beasts and Super-Beasts (1914), The Toys of Peace (1919), and The Square Egg (1924). The Unbearable Bassington (1912) and When William Came (1913) are both novels. In 1914 he enlisted as a trooper and he was killed in France, shot through the head while resting in a shallow crater. His stories include the satiric, the comic, the macabre, and the supernatural, and show a marked interest in the use of animals—wolves, tigers, bulls, ferrets, cats—as agents of revenge upon mankind.

Sakūntalā, see SHAKŪNTALĀ.

SALA, George Augustus (1828–96), journalist and illustrator, began his literary career as editor of *Chat* in 1848, and became a regular contributor to *Household Words* (1851–6); he was sent by *Dickens to Russia as correspondent at the end of the Crimean war and subsequently wrote for the *Daily Telegraph*. He published books of travel and novels.

SALADIN (Salah-ed-Din Yusuf ibn Ayub) (*c*.1138–93), a Kurd who was the founder of the Ayubite dynasty in Egypt. He was established as Caliph there in 1171, and he took possession of southern Syria and Damascus on the death of Noureddin in 1174. After defeat by the Christians in 1177, he made further advances and he defeated their forces led by Guy de Lusignan at the battle of Tiberias at Hattin on 4 July 1187. He then besieged and captured Acre and Jerusalem (Oct. 1187). After several defeats by the forces of the Third Crusade led by *Richard I, Coeur de Lion, he made a truce with them in 1192 which allowed Henry of Champagne, titular king of Jerusalem, a strip of coastal land around Acre and access to Jerusalem itself. But the progress made by his conquests remained considerable at his death in 1193. Largely because of his clemency towards the defeated Christian forces after Tiberias, he is traditionally represented as chivalrous, loyal, and magnanimous: by Boccaccio who represents him thus in two stories in the *Decameron* (Day 1, Tale 3; Day 10, Tale 9); by *Dante who places him in the Limbo of heroes (*Inferno*, iv. 129); and by English writers such as Scott in *The Talisman*. See H. A. R. Gibb, *Studies on the Civilisation of Islam* (1962), pp. 91–107.

Salamander, see PARACELSUS.

Salammbô, a novel by G. *Flaubert.

Salanio and **Salarino,** friends of *Antonio and *Bassanio in Shakespeare's *The Merchant of Venice*.

Salathiel, a novel on the theme of the *Wandering Jew by G. *Croly.

SALINGER, J(erome) D(avid) (1919–), American novelist and short story writer, born in New York, who is best known for his novel *The Catcher in the Rye* (1951), the story of adolescent Holden Caulfield who runs away from boarding-school in Pennsylvania to New York, where he preserves his innocence despite various attempts to lose it. The colloquial, lively, first-person narration, with its attacks on the 'phoniness' of the adult world and its clinging to family sentiment in the form of Holden's affection for his sister Phoebe, made the novel accessible to and popular with a wide readership, particularly with the young. Salinger's other works include *Franny and Zooey* (1961), two long short stories about two members of the eccentric Glass family; and two stories narrated by Buddy Glass appeared originally in the *New Yorker and were published together as *Raise High the Roof-Beam, Carpenters and Seymour: an Introduction* (1963).

SALLUST (Gaius Sallustius Crispus) (86–35 BC), Roman historian whose surviving works are two monographs on *The Conspiracy of Catiline* and *The War Against Jugurtha*. Sallust was one of Julius Caesar's henchmen and as a historian manipulates the truth in favour of the Caesarian party, while his strongly moralistic approach precludes a close analysis of causes. He was popular in the Middle Ages, and his practice of including speeches, gnomic sayings, and character sketches in his narrative was copied by William of Poitiers, the historian of the Norman Conquest, and by the 12th-cent. *William of Malmesbury. The *Jugurtha* was translated by A. *Barclay early in the 16th cent., and T. *Heywood translated both monographs (1608). Sallust's condemnations of corruption were much savoured in the 18th cent. by the architects of the American revolution.

'Sally in our Alley', a ballad by H. *Carey.

Salmantica, in imprints, Salamanca.

SALMASIUS, professional name of Claude de Saumaise (1588–1653), an eminent French scholar, professor at Leyden University in 1649 when Charles II was living at The Hague. At the age of 19 he discovered the Palatine library at Heidelberg and unearthed the 10th-cent. Palatine Anthology (*The Greek *Anthology*). He was commissioned by Charles to draw up a defence of his father and an indictment of the regicide government. This took the form of the Latin *Defensio Regia* which reached England by the end of 1649. *Milton was ordered by the Council in 1650 to prepare a reply to it, and in 1651 issued his *Pro Populo Anglicano Defensio*, also in Latin, a work which brought him an international reputation and attracted great attention, much of it hostile. It is a repetitious and tedious work, a mixture of scholarship and scurrilous invective, but Milton himself was well satisfied with it. Salmasius rejoined in his *Responsio*, which similarly contains much personal abuse, published posthumously in 1660. *Hobbes in his *Behemoth* said he found the two *Defensiones* 'very good Latin both . . . and both very ill reasoning'.

Salome, a play by O. *Wilde, which later formed the basis for the libretto of an opera by R. *Strauss.

Salvation Army, see BOOTH, WILLIAM.

Samient, in Spenser's *Faerie Queene (v. viii), the lady sent by Queen *Mercilla to Adicia, the wife of the *Soldan, received by her with contumely, and rescued by Sir *Artegall.

Sampson, Dominie, a character in Scott's *Guy Mannering. His favourite expression of astonishment is 'Prodigious!'

Samson Agonistes, a tragedy by *Milton, published 1671, in the same volume as *Paradise Regained. Its composition was traditionally assigned to 1666–70, but W. R. Parker in his biography (1968) argues that it was written much earlier, possibly as early as 1647. A closet drama never intended for the stage, it is modelled on Greek tragedy, and has been frequently compared to Prometheus Bound by *Aeschylus or Oedipus at Colonus by *Sophocles: other critics have claimed that its spirit is more Hebraic (or indeed Christian) than Hellenic. Predominantly in blank verse, it also contains passages of great metrical freedom and originality, and some rhyme. Samson Agonistes (i.e. Samson the Wrestler, or Champion) deals with the last phase of the life of the Samson of the Book of Judges when he is a prisoner of the Philistines and blind, a phase which many have compared to the assumed circumstances of the blind poet himself, after the collapse of the Commonwealth and his political hopes.

Samson, in prison at Gaza, is visited by friends of his tribe (the Chorus) who comfort him; then by his old father Manoa, who holds out hopes of securing his release; then by his wife *Dalila, who seeks pardon and reconciliation, but being repudiated shows herself 'a manifest Serpent'; then by Harapha, a strong man of Gath, who taunts Samson. He is finally summoned to provide amusement by feats of strength for the Philistines, who are celebrating a feast to *Dagon. He goes, and presently a messenger brings news of his final feat of strength in which he pulled down the pillars of the place where the assembly was gathered, destroying himself as well as the entire throng. The tragedy, which has many passages questioning divine providence ('Just or unjust, alike seem miserable') ends with the Chorus's conclusion that despite human doubts, all is for the best in the 'unsearchable dispose | Of highest wisdom': its last words, 'calm of mind all passion spent', strike a note of Aristotelian *catharsis, and the whole piece conforms to the *neo-classical doctrine of *Unities.

Samuel Slick, see HALIBURTON, T. C.

Sancho Panza, the squire of *Don Quixote,

who accompanies him in his adventures, shares many of their unpleasant consequences, and attempts to curb his master's enthusiasms by his shrewd common sense.

SAND, George, pseudonym of Amandine-Aurore Lucille Dupin, Baronne Dudevant (1804–76), French novelist. After separating from her husband, the Baron Dudevant, a retired army officer, she went to Paris in 1831 to begin an independent life as a writer. Her fame now largely derives from two groups of novels, of the many that she wrote in a long career. The first, a series of romantic tales, portrayed the struggles of the individual woman against social constraints, especially those of marriage, e.g., Indiana (1832), Lélia (1833), Jacques (1834). The simple, artfully-told idylls of rustic life that compose the second group are set in the region of Berry, where she had a country property at Nohant, and include La Mare au diable (1846), La Petite Fadette (1848), and François le champi (1850). Elle et lui (1859) fictionalizes her liaison with Alfred de *Musset; Un hiver à Majorque (1841) describes an episode in her long relationship with *Chopin. Histoire de ma vie (4 vols, 1854–5) is an autobiography.

SANDBURG, Carl August (1878–1967), American poet, born in Chicago of Swedish Lutheran immigrant stock. He challenged contemporary taste by his use of colloquialism and free verse, and became the principal among the authors writing in Chicago during and after the First World War. He published Chicago Poems (1916), Cornhuskers (1918), Smoke and Steel (1920), Slabs of the Sunburnt West (1922), Good Morning America (1928), and Complete Poems (1950). He also compiled a collection of folksongs, The American Songbag (1927), and wrote stories and poems for children. His major prose work is his monumental life of Abraham Lincoln (6 vols, 1926–39); his novel Remembrance Rock (1948) is on an epic scale and traces the growth of an American family from its English origins and its crossing on the Mayflower to the present day. Always the Young Strangers (1953) is a volume of autobiography.

Sandford and Merton, The History of, see DAY, T.

Sanditon, an unfinished novel by J. *Austen, written 1817.

Mr Parker is obsessed with the wish to create a large and fashionable resort out of the small village of Sanditon, on the south coast. His unquenchable enthusiasm sees crescents and terraces, a hotel and a library, and bathing machines. Charlotte Heywood, an attractive, alert young woman, is invited to stay with the Parkers, where she catches the fancy of Lady Denham, the local great lady. Lady Denham's nephew and niece, Sir Edward and Miss Denham, live nearby, and the second heroine of the novel, Clara Brereton, is staying with her. Edward plans (with a frankness of expression new to the author) to seduce Clara; but his aunt intends him to marry a West Indian heiress, under the care of a Mrs Griffiths and her entourage, whose visit to Sanditon is anticipated shortly. After a ludicrous series of complications, involving both Mrs Griffiths's party and a ladies' seminary from Camberwell, the excited inhabitants of Sanditon find the expected invasion of visitors consists merely of Mrs Griffiths and three young ladies.

This highly entertaining fragment was written in the first three months of 1817, when Jane Austen was already suffering from Addison's disease (of which she died on 18 July); one of its remarkable features is the spirit with which the author satirizes the hypochondria of the sisters and brother of Mr Parker (Diana, Susan, and Arthur) and the scorn she pours on their dependence on patent medicines and tonics for their imaginary illnesses.

Sandra Belloni, a novel by G. *Meredith, originally published 1864 as *Emilia in England*, re-titled 1886.

Emilia Sandra Belloni, an ardent and natural girl, is the daughter of an Italian musician and the possessor of a fine but untrained voice. She leaves home and becomes the protégée of the Poles, a poor family driven by social ambition and consisting of a grasping city merchant, his three affected daughters, and his son Wilfrid, a feeble young man much influenced by propriety and 'good form'. Pericles, a rich Greek and an associate of old Pole, has a passion for beautiful voices, and tries to lure Emilia to train with him in Italy. But the impetuous Emilia falls in love with Wilfrid, and he in his wavering with her. Old Pole, involved in financial speculation, tries to save himself by marrying his children to wealth. Wilfrid is to marry Lady Charlotte Chillingworth; torn between his love for Emilia and the riches and position of Lady Charlotte, Wilfrid finds his wavering exposed by Charlotte to Emilia, whose passionate heart is nearly broken. In her desolation Emilia temporarily loses her voice, and is befriended by Merthyr Powys and his sister. She extracts money from Pericles to save the Poles by promising to go with him to Milan for training, and holds out to Merthyr the hope that she will marry him when her course is completed. The sequel is in the author's *Vittoria.

SANDYS, George (1578–1644), educated at St Mary Hall, Oxford, travelled in Italy and the Near East, and in 1621 went to America as treasurer of the Virginia Company, remaining there probably for ten years. His chief works were a verse translation of *Ovid's *Metamorphoses* (1621–6), a verse *Paraphrase upon the Psalmes* (1636), and *Christ's Passion, a Tragedy*, a verse translation from the Latin of *Grotius (1640). He was a member of *Falkland's circle at Great Tew.

Sanglier, Sir, in Spenser's *Faerie Queene* (v. i), the wicked knight who has cut off his lady's head, and is forced by Sir *Artegall to bear the head before him, in token of his shame. He is thought to represent Shane O'Neill, second earl of Tyrone (?1530–67), a leader of the Irish, who invaded the Pale in 1566. Sanglier in French means 'wild boar'.

Sangreal, see GRAIL.

SANKEY, I. D., see MOODY AND SANKEY.

SANNAZAR, (Jacopo Sannazzaro) (1458–1530), Neapolitan author and rediscoverer of the charms of nature and the rustic life, was author of a pastoral, in prose and verse, the *Arcadia, and of Latin eclogues and other poems.

Sansfoy, Sansjoy, and **Sansloy,** three brothers in Spenser's *Faerie Queene* (I. ii. 25 *et seq.*). Sansfoy ('faithless') is slain by the *Redcrosse Knight, who also defeats Sansjoy ('joyless'), but the latter is saved from death by *Duessa. Sansloy ('lawless') carries off *Una and kills her lion (I. iii). This incident is supposed to refer to the suppression of the Protestant religion in the reign of Queen Mary.

SANSOM, William (1926–76), short story writer, travel writer, and novelist, born in London and educated at Uppingham. He travelled widely as a young man, and worked at various jobs, including that of copy-writer for an advertising agency. His first stories were published in literary periodicals (*Horizon, *New Writing, the *Cornhill, and others) and his first volume, *Fireman Flower and other stories* (1944), reflects his experiences with the National Fire Service in wartime London. This was followed by many other collections of stories, some set in London, others making full use of backdrops from Germany, Scandinavia, and the Mediterranean. His most successful novel, *The Body* (1949), is set in London. A collection of stories, with an introduction by E. *Bowen, appeared in 1963.

Sanskrit, the ancient and sacred language of India, the oldest member of the Indo-European family of languages. The extensive Hindu literature from the Vedas downward is composed in it.

SANTAYANA, George (1863–1952), a Spaniard brought up in Boston and educated at Harvard, where he was professor of philosophy from 1889 to 1912; he then came to Europe, living in France and England and later in Italy, where he died. He was an eminent speculative philosopher, of a naturalist tendency and opposed to German idealism, whose views are embodied in his *The Life of Reason* (1905–6). He holds that the human mind is an effect of physical growth and organization; but that our ideas, though of bodily origin, stand on a higher and non-material plane; that the true function of reason is not in idealistic dreams but in a logical activity that takes account of facts. He analyses religious and other institutions, distinguishing the ideal element from its material embodiment. Thus the wisdom embodied in the ritual and dogmas of religion is not truth about existence, but about the ideals on which mental strength and serenity are founded. He later modified and supplemented his philosophy in a series of four books, *Realms of Being* (1927–40).

Santayana also published poetry, criticism, reviews, memoirs, etc.; his other works include *Soliloquies in England* (1922), essays on the English character; *Character and Opinion in the United States* (1920), one of several studies of American life; and *Persons and Places* (3 vols, 1944–53). His only novel, *The Last Puritan* (1935), describes at length the antecedents and brief life of Boston-born Oliver Alden, 'the child of an elderly and weary man, and of a thin-spun race', whose European wanderings end in death by motor accident just after Armistice day; few perhaps would endorse the comment made by a character to the supposed author, criticizing his fiction: 'Your women are too intelligent, and your men also.' Santayana's style has been variously praised for its richness and condemned for its 'purple passages'.

SAPPER, the pseudonym of Herman Cyril McNeile (1888–1937), creator of Hugh 'Bulldog' Drummond, the hefty, ugly, charming, xenophobic, and apparently brainless British ex-army officer who foils the activities of Carl Peterson, the international crook. He appears in *Bull-dog Drummond* (1920), *The Female of the Species* (1928), and many other popular thrillers; after McNeile's death the series was continued under the same pseudonym by G. T. Fairlie. See R. Usborne, *Clubland Heroes* (1953, 1974).

Sapphics, see METRE.

SAPPHO (b. *c.* mid-7th cent. BC), a Greek lyric poet, born in Lesbos. Like her fellow-countryman and contemporary Alcaeus, she appears to have left Lesbos in consequence of political troubles, gone to Sicily, and died there. The story of her throwing herself into the sea in despair at her unrequited love for Phaon the boatman is mere romance. Thanks to papyrus finds, we now have 12 poems in some form of preservation (see D. L. Page, *Sappho and Alcaeus*, 1955). Her principal subject is always love, which she expresses with great simplicity and a remarkable felicity of phrase.

Sapsea, Mr, in Dickens's *Edwin Drood*, an auctioneer and mayor of Cloisterham.

Sardanapalus, a poetic drama by Lord *Byron, published 1821.

The subject was taken from the *Bibliotheca Historica* of Siculus. Sardanapalus is represented as an effete but courageous monarch. When Beleses, a Chaldean soothsayer, and Arabaces, governor of Media, lead a revolt against him, he shakes off his slothful luxury and, urged on by Myrrha, his favourite Greek slave, fights bravely at the head of his troops. Defeated, he arranges for the safety of his queen, Zarina, and of his supporters, then prepares a funeral pyre round his throne and perishes in it with Myrrha.

Sarpego, a comical pedant in Brome's *The City Witt*, a character modelled on Clove in Jonson's *Every Man out of his Humour*.

Sarras, in the legend of the *Grail, the land to which *Joseph of Arimathea fled from Jerusalem. In the prose *La Queste del Saint Graal*, the three knights who are successful in the Quest, Galaad, Perceval, and Bohort (Bors), are borne there by Solomon's ship, and Galaad dies in ecstasy after seeing openly the ultimate mystery there.

SARRAUTE, Nathalie, see NOUVEAU ROMAN.

SARTORIS, Adelaide, *née* Kemble (?1814–79), singer and author, sister of Fanny *Kemble. After a distinguished operatic career she settled with her husband in Rome. She had many friends in the literary and artistic world, some of whom (notably *Leighton as Kioski) appear in *A Week in a French Country House* (1867), her *roman à clef*.

Sartor Resartus: The Life and Opinions of Herr Teufelsdröckh, by T. *Carlyle, originally published in *Fraser's Magazine* 1833–4, and as a separate volume, at Boston, Mass., 1836 (partly through the intervention of *Emerson, who had visited Carlyle at Craigenputtock in 1833); first English edition 1838.

This work was written under the influence of the German Romantic school and particularly of *Richter. It consists of two parts: a discourse on the philosophy of clothes (*sartor resartus* means 'the tailor re-patched') based on the speculations of an imaginary Professor Teufelsdröckh, and leading to the conclusion that all symbols, forms, and human institutions are properly clothes, and as such temporary; and a biography of Teufelsdröckh himself, which is in some measure the author's autobiography, particularly in the description of the village of Entepfuhl and of the German university (suggested by Ecclefechan and Edinburgh), and still more in the notable chapters on 'The Everlasting No', 'Centre of Indifference', and 'The Everlasting Yea', which depict a spiritual crisis such as Carlyle himself had experienced during his early Edinburgh days. The prose is highly characteristic, dotted with capital letters, exclamation marks, phrases in German, compound words of the author's own invention, wild apostrophes to the Reader, apocalyptic utterances, and outbursts of satire and bathos; an early example of what came to be known as 'Carlylese'.

SARTRE, Jean-Paul (1905–80), French philosopher, novelist, playwright, literary critic, and political activist. He was the principal exponent of *Existentialism in France, and exercised a considerable influence on French intellectual life in the decades following the Second World War. He was educated at the École Normale Supérieure, where he studied philosophy and psychology, and subsequently spent a period studying phenomenology at the French Institute in Berlin. He held various teaching posts in France until the outbreak of war. Mobilized in 1939, taken prisoner in 1940, he was released the following year and played a part in the resistance movement. After the war he devoted himself exclusively to writing and, with varying degrees of intensity, to the pursuit of socialist political objectives. Through the great range of his creative and critical energies, his personal involvement in many of the important issues of his time, and his unceasing concern with problems of freedom, commitment, and moral responsibility, he won a wide audience for his ideas. He made important contributions in many areas: existentialist and Marxist philosophy, *L'Être et le néant* (1943; English trans., *Being and Nothingness*, 1956) and *Critique de la raison dialectique* (1960; *Critique of Dialectical Reason*, 1976); the novel, *La Nausée* (1938; *Nausea*, 1949) and three volumes of a projected tetralogy *Les Chemins de la liberté* (1945–7; *The Roads to Freedom*, 1947–50), comprising *L'Âge de raison*, *Le Sursis*, and *La Mort dans l'âme* (*The Age of Reason*, *The Reprieve*, and *Iron in the Soul*); drama, *Les Mouches* (1943; *The Flies*, 1947), *Huis Clos* (1945; *In Camera*, 1946; *No Exit*, 1947), *Les Mains sales* (1948; *Dirty Hands*, 1949; *Crime Passionnel*, 1949), and *Les Séquestrés d'Altona* (1960; *Loser Wins*, 1960; *The Condemned of Altona*, 1961); biography, with studies of *Baudelaire (1947), *Genet (1952), and *Flaubert (1971–2); literary criticism, *Qu'est-ce que la littérature?* (1948; *What is Literature?* 1949). He was one of the founders of the influential literary and political review *Les Temps Modernes* (1945). His autobiography, *Les Mots* (*Words*), appeared in 1964, in which year he was awarded the *Nobel Prize for literature. His friend and companion from her university days was Simone de *Beauvoir.

SASSOON, Siegfried Louvain (1886–

1967), educated at Marlborough and Clare College, Cambridge, and destined by his mother to be a poet, he lived in Kent and Sussex, following country pursuits and publishing verse in private pamphlets. In the trenches in the First World War he began to write the poetry for which he is remembered; his bleak realism, his contempt for war leaders and patriotic cant, and his compassion for his comrades found expression in a body of verse which was not acceptable to a public revering R. *Brooke. During his first spell in the front line he was awarded the MC, which he later threw away. Dispatched as 'shell-shocked' to hospital, he encountered and encouraged W. *Owen, and organized a public protest against the war. In 1917 he published his war poems in *The Old Huntsman* and in 1918 further poems in *Counter-Attack*, both with scant success. Further volumes of poetry published in the 1920s finally established a high reputation, and collections were published in 1947 and 1961. From the late 1920s Sassoon began to think of himself as a religious poet and was much influenced by G. *Herbert and *Vaughan. The spare, muted poems in *Vigils* (1935) and *Sequences* (1956) are much concerned with spiritual growth. In 1957 he became a Catholic.

Meanwhile he was also achieving success as a prose writer. His semi-autobiographical trilogy (*Memoirs of a Fox-Hunting Man*, 1928; *Memoirs of an Infantry Officer*, 1930; and *Sherston's Progress*, 1936) relates the life of George Sherston, a lonely boy whose loves are cricket and hunting, who grows into a thoughtless young gentleman and eventually finds himself a junior officer in the trenches, where he is brutally thrust into adulthood. The three books were published together as *The Complete Memoirs of George Sherston* in 1937. In 1938 Sassoon published *The Old Century and Seven More Years*, an autobiography of his childhood and youth, and his own favourite among his books. *The Weald of Youth* (1942) and *Siegfried's Journey* (1945) brought his story up to 1920. In 1948 he published an important biography of G. *Meredith. His attachment to the countryside emerges as a major theme in his post-1918 poetry and in most of his prose work. His diaries 1920–2 and 1915–18, ed. R. Hart-Davis, were published 1981 and 1983.

Satanic School, the name under which R. *Southey attacks *Byron and the younger Romantics in the preface to his *A Vision of Judgement.

Satire, from the Latin *satira*, a later form of *satura*, which means 'medley', being elliptical for *lanx satura*, 'a full dish, a hotch-potch'. The word has no connection with 'satyr', as was formerly often supposed. A 'satire' is a poem, or in modern use sometimes a prose composition, in which prevailing vices or follies are held up to ridicule [OED]. In English literature, satire may be held to have begun with *Chaucer, who was followed by many 15th-cent. writers, including *Dunbar. *Skelton used the octosyllabic metre, and a rough manner which was to be paralleled in later times by Butler in *Hudibras, and by *Swift. Elizabethan satirists include *Gascoigne and *Lodge, whereas J. *Hall claimed to be the first to introduce satires based on *Juvenal to England. The great age of English satire began with *Dryden, who perfected the epigrammatic and antithetical use of the *heroic couplet for this purpose. He was followed by *Pope, Swift, *Gay, *Prior, and other satirists of the Augustan period. The same tradition was followed by Charles *Churchill, and brilliantly revived by Byron in *English Bards and Scotch Reviewers. The Victorian age was not noted for pure satire, although the novel proved an excellent vehicle for social satire with *Dickens, *Thackeray, and others. In the early 20th cent. *Belloc, *Chesterton, and R. *Campbell (in his Georgiad) contributed to a moderate revival of the tradition, pursued in various verse forms by P. *Porter, J. *Fuller, Clive James, and other young writers; and prose satire continues to flourish in the works of E. *Waugh, A. *Powell, Angus *Wilson, *Amis, and others. In theatre and television the 'satire boom' of the 1960s is generally held to have been pioneered by the satirical revue Beyond the Fringe (1960) by Alan *Bennett, Jonathan Miller, Peter Cook, and Dudley Moore.

Satire Ménippée (a name derived from the cynic satirist Menippus of Gadara, 3rd cent. BC), a satirical pamphlet, published 1594, attacking the Catholic Ligue in favour of the Protestant claims of Henri IV. Written by a canon of Rouen, Jean Leroy, with five collaborators drawn from the intellectual middle classes, it burlesques the opening of the États Généraux of 1593, parodies the chief spokesmen of the Ligue, and defends anti-aristocratic values.

Satiromastix, or The Untrussing of the Humorous Poet, a comedy by *Dekker, written 1601 (with John *Marston?), printed 1602.

Jonson in his *Poetaster had satirized Dekker and Marston, under the names of Demetrius and Crispinus, while he himself figures as Horace. Dekker here retorts, bringing the same Horace, Crispinus, and Demetrius on the stage once more. Horace is discovered sitting in a study laboriously composing an Epithalamium, and at a loss for a rhyme. Crispinus and Demetrius enter and reprove him gravely for his querulousness. Presently Captain Tucca (of the Poetaster) enters, and turns effectively on Horace the flow of his profanity. Horace's peculiarities of dress and appearance, his vanity and bitterness, are

ridiculed; and he is finally untrussed and crowned with nettles.

The satirical part of the play uses a somewhat inappropriate romantic setting—the wedding of Sir Walter Terill at the court of William Rufus, and the drinking of poison (as she thinks) by his wife, Caelestine, but really of a sleeping-potion, to escape the king's attentions.

Saturday Night and Sunday Morning, the first novel of A. *Sillitoe, published 1958.

Its protagonist, anarchic young Arthur Seaton, lathe operator in a Nottingham bicycle factory, provided a new prototype of the working-class *Angry Young Man; rebellious, contemptuous towards authority in the form of management, government, the army, and neighbourhood spies, he unleashes his energy on drink and women, with quieter interludes spent fishing in the canal. His affair with Brenda, married to his workmate Jack, overlaps with an affair with her sister Winnie, inaugurated in the night that Brenda attempts a gin-and-hot-bath abortion recommended by his Aunt Ada; both relationships falter when he is beaten up by soldiers, one of them Winnie's husband, and he diverts his attention to young Doreen, to whom he becomes engaged (after a fashion) in the penultimate chapter. Arthur's wary recklessness, at once aggressive and evasive, is summed up in his reaction to the sergeant-major who tells him, 'You're a soldier now, not a Teddy boy': 'I'm me, and nobody else; and whatever people think I am, that's what I'm not, because they don't know a bloody thing about me' (ch. 9). A landmark in the development of the post-war novel, with its naturalism relieved by wit, high spirits, and touches of lyricism, the novel provided the screenplay (also by Sillitoe) for Karel Reisz's 1960 film, a landmark in British cinema.

Saturday Review, The, an influential periodical founded in 1855, which ran until 1938. Among the many brilliant contributors of its early days were Sir Henry Maine (1822–88), Sir J. F. *Stephen, J. R. *Green, and *Freeman; it later became more literary in its interests (notably under the editorship of F. *Harris, 1894–8), publishing work by *Hardy, H. G. *Wells, *Beerbohm, Arthur *Symons, and others. G. B. *Shaw was dramatic critic from 1895 to 1898, and *Agate from 1921 to 1923.

Saturninus, the emperor in Shakespeare's *Titus Andronicus, who marries *Tamora.

Satyrane, Sir, in Spenser's *Faerie Queene (I. vi), a knight 'Plaine, faithfull, true, and enimy of shame', son of a satyr and the nymph Thyamis. He rescues *Una from the satyrs, perhaps symbolizing the liberation of the true religion by *Luther.

Satyric Drama, a humorous piece with a chorus of satyrs that authors in the 5th and 4th cents BC were expected to append to tragic trilogies offered for competition. This practice, which had the incidental virtue of providing light relief, may have been due to the fact recorded by *Aristotle (*Poetics*, ch. 4) that Tragedy had its origin in performances by actors dressed as satyrs. The surviving fragments of *Aeschylus' *Diktyoulkoi* (The Net-Drawers) and *Sophocles' *Ichneutai* (The Trackers) reveal sympathy for the promptings of animal impulse and a lyrical feeling for nature. They were both probably superior to the one extant satyric drama, *Euripides' *Cyclops*. J. C. *Scaliger (*Poetics*, 1561) sparked off a controversy when he claimed that Roman satire was descended from Greek satyric drama. The claim was contradicted by *Casaubon who demonstrated that the Latin 'satire' had no connection with satyrs (*De satyra poesi*, 1605), a view that *Dryden was to accept.

Satyricon, see PETRONIUS.

SAUSSURE, Ferdinand de (1857–1913), born in Geneva; he entered the university there in 1875 but moved after a year to Leipzig to study Indo-European languages. After four years in the powerful language department there, he went to Paris in 1881 where he taught for ten years. In 1891 he became professor at Geneva where, between 1907 and 1911, he delivered the three courses of lectures which were reconstructed from students' notes into the *Cours de linguistique générale* (published 1915), a book which is the basis of 20th-cent. linguistics and of much modern literary criticism. His most important and influential idea was the conception of language as a system of signs, arbitrarily assigned and only intelligible in terms of the particular system as a whole. (This idea was applied outside language in the new science called Semiotics.) Language is a *structure* whose parts can only be understood in relation to each other; this *'structuralism' has been very influential in literary criticism and in other fields, such as sociology. Two other sets of distinctions made by Saussure might be noted, as axiomatic for the understanding of modern linguistics: the distinctions between *langage* (the human capacity of using language), *langue* (the particular language as a whole: e.g. English), and *parole* (a particular utterance or occurrence of language); and the division of language study into *synchronic* (the examination of a particular language as a system at one stage of its existence) and *diachronic* (the historical study of the development of a language). Saussure's emphasis was on the value of synchronic study (with which the term 'linguistics' is sometimes used synonymously, as distinct from 'philology' for historical study), rather than the diachronic philology with which

he had previously been concerned. One of the compilers of the *Cours* was Charles Bally (1865–1947), who developed the ideas of Saussure and, with other followers, is sometimes assigned to the 'Geneva School'. Even if all Saussure's ideas were not entirely original with him, his originality and influence cannot easily be exaggerated. See *Course in General Linguistics*, trans. W. Baskin (1959); J. Culler, *Saussure* (1976).

SAVAGE, Richard (*c.*1697–1743), claimed to be the illegitimate son of the fourth Earl Rivers and Lady Macclesfield, but the story of his birth and ill treatment given by Dr *Johnson in his remarkable life (1744, reprinted in *The Lives of the English Poets*) has been largely discredited. (See *Notes and Queries*, 1858.) Johnson describes with much sympathy Savage's career as a struggling writer, his pardon after conviction on a murder charge in 1727, and his poverty-stricken death in a Bristol gaol. Savage wrote two plays (*Love in a Veil*, published 1719, and *The Tragedy of Sir Thomas Overbury*, published 1724), and various odes and satires, but is remembered as a poet for *The Wanderer* (1729) and 'The Bastard' (1728), a spirited attack on his 'Mother, yet no Mother', which contains the well-known line, 'No tenth transmitter of a foolish face'.

Savage Club, a club with strong literary and artistic connections founded in 1857, with *Sala as one of the founder members; it was named after the poet (above). Members have included *Bridie, E. *Wallace, G. and W. *Grossmith, and Dylan *Thomas.

SAVILE, George, see HALIFAX.

SAVILE, Sir Henry (1549–1622), educated at Brasenose College, Oxford, and a fellow and subsequently warden of Merton College and provost of Eton. He was secretary of the Latin tongue to *Elizabeth I, perhaps also teaching her Greek, and one of the scholars commissioned to prepare the authorized translation of the Bible. He translated the *Histories* of *Tacitus (1591) and published a magnificent edition of St John *Chrysostom (1610–13) and of *Xenophon's *Cyropaedia* (1613) at Eton. Savile assisted *Bodley in founding his library and established the Savilian Professorships of geometry and astronomy at Oxford. He left a collection of manuscripts and printed books, now in the Bodleian Library.

Savile Club, founded in 1868 as the Eclectic Club, renamed in 1869 the New Club, and from 1871, when it moved to independent premises in Savile Row, known as the Savile Club. It moved to its present home, 69 Brook Street, in 1927. The club has always had a strong literary tradition; members have included R. L. *Stevenson, *Hardy, *Yeats, L. *Strachey,

H. *James, and S. *Potter. Sean Day-Lewis, in his biography of C. *Day-Lewis, describes the Savile as the home of Potter's invention of the concept of 'Gamesmanship'; and it was in the Savile billiards room that Stevenson is alleged to have said to H. *Spencer 'that to play billiards well was the sign of an ill-spent youth', though other clubs also claim this honour.

SAVONAROLA, Fra Girolamo (1452–98), Dominican monk, an eloquent preacher whose sermons at Florence gave expression to the religious reaction against the artistic licence and social corruption of the Renaissance. Savonarola was leader of the democratic party in Florence after the expulsion of the *Medici, and aroused the hostility of Pope Alexander VI (Rodrigo *Borgia) by his political attitude in favour of Charles VIII of France. His influence was gradually undermined, and he was tried, condemned, and executed as a heretic. There is a careful study of his character in G. Eliot's *Romola.

Savoy, The, a short-lived but important periodical, edited by Arthur *Symons, of which eight issues appeared in 1896, with contributions by *Beardsley, *Conrad, *Dowson, and others.

Savoy Operas, see GILBERT AND SULLIVAN OPERAS.

Sawles Warde, an allegorical work of alliterative prose, found in three manuscripts with the saints' lives called *'The Katherine Group', dating from the end of the 12th cent. and emanating from the West Midlands (probably Herefordshire). It is a loose translation of part of De Anima by Hugh of St Victor, and it presents a morality in which the body is the dwelling-place of the soul and comes under attack by the vices. It has connections then with the morality castle, found from *Grosseteste's Chasteau d'Amour to *The Castle of Perseverance. Its prose has the same virtues—elegance and colloquialism—as *Ancrene Wisse and the Katherine Group. Ed. J. A. W. Bennett, G. V. Smithers, and N. Davis, Early Middle English Verse and Prose (2nd edn, 1968).

Sawyer, Bob, a character in Dickens's *The Pickwick Papers.

SAXO GRAMMATICUS, a 13th-cent. Danish historian, author of the Gesta Danorum, a partly mythical Latin history of the Danes (which contains the *Hamlet story). See A History of the Danes, Vol. I trans. P. Fisher (1970); Vol. II, Commentary, by H. Ellis-Davidson (1980).

SAYERS, Dorothy L(eigh) (1893–1957), daughter of a Fenland clergyman, and married in 1926 to a journalist, O. A. Fleming, worked as a copy-writer in an advertising agency (where she considerably influenced the style of contemporary advertising) till the success of her detective novels gave her financial independence. Her detective fiction is among the classics of the genre, being outstanding for its well-researched backgrounds, distinguished style, observant characterization, and ingenious plotting, and for its amateur detective Lord Peter Wimsey; she reached her peak with Murder Must Advertise (1933) and The Nine Tailors (1934). She also wrote religious plays, mainly for broadcasting, and her learning, wit, and pugnacious personality made her a formidable theological polemicist. Her last years were devoted to a translation of Dante's *Divina Commedia. See James Brabazon, Dorothy L. Sayers (1981).

Scald, Scaldic verse, see SKALDIC VERSE.

Scales, Gerald, a character in Bennett's *The Old Wives' Tale.

SCALIGER, Joseph Justus (1540–1609), the son of J. C. *Scaliger, was the greatest scholar of the Renaissance; he has been described as 'the founder of historical criticism'. His edition of Manilius (1579) and his De Emendatione Temporum revolutionized ancient chronology by insisting on the recognition of the historical material relating to the Jews, the Persians, the Babylonians, and the Egyptians. He also issued critical editions of many classical authors. He incurred the enmity of the Jesuits and retired from France to Lausanne in 1572, and subsequently to Leyden. He was attacked in his old age by Gaspar Scioppius on behalf of the Jesuits, who contested the claim of the Scaligers to belong to the Della Scala family. See Anthony Grafton, Joseph Scaliger: A Study in the History of Classical Scholarship (vol. 1, 1983).

SCALIGER, Julius Caesar (1484–1558), born at Riva on Lake Garda, settled at Agen in France as a physician. Besides polemical works directed against *Erasmus (1531), he wrote a long Latin treatise on poetics, scientific commentaries on botanical works, and a philosophical treatise. These show encyclopaedic knowledge and acute observation, marred by arrogance and vanity. He claimed to belong to the princely family of Della Scala.

SCANNELL, Vernon (1922–), poet and one-time boxer, born in Lincolnshire. His first volume of verse, Graves and Resurrections (1948), was followed by several others including The Masks of Love (1960), A Sense of Danger (1962), and The Loving Game (1975). New and Collected Poems 1950–1980 appeared in 1980. Many of the poems combine informal colloquial language and domestic subjects with a sense of underlying violence: poetry and human love 'build small barriers against confusion' in an essentially hostile world. He has also written several novels and an auto-biography, *The Tiger and the Rose* (1971).

Scapin, in *Les Fourberies de Scapin* by *Molière, the type of rascally resourceful servant who gets out of difficulties by audacious lies. One of these gives the occasion for a much quoted phrase. In order to extract a sum of money needed by his young master from his avaricious father, he tells the latter a cock-and-bull story of the son's having gone on board a Turkish galley, been carried to sea, and held to ransom. The father, gradually convinced by Scapin's eloquence that he will have to produce the ransom, constantly reverts to the question, 'Mais que diable allait-il faire dans cette galère?' The phrase and the scene were taken by Molière from *Le Pédant joué* (II. iv) of *Cyrano de Bergerac.

Scaramouch, adaptation of the Italian *scaramuccia*, 'skirmish', a stock character in *commedia dell'arte, a cowardly and foolish boaster, who is constantly cudgelled by Harlequin. The character was intended in ridicule of the Spanish don, and was dressed in Spanish costume, usually black. The clever impersonation of the part by Tiberio Fiorelli, who brought his company of Italian players to London in 1673, rendered the word very popular in England during the last quarter of the 17th cent. [*OED*]. A comedy entitled *Scaramouch*, by Edward Ravenscroft, was produced in 1677.

Scarlet, or **Scarlock,** or **Scathelocke,** Will, one of the companions of *Robin Hood.

Scarlet Letter, The, a novel by N. *Hawthorne, published 1850.

The scene of the story is the Puritan New England of the 17th cent. An aged English scholar has sent his young wife, Hester Prynne, to Boston, intending to follow her, but has been captured by the Indians and delayed for two years. He arrives to find her in the pillory, with a baby in her arms. She has refused to name her lover, and has been sentenced to this ordeal and to wear for the remainder of her life the red letter A, adulteress, upon her bosom. The husband assumes the name of Roger Chillingworth and makes Hester swear that she will conceal his identity. Hester goes to live on the outskirts of the town, an object of contempt and insult, with her child, Pearl. Her ostracism opens for her a broader view of life, she devotes herself to works of mercy, and gradually wins the respect of the townsfolk. Chillingworth, in the character of a physician, sets out to discover her paramour. Hester's lover is, in fact, Arthur Dimmesdale, a young and highly revered minister whose lack of courage has prevented him from declaring his guilt and sharing Hester's punishment. The author traces the steps by which Chillingworth discovers him, the cruelty with which he fastens on and tortures him, and at the same time the moral degradation that this process involves for Chillingworth himself. When Dimmesdale at the end of seven years is on the verge of lunacy and death, Hester, emancipated by her experience, proposes to him that they shall flee to Europe, and for a moment he dallies with the idea. But he puts it from him as a temptation of the Evil One, makes public confession on the pillory which had been the scene of Hester's shame, and dies in her arms.

Scarlet Pimpernel, The, see ORCZY, BARONESS.

SCARRON, Paul (1610–60), French poet, dramatist, and writer of prose fiction. In 1652 he married Françoise d'Aubigné, who later became the secret wife of Louis XIV by whom she was created Mme de *Maintenon. Besides a number of comedies, Scarron was the author of a collection of short fiction, *Nouvelles tragicomiques* (1661), and a burlesque novel of 17th-cent. provincial life, *Le Roman Comique* (Pt I 1651, Pt II 1657), recounting the adventures of a touring company of actors in the town of Le Mans. His burlesque verse includes *Virgile travesti* (1648–52), a parody of the *Aeneid* in which the ancient gods and heroes speak like ordinary mortals, and which inspired C. *Cotton's popular *Scarronides, or Virgile Travestie* (1664, 1665).

Scenes of Clerical Life, a series of three tales by G. *Eliot, published in two volumes 1858, having appeared in *Blackwood's Magazine* in the previous year.

'The Sad Fortunes of the Rev. Amos Barton' is the sketch of a commonplace clergyman, the curate of Shepperton, without learning, tact, or charm, underpaid, unpopular with his parishioners, who earns their affection by his misfortune—the death from overwork, child-bearing, and general wretchedness of his beautiful gentle wife, Milly.

'Mr Gilfil's Love-Story' is the tale of a man whose nature has been warped by a tragic love experience. Maynard Gilfil was parson at Shepperton before the days of Amos Barton. He had been the ward of Sir Christopher Cheverel and his domestic chaplain, and had fallen deeply in love with Caterina Sastri (Tina), the daughter of an Italian singer, whom the Cheverels had adopted. But Capt. Anthony Wybrow, the heir of Sir Christopher, a shallow selfish fellow, had flirted with Tina and won her heart. At his uncle's bidding he had thrown her over for the rich Miss Assher. The strain of this brought Tina's passionate nature to the verge of lunacy. All this Gilfil had watched with sorrow and unabated love. Tina rallied for a time under his devoted care and finally married him, but died in a few months, leaving Gilfil like a tree lopped of its best branches.

'Janet's Repentance' is the story of a conflict

between religion and irreligion, and of the influence of a sympathetic human soul. The Revd Edgar Tryan, an earnest Evangelical clergyman, comes to the neighbourhood of Milby, an industrial town sunk in religious apathy, which the scanty ministration of the old curate, Mr Crewe, does nothing to stir. His endeavour to remedy this condition is opposed with the utmost vigour and bitterness by a group of inhabitants led by Dempster, a hectoring drunken brute of a lawyer, who beats and bullies his long-suffering wife Janet, until he drives her to drink. She shares her husband's prejudices against the methodistical innovator, until she discovers in him a sympathetic fellow-sufferer. Her husband's ill-treatment, which culminates in an act of gross brutality, causes her to appeal to Tryan for help, and under his guidance her struggle against the craving for drink begins. Dempster dies after a fall from his gig, and Janet gradually achieves self-conquest. The death of Tryan from consumption leaves her bereaved, but strengthened for a life of service.

Scepticism, a philosophical stance which questions the possibility of attaining lasting knowledge about the reality, as distinct from the appearance, of things, and which rejects all dogmatism, fanaticism, and intolerance. As a historical movement, scepticism had its origin in the teaching of some of the *Sophists in the 5th cent. BC. 'Pyrrhonian' scepticism, associated with Pyrrho in the following century, held that any argument supporting one side of a case could be balanced by a contrary argument of equal weight, so that the wise person suspends judgement and cultivates tranquillity and indifference to outward things. 'Academic' scepticism, associated with the Academy of Carneades, held that although the same evidence is always compatible with two contrary conclusions, some beliefs are more reasonable than others and we can act upon the balance of probabilities. *Montaigne and *Bayle in France and *Glanvill in England could combine scepticism with a devout theism, and sceptical techniques have frequently been practised by both supporters and opponents of religion to show that it rests on faith rather than reason. *Hume carried the study to new lengths in his *Treatise of Human Nature* in a detailed analysis of the rational factors which generate scepticism and the psychological factors which allay or moderate it. Since the time of *Descartes critics of scepticism, particularly in religion and morals, have tended to depict it as a form of negative dogmatism, i.e. as seeking actually to deny the existence of anything whose nature is in doubt.

SCÈVE, Maurice, (c.1501–?64), French poet. Long neglected, he has been rediscovered in the 20th cent., and has been called 'the most nearly "metaphysical" of French poets'. His current fame rests largely on his *Délie, object de plus haulte vertu,* an emblematic sequence of 449 *dizains,* primarily concerned with the problems and conflicts of love, published in 1544. He also wrote an eclogue, *Saulsaye* (1547), and *Microcosme* (1562), an epic poem dealing with the history of mankind since the fall of Adam.

Scheherazade, or **Shahrazad,** in the *Arabian Nights,* the daughter of the vizier of King Shahriyar, who married the king and escaped the death that was the usual fate of his wives by telling him the tales which compose that work, interrupting each one at an interesting point, and postponing the continuation till the next night. There is a symphonic suite for orchestra (*Sheherazade*) by Rimsky-Korsakov.

SCHELLING, Friedrich Wilhelm Joseph von (1775–1854), German philosopher, professor of philosophy at Jena, Würzburg, Munich, and Berlin. He was at first a disciple of *Fichte, soon departed from his doctrine. Unlike Fichte, Schelling makes the universe rather than the ego the element of reality. Nature, obedient to the laws of human intelligence, is a single living organism working towards self-consciousness, a faculty dormant in inanimate objects and fully awake only in man, whose being consists in 'intellectual intuition' of the world he creates. Schelling's numerous works include *Ideen zu einer Philosophie der Natur (Ideas towards a Philosophy of Nature,* 1797) and *System des transcendentalen Idealismus (System of Transcendental Idealism,* 1800). His doctrine of the interaction between subject and object, mind and nature, was fruitful for *Coleridge's formulation of the poetic Imagination as the reconciler of opposite qualities (see *Biographia Literaria,* 1817).

SCHILLER, Johann Christoph Friedrich von (1759–1805), German dramatist and lyric poet, the son of an army surgeon, and, with his early play *Die Räuber (The Robbers,* 1781), the chief figure of the *Sturm und Drang period of German literature. In this play Karl von Moor, the heroic robber, takes to the woods to redress the evils of his father's court, in contrast to his wicked brother Franz, who combines some of the characteristics of Shakespeare's *Richard III and Edmund in *King Lear.* The topicality of the theme of authoritarianism and liberty gave the play great popularity. In England *Hazlitt and *Coleridge read it with enthusiasm (see Coleridge's sonnet 'Schiller! That hour I would have wish'd to die', 1794). In his next important play, *Kabale und Liebe (Intrigue and Love,* 1784, the play on which *Verdi based his opera *Luisa Miller*), Schiller attacked contemporary society by showing the forces of a despotic state interfering tragically with the love of a patrician youth and a middle-class girl. There followed the blank verse drama *Don Carlos* (1787), and Schiller achieved his greatest dramatic success with the historical tragedy of *Wallenstein* (1799), composed of three parts, the second and third of which were translated into English verse by Coleridge in 1800. *Maria Stuart* (1800) also dramatizes history, as does *Die Jungfrau von Orleans* (*The Maid of Orleans*, 1801). Schiller then wrote a 'classical' drama with chorus, *Die Braut von Messina* (*The Bride of Messina*, 1803), and his last finished play was *Wilhelm Tell* (1804). All his plays are concerned with the problem of freedom and responsibility, either political, as in the early dramas, or personal and moral.

Schiller was also a fine poet, author of reflective and lyrical poems as well as ballads (he and *Goethe collaborated on a collection of ballads in 1797–8, as Wordsworth and Coleridge did in England at the same time). Some of the best-known poems are 'Die Künstler' ('The Artists'), a poem on the humanizing influence of art; 'Das Ideal und das Leben' ('The Ideal and Life'), a philosophical poem on the unbridgeable gap between the real and the ideal; 'Die Glocke' ('The Bell'); and 'An die Freude' ('Ode to Joy'), which *Beethoven set to music in his Ninth Symphony.

Appointed professor of history at Jena in 1789, Schiller was also the author of historical works on the Revolt of the Netherlands (1788) and the Thirty Years War (the period of *Wallenstein*). He was also a serious student of *Kant's philosophy and the author of *Philosophische Briefe* (*Philosophical Letters*, 1786). Kant influenced his thinking about art, and of his many essays on aesthetics the most important were influential on German Romantic critics like the *Schlegels, and also possibly on Coleridge, who knew and admired his works. These are the *Briefe über die ästhetische Erziehung des Menschen* (*On the Aesthetic Education of Man*, 1795, translated and introduced by E. M. Wilkinson and L. A. Willoughby, 1967); *Über naive und sentimentalische Dichtung* (*On Naïve and Reflective Poetry*, 1795–6), in which Schiller contrasts his own 'modern', reflective mode of writing with Goethe's more 'antique', unselfconscious genius; and several essays on the liberating and moral influence of the theatre.

SCHLEGEL, August Wilhelm von (1767–1845), German Romanticist, critic, and philologist, chiefly known in England for his translation into German, with the assistance of his wife and others, of the plays of Shakespeare. He also became famous for his lectures *Über dramatische Kunst und Literatur* (1809–11), translated by John Black as *Lectures on Dramatic Art and Literature* (1815). *Wordsworth and *Hazlitt praised the lectures dealing with Shakespeare, and *Coleridge almost certainly borrowed from them for his own lectures on Shakespeare. Schlegel was also, with his younger brother Friedrich (below), the author of *Das*

Athenäum (1798–1800), a manifesto of German Romanticism.

SCHLEGEL, Friedrich von (1772–1829), younger brother of A. W. von *Schlegel, notable for his studies of the history of literature, particularly *Geschichte der alten und neuen Literatur*, trans. *Lockhart as *Lectures on the History of Literature, Ancient and Modern* (1818); his recognition of the importance of ancient Hindu poetry, *Sprache und Weisheit der Indier* (*Language and Wisdom of the Indians*, 1808); and his critical fragments and essays, many of them published in the periodical he wrote with his brother, *Das Athenäum* (1798–1800). He contrasted classical and romantic literature, and expounded his theory of 'romantic irony', or the consciousness on the part of the artist of the unbridgeable gap between the ideal artistic goal and the limited possibilities of achievement.

Schlemihl, Peter, in the story or allegory by *Chamisso, the impecunious young man who surrendered his shadow to the devil, a thin elderly gentleman in a grey coat, in exchange for a purse of Fortunatus (see OLD FORTUNATUS). The lack of a shadow exposes Peter to disagreeable notice, and in spite of his wealth he finds himself an outcast from human society.

SCHOENBAUM, Samuel (1927–), American scholar. His *Shakespeare's Lives* (1970) is a history of accounts of Shakespeare's life; his *William Shakespeare: A Documentary Life* (1975) reproduces most of the relevant documents and this has been revised as *William Shakespeare: A Compact Documentary Life* (1977).

SCHOENBERG, Arnold (1874–1951), Austrian composer, theorist, and teacher. As the pioneer of the 'atonal' style in music, and the inventor of the serial, or 12-note, system of composition that grew out of it, Schoenberg has probably been the greatest single influence in the music of the 20th cent. Only two of his works use English literary sources: *Seraphita* (1913), the first of *Four Orchestral Songs*, to a poem of *Dowson translated by Stefan George; and much later, after his removal from Europe to the USA, the setting of *Byron's *Ode to Napoleon Buonaparte* for string quartet, piano, and speaker (1942). In the latter, a strictly serial work, Byron's poem was used by the composer as a framework for the expression of his deep hatred of *Hitler and all contemporary totalitarian régimes.

Towards the end of his life Schoenberg became involved in a quarrel with T. *Mann who, in his novel *Doctor Faustus*, had attributed the invention of the 12-note method of composition to the hero, Adrian Leverkühn, without any mention of Schoenberg's name. The affair achieved some notoriety and weighed heavily on Schoenberg's mind in his last years, though in the end the two men, at least in theory, were reconciled.

'Scholar-Gipsy, The', a poem by M. *Arnold, published 1853. The poem, pastoral in setting, is based on an old legend, narrated by *Glanvill in his *The Vanity of Dogmatizing*, of an 'Oxford scholar poor', who, tired of seeking preferment, joined the gypsies to learn their lore, roamed with them, and still haunts the Oxford countryside. With this is woven a vivid evocation of the places Arnold visited with his Oxford friends (Bagley Wood, Hinksey, the Cumnor moors, etc.) and reflections on the contrast between the single-minded faith of the scholar-gipsy and the modern world, 'the strange disease of modern life, | With its sick hurry, its divided aims'. The tone, as in many of Arnold's best works, is elegiac, but he wrote to *Clough condemning it for failing to 'animate': 'The Gipsy Scholar at best awakens a pleasing melancholy. But this is not what we want.'

Scholasticism, the doctrines of the *Schoolmen, and the predominant theological and philosophical teachings of the period 1100–1500, mainly an attempt to reconcile *Aristotle with the Scriptures, and Reason with Faith. It is characterized too by its dialectical method of argument, first associated with *Abelard. Its greatest monument is the *Summa Theologica* of *Aquinas. In the 14th cent., after *Ockham, Scholasticism had exhausted itself as an intellectual movement. See F. J. Copleston, SJ, *A History of Philosophy*, Vol. 2 (1950).

Scholemaster, The, see ASCHAM, R.

Schoole of Abuse, see GOSSON, S.

School for Scandal, The, a comedy by R. B. *Sheridan, produced 1777.

In this play, generally agreed to be one of the most masterly of English comedies, the author contrasts two brothers: Joseph Surface, the sanctimonious hypocrite, and Charles, the good-natured, reckless spendthrift. Charles is in love with Maria, the ward of Sir Peter Teazle, and his love is returned; Joseph is courting the same girl for her fortune, while at the same time dallying with Lady Teazle. Sir Peter, an old man who has married his young wife six months previously, is made wretched by her frivolity and the fashionable society she inhabits. Members of this society include Sir Benjamin Backbite, Crabtree, Lady Sneerwell, and Mrs Candour, who 'strike a character dead at every word' and chatter with malicious brilliance whenever they meet. Sir Oliver Surface, the rich uncle of Joseph and Charles, returns unexpectedly from India, and decides to test the characters of his nephews before revealing his identity. He visits Charles in the guise of a money-lender, Mr Premium, and Charles, always hard up, cheerfully sells him the family

portraits—but refuses to sell the portrait of 'the ill-looking little fellow over the settee', who is Sir Oliver himself. Thus he unwittingly wins the old man's heart. Meanwhile Joseph receives a visit from Lady Teazle and attempts to seduce her. The sudden arrival of Sir Peter obliges Lady Teazle to hide behind a screen, where she is filled with shame and remorse as she listens to proof of Sir Peter's generosity to her, even though he suspects an attachment between her and Charles. The arrival of Charles sends Sir Peter in turn to hide. Sir Peter detects the presence of a woman behind the screen, but is told by Joseph that it is a little French milliner, so he takes refuge in a cupboard instead. The conversation between Charles and Joseph proves to Sir Peter that his suspicions of Charles were unfounded. On Joseph's leaving the room, Sir Peter emerges and together he and Charles agree to reveal the little French milliner. When Charles flings down the screen he reveals Lady Teazle. Lady Teazle begs Sir Peter's forgiveness and Joseph returns, to be upbraided by both. Sir Oliver then enters in the character of a needy relative, begging for assistance. Joseph refuses, giving as his reason the avarice of his uncle, Sir Oliver, and his character now stands fully revealed. Charles is united to Maria, and Sir Peter and Lady Teazle are happily reconciled.

Schoolmen, the succession of writers, from about the 11th to the 15th cent., who treat of logic, metaphysics, and theology, as taught in the 'schools' or universities of Italy, France, Germany, and England, that is to say on the basis of *Aristotle and the Christian Fathers, whom the schoolmen endeavoured to harmonize. Among the great Schoolmen were Peter *Lombard, *Abelard, *Albertus Magnus, *Aquinas, *Duns Scotus, and *Ockham. (See SCHOLASTICISM.)

Schoolmistress, The, see SHENSTONE, W.

School of Night, a name drawn from a satirical allusion in *Love's Labour's Lost* (IV. iii. 214), and first ascribed by Arthur Acheson in 1903 (*Shakespeare and the Rival Poet*) to a supposed circle of speculative thinkers, led by *Harriot and *Ralegh, and including *Marlowe, *Chapman, Lawrence Keymis, and the 'Wizard Earl' Northumberland. J. Dover *Wilson, G. B. *Harrison in his edition of *Willobie His Avisa* (1926), and M. C. *Bradbrook in *The School of Night* (1936) supported the theory that *Love's Labour's Lost* was an attack upon this coterie, which engaged in free-thinking philosophical debate (not necessarily atheistic) and dabbled in hermeticism, alchemy, and the occult. The existence of such a circle is now much disputed.

SCHOPENHAUER, Arthur (1788–1860), was the author of a pessimistic philosophy embodied in his *Die Welt als Wille und Vorstellung* (*The World as Will and Idea*, 1819). According to this, Will, of which we have direct intuition, is the 'thing-in-itself', the only reality. Will, which is self-consciousness in man, finds its equivalent in the unconscious forces of nature. Will, then, it is that creates the world; and the world is not only an illusion but a malignant thing, which inveigles us into reproducing and perpetuating life. Asceticism, and primarily chastity, are the duty of man, with a view to terminating the evil. Egoism, which manifests itself principally in the 'will to live', must be overcome. Its opposite is compassion, the moral law, based on the intuition of the essential identity of all beings. God, free will, and the immortality of the soul are illusions.

SCHREINER, Olive Emilie Albertina (1855–1920), born in Cape Colony, the daughter of a missionary, began to write while working as a governess, and when she came to England in 1881 had completed her best-known novel, *The Story of an African Farm*, published to much acclaim in 1883 under the pseudonym 'Ralph Iron'. Set in the vividly evoked landscape of her childhood, it recounts the lives of two orphaned cousins, stay-at-home Em and unconventional Lyndall, greeted by feminists as one of the first 'New Women', who breaks away from her Bible-belt origins, becomes pregnant by a lover whom she refuses to marry, and dies after the death of her baby; also of Waldo, son of the farm's German overseer, whose rebellious spirit is aroused (as was Schreiner's) by reading H. *Spencer's First Principles. This novel won her the friendship of Havelock *Ellis, and while in England she moved in progressive literary and political circles, returning in 1889 to South Africa, where she married the politician Samuel Cron Cronwright. In 1914 she came back to England, returning to the Cape to die. Her other novels, both with feminist themes, *From Man to Man* (1927) and *Undine* (1929), appeared posthumously, but during her lifetime she published various other works, including collections of allegories and stories, articles on South African politics, and *Woman and Labour* (1911). Courageous and unconventional as a woman, Schreiner as a writer has been acknowledged as a pioneer both in her treatment of women and in her fictional use of the African landscape. See Ruth First and Ann Scott, *Olive Schreiner* (1980).

SCHUBERT, Franz Peter (1797–1828), Austrian composer and successor to *Haydn, *Mozart, and *Beethoven in the Viennese classical school. In spite of his achievement in the fields of orchestral, chamber, and piano music, it is as a song-writer that Schubert has generally been most highly regarded. Out of more than 600 songs, only 14 are settings of texts of English or British origin (all in German trans-

lations). The most famous of these in Schubert's own lifetime were the W. *Scott songs, especially Ellen's three songs from *The Lady of the Lake* (1825) which include the once rather too popular 'Ave Maria'; from the same source are two part-songs, one of them the beautiful 'Coronach'. Three more Scott songs, 'Lied der Anne Lyle', 'Gesang der Norna', and 'Romanze des Richard Löwenherz' (the king's song from *Ivanhoe*), were written about the same time, though not published till 1828, and there are one or two other English settings, including C. *Cibber's 'The Blind Boy' and the Scottish ballad *Edward*. More famous than any of these, however, are the Shakespeare settings of 1826: the clear freshness of 'Hark, hark, the lark' may have suffered, like the 'Ave Maria', from years of mauling by inadequate singers, but its quality can still be conveyed in a good performance, and no amount of repetition can dim the exquisite simplicity of 'Who is Silvia?' The drinking song from *Antony and Cleopatra*, 'Come! thou Monarch of the Vine', is a less interesting piece.

SCHUMANN, Robert (1810–56), German composer and central figure of the musical Romantic movement. Literary inspiration was very important to Schumann (who was also a writer and musical journalist) and, although this was naturally drawn mainly from works in his own language, there is a sprinkling of English literary associations in the list of his compositions. The first of his major choral works, *Das Paradies und die Peri* (1843), is a setting of a poem from T. Moore's *Lalla Rookh*, treated as a kind of secular oratorio, though without much dramatic sense. Far more successful is the incidental music—an overture and 15 shorter pieces—for Byron's *Manfred* (1849), for which (unlike *Byron himself) he seems to have envisaged a stage presentation: the resulting hybrid is not easy to bring off in performance, though the overture is one of Schumann's best short orchestral works. The later overture to Shakespeare's *Julius Caesar* (1852) does not live up to its own impressive opening.

For many people Schumann is primarily a composer of piano music and songs, and in the latter category there are a number of translations from English, and particularly Scottish, texts: there are nine settings of *Burns (eight included in the *Myrthen* cycle of 1840), several of which happily catch the simple lyricism of the words, and a later group of 5 *Gedichte der Königin Maria Stuart* (1852), written during the onset of his final illness and insanity, and on the whole less successful. There are also two Burns settings as duets, and nine more still (including two separate versions of 'John Anderson, mein Lieb!') for unaccompanied mixed voices. Also in *Myrthen* a single, very beautiful Byron song, 'Mein Herz ist schwer', simpler and more telling than the *Drei Gesänge* of Byron of 1851, and two *Vene-

tianischer Lieder of Moore. One Shakespeare setting, 'When that I was and a little tiny boy' in the new translation by Tieck and *Schlegel, appeared in 1840, and in 1853 a curiosity, *Shelley's *The Fugitives* set as a declamation with piano accompaniment.

Science Fiction is the current name for a class of prose narrative which assumes an imaginary technological or scientific advance, or depends upon an imaginary and spectacular change in the human environment. Although examples exist from the time of *Lucian, and Swift's *Gulliver's Travels*, Mary Shelley's *Frankenstein*, and Bulwer-Lytton's *The Coming Race* are unmistakable precursors, it was not until the end of the 19th cent. that the form emerged as we know it today. The works of *Verne have always been popular in this country, but the first successful English author was H. G. *Wells whose stories include several of the themes later dominant: invasion from outer space (*The War of the Worlds*, 1898), biological change or catastrophe (*The Food of the Gods*, 1904), time travel (*The Time Machine*, 1895), and air warfare (*The War in the Air*, 1908).

Since the Second World War scientific developments and their possible consequences have been reflected in fictional forms by motifs such as interplanetary travel, robots (originally introduced by *Čapek in the 1920s), mechanical brains, and atomic hand weapons; and the destruction of the world as a result of its own technological achievements has proved a favourite theme, often carrying strong *apocalyptic undertones. The literary quality of Science Fiction is extremely variable, ranging from violent strip cartoons in pulp magazines, through the speculative works of the philosopher Olaf Stapledon (1886–1950), to the respectable domestic novels of *Wyndham and the more challenging intellectual ventures of *Ballard, *Aldiss, and *Moorcock. (Moorcock was from 1964 to 1971, editor of an influential magazine, *New Worlds*, which attracted much of the so-called 'New Wave' talent of the period.) Science Fiction elements are present in the 'alternative world' of *Tolkien, the interplanetary stories of C. S. *Lewis, the fantasies of *Burgess and the later works of D. *Lessing. The impact of the Science Fiction genre on film and television has also been enormous; products range from popular children's programmes such as *Dr Who* to *2001: A Space Odyssey* (1968), filmed by Stanley Kubrick from the novel by Arthur C. *Clarke. See K. *Amis, *New Maps of Hell* (1961); B. Aldiss, *Billion Year Spree* (1973).

Scillaes Metamorphosis, a poem by T. *Lodge, later published (1610) under the title *Glaucus and Scilla*. It is the earliest of many Ovidian epyllia, or minor epics, in the Elizabethan period, and describes the sea-god Glaucus's courtship of the nymph Scilla, who is punished for her cruelty to him by being metamorphosed into a lonely rock in the sea. It bears both a generic and a specific relationship to Shakespeare's *Venus and Adonis*, including a brief account of the death of Adonis beginning:

He that hath seene the sweete *Arcadian* boy
Wiping the purple from his forced wound.

SCOGAN, Henry (?1361–1407), a poet whose only surviving literary work is the 'Moral Balade', dedicated to the four sons of Henry IV to whom he was tutor. It is generally agreed that he is the dedicatee of *Chaucer's 'Lenvoy de Chaucer a Scogan', written towards the end of 1393. *Leland says he was a man given to all sort of jocoseness and wit, and he is perhaps mentioned by Shakespeare (2 *Henry IV*, III. ii. 30—though the reference may be to John Scogan, below).

SCOGAN, John, a celebrated jester of Edward IV, whose exploits, real or imagined, are recorded in *The Jestes of Skogyn* (c.1570).

Scoop, a novel by E. *Waugh, published 1938.

Lord Copper, proprietor of *The Beast* (which stands for 'strong mutually antagonistic governments everywhere') is persuaded to send novelist John Boot to cover the war in Ishmaelia, but William Boot, writer of nature notes (torn reluctant and bewildered from his quiet life at Boot Magna), is dispatched by mistake. After many adventures he returns to find himself covered with glory, although in another case of mistaken identity John Boot has been knighted in his stead. Based on Waugh's own experiences in Abyssinia in 1936, where he was writing for the *Daily Mail*, the novel is a brilliantly comic satire of Fleet Street ethics and manners, and on the battle for readership between *The Beast* and *The Brute*.

SCOT, Michael, see SCOTT, M. (c.1175–c.1235).

SCOT, or **SCOTT,** Reginald (?1538–99), educated at Hart Hall, Oxford, and MP for New Romney, 1588–9, was author of *The Discoverie of Witchcraft* (1584). This was written with the aim of preventing the persecution of poor, aged, and simple persons who were popularly believed to be witches, by exposing the impostures on the one hand, and the credulity on the other, that supported the belief in sorcery. He also wrote *A perfite platforme of a hoppe garden* (1574).

Scotist, see DUNS SCOTUS.

Scots is a historical offshoot of the Northumbrian dialect of Anglo-Saxon, sharing with Northern Middle English a strong Norse element in vocabulary and vowel and consonant developments which still mark off northern speech from Standard English. To this Gaelic, French

(Norman and Parisian), and Dutch elements accrued and the political independence of Scotland gave this speech a national status. It became also the vehicle of a considerable literature in *Barbour, *Henryson, *Dunbar, *Douglas, Sir D. *Lindsay, and there was much prose translation as well, but the failure to produce a vernacular Bible at the Reformation, the Union of the Crowns in 1603, and that of the Parliaments in 1707 all helped to extend the bounds of English and prevent the evolution of an all-purpose Scots prose. The 18th-cent. literary revival of Scots under *Ramsay, *Fergusson, and *Burns, who gave it the name of 'Lallans' (Lowlands), was confined to poetry, with prose used merely to represent the colloquy of rustic characters, in Sir W. *Scott, *Hogg, *Galt, R. L. *Stevenson and the *'Kailyard School'. With the renaissance of the period 1920–50, writers like *MacDiarmid, Robert Maclellan (1907–), S. G. *Smith, Douglas Young (1913–), Alexander Scott (1920–), Robert Kemp (1908–), and others, attempted a re-creation of a full canon of Scots to cope with modern themes, which was also called Lallans, the name now connoting the new experimental speech rather than the old historical vernacular which had been rapidly losing ground in the previous 100 years. But Lallans is still defective in prose, and both the name and the practice are at the moment somewhat out of fashion.

Scots Musical Museum, The, (1787–1803), edited by James Johnson, an important collection of songs with music, some genuinely antique, some fake antique, and some new. *Burns made many notable contributions to the later volumes.

'Scots wha hae,' a battle-song by *Burns published in *The Scots Musical Museum.

SCOTT, C. P., see MANCHESTER GUARDIAN.

SCOTT, Geoffrey (1883–1929), poet and biographer, son of a Unitarian manufacturer and nephew of C. P. Scott, editor of the *Manchester Guardian. He was educated at Rugby and New College, Oxford, where he won the Newdigate Prize in 1906 with a poem, 'The Death of Shelley'. His interest in architectural theory was confirmed by his friendship with *Berenson, and culminated in his study The Architecture of Humanism (1914). Scott had great conversational talents, which, combined with what the artist William Rothenstein described as his 'Botticellian' beauty, made him disastrously attractive to women, not least, it would appear, to Berenson's wife Mary. Scott's best-known book is The Portrait of Zélide (1925), an elegant and evocative life of Mme de Charrière (see ZÉLIDE) which his friend Edith *Wharton described as a 'wellnigh perfect' book; Scott wrote in a 'Note', 'I have sought to give her the reality of fiction; but my material is fact.' In the same

year appeared Four Tales by Zélide, translated by Scott's wife Lady Sybil (née Cutting). Scott was working on a biography of *Boswell and an edition of a collection of Boswell papers when he died in New York of pneumonia.

SCOTT, John (1783–1821), educated at the same Aberdeen school as *Byron, was the first editor, 1820–1, of the remarkable *London Magazine; he had by then edited The Champion, and published A Visit to Paris (1814) and Paris Revisited (1816), both books of high repute and admired by many, including *Wordsworth. He began his editorial career approving of *Blackwood's Magazine for its 'spirit of life', and he based the London on roughly the same plan, but with a greater emphasis on books and original writing. He attracted a brilliant set of contributors; de Quincey's *Confessions of an Opium Eater, *Lamb's earlier 'Elia' essays, and much of *Hazlitt's Table-Talk first appeared in the London Magazine, as well as work by *Keats, *Clare, *Hood, *Darley, *Carlyle, *Cunningham, and others. His reviewers aimed to seek out excellence rather than to condemn, and they were permitted no political bias. Scott's own writing on Wordsworth, Sir W. *Scott, *Shelley, Keats, Byron, and other young writers, is of high quality. *Talfourd described him as 'a critic of remarkable candour, eloquence and discrimination'. Eventually he found conflict with Blackwood's impossible to avoid; he came to detest what he saw as its 'scurrility' and 'duplicity and treachery', and he felt obliged to defend his *'Cockney School'. His attacks on Blackwood's, in particular on *Lockhart, led to a series of confusions which culminated in a duel with J. H. Christie, a close friend of Lockhart, in which Scott was killed. There is a biography, Regency Editor (1983), by Patrick O'Leary.

SCOTT, or **SCOT,** Michael (c.1175–c.1235), a Scottish scholar, born at Balwearie, who studied at Oxford, Bologna, and Paris, and was attached to the court of Frederick II at Palermo, probably in the capacity of official astrologer. He translated works of *Aristotle from Arabic to Latin (including De Anima, pre-1220), and perhaps *Averroes' great Aristotelian Commentary, which he certainly began. Because the science he studied was astronomy, legends of his magical power grew up and served as a theme for many writers from *Dante (Inferno, xx. 116) to Sir W. Scott in *The Lay of the Last Minstrel. Works of his on astronomy and alchemy, and various translations, still remain in manuscript. See Lynn Thorndike, Michael Scot (1965).

SCOTT, Michael (1789–1835), was for some years an estate manager in Jamaica, which he left in 1822 to settle in his native Glasgow. Between 1829 and 1833 he published in *Blackwood's Magazine the anonymous Tom Cringle's Log, entertaining sketches of the life he had known in the Caribbean. It was very successful, and *Coleridge found it 'most excellent', yet Scott concealed his identity all his life. In 1834–5 he published *The Cruise of the Midge*, a work with a similar background, equally well received.

SCOTT, Paul Mark (1920–78), novelist, born in north London and educated at Winchmore Hill Collegiate School. He held a commission in the Indian army during the Second World War, and worked for many years in publishing and for a literary agency before becoming a full-time writer. His first novel, *Johnnie Sahib* (1952), was followed by twelve others, most of them dealing with Anglo-Indian relationships, and he is best remembered for the four novels known as the 'Raj Quartet': *The Jewel in the Crown* (1966), *The Day of the Scorpion* (1968), *The Towers of Silence* (1971), and *A Division of the Spoils* (1975). These interwoven narratives, set in India during and immediately after the Second World War, portray political, personal, racial, and religious conflicts in the period leading up to Independence and Partition, presenting events from various points of view in a complex chronological sequence that only gradually reveals a total picture. There are two key episodes in the first volume: the death of a missionary, Edwina Crane, who commits suicide by burning herself to death after a violent incident in which an Indian colleague is killed, and the alleged rape in the Bibighar Gardens of Mayapore of the symbolically named young Englishwoman, Daphne Manners. A group of young Indians, including Daphne's friend, the English-reared and public-school-educated Hari Kumar, is accused, and all are brutally interrogated by ex-grammar-school (and, as it later emerges, repressed homosexual) Ronald Merrick, the district superintendent of police. The affair takes on a political aspect, and its repercussions include, in the fourth volume, Merrick's murder, Daphne having died in childbirth after refusing to implicate Kumar. Other characters in the large canvas include Barbara Batchelor, lonely spinster and retired missionary, who dies insane, haunted by Miss Crane's death; Mildred Layton, hard-drinking wife of prisoner-of-war Colonel Layton of the Pankot Rifles, and their two daughters, sensible Sarah and vain Susan (who marries Merrick as her second husband, after he has lost an arm attempting to rescue her first husband from a blazing tank); Muslim leader and ex-minister Mohammed Ali Kasim, known as MAK, who is imprisoned by the British despite his pro-British sympathies, and his son Ahmed, one of the first victims of the massacres attending Partition; and Count Bronowsky, Russian émigré adviser to the Nawab of Mirat. Scott's last novel, *Staying On* (1977), which was awarded the *Booker Prize, picks up the story of two minor characters

from the Quartet, Colonel 'Tusker' Smalley and his wife Lucy, social misfits who decide to stay on after Independence, surviving on a small pension as they attempt to adjust to the attitudes and conditions of the new India. Although respectfully reviewed during Scott's lifetime, the novels won an increasingly high posthumous reputation, and also gained a popular readership, partly through the televising of the Raj Quartet in 1984 under the title of *The Jewel in the Crown*. J. *Mitchell adapted *Staying On* for television in 1981.

SCOTT, Reginald, see SCOT, R.

SCOTT, Robert Falcon (1868–1912), Antarctic explorer, commanded the National Antarctic Expedition (1900–2), discovering King Edward VII Island, which he recorded in his *The Voyage of the Discovery* (1905). His notable journal, published as *Scott's Last Expedition* (1913), describes his second Antarctic expedition, the last entry of which was made as Scott lay dying, stormbound on his return from the South Pole.

SCOTT, Sir Walter (1771–1832), son of Walter Scott, a writer to the Signet, was born in College Wynd, Edinburgh, educated at Edinburgh High School and University, and apprenticed to his father. He was called to the bar in 1792. His interest in the old Border tales and ballads had early been awakened, and was stimulated by Percy's *Reliques* and by the study of the old romantic poetry of France and Italy and of the modern German poets. He devoted much of his leisure to the exploration of the Border country. In 1797 he published anonymously in *The Chase and William and Helen*, a translation of Bürger's 'Der wilde Jäger' (*'The Wild Huntsman') and *'Lenore', and in 1799 a translation of *Goethe's *Götz von Berlichingen*. In 1797 he married Margaret Charlotte Charpentier (or Carpenter), daughter of Jean Charpentier of Lyon in France, and was appointed sheriff-depute of Selkirkshire in 1799. In 1802–3 appeared the three volumes of Scott's *Minstrelsy of the Scottish Border*; and in 1805 his first considerable original work, the romantic poem *The Lay of the Last Minstrel*. He then became a partner in James *Ballantyne's printing business and published *Marmion* in 1808. This was followed by *The Lady of the Lake (1810), *Rokeby* and *The Bridal of Triermain* (1813), *The Lord of the Isles* (1815), and *Harold the Dauntless* (1817), his last long poem. In 1809 he had entered into partnership with John Ballantyne in the bookselling business known as 'John Ballantyne & Co.', and in 1811 he had purchased Abbotsford on the Tweed, where he built himself a residence. Scott promoted the foundation in 1809 of the Tory *Quarterly Review*—he had been a contributor to the *Edinburgh Review*, but seceded from it owing to its

Whig attitude. In 1813 he refused the offer of the laureateship and recommended *Southey for the honour. Eclipsed in a measure by *Byron as a poet, in spite of the great popularity of his verse romances, he now turned his attention to the novel as a means of giving play to his wide erudition, his humour, and his sympathies. His novels appeared anonymously in the following order: *Waverley (1814); *Guy Mannering (1815); *The Antiquary (1816); *The Black Dwarf and *Old Mortality (1816), as the first series of *Tales of My Landlord; *Rob Roy (1817); *The Heart of Midlothian (1818), the second series of Tales of My Landlord; *The Bride of Lammermoor and *A Legend of Montrose (1819), the third series of Tales of My Landlord; *Ivanhoe (1819); *The Monastery (1820); *The Abbot (1820); *Kenilworth (1821); *The Pirate (1821); *The Fortunes of Nigel (1822); *Peveril of the Peak (1823); *Quentin Durward (1823); *St Ronan's Well (1823); *Redgauntlet (1824); *The Betrothed and *The Talisman (1825), together as Tales of the Crusaders; *Woodstock (1826); *Chronicles of the Canongate (1827, containing *'The Highland Widow', *'The Two Drovers', and *The Surgeon's Daughter); Chronicles of the Canongate (second series): Saint Valentine's Day, or *The Fair Maid of Perth (1828); *Anne of Geierstein (1829); Tales of My Landlord (fourth series): *Count Robert of Paris and *Castle Dangerous (1831). Scott was created a baronet in 1820, and avowed the authorship of the novels in 1827. In 1826 James Ballantyne & Co. became involved in the bankruptcy of Constable & Co., and Scott, as partner of the former, found himself liable for a debt of about £114,000. He shouldered the whole burden himself and henceforth worked heroically, shortening his own life by his strenuous efforts, to pay off the creditors, who received full payment after his death.

Scott's dramatic work, in which he did not excel, includes Halidon Hill (1822), Macduff's Cross (1823), The Doom of Devorgoil, a Melodrama and Auchindrane or the Ayrshire Tragedy (both 1830). Of these Auchindrane is the best. It is founded on the case of Mure of Auchindrane in Pitcairn's Ancient Criminal Trials. Mention must also be made of the important historical, literary, and antiquarian works written by Scott or issued under his editorship: The Works of Dryden with a Life (1808); The Works of Swift with a Life (1814); Provincial Antiquities of Scotland (1819–26); an abstract of the 'Eyrbiggia Saga' in Northern Antiquities (1814); Description of the Regalia of Scotland (1819); Lives of the Novelists prefixed to Ballantyne's Novelist's Library (1821–4); essays on Chivalry (1818), the Drama (1819) and Romance (1824) contributed to the *Encyclopaedia Britannica; The Life of Napoleon Buonaparte (1827); *The Tales of a Grandfather (1827–30); History of Scotland (1829–30); Letters on Demonology and Witchcraft

(1830); Original Memoirs written during the Great Civil War of Sir H. Slingsby and Captain Hodgson (1806); the *Memoirs of Captain George Carleton (1808); the State Papers of Sir Ralph Sadler (1809); the Secret History of James I (1811); and Memorie of the Somervilles (1815). *Paul's Letters to his Kinsfolk appeared in 1816. Scott founded the *Bannatyne Club in 1823. In 1826 he addressed to the Edinburgh Weekly Journal three letters 'from Malachi Malagrowther', 'Thoughts on the proposed Change of Currency', defending the rights of Scotland.

Scott's Life by J. G. *Lockhart, published in 1837–8, has been considered one of the great biographies of English literature. Scott's Journal was published in 1890 and again in 1939–46, in 3 vols, edited by J. G. Tait; there is a modern edition by W. E. K. Anderson, 1972. An edition of his letters in 12 vols was published by H. J. C. Grierson (1932–7) with an index and notes by J. C. Corson, 1979. Sir Walter Scott: the Great Unknown, a biography by Edgar Johnson, 2 vols, was published in 1970.

Scott's influence as a novelist was incalculable; he established the form of the *Historical novel, and, according to V. S. *Pritchett, the form of the short story (with 'The Two Drovers' and 'The Highland Widow'). He was avidly read and imitated throughout the 19th cent., not only by historical novelists such as *Ainsworth and *Bulwer-Lytton, but also by writers like Mrs *Gaskell, G. *Eliot, the *Brontës, and many others, who treated rural themes, contemporary peasant life, regional speech, etc., in a manner that owed much to Scott. His reputation gradually declined (though his medieval and Tudor romances retained a popular readership) until there was a revival of interest from European *Marxist critics in the 1930s (see LUKÁCS), who interpreted his works in terms of historicism. In 1951 three seminal essays were published, David *Daiches's 'Scott's Achievement as a Novelist' (Nineteenth-Century Fiction), Arnold Kettle's chapter in his Introduction to the English Novel (Vol. 1), and S. Stewart Gordon's 'Waverley and the "Unified Design"' (English Literary History, Vol. XVIII); these heralded a considerable upsurge of scholarly activity and reappraisal, most of which concurs in regarding the Scottish 'Waverley' novels (including The Antiquary, Old Mortality, The Heart of Midlothian) as his masterpieces. For a survey of critical attitudes, see Walter Scott: Modern Judgements (1968, ed. D. D. Devlin) and Walter Scott (1982) by T. Crawford.

SCOTT, William Bell (1811–90), poet, artist, and art critic, who taught for many years in Newcastle upon Tyne; his mural Iron and Coal (1862) at Wallington Hall, Northumberland, is one of the earliest representations in art of heavy industry. Scott was a friend of D. G. *Rossetti (who made his acquaintance through an admiring letter) and later of *Swinburne; he was associated with the birth of the *Pre-Raphaelite movement, and contributed to *The Germ. His poems and verses (of which he published several volumes, some illustrated by himself) range from rambling *Pindaric odes to sonnets and medieval-style ballads. His *Autobiographcal Notes* (1892), edited by W. Minto, gave much offence to the Rossetti family.

Scottish Chaucerians, see CHAUCERIANS, SCOTTISH.

Scottish Chiefs, The, a *historical novel by J. *Porter, published 1810.

The story is a romance based on events in the life of William Wallace. The triumphs and setbacks of his career are followed through to his execution, and the story ends with the battle of Bannockburn. The novel was extremely successful, and was translated into German and Russian.

Scottish Enlightenment, a phrase used to describe an intellectual movement originating in Glasgow in the early 18th cent. but reaching fruition mainly in Edinburgh between 1750 and 1800. Several threads are traceable in the attitudes of the scientists, philosophers and *literati associated with the movement, although no single tenet was held by all: a deep concern for the practical implications and social benefits of their enquiries (proclaimed as leading to 'improvement'), an emphasis on the interconnection between separable human practices, and an interest in the philosophical principles underlying them. Several of the group developed an interest in history, and many were at least nominal *Deists.

The main philosophers were *Hutcheson, *Hume, Adam *Smith, A. *Ferguson; for his leadership of the so-called 'common-sense' opposition, *Reid should be mentioned, and later D. *Stewart. The political, economic and social thought of Hume, Smith, and Ferguson was particularly influential in France and America, and the works of Reid and Stewart played a central role in the development of American college education, along with the lectures on rhetoric of H. *Blair. The scientists of the movement included William Cullen, who established chemistry as a discipline in its own right, Joseph Black, who propounded the theories of latent and specific heat, James Hutton, the founder of modern geology, and the Doctors Monro, who were instrumental in establishing the reputation of the Edinburgh Medical School. The names of James Watt, and John Loudon McAdam should also be listed. The literary figures, like their French contemporaries, were often ambivalent towards the theories and practices of their scientific and speculative colleagues, and increasingly distanced themselves towards the end of the century. *Boswell and *Burns were never part of the movement, although Sir W. *Scott is associated with its closing decades. Numerous learned societies and journals flourished during the period, and the founding of the *Encyclopaedia Britannica was in part a product of the movement. (See also ROYAL SOCIETY OF EDINBURGH.)

Scottish Texts Society, The, founded in 1882 for the purpose of printing and editing texts illustrative of the Scottish language and literature, has issued editions of many works of general literary interest, such as *The Kingis Quair, *Barbour's *Bruce,* Gawin *Douglas's *Eneados,* and the *Basilikon Doron,* and the poems of *Dunbar, *Henryson, *Drummond of Hawthornden, and Sir D. *Lindsay. Although the Society's primary concern has been with medieval and Renaissance works, it has also produced a few important editions of later writers, including A. *Ramsay and R. *Fergusson.

SCOTUS, John Duns, see DUNS SCOTUS.

SCOTUS ERIGENA, John (John the Scot) (c.810–77), of Irish origin, was employed as teacher at the court of Charles the Bald, afterwards emperor, c.847. The leading principle of his philosophy, as expounded in his great work *De Divisione Naturae,* is that of the unity of nature; this proceeds from (1) God, the first and only real being (Nature which creates and is not created); through (2) the Creative Ideas (Nature which creates and is created); to (3) the sensible Universe (Nature which is created and does not create); everything is ultimately resolved into (4) its First Cause (immanent, unmoving God: Nature which is not created and does not create). He was one of the originators of the Mystical thought of the Middle Ages, as well as a precursor of *Scholasticism (though with no Aristotelian elements). His originality lies in departing from the mainstream Latin tradition of theology to incorporate into it elements drawn from Pseudo-*Dionysius and others in the *Neoplatonic tradition. He translated the works of Pseudo-Dionysius in 858, as well as of other Neoplatonists, and he wrote a Commentary on the *Celestial Hierarchy* of Pseudo-Dionysius. The presence of a Neoplatonic element in all medieval philosophers, including *Aquinas, owes much to his influence. See *Works,* ed. H. J. Floss in *Migne's *Patrologia Latina,* 122.

Scriblerus Club, an association of which *Swift, *Arbuthnot, T. *Parnell, *Pope, and *Gay were members, and the earl of Oxford (R. *Harley) a regularly invited associate member. The group appears to have met from January to July 1714, though various members later collaborated on joint projects. Its object was to ridicule 'all the false tastes in learning', but nothing was produced under the name of *Martinus Scriblerus for some years. See *Memoirs of* *the Extraordinary Life, Works and Discoveries of Martinus Scriblerus*, ed. C. Kerby-Miller (1950).

Scrooge, a character in Dickens's *A Christmas Carol*.

Scrub, man-of-all-work to Lady Bountiful's household in Farquhar's *The Beaux' Stratagem*.

Scrutiny, a Cambridge periodical which ran for 19 issues, 1932–53, edited by L. C. *Knights, Donald Culver, Denys Thompson, D. W. Harding, and others, but dominated largely by F. R. *Leavis; a 20th issue, with a 'Retrospect' by Leavis, appeared in 1963. Its contributors include Q. D. Leavis, H. A. Mason, E. *Rickword, D. A. Traversi. It published little creative work of importance, with the exception of the posthumous poems of *Rosenberg but was an important vehicle for the views of the new Cambridge school of criticism, and published many seminal essays, particularly in the pre-war years, on J. *Austen, Shakespeare, *Marvell, etc. Its critical standards proved less illuminating when applied to contemporary writing; it ignored most of *Orwell, dismissed G. *Greene, Dylan *Thomas, and most of V. *Woolf (Leavis described *Between the Acts as a work of 'extraordinary vacancy and point-lessness'), and in later years attacked the reputations of *Spender and *Auden, both of whom had been originally greeted as heralds of a Poetic Renascence which, by 1940, Leavis declared not to have taken place. In a preface to *A Selection from Scrutiny* (2 vols, 1968) Leavis deplored the lack of support that this indisputably important periodical had received, which he claimed amounted to 'positively hostile non-recognition of our existence', and went on to blame the British Council, the BBC, the 'intellectuals of literary journalism', etc., for the climate of opinion that had allowed it to perish, while demanding reprints of its back numbers.

Scudamour, Sir, in Spenser's *Faerie Queene* (Bk. IV), the lover of *Amoret, who is reft from him on his wedding-day by the enchanter *Busirane.

SCUDÉRY, Madeleine de (1607–91), author of French heroic romances. Her *Artamène, ou le Grand Cyrus* (10 vols, 1649–53) and *Clélie, historie romaine* (10 vols, 1654–60) consisted of an interweaving of improbable tales of love and war in an antique setting with ingenious systems and codes of contemporary allusions. They had an immense vogue that extended well beyond the frontiers of France, and influenced heroic plays of the court of Charles II.

Scythrop, a character in Peacock's *Nightmare Abbey*, a satirical portrait of the style and literary opinions of *Shelley.

Seafarer, The, an Old English poem of about 120 lines in the *Exeter Book, one of the group known as 'elegies'. The opening section of the poem ostensibly discusses the miseries and attractions of life at sea, before moving by an abrupt transition to moral reflections on the transience of life and ending in an explicitly Christian part (the text of which is uncertain), concluding with a prayer, *Pound made a loose but highly evocative translation of the first half of the poem.

The structure of the poem and the coherence of the relationship between its two halves have been much debated. Some critics regard the didactic second part as an appendage to an earlier secular poem; others see the whole as an allegorical representation of human exile from God on the sea of life. A comparable pattern (though not so sharply divided) can be seen in such poems as *The Wanderer and *The Husband's Message. Whichever view is taken of the coherence of the whole, nobody disputes that the powerful sea description of the opening section is much more appealing than the second half, at least to a post-Romantic readership. Ed. I. L. Gordon (1960).

Seagrim, Molly, a character in Fielding's *Tom Jones*.

Seasons, The, a poem in blank verse, in four books and a final hymn, by J. *Thomson (1700–48), published 1726–30.

'Winter' was composed first, and its first version, of 405 lines, was written and published in 1726; it was gradually expanded to 1,069 lines by 1746 (the other books were also expanded over the years, but less extensively). It describes the rage of the elements and the sufferings of men and animals; two well known episodes are the visit of the redbreast to a family who feed him crumbs from the table, and the death of a shepherd in a snowdrift while his family wait anxiously (the latter much illustrated). Many of the passages are notably *Sublime.

Next came 'Summer' (1727), which sets forth the progress of a summer's day, with scenes of hay-making, sheep-shearing, and bathing, followed by a panegyric to Great Britain and her 'solid grandeur'. It also includes two narrative episodes, one of the lover Celadon whose Amelia is struck by lightning, the other of Damon who beholds Musidora bathing, the latter highly popular, according to *Wordsworth, because it was titillating.

'Spring' (1728) describes the influence of the season on all the natural world, and ends with a panegyric on nuptial love; its opening lines were particularly admired by *Clare.

'Autumn' (1730) gives a vivid picture of shooting and hunting, sports condemned for their barbarity, and of harvesting, wine-making, etc., and ends with a panegyric to the 'pure pleasures of the rural life'. It includes the episode of Palemon who falls in love with Lavinia, a gleaner in his fields, based on the story of Ruth and Boaz. The whole was completed by a Hymn (1730) and illustrations by William Kent.

The work contains many elegant compliments to Thomson's various patrons and their country seats (*Lyttleton, *Dodington, and others). It was immensely popular and went through many editions in the 18th and 19th cents. The text of *Haydn's oratorio *Die Jahreszeiten* (1801) was adapted from Thomson by Baron van Swieten, whose version did not please the composer; he objected to having to represent the croaking of frogs and unpoetic sentiments such as 'Fleiss, O edler Fleiss' ('Oh Industry, noble Industry!'). Ed. J. Sambrook, 1981.

SEATON, Thomas (1684–1741), a fellow of Clare College, Cambridge, founded by legacy the Seatonian Prize at Cambridge for sacred poetry. This is referred to in Byron's *English Bards and Scotch Reviewers*.

Sebastian, (1) *Viola's twin brother in Shakespeare's *Twelfth Night*; (2) in his *The Tempest*, brother to *Alonso whom he tries to murder.

Second Mrs Tanqueray, The, a play by Sir A. *Pinero, first performed 1893.

Tanqueray, knowing of Paula's past reputation, still determines to marry her, in the belief that his love and the generosity of his friends will prove strong enough to counter prejudice and hyprocrisy. Ellean, his young convent-bred daughter from a previous marriage, comes to live with him and Paula; soon Tanqueray begins to realize that Ellean, his friends, and his own suspicions are proving too powerful an opposition to his once-loving marriage. When Paula also realizes that she has lost his love, she kills herself. Because of its daring theme Pinero had great difficulty in having the play accepted for production; but once produced it was an immediate and abiding success.

'Second Nun's Tale', see CANTERBURY TALES, 21.

Secret Agent, The, a novel by *Conrad, published 1907.

A seedy shop in Soho provides cover for Verloc, the secret agent, who is working as a spy for a foreign embassy and as informer for Chief Inspector Heat of Scotland Yard. His wife Winnie has married him chiefly to provide security for her simple-minded younger brother Stevie, and is ignorant of Verloc's spying activities. The shop is a meeting place for a bunch of ill-assorted political fanatics united only in their effort to arouse some extremism in the over-moderate British. We are introduced to the Russian *agent provocateur* Vladimir; the American terrorist 'the Professor'; and Ossipon, Yundt, and Michaelis who easily accommodate their principles to their material needs. The foreign embassy is planning a series of outrages aimed at discrediting the revolutionary groups which will be held responsible. The first target is the Greenwich Observatory and an unwilling Verloc is ordered to engineer the explosion. He uses the poor innocent Stevie as an accomplice and the boy is blown to pieces while carrying the bomb. Winnie, stricken by her brother's death and outraged by Verloc's lack of remorse, kills him with a knife. Fleeing, she encounters Ossipon who flirts with her and they plan to leave the country. But when he discovers Verloc's murder he steals her money and abandons her. Winnie, alone and in terror of the gallows, throws herself overboard from the Channel ferry. Treating this melodramatic theme with ironical humour, Conrad expresses his profound scepticism about the anarchist world.

Secreta Secretorum, a compendium of pronouncements on political and ethical matters, written in Syriac in the 8th cent. AD and claiming to be advice from Aristotle to Alexander. It reached Europe through Arabic and 12th-cent. Hispano-Arabic. The main version in Latin was translated in Spain *c*.1230 and was influential on poets from then until the 16th cent. It influenced in particular the tradition of writing works of advice to kings; it was translated in part by *Lydgate, and Aegidio Collona's *De Regimine Principum* (an important source for *Hoccleve's *Regiment of Princes*) drew on it.

Secret Commonwealth of Elves, Fauns and Fairies, The, a tract on the fairy world, second sight, etc., by Robert Kirk (?1641–92), minister of Aberfoyle, of which the first text, from a MS dating from 1691, dates from 1815; it was printed with a commentary by A. *Lang in 1893 and edited by R. B. *Cunninghame Graham in 1933.

Secret Garden, The, see BURNETT, F. H.

Sedley, Mr, Mrs, Joseph, and Amelia, characters in Thackeray's *Vanity Fair*.

SEDLEY, or **SIDLEY,** Sir Charles (?1639–1701), dramatist and poet, friend of *Rochester and *Dryden, was famous for his wit and urbanity and notorious for his profligate escapades. His tragedy *Antony and Cleopatra* (1677) was followed by two comedies, *Bellamira* (1687) and *The Mulberry Garden* (1668), which was based partly on *Molière's *L'École des maris*. His poems and songs ('Phillis is my only joy', 'Love still has something of the sea', etc.) were published in 1702, with his *Miscellaneous Works*. *Malone identified him as the Lisideius of Dryden's *Of Dramatick Poesie*, who defends the imitation of French drama in English. He also had a hand in a translation of *Corneille's *Pompée* with *Waller, Godolphin, C. *Sackville, and *Filmer.

SEELEY, Sir John Robert (1834–95), educated at the City of London School and Christ's College, Cambridge, was professor of Latin at University College London from 1863 and of modern history at Cambridge from 1869 until his death. In 1865 he published anonymously *Ecce Homo*, a survey of the life of Christ as one of the great religious reformers. His historical works, designed to promote a practical object, the training of statesmen, include: *The Expansion of England in the Eighteenth Century* (1883), which reviews the growth of the Empire as an inevitable process, and infers the imperial mission of Britain from the lessons of the past, a work which met with great success; *The Life and Times of Stein, or Germany and Prussia in the Napoleonic Age* (1878); and *The Growth of British Policy* (1895), tracing the development of British foreign policy from the time of Elizabeth.

SEFERIS, George (1900–71), Greek poet and diplomat, born in Smyrna and educated in Athens. He spent several periods in Britain, including some years as ambassador (1957–62) and in 1963 was awarded the *Nobel Prize. He published several volumes of poetry, from 1931 onwards, much of it strongly imbued with classical mythology: translations include *Poems* (1960), by R. *Warner, and *Collected Poems* (1981), by E. Keeley and P. Sherrard.

Seithenyn, a character in Peacock's *The Misfortunes of Elphin*, the complacent guardian of the sea wall and 'one of the three great drunkards of Wales'.

Sejanus his Fall, a Roman tragedy by *Jonson, performed by the King's Men 1603, with Shakespeare and *Burbage in the cast, printed 1605.

Based mainly on *Tacitus, the play deals with the rise of Sejanus during the reign of Tiberius, his destruction of the family of Germanicus, and his poisoning of Tiberius' son Drusus. Suspecting the scope of his favourite's ambition, Tiberius leaves Rome, setting his agent Macro to spy on him. Tiberius denounces Sejanus in a letter to the senate, which condemns him to death, and the mob, stirred up by Macro, tears him to pieces.

Selborne, Natural History and Antiquities of, see WHITE, G.

SELDEN, John (1584–1654), English historian and antiquary, was born near Worthing, Sussex, and educated at Hart Hall, Oxford, then became an eminent lawyer and bencher of the Inner Temple. His *History of Tythes* (1618) gave offence to the clergy and was suppressed by public authority. In Parliament he took an active part against the Crown until 1649, when he withdrew from public affairs on the principle that 'The wisest way for men in these times is to say nothing.' He won fame as an orientalist with his treatise *De Diis Syris* (1617), and sub-

sequently made a valuable collection of oriental manuscripts, most of which passed at his death to the Bodleian Library. His *Table Talk*, containing reports of his utterances from time to time during the last 20 years of his life, composed by his secretary Richard Milward, appeared in 1689. His works include *Marmora Arundelliana* (1624), *Mare Clausum* (1635), translated by *Nedham, in which he maintained against the *Mare Liberum* of *Grotius that the sea is capable of sovereignty, and *Illustrations* to the first 18 'songs' of Drayton's *Poly-Olbion*. His works were collected by Dr David Wilkins (1726).

Selden Society, The, was founded in 1887 by *Maitland for the publication of ancient legal records.

Select Society, The, an association of educated Scotsmen formed in 1754, whose members met in Edinburgh to discuss philosophical questions. *Hume and W. *Robertson were among its prominent members.

Self-Help, see SMILES, S.

Selima, Horace *Walpole's cat, whose death by drowning in a bowl of goldfish was lamented in a poem by *Gray.

SELINCOURT, Ernest de (1870–1943), scholar and literary critic, educated at Dulwich College and University College, Oxford. From 1908 he was professor of English language and literature at the University of Birmingham, and professor of poetry at Oxford 1928–33. As a scholar he is remembered principally for his editions of the works of Dorothy and William *Wordsworth, which include *The Prelude* (1926); *Letters of William and Dorothy Wordsworth* (6 vols, 1935–9), William's *Poetical Works* (vols 1 and 2, 1940–4), and Dorothy's *Journals* (2 vols, 1941). He also wrote a life of Dorothy, published in 1933.

SELKIRK, Alexander (1676–1721), born in Fife, ran away to sea and joined the privateering expedition of *Dampier in 1703. Having quarrelled with his captain, Thomas Stradling, he was at his own request put ashore on the uninhabited island of Juan Fernandez in 1704, and remained there until 1709 when he was rescued by W. *Rogers. On his return he met *Steele, who published an account of his experiences in *The Englishman* (3 Dec. 1713). Defoe used the story in *Robinson Crusoe* and *Cowper in his poem, 'I am monarch of all I survey'.

Semiotics, see SAUSSURE, F.

Senae, in imprints, Sienna.

SENANCOUR, Etienne Pivert de (1770–1846), French author, now chiefly remembered for his *Obermann* (1804), a lightly fictionalized series of letters to a friend supposed to have been written over a period of years, mostly from a remote alpine valley. The author reflects on the society he has fled and on man, describing his own frustrated inactivity, melancholy, and ennui, his solitude and mystical attachment to Nature. The mental and emotional condition given voice in *Obermann* appealed to many first-generation Romantic writers in France. Senancour was much admired by *Sainte-Beuve and by M. *Arnold, who discerned in his sentimentalism a distinctive 'gravity and severity'. Two well known poems by Arnold, 'Stanzas in Memory of the Author of Obermann' (1852) and 'Obermann Once More' (1867), take the form of meditations that develop from reflecting on Senancour's book in its alpine setting. Arnold also wrote an essay 'Obermann' (*The Academy, 9 Oct. 1869).

SENECA, Lucius Annaeus (*c.*4 BC–AD 65), Roman Stoic philosopher, tragic poet, and, like his father the elder Seneca, a noted rhetorician. He was appointed tutor to the young Nero and, when the latter became emperor, acted as one of his chief advisers, checking his crimes for a period; but, finding this position untenable, he withdrew from the court in AD 62. Three years later he was accused of being implicated in a conspiracy and was forced to commit suicide. His writings consist of tragedies in verse, dialogues, treatises, and letters in prose, which in their different ways all aim to teach *Stoicism. Most of his nine plays are on subjects drawn from Greek mythology and treated in extant Greek dramas, but his manner is very different from that of Greek tragedy. He uses an exaggerated rhetoric, dwells habitually on bloodthirsty details and introduces ghosts and magic; the plays were almost certainly not intended for performance but for reading aloud, probably by the author himself, to a select audience. Senecan drama was familiar in the 16th cent. at a time when Greek tragedies were scarcely known; all the nine plays were translated (1559–81) and imitated by dramatists from the time of *Gorboduc* onwards. For an account of Seneca's influence, see T. S. *Eliot's important essay 'Seneca in Elizabethan Translation' (1927) and his 'Shakespeare and the Stoicism of Seneca' (1927). *Dryden's *Troilus and Cressida* (1679), more than a century later than the Elizabethan imitations, still shows traces of Senecan influence. Seneca's prose writings consist of treatises, some of which are clumsily disguised as dialogues (*De Clementia, De Ira,* etc.) and a collection of what purport to be letters addressed to one Lucilius after the author's retirement, constituting a sort of elementary course in Stoicism. These writings were widely read in the 17th and 18th cents. *L'Estrange's digest of them (1678) reached ten editions by 1711, so that there is an undercurrent of Stoicism in much of early 18th-cent. thinking, visible not only in Addison's *Cato* but also in a wide range of

writers from *Pope to *Duck. In the 19th cent. Stoic morality survived in the public schools, but its influence in serious literature dwindled. (For Senecan drama, see also LUCAN.)

SENIOR, Nassau William (1790–1864), economist, educated at Magdalen College, Oxford, was professor of political economy at Oxford, 1825–30 and 1847–52. Besides writing biographical and critical essays and lectures, he contributed important political articles to the *Edinburgh Review* and other periodicals, and published *Journals, Conversations and Essays relating to Ireland* (1868), *Journals kept in France and Italy* (1871), *Correspondence and Conversations of S. Tocqueville* (1872), *Conversations with M. Thiers, M. Guizot, and other distinguished persons during the Second Empire* (1878), and *Essays on Fiction* (1864), a notable series of reviews of the *Waverley novels.

Sensation, Novel of, a branch of fiction that flourished from *c.*1860 onwards, depicting lurid, implausible, or sensational events, and frequently involving guilty secrets; classics of the genre include Wilkie Collins's *The Woman in White* (1860); Mrs H. *Wood's *East Lynne* (1861); and M. E. *Braddon's *Lady Audley's Secret* (1862). Many of the novels of the period (e.g. those of Mrs *Gaskell and *Dickens) include sensational elements, and the genre later developed into the thriller and detective novel. (See DETECTIVE FICTION.)

Sense and Sensibility, a novel by J. Austen, which grew from a sketch entitled 'Elinor and Marianne'; revised 1797–8 and again 1809; published 1811.

Mrs Henry Dashwood and her daughters Elinor and Marianne, together with the younger Margaret, are left in straitened circumstances, because the estate of which Mrs Dashwood's husband had the life interest has passed to her stepson John Dashwood. Henry Dashwood, before his death, had urgently recommended to John that he look after his stepmother and sisters, but John's selfishness, encouraged by his grasping wife (the daughter of the arrogant Mrs Ferrers), defeats his father's wish. Mrs Henry Dashwood and her daughters accordingly retire to a cottage in Devonshire, but not before Elinor and Edward Ferrers, brother of Mrs John Dashwood, have become much attracted to each other. However, Edward shows a strange uneasiness in his relations with Elinor. In Devonshire Marianne is thrown into the company of John Willoughby, an attractive but impecunious and unprincipled young man, with whom she falls desperately—and very obviously—in love. Willoughby likewise shows signs of a strong affection for her, and their engagement is expected daily. Willoughby suddenly departs for London, leaving Marianne in acute distress. Eventually Elinor and Marianne also go to London, on the invitation of their tactless and garrulous old friend Mrs Jennings. Here Willoughby shows complete indifference to Marianne, and finally, in a cruel and insolent letter, informs her of his approaching marriage to a rich heiress. Marianne makes no effort to hide her great grief. Meanwhile Elinor has learned, under pledge of secrecy, from Lucy Steele (a sly, self-seeking young woman) that she and Edward Ferrers have been secretly engaged for four years. Elinor, whose self-control is in strong contrast to Marianne's demonstrative emotions, silently conceals her distress. Edward's engagement, which had been kept secret because of his financial dependence on his mother, now becomes known to her. In her fury at Edward's refusal to break his promise to Lucy, she dismisses him from her sight, and settles on his younger brother Robert the property that would otherwise have gone to Edward. At this juncture a small living is offered to Edward, and the way seems open for his marriage with Lucy. But Robert, a fashionable young fop, falls in love with Lucy, who, seeing her best interest in a marriage with the wealthier brother, throws over Edward and marries Robert. Edward, immensely relieved to be released from an engagement he has long and painfully regretted, proposes to Elinor and is accepted. Marianne, slowly recovering from the despair that followed her abandonment by Willoughby, eventually accepts the proposal of Colonel Brandon, an old family friend, whose considerable quiet attractions had been eclipsed by his brilliant rival.

Sensibility, see SENTIMENT, NOVEL OF.

Sentences, Master of the, see PETER LOMBARD.

Sentiment, Sensibility, Novel of. The object of this type of novel was to illustrate the alliance of acute sensibility with true virtue. An adherence to strict morality and honour, combined with copious feeling and a sympathetic heart, were (with whatever consequences of failure or humiliation) the marks of the man or woman of sentiment. The cult may be traced particularly to the work of *Marivaux, *Richardson, and S. *Fielding; the most popular and influential novels to which they gave rise were probably H. Brooke's *The Fool of Quality, Sterne's *A Sentimental Journey, and Mackenzie's *The Man of Feeling, together with the work of F. *Brooke, C. *Lennox, and F. *Sheridan. Late in the century *Lamb's The Tale of Rosamund Gray (1798) was in the mainstream of such novels, but the cult was then dying. The early chapters of J. Austen's *Northanger Abbey mock the 'refined susceptibilities' of the Novel of Sentiment, and *Sense and Sensibility was intended to demonstrate the serious consequences of following its standards. (See also NOVEL, RISE OF THE.)

Sentimental Comedy, a type of sentimental drama introduced by *Steele, a reaction from the comedy of the *Restoration. In France it evolved into la comédie larmoyante of La Chaussée (1692–1754). (See KELLY, H.)

Sentimental Journey, A, through France and Italy, by L. *Sterne, published 1768.

The narrator, Parson Yorick (borrowed from *Tristram Shandy), is a man of great charm, sensibility, and gallantry, who sets out to travel through France and Italy. At the end of the book he has gone little further than Lyons, and it is not known whether Sterne intended any further volume. As it is, the work begins by breaking into the middle of a dialogue (with the famous words, 'They order, said I, these matters better in France') and ends ambiguously in mid-sentence: 'So that when I stretch'd out my hand, I caught hold of the Fille de Chambre's—' Sterne referred to the book as his 'Work of Redemption' and declared that its aim was 'to teach us to love the world and our fellow creatures'. The amiable Yorick, who reveres 'Dear sensibility!' and is frequently moved to tears, does indeed find much to commend and little to condemn in France and the French. In parodying fashionable works of travel, he contrasts his own appreciation with Smelfungus (a caricature of *Smollett) and with Mundungus (perhaps a Dr Sharp), both of whom had written disparaging travel books about Europe. Whether Sterne is serious or ironic in describing Yorick's displays of acute sensibility is a matter of conjecture. Certainly the parson is as full of gaiety and irony as of tender feeling. In his journeyings from Calais through Rouen and Paris almost to Lyons, in company with his faithful servant La Fleur, he enjoys many encounters with all manner of men, from marquis to potboy, and, more especially, with pretty women, who range from ladies of wealth and elegance to chambermaids and shop-girls, and include the pathetic Maria from Vol. IX of Tristram Shandy.

The book was no doubt based on Sterne's two journeys abroad in 1762–4 and 1765. It was well received by the public, and in 1769, after Sterne's death, was continued by a *'Eugenius', for long incorrectly assumed to be Sterne's old friend *Hall-Stevenson. A Sentimental Journey is probably the first English novel to survive in the handwriting of its author.

'Sepher Yezirah', Sephiroth, see CABBALA.

Septuagint, The (commonly designated LXX), the Greek version of the OT which derives its name from the story that it was made by 72 Palestinian Jews at the request of Ptolemy Philadelphus (285–246 BC) and completed by them, in seclusion on the island of Pharos, in 72 days; or it may have been so called because it was authorized by the 70 members of the Jewish Sanhedrin (Jebb).

Serious Call, A, to a Devout and Holy Life, see LAW, W.

SERVETUS, Michael (Miguel Serveto) (1511–53), a Spanish physician and theologian, who graduated in medicine in Paris and lectured there on geometry and astrology, and subsequently practised medicine at various places in France. He published in 1531 *De trinitatis erroribus,* directed against the doctrine of the Trinity, and in 1553 *Christianismi restitutio,* in consequence of which he was arrested at Lyons by the Inquisition. He escaped to Geneva, but was arrested and burnt by order of *Calvin.

SERVICE, Robert William (1874–1958), poet, born in Preston and brought up in Glasgow. He emigrated to Canada in 1895 where he observed the gold rush in the Yukon; this inspired his best-known ballads, which include 'The Shooting of Dan McGrew' and 'The Cremation of Sam McGee', published in *Songs of a Sourdough* (1907, Toronto; as *The Spell of the Yukon,* New York). Its sequel, *Ballads of a Cheechako,* followed in 1909. Other volumes include *Rhymes of a Rolling Stone* (1912) and *Rhymes of a Red Cross Man* (1916). *Ploughman of the Moon* (1945) and *Harper of Heaven* (1948) are both autobiographical. Collected volumes appeared in 1933, 1955, and 1960.

SERVIUS HONORATUS, Marius or Maurus (end of 4th cent. AD), Roman grammarian, whose commentary on *Virgil has survived in two versions, the longer of which was not printed till 1600. It preserved a mass of antiquarian, mythographical, and rhetorical information that has done much to forward our understanding of Latin poetry; and it has the further value of showing what was taught about Virgil in Roman schools. It is interesting to note the almost complete absence of what is now regarded as literary criticism.

Sesame and Lilies, see RUSKIN, J.

Sestina, a poem of six six-line stanzas (with an envoy) in which the line-endings of the first stanza are repeated, but in different order, in the other five [OED].

Setebos, a god of the Patagonians, worshipped by Caliban's mother Sycorax (in Shakespeare's *The Tempest*). His purpose in creating the world is worked out by Caliban in R. *Browning's 'Caliban upon Setebos'.

SETTLE, Elkanah (1648–1724), educated at Trinity College, Oxford, was the author of a series of bombastic oriental melodramas which threatened *Dryden's popularity and aroused his hostility. He appears to have written *Cambyses* (1667) while still at Oxford, and his *The Empress of Morocco* (1673) had such a vogue that Dryden, with *Crowne and *Shadwell, wrote a pamphlet of criticism of it. Settle retorted with

an attack on Dryden's *Almanzor and Almahide,* and Dryden vented his resentment by satirizing Settle as Doeg in the second part of *Absalom and Achitophel.* Settle published *Absalom Senior, or Achitophel Transpros'd* in 1682, and *Reflections on several of Mr Dryden's Plays* in 1687. He was appointed city poet in 1691, took to writing *drolls for Bartholomew Fair (as he may have done before his success), and died in the Charterhouse. He also wrote two interesting rogue biographies (see ROGUE LITERATURE).

Seven Champions of Christendom, The Famous History of the, see JOHNSON, R.

Seven Deadly Sins, usually given as Pride, Envy, Anger, Sloth, Covetousness, Gluttony, and Lust; frequently personified in medieval literature (e.g. *Piers Plowman,* B. Passus 5; *Dunbar's 'The Dance of the Sevin Deidly Synnis', and used too in Chaucer's 'Parson's Tale' (*Canterbury Tales,* 24) and in Spenser's *Faerie Queene* where they are personified again. They provide one of the organizing structures for *Dante's *Inferno* and *Purgatorio;* the most important medieval source authority for these literary occurrences is believed to be Guilielmus Peraldus' *Summa seu Tractatus de Viciis* which dates from the mid-13th cent. See M. W. Bloomfield, *The Seven Deadly Sins* (1952).

Seven Lamps of Architecture, The, a treatise by *Ruskin.

Seven Liberal Arts, see QUADRIVIUM and TRIVIUM.

Seven Pillars of Wisdom, The, see LAWRENCE, T. E.

Seven Sages of Rome, The, a metrical romance of the early 14th cent., varying in length in different versions from 2,500 to 4,300 lines. In form it is a framed collection of tales, derived through Latin and French from Eastern collections, the original of which is the Indian *Book of Sindibad* (see SYNTIPAS), of interest as one of the earliest English instances of the form of short verse-story used by Chaucer in *The Canterbury Tales.

The Emperor Diocletian has his son educated by seven sages. His stepmother is jealous of the boy and accuses him to the emperor of attempting to seduce her; the boy is silent for seven days, under the influence of the stepmother's magic, and he is ordered to execution. On each of the seven nights a tale is told by the queen to illustrate the dangers of supplantation of the emperor by his son, and on each of the following mornings a tale is told by one of the sages on the theme of the danger of trusting women. The emperor is alternately persuaded by the queen and the sages. When the seven days are passed, the boy speaks and exposes the stepmother, who is burnt. The most widely attested manuscript version ('A') in 3,974 lines of short couplets has been edited by K. Brunner (EETS os. 191, 1933; reprinted 1971).

Seven Sleepers of Ephesus, seven noble Christian youths of Ephesus who, fleeing from the persecution of Decius (AD 250), concealed themselves in a cavern in a neighbouring mountain. They were ordered by the emperor to be walled up therein, and fell into a deep slumber, which was miraculously prolonged for 187 years. At the end of that time the slaves of one Adolius, to whom the inheritance of the mountain had descended, removed the stones with which the cavern had been walled up, and the seven sleepers were permitted to awake. Under the impression that they had slept a few hours, one of them proceeded to the city for food, but was unable to recognize the place. His singular dress and obsolete speech (or, in some versions, the fact that he tried to buy food with obsolete money) caused him to be brought before a magistrate, and the miracle was brought to light. The people, headed by the bishop, hastened to visit the cavern of the sleepers, 'who bestowed their benediction, related their story, and at the same instant peaceably expired' (Gibbon, *Decline and Fall*, xxxiii). The legend was translated from the Syriac by *Gregory of Tours, and is also given by other authors. It is included in the *Koran, c. xviii, among Muhammad's revelations.

Seven Types of Ambiguity, a critical work by W. *Empson, published 1930, rev. 1947, 1953; one of the most enjoyable and influential offshoots from I. A. *Richards's experiments with *Practical Criticism.

Empson uses the term ambiguity 'in an extended sense', to refer to 'any verbal nuance, however slight, which gives room for alternative reactions to the same piece of language'. The first, or simplest, type of ambiguity he defines as simple metaphor, 'a word or a grammatical construction effective in several ways at once'. The second occurs 'when two or more meanings are resolved into one' (as by 'Double Grammar' in Shakespeare); the third consists of two apparently disconnected meanings given simultaneously, as in a pun, or, by extension, in allegory or pastoral, where reference is made to more than one 'universe of discourse'; the fourth occurs when 'alternative meanings combine to make clear a complicated state of mind in the author' (with examples from Shakespeare, *Donne, and G. M. *Hopkins); the fifth consists of what Empson calls 'fortunate confusion', with examples from *Shelley and *Swinburne, suggesting the possibility that 19th-cent. technique is 'in part the metaphysical tradition dug up when rotten'; the sixth occurs when a statement in itself meaningless or contradictory forces the reader to supply interpretations; and an account of the seventh, which 'marks a division in the author's mind', is accompanied by quotations from *Freud and illustrations from *Crashaw, *Keats, Hopkins. In detail, the work is an interesting example of the rewards of close linguistic analysis, applied to a wide though well-established range of authors; more broadly, it indicates the tendency of the period to elevate intellectual and verbal complexity and richness above simplicity.

Seven Wonders of the World, the seven structures regarded as the most remarkable monuments of antiquity, viz. the Egyptian Pyramids, the Mausoleum at Halicarnassus, the Hanging Gardens of Babylon, the Temple of Artemis at Ephesus, the statue of Zeus by Phidias at Olympia, the Colossus at Rhodes, and the Pharos at Alexandria, or, according to another list, the walls of Babylon.

SEVERN, Joseph (1793–1879), painter, and devoted friend and correspondent of *Keats, of whom he made several drawings and portraits, and of whom he took a death-mask. He won the RA Gold Medal in 1818 but had little public success. He accompanied Keats to Italy in 1820 and attended him at his death. His care of Keats brought him to general notice and for a time he prospered as a painter, especially in English circles in Rome. He attempted fiction, without success, but published *The Vicissitudes of Keats's Fame* in 1863. He was eventually given the British consulship in Rome.

SÉVIGNÉ, Marie de Rabutin-Chantal, marquise de (1626–96), French letter-writer. Orphaned at a very young age, she was brought up by an uncle as a person of wide culture. She frequented the Hôtel de *Rambouillet, made a fashionable marriage in 1644, and was widowed seven years later. Her reputation rests on her lifelong correspondence with her daughter, published posthumously in 1725 and more fully in 1735–54. It gives a portrait of Paris under Louis XIV unique for its charm and vivacity, and for the deftness and intelligence of its observation.

SEWARD, Anna (1747–1809), known as the 'Swan of Lichfield', where she lived from the age of 10, and where her father was canon. Her grandfather John Hunter had taught the young Dr *Johnson and she furnished *Boswell with many details of his early life, while admitting that she did not much care for him. Her literary friends included E. *Darwin, T. *Day, and *Hayley. In 1802 she wrote an admiring letter to Sir W. *Scott, who found some merit in her poetry and edited her works in 3 vols, with a memoir, in 1810, at her suggestion. Her letters were published in 1811 (6 vols) and there is a selection in H. *Pearson's *The Swan of Lichfield* (1936).

SEWELL, Anna (1820–78), wrote only one book, *Black Beauty* (1877), a story for children relating the life of a black mare, which suffers much but eventually finds a happy home. The book, for which she received £20, was published three months before her death; its immediate success and fame survived for many generations, and it became established as a children's classic. There is a life by S. Chitty (1971).

Seyton, Catherine, a character in Scott's *The Abbot*.

Sganarelle, the name of characters in several of *Molière's comedies, notably of Don Juan's pusillanimous servant in *Le Festin de pierre*, and of the hero of *Le Médecin malgré lui*. It is this last who, in the character of the pseudo-doctor, declares that 'Nous avons changé tout cela', when someone suggests that the heart is usually on the left side of the body, and not on the right as Sganarelle supposes.

Shabby Genteel Story, A, a story by *Thackeray, published in *Fraser's Magazine*, 1840. Caroline Gann, the down-trodden daughter of a failed merchant, is tricked into a false marriage by the dashing 'George Brandon' (really Firmin). He abandons her, and her baby dies. The characters reappear in *The Adventures of Philip*.

Shadow, Simon, in Shakespeare's 2 *Henry IV* (III. ii), one of Falstaff's recruits.

Shadow of a Gunman, The, see O'CASEY, S.

SHADWELL, Thomas (?1642–92), dramatist, whose first play *The Sullen Lovers* (1668) was based on *Molière's *Les Fâcheux*; in its preface he proclaimed himself a follower of *Jonson's comedy of humours. He wrote some 14 comedies, including *The Squire of Alsatia* (1688), *The Virtuoso* (1676, a satire on the *Royal Society), *Epsom Wells* (1672), and *Bury Fair* (1689); the last two give an interesting if scurrilous picture of contemporary manners, watering places, and amusements. He also wrote operas, adapting Shakespeare's *The Tempest* as *The Enchanted Island* (1674). A successful dramatist in his day, he has been perhaps unfairly remembered for his quarrel with *Dryden, dating from 1682. He was probably the author of *The Medal of John Bayes* (1682) and other anonymous attacks on Dryden; Dryden's counterattacks include *MacFlecknoe* and the second part of *Absalom and Achitophel*, where Shadwell appears as Og. Shadwell somewhat plaintively defends himself from the charge of dullness in his dedication to *Sedley of his translation of the *Tenth Satire of Juvenal* (1687). As a 'true-blue' Whig, he succeeded Dryden as poet laureate and historiographer at the revolution in 1689; their quarrel had been partly political, for Shadwell had been virtually unable to get his plays performed during the last years of Charles II's reign, or in James II's.

SHAFFER, Peter Levin (1926–), playwright, born in Liverpool, and educated at Trinity College, Cambridge. His first play, *Five Finger Exercise* (1958), a drama of middle-class family life, was followed by many other successes, including *The Royal Hunt of the Sun* (1964, pub. 1965), an epic about the conquest of Peru; *Black Comedy* (1965, pub. 1967), a farce; *Equus* (1973), a drama about an analyst's relationship with his horse-obsessed patient; and *Amadeus* (1979, pub. 1980), which deals with the nature of creativity through a portrayal of the composers *Mozart and Salieri.

His twin brother Anthony Shaffer, author of *Sleuth* (1970, pub. 1971), is also a successful playwright.

SHAFTESBURY, Anthony Ashley Cooper, first Baron Ashley and 1st earl of (1621–83), a statesman prominent on the king's side in the Civil War, as leader of the parliamentary opposition to *Cromwell, after the Restoration as a member of the *Cabal and chancellor. After his dismissal he was leader of the opposition, a promoter of the Exclusion Bill, and a supporter of Monmouth. He died in Holland. He was satirized as Achitophel in Dryden's *Absalom and Achitophel*, by Otway in *Venice Preserv'd*, and by many others.

SHAFTESBURY, Anthony Ashley Cooper, 3rd earl of (1671–1713), excluded by ill-health from active politics after 1702, devoted himself to intellectual pursuits, and in particular to moral and aesthetic philosophy. His principal writings are embodied in his *Characteristics of Men, Manners, Opinions, and Times*, published 1711 (rev. edn, 1714), which included various treatises previously published (notably his *Inquiry concerning Virtue, or Merit*, 1699). Shaftesbury was influenced by *Deism; he was at once a Platonist and a churchman, an opponent of the selfish theory of conduct advocated by *Hobbes. Man has 'affections', Shaftesbury held, not only for himself but for the creatures about him. 'To have one's affections right and entire, not only in respect of oneself, but of society and the public: this is rectitude, integrity, or virtue.' And there is no conflict between the self-regarding and social affections; for the individual's own good is included in the good of society. Moreover, man has a capacity for distinguishing right and wrong, the beauty or ugliness of actions and affections, and this he calls the 'moral sense'. To be truly virtuous, a man must have a *disinterested* affection for what he perceives to be right. Shaftesbury's aesthetic thought, by its attempt to explain nature by the analogy of art and its assertion of a close connection between art and morality, had some influence on later writers, such as *Arbuckle in *Hibernicus's Letters*, and

*Akenside in *The Pleasures of Imagination*. His influence is also seen in the writing of *Fielding, and in the philosophy of *Hutcheson and *Turnbull.

SHAFTESBURY, Anthony Ashley Cooper, 7th earl of (1801–85), philanthropist, active in many movements for the protection of the working classes and the benefit of the poor.

Shafton, Sir Piercie, a character in Scott's *The Monastery*.

Shagpat, *The Shaving of*, see SHAVING OF SHAGPAT, THE.

SHAH, Idries (1924–), writer and teacher, born in the north of India, whose many works have done much to introduce Sufi thought to the West. They include *The Sufis* (1964), *The Tales of the Dervishes* (1967), *Caravan of Dreams* (1968), *The Way of the Sufi* (1968), and *Learning How to Live* (1978, with an introduction by D. *Lessing, 1981). He also collected stories from the *Nasrudin corpus and published other selections of oriental tales. His works are unconventional mixtures of jokes, anecdotes, questions, precepts, and illuminations, inspired by Sufi wisdom and psychology.

Shahrazad, see SCHEHERAZADE.

SHAKESPEARE, William (1564–1616), dramatist, man of the theatre, and poet, was baptized in Holy Trinity Church, Stratford-upon-Avon, on 26 April 1564. His birth is traditionally celebrated on 23 April, which is also known to have been the date of his death. He was the eldest son of John Shakespeare, a glover and dealer in other commodities who played a prominent part in local affairs, becoming bailiff and justice of the peace in 1568, but whose fortunes later declined. John had married c.1557 Mary Arden, who came from a family of higher social standing. Of their eight children, four sons and one daughter survived childhood.

The standard and kind of education indicated by William's writings are such as he might have received at the local grammar school, whose records for the period are lost. On 28 November 1582 a bond was issued permitting him to marry Anne Hathaway of Shottery, a village close to Stratford. She was eight years his senior. A daughter, Susanna, was baptized on 26 May 1583, and twins, Hamnet and Judith, on 2 February 1585. We do not know how Shakespeare was employed in early manhood; the best-authenticated tradition is *Aubrey's: 'he had been in his younger yeares as Schoolmaster in the Countrey.'

Nothing is known of his beginnings as a writer, nor when or in what capacity he entered the theatre. In 1587 an actor of the Queen's Men died through manslaughter shortly before the company visited Stratford. That Shakespeare may have filled the vacancy is an intriguing speculation. The first printed allusion to him is from 1592, in the pamphlet *Greenes Groats-Worth of Witte*, ostensibly by R. *Greene but possibly by *Chettle. Mention of 'an upstart Crow' who 'supposes he is as well able to bombast out a blanke verse as the best of you' and who 'is in his owne conceit the onely Shake-scene in a countrey' suggests rivalry, and parody of a line from 3 *Henry VI* shows that Shakespeare was established on the London literary scene. He was a leading member of the Lord Chamberlain's Men soon after their re-foundation in 1594. With them he worked and grew prosperous for the rest of his career as they developed into London's leading company, occupying the Globe Theatre from 1599, becoming the King's Men on James I's accession in 1603, and taking over the Blackfriars as a winter house in 1608. He is the only prominent playwright of his time to have had so stable a relationship with a single company.

Theatrical life centred on London, which necessarily became Shakespeare's professional base, as various records testify. But his family remained in Stratford. In 1596 his father applied, successfully, for a grant of arms, and so became a gentleman; in August William's son Hamnet died, and was buried in Holy Trinity churchyard. In October Shakespeare was lodging in Bishopsgate, London, and in May of the next year he bought a substantial Stratford house, New Place. His father died in 1601, and in the following year William paid £320 for 127 acres of land in Old Stratford. In 1604 he lodged in London with a Huguenot family called Mountjoy. In the next year he paid £440 for an interest in the Stratford tithes, and there in June 1607 his daughter Susanna married a physician, John Hall. His only granddaughter, Elizabeth Hall, was christened the following February; in 1608 his mother died and was buried in Holy Trinity.

Evidence of Shakespeare's increasing involvement with Stratford at this time suggests that he was withdrawing to New Place, but his name continues to appear in London records; in March 1613, for instance, he paid £140 for a gatehouse close to the Blackfriars theatre, probably as an investment. In the same month he and the actor R. *Burbage received two guineas each for providing an *impresa* to be borne by the earl of Rutland at a court tourney. In February 1616 his second daughter, Judith, married Thomas Quiney, causing her father to make alterations to the draft of his will, which he signed on 25 March. He died, according to the inscription on his monument, on 23 April, and was buried in Holy Trinity. His widow died in 1623 and his last surviving descendant, Elizabeth Hall, in 1670.

Shakespeare's only writings for the press are

the narrative poems *Venus and Adonis and *The Rape of Lucrece, published 1593 and 1594 respectively, each with the author's dedication to Henry Wriothesley, earl of Southampton, and the short poem *'The Phoenix and the Turtle', published 1601 in Robert Chester's Loves Martyr, a collection of poems by various hands. His *Sonnets, dating probably from the mid-1590s, appeared in 1609, apparently not by his agency; they bear a dedication to the mysterious 'Mr W.H.' over the initials of the publisher, Thomas Thorpe. The volume also includes the poem *'A Lover's Complaint'.

Shakespeare's plays were published by being performed. Scripts of only half of them appeared in print in his lifetime, some in reported texts now known as 'bad quartos'. Records of performance are scanty and haphazard: as a result dates and order of composition, especially of the earlier plays, are often difficult to establish. The list that follows gives dates of first printing of all the plays other than those that first appeared in the 1623 *Folio.

Probably Shakespeare began to write for the stage in the late 1580s. The ambitious trilogy on the reign of Henry VI, now known as *Henry VI Parts One, Two, and Three, and its sequel *Richard III, are among his early works. Parts Two and Three were printed in reported texts as The First Part of the Contention betwixt the Two Famous Houses of York and Lancaster (1594) and The True Tragedy of Richard, Duke of York (1595). A bad quarto of Richard III appeared in 1597. Shakespeare's first Roman tragedy is *Titus Andronicus, printed 1594, and his earliest comedies are *The Two Gentlemen of Verona, *The Taming of the Shrew (a derivative play, The Taming of a Shrew, was printed 1594), *The Comedy of Errors (acted 1594), and *Love's Labour's Lost (printed 1598). All these plays are thought to have been written by 1595.

Particularly difficult to date is *King John: scholars still dispute whether a two-part play, The Troublesome Reign of John, King of England, printed 1591, is its source or a derivative. *Richard II, printed 1597, is usually dated 1595. For some years after this, Shakespeare concentrated on comedy, in *A Midsummer Night's Dream and *The Merchant of Venice (both printed 1600), *The Merry Wives of Windsor (related to the later history plays, and printed in a reported text 1602), *Much Ado About Nothing (printed 1600), *As You Like It (mentioned in 1600), and *Twelfth Night, probably written in 1600 or soon afterwards. *Romeo and Juliet (ascribed to the mid-1590s) is a tragedy with strongly comic elements, and the tetralogy begun by Richard II is completed by three comical histories: *Henry IV Parts One and Two, each printed a year or two after composition (Part One 1598, Part Two 1600), and *Henry V, almost certainly written 1599, printed, in a reported text, 1600.

In 1598 *Meres, a minor writer, published praise of Shakespeare in Palladis Tamia: Wit's Treasury, mentioning twelve of the plays so far listed (assuming that by Henry the 4 he means both Parts) along with another, Love's Labour's Won, apparently either a lost play or an alternative title for an extant one.

Late in the century Shakespeare turned again to tragedy. A Swiss traveller saw *Julius Caesar in London in September 1599. *Hamlet apparently dates from a year or two later; it was entered in the register of the *Stationers' Company in July 1602; a bad—very bad—quarto appeared in 1603, and a good text in late 1604 (some copies bear the date 1605). A play that defies easy classification is *Troilus and Cressida, probably written 1602, printed 1609. The comedy *All's Well that Ends Well, too, is probably of this period, as is *Measure for Measure, played at court in December 1604. The tragedy *Othello, played at court the previous month, reached print abnormally late in 1622. *King Lear probably dates, in its first version, from 1605; the quarto printed in 1608, which some regard as a reported text, is gaining acceptance as an authoritative version. The text printed in the Folio appears to represent a revision dating from a few years later. Much uncertainty surrounds *Timon of Athens, printed in the Folio from uncompleted papers, and probably written in collaboration with T. *Middleton. *Macbeth is generally dated 1606, *Antony and Cleopatra 1606–7, and *Coriolanus 1607–9.

Towards the end of his career, though while still in his early 40s, Shakespeare turned to romantic tragi-comedy. *Pericles, printed in a debased text 1609, certainly existed in the previous year; it is the only play generally believed to be mostly, if not entirely, by Shakespeare that was not included in the 1623 Folio. *Forman, the astrologer, records seeing both *Cymbeline and *The Winter's Tale in 1611. *The Tempest was given at court in November 1611.

The last three plays associated with Shakespeare appear to have been written in collaboration with J. *Fletcher. They are *Henry VIII, which 'had been acted not passing 2 or 3 times' before the performance at the Globe during which the theatre burnt down on 29 June 1613; a lost play, *Cardenio, acted by the King's Men in 1613 and attributed to the two dramatists in a Stationers' Register entry of 1653; and *The Two Noble Kinsmen, which appears to derive in part from a 1613 masque by F. *Beaumont, and was first printed 1634. No Shakespeare play survives in authorial manuscript, though three pages of revisions to a manuscript play, Sir Thomas *More, variously dated about 1593 or 1601, are often thought to be by Shakespeare and in his hand.

It may have been soon after Shakespeare died, in 1616, that his colleagues *Heminges and

Condell began to prepare *Mr William Shakespeare's Comedies, Histories, and Tragedies*, better known as the First Folio, which appeared in 1623. Only once before, in the 1616 *Jonson Folio, had an English dramatist's plays appeared in collected form. Heminges and Condell, or their agents, worked with care, assembling manuscripts, providing reliable printed copy when it was available, but also causing quartos to be brought wholly or partially into line with prompt-books. Their volume includes a dedicatory epistle to William and Philip Herbert, earls of Pembroke and Montgomery, an address 'To the Great Variety of Readers' by themselves, and verse tributes, most notably the substantial poem by Jonson in which he declares that Shakespeare 'was not of an age, but for all time'. Above all, the Folio is important because it includes 16 plays which in all probability would not otherwise have survived. Its title-page engraving, by *Droeshout, is, along with the half-length figure bust by Gheerart Janssen erected in Holy Trinity, Stratford, by 1623, the only image of Shakespeare with strong claims to authenticity. The Folio was reprinted three times in the 17th cent.; the second issue (1664) of the third edition adds *Pericles* and six more plays. Other plays, too, have been ascribed to Shakespeare, but few scholars would add anything to the accepted canon except, possibly, parts of *Edward III*, printed anonymously 1596.

Over 200 years after Shakespeare died, doubts were raised about the authenticity of his works (see BACONIAN THEORY). The product largely of snobbery—reluctance to believe that a man of humble origins wrote many of the world's greatest dramatic masterpieces—and of the desire for self-advertisement, they are best answered by the facts that the monument to William Shakespeare of Stratford-upon-Avon compares him with *Socrates and *Virgil, and that Jonson's verses in the Folio identify the author of that volume as the 'Sweet Swan of Avon'.

The documents committed to print between 1593 and 1623 have generated an enormous amount of varied kinds of human activity. The first editor to try to bring them into order, reconcile their discrepancies, correct their errors, and present them for readers of his time was the dramatist *Rowe, in 1709. His 18th-cent. successors include *Pope (1723–5), *Theobald (1733), Dr *Johnson (1765), *Capell (1767–8), and *Malone (1790; third variorum 1821 by *Boswell, out of Malone's edition). The most important 19th-cent. edition is the Cambridge Shakespeare (1863–6, rev. 1891–3), on which the Globe text (1864) was based. The American New Variorum edition, still in progress, began to appear in 1871. Early in the 20th cent. advances in textual studies transformed attitudes to the text. Subsequent editions include the Arden Shakespeare (1899–1924), *Quiller-Couch's and

J. Dover *Wilson's New Shakespeare (Cambridge, 1921–66), G. L. Kittredge's (1936), Peter Alexander's (1951), the New Arden (1951–), and the Riverside (1974). The first volumes in the Oxford English Texts edition appeared in 1982, and Oxford has in active preparation a single-volume edition to be published in both modern and original spelling. Another Cambridge edition in single volumes is also announced.

Great critics who have written on Shakespeare include *Dryden, Samuel Johnson, S. T. *Coleridge, *Hazlitt, A. C. *Bradley, and (less reverently) G. B. *Shaw. The German *Shakespeare Jahrbuch* has been appearing since 1865; other major periodicals are *Shakespeare Survey* (annual from 1948), *Shakespeare Quarterly* (from 1950), and *Shakespeare Studies* (annual from 1965). The standard biographical studies are E. K. *Chambers, *William Shakespeare: A Study of Facts and Problems* (2 vols, 1930) and S. *Schoenbaum, *William Shakespeare: A Documentary Life* (1975). The play scripts have been translated into innumerable languages and have inspired poets, novelists, dramatists, painters, composers, choreographers, film-makers, and other artists at all levels of creative activity. They have formed the basis for the English theatrical tradition, and they continue to find realization in readers' imaginations and, in richly varied transmutations, on the world's stages.

Shakespearean Criticism, a two-volume collection of the lectures of S. T. *Coleridge given between 1808 and 1818, ed. T. M. Raysor, 1907.

Coleridge himself never published these lectures. Vol. I consists of notes and fragments patched together from his papers; vol. II of shorthand reports, and contemporary accounts made by members of his audience. Uneven in quality, at his best Coleridge combines acute insight into details of dramatic psychology, with his broad general theories about the 'organic' form of the Shakespearian play and the process of creating character from 'within'. Coleridge drew heavily on the aesthetics of *Schelling about the role of the Unconscious in art, and on the dramatic criticism of A. W. *Schlegel (1811).

Shakespeare–Bacon controversy, see BACONIAN THEORY.

Shakespeare's Heroines, see JAMESON, A. B.

Shakūntalā, a celebrated Sanskrit drama by *Kālidāsa, translated by Sir W. *Jones. It tells the story of King Dushyanta's love for the maiden Shakūntalā, whom he sees while hunting in the forest; he contracts a summary marriage with her and departs, leaving her a royal ring as a pledge. She is then laid under a curse by the sage Durvasas, who thinks he has been treated with insufficient respect; he decrees that her husband the king shall forget her until he once more sees the ring. Unfortunately she loses the ring while bathing, and when she goes to the palace, she is rejected; she returns to the forest, where she gives birth to Bharata. The ring is shortly recovered by a fisherman from the belly of a fish, the king remembers his lost love, seeks her, and finds her, and they are reunited. Kālidāsa's play was greatly admired by *Goethe.

Shallow, in Shakespeare's 2 *Henry IV* a foolish country justice. He appears again in *The Merry Wives of Windsor*, upbraiding Falstaff for beating his men and killing his deer. This event has been taken as a reference to a poaching incident in Shakespeare's early days.

'Shalott, The Lady of', see LADY OF SHALOTT, THE, and LAUNCELOT OF THE LAKE.

Shamela Andrews, An Apology for the Life of Mrs, a parody by H. *Fielding, published pseudonymously 1741.

Richardson's *Pamela* was published in 1740, and in 1741 Fielding, irritated by what he regarded as the sententious hypocrisy of the book, replied anonymously with the lively travesty *Shamela*. The gullible Parson Tickletext, overcome by the beauty of the person and character of Pamela, writes to his friend, Parson Oliver, commending 'sweet, dear, pretty Pamela'. Oliver, however, has in his possession certain letters which reveal the true nature and history of the heroine. Events and characters remain as in *Pamela*, but all is now seen in a very different light, with Parson Williams appearing as a scheming rogue, Mr B as Mr Booby, Pamela as a calculating hussy, and morality equated with expediency throughout. Richardson was convinced the work was Fielding's and never forgave him.

Shandean, derived from 'shandy', a word of obscure origin, meaning 'crack-brained, halfcrazy', now used to describe anyone or anything reminiscent of Sterne's *Tristram Shandy*.

Shandon, Captain, a character in Thackeray's *Pendennis*.

Shandy, Tristram, Walter, Mrs, and Captain Tobias (Toby), see TRISTRAM SHANDY.

SHARP, Cecil (1859–1924), English folkmusic collector and editor. He began collecting folk-songs in 1903, and soon became the most important of all the workers in this field, transcribing during the course of his life a total of 4,977 tunes of which he published 1,118. Apart from the intrinsic value of this achievement, his work and the enthusiasm he brought to it profoundly influenced a whole school of English composers, of whom *Vaughan Williams and *Holst were the leading figures.

SHARP, James (1618–79), was appointed archbishop of St Andrews in 1661 as a reward for his assistance in restoring episcopacy in Scotland. His treachery to the Presbyterian cause made him obnoxious to the Covenanters, a party of whom murdered him on Magus Muir. Oliver *Cromwell had already nicknamed him 'Sharp of that ilk'. The murder figures in Scott's *Old Mortality*.

Sharp, Rebecca (Becky), a leading character in Thackeray's *Vanity Fair*.

SHARP, William ('Fiona Macleod') (1855–1905), born in Paisley, educated at Glasgow University, wrote under his own name essays, verse, minor novels, and Lives of *Rossetti (1882), *Shelley (1887), *Heine (1888), and R. *Browning (1890). He is chiefly remembered for his mystic Celtic tales and romances of peasant life by 'Fiona Macleod' written in the manner of the *'Celtic twilight' movement. These include *Pharais* (1893), *The Mountain Lovers* (1895), *The Sin Eater* (1895), and plays, including *The House of Usna* (1903) and *The Immortal Hour* (1900). Sharp successfully concealed the identity of 'Fiona Macleod' (including writing a bogus entry in *Who's Who*) until his death.

Shaving of Shagpat, The, an Arabian Entertainment, a series of eastern fantasies by G. *Meredith, published 1856.

The vain, bewhiskered Shagpat is an enchanter who holds a city and its king under a spell by means of one hair on his head, 'The Identical'. It is ordained that Shibli Bagarag, a poor barber, a teller of exotic tales and a juggler of fantastical words, shall become Master of the Event by shaving Shagpat and breaking the spell. In spite of many comical difficulties and humiliations, with the help of his betrothed, Noorna bin Noorka, and many magical happenings he at last succeeds in dispelling the enchantment.

SHAW, (George) Bernard (1856–1950), was born in Dublin, the youngest child of unhappily married and inattentive parents. In 1876 he moved to London, joining his mother and sister, and began his literary career by ghosting music criticism and writing five unsuccessful novels (including *Cashel Byron's Profession*, 1886, and *An Unsocial Socialist*, 1887, both first published in *To-day*, in 1885–6 and 1884 respectively). During his first nine years in London he calculated that he earned less than £10 by his pen. He wrote music, art, and book criticism for the *Dramatic Review* (1885–6), *Our Corner* (1885–6), the *Pall Mall Gazette* (1885–8), *The World* (1886–94), and *The Star* (1888–90, as 'Corno di Bassetto'). His music criticism has been collected in three volumes as *Shaw's Music* (1981, ed. Dan H. Laurence). (See also under MUSIC, LITERATURE OF.) He was a drama critic for *The

Saturday Review (1895–8) and produced a series of remarkable and controversial weekly articles (published in book form as *Our Theatres in the Nineties*, 3 vols, 1932), voicing his impatience with the artificiality of the London theatre and pleading for the performance of plays dealing with contemporary social and moral problems; he was a great admirer of *Ibsen. During these years he took up various causes and joined several literary and political societies, notably the *Fabian Society, serving on the executive committee from 1885 to 1911. Not naturally a good public speaker, he schooled himself to become a brilliant one and gave over 1,000 lectures. He edited and contributed to *Fabian Essays in Socialism* (1889) and wrote many tracts setting down his socialist and collectivist principles. He was a freethinker, a supporter of women's rights, and an advocate of equality of income, the abolition of private property, and a radical change in the voting system. He also campaigned for the simplification of spelling and punctuation and the reform of the English alphabet. He was well known as a journalist and public speaker when his first play, *Widowers' Houses* (pub. 1893), was produced in 1892, but it met with little success. There followed *Arms and the Man* (1894, pub. 1898: later turned into a musical called *The Chocolate Soldier*), *The Devil's Disciple* (perf. NY 1897, pub. 1901), *You Never Can Tell* (1899, pub. 1898), *Caesar and Cleopatra* (pub. 1901, perf. Berlin 1906), *Mrs Warren's Profession* (pub. 1898, perf. 1902), and *John Bull's Other Island* (1904, perf. NY 1907), a play which, thanks to its characteristic 'Shavian' wit, brought his first popular success in London. The critics also were gradually persuaded that the plays were not simply dry vehicles for his reformist zeal.

Shaw was an indefatigable worker, writing over 50 plays, including *Man and Superman* (pub. 1903, perf. 1905), *Major Barbara* (1905, pub. 1907), *The Doctor's Dilemma* (1906, pub. Berlin 1908), *Getting Married* (1908, pub. Berlin 1910), *Misalliance* (1910, pub. Berlin 1911), *Fanny's First Play* (1911, pub. Berlin 1911), *Androcles and the Lion* (pub. Berlin 1912, perf. Hamburg 1913), *Pygmalion* (perf. Vienna 1913, pub. Berlin 1913, later turned into the popular musical *My Fair Lady*), *Heartbreak House* (pub. 1919, perf. 1920, both NY), *Back to Methuselah* (perf. and pub. NY 1921), *Saint Joan* (perf. NY 1923, pub. 1924), *The Apple Cart* (perf. Warsaw 1929, pub. Berlin 1929), *Too True to be Good* (perf. Boston 1932, pub. Berlin 1932), *Village Wooing* (perf. Dallas 1934, pub. 1934), *The Simpleton of the Unexpected Isles* (perf. NY 1935, pub. Berlin 1935), 'In Good King Charles's Golden Days' (perf. and pub. 1939), and *Buoyant Billions* (perf. and pub. Zurich 1948).

These plays were published (some in collections: *Plays Pleasant and Unpleasant*, 1898; *Three Plays for Puritans*, 1901), with lengthy prefaces in which Shaw clearly expresses his views as a non-romantic and a champion of the thinking man. The dramatic conflict in his plays is the conflict of thought and belief, not that of neurosis or physical passion. Discussion is the basis of the plays, and his great wit and intelligence won audiences over to the idea that mental and moral passion could produce absorbing dramatic material. He believed that war, disease, and the present brevity of our lifespan frustrate the 'Life Force' (see under MAN AND SUPERMAN) and that functional adaptation, a current of creative evolution activated by the power of human will, was essential to any real progress, and indeed to the survival of the species. The plays continued to be performed regularly both during and after his lifetime (several were made into films) and his unorthodox views, his humour, and his love of paradox have become an institution. Amongst his other works should be mentioned *The Quintessence of Ibsenism* (1891, revised and expanded 1913), which reveals his debt to Ibsen as a playwright and presents an argument for Fabian Socialism; *The Perfect Wagnerite* (1898); *Common Sense About the War* (1914); *The Intelligent Woman's Guide to Socialism and Capitalism* (1928); and *Everybody's Political What's What* (1944). Shaw was a prolific letter-writer and his correspondence with the actresses Ellen *Terry and Mrs Patrick Campbell, as well as several volumes of collected letters, are available in book form.

In 1898 Shaw married Charlotte Payne-Townshend and, although it seems to have been a marriage of simple companionship, they lived together until her death in 1943. He was a strict vegetarian and never drank spirits, coffee, or tea. He died at the age of 94, as independent as ever and still writing for the theatre. He was awarded the *Nobel Prize in 1925. See *The Bodley Head Collected Plays with their Prefaces* (7 vols, 1970–4).

SHAW, Henry Wheeler (1818–85), who wrote under the pseudonym 'Josh Billings', an American comic essayist and philosopher, who ridiculed humbug of all kinds. He first popularized his work by inventing his own vernacular phonetic spelling.

SHCHEDRIN, N. (Mikhail Evgrafovich Saltykov) (1826–89), Russian satirical writer and polemical journalist. Born in a merchant family near Tver, he was educated at Tsarskoe Selo, outside St Petersburg, and worked in government service while writing reviews for major journals and moving in circles interested in Utopian socialism. After serving as vice-governor of provincial towns, he was retired in 1868 and devoted himself to literature, working first for *The Contemporary* and then for *Notes of the Fatherland*, eventually as editor. His novels often developed from journalistic sketches. With the passage of time he became increasingly radical and in 1884 *Notes of the Fatherland* was closed. *Turgenev (with uncharacteristic exaggeration) called him the Russian *Swift. Shchedrin's major works are *The Story of a Town* (1869–70, English trans., 1980), *The Golovlev Family* (1875–80, trans., 1931), and the semi-autobiographical *Old Times in Poshekhonsk* (1887–89). The first English translation of his work, *Tchinovniks: sketches of provincial life*, appeared in 1861.

SHEBBEARE, John (1709–88), an apothecary and surgeon who gave up his practice in about 1754 to devote himself to writing. He became a pungent and often scurrilous pamphleteer (twice imprisoned for libel), and was a bitter opponent of *Smollett, who satirized him as Ferret in *Sir Launcelot Greaves*. He also wrote many political and medical works, and two novels, *The Marriage Act* (1754) and *Lydia* (1755), in which a wide-ranging miscellany of episodes, reflections, and pugnacious opinions is haphazardly held together by the character of a 'noble savage', the American Indian Cannassetego. (See PRIMITIVISM.)

SHEFFIELD, John, 3rd earl of Mulgrave and afterwards 1st duke of Buckingham and Normanby (1648–1721), a patron of *Dryden and a friend of *Pope, and a statesman who held high offices but was 'neither esteemed nor beloved'. He wrote an *Essay upon Satire* (published anonymously, ?1680), which cost Dryden a beating at the hands of *Rochester's bravoes, and an *Essay upon Poetry* (1682) of no great value. He erected the monument to Dryden in Westminster Abbey.

Sheik, The, a best-selling novel by E(dith) M(aude) Hull, the retiring wife of a Derbyshire pig-farmer. Published in 1919, it had an international success, and was to provide Rudolph Valentino with one of his most famous film roles. It is the erotic and sado-masochistic story of 'proud Diana Mayo', an English girl kidnapped by the Sheik, whose brutal treatment of her finally wins her devotion; at this point it emerges he is not an Arab at all, but, in Claud Cockburn's words, 'son of a tip-top British peer and his beautiful Spanish wife . . . everything is race-wise and class-wise OK.' (*Bestseller: The Books that Everyone Read 1900–1939*, 1972)

SHELDON, Gilbert (1598–1677), was warden of *All Souls College, Oxford, 1626–48, and archbishop of Canterbury from 1663 until his death. As chancellor of Oxford he built and endowed, at his own expense, in 1669, the Sheldonian Theatre, where much of the printing work of the University was conducted until the Clarendon Building was erected in 1713.

SHELLEY, Mary Wollstonecraft (1797–1851), only daughter of W. *Godwin and Mary

*Wollstonecraft. Her mother died a few days after her birth. In 1814 she left England with P. B. *Shelley, and married him in 1816 on the death of his wife Harriet. Only one of their children, Percy, survived infancy. She returned to England in 1823, after Shelley's death. She is best remembered as the author of *Frankenstein, or the Modern Prometheus* (1818), but wrote several other works. *Valperga* (1823), is a romance set in 14th-cent. Italy. *The Last Man* (1826), a novel set in the future, describes England as a republic, and the gradual destruction of the human race by plague; its narrator, Lionel Verney, begins life as a shepherd boy and after many wanderings finds himself as the last survivor amidst the ruined grandeurs of Rome in the year 2100, an interesting variation of the 'noble savage' motif (see PRIMITIVISM). The same motif is seen in *Lodore* (1835); the heroine, Ethel, is taken as a child by her father, Lord Lodore, to the wilds of Illinois and reared amidst the grandest objects of nature, whence she returns to a life of romance and penury in London reminiscent of Mary Shelley's early years. She wrote other novels, several biographies, and many short stories, most of which were published in *The Keepsake*; some have *science fiction elements, others are *Gothic or historical, and many are continental in setting. Her *Rambles in Germany and Italy, in 1840, 1842 and 1843* (1844) was well received. She also edited her husband's poems (1830) and his essays, letters, etc. (1840).

SHELLEY, Percy Bysshe (1792–1822). The eldest son of the MP for Horsham (and later baronet), he was born at Field Place, Sussex, and destined for a parliamentary career. Active, mischievous, and highly imaginative as a child, he was conventionally educated at Syon House Academy, Eton, and University College, Oxford; an upbringing that made him deeply unhappy and rebellious. At school he was mocked and bullied as 'Mad Shelley' and the 'Eton Atheist'; at home he was worshipped by a tribe of younger sisters; a pattern that recurs throughout his life.

Early encouraged in his 'printing freaks', he privately published a series of *Gothic-horror novelettes and verses in his teens: *Zastrozzi* (1810); *Original Poetry by Victor and Cazire* (1810, with his beloved sister Elizabeth); and *St Irvyne or The Rosicrucian* (1811). At Oxford he read radical authors—*Godwin, *Paine, Condorcet—dressed and behaved with provoking eccentricity, and in March 1811 was summarily expelled for circulating a pamphlet, *The Necessity of *Atheism*, written with his friend T. J. *Hogg. He quarrelled violently with his father, and eloped to Scotland with 16-year-old Harriet Westbrook, the daughter of a coffee-house proprietor. They married in Edinburgh in August 1811, though Shelley disapproved of matri-

mony, as well as royalty, meat-eating, and religion. Three years of nomadic existence
followed. At York he tried sharing Harriet with
Hogg; in the Lakes he argued with R. *Southey;
in Dublin he spoke on public platforms, and
published *An Address to the Irish People* (1812)
and *Proposals* for reform associations. He corresponded with Godwin; circulated pamphlets
on vegetarianism and on the free press (*A Letter
to Lord Ellenborough*, 1812); and fly-posted a
democratic broadsheet, *A Declaration of Rights*
(for which his servant was democratically arrested). He tried setting up a radical commune
of 'like spirits' first at Lynmouth, Devon, and
later at Tremadoc, N. Wales. Much of his early
philosophy, both in poetry and politics, is expressed in *Queen Mab* (1813), with its remarkable *Notes*: they show Shelley as the direct
heir to the French and British revolutionary intellectuals of the 1790s.

In 1814 his marriage with Harriet collapsed,
despite the birth of two children and the kindly
intervention of *Peacock. After suicidal scenes,
Shelley eloped abroad with Mary Godwin (see
above), together with her 15-year-old stepsister
Jane 'Claire' Clairmont: their triangular
relationship endured for the next eight years. His
unfinished novella *The Assassins* (1814) reflects
their dreamy travels through post-war France,
Switzerland, and Germany, as does their combined journal, *History of a Six Weeks Tour*
(1817). He returned to London, an annuity of
£1,000, and, after many upheavals, a house
with Mary on the edge of Windsor Great Park.
Here he wrote *Alastor* (1816), a non-political
poem of haunting beauty, which first brought
him general notice and reviews. His favourite
son William was born. The summer of 1816
was spent on Lake Geneva with *Byron. Mary
began *Frankenstein*, and Shelley composed two
philosophic poems much influenced by
*Wordsworth, the 'Hymn to Intellectual
Beauty' (partly about his childhood) and
'Mont Blanc', a meditation on the nature of
power in a Godless universe.

In the autumn of 1816 Harriet drowned herself in the Serpentine. Shelley immediately married Mary and began a Chancery case for the
custody of his first two children, which he lost.
The experience shook him deeply, and is recalled
in many verse fragments, such as the 'Invocation
to Misery', 'Lines: The cold earth slept below
. . .', and the cursing 'To the Lord Chancellor'
(1817—a so-called *'flyting'). However,
friendships developed with Leigh *Hunt,
*Keats, *Hazlitt, and others of the liberal *Exam-
iner* circle; while Peacock, now an intimate
family confidant, drew a portrait of Shelley as
Scythrop Glowry in *Nightmare Abbey*. In 1817
the family settled at Great Marlow, on the
Thames, where Shelley wrote his polemical
'Hermit of Marlow' pamphlets, drafted a self-
searching 'Essay on Christianity', and slowly

composed 'Laon and Cythna', which was published, with alterations to avoid prosecution, as
The Revolt of Islam in 1818.

Harried by creditors, ill-health, and 'social
hatred', Shelley took his household permanently
abroad, to Italy in the spring of 1818, leaving
behind his sonnet 'Ozymandias' and a mass of
unpaid bills. He stayed at Lucca, where he translated Plato's *Symposium* and wrote a daring
essay 'On the Manners of the Ancient Greeks';
and then at Venice and Este, where he composed
*'Julian and Maddalo', based on his friendship
with Byron. He wintered in Naples, where he
wrote the passionately unhappy 'Stanzas Written in Dejection'; he also registered a mysterious
baby, Elena Adelaide Shelley, as his adopted—
or probably illegitimate—child. In the spring of
1819 he was working on *Prometheus Unbound*.

His domestic situation was increasingly
strained. His little daughter Clara had died at
Venice; now his favourite 'Willmouse' died at
Rome and Mary suffered a nervous breakdown.
The shaken family settled in Tuscany: first out-
side Livorno, then at Florence, and finally at
Pisa, which became their more or less permanent
home until 1822.

Yet the twelve months from the summer of
1819 saw Shelley's most extraordinary and
varied burst of major poetry. He completed
the fourth act of *Prometheus* (pub. 1820); wrote
The Mask of Anarchy (Sept. 1819); *'Ode to
the West Wind' (Oct. 1819); the satirical *Peter
Bell The Third* (Dec. 1819); his long political
odes, 'To Liberty' and 'To Naples' (both spring
1820); the lively, intimate 'Letter to Maria Gisborne' (July 1820); and the *'Witch of Atlas'
(Aug. 1820). Much of this work was inspired
by news of political events, which also produced
a number of short, angry, propaganda poems:
'Young Parson Richards', 'Song to the Men of
England', and 'Sonnet: England 1819'. At the
same time he dashed off several pure lyric pieces,
including 'To a Skylark' and 'The Cloud' (both
spring 1820), of dazzling metrical virtuosity;
and completed a verse melodrama, *The Cenci*
(1819). Yet despite this period of creativity, he
could get very little accepted for publication in
England, and he felt increasingly isolated and
despondent. The birth of his youngest son, Percy
Florence, somewhat cheered his domestic life.

The quieter period at Pisa which followed
(1820–1), saw him at work on a number of
prose pieces: *A Philosophical View of Reform*
(1820); the impish 'Essay on the Devil'; and
his famous *Defence of Poetry* (1821). He also
wrote some of his most delicate, low-keyed,
and visually suggestive short poems: 'The Two
Spirits', 'To the Moon', 'The Aziola', and
'Evening: Ponte Al Mare, Pisa'.

In the spring of 1821 news of the death of
Keats in Rome produced *Adonais*. The absence
of Claire and growing restlessness precipitated a
platonic love-affair with Emilia Viviani, a

beautiful 17-year-old heiress 'tyrannized' in a convent at Pisa. Instead of a third elopement this resulted in *Epipsychidion (1821).

In the winter of 1821 Byron also moved to Pisa, and a raffish circle formed round the two poets, including E. J. *Trelawny, Edward and Jane Williams, and eventually Leigh Hunt, who came from England to edit a monthly journal, *The Liberal (1822–4). Shelley was roused again to public utterance: his last completed verse drama, *Hellas (1822), though 'a mere improvise', was inspired by the Greek war of independence. He also began 'Charles I', a political drama of the English Civil War, with its touching song by Archy, the jester, 'A widow-bird sat mourning for her love'.

In April 1822 he moved his household to an isolated beach house on the bay of Lerici. Here Mary suffered a dangerous miscarriage; Claire reacted violently to news of the sudden death of Allegra, her daughter by Byron; and Shelley saw the ghost of a child in the sea. Here he began his last major poem, *The Triumph of Life. At the same time he composed a number of short lyrics, some to Jane Williams, of striking melodic grace: 'When the lamp is shattered', 'With a Guitar, to Jane', and the melancholy 'Lines Written in the Bay of Lerici'. His letters, still full of political hope and magically descriptive of the Italian seascape, are none the less shadowed with personal premonitions. Shelley was drowned in August 1822, in his small schooner the 'Ariel', together with Edward Williams and an English boatboy, on a return trip from visiting Byron and Hunt at Livorno. Overtaken by a violent summer squall, the boat went down without lowering its sails.

His lyric powers and romantic biography have until recently obscured Shelley's most enduring qualities as a writer: his intellectual courage and originality; his hatred of oppression and injustice; and his mischievous, sometimes macabre, sense of humour (especially evident in his light verse and letters). He was widely read in the classics, philosophy, and contemporary science; he translated from Greek (Plato and Homer), Latin (Spinoza), Spanish (Calderón), German (Goethe), Italian (Dante), and some Arabic fragments. His essays—very few published in his lifetime—are highly intelligent, his political pamphlets both angry and idealistic.

His weaknesses as a writer have always been evident: rhetorical abstraction; intellectual arrogance; and moments of intense self-pity. But in great poems like the 'West Wind', or in great prose like passages from the Defence, it is precisely these limitations that he transcends, and indeed explodes. Among the English Romantics, he has recovered his position as an undoubted major figure: the poet of volcanic hope for a better world, of fiery aspirations shot upwards through bitter gloom.

Shelley's Letters have been edited by F. L.

Jones (2 vols, 1964); the standard Life remains that by N. I. White (2 vols, 1947); see also R. Holmes, The Pursuit (1974). The major political re-interpretation of his career is by K. N. Cameron, Young Shelley: Genesis of a Radical (1951) and Shelley: The Golden Years (1974). Excellent modern criticism has been produced by Harold Bloom (1959), Neville Rogers (1967), Judith Chernaik (1972), Timothy Webb (1976), and P. M. Dawson (1980). Among many Selected Poems, that edited by Timothy Webb (1977) best reflects the new appreciation of Shelley. Biographical memoirs by Trelawny, Peacock, and Hogg remain vivid and amusing: everyone under Shelley's influence wrote exceptionally well, including Mary Shelley in her Notes reprinted in the Oxford Standard edition of the Collected Poems.

Shelley, Memoirs of, by *Peacock, published 1858. Not a full-dress biography, it originated as a review of reminiscences by *Trelawny and T. J. *Hogg, which Peacock thought inaccurate, particularly in relation to Shelley's first wife Harriet Westbrook. Peacock's book is polished and reliable, but its reticence and its willingness to question Shelley's veracity have not endeared it to the poet's admirers.

SHENSTONE, William (1714–63), poet, essayist, and landscape gardener of the Leasowes, Halesowen. Educated at Solihull and Pembroke College, Oxford, where he published his Poems Upon Various Occasions (1737), he established his reputation with The Judgement of Hercules (1741) and The Schoolmistress (1742). His poetic works included elegies, odes, songs, ballads, and levities, the most famous being 'A Pastoral Ballad' and 'Lines written at an Inn' (which Dr *Johnson once quoted by heart). From 1743 he transformed the Leasowes, a grazing farm, into a ferme ornée, an early example of a natural landscape garden, beautified with cascades, pools, vistas, urns, and a grove to *Virgil, encircled by a winding walk. His friends included Lord George *Lyttleton from nearby Hagley, *Somervile, Lady Luxborough, Richard *Graves, and *Jago. Later he was befriended by *Dodsley, whose Collection of Poems he helped to edit, and he worked with *Percy on editing the *Reliques of Ancient English Poetry, as well as providing the Birmingham printer *Baskerville with advice. His poetry, mainly pastoral in treatment, was popular in the 18th cent.; his 'Essays on Men and Manners', in the style of *La Rochefoucauld, included his views on 'landskip gardening'; his essay on elegy contributed to the development of that form. Though his way of life was criticized by Johnson and Horace *Walpole, he was respected by friends for his good taste. His correspondence reveals a sensitive, educated man living a provincial semi-rural life.

Shepheardes Calender, The, the earliest important work of *Spenser, published 1579, dedicated to *Sidney. It was illustrated by woodcuts and had accompanying glosses by one 'E.K.' (see KIRKE, E.).

It consists of twelve eclogues, one for each month of the year, written in different metres, and modelled on the eclogues of *Theocritus, *Virgil, and more modern writers, such as *Mantuan and *Marot. They take the form of dialogues among shepherds, except the first and last, which are complaints by 'Colin Clout', the author himself. Four of them deal with love, one is in praise of Elisa (Queen Elizabeth), one a lament for a 'mayden of greate bloud', four deal allegorically with matters of religion or conduct, one describes a singing-match, and one laments the contempt in which poetry is held.

SHEPHERD, Lord Clifford, The, Henry de Clifford, 14th Baron Clifford (?1455–1523), celebrated in *Wordsworth's 'Brougham Castle' and *The White Doe of Rylstone.* His father was attainted and his estates forfeited in 1461. Henry de Clifford was brought up as a shepherd, and restored to his estates and title on the accession of Henry VII.

Shepherd's Calendar, The, a volume of verse by J. *Clare.

Shepherd's Hunting, The, pastorals written by *Wither in the Marshalsea.

Shepherd's Week, The, a series of six pastorals by J. *Gay, published 1714.

They are eclogues in mock-classical style, five of them based more or less closely on *Virgil, but presenting shepherds and milkmaids not of the golden age but of the poet's day, in their earthy simplicity. They were designed to parody those of A. *Philips, but they have a charm and freshness of their own; Gay portrays his rustic characters (Blouzelinda, Bowzybeus, Cloddipole, Grubbinol, etc.) at work as well as at play, paints (in his own words) a 'lively landscape', and includes many references to folklore, games, superstitions, etc. *Empson provides an interesting commentary on mock pastoral in *Some Versions of Pastoral* (1935).

SHEPPARD, John, 'Jack Sheppard' (1702–24), a notorious thief and highwayman, who, after repeated escapes from prison, was hanged at Tyburn. He was the subject of tracts by *Defoe, of many plays and ballads, and of a novel by W. H. *Ainsworth. See NEWGATE CALENDAR.

SHERIDAN, Frances (1724–66), was the wife of Thomas and the mother of R. B. Sheridan (below). She was greatly encouraged in her writing by *Richardson, who arranged for the publication of *The Memoirs of Miss Sydney Biddulph* ('after the manner of *Pamela') in 1761, and in an expanded version in 1767. The novel, which ends not happily but in despair,

describes with honesty and precision the terrible misfortunes and distress of conscience of Sydney, who feels she has not the first claim to her beloved Faulkland. The novel was warmly received and translated into French and German, but Dr *Johnson wondered whether Mrs Sheridan had the moral right to make her readers suffer so. *The Discovery,* a comedy in which *Garrick took part, was very successful in 1763. *The History of Nourjahad,* a much admired and highly moral *Oriental novel, appeared in 1767. An apparently indulgent Sultan permits his friend to indulge all desires, and to enjoy life to eternity; but the liberty is a trick, and retribution falls.

SHERIDAN, Richard Brinsley (1751–1816), the son of Thomas Sheridan, an Irish actor-manager, and Mrs F. *Sheridan. Richard learned early that as a livelihood the theatre was both precarious and ungentlemanly. He was sent to Harrow School, where he was unhappy and regarded as a dunce. In Bath, however, where he joined his family in 1770, he was at once at home. His skit, written for the local paper, on the opening of the New Assembly Rooms, was considered good enough to be published as a separate pamphlet. He fell in love with Eliza Linley, a beautiful and accomplished young singer, with whom he eloped to France and entered into an invalid form of marriage contract, and on whose behalf he fought two farcical duels with her overbearing admirer Captain Matthews. Sheridan's angry father sent him to London to study law, but eventually the fathers withdrew their opposition and in 1773 he was lawfully married to Eliza. Very short of money, he decided to try his hand at a play, and in a very few weeks wrote *The Rivals,* which was produced at Covent Garden in 1775. It was highly successful and established Sheridan in the fashionable society he sought. *The Rivals* was followed in a few months by the farce *St Patrick's Day,* again a success; and in the autumn by *The Duenna,* an operatic play which delighted its audiences. In 1776 Sheridan, with partners, bought *Garrick's half-share in the *Drury Lane Theatre and became its manager. Early in 1777 appeared *A Trip to Scarborough, loosely based on Vanbrugh's *The Relapse, and this again was a success. In March of that year Sheridan was elected a member of the *Club, on the proposal of Dr *Johnson. Meanwhile he was working hard and long on *The School for Scandal,* which was produced, with Garrick's help and with a brilliant cast, in May. The play was universally acclaimed, and all doors, from those of the duchess of Devonshire and Lady Melbourne downwards, were open to the dramatist—whose personal expenses rose accordingly. Although *The School for Scandal* had 73 performances between 1777 and 1789 and made a profit of £15,000, Sheridan's financial anxieties, which were to dog him to the end of his life, became even more acute. In 1779 he became the sole proprietor of Drury Lane, and began to live far beyond his means. Although he seems to have been a sympathetic and creative producer, he found the business side of management increasingly irksome. In 1779 he produced his new play *The Critic, based on *The Rehearsal by Buckingham; once again he enjoyed a huge success, and the world regarded him as the true heir of Garrick. But it was not what he wanted. He had grown up with a positive dislike of the theatre, and he declared he never saw a play if he could help it. He wished to shine only in politics, but he had neither the correct family connections nor the financial stability. He became the friend and ally of *Fox and in 1780 won the seat at Stafford. After only two years as an MP he became the undersecretary for foreign affairs, but he neglected his office work, both as a politician and as the manager of Drury Lane. Fortunately his father had secured both Mrs *Siddons and J. P. *Kemble, who brought the required audiences to the theatre. In 1783 he became secretary to the Treasury and established his reputation as a brilliant orator in the House of Commons. In 1787 *Burke persuaded him into supporting the impeachment of *Hastings, and his eloquent speech of over five hours on the Begums of Oude ensured that he was made manager of the trial. He was by now confirmed an intimate friend of the prince regent and other royal figures. Eliza died in 1792, and in the same year the Drury Lane Theatre was declared unsafe and had to be demolished. Sheridan raised £150,000 for a new theatre with apparent ease, but he was plunging himself yet deeper into debt, and payments to his actors became more uncertain than ever. In 1795 he married Esther Ogle. All through these years he was speaking eloquently in the House and hoping for eventual political advancement. *Pizarro, adapted by Sheridan from *Kotzebue, was performed in 1799 and was successful enough to bring a brief reprieve, but in 1802 the theatre funds were impounded and the bankers put in charge. Enormous sums were owing to the landlord, the architect, the actors, and stage staff. Although he was still speaking daily at the Commons, Sheridan's friendship with Fox was fading, and when Grenville formed the 'ministry of all the talents' in 1806 Sheridan was offered only the treasurership to the navy, without Cabinet rank. The money which came with his appointment to a post with the Duchy of Cornwall was soon spent. In 1809 the new Drury Lane was destroyed by fire, the debts became crushing, and Sheridan was excluded from all aspects of management. In 1811 he lost his seat at Stafford, and in 1813 was arrested for debt. Friends rallied, but he and his wife became ill. His house was discovered to be filthy and denuded of almost all furnishings. He died in July 1816 and was given a fine funeral, with four lords as pallbearers. He wished to be remembered as a man of politics and to be buried next to Fox, but he was laid near Garrick instead. He is remembered chiefly as the author of two superb comedies, but his speeches and letters have also been published. The standard edition of the plays is *The Plays and Poems of Sheridan* (3 vols, 1928), ed. R. C. Rhodes: see also *Harlequin Sheridan* (1933), a life by R. C. Rhodes. The *Letters* were edited by C. Price, 3 vols, 1966.

Sheriffs of Bristol, *A Letter to the,* see LETTER TO THE SHERIFFS OF BRISTOL, A.

SHERLOCK, Thomas (1678–1761), son of W. *Sherlock, succeeded his father as master of the Temple (1704–53), obtained a high reputation as a preacher, and was successively bishop of Bangor, Salisbury, and London. He strongly attacked *Hoadly in the Bangorian controversy. His best-known work was *A Trial of the Witnesses of the Resurrection of Jesus* (1729), a defence of the historical occurrence of miracles.

SHERLOCK, William (1641–1707), became master of the Temple and dean of St Paul's. He was author of *A Practical Discourse concerning Death* (1689), his most popular work, and various controversial treatises. In 1688 he sided with the non-jurors and was suspended, but took the oath in 1690, an act which made him the object of many attacks, vindications, and pasquinades.

SHERRIFF, R(obert) C(edric) (1896–1975), playwright, born in Kingston upon Thames, who worked in a local insurance office and began to write plays to raise money for his rowing club. His best-known play was *Journey's End* (1928, pub. 1929), based on his experiences in the trenches as a captain during the First World War. Realistic and low-key, it was praised by G. B. *Shaw as a 'useful corrective to the romantic conception of war', and has also proved lastingly popular on the stage. It portrays the relationships under stress of Captain Stanhope, new lieutenant Raleigh (who is in love with Stanhope's sister), the reliable second-in-command Osborne, the cowardly Hibbert, etc., and ends in mid-battle after the deaths of Osborne and Raleigh. Other plays include *Badger's Green* (1930), a comedy of village politics and cricket; *St Helena* (1934), about Napoleon's last years; *Home at Seven* (1950), in which a banker suffering from amnesia fears he may have committed a crime; and *The White Carnation* (1953), a ghost story about a conscience-stricken stockbroker. Sherriff also wrote several novels, including *The Fortnight in September* (1931).

SHERWOOD, Mrs Mary Martha (1775–1851), published nearly a hundred books of stories and tracts, many for children and young people. *Susan Gray*, a very successful pious work intended for the poor, appeared in 1802. *Little Henry and his Bearer*, a tale published in 1815 after a period spent in India, was translated into French, German, Hindustani, Chinese, and Sinhalese. The best known of all her works is *The History of the Fairchild Family*, which appeared in 1818, its tremendous success leading to a second part in 1842 and a third in 1847.

She Stoops to Conquer, or *The Mistakes of a Night*, a comedy by *Goldsmith, produced 1773.

The principal characters are Hardcastle, who loves 'everything that's old; old friends, old times, old manners, old books, old wine'; Mrs Hardcastle, and Miss Hardcastle their daughter; Mrs Hardcastle's son by a former marriage, Tony Lumpkin, a frequenter of the Three Jolly Pigeons, idle and ignorant, but cunning and mischievous, and doted on by his mother; and young Marlow, 'one of the most bashful and reserved young fellows in the world', except with barmaids and servant-girls. His father, Sir Charles Marlow, has proposed a match between young Marlow and Miss Hardcastle, and the young man and his friend Hastings accordingly travel down to pay the Hardcastles a visit. Losing their way they arrive at night at the Three Jolly Pigeons, where Tony Lumpkin directs them to a neighbouring inn, which is in reality the Hardcastles' house. The fun of the play arises largely from the resulting misunderstanding, Marlow treating Hardcastle as the landlord of the supposed inn, and making violent love to Miss Hardcastle, whom he takes for one of the servants. This contrasts with his bashful attitude when presented to her in her real character. The arrival of Sir Charles Marlow clears up the misconception and all ends well, including a subsidiary love-affair between Hastings and Miss Hardcastle's cousin Miss Neville, whom Mrs Hardcastle destines for Tony Lumpkin.

The mistaking of a private residence for an inn was said by Goldsmith's sister Mrs Hodson to have been founded on an actual incident in his own youth.

The play was greeted from its opening with immense success, and was seen as a victory in the newly formulated battle against 'that monster called *Sentimental Comedy' (*London Magazine*, 1773).

She wou'd if she cou'd, the second of the comedies by *Etherege, produced 1668.

Sir Oliver Cockwood and his wife, Sir Joslin Jolley and his young kinswomen Ariana and Gatty, come up from the country to London to divert themselves, Sir Oliver and Sir Joslin with dissipation, Lady Cockwood, in spite of her virtuous professions, with an intrigue, and the two spirited young ladies with innocent flirtations. Lady Cockwood pursues Mr Courtal, a gentleman of the town, with her unwelcome attentions. Mr Courtal and his friend Mr Freeman strike up acquaintance with the young ladies, and take them and Lady Cockwood to the Bear in Drury Lane for a dance, where Sir Joslin and Sir Oliver arrive, bent on less innocent pleasures. Sir Oliver gets drunk, dances with his wife, supposing her to be someone quite different, and confusion ensues. The ladies go home. Freeman arrives to console Lady Cockwood. Courtal arrives and Freeman is concealed in a cupboard. Sir Oliver arrives and Courtal is hidden under the table. Sir Oliver drops a 'China orange', which rolls under the table. The two men are discovered, the young ladies are awarded to them, and Lady Cockwood resolves to 'give over the great business of the town' and confine herself hereafter to the affairs of her own family.

Shimei, name for Slingsby Bethel in Dryden's *Absalom and Achitophel*.

'Shipman's Tale, The', see CANTERBURY TALES, 15.

Ship of Fools, The, an adaptation of the famous *Narrenschiff* of Sebastian Brant. The *Narrenschiff* was written in the dialect of Swabia and first published in 1494. It became extremely popular and was translated into many languages. Its theme is the shipping off of fools of all kinds from their native land to the Land of Fools. The fools are introduced by classes and reproved for their folly. The popularity of the book was largely due to the spirited illustrations, which show a sense of humour that the text lacks.

It was translated into English 'out of Laten, Frenche, and Doche' by A. *Barclay, and published in England in 1509; the translation is not literal but is an adaptation to English conditions, and gives a picture of contemporary English life. It starts with the fool who has great plenty of books, 'But fewe I rede, and fewer understande,' and the fool 'that newe garmentes loves, or devyses', and passes to a condemnation of the various evils of the time, notably the misdeeds of officals and the corruption of the courts. The work is interesting as an early collection of satirical types. Its influence is seen in *Cocke Lorells Bote*.

Shipwreck, The, see FALCONER, W.

Shirburn Ballads, The, edited in 1907 by Andrew Clark from a manuscript of 1600–16 (a few pieces are later) at Shirburn Castle, Oxfordshire, belonging to the earl of Macclesfield. The collection contains ballads not found elsewhere, dealing with political events, with legends and fairy-tales, or with stories of domestic life. Some of them are homilies.

Shirley, a novel by C. *Brontë, published 1849.

The scene of the story is Yorkshire, and the

period the latter part of the Napoleonic wars, the time of the *Luddite riots, when the wool industry was suffering from the almost complete cessation of exports. In spite of these conditions, Robert Gérard Moore, half English, half Belgian by birth, a mill-owner of determined character, persists in introducing the latest labour-saving machinery, undeterred by the opposition of the workers, which culminates in an attempt first to destroy his mill, and finally to take his life. To overcome his financial difficulties he proposes to Shirley Keeldar, an heiress of independent spirit, while under the mistaken impression that she is in love with him; he himself loves not her but his gentle and retiring cousin Caroline Helstone, who is pining away for love of him and through enforced idleness in the oppressive atmosphere of her uncle's rectory. Robert is indignantly rejected by Shirley, who is in fact in love with his brother Louis, a tutor in her family, also of proud and independent spirit. The misunderstandings are resolved, and the two couples united.

Despite touches of melodrama (such as the sub-plot, which reveals that Shirley's companion and one-time governess Mrs Pryor is in fact Caroline's long-lost mother) this is Charlotte Brontë's most social novel, intended in her own words to be 'unromantic as Monday morning', and one of its recurrent themes is its plea for more useful occupations for women, condemned by society either to matrimony or, as old maids, to a life of self-denial and acts of private charity. Caroline is forbidden even the career of governess by her uncle, and this career is itself painted by Mrs Pryor as 'sedentary, solitary, constrained, joyless, toilsome'. Shirley herself is an attempt to portray a woman with freedom and power to act; Charlotte told Mrs *Gaskell that she was intended to be what Emily *Brontë might have been 'had she been placed in health and prosperity', but despite certain recognizable characteristics (her relationship with her dog Tartar, her physical courage, her nickname of 'Captain'), the fictitious character for most readers sheds little light on her enigmatic original.

SHIRLEY, James (1596–1666), was born in London and educated at Merchant Taylors' School, St John's College, Oxford, and St Catherine's Hall, Cambridge. His first work appears to have been a poem on the Echo and Narcissus story, published as 'Eccho' in a lost edition of 1618 and as 'Narcissus' in 1646. Shirley took Anglican orders, and was a master at St Albans Grammar School until 1624, when he moved to London. The reason for his departure is said to have been his conversion to Roman Catholicism. His first recorded play, *Love Tricks, or the School of Compliment* (1625), was produced at the Cockpit Theatre, and he continued to write for it, probably under con-

tract, until 1636. In the dedication to his play *The Bird in a Cage* (1632–3), he sarcastically complimented *Prynne, who was then in prison awaiting trial for writing *Histriomastix*. Perhaps because of this dedication, Shirley was made a member of Gray's Inn and invited to supply the literary part of the Inns of Court masque *The Triumph of Peace* (1634).

During the plague closure of 1636–7 he went to Ireland, where he wrote a number of plays for the Dublin theatre, including *St Patrick for Ireland* (c.1639). At his return in 1640 he succeeded *Massinger, recently deceased, as principal dramatist for the King's Men, but the outbreak of the Civil War put an end to this career. He was in the royalist army under the earl of *Newcastle, who was both his patron and a former collaborator on a play (*The Country Captain*, 1639–40). After the defeat of the royalist cause he returned to London and was for a time patronized by T. *Stanley; he then returned to his career as a schoolmaster. Such works as he wrote during the rest of his life seem designed for school performance, though his masque *Cupid and Death* was performed in 1653 before a distinguished audience including the Portuguese ambassador. His *Contention of Ajax and Ulysses* (pub. 1659) was also written during this period; it is largely a dramatic debate interspersed with songs, one of which, 'The glories of our blood and state', was a favourite with Charles II. Shirley and his wife are said to have died as a result of terror and exposure when they were driven from their home by the Great Fire of London.

Shirley wrote some forty dramas, most of which are extant, including *The Traitor* (1631), *Hyde Park* (1632), *The Gamester* (1633), *The Lady of Pleasure* (1635), and *The Cardinal* (1641). He had a considerable reputation in his lifetime and died very well off; Dryden's bracketing of him with *Heywood and *Shadwell in *MacFlecknoe* probably does not represent a considered judgement of his work. His better-known plays are available in modern editions, but the last edition of his collected works was that of Gifford and Dyce in 1833.

SHIRLEY, John (?1366–1456), the scribe of many works of *Chaucer, *Lydgate, and others, whose attributions have been particularly important for the ascriptions to Chaucer of some of the shorter poems, including the Complaints 'To Pity', 'To his Lady', and 'Of Mars'; 'Adam Scriveyn'; 'Truth'; 'Lak of Stedfastnesse'; and 'The Complaint of Venus'. He is said to have been a traveller in various lands, and he translated a number of works from French and Latin, among the latter being 'A full lamentable Cronycle of the dethe and false murdure of James Stewarde, late kynge of Scotys' (see JAMES I OF SCOTLAND).

Shoemaker's Holiday, The, or A pleasant

comedie of the Gentle Craft, a comedy by
*Dekker, written 1599, published 1600.

Rowland Lacy, a kinsman of the earl of Lincoln, loves Rose, the daughter of the lord mayor
of London. To prevent the match the earl sends
him to France in command of a company of
men. Lacy resigns his place to a friend and, disguised as a Dutch shoemaker, takes service with
Simon *Eyre, who supplies the family of the
lord mayor with shoes. Here he successfully pursues his suit, is married in spite of the efforts of
the earl and the lord mayor to prevent it, and is
pardoned by the king. The most entertaining
character in the play is that of Eyre, the cheery,
eccentric master-shoemaker, who becomes
lord mayor of London. See also DELONEY, T.

SHOLOKHOV, Mikhail Alexandrovich
(1905–84), Russian novelist, of mixed Cossack,
peasant, and lower-middle-class background,
who became well known in the West for his
lengthy regional epic novel about Cossack life
in the early 20th cent., *And Quiet Flows the Don*
(4 vols, 1928–40), which has been much admired (despite allegations of plagiarism: he was
accused in some circles of having made use of
the manuscript of a dead White Army officer).
His other works include a novel which has been
described as a classic of *Socialist Realism, *Virgin
Soil Upturned* (1931), which chronicles life
under a Five Year Plan in South Russia.
Sholokhov was awarded the *Nobel Prize in
1965.

SHORE, Jane (d. ?1527), mistress of Edward
IV. She was the daughter of a Cheapside mercer
and wife of a Lombard Street goldsmith, and
exercised great influence over Edward IV by her
beauty and wit. She was afterwards mistress of
Thomas Grey, first marquess of Dorset. She was
accused by Richard III of sorcery, imprisoned,
and made to do public penance in 1483, and
she died in poverty.

She is the subject of a ballad included in
Percy's *Reliques,* of *Churchyard's *Shore's Wife*
in *Mirror for Magistrates,* of a remarkable passage in Sir T. *More's *History of Richard III,*
and of a descriptive note by *Drayton (*Englands
Heroicall Epistles*). The last two passages are
quoted in Percy's *Reliques.* Her adversities are
the subject of a tragedy by *Rowe.

Short, Codlin and, see CODLIN.

Shortest Way with the Dissenters, see
DEFOE, D.

SHORTHOUSE, Joseph Henry (1834–
1903), born into a Birmingham Quaker family,
became an Anglican convert, and the historical
novel by which he is remembered, *John Inglesant*
(1881, privately printed 1880), is an evocation
of 17th-cent. religious intrigue and faith. Inglesant becomes a tool of the Jesuit faction, joins
the court of Charles I, and after the king's death

visits Italy to seek vengeance for his brother's
murder; the most interesting part of the book is
an account of N. *Ferrar's religious community
at *Little Gidding. Inglesant falls in love with
Mary Collet in a wholly fictitious episode, but
the background is on the whole drawn in
accurate detail. The novel had a considerable
vogue in its day, and bears witness to the religious and historical interests revived by the
*Oxford Movement and the *Pre-Raphaelites.

Short-Title Catalogue, see BIBLIOGRAPHICAL
SOCIETY.

Short View *of the Immorality and Profaneness of
the English Stage,* see COLLIER, J.

SHOSTAKOVICH, Dmitri Dimitrievich
(1906–75), Soviet composer, the most distinguished Russian composer of the Soviet era,
was above all a symphonist, though he wrote in
most other forms as well. Among his earlier
operas the best known, and certainly the most
controversial, was *Lady Macbeth of the Mtsensk
district* (1932), from a story by *Leskov, which
in spite of its title has no connection with Shakespeare except for a certain propensity to murder
on the part of the heroine, Katerina Ismailova
(under whose name the work reappeared in a
revised version in 1963). Shakespearian in a
more normal sense is the incidental music for
Hamlet (1964) and *King Lear* (1970), and there
is a group of *Six Songs,* with texts by *Ralegh,
*Burns, and Shakespeare, dating from 1942.

Shropshire Lad, A, see HOUSMAN, A. E.

Shylock, the Jewish usurer in Shakespeare's
**The Merchant of Venice.*

SIBELIUS, Jean (1865–1957), Finnish composer. Sibelius's music was particularly admired
in England in the early and middle decades of
this century, and his influence on contemporary
English composers was considerable (both *Bax
and *Vaughan Williams dedicated their 5th
Symphonies to him, the latter 'with the sincerest
flattery'). Apart from two short songs from
Twelfth Night in a Swedish translation, his only
point of contact with English literature is the
incidental music to *The Tempest* (1925): consisting of a Prelude and 17 other pieces, this is
one of the most extensive works of its kind (for
size of orchestra, too) in the history of the
theatre, though even then it fails to cover all
Shakespeare's expressed musical requirements.
One of Sibelius's last works, it stands in order
of composition between the 7th Symphony and
Tapiola, but cannot compare for musical content
with either of those masterpieces.

Sibylline Leaves, a volume of poems by
S. T. *Coleridge.

SIDDAL, E., see ROSSETTI, D. G.

SIDDONS, Mrs Sarah (1755–1831), the

eldest child of a strolling actor-manager, Roger Kemble (1721–1802), and sister of C. *Kemble, J. P. *Kemble, Stephen, and other theatrical siblings. On her second attempt on London in 1782 she was heralded as a tragic actress without peer, and until her official retirement in 1812 she never fell from that position. Her great roles were in tragic and heroic parts, and she rarely attempted comedy. Jane *Shore, in *Rowe's play of that name, Belvidera in Otway's *Venice Preserv'd, Shakespearian heroines, and in particular Lady Macbeth, were her great roles. *Hazlitt wrote that 'Power was seated on her brow . . . She was tragedy personified.' She returned briefly to the stage in 1819 but was no longer a success. She was a friend of Dr *Johnson, Horace *Walpole, Joshua *Reynolds, and many other eminent figures. Reynolds's portrait of her as 'The Tragic Muse' is at Dulwich, and *Gainsborough's portrait in the National Portrait Gallery.

SIDGWICK, Henry (1838–1900), educated at Rugby and Trinity College, Cambridge, where he became a fellow in 1859, was from 1883 professor of moral philosophy at that university. A follower in economics and politics of J. S. *Mill, his attitude on the question of our knowledge of the external world resembles that of *Reid. But his most important work as a philosophical writer relates to ethics, and his reputation rests on The Methods of Ethics (1874). Here he considers three 'methods' of determining the right course of action: intuitionism, according to which we have direct apprehension of moral principles; egoism, according to which an agent's own interests determine what he should do; Utilitarianism, according to which right and wrong are fixed by considerations of the interests of everyone affected by our actions. Intuitionism and Utilitarianism, Sidgwick believes, combine to form a coherent system; but egoism will sometimes conflict with the other methods, producing practical contradictions which we cannot resolve.

In 1876 Sidgwick married Eleanor Mildred Balfour (1845–1936), who was from 1892 to 1910 principal of *Newnham College, Cambridge; it was partly through their efforts on behalf of women's higher education that the college was founded. She and Sidgwick's brother Arthur wrote a biography of Henry (1906).

SIDNEY, Algernon (1622–83), the grandnephew of Sir P. *Sidney and younger brother of *Waller's 'Sacharissa', took up arms against Charles I and was wounded at Marston Moor. He was employed on government service until the Restoration, but his firm republicanism aroused *Cromwell's hostility. At the Restoration he refused to give pledges to Charles II, and lived abroad in poverty and exile until 1677. He was imprisoned in the Tower after the discovery of the Rye House plot, tried before *Jeffreys, and condemned to death without adequate evidence, though there was little doubt of his guilt. His Discourses concerning Government were published in 1698, and a treatise on Love in 1884. *Burnet described him as 'a man of most extraordinary courage . . . who had set up Marcus Brutus for his pattern'.

SIDNEY, Sir Philip (1554–86), born at *Penshurst Place, eldest son of Sir Henry Sidney (who was thrice lord deputy governor of Ireland), was educated at Shrewsbury School (with his close friend Fulke *Greville), and Christ Church, Oxford, where his contemporaries included *Camden, *Hakluyt, and *Ralegh. He may have spent some time also at Cambridge. Between 1572 and 1575 he travelled in France, where he witnessed the massacre of St *Bartholomew's day in Paris, and in Germany, Austria, and Italy. During his year in Italy, most of it spent in Venice, he was painted by Veronese, but gave most of his time to serious study of history and ethics, and to correspondence with the elderly Protestant statesman Hubert Languet. After his return to England, in spite of a successful embassy to Vienna in 1577, Sidney did not achieve any official post which matched his ambitions until his appointment as governor of Flushing in 1585. His knighthood was awarded for reasons of court protocol in 1582.

Years of comparative idleness enabled him to write and revise the *Arcadia, and to complete the *Defence of Poetry, *The Lady of May, and *Astrophel and Stella. The first Arcadia, and probably other works, were composed while he was staying with his younger sister Mary, countess of *Pembroke, at Wilton. We do not know his exact relations with Penelope Devereux (later *Rich), whose father's dying wish had been that she should marry Philip Sidney. Though this did not happen (Penelope in 1581 marrying Lord Rich, and Philip in 1583 marrying Frances, daughter of Sir Francis Walsingham), verbal and heraldic references leave no room for doubt that she was the 'Stella' of Sidney's sonnet sequence. During these years Sidney also became a notable literary patron, receiving dedications from a variety of authors, the best known being that of Spenser's *The Shepheardes Calender in 1579. Sidney was interested in experimenting with classical metres in English on the lines prescribed by Thomas Drant, but it is unlikely that his discussion of this and other matters with Greville, *Dyer, and *Spenser (the 'Areopagus') amounted to anything so formal as an academy or learned society. The last year of his life was spent in the Netherlands, where his greatest military success was a surprise attack on the town of Axel, in alliance with Count Maurice. On 22 September 1586 he led an attack on a Spanish convoy bringing supplies to the fortified city of Zutphen; he received a musket shot in his thigh and died of infection three weeks later. Greville, who was not present, subsequently told the story of Sidney's death with two famous embellishments, claiming that Sidney left off his thigh-armour deliberately, so as not to be better armed than the marshal of the camp, and that as he was being carried wounded from the field he saw a dying soldier gazing at his water bottle, and gave it to him with the words, 'Thy necessity is yet greater than mine.' Sidney was buried in St Paul's Cathedral, and the almost immediate appearance of volumes of Latin elegies from Oxford, Cambridge, and the Continent testified to the great political and literary promise he had shown. Among many English elegies on him the best known, Spenser's *'Astrophel', was not printed until 1595, among his *Complaints*. This included elegies by Lodowick Bryskett, Matthew Royden, Ralegh, and Dyer. Royden's is unusual in evoking the hero's presence, his 'sweet attractive kind of grace'. Sidney's posthumous reputation, as the perfect Renaissance patron, soldier, lover, and courtier, far outstripped his documented achievements, and can be seen as having a life independent of them which has become proverbial, as when *Yeats paid tribute to Major Robert *Gregory as 'our Sidney and our perfect man'.

None of Sidney's works were published during his lifetime, but Greville and the countess of Pembroke seem to have taken pains to preserve the texts they thought best. The revised *Arcadia* was published in 1590, and again in 1593 with the last three books of the earlier version appended; *Astrophel and Stella* in 1591, first in a pirated and then in an authorized text; and *A Defence of Poetry*, also in two slightly varying texts, in 1595. Editions of the *Arcadia* from 1598 onwards included all the literary works except his version of the Psalms. These were completed posthumously by his sister, and not printed until 1823. *Ruskin admired them and published selections under the title *Rock Honeycomb* (1877). Sidney's complete *Poems* were edited by W. A. Ringler in 1962, the *Old Arcadia* (1973) by Jean Robertson, and *The Miscellaneous Prose* by K. Duncan-Jones and J. van Dorsten (1973); the standard *Life* is by M. W. Wallace (1915).

SIDNEY, Sir Robert (1563–1626), was the younger brother of Sir P. *Sidney. His early career closely followed that of his brother, whom he succeeded as governor of Flushing in 1588, a post he continued to hold for 20 years. He was created Baron Sidney by James I in 1603, Viscount Lisle in 1605, and earl of Leicester in 1618; he held the post of lord chamberlain to Anne of Denmark. It has been claimed that he wrote lyrics for settings by Robert Dowland, who was his godson. An autograph manuscript of his poems, consisting of sonnets, pastorals, songs, and epigrams, apparently written in the mid-1590s, was identified by P. J. Croft in 1973; he has edited them for the Clarendon Press (1983).

'Sidney's sister, Pembroke's mother', see PEMBROKE, COUNTESS OF.

Sidonia, in *Coningsby*, and again in *Tancred*, by Benjamin Disraeli.

Sidrophel, the name (meaning 'star-lover') of the astrologer in Butler's *Hudibras* (II. iii).

Siege of Corinth, The, a poem by Lord *Byron, published 1816.
The poem is founded on the story of the Turkish siege of Corinth, then held by the Venetians, and it was the last of Byron's Eastern tales. The Turks, guided by the fierce and daring renegade Alp, who loves the daughter of the Venetian governor Minotti, make their way into the fortress. Minotti, discovering the betrayal, fires the magazine and violently destroys both victors and defenders, including himself.

Siege of Rhodes, The, one of the earliest attempts at English opera, by *D'Avenant, performed 1656.
Dramatic performances having been suppressed by the Commonwealth government, D'Avenant obtained permission in 1656 to produce at Rutland House an 'Entertainment after the manner of the ancients', in which *Diogenes and *Aristophanes argue against and for public amusements, and a Londoner and Parisian compare the merits of their two cities; this was accompanied by vocal and instrumental music, composed by Henry *Lawes. Immediately after this prologue was given *The Siege of Rhodes* (at first in one, but in 1662 in two parts), a heroic play, the 'story sung in recitative music', which was composed by Dr Charles Coleman and George Hudson. The play deals with the siege of Rhodes by Solyman the Magnificent, and the devotion by which Ianthe, wife of the Sicilian Duke Alphonso, saves her husband and the defenders of the island.

Siege Perilous, see ROUND TABLE.

Sigismonda (Ghismonda), in Boccaccio's *Decameron* (IV. i), daughter of Tancred, prince of Salerno. Her father, having discovered her love for her squire Guiscardo, slew the latter and sent his heart in a golden cup to Sigismonda, who took poison and died. The father, repenting his cruelty, caused the pair to be buried in the same tomb. The story is the subject of *Dryden's 'Sigismunda and Guiscardo', and of Robert Wilmot's *Tancred and Gismund*. James Thomson's *Tancred and Sigismunda* (1745) deals with a different story.

Sigmund, in the *Vǫlsunga saga* and in W. Morris's *Sigurd the Volsung*, the son of King Volsung and the father of Sigurd.

Sigurd the Volsung and the Fall of the Niblungs, The Story of, an epic in anapaestic couplets by W. *Morris, founded on the *Volsunga saga, and published 1876. Although a loose rendering, and at times slack in its versification, it did much to awaken popular interest in Icelandic literature. Morris described its subject as 'the Great Story of the North which should be to all our race what the Tale of Troy was to the Greeks'.

It is in four books; the first, 'Sigmund', is the story of Volsung's son Sigmund and of the fatal marriage of his sister Signy to the king of the Goths; the second and third, 'Regin' and 'Brynhild', deal with Sigmund's son Sigurd, his betrothal to Brynhild, his subsequent marriage (under the influence of a magic potion) to Gudrun, the Niblung king's daughter, and the deaths of Sigurd and Brynhild; the last, 'Gudrun', tells of Gudrun's own death and the fall of the Niblungs. (See also SAGA.)

Sikes, Bill, a character in Dickens's *Oliver Twist.

Silas Lapham, see RISE OF SILAS LAPHAM, THE.

Silas Marner, a novel by G. *Eliot, published 1861.

Silas Marner, a linen-weaver, has been driven out of the small religious community to which he belongs by a false charge of theft, and has taken refuge in the agricultural village of Raveloe. His only consolation in his loneliness is his growing pile of gold. This is stolen from his cottage by the squire's reprobate son Dunstan Cass, who disappears. Dunstan's elder brother Godfrey is in love with Nancy Lammeter, but is secretly and unhappily married to a woman of low class in a neighbouring town. Meditating revenge for Godfrey's refusal to acknowledge her, this woman carries her child one New Year's Eve to Raveloe, intending to force her way into the Casses' house; but dies in the snow. Her child, Eppie, finds her way into Silas's cottage, is adopted by him, and restores to him the happiness which he has lost with his gold. After many years the draining of a pond near Silas's door reveals the body of Dunstan with the gold. Moved by this revelation, Godfrey, now married to Nancy, acknowledges himself the father of Eppie and claims her, but she refuses to leave Silas. The solemnity of the story is relieved by the humour of the rustic travellers at the Rainbow Inn, and the genial motherliness of Dolly Winthrop, who befriends Silas.

Silence, in Shakespeare's 2 *Henry IV, a country justice and cousin to *Shallow.

Silent Woman, The, see EPICENE.

SILKIN, Jon (1930–), poet, born in London, the son of a solicitor, and educated at Wycliffe and Dulwich Colleges. He established

himself as a poet while working as a manual labourer, then as a teacher, and has since lectured extensively. His first volume, The Peaceable Kingdom (1954), was followed by many others, including Nature with Man (1965, which contains many of his piercingly observed 'flower poems'), Amana Grass (1971, with work inspired by visits to Israel and America), and The Principle of Water (1974); his Selected Poems was published in 1980. He founded the literary quarterly *Stand in 1950; his wife, Lorna Tracy, short story writer, is a co-editor.

SILLITOE, Alan (1928–), writer, brought up in Nottingham, one of five children of an illiterate and often unemployed labourer. He started work aged 14 in a bicycle factory, became a cadet, then served in the RAF in Malaya. On demobilization he was found to have tuberculosis and spent 18 months in hospital, during which he began to read widely and to write. He met the American poet Ruth Fainlight (whom he married in 1952), and together they travelled in Europe, spending some years in Majorca, where Robert *Graves encouraged him to write a novel set in Nottingham. His first volume of verse, Without Beer or Bread (1957), was followed by his much praised first novel, *Saturday Night and Sunday Morning (1958), which describes the life of Arthur Seaton, a dissatisfied young Nottingham factory worker. It differed from other provincial novels of the 1950s (see W. COOPER; AMIS; LARKIN; BRAINE; WAIN) in that its hero is a working man, not a rising member of the lower middle class. The title story of The Loneliness of the Long Distance Runner (1959) is a first-person portrait of a rebellious and anarchic Borstal boy who refuses both literally and metaphorically to play the games of the establishment. Many other novels and volumes of prose followed, including the novels The Death of William Posters (1965); A Tree on Fire (1967); and A Start in Life (1970); the semi-autobiographical Raw Material (1972), a vivid evocation of his own family ancestry and working-class attitudes to the First World War and the Depression; Men Women and Children (1973), a collection of short stories; Mountains and Caverns (1975), a collection of autobiographical and critical essays; The Widower's Son (1976, a novel). He has also published several volumes of poetry, including Storm and other poems (1974) and Barbarians and other poems (1974), and written plays and screenplays from his own fiction.

SILONE, Ignazio (Secondo Tranquilli) (1900–78), Italian novelist, critic, and founder member of the Italian Communist Party in 1921. To escape Fascist persecution he went into exile to Switzerland in 1930, where he remained until 1945. The peasant South, its deprivation, and the impact on it of Fascism, are the themes of his best-known novels: *Fontamara* (1930) and *Pane e vino* (published first in English, *Bread and Wine*, 1936; in Italian 1937, rev. 1955 as *Vino e pane*). His memoir in *The God that Failed* (1950) indicates his importance for Anglo-American culture as the type of the European ex-Communist.

Silurist, The, see VAUGHAN, H.

SILVA, Feliciano da (16th cent.), a Spanish romance writer, who composed sequels to *Amadis of Gaul* and *Celestina*, and was ridiculed in *Don Quixote*.

Silver-fork school, see FASHIONABLE NOVEL.

Silvia, in Shakespeare's *The Two Gentlemen of Verona*, the duke of Milan's daughter, who is loved by Valentine. The famous song 'Who is Silvia?' (IV. ii) is addressed to her.

SIMENON, Georges (1903–), Belgian-French popular novelist. One of the most prolific of modern writers, he launched his celebrated detective, Maigret, in 1931. The sympathy and range of his observation of French life, his sensitivity to local atmosphere, his insight into human motives, and the naturalness and accuracy of his use of the French language have earned him a respect rarely accorded to writers in the genre of *detective fiction.

Simile, an object, scene, or action, introduced by way of comparison for explanatory, illustrative, or merely ornamental purpose, e.g. 'as strong as an ox', or more poetically, 'The moon, like a flower | In heaven's high bower | With silent delight | Sits and smiles on the night' (Blake, 'Night', *Songs of Innocence*); or, in more *Modernist vein, 'the evening is spread out against the sky | Like a patient etherised upon a table' (T. S. *Eliot, 'The Love Song of J. Alfred Prufrock'). See also EPIC SIMILE.

Simon Legree, the brutal slave-owner in H. B. *Stowe's *Uncle Tom's Cabin*, who beats Tom to death.

Simon Pure, a character in S. Centlivre's *A Bold Stroke for a Wife*.

Simple Story, A, a romance by Mrs *Inchbald, published 1791.
  The author's avowed purpose in this tale is to show the value of 'a proper education'. She describes the disastrous marriage of Miss Milner, a gay and empty-headed flirt, to Lord Elmwood, formerly a priest and her guardian, and the effects of her behaviour on their daughter Matilda.

Simpliciad, The, an anonymous parody of *Wordsworth, published 1808.

Simplicissimus, The Adventurous, the English title of *Der abenteurliche Simplicissimus Teutsch* (1669), by J. J. C. von *Grimmelshausen: a description of the life of a strange vagabond named Melchior Sternfels von Fuchshaim. The work was first translated into English (with an account of the author) in 1912; its chief interest lies in the fact that it is one of the few existing contemporary records of the life of the people during the Thirty Years War.

SIMPSON, N(orman) F(rederick) (1919–), playwright, whose surreal comedies *A Resounding Tinkle* (perf. 1957) and *One-Way Pendulum* (perf. 1959) established him as a writer of the Theatre of the *Absurd. His work shows an affinity with that of Ionesco, which enjoyed a considerable vogue in Britain in the late 1950s.

SINCLAIR, Catherine, (1800–64), philanthropist and prolific Scottish writer of travel, biography, children's books, novels, essays, and reflections. In *Holiday House* (1839) she produced a classic children's novel that made a conscious stand against the prevailing fashion for moralizing tales for the young and enjoyed success for many years.

SINCLAIR, May (Mary Amelia St Clair Sinclair) (1863–1946), novelist, the youngest daughter of a shipowner who went bankrupt; he died in 1881, and May (who was educated at home, apart from one year at Cheltenham Ladies' College) lived with her mother in London lodgings until her mother's death in 1901. She never married, and supported herself by reviews, translations, etc., and by writing fiction. She was a supporter of *Women's Suffrage, and interested in psychoanalysis; her reviews and novels show considerable knowledge of both *Jung and *Freud. Among the most notable of her 24 novels are *The Divine Fire* (1904), *The Three Sisters* (1914, a study in female frustration with echoes of the *Brontë story), *The Tree of Heaven* (1917), *Mary Olivier: a life* (1919) and *Life and Death of Harriett Frean* (1922). The last two are *stream-of-consciousness novels, taking a woman from girlhood to unmarried middle age, and both show themselves keenly aware (though not necessarily wholly critical) of woman's tendencies towards self-denial; much of *Mary Olivier* (the alcoholic father, the loved but dominating mother, the deaths of several brothers from heart failure, the intellectual curiosity and thirst for unprovided knowledge) is clearly autobiographical. Her novels had a considerable influence on R. *West and R. *Lehmann, but were largely forgotten until their revival (by Virago) in the 1980s. See T. E. M. Boll, *Miss May Sinclair: Novelist* (1973).

SINCLAIR, Upton Beall (1878–1968), American novelist and journalist, born in Baltimore, who paid his way through the College of the City of New York by writing novels, and continued to write prolifically in many genres. He is best known for his novel *The Jungle* (1906), an exposé of the Chicago meat-packing industry to which the public reacted so violently that an investigation of the yards was instituted by the US government; it also marks a conversion to Socialism on the part of its author and of its protagonist, Slav immigrant Jurgis Rudkus. Sinclair's many other works include *The Metropolis* (1908), *King Coal* (1917), *Oil!* (1927), and *Boston* (1928); and a series with international settings featuring Lanny Budd, illegitimate son of a munitions manufacturer, who appears in *World's End* (1940), *Dragon's Teeth* (1942), *The Return of Lanny Budd* (1953), and other works.

Sindbad of the Sea, or *Sindbad the Sailor*, one of the tales of the **Arabian Nights*. Sindbad, a rich young man of Baghdad, having wasted much of his wealth in prodigal living, undertakes a number of sea voyages as a merchant and meets with various marvellous adventures. The best known are those of the Roc, a huge bird that could lift elephants in its claws, and of the Old Man of the Sea. The latter persuades Sindbad to carry him on his shoulders, whereupon he twines his legs round Sindbad, so that Sindbad cannot dislodge him and remains his captive, until at last he gets the Old Man drunk on wine, succeeds in dislodging him, and kills him.

SINGER, Isaac Bashevis (1904–   ), Polish-born Yiddish author, the son and grandson of rabbis, educated at the Warsaw Rabbinical Seminary. In 1935 he emigrated to New York, in the footsteps of his brother, the novelist Israel Joshua Singer (1893–1944), and became a journalist, writing in Yiddish for the *Jewish Daily Forward*, which published most of his short stories. The first of his works to be translated into English was *The Family Moscat* (1950), which was followed by many other works, including *Satan in Goray* (Yiddish, 1935; English, 1955); *The Magician of Lublin* (1960); *The Slave* (1962); *The Manor* (1967) and its sequel *The Estate* (1969). His collections of stories include *Gimpel the Fool* (1957); *The Spinoza of Market Street* (1961); *Zlateh the Goat* (1966); and *A Friend of Kafka* (1970). Singer's work portrays with a colourful intensity and much realistic detail the lives of Polish Jews of many periods of Polish history, illumined by hints of the mystic and supernatural; many of his novels and stories describe the conflicts between traditional religion and rising scepticism, between varying forms of nationalism, and between the primitive, the exotic, and the intellectually progressive. He provides an extraordinarily vivid record to a vanished way of life which lives on in his art; in an interview in **Encounter* (Feb. 1979) he claimed that although the Jews of Poland had died 'something—call it spirit, or whatever—is still somewhere in the universe. This is a mystical kind of feeling, but I feel there is truth in it.' Singer's writings have been increasingly admired internationally, and he was awarded the **Nobel Prize for literature in 1978. There is a life by P. Kresh (1979), and see also *The Brothers Singer* (1983) by Clive Sinclair, which includes an account of the life of the Singers' sister, novelist Esther Kreitman (1891–1954).

Single-Speech Hamilton, see HAMILTON, W. G.

Singleton, *Adventures of Captain*, a romance of adventure by **Defoe, published 1720.

Singleton, the first-person narrator, having been kidnapped in his infancy is sent to sea. Having 'no sense of virtue or religion', he takes part in a mutiny and is put ashore in Madagascar with his comrades; he reaches the continent of Africa and crosses it from east to west, encountering many adventures and obtaining much gold, which he dissipates on his return to England. He takes once more to the sea, becomes a pirate, carrying on his depredations in the West Indies, Indian Ocean, and China Seas, acquires great wealth, which he brings home, and finally marries the sister of a shipmate.

Sinister Street, a novel by C. **Mackenzie.

Sinners, Beware, a 13th-cent. homiletic poem in 354 lines of 6-line rhyming stanzas, concerned with the pains of Hell and the **Seven Deadly Sins. Ed. in *An Old English Miscellany*, ed. R. Morris (EETS 49, 1872: reprinted 1973).

Sir Charles Grandison, a novel by S. **Richardson, published 1754.

Urged by many friends, Richardson had been thinking since about 1749 of the portrayal of a 'Good Man', to balance his female creations in **Pamela and **Clarissa. In his usual manner he took much advice. The novel, again epistolary in form, ranges far more widely in scene and has more characters and a looser plot than his earlier works. It is also the only one set in aristocratic and wealthy society, of which Richardson had little personal knowledge.

Harriet, described as the most beautiful woman in England, attracts many admirers, among them the wealthy and unscrupulous Sir Hargreve Pollexfen. When she refuses his advances he has her abducted from a masquerade, then after the failure of a secret marriage ceremony has her carried off into the country. Sir Charles, hearing her cries from the coach, rescues her and gives her into the care of his kindly married sister. He and Harriet fall in love, but on the day she learns of his love for her he has to set out for Italy. There, in the past, he has become involved with one of the noblest-born women in Europe, Clementina Porretta, but religious differences have kept them apart.

Clementina's unhappiness has deranged her mind, and her parents, now prepared to accept any terms for the cure of their daughter, summon Sir Charles to Italy. As she recovers, however, Clementina reaffirms that she cannot marry a heretic, and Sir Charles, released, returns to England to marry Harriet. Three months later Clementina appears, declaring that she wishes to become a nun but that her parents wish her to marry another suitor. Her parents and suitor then appear, but Sir Charles is able to arrange everything to everyone's satisfaction, and Harriet, he, and Clementina swear eternal friendship.

The book is shorter, faster-moving, and less analytical than Richardson's previous novels, but the 'sense of reality' on which Richardson had so often been complimented is somewhat lacking. Richardson was anxious to avoid all stricture, and as a result Sir Charles is a paragon of honour, wisdom, and all the virtues. However, the book was very popular, and J. *Austen, who held it in high esteem, dramatized scenes from it for family performance: see *Jane Austen's 'Sir Charles Grandison'* (1980), ed. B. Southam.

Sir Courtly Nice, or It Cannot be, a comedy by *Crowne, produced 1685.

This, the best of Crowne's plays, is founded on a comedy by the Spanish dramatist Moreto. Leonora is in love with Farewel, a young man of quality, but her brother Lord Bellguard, owing to a feud between the families, is determined she shall not marry him. Bellguard keeps Leonora under watch by her aunt, 'an old amorous envious maid', and a pair of spies, Hothead and Fanatick, who hold violently opposed views on religious matters and quarrel amusingly. Thanks to the resourcefulness of Crack, who introduces himself in an assumed character into Lord Bellguard's house, Farewel is enabled to carry off and marry Leonora; while her rival suitor Sir Courtly Nice, favoured by Lord Bellguard, a fop whose 'linen is all made in Holland by neat women that dip their fingers in rosewater', is fobbed off with the aunt; and Surly, the rough ill-mannered cynic, gets no wife at all.

Sir Launcelot Greaves, The Life and Adventures of, a novel by T. *Smollett, published 1762.

Smollett's shortest novel, this is a neglected and interesting work, which was written in episodes (many of them in prison in 1760) for Smollett's monthly British Magazine. He describes it as 'an agreeable medley of mirth and madness', but his purpose is serious in examining various states of madness and questioning conventional definitions of sanity. Launcelot is a paragon, handsome, learned, good, robust, but when the book opens he is already crazed by the loss of his love Aurelia, who has been compelled to break with him by her vindictive uncle Darnel. Together with his absurd cowardly squire Crabshaw, and his horse Bronzomarte, the half-mad Launcelot undertakes a quixotic life of knight-errantry, warring against the enemies of virtue and reason. During his adventure on the road between London and York he is involved in many brawls in the cause of justice; he is trapped and abducted; embroiled in a violent election; challenged to a tourney; denounced by the misanthropic charlatan Ferret; and thrown into the prison of the atrocious Judge Gobble. His friends include a lawyer, Tom Clarke, and Clarke's uncle, the nautical Crowe. After a terrible period in a madhouse, Launcelot recovers his sanity and Aurelia is at last restored to him.

The well-known words 'I think for my part one half of the nation is mad—and the other half not very sound' are spoken by Crowe.

Sir Launfal, by Thomas Chestre, a late 14th-cent. *Breton Lay, in 1,044 lines in 12-line, tail-rhyme stanzas. It is one of the two English versions of *Marie de France's Lanval (given in an appendix to Bliss's edition: see below). Launfal is a knight of the Round Table who leaves the court, affronted by tales of *Guinevere's misconduct. He falls in love with a fairy lady, Tryamour. When he returns to Arthur's court Guinevere declares her love for him, but he rejects her, declaring that even his beloved's maids are more beautiful than the queen. The queen accuses him of trying to seduce her and at his trial he is asked to produce the beautiful lady he has boasted of. Tryamour appears and breathes on Guinevere's eyes, blinding her, and the lovers depart happily. The poem has the over-simplicity, but also the narrative liveliness, of its kind and it has been much edited in romance anthologies.

Ed. A. J. Bliss (1960); included in Vol. 1, Medieval Literature, of The New Pelican Guide to English Literature (1982), pp. 440–72.

Sir Patrick Spens, an early Scottish *ballad, included in Percy's *Reliques. The subject is the dispatch of Sir Patrick to sea, on a mission for the king, in winter; his foreboding of disaster; and his destruction with his ship's company. Sir W. *Scott, in his version, makes the object of the expedition the bringing to Scotland of the Maid of Norway (1283–90), who died on her voyage to marry Edward, prince of Wales.

Sir Thomas More, see MORE, SIR THOMAS.

Sirventes, a form of poem or lay, usually satirical, employed by the *troubadours.

SISMONDI, Léonard Simond de (1773–1842), French historian of Italian descent, who lived mainly in Geneva. His famous work was L'Histoire des républiques italiennes du Moyen-Âge (1809–18). He had many friends, including

Mme de *Staël's circle and the duchess of Albany, widow of the Young Pretender, and he was an interesting letter-writer.

SISSON, C(harles) H(ubert) (1914–), poet and translator, born in Bristol, and educated at Bristol University. He worked for many years in the Civil Service, of which he has been at times an outspoken critic. His volumes of poetry include *The London Zoo* (1961), *Numbers* (1965), *Metamorphoses* (1968), and *Anchises* (1976); and *In the Trojan Ditch: Collected Poems and Selected Translations* (1974). Translations include works of *Heine, *Catullus, *Horace, and Dante's *Divina Commedia* (1980). His poetry mingles biblical and classical themes and imagery with Arthurian references drawn from his native Somerset (as in one of his major poems, 'In Insula Avalonia'); many are satiric, but the satire is based on a religious preoccupation with man's fallen nature and a classical view of his limitations. His *Collected Poems* were published in 1984.

Sister Carrie, a novel by T. *Dreiser.

Sister Peg, a political satire published in London in 1760, full title *The History of the Proceedings in the case of Margaret, Commonly called Peg, only lawful Sister to John Bull, Esq.* The work is modelled on *Arbuthnot's *History of John Bull*. It satirizes Anglo-Scottish relations after the Act of Union of 1707 and the cynicism of the politicians in the Scots militia controversy of 1760. *Hume laid claim to the authorship, but most historians follow A. *Carlyle in ascribing the work to A. *Ferguson.

SITWELL, Dame Edith Louisa (1887–1964), was brought up at Renishaw Hall, where an unhappy childhood was made bearable by the company of her brothers, Osbert and Sacheverell (below). She began to write poetry when young, and her first published poem, 'Drowned Suns', appeared in the *Daily Mirror* in 1913. With her brothers she actively encouraged *Modernist writers and artists; she despised much of the work published in *Georgian Poetry*, and from 1916 to 1921 edited *Wheels*, an anti-Georgian magazine, which first published W. *Owen. Her first volume of verse, *The Mother and other poems* (1915), was followed by many others, and she quickly acquired a reputation as an eccentric and controversial figure, confirmed by the first public performance, in 1923, of *Façade*, a highly original entertainment (with music by W. *Walton) with verses in syncopated rhythms. *Gold Coast Customs* (1929), a harsh and powerful work, compared modern Europe with ancient barbaric Africa. Her prose works (which she wrote reluctantly, for money) include a study of *Pope (1930), *English Eccentrics* (1933), and *Victoria of England* (1936). Her only novel, *I Live under a*

Black Sun (1937), was poorly received, but it was followed by a period of great acclaim, aroused by her poems of the blitz and the atom bomb (*Street Songs*, 1942; *Green Song*, 1944; *The Song of the Cold*, 1945; *The Shadow of Cain*, 1947); as J. *Lehmann said, 'The hour and the poet were matched.' Triumphal lecture tours in America followed the war, but in the 1950s her reputation began to fade, as the new austerity of the *Movement became fashionable. She remained, however, a considerable public figure, well known outside literary circles for her theatrical dress and manner (recorded by many artists and photographers) and by her indignant response to real or suspected criticism. *Leavis had claimed in 1932 that 'the Sitwells belong to the history of publicity, rather than that of poetry', but her status as a poet survived this dismissal, although it remains a matter of controversy. See V. Glendinning, *Edith Sitwell* (1981).

SITWELL, Sir (Francis) Osbert (Sacheverell) (1892–1969), brother of Edith and Sacheverell *Sitwell, grew up at Renishaw Hall, Derbyshire, which he later inherited. After Eton he reluctantly served in the First World War, and his early poetry (e.g. *The Winstonburg Line*, 1919) is sharply satirical and pacifist in tone. He produced many volumes of poetry, fiction, biography, and autobiography, and was, with his brother and sister, an outspoken enemy of the *Georgian poets (whom he regarded as philistine) and an ardent supporter of *Pound, T. S. *Eliot, W. *Lewis, and W. *Walton (for whose *Belshazzar's Feast*, 1926, he wrote the words). His prose works include *Triple Fugue* (1924), a collection of satirical stories; *Before the Bombardment* (1926), a novel describing the shelling of Scarborough in 1914 and its effect on the lonely, genteel female society of the town; *Winters of Content* (1932), describing travels in Italy; and *Escape with me!* (1939), describing travels in China and the Far East. His most sustained achievement was his autobiography, in five volumes (*Left Hand! Right Hand!*, 1945; *The Scarlet Tree*, 1946; *Great Morning!*, 1948; *Laughter in the Next Room*, 1949; *Noble Essences*, 1950: with a later addition, *Tales my Father Taught Me*, 1962). These are remarkable for the portrait of the eccentric, exasperating figure of his father, Sir George, and their tone is romantic, acidic, nostalgic, and affectionate in turn. See John Pearson, *Façades* (1978), a biography of all three Sitwells.

SITWELL, Sacheverell (1897–), brother of Osbert and Edith (above). His first volume of verse, *The People's Palace* (1918), was followed by several others; his *Collected Poems*, with an introduction by Edith, appeared in 1936, and a selection, *A Retrospect of Poems*, in 1979. Many of his prose works combine an interest in art and travel; they include *Southern Baroque Art* (1924) and *German Baroque Art* (1927), both written when the baroque was little studied; *Conversation Pieces* (1936), again on a not yet fashionable subject; the monumental *British Architects and Craftsmen* (1945); and *Bridge of the Brocade Sash* (1959), on the arts of Japan. He also wrote biographies of *Mozart (1932) and *Liszt (1934). His imaginative prose includes *The Dance of the Quick and the Dead* (1936), a series of interlocked reflections on literature, art, travel, etc.; *Valse des Fleurs* (1941), a re-creation of a day in St Petersburg in 1868; and *Journey to the Ends of Time* (1959), a macabre and despairing work about the condition of man.

Skaldic Verse (also 'scaldic'), a form of Old Norse poetry distinguished by its elaborate metre, alliteration, consonance, and riddling diction. The most usual skaldic metre is 'dróttkvaett', a strophe which consists of eight six-syllable lines, each ending in a trochee. In regular 'dróttkvaett' each odd line contains two alliterating syllables in stressed positions, and the alliteration is continued on one stressed syllable in each following even line. Odd lines also contain two internal half-rhymes; even lines two full rhymes. The first known skald was Bragi Boddason who probably wrote in the late 9th cent. Skaldic verse flourished in the 10th cent. and on into the 11th, and much of it was composed to commemorate the deeds of chieftains who ruled in Norway at this time. Such verses are preserved mainly in the kings' sagas; many 'lausavísur' or occasional verses, and some love poetry are included in the narratives of family sagas (see SAGA).

E. O. G. Turville-Petre, *Scaldic Poetry* (1976), gives parallel translation and discussion.

SKEAT, W(alter) W(illiam) (1835–1912), one of the greatest of the 19th-cent. editors of Old and Middle English literature. He was educated at Christ's College, Cambridge, where he became a mathematics lecturer in 1864. He devoted much of his time to the study of Early English and in 1878 he was appointed to the chair of Anglo-Saxon at Cambridge. His edition of *Lancelot of the Laik* was one of the first publications of the *Early English Texts Society (no. 6, 1865). He edited *Ælfric, *Barbour's *Bruce*, *Chatterton, and the Anglo-Saxon Gospels; his greatest works were the editions of Langland's *Piers Plowman* (published 1886 after twenty years' work) setting out in parallel the three manuscript versions, the existence of which was Skeat's discovery, and of *Chaucer (7 vols, 1894–7, largely establishing the canon and publishing non-canonical works in vol. 7), both of which have been reprinted throughout the 20th cent. He founded the English Dialect Society in 1873, which led to the appearance of Joseph *Wright's *English Dialect Dictionary* (1896–

1905), and his own *Etymological Dictionary* (1879–82, revised and enlarged 1910) was begun with the object of collecting material for the *New English Dictionary* (see MURRAY, J. A. H.). He also began the systematic study of place-names in English. His autobiography (to that date) can be found in *A Student's Pastime* (1896).

SKEFFINGTON, Sir Lumley St George (1771–1850), fop, playwright, and devoted man of the theatre, who belonged to the Carlton House circle. His most successful works, *The Word of Honour, The High Road to Marriage*, and *The Sleeping Beauty*, were produced in the years 1802–5. He was caricatured by *Gillray, and his dramatic works were described by Byron in *English Bards and Scotch Reviewers* (1809) as 'skeletons of plays'.

SKELTON, John (?1460–1529), was created 'poet-laureate' by the universities of Oxford, Louvain, and Cambridge, an academical distinction. He became tutor to Prince Henry (Henry VIII) and enjoyed court favour despite his outspokenness. He was admitted to holy orders in 1498 and became rector of Diss in Norfolk. From about 1511 until his death he seems to have lived in Westminster. His principal works include: *The Bowge of Courte* (a satire on the court of Henry VII), reprinted by *Wynkyn de Worde; *The Garlande of Laurell* (a self-laudatory allegorical poem, describing the crowning of the author among the great poets of the world); *Phyllyp Sparowe* (a lamentation put into the mouth of Jane Scroupe, a young lady whose sparrow has been killed by a cat, followed by a eulogy of her by Skelton, and a defence of himself and the poem); *Collyn Clout* (a complaint by a vagabond of the misdeeds of ecclesiastics), which influenced *Spenser. Not only this last poem, but also his satires 'Speke Parrot' and *Why come ye nat to Courte*, contained attacks on Cardinal Wolsey, setting forth the evil consequences of his dominating position. However, he seems to have repented of these, for *The Garlande of Laurell* and his poem on the duke of Albany, both of 1523, are dedicated to Wolsey. His most vigorous poem was *The Tunnyng of Elynour Rummyng*. His play *Magnyfycence* is an example of the *Morality. Skelton's *Ballade of the Scottysshe Kynge* is a spirited celebration of the victory of *Flodden. A number of Skelton's poems were printed and reprinted in the 16th cent., most of the extant copies being, though undated, evidently later than the poet's death; in 1568 appeared a fairly full collected edition in one volume. There is a complete edition of the English poems by John Scattergood, 1983. Anecdotes of Skelton appeared in the popular *Merie Tales* (1567) and similar collections.

The verse form now known as 'skeltonic

verse' is derived from his favourite metre, 'a headlong voluble breathless doggrel, which rattling and clashing on through quick-recurring rhymes . . . has taken from the name of its author the title of Skeltonical verse' (J. C. *Collins). As he himself said (*Collyn Cloute*, 53–8):

> For though my ryme be ragged,
> Tattered and jagged,
> Rudely rayne-beaten,
> Rusty and mothe-eaten,
> Yf ye take well therwith,
> It hath in it some pyth.

Skelton's modern admirers include Robert *Graves.

Skeltonic Verse, see SKELTON, J.

Sketches by Boz, a collection of sketches of life and manners, by *Dickens, first published in various periodicals, and in book form in 1836–7 (in one volume, 1839). These are some of Dickens's earliest literary work.

Skewton, The Hon. Mrs, in Dickens's *Dombey and Son*, the mother of Edith, Dombey's second wife.

Skimpole, Harold, a character in Dickens's *Bleak House*.

SKINNER, Cyriack (1627–1700), a grandson of Sir E. *Coke, and a student, then a friend (and possibly also an early biographer) of *Milton. Milton addressed two sonnets to him, written c.1654: 'Cyriack, whose grandsire on the Royal Bench' and 'To Mr Cyriack Skinner upon his Blindness'.

SKINNER, John (1721–1807), an Aberdeenshire minister chiefly remembered as the author of *Tullochgorum* (1776), pronounced by *Burns 'the best Scotch song Scotland ever saw'. His poems and songs were published in Vol. 3 of his *Theological Works* (1809).

Slaughter's Coffee House, opened by Thomas Slaughter in 1692 on St Martin's Lane, was the favourite resort of artists including *Hogarth, *Gainsborough, *Roubiliac, and *Haydon.

Slawkenbergius, the author of a Latin treatise on noses, in Sterne's *Tristram Shandy*.

Slay-good, in Pt. II of Bunyan's *Pilgrim's Progress*, a giant whom Mr *Great-heart killed, rescuing Mr Feeble-mind from his clutches.

Sleary, the circus proprietor in Dickens's *Hard Times*.

Sleeping Beauty, The, a fairy-tale, translated from the French of *Perrault by Robert Samber (1729).

Seven fairies are invited to attend the baptism of the daughter of a king and are received with great honour. An old fairy has been overlooked and comes unbidden. Six fairies bestow on the child every imaginable perfection. The old fairy spitefully pronounces that she shall wound herself with a spindle and die. The seventh fairy, who has purposely kept in the background, amends this fate, converting the death into a sleep of a hundred years, from which the princess will be awakened by a king's son. And so it falls out, and the fairy puts every one in the castle also to sleep so that the princess may not wake up all alone, and makes an impenetrable hedge of trees and briars to grow up round the castle. In due course the prince comes and wakens the princess, which causes the other sleepers to awake.

For analogous legends see A. *Lang, *Perrault's Popular Tales* (1888). It is suggested that the Sleeping Beauty represents the earth awakened from her winter sleep by the kiss of the sun.

'Sleepy Hollow, The Legend of', a story by W. *Irving, included in *The Sketch Book*. Ichabod Crane is a schoolmaster and suitor for the hand of Katrina van Tassel. He meets his death, or, according to another report, leaves the neighbourhood, in consequence of being pursued at night by a headless horseman, an incident for which his rival Brom Bones is suspected of having been responsible.

Slender, Abraham, a cousin of *Shallow's and unsuccessful lover of Anne *Page in Shakespeare's *The Merry Wives of Windsor*.

Slipslop, Mrs, a character in Fielding's *Joseph Andrews*.

SLOANE, Sir Hans (1660–1753), a physician, secretary to the *Royal Society, 1693–1712, and president of the Royal College of Physicians, 1719–35. He purchased the manor of Chelsea in 1712 and endowed the Chelsea Physic Garden. He published (1696) a Latin catalogue of the plants of Jamaica (where he had been physician to the governor, 1687–9). His collection (including a large number of books and manuscripts) was purchased by the nation and placed in Montague House, afterwards the British Museum; the geological and zoological specimens formed the basis of the Natural History Museum in South Kensington, opened in 1881. Sloane Square and Hans Place are named after him.

Slop, Dr, in Sterne's *Tristram Shandy*, a thoroughly incompetent and argumentative physician, now known to be a caricature of Dr John Burton, a male midwife and Tory politician of York, and an enemy of Sterne's. The name was later applied to Sir John Stoddart (1773–1856), who was editor of *The New Times* from 1817 until 1828.

Slope, The Revd Obadiah, a character in Trollope's *The Warden* and *Barchester Towers*.

Slough of Despond, in Bunyan's *Pilgrim's Progress*, a miry place on the way from the City of Destruction to the wicket-gate. 'As the sinner is awakened about his lost condition, there arise in his soul many fears and doubts, and discouraging apprehensions, which all of them get together, and settle in this place.'

Sludge, Dicky, or 'Flibbertigibbet', a character in Scott's *Kenilworth*.

Slumkey, The Hon. Samuel, in Dickens's *Pickwick Papers*, the Blue candidate in the Eatanswill election.

Sly, Christopher, see TAMING OF THE SHREW, THE.

Small House At Allington, The, a novel by A. *Trollope, published 1864, the fifth in the *'Barsetshire' series.

Lily Dale becomes engaged to Adolphus Crosbie, an ambitious civil servant, but Crosbie is invited to a house party at Courcy Castle where he proposes to Lady Alexandrina de Courcy. When news comes back to Allington that Crosbie has jilted her, Lily behaves well, but Johnny Eames, her childhood sweetheart, tries to take some revenge on her behalf by assaulting Crosbie at Paddington station. Crosbie finds that he and his bride are incompatible; Lady Alexandrina returns to her family and travels to Baden, Crosbie taking refuge in wounded bachelordom. Meanwhile Eames's reputation continues to develop. He grows out of his juvenile dissipations, clears up an unfortunate entanglement with the daughter of his London boarding-house keeper, and begins to spend much of his free time at Allington. There he becomes the protégé of Lord de Guest, and at the intercession of Lady Julia renews his suit to Lily. Lily, however, considers herself bound to Crosbie for life.

Lily's sister, Bell, is expected to marry the heir of Squire Dale of the Great House at Allington, but she rejects him in favour of the worthy Dr Crofts.

SMART, Christopher (1722–71), was born in Kent, but educated in Durham and at Pembroke Hall, Cambridge, where he distinguished himself as a classical scholar. In 1749 he came to London and began to write poems and reviews under various pseudonyms, including 'Mrs Midnight', for *Newbery, whose stepdaughter he married in 1752. Newbery published his first collection of verse, *Poems on Several Occasions* (1752), which included a blank-verse georgic in two books, 'The Hop-Garden', and lighter verse. *The Hilliad*, a satire on the quack doctor John Hill, written with the help of A. *Murphy and modelled on *The Dunciad*, appeared in 1753. In 1756 Smart was dangerously ill, and a year later he was admitted to a hospital for the insane; he spent the years 1759–63 in a private

home for the insane in Bethnal Green. His derangement took the form of a compulsion to public prayer, which occasioned the famous comment of Dr *Johnson: 'I'd as lief pray with Kit Smart as anyone else.' After leaving the asylum he published his best-known poem, *A Song to David* (1763), a song of praise to David as author of the psalms, and a celebration of the Creation and the Incarnation; the poem is built on a mathematical and mystical ordering of stanzas grouped in threes, fives, and sevens, and was compared by R. *Browning, one of Smart's few 19th-cent. admirers, to a great cathedral, in both its structure and imagery. Smart also published in these later years translations of the psalms, of *Horace, two oratorios, and poems, and was supported by the friendship of W. *Mason, Dr *Burney, and others (though Mason, on reading *A Song to David*, declared him 'as mad as ever'); however he declined into poverty and debt and died within the 'Rules' of the King's Bench Prison. His work was little regarded until the 1920s, when there was a wave of biographical interest, and his reputation as a highly original poet was confirmed by the publication of his extraordinary work *Jubilate Agno* in 1939 (ed. W. F. Stead as *Rejoice in the Lamb: A Song from Bedlam*). This unfinished work had been composed between 1758/9 and 1763, largely at Bethnal Green; Smart described it as 'my Magnificat', and it celebrates the Creation in a verse form based on the antiphonal principles of Hebrew poetry. It was to consist of parallel sets of verses, one beginning 'Let . . .', with a response beginning 'For . . .' It contains an extremely wide range of references, biblical, botanical, zoological, scientific (Smart was opposed to I. *Newton's view of the universe), personal, and cabbalistic; the most celebrated passage is the one on Smart's cat, which begins 'For I will consider my cat Jeoffrey . . .' This work forms the first volume of a new edition of the complete works, ed. K. Williamson (1980–). There is a biography by A. Sherbo (1967).

Smec, Legion, see SMECTYMNUUS.

Smectymnuus, the name under which five Presbyterian divines, Stephen Marshall, Edmund Calamy, Thomas Young, Matthew Newcomen, and William Spurstow, published a pamphlet in 1641 attacking episcopacy and Bishop J. *Hall. It was answered by Hall, and defended by *Milton (who had been a pupil of Young, the eldest of the five) in his *Animadversions upon the Remonstrant's Defence against Smectymnuus* (1641) and his *An Apology against a Pamphlet call'd A Modest Confutation of the Animadversions upon the Remonstrant against Smectymnuus* (1642). In the latter Milton also defends himself against the allegations of the anonymous *A Modest Confutation* (possibly by Hall's son or by the Revd Robert Duncan, ?1599–?1622), which include the charge that Milton had 'spent his youth in loitering, bezelling and harlotting', and that he had been 'vomited out' of the University: it contains an interesting account of his early studies. From 'Smectymnuus' is derived the 'Legion Smec' in *Hudibras (II. ii), signifying the Presbyterians:

New modell'd the army and cashier'd
All that to Legion Smec adher'd.

SMEDLEY, Francis Edward (1818–64), a cripple from childhood, was for three years editor of *Cruikshank's Magazine* and author of three high-spirited novels of sport, romance, and adventure, including the popular *Frank Fairleigh* (1850), illustrated by *Cruikshank, *Lewis Arundel* (1852), and *Harry Coverdale's Courtship* (1855).

Smelfungus, in Sterne's *A Sentimental Journey, a caricature of *Smollett, who in 1766 had published his *Travels in France and Italy.

SMETANA, Bedřich (1824–84), Czech composer and founder of the Czech national school. The vast majority of Smetana's works depend on subjects or texts from within his own country. He had, however, a special admiration for Shakespeare, and one of his earliest orchestral works is the symphonic poem *Richard III (1858), the first of three written when the composer was still unknown and living in Sweden: constructed on the Lisztian model, with a clearly defined programme, it includes a successful musical portrait of the humpbacked king with his halting, uneven walk. At about the same time Smetana wrote a long piano piece entitled *Macbeth and the Witches*, of considerable originality; it may have been intended for orchestration as another symphonic poem, though it makes an effective virtuoso piano piece as it stands.

From the opposite end of Smetana's career comes the fragment (less than one act) of *Viola*, an opera based on *Twelfth Night on which the composer was working at the time of his death. It would probably have been more interesting than the 'Shakespearian March', a *pièce d'occasion* written 'to accompany a magnificent procession of the most outstanding characters in Shakespeare's plays' at the culmination of the Shakespeare tercentenary concert organized by Smetana in Prague in 1864.

Smike, a character in Dickens's *Nicholas Nickleby.

SMILES, Samuel (1812–1904), son of a Haddington shopkeeper, had a mobile and varied career as surgeon, newspaper editor, secretary for a railway company, etc., and devoted his leisure to the advocacy of political and social reform, on the lines of the *Manchester School, and to the biography of industrial leaders and humble self-taught students. He published a *Life of George Stephenson* (1875), *Lives of the Engineers* (1861–2), *Josiah Wedgwood* (1894), and many similar works, but is now principally remembered for his immensely successful *Self-help* (1859), which was translated into many languages. It preached industry, thrift, and self-improvement, and attacked 'over-government'; it has been much mocked as a work symbolizing the ethics and aspirations of mid-19th-cent. bourgeois individualism. The titles of other works on similar themes (*Character*, 1871; *Thrift*, 1875; *Duty*, 1880) are self-explanatory.

SMITH, Adam (1723–90), born at Kirkcaldy, studied at Glasgow University and as a Snell exhibitioner at Balliol College, Oxford. In 1748 he was appointed to lecture in rhetoric and belles-lettres in Edinburgh where he was associated with the publication of *Hamilton of Bangour's *Poems*. He was appointed professor of logic at Glasgow in 1751, and in 1752 of moral philosophy. He became the friend of *Hume. His contributions to the original *Edinburgh Review* (1755–6) included a critical review of *Johnson's *Dictionary*. In 1759 he published *The Theory of Moral Sentiments*, which brought him into prominence. In 1764 he resigned his professorship and accompanied the young duke of Buccleuch as tutor on a visit to France, where he saw *Voltaire and was admitted into the society of the *physiocrats. After his return he settled down at Kirkcaldy and devoted himself to the preparation of his great work *An Inquiry into the Nature and Causes of the *Wealth of Nations*, published in 1776. This revolutionized the economic theories of the day. Its appearance at the actual date of the 'Declaration of Independence' of the American rebels was of importance if only for the prophecy in Bk IV, 'They will be one of the foremost nations of the world': to obviate the danger he proposed the representation of the colonies in the British Parliament. Smith's edition of the autobiography of Hume in 1777 occasioned some controversy. A projected work on the theatre was never completed, but an essay on the imitative arts was included in his posthumous *Essays on Philosophical Subjects* (1795). He was a member of Johnson's *Club. A critical edition of Smith's works in 6 volumes was published for the University of Glasgow in 1976–80, but the *Correspondence* volume is defective.

SMITH, Alexander (?1830–67), by occupation a lace-pattern designer in Glasgow, published in 1853 *Poems* (including 'A life-drama'), which were received at first with enthusiasm, and satirized, along with other works of the *Spasmodic School, in *Aytoun's *Firmilian*. He published in 1855 sonnets on the Crimean war jointly with S. T. *Dobell; *City Poems* in 1857; and some prose essays, *Dreamthorp*, in 1863. His best prose is to be seen in *A Summer in Skye* (1865), a vivid evocation of the region, its history, and its inhabitants.

SMITH, Charlotte (1748–1806), chiefly a novelist, who also wrote many stories, sketches, and poems, and enjoyed considerable success. She began her career with *Elegaic Sonnets* in 1784 and wrote poetry which Leigh *Hunt found 'natural and touching'. Her novels appeared between 1788 and 1793: *Emmeline*, which was very successful, and admired by Sir W. *Scott, in 1788; three others then appeared; and in 1793 *The Old Manor House*, which Scott, and posterity, considered her best. Orlando, who is favoured by a rich widow, Mrs Rayland, is forced to leave his beloved Monimia, Mrs Rayland's ward, in order to seek a livelihood. He joins the army in America, and after many hardships among battles and Indians returns to find himself Mrs Rayland's heir and to marry Monimia. At her best the author's work is brisk, ironic, and confident.

SMITH, George (1824–1901), joined in 1838 the firm of Smith & Elder, publishers and East India agents, of 65 Cornhill, London, which his father had founded in partnership with Alexander Elder in 1816, soon after coming in youth to London from his native town of Elgin. In 1843 Smith took charge of some of the firm's publishing operations, and on his father's death in 1846 became sole head of the firm. Under his control the business quickly grew in both the India agency and publishing directions. The chief authors whose works he published in his early career were *Ruskin, C. *Brontë, whose *Jane Eyre* he issued in 1848, and W. M. *Thackeray, whose *Esmond* he brought out in 1852. Charlotte Brontë visited Smith and his mother in London on friendly terms, and Smith later acknowledged that 'In *Villette* my mother was the original of "Mrs Bretton", several of her expressions are given verbatim. I myself, I discovered, stood for "Dr John".' ('Recollections of Charlotte Brontë', *Cornhill Magazine*, Dec. 1900.)

In 1853 he took a partner, H. S. King, and after weathering the storm of the Indian Mutiny, founded in 1859 *The Cornhill Magazine*, with Thackeray as editor and numerous leading authors and artists as contributors. In 1865 Smith (with Frederick Greenwood) founded *The Pall Mall Gazette*, a London evening newspaper of independent character and literary quality, which remained his property till 1880. In 1868 he dissolved partnership with King, leaving him to carry on the India agency branch of the old firm's business, and himself taking over the publishing branch, which he thenceforth conducted at 15 Waterloo Place, London. His chief authors now included R. *Browning, M. *Arnold, (Sir) L. *Stephen, and Anne

Thackeray *Ritchie, all of whom were intimate personal friends. He was founder (1882) and proprietor of the *Dictionary of National Biography*.

SMITH, Goldwin (1823–1910), educated at Eton and Christ Church, Oxford, was Regius professor of modern history at Oxford, 1858–66, and subsequently professor of history at Cornell University in America, finally settling at Toronto in 1871. He was an active journalist and vigorous controversialist, supporting the cause of the North in the American Civil War, and the sentiment of national independence in Canada.

Smith (or Gow), Henry, the hero of Scott's *The Fair Maid of Perth*.

SMITH, Horatio (Horace) (1779–1849), brother of James (below), became famous overnight as the joint author, with his brother, of *Rejected Addresses* in 1812, and of *Horace in London* (1813), imitations of certain Odes of *Horace, chiefly written by his brother. He then turned to the writing of historical romance. In 1826 his *Brambletye House*, the story of a young Cavalier and a pale shadow of Scott's *Woodstock* (published in the same year), went through many editions. *The Tor Hill* followed in the same year, and between then and 1846 he wrote nearly 20 further novels, as well as plays and poems and work for the *New Monthly Magazine*.

SMITH, James (1775–1839), elder brother of Horatio (above), was solicitor to the Board of Ordnance, and produced with his brother *Rejected Addresses* in 1812 and *Horace in London* (1813), imitations of certain Odes of *Horace, largely written by James. He also wrote entertainments for the comic actor Charles Mathews.

SMITH, Captain John (1580–1631), set out with the Virginia colonists in 1606 and is said to have been rescued by *Pocahontas when taken prisoner by the Indians. He became head of the colony and explored the coasts of the Chesapeake. He was author of *The General History of Virginia, New England, and the Summer Isles* (1624).

SMITH, John (1618–52), see CAMBRIDGE PLATONISTS.

SMITH, John Thomas (1776–1833), engraver and artist, and eventually keeper of prints and drawings at the British Museum, was particularly interested in the history and character of London. Among other writings he published *Antiquities of London* (1800) and *Vagabondiana* (1817), a description of London's beggars, illustrated by himself. He wrote a remarkably candid life of the sculptor Nollekens, published in 1828, and in 1839 *Cries of London. A Book* *for a Rainy Day, or Recollections of the Events of the Years 1766–1833* (1845), provides a lively account of the literary and artistic life of the time.

SMITH, (Lloyd) Logan Pearsall (1865–1946), man of letters, born in Philadelphia of Quaker stock, spent most of his life in England, devoting himself to the study of literature and the English language; he was (with *Bridges and others) a founder of the *Society for Pure English. One of his sisters became the first wife of Bertrand *Russell, another married *Berenson, and his own circle of literary friends included R. *Fry, H. *James, and C. *Connolly. His works include *Trivia* (1902), *More Trivia* (1921), and *Afterthoughts* (1931), collections of much polished observations and aphorisms; one of his more memorable, 'People say that life is the thing, but I prefer reading', indicates the nature of his success and limitations as an author. See *Recollections of Pearsall Smith* (1949), an unsparing account by R. Gathorne-Hardy.

Smith, Stephen, a character in Hardy's *A Pair of Blue Eyes.*

SMITH, Stevie (Florence Margaret) (1902–71), poet and novelist, who was born in Hull but brought up in Palmers Green, north London, where she spent most of her adult life with an aunt. She wrote three novels, *Novel on Yellow Paper* (1936), *Over the Frontier* (1938), and *The Holiday* (1949), but has been more widely recognized for her witty, caustic, and enigmatic verse, much of it illustrated by her own comic drawings. Her first volume, *A Good Time was Had By All* (1937), was followed by seven others, including *Not Waving But Drowning* (1957), of which the title poem (originally published in *Punch*) is perhaps the best known. She was an accomplished reader of her own verse, and found a new young audience at the poetry readings which flourished in the 1960s. Her *Collected Poems* appeared in 1975; see also *Ivy and Stevie* (1971) by her friend, the novelist Kay Dick.

SMITH, Sydney (1771–1845), educated at Winchester and New College, Oxford, lived for a time as a tutor in Edinburgh, where he became a friend of *Jeffrey and *Brougham with whom he founded the *Edinburgh Review* in 1802. He was himself the original 'projector' of the *Review*, the object of which was to provide a voice for liberal and Whig opinion to balance the Tory *Quarterly*. Smith was a humane man, who campaigned vigorously, in the *Review* and elsewhere, against the Game Laws, transportation, prisons, slavery, and for Catholic emancipation, Church reform, and many other matters. He tried for a time to restrain what he saw as Jeffrey's tendency, as editor of the *Review*, to 'analyse and destroy'; but his own contributions became less frequent, then ceased altogether, as he came to feel that Jeffrey was making it 'perilous' for a cleric to be connected with the *Review*. He came to London in 1803, lectured with great success on moral philosophy at the Royal Institution, and became the wittiest and one of the most beloved of the Whig circle at *Holland House. In 1807 he published *The Letters of Peter *Plymley* in defence of Catholic emancipation, and he published a considerable number of sermons, speeches, essays, and letters. He held the livings, first of Foston in Yorkshire, then of Combe Florey in Somerset, and in 1831 was made a canon of St Paul's. His superb wit was chiefly displayed in his conversation, but may also be found in his numerous letters, reviews, and essays. See biography by H. *Pearson, *The Smith of Smiths* (1934).

SMITH, Sydney Goodsir (1915–75), poet, critic, and journalist, born in New Zealand, who settled in Scotland as a young man and is remembered for his part in the 20th-cent. revival of poetry in the *Scots language. His first volume, *Skail Wind* (1941), was followed by several others, and he also edited various works on Scottish literature.

Smith, W. H., and Son, Ltd, a firm of stationers, newsagents, and booksellers, which originated in a small newsvendor's shop opened in London in Little Grosvenor Street in 1792 by Henry Walton Smith and his wife Anna. He died within a few months, leaving the shop to his widow, who on her death in 1816 left it to her sons; the younger, William Henry Smith (1792–1865), gave the firm its name of W. H. Smith in 1828. When his son, also William Henry (1825–91), became a partner in 1846, the words 'and Son' were added, and have remained ever since. The business prospered, profiting from the railway boom by opening station bookstalls throughout the country (of which the first was at Euston, 1848), and establishing a circulating *library which lasted until 1961; it is now a joint owner (since 1966) of Book Club Associates. In the 20th cent. the wholesale and retail activities of the business expanded greatly, and the name of W. H. Smith is now associated with a wide range of products. The W. H. Smith Literary Award has been awarded annually since 1959, for a work of any genre that constitutes 'the most outstanding contribution to English literature' in the year under review. Past winners include P. *White, L. *Lee, *Gombrich, and *Heaney.

SMITH, Sir William (1813–93), lexicographer, classical scholar, and editor of the *Quarterly Review* (1867–93). He is associated with the revival of classical teaching in England and among his many educational works are his *Dictionary of Greek and Roman Antiquities* (1842), a *Dictionary of Greek and Roman Biography and*

Mythology (1844–9) and a *Dictionary of the Bible* (1860–3).

SMOLLETT, Tobias George (1721–71), the son of a Scots laird, was born near Dunbarton. After attendance at Glasgow University he was apprenticed to a surgeon, but did not prosper and lived in some poverty. He wrote a play, *The Regicide*, which he brought to London in 1739, but he could not get it accepted, then or at any future time. He joined the navy, became surgeon's mate, and sailed in 1741 for the West Indies on an expedition against the Spaniards. He was present at the abortive attack on Cartagena, when the fleet retired, a fact which greatly disturbed Smollett, who later wrote about the failure in *Roderick Random* and (probably) in *A Compendium of . . . Voyages*. While in Jamaica he met Anne Lassells, a young woman of some property and means, whom he married, probably in 1743. In 1744 he set himself up as a surgeon in Downing Street, and began to entertain generously among a wide circle of friends, many of them his Scots compatriots.

Although never a Jacobite, Smollett's first publication, in 1746, was a much-admired poem, 'The Tears of Scotland', elicited by the duke of *Cumberland's cruel treatment of the Scots after 1745. Further poems followed, notably two satires on London life, *Advice* (1746) and *Reproof* (1747). In the course of eight months in 1747 he wrote *The Adventures of *Roderick Random* which was published in 1748 and was a lasting success. The Smolletts' only child, Elizabeth, was born in 1747 or 1748. Smollett toured France and the Low Countries in 1749, the first of various travels in Europe. Back in London he continued to practise as a surgeon, without any great success, and although he laboured hard at various tasks of editing and translation he was chronically short of money. In 1750 he moved to Chelsea, where he kept open board in his fine large house. In the same year he received his MD from Aberdeen, and travelled to Paris, a journey of which he made use in *The Adventures of *Peregrine Pickle* (1751). Long, ferocious, and often savagely libellous, the novel was only reasonably successful; Smollett considerably toned down the second edition of 1758. He may have been the author, in 1752, of the scurrilous pamphlet, *The Faithful Narrative of Habbakkuk Hilding*, attacking *Fielding for plagiarism and on many other counts. He and Fielding conducted intermittent warfare, chiefly in the *Critical Review* and the *Covent Garden Journal*, but Smollett eventually gave his rival handsome praise in his *Continuation of the Complete History* (see below).

In 1753 he published *The Adventures of *Ferdinand Count Fathom*, a story of cruelty and treachery which did not appeal to the public. Smollett was again in financial difficulties, and took on every medical or literary employment

that he could find. In the same year he set out on an extended tour of his native Scotland, and began to exhibit symptoms of consumption. He had long been translating *Cervantes, and in 1755 his *History and Adventures of Don Quixote* appeared, but to his great disappointment received little attention. In 1756 he became cofounder and editor of the *Critical Review*; his stormy and brilliant editorship lasted till 1763, but the *Review* was not a commercial success. *A Compendium of Authentic and Entertaining Voyages*, an anthology of travel, appeared in 1756, and contained an account, probably by his pen, of the retreat at Cartagena. In 1757–8 he published his *Complete History of England* which engendered much angry controversy, but its sales were immense and at last Smollett could feel financially secure. Also in 1757 he had a success at Drury Lane with his naval farce *The Reprisal*, staged by *Garrick. The first volume of the *Continuation of the Complete History* appeared in 1760; and *The Life and Adventures of *Sir Launcelot Greaves*, the story of a quixotic 18th-cent. Englishman, began to appear in instalments in Smollett's new venture, *The British Magazine*, to which *Goldsmith was a major contributor and which ran until 1767. In the same eventful year of 1760 Smollett was fined £100 and sentenced to three months' imprisonment for a libel on Admiral Knowles in the *Critical Review*. His editon of a new translation of *The Works of . . . Voltaire* began to appear in 1761, and in 1762 *Sir Launcelot Greaves* was published in book form, but met with little interest. In 1762–3 Smollett wrote and edited the Tory journal *The Briton*, which was rapidly killed by Wilkes's *The North Briton*.

Smollett's health had long been deteriorating, and he attempted without success to obtain work abroad. In 1763 his daughter died. He gave up his house and all his literary work and left England with his wife and household for France and Italy. They returned in 1765 and in 1766 he published his *epistolary *Travels through France and Italy*, a caustic work which earned him from *Sterne the nickname of Smelfungus. In 1767 he tried again, and again without success, to obtain a consulship abroad. *The Present State of All Nations*, a complex work of geography, history, statistics, and other matters (a long labour in which he was probably assisted by other hands) was finally published in eight volumes in 1768–9.

In 1768 he and his wife left again for Italy, and in 1769 appeared *The Adventures of an *Atom*, a rancorous satire on public men and affairs which was possibly, but not certainly, by Smollett. Meanwhile he had been completing *The Expedition of *Humphry Clinker*, an epistolary novel generally agreed to be Smollett's crowning achievement. It was published in London in 1771, some months before Smollett died at his home near Leghorn.

Smollett's passion for controversy did not always endear him to the literary or fashionable world, but his major novels were admired and successful; his reputation sank considerably in the 19th and early 20th cents, but now stands high. His avowed purpose in writing was to arouse 'generous indignation' against cruelty and injustice, but his relish in the exploits of his 'heroes' sometimes distorts his professed moral purpose. He was greatly attracted by the 'anti-romance' of *Lesage and many of the episodes of his novels are set in scenes of squalor and violence 'where the . . . passions are undisguised by affectation': his works are often (if somewhat loosely) described as *picaresque.

There is a life by L. M. Knapp, *Doctor of Men and Manners* (1949); see also G. M. Kahrl, *Tobias Smollett: Traveler–Novelist* (1945).

Smorltork, Count, in Dickens's *Pickwick Papers*, 'the famous foreigner' at Mrs Leo Hunter's party, 'a well-whiskered individual in a foreign uniform', who is 'gathering materials for his great work on England'.

Snagsby, Mr and Mrs, characters in Dickens's *Bleak House.*

Snailsfoot, Bryce, the pedlar in Scott's *The Pirate.*

Snake, a character in Sheridan's *The School for Scandal.*

Snark, see HUNTING OF THE SNARK, THE.

Sneerwell, Lady, one of the scandal-mongers in Sheridan's *The School for Scandal.*

Snevellicci, Mr, Mrs, and Miss, in Dickens's *Nicholas Nickleby*, actors in Crummles's company.

Snobs of England, see BOOK OF SNOBS, THE.

Snodgrass, Augustus, in Dickens's *Pickwick Papers*, one of the members of the Corresponding Society of the Pickwick Club.

SNORRI STURLUSON (1178–1241), an Icelandic historian and literary antiquarian, the author of *Heimskringla*, the Prose *Edda*, and perhaps *Egils saga*, the biography of a Viking poet. Snorri is the most important figure in Old Icelandic literature; our knowledge of Norse myth and understanding of Old Norse poetry is due largely to him. He was politically ambitious, involved in the chief political intrigues of his time, and at last ignominiously assassinated on the order of King Hákon of Norway.

Snout, Tom, in Shakespeare's *A Midsummer Night's Dream*, an Athenian tinker. He is cast for the part of Pyramus's father in the play of 'Pyramus and Thisbe', but appears as Wall, which gives him nothing to say.

SNOW, C(harles) P(ercy) (Baron Snow of Leicester) (1905–80), novelist, was born and educated in Leicester, the son of a church organist. His early career was devoted to scientific research in Cambridge, but he turned increasingly to administration, and in later life held many important public posts. His first novel was a detective story, *Death under Sail* (1932), followed by *New Lives for Old* (1933) and *The Search* (1934), which deals with the frustrations of a scientist's life. His novel sequence (see ROMAN FLEUVE) *Strangers and Brothers* (the original title of the first volume, 1940, retitled subsequently *George Passant*), spanned 30 years of writing, and more years in the life of its narrator, Lewis Eliot, a barrister who, like Snow himself, rose from lower middle-class provincial origins to enjoy worldly success and influence. The settings of the novels (*The Light and the Dark*, 1947; *Time of Hope*, 1949; *The Masters*, 1951; *The New Men*, 1954; *Homecomings*, 1956; *The Conscience of the Rich*, 1958; *The Affair*, 1959; *Corridors of Power*, 1963; *The Sleep of Reason*, 1968; *Last Things*, 1970) are largely academic or scientific; *The Masters*, a study of the internal politics of a Cambridge college, is perhaps his best known, but he was equally at home writing of crises in the life of a small-town solicitor or a fashionable and wealthy Jewish family. His interest in public affairs is reflected in his work, and his novel on Westminster life, *The Corridors of Power*, added a phrase to the language of the day, as did his Rede Lecture on *The Two Cultures and the Scientific Revolution* (1959). He published several other novels and critical works, including a critical biography of *Trollope (1975), a novelist whose influence is evident in his own work, which consistently avoided modernism and formalism. In 1950 he married Pamela Hansford *Johnson.

Snubbin, Mr Serjeant, in Dickens's *Pickwick Papers*, counsel for the defendant in Bardell v. Pickwick.

Snuffy Davie, or Davie Wilson, in Scott's *The Antiquary*, the hero of a favourite story of Monkbarns, the bibliomaniac who bought *Caxton's *The Game of Chess*, 1474, for two groschen at a stall in Holland.

Snug, in Shakespeare's *A Midsummer Night's Dream*, a joiner, who takes the part of the lion in 'Pyramus and Thisbe'.

SNYDER, Gary, see BEAT GENERATION.

SOANE, Sir John (1753–1837), architect. He was architect to the Bank of England from 1788 to 1833 and founder of the museum in Lincoln's Inn Fields which bears his name and contains his library, antiquities, and works of art. The library is famous for its hoard of architectural drawings by *Wren, the Adam brothers, Dance, and Soane. He published several volumes of his own designs and an extensive description of the museum. His Royal Academy lectures, his only major literary enterprise, were published in 1929.

Social Contract, The, the English title of *Du Contrat Social,* by J. J. *Rousseau.

Socialism, a theory or policy of social organization that aims at the control of the means of production, capital, land, property, etc., by the community as a whole, and their administration or distribution in the interests of all. The early history of the word is obscure, but it was claimed that it was first used in something like the modern sense in 1827 in the Owenite *Co-operative Magazine,* and it is found in the 1830s used in the sense of Owenism. (See OWEN, ROBERT.) One of the most articulate and persistent of British socialists was Bernard Shaw, who published in 1928 *The Intelligent Woman's Guide to Socialism and Capitalism.*

Socialist Realism, a term used to describe the official artistic doctrine adopted at the Congress of Soviet Writers in 1934, approved by *Stalin, *Gorky, N. Bukharin, and A. A. Zhdanov. It required that the creative artist should serve the proletariat by being realistic, optimistic (i.e. by providing positive heroes and positive conclusions), and heroic: it denigrated the bourgeois artist and all forms of experimentalism and formalism as degenerate and pessimistic. (The works of *Joyce were singled out for particular condemnation at this first Congress.) It presented problems for such Marxist critics as *Lukács, and after the hard Stalinist period the use of the term was modified to cover the works of such artistic innovators as *Brecht and *Mayakovsky; but it is still seen in the Western world as an impediment to creativity and freedom of expression. 'Social Realism' is a distinct term, used loosely to describe a realistic, objective, yet socially aware and detailed method of artistic presentation. (See REALISM.)

Society for Promoting Christian Knowledge, see SPCK.

Society for Psychical Research, The, a body founded in 1882 by F. W. H. *Myers, H. *Sidgwick, and others 'to examine without prejudice . . . those faculties of man, real or supposed, which appear to be inexplicable in terms of any recognised hypothesis'. The Society, in a period of intense interest in spiritualism and the supernatural, investigated with high standards of scientific detachment such matters as telepathy, apparitions, etc., and was instrumental in exposing the fraudulent claims of, e.g., Mme *Blavatsky. Its presidents have included A. J. *Balfour, W. *James, and Sir Oliver Lodge (1851–1940, a physicist less sceptical than many of the SPR); members and associates have included *Ruskin, *Tennyson, *Gladstone, and

A. R. *Wallace. See R. Haynes *The Society for Psychical Research 1882–1982* (1982).

Society for Pure English, The, an association of writers and academics, inspired by *Bridges, which included H. *Bradley, Sir W. *Raleigh, and L. P. *Smith in its original committee. The Society was formed in Oxford in 1913, but suspended its activities until the end of the First World War. Between 1919 and 1946 it issued a total of 66 tracts of which the last, by R. W. Chapman, was a retrospective account of its work. The name of the society was somewhat misleading in that the founders had no objections to the entry of foreign words into English, and the writers of its tracts were not for the most part purists in the dogmatic sense. A typical tract would offer an urbane and well-researched enquiry into some question of grammar, pronunciation, etymology, or vocabulary, and there were occasional treatments of quite exotic subjects; for instance, the language of C. M. *Doughty or the pronunciation of *Gladstone.

Society of Antiquaries, The, was founded about the year 1572 at the instance of Archbishop *Parker, but was suppressed on the accession of James I. The present Society was founded in Jan. 1717/18, with Peter Le Neve as president and W. *Stukeley as secretary. Its *Archaeologia* was first printed in 1770. From 1921 it has also published the *Antiquaries' Journal.*

Society of Authors, The, an organization founded in 1884 by W. *Besant to promote the business interests of authors and fight for their rights, especially in copyright. Progress was slow, but by 1914 much had been achieved; Britain had joined the International Copyright Convention (Berne Union), the USA had offered limited protection to foreign authors, while domestic copyright had undergone a major reform under the Copyright Act of 1911. (See Appendix II.) By then too the Society had succeeded in radically improving publishing contracts and in dealing with recalcitrant publishers in and out of the courts.

Besant's example was followed by G. B. *Shaw, who fought arduously for playwrights *vis-à-vis* theatre managers, and to liberalize stage censorship; the League of Dramatists was founded in 1931 as an autonomous section of the Society. Since then the Society has formed other specialized groups, and has also laboured effectively to improve the author's lot with regard to taxation, libel, social security, etc. It conducted a successful 28-year campaign for *Public Lending Right, and has helped to set up the Authors' Lending and Copyright Society, in order to secure income in respect of rights (e.g. photocopying) only possible on a collective basis. Its quarterly publication is *The Author.*

See Victor Bonham-Carter, *Authors by Profession* (2 vols, 1978, 1984).

Society of Friends, see FRIENDS, SOCIETY OF.

Society of Jesus, see LOYOLA and XAVIER.

Socinianism, the doctrine of Lelio Sozini (Socinus) (1525–62) and his nephew Fausto Sozzini (1539–1604) that Jesus was not God but a divine prophet of God's word, and that the sacraments had no supernatural quality. The doctrine was set forth in the Confession of Rakow (1605), and was an influence on early *Unitarianism.

SOCRATES (469–399 BC), the Greek philosopher, was born near Athens, the son of a sculptor or stonemason. He served in the army, saving the life of Alcibiades at Potidea (432 BC). Late in life he held public office, and showed moral courage in resisting illegalities. His wife Xanthippe was reputed to be a scold. He occupied his life with oral instruction, frequenting public places and engaging in discourse designed to reveal truth and expose error. He incurred much enmity, was attacked by *Aristophanes in the *Clouds*, and was finally accused by Meletus, a leather-seller, of introducing strange gods and corrupting youth. He was sentenced to death, and thirty days later took hemlock. Socrates wrote nothing, but his teaching methods are preserved in the Dialogues of *Plato and a more homely account is to be found in *Xenophon's *Memorabilia*. The prominent features of his teaching appear to have been: the view that it is the duty of philosophy to investigate ethical questions; and the view that virtue is knowledge: no one is willingly wicked, for happiness lies in virtue; if a man is wicked, it is from ignorance. He inclined to belief in the immortality of the soul, and thought himself subject to divine promptings. (For Socratic Method see PLATO.)

'Sofa, The', see TASK, THE.

Sofronia, or **Sophronia,** a character in Tasso's *Jerusalem Delivered*.

'Sohrab and Rustum', a poem by M. *Arnold, published 1853. The story is taken from *Firdusi's Persian epic, via a French translation by J. Mohl, *Le Livre des Rois*. It recounts, in blank verse adorned by *epic similes, the fatal outcome of Sohrab's search for his father Rustum, the leader of the Persian forces. Rustum (who believes his own child to be a girl) accepts the challenge of Sohrab, now leader of the Tartars: the two meet in single combat, at first unaware of one another's identity, which is confirmed only when Sohrab has been mortally wounded.

Soldan (from the Arabic *sultan*). The Soldan, or Souldan, in Spenser's *Faerie Queene* (v. viii) represents Philip II of Spain. He is encountered by Prince *Arthur and Sir *Artegall with a bold defiance from Queen *Mercilla (Elizabeth), and the combat is undecided until the prince unveils his shield and terrifies the Soldan's horses, so that they overturn his chariot and the Soldan is torn 'all to rags'. The unveiling of the shield signifies divine interposition.

Solinus, the duke of Ephesus in Shakespeare's *The Comedy of Errors*.

Solmes, a character in Richardson's *Clarissa*.

Solomon Daisy, in Dickens's *Barnaby Rudge*, the parish clerk and bell-ringer at Chigwell.

SOLON, (*c*.638–558 BC), the great Athenian legislator, celebrated for his wisdom. He was appointed archon in 594 BC, and relieved the prevalent distress by his famous ordinance cancelling outstanding debts (σεισάχθεια). He reformed the constitution, introducing some democratic features. The constitution that he set up was overthrown by Peisistratus. Solon was also a successful poet, who used elegy to stir the Athenians to war and also to convey moral instruction.

Solyman and Perseda, *The Tragedye of*, see KYD, T.

SOLZHENITSYN, Alexander Isayevich (1918–   ), Russian prose writer. Born in Kislovodsk in the Caucasus, the son of an army officer, he studied mathematics and physics at the University of Rostov-on-Don. He joined the Red Army in 1941. Arrested in 1945 for remarks critical of *Stalin, he was sent to a labour camp where in 1952 he developed stomach cancer. In 1953 he was released into 'administrative exile'. In 1956 he returned to Ryazan, in central Russia, to work as a teacher. His first published story, *One Day in the Life of Ivan Denisovich* (1962), caused a sensation through its honest and pioneering description of camp life. This was followed by *Matrena's House* (1963) and other stories. His major novels, *The Cancer Ward* (1968) and *The First Circle* (1969), which continue the basic Solzhenitsyn theme of men in extreme situations facing basic moral choices, could only be published abroad, and in late 1969 he was expelled from the Union of Soviet Writers. In 1970 he was awarded the *Nobel Prize for literature. The appearance abroad of the first volume of *The Gulag Archipelago* (1973–5), an epic 'history and geography' of the labour camps, caused the Soviet authorities to deport Solzhenitsyn to West Germany on 13 February 1974. He settled in the United States, where he continued a series of novels begun with *August 1914* (1971), offering an alternative picture of Soviet history.

Some Experiences of an Irish R.M., a collection of stories by *Somerville and Ross, published 1899.

This exuberant and skilful series of stories is narrated by Major Yeates, the resident magistrate, whose misfortune is to attract calamity. With his gallant wife Philippa, he lives at the centre of a vigorous and wily community as the tenant of a dilapidated demesne, Shreelane, which he rents from a well-to-do rogue, Flurry Knox, whose old mother lives in squalid splendour at neighbouring Aussolas, overrun with horses. Frequent rain, flowing drink, unruly hounds, and the eccentricities of the populace contribute to innumerable confusions involving collapsing carts, missed meals, sinking boats, shying horses, and outraged visitors. Yet few of the stories are merely farcical, and some have a sombre echo.

SOMERVILE, William (1675–1742), a country gentleman, is remembered as the author of *The Chace* (1735), a poem in four books of Miltonic blank verse on the pleasures of hunting which had a considerable success. In 1740 he published *Hobbinol*, a mock-heroic account of rural games in Gloucestershire (see COTSWOLD OLIMPICK GAMES), and in 1742 his 'Field Sports', a short poem on hawking, appeared. Dr *Johnson commented in *The Lives of the English Poets* that 'he writes very well for a gentleman'.

SOMERVILLE (Edith) **and ROSS** (Martin). Edith Oenone Somerville (1858–1949) and Violet Martin (1862–1915), were second cousins of Irish families who separately and together wrote some 30 books, mainly set in Ireland, as well as many articles, letters, diaries, and jottings. Their first collaboration, *An Irish Cousin* (1889), was well received. In their most sustained novel, *The Real Charlotte* (1894), Francie Fitzpatrick, a beautiful girl from Dublin, finds herself, on the estate of the wealthy Dysarts, becoming enmeshed with the malign Charlotte Mullen, who is jealous of the attention devoted to Francie by the flash estate manager Lambert. Francie, finding herself in love with a handsome English officer, discovers he is already engaged and marries Lambert, only to be killed riding her horse. In 1897 came *The Silver Fox*, their first book with hunting as a major theme, then *Some Experiences of an Irish R.M.* (1899). The international success of this book led in 1908 to *Further Experiences of an Irish R.M.* and in 1915 to the third of the series, *In Mr Knox's Country*. After Martin Ross's death Edith Somerville wrote another 13 books, the most notable of which was a historical romance, *The Big House at Inver* (1925).

SOMNER, William (1598–1669), antiquary, was author of *The Antiquities of Canterbury* (1640) and of a *Dictionarium Saxonico-Latino-Anglicum* (1659).

'Somnium Scipionis' (Dream of Scipio), is the fable with which *Cicero ends his *De Re*publica*. The only extant manuscript of Cicero's treatise breaks off early in the last book, and the survival of the *Somnium* is due to the accident of its being reproduced by a certain Macrobius, who in the 4th cent. AD furnished it with a *Neoplatonist commentary that interested medieval thinkers.

The fable relates how the younger Scipio saw his grandfather, the elder Scipio, in a dream and was shown the dwelling set aside in the Milky Way for those who follow virtue and especially for those who distinguish themselves in the service of their country. The *Somnium* may have inspired *Petrarch's choice of Scipio Africanus as the hero of his epic *Africa*. Since the fable expressed to perfection the humanist ideal of combining a quest for personal distinction with tranquillity of mind and patriotic effort, it attracted numerous editors during the Renaissance. Chaucer gives a poetical summary of it in *The Parliament of Fowls* and mentions it in other passages.

Song of Solomon, The, otherwise 'The Song of Songs', one of the poetical books of the OT, at one time attributed to King Solomon, now considered on linguistic grounds to be of later date, perhaps of the 4th or 3rd cent. BC. The allegorical interpretations of the work, which took it as an account of God's dealings with the Church or with the individual soul, have been generally abandoned, and it is widely accepted that its original character was erotic.

'Song of the Shirt, The', a poem by T. *Hood, originally published anonymously in *Punch* in 1843. One of Hood's best-known serious poems, it takes the form of a passionate protest by an overworked and underpaid seamstress—'It is not linen you're wearing out | But human creatures' lives.' The poem was a popular theme for illustration, and was treated by *Leech in *Punch* and by the painters Richard Redgrave (1844) and G. F. Watts (1850).

Songs of Experience, see SONGS OF INNOCENCE.

Songs of Innocence, a collection of poems written and etched by W. *Blake, published 1789. Most of the poems are about childhood, some of them written, with apparent simplicity, as if by children (e.g. 'Little lamb, who made thee?' and 'The Chimney Sweeper'); others commenting on the state of infancy ('The Ecchoing Green'); and yet others introducing the prophetic tone and personal imagery of Blake's later work ('The Little Girl Lost', 'The Little Girl Found').

In 1795 Blake issued a further volume, entitled *Songs of Innocence and of Experience: Shewing the Two Contrary States of the Human Soul*, to which he added the 'Songs of Experience', some of them (e.g. 'The Chimney Sweeper' and

'Nurse's Song') bearing identical titles to poems in the first collection, but replying to them in a tone that questions and offsets their simplicities, and manifests with great poetic economy Blake's profoundly original vision of the inter-dependence of good and evil, of energy and restraint, of desire and frustration. They range from fairly straightforward, if highly pro-vocative, attacks on unnatural restraint ('The Garden of Love', 'London') to the extraordinary lyric intensity of 'Infant Sorrow', 'Ah! Sun-Flower', and 'Tyger! Tyger!'

Song to David, A, see SMART, C.

Sonnet, a poem consisting of 14 lines (of 11 syllables in Italian, generally 12 in French, and 10 in English), with rhymes arranged according to one or other of certain definite schemes, of which the Petrarchan and the Elizabethan are the principal, viz.: (1) a b b a a b b a, followed by two, or three, other rhymes in the remaining six lines, with a pause in the thought after the octave (not always observed by English imi-tators, of whom *Milton and *Wordsworth are prominent examples); (2) a b a b c d c d e f e f g g. The *sonnets of Shakespeare are in the latter form.

The sonnet was introduced to England by *Wyatt and developed by *Surrey (see also under METRE) and was thereafter widely used, notably in the sonnet sequences of Shakespeare, *Sidney, *Daniel, *Spenser, and other poets of the *Golden period, most of which are amatory in nature, and contain a certain narrative development: later sonnet sequences on the theme of love include those of D. G. *Rossetti and E. B. *Browning. *Milton, *Donne, *Keats, and *Yeats have all used the form to great and varied effect, and it continues to flour-ish in the 20th cent.

Sonnets from the Portuguese, a sonnet-sequence by E. B. *Browning first published 1850; the so-called 'Reading Edition' of 1847 was a forgery by T. J. *Wise. It describes the growth and development of her love for Robert *Browning, at first hesitating to involve him in her sorrowful invalid life, then yielding to grad-ual conviction of his love for her, and finally rapturous in late-born happiness. The title, chosen to disguise the personal nature of the poems by suggesting that they were a trans-lation, was a secret reference for the Brownings to his nickname for her, 'the Portuguese', based on her poem 'Catarina to Camoens', which Browning particularly admired and which por-trayed a Portuguese woman's devotion to her poet lover.

Sonnets of Shakespeare, The, were printed in 1609 and probably date from the 1590s. In 1598 F. *Meres referred to Shakespeare's 'sugred Sonnets among his private friends', but these are not necessarily identical with the ones we now have. Most of them trace the course of the writer's affection for a young man of rank and beauty: the first 17 urge him to marry to reproduce his beauty, numbers 18 to 126 form a sequence of 108 sonnets, the same number as in Sidney's sequence *Astrophel and Stella. The complete sequence of 154 sonnets was issued by the publisher Thomas Thorpe in 1609 with a dedication to 'Mr W.H., the onlie begetter of these insuing sonnets'. Mr W.H. has been identified as (among others) William, Lord Her-bert, afterwards earl of Pembroke, or Henry Wriothesley, earl of Southampton, and further as the young man addressed in the sonnets. An-other view argues that Mr W.H. was a friend of Thorpe, through whose good offices the manu-script had reached his hands—'begetter' being used in the sense of 'getter' or 'procurer'. Other characters are alluded to in the sequence, in-cluding a mistress stolen by a friend (40–2), a rival poet (78–80 and 80–6), and a dark beauty loved by the author (127–52). Numerous identifications for all the 'characters' involved in the sequence, as well as for Mr W.H., have been put forward: none of them is certain. Perhaps the most ingenious and amusing of these is *Wilde's *The Portrait of Mr W.H.*

For the form of these poems see SONNET.

Sons and Lovers, by D. H. *Lawrence, pub-lished 1913, a closely autobiographical novel set in the Nottinghamshire coalmining village of Bestwood.

Walter Morel has married a sensitive and high-minded woman better educated than him-self. She begins to shrink from his lack of fine feeling and drunkenness; embittered, she turns their marriage into a battle. Morel, baffled and thwarted, is sometimes violent, while Mrs Morel rejects him and turns all her love towards her four children, particularly her two eldest sons, William and Paul. She struggles with the pov-erty and meanness of her surroundings to keep herself and her family 'respectable' and is de-termined that her boys will not become miners. William goes to London to work as a clerk, and Paul also gets a job as a clerk with Mr Jordon, manufacturer of surgical appliances; William de-velops pneumonia and dies. Mrs Morel, numbed by despair, is roused only when Paul also falls ill. She nurses him back to health, and subsequently their attachment deepens. Paul is friendly with the Leivers family of Willey Farm, and a tender-ness grows between him and the daughter Miriam, a soulful, shy girl. They read poetry together, and Paul instructs her in French and even algebra and shows her his sketches. Mrs Morel fears that Miriam will exclude her and tries to break up their relationship, while Paul, himself sickened at heart by Miriam's romantic love and fear of physical warmth, turns away and becomes involved with Clara Dawes, a married woman, separated from her husband Baxter, and a supporter of Women's Rights. Paul is made an overseer at the factory, times are easier, and he now begins to be noticed as a painter and designer. His affair with Clara peters out and she returns to her husband. Meanwhile Mrs Morel is ill with cancer and Paul is in misery at the thought of losing her. At last, unable to bear her suffering, he and his sister Annie put an overdose of morphia in her milk. Paul resists the urge to follow her 'into the darkness' and, with a great effort, turns towards life. *Sons and Lovers* was perhaps the first English novel with a truly working-class background, and certainly Lawrence's first major novel.

Sophia Western, the heroine of Fielding's *Tom Jones.

Sophism, a specious but fallacious argument, used either deliberately to mislead or to display ingenuity in reasoning.

Sophist, in ancient Greece, one who undertook to give instruction in intellectual and ethical matters in return for payment; contrasted with 'philosopher', and frequently used as a term of disparagement.

SOPHOCLES (496–406 BC), the best-liked (in his own day) of the three great Attic tragedians, and the first to increase the number of actors from two to three. Seven of his plays are extant, three of which deal with the unhappy Oedipus and his family. Sophocles has not the epic grandeur of *Aeschylus or *Euripides' radical fire, but he is excellent at drawing character and evoking pathos. His view of the universe is a matter over which scholars disagree. Man's fate depends on the gods, but do the gods share man's moral insights? Though T. *Watson produced a Latin translation of the *Antigone* in 1581, Milton's *Samson Agonistes* was the first work in English to bear the stamp of Sophocles, and it came before its time. *Dryden's *Oedipus* though seven years later is chiefly indebted to *Seneca. It was in the 19th cent. that Sophocles really came into favour. *Shelley read him on his last fatal sailing-trip. *Bulwer-Lytton adapted his *Oedipus the King* (1846). M. *Arnold produced his Sophoclean play *Merope* (1858) and two Sophoclean fragments, an *Antigone* (1849) and a *Dejaneira* (1867). *Swinburne introduced Sophoclean touches into his *Erechtheus* (1876); and during the first decade of the 20th cent. *Freud hit on the term 'Oedipus Complex' to describe certain features of infantile sexuality. This caught the public imagination and led to numerous translations and adaptations of the Theban plays.

Sophonisba, the daughter of Hasdrubal, a Carthaginian general, who avoided captivity by taking poison at the instigation of her betrothed Masinissa, was the subject of several plays,

notably by *Marston, N. *Lee, and James *Thomson. The notorious line 'Oh! Sophonisba, Sophonisba, Oh!' occurs in Thomson's version (1730), was altered to 'Oh Sophonisba, I am wholly thine' in later editions, and parodied by Fielding in *Tom Thumb* as 'O Huncamunca, Huncamunca O!'

Sophy Crewler, in Dickens's *David Copperfield*, 'the dearest girl in the world', whom Traddles marries.

Sorbonne, The, a theological college in Paris founded by Robert de Sorbon about 1257. The name was applied later to the faculty of theology in the old University of Paris, of great importance down to the 17th cent. The Sorbonne is now the seat of the University of Paris and of the faculties of science, literature, and the *hautes études*.

SORDELLO (*c*.1200–?69), a poet born near Mantua but whose political connection with Charles of Anjou, lord of Provence, kept him in Provence for much of his later life. He accordingly wrote 'troubadour' poetry in *Provençal and so became an important link between the love poetry of Provence and that of Italy which was descended from it. *Dante places him in the Ante-Purgatory where he acts as guide to Virgil and Dante, pointing out to them the valley of the Kings in *Purgatorio* vii, a role assigned to him perhaps because of his famous lament for the death of Blacatz. Ed. M. Boni (Bologna, 1954).

Sordello, a narrative poem in iambic pentameter couplets by R. *Browning, published 1840. The poem had taken seven years to complete, and was interrupted by the composition of *Paracelsus* and *Strafford*; Browning intended it to be more 'popular' than the former, but the poem was received with incomprehension and derision by the critics and the public, and its notorious 'obscurity' caused severe and prolonged damage to Browning's reputation. The *Pre-Raphaelites, for whom it became a cult text, were its first defenders, followed later by *Pound; it is now coming to be recognized as one of the finest long poems of the century, and of central importance in the interpretation of Browning's work, particularly its relation to the Romanticism on whose tenets it heavily relies and which, at the same time, it challenges and disputes. Its genuine difficulty springs from the swiftness and compression of the language, the convoluted time-scheme of the narrative, and the fusion of intense specificity (of historical detail, landscape, etc.) with the abstract ideas which form the core of the argument.

The narrative is set in Italy during the period of the Guelf–Ghibelline wars of the late 12th and 13th cents, and traces the 'development of a soul', that of the troubadour Sordello (above), along a path of self-realization where political, aesthetic, and metaphysical ideas reflect each other; all this in the framework of a plot strongly influenced by the elements of fairy-tale (lost heir, wicked stepmother, unattainable princess, etc.). The whole defies summary and demands re-reading.

SORLEY, Charles Hamilton (1895–1915), poet, educated at Marlborough; he spent a year in Germany before returning on the outbreak of war in 1914, when he was commissioned and served in the trenches in France where he was killed. He left only 37 complete poems; his posthumous collection, *Marlborough and Other Poems* (1916), was a popular and critical success in the 1920s, but his verse was then long neglected, despite the efforts of Robert *Graves (who considered him, with W. *Owen and *Rosenberg, 'one of the three poets of importance killed during the War') and of *Blunden. The best known of his poems include 'The Song of the Ungirt Runners', 'Barbury Camp', and the last, bitter 'When you see millions of the mouthless dead'. See *The Letters of Sorley*, ed. W. R. Sorley (1919) and *The Ungirt Runner* (1965) by T. B. Swann.

Sorrel, Hetty, a character in G. Eliot's *Adam Bede*.

Sosia, a character in Dryden's *Amphitryon*.

Soul's Tragedy, A, a play by R. *Browning, published 1846, together with *Luria*, as no. VIII of *Bells and Pomegranates*. Its subtitle—'Act First, being what was called the Poetry of Chiappino's life: and Act Second, its Prose'—indicates both the play's genre, tragi-comedy, and also its unusual form: the division (as opposed to mixture) of verse and prose represents Browning's idiosyncratic adaptation of Elizabethan and Jacobean models (see also PIPPA PASSES).

Chiappino, the 'hero', is a discontented liberal in 16th-cent. Faenza, who, at the climax of Act One, nobly (or egotistically?) takes on himself the punishment for the supposed assassination of the tyrannical Provost by his friend Luitolfo. He expects to be lynched by the Provost's guards, but is instead acclaimed by the people as their liberator, and is unable to resist the temptation of his new-found role. The Provost turns out not to have been killed after all and, just as Chiappino is about to become the new Provost himself, he is unmasked by the papal legate Ogniben, who has sardonically played up to his self-deceiving justification for seizing power. Ogniben, who had arrived in Faenza remarking that he had seen 'three-and-twenty leaders of revolts', utters the famous line 'I have seen *four*-and-twenty leaders of revolts!' as he watches Chiappino fleeing the town after his humiliation.

Sound and the Fury, The, a novel by W. *Faulkner.

SOUTAR, William (1898–1943), Scottish poet, born in Perth, the son of a master-joiner, and educated at Perth Academy. He served in the navy during the First World War, and contracted an illness which, after his subsequent studies at Edinburgh University, left him paralysed for the last 14 years of his life. He published several volumes of poetry from 1923 onwards; he wrote in both *Scots and English, though his Scots work is generally considered more significant. All his poems are short; they include lyrics, epigrams, riddles, pieces for children which he described as 'bairn-rhymes', and other short works which he called 'whig-maleeries'. Several of his poems sing the praises and frustrations of the lost heritage of 'the lawland tongue'. His *Collected Poems* (1948) has an introduction by *MacDiarmid, and his *Diaries of a Dying Man*, ed. A. Scott, were published in 1954.

South, Marty, a character in Hardy's *The Woodlanders*.

SOUTH, Robert (1634–1716), educated at Christ Church, Oxford, a court preacher favoured by Charles II. He was a witty, arresting, and often brutally sarcastic preacher, attacking Dissenters in particular. His *Animadversions* (1690) contain a crushing attack on W. *Sherlock.

SOUTHCOTT, Joanna (1750–1814), a religious fanatic and farmer's daughter who acquired a large following through her doggerel prophecies and supernatural claims.

SOUTHERNE, or **SOUTHERN,** Thomas (1659–1746), of Irish parentage, was educated at Trinity College, Dublin, but came to London in 1680 and settled there. He was a friend of *Dryden, for several of whose plays he wrote prologues and epilogues. His first tragedy, *The Loyal Brother: or the Persian Prince* (1682), was, like Otway's *Venice Preserv'd*, its immediate contemporary, an attack on *Shaftesbury and the Whigs. He wrote several comedies, but is chiefly remembered for his two highly successful tragedies, *The Fatal Marriage* (1694) and *Oroonoko* (1695), both founded on novels by A. *Behn. Remarkably little is known of his long and, in later years, unproductive life, though there are many affectionate references to his good nature by Dryden, *Swift, *Dennis, *Cibber, and other friends. He became known as the Nestor of poets, and William Broome in a letter to *Pope (1725/6), on being asked to supply a preface to one of his late works, commented 'His bays are withered with extreme age . . . It requires some skill to know when to leave off writing.' Southerne is regarded as a successor to *Otway in the art of pathos, and is a link between Restoration tragedy and the sentimental tragedies of the 18th cent. See J. W. Dodds, *Thomas Southerne, Dramatist* (1933).

SOUTHEY, Robert (1774–1843), was the son of a Bristol linen-draper, of a respectable Somerset family. Much of his lonely childhood was spent in the home of an eccentric aunt, Miss Tyler, where he acquired a precocious love of reading; he gives a vivid account of these years in letters written when he was 46 to his friend John May. He was expelled from Westminster School for originating a magazine, *The Flagellant*, and proceeded to Oxford with 'a heart full of poetry and feeling, a head full of Rousseau and Werther, and my religious principles shaken by Gibbon'. He became friendly with S. T. *Coleridge and together they planned their Pantisocratic society (see PANTISOCRACY). At Oxford he wrote a play, *Wat Tyler*, and another with Coleridge, *The Fall of Robespierre*. From this time on his literary output was prodigious. In 1795 he travelled to Portugal, married Elizabeth Fricker (Coleridge married her sister, Sara), and wrote *Joan of Arc* (1796). Between 1796 and 1798 he wrote many ballads, including *'The Inchcape Rock' and 'The Battle of *Blenheim', which had an influence in loosening the constrictions of 18th-cent. verse; he also produced one of his best-known poems, 'The Holly Tree'. In 1800 he went to Spain, and on his return settled in the Lake District, where he remained for the rest of his life as one of the *'Lake Poets'. A narrative poem, *Thalaba, appeared in 1801, but sold poorly. In 1803 he published a translation of *Amadis of Gaul* (revised from an older version); in 1805, *Madoc; and in 1807, the year in which he received a government pension, appeared a version of *Palmerin of England* and *Letters from England by Don Manuel Alvarez Espriella,* purporting to be from a young Spaniard and giving a lively account of life and manners in England. In 1808 he translated the *Chronicle of the Cid* and in 1809 began his long association with the *Quarterly Review*, which provided almost his only regular income for most of the rest of his life. A long poem, *The Curse of Kehama,* appeared in 1810 and *Omniana,* an original commonplace book, with contributions by Coleridge, in 1812. He was appointed in 1813 *poet laureate, a post which he came greatly to dislike, and in the same year published his short but admirable *Life of Nelson*. A narrative poem *Roderick; the Last of the Goths* appeared in 1814. In 1817 he produced an edition of *Malory and had to endure the publication, by his enemies, of his youthful and revolutionary *Wat Tyler*. The final volume of his *History of Brazil* (3 vols, 1810–19) appeared a year before his *Life of Wesley*. In 1821, to commemorate the death of George III, he wrote *A Vision of Judgement,* in the preface to which he vigorously attacked *Byron. Byron's

parody in riposte, *The Vision of Judgement,* appeared in 1822, and Southey is frequently mocked in *Don Juan.* From 1823 to 1832 Southey was working on his *History of the Peninsular War.* In 1824 appeared *The Book of the Church* and in 1825 *A Tale of Paraguay.* His *Sir Thomas More,* in which he converses with the ghost of More, came out in 1829. In the same year appeared *All for Love; and The Pilgrim to Compostella,* and in 1832 *Essays Moral and Political* and the last volume of *History of the Peninsular War* (1823–32), which was overshadowed by *Napier's work on the same subject. Between 1832 and 1837 he worked on a Life and an edition of *Cowper, and on his *Lives of the British Admirals* (1833). In 1835 he was granted a pension of £300 by Peel. His wife died in 1837, and in 1839 he married Caroline Bowles. *The Doctor, etc.* was begun in 1834 (7 vols, 1834–47). Southey's last years were marked by an increasing mental decline.

His longer poems, now little read, were admired by men as diverse as *Fox, Sir W. *Scott, and *Macaulay. The scope of his reading and of his writing was vast, and his clear, firm prose style has been much esteemed; but in no sphere was his work of the highest distinction. Although an honest, generous man (who was particularly kind to Coleridge's abandoned family), he incurred the enmity of many of his contemporaries, in particular *Hazlitt and Byron, who felt that in accepting pensions and the laureateship, and in retracting his youthful Jacobinism, he was betraying principles. In *Melincourt T. L. Peacock caricatures him as Mr Feathernest.

See J. Simmons, *Robert Southey* (1945); *New Letters of Robert Southey* (ed. K. Curry 1965); *Robert Southey: The Critical Heritage* (1972), ed. L. Madden. A selection of verse edited by G. *Grigson appeared in 1970; in the introduction Grigson argues that Southey's best poems belong to 1798–9.

South Sea Company, The, was formed in 1711 by *Harley (later earl of Oxford) to trade with Spanish America under the expected treaty with Spain. An exaggerated idea prevailed of the wealth to be acquired from the trading privileges granted by the Treaty of Utrecht and the Asiento Treaty, and money was readily invested in the Company. A bill was passed in 1720 by which persons to whom the nation owed money were enabled to convert their claims into shares in the Company, and the shares rose in value from £100 to £1,000. The Company shortly afterwards failed. But the scheme meanwhile had given rise to a fever of speculation, of which many unprincipled persons took advantage to obtain subscriptions from the public for the most impossible projects. The collapse of these and of the South Sea scheme caused widespread ruin. The whole affair was known as the South Sea

Bubble. But the original idea of the South Sea Company was a sound one for perfectly honest trade.

The South-Sea House, where the Company had its offices, is the subject of one of Lamb's *Essays of Elia*.

SOUTHWELL, St Robert (?1561–95), was educated by the Jesuits at Douai and Rome. He took Roman orders and came to England in 1586 with Henry Garnett (who was subsequently executed for complicity in the Gunpowder Plot). He became in 1589 domestic chaplain to the countess of Arundel, was captured when going to celebrate mass in 1592, repeatedly tortured, and executed after three years' imprisonment. His poems were mainly written in prison. Of these it was his object to make spiritual love, instead of 'unworthy affections', the subject. His chief work was *St Peters Complaint*, published 1595, a long narrative of the closing events of the life of Christ in the mouth of the repentant Peter, in which the spiritual is contrasted with the material by numerous comparisons and antitheses. He also wrote many shorter devotional poems (some of them collected under the title *Moeoniae*, 1595) of a high order, notably 'The Burning Babe', praised by *Jonson. He was beatified in 1929 and canonized in 1970. His poems were edited by J. H. McDonald and N. P. Brown (1967).

Sowdone of Babylon, The, see FERUMBRAS.

Sowerberry, in Dickens's *Oliver Twist*, an undertaker, to whom Oliver is apprenticed when he leaves the workhouse.

SOYINKA, Wole (1934–), Nigerian dramatist and probably Africa's most versatile author, educated at the Universities of Ibadan and Leeds. He was play reader at the Royal Court Theatre, London, where *The Swamp Dwellers* (1958), *The Lion and the Jewel* and *The Invention* (both 1959) were produced. These already demonstrated his development from simple Nigerian village comedies to a more complex and individual drama incorporating mime and dance. Back in Nigeria from 1960, a variety of university posts and the opportunity of producing and acting in his own plays gave him the self-confidence to undertake even more daring innovations, e.g. in *A Dance of the Forests* (1960), a half-satirical, half-fantastic celebration of Nigerian independence. Soyinka's first novel, *The Interpreters* (1965), captures the idealism of young Nigerians regarding the development of a new Africa—possibly anticipating a new Biafra. In prison for pro-Biafran activity during 1967–9, he produced increasingly bleak verse and prose, *Madmen and specialists* (1970), and his second novel, *Season of Anomy* (1973). A brighter period has followed. *Death and the King's Horseman* (1975), embodies his post-

Biafran cultural philosophy, enunciated in *Myth, Literature and the African World* (1976), of the need for the distinct aesthetics of Africa and Europe to cross-fertilize each other.

SPALDING, John (*fl.* 1650), of Aberdeen, a Scottish historian, author of a valuable history of the troubles in Scotland and England, 1624–45, first published in 1792 and re-edited in 1850 by J. Stuart for the Spalding Club, an antiquarian publishing society founded in his memory in 1839.

Spanish Bawd, The, see CELESTINA.

Spanish Curate, The, a comedy by J. *Fletcher, probably in collaboration with *Massinger, written and performed 1622, and based on *Gerardo, the Unfortunate Spaniard* (1622), translated from the Spanish of Cespedes by L. Digges. It was very popular after the Restoration.

The main plot deals with the intrigues of Don Henrique's mistress Violante, the failure of which leads to the reconciliation of Don Henrique with his divorced wife Jacinta and his brother Don Jamie; Violante is consigned to a nunnery. In the underplot, from which the play takes its name, Leandro, a rich young gentleman, plays on the cupidity of a priest and his sexton, and, with their help, on that of the lawyer Bartolus, the jealous husband of a beautiful wife, Amaranta, to facilitate his intrigue with her.

Spanish Fryar, The, a tragi-comedy by *Dryden, produced and published 1681.

The serious plot is characteristically about a usurpation. Torrismond, though he does not know it, is lawful heir to the throne, and secretly marries the reigning but unlawful queen, who has allowed Torrismond's father, the true king, to be murdered in prison. The sub-plot is dominated by Father Dominic, a monstrous corrupt friar, who uses the cant terms of Dissenters and who pimps for the libertine and whiggish Lorenzo. The latter is a highly dubious character, yet ironically it is through his agency that the lawful Torrismond is rescued. The woman Lorenzo is pursuing, however, turns out to be his sister. The play is like *Mr Limberham* in breaching comic as well as tragic decorum and in its deeply sceptical treatment of religious and political orthodoxies.

Spanish Gipsy, The, (1) a romantic comedy by T. *Middleton and others (1625); (2) a dramatic poem by G. *Eliot (1868).

Spanish Tragedy, The, a tragedy in blank verse by *Kyd, acted and printed 1592.

The political background of the play is the victory of Spain over Portugal in 1580. Lorenzo and Bel-imperia are the children of Don Cyprian, duke of Castile (brother of the king of Spain); Hieronimo is marshal of Spain and

Horatio his son. Balthazar, son of the viceroy of Portugal, has been captured in the war. He courts Bel-imperia, and Lorenzo and the king of Spain favour his suit for political reasons. Lorenzo and Balthazar discover that Bel-imperia loves Horatio; they surprise the couple by night in Hieronimo's garden and hang Horatio on a tree. Hieronimo discovers his son's body and runs mad with grief. He succeeds nevertheless in discovering the identity of the murderers, and carries out revenge by means of a play, *Solyman and Perseda*, in which Lorenzo and Balthazar are killed, and Bel-imperia stabs herself. Hieronimo bites out his tongue before running off stage to kill himself.

*Jonson is known to have been paid for additions to the play, but the additional passages in the 1602 edition do not seem Jonsonian. The play was one of Shakespeare's sources for *Hamlet* and the alternative title given to it in 1615, *Hieronimo is mad againe*, provided T. S. *Eliot with the penultimate line of *The Waste Land*.

SPARK, Muriel (1918–), author, of Scottish–Jewish descent, born and educated in Edinburgh. After spending some years in Central Africa, which was to form the setting for several of her short stories, including the title story of *The Go-Away Bird* (1958) and one of its other tales, 'The Seraph and the Zambesi', she returned to Britain where she worked for the Foreign Office during the Second World War. She began her literary career as editor and biographer, working for the *Poetry Society and editing its *Poetry Review* from 1947 to 1949; the problems of biography and autobiography form the subject of one of her recent novels, *Loitering with Intent* (1981). She turned to fiction after winning the *Observer* short story competition in 1951, and in 1954 became a Roman Catholic. Her first novel, *The Comforters* (1957), was followed by many others, including *Memento Mori* (1959), a comic and macabre study of old age; *The Ballad of Peckham Rye* (1960), a bizarre tale of the underworld, mixing shrewd social observation with hints of necromancy; perhaps her best-known work, *The Prime of Miss Jean Brodie* (1961), a disturbing portrait of an Edinburgh schoolmistress and her group of favoured pupils, her 'crème de la crème'; *The Girls of Slender Means* (1963), a tragi-comedy set in a Kensington hostel in 1945; *The Public Image* (1968); *The Driver's Seat* (1970), about a woman possessed by a death-wish; *The Abbess of Crewe* (1974), a satirical fantasy about ecclesiastical and other kinds of politics; and *The Take Over* (1976), set in Italy, where she settled. Her novels, with the exception of the lengthy and uncharacteristic *The Mandelbaum Gate* (1965), are short, elegant, eccentric, and sophisticated, with touches of the bizarre and the perverse; many have a quality of fable or

parable, and her use of narrative omniscience is highly distinctive. She has also written plays and poems; her *Collected Poems* and *Collected Plays* were both published in 1967.

Sparkish, a character in Wycherley's *The Country Wife*.

Sparkler, Edmund, a character in Dickens's *Little Dorrit*, who marries Fanny, Little Dorrit's sister.

Sparsit, Mrs, a character in Dickens's *Hard Times*.

Spasmodic School, a term applied by *Aytoun to a group of poets which included P. J. *Bailey, J. W. *Marston, S. *Dobell, and Alexander *Smith. Their works for a brief while enjoyed great esteem; this was largely destroyed by Aytoun's attacks and by his parody *Firmilian* (1854), which also satirized their critical champion, *Gilfillan. Spasmodic poems tended to describe intense interior psychological drama, were violent and verbose, and were characterized by obscurity, *pathetic fallacy, and extravagant imagery; their heroes (who owed much to *Byron and *Goethe) were lonely, aspiring, and disillusioned, and frequently poets themselves. See M. A. Weinstein, *W. E. Aytoun and the Spasmodic Controversy* (1968).

Specimens of English Dramatic Poets who lived about the time of Shakespeare, by C. *Lamb, published 1808; an anthology, with brief but cogent and illuminating critical comments, of extracts of scenes and speeches from Elizabethan and Jacobean dramatists, many of them little known or regarded in Lamb's day. His selections include extracts from *Beaumont and *Fletcher, *Jonson, *Marlowe, *Webster, and some dozen others. The book did much to draw the attention of Lamb's contemporaries to this period of drama, which Lamb himself greatly enjoyed 'beyond the diocese of strict conscience'.

SPCK, the Society for Promoting Christian Knowledge, was founded in 1698. One of its primary objects was the setting up of charitable schools for the instruction of poor children in reading, writing, and the catechism, with the addition of arithmetic for boys and sewing for girls. The Society is also a publishing agency for the dissemination of works of a Christian character.

Spectator, The, (1) a periodical conducted by *Steele and *Addison, from 1 March 1711 to 6 Dec. 1712. It was revived by Addison in 1714, when 80 numbers (556–635) were issued, but the first series has been generally considered superior, except by *Macaulay, who found the last volume to contain 'perhaps the finest Essays, both serious and playful, in the English language' (*Edinburgh Review*, July 1843). It appeared daily, and was immensely popular, particularly with the new growing middle-class readership. Addison and Steele were the principal contributors, in about equal proportions; other contributors included *Pope, *Tickell, *Budgell, A. *Philips, *Eusden, and Lady M. W. *Montagu.

It purported to be conducted (see the first two numbers) by a small club, including Sir Roger de *Coverley, who represents the country gentry, Sir Andrew Freeport, Captain Sentry, and Will Honeycomb, representing respectively commerce, the army, and the town. Mr Spectator himself, who writes the papers, is a man of travel and learning, who frequents London as an observer, but keeps clear of political strife. The papers are mainly concerned with manners, morals, and literature. Their object is 'to enliven morality with wit, and to temper wit with morality', and succeeding generations of readers endorsed E. *Young's view that the periodical (which succeeded *The Tatler) provided 'a wholesome and pleasant regimen'; both its style and its morals were considered exemplary by Dr *Johnson, H. *Blair, and other arbiters. There is a five-vol. edition by Donald F. Bond, published 1965.

(2) a weekly periodical started in 1828 by Robert Stephen Rintoul, with funds provided by Joseph Hume and others, as an organ of 'educated radicalism'. It supported Lord John Russell's *Reform Bill of 1831 with a demand for 'the Bill, the whole Bill, and nothing but the Bill'. R. H. *Hutton was joint editor, 1861–97. John St Loe Strachey (1860–1927) was editor and proprietor from 1898 to 1925, and his cousin Lytton *Strachey was a frequent contributor. Other notable contributors in later years include P. *Fleming, G. *Greene, E. *Waugh, L. A. G. *Strong, P. *Quennell, K. *Amis, Bernard Levin, Katharine Whitehorn, and Auberon Waugh.

Speculum Meditantis (*Mirour de l'Omme*), see GOWER, J.

Speculum Stultorum, see WIREKER, N.

SPEDDING, James (1808–81), educated at Trinity College, Cambridge, edited *The Works of Francis Bacon* (7 vols, 1857–9). His *Evenings with a Reviewer* (1848), was a refutation of *Macaulay's 'Essay' on *Bacon which he subsequently developed in his *The Letters and Life of Francis Bacon* (1861–72).

Speed, Valentine's servant in Shakespeare's *The Two Gentlemen of Verona.

SPEED, John (?1552–1629), historian and cartographer, made various maps of English counties, and was encouraged by *Camden, *Cotton, and others to write his *Historie of Great Britaine* (1611). The maps were far more valuable than the history; they began about 1607, and an atlas of them appeared in 1611.

There were several later editions of this (called *The Theatre of the Empire of Great Britain*), and the maps are now constantly detached and sold separately.

Speed the Plough, see MORTON, T.

SPEKE, John Hanning (1827–64), explorer, discovered Lake Victoria Nyanza, Lake Tanganyika, and gave information to Sir S. *Baker which led to the discovery of Lake Albert Nyanza. He published in 1863 his *Journal of the Discovery of the Source of the Nile* and in 1864 *What led to the Discovery of the Source of the Nile*.

SPENCE, Joseph (1699–1768), clergyman, anecdotist, scholar, succeeded T. *Warton as professor of poetry at Oxford in 1728. A man of much generosity, he befriended *Dodsley in his early days, and also S. *Duck, whose life he wrote (1731, reprinted with Duck's poems, 1736). He also wrote a life of the blind poet *Blacklock (1754). He was a close friend of *Pope, whose version of the *Odyssey* he defended, and from 1726 collected anecdotes and recorded conversations with Pope and other literary figures. These, although not published until 1820, were well known and widely quoted during the 18th cent., and were made available to and used by *Warburton and Dr *Johnson. They are usually referred to under the title *Spence's Anecdotes*: an edition by J. M. Osborn appeared in 1966 under the title *Observations, Anecdotes and Characters of Books and Men, Collected from Conversation*.

SPENCER, Herbert (1820–1903), the son of a schoolmaster, was largely self-taught and showed few intellectual interests until he was over 16. He worked as a civil engineer for the London and Birmingham Railway Company, and was discharged on its completion in 1841; he then turned his attention to philosophy and published *Social Statics* (1850) and *Principles of Psychology* (1855); in 1860, after reading C. *Darwin, he announced a systematic series of treatises, to the elaboration of which he devoted the remainder of his life: *First Principles* (1862), *Principles of Biology* (1864–7), *Principles of Sociology* (1876–96), and *Principles of Ethics* (1879–93). Among his other works were *Essays on Education* (1861), *The Classification of the Sciences* (1864), *The Study of Sociology* (1873), *Man versus the State* (1884), and *Factors of Organic Evolution* (1887). His *Autobiography* was published in 1904.

Spencer was the founder of evolutionary philosophy, pursuing the unification of all knowledge on the basis of a single all-pervading principle, that of evolution, which he defines as follows: 'an integration of matter and concomitant dissipation of emotion; during which matter passes from an indefinite incoherent homogeneity to a definite coherent heterogeneity; and during which the retained motion undergoes a parallel transformation'. The process continues until equilibrium is reached, after which the action of the environment will in time bring about disintegration. The law holds good of the visible universe as well as of smaller aggregates, suggesting the conception of past and future evolutions such as that which is now proceeding.

This theory of a physical system leads up to Spencer's ethical system, where he is less successful in producing a consistent whole. He was essentially an individualist, and his first ethical principle is the equal right of every individual to act as he likes, so long as he does not interfere with the liberty of others. His effort is to reconcile utilitarian with evolutionary ethics, but he had to confess that for the purpose of deducing ethical principles 'the Doctrine of Evolution has not furnished guidance to the extent that I had hoped.' Special reference should be made to *Education, Intellectual, Moral and Physical* (1861), a collection of articles previously published in magazines in which he criticized standard methods of teaching Latin and Greek, which crushed the spirit of individual enquiry, and advocated the teaching of the sciences, including social sciences, because they were concerned with the problems of survival. Art, although it had no problem-solving power, was important because it yielded immediate good.

In a literary context Spencer is remembered for his friendship with G. *Eliot, whom he met in 1851; he found her 'the most admirable woman, mentally, I have ever met' and wrote to *Lewes praising *Middlemarch highly, but after her death he was at pains to quell any rumour that they had ever been more than friends. She appears to have been much more strongly attached to him, but transferred her affections to Lewes (c.1852–3). Spencer died a bachelor.

Spence's Anecdotes, see SPENCE, J.

SPENDER, Sir Stephen Harold (1909–   ), poet and critic. His father, E. H. Spender, was a distinguished liberal journalist, and on his mother's side he was partly of German-Jewish descent. He was brought up in Hampstead, and educated at University College School, London, and University College, Oxford, where he became friendly with *Auden and *MacNeice and met *Isherwood. After leaving Oxford he lived in Germany for a period, in Hamburg and near Isherwood in Berlin, an experience which sharpened his political consciousness. In 1930 a small collection of his verse, *Twenty Poems*, was published, and in 1932 some of his work appeared in *New Signatures*; his *Poems* (1933) contained both personal and political poems, including 'I think continually of those who are truly great', 'The Landscape near an Aerodrome', and the notorious 'The Pylons', which gave the nickname of *'Pylon poets' to himself and his friends. He also published a critical work, *The Destructive Element* (1935), largely on H. *James, T. S. *Eliot, and *Yeats and their differing responses to a civilization in decline, which ends with a section called 'In Defence of a Political Subject', in which he discusses the work of Auden and *Upward, and argues the importance of treating 'politico-moral' subjects in literature. During the Spanish Civil War he did propaganda work in Spain for the Republican side, a period reflected in his volume of poems *The Still Centre* (1939). During the Second World War he was a member of the National Fire Service. He was co-editor of *Horizon* (1939–41) and of *Encounter* (1953–67). A gradual shift in his political allegiances may be seen in his poetry, in his critical works (e.g. *The Creative Element*, 1953, which retracts some of his earlier suggestions, laying more stress on the creative power and resistance of the individual), and in his contribution to *The God that Failed*; he also gives an account of his relationship with the Communist Party in his autobiography *World Within World* (1951). His interest in the public and social role and duty of the writer (a duty which he subsequently maintained in his work for the magazine *Index on Censorship*) has tended to obscure the essentially personal and private nature of much of his own poetry, including his elegies for his sister-in-law, in *Poems of Dedication* (1947), and many of the poems in such later volumes as *Collected Poems 1928–1953* (1955). His other works include *Trial of a Judge* (1938), many translations (of *García Lorca, *Rilke, *Schiller, *Toller, and others), *The Thirties and After* (1978, a volume of memoirs), and *Chinese Journal* (1982, an account of a journey taken with and illustrated by David Hockney).

Spenlow, Dora, in Dickens's *David Copperfield*, the hero's 'child-wife'.

Spenlow and Jorkins, in Dickens's *David Copperfield*, a firm of proctors in Doctors' Commons, to whom Copperfield is articled. Jorkins is a gentle, retiring man who seldom appears, but Spenlow makes his partner's supposed intractable character the ground for refusing any inconvenient request.

Spens, Sir Patrick, see SIR PATRICK SPENS.

SPENSER, Edmund (c.1552–99), was the elder son of John Spenser, who was probably related to the Spencers of Althorp, and was described as a journeyman in the art of cloth-making. Edmund Spenser was probably born in East Smithfield, London, and was educated at *Merchant Taylors' School, under *Mulcaster, and Pembroke Hall, Cambridge. In 1569, while still at Cambridge, he contributed a number of 'Visions' and sonnets, from *Petrarch and *Du Bellay, to van der Noodt's *Theatre for Worldlings*. To the 'greener times' of his youth belong also the 'Hymne in Honour of Love' and that of 'Beautie' (not published until 1596), which reflect his study of *Neoplatonism. After possibly spending some time in the north, he became secretary to John Young, bishop of Rochester, in 1578, and in 1579, through his college friend G. *Harvey, obtained a place in Leicester's household. There he became acquainted with Sir P. *Sidney, to whom he dedicated his *Shepheardes Calender* (1579). He probably married Machabyas Chylde in the same year, and also began to write *The Faerie Queene*. In 1580 he was appointed secretary to Lord Grey of Wilton, then going to Ireland as lord deputy. In 1588 or 1589 he became one of the 'undertakers' for the settlement of Munster, and acquired Kilcolman Castle in Co. Cork. Here he settled and occupied himself with literary work, writing his elegy *'Astrophel', on Sidney, and preparing *The Faerie Queene* for the presss. The first three books of it were entrusted to the publisher during his visit to London in 1589. He returned reluctantly to Kilcolman, which he liked to regard as a place of exile, in 1591, recording his visit to London and return to Ireland in *Colin Clouts come home againe* (printed 1595). The success of *The Faerie Queene* led the publisher, Ponsonby, to issue his minor verse and juvenilia, in part rewritten, as *Complaints, Containing sundrie small Poemes of the Worlds Vanitie* (1591). This volume included *'The Ruines of Time', which was a further elegy on Sidney, dedicated to Sidney's sister, the countess of *Pembroke, *'Mother Hubberds Tale', *'Muiopotmos', *'The Teares of the Muses', and *'Virgils Gnat'. Also in 1591 *Daphnaïda* was published, an elegy on Douglas Howard, daughter of Lord Byndon and wife of Sir A. *Gorges. In 1594 he married Elizabeth Boyle, whom he had wooed in his *Amoretti*, and celebrated the marriage in his superb *Epithalamion*: the works were printed together in 1595. He published Books IV–VI of *The Faerie Queene* and his *Fowre Hymnes* in 1596, being in London for the purpose at the house of his friend the earl of Essex, where he wrote his *Prothalamion* and also his well-informed though propagandist *View of the Present State of Ireland*. He returned to Ireland, depressed both in mind and health, in 1596 or 1597. His castle of Kilcolman was burnt in October 1598, in a sudden insurrection of the natives, chiefly O'Neills, under the earl of Desmond; he was compelled to flee to Cork with his wife and three children. We do not know what works, if any, were lost at Kilcolman, but Ponsonby in 1591 had mentioned various other works by Spenser which are not now extant, and in *The Shepheardes Calender* reference is made to his discourse of the 'English Poet'. He died in London in distress, if not actual destitution, at a lodging in King St, Westminster. His funeral expenses were borne by the earl of Essex, and he was buried near his favourite *Chaucer in Westminster Abbey. His monument, set up some 20 years later by Lady Anne Clifford, describes him as 'THE PRINCE OF POETS IN HIS TYME': there have been few later periods in which he has not been admired, and the poetry of both *Milton and *Keats had its origins in the reading of Spenser.

See the Variorum edn of his works, with a biography and full critical commentary, ed. E. Greenlaw, C. G. Osgood, F. M. Padelford, *et al.* (10 vols, 1932–57).

Spenserian stanza, the stanza invented by E. *Spenser, in which he wrote *The Faerie Queene*. It consists of eight five-foot iambic lines, followed by an iambic line of six feet, rhyming a b a b b c b c c.

SPINOZA, Benedict (Baruch) de (1632–77), a Jew of Portuguese origin, born at Amsterdam, who lived there and at The Hague. He was expelled from the Jewish community on account of his criticism of the Scriptures. The principal source of his philosophy was the doctrine of *Descartes, transformed by a mind steeped in the Jewish Scriptures. Spinoza rejected the Cartesian dualism of spirit and matter, and saw only 'one infinite substance, of which finite existences are modes or limitations'. The universe must be viewed 'sub specie aeternitatis', and the errors of sense and the illusions of the finite eliminated. God for him is the immanent cause of the universe, not a ruler outside it. 'By the government of God, I understand the fixed and unalterable order of nature and the interconnection of natural things.' His system is thus in a sense pantheistic. Among his conclusions are determinism, a denial of the transcendent distinction between good and evil, and a denial of personal immortality.

Spinoza's famous *Ethics*, finished about 1665, was not published until 1677, after his death. His morality is founded on the 'intellectual love' of God. Man is moved by his instinct to develop and perfect himself, and to seek this development in the knowledge and love of God. And the love of God involves the love of our fellow creatures. It is by goodness and piety that man reaches perfect happiness: virtue is its own reward.

Spinoza founds his political doctrine on man's natural rights. Man, in order to obtain security, has surrendered part of his rights to the State. But the State exists to give liberty, not to hold in slavery. The sovereign in his own interest must rule with justice and wisdom, nor must the State interfere with freedom of thought. Spinoza's *Tractatus Theologico-politicus* was published in 1670; his unfinished *Tractatus Politicus* in 1677.

Spirit of the Age, The, essays by W. *Hazlitt, published 1825.

The essays are on the work and characters of a selection of Hazlitt's contemporaries, such as *Coleridge, *Wordsworth, and *Lamb, and of writers of the previous half-century. In most cases an incisive character sketch of each writer is interwoven with a discussion of his writing. The essays are written with great conviction, as if intended as a summation, and are generally considered to represent Hazlitt at the height of his powers as writer and critic.

Spiritual Exercises, see LOYOLA.

Spiritual Quixote, The, see GRAVES, RICHARD.

Spleen, The, (1) a poem by Anne Finch, countess of *Winchelsea (1709); (2) a poem by M. *Green (1737).

Splendid Shilling, The, see PHILIPS, J.

Spondee, see METRE.

Sponge, Mr Soapy, see SURTEES, R. S.

Spoonerism, see METATHESIS.

Sport of My Mad Mother, The, a play by A. *Jellicoe.

Sporus, the name under which *Pope satirizes Lord *Hervey in his *Epistle to Dr Arbuthnot* (ll. 305 ff.). The original Sporus was an effeminate favourite of the Emperor Nero.

SPRAT, Thomas (1635–1713), educated at Wadham College, Oxford, was bishop of Rochester and dean of Westminster. Politically he was inclined to be a 'Vicar of Bray'; he sat on James II's objectionable Ecclesiastical Commission in 1686 and allowed the Declaration of Indulgence to be read (amid deep murmurs of disapproval) in the abbey. As a writer he is chiefly remembered for his history of the *Royal Society (1667), of which he was one of the first members, but he was also known as a poet (*The Plague of Athens,* 1659, was his most popular poem) and for his life of his friend *Cowley, which was attached to Cowley's works from 1668 onwards.

SPRING, (Robert) Howard (1889–1968), journalist and novelist, born in Cardiff, where he began his literary career as a newspaper errand boy; he worked for years on the *Manchester Guardian* and as book reviewer on the *Evening Standard.* Of his many novels, the best remembered are his first success *O Absalom!* (1938; published in the US and later in Britain as *My son, my son!*) and *Fame is the Spur* (1940), the latter being the story of a Labour politician's rise to power.

Springrove, Edward, a character in Hardy's *Desperate Remedies.*

Sprung rhythm (or 'abrupt' rhythm), a term invented by G. M. *Hopkins to describe his own idiosyncratic poetic metre, as opposed to normal 'running' rhythm, the regular alternation of stressed and unstressed syllables. It was apparently based partly on Greek and Latin quantitative metre and influenced by the rhythms of Welsh poetry and Old and Middle English *Alliterative verse. Hopkins maintained that sprung rhythm existed, unrecognized, in Old English poetry and in *Shakespeare, *Dryden, and *Milton (notably in *Samson Agonistes*). It is distinguished by a metrical foot consisting of a varying number of syllables. The extra, 'slack' syllables added to the established patterns are called 'outrides' or 'hangers'. Hopkins demonstrated the natural occurrence of this rhythm in English by pointing out that many nursery rhymes employed it, e.g.

Díng, Dóng, Béll,
Pússy's in the wéll.

Conventional metres may be varied by the use of 'counterpoint', by which Hopkins meant the reversal of two successive feet in an otherwise regular line of poetry; but sprung rhythm itself cannot be counterpointed because it is not regular enough for the pattern to be recognized under the variations. Hopkins, an amateur composer, often described his theory in terms of musical notation, speaking of rests, crotchets, and quavers. He felt strongly that his poetry should be read aloud, but seems to have felt that the words themselves were not enough to suggest the intended rhythms, and frequently added various diacritical markings to indicate where a sound was to be drawn out, and where syllables were to be spoken quickly. Some critics have suggested that sprung rhythm is not a poetic metre at all, properly speaking, merely Hopkins's attempt to force his own personal rhythm into an existing pattern, or recognizable variation of one, and that his sprung rhythm is in fact closer to some kinds of free verse or polyphonic prose.

SPURGEON, Caroline (1886–1942), American critic, whose *Shakespeare's Imagery* (1935) was the first detailed study of its subject.

Spurio, a character in *The Revenger's Tragedy.*

Square, a character in Fielding's *Tom Jones.*

Squeers, Wackford, in Dickens's *Nicholas Nickleby,* the headmaster of Dotheboys Hall. He has a heartless wife, who joins him in bullying his miserable pupils, a spiteful daughter, Fanny, and a spoilt son, Wackford.

Squeezum, Justice, a character in *Fielding's *Rape upon Rape.*

SQUIRE, J(ohn) C(ollings) (1884–1958), educated in Devon and at St John's College, Cambridge; he became a highly influential literary journalist and essayist, a skilful parodist, and a poet. He established the *London Mercury* in 1919, and as sometime literary editor of the *New Statesman* and chief literary critic of the *Observer* he exercised considerable power. In the 1920s and 1930s he and his friends formed a literary establishment which was violently opposed by the *Sitwells and the *Bloomsbury group, and was irreverently known as 'the Squirearchy'. Squire edited a large number of successful anthologies, including *A Book of Women's Verse* (1921) and *The Comic Muse* (1925), and between 1921 and 1934 edited three widely popular volumes of *Selections from Modern Poets*. His own *Collected Parodies* appeared in 1921, he was knighted in 1933, and his *Collected Poems*, edited by *Betjeman, were published posthumously in 1959.

Squire of Dames, a humorous character in Spenser's *Faerie Queene* (III. vii). He had been ordered by his lady to 'do service unto gentle Dames' and at the end of twelve months to report progress. At the end of the year he was able to bring pledges of 300 conquests. Thereupon his lady ordered him not to return to her till he had found an equal number of dames who rejected his advances. After three years he had only found three, a courtesan because he would not pay her enough, a nun because she could not trust his discretion, and a 'Damzell' of low degree 'in a countrey cottage found by chaunce'.

Squire of Low Degree, The, a metrical romance, probably mid-15th cent., opening with the much-quoted distich:

It was a squier of lowe degree
That loved the Kings doughter of Hungré.

The squire declares his love to the princess, who consents to marry him when he has proved himself a distinguished knight. But he is seen in his tryst by a steward whom he kills after the steward reports to the king. The squire is imprisoned but finally released because the princess is inconsolable, whereupon he sets out on his quest, proves his worth, and marries the princess. There is no manuscript of the full-length, 1,131-line version, so the romance is known from a printing c.1560 by W. Copland and fragments of a 1520 printing by *Wynkyn de Worde; Wynkyn's edition is dramatically entitled 'Undo youre Dore' from one of its episodes. Ed. D. B. Sands, *Middle English Verse Romances* (1966), pp. 249–78.

'Squire's Tale, The', see CANTERBURY TALES, II.

Squyre Meldrum, *The Historie of,* see LINDSAY, SIR D.

STACPOOLE, H(enry) de Vere (1863–1931), novelist and ship's doctor, of Irish ancestry, whose first publication was a poem in *Belgravia*, but who is remembered for his best-selling romance *The Blue Lagoon* (1908), the story of two cousins, Dick and Emmeline, marooned at the age of eight on a tropical island; they grow up, mature, produce a baby, and are eventually swept away by accident across their lagoon to the ocean and the oblivion of 'the never-wake berries' which they providentially carry with them in their dinghy.

STAËL, Anne-Louise-Germaine Necker, Mme de (1766–1817), French writer. Daughter of the finance minister Necker and mistress of *Constant, she occupied a central place in French intellectual life for over three decades. Her critical study *De la littérature considérée dans ses rapports avec les institutions sociales* (1800) was the first piece of criticism to treat literature as a product of social history and environment. Another study, *De l'Allemagne* (1810), banned on publication by Napoleon, opened French literature to the influence of the German writers and thinkers of the end of the 18th cent. Her two novels, *Delphine* (1802) and *Corinne* (1807), offer to her age a new image of woman. She was a major precursor of French Romanticism.

Stagirite, or **Stagyrite, The,** see ARISTOTLE.

STALIN, Iosif Vissarionovich (I. V. Djugashvili) (1879–1953), ruler of the Soviet Union from the death of *Lenin until his own. A minor member of the Leninist wing of the Russian Social Democratic Party before 1917, he became General Secretary of the Central Committee in 1922, and used this position to oust his rivals after Lenin's death. His main policies as ruler included the forced collectivization of agriculture, rapid expansion of heavy industry, mass terror, including a vast system of concentration camps, patriotism in official propaganda instead of the earlier Communist internationalism, and in his last years xenophobia and anti-Semitism. During his rule literature and the arts were reduced to a position of ever greater servility and abjection through the doctrine of *socialist realism, propagated at the first Congress of the Union of Soviet Writers in 1934, and through the cultural repression reintroduced after the Second World War by his cultural spokesman Andrei Zhdanov (1888–1948). Countless artists perished physically in the purges. Paradoxically, however, Stalin affected a great interest in the arts (many major artists corresponded with him) and personally intervened in the careers of many of them, notably *Bulgakov, *Pasternak ('Do not touch this cloud-dweller'), and *Shostakovich. There is a savage portrait of Stalin, patron of the arts, in *Solzhenitsyn's *The First Circle*.

Stalky & Co., tales of schoolboy life, by **Kipling.

Stand, a literary quarterly founded in 1952 by J. *Silkin, and published from 1965 in Newcastle upon Tyne. It publishes poetry, fiction, and criticism, and contributors have included G. *Hill, G. *MacBeth, Lorna Tracy (also a co-editor), D. *Abse, and many others; it has also published many works in translation by M. Holub (Czechoslovakia), N. Hikmet (Turkey), Brodsky and Yevtushenko (USSR), etc. An anthology, *Poetry of the Committed Individual,* appeared in 1973.

STANFORD, Sir Charles Villiers (1852–1924), British composer and teacher. With *Parry, Stanford was a founder figure of the English musical renaissance in the last decades of the 19th cent.: though his influence as a teacher may have been the most important aspect of his career (his pupils included virtually all the most successful English composers of the following generation, from *Holst and *Vaughan Williams to *Lambert and *Bliss), his list of compositions is long and includes many settings of English texts. Of the choral works the larger ones, like the oratorio *Eden* to words by *Bridges (1891), are now forgotten, but the less pretentious examples, the setting of *Tennyson's 'The Revenge' (1886) or the later *Newbolt cantatas, *Songs of the Sea* (1904) and *Songs of the Fleet* (1910), combine perfect craftsmanship with a racy vigour that has commended them to festivals and choral societies over the years. His nine operas have had little success, with the possible exception of *Shamus O'Brien* (1896, with a text after *Le Fanu); others that perhaps deserved a better fate are *Much Ado About Nothing* (1901), *The Critic* (based on *Sheridan's play, 1916), and, perhaps best, *The Travelling Companion* (1926), with a libretto by Newbolt after H. C. *Anderson. There are many songs and part-songs, often of considerable beauty, which are still occasionally heard.

STANHOPE, Lady Hester (1776–1839), was the niece of the younger *Pitt, in whose house she gained a reputation as a brilliant political hostess. In 1810 she left Europe for good, and in 1814 established herself for the rest of her life in a remote ruined convent at Djoun in the Lebanon. Here she lived in great magnificence among a semi-oriental retinue; her high rank and imperious character gained her some political power in Syria and the desert. In later years her debts accumulated, her eccentricity increased, and she claimed to be an inspired prophetess and mistress of occult sciences. She became a legendary figure, and was visited by many distinguished European travellers, including *Lamartine and *Kinglake.

Stanhope Press, an iron printing-press invented by Charles, third earl Stanhope (1753–1816), the husband of Lady Hester (above). He also devised a stereotyping process, and a microscopic lens which bears his name.

STANLEY, Arthur Penrhyn (1815–81), was educated at Rugby under T. *Arnold (by whom he was much influenced) and at Balliol College, Oxford. On Arnold's death he was commissioned to write a biography by his widow, which appeared in 1844 as *The Life and Correspondence of Thomas Arnold.* Stanley was an ecclesiastical historian, a leader of the *Broad Church movement, and a courageous champion of religious toleration.

STANLEY, Sir Henry Morton (1841–1904), explorer and journalist, born in Wales; he first bore the name John Rowlands. He went to New Orleans as a cabin boy in 1859 where he was adopted by a merchant named Stanley. He fought in the American Civil War and in 1867 joined the *New York Herald.* He went as its correspondent to Abyssinia and Spain, and in 1869 was instructed by his editor Gordon Bennett to find *Livingstone. He first travelled through Egypt for the opening of the Suez Canal, and to Palestine, Turkey, Persia, and India; he found Livingstone at Ujiji in 1871. *How I found Livingstone* (1872) relates these adventures. His further explorations and discoveries in Africa are described in *Through the Dark Continent* (1878) and *In Darkest Africa* (1890). In 1890 he married Dorothy Tennant who edited his autobiography in 1909.

STANLEY, Thomas (1625–78), a descendant of Edward Stanley, third earl of Derby, educated at Pembroke Hall, Cambridge, was author of *The History of Philosophy* (1655–62), an edition of *Aeschylus (1663), and translations from *Theocritus, *Bion, *Ausonius, *Moschus, *Marino, and others, besides original poems.

Stanzaic Life of Christ, The, a 14th-cent. compilation surviving in three 15th-cent. MSS in 10,840 lines of English quatrains, drawn from the *Polychronicon* of *Higden and the *Legenda Aurea* of Jacobus de Voragine (see GOLDEN LEGEND). It was written by a monk of St Werburgh's, Chester, and it was an influence on the Chester *Mystery Plays. Ed. F. A. Foster (EETS os, 166, 1926).

STAPLEDON, Olaf, see SCIENCE FICTION.

Staple of News, The, a comedy by *Jonson, performed 1626, printed 1631.

Pennyboy Junior learns from a beggar, whom he takes on as a servant, that his father has died. He begins to squander his inheritance, buying gaudy clothes, pursuing the rich Lady Pecunia, his miserly uncle's ward, and purchasing a clerkship for his barber at the Staple of News, an office for the collection, sorting, and dissemination of news and gossip, 'authentical and apocryphal'. The beggar reveals that he is Pennyboy's father, and, appalled by his extravagance, disinherits him, but Pennyboy redeems himself, and wins the hand of Lady Pecunia, when he thwarts a plot to ruin his father hatched by the scheming lawyer Picklock. The play is watched throughout by four gossips, Mirth, Tattle, Expectation, and Censure, who sit on the stage and offer an undiscerning commentary at the end of each act.

Stareleigh, Mr Justice, in Dickens's *Pickwick Papers,* the judge in the case of Bardell v. Pickwick.

STARK, Freya (1893–), daughter of a sculptor, was born in Paris, spent her childhood between Devonshire and Italy, and was educated at Bedford College and the School of Oriental Studies, London. In 1927, having mastered Arabic, she began travelling in the Middle East, and in the next decade made adventurous solitary journeys in Luristan, Iran, and the Hadhramaut. During the Second World War she worked for the Ministry of Information in Aden, Cairo, Baghdad, the USA, and India. In 1947 she married the writer Stewart Perowne. Throughout her wanderings her home base was Italy, and she settled in Asolo. She was made a DBE in 1972.
Among her many books on her travels in Iran, Iraq, southern Arabia, and Asia Minor, the most notable are *The Valleys of the Assassins* (1934), *The Southern Gates of Arabia* (1936), *Iona: A Quest* (1954), *The Lycian Shore* (1956). Four volumes of autobiography, including *Traveller's Prelude* (1950), and six volumes of letters appeared in 1950–61 and 1974–81. Her books reveal her as a natural traveller, disregarding discomforts and dangers in spite of poor health, with an unassuming friendliness and curiosity which make her observant and humane descriptions of the life of remote communities memorably lifelike. Her knowledge of classical Arabic and Greek literature gives backbone to her accounts of Middle East travel. Her later works are sometimes diffuse and sententious, without the unaffected charm of her pre-war books. A brilliant photographer, she illustrates her books with portraits of human and architectural splendours and oddities.

STARKE, Mariana, see GRAND TOUR and MURRAY, JOHN.

Starveling, in Shakespeare's *A Midsummer Night's Dream,* a tailor, who is cast for the part of 'Thisby's mother' in the play of 'Pyramus and Thisbe', but appears as 'Moonshine'.

Statesman, The, see TAYLOR, SIR H.

State Trials, a series of reports of important cases in British law, begun by Thomas Salmon in 1719, and repeatedly enlarged.

Stationers' Company, The, was incorporated by royal charter in 1557. No one not a member of the Company might print anything for sale in the kingdom unless authorized by special privilege or patent. Moreover, by the rules of the Company, every member was required to enter in the register of the Company the name of any book that he desired to print, so that these registers furnish valuable information regarding printed matter during the latter part of the 16th cent. The Company's control of the printing trade waned during the 17th cent., to be revived in a modified form under the Copyright Act of 1709. (See Appendix II.)

Statira, see RIVAL QUEENS, THE.

STATIUS, Publius Papinius (AD *c.*45–96), Roman epic poet and Silver Age imitator of *Virgil. The son of a Naples schoolmaster, he made a name for himself winning poetic competitions at an early age. Encouraged by success, he went to Rome, collected rich patrons, and with fulsome flattery won, but failed to keep, the favour of the tyrant Domitian. His surviving works consist of the five books of his *Silvae,* occasional verses which include a famous piece on sleep that inspired *Drummond of Hawthornden, an epic, *Thebais,* in 12 books, relating the bloody quarrel between the sons of Oedipus, and another unfinished epic, the *Achilleis.* Statius' style is mannered and over-ornamental, and his narratives abound in crudely romantic features: magicians, dragons, parted lovers, enchanted woods. These qualities recommended him to medieval taste, and so did the legend of his conversion to Christianity which appears in *Dante. Chaucer based his 'Knight's Tale' (*Canterbury Tales,* 1) on *Boccaccio who had used the *Thebais,* but in the Renaissance Statius was studied rather than imitated. The *Thebais* was not translated till 1648 when Thomas Stephens produced a version of the first five books. The *Achilleis* by Robert Howard appeared in 1660. But although both *Pope and *Gray tried their hands briefly at translating the *Thebais,* it is obvious that Statius had little to offer *Augustan England. *Dryden deplored his 'bladdered greatness: he never thought an expression bold enough if a bolder could be found.'

Staunton, Sir George, alias George Robertson, in Scott's *The Heart of Midlothian,* the lover, and subsequently husband, of Effie Deans.

Staying On, see SCOTT, P.

STEAD, Christina Ellen (1902–83), Australian novelist, born in Sydney and educated at Sydney University Teacher's College. She came to London in 1928 and subsequently worked and travelled in Europe and America with her companion, then husband, the American political economist and ex-broker William J. Blake. In 1953 they settled near London; she returned to Australia on his death in 1968. Her wandering life and her left-wing views (which also raised difficulties for her in Hollywood during the McCarthy period) may have contributed to the neglect of her work, which towards the end of her life received renewed attention and admiration. Her first collection of stories, *The Salzburg Tales* (1934), was followed by several full-length novels, which include her best-known work, *The Man who loved Children* (1940), a bitterly ironic view of American family life and conflict; *For Love Alone* (1945), in which Teresa escapes to Australia to seek her own freedom; *Letty Fox: Her Luck* (1946), a first-person narration describing the adventurous, unconventional and ambitious life of a New York office girl; and *Cotter's England* (1967; US as *Dark Places of the Heart*, 1966) which presents a vivid portrait of post-war working-class Britain, centred on the extraordinary personality of chain-smoking, emotional, destructive Nellie Cook, *née* Cotter, a 'beaky, restless, gabby' and insatiably curious journalist, working on a left-wing London paper. Many of the novels manifest the author's admiration for *Zola, and her feminism and politics are deeply interwoven, independent, and personal.

STEAD, W(illiam) T(homas) (1849–1912), was assistant editor of the *Pall Mall Gazette* in 1880 and during his editórship (1883–8) initiated new and influential political and social movements. He achieved wide notoriety for his 'Maiden Tribute of Modern Babylon' (1885) exposing sexual vice, which led to Parliament raising the age of consent to 16 years. He founded the *Review of Reviews* in 1890 and continued his work for peace, friendship with Russia, and spiritualism (for which he was much ridiculed). He was drowned in the *Titanic* disaster.

STEELE, Sir Richard (1672–1729), was born in Dublin, in the same year as *Addison, and was educated with him at the Charterhouse. He was subsequently at Merton College, Oxford, whence he entered the army as a cadet in the Life Guards. As a result of a poem on Queen Mary's funeral dedicated to Lord Cutts, colonel of the Coldstream Guards, he became his secretary and obtained the rank of captain. He published *The Christian Hero in 1701, in which he first displayed his missionary and reforming spirit. In the same year he produced his first comedy, *The Funeral. Neither this nor his two next comedies, *The Lying Lover* (1703) and *The Tender Husband* (1705), proved very successful. In 1706 he was appointed gentleman waiter to Prince George of Denmark, and in 1707

gazetteer; and in the same year was married to Mary Scurlock ('dear Prue'), his second wife. In 1709 he started *The Tatler, which he carried on with the help of Addison till January 1711. He was made a commissioner of stamps in 1710, but lost the gazetteership after the accession of the Tories. In conjunction with Addison he carried on *The Spectator during 1711–12. This was followed by *The Guardian, to which Addison, *Berkeley, and *Pope contributed, and which was attacked by the Tory *Examiner. Steele next conducted *The Englishman* (1713–14), a more political paper. In 1713 he was elected MP for Stockbridge. In 1714 he published *The Crisis, a pamphlet in favour of the Hanoverian succession, which was answered by *Swift, and led to Steele's expulsion from the House on 18 March 1714. In October of that year he issued his *Apology for Himself and his Writings, and during the same year conducted *The Lover, a paper in the manner of the Spectator. The tide turned in his favour with the accession of George I. He was appointed supervisor of Drury Lane Theatre, and to other posts, and was knighted in 1715. In 1718 he denounced in *The Plebeian Lord Sunderland's Peerage Bill, and was answered by Addison in *The Old Whig. This incident led to the revocation of Steele's Drury Lane patent, and to an estrangement from Addison. He established *The Theatre, a bi-weekly paper, which continued until 1720, in which year he issued pamphlets against the South Sea mania (see SOUTH SEA COMPANY). His last comedy, *The Conscious Lovers, was produced in 1722. Money difficulties forced him to leave London in 1724, and he died at Carmarthen. His letters to his wife, Mary Scurlock, were printed in 1787. Less highly regarded as an essayist than Addison, his influence was nevertheless great; his attacks on *Restoration drama (*Spectator*, 65, on *Etherege, 'I allow it to be Nature, but it is Nature in its utmost Corruption and Degeneracy'); his approval of the 'sober and polite Mirth' of *Terence; his praise of tender and affectionate domestic and family life; and his own reformed and sentimental dramas (described by *Fielding's Parson Adams as 'almost solemn enough for a sermon') did much to create an image of polite behaviour for the new century. There is a Life by George A. Aitken (2 vols, 1889).

Steele Glas, The, a satire in verse by *Gascoigne, published 1576.

The poet's 'steele glas' reveals abuses and how things should be, whereas the common looking-glass only 'shewes a seemely shew', i.e. shows the thing much better than it is. Looking into his 'steele glas' the author sees himself with his faults and then successively the faults of kings; covetous lords and knights; greedy, braggart, and drunken soldiers; false judges;

merchants, and lastly priests. Finally the plough-man is held up as a model:

Behold him (priests) & though he stink of sweat
Disdaine him not: for shal I tel you what?
Such clime to heaven, before the shaven crownes.

Steenson, Willie, 'Wandering Willie', the blind fiddler in Scott's *Redgauntlet*.

Steerforth, James, a character in Dickens's *David Copperfield*.

STEEVENS, George (1736–1800), Shake-spearian commentator, who in 1766 issued in four volumes *Twenty of the Plays of Shakespeare, being the whole Number printed in Quarto during his Lifetime, or before the Restoration,* and in 1773 a complete annotated edition (including notes by Dr *Johnson) in ten volumes, to which a supplementary volume of poems, together with seven plays ascribed to Shakespeare, was added in 1780. He constantly quarrelled with his lit-erary associates and was called by *Gifford 'the Puck of commentators', but was befriended by Johnson and elected a member of the *Club in 1774. He was extremely widely read in Eliza-bethan literature, and supplied to his edition a vast range of illustrative quotations from other works, but was in other respects less scholarly, rejecting as inauthentic various scenes and plays which he appears merely to have disliked. He assisted *Tyrwhitt in his edition of the 'Rowley' poems of *Chatterton, but declared his disbelief in them. He attacked W. H. *Ireland, and satirized literary crazes.

STEIN, Gertrude (1874–1946), American author, born in Pennsylvania into a progressive and intellectual family of German-Jewish origin. She studied psychology at Radcliffe College, where she was a student of W. *James, and then studied the anatomy of the brain at Johns Hop-kins. In 1902 she went with her brother Leo to Paris, where she settled; her home in the rue de Fleurus became a literary salon and art gallery and a home of the avant-garde, attracting painters (including *Picasso, Matisse, and Juan Gris) and writers (including *Hemingway, F. M. *Ford, and S. *Anderson, but not *Joyce, with whom she was not acquainted). Her friend, secretary, and companion from 1907 was San Francisco-born Alice B. Toklas (1877–1967), whom she made the ostensible author of her own memoir, *The Autobiography of Alice B. Toklas* (1933). Her fiction includes *Three Lives* (1909), of which the second portrait, 'Melanctha', was described by R. *Wright as 'the first long serious literary treatment of Negro life in the United States'; *The Making of Americans* (written 1906–8, published 1925), an enormously long work intended as a history of her family; and *A Long Gay Book* (1932). *Tender Buttons* (1914) is an example of her highly idiosyncratic poetry, of which she

said in her *Lectures in America* (1935), 'I struggled with the ridding myself of nouns. I knew that nouns must go in poetry as they had gone in prose if anything that is everything was to go on meaning something.' Her characteristic repetitions and reprises, her flowing, un-punctuated prose, and her attempts to capture the 'living moment' owe much to William James and to *Bergson's concept of time, and represent a highly personal but nevertheless in-fluential version of the *stream-of-consciousness technique. Her many varied published works include essays, sketches of life in France, works of literary theory, short stories, portraits of her friends, a lyric drama called *Four Saints in Three Acts* (first published in *transition*, 1929, and performed in the US, 1934), and *Wars I Have Seen* (1945), a personal account of occupied Paris. For an influential early study of her work, see E. *Wilson, *Axel's Castle* (1931).

STEINBECK, John Ernst (1902–68), Ameri-can novelist, born in California, took his native state as the background for his early short stories and novels and described the lives of those work-ing on the land with realism and understanding. *Tortilla Flat* (1935) was his first success, and he confirmed his growing reputation with two novels about landless rural workers, *In Dubious Battle* (1936) and *Of Mice and Men* (1937), the story of two itinerant farm labourers, one of huge strength and weak mind, exploited and protected by the other. His best-known work, *The Grapes of Wrath* (1939), is an epic account of the efforts of an emigrant farming family from the dust bowl of the West to reach the 'promised land' of California. Among his later novels, which are often marred by senti-mentality and uncertainty of purpose, are *East of Eden* (1952), a family saga, and *The Winter of our Discontent* (1961). He was awarded the *Nobel Prize in 1962, by which time his repu-tation had already declined in his own country.

STEINER, (Francis) George (1929–), American critic and author, born in Paris, and educated at the Sorbonne, the University of Chicago, Harvard, and Oxford. His critical works include *Tolstoy or Dostoevsky: An Essay in the Old Criticism* (1959); *The Death of Tragedy* (1961); *Language and Silence* (1967); *In Blue-beard's Castle: Some Notes Towards the Re-Definition of Culture* (1971); and *After Babel: Aspects of Language and Translation* (1975). Steiner's criticism is wide-ranging and multi-cultural in its references and controversial in its content: one of his recurrent themes is the way in which the 20th-cent. experiences of totalitarianism and world war have, more specifically, of the Holocaust, have destroyed the assumption (self-evident, he claims, to Dr *Johnson, *Coleridge, and M. *Arnold) that literature is a humanizing influence. Silence is the only appropriate response to 20th-cent. horrors. The Holocaust is also the subject of his novella *The Portage to San Cristobal of A.H.* (1979; dramatized by Christopher Hampton, 1982), which puts in the mouth of Hitler (who is supposed to have survived the war and taken refuge in South America) the argument that the Jews (through Monotheism, Christianity, and Marxism) had provoked their own destruction by offering 'the blackmail of transcendence . . . the virus of Utopia'.

Stella, (1) the chaste lady loved by Astrophel in Sidney's sonnet sequence *Astrophel and Stella,* based on Penelope *Rich; (2) Swift's name for Esther Johnson; see SWIFT, and in particular the account there of the *Journal to Stella.*

STENDHAL, pseudonym of Henri Beyle (1788–1842), French novelist, spent his early years in his native Grenoble and later lived for long periods in Italy. His two recognized masterpieces, *Le Rouge et le noir* (1830) and *La Chartreuse de Parme* (1839), the first following the rise and fall of the young provincial Julien Sorel in the France of the Restoration, the second chronicling the fortunes of Fabrice del Dongo at a small Italian court during the same period, figure among the great French novels of the 19th cent. Each is remarkable for its political dimension, for the detail and variety of the experience portrayed, for the energy and passion of the principal characters and for penetrating psychological analysis. Stendhal also wrote studies of music and musicians, and of Italian painting (*Histoire de la peinture en Italie*, 1817), travel books (*Rome, Naples et Florence en 1817*, 1817), and much occasional journalism. *De l'amour* (1822) considers the passion both psychologically and in relation to historical and social conditions. With the two pamphlets entitled *Racine et Shakespeare* (1823, 1825) he entered the Classic–Romantic controversy on the side of the latter. Of his other novels, *Armance* (1822) and *L'Abesse de Castro* (1839) appeared during his lifetime; the unfinished *Lucien Leuwen* (1894) and the fragmentary *Lamiel* (1889) were published posthumously. *La Vie de Henri Brulard* (1890), the *Journal* (1888) of, mainly, the years 1801 to 1815, and *Souvenirs d'Égotisme* (1892), covering the years 1822–30, are all autobiographical.

Stephano, a drunken butler in Shakespeare's *The Tempest.*

STEPHEN, Sir James (1789–1859), father of Sir J. F. *Stephen and Sir L. *Stephen, was under-secretary of state for the colonies (1836–47) and professor of modern history at Cambridge (1849–59), meanwhile contributing articles to the *Edinburgh Review* including an admirable essay on *Wilberforce. He is remembered as author of *Essays in Ecclesiastical Biography* (1849) and *Lectures on the History of France* (1851).

STEPHEN, Sir James Fitzjames (1829–94), son of Sir J. *Stephen and brother of Leslie *Stephen, was a barrister, legal member of council in India (1869–72), and high court judge (1879–91). In 1861 he was counsel for Rowland Williams in the *Essays and Reviews* case. He was a member of the *Apostles and the *Metaphysical Society and vigorously contributed articles on social, moral, and controversial theological subjects to periodicals including *Fraser's Magazine* and the *Cornhill*; he was chief writer for the *Pall Mall Gazette* for five years. Among his works were *A History of the Criminal Law in England* (1883), *Horae Sabbaticae* (1892, collected articles from the *Saturday Review*), and *Liberty, Equality, Fraternity* (1873, re-published 1967) in which he criticized J. S. *Mill's utilitarian position in his essay *On Liberty.* There is a life by Leslie Stephen.

STEPHEN, James Kenneth (1859–92), younger son of Sir J. F. *Stephen and cousin of V. *Woolf, educated at Eton and King's College, Cambridge. He was called to the bar but devoted most of his time to journalism and in 1888 began a weekly paper called *The Reflector*, chiefly written by himself. He was author (as 'J.K.S.') of highly successful parodies and light verse, collected as *Lapsus Calami* and *Quo Musa Tendis* (both 1891). His promising career ended as a result of an accident in 1886 which slowly drove him insane, and he has been suggested as a candidate for the role of *Jack the Ripper. See M. Harrison, *Clarence* (1972).

STEPHEN, Sir Leslie (1832–1904), son of Sir J. *Stephen and brother of Sir J. F. *Stephen, was educated at Eton and Trinity Hall, Cambridge, where he became tutor, having taken orders. From his family he inherited a strong tradition of Evangelicalism and muscular Christianity, and he became a noted mountaineer: he edited the *Alpine Journal*, 1868–72, and the best of his Alpine essays were collected in 1871 as *The Playground of Europe.*

Stephen's reading of J. S. *Mill, *Comte, and *Kant inclined him to scepticism, and by 1865 he had abandoned all belief in even the broadest of *Broad Church doctrine. In 1864 he came to London and embarked on a literary career of prodigious industry and output, contributing articles to many periodicals. In 1871 he became editor of the *Cornhill, a post he held until 1882 when he undertook the editorship of the *Dictionary of National Biography* (the DNB). During these years he published several volumes, some defining his position as an agnostic; his great work, *History of English Thought in the 18th Century* (1876), reviews the Deist controversy of that age, and the intuitional and utilitarian schools of philosophy. He also contributed several biographies to the English Men of Letters series, despite the amount of time consumed by the vast undertaking of the *DNB*, to which he himself contributed almost 400 entries, and from which strain and ill health forced him to resign in 1891. His last important volume was *English Literature and Society in the Eighteenth Century* (1904). Many of his literary judgements are now questioned, but he was one of the most prominent intellectuals of his day (portrayed by his friend *Meredith as Vernon Whitford, 'a Phoebus Apollo turned fasting friar', in *The Egoist*) and his influence was great and lasting.

Stephen's first wife was *Thackeray's daughter 'Minny', who died in 1875. His acute grief, and his second marriage to Julia Duckworth, are both recorded in his autobiographical papers, written for his children by Julia (one of whom was V. *Woolf) and step-children and published in 1977 (ed. A. Bell) as *Mausoleum Book*. V. Woolf portrays some aspects of his character in her portrait of Mr Ramsay in *To the Lighthouse* (1927). See also Noël Annan, *Leslie Stephen: His Thought and Character in Relation to his Time* (1951, rev. 1984).

STEPHENS, James (1882–1950), Irish poet and story-writer, born in poverty, whose best-known work, the prose fantasy *The Crock of Gold* (1912), has overshadowed much other less whimsical work. *Insurrections* (1909) was the first of many volumes of poetry; the *Collected Poems* appeared in 1926, revised 1954. His first novel, *The Charwoman's Daughter* (1912), was followed by *The Demi-Gods* (1914) and *Deirdre* (1923). Many volumes of stories include *Irish Fairy Tales* (1920, illustrated by A. *Rackham); and *Etched in Moonlight* (1928). Stephens became a widely known broadcaster, of stories and verses and conversation. A biography by A. Martin appeared in 1977.

STERLING, John (1806–44), educated at Trinity College and Trinity Hall, Cambridge, a leading member of the *Apostles and a disciple of *Coleridge. With *Maurice he was briefly proprietor of the *Athenaeum* (1828). He was offered in 1834 the curacy of Herstmonceux by his old tutor *Hare, who was vicar, but he resigned the following year. Sterling owes his fame to his close friendship with *Carlyle whose vivid *Life of Sterling* (1851) reveals the tragic history of Sterling's short life, interrupted by persistent ill health necessitating numerous voyages abroad. His monthly meetings of literary friends, from 1838, became known as the Sterling Club; among its members were Carlyle, Hare, J. S. *Mill, and *Tennyson. He contributed to various periodicals and among his few published works were a novel, *Arthur Coningsby* (1833), *Poems* (1839), and *Essays and Tales* (1848) collected and edited with a memoir by J. Hare, to whom with Carlyle his papers were entrusted.

STERNE, Laurence (1713–68), the son of an impoverished infantry ensign (who was, however, the grandson of an archbishop of York), spent his early childhood in various barracks in Ireland and England, where he developed an affection for military men evident in his adult writings. At the age of ten he was sent to school in Yorkshire, under the care of an uncle, and from there proceeded, on a scholarship founded by Archbishop Sterne, to Jesus College, Cambridge, where he encountered and embraced the philosophy of *Locke, and where he made a lifelong friend of *Hall-Stevenson, who was probably the model for *Eugenius. Sterne had by this time already contracted tuberculosis. He took holy orders and obtained the living of the Yorkshire parish of Sutton-on-the-Forest in 1738. In 1741 he became a prebendary of York cathedral, and married Elizabeth Lumley, a cousin of Elizabeth *Montagu, but his domestic and family life was not happy, and of their several children all were stillborn but a daughter, Lydia. He became a JP, earned a reputation as a good country pastor, and his sermons at York Minster were eagerly attended. In 1744 the living of Stillington was added to that of Sutton. For recreation he played the violin, read widely, painted, dined with the local gentry, and, it seems, indulged his considerable interest in women. In 1759, in the course of an ecclesiastical quarrel, he wrote *A Political Romance* (later entitled *The History of a Good Warm Watch Coat*), a satire on local ecclesiastical courts so barbed that the authorities had it burned. In the same year he passed his parish over to the care of a curate and began *Tristram Shandy*. The first version of Vols I and II was rejected by the London printer *Dodsley. At the same time Sterne had to face the deaths of his mother and uncle, and the mental breakdown of his wife. The next version of Vols I and II were 'written under the greatest heaviness of heart', and published in York in 1759, with Dodsley agreeing to take half the printing for sale in London. While waiting for the public's reception of his work, Sterne was enjoying a flirtation with Catherine Fourmantel, a singer then staying in York, who is traditionally (though uncertainly) supposed to be the 'dear Jenny' of *Tristram Shandy*. Early in 1760 Sterne found himself famous. He went to London and (although his book was not liked by Dr *Johnson, *Goldsmith, *Richardson, and others) he was fêted by society, had his portrait painted by *Reynolds, was invited to Court, and saw published a second edition of Vols. I and II. In the same year he was presented with a third Yorkshire living, that of Coxwold, where he happily settled himself into 'Shandy Hall'. He published *The Sermons of Mr Yorick*, a volume whose title caused some scandal, and continued with *Tristram Shandy*. In 1761 four more volumes appeared and *Tristram Shandy* continued its highly successful career. Meanwhile Sterne's health was deteriorating steadily. In 1762 his voice was much affected, and in the hope of improvement he and his wife and daughter left for France, where they lived at Toulouse and Montpelier until 1764, when Sterne returned alone to England, and in 1765 published Vols VII and VIII of *Tristram Shandy*. In 1765 he returned to France, visited his family (who were to remain there permanently), and undertook an eight-month tour of France and Italy, which clearly provided him with much of the material for *A Sentimental Journey through France and Italy*. In 1766 he published two further volumes of sermons. The ninth and last volume of *Tristram Shandy* appeared in 1767. In the same year Sterne met and fell in love with Elizabeth *Draper, the young wife of an official of the East India Company, and after her enforced departure for India began his *Journal to *Eliza*, which he did not publish. He finished and published *A Sentimental Journey* in the same year, but his health rapidly collapsed and he died in London in March 1768. A Shandean fate overtook his body, which was taken by grave-robbers, recognized at an anatomy lecture in Cambridge, and secretly returned to its grave.

A spate of forgeries appeared after Sterne's death, including another volume of *Tristram Shandy*, *Posthumous Works*, and a continuation by 'Eugenius' (an author whose identity is not known, but who was not Hall-Stevenson) of *A Sentimental Journey*.

Sterne is generally acknowledged as an innovator of the highest originality, and has been seen as the chief begetter of a long line of writers interested in the *'stream-of-consciousness'. He acknowledges in *Tristram Shandy* his own debt in this respect to Locke, whose *Essay concerning Human Understanding* seemed to Sterne 'a history-book . . . of what passes in man's own mind'. Throughout his work he parodies, with a virtuosity that has proved inimitable, the developing conventions of the still-new 'novel', and its problems in presenting reality, space, and time. His sharp wit, often sly and often salacious, is balanced by the affection and tolerance he displays towards the delights and absurdities of life. The standard life is by W. D. Cross (1904), and see also A. H. Cash, *Laurence Sterne: the early and middle years* (1975).

STERNHOLD, Thomas (d. 1549), and **HOPKINS,** John (d. 1570), joint versifiers of the Psalms. A collection of 44 of these versified Psalms appeared in 1549; music was first supplied in the Geneva edition of 1556, and by 1640 about 300 editions had been published. In 1562 *The Whole Book of Psalmes*, by Sternhold, Hopkins, Norton, and others, was added to the Prayer Book. This version was ridiculed by Dryden in *Absalom and Achitophel* (II. 403), and it provoked *Rochester's epigram 'Spoken Extempore to a Country Clerk after Having Heard Him Sing Psalms':

> Sternhold and Hopkins had great qualms
> When they translated David's psalms
> To make the heart full glad;
> But had it been poor David's fate
> To hear thee sing, and them translate,
> By God! 'twould have made him mad.

STEVENS, Henry (1819–86), American book-dealer and bibliographical entrepreneur, who came to London in 1845 and became an agent for the *British Museum library, purchasing American books which did much to build up its collection, and also purchasing English books for American collectors. See his own *Recollections of James Lenox and the Formation of his Library* (1886) and W. W. Parker, *Henry Stevens of Vermont* (1963).

STEVENS, Wallace (1878–1955), American poet, born in Pennsylvania and educated at Harvard, where he met *Santayana. He became a lawyer, and from 1916 worked at Hartford, Connecticut, on the legal staff of the Hartford Accident and Indemnity Company, where he remained until his death, becoming vice-president in 1934. Meanwhile, he had begun to publish poems in *Poetry* and elsewhere, his first volume, *Harmonium*, which contains 'Thirteen Ways of Looking at a Blackbird', was published in 1923. This was followed by other collections (including *Ideas of Order*, 1935; *The Man with the Blue Guitar and other Poems*, 1937; *Notes towards a Supreme Fiction*, 1942; *The Auroras of Autumn*, 1950; *Collected Poems*, 1954) which slowly brought him recognition, but it was not until his last years that his enigmatic, elegant, intellectual, and occasionally startling meditations on order and the imagination, on reality, appearance, and art, gained the high reputation that they now enjoy.

STEVENSON, John Hall-, see HALL-STEVENSON, J.

STEVENSON, Robert Louis (originally Lewis) Balfour (1850–94), son of Thomas Stevenson, joint-engineer to the Board of Northern Lighthouses, was born in Edinburgh. A sickly child, he was originally intended for his father's strenuous profession, but ill health encouraged him to abandon the study of engineering at Edinburgh University for the law. He was admitted advocate in 1875, but had already determined to be a writer, and had published in periodicals. He was fascinated by Edinburgh low life, and cultivated a Bohemian style, despite the constraint of financial dependence on his father. In 1875 L. *Stephen introduced him to W. E. *Henley, who became a close friend, and with whom he was to collaborate on four undistinguished plays (*Deacon Brodie*, 1880; *Beau Austin*. 1884; *Admiral Guinea*, 1884; *Macaire*,

1885). From this time on much of his life was spent travelling in search of health; he suffered from a chronic bronchial condition (possibly tuberculosis) and frequent haemorrhages. In France in 1876 he met his future wife, Mrs Fanny Osbourne. *An Inland Voyage*, describing a canoe tour in Belgium and France, appeared in 1878. *Travels with a Donkey in the Cevennes*, the description of a tour taken with his donkey Modestine, appeared in 1879, the year in which he travelled to California by emigrant ship and train in pursuit of Fanny, whom he married shortly after her divorce in 1880; she was ten years his senior, and proved a spirited yet protective companion, caring for him through many bouts of serious illness. After a stay at Calistoga (recorded in *The Silverado Squatters*, 1883) he returned to Europe, settling at Bournemouth for three years in 1884, where he consolidated a friendship with H. *James. By this time he had published widely in periodicals, and many of his short stories, essays, and travel pieces were collected in volume form (*Virginibus Puerisque*, 1881; *Familiar Studies of Men and Books*, 1882; *New Arabian Nights*, 1882). His first full-length work of fiction, *Treasure Island*, published in book form in 1883, brought him fame, which increased with the publication of *The Strange Case of Dr *Jekyll and Mr Hyde* (1886). This was followed by his popular Scottish romances, *Kidnapped* (1886), its sequel *Catriona* (1893), and *The Master of Ballantrae* (1889).

In 1888 Stevenson had set out with his family entourage for the South Seas, becoming a legend in his lifetime. He visited the leper colony at Molokai, which inspired his celebrated defence of Father Damien (1841–89), the Belgian priest who had devoted his life to caring for 700 neglected lepers, himself finally dying of the disease (*Father Damien: an open letter to the Reverend Dr Hyde of Honolulu*, 1890). He finally settled in Samoa at Vailima, where he temporarily regained his health, and gained a reputation as 'Tusitala' or 'The Story Teller'. He died there suddenly from a brain haemorrhage, while working on his unfinished masterpiece, *Weir of Hermiston* (1896).

In addition to the titles mentioned above, Stevenson published many other volumes, including *The Merry Men* (1887, with 'Markheim' and his earliest Scottish story, 'Thrawn Janet'); many travel books; *The Black Arrow* (1888), a historical romance; *Island Nights' Entertainments* (1893), which includes 'The Beach of Falesá'; and *St Ives* (1897, unfinished, completed by *Quiller-Couch). With his stepson Lloyd Osbourne he wrote *The Wrong Box* (1889), *The Wrecker* (1892), and *The Ebb-Tide* (1894). He also published volumes of poetry, including *A Child's Garden of Verses* (1885) and *Underwoods* (1887): his *Collected Poems*, ed. Janet Adam Smith, appeared in 1950. In them, as in many of his prose works, critics have detected beneath the lightness of touch a sense of apprehension, sin, and suffering, and biographers have attributed this darker side to the early influence of Calvinism, as well as to his ill health. The theme of dualism and the *Doppelgänger* recurs in his work, as does an admiration for morally ambiguous heroes or anti-heroes. Although his more popular books have remained constantly in print, and have been frequently filmed, his critical reputation has been obscured by attention to his vivid personality and adventurous life; also by his apparent refusal to take his art seriously. 'Fiction is to grown men what play is to the child', he stated, and his delight in story-telling, swashbuckling romances, and historical 'tushery', as he called it, gave him an audience of readers rather than critics. His weightier admirers include James, G. *Greene and *Borges. See *Vailima letters* (to Sidney Colvin, 1895); *Selected Letters*, ed. Colvin (2 vols, 1899; 4 vols, 1911); lives by G. Balfour (1901); J. C. Furnas (1952); J. Calder (1980). Edinburgh edition of his collected works, ed. Colvin (28 vols, 1894–8); Pentland edition, ed. *Gosse (20 vols, 1906–7).

STEWART, Dugald (1753–1828), was educated at Edinburgh High School and at Edinburgh and Glasgow Universities. He was professor of mathematics at Edinburgh from 1775 to 1785, and then professor of moral philosophy from 1785 to 1810, in which post he exercised a powerful influence on Scottish thought, largely because of his brilliant pedagogy and his elegant prose. Although Stewart considered himself a disciple of T. *Reid, he was an eclectic thinker who borrowed from a wide range of sources. He was particularly indebted to the writings of Adam *Smith, and his lectures on political economy were eagerly attended by the coterie of young Whigs who founded the *Edinburgh Review*. However, in both his lectures and his publications Stewart was primarily concerned with the inculcation of virtue rather than with abstract theorizing, and it cannot be said that he was either an original or a profound thinker. His works, collected by Sir W. *Hamilton (11 vols, 1854–60), include: *Elements of the Human Mind* (1792, 1814, 1827), *Outlines of Moral Philosophy* (1793), *Philosophical Essays* (1810), *Biographical Memoirs* (1810), consisting of lives of Adam Smith, W. *Robertson, and Reid, and his once influential *Dissertation ... Exhibiting a General View of the Progress of Metaphysical and Ethical Philosophy, Since the Revival of Letters in Europe* (1815, 1821), written originally for the *Encyclopaedia Britannica*.

Stewart, Francis, alias Sergeant Bothwell, a character in Scott's *Old Mortality*.

STEWART, J(ohn) I(nnes) M(ackintosh) (1906–), novelist and critic, born in Edinburgh and educated at the Edinburgh Academy and Christ Church, Oxford. Under the pseudonym Michael Innes, he has written many successful works of *detective fiction, beginning with *Death at the President's Lodging* (1936), which introduced his detective, John Appleby of Scotland Yard; they contributed greatly to the vogue for 'donnish' detective stories, rich in literary allusions and quotations. He has also published several novels as J. I. M. Stewart, and has written critical works on Shakespeare, *Joyce, *Peacock, *Kipling, *Hardy, and others.

Stewart of the Glens, James, a character in R. L. Stevenson's *Kidnapped* and *Catriona*; a real character, who was executed in 1752 for a murder which he did not commit, after trial by a jury of Campbells (the foes of his clan).

Steyne, marquis of, a character in Thackeray's *Vanity Fair*.

Stichomythia, in classical Greek drama, dialogue in alternate lines of verse, employed in sharp disputation. The form is sometimes imitated in English drama, e.g. in the dialogue between Richard III and Elizabeth in Shakespeare's *Richard II* (IV. iv).

Stiggins, Mr, a character in Dickens's *Pickwick Papers*.

STILLINGFLEET, Edward (1635–99), fellow of St John's College, Cambridge, and bishop of Worcester from 1689, was a popular preacher and author of the *Irenicum* (1659), suggesting a compromise with the Presbyterians. His erudition was displayed in *Origines Sacrae* (1662) and *Origines Britannicae* (1685).

STIRLING, earl of, see ALEXANDER, SIR W.

Stoicism was a system of thought which originated in Athens during the 3rd cent. BC, flourished in Rome c.100 BC–c. AD 200, exercised a lasting influence on Christianity, and enjoyed a vigorous revival at the time of the Renaissance. It has been said also that Stoicism was the effective religion of the Victorian public schools.

The Stoics' prime concern was always with ethics, but they held that right behaviour had to be grounded on a general understanding of the universe, and their theories extended to cover the nature of the physical world, the arts of discourse (under which they included logic, rhetoric, literature, and grammar), epistemology, and politics. Stoic 'Physics' taught that everything was material, the universe being a continuum, and thought an ethereal form of matter which had the power to shape and control its grosser forms. This ethereal element was considered to possess a coherent set of purposes. Given the name of Providence, it functioned as a World-Soul or immanent God. Man's soul was part of the World-Soul, which made all human beings brothers, and the ethereal element in

Man—his Reason—was in harmony with the purposes of Providence. To be virtuous consisted, therefore, in following Reason undeterred by pain, pleasure, desire, or fear, emotions that belong to a lower level of existence. The weak point in this philosophy was that the Stoics were not agreed on a goal for reason beyond the conquest of the irrational self. The founders of the school insisted that the ends men usually pursue—health, wealth, success, pleasure—had no real importance, so that a wise man had no reason to pursue them either for himself or for others. Their successors of the Middle Stoa, who came under Roman influence, looked more favourably on the qualities that promote civilized life and recommended their exercise. Among the later Stoics some took one line, some another, while the so-called Stoic opposition to the Emperors stressed the importance of freedom. Tyranny was to be condemned on philosophical grounds because it added external difficulties to the internal ones hampering the exercise of reason.

Our knowledge of Stoicism in antiquity is unbalanced. Only fragments have survived of the writings of its founders—Zeno of Citium (336–246 BC), the pious Cleanthes (?331–?232 BC), whose 'Hymn to Zeus' has been preserved, and Chrysippus (c.280–206 BC), the group's system-builder—who all taught in Athens. Information about them comes from later writers like *Diogenes Laertius. The philosophers of the Middle Stoa, Panaetius of Rhodes (189–109 BC) and Posidonius (135–51 BC), have fared a little better. Though their works have been lost, we can learn about their ideas from their disciple *Cicero. The Stoics whose writings survive are those who lived under the Roman Empire: *Seneca, *Epictetus, and *Marcus Aurelius. Their interests were almost exclusively ethical, so that it is as a system of morality that Stoicism was to exercise its greatest influence on later ages.

Extolling Providence, the brotherhood of men, and the need to curb natural desires, Stoicism had much in common with Christianity, and a compilation of Stoic maxims, the *Distichs of Cato*, was the most popular of medieval schoolbooks. *Petrarch in the 14th cent. expounded a Christian Stoicism in his *De remediis fortuitorum*, and in the 16th cent. a life of Marcus Aurelius, supposedly ancient but actually by the Spaniard Antonio de Guevara, proved enormously popular. Translated into French and English in the 1530s, it may have served to promote the Stoic revival which came at the end of the century with *Montaigne's *Essais* (1580) and *Lipsius' *De constantia* (1585). In England the years 1595–1615 saw translations of Lipsius, Montaigne, his disciple Charron, Epictetus, and Seneca, and the influence of Stoicism can be traced in a great number of writers from

*Chapman and Sir William Cornwallis (d. ?1631) to *Addison.

STOKER, Bram (Abraham) (1847–1912), born in Dublin, gave up his career as a civil servant there in 1878 to become Sir H. *Irving's secretary and touring manager for the next 27 years, an experience that produced *Personal Reminiscences of Henry Irving* (1906). Stoker wrote a number of novels and short stories, as well as some dramatic criticism, but is chiefly remembered for *Dracula* (1897), a tale of vampirism influenced by 'Carmilla', one of the stories in Le Fanu's *In a Glass Darkly* (1872).

Stones of Venice, The, by *Ruskin, was published in 3 vols, the first in 1851, the second and third in 1853. It is an architectural study in which immense original scholarship is put to moralistic use.

Volume I sets out first principles for discrimination between good and bad architectural features; there follows, in this and volume II, a criticism of the romantic, *Byronic vision of Venice that blinds the traveller to present misery and disorder. From the remnants of the past Ruskin creates a myth of Venice, where power is decommercialized and desecularized, and religion pre-Catholic. The famous chapter 'The Nature of Gothic' contrasts feudal relations between authority and workman with those resulting from the division of labour and mechanical mass production in English manufacturing: *Clark described it as 'one of the noblest things written in the 19th cent.; even now, when the ideas it expresses are accepted, and the causes it advocates are dead, we cannot read it without a thrill, without a sudden resolution to reform the world', a response which indicates the emotional force of Ruskin's passionate plea for the liberty of the workman. Volume III describes phases in Renaissance architectural history as illustrations of the gradual degradation of Europe.

STOPES, Marie Charlotte Carmichael (1880–1958), distinguished palaeobotanist and pioneer birth control campaigner, whose *Married Love* (1918) was published after the annulment of her first marriage, when, she alleged, she was still a virgin. With the help of her second husband she established the first birth control clinic in England in 1921, in Holloway, London, and she continued to write on such subjects as *Wise Parenthood* (1918, which appeared with a preface by Arnold *Bennett), *Radiant Motherhood* (1920), and sexual fulfilment within marriage. She also published several volumes of plays and of poetry, mostly of a semi-mystical character.

STOPPARD, Tom (1937–), dramatist, born in Czechoslovakia; his family moved to Singapore in 1939, where his father, Dr Eugene

Straussler, was killed, and he subsequently, on settling in England after the war, took his English stepfather's name. He left school at 17 and worked as a journalist before his first play, *A Walk on the Water,* was televised in 1963 (staged in London in 1968 as *Enter a Free Man*). He published a novel, *Lord Malquist and the Moon* (1965), and in 1966 his play *Rosencrantz and Guildenstern are dead* attracted much attention. This was followed by many witty and inventive plays, including *The Real Inspector Hound* (1968, a play-within-a-play which parodies the conventions of the stage thriller); *Jumpers* (1972); *Travesties* (1974); *Dirty Linen* (1976, a satire of political life and parliamentary misdemeanours); *Every Good Boy Deserves Favour* (1977, about a political dissident in a Soviet psychiatric hospital); *Night and Day* (1978), about the dangers of the 'closed shop' in journalism; and *The Real Thing* (1982), a marital tragi-comedy. Stoppard has also written many works for film, radio, and television, including *Professional Foul* (TV, 1977), set in Prague, which portrays the concurrent visits of an English philosopher and an English football team, and dramatizes the inner conflicts of the philosopher, caught between the abstractions of his own discipline and the realities of a régime which stifles free intellectual exchange. Stoppard's work displays a metaphysical wit, a strong theatrical sense, and a talent for pastiche which enables him to move from mode to mode within the same scene with great flexibility and rapidity; yet the plays appear far from frivolous in intention, increasingly posing (though not always choosing to solve) considerable ethical problems.

STOREY, David Malcolm (1933–), novelist and playwright, was born in Wakefield, the third son of a miner; he was educated at the Queen Elizabeth Grammar School, Wakefield, and at the Slade School of Fine Art. He worked as professional footballer, teacher, farm worker, and erector of show tents, acquiring a variety of experience which is evident in his works. His first novel, *This Sporting Life* (1960), describes the ambitions and passions of a young working man, Arthur Machin, a Rugby League player who becomes emotionally involved with his landlady. This was followed by *Flight into Camden* (1960), about the unhappy affair of a miner's daughter with a married teacher, and the highly ambitious *Radcliffe* (1963), a sombre, violent, Lawrentian novel about class conflict, the Puritan legacy, and destructive homosexual passion. Later novels include *Pasmore* (1972, an account of a young lecturer in a state of mental breakdown) and *Saville* (1976, *Booker Prize), an epic set in a South Yorkshire mining village. Meanwhile Storey had also established himself as a playwright, with such works as *In Celebration* (1969), a play in which three educated sons return north to visit their miner father and betray their own dissatisfactions and sense of alienation; *The Contractor* (1970), which presents the audience with the construction, then the dismantling, of a wedding marquee, a spectacle which forms the background for the presentation of the relationship of the contractor Ewbank (who had appeared in *Radcliffe*) with his university-educated son; *Home* (1970), set in a mental home; *The Changing Room* (1972), again using football as a setting; *Life Class* (1974), set in an art college; and *Mother's Day* (1976), a violent black comedy set on a housing estate. Action, in Storey's plays, tends to be offstage, obliquely presented through low-key, episodic encounters in a realistic setting; both plays and novels show a preoccupation with social mobility and the mental disturbance it frequently appears to cause, and an interesting and challenging combination of documentary naturalism with a sense of the symbolic and unspoken.

Story of an African Farm, The, a novel by O. *Schreiner.

Story of my Heart, The, a discourse by R. *Jefferies, published 1883.

Tracing the course of his spiritual and imaginative growth from the age of 18, Jefferies describes his longing for harmony with 'the visible universe' and his sense of 'the great earth speaking through me'. He feels the trees, the grass, the stars 'like exterior nerves and veins', yet acknowledges a frustrating inadequacy in expressing his experience. Long reading in philosophy and many branches of knowledge has convinced him that learning is an encumbrance, that causality and purposive evolution do not exist, that there is a soul-life (represented for him by the ocean) higher than any conception of a god, and that the orthodox Christian deity has no existence. His atheism caused considerable scandal, but the book soon established itself as a significant autobiography and has passed through innumerable editions.

Story of Rimini, The, a poem by Leigh *Hunt published 1816. The work (with which Hunt had assistance from *Byron) is based on *Dante's story of Paolo and Francesca.

On a fine May morning Francesca leaves Ravenna as a bride, and journeys in moonlight to Rimini. The events which overtake her, and the feelings which arise, lead to her adulterous love for Paolo. The lovers are discovered, and their deaths conclude the poem. Although of doubtful quality, the work, with its flexibility of couplets, its use of common speech, and the luxuriance of its southern imagery, suggested new possibilities to the younger Romantic poets. *Blackwood's Magazine*, in attacking 'the Cockney school', derided Hunt's 'glittering and rancid obscenities'. (See ROMANTICISM.)

STOW, John (1525–1605), chronicler and antiquary, followed at first the trade of a tailor, and was admitted a freeman of the Merchant Taylors' Company in 1547. At first his interest was English poetry; then from about 1564 he began to collect and transcribe manuscripts and to compose historical works, the first to be based on systematic study of public records. He was suspected of recusancy, and in 1569 and 1570 was charged with possessing popish and dangerous writings; he was examined before the ecclesiastical commission, but escaped without punishment. He is said to have spent as much as £200 a year on books and manuscripts; he was patronized by the earl of *Leicester and received a pension from the Merchant Taylors. A fine effigy of Stow, erected by his wife, survives in the church of St Andrew Undershaft, Leadenhall Street, London.

As well as assisting M. *Parker with editing historical texts, his chief publications were: *The Workes of Geoffrey Chaucer* (1561)—his further notes on *Chaucer were subsequently printed by T. Speght (1598); *Summarie of English Chronicles* (1565), an original historical work; *The Chronicles of England* (1580), later entitled *The Annales of England*; the second edition of *Holinshed's *Chronicles* (1585–7); and lastly *A Survey of London* (1598 and 1603), invaluable for the detailed information it gives about the ancient city and its customs. It was brought down to his day by J. *Strype in 1720, and modernized and annotated editions have since been published. The fullest edition of the original work was C. L. Kingsford's of 1908.

STOWE, Mrs Harriet Elizabeth Beecher (1811–96), born in Connecticut, sister of Henry Ward Beecher (1813–87, divine, religious author, and journalist), was a schoolteacher in Cincinnati before marrying in 1836 C. E. Stowe, a professor at her father's theological seminary. Her anti-slavery novel *Uncle Tom's Cabin*, which was serialized in the *National Era* in 1851–2 and published in book form in 1852, had a sensational success and stirred up great public feeling. A powerful if melodramatic tale, it describes the sufferings caused by slavery; pious old Uncle Tom, sold by his well-intentioned Kentucky owner Mr Shelby to meet his debts, is bought first by the handsome, idealistic, sensitive Augustine St Clair, in whose New Orleans household he becomes the favourite of the daughter, the saintly little Eva. But both Eva and St Clair die, and Tom is sold again, this time to a brutal cotton plantation owner, Simon Legree, who finally beats the unprotesting Tom to death just before Shelby's son arrives to redeem him. A parallel plot describes the escape to freedom in Canada of Shelby's slave, the beautiful (and almost white) quadroon Eliza, her child, and her husband George. Mrs Stowe's stress on the anguish of parted families was extremely telling, and her contrast between Southern, New England, and Kentucky ways is well observed, but the sensational religiosity of the story and its dubious conclusion (in which most of the survivors, including the once-irrepressible little slave *Topsy, disappear back to Africa to become missionaries) contributed to a shift of attitude which came to use the phrase 'Uncle Tom' pejoratively, to indicate a supine collaboration with the oppressor. The novel's success brought Mrs Stowe to England in 1853, 1856, and 1859, where she was rapturously received, and honoured by Queen *Victoria, although she later alienated British opinion by her *Lady Byron Vindicated* (1870), in which she charged *Byron with incestuous relations with his half-sister. Her other works include *Dred: A Tale of the Dismal Swamp* (1856), which also deals with slavery; *The Minister's Wooing* (1859), a protest against the doctrines of Calvinism; *Old Town Folks* (1869), set in New England; and *Poganuc People* (1878), another tale of New England family life with 'solidly remembered scenes—of candlemakings, quiltings and apple bees, chestnuttings and huckleberryings' praised by E. *Wilson in *Patriotic Gore* (1962).

STRABO (b. c.63 BC), a native of Amasia in Pontus, author of a history, continuing that of Polybius, which is lost, and of an important historical geography of the Roman Empire in 17 books, which is extant almost in its entirety.

STRACHEY, John St Loe, see SPECTATOR, THE.

STRACHEY, (Giles) Lytton (1880–1932), biographer and essayist, born in London; he was the eleventh child of an eminent soldier and public administrator who had served for more than 30 years in India, and he was named after his godfather, the first earl of *Lytton, viceroy of India. After an unhappy and sickly childhood and a miserable year at Liverpool University, he found intellectual stimulus and liberation at Trinity College, Cambridge; he became a member of the *Apostles and a friend of G. E. *Moore, M. *Keynes and L. *Woolf. He was thereafter a prominent member of the *Bloomsbury Group, advocating both in words and life its faith in tolerance in personal relationships: he spent the last 16 years of his life in a *ménage à trois* with the painter Dora Carrington (1893–1932) and her husband Ralph Partridge. He was also, in the First World War, a conspicuous conscientious objector. After an abortive attempt at an academic career, Strachey began to write extensively for periodicals (including the *Spectator*, the *Edinburgh Review*, the *Nation*, and the *Athenaeum*, and, later, *Life and Letters*). His flamboyant *Landmarks in French Literature* appeared in 1912, but he did not achieve fame until 1918, with the publication of *Eminent Victorians*, itself a landmark

in the history of *biography. This was a collection of four biographical essays, on Cardinal *Manning, F. *Nightingale, T. *Arnold, and General Gordon; Strachey's wit, iconoclasm, satiric edge, and narrative powers captured a large (though at times hostile) readership, and *Connolly was later to describe the work as 'the first book of the twenties . . . the light at the end of the tunnel'. His irreverent but affectionate life of Queen *Victoria (1921), which combined careful construction, telling anecdote, and an elegant mandarin style, was also highly successful. His last full-length work, *Elizabeth and Essex: A Tragic History* (1928) is more lurid and pictorial; some critics found it erotic and salacious (E. *Wilson described it as 'slightly disgusting'), and its emphasis on Elizabeth's relationship with her father and its effect on her treatment of Essex shows a clear (and early) debt to *Freud. Various collections of Strachey's essays, on subjects ranging from *Voltaire to the *Muggletonians, appeared during his life and posthumously, and a two-volume critical biography by M. *Holroyd was published in 1967–8.

STRADIVARIUS, the latinized form of the name of Antonio Stradivari (1644–1737), the most famous of all makers of stringed instruments, born at Cremona, a pupil of Nicolo Amati. The name is also applied to violins of the family's making. Antonio Stradivarius is the subject of a poem by G. *Eliot, and *The Lost Stradivarius* is a novel by J. M. *Falkner.

STRAFFORD, Sir Thomas Wentworth, first earl of (1593–1641), English statesman, and from 1639 chief adviser of Charles I. He was impeached by the Commons in 1640, but as it was manifestly impossible to convict him of high treason, a bill of attainder was substituted, and he was executed, after the king's assent, on Tower Hill. His death was the subject of many epitaphs, the best known of which (attributed to *Cleveland) contains the lines 'Strafford, who was hurried hence | Twixt Treason and Convenience'; also of a tragedy by R. *Browning (below).

Strafford, a tragedy in blank verse by R. *Browning, published 1837. It was written at the instigation of *Macready, who produced it at Covent Garden on the day of publication, with himself in the title role. The play received mixed notices and had only a brief run; it has never been professionally revived. Browning drew some of his material from the biography of *Strafford which he helped J. *Forster to write.

The action deals with the events surrounding the impeachment of Strafford; Browning's interest lies in the interplay of love and loyalty between Strafford and the three other main characters: King Charles I, whose weakness causes Strafford's downfall; John Pym, his closest friend until Strafford joined the royalist party and 'betrayed' the people; and Lady Carlisle, whose love for him Strafford, blinded by his devotion to the king, does not perceive. As with his other historical works, Browning's speculations about the characters' motives are idiosyncratic, and the action of the play is only loosely related to the actual course of events.

STRAHAN, or **STRACHAN,** William (1715–85), born in Edinburgh, was by 1738 apprenticed to a printer in London, and became established in the forefront of his trade, aided partly by the printing of *Johnson's *Dictionary*. He was a friend and correspondent of *Hume and of B. *Franklin, and printed work by the leading writers of the age, including *Gibbon, Adam *Smith, *Smollett, and *Warburton, with most of whom he maintained remarkably friendly personal relations. He became *King's Printer in 1770. There is a life by J. A. Cochrane, *Dr Johnson's Printer* (1964).

Strand Magazine, The, a popular illustrated monthly founded in 1891 by G. *Newnes, which included amongst its contributions fiction by A. C. *Doyle (the first appearance of Sherlock Holmes), H. G. *Wells, *Morrison, and a vast number of the short stories of P. G. *Wodehouse. It closed in 1950. See R. Pound, *The Strand Magazine 1891–1950* (1966).

Strange Case of Dr Jekyll and Mr Hyde, The, see JEKYLL.

Strange Story, A, a novel by *Bulwer-Lytton.

STRANGFORD, Percy Clinton, sixth Viscount (1780–1855), born and educated in Dublin, became a highly successful diplomat and public man. Profiting by his first posting to Lisbon, he published in 1803 *Poems from the Portuguese of Camoens*, which went into many editions. He was mocked as 'Hibernian' Strangford by Byron in *English Bards and Scotch Reviewers* (1809), but he was the friend of G. *Moore, *Croker, S. *Rogers, and other literary men, and a contributor to the *Gentleman's Magazine*.

Strap, a character in Smollett's *Roderick Random*.

STRAPAROLA, Giovan Francesco (d. ?1577), Italian author of novelle entitled *Piacevoli Notti* (*Pleasant Nights*), published in two parts, 1550 and 1553. It enjoyed much popularity and introduced various folk-tales to European literature, including the stories of *Puss in Boots and *Beauty and the Beast. Painter, in his *Palace of Pleasure*, drew on Straparola among others.

STRAUSS, David Friedrich (1808–74), German biblical critic, who studied theology at Tübingen. He resigned his teaching post at Tüb-

ingen University in 1833, because of his unorthodox approach to biblical texts. His most famous work was *Das Leben Jesu, kritisch bearbeitet* (*The Life of Jesus, critically examined*, 1835–6), in which Strauss subjected the gospel accounts of the life of Jesus to close historical criticism, finding them based on myth rather than historical fact. G. *Eliot translated the work into English in 1846 (her first published work), and her study of it helped to confirm her break with Christianity.

STRAUSS, Richard (1864–1949), German composer. Strauss's early rise to fame was based almost entirely on the series of orchestral tone-poems that he wrote during the last decades of the 19th century. The first of these in order of composition was *Macbeth*, completed in 1888 though not performed until after its more famous successor, *Don Juan*, in 1890. Strauss only once again returned to Shakespeare, with the three Ophelia songs in the *Sechs Lieder* (1918). The vast majority of Strauss's many song texts are of German origin, though one of the most famous of them all, 'Morgen' (1894), is a setting of a poem written in German by the Scotsman J. H. Mackay. A German version of Tennyson's *Enoch Arden*, for speaker with piano accompaniment, dates from 1897.

With the turn of the century Strauss began what was to be a continuing involvement with opera, and with his third attempt (1905) he achieved a triumph with a German version of *Wilde's *Salome*, a remarkably accurate realization in music of Wilde's *fin-de-siècle* decadence. There was, of course, an element of *scandale* in the *succès*: 'I won't do it, I'm a decent woman', said the original interpreter of the title role at rehearsal, and the Kaiser was later reported as saying, 'I'm sorry Strauss composed this *Salome*. It will do him a lot of damage.' But within two years *Salome* had been performed at 50 opera houses. 'The damage', Strauss observed drily, 'enabled me to build the villa at Garmisch.'

None of the series of operas, beginning with *Elektra* and *Der Rosenkavalier*, which Strauss wrote in collaboration with *Hofmannsthal, used English sources. After Hofmannsthal's death, however, he accepted from the Austrian writer Stefan Zweig a libretto based on Jonson's *Epicene, or the Silent Woman*, which became *Die schweigsame Frau*, one of the wittiest and most brilliant of Strauss's operas, though not perhaps one of the most satisfying. It received four performances in 1935, but was then banned throughout Germany because of the Jewish origin of its librettist.

STRAVINSKY, Igor Fyodorovich (1882–1971), Russian composer, who later adopted French and then American nationality. Most of Stravinsky's earlier works are Russian in origin and background. A more cosmopolitan element manifested itself during the years in France, but it was not until well after his emigration to the USA that he wrote his first and, as it turned out, his most important composition to English words, the three-act opera *The Rake's Progress* (1951). This had the advantage of one of the very best of recent operatic librettos, by *Auden assisted by Chester Kallman, and from the point of view of both text and music the result was a remarkable *tour de force*: both composer and librettist accepted the idea of a strongly marked operatic convention and the 18th-cent. environment imposed by the series of *Hogarth engravings on which this moral tale was based, yet in neither case did this result in pastiche, only in a classical precision of craftsmanship and a great release of vitality.

In the period immediately following *The Rake's Progress* Stravinsky's style of composition underwent a profound change, absorbing certain aspects of the serial practice developed by *Schoenberg and moving away from the tonal principles that had been the essential basis of his music. Among the first works to adopt the new manner were the little *Cantata* (1952), made up of four late medieval English lyrics rather severely set for soloists, chorus, and five solo instruments, and a year later the *Three Songs from William Shakespeare* ('Musick to heare', 'Full Fathom Five', and 'When Daisies Pied') for voice, flute, clarinet, and viola. After *The Rake* Auden had offered him another libretto (a masque entitled *Delia*), but Stravinsky, nervous of repeating himself, turned instead to Dylan *Thomas, who proposed as a subject 'the rediscovery of our planet following an atomic misadventure'. The composer has left a touching account of their one meeting in 1953: the only music that resulted from it, however, was *In Memoriam Dylan Thomas* (1954), a setting of 'Do not go gentle' for tenor, string quartet, and four trombones.

Another 'in memoriam' piece is the miniature *Elegy for J.F.K.* (1964), for which he asked Auden to write a 'very quiet little lyric' which he set for baritone and three clarinets. And a little later the death of his friend T. S. *Eliot produced the short *Introitus*, for male chorus and eight instruments, first heard in April 1965 together with the orchestral *Variations* dedicated to the memory of another close friend, A. *Huxley. Stravinsky's only setting of an actual Eliot text was the short polyphonic *Anthem* for unaccompanied chorus, 'The Dove descending breaks the Air' (1962) to words from the 'Little Gidding' section of *Four Quartets*.

Stravinsky's last work for the stage was written to an English text: the 'musical play' entitled *The Flood* (1962), a 24-minute musical version of part of the York miracle play. His actual last composition, at the age of 84, was a setting for soprano and piano of *Lear's 'The Owl and the Pussy Cat' which he dedicated to his wife.

Straw, Jack, see JACK STRAW.

Strawberry Hill, near Twickenham, about ten miles west of the centre of London. Horace *Walpole settled there in 1747, and with advice from his friends *Chute and Richard *Bentley transformed it into 'a little Gothic castle', housing in it his collection of articles of virtu, and establishing in 1757 a private press; its first printing was of *Gray's *Odes*. Walpole also printed many of his own works. Strawberry Hill now houses St Mary's, a Roman Catholic college. (See also GOTHIC REVIVAL.)

Stream of Consciousness, a phrase coined by W. *James in his *Principles of Psychology* (1890) to describe the flow of thoughts of the waking mind, but now widely used in a literary context to describe the narrative method whereby certain novelists describe the unspoken thoughts and feelings of their characters, without resorting to objective description or conventional dialogue. *Les Lauriers sont coupés* (1888) by the minor French novelist Édouard Dujardin (1861–1949) has been credited (by *Joyce, principally) as a pioneering example of the technique, and it was adapted and developed by Joyce himself, by D. *Richardson, V. *Woolf, *Proust, and others. The ability to represent the flux of a character's thoughts, impressions, emotions, or reminiscences, often without logical sequence or syntax, marked a revolution in the form of the novel, and extended passages of stream of consciousness are now so familiar that they no longer strike a reader as avant-garde. The related phrase 'interior monologue' is also used to describe the inner movement of consciousness in a character's mind: celebrated examples are the opening pages of *Mrs Dalloway*, and Molly Bloom's reflections in the closing pages of *Ulysses*.

STREATFEILD, Noel, see CHILDREN'S LITERATURE.

Streetcar named Desire, A, a play by T. Williams.

Strephon, the shepherd whose lament for his lost Urania forms the opening of Sidney's *Arcadia*. 'Strephon' has been adopted as a conventional name for a rustic lover.

Strether, Lewis Lambert, a character in H. James's *The Ambassadors*.

STRETTON, Hesba, the *nom de plume* of Sarah Smith (1832–1911), a prolific writer of tracts, pamphlets, stories, and booklets, largely published by the Religious Tract Society. *Jessica's First Prayer* (1867) was reprinted innumerable times, brought tears to the eyes of *Kilvert, and remained popular for many years. She also wrote three long novels, which were well received: *Paul's Courtship* (1867), *The Clives of Burcot* (1868), and *Through a Needle's Eye* (1879). She contributed to *Dickens's *All the Year Round*, and to other periodicals.

STRINDBERG, (Johan) August (1849–1912), Swedish playwright and author, born in Stockholm, the son of a steamship agent who married his housekeeper after she had already borne him three sons: hence the title of his autobiography, *The Son of a Servant* (1886). Strindberg achieved theatrical success only after much difficulty and attempts at other careers, and his works, dramatic and non-dramatic, are marked by a deeply neurotic response to religion, social class, and sexuality; he married three times, gained a reputation for anti-feminism and misogyny, and was tried for blasphemy, though acquitted. His first important play, *Master Olof*, written 1872–7, performed 1881, was followed by others, including *The Father* (1887), *Miss Julie* (1888), and *Creditors* (1889), works which combine a highly aggressive and original version of *naturalism with a sense of the extreme and pathological. His later works are tense, symbolic, psychic dramas, marked by a sense of suffering and a longing for salvation and absolution; they include *To Damascus* (1898–1901; 3 parts), *The Dance of Death* (1901), *A Dream Play* (1902), and *The Ghost Sonata* (1907), all distinctive and innovative works which influenced the psychological and symbolic dramas of *O'Neill and the writers of the Theatre of the *Absurd. G. B. *Shaw, who met Strindberg in Stockholm in 1908 and saw a specially arranged performance of *Miss Julie*, was a generous advocate of his work, but it was nevertheless some years before his plays were performed and accepted in England.

Strindberg's non-dramatic works include a novel, *The Red Room* (1879), *Getting Married* (1884, 1885; 2 vols of short stories), and *Inferno* (written and published in French, 1898), an extraordinary account of his life in Paris after the collapse of his second marriage, when, tormented by loneliness and driven to the verge of insanity by guilt and a sense of failure, he studied *Swedenborg, dabbled in alchemy, and suffered severe hallucinations. Many of Strindberg's plays have been translated into English by Michael Meyer, who also published a biography in 1985, and several of his works have been translated by Mary Sandbach.

STRODE, Ralph, minor scholastic philosopher and logician, fellow of Merton College, Oxford, where he was the colleague of *Wyclif with whom he entered into controversy. As 'philosophical Strode' (V. 1857) he was the dedicatee of Chaucer's *Troilus and Criseyde*, along with *Gower.

Strong, Dr, in Dickens's *David Copperfield*, an amiable old schoolmaster, who dotes on his young wife Annie and supports her worthless cousin, Jack Maldon.

STRONG, Emilia Francis (Lady Dilke), see DILKE, SIR C. W.

STRONG, L(eonard) A(lfred) G(eorge) (1896–1958), poet and novelist, born in Devon of half-Irish ancestry. He was educated at Wadham College, Oxford, and later taught for some years in Oxford, before becoming a full-time writer; during this period he befriended the young *Day-Lewis. His many novels (which show a strain of the macabre and violent) include *Dewer Rides* (1929, set in Dartmoor) and *Sea Wall* (1933, set in Dublin). His autobiography of his early years, *Green Memory*, was published posthumously in 1961.

Structuralism, a continental European movement in the human sciences which has had a powerful and controversial influence on literary theory and criticism in the English-speaking world since the 1960s. Its intellectual roots are in the linguistics of *Saussure, and in the work of the Russian Formalists in the Revolutionary period and of the Prague School in the 1930s—*Jakobson being a key figure in both groups. In the 1960s a brilliant generation of French, or French-based, critics, notably Roland Barthes (1915–80), Tzvetan Todorov (1940–), and Gérard Genette (1930–), elaborated and developed structuralist ideas and methods, with particularly successful results in application to narrative. The studies of myth by the anthropologist Claude Lévi-Strauss (1908–) also enhanced the prestige of structuralism at this time.

Structuralism views any cultural phenomenon, from a folk-tale to a menu or an advertisement, as the product of a 'system of signification', or code, and maintains that it is the relationships between the elements of such a system that allow it to signify, rather than the relationships between the elements and 'reality'. All codes of signification are arbitrary, and there is no way of apprehending reality without a code. In its purest form, structuralism tries to do for culture at large what grammar does for natural languages—to identify and define the rules and constraints within which and by virtue of which meaning is generated and communicated. As applied to literary criticism it calls into question the idea that a literary text reflects a reality that is already given, or that it expresses a unique authorial self, and thus challenges the empiricist and humanist assumptions of traditional literary scholarship. This challenge has become more radical in 'post-structuralist' critical theory and practice inspired by the psychoanalyst Jacques Lacan (1901–   ) and the philosopher Jacques Derrida (1930–   ). Critical 'deconstruction', derived from the work of Derrida, aims to show that any and every text inevitably undermines its own claims to a determinate meaning, and emphasizes the role of the reader in the production of meaning. See Terence Hawkes, *Structuralism and Semiotics* (1977); Jonathan Culler, *Structuralist Poetics* (1978); Christopher Norris, *Deconstruction* (1982).

Struldbrugs, see GULLIVER'S TRAVELS.

STRUTT, Joseph (1749–1802), author, artist, engraver, and antiquary, was author of many works valuable for their research and engravings, including a *Chronicle of England* (1777–8), *Dresses and Habits of the English People* (1796–9), and *Sports and Pastimes of the People of England* (1801). An unfinished novel by Strutt was completed by Sir W. *Scott (*Queenhoo Hall*, 1808), and suggested to him the publication of his own *Waverley*.

Struwwelpeter, see HOFFMANN, H.

STRYPE, John (1643–1737), ecclesiastical historian, educated at St Paul's School, Jesus College and St Catharine's Hall, Cambridge, formed a magnificent collection of original documents, mostly of the Tudor period, now in the *Harleian and Lansdowne MSS. He published lives of *Cranmer (1694), *Cheke (1705), Grindal (1710), M. *Parker (1711), and Whitgift (1718). He corrected and enlarged *Stow's *Survey of London* (1720).

STUART, Daniel (1766–1846), journalist, and an early press baron, who in 1795 bought the *Morning Post* and increased its circulation fourfold, later amalgamating with it *The Gazetteer* and *The Telegraph*. In 1796 he bought *The Courier* and when he sold the *Morning Post* in 1803 he proceeded to do for *The Courier* what he had done for his earlier paper. He employed excellent journalists and writers, including *Southey, *Lamb, *Wordsworth, and *Coleridge. Between 1799 and 1802 Coleridge wrote many articles, both political and literary, for the *Post*.

STUBBES, or **STUBBS**, Philip (*fl.* 1583–91), a Puritan pamphleteer, author of *The Anatomie of Abuses* (1583), a denunciation of evil customs of the time which, in the author's opinion, needed abolition. It contains a section on stage plays and is one of the principal sources of information on the social and economic conditions of the period. His account of his wife Katherine, *A Christal Glasse for Christian Women* (1591), was very popular.

STUBBS, John (*c.*1541–90), was educated at Trinity College, Cambridge, and Lincoln's Inn. In August 1579 he published *The Discoverie of a Gaping Gulf whereinto England is like to be Swallowed* against the Queen's marriage to the French king's brother, François, duc d'Alençon. For this he was imprisoned and had his right hand cut off, whereupon he 'put off his hat with his left and said with a loud voice "God save the Queen" '. The pamphlet has been edited by L. E. Berry (1968).

STUBBS, William (1825–1901), historian. Educated at Ripon Grammar School and Christ Church, Oxford, he was elected a fellow of Trinity College, Oxford, in 1848 but resigned in 1850 to take the living of Knavestock, Essex; in 1866 he was appointed Regius professor of modern history at Oxford. He was the first substantial scholar to hold such a chair at either university, and may be said to have created the discipline of English medieval history singlehanded. He showed his supreme professional skill, acquired by the study of contemporary German academic method, in the 18 volumes of medieval texts he edited for the *Rolls Series, and this was the foundation for his great *Constitutional History of [Medieval] England* (3 vols, 1874–8), which has been described as 'one of the most astonishing achievements of the Victorian mind', fit to rank with *Darwin's *Origin of Species*. Together with his *Select Charters and other Illustrations of English Constitutional History to 1307* (1870), it imposed a pattern and a method on the teaching of history in all British universities which survived until the mid-20th cent. (in Oxford longer), though he published nothing more after his elevation to the bishopric of Chester in 1884 and subsequently (1888) Oxford. The chief criticism of his work is that it partook of the attitudes of his time: he assumed that medieval England was a unified nation with common ideals, that her better kings had a formed and consistent plan of constitutional action, and that the development of Parliament was inevitable and evolutionary—ideas which might have had a shorter life had they been put forward by a lesser man.

His letters were published by W. H. Hutton (1904). See Helen Cam, *Stubbs Seventy Years After*, in *Cambridge Historical Journal*, vol. ix (1948); J. G. Edwards, *William Stubbs* (1952); J. W. Burrow, *A Liberal Descent* (1981).

Stukeley, a character in George Peele's *Battle of Alcazar*. The real Thomas Stukeley was said to be a natural son of *Henry VIII. He was an adventurer, who entered the service of the French king, was sent on a spying expedition to England, and betrayed his employer to Cecil.

He next entered the service of Charles V; then embarked on a privateering expedition, for which Queen Elizabeth provided one of his ships, till the remonstrances of foreign powers led to his arrest. He proceeded to Ireland, where his ambitious schemes were distrusted and discountenanced by Elizabeth, then escaped to Spain, having been in treasonable correspondence with Philip II. He joined the king of Portugal's expedition against Morocco and was killed at the battle of Alcazar. Fuller in his *Worthies of England gives an amusing account of a conversation between him and Queen Elizabeth.

STUKELEY, William (1687–1765), antiquary, who started life as a student of law, took a degree as doctor of medicine, and became secretary to the *Society of Antiquaries, which he shared in founding (1718). He wrote on many varied topics, ranging from flute music to earthquakes, but was particularly interested in Druidism, and his discussions of Stonehenge (*Stonehenge: a temple restor'd to the British druids*, 1740) and Avebury (*Abury*, 1743) claimed, (after *Aubrey) that they had been built by the Druids. He believed that the beliefs of the Druids were 'near akin to the Christian doctrine', that they believed in a Trinity, and that their alleged human sacrifices prefigured the Crucifixion; he defended them from the attacks of *Toland who had implied that they were superstitious, debauched, and corrupt. His views may have influenced *Blake's vision of *Albion, and *Wordsworth was also familiar with them. See A. L. Owen, *The Famous Druids* (1962). (See PRIMITIVISM.)

STURLA THORDSSON (c.1214–84), nephew of *Snorri Sturluson, Icelandic historian, author of the *Sturlunga saga*, or contemporary history of the house of Sturla, a vivid picture of old Icelandic life.

Sturm und Drang (Storm and Stress), the name (taken from the title of an absurd romantic drama of the American War of Independence by the German playwright Klinger, 1775) given to a period of literary ferment which prevailed in Germany during the latter part of the 18th cent. It was inspired by *Rousseau's fervent idealism and characterized by a revolt against literary conventions (particularly the *unities in drama), by the cult of genius, and by a return to 'nature'. The principal figures of the movement were the young *Goethe, *Herder, and *Schiller. Many of the plays were translated and adapted for the English stage during the 1790s.

STURT, George (1863–1927), born in Farnham, Surrey, where in 1884 he inherited the long-established family business described in *The Wheelwright's Shop* (1923), which records the traditions of and changes in local craftsman-

ship and relationships. Earlier works, published as 'George Bourne', include *The Bettesworth Book* (1901) and *Change in the Village* (1912). Selections from his journal were edited by G. *Grigson (1941) and E. D. Mackerness (1967).

Stutly, Will, one of the legendary companions of *Robin Hood.

Sublime, the, an idea associated with religious awe, vastness, natural magnificence, and strong emotion which fascinated 18th-cent. literary critics and aestheticians. Its development marks the movement away from the clarity of *Neoclassicism towards *Romanticism, with its emphasis on feeling and imagination; it was connected with the concept of original genius which soared fearlessly above the rules.

Sublimity in rhetoric and poetry was first analysed in an anonymous Greek work, *On the Sublime*, attributed to *Longinus, which was widely admired in England after *Boileau's French translation of 1674. The concept was elaborated by many writers, including *Addison, *Dennis, *Hume, *Burke, and R. *Blair and the discussion spread from literature to other areas. Longinus had described the immensity of objects in the natural world, of the stars, of mountains and volcanoes, and of the ocean, as a source of the sublime, and this idea was of profound importance to the growing feeling for the grandeur and violence of nature. The most widely read work, and most stimulating to writers and painters, was Burke's *Philosophical Enquiry into the Origin of our Ideas of the *Sublime and Beautiful* (1757). Burke put a new emphasis on terror: 'Whatever is fitted in any sort to excite the ideas of pain, and danger . . . or is conversant about terrible objects, or operates in a manner analogous to terror, is a source of the sublime; that is, it is productive of the strongest emotion which the mind is capable of feeling.' Burke saw the sublime as a category distinct from beauty. With the former he associated obscurity, power, darkness, solitude, and vastness and with the latter smoothness, delicacy, smallness, and light. These varied ideas were brought together, and discussed with greater philosophical rigour, by *Kant in the *Critique of Judgement* (1790). Burke's theory was popular, and stimulated a passion for terror that culminated in the Gothic tales of A. *Radcliffe and the macabre paintings, crowded with monsters and ghosts, of Barry, Mortimer, and *Fuseli. The cult drew strength from *Macpherson's Ossianic poems; Ossian took his place beside *Homer and *Milton as one of the great poets of the sublime, whose works were frequently illustrated by painters. The sublime of terror kindled the enthusiasm for wild scenery and cosmic grandeur already apparent in the writings of Addison and *Shaftesbury, and of E. *Young and James *Thomson. Many writers making the *Grand

Tour dwelt on the sublimity of the Alps; they contrasted them with the pictures of *Rosa, whose stormy landscapes provided a pattern for 18th-cent. descriptions of savage nature. By the 1760s, when picturesque journeys in England became popular, travellers sought out the exhilarating perils of the rushing torrent, the remote mountain peak, and the gloomy forest. Many published their impressions in 'Tours', and sublimity became a fashion, pandered to by the dramatic storms shown by de Loutherbourg's Ediophusikon, a small theatre with lantern slides, and later by J. *Martin's vast panoramas of cosmic disaster.

The Romantic poets rejected the categories of 18th-cent. theorists and yet these writers on the sublime were moving, albeit clumsily, towards that sense of the mystery of natural forces that is so powerful in the poetry of *Byron, *Shelley, and *Wordsworth, and in the paintings of *Turner. See S. H. Monk, *The Sublime: A study of critical theories in XVIII century England* (1935).

Sublime, On the, see SUBLIME, THE, and LONGINUS.

Sublime and Beautiful, A Philosophical Enquiry into the Origin of our Ideas of the, a treatise by E. *Burke, published anonymously 1757, with an 'Introduction on Taste' added 1759.

This is one of the earliest of Burke's publications, in which he discusses the distinctions between the *sublime, with its associations of infinity, darkness, solitude, terror, and vacuity, and the beautiful, which consists in relative smallness, smoothness, and brightness of colour. There are interesting sections on pleasure gained from distress (as in tragedy, or in the sight of a conflagration), and his descriptions of 'a sort of delightful horror, a sort of tranquillity tinged with terror' had much influence on the aesthetic theory of the later 18th cent. and in particular on G. E. *Lessing. Aphorisms like 'A clear idea is another name for a little idea' mark the transition from the lucidity admired by *Pope to the sublimity of writers like T. *Gray. Ed. J. T. Boulton (1958).

Subtle, the false alchemist and astrologer of Jonson's *The Alchemist.

SUCKLING, Sir John (1609–41), of an old Norfolk family, was educated at Trinity College, Cambridge. He inherited large estates, travelled in Holland, and was knighted on his return in 1630. In 1631 he was in Germany, as a member of Sir Henry Vane's embassy to Gustavus Adolphus. He returned to London in 1632 and lived at court in great splendour. He became a leader of the royalist party in the early troubles, then fled to France and is said by *Aubrey to have committed suicide in Paris. His chief works are included in *Fragmenta Aurea* (1646) and consist of poems, plays, letters, and tracts, among them the famous 'Ballad upon a Wedding'. His 'Sessions of the Poets', in which various writers of the day, including *Jonson, *Carew, and *D'Avenant, contend for the laurel, appeared in 1637, and is interesting as an expression of contemporary opinion on these writers. Suckling's play *Aglaura* (with two fifth acts, one tragic, the other not) was lavishly staged and printed in 1638 at his own expense. *The Goblins* (1646), a romantic drama in which outlaws disguise themselves as devils, was said by *Dryden to illustrate Suckling's professed admiration for Shakespeare, 'his Reginella being an open imitation of Shakespeare's Miranda; his spirits, though counterfeit, yet are copied from Ariel.' *Brennoralt* (1646), an expansion of the *Discontented Colonell* (1640), a tragedy, is interesting for the light which the melancholy colonel throws on the author himself. The plays are, however, chiefly valuable for their lyrics, and Suckling has enjoyed a steady reputation as one of the most elegant and brilliant of the *Cavalier poets. D'Avenant speaks of his sparkling wit, describing him further as the greatest gallant and gamester of his day. According to Aubrey, he invented the game of cribbage. A two-volume edition of his works, ed. T. Clayton and L. A. Beaurline, appeared in 1971. (See also FALKLAND.)

Suddlechop, Benjamin and Dame Ursula, characters in Scott's *The Fortunes of Nigel.

SUE, Eugène (1804–57), French novelist, a prolific writer of novels of the Parisian underworld. The best-known include *Les Mystères de Paris* (1842–3) and *Le Juif errant* (1844–5): see WANDERING JEW, THE.

SUESS, Eduard (1831–1914), born in London and educated at Prague and Vienna, became professor of geology at Vienna and one of the greatest of recent geologists. His principal work is *Das Antlitz der Erde* (1885–1909), which was translated as *The Face of the Earth* (1904–25) by H. B. C. Sollas.

SUETONIUS (Gaius Suetonius Tranquillus) (AD c.70–c.140), Roman biographer whose major surviving work, the *Lives of the Caesars*, was composed in part while he was in charge of the imperial archives. Suetonius, writing about the Julio-Claudian and Flavian emperors under a new dynasty, saw no reason to treat them as heroes. His aim was to bring out the moral character of his subjects, and for this purpose (and also because he was an inveterate gossip) he paid attention to their private habits as well as to their imperial policy. His method was adopted by later Roman biographers and may be said to have paved the way for the intimate biographies that began to appear in the second half of the 17th cent. But the flavour of his writing has been best caught recently by Robert *Graves in *I, Claudius* and *Claudius the God.*

Suilen, Squire and Mrs, characters in Farquhar's *The Beaux Stratagem.*

SULLIVAN, Sir Arthur (1842–1900), English composer. Such is the popularity of the *Gilbert and Sullivan operas that it is often forgotten that Sullivan made a distinguished career as a composer in his own right, and was considered the leading musician in the period preceding *Parry and *Stanford.

Sullivan's Op. 1, written when he was a 19-year-old student at Leipzig, was a group of 12 pieces of incidental music for *The Tempest*: they seem never to have been used in the theatre, though their first performance in London made Sullivan famous and later, in Paris, he played them in a piano duet version with *Rossini, who apparently liked them very much. He subsequently wrote successful incidental music for other Shakespeare plays—*The Merchant of Venice* (1871), *Henry VIII* (1877), *Macbeth* (1888)—and there are a number of Shakespeare settings in the cantata *Kenilworth* (1865). His *Five Shakespeare Songs* (1866) include the famous setting of 'Orpheus with his lute', and were among the earliest of an enormous number of songs and ballads written for the Victorian drawing room, and he also collaborated with *Tennyson on a song cycle, *The Window, or the Songs of the Wrens* (1871).

The bigger choral works tend to be on sacred subjects, though *The Golden Legend*, which Sullivan himself regarded as his masterpiece, is based on *Longfellow. His one attempt at serious opera, *Ivanhoe* (after Sir W. *Scott, 1891), opened with much publicity but did not last, and certainly could not compare with the brilliance of the comic operas, for which (and perhaps, less happily, for the hymn tune 'Onward, Christian soldiers') he is remembered today.

'Sumer is icumen in', one of the earliest known English lyrics, found in B.M. MS Harley 978, a commonplace book of Reading Abbey from the first half of the 13th cent. The music, and Latin instructions for singing it, are also in the MS.

Summers last will and Testament, a play by T. *Nashe, published 1600, but written in the autumn of 1592 or 1593. It is framed by the jocular comments of Will Summers, *Henry VIII's jester (who died c.1560), and is an allegorical pageant in which Summer, personified as a dying old man, decides to whom to leave his riches. The play reflects fear of the plague, of which there was a prolonged outbreak in 1592–3, in the famous lyric:

> Adieu, farewell earths blisse,
> This world uncertaine is,
> Fond are lifes lustful joyes,

> Death proves them all but toyes,
> None from his darts can flye;
> I am sick, I must dye:
> Lord, have mercy on us.

Summerson, Esther, a character in Dickens's *Bleak House*, and one of the narrators of the tale.

'Summoner's Tale, The', see CANTERBURY TALES, 8.

Sunday Times, The, a Sunday paper founded in 1822 by Henry White, and still in existence, despite several periods of obscurity. It grew greatly in circulation and influence from the 1930s onwards, earning a high reputation for its arts pages and, recently, for its investigative journalism; notable reviewers have included J. *Agate, D. *McCarthy, C. *Connolly, Dilys Powell (film critic, 1936–76), and Sir Harold Hobson (drama critic, 1947–76). The gossip column 'Atticus', started by T. P. *O'Connor, has been written by (among others) J. *Buchan, S. *Sitwell, and I. *Fleming. See *The Pearl of Days* (1972), a memoir of the paper by H. Hobson, P. Knightley, and L. Russell.

Supposes, a comedy in prose, one of the earliest in English, by G. *Gascoigne, translated from *Ariosto's *I Suppositi*, and performed at Gray's Inn in 1566. It concerns a series of disguises and confused identities; the scenes with servants are effectively comic, especially those with the old nurse Balia.

Surface, Joseph and Charles, the two brothers in Sheridan's *The School for Scandal.*

Surgeon's Daughter, The, a novel by Sir W. *Scott, published 1827 as one of the stories in *Chronicles of the Canongate.*

Richard Middlemas, an illegitimate child, has been left in the care of Gideon Gray, surgeon of the village of Middlemas, and brought up in his home, where he and the surgeon's daughter Menie fall in love. On coming of age, Richard, being of an ambitious as well as violent and ill-balanced disposition, leaves the doctor's home to push his fortunes in India. Here he falls under the influence of an adventuress, the Begum Mootee Mahal, otherwise Mme Montreville, and has the unspeakable baseness to fall in with her plan to lure Menie out to India with a view to handing her over to Tippoo Sahib. The plot is defeated by Adam Hartley, Richard's fellow pupil at Dr Gray's, an unsuccessful suitor for Menie's hand. He secures the interposition of Hyder Ali, who orders the release of Menie. By his order also Richard Middlemas is crushed to death by an elephant.

Surly, the choleric gamester of Jonson's *The Alchemist.*

'Surprised by Joy—impatient as the Wind',

a sonnet by *Wordsworth, first published in 1815, suggested by the death of his daughter Catherine in 1812, but written, by his own account, 'long after'.

Surrealism, a movement founded in Paris in 1924 with the publication of A. *Breton's first *Surrealist Manifesto.* It was conceived as a revolutionary mode of thought and action, concerned with politics, philosophy, and psychology as well as literature and art. The *Manifesto* attacked rationalism and narrow logical systems; drawing on *Freud's theories concerning the unconscious and its relation to dreams, it called for the exploration of hidden and neglected areas of the human psyche, not necessarily from the standpoint of psychoanalysis, and the resolution 'of the apparently contradictory states of dream and reality'. The group of writers and painters that gathered round Breton experimented with automatic processes, which were considered the best means of producing the surreal poetic image: the spontaneous coupling of unrelated objects. An extended conception of poetry, which was to be part of, not separate from, life, was central to Surrealism. A great variety of poetry was published by, for example, Breton, *Aragon, *Éluard, Robert Desnos, Benjamin Péret, René Crevel; but much surrealist writing falls outside conventional literary categories, e.g. Aragon's *Paris Peasant* (1926) or Breton's *Communicating Vessels* (1932). Breton's *Nadja* (1928), for instance, both records an intense personal relationship and challenges socially determined definitions of sanity and insanity. Surrealist artists in the 1920s sought equivalents to automatic writing, e.g. André Masson's free ink drawings, Max Ernst's *frottages,* or Joan Miró's field painting. In 1929 *Dali joined the movement, introducing a more illusionistic 'dream' imagery heavily indebted to Freud. In the 1930s writers and artists alike collected or fabricated surrealist objects (often relying on chance), and Breton mixed words and images in his poem-objects. Several surrealists joined the Communist Party and theoretical texts, including Breton's *Surrealist Manifesto* of 1929, try to reconcile Freud and *Marx.

Surrealism was a major intellectual force between the wars, although as it spread internationally in the 1930s interest tended to concentrate on surrealist art. In England the movement attracted some attention among literary circles, but it was only after the International Surrealist Exhibition of 1936 that a surrealist group was established, its members including D. *Gascoyne, H. *Read, Roland Penrose (1900–84), the documentary film-maker Humphrey Jennings (1907–50), and Hugh Sykes Davies (1909–84).

SURREY, Henry Howard, (by courtesy) earl of (?1517–47), poet, was the son of Thomas Howard (afterwards third duke of Norfolk). He married Frances Vere in 1532. He was with the army during the war with France (1544–6), being wounded before Montreuil, and was commander of Boulogne, 1545–6. He was accused of various minor offences, but tried and executed on the charge of treasonably quartering the royal arms. His works consist of sonnets and poems in various metres notable for their elegance of construction. Like *Wyatt he studied Italian models, especially *Petrarch, but his sonnets were predominantly in the 'English' form (a b a b c d c d e f e f g g), later to be used by Shakespeare, which appears to have been his invention. (See SONNET.) A still more durable innovation was his use of blank verse in his translation of the *Aeneid,* Bks II and IV. Forty of his poems were printed in *Tottel's Miscellany* (1557). *Nashe and *Drayton built up a picture of Surrey as the languishing lover of 'Geraldine' (Elizabeth, daughter of the ninth earl of Kildare); but he seems to have done no more than address a single sonnet to this lady, possibly when she was as young as nine.

Surrey's poems were edited together with those of Wyatt by G. F. Nott, 1815–16; and, in selection, by Emrys Jones in 1964.

SURTEES, Robert (1779–1834), educated at Christ Church, Oxford, an antiquary and topographer. He spent his life in collecting materials for his *History of Durham* (1816–40). He is commemorated in the Surtees Society, which publishes original materials relating to the history of the region constituting the old kingdom of Northumbria. Sir W. Scott included in his *Minstrelsy of the Scottish Border* a spurious and spirited ballad by him, 'The Death of Featherstonhaugh'. 'Barthram's Dirge' in the same collection is suspected of being also by Surtees (J. H. Burton, *The Book-Hunter,* 1862).

SURTEES, Robert Smith (1805–64), was born in Durham, the son of a country squire. After attending Durham Grammar School he became articled to a solicitor and practised as a lawyer. From 1830 he built up a reputation as a sporting journalist, contributing to the *Sporting Magazine,* and in 1831 founded, with R. Ackermann the younger, and edited the *New Sporting Magazine* to which he contributed his comic sketches of Mr Jorrocks, the sporting Cockney grocer, later collected as *Jorrocks's Jaunts and Jollities* (1838, illustrated by 'Phiz', H. K. *Browne, and later by H. T. Alken). Jorrocks, whose adventures to some extent suggested the original idea of *Pickwick Papers,* reappears in *Handley Cross* (1843; expanded and illustrated by *Leech, 1854), one of Surtees's most successful novels, and in the less popular *Hillingdon Hall* (1845). His second great character, Mr Soapy Sponge, appears in *Mr Sponge's Sporting Tour*

(1853, illustrated by Leech), which is probably his best work; another celebrated character was Mr Facey Romford, who appears in his last novel, *Mr Facey Romford's Hounds* (1865). Surtees had abandoned his legal practice in 1835, resigned his editorship in 1836, inherited his father's Hamsterley estate in 1838, and thereafter devoted his time to his favourite pursuits of hunting and shooting (he became high sheriff of Durham in 1856) while continuing his literary work. His eight long novels deal mainly with the characteristic aspects of English foxhunting society, but his vivid caricatures, the absurd scenes he describes, the convincing dialect and often repeated catch-phrases, and perceptive social observation distinguish him from other writers of this genre and won him praise from *Thackeray and others; the illustration of his novels by Leech, Alken, and Phiz also contributed to their success. *Young Tom Hall*, originally serialized in the *New Monthly Magazine* in 1853, remained unfinished and was first published in book form in 1926.

Survey of London, A, see STOW, J.

Susan, Lady, the chief character in J. Austen's *Lady Susan*.

Suspicious Husband, The, a comedy by Dr B. *Hoadly and his brother, produced 1747 at Covent Garden, *Garrick taking the part of Ranger.

Strictland, the suspicious husband of a young wife, is guardian of the wealthy Jacintha. She and Bellamy are in love, but Strictland will not hear of the match. So Jacintha, a young lady of spirit, decides to run away with her lover, who provides a rope ladder for the purpose. Clarinda, a sprightly young friend of Mrs Strictland, is staying in her house. Frankly, a friend of Bellamy, who has fallen in love with her at Bath, pursues her to London. Frankly and Bellamy meet outside the house at night, just when Jacintha is about to escape and when Clarinda, after a late whist party, is coming home. A general imbroglio ensues. Bellamy suspects Frankly of an intrigue with Jacintha; Strictland, discovering the latter's attempted flight, goes off in pursuit. Meanwhile Ranger, an adventurous rake and friend of Bellamy and Frankly, happening to pass and seeing a rope ladder hanging from the window, climbs up in search of adventure, and makes his way to the bedroom of Mrs Strictland, whom he has never seen before. The return of Strictland with the captured Jacintha puts him to flight, but he drops his hat in Mrs Strictland's room where it is discovered by her husband, who is now convinced that his suspicions were well founded and sentences his wife to banishment to the country. Meanwhile Ranger, who has taken refuge in another room, discovers Jacintha, and enables her to escape, this time successfully. On the morrow there is a general confrontation and explanation, and all ends happily.

SUTCLIFF, Rosemary, see CHILDREN'S LITERATURE.

Svengali, see TRILBY.

SVEVO, Italo (Ettore Schmitz) (1861–1928), Italian novelist, who also wrote plays, short stories, and criticism, born in Trieste from a Jewish Italo-German background (indicated by his pen-name). His novels are: *Una vita* (*A Life*, 1893), *Senilità* (a title translated by *Joyce as *As a Man Grows Older*, 1898), *La coscienza di Zeno* (*Confessions of Zeno*, 1923), *La novella del buon vecchio e della bella fanciulla* (*The Tale of the Good Old Man and of the Lovely Young Girl*, 1929). He was working on a fifth novel, *Il vecchione* (*The Grand Old Man*, 1967), when he died in a car crash. Svevo's work was unknown until Joyce met him in Trieste and helped him to publish his masterpiece, *Confessions of Zeno*. Svevo's style stood out against prevailing trends based on *D'Annunzio and *Fogazzaro. *Zeno* is a complex and delicately balanced novel in which time and point of view are relative. Arguing with his psychoanalyst, Zeno struggles with chance, time, marriage, and tobacco, disclosing the source of his malady as the Oedipus complex.

Swan of Avon, The Sweet, see AVON, THE SWEET SWAN OF.

Swan of Lichfield, see SEWARD, A.

SWEDENBORG, Emanuel (1688–1772), born Swedberg, Swedish philosopher, scientist, and mystic, was the son of a professor of theology at Uppsala. He studied at Uppsala, and travelled extensively in England, where he was influenced by Henry More, J. *Locke, and I. *Newton. He was appointed to a post on the Swedish Board of Mines in 1716, and in his capacity as scientist and engineer anticipated many subsequent hypotheses and inventions. He was gradually led to seek a comprehensive scientific explanation of the universe, attempting to demonstrate that it had, essentially, a spiritual structure, and in his later years he began to experience visions and to converse with angels, not only in his dreams, but, he claimed, in his waking life. According to his theosophic system, God, as Divine Man, is infinite love and infinite wisdom, from whom emanate the two worlds of nature and spirit, distinct but closely related. God is not a 'windy or ethereal spirit', but 'very Man. In all the Heavens, there is no other idea of God, than that of a Man' (*Divine Love and Wisdom*, 1763). The end of creation is the approximation of Man to God; this end having been endangered by evil spirits, Jehovah descended into nature, restored the connection between God and Man, and left the Scriptures as his testimony, with Swedenborg as his appointed interpreter. Swedenborg died in London, and his followers there organized themselves into the New Church, of which *Blake was for a while an active member. Blake was deeply influenced by Swedenborg's writings, which began to appear in English from 1750, a printing society being founded in Manchester in 1782 to propagate his works: Blake's pencilled annotations to Swedenborg's *Wisdom of Angels concerning Divine Love and Divine Wisdom*, written c.1789, survive. See J. G. Davies, *The Theology of William Blake* (1948) and K. *Raine, *Blake and Tradition* (2 vols, 1969). Swedenborg also had a considerable influence on other writers, including *Strindberg and the French *Symbolists.

Sweedlepipe, Paul or Poll, in Dickens's *Martin Chuzzlewit*, bird-fancier and barber, Mrs Gamp's landlord.

Sweeney Agonistes, a poetic drama by T. S. *Eliot.

SWEET, Henry (1845–1912), a great phonetician and (after A. J. Ellis) one of the founders of that study in England, was educated at Heidelberg University and Balliol College, Oxford, where he got a Fourth Class in Lit. Hum. (1873). He lived in Oxford from 1895 until his death, but he never fully received the recognition there that his eminence warranted; the readership in phonetics he was accorded in 1901 was a poor compensation for his failure to gain a number of chairs, especially the chair of comparative philology on the death of *Max Müller in 1901. He is said to be the inspiration for Shaw's Henry Higgins in *Pygmalion*, though Higgins's hypersensitivity about judgements on him is lighter than the original's. His works are still a staple of the study of Old English and the philology of English; the most celebrated are *History of English Sounds* (1874, 1888); *Anglo-Saxon Reader* (1876); *Anglo-Saxon Primer* (1882); *A New English Grammar* (1892, 1898); *The History of Language* (1900); and *The Sounds of English: an Introduction to Phonetics* (1908).

SWIFT, Jonathan (1667–1745), was born in Dublin after his father's death. He was son of Jonathan Swift by Abigail (Erick) of Leicester, and grandson of Thomas Swift, the well known royalist vicar of Goodrich, descended from a Yorkshire family. He was a cousin of *Dryden. He was educated with *Congreve, at Kilkenny Grammar School, then at Trinity College, Dublin, where he was censured for offences against discipline, obtaining his degree only by 'special grace'. He was admitted (1689) to the household of Sir W. *Temple, and there acted as secretary. He was sent by Temple to William III to convince him of the necessity of triennial Parliaments, but his mission was not successful. He

wrote pindarics, one of which, printed in the *Athenian Mercury* (1692), provoked, according to Dr *Johnson, Dryden's remark, 'Cousin Swift, you will never be a poet.' Chafing at his position of dependence, and indignant at Temple's delay in getting him preferment, he returned to Ireland, was ordained (1694), and received the small prebend of Kilroot. He returned to Temple at Moor Park in 1696, where he edited Temple's correspondence, and in 1697 wrote *The Battle of the Books*, which was published in 1704 together with *A Tale of a Tub*, his celebrated satire on 'corruptions in religion and learning'. At Moor Park he first met Esther Johnson ('Stella'), the daughter of a servant or companion of Temple's sister. On the death of Temple in 1699, Swift went again to Ireland, where he was given a prebend in St Patrick's, Dublin, and the living of Laracor. He wrote his *Discourse of the Contests and Dissensions between the nobles and the commons in Athens and Rome*, with reference to the impeachment of the Whig lords, in 1701. In the course of numerous visits to London he became acquainted with *Addison, *Steele, Congreve, and Halifax. He was entrusted in 1707 with a mission to obtain the grant of Queen Anne's Bounty for Ireland, and in 1708 began a series of pamphlets on church questions with his ironical *Argument against Abolishing Christianity*, followed in the same year by his *Letter concerning the Sacramental Test*, an attack on the Irish Presbyterians which injured him with the Whigs. Amid these serious occupations, he diverted himself with the series of squibs upon the astrologer John Partridge (1708–9, see under BICKERSTAFF), which have become famous, and his 'Description of a City Shower' and 'Description of the Morning', poems depicting scenes of London life, which were published in *The Tatler* (1709). Disgusted at the Whig alliance with Dissent, he went over to the Tories in 1710, joined the *Brothers' Club, attacked the Whig ministers in *The Examiner*, which he edited, and in 1711 wrote *The Conduct of the Allies* and *Some Remarks on the Barrier Treaty*, pamphlets written to dispose the mind of the nation to peace. He became dean of St Patrick's in 1713. He had already begun his *Journal to Stella*, a series of intimate letters (1710–13) to Esther Johnson and her companion Rebecca Dingley, who had moved to Ireland in 1700/1; it is written partly in baby language, and gives a vivid account of Swift's daily life in London where he was in close touch with Tory ministers. Swift's relations with Stella remain obscure; they were intimate and affectionate, and some form of marriage may have taken place. Another woman, Esther Vanhomrigh (pron. 'Vanummery'), entered his life in 1708; his poem *Cadenus and Vanessa* suggests that she fell deeply in love with him ('She wished her Tutor were her Lover') and that he gave her some encouragement. She is said to have died of shock in 1723 after his final rupture with her, inspired by her jealousy of Stella. Stella died in 1728.

Swift wrote various political pamphlets, notably *The Importance of the Guardian considered* (1713) and *The Public Spirit of the Whigs* (1714), in reply to Steele's *Crisis*; and about the time of the queen's death in 1714 and the fall of the Tory ministry, several papers (published much later) in defence of the latter. In the same year he joined *Pope, *Arbuthnot, *Gay, and others in the celebrated *Scriblerus Club. He returned to Ireland in August 1714 and occupied himself with Irish affairs, being led by his resentment of the policy of the Whigs to acquire a sense of their unfair treatment of Ireland. By his famous *Drapier's Letters* (1724) he prevented the introduction of 'Wood's Halfpence' into Ireland. He came to England in 1726, visited Pope and Gay, and dined with Sir R. *Walpole, to whom he addressed a letter of remonstrance on Irish affairs with no result. He published *Gulliver's Travels* in the same year, and paid a last visit to England in 1727, when the death of George I created for a moment hopes of dislodging Walpole. He wrote some of his most famous tracts and characteristic poems during his last years in Ireland, *The Grand Question Debated* (1729); *Verses on the Death of Dr Swift* (1731, pub. 1739), in which with mingled pathos and humour he reviews his life and work; *A Complete Collection of Polite and Ingenious *Conversation* (1738); and the ironical *Directions to Servants* (written about 1731 and published after his death). He kept up his correspondence with *Bolingbroke, Pope, Gay, and Arbuthnot, attracted to himself a small circle of friends, and was adored by the people. He spent a third of his income on charities, and saved another third to found St Patrick's Hospital for imbeciles (opened 1757). The symptoms of the illness from which he suffered for most of his life (now thought to have been Ménière's disease) became very marked in his last years, and he suffered the decay of his faculties to such a degree that many considered him insane, though modern biographical opinion rejects this view. He was buried by the side of Stella, in St Patrick's, Dublin, his own famous epitaph 'ubi saeva indignatio ulterius cor lacerare nequit' being inscribed on his tomb. Nearly all his works were published anonymously, and for only one, *Gulliver's Travels*, did he receive any payment (£200). Dr Johnson, *Macaulay, and *Thackeray, among many other writers, were alienated by his ferocity and coarseness, and his works tended to be undervalued in the late 18th–19th cents. The 20th cent. has seen a revival of biographical and critical interest, stressing on the whole Swift's sanity, vigour, and satirical inventiveness rather than his alleged misanthropy.

Swift published a great number of works. Besides the more important, referred to above, mention may be made of the following:

Political writings: *The Virtues of Sid Hamet the Magician's Rod* (1710), an attack on Godolphin; *The W—ds—r Prophecy* (1711), attacking the duchess of Somerset; *A short Character of T[homas] E[arl] of W[harton]* (1711); *The Fable of Midas* (1711); *Some Advice humbly offered to the Members of the *October Club*, the extreme Tories (1712); *Some Free Thoughts upon the present state of affairs* (1714); *Traulus* (1730), attacking Lord Allen; and the *History of the Four Last Years of the Queen* [Anne] (1758), which contains his famous character of *Harley.

Pamphlets relating to Ireland: *A Proposal for the Universal Use of Irish Manufacture* (1720); *The Swearer's-Bank* (1720); *The Story of the Injured Lady* (?1746); *A Short View of the State of Ireland* (1728); *A Modest Proposal* (1729); *An Examination of certain Abuses, Corruptions and Enormities in the City of Dublin* (1732); *The Legion Club* (the Irish Parliament, 1736).

Pamphlets on Church questions: *The Sentiments of a Church of England Man with respect to Religion and Government* (1708); *A Project for the Advancement of Religion and the Reformation of Manners* (1709); *A Preface to the B——p of S—— r——m's Introduction*, an attack on Bishop *Burnet (1713); *Mr C——ns's Discourse on Free Thinking*, a satire on Anthony *Collins (1713); *A Letter to a Young Gentleman, lately entered into Holy Orders* (1721). Swift's *Sermons* (of which four were published in 1744), are marked by the author's usual characteristics of vigour and common sense.

Miscellaneous verses and other writings: 'Mrs Frances Harris's Petition', a servant who has lost her purse, an amusing burlesque (1709); *Baucis and Philemon* (1709); 'On Mrs Biddy Floyd' (1709); 'A Meditation upon a Broom-Stick' (1710); *A Proposal for Correcting, Improving and Ascertaining the English Tongue* (1712); imitations of the Seventh Epistle of the First Book of *Horace and the First Ode of the Second Book of Horace (1738); *A Letter of Advice to a Young Poet* (1721); a 'Letter to a very young Lady on her Marriage' (1727); the 'Journal of a Dublin Lady' (1729); *The Lady's Dressing-Room* (1732); *The Beasts Confession to the Priest* (1732), a satire on 'the universal folly of mankind in mistaking their talents'; *A serious and useful scheme to make an Hospital for Incurables*—whether the incurable disease were knavery, folly, lying, or, infidelity (1733); *On Poetry, a Rhapsody* (1733), satirical advice to a poet; *A Beautiful Young Nymph Going to Bed*; and *Strephon and Chloe* (1734).

The *Prose Works* have been edited by Herbert Davis (16 vols, 1939–74); *Journal to Stella* by H. Williams (2 vols, 1948); *Poems* by H. Williams (1937); *Correspondence* by H. Williams (5 vols, 1963–5); *Complete Poems* (Penguin, 1983), ed. P. Rogers, with an important commentary. See also Irvin Ehrenpreis, *Swift: The Man, His Works and the Age* (3 vols, 1962–

83) and a useful short study by R. Quintana, *Swift, an Introduction* (1955).

SWINBURNE, Algernon Charles (1837–1909), of an old Northumbrian family, spent much of his childhood in the Isle of Wight, where he acquired a lasting love of the sea, reflected in much of his work. He was educated at Eton, where he developed an equally lasting interest in flagellation, and at Balliol College, Oxford, where he was associated with *Rossetti and the *Pre-Raphaelite circle. His first published volume, *The Queen-Mother; Rosamund* (1860), shows the influence of Elizabethan dramatists, notably of *Chapman, and attracted little attention, but *Atalanta in Calydon* (1865), a drama in classical Greek form, with choruses (e.g. 'When the hounds of spring are on winter's traces') that revealed his great metrical skills, brought him celebrity; *Tennyson wrote praising his 'wonderful rhythmic invention'. *Chastelard*, the first of three dramas on the subject of *Mary Queen of Scots, which appeared the same year, raised some doubts about the morality of Swinburne's verse, doubts reinforced by the first series of *Poems and Ballads* (1866), which brought down a torrent of abuse from R. *Buchanan, J. *Morley, and others. The volume contains many of his best as well as his most notorious poems (*'Dolores', 'Itylus', 'Hymn to Proserpine', 'The Triumph of Time', 'Faustine', 'Laus Veneris', etc.) which clearly demonstrate the preoccupation with de *Sade, masochism, and *femmes fatales* which he shared with a circle of friends which by now included M. *Milnes and Richard *Burton: also his outspoken repudiation of Christianity, which was to impress *Hardy and his heroine Sue Bridehead (in *Jude the Obscure*). *A Song of Italy* (1867) and *Songs before Sunrise* (1871) express his support for Mazzini in the struggle for Italian independence, and a hatred of authority which owes much to *Blake. *Bothwell* (1874) and a second Greek drama, *Erechtheus* (1876), were followed by the more subdued *Poems and ballads: second series* (1878), which contains 'A Forsaken Garden'. By this time Swinburne's health, always delicate and subject to fits of intense nervous excitement, was seriously undermined by heavy drinking and other excesses. In 1879 he moved to Putney with his friend *Watts-Dunton, who gradually weaned him from drink and restored his health. He published many more volumes, including *Mary Stuart* (1881), *Tristram of Lyonesse and other poems* (1882), *Marino Faliero* (1885, a tragedy on the same subject as Byron's of the same title), and *Poems and ballads: third series* (1889), but they lack the force of his earlier work, and often fall into a kind of self-parody which he himself referred to as 'a tendency to the dulcet and luscious form of verbosity which has to be guarded against'. Swinburne commanded an impressive variety of verse forms, writing in classical metres, composing burlesques, modern and mock-antique ballads, roundels, etc.; he also translated the ballads of *Villon. His published prose works include two novels, *A Year's Letters* (serialized pseudonymously 1877, republished 1905 as *Love's Cross Currents*) and *Lesbia Brandon* (ed. R. Hughes, 1952). His influence on fellow aesthetes like *Pater and a later generation of poets was considerable, and was deplored by T. S. *Eliot and *Leavis. Swinburne himself was a critic of perception and originality; his studies of Chapman (1875), *Marlowe (1883, *Encyclopaedia Britannica*). *Middleton (1887), *Tourneur (1889, *E.B.*), and others were the first important successors to *Lamb in the revival of interest in Elizabethan and Jacobean drama, and those of Blake (1868) and the *Brontës (1877, 1883, etc.) in many ways laid the foundation of modern appreciation.

His letters were edited in 6 vols, 1959–62, by C. Y. Lang, and the most recent of several biographies is by P. Henderson, 1974. Many of his writings remain unpublished, presumably unpublishable.

Swing, Captain, an imaginary person to whom about 1830–3 were attributed a number of outrages against farmers who had adopted the use of agricultural machinery.

SWINNERTON, Frank (1884–1982), critic and prolific novelist, left school at 14 and worked as office boy, proofreader, then editor at Chatto and Windus. His novels, often set in contemporary London, include *Nocturne* (1917, his greatest success) and *Harvest Comedy* (1937). He was literary critic of *Truth and Nation, The Evening News* and the *Observer* and a familiar figure in the literary life of the first half of this century, Arnold *Bennett and *Galsworthy being among his friends. His knowledge of the period provided material for his literary reminiscences, notably *The Georgian Literary Scene* (1935), and two autobiographical works, *Swinnerton: An Autobiography* (1937) and *Reflections from a Village* (1969). *Arnold Bennett: A Last Word* (1978) appeared in his 94th year. He was president of the *Royal Literary Fund (1962–6).

Swiss Family Robinson, The, the romance of a family wrecked on a desert island, written in German by Johann David Wyss (1743–1818), a Swiss pastor. It was published in two parts in Zurich in 1812–13 and the first English translation was a year later.

Swiveller, Dick, a character in Dickens's *The Old Curiosity Shop.

Sword-dance, a medieval folk custom, of ritual origin, probably symbolizing the death and resurrection of the year. The stock characters were the fool, dressed in the skin of an animal, ind the 'Bessy', a man dressed in woman's clothes. In many of the extant dances one of the characters is surrounded with the swords of the other dancers or slain. The characters were introduced in rhymed speeches. The sword-dance is one of the origins of the *Mummers' play and so of English drama. See also REVESBY PLAY.

Sword of Honour, a trilogy by E. *Waugh, published under this title in 1965.

Men at Arms (1952) introduces 35-year-old divorced Catholic Guy Crouchback, who after much effort succeeds in enlisting in the Royal Corps of Halberdiers just after the outbreak of the Second World War. Much of the plot revolves around his eccentric fellow-officer Apthorpe, an old Africa hand who suffers repeatedly from 'Bechuana tummy', is deeply devoted to his 'thunder box' (or chemical closet), and dies in West Africa at the end of the novel of some unspecified tropical disease, aggravated by Guy's thoughtful gift of a bottle of whisky. Other characters include Guy's ex-wife, the beautiful socialite Virginia Troy, her second (but not her final) husband, Tommy Blackhouse, and the ferocious one-eyed Brigadier Ritchie-Hook, who involves Guy in a near-disastrous escapade.

Officers and Gentlemen (1955) continues Waugh's semi-satiric, semi-emotional portrayal of civilian and military life with an account of Guy's training on the Hebridean island of Mugg with a Commando unit, and of the exploits of ex-hairdresser Trimmer, now Captain Mc-Tavish, which include an affair with Virginia and the blowing up of a French railway; the action moves to Alexandria, then to the with-drawal from Crete, with all but four of 'Hook-force' taken prisoner.

Unconditional Surrender (1961) opens with a frustrated and disillusioned Captain Guy Crouchback in London, working at Hazardous Offensive Operations Headquarters: he then in-jures himself learning to parachute, and on his sickbed is wooed by Virginia, now pregnant by Trimmer, and conscious that Guy has inherited his father's fortune. He remarries her out of a sense of chivalry and compassion, is transferred to the chaos and conflicts of Yugoslavia as a liaison officer with the Partisans, and there learns that Virginia has given birth to a son, then that she has been killed in an air raid. The baby sur-vives, and an Epilogue informs us that Guy mar-ries again, and has more children of his own.

Sybil, or *The Two Nations,* a novel by B. *Dis-raeli, published 1845.

This is the second book of the trilogy *Con-ingsby—Sybil—*Tancred. It was written, like *Coningsby,* to celebrate the ideas of the 'Young England' Tories and was designed to describe the Condition of the People' and of the 'Two Nations of England, the Rich and the Poor'. An ambitious, crowded book, it points to reforms a generation before Disraeli's government was able to introduce them. Poverty and oppression are described with feeling, and the radical *Chartist spirit is sympathetically shown in Ger-ard, Morley, and others; aspects of the wealthy social and political world, particularly as seen in Mowbray Castle, are described with irony and contempt.

After a long historical introduction, setting the background in the prime ministership of *Wellington, the story of the Marneys begins. Charles Egremont, the younger brother of the pitiless landowner Lord Marney, master of splendid Marney Abbey, meets in the starlit ruins of the old abbey the beautiful young novice Sybil. She is the daughter of the Chartist Walter Gerard (who becomes Egremont's friend) and is beloved by Stephen Morley, a radical and athe-ist; all three live in the oppressed industrial town of Mowbray some miles away. Egremont falls in love with Sybil, and when she refuses him because of his rank, begins to live a life pain-fully divided between the poverty-stricken town of Mowbray, the glittering life of his brother's Abbey, and his parliamentary life in London. His brother's plan to marry him into the Fitzwarene family, which owns Mowbray Castle and most of Mowbray, is indignantly resisted, as he sets himself earnestly to discover the true condition of the poor in Mowbray and to understand the feelings of the Chartists and incendiaries. Events of the present are seen in a long historical perspective. The plight of the poor, whose land has been taken by the rich, is compared with that of the Saxons despoiled by the Normans, and Sybil's ancestry provides her with rights to the lands of Marney which had been confiscated from her family at the Reformation. Much of the narrative is concerned with the development of the Chartist rising, Gerard's imprisonment, the activities of Morley, the radical parson St Lys, the good employer Trafford, and many others less principled; and with Egremont's struggle in the House of Commons to secure reforms and his failure to win Sybil. Five years pass of increasing poverty and unrest. The riots in which they culminate are of great violence; Sybil and St Lys, in Mowbray Castle, fail to persuade the mob to disperse, while Morley searches for the Marney deeds which are right-fully Sybil's. The yeomanry arrive, Gerard is killed, Lord Marney stoned to death by rioters, Morley shot, and the castle burned down. Egre-mont rescues Sybil and the true heir marries the new earl of Marney.

Sycorax, in Shakespeare's *The Tempest* a witch, the mother of *Caliban; she does not appear in the play.

Syllepsis, a figure of speech by which a word, or a particular form or inflection of a word, is made to refer to two or more words in the same sentence, while properly applying to them in different senses: e.g. 'Miss Bolo . . . went home in a flood of tears and a sedan chair' (Dickens, *Pickwick Papers, ch. 35). Cf. *zeugma.

Sylphs, see PARACELSUS.

Sylva, a book on arboriculture by J. *Evelyn.

SYLVANUS URBAN, the pseudonym of E. *Cave.

SYLVESTER, Joshua (c.1563–1618), was a London merchant, whose translation into rhyming couplets of The Divine Weeks and Works of *Du Bartas was, according to John Davies of Hereford, 'admir'd of all'. The first instalment appeared in 1592, more in 1598, further parts in 1605–7, and a complete translation in 1608, which was reprinted for the fifth time in 1641. The edition of 1621 contained many of Sylvester's other works, including his poems in the important collection Lachrymae Lachrymarum (1613). This contained elegies by John Hall and *Donne, among others, on Prince Henry, to whom Sylvester had attached himself. His translation of Du Bartas has been edited by Susan Snyder (1979).

Sylvia's Lovers, a novel by Mrs *Gaskell, published 1863.

The scene is the whaling port of Monkshaven (based on Whitby in Yorkshire) during the Napoleonic wars, and the plot hinges on the activities of the press-gangs whose seizure of Monkshaven men to man naval warships provokes bitter resentment. Sylvia's father, the farmer Daniel Robson, leads a mob attack on the press-gang's headquarters, and he is tried and hanged for this. Her lover, the 'specksioneer' (harpooner) Charley Kinraid, is carried off by the press-gang, but sends her a message promising constancy and return by Sylvia's cousin, the pedantic, hard-working shopkeeper Philip Hepburn, who has long loved Sylvia. Philip yields to the temptation of concealing the message, and Sylvia, believing Charley dead, and left in poverty after her father's execution, agrees to marry Philip. Years later, Charley returns and Philip's treachery is revealed to Sylvia, who swears never to forgive him. He flees from Monkshaven and enlists, but eventually returns disfigured and beggared, and—recognized on his death-bed—dies in the arms of the now repentant Sylvia. The last few chapters of the book, full of heroic rescues, improbable encounters, and death-bed reunions, are notably inferior to the earlier part of the novel, which is remarkable for its vivid reconstruction of life in the little town dominated by the whaling industry (which Mrs Gaskell carefully researched) and at the farm where noisy, unreasonable Daniel Robson, his quiet, devoted wife, and their sturdy old servant Kester, combine to cherish the much-loved and lovely but hapless Sylvia.

Symbolism, Symbolists (Symbolisme, les Symbolistes), a group of French writers of the 19th cent. The term is widely applied, but in its most useful and restricted sense refers to the period c.1880–95. The movement may be seen as a reaction against dominant *realist and *naturalist tendencies in literature generally and, in the case of poetry, against the descriptive precision and 'objectivity' of the *Parnassians. The symbolists stressed the priority of suggestion and evocation over direct description and explicit analogy (cf. *Mallarmé's dictum, 'Peindre, non la chose, mais l'effet qu'elle produit'), and to the symbol was ascribed a pre-eminent function in the effort to distil a private mood or to evoke the subtle affinities which were held to exist between the material and spiritual worlds. Symbolist writers were particularly concerned to explore the musical properties of language, through the interplay of connotative sound relationships, but were deeply interested in all the arts and much influenced by the synthesizing ideals of *Wagner's music dramas. Other influences on the movement were the mystical writings of *Swedenborg, and the poetry of *Nerval, *Baudelaire (see the sonnet 'Correspondances'), and *Poe.

Generally associated with the symbolist movement are: the poets Mallarmé, *Verlaine, *Rimbaud, and *Laforgue; the dramatists *Villiers de l'Isle-Adam (Axël, 1890) and *Maeterlinck, whose Pelléas et Mélisande (1892) was the source of *Debussy's opera of that name; and the novelists *Huysmans (A rebours, 1884) and Édouard Dujardin, whose Les Lauriers sont coupés (1888) influenced *Joyce. The movement exercised an influence on painting (Odilon Redon, Gustave Moreau) and on a wide range of 20th-cent. writers, including *Pound, T. S. *Eliot, W. *Stevens, *Yeats, Joyce, V. *Woolf, *Claudel, *Valéry, Stefan George, and *Rilke. It was the subject of A. W. *Symons's The Symbolist Movement in Literature (1899) and played a part in the development of the Russian symbolist movement and of the modernista movement in Latin America.

SYMONDS, John Addington (1840–93), born in Bristol, the son of an eminent physician, was educated at Harrow and Balliol College, Oxford, where he won the Newdigate prize and became a fellow of Magdalen. He suffered from tuberculosis, and spent much of his life in Italy and Switzerland. He was much attracted by the Hellenism of the Renaissance, and both his prose and poetry are coloured by his concept of *Platonic love and his admiration for male beauty. His largest work, Renaissance in Italy (1875–86), is more picturesque than scholarly and at times overburdened with detail and anecdote, but remains a valuable source of information. His works include volumes on *Jonson, *Sidney, *Shelley, *Whitman, and *Michelangelo; collections of travel sketches and impressions; several volumes of verse (including *Many Moods*, 1878; *New and Old*, 1880); a translation of the autobiography of *Cellini (1888); and translations of Greek and Italian poetry. He had a wide circle of literary friends (among them *Lear, *Swinburne, L. *Stephen, and R. L. *Stevenson), and his aesthetic prose had its admirers, but his life was marked by physical and mental stress. He married in 1864, but acknowledged increasingly his own homosexuality, and campaigned, albeit discreetly, for legal reform and more outspoken recognition of inversion, which he saw as a congenital condition. His privately printed pamphlets *A problem in Greek ethics* (1883) and *A problem in modern ethics* (1891) were reproduced in part by H. *Ellis in *Sexual Inversion* (1897), a work originally planned as a collaboration. See Phyllis Grosskurth, *John Addington Symonds* (1964).

SYMONS, A(lphonse) J(ames) A(lbert) (1900–41), bibliographer, bibliophile, dandy, and epicure, who became an authority on the literature of the 1890s and published *An anthology of 'Nineties' verse* in 1928. He wrote several biographies, but is best remembered for *The Quest for Corvo: an experiment in biography* (1934), a life of F. W. *Rolfe. *A. J. A. Symons: His Life and Speculations* (1950), by his brother, novelist and critic Julian (Gustave) Symons (1912–), is a vivid evocation of his paradoxical personality, diverse interests, and social ambitions.

SYMONS, Arthur William (1865–1945), son of a West Country Methodist minister, moved to London when a young man and quickly abandoned his narrow upbringing for city life. He became a friend of *Yeats, G. A. *Moore, and H. *Ellis, and attended the *Rhymers' Club; his early volumes of poetry (*Days and Nights,* 1889; *London Nights,* 1895) were very much of their time in their celebration of decadence and the *demi-monde* of stage, street, and *Café Royal. He was editor of *The Savoy*, 1896, and published *Beardsley, *Conrad, *Dowson, L. P. *Johnson, etc. His *The Symbolist movement in literature* (1899) was an attempt to introduce French *Symbolism to England, and he wrote many other critical studies, of *Blake, *Baudelaire, *Pater, *Wilde, and others; but his fascination with the morbid and the extreme took its revenge when, in 1908–9, he suffered a complete nervous collapse, from which he largely recovered through the ministrations of his friends (including *Gosse and Augustus *John) and the help of the *Royal Literary Fund. He is largely remembered as a leading spirit in the Decadent movement, a defender of *'Art

for Art's Sake', although his biographer Roger Lhombreaud (*Arthur Symons: A Critical Biography*, 1963) argues for a more modest but wider role.

Symkyn, Symond, the miller of Trumpington in *Chaucer's 'The Reeve's Tale' (see CANTERBURY TALES, 3).

Symposium, The, or 'The Banquet', the title of a dialogue in which *Plato describes a drinking party where *Socrates, *Aristophanes, and others propound their views of love and distinguish three forms of the emotion: the sensual, the altruistic, and the wisdom-oriented. Written soon after 371 BC, the dialogue appears to have had for its aim the rehabilitation of Socrates against the charge of corrupting the young, but its influence, once it had been translated into Latin by *Ficino (1482), had a far wider scope. It popularized the identification of love with a quest for the highest form of spiritual experience, and although the love discussed in Plato's dialogue was primarily a homosexual one, the exalted claims made on its behalf were easily transferred to heterosexual relationships and came to be linked with the conventions of courtly love. Another idea in the *Symposium* that gained wide currency was the fanciful notion advanced by Aristophanes in his speech that each human being is a male or female half of a whole which was originally hermaphrodite, and that every person necessarily seeks his or her lost half. The belief that every person has a single predestined mate was to become a romantic commonplace. (See also PLATONIC LOVE.)

Synecdoche (pron. 'sinekdoki'), a figure of speech by which a more comprehensive term is used for a less comprehensive or vice versa, as whole for part or part for whole, e.g. 'There were six guns out on the moor' where 'guns' stands for shooters; and 'Oxford won the match', where 'Oxford' stands for 'the Oxford eleven'.

SYNGE, (Edmund) John Millington (1871–1909), Irish playwright, born near Dublin; his father was a barrister, and died when Synge was an infant. He was educated at Trinity College, Dublin, and then spent some years in Paris, where he met W. B. *Yeats in 1896. Following a suggestion from Yeats, he went to the Aran islands in order to write of Irish peasant life, and stayed there annually from 1898 to 1902; his description, *The Aran Islands*, was published in 1907. The first of his plays, *In the Shadow of the Glen*, was performed in 1903; it is a grim one-act peasant comedy, in which an elderly husband feigns death to test his wife's fidelity. *Riders to the Sea*, an elegiac tragedy in which an elderly mother, Maurya, stoically anticipates 'a great rest' after the death of the last of her six sons, followed in 1904; both were published, as was

The Well of the Saints, in 1905. His best-known play, and in its time the most controversial, *The Playboy of the Western World, was performed in 1907; the anti-clerical The Tinker's Wedding, was published in 1908. All except the last were performed at the *Abbey Theatre, of which Synge became a director in 1906. His Poems and Translations (many of which foreshadow his imminent death) appeared in 1909. From 1897 Synge had suffered from Hodgkin's disease, and he virtually completed his last play, Deirdre of the Sorrows, as he was dying; it was performed and published posthumously, in 1910. In this, as in his other work, Synge uses a spare, rhythmic, lyric prose to achieve effects of great power and resonance; both tragedies and comedies display the ironic wit and realism which many of his countrymen found offensive. Yeats commented in his preface to Poems and Translations, 'He was but the more hated because he gave his country what it needed, an unmoved mind', and described him in 'In Memory of Major Gregory' as one who had come 'Towards nightfall upon certain set apart | In a most desolate stony place, | Towards nightfall upon a race | Passionate and simple like his heart'. The authorized biography is J. M. Synge 1871–1909 (1959) by D. H. Greene and E. M. Stephens, and the Collected Works (4 vols, 1962–8) were edited by Robin Skelton; his Collected Letters, edited by Ann Saddlemyer, appeared 1983–4.

Synoptic Gospels, those of Matthew, Mark, and Luke, so called as giving an account of the events from the same point of view, or under the same general aspect.

Syntax, Dr, see COMBE, W.

Syntipas, the Greek form of the name Sindabar, Sandabar, or Sindibad, an Indian philosopher, said to have lived about 100 BC, the supposed author of a collection of tales generally known as The Seven Wise Masters. Their main outline is the same as that of *The Seven Sages of Rome, though details of the several stories vary. 'Syntipas' was translated from Greek into Latin (under the title 'Dolopathos') in the 12th cent., and thence into French. The names Syntipas, Sindabar, etc., are probably corruptions of the original Sanskrit word from which *Bidpai and Pilpay are derived.

T

TACITUS, Cornelius (c. AD 55–after 115), the greatest historian of Imperial Rome. His first work was a dialogue that discussed the shortcomings of contemporary oratory. He followed this by a biography of his father-in-law Julius Agricola (c.98) and by an ethnographical account of the German tribes. The former provides a useful description of Roman Britain, the latter contains one of the earliest representations of the Noble Savage (see PRIMITIVISM). His fame rests however on his *Annals* (18 books, of which 11 and part of a 12th survive) and his *Histories* (12 books, of which 4 and part of a 5th survive), which related events from the death of Augustus to the Flavian period. Tacitus' avowed aim was to keep alive the memory of virtuous and vicious actions so that posterity could judge them, and his great achievement was to have drawn a picture of how men must live under tyranny. Little known in the Middle Ages, Tacitus was rediscovered by *Boccaccio in the 14th cent., but he did not become widely popular till the age of autocracy 200 years later. The *Agricola* and the *Histories* were translated into English by Sir H. *Savile (1591), the *Germania* and *Annals* by R. Greneway (1598); and after this Tacitus became in *Donne's phrase the 'Oracle of Statesmen' or at any rate the model for historians like F. *Bacon in his *History of Henry VII* (1622) and Sir John *Hayward. He was also influential as a stylist in the 17th cent., when attempts were made to imitate his concision and trenchancy.

Tadpole and **Taper,** in Disraeli's *Coningsby* and *Sybil*, typical party wire-pullers. 'Tadpole worshipped registration; Taper adored a cry.'

TAGORE, Rabindranath (1861–1941), most eminent modern Bengali poet, was also critic, essayist, composer, and author of short fiction innovative in Bengali literature. He is known outside India principally in English translation. *Gitanjali: Song Offering* (1912), his free verse re-creations of his Bengali poems modelled on medieval Indian devotional lyrics, won the *Nobel Prize for literature in 1913, its first award to an Asian. Representative translations followed, of philosophical plays such as *Chitra* (1913) and *The King of the Dark Chamber* (1914), and of his novels *The Home and the World* (1919) and *Gora* (1924). His short fiction often comments powerfully and courageously on Indian national and social concerns, in the collections *Hungry Stones* (1916), *Broken Ties*

(1925), and *The Housewarming* (1965), and in the novella *The Broken Nest* (1971). Tagore had an excellent command of English, but he wrote primarily in Bengali and tirelessly encouraged writers of the Indian vernaculars.

TAILLEFER (Incisor Ferri), a minstrel in the army of William the Conqueror who (according to the *Carmen de Hastingae Proelio* and to *Henry of Huntingdon and *Gaimar) marched in front of the army at Hastings, singing of the deeds of *Roland to encourage the Normans.

Tail-rhyme, translated from the Latin *rhythmus caudatus*, the measure associated in particular with a group of Middle English romances in which a pair of rhyming lines is followed by a single line of different length and the three-line pattern is repeated to make up a six-line stanza. Chaucer's 'Sir Thopas' (see CANTERBURY TALES, 17) is an example; six are edited by M. Mills in *Six Middle English Romances* (1973).

Tain-Bo-Cuailgne, the chief epic of the Ulster cycle of Irish mythology, the story of the raid of Queen *Maeve of Connaught to secure the Brown Bull of Cuailgne (pron. 'Cooley'), and her defeat by *Cuchulain. There is a modern translation by T. Kinsella (1969).

TAINE, Hippolyte (1828–93), French philosopher, historian, and critic, the leading exponent in his age of the view that historical and artistic phenomena are susceptible of explanation by the application of the methods of natural science. Taine's determinist and mechanistic theory of mental activity is fully set out in *De l'intelligence* (1870). Its moral corollary was given a provocative formulation in the Introduction to his *Histoire de la littérature anglaise* (3 vols, 1863; trans. H. Van Laun, 1871): 'vice and virtue are products like vitriol and sugar.' In the same Introduction he laid down the principle that hereditary, environmental, and historical factors ('la race, le milieu, le moment') could sufficiently account for the entire range and character of a national literature. Taine wrote widely on art and aesthetics, e.g. *Philosophie de l'art* (1865), *De l'idéal dans l'art* (1867), as well as books on the art of Italy, Greece, and the Low Countries. *Les Origines de la France contemporaine* (6 vols, 1875–94) is a history of France in the late 18th and early 19th cents, centring on the revolutionary period and deploring the centralizing tendency of which, to his mind, the revolution was an expression. Taine's numerous travel books include *Notes sur l'Angleterre* (1872), impressions of the country and of life and manners gathered during his stays in England, together with reflections on the English mind, system of government, etc.

Tale of a Tub, A, a comedy by *Jonson, performed 1633, printed 1640.

It concerns the attempts, in the course of St Valentine's Day, of various suitors to marry Audrey, the daughter of Toby Turf, high constable of Kentish Town. Her father wishes to marry her to John Clay, tile-maker, and he and the wedding-party set off for the church. But his intention is defeated by Squire Tub and Canon Hugh the vicar, by means of a bogus story of a highway robbery, of which John Clay is accused. Squire Tub's desire to marry Audrey is in turn frustrated by Justice Preamble, who conspires with Hugh to get her for himself. Tub warns Toby Turf, who recovers his daughter. But she is presently lured away from him again (together with £100) by the Justice, is intercepted by Tub, and finally carried off and married out of hand by Pol Martin, usher to Tub's mother, 'a groom was never dreamt of'. This was Jonson's last completed play.

Tale of a Tub, A, a satire in prose by *Swift, written, according to his own statement, about 1696, but not published until 1704.

The author explains in a preface that it is the practice of seamen when they meet a whale to throw out an empty tub to divert him from attacking the ship. Hence the title of the satire, which is intended to divert Hobbes's *Leviathan* and the wits of the age from picking holes in the weak sides of religion and government. The author proceeds to tell the story of a father who leaves as a legacy to his three sons Peter, Martin, and Jack a coat apiece, with directions that on no account are the coats to be altered. Peter symbolizes the Roman Church, Martin (from Martin *Luther) the Anglican, Jack (from John *Calvin) the Dissenters. The sons gradually disobey the injunction, finding excuses for adding shoulder-knots or gold lace according to the prevailing fashion. Finally Martin and Jack quarrel with the arrogant Peter, then with each other, and separate. The satire is directed with especial vigour against Peter, his bulls and dispensations, and the doctrine of transubstantiation. But Jack is also treated with contempt. Martin, as representing the church to which Swift himself belonged, is spared, though not very reverently dealt with. The narrative is freely interspersed with digressions, on critics, on the prevailing dispute as to ancient and modern learning, and on madness—this last an early example of Swift's love of paradox and of his misanthropy.

Tale of Chloe, The, a short novel by G. *Meredith published 1879.

This tragic story is described by the author as an episode in the history of Beau Beamish, 'the King of Bath'. The generous Chloe has given her fortune to redeem from prison the unprincipled Caseldy, whom she loves. But he then leaves Bath, while she lives on there, enjoying the esteem of Beamish yet still faithful to Caseldy. An old duke who has married a young dairymaid, Susan Barley, entrusts her for a month to the care of Beamish, and he to Chloe. Caseldy now returns to Bath, but for the sake of Susan and not for Chloe. He seduces Susan, and Chloe, heartbroken, determines to save her. This she finally does by hanging herself in the doorway through which the young duchess is about to elope with the treacherous Caseldy.

Tale of Genji, The, a classic Japanese novel written *c.* AD 1001–15 by Lady Murasaki (?978–?1031) and translated in a slightly abridged version by A. *Waley in 6 vols (1925–33): I 'The Tale of Genji', II 'The Sacred Tree', III 'A Wreath of Cloud', IV 'Blue Trousers', V 'The Lady of the Boat', VI 'The Bridge of Dreams'.

Prince Genji is an illegitimate son of the emperor, living about the time of the authoress's childhood, and volumes I–IV are mainly concerned with the rivalry between the various women whom he loved. Between volumes IV and V there is a gap in the narrative of eight years, during which time Genji has died, and the last two volumes deal with the rivalry in love between Kaoru, Genji's supposed son, and Niou, Genji's grandson.

The authoress, who became lady-in-waiting to the empress *c.*1005 and spent a certain amount of her time at court, was nicknamed 'Murasaki' in allusion to the heroine of her book: her real name remains unknown. A fuller translation by E. G. Seidensticker appeared in 1976.

Tale of Two Cities, A, a novel by *Dickens, published 1859.

The 'two cities' are Paris, in the time of the French revolution, and London. Dr Manette, a French physician, having been called in to attend a young peasant and his sister in circumstances that made him aware that the girl had been outrageously treated and the boy mortally wounded by the marquis de St Évremonde and his brother, has been confined for 18 years in the Bastille to secure his silence. He has just been released, demented, when the story opens; he is brought to England, where he gradually recovers his sanity. Charles Darnay, who conceals under the name the fact that he is a nephew of the marquis, has left France and renounced his heritage from detestation of the cruel practices of the old French nobility; he falls in love with Lucie, Dr Manette's daughter, and they are happily married. During the Terror he goes to Paris to try to save a faithful servant, who is accused of having served the emigrant nobility. He is himself arrested, condemned to death, and saved only at the last moment by Sydney Carton, a reckless wastrel of an English barrister, whose character is redeemed by his generous devotion to Lucie. Carton, who strikingly resembles Darnay in appearance, smuggles the latter out of prison, and takes his place on the scaffold.

The book gives a vivid picture (modelled on Carlyle's *The French Revolution) of Paris at this period. Critics complained on publication of its lack of humour, but it later achieved wide popularity, partly through successful dramatizations and film adaptations.

Tales in Verse, a collection of poems by *Crabbe, published 1812.

There is humour and tenderness, as well as horror, in these 21 tales, whose object is largely to reveal the destruction of happiness by uncontrolled passions.

Tales of a Grandfather, The, a history of Scotland to the close of the rebellion of 1745–6, by Sir W. *Scott, published 1827–9. A later series (1831) deals with the history of France.

The 'Tales' were designed in the first instance for the author's grandson, John Hugh Lockhart ('Hugh Littlejohn'). After a prefatory chapter on the period of the Roman occupation, the tales proceed to the period of Macbeth, and thence through Wallace and Bruce right through the history of Scotland down to the '45.

Tales of My Landlord, four series of novels by Sir W. *Scott: *The Black Dwarf, *Old Mortality (1st Series); *The Heart of Midlothian (2nd Series); *The Bride of Lammermoor, *A Legend of Montrose (3rd Series); *Count Robert of Paris, *Castle Dangerous (4th Series). Jedediah Cleishbotham, schoolmaster and parish clerk of Gandercleugh, by a fiction of Scott, sold these tales to a publisher. They were supposed to be compiled by his assistant Peter Pattieson. The title of the series is a misnomer as Scott himself admitted, for the tales were not told by the landlord; nor did the landlord have any hand in them at all.

Tales of the Crusaders, two novels by Sir W. *Scott, *The Betrothed and *The Talisman.

Tales of the Hall, a collection of poems by *Crabbe, published 1819.

The work shows a falling-off in care and skill, but is otherwise very similar in character to *Tales in Verse.

TALFOURD, Sir Thomas Noon (1795–1854), son of a Reading brewer, was a judge and member of Parliament but also a literary critic and author of Ion (1836), The Athenian Captive (1838), and other lifeless tragedies in insipid blank verse, for which only *Macready's acting secured momentary celebrity. Talfourd is, however, remembered for his editing of the letters of his friend Charles *Lamb, and for having introduced an Act securing real legal protection for authors' copyright. The friendships of this warm-hearted though excessively loquacious man spanned the literary generation from Lamb and *Coleridge to M. R. *Mitford and *Dickens, who dedicated *Pickwick Papers to him. See J. A. Brain, An Evening with Thomas Noon Talfourd (1889).

Talgol, the name (meaning 'cut-throat') of a butcher who appears among the bear-baiting mob in Butler's *Hudibras.

TALIESIN (fl. 550), a British bard, perhaps a mythic personage, first mentioned in the Saxon Genealogies appended to the Historia Britonum (c.690). A mass of poetry, probably of later date, has been ascribed to him, and the Book of Taliesin (14th cent.) is a collection of poems by different authors and of different dates. The village of Taliesin in Cardiganshire sprang up near the supposed site of his grave. Taliesin figures prominently in Peacock's *The Misfortunes of Elphin, and he is mentioned in Tennyson's *Idylls of the King as one of the Round Table.

Talisman, The, a novel by Sir W. *Scott, published 1825, forming part of the *Tales of the Crusaders.

The Crusaders, led by Richard I of England, are encamped in the Holy Land, and torn by the dissensions and jealousies of the leaders, including, besides Cœur de Lion himself, Philip of France, the duke of Austria, the marquis of Montferrat, and the Grand Master of the Templars. The army's impotence is accentuated by the illness of Richard. A poor but doughty Scottish crusader, known as Sir Kenneth or the Knight of the Leopard, on a mission far from the camp encounters a Saracen emir, with whom, after an inconclusive combat, he strikes up a friendship. This emir proves subsequently to be Saladin himself, and he presently appears in the Christian camp in the disguise of a physician sent by the Soldan to Richard, whom he quickly cures. Meanwhile Sir Kenneth is lured from his post by Queen Berengaria, Richard's wife, who in a frolic sends him an urgent message purporting to come from Edith Plantagenet, between whom and the knight there exists a romantic attachment. During his brief absence his faithful hound is wounded, and the English flag torn down. Sir Kenneth, thus dishonoured, narrowly escapes execution at Richard's order by the intervention of the Moorish physician, who receives him as his slave. Kindly and honourably treated by Saladin, he is sent, in the disguise of a black mute attendant, to Richard, whom he saves from assassination. Richard pierces Kenneth's disguise and gives him the opportunity he desires of discovering who wounded the hound and tore down the standard.

As the Christian princes and their forces file past the re-erected standard, the hound springs on Conrade of Montferrat and tears him from his horse. A trial by combat is arranged in which Sir Kenneth defeats and wounds Montferrat, and is revealed to be Prince David of Scotland. The obstacle which his supposed lowly birth presented to his union with Edith Plantagenet is thus removed.

The Talisman of the title is the amulet by which Saladin effects the cure of Richard and which he presents to the Scottish knight. The incident has some historical basis in the amulet, known as the Lee-penny, obtained by Sir Simon Lockhart in a crusade, and long preserved (perhaps still) in the ancient family of the Lockharts of the Lee in Lanarkshire.

TALLIS, Thomas (c.1505–85), composer and organist and colleague of W. *Byrd, largely known for his church music and for the tune known as 'Tallis's Canon' which he composed for M. *Parker's *Whole Psalter* (1567).

Talmud, The, in the wide sense, the body of Jewish civil and ceremonial traditionary law, consisting of the Mishnah or binding precepts of the elders, additional to and developed from the Pentateuch, and the later Gemara or commentary upon these. The term was originally applied to the Gemara, of which two recensions exist, known respectively as the Jerusalem (Palestinian) and the Babylonian Talmud. The precepts of the Mishnah were codified about AD 200; the redaction of the Jerusalem Talmud had reached almost its present form by AD 408, that of the Babylonian Talmud extended from AD 400 to 500 [*OED*].

Talus, a character in Spenser's *Faerie Queene*. When Astraea left the world and returned to heaven, she

> left her groome
> An yron man, which did on her attend
> Always to execute her steadfast doome.
> (Bk v. i. 12)

He thus represents the executive power of government. He attends on *Artegall, wielding an iron flail, with which he dispatches criminals.

TAMBIMUTTU, see POETRY LONDON.

Tamburlaine the Great, a drama in blank verse by *Marlowe, written not later than 1587, published 1590. It showed an immense advance on the blank verse of *Gorboduc and was received with much popular approval. The material for it was taken by the author from Pedro Mexia's Spanish Life of Timur, of which an English translation had appeared in 1571.

Part I of the drama deals with the first rise to power of the Scythian shepherd-robber Tamburlaine; he allies himself with Cosroe in the latter's rebellion against his brother, the king of Persia, and then challenges him for the crown

and defeats him. Tamburlaine's unbounded ambition and ruthless cruelty carry all before him. He conquers the Turkish emperor *Bajazet and leads him about, a prisoner in a cage, goading him and his empress Zabina with cruel taunts till they dash out their brains against the bars of the cage. His ferocity is softened only by his love for his captive Zenocrate, the daughter of the Soldan of Egypt, whose life he spares in deference to the pleadings of Zenocrate when he captures Damascus.

Part II deals with the continuation of his conquests, which extend to Babylon, whither he is drawn in a chariot dragged by the kings of Trebizond and Soria, with the kings of Anatolia and Jerusalem as relay, 'pampered Jades of *Asia*' (a phrase quoted by Pistol in Shakespeare, 2 *Henry IV*, II. iv); it ends with the death of Zenocrate, and of Tamburlaine himself.

Tamerlane, a tragedy by *Rowe, produced 1701, of some historical interest because under the name of Tamerlane the author intended to characterize William III, while under that of Bajazet he held up Louis XIV to detestation. The play was, for more than 100 years, annually revived on 5 Nov., the date of William III's landing.

Taming of the Shrew, The, a comedy by *Shakespeare, first printed in the *Folio of 1623, probably written c.1592 and based in part on the *Supposes adapted by G. Gascoigne from *Ariosto. In 1594 a quarto text called 'The Taming of a Shrew' was published; this was once thought to be Shakespeare's source, but it is now considered to be a corrupt version of his play compiled by the actor who played Grumio and an unknown playwright.

The play begins with an induction in which Christopher Sly, a drunken Warwickshire tinker, picked up by a lord and his huntsmen on a heath, is brought to the castle, sumptuously treated, and in spite of his protestations is assured that he is a lord who has been out of his mind. He is set down to watch the play that follows, performed solely for his benefit by strolling players. Sly appears again at the end of I. ii, disappears after that in the folio text; in the bad quarto he is given five more short scenes throughout the play.

Baptista Minola of Padua has two daughters, Katherina the Shrew, who is the elder of the two and Bianca, who has many suitors, but who may not marry until a husband has been found for Katherina. Petruchio, a gentleman from Verona, undertakes to woo the shrew to gain her dowry and to help his friend Hortensio win Bianca. To tame her he pretends to find her rude behaviour courteous and gentle and humiliates her by being late for their wedding and appearing badly dressed. He takes her off to his country house and, under the pretext that nothing there is good enough for her, prevents her from eating or sleeping. By the time they return to Baptista's house, Katherina has been successfully tamed, and Lucentio, a Pisan, has won Bianca by disguising himself as her schoolmaster, while the disappointed Hortensio has to console himself with marriage to a rich widow. At the feast which follows the three bridegrooms wager on whose wife is the most docile and submissive. Katherina argues that 'Thy husband is thy lord, thy life, thy keeper, | Thy head, thy sovereign' and Petruchio wins the bet.

A play by J. Fletcher, *The Woman's Prize, shows Petruchio tamed in a second marriage after Kate's death. Petruchio's three times repeated request 'kiss me, Kate' supplied the title for Cole Porter's popular musical of 1948.

Tam Lin, the subject of an old *ballad. Janet wins back to mortal life her elfin lover, Tam Lin, from the queen of the fairies, who has captured him.

Tamora, queen of the Goths in Shakespeare's *Titus Andronicus.

'Tam o' Shanter', a narrative poem by *Burns, published 1791.

Tam, a farmer, spends the cold evening of Ayre's market-day in a snug alehouse, where he becomes tipsy and amorous ('Tam was glorious'). Eventually riding home, he passes the Kirk of Alloway. Seeing it mysteriously lighted, he stops and looks in. Weird warlocks and witches are dancing to the sound of the bagpipes, played by Old Nick, the Devil. Roused by the sight of one 'winsome wench' among the old beldams, Tam shouts to her. At once the lights go out and the horde of witches rush out in pursuit of Tam. Terrified, he wildly spurs his grey mare, Meg, and just reaches the middle of the bridge over the Doon before the girl catches him. Once over the middle of the bridge he is out of her power, but his mare's tail is still within the witches' jurisdiction, and this the girl pulls off. The narrative is swift, and both the humour and the horror are effectively conveyed.

Tanaquil, in Roman legend, the wife of Tarquinius Priscus, the first of the Tarquin (Etruscan) kings of Rome. Spenser uses the name to signify Queen Elizabeth in the introduction to Book I of *The Faerie Queene.

Tancred, one of the Norman heroes of the first Crusade, figures in Tasso's *Jerusalem Delivered as one of the principal knights serving under Godfrey de *Bouillon.

Tancred, or the New Crusade, a novel by B. *Disraeli, published 1847.

This is the last of the trilogy *Coningsby—*Sybil—Tancred. Much of the novel is devoted to an attempt to resolve the antagonism between Judaism and Christianity and to establish a role for a reforming faith and revitalized church in a progressive society. Tancred, whose brilliant social and political future is assured, declares to his bewildered parents, Lord and Lady Montacute, that he must reject their plans for him and seek a faith and philosophy for himself in the Holy Land, where the secrets of the 'Asian mystery' may be revealed to him. He abandons the London of society hostesses and the young bloods of White's, travels to Jerusalem, and thence to Sinai, where he receives a revelation from the Angel of Arabia of 'a common Father'. But he soon becomes embroiled in war and intrigue between the Druses and the Maronites, and is used as a pawn to increase the power and prestige of the fiery Fakredeen, a dissembling and brilliant emir, who manœuvres Tancred into battle. Tancred, wounded and captured, is saved by a potion given him by the beautiful Jewess Eva, with whom he falls in love. This, and his conviction that Christianity owes everything to the Jews, leads him to beg her to marry him. But his parents, the duke and duchess, arrive at Jerusalem to claim him.

Tancred and Gismund, The Tragedie of, or Gismond of Salerne, a play by R. Wilmot (fl.c.1566–1608) and others, published 1591 but dating from 1566 or 1568. Act II is by Henry Noel, Act IV by *Hatton. The play is founded on a tale by *Boccaccio (see SIGISMONDA).

Tancred and Sigismunda, a tragedy by J. *Thomson, published 1745, produced (with *Garrick as Tancred) 1752.

It is based on the story inserted in *Lesage's Gil Blas, IV. iv, in which Tancred, the heir to the kingdom of Sicily, is lured by the cunning Siffredi into accepting with the throne a bride, Constantia, whom he does not love, and abandoning Siffredi's daughter Sigismunda, whom he does. The latter, in despair at her desertion, consents to marry Osmond, her father's choice. But Tancred does not give up his lady-love so easily. He kills Osmond, but not before the latter has fatally stabbed Sigismunda.

Tanglewood Tales, see HAWTHORNE, N.

TANNAHILL, Robert (1774–1810), born in Paisley, became an apprenticed handloom weaver to his father at the age of 12 and showed signs of talent in poetic composition. At 17 he paid homage to *Burns in Ayrshire and was inspired to write his first song 'My Ain Kind Dearie O'. From 1805 his work began to appear in newspapers and journals and in 1807 he published by subscription a volume of Poems and Songs, some of which were harshly criticized. Bitterly grieved on having a revised edition declined by a publisher, he burnt his manuscripts and drowned himself in a culvert near Paisley.

TANNHÄUSER, a German *Minnesinger of

the 13th cent. and the subject of the legend embodied in the 16th-cent. ballad, the *Tannhäuserlied*, in which he becomes enamoured of a beautiful woman who beckons him into the grotto of Venus in the 'Venusberg' (located in Thuringia), where he spends seven years in revelry. When he emerges he goes to Rome to seek absolution from the pope, who replies that it is as impossible for Tannhäuser to be forgiven as for his dry staff to burgeon. Tannhäuser departs in despair. After three days the pope's staff breaks into blossom, and he urgently sends for Tannhäuser, but he is not to be found, having returned to Venus. The story is the subject of an opera by *Wagner (perf. 1845), and of *Swinburne's poem 'Laus Veneris' (1866), a characteristically over-heated dramatic monologue of guilt, passion, and sensual abandon, which provided the basis for some of *Beardsley's best-known illustrations.

Tanqueray, Paula, see SECOND MRS TANQUERAY, THE.

Tapley, Mark, see MARK TAPLEY.

Tappertit, Simon, in Dickens's *Barnaby Rudge*, Gabriel Varden's apprentice.

Targum, a word meaning 'interpretation' the name given to several Aramaic translations, interpretations, paraphrases of the various divisions of the OT, made after the Babylonian captivity, at first preserved by oral transmission, and committed to writing from about AD 100 onwards [*OED*].

Tarka the Otter, see WILLIAMSON, H.

TARKINGTON, (Newton) Booth (1869–1946), American novelist, whose works include *The Gentleman from Indiana* (1899), *Monsieur Beaucaire* (1900, a historical romance which first won him popularity), *The Magnificent Ambersons* (1918, a chronicle of the Midwest), *The Plutocrat* (1927, a study of a self-made business man abroad), and *The Heritage of Hatcher Ide* (1941), portraying the Depression in the Midwest. He also wrote for children; *Penrod* (1914) and its sequels describe the adventures of an American boy and his gang of friends in a small Midwestern city.

TARLTON, Richard (d. 1588), actor, a man of humble origin and imperfect education, who attracted attention by his '*happy unhappy* answers' and was introduced to Queen Elizabeth through the earl of *Leicester. He became one of the queen's players in 1583, and attained an immense popularity by his jests, comic acting, and improvizations of doggerel verse. He led a dissipated life and died in poverty. He is perhaps to be identified with *Spenser's 'Pleasant Willy' (see 'Teares of the Muses') and Shakespeare's *Yorick. Many fictitious anecdotes connected with him were published, notably *Tarlton's Jests*, in three

parts (1613) and *Tarltons Newes out of Purgatorie* (1590).

Tarot Cards, a set of playing-cards first used in Italy in the 14th cent.; from *tarocchi*, a word of unknown origin. 'Play at Ombre and Taroc, a game with seventy-two cards all painted with suns and moons, devils and monks' (*Gray, letter to R. West, 1739). Use is made of the Tarot symbols in T. S. Eliot's *The Waste Land*.

Tartar, Mr, a character in Dickens's *Edwin Drood*.

Tartuffe, Le, in Molière's comedy of that name, an odious hypocrite, who, under an assumption of piety, introduces himself into the household of the credulous Orgon, attempts to seduce his wife, and being repulsed, endeavours to ruin the family. The normal spelling is *tartufe*.

Tarzan, see BURROUGHS, E. R.

Task, The, a poem in six books by *Cowper, published 1785.

Cowper's friend Lady Austen (whom he met in 1781) having suggested to him the sofa in his room as the subject of a poem in blank verse, the poet set about 'the task'. Its six books are entitled 'The Sofa', 'The Time-piece', 'The Garden', 'The Winter Evening', 'The Winter Morning Walk', and 'The Winter Walk at Noon'. Cowper opens with a mock-heroic account of the evolution of the sofa ('I sing the sofa') and thence digresses to description, reflection, and opinion. The poem stresses the delights of a retired life ('God made the country, and man made the town', Bk 1, 749); describes the poet's own search for peace ('I was a stricken deer, that left the herd', Bk 3, 108); and evokes the pleasures of gardening, winter evenings by the fire, etc. The moral passages condemn blood sports, cards, and other diversions; the poet manifests tenderness not only for his pet hare, but even for worms and snails. The poem was extremely popular: *Burns found it 'a glorious poem' that expressed 'the Religion of God and Nature', and it helped to create and supply the growing demand for natural description and tender emotion that found a fuller expression in Wordsworth's *Prelude*, a poem which contains many echoes of Cowper.

TASSO, Torquato (1544–95), son of Bernardo Tasso (author of an epic on *Amadis of Gaul), was born at Sorrento and spent many years at the court of Ferrara. He was from early life in constant terror of persecution and adverse criticism, and his conduct at Ferrara was such as to make it necessary for the duke, Alphonso II of Este, to lock him up as mad from 1579 to 1586. The legend of his passion for Leonora d'Este, the duke's discovery of it, and his consequent imprisonment, is no longer credited, but was for long widely believed; *Milton refers to it (in a Latin poem), Byron's *The Lament of Tasso* is based on it, and *Goethe's *Torquato Tasso* (1789) supports it, as does *Donizetti's opera (1833) of the same title. Tasso was released on the condition that he would leave Ferrara, and he spent the rest of his life wandering from court to court, unhappy, poverty-stricken, and paranoid, though widely admired. He died in Rome.

His chief works were *Rinaldo*, a romantic epic (1562); a pastoral play, *Aminta* (1573), which had a great success; *Jerusalem Delivered* (1580–1); and a less successful tragedy, *Torrismondo* (1586). He also wrote *Pindaric odes, and Spenser used his sonnets in many of his *Amoretti*. Tasso's epics and his critical works (*Discorsi dell'arte poetica*, *Discorsi del poema eroica*) had a great influence on English literature, displayed in the works of *Daniel, Milton, Giles and Phineas *Fletcher, *Cowley, *Dryden, and others; Milton refers to his theory of the epic in *The Reason of Church Government* and *Of Education*. *Fairfax's translation of *Jerusalem Delivered* (1600) also had an influence in its own right; according to Dryden, *Waller said that he 'derived the harmony of his numbers' from it. In the following century, *Gray translated a passage (Book XIV, 32–9), and *Collins recorded ('Ode on the Popular Superstitions of the Highlands') his great admiration for both Tasso and Fairfax: 'How have I trembled, when at Tancred's stroke | Its gushing blood, the gaping Cypress pour'd.'

Taste of Honey, A, see DELANEY, S.

TATE, (John Orley) Allen (1899–1979), American poet and critic, born in Tennessee, who began his literary career as editor of the little magazine *The Fugitive* (1922–5), published at Nashville, Tennessee, which published work by J. C. *Ransom, L. *Riding, R. P. *Warren, and others and supported a sense of regionalism as a defence against the 'all-destroying abstraction America'. He is best known for his poetry; his collections include *Mr Pope and Other Poems* (1928), *Poems 1928–1931* (1932), and *Collected Poems* (1977). As a critic he is associated with the *New Criticism.

TATE, Nahum (1652–1715), playwright, most of whose dramatic works were adaptations from earlier writers; his version of *King Lear* omits the Fool, makes Edgar and Cordelia lovers, and ends happily. It was highly popular; Dr *Johnson defended it on the grounds that the original is too painful, and the full text was not restored until the 19th cent.: *Kean was the first actor to conclude with Lear's death. Tate also wrote, with *Dryden, the second part of *Absalom and Achitophel*; also the libretto of *Purcell's *Dido and Aeneas*. In 1696 he published with Nicholas Brady the well-known metrical version of the psalms that bears their name. He was appointed poet laureate in 1692, and was pilloried by Pope in *The Dunciad*.

TATE and BRADY, see TATE, N.

Tatler, The, a periodical founded by R. *Steele, of which the first issue appeared on 12 April 1709; it appeared thrice weekly until 2 Jan. 1711.

According to No. 1, it was to include 'Accounts of Gallantry, Pleasure and Entertainment . . . under the Article of White's Chocolate House'; poetry under that of Will's Coffee House; foreign and domestic news from St James's Coffee-house; learning from the Grecian; and so on. Gradually it adopted a loftier tone; the evils of duelling and gambling are denounced in some of the earlier numbers, and presently all questions of good manners are discussed from the standpoint of a more humane civilization, and a new standard of taste is established. The ideal of a gentleman is examined, and its essence is found to lie in forbearance. The author assumes the character of Swift's *Bickerstaff, the marriage of whose sister, Jenny Distaff, with Tranquillus gives occasion for treating of happy married life. The rake and the coquette are exposed, and virtue is held up to admiration in the person of Lady Elizabeth Hastings (1682–1739), somewhat inappropriately named Aspasia—'to love her is a liberal education.' Anecdotes, essays, and short stories illustrate the principles advanced.

From an early stage in the history of *The Tatler* Steele had the collaboration of *Addison, who contributed notes, suggestions, and a number of complete papers. It was succeeded by *The Spectator*, which they edited jointly.

Tattle, a character in Congreve's *Love for Love*.

Tattycoram, in Dickens's *Little Dorrit*, a foundling brought up in the Meagles household.

TAUCHNITZ, Christian Berhard von (1816–95), the founder of a publishing house at Leipzig which in 1841 began to issue piratically, then from 1843 to 1943 by sanction or copyright, a series of 5,370 volumes eventually designated 'Collection of British and American Authors'. This and other textually significant English-language 'collections', though specified for sale only on the Continent, were distributed worldwide and reportedly exceeded 40 million copies. Post-war Tauchnitz editions have been issued from Hamburg (1946–9) and Stuttgart (1952–5).

Taurinum, in imprints, Turin.

Taverner's Bible, see BIBLE, THE ENGLISH.

TAWNEY, R(ichard) H(enry) (1880–1962), educated at Rugby and Balliol College, Oxford; historian, socialist (of the *Ruskin, *Morris, and Christian Socialist tradition), and teacher and activist in the *Workers' Educational Association. He joined the executive committee of the WEA in 1905, remained on it for 42 years, and was profoundly affected by the movement, as well as himself influencing its course. From 1917 he was attached to the London School of Economics, becoming professor of economic history in 1931. His works include *The Acquisitive Society* (1921), *Religion and the Rise of Capitalism* (1926), and *Land and Labour in China* (1932).

TAYLOR, A(lan) J(ohn) P(ercivale) (1906–), historian, educated at Bootham School, York, and Oriel College, Oxford. His many publications include *The Habsburg Monarchy* (1941), *The Troublemakers* (1957, from his Ford lectures), *The Origins of the Second World War* (1961), and a life of *Beaverbrook (1972). He also became widely known as a journalist and television personality, and his autobiography, *A Personal History* (1983), gives a lively and frequently iconoclastic account of his colleagues and acquaintances (including a hostile portrait of Dylan *Thomas), and traces the evolution of his political sympathies from his support of the workers in the General Strike to his support of the Campaign for Nuclear Disarmament.

TAYLOR, Edward (*c*.1644–1729), American poet and divine, born in England, emigrated to Boston in 1668, and was educated at Harvard. His devotional poems remained in manuscript, at his own request, and were not published until 1937, when their importance to the history of early American letters, and their own considerable quality, were at once recognized. He belongs to the metaphysical tradition of G. *Herbert and *Quarles. A full edition of his works, ed. D. E. Stanford, was published in 1960.

TAYLOR, Elizabeth (1912–75), writer, was educated in Reading, then worked locally as tutor and librarian until she married in 1936. Her first novel, *At Mrs Lippincote's* (1945), was followed by many others, most of them delicate but shrewd observations of middle-class life in the stockbroker belt, written in the Austen–Forster tradition. Amongst the best known are *A Wreath of Roses* (1950), in which Camilla Hill, a reserved school secretary on the brink of middle age, becomes involved with a handsome but suspect young man, and *Mrs Palfrey at the Claremont* (1972), a study of the pathos of impoverished but genteel old age. Her collection of short stories, *Hester Lilly* (1954), *The Blush* (1958), *A Dedicated Man* (1965), and *The Devastating Boys* (1972), are also much admired.

TAYLOR, Sir Henry (1800–86), held an appointment in the Colonial Office from 1824 to 1872, during which time he published a number of verse dramas which had a considerable vogue in their day, but are now largely forgotten. The most admired was *Philip van Artevelde* (1834), a lengthy work set in Flanders in the 14th cent.;

he describes its hero, a retiring citizen raised to prominence during the power struggles between Ghent and Bruges, as 'a statesman and a man of business'. His only work with any lasting reputation is *The Statesman* (1836), an ironical exposition of the arts of succeeding as a civil servant; its apparent cynicism shocked many of its readers, but recent editors (H. J. Laski, 1927; L. Silberman, 1957) find it a shrewd and interesting commentary on the changing and expanding role of the civil service. Taylor was a friend of *Southey and his literary executor. His *Autobiography 1800–75* was published in 1885 (privately printed 1877) and his complete works in 5 vols appeared in 1877–8.

TAYLOR, Jane (1783–1824) and Ann (1782–1866), authors of books for children. In 1804 they published *Original Poems for Infant Minds*, which was translated into German, Dutch, and Russian, and ran into 50 editions in England alone. In 1806 followed *Rhymes for the Nursery*, which included one of the most famous poems in the English language, 'Twinkle, twinkle little star'. Other nursery rhymes and stories followed, and in 1810 *Hymns for Infant Minds*. In 1816 Jane produced *Essays in Rhyme*, and until 1822 contributed regularly to *Youth's Magazine*. Both Sir W. *Scott and R. *Browning expressed admiration for the Taylors' work.

TAYLOR, Jeremy (1613–67), was born at Cambridge, and was the son of a barber. He was educated at Gonville and Caius College, Cambridge. Having attracted *Laud's attention as a preacher, he was sent by him to Oxford and became a fellow of All Souls College. He was chaplain to Laud and Charles I, and was appointed rector of Uppingham in 1638. He was taken prisoner in the royalist defeat before Cardigan Castle in 1645, and retired to Golden Grove, Carmarthenshire, where he wrote most of his greater works. After the Restoration he was made bishop of Down and Connor, and subsequently of Dromore. He died at Lisburn and was buried in his cathedral of Dromore. His fame rests on the combined simplicity and splendour of his style, of which *The Rule and Exercises of Holy Living* (1650) and *The Rule and Exercises of Holy Dying* (1651) are perhaps the best examples. Among his other works, *The Liberty of Prophesying*, an argument for toleration, appeared in 1647; his *Eniautos*, or series of sermons for the Christian Year, in 1653; *The Golden Grove*, a manual of daily prayers, in 1655; his *Ductor Dubitantium*, 'a general instrument of moral theology' for determining cases of conscience, in 1660; and *The Worthy Communicant* in the same year.

TAYLOR, John (?1578–1653), the 'water-poet', born of humble parentage in Gloucester, was sent to Gloucester Grammar School, but becoming 'mired' in his Latin accidence was apprenticed to a waterman, pressed for the navy, and was present at the siege of Cadiz. He then became a Thames waterman, and increased his earnings by writing rollicking verse and prose; he obtained the patronage of *Jonson and others, and diverted both court and city. He went on foot from London to Braemar, visited the Continent, started from London to Queenborough in a brown-paper boat and narrowly escaped drowning, and accomplished other journeys, each one resulting in a booklet with an odd title. He published in 1630 a collective edition of his works, *All the Workes of John Taylor, the Water Poet* (reprinted, with other pieces, by the Spenser Society, 1868–78), but continued to write a good deal after this, notably royalist ballads and news-sheets.

TAYLOR, John (1781–1864), first distinguished himself, amid much controversy, by identifying *'Junius' as Sir P. *Francis in 1813. After the death of J. *Scott, he became the editor of the *London Magazine*, 1821–4, and he became a very perceptive partner in the publishing firm of Taylor and Hessey. He published the work of *De Quincey, *Lamb, *Hazlitt, *Keats, *Clare, *Carey, and others, many of whom had already appeared in the *London Magazine*. He greatly encouraged and assisted Clare, published his first volume of *Poems* in 1820, and raised a subscription, to which he contributed generously himself, for the joint benefit of the indigent Clare and Keats. But Clare felt that the comparative failure of *The Shepherd's Calendar* in 1827 was Taylor's fault, and although Taylor offered Clare all the remaining copies to sell for his own benefit, he advanced no more money to the poet and was not the publisher of *The Rural Muse* (1835). He caused some offence to Keats, and to other writers, by his occasional 'revisions' of their works. He held regular dinners for writers, lent money to Keats to travel to Italy, and seems generally to have happily combined the qualities of businessman and friend.

TAYLOR, Philip Meadows (1808–76), Anglo-Indian novelist and historian, born in Liverpool, joined the Indian Army and became a correspondent for *The Times* from 1840 to 1853. He was author of the successful *Confessions of a Thug* (1839), a result of his investigation into Thuggism, the secret terrorist movement in India. His reputation rests mainly on stories written after his retirement to England in 1860, notably the trilogy *Tara: a Mahratta Tale* (1843), *Ralph Darnell* (1865), and *Seeta* (1872), which delineate epochs of Indian history from the 17th cent. to his own time. His autobiography, edited by his daughter, appeared in 1877.

TAYLOR, Thomas (1758–1835), classical scholar, mathematician, and *Neoplatonist, was the friend of T. L. *Peacock and other literary men and painters. He was the first to embark on a systematic translation and exposition of Orphic and Neoplatonic literature, and he also devoted himself to the metaphysical aspect of mathematics. He published a great many works covering these interests.

TAYLOR, Tom (1817–80), educated at Trinity College, Cambridge, of which he became a fellow, was editor of *Punch*, 1874–80. He produced a number of successful plays (some in collaboration with C. *Reade), most of them adaptations. His comedy *Our American Cousin* (1858) contained the character of the brainless peer Lord Dundreary, who was played with great panache by E. A. Sothern. He edited *Haydon's autobiography in 1853.

TAYLOR, William (1765–1836), born in Norwich, author and translator, who did much to popularize German literature through his translations of Bürger's ballads (see LENORE), and of G. E. *Lessing's *Nathan der Weise* (1791) and *Goethe's *Iphigenia in Tauris* (1793): also through his *Historic Survey of German Poetry* (3 vols, 1828–30) and many contributions on the subject to the *Monthly Magazine*, for which he wrote over 800 reviews, essays, and translations. He was a friend of *Southey, his correspondence with whom is printed in a *Memoir* by J. W. Robberds (1843).

TCHAIKOVSKY, Peter Ilich (1840–93), Russian composer, and probably the man who has most nearly brought 'classical' music (though in his case it was actually profoundly Romantic) into the world of popular musical understanding. Along with the Piano Concerto in B flat minor, the 'Pathétique' Symphony, and the *Swan Lake* and *Sleeping Beauty* ballet scores, the Fantasy Overture *Romeo and Juliet* (1869) is a piece which has reached out to a wide audience—perhaps wider than any other musical composition inspired by Shakespeare—and yet retains its inherent qualities as a serious work of art. It was Tchaikovsky's first masterpiece (revised in 1870 and again in 1880), brilliantly integrating the dramatic and passionate elements of Shakespeare's play into the requirements of a compact musical structure. In the last months of his life Tchaikovsky used the Love Theme (one of the most ravishing of his melodic ideas and one of the most famous) as the basis for a duet version of the opening of Shakespeare's Act III, sc. v, but he left it incomplete, and there is no evidence that he ever seriously considered making an opera out of the play. There are, however, two other important Shakespearian orchestral works: the Symphonic Fantasia *The Tempest* (1873), and the Fantasy Overture *Hamlet* (1888).

On the one other occasion when Tchaikovsky

turned to an English poet for a subject he produced what is usually regarded, with the 6th Symphony, as his finest orchestral work, the *Manfred* symphony after *Byron (1886). It cost him a great deal: 'the symphony has turned out to be huge, serious, difficult', he wrote, 'absorbing all my time, sometimes to my utter exhaustion', yet almost nowhere else did he realize a large musical form with such success. *Manfred* is one of the great programme symphonies of the 19th cent.

TCHEKHOV, see CHEKHOV.

'Teares of the Muses, The', a poem by *Spenser, included in the *Complaints*, published 1591. In this the poet deplores, through the mouth of several Muses, the decay of literature and learning.

Tearsheet, Doll, *Falstaff's mistress in Shakespeare's 2 *Henry IV*.

Teazle, Sir Peter and Lady, characters in Sheridan's *The School for Scandal.*

'Te Deum', a Latin hymn of praise to God, so called from its opening words. Its authorship used to be ascribed to St *Ambrose and associated with the conversion by him of St *Augustine of Hippo; but modern scholars attribute it to Ambrose's younger contemporary Niceta of Remesiana.

TEILHARD DE CHARDIN, Pierre (1881–1955), French palaeontologist and Jesuit priest, author of a series of posthumously-published works, notably *Le Phénomène humain* (1955), in which he elaborated a system of cosmic evolution. In Teilhard's conception, every physical being was endowed with an inner consciousness whose concentration varied in direct proportion to its material complexity. All matter and material systems were continually and irreversibly evolving along related and converging paths towards physical synthesis and spiritual perfection. The appearance of man in evolutionary history marks the emergence of self-consciousness and has added to the earth, superimposed as it were upon the biosphere, a new dimension, the noosphere, or domain of thought. The development of this specifically human sphere of activity initiates a critical phase in the process of simultaneous complexification and integration, which is to attain its natural term in the unification of cultures, together with a concomitant intensification of collective consciousness to a 'hyperpersonal' level. Evolutionary integration thus reaches its ultimate stage, the point of maximum differentiated unity, which is designated as Omega, and which is arrived at simultaneously with a full realization of the principle of love inherent in the universe.

TELFORD, Thomas (1757–1834), civil engineer and architect, who loved literature and

versifying. He was interested in *Goethe and *Kotzebue and was a close friend of *Southey and *Campbell. He is said to have assisted Campbell in the composition of 'Hohenlinden', and he travelled in Scotland with Southey. He built over 1,000 miles of road, 1,200 bridges, churches, docks, aqueducts, and canals, notably the Caledonian. His *Life*, a long and detailed autobiography, was published in 1838.

Tell, William, a legendary hero of the liberation of Switzerland from Austrian oppression. The stories concerning him differ in details, but in its generally accepted form the legend represents him as a skilled Swiss marksman who refused to do honour to the hat of Gessler, the Austrian bailiff of Uri, placed on a pole, and was in consequence arrested and required to hit with an arrow an apple placed on the head of his little son. This he successfully did, and with a second arrow shot Gessler, subsequently stirring up a rebellion against the oppressors. Another version relates how Tell, being carried a prisoner across the lake to Gessler's castle, was given the tiller, on account of his strength, when a storm arose. He steered the boat on to a ledge of rock, subsequently called Tell's Platte, sprang ashore, and shot the bailiff. These events are placed in the 14th cent. Swiss historians have shown that there is no evidence for the existence of a real William Tell. The story is first found in writings of the 15th cent. William Tell is the subject of a play by *Schiller and an opera by *Rossini.

Similar legends of marksmen shooting at an object placed on the head of a man or child are of widespread occurrence, e.g. in Norway and England (Egil, Clym of the Clough, William of Cloudesley).

TÉLLEZ, Gabriel (1583–1648), who wrote under the pseudonym Tirso da Molina, a Spanish dramatist, famous outside Spain principally as the creator of the prototype of *Don Juan in his play *El Burlador de Sevilla* (1630, *The Seville Deceiver* or *Jester*).

Temora, see FINGAL.

Tempest, The, a romantic drama by *Shakespeare probably written in 1611, when it was performed before the king at Whitehall; in 1613 it was included in the wedding celebrations for the Princess Elizabeth and the Elector Palatine. It was not printed until 1623 when it appeared as the first play in the First *Folio. It is usually taken to be his last play written without a collaborator for the London stage before his retirement to Stratford. Although there are several analogues for the story of *The Tempest*, and contemporary accounts of the shipwreck of the *Sea-Venture* in 1609 on the Bermudas and passages from *Golding's Ovid and *Florio's Montaigne contribute details to the play, no single source for it is known. As Dr *Johnson observed, *The

Tempest's 'plan is regular', that is, it conforms to the *unities.

Prospero, duke of Milan, ousted from his throne by his brother Antonio, and turned adrift on the sea with his child Miranda, has been cast upon a lonely island. This had been the place of banishment of the witch Sycorax. Prospero, by his knowledge of magic, has released various spirits (including Ariel) formerly imprisoned by the witch, and these now obey his orders. He also keeps in service the witch's son Caliban, a misshapen monster, the sole inhabitant of the island. Prospero and Miranda have lived thus for twelve years. When the play begins a ship carrying the usurper, his confederate Alonso, king of Naples, his brother Sebastian and son Ferdinand, is by the art of Prospero wrecked on the island. The passengers are saved, but Ferdinand is thought by the rest to be drowned, and he thinks this is their fate. According to Prospero's plan Ferdinand and Miranda are thrown together, fall in love, and plight their troths. Prospero appears to distrust Ferdinand and sets him to carrying logs. On another part of the island Sebastian and Antonio plot to kill Alonso and Gonzalo, 'an honest old Councellor' who had helped Prospero in his banishment. Caliban offers his services to Stephano, a drunken butler, and Trinculo, a jester, and persuades Sebastian and Antonio to try to murder Prospero. As their conspiracy nears him, Prospero breaks off the masque of Iris, Juno, and Ceres, which Ariel has presented to Ferdinand and Miranda. Caliban, Stephano, and Trinculo are driven off and Ariel brings the king and his courtiers to Prospero's cell. There he greets 'My true preserver' Gonzalo, forgives his brother Antonio, on the condition that he restores his dukedom to him, and re-unites Alonso with his son Ferdinand, who is discovered playing chess with Miranda. While Alonso repents for what he has done, Antonio and Sebastian do not speak directly to Prospero, but exchange ironical and cynical comments with each other. The boatswain and master of the ship appear to say that it has been magically repaired and that the crew is safe. Before all embark for Italy Prospero frees Ariel from his service, renounces his magic, and leaves Caliban once more alone on the island.

The Tempest has inspired numerous other works of art, including Milton's *Comus*, an incomplete opera by *Mozart, *Shelley's 'Ariel to Miranda' (see also under ARIEL), *Browning's 'Caliban upon Setebos', music by *Berlioz and *Tchaikovsky, and more recently W. H. *Auden's series of poetic meditations *The Sea and the Mirror* and an excellent science fiction film, *Forbidden Planet* (1954).

Templars, Knights, an order founded about 1118, consisting originally of nine knights whose profession was to safeguard pilgrims to Jerusalem, and who were granted by Baldwin, king of Jerusalem, a dwelling-place in his palace near the temple. Many noblemen from all parts of Christendom joined the order, and it acquired great wealth and influence in France, England, and other countries. Active always in the field, they were really a source of weakness to the Christian king of Jerusalem from their direct dependence on the Pope and their constant violation of treaties with the Muslim powers. After the battle of 1187 *Saladin made an example of the Templars and the (much less guilty) Hospitallers who became his prisoners, and beheaded them all, about 200 in number, while sparing nearly all his other prisoners. The knights were organized in commanderies, under a preceptor in each province, and a grand master at the head of the order. From a state of poverty and humility (their seal represents two of them riding on the same horse) they became so insolent that the order was suppressed. They were accused of blasphemy, sorcery, and other crimes. The order was crushed by the kings of Europe in their various dominions with circumstances, especially in France, of great cruelty. It was also officially suppressed by the Pope and the Council of Vienne (1312). *Browning's poem 'The Heretic's Tragedy' alludes to the burning of Jacques de Bourg-Molay, the grand master, in 1314. See P. Partner, *The Murdered Magicians, the Templars and their Myth* (1982).

Temple, Miss, a character in C. Brontë's *Jane Eyre*.

TEMPLE, Sir William (1628–99), educated at Emmanuel College, Cambridge, was envoy at Brussels in 1666, and visited The Hague, where he effected the triple alliance between England, Holland, and Sweden, aiming at the protection of Spain from French ambition. He went again to The Hague in 1674, where he brought about the marriage between William of Orange and Mary. In 1655 he married Dorothy *Osborne, whose letters to him give a vivid picture of the times. He settled first at Sheen, then at Moor Park, near Farnham, where he was much occupied with gardening, and where *Swift was an inmate of his household. His principal works include *Observations upon . . . the Netherlands* (1672), an essay upon *The Advancement of Trade in Ireland* (1673), and three volumes of *Miscellanea* (1680, 1692, 1701). The second of these contains 'Of Ancient and Modern Learning', an essay which, by its uncritical praise of the spurious epistles of *Phalaris, exposed Temple to the censure of *Bentley and led to a vigorous controversy. The *Miscellanea* also include 'Upon the Gardens of Epicurus', 'Of Health and Long Life', 'Of Heroic Virtue', and 'Of Poetry'. Temple's letters were published by Swift, 1700–3, after Temple's death. His *Memoirs*, relating to the period 1672–9, published in 1692, are an interesting blend of public and private affairs.

Tenant of Wildfell Hall, The, a novel by A. *Brontë, published 1848.

The narrator, Gilbert Markham, a young farmer, falls in love with Helen Graham, a young widow and talented painter newly arrived in the neighbourhood with her son Arthur, and the tenant of the title. Her youth, beauty, and seclusion, and her mysterious relationship with her landlord Lawrence, give rise to local gossip, which Markham refuses to credit until he himself overhears Helen and Lawrence in intimate conversation. He violently assaults Lawrence, and Helen, distressed at the threatened rupture of their friendship, reveals the truth of her past to him through a lengthy document. Despite the warnings of her family, she had married Arthur Huntingdon, who, after a period of initial happiness, had relapsed, despite her efforts, into a life of drinking, debauchery, and infidelity. She had fled, to protect her child, to Wildfell Hall, provided for her by Lawrence, who is in fact her brother. Shortly after the revelation of this secret, Helen returns to nurse her husband through a fatal illness, his death hastened by his intemperance, and the way is left clear for Markham successfully to renew his suit. In her 'Biographical Notice' (1850) Charlotte *Brontë suggested that the portrait of the dissolute Huntingdon was based on their brother Branwell, in whom Anne Brontë had had ample opportunity to observe 'the terrible effects of talents misused and faculties abused', and the novel was generally considered (with *Wuthering Heights) as excessively morbid. The author defended it in a preface to the second edition: 'I am at a loss to conceive how a man should permit himself to write anything that would be really disgraceful to a woman, or why a woman should be censured for writing anything that would be proper and becoming for a man.'

Ten Days that Shook the World, an eyewitness account of the Russian revolution by American journalist and socialist John Reed (1887–1920), published 1919. It was published in England by the British Communist Party in 1926, with an introduction by *Lenin.

Tender is the Night, a novel by F. S. *Fitzgerald.

TENIERS, David, the younger (1610–90), Flemish painter, chiefly of genre scenes of peasants and topers. His father David Teniers the elder (1582–1649), painted chiefly religious subjects, and his son, David (1638–85), was also a painter, often imitating his father.

TENNANT, Emma (1938–), novelist, born in London but brought up largely in Scotland. She founded and edited the literary review *Bananas, and her novels (which have been variously described as Neo-*Gothic and *Magic Realist, and which are written in a powerful poetic prose) include *Hotel de Dream* (1976); *The Bad Sister* (1978); *Wild Nights* (1979); *Alice Fell* (1980); and *Woman Beware Woman* (1983).

TENNANT, William (1784–1848), educated at St Andrews University, a parish schoolmaster (at Anstruther in Fife) learned in oriental languages, of which he became professor at St Andrews. He is remembered in a literary connection for his poem in six cantos *Anster Fair* (1812), a mock-heroic description of the humours of the fair (in James V's reign) and of the courting, with fairy interposition, of Maggie Lauder by Rob the Ranter.

TENNIEL, Sir John (1820–1914), illustrator. He worked for *Punch from 1850, and from 1864 succeeded *Leech as its chief cartoonist; 'Dropping the Pilot' (1890), referring to Bismarck's resignation, is one of his best-known cartoons. His illustrations for *Alice's Adventures in Wonderland* (1865) and *Through the Looking Glass* (1871) are perfect examples of the integration of illustration with text.

TENNYSON, Alfred, first Baron Tennyson (1809–92), was born at Somersby, Lincolnshire, the third surviving son of the rector, George Tennyson. He was educated partly by his father, then at Trinity College, Cambridge, where he joined the *Apostles and became acquainted with A. H. *Hallam. In 1829 he won the chancellor's medal for English verse with 'Timbuctoo', the first poem in blank verse to win. *Poems by Two Brothers* (1827) contains some early work that he chose not to reprint even in his Juvenilia, as well as poems by his brothers Charles and Frederick (below). *Poems, Chiefly Lyrical* (1830, including *'Mariana') was unfavourably reviewed by *Lockhart and John *Wilson. In 1832 he travelled with Hallam on the Continent, visiting among other places Cauteret, a landscape that was to be a lasting inspiration. Hallam died abroad in 1833, and in that year Tennyson began *In Memoriam, expressive of his grief for his lost friend.

He became engaged to Emily Sellwood, to whom, however, he was not married until 1850; poverty caused by the disinheritance of the Somersby Tennysons in favour of his socially ambitious uncle Charles Tennyson (D'Eyncourt) was long accepted as the principal reason for this delay, but R. B. Martin suggested (*Tennyson: The Unquiet Heart*, 1980) that Alfred feared the 'black blood' of the Tennysons, a notoriously melancholic and unstable family, and suspected that he, like his father, suffered from epilepsy. (George Tennyson, a violent alcoholic, had died in 1831.) In December 1832 he published a further volume of *Poems* (dated 1833), which included 'The Two Voices', 'Oenone', 'The Lotos-Eaters', and 'A Dream of Fair Women'; *'Tithonus', published 1860, was composed

1833–4. In 1842 appeared a selection from the previous two volumes, many of the poems much revised, with new poems, including *'Morte d'Arthur' (the germ of the *Idylls*), *'Locksley Hall', *'Ulysses', and 'St Simeon Stylites'. From 1845 until his death he received a civil list pension of £200 per annum. In 1847 he published *The Princess* and in 1850 *In Memoriam*, and in the latter year he was appointed poet laureate in succession to *Wordsworth. He wrote his 'Ode' on the death of *Wellington in 1852 and *'The Charge of the Light Brigade' in 1854, having at this time settled in Farringford on the Isle of Wight.

Tennyson's fame was by now firmly established, and *Maud, and other Poems* (1855, see MAUD) and the first four *Idylls of the King* (1859) sold extremely well. Among the many friends and admirers who visited Farringford were E. *Fitzgerald, who had helped him financially in early years, *Lear, *Patmore, *Clough, F. T. *Palgrave, and *Allingham. Prince Albert called in 1856, but despite the high esteem with which she regarded him Queen *Victoria never visited him, preferring to summon him to Osborne or Windsor. Although suspicious of unknown admirers, Tennyson was a sociable man, with a fondness for declaiming his work to a respectful audience; his wife and his son Hallam protected him from hostile criticism, to which he was highly sensitive. In London he frequented the literary and artistic salon of Mrs Prinseps at Little Holland House; her sister, the photographer Julia Margaret *Cameron, moved to the Isle of Wight in 1860, where she frequently used Tennyson and his family as subjects. *Enoch Arden Etc.* (see ENOCH ARDEN) appeared in 1864, *The Holy Grail and Other Poems* (including 'Lucretius') in 1869 (dated 1870), 'The Last Tournament' in the *Contemporary Review* in 1871, and *Gareth and Lynette, etc.* in 1872. Tennyson began building his second residence, Aldworth, near Haslemere in Surrey, in 1868. His dramas *Queen Mary* and *Harold* were published in 1875 and 1876, and *The Falcon, *The Cup, and *Becket in 1884, in which year he was made a peer. H. *Irving and Ellen *Terry appeared in *The Cup* in 1881 and, with much success, in *Becket* in 1893. In 1880 appeared *Ballads and Other Poems*, including 'The Voyage of Maeldune', *'Rizpah', and 'The Revenge'. He published *Tiresias, and Other Poems* (see TIRESIAS) in 1885, and *The Foresters* appeared in 1892. He was buried in Westminster Abbey, and a life by his son Hallam appeared in 1897.

In his later years there were already signs that the admiration Tennyson had long enjoyed was beginning to wane; the *Idylls*, although admired by readers as various as *Longfellow, Clough, *Macaulay, *Thackeray, *Gladstone, and Queen Victoria, were found by *Carlyle, despite their 'finely elaborated execution' to express 'the inward perfectn. of *vacancy*', and *Swinburne referred to them as 'Morte d'Albert, or Idylls of the Prince Consort'. *Bagehot found 'Enoch Arden' 'ornate' and G. M. *Hopkins found it 'Parnassian'. In 1870 A. *Austin described Tennyson's work as 'poetry of the drawing room'. Critical opinion has tended to endorse *Auden's view that 'his genius was lyrical', and that he had little talent for the narrative, epic, and dramatic forms to which he devoted such labour. T. S. *Eliot called him 'the great master of metric as well as of melancholia', who has 'the finest ear of any English poet since Milton', and *Leavis suggested that his influence, like *Milton's, was unfortunate. More recently there has been a revival of interest in some of the longer poems, e.g. 'Locksley Hall', *The Princess*, and 'Enoch Arden'. There is an excellent annotated edn by C. Ricks (1969); see also his *Tennyson* (1972).

TENNYSON, Frederick (1807–98), elder brother of A. *Tennyson, contributed to the *Poems by Two Brothers* (1827), and published *Days and Hours* (1854), *The Isles of Greece* (1890), and other volumes of verse.

TENNYSON TURNER, Charles (1808–79), elder brother of A. *Tennyson, contributed to *Poems by Two Brothers* (1827) and published from time to time volumes of sonnets (1830–80), simple and restrained in manner, some of them depicting the rustic aspects of the Lincolnshire wolds.

Ten Thousand a Year, see WARREN, S.

TERENCE (Publius Terentius Afer) (*c.*190 or *c.*180–159 BC), Roman comic poet, supposedly an African and a slave at birth, whose good looks and intelligence led to his being educated and then freed by his master. As a young man he found patrons among the cultured nobility. His six plays (all extant) owed a great deal to the Greek New Comedy, but as their models have been lost it is impossible to assess the measure of his debt or the truth of the belief that he habitually combined the plots of two existing plays. He may have done no more than to borrow scenes from several sources. Although he employs the same limited range of characters that is found in *Plautus, he gives them greater depth and presents a world of genuine relationships. He was famed already in antiquity for the elegance and colloquial character of his Latin. It was as a stylist that he was studied in the Middle Ages and figured in the curriculum of most Tudor schools: there is an early translation of the *Andria*, probably by *Rastell (*c.*1520), a later one specifically for schools by M. Kyffin (1588), and an English version of all the six comedies by R. Bernard (1598). But Terence was known more through imitations than through translations. Along with Plautus, he contributed plots, characters, and tone to the mainstream of Renaissance comedy in 16th-cent. Italy, then (with original features) in the France of *Corneille and *Molière, from where it spread to Restoration London.

TERESA, St, see THERESA.

TERRY, Ellen Alice (1847–1928), celebrated actress, and member of a distinguished theatrical family. She married the painter G. F. Watts in 1864, when only sixteen, a union that soon ended, and had two children by E. W. Godwin (1833–86), the architect and theatrical designer, one of whom was Gordon *Craig. She was H. *Irving's leading lady during his brilliant management of the Lyceum Theatre.

TERSON, Peter, the pseudonym of Peter Patterson (1932–), playwright, born in Newcastle upon Tyne; he was associated with the Victoria Theatre, Stoke-on-Trent, with its tradition of social documentary and theatre-in-the-round, then with the National Youth Theatre, where he excelled in writing for large casts. His works include *Mooney and his Caravans* (TV 1966, pub. 1970), a poignant play about a young and inadequate couple victimized by the owner of a caravan site; *Zigger Zagger* (1967, pub. 1970), about a football fan, which skilfully incorporates the drama of the football terraces; and *Good Lads at Heart* (1971), set in a Borstal.

TERTULLIAN (b. *c*.150), one of the greatest of the early Christian writers in Latin, author of the *Apologeticus* (197), an eloquent appeal to Roman governors on behalf of the Christians, and of many treatises on the Christian life. He was opposed to the introduction of classical authors into Christian schools, and posed that famous question adapted by St *Jerome and *Alcuin: 'What has Athens to do with Jerusalem?' (*De Spectaculis*).
   Disciplinary, Moral and Ascetical Works (including *De Spectaculis*), trans. R. Arbesmann, E. J. Daly, and E. A. Quain (1959); *The Apology*, trans. T. H. Bindley (1890).

Terza rima, the measure adopted by Dante in the *Divina Commedia*, consisting of lines of five iambic feet with an extra syllable, in sets of three lines, the middle line of each rhyming with the first and third lines of the next set (a b a, b c b, c d c, etc.).

Tess of the D'Urbervilles; A Pure Woman, a novel by T. *Hardy, published 1891.
   The subtitle was important to Hardy's purpose. Tess Durbeyfield is the daughter of a poor villager of Blackmoor Vale, whose head is turned by learning that he is descended from the ancient family of D'Urberville. Tess is cunningly seduced by Alec, a young man of means, whose parents, with doubtful right, bear the name of D'Urberville. Tess gives birth to a child, which dies after an improvised midnight baptism by its mother. Later, while working as a dairymaid on a prosperous farm, in a beautiful summer, she becomes blissfully engaged to Angel Clare, a clergyman's son. On their wedding night she confesses to him the seduction by Alec; and Angel, although himself no innocent, cruelly and hypocritically abandons her. Misfortunes and bitter hardships come upon her and her family, and accident throws her once more in the path of Alec D'Urberville. He has become an itinerant preacher, but his temporary religious conversion does not prevent him from persistently pursuing her. When her pathetic appeals to her husband, now in Brazil, remain unanswered, she is driven for the sake of her family to become the mistress of Alec. Clare, returning from Brazil and repenting of his harshness, finds her living with Alec in Sandbourne. Maddened by this second wrong that has been done her by Alec, Tess stabs and kills him to liberate herself. After a brief halcyon period of concealment with Clare in the New Forest, Tess is arrested at Stonehenge, tried, and hanged. Hardy's final sentence reads: '"Justice" was done, and the President of the Immortals (in Aeschylean phrase) had ended his sport with Tess.'
   The publication of the novel created a violent sensation (see also JUDE THE OBSCURE). Some reviewers were deeply impressed, but most considered the work immoral, pessimistic, extremely disagreeable, and, as H. *James wrote, 'chockful of faults and falsity'.

Testament of Beauty, The, see BRIDGES, R.

Testament of Cresseid, The, a poem in 616 lines of rhyme-royal by *Henryson. The poet describes in the Prologue how he took up Chaucer's *Troilus and Criseyde* and proceeded to tell of the retribution that came upon Cresseid. Diomede grows tired of Cresseid and leaves her; she takes refuge with her father Calchas and bitterly reproaches Venus and Cupid. A council of the gods discusses the punishment for her blasphemy; Saturn deprives her of joy and beauty, and the Moon strikes her with leprosy. As she sits by the roadside with her leper's cup and clapper, Troilus rides by with a party of victorious Trojans and, though the leper brings Cresseid to his mind, he does not recognize her. Neither does she recognize him, but she receives alms from him and then learns who he is. She dies after sending him a ring he had once given her.

Testament of Love, The, see USK, T.

Tetrachordon, the third of *Milton's pamphlets on divorce, published 1645, a substantial work of 110 pages. It deals with four sets of passages on marriage and nullities in marriage from Genesis, Deuteronomy, St Matthew, and the First Epistle to the Corinthians. Milton seeks to reconcile the passages and to prove their essential harmony. (A tetrachordon was a four-stringed Greek lyre.) Milton wrote two sonnets in defence of his views on divorce, attacking his detractors; one is specifically related to *Tetra-chordon*, which, he says, 'walk'd the Town a while, | Numbring good intellects; now seldom por'd on'.

Teufelsdröckh, Herr Diogenes, the fictitious mystical German philosopher from the University of Weissnichtwo whose life and opinions are described in Carlyle's *Sartor Resartus.*

THACKERAY, Anne Isabella, see RITCHIE, A. I.

THACKERAY, William Makepeace (1811–63), was born in Calcutta, the son of Richmond Thackeray, a Collector in the East India Company's service. His father died when he was three, and Thackeray was sent home to England in 1817, to be rejoined by his mother, who had married again, in 1820. Thackeray was educated at Charterhouse, where he was not happy, and at Trinity College, Cambridge, where he became a close friend of E. *Fitzgerald. He left Cambridge in June 1830 without taking a degree, having lost some of his inheritance through gambling. He visited Paris, and spent the winter of 1830–1 in Weimar, where he met *Goethe. He entered the Middle Temple, but he had little enthusiasm for the law, and never practised as a barrister. He began his career in journalism by becoming the proprietor of a struggling weekly paper, the *National Standard*, in 1833. It ceased publication a year later, but the experience had given Thackeray an entrée to the London literary world. He also pursued his other enthusiasm, for art, and studied in a London art school and a Paris atelier. By the end of 1833 virtually all his inherited money had been lost, probably in the collapse of the Indian agency-houses. Thackeray lived in Paris from 1834 until 1837, making a meagre living from journalism. For a short while he had a regular income as Paris correspondent of the *Constitutional*, a newspaper bought by his stepfather, and he married Isabella Shawe in 1836, the year in which his first publication in volume form, *Flore et Zephyr*, appeared. The *Constitutional* failed, and the Thackerays returned to London, where their first child Anne (Anne Thackeray *Ritchie) was born in 1837. Thackeray began to contribute regularly to *Fraser's Magazine*, and also wrote for many other periodicals, including the *Morning Chronicle*, the *New Monthly Magazine*, and *The Times.* A second daughter born in 1839 did not live long, and after the birth of their third child, Harriet Marian (later the first wife of Leslie *Stephen), in 1840 Isabella Thackeray suffered a mental breakdown which proved permanent.

Thackeray was forced to place her first in the care of a French doctor, later in a private home in England, and to send his children to live with his mother in Paris.

During the 1840s Thackeray began to make his name as a writer. He first came to the attention of the public with *The Yellowplush Papers*, which appeared in *Fraser's Magazine* in 1837–8, followed by *Catherine* in 1839 and *A Shabby Genteel Story* in 1840. His first full-length volume, *The Paris Sketch Book*, appeared in the same year, and *The Great Hoggarty Diamond* in 1841, both under his most familiar pseudonym, Michael Angelo *Titmarsh. In 1842–3 he wrote, as 'George Savage Fitz-Boodle', *The FitzBoodle Papers* and *Men's Wives*, and FitzBoodle is also the 'editor' of *The Luck of Barry Lyndon* which appeared in 1844. *The Irish Sketch Book* of 1843 has a preface signed, for the first time, with Thackeray's own name.

Thackeray began his association with *Punch* in 1842, and contributed to it caricatures as well as articles and humorous sketches. *The Snobs of England* (later republished as *The Book of Snobs*) appeared there in 1846–7, and *Mr Punch's Prize Novelists*, parodies of the leading writers of the day, in 1847. His children returned to live with him in 1846. In 1847 his first major novel, *Vanity Fair*, began to appear in monthly numbers, with illustrations by the author. *Pendennis* followed in 1848–50. In 1841 Thackeray's increasing love for Jane Brookfield, the wife of an old Cambridge friend, led to a rupture in their friendship, and his next novel *The History of Henry Esmond* shows signs, as Thackeray confessed, of his melancholy at this time. It was published in three volumes in 1852, and was followed by *The Newcomes*, published in numbers in 1853–5. As well as the major novels, Thackeray continued to produce lighter work; he wrote for *Punch* until 1854, and produced a series of 'Christmas Books' which he illustrated himself. In 1851 he gave a series of lectures on *The English Humourists of the Eighteenth Century*, and in 1855–7 he lectured on *The Four Georges.* He twice visited the United States to deliver his lectures, in 1851–3 and 1855–6. *The Virginians*, set partly in America, appeared in numbers in 1857–9. In 1860 he became the first editor of the *Cornhill Magazine*, for which he wrote his *Roundabout Papers. *Lovel the Widower, *The Adventures of Philip*, and the unfinished *Denis Duval* all first appeared in the *Cornhill.* Thackeray died suddenly on Christmas Eve 1863.

There is an authoritative biography of Thackeray by Gordon Ray in two volumes: *Thackeray: The Uses of Adversity* (1955) and *Thackeray: The Age of Wisdom* (1958). Dr Ray has also edited Thackeray's *Letters and Private Papers* (1945–6), and his study of the relation between Thackeray's fiction and his life, *The Buried Life*, was published in 1952. Anne Thackeray Ritchie published *Chapters from some Memoirs* in 1894, and her introductions to the *Biographical Edition* (1899) of her father's works contain many anecdotes about his life.

Thaddeus of Warsaw, a *historical novel by J. *Porter, published 1803.

Thaddeus, a young nobleman of the family of the king of Poland, accompanies his grandfather to join the army of King Stanislaus, which is led by Prince Poniatowski and General Kosciuszko against the invading Russians. The grandfather is killed, the Polish forces defeated, the king's castle burned, and Thaddeus driven into exile. He comes to England, where after much suffering he is discovered to be the son of an English gentleman. The work was very successful, and led to friendship with General Kosciuszko. It is interesting as an early example of the historical novel, written before the form was established by Sir W. *Scott.

Thaisa, in Shakespeare's *Pericles*, the wife of Pericles.

Thalaba the Destroyer, a narrative poem by R. *Southey, published 1801.

Thalaba, a young Muslim, sets himself to destroy the kingdom of the magicians, Domdaniel, under the sea. With the aid of a magic ring he overcomes his enemies, and destroys the sorcerers and their kingdom. He sacrifices his life in doing so, but is reunited in Paradise with his wife. The poem was attacked by the *Edinburgh Review*, and sales were poor.

Thatched House Club, at the lower end of St James's Street, London, was originally a tavern much frequented by politicians and men of fashion. The tavern was demolished in 1814.

Theatre, The, see BURBAGE, J.

Theatre of the Absurd, see ABSURD, THEATRE OF THE.

Thel, *The Book of*, see BLAKE, W.

Thelema, Abbey of, in *Rabelais, I. lii *et seq.*, was built and endowed by Gargantua to reward the bold Friar John (Jean des Entommeures) for his prowess in the war with Picrochole. It was to be in every way the opposite of ordinary monasteries and convents. Only men and women favourably endowed by nature were to be admitted to it; it was not to be walled in; it was to contain a magnificent library filled with the works of the humanists. The only rule was to be 'Fay ce que vouldras' ('Do what you like'); because persons who are free, well born, well educated, and associate with honourable companions, are naturally virtuous and averse from vice. See MEDMENHAM.

THELWALL, John (1764–1834), English radical, who in 1794 was arrested with *Tooke

for his revolutionary views, and subsequently tried and acquitted. He published several volumes of verse, political essays, tracts on elocution, etc. He was an acquaintance of *Wordsworth and *Coleridge, whom he visited in Somerset in 1797, having walked on foot from London, a journey described in part (although anonymously) in the *Monthly Magazine*, 1799.

Thenot, (1) a shepherd in Spenser's *The Shepheardes Calender*; (2) a character in Fletcher's *The Faithfull Shepherdess*.

THEOBALD, Lewis (1688–1744), Shakespearian scholar and author of poems, essays, and dramatic works. His *Shakespeare Restored* (1726) exposed *Pope's incapacity as an editor of Shakespeare; Pope retaliated with his devastating portrait of Theobald as hero of his *Dunciad*. Nevertheless Pope incorporated many of Theobald's corrections in his second edition, and Theobald's 1733–4 edition of Shakespeare surpassed that of his rival. Over 300 emendations made to the texts by Theobald are still accepted by most modern editors and he was a pioneer in the study of Shakespeare's sources. *Double Falshood* (1728), a dramatization of *Cardenio, bears the inscription on the title page: 'Written Originally by W. Shakespeare; and now Revised and Adapted to the Stage By Mr. Theobald.' *Cardenio*, a lost play, had been entered in the Stationers' Register in 1653 as 'by Mr. Fletcher and Shakespeare' and it is likely that *Double Falshood* is Theobald's attempt at establishing a vital relationship between Shakespeare and *Cervantes. The fact that Theobald failed to publish the original or comment on it in any detail in his 1733–4 edition subjected him to further ridicule by, among others, *Fielding in his *A Journey from this World to the Next*.

THEOCRITUS (*c*.308–*c*.240 BC) born in Sicily, was the most important of the Greek bucolic poets and the one who established for the *pastoral the formal characteristics, setting, and tone, which it was to retain for centuries. His most distinctive poems evoke the life and rustic arts of the shepherds on his native island, maintaining a successful balance between idealization and realism. Remembered primarily as a pastoral poet, he was in fact a most versatile writer, and a bridal hymn, a panegyric, and a mime describing two middle-class women at a showy religious ceremony are among his best pieces. Theocritus wrote in the Doric dialect, and the difficulties this produced for his readers led to his comparative neglect during the Renaissance. Editions of his text did not appear in substantial numbers until the end of the 18th cent., and modern writers of pastoral from *Petrarch to *Pope tended rather to take *Virgil for a model. There was however an excellent anonymous translation of six of Theocritus' idylls in 1588, and in 1684 Thomas Creech put all his works into English, a year before *Dryden (whose preface praised Theocritus' 'tenderness and naturalness') contributed some stilted and artificial renderings to *Tonson's *Miscellany*. By the 19th cent. the vogue of the pastoral as a genre was at an end. Admirers of Theocritus were concerned merely to re-create his world of pastoral delights, and like *Tennyson in 'The Lotos-Eaters' (1833) most of them over-emphasized its sensuous aspects.

Theodora, in *Lothair* by B. Disraeli.

THEODORE (602–90), archbishop of Canterbury, a native of Tarsus in Cilicia, studied at Athens, and was well versed in Greek and Latin literature. He was consecrated archbishop of Canterbury by Pope Vitalius in 668. He imposed the Roman order and was the first archbishop to whom (according to *Bede) the whole English church agreed in submitting after the divisions leading up to the Synod of Whitby (663/4). He founded a school of learning at Canterbury, and created many new bishoprics. Theodore was a great organizer, the effects of his work surviving to the present day; and was author, at least in part, of the *Poenitentiale*, of considerable ecclesiastical and historical interest. See ed. A. W. Haddan and W. Stubbs, *Councils and Ecclesiastical Documents relating to Great Britain and Ireland* (1871), iii. 173–204.

Theodoric, see DIETRICH OF BERN.

THEOPHRASTUS (*c*.372–287 BC), Greek philosopher, head of the Peripatetic School after *Aristotle. He is reputed to have written on style, and two of his works on plants survive. But his interest for English literature derives from his *Characters*, brief sketches of human types embodying particular faults: the toady, the over-proud, the churlish. The popularity of Theophrastus in modern times dates from the edition of his *Characters* with Latin translations by I. *Casaubon in 1592. An English rendering by John Healey appeared in 1616, but before then J. *Hall enlarged Theophrastus' scope, adding good qualities to bad in his Characters of *Virtues and Vices* (1608), and Sir T. *Overbury produced, in collaboration with J. *Webster, *Dekker, and *Donne, a volume of *Characters* that, enlarged after his death, ran into a great number of editions (1614). The genre remained popular throughout the century. (See also CHARACTER WRITING.)

Theophrastus Such, see IMPRESSIONS OF THEOPHRASTUS SUCH, THE.

Theory of Moral Sentiments, The, a philosophical work by Adam *Smith, published 1759, and originally delivered in the form of lectures at Glasgow.

The author advances the view that all moral sentiments arise from sympathy, the principle which gives rise to our notions of the merit or demerit of the agent. The basis of morality is pleasure in mutual sympathy, which moderates our natural egocentricity. The desire for such pleasure requires us to see ourselves 'in the light in which others see us', a thought quoted admiringly by *Burns ('To a Louse'):

O wad some Pow'r the giftie gie us
To see oursels as others see us.

Smith's account of the role of the imagination in the operation of sympathy influenced *Sterne, in *A Sentimental Journey*, and other contemporary writers.

Theosophical Society, see BLAVATSKY.

Theosophy, from a Greek word meaning wisdom concerning God or things divine, a term applied in the 17th cent. to a kind of speculation, such as is found in the Jewish *Cabbala, which sought to derive from the knowledge of God contained in secret books, or traditions mystically interpreted, a profounder knowledge and control of nature than could be obtained by the current philosophical methods. It was often applied specifically to the system of *Boehme.

In more recent times, it is more commonly applied to the movement associated with Mme *Blavatsky.

THERESA, or **TERESA, St** (Teresa of Ávila) (1515–82), a Spanish saint and author, who entered the Carmelite sisterhood and became famous for her mystic visions. Her works include *El Camino de la Perfección* and *El Castillo interior*. She was great not only as a mystic, but as an energetic reformer of the Carmelite order and a foundress of new convents. Her *Book of the Foundations* narrates her ceaseless journeys for this purpose and the continually growing labour of organization. She is the subject of *Crashaw's 'Hymne to Sainte Teresa', which relates her childish attempt to court martyrdom by preaching to the Moors (an incident taken from her own spiritual autobiography) and her progress towards a state of mystic ecstasy or spiritual 'marriage'. She is also the subject of Bernini's celebrated erotic masterpiece, the *Ecstasy of Saint Teresa* (1645) in S. Maria della Vittoria, Rome. She is commemorated on 15 Oct.

Thersites, the most querulous and ill-favoured of the Greek host in the Trojan War. He was killed by Achilles for laughing at the latter's grief over the death of Penthesilea, the queen of the Amazons. He figures in Shakespeare's *Troilus and Cressida* as a scabrous cynic.

Theseus, a son of Poseidon, or, according to later legend, of Aegeus, king of Athens. His exploits (in association with Medea, the Minotaur, Ariadne, Phaedra, etc.) form the basis of many literary works, and he appears as the duke of

Athens in Shakespeare's *A Midsummer Night's Dream*, with his newly-won bride *Hippolyta, and also in Fletcher's *The Two Noble Kinsmen*.

Thierry King of France, and his brother Theodoret, The Tragedy of, a play by J. *Fletcher, with the collaboration probably of *Massinger and possibly of *Beaumont, published 1621.

Theodoret, king of Austrasia, reproves his mother, Brunhalt, for her licentiousness, and to revenge herself she attempts to sow enmity between him and his younger brother Thierry, but fails. With the assistance of her paramour Protaldy, and a physician, specialist in poisons, she destroys the happiness of Thierry and his young bride Ordella, then has Theodoret assassinated, then attempts to procure the death of Ordella, and finally poisons Thierry. Vengeance then falls upon Brunhalt and her accomplices. There are incidents in the play which may be allusions to the queen-regent of France, Marie de Médicis, and her favourite Concini (murdered in 1617).

Things As They Are, see CALEB WILLIAMS.

THIONG'O, Ngugi Wa, formerly known as James T. Ngugi (1938–), Kenyan novelist, born at Limuru, Kenya, and educated at the University of Makerere and at Leeds University. *Weep Not, Child* (1964), a novel of childhood that draws largely from his own upbringing and mission-school education, ends by rejecting the romantic individualism of its protagonist. *The River Between* (1965; the first written, though the second to be published, of his novels) also ends with a reversal, in which Waiyaki recognizes on his deathbed the need for political activity if clannish divisions and cultural fragmentation are to be overcome; education can bring individual but not national advancement. *A Grain of Wheat* (1967) blends the realism and compassion of his undergraduate short stories with the messianic political search of his first two novels. When Ngugi took to writing in his own language, Gikuyu, his government arrested him in 1977, and he wrote his first Gikuyu novel largely in prison; it was translated as *Devil on the Cross* (1982), after being published in Nairobi in 1980 in its original version. *Detained: A Prison Writer's Diary* (1981) was, however, written in English. Several extracts from works banned in Kenya have appeared in *Index on Censorship.

Third Man, The, see GREENE, G.

THIRLWALL, Connop (1797–1875), educated at Charterhouse and Trinity College, Cambridge, where he became a fellow in 1818. He was called to the bar in 1823, then began an ecclesiastical career and was ordained priest in 1828. He translated Schleiermacher's *Essay on the Gospel of St Luke* (1825) and his Introduction to this work was remarkable for its acquaintance with German theology. This was followed by a translation with *Hare of *Niebuhr's *History of Rome* (1828–42) and their *Vindication of Niebuhr's History* (1829). Also with Hare he edited the *Philological Museum* (1832–3) which contained Thirlwall's important essay on 'The Irony of Sophocles'. In 1832 he was appointed assistant tutor at Trinity College but was forced to resign his university posts in 1834 owing to his denunciation of compulsory attendance in chapel in the controversy over the admission of Dissenters to the universities. He was immediately offered the living of Kirby Underdale where he wrote his chief work, the *History of Greece* (1835–44, for Lardner's Cyclopaedia, rev. 1847–52). In 1840 Lord Melbourne appointed him bishop of St David's. He supported the admission of Jews to Parliament, the disestablishment of the Irish Church, and allowed Bishop *Colenso to preach in his diocese. These subjects and the *Essays and Reviews* controversy are dealt with in his 'Charges' (published in *Remains, Literary and Theological,* 1877–8). He was buried in Westminster Abbey in the same grave as *Grote.

This Sporting Life, see STOREY, D.

Tholosa, in imprints, Toulouse.

THOMAS, Ambroise (1811–96), French composer, mainly of opera. The only works by Thomas that are remembered today are *Mignon* (a sentimentalized version of *Goethe's *Wilhelm Meister*, written in emulation of *Gounod's *Faust*), and its successor *Hamlet* (1868), a travesty of Shakespeare by the Parisian librettists Barbier and Carré, emulating Gounod's *Roméo et Juliette*. Though composed in a style that is singularly unsuited to its subject, and burdened with an absurdly inflated coloratura role for Ophelia, *Hamlet* does still have its Shakespearian moments (and was sharply criticized for them on its first appearance): the earlier *Le Songe d'une nuit d'été* (1850) does not. This opera has nothing to do with Shakespeare's play, but includes parts for Falstaff, Queen Elizabeth I, and Shakespeare himself, who gets drunk in front of the queen and is conveyed to Richmond Park where the queen, appearing as his muse, recalls him to the poetic destiny that will bring glory to his name and country. Thomas's last work for the stage was also Shakespearian, the 'ballet fantastique' *La Tempête* (1889), which met with little success.

THOMAS, (Walter) Brandon, see CHARLEY'S AUNT.

THOMAS, D(onald) M(ichael) (1935–), poet, novelist, and translator, was born in Cornwall and educated there, in Australia, and at New College, Oxford; he learned Russian while doing his National Service, and his work has been much influenced and enriched by his familiarity with Russian literature. He subsequently worked as a lecturer in English at Hereford College of Education. His translations include two volumes of the poems of *Akhmatova (1976, 1979) and *Pushkin's The Bronze Horseman and other poems (1982); his own volumes of poetry include Two Voices (1968), Logan Stone (1971), Love and other Deaths (1975), The Honeymoon Voyage (1978), Dreaming in Bronze (1981), and Selected Poems (1983). His first novel, The Flute-Player (1979), is a surreal fantasy set in a totalitarian state, in which flute-player Elena represents in part the persecuted creative spirit of the Russian poets (*Mandelstam, *Pasternak, *Tsvetaeva, and Akhmatova) to whom the book is dedicated. Birthstone (1980), set in Cornwall, is an idiosyncratic blend of fantasy, comedy, realism, eroticism, and magic. With The White Hotel 1981) he achieved international success. The novel combines an invented but carefully-documented case history of one of *Freud's patients, Russian-Jewish Lisa Erdman, with her erotic and nightmare fantasies in prose and verse, a realistic account of her cure, her career as opera singer and subsequent marriage, and the steps that lead her and her stepson Kolya to their dream-foreseen death in the 1941 massacre at Babi Yar. Ararat (1983) shows a similar brooding on the theme of holocaust (this time of the Armenians) and on the relationship between sex and death, and a similar narrative complexity: Russian poet Sergei Rozahov, grandson of an Armenian story-teller improvises one night in Gorky to a blind admirer a tale of improvisation within improvisation, with a central section inspired by Pushkin's unfinished Egyptian Nights, in which Cleopatra offers a night of love in exchange for death.

THOMAS, Dylan Marlais (1914–53), poet, was born in Swansea, the son of the English master at Swansea Grammar School, where he himself was educated; he knew no Welsh. He began to write poetry while still at school, and worked in Swansea as a journalist before moving to London in 1934; his first volume of verse, 18 Poems, appeared in the same year. He then embarked on a Grub Street career of journalism, broadcasting, and film-making, spending much time in the flourishing afternoon drinking clubs of the era, and rapidly acquiring a reputation for exuberance and flamboyance, as both poet and personality. In 1937 he married Caitlin Macnamara; they settled for a while at Laugharne in Wales, returning there permanently after many wanderings in 1949. Despite some allegations of deliberate obscurity, Thomas's romantic, affirmative, rhetorical style gradually won a large following; it was both new and influential and much imitated by his contemporaries of the *New Apocalypse movement), and the publication of Deaths and Entrances (1946), which contains some of his best-known work (in-

cluding 'Fern Hill' and 'A Refusal to Mourn the Death by Fire of a Child in London') established him with a wide public: his Collected Poems 1934–1952 (1952) sold extremely well. His work sheets, minutely and continually laboured over, reveal him as an impassioned, even obsessional, craftsman; a great part of his mature work consists of the reworking of the early poetic outbursts of his youth, controlled by a strict discipline.

Thomas also wrote a considerable amount of prose. The Map of Love (1939) is a collection of prose and verse; Portrait of the Artist as a Young Dog (1955) is a collection of largely autobiographical short stories; Adventures in the Skin Trade (1955) is a collection of stories, including the unfinished title story (also edited separately by his friend V. *Watkins, 1955); A Prospect of the Sea (1955) is a collection of stories and essays. He was a popular entertainer on radio and with students; in 1950 he undertook the first of his lecture tours to the United States, and he died there on his fourth visit, as legend grew about his wild living and hard drinking. Shortly before his death he took part in a reading in New York of what was to be his most famous single work, *Under Milk Wood. His Notebooks (ed. R. N. Maud) were published in 1968, and a new edition of The Poems of Dylan Thomas (1971) is enriched by authoritative critical notes and personal comments by his friend and early collaborator, the composer Daniel Jones (1912–). See also a life by C. Fitzgibbon (1965), who also edited his Selected Letters (1960).

THOMAS, (Philip) Edward (1878–1917), poet, was born in Lambeth and educated at St Paul's and Lincoln College, Oxford. He married young and moved to Kent, supporting his family by producing many volumes of prose, much of it topographical and biographical, including a biography of R. *Jefferies (1909), who profoundly influenced him. In 1913 *Hodgson introduced him to *Frost, with whose encouragement he turned to poetry. In 1915 Frost returned to America and Thomas enlisted in the army. He was killed at Arras. Most of his poetry was published posthumously, though a few pieces appeared under the pseudonym 'Edward Eastaway' between 1915 and 1917. Various collections followed, the fullest, Collected Poems, edited by R. George Thomas, 1978. His work shows a loving and accurate observation of the English pastoral scene, combined with a bleak and scrupulous honesty and clarity. Both he and Frost advocated the use of natural diction, and of colloquial speech rhythms in metrical verse. *Leavis singled him out as 'an original poet of rare quality, who has been associated with the Georgians by mischance' and his work is now highly regarded. There are memoirs by his widow Helen Thomas, As It Was (1926) and *World Without End* (1931), and by E. *Farjeon. See also A. Motion, *The Poetry of Edward Thomas* (1980).

THOMAS, R(onald) S(tuart) (1913–), poet and clergyman, born in Cardiff, and educated at St Michael's College, Llandaff, and University College, Bangor; he was ordained as clergyman in the Church of Wales in 1936. From 1942 to 1954 he was rector of Manafon, Montgomeryshire, and subsequently was vicar of Eglwysfach, then of St Hywyn, Aberdaron, with Y Rhiw and Llanfaelrhys; he retired in 1978. His first volume of poems, *The Stones of the Field* (1946), was followed by many others, including *Song at the Year's Turning* (1955), *Tares* (1961), *Pietà* (1966), *Not that he brought flowers* (1968), and *Laboratories of the Spirit* (1975); his *Selected Poems 1946–68* was published in 1973. His poetry is deeply coloured by his experience of working in remote rural communities, where some of the churches had tiny congregations and where life was harsh and the landscape bleak; he has created his own form of bleak Welsh pastoral, streaked with indignation over the history of Wales and the Welsh—'an impotent people, | Sick with inbreeding | Worrying the carcase of an old song' ('Welsh Landscape', 1955). The poet's evocation of his peasant parishioners (who are frequently portrayed as vacant, sullen, miserly, mean-spirited) is unsparing: 'There is no love | For such, only a willed | gentleness' ('They'). Many of the poems unite religious and rural imagery (see the title poem of *Pietà*), but the religious affirmation is always hard won. Thomas has also edited various anthologies, including *The Penguin Book of Religious Verse* (1963), and selections from E. *Thomas (1964), G. *Herbert (1967), and *Wordsworth (1971).

THOMAS À BECKET, see BECKET, ST THOMAS.

THOMAS À KEMPIS (Thomas Hämmerlein or Hämmerken) (1380–1471), born of humble parents at Kempen near Cologne. He became an Augustinian monk and wrote Christian mystical works, among which is probably to be included the famous *De Imitatione Christi*, which has been translated from the Latin into many languages (into English in the middle of the 15th cent.). This work was at one time attributed to Jean Charlier de Gerson, a French theologian. It traces in four books the gradual progress of the soul to Christian perfection, its detachment from the world and its union with God; and obtained wide popularity by its simplicity and sincerity and the universal quality of its religious teaching.

THOMAS BECKET, see BECKET, ST THOMAS.

THOMASON, George (d. 1666), a London bookseller and publisher and friend of *Prynne and *Milton; Milton's sonnet 'When Faith and Love which parted from thee never' was written in 1646 on the death of Thomason's wife Katherine. Thomason's collection of political tracts and broadsides published between the outbreak of the Civil War and the Restoration was presented to the British Museum in 1762; it includes four items donated by Milton personally. The tracts were catalogued in 1908 by George Fortescue.

Thomas the Rhymer, see ERCELDOUNE.

Thomist (pron. 'Tomist'), a follower of the *scholastic philosopher St Thomas *Aquinas.

THOMPSON, E(dward) P(almer) (1924–), historian, educated at Corpus Christi College, Cambridge, and for many years (1948–65) an extramural lecturer at Leeds University. His works include a study of W. *Morris (1955) and *The Making of the English Working Class* (1963), a work in which he sought 'to rescue the poor stockinger, the Luddite cropper, the "obsolete" hand-loom weaver, the "utopian" artisan, and even the deluded follower of Joanna Southcott, from the enormous condescension of posterity'. He has also written and lectured in support of the Campaign for Nuclear Disarmament.

THOMPSON, Flora Jane, *née* Timms (1876–1947), the daughter of a builder's labourer, was born at Juniper Hill, near Brackley, a hamlet on the borders of Oxfordshire and Northamptonshire. She left school at fourteen, and worked as a post-office clerk before marrying John Thompson, who became a postmaster. They lived from 1916 at Liphook in Hampshire, moving in 1928 to Dartmouth. In the early years she supplemented their meagre income with journalism, writing nature essays for *The Catholic Fireside*, the *Daily News*, *The Lady*, and other papers, and in 1921 she published a volume of verse, *Bog-myrtle and peat*. She is remembered for her autobiographical trilogy *Lark Rise to Candleford* (1945), published originally as *Lark Rise* (1939), *Over to Candleford* (1941), and *Candleford Green* (1943), works which evoke through the childhood memories and youth of third-person 'Laura' a vanished world of agricultural customs and rural culture. There is a selection of works by Margaret Lane, *A Country Calendar and other writings* (1979), with a biographical introduction.

THOMPSON, Francis (1859–1907), son of a Roman Catholic doctor, was born in Preston, Lancashire, and educated at Ushaw College. He was intended for the priesthood, but was judged not to have a vocation. He also failed to qualify as a doctor, and in 1885 left home to spend three years of homeless and opium-addicted destitution in London, till he was rescued by Wilfrid and Alice *Meynell, who secured him literary recognition and organized his life in London lodgings and monasteries in Sussex and Wales. He never married, and never for long freed himself from opium which, together with tuberculosis, caused his early death. His best-known poems are 'The Hound of Heaven' and 'The Kingdom of God'; he published three volumes of verse, in 1893, 1895, and 1897, and much literary criticism in Meynell's *Merry England*, *The Academy*, and the *Athenaeum*. His finest work conveys intense religious experience in imagery of great power, but some of his poetry sounds ornate, over-heated, and derivative; he was influenced especially by *Shelley, *De Quincey, and *Crashaw. His poetry has been more popular with the general public (especially with Catholic readers) than with the critics.

The standard life is by Everard Meynell (1913): see also J. C. Reid, *Francis Thompson, Man and Poet* (1959), which gives a full and scholarly account of the poet's opium addiction, and John Walsh, *Strange Harp, Strange Symphony* (1968), which has the fullest account of his personal life.

THOMS, William John (1803–85), antiquary, who became successively clerk and deputy librarian to the House of Lords. He was author of several works including *The Book of the Court* (1838), and edited a number of volumes including a collection of *Early Prose Romances* (1827–8) and *The History of Reynard the Fox* (1844) for the *Percy Society. He was secretary of the *Camden Society from 1838 to 1873. In 1846, in an article in the *Athenaeum headed 'Folk Lore' he introduced this term into the English language. Encouraged by *Dilke he founded *Notes and Queries* in 1849.

THOMSON, James (1700–48), born at Ednam on the Scottish border, the son of a minister, and educated at Edinburgh University, where he already showed promise as a poet. Encouraged by his friend *Mallet, he came to London in 1725, and wrote 'Winter', the first of *The Seasons*, which appeared successively in 1726–30. He made the acquaintance of *Arbuthnot, *Gay, and *Pope, found patrons, and eventually, through the influence of Lord *Lyttleton, received a sinecure. He travelled in France and Italy as tutor to Charles Talbot, son of the solicitor-general, and in 1735–6 published his long patriotic poem *Liberty*, in which *Liberty narrates her progress through the ages in Greece, Rome, and Britain. He produced a series of tragedies, *Sophonisba* (1730), *Agamemnon* (1738), *Edward and Eleanora* (1739); *Tancred and Sigismunda* (published 1745) and *Coriolanus* (1749) were produced after his death. In 1740 was performed the masque of *Alfred* by Thomson and Mallet, containing 'Rule, Britannia', probably written by Thomson. In

1748, a few weeks before his death, appeared *The Castle of Indolence*, which contains a portrait of himself ('A bard here dwelt, more fat than bard beseems') supposed to have been written by Lyttleton, the first line by J. *Armstrong, which affectionately mocks the poet's notorious love of idleness. He was buried in Richmond church; his friend William *Collins, also then living at Richmond, wrote an elegy, 'In yonder Grave a Druid lies' (1749). *The Seasons*, one of the most popular (and frequently reprinted and illustrated) of English poems, was immensely influential, offering both in style and subject a new departure from the urbanity of Pope and developing in a highly distinctive manner the range of *topographical poetry; *Wordsworth recognized Thomson as the first poet since *Milton to offer new images of 'external nature'. Yet most of the Romantics and, later, *Tennyson deplored his artificial diction. *Coleridge's summary was 'Thomson was a great poet, rather than a good one; his style was as meretricious as his thoughts were natural.' He contributed greatly to the vogue for the *picturesque and his landscapes were influenced by those of *Claude, *Poussin, and *Rosa; he was himself greatly admired by J. M. W. *Turner, who drew inspiration from his works. See *Poetical Works*, ed. J. L. Robertson, 1908, 1951.

THOMSON, James (1834–82), born in Scotland, the son of a poor merchant seaman, attended the Royal Caledonian Asylum school when the family moved to London. He was trained as an army schoolmaster, in which capacity he was sent in 1851–2 to Ireland, where he met *Bradlaugh, who became his staunch friend, and also a young girl, Matilda Weller, who died in 1853 but who became an important symbolic figure in Thomson's later poetry. Between 1852 and 1862 he worked at army stations in England and Ireland and wrote much poetry, some of which was accepted by various journals, including Bradlaugh's *National Reformer*. For his early work he used the pseudonym 'B.V.', representing his admiration for *Shelley with 'Bysshe' and for the German poet *Hardenberg ('Novalis') with 'Vanolis'. Signs of growing alcoholism appeared in the late 1850s and in 1862 Thomson was discharged from the army, probably for drunkenness. He came to London, and until 1868 lodged with the Bradlaughs. He took various jobs and wrote poems, essays, and translations for several magazines, publishing among other work 'Vane's Story', 'Sunday up the River', and 'Sunday at Hampstead'. 'Weddah', a long poem relating a tragic Arabian love-story, appeared in 1871, and led to friendship with W. M. *Rossetti. For part of 1872 Thomson was with a gold company in Colorado, and in 1873 in Spain as a war reporter; on his return he completed his best-known poem, 'The City of Dreadful Night', which appeared in the *National Reformer* in 1874, and received some favourable notice, including encouragement from G. *Eliot and later from *Meredith. This long poem, which much influenced the mood of *fin-de-siècle* poetic pessimism, is a powerful evocation of a half-ruined city, a 'Venice of the Black Sea', through which flows the River of the Suicides; the narrator, in vain search of 'dead Faith, dead Love, dead Hope' encounters tormented shades wandering in a Dantesque vision of a living hell, over which presides the sombre and sublime figure of Melancolia (based on *Dürer's engraving of 1514). In 1880 his first volume of verse, *The City of Dreadful Night and Other Poems*, and a second volume later in the same year, were well received. *Essays and Phantasies* appeared in 1881. But his alcoholism was by now out of control; *Satires and Profanities* was published posthumously in 1884. There is a life by H. S. Salt, 1889; see also *Poems and Some Letters of James Thomson* (1963) edited with a biographical introduction by Anne Ridler.

THOMSON, Sir William, first Baron Kelvin (1824–1907), educated at Glasgow, where he later became professor of natural philosophy, and at Peterhouse, Cambridge. His formulation of the second law of thermodynamics, predicting that the world would sooner or later suffer a heat death as a result of entropy, contributed significantly to late 19th-cent. pessimism. The ignorance of this law displayed by most 20th-cent. literary intellectuals was used as an illustration of the gap between the *'Two cultures' by C. P. *Snow.

'Thopas, The Tale of Sir', see CANTERBURY TALES, 17.

THOREAU, Henry David (1817–62), American author, born in Concord, Massachusetts, and educated at Harvard. He became a follower and friend of *Emerson, and was, in his own words, 'a mystic, a transcendentalist, and a natural philosopher to boot'. He supported himself by a variety of occupations, as lead-pencil-maker (his father's trade), as schoolteacher, tutor, and surveyor; a few of his poems were published in *The Dial*, but he made no money from literature, and published only two books in his lifetime. The first, *A Week on the Concord and Merrimack River* (1849), described a journey undertaken in 1839 with his brother; the second, *Walden, or Life in the Woods* (1854), attracted little attention, but has since been recognized as a literary masterpiece and as one of the seminal books of the century. It describes his two-year experiment in self-sufficiency (1845–7) when he built himself a wooden hut on the edge of Walden Pond, near Concord; he describes his domestic economy, his agricultural experiments, his visitors and neighbours, the plants and wild life, and his sense of the Indian past, with a deeply challenging directness that questions the materialism and the prevailing work ethic of the age. Yet he is constantly aware of the surrounding world, to which he eventually returns; he can hear from his hut 'the rattle of railroad cars, now dying away and then reviving like the beat of a partridge'. The work is studded with apparently casual illuminations ('The mass of men lead lives of quiet desperation') and with lines of poetic sensibility ('A field of water betrays the spirit that is in the air') Equally influential in future years was his essay on 'Civil Disobedience' (1849; originally entitled 'Resistance to Civil Government'), in which he argues the right of the individual to refuse to pay taxes when conscience dictates, as he and Bronson Alcott had done in 1843, in protest against the Mexican War and slavery, for which he had in 1845 been briefly imprisoned. Thoreau's reputation as philosopher and political thinker, as well as naturalist, was strengthened by a biography (1890) by the British socialist Henry C. Salt, and by the admiration of E. *Carpenter and H. *Ellis in Britain; his technique of passive resistance, as described in 'Civil Disobedience', was adopted by *Gandhi. He has also been hailed as a pioneer ecologist. His *Journal* (14 vols) was published in 1906, his collected *Writings* (20 vols) also in 1906, and a new scholarly edition of works began publication in 1971.

Thornberry, Job, (1) in *Endymion* by B. Disraeli; (2) in *John Bull* by *Colman the younger, an honest, kindly English tradesman, supposed to typify the national character.

Thornhill, Squire and Sir William, characters in Goldsmith's *The Vicar of Wakefield*.

Thorpe, John and Isabella, characters in J. Austen's *Northanger Abbey*.

Thoughts on the Cause of the Present Discontents, see PRESENT DISCONTENTS.

Thousand and One Nights, The, see ARABIAN NIGHTS ENTERTAINMENTS.

THRALE, Hester Lynch, Mrs, *née* Salusbury (1741–1821), was married against her inclinations in 1763 to Henry Thrale, the son of a wealthy brewer. The following year they met Dr *Johnson, who became very friendly with both. He wrote election addresses for Thrale, and spent much time in their company, at one period becoming almost domesticated at their house in Streatham Place. Mrs Thrale, a lively and intelligent woman, bore several children, of whom only four daughters survived to maturity. Three years after Thrale's death in 1781, and amid much opposition from family and friends (including F. *Burney), she married Gabriel Piozzi, an Italian musician; this drew from Johnson a letter of anguished protest, which he regretted, but their intimacy was at an end, and there is evidence that Mrs Thrale had already begun to find him a demanding guest. She published several works, including *Anecdotes of the late Samuel Johnson* (1786); *Thraliana*, a mixture of diary, anecdotes, poems, and jests, covering the period 1776–1809, was edited in 1942, 2 vols, by K. C. Balderston.

Three Clerks, The, a novel by A. *Trollope, published 1858.

The three clerks are Harry Norman, Alaric Tudor, and Alaric's gauche cousin Charley. In the course of the novel each marries one of the daughters of Mrs Woodward, a widow living near Hampton Court. At first Harry and Alaric vie for the attentions of the eldest daughter, Gertrude, and in this, as in every other matter where the two come into competition, Alaric gets his way. Alaric, clever and dynamic, profits from the new system of promotion by examination in the Civil Service; but with responsibility comes temptation, and Alaric falls. He is arrested for the abuse of a trust fund, is tried, and, despite the best efforts of his counsel, Chaffanbrass, imprisoned. His wife Gertrude, and the dependable Harry Norman, help him through the ordeal and into Australian exile.

Meanwhile Charley has built up a literary reputation, won promotion, and settled down to married life. Charley's experiences reflect Trollope's own in his early days as a clerk at the Post Office.

Three Hours After Marriage (1717), a comedy by *Arbuthnot, *Gay, and *Pope.

Three Men in a Boat, see JEROME, J. K.

Three Musketeers, The (*Les Trois Mousquetaires*), one of the most popular of the romances of *Dumas père, published 1844–5.

With its sequels *Twenty Years After* and *The Vicomte de Bragelonne* it deals with the life of a poor Gascon gentleman, d'Artagnan, who comes to Paris in the reign of Louis XIII to join the king's musketeers, gets involved in duels with three valiant members of that force, Athos, Porthos, and Aramis, and thereafter becomes their friend and shares their fortunes and their many heroic adventures. *The Three Musketeers* is more particularly concerned with the love of Anne of Austria and the duke of Buckingham, and the life of Miladi at whose instigation Felton stabs the duke.

The original d'Artagnan was a Gascon gentleman, born *c*.1620 and killed at the siege of Maastricht, 1673, as captain of the king's musketeers.

Threepenny Opera, The (*Die Dreigroschenoper*), *Brecht's updated version of *The Beggar's Opera*.

Three Weeks after Marriage, a comedy by

*Murphy, performed 1764. It satirizes the parvenu tastes of a rich retired tradesman, Mr Drugget, who has married his eldest daughter to Sir Charles Rackett, and proposes to marry his second daughter to another penniless man of fashion, Lovelace. But his experiences with the recently wedded couple resolve him to abjure all dealings with fashionable society.

Thrie Estaitis, *Satyre of the,* see PLEASANT SATYRE OF THE THRIE ESTAITIS, ANE.

Through the Looking-Glass and *What Alice Found There,* a book for children by Lewis Carroll (see DODGSON), published 1872.

Alice (see ALICE'S ADVENTURES IN WONDERLAND) walks in a dream through the looking-glass into Looking-Glass House, where she finds that the chessmen, particularly the red and white queens, are alive; meets with Tweedledum and Tweedledee and Humpty-Dumpty; and so forth. The story ends with Alice, who has the red queen in her arms, 'shaking her into a kitten' (for she had gone to sleep playing with the black and white kittens). The well known verses about the *Jabberwock and the Walrus and the Carpenter occur in the course of the story.

THUCYDIDES (*c*.460–*c*.395 BC), Athenian historian who left a brilliant account of the disastrous war Athens waged against Sparta. Outstanding talent as a writer enabled him to bestow on his subject the inevitable character of a tragedy. He was prepared to trace effects to rational causes; his handling of eyewitness accounts (all important in a contemporary history) was securely scientific; and although his obvious desire to trace the psychological laws underlying political action has been held to have damaged his standing as a pure historian, some readers have found his political speculations of interest. Like other difficult Greek authors, Thucydides was little read before the 19th cent., although there was a translation by T. Nichols (1550) and one by *Hobbes (1629) which he said was intended to display the follies of democracy. Then in 1829 S. T. Bloomfield produced an annotated translation. In 1830–5 T. *Arnold published a commentary in which he tried to derive lessons for his own time from the text of Thucydides, and *Jowett's elegant translation followed in 1881.

Thunderer, The, a nickname given to *The Times* in the middle of the 19th cent., in allusion to the style of writing of Edward Sterling (1773–1847), a member of its staff, and father of John *Sterling. *Trollope similarly alludes in some of his novels to *The Times* as 'The Jupiter' (from Jupiter Tonans).

THURBER, James Grove (1894–1961), American humorist, many of whose essays, stories, and sketches appeared in the *New Yorker*, including one of his best-known short stories, 'The Secret Life of Walter Mitty' (1932), which describes the colourful escapist fantasies of a docile husband.

Thurio, 'a foolish rivall to Valentine' as *Silvia's suitor in Shakespeare's *The Two Gentlemen of Verona.*

THURLOW, Edward, second Baron Thurlow (1781–1829), public servant and minor writer, who contributed frequently to the *Gentleman's Magazine.* In 1810 he published an edition of Sidney's *A Defence of Poetry* and in 1813 his own *Poems,* followed by further volumes. In 1822 he published *Angelica,* an attempted continuation of Shakespeare's *The Tempest.*

Thwackum, a character in Fielding's *Tom Jones.*

THWAITE, Anthony Simon (1930–   ), poet and critic, born at Chester, and educated at Christ Church, Oxford. His varied literary career has included academic posts in Japan (1955–7), Libya (1965–7), and Kuwait (1974); some years as producer for the BBC, and as literary editor (1962–5) of the *Listener;* he has been co-editor of *Encounter* since 1973. His volumes of poetry include *Home Truths* (1957), *The Stones of Emptiness* (1967), and *A Portion for Foxes* (1977). An early allegiance to *Larkin has expanded into a wide range of theme and subject matter, ranging from the domestic to the exotic: *Victorian Voices* (1980) is a collection of fourteen dramatic monologues which takes as subjects such lesser Victorian figures as P. H. Gosse (father of E. *Gosse), J. C. *Collins, and Alma-Tadema. His collected *Poems 1953–1983* was published in 1984.

'Thyrsis, A Monody, to commemorate the author's friend, Arthur Hugh Clough, who died at Florence, 1861', a poem by M. *Arnold, first published in *Macmillan's Magazine,* 1866. The poem is a pastoral elegy lamenting *Clough as Thyrsis, recalling his 'golden prime' in the days when he and Arnold wandered through the Oxfordshire countryside, their youthful rivalry as poets, and Clough's departure for a more troubled world, where his poetry took on 'a stormy note | Of men contention-tossed'. It invokes the *Scholar-Gipsy as an image of hope and perpetual quest: 'Roam on! | The light we sought is shining still.'

Tibert, the cat in *Reynard the Fox. The name is the same as Tybalt (see the exchange between Mercutio and Tybalt in *Romeo and Juliet,* III. i. 75 ff: 'Tybalt, you rat-catcher . . . Good King of Cats, nothing but one of your nine lives').

TIBULLUS, Albius (*c.*48–19 BC), Roman elegiac poet, noted for his gentleness and his love of country life. Born of well-to-do parents, moving effortlessly in the best society, friendly with all the recognized poets of his day, many of whom seem to have been deeply attached to him, he wrote verses of great elegance, marked by a fastidious melancholy. Of the three books of poems that bear his name, the first two, published in his lifetime were his work. The third, published after his death, is largely, if not entirely, by other hands. Known as the 'Corpus Tibullianum', it is the product of the literary circle that gathered round Tibullus' patron Messala, and included Messala's niece, the poetess Sulpicia. Most English poets of the 16th and 17th cents had read their Tibullus, but his style was too muted and not clearly enough distinguished from the styles of his fellow elegists for his influence to be easily traced. Something of his gentleness survives in *Campion, something of his contentment with country life is met in *Herrick, but *Dryden's likening him to *Sedley appears unjustified.

TICKELL, Thomas (1685–1740), educated at The Queen's College, Oxford, contributed verse to the *Guardian, the *Spectator and other publications, and was author of various poems, including *Oxford* (1707), *On the Prospect of Peace* (1713), and *Kensington Garden* (1722); his sentimental *ballad *Lucy and Colin* (1725) was much admired by *Gray and *Goldsmith. But he is chiefly remembered as a friend and supporter of *Addison; he may have occasioned the quarrel between *Pope and Addison by publishing in 1715 a translation of the first book of the *Iliad* at the same time as Pope, at Addison's instigation, as Pope supposed. He edited Addison's works (1721), publishing in the first volume an elegy on Addison's death.

Tietjens, Christopher, a character in *Parade's End,* by F. M. Ford.

Tigg, Montague, a character in Dickens's *Martin Chuzzlewit.*

Tilburina, the heroine of Mr Puff's tragedy 'The Spanish Armada' in Sheridan's *The Critic.* It is she who observes that even an oyster may be crossed in love.

Till Eulenspiegel, see EULENSPIEGEL.

TILLOTSON, John (1630–94), educated at Clare Hall, Cambridge, a latitudinarian who became archbishop of Canterbury. His sermons, which were very popular, show a marked difference from the earlier *metaphysical style of *Donne and *Andrewes; they were both plainer and shorter, and were extolled as models of lucidity and good sense through most of the 18th cent.

TILLYARD, E(ustace) M(andeville) W(etenhall) (1889–1962), scholar and critic. Among weightier publications such as *Milton* (1930), *Shakespeare's last plays* (1938), *Shakespeare's history plays* (1944), and *Shakespeare's problem plays* (1950), probably his short essay *The Elizabethan

World Picture (1943) has been the most influential. *The Personal Heresy*, his debate with C. S. *Lewis about the value of searching for a writer's true state of mind through his works, was first published in 1939.

Tilney, General, his sons Henry and Frederick, and his daughter Eleanor, characters in J. Austen's *Northanger Abbey*.

Timber, *or Discoveries Made upon Men and Matter*, by *Jonson, printed in the folio of 1640, a collection of notes, extracts, and reflections on miscellaneous subjects, made in the course of the author's wide reading, varying in length from a single sentence to short essays. They are, for the greater part, adapted from Latin writers.

Time and Tide: *An Independent Non-Party Weekly Review*, a periodical founded in 1920 by Viscountess Rhondda (Margaret Haig Thomas, 1883–1958), with the support of R. *West, Cicely Hamilton, and others. Originally a strongly left-wing and feminist publication, under the editorship of Helen Archdale, it went through many shades of political opinion before its disappearance in 1977. Its contributors included D. H. *Lawrence, V. *Woolf, S. *Jameson, G. B. *Shaw, and Robert *Graves; in 1929 it serialized E. M. *Delafield's *Diary of a Provincial Lady*; *Betjeman's poem 'Caprice' describes how he was sacked from his post as its literary adviser in 1953.

Time Machine, The, see WELLS, H. G.

Times, The, was founded under the name of 'The Daily Universal Register' on 1 Jan. 1785 by John Walter, the name being changed to *The Times* in 1788. The founder and his son, also John Walter, introduced great improvements both in the mechanism of newspaper printing and in the collection of intelligence. Among the famous editors of *The Times* have been Thomas Barnes (1817–41) and John Thaddeus Delane (1841–77). The latter was followed by Thomas Chenery, and in 1884 by G. E. Buckle. *The Times* was one of the first papers to employ special foreign correspondents (H. C. *Robinson was sent to North Germany in this capacity in 1807) and war correspondents (W. H. *Russell in the Crimea). Among notable men of letters who contributed to *The Times* in early days were *Borrow (from Spain), Leigh *Hunt, and B. *Disraeli ('Runnymede Letters'). In the 20th cent. *The Times* has been edited by G. Robinson (1912–19); H. W. Steed (1919–22); G. Dawson (1922–41); R. M. Barrington Ward (1941–8); W. F. Casey (1948–52); W. Haley (1952–66); W. Rees-Mogg (1967–81); C. Douglas-Home (1982–). The most dramatic change in the appearance of the paper during this period was the removal, on 3 May 1966, of the column marked 'Personal' from the front page, and its replacement by

news. Of the three weekly supplements published by *The Times* group, *The Times Literary Supplement* was founded in 1901, *The Times Educational Supplement* in 1910, and *The Times Higher Educational Supplement* in 1971. In 1967 both *The Times* and the *Sunday Times* came under the control of Times Newspapers Limited, a group set up by Lord Thomson of Fleet (1894–1976). Because of strike action both papers and the supplements closed down for some months in 1978–9; in 1981 they were all acquired by The News Corporation Limited, of which Rupert Murdoch is Chief Executive.

Times Literary Supplement, The (1902–), a weekly literary periodical of high international standing, first appeared with *The Times* in 1902, then in 1914 became a separate publication. The first editor, Bruce *Richmond (later knighted), supported and encouraged many writers of his time, including V. *Woolf, T. S. *Eliot, J. M. *Murry, E. *Blunden, the historians *Namier and E. H. Carr, and many others, both by commissioning articles from them and by giving publicity to their own works. Reviews continued to be anonymous until 1974 when under the editorship of John Gross they began to be signed. The journal endeavours to cover most of the important works of literature and scholarship, and remains highly influential.

Timias, in Spenser's *Faerie Queene*, Prince *Arthur's squire, may represent *Ralegh. When wounded (III. v), he is healed by *Belphoebe. The incident of Timias and *Amoret, in IV. vii. 35 and 36, may allude to Ralegh's relations with Elizabeth Throckmorton.

Timon, a misanthropical citizen of Athens who lived about the time of the Peloponnesian War, the subject of (1) one of *Lucian's finest Dialogues; (2) of Shakespeare's *Timon of Athens*. Pope's Timon, in *Moral Essays* IV. 98, an example of ostentatious wealth without sense or taste, was said to be drawn from the duke of Chandos, but Pope repudiated this charge, apparently to the duke's satisfaction, and it is more likely to be a composite portrait.

Timon of Athens, a drama by *Shakespeare, possibly in collaboration with *Middleton, written probably about 1607 and apparently left unfinished; it was not printed until the First *Folio of 1623. The material for the play is in *Plutarch's *Life of Antony*, Painter's *Palace of Pleasure*, *Lucian's *Timon, or the Misanthrope*, and possibly an anonymous play *Timon* among the Dyce MSS in the Victoria and Albert Museum.

Timon, a rich and noble Athenian of good and gracious nature, having ruined himself by his prodigal liberality to friends, flatterers, and parasites, turns to the richest of his friends for assistance in his difficulties, and is denied it and deserted by all who had previously frequented him. He surprises these by inviting them once more to a banquet; but when the covers are removed from the dishes (Timon crying, 'Uncover, dogs, and lap', III. vi), they are found to contain warm water, which with imprecations he throws in his guests' faces. Cursing the city, he betakes himself to a cave, where he lives solitary and misanthropical. While digging for roots he finds a hoard of gold, which has now no value for him. His embittered spirit is manifested in his talk with the exiled Alcibiades, the churlish philosopher Apemantus, the thieves and flatterers attracted by the gold, and his faithful steward Flavius. When the senators of Athens, hard pressed by the attack of Alcibiades, come to entreat him to return to the city and help them, he offers them his fig-tree, on which to hang themselves as a refuge from affliction. Soon his tomb is found by the sea-shore, with an epitaph expressing his hatred of mankind.

Tina Sastri, a character in G. Eliot's 'Mr Gilfil's Love-Story' (see SCENES OF CLERICAL LIFE).

TINDAL, Matthew, see DEISM.

TINDAL, William, see TYNDALE.

Tintagel, a castle on the north coast of Cornwall, of which ruins remain. It figures in *Malory as the castle where *Uther Pendragon was wedded to Igraine, and subsequently as the home of King Mark of Cornwall.

'Tintern Abbey, Lines composed a few miles above, on revisiting the banks of the Wye during a tour', a poem by *Wordsworth published in the first edition of the *Lyrical Ballads, 1798.

Wordsworth had visited Tintern in 1793; the second visit recorded in this work was with his sister Dorothy, who is addressed in its closing passage, and the poem was composed as they walked towards Bristol. Written in blank verse, its style is far removed from the deliberately 'low' manner of the ballads, and Wordsworth himself referred to 'the impassioned music of the versification', which resembled the elevation of an ode. It is a central statement of Wordsworth's faith in the restorative and associative power of nature; he describes the development of his own love of nature from the 'coarser pleasures' of boyhood, through the 'aching joys' and 'dizzy raptures' of young manhood, to the more reflective, moral, philosophic pleasures of maturity, informed by 'the still, sad music of humanity'.

Tinto, Dick, a poor artist and sign-painter, who, by a fiction of Scott, supplied notes out of which Peter Pattieson compiled *The Bride of Lammermoor.

TIPPETT, Michael (1905–), English composer, and, with *Britten, one of the most important to reach maturity after the Second World War. He made his first substantial impression with the oratorio *A Child of our Time* (1944). At an early stage in its creation he had interested T. S. *Eliot in writing the libretto, but Eliot finally declined, suggesting Tippett would do better to write the words himself. He followed this advice with conspicuous success, and adopted the same procedure in the four operas of his maturity, *The Midsummer Marriage* (1955), *King Priam* (1962), *The Knot Garden* (1970), and *The Ice Break* (1977).

There are two important song settings from the earlier period, both for solo voice and piano: the cantata *Boyhood's End* (1943), to words by *Hudson, and the passionate song cycle *The Heart's Assurance* (1951), poems by A. *Lewis and *Keyes. His choral works include settings of E. *Sitwell (the motet *The Weeping Babe*, 1944), C. *Fry (the cantata *Crown of the Year*, 1958), *Shelley and *Yeats (*Music for Words Perhaps*, 1960). But perhaps Tippett's most important work to date is *The Vision of St Augustine* (1965), a dense and complex setting of words from St *Augustine and the Bible, arranged by the composer himself as a mystical testament of his own beliefs.

'Tiresias', a dramatic monologue in blank verse by *Tennyson, published 1885, but composed in 1833. The prophet Tiresias, blinded and doomed to 'speak the truth that no man may believe' as a consequence of glimpsing Athene naked, urges Menoeceus, son of Creon, to sacrifice himself for Thebes.

'Tis Pity She's a Whore, a tragedy by J. *Ford, printed 1633.

The play deals with the guilty passion of Giovanni and his sister Annabella for each other. Being with child, Annabella marries one of her suitors, Soranzo, who discovers her condition. She refuses to name her lover, though threatened with death by Soranzo. On the advice of Vasques, his faithful servant, Soranzo feigns forgiveness, Vasques undertaking to discover the truth, which he does. Soranzo invites Annabella's father and the magnificoes of the city, with Giovanni, to a sumptuous feast, intending to execute his vengeance. Although warned of Soranzo's intentions, Giovanni boldly comes. He has a last meeting with Annabella just before the feast and, to forestall Soranzo's vengeance, stabs her himself. He then enters the banqueting-room with her heart on his dagger, defiantly tells what he has done, fights with and kills Soranzo, and is himself killed by Vasques.

'Tis Pity is an obsessive, passionate play, focusing on the sensationalist incest taboo, but treating it seriously and with penetrating honesty (see I. ii). It is portrayed, with rich symbolic imagery, as doomed but intensely beautiful, and this has made it Ford's most famous play, in the study and on the stage.

Titania, in Shakespeare's *A Midsummer Night's Dream*, the queen of the fairies, and wife of Oberon.

The name is given by *Ovid in the *Metamorphoses* to Latona, Pyrrha, Diana, and Circe, as descendants of the Titans.

Tit-Bits, a popular weekly magazine, still in existence, founded in 1881 by G. *Newnes. The original formula included jokes, quizzes, correspondence, short stories and serialized fiction, snippets of news, etc., 'from all the Most Interesting Books, Periodicals and Contributors in the World', and over the years such ingredients as comic strips, cartoons, and sports coverage have been added. In its early years it attracted short stories by Arnold *Bennett, *Conrad, and other aspiring literary figures.

'Tithonus', a dramatic monologue in blank verse by *Tennyson, published in the *Cornhill* in 1860, then in 1864, but composed in 1833 and described by the poet as 'originally a pendent to the "Ulysses" in my former volume'. Tithonus is granted perpetual life but not perpetual youth by Aurora, and in a dramatic monologue he longs for death; like *In Memoriam*, the poem reflects Tennyson's anxiety about the nature of personal immortality.

TITIAN (*c.*1487–1576), the most brilliant of the Venetian painters and among the most celebrated of all great artists; his handling of oil paint is unrivalled. Titian's output was prodigious and he excelled in every kind of painting; in religious and history paintings, scenes from allegory and mythology; landscape and portraiture. He was a close friend of *Aretino, whose letters and poems describe his works. Titian's early pictures were influenced by *Giorgione and Bellini (*The Three Ages of Man*, *c.*1512; on loan to the National Gallery of Scotland, Edinburgh); his mature works are more dramatic and glow with rich colour (*The Assumption of the Virgin*, 1516–18, Venice, Frari); the pagan subjects, such as the *Bacchus and Ariadne* (1523, London, National Gallery), are radiantly sensuous and joyful. The *Death of St Peter Martyr* (completed 1530), once his most famous picture, was destroyed by fire in 1867. From 1532 the Emperor Charles V became a powerful patron; for him and for the Farnese family Titian created increasingly opulent portraits and, for Philip II of Spain, a series of erotic 'poesie'. His late style is characterized by its extraordinarily free and expressive handling and tragic mood (*Pietà*, Venice, Accademia). 'Titian's warmth divine' (*Pope: 'Epistle to Mr Jervas') has always been popular with the literary English; E. Panofsky suggested that Shakespeare's interpretation of Adonis as a reluctant lover (*Venus and Adonis*, st. 136) may have been inspired by Titian's *Adonis taking leave from Venus* (Madrid, Prado). Travellers on the *Grand Tour invariably commented on the

Venus of Urbino (1538, Uffizi, Florence) which then hung in the Tribuna with the *Medici Venus*. The Romantics—*Haydon, *Hazlitt, Sir T. *Lawrence—admired the *Bacchus and Ariadne*; this picture inspired *Keats's description of the 'swift bound of Bacchus' in *Sleep and Poetry*. G. *Eliot and H. *James were enthusiastic admirers and refer to his pictures in their novels.

Titmarsh, (1) Michael Angelo, a pseudonym used by *Thackeray for much of his early journalism. 'Michael Angelo' is a comic reference to his broken nose and to his aspirations to be an artist. (2) Samuel, a character in his *The Great Hoggarty Diamond*.

Tito Melema, a character in G. Eliot's *Romola*.

Titurel, a German *Grail legend of the 13th cent., left incomplete by *Wolfram von Eschenbach. Titurel (the great-grandfather of Parsifal) is entrusted from Heaven with the guardianship of the Grail, and he builds a chapel at Mount Selvagge (Montsalvatsch) where he reposes it and organizes a band of defenders for it.

Titus Andronicus, a tragedy by *Shakespeare. It is probably his earliest tragedy and may date from 1590; in 1594 it was published in a quarto which was reprinted twice before its appearance in the First *Folio of 1623, with an added scene (III. ii). Shakespeare's authorship has been questioned, but it is now generally agreed that he was responsible for the whole play. Various sources for *Titus Andronicus* have been put forward, including the *Hecuba* of *Euripides. *Seneca's *Thyestes* and *Troades* contributed to the plot, as did *Ovid's version of 'the tragic tale of Philomel', in *Metamorphoses* Book XIII, and *Plutarch.

The first half of the play deals with the return of Titus Andronicus to Rome after his sixth victory over the Goths. He brings with him their Queen Tamora and her three sons, the eldest of whom, Alarbus, is sacrificed to avenge his own sons' deaths. Titus is offered the imperial mantle, but gives it instead to the late emperor's son Saturninus, to whose marriage with his daughter, Lavinia, Titus consents. Saturninus' brother claims Lavinia as his own and, while taking her off, Titus kills his son Mutius, who had tried to block his way. Saturninus now changes his mind, renounces Lavinia, and marries Tamora, who engineers a false reconciliation between the emperor and Titus, whom she plans to destroy. She does this with the help of her lover Aaron, the Moor, who gets Tamora's sons Chiron and Demetrius to murder Bassianus, whose body is thrown into a pit, rape Lavinia, and cut off her tongue and hands. Titus' sons Quintus and Martius are then lured by Aaron to fall into the pit, where they are found and accused of Bassianus' murder. Aaron tells Titus that his sons will not be executed if he sacrifices his hand and sends it to the emperor. Titus does this, but gets it back again with the heads of his two sons.

In the second half of the play Titus discovers who raped and mutilated his daughter, and with his brother Marcus, and last remaining son Lucius, vows revenge. Lucius leaves Rome, but returns with an army of Goths, which captures Aaron and his child by Tamora. Tamora and her sons Demetrius and Chiron visit Titus disguised as Revenge, Rapine, and Murder and ask him to have Lucius banquet at his house, where the emperor and the empress and her sons will be brought. Titus recognizes his enemies and with the help of Lavinia slits the throats of Chiron and Demetrius and uses their flesh in a pie, some of which Tamora eats at the banquet before Titus kills her. He also stabs Lavinia, but is killed by Saturninus, who is in turn killed by Lucius. He is elected emperor and sentences Aaron to be buried breast-deep in the ground and starved to death.

Critical judgement of the play has tended to be unfavourable. It was dismissed by its Restoration adapter Edward Ravenscroft, with the sentence: 'It seems rather a heap of Rubbish than a Structure.' More recent critics have related the play to *Revenge Tragedy, and praised it for its anticipation of Shakespeare's great tragedies, in particular *Othello and *King Lear. A drawing ascribed to Henry *Peacham depicting 'Tamora pleadinge for her sonnes going to execution' dated 1595 is at Longleat and is the first known surviving illustration of one of Shakespeare's plays.

(Andronicus in the play is accentuated thus, on the second syllable; in Latin it is Andronicus.)

Titus Groan, see PEAKE, M. L.

TITUS LIVIUS FOROJULIENSES, an Italian in the service of Duke *Humphrey of Gloucester, who wrote, about 1440, a chronicle of the reign of Henry V.

Toad of Toad Hall, a dramatic adaptation by A. A. *Milne of K. *Grahame's The Wind in the Willows.

'To Autumn', a poem by *Keats, written Sept. 1819, published 1820. It was his last major poem, and although usually included in a discussion of the Odes, it was not so labelled by Keats himself.

The poem, in three stanzas, is at once a celebration of the fruitfulness of autumn (lightly personified as a figure in various autumnal landscapes) and an elegy for the passing of summer and the transience of life, and its mood has been generally taken to be one of acquiescence. The association of autumn and early death in the mind of Keats is poignantly revealed in a letter to Reynolds (21 Sept. 1819), written immediately

after the composition of the poem, in which he says, 'I always somehow associate Chatterton with the autumn.'

Toboso, Dulcinea del, see DULCINEA DEL TOBOSO.

Toby, Uncle, Captain Tobias Shandy, in Sterne's *Tristram Shandy.

TOCQUEVILLE, Alexis de (1805–59), French sociologist and historian. Until the coup d'état of 1851 he was active in the judicature and in politics, serving for a time as foreign minister. An official visit to the United States in 1851 produced the first of his two classic works, La démocratie en Amérique (1835 and 1840), a subtle and prescient analysis of the strengths and weaknesses of a democratic society in evolution. The second, L'Ancien Régime (1856), is a profound social and political study of pre-revolutionary France, regarded as the source rather than the contradiction of the revolution that destroyed it. No 19th-cent. historian discerned with greater exactness the tensions hidden in large-scale contemporary communities. He corresponded extensively with J. S. *Mill.

Todgers, Mrs, in Dickens's *Martin Chuzzlewit, mistress of a boarding-house.

TOKLAS, Alice B., see STEIN, G.

TOLAND, John (1670–1722), freethinker, was born on Inishowen in Donegal (Ireland). 'Educated from the cradle in the grossest superstition', as he says in his Apology (1697), he threw off Roman Catholicism at the age of 15. After studying at universities in Scotland and Holland, he settled in Oxford where he completed Christianity not Mysterious (1696), which made him notorious. It also began the Deist controversy (see DEISM) and initiated the one great epoch of Irish philosophy.

In 1702 he travelled to Berlin, where he discussed theology with the queen of Prussia. To her he addressed his Letters of Serena (1704), whose materialistic pantheism—he coined the word 'pantheist' in 1705—he flamboyantly expressed in Pantheisticon (1720). He was a prolific controversialist. In 1698 he wrote a life of *Milton and edited his prose works. Toland's Tetradymus (1720) contains perhaps the first essay on the esoteric/exoteric distinction. *Pope ridiculed him; *Swift called him 'the great Oracle of the Anti-Christians'.

Tolbooth, originally a booth or stall where customs were collected, came to mean a town hall or town prison (formerly consisting of cells under the town hall). The Tolbooth at Edinburgh figures prominently in Scott's *The Heart of Midlothian.

TOLKIEN, J(ohn) R(onald) R(euel) (1892–1973), Merton professor of English language

nd literature at Oxford, 1945–59. He pub-
ished a number of philological and critical
tudies, such as 'Beowulf: the Monsters and the
Critics' (in *Proceedings of the British Academy*,
1936), and became internationally known for
two books based on a mythology of his own:
The Hobbit (1937) and its sequel *The Lord of the
Rings* (3 vols, 1954–5). *The Silmarillion* (1977),
which has an earlier place in this sequence of
tories, was published posthumously. A Life by
Humphrey Carpenter was published in 1977.

TOLLER, Ernst (1893–1939), German revo-
utionary poet and dramatist, associated with the
hort-lived Bavarian Communist government
of 1918. He was imprisoned for five years after
he war, during which period he wrote *Expressionist plays such as *Die Maschinenstürmer*
1922; *The Machine Wreckers*). After the rise
of Hitler he moved to New York, where he
committed suicide, an act commemorated in an
elegy by *Auden ('In Memory of Ernst Toller')
who had met Toller in 1936 in Portugal and
translated the lyrics for his satirical musical play
Nie wieder Friede! (*No More Peace!*, 1937).

TOLSTOY, Count Lev Nikolaevich (1828–
910), Russian prose writer. He was born at
Yasnaya Polyana, in central Russia, which he
inherited in 1847. His first published work was
Childhood (1852), the first part of a remarkably
perceptive trilogy on his early years completed
by *Boyhood* (1854) and *Youth* (1857). His Cau-
asian tale *The Raid* appeared in 1853. He served
n the army and took part in the Crimean war:
is *Sevastopol Sketches* (1855–6), are marked by
n unromantic view of war indebted to *Stendhal. He then published *Family Happiness* (1859)
nd *The Cossacks* (1863), but the next decade
was mainly engaged in the creation of *War and
Peace* (1863–9), an epic novel of the Napoleonic
nvasion and the lives of three aristocratic fam-
lies. This was followed by *Anna Karenina*
1873–7), the story of a married woman's pas-
ion for a young officer and her tragic fate. From
bout 1880 Tolstoy's constant concern with
moral questions developed into a spiritual crisis
which led to radical changes in his life and to
he writing of such works as *A Confession*
1879–82), *What Men Live By* (1882), *What I
Believe* (1883), and *What is Art?* (1898). The
major fictional works of this late period, bearing
he imprint of changes in his thinking, are *The
Death of Ivan Illich* (1886), *The Kreutzer Sonata*
1889), *Master and Man* (1895), *Resurrection*
1899), and *Hadji Murad* (1904). Tolstoy's
moral positions, involving non-resistance to evil,
he renunciation of property, the abolition of
governments and churches, but a belief in God
nd love of men, led to the banning of many of
is works by the censorship, and to his excommunication by the Orthodox Church in
901. But they also brought him a unique

moral authority and influence, and Yasnaya
Polyana became a place of pilgrimage. He died
at Astapovo railway station after having fled his
home. *The Cossacks* appeared in English translation in 1878, and there were a large number
of translations in the 1880s. His collected works
were translated 1899–1902 and have been re-
translated many times since. Among those who
played a part in establishing his English reputation were M. *Arnold, G. B. *Shaw, *Galsworthy, E. M. *Forster, and D. H. *Lawrence.

Tom and Jerry, the two chief characters in
*Egan's *Life in London*; hence used in various
allusive senses, e.g. of riotous behaviour.

Tom Brown's Schooldays, see HUGHES, T.

Tom Folio, see RAWLINSON, T.

Tom Jones, *The History of*, a novel by H.
*Fielding, published 1749.
   Although very long, the novel is highly organized, and was thought by *Coleridge to have
one of the three great plots of all literature. The
kindly, prosperous Mr Allworthy, a widower,
lives in Somerset with his ill-humoured unmarried sister Bridget. Late one evening Allworthy finds a baby boy lying on his bed. He is
charmed with the mysterious baby, names it
Tom, and adopts it, adding the surname Jones
on the assumption that the mother is Jenny Jones,
a maidservant to the wife of the schoolmaster
Partridge, who is eventually accused of being
the father and dismissed his post. Both Jenny
and Partridge vanish from the neighbourhood.
Meanwhile Bridget marries the obnoxious Captain Blifil and they have a son, Master Blifil,
who is brought up with Tom. They are taught
by the brutish chaplain Thwackum, and the
philosopher Square, and have as family neighbours the bluff fox-hunting Squire Western, his
sister, and his daughter Sophia, as well as
Allworthy's gamekeeper, Black George
Seagrim, and his wife and daughters.
   The story moves on to the point when Tom
is 19, and begins to find that his childhood affection for the beautiful and sweet-natured Sophia
(whose portrait Fielding founded upon his own
wife) has grown into adult love. However,
Sophia is destined by her father for Master Blifil,
and Tom allows himself to be distracted by the
charms of Molly Seagrim. By clever mis-
representation the scheming young Blifil converts Allworthy's affection for Tom into anger,
and with the help of Thwackum and Square
he succeeds in having the harum-scarum Tom
expelled from the house. Filled with despair that
he has alienated his beloved foster-father and is
leaving all he loves, Tom sets off for Bristol
intending to go to sea. Meanwhile Sophia, disgusted by Blifil's courtship, runs away with her
maid Honour, hoping to find her kinswoman
Lady Bellaston in London. Amid numerous ad-

ventures on the road, during which he falls in with redcoats and is deflected from his plan of going to sea, Tom encounters Partridge, once supposed to be his father, who is now travelling the country as a barber-surgeon. Unknown to Tom, he and Sophia both find themselves in an inn at Upton, but because of Partridge's malicious stupidity Sophia believes that Tom (now in bed with Mrs Waters, of whom we are to hear more) no longer loves her, and flees on towards London. Tom follows, and in London is ensnared by the rich and amorous Lady Bellaston. She and her friend Lord Fellamar, who is in pursuit of Sophia, contrive together to keep Tom away from his love, but the abrupt eruption of Squire Western saves Sophia from Fellamar's snare. Partridge now reveals that Mrs Waters is none other than Jenny Jones, supposed to be Tom's mother, and for a brief period Tom believes he has committed incest. But Jenny reveals that Tom's mother was really Bridget Allworthy (later Blifil), who has confessed all to her brother on her death-bed, and that his father was a young man long since dead. Lady Bellaston and Lord Fellamar attempt to have Tom pressganged, but instead he is arrested and imprisoned after a fight in which it first appears he has killed his assailant. Sophia cannot forgive his entanglement with Lady Bellaston and Tom's fortunes are at their lowest ebb. Blifil arranges that the gang shall give evidence against Tom, but, with the help of a long letter from Square to Allworthy, Blifil's envious machinations, dating from their earliest boyhood, are finally revealed, and Tom is reinstated in his repentant uncle's affection. He meets Sophia again at last, learns that she loves him, and receives the hearty blessing of her father. In the generosity of his heart, Tom forgives all who have wronged him, even including the detestable Blifil.

In Chapter One, 'Bill of Fare', Fielding informs the reader that 'The provision . . . we have here made is no other than Human Nature' and in his Dedication to *Lyttleton declares, 'that to recommend goodness and innocence hath been my sincere endeavour in this history'. The book was enthusiastically received by the general public of the day, although Fielding's robust distinctions between right and wrong (which, for instance, permit his high-spirited hero various sexual escapades before his final blissful marriage) were a severe irritant to many, including Dr *Johnson. The book is generally regarded as Fielding's greatest, and as one of the first and most influential of English novels.

TOMKINS, Thomas (1572–1656), Welsh composer and organist, who studied under *Byrd. He is chiefly remembered as a composer of *madrigals, but also wrote many sacred works, published posthumously as *Musica Deo Sacra* (1668).

TOMKIS, Thomas (?1580–?1634), fellow of Trinity College, Cambridge, and author of two university comedies, *Lingua, or the Combat of the Tongue and the five Senses for Superiority* (1607) and *Albumazar*. The latter was acted before James I at Cambridge. Albumazar (historically an Arabian astronomer, 805–85) is a rascally wizard who transforms the rustic Trincalo into the person of his master, with absurd consequences. It was revived (1668) with a prologue by *Dryden, wrongly charging *Jonson with adopting it as a model for *The Alchemist*. It was again revived by *Garrick.

TOMLINSON, (Alfred) Charles (1927–), poet and artist, born in Stoke-on-Trent and educated locally and at Queens' College, Cambridge, where he was taught by D. *Davie. His aspirations as a painter are reflected in the visual qualities of his verse, which also shows the influence of W. *Stevens, W. C. *Williams, and M. *Moore. His first volume, *Relations and Contraries* (1951), was followed by several others including *Seeing is Believing* (US 1958; London 1960), *The Way of the World* (1969), *Written on Water* (1972), *The Way In and Other Poems* (1974), and *The Flood* (1981).

TOMLINSON, H(enry) M(ajor) (1873–1958), novelist and journalist, born in Poplar, the son of a foreman at the West India Dock; his early love of ships and the sea is reflected in his life and works, e.g. *The Sea and the Jungle* (1912, an account of a voyage to Brazil and up the Amazon), *London River* (1921, essays and reflections), and his first novel, *Gallions Reach* (1927). *All Our Yesterdays* (1930) is an anti-war novel about the First World War. As a journalist he contributed to the radical *Morning Leader* and the *English Review*, and was literary editor of the *Nation* from 1917 to 1923.

Tom o' Bedlam, a wandering beggar. After the dissolution of the religious houses, where the poor used to be relieved, there was for long no settled provision for them. In consequence they wandered over the country, many assuming disguises calculated to obtain them charity. Among other disguises some affected madness, and were called Bedlam Beggars (so in *Gammer Gurtons Nedle* 'Diccon the Bedlam'). Edgar, in *King Lear*, II. iii, adopts this disguise:

> Of Bedlam beggars, who, with roaring voices,
> Strike in their numb'd and mortified bare arms
> Pins, wooden pricks, nails, sprigs of rosemary.

In *Dekker's *Bellman of London* (1616) 'Tom of Bedlam's band of mad caps' are enumerated among the species of beggars. Some of these Bedlam beggars sang mad songs, examples of which are given in Percy's *Reliques*. They were also called 'Abraham-men', from the name, it is said (Brewer), of one of the wards in Bedlam.

Tom Sawyer, *The Adventures of*, a novel by Mark *Twain, published 1876.

Tom, a lively and adventurous lad, lives with his priggish brother Sid and his good-hearted Aunt Polly in the quiet town of St Petersburg, Missouri. His companion is the irrepressible Huckleberry Finn, and together they embark on many exploits, during one of which they happen to observe Injun Joe stab the town doctor to death and attempt to incriminate the drunken Muff Potter; Tom is later able to absolve Potter at his trial. Tom and his sweetheart Becky Thatcher wander away from a school picnic and are lost for three days in a cave, where Tom spies Injun Joe; after the children are rescued Injun Joe is found dead and his treasure is divided between Tom and Huck. Huck's subsequent escapades become the subject of the classic sequel *The Adventures of* *Huckleberry Finn.*

Tom's Coffee House, named after Thomas West, its landlord, was situated in Russell Street, Covent Garden, and frequented by the best company after the play; its patrons included Dr *Johnson, *Goldsmith, *Garrick, *Murphy, and *Steevens. It became a subscription club *c.*1768.

There were several other coffee houses by the name of 'Tom's', including one in Birchin Lane, Cornhill.

Tom Thumb, a Tragedy, a farce by H. *Fielding, performed and published 1730, and published in a different version 1731 under the title of *The Tragedy of Tragedies, or, The Life and Death of Tom Thumb the Great.*

The most successful of Fielding's many plays, this is an exuberant farce in the mock-heroic manner, ridiculing the 'Bombastic Greatness' of the fashionable grandiose tragedies of authors such as N. *Lee and J. *Thomson, and similar in form to Buckingham's *The Rehearsal.* It was published with a heavy apparatus of absurd scholarly notes, and a frontispiece by *Hogarth. *Swift declared that he had laughed only twice in his life, once at a Merry-Andrew and once at a performance of *Tom Thumb.*

Tono-Bungay, see WELLS, H. G.

TONSON, Jacob (1656–1737), publisher and bookseller, the son of a barber-surgeon; he established himself in 1678 with his brother Richard (d. 1689) and eventually took his nephew Jacob into the business, in whose favour he resigned in 1720; the firm was continued by a great-nephew of the same name. He published the foremost poets and playwrights of the age; his long association with *Dryden began in 1679, with the publication of his version of *Troilus and Cressida,* and his other writers included A. *Behn, *Otway, *Cowley, *Rowe, *Addison, and *Pope; he also acquired the profitable copyright of *Paradise Lost.* He was well known for his *Miscellanies,* in six parts, of which the earliest were edited and largely written by Dryden; they appeared between 1684 and

1709, and contained translations from *Horace, *Ovid, *Lucretius, *Virgil, etc., as well as original work by *Pope, A. *Philips, *Swift, and others. A conspicuous figure in literary society, he was secretary of the *Kit-Cat Club (which occasionally met at his home in Barnes) and the butt of satire from Dryden (who mocked his 'two left legs, and Judas-coloured hair') and Pope, who took up the theme of his ungainly legs in the *Dunciad.*

Tony Lumpkin, a character in Goldsmith's *She Stoops to Conquer.*

Toodle, Polly and Robin ('Rob the Grinder'), her son, characters in Dickens's *Dombey and Son.* Polly was Paul Dombey's foster-mother.

TOOKE, John Horne (1736–1812), radical politician, and the son of a poulterer named Horne; he added the name of his friend William Tooke of Purley to his own in 1782. He vigorously supported *Wilkes in connection with the Middlesex election, but later quarrelled with him. He was more than once in conflict with the authorities, and was (with *Holcroft) tried for high treason and acquitted in 1794. His varied acquaintance included *Boswell, *Bentham, *Godwin, *Paine, and *Coleridge. His principal work, "Ἔπεα πτερόεντα, or the Diversions of Purley (1786–1805, two volumes of a planned three) established his reputation as a philologist and was extremely popular; it was much admired by James *Mill and the Utilitarians, but its philosophical (rather than historical or philological) approach to language and grammar, and its wildly speculative etymologies delayed for decades, it has been alleged, the introduction of the new and sounder philology from the Continent. See H. Aarsleff, *The Study of Language in England, 1780–1860* (1967).

Toots, Mr, a character in Dickens's *Dombey and Son.*

TOPLADY, Augustus Montague (1740–78), from 1768 vicar of Broad Hembury, is remembered for his hymns, especially 'Rock of Ages', published in the *Gospel Magazine* in 1775. At first influenced by *Wesley, he later became his bitter opponent, and an extreme Calvinist.

Topographical Poetry, described by Dr *Johnson as 'local poetry, of which the fundamental object is some particular landscape . . . with the addition of . . . historical retrospection or incidental meditation'. *Cooper's Hill* (1642) by *Denham is an early example of a genre that flourished principally in the 18th cent.: see DYER, GARTH, JAGO, THOMSON, J., for example. Many topographical poems are also 'prospect poems', i.e. written from a high point, surveying a large view, and many were written in praise of particular parks, estates, and gardens, evidently in the hope of patronage. The genre had a renewed vogue in the late 20th cent., when the emphasis has been less on the country estate, more on the vanishing rural scene; distinguished examples include *Remains of Elmet* (1979) and the less precisely located *River* (1983), both by Ted *Hughes.

Topsy, the lively little slave girl in H. B. *Stowe's *Uncle Tom's Cabin*, who asserted that she had neither father nor mother, and being asked who made her, replied, 'I 'spect I grow'd'. One of Mrs Stowe's most original creations, she forms a contrast to the virtuous ethereal *Little Eva, and is carried off to Vermont after Eva's death by Eva's aunt, the orderly Miss Ophelia.

TORQUEMADA, Tomás de (1420–98), a Spanish Dominican monk, appointed in 1483 the first inquisitor-general by Ferdinand and Isabella. He was famous for the untiring energy with which the work of the Inquisition in Spain was carried on under his direction. Hence his name became a synonym for a cruel persecutor. But Torquemada's code of instructions for the application of torture was relatively moderate by the standards of his time, and the number of burnings during his term of office has been greatly exaggerated; it is now usually given at about 2,000.

Torquil of the Oak, a character in Scott's *The Fair Maid of Perth*.

Torre, Sir, in *Malory, the illegitimate son of a cowherd's wife and King *Pellinore; his knighting before Gawain by Arthur causes further rancour amongst the sons of King Lot whose father had been slain by Torre's father Pellinore, developing the long feud between their two houses.

Torrismond, hero of Dryden's *The Spanish Fryar*.

To the Lighthouse, a novel by V. *Woolf, published 1927, which draws powerfully on the author's recollections of family holidays at St Ives, Cornwall, although the setting is ostensibly the Hebrides; her parents, as she acknowledged, provided the inspiration for the maternal, managing, gracious, much-admired Mrs Ramsay, and the self-centred, self-pitying, poetry-reciting, absurd, and tragic figure of the philosopher, Mr Ramsay, who become the focus of one of her most profound explorations of the conflict between the male and female principles.

The novel is in three sections, of which the first and longest, 'The Window', describes a summer day, with the Ramsays on holiday with their eight children and assorted guests, who include the plump and lethargic elderly poet Augustus Carmichael; the painter Lily Briscoe (who represents in part the struggle and cost of

female creativity); and the graceless lower-middle-class academic Charles Tansley. Family tension centres on the desire of the youngest child, James, to visit the lighthouse, and his father's apparent desire to thwart him: the frictions of the day are momentarily resolved around the dinner table, and a triumphant *boeuf en daube*, as Mrs Ramsay reflects that 'something . . . is immune from change, and shines out . . . in the face of the flowing, the fleeting, the spectral, like a ruby.' The second section, 'Time Passes', records with laconic brevity the death of Mrs Ramsay and of her son Andrew, killed in the war, and dwells with a desolate lyricism on the abandoning of the family home, and its gradual post-war reawakening; it ends with the arrival of Lily Briscoe and Mr Carmichael. The last section, 'The Lighthouse', describes the exhausting but finally successful efforts of Lily, through her painting, to recapture the revelation of shape-in-chaos which she owes to the vanished Mrs Ramsay, and the parallel efforts of Mr Ramsay, Camilla, and James to reach the lighthouse, which they also accomplish, despite the undercurrents of rivalry, loss, and rebellion that torment them. The novel represents a heroic exploration and re-creation of the bereavements and (real or imagined) tyrannies of the past; it also displays Woolf's technique of narrating through *stream of consciousness and imagery at its most assured, rich, and suggestive.

TOTTEL, Richard (*c.*1530–94), a publisher who carried on business at 'The Hand and Star' within Temple Bar from 1553 to 1594, is chiefly known as the compiler (with *Grimald) of *Songs and Sonnets*, known as *Tottel's Miscellany* (1557), comprising the chief works of *Wyatt and *Surrey. He also published, besides law-books, Sir T. *More's *Dialoge of Comfort* (1553) and *Surrey's *Aeneid* (1557).

Slender, in Shakespeare's *The Merry Wives of Windsor*, had 'rather than forty shillings' he had Tottel's 'book of Songs and Sonnets' with him when courting Anne Page; and the gravedigger in *Hamlet* mumbles Lord *Vaux's song from the same collection.

Touchett, Mr, Mrs, and Ralph, characters in H. James's *The Portrait of a Lady*.

Touchstone, the jester to the exiled Duke Frederick's court in Shakespeare's *As You Like It*.

Touchwood, (1) Lord, a character in Congreve's *The Double Dealer*; (2) Mr Scrogie, a character in Scott's *St Ronan's Well*.

TOURNEUR, Cyril (?1575–1626), dramatist. Practically nothing is known of his life. He appears to have worked for a time in the Netherlands, and died at Kinsale in Ireland after accompanying Sir Edward Cecil to Cadiz in

1625 on an unsuccessful raid of Spanish treasure ships. His small known output includes an allegorical poem, *The Transformed Metamorphosis* (1600), a lost play, *The Nobleman* (1612), *The Atheist's Tragedy* (1611), an elegy on the death of Prince Henry (1613), and several minor and disputed works. *The Revenger's Tragedy*, printed anonymously in 1607, was first ascribed to him in 1656 by Edward Archer in a play list, and was generally accepted as his until the end of the 19th cent., when *Middleton was proposed as the author. Since then there has been prolonged debate over attribution, with Middleton gradually emerging as the most likely candidate, a view confirmed by recent statistical analysis, though some critics and editors still favour Tourneur. G. Parfitt, after a brief summary of the arguments in his edition *The Plays of Cyril Tourneur* (1978), concludes that 'unless new evidence emerges . . . the play has to be regarded as anonymous.' The *Complete Works* were edited by Allardyce Nicoll, 1930. (See also REVENGE TRAGEDY.)

TOUSSAINT L'OUVERTURE, François (1743–1803), to whom *Wordsworth addressed a sonnet, was a Negro revolutionary who made himself master of the French colony of San Domingo (Haiti) when the decree of 1791 freeing the Negroes was revoked. For some years he administered the island with great success, but he was overcome by a military expedition sent by Napoleon and transported to France, where he died. He remained a hero to radical writers: H. *Martineau published a Life in 1840.

Towneley Plays, see under MYSTERY PLAYS.

TOWNLEY, Revd James (1714–78), educated at *Merchant Taylors' school and St John's College, Oxford, was headmaster of Merchant Taylors' from 1760. He was a friend of *Garrick, and author of the successful farce *High Life below Stairs* (1759).

Townly, Lord, in Vanbrugh and Cibber's *The Provok'd Husband*, the title character.

Town Mouse and Country Mouse, a fable told by *Horace (Sat. II. vi) and by *La Fontaine (though the latter substitutes rats for mice). The city mouse, contemptuous of the country mouse's cave and humble fare, invites it to a sumptuous supper in its palace. But the feast is disturbed by an alarm, and the mice scurry away. The country mouse concludes that it prefers its safe wood and cave and its homely fare.

M. *Prior was part-author of *The Hind and the Panther Transvers'd to the Story of the Country Mouse and the City Mouse*.

TOWNSHEND, Aurelian (?1583–?1643), travelled in France and Italy, then appears in 1632 as a writer of court *masques. He seems to have collaborated with I. *Jones in *Albion's Triumph* and to have contributed verses for the queen's masque of *Tempe Restored*. He enjoyed favour at the court of Charles I, as his lyric 'On his hearing Her Majesty sing' records. His poems were not collected, but scattered through various miscellanies, until E. K. *Chambers's edition, *Poems and Masks* (1912).

TOWNSHEND, Charles, second Viscount Townshend (1674–1738), a distinguished statesman of the reign of George I. He carried on at Rainham agricultural experiments which earned him his nickname of 'Turnip' Townshend. *Pope (*Imitations of Horace*, Ep. II. ii. 273) refers to Townshend's turnips, and in a footnote states that 'that kind of rural improvement which arises from turnips' was 'the favourite subject of Townshend's conversation'.

Tow-wouse, Mr and Mrs, characters in Fielding's *Joseph Andrews*.

Toxophilus, see ASCHAM, R.

TOYNBEE, Arnold Joseph (1889–1975), historian, educated at Winchester and Balliol College, Oxford. He was professor of Byzantine and modern Greek language, literature, and history at King's College, London, 1919–24, the director of studies at the Royal Institute of International Affairs, and research professor of international history until he retired in 1955. His great work *A Study of History*, published in 10 vols between 1934 and 1954, is a survey of the chief civilizations of the world, and an enquiry into cycles of creativity and decay. His view that the fragmentation and waning of Western civilization could already be detected, and that hope lay in a new universal religion which would recapture 'spiritual initiative', aroused much controversy. His other works include *Civilization on Trial* (1948) and *The World and the West* (1953). *Comparing Notes: a Dialogue across a generation* (1963) was written with his son, novelist, critic, and journalist Philip Theodore Toynbee (1916–81).

T.P.'s Weekly, see O'CONNOR, T. P.

Tractarian Movement, Tracts for the Times, see OXFORD MOVEMENT.

Traddles, a character in Dickens's *David Copperfield*.

TRADESCANT, John (d. ?1637), traveller, naturalist, and gardener, probably author of *A voiag of ambasad* (1618) describing a voyage under Sir Dudley Digges to Archangel, containing the earliest known account of Russian plants. From the expedition (1620) against the Algerine pirates he brought back the 'Algier apricot'. He established a physic garden at Lambeth. His son John Tradescant (1608–63) was likewise a traveller and gardener. He published *Museum Tradescantianum* in 1656, and gave his collection to *Ashmole, who presented it to the University of Oxford. Both Tradescants held the appointment of gardener to Charles I. See Mea Allen, *The Tradescants* (1964).

Tragedy, a word of uncertain derivation, applied, broadly, to dramatic (or, by extension, other) works in which events move to a fatal or disastrous conclusion. Aristotle's *Poetics* was the first attempt to define the characteristics of tragedy and its effect upon the spectator, and it profoundly influenced the neo-classic concept of tragedy in France and England. Shakespeare and other English dramatists of the Elizabethan period evolved new tragic conventions (see REVENGE TRAGEDY), partly derived from *Seneca, and the genre continued to flourish in the Jacobean period (see WEBSTER, J.; MIDDLETON, T.; BEAUMONT, F.; FLETCHER, J.). A period of predominantly dull and frigid *neo-classicism followed, and tragedy as a form, with odd exceptions, did not seriously revive until the 20th cent., when the works of *Ibsen, *Strindberg, *O'Neill, A. *Miller, T. *Williams, and S. *Beckett brought it a new seriousness, relevance, and urgency.

Tragedy of Tragedies, see TOM THUMB.

Tragic Comedians, The, a novel by G. *Meredith, published 1880.

The story is based on the account given by Hélène von Dönniges of her love-affair with Ferdinand Lassalle (1825–64), the German socialist. Hélène appears in the novel as 'Clotilde', a high-born young woman who falls in love with the writer and rebel Alvin (Lassalle), and is prepared to defy her family to marry him. But he insists she go back to them to obtain their free consent to the match. So Clotilde returns, and is bullied and deceived into accepting a more conventional suitor, Marko. Alvin, infuriated, writes an insulting letter to Clotilde's father. Marko then fights Alvin, kills him, and marries Clotilde.

TRAHERNE, Thomas (1637–74), son of a shoemaker in Hereford. It seems possible that both his parents died while he and his brother Philip were infants, and the boys were brought up by a wealthy innkeeper, Philip Traherne, twice mayor of Hereford. They evidently had a good education, but no record exists of their attending Hereford Cathedral School. Thomas went up to Brasenose College, Oxford, as a commoner in March 1653 and took his BA in October 1656. In 1657 the parliamentary commissioners appointed him rector of Credenhill, Herefordshire, but he seems not to have resided there until 1661. He was ordained in 1660, and the following year took his Oxford MA. At Credenhill he joined the religious circle

centring on Susanna Hopton at Kington, for whom he was to write the *Centuries*. During this period he evidently travelled to Oxford to work on *Roman Forgeries* in the Bodleian. Probably in recognition of this work he gained his BD in 1669, and also his appointment the same year as chaplain to Sir Orlando Bridgeman, lord keeper of the Great Seal, which necessitated his moving to London. He was buried at Teddington.

Traherne led a 'single and devout life', according to A. *Wood. He left five houses in Hereford in trust for the poor people of All Saints parish. He told *Aubrey that he had visions, seeing, on one occasion, the phantom of an apprentice who was asleep in the same house, and on another a basket of fruit sailing in the air over his bed. Traherne's *Centuries* and many of his poems were discovered in a notebook (now in the Bodleian) which was picked up for a few pence on a London bookstall in the winter of 1896–7 by W. T. Brooke. Bertram Dobell identified Traherne as the author, and edited the *Poetical Works* (1903) and the *Centuries of Meditation* (1908). More poems, prepared for publication by Traherne's brother Philip 'Poems of Felicity', were discovered in a British Museum manuscript and published by H. I. Bell in 1910. A further manuscript of *Select Meditations* has since come to light, and is in the collection of the late J. M. Osborne. In his lifetime Traherne published *Roman Forgeries* (1673), which exposes the falsifying of ecclesiastical documents by the church of Rome, concentrating in the mid-9th-cent. collection known as the 'False Decretals' which had, in fact, already been decisively discredited by several 16th-cent. scholars. His *Christian Ethicks* (1675) was prepared for the press before he died. But his major achievement comprises the *Centuries*, the poems, and the Thanksgivings, written in exuberant, unconventional verse, and at times foreshadowing *Whitman, which appeared in 1699. He expresses a rapturous joy in creation unmatched by any other 17th-cent. writer, and his memories, in the *Centuries*, of his own early intuitions are the first convincing depiction of childhood experience in English literature. He is also among the first English writers to respond imaginatively to new ideas about infinite space, and at times virtually equates infinite space with God. The boundless potential of man's mind and spirit is his recurrent theme, as is the need for adult man to regain the wonder and simplicity of the child. In both, his thought is influenced by *Neoplatonism, especially by the Hermetic books.

Centuries, Poems and Thanksgivings, ed. H. M. Margoliouth (2 vols, 1958); *Christian Ethicks*, ed. C. L. Marks and G. R. Guffey (1968); G. Wade, *Thomas Traherne* (1944); K. W. Salter, *Thomas Traherne, Mystic and Poet* (1964).

TRAILL, Henry Duff (1842–1900), journalist and first editor of *Literature* (1897–1900). His published works include two volumes of satiric verse, *Recaptured Rhymes* (1882) and *Saturday Songs* (1890), *The New Lucian: dialogues of the dead* (1884), lives of William III (1888) and Sir John *Franklin (1896), biographical and critical works, and some excellent political satires in verse. He was general editor of *Social England* (1893–7).

Traitor, The, a tragedy by J. *Shirley, acted 1631, printed 1635.

This play was highly successful both before and after the Civil War; *Pepys saw it several times and praised it highly. It is based on the assassination of the Florentine Duke Alessandro de' Medici by his kinsman Lorenzo. Unlike the hero of the best-known play on this subject, de *Musset's *Lorenzaccio*, Shirley's Lorenzo is a scheming villain who talks of republicanism and liberty only to gain the support of others. The plot interweaves a number of devices already used by earlier dramatists. Lorenzo encourages the duke's lust for Amidea, sister of Sciarrha, while simultaneously urging Sciarrha to take revenge on the duke. The duke, though unmoved by a moral masque presented him by Sciarrha, is nearly converted by Amidea's courageous virtue. Later, however, Lorenzo persuades him to blackmail her into yielding to save her brother's life. Sciarrha, to test Amidea's virtue, threatens to kill her unless she accepts this proposal; she, to save him from the guilt of murder, pretends to accept, whereupon he stabs her for dishonouring him. Her final act of virtue is to pretend that her death was suicide. When the duke comes to her bed, he finds only a corpse. Lorenzo then seizes the opportunity to kill him, and he and Sciarrha kill each other in the ensuing scuffle.

Trajectum ad Rhenum, also Ultrajectum, in imprints, Utrecht.

Tranio, *Lucentio's servant in Shakespeare's *The Taming of the Shrew*.

Transatlantic Review, a literary periodical edited from Paris by F. M. *Ford, from Jan. 1924 to Jan. 1925, in which he published *Joyce, E. E. *Cummings, and others. B. *Bunting worked for a while as sub-editor. The title was revived in 1959 by J. McCrindle: the new *Transatlantic Review* (of which B. S. *Johnson was for a time poetry editor) publishes fiction, poetry, interviews, etc., and contributors have included W. *Trevor, I. *Murdoch, J. G. *Ballard, A. *Burgess, D. M. *Thomas, and J. *Arden.

Transcendental Club, a group of American intellectuals who met informally for philosophical discussion at *Emerson's house and elsewhere during some years from 1836, the embodiment of a movement of thought, philo-

sophical, religious, social, and economic, produced in New England between 1830 and 1850 by the spirit of revolutionary Europe, German philosophy, and *Wordsworth, *Coleridge, and *Carlyle. The philosophical views of this Transcendentalism may be gathered from Emerson's short treatise *Nature* (1836). Its literary organ was *The Dial*.

Its social and economic aspects took form in the Brook Farm Institute (1841–7) of George Ripley, a self-supporting group of men and women, who shared in manual labour and intellectual pursuits.

transition: *an international quarterly for creative experiment*, a periodical founded in 1927 in Paris by Eugène and Maria Jolas, and edited for some ten years by Jolas and Elliot Paul. It proclaimed 'the revolution of the word', and published new and experimental work by *Joyce, G. *Stein, Dylan *Thomas, *Durrell, *Beckett, etc.; its distinguished art coverage included work by Duchamp, Miró, and Man Ray.

Transome, Harold, a character in G. Eliot's *Felix Holt*.

Trapbois, and his daughter Martha, characters in Scott's *The Fortunes of Nigel*.

Traveller, The, or a Prospect of Society, a poem by *Goldsmith, published 1764, and the first production under his own name. It is dedicated and addressed to his brother, a country clergyman.

The poet as traveller, from a vantage point in the Alps, surveys and compares the social, political, and economic conditions of the various countries spread before his eyes and his imagination, and endeavours to illustrate that (in the words of his preface) 'there may be equal happiness in states, that are differently governed from our own.' The vividly drawn landscapes of Italy, the Loire valley, and the 'slow canals' of Holland are clearly based on Goldsmith's own continental tour in 1755. The poem ends with a lament for rural decay in the face of growing commerce that foreshadows the theme of *The Deserted Village*. Dr *Johnson, who greatly admired the poem, contributed nine lines to it, ll. 420, 429–34, 437–8.

Travels in Arabia Deserta, see DOUGHTY, C. M.

Travels in France, a record of travel in that country during the years 1787–90, by A. *Young, published 1792. The first journey takes him through the south-west (Berri, Poitou, Languedoc), the second through Brittany and Anjou, the third through Alsace-Lorraine, the Jura, Burgundy, and Provence. Visiting France shortly before and during the revolution, Young draws attention to the defective social and economic conditions of the *ancien régime*. The work was translated into various languages and has always been highly valued in France. It contains the famous phrase, 'The magic of property turns sand into gold.' It was edited by M. Betham-Edwards (1892) and C. Maxwell (1929).

Travels through France and Italy, a work by *Smollett, published 1766.

The book covers the period of Smollett's main sojourn abroad, between mid-1763 and mid-1765. It is sharply observant, prejudiced and idiosyncratic, often highly entertaining, and almost universally derogatory about all levels of French and Italian society. Smollett's attitude induced *Sterne to describe him in *A Sentimental Journey* as 'the learned Smelfungus'. In search of better health, Smollett travelled with his wife and a party of three others, starting at Boulogne, proceeding to Paris, Lyons, Montpellier, and eventually to Nice. In that distance he asserts he met only one pleasant innkeeper. But although manners, arts, and religion are generally deprecated (sometimes with humour but more often with disgust), Smollett's enjoyment of food, drink, and the company of other travelling or expatriate Britons is conveyed with relish. His party was based in Nice, where the scenery, walking, bathing, riding, and the bounty of the countryside delighted him, and where his health intermittently improved. During this time he travelled for two months in Italy, visiting Pisa, Florence, and Rome, in all of which the art and architecture greatly impressed him. After many wearisome episodes on road and sea, they returned to Nice, and then with relief to England. The *Travels* were reviewed kindly, sold well, quickly reprinted, and translated into German; but not into French or Italian.

Travels with a Donkey, see STEVENSON, R. L.

Traven, B. (?1882–1969), novelist and short story writer, whose first stories appeared in German in Berlin in 1925 as *Die Baumwollpflücker* (*The Cottonpickers*) followed by his highly successful novel *The Death Ship* (1925). It recounts the wanderings of an American seaman after the First World War, bereft of passport and nationality. Traven, whose identity remained for many years shrouded in mystery, went to Mexico in the 1920s, whence appeared some 12 novels and collections of stories, including *The Treasure of Sierra Madre* (1934) filmed by John Huston in 1947. *The Man who was B. Traven* (1980) by W. Wyatt established that he was Albert Otto Max Feige, later known as Ret Marut, born in Swiebodzin, a Polish town then in Germany, of working-class origins, a radical pamphleteer and survivor of the German revolution of 1919. He eschewed publicity, appearing in later years to visitors under the guise of his own 'translator', Hal Croves.

TRAVERS, Ben (1886–1980), novelist and playwright, chiefly known for his 'Aldwych farces' of the 1920s, which include *A Cuckoo in the Nest* and *Rookery Nook* (both produced in 1926) and *Thark* (1927). A new comedy, *The Bed Before Yesterday*, was successfully produced in 1975, his 90th year.

Travesties, a comedy by T. *Stoppard, performed 1974, published 1975.

The play is largely set, with various time shifts, in Zurich during the First World War, where *Lenin, *Joyce, and Tristan Tzara happened to be residing; they appear as characters, as does the marginally historical figure of Henry Carr (1894–1962), through whose memories much of the action is portrayed. Stoppard takes a minor incident from *Ellman's life of Joyce, describing a semi-amateur performance in Zurich in 1918 of *The Importance of Being Earnest*, in which both Joyce and Carr were involved, and builds from it an extravaganza which plays on *Wilde's original (in terms of stylistic parody and of the plot of assumed and mistaken identities) to produce a theatrical, informative, and witty commentary on the birth of *Dada, the writing of *Ulysses, and the genesis of the doctrine of *socialist realism, and on the nature of the artist as revolutionary or conformist. Stoppard uses a dazzling range of literary and theatrical effects, from Wildean epigram to a scene written entirely in limericks, from a suggestion of strip-tease to a lecture on Marxist theory.

Treasure Island, a romance by R. L. *Stevenson, published in book form 1883. It had previously appeared in *Young Folks*, July 1881–June 1882, under the title 'The Sea Cook or Treasure Island', and the concept grew from a map that Stevenson and his stepson Lloyd Osbourne devised together on holiday in Scotland. The flamboyant one-legged anti-hero Long John Silver was suggested by Stevenson's friend *Henley.

The narrator is Jim Hawkins, whose mother keeps the Admiral Benbow inn somewhere on the coast in the west of England in the 18th cent. An old buccaneer takes up his quarters at the inn. He has in his chest information, in the shape of a manuscript map, as to the whereabouts of Capt. Flint's treasure. Of this his former confederates are determined to obtain possession, and a body of them, led by the sinister blind pirate Pew, makes a descent on the inn. But Jim Hawkins outwits them, secures the map, and delivers it to Squire Trelawney. The Squire and his friend Dr Livesey set off for Treasure Island in the schooner *Hispaniola* taking Jim with them. Some of the crew are the squire's faithful dependants, but the majority are old buccaneers recruited by Long John Silver. Their design to seize the ship and kill the squire's party is discovered by Jim, and after a series of thrilling fights and adventures is completely thwarted; and the squire, with the help of the marooned pirate Ben Gunn, secures the treasure.

Treatise of Human Nature, A, a philosophical work by *Hume, written in France 1734–7, published in three volumes in London 1739–40. The work was recast as three separate and simpler works published between 1748 and 1757: *An Enquiry* (originally *Philosophical Essays*) *concerning Human Understanding, An Enquiry concerning the Principles of Morals*, and *A Dissertation on the Passions*. Scholars differ as to whether these recastings involve any significant changes in Hume's philosophical position.

Hume's work has been traditionally depicted as the culmination of one of two philosophical traditions. His contemporary critic T. *Reid established the common view that Hume was heir to a tradition set by *Locke and *Berkeley, notwithstanding Berkeley's rejection of the central theses of Locke's philosophy. Equally influential in the 20th cent. has been the view of Kemp Smith (1941) that Hume sought to extend and redirect the philosophy of *Hutcheson. Hume indicates his familiarity with their writings, and with the writings of other (otherwise incompatible) British predecessors like B. de *Mandeville and J. *Butler, but cites them mostly for their pioneer work on the science of human nature. Current biographical research suggests that the main formative influences on Hume's thought were his reading of *Cicero (on *Stoicism and *scepticism), *Descartes, Nicolas Malebranch (1638–1715), and *Bayle.

Hume saw the disputes of philosophers as centred upon the conflicting roles of reason and instinct or sentiment, and tried to define these roles for metaphysics in Book I of the *Treatise* and for the passions and morals in Books II–III. He agreed with Locke, against Descartes, that there are no innate ideas, and that all the data of reason stem from experience, and derived from Descartes the thesis that whatever may be conceived distinctly may be distinct. He argued that reason has insufficient data in experience to form adequate ideas of the external world, distance, bodily identity, causality, the self, and other minds, and that any beliefs we form about these must fall short of knowledge. Reason can attain certainty only in abstract mathematics—from which, in the *Treatise*, he even excluded geometry, owing to the empirical basis of our idea of space. We also employ reason when we use the experience of acquired associations to identify causes and effects, past events and future contingencies; this does not warrant the name 'certainty' and the process cannot be independently justified. It ceases to be rational altogether, and is then due to the imaginative faculty, when, as in religion, it involves inferences beyond the bounds of familiar experience.

Compensating for the inadequate data of experience and the infirmity of unaided reason are certain 'natural instincts' by which the imagination forges its own links between distinct ideas according to certain principles of association and habituation. Through these acquired but unavoidable associations, which Hume assumed to be explainable in terms of the brain science of the day, we project on to the world a sense of the continuity and externality of bodies, or of the necessity which we feel when some particular sequence of cause and effect has become habitual with us. In calling these mental constructions 'fictions' Hume meant only that they are not directly given in experience. Taken on their own, they can indeed lead us into false judgements, e.g. in misidentifying our sense impressions as the external object. But 'philosophical decisions are nothing but the reflections of common life, methodized and corrected' by the balanced interplay of reason, sense, and natural instinct, a standpoint Hume characterized in the first *Enquiry* as 'mitigated scepticism'. Hume was, however, dissatisfied with his account of the self as 'a bundle or collection of different perceptions' appropriately associated, because he thought this failed to explain the sense each person has of the unity of consciousness.

In regard to morals, Hume again argued for an accommodation between reason and experience on the one hand (in determining facts and consequences) and sentiment on the other (in so far as moral distinctions are felt, not judged). Hume shared Hutcheson's belief in a moral sense, but not the theological framework or the psychological simplicity of Hutcheson's theory. In so far as there is a common structure of human nature, which approves whatever quality or character gives happiness to the parties affected without giving unhappiness to others, and enables us by the mechanisms of association or sympathy to share the sentiments of others, there is general consensus as to the motives and acts that are accounted morally virtuous and vicious. Hume's distinction between natural and artificial virtues was widely misconstrued in his lifetime: artificial virtues, e.g. justice, involve the determination and application of appropriate conventions in circumstances of need, where merely spontaneous virtues like benevolence are inadequate.

TREECE, Henry, see NEW APOCALYPSE.

Trelawney, see HAWKER, S.

TRELAWNY, Edward John (1792–1881), a friend of *Shelley who was present at Leghorn when Shelley was drowned, was author of the notable *Adventures of a Younger Son* (1831) and of *Records of Shelley, Byron, and the Author* (1858).

Tremendous Adventures of Major Gaha-

gan, The, a story by *Thackeray, published in the *New Monthly Magazine*, 1838–9. The Major is an Irish *Munchausen whose adventures as an officer in the Indian Army burlesque military memoirs.

TRENCH, Frederic Herbert (1865–1923), born in Co. Cork and educated at Keble College, Oxford, travelled widely in southern Europe and the near east, and was from 1909 to 1911 artistic director of the Haymarket Theatre. His own plays had little success. Of his various poetic works, the most interesting is 'Apollo and the seaman' (1907), a haunting narrative poem with echoes of the *Ancient Mariner*, in which Apollo and the seaman debate the sinking of the great ship, Lost Immortality, and the future of the soul.

TRENCH, Richard Chenevix (1807–86), educated at Trinity College, Cambridge, and afterwards dean of Westminster and archbishop of Dublin. He was the author of works dealing with history and literature, poetry, divinity, and philology. As a philologist, and notably by his *On the Study of Words* (1851) and *English Past and Present* (1855), he popularized the scientific study of language. The scheme of the *Oxford English Dictionary* originated in a resolution passed at his suggestion in 1858 by the *Philological Society. He also published several volumes of poetry, and his anthology *Sacred Latin Poetry, chiefly lyrical* (1849) drew attention to the masterpieces of Latin hymnody.

Trent, the detective in E. C. *Bentley's *Trent's Last Case* (1913).

Trent, Fred, a character in Dickens's *The Old Curiosity Shop*. His sister is 'Little Nell'.

TRESSELL, Robert, the pen-name of Robert Noonan (?1870–1911), a house-painter of Irish extraction, is remembered for his posthumously published novel *The Ragged Trousered Philanthropists*, which first appeared in 1914, edited from a manuscript left in the care of his daughter. It draws on his experiences while working for a builder in Hastings, where he settled in 1902 after various wanderings. He died of tuberculosis in Liverpool. An abridged edition of his novel appeared in 1918, but on the discovery of the original handwritten manuscript in 1946 it became clear that the author's intentions had been widely altered, and it reappeared, ed. by F. C. Ball, in 1955.

The action takes place during one year in the lives of a group of working men in the town of Mugsborough, and the novel is a bitter but spirited attack on the greed, dishonesty, and gullibility of employers and workers alike, and on the social conditions that gave rise to these vices. Debates on socialism, competition, employment, and capitalism are skilfully interwoven with a realistic and knowledgeable portrayal of skilled and unskilled labour in the decorating and undertaking business, and with the human stories of the families of the workers. Principal characters include Frank Owen, socialist craftsman and atheist; Barrington, socialist son of a wealthy father, intent on first-hand experience of labour; the inadequate but well-intentioned Eastons with their unfortunate baby whom they feed on fried bacon; and Slyme, a canting and unprincipled teetotaller. Noonan's coining of names for local worthies—Sweater, Didlum, Grinder, Botchit, etc.—indicates his attitude towards the widespread corruption and hypocrisy that he exposes, and the book has become a classic text of the Labour movement. The ironically named 'philanthropists' of the title are the workers who for pitiful wages 'toil and sweat at their noble and unselfish task of making money' for their employers, while making no effort to understand or better their lot.

Tressilian, Edmund, a character in Scott's *Kenilworth*.

TREVELYAN, G(eorge) M(acaulay) (1876–1962), historian, son of Sir G. O. *Trevelyan, was educated at Harrow and Trinity College, Cambridge, where he became a member of the *Apostles. He was appointed Regius professor of modern history at Cambridge in 1927, and master of Trinity in 1940. He was author of three remarkable works on Garibaldi, *Garibaldi's Defence of the Roman Republic* (1907), *Garibaldi and the Thousand* (1909), and *Garibaldi and the Making of Italy* (1911), which owe some of their vividness of narrative and description to the fact that Trevelyan himself, a tireless walker, retraced on foot every mile of the scenes of campaign. His many other works include lives of John Bright (1913), Lord Grey (1920), and Grey of Falloden (1937); a three-volume work on *England under Queen Anne* (1930–4); and his popular and nostalgic *English Social History* (1944). In *Layman's Love of Letters* (1954), delivered in 1953 as the Clark lectures, he speaks warmly of R. *Browning, Sir W. *Scott, *Meredith, *Housman, the poetry of mountaineering, etc., and mildly deplores the professional view of literature as 'a set of intellectual conundrums, to be solved by certain rules. It is joy, joy in our inmost heart.'

TREVELYAN, Sir George Otto (1838–1928), nephew of *Macaulay, educated at Harrow and Trinity College, Cambridge, entered Parliament as a Liberal in 1865 and held several important offices. Some of his early humorous writings were collected in *The Ladies in Parliament* (1869), others mainly about India included *The Dawk Bungalow* (1863, a comedy), *The Competition Wallah* (1864), and *Cawnpore* (1865). The first of his great works, *The Life and Letters of Lord Macaulay*, appeared in 1876, and was followed by *The Early History of George the Third and Charles Fox* (1912–14).

TREVISA, John of (?1340–1402), born in Cornwall, was a fellow of Exeter (1362–9) and The Queen's (1369–79) Colleges, Oxford. He was expelled from Oxford for 'unworthiness' and became vicar of Berkeley. In 1387 he translated the *Polychronicon* of *Higden, adding a short continuation and an introduction; part of this has become famous as an account of the state of the English language in its time (see K. Sisam, *Fourteenth Century Verse and Prose*, 1921, no. XIII). The *Polychronicon* translation is written in a vigorous and colloquial style, though he also has claims to a more elaborate manner; his principles of translation are declared in two short essays prefixed to the *Polychronicon*. He also translated Egidio Colonna's *De Regimine Principum*, one of the sources of *Hoccleve's *Regiment of Princes*, and in 1398 the *De Proprietatibus Rerum* of *Bartholomaeus Anglicus. In the edition of his *Dialogus* by A. J. Perry (EETS os 167, 1925—also containing works by other writers) there is a good account of his life.

TREVOR, William (William Trevor Cox) (1928–), Anglo-Irish novelist and short story writer, born in Co. Cork and educated at Trinity College, Dublin; he has spent much of his life in Ireland, which provides the setting for many of his works. His novels include *The Old Boys* (1964), *Mrs Eckdorf in O'Neill's Hotel* (1969), *Elizabeth Alone* (1973), and *Fools of Fortune* (1983); collections of short stories include *The Day We Got Drunk on Cake* (1969), *Angels at the Ritz* (1975), and *Beyond the Pale* (1981). A Penguin collection of his stories appeared in 1983. The title story of *The Ballroom of Romance* (1972), which like many of Trevor's works, has been successfully televised, is a characteristically low-key, poignant evocation of a rural Ireland where men drink and women wait, whereas that of *Lovers of their Time* (1978) deals with middle-aged romance in a hotel bathroom at Paddington, and the novel *The Children of Dynmouth* (1976) describes an English seaside resort terrorized by a delinquent teenager. Trevor writes with insight of the elderly, the lonely, and the unsuccessful, and his more recent works (e.g. 'Attracta', 1978, the story of an ageing schoolmistress) show an increasing preoccupation with the effects of terrorism in Northern Ireland.

Triamond, in Spenser's *Faerie Queene* (iv. iii. iv), the Knight of Friendship. After an inconclusive fight with *Cambello in the contest to decide to which of her suitors Canacee is to be awarded, *Triamond and Cambello swear eternal friendship. In the tournament arranged by *Satyrane, Triamond, though wounded, returns to rescue Cambello. He marries *Canacee, Cambello's sister.

Tribrach, see METRE.

Tribulation Wholesome, the fanatical Puritan elder in Jonson's *The Alchemist*.

Tridentum, in imprints, Trent.

Trifaldi, the countess of, in *Don Quixote, the 'Afflicted Duenna', whose adventure Don Quixote undertakes (Pt II, ch. xxxvi–xli).

Trilby, a novel written and illustrated by George *du Maurier, published 1894.
  The setting of the story reflects the writer's years as an art student in Paris, and the three student friends of Trilby O'Ferrall (the Laird, Little Billee, and Taffy) are portraits of friends. The charming Trilby, an artist's model, slowly falls under the mesmeric spell of Svengali, a German–Polish musician, who trains her voice and establishes her as a famous singer. His power over her is such that when he dies her voice collapses, she loses her eminence, languishes, and finally dies herself. The novel was immensely popular for many years, and in 1895 was dramatized with Beerbohm Tree as Svengali. Trilby's hat, a soft felt with an indented crown, is the origin of the 'trilby'.

TRILLING, Lionel (1905–75), American critic, whose many works include *The Liberal Imagination* (1950), *The Opposing Self* (1955), and *Sincerity and Authenticity* (1972). His works are written from the standpoint of liberal humanism (increasingly conceived as being under threat) and manifest a marked admiration for *Freud, 'one of the few great Plutarchian characters of our time', without in any way committing themselves to doctrinaire *Freudian criticism. Trilling's wide range of subjects includes *Keats, H. *James, J. *Austen, *Wordsworth, F. S. *Fitzgerald, S. *Anderson, etc. His works appeared in a 12-volume edition, 1978–80. He also wrote one novel, *The Middle of the Journey* (1947).

Trilogy, in Greek antiquity, a series of three tragedies (originally connected in subject) performed at Athens at the festival of Dionysus. Hence any series of three related dramatic or other literary works.

Trim, Corporal, the devoted servant of Toby in Sterne's *Tristram Shandy*.

Trimalchio, see PETRONIUS.

Trimeter, see METRE.

Trimmer, originally applied to one who trims between opposing parties in politics; hence, one who inclines as his interest dictates. But *Halifax in his *Character of a Trimmer* (1682) accepted the nickname in the sense of 'one who keeps even the ship of state'.

Trimmer, *Character of a*, see HALIFAX.

TRIMMER, Mrs Sarah, *née* Kirby (1741–1810), known as 'Good Mrs Trimmer', was the author of the popular children's book *The History of the Robins*, originally entitled *Fabulous Histories* (1786), and of many exemplary tales, educational works, and textbooks for charity schools. In her periodical *The Guardian of Education* (1802–6) she attacked traditional children's literature, and in particular fairy-stories, describing *Cinderella as a tale inculcating 'envy, jealousy, a dislike for mothers-in-law and half-sisters, vanity, a love of dress'.

Trinculo, companion to *Stephano in Shakespeare's *The Tempest.*

Trinity College, Cambridge, the largest college of Cambridge University, founded by Henry VIII in 1546, in place of several older foundations. The library was built by Sir C. *Wren. Among the distinguished men of letters educated there may be mentioned F. *Bacon, *Herbert, *Cowley, *Dryden, *Newton, *Porson, *Byron, *Macaulay, *Thackeray, and *Tennyson. *Bentley and *Whewell were masters of Trinity.

Triolet, a poem of eight lines, with two rhymes, in which the first line is repeated as the fourth and seventh, and the second as the eighth.

Triplet, three successive lines of verse rhyming together, occasionally introduced among heroic couplets, e.g. by *Dryden.

Triptolemus Yellowley, and his sister Barbara, characters in Scott's *The Pirate.*

Trip to Scarborough, A, a musical play by R. B. *Sheridan, produced 1777. The play is based on Vanbrugh's *The Relapse*, but it was considerably rewritten, coarse language was carefully expunged, and music and songs were added. In Sheridan's version Berinthia is no longer altogether an unscrupulous coquette; she tempts Loveless in order to punish Towneley (the Worthy of the earlier play) for deserting her in favour of Amanda, Loveless's wife.

Eventually it is his sense of shame and honour, and not the threat of exposure, that restores Loveless to Amanda.

Trismegistus, SEE HERMES TRISMEGISTUS.

TRISTAN L'HERMITE, Louis, historically, an adviser of Louis XI of France, who appears in Scott's *Quentin Durward.*

'Tristram and Iseult', a poem in three parts by M. *Arnold, published 1852. This is the first modern version of the story that was made familiar by *Wagner and *Tennyson; it deals with the death of Tristram (Tristan, in earlier editions of the same work), who lies dying, watched over by Iseult of Brittany, and dreaming in his fever of his love for Iseult of Ireland, the wife of Marc. She arrives, and after a brief passionate dialogue he dies. In Part III Iseult of Brittany tells her children the story of Merlin, entranced by Vivian.

Tristram and Isoud (*Tristan and Isolde*); the long story of Tristram de Lyones is the fifth of Vinaver's eight *Works* of *Malory. The love of Tristram and Isoud is much older than the corresponding Arthurian story of the love of Launcelot and Guinevere, and it was incorporated into the Arthurian legends only at a late stage. Denis de Rougemont (*Passion and Society,* 1940) declares Tristan to be the prototype of the courtly lover, a view corroborated by repeated references to him in courtly love lyrics and romances (see COURTLY LOVE). It is thought likely that there was a *Tristan* romance (since lost) by *Chrétien de Troyes in the 1170s, and it is possible, judging from repeated references in the poetry of the troubadours, that there was an early Provençal *Tristan*. There are three versions surviving from the 12th cent.: Béroul's fragment of the 4,485 lines (*c.* ?1190) in the Norman dialect; Thomas's French fragment (*c.*1170); and the version in literary Rhenish German by Eilhart (*c.*1170). The most authoritative medieval version is by Gottfried von Strassburg (*c.*?1200; nothing is known of his life) in German, of which the last sixth is missing and which is based to some extent on Thomas. The best English translation (by A. T. Hatto, 1960) supplies the last sixth from Thomas's version. The first English version is *Sir Tristrem,* a northern 3,344-line romance in 11-line stanzas, dating from *c.*1300 (unpersuasively attributed to Thomas of *Ercelldoune). In Malory, Tristram is the child of Meliodas, king of *Lyonesse, and Elizabeth, the sister of King Mark of Cornwall, who dies soon after his sorrowful birth. The sad child is brought up at the court of King Mark whose attitude to the boy varies in different versions from great affection to jealousy. Tristram defeats and kills Sir Marhalt (Marhaus), the brother of Isoud, queen of Ireland. Tristram is sent to Ireland to be cured of his wounds by Isoud the queen, and he falls in love with her daughter Isoud; when the queen discovers that this knight (whom she too holds in special esteem) is the slayer of her brother, Tristram returns to Cornwall. Later King Mark sends Tristram as ambassador in seeking for him the hand of the younger Isoud. The princess and her maid Brangwayn return by ship to Cornwall; Brangwayn has been given a love-potion by Queen Isoud to be given on their wedding-night to Isoud and King Mark, which will bind them in unending love. By mistake the love-potion is drunk by Tristram and Isoud who are bound thereafter in endless passion, though Isoud has to marry Mark. The rest of the story is concerned with the fated love of Tristram and Isoud (in a manner broadly reminiscent of the Irish epic stories of *Þeirdre and the sons of Usna, and Diarmid and *Gráinne), and the subterfuges (often ingenious and morally reprehensible) which the lovers have to adopt; as in Chrétien's *Lancelot*, love is represented as a value that transcends morality. Tristram leaves Mark's court and, while fighting for Howel of Brittany, falls in love with and marries a third Isoud (Isolde of the White Hands). But, on the invitation of Isoud of Ireland, he returns to Cornwall where he is killed by Mark while playing his harp before Isoud. In some versions his death is not mentioned at all; in the most celebrated (adopted by *Wagner) Tristram sends for Isoud while he lies dying in Brittany. If she is on the ship when it returns, a white flag is to be flown; if not, a black one. The flag is white, but Isoud of the White Hands tells Tristram it is black, whereupon he dies. When Isoud comes to his bedside, she dies too. The story is the classic of medieval romance (with its strong mythical overtones and themes which recur in the romance, such as Tristram's madness, his harping, and the blood from his betraying wound) and of medieval love poetry. See D. de Rougemont, *Passion and Society* (1940; trans. of French *L'Amour et L'Occident*, 1939). W. T. H. Jackson, *The Anatomy of Love. The Tristan of Gottfried von Strassburg* (1971).

Tristram of Lyonesse, a poem in heroic couplets by *Swinburne, published 1882, which tells the story of Tristram's love for Queen Iseult, his marriage to Iseult of Brittany, and his death. W. *Morris, whose own medieval romances had much influenced Swinburne, was prompted by it to comment that his friend's work 'always seemed to me to be founded on literature, not on nature'.

Tristram Shandy, The Life and Opinions of, by L. *Sterne, published 1759–67.

This unique work, although itself the culmination of experiments by lesser authors, is generally regarded as the progenitor of the 20th-cent. *stream-of-consciousness novel. It owes much to *Rabelais, to Robert *Burton, and to Locke's *Essay concerning Human Understanding*. The word 'shandy', of obscure origin, means 'crack-brained, half-crazy', and Tristram in Volume VI of his book declares that he is writing a 'civil, nonsensical, good humoured *Shandean* book'.

Set in the Shandys' small parlour and garden, the book, erratically narrated by Tristram, consists of a slim line of narrative constantly and flagrantly interrupted by exuberant digressions, exploiting the relativity of time in human experience by deliberately disordering the sequence and emphasis of events. Parodying the new 'novel' form of his contemporaries, the narrator mocks the absurdity of development in narrative, insisting on beginning at the moment of his own conception, and deliberately pro-

viding no consistent plot or conclusion. Sterne's wayward typography, which includes rows of asterisks, dashes, diagrams, blank pages, various typefaces and other devices, paradoxically emphasizes his cheerful view of the unreality of the 'novel' form which he is himself using.

The chief character of the book is the narrator, Tristram, through whose thoughts, feelings, and observations we encounter the people and events about which he writes. He is shrewd and bawdy, delighting in the idiosyncrasy of the Shandy household, and filled with such vitality his words can scarcely keep up with his headlong thought. The main characters he introduces are his excitable and devoted father, Walter, whose flamboyant eloquence flows on through philosophy, paradox, and hypothesis, filled with references to the classics, history, science, medicine, law, the arts, and all learning run wild; Uncle Toby, Walter's soldier brother, whose portrait *Hazlitt described as 'one of the finest compliments ever paid to human nature', a man benign and practical, whose most passionate interest is aroused only by the problems of military fortifications and, more fleetingly, by the widow Wadman; Corporal Trim, Toby's devoted and loquacious servant, who shares his master's passion for fortifications; the bewildered Mrs Shandy; the impulsive and argumentative parson, Yorick; Dr *Slop, an incompetent physician; the Shandys' neighbour, Mrs Wadman, who designs to marry Toby; and the irrepressible household servant, Obadiah. Tristram's persistent interest and amusement in sexual matters (such as his own conception or Toby's wound in the groin) is demonstrated in frequent ironical parades of discretion, indiscretion, and innuendo.

A sketch of the 'story' may be attempted but cannot be very helpful. In Volume I Tristram is noted as arriving in 'the scurvy and disastrous world', and with much learned digression and other distraction his family and friends are introduced and described. Volume II concentrates chiefly on the past military experiences of Toby and Corporal Trim, and their present enthusiasms, and on a lengthy discussion of a controversial sermon read aloud by Trim. Tristram's birth is now fully described in Volume III, but only after many diversions and asides, including the mighty curse of Ernulphus of Rochester—at which time the author finds occasion to produce his overdue Preface. Volume IV contains Walter's exposition to his bewildered brother Toby of Slawkenbergius's Latin treatise on noses (for which the Shandys are famous), and an account of the misnaming of the infant 'Tristram' instead of 'Trismegistus'. Volume V covers the death of Tristram's brother Bobby and Walter's response, the reflections of Trim on death, and the devising of the *Tristapaedia* for Tristram's education. Volume VI relates the pathetic tale of Lieutenant Le Fever and his son, together with Toby's great kindness to them; includes the ludicrous bedtime discussion between Mr and Mrs Shandy on the putting of Tristram into breeches; describes the tremendous model of military earthworks constructed by Toby and Trim in the garden; and begins the story of Toby's amour with the widow Wadman. In Volume VII the Shandy family narrative is broken by a description of Tristram's travels and adventures in France. Volume VIII follows the complex emotions developing between Toby and Mrs Wadman, and Trim's attempt to tell his story of the king of Bohemia. Volume IX includes the pathetic tale of mad Maria (who appears again in *A Sentimental Journey) and continues the story of Toby's love-affair, until its sad collapse. The final brief episode of the book contains a confused conversation about Walter's bull. 'L—d! said my mother, what is all this story about?—A COCK and a BULL, said Yorick—And one of the best of its kind, I ever heard.'

The first version of Volumes I and II were rejected by *Dodsley, and Sterne had a revised version of them published in York in 1759. The rest of the work was published in London between 1761 and 1767 and enjoyed great general success, although Dr *Johnson, *Richardson, *Goldsmith, and certain other literary figures expressed their reservations on both literary and moral grounds.

Triumph of Life, The, an unfinished visionary poem by P. B. *Shelley, written in the bay of Lerici in summer 1822, published from rough drafts 1824.

Composed in *terza rima, the poem is strongly influenced by *Dante's Inferno, *Petrarch's Trionfi, and the carvings of Roman triumphal processions Shelley had seen in the Forum. The 'triumph' or masquerade (as the *'Mask of Anarchy') belongs to the cruel Chariot of Life, here shown as one of Shelley's Tyrant-figures. Life appears to vanquish the hope and ideals of all men, dragging in its train even the greatest, like Plato, Alexander, or Napoleon. Only the 'sacred few', like Jesus and Socrates, who early 'Fled back like eagles to their native noon', escape compromise and captivity. The poetry has a bitter, lucid directness that is new to Shelley; it contains a grim and masterful passage about growing old and sexually disillusioned (ll. 137–69). But it is impossible to know how he would have concluded the vision, had he lived.

The poet is conducted by the spirit of *Rousseau (as Dante is led through Hell by Virgil); he observes that most men do not know themselves truly, and are destroyed by 'the mutiny within'. The atmosphere of the poem, full of images drawn from the sea, is darkly hypnotic.

Triumph of Peace, The, a masque by J. *Shirley, acted and printed 1634.

This was the best known of all 17th-cent.

*masques, mainly because of the spectacular torchlight procession (or 'triumph') of the masquers, from Holborn to Whitehall, which preceded the masque proper. It was an expression of loyalty to the Crown on the part of the four Inns of Court, after *Prynne—a member of Lincoln's Inn—had published his Histriomastix (1633) with a dedication to his fellow-benchers at the Inn. Shirley's plot is simple: the chief antimasquer, Fancy, presents a series of interludes showing the benefit and abuses of Peace; these are finally driven away by the entry of Peace, Law, and Justice—qualities which, the lawyers were eager to point out, cannot flourish apart from one another. The masque was designed by I. *Jones, and its score (by W. *Lawes and Simon Ives) is among the few examples of masque music that have survived.

TRIVET, Nicholas, (c.1258–?1334), of a family with connections in Norfolk and Somerset, a Dominican who studied at Oxford and Paris. He made early commentaries on a number of classical texts, including *Boethius, but he is most celebrated as the writer of three histories in the 1320s: his Anglo-Norman Chronicle, extending from the Creation to 1285, surviving in eight manuscripts and containing the tale of Constance, told by *Gower in Confessio Amantis and by Chaucer's Man of Law (*Canterbury Tales, 5); secondly, Annals of Six Kings of England 1136–1307, pro-Angevin and particularly useful for the reign of Edward I; and third, the Historia ab orbe Condita (1327–9), an encyclopaedic history influenced by *Vincent of Beauvais.

Trivia, or The Art of Walking the Streets of London, a poem by J. *Gay in three books, published 1716. It is a town eclogue, owing 'some hints' to *Swift, whose 'City Shower' (1710) is in the same vein. Gay conducts the reader through the streets of London, by day and then by night, offering advice on coats and boots (Book I contains a mock-heroic derivation of the word 'patten'), on the hazards of pavement, gutters, and rubbish, and on the characters he will encounter—boot-boys, ballad-singers, footmen, bullies, fishwives, etc. It is a lively, affectionate, and entertaining piece, and a mine of information. 'Trivia' means 'streets', from the root meaning of 'road junction', and Gay, who invokes Trivia as a goddess of the highways, also refers to the murder of Laius by Oedipus at the crossroads in Book 3, l. 217.

Trivium, the lower division of the Seven Liberal Arts, consisting of the methodological subjects Grammar, Rhetoric, and Logic, as distinct from the mathematically based sciences of the *Quadrivium. The Trivium had great importance throughout the period of the Roman Empire, and it was taught from the time of Aristotle in Greek. Its period of greatest importance was the 11th and 12th cents, at

Chartres and in such writers as *John of Salisbury. Gradually logic became the all-important member, so that in the 12th cent. the Trivium was redefined as grammar, rhetoric, and dialectic, regarded as sub-sections of logic; in the 13th cent. concern for argumentative precision meant that the literary aspects of the Trivium disappeared almost entirely, and grammar and rhetoric as expressive skills ceased to be taught. The derogatory adjective 'trivial' (first found in English in the 16th cent.) reflects this progressive decline.

TROCCHI, Alexander, see UNDERGROUND POETRY.

Trochee, see METRE.

Troil, Magnus, Minna, Brenda, and Ulla (Norna), characters in Scott's *The Pirate*.

Troilus and Cressida, a tragedy by *Shakespeare probably written 1602, perhaps with a performance at one of the Inns of Court in mind. It was first printed 1609, in a quarto of which there are two issues, with different title-pages, one of which has a prefatory Epistle, 'A never writer, to an ever reader. News.' This was not included in the First *Folio, where *Troilus and Cressida* is the first play in the section of tragedies. As well as *Homer's and *Chaucer's handling of material concerning the lovers and the siege of Troy, Shakespeare knew of Henryson's *Testament of Cresseid, *Caxton's Recuyell of the Historyes of Troye, and *Lydgate's Troy Book, and drew on *Ovid's Metamorphoses Books XI and XII and R. *Greene's Euphues his Censure to Philautus (1587).

Shakespeare's treatment of the love of Troilus and Cressida and its betrayal, against the setting of the siege of Troy by the Greeks, is conventional. The play contains much formal debate, and takes the story up to the death of Hector at the hands of Achilles: Troilus fails to kill his rival Diomedes, and the cynically railing Thersites escapes death. Modern criticism has tended to agree with *Coleridge's view that 'there is none of Shakespeare's plays harder to characterize'.

Troilus and Criseyde, *Chaucer's longest complete poem, in 8,239 lines of rhyme-royal, probably written in the second half of the 1380s (J. D. North, RES, 1969, has shown that the events of the poem take place in calendar circumstances corresponding on astrological evidence to dates between 1385 and 1388). Chaucer takes his story from *Boccaccio's Il Filostrato, adapting its twelve books to five and changing the characters of Criseyde and *Pandarus. In Boccaccio Troilo falls in love with Criseida whose cousin, Troilo's friend Pandaro, persuades her, not unwillingly, to become Troilo's lover. In the end Criseida has to leave the Trojan camp to join her father who had

defected to the Greeks; in the Greek camp she betrays Troilo by falling in love with Diomede. While following the same narrative pattern, Chaucer deepens the sense of seriousness in the story by making Pandaro Criseida's uncle and guardian, by showing her deliberating at more length (this series of exchanges between uncle and niece in Book II is one of the most admired and anthologized parts of the poem), and by introducing deliberative material, principally from *Boethius, calling into question the lovers' freedom of action. The poem ends with an adjuration to the young to repair home from worldly vanity and to place their trust, not in unstable fortune as Troilus did, but in God. Discussion of the poem has centred largely on the appropriateness of the epilogue to the preceding action, on the attitudes to love (*courtly love in particular) in the poem, and on the personality of the narrator and his effect on the narrative. The love story has no basis in classical antiquity but is the invention of *Benoît de Sainte-Maure in his Roman de Troie, which was based on the pretended histories of Troy by *Dares Phrygius and *Dictys Cretensis. Boccaccio's intermediate source was *Guido delle Colonne (see TROPHEE). After Chaucer, the story was treated by Henryson in *The Testament of Cresseid and by Shakespeare in *Troilus and Cressida.

N. R. Havely, Chaucer's Boccaccio (1980); I. Bishop, Chaucer's 'Troilus and Criseyde': A Critical Study (1981); M. B. Salu, Essays on Troilus and Criseyde (1979); ed. S. A. Barney, Chaucer's Troilus: Essays in Criticism (1980).

TROLLOPE, Anthony (1815–82), was born in London. His Autobiography, written 1875–6, published posthumously 1883, describes his life with a characteristic blend of candour and reticence. His father, a fellow of New College, Oxford, before his marriage, failed both as a lawyer and as a farmer. The family's poverty made Trollope miserable at school (he went to both Harrow and Winchester), and when financial difficulties became acute, the family moved to Belgium, where Trollope's father died. Mrs Frances *Trollope had already begun to support the family through her belated career as an author; she was already in her fifties when her successful Domestic Manners of the Americans was published in 1832. Trollope became a junior clerk in the General Post Office in London in 1834, but only began to make any professional progress when transferred to Ireland in 1841. He married Rose Heseltine in Ireland in 1844; they had two sons, the younger of whom was to settle in Australia. Trollope did not return permanently to England until 1859, although he travelled extensively on Post Office business; he undertook important postal missions at various times to Egypt, the West Indies, and the United States. By the end of his professional career Trollope had become a successful and important if also highly individual civil servant. Among his achievements is the introduction in Great Britain of the pillar-box for letters. He resigned from the Post Office in 1867, and stood unsuccessfully for Parliament as a Liberal in 1868. Trollope thought that a seat in Parliament ought to be 'the highest object of ambition to every educated Englishman'. He edited the *St Paul's Magazine*, 1867–70.

His literary career began with the appearance of *The Macdermots of Ballycloran* in 1847, but not until his fourth novel, *The Warden* (1855), did he establish the manner and material by which he is best known. This, the first of the 'Barsetshire' series, was followed by *Barchester Towers* (1857), *Doctor Thorne* (1858), *Framley Parsonage* (1861), *The Small House at Allington* (1864), and *The Last Chronicle of Barset* (1867). The action of these novels is for the most part set in the imaginary west country county of Barset and its chief town, Barchester, of which Trollope says in the *Autobiography*, 'I had it all in my mind,—its roads and railroads, its towns and parishes, its members of Parliament, and the different hunts which rode over it. I knew all the great lords and their castles, the squires and their parks, the rectors and their churches . . . Throughout these stories there has been no name given to a fictitious site which does not represent to me a spot of which I know all the accessories, as though I had lived and wandered there.' Trollope regarded *The Last Chronicle of Barset* as his best novel, taken as a whole. The Barset novels are also interconnected by characters who appear in more than one of them, and Trollope developed this technique in his second series, known as the 'Political' novels or—perhaps more appropriately—as the 'Palliser' novels, after Plantagenet Palliser, who appears in all of them. This series began with *Can you Forgive Her?* (1864) and continued with *Phineas Finn* (1869), *The Eustace Diamonds* (1873), *Phineas Redux* (1876), *The Prime Minister* (1876), and *The Duke's Children* (1880). The two series taken together thus span over twenty years of Trollope's writing life. Trollope established the novel-sequence in English fiction. His use of reappearing characters had been anticipated by *Balzac (who uses them on an even grander scale), but there is no evidence that Trollope was in any way indebted to the French author. The characters of Palliser and his wife Lady Glencora, together with that of Mr Crawley from *The Last Chronicle of Barset*, seemed to Trollope to give his work its best chance of survival. The Palliser novels also allowed Trollope to express his views on political matters.

Although modest in claiming literary excellence, Trollope prided himself on his workmanlike attitude towards his art, as well as on its sheer quantity. He attributed his remarkable output, which included 47 novels, several travel books, biographies, as well as collections of short stories and sketches, to a disciplined regularity of composition. He trained himself to produce a given number of words an hour in the early morning before going off to his post office duties (which he also managed to combine with an almost fanatical devotion to hunting). He also wrote when travelling by rail and sea, and as soon as he finished one novel began another. He was always much more concerned with character than with plot, and made the degree to which an author really knows his characters a fundamental test of his or her merit. In the *Autobiography* Trollope writes eloquently of the novelist's need to live with his creatures 'in the full reality of established intimacy. They must be with him as he lies down to sleep, and as he wakes from dreams.' He also stresses the importance of recording change and the effects of time: 'On the last day of each month recorded, every person in his novel should be a month older than on the first.' Trollope attributed whatever success he had obtained to the intimacy with which he himself had lived with the characters in his lifelike imagination. His popularity was at its peak during the 1860s; readers admired his treatment of family and professional life, the variety and delicacy of his heroines, and the photographic accuracy of his pictures of social life.

Apart from the two series, Trollope's other principal novels include: *The Three Clerks* (1857), *The Bertrams* (1859), *Orley Farm* (1862), *The Belton Estate* (1866), *The Claverings* (1867), *He Knew He Was Right* (1869), *The Vicar of Bullhampton* (1870), *The Way we Live Now* (1875), *The American Senator* (1877), *Doctor Wortle's School* (1881), *Ayala's Angel* (1881), *Mr Scarborough's Family* (1883). The *Autobiography* records that, down to 1879, his publications had brought him some £70,000, which he thought 'comfortable, but not splendid'. Despite a sometimes overbearing public manner, Trollope became a popular figure in London and literary society in his later years. He was on good terms with the major novelists of his day: he greatly admired *Thackeray, of whom he nevertheless wrote a clearsighted study (1879), and was a close friend of G. *Eliot and G. H. *Lewes. In an obituary essay on Trollope written in 1883, H. *James summed up his achievement by saying that 'His great, his inestimable merit was a complete appreciation of the usual . . . Trollope's great apprehension of the real, which was what made him so interesting, came to him through his desire to satisfy us on this point—to tell us what certain people were and what they did in consequence of being so.' See *The Critical Heritage* (1969), ed. D. Smalley; *Letters* (2 vols, 1983), ed. N. John Hall.

TROLLOPE, Frances (1780–1863), a

woman, and writer, of indefatigable energy, who made an unfortunate marriage, conducted several ventures into, for instance, farming, and when she was past 50 wrote the first of over forty books, by which she proceeded to support her large family, and eventually achieved wealth and fame. After the failure of their farm at Harrow (later to appear in her son Anthony *Trollope's *Orley Farm*) she took her three youngest children to America to assist in the founding of the city of New Harmony, Memphis. This venture failing, she travelled for fifteen months in America, then in 1832, back in England, published her caustic *Domestic Manners of the Americans*. Its resounding success brought contracts to write on the Belgians, the French, the Austrians, and others, and she lived for the next few years on the Continent. *Paris and the Parisians* appeared with great success in 1835, *Vienna and the Austrians* in 1838, and in 1842 *A Visit to Italy* (where she became the friend of the *Brownings, *Dickens, and *Landor). Meanwhile, by working both early and late every day, she was writing a long sequence of popular (though little remembered) novels, and by the early 1840s was earning a considerable income. She built a house at Penrith, and was invited to meet the elderly *Wordsworth (whom she disliked). Shortly before her death she was astonished to receive Anthony's first novel. See a Life by H. Heinemann, 1979.

Trompart, in Spenser's *Faerie Queene* (II. iii),

> wylie witted, and growne old
> In cunning sleights and pratick knavery,

attends *Braggadochio as his squire, and with him is finally exposed and beaten out of court.

Trophee, an unknown writer mentioned by *Chaucer in 'The Monk's Tale' (*Canterbury Tales*, 19):

> At bothe the wordles endes, seith Trophee,
> In stide of boundes he (i.e. Hercules) a pileer sette.
> (CT VII, 2,117–18)

A marginal note in the Ellesmere and Hengwrt manuscripts says 'Ille vates Chaldeorum Tropheus'. *Lydgate says that Chaucer in his youth made a translation of a book called in the Lombard tongue *Trophe*, and that he later named it 'Troilus and Cressida'. No such book, or author, is known; of the explanations offered, the most likely is either that the Latin word for the pillars (of Hercules), *trophea*, has been interpolated and interpreted as an author's name, or that *Trophea* represents *Guido delle *Colonne ('Pillars') and that it is he that Chaucer is indicating.

Trotcosey, in Scott's *The Antiquary*, a favourite subject of reference by Jonathan Oldbuck; the house of Monkbarns stood on the lands of the ancient abbey of Trotcosey. Scott prepared in his later years *Reliquiae Trottcosienses*, a cata-

logue raisonné, of the most curious articles in the library and museum at Abbotsford.

TROTSKY, Lev Davidovich (1879–1940), Russian politican, born Bronstein. Having joined the Social-Democratic Party in early youth and at first supported *Lenin, from 1903 to 1917 he opposed Lenin's dictatorial methods within the party. He joined the Bolshevik party in 1917, however, when Lenin substantially accepted his idea of 'permanent revolution', i.e. of making a 'socialist' revolution immediately follow the 'bourgeois' one of March 1917. He took the leading part in the Bolshevik seizure of power and in the ensuing civil war directed the Red Army, whose success owed much to his leadership. In the struggle among the party leaders after Lenin's death, he was defeated by *Stalin and expelled from the Soviet Union. He was murdered in Mexico by Stalin's agents. Among Communist leaders Trotsky was comparatively liberal in cultural policy and perceptive as a literary critic, as is evident from his influential *Literature and Revolution* (1924).

Trotter, Job, in Dickens's *Pickwick Papers*, Jingle's servant.

Trotwood, Betsey, a character in Dickens's *David Copperfield*.

Troubadours, poets composing in Provençal during the 12th and early 13th cents (and perhaps earlier). They were famous for the complexity of their verse forms in the lyric, and for the conception of *Courtly Love which is founded to an important degree in their poems. Guilhem IX (1071–1127), count of Poitiers and duke of Aquitaine, is the first known troubadour; Jaufre Rudel (d. before 1167) developed the theme of 'amor de lonh', love from afar. The most admired troubadour love poets are Bernart de Ventadorn (*fl.* 1140–75), Raimbaut d'Aurenga (*c*.1144–73), Guiraut de Borneil (*c*.1165–1212: the most admired in his own time, the 'maestre dels trobadors'), and Arnaut Daniel (*fl.* 1180–1200), whom *Dante and *Petrarch admired most, an admiration shared in the 20th cent. by *Pound, who composed excellent translations of Daniel. The troubadours flourished in the courts of Spain, Italy, and northern France, as well as in the south of France, and courtly poetry in Provençal was being written and cultivated in Italy in the later 13th cent. (see SORDELLO and DANTE) when it was disappearing in the Midi. Through their influence on the Northern French poets (such as *Chrétien, and the writers of the *Roman de la Rose*) and on the German poets of the *Minnesang* (see MINNESINGERS) they had a major effect on all the subsequent development of European lyric poetry. Though love was their major subject, it was not their only one; they also composed moralizing, satirical, and political poems called *sirventes* (of which Guiraut de Borneil was the recognized master), and military poems in which Bertran de Born excelled. See A. R. Press ed. and trans., *Anthology of Troubadour Lyric Poetry* (1971: parallel text); L. T. Topsfield, *Troubadours and Love* (1975).

Trouvères, poets composing narrative, dramatic, satyric, comic, and especially lyric verse in the north of France during the late 12th and 13th cents. They were either professional entertainers (overlapping with *jongleurs*), *clercs*, or (when courtly society developed and the lyrics lost their energy) feudal lords composing fashionable verse. *Chrétien de Troyes was a *clerc*; other prominent trouvères were Conon de Béthune (d. *c.*1224), a Picard nobleman who composed crusading songs, Gâce Brulé (d. *c.*1220), *Blondel de Nesle (late 12th cent.), and Thibaut de Champagne, count of Champagne and king of Navarre. Their poetry was much influenced by that of the Provençal *troubadours (which however it never equalled) one of whom, Bernart de Ventadorn, came north to the court of *Eleanor of Aquitaine who was herself the granddaughter of Guilhem IX of Aquitaine, the first known troubadour. The most successful poets are those around 1200, particularly Gâce Brulé; thereafter their poetry becomes feebler and less inspired.

Troy, Sergeant, a character in Hardy's *Far from the Madding Crowd.*

Troynovant, see BRUT.

True Law of Free Monarchies, a political treatise attributed to James I, published 1598, and written to combat the Calvinist theory of government advocated by G. *Buchanan in his *De Jure Regni* (1579). It sets forth the doctrine of the divine right of kings and of the king's responsibility to God alone.

Truewit, the gallant and chief wit of Jonson's *Epicene*, a model for the wits of *Restoration comedy.

Trulla, the name (meaning 'a whore') of one of the bear-baiters in Butler's *Hudibras.*

Trulliber, Parson, a character in Fielding's *Joseph Andrews.*

Trumpet Major, The, a novel by T. *Hardy, published 1882. The story is set during the Napoleonic wars, at a time in which there were busy preparations against the threat of invasion. It tells of the wooing of Anne Garland, whose mother is tenant of a part of Overcombe Mill, where the dragoons come down from the nearby camp to water their horses. One of these dragoons is John Loveday, the trumpet-major, the gentle, unassuming son of the miller. He loves Anne Garland, but has a rival in his brother Bob, a cheerful, lighthearted sailor. Her third

suitor is the boorish yeoman Festus Derriman. In the course of events Anne meets King George III, on a military inspection, and later watches the departure of the *Victory* for Trafalgar. The story ends with the discomfiture of Festus and the success of Bob's courtship, while John marches off with his dragoons, to die on a battlefield in Spain.

Trunnion, Commodore Hawser and Mrs, characters in Smollett's *Peregrine Pickle.*

Tryamour, see SIR LAUNFAL.

Tryan, the Revd Edgar, a character in G. Eliot's 'Janet's Repentance' (see SCENES OF CLERICAL LIFE).

TSVETAEVA, Marina Ivanovna (1892–1941), Russian poet and prose writer. Born in Moscow, the daughter of a professor of art and a gifted pianist, she spent much of her childhood in Western Europe. She published her poetry of 1907–9 privately as *Evening Album* (1910) with great success. In 1912 she married Sergei Yakovlevich Efron, who became an officer in the Tsarist army, and published a second book of poetry. She totally rejected the October revolution and wrote a cycle of poems *The Encampment of the Whites* (Munich 1957, English trans. Robin Kemball, 1980), glorifying the White army. At the end of the Civil War she got permission to join her husband (whom she had thought dead) in Prague, and in 1922 much of her poetry appeared in Moscow and Berlin, consolidating her reputation. In exile she engaged in an exalted correspondence with *Rilke and *Pasternak, two poets whom she admired inordinately. In 1925 she moved to Paris, and in March 1926 she spent two weeks in London. She became increasingly estranged from the Emigration and, finding it ever more difficult to publish, lived in great poverty, while continuing to write poetry and critical prose of lasting importance. Her husband became more and more pro-Soviet, and on the orders of the Soviet Secret Police he assassinated a Soviet official who had defected in the West, then fled to the USSR. Ostracized by the Emigration, Tsvetaeva decided, despite her better judgement, to return to Russia. She arrived in Moscow in June 1939 to be shunned by most of her former friends, and later that year her daughter Ariadna was arrested and her husband arrested and shot. During the war she was evacuated to Elabuga, in the Tatar Autonomous Republic, where in despair she hanged herself. Much of her poetry has been republished in the Soviet Union since 1961, and both there and elsewhere her passionate yet articulate and precise work, with its daring linguistic experimentation, has brought her increasing recognition as a major 20th-cent. poet. She has been much translated into English, notably in *Selected Poems* (trans. E. *Feinstein,

1971, 1981) and in *A Captive Spirit: Selected Prose* (trans. J. Marin King, 1980).

Tuatha Dé Danann, in Gaelic mythology, the gods, the 'Folk of the goddess Danu', the enemies of the *Fomors. They are represented as invaders of Ireland, subsequent to the Fomors and the Fir Bolgs. They rout the Fomors at the battle of Moytura, and are ousted in their turn by the *Milesians. Conspicuous among the Tuatha Dé Danann are Lugh, the Gaelic sun-god, their leader; and *Lêr, the god of the sea.

Tucca, Captain Pantilius, the swaggering bully of Jonson's *Poetaster*, who reappears in Dekker and Marston's *Satiromastix*.

Tuck, Friar, see FRIAR TUCK.

TUCKER, Abraham (1705–74), a country gentleman and one of the first writers of the utilitarian school of philosophy. In his great work *The Light of Nature Pursued*, of which three volumes were published in 1768 and three after his death in 1778, he rejects the moral sense theory of *Shaftesbury and *Hutcheson and finds the criterion of moral conduct in general happiness, and the motive of the individual in his own happiness. The coincidence of these two is almost, but not quite, complete. There comes a point where virtue requires a self-sacrifice that prudential motives do not justify. Here Tucker finds the place for religion and its promise of a future life, where 'the accounts of all are to be set even', and the sacrifice of personal happiness required by virtue is to be made good.

Tucker's writings are diffuse and unmethodical, but marked by humour and quaint illustration and comment. His theories were systematized by *Paley.

Tuirenn, *The Fate of the Sons of,* one of the 'three sorrowful tales of Erin', a mythological tale in which the three sons of Tuirenn are punished for killing Cian, the father of the hero-god Lugh, by being required, by way of fine, to achieve a number of quests, in the last of which they perish.

Tulkinghorn, a character in Dickens's *Bleak House*.

Tulliver, Mr and Mrs, Tom and Maggie the principal characters in G. Eliot's *The Mill on the Floss*.

Tullochgorum, see SKINNER, J.

Tully, see CICERO.

Tully-Veolan, in Scott's *Waverley*, the castle of the baron of Bradwardine.

Tunnyng of Elynour Rummyng, The, a poem by *Skelton, is a vigorous Hogarthian description of contemporary low life. Elinour Rumming is an alewife who dwells beside

Leatherhead and brews 'noppy ale' for 'travellars, to tynkers, | to sweters, to swynkers, | And all good ale drynkers', and the poem, coarse but full of humour and life, describes the mixed company who throng to drink it.

Tupman, Tracy, in Dickens's *Pickwick Papers*, one of the members of the Corresponding Society of the Pickwick Club.

TUPPER, Martin Farquhar (1810–89), prolific writer of verse and prose, was educated at Christ Church, Oxford. His *Proverbial Philosophy* (1838–76, 4 series), presenting maxims and reflections couched in vaguely rhythmical form, became the favourite of millions who knew nothing about poetry, and remained a best-seller in Britain and America for more than a generation. His two novels, *The Crock of Gold* (1844) and *Stephan Langton* (1858), and his numerous other published works are now forgotten.

TURBERVILLE, George (*c.*1544–*c.*1597), scholar of Winchester and fellow of New College, Oxford, published *Epitaphes, Epigrams, Songs and Sonets* (1567); *The Books of Faulconrie* (1575), and various translations from *Ovid and *Mantuan, including Mantuan's eclogues (1567); and an account of the state of 'Muscovia', later reprinted by *Hakluyt. *The Noble Art of Venerie or Hunting* (1575) is also attributed to him (reprinted 1908). His poems reflect the use of Italian models and show the influence of *Wyatt and *Surrey.

TURGENEV, Ivan Sergeevich (1818–83), Russian novelist and playwright. He was born in Orel, in central Russia, and studied at Moscow and St Petersburg Universities. He published some poetry in 1838 and studied in Berlin, 1838–41. On returning to Russia he served briefly in the Civil Service, but from 1845 he devoted himself to literature. He also fell in love with the singer Pauline Garcia Viardot, and partly for this reason was to live much of his life abroad, mainly in Baden-Baden and Paris, where he died. His first important prose work was *A Hunter's Notes* (1847–51), the limpid prose of which, in such masterpieces as 'Bezhin Meadow' and 'The Living Relic', is one of his greatest achievements. This was followed by a series of novels in which individual lives are examined to illuminate the social, political, and philosophical issues of the day: *Rudin* (1856), *A Nest of Gentlefolk* (1859), *On the Eve* (1860), *Fathers and Sons* (1862), in which, in Bazarov, he created a *Nihilist hero, *Smoke* (1867), and *Virgin Soil* (1877). His greatest short stories are 'Asya' (1858), 'First Love' (1860), and 'Torrents of Spring' (1870). His best play is *A Month in the Country* (1850). Turgenev was the first major Russian writer to find success in the rest of Europe. This resulted partly from his living largely in Western Europe, where he was personally acquainted with *Flaubert, G. *Sand, *Mérimée, and others, but also from the fact that he was closer in both sensibility and literary practice to Western Europe than his contemporaries *Tolstoy and *Dostoevsky. Turgenev first visited England in 1847 and returned many times up to 1881: *Fathers and Sons* was planned on the Isle of Wight. He received an honorary DCL at Oxford in 1879 for 'advancing the liberation of the Russian serfs'. He was extremely widely read in English literature, and admired Shakespeare inordinately, comparing him to 'Nature, simple yet infinitely complex, harmonious, wise and free'. Of his English contemporaries, he most valued *Dickens and G. *Eliot, both of whom he knew. He was acquainted with *Thackeray, *Trollope, *Carlyle, R. *Browning, *Tennyson, the *Rossettis, and *Swinburne, and in correspondence with *Gissing. He was one of the earliest admirers of H. *James, who first met him in Paris in 1875 and on whom he had a substantial influence. Perhaps the greatest English debt to him is owed by G. A. *Moore, who said, 'a sort of Jesus of Nazareth he was in art', whose whole mature career was given shape by the discovery of Turgenev's artistry, and who, in *The Lake* (1905), came as close as anyone to writing a Turgenev novel in English. *A Hunter's Notes* was translated into English by J. D. Meiklejohn in 1855, and by 1890 most of Turgenev's major work had appeared in English. The most complete early translation is C. *Garnett's *Turgenev—The Novels and Tales* (1894–9), the edition through which he exerted his influence on such writers as *Galsworthy, *Conrad, and V. *Woolf.

TURGOT, Anne-Robert-Jacques, see PHYSIOCRATS.

Turkish Spy, *Letters written by a,* eight vols, published ?1687–94. The first is a translation of 'L'Espion du Grand Seigneur' by Giovanni Paolo Marana, a Genoese residing in Paris, published in French in 1684–6, partly itself a translation from an Italian version. The work inaugurated a new genre in European literature, the pseudo-foreign letter, of which the *Lettres persanes* of *Montesquieu is the chief example.

A continuation to the *Letters,* probably by *Defoe, was published in England in 1718.

TURNBULL, George (1698–1748), educated at Edinburgh, regent at Marischal College, Aberdeen, 1721–7, and teacher of T. *Reid. He was an early member of the *Rankenian club, and his published lectures (*Principles of Moral and Christian Philosophy,* 2 vols, 1740) and surviving correspondence show him as an ardent follower of *Shaftesbury in his advocacy of civic virtue and educational reform, and the prominence he attached to the sense of beauty. He sought to turn natural science to the service of

religion, and to construct a moral science based on experimental laws of human nature, in which the association of ideas had a central role. His *Treatise on Ancient Painting* (1739), which figures in a caricature by *Hogarth, discusses the place of the fine arts in education. Turnbull stresses the links between the sense of beauty and the moral sense, and between beauty and truth, and sees a close parallel between the didactic moral function of good painting and good poetry.

TURNER, J(oseph) M(allord) W(illiam) (1775–1851), major English landscape painter, whose mature works convey a profoundly Romantic vision of the magnificence of nature and the violence of the elements—storms at sea, floods, fires, avalanches, snow, and wind. He travelled in England and in France, Switzerland, and Italy, and his subjects and styles are astonishingly varied. He moved from conventional topographical watercolours of *picturesque subjects to historical landscapes which vie with the grandeur of *Poussin and *Claude; in his late, increasingly violent, and almost abstract works (*Snowstorm at Sea,* 1842; *Rain, Steam and Speed,* 1844, both London, National Gallery) forms are dissolved in the sweep of light and brilliant colour patterning the surface of the canvas. Turner was devoted to the 18th-cent. doctrine of *Ut Pictura Poesis* ('as is painting, so is poetry': *Horace, *Ars Poetica,* 361) and was often inspired by contemporary poetry. He was committed to the values of the *Royal Academy, where he was appointed professor of perspective in 1807 and lectured in 1811, and sought to ennoble the genre of landscape painting by suggesting that it could attain the imaginative power and complexity of poetry. From 1798 many of his pictures exhibited at the Royal Academy were accompanied by verses printed in the catalogue; from 1800 he added lines composed by himself. His quotations are frequently from James *Thomson, who deeply influenced his literary style, and in 1811 his picture *Thomson's Aeolian Harp* was accompanied by 32 lines honouring the poet. *Snowstorm; Hannibal and his army crossing the Alps* (1812, London, Tate Gallery) was exhibited with the first quotation taken from his gloomy 'M. S. P. Fallacies of Hope'. There is no trace of this projected epic poem beyond excerpts in Royal Academy catalogues; it was influenced by Akenside's *Pleasures of Imagination* and Campbell's *Pleasures of Hope.* Between 1806 and 1815 Turner frequently wrote poems beside the drawings in his sketchbooks; they have been transcribed by Jack Lindsay in *The Sunset Ship* (1968). In the 1830s Turner did many designs for book illustrations, amongst them charming and highly successful vignettes for *Rogers's *Italy* (1830) and *Poems* (1834). He also illustrated works by *Milton, *Byron, Sir W. *Scott, and T. *Campbell.

Turner endured much ridicule, including *Hazlitt's famous description of his work as 'pictures of nothing and very like', but *Ruskin became his passionate admirer and the first volume of *Modern Painters* (1843) was written in his defence.

TURNER, Sharon (1768–1847), a lawyer who became an enthusiastic student of Icelandic and Anglo-Saxon literature, and found much new material, especially among the unexplored Cottonian MSS (see COTTON, R. B.). His interest was, however, more historical than literary. Between 1799 and 1805 he published his *History of the Anglo-Saxons from the earliest period to the Norman Conquests*, which was greatly admired, by H. *Hallam, *Southey, and Sir W. *Scott, among others. He continued his histories up to the death of Queen Elizabeth I. His insistence on the use of original first sources was important to the future writing of history. He wrote also on many religious and literary subjects. He has a place in literary history as the legal adviser to J. *Murray and was much embroiled in the controversies surrounding the publication of Byron's *Don Juan*. He was also legal adviser to the *Quarterly Review*.

TURNER, Walter James Redfern (1889–1946), born in Melbourne, came to London when he was seventeen. He was music critic of the *New Statesman*, drama critic of the *London Mercury*, and literary editor of the *Spectator*. He wrote novels, including *The Aesthetes* (1927), *Blow for Balloons* (1935), and *The Duchess of Popocatapetl* (1939); volumes of verse, including *The Dark Fire* (1918), *Pursuit of Psyche* (1931), and *Songs and Incantations* (1936); a play, *The Man who ate the Popomack* (1922); and books on *Beethoven, *Mozart, and *Wagner.

Turn of the Screw, The, a ghost story by H. *James, published 1898.

The narrator is a young governess, sent off to a country house, Bly, to take charge of two orphaned children. She has been engaged by their uncle, a handsome man to whom she feels attracted, on the understanding that she takes all responsibility for the children and the entire household. She finds a pleasant house and a comfortable housekeeper, Mrs Grose, while the children, Miles and Flora, are unusually beautiful and charming. But she soon begins to feel the presence of intense evil, and sees the figure of the ex-valet Peter Quint and that of her own predecessor Miss Jessel. In fact they are both dead, and she learns of the guilty liaison that existed between them. For the young woman these apparitions emanate a fearful wickedness and she becomes convinced that, despite their denials, Miles and Flora are communicating with them. These terrible figures have returned to claim the children, to draw them into their web of sin and evil, and the governess is determined

to exorcize them. After a dramatic scene by the pond, where the narrator believes that Flora is meeting Miss Jessel, the little girl is taken off to safety by the housekeeper, and Miles, left with the governess, dies in her arms as she battles for his soul with the apparition of Peter Quint. It is left to the reader to decide whether these ghosts and their designs exist for anyone else in the story, or whether they are simply the hysterical fantasies of the young governess. James himself described this story as 'a trap for the unwary'.

Turonum, or **Turonium**, in imprints, Tours.

Turveydrop, father and son, characters in Dickens's *Bleak House*.

TUSSER, Thomas (?1524–80), agricultural writer and poet, was educated at St Paul's School, Eton, King's College and Trinity Hall, Cambridge. He farmed at Cattawade, Suffolk, and introduced the culture of barley to England. He published his *Hundreth good pointes of husbandrie* in 1557 (amplified in later editions) in verse of quaint and pointed expression, many proverbs being traceable to this work. It is a collection of instructions on farming, gardening, and housekeeping, together with humorous and wise maxims on conduct in general.

'Twa Dogs, The', a poem by *Burns, published 1786.

Caesar, the gentleman's dog of exotic foreign breed, and Luath, the ploughman's rough collie, converse on the comparative happiness of the lives of their masters, concluding that for all his poverty and toil the ploughman's is best. When the sun goes down:

> up they gat, and shook their lugs,
> Rejoiced they were na men but dogs.

TWAIN, Mark, pseudonym of Samuel Langhorne Clemens (1835–1910), American writer, born in Florida of a Virginian family, and brought up in Hannibal, Missouri. After his father's death in 1847 he was apprenticed to a printer, and wrote for his brother's newspaper; from 1857 to 1861 he was a pilot on the Mississippi, and from 1862 worked as a newspaper correspondent for various Nevada and Californian magazines, adopting the pseudonym 'Mark Twain', familiar to him as the leadsman's call on the Mississippi. Under this name he published his first successful story, 'Jim Smiley and his Jumping Frog', in 1865 in the New York *Saturday Press*. This comic version of an old folk-tale became the title story of *The Celebrated Jumping Frog of Calvaleras County, and other Sketches* (1867), which established him as a leading humorist, a reputation consolidated by *The Innocents Abroad* (1869), an account of a voyage through the Mediterranean. *Roughing It* (1872), an account of his adventures as miner and journalist in Nevada, appeared in the year of his first English lecture tour; England provided the background for his democratic historical fantasy *The Prince and the Pauper* (1882), in which Edward VI as a boy changes places with Tom Canty, a beggar, and for *A Connecticut Yankee in King Arthur's Court* (1889), a disturbing and not wholly amiable fantasy that satirizes both past and present. Meanwhile appeared his most famous works, both deeply rooted in his own childhood, *The Adventures of *Tom Sawyer* (1876) and its sequel *The Adventures of *Huckleberry Finn* (1885), which paint an unforgettable picture of Mississippi frontier life, and combine picaresque adventure with challenging satire and great technical innovative power. *Life on the Mississippi* (1883), an autobiographical account of his life as a river pilot, contains a notable attack on the influence of Sir W. *Scott, whose romanticism ('silliness and emptinesses, sham grandeurs, sham gauds and sham chivalries') did 'measureless harm' to progressive ideas and progressive works, creating, Twain alleges, the myth of the Southern gentleman that did much to precipitate the Civil War.

In the last two decades of his life Clemens was beset with financial anxieties and dissipated time and money on chimerical business enterprises, trying to recoup by lecture tours (in 1895–6 he toured New Zealand, Australia, India, and South Africa) and by writing potboilers; his pessimism and bitterness were increased by the death of his wife in 1904, of two of his three daughters, and by other family troubles. In these last years, however, he wrote some memorable if sombre works, including *The Man that Corrupted Hadleyburg* (1900), a fable about the venality of a smug small town, and *The Mysterious Stranger* (published posthumously in 1916, in a much-edited version), an extraordinary tale set in 16th-cent. Austria, in which Satan appears as a morally indifferent but life-enhancing visitor, to reveal the hypocrisies and stupidities of the village of Eseldorf. He dictated his autobiography during his last years to his secretary A. B. Paine, and various versions of it have appeared.

Twelfth Night, *Or What You Will*, a comedy by *Shakespeare probably written 1601. John Manningham saw a performance of it in the Middle Temple in February 1602; it was first printed in the *Folio of 1623. Shakespeare's immediate source for the main plot was 'The History of Apolonius and Silla' in B. *Rich's *Riche his Farewell to Militarie Profession* (1581). This is derived from Belleforest's version, which by way of *Bandello can be traced back to a Sienese comedy *Gl'Ingannati* (*The Deceived*), written and performed 1531.

Sebastian and Viola, twin brother and sister and closely resembling one another, are separated in a shipwreck off the coast of Illyria. Viola, brought to shore in a boat, disguises herself as a youth, Cesario, and takes service as page with Duke Orsino, who is in love with the lady Olivia. She rejects the duke's suit and will not meet him. Orsino makes a confidant of Cesario and sends her to press his suit on Olivia, much to the distress of Cesario, who has fallen in love with Orsino. Olivia in turn falls in love with Cesario. Sebastian and Antonio, captain of the ship that had rescued Sebastian, now arrive in Illyria. Cesario, challenged to a duel by Sir Andrew Aguecheek, a rejected suitor of Olivia, is rescued from her predicament by Antonio, who takes her for Sebastian. Antonio, being arrested at that moment for an old offence, claims from Cesario a purse that he had entrusted to Sebastian, is denied it, and haled off to prison. Olivia coming upon the true Sebastian, takes him for Cesario, invites him to her house, and marries him out of hand. Orsino comes to visit Olivia. Antonio, brought before him, claims Cesario as the youth he has rescued from the sea; while Olivia claims Cesario as her husband. The duke, deeply wounded, is bidding farewell to Olivia and the 'dissembling cub' Cesario, when the arrival of the true Sebastian clears up the confusion. The duke, having lost Olivia, and becoming conscious of the love that Viola has betrayed, turns his affection to her, and they are married.

Much of the play's comedy comes from the sub-plot dealing with the members of Olivia's household: Sir Toby Belch, her uncle, Sir Andrew Aguecheek, his friend, Malvolio, her pompous steward, Maria, her waiting-gentlewoman, and her clown Feste. Exasperated by Malvolio's officiousness, the other members of the household make him believe that Olivia is in love with him and that he must return her affection. In courting her he behaves so outrageously that he is imprisoned as a madman. Olivia has him released and the joke against him is explained, but he is not amused by it, threatening, 'I'll be reveng'd on the whole pack of you.'

The play's gentle melancholy and lyrical atmosphere are captured in Feste's two beautiful songs 'Come away, come away, death' and 'When that I was and a tiny boy, | With hey, ho, the wind and the rain'.

Twentieth Century, The, see NINETEENTH CENTURY.

Twitcher, Jemmy, in Gay's *The Beggar's Opera*, one of Captain Macheath's associates, who betrays him. The nickname was given to the fourth earl of Sandwich (1718–92), who had been associated with *Wilkes in the *Medmenham 'brotherhood' and yet, when Wilkes's papers were seized, was active in collecting evidence against him. The allusion is to a line in the play: 'That Jemmy Twitcher should peach me, I own surprised me.'

Two Cultures and the *Scientific Revolution, The*.

The Two Cultures' is a phrase coined by C. P. *Snow in the Rede Lecture delivered at Cambridge in 1959 and published the same year. In it, he contrasts the culture of 'literary intellectuals' and that of 'scientists', and as the most representative, physical scientists'. He describes the increasing gulf between them, claiming that thirty years earlier the two sides could at least manage 'a frozen smile' but are now incapable of communication. His analysis of the educational attitudes that produced this situation and his recommendations for change were strongly attacked by *Leavis in the TLS, 23 April 1970. (See also THOMSON, SIR W., and second law of thermodynamics.)

Two Drovers, The', a short story by Sir W. *Scott, one of the *Chronicles of the Canongate, published 1827.

The story is designed to illustrate the Highland character. Robin Oig M'Combich, a Highland drover of good family, sets out for England with his cattle, in company with his friend, a Yorkshire drover, Harry Wakefield. When they reach Cumberland the latter, annoyed over some trivial affair of accommodation for the cattle, fixes a quarrel on Robin in an inn, where the whole company join in insulting the Highlander. When Robin refuses to fight with his fists, as beneath the dignity of a Highland gentleman, Wakefield knocks him down. Robin walks twelve miles to fetch his dirk, which he has left with a comrade, returns to the inn, and in the presence of all plunges the dirk in Harry's breast. He then gives himself up, ready to give a life for the life he took.

Two Foscari, The, a poetic drama by *Byron, published 1821.

Jacopo, son of the doge of Venice, Francesco Foscari, has twice been exiled, once for venality and once for complicity in murder. He has been brought back from exile on a charge of treasonable correspondence, and the play opens with his examination on the rack. The doge his father, broken-hearted at his disgrace, signs the sentence for his third perpetual exile. But Jacopo's love for Venice is so intense that he dies with horror at the prospect of yet another banishment. The Council of Ten meanwhile decide to require the abdication of the old doge. He at once leaves the palace, and as he descends the steps he falls and dies.

Two Gentlemen of Verona, The, a comedy by *Shakespeare, probably written about 1592–. There is no record of a performance before the Restoration. It was first printed in the *Folio of 1623, where it is the second play in the section of comedies. The play's main source is the story of Felix and Felismena in the Diana of Montemayor.

The two gentlemen of Verona are the friends Valentine and Proteus. Proteus is in love with

Julia, who returns his affection, Valentine leaves Verona for Milan 'to see the wonders of the world abroad', and there falls in love with Silvia, the duke of Milan's daughter. Presently Proteus is sent also on his travels, and exchanges vows of constancy with Julia before starting. But arriving at Milan, Proteus is at once captivated by Silvia, and, betraying both his friend and his former love, reveals to the duke the intention of Valentine to carry off Silvia. Valentine is banished and becomes a captain of outlaws and Proteus continues his courting of Silvia. Meanwhile Julia, pining for Proteus, comes to Milan dressed as a boy and takes service as Proteus' page, unrecognized by him. Silvia, to escape marriage with Thurio, her father's choice, leaves Milan to rejoin Valentine, is captured by outlaws and rescued from them by Proteus. Proteus is violently pressing his suit on Silvia when Valentine comes on the scene. Proteus is struck with remorse, and his contrition is such that Valentine is impelled to surrender Silvia to him, to the dismay of Proteus' page, the disguised Julia. She swoons, and is then recognized by Proteus, and the discovery of her constancy wins back his love. The duke and Thurio arrive. Thurio shows cowardice in face of Valentine's determined attitude, and the duke, approving Valentine's spirit, accords him Silvia and pardons the outlaws. Launce, the clownish servant of Proteus, and his dog Crab, 'the sourest-natured dog that lives', provide much humour.

Two Nations, The, see Disraeli's *Sybil.

Two Noble Kinsmen, The, a tragi-comedy attributed to J. *Fletcher and Shakespeare, published 1634. In spite of its absence from the First *Folio (1623), recent studies of the play suggest that it is probably a genuine work of collaboration between Fletcher and Shakespeare, taking more or less equal shares, written in about 1613. Modern collected editions of Shakespeare do not regularly include it, but the Riverside edition (1974) is a notable exception.

The play is closely based on Chaucer's 'Knight's Tale' (*Canterbury Tales, 1), which Shakespeare had drawn on before in *A Midsummer Night's Dream. The main addition to the plot is the jailer's daughter who falls in love with Palamon, runs melancholy mad, and is cured by a lower-class wooer pretending to be Palamon. The overall tone is considerably lighter than in Chaucer's poem, the play being diversified with songs and lyrical passages such as Emilia's reminiscence of her friendship with Flavina (I. iii. 55–82); there is also a country festival with morris dancing, presided over by a pedantic schoolmaster (III. v). Theseus is a much less weighty and ominous figure than in Chaucer, and Arcite's death is rapid and dignified.

The play has rarely been performed in modern times.

Two on a Tower, a novel by T. *Hardy, published 1882.

Lady Constantine, whose disagreeable husband is away, falls in love with Swithin St Cleeve, an astronomer, younger than herself, who works at the top of a tower, where many of the scenes of the novel occur. Hearing her husband has died, Lady Constantine secretly marries Swithin, but later learns, first, that by so doing she had deprived him of a legacy; and, second, that her husband, though now dead, was alive when she married Swithin. Thus her marriage to Swithin is void, and she nobly insists on his leaving her, to take up employment abroad. She then finds she is pregnant by him; under pressure from her brother she accepts an offer of marriage from Bishop Helmsdale and a son is born. Swithin returns after the bishop's death, and is appalled that she is no longer a young woman. Eventually he offers to marry her, but the joy is too great and she falls dead in his arms.

Hardy's object was 'to set the history of two infinitesimal lives against the tremendous background of the stellar universe' and to show 'that of these contrasting magnitudes the smaller might be the greater to them as men'. But, as he acknowledged, the effect of the novel falls far short of his ambitions.

Two Poets of Croisic, The, see LA SAISIAZ.

Two Years Ago, a novel by C. *Kingsley, published 1857.

In the last of his reforming novels, Kingsley describes the descent of cholera upon the little West Country fishing village of Aberalva, attacks the poor sanitary conditions and public apathy that allowed it to take hold, and praises the gallantry and dedication of various of the inhabitants. These include the much-travelled doctor, Tom Thurnall, rescued from shipwreck in the second chapter by the noble Nonconformist schoolmistress Grace Harvey, who converts him to Christianity and whose love he wins by the end of the novel, and Frank Headley, the High-Church curate, also redeemed by the love of a good woman, who finally wins the confidence of his Dissenting flock. A secondary plot involves a denunciation of slavery in the United States, influenced by H. B. *Stowe's Uncle Tom's Cabin, and there are also many references to the Crimean war, which brings about a crisis in Thurnall's spiritual life. Contrasted with the practical Thurnall is Elsley Vavasour (once an apothecary's assistant under his real name, John Briggs) an opium-taking poet evidently of the *Spasmodic school, who is condemned for preferring Art to Action, and who demonstrates the dangers of unleashed emotion by running wild on Snowdon in the aptly titled Chapter XXI, 'Nature's Melodrama', before a deathbed scene in which he desires that his poetry be burned and his children be prevented

ever from writing verse. This portrait caused a temporary rift with *Tennyson, who wrongly took it to be aimed at him.

Tybalt, a Capulet in Shakespeare's *Romeo and Juliet who is killed by *Mercutio. For the allusion in the play to cats in connection with his name, see TIBERT.

TYLER, Wat (d. 1381), the leader of the peasants' revolt of 1381, who with *Jack Straw led the peasants of Kent and Essex to London. He was killed by William Walworth, the lord mayor of London, in the course of a discussion with Richard II at Smithfield. He is the subject of a drama by *Southey.

TYNAN, Katharine (1861–1931), poet and novelist, born in Dublin, is now remembered principally for her association with the *Irish revival and as a friend of *Yeats. Her first volume of verse, Louise de la Vallière and other poems (1885), was followed by many volumes of poems, fiction, and autobiography; Yeats's Letters to Katharine Tynan, ed. R. McHugh, was published in 1953.

TYNAN, Kenneth Peacock (1927–80), dramatic critic, educated at Magdalen College, Oxford. He wrote for various papers, most influentially for the *Observer (1954–63), and championed the plays of *Osborne, *Wesker, S. *Delaney, N. F. *Simpson, *Beckett, and others, playing a leading role in the shift of taste from drawing-room comedy and the poetic drama of T. S. *Eliot and C. *Fry (which he disliked) to naturalism and 'working class drama'. (See KITCHEN SINK DRAMA.) He also vigorously attacked theatre censorship and the Lord Chamberlain ('The Royal Smut-Hound', 1965). His various collections of reviews and essays include Curtains (1967), The Sound of Two Hands Clapping (1975), and A View of the English Stage (1976), which pay tribute to the role of the *English Stage Company in the development of British theatre. Tynan was also a moving force in the creation of the National Theatre, and its literary manager from 1963 to 1969.

TYNDALE, William (c.1495–1536), the translator of the *Bible, studied at Oxford and Cambridge. About 1522 he formed the project of translating the Scriptures into the vernacular but finding difficulties in England went to Hamburg for the purpose. He visited *Luther at Wittenberg, and commenced printing his translation of the New Testament at Cologne in 1525. He completed the work at Worms and introduced copies into England, which were denounced by the bishops and destroyed. He eventually settled at Antwerp, became a Zwinglian and an active pamphleteer, and engaged in controversy with Sir T. *More, writing An Answere unto Sir Thomas Mores dialoge in 1530. He was betrayed to imperial officers and arrested for heresy, imprisoned at Vilvorde in 1535, and strangled and burnt at the stake there, in spite of Cromwell's intercession. Tyndale was one of the most remarkable of the *Reformation leaders; his original writings show sound scholarship, but his translation of the Bible—consisting of the New Testament (1525), Pentateuch (1530), and Jonah (1531)—the accuracy of which has been endorsed by the translators of the Authorized Version, is his surest title to fame.

TYNDALL, John (1820–93), professor of natural history at the Royal Institution in 1853, and later superintendent there, did much in his writings and lectures to popularize science. He had many friends in literary and scientific circles, including *Tennyson, C. *Darwin, H. *Spencer, and L. *Stephen. His famous address to the British Association in Belfast in 1874, on the relation between science and theology, gave rise to acute controversy.

Typee or a Peep at Polynesian Life, a novel by H. *Melville, published 1846, first in Britain by John *Murray, under the non-fiction title *Narrative of a Four Months Residence among the Natives of a Valley of the Marquesas Islands,* and shortly after by Harpers in New York, who censored some 'sea freedoms' and satirical attacks on imperialism and missionaries. It was Melville's first book, and his most popular during his lifetime.

Like Melville himself, *Typee's* hero Tommo and his friend Toby jump ship in the Marquesas, but the *Defoe-like factual account masks a symbolic tale of the ambiguity of innocence. Hoping to find the Johnsonian 'Happy Valley' (see RASSELAS) of the peaceful Happars, Toby and the injured Tommo stumble instead upon the cannibalistic Typees, who live in an apparent Eden of sensuous plenty yet lack respect for life.

'Typhoon', a story by J. *Conrad, published 1903.

The unimaginative and imperturbable Captain MacWhirr pilots his steamer *Nan-Shan* through a typhoon of such violence that even he is moved to doubt the possibility of survival. Nevertheless, to avoid trouble between decks, he sends his appalled chief mate Mr Jukes down to confiscate the money of his 200 Chinese passengers. Later, the money redistributed and the ship safe in Fu-chau harbour, Jukes is forced to conclude that MacWhirr 'got out of it very well for a stupid man'.

Tyranipocrit Discovered, one of the best-written of the radical pamphlets of the Commonwealth, published anonymously in Rotterdam, 1649. The writer attacks the 'White Devil' of hypocrisy, which cloaks tyrannical power, idleness, and greed with Christian piety, finding it yet more pernicious than the 'Black

Devil' of undisguised oppression, or the petty crimes of the poor. It is an eloquent plea for equality: 'O to give unto everyone with discretion, as near as may be, an equal portion of earthly goods, to maintain him in this life, that is the greatest actuall justice that man can doe.' Extracts are printed in Orwell and Reynolds, *British Pamphleteers* (1948).

Tyrannick Love, or the Royal Martyr, a heroic play by *Dryden, produced and published 1669.

Based on the legend of the martyrdom of St Catharine by the Roman emperor Maximin, it contains some of Dryden's most extravagant heroic verse. Possibly deliberately comic at times, it is also seriously concerned with contrasting Lucretian and Christian conceptions of God. It was ridiculed in *The Rehearsal,* and by *Shadwell. Dryden himself satirizes its excesses in *MacFlecknoe.

Tyrrel, Francis, a character in Scott's *St Ronan's Well.

TYRRELL, George (1861–1909), a modernist theologian, joined the Roman Church in 1879 and the Society of Jesus in 1880. He made his name by publishing *Nova et Vetera* (1897) and *Hard Sayings* (1898), both collections of Meditations. He was dismissed from his order in 1906 for his unorthodox 'Letter to a Professor of Anthropology', published as *A much abused Letter.* In spite of his expulsion he continued his literary activities which included *Medievalism* (1908), a bitter attack on Cardinal Mercier denouncing the contemporary Roman Catholic Church, and *Christianity at the Cross-Roads* which appeared posthumously in 1909.

TYRWHITT, Thomas (1730–86), scholar and editor, had an early career in politics (clerk of the House of Commons, 1762–8), but is remembered partly for his edition and exposure of *Chatterton's Rowley poems; he published them in 1777, then in an appendix in 1778 stated authoritatively that they were modern, not ancient, a view he elaborated in his *Vindication* (1782). His *Observations and Conjectures upon Some Passages of Shakespeare* (1765, dated 1766) insisted on the importance of careful collation, and criticized Dr *Johnson's edition for its lack of attention to the early texts. His greatest contribution was his edition of Chaucer's *Canterbury Tales* (4 vols, 1775, vol. 5 with Glossary, 1778), which expounded *Chaucer's versification and helped to establish the canon.

TYRWHITT-WILSON, see BERNERS.

TYTLER, Patrick Fraser (1791–1849), Scottish lawyer and historian, joint founder with Sir W. *Scott of the *Bannatyne Club and its poet laureate. He was the author of several biographies, but most notably of the *History of Scotland* from the reign of Alexander III to the year 1603 (1828–43) and of *England under the Reign of Edward VI and Mary* (1839).

TYUTCHEV, Fedor Ivanovich (1803–73), Russian lyric poet, who served as a diplomat in Munich (1822–37), where he was a friend of *Heine. From 1858 until his death he worked as president of the committee of foreign censorship. His first poetry appeared in 1819 and throughout the 1820s and 1830s he was widely published; he was praised by *Nekrasov and *Turgenev in the 1850s, and his first volume of poetry appeared in 1854. His poetry is notable for the delicacy and profundity of its analysis of often paradoxical or overtly tragic human feeling, and for its analysis of man's position in nature. Tyutchev's reputation waned in the period 1860–90, only to rise again in the early 20th cent. when the Russian Symbolists, including *Blok, acknowledged him as a significant influence.

U

Ubi sunt, derived from the opening words of a type of Medieval Latin poem ('Where are they?'), taken up in Old English poems such as *Beowulf* and particularly *The Wanderer* (ll. 92–3) and in many Middle English lyrics (especially the one beginning 'Where beth they, beforen us weren', *c.*1300). Many later medieval French poems use the theme, most famously *Villon's 'Ballade des Dames du Temps Jadis' with its refrain, 'Mais où sont les neiges d'antan?'—'Where are the snows of yesteryear?'

UDALL, or UVEDALE, Nicholas (1504–56), dramatist and scholar, educated at Winchester and Corpus Christi College, Oxford, successively headmaster of Eton and Westminster. He was author of *Ralph Roister Doister*, the earliest known English comedy. He translated selections from *Terence and other works, and wrote Latin plays on sacred subjects. *Tusser (*Five hundreth pointes*) complains of having been severely flogged by Udall 'For fault but small, or none at all'. Udall got into grave trouble at Eton and was sent to the Marshalsea by the Privy Council. He figures in F. M. *Ford's novel *The Fifth Queen* (1906).

Udolpho, *The Mysteries of,* see MYSTERIES OF UDOLPHO, THE.

UGOLINO DELLA GHERARDESCA

(d. 1289), an Italian Guelf leader who twice made himself master of Pisa by treachery, in 1284 and 1288, by forming an intrigue with the Ghibelline leader Ruggieri degli Ubaldini. But Ruggieri betrayed him in turn, and he was locked with his two sons and two of his grandsons in a tower and starved to death. The story is told by Ugolino himself in *Dante's *Inferno*, xxxiii, and it is told among the tragedies of Fortune in Chaucer's 'The Monk's Tale' (*Canterbury Tales*, 19; VII, 2407–62); though he knew the source was Dante, Chaucer tells of three sons and says the youngest was five years old, although three of the four in Dante were grown men. The story was used again as the basis for a poem in *Heaney's *Field Work* (1981).

ULFILAS, or WULFILA (AD 311–81), a Christian of Cappadocian origin, was consecrated bishop of the Arian Visigoths in 341, and subsequently migrated with them to the neighbourhood of Nicopolis in Moesia. He translated the Bible into Gothic from the Greek,

inventing, it is said, an alphabet for the purpose. Fragments of this translation, chiefly of the NT, survive (e.g. the Codex Argenteus at Uppsala), and are of great value to the philological science of the Germanic languages.

Ulrica, in Scott's *Ivanhoe*, the old sibyl who sets fire to the castle of Torquilstone and perishes in the flames.

Ultrajectum, also Trajectum ad Rhenum, in imprints, Utrecht.

'Ulysses', a poem by *Tennyson, composed 1833, published 1842. In a dramatic monologue Ulysses describes how he plans to set forth again from Ithaca after his safe return from his wanderings after the Trojan war, 'to sail beyond the sunset'. The episode is based not on *Homer but on *Dante (*Inferno*, xxvi), which Tennyson probably read in the translation of *Cary, and expresses the poet's sense of 'the need of going forward and braving the struggle of life' after the death of A. H. *Hallam.

Ulysses, a novel by J. *Joyce, serialized in the *Little Review* from 1918, published in Paris 1922. Copies of the first English edition were burned by the New York post office authorities, and the Folkestone Customs authorities seized the second edition in 1923. Various later editions appeared abroad, and, after the United States District Court found the book not obscene in 1933, the first English edition appeared in 1936, and the first unlimited edition in America and England in 1937.

The novel deals with the events of one day in Dublin, 16 June 1904 (the anniversary of Joyce's first walk with Nora Barnacle, who became his wife), now known as 'Bloomsday'.

The principal characters are Stephen Dedalus (the hero of Joyce's earlier, largely autobiographical, *A Portrait of the Artist as a Young Man*); Leopold Bloom, a Jewish advertisement canvasser; and his wife Molly. The plot follows the wanderings of Stephen and Bloom through Dublin, and their eventual meeting. The last chapter is a monologue by Molly Bloom, The various chapters roughly correspond to the episodes of Homer's *Odyssey*, Stephen representing Telemachus, Bloom Odysseus, and Molly Penelope. In the course of the story a public bath, a funeral, a newspaper office, a library, public houses, a maternity hospital, and a brothel are visited. A number of other Dublin scenes and characters are introduced. The style is highly allusive and employs a variety of techniques, especially those of the *stream of consciousness and of parody, and ranges from extreme realism to fantasy.

Joyce described the theme of the *Odyssey* to one of his students in 1917 as 'the most beautiful, all-embracing theme . . . greater, more human, than that of *Hamlet, Don Quixote*, Dante, *Faust*', and refers to Ulysses himself as pacifist, father, wanderer, musician, and artist: 'I am almost afraid to treat such a theme; it's overwhelming.'

Ulysses, a Greek commander in Shakespeare's *Troilus and Cressida*. His speech on order and 'degree' occurs in I. iii.

Ulyssipo, in imprints, Lisbon.

Umbriel, 'a dusky melancholy sprite' in Pope's *The Rape of the Lock*.

Una, in Bk I of Spenser's *Faerie Queene*, typifies singleness of the true religion. She is separated from the *Redcrosse Knight of Holiness (the Anglican Church) by the wiles of *Archimago, but meets and is protected by a lion, until the latter is killed by *Sansloy, who carries Una off to a forest. She is rescued by fauns and satyrs, and is finally united to the Redcrosse Knight.

UNAMONO Y JUGO, Miguel de (1864–1936), Spanish writer and philosopher, born at Bilbao, and educated at the University of Madrid. He became professor of Greek at the University of Salamanca in 1892 and later became rector. A fierce and often eccentric critic of Spanish intellectual, social, and political life, who was at one point exiled for his views, nevertheless opposed thoughtless 'Europeanization'. He wrote plays, poems, novels, travel books, and short stories, but is perhaps best known in English-speaking countries for his philosophical essays, which show the influence of *Kierkegaard, W. *James, and *Bergson. *La Vida de Don Quijote y Sancho* (1905) is, in his own words, 'a free and personal exegesis' which perceives *Don Quixote as the embodiment of the Spanish genius; *Del Sentimiento tragico de la vida* (1912; English trans. *The Tragic Sense of Life*, 1921) is a deeply unorthodox meditation on man's religious aspirations, which suggests that 'God is not the cause, but the consequence of man's longing for immortality', and concludes that all dogma, religious or anti-religious, is false: the only tenable philosophical position is that of doubt and wonder.

Uncle Remus, see HARRIS, J. C.

Uncle Silas, a novel by J. S. *Le Fanu, published 1864.

Maud Ruthyn, aged 17, is the only child of Austin Ruthyn, an elderly recluse of considerable wealth. Her mother, whom he married late in life, is dead. Austin has a younger brother, Silas, suspected by many of the murder of a wealthy gambler who, years before, was found with his throat cut in mysterious circumstances at Bartram-Haugh, Silas's Derbyshire home. Believing in Silas's innocence, Austin at his death leaves a will designed to demonstrate his confidence in his brother: Silas is made Maud's guardian, and her entire fortune is to go to him if she dies under age. Uncle Silas, who has been involved in many scandals and is heavily in debt, loses no time in summoning Maud to Bartram-Haugh, where he attempts to marry her to his boorish son Dudley, who is in fact already secretly married. When she refuses, he pretends that he is sending her to school in France; but when, after two days' travel, she wakes up believing she is in Dover, she finds herself a prisoner back at Bartram-Haugh, where Silas and Dudley, aided by a grotesque and sinister French governess, Mme de la Rougierre, attempt to murder her. The plot miscarries and the governess is horribly murdered by Dudley in mistake for Maud, who escapes. The tale is one of suspense, without any supernatural element; but Maud's mounting terror at these events, seen through her eyes, is conveyed to the reader in a masterly manner. Uncle Silas himself is a fearful figure, tall, marble-faced, with black eyebrows and long silver hair, a laudanum-taker prone to strange cataleptic trances.

Uncle Toby, see TOBY, UNCLE.

Uncle Tom's Cabin, a novel by Mrs H. E. B. *Stowe.

UNDERDOWNE, Thomas (*fl.* 1566–87), translated the *Aethiopica* of Heliodorus under the title *An Aethiopian Historie* (?1569).

Underground Poetry, a phrase used to describe the work of a number of writer-performers active in Britain between the late 1950s and mid-1970s, including A. *Mitchell, Jeff Nuttall (1933–), Tom Pickard (1946–), Alexander Trocchi (1923–84), Heathcote Williams (1941–), and the *Liverpool poets. The open forms and protest or folk-song bias of this poetry reflected the experimental, anti-war aspirations of the 'alternative society' of the 1960s, and found its public largely through readings, events, and little magazine publications. Michael Horovitz's populist magazine *New Departures*, founded in 1959, and his Penguin anthology *Children of Albion: Poetry of the 'Underground' in Britain* (1969), record the mood of the movement and Horovitz's tribute to the liberating spirit of *Blake: see also Mitchell's 'Poetry Explodes' (*The Listener*, 14 May 1970); and under JAZZ POETRY.

UNDERHILL, Evelyn (1875–1941), writer on religious subjects, and notably on the Mystics;

she was much influenced by F. *von Hügel, whom she met after the publication of her study *Mysticism* (1911); she became a practising Anglican in 1921. She produced editions of *The Cloud of Unknowing* (1912) and W. *Hilton's *The Scale of Perfection* (1923), and wrote many books, meditations, and pamphlets on the spiritual life.

Under Milk Wood, a radio drama by Dylan *Thomas, first broadcast by the BBC on 25 Jan. 1954 and subsequently adapted for the stage; the published version was completed shortly before his death, although he was still at work on the text.

Set in the small Welsh seaside town of Llareggub, it evokes the lives of the inhabitants—Myfanwy Price the dressmaker, and her lover Mog Edwards the draper; twice-widowed Mrs Ogmore-Pritchard; Butcher Beynon and his daughter Gossamer; the Reverend Eli Jenkins; the romantic and prolific Polly Garter; nostalgic Captain Cat, dreaming of lost loves; and many others. The poetic, alliterative prose is interspersed with songs and ballads. An earlier version of the first part of this play appeared in *Botteghe Oscure* in 1952 under the title 'Llareggub'.

Under the Greenwood Tree, a novel by T. *Hardy, published 1872.

This is a gentle, humorous novel, skilfully interweaving the love story of Dick Dewy and Fancy Day with the fortunes and misfortunes of a group of villagers, many of whom are musicians and singers in Mellstock church. Dick Dewy, the son of the local 'tranter', or carrier, falls in love with the new schoolmistress, the pretty and capricious Fancy Day. Her other two suitors (Shiner, a rich local farmer, and Maybold, the vicar in charge of the school) are rejected, after a series of vicissitudes, and in spite of the opposition of Fancy's father, in favour of Dick. Dick and his father are among the small band of musicians who have always sung and played the music in the gallery of Mellstock church, and who find themselves ousted by the new-fangled organ. This story of the displaced musicians reflected the true story of the Hardy's own church at Stinsford, and Hardy originally wished to call his book 'The Mellstock Choir'. The novel marks the first appearance of Hardy's village rustics, who drew much critical comment, both favourable and unfavourable, and who were to reappear frequently in later novels.

Under the Volcano, a novel by M. *Lowry, published 1947, considered his masterpiece.

It opens in Quauhnahuac, Mexico, on the Day of the Dead, November 1939, as film-maker Jacques Laruelle looks back on the dramatic events of the same day in the preceding year, which occupy with many flashbacks and shifts of time sequence the main action of the book.

The characters are the British ex-consul Geoffrey Firmin, an alcoholic, his wife Yvonne, an ex-film star who has returned after a year's estrangement, Laruelle, with whom she has had an affair, and the consul's half-brother Hugh, an anti-Fascist journalist much preoccupied by the Spanish Civil War. The theme of self-destruction is linked with the menace to Western civilization, and the mood grows increasingly sombre, ending with the consul's death. The narrative technique is complex, showing debts to *Conrad, *Joyce, and *Faulkner, and the text is packed with allusions to classical, Elizabethan, and Jacobean tragedy and to 'poètes maudits' such as *Swinburne and *Baudelaire. The Mexican landscape, over which brood the two volcanoes Popocatapetl and Ixtaccihuatl, is described with much vividness. Half-way through the book the consul reflects that 'It was already the longest day in his entire experience, a lifetime', and Lowry's control over the consul's confused and alcoholic sense of time and memory is remarkable. Like most of his work, the novel is highly autobiographical.

Under Western Eyes, a novel by J. *Conrad.

Underwood, The, or **Underwoods,** a collection of poems by *Jonson, printed in the folio of 1640. It includes 'A Celebration of Charis', 'An Ode to Himself', 'An execration upon Vulcan' (concerning the fire in Jonson's library in 1623), 'An Epigram on the Court Pucelle', and the ode to Sir Lucius Cary and Sir Henry Morison. Like Jonson's *The Forest* and *Timber, the title was suggested by Latin *silva*, which meant both 'collection' and 'wood'.

Underwoods (1887) is also the name (confessedly adopted from Jonson) of a book of poems by R. L. *Stevenson.

Undine, a fairy romance published in 1811 by Friedrich, baron de la Motte Fouqué (1777–1843), German officer of cuirassiers and prolific writer of poetry, drama, and prose fiction. The story was suggested to him by a story in *Paracelsus, and Undine is a nymph, the personification of the watery element. She is brought up and adopted by a humble fisherman and his wife, who have lost their own child through drowning. She falls in love with a knight, Huldbrand, who takes shelter in their cottage; they are married, and she thus receives a human soul. But Huldbrand begins to neglect his wife, and falls in love with the haughty Bertalda, believed at first to be a duke's daughter, but in fact the long-lost child of the fisherman and his wife. One day as they sail on the Danube, Huldbrand, tormented by Undine's kindred, angrily rebukes his wife and she is snatched away into the water. As Huldbrand is about to marry Bertalda, Undine reappears and kills him with a kiss. The story was used as a libretto by E. T. A.

*Hoffmann (1816) and Lortzing (1845), and adapted as a play by *Giraudoux (*Ondine*, 1939).

Unfortunate Traveller, The, or *The life of Jacke Wilton*, a prose tale of adventure by T. *Nashe, published 1594, the earliest picaresque romance in English, and the most remarkable work of the kind before *Defoe. It is dedicated to the earl of Southampton.

Jack Wilton is 'a certain kind of an appendix or page' attending on the court of Henry VIII at the time of the siege of Tournay. He lives by his wits, playing tricks on a niggardly old victualler and other gullible occupants of the camp, and gets whipped for his pains. He goes to Münster, which the Anabaptists are holding against the emperor, and sees John of Leyden hanged. The earl of Surrey, the lover of the Fair Geraldine, takes him to Italy as his page. During their travels they meet Erasmus, Sir Thomas More, Cornelius Agrippa, and Aretino. They hear Luther disputing at Wittenberg. Wilton passes himself off as the earl of Surrey and runs away with an Italian courtesan. There is a pleasant scene where the true earl discovers them and treats the escapade with singular good humour. After a tourney at Florence, where the earl defeats all comers in honour of the Fair Geraldine, Wilton leaves him, and is at Rome during an outbreak of the plague. Here, turning from lighter themes, he depicts scenes of violence and tragedy, rapes, murders, tortures, and executions. Depressed by what he has seen, he is converted to a better way of life, marries his courtesan, and is last seen at the Field of the Cloth of Gold, in the king of England's camp. The book includes much literary parody and pastiche.

UNGARETTI, Giuseppe (1888–1970), Italian poet. He founded *hermeticism with his first two collections of poems *L'allegria* (*Gaiety*, 1914–15) and *Il porto sepolto* (*The Buried Port*, 1916), in which he used neither rhyme nor punctuation. His later poems, of which the best are in *Il dolore* (*Sorrow*, 1947) and *Sentimento del tempo* (*The Feeling of Time*, 1950), depart from hermeticism by reviving the tradition of *Leopardi and *Petrarch. He translated *Blake's visionary poems (*Visioni di William Blake*, 1965) and has himself been translated by R. *Lowell.

Unitarianism, a Christian body which rejects the Trinity and the divinity of Christ in favour of the single personality of the Godhead. As an organized community it became established in Poland, Hungary, and England in the 16th–17th cents. In England John Biddle (1615–62) published Unitarian tracts in 1652–4 and from 1652 his followers (Biddelians, *Socinians, or 'Unitarians') began regular Sunday worship. More than 100 years later Joseph *Priestley in his *Appeal to the Serious and Candid Professors of Christianity* (1770) defended Unitarian principles, and in 1773 Theophilus Lindsey (1723–1808) formed the first Unitarian denomination, opening in 1774 Essex Chapel in London. Both Priestley and his friend R. *Price became original members of the Unitarian Society in 1791. In the 18th cent. Dissenting congregations, including the English Presbyterians, turned to Unitarian views. Later in the 19th cent. J. *Martineau influenced the organization of the Unitarian body in England and Ireland and led the advance from biblical to rational Unitarianism.

Unities, The, principles of dramatic composition supposedly derived from Aristotle's *Poetics*. Recording the practice of the tragedians whose works he knew, Aristotle states that a play should have the unity of a living organism, and that the action it represents should last, if possible, no longer than a single revolution of the sun. It was from these hints that 16th-cent. critics developed the rule of the three unities: action, time, and place. The most influential of these critics, *Castelvetro, had a low opinion of the imaginative powers of the average audience and held that they would be upset by the time of the action lasting longer than the time of its performance and that they could not be made to accept changes of scene. Castelvetro's ideas left their mark on neo-classical drama, especially in France, but they did not go unchallenged. The exclusion of sub-plots became the rule in France only after the controversy over *Corneille's *Le Cid* (1637). The time allowed for the action of a tragedy was extended by common consent to 24 hours. The place the stage represented was allowed to shift from one point to another within a larger area: a palace or even a city. Moreover, dramatists learnt to circumvent the limitations of the unities by avoiding the mention of specific times and places. The impact of *neo-classicism on English tragedy was delayed by the disturbances connected with the Civil War and was weakened by the taste for exciting action that was a legacy from the Jacobean stage. Dryden's essay *Of Dramatick Poesy* (1668) offers the unities only half-hearted support, and in spite of the efforts of French-inspired critics like *Rymer and *Dennis, and the success of Addison's *Cato* (1713), neo-classical drama never took firm root in England.

University presses. The appointment of printers by European academies to produce learned books under some control and protection was common by the end of the 16th cent. As early as 1470 Jean Heynlin, prior of the Sorbonne, brought printers from Germany to work in the college; but his press had no sanction from the University of Paris and lasted only two years. A printer worked at Oxford from *c*.1478 until 1486, but his relation to the University is not known.

With the advent of the 'new learning' universities needed new texts and printers needed help and protection for issuing them. The University of Leipzig, devoted to humane studies since 1502, took the lead in attracting printers, directing them to Greek and elegant Latin, and defending their books from attack by conservative authorities. The advantages of printing in a university were exemplified in the polyglot Bible produced in 1502–22 at Alcalá de Henares.

The modern conception of a university press owes much to Leyden. The academy founded there in 1575 appointed an official printer from the first, and was served in that capacity by Christophe Plantin (in 1584–5), by the erudite Raphelengius (d. 1595), and three generations of Elzeviers. Their books, edited or approved by the resident professors and well corrected at the press, established the benefits of authority, continuity, and universality that a university can bestow in publishing.

In England the University of Cambridge had power by royal charter to appoint printers to work in its precinct and sell books anywhere since 1534, mainly, no doubt, with a view to propagating defence against heresy (see CAMBRIDGE UNIVERSITY PRESS). It exercised the power from 1583, and Oxford followed the year after (see OXFORD UNIVERSITY PRESS), apparently with only verbal warrant from the queen. Costly conflicts with vested interests contesting the universities' right to override private monopolies in such lucrative works as the *Bible in English, the Book of *Common Prayer, and the Metrical Psalms, induced both universities to forego this privilege in return for money during most of two centuries and to sponsor only works of scholarship.

The press owned, financed, and conducted by a university, as distinct from one censored and protected by it but privately financed and managed, had its origin in England and is still confined to English-speaking countries. Oxford acquired such a press in 1690, when the printing equipment and rights in copy of *Fell came to it by bequest from him. Cambridge took immediate control of its printing in 1698 and exercises it through a board of Syndics.

The style of 'university press' is used by many publishing firms, particularly in Great Britain, the USA, and Canada, some of which also print. They are variously related to the academies from which they take their names. In the USA Cornell opened a small press in 1869, which lasted until 1894, and Johns Hopkins established an agency for publishing in 1875. The University of Chicago has owned its printing and publishing office since 1894. Harvard, Yale, Princeton, Columbia, California, Toronto, among other North American universities, are equipped to print at least some of their publications.

University Wits, name given by *Saintsbury

to a group of Elizabethan playwrights and pamphleteers, of whom *Nashe, R. *Greene, *Lyly, and T. *Lodge were the chief.

Unknown, The Great, title applied to Sir W. *Scott by his contemporaries.

Unquiet Grave, The, (1) a ballad included in *Child's collection, in which a lover laments his dead love for a twelvemonth and a day, at the end of which time she speaks to him from the grave, telling him to content himself and let her sleep; (2) see CONNOLLY, C.

Unreason, Abbot of, see MISRULE.

Unto this Last, see RUSKIN, J.

UPDIKE, John Hoyer (1932–), American novelist, short story writer, and poet, born in Pennsylvania (where his early works are set) and educated at Harvard. His novels include the trilogy *Rabbit, Run* (1960), *Rabbit Redux* (1971), and *Rabbit is Rich* (1981), a small-town domestic tragi-comedy which traces the career of ex-basketball champion Harry Angstrom from the early days of his precarious (but, as it turns out, lasting) marriage to alcoholic Janice, through the social and sexual upheavals of the 1960s, to the compromises of middle age. *The Centaur* (1963) uses a mythological framework to explore the relationship of a schoolmaster father and his teenage son and *Couples* (1968) is a portrait of sexual passion and realignment amongst a group of young suburban married couples in Tarbox, Mass., a town which in this and succeeding works takes on an archetypal quality. Updike's characteristic preoccupations are with the erotic, with the pain and striving implicit in human relationships, and with the sacred (at times explicitly religious) in daily life; these are conveyed in an ornate, highly-charged prose which reaches its most flamboyant in an atypical work, *The Coup* (1979), an exotic first-person narration by the ex-dictator of a fictitious African state. His volumes of short stories (many of which were first published in the *New Yorker*, and several of which feature the representative and recurring marital crises of a couple called the Maples) include *Pigeon Feathers and other stories* (1962), *Museums and Women* (1972), and *Problems and other stories* (1979).

UPWARD, Edward Falaise (1903–), novelist, born in Essex, and educated at Repton and Corpus Christi College, Cambridge, with *Isherwood, whose lifelong friend he became; at Cambridge they both wrote *Barbellion-inspired diaries, and invented the surreal imaginary world of 'Mortmere'. A long Mortmere fragment appeared in Upward's *The Railway Accident and other stories* (1969) and its fantasies are described in Isherwood's *Lions and Shadows* (1938), in which Upward appears as Allen

Chalmers. Upward's *Journey to the Border* (1938) describes the progress of a neurotic tutor in an upper-middle-class household towards commitment to the worker's movement (Upward was for some years a member of the Communist Party); his trilogy *In the Thirties* (1962), *The Rotten Elements* (1969), and *No Home but the Struggle* (1977), published together in 1977 as *The Spiral Ascent*, describe the alternating political and artistic conflicts, over some decades, in the life of Marxist poet and schoolmaster Alan Sebri·l. The last, and most introspective, volume affi·rns the narrator's need for a union of per-so:.al and political commitment in his work.

URBAN, Sylvanus, the pseudonym of E. *Cave and, by succession, of the later editors of the *Gentleman's Magazine*.

URFÉ, Honoré D', see D'URFÉ, H.

Urgan, see ALICE BRAND.

Urizen, a principal character in the symbolic books of *Blake, represented as God of Reason and law-maker, to some extent to be identified with the Hebrew Jehovah; Dorothy Plowman (facsimile edn, *The Book of Urizen*, 1929) suggests his name is taken from the Greek οὐρίζειν, to limit. *The Book of Urizen* (1794) is Blake's version of the myth of Genesis, describing the creation of the material world by Urizen from the 'abominable void', from which is engendered Urizen's opponent, *Los, and Pity, the first female form, who is named *Enitharmon. The spirit of the book is of anguish, revolt, and suffering, and Urizen, after long struggles with Los, surveys his creation in a sorrow that engenders a web, 'The Net of Religion'. In the first plate of *Europe*, Urizen is portrayed majestically as an aged, Newtonian figure leaning down from the sun with a great pair of compasses to create the world.

Urn Burial, see HYDRIOTAPHIA.

URQUHART, Sir Thomas (1611–60), of Cromarty, educated at King's College, Aberdeen, fought at Turriff against the Covenanters, withdrew to London, and was knighted in 1641. He followed Prince Charles to Worcester, where many of his manuscripts were lost, was imprisoned 1651–2, and died abroad. His best-known work is a translation of the first three books of *Rabelais, the first two 1653, the third 1693 (completed by *Motteux). He wrote a number of curious treatises on mathematics, linguistics, etc., with strange Greek titles, collected in 1774 and 1834; among them is *Ekskubalauron* (1651, known as 'The Jewel'), which contains in his 'Vindication of the Honour of Scotland' the story of the 'Admirable' *Crichton. A modern edn, *The Jewel*, ed. R. D. S. Jack and R. J. Lyall, was published in 1984.

Ursula, (1) the pig-woman in Jonson's *Bartholomew Fair*; (2) Hero's maidservant in Shakespeare's *Much Ado About Nothing*; (3) one o' the Brangwen sisters in D. H. Lawrence's *The Rainbow* and *Women in Love*.

Ursula, St, a British saint and martyr, daughte: of a Christian king of Britain, who, according to a 12th-cent. legend, was put to death with 11,000 virgins by the Huns who captured her on pilgrimage near Cologne. The story finds it most distinguished expression in the series o' paintings by Carpaccio in the Galleria in Venice S. *Baring-Gould (in *Curious Myths of the Middle Ages*, 1866–8) traces her to the Swabian moon-goddess Hörsel, the wandering Isis.

'Usher, Fall of the House of', see POE, E. A.

USK, Thomas (d. 1388), the author of *The Testament of Love*, formerly ascribed to *Chaucer and included in Skeat's *Chaucerian and Other Pieces* appended to his edition of Chaucer as Vol. vii. He was under-sheriff of London ir 1387, by the mandate of Richard II, and he wa proceeded against and executed by the 'Merciles Parliament' in 1388. *The Testament of Love* i an allegorical prose-work perhaps written by Usk in prison to elicit sympathy; it is sometime dated in 1385, though this seems too early fo the borrowings from *Troilus and Criseyd which it contains (as well as from *Piers Plow man). Skeat noticed that the first letters of th sections formed an acrostic reading 'Margare of virtu have merci on TSKNVI', and Henry Bradley rearranged the text so that the last letter read THINUSK, i.e. 'thine Usk'. This crypticism is typical of the allusiveness of the poem part of which is now impenetrable. C. S. *Lewi (*The Allegory of Love*, 1936, pp. 222–31) regards the way Margarite is at once real and symbolic as the great interest of the work, while attributing its flaws in style to the excessive influence of Chaucer's *Boece* from which the work borrows its form as instructive debate.

Usnach, The Sons of, see DEIRDRE.

USSHER, James (1581–1656), a scholar o the newly-founded Trinity College, Dublin, be came archbishop of Armagh in 1625. He came to London in 1640. He wrote much on theo logical subjects, and was learned in patristi literature and ancient Irish history. His chie work is the *Annales Veteris et Novi Testamenti*, a chronological summary in Latin of the history of the world from the Creation to the dispersior of the Jews under Vespasian, said to be the source of the dates later inserted in the margins of the Authorized Version of the Bible, which fix the Creation at 23 Oct. 4004 BC. He bequeathed hi collection of books and manuscripts to Trinity College, Dublin.

Uther Pendragon, in the Arthurian legend

king of the Britons and father of *Arthur. Pendragon means 'chief dragon', and Uther has been variously explained; it may be a misreading as a proper name of the Welsh word *uthr*, 'terrible' (an interpretation that squares with *Geoffrey of Monmouth's calling him 'Utherpendragon', undivided). After he became king of the Britons, he lusted after Ygerna, wife of Gorlois, duke of Cornwall. He picked a quarrel with Gorlois and was transformed by Merlin's magic into his shape, whereupon he slept with Ygerna. After the death of Gorlois he married Ygerna who bore him two children, Arthur and Anna. (See IGRAINE.) See Geoffrey of Monmouth, *The History of the Kings of Britain*, trans. L. Thorpe (1966), pp. 151–211 (summary pp. 368–9).

Utilitarianism, an essay by J. S. *Mill, first published in a series of articles in *Fraser's Magazine* in 1861, in book form 1863. The term 'utilitarian' was first adopted by Mill in 1823, from Galt's *Annals of the Parish*. In this work, Mill, while accepting the Benthamite principle (see BENTHAM) that Utility, or the greatest happiness of the greatest number, is the foundation of morals, departs from it by maintaining that pleasures differ in kind or quality as well as in quantity, 'that some *kinds* of pleasure are more desirable and more valuable than others'; also by recognizing in 'the conscientious feelings of mankind' an 'internal sanction' to be added to Bentham's 'external sanctions'. 'The social feelings of mankind, the desire to be in unity with our fellow creatures' constitute 'the ultimate sanction of the greatest happiness, morality'.

Utopia, the principal literary work of Sir T. *More, is a speculative political essay written in Latin. The work was published in 1516 at Louvain, *Erasmus supervising the printing. The form was probably suggested by the narrative of the voyages of Vespucci, printed 1507. The subject is the search for the best possible form of government. More meets at Antwerp a traveller, one Raphael *Hythloday, who has discovered 'Utopia', 'Nowhere land'. Communism is there the general law, a national system of education is extended to men and women alike, and the freest toleration of religion is recognized. The work at once became popular, and was translated by Ralph Robinson into English in 1551, and into French (in 1550), German, Italian, and Spanish. The rapid fame of the book is shown by the reference to Utopians by *Rabelais (III. i, published 1546).

The name 'Utopia' ('no place'), coined by More, passed into general usage, and has been used to describe, retrospectively, Plato's *Republic, and many subsequent fictions, fantasies, and blueprints for the future, including Bacon's *New Atlantis, Harrington's *The Commonwealth of Oceana, Morris's *News from Nowhere, and Bellamy's *Looking Backward. Satirical Utopias include Swift's *Gulliver's Travels and Samuel Butler's *Erewhon, and the word 'dystopia' ('bad place') has been coined to describe nightmare visions of the future, such as Huxley's *Brave New World, *Zamyatin's *We, and Orwell's *Nineteen Eighty-Four, in which present-day social, political, and technological tendencies are projected in an extreme and unpleasant form. Many works of *Science Fiction use the Utopian and Dystopian forms.

UTTLEY, Alison (1884–1976), born on a farm in rural Derbyshire, published many popular children's books, and is best remembered for her 'Little Grey Rabbit' series (of which the first was published in 1929) and for her 'Sam Pig' series (1940 onwards). *The Country Child* (1931) is a vivid and largely autobiographical account of a country childhood. (See also CHILDREN'S LITERATURE.)

V

Vainlove, a character in Congreve's *The Old Bachelor.*

Vala, see FOUR ZOAS, THE.

Valence, Aymer de, in Scott's *Castle Dangerous,* lieutenant to Sir John de Walton.

Valentine, (1) one of *The Two Gentlemen of Verona* in Shakespeare's play; (2) one of *Orsino's court in his *Twelfth Night.*

Valentine and Orson, the subject of an early French romance. Bellisant, sister of King Pepin, is married to Alexander, emperor of Constantinople. The archpriest treacherously accuses Bellisant to her husband and she is banished. A bear carries away one of her children (Orson), who is reared as a wild man. The other (Valentine) is found by Pepin and brought up as a knight. Valentine meets Orson, conquers him, brings him to the court, and tames him. Numerous adventures follow, the principal of which is the imprisonment of Valentine and Orson and their mother Bellisant in the castle of Clerimond, sister of the giant Ferragus, and their rescue by Pacolet, the dwarf messenger of Ferragus, who has a little magic horse of wood which conveys him instantly wherever he wishes.

The story appeared in English about 1550 as the 'History of two Valyannte Brethren, Valentyne and Orson', by Henry Watson. A ballad in Percy's *Reliques* deals with it.

Valentinian, The Tragedy of, a play by J. *Fletcher, performed between 1610 and 1614, published 1647.

A sensational drama with elements of *revenge tragedy, it deals with the vengeance of Maximus, a general under Valentinian III, for the dishonour of his wife by the emperor, and her suicide. A dense web of intrigue and treachery results in the slow death of Valentinian by poisoning (to the accompaniment of the well-known lyric 'Care charming sleep'), and the subsequent death of Maximus, poisoned, again to musical accompaniment, by the widowed empress Eudoxa, as he is inaugurated as Valentinian's successor.

Vale Press, see PRIVATE PRESSES.

Valerian, the husband of St Cecilia, whose story is told in Chaucer's 'The Second Nun's Tale' (*Canterbury Tales, 21).

VALERIUS MAXIMUS, Latin writer of the reign of Tiberius (AD 14–37), who compiled a commonplace book of historical anecdotes. What we possess is an epitome of his work. Widely used during the Middle Ages and the Renaissance, the collection did much to encourage the idea that history is a storehouse of moral examples.

VALÉRY, Paul (1871–1945), French poet, essayist, and critic. As a young man he was deeply influenced by the *Symbolists and, in particular, by the work of *Mallarmé. He became widely known for the poetry of *La Jeune Parque* (1917) and the collection *Charmes* (1922). The latter contains 'Le Cimetière marin' (English trans., 'The Graveyard by the Sea', 1932, and, by *Day-Lewis, 1946). He wrote little poetry after 1922, but published essays on a variety of literary, philosophical, and aesthetic subjects (*Variété,* 1924–44) and two Socratic dialogues, *Eupalinos ou l'architecte* and *L'Âme et la danse* (1923). His notebooks (*Cahiers*), covering the years 1894 to 1945, were published posthumously.

Valley of Humiliation, in Bunyan's *Pilgrim's Progress,* the place where *Christian encounters *Apollyon. There is a beautiful description of it in Pt II, where Mr *Great-heart explains its true character.

Valley of the Shadow of Death, see Psalm 23: 4. Christian, in Bunyan's *Pilgrim's Progress,* passes through it, 'a very solitary place', with a dangerous quag on one side and a deep ditch on the other, and the mouth of hell is close by one side of it, from which issue flames and fiends.

VALLON, Annette, see WORDSWORTH, W.

Valmouth, see FIRBANK, R.

VANBRUGH, Sir John (1664–1726), dramatist and architect, was son of a London tradesman, whose father, a merchant of Ghent, had fled to England from Alva's persecutions. He was imprisoned in France between 1688 and 1692 for spying. In 1696 he produced *The Relapse, or Virtue in Danger,* with immense success, and *The Provok'd Wife* in 1697. His other principal comedies are *The Confederacy* (1705) and *The Provok'd Husband,* which he left unfinished and C. *Cibber completed and brought out in 1728. His collected dramatic works appeared in 1730. He, together with

*Congreve, was specially attacked by Jeremy *Collier in his *Short View*.

Vanbrugh's first building was Castle Howard, 1699–1726. This already shows the grandeur and dramatic quality of his style, which reaches its climax in Blenheim Palace. Hawksmoor assisted him in many of his projects. Vanbrugh was Clarenceux king-of-arms and in 1714 was the first man knighted by George I. (See RESTORATION.)

VAN DER POST, Sir Laurens Jan (1906–), writer, soldier, farmer, and explorer, born in South Africa, whose many works of travel, anthropology, and adventure (much influenced by *Jung) include *The Lost World of the Kalahari* (1958), *The Heart of the Hunter* (1961), *A Story like the Wind* (1972), and *A Far-Off Place* (1974).

VAN DYCK, Sir Anthony (1599–1641), Flemish painter, born in Antwerp. He began to work in *Rubens's studio when a youth, and soon became his chief assistant. He spent a short time in the winter of 1620–1 in the service of James I, but returned to Flanders and was in Italy from 1621 to 1625. In 1632 he came to England as court painter to Charles I. He was knighted and had great success, painting many portraits of the royal family and the Court. He married a lady of the Scottish house of Ruthven in 1640. In England there was little patronage for religious and history painting, and Van Dyck's output was almost exclusively portraits. But, a painter of international repute with a knowledge of the best continental work, he widened the horizons of English art and set the style of the grand portrait for nearly two centuries. He died in England and was buried in Old St Paul's.

Van Dyck's success lay in his ability to portray the poetic ideals that sustained the Caroline court. He painted the king both as warrior monarch and as the perfect gentleman; his mythological portraits (Venetia, Lady Digby, as Prudence; private collection) and those which convey an Arcadian mood—as *Sir John Suckling* (Frick coll., New York)—suggest the atmosphere of the *masque. Van Dyck was a courtier-artist, the friend of men of letters and of the most cultivated patrons of his day; among others, he painted the earl of Arundel, *Laud, E. *Porter, T. *Killigrew the elder, and *Suckling. He was eulogized by *Cowley; *Herrick called him 'the glory of the World, Vandike'; *Waller praised his portraits for showing 'Not the form alone, and grace. | But art and power of a face'.

VANE, Frances Anne, Viscountess, *née* Hawes (1713–88), was the source of the notorious Chapter 81 of *Peregrine Pickle*, 'Memoirs of a Lady of Quality', in which the said lady relates her scandalous adventures to Peregrine. It is probable that *Smollett compiled the memoirs for her, though whether from a written or verbal account remains uncertain. Horace *Walpole referred to Lady Vane as 'that living academy of love-life'.

Vanessa, *Swift's name for Esther Vanhomrigh.

VANHOMRIGH, Esther, see SWIFT, J.

Vanity Fair, in Bunyan's *Pilgrim's Progress*, a fair set up by *Beelzebub, *Apollyon, and Legion in the town Vanity, through which pilgrims passed on their way to the Eternal City. The town was so called because it was 'lighter than vanity', and in the fair were sold all kinds of vanity—houses, honours, kingdoms, and all sorts of delights. There *Faithful was burnt to death; but there, in Pt II, were found some pious persons who could now show their heads, for the blood of Faithful lay as a load upon his oppressors.

Vanity Fair, a novel by *Thackeray, published in numbers 1847–8, illustrated by the author.

The story is set at the time of the Napoleonic wars, and gives a satirical picture of a worldly society, which Thackeray intended to be applied also to his own times. It follows the fortunes of two sharply contrasted characters, Rebecca (Becky) Sharp, the penniless orphaned daughter of an artist and a French opera dancer, and Amelia Sedley, the sheltered child of a rich City merchant. The two girls, as unlike in character as they are in fortune, have been educated at Miss Pinkerton's Academy for young ladies. Becky, having failed to force a proposal of marriage from Amelia's elephantine brother Jos, 'the Collector of Boggley Wallah', becomes governess to the children of Sir Pitt Crawley, a coarse, brutal old man who bullies his fading second wife. Becky manages to charm the Crawley family, and becomes a favourite of Miss Crawley, Sir Pitt's rich and capricious sister. When his wife dies Sir Pitt proposes to Becky, but she has to confess that she is already married, to his younger son Rawdon. The young couple abruptly fall from favour with Miss Crawley, and have to live on Becky's wits.

Meanwhile Amelia's apparently secure life has been disrupted. Her father has lost all his money, and her engagement to George Osborne, the handsome but vain and shallow son of another City magnate, has been broken off in consequence. William Dobbin, George's awkward, loyal friend, who is secretly in love with Amelia, persuades George to defy his father and go on with the marriage, and Mr Osborne disinherits his son.

George, Rawdon, and Dobbin are all in the army, and Amelia and Becky accompany their husbands to Belgium, where Becky carries on an intrigue with George Osborne. George is killed at Waterloo, and Amelia, with her baby son Georgy, goes to live in poverty with her parents, while Becky and Rawdon manage to make a brilliant display in London society on 'nothing a year'. Amelia's devotion to her son is contrasted with Becky's neglect of hers, but she is finally forced by poverty to part with Georgy, who is growing up to be much like his father, to his grandfather. Dobbin, despairing of ever winning Amelia's love, for she is dedicated to the memory of her husband, has spent ten years in India. Becky and Rawdon part, after Rawdon has discovered his wife in a compromising situation with Lord Steyne, who has, it turns out, been paying for Becky's extravagances. Becky leads an increasingly disreputable life on the Continent, and it is hinted that she may be responsible for the death of Jos Sedley, who has insured his life in her favour. Rawdon, who has become governor of Coventry Island, dies of fever. Amelia steadfastly refuses to marry Dobbin, until a chance meeting with Becky, who tells her of George Osborne's infidelity. Disillusioned, she marries Dobbin, but by then his love for her has lost much of its intensity.

Vanity of Human Wishes, The, a poem by Dr *Johnson, published 1749, in imitation of the Tenth Satire of *Juvenal. Less topical than his other long poem, *London*, it owes its success to its moral seriousness and to its weighty but well-illustrated generalizations. Johnson comments on the vanities of various ambitions—for power, learning, military glory, and beauty—and cites the examples of Wolsey, *Clarendon, *Laud, and others: the passage on Charles XII of Sweden is perhaps the finest in the poem, 'quite perfect in form', according to T. S. *Eliot. Johnson's deep religious faith transforms the *Stoicism of the original's conclusion: 'Still raise for good the supplicating voice, | But leave to heav'n the measure and the choice.' This was the first work to which he put his name.

VANSITTART, Peter (1920–), educated at Haileybury and Worcester College, Oxford, was a schoolteacher for 25 years before becoming a full-time writer. His novels range from experimental historical narratives (*Pastimes of a Red Summer*, 1969; *Lancelot*, 1978) to portraits of contemporary life, which include *Landlord* (1970) and *Quintet* (1976).

Varden, Gabriel, a character in Dickens's *Barnaby Rudge*, father of Dolly Varden.

Variorum, or **Variorum Edition,** an edition, especially of the complete works of a classical author, containing the notes of various editors or commentators [*OED*].

Varney, Richard, a character in Scott's *Kenilworth*.

VASARI, Giorgio (1511–74), Italian painter, architect, and author of *The Lives of the most excellent Italian Architects, Painters and Sculptors*

(1550 and 1568), for generations the main source for the history of Italian art. A selection translated by G. Bull appeared in 1965.

VASCO DA GAMA, see GAMA, VASCO DA.

Vathek, an *Arabian Tale*, by W. *Beckford, published in English 1786. The book was written in French and translated into English, with the author's assistance, by Samuel Henley. It was one of the most successful of the *oriental tales then in fashion.

The cruel and sensual Caliph Vathek, whose eye can kill with a glance, is compelled, by the influence of his sorceress mother and by the unbridled pride of his own nature, to become a servant of Eblis, the Devil. He makes a sacrifice of fifty children, and sets off from his capital, Samarah, to the ruined city of Istakar, where he is promised the sight of the treasures of the pre-Adamite sultans. On the way he falls in love with Nouronihar, the exquisite daughter of one of his emirs, who accompanies him on his journey. After various exotic and terrifying incidents, he obtains admission to the great subterranean halls of Eblis, only to discover the sickening worthlessness of the riches that he sees there, and to receive the penalty of his sin, when his own heart and the hearts of all the damned burst into flame in their living bodies. The febrile excitement of the story is sustained by the use of rapid action, exotic locales, and exaggerated passions, often cruel or prurient. *Hazlitt objected to 'the diabolical levity of its contempt for mankind', but critics disagree as to whether the tale is related with a sly irony. Beckford wrote three further 'Episodes' (the last unfinished) for insertion in the story, and included them in his French version of 1815.

Vaudeville, a light popular song or a stage performance of a light and amusing character interspersed with songs, from *vau de vire*, in full *chanson du Vau de Vire*, a song of the Valley of the Vire (in Calvados, Normandy). The name is said to have been first given to songs composed by Olivier Basselin, a fuller of Vire (15th cent.).

'Vaudracour and Julia', see WORDSWORTH, W.

VAUGHAN, Henry (1621–95), was born at Newton-upon-Usk, Breconshire, the son of a Welsh gentleman, Thomas Vaughan of Tretower, and his wife Denise. Henry's twin brother Thomas (below) became a 'natural magician' of repute, publishing several alchemical and Hermetic treatises. Probably in 1628 a third brother William was born. Henry and Thomas were tutored by Matthew Herbert, a noted schoolmaster at Llangattock. By May 1638 Thomas was at Jesus College, Oxford, and Henry almost certainly accompanied him, though his residence is not recorded. Around 1640 Henry probably went to London to study law, though it is not known which Inn admitted him. He may have come within the orbit of the literary set of which *Jonson had been the leader. He returned to Breconshire, probably at the outbreak of the Civil War, and after a spell as clerk to Sir Marmaduke Lloyd, chief justice of the sessions, he may have seen military service on the royalist side. About 1646 he married Catherine Wise. They had a son, Thomas, and three daughters. His wooing of Catherine is apparently recalled in the poem 'Upon the Priory Grove' printed in *Poems with the Tenth Satire of Juvenal Englished* (1646), his first collection. His second, *Olor Iscanus* ('The Swan of Usk'), has a dedication bearing the date 1647, but was not published till 1651. The poems in these two volumes are almost wholly secular, including fashionable love verses and translations from *Ovid, *Ausonius, *Boethius, and the Polish Jesuit Latin poet Casimir Sarbiewski (1595–1640). There is little in them that anticipates the great religious poetry of Vaughan's next volume, *Silex Scintillans* (1650). Some profound spiritual experience, possibly connected with the death of his brother William in 1648 and the defeat of the royalist cause, has been conjectured to account for this change. Further devotional works followed: *The Mount of Olives, or Solitary Devotions* (1652) and *Flores Solitudinis* (1654), which consists of three pious prose translations and a life of St Paulinus of Nola. In 1655 appeared the second edition of *Silex Scintillans*, with a second part added, and also a translation of the *Hermetical Physick* of Henry Nollius. A translation of *The Chymists Key* by the same author followed in 1657. Vaughan's first wife having died, he married her younger sister Elizabeth, probably in 1655. They had a son, Henry, and three daughters. According to a letter he sent to *Aubrey in 1673 he had by that date been practising physic 'for many years with good success'. There is no record of a medical degree, but he may have begun practice as early as the 1640s. His brother Thomas died in 1666, and in 1678 *Thalia Rediviva*, containing poems by both twins, was published.

Vaughan's religious poetry is uneven, but its best moments, like the start of 'The World' ('I saw Eternity the other night') have a limpid, ethereal quality which is wholly distinctive, and which has prevailed with critics to class him as a 'mystic'. He was seized with the idea of childish innocence, and the child's recollections of pre-natal glory. He writes, in 'The Retreat', of his own 'Angel-infancy', when he would muse on clouds and flowers and see in them 'Some shadows of eternity'. He acknowledged, in the preface to the second part of *Silex Scintillans*, his great debt to G. *Herbert, 'whose holy life and verse gained many pious Converts, (of whom I am the least)'. Vaughan's profound fascination with *Hermeticism, and particularly with the idea of sympathetic bonds uniting microcosm and macrocosm, is clear in his poems, many

of which share ideas and even phrases with his brother Thomas's treatises. On the title-pages of *Olor Iscanus* and *Silex Scintillans* Vaughan calls himself a 'Silurist', presumably because his native Brecon was anciently inhabited by the British tribe of Silures.

Works (ed. L. C. Martin, 2nd edn, 1957); Complete Poems (ed. Alan Rudrum, 1976); F. E. Hutchinson, *Henry Vaughan: A Life and Interpretation* (1947; corrected repr. 1971).

VAUGHAN, Thomas (1621–66), twin brother of Henry *Vaughan, whose entry gives details of his background, education, etc. Thomas, a disciple of Cornelius *Agrippa, published various treatises on alchemy, magic, and mysticism, including *Anima Magica Abscondita: or a Discourse on the Universall Spirit of Nature* (1650) and *Magia Adamica; or the Antiquity of Magic* (1650); *Aula Lucis, or the House of Light* (1652); and a Preface to a *Rosicrucian work, *The Fame and Confession of the Fraternity of R.C., commonly, of the Rosie Cross* (1652). Most of his works were published under the pseudonym of 'Eugenius Philalethes'. He was satirized by S. *Butler in his 'Character of a Hermetic Philosopher' (published posthumously) and is said to have suggested some aspects of Ralpho in *Hudibras. Works, ed. A. Rudrum (1984).

VAUGHAN WILLIAMS, Ralph (1872–1958), English composer, and the central figure in the English musical renascence of the first half of the 20th cent. His interest in folk-song, the tradition of amateur music-making, and the works of *Byrd and *Purcell enabled him to escape from the European romantic inheritance of his predecessors and create a new and personal style which created the conditions in which others could do the same.

Vaughan Williams made a large number of settings of the English language: his first published work, the song 'Linden Lea' (1901), to words by W. *Barnes, achieved early popularity, as did other solo settings of this period, including 'Silent Noon', from D. G. Rossetti's *The House of Life, and Songs of Travel, from R. L. *Stevenson. A landmark in the development of his style was the *Housman cycle *On Wenlock Edge* (1909); two years later the *Five Mystical Songs* for baritone, chorus, and orchestra, to poems by G. *Herbert, brought out the visionary quality that was to be characteristic of his mature work. In the 1920s came settings of *Chaucer, Shakespeare, and *Whitman, another Housman cycle, and, after a long gap, the *Ten Blake Songs* (1957) for voice and oboe and *Four Last Songs* (1954–8), settings of poems by the composer's second wife, Ursula Wood.

On a larger scale the first considerable choral work *Toward the Unknown Region* (1907) and *A Sea Symphony* (1909) are both settings of Whitman, who reappears in the cantata *Dona*

Nobis Pacem (1936). The *Five Tudor Portraits* (1935) are made up of extracts from *Skelton, racy, boisterous, and delicate by turns. *Serenade to Music* (1938) is a setting for 16 solo singers and orchestra of Lorenzo's speech from the last act of *The Merchant of Venice*. There is an effective experiment with speaker, chorus, and orchestra in *An Oxford Elegy* (1949, words from Arnold's *'The Scholar-Gipsy' and *'Thyrsis'), and the Christmas cantata *Hodie* (1954) has texts from *Milton, *Hardy, Herbert, and others.

Vaughan Williams also contributed to the liberation of English opera. *Hugh the Drover* (1924) was a pioneering work, leaning heavily on folk-song, and *Sir John in Love* (1929) counterposed an English *Falstaff to *Verdi and *Nicolai. *Riders to the Sea* (1937), an intense and economical setting of *Synge's tragedy, is highly successful. Vaughan Williams's last opera, *The Pilgrim's Progress* (1951) based on *Bunyan, had been in the composer's mind at least since 1909, and one episode, 'The Shepherds of the Delectable Mountains', had been performed as early as 1922.

Vautrin, the master-criminal, one of the most powerful characters of *Balzac's series of novels *La Comédie humaine*. He makes his first appearance in *Le Père Goriot*.

VAUVENARGUES, Luc de Clapiers, marquis de (1715–47), French moralist. After serving as an army officer in the War of the Austrian Succession, he was forced by broken health into premature retirement. His *Introduction à la connaissance de l'esprit humain, suivie de réflexions et de maximes* (1746) put him in the literary tradition of *Pascal and *La Rochefoucauld. Less sceptical than the first and less cynical than the second, he sought in the natural feelings of men and women the source of their best thought and the springs of their moral energy.

Vaux, (1) Roland de, the baron of Triermain, in Scott's *The Bridal of Triermain*; (2) Roland of, in Coleridge's *'Christabel', the estranged friend of the heroine's father.

VAUX, Thomas, second Baron Vaux of Harrowden (1509–56), educated at Cambridge and employed by Wolsey and Henry VIII until 1536, when he fell out of favour until Mary's accession, was a contributor to *Tottel's Miscellany* and *The Paradyse of Daynty Devises*. He is chiefly remembered now as the author of 'The aged Lover renounceth Love', the song mumbled by the grave-digger in *Hamlet*, v. i. His poems were edited by L. P. Vonalt (1960).

Vauxhall, or Fox Hall, originally 'Falkes Hall' (said to be from Falkes de Breauté, captain of John's mercenaries, and lord of the manor in the early 13th cent.), famous for the gardens laid out there in the middle of the 17th cent., and at first called 'The New Spring Gardens', because they replaced the old Spring Gardens adjoining St James's Park. Vauxhall Gardens are frequently referred to from that time by dramatists and other writers, including *Pepys. Sir Roger de Coverley visited them with Mr Spectator (he commented on the scarcity of nightingales in the gardens as compared with less desirable visitors—*Spectator*, No. 383). Thackeray in ch. vi of *Vanity Fair* and Fanny Burney in *Evelina* describe the visits to them of certain of their characters. The gardens were finally closed in 1859.

Veal, (1) Captain, the ship's captain in Fielding's *Journal of a Voyage to Lisbon*; (2) Mrs, see DEFOE, D.

VEGA, Garcilaso, see GARCILASO DE LA VEGA.

VEGA CARPIO, Lope Felix de (1562–1635), Spanish poet and playwright, born in Madrid. He took part in the expedition to the Azores in 1582, and later sailed with the Armada in 1598, an experience which inspired one of his less-regarded works, an epic in 10 cantos, *La Dragontea* (1598), which violently attacks England and *Drake. His personal life was passionate and turbulent; his many love poems are addressed to several mistresses. He was immensely prolific and versatile in many genres, and is regarded as the founder of Spanish drama; he claimed to have written 1,500 plays, of which several hundred survive. These include dramas of intrigue and chivalry, historical dramas, sacred dramas, plays of peasant life, and plays on biblical subjects. His other works include pastoral romances, imitations of *Tasso, and a novel in dialogue called *La Dorotea* (1632). The immense energy and fecundity of his imagination made a profound impact not only in Spain, but on European literature in general, particularly that of France.

Vendice, or Vindice, see REVENGER'S TRAGEDY, THE.

Veneering, Mr and Mrs, in Dickens's *Our Mutual Friend*, types of flashy social parvenus.

Venetia, a novel by B. *Disraeli, published 1837.

Largely written in seclusion, to avoid arrest for debt after Disraeli's heady success in the London society of 1834–5, the novel celebrates, in the author's words, 'two of the most renowned and refined spirits', *Byron and *Shelley. But the story is placed in the 18th cent., and parallels between the lives of Byron/Carducis and Shelley/Herbert are intermittent and subdued to the story of Venetia. She is the daughter of Marmion Herbert and Lady Annabel, who detests her husband's subversive beliefs and lives in England, while he lives in Italy. Venetia becomes obsessed with thoughts of her absent father, and when her childhood friend, the brilliant and moody Carducis, who lives in a neighbouring 'abbey', eventually wishes to marry her, her mother objects to his advanced views, and Venetia herself feels too devoted to her absent father. Venetia and her mother enter society, where she and Carducis enjoy sensational success. But Venetia becomes ill, and she and her mother travel to Italy. On the shore near Spezia they encounter Venetia's father, and he and her mother become reconciled. Carducis and Venetia are joyfully reunited, but he and Herbert are drowned in a squall in the bay of Spezia. After a long illness, and the return home, Venetia marries Carducis's devoted brother.

Venice Preserv'd, or a Plot Discovered, a tragedy in blank verse by *Otway, produced 1682.

Jaffeir, a noble Venetian youth, has secretly married Belvidera, daughter of a proud senator, Priuli, who has repudiated her. Jaffeir, reduced to poverty, begs Priuli for assistance, but is met with insults. Pierre, a foreign soldier with a grievance against the Venetian republic, stimulates Jaffeir's desire for revenge, confides to him a plot that is hatching against the State, and introduces him to the conspirators. As a pledge of his loyalty to them Jaffeir places Belvidera in the charge of their leader, Renault, but without explaining the reason. Renault tries to rape her in the night. She escapes to her husband, who, in spite of his pledge to the contrary, makes known to her the conspiracy. To save her father, who as one of the senators is to be killed, she persuades Jaffeir to reveal the plot to the Senate, but to claim as reward the lives of the conspirators. These are arrested. Jaffeir, loaded by them with insults, is overwhelmed with remorse. The senators, in spite of their promise, condemn the conspirators to death. Jaffeir threatens to kill Belvidera unless she secures their pardon from her father. She succeeds, but Priuli's intervention is too late. Belvidera goes mad. Jaffeir stabs his friend Pierre on the scaffold and then himself, and Belvidera dies broken-hearted.

The play, with *Betterton as Jaffeir and Mrs *Barry as Belvidera, was very well received and frequently revived. It was popular throughout the 18th and early 19th cents, and is still occasionally performed. The bawdy comic scenes in which the masochistic senator Antonio is kicked and abused by his whore Aquilina ('Nicky-Nacky') are strikingly different in tone from the rest of the play, and were at first popular, though by 1750 it was customary to cut them. Antonio is a caricature of *Shaftesbury.

Venn, Diggory, a character in Hardy's *The Return of the Native.

Ventidius, (1) in Shakespeare's *Timon of Athens,* one of the faithless friends of Timon; (2)

in his *Antony and Cleopatra* and in Dryden's *All for Love, one of Antony's generals.

Venus, Mr, in Dickens's *Our Mutual Friend,* a preparer of anatomical specimens and for a time an ally of Silas Wegg.

Venus and Adonis, an Ovidian poem by *Shakespeare, published 1593, the same year in which Marlowe's *Hero and Leander was registered, and dedicated to Henry Wriothesley, earl of Southampton, who has been connected with the *Sonnets. The poem is written in sesta rima, a quatrain followed by a couplet, which Spenser used in *Astrophel (1595) and Lodge in *Scillaes Metamorphosis (1589). Shakespeare's poem was probably his first publication, and was first printed by Richard Field, another Stratford man, in 1593: it was extremely popular, being reprinted at least 15 times before 1640.

Venus, in love with the youth Adonis, detains him from the chase and woos him, but cannot win his love. She begs him to meet her the next day, but he is then to hunt the boar. She tries in vain to dissuade him. When the morning comes she hears his hounds at bay; filled with terror she goes to look for him and finds him killed by the boar.

Vercelli Book, The, an Old English manuscript, made in England before the year 1000, now in the possession of the chapter of Vercelli in North Italy. It contains prose sermons and about 3,500 lines of Old English poetry; its most distinguished contents are the poems *The Dream of the Rood and *Andreas, and two of the four signed poems of *Cynewulf: Elene and The Fates of the Apostles.

ASPR II. The Vercelli Book Poems, ed. F. P. Magoun (1960).

Verdant Green, The Adventures of, see BRADLEY, E.

VERDI, Giuseppe (1813–1901), Italian composer, mainly of operas. Of his 28 works in this form, three are based on Shakespeare and two on *Byron. I Due Foscari (The Two Foscari, 1844) and Il Corsaro (The Corsair, 1848) are relatively early works, of which the former is notable for a certain delicacy of style in comparison with preceding works. Macbeth (1847), the most serious of the operas before Rigoletto, is in a different class. Verdi gave his librettist (Francesco Piave) a more than usually rough passage in his determination to get the text as he wanted it; he took immense pains over the first production, watched over the opera's subsequent career with interest, and subjected it to a thorough revision for Paris in 1865. The Paris version, in which the opera is now heard, betrays its dual origin, yet remains a work of great nobility, and Verdi was stung by Parisian criticism that he did not know his Shakespeare: 'Maybe I haven't done Macbeth justice', he wrote, 'but that I don't know, don't feel, don't understand Shakespeare—no, for God's sake no . . . I have had him in my hands from earliest youth, and I read and re-read him continually.'

This preoccupation with Shakespeare continued throughout Verdi's life, although his next project—an attempt at *King Lear, at which he was to struggle for many years—proved abortive, probably because of dissatisfaction with the text. It was above all the problem of the libretto that made Verdi hesitate to set Shakespeare. But at the end of his life, when he had apparently concluded his career with *Aida* and settled into retirement, he found a librettist who was capable of overcoming the problems and providing him with the framework he needed. The story of Verdi's collaboration with *Boito is touching, and its outcome the two greatest of all operatic settings of Shakespeare. *Otello* (1887) is perhaps the more remarkable achievement: it is rare to find passion and jealousy evoked with such intensity by a man in his seventies. Yet the fleeting, boisterous, tender wisdom of *Falstaff* (1893, after *The Merry Wives of Windsor*), and the technical perfection of its musical realization, provide perhaps Verdi's most personal expression of love for the English poet.

Vere, (1) Arthur de, see DE VERE, ARTHUR; (2) Aubrey de, see DE VERE, AUBREY; (3) Isabella, a character in Scott's *The Black Dwarf.

VERGA, Giovanni (1840–1922), Italian novelist, dramatist, and writer of short stories, born at Catania. His finest works portray life at the lower levels of society in his native Sicily. The novels *I Malavoglia* (1881) and *Mastro-don Gesualdo* (1889) deal respectively with a family of poor Sicilian fisherfolk and an ambitious master stone-mason in economic competition with the local gentry. The story 'Cavalleria rusticana' ('Rustic Chivalry', 1880), after being dramatized by the author, was adapted as a libretto for Mascagni's opera. True to the principles of *verismo*, Verga sought to eliminate from his works all trace of his own personality and outlook, and perfected a unique narrative style, which combined the literary language with idioms and constructions from popular and dialect speech. His English translators include D. H. *Lawrence, whose *Little Novels of Sicily* (1925) and *Cavalleria rusticana and Other Stories* (1928) contain the best of Verga's tales. Lawrence also translated the second of the great Sicilian novels under the title *Master don Gesualdo* (1923).

Verges, head borough or petty constable to *Dogberry's constable in Shakespeare's *Much Ado About Nothing*; his name suggests a possible spelling of 'verjuice' and so his sourness.

VERGIL, the Roman poet, see VIRGIL.

VERGIL, Polydore (?1470–?1555), a native of Urbino, who came to England in 1502 as

sub-collector of Peter's pence, and held various ecclesiastical preferments; he was archdeacon of Wells 1508–54. He was a friend of Sir T. *More and other English humanists. He published his *Anglicae Historiae Libri XXVI* in 1534–55, a chronicle of special value for the reign of Henry VII. He was also author of a *Proverbiorum Libellus* (Venice, 1498) anticipating the *Adagia* of *Erasmus.

Verismo, a movement in 19th-cent. Italian literature akin to *Naturalism, whose greatest writer was the Sicilian *Verga. The affirmation of dialects, after the Unity of Italy (1870) ran counter both to State policies for linguistic unification and to *Manzoni's literary programme for a standard language. Literature was to document social conditions—particularly the 'southern question' which arose in the unified country because of exploitation of southern resources by the industrializing north. *Verismo* influenced the early works of the southern writers *D'Annunzio and *Pirandello, and it relates to post-war *Neo-realism.

Verisopht, Lord Frederick, a character in Dickens's *Nicholas Nickleby.

VERLAINE, Paul (1844–96), French poet. Some of his poems appeared in *Le Parnasse contemporain* of 1866; his *Poèmes saturniens* were published in the same year, and his *Fêtes galantes* in 1869. From the end of 1871 he came under the influence of *Rimbaud and their problematical relationship culminated in Verlaine's arrest and imprisonment, in 1873, for wounding Rimbaud with a revolver. His most interesting work, characterized by an intense musicality and metrical inventiveness, appeared in *Romances sans paroles* in 1874. His influential 'Art poétique' ('De la musique avant toute chose') dates from the same time, but remained unpublished for ten years. *Sagesse* appeared in 1881, *Jadis et naguère* in 1884, and in the same year he published a number of short studies of contemporary poets (including *Mallarmé and Rimbaud) under the title *Les Poètes maudits*. Verlaine's relationship with Rimbaud is the subject of a play by Christopher Hampton, *Total Eclipse* (perf. 1968, pub. 1969).

Verloc, a character in Conrad's *The Secret Agent.

VERNE, Jules (1828–1905), French novelist, who achieved great popularity with a long series of books combining adventure and popular science. Among his most successful stories are: *Voyage au centre de la terre* (1864), *Vingt mille lieues sous les mers* (1869, the adventures of Captain Nemo and his crew aboard the submarine *Nautilus*), and *Le tour du monde en quatre-vingts jours* (1873, recounting the travels of the Englishman Phileas Fogg and his valet Passepartout).

VERNER, Karl Adolph (1846–96), a philologist of Copenhagen, the son of a German father and Danish mother. 'Verner's Law', which completes 'Grimm's Law' (see GRIMM, J. L. C.) of consonantal variations in the Aryan languages, was a notable advance in the science of comparative philology.

Vernon, Diana, the heroine of Scott's *Rob Roy*.

Vers de société, a term applied to a form of light verse dealing with events in polite society, usually in a satiric or playful tone, sometimes conversational, sometimes employing intricate forms such as the *villanelle or the *rondeau. English writers noted for their *vers de société* include *Prior, *Goldsmith, *Praed, *Calverley, *Dobson, and *Locker-Lampson.

Vers libre, a term used to describe many forms of irregular, syllabic, or unrhymed verse, in which the ordinary rules of prosody are disregarded: *Whitman pioneered a form of *vers libre* in America, and its independent evolution in France and Belgium (in the works of *Laforgue, *Maeterlinck, and others in the 1890s) had a great influence on the early *Modernists such as T. S. *Eliot and *Pound.

VERTUE, George (1684–1756), engraver and antiquary, whose notes for a history of the arts in Britain are a major source of information. His notebooks were sold to Horace *Walpole, who used them as a basis for his *Anecdotes of Painting in England*: they were published separately by the Walpole Society (6 vols, 1929–52).

Verver, Adam and his daughter Maggie, characters in *The Golden Bowl* by H. James.

Very Woman, A, see MASSINGER, P.

VESEY, Mrs Elizabeth (?1715–91), an Irish woman, the first, and perhaps the most loved and successful, of the *Blue Stocking hostesses. In the early 1750s she determined, with the support of her husband, who was an Irish MP, to open her doors to literary and fashionable society for an entirely new kind of evening party. Vivacious, intelligent, but always modest, she liked to break her parties into small, ever-changing groups; Horace *Walpole, a devoted attender at all Blue Stocking functions, described her gatherings as 'Babels'. She set the pattern of Blue Stocking evenings for the next 50 years and, according to Hannah *More in her poem *Bas Bleu*, shared with Mrs *Montague and Mrs *Boscawen 'the triple crown' among Blue Stocking hostesses.

Vesey, Sir John, a character in Bulwer-Lytton's comedy *Money*.

Vestiges of Creation, see CHAMBERS, R.

Vholes, a lawyer in Dickens's *Bleak House*.

VIAN, Boris, see ABSURD, THEATRE OF THE.

'Vicar of Bray, The', a well-known song of unknown authorship, dating from the 18th cent. The subject is a time-serving parson, who boasts that he has accommodated himself to the religious views of the reigns of Charles, James, William, Anne, and George, and that 'whatsoever king may reign' he will remain vicar of Bray.

Various suggestions have been made as to who this vicar was. Haydn (*Dictionary of Dates*) quotes *Fuller as stating that Symon Symonds, vicar of Bray, Berks., in the reigns of Henry VIII, Edward VI, Mary, and Elizabeth, was twice a Papist and twice a Protestant. When charged with being a time-server he is said to have replied, 'Not so, neither, for if I changed my religion, I am sure I kept true to my principle, which is to live and die the vicar of Bray' (see *D'Israeli, *Curiosities of Literature*, s.v. Vicar of Bray).

Vicar of Bullhampton, The, a novel by A. *Trollope, published 1870.

Carry Brattle is a 'fallen woman', and her brother Sam is accused of the murder of a local farmer, Trumbull. The arbitrary old marquis of Trowbridge does his best to have them evicted from his land, but reckons without the efforts of Frank Fenwick, one of the best of Trollope's wordly and energetic clergymen. Fenwick solves the murder mystery, clears Sam's name, and restores Carry to society. A sub-plot concerns the love of Fenwick's friend Harry Gilmore for Mary Lowther. Mary and Gilmore are engaged to be married, but the latter nobly steps down when Mary's previous suitor, the ruined Walter Marrable, unexpectedly comes into the family estate.

Vicar of Christ, a papal title, first assumed by Innocent III (1198–1216).

Vicar of Hell, see BRYAN, F.

Vicar of Wakefield, The, a novel by *Goldsmith, published 1766.

This minor classic was sold for £60 by Dr *Johnson on Goldsmith's behalf, to prevent the author's arrest for debt. The plain, detached manner of the narrative carries considerably greater force than the exclamatory style of many novels of *sentiment of the time. In his *Advertisement* Goldsmith describes the vicar, Dr Primrose, as combining 'the three greatest characters upon earth; he is a priest, an husbandman, and the father of a family', who is 'simple in affluence and majestic in adversity'.

Dr Primrose and his wife Deborah live an idyllic life in a country parish with their six children, the most important of whom are George and Moses, Olivia and Sophia. On the eve of their son George's wedding to Arabella Wilmot, the vicar loses all his money through the bankruptcy of a merchant, and the young people cannot marry. George is sent away to town, and the family move to a meagre living on the land of a Squire Thornhill. In the course of the story references are made to the reputed worthiness of the Squire's uncle, Sir William Thornhill. A poor, eccentric friend, Mr Burchell, rescues Sophia from drowning, but her attraction to him is not encouraged by her ambitious mother. Another period of frugal happy family life is disrupted by the attentions of the dashing Squire, who captivates Olivia and encourages the social pretensions of Mrs Primrose and her daughters to a ludicrous degree. Two fashionable ladies from London, friends of Thornhill, offer 'places' to Olivia and Sophia, and the girls angrily dismiss Burchell's warnings. (In a celebrated episode the second son, Moses, sells the family colt in order to raise money for London outfits, but then spends his gains on a 'bargain' of a gross of green spectacles.) Then the girls hear, to their indignation, that because of a letter of Burchell's the London offer has been withdrawn.

Shortly, Olivia is reported as having fled, and Burchell is suspected. The vicar's useless and anguished pursuit ends in three weeks of fever, after which he encounters Arabella at an inn, and falls in with a travelling theatre company. One of the players turns out to be his long-lost son George, who has been travelling abroad seeking a livelihood, and has recently returned. Thornhill reappears, now seriously courting Arabella, and obtains a commission in the army for his rival, George. Further along the road home Dr Primrose observes a distraught young woman being ejected from an inn, and discovers she is his daughter Olivia. Thornhill had pretended to marry her, seduced her, and later cast her off, intending to add her to his other abandoned 'wives', now all prostitutes, but she had escaped. She exonerates Burchell, who had warned her against Thornhill. The vicar receives her with loving joy, and they proceed home, only to find a terrible fire destroying their house.

A period of grim poverty is alleviated by the kindness of parishioners. Thornhill reappears, unrepentant, and offers to find a husband for the ailing Olivia. When he is rejected he demands his rent, which the vicar cannot pay, so he takes all the family's cattle instead. He then has the vicar removed to the debtors' prison where Primrose encounters every degradation, but within a week captures the attention and even the repentance of many of his fellow inmates. But misfortunes crowd in upon him; he hears of Olivia's death, he is told that Sophia has been abducted, and he finds that George has been brought bleeding and half-dead into the prison, having been set upon by Thornhill's servants. At this point Sophia appears with Burchell. She explains how he rescued her from abduction by Thornhill, and in his gratitude the vicar offers

her to Burchell as his wife. Meanwhile George has recognized Burchell as none other than the good Sir William Thornhill. The nephew is denounced as a scheming villain, and Arabella, disabused, is united with George. Olivia, who is not after all dead, was apparently legally wed to Thornhill after all, and he thus loses Arabella's fortune. All proceed home, where Sophia and Sir William, Arabella and George, are married at a double ceremony, the hilarity of which the good vicar is not entirely able to control.

The well-known poems 'The Hermit', the 'Elegy on the Death of a Mad Dog', and 'When lovely woman stoops to folly' are placed at three turning-points of the story.

Vice, The, a fool or buffoon introduced into some of the *interludes and later *Moralities as a figure of evil. The descent of the figure from characters in *Mystery cycles and Morality Plays (such as 'The Vices', the *Seven Deadly Sins) is likely, though they are related too to the mischievous devil figure. See L. W. Cushman, *The Devil and the Vice in the English Dramatic Literature before Shakespeare* (1900; 1970); B. Spivack, *Shakespeare and the Allegory of Evil* (1958).

VICO, Giambattista (1668–1744), Italian philosopher and classical scholar. The son of a poor Neapolitan bookseller, he suffered penury until his appointment in 1734 as royal historian. His most important work is *Principii di una scienza nuova intorno alla natura delle nazioni* (*Principles of a New Science of Nations*, 1725, rev. 1729–30, 1744), in which he developed his theory of historical change as a redemptive design based on 'corsi' and 'ricorsi'—recurring cycles of barbarism, heroism, and reason. To each of these phases correspond cultural, linguistic, and political modes, and at the end of each cycle of phases there is a fall into disorder from which the next cycle is born. The language of poetry, being metaphoric and sensuous, flourishes in the heroic age. It is typified by the Homeric epics, for which Vico was first to postulate collective authorship. Prose enters with the age of reason. This scheme of cycles was put to artistic use by *Joyce.

VICTORIA (1819–1901), queen of England from 1837, wrote innumerable letters and accumulated over 100 volumes of diaries and journals, kept from the age of 13 until shortly before her death. Much was excised by her family, at her wish, but many selections have been published. They are factual and practical, but observant and often vivid in detail. Her only writings published in her lifetime were *Leaves from a Journal of our Life in the Highlands 1848–61*, which appeared in 1868. In spite of a limited vocabulary, the queen's love of Scotland comes clearly through her observations on the views, the weather, and the domestic events of her holidays. Expeditions, such as that up Lochnagar, are undertaken in all weathers, by pony and on foot, with lengthy pauses for spartan picnics and to watch Prince Albert shoot. *More Leaves* covered the years 1862–3 and appeared in 1883. Apart from her huge official correspondence, the queen's lively and heavily underlined letters to her eldest daughter, Vicky, have been published, and also a selection of her daughter's replies.

In her diaries the queen notes her reading, which included many sermons; some Shakespeare; some *Macaulay; F. *Burney and J. *Austen. She took an interest in the novelists of her own reign, including Sir W. *Scott, *Dickens, the *Brontës, Mrs *Gaskell, G. *Eliot, and *Disraeli. But she preferred poetry ('in all shapes'), a preference which led to her friendship with *Tennyson, whom she regarded as the perfect poet of 'love and loss'. Their correspondence has been published. Among many biographical studies, mention may be made of L. *Strachey's highly unauthorized *Life* (1921) and E. Longford's authorized version (1964).

Vignette, an ornamental design on a blank space in a book, especially at the beginning or end of a chapter, of small size, and unenclosed in a border. The word is a diminutive of the Fr. *vigne*, a vine; originally meaning an ornament of leaves and tendrils. It is now, by extension, used for any miniature work, visual, verbal, or musical.

VIGNY, Alfred de (1797–1863), French poet. His ten-year career as an army officer was undistinguished, and he was discharged in 1827. His career as a poet, however, consistently enacted a basic romantic value: stoic pride as the only valid response to the inflexibility of Divine Justice. His historical novel *Cinq-Mars* (1826), based on a conspiracy against Cardinal *Richelieu, his three tales *Servitude et grandeur militaires* (1835), illustrating the self-sacrifice of Napoleon's armies, and his play *Chatterton* (1835), on the fate of the solitary poet in the world, form part of what he called his 'epic of disillusionment' which argued in favour of a reasoned pessimism as a condition for survival. A number of powerful individual poems, such as 'La mort du loup', 'Le mont des oliviers', and 'La bouteille à la mer' (collected posthumously in 1863), proclaim a more positive, though equally romantic, faith in 'man's unconquerable mind'.

Village, The, a poem by *Crabbe, published 1873.

The poet contrasts the cruel realities of country life with the Arcadian pastoral favoured by poets. He was assisted in the writing of the work (which Dr *Johnson found 'original, vigorous, and elegant') both by his patron *Burke and by Johnson. The poem established Crabbe's reputation as a writer.

'Village Blacksmith, The', a poem by *Longfellow.

Villanelle, a poem, usually of a pastoral or lyrical nature, consisting normally of five three-lined stanzas and a final quatrain, with only two rhymes throughout. The first and third lines of the first stanza are repeated alternately in the succeeding stanzas as a refrain, and form a final couplet in the quatrain [*OED*]. The form has been much employed in light verse and *vers de société* by A. *Lang, A. *Dobson, and others, and in the 20th cent. was used to more serious purpose by *Auden, *Empson ('Slowly the poison the whole blood stream fills'), Dylan *Thomas ('Do not go gentle into that good night'), and others.

VILLEHARDOUIN, Geoffroi de (*c*.1152–1212), a member of a powerful French crusading family which ruled over a great court at Achaea, marshal of Champagne, was an eyewitness of the events described in his *Conquête de Constantinople,* an account of the so-called fourth Crusade, the first great literary work in French prose. Villehardouin relates with vigour and picturesqueness the negotiations with the doge of Venice, the departure of the crusading host, its diversion from its proper purpose to various more secular undertakings, including the capture of Constantinople, the subsequent dissensions and intrigues, culminating in the crowning of Baldwin of Flanders as emperor of the East, and the grant of the kingdom of Macedonia to Boniface of Montferrat. See M. R. B. Shaw, *Chronicles of the Crusades: Joinville and Villehardouin* (1963).

Villette, a novel by C. *Brontë, published 1853.

The novel, like its predecessor * *The Professor* (then unpublished), is based on the author's experiences in Brussels, here renamed Villette, and also has as its centre a pupil–teacher relationship. The narrator, Lucy Snowe, poor, plain, and friendless, finds herself a post as teacher in a girls' school in Villette, where she wins the respect of the capable, if unscrupulous, headmistress, Madame Beck, and gains authority over the boisterous girls. She becomes deeply attached to the handsome John Bretton, the school's English doctor, in whom she recognizes an acquaintance from her childhood, the son of her own godmother; she watches his infatuation with the shallow and flirtatious Ginevra Fanshawe, followed by a happier love for his childhood friend Pauline Home, and represses her own strong feelings for him. These feelings gradually attach themselves to the waspish, despotic, but goodhearted little professor, M. Paul Emmanuel, Mme Beck's cousin, whose own response to her changes from asperity to esteem and affection, despite Mme Beck's attempts to discourage the friendship. His generosity leaves her mistress of her own school when he is called away on business to the West Indies; the ending is ambiguous, and the reader is left to decide whether he returns to marry her or is drowned on his way home. The novel combines a masterly portrayal of Belgian daily life with a highly personal use of the elements of *Gothic fiction; Charlotte Brontë uses hints of the supernatural (the story of a ghostly nun, a visit to the mysterious and deformed Mme Walravens) to heighten the impression of her heroine's nervous isolation and heroic fortitude; but all the apparitions are found to have realistic explanations, and in Paul Emmanuel she successfully creates an unromantic hero very far removed from the *Byronic Rochester of *Jane Eyre.

VILLIERS DE L'ISLE-ADAM, Philippe-Auguste (1838–89), French novelist, dramatist, and aesthete. His best-known work, the visionary drama Axël (1890, English trans. Fineberg, 1925), which first appeared in symbolist reviews, is a Wagnerian narrative of love and death set in an isolated German castle, which enshrines *Rosicrucian mysteries. Its symbolic subtleties have exerted an influence on English writing which has only recently begun to be recognized; it provided a title for E. *Wilson's study of symbolist writers, Axel's Castle (1931).

VILLON, François (1431–after 1463), French poet. He studied at the University of Paris, gaining a master's degree in 1452. The little that is known of his life suggests nearly constant turmoil: he was imprisoned several times for violent crime and theft, and narrowly escaped death by hanging in 1463. His surviving work consists mainly of Le Lais (or Petit Testament) and Le Testament (or Grand Testament); the latter contains the famous 'Ballade des dames du temps jadis', with its refrain, 'Mais où sont les neiges d'antan?' In addition to these two works a number of short poems survive, including Villon's own epitaph, 'Frères humains qui après nous vivez', written under sentence of death. He is now recognized as pre-eminent among the poets of medieval France. He has been frequently translated into English since the 19th cent.; there are versions of individual poems by *Rossetti, *Swinburne, and R. *Lowell, among others.

Vincentio, (1) Lucentio's father in Shakespeare's *The Taming of the Shrew; (2) the duke in his *Measure for Measure.

VINCENT OF BEAUVAIS, the Dominican author of Speculum Naturale, Historiale, Doctrinale (c.1250), an enormous compilation of all the knowledge known at the time. He is mentioned by Chaucer in one version of the Prologue to *The Legend of Good Women (G 307).

Vincy, Fred and Rosamond, characters in G. Eliot's *Middlemarch.

Vindication of a Natural Society, A, a treatise by E. *Burke, published anonymously 1756, his first substantial work. It is an ironical answer to *Bolingbroke's indictment of revealed religion, in imitation of his style and in the form of a reductio ad absurdum; it was so successful a parody that even *Warburton was deceived by it, and in 1765 Burke published another edition with a preface explaining his ironical stance. Bolingbroke had exalted the claims of natural religion by pointing to the unfortunate results of religious creeds; Burke points to the evil results of artificial society and the artificial division of rich and poor, but expects his exposition to reinforce 'the necessity of political institutions, weak and wicked as they are'.

Vindication of the Rights of Woman, A, by M. *Wollstonecraft, published 1792.
    In this work the author attacks the educational restrictions and 'mistaken notions of female excellence' that keep women in a state of 'ignorance and slavish dependence'. She argues that girls are forced into passivity, vanity, and credulity by lack of physical and mental stimulus, and by a constant insistence on the need to please; she attacks the educational theories of the 'unmanly, immoral' *Chesterfield, of *Rousseau (who in her view made false and discriminatory distinctions in his approach to the sexes in Émile), and of other writers, concluding that 'From the tyranny of man . . . the greater number of female follies proceed.' The work was much acclaimed, but also inevitably attracted hostility; Horace *Walpole referred to its author as 'a hyena in petticoats'.

Vindice, see REVENGER'S TRAGEDY, THE.

Vindobona, in imprints, Vienna.

Vinegar, Captain Hercules and family, introduced by Fielding in *The Champion.

Vinegar Bible, The, an edition of the Bible printed by *Baskett at Oxford in 1716–17, so called from the substitution or misprint of the word 'vinegar' for 'vineyard' in the heading of Luke 20.

VINER, Charles (1678–1756), published A General Abridgement of Law and Equity in 23 vols (1742–53), and the Vinerian professorship at Oxford, first held by *Blackstone in 1758, was founded from his bequests.

Violenta, one of the dramatis personae of Shakespeare's *All's Well that Ends Well who appears only once (III. v) in the play and does not speak; sometimes referred to as a typical nonentity.

Virago Press, see FEMINIST CRITICISM.

Virelay, a song or short lyric piece, of a type originating in France in the 14th cent., usually consisting of short lines arranged in stanzas with only two rhymes, the end-rhyme of one stanza being the chief one of the next [OED].

Virgidemiarum, Sex Libri, by J. *Hall, two volumes of English satires, 1597 and 1598. The first volume, called 'Toothless', treats mildly certain literary conventions in the spirit of *Martial and *Horace; the second volume, Juvenalian in character, 'bites' fiercely into such ills as sexual promiscuity, ostentatious piety, impostures in astrology and genealogy, economic injustices, etc. The title means 'a sheaf of rods', with which the satirist delivers his blows. The books were condemned by the High Commission in 1599, along with satires by *Marston, *Nashe, and others; but Hall's books were reprieved.

VIRGIL (Publius Vergilius Maro) (70–19 BC), the greatest of Roman poets, valued particularly for his craftsmanship, love of nature, and sense of pathos. Maturing at a time when the Romans were struggling to produce a literature that would match the Greek, he imitated successively the pastorals of *Theocritus, the didactic poems of *Hesiod and Aratus, and the epics of *Homer, making original contributions to all three genres. In his *Eclogues* he added a new level of meaning to the pastoral's idealization of country life by alluding to topics of contemporary interest; in the *Georgics* he transformed the bald didacticism of his models into a panegyric of Italy and the traditional ways of rural life; and in the *Aeneid* he committed the epic to the presentation of a major patriotic theme. He began like most poets of his generation by working within the conventions of *Hellenistic poetry, but later, when he came to enjoy the patronage of Augustus, he widened his stylistic range and, drawing also on earlier and more naïve authors, created a diction and a manner of presentation that were all his own.

Everyone who could read Latin (and until the latter half of the 19th cent. that covered all educated persons) read Virgil; and although it is easy to trace borrowings from his works, these fall far short of representing the totality of his influence, which was pervasive rather than specific. Many generations found in him their main gateway to the *Sublime. In the Middle Ages he was regarded as a seer and a magician, and the 'Messianic Eclogue' (below) led *Dante to choose him as a guide through Hell and Purgatory. His *Aeneid* served as a model for all the Latin epics of the medieval period and then for the new classical epic of the Renaissance. There are Virgilian similes in *Spenser, Virgilian motifs in Shakespeare's *Rape of Lucrece* and Milton's *Paradise Lost*. The *Georgics*, comparatively neglected earlier, came into their own in the 18th cent., when they provided a model for descriptive poets like J. *Thomson and were seriously discussed by writers on agriculture. In the 19th cent. came *Wordsworth's 'Laodamia' and

*Tennyson's avowal in 'To Virgil' of an indebtedness beyond the obvious.

A legion of translators was attracted to Virgil. *Dryden's version of his works (1697) remains probably the finest in spite of its occasional defects. Gavin *Douglas, writing in Scots, produced a vivid *Aeneid* (1513) and W. *Morris a ponderously medieval one (1885). Recently there have been interesting translations by C. *Day-Lewis of the *Georgics* (1940) and the *Aeneid* (1952).

Virgilia, in Shakespeare's *Coriolanus*, the wife of Coriolanus.

Virgil's Fourth or Messianic Eclogue, written 40 BC, celebrated the coming birth of a child who would bring back the Golden Age. This was taken in the Middle Ages to be a prophecy of the birth of Christ, and the interpretation appeared the more plausible because the poem contains imagery reminiscent of the Bible. The voluminous literature provoked by this work has focused on two problems: the first, the identity of the child (Augustus'? Antony's?); the second, the puzzle of the language. Was Virgil acquainted with Hebrew tradition? And if so, why did he choose to draw on it here? A plausible explanation advanced recently is that Virgil's source was not the Bible, but Sibylline writings originating in a South Italian culture that had come under Phoenician influence.

'Virgils Gnat', a poem by *Spenser, published 1591, and adapted from the *Culex* attributed to *Virgil. A shepherd sleeping in the shade is about to be attacked by a serpent, when a gnat, to warn him, stings him on the eyelid. The shepherd crushes the gnat, and sees and kills the serpent. The next night the ghost of the gnat reproaches him for his cruelty. The shepherd, filled with remorse, raises a monument to the gnat. In what way the poem reflects Spenser's relations with the earl of Leicester, to whom it was dedicated 'Long since', will probably never be known.

Virginia, a daughter of the centurion Lucius Virginius. Appius Claudius, the decemvir, became enamoured of her and sought to get possession of her. For this purpose she was claimed by one of his favourites as daughter of a slave, and Appius in the capacity of a judge gave sentence in his favour and delivered her into the hands of his friend. Virginius, informed of these proceedings, arrived from the camp, and plunged a dagger into his daughter's breast to save her from the tyrant. He then rushed to the camp with the bloody knife in his hand. The soldiers, incensed against Appius Claudius, marched to Rome and seized him. But he destroyed himself in prison and averted the execution of the law. This incident led to the abolition of the decemviral power. The story (which is in *Livy, iii. 44 *et seq.*) is the basis of two plays called *Appius and Virginia*, one by *Webster and/or *Heywood, one by *Dennis; of *Knowles's tragedy *Virginius*; and of *Macaulay's lay 'Virginia'.

Virginians, The, a novel by *Thackeray, published in numbers, 1857–9.

The novel takes up the story of the Esmond family a generation after the events of *The History of Henry Esmond*, and mainly concerns the fortunes of Esmond's twin grandsons, George and Harry Warrington, in America and England. Their mother, Esmond's only daughter Rachel, favours her younger son Harry, and is capricious and autocratic in her treatment of George. The boys are alike in appearance, but totally different in character, George being serious and scholarly, Harry cheerful, volatile, and attractive. However, they always remain close friends. When George disappears in a military expedition against the French and is presumed dead, Harry, now the heir, visits England, and meets his Castlewood relations, whose corrupt behaviour is in marked contrast to Harry's New World innocence. Under their influence Harry plunges into gambling and dissipation, and is inveigled into an engagement to his much older cousin, Maria. He is arrested for debt and imprisoned in a spunging-house. He is rescued by the sudden reappearance of George, who has escaped from the French and come to England. Maria releases Harry from his engagement, since he is no longer heir to a fortune. But when George falls in love with and marries Theo, the daughter of a poor soldier, General Lambert, rather than an American heiress, his mother cuts off his allowance, and he is only saved from penury by becoming the heir of Sir Miles Warrington, of the English branch of the family. Harry has become a favourite of the rakish old Baroness Bernstein, the former Beatrix Esmond, and she leaves money to him in her will. Harry joins the army, and is with Wolfe at the capture of Quebec. He falls in love with Fanny Mountain, the daughter of his mother's housekeeper, and marries her rather than Hetty Lambert, Theo's sister, who is in love with him. When the War of Independence breaks out, Harry joins Washington, and George, who is in the British army, resigns his commission rather than run the risk of fighting against his brother. He settles on the Warrington estates in England, and gives up the Virginian property to Harry.

Virgin Martyr, The, a tragedy by *Massinger and *Dekker, printed 1622.

The Emperor Diocletian bids his daughter Artemia choose whom she will marry. She chooses Antoninus, a brave soldier, son of Sapritius, governor of Caesarea. He declines the dangerous honour, being moreover devoted to Dorothea, a maid of the Christian sect, which is at the time subject to persecution. Theophilus, a zealous persecutor, and his secretary Harpax, 'an evil spirit', betray Antoninus and Dorothea to Artemia, who finds them together, and at once orders them to execution, but presently allows Theophilus to send his daughters to Dorothea to convert her to the pagan religion. The daughters, instead, are converted by Dorothea to Christianity, and on their boldly professing it are killed by their own father. Dorothea, attended by her 'good spirit' Angelo, is subjected to extremes of torture and indignity and finally executed, Antoninus dying by her side. In the last act, Angelo and Harpax, the good and evil spirits, contend for the soul of Theophilus. Theophilus, summoned before Diocletian, proclaims his conversion to Christianity, courageously suffers torture, and dies. The same story has been treated in poems by *Swinburne and G. M. *Hopkins.

Virgin Queen, a name for Queen *Elizabeth I.

Virtuosi, see LITERATI.

Vision of Judgement, A, a poem in hexameters by R. *Southey, published 1821, at the time when Southey was poet laureate.

The preface, written in defence of this metrical innovation, contains, in a digression, a violent attack on the works of *Byron, 'those monstrous combinations of horrors and mockery, lewdness and impiety'. Byron retorted with his parody *The Vision of Judgement* (below).

The poet in a trance sees George III (who had died in 1820) rise from the tomb and, after receiving from the shade of Perceval news of affairs in England, proceed to the gates of Heaven. The Devil, accompanied by *Wilkes, comes forward to arraign him, but retires discomfited, and the king, after receiving a eulogy from Washington, is admitted to Paradise, where he is greeted by previous English sovereigns, the worthies of England, and finally by his family.

Vision of Judgement, The, a satirical poem by Lord *Byron, published in *The Liberal*, 1822.

In 1821 there appeared *A Vision of Judgement* by the poet laureate, *Southey, containing in the Preface a violent attack on Byron's works, and describing Byron as the leader of the 'Satanic school' of poetry. Byron replied with an exuberant travesty of Southey's poem. George III, at the celestial gate, is on his way to Heaven, but is hindered by Satan's claim to his soul. Byron, attacking the pomposity and sycophancy of Southey, gives to Satan and his witnesses a lively and formidable indictment of the king's reign. Southey is swept up from the Lake District by one of the devils, which, with Tory angels, enliven the story. He offers to write Satan's biography and is in all respects treated to the author's derision. When he attempts to read aloud his own 'Vision' he is knocked back down to his Lakes, and George slips into Heaven. While departing very little from its form, Byron totally transforms the tone and import of Southey's poem, substituting his own values and beliefs with verve and comic brilliance.

'Vision of Mirzah, The', an allegory by *Addison, published in *The Spectator* (No. 159). Mirzah has a vision of human life as a bridge over which multitudes are passing, some dropping through concealed trap-doors into the flood beneath; he also sees the happy islands of the virtuous dead.

Vita Nuova, see DANTE.

VITRUVIUS POLLIO (*fl.* 40 BC), Roman architect and author of *De architectura,* the only surviving classical treatise on architecture. It was much studied by Renaissance and later architects; the first printed editon was published in 1486.

Vittoria, a novel by G. *Meredith, published 1867.

The continuation of *Sandra Belloni,* this crowded novel was Meredith's attempt 'to put blood into history' and to write something that was 'all story . . . no Philosopher present'. It is set in northern Italy during the failed revolution of 1848–9, led by Mazzini, who appears as a heroic figure. The ardent Sandra, now a singer, throws herself into the cause of Italian independence, singing (under the name of Vittoria) in the opera in Milan the song which is the signal of revolt. But her continuing involvement with her English friends, particularly with Wilfrid Pole (now an officer in the Austrian army), brings her under suspicion. This, together with various other enmities, involves her and the gallant Carlo, whom she marries, and Wilfrid himself, in a series of dangers from which she emerges widowed. Merthyr Powys reappears as her devoted friend and protector.

Vittoria Corombona, see WHITE DEVIL, THE.

Vivian Grey, a novel by B. *Disraeli, published 1826, with a continuation in 1827.

This was the first of Disraeli's novels, published anonymously when he was 22 and written, as he later observed, 'with imagination acting upon knowledge not acquired by experience'. The first of a group of three novels (see ALROY and CONTARINI FLEMING), it represented, in its author's words, 'my active and real ambition'. Vivian, a brilliant and difficult boy, is expelled from school, and discovers that by clever manipulation of his charm and social skills he can advance himself in the world of politics. He becomes the protégé of the marquis of Carabas, a powerful but disappointed politician, and by cynically playing on the follies of various discontented peers and MPs builds a faction round the marquis. His secret efforts to create a new

party are exposed by the tempestuous Mrs Lorraine (a reminiscence of Lady Caroline *Lamb). Vivian is challenged to a duel by the outraged Cleveland, leader-designate of the party, whom Vivian kills. All hopes destroyed, the young man leaves England and begins a desultory life of intrigue, adventure, and lost love among German princelings and principalities. The last four Books were added by popular demand in 1827.

Disraeli came to dislike the novel, which he regarded as 'puerile'. The character of the unprincipled Vivian dogged him for many years, and he tried to suppress the book, but pirated editions abroad forced him to reprint, and in 1853 he drastically revised the work. Among various identifications, the kindly, scholarly Mr Grey represents Disraeli's father, Isaac *D'Israeli, the dashing Lord Alhambra has something of *Byron, the marquis of Carabas of John *Murray (who was extremely angry), and Cleveland of *Lockhart.

VIZETELLY, Henry (1820–94), son of a publisher and engraver, of a family Italian in origin, but long settled in England; he became an engraver, publisher, journalist, and editor, whose defiance of censorship and policy of issuing cheap reprints had a considerable impact on the literary scene. In 1885 he joined forces with G. A. *Moore to publish a cheap one-volume edition of *A Mummer's Wife,* an act which did much to break the power of the circulating *libraries and the three-decker novel; in 1886 with H. *Ellis he founded the *Mermaid Series of unexpurgated reprints of 'Best Plays of the Old Dramatists'. He also published translations of *Flaubert, *Gogol, *Tolstoy, the *Goncourts, etc., and 17 novels by *Zola; it was his publication of Zola's *La Terre* that led to his three-month imprisonment in 1888 on an obscenity charge, despite the protests of *Bradlaugh, *Gosse, Ellis, and others. This bankrupted his publishing company. Vizetelly had many friends in the artistic and literary world, including *Thackeray, *Doré, and *Sala, and his memoirs, *Glances Back through Seventy Years* (1893), give a lively portrait of 19th-cent. Bohemia.

VOLNEY, Constantin François de Chasseboeuf, comte de (1757–1820), French historian, travel-writer, and *philosophe,* author of *Les ruines, ou Méditation sur les révolutions des empires* (1791), in which contemplation of the ruins of Palmyra becomes the occasion for reflections on the rise, progress, and decline of ancient civilizations and the prospect for modern ones. The soul of the narrator, enlightened by a spirit, the Genius of Tombs and Ruins, comprehends through a conspectus of human history that man's miseries have at all times been the result of his ignorance, greed, and neglect of natural law; but that, guided by Nature and Reason, he will at last come to know his own best interest. Putting aside the dual tyranny of religious superstition and political despotism, he will perfect his nature and establish freedom, equality, and justice. *Les ruines* was translated into English in 1795 and (generally known as *Ruins of Empire*) had a certain currency in England through the early 19th cent., especially among rationalists and freethinkers. It was a favourite book of *Shelley's, providing the plan for his *Queen Mab*; in Mary Shelley's *Frankenstein* it is one of four books by means of which the monster receives his education.

Volpone, or *The Fox*, a comedy by *Jonson, performed by the King's Men in 1605–6, printed 1607.

Volpone, a rich Venetian without children, feigns that he is dying, in order to draw gifts from his would-be heirs. Mosca, his parasite and confederate, persuades each of these in turn that he is to be the heir, and thus extracts costly presents from them. One of them, Corvino, even attempts to sacrifice his wife to Volpone in hope of the inheritance. Finally Volpone overreaches himself. To enjoy the discomfiture of the vultures who are awaiting his death, he makes over his property by will to Mosca and pretends to be dead. Mosca takes advantage of the situation to blackmail Volpone, but rather than be thus defeated Volpone chooses to reveal all to the authorities. They direct that Volpone shall be cast in irons until he is as infirm as he pretended to be, Mosca whipped and confined to the galleys, Corvino made to parade in ass's ears, and his wife be returned to her family with a trebled dowry. A secondary plot involves Sir Politic Would-be, an English traveller who has absurd schemes for improving trade and curing diseases, and his Lady, a loquacious, hectoring pedant. Sir Politic is chastened when Peregrine, a wiser English traveller, pretends to have him arrested for treason. The names of the principal characters, Volpone (the fox), Mosca (the fly), Voltore (the vulture), Corbaccio (the crow), Corvino (the raven), indicate their roles and natures.

Volscius, Prince, a character in Buckingham's *The Rehearsal*. He is torn between love and honour, and comes on the stage with one boot on and one off, his legs illustrating his distraction.

Volsunga saga, a prose version of a lost cycle of heroic songs of which fragments survive in the poetic *Edda, dealing with the families of the Volsungs and the Niblungs. It has been translated by W. *Morris and E. Magnusson (1888). For the treatment in it of the story of Sigurd and Brunhild, see SIGURD THE VOLSUNG.

VOLTAIRE, pseudonym of François-Marie Arouet (1694–1778), French satirist, novelist, historian, poet, dramatist, polemicist, moralist, critic, and correspondent. Voltaire was the universal genius of the *Enlightenment. Welcomed in the free-thinking circles of Parisian society, he was committed to the Bastille for his satires in 1717–18, and again exiled to England in 1726–9. The remainder of his life was divided between long periods of retreat in the provinces (first in Champagne with Mme du Châtelet, finally at Ferney near Geneva) and brief returns to metropolitan centres (Paris, Versailles, Berlin). His literary principles were fundamentally neoclassical: his epic poem *La Henriade* (1723 and 1728), on the career of Henry of Navarre, and his heroic tragedies, notably *Zaïre* (1732), a Turkish tale of fated love, exhibit all the formality, decorum, artificiality, and lucidity of the mode. His political principles were essentially liberal. The *Lettres philosophiques* (1734, English version 1733), inspired by his residence in England, attack the abuses of the *ancien régime* in the name of tolerance and liberty, while his history *Le Siècle de Louis XIV* (1751) disregards providence as an explanatory principle, seeking instead evidence of social and moral progress. His most characteristic works, however, were his philosophical tales, notably *Zadig* (1747) and *Candide* (1759) in which the rapidity, cleverness, and precision of his mind are put to the service of elaborating a rational protection against the basic evils of life. His relentless mockery of the cruelty and obscurantism of the civil and ecclesiastical establishments was the source of both his persecution and his immense prestige.

Volumnia, in Shakespeare's *Coriolanus, the mother of Coriolanus. A proud, imperious Roman matron, she rejoices in her son's exploits; but it is her eloquence that saves Rome from the Volscians, at her son's expense.

VON ARNIM, Elizabeth (1866–1941), novelist and cousin of K. *Mansfield, was born Mary Annette Beauchamp in Sydney, Australia. In 1890 she married Count Henning August von Arnim-Schlagenthin, who appears as 'the Man of Wrath' in her best-known work, *Elizabeth and her German Garden*, published anonymously in 1898; it describes her family life and the garden she created at Nassenheide in Pomerania. E. M. *Forster and Hugh *Walpole were tutors to her children there. After von Arnim's death she was married in 1916 to Bertrand *Russell's brother, the second Earl Russell. She published several novels, including *Pastor's Wife* (1912) and *Vera* (1921).

VON HÜGEL, Friedrich, baron of the Holy Roman Empire (1852–1925), Roman Catholic theologian and philosopher. He was born in Florence and after a cosmopolitan education settled in England in 1867. He studied natural science, philosophy, and religious history, adopting the critical views of the Old Testament. In 1905 he founded the London Society for the

Study of Religion, which brought him into touch with thinkers and scholars of the most diverse views. His works include *The Mystical Element of Religion* (1908), *Eternal Life* (1912), and *The Reality of God* (published posthumously, 1931).

VONNEGUT, Kurt (1922–), American novelist and short story writer, whose works mingle realism, *Science Fiction, fantasy, and satire. They include *Player Piano* (1952), *Cat's Cradle* (1963), and *Slaughterhouse-Five; or The Children's Crusade* (1969), a novel inspired by Vonnegut's own experience of the bombing of Dresden in the Second World War.

VORAGINE, Jacobus de, see GOLDEN LEGEND.

Vorticism, an aggressive literary and artistic movement that flourished 1912–15; it attacked the sentimentality of 19th-cent. art and celebrated violence, energy, and the machine. The Vorticists, dominated by W. *Lewis, included *Pound, *Gaudier-Brzeska, the painters C. R. Nevison and Edward Wadsworth; they were associated with T. E. *Hulme, F. M. *Ford, and the sculptor Jacob Epstein (*Rock Drill*, 1913, Tate Gallery, London). In the visual arts this revolutionary fervour was expressed in abstract compositions of bold lines, sharp angles, and planes; the Vorticist style was indebted to *Cubism and *Futurism, although Lewis mocked the Futurist obsession with speed (E. Wadsworth, *Abstract Composition*, 1915, Tate Gallery, London; Wyndham Lewis, *Composition*, 1913, Tate Gallery, London). *Blast: the Review of the Great English Vortex*, published in June 1914 and edited by Lewis, was an ambitious attempt to establish in England a magazine dedicated to the modern movement and to draw together artists and writers of the avant-garde. Its long lists of the blasted and blessed, its mixture of flippancy and rhetoric, and its provocative title and typography were designed to jolt the English out of their complacent insularity. Several artists adapted the Vorticist style to First World War subjects, but the real impetus petered out after the Vorticist Exhibition held at the Doré Gallery in 1915.

Vortigern, a legendary 5th-cent. king of Britain who is reputed to have enlisted Hengist and Horsa against his former allies the Picts, thus causing the transfer of Britain to the Anglo-Saxons. He marries Renwein (Rowena), the daughter of Hengist. After a lifetime of feuds and alliances with the Germanic invaders, in the course of which he meets Merlin and is astonished by his prophecies, he is burnt alive in the tower in Wales to which he had retired. The story is told in *Geoffrey of Monmouth's *History* (vi. 6–viii. 2) and in *Laȝamon's *Brut*, 14,255–396.

Vortigern and Rowena, see IRELAND, W. H.

Voss, a novel by P. *White.

VOSSIUS, Gerhard John (1577–1649), and Isaac (1618–89), his son, eminent Dutch scholars. The father, who was invited to England and made a canon of Canterbury, was professor of history at Amsterdam and author of *Historia Pelagiana*. The son came to England and was a canon of Windsor 1673–89. He published editions of *Catullus and *Juvenal and *Observations* on classical subjects.

Vox Clamantis, see GOWER, J.

VOYNICH, Ethel Lillian, *née* Boole (1864–1960), novelist, born in Cork, remembered for her revolutionary novel *The Gadfly* (1897), set in pre-1848 Italy, which sold in vast quantities in translation in the Soviet Union. She married a Polish revolutionary, and worked in London for the periodical *Free Russia*.

Vril, see COMING RACE, THE.

Vulgar Errors, see PSEUDODOXIA EPIDEMICA.

Vulgate, The, from the Latin *vulgatus*, 'made public or common', a term applied more particularly to St *Jerome's Latin version of the Bible completed in *c*.404. The Clementine text of this, a recension made by order of Clement VIII (1592–1605), is the authorized Latin text of the Roman Catholic Church. See BIBLE.

Vulgate Cycle, The, a very important group of Arthurian romances in French prose, dating from 1215–30. It comprises the three romances which make up the Prose *Lancelot* (*Lancelot* itself, the *Queste del Saint Graal*, and *Mort Artu*) and two others: the *Estoire del Saint Graal*, and a version of Robert de *Boron's partially surviving *Merlin*. The group is the most influential version of the Arthurian legends between *Geoffrey of Monmouth and *Malory. Ed. H. O. Sommer (7 vols, 1908–13); see ch. 22–3 by J. Frappier and H. Micha in *Arthurian Literature in the Middle Ages* (1959).

VYAZEMSKY, Prince Pyotr Andreevich (1792–1878), Russian poet and intimate friend of *Pushkin. His poetry is elegant, polished, and witty; as a critic he is one of the main theorists of Russian Romanticism. His use of the term in an article of 1817 is considered to be the first mention of it in Russia. He was a great admirer of *Byron and Sir W. *Scott, and did much to advance their reputation in Russia. In 1838 Vyazemsky visited England, taking a cure of sea-bathing at Brighton, spending time in the circle of Lady *Morgan and meeting Horace *Smith. He visited the Royal Pavilion, discussed the woman question with Lady Morgan in the light of her book *The Woman and her Master*, listened to the Chartist O'Connor, visited the duke of Norfolk's estate at Arundel and the Isle of Wight, read *The Spectator* and discussed the

Irish question (Vyazemsky's mother was an Irishwoman by the name of O'Reilly, and he made vague attempts to trace his ancestors). He then spent some time in London, visiting Westminster, Newgate Prison, and Drury Lane. His impressions of England are contained in the thirteenth of his 'Notebooks'. His conclusion is uncannily like that of *Zamyatin eighty years later: 'In English life there is nothing unexpected, *imprévu*, and therefore the general result must be boredom.'

Vye, Eustacia, a character in Hardy's *The Return of the Native.*

W

WACE (*c.*1100–after 1171), wrote in French verse of 15,000 short couplets the *Roman de Brut* (or *Geste des Bretons*), completed 1155 and dedicated to *Eleanor of Aquitaine, which is based on *Geoffrey of Monmouth's *Historia Regum Britanniae*. This work was the principal source of *Laȝamon's *Brut*. He also wrote a *Roman de Rou* (i.e. Rollo) (or *Geste des Normands*), a history of the dukes of Normandy in the course of which he provided some apparently autobiographical information. He was made a canon of Bayeux by Henry II. The *Roman de Brut* is circumstantial, commonsensical, and well written, adding substantially to Geoffrey's version. It survives in 22 manuscripts, including the four manuscripts of *Gaimar in which Wace's poem has been substituted for Gaimar's account of the *Historia*. It retained considerable influence up to the 14th cent.

Ed. I. Arnold (2 vols, 1938–40); trans. in E. Mason, *Arthurian Chronicles* (1912).

Wackles, Mrs and the Misses Melissa, Sophy, and Jane, in Dickens's *The Old Curiosity Shop*, kept a 'Ladies' Seminary' at Chelsea.

WADDELL, Helen Jane (1889–1965), medieval scholar and translator, born in Tokyo, and educated at Queen's University, Belfast. She is best remembered for her popular study of the 'vagantes' of the Middle Ages, *The Wandering Scholars* (1927), for her anthology of imaginative but sometimes misleading translations from their works in her *Medieval Latin Lyrics* (1929), and for her novel *Peter Abelard* (1933), based on the life of *Abelard.

Wade, Miss, a character in Dickens's *Little Dorrit*, a suspicious, venomous woman who entices away Tattycoram from the Meagles family.

Wade's boat in *Chaucer's 'The Merchant's Tale' (*Canterbury Tales*, 10):

> And eek thise olde wydwes, God it woot,
> They konne so muchel craft on Wades boot,
> So muchel broken harm, whan that hem leste
> (IV. 1423–5).

According to *Skeat's note, Wade was a famous hero of antiquity who is mentioned in various poems and in *Malory (Caxton VII, ix; interestingly, it appears to be Caxton's addition, not being in Vinaver's *Sir Gareth* from the Winchester manuscript: *Works*, p. 188). The 'tale of Wade' is also mentioned in *Troilus and Criseyde*, iii. 614. Speght in his 1598 edition of the Tales forbears from telling the story of Wade on the ground that it is too familiar. Wade (mentioned in the Old English *Widsith, 22) was the father of Wayland, who in Norse legend built a famous boat to escape his pursuers; Robinson in his note on these lines suggests that the boat may have become transferred to the son (1957 edn, p. 714). But its meaning in Chaucer's context here becomes obscure.

Wadman, Widow, or Mrs, in Sterne's *Tristram Shandy*.

Wagg, Mr, in Thackeray's *Vanity Fair* and *Pendennis*, a parasitical journalist and diner-out, based on T. *Hook.

Waggoner, The, a poem by *Wordsworth, composed 1805, published 1819 with a dedication to Charles *Lamb.

It tells how Benjamin the Waggoner, driving home his team of eight horses through the night among the Lakeland hills, escapes the temptation of the Swan Inn, but falls victim to that of the Cherry-Tree, and loses his place in consequence. But no one else can drive the team, and Lakeland loses both waggoner and wain.

Wagner, the attendant of Faust in Marlowe's *Dr Faustus* and in *Goethe's *Faust*.

WAGNER, Richard (1813–83), German composer, dramatist, and writer, whose theories and works were the subject of vigorous controversy throughout the second half of the 19th cent. He set himself to create, out of materials inherited from the German Romantic tradition and from French and Italian grand opera, a new and compelling synthesis of music and drama (for which he wrote both words and music). His ideas, like his personality, were on the grandest scale; Der *Ring des Nibelungen (based on the *Nibelungenlied), planned as a single drama, developed backwards (each episode requiring previous explanation for its proper understanding) until the finished work required four separate evenings and eventually the construction of a new type of theatre for its complete performance.

His theoretical writings reached beyond the musical field: a revolutionary in 1848–9, he later came under the influence of *Schopenhauer, and his writings include much that has social, political, and more generally cultural implications. His first champion in this country was G. B. *Shaw; later Ernest Newman became the 'Perfect Wagnerite'. (See MUSIC, LITERATURE OF.) The composer's complete prose works were translated into English by W. Ashton Ellis (8 vols, 1892–9). Among the English musical public early resistance gave way to a passionate involvement, and the literary world also felt the shock of his achievement: *Swinburne wrote poems on the preludes to Lohengrin and Tristan and an elegy, 'The Death of Richard Wagner' (all in A Century of Roundels, 1883), and D. H. *Lawrence's The Trespasser (originally entitled The Saga of Siegmund) is deeply Wagnerian in its symbolism, as is much of Lawrence's later work. G. A. *Moore and C. *Morgan also make substantial reference to Wagner as do three of the most influential literary works of the 20th cent., *The Waste Land, *Ulysses, and *Finnegans Wake, all of which quote directly from Wagner's operas.

The music of Wagner's mature operas is indissolubly linked with the text, and the subjects are in all cases German in origin. Of his early works, however, his third opera, Das Liebesverbot (1836), is an adaptation of *Measure for Measure (after mainly French and Italian models). Its successor, Rienzi, modelled more obviously on French grand opera, is based on *Bulwer-Lytton's novel and, to some extent, on M. R. *Mitford's drama of the same name. The later masterpieces, Tristan und Isolde and Parsifal, are drawn entirely from German sources, and can claim only a generic connection with British legend.

WAIN John Barrington (1925–), poet, critic, and novelist, born in Stoke-on-Trent and educated at Newcastle under Lyme and St John's College, Oxford. He lectured at Reading, 1947–55, and was professor of poetry at Oxford 1973–8. His first novel, Hurry On Down (1953), is an episodic and picaresque account of the career of Charles Lumley, who, on leaving university, rejects his lower-middle-class origins by working as window-cleaner, crook, hospital orderly, chauffeur, and bouncer. It has been linked with the novels of W. *Cooper, K. *Amis, and J. *Braine as a manifestation of the spirit of the *'angry young men' of the 1950s. Other novels include The Contenders (1958), A Travelling Woman (1959), and Strike The Father Dead (1962), again a novel about a rebellious young man, who runs away from school and the expectations of his 'red-brick' professor father to become a jazz pianist. As a poet Wain was associated with the *Movement and contributed to *New Lines. He published several volumes of verse, collected in Poems 1949–79 (1981), a volume of autobiography, Sprightly Running (1962), and a biography of Dr *Johnson (1974). Later fiction includes The Young Visitors (1965), The Pardoner's Tale (1978), and Young Shoulders (1982).

WAINEWRIGHT, Thomas Griffiths (1794–1852), apprentice painter, soldier, then art journalist. He wrote as an art critic for the *London Magazine, 1820–3, and became the friend of *Hazlitt, *Lamb, *De Quincey, and others. He exhibited at the *Royal Academy, 1821–5, began to live far beyond his means, and forged an order on the bank. In 1827 he published The Life of Egomet Bonmot Esq., largely consisting of sneers at writers. After insurance frauds, a poisoning, and prison in Paris, he was tried and transported to Tasmania, where he died. He is the original of Varney in *Bulwer-Lytton's Lucretia and the victim in *Dickens's story 'Hunted Down'.

Waiting for Godot, the first stage play of S. *Beckett, published in French as En attendant Godot, 1952, staged in French in Paris, 1953, first staged in English in Cambridge, 1955.

One of the most influential plays of the post-war period, it portrays two tramps, Estragon and Vladimir, trapped in an endless waiting for the arrival of a mysterious personage named Godot, while disputing the appointed place and hour of his coming. They amuse themselves meanwhile with various bouts of repartee and word-play, and are for a while diverted by the arrival of whip-cracking Pozzo, driving the oppressed and burdened Lucky on the end of a rope. Towards the end of each of the two acts, a boy arrives, heralding Godot's imminent appearance, but he does not come; each act ends with the interchange between the two tramps, 'Well, shall we go?' 'Yes, let's go', and the stage direction, 'They do not move.' There are strong biblical references throughout, but Beckett's powerful and symbolic portrayal of the human condition as one of ignorance, delusion, paralysis, and intermittent flashes of human sympathy, hope, and wit has been subjected to many varying interpretations. The theatrical vitality and versatility of the play have been demonstrated by performances throughout the world. (See also ABSURD, THEATRE OF THE.)

Wakefield, Harry, the English drover in Scott's *The Two Drovers.

Wakefield Master, Wakefield (or Towneley) **Plays,** see MYSTERY PLAYS.

Wakem, Mr and Philip, characters in G. Eliot's *The Mill on the Floss.

WALCOTT, Derek Alton (1930–), poet and playwright, born in St Lucia, in the West Indies, and educated at the University College of the West Indies. He founded the Trinidad Theatre Workshop in 1959, and many of his own plays had their first performances there. These include Dream on Monkey Mountain (1967, pub. 1971), The Joker of Seville (1974, pub. 1978; based on Tirso da Molina's El Burlador de Sevilla; see TÉLLEZ), and O Babylon!

(1976, pub. 1978; set amongst a Rastafarian community in Kingston, Jamaica). His collections of poetry include *In a Green Night: Poems 1948–60* (1962), *The Castaway and other poems* (1965), *Sea Grapes* (1976), and *The Fortunate Traveller* (1982). Both plays and poetry show a preoccupation with the national identity of the West Indies and their literature, and with the conflict between the heritage of European and West Indian culture ('the choice of home or exile, self-realisation or spiritual betrayal of one's country', in his own words). Walcott's plays mingle verse and prose, Creole vocabulary and the rhythms of calypso, and his poems, many of which are confessional and self-questioning, are rich in classical allusion and evoke with equal vividness both Caribbean and European landscapes.

Waldeck, Martin, the subject of a legend from the German interposed in Scott's *The Antiquary*, a charcoal-burner enriched by gold obtained from the demon of the Harz Mountains, and brought to an evil end by his wealth.

Walden, or *Life in the Woods,* see THOREAU, H. D.

Waldenses, or **Waldensians** (in French, *Vaudois*), the adherents of a religious sect which originated in the south of France about 1170 through the preaching of Peter Waldo, a rich merchant of Lyons. They rejected the authority of the pope and various rites, and were excommunicated in 1184 and subjected to persecution. But they survived and eventually became a separately organized church, which associated itself with the Protestant Reformation of the 16th cent. and still exists, chiefly in northern Italy and the adjacent regions. Their persecution by the duchess-regent of Savoy in 1655 led to *Milton's sonnet, 'Avenge, O Lord, thy slaughtered saints', and caused *Cromwell to insist on his new ally, France, putting an instant stop to the massacre.

'Waldhere', the name given to two short fragments of an Old English poem in a manuscript of the late 10th cent., totalling 63 lines. It is thought that the poem they come from is an epic of considerable length, perhaps 1,000 lines. The manuscript is in the Royal Library at Copenhagen. We know from other sources that Waldhere was the son of a king of Aquitaine, who was given up to Attila the Hun and became one of his generals. He escapes with Hiltgund, a Burgundian princess to whom he had been betrothed as a child. In the course of their flight they are attacked, and Waldhere, after slaying his assailants in a first fight, is ambushed and wounded the next day. But they are able to continue the journey and are finally married. It is paralleled by the 10th-cent. Latin poem *Waltharius*. Ed. F. Norman (1933; rev. 1949).

WALEY, Arthur David (1889–1966), poet and authority on Chinese and Japanese literature, which he introduced to a wide public through his well known translations. He taught himself the languages while working in the Print Room at the British Museum, and in 1918 published *A hundred and seventy Chinese poems*, which went into several editions, appealing (in his own words) 'to people who do not ordinarily read poetry', largely through their emphasis on the concrete and particular. His translations are unrhymed, elegant, and lucid; his use of stressed and unstressed syllables had, he believed, something in common with G. M. Hopkins's *Sprung Rhythm. His other translations in prose and verse include *The Tale of Genji* (1925–33), *The Pillow-book of Sei Shonagon* (1928, from the diary of a 10th-cent. Japanese court lady), and *Monkey* (1942, translation of a 16th-cent. Chinese novel). He also published many works on oriental art, history, and culture, but despite frequent invitations, never visited the Far East. He spent most of his life in Bloomsbury, where he was on friendly terms with many of the *Bloomsbury Group and the *Vorticists. See Alison Waley, *A Half of Two Lives: A Personal Memoir* (1982).

WALKER, Thomas (1784–1836), of Trinity College, Cambridge; called to the bar 1812; magistrate of Lambeth Police Court 1829. He is noted as the author of a weekly periodical, *The Original*, of which 29 numbers appeared (20 May to 2 Dec. 1835). Each number contains short articles on a variety of subjects; its purpose was to raise 'the national tone in whatever concerns us socially or individually', and it is especially remembered for Walker's admirable papers on health and gastronomy.

WALLACE, Alfred Russel (1823–1913), left school at 14, was apprenticed to a schoolmaster in Leicester, then accompanied the naturalist Henry Walter Bates on a trip to the Amazon in 1848, an expedition described in Wallace's *Travels on the Amazon and Rio Negro* (1853). A further voyage to the Malay archipelago is described in *The Malay Archipelago* (1869). In 1858, during an attack of fever at Ternate in the Moluccas, the idea of natural selection as the solution to the problem of evolution flashed upon him, and he at once communicated it to C. *Darwin. The outcome, a testimony to the generosity of both, was the famous joint communication to the *Linnean Society on the theory of evolution. He published numerous other works and scientific papers and in 1905 his autobiography, *My Life*.

WALLACE, (Richard Horatio) Edgar (1875–1932), a very successful and prolific writer of thrillers, which include *The Four Just Men* (1905), *The Crimson Circle* (1922), and *The Green Archer* (1923). He also wrote successful plays, and died in Hollywood, where he had been working on the screenplay of *King Kong*, which was produced after his death.

WALLACE, Sir William (?1272–1305), Scottish patriot of the time of Edward I, who devoted his life to resistance to the English and was finally captured by treachery and executed in London. He is the subject of a long poem by *Henry the Minstrel.

WALLENSTEIN, Albrecht Eusebius von (1583–1634), an Austrian general celebrated for his campaigns in the Thirty Years War. After many victories he was defeated by Gustavus Adolphus at Lützen in 1632. He now prepared to abandon the Imperial cause; but Ferdinand II, suspecting his intention, removed him from his command. Wallenstein was murdered by some of his officers when he was believed to be on the point of going over to the Swedes. His career is the subject of a great historical trilogy by *Schiller, of which the two last parts were translated by *Coleridge.

WALLER, Edmund (1606–87), educated at Eton and King's College, Cambridge, entered Parliament early and was at first an active member of the opposition. In 1631 he married a London heiress who died in 1634. Later he became a royalist, and in 1643 was leader in a plot to seize London for Charles I. For this he was imprisoned, fined, and banished. He made his peace with *Cromwell in 1651, returned to England, and was restored to favour at the Restoration. After the death of his first wife he unsuccessfully courted Lady Dorothy Sidney, 'Sacharissa' of his poems; he married Mary Bracey as his second wife in 1644. Waller was a precocious poet; he wrote, probably as early as 1625, a complimentary piece on *His Majesty's Escape at St Andere* (Prince Charles's escape from shipwreck at Santander) in heroic couplets, one of the first examples of a form that prevailed in English poetry for some two centuries. His verse, much of it occupied with praise of Sacharissa, Lady Carlisle and others, is of a polished simplicity; *Dryden repeatedly praised his 'sweetness', describing him as 'the father of our English numbers', and linking his name with *Denham's as poets who brought in the *Augustan age. His early poems include 'On a Girdle' and 'Go, lovely rose'; his later *Instructions to a Painter* (1666, on the battle of Sole Bay) and 'Of the Last Verses in the Book', containing the famous lines, 'The Soul's dark cottage, battered and decayed, | Lets in new light through chinks that time hath made.' His *Poems* first appeared in 1645, *Divine Poems* in 1685, *Poems*, ed. G. Thorn-Dury, 2 vols, 1893.

WALLIS, John (1616–1703), mathematician and founder member of the *Royal Society, was Savilian professor of geometry at Oxford,

1649–1703. His *Arithmetica Infinitorum* (1655) contained the germs of differential calculus.

WALPOLE, Horace, fourth earl of Orford (1717–97), fourth son of Sir Robert *Walpole, was educated at Eton, where he formed a happy 'Quadruple Alliance' with friends of like tastes, T. *Gray, R. *West, and Thomas Ashton; then at King's College, Cambridge. In 1737 his mother, to whom he was deeply attached, died, and six months later his father married his long-term mistress Maria Skerrett. In 1739–41 Walpole travelled in France and Italy with Gray, and met in Florence H. *Mann, who became one of his most valued correspondents. At Reggio he and Gray quarrelled and parted company, for reasons which have given rise to much inconclusive discussion, and were probably connected with Walpole's more sociable and less studious notions of entertainment. Walpole was MP successively for Callington, Castle Rising, and Lynn, 1741–67. From 1741 he spent some time at his father's new home at Houghton, where the dullness of country life was alleviated by the excellent collection of paintings, which he catalogued and described in *Aedes Walpolianae* (1747). His father died in 1745, and in 1747 Walpole, supported by various sinecures, settled in Twickenham in the house he made known as *Strawberry Hill: he made it into 'a little Gothic castle', aided by his fellow enthusiasts *Chute and R. *Bentley (the younger), and in it collected articles of virtu. In 1748 he had three poems published in *Dodsley's *Collection*, and in 1757 he established his own printing press at Strawberry Hill. His first publication was Gray's Pindaric odes; he and Gray had been lastingly reconciled in 1745. In 1758 he printed his own *A Catalogue of the Royal and Noble Authors of England*, a light-hearted work which later attracted much censure when it reached a wider public through a London bookseller. In the same year he printed several minor poems, essays, etc., as *Fugitive Pieces in verse and prose*, and in 1762 his *Anecdotes of Painting in England*. His Gothic novel *The Castle of Otranto* (1764) appeared at first pseudonymously, purporting to be a translation from an Italian work of 1529. In 1765 he paid the first of several visits to Paris, where he received a warm welcome, and met Mme du *Deffand, with whom he formed a lasting friendship; he was less enchanted (though not himself religious) with the prevailing atmosphere of rationalism and freethinking. In 1768 he published *Historic Doubts on the Life and Reign of King Richard the Third*, in which he attempted to acquit Richard of the crimes imputed to him by history, and in the same year appeared his tragedy *The Mysterious Mother*. In 1787/8 he met the sisters Agnes and Mary Berry, who became intimate friends of his last years; in 1791 they settled at Little Strawberry Hill, where Mrs *Clive had been his neighbour until her death six years earlier. In the same year he succeeded his nephew to the earldom, and inherited an estate loaded with debt. Although he had been plagued by severe gout for many years, and was increasingly dependent on Mary Berry's company for his good spirits, he seems to have remained cheerful and mentally active until the end of his life.

Walpole left his Memoirs ready for publication in a sealed chest, which was opened in 1818. *Memoires of the last ten years of the Reign of George II* was edited by Lord Holland, 2 vols, 1822, and *Memoirs of the Reign of King George the Third* by D. Le Marchant, 4 vols, 1845. His literary reputation rests largely on his letters, which are remarkable for their charm, their wit, and their autobiographical, political, and social interest. His model was Mme de *Sévigné, whose letters he greatly admired, and he clearly wrote for posterity as well as for his correspondents, who included Mann, his cousin Henry Seymour Conway, the countess of Upper Ossory, George Montagu, Mary Berry, and others to whom he could express his many varied interests. His letters to Mme de Deffand were destroyed at his own wish, possibly because he was ashamed of his imperfect French; hers to him were edited by Mrs Paget Toynbee in 1912. Some of his correspondence appeared with his works in 1798, ed. by Mary Berry in her father's name: Mrs P. Toynbee's edition (16 vols, 1903–5, plus various later vols) has been followed by the monumental Yale edition, ed. W. S. Lewis et al. (42 vols, 1937–81, with one vol. additions and corrections and 5 vols index to follow). These later editions, with recent biographies (e.g. R. W. Ketton-Cremer, *Horace Walpole*, 1946) have done much to dispel the 19th-cent. image of Walpole, inspired by *Macaulay's famous attack in the *Edinburgh Review*, 1833, as a malicious and affected gossip, though even Macaulay had allowed that he possessed 'irresistible charm'. His name has now also been cleared of the accusation that he hastened *Chatterton's suicide by his neglect: initially deceived by a fake manuscript sent to him by Chatterton in 1769, he later suspected a hoax and withdrew his active support, for which Chatterton bitterly reviled him, although Walpole was in no way to blame for the incident and indeed throughout treated Chatterton with consideration, and spoke of him after his death with much respect.

WALPOLE, Sir Hugh Seymour (1884–1941), novelist, was born in New Zealand, the son of a bishop, and came to England aged five. He was educated at King's School, Canterbury, and Emmanuel College, Cambridge; his short experience of teaching is reflected in his third novel, *Mr Perrin and Mr Traill* (1911), which set a vogue for novels and plays about schoolmasters. *The Dark Forest* (1916) is based on his wartime service with the Russian Red Cross.

Other works include *Jeremy* (1919), the first of three stories about a young boy, and the *Herries Chronicle*, a historical sequence set in Cumberland (where Walpole lived from 1924), consisting of *Rogue Herries* (1930), *Judith Paris* (1931), *The Fortress* (1932), and *Vanessa* (1933). Although proud of his popularity, he worried that his work was 'old-fashioned' and expressed envy of the *modernism of his friend and correspondent V. *Woolf; he was deeply offended by *Maugham's portrait of him as Alroy Kear, a hypocritical literary careerist, in *Cakes and Ale* (1930). There is a life by R. Hart-Davis (1952).

WALPOLE, Sir Robert, first earl of Orford (1676–1745), father of Horace *Walpole, and the leader of the Whig party, was prime minister and chancellor of the exchequer 1715–17, and again 1721–42. His longstanding relationship with his mistress Maria Skerrett (whom he married on his wife's death in 1737) is satirized in Gay's *The Beggar's Opera* ('How happy could I be with either'), as are his quarrels with *Townshend in the quarrel between Peachum and Lockit. In 1737, provoked by this and other satirical attacks in the theatre (by *Fielding in particular) he introduced the Licensing Act, which was bitterly attacked by writers of the time and has been blamed for the decline of the drama in the 18th cent. (See Appendix I.)

WALSH, William (1663–1708), poet, was author of various pastorals, elegies, and songs, but is chiefly remembered for his encouragement of and influence on the young *Pope, whose 'Pastorals' he praised; according to *Spence, he imparted to Pope the desire to make correctness his 'study and aim'. Pope praised him in his *Essay on Criticism* as 'the Muse's judge and friend'.

WALTON, Izaak (1593–1683), born at Stafford, was apprenticed in London to a kinsman who was a draper and a member of the Ironmongers' Company, and later carried on trade there on his own account. He was a friend of *Donne and *Wotton and of Bishops Morley, Sanderson, and *King. He was twice married, and spent the latter part of his life at Winchester, where his son-in-law was prebendary. His biographies of Donne (1640), Wotton (1651), *Hooker (1665), G. *Herbert (1670), and Sanderson (1678) are gentle and admiring in tone. He is chiefly known for *The Compleat Angler*, first published 1653, and largely rewritten for the second edition (1655), which is half as long again. Often reprinted, this work combines practical information about angling with folklore, quotations from writers as diverse as *Pliny, *du Bartas and Herbert, pastoral interludes of songs and ballads, and glimpses of an idyllic rural life of well-kept inns and tuneful milkmaids. (See also COTTON.)

Walton, Sir John de, in Scott's *Castle Danger-ous*, governor of Douglas Castle.

WALTON, Sir William Turner (1902–83), English composer. Walton's early association with the *Sitwell family was the background to the work by which he first became known, the brilliant and witty 'entertainment' *Façade* (1922) for reciter with six instrumental soloists. Twenty-one poems of Edith Sitwell (recited at earlier performances by the poet herself) were accompanied by a score which took its point of departure entirely from the rhythms, sounds, and allusions of the words: the first public performance provoked a scandal ('Drivel They Paid To Hear' ran one headline the next morning), but the piece has since come to be regarded as a minor classic of 20th-cent. English music. (Walton later arranged two orchestral suites from *Façade*, though without reference to the texts that originally gave them birth.) Three poems of Edith Sitwell were also set as independent songs, but the other main Sitwell contribution to Walton's musical output was the text of the dramatic cantata *Belshazzar's Feast* (1931), skilfully arranged by Osbert Sitwell from biblical sources. A later choral work, *In Honour of the City of London* (1937), is a setting of *Dunbar. Walton came to opera late in life with *Troilus and Cressida* (1954), an adaptation of *Chaucer. He only made one other experiment in this field (a one-act setting of *Chekhov's *The Bear* in 1967), but he wrote excellent incidental music for Laurence Olivier's three Shakespeare films: *Henry V* (1944), *Hamlet* (1947), and *Richard III* (1955). Of these, only three pieces from *Henry V* have been published, the composer feeling that his film music should only be heard in its original context. The same restriction applies to the score which he wrote for a stage production of *Macbeth* (1941). To the later period of his career belong two short song cycles, *Anon in Love* with accompaniment for guitar (1960) and *A Song for the Lord Mayor's Table* (1962), six songs to words by various poets.

WALWYN, William (*fl.* 1649), pamphleteer and a leader of the Leveller movement, came from an upper-middle-class background in Worcestershire and prospered as a cloth merchant. He was imprisoned in 1649 with *Lilburne, *Overton, and T. Prince as one of the authors of *England's New Chains discovered*, and was accused of communism and atheism. He was released later that year, after the publication of *Walwyn's Just Defence*. A well-read man, he advocated in his many tracts liberty of conscience and voluntary community of property, quoting *Montaigne in support of his own humane rationalism.

Wamba, in Scott's *Ivanhoe*, 'the son of Witless', the devoted and heroic jester of Cedric the Saxon.

Wanderer, The, an Old English poem of 115 lines in the *Exeter Book, one of the group known as 'elegies', telling of the hardships of a man who has lost his lord. It is a plangent lament for the transience of life, culminating towards its end in a powerful *'ubi sunt' passage. It begins and ends with a brief and bald statement of Christian consolation, but that is not the prevailing sentiment of the poem. It is paralleled in spirit and structure by the *Seafarer, particularly in the latter's first half, and similar arguments have been advanced for and against the coherence of organization in both poems. The poem was admired by *Auden, among other modern poets, and he translated it loosely. Ed. R. F. Leslie (1966), A. J. Bliss and T. P. Dunning (1969).

Wanderer, The, a poem in five cantos by R. *Savage (1729); some of it has been attributed to his friend A. *Hill. Its design is obscure; its message, conveyed to the Wanderer by a Hermit, appears to be that 'affliction purifies the mind', but its most noteworthy passages are descriptive, and it contains some fresh observations of nature and landscape. Dr *Johnson observed that it was 'a heap of shining materials thrown together by accident, which strikes . . . with the solemn magnificence of a stupendous ruin'.

Wanderer, The, or *Female Difficulties*, a novel by F. *Burney.

Wandering Jew, the, a Jew condemned to wander about the world until Christ's second coming because, according to the legend, as Christ bore the cross to Calvary the Jew chid him, and urged him to go faster.

A pamphlet was published in Leyden in 1602, relating that Paulus von Eizen, bishop of Schleswig, had in 1542 met a man named Ahasuerus, who declared that he was the Jew in question. The story, which had previously flourished in Spain and Italy, became popular, and many instances of the Wandering Jew are recorded from the 16th to the 19th cents.

But a somewhat similar story is told much earlier by *Roger of Wendover, in his *Flores Historiarum*. An Armenian archbishop visited England in 1228, and, while being entertained at St Albans, was asked if he had ever seen or heard of Joseph, who was present at the Crucifixion, and was said to be still alive, as a testimony to the Christian faith. The prelate replied that the man had recently dined at his own table. He had been Pontius Pilate's porter, by name Cartaphilus, who, when they were dragging Jesus from the Judgement Hall, had struck him on the back, saying, 'Go faster, Jesus, why dost thou linger?', to which Jesus replied, 'I indeed am going, but thou shalt tarry till I come.' This man had been converted soon after and named Joseph. He lived for ever, and was now a very grave and holy person.

The legend of the Wandering Jew has been

the subject of many German works; *Goethe contemplated (but did not write) a poem on the subject of a meeting of Ahasuerus and *Spinoza, and C. F. D. Schubart (1739–91) wrote a romantic version identifying the Jew with the turmoil of wild nature. There are elements of the story in Lewis's *The Monk and Maturin's *Melmoth the Wanderer, a ballad on the subject is in Percy's *Reliques, and *Croly wrote a version called Salathiel: a story of the past, the present and the future (1828), in which the Wanderer takes on a tragic nationalist grandeur. Other treatments include *Sue's Le Juif errant (1844–5) and *Kingsmill's 'W.J.' (The Dawn's Delay, 1924). See The Haunted Castle (1927) by Eino Railo, and 'The Changing Myth of the Jew', in Speaking of Literature and Society (1982) by L. *Trilling.

Wandering Willie, (1) Willie Steenson, the blind fiddler in Scott's *Redgauntlet. 'Wandering Willie's Tale' is an episode in the novel, an example of the author's successful use of the supernatural. (2) the name of a song by *Burns.

WANLEY, Humfrey (1672–1726), began life as a draper's assistant at Coventry, but read widely and went to Oxford in 1695, and was an assistant in the Bodleian Library in 1696. He displayed remarkable skill in palaeography and assisted Edward Bernard in the preparation of the Catalogi Librorum Manuscriptorum Angliae et Hiberniae (1697). He produced in 1705 a catalogue of Anglo-Saxon manuscripts, which is still the standard work. He was librarian to the first and second earls of Oxford, and began the catalogue of the *Harleian MSS, a work on which he was engaged when he died.

WANLEY, Nathaniel (1634–80), divine and compiler, and father of Humfrey *Wanley. He published The Wonders of the Little World (1678), a collection of tales and superstitions in which R. *Browning found the story of the 'Pied Piper of Hamelin' and other oddities. His poems, some in the vein of H. *Vaughan, were edited by L. C. Martin (1928).

War and Peace, a novel by *Tolstoy.

WARBURTON, Eliot (Bartholomew Eliott George) (1810–52), an Irish barrister who gave up his profession for travel and the literary life. He is remembered for his account of an eastern tour, The Crescent and the Cross: or romance and realities of Eastern travel (1845), a highly successful work which covered much the same ground as his friend *Kinglake's Eothen. He also wrote two historical novels, Reginald Hastings (1850) and Darien (1852). He died at sea, when the ship on which he had embarked for the West Indies caught fire off Land's End.

WARBURTON, John (1682–1759), herald and antiquary. He was an indefatigable collector and owned many rare manuscripts. Most of the rare Elizabethan and Jacobean plays in his possession were through his own 'carelessness and the ignorance' of Betsy Baker, his servant, 'unluckily burned or put under pye bottoms'. A list in his handwriting of the 55 destroyed and those saved, three and a fragment, has been preserved. Some of the burnt manuscripts were unique.

WARBURTON, William (1698–1779), rose to be bishop of Gloucester in 1759. He was much engaged in theological controversy, writing with vigour and arrogance. His most famous work was The Divine Legation of Moses (1738–41), a paradoxical argument that the very absence in the Mosaic law of any reference to a future life, a necessary element in a scheme of morality, is a proof of the divine mission of the lawgiver. A View of Lord Bolingbroke's Philosophy (1754) attacked *Bolingbroke's views on natural religion and The Doctrine of Grace (1762) the 'enthusiasm' of *Wesley. He brought out in 1747 an edition of Shakespeare in 8 volumes which was sharply criticized as unscholarly, and in 1751 an edition of *Pope's works. He was Pope's literary executor, and is said to have encouraged him in the composition of The New Dunciad. A quarrelsome man who made many enemies, he was nevertheless admired by Dr *Johnson, who remained grateful for his early praise of his essay on Macbeth (1747): 'He praised me at a time when praise was of value to me.'

WARD, Artemus, see BROWNE, C. F.

WARD, Edward ('Ned') (1667–1731), tavern keeper and writer (under various pseudonyms) of *Hudibrastic sketches of London life. Some of the best of these are contained in The London-Spy (1698–1709), a simply told tale of a country resident who visits London, meets a cockney acquaintance, and with him ranges about the town noting sights, sounds, smells, and odd characters. His Hudibras Redivivus, a burlesque poem, was published in 1705–7.

WARD, John (1571–1638), English composer, remembered chiefly as a composer of *madrigals, including 'Come, sable night' and 'If the deep sighs'.

WARD, Mary Augusta, better known as Mrs Humphry Ward (1851–1920), was granddaughter of T. *Arnold of Rugby, and daughter of Thomas Arnold, inspector of schools, whose conversion to Roman Catholicism, return to the Anglican faith, and subsequent reconversion to Catholicism caused his family much distress. In 1872 she married Thomas Humphry Ward, then an Oxford don, and later on the staff of *The Times in London. Her most famous novel, Robert Elsmere, is in part a vivid evocation of the Oxford of *Pater, *Pattison, and T. H. *Green, and of the many varieties of religious faith and doubt which succeeded the ferment of the *Oxford Movement. Its protagonist, an earnest but questioning clergyman, resigns his orders for a life of social service in the East End, to the distress of his devout wife Catherine. The novel sold extremely well, was reviewed by *Gladstone, and initiated much debate; she herself compared it to *Froude's *The Nemesis of Faith* and *Newman's *Loss and Gain*, novels which also dealt with the crisis of mid-Victorian faith. Most of her other novels deal with social and religious themes, frequently contrasting traditional belief with the values of progress and intellectual freedom; they include *The History of David Grieve* (1892), *Marcella* (1894), *Helbeck of Bannisdale* (1898), *Lady Rose's Daughter* (1903), and *The Marriage of William Ashe* (1905). She inherited the Arnold sense of high moral purpose, was an active philanthropist and a leading figure in the intellectual life of her day; she supported the movement for higher education for women, but opposed women's suffrage, on the grounds that women's influence was stronger in the home than in public life. Her *A Writer's Recollections* (1918) draws a striking picture of Oxford life and of the domestic influence of W. *Morris, *Burne-Jones, and Liberty prints; it also contains portraits of *Jowett, Pater, H. *James, and other friends.

WARD, Plumer (formerly Robert) (1765–1846), a lawyer and MP who held minor government posts and wrote much on legal and political matters. When he was sixty he became, somewhat eccentrically, an exponent of the *Fashionable novel with the publication of his first novel, *Tremaine, or a Man of Refinement* (1825). He hoped that his works of fiction (which he did not care to call 'novels') would display 'Philosophy teaching by examples', and demonstrate how the standards of public and private morality could be upheld amid the luxury and dissipation of the times. In 1827 appeared *De Vere, or the Man of Independence* and in 1841 *De Clifford, or the Constant Man*. All are lengthy, ponderous works, in which (to use the author's own words of *Tremaine*) 'variety and incident are equally wanting'.

WARD, William George (1812–82), theologian, fellow of Balliol College, Oxford, and a follower of *Newman. In 1844 he published *The Ideal of a Christian Church* in praise of the Roman Catholic Church from which he gained the title 'Ideal' Ward. He was subsequently deprived of his degrees for heresy, and in 1845 joined the Roman Catholic Church. In later life he became increasingly controversial in his writings and joined the Ultramontane party, which upheld anti-liberal views and papal infallibility.

Warden, The, a novel by A. *Trollope, published in 1855, and the first in the *'Barsetshire' series.

The income of Hiram's Hospital, a charitable institution, has grown in real terms down the centuries, but the twelve old bedesmen have not benefited. The surplus has created a pleasant sinecure for the mild-mannered old Warden, the Revd Septimus Harding, a fact which John Bold, a local surgeon with a passion for causes, makes known to the national press. Harding finds himself the object of unpleasant publicity, and his son-in-law, the combative Archdeacon Grantly, bullies him to dispute the case along party lines. But Harding is not the man for the fight, sees the anomaly in his position, and with considerable personal courage resigns. The novel ends in an atmosphere of quiet goodwill, with Bold withdrawing his accusations and marrying the Warden's daughter Eleanor, and Harding receiving a new preferment in the Cathedral Close.

Warden, Henry, in Scott's *The Monastery* and *The Abbot*, an earnest Protestant divine.

Wardle, Mr, a character in Dickens's *Pickwick Papers*.

Wardour, Sir Arthur, and his son and daughter Captain Reginald and Isabella, characters in Scott's *The Antiquary*.

Wardour Street English, a term used to describe the pseudo-archaic diction frequently affected by historical novelists (otherwise referred to in R. L. *Stevenson's coinage as 'tushery'); it derives from the days when Wardour Street was a centre not as now of the film industry but of the antique and mock-antique furniture trade.

WARLOCK, Peter, pseudonym of Philip Heseltine (1894–1930), English composer, almost entirely of songs. Under his own name he made a distinguished contribution to musical scholarship, particularly in the Elizabethan and Jacobean periods: some of his songs, like the lovely setting of 'Sleep' (1922, poem by *Fletcher), reflect this interest in their musical style, but in many others the influence of his friend and mentor *Delius produced a richer harmonic idiom, while in others again the extrovert, even bawdy, side of Warlock's character finds ebullient expression. His choice of poetic texts was varied: many of them come from the earlier periods of English literature, though some of the best of his later songs are settings of Arthur *Symons, *Belloc, and Bruce Blunt. The intense and haunting setting of 'The Curlew' (1922), with words by *Yeats, is considered by many his masterpiece, and reveals a desolation of spirit perhaps not unconnected with his eventual suicide.

WARNER, Rex (1905–), poet, novelist, and translator, educated at Wadham College, Oxford, where he was a close friend of *Auden and *Day-Lewis. His first volume of poetry,

Poems (1937), shares their Messianic revolutionary fervour, and the fourth of Auden's six 'Odes' in *The Orators* (1932) is a buoyant address to Warner's infant son John. Warner's early novels, which include *The Wild Goose Chase* (1937), *The Professor* (1938), and *The Aerodrome* (1941; ironically subtitled 'A Love Story'), are more sombre, Kafkaesque political parables, which reflect the gathering gloom of the 1930s, and in which the matter-of-fact and the uncanny mingle with disturbing effect. His later fiction is based largely on Greek or Roman historical subjects, and he also translated the *Medea* (1944), *Hippolytus* (1950), and *Helen* (1951) of *Euripides, and the *Prometheus Bound* (1947) of *Aeschylus.

WARNER, Sylvia Townsend (1893–1978), novelist and poet, born in Harrow, the daughter of a housemaster at Harrow School. She worked as one of the editors of *Tudor Church Music* (10 vols, 1922–9) and her love of early music is reflected in her later fiction. Her first volume of verse, *The Espalier* (1925), was followed by several others, including *Whether a Dove or a Seagull* (1933), written in collaboration with her friend and companion Valentine Ackland, and the posthumous *Twelve Poems* (1980); her *Collected Poems* appeared in 1982. Her poetry shows her admiration for *Hardy, *Crabbe, and E. *Thomas. Her original voice is heard more strongly in her novels, which include *Lolly Willowes* (1926), a tale of the supernatural in which a maiden aunt realizes her vocation as a witch; *Mr Fortune's Maggot* (1927), which describes the visit of ex-clerk missionary Timothy Fortune to the remote South Sea island of Fanua, where he makes only one doubtful convert and in the process loses his own faith through his love of the islanders; and *The True Heart* (1929), set in the Essex marshes, which retells the story of Cupid and Psyche through the medium of a Victorian orphan, Sukey Bond. Her later works include a biography of T. H. *White (1967), and various collections of short stories, many previously first published in the *New Yorker. Her *Letters* (1982, ed. W. Maxwell) describe her brief friendships, notably with T. F. *Powys, and her love for Valentine Ackland, with whom she lived for many years, mainly in Dorset.

WARNER, William (*c.*1558–1609), was an attorney in London. He published *Pan his Syrinx*, seven prose tales (1584), and a translation of the *Menaechmi* of *Plautus (1595) may be his. His chief work was *Albions England*, a metrical British history, with mythical and fictitious episodes, extending in the first edition (1586) from Noah to the Norman Conquest. It was brought up to Elizabeth's reign in 1592; and a complete edition, reaching James I, was published posthumously (1612). *Meres, in his *Palladis Tamia* (1598), claimed to have heard Warner

called 'our English *Homer*', and *Drayton praised him in his elegy *To Henery Reynolds*; the assessment of C. S. *Lewis, in more modern times, was that 'The good things in *Albion's England* are as far divided as the suns in space.'

War of the Worlds, The, a *Science Fiction fantasy by H. G. *Wells, published 1898, and written while he was living in Woking; it describes the arrival of the Martians in Woking, driven from their own planet by its progressive cooling to take refuge in a warmer world. In a letter Wells described his plan for the work, in which: 'I completely wreck and sack Woking—killing my neighbours in painful and eccentric ways—then proceed via Kingston and Richmond to London, selecting South Kensington for feats of peculiar atrocity'; much of the novel's power depends on the contrast between the familiar stupid bourgeois complacent reactions of the humans and the terrifying destructive intelligence of the Martians, which consist of round bodies, each about 4 feet in diameter, each body containing a huge brain. They live by the injection into themselves of the fresh living blood of other creatures, mostly of human beings, and they devastate the country before eventually falling victims to terrestrial bacteria. A broadcast by Orson Welles of a dramatization of the novel in the US on 30 Oct. 1938 caused a furore, many of its millions of listeners taking it for a factual report of the invasion by Martians of New Jersey.

WARREN, John Byrne Leicester, Baron de Tabley (1835–95), educated at Christ Church, Oxford, published some volumes of verse under the pseudonyms 'George F. Preston' (1859–62) and 'William Lancaster' (1863–8), and two tragedies, also under pseudonyms, *Philoctetes* (1866) and *Orestes* (1867). In 1893–5 he published under his own name two series of *Poems, dramatic and lyrical*; also *A guide to the study of book plates* (1880). He was a botanist, and his best poems manifest his close observation of nature.

WARREN, Robert Penn (1905–   ), American poet, novelist, and critic, born in Kentucky and educated at the Universities of California, Yale, and Harvard. His novels include *All the King's Men* (1946), a study of a power-crazed, corrupt Southern politician, Willie Stark, and his volumes of poetry include *Selected Poems 1923–43* (1944) and *Promises* (1957). His critical works are associated with the *New Criticism, and include two anthologies-with-commentaries, compiled in collaboration with Cleanth Brooks, *Understanding Poetry* (1938) and *Understanding Fiction* (1943).

WARREN, Samuel (1807–77), after studying medicine at Edinburgh, became successively barrister, recorder of Hull, MP for Midhurst, and master of lunacy. From early youth he aimed for literary fame. His first publication, the morbid, melodramatic *Passages from the Diary of a Late Physician* (1832–8, first published in *Blackwoods), provoked criticism from the *Lancet* for revealing professional secrets. Warren is chiefly remembered as the author of the sensationally popular *Ten Thousand a Year* (1840–1), a story of greed and imposture concerning Mr Titlebat Titmouse, a draper's assistant who inherits a vast fortune by way of documents forged by the lawyers Quirk, Gammon, and Snap, and whose unexpected elevation to wealth leads to absurd consequences; he marries Lady Cecilia, daughter of Lord Dredlington, but when the fraud is finally exposed he is discovered to be illegitimate, is imprisoned for debt, goes mad, and is confined to a lunatic asylum. Both novels went through many editions and were translated into several European languages, but his third novel, *Now and Then* (1847), was less successful. He also wrote a number of technical legal works.

Warrington, George, a character in Thackeray's *Pendennis, and *The Newcomes. He is a descendant of the Warringtons in *The Virginians.

Wart, Thomas, in Shakespeare's 2 *Henry IV, one of the recruits for Falstaff's force.

WARTON, Joseph (1722–1800), son of Thomas *Warton and brother of Thomas *Warton the younger, held various livings and was a conspicuously unsuccessful headmaster of *Winchester (1766–93), forced into retirement by the protests of his pupils. He published various poems and odes (including *The Enthusiast: or the lover of nature,* 1744; *An Ode to Evening,* 1749), but is better remembered as a critic of wide knowledge and independent judgement. His *An Essay on the Writings and Genius of Pope* (1756, 1782) distinguishes between the poets of 'the sublime and pathetic' (see SUBLIME) and the 'men of wit and sense', Shakespeare, *Spencer, and *Milton belonging to the first and higher category, and *Pope to the second: 'wit and satire are transitory and perishable, but nature and passion are eternal.' He contributed to *The Adventurer* at Dr *Johnson's request (1752–4), and was elected member of the *Club in 1777.

WARTON, Thomas (c.1688–1745), father of Joseph and Thomas *Warton, was from 1718 to 1728 professor of poetry at Oxford; his poems, including some 'runic odes', were published posthumously in 1748, edited by his son Thomas.

WARTON, Thomas (1728–90), son of Thomas *Warton the elder and brother of Joseph *Warton, was professor of poetry at Oxford (1757–67), and became poet laureate in 1785, an appointment celebrated in the

Probationary Odes (see ROLLIAD). His many poetic works included odes, sonnets (a form then unfashionable, which he did much to revive), and light verse; he edited the early poems of *Milton (1785), and his own work shows the marked influence of *'Il Penseroso'. He also edited *The Oxford Sausage* (1764), a celebrated miscellany of university verse. He was a friend of Dr *Johnson, contributed three numbers to *The Idler* (nos. 33, 93, 96), and was elected to the *Club in 1782. He is, however, best remembered for his valuable work *The History of English Poetry* (3 vols, 1774–81), the first literary history of any real scope, which combines a respect for classicism with a warm admiration for *Chaucer, the Scottish *Chaucerians, *Dante, *Spenser, and other early poets. It lacks method, but throws much light on the taste of the time and the interest in *primitivism, and has been seen as an important stage in the transition towards *Romanticism.

Warwick, Mrs, the heroine of Meredith's *Diana of the Crossways.

WASHINGTON, Booker T(aliaferro) (1856–1915), son of a black slave and a white man, was born into slavery on a Virginia plantation. Freed, he taught himself to read, studied at the Hampton Institute in Virginia, and became the founder and head of the Tuskegee Institute, Alabama, a school for blacks. He was an eloquent speaker and a voluminous writer, and became a spokesman for his people. His works include an autobiography, *Up from Slavery* (1901), and *Working with the Hands* (1904).

Washington Square, a novel by H. *James, published 1881.
   Catherine Sloper lives in Washington Square with her widowed father, a rich physician. She is plain, shy, without social graces or conversation. Dr Sloper cannot conceal his disappointment that she has nothing of her dead mother's beauty and wit. When the handsome, but penniless and indolent, Maurice Townsend begins to court her, he casts him, correctly, as a fortune-hunter. Both Catherine's romantic hopes and Maurice's pecuniary ones are encouraged and abetted by the girl's silly aunt, Lavinia Penniman. Dr Sloper will disinherit Catherine if she marries Maurice, and although she has a certain fortune in her own right it is not enough for the greedy Maurice and he jilts her. Even the dull Catherine is not deceived by his assertion that he is renouncing her to preserve her inheritance. Life in Washington Square continues soberly. Catherine, despised by her father, pitied by her aunt, refuses later chances of a suitable match and withdraws into a lonely humdrum life. After her father's death (cautiously, he has largely disinherited her in any case) Maurice reappears to try his luck again. His continued lack of success has made him less ambitious. But

Catherine finds no charm in this balding middle-aged stranger. With some bitter reminders of his past cruelty, she turns him away. This novel has been filmed and re-entitled *The Heiress*.

Waste Land, The, a poem by T. S. *Eliot, first published 1922 in *The Criterion*. It consists of five sections, 'The Burial of the Dead', 'A Game of Chess', 'The Fire Sermon', 'Death by Water', and 'What the Thunder Said', together with Eliot's own 'Notes' which explain his many varied and multicultural allusions, quotations, and half-quotations (from *Webster, *Dante, *Verlaine, *Kyd, etc.), and express a general indebtedness to the Grail legend (see in this connection GRAIL, HOLY, and BALYN) and to the vegetation ceremonies in *Frazer's *The Golden Bough*. (Eliot himself was later to describe these 'Notes' as 'a remarkable exposition of bogus scholarship', written to pad out the text of the poem when it first appeared as a little book; he admits that they were a temptation to critics, and had achieved 'almost greater popularity than the poem itself': 'The Frontiers of Criticism', 1956.) The poem was rapidly acclaimed as a statement of the post-war sense of depression and futility; it was seriously praised by I. A. *Richards as 'a perfect emotive description of a state of mind which is probably inevitable for a while to all meditative people' (*Science and Poetry*, 1926), and less seriously but significantly chanted as a kind of protest against the older generation by the undergraduates of the day. Complex, erudite, cryptic, satiric, spiritually earnest, and occasionally lyrical, it became one of the most recognizable landmarks of *modernism, an original voice speaking through many echoes and parodies of echoes. *The Waste Land: A Facsimile and Transcript of the Original Drafts* (1971), edited by Valerie Eliot, sheds much light on the circumstances of the poem's composition, and particularly on the well-heeded and detailed textual advice offered by *Pound (through which the poem's length was very considerably reduced); it also quotes a remark by Eliot himself, that the poem could be seen not so much as 'an important bit of social criticism', but as 'the relief of a personal and wholly insignificant grouse against life; it is just a piece of rhythmical grumbling.'

Watchman, The (1796), a political and literary journal, of ten issues only, produced by *Coleridge. The journal was pacifist and anti-*Pitt, and included literary contributions from, among others, *Beddoes and *Poole.

Water-Babies, The: *A Fairy Tale for a Land-Baby*, serialized in *Macmillan's Magazine* 1862–3, published in book form 1863, with illustrations by (Sir) Noel Paton.

Kingsley wrote this, his best-loved work, for his youngest son Grenville. Despite considerable didactic and satiric content, Kingsley's imagination works with unusual ease and freedom, and the tale displays as its most attractive his knowledgeable love of the underwater world of river and sea, his sense of landscape, his open-minded interest in evolutionary theory, and his philanthropic concern. The story tells of the adventures of Tom, the chimney-sweep, employed by the bully Mr Grimes. Tom stumbles down a chimney into the bedroom of a little girl, Ellie, and for the first time he becomes aware of his own grimy body; he runs away, hounded by the household, falls into a river, and is transformed into a water-baby. In his underwater life he makes the acquaintance of many vividly realized creatures, from caddis flies to salmon, and also of Mrs Doasyouwouldbedoneby and Mrs Bedonebyasyoudid, who play a large part in the moral re-education which finally unites him with Ellie. The story was a favourite with Queen *Victoria, who read it to her children, and it remains popular with children today, though it also provides rich opportunities for psychoanalytic interpretation, much of it based on Kingsley's obsession with water, washing, and the public-school cold bath.

WATERHOUSE, Keith Spencer (1929–), journalist, novelist, and dramatist, born and educated in Leeds. He had a considerable success with his second novel, *Billy Liar*, a regional comedy about a youth who attempts to escape his dull family life through fantasy, which he adapted for the stage in collaboration with W. *Hall (1960). Waterhouse and Hall subsequently worked together on many stage, screen, and television plays, adaptations, and musicals, including the film *Whistle Down the Wind* (1961). Waterhouse also wrote the screenplay of S. *Barstow's *A Kind of Loving* (1960).

Waterloo, see WELLINGTON.

Water-Poet, The, see TAYLOR, JOHN.

Watier's, a club founded at 81 Piccadilly, at the suggestion of the prince regent, by Watier, the prince's chef, as a dinner club, noted for its elaborate cooking. It was frequented by men of fashion (including *Brummell), became a gambling centre, and was closed about 1819.

WATKINS, Vernon Phillips (1906–67), poet, born in Wales of Welsh-speaking parents, and educated at Magdalene College, Cambridge. He lived most of his life in and near Swansea, working as a bank clerk before taking various teaching posts, and was for many years a friend of Dylan *Thomas. Their relationship is recorded in *Dylan Thomas: Letters to Vernon Watkins* (1957). Although in his early years he was associated with the poets of the *New Apocalypse, his poetry was, as *Larkin was to record, 'much more controlled than theirs and reached further back to the symbolist poets of

Europe' ('An Encounter and a Re-encounter', a memorial essay in *Vernon Watkins*, 1970, by Leslie Norris). His first volume demonstrated his range; the title poem of *The Ballad of the Mari Lwyd* (1941) is a long, rhetorical piece rooted in Welsh folklore and mythology, whereas 'The Collier' and other poems in the collection are marked by simplicity and a restrained compassion. Watkins's lyric gift was developed in many subsequent volumes, including *The Lamp and the Veil* (1945), *Cypress and Acacia* (1959), and *Fidelities* (1968), and his *Selected Poems 1930–60* appeared in 1967. His work shows an awareness of, and was influenced by, German and French poetry, and he translated two cycles of poems of *Heine (*The North Sea*, 1955), and paid tributes in his own verse to *Hölderlin, *Rilke, *Baudelaire, and others, some of whose work he also translated.

Watson, Dr, companion of Sherlock *Holmes, a character created by A. C. *Doyle.

WATSON, John, see KAILYARD SCHOOL.

WATSON, Richard (1737–1816), from 1782 bishop of Llandaff, wrote a notable *Apology for Christianity* (1776), in reply to *Gibbon (who responded with respect), and an *Apology for the Bible* (1796), in reply to *Paine. *Wordsworth's long *Letter to the Bishop of Llandaff*, in which he supports the French republicans and attacks *Burke and the British constitution, was written in 1793 but not published until 1876; it was a reply to Watson's sermon on 'The Wisdom and Goodness of God in having made both Rich and Poor'.

WATSON, Thomas (c.1557–92), was possibly educated at Oxford, and was a law student in London. He published a Latin version of the *Antigone* of *Sophocles, with an appendix of Latin allegorical poems and experiments in classical metres (1581). His most important work was The 'Εκατομπα Θια or *Passionate Centurie of Love* (1582), 18-line poems, called sonnets, often based on classical, French, and Italian sources, and accompanied by learned explanatory notes. He published Latin versions of *Tasso's *Aminta* (1585), which was translated without authority by Abraham Fraunce (1587), and *Raptus Helenae* from the Greek of Coluthus (1586). He also published *The first Sett of Italian Madrigalls Englished* (1590), which were set to music by W. *Byrd and an *Eglogue*, in Latin and English versions, on the death of Sir Francis Walsingham (1590). His Latin pastoral *Amintae Gaudia* appeared posthumously (1592), and a few previously unpublished poems by him were included in *The Phoenix Nest* and *Englands Helicon*. He was a close friend of *Marlowe, and was mentioned as 'Amyntas' in Spenser's *Colin Clouts come home againe*. His 'sonnets', among

the earliest in English, were an influence on Shakespeare and others.

WATSON, Sir William (1858–1935), poet, born in Yorkshire, gained a certain reputation with *Wordsworth's Grave and other poems* (1890) and *Lachrymae musarum* (1892, verses on the death of *Tennyson), but his many subsequent volumes of derivative, verbose, post-Tennysonian verse are now forgotten, and his memory lingers largely in his anthology piece, 'April, April, | Laugh thy girlish laughter'. See J. M. Wilson, *I was an English poet* (1982).

Watsons, The, an unfinished novel by J. *Austen, written some time between 1804 and 1807.

This story is regarded by some, with little justification, as an early version of *Emma. Although it is only a fragment, probably never revised, the characters are fully realized. The story is set at a social level below that of the other novels, and largely concerns the unremitting efforts of Emma's three sisters to get themselves married. Emma Watson, who has been brought up by a well-to-do aunt, returns to her family, who live unfashionably in genteel poverty in a Surrey village. A pretty, sensible girl, Emma is here surrounded by people in every way inferior to herself. Even her good-natured sister Elizabeth is as intent on a good match as her unpleasant sisters Margaret and Penelope. The other principal characters are Lady Osborne, handsome and dignified; her son, Lord Osborne, a fine but cold young man; Mr Howard, a gentlemanly clergyman; and Tom Musgrave, a cruel and hardened flirt. The intention appears to have been that the heroine should marry Mr Howard, but the author left no hint as to the future course of events, or why she abandoned the novel.

WATT, A. P., see AGENTS, LITERARY.

WATT, Robert (1774–1819), Scottish bibliographer, who began life as a farm and road labourer, and in his boyhood met *Burns—'an extraordinary character'. He learned Greek and Latin, and proceeded to Glasgow and then Edinburgh University, where he studied classics, anatomy, and divinity. He became a very successful doctor, but the work for which he is remembered, and on which he spent over thirty years, is his remarkable *Bibliotheca Britannica, or a general Index to British and Foreign Literature*, published in 1824.

WATTEAU, Jean-Antoine (1684–1721), French rococo painter who invented the 'fête-galante'—small pictures where elegant men and women, among them exotic players from the *commedia dell'arte, picnic, play music, and make love in a soft and dreamy parkland; the most famous of them is *The Embarkation for Cythera* (1717). Watteau died young, of consumption, and was notorious for his discontent and restlessness; his popularity declined in the late 18th cent., but Romantic writers, among them *Gautier and *Nerval, created around him an aura of mystery; they saw him as the tragic artist whose work is touched with melancholy and the transience of human pleasure. A vision of the enchanted, aristocratic 18th cent. in contrast to the bourgeois 19th cent. (expressed, notably, in an evocative essay by the *Goncourt brothers in L'art du dix-huitième siècle), inspired many fin-de-siècle poets and artists, including *Dobson, *Beardsley, *Ricketts, and Michael *Field; *Pater's story 'A Prince of Court Painters' (in Imaginary Portraits, 1877), a study of ill-fated genius, is based on Watteau's life.

WATTS, Isaac (1674–1748), the son of a Nonconformist Southampton tradesman and keeper of a boarding school, was educated at the Stoke Newington Academy 1690–4, became a minister, but was forced into early retirement by ill health. He published four collections of verse, Horae Lyricae (1706), Hymns and Spiritual Songs (1707), Divine Songs for the Use of Children (1715), and The Psalms of David Imitated (1719). He also wrote a number of theological and educational works. He is chiefly remembered for his hymns, which include 'O God, our help in ages past' and 'When I survey the wondrous Cross', and for his songs for children ('How doth the little busy bee'), some of which foreshadow those of *Blake; they became widely enough known to be parodied in the 'Alice' books of Lewis Carroll (C. L. *Dodgson). But he was also the author of Pindaric Odes, blank verse, and of daring technical experiments such as his alarming 'The Day of Judgement' (1706), in English Sapphics. He was included in *The Lives of the English Poets at Johnson's own suggestion.

WATTS-DUNTON, (Walter) Theodore (1832–1914), born Watts, from 1896 by deed poll Watts-Dunton, gave up his profession as solicitor to devote himself to literature. He reviewed for the *Examiner, and then from 1876 to 1902 without a break was one of the most influential writers for the *Athenaeum, and its chief poetry reviewer, in which capacity he supported the work of his friends in the *Pre-Raphaelite movement. Like *Borrow, whom he met in 1872, he was much interested in the gypsies, and republished in The Coming of Love (1898) scenes in verse previously printed in the Athenaeum, in which the gypsy girls Rhona Boswell and Sinfi Lovell feature prominently. These characters reappear in his novel Aylwin (1898), a curious work which he was many years writing; it recounts the love of Henry Aylwin for a Welsh girl, Winifred, his separation from her through a Gnostic curse, and his pursuit of her until their final reunion (with Sinfi

Lovell's aid) on Snowdon. Its romantic mysticism and sensational plot brought it much success.

His other works include introductions to Borrow's *Lavengro (1893) and *The Romany Rye (1900), reminiscent sketches of *Rossetti, *Tennyson, etc., collected as Old Familiar Faces (1916), an article on 'Poetry' in the EB (9th edn, 1885) and an essay, 'The Renascence of Wonder in English Poetry' (in Chambers's Cyclopaedia of English Literature, Vol. iii, 1901), in which he strongly defends the Romantic movement. He is probably best remembered, however, for his loyal support of *Swinburne, whom he rescued from declining health, and who lived with him from 1879 until his death at The Pines, Putney, in an intimacy little interrupted by Watts-Dunton's late marriage, in 1905, to a woman much younger than himself.

WAUGH, Alec (Alexander Raban) (1898–1981), novelist and travel writer, brother of Evelyn *Waugh. His first novel, The Loom of Youth (1917), became a succès de scandale through its colourful suggestions of public-school homosexuality. It was followed by many others, including the late success Island in the Sun (1956), and several autobiographical volumes, including My Brother Evelyn and Other Profiles (1967).

WAUGH, Evelyn Arthur St John (1903–66), novelist, born in Hampstead, the son of a publisher, Arthur Waugh. He was educated at Lancing and Hertford College, Oxford, where he devoted himself more to social than to academic life; his literary and artistic interests were strengthened by new friendships, notably with H. *Acton. He took a third-class degree, then worked for some years (unhappily) as assistant schoolmaster in various posts which provided material for *Decline and Fall (1928), his first and immensely successful novel, which followed the publication of an essay on the *Pre-Raphaelites (1926). In 1928 he married Evelyn Gardner; in 1930 he was divorced, and received into the Roman Catholic Church. His career as a novelist prospered, with Vile Bodies (1930, set in Mayfair), Black Mischief (1932, set in Africa), *A Handful of Dust (1934), and *Scoop (1938), works of high comedy and social satire which capture the brittle, cynical, determined frivolity of the post-war generation. He also established himself as journalist and travel writer with accounts of a journey through Africa (Remote People, 1931), a journey though South America (Ninety-two Days, 1934), and Mussolini's invasion of Abyssinia (Waugh in Abyssinia, 1936). In 1937 he married Laura Herbert, a cousin of his first wife, and from this time made his home in the West Country, first at Piers Court in Gloucestershire, then at Combe Florey in Somerset, where he cultivated the image of the country squire, with, eventually, a family of six children.

The war, however, intervened; *Put Out More Flags* (1942) was written while he was serving in the Royal Marines, and his wartime experiences in Crete and Yugoslavia appear in his trilogy *Sword of Honour* (1965), originally published as *Men at Arms* (1952), *Officers and Gentlemen* (1955), and *Unconditional Surrender* (1961). In the interim appeared one of his most popular works, *Brideshead Revisited* (1945), which struck a more serious note, and a macabre comedy about Californian funeral practices, *The Loved One* (1948). *The Ordeal of Gilbert Pinfold* (1957) is a bizarre novel about a famous 50-year-old Roman Catholic novelist, corpulent, heavy-drinking, insomniac, out of tune with modern life, plagued by disgust and boredom, who sets off on a cruise to Ceylon to escape growing hallucinations, but becomes increasingly paranoid, imagining himself accused of being homosexual, Jewish, Fascist, alcoholic, a social climber, etc.; it is a self-caricature which ends in salvation. He casts an equally cold eye on himself in his revealing *Diaries* (1976, ed. M. Davie); see also *Evelyn Waugh* (1975) by Christopher Sykes. Waugh's other works include biographies of E. *Campion (1935) and R. *Knox (1959), and a volume of autobiography, *A Little Learning* (1964); his *Letters*, ed. M. Amory, appeared in 1980.

Waverley, the first of the novels of Sir W. *Scott, published 1814. Much of it had been written, and thrown aside, some years before.

Edward Waverley, a romantic young man ('a sneaking piece of imbecility' Scott himself, with perhaps excessive severity, called him), has been brought up in part by his father, a Hanoverian in politics, in part by his uncle Sir Everard Waverley, a rich landowner of Jacobite leanings. Obtaining a commission in the army in 1745, he joins his regiment in Scotland, and there, while on leave, visits his uncle's friend, the baron of Bradwardine, a kind-hearted but pedantic old Jacobite, and attracts the favourable notice of the gentle Rose, his daughter. Impelled by curiosity, he visits Donald Bean Lean, a Highland freebooter, in his lair, and Fergus Mac-Ivor Vich Ian Vohr of Glennaquoich, a young Highland chieftain, active in the Jacobite interest. He falls in love with Fergus's sister Flora, whose beauty and ardent loyalty to the Stewart cause appeal to his romantic disposition. These visits, injudicious in an officer of the British army at a time of acute political tension, compromise Edward with his colonel. He moreover falls a victim to Jacobite intrigues, finds himself accused of fomenting mutiny in his regiment, and is finally cashiered and arrested. Rescued by the action of the devoted Rose, and under the influence of a sense of unjust treatment, Flora's enthusiasm, and a gratifying reception by Prince Charles Edward, he joins the Jacobite forces. At the battle of Prestonpans he has the good fortune to save from death Colonel Talbot, a distinguished English officer and friend of his family, and the latter, after the final defeat and dispersal of the Pretender's army, secures Edward's pardon and the rehabilitation of the baron. Meanwhile Edward has been decisively rejected by the spirited Flora, and has turned his affections to Rose, to whom in due course he is married. Fergus is convicted of high treason and bravely meets his end, and Flora retires to a convent.

Among the minor characters may be mentioned bailie Duncan Macwheeble, Bradwardine's 'prime minister'; Davie Gellatley, the 'innocent', the mouthpiece of some of Scott's most beautiful lyrics; and the laird of Balmawhapple, the quarrelsome sportsman who falls foul of Edward and contributes to his early discomfiture. For Colonel Gardiner, Edward Waverley's commanding officer, see under DODDRIDGE.

Waves, The, a novel by V. *Woolf, published 1931, and regarded by many as her masterpiece.

It traces the lives of a group of friends (Bernard, Susan, Rhoda, Neville, Jinny, and Louis) from childhood to late middle age, evoking their personalities through their reflections on themselves and on one another: the effect is not so much of *stream of consciousness as of what *Daiches has called 'recitative', in that each character speaks formally his or her own thoughts, within inverted commas. There is no attempt to differentiate the speech patterns of the six friends; their individuality is presented through a highly patterned sequence of recurring phrases and images, and what we learn of their daily lives (that Susan marries a farmer, that Bernard's ambitions as a writer are disappointed, that Louis becomes a man of power and wealth) we learn obliquely. The organization of the novel is highly formal: the main text is introduced and divided by sections of lyrical prose describing the rising and sinking of the sun over a seascape of waves and shore. There is one additional character, Percival, whose thoughts are never directly presented: his death in India in his mid-twenties, half-way through the novel, becomes the focus for fears and defiance of death and mortality. One of the dominant images of the novel, used by phrasemaker Bernard, is that of a fin breaking over the water; this was, as Woolf's diary reveals, her starting-point for the work ('One sees a fin passing far out', 30 Sept. 1926) and on 7 Feb. 1931, having just written the last words, she recorded in her diary, 'I have netted that fin . . . ' It is the most intense and poetic of all her works, and after it, significantly, she turned to a much less concentrated form in *The Years.*

Way of All Flesh, The, a novel by S. *Butler, published posthumously 1903.

In this study of four generations, dissecting the stultifying effects of inherited family traits and attitudes, many experiences of Butler's life are clearly visible. He completed the book some 17 years before his death, but he never revised the second half. The story (narrated by a family friend, Overton) was originally called *Ernest Pontifex*; Ernest is the awkward and unhappy great-grandson of John Pontifex, a village carpenter, whose natural instinctive character he comes to revere. His own father, Theo, is a tyrannical, canting parent, repeating the attitudes of Ernest's grandfather, George. After his ordination the inept Ernest, taking a respectable woman for a prostitute, is sentenced to prison, where he begins to try to free himself from his immediate forbears and return to the simplicity of Old Pontifex. On his release he plunges into a disastrous union with Ellen, a drunken maidservant, and with her engages in tailoring and running a shop. Fortunately she turns out to be already married, and Ernest's beloved aunt Alethea leaves him sufficient money to devote himself to literature.

Aunt Alethea was based on Butler's friend Miss Savage, who gave him much help with the first half of the book before her death. The book received much praise, led by G. B. *Shaw, and reached the height of its success in the 1920s.

Way of the World, The, a comedy by *Congreve, produced 1700. This is the most finished of Congreve's comedies, but it was not very well received.

Mirabell is in love with Millamant, a niece of Lady Wishfort, and has pretended to make love to the aunt in order to conceal his suit of the niece. The deceit has been revealed to Lady Wishfort by Mrs Marwood to revenge herself on Mirabell, who has rejected her advances. Lady Wishfort, who now hates Mirabell 'more than a quaker hates a parrot', will deprive her niece of the half of the inheritance which is in her keeping if Millamant marries Mirabell. The latter accordingly contrives that his servant Waitwell shall personate an uncle of his, Sir Rowland, make love to Lady Wishfort, and pretend to marry her, having, however, first married Lady Wishfort's woman Foible. He hopes by this deception to force Lady Wishfort to consent to his marriage to her niece. The plot is discovered by Mrs Marwood, and also the fact that Mirabell has in the past had an intrigue with Mrs Fainall, daughter of Lady Wishfort. She conspires with Fainall, her lover and the pretended friend of Mirabell, to reveal these facts to Lady Wishfort, while Fainall is to threaten to divorce his wife and discredit Lady Wishfort, unless he is given full control of Mrs Fainall's property and Millamant's portion is also handed over to him. The scheme, however, fails. Mrs Fainall denies the charge against her and brings proof of Fainall's affair with Mrs Marwood, while Mirabell pro-

duces a deed by which Mrs Fainall, before her last marriage, made him trustee of her property. Lady Wishfort, in gratitude for her release from Fainall's threats, forgives Mirabell and consents to his marriage to Millamant.

Congreve enlivens the action with a fine gallery of fools, including Sir Wilfull Witwoud, Lady Wishfort's boisterous and good-natured country nephew; they serve to highlight the central contrast between the passionate and grasping relationship of Fainall and Mrs Marwood and the delicate process by which Mirabell persuades Millamant that even in such a mercenary society, love can survive into marriage. The dialogue is exceptionally brilliant, and many critics also consider the play a study of the battle between good and evil, rather than of the characteristically *Restoration conflict between the witty and the foolish.

Way We Live Now, The, a novel by A. *Trollope, published 1875.

Augustus Melmotte has the reputation of a great financier, and huge quantities of money pass through his hands. He entertains the emperor of China, and is offered a seat in Parliament. Yet no one thinks to examine the nature of the Melmotte millions until Melmotte is caught forging the title deeds to one of the estates he is buying up. Subsequent inquiries into Melmotte's prize speculation, a Central American railway, prove it to be a gigantic confidence trick, and when it becomes clear that the 'great financier' has tampered with his daughter's trust fund, his disgrace is absolute. After a drunken appearance in the House of Commons he commits suicide. The sordidness of Melmotte's career is matched by his daughter Marie's experiences in the marriage-mart. She is treated as a commodity by the cautious Lord Nidderdale, and as a diversion by the shamelessly dissipated Sir Felix Carbury. When Carbury entices Marie to elope with him she steals the money necessary for the elopement, only to find that Carbury does not keep his appointment, having gambled the money away. At the end of the novel she marries the stockjobber Hamilton K. Fisker, a leading promoter of the American railway scheme.

Trollope conceived the novel as an attack on 'the commercial profligacy of the age', and his perspective is shared by the upright Roger Carbury, head of the dissolute Carbury family. Lady Carbury's shifts as a glib authoress lead to an exposition of the lower levels of contemporary literary life.

We, a novel by *Zamyatin.

Weak ending, the occurrence of an unstressed or proclitic monosyllable (such as a preposition, conjunction, or auxiliary verb) in the normally stressed place at the end of an iambic line.

Wealth of Nations, *Inquiry into the Nature and Causes of the,* a treatise on political economy by Adam *Smith, published 1776, originally delivered in the form of lectures at Glasgow.

Smith's work is the first comprehensive treatment of the whole subject of political economy, and is remarkable for its breadth of view. Smith shared the objection of the French *physiocrats to the mercantile system, but he did not share their view that land is the sole source of wealth. The *Wealth of Nations* sets out with the doctrine that the labour of the nation is the source of its means of life. It insists on the value of the division of labour. Labour is the standard of value, and originally was the sole determinant of price; but in a more advanced state of society three elements enter into price—wages, profit, and rent—and these elements are discussed separately.

The second book deals with capital, its nature, accumulation, and employment. With the increase of capital there is an increase of productive labour and a decrease in the rate of interest.

After this exposition the author proceeds to an elaborate attack on the mercantile system, and an advocacy of freedom of commerce and industry. His political economy is essentially individualistic; self-interest is the proper criterion of economic action. But the universal pursuit of one's own advantage contributes, in his view, to the public interest.

'Wearin' of the Green, The', an Irish national folk-ballad, attributed to the last decade of the 18th cent.

WEBB, Beatrice, *née* Potter (1858–1943), born into a wealthy and well-connected family, was from an early age deeply interested in both the theoretical and practical aspects of social reform, political economy, and sociology, concerns that were shared by her husband, Sidney Webb (1859–1947), the son of a London shopkeeper, whom she married in 1892. Both were leading spirits in the *Fabian Society, and they produced jointly numerous works on social history, served on many royal commissions, and helped to found the London School of Economics. Beatrice also wrote two autobiographical works (*My Apprenticeship,* 1926; *Our Partnership,* 1948), and kept a remarkable diary, of which selections were published in 1952 and 1956, ed. M. Cole; the first volume of a fuller four-volume edition, ed. N. and J. Mackenzie, appeared in 1982. These show the width of her human and intellectual interests and considerable literary skill, and are a valuable record of social life and progressive thought of the period. Sidney and Beatrice Webb appear in H. G. *Wells's novel *The New Machiavelli* (1911) as the Baileys, 'two active self-centred people, excessively devoted to the public service . . . the most formidable and distinguished couple conceivable' (Book 2, ch. 2, 'Margaret in London').

WEBB, (Gladys) Mary *née* Meredith (1881–1927), novelist, born in Shropshire, the daughter of a schoolmaster. In 1912 she married Henry Bertram Law Webb, also a schoolmaster; they lived for some years in Shropshire, working as market gardeners and selling their produce at Shrewsbury market, before moving to London in 1921. She had contracted Graves' disease while still young, an affliction which found its fictional counterpart in the hare-lip of Prudence Sarn, the narrator of her most famous novel, *Precious Bane* (1924). Her other works include *The Golden Arrow* (1916), *Gone to Earth* (1917), and *The House in Dormer Forest* (1920). They are tales of rustic life, romantic, passionate, morbid, and frequently naïve, written in a fervid prose easily ridiculed by Stella Gibbons in *Cold Comfort Farm,* but they nevertheless retain a certain emotional power. They had little success in her lifetime; her great posthumous success was due largely to the championship of Stanley Baldwin, who spoke warmly of her at a *Royal Literary Fund dinner after her death, and wrote an introduction to a reprint of *Precious Bane* in 1928 in which he praised her lyrical intensity, her evocation of the Shropshire landscape, and her 'blending of human passion with the fields and skies'.

WEBB, Sidney, see WEBB, BEATRICE.

WEBER, Carl Maria von (1786–1826), German composer, and one of the founders of the Romantic movement in Germany. After the success of *Der Freischütz* in 1821, Weber's reputation was assured, though ill-health limited his creative activity and more than two years passed before his next opera, *Euryanthe.* Until this period, apart from a single setting, for vocal trio with guitar of a German translation of 'Tell me, where is fancy bred?', he had made no use of texts from English sources, nor had any particular contacts with England.

In 1824 he was asked by Charles *Kemble to write and conduct an opera for the 1825 season at Covent Garden and, largely for financial reasons, accepted, at once beginning a crash course of English lessons, of which he took 153 and acquired reasonable proficiency in the language. (This stood him in good stead when he temporarily took over a task previously done by *Haydn and *Beethoven and provided instrumental accompaniments for 12 Scottish folk-songs early in 1825.) Meanwhile, he had received the first instalment of *Oberon: or the Elf King's Oath* from *Planché: based on an 18th-cent. English translation of *Wieland's *Oberon* (itself a reworking of the medieval French epic *Huon de Bordeaux*), the libretto's only link with Shakespeare is the quarrel between Oberon and Titania (already incorporated by Wieland from *A Midsummer Night's Dream*), and the names of Oberon and Puck—not Titania—among the *dramatis personae*. For this unpromising jumble of the chivalric, the oriental, and the enchanted, in a lavishly spectacular framework with over-tones of the English pantomime, Weber suc-ceeded in producing music which, though inevitably uneven, includes much that is among the most poetic, and indeed prophetic, that he ever wrote. As a result *Oberon* (1826) remains one of the great 'sports' in the history of English opera.

WEBSTER, Daniel (1782–1852), born in New Hampshire, rose to great eminence as an orator, in the law courts, in the American House of Representatives and Senate, and in public speeches, when he urged the union of the American States. He was twice secretary of state. His speeches, even in ordinary criminal trials, show a rare literary quality comparable to that of speeches by *Burke. Among the best known are the Discourse on the 200th anniversary of the landing of the Pilgrims (1825), the Bunker Hill oration (1825), and the Adams and Jefferson speech (1826).

WEBSTER, John (*c*.1578–*c*.1632), the son of a prosperous London coachmaker of Smithfield, was himself admitted by patrimony to the Merchant Taylors' Company, and combined the careers of coachmaker and playwright. He wrote several plays in collaboration with other dramatists; these include *Westward Hoe* and *Northward Hoe*, with *Dekker, written 1604 and 1605, both printed 1607; *A Cure for a Cuckold* (printed 1661, written ?1625), prob-ably with *Rowley (and possibly *Heywood); and a lost play with *Ford entitled *A Late Murder of the Son upon the Mother* (1624). It has also been suggested that he had a hand in *Middleton's *Anything for a Quiet Life* (1661, written ?1621) and *Fletcher's *The Faire Maide of the Inne* (1625). He expanded Marston's *The Malcontent* for the *King's Men in 1604, and published elegies on Prince Henry in 1613 with Heywood and *Tourneur. In 1615 he contributed several sketches to the sixth im-pression of *Overbury's *Characters. The Devil's Law Case*, a tragi-comedy, published 1623, written 1617–21, mentions in its dedication a lost play, *Guise*, which would have brought Webster's total of single-handed plays up to four; as it is, his great reputation rests on his two major works, *The White Devil* (which dates from between 1609 and 1612, when it was published) and *The Duchess of Malfi* (published 1623, written 1612/13). With these two tragedies Webster has achieved a reputation second only to Shakespeare's; they have been revived in this century more frequently than those of any other of Shakespeare's con-temporaries. However, critics have by no means agreed on his virtues. Attempts by N. *Tate and *Theobald to accommodate the plays to

18th-cent. taste were followed in 1808 by *Lamb's influential *Specimens*, which singled out the 'beauties', in terms of poetic passages, and many 19th-cent. critics continued to complain about Webster's poor sense of structure, his inconsistencies, his excessive use of horror. (*Saintsbury, 1887, on *The Duchess*: 'the fifth act is a kind of gratuitous appendix of horrors stuck on without art or reason.') The 20th cent. has seen a strong revival of interest in the plays as drama, and in Webster as satirist and moralist. The works were edited by F. L. *Lucas (4 vols, 1927).

WEBSTER, Noah (1758–1843), American lexicographer and philologist, born in Con-necticut, was educated at Yale University, and worked subsequently as teacher, lawyer, and journalist. The chief work for which he is remembered is his great and scholarly *An Amer-ican Dictionary of the English Language* (2 vols, 1828), in which he challenged the parochialism of British dictionaries and, with a strong national pride and spirit, established Americanisms and American usages. He revised and expanded it himself in 1840, and it has been through several subsequent revisions. (See also DICTIONARY.)

WEDDERBURN, John (?1500–56), with his brother Robert (?1510–?57), produced a metri-cal translation from German Protestant sources of 22 Psalms. The earliest known edition is of 1567–8 and the collection became known as the 'Dundee Psalms'.

WEDGWOOD, Josiah (1730–95), the first English potter with an international reputation, was founder of the pottery at Etruria, Stafford-shire, where he produced both useful and orna-mental ware, maintaining high standards of quality despite large-scale production. He con-tributed much to the taste for *Neo-classicism in design, and was a generous patron; *Flaxman worked for him from 1775 to 1787.

Thomas Wedgwood (1771–1805), son of Josiah, was the first to produce (unfixed) photo-graphs, and was a patron of S. T. *Coleridge.

WEDGWOOD, Dame (Cicely) Veronica (1910–), historian, educated privately and at Lady Margaret Hall, Oxford. Her publications include *Strafford* (1935), *The Thirty Years' War* (1938), *Oliver Cromwell* (1939, rev. 1973), *The King's Peace* (1955), *The King's War* (1958), and *The Great Rebellion* (1966).

WEELKES, Thomas (?1576–1623), English composer. With *Wilbye, he was the most im-portant of the English madrigalists who fol-lowed the lead given by *Morley in 1593 and 1594. Little is known of his life before the pub-lication of his *Madrigals to 3. 4. 5. & 6. Voyces* in 1597; in the next year he became organist at Winchester College and later held the same post at Chichester Cathedral. *The Balletts and Mad-*

rigals to Five Voyces came out in 1598, and the best of his works, the *Madrigals of 5. and 6. Parts, apt for the Viols and Voices*, in 1600. He contributed one of the finest *madrigals to *The Triumphes of Oriana* in 1601, but his last collection, *Ayeres or Phantasticke Spirites for Three Voices* (1608), is less interesting.

In the best of Weelkes's madrigals the Italianate manner of Morley is developed into a more characteristically English style, often more serious in content and laid out for larger forces with great contrapuntal brilliance and expressive richness of harmony. As with most of the madrigalists, the authors of the texts are generally not known, though Weelkes is one of the composers whose imagination is most evidently fired by the bold and vivid imagery of the age of *Donne.

'Wee Willie Winkie', a short story by Rudyard *Kipling; see also NIGHT AND DAY.

Wegg, Silas, in Dickens's *Our Mutual Friend*, a one-legged impudent old rascal, with a smattering of education, who becomes reader to Mr Boffin and attempts to blackmail him.

WEIL, Simone (1909–43), French essayist and thinker. Equally independent in her life and her work, she devoted herself to resisting the oppression inherent in organized institutions and to achieving identification with the sufferings of its victims. Although an *agrégée de philosophie*, she worked for a year on the shop floor of the Renault factory, joined the International Brigade in 1936, and after the outbreak of war found employment as a farm servant. Broken by her voluntary privations, she died in England where she had been engaged by the Provisional French Government. Her moral intellectual authority became generally apparent only posthumously. *Le Pesanteur et la Grâce* (1947), *L'Attente de Dieu* (1949), and *Cahiers* (1951–6) have earned her a unique respect for their intensity of thought, their moral commitment, and their religious inwardness.

WEILL, Kurt (1900–50), German composer, most famous for the music he wrote for *Brecht's *Threepenny Opera* (1928) and *Mahagonny* (1930), in which, in keeping with Brecht's break with dramatic tradition and attack on the bourgeoisie, Weill mingled popular songs and jazz of the 1920s with ironic echoes of Wagnerian opera. Weill settled in New York in 1935.

Weir of Hermiston, an unfinished novel by R. L. *Stevenson, published 1896, which contains some of Stevenson's finest work.

Archie Weir is the only child of Adam Weir, Lord Hermiston, the lord justice clerk, a formidable 'hanging judge', based on the character of Robert Macqueen, Lord Braxfield (1722–99), known as 'the Jeffrey of Scotland'. His mother, a pale, ineffectual, religious woman, dies young, leaving Archie to the care of a father he dreads and dislikes. The conflict between the two comes to a head when Archie wi lesses his father hounding a wretched criminal tc death at a trial with sadistic glee; he publicly confronts his father, speaking out against capital punishment, and is banished to Hermiston, a remote Lowland village. There he lives as a recluse with Kirstie, his devoted housekeeper and distant relative, who is aunt to four notable brothers, the 'Black Elliotts', famed for hunting down their father's murderer. Archie falls in love with their sister, and Kirstie's niece, Christina. The novel ends as Archie, warned by the jealous Kirstie, tells Christina that their secret meetings must end. We know from Stevenson's notes that the novel was to end with another confrontation between father and son, in which Archie is on trial for his life for the alleged murder of Christina's seducer, Frank Innes. Archie and Christina escape to America, but the old man dies of shock. In this novel, Stevenson returns to the Edinburgh and Lowland landscapes of his youth, which he evokes with a grim but poetic power, and many have seen in Archie's rebellion Stevenson's rejection of his own Calvinist ancestry, though in real life he was able to achieve a reconciliation and understanding with his parents, and their approval of his career as a writer. Critics agree that it promised to be the most ambitious and profound of his works.

WELCH, (Maurice) Denton (1915–48), born in Shanghai, spent part of his childhood in China, and was educated at Repton and Goldsmith's School of Art. He intended to be a painter, but in 1935 was severely injured in a bicycle accident; he spent months in hospital and a sanatorium, and was an invalid for the rest of his life. A volume of autobiography, *Maiden Voyage* (1943), was followed by a novel about adolescence, *In Youth is Pleasure* (1944), and a volume of short stories, *Brave and cruel, and other stories* (1949). His most distinctive work is the unfinished, autobiographical, posthumously published *A Voice Through a Cloud* (1950), a vivid, heightened, and at times painfully sensitive account of accident and illness.

WELDON, Fay, *née* Birkinshaw (1933–), novelist, dramatist, and television screenwriter, born in Worcester and educated at the University of St Andrews; she worked for some time in advertising before becoming a full-time writer. She is perhaps best known for her novels, which express the rising feminist consciousness of the 1970s, and which deal, frequently in tragi-comic vein, with women's troubled relationships with parents, men, and children and with one another; these include *The Fat Woman's Joke* (1967), *Down Among the Women* (1971), *Female Friends* (1975), *Praxis* (1978), and *Puffball* (1980). Her gift for realistic dialogue is manifested both in her fiction and in her many plays for television.

Well-Beloved, The, a novel by T. *Hardy, published serially 1892, revised and reissued 1897.

The scene is the Isle of Slingers (i.e. Portland). The central figure is Jocelyn Pierston, a sculptor of the Isle, who falls in love successively with three generations of island women; Avice Caro, her daughter, and her granddaughter, all of the same name. He is seeking in each the perfect form in woman, as he seeks it in stone. Perversity of circumstances, and the varying natures of the women, prevent him from marrying any of them. Despairing of the pursuit of art and beauty, he eventually marries an elderly widow, Marcia, when both he and she have been, like the rock of Portland, subjected to the raspings and chisellings of time.

Wellborn, Frank, a character in Massinger's *A New Way to pay Old Debts.

Weller, Samuel, in Dickens's *Pickwick Papers, Mr Pickwick's devoted servant, formerly boots at the White Hart in the Borough, a cheerful, facetious, and resourceful character, with an endless store of humorous illustrations apposite to the various incidents of life; and his father Tony, a coach-driver.

WELLESLEY, Arthur, see WELLINGTON.

WELLESLEY, Dorothy Violet, duchess of Wellington, *née* Ashton (1889–1956), is remembered as a poet chiefly through the admiration of *Yeats, who included a disproportionate number of her poems in his *Oxford Book of Modern Verse* (1936). His *Letters on Poetry*, originally written to her, were published in 1940. She herself published several volumes of poetry, collected in 1955 as *Early Light*. She was a friend of V. *Sackville-West, and sponsored and edited the Hogarth Living Poets series for the *Hogarth Press.

WELLINGTON, Arthur Wellesley, first duke of (1769–1852), soldier and statesman, who fought in the Indian Campaign (1799–1803), the Peninsular Campaign (1808–14), and was the hero of the battle of Waterloo (18 June 1815) at which Napoleon was decisively defeated. He first became a national figure with the victory of Talavera in 1809, and was created marquess of Douro and duke of Wellington in 1814. He was prime minister 1828–30, and secretary of state for foreign affairs 1834–5. Known as the 'Iron Duke', or, more familiarly, as 'Old Nosey', he was much portrayed by caricaturists, notably John Doyle (father of R. *Doyle) and William Heath ('Paul Pry', 1795–1840). Although a less romantic figure than Napoleon, his exploits and his phlegmatic utterances (e.g. 'Publish and be damned',

attributed to him) caught the imagination of contemporary and later writers: the battle of Waterloo is depicted in Byron's *Childe Harold's Pilgrimage* (Canto 3, xxi, 'There was a sound of revelry by night') and in *Vanity Fair*; he inspired much of the Juvenilia of C. *Brontë; and he appears in historical novels by A. C. *Doyle, *Henty, and others. By the queen's wishes he was given the most magnificent state funeral ever accorded to a subject, a pageant commemorated in *Tennyson's 'Ode on the Death of the Duke of Wellington' (1852). There is a biography (2 vols, 1969, 1973) by Elizabeth Longford.

Well of Loneliness, The, see HALL, R.

WELLS, Charles Jeremiah (1800–79), author (under the pseudonym of H. L. Howard) of *Joseph and his Brethren: a Scriptural Drama* (1824), a verse play much admired by *Rossetti, republished in 1876 with an essay by *Swinburne, and again in 1908 by the *World's Classics.

WELLS, H(erbert) G(eorge) (1866–1946), born in Bromley, Kent, the son of an unsuccessful small tradesman and professional cricketer, was apprenticed to a draper in early life, a period reflected in several of his novels. He then became assistant teacher at Midhurst Grammar School, studying by night and winning a scholarship in 1884 to the Normal School of Science in South Kensington, where he came under the lasting influence of T. H. *Huxley. For some years, in poor health, he struggled as a teacher, studying and writing articles in his spare time; his marriage in 1891 to his cousin Isabel proved unhappy, and he eloped with his student Amy Catherine ('Jane') Robbins, whom he married in 1895 (though this did not prevent him from embarking on further liaisons, and continuing to criticize conventional marriage). In 1903 he joined the *Fabian Society, but was soon at odds with it, his sponsor G. B. *Shaw, and Sidney and Beatrice *Webb; impatient and turbulent, his career as writer and thinker was marked by a provocative independence.

His literary output was vast and extremely varied. As a novelist he is perhaps best remembered for his scientific romances, among the earliest products of the new genre of *science fiction. The first, *The Time Machine* (1895), is a social allegory set in the year 802701, describing a society divided into two classes, the subterranean workers, called Morlocks, and the decadent Eloi. This was followed by *The Wonderful Visit* (1895), *The Island of Doctor Moreau* (1896), *The Invisible Man* (1897), *The War of the Worlds* (1898, a powerful and apocalyptic vision of the world invaded by Martians), *When the Sleeper Wakes* (1899), *The First Men in the Moon* (1901), *Men Like Gods* (1923), and others. These combine, in varying degrees, political satire, warnings about the dangerous new powers of science, and a desire to foresee a possible future (see also *A Modern Utopia*, 1905); Wells's preoccupation with social as well as scientific progress distinguishes them from the fantasies of *Verne.

Another group of novels evokes in comic and realistic style the lower-middle-class world of his youth. *Love and Mr Lewisham* (1900) tells the story of a struggling teacher; *Kipps* (1905) that of an aspiring draper's assistant, undone by an unexpected inheritance and its consequences; *The History of Mr Polly* (1910) recounts the adventures of Alfred Polly, an inefficient shopkeeper who liberates himself by burning down his own shop and bolting for freedom, which he discovers as man-of-all-work at the Potwell Inn.

Among his other novels, *Ann Veronica* (1909) is a feminist tract about a girl who, fortified by the concept of the *'New Woman', defies her father and conventional morality by running off with the man she loves. *Tono-Bungay* (1909), one of his most successful works (described by himself as 'a social panorama in the vein of Balzac') is a picture of English society in dissolution, and of the advent of a new class of rich, embodied in Uncle Ponderevo, an entrepreneur intent on peddling a worthless patent medicine. *The Country of the Blind, and other stories* (1911), his fifth collection of short stories, contains, as well as the well known title story, originally published in 1904, the memorable 'The Door in the Wall' (originally published 1906). *The New Machiavelli* (1911), about a politician involved in sexual scandal, was seen to mark a decline in his creative power, evident in later novels, which include *Mr Britling Sees It Through* (1916) and *The World of William Clissold* (1926). He continued to reach a huge audience, however, notably with his massive *The Outline of History* (1920) and its shorter offspring *A Short History of the World* (1922), and with many works of scientific and political speculation (including *The Shape of Things to Come*, 1933) which confirmed his position as one of the great popularizers and one of the most influential voices of his age; the dark pessimism of his last prediction, *Mind at the End of its Tether* (1945), may be seen in the context of his own ill health and the course of the Second World War. One of his last statements (made after Hiroshima) was an exhortation to man to confront his 'grave and tragic' destiny with dignity and without hysteria.

His *Experiment in Autobiography* (1934) is a striking portrait of himself, his contemporaries (including Arnold *Bennett, *Gissing, and the Fabians) and their times. See also a life by N. and J. Mackenzie, *The Time Traveller* (1973), and a memoir by his son by Rebecca *West, Anthony West (1914–), *Aspects of a Life* (1984).

WELSH, Jane, see CARLYLE, J. B. W.

Wemmick, in Dickens's *Great Expectations*, clerk to Mr Jaggers the lawyer, and Pip's good friend.

Wen, The, Cobbett's name for London (see RURAL RIDES).

Wentworth, Captain, a character in J. Austen's *Persuasion*.

WENTWORTH, Sir Thomas, see STRAFFORD.

Werner, a poetic drama by Lord *Byron, published 1822, founded on 'The German's Tale' in Sophia and Harriet *Lee's *Canterbury Tales*.

The outlawed son of Count Siegendorf, bearing the assumed name of Werner, finds himself in the same house as his enemy Count Stralenheim, and on a sudden impulse robs him. Werner's son Ulric then murders Stralenheim to conceal his father's dishonour, and throws the appearance of guilt on the Hungarian, Gabor, who accuses Ulric of the crime. Ulric seeks to kill Gabor, but is prevented by Siegendorf, who shrinks from assassination, and dies brokenhearted at his own infamy and his son's crime. Byron dedicated the work to *Goethe.

Wertherism, a cultural phenomenon resulting from the fame throughout Europe of *Goethe's early novel *Die Leiden des jungen Werthers* (*The Sorrows of Young Werther*, 1774). This was a semi-autobiographical work about a sensitive artist, melancholy, at odds with society, and hopelessly in love with a girl, Charlotte, who was engaged to someone else. Its combination of the hero's 'Weltschmerz' (sense of ill-ease with the world) and 'Ichschmerz' (dissatisfaction with self), together with the scandalous suicide of Werther, made the work a huge success throughout Europe. Young men wore blue coats and yellow breeches in imitation of Werther, china tea-sets were produced with scenes from the novel depicted on them, and perfumes named after Werther were sold. Goethe was later much embarrassed by this early work and by the assumption that it was autobiographical. *Thackeray wrote a well-known sardonic poem about Werther and Charlotte, and the term 'Wertherism' became current in English to describe a man's early self-indulgent moods of melancholy (for example, C. *Kingsley accused his brother-in-law J. A. *Froude of catching the disease of Wertherism in his youthful novel *The Nemesis of Faith*, 1849).

WESKER, Arnold (1932–), playwright, born in Stepney of Jewish immigrant parents, and educated in Hackney. He left school at sixteen and worked at various jobs (including furniture-maker's apprentice and pastry cook) before making his name as a playwright. His early work was closely associated with the *English Stage Company, although his first play to be performed, *Chicken Soup with Barley* (1958), transferred there from the Belgrade Theatre, Coventry, which also put on the first productions of *Roots* (1959) and *I'm Talking about Jerusalem* (1960), three plays now grouped together as the Wesker Trilogy (see below). *The Kitchen* (1959) which first appeared at the Royal Court, shows the stresses and conflicts of life behind the scenes in a restaurant, which culminate in tragedy; its use of the rhythms of working life was highly innovative and did much to stimulate the growth of what was to be known (though in a slightly different sense) as *kitchen sink drama. Wesker's political commitments were also manifested in 1960–1 in his efforts to establish Centre 42, a movement which aimed to popularize the arts through trade union support. His subsequent plays include *Chips with Everything* (1962), a study of class attitudes in the RAF during National Service; *The Four Seasons* (1965), about a love affair; *Their Very Own and Golden City* (1966) and *The Friends* (1970), both of which deal in different ways with the disappointment of political and social hope; *The Merchant* (1977), which treats the story of *Shylock in a manner that constitutes an attack on anti-Semitism; and *Caritas* (1981), which shows the spiritual anguish of a 14th-cent. anchoress who realizes she has mistaken her vocation. Wesker has also published essays, screenplays, and volumes of short stories; the title story of *Love Letters on Blue Paper* (1974), about the relationship of a dying trade unionist and his wife, was televised and adapted (1978) for the stage.

Wesker Trilogy, The, the name given to three plays by A. *Wesker, directed as a sequence for the first time by the *English Stage Company in 1960.

Chicken Soup with Barley (1958) introduces the Kahn family in their East London home in 1936; Sarah Kahn, a warm-hearted Communist Jewish matriarch, energetically supports Socialist opposition to the Fascist marches, but her weak husband Harry is less enthusiastic. The play spans two decades; Harry becomes physically enfeebled by successive strokes, but Sarah battles for her ideals, manifested in the second generation in her daughter Ada and her emotional and volatile son Ronnie, who returns at the end of the play from working as a cook in Paris with many of his illusions about brotherly love shattered. Sarah rallies her own faith, which has suffered many bureaucratic blows in the new world of the Welfare State, and urges him to keep fighting: 'You've got to care or you'll die.'

Roots (1959), set in Norfolk, portrays the effects of Ronnie's infectious idealism in his fiancée, Beatie Bryant, daughter of an agricultural labourer; she returns to her family for a visit, full of his praises and his notions, which she tries to convey to her highly resistant sister and

mother. She is full of second-hand Socialism, classical music, and the *Manchester Guardian*; they retaliate (in acutely observed and realistic dialect) with second-hand talk of pop songs and gossip about operations and illnesses. In the last act Beatie is playfully trying to stir her family to some intellectual exertion while awaiting Ronnie's visit, when a letter arrives from him breaking off their engagement; after her initial despair, Beatie finds her own voice as she attacks her family for its acceptance of the third-rate and the dull, and realizes triumphantly that she is no longer quoting Ronnie, but speaking for herself.

I'm Talking about Jerusalem (1960) opens in 1946 in Norfolk, as newly-demobbed Dave (who fought in the Spanish Civil War and the Second World War) and Ada, helped by Sarah and Ronnie, move into their new home, where they hope to create a William Morris oasis of independence, with Dave working as a craftsman-carpenter, but over the next two acts (which span the years 1947–59) they are defeated by economic and social reality, and the last act sees them, again aided by Sarah and a deeply distressed and possibly embittered Ronnie, packing to leave.

WESLEY, Charles (1707–88), brother of John *Wesley, and also an active member of the Oxford Methodists. He accompanied John to Georgia in 1735, and like him was influenced by the Moravians, though he remained faithful to the Anglican church and regretted his brother's departure from it. He composed many thousands of hymns, including such favourites as 'Jesu, lover of my soul'. He left a *Journal*, published in 1849.

WESLEY, John (1703–91), the fifteenth child of the Revd Samuel Wesley, was educated at Oxford, and became fellow of Lincoln College in 1726. In Oxford he was the centre of a group of devout Christians (including his brother Charles, above, and *Whitefield); they practised severe self-discipline and self-examination, and were nicknamed the 'Holy Club' or 'Methodists'. On his father's death in 1735 he went to Georgia on an (unsuccessful) mission; he became a member of the Moravian society at Fetter Lane. He visited the Moravian colony at Herrnhut in 1738, and appointed his first lay preacher in the same year. He then began field preaching and opened a Methodist chapel at Bristol, and for the rest of his life conducted his ministry with extraordinary energy, preaching 40,000 sermons, and travelling thousands of miles a year, mainly on horseback. His literary output was also prodigious. He published from 1737 many collections of hymns; the singing of hymns to familiar tunes by the whole congregation was a new practice and contributed greatly to the fervent Methodist spirit. He wrote educational works, practical treatises, edited *Thomas à Kempis (1735), published selections from W. *Law, by whom he was deeply influenced, and kept a *Journal* (standard edn ed. N. Curnock, 1909–11) remarkable not only as a record of his spiritual life and tireless organizational activities, but also for its pathos and humour. Dr *Johnson found him a good conversationalist, but 'never at leisure'. Wesley's impact on public and private life, notably in his concern for the illiterate industrial poor, was enormous, and has even been credited (or discredited) with preventing a proletarian revolution. An edition of his complete works (ed. F. Baker, 34 vols), containing some unpublished material, began to appear in 1975.

Wessex, the name used by *Hardy to designate the south-west counties, principally Dorset, which form the setting of many of his works.

WEST, Nathaniel, the pseudonym of Nathan Wallenstein Weinstein (1903–40), American novelist, born in New York. He is known principally for two macabre and tragic novels, *Miss Lonelyhearts* (1933), the story of a heavy-drinking agony columnist who becomes involved in the life of one of his correspondents, and *The Day of the Locust* (1939), a satire of Hollywood life based on West's own experiences as a scriptwriter. He was killed in a car crash.

WEST, Dame Rebecca, the adopted name of Cecily Isabel Fairfield (1892–1983), daughter of Charles Fairfield, of Anglo-Irish descent, who became known in London for his witty defence of extreme individualism in debates with H. *Spencer and G. B. *Shaw. He moved his family to Edinburgh, where he died, leaving his widow and four daughters in straitened circumstances. Rebecca (who adopted this name, after *Ibsen's heroine in *Rosmersholm*, at 19) was educated in Edinburgh, trained briefly for the stage in London, then became a feminist and journalist, much influenced at this stage by the Pankhursts (see WOMEN'S SUFFRAGE); from 1911 she wrote for *The Freewoman*, *The New Freewoman*, and *The Clarion*. Many of her shrewd, witty, and combative pieces have been collected and reprinted as *The Young Rebecca* (1982, ed. Jane Marcus); this includes her outspoken review of H. G. *Wells's *Marriage* (1912), which led to a ten-year love affair and the birth of a son, Anthony West. Her first novel, *The Return of the Soldier* (1918), which describes the return home of a shell-shocked soldier, was followed by *The Judge* (1922), *The Strange Necessity* (1928), *Harriet Hume* (1929), and *The Thinking Reed* (1936); then, after a long gap, *The Fountain Overflows* (1956) and *The Birds Fall Down* (1966). Meanwhile, in 1930, she had married a banker, Henry Maxwell Andrews, who accompanied her on the journey which produced her two-volume study of the Yugoslav nation, *Black Lamb and Grey Falcon* (1941). She was present at the Nuremberg trials, and *The Meaning of Treason* (1949) grew out of articles originally commissioned by the *New Yorker*; an updated version in 1965 added accounts of more recent spy scandals (e.g. Vassall and Ward) to her study of 'Lord Haw Haw' (William Joyce) and others. She continued to write and to review with exceptional vigour almost until her death, at 90. The reputation of her novels tends to have been eclipsed somewhat by the aggressive panache of her reportage and journalism, and they have frequently been described as 'too intellectual', but feminist re-assessments in the 1980s have admired her strong and unconventional heroines, and her fine craftsmanship.

WEST, Richard (1716–42), son of a lawyer, became at Eton a close friend of T. *Gray and Horace *Walpole. Gray wrote a moving sonnet on his early death, 'In vain to me the smileing Mornings shine', first printed in 1775, which *Wordsworth used to illustrate his views on poetic diction in the *Preface* of 1800 to the *Lyrical Ballads*.

Western, Squire, and Sophia, characters in Fielding's *Tom Jones*.

West Indian, The, a comedy by R. *Cumberland, produced 1771.

Stockwell, having secretly married in Jamaica the daughter of his rich employer, old Belcour, has had a son by her, who has been passed off on old Belcour as a foundling, been brought up by him, and has inherited his property. Young Belcour, as he is called, comes home, but Stockwell postpones recognizing him as his son until he has made trial of his character. Young Belcour, a Rousseauesque child of nature, falls in love with Louisa, daughter of the impecunious Captain Dudley, but is misled into thinking her the mistress of Charles, who is actually her brother. Charles is in love with his rich cousin Charlotte, but because of his poverty will not confess his love, although it is returned. Belcour generously comes to the financial assistance of Captain Dudley, but his impetuous gift to Louisa of some jewels entrusted to him for Charlotte leads to grave complications. The imbroglio is eventually cleared up; Belcour discovers his mistake, is pardoned by Louisa and obtains her hand, and is acknowledged by his father, Stockwell. Charles is discovered to be the real heir of his grandfather's property, and marries Charlotte. Belcour's generosity and simplicity are favourably contrasted with the civilized decadence of London. (See PRIMITIVISM.) The play was produced by *Garrick, and enjoyed great success.

Westlock, John, a character in Dickens's

*Martin Chuzzlewit, at one time pupil of Mr Pecksniff.

'Westminster Bridge, Composed upon', a sonnet by *Wordsworth ('Earth hath not anything to show more fair'), written 1802, published 1807.

Westminster Review, The (1824–1914), was established by J. *Mill, an ardent supporter of *Bentham, as the journal of the 'philosophical radicals', in opposition to the *Edinburgh Review and the *Quarterly Review. The conservatism of the Quarterly and the quality of the Edinburgh reviewers both came under attack. *Byron, *Coleridge, *Tennyson, and *Carlyle were among the literary figures it supported, but political and philosophical attitudes were always put first. The journal survived several changes of name and ownership, and under the editorship of John *Chapman from 1851 (when G. *Eliot became the assistant editor) published *Froude, *Pattison, *Pater, George Eliot herself, and other important writers. It became a monthly in 1887, and in this century dropped its literary interests.

Westminster School was founded by *Elizabeth I in 1560. Among its famous pupils have been *Jonson, G. *Herbert, *Locke, *Dryden, *Wren, *Bentham, *Gibbon, *Cowper, *Southey, and A. *Wilson.

Westward for Smelts, a collection of tales borrowed from *The Decameron and similar sources, recounted by seven fishwives who embark after selling their fish in London; by 'Kinde-Kit of Kingston' (?1603, 1620).

Westward Ho!, see KINGSLEY, C.

Westward Hoe, a comedy by *Webster and *Dekker, printed 1607.
    The main plot deals with an escapade of three merry wives and their gallants to Brentford, where their husbands find them at an inn, but their innocence is established. In the sub-plot Justiniano, an Italian merchant, convinced of his wife's infidelity, abandons her and lives disguised, enjoying the comedy of London life. Mistress Justiniano is involved in an intrigue with a profligate earl, but conscience intervenes and repentance and reconciliation follow.

WEYMAN, Stanley John (1855–1928), established his reputation as a historical novelist with A Gentleman of France (1893, dealing with the period of Henry of Navarre) followed by a number of other romances of a similar character, including The Red Cockade (1895), Under the Red Robe (1896, afterwards successfully dramatized at the Haymarket), Count Hannibal (1901, based on the Massacre of St *Bartholomew), and Chippinge (1906, in an English setting, at the time of the *Reform Bill).

Weymouth Sands, a novel by J. C. *Powys.

WHARTON, Edith, née Newbold Jones (1862–1937), American novelist and short story writer, born in New York of a distinguished and wealthy New York family. She was educated privately at home and in Europe, where she travelled widely; she married Edward Robbins Wharton in 1885 and they settled in France in 1907. The marriage was not happy; she suffered from nervous illnesses, and her husband's mental health declined in later years. They were divorced in 1913. She devoted her considerable energy to a cosmopolitan social life, which included a close friendship with H. *James, and to a literary career, which began with the publication of poems and stories in Scribner's Magazine. Her first volume of short stories, The Greater Inclination (1899), was followed by a novella, The Touchstone (1900), but it was The House of Mirth (1905), the tragedy of failed social climber Lily Bart, which established her as a leading novelist. Many other works followed, including the less characteristic but much admired Ethan Frome (1911), a grim and ironic tale of passion and vengeance on a poor New England farm; Madame de Treymes (1907), which describes American-born marquise de Malrive's adjustments to aristocratic Parisian society; The Reef (1912), also set in France, at the château of Givré, where widowed Anna Leath's expectations of a happy second marriage are frustrated when she learns of her fiancé's fleeting past dalliance with her daughter's governess; *The Custom of the Country (1913). The Age of Innocence (1920) describes the frustrated love of a New York lawyer, Newland Archer, for Ellen Olenska, the separated wife of a dissolute Polish count; her unconventional and artistic nature is contrasted with the timid but determined calculations of Archer's fiancée May, who, backed by all the authority of society, keeps him within her grasp and marries him. The Mother's Recompense (1925) concerns the struggle between runaway mother Kate Clephane and her daughter Anne for the hand of the same young man, and Hudson River Bracketed (1929) contrasts Middle West with New York society. She also published many volumes of short stories, various travel books, and an autobiography, A Backward Glance (1934). Edith Wharton's chief preoccupation is with the conflict between social and individual fulfilment which frequently leads to tragedy. Her observant, satiric, witty portrayal of social nuance, both in America and Europe, shows her keen interest in anthropology and in what she called the 'tribal behaviour' of various groups. There is a full biography by R. W. B. Lewis, published in 1975.

WHATELY, Richard (1787–1863), educated at Oriel College, Oxford, of which he became fellow and tutor. He contributed to the *Quar-

terly Review 1820–1. From 1829 to 1831 he was professor of political economy at Oxford, and was then appointed archbishop of Dublin. He was active in Irish cultural and political life, founding a professorship of political economy at Dublin in 1832 and 15 years later a Statistical Society, and involving himself in educational reform at all levels. He published a great number of works on philosophy and religion, supporting *Broad Church views, but his reputation rested largely on his *Logic* (1826) and *Rhetoric* (1828).

What Maisie Knew, a novel by H. *James, published 1897.

With insight and humour James takes us into the world of Maisie, the child of divorced parents who use her, neglect her, and expose her to their own world of emotional chaos.

Her father, Beale Farrange, marries Maisie's governess, Miss Overmore, while her mother marries a handsome, weak, and younger man, Sir Claude, to whom Maisie becomes devoted. These new marriages collapse, the step-parents become lovers, and her parents enter into new amorous entanglements. A new governess, Mrs Wix, appears to offer support, but also becomes infatuated with Sir Claude. Maisie is used as a pawn in the power games of the adults who surround her; her perception of their corrupt lives leads her to an odd and disconcerting maturity, yet she is not of their world and retains a fundamental honesty and innocence.

What You Will, the sub-title of Shakespeare's *Twelfth Night*; it is his only play (with the possible exception of *King *Henry VIII*) with an alternative title—its meaning is 'whatever you want to call it'. It is clearly connected, in some way, with *Marston's *What You Will* which probably appeared in 1601.

WHEATLEY, Dennis Yates (1897–1977), novelist of the occult, who worked for some years in the family wine business before selling it in 1931 to become a writer. His Satanic thrillers and romances (*The Devil Rides Out*, 1935; *To the Devil—a Daughter*, 1953, etc.), of which he sometimes produced several a year, were extremely popular.

WHEATLEY, Phillis (?1735–84), a black poet born in Africa and shipped as a child to the slave-market of Boston, where she was purchased by John Wheatley, who encouraged her literary talent. Her *Poems on Various Subjects, Religious and Moral* were first published in London in 1773.

'When lovely woman stoops to folly', a poem by Goldsmith, from *The Vicar of Wakefield*.

Where Angels Fear to Tread, E. M. *Forster's first novel, published 1905.

It is a tragi-comedy describing the conse-quences of the marriage of Lilia Herriton, an impulsive young widow, to an Italian dentist, Gino Carella, whom she meets while touring in Tuscany, ineffectively chaperoned by 'charming, sober' Caroline Abbott. Lilia's mother-in-law in suburban Sawston, outraged by news of the engagement, dispatches her young son Philip Herriton, barrister and aesthete, to break off the match, but he arrives too late, for the couple are already married. Lilia dies shortly afterwards in childbirth, and Philip is once more dispatched, this time accompanied by his sister Harriet, to rescue the baby from imagined disasters. They meet Miss Abbott in Monteriano, and both she and Philip find their intentions waver as they fall under the spell of Italy (there is a fine description of an enthusiastic Italian audience watching *Lucia di Lammermoor*) and become aware of Gino's strong feelings for and determination to keep his son; once more they admit defeat, recognizing, and in Miss Abbott's case much moved by, Gino's passion. Without their knowledge Harriet kidnaps the baby, who is accidentally killed when their carriage over-turns. Gino, hearing the news, breaks Philip's arm, but the two are reconciled, after a fashion, through Miss Abbott's concern for both. As Philip and Miss Abbott travel back to England, he realizes that he has learned to love her, but she reveals that she loves Gino, and appears to be resigning herself to a spinster's life of good works in Sawston.

WHETSTONE, George (1550–87), author of miscellaneous verse, especially elegies, and prose tales, is principally remembered for his *Promos and Cassandra* (1578), a play in rhymed verse (based on a tale in *Cinthio's *Hecatommithi*), which provided the plot for Shakespeare's *Measure for Measure* and is an early example of English romantic comedy. There is a life by T. C. Izard (1942).

WHEWELL, William (1794–1866), the son of a carpenter, educated at Lancaster Grammar School and Trinity College, Cambridge. A philosopher and scientist of wide range and copious output, he was professor of moral philosophy at Cambridge from 1838 to 1855 and master of Trinity College from 1841 till his death. His principal works were *The History* (1837) and *The Philosophy* (1840) *of the Inductive Sciences* and *Astronomy and Physics in reference to Natural Philosophy* (1833). He published and edited many other works in natural and mathematical science, philosophy, and theology, including *Lectures on Systematic Morality* (1846) and *Lectures on the History of Moral Philosophy in England* (1852).

WHICHCOTE, Benjamin, see CAMBRIDGE PLATONISTS.

Whig Examiner, The, a literary and political

periodical published by *Addison. Five numbers appeared, Sept.–Oct. 1710.

Whiskerandos, Don Ferolo, a character in Sheridan's *The Critic.

WHISTLER, James Abbott McNeill (1834–1903), an American painter, who moved between Paris and London; his art and ideas were an important link between the two capitals. He was first influenced by Courbet's Realism, but later emphasized that a painting is 'an arrangement of line, form and colour first'. His most famous works are the *Nocturnes,* paintings in delicate tones of the Thames at dusk, when 'the evening mist covers the riverside with poetry'. G. du Maurier's *Trilby describes his bohemian life as a student in Paris (1855–9). Whistler moved to London in 1859; he mixed in *Pre-Raphaelite circles, and discussed his ideas on art with *Swinburne; Swinburne dedicated a poem to the *Little White Girl* (1864, London, Tate Gallery). Whistler, notorious as a dandy and wit, was at the centre of the Aesthetic Movement. In 1877 *Ruskin attacked him for 'flinging a pot of paint into the public's face'; Whistler sued him, won, and was awarded a farthing damages. The trial stimulated Whistler's gifts as a polemicist; he wrote a series of pamphlets and vituperative letters to the press, later published together in *The Gentle Art of Making Enemies* (1890). His most serious and elegant attack on Ruskin's belief in the moral purpose of art was his *Ten O'Clock Lecture.* He had discussed many of his ideas with *Wilde, whom he later accused of plagiarism; Whistler's influence is evident in Wilde's lectures in America (1882) and in 'The Decay of Lying' and 'The Critic as Artist'. After 1891 Whistler again lived in Paris, where both his writing and the shadowy, mysterious beauty of his pictures were deeply admired by Symbolist writers. *Mallarmé, a close friend, translated his *Ten O'Clock Lecture* (1888). *Proust's Elstir is generally considered to be drawn from the characters of Whistler and Monet.

WHITAKER, Joseph (1820–95), publisher and at one time editor of *The Gentleman's Magazine* (1856–9). He founded the *Educational Register* (1850), *Whitaker's Clergyman's Diary* (1850), *The Artist* (1855), *The Bookseller,* (1858), and *Whitaker's Almanack* (1868), a compendium of general information regarding the government, finances, population, and commerce of the world, with special reference to the British Commonwealth and the United States. (See ALMANACS.)

Whitaker's Almanack, see WHITAKER, J.

WHITE, Antonia (1899–1979), novelist and translator, was the daughter of C. G. Botting, a classics master at St Paul's School. She was educated at the Convent of the Sacred Heart, Roehampton, and at St Paul's School for Girls. In 1930 she married H. T. Hopkinson, later editor of *Picture Post.* Her convent childhood is described in her first autobiographical novel, *Frost in May* (1933), which she began to draft when she was 16. The heroine of this work, Nanda Grey, becomes Clara Batchelor in her three subsequent novels, also largely autobiographical, *The Lost Traveller* (1950), *The Sugar House* (1952), and *Beyond the Glass* (1954), which give a vivid account of her experiences as an actress in provincial repertory, her struggles as a freelance copy-writer attempting to write seriously at the same time, her complex relationship with her possessive father, and her descent into mental illness and confinement in an asylum. Clara is named after Clara Middleton of Meredith's *The Egoist,* a novel much admired by her father. Antonia White also translated many of the novels of *Colette (whose love of the sensuous, the eccentric, and the bohemian is reflected in her own work), and published an account of her reconversion to Catholicism, *The Hound and the Falcon* (1966).

WHITE, Gilbert (1720–93), born at Selborne in Hampshire, became fellow of Oriel College, Oxford, but spent most of his life as curate of Selborne, refusing various livings in order to remain in his beloved birthplace. He began in 1751 to keep a 'Garden Kalendar' and later a 'Naturalist's Journal'. He made the acquaintance of two distinguished naturalists, Thomas *Pennant and Daines *Barrington, with whom he carried on a correspondence from 1767 which formed the basis of his *Natural History and Antiquities of Selborne* (published Dec. 1788, title page 1789), a work which displays his affectionate and detailed observations of wild life and nature, and his love of the *picturesque in landscape. It slowly gathered a wide reputation, with both scientists (C. *Darwin read it with enthusiasm as a boy) and general readers, went through many editions, and remains a classic. *A Naturalist's Calendar,* ed. Dr John Aikin, appeared in 1795, and his *Journals,* ed. W. Johnson, in 1931.

WHITE, Henry Kirke (1785–1806), son of a butcher, articled to a lawyer in Nottingham. His volume of verses in 1803 attracted the attention of *Southey, who encouraged and assisted him. He obtained a sizarship at Cambridge, where overwork helped to bring about his early death. Southey collected his works, with a memoir, and published them in 1807. Little is remembered of his work except a few hymns, such as 'Oft in danger, oft in woe'.

WHITE, Joseph Blanco (1775–1841), born in Seville, became a Catholic priest, soon abandoned the priesthood, and came to England in 1810. With the help of Lord Holland (see HOLLAND HOUSE) he started a journal, *El Español,* which ran from 1810 to 1814. He wrote for the *New Monthly Magazine* and later for J. S. Mill's *London Review*. He went to study at Oxford and became an Anglican cleric, and the friend of *Whately, *Newman, *Pusey, and *Froude. His *Evidences against Catholicism* appeared in 1825. His other publications include *Observations on Heresy and Orthodoxy* (1835), translations into Spanish of *Paley's *Evidences*, and other ecclesiastical works. In 1828 the *Bijou* published his sonnet 'Night and Death', which *Coleridge declared 'the finest . . . sonnet in our language'.

WHITE, Patrick Victor Martindale (1912–), Australian novelist, born in England; he was taken to Australia (where his father owned a sheep farm) when he was six months old, but educated in England, at Cheltenham College and King's College, Cambridge. He settled in London, where he wrote several unpublished novels, then served in the RAF during the war; he returned after the war to Australia with Manoly Lascaris, who was to be his lifelong companion. His first published novel, *Happy Valley* (1939), set in New South Wales, was followed by *The Living and the Dead* (1941), set in pre-war London, and *The Aunt's Story* (1948), a comic and sympathetic account of the travels of an independent Australian spinster, Theodora Goodman. *The Tree of Man* (1955) is an epic account of a young farmer Stan Parker at the beginning of the 20th cent., and his struggles to build himself a life and a family in the Australian wilderness; the epic theme was continued in *Voss* (1957), which returns to the heroic Australian past in its description of the doomed attempt of a Nietzschean German visionary and aspiring hero, Johann Voss, to lead an expedition across the continent in 1845. The sufferings of his band in the hostile terrain are chronicled with great power; he is bound in a form of mystic communion with Laura Trevelyan, who, at home in Sydney, suffers with him and is released from fever at the moment when, already *in extremis*, he is decapitated by the aboriginal boy Jackie. Voss lives on as an increasingly legendary, martyred figure. The story was suggested by the true record of Ludwig Leichardt, who died in the desert in 1848. These two novels gave White an international reputation, which he strengthened with several subsequent works, including *Riders in the Chariot* (1961); *The Solid Mandala* (1966); *The Vivisector* (1970, about a painter, Hurtle Duffield, and and 'wet, boiling, superficial, brash, beautiful, ugly Sydney'); *The Eye of the Storm* (1973); *A Fringe of Leaves* (1976, a tale of shipwreck on the Australian coast in 1836); and *The Twyborn Affair* (1979), a baroque novel with an international canvas, which ends apocalyptically in the London blitz; he has also published *Four Plays* (1965), volumes of short stories, and a frank self-portrait, *Flaws in the Glass* (1981), which contains a brief and

revealing account of his allegedly 'ungracious' reception of the *Nobel Prize for literature in 1973, which he persuaded his friend, the artist Sidney Nolan, to accept in Stockholm on his behalf.

WHITE, T(erence) H(anbury) (1906–64), is best known for his novels on the Arthurian legend, published under the title *The Once and Future King* (1958). The first book in this sequence, *The Sword in the Stone*, originally published separately in 1937, is a classic children's novel, as is *Mistress Masham's Repose* (1947). He also wrote several adult novels. *The Goshawk* (1951), is an account of how he trained a hawk. *The Book of Beasts* (1954) is a translation from a 12th-cent. Latin *bestiary. There is a life by S. T. *Warner, published in 1967.

WHITE, William Hale (1831–1913), known as a writer under the pseudonym of 'Mark Rutherford', was born in Bedford, the son of William White, Dissenter, bookseller, and later a well known doorkeeper in the House of Commons and author of *The Inner Life of the House of Commons* (1897). Hale White was educated with a view to becoming an independent minister, but disillusion with his teachers and growing religious doubts led him to abandon this course, and in 1854 he entered the Civil Service, rising to a responsible post as assistant director of contracts at the Admiralty. He supplemented his income by parliamentary and literary journalism, and in 1881 published *The autobiography of Mark Rutherford, dissenting minister*. This relates the spiritual development of a young Dissenter, supposedly edited after his death by his friend Reuben Shapcott; Rutherford, born in a small Midlands town, attends a Dissenting college and then becomes a minister, but is beset both by theological doubts and by distress at the narrowness and hypocrisy of his colleagues and congregations. Loneliness makes him an easy prey to melancholy, and he gradually loses his faith, becoming as disillusioned by the Unitarians as he was by his own church. It is a compact and powerful account of the progress of 19th-cent. doubt; Rutherford cannot believe in personal immortality (though he is somewhat reassured by Wordsworthian pantheism), and finally sees himself as one born a hundred years too late, for whom it would be 'a mockery to think about love for the only God whom I knew, the forces that maintained the universe'. The book was well received, and was followed by other imaginative works, all under the same pseudonym: these were Mark Rutherford's *Deliverance* (1885), *The Revolution in Tanner's Lane* (1887, a novel which draws an intimate and sympathetic portrait of Dissenting circles, radical politics, and working men's lives earlier in the century), *Miriam's Schooling and other Papers* (1893), *Catherine Furze* (1893), and *Clara Hopgood* (1896). His other pseudonymous works include *Pages from a Journal* (1900), a collection of essays and stories, *More Pages from a Journal* (1910), and *Last Pages from a Journal* (1915); works published under his own name include a life of *Bunyan (1905), a writer who profoundly influenced him. His own life was overshadowed by the prolonged illness of his wife, who died in 1891, and whose patient suffering he saw as 'salvation through Crucifixion'. See a biography by C. D. Maclean, published in 1955.

Whiteboy, a member of a secret agrarian association formed in Ireland in 1761, so called from the fact that its members wore a shirt over their clothes to distinguish each other at night. The Whiteboys figure in *Tales by the O'Hara Family* by *Banim.

White Devil, The (*The White Divel: or the tragedy of . . . Brachiano, with the life and death of Vittoria Corombona*), a tragedy by *Webster, written between 1609 and 1612, when it was published.

The duke of Brachiano, husband of Isabella, the sister of Francisco, duke of Florence, is weary of her and in love with Vittoria, wife of Camillo. The *Machiavellian Flamineo, Vittoria's brother, helps Brachiano to seduce her, and contrives (at her suggestion, delivered indirectly in a dream) the death of Camillo: Brachiano causes Isabella to be poisoned. Vittoria is tried for adultery and murder in the celebrated central arraignment scene (III. ii), and defends herself with great spirit; *Lamb's phrase for her manner was 'innocence-resembling boldness', and *Hazlitt found in her 'that forced and practised presence of mind' of the hardened offender, pointing out that she arouses sympathy partly through the hypocrisy of her accusers. She is sentenced to confinement in 'a house of penitent whores', whence she is carried off by Brachiano, who marries her. Flamineo quarrels with his younger brother, the virtuous Marcello, and kills him; he dies in the arms of their mother Cornelia, who later, driven out of her wits by grief, sings the dirge 'Call for the robin redbreast, and the wren', a scene which elicits from Flamineo a speech of remorse. ('I have a strange thing in me to the which | I cannot give a name, without it be | Compassion.') Meanwhile Francisco, at the prompting of Isabella's ghost (see REVENGE TRAGEDY) avenges her death by poisoning Brachiano, and Vittoria and Flamineo, both of whom die Stoic deaths, are murdered by his dependants. Whether or not Vittoria qualifies as a tragic heroine has been much debated.

WHITEFIELD, George (1714–70), the popular evangelical preacher, came under the influence of John and Charles *Wesley while at Oxford, and followed them on a mission to Georgia, where he founded an orphanage. On his return he attracted much attention at large open-air meetings by his fervent and emotional sermons. His views diverged from those of the Wesleys, as he became increasingly Calvinistic. He became domestic chaplain to Lady *Huntingdon and through her patronage opened a Tabernacle in Tottenham Court Road; she was the founder of the body of Calvinistic Methodists known as 'Lady Huntingdon's Connection', and she warmly supported Whitefield in his disputes with Wesley. Whitefield died near Boston on the last of several evangelical visits to America. His Journals were published in 7 parts, 1738–41, and *Hymns for Social Worship* in 1753. He was ridiculed by *Foote in his play *The Minor* and satirized by Graves in *The Spiritual Quixote*. *Garrick was said to have greatly admired his preaching, but Dr *Johnson, while respecting his ministry, found he had more 'familiarity and noise' than 'knowledge, art and elegance'.

WHITEHEAD, A(lfred) N(orth) (1861–1947), educated at Sherborne and Trinity College, Cambridge, professor of applied mathematics in the Imperial College of Science and Technology (1911–24), professor of philosophy at Harvard University (1924–36). He was the author of many important philosophical and mathematical works, including *Principia Mathematica* (with B. *Russell, 1910), *Science and the Modern World* (1925), *Religion in the Making* (1926), *Symbolism* (1927), *Process and Reality* (1929), *Adventures of Ideas* (1933).

WHITEHEAD, Charles (1804–62), poet, novelist, and dramatist, published in 1831 *The Solitary*, a poem which met with warm approval. His quasi-historical romances, *The Autobiography of Jack Ketch* (1834) and *Richard Savage* (1842), and his play *The Cavalier* (1836), were also successful. His career was ruined by intemperance and he died miserably in Australia.

WHITEHEAD, William (1715–85), educated at Winchester and Clare Hall, Cambridge, published in 1741 a verse epistle, *The Danger of Writing Verse*, in which he describes the temerity of those embarking on a literary career, and the hazards of neglect, notoriety, and the whims of patrons. In his day he was best known for his successful *neo-classical tragedy *The Roman Father* (1750), a version of *Corneille's *Horace*; this was followed by another tragedy, *Creusa* (1754), and a comedy, *The School for Lovers* (1762). In 1757 he was appointed poet laureate, an elevation which caused much satiric comment, notably from Charles *Churchill; he replied both to his detractors and to his own first publication in another verse epistle, *A Charge to the Poets* (1762), in which he recommends his fellow poets to remain calm in the face of hostile and favourable criticism alike, and to see themselves as 'the firm spectators of a bustling world'. His *Plays and Poems* were collected in 1774, and a complete edition of his poems appeared in 1788.

White Hotel, The, a novel by D. M. *Thomas.

White Lady of Avenel, The, a supernatural being introduced by Scott in *The Monastery.

White's, a chocolate-house in St James's Street, London, started in 1697 by Francis White. The first number of *The Tatler* announced that accounts of gallantry, pleasure, and entertainment would emanate from White's Chocolate House. It was taken over by Arthur (the founder of Arthur's Club) and converted into a club, which became a celebrated gaming centre. The present clubhouse, with its bay window (associated with *Brummell), dates from 1755, though much altered inside and out.

Whitford, Vernon, a character in Meredith's *The Egoist.

WHITING, John (1917–63), playwright, whose plays, at first ill-received, marked a historic break from the prevailing vogue for drawing-room comedy. *A Penny for a Song* (1956, pub. 1969), *Saint's Day* (perf. and pub. 1951), *Marching Song* (perf. and pub. 1954), and *The Gates of Summer* (1956, pub. 1969) show a powerful and individual talent, but he did not achieve popular success until *The Devils,* adapted from *The Devils of Loudun* by A. *Huxley, was performed by the Royal Shakespeare Company in 1961. A highly theatrical piece, influenced by *Brecht, it deals with a case of hysterical demonic possession in a French nunnery. His *Collected Plays* (1969, ed. R. Hayman) includes several performed posthumously.

WHITMAN, Walt (1819–92), born on Long Island, New York, and brought up partly in Brooklyn. He had little formal education, and started work as an office boy; he subsequently worked as printer, wandering schoolteacher, and contributor to and editor of various magazines and newspapers, entering politics as a Democrat, and travelling in 1848 to New Orleans, where he wrote for the *Crescent.* He returned to New York and the *Brooklyn Times* via St Louis and Chicago, and the experience of the frontier merged with his admiration for *Emerson to produce the first edition of *Leaves of Grass,* twelve poems saturated, as he describes it 'with the vehemence of pride and audacity of freedom necessary to loosen the mind of still-to-be-form'd America from the folds, the superstitions, and all the long, tenacious and stifling anti-democratic authorities of Asiatic and European past'. When Emerson was sent a copy he replied hailing the work, with good reason, as 'the most extraordinary piece of wit and wisdom that America has yet contributed'. The second edition (1856) added 21 poems, and the third edition (1860) 122, including the group entitled 'Calamus', which has been taken as a reflection of the poet's homosexuality, although in his own words they celebrate the 'beautiful and sane affection of man

for man'. The six further editions that appeared in Whitman's lifetime were revised or added to, the work enlarging as the poet developed. During the Civil War Whitman worked as a clerk in Washington, but his real business was as a volunteer hospital visitor among the wounded, an experience which affected him deeply, as can be seen in his prose *Memoranda during the War* (1875) and in the poems published under the title of *Drum-Taps* in 1865. In the *Sequel* to these poems (1865–6) appeared the great elegy on *Lincoln, 'When Lilacs Last in the Dooryard Bloom'd'. In spite of his achievement, and his efforts at self-publicity, Whitman was disregarded by the public at large, some of whom were offended by his outspokenness on sexual matters, some by his pose as rough working man; his reputation began to rise after recognition in England by W. G. *Rossetti, *Swinburne (who compared him to *Blake, Mrs *Gilchrist, and E. *Carpenter. After a paralytic stroke in 1873 he left Washington and lived quietly in Camden, New Jersey, still writing, though without the originality of his early years. The free, vigorous sweep of his verse conveys subjects at once national ('Pioneers! O Pioneers!', 1865), mystically sexual ('I sing the body electric', 1855), and deeply personal ('Out of the Cradle Endlessly Rocking', 1860), and his work proved a liberating force for many of his successors, including H. *Miller, D. H. *Lawrence, H. *Crane, and the poets of the *Beat Generation.

WHITNEY, Geoffrey, see EMBLEM BOOKS.

WHITTIER, John Greenleaf (1807–92), American poet, was born of Quaker parents at Haverhill, Massachusetts, where Thomas Whittier, his Puritan ancestor, had built the oak farmhouse described in *Snow-Bound.* He began life as a farmer's boy, and supported himself while at Haverhill Academy by shoemaking and teaching. He became an ardent Abolitionist, and wrote tracts and edited various periodicals for the cause, as well as writing poems on the subject of slavery, collected as *Voices of Freedom* (1846). He was a regular contributor to the *Atlantic Monthly,* which he helped to found. A prolific and popular poet, he wrote in many genres; his first book, *Legends of New-England in Prose and Verse* (1831), which demonstrates his lifelong interest in local history, was followed by many volumes of verse on political and rural themes, by verse narratives, sonnets, and ballads. Among his best-known works are 'The Barefoot Boy' (1856), a celebration of rural boyhood which manifests his admiration for *Burns, and *Snow-Bound* (1866), a recollection of winter evenings with his family in the old homestead.

WHITTINGTON, Richard (d. 1423), son of Sir William Whittington, a mercer in London. He rose to be lord mayor of London, 1397–8, 1406–7 (a year of plague), and 1419–20. He was a liberal benefactor of the city, leaving legacies for rebuilding Newgate prison and other purposes (including a city library). The popular legend of Whittington and his cat, the germ of which is probably of very remote origin, is not known to have been narrated before 1605, when a dramatic version and a ballad were licensed for the press. The story of a cat helping its owner to fortune has been traced in many countries of Europe. It is also suggested that it is based on a confusion between 'a cat' and the French *achat*, in the sense of 'trade'. According to the story, Whittington, when in the service of Mr Fitzwarren, a London merchant, sent his cat, the only thing he possessed, as part of one of his master's trading ventures; the king of Barbary, who was plagued with rats and mice, purchased the cat for an enormous sum. Meanwhile Whittington, ill-treated by the cook under whom he served as scullion, ran away. He rested at Holloway, and hearing Bow Bells ringing, as he fancied, the words,

Turn again, Whittington, Lord Mayor of London,

returned to Fitzwarren's house.

Whole Duty of Man, The, a devotional work published 1658, in which man's duties in respect of God and his fellow men are analysed and discussed in detail. The book was at one time attributed to Lady Dorothy Pakington (d. 1679). She was, however, probably only the copyist. The book, by internal evidence, is the work of a practised divine, acquainted with Hebrew, Syriac, and Arabic, perhaps Richard Allestree (1619–81), chaplain in ordinary to the king, Regius professor of divinity, and provost of Eton. It had enormous popularity, lasting for over a century; it is comparable in this respect to *Thomas à Kempis' De Imitatio Christi* and *Law's Serious Call*. Some of the injunctions in it belong to a sterner age than the present, e.g. 'But of all the acts of disobedience that of marrying against the consent of the parent is one of the highest.'

Who's Who, an annual biographical dictionary of contemporary men and women. It was first issued in 1849 but took its present form in 1897, when it incorporated material from another biographical work, *Men and Women of the Time*; earlier editions of *Who's Who* had consisted merely of professional lists, etc. The entries are compiled with the assistance of the subjects themselves, and contain some agreeable eccentricities particularly in the section labelled 'Recreations'.

The first *Who Was Who 1897–1916* appeared in 1920, and the seventh (1971–1980) in 1981. These decennial volumes contain the biographies removed from *Who's Who* on account of death, with final details and date of death added.

WHYTE-MELVILLE, George John (1721–78), born in Fife, educated at Eton, joined the 93rd Highlanders, then the Coldstream Guards, and served in the Crimean war. He then returned to England and devoted his time to field sports on which he was an authority. Most of his literary works were novels, sometimes historical, and hunting figures largely in many of them. His first, *Digby Grand*, was published in 1853; *Galsworthy, at Oxford, fell under the spell of the 'Bright Things' in Whyte-Melville's novels and Digby Grand was Jolyon's (in *The Forsyte Saga*) first idol. He achieved fame with *Holmby House* (1859) a historical romance describing the Civil War. *Market Harborough* (1861) and *The Gladiators* (1863), also very popular, were followed by several others. In 1869 he published his *Songs and Verse*, and *Riding Recollections* (1879) was a notable book on horsemanship. He was killed in a hunting accident.

WHYTHORNE, Thomas (1528–96), educated at Magdalen College, Oxford. After three years as 'servant and scholar' in the household of J. *Heywood he became a teacher of music and composer of madrigals. His autobiography, *A Book of Songs and Sonetts*, discovered in manuscript in 1955, was edited by James M. Osborn and published in 1961. It is not only an interesting document of Tudor life, poetry, and music, but also, because Whythorne wrote in his own phonetic system, a key to the pronunciation of his day.

Wickfield, Mr and Agnes, characters in Dickens's *David Copperfield*.

WICKHAM, Anna, pseudonym of Edith Alice Mary Harper (1884–1947), poet, born in Wimbledon, and educated in Queensland and New South Wales, Australia. She returned to London in 1905 to study singing, went to Paris to be coached for opera by de Reszke, but married in 1906 Patrick Hepburn, solicitor and astronomer, by whom she had four sons. More popular in the US and France than at home, she was an original and copious poet; in imagery and subject matter in advance of her time, she charted the struggle of a woman artist to achieve freedom to work as well as to fulfil herself as wife and mother. Her friends included D. H. *Lawrence, M. *Lowry, Dylan *Thomas, and Kate O'Brien. Her publications include *The Contemplative Quarry* (1915), *The Little Old House* (1921), and *Thirty-Six New Poems* (1936); a collection, *The Writings of Anna Wickham* (1984), was edited by R. D. Smith.

'Widdicombe Fair', the title of a popular song. 'For some reason or other, not exactly known', writes S. *Baring-Gould in *English Minstrelsie*, 'this has become the accepted Devonshire song ... The date of words and tune is probably the end of the last [18th] century.'

Tom Pearse lends his grey mare to carry a party (including Old Uncle Tom Cobbleigh) to Widdicombe Fair, but the mare takes sick and dies, and is still to be seen haunting the moor at night. Widdicombe, or Widecombe-in-the-Moor, is near Ashburton.

Widmerpool, a character in A. *Powell's *A Dance to the Music of Time*.

Widowers' Houses, a play by Bernard *Shaw, first performed 1892, published 1893, and published (with *The Philanderer* and *Mrs Warren's Profession*) in *Plays Unpleasant* (1898). It is designed to show the manner in which the capitalist system perverts and corrupts human behaviour and relationships, through a demonstration, in Shaw's words, of 'middle-class respectability and younger son gentility fattening on the poverty of the slum as flies fatten on filth'. Dr Harry Trench, on a Rhine holiday, meets Blanche Sartorius, travelling with her wealthy father, and proposes marriage to her: Sartorius is willing to permit the match if Trench's family (including his aunt Lady Roxdale) agrees to accept her as an equal. All seems well, until it is revealed in Act II that Sartorius is a slum landlord. Trench is horrified, refuses to accept Sartorius's money, suggests that he and Blanche should live on his £700 a year, and is even more horrified when Sartorius points out that this income is derived from a mortgage of Sartorius's property, and that he himself and his miserable rent collector Lickcheese are merely intermediaries: 'You are the principal.' Blanche, revealing a passionate and violent nature, rejects Trench for his hesitations. In the third act Lickcheese, himself now rich through dubious dealings in the property market, approaches Sartorius with an apparently philanthropic but in fact remunerative proposition, which involves Lady Roxdale as ground landlord and Trench as mortgagee. Trench, now considerably more cynical, accepts the deal, and he and Blanche are reunited.

Widsith, a poem of 143 lines in Old English, named from its opening word, in the *Exeter Book*. It is constructed around three 'thulas' (i.e. mnemonic name-lists), connected by the ostensible experience of the eponymous minstrel: the first names great rulers; the second lists the tribes among whom the minstrel claims to have travelled; and the third speaks of people that the minstrel sought out. The poem, although it contains some later interpolations, is thought to date substantially from the 7th cent. and thus to be the earliest poem in the language. Both the editions are important, and Malone's contains a very full bibliography. Ed. R. W. Chambers (1912); K. Malone (Copenhagen, 1962).

WIELAND, Christoph Martin (1733–1813), German poet and writer of romances, whose best-known works are light ironic verse-tales drawn from medieval or oriental sources, of which *Oberon* (on the story of *Huon of Bordeaux*, 1780) is a good example. Wieland translated eleven of Shakespeare's plays into German prose, and *A Midsummer Night's Dream* into verse.

Wife of Bath, (1) see CANTERBURY TALES, 6; (2) the title of an unsuccessful comedy by J. *Gay (1713).

Wife of Usher's Well, The, a ballad of the Scottish border. The wife sends her three sons to sea, and soon gets tidings of their death. Their ghosts come back on one of the long nights of Martinmas, and the mother, deceived by the apparitions, orders a feast; but at cock-crow they disappear.

WIGGLESWORTH, Michael (1631–1705), colonial American poet and divine, born in Yorkshire, England, who emigrated in 1638. He is known chiefly for his long Calvinistic poem in ballad metre, *The Day of Doom: A Poetical Description of the Great and Last Judgment* (1662), a work of little literary merit which had a great success both in America and England. See R. Crowder's life, *No Feather Bed to Heaven* (1962).

WILBERFORCE, William (1759–1833), educated at St John's College, Cambridge, and an MP for Yorkshire, devoted himself to the abolition of the slave-trade and to other philanthropic projects. He published in 1797 *A Practical View of the Prevailing Religious System of Professed Christians*, a work which was influential and widely read. He was the leading layman of the evangelical *'Clapham Sect', and he lived just long enough to see carried the second reading of the Bill abolishing slavery.

WILBUR, Richard Purdy (1921–), American poet, born in New York City, and educated at Amherst College and Harvard. His elegant, urbane, and witty poetry appears in several collections, from *Ceremony* (1950) to *Seven Poems* (1981), and he has also translated several plays by *Molière into English verse.

WILBYE, John (1574–1638), English composer, with *Weelkes, the most important of the English madrigalists who followed the lead given by *Morley in 1593 and 1594. Born in Norfolk, Wilbye spent most of his life in the service of the Kytson family at Hengrave Hall, in Suffolk; he published only two sets of *madrigals, the first in 1598, the second in 1609, and contributed one madrigal to *The Triumphes of Oriana* in 1601. His other works are of little interest.

As a madrigalist Wilbye, at least in the first collection, stays closer than Weelkes to the Italianate manner pioneered by Morley: 'Adieu, sweet Amaryllis' is a perfect, as well as a very famous, example of the delicate balance he achieved in this style. In the second set, generally regarded as the finest of all the English madrigal collections, he went further and brought together a poetic understanding, purity of style, musical expressiveness, subtlety and variety of texture, and structural power, that put madrigals like the 6-part 'Draw on sweet night' among the greatest things in English music.

WILCOX, Ella Wheeler (1850–1919), American poet, born in Wisconsin, whose many volumes of romantic, sentimental, and mildly erotic verse (with titles such as *Poems of Passion* and *Poems of Cheer*) brought her a vast readership. She also wrote short stories and novels, and two volumes of autobiography.

WILD, Jonathan (?1682–1725), worked as a buckle-maker in London. He became head of a large corporation of thieves, and opened offices in London for the recovery and restoration of property stolen by his dependants. He gained notoriety as a thief-taker, and was ultimately hanged at Tyburn. His 'Life and Actions' were related by *Defoe (1725). For Fielding's satire, see JONATHAN WILD THE GREAT. There is a Life by G. Howson, *Thief-Taker General* (1970).

Wildair, Sir Harry, a character in Farquhar's *The Constant Couple* and in its sequel, *Sir Harry Wildair*.

WILDE, Oscar Fingal O'Flahertie Wills (1854–1900), was born in Dublin, the son of Sir William Wilde, Irish surgeon, and Jane Francesca Elgee, well known as writer and literary hostess under the pen-name 'Speranza'. A brilliant classical scholar, Wilde studied at Trinity College, Dublin, then at Magdalen College, Oxford, where in 1878 he won the Newdigate Prize for his poem 'Ravenna'. His flamboyant aestheticism attracted attention, much of it hostile; he scorned sport, collected blue china and peacock's feathers, and proclaimed himself a disciple of *Pater and the cult of *'Art for Art's sake' mocked in *Gilbert and Sullivan's *Patience* (1881). Wilde successfully lived up to the image of the satire, and its impetus took him on a lecture tour of the United States in 1882, after the publication of his first volume of *Poems* (1881). In 1883 he attended the first night of his play *Vera* in New York but it was not a success. In 1884 he married, and in 1888 published a volume of fairy-stories, *The Happy Prince and other tales*, written for his sons. In 1891 followed *Lord Arthur Savile's Crime, and other stories* and his only novel, *The Picture of Dorian Gray*, a Gothic melodrama which had aroused scandalized protest when it appeared in *Lippincott's Magazine* (1890). Wilde claimed in his preface, 'There is no such thing as a moral or an immoral book. Books are well written or badly written. That is all.' In 1891 he published more fairy-stories, *A House of Pomegranates*. His second play, *The Duchess of Padua* (1891), is a dull verse tragedy, but epigrammatic brilliance

and shrewd social observation brought theatrical success with *Lady Windermere's Fan* (1892), *A Woman of No Importance* (1893), and *An Ideal Husband* (1895). His masterpiece was *The Importance of Being Earnest* (1895), *Salomé* (now known chiefly by R. *Strauss's opera), written in French, was refused a licence, but performed in Paris by *Bernhardt in 1896 and published in 1894 in an English translation by Lord Alfred *Douglas with illustrations by *Beardsley. Lord Alfred's father, the marquess of Queensberry, disapproved of his son's friendship with Wilde and publicly insulted the playwright. This started a chain of events which led to Wilde's imprisonment for homosexual offences in 1895. He was declared bankrupt while in prison and wrote a letter of bitter reproach to Lord Alfred, published in part in 1905 as *De Profundis*: in it he provided an apologia for his own conduct, claiming to have stood 'in symbolic relations to the art and culture' of his age. He was released in 1897 and went to France where he wrote *The Ballad of Reading Gaol* (1898), inspired by his prison experience. In exile he adopted the name Sebastian Melmoth, after the romance by *Maturin. He died in Paris. His other writings include critical dialogues ('The Decay of Lying' and 'The Critic as Artist', in *Intentions*, 1891) and *The Soul of Man under Socialism*, a plea for individualism and artistic freedom, which Wilde wrote after hearing G. B. *Shaw speak, and which was first published in the *Fortnightly Review* in 1891.

A volume of letters, ed. R. Hart-Davis, appeared in 1962 and there is a biography by H. *Pearson (1946).

Wilde-Goose Chase, The, a comedy by J. *Fletcher, acted with great success in 1621, printed 1652; it was very popular on the *Restoration stage.

Mirabell, the 'wild goose', a boastful Don Juan with an aversion to marriage, is 'chased' by Oriana, his betrothed, who tries various wiles to bring him to the altar. She feigns madness for love of him, but he sees through the pretence, and she finally traps him in the disguise of a rich Italian lady. His two companions, Pinac and Belleur, with less assurance and more at the mercy of their high-spirited mistresses, alternately pursue and are pursued by Rosalura and Lillia-Bianca. *Farquhar's comedy *The Inconstant* is based on this play.

WILDER, Thornton Niven (1897–1975), American novelist and dramatist, born in Wisconsin. *The Bridge of San Luis Rey* (1927) is the best-known of his novels, but *The Ides of March* (1948), among others, is also notable. He scored considerable success in the theatre with *Our Town* (1938), *The Skin of Our Teeth* (1942), and *The Merchant of Yonkers* (1938), a comedy which was revised as *The Matchmaker* (1954) and adapted as the musical comedy *Hello, Dolly!* (1963).

Wildeve, Damon, a character in Hardy's *The Return of the Native.*

Wildfell Hall, see TENANT OF WILDFELL HALL, THE.

Wildfire, Madge, see MURDOCKSON.

Wild Huntsman, The, a spectral huntsman of German folklore, the subject of a ballad ('Der wilde Jäger') by Gottfried August Bürger (1747–94), imitated by Sir W. *Scott. Scott's version was included in *The Chase and William and Helen: two ballads from the German,* published anonymously in 1797. The legend is that a wildgrave (keeper of a royal forest), named Falkenburg, not only hunted on the Sabbath but also tyrannized over the peasants under his authority. After his death he continued to haunt the forest, and he and his hounds might be heard, though rarely seen. (See also LENORE.)

Wild Oats, a play by J. *O'Keeffe.

Wildrake, Roger, a character in Scott's *Woodstock.*

Wilfer Family, characters in Dickens's *Our Mutual Friend.*

Wilhelmine, old Kaspar's granddaughter in 'The Battle of *Blenheim' by R. *Southey.

Wilhelm Meisters Lehrjahre and *Wanderjahre,* see GOETHE.

WILKES, John (1727–97), the son of a Clerkenwell distiller, studied at Leyden, and after marrying an heiress ten years older than himself (who bore him his much-loved daughter Polly) led a life of dissipation and became a member of the *Medmenham Abbey fraternity. He was elected MP for Aylesbury in 1757 and in 1762 founded *The North Briton* in which, aided by his friend Charles *Churchill, he attacked Bute's government. In the notorious No. 45 he denounced the King's Speech, and was arrested for libel on a general warrant, but released; he was then expelled from Parliament for publishing an obscene libel, the *Essay on Woman* (a parody of *Pope), and retired to Paris. (For Lord Sandwich's role in this affair, see TWITCHER.) He returned in 1768, and after various setbacks (see PRESENT DISCONTENTS) took his seat unopposed as MP for Middlesex in 1774, in which year he was also lord mayor of London.

A man of wit, learning, and ability, and a popular hero in the cause of liberty, he secured important legal rights, including the illegality of general warrants, the freedom of choice of the electorate, and the freedom of the press. His friendly meeting over dinner with his old political adversary Dr *Johnson, on 15 May 1776, provides one of the finest moments of *Boswell's *Life.*

WILKIE, William (1721–72), author of *The Epigoniad,* an epic poem in nine books modelled on *Homer, which went into two editions (1757, 1759) and was highly regarded by *Hume and by Adam *Smith. Raised on a Scottish farm, Wilkie never fully mastered literary English, but was a skilled classicist and mathematician and became professor of natural philosophy at St Andrews. He was a member of the *Select Society.

Wilkins, Peter, see PETER WILKINS.

Willet, John, in Dickens's *Barnaby Rudge,* the host of the Maypole Inn, and Joe his son, finally the successful wooer of Dolly Varden.

'William and Helen', see LENORE.

'William and Margaret', a ballad by *Mallet in the 18th-cent. mock-antique style, written 1723, and published in A. *Hill's *Plain Dealer,* No. 36, July 1724. It is included in Percy's *Reliques* under the title 'Margaret's Ghost'.

Margaret's 'grimly ghost' visits her faithless lover William just before dawn and summons him to visit her grave; he lays his cheek upon her grave 'and word spake never more'.

William of Cloudesley, see ADAM BELL.

WILLIAM OF MALMESBURY (c.1095–1143), the first full-scale writer of history in England after *Bede, was educated at Malmesbury Abbey in Wiltshire of which he became librarian. He was a polymath who may have been influenced by the historiographical traditions of Worcester and Evesham. His major works were the *Gesta Regum Anglorum,* a history of England from 449 to 1120; the *Gesta Pontificum Anglorum,* an ecclesiastical history of England from 597 to 1125; the *Historia Novella,* the sequel to the *Gesta Regum,* dealing with 1128 to 1142 and left unfinished at his death in 1143; *De Antiquitate Glastoniensis Ecclesiae* (a work which has led to the speculation that he may have lived at Glastonbury, written between 1129 and 1139); and the *Life of St Dunstan,* a hagiographical work. As well as being an authoritative and serious historian, William was a picturesque and circumstantial writer who enlivened his narrative with topographical observation, anecdote, reminiscence, and comment. The *Gesta Regum* has two stories about *Arthur whom William regards as a great warrior while discrediting many of the stories about him. See A. Gransden, *Historical Writing in England, c.550–c.1307* (1974), ch. 9, pp. 166–85; H. Farmer, 'William of Malmesbury's Life and work' in *Journal of Ecclesiastical History,* xiii (1962), pp. 39–54.

WILLIAM OF NEWBURGH (1135/6–

?98), a canon of the priory of Newburgh (near Richmond) in Yorkshire who began in 1196 his *Historia Rerum Anglicarum*, suddenly abandoned in 1198, presumably at his death. The work was commissioned by Ernald, abbot of the Cistercian abbey of Rievaulx. The *Historia* deals with events from 1066 to 1198, especially the reigns of Stephen (with its hardships) and Henry II. It is a well-written, critical, and personal work with regard for historicity; it exposes the *Historia*, of *Geoffrey of Monmouth, for instance, as legend rather than fact.

William of Palerne, one of the earliest of the 14th-cent. English romances of the *Alliterative Revival, of 5,540 lines in a West Midland dialect. It was written for Humphrey de Bohun, based on the late 12th-cent. French *Roman de Guillaume de Palerne*.

William is a prince of Apulia who is saved from his uncle's attempts to poison him by a werewolf who is really a prince of Spain turned into that shape by his wicked stepmother. William falls in love with and wins the daughter of the Roman emperor and finally defeats the king of Spain, forcing the queen to undo her dastardly magic and restore the prince to his rightful form. While William and his love, Melior, are fleeing, they disguise themselves as bears and deer. Within this improbable framework, the poet has incorporated a discussion of courtliness and love which is not without sophistication.

Ed. W. W. Skeat, EETS es 1 (1867; reprinted Kraus, 1973).

WILLIAM OF WYKEHAM (1324–1404), bishop of Winchester and chancellor of England, founder of New College, Oxford (1379), and *Winchester College (1382). He was first employed as clerk of the king's works at Windsor, and he administered the rebuilding of Windsor Castle for Edward III. He became chancellor in 1367 but was dismissed, as a symbol of the clerical establishment, in 1371. He was one of the leaders of the bishops who opposed *John of Gaunt, and he was a lifelong opponent of Wyclifitism. His political power waned with the ascendance of Gaunt, who seized Wykeham's lands, after the death of Edward III in 1377.

Williams, Parson, a character in Richardson's *Pamela*.

WILLIAMS, Charles Walter Stansby (1886–1945), poet, novelist, and theological writer who worked for many years at the Oxford University Press. His novels, which have been described as supernatural thrillers, include *War in Heaven* (1930), *Descent into Hell* (1937), and *All Hallows Eve* (1944). Of his theological writings the most important was *The Descent of the Dove* (1939). His literary criticism included a study of *Dante, *The Figure of Beatrice* (1943). In verse he wrote a number of plays on religious themes, including *Thomas Cranmer* (1936) and *Seed of Adam* (1948), but his most original poetic achievement is perhaps his cycle on the Arthurian legend, *Taliessin through Logres* (1938) and *The Region of the Summer Stars* (1944), afterwards reissued in one volume (1974) together with *Arthurian Torso*, a study of Williams's poetry by his friend C. S. *Lewis. He was a member of Lewis's group 'the *Inklings'.

WILLIAMS, Heathcote, see UNDERGROUND POETRY.

WILLIAMS, Helen Maria (1762–1827), published her first poem, a ballad, *Edwin and Eltruda* in 1782, and travelled in 1788 to Paris, where she was chiefly to reside. She became friendly with the leading Girondists, and made the acquaintance of M. *Wollstonecraft; her *Letters* (1790–5) contain interesting information on the state of Paris and France just before and during the Revolution. She was a friend of *St Pierre, whose *Paul et Virginie* she translated (1795); she also translated A. von *Humboldt's travels (1814–29). *Wordsworth's first printed poem was 'Sonnet on seeing Miss Helen Maria Williams Weep at a Tale of Distress' (1787, under the pseudonym 'Axiologus'), but despite its title he appears not to have met her until 1820 in Paris.

WILLIAMS, Isaac (1802–65), poet and theologian, educated at Trinity College, Oxford, where he was influenced by *Keble and participated in the *Oxford Movement. He was author of poems in *Lyra Apostolica* and other poetical works including *The Cathedral* (1838) and *The Baptistery* (1842). His contribution to *Tracts for the Times* on 'Reserve in communicating Religious Knowledge' lost him the election to the chair of poetry (1842). His autobiography (edited by Sir G. Prevost, 1892) is an interesting record of the days of the Oxford Movement.

WILLIAMS, John, known as Anthony Pasquin (1761–1818), was a voluminous satirist and miscellaneous writer, often threatened with prosecution for libel. *The Children of Thespis* (1786–8) was his most successful poem, but he produced various volumes of poetry, biography, politics, satire, and plays.

WILLIAMS, Raymond Henry (1921–), critic and novelist, was born in the Welsh border village of Pandy, the son of a railway signalman, and educated at Abergavenny Grammar School and Trinity College, Cambridge. He edited *Politics and Letters* (1947–8) and was later general editor of the New Thinker's Library; from 1974 to 1983 he was professor of drama at Cambridge. His two novels are *Border Country* (1960) and *Second Generation* (1964), and his critical works, which explore the relationship of literature and society from an increasingly Marxist viewpoint, include *Culture and Society 1780–1950* (1958), *The Long Revolution* (1961), *Modern Tragedy* (1966), and *The Country and the City* (1973). (See also MARXIST LITERARY CRITICISM.)

WILLIAMS, Tennessee (Thomas Lanier Williams) (1911–83), American dramatist, born in Mississippi, the son of a travelling salesman, and brought up there and in St Louis; he studied at the Universities of Washington and Iowa, and in New York, while embarking on a career as a playwright with *American Blues* (1939, pub. 1948) and *Battle of Angels* (1940, pub. 1945, revised 1957 as *Orpheus Descending*). He achieved success with the semi-autobiographical *The Glass Menagerie* (1944, pub. 1945), a poignant and painful family drama set in St Louis, in which a frigid and frustrated mother's dreams of her glamorous past as a Southern belle conflict with the grimness of her reduced circumstances, as she persuades her rebellious son Tom to provide a 'gentleman caller' for her crippled daughter, Laura. His next big success was *A Streetcar named Desire* (1947), a study of sexual frustration, violence, and aberration, set in New Orleans, in which Blanche Dubois' fantasies of refinement and grandeur are brutally destroyed by her brother-in-law, Stanley Kowalski, whose animal nature fascinates and repels her. Williams continued to write prolifically, largely in a Gothic and macabre vein, but with insight into human passion and its perversions, and a considerable warmth and compassion; his other works include *The Rose Tattoo* (1950), a comedy about a Sicilian woman and her quest for love; the symbolic and anti-naturalistic *Camino Real* (1953); *Cat on a Hot Tin Roof* (1955), a Freudian family drama which takes place at wealthy cotton planter Big Daddy's 65th birthday, while his daughter-in-law Maggie fights to save her marriage to the alcoholic and despairing Brick; *Suddenly Last Summer* (1958); *Sweet Bird of Youth* (1959); *The Night of the Iguana* (1962); and a novella, *The Roman Spring of Mrs Stone* (1950), about an ageing actress's affair with a gigolo. He also published collections of poems, and his *Memoirs* appeared in 1975.

WILLIAMS, William Carlos (1883–1963), American poet, novelist, short story writer, and, for many years, a pediatrician in his home town of Rutherford, New Jersey; his profession as doctor deeply affected his literary life, giving him, in his own words, an entry into 'the secret gardens of the self . . . a badge to follow the poor, defeated body into those gulfs and grottos' (*Autobiography*, 1951). In his student days he was a friend of *Pound and H. *Doolittle, and his early poems (*Poems*, 1909; *The Tempers*, 1913) are Imagist, although he was to move from *Imagism to what he called Objectivism.

His poems range from the minimal, eight-line, sixteen-word 'The Red Wheelbarrow' (1923) to his most ambitious production, *Paterson* (1946–58), a long, five-part, free-verse, collage-mixed evocation of a characteristic industrial city, with the mystic motif, 'man is himself a city'. The title of his last collection, *Pictures from Brueghel* (1963), suggests the plain, poverty-stricken subjects of some of his verse and prose; and his skill at painting the ordinary with freshness and compassion is manifested in his short stories, collected as *The Farmers' Daughters* (1961). Other prose works include *In the American Grain* (1925), an important series of essays exploring the nature of American literature and the influence of Puritanism in American culture, and urging his own faith that 'all art begins in the local.' Despite his growing reputation at home, Williams's work was more or less disregarded in Britain until the 1950s; *Leavis in 1933 somewhat prematurely dismissed it as already outdated, and only a handful of writers, such as D. H. *Lawrence and B. *Bunting, took him seriously. Recently interest has increased considerably, and he is now established as one of the masters of *Modernism.

WILLIAMSON, Henry (1895–1977), born in south London, the son of a bank clerk, was educated at Colfe's Grammar School, Lewisham. He joined the army in the First World War and was commissioned in 1915; his experience of warfare permanently affected him convincing him of the futility of war and the need for understanding between nations. After the war he worked briefly in Fleet Street while writing his first novel, *The Beautiful Year* (1921: Vol. I of *The Flax of Dreams* quartet). In 1921 he moved to North Devon, and embarked on a modest country life (much influenced by R. *Jefferies) which produced his most widely known work, *Tarka the Otter* (1927), a remarkably observed, unsentimental tale which was much admired and remains a popular classic. This was followed by other tales of wild-life and the countryside, including *Salar the Salmon* (1935). In the 1930s Williamson became an admirer of Hitler and Sir Oswald Mosley, addressing Hitler in a notorious foreword to *The Flax of Dreams* (1936) as 'the great man across the Rhine, whose life symbol is the happy child'. This led, in the short term, to a brief internment at the outbreak of the Second World War, and in the long run, his admirers maintain, to the neglect of his most ambitious work, a series of fifteen novels known under the collective title *Chronicle of Ancient Sunlight*, a panoramic survey which opens in the mid-1890s with *The Dark Lantern* (1951) and closes with *The Gale of the World* (1969). This traces the career of Phillip Maddison, writer, from birth to the aftermath of the Second World War and the point at which he resolves to write a series of novels 'to reveal the past' of his own generation to the next, and to explain the true meaning of his Mosley–Birkin character's philosophy. Less politically tendentious is Williamson's short, devastating account of trench warfare, *A Patriot's Progress* (1930), seen through the eyes of a naïve, suffering Everyman, City clerk John Bullock, which was one of the most telling of the anti-war novels of the 1930s, and admired by T. E. *Lawrence. Williamson wrote about his friend-ship and correspondence with Lawrence in *Genius of Friendship* (1941).

Willobie his Avisa, one of the books which, with G. *Harvey's and T. *Nashe's satirical works, was called in by the High Commission in 1599. The poem, first published in 1594, consists of 74 serviceable but uninspired songs and a few other poems by Henry Willoby (?1574–?96). They narrate the unsuccessful courting of Avisa, a country inn-keeper's wife, by a nobleman before her marriage, and by four foreign suitors after it. The last of these has a 'familiar friend W.S.' as a companion; he has been identified with Shakespeare, who is also mentioned as author of *The Rape of Lucrece* in prefatory verses.

Willoughby, (1) Sir Clement, a character in F. Burney's *Evelina*; (2) John, a character in J. Austen's *Sense and Sensibility*.

WILLS, W(illiam) G(orman) (1828–91), a highly successful but unremembered Irish verse dramatist, whose first play, *A Man and his Shadow*, was produced in London in 1865. A long succession of popular plays led to his appointment as 'Dramatist to the Lyceum', for which he wrote many historical dramas, including *Charles I* (1872, with H. *Irving). He produced a version of *Faust in 1885, and a long poem, *Melchior*, dedicated to R. *Browning, in the same year. His chief interest, however, was in portrait painting, at which he was also eminently successful.

Will's Coffee House, called after William Un-win, its proprietor, was at No. 1, Bow Street, at the corner of Russell Street. It was frequented in the 17th and 18th cents by authors (notably by *Wycherley, *Addison, *Pope, and *Con-greve), wits, and gamblers, and is particularly associated with *Dryden; Dr Johnson in his *Lives of the English Poets* recalls that at Will's, Dryden's 'armed chair, which in the winter had a settled and prescriptive place by the fire, was in the summer placed in the balcony', and that he there presided over all literary disputes. The first number of *The Tatler* announced that all poetry appearing in it would be under the article of Will's Coffee House.

WILMOT, John, see ROCHESTER.

WILMOT, Robert, see TANCRED AND GISMUND.

Wilson, a character in Smollett's *Humphry Clinker*.

Wilson, Alison, in Scott's *Old Mortality*, the housekeeper of Silas Morton of Milnwood.

WILSON, Sir Angus Frank Johnstone (1913–), novelist and short story writer, born in Durban, South Africa, and educated at Westminster and Merton College, Oxford. He worked for some time in the Foreign Office (1949–55), then as deputy superintendent of the Reading Room of the British Museum. His first two volumes, *The Wrong Set* (1949) and *Such Darling Dodos* (1950), were of short stories, followed by *Hemlock and After* (1952), a novel about the doomed attempts of a middle-aged novelist, Bernard Sands, to establish a writer's centre in a country house. *Anglo-Saxon Attitudes* (1956, novel) also has a middle-aged pro-tagonist, historian Gerald Middleton, separated from his grotesque Danish wife and his ex-mistress Dolly, and involved in an attempt to reconstruct and understand the past, including the mystery of a possible archeological forgery, reminiscent of the Piltdown case. *A Bit off the Map* (1957, short stories) was followed by *The Middle Age of Mrs Eliot* (1958) a novel about the reversed fortunes of Meg Eliot, the sociable, handsome, and contented wife of an apparently wealthy barrister, who finds herself suddenly widowed in reduced circumstances. *The Old Men at the Zoo* (1961), about a doomed attempt to set up a large natural reservation for wild animals, reflects Wilson's concern with conflicts between the wild and the tame, the disciplined and the free, and ends with a portrayal of Europe at war. *Late Call* (1964), set with telling ac-curacy in a New Town, tells of the search for purpose and understanding of the retired hotel manageress Sylvia Calvert, obliged to live with her widowed headmaster son Harold and his family. *No Laughing Matter* (1967), his most ambitious novel, is a family saga covering some fifty years in the history of the Matthews family, but despite its subject it marks a departure from the realism of earlier works, mingling parody and dramatization with direct narration in a rich and complex evocation of family politics and neuroses. *As if by Magic* (1973) follows through various parts of the world the adventures of Hamo Langmuir, breeder of 'magic' rice, and his god-daughter Alexandra Grant, ex-student, involved in a sexual triangle and a search for purpose. *Setting the World on Fire* (1980) is a more tightly-constructed novel, contrasting the characters and destinies of two brothers, one a theatre director in love with artistic daring, the other a lawyer dismayed by disorder and en-croaching chaos. Wilson has also written on *Zola (1950), *Dickens (1970), and *Kipling (1977), and an interesting account of his own sources and creative processes, *The Wild Garden*

(1963). His works display a brilliant satiric wit, acute social observation, and a love of the macabre and the farcical, combined with humanity, compassion, and a lively interest in human affairs. His *Diversity and Depth in Fiction: selected critical writings* was published in 1983.

WILSON, Colin Henry (1931–   ), born and brought up in Leicester, left school at sixteen, and after working at a variety of jobs and reading widely in his spare time, published *The Outsider* (1956), a work which enjoyed a considerable vogue. It describes the sense of alienation of the man of genius, using a mixture of texts, from Barbusse, *Camus, *Sartre, T. E. *Lawrence, *Hesse, etc. and did much to popularize a version of *Existentialism in Britain; it appeared in the same week as *Osborne's *Look Back in Anger*, and Wilson was promptly labelled an *Angry Young Man, though he had little in common with others allocated to the same group. Wilson has since written many works on mysticism, existentialism, the occult, etc., and published many novels in various genres (*Ritual in the Dark*, 1960; *The Philosopher's Stone*, 1969; *The Space Vampires*, 1976, etc.).

WILSON, Edmund (1895–1972), American author, born in New Jersey, and educated at Princeton (where A. *Noyes, whom he did not admire, was at the time professor of poetry). He served abroad during the First World War, an experience which inspired verse and short stories published in a lively and eccentric little anthology about death, *The Undertaker's Garland* (1922, with his friend J. P. *Bishop). He then worked for various magazines, including *Vanity Fair* (1920–1), the *New Republic* (1926–31) and the *New Yorker* (1944–8). His novel *I Thought of Daisy* (1929, rev. 1967) is set in bohemian literary New York, and his short stories, *Memoirs of Hecate Country* (1946) are also set largely in New York. He is principally known for his influential, wide-ranging, and independent works of literary and social criticism, which include *Axel's Castle* (1931), a study of *Symbolist literature (*Yeats, *Valéry, G. *Stein, and others, including *Villiers de L'Isle-Adam, whose play *Axël* gave the volume its title); *The Triple Thinkers* (1938); *To the Finland Station* (1940), which traces socialist and revolutionary theory from *Michelet and R. *Owen through *Marx to *Lenin; *The Wound and the Bow* (1941), a series of studies with a *Freudian angle, taking its title from an essay on the *Philoctetes* of *Sophocles; and *Patriotic Gore: Studies in the Literature of the American Civil War* (1962), a comprehensive survey of major and minor writers of the period, and the war's roots in the national psyche. His other works include experimental plays, collections of articles and reviews, and memoirs of early and later life (*A*

Prelude, 1967; *Upstate*, 1971). His third wife was the novelist Mary *McCarthy, and he was a friend from college days of F. S. *Fitzgerald, whose posthumously published works he edited.

WILSON, Frank Percy (1889–1963), scholar and Merton professor of English literature at Oxford University (1947–57). Apart from his general editorship from 1935 of the Oxford History of English Literature and revision of *The Oxford Dictionary of English Proverbs* (1970), almost all his work was concerned with Elizabethan and Jacobean literature. His most important works were *The Plague in Shakespeare's London* (1927, rev. 1963), *Shakespeare and the New Bibliography* (1927, rev. 1970), and his revision of *McKerrow's edition of *Nashe's works (1958).

WILSON, Harriette, *née* Dubochet (1786–1846), courtesan, daughter of a Swiss-born London shopkeeper, who left a spirited account of her adventures and amours in the fashionable Regency world in *Memoirs of Harriette Wilson, written by herself* (1825), which went through many editions. It opens with panache, with the sentence 'I shall not say why and how I became at the age of fifteen, the mistress of the earl of Craven', and proceeds to describe with much frankness and some art her impressions of and friendships with *Brummell, Prince Esterhazy, the dukes of *Wellington, Argyle, Beaufort, Leinster, etc. She also wrote two slight novels, *Paris Lions and London Tigers* (1825) and *Clara Gazul* (1830), both *romans à clef*.

WILSON, John (?1627–96), educated at Oxford, became recorder of Londonderry. His two principal plays, of which the first was popular, are *The Cheats* (1663) and *The Projectors* (printed 1665, no recorded performance); they are Jonsonian satires in which sharks, gulls, usurers, and astrologers are vigorously and effectively displayed.

WILSON, John (1785–1854), enjoyed a brilliant university career at Glasgow and Oxford, and was in youth a friend of *Wordsworth and *Coleridge (to whose *The Friend* he contributed). He joined the editorial staff of *Blackwood's* shortly after its foundation and became its most copious single contributor. For the 'Maga' he provided more than half the series *Noctes Ambrosianae*, in which he appears as 'Christopher North'; he was part-author of the notorious *Chaldee MS*; he wrote a ferocious attack on Coleridge's *Biographia Literaria*; joined in *Lockhart's prolonged onslaught on the *Cockney school. He supported *Shelley, and dubbed Wordsworth, Sir W. *Scott, and *Byron, as poets, 'the three great master-spirits of our day'. But his praise alternated bewilderingly with derision and he declared, 'I like to abuse my friends.' He wrote some poetry and three sentimental novels of Scottish life, *Lights and Shadows of Scottish Life* (1822), *The Trials of Margaret Lyndsay* (1823); and *The Foresters* (1825), which Wordsworth described as 'mawkish stuff'. In 1820 he was appointed, for political reasons, to the chair of moral philosophy at Edinburgh, but his inadequacy was such that for many years a friend wrote his lectures for him.

WILSON, John Dover (1881–1969), Shakespearian scholar and editor. Using the methods of the new bibliography, he was responsible for editing most of the plays in the New Cambridge Shakespeare series which was begun in 1921. As well as this and many other scholarly works he produced several popular and influential books about Shakespeare, notably the 'biographical adventure' *The Essential Shakespeare* (1932), *What Happens in Hamlet* (1935), and *The Fortunes of Falstaff* (1943).

WILSON, Thomas (*c*.1525–81), educated at Eton and King's College, Cambridge, was privy councillor and secretary of state in 1578. He published *The Rule of Reason*, a work on logic (1551); and the *Arte of Rhetorique* (1553; revised and improved, 1560). The *Arte* is a notable landmark in the history of English prose. Wilson provides interesting examples of epistles and orations in a variety of English styles. Most of them are for emulation, but some of the more amusing, such as the famous *'ink-horn' letter from a Lincolnshire clergyman seeking preferment, exhibit the worst excesses of Latinism and affectation:

There is a Sacerdotall dignitie in my native Courey contiguate to me, where I now contemplate: vhich your worshipfull benignitie could sone impetrate for mee, if it would like you to extend your edules, and collaude me in them to the right honourble lord Chaunceller, or rather Archgrammacian of Englande.

The *Arte of Rhetorique* was edited by G. H. Mair 1909).

Wilton, Jacke, see UNFORTUNATE TRAVELLER, THE.

Wilton House, in Wiltshire, seat of the earls of Pembroke, is associated with Sir P. *Sidney, who is said to have written much of the first version of the *Arcadia there while staying with his sister Mary, countess of *Pembroke. According to *Aubrey, 'In her time Wilton house was like a College, there were so many earned and ingeniose persons.' She was undoubtedly a literary patroness, but the claim made to W. J. *Cory in 1865 that Shakespeare vas her guest and that *As You Like It* was performed there before James I has never been confirmed.

Wimble, Will, in *The Spectator*, a friend of Sir Roger de *Coverley, introduced in No. 108 as a good-natured fellow 'who hunts a pack of dogs better than any man in the country' and is generally esteemed for the obliging services he renders to all.

Wimsey, Lord Peter, the detective hero of most stories by D. L. *Sayers.

Winchester College, was founded by *William of Wykeham in 1382, its pupils, past or present, being known as Wykehamists. Among Wykehamists famous in a literary connection may be mentioned *Grocyn, *Udall, Sir H. *Wotton, Sir T. *Browne, *Otway, W. *Somerville, E. *Young, William *Collins, J. *Warton, Sydney *Smith, T. *Arnold, A. *Trollope, L. *Johnson, and J. *Mitchell.

WINCHILSEA, Anne Finch, countess of, *née* Kingsmill (1661–1720), poet, was a maid of honour to Mary of Modena and in 1684 married Colonel Heneage Finch. She was a friend of *Pope, *Swift, *Gay, and *Rowe. Her *Miscellany poems on several occasions* appeared in 1713; they were admired by *Wordsworth, who found affinities in them, and chose a selection for an album (1819). Her best-known poem is *The Spleen*; her couplet about the jonquil and 'aromatic pain' was echoed by Pope in his *Essay on Man*, and J. M. *Murry, in his preface to his 1928 selection, singles out from the same poem the lines 'Nor will in fading silks compose | Faintly the inimitable rose.' V. *Woolf in *A Room of One's Own* (1928) concluded that she 'suffered terribly from melancholy'.

WINCKELMANN, Johann Joachim (1717–68), the son of a German shoemaker, became the founder of the modern study of Greek sculptures and antiquities. By his understanding of the ideal of Greek art, its spiritual quality, its sense of proportion, and its 'noble simplicity and quiet grandeur', he exerted an immense influence on subsequent thought and literature (e.g. on *Goethe and *Schiller). *Nietzsche later rebelled against Winckelmann's 'Apollonian' view of Greek culture in his first work, *The Birth of Tragedy*.

Winckelmann's principal works were the *Gedanken über die Nachahmungen der griechischen Werke in der Malerei und Bildhauerkunst* (*Thoughts on Greek Works of Painting and Sculpture*, 1755) and the *Geschichte der Kunst des Altertums* (*History of the Art of Antiquity*, 1764). Winckelmann was the subject of an essay by *Pater and of *The Conversion of Winckelmann* by A. *Austin.

Wind in the Willows, The, see GRAHAME, K.

Windsor Forest, a *topographical poem by *Pope in the genre of *Cooper's Hill* by *Denham. Begun in 1704, it was published in 1713 to celebrate the Peace of Utrecht; it combines description of landscape with historical, literary, and political reflections.

WING, Donald Goddard (1904–), American scholar, librarian, and bibliographer, who was responsible for compiling the *Short-Title Catalogue of Books Printed in England, Scotland, Ireland, Wales and British America, and of English Books Printed in Other Countries 1641–1700*, published by the Index Society in 1945. A second edition, revised and enlarged, appeared in 1972.

Wings of the Dove, The, a novel by H. *James published 1902.

In this novel James, for the first time, takes passionate human love as his central theme. The handsome and clever Kate Croy allows herself to be taken up by her rich aunt, Maud Lowder. Fearful of the poverty surrounding her disgraced father and widowed sister, she is as determined to feather her nest as she is genuinely in love with Merton Densher, a journalist without bright financial prospects. While on a visit to New York Densher meets Milly Theale, an orphaned, gentle girl who is immensely rich. Her wings are weighted with gold. Milly travels to Europe with her friend Susan Stringham, and in London she is gathered into Mrs Lowder's circle. She is anxious to meet Densher again and is disturbed to learn, from a disapproving Mrs Lowder, of his interest in Kate. While in London she learns that she is doomed and is advised by the sympathetic doctor Sir Luke Strett to seize what joy she can from life. She installs herself in a palazzo in Venice, and with their varying motives her friends gather round her: Kate and Mrs Lowder, Densher, the fortune-hunting Sir Mark, the faithful Susan Stringham, and even the London doctor. Kate and Densher become lovers while Milly is deliberately misled into believing that Kate does not return Densher's interest. The predatory Kate persuades a reluctant Densher to make a show of love for Milly in the hope that, dying, she will provide for him—and for them. After Milly's death Densher does indeed discover that she has done so. But Kate has reckoned without his growing unease and distaste for the role he has been forced to play; Densher finds himself unable to accept the money, and Kate. Their very success in this dreadful game has brought about the death of their relationship.

Winkle, Nathaniel, in Dickens's *Pickwick Papers*, one of the members of the Corresponding Society of the Pickwick Club.

'Winkle, Rip Van', see RIP VAN WINKLE.

Winner and Waster, see WYNNERE AND WASTOUR.

Winnie-the-Pooh, the bear of very little brain, and friend of Piglet, Eeyore, and others, in the popular stories of A. A. *Milne.

WINSTANLEY, Gerrard (c.1609–76), radical pamphleteer and leader of the Diggers, or True Levellers, was born in Wigan, the son of a mercer, went to London as a clothing apprentice in 1630, and set up for himself in 1637, unsuccessfully; by 1643 he described himself as 'beaten out of both trade and estate', and he worked subsequently as a hired labourer. He published several religious pamphlets in 1648, and in 1649 with a group of comrades started digging and planting crops on St George's Hill, in Surrey, in a bold but short-lived attempt to claim the common land for 'the common people of England'. His first Digger manifesto, *The True Levellers' Standard Advanced*, is dated 20 April 1649, and it was followed by others putting forward his political and collectivist programme, e.g. *A Watchword to the City of London, and the Army* (1649), *Fire in the Bush* (1650), ending with his last and most systematic work, *The Law of Freedom, in a Platform* (1652), which also expresses his disillusion at the collapse of his agrarian experiment. He believed that the sin of covetousness had brought mankind into bondage, and his work expresses a deep compassion for the poor, while remaining remarkably fair-minded and free of sectarian virulence. His prose is powerful and lucid, addressed to plain readers, and avoiding 'the traditional, parrot-like speaking' of the universities, which in his view drew a veil over truth with 'dark interpretation and glosses': many of his metaphors are drawn from daily life, but he can also express himself with poetic and passionate intensity, and with a personal and inventive use of biblical imagery that prefigures *Blake. Nothing is known of his later years, and his contribution to literature and political thought was neglected until the 20th cent., no doubt because of the apparent failure of his ideas, but there has been a considerable revival of interest, and he is now acclaimed by many as one of the most original and prophetic writers of his time. See *The Works of Gerrard Winstanley*, ed. G. H. Sabine (1941); Winstanley, *The Law of Freedom and Other Writings*, ed. C. *Hill (Penguin, 1973).

Winterborne, Giles, a character in Hardy's *The Woodlanders*.

WINTERS, (Arthur) Yvor (1900–68) American poet and critic, whose own poem exemplify his critical doctrine of classicism, restraint, moral judgement, and 'cold certitude' (See NEW CRITICISM.) His *In Defense of Reason* (1947) contains three earlier works, *Primitivism and Decadence* (1937), *Maule's Curse* (1938), and *The Anatomy of Nonsense* (1943), all of which attack obscurantism and *Romanticism, and an essay on his friend, the highly dissimilar Hart *Crane, for whom he also wrote an elegy 'Orpheus'.

Winter's Tale, The, a play by *Shakespeare written 1610 or 1611, in which year it wa performed at the Globe. It was one of the play put on to celebrate the marriage of Princess Elizabeth and the Elector Palatine in 1612–13 and was first printed in the *Folio of 1623 where it is the last play in the section of comedies. Its main source is Greene's *Pandosto.

Leontes, king of Sicily, and Hermione, his virtuous wife, are visited by Leontes' childhood friend Polixenes, king of Bohemia. Leontes presently convinces himself that Hermione and Polixenes are lovers, attempts to procure the death of the latter by poison, and on his escape imprisons Hermione, who in prison gives birth to a daughter. Paulina, wife of Antigonus, a Sicilian lord, tries to move the king's compassion by bringing the baby to him, but in vain. He orders Antigonus to leave the child on a desert shore to perish. He disregards a Delphian oracle declaring Hermione innocent. He soon learns that his son Mamillius has died of sorrow for Hermione's treatment, and shortly after that Hermione herself is dead, and is filled with remorse. Meanwhile Antigonus leaves the baby girl, Perdita, on the shore of Bohemia, and is himself killed by a bear. Perdita is found and brought up by a shepherd. Sixteen years pass. When she grows up, Florizel, son of King Polixenes, falls in love with her, and his love is returned. This is discovered by Polixenes, to avoid whose anger Florizel, Perdita, and the old shepherd flee from Bohemia to the court of Leontes, where the identity of Perdita is discovered, to Leontes' great joy, and the revival of his grief for the loss of Hermione. Paulina offers to show him a statue that perfectly resembles Hermione, and when the king's grief is intensified by the sight of this, the statue comes to life and reveals itself as the living Hermione, whose death Paulina had falsely reported in order to save her life. Polixenes is reconciled to the marriage of his son with Perdita, on finding that the shepherd-girl is really the daughter of his former friend Leontes. The rogueries of Autolycus, the pedlar and 'snapper-up of unconsidered trifles', add amusement to the later scenes of the play; and his songs 'When daffodils begin to peer' and 'Jog on, jog on, the footpath way' are famous.

WIREKER, Nigel (*fl.* 1190), precentor of Christ Church, Canterbury, author of *Burnellus* or *Speculum Stultorum*, a satire on monks recounting the adventures of *Burnell the ass. It is found in *Anglo-Latin Satirical Poets of the Twelfth Century*, ed. T. Wright (Rolls Series, 1872, I). (See also ANGLO-LATIN LITERATURE.)

Wisden, A Cricketer's Almanac, first published under this title by John Wisden and Co. in 1870 (previously known, 1864–9, as *The Cricketer's Almanac*). The first number contains the laws of cricket, scores of 100 and upwards from 1850 to 1863, records of extraordinary matches, etc. The publication continues, and it remains the cricket enthusiast's vade-mecum.

Wisdom (also *Mind, Will and Understanding* or *Wisdom, who is Christ*), a *Morality play from c.1460, one of the group called *Macro plays, describing the seduction by Lucifer of Mind, Will, and Understanding in a series of dances. Ed. Mark Eccles in *The Macro Plays* (EETS 262, 1969).

Wisdom of Solomon, one of the books of the Apocrypha, attributed by tradition to Solomon's authorship, but probably from a Greek original of a period little anterior to Christianity. It is an eloquent eulogy of wisdom, with illustrations of its beneficent influence and a condemnation of idolatry.

WISE, Thomas James (1859–1937), bibliographer, collector, and editor, who formed the great *Ashley Library. In 1934 his credit as a bibliographer was gravely damaged by the publication of a book (*An enquiry into the nature of certain 19th-century pamphlets* by J. Carter and G. Pollard) which proved that a large number of rare pamphlets whose authenticity depended upon Wise's statements were in fact forgeries—in particular an edition of E. B. Browning's *Sonnets from the Portuguese* said to have been published in Reading in 1847.

WISHART, William (*c.*1692–1753), Scots cleric and controversialist, and co-founder of the *Rankenian club. An early collaborator with *Arbuckle, *Turnbull, and *Hutcheson, he was an energetic exponent of the moral sense philosophy of *Shaftesbury and Hutcheson. In addition to sermons, he published anonymous satires on *Berkeley's *Alciphron* in 1734 and *Doddridge's *Life of Col. Gardiner* in 1747. As principal of Edinburgh University, he led the successful opposition to *Hume's appointment as a professor in 1744–5.

Wishfort, Lady, a character in Congreve's *The Way of the World*.

Witch, The, a play by T. *Middleton, written before 1616, not printed until 1778.

The principal part of the plot is based on the story of the revenge of Rosamund on Alboin in the history of the kings of Lombardy. In Middleton's play the duchess is obliged by her husband to drink a health at a banquet out of a cup made from her father's skull and, to avenge herself, purchases by her pretended favours the help of a courtier Almachides, to kill her husband. (The same subject is treated in *D'Avenant's *Albovine*, and in *Swinburne's *Rosamund, Queen of the Lombards*.) In this and the subordinate intrigue, the assistance of the witch Hecate is called in, and part of the interest of the play lies in the comparison between Middleton's Hecate and the witches in Shakespeare's *Macbeth*. *Lamb in his *Specimens* indicated the difference between them.

Witchcraft, The Discoverie of, see SCOT, R.

'Witch of Atlas, The', a fantasy poem by P. B. *Shelley, written in the summer of 1820, on his return from a solitary pilgrimage to Monte San Peligrino, Lucca, in Italy, published 1824.

Shelley composed this playful work of 78 stanzas in *ottava rima* within the space of three days. The beautiful Witch (whom he had presumably met on his pilgrimage) is the daughter of Apollo, and the spirit of mischief and poetry. She besports herself amid pyrotechnic imagery of magic boats, airships, storms, and fireballs. Her mysterious companion is the Hermaphrodite, and together they circle the globe, weaving spells over recalcitrant kings, priests, soldiers, and young lovers (whose inhibitions are blissfully dissolved). Mary *Shelley disliked the poem; Shelley replied in verse, asking if she were 'critic-bitten'.

Witch of Edmonton, The, a tragi-comedy by *Dekker, *Ford, *Rowley, 'etc.' (possibly *Webster?), first performed probably 1621, not published until 1658. It is partly based on the story of Elizabeth Sawyer, who was hanged as a witch in April 1621.

Frank Thorney marries his fellow servant Winifred, without his father's knowledge and against his will. To save himself from being disinherited, at his father's bidding he also marries Susan Carter, and presently, to extract himself from his embarrassment, murders her and attempts to throw the guilt on her two rejected suitors, but is discovered and in due course executed.

The old woman of Edmonton is persecuted by her neighbours because she is, in her own words, 'poor, deform'd and ignorant', and to revenge herself she sells her soul to the devil, who appears to her in the form of a dog. 'Some call me witch; | And being ignorant of my self, they go | About to teach me how to be one.' Her character is notable for the characteristic sympathy shown by Dekker for the poor outcast, and the tone of the play is markedly humane. Both plots reflect the theme of revenge, but are otherwise little connected. T. S. *Eliot praised the play, and found the clown, Cuddy Banks, 'worthy to rank with clowns of Shakespeare'. It has been successfully staged several times in recent decades.

WITHER, George (1588–1667), poet and pamphleteer, was born at Bentworth in Hampshire, and educated at Magdalen College, Oxford. His satires *Abuses stript and whipt,* published 1613, in spite of the innocuous character of their denunciations of Avarice, Gluttony, and so forth, earned him imprisonment in the Marshalsea. There he wrote five pastorals under the title of *The Shepheards Hunting,* a continuation of *The Shepheard's Pipe,* which he had written

in conjunction with William *Browne, the 'Willie' of these verses. In the second of these, Wither (in the character of Philarete) describes the 'hunting of foxes, wolves and beasts of prey' (the abuses) which got him into trouble with the government. His *Fidelia,* a poetical epistle from a faithful nymph to her inconstant lover, appeared in 1617 (privately printed 1615) and again, with the famous song 'Shall I, wasting in despair', in 1619; it was this song, printed by Percy in his *Reliques,* that was to rescue Wither's reputation from a century of neglect.

Wither's self-aggrandizing Motto: *Nec habeo, nec careo, nec curo* (1621) led to another, but not his last, spell of imprisonment. In 1622 appeared *Faire-Virtue, the mistresse of Phil'arete,* a long sequence of poems in various verse forms (octo-syllabics, sonnets, diamond-shaped verses, etc.) in praise of his semi-allegorical mistress. From this time Wither's poetry became increasingly religious and satirical in tone, which led to accusations that he was a Puritan, and his portrayal as 'Chronomastix' in *Jonson's masque *Time Vindicated* (1623). He published *The hymnes and songs of the Church* in 1623, a poem on the plague in 1628, a book of *emblems in 1634–5, and *Heleluiah* in 1641. During the Civil War he raised a troop of horses and wrote many pamphlets for Parliament, and in 1642 was captain and commander of Farnham Castle, but after the war devoted much energy to petitions and litigation on behalf of his own lost property. C. S. Hensley, in *The Later Career of George Wither* (1969), challenged the traditional view that Wither's powers declined rapidly after his early pastoral phase, and presents him as 'a fair-minded man, constantly devoted to toleration and moderation', with a commitment to the plain or Puritan style of verse and prose.

No complete edition of Wither's work has been published, but several collections were printed by the Spenser Society from 1871, and there is a two-volume edition with a biographical introduction by F. Sidgwick, 1902.

Wititterly, Mr and Mrs, in Dickens's *Nicholas Nickleby,* typical snobs.

Wits, The, a comedy by *D'Avenant, published 1636, revised by him after the Restoration, and generally considered his best comedy.

Young Pallatine, a wit, who lives in London on an allowance, but finds it unequal to his wants, is in love with Lucy, who sells her jewels to provide him with money and is in consequence turned out by her cruel aunt, who suspects her of misconduct. She takes refuge with Lady Ample, the rich ward of Sir Tyrant Thrift, who proposes to force an unwelcome marriage on his ward before he loses control over her. Meanwhile Pallatine's wealthy elder brother comes to town, with old Sir Morglay Thwack, for a spell of dissipation. He tells young Pallatine that he will never more give him money, but that he must live by his wits, as he himself and Thwack propose to do. In pursuit of this purpose they become involved in a series of adventures, are thoroughly fooled, and the elder Pallatine is released from his troubles only on making liberal provision for his brother and Lucy. Thrift is likewise fooled and held to ransom.

WITTGENSTEIN, Ludwig Josef Johann (1889–1951), born in Vienna, and educated at Linz and Berlin, came to England in 1908; he lived most of his adult life in Cambridge, where he was professor of philosophy (1939–47). Trained as an engineer, he came to philosophy through the study of the philosophy of mathematics with B. *Russell. He himself published only the *Tractatus Logico-Philosophicus* (1922); in this aphoristic and difficult book he presents the view that the only meaningful use of language is as a picture of empirical, scientific fact; otherwise language will be tautological, as in logic and mathematics, or nonsensical, as in metaphysics and judgements of value. About 1930 he began to doubt the correctness of this approach; he gradually developed the view that language had a vast multiplicity of uses, which he likened to the multiplicity of tools in a carpenter's tool-bag, and that the traditional problems of philosophy arose from a misunderstanding of the use of those concepts in terms of which the problems arose; this misunderstanding he likened to mental cramp or bewilderment, and held that the problems could be dissolved by carefully bringing out the true character of the language in which they were framed. Thus there were no philosophical results, in the form of answers to questions, but only the growth and dissolution of philosophical puzzlement. Among other posthumously published writings, the *Philosophical Investigations* (1953) contain a full account of this later position.

Wittol, Sir Joseph, a character in Congreve's *The Old Bachelor.*

Witwoud, and his half-brother Sir Wilfull Witwoud, characters in Congreve's *The Way of the World.*

Wives and Daughters, the last and unfinished novel of E. *Gaskell, published in the *Cornhill Magazine,* 1864–6, and in volume form 1866.

This novel, Mrs Gaskell's masterpiece, centres on two families, the Gibsons and the Hamleys. Mr Gibson, surgeon in the little country town of Hollingford, is a widower with one daughter, Molly, who is a child when the story starts, but as she grows up her father feels he ought to marry again for her sake, and proposes to a widow, Mrs Kirkpatrick, formerly governess in the family of Lord Cumnor, the local magnate. Molly passionately resents her father's marriage,

and is made unhappy by her graceful stepmother's shallow selfishness, but she loyally tries to accept the new situation, and her lot is improved when her stepmother's daughter by her previous marriage, Cynthia, who has been brought up in France, joins the household. Cynthia is a fascinating beauty, more sincere than her mother, but with few moral principles.

The Hamleys are an ancient county family—the proud and hot-tempered Squire, his invalid wife, their elder son Osborne who is handsome and clever and his parents' favourite, and a younger son, Roger, sturdy, honest, and a late developer. Molly Gibson often stays with the Hamleys, and discovers by accident that Osborne is secretly married to a French nursery-maid. Molly, who at first found Roger unattractive, has begun to love and admire him, but he becomes engaged to Cynthia, and, being by now a successful scientist, goes off on an expedition to Africa. Cynthia is in fact already secretly engaged to Preston, Lord Cumnor's clever but ill-bred agent, and she enlists Molly's help in extricating herself from this entanglement, by a series of secret meetings which compromise Molly's reputation. The secret of Osborne Hamley's marriage comes out, causing a bitter estrangement with his father, but when Osborne dies Squire Hamley, deeply repenting his harshness, adopts Osborne's baby son. Cynthia throws over Roger Hamley and marries a man more suited to her, and when Roger returns he has realized that it is Molly whom he really loves. Like the plants and insects that Roger shows Molly through his microscope, the habits, loyalties, prejudices, petty snobberies, rumours, adjustments of a whole countryside hierarchy are displayed by Mrs Gaskell with minute and loving observation, equally acute for the aristocratic Lady Cumnor and her satirical and kind-hearted daughter Lady Harriet, who befriends Molly, and for old Silas, Squire Hamley's dying gamekeeper. Unlike some of Mrs Gaskell's earlier novels, *Wives and Daughters* is expertly constructed, convincing in all its incidents and dialogues, and peopled by fully realized characters.

WODEHOUSE, Sir P(elham) G(renville) (1881–1975), born in Guildford, the son of a civil servant who became a judge in Hong Kong. He spent much of his childhood in England in the care of various aunts, and was educated at Dulwich College, which he always remembered with affection. He soon abandoned a career in banking in Hong Kong for literature; he began by writing short stories for boys' magazines, and later published extensively in the *Strand Magazine,* *Punch,* etc., establishing himself as one of the most widely-read humorists of his day. His first novel was published in 1902, and his prolific output, of over 120 volumes, included *The Man with Two Left Feet* (1917), the collection of stories which first introduced *Jeeves and Bertie *Wooster; a series of Jeeves volumes (*My Man Jeeves*, 1919; *The Inimitable Jeeves*, 1923; *Carry On, Jeeves*, 1925, etc.); and other works featuring such favourite characters as Lord Emsworth (and his prize sow, the Empress of Blandings), Mr Mulliner, Psmith, several redoubtable aunts, and many patrons of the Drones Club. Wodehouse's amiable career, which also embraced successes in musical comedy, the theatre, and Hollywood, was interrupted by the Second World War, when he was captured by the Germans at Le Touquet in 1940. He was interned and then released, but not allowed to leave Germany, and unwisely accepted an invitation to broadcast to America. Despite the innocuous nature of the broadcasts, this caused a scandal in England, and after the war he settled in America (where he had previously lived for some years) taking American citizenship in 1955. He continued to write prolifically until the end of his life, and to retain the warm admiration of his many admirers. See Frances Donaldson, *P. G. Wodehouse* (1982).

WODROW, Robert (1679–1734), was minister of Eastwood, near Glasgow, and university librarian of Glasgow. His works include a *History of the Sufferings of the Church of Scotland from the Restoration to the Revolution* (1721–2). He also kept private notebooks (partly in cipher) published by the Maitland Club in 1842–3 as *Analecta, or materials for a history of remarkable providences*. He was a great book-collector, and left a valuable collection of broadsides and pasquinades (see J. H. Burton, *The Book-hunter*, 1862). He is commemorated in the Wodrow Society, devoted to the history of Presbyterianism and the works of eminent Presbyterians.

Woeful Countenance, The Knight of the, *Don Quixote.

WOFFINGTON, Peg (Margaret) (*c.*1714–60), the celebrated actress, was daughter of a Dublin bricklayer. She was engaged by J. *Rich for Covent Garden in 1740, and was immediately successful, acting in a great number of leading comic roles. She had many lovers, and lived for some time with *Garrick. She is the subject of *Masks and Faces* (1852), a play by C. *Reade and Tom *Taylor, on which Reade based his novel *Peg Woffington* (1853).

WOLCOT, John (1738–1819), 'Peter Pindar', began his career as a physician, took holy orders, then returned to the practice of medicine until 1778, when he came to London and began the writing of vigorous and witty satirical verses. Among these were *Lyric Odes to the Royal Academicians* (1782–5), mocking their painting; a mock-heroic poem, *The Lousiad*, published in five cantos between 1785 and 1795, and various other satires on George III. *Bozzy and Piozzi*, in which *Boswell and Mrs *Thrale set forth their reminiscences of Dr *Johnson, appeared in 1786, as did his *Poetical and Congratulatory Epistle to James Boswell*. In 1787 appeared *Instructions to a Celebrated Laureate*, which professes to teach *Warton how he should celebrate the visit of George III to Whitbread's brewery.

WOLF, Hugo (1860–1903), Austrian composer, the last exponent of the German *lied* in succession to *Schubert, *Schumann, and *Brahms. By far the largest part of Wolf's output is made up of songs, almost exclusively to German texts, or to Spanish or Italian texts in German translations. There is, however, one group of *Vier Gedichte nach Heine, Shakespeare und Lord Byron* (1888–96) which belong to the very end of his composing career: the *Byron settings are 'Sonne der Schlummerlosen' ('Sun of the sleepless!') and 'Keine gleich von allen Schönen' ('There be none of Beauty's daughters'); the Shakespeare is an interpretation of Bottom 'translated'. An *Elfenlied* ('You spotted snakes with double tongue'), for soprano solo, women's chorus, and orchestra, dates from about the same period and, like the Bottom song, was probably associated with a project for an opera based on *A Midsummer Night's Dream*.

WOLFE, Charles (1791–1823), educated at Trinity College, Dublin, was curate of Donoughmore, Co. Down, from 1818 to 1821. He was the author of the well known lines on 'The Burial of Sir John Moore', his only poem of note, apparently based on *Southey's narrative in the *Annual Register*, and first published in the *Newry Telegraph* in 1817. His *Poems*, with a memoir by C. L. Falkiner, were published in 1903.

WOLFE, Reyner or Reginald (d. 1573), bookseller and printer, who came from Strasburg and established himself in London at St Paul's Churchyard. He was the first printer in England to possess a large stock of Greek type of good quality, and he printed in 1543, with Greek and Latin text, the *Homilies* of *Chrysostom, edited by *Cheke, the first Greek book printed in this country. In 1547 he was appointed King's Printer in Latin, Greek, and Hebrew. He also came under the patronage of Archbishop *Parker. His son John Wolfe (d. 1601) inherited the business.

WOLFE, Thomas Clayton (1900–38), American novelist, born in North Carolina, the son of a stonecutter, and educated at University there and at Harvard, where he studied playwriting. He made his name with his autobiographical novel *Look Homeward, Angel* (1929), which describes at length and with much intensity the adolescence of Eugene Gant; this was followed by a sequel, *Of Time and the River* (1935), and various posthumous works, which include *The Web and the Rock* (1939) and its sequel *You Can't Go Home Again* (1940). Passionate, prolix, rhetorical, and shapeless, Wolfe's novels lacked discipline; he was unable or unwilling to prune his own work, which owed much in its published form to editorial assistance, but its emotional power won many readers, particularly among the young. He died of an infection following pneumonia.

WOLFRAM VON ESCHENBACH (*fl.* c.1200–20), a Bavarian knight and a great German epic poet, whose principal works were the epics *Parsifal* and *Willehalm*. He also composed fragments of *Titurel* and several *Tagelieder* (dawn pieces) the most famous of which begins 'Sîne klâwen'. Wolfram appears as a character in *Wagner's Parsifal*. (See MINNESINGERS.)

Wolf Solent, a novel by J. C. *Powys.

WOLLSTONECRAFT, Mary (1759–97), after an unsettled childhood, opened a school at Newington Green in 1784 with her sister Eliza and a friend; there she made the acquaintance of R. *Price and other eminent Dissenters. In 1786, after writing *Thoughts on the Education of Daughters* (1787), she went to Ireland as governess to Lord Kingsborough's children; she returned in 1788 and spent some years writing reviews and translations for the radical publisher J. *Johnson, who published her novel *Mary* (1788), her *A Vindication of the Rights of Men* (1790, a reply to *Burke), and her most famous work, *A Vindication of the Rights of Woman* (1792). During these years she met the members of Johnson's circle, which included W. *Godwin, *Holcroft, and *Fuseli. In 1792 she went to Paris, where she met Gilbert Imlay, an American writer, by whom she had a daughter, Fanny, in 1794; in the same year she published her 'View' of the French revolution. She returned to London in 1795, where Imlay's neglect drove her to two suicide attempts; in 1797 she married Godwin, and she died from septicaemia shortly after the birth of her daughter, the future Mary *Shelley. Godwin published a memoir in 1798, edited her *Posthumous Works* in the same year, and portrayed her in his novel *St Leon* (1799). See C. Tomalin, *The Life and Death of Mary Wollstonecraft* (1974).

Wolsey, The Life and Death of Cardinal, see CAVENDISH, G.

Woman in the Moone, The, a prose play by *Lyly, published 1597. The shepherds of Utopia ask Nature to provide a woman to comfort their 'sole estate'. Nature creates Pandora, endowing her with the qualities of the Seven Planets. Pandora's moods and actions vary as the planets in turn assume the ascendant, with consequent complications among the shepherds.

Woman in White, The, a novel by Wilkie *Collins, published 1860.

The narrative, related in succession by Walter Hartright and other characters in the story, starts with his midnight encounter on a lonely road with a mysterious and agitated woman dressed entirely in white, whom he helps to escape from pursuers. When working as a drawing-master in the family of Mr Fairlie, a selfish valetudinarian, he falls in love with his niece Laura, who strikingly resembles the woman in white. She returns his love, but is engaged to Sir Percival Glyde, whom she marries. It comes to light that Sir Percival, whose affairs are embarrassed, has married Laura to get possession of her wealth, that he was responsible for the confinement of the woman in white, Anne Catherick, in an asylum, and that Anne Catherick and her mother know a secret concerning Sir Percival, the revelation of which he is determined to prevent. Unable to obtain Laura's signature to the surrender of her money, Sir Percival and his friend Count Fosco (a fat, smooth villain, admirably conceived) contrive to get Laura confined in an asylum as Anne Catherick, while Anne Catherick, who dies, is buried as Laura Glyde. The device is discovered by the courage and resource of Marian Halcombe, Laura's half-sister, and Laura is rescued. Hartright, who has been abroad, returns and takes Laura and Marian under his care, and discovers Sir Percival's secret (that he was born out of wedlock and has no right to the title). Sir Percival is burnt to death while tampering with a parish register in a last effort to save his position. Fosco is forced to supply the information which restores Laura to her identity, and is killed by a member of an Italian secret society which he has betrayed.

Woman Killed with Kindness, A, a domestic tragedy by T. *Heywood, acted about 1603, printed 1607.

Frankford, a country gentleman, is the husband of Anne, a 'perfect' wife. But his happiness is ruined by the treachery of Wendoll, a guest to whom Frankford has shown every kindness and hospitality. Frankford discovers Anne in the arms of Wendoll, but instead of taking immediate vengeance on her, he determines to 'kill her even with kindness'. He sends her to live in comfort in a lonely manor-house, only prohibiting her from seeing him or her children again. She dies from remorse, after having sent for Frankford to ask forgiveness on her deathbed and received it.

The sub-plot, in which Susan Mountford is used as a pawn to redeem her bankrupt brother from prison, but finds herself loved by her new husband, offers interesting perspectives on the main plot. The play is one of the most successful examples of English domestic tragedy.

Woman's Prize, The, or the *Tamer Tamed,* a

comedy by J. *Fletcher, written 1604–?17, printed 1647. It shows the second marriage of Petruchio, from Shakespeare's *The Taming of the Shrew*; Katharine is dead, and he marries Maria, who locks him out of his house on his wedding night, and further humiliates him until he is thoroughly subdued.

Woman Who Did, The, see ALLEN, G.

Women Beware Women, a tragedy by T. *Middleton, published 1657, thirty years after his death; a composition date has not been established.

Set in Florence, the action involves two interwoven plots. The sub-plot is concerned with the guilty love of Hippolito for his niece Isabella. Hippolito's sister Livia acts as go-between, persuading Isabella she is no blood relation of her uncle: Isabella then consents to marry a foolish young heir as a screen for her own passion for Hippolito.

The main plot is loosely based on the life of the historical Bianca Cappello, who became the mistress, and then the consort, of Francesco de' Medici (1541–87), second grand duke of Tuscany. In Middleton's version, she is at the opening of the play innocently but secretly married to the poor but honest young Leantio, a merchant's clerk. The duke sees her at a window and falls in love with her: in Act II. ii, while Livia outwits Leantio's mother at chess (a scene invoked by T. S. *Eliot in *The Waste Land*), the duke gains access to Bianca and seduces her. Thereafter both she and Leantio are plunged into the corruption of the court, and consumed by it. Bianca becomes the duke's mistress: the duke, reproved by the cardinal, his brother, for his sin, contrives the death of Leantio, who has sworn everlasting enmity to Bianca, and accepted both financial and amorous compensation for her loss. These various crimes, in the last act, meet with retribution in a wholesale massacre of the characters, through the theatrical medium of a masque accompanied by poisoned incense: Bianca destroys herself by drinking deliberately from a poisoned cup.

Women in Love, a novel by D. H. *Lawrence, published in London 1921.

The sisters Ursula and Gudrun Brangwen (who first appeared in *The Rainbow*) live in Beldover, a Midlands colliery town. Ursula has been teaching for some years at the Grammar School and Gudrun has just returned from art school in London. Ursula is in love with Rupert Birkin (a self-portrait of Lawrence), a school-inspector involved in an unsatisfactory affair with Hermione Roddice, an eccentric and dominating literary hostess. Gudrun meets Gerald Crich, friend of Birkin and son of the local colliery owner. As a boy Gerald accidently killed his brother and now he feels responsible when his sister Diana is drowned. His father, Walter, is

dying and he takes over management of the mine, his ruthless efficiency being both feared and respected by the miners; but with Gudrun he becomes increasingly helpless. Birkin breaks free from Hermione and her demanding love and hopes to find with Ursula the complete union between man and woman in which he believes. Gerald suffers in his relationship with Gudrun, his mixture of violence and weakness arousing a destructive demon in her. Birkin recognizes an emptiness in Gerald, and offers him love and friendship to be based on a new intimacy between men, but Gerald is unable to accept. Ursula and Birkin are married and together with Gudrun and Gerald they take a trip to the Alps where they meet the corrupt sculptor Loerke, the 'wizard rat', with whom Gudrun flirts. While Ursula and Birkin move towards a real tenderness and fulfilment the relationship between Gudrun and Gerald becomes purely destructive until finally, in blankness and despair, Gerald wanders off into the snow and dies. Lawrence completed *Women in Love* in 1916 but was unable to find a publisher until 1920 in the USA and the following year in London where it was described by a reviewer as an 'analytical study of sexual depravity' and an 'epic of vice'. Lawrence himself thought it his best book.

Women's Press, The, see FEMINIST CRITICISM.

Women's Suffrage. The campaign for women's suffrage began in 1866 when a group of women presented a petition to J. S. *Mill requesting female enfranchisement. Mill moved an amendment to the *Reform Act of 1867 to include women, which was defeated. Thereafter organizations sprang up all over the country and joined forces to form the National Union of Women's Suffrage Societies (NUWSS). Owing to their agitation and to that of the female textile workers, by the end of the century a majority of MPs had pledged themselves to vote for women's suffrage bills, which passed their second readings three times only to be blocked by governments.

To invigorate the campaign Mrs Emmeline Pankhurst (1858–1928) founded in 1903 the Women's Social and Political Union (WSPU), and her daughter Christabel (1880–1958) in 1905 initiated mildly militant tactics, designed to make the incoming Liberals take the women's demand seriously. Because of their youthfulness militants were known as suffragettes, and members of the NUWSS, led by Millicent Garrett Fawcett (1847–1929), as suffragists.

In 1912, when it became evident that other means were failing to break Asquith's resistance, the Pankhursts resorted to destruction of empty property on a massive scale, which antagonized the public. The war brought the campaign virtually to an end; women's patriotism (coupled with a fear of renewed militancy) induced Parliament in 1918 to enfranchise women over 30, provided they occupied or were the wives of occupiers of premises of not less than £5 annual value.

The campaign was supported by many writers; in 1908 the Women Writers Suffrage League was founded by Cicely Hamilton (1872–1952), journalist, playwright, and novelist, and journalist Bessie Hatton. Its president was Elizabeth Robins (1862–1952), who under the pseudonym 'C. E. Raimond' had written several novels; her play Votes for Women (1907) was highly influential. Other supporters included O. *Schreiner, M. *Sinclair, A. *Meynell, S. *Grand, R. *West, and V. *Hunt. Suffragists and suffragettes were widely portrayed in the literature of the period: see V. *Woolf's Night and Day, H. G. *Wells's Ann Veronica, G. B. *Shaw's Press Cuttings, and many other works. Accounts of the movement were also written by leading feminists, including the Pankhursts and E. Pethick-Lawrence (1867–1954). It produced many periodicals, including Women's Suffrage Journal, The Common Cause, Votes for Women, and Women's Dreadnought.

WOOD, Anthony, or, as he latterly called himself, Anthony à Wood (1632–95), historian and antiquary, was educated at New College School, Oxford, Thame School, and Merton College, Oxford. He prepared a treatise on the history of the University of Oxford, which was translated into Latin and edited (with alterations) by *Fell and published as Historia et Antiquitates Univ. Oxon. (1674). Of this an English version by Wood, issued by John Gutch, is the standard edition. He received much ill-acknowledged help from *Aubrey. Wood published Athenae Oxonienses (1691–2), a biographical dictionary of Oxford writers and bishops, containing severe judgements on some of these, and was expelled from the University in 1693 at the instance of Henry Hyde, for a libel which the work contained on his father, the first earl of *Clarendon. Several antiquarian manuscripts left by Wood were published posthumously. His Life and Times, ed. A. Clark, occupy five volumes of the Oxford Historical Society's publications (1891–1900) in which series, also edited by Clark, appeared his History of the City of Oxford (3 vols, 1889–99).

WOOD, Ellen, née Price, better known as Mrs Henry Wood (1814–87), daughter of a glove manufacturer, lived till her marriage at Worcester, whose neighbourhood she used as the background for her Johnny Ludlow short story series (1868–89). In 1836 she married Henry Wood, a banker, and lived in the Dauphiné till she returned in 1856 to spend the rest of her life in London. She had an immense success with her first novel East Lynne (1861). She subsequently owned and edited the magazine *The Argosy, and wrote nearly 40 novels, among the best of which are Mrs Halliburton's Troubles (1862), The Channings (1862), and The Shadow of Ashlydyat (1863). Her ingenious plots about murders, thefts, and forgeries, her numerous court scenes and well-planted clues, make her in such novels as Lord Oakburn's Daughters (1864), Elster's Folly (1866), and Roland Yorke (1869) one of the forerunners of the modern *detective story. The sensational, and occasionally supernatural, events in her novels are presented in solidly detailed settings of middle-class country-town communities of doctors and lawyers, bankers and manufacturers. She often used industrial and trade union problems—slumps, unemployment, strikes—in her novels; her hostile description of a strike in A Life's Secret (1867) caused her publisher's office to be besieged by an angry mob. In spite of a commonplace style and a strong element of moralizing, many of her novels were world best-sellers, outstripping even *Dickens in Australian sales. East Lynne was repeatedly dramatized and filmed, and translated into many languages, from Welsh to Hindustani. See C. W. Wood, Memorials of Mrs Henry Wood (1894).

Woodall, the hero of Dryden's *Mr Limberham.

Woodcock, Adam, the falconer in Scott's *The Abbot.

Woodcourt, Allan, a character in Dickens's *Bleak House.

WOODFORDE, the Revd James (1740–1803), fellow of New College, Oxford, held curacies in Somerset, then was rector of Weston Longeville, Norfolk, from 1774 (in residence from 1776) until his death. His diary, known as The Diary of a Country Parson (5 vols, ed. J. Beresford, 1924–31), was published in extracts, and covers the period of the American War of Independence and the French revolution, but in the main the life he describes is matter-of-fact, concerned with local friends, minor travels, and daily events. His love of food and drink is recorded in frequent descriptions of meals ('Fowls boiled, Rabbitts smothered in onions', etc.). He is uninterested in literary matters, or in landscape and the natural world (though he writes of agricultural matters). The prose is not distinguished, and the abiding popularity of the work is due more to its social interest and period charm than to its literary qualities.

Woodhouse, Mr, the heroine's father in J. Austen's *Emma.

Woodlanders, The, a novel by T. *Hardy, published 1887.

The scene is set in Little Hintock, a village deep in the woods of Dorset. In this luxuriant woodland country, lovingly described, live a group of native woodlanders, whose living depends upon trees, and certain outsiders with whom their lives become entwined. Giles Winterbourne, who tends trees and travels in the autumn with his cider-press, loves and is betrothed to Grace Melbury, daughter of a well-to-do Hintock timber merchant. But when she returns from her finishing school she appears as the social superior of Giles. At about the same time Giles suffers financial misfortune, and these facts together induce Grace's father to bring the engagement to an end and to press his daughter into marriage with Edred Fitzpiers, a handsome and attractive young doctor who has settled nearby. Meanwhile Marty South, a village girl who had always loved Giles, has to sell her splendid hair to help herself and her sick father to live. Fitzpiers is soon lured away from Grace by a wealthy widow, Felice Charmond, who has come to live in the great house. The hope of divorce brings Grace and the faithful Giles together again. But the hope is illusory, and when Fitzpiers returns from his travels with Mrs Charmond Grace flies for refuge to Giles's cottage in the woods. Not wishing to offend her by remaining in the cottage, Giles, although ill, makes for himself a shelter of hurdles, where a few days later he dies. The loving, faithful Marty meets Grace by Giles's deathbed, and together they regularly visit his burial-place. With Mrs Charmond's death Grace and Fitzpiers are reconciled, and Marty is left alone to tend Giles's grave.

Writing to a friend in 1912, Hardy said of *The Woodlanders*, 'I think I like it, *as a story*, the best of all.'

Wood's half-pence, see DRAPIER'S LETTERS, THE.

Woodstock; or, *The Cavalier. A tale of the year 1651,* a novel by Sir W. *Scott, published 1826. The work was written when misfortunes were heaping themselves upon the author: his financial ruin, the death of his wife, and the serious illness of his beloved grandson.

The period is that of the Civil War, and the story centres in the escape of Charles II from England after the battle of Worcester. The scene is the royal lodge and park of Woodstock, near Oxford, of which the gallant old cavalier Sir Henry Lee is ranger. His nephew, Colonel Markham Everard, has, for reasons of conscience, adopted the parliamentary cause, distinguished himself as a soldier, and earned the favour of Cromwell. On the other hand he has incurred the displeasure of the fiery old Lee, and the course of his love for Lee's daughter Alice has been gravely impeded. Parliamentary commissioners are sent to sequestrate Woodstock, but through Everard's influence with Cromwell are withdrawn, for Cromwell hopes that the fugitive Charles II will take refuge in the old

lodge, and be captured there. Charles indeed arrives, disguised as the page of Colonel Albert Lee, Sir Henry's son; and during his residence at the lodge makes ardent love to the unwilling Alice, first in the character of page and, when this fails, of king. This brings about a fierce dispute between Everard and Charles, and bloodshed is prevented only by the interposition of Alice. The king relieves the anguish caused to Everard by the preference apparently shown by Alice to his rival, by revealing his identity; and Everard promises not to betray him. Cromwell, advised by a spy of the presence of Charles at Woodstock, now arrives with a force to capture him, arrests Everard, and prepares to surround the lodge. The king receives warning and flees, leaving Albert to personate him and thus delay the pursuit. After an exciting search Albert is captured and the escape of the king revealed. Cromwell, after having in his fury ordered the immediate execution of Everard, Sir Henry Lee, and his other prisoners, presently relents and pardons them. The reconciliation of Everard and Sir Henry, and the marriage of Everard and Alice, are brought about by a parting message from Charles. An important feature in the story is the supposed haunting of Woodstock. The royalists take advantage of it by 'playing at ghosts' in the secret passages of the old mansion, in order to defeat the intended sequestration.

The portrait of Cromwell has been criticized; the author makes, it is said, the mistake of representing Oliver as being in supreme power before he became lord protector in 1653. But the work gives a vivid picture of a reckless cavalier, Roger Wildrake; of the Revd Nehemiah Holdenough, Presbyterian minister of the town of Woodstock; of Puritan soldiers and preachers (including Joseph Tomkins, the steward of the parliamentary commissioners, a mixture of hypocrisy and enthusiasm); and of plotters and spies on both sides.

WOOLF, Leonard Sidney (1880–1969), author, Fabian, and social reformer, the second son of a Jewish barrister who died in 1892. He was educated at St Paul's, then at Trinity College, Cambridge, where he became a member of the *Apostles and was much influenced by G. E. *Moore. He entered the colonial service and in 1904 went to Ceylon, which was to form the background for his first novel, *The Village in the Jungle* (1913), a sympathetic study of the difficulties and dangers of rural life, threatened by superstition, drought, disease, and the encroaching jungle: the effect of imperial government is shown as minimal. Woolf returned to England on leave in 1911, and in 1912 left the colonial service to marry Virginia Stephen (see below). After the publication of his second and last novel, *The Wise Virgins* (1914), he devoted himself to social studies, journalism, and political writing, although he and his wife continued to share a close intellectual comradeship and a commitment to the *Hogarth Press; her delicate mental health exacted constant care and attention, but despite this his energy and output remained impressive. He wrote on the Co-operative Movement, Socialism, imperialism, the League of Nations, and international affairs, was literary editor of the *Nation* (1923–30), and co-founder and joint editor of the *Political Quarterly* (1931–59). *After the Deluge* (2 vols, 1931 and 1939) and *Principia Politica* (1953) were his most concerted attempt to formulate a political philosophy, but the five volumes of his autobiography, written after his wife's death, have reached a much wider audience: *Sowing* (1960), *Growing* (1961), *Beginning Again* (1964), *Downhill All the Way* (1967), and *The Journey not the Arrival Matters* (1969) together constitute a remarkably clear-sighted view of a life devoted (despite disappointments) to social progress and international understanding, and rich in intellectual and literary friendships. See D. Wilson, *Leonard Woolf: A Political Biography* (1978) for an account of Woolf's political thought and writings.

WOOLF, (Adeline) Virginia (1882–1941), daughter of Leslie *Stephen and Julia Duckworth (1847–95), was born at Hyde Park Gate, where she lived with her sister Vanessa (later Vanessa *Bell) and her brothers until her father's death in 1904. The Stephen children then moved to Bloomsbury, where they formed the nucleus of the *Bloomsbury Group. In 1905 she began to write for the *Times Literary Supplement*, a connection which lasted almost until her death. In 1912 she married Leonard *Woolf; she was already working on her first novel, *The Voyage Out*, published in 1915. Realistic in form but already foreshadowing the lyric intensity of her later work, it describes the voyage to South America of a young Englishwoman, Rachel Vinrace; her engagement there to St John Hirst; and her subsequent fever and rapid death. Virginia herself had meanwhile experienced one of the bouts of acute mental disturbance from which she had suffered since her mother's death, and it was partly as therapy for her that she and Leonard founded, in 1917, the *Hogarth Press; its first production was *Two Stories*, one by each of them. Her second novel, also realistic, *Night and Day* (1919), set in London, centres on Katherine Hilbery, daughter of a famous literary family (modelled on Vanessa), whose pursuits are contrasted with her friend Mary's involvement with *Women's Suffrage. *Jacob's Room* (1922), a novel evoking the life and death (in the First World War) of Jacob Flanders (clearly related to the death of her brother Thoby in 1906) was recognized as a new development in the art of fiction, in its indirect narration and poetic impressionism; it was hailed by friends such as

T. S. *Eliot ('you have freed yourself from any compromise between the traditional novel and your original gift') and attacked by, e.g., J. M. *Murry for its lack of plot. Shortly afterwards she published one of her important statements on modern fiction, 'Mr Bennett and Mrs Brown', in the *Nation and Athenaeum*, 1 Dec. 1923 (afterwards revised and reprinted in various forms), which attacked the realism of Arnold *Bennett and advocated a more fluid, internal approach to the problem of characterization, etc. From this time onwards she was regarded as one of the principal exponents of *Modernism, and her subsequent major novels, *Mrs Dalloway* (1925), *To the Lighthouse* (1927), and *The Waves* (1931), established her reputation securely. The intensity of her creative work was accompanied by mental suffering and ill health, but she was able to intersperse her more serious works with more playful productions, such as *Orlando* (1928), a fantastic biography inspired by her friend V. *Sackville-West, which traces the history of the youthful, beautiful, and aristocratic Orlando through four centuries and both male and female manifestations; *Flush* (1933), a slighter work, is the 'biography' of E. B. *Browning's spaniel. *The Years* (1937) is in form a more conventional novel, whereas her last work, *Between the Acts* (1941), is again highly experimental. It was shortly after finishing it, and before its publication, that the last of her attacks of mental illness led to her drowning herself in the Ouse, near her home at Rodmell, Sussex.

Virginia Woolf is now acclaimed as one of the great innovative novelists of the 20th cent., many of whose experimental techniques (such as the use of the *stream of consciousness, or interior monologue) have been absorbed into the mainstream of fiction; her novels have been particularly highly regarded from the 1970s onwards by the new school of *feminist criticism. She was also a literary critic and journalist of distinction. *A Room of One's Own* (1929) is a classic of the feminist movement; a sequel, *Three Guineas*, appeared in 1938. Her critical essays were published in several collections, including *The Common Reader* (1925; Second Series, 1932), and the posthumous *The Death of the Moth* (1942), *The Captain's Death Bed* (1950), and *Granite and Rainbow* (1958). A volume of short stories, *A Haunted House* (1943), collects earlier stories and some not previously published. She was also a tireless letter-writer and diarist. Her letters (ed. Nigel Nicolson and J. Trautmann, 6 vols, 1975–80) are a dazzling, at times malicious evocation of a world of literary and social friendships and intrigues, with a cast list that includes *Strachey, the *Sitwells, Ottoline *Morrell, R. *Fry and many others; her diaries (5 vols, ed. Anne Olivier Bell and A. McNeillie, 1977–84) are a unique record of the joys and pains of the creative process. See also

Virginia Woolf (2 vols, 1972), a biography by her nephew Quentin Bell, and *Deceived with Kindness* (1984), by her niece Angelica Bell.

WOOLMAN, John (1720–72), American Quaker, who travelled during many years preaching the faith, and both wrote and spoke against slavery. He is best remembered for his *Journal* (1774), notable for its purity and simplicity of style. *Lamb wrote, 'Get the writings of John Woolman by heart, and love the early Quakers.'

WOOLNER, Thomas (1825–92), poet and sculptor, one of the original *Pre-Raphaelite brethren, who contributed to *The Germ* two cantos of what was to become *My Beautiful Lady* (1863). At first he met with small success as a sculptor, and in 1852 sailed for the Australian gold fields (his departure inspiring Ford Madox Brown's picture *The Last of England*), but returned in 1854 and became a prosperous portrait sculptor, doing busts and statues of (among many others), *Tennyson, *Newman, C. *Kingsley, and J. S. *Mill. His other poems include the blank verse *Pygmalion* (1881). 'The Piping Shepherd', which appears as a frontispiece to *Palgrave's *Golden Treasury*, is by him.

Wooster, Bertram (familiarly known as 'Bertie'), an amiable, vacuous young man-about-town in the stories of P. G. *Wodehouse; the employer of *Jeeves.

Wopsle, Mr, in Dickens's *Great Expectations*, a parish clerk who turns actor and plays Hamlet with indifferent success.

WORDE, Winkyn de, see WYNKYN DE WORDE.

WORDSWORTH, Dorothy (1771–1855), was the sister of William *Wordsworth and his treasured companion throughout their adult lives. After an unsettled and partly orphaned childhood, away from her three brothers, Dorothy settled with William in 1795, and from that time they lived together, through William's marriage until his death. After a short time in Dorset they moved to Alfoxden in Somerset, to be near *Coleridge at Nether Stowey. Here in 1798, when she, William, and Coleridge walked and talked, as Coleridge wrote, 'as three persons with one soul', she began her first journal. This was the *Alfoxden Journal*, but the MS has disappeared and only the months Jan.–April 1798 remain. It is, however, valuable, not only for its close description of the Quantocks and the sea, but for the revelation of the companionship of the three friends in the heady year of the *Lyrical Ballads*. In 1799 William and Dorothy moved to Dove Cottage at Grasmere in the Lake District. The *Grasmere Journal* covers the years 1800–3 and was begun 'because I shall give William pleasure by it'. The entries are again filled with her love of landscape,

season, walking, and weather; her skill with words is evident both in the precise descriptions of the world about them and of the daily events of life in Dove Cottage.

Dorothy kept several other journals of travels and expeditions, which also were not published until after her death. She wrote a brief Journal of a *Visit to Hamburgh and a Journey . . . to Goslar 1798–99*. In 1805 she finished *Recollections of a Tour made in Scotland 1803*, which exists in five MSS; the earlier, less formal, versions vividly describe the wild countryside and weather, the tremulous horse, the uneatable oatcake, and the wet sheets. (Coleridge, overwhelmed, abandoned the expedition at Loch Long.) Her spirited accounts of *An Excursion on the Banks of Ullswater 1805* and *An Excursion up Scawfell Pike 1818* were both used by Wordsworth in his *Guide to the Lakes* (1823). A long *Journal of a Tour on the Continent 1820* conveys her intoxication with, especially, Switzerland, and the rubs of life on the road with William. A sprightly *Journal of a Second Tour in Scotland* followed in 1822, and a *Journal of a Tour in the Isle of Man* in 1828.

It is clear from passages in her notes and from certain of his poems (for instance, the untitled 'Daffodils') that Wordsworth made use of his sister's journals. Coleridge seems also to have used the Alfoxden journal for certain passages in *'Christabel'. Several of Wordsworth's poems, as well as the famous closing lines of *'Tintern Abbey', are addressed to Dorothy, including 'The Glow Worm', 'Ode to Lycoris', and 'To the Same'. Dorothy died, after many years of illness and senility, from arteriosclerosis. In his *Life* (1933) her editor de *Selincourt finds her 'probably . . . the most distinguished of English writers who never wrote a line for the general public'.

WORDSWORTH, William (1770–1850), born at Cockermouth, Cumbria, the son of an attorney; he attended (with Mary Hutchinson, his future wife) the infants' school in Penrith and, from 1779 to 1787, Hawkshead Grammar School. His mother died in 1778, his father in 1783, losses recorded in *The Prelude*, which describes the mixed joys and terrors of his country boyhood with a peculiar intensity. He attended St John's College, Cambridge, but disliked the academic course. In 1790 he went on a walking tour of France, the Alps, and Italy, and returned to France late in 1791, to spend a year there; during this period he was fired by a passionate belief in the French revolution and republican ideals, and also fell in love with the daughter of a surgeon at Blois, Annette Vallon, who bore him a daughter (see E. Legouis, *William Wordsworth and Annette Vallon*, 1922). (This love affair is reflected in 'Vaudracour and Julia', composed ?1804, published 1820, incorporated somewhat anomalously in Book IX of *The Prelude*.) After his return to England he published in 1793 two poems in heroic couplets, *An Evening Walk* and *Descriptive Sketches*, both conventional attempts at the *picturesque and the *sublime, the latter describing the Alps. In this year he also wrote (but did not publish) a *Letter to the Bishop of Llandaff* (see WATSON, R.) in support of the French Republic. England's declaration of war against France shocked him deeply, but the institution of the Terror marked the beginning of his disillusion with the French revolution, a period of depression reflected in his verse drama *The Borderers* (composed 1796–7, published 1842) and in 'Guilt and Sorrow' (composed 1791–4, published in part in 1798 as 'The Female Vagrant'). In 1795 he received a legacy of £900 from his friend Raisley Calvert, intended to enable him to pursue his vocation as a poet, which also allowed him to be reunited with his sister Dorothy (above); they settled first at Racedown in Dorset, then at Alfoxden in Somerset, where they had charge of the son of their friend Basil *Montagu. The latter move (aided by T. *Poole) was influenced by a desire to be near *Coleridge, then living at Nether Stowey, whom Wordsworth had met in 1795. This was a period of intense creativity for both poets, which produced the *Lyrical Ballads* (1798), a landmark in the history of English *Romanticism. (See ANCIENT MARINER, IDIOT BOY, TINTERN ABBEY.) The winter of 1798–9 was spent in Goslar in Germany, where Wordsworth wrote sections of what was to be *The Prelude* and the enigmatic *'Lucy' poems. In 1799 he and Dorothy settled in Dove Cottage, Grasmere; to the next year belong 'The Recluse', Book I (later *The Excursion*), 'The Brothers', *'Michael', and many of the poems included in the 1800 edition of the *Lyrical Ballads* (which, with its provocative Preface on *poetic diction, aroused much criticism). In 1802 Wordsworth and Dorothy visited Annette Vallon in France, and later that year William married Mary Hutchinson, his financial position having been improved by the repayment of a debt on the death of Lord Lonsdale. In the same year he composed *'Resolution and Independence', and began his ode on *'Intimations of Immortality from Recollections of Early Childhood', both of which appeared in *Poems in Two Volumes* (1807), along with many of his most celebrated lyrics. To the same period belong the birth of five children (of whom the eldest, John, was born in 1803), travels with Dorothy and Coleridge, and new friendships, notably with Sir W. *Scott, Sir G. *Beaumont, and *De Quincey. Wordsworth's domestic happiness was overcast by the death of his sailor brother John in 1805 (which inspired several poems, including 'Elegiac Stanzas suggested by a Picture of Peele Castle', 1807), the early deaths of two of his children (one of which inspired his sonnet 'Surprised by joy', 1815), and the physical deterioration of Coleridge, from whom he was for some time estranged,

and with whom he was never entirely reconciled. But his productivity continued, and his popularity gradually increased. *The Excursion* was published in 1814, *The White Doe of Rylstone* in 1815, two volumes of *Miscellaneous Poems* in 1815, and *Peter Bell* and *The Waggoner* in 1819. In 1813 he had been appointed Stamp Distributor for Westmorland, a post which brought him some £400 a year, and in the same year moved from Allan Bank (where he had lived from 1808) to Rydal Mount, Grasmere, where he lived the rest of his life. The great work of his early and middle years was now over, and Wordsworth slowly settled into the role of patriotic, conservative public man, abandoning the radical politics and idealism of his youth. Much of the best of his later work was mildly topographical, inspired by his love of travel; it records journeys to Scotland, along the river Duddon, to the Continent, etc. He was left a legacy by Sir George Beaumont in 1827, and in 1842 received a civil list pension of £300 a year; in 1843 he succeeded *Southey as poet laureate. He died at Rydal Mount, after the publication of a finally revised text of his works (6 vols, 1849–50), and *The Prelude* was published posthumously in 1850. His prose works include an essay, *Concerning the Relations of Great Britain, Spain and Portugal . . . as affected by the Convention of Cintra* (1809), castigating the supine English policy, and *A Description of the Scenery of the Lakes in the North of England*, written in 1810 as an introduction to Wilkinson's *Select Views of Cumberland*.

De Quincey wrote of Wordsworth in 1835, 'Up to 1820 the name of Wordsworth was trampled underfoot; from 1820 to 1830 it was militant; from 1830 to 1835 it has been triumphant.' Early attacks in the *Edinburgh Review* and by the anonymous author of a parody, *The Simpliciad* (1808), were followed by criticism and satire by the second generation of Romantics; *Byron and *Shelley mocked him as 'simple' and 'dull', *Keats distrusted what he called the *'egotistical sublime', and *Hazlitt and later *Browning, deplored him as *'The Lost Leader', who had abandoned his early radical faith. But these doubts were counterbalanced by the enormous and lasting popularity of much of his work, which was regarded by writers such as M. *Arnold and J. S. *Mill with almost religious veneration, as an expression in an age of doubt of the transcendent in nature and the good in man. A great innovator, he permanently enlarged the range of English poetry, both in subject matter and in treatment (a distinction he would not himself have accepted).

Wordsworth's *Poetical and Prose Works*, together with Dorothy Wordsworth's *Journals*, ed. W. Knight, appeared in 1896, and his *Poetical Works* (ed. E. de *Selincourt and H. Darbishire, 5 vols) in 1940–9 and 1952–4. *Letters of the Wordsworth Family 1787–1855* were edited by W.

Knight in 1907, and *Letters of William and Dorothy Wordsworth* (ed. de Selincourt) appeared in 1935–9. His biography by M. Moorman was published in 1968 (2 vols), and a long-lost collection of letters between Mary and William appeared as *The Love Letters of William and Mary Wordsworth*, ed. B. Darlington (1982).

Workers' Educational Association, a movement founded in 1903 by Albert Mansbridge (1876–1952) to promote 'the Higher Education of Working Men', which soon received recognition from most universities. It provided tutorial classes (one of the pioneer tutors being R. H. *Tawney), and continues its work today, providing day and evening classes for democratically organized voluntary groups, with courses worked out in partnership between tutor and students.

World, The, by 'Adam Fitz-Adam', a weekly 'paper of entertainment', owned by R. *Dodsley, and edited by E. *Moore. It ran from 1753 to 1756, and its contributors included *Chesterfield, Horace *Walpole, and *Jenyns.

Worldly Wiseman, Mr, in Bunyan's *Pilgrim's Progress*, an inhabitant of the town of Carnal Policy, who tries to dissuade *Christian from going on his pilgrimage.

World's Classics, The, a series of cheap reprints of standard works of English literature, launched in 1901 by G. *Richards; its first titles included *Jane Eyre*, * The Vicar of Wakefield*, and *Barham's *The Ingoldsby Legends*, and the spine decoration of the series was designed by L. *Housman. In 1905 the series was bought by Henry Frowde for the *Oxford University Press; he introduced pocket editions on thin paper and by 1907 the ordinary edition was available in eight different styles, at prices ranging from 1/– to 5/6d. The series (which includes some translations, e.g. of *Tolstoy, *Montaigne, and others) was relaunched in paperback in 1980.

Worthies of England, The History of the, by T. *Fuller, published 1662, after his death.
   The work is a kind of gazetteer of England, in which the author takes the counties one by one, describes their physical characteristics, natural commodities, and manufactures, with quaint comments on each, some his own aphorisms ('Knives . . . are the teeth of old men'), some proverbial ('Bean-belly Leicestershire, so called from the great plenty of that grain growing therein'). After these come short biographies of the local saints, Protestant martyrs, prelates, statesmen, writers, etc., and lists of the gentry and sheriffs. This work (which was used without acknowledgement by A. *Wood) is the source of many well known anecdotes, such as that of *Ralegh laying his cloak for the queen in 'a plashy place'.

Worthies of the World, The Nine, were 'three Paynims, three Jews, and three Christian men', viz. Hector of Troy, Alexander the Great, and Julius Caesar; Joshua, David, and Judas Maccabaeus; Arthur, Charlemagne, and Godefroi de Bouillon. (Caxton, Preface to *Le *Morte D'Arthur*). The list of worthies in Shakespeare's *Love's Labour's Lost*, v. ii. is not quite the same, for it includes Pompey and Hercules.

WOTTON, Sir Henry (1568–1639), was educated at Winchester and New and Queen's Colleges, Oxford, where he became a close friend of *Donne. He entered the Middle Temple, then became agent and secretary to the earl of Essex, 1595, and was employed by him in collecting foreign intelligence. He was ambassador at the court of Venice and employed on various other diplomatic missions from 1604 to 1624. While on a visit to Augsburg he wrote in his host's album his famous definition of an ambassador, 'vir bonus peregre missus ad mentiendum Reipublicae causa', 'which he would have been content should have been thus englished "An Ambassador is an honest man, sent to lie abroad for the good of his country" '(I. *Walton); Scioppius mentioned this in his printed diatribe against James I (1611). Wotton was provost of Eton, 1624–39. He published *Elements of Architecture* (1624). A collection of his poetical and other writings appeared under the title *Reliquiae Wottonianae*, containing his famous 'Character of a Happy Life' and 'On his Mistress, the Queen of Bohemia' ('You meaner beauties of the night') in 1651 (enlarged eds, 1672, 1685). His *Life* was written by his friend Izaak Walton (1670). His poems appeared in J. Hannah's edition *The Courtly Poets from Raleigh to Montrose* (1870) and *Life and Letters*, by L. Pearsall *Smith, appeared in 1907.

Would-be, Sir Politic and Lady, the foolish traveller and his garrulous wife in Jonson's *Volpone*.

Wound and the Bow, The, see WILSON, E.

Wrayburn, Eugene, a character in Dickens's *Our Mutual Friend*.

'Wreck of the Deutschland, The', see HOPKINS, G. M.

'Wreck of the Hesperus, The', a poem by *Longfellow.

WREN, Sir Christopher (1631–1723), son of Christopher Wren, dean of Windsor, 1635–58, and nephew of Matthew Wren, bishop of Ely (who was imprisoned in the Tower, 1642–60). Wren was educated at Westminster School and Wadham College, Oxford. He became a member of All Souls in 1653 and was a prominent member of the circle of scholars who later were founder members of the *Royal Society. With them he studied anatomy, mathematics, and astronomy, being appointed professor of anatomy at Gresham College, London, in 1657 and Savilian professor of astronomy at Oxford in 1661. His first architectural works were the chapel of Pembroke College, Cambridge (1663–5), and the Sheldonian Theatre, Oxford (1664–9). A few days after the Fire of London in 1666, he presented a plan for rebuilding the City, but it was not adopted. He was, however, made surveyor in charge of the City churches, and designed 52 of them. He had prepared a scheme for repairing St Paul's before the fire, and when it became clear in 1668 that it must be rebuilt he prepared designs: work began on the new building in 1675 and it was finished in 1710. Wren also designed many other buildings, including the library of Trinity College, Cambridge, and Tom Tower, Christ Church, Oxford. *Parentalia, or Memories of the Family of the Wrens* (1750) is a collection of family documents made by Wren's son Christopher.

Wren, Jenny, the business name of the doll's dressmaker in Dickens's *Our Mutual Friend.* Her real name was Fanny Cleaver.

WREN, P(ercival) C(hristopher) (1885–1941), born in Devon and educated at Oxford, had a varied and much-travelled life, working at one time as a member of the French Foreign Legion, and later for some years in India as assistant director of education. His first book of stories, *Dew and Mildew* (1912), was set in India, but he did not achieve popular success until the publication of *Beau Geste* (1924), the first of his Foreign Legion novels, a romantic adventure story which became a best-seller, and which was followed by *Beau Sabreur* (1926), *Beau Ideal* (1928), etc.

WRIGHT, Joseph, of Derby (1734–97), English painter, who worked mainly in Derby. Wright's subjects are novel—scientific experiments, industrial activity—and he was celebrated for effects of light—candlelight, moonlight, the flames of a forge, the windows of a mill at night. Wright was patronized by J. *Wedgwood and Arkwright, and his works reflect the scientific curiosity that dominated intellectual life in the industrial Midlands. He was a friend of E. *Darwin, whose poem *The Botanic Garden* is close in subject and feeling to Wright's pictures; painter and poet move easily from modern engineering to classical allegory. In the 1770s and 1780s Wright, a friend of W. *Hayley, began to choose his subjects from literature; he was attracted by the macabre and by the Romantic melancholy of contemporary literature. He painted scenes from Shakespeare, *Milton, and from contemporary writers, including *Beattie, *Sterne, and *Langhorne. *The Dead Soldier,* from Langhorne, was engraved and widely popular.

WRIGHT, Joseph (1855–1930), lexicographer and philologist, of working-class Yorkshire origins and largely self-educated; editor (1891–1905) of the *English Dialect Dictionary* (published at his own expense) and author of the *English Dialect Grammar* (1905) and several primers and grammars of Old and Middle English, Old and Middle High German, and Gothic; his wife Elizabeth Mary Wright was his collaborator in several of his works.

WRIGHT, Richard (1908–60), black American writer, brought up in Memphis, and largely self-educated; he joined the Communist Party in the 1930s, but left in the 1940s, as he records in *The God that Failed* (1950). His best-known novels are the powerful and violent *Native Son* (1940) and *The Outsider* (1953), both of which deal with tragedy in the lives of black victims of poverty and politics.

WRIGHT, Thomas (1810–77), educated at Trinity College, Cambridge, was instrumental in founding the *Camden, *Percy, and Shakespeare Societies. His published works, mainly on historical, literary, and antiquarian subjects, included *Biographia Literaria* (1842–6) and *A History of Domestic Manners and Sentiments in England during the Middle Ages* (1862). Among the many volumes he edited are *Queen Elizabeth and her Times* (1838), *The Vision and the Creed of Piers Plowman* (1842), *Anecdota Literaria* (1844).

Wronghead, Sir Francis, a character in Vanbrugh and Cibber's *The Provok'd Husband.*

'Wulf and Eadwacer', an Old English poem in 19 lines of varying length, one of the group called 'Elegies' from the *Exeter Book. Its theme seems to be the separation of lovers, but it is very unclear, despite its powerfully suggestive atmosphere. It is often translated by modern poets, including Craig Raine in *Rich* (1984). See also *The Old English Elegies* (1983), ed. M. Green.

WULFILA, see ULFILAS.

WULFSTAN (d. 1023), archbishop of York, author of homilies in English including the famous 'Address to the English', *Sermo Lupi ad Anglos,* in which he describes the desolation of the country brought about by the Danish raids and castigates the vices and demoralization of the people. Like his predecessor Oswald he held the sees of Worcester and York simultaneously from 1002 to his death (whereupon he was buried at Ely); this pluralism is possibly the reason why he is called *reprobus* and *impius* by some contemporary commentators. He was bishop of London in 996 and he reformed the monastery of St Peter's, Gloucester, in 1022. He had contacts with *Ælfric, with whom he shares a distinction as a writer of sermons in rhythmical, alliterative prose; only four sermons and one

Pastoral Letter can be ascribed to him with any probability, on stylistic grounds. He drafted codes of Laws for Ethelred from 1008 to 1015, and for Cnut (*Canute), despite his earlier deploring of the Danish raids, from his accession in 1016 to Wulfstan's death in 1023.
Ed. D. Whitelock, *Sermo Lupi ad Anglos* (1939; rev. 1963); ed. D. Bethurum, *Homilies* (1957).

Wuthering Heights, a novel by E. *Brontë, published 1847.
The story is narrated by Lockwood, temporary tenant of Thrushcross Grange, who at the opening of the novel stumbles unsuspecting into the violent world of Wuthering Heights, the home of his landlord Heathcliff. The narration is taken up by the housekeeper, Nelly Dean, who had been witness of the interlocked destinies of the original owners of the Heights, the Earnshaw family, and of the Grange, the Linton family. In a series of brilliantly handled flashbacks and time shifts, Emily Brontë unfolds a tale of exceptional emotional and imaginative force. Events are set in motion by the arrival at the Heights of Heathcliff, picked up as a waif of unknown parentage in the streets of Liverpool by the elder Earnshaw, who brings him home to rear as one of his own children. Bullied and humiliated after Earnshaw's death by his son Hindley, Heathcliff's passionate and ferocious nature finds its complement in Earnshaw's daughter Catherine. Their childhood collusions develop into an increasingly intense though vexed attachment, but Heathcliff, overhearing Catherine tell Nelly that she cannot marry him because it would degrade her, and failing to stay to hear her declare her passion for him, leaves the house. He returns three years later, mysteriously enriched, to find Catherine married to the insignificant Edgar Linton. Heathcliff is welcomed by Hindley, by now widowed with a son, Hareton, and a hardened gambler. Heathcliff's destructive force is now unleashed; he marries Edgar's sister Isabella and cruelly ill-treats her, hastens Catherine's death by his passion as she is about to give birth to a daughter, Cathy, and brings Hareton and Hindley under his power, brutalizing the latter in revenge for Hindley's treatment of himself as a child. Edgar Linton dies, after doing his best to prevent a friendship between Cathy and Heathcliff's son Linton; Heathcliff then lures Cathy to his house, and forces a marriage between her and young Linton in order to secure the Linton property. Young Linton, always sickly, also dies, and an affection springs up between her, an unwilling prisoner at the Heights, and the ignorant Hareton, whom she does her best to educate. Heathcliff's desire for revenge has now worn itself out, and he longs for the death that will reunite him with Catherine; at his death there is a promise that the two contrasting worlds and moral orders

represented by the Heights and the Grange will be united in the next generation, in the union of Cathy and Hareton.
Early reviewers tended to dwell on the novel's morbid and painful aspects, but their neglect has been overtaken by what is now a general recognition of the mastery of an extremely complex structure, acute evocation of place, poetic grandeur of vision, and a highly original handling of *Gothic and Romantic elements inherited from lesser works.

WYATT, Sir Thomas (1503–42), came from a Yorkshire family, and was educated at St John's College, Cambridge. He held various diplomatic posts in the service of Henry VIII in France, Italy, Spain, and the Netherlands. His first visit to Italy in 1527 probably stimulated him to translate and imitate the poems of *Petrarch. In the same year he made a version of a *Plutarch essay, based on Budé's French translation, *The Quyete of Mynde*, which he dedicated to the queen (Catherine of Aragon) whom the king was in process of divorcing. Wyatt's relationship with *Henry VIII's next bride, Anne Boleyn, was more problematic. He was certainly closely acquainted with her before her marriage and, according to three 16th-cent. accounts, confessed to the king that she had been his mistress and was not fit to be a royal consort. Possibly this frankness explains why Wyatt was not executed, along with Anne's other lovers, in 1536, suffering only a period of imprisonment in the Tower. After his release his career soon recovered; he became a sheriff of Kent, and in 1537–9 held the important post of ambassador to Charles V's court in Spain. He celebrated his departure from Spain, June 1539, in the epigram 'Tagus, farewell'. In 1540 the tide of Wyatt's fortunes turned, with the execution of his friend and patron Thomas Cromwell, which is probably referred to in the sonnet (based on Petrarch) 'The piller pearisht is whearto I lent'. Wyatt himself was arrested, on charges of treason, in July 1541; though released two months later he never fully regained favour. He died in September 1542, of a fever contracted by hard riding on a last diplomatic errand for the king.
Wyatt's poetry is beset by problems in three main areas; authorship, biographical relevance, and artistic aims. Though the canon of Wyatt's poems is generally taken to include all the poems in the Egerton manuscript, even this cannot be proved with certainty, and there are many other poems whose attribution to him depends mainly upon association. The authenticated poems and translations include sonnets, rondeaux, epigrams, satires, lute songs, and a version (based on *Aretino) of the seven Penitential Psalms, whose framing poems depict David repenting of his adulterous love for Bathsheba. Much controversy surrounds Wyatt's artistic purpose in making translations from Italian poems. His metre

must have been perceived as irregular even twenty years later, since *Tottel in his *Songes and Sonettes* (1557) adapted many of Wyatt's poems to conventional iambic stress, including 'They fle from me that sometyme did me seke'. Critical estimates of Wyatt's poetry in the 20th cent. have varied widely. C. S. *Lewis called him 'the father of the Drab Age', but others have viewed him as a complex and original writer whose love poems anticipate those of *Donne. The poems have been frequently edited, for instance by K. Muir and P. Thomson (1969), by Joost Daalder (1975), and by R. A. Rebholz (Penguin, 1978). Muir and Thomson's *Life and Letters* (1962) assembles most of the biographical material; Thomson's *Critical Heritage* collection (1974) assembles critical views through the ages.

WYCHERLEY, William (1641–1715), of a Shropshire family, was educated first in France, then at The Queen's College, Oxford, but he never matriculated, afterwards enrolling as a student in the Inner Temple. His first play, *Love in a Wood, or, St James's Park*, a comedy of intrigue set in St James's Park, was probably acted in 1671, and published in 1672, and brought him the favour of the duchess of Cleveland, the king's mistress. In 1679 he secretly married the widowed countess of Drogheda, daughter of the first earl of Radnor, and incurred thereby the displeasure of Charles II, who had offered him the tutorship of his son, the duke of Richmond. His second play, *The Gentleman Dancing-Master*, was probably acted 1671, published 1673; *The Country Wife* was published and probably first acted 1675; his last play, *The Plain-Dealer*, was probably acted 1676, published 1677. His *Miscellany Poems* (1704) led to a friendship with *Pope, who revised many of his writings. His *Posthumous Works* appeared in 1728.

Wycherley's plays, admired by *Lamb but condemned by *Macaulay as licentious and indecent, are highly regarded for their acute social criticism, particularly of sexual morality and the marriage conventions; his characterization and thematic organization are also strong, and his last two plays have been successfully revived many times. The standard edition is by A. Friedman (1979). (See also RESTORATION.)

WYCLIF, John (c.1330–84), probably born in Hipswell (near Wycliffe), a village near Richmond in North Yorkshire. He came to Oxford in 1354 and was connected with Merton, Balliol, and The Queen's Colleges during his period there, from 1354 to 1381. He was a protégé of *John of Gaunt, and it was probably at his instance that he preached against *William of Wykeham and the Good Parliament in 1376. He was a trained scholastic who lectured and wrote on logic, 1361–72, and modern accounts

of him often stress the philosophical (in which area he could be called an extreme exponent of *Realism) rather than the radically reforming side of him. His attacks on the authority and abuses in the Church, and ultimately his denial of Transubstantiation, led to repeated attempts to condemn him from at least 1378 onwards; he was finally condemned in 1380, and in 1381 he retired to Lutterworth, the living of which he had held since 1374, where he remained until his death on 31 Dec. 1384. His followers were known as *Lollards, and many of them were executed in the first quarter of the 14th cent. (such as *Oldcastle in 1417 and John Badby in 1410: for the latter, see *Hoccleve's *Regiment of Princes*, 285–7). He was also an influence on John Huss and his followers in Bohemia, and through them perhaps ultimately on *Luther. His great significance lies in the Bible translations which he instigated and in the importance he and his followers have in the writings of such poets as *Chaucer and *Langland. Modern authorities, such as Anne Hudson, are reluctant to attribute particular English works, at least in the versions in which they survive, to Wyclif himself rather than to the Wyclifites in general. The earliest versions of Bible translations come from the 1380s and are traditionally associated with Purvey and Nicholas of Hereford. Recently such works as the 294-item Wyclifite sermon cycle have come under scholarly scrutiny, but Hudson says their literary merit is slight.

H. B. Workman, *John Wyclif* (2 vols, 1926); K. B. McFarlane, *John Wycliffe and the Beginning of English Nonconformity* (1952); G. Leff, *Heresy in the Later Middle Ages* (1967), ii, 494–605; A. M. Hudson ed., *Selections from English Wycliffite Writings* (1978).

Wycliffe, Oswald and Wilfrid, characters in Scott's *Rokeby*.

WYKEHAM, William of, see WILLIAM OF WYKEHAM.

Wykehamist, see WINCHESTER COLLEGE.

WYLIE, Elinor Morton Hoyt (1885–1928), American poet and novelist, who left her first husband to elope with Horace Wylie, and left Wylie to marry the poet William Rose Benét (1886–1950), brother of S. V. *Benét. Her works include *Nets to Catch the Wind* (1921, poems); *The Venetian Glass Nephew* (1925, novel); and *The Orphan Angel* (1926; in England as *Mortal Image*, 1927), a novel based on *Shelley's life after his supposed rescue from drowning, infused by her 'patent adoration' of Shelley, which E. *Garnett tried to dissuade her from publishing. Her *Collected Poems* appeared in 1932. Beautiful, vain, and histrionic, she aroused both passionate admiration and passionate hostility; the latter, notably, from V.

*Woolf, whom she met in London in 1926. See S. Olson, *Elinor Wylie; A Life Apart* (1979).

Wynd, Hal o' the, Henry Smith, the hero of Scott's *The Fair Maid of Perth.*

WYNDHAM, John, the best-known pseudonym of John Wyndham Parkes Lucas Beynon Harris (1903–69), son of a barrister, who pursued several different careers before settling to a successful life as a writer, principally of *Science Fiction, a genre to which he was attracted partly through his early admiration of H. G. *Wells and *Verne. He preferred the description 'logical fantasy' for his own works, which included *The Day of the Triffids* (1951), *The Kraken Wakes* (1953), *The Chrysalids* (1955), and *The Midwich Cuckoos* (1957). Several of his works were filmed; most are distinguished by the contrast between a comfortable English background and the sudden invasion of catastrophe, usually of a fantastic or metaphysical rather than a technologically suggestive nature.

The word 'triffid' has passed into the language to describe almost any kind of imaginary hostile and dangerous plant: Wyndham's species, lethal and mobile monsters on average 7 feet high were so called because of their three-pronged roots, on which they propelled themselves.

WYNKYN DE WORDE (d. 1535), printer from Wörth in Alsace, probably met *Caxton in Cologne and was brought by him to London in 1476. He was Caxton's principal assistant until his death in 1491/2 whereupon Wynkyn succeeded to the printing business which he managed until his death, moving it to Fleet Street. He printed many important literary works in the 1490s, and the catalogue of his works is evidence of bibliographical demand between 1490 and 1535: for instance he sometimes printed several editions of the same

grammar in a single year. See H. R. Plomer, *Wynkyn de Worde and His Contemporaries* (1925); J. Moran, *Wynkyn de Worde* (London, Wynkyn de Worde Society, 1960).

Wynnere and Wastour, an alliterative dream-poem of about 500 lines in a North-West Midland dialect, based on events of 1352–3 and thought to have been written shortly after that, discussing the economic problems of the day. The poet says that he saw in his dream two opposing armies drawn up against each other on the plain, with Edward III encamped above them. The king sends his son, the *Black Prince, to intervene and prevent the battle. The leaders of the two armies explain their causes: with Winner (the gainer of wealth in society) are the pope and the traditionally avaricious friars; with Waster (the prodigal spender) are the nobility and the soldiery. In the king's judgement speech (which is unfinished), he sends Waster to the markets of London to stimulate the economy and Winner to the rich courts of the pope and the cardinals. In its concerns and methods, the poem has often been compared to, and said to be an influence on, *Piers Plowman*. Ed. F. Berry in *The Age of Chaucer*, ed. B. Ford (1959).

WYNTOUN, Andrew of (*c.*1350–*c.*1425), a canon regular of St Andrews and author of *The Orygynale Cronykil* (*c.*1420), a metrical history of Scotland in octosyllabics, from the beginning of the world to the accession of James I. He becomes a valuable authority later in the work; among his stories is that of Macbeth and the witches, and of Macduff and Malcolm. The chronicle was first published in 1795. (See HUCHOWN.) Ed. F. J. Amours (Scottish Texts Society, 6 vols, 1902–5, 1914).

X

Xanadu, in Coleridge's *'Kubla Khan', the place where the Khan decreed 'a stately pleasure-dome'.

XAVIER, St Francis (1506–52), a Spaniard, one of the founders of the Society of Jesus, and a famous missionary in the Far East. He died on his way to China and is buried in Goa. He is commemorated on 3 December.

XENOPHON (*c*.430–352 BC), Athenian writer who may fairly be called the world's earliest journalist. He left an account of a military expedition in which he participated (*Anabasis*), a history of his own times (*Hellenica*), a panegyric on a contemporary monarch (*Agesilaus*), chatty memoirs about *Socrates (*Memorabilia, Symposium*), and treatises on domestic economy, horsemanship, and hunting. His most popular work was however the *Cyropedia*, a fictionalized biography of the Persian king Cyrus. This created a vogue for such biographies in which the fictional element became progressively greater until the world saw the emergence of a new genre—the novel. The *Cyropedia* was translated into English by W. Baker, *c*.1560, contributed a story to Painter's *Palace of Pleasure* (1566), and was described by *Sidney as an 'absolute historicall poem'. *Milton, on the other hand, spoke highly of the *Memorabilia*, whose account of Socrates he placed on a level with *Plato's.

Ximena (in French Chimène), the wife of the *Cid. C. *Cibber wrote an adaptation of *Corneille's *Le Cid*, called *Ximena, or the heroick daughter* (1712).

XIMENES, Francisco (1436–1517), a Spanish cardinal and statesman, who printed the Complutensian *Polyglot Bible and founded the University of Alcalá. But he also destroyed countless Arabic works of learning, especially after the taking of Granada.

Y

Yahoo, see GULLIVER'S TRAVELS.

Yakimov, a character in O. *Manning's *Balkan Trilogy.*

Yale University, originally founded as a school at Saybrook, Connecticut, in 1701, was transferred to New Haven, Connecticut, in 1716 and called Yale College in consequence of benefactions received from Elihu Yale (1648–1721), a native of Boston, Massachusetts, who came to England, entered the service of the East India Company, and became governor of Madras. It received a new charter in 1745 and assumed the name of Yale University in 1887. The *Hartford Wits were all either graduates or associates of Yale.

'Yardley-Oak', a poem by *Cowper.

Yarico, see INKLE AND YARICO.

YATES, Dornford, the pseudonym of Cecil William Mercer (1885–1960), whose sequence of stories about 'Berry' Pleydell and his family includes *The Brothers of Daphne* (1914), *Berry and Co.* (1920), and *The House that Berry Built* (1945). Both this group, and Yates's 'Chandos' thrillers (*Blind Corner*, 1927, etc.) were much influenced by Anthony Hope (*Hawkins); both reflect a world of wealth and idleness and were immensely popular between the wars. See R. Usborne, *Clubland Heroes* (1953, 1974) and a life by A. J. Smithers (1982).

YATES, Dame Frances Amelia (1899–1981), Renaissance scholar, educated at University College London. Some of her most important work was on *Neoplatonism and the *Rosicrucian tradition in Renaissance thought, and their connections with literature and the drama: her publications include a study of *Bruno (1964), *The Rosicrucian Enlightenment* (1972), and *Elizabethan Neoplatonism Reconsidered* (1977).

Year at Hartlebury, A, or *the Election*, a novel by Sarah and Benjamin *Disraeli, published in 1834 under the pseudonyms 'Cherry' and 'Fair Star'.

This hitherto anonymous and unattributed novel was discovered in 1979 by the Disraeli Project in Kingston, Ontario, to be by the Disraelis, brother and sister. Clearly intending to disown it, Disraeli never gave any hint of his authorship. It seems probable that the first volume, describing the village, the inhabitants, and the pretty countryside of Hartlebury, is by

Sarah; and the second, a vigorous narrative, much of which is given over to a hectic election, by Benjamin.

Helen Molesworth, the daughter of a local landed gentleman, is beloved by the gentle young cleric Arthur Latimer and by George Gainsborough, the son of a wealthy farmer. The heir of Hartlebury Castle, the wealthy and dashing Aubrey Bohun, is almost unknown in the village until he decides to stand for Parliament. Then he too falls in love with Helen, and after much manœuvring and suspense is returned to the House, where he becomes a great orator. Helen is attracted and flattered, but George discovers that Bohun is already married. The young squire persists in his attentions, but soon after is found murdered in a ditch, and George is clearly guilty. At this point the book abruptly ends.

Year Books, reports of English common law cases for the period 1292–1534, of great interest from a historical as well as a legal standpoint. They were succeeded by the law 'Reports', F. W. *Maitland began editing them, and the work is still going on.

Years, The, a novel by V. *Woolf, published 1937.

Her longest novel, and the most traditional of her later works, it traces the history of a family, opening in 1880 as the children of Colonel and Mrs Pargiter, living together in a large Victorian London house (later described by one of them as 'Hell') wait for their mother's death and the freedom it will bring; it takes them through several carefully dated and documented sections to the 'Present Day' of 1936, and a large family reunion, where two generations gather. Its composition caused the author much difficulty, and she was even more than usually apprehensive about its reception, fearing that her return to the 'novel of fact' would be seen as a false step in her career; many of her friends were critical, but it was on the whole well reviewed, and sold well.

YEARSLEY, Ann, *née* Cromartie (1752–1806), was born at Clifton, Bristol, the daughter of a dairywoman, and pursued her mother's trade, marrying in 1774 and producing several children. She published three collections of poems (*Poems, on several occasions*, 1785; *Poems on various subjects*, 1787; *The Rural Lyre*, 1796). She was initially patronized by

Hannah *More, whom she addressed as 'Stella' in the persona of 'Lactilla', but the friendship ended in some bitterness. She also wrote a play, *Earl Goodwin* (1791), and a *Gothic historical novel, *The Royal Captives* (1795), based on the story of the Man in the Iron Mask. See R. *Southey, *Lives of the uneducated poets* (1836; ed. J. S. Childers, 1925) and *The Polite Marriage* ('The Bristol Milkwoman') (1938) by J. M. S. Tomkins. See also PRIMITIVISM.

Yeast, a novel by C. *Kingsley, published in *Fraser's Magazine* 1848, in volume form 1851.

This was the first of Kingsley's novels and is crude as a literary work. It deals with some of the social and religious problems of the day (the miserable conditions of the rustic labourer, the game laws, and Tractarianism: see OXFORD MOVEMENT), largely by means of dialogues between the hero and various other characters. The story is that of the reactions of the generous but undisciplined nature of Lancelot Smith to the influences exercised on him by the philosophical Cornish gamekeeper Tregarva, the worldly Colonel Bracebridge, the Romanizing curate Luke, Lancelot's orthodox love Argemone Lavington, and the philanthropic banker Barnakill; he is seen suffering the loss, first of his fortune, and then of Argemone. The story ends in a vague and semi-mystical indication that Lancelot is to seek his salvation in contribution to the regeneration of England.

YEATS, Jack Butler (1871–1957), painter and illustrator, brother of W. B. *Yeats, who contributed for many years to *Punch* (1910–41) under the pseudonym 'W. Bird', and also did many illustrations for the *Cuala Press, although he remains better known for his oil paintings of Irish life and landscape.

YEATS, John Butler (1839–1922), Irish portrait painter, father of W. B. and J. B. *Yeats; his *Letters to His Son W. B. Yeats and Others, 1869–1922* (ed. J. Hone, 1946) give a vivid portrait of cultural life in Ireland, in London (where he lived for some years from 1887 in Bedford Park), and in New York, where he spent his last 14 years, renowned, in Hone's words, less as a painter than as 'a critic, philosopher and conversationalist'.

YEATS, William Butler (1865–1939), eldest son of J. B. *Yeats and brother of Jack *Yeats, both celebrated painters, was born in Dublin and educated at the Godolphin School, Hammersmith, and the High School, Dublin. For three years he studied at the School of Art in Dublin, where with a fellow student, G. *Russell (Æ), he developed an interest in mystic religion and the supernatural. At 21 he abandoned art as a profession in favour of literature, writing *John Sherman and Dhoya* (1891) and editing *The*

Poems of William Blake (1893), *The Works of William Blake* (with F. J. Ellis, 3 vols, 1893), and *Poems of Spenser* (1906). A nationalist, he helped to found an Irish Literary Society in London in 1891 and another in Dublin in 1892; and he subsequently applied himself to the creation of an Irish national theatre, an achievement which, with the help of Lady *Gregory and others, was partly realized in 1899 when his play *The Countess Cathleen* (1892) was acted in Dublin. The English actors engaged by the *Irish Literary Theatre gave place in 1902 to an Irish amateur company, which produced Yeats's *Cathleen ni Houlihan* in that year. The Irish National Theatre Company was thereafter created, and, with the help of Miss A. E. *Horniman, acquired the *Abbey Theatre in Dublin. Yeats's early study of Irish lore and legends resulted in *Fairy and Folk Tales of the Irish Peasantry* (1888), *The Celtic Twighlight* (1893), and *The Secret Rose* (1897). Irish traditional and nationalist themes and the poet's unrequited love for Maude Gonne, a beautiful and ardent revolutionary, provided much of the subject matter for *The Wanderings of Oisin and other Poems* (1889), *The Land of Heart's Desire* (1894), *The Wind among the Reeds* (1899), *The Shadowy Waters* (1900), and such of his later plays as *On Baile's Strand* (1904) and *Deirdre* (1907).

With each succeeding collection of poems Yeats moved further from the elaborate, *Pre-Raphaelite style of the 1890s. *In the Seven Woods* (1903) was followed by *The Green Hamlet and Other Poems* (1910), *Poems Written in Discouragement* (1913), *Responsibilities: Poems and a Play* (1914), and *The Wild Swans at Coole* (1917). His mounting disillusionment with Irish politics came to a head in 1912 and 1913 with the controversy over the Lane Bequest of French Impressionist paintings. The Easter Rising of 1916, however, restored his faith in the heroic character of his country. The following year he married Georgie Hyde-Lees, who on their honeymoon attempted automatic writing, an event that exercised a profound effect on his life and work. His wife's 'communicators' ultimately provided him with the system of symbolism described in *A Vision* (1925) and underlying many of the poems in *Michael Robartes and the Dancer* (1921), *Seven Poems and a Fragment* (1922), *The Cat and the Moon and Certain Poems* (1924), *October Blast* (1927), *The Tower* (1928), *The Winding Stair* (1929), *Words for Music Perhaps and Other Poems* (1932), *Wheels and Butterflies* (1934), *The King of the Great Clock Tower* (1934), *A Full Moon in March* (1935), *New Poems* (1938), and *Last Poems and Two Plays* (1939). In the poems and plays written after his marriage he achieved a spare, colloquial lyricism wholly unlike his earlier manner, although many themes of his early manhood reach their full flowering in the later period.

Yeats served as a senator of the Irish Free State from 1922 to 1928; was chairman of the commission on coinage; and in 1923 received the *Nobel Prize for literature. He died in the south of France, but in 1948 his body was brought back to Ireland and interred at Drumcliff in Sligo, where much of his childhood had been spent.

Yeats's other publications include such collections of essays as *Ideas of Good and Evil* (1903), *Discoveries* (1907), *Per Amica Silentia Lunae* (1918), *The Cutting of an Agate* (1919), and *On the Boiler* (1939). Most important of the many books he edited and introduced was *The Oxford Book of Modern Verse* (1936), a somewhat eccentric and personal selection. He wrote good letters, and five major collections have been made: *Letters on Poetry from W. B. Yeats to Dorothy Wellesley* (1940), *Florence Farr, Bernard Shaw and W. B. Yeats* (1941), *W. B. Yeats and T. Sturge Moore: Their Correspondence 1901–37* (1953), *W. B. Yeats: Letters to Katharine Tynan* (1953), and Allan Wade's notable edition of *The Letters of W. B. Yeats* (1954). Also posthumously published were his *Collected Poems* (1950), *Collected Plays* (1952), *Autobiographies* (1955), *The Variorum Edition of the Poems* (1957), *Mythologies* (1959), *Essays and Introductions* (1961), *The Senate Speeches of W. B. Yeats* (1961), and *Explorations* (1962). There are biographies by Joseph Hone, *W. B. Yeats 1865–1939* (1942), and A. N. Jeffares, *W. B. Yeats, Man and Poet* (1949, rev. 1962). See also *Yeats: The Man and the Masks* (1948, rev. 1979) by R. *Ellmann. A second edition, rev. R. Hart-Davis, of Allan Wade's *A Bibliography of the Writings of W. B. Yeats* was published in 1958. R. J. Finneran's controversial edn, *The Poems: a new edition*, appeared in 1984.

'Ye Banks and Braes', a lyric by *Burns.

Yellow-backs, cheap editions of novels, so called from being bound in yellow boards. They were the ordinary 'railway novels' of the 1870s and 1880s.

Yellow Book, The (1894–7), a handsome, short-lived publication, startling in its time and immediately notorious, devoted to literature and art. Published by J. *Lane and edited by H. *Harland, with the initial assistance of *Beardsley as art editor, its first issue (which included *Beerbohm's essay 'A Defence of Cosmetics') provoked a public storm which did not subside during the three years of the *Book*'s life. Writers published included H. *James, *Gosse, *Le Gallienne, Arnold *Bennett, and *Dowson; among artists represented were Beardsley, Walter Sickert, and Wilson Steer.

Yellowley, Triptolemus and Barbara, characters in Scott's *The Pirate.

Yellowplush Papers, The, sketches by *Thackeray, published in *Fraser's Magazine* in 1837–8. The narrator is a footman who observes and comments on the lives of his employers and their friends in a comic mixture of malapropisms and misspellings.

Yeobright, Clym, Thomasin, and Mrs, characters in Hardy's *The Return of the Native.

'Yeoman's Tale, The', see CANTERBURY TALES, 22.

Yiddish, derived, either directly, or through the German-Jewish *jiddisch*, from the German *jüdisch*, Jewish; the language used by Jews in Europe and America, consisting mainly of German, with Balto-Slavic or Hebrew words, and printed in Hebrew characters. One of the few Yiddish writers to achieve an international reputation is I. B. *Singer.

YONGE, Bartholomew (1560–1612), travelled in Spain in 1578–80, and subsequently translated the Spanish romance *Diana* by *Montemayor; his version was published in 1598, with a dedication to Lady *Rich. It has been edited by J. M. Kennedy (1968).

YONGE, Charlotte M(ary) (1823–1901), daughter of an army officer, was born and lived all her life in the Hampshire village of Otterbourne, and was educated at home by her parents. In 1838 she came under the influence of *Keble, then rector of the neighbouring parish of Hursley, and absorbed the Tractarian religious views which thereafter coloured all her writings. Her best-known novel is *The Heir of Redclyffe* (1853); her other novels of contemporary life include *Heartsease* (1854), *The Daisy Chain* (1856), *Dynevor Terrace* (1857), *Hopes and Fears* (1860), *The Trial* (1864), *The Clever Woman of the Family* (1865), *The Pillars of the House* (1873), and *Magnum Bonum* (1879). She also wrote many historical romances for children (including *The Little Duke*, 1854; *The Dove in the Eagle's Nest*, 1866; and *The Chaplet of Pearls*, 1868) and numerous historical textbooks, short stories of village life, and a biography of Bishop Patteson (1874). For 40 years she edited a girls' magazine, *The Monthly Packet*.

Her chief excellence as a novelist was her loving depiction of life in large families, particularly sibling relationships, presented with convincing dialogue and unstinted incident. Her novels of her own times are incidentally a mine of information about social mobility, ecclesiastical change, and developments in education and housing. She wrote mainly for young women readers, of whom she had a world-wide following, but her books were also admired by *Tennyson, *Kingsley, *Rossetti, and W. *Morris, and were said to have been the favourite reading of young officers in the Crimean war. See G. Battiscombe, *Charlotte Mary Yonge* (1943); M. Mare and A. C. Percival, *Victorian*

Best-Seller: The World of Charlotte M. Yonge (1947).

Yorick, (1) in Shakespeare's *Hamlet,* (v. i), the king's jester, whose skull the grave-diggers throw up when digging Ophelia's grave; (2) in Sterne's *Tristram Shandy,* 'the lively, witty, sensible, and heedless parson', of Danish extraction, and probably a descendant of Hamlet's Yorick. Sterne adopted 'Yorick' as a pseudonym in his *Sentimental Journey.*

***Yorick to Eliza,** Letters from,* by *Sterne, published 1773.
A collection of ten brief letters from Sterne to Mrs E. *Draper, written in 1767, and following the course of his growing passion for her.

York Plays, see MYSTERY PLAYS.

Yorkshire Tragedy, A, a play published 1608, stated in the title to be by Shakespeare, but internal evidence and the late date make it extremely improbable that he had any part in its authorship.
The play is based on certain murders actually committed in 1605. The husband, a brutal and depraved gamester, suddenly filled with remorse when he realizes his shame, murders his two children and stabs his docile and devoted wife. It is extremely brief and probably formed part of a composite programme of *Four Plays in One.*

YOUNG, Andrew John (1885–1971), born in Scotland, educated at school and university in Edinburgh, ordained a minister of the Free Church in 1912. In 1910 his father paid for the publication of his *Songs of Night,* the first of many slim volumes of poetry which were greatly admired by an ever-widening circle. The first *Collected Poems* appeared in 1936 and the verse-play *Nicodemus* in 1937. In 1939 Young was ordained in the Church of England. *The Green Man* (1947) is sometimes considered his best collection. In 1952 he published a long, disturbing poem, 'Into Hades', which was later combined with the visionary 'A Traveller in Time' to create *Out of the World and Back* (1958), his most ambitious work. His lifelong interest in botany was reflected in a prose account of his travels and searches, *A Prospect of Flowers* (1945), but also in many lyrics, whose subjects also included many aspects of the natural world, as well as brief lapidary reflections on God and man. His spare line, sharp specific imagery, quiet concision, and skill with conceit, brought him much critical and public admiration. The influence of literary fashions barely touched him, but he acknowledged a particular debt to *Hardy, and to *Crabbe and G. *Herbert. The *Complete Poems* were revised in 1974.

YOUNG, Arthur (1741–1820), the son of a Suffolk clergyman, became well known as an agricultural theorist, though unsuccessful as a practical farmer. He wrote a large number of works on agricultural subjects and edited the periodical *The Annals of Agriculture* (1784–1809), which extended to 47 volumes (parts of another volume were published in 1812 and 1813). His power of political and social observation is shown by his *Political Arithmetic* (1774) and his *Tour in Ireland* (1780), the latter highly praised as a true account of the country by M. *Edgeworth, but his fame rests chiefly on *Travels in France* (1792). Young was connected with the *Burneys, and his country house, Bradfield Hall, Suffolk, is described in Fanny Burney's *Camilla.* He took her to hear *Hastings's trial in Westminster Hall and she was charmed with him. The death of a much-loved daughter in 1797, and a growing religious melancholia (influenced by his friend W. *Wilberforce), darkened his later years, and he went blind about 1811. His autobiography, edited by M. Betham-Edwards, appeared in 1898, and there is a life by J. G. Gazley (1973).

YOUNG, Edward (1683–1765), born near Winchester and educated there and at Oxford. His early works include the tragedies *Busiris,* successfully produced at Drury Lane in 1719, and *The Revenge,* produced at the same theatre in 1721. In 1725–8 he published a series of satires under the title *The Universal Passion* (the love of fame), which were much admired until eclipsed by those of *Pope, who was a few years younger. Disappointed in more worldly ambitions, he took orders and became rector of Welwyn in 1730, where he spent the remainder of his long life; in 1731 he married Elizabeth Lee, daughter of the second earl of Lichfield, who died in 1740. Young's most celebrated poem, *The Complaint, or Night Thoughts on Life, Death and Immortality* (1742–5, see NIGHT THOUGHTS), is thought to commemorate her, her daughter by a previous marriage, and her son-in-law. A noted example of the *graveyard genre, it was extremely popular both in England and Europe. *The Brothers,* a tragedy written decades earlier, was performed and published in 1753, and *Resignation,* his last considerable poem, with a preface to Mrs *Boscawen, appeared in 1762. He was a friend of *Richardson, with whom he corresponded for many years. Dr *Johnson concludes his life with the words, 'But, with all his defects, he was a man of genius and a poet.'

YOUNG, Francis Brett (1884–1954), novelist, short story writer, poet, and doctor, was educated at the University of Birmingham, practised for some years in Devon, and served during the First World War in East Africa. He is remembered largely for his solid, traditional novels of the West Midlands, which include

Portrait of Clare (1927) and *My Brother Jonathan* (1928), but he also wrote novels based on his African experiences, including *Jim Redlake* (1930) and *They seek a Country* (1937). Poems *1916–1918* (1919) was written in Africa while he was convalescing from what proved permanent damage to his health, and *The Island* (1944) is a verse history of England, employing the verse forms of succeeding periods in strict chronological sequence.

Young Duke, The, a novel by B. *Disraeli, published 1831.

The second of Disraeli's novels, this offered its hero as 'a model for our youth'. George, duke of St James, is left on the death of his parents under the guardianship of the quiet, country-loving Dacres, but his foolish uncle, Lord Fitzpompey, takes over the boy, encourages his vanity and social graces, and eventually launches him in London society. For a while the duke is captivated by the life of soirées, clubs, racing, gambling, and beautiful women. But he becomes weary of it, and falls in love with Dacres's daughter May, his childhood friend. When he is rejected he returns to high living, and begins to spend incalculable sums on renovating and building a castle and a 'palace'. In despair at his increasing debts he takes to heavy gambling but loses everything, and is ousted as the leader of the 'dandies'. Eventually he rushes back to Dacres, who without recrimination sets about restoring the duke's finances. During the long period George spends in the country at Castle Dacre he discovers that May loves him. The great buildings are sold, the creditors paid, and George and May settle into quiet country life. The book was successful, although the author's bewildered father, Isaac *D'Israeli, is said to have asked, 'What does Ben know of Dukes?' and *Borrow damned it as 'the most unexceptionally genteel book ever written'. Writing in 1853,

Disraeli apologized for its 'affectations and conceit' and pleaded the excuse of youth.

Younger Son, *The Adventures of a,* see ADVENTURES OF A YOUNGER SON, THE.

Ywain and Gawain, a northern romance from the first half of the 14th cent. of 4,032 lines in short couplets, surviving in a single manuscript. In spite of its title, the poem is principally concerned with Ywain, being a translation (with variations) from the 6,818 lines of *Yvain* by *Chrétien de Troyes. As well as being briefer, the English translation (which is about 150 years later than the original) has some elements in common with other versions of the Ywain story (such as the Welsh *Owein*), and there has been much discussion of the relation it bears to the original. The English romance is much admired for its narrative life and clarity of diction.

Ywain kills the knight of a castle who seems to have magical connections with the weather, and, aided by her serving-lady Lunet, marries his widow Alundyne (Lunete and Laudine in Chrétien). Gawain persuades him to go, assisted by a lion, in search of adventure, abandoning his lady. The two knights have many adventures, ending by fighting each other incognito; but they recognize each other and are reconciled. At the end, Ywain is reconciled to Alundyne, again by the skills of Lunet. Many of the incidental themes in Chrétien (such as his commenting on courtly love by cross-reference to Lancelot, his explanation of the name of Lunete by reference to the moon, and his general interest in the characters' motivation) are played down or entirely suppressed in the English version.

Ed. A. B. Friedman and N. T. Harrington, EETS os 254 (1964); extracts in A. V. C. Schmidt and N. Jacobs, *Medieval English Romances*, 2 (1980).

Z

ZAMYATIN, Evgeny Ivanovich (1884–1937), Russian prose writer, critic, and playwright. He was born in Lebedyan in central Russia, the son of a teacher. From 1902 he studied in St Petersburg and soon after joined the Bolshevik Party (which he later left). He was arrested and exiled in 1905 and his first story dates from 1908. From 1911 he lectured in naval architecture at the St Petersburg Polytechnic Institute while continuing to write. He spent 18 months in Newcastle upon Tyne, 1915–16, supervising the construction of Russian ice-breakers, and the two stories that sprang from this experience, 'Islanders' (1917) and 'The Fisher of Men' (1918), are devastating assessments of English life. After the revolution Zamyatin produced a steady flow of stories while working in various literary organizations, as well as editing collections by H. G. *Wells, G. B. *Shaw, Jack *London, and O. *Henry. His novel *We* (1920–1) was published abroad in the late 1920s, leading to a vicious campaign against him; he wrote to *Stalin in June 1931 asking permission to emigrate and left Russia in November, eventually settling in Paris. Among Zamyatin's best stories are 'The North' (1918), 'The Cave' (1920), 'Mamai' (1920), 'The Yawl' (1928), and 'The Flood' (1929), in which his major theme, the cult of obsession and the primitive, is apparent, but he is best known for the anti-Utopian satire *We*. (See UTOPIA.) Indebted to Wells, in particular *The Time Machine*, it was in turn acknowledged by *Orwell as an influence on *Nineteen Eighty-Four*, though its widely suggested influence on *Brave New World* was denied by A. *Huxley. *We* was first translated by Gregory Zilboorg in 1924. The major collection of Zamyatin's stories in English is *The Dragon: Fifteen Stories* (trans. Mirra Ginzburg, 1966).

ZANGWILL, Israel (1864–1926), was a noted Jewish spokesman, writer, and translator. The popular novel *Children of the Ghetto* (1892) established his reputation by its realistic and sympathetically critical portrayal of London's poor Jews, when alien immigration was a burning issue. *Ghetto Tragedies* (1899), *Ghetto Comedies* (1907), and *The King of Schnorrers* (1894), a *jeu d'esprit*, contain vignettes of Jewish life. The historical *Dreamers of the Ghetto* (1898) testifies both to Judaism's inner strength and to its role in civilization. *The War for the World* (1916) and *The Voice of Jerusalem* (1920) combine apologia

with polemic. His plays are vehicles for ideas, notably *The Melting Pot* (1909), which coined the phrase.

Zanzis (or possibly 'Zauzis'), a wise writer referred to by Chaucer in *Troilus and Criseyde* (IV. 414), referring to Zeuxis who is a sage in the Alexander story. The form may come from a misreading of the text of *Boccaccio that Chaucer is following; but this is unlikely, since the Athenian painter Zeuxis is called 'Zanzis' in 'The Physician's Tale' (*Canterbury Tales*, 13; VI. 16).

Zapolya, a 'dramatic poem . . . in humble imitation of "The Winter's Tale" of Shakespeare', by S. T. *Coleridge, published 1817. Zapolya is a dowager queen of Illyria driven from the throne by the usurper Emerick. After an interval of twenty years she returns to power with her son Bethlen.

Zarathustra, see ZOROASTER.

Zarathustra, *Thus spake*, see NIETZSCHE.

Zastrozzi, see SHELLEY, P. B.

Zeal-of-the-land Busy, in Jonson's *Bartholomew Fair*, a canting, gluttonous Puritan, 'a Banbury man'.

Zeitgeist, German, the spirit of genius which marks the thought or feeling of a period.

ZÉLIDE, the name given to herself in a self-portrait by Isabella van Tuyll van Serooskerken, also known as Mme de Charrière (1740–1805), a Dutchwoman of good family, great intelligence and originality, and considerable beauty. She numbered among her many suitors *Boswell, who quickly reconciled himself to her rejection of his hand. Declining more brilliant matches, she married her brother's Swiss tutor, the dull but worthy M. de Charrière. Her unhappy married life was brightened by an ardent intellectual friendship with *Constant, until she was ousted by Mme de *Staël. She wrote in French a number of novels, of which the best known are *Lettres Neuchâteloises* (1784), *Mistress Henley* (1784), and *Lettres écrites de Lausanne* (1787). There is an interesting account of her life in G. *Scott's *Portrait of Zélide*.

Zelmane, in Sidney's *Arcadia*, the name assumed by Pyrocles when disguised as a woman.

Zeluco, a novel by Dr J. *Moore, published 1786.

In the author's words, this novel 'traces the windings of vice' through the life of a wholly wicked man. Zeluco, a Sicilian noble, exhibits from childhood a character of cruelty, treachery, lust, and violence. He tyrannizes, maims, and murders, even killing his own child and driving its mother mad. In the end he is himself killed. The savagery is curiously interspersed with humorous episodes, several of which involve two comic Scotsmen, Buchanan and Targe.

ZENO (1) of Citium (336–246 BC), see STOI-CISM; (2) of Elia (early 5th cent. BC), a monistic philosopher famous for his paradoxes which, revealing the inconsistencies in man's picture of the universe, were intended to discredit belief in the multiplicity of entities. Sir T. Browne was to attack his paradoxes in the *Pseudodoxia Epidemica* (1646).

Zenobia, a character in Hawthorne's *The Blithedale Romance*.

Zenocrate, the wife of Tamburlaine, in *Marlowe's play of that name.

Zerbino, in *Orlando Furioso*, a Scottish prince and perfect knight, of whom it was said that Nature broke the mould in which he had been fashioned. He was the lover of *Isabella. He was rescued by Orlando when about to be executed on a false charge, but was killed by *Mandricardo when attempting to defend the arms that Orlando in his madness had thrown away.

Zeugma, a figure of speech by which a single word is made to refer to two or more words in a sentence, when properly applying in sense to only one of them; e.g. 'See Pan with flocks, with fruits Pomona crowned'. Cf. SYLLEPSIS.

ZHUKOVSKY, Vasily Andreevich (1783–1852), Russian poet, regarded as the founder of the Golden Age of Russian poetry. His 1802 translation of Gray's *'Elegy', his first publication, is seen as ushering in the new age. His first ballads, 'Lyudmila' and 'Svetlana' (1808, his most famous work), both based on Bürger's *'Lenore', gave rise to a fashion for the ballad. Zhukovsky served in the army, and later was tutor to the future Alexander II. He met and befriended both *Pushkin and *Gogol. He wrote a small number of elegies, ballads, lyrics, and humorous epistles, and his lasting influence on Russian poetry depends on his metrical and linguistic innovations and his moves towards the direct expression of feeling in poetry. But perhaps his most important achievement in the history of Russian literature lies in his translations of the *Odyssey (from a German translation), German poets including Uhland and *Schiller and, from the English, *Dryden ('Alexander's Feast'), James *Thomson, *Gray, *Southey, Sir W. *Scott, T. *Moore (*Lalla Rookh), T. *Campbell, and *Byron (*The Prisoner of Chillon). The first translations of Zhukovsky's works into English, by John Bowring, appeared in 1821 and 1823.

Zimri, name for the duke of *Buckingham in Dryden's *Absalom and Achitophel.

'Zohar', see CABBALA.

ZOILUS, a grammarian of Amphipolis, of the period of Philip of Macedon. His name became proverbial as that of a carping critic, on account of his strictures on *Homer, *Plato, and Isocrates.

ZOLA, Émile (1840–1902), the leading figure in the French school of *naturalistic fiction, of which *Thérèse Raquin* (1867) is his earliest example. The first volume (*La Fortune des Rougon*) of his principal work, *Les Rougon-Macquart*, which he termed the 'natural and social history of a family under the Second Empire', appeared in 1871; nineteen more volumes followed, the last (*Le Docteur Pascal*) in 1893. In this series of novels, which was influenced by contemporary theories of heredity and experimental science, Zola chronicles the activities of the two branches (the Rougons and the Macquarts) of a family, whose conduct is seen as conditioned through several generations by environment and inherited characteristics, chiefly drunkenness and mental instability. The result is a panorama of mid-19th-cent. French life, especially in the middle and working classes, carefully documented and focusing attention on vice, misery, and the powerful claims of human appetites and instincts. *Germinal* (1885) depicts the life of a mining community, *La Terre* (1887) the life of the agricultural peasant, *Le Ventre de Paris* (1873) the markets of the metropolis, *L'Assommoir* (1877) its taverns, *Au bonheur des dames* (1883) the world of the great department store, *La Débâcle* (1892) the catastrophe of the war of 1870. The prevailing pessimism of the cycle is relieved by passages of lyrical beauty (e.g. in *La Faute de l'abbé Mouret*, 1875) and by faith in scientific and social meliorism. The essays of *Le Roman expérimental* (1880) establish an analogy between the novelist's aims and practices and those of the scientist. In the later trilogy *Les Trois Villes* (*Lourdes*, 1894; *Rome*, 1896; *Paris*, 1898) Zola examines, in a mode of heightened symbolism, the claims of the religious and social organizations of the day to minister to human needs. The novels of his final, unfinished, work, *Les Quatre Evangiles* (*Fécondité*, 1899; *Travail*, 1901; *Vérité*, 1903) are optimistic presentations of social ideals. The last of these refers to the *Dreyfus case in which Zola intervened with trenchant vigour, notably in his letter to the newspaper *L'Aurore*, 'J'Accuse'. To foil the sentence of imprisonment for libel that followed the publication of the letter, he spent 11 months in exile in England (1898–9). Zola's works were themselves the cause of the imprisonment in 1888 of his English publisher, *Vizetelly. (See ROMAN FLEUVE.)

Zoroaster, the Greek form of Zarathustra, the founder of the Magian system of religion, probably a historical personage who has become the subject of legends; a Persian who is believed to have lived in the 6th cent. BC during the reigns of Cyrus, Cambyses, and Darius.

The Zoroastrian religion was founded on the old Aryan folk-religion, but the polytheistic character of the latter was completely changed. The essential feature of Zoroastrianism is the existence of two predominant spirits: Ahura-Mazda (Ormazd) the wise one, the spirit of light and good; and Ahriman, the spirit of evil and darkness. The conflict between these two is waged in this world, and centres in man, created a free agent by Ormazd. (See also NIETZSCHE.)

Zuleika, (1) according to Muslim tradition (Sale's *Koran*, xii), the name of Potiphar's wife; (2) the heroine of Byron's *The Bride of Abydos*.

Zuleika Dobson, the eponymous heroine of *Beerbohm's novel, a great beauty who pays a fatal visit to her uncle, the warden of Judas College, Oxford, in Eights Week. All the young men fall madly in love with her and, when rejected, they rush 'like lemmings' and drown themselves in the Isis. The only survivor is the less agile Noaks, who trips on the way.

ZWINGLI, Ulrich (1485–1531), a famous Swiss leader of the Reformation. He first found his inspiration in *Erasmus and *Luther, but soon drew away from the latter, and by 1525 had rejected the mass altogether; this split Switzerland into Catholic and Protestant cantons. To Zwingli the Eucharist was purely symbolic; there was no 'real presence' at all, not even in the (later) Calvinistic sense, still less in the Lutheran sense of 'consubstantiation'. The conflict ended in civil war, in which Zwingli was killed in battle.

APPENDIX I

CENSORSHIP AND THE LAW OF THE PRESS

§ 1. *The control of the press*

THE introduction of printing immensely increased facilities for the spread of sedition and heresy, grave dangers always threatening the life of government and church; and as the industry of the press developed in the 16th century we find the publication of subversive matter a cause of increasing concern to the authorities. Proclamations against heretical and seditious books began under Henry VIII in 1529, and the requirement that books should be licensed for printing by the privy council or other royal nominees was introduced in 1538. Edward VI in 1547 and 1549 issued orders against the use of popish books of prayer and instruction. Mary, by proclamation in the first year of her reign, forbade the printing of any book or other matter without her special licence, and endeavoured, notably by a proclamation of 1555, to prevent the importation from abroad of the works of the reformers. A notable date in the history of the subject is 1557, when the Stationers obtained a charter of incorporation (see App. II, COPYRIGHT). Thereafter only members of the Stationers' Company or other persons holding a special patent might print any work for sale in the kingdom. (The sale in the kingdom of foreign-printed books had been regulated by an Act of 1533. In 1564 Elizabeth addressed a letter to the Bishop of London directing him to make arrangements for the seizure of any subversive books brought from overseas to London or other ports. In 1586 we find the Archbishop of Canterbury, Whitgift, issuing to Ascanius de Renialme, merchant bookseller, a licence to bring in from foreign parts some few copies of sundry books, which though popish and seditious, are yet in many respects expedient to be had by some of the learned of this realm; these copies to be delivered to approved persons only.) The incorporation was advantageous both to the book trade and the State, for the craft gained in dignity and organization, while the facilities for the supervision of printed matter were improved. The charter did not transfer to the Stationers the responsibility in the matter of undesirable publications, but it seems probable that the wardens exercised some discretion, at any rate before the Star Chamber orders of 1586, as to the need for seeing the 'hand' of an official licenser before recording a copyright. In 1559 Elizabeth, in the first year of her reign, issued 'Injunctions' requiring that no book should be printed unless licensed by her majesty, six of her privy council, or certain specified dignitaries of the Church, and that the names of those licensing the work should be printed at the end of it. The injunction must have proved largely ineffective, for, in spite of renewed orders, a multitude of unauthorized pamphlets continued to issue from the press. In 1586, at the instance of Archbishop Whitgift, a further effort was made to enforce State control: an ordinance of the Star Chamber directed that no printing press should be set up in any place other than London, apart from one in each of the university towns of Oxford and Cambridge, and that no more presses should be set up at all until those already existing had through natural causes been reduced to such number as the Archbishop of Canterbury and the Bishop of London thought sufficient for the needs of the realm. The ordinance again forbade the printing of unlicensed works. In 1588 Whitgift appointed twelve persons to license books for printing; he was especially concerned to check the flow of Puritan pamphlets which at this time were attacking the episcopal system. The conflict between bishop and Puritan continued, and has left its trace in English literature in the Marprelate tracts (see MARTIN MARPRELATE). In 1599 an edict was issued requiring that certain satirical works, notably those of Gabriel *Harvey and Thomas *Nashe, should be burnt, and that no satires or epigrams should be printed thereafter.

A further stringent decree (1637), imposing severe penalties on offending printers, was among the last measures of the Star Chamber; but the abolition of the Chamber by the Long Parliament in 1641 did not carry with it any liberation of the press. On the contrary, Parliament during 1642 was much occupied with offences by writers and printers, and in 1643 issued an Ordinance requiring that no book should be printed unless previously licensed by an officer named by them, and appointed a licenser. It was this activity which in 1644 called forth Milton's noble protest, the *Areopagitica. But the protest fell on deaf ears, and the licensing system continued throughout the Commonwealth period; indeed we find Milton himself acting as a licenser in 1651-2.

By this time journalism, a new element in English letters, had come into existence (see NEWSPAPERS, ORIGINS OF). It had its origin in the manuscript newsletters which, after the introduction of regular postal services, were dispatched to subscribers from the metropolis. The licensing system and the Star Chamber decrees, as well as the royal prerogative in the distribution of news, proved for a long time an impediment to the publication of any sort of printed journal. In 1622 authority was first given to certain stationers for the issue of periodical pamphlets relating the course of foreign wars (the Thirty Years War was then in progress and was being watched with intense interest). Such pamphlets were known as Corantos. In 1632 the Star Chamber prohibited the publication of news from abroad, and the interdict on Corantos was not raised until 1638, when Nathaniel Butler and Nicholas Bourne were granted a monopoly of the printing of foreign news. These later Corantos in turn vanished after a few years, and in 1641 appeared the first authorized 'newsbooks' or printed 'Diurnalls' of parliamentary proceedings and other domestic intelligence. It is not surprising that at this period of political excitement similar but unauthorized newsbooks were soon produced in great numbers, supplementing or replacing the newsletters of the scriveners. These printed newsbooks, unlike the manuscript newsletters, came under the censorship established by the Long Parliament, and we read of many suppressions and imprisonments, until Cromwell in 1655 put an end to all unofficial periodicals. Licensed newsbooks were allowed afresh by the Rump Parliament in April 1659, but at the end of the same year permission for their issue was restricted to certain journalists.

Under the Restoration the control and licensing of the press were continued. In 1662 a Licensing Act was passed for two years, then extended to 1679. It forbade the printing of any book or pamphlet contrary to the doctrine and discipline of the Church of England or tending to the scandal of Church or government; and it required that all books and pamphlets should be licensed by persons appointed for the purpose. It empowered the king's messengers by warrant under the sign manual or under the hand of the Secretaries of State or of the Master and Wardens of the Stationers' Company to search houses and shops for unlicensed books and to bring before the authorities any which they suspected to contain seditious or heretical matter, and it also regulated the conduct of the book trade. Under this Act Roger *L'Estrange was in 1663 appointed surveyor of printing presses and licenser. After 1679 came a period during which the press was controlled by the prosecution of offenders under the ordinary law. In 1685 the Licensing Act was revived until 1694, in which year Parliament refused to renew it, and the licensing system (so far as the press was concerned) came finally to an end. The case against the Act was prepared by John *Locke: it was pointed out that the Act had not served the purpose for which it was made, which was to prevent the publishing of seditious matter; it had appointed no penalties for offences, but had left transgressors to the common law, which already had sufficient powers to deal with them; moreover licensers had not been free from partiality. The abandonment of the Act was not due to any change of opinion in Parliament or government in favour of the liberty of expression. Various bills restraining the press were introduced in the following years, but failed to obtain approval. Other measures were resorted to. The detection of the authors and publishers of libels was entrusted to two salaried 'messengers of the press', assisted by informers in the service of the government and by the presentments of grand juries. Both Houses of Parliament were also active in drawing the attention of government to obnoxious publications and even carried out examinations and committed offenders to prison. The Solicitor to the Treasury was charged with the duty of examining alleged libellous matter, which term may be said to have included anything published with the intent of causing a breach of the peace, or likely to bring the king, the government, Parliament, or the administration of justice into contempt, or to incite to the alteration of anything in Church or State by illegal means. Upon the Solicitor's advice the Secretaries of State issued warrants for the arrest of the suspected parties. These were examined, and as a consequence might be committed to prison and prosecuted. The usual punishments were the pillory, imprisonment, fines, and the requirement of security for future good behaviour. But John Matthews was hanged for high treason in 1719 in consequence of his pamphlet 'Vox Populi Vox Dei', in which he asserted that James III was the rightful king of England. *Defoe was arrested in 1703 for his pamphlets on ecclesiastical matters, imprisoned and pilloried. Even if prosecution did not follow examination, the power of arrest, accompanied by seizure of papers and type, frequently repeated, enabled the government to harass and even ruin obnoxious printers. The *Freeholder's Journal* and the *True Briton* were thus brought to an end in 1723 and 1724. Ordinary warrants issued by the Secretary of State specified the charge against the person named in them. But in the first half of the 18th century the Secretary of State also issued general warrants, which might authorize the arrest of a person unnamed, and the seizure of unspecified papers. Their use for the former purpose became impracticable owing to a decision of the courts in 1765 and was further declared illegal by the Commons in 1766; their use for the latter purpose was declared illegal by the courts in 1763 in connection with the case of No. 45 of the *North Briton*. *Wilkes had started this paper in 1762 in opposition to Bute's *The Briton*, and in it had attacked the government with increasing audacity. No. 45, imputing deliberate untruth to the authors of the recent speech from the throne, gave an opportunity for legal proceedings, and a general warrant was issued for the arrest of the authors, printers, and publishers of the number. When this had been executed, Wilkes brought an action against Wood, the Under-Secretary concerned, on the ground that the seizure of his papers under the warrant had been illegal, and the jury by direction of Lord Chief Justice Pratt (later Lord Camden) returned a verdict in his favour.

Wilkes was concerned in another important reform. In trials for libel the province of the jury was at first restricted to deciding the fact of publication and interpreting the innuendoes that the alleged libels might contain. It was left to the judge to determine whether the publication was libellous or not. This restriction of the jury's province had been questioned from time to time, and the right of the jury to decide the whole issue was asserted by Bolingbroke in the *Craftsman* (see below), and maintained by Lord Camden and by Wilkes. The restriction was removed by Fox's Libel Act of 1792.

Another of the government's measures, designed in part to reduce the number of libels, was the Stamp Act of 1712, which imposed a duty of $\frac{1}{2}d$. on every periodical of half a sheet or less, and of 1d. on every whole sheet (altered by an Act of 1725 to a halfpenny on every half-sheet). This for a time lessened the number of periodicals but it discouraged publications favourable to the government at least as much as those of the opposition; ultimately there was no considerable reduction in the number of papers published.

In general, executive interference with the press diminished in the course of the 18th century. The government relied in part, for meeting the attacks made upon it, on its own pamphlets and journals, notably for a time on the *London Gazette* (which Steele was appointed to conduct, 1707–10), on Defoe's *Review* (1704–13), and on the *Examiner* (to which Matthew Prior and Swift were contributors). At a later period we find Bute's *The Briton* (edited by Smollett) employed to meet the attacks of *The Monitor*. The government sometimes bought up an opposition paper (such as the *London Journal*), or subsidized pro-government prints (such as the *Daily Courant* and *Free Briton*, and later the *Daily Gazetteer*) and had these distributed gratis over the kingdom. The ablest of the opposition papers, the *Craftsman*, long defied the resentment of the government. Bolingbroke and Pulteney were its best-known contributors. Its publisher was tried in 1729 and acquitted, but in 1731 was sentenced to imprisonment and fine.

The attempt of Charles I to arrest the five members had left Parliament disinclined to the publication of its proceedings. It was held accordingly a breach of privilege to print without permission the proceedings of either House or even to mention the names of members of Parliament in the press. A dry summary of the proceedings, known as the 'Votes', was allowed to appear, but it contained no account of the debates and entirely failed to meet the demands of the public at times of political excitement. From the accession of Anne some discreet account of the proceedings was introduced in Abel Boyer's *The Political State of Great Britain*, and from 1716 in the *Historical*

Register. In 1732 the *Gentleman's Magazine* and the *London Magazine* began reporting debates (Johnson's editorship of these in the *Gentleman's Magazine* is famous). In 1738 the House of Commons by resolution reaffirmed its privilege and threatened the utmost severity against offenders. But the reports of debates continued, under such transparent disguises as accounts of proceedings in the senate of Lilliput. A last and unsuccessful attempt to enforce the privilege was made in 1771, when the House of Commons took action against the printers of certain journals. Here again we find Wilkes taking part in the conflict, on the side of the liberty of the press.

The application of the law in the later 18th and early 19th centuries in restraint of the press may be illustrated by the cases of Thomas *Paine, who was brought in danger of arrest by what was regarded as his subversive work *The Rights of Man* (1791-2), and fled the country in consequence; and of *Cobbett, who in 1810 received a sentence of two years' imprisonment and a fine of £1,000 for a denunciation of flogging in the army. The last special restriction on the newspaper press, the Stamp Duty, was abolished in 1855; the stamp, for postal purposes, was retained until 1870. With the lapse of the Licensing Act in 1694 the importance of the Stationers' Company in connection with the control of the press came to an end, though registration at Stationers' Hall continued necessary for certain purposes in relation to copyright (see App. II).

§ 2. *Control of dramatic performances*

In the 16th century companies of players were attached to the court and to households of the nobility. Some of these companies travelled about the country giving performances at private houses and to the public. In addition, there were wandering troupes of miscellaneous players under no patronage. In the larger towns the guilds continued to present Corpus Christi plays, and similar performances were given sporadically in smaller places, but the performers of these probably remained amateurs. Some measure of control over stage performances was exercised in the interests of public order from about the middle of the century. The licensing of individual plays, in one form or another, began in 1549 if not earlier; and the subjection of players, unless 'protected', to the laws relating to vagabonds dates at least from 1554, and was probably enforced in practice even earlier. These measures were re-enacted in the reign of Elizabeth. By the Injunctions of 1559 already referred to she directed that no interlude should be played unless previously licensed by the mayor of the town, or in the country by the lord lieutenant or two justices of the peace; and no plays were to be so licensed which treated of matters of religion or of the governance of the country. By an Act of 1572 all players were to be deemed rogues and vagabonds unless they belonged to a baron of the realm or person of higher degree, or were licensed by two justices. The mayor and corporation of London, who under the Injunctions of 1559 had jurisdiction over stage plays in the city of London, the chief centre of theatrical activity, were in general hostile to dramatic performances, partly from Puritan sentiment, partly because the performances were apt to give rise to overcrowding and tumults, and moreover tended to spread infection in the frequently recurring periods of plague. The court on the other hand, and

Elizabeth herself, favoured the players, and the grant in 1574 of a patent to the Earl of Leicester's company, authorizing them to play in all towns without hindrance by the local authorities, conflicted with the powers previously conferred on the corporation. The latter retorted with an act of Common Council requiring all players to be licensed by the corporation and all plays allowed by it. The conflict between court and city was keen and prolonged, and during certain periods the corporation prohibited all performances within the city boundaries. In consequence, the first permanent playhouse in London was erected in Finsbury fields, outside the Lord Mayor's jurisdiction. Another issue of the conflict was to bring the players increasingly under the authority of the Master of the Revels, a court official, and from about 1574 no plays might be performed in England without his licence. His authority was gradually extended: in 1581 he was given power to commit offenders to prison; after 1606 he is found issuing licences for the printing as well as the performance of plays; also for various non-dramatic performances, such as those of acrobats and displays of animals. Under James I and Charles I the London companies of players worked under royal patents; companies protected by nobles are still found in the provinces. It should be emphasized that at this time the official control over the drama was directed to the exclusion of matters of religion and government, and was exercised in the interests of Church and State, not of morality. Jonson came under suspicion of papacy and treason for his *Sejanus and (together with Marston and Chapman) got into trouble for disparaging allusions to the Scots in *Eastward Hoe. Daniel incurred suspicion of allusion to Essex's plot in his *Philotas. Other famous examples of official interference with the Elizabethan drama may be mentioned. The original name of the fat knight in Shakespeare's *Henry IV was Sir John Oldcastle. To avoid offence to members of the family of that name, Shakespeare was required to change it, and substituted Falstaff. In the play *Sir Thomas More the part relating to the insurrectionary movement in London was required by the Master of the Revels to be omitted. The performance of Middleton's *A Game at Chesse was prohibited on the complaint of the Spanish Ambassador. But the attitude of the Puritans to the drama was quite different from that of the government. They regarded the stage as an immoral institution; the character of their hostility to it may be gathered from Histriomastix (1632), in which *Prynne asserted that stage plays, from their origin in the Devil onwards, had been the source of every possible crime. The work was held by the Star Chamber to reflect on Charles I and his queen, and Prynne was sentenced to lose his ears, to imprisonment, and to a heavy fine. The drama, on the other hand, was full of contemptuous references to the Puritans. In 1642 the Long Parliament put an end to all dramatic performances. The prohibition was to some extent evaded, was repeated in 1647, and towards the end of the Commonwealth period was in part relaxed, for *D'Avenant was then allowed to present certain semi-dramatic entertainments accompanied by music.

After the Restoration Charles II issued patents to D'Avenant and Thomas *Killigrew the elder, authorizing them to form two companies of actors with exclusive rights of performance in London and Westminster, and enjoining on them to expunge all profaneness and scurrility from the plays that should be acted. But Sir Henry Herbert, who had been Master of the Revels under

Charles I, asserted his right to grant licences, and many quarrels resulted. Finally an arrangement was arrived at between Herbert and Killigrew for sharing the control of the stage, and on Herbert's death Killigrew succeeded him as Master of the Revels. In the reaction which followed the period of Puritan austerity, the administration of the censorship was very lax. Not only was gross indecency tolerated, but references to political and religious matters were inadequately controlled. In course of time, after the death of Charles II, the public mood changed, and there was a revolt against the previous licentiousness. Jeremy *Collier's attack 'on the profaneness and immorality of the stage' (1697) found a wide measure of sympathy. It was followed in 1698 by a royal order prohibiting the acting of anything contrary to religion and good manners and forbidding the Master of the Revels to license plays containing anything of the kind. The attention of the censor was thus specifically directed to moral supervision. But the gradual chastening of the drama which followed and which led to such plays as those of Rowe, Addison, and Steele, may be attributed more to a change of public sentiment than to the action of the censor.

In the early part of the 18th century the control of the stage appears to have been exercised largely by the Lord Chamberlain himself. Little of importance in its history is recorded until Rich in 1728 produced Gay's *The Beggar's Opera, a play containing social and political satire and obvious allusions to Walpole and Townshend. The performance of its sequel, Polly, was prohibited by the Lord Chamberlain. In 1736 and 1737 *Fielding, in his Pasquin and The Historical Register for 1736, carried political satire and personal allusion to greater lengths; and it was no doubt to some extent in consequence of these plays that Walpole took statutory powers, by the Licensing Act of 1737 (10 Geo. II, cap. 28), to control dramatic performances. This Act made the Lord Chamberlain licenser of theatres in London and Westminster and in other places of residence of the sovereign; it imposed penalties on the performance for hire anywhere in Great Britain of plays not licensed by him, and required that a copy of every new play proposed to be performed should be sent to him. For the purpose of his duties under the Act the Lord Chamberlain appointed an Examiner of Plays as his official subordinate. The Act was unpopular with the public and was evaded in various ways. Brooke's Gustavus Vasa was one of the first plays censored, owing to a supposed allusion in it to Walpole; Johnson's ironical 'Compleat Vindication of the Licenser of Plays' on this occasion (1739) reflected the popular resentment. Edward and Eleanora, a play about Edward I and Eleanor of Castile, by James *Thomson, was similarly prohibited on account of its political allusions. It is more difficult to understand why Charles Macklin's *The Man of the World should for many years have been refused a licence. Another well-known incident was the prohibition of A Trip to Calais by Samuel Foote, until he had removed from it the character of Lady Kitty Crocodile, in which the Duchess of Kingston was ridiculed.

The most interesting of the appointments to the post of Examiner of Plays in the early 19th century was that of George *Colman the Younger, who held the office from 1824 to 1836. Some of his plays and poems had shown him no strait-laced moralist, and one of his proposed productions at the Haymarket had even been forbidden by the Lord Chamberlain. The severity with which he now exercised his duties as censor and prohibited expletives and scriptural allusions was therefore a surprise to authors and managers. He tempered this severity, however, by letting his opinion be known that it was no part of his duties to spy on the theatre and to see that plays were performed in accordance with his obliterations. He was succeeded by Charles Kemble the actor, and the latter in 1840 by his son John Mitchell Kemble. William Bodham Donne was appointed Examiner of Stage Plays in 1857, E. F. S. Pigott in 1874, G. A. Redford in 1895, C. H. E. Brookfield in 1912; he died in the following year and G. S. Street held the office 1913–36.

In 1832 a Select Committee of the House of Commons was appointed under the chairmanship of Edward *Bulwer-Lytton to consider the working of the Act of 1737. The recommendations of this committee led to the passing in 1843 of an Act (6 & 7 Vict. cap. 68) whose provisions left the censorship of the drama in the hands of the Lord Chamberlain and empowered him to forbid the acting for hire of any play or part thereof 'whenever he shall be of opinion that it is fitting for the preservation of good manners, decorum, or the public peace so to do'. The administration of the censorship under this Act at times gave rise to much criticism; in particular the refusal of a licence to certain plays by distinguished authors (such as Maeterlinck, Ibsen, and Bernard Shaw) evoked strong protests. In 1909 the matter was considered by a Select Committee of both Houses. The evidence given before it showed a large measure of agreement among dramatic authors that the censorship should be abolished or modified; among managers of theatres, on the other hand, that some form of licensing plays before their production should be retained. The Committee's principal recommendations were that the Lord Chamberlain should remain the licenser of plays, that it should be optional to submit a play for licence and legal to perform an unlicensed play. The Committee enumerated the various grounds (indecency, offence to the sentiment of religious reverence, offence to a foreign power, etc.) on which the Lord Chamberlain should refuse a licence; and it recommended the action to be taken if a play produced without a licence should appear to the Attorney-General improper to be played on any of these grounds, or to the Director of Public Prosecutions improper to be played on the ground of indecency. No legislative action followed the report of the Committee until the passing of the Theatres Act in 1968 (see below).

§ 3. The present law of the press and drama

The following are the chief heads under which the law today punishes the publication of illegal matter:

1. *Libel as a civil injury*, the publication of matter defamatory of the plaintiff, that is, 'calculated to convey to those to whom it is published an imputation on the plaintiff injurious to him in his trade, or holding him up to hatred, contempt, or ridicule',

   (a) unless it appears that the publication is privileged, either

   (i) absolutely (this applies to Reports and Proceedings published under the authority of either House of Parliament, documents used in judicial proceedings, and reports of State officials to their superiors; but not necessarily to the reproduction of any of the above in newspapers);

or (ii) partially (this applies to reports of parliamentary, judicial, or other public proceedings, provided that the report is fair and accurate and was not published maliciously, that the matter is of public concern and its publicity for the public benefit, and that the defendant has not refused on request to publish in the newspaper in which the publication complained of was made a reasonable contradiction or explanation);

(b) or unless the defendant can prove the defamatory matter to be true (if a statement of fact) or fair and honest comment on a subject of public interest (if a matter of opinion).

Everyone who is party to producing, printing, and issuing the libel (author, proprietor of a newspaper, printer, publisher, and in certain circumstances the vendor) is liable in respect of it.

2. *Libel as a criminal offence*, i.e. as calculated to provoke a breach of the peace or to outrage public feeling or morality, or to endanger the State:

(a) libels defamatory of private character. Here in order to establish justification, it is necessary to prove not only that the defamatory statement is true, but also that its publication is for the public benefit;

(b) libels (not in the popular sense of the word, but publications which the State for public purposes prohibits) that are

(i) obscene, i.e. matter tending to deprave and corrupt those whose minds are open to such immoral influences, and into whose hands the matter is likely to fall. The Act 20 & 21 Vict. cap. 83 was passed for the purpose of preventing the sale of obscene books, etc. An instance of action by the government to restrain the sale of printed matter on the score of alleged obscenity is afforded by the well-known case of Joyce's *Ulysses*. An edition of 500 numbered copies, published by John Rodker, Paris, for the Egoist Press, London, in January 1923, was confiscated (with, it is said, the exception of one copy) by the British Customs authorities, and this action effectively prohibited publication in Great Britain so long as the government's policy remained unchanged. Under the Obscene Publications Act 1959 a book 'is deemed to be obscene if its effect . . . if taken as a whole, is such as to tend to deprave and corrupt persons who are likely, having regard to all relevant circumstances, to read . . . the matter contained . . . in it'. Sect. 2 reads shortly as '. . . any person who, whether for gain or not, publishes an obscene article shall be liable upon conviction' to certain penalties. Sect. 4 reads, 'A person shall not be convicted of an offence against Section 2 if it is proved that publication of the article in question is justified as being for the public good on the ground that it is in the interests of science, literature, art, or learning, or of other subjects of general concern.' Before the passing of the 1959 Statute defendants were not allowed by law to call any evidence with regard to the literary or other merits of the book. Sub-sect. 2 (of sect. 4) reads, 'that the opinion of experts as to the literary, artistic,

scientific, or other merits of an article may be admitted in any proceedings under this Act to establish or to negative the said ground.'
Lady Chatterley's Lover by D. H. Lawrence was the subject of the
case *Regina* v. *Penguin Books Limited*, heard at the Old Bailey in 1960
(20 Oct.-2 Nov.). The case, which resulted in the acquittal of Penguin
Books and the release of the book for sale, was interesting because for
the first time the defendants were allowed to bring witnesses to give
evidence on the literary and moral qualities of the book. In 1964 an
amending act, aimed at traffic in and display of pornography, created
a new offence of '*having* an obscene article for publication for gain',
a clause which was applied in 1967 in the conviction of a bookseller
for stocking H. Selby Jnr.'s *Last Exit to Brooklyn*. This decision
was reversed on appeal in 1968, and in 1976 the 'not guilty' verdict
on a paperback called *Inside Linda Lovelace* convinced prosecuting
authorities that the pursuit of written works with the slightest preten-
sion to serious purpose would be counter-productive;

(ii) blasphemous, i.e. written or published with the malicious intent of
outraging Christian sentiment or of misleading the uneducated on a
sacred subject. 'If the decencies of controversy are observed, even the
fundamentals of religion may be attacked without a person being
guilty of blasphemous libel' (Lord Coleridge). In 1977 the crime of
blasphemous libel was deployed for the first time since 1922 by a
private prosecutor to obtain the conviction of the editor of *Gay News*
for publishing a poem by J. *Kirkup; it was held that indecent writing
which vilifies sacred personages can amount to blasphemy, the crime
lying in the scurrility of the expression rather than in the message
imparted. The opinions of experts on the poem's literary merits were
ruled inadmissible;

(iii) seditious, i.e. matter tending to bring into hatred or contempt the
sovereign, the government and constitution, or either House of Parliament, or to excite to the alteration of anything in Church or State
by unlawful means, or to raise discontent and disaffection among the
king's subjects, or to promote ill-will and hostility between different
classes of them.

In a trial for criminal libel a defendant presumptively responsible for the
publication (such as a newspaper proprietor) who is able to prove that such
publication was made without his authority, consent, or knowledge, and that
the publication did not arise from want of due care on his part, is freed from
criminal responsibility.

3. *Infringement of copyright* (see App. II).

4. *Slander of property*, i.e. the publication of a statement referring to the
property or trade of another which is false and is calculated to cause, or has
caused, damage.

5. *Contempt of Parliament or Court*, i.e. the publication of matter defamatory of or insulting to either House of Parliament, or reflecting on any
member of such House in his character of member, or of any matter reflecting
on one of the Superior Courts of Record or referring to the parties concerned

in causes therein, if the matter is calculated to prejudice the public against the parties before the cause is heard, or to interfere with the due administration of the law. In 1977 the *Sunday Times* successfully appealed to the European Court against the suppression of a series of articles on the negligent manufacture of the drug thalidomide, a suppression ordered on the basis that the articles would pre-judge issues to be tried in court; this judgement led to the 1981 Contempt Act which provides a special defence whereby publication made as part of a discussion in good faith of public affairs or other matters of general public interest is not contempt if the risk of impediment or prejudice to particular legal proceedings is merely incidental to the discussion.

6. The *Official Secrets Act*, introduced in the Agadir crisis of 1911, was designed to protect the nation's secrets from enemy agents. It has theoretical breadth and formidable powers: Section 2, which was drafted to prevent leakage of official information to the Press, created more than 2,000 offences. It is rarely invoked, its use being circumscribed by political considerations.

7. *Breach of Confidence.* The courts have power to restrain publications which divulge information obtained in breach of the plaintiff's right to confidentiality: this can be defeated by proof that there is a 'public interest' that strongly justifies disclosure.

The printer is required to put his name and address on every copy of every paper or book printed by him to be published or dispersed (2 & 3 Vict. cap. 12).

Dramatic performances. The Act of 6 & 7 Vict. cap. 68 (1843) required that a copy of new plays and additions to old plays intended to be acted for hire should be sent at least seven days before the first acting thereof, together with the prescribed fee (which was not to exceed two guineas in any case), to the Lord Chamberlain, who might forbid the acting of any play or of any part thereof anywhere in Great Britain. Penalties for infringement were prescribed, and the meaning of 'acted for hire' was defined. The Act further required that theatres should be authorized either by letters patent or by the Lord Chamberlain or (outside London and other places of royal residence) by justices of the peace (this last provision was modified by Local Government Acts). The Theatres Act of 1968 abolished the Lord Chamberlain's responsibilities with regard to theatrical censorship, and plays are no longer required to be licensed. In 1982 a private prosecution was brought against Howard Brenton's play *The Romans in Britain*, in performance at the National Theatre, alleging that the director had procured an act of gross indecency (an act of simulated homosexual rape) contrary to Section 13 of the Sexual Offences Act: the prosecution collapsed on technical grounds.

Television, radio, film, and video. The government has certain direct legal powers over BBC radio and television, contained in the License Agreement which forms part of the Corporation's charter; the Home Secretary, for example, has the right to prohibit the BBC from transmitting any item at any time, under Section 13 (4) of the Licence, with the safeguard that the BBC 'may' (not 'must') tell the public that it has received such an order.

Commercial radio and television are supervised by a government-appointed licensing body called the Independent Broadcasting Authority, which has wide powers (dating from 1954) to control programme content. It comprises a Board of 18 government appointees, with a staff of several hundred, and one subsidiary company responsible for running Channel 4. The IBA has the duty to vet programmes to ensure that they are neither offensive nor biased.

The cinema is subject to the British Board of Film Censors, a body which has no standing in law, but which exercises considerable influence over the way the law is enforced. It is financed by the film industry, and will grant certificates only to films which it considers are within the limits of public acceptability. In practice the Director of Public Prosecutions does not prosecute films with BBFC certificates. The BBFC has taken on an even greater importance with the advent of cable television and video cassettes. Cable stations are bound, by their Home Office licences, to show only those feature films which have BBFC certificates, and videos which deal with matters of sex and violence can legally be publicly distributed only if they have a BBFC certificate.

APPENDIX II

NOTES ON THE HISTORY OF ENGLISH COPYRIGHT

By Sir Frank Mackinnon[1]

'No man but a blockhead ever wrote except for money', said the great man. In order to increase the number of books worth reading, mankind has been concerned to see that writers may get some reward for their industry. And so there came to be devised that security for them which we call Copyright.

The first English Copyright Act was the celebrated Statute[2] of 1709. But something akin to the protection of copyright had existed for at least a century and a half before that date. This had two principal sources and means of support, firstly, the prerogative rights of the Crown, and secondly, the domestic arrangements of London booksellers under the rule of the Stationers' Company.

The action of the Crown was part of its practice to grant monopolies in general, but from an early date after Caxton printed his first book[3] at Westminster in 1477, it claimed especial rights as to printed books. There are indeed traces of a claim that all printing was the king's prerogative. There is, for example, a record[4] of a privilege granted in 1597 to the queen's footman to print certain schoolbooks for 14 years; and as late as 1631 of a grant[5] to one Weckherlin of the sole right to print some of the Latin classics.

But a royal grant of the sole privilege to print new books was much more common. In 1518 Richard Pynson, the second holder of the office of King's Printer, produced the first English book in Roman type, and on its title-page is inscribed, 'Cum privilegio impressa a rege indulto, ne quis hanc orationem intra biennium in regno Angliae imprimat aut alibi impressam et importatam in eodem regno Angliae vendat'. Pynson's later books are only inscribed, 'Cum privilegio a rege indulto'.

The Act[6] of 1623 abolished monopolies; but sect. 5 of it excepts Letters Patent for new inventions, and sect. 10 provides that the Act shall not extend to any Letters Patent that concern Printing, Saltpetre, Gunpowder, and Ordnance.

For more than two centuries after Pynson's grant in 1518 it was common for such a privilege to be obtained from the Crown. For example, Loggan's *Oxonia Illustrata* (Oxon. e Theatro Sheldoniano, 1675) has printed in it a

---

[1] The paragraphs concerning the Copyright Act of 1956 and the last two paragraphs under the heading *International Copyright* were contributed by Kenneth Ewart, further revised.

[2] 8 Anne, cap. 19.

[3] There exists in the Record Office a lease dated 10 May 1482 of premises in St Mark's Alley, St Clement's Lane, to Henry Franckenbergk and Bernard Van Stondo 'merchants of printed books'. The Act of 1483 (1 Rich. III, cap. 9) to prevent aliens trading within the realm, by sect. 12 made an exception in favour of any Artificer or Merchant Stranger bringing into this Realm or selling any Books written or printed. The demand for the new luxury evidently exceeded the native supply. This foreigner's privilege was repealed in 1533 by 25 Hen. VIII, cap. 15.

[4] S. P. Dom. (1595–7), p. 352.

[5] S. P. Dom. (1629–34), pp. 514, 557.

[6] 21 James I, cap. 3.

grant by Charles II giving Loggan 'the sole Priviledge of printing the aforesaid Delineations for the term of 15 years next ensuing the date of this our License'. And the practice became so inveterate that it was often continued after the Act of Anne was passed in 1709. So when in 1741 the bookseller Austin was minded to publish a second edition of Stackhouse's *History of the Bible* (first published in 1732) he got Letters Patent from George II giving him the sole privilege of printing his edition for 14 years. And the early editions of Warburton's Pope have printed in them a licence or grant from George II, dated 24 July 1759, giving Warburton 'our Royal Privilege and License for the sole printing and publishing the said Works' for 14 years.

There was a second way in which the Crown was concerned with copyright. In certain classes of books it claimed an especial prerogative right, and granted the sole privilege of printing them. These were State documents, like Acts of Parliament and Orders in Council, Bibles and Prayer Books, the Year Books, and Almanacs.[1] Except as to the Year Books and Almanacs, this right was a real one, and survives today. The Queen's Printers are still, by Letters Patent, empowered to print Acts of Parliament, Bibles, and Prayer Books. That the University Presses of Oxford and Cambridge share the right with them arises solely from the fact that each of the Universities possesses an early Charter (that of Oxford 1636), which authorizes it 'to print all manner of books'.

A third way in which the Crown may be said to have been concerned in the maintenance of the rights of authors and their publishers was in connection with the licensing of publications. But this part of the Crown's activity is to a large extent combined with the working of the Stationers' Company as the controlling power over the publication of books.

In 1557 a charter of Queen Mary incorporated 97 named persons to constitute the Company of Stationers. The motive for this creation was very little concerned with the protection of authors and their copyright. It was in fact because 'certain seditious books . . . are daily printed, renewing and spreading great and detestable heresies against the catholic doctrine of the holy Mother Church'. It was ordered that no one should exercise the art of printing unless he was a freeman of the Company, and the Master and Wardens were authorized to seize and destroy prohibited books, and to imprison anyone printing contrary to their orders. The Company was further empowered to make by-laws for regulating the trade.

This charter was confirmed by Queen Elizabeth in 1559; and in the same year a Royal Injunction required that a licence for the printing of any book must be obtained from some authority (see App. I, CENSORSHIP).

From a very early date after 1557 the Stationers' Company began to keep registers of the proprietors of 'copy', and books were entered in these by the printers to whom authors had sold them. From 1576 to 1595 more than 2,000 'copies' of books were registered, entirely or in shares, as the property of particular members. As only members of the Company could legally print, the entry in the register showed which member had the right to print a particular book, and any infringement of this by another printer-member could be prevented, or remedied, by fines imposed by the Company. Any

[1] The royal claim to almanacs may have been based on their being derived from the Tables in the Prayer Book. That it was without foundation was eventually decided in *Stationers' Co.* v. *Carnan* (1775), 2 W. Bl. 1002.

printing by a piratical printer, not a member, could be stopped by the Company's power to destroy his press altogether. The State Papers of the 16th and 17th centuries, especially in reference to the Star Chamber and the High Commission Court, contain many references to the activity of the Company in both these ways.

Not unnaturally the richer members of the Company came to own the largest number of 'copies', and this caused discontent among the smaller men. A royal decree of 1585 confirmed the charter of the Company, but recited that many of the richer members[1] had yielded divers of their copies to the Company for the benefit and relief of the poorer members. This process would make the Company itself the proprietor of certain works.

The effect of all this was that by 1600 the sole right of printing a particular book, not yet called 'copyright',[2] was protected in two ways, first by virtue of Royal Grants giving the grantee a sole right of printing for a specified number of years, and secondly by the rules and by-laws of the Stationers' Company. There is, however, no record of any case in the law courts in which this right was enforced or recognized. The fact that it could be so thoroughly upheld by the domestic powers of the Company is no doubt the reason for this.

These two sources of the sole right to print are recognized by the decree of the Star Chamber in 1637 'touching the Regulation of Printers and Founders of Letters'. That enacted by sect. 2 that every book should be licensed and entered in the Register Book of the Stationers' Company; and by sect. 7 that no person should print or import any copy which the Company of Stationers, or any other person, has by any letters patent, order, or entrance in their Register Book, the right or allowance solely to print.

The Star Chamber having been abolished in 1641, an Ordinance of 1641 prohibited printing without the consent of the owner of the 'copy' of any book. And this was followed by the famous Ordinance of the Long Parliament of 1643. This provided that no book should be printed unless licensed. It also enacted that no book, of which the copy had been granted to the Stationers' Company 'for their relief and the maintenance of their poor', be printed by any one without the licence of the Company. It also renewed to the Company the power to break up unlicensed presses, and to search for, and confiscate, unlicensed books.

But here again, as in Queen Mary's Charter to the Company of 1557, the primary motive was not the protection of authors. For the preamble to the Ordinance recites that 'many false, scandalous, seditious, and libellous' works have been lately published, 'to the great defamation of Religion and Government'; and that many private presses have been set up. It was the part of this Ordinance that required all books to be licensed that gave rise to Milton's *Areopagitica*. 'For that part', he says, 'which preserves justly every man's copy to himself, or provides for the poor, I touch not, only wish they be not made pretences to abuse and persecute honest and painful men, who offend not in either of these particulars.' And near the end he speaks of 'the just retaining of each man his several copy, which God forbid should be gainsaid'.

---

[1] Mr Tottell surrendered *Romeo et Julietta, inter alia.*
[2] The earliest quotation for the word 'Copyright' in the *OED* is dated 1767 from *Blackstone's Commentaries.*

There were further Ordinances to the same effect in 1647, 1649, and 1652. And after the Restoration an Act[1] of 1662 was again passed 'for preventing the frequent abuses in printing seditious, treasonable, and unlicensed books and pamphlets'. This again incidentally dealt with copyright. By sect. 3 all books are to be entered in the Register of the Stationers' Company, and by sect. 6 'no person shall print or import any book which any person by virtue of letters Patent, or of entries duly made in the Register Book of the Company . . . has, or shall have, the right, privilege, authority, or allowance solely to print without the consent of the owner or owners'.

In 1684 a new charter was granted to the Company, which recited the ownership of 'copies' according to the Register by members of the Company, and went on, 'We, willing and desiring to confirm and establish every member in their just rights and properties, do well approve of the said Register, and declare that every member of the Company, who shall be the proprietor of any book, shall have and enjoy such sole right, power, privilege, and authority of printing such book or copy as in that case hath been usual heretofore.'

These Licensing Acts were several times re-enacted, but the last of them lapsed in 1694. The effect of this was that there remained no Act of Parliament recognizing the sole right to print, and this was no doubt one of the reasons for the passing of the Act of 1709.

It is of great importance to observe that, though Letters Patent from the Crown used to specify a period, usually 14 years, for the sole right of printing, there is nowhere any trace of any limitation of time in regard to the ownership of 'copy' by registration with the Company. In the year 1700 there can be no doubt that this was universally recognized as a perpetual right. The Tonsons, for example, through most part of the 18th century were regarded as the undoubted owners of the copyright in *Paradise Lost, under an assignment from Milton dated 1667, duly entered in the Register. They were also regarded as the proprietors of Shakespeare's plays, though I do not know that they had any assignment from the author on which to rely. And the Special Verdict in Millar v. Taylor in 1769 stated 'that before the reign of her late Majesty, Queen Anne, it was usual to purchase from authors the perpetual copyright of their books and to assign them from hand to hand for valuable considerations, and to make the same the subjects of family settlements for the provision of wives and children'.

In short, in 1700 it was the universal belief of the trade, and probably of lawyers, that by the common law an author, or his bookseller-assignee, had a perpetual copyright in any book.

The Act of 1709 was probably the result of petitions from the Booksellers in 1703, 1706, and 1709. What they desired was not the creation of copyright— as to that they had no doubt, nor as to its duration—but the provision of machinery by which it could be more readily enforced. This they had enjoyed, under the Licensing Act which expired in 1694, by the power to seize unlicensed and unregistered books.

The title of the Act of 1709 was 'An Act for the encouragement of Learning, by vesting[2] the copies of printed books in the authors or purchasers of such

---

[1] 13 & 14 Car. II, cap. 33.
[2] In the original Bill this was 'securing'.

copies during the times therein mentioned'. The Preamble recited that persons have of late frequently taken the liberty of printing books without the consent of the authors, or proprietors, of such books, to their great detriment and too often to the ruin of them and their families. The first section enacted that from 10 April 1710 an author of a book already printed, or the bookseller who had bought his copy, should have the sole right and liberty of printing such book for the term of 1 and 20 years, and no longer; and an author of any book not yet published should have the sole liberty of printing it for the term of 14 years from its publication, and no longer. If anyone printed a book in breach of these rights, the offender should forfeit the book, and be liable to pay a penalty of a penny for every sheet found in his possession. Sect. 2 provided that no offender should be liable to such forfeiture or penalties unless the title to the copy of the book should be entered in the Register of the Stationers' Company. Sect. 4 provided a cumbrous machinery for fixing fair prices for books in case of a complaint by anyone that a bookseller was asking an unreasonable price.[1] Sect. 5 provided for the delivery of copies for certain libraries: I refer to this later. Sect. 7 provided that nothing in the Act should extend to prohibit the importation and sale of any books in Greek, Latin, or any other foreign language, printed beyond the seas.

Sect. 9 was, 'Provided that nothing in this Act contained shall extend, or be construed to extend, either to prejudice or confirm any right that the said Universities, or any of them, or any person or persons have, or claim to have, to the printing or reprinting any book or copy already printed, or hereafter to be printed.' And the final sect. 11 was, 'Provided always that after the expiration of the said term of fourteen years, the sole right of printing or disposing of copies shall return to the author thereof, if they are then living, for another term of fourteen years.'

The great 'Question of Literary Property' which reverberates through the second half of the 18th century, and has its echo in the pages of Boswell, was whether the perpetual copyright, at common law, of an author or his bookseller-assignee survived the passage of this Act, or was destroyed by it. Until their final discomfiture in 1774 the Booksellers were confident that it survived. They regarded the Act as only designed to provide, for the periods named, machinery for enforcing the right by forfeiture and penalties; and they relied confidently on the proviso in clause 9. But ultimately the words 'and no longer' in clause 1 proved fatal to them.

The question could hardly arise until the expiration of the 21 years in 1731. And for a time the Booksellers were successful, especially in applications for injunctions in the Court of Chancery. For example, in 1735 the proprietor of *The Whole Duty of Man*, claiming under an assignment of 1657 (from what author is not apparent), successfully restrained a rival from printing it. And

---

[1] There was precedent for this in an Act of 1533 (25 Hen. VIII, cap. 15) which provided that if English printers increase the price of books at too high and unreasonable prices the Lord Chancellor, Lord Treasurer, or two Chief Justices may hold an inquiry with 12 jurors and limit the prices. The Act of 1709 in the above clause gave power to limit prices, in England, to the Archbishop of Canterbury, the Lord Chancellor, the Bishop of London, the two Chief Justices, the Chief Baron, and the Vice-Chancellors of Oxford and Cambridge; and in Scotland, to the Lord President, the Lord Justice General, the Lord Chief Baron, and the Rector of Edinburgh University. Nothing is provided as to Ireland.

in 1736, before Lord Hardwicke, 'Tonson and Others' vindicated their 'copy' in *Paradise Lost* under the assignment from Milton of 1667.

In 1769 the question came before a Court of Law in the famous case of *Millar v. Taylor*. It concerned Thomson's *Seasons*, published 1726-30. Thomson's 28 years under clauses 1 and 11 of the Act of 1709 had therefore expired by 1758. He had sold all his rights to Millar. In 1763 Taylor reprinted the work, and in 1766 Millar sued him in the King's Bench. In 1769 the Court delivered judgement, and it was one of the few occasions on which that Court, during the 32 years of Lord Mansfield's reign as Chief Justice, was not unanimous. Lord Mansfield, Mr Justice Willes, and Mr Justice Aston decided in favour of Millar. Mr Justice Yates (after a 'very decent preface', as the reporter, Burrow, records) delivered a lengthy dissentient judgement in favour of Taylor. So, for the time, the Booksellers won.

The chief source of trouble to the London Booksellers was the activity of printers in Ireland and Scotland. For some reason they do not seem to have attempted to take action in Dublin,[1] and those who read booksellers' catalogues are aware that Dublin reprints of all the important books in the 18th century are numerous. But they did attack those whom they no doubt regarded as the Edinburgh 'pirates', and this was eventually their undoing.

The first edition of Stackhouse's *History of the Bible* was published in 1732. A second edition[2] was published by his assignee, Austin, in 1744. Stackhouse died in 1752, so his 28 years under the Act expired in 1760. In 1767 Donaldson, an Edinburgh bookseller, reprinted the book. In 1770 Hinton, a London bookseller, and the assignee of Austin, sued Donaldson in the Court of Session. Ilay Campbell was Donaldson's advocate, and James Boswell was his junior. On 28 July 1773 the Court of Sessions, by eleven to one, decided in favour of Donaldson. The eleven included Lord Auchinleck, Lord Hailes, and Lord Kames: the one dissentient was Lord Monboddo. So the London booksellers had won in London in 1769 and had lost in Scotland in 1773.

In 1774 came *Donaldson v. Beckett* in the House of Lords. This again concerned Thomson's *Seasons*. Beckett had bought from Millar's executors the copyright that had been upheld in *Millar v. Taylor* in 1769. And Beckett made his claim in the English Court of Chancery against the Edinburgh 'pirate' Donaldson, who had reprinted *The Seasons*. Lord Chancellor Bathurst granted a perpetual injunction against Donaldson, whereupon Donaldson appealed to the House of Lords. The hearing began[3] 4 February 1774. The judges, then twelve in number, being summoned, they all attended with the exception of Lord Mansfield: it was not the etiquette for him to advise the House; as a peer himself, if he were present, he would form part of the

---

[1] One of the pamphlets ('A Letter from a gentleman in Edinburgh to his friend in London concerning Literary Property', 1769) referring to Blackstone's support of the perpetual right at common law (*Commentaries*, ii. 406) says, 'His book has been reprinted in Ireland, copies have been smuggled over to Britain, and a good many of them, it is said, were seized some time ago by the Doctor's agents in the port of London; but if he really believes he has any right at common law, why does he not sue the Irish printers for piracy, robbery, or theft, in virtue of this *common law right?*'

[2] It was for this edition that Austin got the Letters Patent from George II, mentioned *supra* p. 1114, giving him the sole privilege of printing it for 14 years.

[3] Johnson wrote to Boswell, 7 Feb. 1774: 'The question of Literary Property is this day before the Lords. Murphy drew up the Appellant's case, that is the plea against the perpetual right. I have not seen it, nor heard the decision. I would not have the right perpetual.' Boswell, *Life*, ii. 272.

tribunal. Five questions were submitted to the judges, to which they gave answers by varying majorities. But to the most vital question—'Whether by the Statute of 1709 an author is precluded from every remedy, except on the foundation of the said statute, or on the terms and conditions prescribed therein'—six answered 'Yes', and five answered 'No'.

Lord Mansfield, who might have sat, and upheld the view he had taken in *Millar v. Taylor* five years before, did not attend the House. And on the motion of Lord Camden, on 22 February, the House decided in favour of the appellant, Donaldson,[1] and *Millar v. Taylor* was overruled. The English booksellers had found their Bannockburn.

They attempted to get relief from Parliament, but a Bill for that purpose, having passed the Commons, was rejected by the Lords. But the Universities of Oxford, Cambridge, St Andrews, Glasgow, Aberdeen, and Edinburgh, and the Colleges of Winchester, Eton, and Westminster got an Act[2] in 1775 giving them perpetual copyright 'in books given or bequeathed to the said Universities and Colleges for the advancement of useful learning, and other purposes of education'. This was subject to the condition that such books be printed at their own private presses, which Oxford and Cambridge alone possessed!

In 1814 the author's period of 14 years, with a second 14 years, if he was alive at the end of the first, under the Act of 1709 was altered when, by 54 Geo. III, cap. 156, the author was given 28 years, and, if he were living at the end of that period, the term of his life.

So matters remained until Serjeant Talfourd in 1837 began his efforts to secure an increased period of copyright in the interests of authors. He was removed from the House of Commons, by being made a judge, before his crusade was successful in 1842. Sixty years was his proposal, in the Bill he introduced without success in 1838. The question was further debated in 1841 and 1842, and was made memorable by two famous speeches of Macaulay. His proposal, supported by a wealth of historical instances, was that the period should be 42 years, or the life of the author, whichever was the longer. The House was convinced by his eloquence. Sir George Trevelyan, in his *Life of Macaulay*,[3] says: 'Never has any public man, unendowed with the authority of a minister, so easily moulded an important piece of legislation into a shape which so accurately accorded with his own views as did Macaulay the Copyright Act of 1842.'

Sir Robert Peel successfully moved one amendment, by which seven years was added to the author's life. In the result the Act[4] of 1842 gave copyright for the period of 42 years from the date of publication, or until seven years after the author's death, whichever was the longer. Sect. 5 of the Act empowered the Judicial Committee of the Privy Council to authorize, after the author's death,

[1] When Mr Dempster said, 'Donaldson, Sir, is anxious for the encouragement of literature. He reduces the prices of books so that poor students may buy them', Dr Johnson said (laughing), 'Well, Sir, allowing that to be his motive, he is no better than Robin Hood, who robbed the rich in order to give to the poor.' Boswell, *Life*, i. 438.

[2] 15 Geo. III, cap. 53. Sect. 33 of the Copyright Act 1911 provides that 'Nothing in this Act shall deprive any of the Universities and Colleges mentioned in the Act of 1775 of any copyright they already possess under that Act.' But the Act of 1775 itself is repealed by the Act of 1911, so that none of the Universities or Colleges can acquire a perpetual copyright in the future.

[3] Vol. ii, p. 132.

[4] 5 & 6 Vict. cap. 45.

the reprinting of a book which the proprietor of the copyright refused to permit. Sect. 11 continued the Registry at Stationers' Hall, and provided that certificates issued there should be *prima facie* proof in any court of the ownership of the copyright. And by sect. 24 no action for infringement could be begun unless the work had been entered in the Registry before the writ was issued. This meant that the Registry was not necessarily a complete record of publications, though the great majority were entered. But a publisher could abstain from registering altogether, unless he came to want to sue for an infringement, when he must register before starting his suit.

This Act, like all previous ones, dealt with copyright as from the time of publication. There never was any doubt that by the common law the author of any writing, or his personal representative after his death, had complete and perpetual power over his work so long as it remained unpublished. This applied to letters. The recipient of a letter had the property in the paper, but, unless he had express or implied authority from the writer (as the editor of a newspaper, for example), he had no right to publish copies of it. In pure theory the purchaser of an unpublished letter of Samuel Johnson could have been restrained from publishing it by his then personal representative, who would be found in a line of successive executors from Lord Stowell, the survivor of his three executors.[1]

This Act of 1842 provided for English literary copyright until it was replaced by the Act[2] of 1911. This effected three momentous changes. Firstly, it increased the period of copyright to the life of the author and 50 years after his death. This got rid of difficult questions that used to arise when the period of copyright began from the date of publication.[3] In the case of a posthumous work, however, copyright was (by sect. 17) to subsist for 50 years from publication. Secondly, the Act tacitly abolished the Register at Stationers' Hall, since it no longer made registration there necessary for any purpose. And so those records, which had been kept for three and a half centuries, came to an end.[4] Thirdly, the Act altered the nature of the perpetual common law right of an author, and his personal representatives, in an unpublished work. For its definition of 'copyright' includes the right, if a work is unpublished, to publish it, or any substantial part of it. Thus the right became part of the personal property of the deceased author.

In regard to the unpublished manuscript of a deceased author two questions may follow: (1) Who is the owner of the manuscript? and (2) Who is proprietor of the right to publish it? As to the latter it was provided by sect. 17 (2) that the ownership of an unpublished manuscript after the author's death, when acquired pursuant to a will made by the author, should be *prima facie* proof

---

[1] In the early 20th cent., in litigation between two publishers about some letters of Charles Lamb, one of the parties, in order to strengthen his case, got hold of Lamb's personal representative (in a line from his executor, Moxon), caused him to take out letters of administration *de bonis non*, and took an assignment of the right to publish from him.

[2] 1 & 2 Geo. V, cap. 46.

[3] Possibly it was an inducement to the inferior publisher to indulge in that reprehensible practice of putting no date on a title-page.

[4] In fact the registration of books at Stationers' Hall continued until Dec. 1923. This was done with the object of securing copyright in Canada, since the Act of 1911 was not (by sect. 25) to apply to a self-governing Dominion until made to do so by domestic legislation. This was not passed in Canada, but the result of two Canadian statutes of 1921 and 1923 (on similar lines to the English Act of 1911) caused the final closing of the Stationers' Hall Register.

of the copyright being vested in the owner of the manuscript. Apart from this, the proprietor was the express devisee of the copyright, or copyrights in general, of the deceased, or his residuary legatee.

By sect. 2 it was an infringement to produce or reproduce a work, or any substantial part thereof, in any material form, without the consent of the owner of the copyright. But a proviso adds that certain acts should not constitute an infringement, in particular (i) any fair dealing with any work for the purposes of private study, research, criticism, review, or newspaper summary; and (ii) the reading or recitation in public by one person of any reasonable extract from any published work.

Sect. 4 of the Act re-enacted the provision of sect. 5 of the 1842 Act as to the power of the Judicial Committee of the Privy Council to authorize the reprinting of a book unreasonably withheld by the owner of the copyright.[1]

A proviso to sect. 3 of the Act introduced a novelty by enacting that on the expiration of 25 years from the death of the author of a published work anyone might reproduce it if he gave notice of his intention to the owner of the copyright, and paid him royalties at the rate of ten per cent. on the price at which he published the book. Another novelty was contained in a clause in sect. 2. It was not to be an infringement of copyright to publish, in a collection mainly composed of non-copyright matter, bona fide intended for the use of schools and so described on the title-page and in any advertisements of the book . . . short passages from published literary works not themselves published for the use of schools . . . provided that not more than two of such passages from works by the same author were published by the same publisher within five years, and that the source from which such passages are taken was acknowledged.

The next milestone was the Copyright Act (1956, 4 & 5 Eliz. II, cap. 74), passed as the result of the labours of the Copyright Committee, which presented a valuable report in October 1952. It modified the 1911 Act considerably to bring it into line with current conditions, in particular the development of broadcasting, and with the requirements of two new international Conventions, viz., the 1948 Brussels revision of the Berne Convention, and the Universal Copyright Convention of 1952. Some of the changes introduced by the 1911 Act were themselves swept away, and, in particular, sect. 4 (which had never in fact been used) and the proviso to sect. 3 which have already been noted.

The Act also recognized that scope should be given to certain libraries to make research and private study easier by providing students with copies of articles in periodicals, and copies of parts of published works (sect. 7)—the 1911 Act would only have protected the student who made his own copies of the extracts he required. But perhaps the most extensive amendment is contained in sect. 7 (6) which provides that where, at a time more than 50 years from the author's death and more than 100 years from the time it was made, there is a manuscript or copy of an unpublished work which is open to public inspection then the work may be reproduced 'for purposes of research or private study, or with a view to publication'. The words 'or with a view to

---

[1] The equivalent of this power of a public authority to prevent the suppression of books, or the demand of an excessive price for them, has thus been continuous since 1533. I am not aware that the power has ever been invoked.

publication' have to be considered in the light of subsect. (7); and subsect. (6) does not in any way deprive the owner of the copyright in the document of his rights. Under the provisions of sect. 17 (2) of the Copyright Act 1911 (which are substantially re-enacted by sect. 38 of the Act of 1956), for example, the bequest of an unpublished work by Will gave the legatee the copyright in the unpublished work. It follows that there is a mass of historical or literary material, open to inspection by the public, in libraries throughout the country which remains unpublished because it is difficult or impossible to find the owner of the copyright with a view to obtaining permission to publish. Sect. 7 (7) of the 1956 Act, read in conjunction with sect. 7 (6) seeks to remove the difficulty by providing that where an author seeks to publish a new work in which he incorporates the whole or part of such material he may not publish the new work without satisfying two conditions, viz., (1) he must establish that the identity of the owner of the copyright in the old work is not known to the proposed publisher of the new work and (2) that notice of the intended publication is given in such form as may be prescribed by regulations made by the Board of Trade, called 'The Copyright (Notice of Publication) Regulations, 1957' and contained in 'Statutory Instruments 1957. No. 865', obtainable at HMSO. These conditions are, of course, intended to ensure that only if the copyright owner cannot be traced, and fails to materialize as the result of the publication of the prescribed notice will the publication of the new work be regarded as other than an infringement of copyright. If the owner is thus brought to light the new work can only be published with his consent.

During the period since 1956 the Act has become seriously out of date, due in particular to the 1971 Paris revision of the Berne Convention and also to a number of problems created by the rapid advance of technology. These include the increasing use of reprographic machines (such as photocopiers), audio and video recording equipment, and computers. In 1977 the Whitford Report on Copyright and Designs Law (Cmnd. 6732) was presented to Parliament, containing numerous recommendations for revising the law. Although in 1981 the Government published a Green Paper (Cmnd. 8302) dealing with some of these, by the General Election of 1983 no comprehensive new legislation had been introduced.

International Copyright

This is a most complicated topic, which can only be noticed very briefly. Following upon an abortive Act[1] of 1838, the Act[2] of 1844 empowered Her Majesty by Order in Council to direct that foreign authors should have British copyright to the same extent as British subjects. Such Orders were issued as to countries which had given, or were prepared to give, similar protection to British authors. Between 1846 and 1886 sixteen Orders in Council were issued as to various European states, and they resulted in considerable complication.

In 1885 the Berne Convention providing for a uniform international system was arranged, and this was given effect to by the Act[3] of 1886. Most States

---

[1] 1 & 2 Vict. cap. 59.
[2] 7 Vict. cap. 12.
[3] 49 & 50 Vict. cap. 33.

with any pretensions to civilization and culture became parties to the Convention, but the United States (with whom no arrangement under the Act of 1844 had been possible) did not.

The Berne Convention was revised successively in Berlin (1908), Rome (1928), Brussels (1948), Stockholm (1967), and finally in Paris in 1971. It now has over 70 member states including most of the principal countries of the world with the important exceptions of the USA, the USSR, and the People's Republic of China.

Up to 1891 printers and publishers in the United States dealt as they liked with the works of British authors. In that year the Chace Act was passed, partly in the interests of foreign authors, but at least as much for the benefit of American printers. It enabled a foreign author to enjoy copyright in the United States, provided that he delivered two copies of his work on publication to the Librarian of Congress, and provided those two copies were printed from type set within the limits of the United States.

A revised United States law was passed in March 1909. Sect. 15 of this provided that of any printed book, except the original text of a book of foreign origin in a language other than English, the text of all copies accorded protection under this Act . . . shall be printed from type set within the limits of the United States . . . and the printing of the text and binding of the said book shall be performed within the limits of the United States.[1] A noble concession to humanity provided that this requirement should not apply to works in raised characters for the use of the blind.

Many of the restrictions contained in the United States law were progressively released, particularly after 1945, but a very real step forward in the sphere of international relations was taken with the passing of the Universal Copyright Convention, the product of UNESCO, in 1952. It established the principle of mutual protection of copyright throughout the contracting States, upon the same basis as each contracting State protects the works of its own nationals. Further (and most important) it provides in Article 3 that works first published outside a contracting State are to enjoy protection throughout the remaining contracting States without any formality such as registration, if all copies published 'bear the symbol © accompanied by the name of the copyright proprietor and the year of first publication, placed in such manner and location as to give reasonable notice of claim of copyright'. The USA joined in 1955; and the UK in 1957, with the result that for the first time works by British authors were protected in the US without other formalities, or the need to be manufactured there, for a period of 28 years from first publication.

The Universal Copyright Convention did not abrogate the Berne Union, which continues to operate between the contracting parties, but it did bring in, not only the USA, but a large number of States which had hitherto not

---

[1] The law of 1891 required the copies to be printed from type set within the limits of the United States. This made it possible for plates to be made there, and the actual printing from them, and the bookbinding, to be done in this country. The law of 1909 effectively puts an end, so far as books in English are concerned, to so nefarious a practice. By sect. 21, as amended in 1919, the deposit within 60 days of publication of one copy printed abroad will secure an interim copyright for four months. If the American printed copies are not deposited within that time all protection will cease.

entered into copyright relations with the European countries, e.g., most of the South American Republics and, in 1973, the USSR.

A comprehensive new US Copyright Act was passed in 1976 and came into force on 1 January 1978. It extended the period of protection for existing works, although to obtain the renewal period of protection after the initial 28 years, application still had to be made to the Library of Congress. Works created from 1978 onwards, however, are automatically protected for the author's lifetime and for 50 years after the author's death (the period which applies in countries which are members of the Berne Union).

However, the new law still requires the UCS copyright notice (see above) to be printed on all copies of a work and it is obligatory, although not a condition of copyright, to deposit two copies of a work with the Library of Congress when publication takes place in the US.

Delivery of Copies to Libraries

By an Act[1] of 1666 every printer was required to deliver three copies of the best and largest paper of each book printed by him to the Master of the Stationers' Company for the use of the King's Library, and the two Universities, under a penalty for not doing so.

Bentley, in the Preface to his *Dissertation on the Letters of Phalaris* (1699), says that as Keeper of the King's Library he procured nearly a thousand volumes under this. But some booksellers refused to comply; and one named Bennet in particular declared that 'he knew not what right the Parliament had to give away any man's property; that he hoped the Company of Stationers would refuse, and try it out at law; that they were a Body, and had a common Purse, and more to this purpose'.

The Act of 1709 by clause 5 required nine copies to be delivered at Stationers' Hall for the Royal Library, the two English and four Scottish Universities, Sion College, and the Advocates' Library in Edinburgh. According to a Cambridge pamphlet[2] of 1770, under this provision 'very few books of value have been obtained, the booksellers . . . chusing rather to forfeit all the benefit of the Act, and trust one another, by never entering their books in the Register . . .; or when this method is not safe enough, entering only one Volume of each Sett'.

After the Union these nine copies were, by 41 Geo. III, cap. 107, increased to eleven by the addition of Trinity College, Dublin, and the King's Inn, Dublin. Sion College, the four Scottish Universities, and the King's Inn, Dublin, lost this right to copies in 1836, but by other sections of the Act[3] were given an annual payment out of the Consolidated Fund by way of compensation, the money to be spent on books for their libraries. This, I think, they still enjoy.

The Act of 1842 by sects. 6 and 7 required one copy to be delivered at the British Museum, and by sect. 8 four copies at Stationers' Hall, for the Bodleian, the Cambridge University Library, the Advocates' Library, and the Library of Trinity College, Dublin.

[1] 17 Car. II, cap. 4.
[2] 'Observations occasioned by the Contest about Literary Property.'
[3] 6 & 7 Will. IV, cap. 110.

Finally the Act of 1911 by sect. 15 requires the delivery of copies for the same five libraries,[1] and a sixth for the National Library of Wales. Every book must be sent to the British Museum, but to the other libraries only those for which a written demand, by the authorities of any of the libraries, is made within a year of publication. And the books to be delivered to the National Library of Wales shall not include books of such classes as may be specified in regulations to be made by the Board of Trade.

Despite representations made by the publishers to the 1952 Copyright Committee that this compulsory delivery to libraries was unfair the Copyright Act 1956 did not remove the requirement.

---

[1] The 'National Library of Scotland' is substituted for the 'Advocates Library' by 15 & 16 Geo. V, cap. 73.

APPENDIX III

THE CALENDAR

ENGLISH historical documents and literary remains are dated in various ways, and the tables below are designed to make it easier to convert their dates into terms of the modern calendar. While the only era that has been in common use has been the era of the Incarnation, popularized by the writings of the Venerable Bede, from the latter part of the twelfth century legal documents, especially those emanating from the royal government, have often been dated, not by the year of Our Lord, but by the regnal year of the ruling monarch; this practice survives in the dating of acts of parliament. Both in narratives and private and public documents of the Middle Ages it was usual to express a particular date within a year by reference to a saint's day or feast of the Church; while in ecclesiastical records the Roman calendar (see below) was sometimes used to indicate the day of the month.

Most of the errors made in translating dates into modern terms arise from doubt about the starting-point of the year of the Incarnation (also known as the Year of Grace, or Year of Our Lord). For there was wide variation of practice until the reform of the calendar introduced in England in 1751 by the Act 24 Geo. II, cap. 23 ('Lord Chesterfield's Act'). Before this time records of different types are found to have employed simultaneously different methods of reckoning. In classical Rome, according to the calendar established by Julius Caesar and known as the Julian calendar, the year began on 1 January. Although, in the Middle Ages, under Christian influences other dates were chosen for beginning the year, the pagan usage survived, the Church calculated its calendar within the framework of a solar year beginning on 1 January, and 'New Year' gifts were given on that day. Early English chroniclers usually preferred a year beginning on Christmas Day. From the latter part of the twelfth century, according to a mode of reckoning which started on the Continent, the feast of the Annunciation ('Lady Day', 25 March) became the starting-point of the year for most purposes in England, and this remained the legal and official mode of reckoning until the reform of the calendar in 1751. Even so, in the Middle Ages Benedictine chroniclers continued to date their year from Christmas, and both then and later a private person, drawing up a will or writing a letter, might use the same method. After 1582 Englishmen had to reckon with the fact that some continental countries (and Scotland, in 1600) had agreed to begin the year on 1 January; and English writers of the next century and a half sometimes give a double year-date for days from 1 January to 24 March. Eventually, Lord Chesterfield's Act, in 1751, provided that the day after 31 December 1751 should be, throughout the dominions of the British Crown, 1 January 1752.

Lord Chesterfield's Act also made a major reform by substituting the Gregorian calendar ('New Style') for the Julian ('Old Style'), so bringing England into line with most European countries, excepting Greece, the Balkans, and Russia. When Pope Gregory XIII ordered this reform in 1582, it had involved the omission of ten days after 4 October 1582 (see *Calendar*). By 1752 the discrepancy between the Old and New Styles had increased, and the Act provided that the eleven days between 2 September and 14 September 1752 should be omitted.

The Roman Calendar. The Julian calendar, like ours, divided the year into twelve months, each containing the same number of days as the corresponding month in our calendar. In each month there were three special days, known respectively as the Kalends, the Nones, and the Ides. The Kalends were the first day of the month; the Nones and Ides were the 5th and 13th respectively, except in March, May, July, and October, when they were the 7th and 15th. The other days of the month were numbered with reference to the Kalends, Nones, or Ides, as being so many days *before* one or other of them, but in this reckoning the first and last days of the series were both included. Thus A.D. (*ante diem*) V Kal. Jun. (the fifth, or as we should say, the fourth day before 1 June) was the designation of 28 May; A.D. IV Id. Jun. = 10 June; Prid. (*pridie*) Id. June. = 12 June. Every fourth year an additional day was introduced by doubling 24 February (the 24th became *bis VI Kal. Mart.*, the 25th became *VI Kal. Mart.*, so that these years were known as 'bissextile' years).

Indictions. The indiction was a fiscal period of 15 years, at the beginning of which the property tax in the Roman Empire was reassessed. It was instituted by the Emperor Constantine and was reckoned from 1 September 312. At a time when other eras were not in use, it was a useful element in dating: the expression 'indiction 5' signified the fifth year in an unspecified cycle of fifteen years. The Papacy maintained the practice of using the indiction for dating, either by itself or in conjunction with the pontifical year or year of grace; some other chanceries used it in the Middle Ages for the elaborate dating of their most formal documents. Their calculations were not always correct, and the historian is sometimes hampered by not knowing whether 1 September, 24 September, or 25 December was chosen as the opening date.

The **Dominical Letter** (from *dies dominica*, Latin for Sunday) is a convention adopted in chronological tables to indicate the day in January on which the first Sunday falls in any particular year; from which the day of the week for every day in that year can readily be found. The letters A to G, corresponding to the numbers 1 to 7, are taken for this purpose, so that if the first Sunday falls on 1 January, the Dominical Letter of the year is A; if on 2 January, the Dominical Letter is B, and 1 January in that year is a Saturday; if on 7 January, the Dominical Letter is G, and 1 January is a Monday. The first day of successive ordinary years falls on successive days of the week, and their Dominical Letters are consequently in the reverse order of the alphabet. In leap years the interposition of 29 February has the effect of making 1 March and the remaining days of the year fall one day later in the week than if the year had been ordinary. Accordingly a leap year is treated as if composed of January and February of an ordinary year, and of March–December of the succeeding ordinary year, and two Dominical Letters are assigned to it, viz. those appropriate to the two years in question. Thus the year 1216, being a leap year, has the Dominical Letters CB, because the first Sunday in 1216 fell on 3 January, while the days of the months from March to December fall on days of the week corresponding to a first Sunday, in an ordinary year, on 2 January.

In TABLE I below, the years in the first, fifth, and sixth columns are 'historical' years (1 January–31 December). The dates of Easter Day and of the beginning[1] and ending of regnal years, from 1066 to 1752 inclusive, are according to the Julian Calendar or Old Style. From 1583 to 1752 the date of Easter according to the Gregorian Calendar or New Style is added in a separate column. From 1753 all

---

[1] From the time of Edward VI a reign was reckoned as beginning on the day of the predecessor's death. For the reigns from Richard I to Henry VIII the date of commencement given below is that on which, according to public records, the reign was regarded as having begun. The practice for the first century after the Norman Conquest, when the regnal year was seldom employed, is uncertain. Here the coronation date is given.

dates are New Style. The date of Easter connects this table with Table III, and the Dominical Letter connects it with Table V.

TABLE II is an abbreviated calendar for 1752, in which year the change from Old Style to New Style was made.

TABLE III gives the dates of the principal movable Feasts according to the various dates on which Easter Day may fall. The Dominical Letter connects this table with Table V.

TABLE IV gives the dates Feasts and Saints' Days most frequently used in dating documents.

TABLE V, used in conjunction with Table I, makes it easy to find the day of the week on which any day of the month fell in any year from 1066 onwards.

TABLE I

Leap years are shown in heavy type and by double Dominical Letter

Year	Domi-nical Letter	Easter Day	Regnal Years No.	Regnal Years Beginning	Regnal Years Ending
1066	A	16 Apr.	1 Will. I	25 Dec. 1066*	24 Dec. 1067
1067	G	8 Apr.	2 Will. I	25 Dec. 1067	24 Dec. 1068
1068	FE	23 Mar.	3 Will. I	25 Dec. 1068	24 Dec. 1069
1069	D	12 Apr.	4 Will. I	25 Dec. 1069	24 Dec. 1070
1070	C	4 Apr.	5 Will. I	25 Dec. 1070	24 Dec. 1071
1071	B	24 Apr.	6 Will. I	25 Dec. 1071	24 Dec. 1072
1072	AG	8 Apr.	7 Will. I	25 Dec. 1072	24 Dec. 1073
1073	F	31 Mar.	8 Will. I	25 Dec. 1073	24 Dec. 1074
1074	E	20 Apr.	9 Will. I	25 Dec. 1074	24 Dec. 1075
1075	D	5 Apr.	10 Will. I	25 Dec. 1075	24 Dec. 1076
1076	CB	27 Mar.	11 Will. I	25 Dec. 1076	24 Dec. 1077
1077	A	16 Apr.	12 Will. I	25 Dec. 1077	24 Dec. 1078
1078	G	8 Apr.	13 Will. I	25 Dec. 1078	24 Dec. 1079
1079	F	24 Mar.	14 Will. I	25 Dec. 1079	24 Dec. 1080
1080	ED	12 Apr.	15 Will. I	25 Dec. 1080	24 Dec. 1081
1081	C	4 Apr.	16 Will. I	25 Dec. 1081	24 Dec. 1082
1082	B	24 Apr.	17 Will. I	25 Dec. 1082	24 Dec. 1083
1083	A	9 Apr.	18 Will. I	25 Dec. 1083	24 Dec. 1084
1084	GF	31 Mar.	19 Will. I	25 Dec. 1084	24 Dec. 1085
1085	E	20 Apr.	20 Will. I	25 Dec. 1085	24 Dec. 1086
1086	D	5 Apr.	21 Will. I	25 Dec. 1086	9 Sep. 1087
1087	C	28 Mar.	1 Will. II	26 Sep. 1087*	25 Sep. 1088
1088	BA	16 Apr.	2 Will. II	26 Sep. 1088	25 Sep. 1089
1089	G	1 Apr.	3 Will. II	26 Sep. 1089	25 Sep. 1090
1090	F	21 Apr.	4 Will. II	26 Sep. 1090	25 Sep. 1091
1091	E	13 Apr.	5 Will. II	26 Sep. 1091	25 Sep. 1092
1092	DC	28 Mar.	6 Will. II	26 Sep. 1092	25 Sep. 1093
1093	B	17 Apr.	7 Will. II	26 Sep. 1093	25 Sep. 1094
1094	A	9 Apr.	8 Will. II	26 Sep. 1094	25 Sep. 1095
1095	G	25 Mar.	9 Will. II	26 Sep. 1095	25 Sep. 1096
1096	FE	13 Apr.	10 Will. II	26 Sep. 1096	25 Sep. 1097
1097	D	5 Apr.	11 Will. II	26 Sep. 1097	25 Sep. 1098
1098	C	28 Mar.	12 Will. II	26 Sep. 1098	25 Sep. 1099
1099	B	10 Apr.	13 Will. II	26 Sep. 1099	2 Aug. 1100
1100	AG	1 Apr.	1 Hen. I	5 Aug. 1100*	4 Aug. 1101
1101	F	21 Apr.	2 Hen. I	5 Aug. 1101	4 Aug. 1102
1102	E	6 Apr.	3 Hen. I	5 Aug. 1102	4 Aug. 1103
1103	D	29 Mar.	4 Hen. I	5 Aug. 1103	4 Aug. 1104
1104	CB	17 Apr.	5 Hen. I	5 Aug. 1104	4 Aug. 1105
1105	A	9 Apr.	6 Hen. I	5 Aug. 1105	4 Aug. 1106
1106	G	25 Mar.	7 Hen. I	5 Aug. 1106	4 Aug. 1107
1107	F	14 Apr.	8 Hen. I	5 Aug. 1107	4 Aug. 1108
1108	ED	5 Apr.	9 Hen. I	5 Aug. 1108	4 Aug. 1109
1109	C	25 Apr.	10 Hen. I	5 Aug. 1109	4 Aug. 1110
1110	B	10 Apr.	11 Hen. I	5 Aug. 1110	4 Aug. 1111
1111	A	2 Apr.	12 Hen. I	5 Aug. 1111	4 Aug. 1112
1112	GF	21 Apr.	13 Hen. I	5 Aug. 1112	4 Aug. 1113
1113	E	6 Apr.	14 Hen. I	5 Aug. 1113	4 Aug. 1114
1114	D	29 Mar.	15 Hen. I	5 Aug. 1114	4 Aug. 1115
1115	C	18 Apr.			

* Date of coronation.

Year	Dominical Letter	Easter Day	Regnal Years		
			No.	Beginning	Ending
1115	C	18 Apr.	16 Hen. I	5 Aug. 1115	4 Aug. 1116
1116	BA	2 Apr.	17 Hen. I	5 Aug. 1116	4 Aug. 1117
1117	G	25 Mar.	18 Hen. I	5 Aug. 1117	4 Aug. 1118
1118	F	14 Apr.	19 Hen. I	5 Aug. 1118	4 Aug. 1119
1119	E	30 Mar.	20 Hen. I	5 Aug. 1119	4 Aug. 1120
1120	DC	18 Apr.	21 Hen. I	5 Aug. 1120	4 Aug. 1121
1121	B	10 Apr.	22 Hen. I	5 Aug. 1121	4 Aug. 1122
1122	A	26 Mar.	23 Hen. I	5 Aug. 1122	4 Aug. 1123
1123	G	15 Apr.	24 Hen. I	5 Aug. 1123	4 Aug. 1124
1124	FE	6 Apr.	25 Hen. I	5 Aug. 1124	4 Aug. 1125
1125	D	29 Mar.	26 Hen. I	5 Aug. 1125	4 Aug. 1126
1126	C	11 Apr.	27 Hen. I	5 Aug. 1126	4 Aug. 1127
1127	B	3 Apr.	28 Hen. I	5 Aug. 1127	4 Aug. 1128
1128	AG	22 Apr.	29 Hen. I	5 Aug. 1128	4 Aug. 1129
1129	F	14 Apr.	30 Hen. I	5 Aug. 1129	4 Aug. 1130
1130	E	30 Mar.	31 Hen. I	5 Aug. 1130	4 Aug. 1131
1131	D	19 Apr.	32 Hen. I	5 Aug. 1131	4 Aug. 1132
1132	CB	10 Apr.	33 Hen. I	5 Aug. 1132	4 Aug. 1133
1133	A	26 Mar.	34 Hen. I	5 Aug. 1133	4 Aug. 1134
1134	G	15 Apr.	35 Hen. I	5 Aug. 1134	4 Aug. 1135
1135	F	7 Apr.	36 Hen. I	5 Aug. 1135	1 Dec. 1135
			1 Steph.	22 Dec. 1135*	21 Dec. 1136
1136	ED	22 Mar.	2 Steph.	22 Dec. 1136	21 Dec. 1137
1137	C	11 Apr.	3 Steph.	22 Dec. 1137	21 Dec. 1138
1138	B	3 Apr.	4 Steph.	22 Dec. 1138	21 Dec. 1139
1139	A	23 Apr.	5 Steph.	22 Dec. 1139	21 Dec. 1140
1140	GF	7 Apr.	6 Steph.	22 Dec. 1140	21 Dec. 1141
1141	E	30 Mar.	7 Steph.	22 Dec. 1141	21 Dec. 1142
1142	D	19 Apr.	8 Steph.	22 Dec. 1142	21 Dec. 1143
1143	C	4 Apr.	9 Steph.	22 Dec. 1143	21 Dec. 1144
1144	BA	26 Mar.	10 Steph.	22 Dec. 1144	21 Dec. 1145
1145	G	15 Apr.	11 Steph.	22 Dec. 1145	21 Dec. 1146
1146	F	31 Mar.	12 Steph.	22 Dec. 1146	21 Dec. 1147
1147	E	20 Apr.	13 Steph.	22 Dec. 1147	21 Dec. 1148
1148	DC	11 Apr.	14 Steph.	22 Dec. 1148	21 Dec. 1149
1149	B	3 Apr.	15 Steph.	22 Dec. 1149	21 Dec. 1150
1150	A	16 Apr.	16 Steph.	22 Dec. 1150	21 Dec. 1151
1151	G	8 Apr.	17 Steph.	22 Dec. 1151	21 Dec. 1152
1152	FE	30 Mar.	18 Steph.	22 Dec. 1152	21 Dec. 1153
1153	D	19 Apr.	19 Steph.	22 Dec. 1153	25 Oct. 1154
1154	C	5 Apr.	1 Hen. II	19 Dec. 1154†	18 Dec. 1155
1155	B	27 Mar.	2 Hen. II	19 Dec. 1155	18 Dec. 1156
1156	AG	15 Apr.	3 Hen. II	19 Dec. 1156	18 Dec. 1157
1157	F	31 Mar.	4 Hen. II	19 Dec. 1157	18 Dec. 1158
1158	E	20 Apr.	5 Hen. II	19 Dec. 1158	18 Dec. 1159
1159	D	12 Apr.	6 Hen. II	19 Dec. 1159	18 Dec. 1160
1160	CB	27 Mar.	7 Hen. II	19 Dec. 1160	18 Dec. 1161
1161	A	16 Apr.	8 Hen. II	19 Dec. 1161	18 Dec. 1162
1162	G	8 Apr.	9 Hen. II	19 Dec. 1162	18 Dec. 1163
1163	F	24 Mar.	10 Hen. II	19 Dec. 1163	18 Dec. 1164
1164	ED	12 Apr.	11 Hen. II	19 Dec. 1164	18 Dec. 1165
1165	C	4 Apr.	12 Hen. II	19 Dec. 1165	18 Dec. 1166
1166	B	24 Apr.			

* The date of Stephen's coronation according to William of Malmesbury.
† Date of coronation.

Year	Domi-nical Letter	Easter Day	Regnal Years		
			No.	Beginning	Ending
1166	B	24 Apr.	13 Hen. II	19 Dec. 1166	18 Dec. 1167
1167	A	9 Apr.	14 Hen. II	19 Dec. 1167	18 Dec. 1168
1168	GF	31 Mar.	15 Hen. II	19 Dec. 1168	18 Dec. 1169
1169	E	20 Apr.	16 Hen. II	19 Dec. 1169	18 Dec. 1170
1170	D	5 Apr.	17 Hen. II	19 Dec. 1170	18 Dec. 1171
1171	C	28 Mar.	18 Hen. II	19 Dec. 1171	18 Dec. 1172
1172	BA	16 Apr.	19 Hen. II	19 Dec. 1172	18 Dec. 1173
1173	G	8 Apr.	20 Hen. II	19 Dec. 1173	18 Dec. 1174
1174	F	24 Mar.	21 Hen. II	19 Dec. 1174	18 Dec. 1175
1175	E	13 Apr.	22 Hen. II	19 Dec. 1175	18 Dec. 1176
1176	DC	4 Apr.	23 Hen. II	19 Dec. 1176	18 Dec. 1177
1177	B	24 Apr.	24 Hen. II	19 Dec. 1177	18 Dec. 1178
1178	A	9 Apr.	25 Hen. II	19 Dec. 1178	18 Dec. 1179
1179	G	1 Apr.	26 Hen. II	19 Dec. 1179	18 Dec. 1180
1180	FE	20 Apr.	27 Hen. II	19 Dec. 1180	18 Dec. 1181
1181	D	5 Apr.	28 Hen. II	19 Dec. 1181	18 Dec. 1182
1182	C	28 Mar.	29 Hen. II	19 Dec. 1182	18 Dec. 1183
1183	B	17 Apr.	30 Hen. II	19 Dec. 1183	18 Dec. 1184
1184	AG	1 Apr.	31 Hen. II	18 Dec. 1184	18 Dec. 1185
1185	F	21 Apr.	32 Hen. II	19 Dec. 1185	18 Dec. 1186
1186	E	13 Apr.	33 Hen. II	19 Dec. 1186	18 Dec. 1187
1187	D	29 Mar.	34 Hen. II	19 Dec. 1187	18 Dec. 1188
1188	CB	17 Apr.	35 Hen. II	19 Dec. 1188	6 Jul. 1189
1189	A	9 Apr.	1 Ric. I	3 Sep. 1189*	2 Sep. 1190
1190	G	25 Mar.	2 Ric. I	3 Sep. 1190	2 Sep. 1191
1191	F	14 Apr.	3 Ric. I	3 Sep. 1191	2 Sep. 1192
1192	ED	5 Apr.	4 Ric. I	3 Sep. 1192	2 Sep. 1193
1193	C	28 Mar.	5 Ric. I	3 Sep. 1193	2 Sep. 1194
1194	B	10 Apr.	6 Ric. I	3 Sep. 1194	2 Sep. 1195
1195	A	2 Apr.	7 Ric. I	3 Sep. 1195	2 Sep. 1196
1196	GF	21 Apr.	8 Ric. I	3 Sep. 1196	2 Sep. 1197
1197	E	6 Apr.	9 Ric. I	3 Sep. 1197	2 Sep. 1198
1198	D	29 Mar.	10 Ric. I	3 Sep. 1198	6 Apr. 1199
1199	C	18 Apr.	1 John	27 May 1199†	17 May 1200
1200	BA	9 Apr.	2 John	18 May 1200	2 May 1201
1201	G	25 Mar.	3 John	3 May 1201	22 May 1202
1202	F	14 Apr.	4 John	23 May 1202	14 May 1203
1203	E	6 Apr.	5 John	15 May 1203	2 Jun. 1204
1204	DC	25 Apr.	6 John	3 Jun. 1204	18 May 1205
1205	B	10 Apr.	7 John	19 May 1205	10 May 1206
1206	A	2 Apr.	8 John	11 May 1206	30 May 1207
1207	G	22 Apr.	9 John	31 May 1207	14 May 1208
1208	FE	6 Apr.	10 John	15 May 1208	6 May 1209
1209	D	29 Mar.	11 John	7 May 1209	26 May 1210
1210	C	18 Apr.	12 John	27 May 1210	11 May 1211
1211	B	3 Apr.	13 John	12 May 1211	2 May 1212
1212	AG	25 Mar.	14 John	3 May 1212	22 May 1213
1213	F	14 Apr.	15 John	23 May 1213	7 May 1214
1214	E	30 Mar.	16 John	8 May 1214	27 May 1215
1215	D	19 Apr.	17 John	28 May 1215	18 May 1216
1216	CB	10 Apr.	18 John	19 May 1216	19 Oct. 1216
			1 Hen. III	28 Oct. 1216*	27 Oct. 1217
1217	A	26 Mar.	2 Hen. III	28 Oct. 1217	27 Oct. 1218
1218	G	15 Apr.			

* Date of coronation.

† John was crowned on Ascension Day 1199; his regnal years run from one Ascension Day to the eve of the next and are therefore irregular.

Year	Dominical Letter	Easter Day	Regnal Years		
			No.	Beginning	Ending
1218	G	15 Apr.	3 Hen. III	28 Oct. 1218	27 Oct. 1219
1219	F	7 Apr.	4 Hen. III	28 Oct. 1219	27 Oct. 1220
1220	ED	29 Mar.	5 Hen. III	28 Oct. 1220	27 Oct. 1221
1221	C	11 Apr.	6 Hen. III	28 Oct. 1221	27 Oct. 1222
1222	B	3 Apr.	7 Hen. III	28 Oct. 1222	27 Oct. 1223
1223	A	23 Apr.	8 Hen. III	28 Oct. 1223	27 Oct. 1224
1224	GF	14 Apr.	9 Hen. III	28 Oct. 1224	27 Oct. 1225
1225	E	30 Mar.	10 Hen. III	28 Oct. 1225	27 Oct. 1226
1226	D	19 Apr.	11 Hen. III	28 Oct. 1226	27 Oct. 1227
1227	C	11 Apr.	12 Hen. III	28 Oct. 1227	27 Oct. 1228
1228	BA	26 Mar.	13 Hen. III	28 Oct. 1228	27 Oct. 1229
1229	G	15 Apr.	14 Hen. III	28 Oct. 1229	27 Oct. 1230
1230	F	7 Apr.	15 Hen. III	28 Oct. 1230	27 Oct. 1231
1231	E	23 Mar.	16 Hen. III	28 Oct. 1231	27 Oct. 1232
1232	DC	11 Apr.	17 Hen. III	28 Oct. 1232	27 Oct. 1233
1233	B	3 Apr.	18 Hen. III	28 Oct. 1233	27 Oct. 1234
1234	A	23 Apr.	19 Hen. III	28 Oct. 1234	27 Oct. 1235
1235	G	8 Apr.	20 Hen. III	28 Oct. 1235	27 Oct. 1236
1236	FE	30 Mar.	21 Hen. III	28 Oct. 1236	27 Oct. 1237
1237	D	19 Apr.	22 Hen. III	28 Oct. 1237	27 Oct. 1238
1238	C	4 Apr.	23 Hen. III	28 Oct. 1238	27 Oct. 1239
1239	B	27 Mar.	24 Hen. III	28 Oct. 1239	27 Oct. 1240
1240	AG	15 Apr.	25 Hen. III	28 Oct. 1240	27 Oct. 1241
1241	F	31 Mar.	26 Hen. III	28 Oct. 1241	27 Oct. 1242
1242	E	20 Apr.	27 Hen. III	28 Oct. 1242	27 Oct. 1243
1243	D	12 Apr.	28 Hen. III	28 Oct. 1243	27 Oct. 1244
1244	CB	3 Apr.	29 Hen. III	28 Oct. 1244	27 Oct. 1245
1245	A	16 Apr.	30 Hen. III	28 Oct. 1245	27 Oct. 1246
1246	G	8 Apr.	31 Hen. III	28 Oct. 1246	27 Oct. 1247
1247	F	31 Mar.	32 Hen. III	28 Oct. 1247	27 Oct. 1248
1248	ED	19 Apr.	33 Hen. III	28 Oct. 1248	27 Oct. 1249
1249	C	4 Apr.	34 Hen. III	28 Oct. 1249	27 Oct. 1250
1250	B	27 Mar.	35 Hen. III	28 Oct. 1250	27 Oct. 1251
1251	A	15 Apr.	36 Hen. III	28 Oct. 1251	27 Oct. 1252
1252	GF	31 Mar.	37 Hen. III	28 Oct. 1252	27 Oct. 1253
1253	E	20 Apr.	38 Hen. III	28 Oct. 1253	27 Oct. 1254
1254	D	12 Apr.	39 Hen. III	28 Oct. 1254	27 Oct. 1255
1255	C	28 Mar.	40 Hen. III	28 Oct. 1255	27 Oct. 1256
1256	BA	16 Apr.	41 Hen. III	28 Oct. 1256	27 Oct. 1257
1257	G	8 Apr.	42 Hen. III	28 Oct. 1257	27 Oct. 1258
1258	F	24 Mar.	43 Hen. III	28 Oct. 1258	27 Oct. 1259
1259	E	13 Apr.	44 Hen. III	28 Oct. 1259	27 Oct. 1260
1260	DC	4 Apr.	45 Hen. III	28 Oct. 1260	27 Oct. 1261
1261	B	24 Apr.	46 Hen. III	28 Oct. 1261	27 Oct. 1262
1262	A	9 Apr.	47 Hen. III	28 Oct. 1262	27 Oct. 1263
1263	G	1 Apr.	48 Hen. III	28 Oct. 1263	27 Oct. 1264
1264	FE	20 Apr.	49 Hen. III	28 Oct. 1264	27 Oct. 1265
1265	D	5 Apr.	50 Hen. III	28 Oct. 1265	27 Oct. 1266
1266	C	28 Mar.	51 Hen. III	28 Oct. 1266	27 Oct. 1267
1267	B	17 Apr.	52 Hen. III	28 Oct. 1267	27 Oct. 1268
1268	AG	8 Apr.	53 Hen. III	28 Oct. 1268	27 Oct. 1269
1269	F	24 Mar.	54 Hen. III	28 Oct. 1269	27 Oct. 1270
1270	E	13 Apr.	55 Hen. III	28 Oct. 1270	27 Oct. 1271
1271	D	5 Apr.	56 Hen. III	28 Oct. 1271	27 Oct. 1272
1272	CB	24 Apr.	57 Hen. III	28 Oct. 1272	16 Nov. 1272

Year	Domi-nical Letter	Easter Day	Regnal Years No.	Beginning	Ending
1272	CB	24 Apr.	**1 Edw. I***	20 Nov. 1272†	19 Nov. 1273
1273	A	9 Apr.	2 Edw. I	20 Nov. 1273	19 Nov. 1274
1274	G	1 Apr.	3 Edw. I	20 Nov. 1274	19 Nov. 1275
1275	F	14 Apr.	4 Edw. I	20 Nov. 1275	19 Nov. 1276
1276	ED	5 Apr.	5 Edw. I	20 Nov. 1276	19 Nov. 1277
1277	C	28 Mar.	6 Edw. I	20 Nov. 1277	19 Nov. 1278
1278	B	17 Apr.	7 Edw. I	20 Nov. 1278	19 Nov. 1279
1279	A	2 Apr.	8 Edw. I	20 Nov. 1279	19 Nov. 1280
1280	GF	21 Apr.	9 Edw. I	20 Nov. 1280	19 Nov. 1281
1281	E	13 Apr.	10 Edw. I	20 Nov. 1281	19 Nov. 1282
1282	D	29 Mar.	11 Edw. I	20 Nov. 1282	19 Nov. 1283
1283	C	18 Apr.	12 Edw. I	20 Nov. 1283	19 Nov. 1284
1284	BA	9 Apr.	13 Edw. I	20 Nov. 1284	19 Nov. 1285
1285	G	25 Mar.	14 Edw. I	20 Nov. 1285	19 Nov. 1286
1286	F	14 Apr.	15 Edw. I	20 Nov. 1286	19 Nov. 1287
1287	E	6 Apr.	16 Edw. I	20 Nov. 1287	19 Nov. 1288
1288	DC	28 Mar.	17 Edw. I	20 Nov. 1288	19 Nov. 1289
1289	B	10 Apr.	18 Edw. I	20 Nov. 1289	19 Nov. 1290
1290	A	2 Apr.	19 Edw. I	20 Nov. 1290	19 Nov. 1291
1291	G	22 Apr.	20 Edw. I	20 Nov. 1291	19 Nov. 1292
1292	FE	6 Apr.	21 Edw. I	20 Nov. 1292	19 Nov. 1293
1293	D	29 Mar.	22 Edw. I	20 Nov. 1293	19 Nov. 1294
1294	C	18 Apr.	23 Edw. I	20 Nov. 1294	19 Nov. 1295
1295	B	3 Apr.	24 Edw. I	20 Nov. 1295	19 Nov. 1296
1296	AG	25 Mar.	25 Edw. I	20 Nov. 1296	19 Nov. 1297
1297	F	14 Apr.	26 Edw. I	20 Nov. 1297	19 Nov. 1298
1298	E	6 Apr.	27 Edw. I	20 Nov. 1298	19 Nov. 1299
1299	D	19 Apr.	28 Edw. I	20 Nov. 1299	19 Nov. 1300
1300	CB	10 Apr.	29 Edw. I	20 Nov. 1300	19 Nov. 1301
1301	A	2 Apr.	30 Edw. I	20 Nov. 1301	19 Nov. 1302
1302	G	22 Apr.	31 Edw. I	20 Nov. 1302	19 Nov. 1303
1303	F	7 Apr.	32 Edw. I	20 Nov. 1303	19 Nov. 1304
1304	ED	29 Mar.	33 Edw. I	20 Nov. 1304	19 Nov. 1305
1305	C	18 Apr.	34 Edw. I	20 Nov. 1305	19 Nov. 1306
1306	B	3 Apr.	35 Edw. I	20 Nov. 1306	7 Jul. 1307
1307	A	26 Mar.	1 Edw. II	8 Jul. 1307	7 Jul. 1308
1308	GF	14 Apr.	2 Edw. II	8 Jul. 1308	7 Jul. 1309
1309	E	30 Mar.	3 Edw. II	8 Jul. 1309	7 Jul. 1310
1310	D	19 Apr.	4 Edw. II	8 Jul. 1310	7 Jul. 1311
1311	C	11 Apr.	5 Edw. II	8 Jul. 1311	7 Jul. 1312
1312	BA	26 Mar.	6 Edw. II	8 Jul. 1312	7 Jul. 1313
1313	G	15 Apr.	7 Edw. II	8 Jul. 1313	7 Jul. 1314
1314	F	7 Apr.	8 Edw. II	8 Jul. 1314	7 Jul. 1315
1315	E	23 Mar.	9 Edw. II	8 Jul. 1315	7 Jul. 1316
1316	DC	11 Apr.	10 Edw. II	8 Jul. 1316	7 Jul. 1317
1317	B	3 Apr.	11 Edw. II	8 Jul. 1317	7 Jul. 1318
1318	A	23 Apr.	12 Edw. II	8 Jul. 1318	7 Jul. 1319
1319	G	8 Apr.	13 Edw. II	8 Jul. 1319	7 Jul. 1320
1320	FE	30 Mar.	14 Edw. II	8 Jul. 1320	7 Jul. 1321
1321	D	19 Apr.	15 Edw. II	8 Jul. 1321	7 Jul. 1322
1322	C	11 Apr.	16 Edw. II	8 Jul. 1322	7 Jul. 1323
1323	B	27 Mar.	17 Edw. II	8 Jul. 1323	7 Jul. 1324
1324	AG	15 Apr.			

* The distinguishing numbers of Edward I, Edward II, and Edward III are often omitted. A king described in a document as 'Edward' is not necessarily Edward I.
† Date of proclamation.

Year	Dominical Letter	Easter Day	Regnal Years No.	Beginning	Ending
1324	AG	15 Apr.	} 18 Edw. II	8 Jul. 1324	7 Jul. 1325
1325	F	7 Apr.	} 19 Edw. II	8 Jul. 1325	7 Jul. 1326
1326	E	23 Mar.	} 20 Edw. II	8 Jul. 1326	20 Jan. 1327*
1327	D	12 Apr.	} **1 Edw. III**	25 Jan. 1327	24 Jan. 1328
1328	CB	3 Apr.	} 2 Edw. III	25 Jan. 1328	24 Jan. 1329
1329	A	23 Apr.	} 3 Edw. III	25 Jan. 1329	24 Jan. 1330
1330	G	8 Apr.	} 4 Edw. III	25 Jan. 1330	24 Jan. 1331
1331	F	31 Mar.	} 5 Edw. III	25 Jan. 1331	24 Jan. 1332
1332	ED	19 Apr.	} 6 Edw. III	25 Jan. 1332	24 Jan. 1333
1333	C	4 Apr.	} 7 Edw. III	25 Jan. 1333	24 Jan. 1334
1334	B	27 Mar.	} 8 Edw. III	25 Jan. 1334	24 Jan. 1335
1335	A	16 Apr.	} 9 Edw. III	25 Jan. 1335	24 Jan. 1336
1336	GF	31 Mar.	} 10 Edw. III	25 Jan. 1336	24 Jan. 1337
1337	E	20 Apr.	} 11 Edw. III	25 Jan. 1337	24 Jan. 1338
1338	D	12 Apr.	} 12 Edw. III	25 Jan. 1338	24 Jan. 1339
1339	C	28 Mar.	} 13 Edw. III	25 Jan. 1339	24 Jan. 1340
1340	BA	16 Apr.	} 14 & 1 Edw. III†	25 Jan. 1340	24 Jan. 1341
1341	G	8 Apr.	} 15 & 2 Edw. III	25 Jan. 1341	24 Jan. 1342
1342	F	31 Mar.	} 16 & 3 Edw. III	25 Jan. 1342	24 Jan. 1343
1343	E	13 Apr.	} 17 & 4 Edw. III	25 Jan. 1343	24 Jan. 1344
1344	DC	4 Apr.	} 18 & 5 Edw. III	25 Jan. 1344	24 Jan. 1345
1345	B	27 Mar.	} 19 & 6 Edw. III	25 Jan. 1345	24 Jan. 1346
1346	A	16 Apr.	} 20 & 7 Edw. III	25 Jan. 1346	24 Jan. 1347
1347	G	1 Apr.	} 21 & 8 Edw. III	25 Jan. 1347	24 Jan. 1348
1348	FE	20 Apr.	} 22 & 9 Edw. III	25 Jan. 1348	24 Jan. 1349
1349	D	12 Apr.	} 23 & 10 Edw. III	25 Jan. 1349	24 Jan. 1350
1350	C	28 Mar.	} 24 & 11 Edw. III	25 Jan. 1350	24 Jan. 1351
1351	B	17 Apr.	} 25 & 12 Edw. III	25 Jan. 1351	24 Jan. 1352
1352	AG	8 Apr.	} 26 & 13 Edw. III	25 Jan. 1352	24 Jan. 1353
1353	F	24 Mar.	} 27 & 14 Edw. III	25 Jan. 1353	24 Jan. 1354
1354	E	13 Apr.	} 28 & 15 Edw. III	25 Jan. 1354	24 Jan. 1355
1355	D	5 Apr.	} 29 & 16 Edw. III	25 Jan. 1355	24 Jan. 1356
1356	CB	24 Apr.	} 30 & 17 Edw. III	25 Jan. 1356	24 Jan. 1357
1357	A	9 Apr.	} 31 & 18 Edw. III	25 Jan. 1357	24 Jan. 1358
1358	G	1 Apr.	} 32 & 19 Edw. III	25 Jan. 1358	24 Jan. 1359
1359	F	21 Apr.	}33 & 20 Edw. III	25 Jan. 1359	24 Jan. 1360
1360	ED	5 Apr.	{34 & 21 Edw. III	25 Jan. 1360	8 May 1360†
			} 34 Edw. III	9 May 1360	24 Jan. 1361
1361	C	28 Mar.	} 35 Edw. III	25 Jan. 1361	24 Jan. 1362
1362	B	17 Apr.	} 36 Edw. III	25 Jan. 1362	24 Jan. 1363
1363	A	2 Apr.	} 37 Edw. III	25 Jan. 1363	24 Jan. 1364
1364	GF	24 Mar.	} 38 Edw. III	25 Jan. 1364	24 Jan. 1365
1365	E	13 Apr.	} 39 Edw. III	25 Jan. 1365	24 Jan. 1366
1366	D	5 Apr.	} 40 Edw. III	25 Jan. 1366	24 Jan. 1367
1367	C	18 Apr.	} 41 Edw. III	25 Jan. 1367	24 Jan. 1368
1368	BA	9 Apr.	} 42 Edw. III	25 Jan. 1368	24 Jan. 1369
1369	G	1 Apr.	} 43 Edw. III	25 Jan. 1369	10 Jun. 1369
			}43 & 30 Edw. III§	11 Jun. 1369	24 Jan. 1370
1370	F	14 Apr.	} 44 & 31 Edw. III	25 Jan. 1370	24 Jan. 1371
1371	E	6 Apr.	} 45 & 32 Edw. III	25 Jan. 1371	24 Jan. 1372
1372	DC	28 Mar.			

* Date of deposition.
† In 1340 Edward III asserted his claim to the French crown and added his French regnal years to his English regnal years. In 1360 he undertook to renounce his claim to the throne of France and dropped the French regnal years in dating.
§ In 1369 Edward III resumed his claim to the French crown, counting in the years 1360–9 during which his claim had been in abeyance.

Year	Dominical Letter	Easter Day	Regnal Years		
			No.	Beginning	Ending
1372	DC	28 Mar.	} 46 & 33 Edw. III	25 Jan. 1372	24 Jan. 1373
1373	B	17 Apr.	} 47 & 34 Edw. III	25 Jan. 1373	24 Jan. 1374
1374	A	2 Apr.	} 48 & 35 Edw. III	25 Jan. 1374	24 Jan. 1375
1375	G	22 Apr.	} 49 & 36 Edw. III	25 Jan. 1375	24 Jan. 1376
1376	FE	13 Apr.	} 50 & 37 Edw. III	25 Jan. 1376	24 Jan. 1377
1377	D	29 Mar.	} 51 & 38 Edw. III	25 Jan. 1377	21 Jun. 1377
1378	C	18 Apr.	} **1 Ric. II**	22 Jun. 1377	21 Jun. 1378
1379	B	10 Apr.	} 2 Ric. II	22 Jun. 1378	21 Jun. 1379
1380	AG	25 Mar.	} 3 Ric. II	22 Jun. 1379	21 Jun. 1380
1381	F	14 Apr.	} 4 Ric. II	22 Jun. 1380	21 Jun. 1381
1382	E	6 Apr.	} 5 Ric. II	22 Jun. 1381	21 Jun. 1382
1383	D	22 Mar.	} 6 Ric. II	22 Jun. 1382	21 Jun. 1383
1384	CB	10 Apr.	} 7 Ric. II	22 Jun. 1383	21 Jun. 1384
1385	A	2 Apr.	} 8 Ric. II	22 Jun. 1384	21 Jun. 1385
1386	G	22 Apr.	} 9 Ric. II	22 Jun. 1385	21 Jun. 1386
1387	F	7 Apr.	} 10 Ric. II	22 Jun. 1386	21 Jun. 1387
1388	ED	29 Mar.	} 11 Ric. II	22 Jun. 1387	21 Jun. 1388
1389	C	18 Apr.	} 12 Ric. II	22 Jun. 1388	21 Jun. 1389
1390	B	3 Apr.	} 13 Ric. II	22 Jun. 1389	21 Jun. 1390
1391	A	26 Mar.	} 14 Ric. II	22 Jun. 1390	21 Jun. 1391
1392	GF	14 Apr.	} 15 Ric. II	22 Jun. 1391	21 Jun. 1392
1393	E	6 Apr.	} 16 Ric. II	22 Jun. 1392	21 Jun. 1393
1394	D	19 Apr.	} 17 Ric. II	22 Jun. 1393	21 Jun. 1394
1395	C	11 Apr.	} 18 Ric. II	22 Jun. 1394	21 Jun. 1395
1396	BA	2 Apr.	} 19 Ric. II	22 Jun. 1395	21 Jun. 1396
1397	G	22 Apr.	} 20 Ric. II	22 Jun. 1396	21 Jun. 1397
1398	F	7 Apr.	} 21 Ric. II	22 Jun. 1397	21 Jun. 1398
1399	E	30 Mar.	} 22 Ric. II	22 Jun. 1398	21 Jun. 1399
			} 23 Ric. II	22 Jun. 1399	29 Sep. 1399
1400	DC	18 Apr.	} **1 Hen. IV**	30 Sep. 1399	29 Sep. 1400
1401	B	3 Apr.	} 2 Hen. IV	30 Sep. 1400	29 Sep. 1401
1402	A	26 Mar.	} 3 Hen. IV	30 Sep. 1401	29 Sep. 1402
1403	G	15 Apr.	} 4 Hen. IV	30 Sep. 1402	29 Sep. 1403
1404	FE	30 Mar.	} 5 Hen. IV	30 Sep. 1403	29 Sep. 1404
1405	D	19 Apr.	} 6 Hen. IV	30 Sep. 1404	29 Sep. 1405
1406	C	11 Apr.	} 7 Hen. IV	30 Sep. 1405	29 Sep. 1406
1407	B	27 Mar.	} 8 Hen. IV	30 Sep. 1406	29 Sep. 1407
1408	AG	15 Apr.	} 9 Hen. IV	30 Sep. 1407	29 Sep. 1408
1409	F	7 Apr.	} 10 Hen. IV	30 Sep. 1408	29 Sep. 1409
1410	E	23 Mar.	} 11 Hen. IV	30 Sep. 1409	29 Sep. 1410
1411	D	12 Apr.	} 12 Hen. IV	30 Sep. 1410	29 Sep. 1411
1412	CB	3 Apr.	} 13 Hen. IV	30 Sep. 1411	29 Sep. 1412
1413	A	23 Apr.	} 14 Hen. IV	30 Sep. 1412	20 Mar. 1413
1414	G	8 Apr.	} **1 Hen. V**	21 Mar. 1413	20 Mar. 1414
1415	F	31 Mar.	} 2 Hen. V	21 Mar. 1414	20 Mar. 1415
1416	ED	19 Apr.	} 3 Hen. V	21 Mar. 1415	20 Mar. 1416
1417	C	1 Apr.	} 4 Hen. V	21 Mar. 1416	20 Mar. 1417
1418	B	27 Mar.	} 5 Hen. V	21 Mar. 1417	20 Mar. 1418
1419	A	16 Apr.	} 6 Hen. V	21 Mar. 1418	20 Mar. 1419
1420	GF	7 Apr.	} 7 Hen. V	21 Mar. 1419	20 Mar. 1420
1421	E	23 Mar.	} 8 Hen. V	21 Mar. 1420	20 Mar. 1421
			} 9 Hen. V	21 Mar. 1421	20 Mar. 1422
1422	D	12 Apr.	} 10 Hen. V	21 Mar. 1422	31 Aug. 1422
			} **1 Hen. VI**	1 Sep. 1422	31 Aug. 1423
1423	C	4 Apr.	} 2 Hen. VI	1 Sep. 1423	31 Aug. 1424
1424	BA	23 Apr.			

Year	Domi-nical Letter	Easter Day	Regnal Years		
			No.	Beginning	Ending
1424	BA	23 Apr.	} 3 Hen. VI	1 Sep. 1424	31 Aug. 1425
1425	G	8 Apr.	} 4 Hen. VI	1 Sep. 1425	31 Aug. 1426
1426	F	31 Mar.	} 5 Hen. VI	1 Sep. 1426	31 Aug. 1427
1427	E	20 Apr.	} 6 Hen. VI	1 Sep. 1427	31 Aug. 1428
1428	DC	4 Apr.	} 7 Hen. VI	1 Sep. 1428	31 Aug. 1429
1429	B	27 Mar.	} 8 Hen. VI	1 Sep. 1429	31 Aug. 1430
1430	A	16 Apr.	} 9 Hen. VI	1 Sep. 1430	31 Aug. 1431
1431	G	1 Apr.	} 10 Hen. VI	1 Sep. 1431	31 Aug. 1432
1432	FE	20 Apr.	} 11 Hen. VI	1 Sep. 1432	31 Aug. 1433
1433	D	12 Apr.	} 12 Hen. VI	1 Sep. 1433	31 Aug. 1434
1434	C	28 Mar.	} 13 Hen. VI	1 Sep. 1434	31 Aug. 1435
1435	B	17 Apr.	} 14 Hen. VI	1 Sep. 1435	31 Aug. 1436
1436	AG	8 Apr.	} 15 Hen. VI	1 Sep. 1436	31 Aug. 1437
1437	F	31 Mar.	} 16 Hen. VI	1 Sep. 1437	31 Aug. 1438
1438	E	13 Apr.	} 17 Hen. VI	1 Sep. 1438	31 Aug. 1439
1439	D	5 Apr.	} 18 Hen. VI	1 Sep. 1439	31 Aug. 1440
1440	CB	27 Mar.	} 19 Hen. VI	1 Sep. 1440	31 Aug. 1441
1441	A	16 Apr.	} 20 Hen. VI	1 Sep. 1441	31 Aug. 1442
1442	G	1 Apr.	} 21 Hen. VI	1 Sep. 1442	31 Aug. 1443
1443	F	21 Apr.	} 22 Hen. VI	1 Sep. 1443	31 Aug. 1444
1444	ED	12 Apr.	} 23 Hen. VI	1 Sep. 1444	31 Aug. 1445
1445	C	28 Mar.	} 24 Hen. VI	1 Sep. 1445	31 Aug. 1446
1446	B	17 Apr.	} 25 Hen. VI	1 Sep. 1446	31 Aug. 1447
1447	A	9 Apr.	} 26 Hen. VI	1 Sep. 1447	31 Aug. 1448
1448	GF	24 Mar.	} 27 Hen. VI	1 Sep. 1448	31 Aug. 1449
1449	E	13 Apr.	} 28 Hen. VI	1 Sep. 1449	31 Aug. 1450
1450	D	5 Apr.	} 29 Hen. VI	1 Sep. 1450	31 Aug. 1451
1451	C	25 Apr.	} 30 Hen. VI	1 Sep. 1451	31 Aug. 1452
1452	BA	9 Apr.	} 31 Hen. VI	1 Sep. 1452	31 Aug. 1453
1453	G	1 Apr.	} 32 Hen. VI	1 Sep. 1453	31 Aug. 1454
1454	F	21 Apr.	} 33 Hen. VI	1 Sep. 1454	31 Aug. 1455
1455	E	6 Apr.	} 34 Hen. VI	1 Sep. 1455	31 Aug. 1456
1456	DC	28 Mar.	} 35 Hen. VI	1 Sep. 1456	31 Aug. 1457
1457	B	17 Apr.	} 36 Hen. VI	1 Sep. 1457	31 Aug. 1458
1458	A	2 Apr.	} 37 Hen. VI	1 Sep. 1458	31 Aug. 1459
1459	G	25 Mar.	} 38 Hen. VI	1 Sep. 1459	31 Aug. 1460
1460	FE	13 Apr.	} 39 Hen. VI	1 Sep. 1460	4 Mar. 1461*
1461	D	5 Apr.	} 1 **Edw. IV**	4 Mar. 1461*	3 Mar. 1462
1462	C	18 Apr.	} 2 Edw. IV	4 Mar. 1462	3 Mar. 1463
1463	B	10 Apr.	} 3 Edw. IV	4 Mar. 1463	3 Mar. 1464
1464	AG	1 Apr.	} 4 Edw. IV	4 Mar. 1464	3 Mar. 1465
1465	F	14 Apr.	} 5 Edw. IV	4 Mar. 1465	3 Mar. 1466
1466	E	6 Apr.	} 6 Edw. IV	4 Mar. 1466	3 Mar. 1467
1467	D	29 Mar.	} 7 Edw. IV	4 Mar. 1467	3 Mar. 1468
1468	CB	17 Apr.	} 8 Edw. IV	4 Mar. 1468	3 Mar. 1469
1469	A	2 Apr.	} 9 Edw. IV	4 Mar. 1469	3 Mar. 1470
1470	G	22 Apr.	} { 10 Edw. IV	4 Mar. 1470	3 Mar. 1471
			} { 49 & 1 Hen. VI†	9 Oct. 1470	14 Apr. 1471
1471	F	14 Apr.	} 11 Edw. IV	4 Mar. 1471	3 Mar. 1472
1472	ED	29 Mar.	} 12 Edw. IV	4 Mar. 1472	3 Mar. 1473
1473	C	18 Apr.	} 13 Edw. IV	4 Mar. 1473	3 Mar. 1474
1474	B	10 Apr.			

* Date of deposition of Henry VI and recognition of Edward IV.
† The period of the restoration of Henry VI (1 Oct. 1470–11 Apr. 1471) was described as follows: 'Anno ab inchoatione regni nostri quadragesimo nono et readeptionis nostrae regiae potestatis anno primo.' The reckoning of the regnal years of Edward IV was not altered on account of this restoration.

Year	Dominical Letter	Easter Day	Regnal Years		
			No.	*Beginning*	*Ending*
1474	B	10 Apr.	14 Edw. IV	4 Mar. 1474	3 Mar. 1475
1475	A	26 Mar.	15 Edw. IV	4 Mar. 1475	3 Mar. 1476
1476	GF	14 Apr.	16 Edw. IV	4 Mar. 1476	3 Mar. 1477
1477	E	6 Apr.	17 Edw. IV	4 Mar. 1477	3 Mar. 1478
1478	D	22 Mar.	18 Edw. IV	4 Mar. 1478	3 Mar. 1479
1479	C	11 Apr.	19 Edw. IV	4 Mar. 1479	3 Mar. 1480
1480	BA	2 Apr.	20 Edw. IV	4 Mar. 1480	3 Mar. 1481
1481	G	22 Apr.	21 Edw. IV	4 Mar. 1481	3 Mar. 1482
1482	F	7 Apr.	22 Edw. IV	4 Mar. 1482	3 Mar. 1483
1483	E	30 Mar.	23 Edw. IV	4 Mar. 1483	9 Apr. 1483
			1 **Edw. V**	9 Apr. 1483	25 Jun. 1483
			1 Ric. III	26 Jun. 1483	25 Jun. 1484
1484	DC	18 Apr.	2 Ric. III	26 Jun. 1484	25 Jun. 1485
1485	B	3 Apr.	3 Ric. III	26 Jun. 1485	22 Aug. 1485
1486	A	26 Mar.	1 **Hen. VII**	22 Aug. 1485	21 Aug. 1486
1487	G	15 Apr.	2 Hen. VII	22 Aug. 1486	21 Aug. 1487
1488	FE	6 Apr.	3 Hen. VII	22 Aug. 1487	21 Aug. 1488
1489	D	19 Apr.	4 Hen. VII	22 Aug. 1488	21 Aug. 1489
1490	C	11 Apr.	5 Hen. VII	22 Aug. 1489	21 Aug. 1490
1491	B	3 Apr.	6 Hen. VII	22 Aug. 1490	21 Aug. 1491
1492	AG	22 Apr.	7 Hen. VII	22 Aug. 1491	21 Aug. 1492
1493	F	7 Apr.	8 Hen. VII	22 Aug. 1492	21 Aug. 1493
1494	E	30 Mar.	9 Hen. VII	22 Aug. 1493	21 Aug. 1494
1495	D	19 Apr.	10 Hen. VII	22 Aug. 1494	21 Aug. 1495
1496	CB	3 Apr.	11 Hen. VII	22 Aug. 1495	21 Aug. 1496
1497	A	26 Mar.	12 Hen. VII	22 Aug. 1496	21 Aug. 1497
1498	G	15 Apr.	13 Hen. VII	22 Aug. 1497	21 Aug. 1498
1499	F	31 Mar.	14 Hen. VII	22 Aug. 1498	21 Aug. 1499
1500	ED	19 Apr.	15 Hen. VII	22 Aug. 1499	21 Aug. 1500
1501	C	11 Apr.	16 Hen. VII	22 Aug. 1500	21 Aug. 1501
1502	B	27 Mar.	17 Hen. VII	22 Aug. 1501	21 Aug. 1502
1503	A	16 Apr.	18 Hen. VII	22 Aug. 1502	21 Aug. 1503
1504	GF	7 Apr.	19 Hen. VII	22 Aug. 1503	21 Aug. 1504
1505	E	23 Mar.	20 Hen. VII	22 Aug. 1504	21 Aug. 1505
1506	D	12 Apr.	21 Hen. VII	22 Aug. 1505	21 Aug. 1506
1507	C	4 Apr.	22 Hen. VII	22 Aug. 1506	21 Aug. 1507
1508	BA	23 Apr.	23 Hen. VII	22 Aug. 1507	21 Aug. 1508
1509	G	8 Apr.	24 Hen. VII	22 Aug. 1508	21 Apr. 1509
1510	F	31 Mar.	1 **Hen. VIII**	22 Apr. 1509	21 Apr. 1510
1511	E	20 Apr.	2 Hen. VIII	22 Apr. 1510	21 Apr. 1511
1512	DC	11 Apr.	3 Hen. VIII	22 Apr. 1511	21 Apr. 1512
1513	B	27 Mar.	4 Hen. VIII	22 Apr. 1512	21 Apr. 1513
1514	A	16 Apr.	5 Hen. VIII	22 Apr. 1513	21 Apr. 1514
1515	G	8 Apr.	6 Hen. VIII	22 Apr. 1514	21 Apr. 1515
1516	FE	23 Mar.	7 Hen. VIII	22 Apr. 1515	21 Apr. 1516
1517	D	12 Apr.	8 Hen. VIII	22 Apr. 1516	21 Apr. 1517
1518	C	4 Apr.	9 Hen. VIII	22 Apr. 1517	21 Apr. 1518
1519	B	24 Apr.	10 Hen. VIII	22 Apr. 1518	21 Apr. 1519
1520	AG	8 Apr.	11 Hen. VIII	22 Apr. 1519	21 Apr. 1520
1521	F	31 Mar.	12 Hen. VIII	22 Apr. 1520	21 Apr. 1521
1522	E	20 Apr.	13 Hen. VIII	22 Apr. 1521	21 Apr. 1522
1523	D	5 Apr.	14 Hen. VIII	22 Apr. 1522	21 Apr. 1523
1524	CB	27 Mar.	15 Hen. VIII	22 Apr. 1523	21 Apr. 1524

Year	Dominical Letter	Easter Day	Regnal Years No.	Beginning	Ending
1524	CB	27 Mar.	16 Hen. VIII	22 Apr. 1524	21 Apr. 1525
1525	A	16 Apr.	17 Hen. VIII	22 Apr. 1525	21 Apr. 1526
1526	G	1 Apr.	18 Hen. VIII	22 Apr. 1526	21 Apr. 1527
1527	F	21 Apr.	19 Hen. VIII	22 Apr. 1527	21 Apr. 1528
1528	ED	12 Apr.	20 Hen. VIII	22 Apr. 1528	21 Apr. 1529
1529	C	28 Mar.	21 Hen. VIII	22 Apr. 1529	21 Apr. 1530
1530	B	17 Apr.	22 Hen. VIII	22 Apr. 1530	21 Apr. 1531
1531	A	9 Apr.	23 Hen. VIII	22 Apr. 1531	21 Apr. 1532
1532	GF	31 Mar.	24 Hen. VIII	22 Apr. 1532	21 Apr. 1533
1533	E	13 Apr.	25 Hen. VIII	22 Apr. 1533	21 Apr. 1534
1534	D	5 Apr.	26 Hen. VIII	22 Apr. 1534	21 Apr. 1535
1535	C	28 Mar.	27 Hen. VIII	22 Apr. 1535	21 Apr. 1536
1536	BA	16 Apr.	28 Hen. VIII	22 Apr. 1536	21 Apr. 1537
1537	G	1 Apr.	29 Hen. VIII	22 Apr. 1537	21 Apr. 1538
1538	F	21 Apr.	30 Hen. VIII	22 Apr. 1538	21 Apr. 1539
1539	E	6 Apr.	31 Hen. VIII	22 Apr. 1539	21 Apr. 1540
1540	DC	28 Mar.	32 Hen. VIII	22 Apr. 1540	21 Apr. 1541
1541	B	17 Apr.	33 Hen. VIII	22 Apr. 1541	21 Apr. 1542
1542	A	9 Apr.	34 Hen. VIII	22 Apr. 1542	21 Apr. 1543
1543	G	25 Mar.	35 Hen. VIII	22 Apr. 1543	21 Apr. 1544
1544	FE	13 Apr.	36 Hen. VIII	22 Apr. 1544	21 Apr. 1545
1545	D	5 Apr.	37 Hen. VIII	22 Apr. 1545	21 Apr. 1546
1546	C	25 Apr.	38 Hen. VIII	22 Apr. 1546	28 Jan. 1547
1547	B	10 Apr.	1 Edw. VI	28 Jan. 1547	27 Jan. 1548
1548	AG	1 Apr.	2 Edw. VI	28 Jan. 1548	27 Jan. 1549
1549	F	21 Apr.	3 Edw. VI	28 Jan. 1549	27 Jan. 1550
1550	E	6 Apr.	4 Edw. VI	28 Jan. 1550	27 Jan. 1551
1551	D	29 Mar.	5 Edw. VI	28 Jan. 1551	27 Jan. 1552
1552	CB	17 Apr.	6 Edw. VI	28 Jan. 1552	27 Jan. 1553
1553	A	2 Apr.	7 Edw. VI	28 Jan. 1553	6 Jul. 1553
			1 Jane	6 Jul. 1553	19 Jul. 1553
			1 Mary	19 Jul. 1553*	5 Jul. 1554
1554	G	25 Mar.	2 Mary	6 Jul. 1554	24 Jul. 1554
			1 & 2 P. & M.	25 Jul. 1554†	5 Jul. 1555
1555	F	14 Apr.	1 & 3 P. & M.	6 Jul. 1555	24 Jul. 1555
			2 & 3 P. & M.	25 Jul. 1555	5 Jul. 1556
1556	ED	5 Apr.	2 & 4 P. & M.	6 Jul. 1556	24 Jul. 1556
			3 & 4 P. & M.	25 Jul. 1556	5 Jul. 1557
1557	C	18 Apr.	3 & 5 P. & M.	6 Jul. 1557	24 Jul. 1557
			4 & 5 P. & M.	25 Jul. 1557	5 Jul. 1558
1558	B	10 Apr.	4 & 6 P. & M.	6 Jul. 1558	24 Jul. 1558
			5 & 6 P. & M.	25 Jul. 1558	17 Nov. 1558
			1 Eliz. I	17 Nov. 1558	16 Nov. 1559
1559	A	26 Mar.	2 Eliz. I	17 Nov. 1559	16 Nov. 1560
1560	GF	14 Apr.	3 Eliz. I	17 Nov. 1560	16 Nov. 1561
1561	E	6 Apr.	4 Eliz. I	17 Nov. 1561	16 Nov. 1562
1562	D	29 Mar.	5 Eliz. I	17 Nov. 1562	16 Nov. 1563
1563	C	11 Apr.	6 Eliz. I	17 Nov. 1563	16 Nov. 1564
1564	BA	2 Apr.	7 Eliz. I	17 Nov. 1564	16 Nov. 1565
1565	G	22 Apr.	8 Eliz. I	17 Nov. 1565	16 Nov. 1566
1566	F	14 Apr.			

* Mary reckoned the beginning of her second and succeeding regnal years as though Jane had not been queen.
† Date of Mary's marriage to Philip, king of Naples and Jerusalem and (after 16 Jan. 1556) Spain.

Year	Domi- nical Letter	Easter Day Old Style	Easter Day New Style	Regnal Years No.	Regnal Years Beginning	Regnal Years Ending
1566	F	14 Apr.		9 Eliz. I	17 Nov. 1566	16 Nov. 1567
1567	E	30 Mar.		10 Eliz. I	17 Nov. 1567	16 Nov. 1568
1568	DC	18 Apr.		11 Eliz. I	17 Nov. 1568	16 Nov. 1569
1569	B	10 Apr.		12 Eliz. I	17 Nov. 1569	16 Nov. 1570
1570	A	26 Mar.		13 Eliz. I	17 Nov. 1570	16 Nov. 1571
1571	G	15 Apr.		14 Eliz. I	17 Nov. 1571	16 Nov. 1572
1572	FE	6 Apr.		15 Eliz. I	17 Nov. 1572	16 Nov. 1573
1573	D	22 Mar.		16 Eliz. I	17 Nov. 1573	16 Nov. 1574
1574	C	11 Apr.		17 Eliz. I	17 Nov. 1574	16 Nov. 1575
1575	B	3 Apr.		18 Eliz. I	17 Nov. 1575	16 Nov. 1576
1576	AG	22 Apr.		19 Eliz. I	17 Nov. 1576	16 Nov. 1577
1577	F	7 Apr.		20 Eliz. I	17 Nov. 1577	16 Nov. 1578
1578	E	30 Mar.		21 Eliz. I	17 Nov. 1578	16 Nov. 1579
1579	D	19 Apr.		22 Eliz. I	17 Nov. 1579	16 Nov. 1580
1580	CB	3 Apr.		23 Eliz. I	17 Nov. 1580	16 Nov. 1581
1581	A	26 Mar.		24 Eliz. I	17 Nov. 1581	16 Nov. 1582
1582	G	15 Apr.		25 Eliz. I	17 Nov. 1582	16 Nov. 1583
1583	F	31 Mar.	10 Apr.	26 Eliz. I	17 Nov. 1583	16 Nov. 1584
1584	ED	19 Apr.	1 Apr.	27 Eliz. I	17 Nov. 1584	16 Nov. 1585
1585	C	11 Apr.	21 Apr.	28 Eliz. I	17 Nov. 1585	16 Nov. 1586
1586	B	3 Apr.	6 Apr.	29 Eliz. I	17 Nov. 1586	16 Nov. 1587
1587	A	16 Apr.	29 Mar.	30 Eliz. I	17 Nov. 1587	16 Nov. 1588
1588	GF	7 Apr.	17 Apr.	31 Eliz. I	17 Nov. 1588	16 Nov. 1589
1589	E	30 Mar.	2 Apr.	32 Eliz. I	17 Nov. 1589	16 Nov. 1590
1590	D	19 Apr.	22 Apr.	33 Eliz. I	17 Nov. 1590	16 Nov. 1591
1591	C	4 Apr.	14 Apr.	34 Eliz. I	17 Nov. 1591	16 Nov. 1592
1592	BA	26 Mar.	29 Mar.	35 Eliz. I	17 Nov. 1592	16 Nov. 1593
1593	G	15 Apr.	18 Apr.	36 Eliz. I	17 Nov. 1593	16 Nov. 1594
1594	F	31 Mar.	10 Apr.	37 Eliz. I	17 Nov. 1594	16 Nov. 1595
1595	E	20 Apr.	26 Mar.	38 Eliz. I	17 Nov. 1595	16 Nov. 1596
1596	DC	11 Apr.	14 Apr.	39 Eliz. I	17 Nov. 1596	16 Nov. 1597
1597	B	27 Mar.	6 Apr.	40 Eliz. I	17 Nov. 1597	16 Nov. 1598
1598	A	16 Apr.	22 Mar.	41 Eliz. I	17 Nov. 1598	16 Nov. 1599
1599	G	8 Apr.	11 Apr.	42 Eliz. I	17 Nov. 1599	16 Nov. 1600
1600	FE	23 Mar.	2 Apr.	43 Eliz. I	17 Nov. 1600	16 Nov. 1601
1601	D	12 Apr.	22 Apr.	44 Eliz. I	17 Nov. 1601	16 Nov. 1602
1602	C	4 Apr.	7 Apr.	45 Eliz. I	17 Nov. 1602	23 Mar. 1603
1603	B	24 Apr.	30 Mar.	1 & 36 Jac. I*	24 Mar. 1603	23 Jul. 1603
				1 & 37 Jac. I	24 Jul. 1603	23 Mar. 1604
1604	AG	8 Apr.	18 Apr.	2 & 37 Jac. I	24 Mar. 1604	23 Jul. 1604
				2 & 38 Jac. I	24 Jul. 1604	23 Mar. 1605
1605	F	31 Mar.	10 Apr.	3 & 38 Jac. I	24 Mar. 1605	23 Jul. 1605
				3 & 39 Jac. I	24 Jul. 1605	23 Mar. 1606
1606	E	20 Apr.	26 Mar.	4 & 39 Jac. I	24 Mar. 1606	23 Jul. 1606
				4 & 40 Jac. I	24 Jul. 1606	23 Mar. 1607
1607	D	5 Apr.	15 Apr.	5 & 40 Jac. I	24 Mar. 1607	23 Jul. 1607
				5 & 41 Jac. I	24 Jul. 1607	23 Mar. 1608
1608	CB	27 Mar.	6 Apr.	6 & 41 Jac. I	24 Mar. 1608	23 Jul. 1608
				6 & 42 Jac. I	24 Jul. 1608	23 Mar. 1609
1609	A	16 Apr.	19 Apr.	7 & 42 Jac. I	24 Mar. 1609	23 Jul. 1609
				7 & 43 Jac. I	24 Jul. 1609	23 Mar. 1610
1610	G	8 Apr.	11 Apr.	8 & 43 Jac. I	24 Mar. 1610	23 Jul. 1610
				8 & 44 Jac. I	24 Jul. 1610	23 Mar. 1611
1611	F	24 Mar.	3 Apr.	9 & 44 Jac. I	24 Mar. 1611	23 Jul. 1611

* The Scottish regnal year of James I (reckoned from his accession in Scotland on 24 July 1567) is generally given in documents as well as his English regnal year.

Year	Dominical Letter	Easter Day Old Style	Easter Day New Style	Regnal Years No.	Regnal Years Beginning	Regnal Years Ending
1611	F	24 Mar.	3 Apr.	9 & 45 Jac. I	24 Jul. 1611	23 Mar. 1612
				10 & 45 Jac. I	24 Mar. 1612	23 Jul. 1612
1612	ED	12 Apr.	22 Apr.	10 & 46 Jac. I	24 Jul. 1612	23 Mar. 1613
				11 & 46 Jac. I	24 Mar. 1613	23 Jul. 1613
1613	C	4 Apr.	7 Apr.	11 & 47 Jac. I	24 Jul. 1613	23 Mar. 1614
				12 & 47 Jac. I	24 Mar. 1614	23 Jul. 1614
1614	B	24 Apr.	30 Mar.	12 & 48 Jac. I	24 Jul. 1614	23 Mar. 1615
				13 & 48 Jac. I	24 Mar. 1615	23 Jul. 1615
1615	A	9 Apr.	19 Apr.	13 & 49 Jac. I	24 Jul. 1615	23 Mar. 1616
				14 & 49 Jac. I	24 Mar. 1616	23 Jul. 1616
1616	GF	31 Mar.	3 Apr.	14 & 50 Jac. I	24 Jul. 1616	23 Mar. 1617
				15 & 50 Jac. I	24 Mar. 1617	23 Jul. 1617
1617	E	20 Apr.	26 Mar.	15 & 51 Jac. I	24 Jul. 1617	23 Mar. 1618
				16 & 51 Jac. I	24 Mar. 1618	23 Jul. 1618
1618	D	5 Apr.	15 Apr.	16 & 52 Jac. I	24 Jul. 1618	23 Mar. 1619
				17 & 52 Jac. I	24 Mar. 1619	23 Jul. 1619
1619	C	28 Mar.	31 Mar.	17 & 53 Jac. I	24 Jul. 1619	23 Mar. 1620
				18 & 53 Jac. I	24 Mar. 1620	23 Jul. 1620
1620	BA	16 Apr.	19 Apr.	18 & 54 Jac. I	24 Jul. 1620	23 Mar. 1621
				19 & 54 Jac. I	24 Mar. 1621	23 Jul. 1621
1621	G	1 Apr.	11 Apr.	19 & 55 Jac. I	24 Jul. 1621	23 Mar. 1622
				20 & 55 Jac. I	24 Mar. 1622	23 Jul. 1622
1622	F	21 Apr.	27 Mar.	20 & 56 Jac. I	24 Jul. 1622	23 Mar. 1623
				21 & 56 Jac. I	24 Mar. 1623	23 Jul. 1623
1623	E	13 Apr.	16 Apr.	21 & 57 Jac. I	24 Jul. 1623	23 Mar. 1624
				22 & 57 Jac. I	24 Mar. 1624	23 Jul. 1624
1624	DC	28 Mar.	7 Apr.	22 & 58 Jac. I	24 Jul. 1624	23 Mar. 1625
				23 & 58 Jac. I	24 Mar. 1625	27 Mar. 1625
1625	B	17 Apr.	30 Mar.	1 Car. I	27 Mar. 1625	26 Mar. 1626
1626	A	9 Apr.	12 Apr.	2 Car. I	27 Mar. 1626	26 Mar. 1627
1627	G	25 Mar.	4 Apr.	3 Car. I	27 Mar. 1627	26 Mar. 1628
1628	FE	13 Apr.	23 Apr.	4 Car. I	27 Mar. 1628	26 Mar. 1629
1629	D	5 Apr.	15 Apr.	5 Car. I	27 Mar. 1629	26 Mar. 1630
1630	C	28 Mar.	31 Mar.	6 Car. I	27 Mar. 1630	26 Mar. 1631
1631	B	10 Apr.	20 Apr.	7 Car. I	27 Mar. 1631	26 Mar. 1632
1632	AG	1 Apr.	11 Apr.	8 Car. I	27 Mar. 1632	26 Mar. 1633
1633	F	21 Apr.	27 Mar.	9 Car. I	27 Mar. 1633	26 Mar. 1634
1634	E	6 Apr.	16 Apr.	10 Car. I	27 Mar. 1634	26 Mar. 1635
1635	D	29 Mar.	8 Apr.	11 Car. I	27 Mar. 1635	26 Mar. 1636
1636	CB	17 Apr.	23 Mar.	12 Car. I	27 Mar. 1636	26 Mar. 1637
1637	A	9 Apr.	12 Apr.	13 Car. I	27 Mar. 1637	26 Mar. 1638
1638	G	25 Mar.	4 Apr.	14 Car. I	27 Mar. 1638	26 Mar. 1639
1639	F	14 Apr.	24 Apr.	15 Car. I	27 Mar. 1639	26 Mar. 1640
1640	ED	5 Apr.	8 Apr.	16 Car. I	27 Mar. 1640	26 Mar. 1641
1641	C	25 Mar.	31 Mar.	17 Car. I	27 Mar. 1641	26 Mar. 1642
1642	B	10 Apr.	20 Apr.	18 Car. I	27 Mar. 1642	26 Mar. 1643
1643	A	2 Apr.	5 Apr.	19 Car. I	27 Mar. 1643	26 Mar. 1644
1644	GF	21 Apr.	27 Mar.	20 Car. I	27 Mar. 1644	26 Mar. 1645
1645	E	6 Apr.	16 Apr.	21 Car. I	27 Mar. 1645	26 Mar. 1646
1646	D	29 Mar.	1 Apr.	22 Car. I	27 Mar. 1646	26 Mar. 1647
1647	C	18 Apr.	21 Apr.	23 Car. I	27 Mar. 1647	26 Mar. 1648
1648	BA	2 Apr.	12 Apr.	24 Car. I	27 Mar. 1648	30 Jan. 1649
1649	G	25 Mar.	4 Apr.			

Year	Dominical Letter	Easter Day		Regnal Years		
		Old Style	New Style	No.	Beginning	Ending
1649	G	25 Mar.	4 Apr.	[1 Car. II]*	[30 Jan. 1649]	[29 Jan. 1650]
1650	F	14 Apr.	17 Apr.	[2 Car. II]	[30 Jan. 1650]	[29 Jan. 1651]
1651	E	30 Mar.	9 Apr.	[3 Car. II]	[30 Jan. 1651]	[29 Jan. 1652]
1652	DC	18 Apr.	31 Mar.	[4 Car. II]	[30 Jan. 1652]	[29 Jan. 1653]
1653	B	10 Apr.	13 Apr.	[5 Car. II]	[30 Jan. 1653]	[29 Jan. 1654]
1654	A	26 Mar.	5 Apr.	[6 Car. II]	[30 Jan. 1654]	[29 Jan. 1655]
1655	G	15 Apr.	28 Mar.	[7 Car. II]	[30 Jan. 1655]	[29 Jan. 1656]
1656	FE	6 Apr.	16 Apr.	[8 Car. II]	[30 Jan. 1656]	[29 Jan. 1657]
1657	D	29 Mar.	1 Apr.	[9 Car. II]	[30 Jan. 1657]	[29 Jan. 1658]
1658	C	11 Apr.	21 Apr.	[10 Car. II]	[30 Jan. 1658]	[29 Jan. 1659]
1659	B	3 Apr.	13 Apr.	[11 Car. II]	[30 Jan. 1659]	[29 Jan. 1660]
1660	AG	22 Apr.	28 Mar.			29 May 1660†
				12 Car. II	[30 Jan. 1660]	29 Jan. 1661
1661	F	14 Apr.	17 Apr.	13 Car. II	30 Jan. 1661	29 Jan. 1662
1662	E	30 Mar.	9 Apr.	14 Car. II	30 Jan. 1662	29 Jan. 1663
1663	D	19 Apr.	25 Mar.	15 Car. II	30 Jan. 1663	29 Jan. 1664
1664	CB	10 Apr.	13 Apr.	16 Car. II	30 Jan. 1664	29 Jan. 1665
1665	A	26 Mar.	5 Apr.	17 Car. II	30 Jan. 1665	29 Jan. 1666
1666	G	15 Apr.	25 Apr.	18 Car. II	30 Jan. 1666	29 Jan. 1667
1667	F	7 Apr.	10 Apr.	19 Car. II	30 Jan. 1667	29 Jan. 1668
1668	ED	22 Mar.	1 Apr.	20 Car. II	30 Jan. 1668	29 Jan. 1669
1669	C	11 Apr.	21 Apr.	21 Car. II	30 Jan. 1669	29 Jan. 1670
1670	B	3 Apr.	6 Apr.	22 Car. II	30 Jan. 1670	29 Jan. 1671
1671	A	23 Apr.	29 Mar.	23 Car. II	30 Jan. 1671	29 Jan. 1672
1672	GF	7 Apr.	17 Apr.	24 Car. II	30 Jan. 1672	29 Jan. 1673
1673	E	30 Mar.	2 Apr.	25 Car. II	30 Jan. 1673	29 Jan. 1674
1674	D	19 Apr.	25 Mar.	26 Car. II	30 Jan. 1674	29 Jan. 1675
1675	C	4 Apr.	14 Apr.	27 Car. II	30 Jan. 1675	29 Jan. 1676
1676	BA	26 Mar.	5 Apr.	28 Car. II	30 Jan. 1676	29 Jan. 1677
1677	G	15 Apr.	18 Apr.	29 Car. II	30 Jan. 1677	29 Jan. 1678
1678	F	31 Mar.	10 Apr.	30 Car. II	30 Jan. 1678	29 Jan. 1679
1679	E	20 Apr.	2 Apr.	31 Car. II	30 Jan. 1679	29 Jan. 1680
1680	DC	11 Apr.	21 Apr.	32 Car. II	30 Jan. 1680	29 Jan. 1681
1681	B	3 Apr.	6 Apr.	33 Car. II	30 Jan. 1681	29 Jan. 1682
1682	A	16 Apr.	29 Mar.	34 Car. II	30 Jan. 1682	29 Jan. 1683
1683	G	8 Apr.	18 Apr.	35 Car. II	30 Jan. 1683	29 Jan. 1684
1684	FE	30 Mar.	2 Apr.	36 Car. II	30 Jan. 1684	29 Jan. 1685
1685	D	19 Apr.	22 Apr.	37 Car. II	30 Jan. 1685	6 Feb. 1685
				1 Jac. II	6 Feb. 1685	5 Feb. 1686
1686	C	4 Apr.	14 Apr.	2 Jac. II	6 Feb. 1686	5 Feb. 1687
1687	B	27 Mar.	30 Mar.	3 Jac. II	6 Feb. 1687	5 Feb. 1688
1688	AG	15 Apr.	18 Apr.	4 Jac. II	6 Feb. 1688	11 Dec. 1688
1689	F	31 Mar.	10 Apr.	Interregnum	12 Dec. 1688	12 Feb. 1689
1690	E	20 Apr.	26 Mar.	1 Wm. & Mar.	13 Feb. 1689	12 Feb. 1690
1691	D	12 Apr.	15 Apr.	2 Wm. & Mar.	13 Feb. 1690	12 Feb. 1691
1692	CB	27 Mar.	6 Apr.	3 Wm. & Mar.	13 Feb. 1691	12 Feb. 1692
1693	A	16 Apr.	22 Mar.	4 Wm. & Mar.	13 Feb. 1692	12 Feb. 1693
				5 Wm. & Mar.	13 Feb. 1693	12 Feb. 1694
1694	G	8 Apr.	11 Apr.	6 Wm. & Mar.	13 Feb. 1694	27 Dec. 1694‡
1695	F	24 Mar.	3 Apr.	6 Wm. III	28 Dec. 1694	12 Feb. 1695

COMMONWEALTH

* Charles II reckoned his regnal years from 30 Jan. 1649 (the date of the execution of Charles I) but did not reign in England and rarely used regnal years in dating until his restoration, 29 May 1660. During the Commonwealth public documents were dated according to the year of our Lord. Oliver Cromwell died 3 Sept. 1658. Richard Cromwell abdicated 24 May 1659, after which the government was carried on by Parliament and the Army until the restoration.

 † Date of the restoration of Charles II. ‡ Queen Mary died in the night of 27–28 Dec.

Year	Dominical Letter	Easter Day Old Style	Easter Day New Style
1695	F	24 Mar.	3 Apr.
1696	ED	12 Apr.	22 Apr.
1697	C	4 Apr.	7 Apr.
1698	B	24 Apr.	30 Mar.
1699	A	9 Apr.	19 Apr.
1700	GF	31 Mar.	11 Apr.
1701	E	20 Apr.	27 Mar.
1702	D	5 Apr.	16 Apr.
1703	C	28 Mar.	8 Apr.
1704	BA	16 Apr.	23 Mar.
1705	G	8 Apr.	12 Apr.
1706	F	24 Mar.	4 Apr.
1707	E	13 Apr.	24 Apr.
1708	DC	4 Apr.	8 Apr.
1709	B	24 Apr.	31 Mar.
1710	A	9 Apr.	20 Apr.
1711	G	1 Apr.	5 Apr.
1712	FE	20 Apr.	27 Mar.
1713	D	5 Apr.	16 Apr.
1714	C	28 Mar.	1 Apr.
1715	B	17 Apr.	21 Apr.
1716	AG	1 Apr.	12 Apr.
1717	F	21 Apr.	28 Mar.
1718	E	13 Apr.	17 Apr.
1719	D	29 Mar.	9 Apr.
1720	CB	17 Apr.	31 Mar.
1721	A	9 Apr.	13 Apr.
1722	G	25 Mar.	5 Apr.
1723	F	14 Apr.	28 Mar.
1724	ED	5 Apr.	16 Apr.
1725	C	28 Mar.	1 Apr.
1726	B	10 Apr.	21 Apr.
1727	A	2 Apr.	13 Apr.
1728	GF	21 Apr.	28 Mar.
1729	E	6 Apr.	17 Apr.
1730	D	29 Mar.	9 Apr.
1731	C	18 Apr.	25 Mar.
1732	BA	9 Apr.	13 Apr.
1733	G	25 Mar.	5 Apr.
1734	F	14 Apr.	25 Apr.
1735	E	6 Apr.	10 Apr.
1736	DC	25 Apr.	1 Apr.
1737	B	10 Apr.	21 Apr.
1738	A	2 Apr.	6 Apr.
1739	G	22 Apr.	29 Mar,
1740	FE	6 Apr.	17 Apr.
1741	D	29 Mar.	2 Apr.
1742	C	18 Apr.	25 Mar.
1743	B	3 Apr.	14 Apr.
1744	AG	25 Mar.	5 Apr.
1745	F	14 Apr.	18 Apr.
1746	E	30 Mar.	10 Apr.
1747	D	19 Apr.	2 Apr.
1748	CB	10 Apr.	14 Apr.
1749	A	26 Mar.	6 Apr.

Regnal Years

No.	Beginning	Ending
7 Wm. III	13 Feb. 1695	12 Feb. 1696
8 Wm. III	13 Feb. 1696	12 Feb. 1697
9 Wm. III	13 Feb. 1697	12 Feb. 1698
10 Wm. III	13 Feb. 1698	12 Feb. 1699
11 Wm. III	13 Feb. 1699	12 Feb. 1700
12 Wm. III	13 Feb. 1700	12 Feb. 1701
13 Wm. III	13 Feb. 1701	12 Feb. 1702
14 Wm. III	13 Feb. 1702	8 Mar. 1702
1 Anne	8 Mar. 1702	7 Mar. 1703
2 Anne	8 Mar. 1703	7 Mar. 1704
3 Anne	8 Mar. 1704	7 Mar. 1705
4 Anne	8 Mar. 1705	7 Mar. 1706
5 Anne	8 Mar. 1706	7 Mar. 1707
6 Anne	8 Mar. 1707	7 Mar. 1708
7 Anne	8 Mar. 1708	7 Mar. 1709
8 Anne	8 Mar. 1709	7 Mar. 1710
9 Anne	8 Mar. 1710	7 Mar. 1711
10 Anne	8 Mar. 1711	7 Mar. 1712
11 Anne	8 Mar. 1712	7 Mar. 1713
12 Anne	8 Mar. 1713	7 Mar. 1714
13 Anne	8 Mar. 1714	1 Aug. 1714
1 Geo. I	1 Aug. 1714	31 Jul. 1715
2 Geo. I	1 Aug. 1715	31 Jul. 1716
3 Geo. I	1 Aug. 1716	31 Jul. 1717
4 Geo. I	1 Aug. 1717	31 Jul. 1718
5 Geo. I	1 Aug. 1718	31 Jul. 1719
6 Geo. I	1 Aug. 1719	31 Jul. 1720
7 Geo. I	1 Aug. 1720	31 Jul. 1721
8 Geo. I	1 Aug. 1721	31 Jul. 1722
9 Geo. I	1 Aug. 1722	31 Jul. 1723
10 Geo. I	1 Aug. 1723	31 Jul. 1724
11 Geo. I	1 Aug. 1724	31 Jul. 1725
12 Geo. I	1 Aug. 1725	31 Jul. 1726
13 Geo. I	1 Aug. 1726	11 Jun. 1727
1 Geo. II	11 Jun. 1727	10 Jun. 1728
2 Geo. II	11 Jun. 1728	10 Jun. 1729
3 Geo. II	11 Jun. 1729	10 Jun. 1730
4 Geo. II	11 Jun. 1730	10 Jun. 1731
5 Geo. II	11 Jun. 1731	10 Jun. 1732
6 Geo. II	11 Jun. 1732	10 Jun. 1733
7 Geo. II	11 Jun. 1733	10 Jun. 1734
8 Geo. II	11 Jun. 1734	10 Jun. 1735
9 Geo. II	11 Jun. 1735	10 Jun. 1736
10 Geo. II	11 Jun. 1736	10 Jun. 1737
11 Geo. II	11 Jun. 1737	10 Jun. 1738
12 Geo. II	11 Jun. 1738	10 Jun. 1739
13 Geo. II	11 Jun. 1739	10 Jun. 1740
14 Geo. II	11 Jun. 1740	10 Jun. 1741
15 Geo. II	11 Jun. 1741	10 Jun. 1742
16 Geo. II	11 Jun. 1742	10 Jun. 1743
17 Geo. II	11 Jun. 1743	10 Jun. 1744
18 Geo. II	11 Jun. 1744	10 Jun. 1745
19 Geo. II	11 Jun. 1745	10 Jun. 1746
20 Geo. II	11 Jun. 1746	10 Jun. 1747
21 Geo. II	11 Jun. 1747	10 Jun. 1748
22 Geo. II	11 Jun. 1748	10 Jun. 1749

Year	Domi-nical Letter	Easter Day Old Style	Easter Day NewStyle	Regnal Years No.	Beginning	Ending
1749	A	26 Mar.	6 Apr.	23 Geo. II	11 Jun. 1749	10 Jun. 1750
1750	G	15 Apr.	29 Mar.	24 Geo. II	11 Jun. 1750	10 Jun. 1751
1751	F	7 Apr.	11 Apr.	25 Geo. II	11 Jun. 1751	10 Jun. 1752
1752*	EDA*	29 Mar.	2 Apr.	26 Geo. II	11 Jun. 1752	21 Jun. 1753†
1753	G	22 Apr,		27 Geo. II	22 Jun. 1753	21 Jun. 1754
1754	F	14 Apr.		28 Geo. II	22 Jun. 1754	21 Jun. 1755
1755	E	30 Mar.		29 Geo. II	22 Jun. 1755	21 Jun. 1756
1756	DC	18 Apr.		30 Geo. II	22 Jun. 1756	21 Jun. 1757
1757	B	10 Apr.		31 Geo. II	22 Jun. 1757	21 Jun. 1758
1758	A	26 Mar.		32 Geo. II	22 Jun. 1758	21 Jun. 1759
1759	G	15 Apr.		33 Geo. II	22 Jun. 1759	21 Jun. 1760
1760	FE	6 Apr.		34 Geo. II	22 Jun. 1760	25 Oct. 1760
1761	D	22 Mar.		1 Geo. III	25 Oct. 1760	24 Oct. 1761
1762	C	11 Apr.		2 Geo. III	25 Oct. 1761	24 Oct. 1762
1763	B	3 Apr.		3 Geo. III	25 Oct. 1762	24 Oct. 1763
1764	AG	22 Apr.		4 Geo. III	25 Oct. 1763	24 Oct. 1764
1765	F	7 Apr.		5 Geo. III	25 Oct. 1764	24 Oct. 1765
1766	E	30 Mar.		6 Geo. III	25 Oct. 1765	24 Oct. 1766
1767	D	19 Apr.		7 Geo. III	25 Oct. 1766	24 Oct. 1767
1768	CB	3 Apr.		8 Geo. III	25 Oct. 1767	24 Oct. 1768
1769	A	26 Mar.		9 Geo. III	25 Oct. 1768	24 Oct. 1769
1770	G	15 Apr.		10 Geo. III	25 Oct. 1769	25 Oct. 1770
1771	F	31 Mar.		11 Geo. III	25 Oct. 1770	24 Oct. 1771
1772	ED	19 Apr.		12 Geo. III	25 Oct. 1771	24 Oct. 1772
1773	C	11 Apr.		13 Geo. III	25 Oct. 1772	24 Oct. 1773
1774	B	3 Apr.		14 Geo. III	25 Oct. 1773	24 Oct. 1774
1775	A	16 Apr.		15 Geo. III	25 Oct. 1774	24 Oct. 1775
1776	GF	7 Apr.		16 Geo. III	25 Oct. 1775	24 Oct. 1776
1777	E	30 Mar.		17 Geo. III	25 Oct. 1776	24 Oct. 1777
1778	D	19 Apr.		18 Geo. III	25 Oct. 1777	24 Oct. 1778
1779	C	4 Apr.		19 Geo. III	25 Oct. 1778	24 Oct. 1779
1780	BA	26 Mar.		20 Geo. III	25 Oct. 1779	24 Oct. 1780
1781	G	15 Apr.		21 Geo. III	25 Oct. 1780	24 Oct. 1781
1782	F	31 Mar.		22 Geo. III	25 Oct. 1781	24 Oct. 1782
1783	E	20 Apr.		23 Geo. III	25 Oct. 1782	24 Oct. 1783
1784	DC	11 Apr.		24 Geo. III	25 Oct. 1783	24 Oct. 1784
1785	B	27 Mar.		25 Geo. III	25 Oct. 1784	24 Oct. 1785
1786	A	16 Apr.		26 Geo. III	25 Oct. 1785	24 Oct. 1786
1787	G	8 Apr.		27 Geo. III	25 Oct. 1786	24 Oct. 1787
1788	FE	23 Mar.		28 Geo. III	25 Oct. 1787	24 Oct. 1788
1789	D	12 Apr.		29 Geo. III	25 Oct. 1788	24 Oct. 1789
1790	C	4 Apr.		30 Geo. III	25 Oct. 1789	24 Oct. 1790
1791	B	24 Apr.		31 Geo. III	25 Oct. 1790	24 Oct. 1791
1792	AG	8 Apr.		32 Geo. III	25 Oct. 1791	24 Oct. 1792
1793	F	31 Mar.		33 Geo. III	25 Oct. 1792	24 Oct. 1793
1794	E	20 Apr.		34 Geo. III	25 Oct. 1793	24 Oct. 1794
1795	D	5 Apr.		35 Geo. III	25 Oct. 1794	24 Oct. 1795
1796	CB	27 Mar.		36 Geo. III	25 Oct. 1795	24 Oct. 1796
1797	A	16 Apr.		37 Geo. III	25 Oct. 1796	24 Oct. 1797
1798	G	8 Apr.		38 Geo. III	25 Oct. 1797	24 Oct. 1798
1799	F	24 Mar.		39 Geo. III	25 Oct. 1798	24 Oct. 1799
1800‡	E	13 Apr.		40 Geo. III	25 Oct. 1799	24 Oct. 1800

* See Table II.
† To make up for the eleven days omitted in Sept. 1752, eleven days (11–21 June) were added at the end of the regnal year. ‡ The year 1800 was not a leap year.

Year	Dominical Letter	Easter Day
1800	E	13 Apr.
1801	D	5 Apr.
1802	C	18 Apr.
1803	B	10 Apr.
1804	AG	1 Apr.
1805	F	14 Apr.
1806	E	6 Apr.
1807	D	29 Mar.
1808	CB	17 Apr.
1809	A	2 Apr.
1810	G	22 Apr.
1811	F	14 Apr.
1812	ED	29 Mar.
1813	C	18 Apr.
1814	B	10 Apr.
1815	A	26 Mar.
1816	GF	14 Apr.
1817	E	6 Apr.
1818	D	22 Mar.
1819	C	11 Apr.
1820	BA	2 Apr.
1821	G	22 Apr.
1822	F	7 Apr.
1823	E	30 Mar.
1824	DC	18 Apr.
1825	B	3 Apr.
1826	A	26 Mar.
1827	G	15 Apr.
1828	FE	6 Apr.
1829	D	19 Apr.
1830	C	11 Apr.
1831	B	3 Apr.
1832	AG	22 Apr.
1833	F	7 Apr.
1834	E	30 Mar.
1835	D	19 Apr.
1836	CB	3 Apr.
1837	A	26 Mar.
1838	G	15 Apr.
1839	F	31 Mar.
1840	ED	19 Apr.
1841	C	11 Apr.
1842	B	27 Mar.
1843	A	16 Apr.
1844	GF	7 Apr.
1845	E	23 Mar.
1846	D	12 Apr.
1847	C	4 Apr.
1848	BA	23 Apr.
1849	G	8 Apr.
1850	F	31 Mar.
1851	E	20 Apr.
1852	DC	11 Apr.
1853	B	27 Mar.
1854	A	16 Apr.
1855	G	8 Apr.

Regnal Years No.	Beginning	Ending
41 Geo. III	25 Oct. 1800	24 Oct. 1801
42 Geo. III	25 Oct. 1801	24 Oct. 1802
43 Geo. III	25 Oct. 1802	24 Oct. 1803
44 Geo. III	25 Oct. 1803	24 Oct. 1804
45 Geo. III	25 Oct. 1804	24 Oct. 1805
46 Geo. III	25 Oct. 1805	24 Oct. 1806
47 Geo. III	25 Oct. 1806	24 Oct. 1807
48 Geo. III	25 Oct. 1807	24 Oct. 1808
49 Geo. III	25 Oct. 1808	24 Oct. 1809
50 Geo. III	25 Oct. 1809	24 Oct. 1810
51 Geo. III	25 Oct. 1810	24 Oct. 1811
52 Geo. III	25 Oct. 1811	24 Oct. 1812
53 Geo. III	25 Oct. 1812	24 Oct. 1813
54 Geo. III	25 Oct. 1813	24 Oct. 1814
55 Geo. III	25 Oct. 1814	24 Oct. 1815
56 Geo. III	25 Oct. 1815	24 Oct. 1816
57 Geo. III	25 Oct. 1816	24 Oct. 1817
58 Geo. III	25 Oct. 1817	24 Oct. 1818
59 Geo. III	25 Oct. 1818	24 Oct. 1819
60 Geo. III	25 Oct. 1819	29 Jan. 1820
1 Geo. IV	29 Jan. 1820	28 Jan. 1821
2 Geo. IV	29 Jan. 1821	28 Jan. 1822
3 Geo. IV	29 Jan. 1822	28 Jan. 1823
4 Geo. IV	29 Jan. 1823	28 Jan. 1824
5 Geo. IV	29 Jan. 1824	28 Jan. 1825
6 Geo. IV	29 Jan. 1825	28 Jan. 1826
7 Geo. IV	29 Jan. 1826	29 Jan. 1827
8 Geo. IV	29 Jan. 1827	28 Jan. 1828
9 Geo. IV	29 Jan. 1828	28 Jan. 1829
10 Geo. IV	29 Jan. 1829	28 Jan. 1830
11 Geo. IV	29 Jan. 1830	26 Jun. 1830
1 Wm. IV	26 Jun. 1830	25 Jun. 1831
2 Wm. IV	26 Jun. 1831	25 Jun. 1832
3 Wm. IV	26 Jun. 1832	25 Jun. 1833
4 Wm. IV	26 Jun. 1833	25 Jun. 1834
5 Wm. IV	26 Jun. 1834	25 Jun. 1835
6 Wm. IV	26 Jun. 1835	25 Jun. 1836
7 Wm. IV	26 Jun. 1836	20 Jun. 1837
1 Vic.	20 Jun. 1837	19 Jun. 1838
2 Vic.	20 Jun. 1838	19 Jun. 1839
3 Vic.	20 Jun. 1839	19 Jun. 1850
4 Vic.	20 Jun. 1840	19 Jun. 1841
5 Vic.	20 Jun. 1841	19 Jun. 1842
6 Vic.	20 Jun. 1842	19 Jun. 1843
7 Vic.	20 Jun. 1843	19 Jun. 1844
8 Vic.	20 Jun. 1844	19 Jun. 1845
9 Vic.	20 Jun. 1845	19 Jun. 1846
10 Vic.	20 Jun. 1846	19 Jun. 1847
11 Vic.	20 Jun. 1847	19 Jun. 1848
12 Vic.	20 Jun. 1848	19 Jun. 1849
13 Vic.	20 Jun. 1849	19 Jun. 1850
14 Vic.	20 Jun. 1850	19 Jun. 1851
15 Vic.	20 Jun. 1851	19 Jun. 1852
16 Vic.	20 Jun. 1852	19 Jun. 1853
17 Vic.	20 Jun. 1853	19 Jun. 1854
18 Vic.	20 Jun. 1854	19 Jun. 1855